Key to Highways in *The MILEPOST*®

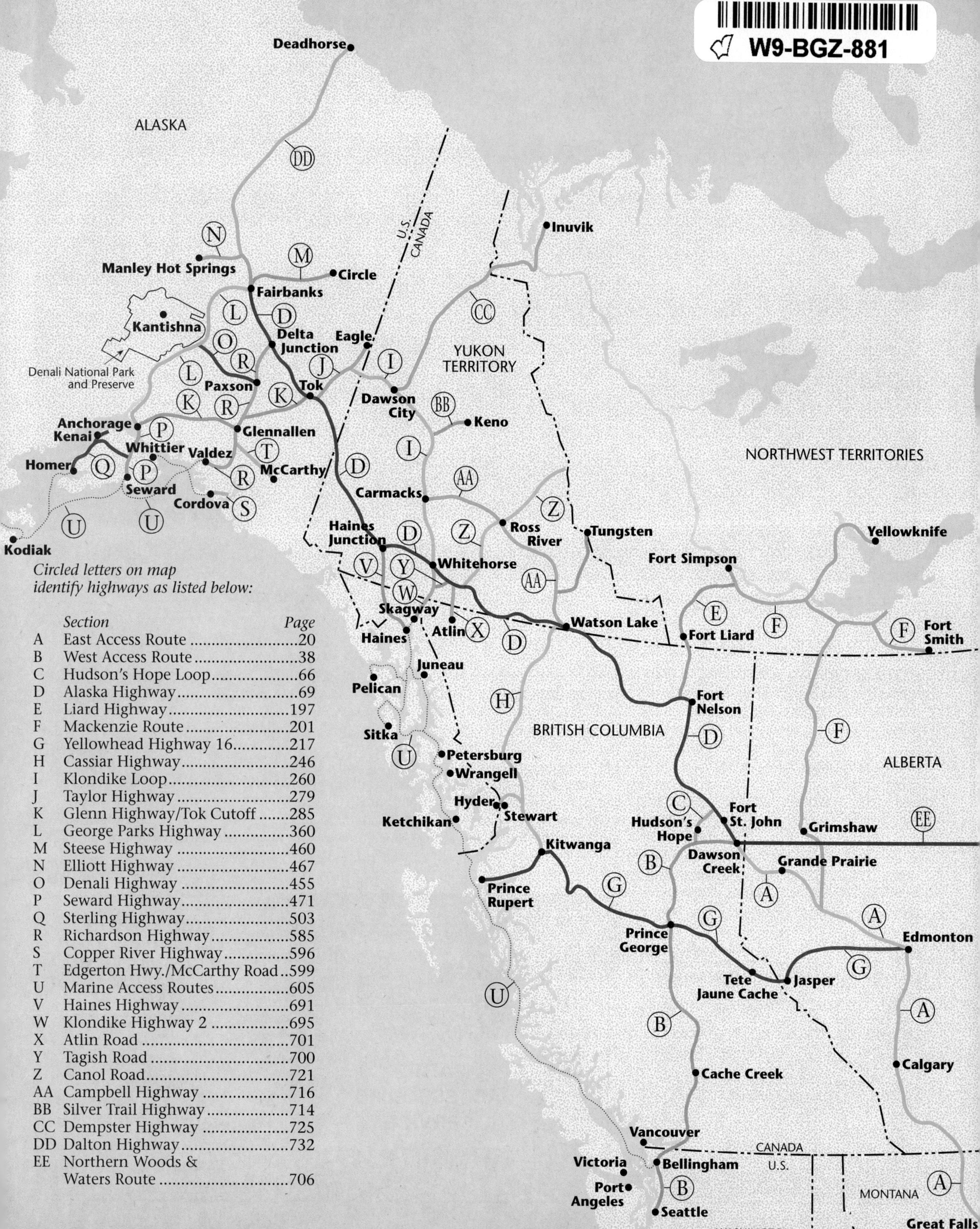

Planning Your Trip

Driving the Top of the World Highway between Dawson City, YT, and the Taylor Highway in Alaska. (© John K. Nakata)

The first thing to think about in planning your trip North is how you wish to travel—by highway, by ferry, by cruise ship, by airplane, by rail, on your own or with a tour. You may want to use more than one form of transportation, such as driving the Alaska Highway one way and taking the Alaska Marine Highway (the state ferry system) the other way.

Regardless of how you travel, *The MILEPOST®* works the same way. Information in *The MILEPOST®* is organized into sections: Highways, Major Attractions, Railroads, Marine Access Routes, Inside Passage and General Information. All sections are listed on the Contents page.

If you are driving from Anchorage to Denali National Park, for example, turn to the George Parks Highway section for the log of the highway and the Denali National Park section for a description of the park and its facilities. Pertinent sections are always cross-referenced in capital letters in the log at the appropriate junction, so, when you reach the turnoff for Denali National Park on the George Parks Highway, the log entry reads "see DENALI NATIONAL PARK section for details." The quickest way to find another section is to refer back to the Contents page. Place names and highways are also indexed in the back of the book.

The second thing to consider in planning your trip North is your itinerary.

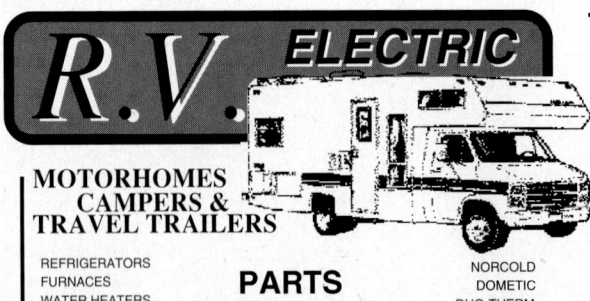

Totems at Saxman Totem Park near Ketchikan. (© Chris Sharp)

Contents

Highways

Highways in blue are Alaskan; green are Canadian; red are International.

Major Attractions

Railroads

Marine Access Routes

Inside Passage

How to Read a Highway Log

To the right is an abbreviated version of part of the George Parks Highway log, keyed to help you understand how to read all highway logs in *The MILEPOST®*.

1. A boldface paragraph appears at the beginning of each highway log in *The MILEPOST®* that explains what beginning and ending destinations are used, and what boldface letters represent those destinations. In this log A represents **Anchorage, F** is **Fairbanks.**

2. In the log, the boldface numbers represent the distance in miles from the beginning and ending destinations, and the lightface numbers are the metric equivalent in kilometers (unless otherwise noted). For example, the entrance to Denali National Park and Preserve is 237.3 miles, or 381.9 kilometers, from Anchorage.

3. References to other sections in *The MILEPOST®* are always uppercased. In this example, the DENALI NATIONAL PARK section is referenced. Refer to the Contents page to quickly find other sections.

4. Display advertisements are keyed in the log by a boldface entry at their highway locations, followed by the words "See display ad this section." Their advertisement will appear near this entry.

5. "Log" advertisements are classified-type advertisements that appear in the text. These are identified by the boldface name of the business at the beginning of the entry and "[ADVERTISEMENT]" at the end. These log advertisements are written by the advertisers.

George Parks Highway Log

1 — **ALASKA ROUTE 1**
Distance from Anchorage (A) is followed by distance from Fairbanks (F).

A 231.3 (372.2 km) **F 126.7** (203.9 km) Crabb's Crossing, second bridge northbound over the Nenana River.

A 233.1 (375.1 km) **F 124.9** (201 km) Gravel turnout to east.

A 234.1 (376.7 km) **F 123.9** (199.4 km) Double-ended turnout with litter barrels to east; scenic viewpoint. No overnight parking or camping. Mount Fellows (elev. 4,476 feet/1,364m) to the east. The constantly changing shadows make this an excellent camera subject.

A 235.1 (378.4 km) **F 122.9** (197.8 km) *CAUTION: Railroad crossing.*

A 237.2 (381.7 km) **F 120.8** (194.4 km) Riley Creek bridge.

2 — **A 237.3** (381.9 km) **F 120.7** (194.2 km) Entrance to Denali National Park and Preserve (formerly Mount McKinley National Park) to west. Fresh water fill-up hose and dump station 0.2 mile/0.3 km from junction on Park Road; Visitor Center is 0.5 mile/0.8 km from the highway junction. See DENALI NATIONAL PARK section for details. — 3

A 238 (383 km) **F 120** (193.4 km) Third bridge northbound over the Nenana River.

A 238.1 (383.2 km) **F 119.9** (193 km) **Denali Raft Adventures.** See display ad this section. — 4

A 238.3 (383.5 km) **F 119.7** (192.6 km) Kingfisher Creek.

A 238.5 (383.8 km) **F 119.5** (192.3 km) **McKinley/Denali Steakhouse and Salmon Bake.** Satisfy that hearty Alaskan appetite at a real home-style barbecue restaurant. Rustic heated indoor seating with majestic view of mountains. Free shuttle from all local hotels. Sourdough breakfasts. Large selection of postcards in our upstairs gift shop. T-shirts, sweatshirts and ice for sale. Pay phone. Open daily 5 A.M. to 11 P.M. in summer. [ADVERTISEMENT]

5

It may also help you to know how our field editors log the highways. *The MILEPOST®* field editors drive each highway, taking notes on facilities, features and attractions along the way and noting the mile at which they appear. Mileages are measured from the beginning of the highway, which is generally at a junction or the city limits, to the end of the highway, also usually a junction or city limits. Most highways in *The MILEPOST®* are logged either south to north or east to west. If you are traveling the opposite direction of the log, you will read the log back to front.

To determine driving distance between 2 points, simply subtract the first mileage figures. For example, the distance from Crabb's Crossing at **Milepost A 231.3** to the park entrance at **Milepost A 237.3** is 6 miles.

Physical mileposts (usually steel rods with a mileage flag at the top) are found on most highways in Alaska. Kilometreposts are up along most highways in Canada.

Managing Editor, Kris Valencia Graef
Editorial Assistants: Michelle Arab, Heidi Roe
Field Editors and Advertising Representatives: Ardythe Arnold, Earl L. Brown, Lynn Owen, Jerrianne Lowther, Judy Parkin
Production Manager, Jon Flies
Advertising and Production Coordinator, Alexa Peery
Production Supervisor, David Ranta
Page Designer, Pam Smith
Graphic Designer, Sisi Mereness
Advertising Designer, Lillian Newman
Prep Supervisor, George Eccard
Fulfillment Manager, Tina L. Boyle
Associate Publisher, Michele Andrus Dill
Publisher, Geoffrey P. Vernon

ISSN 0361-1361 ISBN 1-878425-28-5
Key title: The Milepost
Printed in U.S.A. on recycled stock.

Vernon Publications Inc.
3000 Northup Way, Suite 200
Bellevue, WA 98004
(206) 827-9900
1-800-726-4707
Fax (206) 822-9372

Publishers of:
The MILEPOST®, ALASKA A to Z
NORTHWEST MILEPOSTS®
The ALASKA WILDERNESS GUIDE
The MILEPOST® Souvenir Logbook

COVER: Matanuska Glacier.
(© Michael DeYoung)
INSET: Sourdough in stream panning for gold. (Courtesy of Alaska State Library, Skinner Foundation, #44-3-15)
Cover Design: David Ranta

Vernon Publications Inc.
Geoffrey P. Vernon, Chairman, President & CEO
Michele Andrus Dill, Vice President
Judy Vernon, Secretary
Fred W. Gallimore, Treasurer
Bill R. Vernon, Chairman Emeritus

Deciding what you want to see and do will help narrow down the choices on what routes to take. Pull out the Plan-A-Trip map for an overview of the North Country and the access routes leading north. Begin a list of places or activities you want to include on your trip. (Remember, you can find specific places by checking the index in the back of the book.) Thumb through the pages of *The MILEPOST®* for photos, advertisements and stories about other wonderful attractions, big and small. Enhance your trip by taking a tour off the beaten path; there are many to choose from.

If you are driving the Alaska Highway, consult 1 of the 2 access routes to the Alaska Highway logged in *The MILEPOST®* and the Alaska Highway section. If you are taking the water route to Alaska, refer to the Marine Access Routes section for cruise ship and ferry information; read the descriptions of communities accessible by ferry in the Inside Passage section; and refer to the Haines Highway and Klondike Highway 2 logs for road connections for ferry travelers. For an overview of the ferry and cruise ship routes, see the maps in the Marine Access Routes section. For a detailed look at the Inside Passage, study the maps on pages 630-634.

Highlights of—and hints about—each method of transportation are discussed in the following pages. Becoming familiar with what's available by highway, by water, by air and by packaged tour will also help you work out an itinerary.

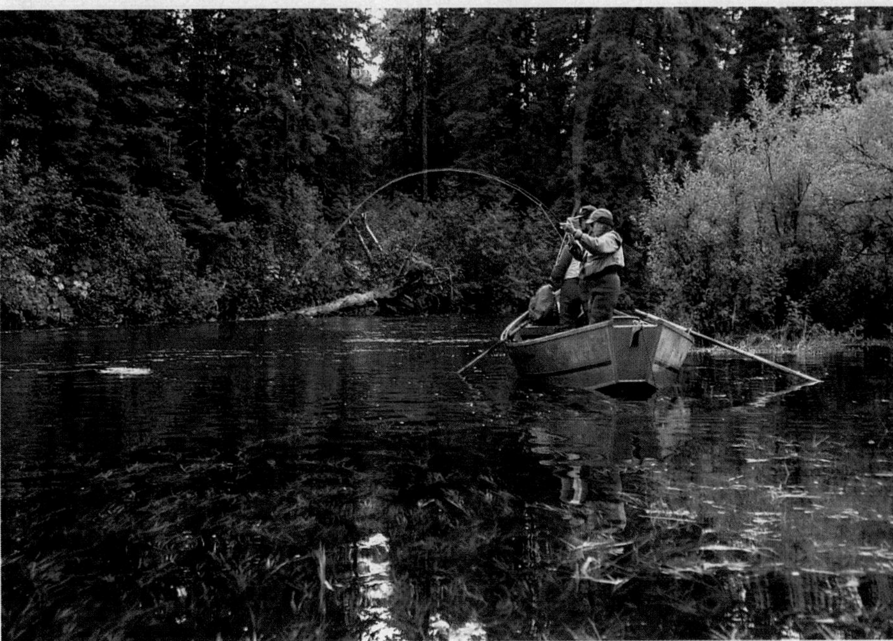

Yakutat's Situk River is a world-renowned fishing spot. (© Michael DeYoung)

By Highway

For highway travelers, *The MILEPOST®* includes mile-by-mile logs and detailed maps of all highways in Alaska and northwestern Canada. The highway logs include campgrounds, businesses offering food, gas, lodging and other services, attractions, fishing spots, and the geography and history of the land. Descriptions of highway communities are included in the highway logs.

The Key to Highways map on page 5 shows you what highways are covered in *The MILEPOST®*. How to Read a Highway Log on page 4 gives a detailed explanation of the highway logging system.

When planning your trip, read the introduction to each highway section for a general description of the road, including type of surfacing, length in miles, travel advisories, special features and history. For a mile-by-mile look at the road, read through the log. Depending on where you want to stop and how much time you have to spend, you can count on driving anywhere from 150 to 500 miles a day! On most roads in the North, you can figure on comfortably driving 250 to 300 miles a day.

Mileages are keyed on the highway strip maps which accompany each highway section. By using the mileage boxes on these maps, you can figure out exact mileages between points. You can also approximate mileages for your trip by referring to the Mileage Chart on the back of the Plan-A-Trip map for mileages between principal points (via most direct route).

To figure approximate gas costs, use the charts under Driving in the General Information section (see page 739). This

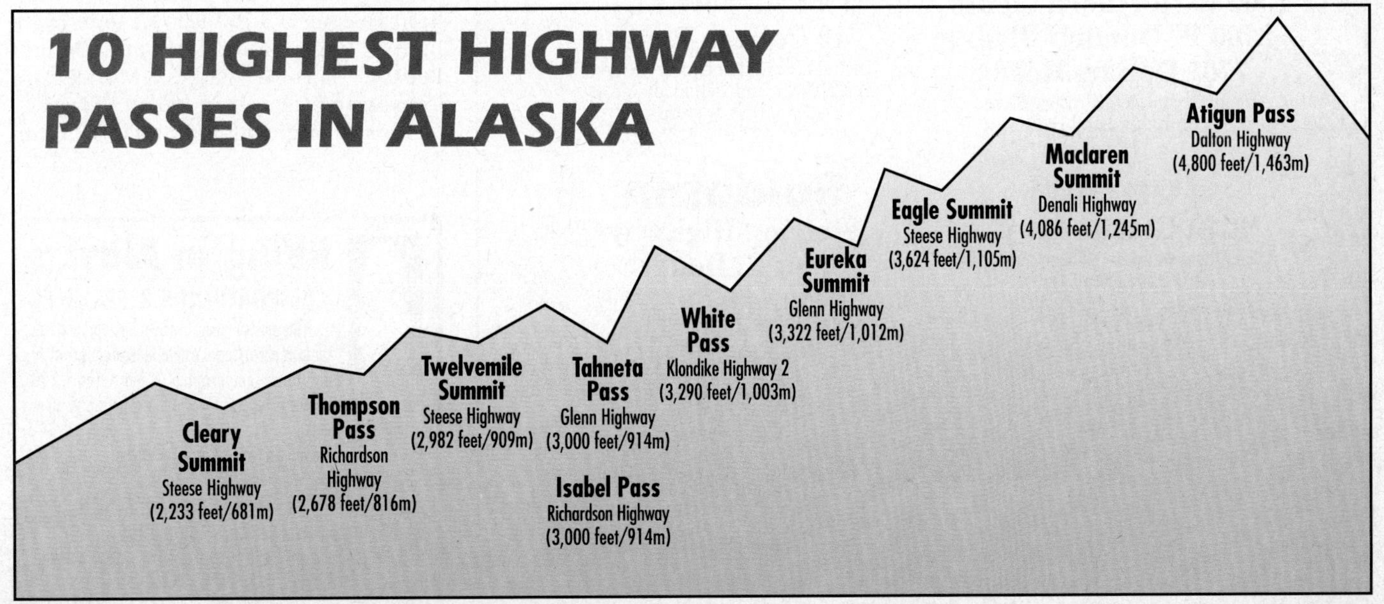

section also has other helpful information on driving in the North.

Finally, to help you plan your trip, following are brief descriptions of each highway covered in *The MILEPOST®*, in order from south to north, and a few of the highlights. Again, for a more detailed look at each highway refer to the individual highway sections.

East Access Route (749 miles/1,205 km) One of 2 access routes to the Alaska Highway included in *The MILEPOST®*, this route leads from Great Falls, MT, through Alberta to Dawson Creek, BC. Highlights: Calgary, Edmonton. *Interstate 15, Alberta Highways 4,3,2,43 and 34.*

West Access Route (817 miles/1,315 km) The other Alaska Highway access route, this one heads from Seattle, WA, to Dawson Creek, BC. Highlights: Fraser and Thompson river canyons, Barkerville side trip. Highest summit is Pine Pass (elev. 3,068 feet/935m). *Interstate 5, Trans-Canada Highway 1, BC Highway 97.*

Hudson's Hope Loop (87 miles/140 km) Popular side trip between West Access Route and the Alaska Highway. Highlights: W.A.C. Bennett Dam, Peace Canyon Dam, Moberly Lake. *BC Highway 29.*

Alaska Highway (1,488 miles/2,395 km) Historic pioneer road from Dawson Creek, BC, to Fairbanks, AK. Asphalt-surfaced and straightened out over the years (the original distance was 1,520 miles/2,446 km). The highest summit is at Summit Lake, elev. 4,240 feet/1,292m. Highlights: Muncho Lake, Watson Lake signforest, Silver City, Whitehorse, Kluane Lake, Kluane National Park, Tanana River pipeline crossing. *BC Highway 97, Yukon Highway 1, Alaska Route 2.*

Yellowhead Highway 16 (906 miles/1,458 km) Transprovincial highway which leads west from Edmonton, AB, across the Canadian Rockies to Prince Rupert, BC, departure point for BC and Alaska ferries. Highest summit is Yellowhead Pass, elev. 3,760 feet/1,146m. Highlights: Jasper National Park, Mount Robson, Fort St. James, Moricetown Canyon and Falls, 'Ksan Indian Village.

Cassiar Highway (456 miles/733 km)

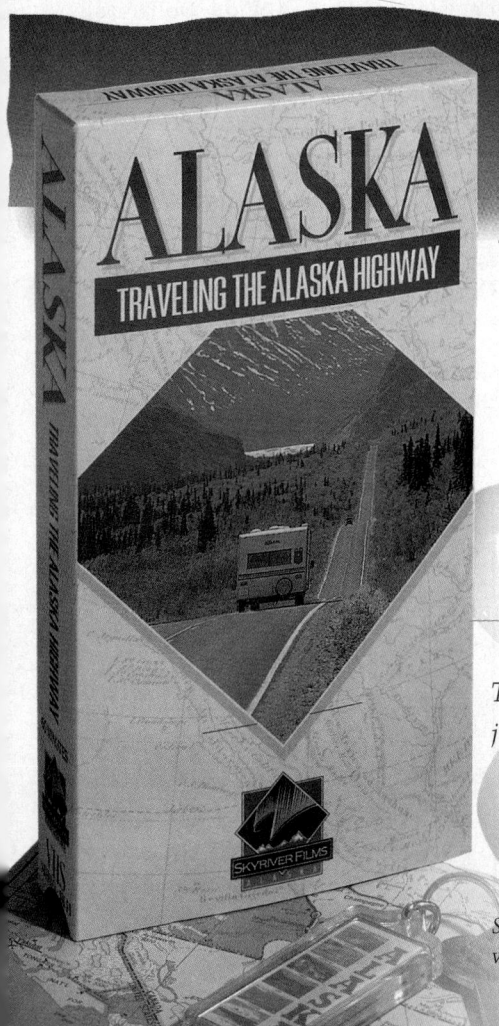

This paved and gravel road—with lots of mountain scenery—connects Yellowhead Highway 16 and the Alaska Highway. Highlights: Stewart, BC/Hyder, AK, Telegraph Creek side trip. *BC Highway 37.*

Northern Woods & Waters Route (490 miles/789 km) Major east-west route from the Alberta–Saskatchewan border to Dawson Creek, BC. Highlights: Oil Sands Interpretive Center in Fort McMurray.

Liard Highway (244 miles/393 km) Gravel highway connecting the Alaska Highway near Fort Nelson, BC, with the Mackenzie Highway in Northwest Territories. Highlights: Fort Liard crafts, flightseeing Nahanni National Park, Liard River and Nahanni Butte views. *BC Highway 77, NWT Highway 7.*

Mackenzie Route (1,330 miles/2,140 km) Umbrella title for the road system of western Northwest Territories, including the Mackenzie Highway and access route in Alberta. More than half the miles are paved and more paving is planned. Includes new 137-mile/221-km road to Wrigley. Highlights: Yellowknife, boat trips from Fort Simpson, Nahanni National Park, Wood Buffalo National Park. *Alberta Highways 43 and 35, NWT Highways 1,2,3,4,5,6.*

Campbell Highway (373 miles/600 km) Gravel wilderness highway in Yukon connects Alaska Highway at Watson Lake with the Klondike Highway near Carmacks. Highlights: Ross River, Faro. *Yukon Highway 4.*

Canol Road (513 miles/826 km) Winding gravel road built during the WWII oil pipeline project. Highlights: Relics from WWII construction days. *Yukon Highway 6.*

Atlin Road (58 miles/93 km) Gravel road connects the Alaska Highway in Yukon with beautiful Atlin, BC. Highlights: Atlin Lake, gold mining. *Yukon/BC Highway 7.*

Tagish Road (34 miles/54 km) Gravel connecting road between Klondike Highway 2 and Atlin Road. Highlights: Marsh and Tagish lakes, fall colors. *Yukon Highway 8.*

Klondike Highway 2 (99 miles/159 km) Paved road connecting Skagway, AK, with the Alaska Highway south of Whitehorse, YT, via White Pass (elev. 3,290 feet/1,003m); also crosses through British Columbia. Highlights: Tormented Valley, Carcross, Emerald Lake.

Haines Highway (152 miles/244 km) Paved road connecting Haines, AK, with the Alaska Highway at Haines Junction, YT, via Chilkat Pass (elev. 3,493 feet/1,065m). Highlights: Eagle viewing on Chilkat River, Million Dollar Falls, Kluane National Park. *Alaska Route 7, BC Highway 4, Yukon Highway 3.*

Klondike Loop (567 miles/912 km) Paved continuation of Klondike Highway 2 from the Alaska Highway north of Whitehorse to the territory's first capital, Dawson City. Connects with gravel Top of the World Highway to Alaska. Highlights: Five Finger Rapids, Yukon River, No. 4 Dredge, Discovery Claim. *Yukon Highways 2 and 9.*

Silver Trail (69 miles/111 km) Gravel side road off the Klondike Loop leads to the mining communities of Mayo, Elsa

and Keno City. Highlights: Keno Mining Museum. *Yukon Highway 11.*

Dempster Highway (456 miles/734 km) All-gravel road leads from the Klondike Loop to the western Arctic community of Inuvik, NWT. Highlights: erosion pillars, "Lost Patrol" gravesite, Igloo Church, Northern arts and crafts. *Yukon Highway 5, NWT Highway 8.*

Taylor Highway (161 miles/259 km) Gravel road from the Alaska Highway to Eagle, AK. Junctions with the Top of the World Highway to Dawson City, YT. Highlights: Chicken, Fortymile River, Jack Wade No. 1 dredge, historic Eagle and Fort Egbert. *Alaska Route 5.*

Glenn Highway (328 miles/528 km) Principal access route from the Alaska Highway at Tok west to Anchorage. Lots of mountain scenery. Access to Wrangell–St. Elias National Park via Nabesna Road. Highlights: Copper River Valley, Lake Louise, Matanuska Glacier, musk-oxen, Independence Mine at Hatcher Pass, Alaska State Fair at Palmer, Chugach State Park, Anchorage. *Alaska Route 1.*

Seward Highway (127 miles/204 km) Very scenic all-weather route connects Anchorage with Seward (site of the Mount Marathon Race and Silver Salmon Derby) on the Kenai Peninsula; accesses Hope Highway. Highlights: Turnagain Arm, Alyeska Resort, Crow Creek Mine, Portage Glacier, Exit Glacier, Kenai Fjords National Park. *Alaska Routes 1 and 9.*

Sterling Highway (143 miles/229 km) Connects the Seward Highway with Homer, AK. The Sterling Highway accesses the Kenai Peninsula's famous fishing spots and canoe trails. Highlights: River rafting, salmon fishing, halibut fishing, Fort Kenay, Russian Orthodox churches, Homer Spit, Gull Island, Seldovia. *Alaska Route 1.*

Copper River Highway (48 miles/77 km) A paved and gravel dead-end road leading from the Prince William Sound community of Cordova through the Copper River Delta. Highlights: Dusky Canada geese, Chugach National Forest recreation areas, Childs Glacier, Million Dollar Bridge. *Alaska Route 10.*

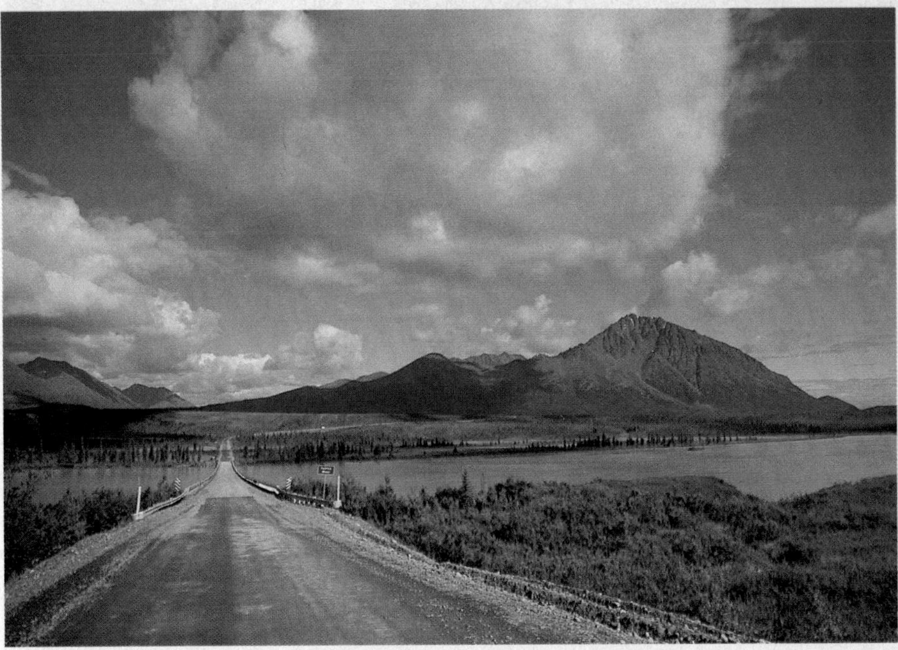

The Denali Highway is a mostly gravel road connecting the Richardson Highway with the George Parks Highway, both of which are paved. (© Doug Wilson)

Richardson Highway (368 miles/592 km) A very scenic paved highway connecting the Prince William Sound community of Valdez (jump-off spot for Columbia Glacier sightseeing trips) with Fairbanks in the Interior. Highlights: Thompson Pass, Worthington Glacier, Copper Center, trans-Alaska pipeline. *Alaska Route 4.*

Edgerton Highway/McCarthy Road (93 miles/150 km) The paved Edgerton

Aerial view of Glacier Bay's Marble Islands and Muir Inlet. (© Michael DeYoung)

Highway leads off the Richardson Highway to Chitina on the Copper River. The gravel McCarthy Road continues east to McCarthy and Kennicott, 2 increasingly popular wilderness spots. Highlights: Liberty Falls, Copper River dip-net fishery, Kennecott Mine. *Alaska Route 10.*

Denali Highway (135 miles/218 km) Mostly gravel highway that connects the Richardson Highway with the George Parks Highway near Denali National Park. This was the original route to the park. Lots of mountain scenery as it travels along the southern flank of the Alaska Range. Second highest highway pass in Alaska. Highlights: Grayling fishing, bird watching, Tangle Lakes. *Alaska Route 8.*

George Parks Highway (323 miles/520 km) Busy all-weather route connecting Anchorage with Denali National Park and Fairbanks. Highlights: Iditarod Headquarters, museums (pioneer, transportation, sled dogs), Big Lake, Nancy Lake, Talkeetna, Denali National Park, Alaska Veterans Memorial, Nenana, Ester gold camp, Fairbanks. *Alaska Route 3.*

Steese Highway (162 miles/261 km) Paved and gravel road from Fairbanks to Circle city on the Yukon River. Great scenery; accesses Chena Hot Springs Road and Circle Hot Springs Road. Has 3 of the highest highway passes in the state. Highlights: Gold Dredge No. 8, Chena Hot Springs, Circle Hot Springs, Davidson Ditch. *Alaska Route 6.*

Elliott Highway (152 miles/245 km) Gravel road from the Steese Highway junction to Manley Hot Springs. Highlights: Little Eldorado Gold Mine, Minto Flats, Manley. *Alaska Route 2.*

Dalton Highway (414 miles/666 km) Gravel road from the Elliott Highway junction to Deadhorse; crests the Brooks Range at Atigun Pass (highest highway pass in the state). Can be dusty, limited services. This former haul road for Prudhoe Bay oil companies is open to the public to Deadhorse. Highlights: Trans-Alaska pipeline, Arctic Circle crossing, caribou herds. *Alaska Route 11.*

By Air

Slightly more than half of all visitors to Alaska arrive by air. Air travel is also one of the most common forms of transportation in the North. You can fly just about anywhere. If there is no scheduled service, you can charter a plane. A list of scheduled air operators to and within the North, a map of air mileages between major points in Alaska, and a chart of flight times between selected cities are included in the General Information section (see page 739). Also read the information on air transportation in each community description in *The MILEPOST®*.

Travelers flying into one of Alaska's hub cities can rent a car or motorhome, join a packaged land tour, or just keep flying. Check the advertisements in the communities and along the highways throughout *The MILEPOST®* for airlines and charter services offering something to meet every interest or need: an afternoon of flightseeing, drop-off and pickup at a remote river, a day tour to Barrow, or an overnight to Kotzebue or Nome. (Also check the advertisements in Anchorage, Fairbanks, Whitehorse and other major cities for rental car agencies and motorhome rentals. In planning your trip, keep in mind that renting a vehicle in Canada and dropping it off in Alaska is prohibitively expensive. Drop-off charges within Alaska can also increase costs significantly. Be sure to inquire if there are any restrictions on roads that can be driven; some car rental agencies will not rent passenger cars for traveling the Dalton Highway, for example.)

Highway logs in Alaska and northwestern Canada also include information on airstrips for private pilots.

By Water

Travel to and within Alaska by water is described in *The MILEPOST®* in the Marine Access Routes section. Major water carriers are the Alaska State ferries, BC Ferries and cruise ships. Descriptions of each—ports-of-call, schedules and fares—are covered in detail, starting on page 605.

Both ferries and cruise ships use the Inside Passage to Alaska, and each offers a uniquely different experience. Which method to use—ferry or cruise ship—is a personal preference. More than 25 percent of the visitors arriving in Alaska arrive by cruise ship. If you know you like cruising, read through the list of cruise ships on page 628 to get a general idea of the itineraries available. You'll need to work with a travel agent or contact the cruise line for more details on cruise itineraries, land tour options and add-ons, airfares from gateway cities, deck plans and cruise pricing.

There is great variety in the cruise options available (see also By Packaged Tour this section). You can cruise the entire length of the Inside Passage plus cruise across the Gulf of Alaska to Prince William Sound, or cruise just part of the Inside Passage. You can sail on large cruise ships that carry a thousand passengers or more, or go on 90-passenger yachts. You can stay on the cruise ship for the entire trip or cruise one way and fly the other.

A tour bus stops for photos of Worthington Glacier on the Richardson Highway.
(© Bruce M. Herman)

There is a cruise to suit every taste.

The Alaska Marine Highway through the Inside Passage is the transportation choice of many independent travelers to Alaska, especially those with vehicles. Travelers may embark at either Bellingham, WA, or Prince Rupert, BC, and connect with the Alaska Highway from either Skagway, AK, via Klondike Highway 2, or Haines, AK, via the Haines Highway. If you get off at Skagway, it is 507 miles/815 km to Tok, AK, and you will drive through Whitehorse, YT. If you get off at Haines, it is 449 miles/722 km from Haines to Tok. (From Tok, it is 206 miles/331 km to Fairbanks, or 328 miles/528 km to Anchorage.)

Bellingham, WA, is about a 1½-hour drive north of Seattle. If you are traveling without a vehicle, train and bus service to Bellingham's Fairhaven Station is available from Seattle. Prince Rupert is served by BC Ferries out of Port Hardy, on the tip of Vancouver Island, and is also accessible via the Yellowhead Highway 16 from Prince George. It is approximately 1,033 miles/1,662 driving miles from Seattle, WA, to Prince Rupert, BC.

Alaska's ferry system also provides transportation to communities in the Southcentral and Southwest regions of the state. If you wish to visit Cordova, Kodiak or Seldovia, for example, you'll need to take a ferry (unless you fly). These systems are described in detail in the Marine Access Route section.

Familiarize yourself with the sights of the Inside Passage by reading the descriptions of communities in southeastern Alaska (beginning on page 629).

Probably the most important part of planning your trip by water is making reservations as soon as possible. Ferries on the Southeast/Inside Passage marine highway system fill up quickly for the summer. Reservations are also required on the Southcentral and Southwest systems. Reservations are strongly recommended for the BC Ferries between Port Hardy and Prince Rupert.

By Packaged Tour

Tours have become so popular in recent years that tour companies have

(Continues on page 16)

KLONDIKE GOLD RUSH CENTENNIAL 1896–1996 "THE DISCOVERY"

Klondike Gold Rush Centennial celebrations will begin in 1996 in Alaska, Yukon Territory and Seattle, WA, marking the discovery of gold on a small tributary of the Klondike River in Canada in 1896. The Centennial will continue over the next several years, recognizing various anniversaries related to the gold rush and the development of the North, including the formation of Yukon Territory in 1898, the completion of the White Pass & Yukon Route in 1900, and succeeding gold rushes in Alaska at Nome and Fairbanks.

Although gold and the North had drawn prospectors and dreamers throughout the 1800s, it was the Klondike gold rush that captured the imagination of the Western world. It was also the "most concentrated mass movement of American citizens onto Canadian soil in all our history," according to Canadian historian Pierre Berton. And it began on Aug. 16, 1896, when an American, George Washington Carmack, panning for gold on Rabbit Creek, discovered the richest goldfield in the North.

The Klondike Gold Rush

When the steamer *Excelsior* sailed into the port of Seattle in the spring of 1897, the city's newspaper reported that it carried "a ton of gold." In fact there were more than 2 tons aboard. Following George Carmack's gold strike on Rabbit Creek in the Yukon the previous year, several hundred prospectors already in the area had immediately set to work mining. After the spring cleanup, the majority returned to the mainland with suitcases, sacks and every conceivable kind of container stuffed full of gold dust.

The "ton of gold" phrase was wired to newspapers around the world, and soon thousands of people who had never dreamed of prospecting—and knew nothing about the trade—dropped everything and outfitted for the Klondike. Seattle's population nearly doubled that summer as people rushed West; hotels filled, and transportation and supply companies prospered. Even the mayor of Seattle resigned his post and headed north.

Actually reaching the Klondike was far more difficult than most knew. Of the 3 major routes north, the all-water route was considered the easiest by many. For those who had money, it offered what seemed to be a comfortable, though long, steamer journey: 3,000 miles from Seattle to St. Michael, AK, on Alaska's west coast, and 1,700 miles east up the Yukon River to Dawson City. Yet few had expected such difficult waters to navigate as they found on the Yukon River. Of the 1,800 stampeders who chose this route, only 43 reached Dawson City, and of these, 35 had to turn back for lack of supplies. The majority of boats were frozen into the Yukon and had to await the spring breakup.

The 2 major land routes were by the Chilkoot Pass and White Pass. In appearance, the White Pass seemed a less arduous trail over the mountains than the steep Chilkoot. Beginning from Skagway, AK, the first several miles of White Pass were on a good road, wide enough for pack animals, with a gentle upward grade. Following this, however, was a series of narrow climbs on a rocky, switchback path. Eventually the pass would earn the name Dead Horse Trail, for the scores of pack animals which died on the path.

Just north of Skagway, at Dyea, the 33-mile Chilkoot Pass, with forbiddingly steep grades, turned out to be the most expedient route to the goldfields. Some 22,000 men, all loaded with 100-lb. packs, attempted the trail in the fall of 1897. A human chain stretched across the entire length of the pass, and those who paused to rest often were unable to re-enter the line for hours.

Those who did make it across one of the land trails, then had to construct their own boats and navigate 500 miles down the Yukon to Dawson City. The North West Mounted Police, patrolling the border on both mountain passes, enforced the rule that all those heading to the goldfields had to import at least 1 ton of supplies. Most men hired Indian packers at exorbitant rates, while others with less money shuttled bit by bit across the trail, making as many as 30 trips. Many stampeders, though, either lost their goods on the rapids of the Yukon, or abandoned their packs on the difficult journey.

It is estimated that over 100,000 gold seekers left for the Klondike. Almost none made it to Dawson by the first winter of 1897; the few who did arrive faced starvation in the ill-supplied town. Less than half reached Dawson by the fall of 1898, briefly transforming it into a boomtown of 40,000. Only a fraction of those who arrived still had the desire to look for gold, and most returned home. A mere handful of people, excluding those who originally staked Klondike claims in the winter of 1896, made any fortune at all.

Alaska Gold Rushes

The Klondike wasn't the North's first big gold strike, or even its last. There were earlier gold strikes all over Alaska, many of which led to a permanent settlement, others that didn't even leave a ghost town to commemorate the event (see the time line).

Southeast Alaska had its share of gold strikes, and more than its share of gold stampeders, as prospectors journeyed North via the Inside Passage to reach the goldfields at Cassiar, at Sitka, at Juneau and later the Klondike. In 1880, a Sitka mining engineer named George Pilz hired 2 prospectors—Joe Juneau and Richard Harris—to look for gold in Silver Bow Basin, a spot suggested to him by Chief Kowee of the Auk tribe. On Oct. 3, the men struck gold on what they were to call Gold Creek. As gold stampeders followed, a new city sprouted near the

Mining on the beach at Nome. *(Courtesy of Alaska State Library, Skinner Foundation, 44-11-3)*

discovery site, first known as Harrisburgh and later renamed Juneau.

One of the earliest and richest gold mining areas in Alaska was the Fortymile River country near the Canadian border. The Fortymile River, a tributary of the Yukon River, was named by prospectors because it was 40 miles below the former Hudson's Bay post of Fort Reliance. Gold was discovered here on Sept. 7,1886, by a prospector named Howard Franklin, who worked the river bars of the Fortymile and a small tributary stream that was later named for him. The resulting rush created a number of long-gone mining camps. Prospectors filed claims in both Canada and Alaska because of uncertainties about the location of the international boundary.

In 1893, gold was discovered on Birch Creek in the Yukon–Tanana Highlands northwest of the Fortymile Mining District. Nearby Circle, a mining supply town first established in 1887 by L.N. McQuesten as a trading post, boomed as prospectors poured into area.

With each new gold strike, boom towns and ghost towns were created, as stampeders left the old strike for the promise of new riches. Gold strikes on the Kenai Peninsula in 1895 created Hope City at the mouth of Resurrection Creek, and a year later nearby Sunrise City, upstream from a gold find at the mouth of Sixmile Creek. A newspaper at the time reported that the Cook Inlet stampede was "almost as great" as the Circle strike. But the settlements prospered only a couple of years. By 1897, with the Klondike gold rush beginning, only 80 people lived in Hope and 150 lived in Sunrise. By 1900, Sunrise had all but disappeared.

Even at the height of the Klondike Gold Rush in 1898, thousands of gold stampeders turned toward Alaska's Bering Sea coast, when news spread of a gold strike on Anvil Creek near Nome. In 1899, an estimated 15,000 prospectors landed in Nome between June and October. That same year gold was found on the beaches of Nome, and by the following year, some 20,000 people were living in Nome, including Wyatt Earp (he opened a saloon). The Discovery Claim on Anvil Creek produced the largest gold nugget ever found in Alaska, weighing 155 troy ounces and measuring 7 inches long, 4 inches wide and 2 inches thick.

In 1901, an entreprenuer named E.T. Barnette landed at the mouth of the Chena River and established a trading post. A year later, on July 22, an Italian immigrant named Felix Pedro found gold on a creek just north of Barnette's trading post. Thanks to Barnette's promotional efforts, as much as the gold discovery itself, there was a stampede to the area and Barnette's trading post became the town of Fairbanks.

Along Today's Gold Rush Trail

While the Klondike Gold Rush was incandescently brief, it left behind a wealth of memorabilia. Dawson City is a must-stop during the centennial celebrations. Parks Canada offers walking tours of the town, the old Palace Grand Theatre, Dredge No. 4, and the Bear Creek historical site. The annual Discovery Days Festival (August 16–19, 1996) will include a dedication of the Discovery Claim Interpretive Site at Bonanza (Rabbit) Creek this year. See the KLONDIKE LOOP section for details on Dawson City and gold rush sites along the Klondike Highway.

Alaska's gold rush history also lies alongside today's highways. The Taylor Highway travels through the historic Fortymile Mining District, passing active mining sites and one of the first bucket-line dredges used in the area. The Steese Highway travels through the still-active Circle Mining District, passing Gold Dredge No. 8, Chatanika Camp and the Davidson Ditch, on its way to Circle City on the Yukon River. Drive down the Seward Highway to visit the tiny town of Hope, Crow Creek Mine and Indian Valley Mine.

Fairbanks celebrates its gold rush heritage with Golden Days (July 8–21, 1996), which includes a Felix Pedro look-alike contest, and the University of Alaska Fairbanks Museum has the state's largest gold display.

The Alaska State Museum in Juneau will have a special exhibit in 1996 commemorating the Alaska–Yukon gold rush. Juneau visitors also may see old mine ruins around the city. A 6-block section of the town of Skagway is a living museum. Designated as part of Klondike Gold Rush National Historical Park, downtown Skagway offers visitors a look at a genuine gold rush boom town. Skagway's Trail of '98 Museum is also a must-stop.

The MILEPOST® includes details on all these attractions and more. Additional features in this edition on the Klondike Gold Rush Centennial may be found on pages 38, 265 and 272. *The MILEPOST®* will continue coverage of the centennial in 1997 and 1998.

GOLD RUSH TIME LINE

1849—Russian gold discovery on the Kenai Peninsula
1870—Gold found at Sumdum Bay, Southeast Alaska
1871—Gold discovered at Indian River near Sitka
1872—Cassiar (BC) district gold discovery near Wrangell
1874—Windam Bay gold strike near Juneau
1880—Joe Juneau and Richard Harris make major gold strike on Gold Creek
1886—Fortymile River gold strike in Alaska
1887—Yakutat beach and Lituya Bay gold discoveries
1893—Birch and Mastodon creeks gold rush; Circle City founded
1895—Sunrise gold rush, Sixmile Creek, Kenai Peninsula
1896—Resurrection Creek gold strike near Hope, AK; George Carmack discovers gold on Rabbit Creek (renamed Bonanza Creek) in the Yukon
1897—Klondike gold reaches the Outside aboard the SS *Excelsior* (to Seattle, WA) and the SS *Portland* (to San Francisco); Klondike gold rush begins
1898—65 stampeders die in Palm Sunday Avalanche on the Chilkoot Trail; construction of the White Pass & Yukon Route Railroad begins in May; Anvil Creek gold discovery, Seward Peninsula, AK; Atlin gold discovery, BC
1899— Beach mining begins in Nome
1900—White Pass & Yukon Route Railroad completed between Skagway, AK, and Whitehorse, YT. Porcupine Mining District gold strike, Haines
1902—Felix Pedro discovers gold on Pedro Creek; leads to founding of Fairbanks
1905—Kantishna Hills gold discovery; Kantishna mining camp established
1906—Chandalar mining camp established
1907—Gold discovered at Ruby; first rush of prospectors to Innoko
1909—Iditarod gold discovery
1911—Town of Ruby established with gold stampede to Long Creek; mining activity on Wiseman Creek leads to establishment of Wiseman
1913—Marshall (also known as Fortuna Ledge) becomes a placer mining camp when gold is discovered on nearby Wilson Creek
1914—Gold discovered at Livengood near Fairbanks

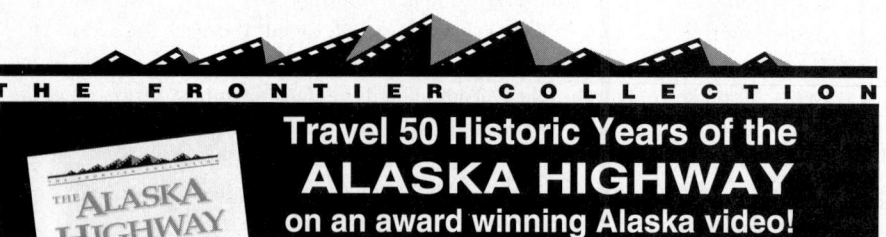

Tour boats out of Seward visit Kenai Fjords National Park. (© Beth Davidow)

(Continued from page 13)
designed packages to meet the requirements of almost anyone. While the packaged tour takes the worry and planning out of arranging for accommodations and transportation, you still have to choose which packaged tour you want.

When planning a trip by packaged tour, decide which areas you wish to see, your preference for mode of travel and what will fit your pocketbook and calendar, then check what the tour companies have to offer. You'll need to carefully read through the tour company brochures for details on itineraries, dates and prices. Brochures are available from travel agents or by contacting the company (see Cruise Ships on page 628).

At the high end of available tours are the 2-week cruisetours, which can cost anywhere from $3,500 (minimum category stateroom, May departure) to a high of almost $6,000 (deluxe stateroom, July departure), per person double-occupancy. Airfare from gateway cities is additional.

Here is just a sampling of what 3 of the major tour companies offer in the cruisetour category.

- Alaska Sightseeing/Cruise West, which specializes in small-ship cruises and land tours, has a 15-day, 14-night cruisetour from Seattle, WA, which includes: 7 days exploring Inside Passage; jet to Fairbanks for sightseeing and stern-wheeler cruise; Alaska Railroad to Denali National Park for wildlife tour; motorcoach to Anchorage for sightseeing; motorcoach to Valdez and board boat for a day of sightseeing Prince William Sound; return to Anchorage via Whittier.
- Princess Tours, which has several large cruise ships, has a 14-day cruisetour from Vancouver, BC, which includes: 8 days cruising the Inside Passage and across Prince William Sound to Seward; motorcoach to Kenai Princess Lodge for 2 nights; motorcoach to Anchorage for sightseeing; board Midnight Sun Express railcar to Denali National Park; overnight at Denali Princess Lodge, tour park; continue by rail to Fairbanks for 2 nights; sightsee Fairbanks, gold camp and pipeline; fly back to Seattle.
- Holland America Westours has a 12-day cruisetour from Vancouver, BC, which includes: 7 days cruising the Inside Passage to Seward via Harriman and Hubbard glaciers; motorcoach to Anchorage for 1 night, city tour; board the McKinley Explorer railcar to Denali National Park; overnight at park, natural history tour; continue by rail to Fairbanks for 2 nights; sightsee Fairbanks and riverboat cruise; fly back to Seattle.

Remember that tours come in all shapes and sizes. Look through the pages of *The MILEPOST®* for advertised tours in the areas you are interested in; there is something for everyone.

By Railroad

Although no railroads connect Alaska or the Yukon with the Lower 48, travel by rail can be combined with other methods of transportation in your itinerary.

If you arrive by ferry or air in Skagway, AK, the White Pass & Yukon Route offers passenger through-service from Skagway to Whitehorse, YT, via rail and motorcoach. Or you can simply enjoy a roundtrip excursion rail trip out of Skagway to White Pass. See the White Pass & Yukon Route section for details.

The Alaska Railroad offers passenger service between Anchorage, Denali Park, Fairbanks and Seward, and shuttle service for passengers and vehicles from the Seward Highway to Whittier, port for Alaska state ferries crossing Prince William Sound. Travelers can easily combine a rail trip with their air or highway itinerary. Rail travel is also included on many packaged tours. See the Alaska Railroad section for details.

Welcome to the North Country

Canoeist enjoys an Alaska sunset from the shore of Byers Lake. (© Michael DeYoung)

The North Country is the land north of 51° 16′ latitude. Geographically, it encompasses Alaska, Yukon Territory, western Northwest Territories, northern British Columbia and Alberta. Following are some facts and figures about each of these areas. *The MILEPOST®* covers this immense region in detail. Read through each of the sections listed on the Contents page for a closer look at the land.

Alaska

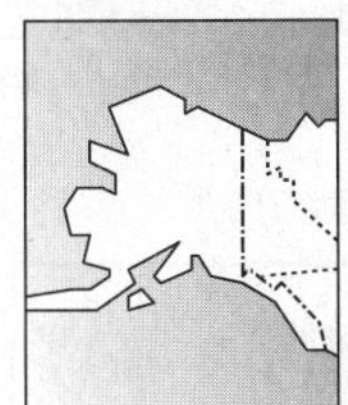

Capital: Juneau
Population: 550,043
Area: 587,878 square miles/ 1,522,596 square km

Alaska became the 49th state on January 3, 1959. It is the largest state in the union in area (twice the size of Texas), but ranks 49th in population, based on the 1990 census. (Only Wyoming has fewer residents.) Approximately 15 percent of the population is Native: Eskimo, Aleut and Indian (Athabascan, Tlingit, Haida, Tsimshian).

Alaska has 17 of the 20 highest mountains in the United States, including the highest peak in North America—Mount McKinley (Denali). Chief industries are fishing, timber, tourism and mining (oil and gas). Geographically, the state falls into roughly 6 distinct natural regions: Southeastern, Southcentral, the Interior, Southwestern, Western and the Brooks Range/Arctic.

Southeastern Alaska is a moist, luxuriantly forested panhandle extending some 500 miles/805 km from Dixon Entrance south of Ketchikan to Icy Bay on the Gulf of Alaska coast. This narrow strip of coast, separated from the mainland and Canada by the Coast Mountains, and the hundreds of islands of the Alexander Archipelago, form the Inside Passage water route used by ships and ferries. Cruise ships bring thousands of passengers through the Inside Passage each summer.

The Southcentral region of Alaska curves 650 miles/1,046 km north and west from the Gulf of Alaska coast to the Alaska Range. This region's tremendous geographic variety includes the Matanuska–Susitna river valleys, the Chugach and Wrangell–St. Elias mountain ranges, the Kenai Peninsula and the glaciers of Prince William Sound. Anchorage, the state's largest city, is the hub of Southcentral.

Interior Alaska lies cradled between the Brooks Range to the north and the Alaska Range to the south, a vast area that drains the Yukon River and its tributaries. It is a climate of extremes, holding both the record high (100°F at Fort Yukon) and the

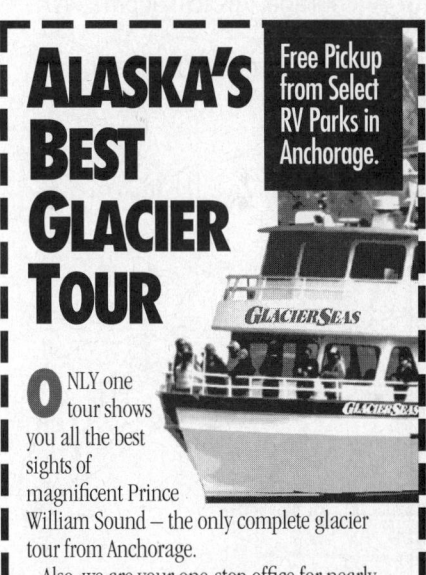

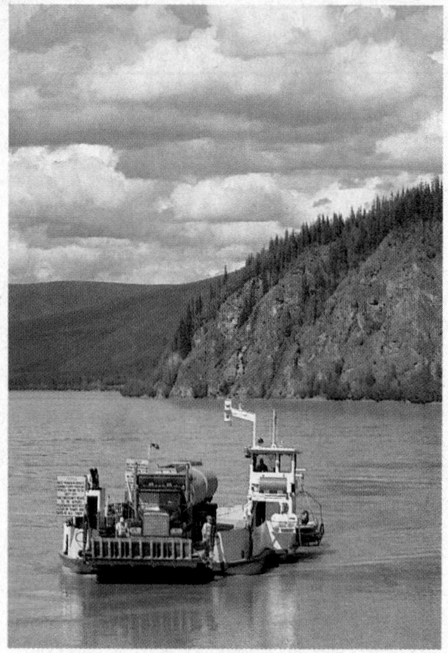

Yukon River ferry at Dawson City, YT.
(© Doug Wilson)

record low (-80°F at Prospect Creek). Fairbanks is the hub of the Interior and a jump-off point for bush communities in both the Interior and Arctic.

Southwestern Alaska takes in Kodiak Island, the Alaska Peninsula and Aleutian Islands. Kodiak, less than an hour's flight from Anchorage and about 10 hours by ferry from Homer, is the largest island in Alaska. Kodiak was Russian Alaska's first capital city. Brown bear viewing is an attraction on Kodiak and at Katmai National Park and Preserve near King Salmon. The Southwest ferry system provides service from Kodiak to Unalaska/Dutch Harbor.

Western Alaska stretches from the head of Bristol Bay north along the Bering Sea coast to the Seward Peninsula near the Arctic Circle. This region extends inland from the coast to encompass the Yukon-Kuskokwim Delta. Nome is perhaps one of the best known destinations in Western Alaska.

Arctic Alaska lies above the Arctic Circle, between the Brooks Range to the south and the Arctic sea coast to the north, and from the Canadian border to the east westward to Kotzebue. Arctic day and overnight trips to destinations such as Kotzebue, Barrow and Prudhoe Bay are popular packages offered out of both Anchorage and Fairbanks.

If you include the Marine Highway, all regions of Alaska are connected by highway with the exception of Western Alaska. And that region's hub cities—Bethel and Nome—are less than 2 hours from Anchorage by air.

Bush travel in all regions of Alaska is covered in detail in our companion guide, *The ALASKA WILDERNESS GUIDE*. For ordering information, see page 11.

Yukon Territory

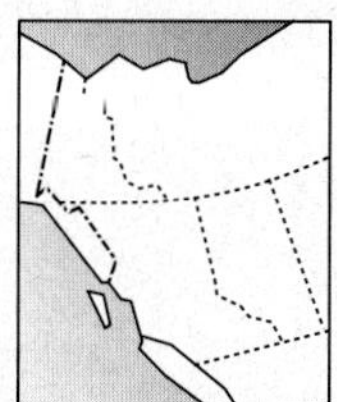

Capital: Whitehorse
Population: 27,797
Area: 186,661 square miles/483,450 square km

Shaped somewhat like a right triangle, Yukon Territory is bordered on the west by Alaska at 141° longitude and on the south by British Columbia at latitude 60°. The northern boundary is the Beaufort Sea in the Arctic Ocean and the eastern boundary is the Mackenzie Mountains that separate Yukon Territory from Northwest Territories.

Yukon Territory is larger than all the New England states combined. Canada's highest peak, Mount Logan (elev. 19,524 feet/5,951m), is located in Yukon's St. Elias Mountains.

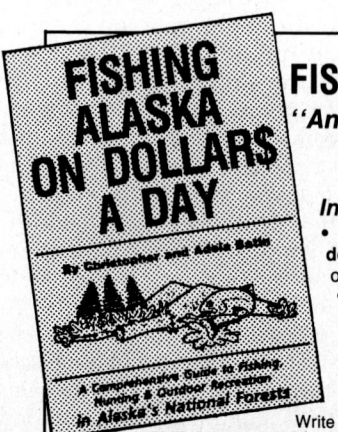

The Yukon was made a district of the Northwest Territories in 1895 and became a separate territory in June of 1898. The territory's first capital was Dawson City, site of the great Klondike gold rush, which brought thousands of gold seekers to the Yukon and Alaska in 1897–98. The

Klondike gold rush begins celebrating its centennial in 1996 (see pages 14–15), marking the discovery of gold on Bonanza Creek on August 16, 1896. At the height of the gold rush, an estimated 40,000 people lived in Dawson City. By 1903, as other gold stampedes drew off much of Dawson's population, the city's boom days were over, although mining continued to support the community for many years. On March 31, 1953, Whitehorse—on the railway and the highway, with a large airport—replaced Dawson City as capital of Yukon Territory.

Today, Yukon's chief industries are mining (zinc, gold, lead, silver) and tourism.

Northwest Territories

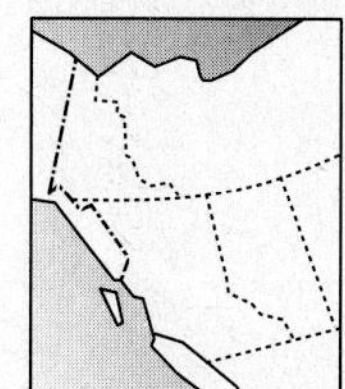

Capital: Yellowknife
Population: 57,649
Area: 1,322,910 square miles/3,426,320 square km

Covering about one-half of Canada, Northwest Territories is nearly twice the size of Alaska with a quarter of the population of Anchorage. A majority of the population is Native: Dene (Indian), Inuit (Eskimo) and Metis (mixed ancestry). There are about 4 people for every 100 square miles. Northwest Territories' Wood Buffalo National Park is the second largest national park in the world.

A major road-building project in the 1960s constructed most of the highway system in western Northwest Territories. (Road improvement continues with paving of the existing gravel roads.) Access to Northwest Territories is from Alberta via the Mackenzie Highway system, from British Columbia via the Liard Highway, and from Yukon Territory via the Dempster Highway.

Chief industries are mining (gold, petroleum, zinc and diamonds), manufacturing and fishing.

On April 1, 1999, Northwest Territories will be divided into 2 territories. Passed by popular vote in 1982 and approved by the Canadian Parliament in 1993, this division will create Nunavut in what will be the former eastern half of Northwest Territories.

British Columbia

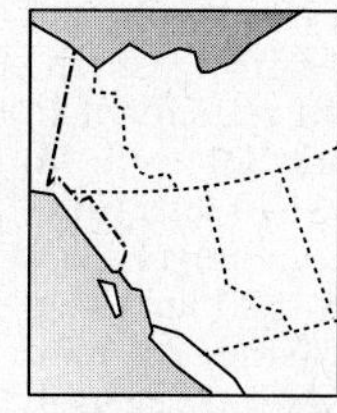

Capital: Victoria
Population: 3,282,061
Area: 365,900 square miles/947,800 square km

Canada's most westerly—and 3rd largest—province, British Columbia stretches 813 miles/1,300 km from its southern border with the United States to the north boundary with Yukon Territory. It is bounded on the east by Alberta and on the west by the Pacific Ocean. The province encompasses the Queen Charlotte Islands and Vancouver Island, site of the capital city of Victoria. Approximately half the province's population resides in the Victoria–Vancouver area.

British Columbia entered the Dominion of Canada on July 20, 1871, as the 6th province. An important region in the early fur trade, expansion of the province came with the 1860s Cariboo gold rush followed by the completion of Canada's first transcontinental railway—the Canadian Pacific. Today, the province has a diverse economy based on agriculture, fishing, forestry, manufacturing, mining and services.

Mile Zero of the Alaska Highway is located in Dawson Creek, BC (not to be confused with Dawson City, YT), in the northeastern corner of the province.

Many small lakes make up the Mackenzie River Delta near Inuvik, NWT. (© Michael DeYoung)

Alberta

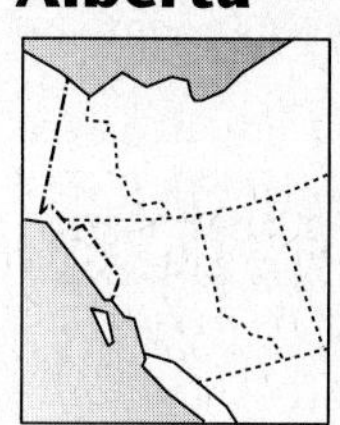

Capital: Edmonton
Population: 2,545,553
Area: 255,287 square miles/661,190 square km

More than half of Alberta's population lives in its 2 largest cities—Calgary and Edmonton. Alberta provides most of Canada's natural gas and some 80 percent of its petroleum. The province also grows more barley and oats than any other province or state, and is a leading producer of beef cattle and rye.

Alberta has both the world's largest shopping center (West Edmonton Mall), and the world's largest Easter egg (at Vegreville), made of aluminum and measuring 26 feet long. Alberta became a province on September 1, 1905.

Alaska Highway via EAST ACCESS ROUTE

Great Falls, Montana, to Dawson Creek, British Columbia via Calgary and Edmonton, Alberta Interstate Highway 15 and Provincial Highways 4, 3, 2, 43 and 34

(See maps, pages 21–22)

The East Access Route is logged in *The MILEPOST®* as one of the 2 major access routes (the other is the West Access Route) to the Alaska Highway.

When the Alaska Highway opened to civilian traffic in 1948, this was the only access route to Dawson Creek, BC, the start of the highway. At that time the route led from Great Falls, MT, through Calgary to Edmonton. From Edmonton, it continued north to Clyde and from there to Athabasca via Highway 2 or Smith via Highway 44. At Triangle, the junction of Highways 2 and 2A (then Highway 34), motorists either headed north to McLennan and Peace River, or south via Valleyview to Grande Prairie, another 110 miles. In late 1955, Highway 43 was completed connecting Edmonton and Valleyview via Whitecourt.

Highways on this route are all paved primary routes, with visitor services readily available along the way. Total driving distance from Great Falls, MT, to Dawson Creek, BC, is approximately 867 miles/ 1394 km.

INTERSTATE HIGHWAY 15

The East Access Route begins in **GREAT FALLS** (pop. 55,097; elev. 3,333 feet/ 1,016m), Montana's second largest city. Head north through northcentral Montana on Interstate 15. From Great Falls to the Canadian border it is 117 miles/188.3 km. *The MILEPOST®* log begins at the Canadian border.

A dinosaur model at the Milk River Information and Interpretive Centre makes a good photo stop. *(Judy Parkin, staff)*

East Access Route Log

HIGHWAY 4

The East Access Route log is divided into 2 sections: Canadian border to Edmonton, and Edmonton to Dawson Creek.

This section of the log shows distance from the Canadian border (CB) followed by distance from Edmonton (E).

CB 0 E 382.2 (615 km) U.S.–Canada border, **COUTTS** border crossing; customs and immigration open 24 hours a day. Food, gas and lodging at border. Duty-free shop.

CB 11.7 (18.9 km) **E 370.5** (596.2 km) Milk River Travel Information and Interpretive Centre; picnic tables, dump station, souvenir shop, ice cream shop and travel information. The large dinosaur model on display here makes a good photo subject.

CB 13 (21 km) **E 369.2** (594.1 km) **MILK RIVER** (pop. 900) has food, gas, stores, lodging and a small public campground (6 informal sites; no hookups). The 8 flags flying over the campground represent 7 countries and the Hudson's Bay Co., all of which once laid claim to the Milk River area. Grain elevators are on the west side of the highway, services are on the east side. ▲

CB 13.5 (21.7 km) **E 368.7** (593.3 km) **Junction** with Secondary Road 501 east to Writing-on-Stone Provincial Park, 26 miles/ 42 km; camping, Indian petroglyphs.

CB 16.3 (26.3 km) **E 365.9** (588.8 km) Stop of interest sign about Milk River Ridge.

CB 24.4 (39.2 km) **E 357.8** (575.8 km) Road west to community of **WARNER** (pop. 434); store, gas, restaurant. Warner is the gateway to Devil's Coulee, where dinosaur eggs and fossilized fish and reptiles were discovered in 1987. Still under excavation, visits to Devil's Coulee are by tour bus only. The tour buses leave the Dinosaur Egg Interpretive Centre in Warner from June to mid-September.

CB 24.6 (39.6 km) **E 357.6** (575.5 km) **Junction** with Highway 36A north to Taber, centre of Alberta's sugar beet industry.

CB 36.8 (59.2 km) **E 345.4** (555.8 km) Small community of New Dayton.

CB 41.5 (66.8 km) **E 340.7** (548.3 km) **Junction** at Craddock elevators with Highway 52 west to Raymond (10 miles/16 km), site of the annual Stampede and Heritage Days; Magrath (20 miles/32 km); Cardston (46 miles/74 km); and Waterton Lakes National Park (74 miles/119 km).

CB 46.1 (74.2 km) **E 336.1** (540.9 km) Small community of Stirling to west; municipal campground with 15 sites, some with power and water, dump station, showers and tennis court. Grain elevators and rail yards alongside highway. Stirling is the oldest best preserved Mormon settlement in Canada and a National Historic Site. ▲

CB 46.6 (75 km) **E 335.6** (540 km) **Junction** with Highway 61 east to Cypress Hills.

CB 57.2 (92.1 km) **E 325** (523 km) Stop of interest sign on west side of road describes how large-scale irrigation began in this area in 1901.

CB 61.1 (98.4 km) **E 321.1** (516.7 km) **LETHBRIDGE** (pop. 63,000), Alberta's third largest city, is located in the heart of South-

EAST ACCESS ROUTE *Great Falls, MT, to Edmonton, AB*

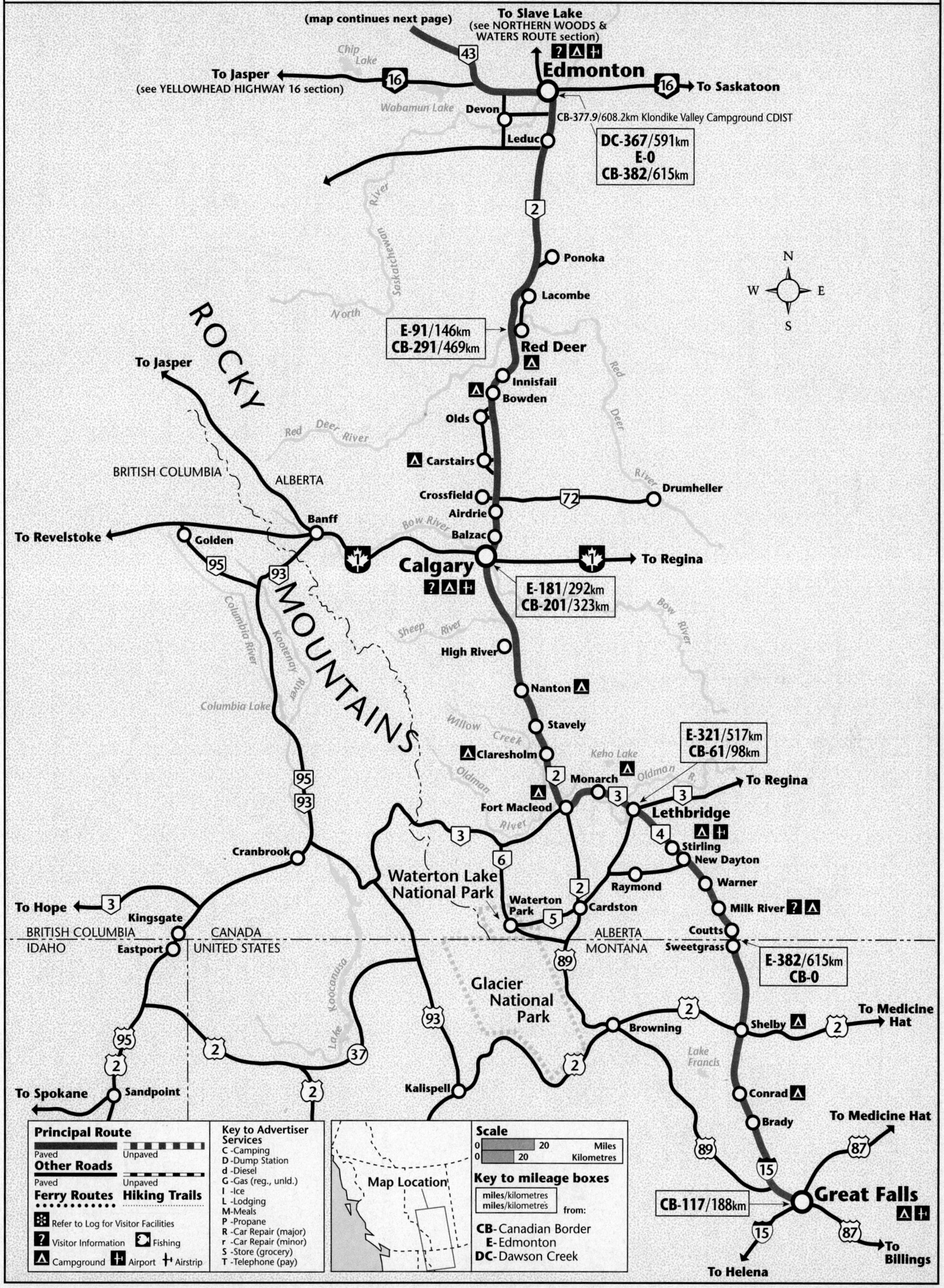

EAST ACCESS ROUTE *Edmonton, AB, to Dawson Creek, BC*

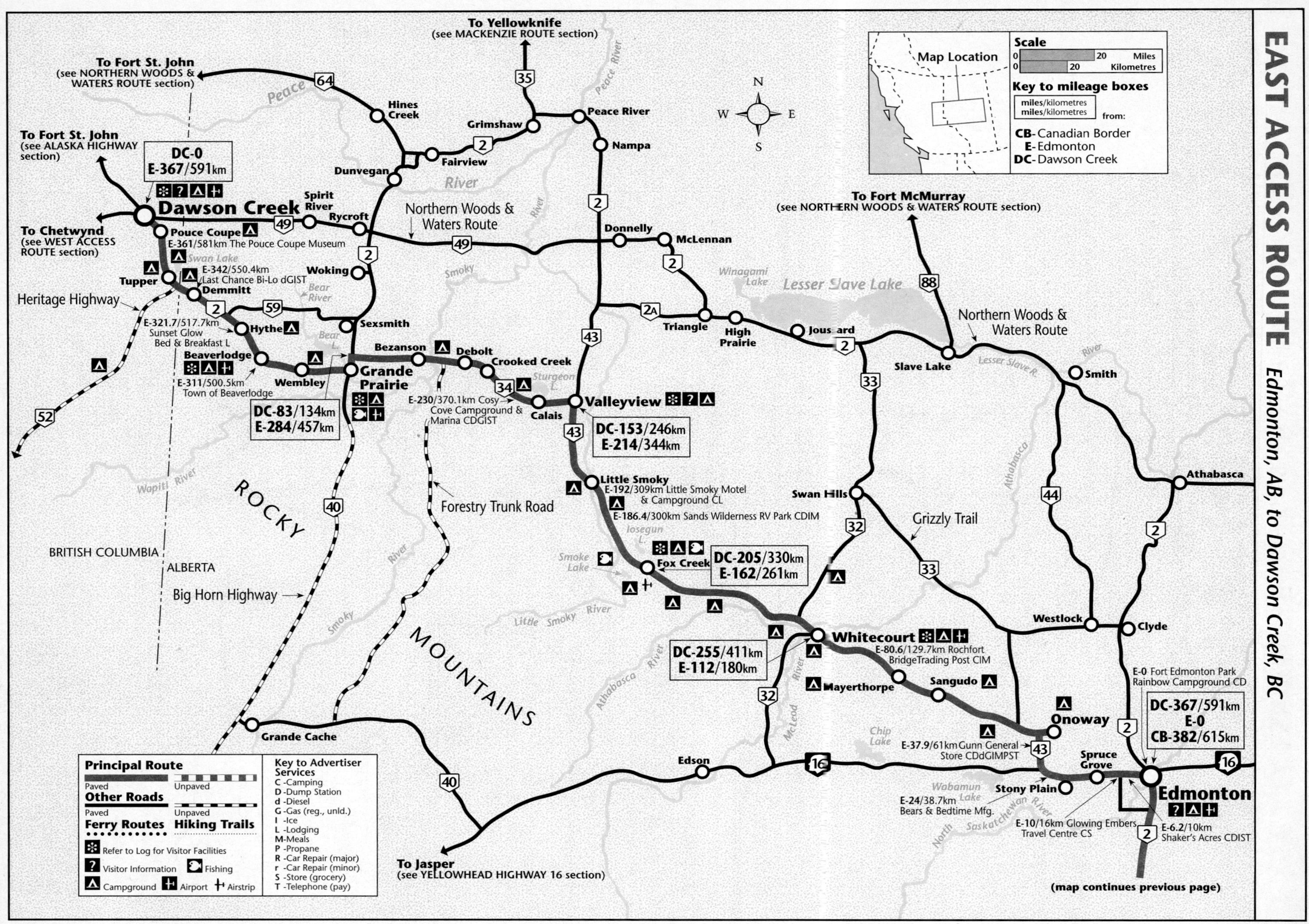

western Alberta. The city has complete facilities, including department stores, shopping malls, a wide choice of restaurants and hotel/motel accommodations. There are 2 campgrounds in Lethbridge and many more in the surrounding area. Watch for the tourist information centres (see **Milepost CB 62.9**). For additional information on Southwestern Alberta, phone 1-800-661-1222. ▲

Private Aircraft: Airport 4 miles/6.4 km southeast; elev. 3,047 feet/929m; length 6,500 feet/1,981m; paved, fuel 80, 100, jet. FSS, customs.

Founded in 1870 on the wealth of nearby coal mines, its economy today is based upon grain, livestock, sugar beets, oil and gas. It is home to Canada's largest agricultural research station. Attractions include Indian Battle Park (exit west on Whoop-up Drive from Highway 4), which contains a replica of Fort Whoop-Up, one of the whiskey-trading posts instrumental in bringing the North West Mounted Police to the West.

Attractions within the city include Nikka Yukko Japanese Gardens, Helen Schuler Coulee Center, High Level Bridge, Fort Whoop-up Interpretive Centre, Sir Alexander Galt Museum and the Southern Alberta Art Gallery.

There are a wealth of attractions located within a short drive from the city. Waterton Lakes National Park in the Rocky Mountains offers spectacular scenery and recreation. Head-Smashed-In Buffalo Jump Interpretive Center, located outside of Fort Macleod (see **Milepost CB 100.4**), is a UNESCO World Heritage Site. Other sites of interest include the Remington Alberta Carriage Center in Cardston and the Alberta Birds of Prey Centre in Coaldale.

CB 62.9 (101.3 km) **E 319.3** (513.8 km) **Junction** with Highway 5 south to Cardston and Waterton Park in Waterton Lakes National Park. Mayor Magrath Drive to east provides access to motels, hotels and Henderson Lake Park. Alberta's Waterton Lakes, and adjoining Glacier National Park in Montana, form Waterton–Glacier International Peace Park. The park offers spectacular mountain and lake scenery.

Chinook County Tourist Information Centre, on the north side of the intersection of Highway 4 and Mayor Magrath Drive, has RV parking, restrooms, picnic shelter, dump station and dumpster; open year-round. Phone (403) 329-6777 or 1-800-661-1222 for information on attractions and facilities in Southwestern Alberta.

CB 66.6 (107.2 km) **E 315.6** (507.9 km) Tourist information centre beside Brewery Gardens.

Highway 4 ends northbound. Route now follows Highway 3 (Crowsnest) west.

HIGHWAY 3

CB 69.5 (111.8 km) **E 312.7** (503.2 km) **Junction** with Highway 25. Access to **Park Lake** Provincial Park (9 miles/14 km north); 53 campsites, swimming, boat launch, fishing, playground.

CB 72 (115.9 km) **E 310.2** (499.2 km) Community of Coalhurst just north of highway; gas station.

CB 73.5 (118.3 km) **E 308.7** (496.8 km) CPR marshalling yards at Kipp.

CB 80.3 (129.2 km) **E 301.9** (485.8 km) **Junction** with Highway 23 north. Continue west on Highway 3 for Fort Macleod.

CB 81.5 (131.2 km) **E 300.7** (483.9 km) Community of Monarch; hotel, gas.

Westbound, the highway enters Oldman River valley. Good view west of the Rockies on a clear day.

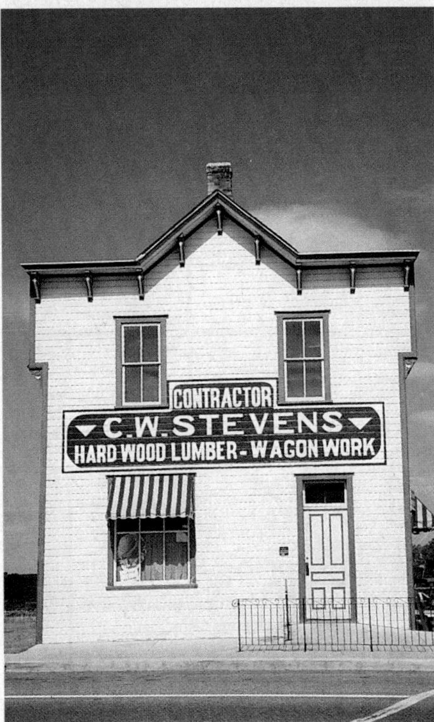

Fort Macleod's downtown area is Alberta's first designated historic site. (Brian Stein)

CB 96.1 (154.7 km) **E 286.1** (460.4 km) **Junction** with Highway 2 south to the U.S. border and access to Waterton Lakes and Glacier national parks.

Highway 3 continues through **FORT MACLEOD** (pop. 3,100; elev. 3,300 feet/1,006m). There are several hotels and motels, restaurants, shopping facilities and gas stations. This community's main street is a designated historic site. The main attraction in Fort Macleod is the Fort Museum, a replica of the original fort built in 1874, the first outpost of the North West Mounted Police (later the RCMP) in western Canada. During July and August, the museum features a local re-creation of the RCMP Musical Ride: Youth in RCMP uniforms execute drills on horseback in a colorful display. The museum is open daily from May to mid-Oct.; open weekdays except holidays mid-Oct. through April.

CB 99 (159.4 km) **E 283.2** (455.8 km) **Junction** with Highway 2 north to Calgary and Edmonton. Highway 3 (Crowsnest) continues west to Hope, BC. Tourist information booth east side of town; open May to Sept. Access to private campground. ▲

HIGHWAY 2

CB 100 (160.8 km) **E 282.2** (454.1 km) **Oldman River** bridge. Alberta government campground to southwest with 10 campsites, dump station, playground, fishing and swimming. North of the river is the largest turkey farm in Alberta.

CB 100.4 (161.6 km) **E 281.8** (453.5 km) Side road leads 10 miles/16 km to Head-Smashed-In Buffalo Jump, a World Heritage Site; open 9 A.M. to 8 P.M., May 15 to Labour Day, 9 A.M. to 5 P.M., the remainder of the year. Closed Mondays, Nov. to March. Admission charged. The interpretive centre is built into the cliff and features displays on seven levels.

CB 111.2 (179 km) **E 271** (436.1 km) Road east to Granum, a small settlement dominated by grain elevators. Recreation park in town with 41 campsites. ▲

CB 116.2 (187 km) **E 266** (428 km) Community of Woodhouse.

CB 121.8 (196 km) **E 260.4** (419.1 km) **CLARESHOLM** (pop. 3,500), a prosperous ranching centre with all visitor facilities. The old railway station houses a museum. Camping at Centennial Park; 15 sites, dump station, playground. ▲

CB 125.9 (202.6 km) **E 256.3** (412.5 km) Stop of interest sign commemorating The Leavings, a stopping place on the Fort Macleod–Calgary trail in 1870.

CB 131.3 (211.3 km) **E 250.9** (403.8 km) Community of Stavely to the east.

CB 132.1 (212.6 km) **E 250.1** (402.5 km) Access road west to **Willow Creek** Provincial Park; 150 campsites, swimming, fishing.

CB 138.4 (222.8 km) **E 243.8** (392.3 km) Small settlement of Parkland.

CB 145.9 (234.8 km) **E 236.3** (380.3 km) Nanton campground (75 sites) at junction with Secondary Road 533, which leads west to Chain Lakes Provincial Park. ▲

CB 146.8 (236.3 km) **E 235.4** (378.8 km) **NANTON** (pop. 1,700); all visitor facilities. Nanton is famous for its springwater, which is piped from Big Spring in the Porcupine Hills, 6 miles/10 km west of town, to a large tap located in town centre. Springwater tap operates mid-May to Sept. WWII Lancaster bomber on display at Centennial Park.

CB 151.1 (243.2 km) **E 231.1** (371.9 km) **Junction** with Highway 2A, which parallels Highway 2 northbound.

CB 162.8 (262 km) **E 219.4** (353.1 km) **Junction** with Highway 23 west to **HIGH RIVER** (pop. 6,600) located on Highway 2A. All visitor facilities. Once the centre of a harness-making industry, High River has elegant sandstone buildings and the Museum of the Highwood (open in summer).

CB 164 (264 km) **E 218.2** (351.1 km) Stop of interest commemorating Spitzee Post, built in 1869.

CB 170 (273.6 km) **E 212.2** (341.5 km) Stop of interest sign about cattle brands.

CB 171.6 (276.1 km) **E 210.6** (338.9 km) **Junction** at Aldersyde with Highways 2A and 7 to Okotoks, Black Diamond and Turner Valley (18.5 miles/30 km). Stop of interest commemorating the Turner Valley oil fields.

CB 173.3 (278.9 km) **E 208.9** (336.2 km) Sheep Creek bridge. **Sheep Creek** Provincial Park has a picnic area, playground, swimming and fishing.

CB 183 (294.5 km) **E 199.2** (320.6 km) Junction with Highway 2A to **OKOTOKS** (5 miles/8 km west), which has a general store, RV repair and a tea room. Near Okotoks is Spruce Meadows Equestrian Center, which hosts the International Horse Show, June to Sept.; phone (403) 974-4200.

CB 184.6 (297.2 km) **E 197.6** (318 km) Gas station to east with diesel and propane.

CB 188.6 (303.5 km) **E 193.6** (311.6 km) Calgary southern city limits. Private RV park to east. ▲

NOTE: To bypass downtown Calgary, exit at Marquis of Lorne Trail and continue to Highway 2 (Deerfoot Trail) north.

CB 196.5 (316.2 km) **E 185.7** (298.8 km) Exit for Glenmore Trail, the southwest bypass route that connects with Trans-Canada Highway 1 west to Banff and Vancouver, BC.

Calgary

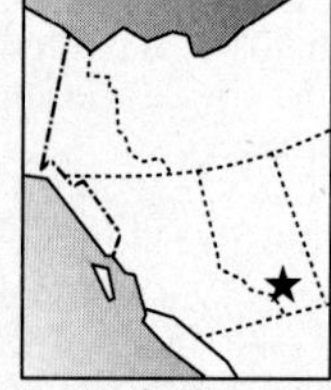

CB 200.8 (323.1 km) **E 181.4** (291.9 km) Located at the confluence of the Bow and Elbow rivers. **Population:** 738,000. **Elevation:** 3,440 feet/1,049m. **Emergency Services:** Phone 911 for emergency services. **Hospitals:** Bow Valley Centre, 841 Centre Ave. NE; Foothills, 1403 29th St. NW; Rockyview, 7007 14th St. SW; Peter Lougheed Center, 3500 26th Ave. NE.

Visitor Information: In the downtown area at the base of Calgary Tower, and at the Calgary Airport; both are open year-round. A visitor centre at Canada Olympic Park is open in summer only. Or call Calgary Convention & Visitors Bureau at (403) 263-8510 or 1-800-661-1678 (toll-free in North America).

Private Aircraft: Calgary International Airport, 4 miles/6.4 km northeast; elev. 3,557 feet/1,084m; 3 runways. See Canadian Flight Supplement.

This bustling city is one of Alberta's 2 major population and business centres. A great influx of homesteaders came to Calgary with the completion of the Canadian Pacific Railway in 1883. It grew as a trading centre for surrounding farms and ranches. Oil and gas discovered south of the city in 1914 contributed to more growth.

Perhaps the city's best-known attraction is the annual Calgary Stampede, which takes place at the Exhibition Grounds, July 5-14, 1996. The 10-day event includes a parade and daily rodeo; phone 1-800-661-1260 for Stampede information and tickets.

Some other major attractions are: Alberta Science Centre, 11th Street and 7th Avenue; the Glenbow Museum, which presents a lively journey into the heritage of the Canadian West, 130 9th Avenue SE; the Eau Claire Market, adjacent to Prince's Island in the downtown area; the Calgary Chinese Cultural Centre, 197 1st St. SW; the Energeum, at the Energy Resources Bldg., 640 5th Ave. SW; Fort Calgary interpretive centre, 750 9th Ave. SE; Calgary Zoo, off Memorial Drive, has a prehistoric park with life-sized replicas of dinosaurs; and Heritage Park, west of 14th Street and Heritage Drive SW, a re-creation of Calgary's pioneer eras. Visitors may recognize the distinctive Saddledome, located at the Exhibition Grounds, which was the site of the 1988 Winter Olympics skating and hockey events. Canada Olympic Park (site of ski jumping, luge and bobsled) is on Trans-Canada Highway 1, west of Sarcee Trail.

Calgary has large shopping malls, department stores, restaurants and many hotels and motels. Most lodging is downtown or on Highway 2 south (Macleod Trail), Trans-Canada Highway 1 north (16th Avenue) and Alternate 1A (Motel Village). There are several campgrounds in and around the city. ▲

East Access Route Log

(continued)

CB 211.3 (340 km) **E 170.9** (275 km) Calgary northern city limits.

Highway 2 from Calgary to Edmonton bypasses most communities. Except for a few service centres built specially for freeway traffic, motorists must exit the freeway for communities and gas, food or lodging.

CB 211.9 (341 km) **E 170.3** (273 km) Exit to community of **BALZAC**. Private RV park with dump station. ▲

CB 217.9 (350.7 km) **E 164.3** (264.4 km) Road west to **AIRDRIE** (pop. 13,000). Visitor facilities include hotels and motels.

CB 225 (362 km) **E 157.2** (253 km) Dickson–Stephensson Stopping House on Old Calgary Trail; rest area, tourist information.

CB 232.2 (373.6 km) **E 150** (241.4 km) **Junction** with Highway 2A west to Crossfield and Highway 72 east to Drumheller, 60 miles/97 km, site of Alberta's Badlands. The Badlands are famous for the dinosaur fossils found there. Fossil displays at world-renowned Tyrrell Museum of Paleontology in Drumheller.

CB 232.6 (374.4 km) **E 149.6** (240.7 km) Stop of interest sign about the buffalo that once darkened the prairies here. Gas and restaurant at turnout.

CB 235.1 (378.3 km) **E 147.1** (236.7 km) Exit to **CROSSFIELD**; gas, hotel, food.

CB 243.1 (391.2 km) **E 139.1** (223.9 km) Exit west for **CARSTAIRS** (pop. 1,725), a farm and service community with tourist information centre and campground. The campground has 28 sites, electric hookups, hot showers and dump station. Services here include groceries, liquor store, banks, a motel, propane and gas stations. ▲

CB 252.7 (406.6 km) **E 129.5** (208.4 km) **Junction** with Highway 27 west to **OLDS** (pop. 4,888); all visitor facilities, museum and information booth.

CB 268.8 (432.5 km) **E 113.4** (182.5 km) **Junction** with highway west to Bowden and Red Lodge Provincial Park (8.5 miles/14 km); 110 campsites, playground, swimming and fishing. **BOWDEN** (pop. 1,000) is the site of a large oil refinery and Alberta Nurseries and Seeds Ltd., a major employer. Most visitor services available. ▲

Heritage rest area with 24 campsites, dump station and tourist information booth at highway junction. ▲

CB 276 (444 km) **E 106.2** (171 km) **Junction** with Highway 54 west to **INNISFAIL** (pop. 5,500); all visitor facilities. South of Innisfail 3 miles/5 km is the RCMP Dog Training Centre, the only one in Canada; open to the public daily year-round from 9 A.M. to 4 P.M.

CB 278.8 (448.7 km) **E 103.4** (166.4 km) Stop of interest sign about explorer Anthony Henday.

CB 285.6 (459.6 km) **E 96.6** (155.4 km) **Junction** with Highway 42 west to Penhold, a service community for the nearby Air Force base.

CB 290 (466.8 km) **E 92.2** (148.3 km) Tourist service area with gas stations and restaurants.

CB 290.5 (467.5 km) **E 91.7** (147.6 km) Tourist information booth.

CB 291.4 (468.9 km) **E 90.8** (146.1 km) **Junction** with Highway 2A east to **RED DEER** (pop. 60,000), in the centre of cattle ranching and grain growing, with a burgeoning oil and gas industry and nearby ethylene plants. All visitor facilities available. Camping at Lions Municipal Campground on Riverside Drive; 62 sites, dump station, laundry, picnic area, playground. ▲

Private Aircraft: Airport 6 miles/9.6 km southwest; elev. 2,968 feet/905m; length 5,528 feet/1,685m; fuel 100, jet. FSS.

CB 298 (479.6 km) **E 84.2** (135.5 km) **Junction** with Highway 11 to Sylvan Lake (10 miles/16 km) and Rocky Mountain House (51 miles/82 km). Sylvan Lake Provincial Park has picnicking and swimming. Private campgrounds and waterslide nearby. ▲

CB 302.5 (486.8 km) **E 80.2** (129.1 km) Access road east to community of **BLACKFALDS** (pop. 1,500). Tourist services and accommodations.

CB 309.1 (497.4 km) **E 73.1** (117.6 km) **Junction** with Highway 12. Exit east for **LACOMBE** (pop. 6,000); all visitor facilities. Camping at Michener Park; 21 sites. Site of the Federal Agricultural Research Station; open to the public weekdays, 8 A.M. to 4:30 P.M.

Exit west on Highway 12 for Aspen Beach Provincial Park at Gull Lake (6 miles/10 km); camping, swimming. ▲

CB 325 (524.7 km) **E 56.2** (90.4 km) **Junction** with Highway 53 east to **PONOKA** (pop. 5,000); all visitor facilities. Camping at Ponoka Stampede Trailer Park, May to Oct. Ponoka's Stampede is held June 29 to July 3 at Stampede Park. ▲

CB 340.7 (548.3 km) **E 41.5** (66.8 km) Northbound-only access to Wetaskiwin rest area with picnic tables and information centre (open May to Sept.); restrooms, gas service and groceries.

CB 345.3 (555.7 km) **E 36.9** (59.4 km) **Junction** of Highway 13 east to Wetaskiwin, site of the Reynolds-Alberta Museum and Aviation Hall of Fame.

CB 356 (572.9 km) **E 26.2** (42.2 km) Turnout to east with litter barrels and pay phone.

CB 366 (589 km) **E 16.2** (26.1 km) Exit for Edmonton bypass route (see NOTE) and access to **LEDUC** (pop. 12,500), founded and named for the Leduc oil well, which blew in on Feb. 13, 1947; all visitor facilities.

NOTE: Northbound motorists wishing to avoid heavy traffic through Edmonton may exit west on Highway 39 for Devon Bypass. Drive 6.8 miles/11 km west on Highway 39, then 20 miles/32 km north on Highway 60 to junction with Yellowhead Highway 16, 10 miles/16 km west of Edmonton (see ***Milepost E 10*** *this section).*

CB 372 (598.6 km) **E 10.2** (16.4 km) **Junction** with Highway 19 west to community of Devon, Devon Bypass and University of Alberta Devonian Botanic Garden, open daily May through Sept., 10 A.M. to 6 P.M. From Devon continue north on Highway 60 to bypass Edmonton and rejoin this route at **Milepost E 10** on Yellowhead Highway 16 west of the city.

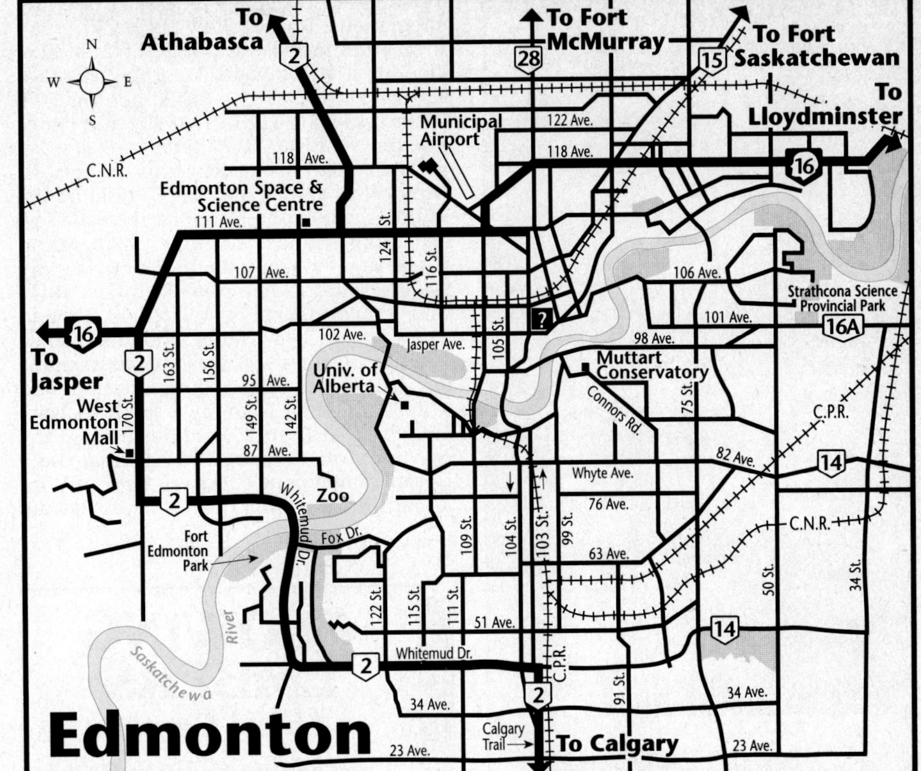

Highway 2 northbound becomes Calgary Trail. Access to Edmonton International Airport.

CB 377.9 (608.2 km) **E 4.3** (6.9 km) Stoplight at Ellerslie (grain elevator). Turn left then immediately south on service road for private campground. ▲

Klondike Valley Campground. See display ad this section. ▲

CB 382.2 (615 km) **E 0 Junction** with Whitemud Drive. Turn east for Highway 16 East, turn west for Highway 16 West (see YELLOWHEAD HIGHWAY 16 section). Continue north for Edmonton city centre (description follows).

Whitemud Drive west continues as Highway 2, crossing the North Saskatchewan River, then turns north to become 170 Street. Access to West Edmonton Mall on 170 Street.

Edmonton

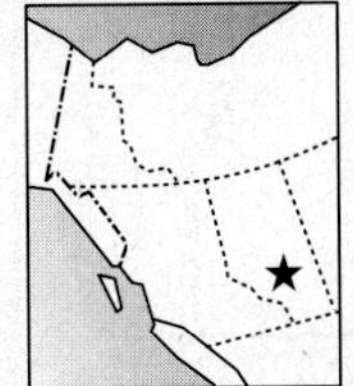

E 0 DC 367 (590.6 km) Capital of Alberta, 1,853 miles/2982 km from Fairbanks, AK. **Population:** 627,000; area 850,000. **Elevation:** 2,182 feet/668m. **Emergency Services:** Phone 911 for all emergency services. **Hospitals:** Grey Nun's, 34th Avenue and 66th Street; Misericordia, 16940 87th Ave.; Royal Alexandra, 10240 Kingsway Ave.; University, 84th Avenue and 112th Street.

Visitor Information: Edmonton Tourism operates visitor information centres downtown and on Highway 2 south. Or write Edmonton Tourism, Dept. MI 96, 9797 Jasper Ave. #104, Edmonton, AB T5J 1N9; phone (403) 496-8400 or 1-800-463-4667 for information.

Private Aircraft: Edmonton International Airport 14 miles/22.5 km southwest and Edmonton Municipal north side of downtown. See Canadian Flight Supplement.

The North Saskatchewan River winds through the centre of Edmonton, its banks lined with public parks. Major attractions include the Edmonton Space & Science Centre, Muttart Conservatory, Alberta Legislature Building, the Provincial Museum of Alberta and Fort Edmonton Park.

A reconstruction of the Hudson's Bay Company headquarters, Fort Edmonton Park features 12 buildings inside the fort walls with costumed historical interpreters. The original fort was established in 1795 as part of the westward expansion of the fur trade, and by 1846 its main function was to prepare the pemmican and build the York boats necessary to make the journey to York Factory on the Hudson Bay to bring out furs and return with trade goods each summer. Contact Fort Edmonton Park, Box 2359, Edmonton, AB T5J 2R7; phone (403) 496-8787.

Also on the list of major attractions for visitors to Edmonton is the world's largest shopping mall—West Edmonton Mall. The mall features some 800 stores and services, a waterpark, ice arena, aquariums, aviaries and some 90 eating establishments. Located on 87 Avenue at 170 Street, the shopping mall is open 7 days a week.

Known as Canada's festival city, Edmonton hosts a number of events throughout the year. These include: Northern Alberta

Children's Festival (May-June TBA); Jazz City International Festival (June 28–July 7, 1996); Street Performers Festival (July 12–21, 1996); Klondike Days (July 18–27, 1996); Heritage Festival (Aug. 3–5, 1996); Edmonton Folk Music Festival (Aug. 8–11, 1996); and Fringe Theatre Event (Aug. 16–25, 1996).

There are 80 hotels and motels in Edmonton and some 2,000 restaurants. Within the Edmonton vicinity there are several campgrounds. Rainbow Campground has 85 sites, hookups, dump station, laundry facilities and showers; from Highway 2 drive west 2 miles/3.2 km on Whitemud Drive to 119 Street and 45 Avenue. Klondike Valley Campground has 155 sites, hookups, showers, laundry facilities, dump station and store. Located on Highway 2 south (Calgary Trail), west at Ellerslie Road. Just west of the city limits off Highway 16 West there are 2 private campgrounds: Shakers Acres, at Winterburn Road, with 177 sites; and Glowing Embers, at the Devon Overpass, with 273 sites and all facilities. ▲

Fort Edmonton Park. See display ad this section.

Rainbow Campground. See display ad this section. ▲

East Access Route Log

(continued)

HIGHWAY 16 WEST

This section of the log shows distance from Edmonton (E) followed by distance from Dawson Creek (DC).

E 0 DC 367 (590.6 km) Downtown Edmonton. Take Jasper Avenue westbound (becomes 16A then Yellowhead 16 at city limits).

E 6.2 (10 km) **DC 360.8** (580.6 km) Exit 215 Street/Winterburn Road. Access to private campground. ▲

Shakers Acres Campground. See display ad this section. ▲

E 10 (16 km) **DC 357** (574.5 km) **Junction** of Highways 16 West and 60 (Devon Overpass); access to private campground. ▲

Glowing Embers Travel Centre. See display ad this section. ▲

NOTE: Southbound travelers may bypass Edmonton by taking Highway 60 south, then either Highway 19 or 39 east to Highway 2.

E 18 (29 km) **DC 349** (561.6 km) SPRUCE GROVE (pop. 13,076). All visitor facilities including motels, restaurants, gas and service stations, grocery stores, farmer's market, shopping malls and all emergency services. Recreational facilities include a golf course, swimming pool, skating and curling

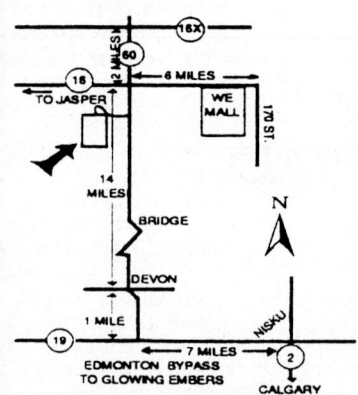

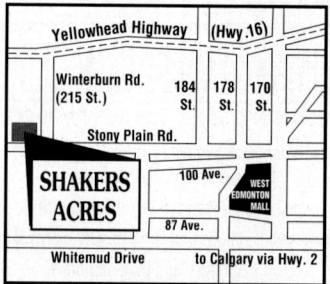

rinks, parks and extensive walking and cycling trails. The chamber of commerce tourist information booth, located on Highway 16, is open year-round; phone (403) 962-2561.

E **24** (38.7 km) **DC 345** (555.2 km) **STONY PLAIN** (pop. 7,405). All visitor facilities including hotels, restaurants, supermarkets, shopping mall and gas stations with major repair service; RCMP and hospital; outdoor swimming pool, tennis courts and 18-hole golf course. The Multicultural Heritage Centre here has historical archives, a craft shop and home-cooked meals. Other attractions include 16 outdoor murals; Oppertshauser Art Gallery; the Andrew Wolf Winery; and the Pioneer Museum at Exhibition Park. Visitor information centre at Rotary Park rest area. Camping at Lions RV Park and Campground; 26 sites. ▲

E **25.6** (41.2 km) **DC 341.4** (549.4 km) Edmonton Beach turnoff to south; campground. ▲

E **26.1** (42 km) **DC 340.9** (548.6 km) Hubbles Lake turnoff to north.

E **27.2** (43.8 km) **DC 339.8** (546.8 km) Restaurant, gas station and store to north.

E **27.7** (44.6 km) **DC 339.3** (546 km) Andrew Wolf Wine Cellars; visitors welcome.

E **28** (45 km) **DC 334** (545.6 km) Multicultural Heritage Centre, a regional museum, with restaurant and crafts shop. Open daily.

E **31** (49.9 km) **DC 336** (540.7 km) **Junction** of Yellowhead Highway 16 and Highway 43. Turn north onto Highway 43. (If you are continuing west on Yellowhead Highway 16 for Prince George or Prince Rupert, BC, turn to the YELLOWHEAD HIGHWAY section.)

HIGHWAY 43

E **36.9** (59.4 km) **DC 330.1** (531.2 km) **Junction** of Highways 43 and 33 (Grizzly Trail). The Grizzly Trail junctions with Highway 2; see NORTHERN WOODS & WATERS ROUTE section. Continue on Highway 43.

E **37.3** (60 km) **DC 329.7** (530.6 km) Turnout to east with litter barrel and historical information sign about construction of the Alaska Highway.

E **37.9** (61 km) **DC 329.1** (529.6 km) **Gunn General Store and Campground**. See display ad this section. ▲

E **38.7** (62.3 km) **DC 328.3** (528.3 km) Gas station to east.

E **39.2** (63.1 km) **DC 327.8** (527.5 km) Highway 633 west to Alberta Beach Recreation Area on Lac Ste. Anne. Facilities include a municipal campground (open May 15 to Sept. 15) with 115 sites. ▲

E **41.6** (66.9 km) **DC 325.4** (523.7 km) **ONOWAY** (pop. 671) has a medical clinic, dentist and veterinary clinic. Other services include gas, propane, banks and bank machine, grocery stores, laundromat, restaurants, motel, car wash, post office, pharmacy, RV park with hookups and dump station. Information booth and Elks campground with 8 sites. ▲

Highway 43, completed in 1955, is known as the Flag Route to Alaska.

(Earl L. Brown, staff)

E **45.4** (73.2 km) **DC 321.5** (517.4 km) Alberta government campground with dump station, water, toilets and stoves. ▲

E **45.9** (73.9 km) **DC 321.1** (516.7 km) Restaurant and gas station.

E **48** (77.2 km) **DC 318.9** (513.2 km) **Lessard Lake** county campground; water, stoves, boat launch, fishing for pike and perch. Golf course to west. ▲

E **63.7** (102.5 km) **DC 303.3** (488.1 km) Gas station.

E **72** (115.8 km) **DC 295** (474.8 km) **SANGUDO** (pop. 405) is on a 0.3-mile/0.4-km side road. Restaurants, motel and hotel accommodations; gas station with garage open 7 days a week; grocery, clothing and liquor stores; antique shop; banks, post office, pharmacy, laundromat and car wash. Oval race car track with racing in summer; shale baseball diamonds; elk farm tours. A public campground with 14 sites, showers and flush toilets, is located at the sportsground. ▲

E **74.4** (119.7 km) **DC 292.6** (470.9 km) Pembina River bridge.

E **75.4** (121.3 km) **DC 291.6** (469.3 km) Gas station and restaurant to south.

E **79.5** (128 km) **DC 287.5** (462.7 km) Second longest wooden railway trestle in the world crosses highway and Paddle River. The C.N.R. Rochfort Bridge trestle is 2,414 feet/736m long and was originally built in 1914.

E **80.6** (129.7 km) **DC 286.4** (460.9 km) **ROCHFORT BRIDGE.** Trading post (open daily, year-round) with gas, convenience store, gift shop, restaurant and Lac St. Anne Pioneer Museum. Camping. ▲

E **83.1** (133.7 km) **DC 283.9** (456.1 km) Paved turnouts with litter barrels both sides of highway.

E **85** (136.8 km) **DC 282** (453.8 km) **MAYERTHORPE** (pop. 1,615). One mile/1.6 km from the highway on a paved access road. Hotel, motel, restaurant, grocery store, gas stations with repair service, car wash, hospital, laundromat, post office, RCMP and banks. A public campground with 30 sites (no hookups, pit toilets) and 9-hole golf course are located 1 mile/1.6 km south of town. Airstrip located 2 miles/3.2 km southwest of town; no services. (Most northbound air travelers use Whitecourt airport, which has fuel.) ▲

E **87** (140 km) **DC 280** (450.6 km) Gas station and restaurant at junction with Highway 658 north to Goose Lake.

E **109** (175.4 km) **DC 258** (415.2 km) Lions Club Campground; 74 sites, flush toilets, showers, water, tables and firepits. Fee charged. ▲

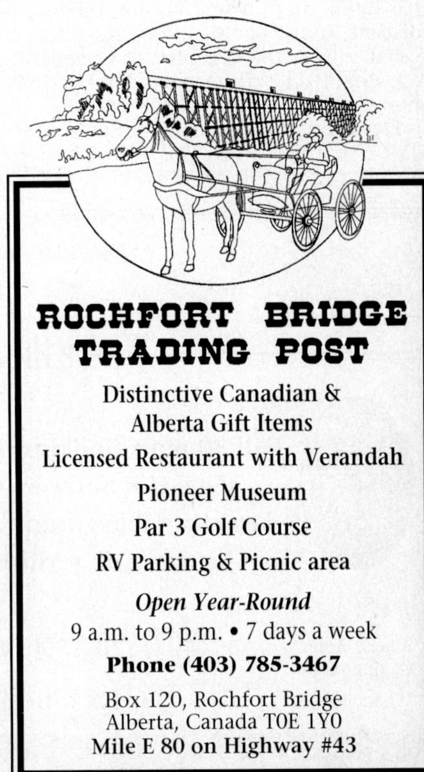

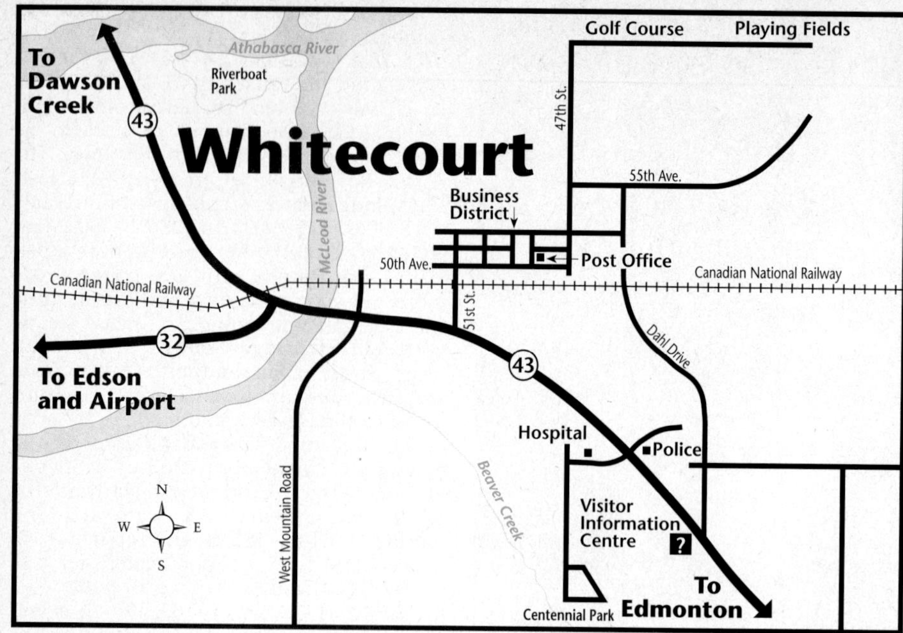

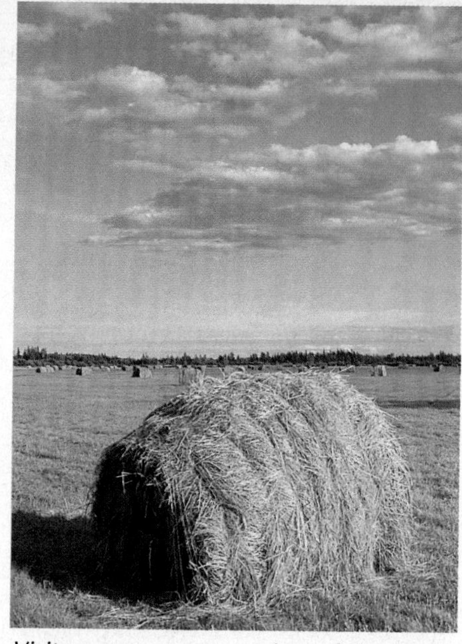
Visitors may note a variety of sizes and shapes of hay bales on the Canadian prairies. (Judy Parkin, staff)

Whitecourt

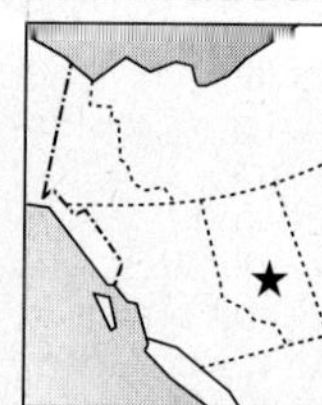

E 111.8 (179.9 km) DC 255.2 (410.7 km). Located two hours from Edmonton. **Population:** 7,100. **Emergency Services: Police,** phone (403) 778-5454. **Fire Department,** phone (403) 778-2311. **Hospital** located on Hilltop, phone (403) 778-2285. Ambulance service available.

Visitor Information: Tourist information booth on Highway 43 west at the traffic lights. The helpful staff will assist with travel plans and directions to Whitecourt sights and activities. The booth is fully stocked with pamphlets and brochures. Open daily, 9 A.M. to 7 P.M., May 1 to Sept. 1; weekdays only, 9 A.M. to 5 P.M., Sept. through April. Free dump station and freshwater fill-up adjacent tourist booth. Information is also available from the Chamber of Commerce, P.O. Box 1011, Whitecourt, AB T7S 1N9; phone (403) 778-5363, fax 778-2351..

Elevation: 2,567 feet/782m. **Radio:** 1400 CJYR-AM, 107.5 SKUA-FM. **Television:** 10 channels. **Newspaper:** *Whitecourt Star* (weekly); *Whitecourt Advertiser* (biweekly).

Private Aircraft: Airport 4 miles/6.4 km south on Highway 32; elev. 2,567 feet/782m; length 5,800 feet/1,768m; paved; fuel 80, 100, jet (24-hour, self-serve). Aircraft maintenance, 24-hour flight service station, all-weather facility.

Transportation: Air–Local charter air service available; helicopter and fixed-wing aircraft. **Bus**–Greyhound service to Edmonton, Grande Prairie, Peace River and points north.

Located at the junction of Highways 43 and 32, Whitecourt dubs itself the "Gateway to the Alaska Highway and the fabulous North." Established as a small trading, trapping and forestry centre, Whitecourt became an important stop for Alaska Highway travelers when a 106-mile section of Highway 43 connecting Whitecourt and Valleyview was completed in October 1955. This new route was 72 miles shorter than the old Edmonton to Dawson Creek route via Slave Lake.

Several major forest industries operating in and around Whitecourt offer tours. Visitors may observe state-of-the-art technologies at sawmills, medium density fiberboard production, and pulp and paper manufacturing plants. Check with the tourist information booth or chamber of commerce for tour times.

The Eric S. Huestis Demonstration Forest, northwest of town on Highway 32 (see **Milepost E 117.1**), has 4.3 miles/7 km of self-guided trails with interpretive sites and information signs describing forest manage-

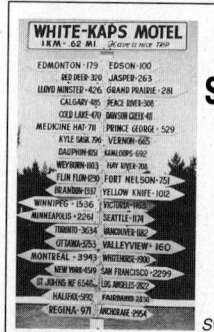

WHITECOURT ADVERTISERS

CJ's Liquor ....Mountain Shopping Strip
Fas Gas & am pm...............................Hwy. 43
McDonald's ....Hwy. 43
Renford Inn.......................Ph. (403) 778-3133
Robin's Donuts...................................Hwy. 43
Sagitawah Tourist Park.....Ph. (403) 778-3734
Tags Food & Gas/A&W ....3711 Highway St.
White-Kaps Motel & RV Parking.....Next to Hilltop Shopping Center
Whitecourt Dairy Queen ....At the Stoplights
Whitecourt Lions Club Campground...............................Hwy. 43

ment techniques and the forest life-cycle; phone (403) 778-7165.

Recreational activities include an excellent 18-hole public golf course and fishing in area creeks, rivers and lakes (boat rentals at Carson–Pegasus Provincial Park). Swimming, rollerskating, tennis and gold panning are also enjoyed in summer. Other attractions available: an exotic animal farm; a guest ranch with arts and crafts; horseback riding; and river boating. In the fall, big game hunting is very popular. During the winter there is ice fishing, snowmobiling and cross-country skiing on area trails, downhill skiing at a local facility, skating and curling, bowling, and swimming at the indoor pool.

There are 14 hotels/motels, 29 restaurants, 14 gas stations, several laundromats, 2 malls, 6 liquor stores and 5 banks. Most services are located on the highway or 2 blocks north in the downtown business district. Some gas stations and restaurants are open 24 hours.

This full-service community also supports a library and 7 churches. The Legion, located in the business district, is open year-round. Service clubs (Lions, Kinsmen) and community organizations (Masons, Knights of Columbus) welcome visitors.

A popular wilderness area nearby is Carson–Pegasus Provincial Park, located 14.6 miles/23.5 km west and north of town on Highway 32 (paved). The park has 182 campsites, electrical hookups, dump station, boat launch, boat rentals, concession, convenience store, hot showers and laundry facilities. Powered sites and showers are open year-round. There are 2 lakes at the park: **McLeod (Carson) Lake**, stocked with rainbow trout, has a speed limit of 12 kmph for boaters; **Little McLeod (Pegasus) Lake** has northern pike and whitefish, electric motors and canoes only. Eagle River Outfitting (phone 403/778-3251), located 7 miles/11.3 km south of town via Highway 32, offers camping and wilderness activities

East Access Route Log

(continued)

E 111.9 (180.1 km) **DC 255.1** (410.5 km) Beaver Creek bridge.

CAUTION: The highway between Whitecourt and Valleyview is known locally as "Moose Row" and "Moose Alley." Several moose-vehicle accidents occur yearly. Northbound travelers, watch for moose on road, especially at dusk and at night.

E 112.4 (180.9 km) **DC 254.6** (409.7 km) McLeod River.

E 112.6 (181.2 km) **DC 254.4** (409.4 km) Railroad crossing.

E 112.7 (181.4 km) **DC 254.3** (409.2 km) **Junction** with Highway 32 South (paved). Access to Eagle River Outfitting, 7 miles/11.3 km south; camping, wilderness activities.

Canada is on the metric system; see the conversion chart in GENERAL INFORMATION.

Highway 32 leads 42 miles/68 km to Yellowhead Highway 16 (see **Milepost E 97.5** in the YELLOWHEAD HIGHWAY section). ▲

E 112.9 (181.7 km) **DC 254.1** (408.9 km) Gas stations both sides of highway.

E 113.4 (182.5 km) **DC 253.6** (408.1 km) Turnoff to north for Sagitawah Tourist Park (RV camping) and Riverboat Park, both at the confluence of the McLeod and Athabasca rivers. Riverboat Park has a boat launch, picnic area and toilets. ▲

E 113.6 (182.8 km) **DC 253.4** (407.8 km) Athabasca River bridge.

E 115.6 (186 km) **DC 251.4** (404.6 km) Vehicle inspection station to north.

E 117.1 (188.4 km) **DC 249.9** (402.2 km) **Junction** with Highway 32 North (paved). Access to Eric S. Huestis Demonstration Forest (self-guided trails) and Carson–Pegasus Provincial Park. The provincial park, 9.3 miles/15 km north, has 182 campsites, electrical hookups, group camping area, tables, flush toilets, showers, water, dump station, firewood, store, laundromat and playground. (Powered sites and showers open year-round.) Boat launch, boat rentals and rainbow trout fishing are available. ▲

E 117.6 (189.2 km) **DC 249.4** (401.4 km) Alberta Newsprint Co. to south.

E 122 (196.3 km) **DC 245** (394.3 km) Turnout with litter barrel.

E 122.5 (197.1 km) **DC 244.5** (393.5 km) Chickadee Creek government campground; 7 sites, pit toilets, water, tables and firepits. ▲

E 124.3 (200 km) **DC 242.7** (390.6 km) Chickadee Creek.

E 131.8 (212.1 km) **DC 235.2** (378.5 km) Turnouts with litter barrels both sides of highway.

E 140.5 (226.1 km) **DC 226.5** (364.5 km) Two Creeks government campground; 8 campsites, pit toilets, water, picnic tables and firepits. ▲

E 142.5 (229.3 km) **DC 224.5** (361.3 km) Turnout with litter barrel to south.

E 143 (230.1 km) **DC 224** (360.5 km) Turnout with litter barrel to north.

E 152 (244.6 km) **DC 215** (346 km) Iosegun Creek government campground; 12 sites, pit toilets, water, tables and firepits. ▲

E 159 (255.9 km) **DC 208** (334.7 km) Fox Creek airport.

Fox Creek

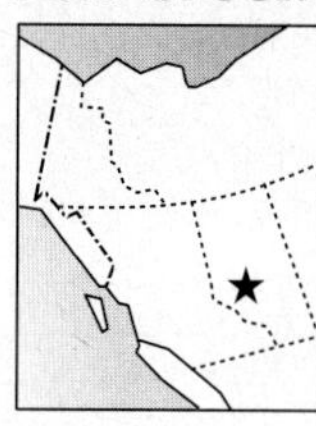

E 162 (260.7 km) **DC 205** (329.9 km) **Population:** 2,259. **Elevation:** 2,800 feet/853m. **Emergency Services: RCMP,** phone (403) 622-3740. **Hospital,** phone (403) 622-3545. **Visitor Information:** Tourist Information Centre at the Rig Earth Resource Park, open in summer; phone (403) 622-2000.

Private Aircraft: Fox Creek airport, 3 miles/4.8 km south on Highway 43; elev. 2,840 feet/866m; length, 2,950 feet/899m; paved; no fuel. Unattended.

All visitor facilities including a hotel, 3 motels, gas stations with repair service, a grocery and deli, pharmacy, banks and bank machines, hospital and medical clinic, and a 9-hole golf course with driving range. Municipal campground with 17 sites, full hookups. Dump station located at north end of town. Shops open Friday evening, closed Sunday.

Centre of oil and gas exploration and production, North America's largest known natural gas field is here. There are 3 major gas plants in the area (Amoco, Chevron, Petro–Canada) and a full range of related industrial services.

Fox Creek is in the heart of big game country, and hunting guides are available. Two local lakes popular with residents and visitors are Iosegun and Smoke. Camping, boat launch and fishing at **Iosegun Lake,** 6.8 miles/11 km north on good gravel road; walleye, northern pike and perch. Camping, boat launch and fishing at **Smoke Lake,** 8 miles/13 km southwest; northern pike, perch and pickerel. ▲

FOX CREEK ADVERTISERS

Alaskan Motel, The ....Ph. (403) 622-3073
Fox Creek R.V. Campground ....Ph. (403) 622-3896
Regal Motor Inn ....Ph. (403) 622-3333

East Access Route Log

(continued)

E 167 (268.7 km) **DC 200** (321.9 km) Turnout with litter barrel.

E 169.5 (272.8 km) **DC 197.5** (317.8 km) Turnouts with litter barrels both sides of highway.

E 172 (276.8 km) **DC 195** (313.8 km) Pines government campground; 25 sites, shelter, firewood, pump water, tables and pit toilets. ▲

E 182.1 (293 km) **DC 184.9** (297.6 km) Turnout with litter barrel.

E 186.4 (300 km) **DC 180.6** (290.6 km) **Sands Wilderness R.V. Park.** 24-hour security campground. Power and unserviced sites, tenting area. Spacious pull-throughs with power. Water fill-up and dump station. Laundromat, showers. Concession; hot and cold snacks. Horseshoe pits and mini-golf. Children's playground. Free firewood. Guests have said, "One of the nicest campgrounds in Canada." Outdoor adventures—trail rides and raft trips. Your hosts—"Wild Bill" and Agnes Sands, Box 511, Valleyview, AB T0H 3N0. Phone (403) 524-2207, Fax (403) 524-3288. [ADVERTISEMENT] ▲

E 192 (309 km) **DC 175** (281.6 km) **LITTLE SMOKY** (pop. about 50). Motel, RV park, tea house, gift shop, pay phone, propane, grocery store, service station and post office. ▲

Little Smoky Motel & Campground. See display ad this section. ▲

E 192.2 (309.3 km) **DC 174.8** (281.3 km) Little Smoky River bridge.

E 193.5 (311.4 km) **DC 173.5** (279.2 km) Waskahigan (House) River bridge at confluence with Smoky River. Government campground with 24 sites, pit toilets, water, tables and firepits. ▲

E 197 (317 km) **DC 170** (273.6 km) Turnout.

E 206.7 (332.6 km) **DC 160.3** (258 km) Turnout with litter barrel.

E 208.5 (335.5 km) **DC 158.5** (255.1 km) Peace pipeline storage tanks.

E 210.8 (339.2 km) **DC 156.2** (251.4 km) Valleyview Riverside golf course.

E 213.2 (343.1 km) **DC 153.8** (247.5 km) Valleyview tourist information centre (phone 403/524-4129); pay phone, postal service, souvenirs, picnic tables, flush toilets. Open daily in summer, 8 A.M. to 8 P.M.

E 213.4 (343.4 km) **DC 153.6** (247.2 km) Valleyview airport to west.

Private Aircraft: Valleyview airport; elev. 2,434 feet/742m; length, 3,300 feet/1,006m; paved; no fuel. Unattended.

CAUTION: The highway between Valleyview and Whitecourt is known locally as "Moose Row" and "Moose Alley." Several moose-vehicle accidents occur yearly. Southbound travelers, watch for moose on road, especially at dusk and at night.

Valleyview

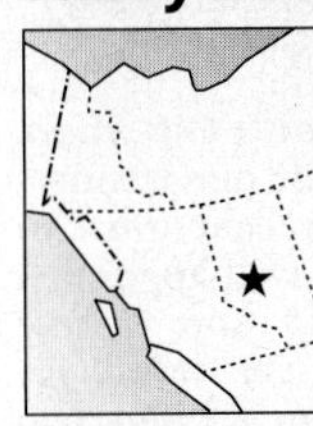

E 214.1 (344.4 km) **DC 152.9** (246.1 km) **Junction** of Highways 43 and 34, approximately 4 hours drive time from Edmonton. **Population:** 2,218. **Emergency Services: RCMP**, phone (403) 524-3343. **Fire Department**, phone (403) 524-3211. **Ambulance**, phone (403) 524-3916. **Hospital**, Valleyview General, 45 beds, phone (403) 524-2256.

Visitor Information: Major tourist information centre and rest stop located 0.9 mile/1.5 km south of Valleyview on Highway 43. Open daily, 8 A.M. to 8 P.M. from May through Labour Day weekend; phone (403)524-4129. Postal service, souvenirs and refreshments, as well as regional travel and community events and services information. For information on small business opportunities, contact the Valleyview Regional Economic Development Board office at (403)524-3942.

Elevation: 2,400 feet/732m. **Newspaper:** *Valley Views* (weekly). **Transportation: Air**–Airport 0.7 mile/1.1 km south (see **Milepost E 213.4**). **Bus**–Greyhound.

Valleyview, known as the "Portal to the Peace Country" of northwestern Alberta, is located at the junction of Highways 43 and 34. From Valleyview, Highway 34 leads west to Grande Prairie and Dawson Creek. Highway 43 continues north to Peace River. From Peace River, travelers have the option of continuing on the Mackenzie Highway to Northwest Territories, or heading west via Highway 64 to Fort St. John. (See the MACKENZIE ROUTE and NORTHERN WOODS & WATERS ROUTE sections for details.)

Highway 43 also connects with Highway 2 east to Athabasca, the Slave Lake route from Edmonton used by Alaska Highway travelers until 1955, when Highway 43 was completed to Whitecourt.

Sunset on Sturgeon Lake west of Valleyview. There is camping, fishing and a marina at the lake. (Earl L. Brown, staff)

VALLEYVIEW ADVERTISERS

Horizon Motel, Restaurant & Gift Shop..................Ph. (403) 524-3904
Lion's Den Trailer Park and Campground, The.....W. edge of town
Sherk's R.V. Park ....Ph. (403) 524-4949
Town of Valleyview ....Ph. (403) 524-5150
Valleyview Esso Service ....Ph. (403) 524-3504

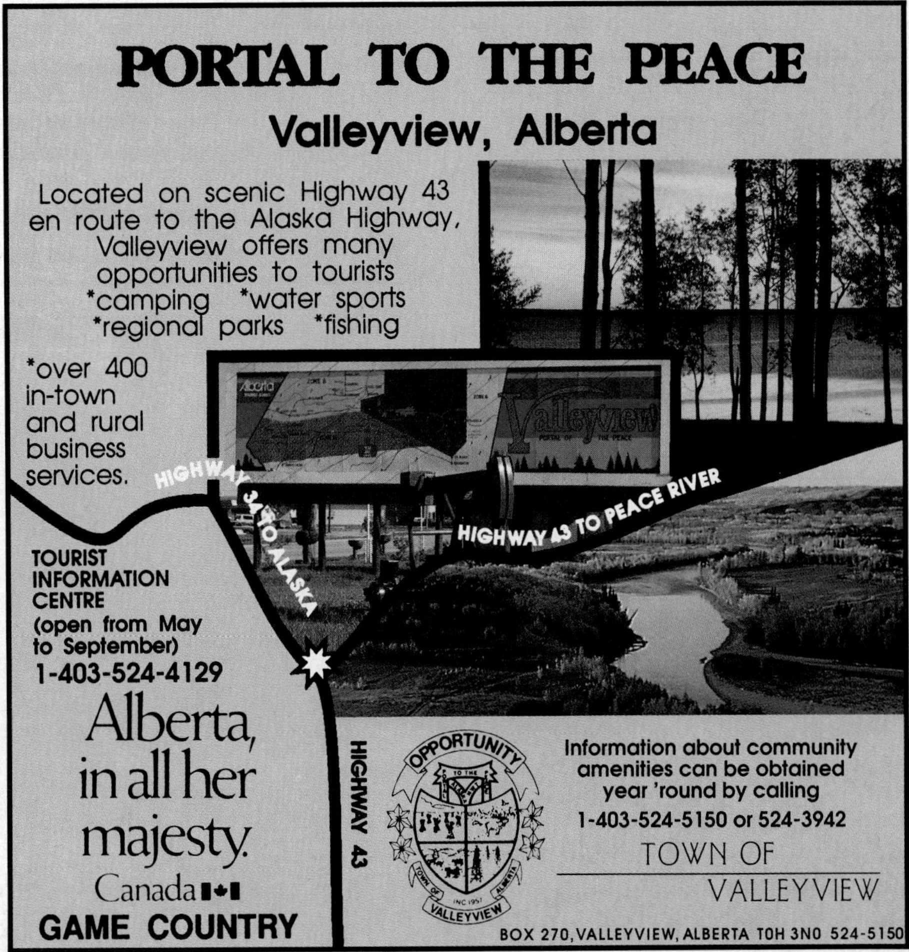

Originally called Red Willow Creek when it was homesteaded in 1916, Valleyview boomed with the discovery of oil and gas in the 1950s, and services grew along with the population. Today, Valleyview's economy has diversified to include the oil and gas industry, forestry, tourism, agriculture and government services. Farming consists mainly of grain, oilseed, beef cattle and forage production.

The community has a full range of services including banks (automatic teller machine at Alberta Treasury Branch), post office, a library, several churches and a veterinary clinic.

All visitor facilities including 5 motels and hotels, several restaurants, gas stations (many with major repair service, propane and diesel), laundromat, grocery, liquor store, clothing and hardware stores, a bakery, gift shops and a golf course. Some gas stations and restaurants open 24 hours a day.

The area boasts many lakes and streams, abundant wildlife, and lush vegetaton, including berries. Summer travelers can take advantage of the long summer days here by attending local rodeos, fairs and festivals; playing a round of golf on one of the local golf courses; visiting one of the provincial parks along Sturgeon lake; taking a dip in the outdoor swimming pool in town; or exploring the wilderness by all-terrain vehicle, horse, canoe or hiking trail.

Horizon Motel, Restaurant & Gift Shop. At the Horizon, we have built our business on loyalty and customer satisfaction. An Alberta Best property, clean, well-appointed rooms, several nonsmoking and deluxe family suites available, reasonable rates. Our Westside Cafe, "where to turn when you simply must have a good meal...", tastefully decorated, featuring Western and Chinese menu. Open daily 6 A.M. to 10 P.M. Tour

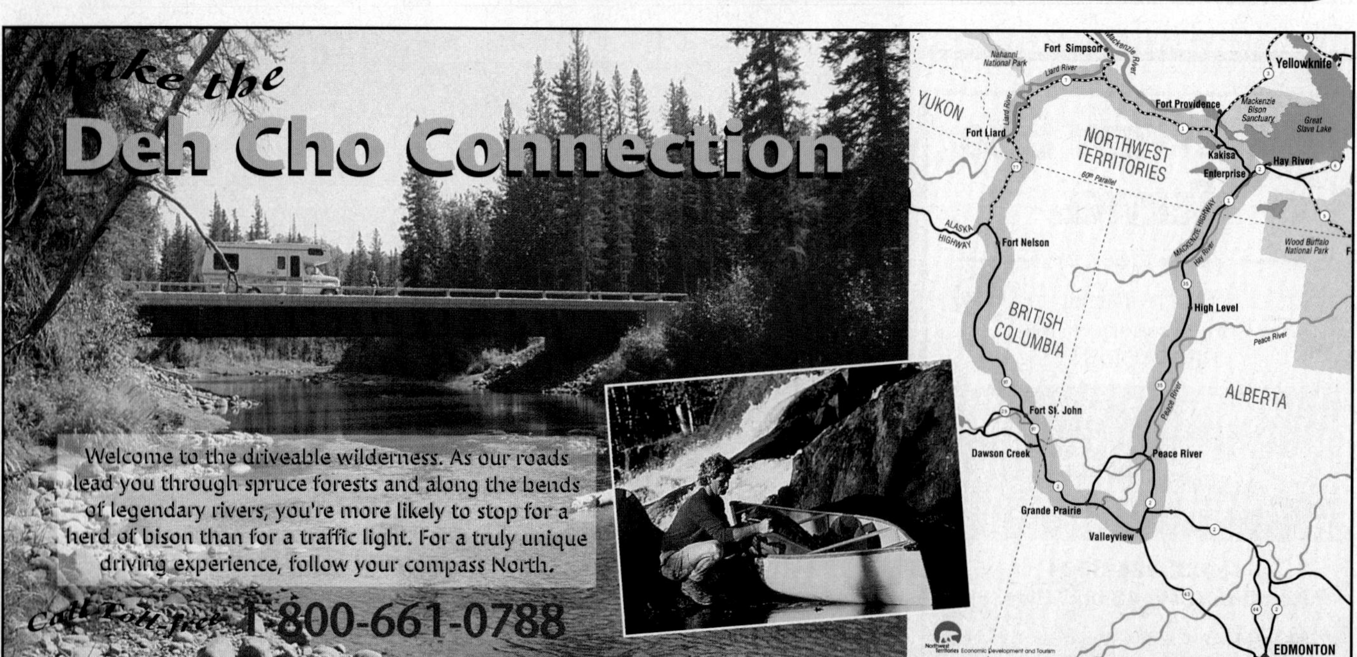

buses welcome. Quality souvenirs and gifts. Bank rate of exchange paid on U.S. funds. We take pride in our service; stop in and experience for yourself! Phone (403) 524-3904. Fax (403) 524-4223. [ADVERTISEMENT]

Lion's Den Campground, west end of town, has 19 sites with hookups, tables, showers and toilets. Private campground on west edge of town with 56 sites. ▲

East Access Route Log

(continued)

E 216 (347.6 km) **DC 151** (243 km) Highway 43 continues north 86 miles/138.4 km to **PEACE RIVER** (pop. 6,690). Highway 43 **junctions** with the Mackenzie Highway 12 miles/19 km west of Peace River. See the MACKENZIE ROUTE section for a description of Peace River and the log of the Mackenzie Highway to Northwest Territories. The Mackenzie Highway is connected to the Alaska Highway via the Liard Highway (see the LIARD HIGHWAY section for details). From Peace River, travelers may also connect with the Alaska Highway at Fort St. John via Highway 64 (see NORTHERN WOODS & WATERS ROUTE section).

Highway 34 begins westbound from Valleyview; continue west on Highway 34.

HIGHWAY 34

E 222.6 (358.2 km) **DC 144.4** (232.4 km) 24-hour convenience store and gas.

E 224.7 (361.6 km) **DC 142.3** (229 km) Access north to **Sturgeon Lake**; fishing and camping. Williamson Provincial Park (1.2 miles/2 km) has 60 campsites, boat launch, showers and dump station. Sturgeon Lake Campground has 102 sites, some hookups, tables, showers, laundry, dump station and store. Fishing for perch, pickerel, northern pike and whitefish. ▲

E 227 (365.3 km) **DC 140** (225.3 km) **CALAIS** (pop. about 550); post office and grocery store.

E 230 (370.1 km) **DC 137** (220.5 km) Private campground and marina on **Sturgeon Lake**; fishing, boat rentals. ▲

Cosy Cove Campground & Marina. See display ad this section. ▲

E 232 (373.3 km) **DC 135** (217.3 km) Sturgeon Heights. Turnoff for Youngs Point Provincial Park, 6 miles/10 km northeast; 97 campsites (some with electrical hookups), firewood, showers, playground, hiking trails, dump station, boat launch, fish cleaning station, beach, fishing in **Sturgeon Lake.** ▲

E 235 (378.2 km) **DC 132** (212.4 km) Turnouts both sides of highway.

E 240 (386.2 km) **DC 127** (204.4 km) **CROOKED CREEK** (pop. 10); gas station, grocery, post office and pay phone.

E 246 (395.9 km) **DC 121** (194.7 km) **DeBOLT**, a small farming community north of highway with a general store and district museum. Garage with gas on highway.

E 253.8 (408.7 km) **DC 113.2** (181.9 km) **Junction.** Forestry Trunk Road leads 632 miles/1017 km south, intersecting Yellowhead Highway 16 and Trans-Canada Highway 1, to Highway 3.

E 255.2 (410.7 km) **DC 111.8** (179.9 km) Microwave towers to east.

E 259.5 (417.6 km) **DC 107.5** (173 km) Smoky River bridge and government campground; 30 sites, shelter, firepits, firewood, tables, pit toilets, water pump and boat launch. ▲

E 264 (424.9 km) **DC 103** (165.7 km) **BEZANSON.** Post office, gas station with

(continues on page 35)

Bighorn Highway 40 Log

This 207-mile/333.2-km highway connects Yellowhead Highway 16 and Highway 2, and the communities of Hinton, Grande Cache and Grande Prairie. The highway is paved between its junction with Yellowhead Highway 16 and Grande Cache. Between Grande Cache and Grande Prairie, the highway was undergoing paving from both ends in 1995, and is scheduled to be paved in its entirety in 1996.

Distance from Yellowhead Highway 16 junction (Y) is followed by the distance from Grande Prairie (GP).

Y 0 GP 207 (333.2 km) **Junction** of Highways 16 and 40. (See **Milepost E 177** in the YELLOWHEAD HIGHWAY 16 section.) Log follows Highway 40 northbound.

Y 2.1 (3.4 km) **GP 204.9** (329.8 km) Community of **ENTRANCE** (pop. 79) to west.

Y 3 (4.8 km) **GP 204** (328.4 km) Athabasca River bridge.

Y 3.7 (5.9 km) **GP 203.3** (327.3 km) Access road to west leads 10 miles/16 km to the community of **BRULE** (pop. 161), which has a guest ranch with trail riding, fishing, and cross-country skiing in winter.

Y 8.5 (13.6 km) **GP 198.5** (319.6 km) Access road leads west 4 miles/7 km to Athabasca Lookout Nordic Centre; cross-country and biathlon skiing, hiking trails, and day lodge.

Y 8.9 (14.3 km) **GP 198.1** (318.9 km) Turnout to east with litter barrels and information sign about William A. Switzer Provincial Park.

Y 9.1 (14.7 km) **GP 197.9** (318.5 km) Entering William A. Switzer Provincial Park northbound.

Y 9.8 (15.8 km) **GP 197.2** (317.4 km) Access road leads east to Jarvis Lake day-use area; pump water, public phone, beach and boat launch.

Y 12.8 (20.5 km) **GP 194.2** (312.7 km) Kelley's Bathtub day-use area to west; hiking trail, public phone, swimming.

Y 15.2 (24.5 km) **GP 191.8** (308.7 km) Winter Creek.

Y 15.3 (24.7 km) **GP 191.7** (308.5 km) Side road to east leads 1.2 miles/2 km to Cache Lake and 2.4 miles/4 km to Graveyard Lake. Cache Lake campground has 14 sites, sewer hookups, water pump, picnic tables, shelter, children's playground, camping fee $7.50. Graveyard campground has 16 sites, sewer hookups, water available at Cache Lake campground, camping fee $7.50. ▲

Y 16.8 (27 km) **GP 190.3** (306.2 km) Access road to east leads to **Gregg Lake** day-use area and campground; 164 sites, sewer hookups, tap water, picnic tables, shelter, children's playground, fish-cleaning stand, beach, hiking trails, public phone. Camping fee $13. ▲

Y 17.6 (28.4 km) **GP 189.4** (304.8 km) Turnout to west with litter barrels and information sign about William A. Switzer Provincial Park for southbound travelers.

Y 22.9 (36.9 km) **GP 184.1** (296.3 km) Wildhay River bridge.

Y 25.6 (41.2 km) **GP 181.4** (292 km) Side road to west leads 20 miles/32 km to Rock Lake campground on Rock Lake; 96 sites, sewer hookups, water pump, picnic tables, shelter, hiking trails, boat launch, camping fee $7.50. ▲

Y 28.9 (46.5 km) **GP 178.1** (286.7 km) Entering Grande Cache ranger district northbound.

Y 30.6 (49.3 km) **GP 176.4** (283.9 km) Fred Creek.

Y 36.3 (58.5 km) **GP 170.7** (274.7 km) Pinto Creek.

Y 40.5 (65.2 km) **GP 166.5** (268 km) Bridge over the Little Berland River.

Y 43.2 (69.6 km) **GP 163.8** (263.6 km) Fox Creek.

Y 47.4 (76.3 km) **GP 159.6** (256.9 km) Small airstrip to east.

Y 48.4 (77.9 km) **GP 158.6** (255.3 km) Bridge over the Big Berland River. Big Berland River government campground at north end of bridge to west has 12 sites, sewer hookups, water pump, picnic tables, shelter, camping fee $7.50. ▲

Y 52.9 (85.2 km) **GP 154.1** (248 km) Hendrickson Creek.

Y 56.4 (90.7 km) **GP 150.6** (242.5 km) Access road to east leads 1.8 miles/3 km to Hucklebury Tower.

Y 57.4 (92.3 km) **GP 149.6** (240.9 km) Shand Creek.

Y 61.3 (98.6 km) **GP 145.7** (234.6 km) Burleigh Creek.

Y 65.2 (105 km) **GP 141.8** (228.2 km) Pierre Grey's Lakes government campground to east; 83 sites, sewer hookups, pump water, picnic tables, shelter, fireplaces, firewood, hiking trails, boat launch, camping fee $7.50. ▲

Y 66.1 (106.4 km) **GP 140.9** (226.8 km) Entering **MUSKEG RIVER** (pop. 22) northbound; pay phone.

Y 66.7 (107.3 km) **GP 140.3** (225.9 km) Highway maintenance station to north.

Y 67 (107.8 km) **GP 140** (225.4 km) Lone Teepee Creek.

Y 67.9 (109.3 km) **GP 139.1** (223.9 km) **Junction** with Highway 734 (Forestry Trunk Road, gravel) which leads north 116 miles/187 km to Highway 34. There are no services along the highway.

Y 69.4 (111.7 km) **GP 137.6** (221.5 km) Turnout to south.

Y 70 (112.6 km) **GP 137** (220.6 km) Veronique River bridge.

Y 72.3 (116.4 km) **GP 134.7** (216.8 km) Findley Creek.

Y 74.1 (119.3 km) **GP 132.9** (213.9 km) Muskeg River bridge.

Y 74.9 (120.6 km) **GP 132.1** (212.6 km) Mason Creek day-use area; picnic facilities and hiking trail to the Muskeg River.

Y 75.1 (120.8 km) **GP 131.9** (212.3 km) Mason Creek.

Y 75.7 (121.8 km) **GP 131.3** (211.4 km) Grande Cache airport to south.

Y 80.8 (130.1 km) **GP 126.2** (203.1 km) Susa Creek.

Y 82 (132 km) **GP 125** (201.2 km) Washa Creek.

Y 84.1 (135.3 km) **GP 122.9** (197.9 km) Carconte Creek.

Y 84.5 (136 km) **GP 122.5** (197.2 km) Grande Cache Lake to south; picnic area, swimming, boat launch.

Y 85.3 (137.3 km) **GP 121.7** (195.9 km) Allen Creek.

Y 86.7 (139.5 km) **GP 120.3** (193.7 km) **Victor Lake** to south; canoeing and fishing.

Y 88.1 (141.7 km) **GP 118.9** (191.5 km) Entering Grande Cache northbound. Visitor information centre to east.

Grande Cache

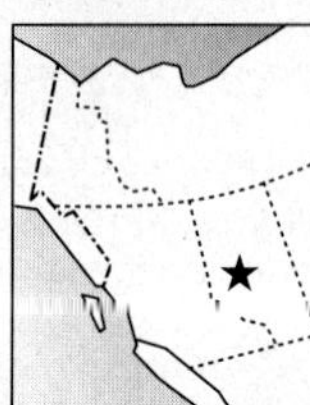

Y 88.2 (142 km) **GP 118.8** (191.2 km) Located 116 miles/188 km south of Grande Prairie. **Population:** 3,842. **Emergency services:** RCMP, phone (403) 827-2222. **Hospital**, phone (403) 827-3701. **Ambulance**, phone (403) 827-3600. **Fire department**, phone (403) 827-3600. **Visitor information:** Tourist information centre is located on 100th Street (Highway 40) at the south entrance into town, open 8:30 A.M. to 9 P.M. July 1 through Labour Day.

Elevation: 4,200 feet/1,280m. **Private Aircraft:** Grande Cache airport, 12 miles/19 km east on Highway 40; elev. 4,117 feet/1,255m; length 5,000 feet/1,524m; asphalt; no fuel available.

Grande Cache was established in 1969 in conjunction with resource development by McIntyre Porcupine Coal Ltd. In 1980 a sawmill was constructed by British Columbia Forest Products Ltd. and in 1984 a medium security correctional centre was built.

Historically, the location was used as a staging area for fur trappers and natives prior to their departure to trap lines in the valleys and mountain ranges now known as Willmore Provincial Park. Upon their return, they stored large caches of furs while waiting for transportation opportunities to trading posts.

Today Grande Cache, nestled on the leeward side of the Rocky Mountains, is a picturesque and vibrant community. Visitor facilities include 2 hotels, 4 motels, 2 banks, restaurants, laundromats, service stations with repair facilities, car washes and a library. Shopping facilities include several small shopping centres, 2 supermarkets, a bakery, sporting goods store and department store.

Recreational facilities include a recreation centre which houses a curling rink, swimming pool, skating rink, fitness rooms and saunas. Grande Cache Golf and Country Club, located in the northeast part of town, has 9 holes, grass greens, club house, pro shop, food and beverages, and banquet facilities.

Camping at Marv Moore municipal campground on the south side of the highway, at the north end of town just past the golf course. There are 55 sites, all hookups, showers, flush toilets, public phone, children's playground. Camping fee from $8.

Big Horn Highway log

(continued)

Y 88.7 (142.7 km) **GP 118.3** (190.5 km) Highway 40 descends northbound to the Smoky River.

Y 91.3 (146.9 km) **GP 115.7** (186.3 km) Blue Bridge provincial campground to south has 22 sites, sewer hookups, no water, shelters, firewood, firepits, tables, pit toilets, boat launch. Camping fee $7.50. Trail access to Willmore Wilderness Park.

Y 91.5 (147.2 km) **GP 115.5** (186 km) **Smoky River** bridge, fishing for arctic grayling, Dolly Varden and whitefish.

Y 92.3 (148.6 km) **GP 114.7** (184.6 km) Turnoff to south for Willmore Wilderness Park and Hell's Gate campground (4 miles/6.4 km south) with 10 sites, sewer hookups, horse holding areas, camping fee $5.50.

Y 95.3 (153.4 km) **GP 111.7** (179.8 km) Grande Cache gun range to east. Northbound, the highway parallels the Northern Alberta Resource Railroad and the Smoky River.

Y 100.8 (162.2 km) **GP 106.2** (171 km) Turnout to east overlooks Smoky River Coal Ltd. and H.R. Milner Generating Station.

Y 104.8 (168.7 km) **GP 102.2** (164.5 km) Entering Grande Prairie Forest northbound, entering Edson Forest southbound.

Y 106.7 (171.7 km) **GP 100.3** (161.5 km) Turnoff to east for Sheep Creek day-use area; shaded picnic tables, water pump, firepits, firewood, litter barrels, outhouses, and gravel parking areas. Boat launch on the Smoky River.

Y 107.1 (172.4 km) **GP 99.9** (160.8 km) Sheep Creek. Sheep Creek campground to east; 9 sites, sewer hookups, water pump, camping fee $5.50.

Y 108.4 (174.5 km) **GP 98.6** (158.7 km) Entering Game Country Tourist Zone northbound, Evergreen Tourist Zone southbound.

Y 110.1 (177.2 km) **GP 96.9** (156 km) Wayandie Road. Highway ascends steep hill northbound, some sections of 7 percent grade.

Y 115.9 (186.5 km) **GP 91.1** (146.7 km) Small turnout to east.

Y 125.1 (201.3 km) **GP 81.9** (131.9 km) Southview recreation area to east; gravel parking area, shaded picnic tables, litter barrels, outhouses, highbush cranberries in season.

Y 128.5 (206.8 km) **GP 78.5** (126.4 km) *CAUTION: logging trucks next 36 miles/60 km northbound.*

Y 130.4 (209.8 km) **GP 76.6** (123.4 km) 16th base line sign marks north-south hunting boundary.

Y 142 (228.6 km) **GP 65** (104.6 km) Distance marker indicates Grande Prairie 62 miles/100 km.

Y 145.6 (234.3 km) **GP 61.4** (98.9 km) Kakwa River bridge.

Y 145.9 (234.8 km) **GP 61.1** (98.4 km) Turnoff for **Kakwa River** campground and day-use area; 14 sites, sewer hookups, picnic tables, firewood, firepits, water pump, litter barrels, outhouses, gravel parking area. Camping fee $5.50. Fishing for arctic grayling.

Y 155.2 (249.7 km) **GP 51.8** (83.5 km) Side road to west leads 7 miles/11 km to Unocal oil field office.

Y 158.4 (254.9 km) **GP 48.6** (78.3 km) Highway construction and maintenance camp to east.

Y 159.1 (256.1 km) **GP 47.9** (77.1 km) Access road to east leads 3.6 miles/6 km to **Musreau Lake** campground and day-use area. There are 50 picnic sites, 69 campsites, sewer hookups, picnic tables, firewood, firepits, waterpump, litter barrels, outhouses, equestrian trails, boat launch and fishing.

Y 161.8 (260.4 km) **GP 45.2** (72.8 km) Sheep Creek.

Y 164.3 (264.4 km) **GP 42.7** (68.8 km) Cutbank River bridge. River access at north end of bridge.

Y 165.6 (266.5 km) **GP 41.4** (66.7 km) Elk Creek.

Y 165.8 (266.8 km) **GP 41.2** (66.4 km) *CAUTION: logging trucks next 36 miles/60 km southbound.*

Y 172.2 (277.1 km) **GP 34.8** (56.1 km) Distance marker indicates Grande Prairie 31 miles/50 km.

Y 179.5 (288.9 km) **GP 27.5** (44.3 km) Canfor Road leads east to Gold Creek Gas Plant and Highway 734.

Y 180.9 (291.1 km) **GP 26.1** (42.1 km) Big Mountain Creek.

Y 182.8 (294.1 km) **GP 24.2** (39.1 km) Bald Mountain Creek.

Y 189.4 (304.5 km) **GP 17.6** (28.5 km) Access road leads west 0.1 mile/0.2 km to picnic area and 7 miles/11 km to Grovedale.

Y 191.1 (307.5 km) **GP 15.9** (25.7 km) Bent Pipe Creek.

Y 199.7 (321.3 km) **GP 7.3** (11.8 km) **Junction** with Highway 666 which leads southwest to O'Brien Provincial Park and day-use area; water pump, firewood, playground, hiking trails. Also access to Nitehawk ski resort, which has a 460-foot/140-m rise, 3 runs, ski lifts and food service. Highway 666 continues from this junction 5 miles/8 km to Grovedale.

Y 199.8 (321.5 km) **GP 7.2** (11.6 km) Wapiti River bridge.

Y 200.1 (322 km) **GP 6.9** (11.1 km) Entering Grovedale ranger district southbound.

Y 201.6 (324.4 km) **GP 5.4** (8.7 km) Access road leads east 15 miles/25 km to the Dunes golf and winter club; 18 holes, grass greens, driving range, pro shop.

Y 207 (333.2 km) **GP 0 Junction** of Highways 40 and 2 at Grande Prairie.

Return to Milepost E 284
East Access Route

The *Original* MILEPOST PLAN-A-TRIP MAP

· ALASKA ·

YUKON TERRITORY · NORTHWEST TERRITORIES
BRITISH COLUMBIA · ALBERTA

© Michael DeYoung

Alaska State Library (Skinner) #44-3-15

$4.95 / $7.95 Laminated U.S.

The complete guide to Alaska, the Alaska Highway and other Northern roads.

This fold-out, full color PLAN-A-TRIP Map is from the publishers of The MILEPOST®, the best-selling All-The-North Travel Guide® to the Alaska Highway and the highways of Alaska, Yukon Territory, Northwest Territories, Alberta and British Columbia.

The MILEPOST®, which began in 1949, was the first reliable guide to the rugged Alcan Highway, which had opened to civilian traffic in 1948. Often referred to as the "bible of North Country travel," The MILEPOST® takes its name from the mileage markers found along Northern roads. Today, The MILEPOST® is more than 700 pages and covers 15 routes in Alaska, all highways in Yukon Territory and western Northwest Territories, and major access routes in British Columbia and Alberta—in addition to transportation by ferry system, train, cruise ship, airplane, and motorcoach.

The MILEPOST® is available in bookstores or from the publisher for $21.95 U.S., ($24.95 Canadian funds). Additional copies of this map are available for $4.95 U.S. funds ($5.95 Canadian). To order call Vernon Publications Inc., (206) 827-9900 or toll-free 1-800-726-4707. ◆

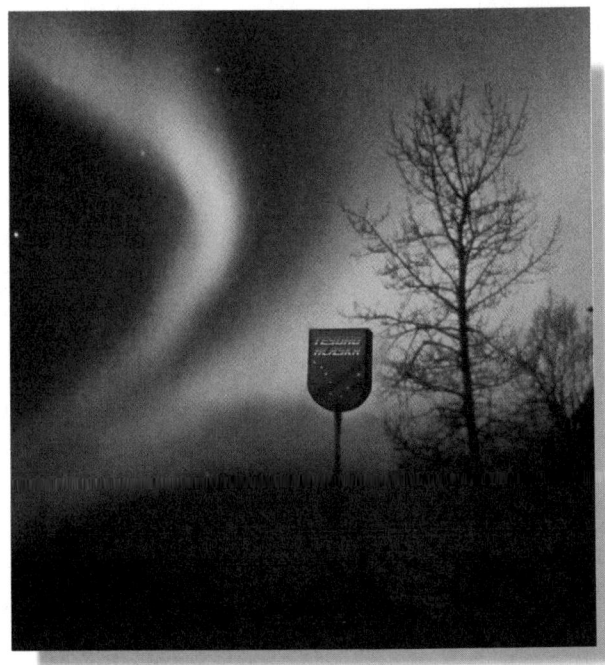

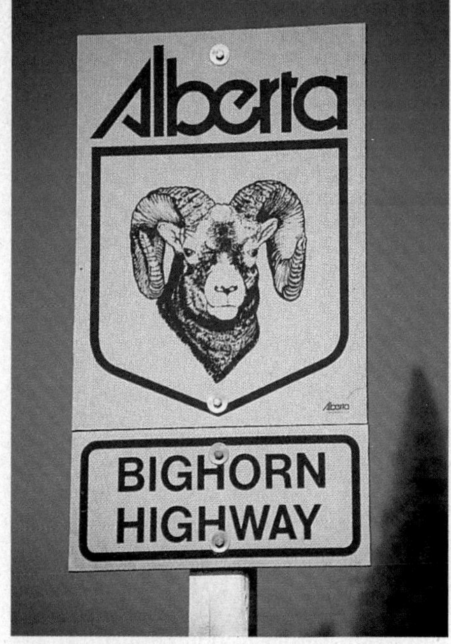

Big Horn Highway sign at Grande Prairie. (Earl L. Brown, staff)

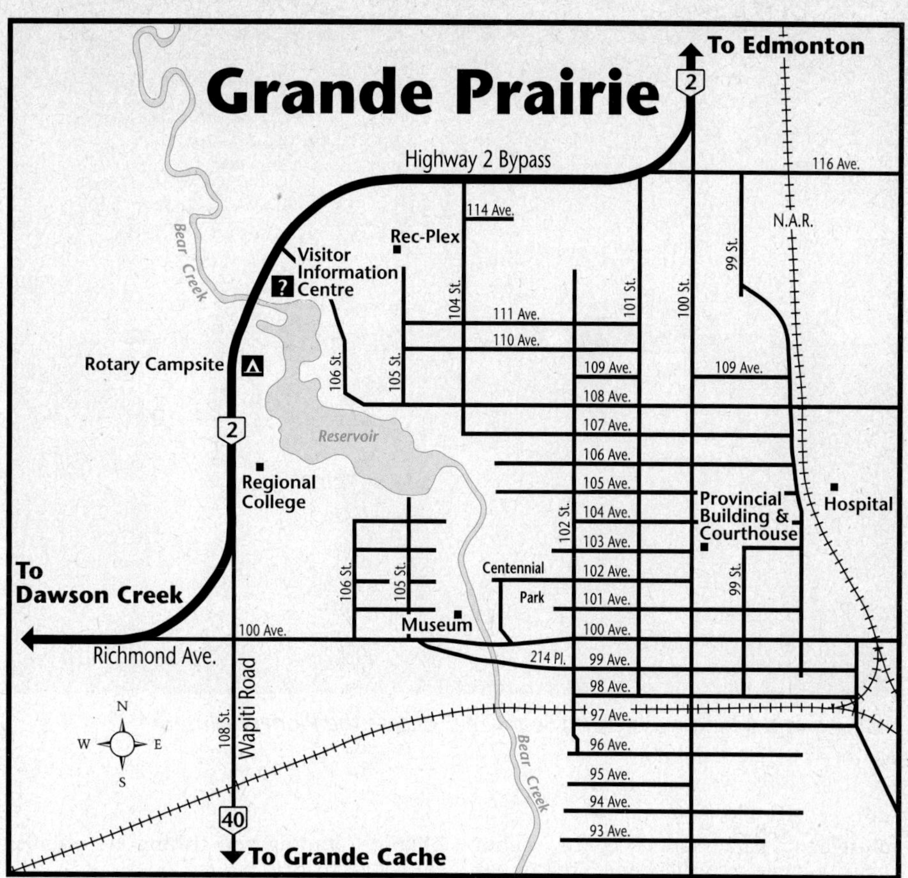

minor repair service, grocery, general store, propane.

E 269 (432.9 km) **DC 98** (157.7 km) Kleskun Hills Park to north 3 miles/5 km. The park features an ancient sea bottom with fossils of dinosaurs and marine life.

E 270.6 (435.5 km) **DC 96.4** (155.1 km) Turnout to north with historical sign about the Kleskun Hills.

E 283.5 (456.2 km) **DC 83.5** (134.4 km) Weigh scales to north.

E 283.8 (456.7 km) **DC 83.2** (133.9 km) Railroad crossing.

E 284 (457 km) **DC 83** (133.6 km) **Junction**, Highways 34 and 2. Westbound travelers turn south for Grande Prairie and Highway 2 to Dawson Creek (log follows). Turn north on Highway 2 for Sexsmith (8.5 miles/13.7 km) and Rycroft (43.2 miles/69.5 km), and Highway 49 west to Dawson Creek (see log in NORTHERN WOODS & WATERS ROUTE section). Continue north from Rycroft on Highway 2 for Highway 64 west to Fort St. John (see log in NORTHERN WOODS & WATERS ROUTE). Continue on Highway 2 north to Grimshaw, to connect with the Mackenzie Highway to Northwest Territories (see MACKENZIE ROUTE section). **SEXSMITH** has a hotel, restaurants, 13-site campground, banks, gas station and golf courses. The Sexsmith Blacksmith Shop is cited as one of the best examples of a working pioneer smithy in Alberta; open daily May to Sept. ▲

HIGHWAY 2

From its junction with Highway 34, Highway 2 leads south into Grande Prairie (description follows). To reach Grande Prairie city centre, keep straight ahead on Highway 2 (Clairmont Road) as it becomes 100th Street and follow it downtown. To skirt the downtown area, take the Highway 2 Bypass. Highway 2 becomes 100th Avenue (Richmond Avenue) on the west side of Grande Prairie.

NOTE: Bighorn Highway 40 connects Grande Prairie with Grande Cache and Yellowhead Highway 16. To reach the Bighorn Highway, follow Wapiti Road (108th Street) south from Highway 2 on the west side of Grande Prairie. See BIGHORN HIGHWAY log page 33.

Grande Prairie

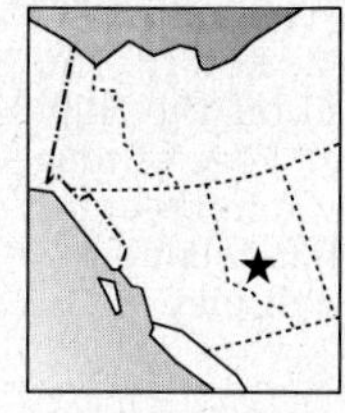

E 288 (463.5 km) **DC 79** (127.1 km). Located at **junction** of Highways 2 and 34. **Population:** 30,000. **Emergency Services: RCMP,** phone (403) 538-5700. **Fire Department,** phone (403) 532-2100. **Ambulance,** phone (403) 532-9511. **Hospital,** Queen Elizabeth, 10409 98th St., phone (403) 538-7100.

Visitor Information: Chamber of Commerce office at 10011 103rd Ave.; open weekdays 8:30 A.M. to 4:30 P.M. Visitor service center located off Highway 2 Bypass on 106th Street at Bear Creek Reservoir, open 9 A.M. to 9 P.M. in July and August, shorter hours in June.

Private Aircraft: Airport 3 miles/4.8 km west; elev. 2,195 feet/669m; length 6,500 feet/1,981m; paved; fuel 80, 100, jet. 24-hour flight service station.

Elevation: 2,198 feet/670m. **Transportation: Air**–Scheduled air service to Vancouver, BC, Edmonton, Calgary, and points north. **Bus**–Greyhound.

Grande Prairie was first incorporated as a village in 1914, as a town in 1919, and as a city in 1958, by which time its population had reached nearly 8,000.

With a strong and diverse economy based on agriculture (cereal grains, fescue, honey, livestock), forestry (a bleached kraft pulp mill, sawmill and oriented strand board plant), and oil and gas, Grande Prairie is a regional centre for much of northwestern Alberta and northeastern British Columbia. The trumpeter swan is the symbol of Grande Prairie and is featured throughout the city.

A variety of shopping is available at 2 major malls, several strip malls and a well-developed downtown area. Visitor facilities include several restaurants, hotels, motels and bed and breakfasts. Recreation facilities include 2 swimming pools, 3 18-hole golf courses, a par 3 golf course, ball diamonds,

Walking and biking trails along Bear Creek access the Pioneer Museum.
(Earl L. Brown, staff)

amusement park, tennis courts, public library, a public art gallery and 3 private galleries. Churches representing almost every denomination are located in Grande Prairie. There are several public schools and a regional college.

Area attractions include Muskoseepi Park, which follows the Bear Creek corridor. The park includes 9 miles/15 km of paved walking and biking trails, a bird sanctuary at Crystal Lake, picnic areas, swimming pool, lawn bowling, mini-golf, a stocked pool, playground and canoe, paddleboat and bike rentals. Visitor services are available in the Pavilion. Nearby is the Grande Prairie Museum & Pioneer Village and the Regional College, a unique circular facility designed by Douglas Cardinal. Several of the downtown buildings have murals by local artists.

Weyerhaeuser offers tours of their pulp mill and sawmill in summer; phone (403)539-8213 for details.

The area has prime hunting for both migratory birds and big game. Area lakes are the nesting sites of the trumpeter swan. Hiking, camping and fishing are popular outdoor activities.

Annual events include the Stompede the first weekend in June, several smaller rodeos, Canada Games, Highland games, pari-mutuel racing during July, the County Fair, Heritage Day and the Dinosaur Festival. Contact the visitor information center for more information.

Two campsites within the city limits offer showers and full hookups. Rotary Park public campground is located off the Highway 2 Bypass at the northwest edge of town near the college. Bear Creek Campground is located at the south end on 100 Avenue. ▲

the Lodge Motor Inn. See display ad this section.

East Access Route Log

(continued)

HIGHWAY 2 WEST

E 298 (479.6 km) **DC 69** (111 km) Saskatoon Island Provincial Park is 1.9 miles/3 km north on park road; 96 campsites, dump station, boat launch, swimming, playground; Saskatoon berry picking in July; game preserve for trumpeter swans. ▲

E 299 (481.2 km) **DC 68** (109.4 km) **WEMBLEY** (pop. 1,424) has a hotel (banking service and liquor store at hotel), post office, 2 grocery stores, gas stop, car wash and restaurants. Picnicking and camping at Sunset Lake Park in town. Camping May 1 to Oct. 15 at Pipestone Creek County Park, 9 miles/14.5 km south; 99 sites, showers, flush toilets, dump station, boat launch, firewood, fishing, playground, fossil display and an 18-hole golf course with grass greens nearby. ▲

Beaverlodge

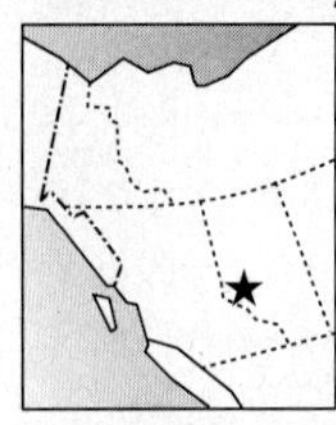

E 311 (500.5 km) **DC 56** (90.1 km) **Population:** 1,808. **Elevation:** 2,419 feet/737m. **Emergency Services: RCMP,** phone (403) 354-2485. **Ambulance,** phone (403) 354-2154. **Hospital,** Beaverlodge Municipal Hospital, phone (403) 354-2136.

Visitor Information: Located in the restored Lower Beaver Lodge School at Pioneer Campsite on the north side of Highway 2 at the west end of town.

Private Aircraft: DeWit Airpark 2 miles/3.2 km south; elev. 2,289 feet/1,698m; length 3,000 feet/914m; paved; no fuel.

Beaverlodge is a service centre for the area with a provincial courthouse, RCMP, hospital, medical and dental clinic. There are 9 churches, schools, a swimming pool and tennis courts.

Visitor services include 3 motels, 8 restaurants and gas stations. There are supermarkets, banks, a drugstore, car wash and sporting goods store. Beaverlodge Area Cultural Centre, at the south end of town, features local arts and crafts as well as a tea room. South Peace Centennial Museum is west of town (see **Milepost E 312**). Camping is available at the municipal Pioneer Campsite (19 sites, showers, dump station, electrical hookups, tourist information). The Beaverlodge Airpark, 2 miles/3.2 km south of town, is becoming a popular stopover on the flying route to Alaska. ▲

Beaverlodge is the gateway to Monkman Pass and Kinuseo Falls. Beaverlodge is also home to Canada's most northerly Agricultural Research Station (open to the public), and serves as regional centre for grain transportation, seed cleaning and seed production. Cereal grains, such as wheat, barley and oats, are the main crops in the area.

Town of Beaverlodge. See display ad this section.

East Access Route Log

(continued)

E 312 (502.1 km) **DC 55** (88.5 km) South Peace Centennial Museum to east, open daily in summer; phone (403) 354-8869. The museum features 15 display buildings and working steam-powered farm equipment from the early 1900s. Open 10 A.M. to 8 P.M., mid-May through mid-Oct. The annual Pioneer Day celebration, held here the third Sunday in July, attracts several thousand visitors.

E 312.4 (502.7 km) **DC 54.6** (87.9 km) Turnoff for Driftwood Ranch Wildlife Haven, 14.3 miles/23 km west, a private collection of exotic and endangered animals. Opens May 1 for season; phone (403)356-3769 for more information.

E 314.3 (505.8 km) **DC 52.6** (84.8 km) Golf course. This joint project of Hythe and Beaverlodge residents has a clubhouse that was once an NAR station. The 9-hole par 35 course has grass greens. Visitors are welcome; rentals available.

E 320 (515 km) **DC 47** (75.6 km) **HYTHE** (pop. 681) is an agricultural service community and processing center for fruit and berry crops, especially saskatoon berries. Canola is also a major crop. The town has a motel, a bed and breakfast, restaurant, laundromat, gas station, tire repair, car wash, outdoor covered heated swimming pool, complete shopping facilities and a hospital. Municipal campground in town with 17 sites, showers, dump station and playground. The information centre is housed in the Tags Food and Gas store. Inquire locally for directions to Riverside Bison Ranch. An old 1910 tack shop, staffed by volunteers in summer, is located between the highway and railroad tracks. ▲

E 321.7 (517.7 km) **DC 45.3** (72.9 km) **Sunset Glow Bed & Breakfast.** Enjoy our fresh country air and quiet atmosphere on a working farm. Friendly outdoor dogs, cats, cows and horses. Three guest bedrooms (smoking allowed outside). Hearty farm breakfast or ducks breakfast available. Vegetables organically grown in our garden and greenhouse. Wir sprechen Deutsch. Your hosts—the Jantzens. Phone (403)356-2520. [ADVERTISEMENT]

E 329 (529.4 km) **DC 38** (61.1 km) **Junction** with Highway 59 east to Sexsmith.

E 337 (542.3 km) **DC 30** (48.3 km) **DEMMITT**, an older settlement, site of a sawmill (worth a visit), postal service and gas.

E 340 (547.2 km) **DC 27** (43.4 km) Railway crossing.

E 341 (548.8 km) **DC 26** (41.8 km) Public campground to east; 15 sites, shelter, firewood, tables, pit toilets, pump water and playground. ▲

E 341.3 (549.2 km) **DC 25.7** (41.3 km) Vehicle inspection station to west.

E 342 (550.4 km) **DC 25** (40.2 km) Gas, diesel and convenience store.

Last Chance Bi-Lo. See display ad this section.

E 343.3 (552.5 km) **DC 23.7** (38.1 km) Alberta–British Columbia border. Turnout with litter barrels and pay phone.

TIME ZONE CHANGE: Alberta is on Mountain time; most of British Columbia is on Pacific time.

E 345.1 (555.4 km) **DC 21.9** (35.2 km) **Junction** with Heritage Highway 52 (gravel surface) which leads 18.5 miles/30 km south to **One Island Lake** Provincial Park (30 campsites, fee charged, rainbow and brook trout fishing) and 92 miles/148 km southwest from Highway 2 to Tumbler Ridge townsite, built in conjunction with the North East Coal development. Monkman Provincial Park, site of spectacular Kinuseo Falls, lies south of Tumbler Ridge. A campground with viewing platform of falls is accessible via a 25-mile/40-km road from Tumbler Ridge. Heritage Highway loops north 59.5 miles/96 km from Tumbler Ridge to join Highway 97 just west of Dawson Creek (see **Milepost PG 237.7** in the WEST ACCESS ROUTE section).

E 345.7 (556.3 km) **DC 21.3** (34.3 km) Tupper Creek bridge.

E 347 (558.5 km) **DC 20** (32.1 km) Swan Lake Provincial Park, with 41 campsites, picnic area, playground and boat launch, is 1.2 miles/2 km north of the tiny hamlet of **TUPPER**, which has a general store. ▲

Historic 1910 tack shop in Hythe houses visitor information in summer.
(Earl L. Brown, staff)

E 347.9 (559.9 km) **DC 19.1** (30.7 km) Sudeten Provincial Park day-use area; 8 picnic tables. Plaque tells of immigration to this valley of displaced residents of Sudetenland in 1938–39.

E 348.9 (561.5 km) **DC 18.1** (29.1 km) Tate Creek bridge.

E 349.7 (562.7 km) **DC 17.3** (27.8 km) Side road west to community of Tomslake.

E 356.3 (573.4 km) **DC 10.7** (17.2 km) Turnout to east with litter barrel.

E 358 (576.1 km) **DC 9** (14.5 km) Historic sign tells of Pouce Coupe Prairie.

E 359.4 (578.4 km) **7.6** (12.2 km) Railway crossing.

E 360 (579.3 km) **DC 7** (11.2 km) Weigh scales to east.

E 360.4 (580 km) **DC 6.6** (10.6 km) Bissett Creek bridge. Regional park located at south end of bridge.

E 361 (581 km) **DC 6** (9.6 km) **POUCE COUPE** (pop. 832; elev. 2,118 feet/646m). **Visitor Information:** Tourist Bureau Office located in Pouce Coupe Museum, 5006 49th Ave. (1 block south of Highway 2). Open 9 A.M. to 5 P.M., May 15 to Sept. 15. Phone (403)786-5555.

The Pouce Coupe area was first settled in 1898 by a French Canadian, who set up a trading post in 1908. The Edson Trail, completed in 1911, brought in the main influx of settlers from Edmonton in 1912. Historical artifacts are displayed at the Pouce Coupe Museum, located in the old NAR railroad station, 1 block south of Highway 2; open 8 A.M. to 5 P.M.

The village has 2 motels, a hotel, restaurant, post office, gas station, dump station, car wash, garage and food store. Camping at Regional Park, open mid-May to mid-Sept.; hookups. ▲

The Pouce Coupe Museum. See display ad this section.

E 364.5 (586.6 km) **DC 2.5** (4 km) Dawson Creek airport.

E 367 (590.6 km) **DC 0 DAWSON CREEK**, the beginning of the Alaska Highway. For details turn to the ALASKA HIGHWAY section.

Alaska Highway via
WEST ACCESS ROUTE

Seattle, Washington, to Dawson Creek, British Columbia via Cache Creek and Prince George, British Columbia Interstate Highway 5, Trans-Canada Highway 1 and BC Highway 97

(See maps, pages 39-40)

The West Access Route links Interstate 5, Trans-Canada Highway 1 and BC Highway 97 to form the most direct route to Dawson Creek, BC, for West Coast motorists. This has been the major western route to the start of the Alaska Highway since 1952, when the John Hart Highway connecting Prince George and Dawson Creek was completed.

The West Access Route junctions with Yellowhead Highway 16 at Prince George. This east–west highway connects with the Alaska State Ferry System and BC Ferries at Prince Rupert, and with the East Access Route to the Alaska Highway at Edmonton. Turn to the YELLOWHEAD HIGHWAY 16 section for a complete log of that route.

INTERSTATE HIGHWAY 5

The West Access Route begins in the city of **SEATTLE, WA** (pop. 493,846), the Alaska gateway city since the Klondike gold rush days, when it became the major staging and departure point for most of the gold seekers. Seattle was also southern terminus of the Alaska Marine Highway System until 1989, when the Alaska state ferries moved to the Fairhaven Terminal at Bellingham, WA (Interstate 5, Exit 250). Seattle–Tacoma International Airport is the departure point for jet flights to Alaska. The air terminal is located 10 miles/16 km south of city center via Interstate 5 (Exit 154).

Like most interstate routes in the United States, Interstate 5 has physical mileposts along its route and corresponding numbered exits. Exit numbers and physical mileposts reflect distance from Mile 0 at the OR–WA border. Interstate 5 in Oregon and Washington is logged in *Northwest Mileposts®*, available from Vernon Publications Inc.; phone 1-800-726-4707.

From Seattle, drive 92 miles north on Interstate 5 to Bellingham and turn off onto Highway 539 north (Exit 256), which goes north 12 miles to Highway 546, which will take you another 13 miles to Sumas, WA, and the U.S.–Canada border (customs open 24 hours a day). *The MILEPOST®* log begins on Trans-Canada Highway 1 near Abbotsford.

From Seattle to Abbotsford via Sumas it is 120 miles. From Abbotsford to Cache Creek, it is 170 miles; from Cache Creek to Prince George, 277 miles; and from Prince George to Dawson Creek it is 250 miles.

KLONDIKE GOLD RUSH NATIONAL HISTORICAL PARK
SEATTLE, WA

Located in Seattle's historic Pioneer Square, this unique museum and visitor center is 1 of 4 units in Klondike Gold Rush National Historcial Park that help preserve and interpret the great gold rush of 1897-98. The rest of the park is in Alaska and consists of a 6-block historical district in Skagway and land corridors along the historic Chilkoot and White Pass trails into Canada.

Summit of Chilkoot Pass.
(Photo courtesy of Alaska State Library, Winter & Pond Photographers)

It was in the spring of 1897 that the *Excelsior* sailed into the port of Seattle carrying 2 tons of gold from the Klondike. As word spread across the country, thousands of gold seekers poured into Seattle, which was touted as the "only place" that stampeders could outfit themselves for the gold fields.

Although not a large building, the Seattle unit of Klondike Gold Rush National Historical Park offers an excellent overview of the gold rush and Seattle's role as a staging area in 1897-98. One exhibit shows the recommended year's supplies for stampeders. Films such as *Seattle: Gateway To The Goldfields, Hiking the Chilkoot Trail* and *City of Gold* are shown several times daily in the small theatre. Open daily, 9 a.m. to 5 p.m. year-round, the park has a full schedule of interpretive events from June to September. These include gold panning demonstrations and ranger-led walking tours of the historic Pioneer Square district. The park is located at 117 South Main Street in Seattle, between First Avenue and Occidental Street; phone (206) 553-7220.

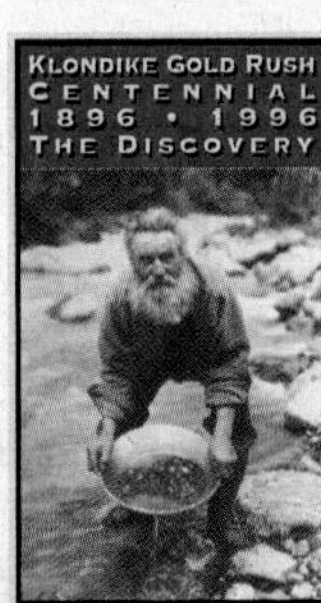

West Access Route Log

TRANS-CANADA HIGHWAY 1

The West Access Route log is divided into 3 sections: Abbotsford to Cache Creek; Cache Creek to Prince George; and Prince George to Dawson Creek.

This section of the log shows distance from Abbotsford (A) followed by distance from Cache Creek (CC).

A 0 CC 170 (273.6 km) Exit 92. **Junction** of Trans-Canada Highway 1 and Highway 11 south to the international border crossing at Sumas–Huntingdon. Highway 11 north to **ABBOTSFORD** (pop. 60,400), all visitor services. Abbotsford is the "Raspberry Capital of Canada" and is the home of the Abbotsford International Airshow in August.

Highway 11 north crosses the bridge over the Fraser River to Mission, and connects with Highway 7 to Harrison Hot Springs. This 2-lane highway traverses the rural farmland on the north side of the Fraser River, rejoining Trans-Canada Highway 1 at Hope (see HIGHWAY 7 log on page 41).

A 1.9 (3 km) **CC 168.1** (270.5 km) Exit 95 to Whatcom Road and westbound exit to Sumas River rest area. Access to Sumas Mountain Provincial Park; hiking.

A 5.3 (8.5 km) **CC 164.7** (265.1 km) Exit 99 to Sumas River rest area (eastbound only); tables, toilet, pay phones.

A 8.8 (14.2 km) **CC 161.2** (259.4 km) Exit 104 to small farming community of Yarrow and road to Cultus Lake. The Lower Fraser Valley is prime agricultural land.

CAUTION: Watch for farm vehicles crossing freeway.

A 15 (24.1 km) **CC 155** (249.4 km) Exit 116 to Lickman Road; access south to tourist infocentre, open daily in summer, and Cottonwood Meadows RV park. Chilliwack Antique Powerland museum located behind

WEST ACCESS ROUTE *Seattle, WA, to Lac La Hache, BC*

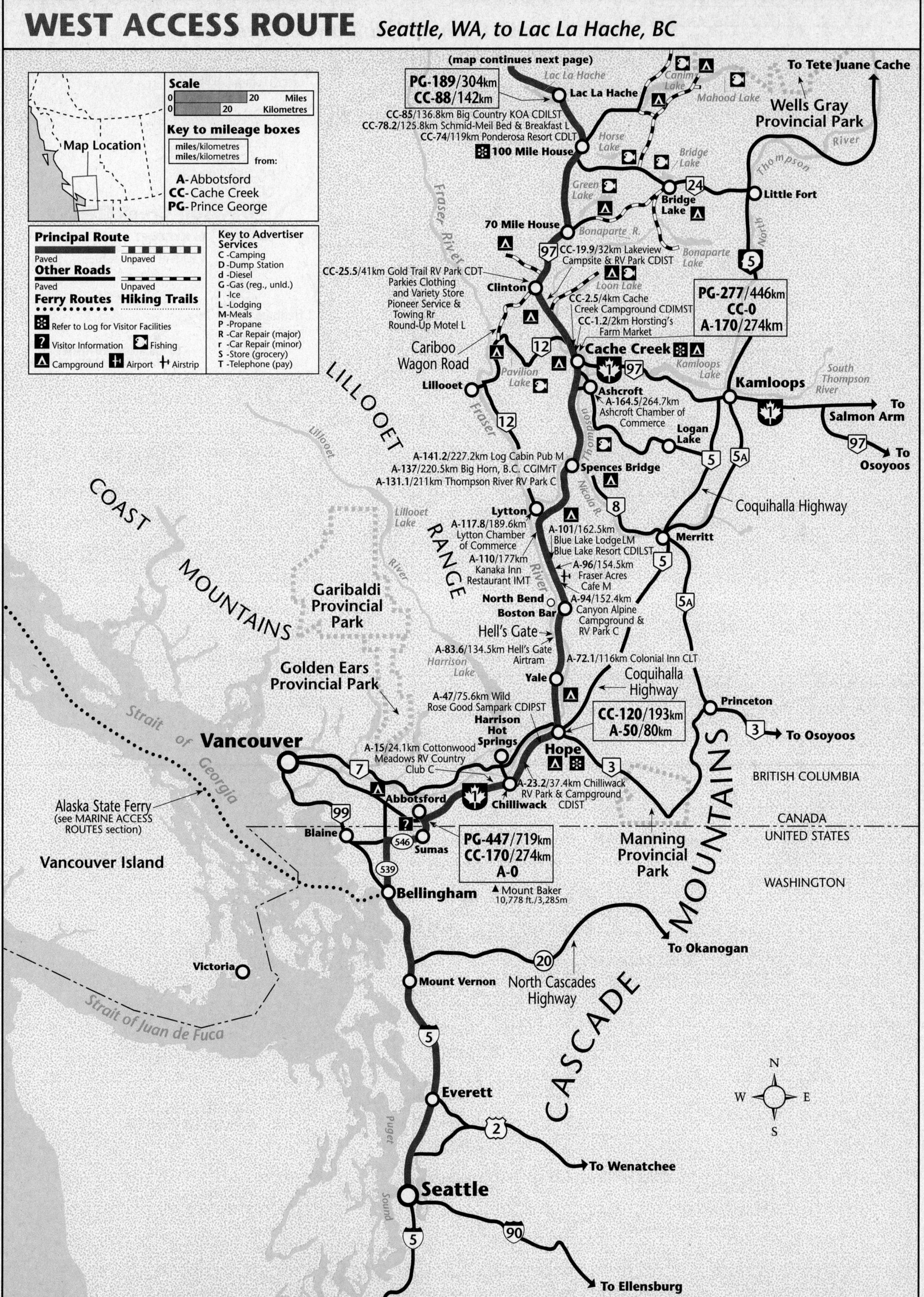

WEST ACCESS ROUTE *Lac La Hache, BC, to Dawson Creek, BC*

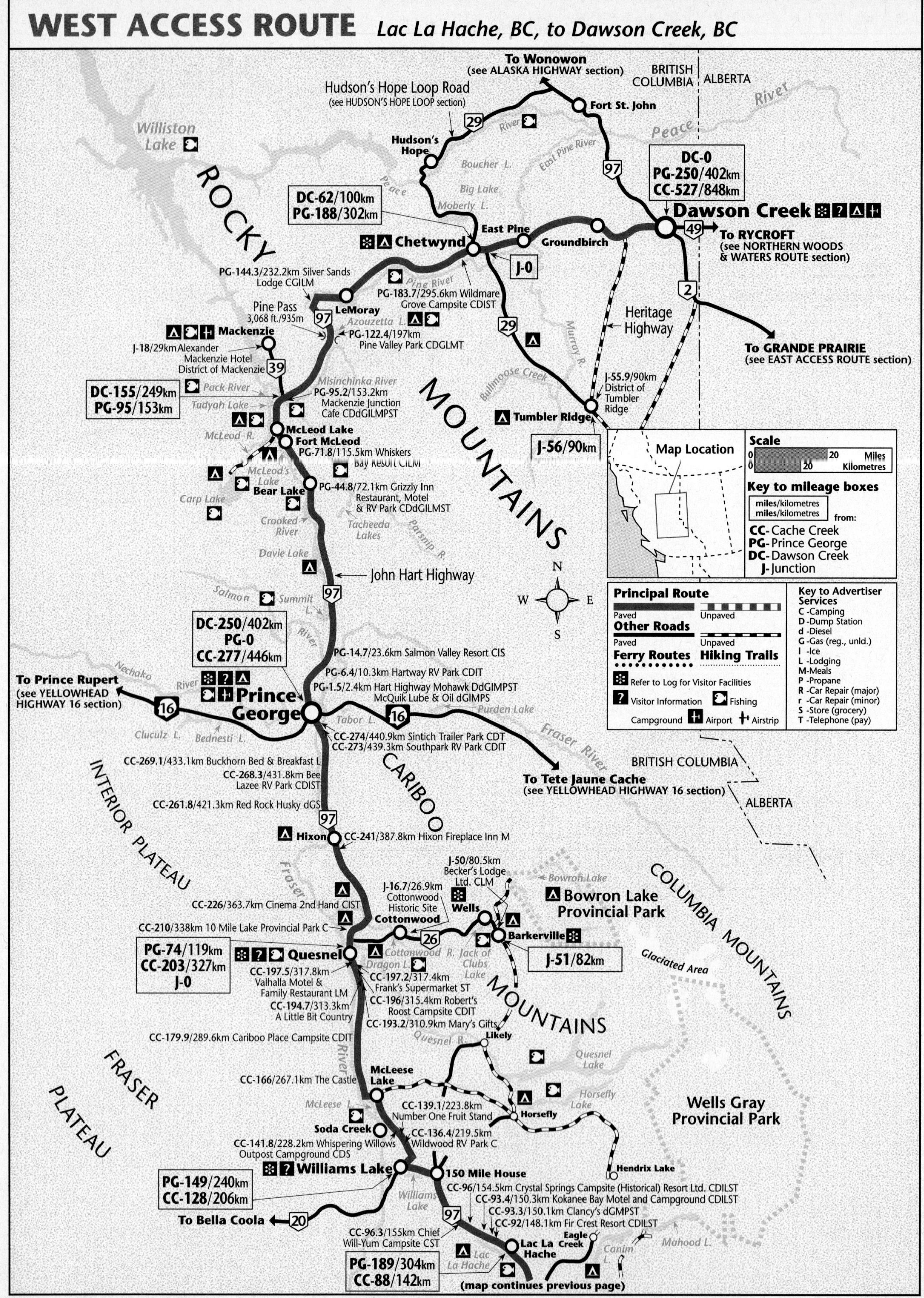

the infocentre. ▲

Cottonwood Meadows RV Country Club. Exit 116. Highly rated and recommended by Good Sam, Woodalls, Tourism B.C. New, secure, clean, well-maintained, full service park. Easy access, electronic gates, well lit and well managed. Lazy stream, full hooks, cable TV, wide level sites, paved roadways. Nicest washrooms, laundromat, clubhouse, jacuzzi, pay phone. Near U.S. border crossing, shopping centers, golf-courses. Pets on leash only. Open end of March to early November. VISA, MasterCard. 44280 Luckakuk Way, Chilliwack, BC V2R 4A7. Telephone (604) 824-PARK (7275). [ADVERTISEMENT] ▲

A 16.8 (27.1 km) **CC 153.2** (246.5 km) Highway 119B to Chilliwack Airport.

A 17 (27.4 km) **CC 153** (246.2 km) Exit 119 north to Chilliwack (all services, description follows) and south to Sardis (all services) and Cultus Lake Provincial Park.

Cultus Lake Provincial Park has 300 campsites; water, flush and pit toilets, showers, firewood, water, boat launch, swimming, fishing, canoeing, kayaking, and hiking and walking trails. Cultus Lake resort area also offers water slides, go-carts and other activities. ▲

CHILLIWACK (pop. 63,000) has motels, restaurants, shopping malls, banks, gas stations, RV parks and other services. There is a library, 2 movie theatres and an arts centre. The Canadian Military Engineers Museum is located off Vedder Road. Recreational attractions include golf and the popular Cultus Lake area with water park, boat rentals, horseback riding and camping. ▲

A 18 (29 km) **CC 152** (244.6 km) Exit 123 Prest Road north to Rosedale, south to Ryder Lake.

A 23.2 (37.4 km) **CC 146.8** (236.2 km) Exit 129 for Annis Road and RV park. ▲

Chilliwack RV Park & Campground. See display ad this section. ▲

A 26.5 (42.5 km) **CC 143.5** (230.9 km) Exit 135 to Highway 9 east to Harrison Hot Springs and alternate route Highway 7 to Hope and Vancouver (see HIGHWAY 7 log this section). Westbound exit for Bridal Veil Falls. Also exit here for access to Minter Gardens, which rivals Victoria's famous Butchart Gardens for beauty. The 27 acres of floral displays feature 11 themed gardens, topiary figures and a rare collection of Chinese Penjing Rock Bonsai. Open daily, April through Oct., 9 A.M. to dusk. Entertainment is scheduled Sundays and holidays, weather permitting.

Exit north for Cheam Lake Wetlands Regional Park. Once mined for its marl deposits, Cheam Lake is now a wildlife habitat; interpretive trails, good bird watching.

Highway 7 Log

An older route than Trans-Canada Highway 1, Highway 7 connects Vancouver and Hope via the north bank of the Fraser River. This log follows Highway 11 to its junction with Highway 7 at Mission, then Highway 7 to Hope via Harrison Hot Springs. This route is a scenic—and slower—alternative to Trans-Canada Highway 1.

Distance is measured from junction (J) of Trans-Canada Highway 1 and Highway 11 at Abbotsford.

J 0 Junction of Highways 1 and 11 at Abbotsford (Exit 92). Follow signs for Highway 11 North. This is a 2-lane road, with passing lanes, through a scenic valley of agricultural lands.

J 5.5 (8.9 km) Matsqui Trail Regional Park; 6 miles/10 km of Fraser River dikes for walking.

J 6.8 (10.9 km) Fraser River bridge.

J 7.4 (11.9 km) Exit to **MISSION** (pop. 31,000), named for a Roman Catholic mission built in 1861. Facilities include 2 motels, bed and breakfasts, restaurants and gas stations. The major attraction here is the Westminster Abbey, a Benedictine seminary completed in 1982 and known for its view and stained glass. The ruins of the original mission and school are located in Fraser River Heritage Park.

Follow signs northeast to Highway 7.

J 8.5 (13.7 km) **Junction** with Highway 7; follow signs east for Agassiz and Harrison Hot Springs.

9.1 (14.7 km) Access to Fraser River Heritage Park, site of the ruins of St. Mary's Mission and Indian school, a day-use area with good views of the Fraser River valley and Mount Baker. Norma Kenney House on park grounds has a gift shop and food service.

J 9.4 (15.1 km) Travel Infocentre; parking, restrooms.

J 10.9 (17.5 km) Turnoff for Nielson Regional Park and Hatzic Lake; picnic tables, swimming.

J 11 (17.7 km) Hatzic Rock, an important spiritual and habitation site for the people of the Stolo nation; open 8 A.M. to dusk.

J 11.1 (17.8 km) Hatzic Lake turnoff. Watch for fruit and vegetable stands in summer.

J 13 (20.9 km) Inch Creek Fish Hatchery turnoff.

J 13.2 (21.3 km) Dewdney; general store, post office and grocery.

J 13.4 (21.6 km) Nicomen Slough bridge.

J 20 (32.2 km) Deroche; general store and gas.

J 25.5 (41.1 km) Squaqum Park; picnicking.

J 25.7 (41.6 km) Harrison Bay ("Sasquatch country"); store, camping, gas.

J 26.5 (42.7 km) Harrison Mills (unincorporated).

J 27.4 (44.1 km) Morris Valley Road north to Hemlock Valley ski area and Chehalis River Hatchery.

J 27.7 (44.6 km) Gas station to north.

J 28 (45 km) Swing bridge over Harrison River.

J 29 (46.6 km) Kennedy Road. Turn south for Kilby General Store and Farm, a BC Heritage site, and Kilby Provincial Historic Park; picnicking and a fully stocked 1928 general store museum (open daily in summer).

View of Harrison Lake from Harrison Hot Springs Resort. *(Judy Parkin, staff)*

J 31.9 (51.3 km) Brio Springs; stop for spring water.

J 32.4 (52.1 km) Stop-of-interest plaque about Fraser River Delta.

Begin 11 percent downgrade eastbound; 3 lanes.

J 35.2 (56.6 km) Gas station.

J 37.2 (59.8 km) **Junction** with Highway 9 south to Agassiz. Turnoff to north for **HARRISON HOT SPRINGS** (pop. 700), 4 miles/6.4 km. Known as the "Spa of Canada," this resort town on the shore of Harrison Lake has 2 hot mineral springs. Harrison public hot pool is open daily. Motels, restaurants and other services available. Boat tours of the lake depart from the Harrison Hotel. Beach, good windsurfing and other water sports. Camping, picnicking and hiking at Sasquatch Provincial Park north of town.

There are several private campgrounds on Highway 7 north to Harrison Hot Springs.

J 44.6 (71.8 km) Turnout to south overlooking Fraser River valley.

J 46 (74 km) Johnson Slough. Rest area to north.

J 48.3 (77.7 km) Ruby Creek bridge.

J 55.7 (89.7 km) **Junction** with Trans-Canada Highway 1 north of Hope (see **Milepost A 51.5** this section).

Return to Milepost AO or A 51.5 West Access Route

A 27.3 (43.9 km) **CC 142.7** (229.6 km) Exit 138 to Popkum Road. Eastbound access to Bridal Veil Falls Provincial Park to south; picnicking, trail to base of falls. Also access to small community of Popkum and various roadside attractions, including water slide, Sandstone Gallery rock and gem museum, and prehistoric-themed amusement park. Food, gas and lodging.

A 34.5 (55.5 km) **CC 135.5** (218.1 km) Exit 146 Herrling Island, a cottonwood tree farm (no access or services), visible from highway.

A 40.5 (65.2 km) **CC 129.5** (208.4 km) Exit 153 to Laidlaw (no services) and access to Jones (Wahleach) Lake. Although F.H. Barber Provincial Park is noted here on BC provincial park maps, travelers should be aware that the park is totally undeveloped and has no access and no facilities.

A 42.5 (68.4 km) **CC 127.5** (205.2 km) Truck weigh scales; public phone.

A 44.7 (71.9 km) **CC 125.3** (201.6 km) Exit 160 to Hunter Creek rest area; tables, toilet and pay phone. Hunter Creek Travel Infocentre operates here daily, 9 A.M. to 5 P.M., mid-May to Labour Day weekend.

A 45.5 (73.2 km) **CC 124.5** (200.4 km) Exit 165 to Flood/Hope Road. Access to RV parks and Hope airport. Vancouver Soaring Assoc. is located at Hope Airport and offers glider rides on summer weekends; phone (604) 521-5501 for cost and schedule. Also access this exit to Silver Skagit Road (see **Milepost A 48.5**). ▲

A 47 (75.6 km) **CC 123** (197.9 km) **Wild Rose Good Sampark.** On Highway 1 east (from Vancouver) 4.8 km (3 miles) west of Hope; take Flood–Hope Road exit 165. On Highway 1 west (from Hope) take Flood–Hope Road exit 168. Full hookups, 15–30 amps, tenting, level grassy sites in parklike setting, 60-foot pull-throughs, free cable TV, free hot showers, laundry, playground, clubroom, horseshoes, firepits, picnic tables, a limited store. Ice, wood, pay phone, sani-station, near restaurant. Senior citizen discount, weekly rates, MasterCard, VISA. Small pets. Cancellation policy—two days. Open March 15 to Oct. 15. Phone (604) 869-9842, fax 869-3171. Toll-free reservations in Canada and U.S.A. Phone 1-800-463-7999. [ADVERTISEMENT] ▲

A 48.5 (78.1 km) **CC 121.5** (195.5 km) Exit 168 to Silverhope Creek (eastbound only). Access to RV park. Also access to Silver Skagit Road which leads south 37 miles/60 km through the Skagit Valley past Silver Lake Provincial Park and Skagit Valley Recreation Area. ▲

A 48.7 (78.4 km) **CC 121.3** (195.2 km) Silver Creek, Flood-Hope Road exit.

A 50 (80.5 km) **CC 120** (193.1 km) **Junction** of Trans-Canada Highway 1, Highway 3 (Crowsnest Highway) and Highway 5 (Coquihalla Highway). Use Exit 170 northbound for Trans-Canada Highway 1 to Hope.

Hope

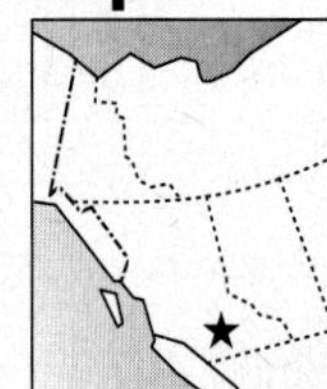

A 50.2 (80.8 km) **CC 119.8** (192.8 km) **Population:** 6,850. **Elevation:** 140 feet/43m. **Emergency Services: RCMP, Fire Department, Ambulance,** phone 911. **Hospital,** 1275 7th Ave., phone (604) 869-5656. **Visitor Information:** Visitor InfoCentre and museum building, corner of Hudson Bay Street and Water Avenue, on the right northbound as you enter town. Open daily 8 A.M. to 8 P.M. in July and Aug., 9 A.M. to 5 P.M. in May, June and Sept.; weekdays only, 10 A.M. to 4 P.M., rest of the year.

Hope is on a bend of the Fraser River where it flows through a picturesque gap in the forested Coast Mountains near Mount Hope (elev. 6,000 feet/1,289m). It is a popular tourist stop with complete services. About 20 motels and resorts are in Hope or just outside town on Trans-Canada Highway 1 and on Highway 3. Other facilities include auto body shops, service stations, department stores, restaurants and grocery stores.

Hope has some 20 wood carvings throughout downtown. These cougars are in Memorial Park. (© Carmen Scott)

Hope is rapidly becoming known for its collection of locally crafted chain saw carvings. There are approximately 20 of these large wooden carvings throughout the downtown area. Ask at the Visitor InfoCentre for directions to see all the carvings.

The major attraction in the Hope area is the Coquihalla Canyon Provincial Recreation Area, the focus of which is the Othello Quintette Tunnels. The 5 rock tunnels which cut through the tortuous canyon were part of the Kettle Valley Railway. This stretch of railway has been restored as a walking trail through the tunnels and across bridges. The tunnels are accessible from downtown Hope via Kawkawa Lake Road and Othello Road, about a 10-minute drive.

The Coquihalla Highway, completed in 1987, connects Hope with the Trans-Canada Highway just west of Kamloops, a distance of 118 miles/190 km. This is a 4-lane divided highway; toll charged.

There are private campgrounds on all roads into town. The town campground on Kawkawa Lake Road has 31 RV sites, 81 tent sites, coin showers and sani-station. ▲

HOPE ADVERTISERS

West Access Route Log
(continued)

A 50.7 (81.6 km) **CC 119.3** (191.9 km) Bridge over Fraser River. Turnout at north end, access to pedestrian bridge across the Fraser.

A 51.5 (82.8 km) **CC 118.5** (190.7 km) **Junction** with Highway 7, which leads west to Harrison Hot Springs and Vancouver.

A 53.1 (85.5 km) **CC 116.9** (188.1 km) Rest area (westbound access only) with picnic tables to west by Lake of the Woods.

A 60.8 (97.8 km) **CC 109.2** (175.7 km) Easy-to-miss turnoff (watch for sign 400m before turn) for Emory Creek Provincial Park east of highway; 34 level gravel sites in trees, water, fire rings, picnic tables, firewood, flush and pit toilets, and litter barrels. Camping fee April to Oct. Hiking and walking trails. Gold panning and fishing in **Fraser River.** ▲

Very much in evidence between Hope and Cache Creek are the tracks of the Canadian National and Canadian Pacific railways. Construction of the CPR—Canada's first transcontinental railway—played a significant role in the history of the Fraser and Thompson river valleys. Begun in 1880, the CPR line between Kamloops and Port Moody was contracted to Andrew Onderdonk.

A 64.8 (104.3 km) **CC 105.2** (169.3 km) **YALE** (pop. 500; elev. 250 feet/76m). **Emergency Services: Police, Fire Department, Ambulance,** phone 911. **Visitor Information:** In the museum, phone (604) 863-2324. Visitor facilities include motels, stores, gas stations and restaurants.

Yale was the head of navigation for the Lower Fraser River and the beginning of the overland gold rush trail to British Columbia's goldfields. The Anglican Church of Saint John the Divine here was built for the miners in 1859 and is the oldest church still on its original foundation in mainland British Columbia. Next to the church is Yale Museum and a bronze plaque honouring Chinese construction workers who helped build the Canadian Pacific Railway. Walking around town, look for the several plaques relating Yale's history. Daily guided walking tours of historic Yale are offered in summer; fee charged, includes admission to museum and church. Phone (604) 863-2428 for more information.

A 65.6 (105.5 km) **CC 104.5** (168.2 km) Entering Fraser Canyon northbound. The Fraser River and canyon were named for Simon Fraser (1776–1862), the first white man to descend the river in 1808. This is the dry forest region of British Columbia, and it can be a hot drive in summer. The scenic Fraser Canyon travelers drive through today was a formidable obstacle for railroad engineers in 1881.

A 66 (106.2 km) **CC 104** (167.4 km) Yale Tunnel, first of several northbound through the Fraser Canyon.

A 67.3 (108.3 km) **CC 102.7** (165.2 km) Turnout to east with plaque about the Cariboo Wagon Road, which connected Yale with the Cariboo goldfields near Barkerville. Built between 1861 and 1863 by the Royal Engineers, it replaced an earlier route to the goldfields—also called the Cariboo Wagon Road—which started from Lillooet.

A 68.4 (110.1 km) **CC 101.6** (163.5 km) Saddle Rock Tunnel. This 480-foot-/146-m-long tunnel was constructed in 1957–58.

A 72.1 (116 km) **CC 97.9** (157.5 km) **Colonial Inn.** In scenic Fraser Canyon. Cabin-style sleeping and kitchen units with showers and satellite TV. Pay phones. Picnic area with barbecues. Mountain views. Campground with full hookups and showers. For reservations call (604) 863-2277 or write RR #1, Yale, BC V0K 2S0. Stop and smell the flowers. [ADVERTISEMENT] ▲

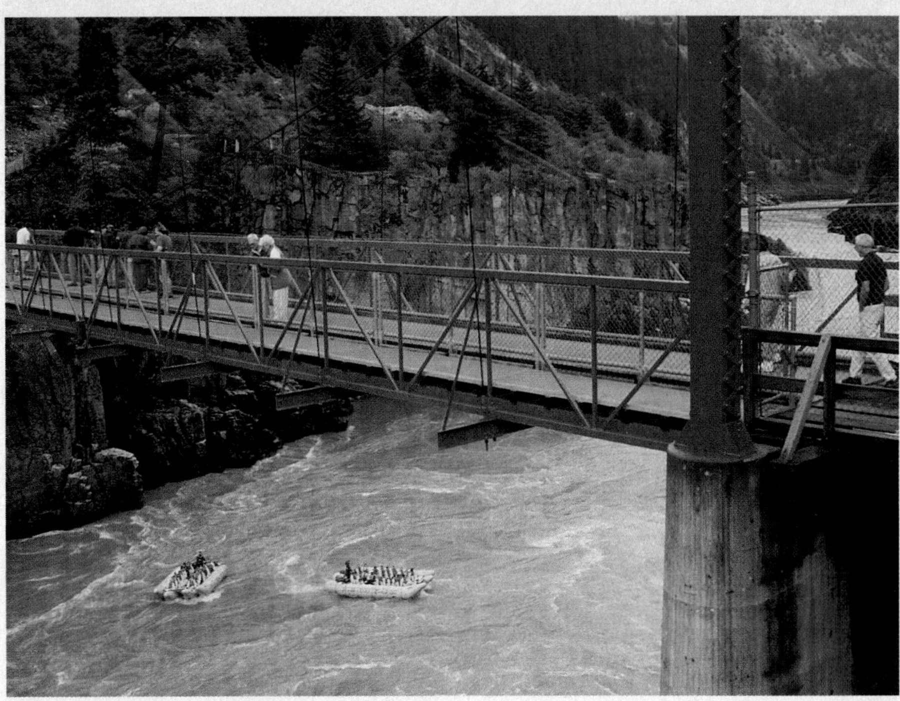

View of rafters in the swirling Fraser River from footbridge at Hells Gate, Milepost A 83.6. (Judy Parkin, staff)

A 72.3 (116.3 km) **CC 97.7** (157.2 km) Sailor Bar Tunnel, nearly 984 feet/300m long. There were dozens of bar claims along the Fraser River in the 1850s bearing colourful names such as Sailor Bar.

A 76.5 (123.1 km) **CC 93.5** (150.5 km) Spuzzum (unincorporated), gas station and food.

A 77.1 (124.1 km) **CC 92.9** (149.5 km) Stop of interest at south end of Alexandra Bridge, built in 1962, the second largest fixed arch span in the world at more than 1,640 feet/500m in length.

A 77.5 (124.8 km) **CC 92.5** (148.9 km) Alexandra Bridge Provincial Park, picnic areas and interpretive displays on both sides of highway. Hiking trail down to the old Alexandra Bridge, still intact. This suspension bridge was built in 1926, replacing the original built in 1863.

A 77.8 (125.2 km) **CC 92.2** (148.4 km) Historic Alexandra Lodge is the last surviving original roadhouse on the Cariboo Wagon Road.

A 79.5 (128 km) **CC 90.5** (145.6 km) Alexandra Tunnel.

A 80.5 (129.5 km) **CC 89.5** (144 km) Rest area by Copper Creek to east.

A 82.6 (133 km) **CC 87.4** (140.7 km) Hells Gate Tunnel (328 feet/100m long).

A 83.3 (134 km) **CC 86.7** (139.5 km) Ferrabee Tunnel (328 feet/100m long).

A 83.6 (134.5 km) **CC 86.4** (139 km) Hells Gate, the narrowest point on the Fraser River and a popular attraction. (Northbound traffic park at lot immediately south of attraction on east side of road; southbound traffic park on west side of road at attraction.) Two 25-passenger airtrams take visitors some 500 feet down across the river to a restaurant and shop complex. Footbridge across river to view fishways where some 2 million salmon pass through each year. A display details the life cycle of the salmon, the construction of the International Fishways and the history of Hells Gate. Trams operate daily, April 5 to Oct. 24, 1996. There is also a steep trail down to the fishways; strenuous hike.

Hells Gate was well named. It was by far the most difficult terrain for construction of both the highway and the railway. To haul supplies for the railway upstream of Hells Gate, Andrew Onderdonk built the sternwheel steamer *Skuzzy*. The *Skuzzy* made its way upstream through Hells Gate in 1882, hauled by ropes attached to the canyon walls by bolts.

Hell's Gate Airtram. See display ad this section.

A 83.8 (134.9 km) **CC 86.2** (138.7 km) Hells Gate turnaround for travelers who miss

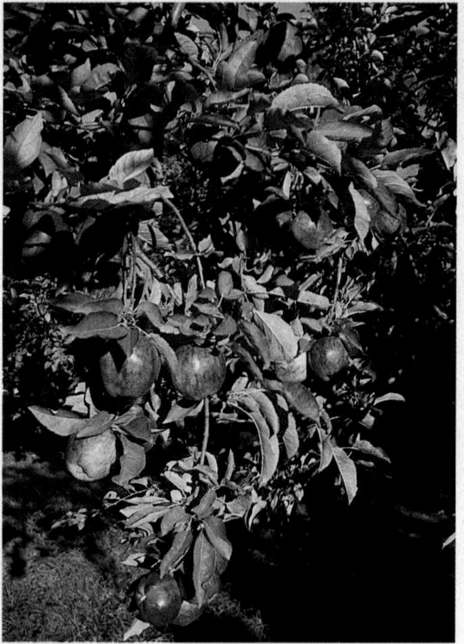

Apple orchard in the Thompson River valley. Watch for fruit stands along the highway. (Judy Parkin, staff)

the Hells Gate parking lot.

A 85.7 (137.9 km) **CC 84.3** (135.7 km) China Bar Tunnel, built in 1960. It is almost 2,300 feet/700m long, one of the longest tunnels in North America. Point of interest sign at south end about Simon Fraser.

A 91 (146.5 km) **CC 79** (127.1 km) **BOSTON BAR** (pop. 885; elev. 400 feet/122m). **Emergency Services: Police, Fire Department, Ambulance**, phone 911. Services include gas stations, cafes, grocery stores, motels and private RV parks. Site of the J.S. Jones Timber Mill; tours may be available in summer, phone (604) 867-9214 for information. Boston Bar was the southern landing for the steamer *Skuzzy*, which plied the Fraser River between here and Lytton during construction of the CPR.

North Bend, located across the river from Boston Bar, is a former railway community with a picturesque old station and roundhouse. Old cable cage from the aerial car ferry that once served North Bend is on display by the bridge.

A 94 (151.3 km) **CC 76** (122.3 km) **Canyon Alpine RV Park & Campground.** Still the best-kept secret in the Fraser Canyon, but quickly being discovered and described as "...one of the nicest parks on the Alaskan route." Secure RV parking and tenting 3 miles North of Boston Bar. 31 Level, pull-through sites, fully serviced with 30 amp, water, sewer and cable TV. Easy access and turnarounds for rigs over 35 feet. 14 foot entrance gate clearance. Away from traffic noise and railroads. Clean washrooms. Hot showers. Shaded sites. Fire rings. Free firewood. 50 yards south of restaurant, store, laundromat and telephones. Pets on leash welcome. 10 minutes from world famous Hell's Gate Airtram. Open April 15 to Oct. 15. 50490 Trans-Canada Highway. Phone/fax (604) 867-9734. Your friendly hosts, Martha and Fred Jost. [ADVERTISEMENT] ▲

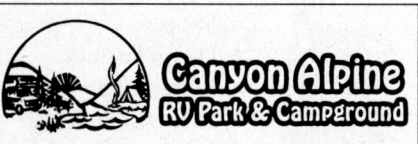

A 96 (154.5 km) **CC 74** (119.1 km) **Fraser Acres Cafe**. We make our soup and buns fresh each morning. We also serve daily specials—fresh salmon is our specialty. Our home-baked fruit pies are a favourite. We offer local Native arts and crafts for sale. Open early May to end of October. Drive-through parking lot. Box 369, Boston Bar, BC, V0K IC0. (604) 867-9266. [ADVERTISEMENT]

A 101 (162.5 km) **CC 69** (111 km) Turnoff for Blue Lake Lodge and Blue Lake Resort, 0.6 mile/1 km gravel road (first 0.3 mile/0.5 km steep and winding).

Blue Lake Lodge. Log lodge (non-smoking bedrooms) twin, queen and 1 king-sized bed. Shared bathrooms. Continental breakfast included. Full menu service with gourmet dinners. Licensed beer, wine, liquors. Outdoor patio with hot tub. Service, pampering and serenity is our specialty. On the same property as Blue Lake Resort. Swimming in crystal clear lake. Boat and canoe rentals. Hiking and trout fishing. Phone/fax (604) 867-9202. [ADVERTISEMENT]

Blue Lake Resort. 1 km off highway on quiet, family oriented, private trout lake. Wooded RV/tent sites, power, water, some sewer, pull-thrus, pet area, sani-dump. Rustic wilderness cabins (need bedding), kitchenettes, central washrooms, laundry, free showers. Boat and canoe rentals, store, playground, summer activities. Swimming, hiking, abundant wildlife. Security gate closed 10 P.M.–7 A.M. Phone/fax (604) 867-9246. [ADVERTISEMENT] ▲

A 110 (177 km) **CC 60** (96.6 km) Kanaka Bar; restaurant.

Kanaka Inn Restaurant—Located at Historic Kanaka Bar. Large well-lit parking lot for big rigs on west side of highway. Popular with truckers. Licensed. Daily lunch and dinner specials. Canadian and Chinese cuisine. Seating for up to 100. Open year-round from 6 A.M. to midnight daily. VISA, MasterCard, American Express, Diner's Club. (604) 455-6649. P.O. Box 309, Lytton, BC V0K 1Z0. [ADVERTISEMENT]

A 112.8 (181.5 km) **CC 57.2** (92.1 km) Viewpoint to west overlooking the Fraser River.

A 114.6 (184.5 km) **CC 55.4** (89.2 km) Skupper rest area (northbound only); toilets, tables, litter barrels.

A 117.8 (189.6 km) **CC 52.2** (84 km) **Junction** with Highway 12 to Lillooet. Turn west here for community of Lytton (description follows).

LYTTON (pop. 400; elev. 561 feet/171m). **Emergency Services: RCMP**, phone (604) 455-2225. **Fire Department**, phone (604) 455-2333. **Ambulance**, phone 1 (604) 374-5937. **Hospital**, St. Bartholomew's, phone (604) 455-2221. **Visitor Information**: Travel Infocentre, 400 Fraser St., phone (604) 455-2523. Located at the confluence of the Thompson and Fraser rivers, Lytton acts as headquarters for river raft trips. All visitor facilities are available. Sand bars at Lytton yielded much gold, and river frontage has been set aside for recreational gold panning. Lytton has recorded the highest temperature in British Columbia, 111°F/44°C.

Lytton. Rafting capital of British Columbia in the scenic Fraser Canyon. Public pool at Infocentre. Whitewater rafting on the Thompson River with raft rides through Hells Gate on the Fraser during August and September. Hiker access to the Stein and Botannie valleys. Many other natural attractions from Spences Bridge to Yale. Visit the Infocentre: view the "jellyroll"—a rare geological formation, get highway and local travel information, arrange for sawmill and woods tours. At the confluence of the Thompson and Fraser rivers. Pan for gold at water's edge. Infocentre, 400 Fraser St., phone (604) 455-2523. [ADVERTISEMENT]

A 113.6 (182.9 km) **CC 56.4** (90.7 km) Canadian National and Canadian Pacific railways cross over the Fraser River here; a favorite spot for photos. Gravel turnout to east.

A 121.2 (195.2 km) **CC 48.8** (78.4 km) Rafting centre. Watch for rafters in the river during the summer months.

A 122.8 (197.6 km) **CC 47.2** (76 km) Skihist Provincial Park to east; 58 campsites on east side of highway with water, flush and pit toilets, firewood and dump station. Picnic area on west side of highway (good place to watch the trains go by); wheelchair-accessible restrooms. ▲

A 131.1 (211 km) **CC 38.9** (62.6 km) **Thompson River RV Park**. See display ad this section. ▲

A 134.7 (216.8 km) **CC 35.3** (56.8 km) Goldpan Provincial Park to west alongside river; 14 campsites, picnic area, water, firewood, canoeing, kayaking, fishing. ▲

A 136 (218.9 km) **CC 34** (54.7 km) In summer, watch for fruit stands selling locally grown produce along the highway. Watch for bighorn sheep on the hillsides in the fall.

A 137 (220.5 km) **CC 33** (53.1 km) **Big Horn, BC**. Bring your binoculars! Depending on month and season, you may see eagles, osprey, bears, deer or big horn sheep on our mountain face. Large viewing windows in our cafe. Enjoy our extra-deep-dish pies, custom burgers. Vegetarian dishes available. We also sell fishing tackle, fresh fruit (June–Sept.), local rocks and minerals, fireworks, souvenirs. Trading post. Fuel. 24-hour towing. Tire shop. Dry overnight parking. Family operated. Box 98, Spences Bridge, BC, V0K 2L0. (604) 458-2333. [ADVERTISEMENT] ▲

A 140 (225.3 km) **CC 30** (48.3 km) **Junction** with Highway 8 to Merritt and south

3 Minute "Detour It!" Through

HISTORIC ASHCROFT

Experience the drive through the true Old West — historic Ashcroft — a village that was the major wagon team centre of transportation activity on the "Gold Rush Trail". (A downtown revitalization is in process to return this town to its historic past of the 1885 - 1915 era.)

Ashcroft has undergone many changes in past. The native Indians called the area Tuk Tuk Chim. The first pioneers referred to it as Harper's Mill. The CPR's Mr. Van Horne noted it as St. Cloud in his records, although freighters and prospectors called it Barnes Station. The name that finally stayed with the town was "Ashcroft", a name used by the Cornwall brothers for their nearby home and post office which recalled an estate in England.

The Cornwalls established Ashcroft Manor and Ashcroft's first industries in 1862-63. Mr. Clement Cornwall then went on to become B.C.'s first Lieutenant Governor in 1881.

Ashcroft as we know it began with the construction of the Thompson River Hotel in 1883. Today there is a new hotel on the Thompson River, Ashcroft's River Inn. As well, the first bridge was built in 1886. Today we see the newly constructed bridge, opened in August 1991.

The great fire of 1916 saw the large Chinese community become very prosperous, building several general stores, restaurants and new hotels to replace those lost in the fire. They were so successful that Dr. Sun Yat Sen spent an entire week in Ashcroft when travelling Canada to raise money to overthrow the Manchu Dynasty in China. Their graveyard, still intact, is a reminder of their deep rooted history; many were responsible for the building of the great Canadian railways — the routes over which both Canadian National and Canadian Pacific Railways travel.

Ashcroft became famous for its crops of delicious potatoes and tomatoes, grown and produced by the Chinese. Its excellent Canada-wide reputation led to the nickname "Spud City". However, tomatoes soon became the most lucrative crop and the cannery of 1924 became Canada's largest. By 1930 Canadian Canners marketed Ashcroft-grown Aylmer Brand tomatoes, shipping 30,000 cases per season, each season attracting 100's of Chinese from Vancouver to cultivate and harvest the crops. With the closing of the cannery in 1957, the future looked bleak. However, just five years later the copper mine came into existence, followed by 20 years of prosperity. The price of copper dropping in the 80s and the Coquihalla Highway going through spelled bad news for the entire area. Fortunes have, however, been revived. Ashcroft is now the business and trading centre for the residents of the area, and is becoming a retirement settlement for seniors.

The first newspaper, The Journal, established in 1885, continues to serve Ashcroft and area today. Pick up your copy of the historical publication *Out of the Sagebrush* or *Bittersweet Oasis*, a book that tells it all! Historic Ashcroft is on its way to becoming an number one attraction — "NOT TO BE MISSED!"

Sand and sage and the magical moods of the desert hills create a healthy sunshine location where the oasis named Ashcroft, with the Thompson River flowing through, becomes a place to discover and spend time at the full facility LEGACY PARK CAMPSITE. Near Ashcroft are some of the best fishing lakes in B.C. — as well as the Thompson River's steelhead fishing, grouse hunting, birdwatching, river rafting, and mountain biking.

For further information, come and visit the VISITOR INFOCENTRE in the Museum on Fourth Street.

SOME EVENTS & ATTRACTIONS NOT TO MISS...

- ✯ NL'AKAPXM EAGLE MOTORPLEX holds 15 drag races a season.
- ✯ Among them are the Oldtime Drag races in June with classic cars & the Winston Cup in September with over $100,000.00 in prize money.
- ✯ ASHCROFT & DISTRICT RODEO & PARADE 3nd week in June.
- ✯ ASHCROFT MUSEUM at the corner of 4th & Brink Streets, open daily.

SPONSORED BY:
Village of Ashcroft, Ashcroft Chamber of Commerce and Associated Businesses

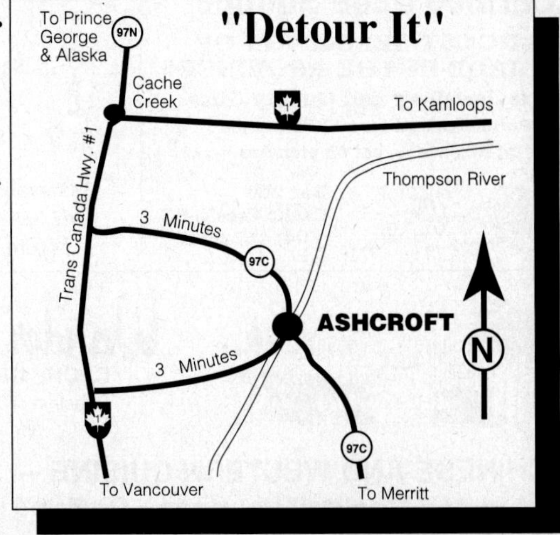

Black plastic mesh tarps cover fields of ginseng, an Asian medicinal root crop grown in this area. (Liz Bryan)

access to Spences Bridge. Plaque here about the great landslide of 1905.

A 141.2 (227.2 km) **CC 28.8** (46.3 km) North access to **SPENCES BRIDGE** (pop. 300; elev. 760 feet/231m) located at the confluence of the Thompson and Nicola rivers. Services include a cafe, pub and grocery with ice, bait, tackle and fishing licenses. A record 30-lb., 5-oz. steelhead was caught in the Thompson River in 1984. Look for an osprey nest atop the hydroelectric pole on the east side of the river.

Log Cabin Pub. Labeled the "Unofficial museum of Spences Bridge." You will appreciate this unique log structure. The logs were specially selected and prepared locally. Some spanning 50 feet. It features an assortment of antique guns, traps, and stuffed animals. An eye-catching 20-foot rock fireplace. 3,500 patrons have left their signatures on money which now decorates the walls. The pub offers spirits, beverages and a light menu. Beer and coolers to go. April–Dec. Sunday–Thursday 11 A.M.–12:30 A.M., Friday–Saturday 11 A.M.–1:30 A.M. (604) 458-2215. [ADVERTISEMENT]

A 153.4 (246.9 km) **CC 16.6** (26.7 km) Viewpoint overlooking Thompson River with plaque about the Canadian Northern Pacific (now the Canadian National Railway), Canada's third transcontinental railway, completed in 1915.

A 158.4 (255 km) **CC 11.6** (18.7 km) Red Hill rest area to east; tables, toilets, litter barrels, pay phone.

A 164.3 (264.4 km) **CC 5.7** (9.2 km) Stop of interest sign to east describes Ashcroft Manor, a roadhouse on the Cariboo Wagon Road. Summer temperatures in this dry and desertlike region typically reach the high 80s and 90s (26°C to 32°C).

Fields under black plastic mesh tarps—which may be seen as the highway descends northbound—are ginseng, an Asian medicinal root crop. The world supply of North American ginseng, which takes 4 years to mature, is grown in the southern Cariboo.

A 164.5 (264.7 km) **CC 5.5** (8.9 km) **Junction** with road to **ASHCROFT**, a small village on the Thompson River with full tourist facilities just east of the highway. Historic Ashcroft supplanted Yale as gateway to the Cariboo with the arrival of the Canadian Pacific Railway in 1885. There are a number of original buildings with distinctive architectural details. Ashcroft Museum houses a fine collection of artifacts tracing the history of the region. Logan Lake, east of Ashcroft, is the site of the second largest open-pit copper mine in North America (tours available).

Ashcroft Chamber of Commerce. See display ad this section.

Also **junction** with Highway 97C to Logan Lake and Merritt.

A 168.2 (270.7 km) **CC 1.8** (2.9 km) Second turnoff northbound for Ashcroft and road to Logan Lake.

Cache Creek

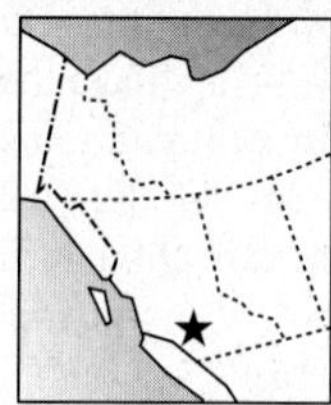

A 170 (273.6 km) **PG 277** (445.8 km) Located at the junction of Trans-Canada Highway 1 and Highway 97. **Population:** 1,200. **Elevation:** 1,508 feet/460m. **Emergency Services:** RCMP, phone (604) 453-2216. **Ambulance,** phone 1-604-374-5937. **Hospital,** phone (604) 453-5306.

Visitor Information: Write Box 460, Cache Creek, BC V0K 1H0; fax (604) 457-9669.

Cache Creek has ample facilities for the traveler (most located on or just off the main highways), including motels, restaurants, service stations and grocery store. Private campgrounds are available east of Cache Creek on Trans-Canada Highway 1 (across from the golf course) and just north of town on Highway 97.

A post office and bus depot are on Todd Road. Nearby, Cariboo Jade Shoppe offers free stone-cutting demonstrations in summer. On display out front is a 2,850-lb. jade boulder. Public park and swimming pool on the Bonaparte River, east off Highway 97 at the north edge of town.

The settlement grew up around the con-

CACHE CREEK ADVERTISERS

Bonaparte Motel ....Ph. (604) 457-9693
Brookside Campsite ....1 km E. of jct.
Cache Creek Campground ....4 km N. on Hwy. 97
Cariboo Jade & Gift Shoppe ....Ph. (604) 457-9566
Desert Motel.....................Ph. (604) 457-6226
Horsting's Farm Market...2 km N. on Hwy. 97
Wander-Inn Restaurant ....Ph. (604) 457-6511

fluence of the creek and the Bonaparte River. The Hudson's Bay Co. opened a store here, and Cache Creek became a major supply point on the Cariboo Wagon Road. Today, hay and cattle ranching, ginseng farming, mining, logging and tourism support the community. Area soils are dry but fertile. Residents claim that with irrigation, nearly anything can be grown here.

From the junction, Highway 97 leads north 277 miles/445.8 km to Prince George. Kamloops is 52 miles/83.7 km east via Trans-Canada Highway 1. Traveling north from Cache Creek the highway generally follows the historic route to the Cariboo goldfields.

Brookside Campsite. 1 km east of Cache Creek on Highway 1, full (30 amp) and partial hookups, pull-throughs, tent sites, super clean heated wash and laundry rooms, free showers, sani-stations, store, playground, nature path, heated pool, golf course adjacent, pets on leash, pay phones. VISA, MasterCard, C.P. two days. Good Sam. Box 737, Cache Creek, BC V0K 1H0. Phone: (604) 457-6633. [ADVERTISEMENT] ♿▲

Cariboo Jade & Gift Shoppe—Jade has been prized for over 7,000 years, and has at times been more valued than gold. Even today, it is reputed to bring its possessor good health and fortune. Nephrite jade, British Columbia's provincial gem stone, is very tough (4 times harder than marble) and difficult to work; but the finished piece always reveals unforgettable beauty. The Cariboo Jade & Gift Shoppe has the largest selection of BC jade in Canada; some items are crafted on-premise. Its 30 year reputation has been built on the variety, quantity, and quality of hand-picked semi-precious stone gift items from around the world. Stop by to see the 2,850-lb. jade boulder standing out front, and find out why so many visitors rave about this shop. At the junction in centre of Cache Creek. [ADVERTISEMENT]

West Access Route Log

(continued)

HIGHWAY 97/CARIBOO HIGHWAY

From Cache Creek, continue north on BC Highway 97 for Dawson Creek. Kilometreposts on this section of highway are located on the east side of the highway facing west, so that they may be seen by traffic traveling in either direction. Highway 97 between Cache Creek and Prince George is called the Cariboo Highway, and the region is locally referred to as "Super, Natural Cariboo Country." Contact the Cariboo Tourist Assoc., P.O. Box 4900, Williams Lake, BC V2G 2VB; phone toll-free 1-800-663-5885.

This section of the log shows distance from Cache Creek (CC) followed by distance from Prince George (PG).

CC 0 PG 277 (445.8 km) Cache Creek, **junction** of Trans-Canada Highway 1 and Highway 97.

CC 1.2 (2 km) **PG 275.8** (443.8 km) **Horsting's Farm Market**. See display ad this section.

CC 2.5 (4 km) **PG 274.5** (441.8 km) **Cache Creek Campground**, 3 km north of Cache Creek on Highway 97 north. Full hookups, pull-throughs and tenting, sani-station, store, country kitchen restaurant, laundromat, coin showers, heated washrooms. Outdoor pool and whirlpool (no charge). 18-hole mini-golf, horseshoes, seasonal river swimming and fishing. P.O. Box 127, Cache Creek, BC V0K 1H0. For reservations, phone (604) 457-6414. [ADVERTISEMENT] ▲

CC 7 (11.3 km) **PG 270** (434.5 km) **Junction** with Highway 99 west to Lillooet (46.5 miles/75 km) and Vancouver (209 miles/336.5 km) via Whistler and Blackcombe ski areas. (Formerly Highway 12, this route was designated as part of Highway 99 when the logging road between Lillooet and Pemberton was paved, making it possible to drive to the Cariboo from Vancouver via Squamish. Highway 99, promoted as the "Sea to Sky Highway," is logged in *Northwest Mileposts®*, available from Vernon Publications Inc.; phone 1-800-726-4707.)

Drive 0.4 mile/0.7 km west on Highway 99 for Hat Creek Heritage Ranch, a restored Cariboo Trail roadhouse and farm with reconstructed barn, working blacksmith shop, wagon and trail rides, and tours. Open daily 10 A.M. to 6 P.M., mid-May to mid-Oct. Phone (604) 457-9722 for current information.

Marble Canyon Provincial Park, 17.5 miles/28 km west on Highway 99, has 34 campsites, picnicking, swimming and hiking trails. ▲

CC 10 (16 km) **PG 267** (430 km) Gravel turnout with plaque about the BX stagecoaches that once served Barkerville. Formally known as the BC Express Company, the BX served the Cariboo for 50 years.

CC 13.6 (21.9 km) **PG 263.4** (423.9 km) Paved road leads east to **Loon Lake**, rainbow fishing, boat launch. Camping at Loon Lake Provincial Park (16 miles/26 km); 14 sites, water, pit toilets, firewood. ▲

CC 16.6 (26.7 km) **PG 260.4** (419.1 km) Carguile rest area.

CC 19.9 (32 km) **PG 257.1** (413.7 km) **Lakeview Campsite & RV Park**. See display ad this section. ▲

CC 25 (40.2 km) **PG 252** (405.5 km) **Junction** with Pavilion Mountain Road west to Pavilion via Kelly Lake. Camping at Downing Provincial Park (11 miles/18 km); 25 sites, swimming, fishing. ▲

CC 25.5 (41 km) **PG 251.5** (404.7 km) CLINTON (pop. 900, area 4,000; elev. 2,911 feet/887m). **Visitor Information**: Available at various local businesses; look for signs. All visitor facilities are available, including 3 motels, campground, gas stations, 24-hour towing and stores. Originally the site of 47 Mile Roadhouse, a gold-rush settlement on the Cariboo Wagon Road from Lillooet, today Clinton is called the "guest Ranch Capital of British Columbia." The museum, housed in a building of local, handmade red brick that once served as a courthouse, has fine displays of pioneer tools and items from the gold rush days, and a scale model of the Clinton Hotel. Clinton pioneer cemetery just north of town. Clinton boasts the oldest continuously held event in the province, the Clinton Ball (in May the weekend following Victoria Day), an annual event since 1868.

Clinton has its own sign forest. Visitors may sign a wooden slab (donated by the local sawmill) and add it to the sign forest.

Round-up Motel. See display ad this section.

Parkies Clothing and Variety Store. The largest selection of moccasins in the Cariboo. 30 minute photo developing. Deli and freshly-made submarine sandwich counter. Colour laser copies and fax service. Fishing tackle. Fishing and hunting licenses. Souvenirs. Large assortment of wildlife T-shirts, sweatshirts and western hats. Video rentals. Historical books and *The MILEPOST®* for sale. The friendly place where the flags are flying. VISA and MasterCard accepted. Box 538, Clinton, BC V0K 1K0. Phone/fax (604) 459-2535. Super, Natural Cariboo. [ADVERTISEMENT]

Pioneer Service and Towing. 24-hour towing service including RV's, trailers and motorcycles. Contract towing for BCAA/CAA/AAA. Complete major and minor repairs during regular shop hours: oil, lube, tire sales and repairs, brakes, tune-ups, air conditioning. In Clinton next to PetroCan. (604) 459-2253. Super, Natural Cariboo. [ADVERTISEMENT]

Gold Trail RV Park. Fully serviced sites, 30-amp power. Pull-throughs. Immaculate. Washrooms with flush toilets, handicap-equipped. Free hot showers for guests. On highway in town; easy walking to all amenities. Well-lit level sites. Grassed and landscaped. Sani-station. 1620 Cariboo Highway North, Clinton, BC V0K 1K0. (604) 459-2519. [ADVERTISEMENT]

CC 31 (49.9 km) **PG 246** (395.9 km) Dirt and gravel road leads 21 miles/34 km west to **Big Bar Lake** Provincial Park; 33 campsites, water, pit toilets, firewood, swimming, fishing and boat launch.

Clinton Lookout and Big Bar rest area to east just north of turnoff; toilets, tables, litter barrels.

CC 35 (56.3 km) **PG 242** (389.5 km) Loop road leads east 3 miles/5 km to Painted Chasm geological site and Chasm Provincial Park picnic area. This 1-mile-/1-.6-km-long bedrock box canyon was cut by glacial meltwaters.

CC 45 (72.4 km) **PG 232** (373.4 km) **70 MILE HOUSE** (unincorporated), originally a stage stop named for its distance from Lillooet, Mile 0. General store, post office, restaurant, motel, gas station with diesel and bus depot.

North Bonaparte Road leads east 7.5 miles/12 km to Green Lake Provincial Park; 121 campsites, water, toilets, firewood, dump station, swimming and boat launch. Rainbow and kokanee fishing at **Green Lake.** Paved road leads north to Watch Lake, east to Bonaparte Lake, and northeast to join Highway 24 at Bridge Lake.

CC 58.8 (94.7 km) **PG 218.2** (351.1 km) **83 MILE HOUSE**; restaurant, gas, propane, store, public phone. Turnoff for Green Lake.

CC 66 (106.2 km) **PG 211** (339.6 km) **Junction** with Highway 24 East to Lone Butte Bridge Lake and Little Fort (60 miles/96.5 km) on Yellowhead Highway 5. Highway 24 provides access to numerous fishing lakes and resorts, including **Bridge Lake** Provincial Park (31 miles/50 km east) with 20 campsites.

100 Mile House

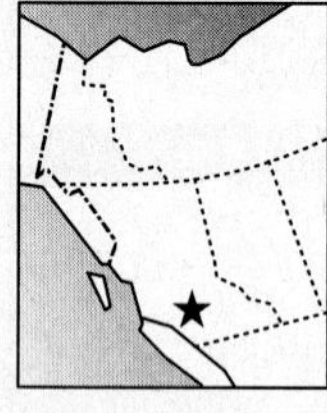

CC 72 (115.9 km) **PG 205** (329.9 km) **Population:** 1,900. **Elevation:** 3,050 feet/930m. **Emergency Services: Police,** phone (604) 395-2456. **Ambulance,** phone 1-604-374-5937. **Hospital,** phone (604) 395-2202. **Visitor Information:** At the log cabin by 100 Mile House Marsh (a bird sanctuary at the south edge of town); phone (604) 395-5353, fax 395-4085. Look for the 39-foot-/12-m-long skis! Or contact the Cariboo Tourist Assoc., P.O. Box 4900, Williams Lake, BC V2G 2VB; phone toll-free 1-800-663-5885.

This large, bustling town was once a stop for fur traders and later a post house on the Cariboo Wagon Road to the goldfields. In 1930, the Marquess of Exeter established the 15,000-acre Bridge Creek Ranch here. Today, 100 Mile House is the site of 2 lumber mills, and an extensive log home building industry.

Visitor services include restaurants, motels, a campground, gas stations with repair service, stores, a post office, 2 golf courses, a government liquor store, 2 supermarkets and banks. Shopping malls and the downtown area are located east of the highway. Centennial Park in town has picnic sites and walking trails.

100 Mile House is a popular destination for snowmobiling and cross-country skiing in winter. It is also the jumping-off point for fishermen headed for Canim Lake and Mahood Lake in Wells Gray Provincial Park. (Well-known for its spectacular waterfalls, including 460-foot/140-m Helmcken Falls, 4th largest in Canada, Wells Gray main entrance is from Yellowhead Highway 5 at Clearwater. Yellowhead Highway 5 is logged in *Northwest Mileposts®*, available from Vernon Publications Inc.; phone 1-800-726-4707.)

Horse Lake Road leads east from 100 Mile House to **Horse Lake** (kokanee) and other fishing lakes of the high plateau.

Farmhouse Collectables—Past to present: old license plates, "only-in-Canada" Wade Nursery Rhyme ornaments, railway collectables, old books and Canadiana, Depression glass, bottles, tins, jewellery, second-hand kitchenware, and more. Big parking lot. Open year-round, Monday–Saturday 9:30 A.M.–5 P.M. Highway. 97 on 99 Mile Hill. P.O. Box 45, 100 Mile House, BC V0K 2E0. (604) 395-4258. [ADVERTISEMENT]

99 Mile Motel. Air-conditioned sleeping and housekeeping units. Fridges in all units, housekeeping units with microwave ovens. DD touchtone phones, remote control cable TV, super channel and TSN, courtesy in-room coffee and tea. Carports, winter plug-ins, freezer available for guests, bowling, legion supermarket and cross-country ski trails. Senior citizens discount, commercial rates, partially wheelchair accessible, small dogs only. Highway 97, 100 Mile House, BC V0K 2E0. (604) 395-2255 (call collect). Super, Natural Cariboo. [ADVERTISEMENT]

100 Mile Motel and RV Park. 310 Highway 97. Downtown. Ground level sleeping and housekeeping units. DD phones, cable TV, seniors' rates, campground and RV park with hookups, showers, flush toilet (open mid-April to end of Oct.), hiking trail, shopping and restaurants nearby. P.O. Box 112, 100 Mile House, BC V0K 2E0. Phone (604) 395-2234. Super, Natural Cariboo. [ADVERTISEMENT]

The Loon Complex. Major and minor automotive and RV repairs provided by qualified, conscientious mechanics. Oversized pressure wash bays where you do the washing, or we can do it for you. Special detail bay for shampooing, hand waxing and interior cleaning. Car rentals. 755 Alder Ave., adjacent to Highway. 97 on south side of town. (604) 791-3394. [ADVERTISEMENT]

100 MILE HOUSE ADVERTISERS

Farmhouse Collectables....Ph. (604) 395-4258
Happy Landing Restaurant ....On the 99 Mile Hill
Loon Complex, The ....755 Alder Ave.
99 Mile Motel ....Ph. (604) 395-2255
100 Mile Motel ....Ph. (604) 395-2234

West Access Route Log

(continued)

CC 74 (119 km) **PG 203** (326.7 km) **Junction** with road east to **Ruth, Canim** and **Mahood lakes.** Resorts and fishing at all lakes. Camping at Canim Beach Provincial Park (27 miles/43 km); 16 sites, water, pit toilets, swimming. Access to Canim Falls.

Ponderosa Resort. See display ad this section.

CC 78.2 (125.8 km) **PG 198.8** (319.9 km) 108 Mile Ranch, a recreational community built in the 1970s, was once a cattle ranch. Motel and golf course.

Schmid-Meil Bed & Breakfast. Bavarian-Canadian guest house. Enjoy a restful visit. Stay in our main house or in our separate

guest house overlooking 108 Mile Lake and golf course. Spacious deluxe non-smoking rooms, most with private baths. Our generous breakfasts are a favourite. Outdoor pool, hot tub, sauna, patio, movie channel and free movie service. German news all day. Excellent restaurants nearby. Golfing, horseback riding, swimming, hiking, fishing and cross-country skiing. Open year-round. (604) 791-5644. Fax (604) 791-5645. Comp. 749, S 41 and R59 Telqua Drive, 108 Mile Ranch, BC V0K 2Z0. [ADVERTISEMENT]

CC 80.5 (129.5 km) **PG 196.5** (316.2 km) Rest area to west beside 108 Mile Lake. Alongside is 108 Heritage Site with some of

108 Heritage Site at Milepost CC 80.5 includes original log buildings from the 1860s. (Judy Parkin, staff)

the original log buildings from 108 Mile Ranch, and others relocated from 105 Mile. Guided tours; open May to early Sept.

CC 85 (136.8 km) **PG 192** (309 km) **Big Country KOA.** Located on 60 acres of rolling ranchland 3 miles south of Lac La Hache. Heated swimming pool, free showers, store, gift shop, laundromat, games room. Extra-long shady pull-throughs; shaded grassy tent sites; camping cabin. Full hookup facilities, sani-dump, phone. Pets welcome. VISA, MasterCard. (604) 396-4181. Box 68, Lac La Hache, BC V0K 1T0. [ADVERTISEMENT] ▲

CC 88 (141.6 km) **PG 189** (304.2 km) **LAC LA HACHE** (pop. 400; elev. 2,749 feet/838m), unincorporated. Motels, stores, gas stations and a museum. The community holds a fishing derby in July and a winter carnival in mid-February. Lac La Hache is French for "Ax Lake." There are many stories of how the lake got its name, but Molly Forbes, local historian, says it was named by a French–Canadian *coureur de bois* (voyageur) "because of a small ax he found on its shores."

Lac La Hache, lake char, rainbow and kokanee; good fishing summer and winter (great ice fishing).

CC 92 (148.1 km) **PG 185** (297.7 km) **Fir Crest Resort** (Good Sam). Quiet parklike setting just two minutes from Highway 97, but away from traffic noise. Full hookups including pull-throughs, camping and cabins on the lakeshore. Sandy beach, swimming, games room, groceries, sani-dump, laundromat. Full marina with boat, motor, canoe and tackle rentals. Enjoy the Super, Natural Cariboo. Show this ad for a 10 percent discount. Phone (604) 396-7337. [ADVERTISEMENT] ▲

CC 93.3 (150.1 km) **PG 183.7** (295.6 km) **Clancys'** restaurant, truck stop (full-serve gas, diesel, propane), convenience store and gifts. Open 7 A.M.–12 A.M. 2 acres, paved parking, air-conditioned, licensed with home cooking and homemade desserts. Very easy access to pumps for any length of vehicle. American exchange. Clancys', located Mile 122, Highway 97 at Kokanee Bay. [ADVERTISEMENT]

CC 93.4 (150.3 km) **PG 183.6** (295.4 km) **Kokanee Bay Motel and Campground.** Relaxation at its finest right on the lakeshore. Fish for kokanee and char or take a refreshing dip. We have a modern, comfortable motel, cabins. Full trailer hookups, grassy tenting area, hot showers, laundromat. Aquabike, boat and canoe rentals. Fishing tackle and ice. Phone (604) 396-7345. Fax (604) 396-4990. Super, Natural Cariboo. [ADVERTISEMENT] ▲

CC 96 (154.5 km) **PG 181** (291.3 km) **Crystal Springs Campsite (Historical) Resort Ltd.** Visit the Cariboo's best. We honour Good Sam, AAA and are a Good Neighbor Park. 8 miles north of Lac La Hache. Parklike setting on lakeshore. Showers, flush toilets, laundromat, full (20- and 30-amp pull-throughs) and partial hookups, boat rentals. New chalets, winterized. Groceries, tackle, camping supplies, handicrafts. Games room, playground, picnic shelter. Pets on leash. Public beach and boat launch adjacent, fishing. Your hosts, Doug and Lorraine Whitesell. Phone (604) 396-4497. Super, Natural Cariboo. [ADVERTISEMENT] ▲

CC 96 (154.5 km) **PG 181** (291.3 km) **Lac La Hache** Provincial Park; 83 campsites, lakeshore picnic area, water, flush and pit toilets, firewood, dump station, boat launch, swimming, hiking trail and fishing. Camping on east side of highway, picnicking and boat launch on west side of highway. ▲

CC 96.3 (155 km) **PG 180.7** (290.8 km) **Chief Will-Yum Campsite**. See display ad this section. ▲

CC 97 (156.1 km) **PG 180** (289.7 km) San Jose River parallels highway to west. Canadian artist A.Y. Jackson painted in this valley.

CC 104.4 (168 km) **PG 172.6** (277.7 km) Stop of interest sign commemorating the miners, traders and adventurers who came this way to the Cariboo goldfields in the 1860s.

CC 116.6 (187.6 km) **PG 160.4** (258.1 km) 148 Mile Ducks Unlimited conservation area. This is an important waterfowl breeding area in Canada and offers good bird watching for bald eagles, osprey, great horned owls, American kestrels and pileated woodpeckers.

CC 118.5 (190.7 km) **PG 158.5** (255.1 km) **150 MILE HOUSE,** so named because it was 150 miles from Lillooet on the old Cariboo Wagon Road. The post office, which serves about 1,200 people in the area, was established in 1871. Hotel, restaurant, pub, gas station with repair service and a store open daily. Hunting and fishing licenses available at the store.

CC 119.1 (191.7 km) **PG 157.9** (254.1 km) **Junction** with road to **Quesnel** and **Horsefly lakes.** Horsefly Lake Provincial Park (40 miles/65 km) has 22 campsites. Fishing for rainbow and lake trout. ▲

Williams Lake

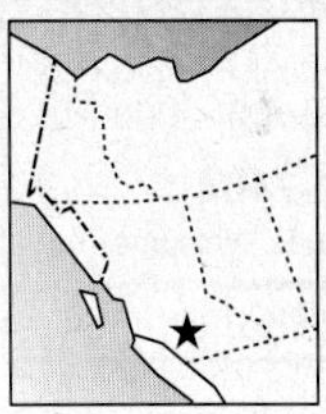

CC 128 (206 km) **PG 149** (239.8 km) Located at the junction of Highway 97 and Highway 20 to Bella Coola. **Population:** 20,000. **Elevation:** 1,964 feet/599m. **Emergency Services: Police,** phone (604) 392-6211. **Hospital,** phone (604) 392-4411.

Visitor Information: Travel Infocentre

WILLIAMS LAKE ADVERTISERS

Fraser Inn..........................Ph. (604) 398-7055
Museum of the Cariboo Chilcotin........Ph. (604) 392-7404
Williams Lake & District Chamber of Commerce..............Ph. (604) 392-5025

Distinctive Cariboo fence along Highway 20 west of Williams Lake. (Liz Bryan)

located on east side of highway just south of the junction of Highways 97 and 20, open year-round; phone (604) 392-5025. Or contact the Cariboo Tourist Assoc., P.O. Box 4900, Williams Lake, BC V2G 2VB; phone toll-free 1-800-663-5885.

The administrative and transportation hub of the Cariboo–Chilcotin region, Williams Lake has complete services, including hotels/motels, restaurants, an 18-hole golf course and par 3 golf course, a twin sheet arena and pool complex. Highway 97 bypasses the business and shopping districts of downtown Williams Lake, which are situated to the west of the highway. Motels, gas stations and fast-food restaurants are located on frontage roads paralleling Highway 97 on the south side of town.

A museum featuring the ranching and rodeo history of the region is located at the corner of 4th Avenue and Borland; open year-round.

The airport, 7 miles/11 km north of town on Highway 97, is served by daily flights to Vancouver and other interior communities.

Located on the shore of the lake of the same name, it was named for Shuswap Indian Chief Willyum. The town grew rapidly with the advent of the Pacific Great Eastern Railway (now B.C. Railway) in 1919, to become a major cattle marketing and shipping centre for the Cariboo–Chilcotin. Today the city has the largest and most active cattleyards in the province. Lumber and mining for copper-molybdenum are the mainstays of the economy.

The famous Williams Lake Stampede, British Columbia's premier rodeo, is held here annually on the July 1 holiday. The 4-day event draws contestants from all over Canada and the United States. The rodeo grounds are located in the city.

At the north end of Williams Lake is Scout Island Nature Center. This island is reached by a causeway, with boardwalks providing access to the marshes. A nature house is open May to Aug.

Highway 20 travels west from Williams Lake 282 miles/454 km to Bella Coola, giving access to the Chilcotin country's excellent fishing, Tweedsmuir Provincial Park, and the remote central coast. The highway is paved for the first 112.5 miles/181 km. At Heckman Pass (elev. 5,000 feet/1,524m), 218.5 miles/352 km west of Williams Lake, the highway descends a section of narrow, switchbacked road with an 18 percent grade for about 12 miles/19 km. Beyond "the hill," the road is paved to Bella Coola. Highway 20, the Chilcotin Highway, is logged in *Northwest Mileposts®* (Vernon Publications Inc.; phone 1-800-726-4707).

West Access Route Log

(continued)

CC 136.4 (219.5 km) **PG 140.6** (226.3 km) Wildwood Road; gas station, store, access to private campground. ▲

Wildwood RV Park. See display ad this section. ▲

CC 139.1 (223.8 km) **PG 137.9** 221.9 km) **Number One Fruit Stand.** Fresh fruit and produce in season. Free fruit samples for customers. Succulent hot buttered corn from June–October. Sweet, yellow-fleshed watermelon. Syrups and jams from local fruit. Local honey. Soft drinks. Snacks. Fair U.S. exchange. Proposed for 1996: open year-round with convenience items. (604) 458-2493. [ADVERTISEMENT]

C 141.3 (227.3 km) **PG 135.7** (218.4 km) Turnout with litter barrel.

CC 141.8 (228.2 km) **PG 135.2** (217.6 km) **Whispering Willows Outpost Campground and Store.** RV pull-throughs, sani-dump. Power and water hookups, free hot showers, flush toilets. Level spacious treed area for camping. Safe firepits, wood available. Teepee for rent. Play area. Convenience store. Pets and horse trailers welcome, corrals available. Deep Creek runs by Whispering Willows Campground, RR 4, Site 12, Comp. 46, Williams Lake, BC V2G 4M8. (604) 989-0359. Super, Natural Cariboo. [ADVERTISEMENT] ▲

CC 145.3 (233.9 km) **PG 131.7** (211.9 km) Turnout with litter barrel.

CC 147.8 (237.9 km) **PG 129.2** (207.9 km) Replica of a turn-of-the-century roadhouse (current status of services unknown) at junction with side road to which leads west 2.5 miles/4.5km tiny settlement of **SODA CREEK**. The original wagon road to the goldfields ended here and miners went the rest of the way to Quesnel by river steamboats. Soda Creek became an important transfer point for men and supplies until the railway went through in 1920. Soda Creek was so named because the creek bed is carbonate of lime and the water bubbles like soda water.

CC 155 (249.4 km) **PG 122** (196.4 km) **McLEESE LAKE,** small community with gas stations, cafe, post office, store, pub, private campground and motel on McLeese Lake. The lake was named for a Fraser River steamboat skipper. **McLeese Lake,** rainbow to 2 lbs., troll using a flasher, worms or flatfish lure. ▲

Junction with road to Beaver Lake and on to Likely. Historic Quesnelle Forks, a heritage site with a Forestry campsite, is located near Likely. Travelers may continue north from Likely to Barkerville and rejoin Highway 97 at Quesnel.

CC 155.5 (250.2 km) **PG 121.5** (195.5 km) Rest area to west overlooking McLeese Lake.

CC 160 (257.5 km) **PG 117** (188.3 km) Turnout with litter barrel to west with plaque about Fraser River paddle-wheelers.

CC 166 (267 km) **PG 111** (178.6 km) Glass sculpture museum and rock shop.

the Castle. See display ad this section.

CC 166.5 (267.9 km) **PG 110.5** (177.8 km) Marguerite rest area. View upriver to Marguerite reaction cable ferry across the Fraser River. Ferry crossing takes 10 minutes, operates 7 A.M. to 6:45 P.M.; 2 cars and 10 passengers, no charge.

CC 168.5 (271.2 km) **PG 108.5** (174.6 km) Basalt columns to east create a formation known as the Devil's Palisades. Cliff swallows nest in the columns.

CC 169.8 (273.2 km) **PG 107.2** (172.5 km) Stone cairn commemorates Fort Alexandria, the last North West Co. fur-trading post established west of the Rockies, built in 1821. The actual site of the fort is across the river. Cairn also marks the approximate farthest point reached by Alexander Mackenzie in his descent of the Fraser in 1793.

CC 179.9 (289.6 km) **PG 97.1** (156.2 km) **Cariboo Place Campsite.** We have the Cariboo in the palm of our hands. Beautiful natural park setting. A convenient and delightful stop, just off Highway 97. Pull-through bays for large units, tenters welcome. Exceptionally clean showers and washrooms. Laundromat. Picnic tables and firepits. Sani-dump station. Electrical hookups. Drinking water. Pets welcome but must be leashed. Rates $13–$14 plus tax. Electrical extra. Open 24 hours. [ADVERTISEMENT]. ▲

CC 180 (289.7 km) **PG 97** (156.1 km) Australian rest area to west with toilets,

Dragon Lake Road, south of Quesnel at Milepost CC 196, loops east to golf course, camping and fishing. (Judy Parkin, staff)

tables and litter barrels. Private campground to east. ▲

CC 188.5 (303.4 km) **PG 88.5** (142.4 km) Kersley (unincorporated), gas and food.

CC 188.6 (303.6 km) **PG 88.4** (142.3 km) Restaurant, gas and private campground. ▲

CC 193.2 (310.9 km) **PG 83.8** (134.9 km) **Mary's Gifts,** located 100 yards east of Highway 97 on Dragon Lake Road. Exciting wonderland of Canadian handcrafted gifts. Moccasins, gold and pewter jewellery, gourmet products, pottery and framed prints. Official Bradford Exchange dealer. Canadian souvenirs. Open daily 9 A.M. to 5 P.M. Easy RV access. Mail orders. Box 32, Dragon Lake Road, RR 1, Quesnel, BC V2J 3H5. (604) 747-2993. Super, Natural Cariboo. [ADVERTISEMENT]

CC 194.7 (313.3 km) **PG 82.3** (132.4 km) **A Little Bit Country.** Come in and choose from our hand-picked assortment of antiques and collectables, including Depression glass, china, hand tools, antique furniture and farmhouse collectables. Enjoy a trip down memory lane. P.O. Box 73, Jasper Rd., Quesnel, BC V2J 4P2. (604) 747-3919. On Highway 97; access on Jasper Road. [ADVERTISEMENT]

CC 196 (315.4 km) **PG 81** (130.4 km) South end of loop road east to **Dragon Lake,** a small, shallow lake popular with Quesnel families. Camping and fishing for rainbow. ▲

CC 196 (315.4 km) **PG 81** (130.4 km) **Robert's Roost Campsite** located 6 km south of Quesnel and 2 km east of Highway 97 in a parklike setting on beautiful Dragon Lake. Grass sites, both partial and fully serviced. 15- and 30-amp service. Sani-dump, fishing, boat rental, swimming, horseshoes, playground, coin-operated showers, flush toilets and laundromat. Can accommodate any length unit. Limited accommodation. Approved by Tourism BC. Hosts: Bob and Vivian Wurm, 3121 Gook Road, Quesnel, BC V2J 4K7. Phone (604) 747-2015. Super, Natural Cariboo. [ADVERTISEMENT] ▲

CC 197.2 (317.4 km) **PG 79.8** (128.4 km) **Frank's Supermarket.** Just about everything for the fisherman and hunter. Extensive selection of fishing tackle and hunting supplies. Hunting and fishing licenses. Tents, backpacks, sleeping bags and camping accessories. Grocery store. Post office. Open daily. Easy RV access on frontage road. 2310 Hydraulic Rd., Quesnel, BC V2J 4C4. (604) 747-2092. [ADVERTISEMENT]

CC 197.5 (317.8 km) **PG 79.5** (127.9 km) **Valhalla Motel and Family Restaurant.** Quietly situated at the top of Dragon Hill 3 km (2 miles) south of Quesnel. All rooms have air conditioning, individual electric heat, combination bath/showers, new remote colour cable televisions, direct dial touch tone telephones with free local calls, new queen beds, and refrigerators. Some non-smoking rooms available. Complete family dining facilities. Complimentary coffee. Complimentary guest laundry. Some newly renovated rooms. Winter plug-ins. Large vehicle parking. Close to fairgrounds, recreation centre and racing oval. Shopping

Gateway to Barkerville...

Quesnel, B.C. - Goldpan City

FOR MORE INFORMATION WRITE QUESNEL TRAVELINFO CENTRE, STN. A, 703 CARSON AVENUE, QUESNEL, BC V2J 2B6
1-800-992-4922

Kennedy's Lazy Daze Lakeside Resort

• Boat launch • Boat Rentals • Year round pull-through hook-ups • • 30 amp service • Sani- dump • Treed dry and tent sites • • Cabins • Convenience store • Laundry • Play area • • Free hot showers for guests • Picnic shelter •

Your hosts, Joanne and John Kennedy welcome you.

Telephone (604) 992-3282
R.R.8, Box 29, Best Site, Quesnel, B.C. Canada V2J 5E6

Dragon Lake Golf Course & Campsite

9 Hole Course and Driving Range

Situated on edge of Dragon Lake at $10/night

•Flush toilets •Showers •Sani-Dump •Wharf •Trout Fishing •Snack Bar •Lounge •Located off Highway 97 just 10 minutes south of City Centre

1692 Flint Ave., Quesnel BC Canada • (604) 747-1358

Mary's Gift Shop

CANADIAN HANDCRAFTED GIFTS

• Gold & Pewter Jewelry • Moccasins • Pottery •
Bradford Plates and Dolls

Shop located 100 yds off Hwy. 97 S on Dragon Lake Road

EASY R.V. ACCESS

SUPPER SPECIALS EVERY EVENING!

NOW OPEN
7 am - 9 pm every day!

Heritage House

102 Carson Ave., Quesnel, B.C.
992-2700

"Home of the World Famous A&W Rootbeer"

• Full Breakfast • Burgers • Fries •
Onion Rings • Chicken Grill • Chicken Chunks
2 Locations serving you better
Hwy 97 N - 3 Mile Flat & West Park Mall
992-5778 992-8336

Calendar of Events

QUESNEL

July 18-21, 1996
Over 150 Events for the Whole Family
For your Free Program of Events, write Box 4441, Quesnel, BC, V2J 3J4 or phone (604) 992-1234

Barlow Creek Music Festival
July 26-28, 1996

Great Canadian Snowmobile Hillclimb
April 8, 1996

Quesnel/Wells Winter Carnival
January 27-29, 1996

Gold Rush Trail Dog Sled Race
(Iditarod Qualifier)
January 27-29, 1996

FOUNTAIN MOTEL

•34 Modern Units •Heated Indoor Pool •Sauna
CAA Color Cable TV • TSN & Movie Channel • DD Phones •Air Conditioned •
•Non-smoking rooms available •FREE coffee and ice•

Senior's Discount

(604) 992-7071 1-800-665-6995 Fax 992-2873
524 Front Street, Quesnel, BC V2J 2K6

SYLVAN MOTEL

(604) 992-5611 - QUESNEL, BC
•26 Kitchen and Sleeping Units
•Super Channel •Free Coffee

VISA

•River Views •Restaurant Nearby

TOWER INN

NEW AAA

SUITES & HOTELS
AFFORDABLE EXCELLENCE
500 Reid St., Quesnel, B.C.
Canada V2J 2M9
Telephone (604) 992-2201
Fax (604) 992-5201
Reservations 1-800-663-2009

VISIT OUR FAMOUS BEGBIE'S RESTAURANT & LOUNGE

MARTIN & ELLEN DILLABOUGH

(604) 998-4746

Discover Beautiful Ahbau Country and More! Guided Rides.

LOCATION: 30 Km North of Quesnel or 100 Km South of P.G. on Hwy. 97
BOX 4767, QUESNEL, B.C. V2J 3J9 "WATCH FOR THE SIGN!"

Talisman Inn

• Direct Dial Telephones •
• Extra Long Queensize Beds •
• Fully Air Conditioned Units •
• Modern Kitchen Units •
753 Front Street, Quesnel, B.C.
Phone 992-7247 Fax 992-3126
or 1-800-663-8090
CAA - AAA Major Credit Cards Accepted

centre nearby. Large lawn area. Senior discount. Pets welcome. Major credit cards. 2010 Valhalla Rd., Highway. 97 South, Quesnel, BC V2J 4CI. (604) 747-1111. Super, Natural Cariboo. [ADVERTISEMENT]

Quesnel

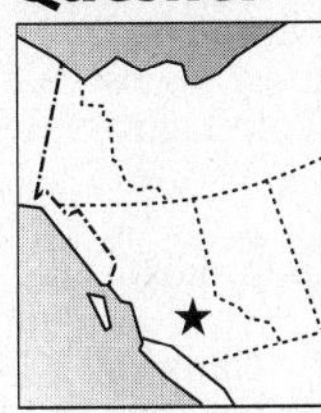

CC 203 (326.7 km) **PG 74** (119.1 km). Located at the confluence of the Fraser and Quesnel rivers. **Population:** 8,145. **Elevation:** 1,789 feet/545m. **Emergency Services:** Emergency only, phone 911. **RCMP**, phone (604) 992-9211. **Ambulance**, phone (604) 992-3211. **Hospital**, phone (604) 992-2181.

Visitor Information: Located on the west side of the highway just north of Quesnel River bridge, in LeBourdais Park. Open year-round. Write Quesnel Travel Infocentre, Stn. A, 703 Carson Ave., Quesnel, BC V2J 2B6; phone (604) 992-8716, or toll-free 1-800-992-4922. For information on the Cariboo Tourist Region, contact the Cariboo Tourist Assoc., P.O. Box 4900 Williams Lake, BC V2G 2VB; phone toll-free 1-800-663-5885.

Quesnel (kwe NEL) began as a supply town for the miners in the gold rush of the 1860s. The city was named for fur trader Jules Maurice Quesnel, a member of Simon Fraser's 1808 expedition and later a political figure in Quebec. Today, forestry is the dominant economic force in Quesnel, with 2 pulp mills, a plywood plant, and 5 sawmills and planer mills. Check with the Tourist Infocentre about tours.

Accommodations include 3 hotels, 15 motels, 5 bed and breakfasts and 8 campgrounds. There are gas stations (with diesel and propane), 2 shopping malls and 45 restaurants offering everything from fast food to fine dining. Golf and a recreation centre with pool are available.

Visitors can take a walking tour of the city along the Riverfront Park trail system. The 3.1-mile/5-km north Quesnel trail starts at Ceal Tingley Park at the confluence of the Fraser and Quesnel rivers. The west Quesnel trail is a 2.7-mile/4.3-km walk through a residential area. Trail information is available at the Tourist Infocentre.

Local attractions include the Quesnel Museum, located adjacent the Tourist Infocentre, which boasts the largest collection of Chinese artifacts west of Ottawa.

There are some interesting hoodoo formations and scenic canyon views at Pinnacles Provincial Park, 5 miles/8 km west of Highway 97; picnicking. It is a 1.1-mile/1.8-km walk round-trip from the parking area to the pinnacle viewpoints.

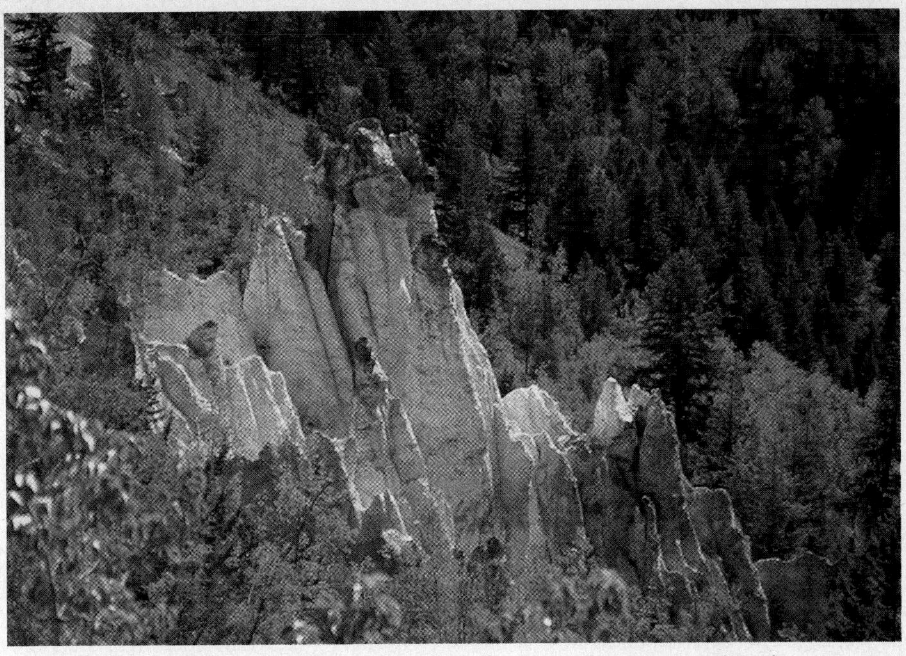

Interesting hoodoo formations may be seen at Pinnacles Provincial Park, 5 miles/8 km west of Quesnel. (© Carmen Scott)

A worthwhile side trip is Highway 26, which intersects Highway 97 at **Milepost CC 206.** This 51-mile/82-km paved highway leads to Barkerville Provincial Historic Park, a reconstructed and restored Cariboo gold rush town. (See HIGHWAY 26 side road log next page.) Gold Pan City Stage Lines offers charter and scheduled tours of Barkerville and surrounding area from Quesnel.

Billy Barker Days, a 4-day event held the third full weekend in July, commemorates the discovery of gold at Barkerville in 1862. Held in conjunction with the Quesnel Rodeo, Billy Barker Days is the third largest outdoor family festival in the province. For more information, write Box 4441, Quesnel, BC V2J 3J4. The Barlow Creek Music Festival takes place on Highway 26 the weekend after Billy Barker Days.

QUESNEL ADVERTISERS

West Access Route Log

(continued)

CC 206 (331.5 km) **PG 71** (114.3 km) Quesnel airport. **Junction** with Highway 26 to Barkerville and Bowron Lake. See HIGHWAY 26 side road log on pages 54-55.

CC 210 (338 km) **PG 67** (107.8 km) **Ten Mile Lake** Provincial Park; 142 campsites, flush toilets, picnic area, boat launch, good swimming beach, nature trails, dump station. Self-guided trail to beaver colony, good bird watching (pileated woodpeckers, warblers, snowy owls). Good fishing for rainbow to 3 lbs.

10 Mile Lake Provincial Park—Clean, friendly park one paved kilometer from Highway. 97. Quiet, treed sites with table and firepit. Some pull-throughs available. Coin operated hot showers. Security gates closed 11 P.M.–7 A.M. 30 kms of hiking and maintained mountain bike trails. Playground. Only 1 hour to Barkerville. [ADVERTISEMENT]

CC 214.2 (344.7 km) **PG 62.8** (101.1 km) Cottonwood River bridge. Turnout with litter barrels and stop of interest sign at south end of bridge describes railway bridge seen upriver.

CC 218.7 (352 km) **PG 58.3** (93.8 km) Hush Lake rest area to west; toilets, tables, litter barrels.

CC 226 (363.7 km) **PG 51** (82 km) **Cinema 2nd Hand.** General store, groceries. Movie rentals, souvenirs. Local artwork, circle drive. 9 A.M.–9 P.M. every day. Free camping, picnic tables, firepits and wood, toilet, some long pull-throughs, some shady sites, hiking trail, phone. Welcome to friendly Cinema, BC. Vic and Theresa Olson, RR 1 Box 1, Site 10, Hixon, BC V0K 1S0. (604) 998-4774. [ADVERTISEMENT]

CC 229.6 (369.5 km) **PG 47.4** (76.3 km) Strathnaver (unincorporated), no services.

CC 241 (387.8 km) **PG 36** (58 km) **HIXON** (pop. 1,500) has a post office, 2 motels, gas stations, grocery stores, 2 restaurants (1 with licensed premises), a pub and private campground. Hixon is the Cariboo's most northerly community. Extensive placer mining took place here in the early 1900s. Southbound motorists watch for roadside display about points of interest in the Cariboo region located just north of Hixon.

Hixon Fireplace Inn. See display ad this section.

CC 247.6 (398.5 km) PG 29.4 (47.3 km) Woodpecker rest area to west; toilets, tables,

(Continues on page 56)

Highway 26 Log

This 51-mile/82-km paved road leads to Barkerville Historic Town in the historic Cariboo gold fields (active mining under way). Gas available in Wells.

Distance from Highway 97 junction (J) is shown.

J 0 Junction with Highway 97 at **Milepost CC 206.** Travel Infocentre on southeast side of junction.

J 0.8 (1.3 km) Barlow Creek residential area; grocery, food and fuel. Eastbound, Highway 26 accesses local roads. Watch for deer.

J 13 (21 km) Rest area and interpretive trails to south. Wooden rail "snake" and wire fences with wooden top rail allow deer and moose to safely jump them, while penning domestic livestock.

J 15.2 (24.5 km) Cottonwood River bridge. The river is named for the black cottonwood trees growing alongside it.

J 16.7 (26.9 km) Cottonwood House Historic Site, a restored and furnished log roadhouse built in 1864. Gift shop, coffee shop, picnicking and guided tours by costumed docents. Open May to Sept.

Cottonwood House Historic Site. Visit the general store for unusual, quality gifts and crafts or try our old-fashioned, homemade fudge. Coffee shop and bakery fare, made in our own bakery, includes muffins, soup and bunwiches, bread, pies and pastries. Take a guided tour of the house, help feed the farm animals or stroll the river trail. Overnight parking for self-contained RVs at reasonable rates. Admission $2/adult; $4/family. Open 8 A.M.–5 P.M. Box 65, R.R. #4, Cottonwood Site, Quesnel, B.C. V2J 3H8. (604) 992-3997. [ADVERTISEMENT]

J 20.1 (32.4 km) Swift River Forest Road leads 0.2 mile/0.3 km to Lightning Creek Forest Service recreation site (first turn on left); free camping, 14-day limit. *CAUTION: Active logging road, drive with headlights on.* ▲

J 21.4 (34.5 km) Lover's Leap viewpoint and Mexican Hill Summit, one of the steepest grades on the original Cariboo Wagon Road, to the south.

J 27.1 (43.6 km) Historical stop of interest marker for Charles Morgan Blessing's grave. Blessing, from Ohio, was murdered on his way to Barkerville in 1866. His killer, John Barry, was caught when he gave Blessing's keepsake gold nugget stickpin, in the shape of a skull, to a Barkerville dance-hall girl. John Barry was the only white man hanged in the Cariboo during the gold rush.

J 37.3 (60.1 km) Stanley Road and Boulder Gold Mines (active claim). Stanley Road is a 1.9-mile/3-km loop road that leads past the gold-rush ghost towns of Stanley and VanWinkle, the old Lightning Hotel, and gold rush-era gravesites. A worthwhile sidetrip.

J 38.6 (62.2 km) Stanley (Loop) Road, Chisholm Creek.

J 40.2 (64.7 km) Devil's Canyon paved turnout to south. This was the highest point on the Cariboo Wagon Road.

J 42.9 (69 km) Slough Creek, site of much hydraulic mining activity after Joe Shaw discovered gold here in 1870.

J 44.9 (72.2 km) Paved turnout to litter barrel to south. **Jack o' Clubs Lake;** fishing for rainbows, lake trout and Dolly Varden.

J 45.2 (72.7 km) Rest area on peninsula to south with picnic tables, pit toilets and boat launch.

J 45.7 (73.6 km) Paved turnout with litter barrels to south.

J 46.1 (74.2 km) Lakeshore turnout with area information sign.

J 46.7 (75.2 km) **WELLS** (pop. 300) offers all visitor facilities, including motels, restaurants, liquor outlet, automatic teller machine, groceries and gas. Wells dates to the 1930s when the Cari-

WELLS ADVERTISERS

Amazing Space............Ph. (604) 994-2332
Hubs Motel..................Ph. (604) 994-3313
Northwood Family Restaurant..............Ph. (604) 994-3225
St. George's Gallery.....Ph. (604) 994-3492
Sunshine Cottage........Ph. (604) 994-3342
Wells Hotel & Mom's Diner......................Ph. (604) 994-3427
Wells Service Station...Ph. (604) 994-3224
White Cap Motor Inn & RV Park..................Ph. (604) 994-3489

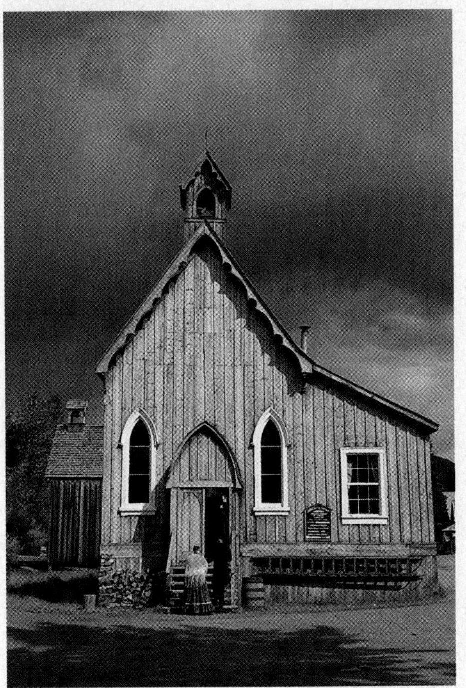

Historic church in Barkerville. Costumed performers represent citizens of the 1870s town. *(©Stephanie Satter)*

boo Gold Quartz Mine, promoted and developed by Fred Wells, brought hundreds of workers to this valley. The mine closed in 1967, but the town has continued as a service centre and attraction for tourists. There are numerous art galleries and gift shops, some housed in refurbished buildings from the 1930s. Guided and self-guided tours of the town are available. A museum with displays of local mining history is open daily from June to Sept.

Recreation in the area includes hiking, skiing, curling and snowmobiling. The local Legion hosts horseshoes and bocci tournaments, has a pub, and offers potluck suppers throughout the year.

J 49.6 (79.8 km) Barkerville Provincial Park Forest Rose Campground to north. Lowhee Campground to south; 170 campsites, picnic areas and dump stations. ▲

J 50 (80.5 km) Gravel road leads north 18 miles/29 km to **Bowron Lakes** Provincial Park, noted for its interconnecting chain of lakes and the resulting 72-mile/116-km canoe circuit which takes from 7 to 10 days to complete. Visitor information available at registration centre next to main parking lot where canoeists must register and pay circuit fees. Reservations recommended in July and August (required for 7 or more people); phone (604) 992-3111.

Airfield at junction with 2,500-foot/762-m paved runway, elev. 4,180 feet/1,274m.

There are 2 private lodges at the north end of the lake with restaurants, a general store and canoe rentals. Provincial park campground has 25 sites, water, pit toilets, firewood and a boat launch. Swimming, fishing, canoeing, kayaking and hiking. ▲

Becker's Lodge. See display ad this section.

J 50.1 (80.7 km) Entrance to Barkerville; admission charged. Admisssion fees in 1995 for a 2-day pass were: Adults, $5.50; youth and seniors, $3.25; children, $1; and families, $10.75.

J 50.3 (81.7 km) Former site of Cameronton, named for John A. "Cariboo" Cameron who found gold in this area. Also in this area is Williams Creek, the richest gold-producing creek during the gold rush.

J 50.9 (81.9 km) Turnoff on 1.8-mile/2.9-km side road for gold rush cemetery and Government Hill Campground (0.2 mile/0.4 km), New Barkerville (0.4 mile/0.7 km), and Grubstake Store (0.7 mile/1.1 km). ▲

J 51 (82.1 km) **BARKERVILLE,** a provincial historic town; open year-round, phone (604) 994-3332. Visitor information at Reception Centre.

Barkerville was named for miner Billy Barker, who struck gold on Williams Creek. The resulting gold rush in 1862 created Barkerville. Virtually a ghost town when the provincial government began restoration in 1958, today Barkerville's buildings and boardwalks are faithful restorations or reconstructions from the town's heyday. Visitors can pan for gold, shop at the old-time general store, watch a blacksmith at work, or take in a show at the Theatre Royal. Restaurants and food service available. It is best to visit between June 1st and Labour Day, when the Theatre Royal offers performances and all exhibits are open.

The Theatre Royal is extremely popular with visitors. The half-hour spring show plays daily (except Saturdays) from 12:45 to 1:15 P.M. between May 12 and June 15, 1996. Regular season begins June 16, 1996, with 1800s-style musical dramas playing daily (except Fridays) at 1 and 4 P.M. Regular season shows continue until Labour Day. Between July 1 and Labour Day there is also an 8 P.M. show on Saturdays and Sundays that is fashioned after a 1930s-style radio show. Admission is charged at all shows.

History comes alive at Barkerville thanks to interpreters and street performers who represent actual citizens of the town in 1870, discuss "current" events with visitors, conduct tours and stage daily dramas throughout the summer.

Beyond Main Street, the Cariboo Wagon Road leads on (for pedestrians only) to Richfield, 1 mile/1.6 km, to the courthouse of "Hanging" Judge Begbie.

**Return to Milepost CC 206
West Access Route**

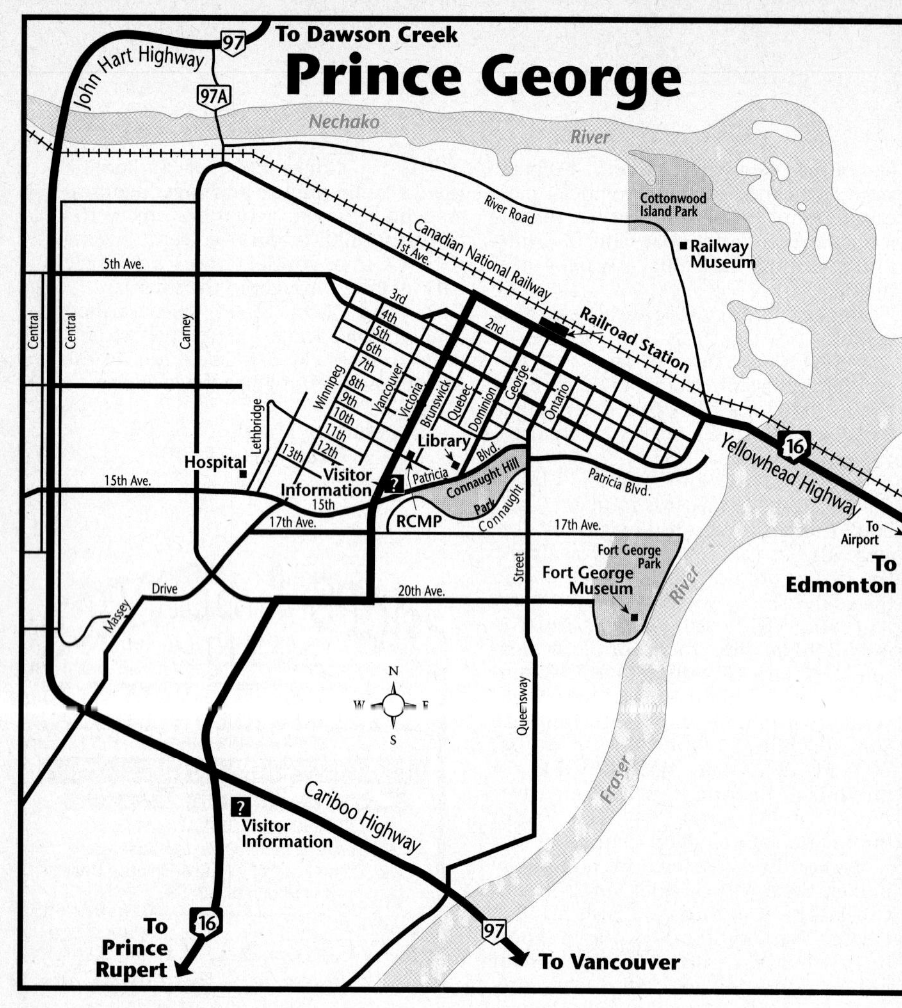

litter barrels.

CC 257.7 (414.7 km) **PG 19.3** (31 km) Stoner (unincorporated), no services.

CC 261.8 (421.3 km) **PG 15.2** (24.5 km) Red Rock (unincorporated); ice; gas station with diesel; pay phone.

Red Rock Husky. See display ad this section.

CC 268.3 (431.8 km) **PG 8.7** (14 km) **Bee Lazee RV Park, Campground & Honey Farm.** See display ad this section. ▲

CC 269.1 (433.1 km) **PG 7.9** (12.7 km) **Buckhorn Bed and Breakfast.** 1 km east off Highway 97 on Buckhorn Lake Road, 14900 Buckhorn Place. Guest lounge, private entrance, kitchenette, porch. Queen and single bed and private bathroom each room. Wheelchair accessible. Enjoy quiet country setting close to town. Single $40. Double $50. RR7 S25 C28, Prince George, BC V2N 2J5. (604) 963-8884. [ADVERTISEMENT] ♿

CC 270.6 (435.5 km) **PG 6.4** (10.3 km) Junction with bypass road to Yellowhead 16 East. Keep left for Prince George; continue straight ahead for Jasper and Edmonton. If you are headed east on Yellowhead Highway 16 for Jasper or Edmonton, turn to **Milepost E 450** in the YELLOWHEAD HIGHWAY 16 section and read the log back to front.

CC 273 (439.3 km) **PG 4** (6.4 km) **Southpark RV Park.** See display ad this section. ▲

CC 273.4 (440 km) **PG 3.6** (5.8 km) Access to Prince George airport to east.

CC 274 (440.9 km) **PG 3** (4.8 km) **Sintich Trailer Park.** See display ad this section. ▲

CC 275.2 (442.8 km) **PG 1.8** (2.8 km) Bridge over the Fraser River. Turn right at north end of bridge then left at stop sign for city centre via Queensway. This is the easiest access for Fort George Park; follow Queensway to 20th Avenue and turn east.

Continue straight ahead for Highway 16 entrance to city.

CC 276 (444.1 km) **PG 1** (1.6 km) **Junction** of Highway 97 with Yellowhead 16 West. Description of Prince George follows. If you are headed west on Yellowhead Highway 16 for Prince Rupert, turn to **Milepost PG 0** in the YELLOWHEAD HIGHWAY 16 section. Prince Rupert is port of call for Alaska state ferries and BC Ferries (see MARINE ACCESS ROUTES section for details).

Prince George

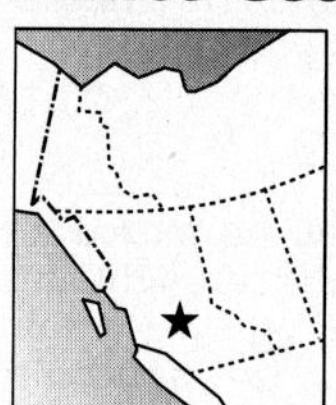

CC 277 (445.8 km) **Population:** 75,000, area 160,000. **Emergency Services: RCMP,** phone (604) 562-3371, emergency only, phone 911. **Fire Department,** phone 911. **Ambulance,** 24-hour service, phone 911. **Poison Control Centre,** phone (604) 565-2442. **Hospital,** Prince George Regional, phone (604) 565-2000; emergency, phone (604) 565-2444.

Visitor Information: Tourism Prince George, Dept. MP, 1198 Victoria St., phone (604) 562-3700 or fax 563-3584, or toll-free 1-800-668-7646. Open year-round, 8:30 A.M. to 5 P.M. weekdays Sept. to June, daily in July and August. Visitor centre, junction Yellowhead 16 and Highway 97; open daily mid-May to Labour Day, 9 A.M. to 8 P.M., phone

(604) 563-5493.

Elevation: 1,868 feet/569m. **Climate:** The inland location is tempered by the protection of mountains. The average annual frost-free period is 85 days, with 1,793 hours of bright sunshine. Dry in summer; chinooks off and on during winter which, accompanied by a western flow of air, break up the cold weather. Summer temperatures average 72°F/22°C with lows to 46°F/8°C. **Radio:** CKPG 550, CJCI 620, BC-FM 94.3, CBC-FM 91.5, C-101 FM. **Television:** 36 channels via cable. **Newspaper:** *The Citizen* (daily except Sunday); *Prince George This Week* (Sunday); *Free Press* (Sunday).

Prince George is located at the confluence of the Nechako and Fraser rivers, near the geographical centre of British Columbia. It is the fourth largest city in British Columbia. Hub of the trade and travel routes of the province, Prince George is located at the junction of Yellowhead Highway 16—linking Prince Rupert on the west coast with the Interior of Canada—and Highway 97, which runs south to Vancouver and north to Dawson Creek.

In the early 1800s, Simon Fraser of the North West Trading Co. erected a post here which he named Fort George in honour of the reigning English monarch. In 1906, survey parties for the transcontinental Grand Trunk Pacific Railway (later Canadian National Railways) passed through the area, and with the building of the railroad a great land boom took place. The city was incorporated in 1915 under the name Prince George. Old Fort George is now a park and picnic spot and the site of Fort George Museum.

Connaught Hill Park offers formal gardens, shaded picnic areas and vistas of downtown Prince George. (Judy Parkin, staff)

Prince George is primarily an industrial centre, fairly dependent on the lumber industry, with 3 pulp mills, sawmills, planers, dry kilns, a plywood plant and 2 chemical plants to serve the pulp mills. Oil refining, mining and heavy construction are other major area industries. The Prince George Forest Region is the largest in the province.

Prince George is the focal point of the central Interior for financial and professional services, equipment and wholesale firms, machine shops and many services for the timber industry. Canada's newest university

PRINCE GEORGE ADVERTISERS

Arctic RV Service Centre ....Mile 2.5 Hart Hwy.
Bed & Breakfast Assn. of Prince George.............Ph. (604) 561-2337
Blue Spruce RV Park & Campground..........Yellowhead Hwy. 16W
Celeste's RV Center Ltd. ...Ph. (604) 962-2049
Cozy Corner Bed & Breakfast.................Ph. (604) 964-7550
Dutch Maid Laundromat ....5th Ave. & Harper
Esther's Inn..............10th Ave. & Commercial
Goldcap Motor Inn..........Ph. (604) 563-0666
Grama's Inn..........................901 Central Ave.
Inland Spring and Axle Ltd. ....1936 Quinn St.
P.G. Hi-Way Motel..................1737 20th Ave.
Tourism Prince George..........1198 Victoria St.

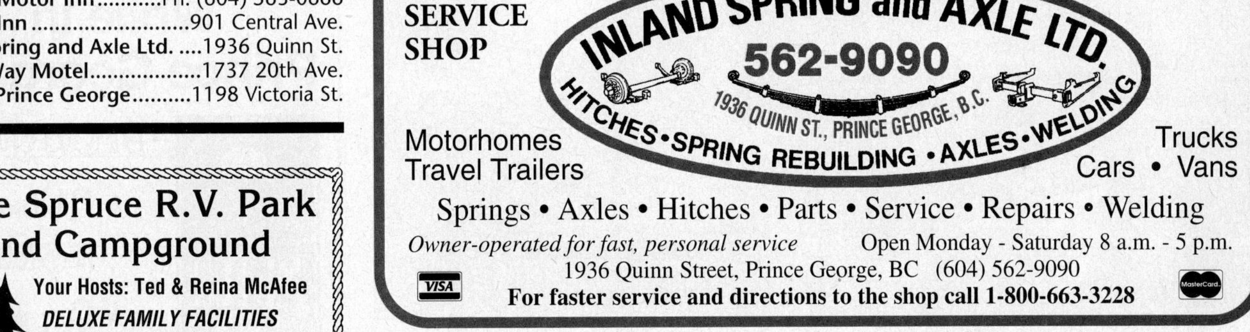

opened here in the fall of 1994. The campus of the University of Northern British Columbia is located at the top of Cranbrook Hill.

Agriculture in central British Columbia is basically a forage-livestock business, for which the climate and soils are well suited. Dairying and beef are the major livestock enterprises, with minor production in sheep and poultry.

ACCOMMODATIONS/VISITOR SERVICES

Prince George offers 5 hotels, 17 motels, 9 RV parks and more than 2 dozen bed and breakfasts. Most accommodations are within easy reach of the business district. There are more than 80 restaurants in the city. Most stores are open 7 days a week. The usual hours of operation are: Sunday, noon to 5 P.M.; Saturday and Monday through Wednesday, 9:30 A.M. to 6 P.M.; Thursday and Friday, 9:30 A.M. to 9 P.M.

Cozy Corner Bed & Breakfast. Friendly hosts offer a warm welcome, relaxing hot tub, 2 guest rooms with TVs, one with queen bed, one has twin beds with sitting area. Enjoy a delicious breakfast. Reasonable rates. Reservations: Linda Malcolm, 7131 Harvard Crescent, Prince George, BC V2N 2V6. Phone (604) 964-7550; fax (604) 562-8252. [ADVERTISEMENT]

TRANSPORTATION

Air: Prince George airport is southeast of the city, serviced by Canadian Airlines International, Air BC and Central Mountain Air. Limousine service to and from the airport.

Railroad: VIA Rail connects Prince George with Prince Rupert and Jasper, AB. Passenger service south to Vancouver via British Columbia Railway 3 days a week.

Bus: Greyhound. City bus service is provided by Prince George Transit & Charter Ltd.

ATTRACTIONS

City View: Follow Connaught Drive to the viewpoint at Connaught Hill Park for a panoramic view of the city.

City Landmarks: Centennial Fountain at the corner of 7th Avenue and Dominion Street depicts the early history of Prince George in mosaic tile. A cairn at Fort George Park commemorates Sir Alexander Mackenzie.

Prince George Art Gallery on 15th Avenue features regional, national and international artists.

Fort George Park is the largest park in Prince George and a good stop for travelers with its playgrounds, picnic tables, barbecue facilities and museum. The Fort George Regional Museum displays artifacts from the pioneer days through 1920. The museum is open daily in summer from 10 A.M. to 5 P.M.; phone (604) 562-1612. The Fort George Railway operates on weekends and holidays at the park from a railway building patterned after the original Grand Trunk Pacific stations.

Cottonwood Island Park, located on the Nechako River (see city map), has picnic facilities and extensive nature trails.

Giscome Portage Regional Park contains the historic Huble Homestead. Tour the Huble House, built in 1912, and the other carefully reconstructed farm buildings in this beautiful setting. Located north of Prince George on Highway 97; turn off highway at **Milepost PG 26.9.**

Prince George Railway Museum, located adjacent Cottonwood Island Park, has an excellent selection of antique rail stock. Attractions include a 1914 Grand Trunk Railway station and restored dining car.

Golf Courses. Aspen Grove Golf Club is 9 miles/14.5 km south of the city; Yellowhead Grove Golf Club, Pine Valley Golf Club and Prince George Golf and Curling Club are on Yellowhead Highway 16 West.

Swimming. Four Seasons Swimming Pool at the corner of 7th Avenue and Dominion Street has a pool, water slide, diving tank and fitness centre. Open to the public afternoons and evenings.

Rockhounding. The hills and river valleys in the area provide abundant caches of Omineca agate and Schmoos. For more information, contact Prince George Rock and Gem Club, phone (604) 562-4526; or Spruce City Rock and Gem Club, phone (604) 562-1013.

Tennis Courts. A total of 20 courts currently available to the public at 3 places: 20th Avenue near the entrance to Fort George Park; at Massey Drive in Carrie Jane Gray Park; and on Ospika Boulevard in the Lakewood Secondary School complex.

Industrial Tours are available from mid-May through August by contacting Tourism Prince George at (604) 562-3700. Tours, which are on weekdays only, include Northwood Pulp and Timber, and North Central Plywoods. Tours of Prince George Pulp and Intercon Pulp are available on request.

Special Events: Elks May Day celebration; Prince George Regional Forest Exhibition in May (even years); Folkfest on July 1, Canada Day; Prince George Live, Sunday through Thursday during July and August; International Food Festival in August; Annual Sandblast Skiing in August; Prince George Airshow in August; Prince George Exhibition in July; Oktoberfest in October; and the winter Mardi Gras Festival in mid-February. Details on these and other events are available from Tourism Prince George; phone (604) 562-3700.

Side Trips: Prince George is the starting point for some of the finest holiday country in the province. There are numerous lakes and resorts nearby, among them: Bednesti Lake, 30 miles/48 km west of Prince George; Cluculz Lake, 44 miles/71 km west; Purden Lake, 42 miles/68 km east; and Tabor Lake, 6 miles/10 km east. Day-use only sandy beaches are found at Bear Lake, 40 miles/66 km north, and West Lake, 15 miles/25 km west.

AREA FISHING: Highways 16 and 97 are the ideal routes for the sportsman, with year-round fishing and easy access to lakes and rivers. Hunters and fishermen stop over in Prince George as the jumping-off place for some of North America's finest big game hunting and fishing. For more information contact Fish & Wildlife at (604) 565-6145, or Tourism Prince George, phone (604) 562-3700.

West Access Route Log

(continued)

HIGHWAY 97/HART HIGHWAY

The John Hart Highway, completed in 1952, was named for the former B.C. premier who sponsored its construction. The highway is a 2-lane paved highway with both straight stretches and winding stretches.

This section of the log shows distance from Prince George (PG) followed by distance from Dawson Creek (DC).

PG 0 DC 250 (402.3 km) John Hart Bridge over the Nechako River. The 4-lane highway extends 6.5 miles/10.5 km northbound through the commercial and residential suburbs of Prince George.

PG 1.5 (2.4 km) **DC 248.5** (399.9 km) Truck weigh scales to west. Gas station and lube and oil service.

Hart Highway Mohawk. See display ad this section.

McQuik Lube & Oil. See display ad this section.

PG 2.5 (4 km) **DC 247.5** (398.3 km) RV service centre.

PG 6.4 (10.3 km) **DC 243.6** (392 km) **Hartway RV Park**. Shaded, fully-serviced sites. Pull-throughs. Free hot showers, laundromat, 30-amp, cable TV. Groceries nearby. Phone. On-site antique and gift shop. On south Kelly Road adjacent to highway.

Access at stop light (Handlen Road Junction); south of RV park. 7729 South Kelly Rd., Prince George, BC V2K 3H5. (604) 962-8848. [ADVERTISEMENT] ▲

PG 6.5 (10.5 km) **DC 243.5** (391.9 km) Two-lane highway (with passing lanes) begins abruptly northbound.

PG 14.6 (23.5 km) **DC 235.4** (378.8 km) Salmon River bridge. Litter barrel and river access to west at north end of bridge.

PG 14.7 (23.6 km) **DC 235.3** (378.7 km) **Salmon Valley Resort** campgrounds and convenience store, on over 20 acres along the scenic Salmon River. All facilities are

wheelchair accessible including showers. 50 treed sites, 8 pull-throughs, all with fire rings, tables, laundry. Limited water and power 15-30 amp. Swimming and camping on the Salmon that's second to none. Fair fishing for rainbows, grayling and spring salmon. "Home of the Happy Camper." Phone (604) 971-2212. Fax (604) 971-2229. [ADVERTISEMENT] ▲

PG 16.4 (26.4 km) **DC 233.6** (375.9 km) Highway overpass crosses railroad tracks.

PG 22 (35.4 km) **DC 228** (366.9 km) Gravel turnouts both sides of highway.

PG 26.5 (42.6 km) **DC 223.5** (359.7 km) Paved turnout to east with litter barrels and point of interest sign about Crooked River Forest Recreation Area.

PG 26.9 (43.3 km) **DC 223.1** (359 km) Access west to Giscome Portage regional park via Mitchell Road; narrow road. Site of Huble Farm, a 1912 homestead.

PG 28.2 (45.4 km) **DC 221.8** (356.9 km) Turnoff to west for **Summit Lake**, a resort area popular with Prince George residents; lake char and rainbow fishing spring and fall.

PG 29.3 (47.2 km) **DC 220.7** (355.2 km) Westcoast Energy compressor station.

PG 30.7 (49.4 km) **DC 219.3** (352.9 km) Second turnoff to west for Summit Lake.

PG 36.6 (58.9 km) **DC 213.4** (343.4 km) Cottonwood Creek.

PG 38.8 (62.4 km) **DC 211.2** (339.9 km) Paved turnout with litter barrel.

PG 40.6 (65.3 km) **DC 209.4** (337 km) Railroad crossing.

PG 42 (67.6 km) **DC 208** (334.7 km) Slow down for sharp turn across railroad tracks.

PG 43.9 (70.6 km) **DC 206.1** (331.7 km) Turnoff to west for Crooked River Provincial Park; 90 campsites, picnic area, flush toilets, tables, firepits, dump station. Camping fee charged. Also horseshoe pits, volleyball, playground, trails, swimming and paddleboat rentals. Powerboats prohibited. Picnic shelter with wood stove. **Crooked River** and area lakes have fair fishing for rainbow, Dolly Varden, grayling and whitefish. ▲

Highway 97 follows the Crooked River north to McLeod Lake.

PG 44.8 (72.1 km) **DC 205.2** (330.1 km) **BEAR LAKE** (unincorporated); gas, diesel, propane, grocery, restaurant, motel, RV park, gift shop, post office and ambulance station. Highway maintenance camp. ▲

Grizzly Inn, Restaurant, Motel & RV Park. See display ad this section. ▲

PG 50.7 (81.6 km) **DC 199.3** (320.7 km) Angusmac Creek.

PG 54.2 (87.2 km) **DC 195.8** (315.1 km) Tumbler Ridge branch line British Columbia Railway connects Tumbler Ridge with the B.C. Railway and Canadian National Railway, allowing for shipments of coal from Tumbler Ridge to Ridley Island near Prince Rupert.

PG 55.6 (89.5 km) **DC 194.4** (312.8 km) Large gravel turnout with litter barrel to west.

PG 56.1 (90.3 km) **DC 193.9** (312 km) Large gravel turnout with litter barrel to west.

PG 57 (91.7 km) **DC 193** (310.6 km) Large gravel turnout with litter barrel to west.

PG 60.8 (97.8 km) **DC 189.2** (304.5 km) Turnout with litter barrel to east.

PG 62.4 (100.4 km) **DC 187.6** (301.9 km) Large gravel turnout with litter barrel to east.

PG 65.2 (104.9 km) **DC 184.8** (297.4 km) Lomas Creek.

PG 67.9 (109.3 km) **DC 182.1** (293 km) Large, double-ended, paved rest area to west beside small lake; litter barrels, picnic tables and pit toilets.

PG 68.8 (110.7 km) **DC 181.2** (291.6 km) 42 Mile Creek.

PG 71.8 (115.5 km) **DC 178.2** (286.8 km) **Whiskers Bay Resort** has beautiful lakeside camping spots on a quiet bay, some with electricity and water. Hot showers. Cabins with showers, fridges and cooking facilities. Fishing is right off our dock or in the many surrounding lakes. Sunsets are sensational and hummingbirds are bountiful. The cafe offers breakfast, lunch, wonderful burgers, homemade pies, soups, the best coffee on the highway, and real northern hospitality. Come visit us! [ADVERTISEMENT] ▲

PG 76.6 (123.3 km) **DC 173.4** (279.1 km) First view northbound of McLeod Lake and view of Whisker's Point.

PG 77.7 (125 km) **DC 172.3** (277.3 km) Turnoff to west for Whisker's Point Provincial Park on McLeod Lake. This is an exceptionally nice campground with a paved loop road, 69 level gravel sites, a dump station, tap water, flush toilets, boat ramp, fire rings, firewood and picnic tables. Also horseshoe pits, volleyball, playground and picnic shelter. Camping fee charged. Boat launch, swimming, sandy beach and fishing. ▲

McLeod Lake has fair fishing for rainbow, lake char and Dolly Varden, spring and fall, trolling is best.

PG 81.4 (131 km) **DC 168.6** (271.3 km) Lodge (closed).

PG 84 (135.2 km) **DC 166** (267.1 km) Food, gas, camping and lodging. ▲

PG 84.5 (136 km) **DC 165.5** (266.3 km) **FORT McLEOD** (unincorporated) has a gas station, grocery, motel and cafe. A monument here commemorates the founding of Fort McLeod, oldest permanent settlement west of the Rockies and north of San Francisco. Founded in 1805 by Simon Fraser as a trading post for the North West Trading Co., the post was named by Fraser for Archie McLeod.

PG 84.7 (136.3 km) **DC 165.3** (266 km) **McLEOD LAKE** (unincorporated), post office, store and lodging.

PG 85 (136.8 km) **DC 165** (265.5 km) Turnoff for Carp Lake Provincial Park, 20 miles/32 km west via a gravel road; 105 campsites on Carp and War lakes, limited island camping, picnic tables, firepits, boat launch, fishing and swimming. Also tap water, dump station, horseshoe pits, playground and picnic shelter with wood stove. Ten-minute walk to scenic War Falls. Camping fee charged. Park access road follows the McLeod River to Carp Lake. ▲

Carp Lake, rainbow June through Sept.; special restrictions in effect, check current posted information. **McLeod River**, rainbow from July, fly-fishing only.

PG 85.6 (137.8 km) **DC 164.4** (264.6 km) Paved turnout with litter barrel to west.

PG 87.6 (141 km) **DC 162.4** (261.4 km) Westcoast Energy compressor station and McLeod Lake school.

PG 89.8 (144.5 km) **DC 160.2** (257.8 km) Turnoff to west for Tudyah Lake Provincial Park; 36 campsites, picnic tables, fire rings, firewood, pit toilets, drinking water. Also swimming, boat ramp, fishing. Camping fee charged. ▲

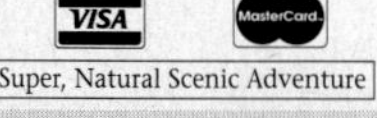

Tudyah Lake, shore access, rainbow, Dolly Varden and some grayling in summer and late fall. **Pack River** (flows into Tudyah Lake), fishing for: grayling (catch-and-release only), June 1 to July 1; rainbow, June 10 to Nov.; large Dolly Varden, Sept. 15 to Oct. 10, spinning.

PG 89.9 (144.7 km) **DC 160.1** (257.6 km) Bear Creek bridge.

PG 93.9 (151.1 km) **DC 156.1** (251.2 km) Gas, food and lodging (open year-round).

PG 94.7 (152.4 km) **DC 155.3** (249.9 km) Parsnip River bridge. This is the Rocky Mountain Trench, marking the western boundary of the Rocky Mountains. Northbound motorists begin gradual climb through the Misinchinka then Hart ranges of the Rocky Mountains.

Parsnip River, good fishing for grayling and Dolly Varden, some rainbow, best from Aug. to Oct.; a boat is necessary.

PG 95.2 (153.2 km) **DC 154.8** (249.1 km) **Junction** with Highway 39 (paved), which leads 18 miles/29 km to the community of Mackenzie (description follows). Food, gas, lodging, camping and tourist information at junction. Signed trailheads along Highway 39 are part of the Mackenzie Demonstration Forest. There are 8 self-guiding trails in the demonstration forest, each focusing on an aspect of forest management. Interpretive signs are posted along each trail.

Mackenzie Junction Cafe. See display ad this section. ▲

Mackenzie

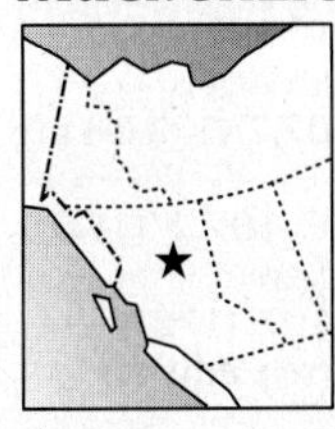

J 18 (29 km) Located 18 miles/29 km northwest of the John Hart Highway 97 via Highway 39. **Population:** 5,796. **Emergency Services:** Emergency only, phone 911. **RCMP**, phone (604) 997-3288. **Hospital**, 12 beds. **Ambulance**, phone 1-604-563-5433.

Visitor Information: Infocentre in the railway caboose located at the junction of Highways 97 and 39. Or write the Chamber of Commerce, Box 880, Mackenzie, BC V0J 2C0; (604) 997-5459.

Elevation: 2,300 feet/701m. **Radio:** CKMK 1240, CKPG 1240; CBC-FM 990. **Television:** Channels 3, 13 and cable.

A large, modern, planned community, Mackenzie was built in 1965. It lies at the south end of Williston Lake, the largest manmade reservoir on the continent. Construction of the new town in what had been just wilderness was sparked by the Peace River Dam project and the need to attract skilled employees for industrial growth. Mackenzie was incorporated in May 1966 under "instant town" legislation; the first residents moved here in July 1966. Industry here includes mining and forestry, with 5 sawmills, a paper mill and 2 pulp mills. Inquire about mill tours at the Infocentre.

On display in Mackenzie is the "world's largest tree crusher." The 56-foot-long electrically powered Le Tourneau G175 tree crusher was used in clearing land at the Peace River Power Project in the mid-1960s.

Attractions include swimming, waterskiing, fishing and boating at Morfee Lake, a 10-minute walk from town. There are boat launches on both Morfee Lake and Williston Lake reservoir. Good view of Mackenzie and Williston Lake reservoir from the top of Morfee Mountain (elev. 5,961 feet/1,817m); check with Infocentre for directions. There are self-guided hiking trails at John Dahl Regional Park, located behind the recreation centre. The big summer event here is the Blue Grass Festival, held in August.

Mackenzie has all visitor facilities, including motels, restaurants, shopping malls, gas stations, swimming pool, tennis courts, 9-hole golf course and other recreation facilities. There is also a paved 5,000-foot/1,524-m airstrip.

There is a municipal RV park with 20 sites, flush toilets, showers and sani-dump.

World's largest tree crusher in Mackenzie. This planned community at the south end of Williston Lake is an 18-mile side trip. (Earl L. Brown, staff)

Fishing for rainbow, Dolly Varden, arctic char and grayling in **Williston Lake.** ▲

Alexander Mackenzie Motel. See display ad this section.

District of Mackenzie. See display ad this section.

West Access Route Log

(continued)

PG 95.2 (153.2 km) **DC 154.8** (249.1 km) **Junction** with Highway 39 to Mackenzie; food, gas, lodging and tourist booth.

PG 95.5 (153.7 km) **DC 154.5** (248.6 km) Highway crosses railroad tracks.

PG 98.9 (158.2 km) **DC 151.1** (243.2 km) Gravel turnout with litter barrel to east.

PG 106 (170.6 km) **DC 144** (231.7 km) Turnout with litter barrel to east.

PG 108.4 (174.4 km) **DC 141.6** (227.9 km) Highway maintenance yard.

PG 108.5 (174.6 km) **DC 141.5** (227.7 km) Bridge over Honeymoon Creek.

PG 109.6 (176.4 km) **DC 140.4** (225.9 km) Powerlines crossing highway carry electricity south from hydro dams in the Hudson Hope area. (See HUDSON'S HOPE LOOP section.)

PG 110.5 (177.8 km) **DC 139.5** (224.5 km) Slow down for sharp curve across railroad tracks.

PG 112.3 (180.7 km) **DC 137.7** (221.6 km) Bridge over Rolston Creek; dirt turnout by small falls to west.

CAUTION: Rough pavement. Watch for frost heaves next 9 miles/14.6 km northbound.

PG 115.3 (185.6 km) **DC 134.7** (216.8 km) Bijoux Falls Provincial Park; pleasant picnic area adjacent falls on west side of highway. This day-use area has paved parking for 50 cars, pit toilets and picnic tables. Good photo opportunity.

Misinchinka River, southeast of the highway; fishing for grayling, whitefish and Dolly Varden.

PG 116.3 (187.2 km) **DC 133.7** (215.2 km) Highway crosses under railroad.

PG 119.3 (191.8 km) **DC 130.8** (210.5 km) Crossing Pine Pass (elev. 3,068 feet/935m), the highest point on the John Hart-Peace River Highway. Beautiful view of the Rockies to the northeast. Good highway over pass; steep grade southbound.

PG 119.4 (192.2 km) **DC 130.6** (210.2 km) Turnoff to Powder King Ski Village. Skiing Nov. to late April; chalet with ski shop, cafeteria, restaurant and lounge, hostel-style hotel. This area receives an annual average snowfall of 495 inches. Campground at Powder King Ski Village, open in summer. ▲

PG 121.4 (195.4 km) **DC 128.6** (207 km) Viewpoint to east with point of interest sign about Pine Pass and view of Azouzetta Lake. Pit toilet and litter barrels.

Watch for frost heaves next 9 miles/14.6 km southbound.

PG 122.4 (197 km) **DC 127.6** (205.3 km) Pine Valley Park, open year-round; gas station, propane, cafe, lodge, campground on **Azouzetta Lake.** Very scenic spot. Spectacular hiking on Murray Mountain Trail; inquire at lodge for details. A scuba diving school operates at Azouzetta Lake in summer. Fishing for rainbow (stocked lake) to 1½ lbs., flies or lures, July to Oct. Boat launch. ▲

Pine Valley Park. See display ad this section. ▲

PG 125.5 (202 km) **DC 124.5** (200.3 km) Microwave station and receiving dish to west.

PG 125.7 (202.3 km) **DC 124.3** (200 km) Westcoast Energy compressor station.

PG 128.7 (207.1 km) **DC 121.3** (195.2 km) Power lines cross highway.

PG 131.1 (211 km) **DC 118.9** (191.3 km) Turnout with litter barrel.

PG 140.6 (226.3 km) **DC 109.4** (176.1 km) Bridge over Link Creek.

PG 141.4 (227.5 km) **DC 108.6** (174.8 km) Gravel turnout with litter barrels.

PG 142.3 (229 km) **DC 107.7** (173.3 km) Bridge over West Pine River.

PG 142.8 (229.8 km) **DC 107.2** (172.5 km) Bridge over West Pine River.

PG 143 (230.1 km) **DC 107** (172.2 km) Paved rest area with litter barrels and pit toilets beside Pine River.

PG 143.4 (230.8 km) **DC 106.6** (171.6 km) Bridge over West Pine River, B.C. Railway overpass.

PG 144.3 (232.2 km) **DC 105.7** (170.1 km) Food, gas, towing, lodging and camping; autotel 784-9443. ▲

Silver Sands Lodge. See display ad this section. ▲

PG 146.1 (235.1 km) **DC 103.9** (167.2 km) Cairns Creek.

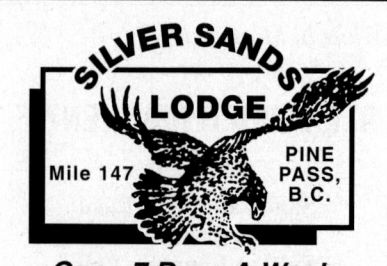

PG 146.9 (236.4 km) **DC 103.1** (165.9 km) Gravel access road to Pine River to south.

PG 148.2 (238.5 km) **DC 101.8** (163.8 km) LeMoray (unincorporated). Lodge to north of highway was closed in 1995, current status unknown. Highway maintenance camp.

PG 148.3 (238.7 km) **DC 101.7** (163.7 km) Gravel turnout to south.

PG 148.8 (239.5 km) **DC 101.2** (162.9 km) Lillico Creek.

PG 149.7 (240.9 km) **DC 100.3** (161.4 km) Marten Creek.

PG 150.4 (242 km) **DC 99.6** (160.3 km) Big Boulder Creek.

PG 156.2 (251.4 km) **DC 93.8** (151 km) Fisher Creek.

PG 156.9 (252.5 km) **DC 93.1** (149.8 km) Large gravel turnout with litter barrel to south beside Pine River.

PG 159.9 (257.3 km) **DC 90.1** (145 km) Crassier Creek.

PG 161.7 (260.2 km) **DC 88.3** (142.1 km) Westcoast Energy compressor station.

PG 163.6 (263.3 km) **DC 86.4** (139 km) Pine Valley rest areas, both sides of highway, with picnic tables and pit toilets. View of Pine River to south.

PG 169.5 (272.8 km) **DC 80.5** (129.5 km) Turnout with picnic tables, pit toilets and litter barrel to south overlooking the beautiful Pine River valley.

PG 172.4 (277.4 km) **DC 77.6** (124.9 km) Westcoast Energy (natural gas), Pine River plant. View of the Rocky Mountain foothills to the south and west.

PG 177.4 (285.5 km) **DC 72.6** (116.8 km) Turnout with litter barrel.

PG 181.9 (292.7 km) **DC 68.1** (109.6 km) Bissett Creek.

PG 183.6 (295.5 km) **DC 66.4** (106.9 km) Turnout with litter barrels at Wildmare Creek.

PG 183.7 (295.6 km) **DC 66.3** (106.7 km) **Wildmare Grove Campsite.** 50 sites. 32 long pull-throughs, back-ins, tent sites with full hookups, firepits and picnic tables. Quiet, beautifully treed with easy access to and from the highway. Hot showers, flush toilets, coin laundry, sani-station, variety store and pay phone. 3 miles west of Chetwynd on Highway 97. Phone (604) 788-2747. Box 42, Chetwynd, BC V0C 1J0. Enjoy Super, Natural Scenic Adventure. [ADVERTISEMENT] ▲

PG 184.1 (296.3 km) **DC 65.9** (106 km) Truck stop; gas, diesel, food and lodging.

Chetwynd

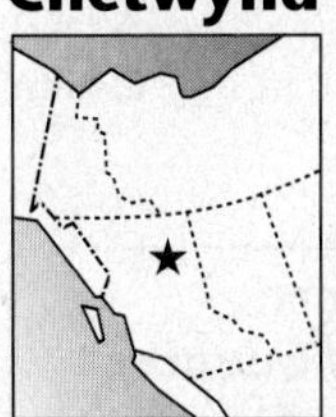

PG 187.6 (301.9 km) **DC 62.4** (100.4 km) Located on Highway 97 at the junction with Highway 29 north to the Alaska Highway via Hudson's Hope, and south to Tumbler Ridge. **Population:** 3,000, area 8,000. **Emergency Services: RCMP**, phone (604) 788-9221. **Hospital, Poison Control Centre** and **Ambulance**, phone (604) 788-3522. **Fire Department**, phone (604) 788-2345.

Visitor Information: Chamber of Commerce, open 8 A.M. to 8 P.M. July 1 to Labour Day weekend; open 9 A.M. to 4 P.M. rest of year. Write Box 1000, Chetwynd V0C 1J0, or phone (604) 788-3345 or 788-3655; fax 788-7843. Chetwynd Infocentre is located on the North Access Road adjacent to Highway 97 at the west end of town (watch for signs).

Elevation: 2,017 feet/615m. **Radio:** CFGP 105, CISN-FM 102, CJDC 890, CKNL 560, CBC 1170, CFMI-FM 103.9. **Television:** 7 channels (includes CBC, BCTV, ABC, CBS and NBC) plus pay cable.

The town was formerly known as Little Prairie and is a division point on the British Columbia Railway. The name was changed to honour the late British Columbia Minister of Railways Ralph Chetwynd, who was instrumental in the northward extension of the province-owned railway. In recent years, Chetwynd's collection of chainsaw sculptures has earned it the title, "Chain Saw Sculpture Capital of the World." The Infocentre has a map showing locations of the sculptures in town.

Chetwynd lies at the northern end of one of the largest known coal deposits on earth. Access from Chetwynd south to Tumbler Ridge and the resource development known as the North East Coal is via Highway 29 south, a 56-mile/90-km paved road (see HIGHWAY 29 SOUTH side road log this section). Forestry, mining, natural gas processing, ranching and farming are the main industries in Chetwynd. Louisiana Pacific has a modern nonpolluting pulp mill here. Free guided tours are available of Canadian Forest Products (604/788-2231) and Chetwynd Forest Industries (604/788-2686) soft wood sawmills.

Chetwynd has several large motels, restaurants, banks and 2 bank machines, post office, 2 laundromats, gas stations, supermarkets, art gallery and golf courses.

CHETWYND ADVERTISERS

Country Squire Motor Inn ....Ph. (604) 788-2276
District of Chetwynd ....Ph. (604) 788-2281
Pine Cone Motor Inn ....Ph. 1-800-663-8082
Robert's Towing ....Ph. (604) 788-9194
Stagecoach Inn ....Ph. (604) 788-9666
Swiss Inn Restaurant, The....0.5 mile E. of traffic light

Good traveler's stop with easy access to all services. (Heavy commercial and industrial traffic often fill up local motels and campgrounds; reserve ahead.) Chetwynd & District Leisure Pool has a wave machine, whirlpool, sauna and weight room; open daily 6 A.M. to 10 P.M., visitors welcome.

The Little Prairie Heritage Museum, located on Highway 97 at the west end of town, features the region's pioneer days; inquire at infocentre for directions. The museum is open from the first Tuesday in July to the last Saturday in August.

Free municipal campground in town with 20 sites and dump station. There's also

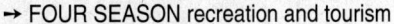

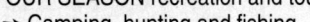

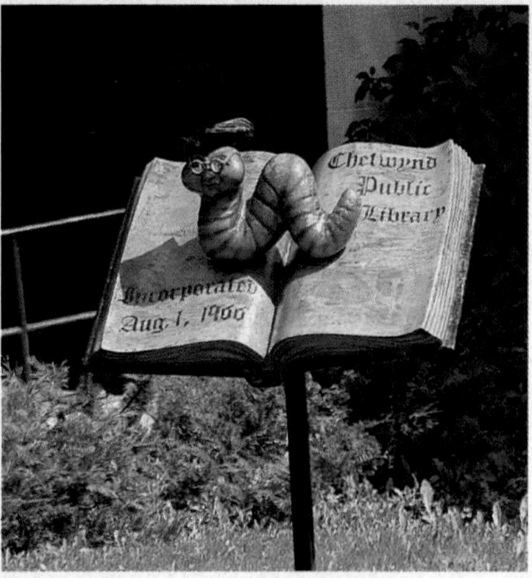

Chain saw sculpture at Chetwynd's public library. (Earl L. Brown, staff)

a dump station at the 51st Avenue car/truck wash. There are also private tent and trailer parks in town and at Moberly Lake. Moberly Lake Provincial Park is 12 miles/19.3 km north of Chetwynd via Highway 29 north (see **Milepost PG 187.9**) and 1.9 miles/3 km west via a gravel road. The park has 109 campsites, beach, picnic area, playground, nature trail, boat launch and a private marina next door with boat rental and concession. There's good swimming at huge Moberly Lake on a warm summer day. Worth the drive. ▲

West Access Route Log

(continued)

PG 187.8 (302.2 km) **DC 62.2** (100.1 km) Highway crosses railroad tracks.

PG 187.9 (302.4 km) **DC 62.1** (99.9 km) **Junction** with Highway 29 north, which leads 12 miles/19.3 km to Moberly Lake, 36.5 miles/58.7 km to Peace River Provincial Recreation Area and Peace Canyon dam, and 40.4 miles/64.9 km to community of Hudson's Hope and access to W.A.C. Bennett Dam; Highway 29 north connects with the Alaska Highway 53.7 miles/86.4 km north of Dawson Creek. (See HUDSON'S HOPE LOOP section for details.)

Highway climbs next 12 miles/19 km for Dawson Creek-bound motorists.

PG 189.4 (304.8 km) **DC 60.6** (97.5 km) **Junction** with Highway 29 (paved) south to Gwillim Lake and Tumbler Ridge (see HIGHWAY 29 SOUTH side road log this section). Tumbler Ridge is also accessible from **Milepost PG 237.7** via the Heritage Highway.

PG 199.3 (320.7 km) **DC 50.7** (81.6 km) Gravel turnouts with litter barrels both sides of highway.

PG 201.2 (323.8 km) **DC 48.8** (78.5 km) Slow down for sharp curve across railroad tracks.

PG 205.6 (330.9 km) **DC 44.4** (71.5 km) Turnout with litter barrel and a commanding view of the East Pine River valley to the south.

PG 206.5 (332.3 km) **DC 43.5** (70 km) Sharp curves approximately next 2 miles/3.2 km as highway descends toward Dawson Creek. View of Table Mountain.

PG 207.9 (334.6 km) **DC 42.1** (67.7 km) Highway crosses under railroad.

PG 208.1 (334.9 km) **DC 41.9** (67.4 km) Sharp turn to south at west end of bridge for East Pine Provincial Park (0.5 mile on gravel road); picnicking and boat launch on Pine River. Turnout with litter barrel at park entrance.

From East Pine Provincial Park, canoeists may make a 2-day canoe trip down the Pine River to the Peace River; take-out at Taylor Landing Provincial Park (at **Milepost DC 34** on the Alaska Highway).

PG 208.2 (335.1 km) **DC 41.8** (67.3 km) Bridge across East Pine River. Railroad also crosses river here.

PG 208.3 (335.2 km) **DC 41.7** (67.1 km) Turnout with litter barrel to south.

PG 209.8 (337.6 km) **DC 40.2** (64.7 km) East Pine (unincorporated) has a store, gas station and distinctive treehouse.

PG 211.7 (340.7 km) **DC 38.3** (61.6 km) Turnout with litter barrel to north.

PG 221.5 (356.5 km) **DC 28.5** (45.9 km) Turnouts with litter barrels both sides of highway.

PG 222 (357.3 km) **DC 28** (45 km) Groundbirch (unincorporated); store, liquor outlet, gas, propane, diesel, post office and camping. ▲

PG 230.7 (371.3 km) **DC 19.3** (31.1 km) Progress (unincorporated), highway maintenance yard, cairn and pay phone.

PG 234.4 (377.2 km) **DC 15.6** (25.1 km) Turnout with litter barrels to north.

PG 237.7 (382.5 km) **DC 12.3** (19.8 km) **Junction** with Heritage Highway, which leads 59.5 miles/96 km (paved) south to the community of Tumbler Ridge and access roads to the North East Coal Development. (Tumbler Ridge is also accessible via Highway 29 south from Chetwynd. See side road log this section.)

From Tumbler Ridge, the Heritage Highway continues 92 miles/148 km (123 km gravel, 25 km paved) east and north to connect with Highway 2 southeast of Dawson Creek. Inquire locally about road conditions.

PG 238 (383 km) **DC 12** (19.3 km) Kiskatinaw River bridge.

PG 240.7 (387.4 km) **DC 9.3** (15 km) Arras (unincorporated), cafe and gas station.

PG 247.9 (398.9 km) **DC 2.1** (3.4 km) Small turnout with litter barrel and point of interest sign to south.

PG 248 (399.1 km) **DC 2** (3.2 km) Private RV Park. ▲

PG 249.9 (402.2 km) **DC 0.1** (0.2 km) Entering Dawson Creek. Private campground on south side of highway; Rotary Lake Park and camping on north side of highway. ▲

PG 250 (402.3 km) **DC 0 Junction** of the Hart Highway and Alaska Highway; turn right for downtown Dawson Creek. See description of Dawson Creek in the ALASKA HIGHWAY section.

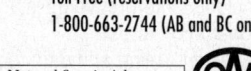

Highway 29 South Log

Highway 29 South is a paved road that leads 55.9 miles/90 km from **Milepost PG 189.4** to the community of Tumbler Ridge. Travelers may return to Highway 97 via Highway 29, or via the Heritage Highway, a paved road that leads 59.5 miles/95 km from Tumbler Ridge to junction with Highway 97 at **Milepost PG 237.7.**

Distance from Highway 97 junction (J) is shown.

J 0 Junction with Highway 97 at **Milepost PG 189.4.**

J 0.1 (0.2 km) Turnout with litter barrels to east.

Highway 29 climbs next 2.3 miles/3.7 km southbound.

J 1.9 (3.1 km) Distance marker indicates Tumbler Ridge 88 km.

J 2.8 (4.5 km) Sign: Trucks check brakes, steep hill ahead.

J 3 (4.8 km) Large gravel turnouts with litter barrels both sides of highway.

J 5.5 (8.8 km) Twidwell Bend bridge.

J 5.6 (9 km) Access road east to Long Prairie (8 miles/12.9 km).

J 6.6 (10.6 km) Highway parallels Sukunka River to west.

J 8.2 (13.2 km) Zonnebeke Creek.

J 8.5 (13.7 km) Natural Springs Resort; 9-hole golf course.

J 9 (14.5 km) Kilometrepost 15.

J 10.6 (17 km) Bridge over Dickebush Creek.

J 11 (17.7 km) Sanctuary River.

J 13.7 (22 km) **Junction** with Sukunka Forest Road, which leads west 11 miles/17.7 km to Sukunka Falls. *NOTE: Radio-controlled road, travellers must monitor channel 151.325 MHz.*

J 13.8 (22.2 km) Highway climbs next 3 miles/4.8 km southbound.

J 16.7 (26.9 km) Turnouts with litter barrels both sides of highway.

J 21.6 (34.8 km) Turnout with litter barrels to east.

J 26.9 (43.3 km) Turnouts with litter barrels both sides of highway.

J 28.4 (45.7 km) Paved road leads east 1.2 miles/1.9 km to **Gwillum Lake** Provincial Park (gate closed 11 P.M. to 7 A.M.); 53 campsites, picnic tables, firewood and firepits. Day-use area and boat launch. Fishing for lake trout, grayling and pike. Camping fee $7 to $12. ▲

J 40.8 (65.6 km) Access road leads west 9 miles/14.5 km to Bullmoose Mountain and mine. Mine tours may be available; phone (604) 242-5221 for current information.

J 41.1 (66.1 km) Turnout to east.

J 41.5 (66.8 km) Bridge over Bullmoose Flats River.

J 46.1 (74.2 km) Turnout with litter barrels to east. Phillips Way Summit, elev. 3,695 feet/1,126m.

J 51.4 (82.7 km) Bullmoose Creek bridge.

J 52.6 (84.3 km) Wolverine River bridge.

J 54.1 (87 km) Murray River bridge.

J 54.8 (88.2 km) Flatbed Creek bridge.

J 54.9 (88.3 km) Flatbed Creek Campground; 40 sites, hookups, water, flush toilets, showers, dump station, picnic tables and playground. Camping fee $10. ▲

J 55.9 (90 km) Turnoff for community of Tumbler Ridge (description follows).

Tumbler Ridge

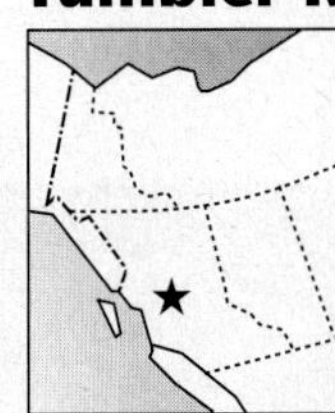

Located 116.5 miles/187.5 km southwest of Dawson Creek via Highways 97 and 29. **Population:** 4,550. **Emergency Services: RCMP**, phone (604) 242-5252. **Medical Centre**, phone (604) 242-5271. **Ambulance**, phone 1-800-461-9911. **Fire Department**, phone (604) 242-5555.

Visitor Information: Located in town at Southgate Road and Front Street, across from the hospital. Open year-round, limited hours in winter. Write the Chamber of Commerce, Box 606, Tumbler Ridge, BC V0C 2W0, or phone (604) 242-4702, fax 242-5159.

Elevation: 3,000 feet/914m. **Private Aircraft**: 9 miles/15 km south; elev. 3,150 feet/960m, length 4,000 feet/1,218m; asphalt; fuel 80, 100, Jet B.

Tumbler Ridge was built in conjunction with development of the North East Coal resource. Construction of the townsite began in 1981. It is British Columbia's newest community, incorporated June 1, 1984.

Visitor facilities include a motel, restaurants, retail and grocery outlets, service stations with major repairs, car wash and a laundromat. Camping at Flatbed Creek Campground just outside of town and at Monkman RV Park in town. Recreational facilities include a community centre with arena, curling rink, weight room, indoor pool and a library. Outdoor facilities include tennis courts and a 9-hole golf course. ▲

Major attraction in the area is Monkman Provincial Park, site of spectacular 225-foot/69-m Kinuseo (keh-NEW-see-oh) Falls. The falls and a 42-site campground are accessible from Tumbler Ridge via a 37-mile/60-km dirt road (watch for trucks) south from town. Viewing platform of falls is a short walk from the campground. For more information on the park, contact BC Parks in Fort St. John, phone (604) 787-3407. ▲

Coal mine tours may be available at Quintette Mine south of town and at Bullmoose Mine (see **Milepost J 40.7** on Highway 29); inquire locally.

District of Tumbler Ridge. See display ad this section.

Return to Milepost PG 189.4
West Access Route

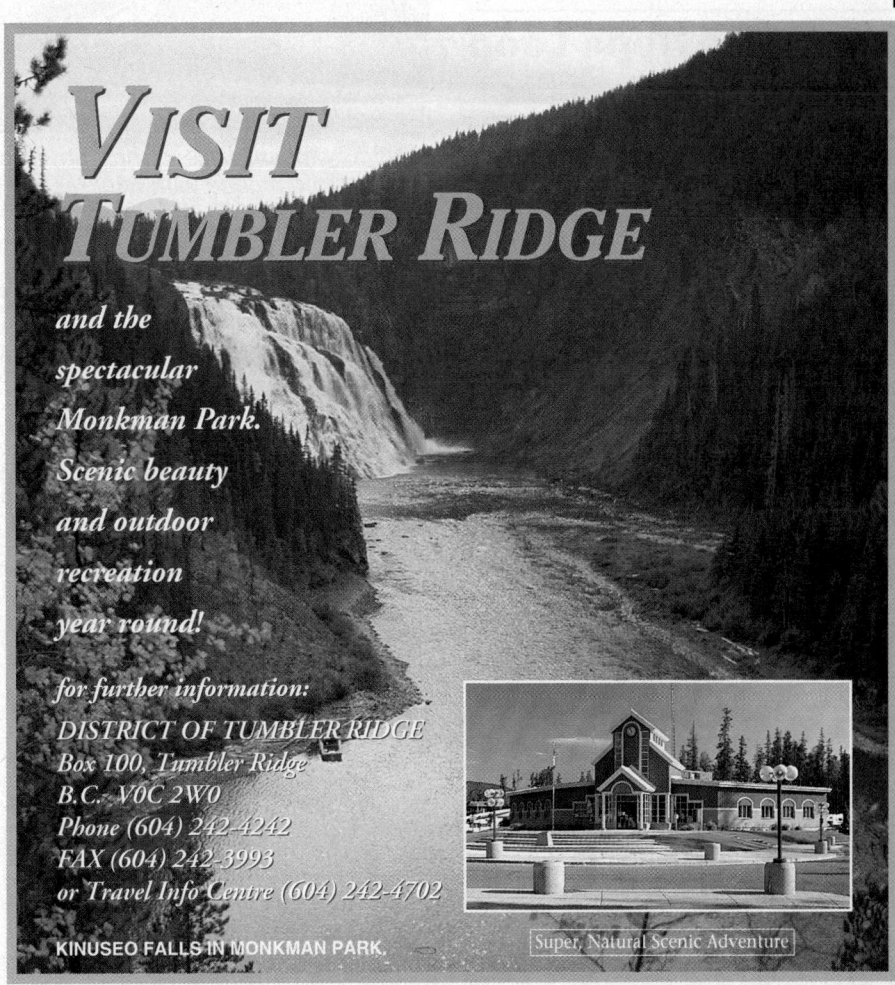

HUDSON'S HOPE LOOP

Chetwynd, British Columbia, to the Alaska Highway
BC Highway 29

Beautiful Moberly Lake, a short drive from Chetwynd, offers camping, picnicking, fishing and a marina with boat rentals. *(Earl L. Brown, Staff)*

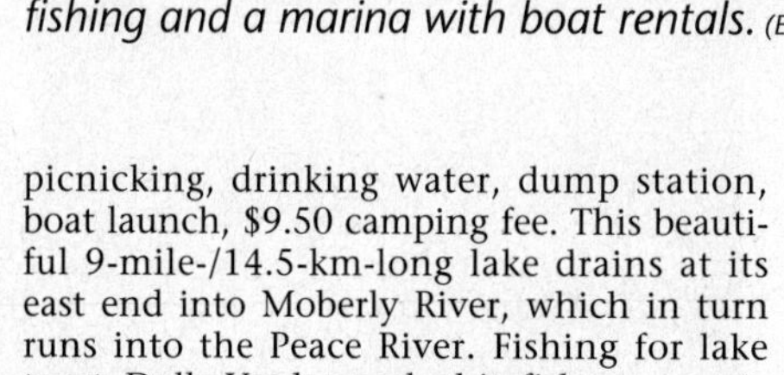

The Hudson's Hope Loop links the John Hart Highway (Highway 97) with the Alaska Highway (also Highway 97). This 86.9-mile/139.8-km paved loop road provides year-round access to the town of Hudson's Hope, W.A.C. Bennett Dam, Peace Canyon Dam and Moberly Lake. As a shortcut bypassing Dawson Creek, the Hudson's Hope Loop saves 28.9 miles/46.5 km. Highway 29 is a good scenic 2-lane road but is steep and winding in places.

A popular side trip with Alaska Highway travelers today, and an alternate access route to the Alaska Highway, Highway 29 was only a 53-mile/85.3-km side road to the Hudson Hope Coal Mines in the 1950s. In the 1960s, with construction of the W.A.C. Bennett Dam under way, Alaska Highway travelers drove the side road to see the Peace River dam site. The highway was completed to Chetwynd in 1968.

Hudson's Hope Loop Log

Distance from Chetwynd (C) is followed by distance from Alaska Highway junction (AH).

C **0** AH **86.9** (139.8 km) **Junction** of Highways 29 and 97 at Chetwynd (see **Milepost PG 187.6** in the WEST ACCESS ROUTE section for description of Chetwynd).

C **0.5** (0.8 km) **AH 86.4** (139 km) Truck weigh scales to west.

C **2.3** (3.7 km) **AH 84.6** (136.1 km) Jackfish Road to east.

C **5** (8 km) **AH 81.9** (131.8 km) Turnout with litter barrel to west.

C **12** (19.3 km) **AH 74.9** (120.5 km) Gravel access road leads 2 miles/3.2 km west to **Moberly Lake** Provincial Park on south shore; 109 campsites, swimming, waterskiing, picnicking, drinking water, dump station, boat launch, $9.50 camping fee. This beautiful 9-mile-/14.5-km-long lake drains at its east end into Moberly River, which in turn runs into the Peace River. Fishing for lake trout, Dolly Varden and whitefish. ▲

Moberly Lake Marina & Resort. See display ad this section.

C **12.2** (19.6 km) **AH 74.7** (120.2 km) Moberly River bridge; parking area with litter barrel at south end.

C **15.9** (25.6 km) **AH 71** (114.3 km) Highway cairn is memorial to John Moberly, fur trader and explorer who first landed here in 1865.

C **16.4** (26.4 km) **AH 70.5** (113.5 km) Spencer Tuck Regional Park; picnic tables, swimming, fishing and boat launch.

C **17.4** (28 km) **AH 69.5** (111.8 km) **Harv's Resort,** on the north shore of beautiful Moberly Lake. Treed picnic sites, large grass picnic field, cabins, campsites and full hookups. Swimming, fishing, pay phone, laundromat and showers. Store, restaurant. Gas, oils, propane, hunting and fishing licenses. Boat launch and golf course nearby. Your hosts, Harve and Darlene Evans. Open till 10 P.M. daily. Phone (604) 788-9145. [ADVERTISEMENT] ▲

C **18.3** (29.5 km) **AH 68.6** (110.4 km) **MOBERLY LAKE.** Post office, cafe, store and pay phone.

C **18.5** (29.8 km) **AH 68.4** (110.1 km) Moberly Lake and District Golf Club, 0.7 mile/1.1 km from highway; 9 holes, grass greens, rentals, clubhouse, licensed lounge. Open May to Sept.

C **25.4** (40.9 km) **AH 61.5** (99 km) Cameron Lake camping area; tables, water, toilets, firewood, playground, horseshoe pits, boat launch (no motorboats) and swimming. Camping fee by donation. ▲

C **30.7** (49.4 km) **AH 56.2** (90.4 km) Gravel turnout with litter barrel to east. Highway descends northbound to Hudson's Hope.

C **35.9** (57.8 km) **AH 51** (82.1 km) Suspension bridge over Peace River; paved turnouts at both ends of bridge with concrete totem pole sculptures. View of Peace Canyon Dam.

C **36.5** (58.7 km) **AH 50.4** (81.1 km) Turnoff to west for Dinosaur Lake Campground and B.C. Hydro Peace Canyon Dam. The dam's visitor centre, 0.6 mile/1 km on paved access road, is open from 8 A.M. to 4 P.M. daily from late May through Labour Day; Monday through Friday the rest of the year (closed holidays). Self-guided tour includes a full-scale model of duck-billed dinosaurs (hadrosaurs), a tableau portraying Alexander Mackenzie's discovery of the

HUDSON'S HOPE LOOP *Chetwynd, BC, to Milepost DC 53.7 Alaska Highway*

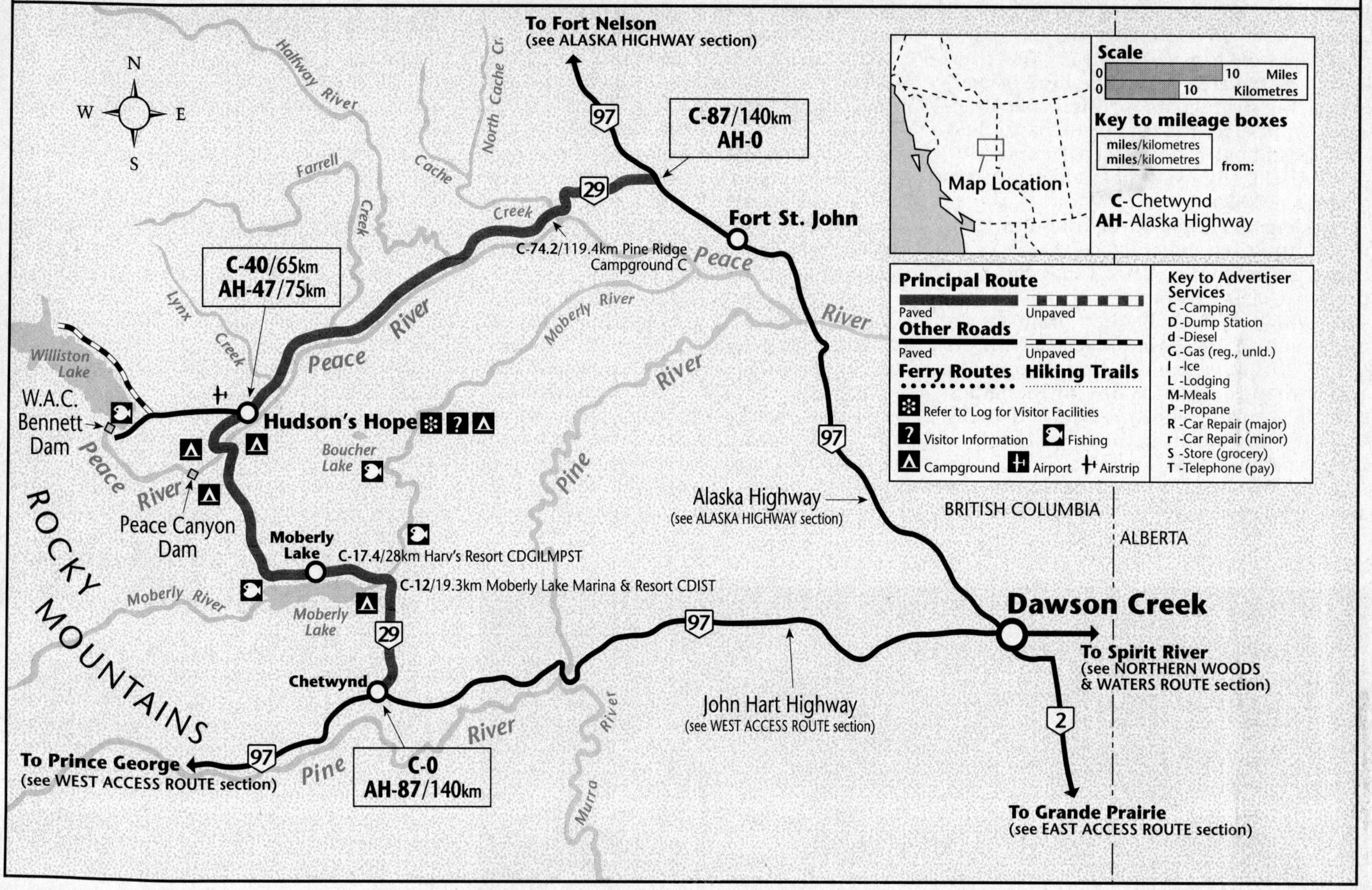

To Fort Nelson (see ALASKA HIGHWAY section)
C-87/140km AH-0
Fort St. John
C-74.2/119.4km Pine Ridge Campground C
C-40/65km AH-47/75km
W.A.C. Bennett Dam
Hudson's Hope
Williston Lake
Boucher Lake
Peace Canyon Dam
ROCKY MOUNTAINS
Moberly Lake
C-17.4/28km Harv's Resort CDGILMPST
C-12/19.3km Moberly Lake Marina & Resort CDIST
Chetwynd
C-0 AH-87/140km
To Prince George (see WEST ACCESS ROUTE section)
John Hart Highway (see WEST ACCESS ROUTE section)
Alaska Highway (see ALASKA HIGHWAY section)
Dawson Creek
To Spirit River (see NORTHERN WOODS & WATERS ROUTE section)
To Grande Prairie (see EAST ACCESS ROUTE section)
BRITISH COLUMBIA
ALBERTA
Halfway River, Farrell Creek, Cache Creek, North Cache Cr., Lynx Creek, Peace River, Moberly River, Pine River, Murra River

Scale 0 10 Miles; 0 10 Kilometres
Key to mileage boxes: miles/kilometres from: C-Chetwynd, AH-Alaska Highway
Map Location

Principal Route: Paved, Unpaved
Other Roads: Paved, Unpaved
Ferry Routes; Hiking Trails
Refer to Log for Visitor Facilities; Visitor Information; Fishing; Campground; Airport; Airstrip

Key to Advertiser Services
C -Camping
D -Dump Station
d -Diesel
G -Gas (reg., unld.)
I -Ice
L -Lodging
M -Meals
P -Propane
R -Car Repair (major)
r -Car Repair (minor)
S -Store (grocery)
T -Telephone (pay)

Peace River canyon and a section on local pioneering. A pictorial display traces the construction of the Peace Canyon Dam. You may view the dam spillway from the visitor centre. Get permission before walking across top of dam. Phone (604) 783-9943 for a guided tour (groups of 8 or more).

Dinosaur Lake Campground, on Dinosaur Lake, has 30 campsites with firepits, water, toilets and tables. Boat launch and swimming area. Camping fee by donation.▲

C 38.3 (61.6 km) **AH 48.6** (78.2 km) Alwin Holland Memorial Park (0.5 mile/0.8 km east of highway) is named for the first teacher in Hudson's Hope, who willed his property, known locally as The Glen, to be used as a public park. There are 17 campsites, picnic grounds, barbecues and water. Camping fee by donation. ▲

C 38.9 (62.6 km) **AH 48** (77.2 km) Welcome to Hudson's Hope sign.

C 39 (62.8 km) **AH 47.9** (77.1 km) King Gething Park; small campground with 15 grassy sites, picnic tables, cookhouse, flush toilets, showers and dump station east side of highway. Camping fee by donation. ▲

Hudson's Hope

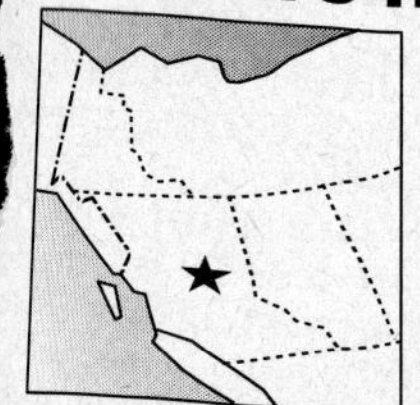

C 40.4 (65 km) AH 46.5 (74.8 km) **Population:** 1,005. **Emergency Services:** RCMP, phone (604) 783-5241. **Fire Department,** phone (604) 783-5700. **Ambulance,** phone 112-562-7241. **Medical Clinic,** phone (604) 783-9991.

Visitor Information: A log building houses the tourist information booth at Beattie Park, across from the museum and St. Peter's Anglican United Church. Open daily mid-May to the end of August, hours are 8 A.M. to 5:30 P.M. Phone (604) 783-9154 or write Box 330, Hudson's Hope, BC V0C 1V0. (Off-season, phone the district office at 604/783-9901.)

Elevation: 1,707 feet/520m. **Climate:** Summer temperatures range from 60°F/16°C to 90°F/32°C, with an average of 135 frost-free days annually. **Radio:** CBC, CKNL 560, CJDC 870. **Television:** Channels 2, 5, 8, 11 and cable.

Private Aircraft: Hudson's Hope airstrip, 3.7 miles/6 km west; elev. 2,200 feet/671m; length 5,200 feet/1,585m; asphalt.

Hudson's Hope is the third oldest perma-

HUDSON'S HOPE ADVERTISERS

B.C. Hydro ....Ph. (604) 783-5211 or 9943
District of Hudson's Hope ....Ph. (604) 783-9901
Hudson's Hope Gourmet Pizza ......Across from Beattie Park
Hudson's Hope Museum ....Across from Info Centre

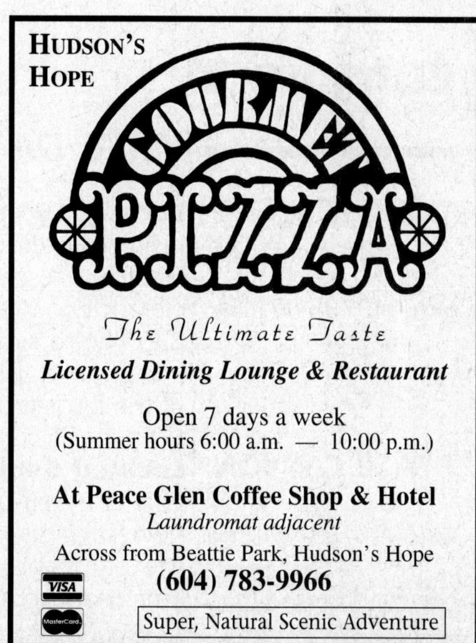

nently settled community in British Columbia. The site was first visited in 1793 by Alexander Mackenzie. In 1805 a Hudson's Bay trading post was established here by Simon Fraser. In 1916, after the fur-trading days were over, a major influx of settlers arrived in the area. It was the head of navigation for steamboats on the lower Peace River until 1936, the year of the last scheduled steamboat run. Area coal mines supplied Alaska Highway maintenance camps during the 1940s.

Modern development of Hudson's Hope was spurred by construction of the Peace Power project in the 1960s. Today the area's principal claim to fame is the 600-foot-/183-m-high W.A.C. Bennett Dam at the upper end of the Peace River canyon, 15 miles/24.1 km west of Hudson's Hope. The 100-million-ton dam is one of the largest earth-fill structures in the world and Williston Lake, behind it, is the largest body of fresh water in British Columbia. Tours of the Gordon M. Shrum generating station are available daily from mid-May to the end of September, weekdays only the remainder of the year (closed holidays). Tours are available each hour on the half hour from 9:30 A.M. to 4:30 P.M. Self-guided tours are available at the Peace Canyon Dam.

Also of interest is the Hudson's Hope Museum on Highway 29 in town. The museum has a fine collection of artifacts and dinosaur fossils from the Peace District. It offers hands-on paleontology and dinosaur activities and is well worth a visit. Souvenir shop in the museum. The active congregation of the log-constructed St. Peter's Anglican United Church (next to the museum) welcomes visitors to look inside.

Visitor services in Hudson's Hope include a motel, hotel, 3 restaurants, 2 service stations, a laundromat, supermarket, bakery, and convenience and hardware stores. There are also a bank, post office, fitness centre, liquor store, community hall, library, swimming pool, tennis courts, and numerous parks and playgrounds. Sightseeing and flightseeing tours are available locally. The main business district is along Highway 29 and adjoining streets. The RCMP office is at the corner of 100th Street and 100th Avenue.

Hudson's Hope Loop Log

(continued)

C 41.2 (66.3 km) **AH 45.7** (73.5 km) Turnout to north with Hudson's Hope visitor map.

CAUTION: Watch for deer between here and the Alaska Highway, especially at dusk and at night.

C 44 (70.8 km) **AH 42.9** (69 km) Lynx Creek bridge.

C 48.3 (77.7 km) **AH 38.6** (62.1 km) Pay phone, north side of road.

C 48.4 (77.9 km) **AH 38.5** (62 km) Turnout to north for view of the Peace River.

C 50.9 (81.9 km) **AH 36** (57.9 km) Farrell Creek bridge and picnic site.

C 56.6 (91.1 km) **AH 30.3** (48.8 km) Pull-through turnout with litter barrels. View of Peace River valley.

C 57.1 (91.9 km) **AH 29.8** (48 km) Turnout to south with litter barrels and view of Peace River valley.

C 59.3 (95.4 km) **AH 27.6** (44.4 km) Turnout to south with litter barrels.

C 64.7 (104.1 km) **AH 22.2** (35.7 km) Halfway River.

C 67.2 (108.1 km) **AH 19.7** (31.7 km) Rest area to south with point of interest sign, litter barrel and toilet. A slide occurred here on May 26, 1973, involving an estimated 10 million to 15 million cubic yards of overburden. Slide debris completely blocked the river channel for some 12 hours, backing up the river an estimated 24 feet/7.3m above normal level.

C 68.4 (110.1 km) **AH 18.5** (29.8 km) Milepost 19.

C 71.1 (114.4 km) **AH 15.8** (25.4 km) Turnout to north.

C 71.4 (114.9 km) **AH 15.5** (24.9 km) Milepost 16.

C 73.5 (118.3 km) **AH 13.4** (21.6 km) Beaver dam to north.

C 74.2 (119.4 km) **AH 12.7** (20.4 km) **Pine Ridge Campground.** A relaxing owner-operated campground, halfway between Fort St. John and Hudson's Hope. 100 spacious sites, some with power. Showers, washer and dryer, spring water and confectionary. Cooking shelter, fire pits and firewood, horseshoe pits, ping pong, ball diamonds, child-proof fence. Very reasonable rates. Gates open 7 A.M.–10 P.M. (Pets on a leash please.) Your hosts, the Bentley's, (604) 262-3229 mid-May to mid-September. Super, Natural Scenic Adventure. [ADVERTISEMENT] ▲

C 74.6 (120.1 km) **AH 12.3** (19.8 km) Cache Creek 1-lane bridge. Turnout to north at east end of bridge for picnic area with litter barrels.

C 76.6 (123.3 km) **AH 10.3** (16.6 km) Turnout with litter barrel to north overlooking Bear Flat in the Peace River valley. Highway begins climb eastbound. *CAUTION: Switchbacks.*

C 78.1 (125.7 km) **AH 8.8** (14.2 km) Highest point on Highway 29 (2,750 feet/838m) overlooking Peace River Plateau. Highway descends on a 10 percent grade westbound. *CAUTION: Switchbacks.*

C 86.9 (139.8 km) **AH 0 Junction** with the Alaska Highway, 6.7 miles/10.8 km north of Fort St. John (see **Milepost DC 53.7** in the ALASKA HIGHWAY section).

CAUTION: Watch for deer on the highway between here and Hudson's Hope, especially at dusk and at night.

ALASKA HIGHWAY

Dawson Creek, British Columbia, to Fairbanks, Alaska BC Highway 97, Yukon Highway 1 and Alaska Route 2 *(See maps, pages 70-74)*

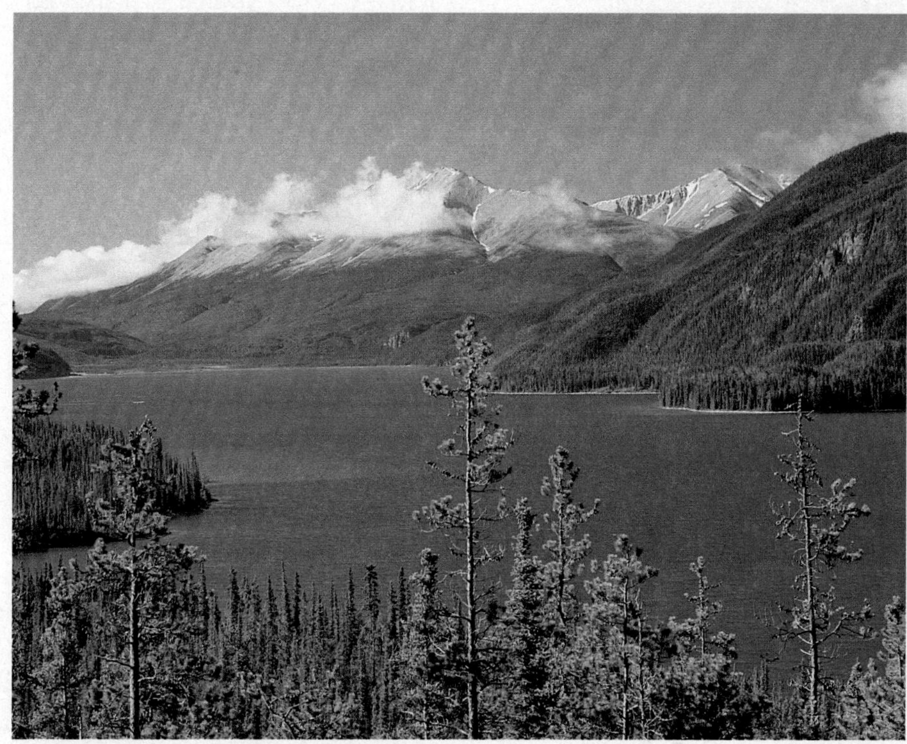

The Alaska Highway winds along the east shore of 7-mile-long Muncho Lake, known for its beautiful, deep green-and-blue waters. (Wes Bergen, Diarama)

The Alaska Highway stretches in a northwesterly direction from Mile 0 at Dawson Creek, BC, through Yukon Territory to Mile 1520 at Fairbanks, AK. Although the Alaska Highway does not compare with highways in the Lower 48, it is no longer a wilderness road but rather a road through the wilderness. The Alaska Highway is driven by thousands of people each year in all sorts of vehicles. The highway is open and maintained year-round.

For more information, contact Peace River Alaska Highway Tourist Assoc., P.O. Box 6850M, Fort St. John, BC V1J 4J3; phone (604) 785-2544, fax 785-4424.

Road Conditions

All of the Alaska Highway between Dawson Creek, BC, and Fairbanks, AK, is asphalt-surfaced. Repaving and highway improvement continue. Surfacing of the Alaska Highway ranges from poor to excellent.

There are still some stretches of poor surfacing with many chuckholes, gravel breaks (sections of gravel ranging from a few feet to several miles), hardtop with loose gravel, deteriorated shoulders and bumps. On the northern portion of the highway—in Yukon Territory and on into Alaska—watch for frost heaves. This rippling effect in the pavement is caused by the freezing and thawing of the ground. Drive slowly in sections of frost heaves to avoid breaking an axle or trailer hitch.

Surfacing on much of the highway is fair, with older patched pavement and a minimum of gravel breaks and chuckholes. There are also sections of excellent surfacing where highway maintenance crews have recently upgraded the road.

Loose gravel patches are common on the Alaska Highway and are often signed. *CAUTION: Slow down for loose gravel! Excessive speeds can lead to loss of control of your vehicle.*

Travelers should keep in mind that road conditions are subject to change! Weather and traffic may cause deterioration of newer pavement, while construction may improve older sections. Always be alert for bumps and holes in the road and for abrupt changes in highway surfacing. There are stretches of narrow, winding road without shoulders. Also watch for soft shoulders.

Always watch for construction crews along the Alaska Highway. Extensive road construction may require a detour or travelers may be delayed while waiting for a pilot car to guide them through the construction. Motorists may encounter rough driving at construction areas, and muddy roadway if there are heavy rains while the roadbed is torn up.

For current road conditions from Dawson Creek to the BC–YT border, phone the Peace River Alaska Highway Tourist Assoc. in Fort St. John at (604) 785-2544, or the Dawson Creek Tourist Infocentre at (604) 782-9595. The BC Ministry of Highways provides a recorded message on road conditions on the Alaska Highway in BC; phone (604) 774-7447. For recorded message on current road conditions on the Alaska Highway and other highways in Yukon Territory, phone (403) 667-8215 for daily road report.

Detailed weather information for the Canadian portion of the Alaska Highway is available from Atmospheric Environment Service of Environment Canada. For 24-hour recorded weather information between Dawson Creek and Sikanni Chief, phone (604) 784-2244 or 785-7669; for detailed weather information, phone the weather office at (604) 785-4304 between 6:15 A.M. and 4:45 P.M.; or for weather broadcasts, tune to 580 AM. Between Sikanni Chief and the BC–YT border, phone (604) 774-6461 for 24-hour recorded message; for detailed weather information phone (604) 774-2302 between 3 A.M. and 6:15 P.M.; or tune your radio to 590 AM for weather broadcasts. Between the BC–YT border and the YT–AK border, phone (403) 668-6061 for 24-hour recorded message; for detailed weather information phone (403) 667-8464 (24 hours a day); or tune your radio to CBC Yukon (570 AM) for weather broadcasts. Regional weather forecasts are also supplied to local visitor information centres, local hotels and motels, and lodges along the highway.

Road conditions along the Alaska Highway may be summarized as follows. Good pavement first 300 miles/483 km (through Fort Nelson) with recent resurfacing improving some sections. Watch for surface changes and continued construction in some areas. Between Fort Nelson and the BC–YT border, the Alaska Highway crosses the Rocky Mountains, so be prepared for narrow, winding road and some rough spots in surfacing due to deterioration from weather and traffic. Also watch for construction projects on this stretch. Between the BC–YT border and Haines Junction, expect fair to excellent road with a few rough spots and sections of narrow, winding road. From Haines Junction to the YT–AK border, the road is in fair condition with some narrow, winding sections without shoulders. Between **Historical Mile 1118** (Kluane Wilderness Village) and Beaver Creek there are both improved road and rough road, with some gravel patches and winding road; watch for continued road construction in 1996. The highway between Beaver Creek

(continues on page 75)

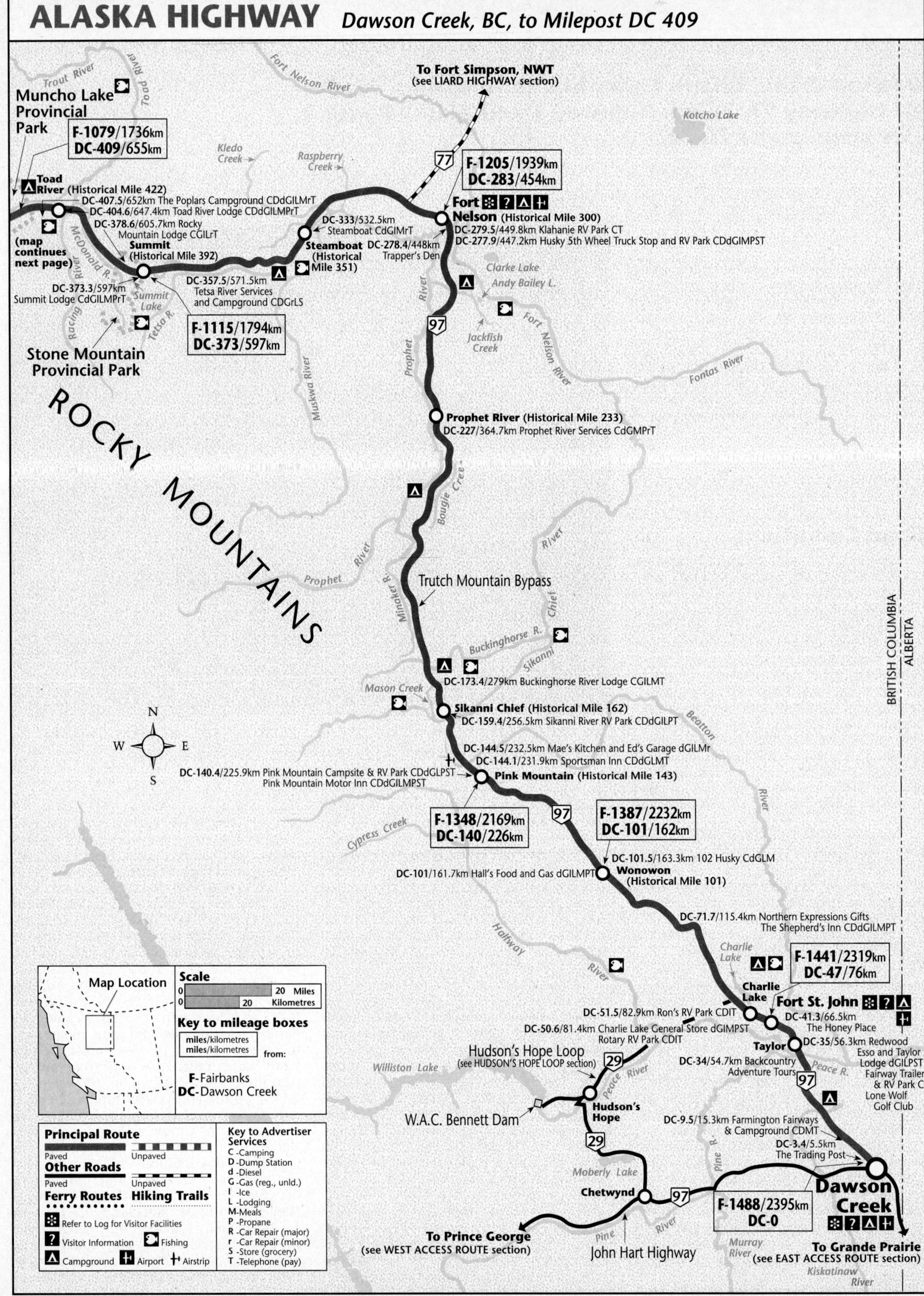
ALASKA HIGHWAY Dawson Creek, BC, to Milepost DC 409
To Fort Simpson, NWT
(see LIARD HIGHWAY section)
Muncho Lake Provincial Park
F-1079/1736km
DC-409/655km
Toad River (Historical Mile 422)
DC-407.5/652km The Poplars Campground CDdGILMrT
DC-404.6/647.4km Toad River Lodge CDdGILMPrT
DC-378.6/605.7km Rocky Mountain Lodge CGILrT
(map continues next page)
Summit (Historical Mile 392)
DC-373.3/597km Summit Lodge CdGILMPrT
DC-357.5/571.5km Tetsa River Services and Campground CDGrLS
F-1115/1794km
DC-373/597km
Stone Mountain Provincial Park
DC-333/532.5km Steamboat CdGIMrT
Steamboat (Historical Mile 351)
DC-278.4/448km Trapper's Den
F-1205/1939km
DC-283/454km
Fort Nelson (Historical Mile 300)
DC-279.5/449.8km Klahanie RV Park CT
DC-277.9/447.2km Husky 5th Wheel Truck Stop and RV Park CDdGIMPST
Trout River
Toad River
Fort Nelson River
Kledo Creek
Raspberry Creek
Kotcho Lake
Clarke Lake
Andy Bailey L.
Jackfish Creek
Fort Nelson River
Fontas River
McDonald R.
Racing River
Summit Lake
Tetsa R.
Muskwa River
Prophet River
ROCKY MOUNTAINS
Prophet River (Historical Mile 233)
DC-227/364.7km Prophet River Services CdGMPrT
Bougie Creek
Prophet River
Minaker R.
Trutch Mountain Bypass
Buckinghorse R.
Sikanni Chief
DC-173.4/279km Buckinghorse River Lodge CGILMT
Mason Creek
Sikanni Chief (Historical Mile 162)
DC-159.4/256.5km Sikanni River RV Park CDdGILPT
Beatton River
DC-144.5/232.5km Mae's Kitchen and Ed's Garage dGILMr
DC-144.1/231.9km Sportsman Inn CDdGLMT
DC-140.4/225.9km Pink Mountain Campsite & RV Park CDdGLPST
Pink Mountain Motor Inn CDdGILMPST
Pink Mountain (Historical Mile 143)
F-1348/2169km
DC-140/226km
F-1387/2232km
DC-101/162km
Cypress Creek
DC-101.5/163.3km 102 Husky CdGLM
DC-101/161.7km Hall's Food and Gas dGILMPT
Wonowon (Historical Mile 101)
Halfway River
DC-71.7/115.4km Northern Expressions Gifts
The Shepherd's Inn CDdGILMPT
Charlie Lake
F-1441/2319km
DC-47/76km
Charlie Lake
Fort St. John
DC-51.5/82.9km Ron's RV Park CDIT
DC-50.6/81.4km Charlie Lake General Store dGIMPST
Rotary RV Park CDIT
DC-41.3/66.5km The Honey Place
Taylor
DC-35/56.3km Redwood Esso and Taylor Lodge dGILPST
Fairway Trailer & RV Park C
Lone Wolf Golf Club
DC-34/54.7km Backcountry Adventure Tours
Peace R.
Hudson's Hope Loop
(see HUDSON'S HOPE LOOP section)
Williston Lake
Peace River
Hudson's Hope
W.A.C. Bennett Dam
DC-9.5/15.3km Farmington Fairways & Campground CDMT
DC-3.4/5.5km The Trading Post
Moberly Lake
Chetwynd
Pine R.
F-1488/2395km
DC-0
Dawson Creek
To Prince George
(see WEST ACCESS ROUTE section)
John Hart Highway
Pine River
Murray River
To Grande Prairie
(see EAST ACCESS ROUTE section)
Kiskatinaw River
BRITISH COLUMBIA
ALBERTA
N
W
E
S
Map Location
Scale
0 20 Miles
0 20 Kilometres
Key to mileage boxes
miles/kilometres
miles/kilometres
from:
F-Fairbanks
DC-Dawson Creek
Principal Route
Paved
Unpaved
Other Roads
Paved
Unpaved
Ferry Routes
Hiking Trails
Refer to Log for Visitor Facilities
Visitor Information
Fishing
Campground
Airport
Airstrip
Key to Advertiser Services
C -Camping
D -Dump Station
d -Diesel
G -Gas (reg., unld.)
I -Ice
L -Lodging
M-Meals
P -Propane
R -Car Repair (major)
r -Car Repair (minor)
S -Store (grocery)
T -Telephone (pay)

ALASKA HIGHWAY *Milepost DC 409 to Teslin, YT*

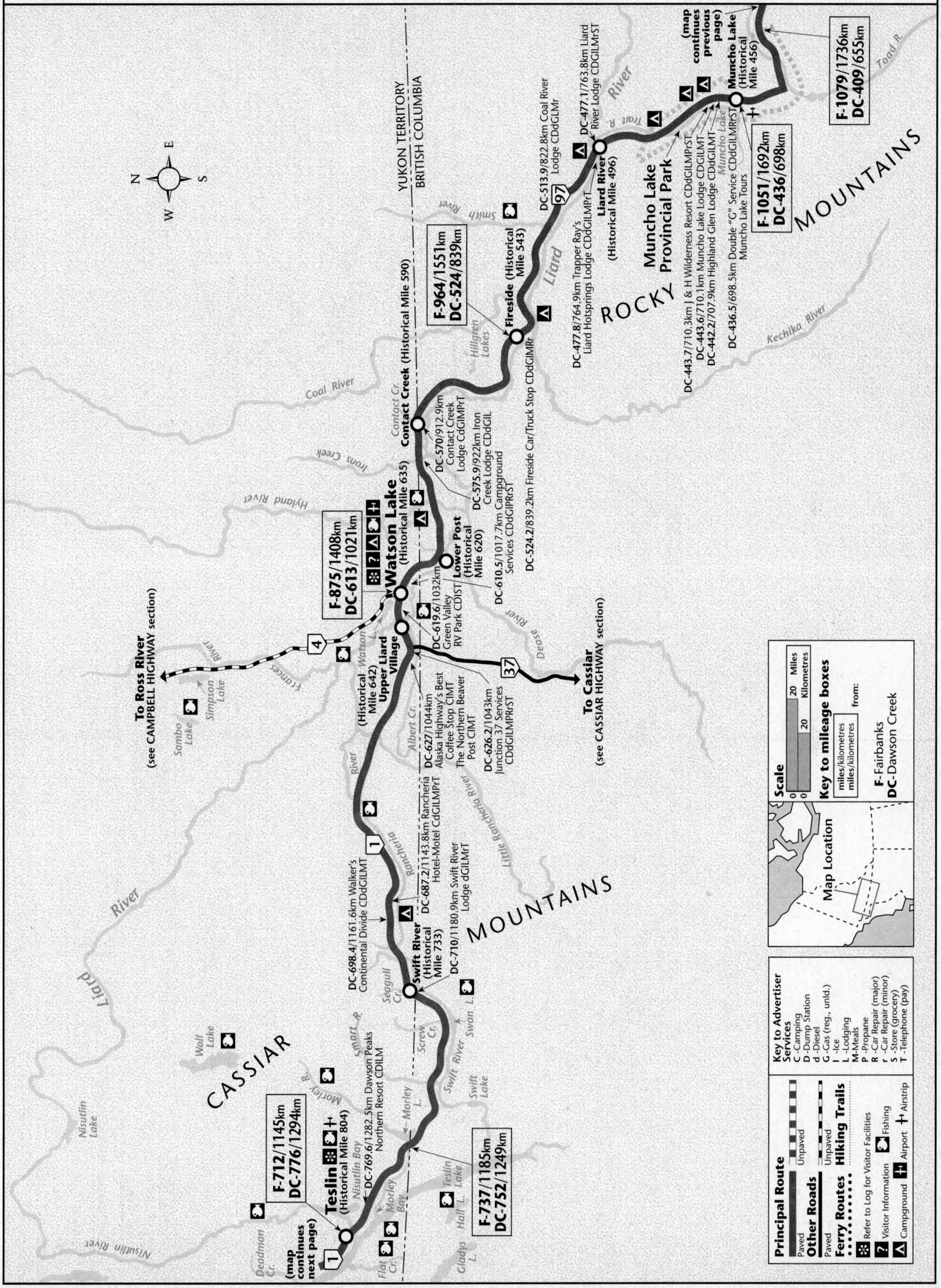

(map continues next page)
F-712/1145km
DC-776/1294km
Teslin (Historical Mile 804)
DC-769.6/1282.5km Dawson Peaks Northern Resort CDILM
F-737/1185km
DC-752/1249km
Swift River (Historical Mile 733)
DC-710/1180.9km Swift River Lodge dGILMrT
DC-698.4/1161.6km Walker's Continental Divide CDdGILMT
DC-687.2/1143.8km Rancheria Hotel-Motel CdGILMPrT
DC-627/1044km Alaska Highway's Best Coffee Stop CIMT The Northern Beaver Post CIMT
DC-626.2/1043km Junction 37 Services CDdGILMPRrST
Upper Liard Village (Historical Mile 642)
DC-619.6/1032km Green Valley RV Park CDIST
F-875/1408km
DC-613/1021km
Watson Lake (Historical Mile 635)
Lower Post (Historical Mile 620)
DC-610.5/1017.7km Campground Services CDdGIPRrST
DC-575.9/922km Iron Creek Lodge CDdGIL
DC-570/912.9km Contact Creek Lodge CdGIMPrT
Contact Creek (Historical Mile 590)
F-964/1551km
DC-524/839km
Fireside (Historical Mile 543)
DC-524.2/839.2km Fireside Car/Truck Stop CDdGIMRr
DC-513.9/822.8km Coal River Lodge CDdGLMr
DC-477.8/764.9km Trapper Ray's Liard Hotsprings Lodge CDdGILMPrT
DC-477.1/763.8km Liard River Lodge CDGILMrST
Liard River (Historical Mile 496)
Muncho Lake Provincial Park
DC-443.7/710.3km J & H Wilderness Resort CDdGILMPrST
DC-443.6/710.1km Muncho Lake Lodge CDGILMT
DC-442.2/707.9km Highland Glen Lodge CDdGILMT
DC-436.5/698.5km Double "G" Service CDdGILMRrST Muncho Lake Tours
Muncho Lake (Historical Mile 456)
F-1051/1692km
DC-436/698km
(map continues previous page)
F-1079/1736km
DC-409/655km

To Ross River (see CAMPBELL HIGHWAY section)
To Cassiar (see CASSIAR HIGHWAY section)
YUKON TERRITORY
BRITISH COLUMBIA
CASSIAR MOUNTAINS
ROCKY MOUNTAINS
N E S W

Nisutlin River, Nisutlin Lake, Liard River, Deadman Cr., Wolf Lake, Morley R., Nisutlin Bay, Smart R., Flat Cr., Morley Bay, Morley L., Seagull Cr., Screw Cr., Teslin Lake, Gladys L., Hall L., Swift River, Swan L., Swift Lake, Rancheria River, Little Rancheria River, Albert Cr., Sambo Lake, Simpson Lake, Frances River, Watson L., Hyland River, Irons Creek, Coal River, Dease River, Contact Cr., Hillgren Lakes, Smith River, Liard, Trout R., River, Muncho Lake, Kechika River, Toad R.

Principal Route Paved / Unpaved
Other Roads Paved / Unpaved
Ferry Routes **Hiking Trails**
Refer to Log for Visitor Facilities
Visitor Information
Fishing
Campground
Airport
Airstrip

Key to Advertiser Services
C -Camping
D -Dump Station
d -Diesel
G -Gas (reg., unld.)
I -Ice
L -Lodging
M-Meals
P -Propane
R -Car Repair (major)
r -Car Repair (minor)
S -Store (grocery)
T -Telephone (pay)

Map Location

Scale
0 — 20 Miles
0 — 20 Kilometres

Key to mileage boxes
miles/kilometres
miles/kilometres from:
F-Fairbanks
DC-Dawson Creek

ALASKA HIGHWAY *Teslin, YT, to Milepost DC 1136*

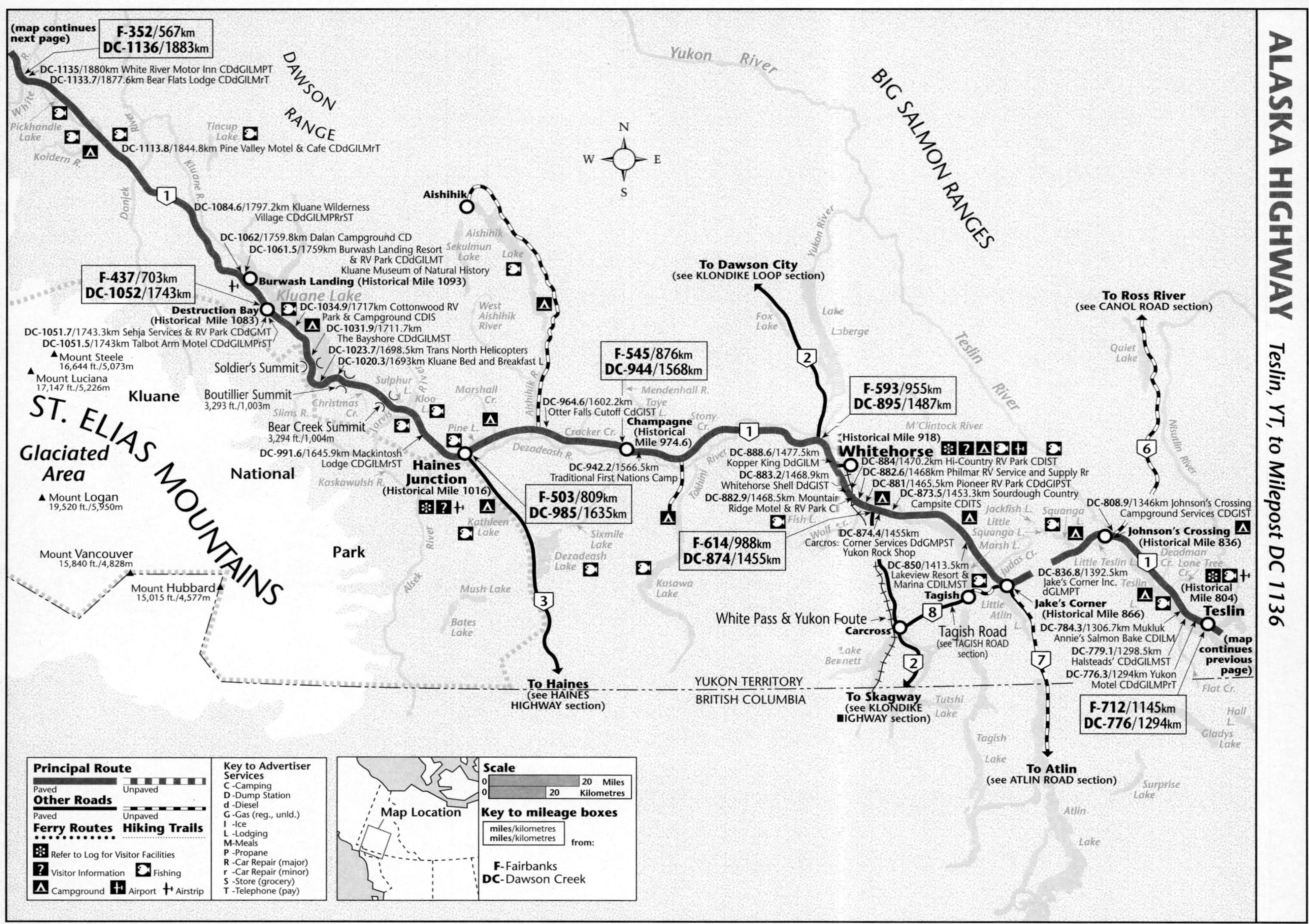

ALASKA HIGHWAY *Milepost DC 1136 to Milepost DC 1378*

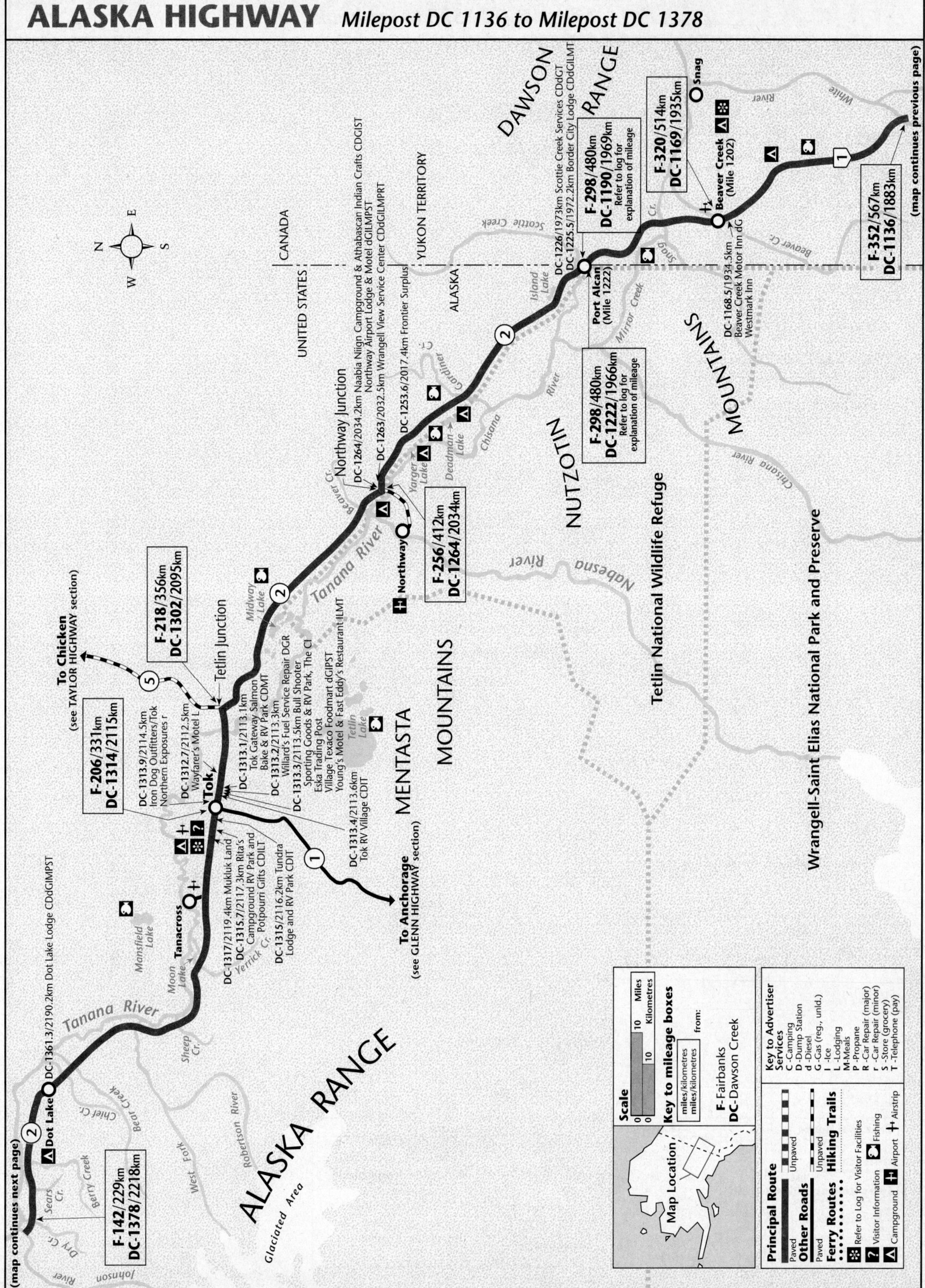

ALASKA HIGHWAY *Milepost DC 1378 to Fairbanks, AK*

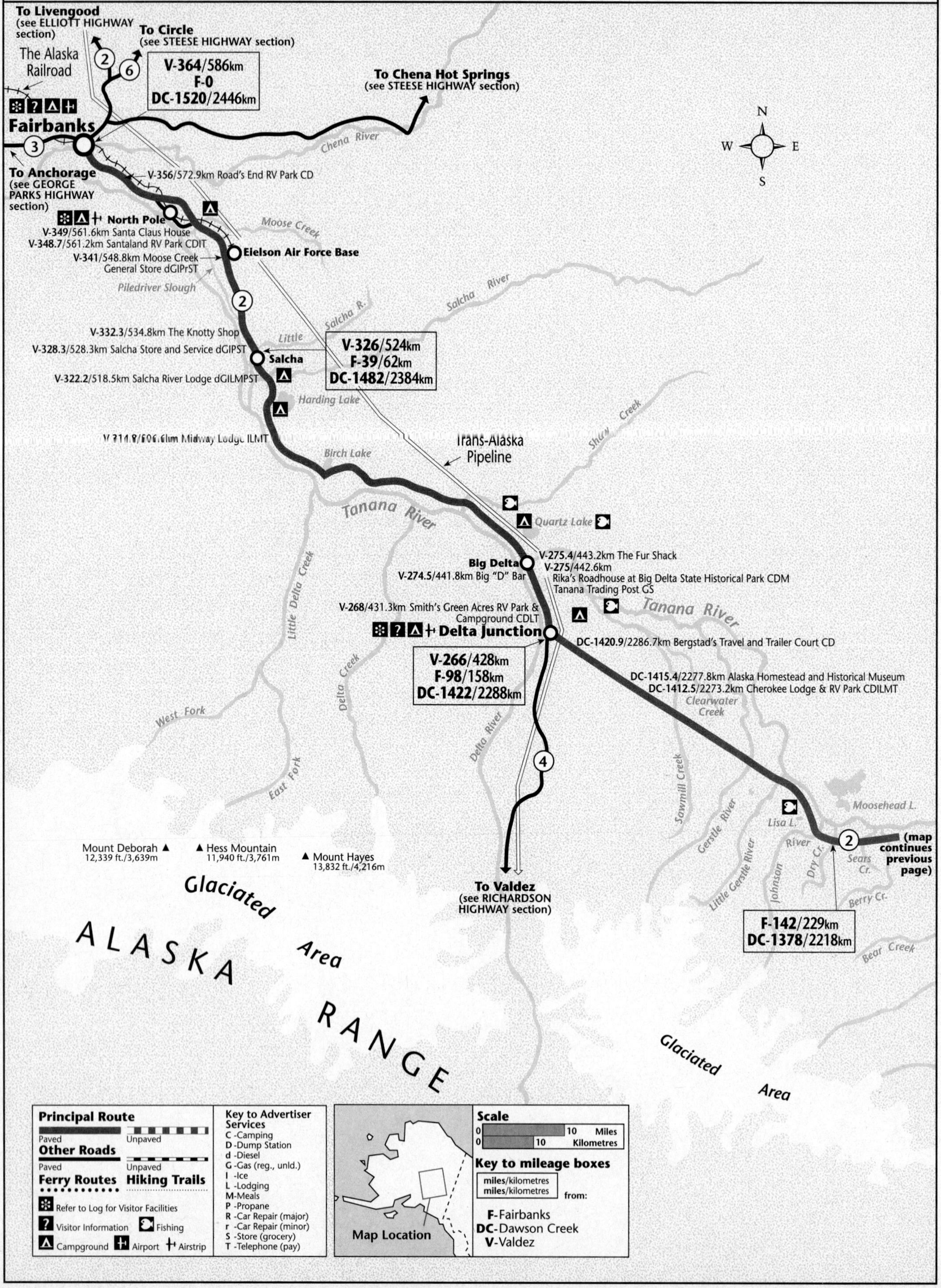

To Livengood
(see ELLIOTT HIGHWAY section)

To Circle
(see STEESE HIGHWAY section)

The Alaska Railroad

V-364/586km
F-0
DC-1520/2446km

To Chena Hot Springs
(see STEESE HIGHWAY section)

Fairbanks

Chena River

N
W E
S

To Anchorage
(see GEORGE PARKS HIGHWAY section)

V-356/572.9km Road's End RV Park CD

North Pole

V-349/561.6km Santa Claus House
V-348.7/561.2km Santaland RV Park CDIT
V-341/548.8km Moose Creek General Store dGIPrST

Moose Creek

Eielson Air Force Base

Piledriver Slough

Salcha River

Little Salcha R.

V-332.3/534.8km The Knotty Shop
V-328.3/528.3km Salcha Store and Service dGIPST

Salcha

V-322.2/518.5km Salcha River Lodge dGILMPST

V-326/524km
F-39/62km
DC-1482/2384km

Harding Lake

Shaw Creek

V-314.8/506.6km Midway Lodge ILMT

Trans-Alaska Pipeline

Birch Lake

Tanana River

Quartz Lake

Little Delta Creek

Big Delta

V-275.4/443.2km The Fur Shack
V-275/442.6km
Rika's Roadhouse at Big Delta State Historical Park CDM
Tanana Trading Post GS

V-274.5/441.8km Big "D" Bar

Tanana River

V-268/431.3km Smith's Green Acres RV Park & Campground CDLT

Delta Junction

DC-1420.9/2286.7km Bergstad's Travel and Trailer Court CD

V-266/428km
F-98/158km
DC-1422/2288km

DC-1415.4/2277.8km Alaska Homestead and Historical Museum
DC-1412.5/2273.2km Cherokee Lodge & RV Park CDILMT

Clearwater Creek

Delta Creek

West Fork

East Fork

Delta River

Sawmill Creek

Gerstle River

Little Gerstle River

Johnson River

Dry Cr.

Lisa L.

Moosehead L.

Sears Cr.

Berry Cr.

Bear Creek

(map continues previous page)

Mount Deborah ▲ 12,339 ft./3,639m
▲ Hess Mountain 11,940 ft./3,761m
▲ Mount Hayes 13,832 ft./4,216m

To Valdez
(see RICHARDSON HIGHWAY section)

F-142/229km
DC-1378/2218km

Glaciated Area

ALASKA RANGE

Glaciated Area

Principal Route
Paved
Unpaved
Other Roads
Paved
Unpaved
Ferry Routes
Hiking Trails
Refer to Log for Visitor Facilities
Visitor Information
Fishing
Campground
Airport
Airstrip

Key to Advertiser Services
C -Camping
D -Dump Station
d -Diesel
G -Gas (reg., unld.)
I -Ice
L -Lodging
M-Meals
P -Propane
R -Car Repair (major)
r -Car Repair (minor)
S -Store (grocery)
T -Telephone (pay)

Map Location

Scale
0 10 Miles
0 10 Kilometres

Key to mileage boxes
miles/kilometres
miles/kilometres
from:
F-Fairbanks
DC-Dawson Creek
V-Valdez

and the YT–AK border was under construction in 1995; continue to watch for rough spots, gravel surface and road construction in 1996. On the Alaska portion of the Alaska Highway, expect fair to good surfacing, but watch for frost heaves and narrow sections of road without shoulders. Also watch for continued road construction on the highway between the YT–AK border and Tok in 1996.

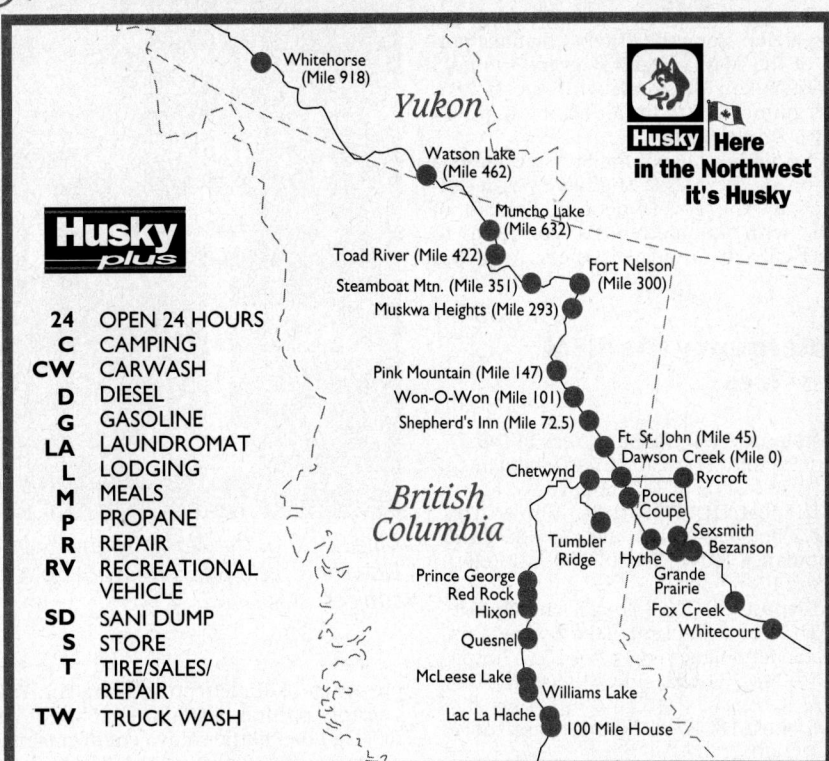

Driving Information

The Alaska Highway is a 2-lane highway that winds and rolls across the wilderness. There are sections of road with no centerline and stretches of narrow highway with little or no shoulder. The best advice is to take your time; drive with your headlights on at all times; keep to the right on hills and corners; watch for wildlife on the road; and—as you would on any highway anywhere else—drive defensively.

There are relatively few steep grades on the Alaska Highway. The highest summit on the highway is at Summit Lake, elev. 4,250 feet/1,295m.

Dust and mud may be a problem in construction areas and on some stretches of the highway. Gravel road is treated with calcium chloride to keep the dust down. This substance corrodes paint and metal: Wash your vehicle as soon as possible. In heavy rains, calcium chloride and mud combine to make a very slippery road surface; drive carefully! Flying gravel—which may damage headlights, radiators, gas tanks, windshields and paint—is still a problem. There are many sections of hardtop with loose gravel and gravel breaks along the highway. Side roads and access roads to campgrounds and other destinations are generally not paved. Keep in mind that many highways in the Yukon and some highways in Alaska are gravel.

Travelers with trailers should be especially cautious in areas of frost heaving. This corrugated road surface can be especially hard on trailer hitches.

Gas, food and lodging are found along the Alaska Highway on an average of every 20 to 50 miles. (The longest stretch without services is about 100 miles.) Not all businesses are open year-round, nor are most services available 24 hours a day. There are dozens of government and private campgrounds along the highway.

Remember that you will be driving in 2 different countries that use 2 different currencies: For the best rate, exchange your money at a bank. There are banks in Dawson Creek, Fort St. John, Fort Nelson, Watson Lake, Whitehorse, Tok, Delta Junction and Fairbanks. Haines Junction has banking service at the general store. See GENERAL INFORMATION in the back of the book for more details on Customs Requirements, Driving Information, Holidays and Money/Credit Cards.

Mileposts and Kilometreposts

Mileposts were first put up at communities and lodges along the Alaska Highway in the 1940s to help motorists know where they were in this vast wilderness. Today, those original mileposts remain a tradition with communities and businesses on the highway and are still used as mailing addresses and reference points, although the figures no longer accurately reflect driving distance.

When Canada switched to the metric system in the mid-1970s, the mileposts were replaced by kilometreposts. These posts are located on the right-hand side of the highway (Alaska-bound). Kilometreposts, consisting of reflective white numerals on green signs, are up along the British Columbia portion of the Alaska Highway every 3 miles/5 km. In Yukon Territory, white posts with black numerals are up along the highway every 1.2 miles/2 km.

The kilometerage of the British Columbia portion of the Alaska Highway was recalibrated by the government in the fall of 1990, with kilometreposts corrected to reflect current driving distances. As of our press time, kilometreposts along the Yukon Territory portion of the Alaska Highway still reflected the metric equivalent of the historical mileposts. Thus, at the BC–YT border (Historical Mile 627) the kilometerage from Dawson Creek is given as 967.6 km on the BC side and 1009 km on the YT side.

The MILEPOST® log of the Alaska Highway gives distance from Dawson Creek to the AK–YT border as actual driving distance in miles from Dawson Creek followed by kilometre distance based on the kilometreposts. Use our mileage figure from Dawson Creek to figure correct distance between points on the Alaska Highway in Canada. Use our kilometre figure from Dawson Creek to pinpoint location in reference to physical kilometreposts on the Alaska Highway in Canada. On the Alaska portion of the highway, mileposts are based on historical miles, so distance from Dawson Creek in the log is given according to the mileposts up along the road. This figure is followed by the metric equivalent in kilometres.

Traditional milepost figures in Canada are indicated in the text as **Historical Mile**. Where the governments of British Columbia, Yukon and Alaska have installed commemorative mileposts, the text reads **Historic Milepost.** Restored in 1992 to commemorate the 50th anniversary of the construction of the Alaska Highway, many of these historic markers are accompanied by signs and interpretive panels. These mileposts reflect the original or traditional mileage and do not reflect actual driving distance.

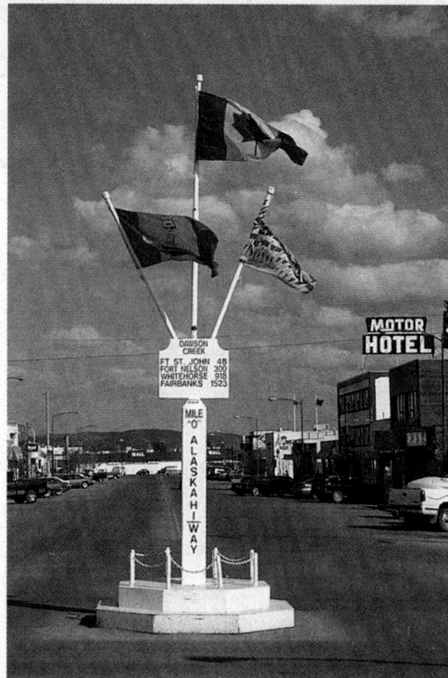

Milepost 0 of the Alaska Highway in Dawson Creek, BC, is a favorite photo subject. (Michael N. Dill)

Emergency Medical Services

Milepost DC 0 Dawson Creek to **DC 47** Fort St. John. Dawson Creek ambulance (604) 782-2211; RCMP (604) 782-5211.

Milepost DC 47 Fort St. John to **DC 222.3** Bougie Creek bridge. Fort St. John ambulance (604) 785-2079; RCMP (604) 785-6617.

Milepost DC 222.3 Bougie Creek bridge to **DC 373.3** Summit Lake Lodge. Fort Nelson ambulance (604) 774-2344, hospital (604) 774-6916; RCMP (604) 774-2777.

Milepost DC 373.3 Summit Lake Lodge to **DC 605.1** BC–YT border. Toad River ambulance (604) 232-5351; Fort Nelson RCMP (604) 774-2777.

Milepost DC 605.1 BC–YT border to **DC 710** Swift River. Watson Lake ambulance (403) 536-4444; RCMP (403) 536-5555 or (403) 667-5555.

Milepost DC 710 Swift River to **DC 821** Squanga Lake. Teslin ambulance (403) 390-4444 or (403) 667-3333; RCMP (403) 390-5555 or (403) 667-5555.

Milepost DC 821 Squanga Lake to **DC 936.8** Mendenhall River bridge. Whitehorse ambulance (403) 667-3333; RCMP (403) 667-5555.

Milepost DC 936.8 Mendenhall River bridge to **DC 1023.7** Kluane Lake Lodge. Haines Junction ambulance (403) 634-4444 or (403) 667-3333; RCMP (403) 634-5555 or (403) 667-5555.

Milepost DC 1023.7 Kluane Lake Lodge to **DC 1122.7** Longs Creek. Destruction Bay ambulance (403) 841-3333 or 1-403-667-3333; RCMP (403) 634-5555 or (403) 667-5555.

Milepost DC 1122.7 Longs Creek to **DC 1189.8** YT–AK border. Beaver Creek RCMP (403) 862-5555 or (403) 667-5555; Ambulance (403) 862-3333 or (403) 667-3333.

Milepost DC 1221.8 YT–AK border to **DC 1314.2** Tok. Northway EMS (907) 778-2211. Port Alcan Rescue Team (Alaska Customs) (907) 774-2252.

Milepost DC 1314.2 Tok to **DC 1361.3** Dot Lake. Tok ambulance (907) 883-2300 or 911.

Milepost DC 1361.3 to **DC 1422** Delta Junction. Delta Rescue Squad phone 911 or (907) 895-4600; Alaska State Troopers (907) 895-4800.

Milepost DC 1422 Delta Junction to **DC 1520** Fairbanks. Dial 911.

See the GENERAL INFORMATION section for details on Customs Requirements, Driving Information, Holidays, Money and Metric Conversion Chart.

A Brief History of the Alaska Highway

Construction of the Alaska Highway officially began on March 8, 1942, and ended eight months and 12 days later on Oct. 25, 1942. But an overland link between Alaska and the Lower 48 had been studied as early as 1930 under President Herbert Hoover's authorization. It was not until the bombing of Pearl Harbor in December 1941 that construction of the highway was deemed a military necessity. Alaska was considered vulnerable to a Japanese invasion. On Feb. 6, 1942, approval for the Alaska Highway was given by the Chief of Staff, U.S. Army. On Feb. 11, President Roosevelt authorized construction of the pioneer road.

The general route of the highway, determined by the War Department, was along a line of existing airfields from Edmonton, AB, to Fairbanks, AK. This chain of airfields was known as the Northwest Staging Route, and was used to ferry more than 8,000 war planes from Great Falls, MT, to Ladd Air Force Base in Fairbanks, AK, as part of the Russian–American Lend Lease Program. The planes were flown from Fairbanks to Nome, then on to Russia.

In March 1942, rights-of-way through Canada were secured by formal agreement between the 2 countries. The Americans agreed to pay for construction and turn over the Canadian portion of the highway to the Canadian government after the war ended. Canada furnished the right-of-way, and waived import duties, sales taxes, income taxes and immigration regulations, and provided construction materials along the route.

A massive mobilization of men and equipment began. Regiments of the U.S. Army Corps of Engineers were moved north to work on the highway. By June, more than 10,000 American troops had poured into the Canadian North. The Public Roads Administration tackled the task of organizing civilian engineers and equipment. Trucks, roadbuilding equipment, office furniture, food, tents and other supplies all had to be located and then shipped north.

Road work began in April, with crews working out of the 2 largest construction camps, Whitehorse and Fort St. John. The highway followed existing winter roads, old Indian trails, rivers and, on occasion, "sight" engineering.

For the soldiers and civilian workers, it was a hard life. Working 7 days a week, they endured mosquitoes and black flies in summer, and below zero temperatures in winter. Weeks would pass with no communication between headquarters and field parties. According to one senior officer with the Public Roads Administration, "Equipment was always a critical problem. There never was enough."

In June 1942, the Japanese invaded Attu and Kiska islands in the Aleutians, adding a new sense of urgency to completion of the road. Crews working from east and west connected at Contact Creek on Sept. 25. By October, it was possible for vehicles to travel the entire length of the highway. The official opening of the Alaska Highway was a ribbon-cutting ceremony held Nov. 20, 1942, on Soldier's Summit at Kluane Lake. (A rededication ceremony was held Nov. 20, 1992, as part of the 50th anniversary celebration of the Alaska Highway.)

Dawson Creek

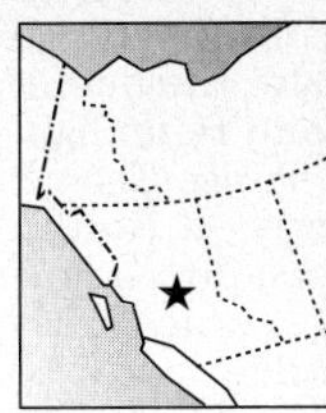

Milepost 0 of the Alaska Highway. **Population:** 12,000, area 66,500. **Emergency Services: RCMP,** phone (604) 782-5211. **Fire Department,** phone (604) 782-5000. **Ambulance,** phone (604) 782-2211. **Hospital and Poison Centre,** Dawson Creek and District Hospital, 11000 13th St., phone (604) 782-8501.

Visitor Information: At NAR (Northern Alberta Railway) Park on Alaska Avenue at 10th Street (one block west of the traffic circle), in the building behind the railway car. Open year-round, 8 A.M. to 8 P.M. daily in summer, 10 A.M. to 4 P.M. Monday through Saturday in winter. Phone (604) 782-9595. Plenty of public parking in front of the refurbished grain elevator that houses the Dawson Creek Art Gallery and Museum.

Elevation: 2,186 feet/666m. **Climate:** Average temperature in January is 0°F/-18°C; in July it is 60°F/15°C. The average annual snowfall is 72 inches with the average depth of snow in midwinter at 19.7 inches. Frost-free days total 97, with the first frost of the year occurring about the first week of September. **Radio:** CJDC 890. **Television:** 13 channels via cable including pay TV. **Newspapers:** *Peace River Block News* (daily); *The Mirror* (biweekly).

Private Aircraft: Dawson Creek airport, 2 miles/3.2 km southeast; elev. 2,148 feet/655m; length 5,000 feet/1,524m; asphalt; fuel 100, jet. Floatplane base parallels runway.

Dawson Creek lies 367 miles/591 km northwest of Edmonton, AB, and 250 miles/402 km northeast of Prince George, BC.

Dawson Creek (like Dawson City in the Yukon Territory) was named for George Mercer Dawson of the Geological Survey of Canada, whose geodetic surveys of this region in 1879 helped lead to its development as an agricultural settlement. The open level townsite is surrounded by rolling farmland, part of the government-designated Peace River Block.

The Peace River Block consists of 3.5 million acres of arable land in northeastern British Columbia, which the province gave to the Dominion Government in 1883 in return for financial aid toward construction of the Canadian Pacific Railway. (While a route through the Peace River country was surveyed by CPR in 1878, the railroad was eventually routed west from Calgary through Kicking Horse Pass.) The Peace River Block was held in reserve by the Dominion Government until 1912, when some of the land was opened for homesteading. The federal government restored the Peace River Block to the province of British Columbia in 1930.

Today, agriculture is an important part of this area's economy. The fields of bright yellow flowers (in season) in the area are canola, a hybrid of rapeseed that was developed as a low cholesterol oil seed. Raw seed is processed in Alberta and Japan. The Peace River region also produces most of the province's cereal grain, along with fodder, cattle and dairy cattle. Other industries include the production of honey, hogs, eggs and poultry. Some potato and vegetable farming is also done here.

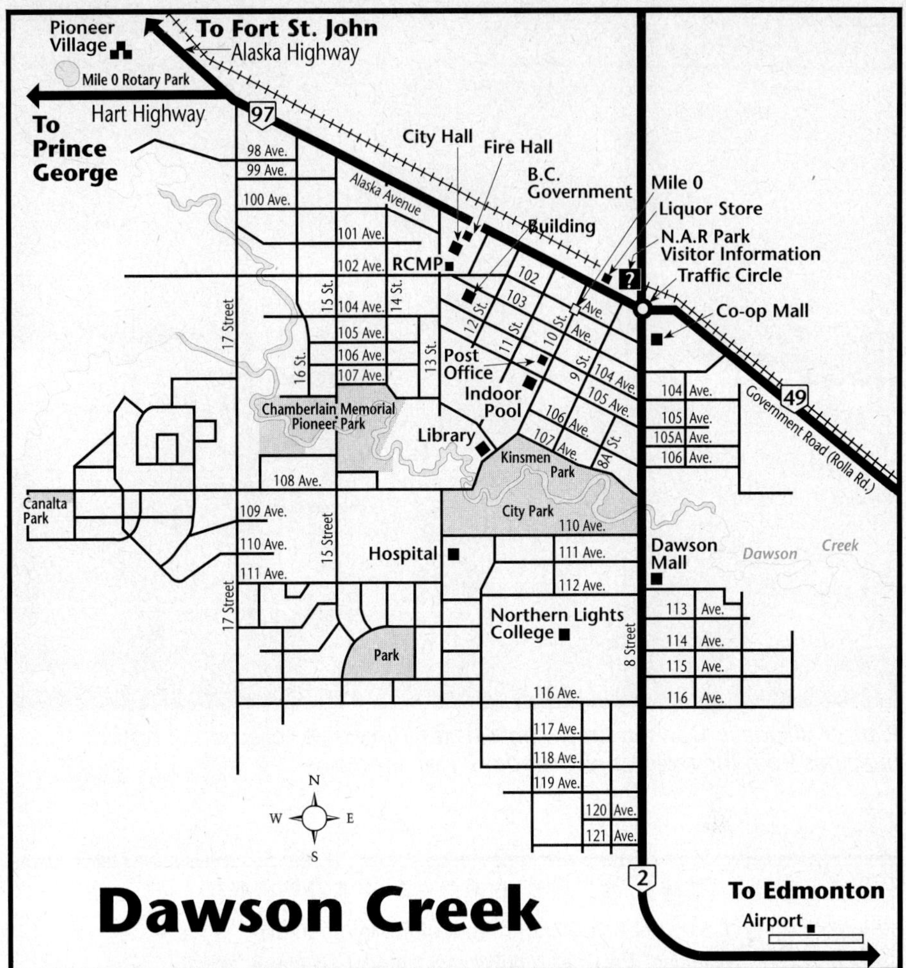

Pioneer Village in Dawson Creek contains an impressive collection of historic buildings from the region's pioneer days. (Earl L. Brown, staff)

On the British Columbia Railway line and the western terminus of the Northern Alberta Railway (now Canadian National Railway), Dawson Creek is also the hub of four major highways: the John Hart Highway (Highway 97 South) to Prince George; the Alaska Highway (Highway 97 North); Highway 2, which leads east to Grande Prairie, AB; and Highway 49, which leads east to Spirit River and Donnelly.

The Northern Alberta Railway reached Dawson Creek in 1930. As a railhead, Dawson Creek was an important funnel for supplies and equipment during construction of the Alaska Highway in 1942. Some 600 carloads arrived by rail within a period of five weeks in preparation for the construction program, according to a report by the Public Roads Administration in 1942. A "rutted provincial road" linked Dawson Creek with Fort St. John, affording the only approach to the southern base of operations.

DAWSON CREEK ADVERTISERS

Alahart RV Park.................Ph. (604) 782-4702
Alaska Hotel Cafe & Dew Drop Inn Pub.........55 paces south of Mile 0 Post
Bed & Breakfast Inn Margaree.....................Ph. (604) 782-4319
Blue Goose Caboose, The.................NAR Park
Boston Pizza..........................1525 Alaska Ave.
Corlane Sporting Goods Ltd. ....2 blks from Mile 0 Post
Dawson Creek Art Gallery ....NAR Park
Dawson Creek Coin Laundry Ltd..........5 blocks S. of traffic circle
Dawson Creek Tourist Information Bureau.....Ph. (604) 782-9595
George Dawson Inn,The ..Ph. (604) 782-9151
Joy Propane ....4805 S. Access Rd.
King Koin Laundromat.................Across from BC Government Bldg.
Lodge Motor Inn, The ......Ph. (604) 782-4837
Loiselle's Bed & Breakfast......................Ph. (604) 782-4965
Mile 0 Campsite......................Adjacent Walter Wright Pioneer Village
Northern Lights Bed & Breakfast...........Ph. (604) 782-3197
Northern Lights R.V. Park Ltd........1 mile from Alaska Hwy. Jct. on Hwy. 97 S.
Northwinds Motel ....1 block E. Co-op Mall
Organic Farms Bakery.......Ph. (604) 782-6533
Peace Villa Motel..................1641 Alaska Ave.
TLC Car Wash................Across from Northern Lights College
Trail Inn, The ....Ph. (604) 782-8595
Treasure House Imports ....10109 10th St.
Tubby's R.V. Park...................1913 Hart Hwy.
United Spring & Brake Ltd..........Directly behind McDonald's
Voyageur Motor Inn.......................Across from Dawson Mall
Yarn Barn, The ....Across from Provincial Bldgs.

Field headquarters were established at Fort St. John and Whitehorse. Meanwhile, men and machines continued to arrive at Dawson Creek. By May of 1942, 4,720 carloads of equipment had arrived by rail at Dawson Creek for dispersement to troops and civilian engineers to the north.

With the completion of the Alaska Highway in 1942 (and opening to the public in 1948) and the John Hart Highway in 1952, Dawson Creek expanded both as a distribution centre and tourist destination. Dawson Creek was incorporated as a city in 1958.

The development of oil and natural gas exploration in northeastern British Columbia, and related industries such as pipeline construction and oil storage, has contributed to the economic expansion of Dawson Creek. The city is also one of the major supply centres for the massive resource development known as North East Coal, southwest of Dawson Creek. Access to the coal development and the town of Tumbler Ridge is via the Heritage Highway, which branches off the John Hart Highway just west of Dawson Creek and also branches off Highway 2 southeast of the city. Highway 29 extends south from Chetwynd to Tumbler Ridge.

Provincial government offices and social services for the South Peace region are located in Dawson Creek. The city has a modern 100-bed hospital, a public library and a college (Northern Lights). There are also an indoor swimming pool, 2 skating arenas, a curling arena, bowling alley, golf course, art gallery, museum, tennis and racquetball courts. There are numerous churches in Dawson Creek (check at the visitor infocentre for location and hours of worship).

ACCOMMODATIONS/VISITOR SERVICES

There are 14 hotels/motels, several bed and breakfasts and dozens of restaurants. Department stores, banks, grocery, an organic bakery, drug and hardware stores and many specialty shops are located both downtown and in the 2 shopping centres, Co-op Mall and Dawson Mall. Visitors will also find laundromats, car washes, gas stations and automotive repair shops. The liquor store is adjacent the NAR visitor information centre on Alaska Avenue.

There are 4 campgrounds in Dawson Creek, 2 located on either side of the Hart Highway at its junction with the Alaska Highway and 2 located on Alaska Avenue. There is a private campground on the Hart Highway, 2 miles/3.2 km west from the Alaska Highway junction. There are also campgrounds (both private and provincial) north of Dawson Creek on the Alaska Highway. ▲

The Alaska Hotel Cafe & Dew Drop Inn Pub combines the spirit of northern adventure with Old World charm. *Where to Eat in*

Canada, which lists the 500 top restaurants, suggests "it is a good idea to start out on the Alaska Highway with a good meal under your belt and there's no better place than the Alaska Cafe." The Cafe also holds membership in World Famous Restaurants International; a definite must to experience! Open daily for breakfast, brunch, lunch, dinner and snacks. American Express, VISA and MasterCard. Located 55 paces south of the Mile "0" Post. In days of old, the Hotel Alaska proclaimed, "When you drop in to Dawson Creek, do drop in to the Dew Drop Inn." The pub features live entertainment nightly, a hot spot in town. The Alaska's "rooms with charm," from $25, have been renovated in the "old style"—in addition to original furnishings, the building provides a perfect backdrop for the Kux-Kardos collection of antiques and works of art. At the Alaska, our philosophy is Deluxe Evolution-

ary ... "Always changing for the better." Phone (604) 782-7998. Enjoy Super, Natural Scenic Adventure. [ADVERTISEMENT]

Northern Lights RV Park. Peaceful surroundings, just 1½ miles from town. Spacious pull-throughs with your own lawn and picnic table. Full and partial hookups, 20-30 amp services, clean washrooms, free hot showers. We'll pamper you and your rig to get you ready for your Super, Natural Scenic Alaska Highway Adventure. Caravans welcome! Your hosts—the Bates family. (604) 782-9433. [ADVERTISEMENT] ▲

Organic Farms Bakery. Using grain crops from our family farm, 100 percent certified organic stoneground flour. Specializing in German-style rye, spelt and whole wheat breads, buns, pretzels, croissants and pastries. Flours and spelt pastas. Taste the difference! 1425 – 97 Ave., Dawson Creek. (Look for our colourful bakery). Just off Alaska Ave. (604) 782-6533. [ADVERTISEMENT]

TRANSPORTATION

Air: Scheduled service from Dawson Creek airport to Prince George, Vancouver, Edmonton, Grande Prairie and Calgary via Air BC. The airport is located 2 miles/3.2 km south of the Alaska Avenue traffic circle via 8th Street/Highway 2; there is a small terminal at the airport. There is also a floatplane base.

Railroad: Canadian National Railroad and British Columbia Railway provide freight service only. B.C. Railway provides passenger service from Vancouver to Prince George.

Bus: Greyhound service to Prince George and Vancouver, BC; Edmonton, AB; and Whitehorse, YT. Dawson Creek also has a city bus transit system.

ATTRACTIONS

NAR Park, on Alaska Avenue at 10th Street (near the traffic circle), is the site of the Tourist Information Bureau, which is housed in a restored railway station; phone (604) 782-9595. The tourist bureau offers a self-guided historical walking tour with descriptions of Dawson Creek in the early 1940s during construction of the Alaska Highway.

Also at the station is the Dawson Creek Station Museum, operated by the South Peace Historical Society, which contains pioneer artifacts and wildlife displays.

In front of the station is a 1903 railway car, called "The Blue Goose Caboose," serving snacks and ice cream. Adjacent the station is a huge wooden grain elevator, which has been refurbished; its annex now houses an art gallery that features art shows throughout the summer. The last of Dawson Creek's old elevators, it was bought and moved to its present location by the art society in 1982.

Inquire at the Tourist Information Bureau for the location of Bear Mountain Community Forest. This Ministry of Forests recreation area features interpretive trails on the flora and fauna of the area. It is located 6 miles/10 km south of the city.

Recreational facilities in Dawson Creek include a bowling alley, miniature golf, indoor pool, 2 ice arenas, curling rink, 18-hole golf course, tennis courts, and an outdoor pool at Rotary Lake Park.

Walter Wright Pioneer Village and Mile 0 Rotary Park are a must-see attraction. The pioneer village contains an impressive collection of local pioneer buildings, including: a teahouse; a photo studio; a dried flowers, antiques and collectibles shop; and a general store. Admission is by donation. Food service available at the Mile 1 Cafe. Adjacent to the village is the Sudeten Memorial Hall. "A Mile Zero Welcome," a presentation about Dawson Creek, then and now, by Marilyn Croutch, is held either in Sudeten Hall or the old Dawson School in summer; phone (604) 782-7144. Check with Tourist Information for details on entertain-

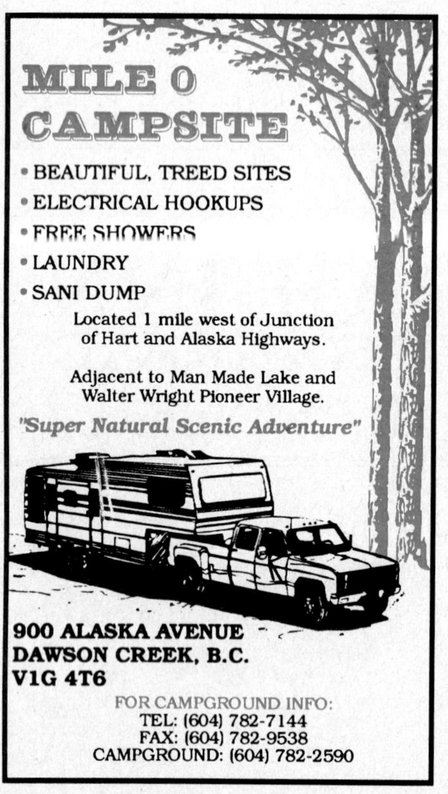

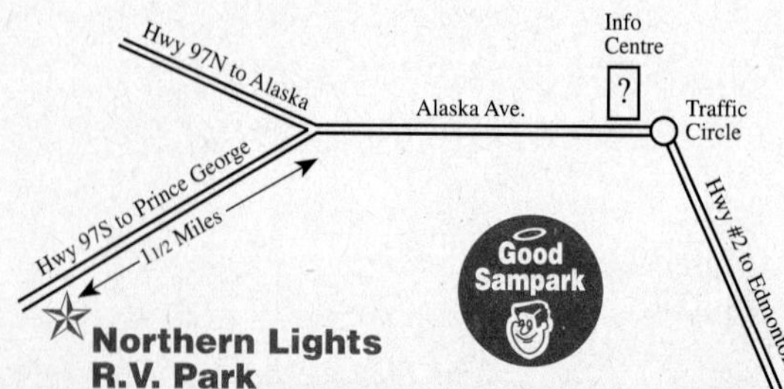

ment offerings. Also located here is Rotary Lake, an outdoor man-made swimming facility.

Tumbler Ridge Side Trip. To reach Tumbler Ridge, drive west from Dawson Creek 12 miles/20 km on Highway 97 to junction with the Heritage Highway (see **Milepost PG 237.7** in the WEST ACCESS ROUTE section), or drive west 60.6 miles/97.5 km to junction with Highway 29 South (see **Milepost PG 189.4** in the WEST ACCESS ROUTE section). Heritage Highway 52 (paved) leads south 59.5 miles/96 km to the community of Tumbler Ridge. Highway 29 South is a paved maintained road all the way to Tumbler Ridge. Tumbler Ridge is the townsite for Quintette Coal Limited's large-scale surface mines, and also serves workers of the Bullmoose Mine. Tours of Quintette and Bullmoose mines are available; inquire at the information centre in Tumbler Ridge. The huge coal processing plant and overhead conveyor are visible from the road. Monkman Provincial Park, site of spectacular 225-foot/69-m Kinuseo (Keh-NEW-see-oh) Falls, lies south of Tumbler Ridge. Contact BC Parks in Fort St. John (phone 604/787-3407) or Tumbler Ridge Infocentre (604/242-4702) for more information.

At Tumbler Ridge, motorists have a choice: return to Highway 97 via Highway 52; return to Highway 97 via Highway 29 South to Chetwynd; or continue on the Heritage Highway loop, 76 miles/123 km via all-gravel road and 16 miles/25 km via paved road, to Highway 2 southeast of Dawson Creek. (Highway 29 South offers the best road surface.) There are no services on the Heritage Highway except at Tumbler Ridge, which has a motel, campgrounds, restaurants, a bank and shopping. On gravel stretches of the road, watch for poor road conditions in wet weather.

Kiskatinaw River bridge at Milepost DC 20.9 replaced historic, curved wooden bridge on old Alaska Highway at Milepost DC 17.3. (Earl L. Brown, staff)

Alaska Highway Log

BC HIGHWAY 97
Distance* from Dawson Creek (DC) is followed by distance from Fairbanks (F). Original mileposts are indicated in the text as Historical Mile.
*Mileages from Dawson Creek are based on actual driving distance. Kilometres from Dawson Creek are based on physical kilometreposts. Read Mileposts and Kilometreposts in the introduction on page 71 for an explanation of how this highway is logged.

DC 0 F 1488 (2394.6 km) **Mile 0** marker of the Alaska Highway on 10th Street in downtown Dawson Creek.

Northbound: Good pavement approximately next 284 miles/457 km (through Fort Nelson). Watch for road construction and surface changes from Pink Mountain north.

DC 1.2 (1.9 km) **F 1486.8** (2392.7 km) **Junction** of the Alaska Highway and John Hart Highway.

Prince George-bound travelers turn to the end of the WEST ACCESS ROUTE section and read log back to front. Alaska-bound travelers continue with this log.

DC 1.5 (2.4 km) **F 1486.5** (2392.2 km) Mile 0 Rotary Park, Walter Wright Pioneer Village and Mile 0 Campground to west. ▲

DC 1.7 (2.7 km) **F 1486.3** (2391.9 km) **Historic Milepost 2.** Sign about Cantel Repeater Station. Cantel telephone–teletype lines stretched from Alberta to Fairbanks, AK, making it one of the world's longest open wire toll circuits at the time.

DC 2 (3.2 km) **F 1486** (2391.4 km) Recreation centre and golf course to west. Louisiana Pacific waferboard plant to east.

DC 2.7 (4.3 km) **F 1485.3** (2390.3 km) Truck scales and public phone to east. Truck stop to west; gas, cafe.

DC 2.9 (4.7 km) **F 1485.1** (2390 km) Northern Alberta Railway (NAR) tracks.

DC 3.3 (5.3 km) **F 1484.7** (2389.3 km) Turnout with litter barrel to east. **Historic Milepost 3**; historic sign marks Curan & Briggs Ltd. Construction Camp, U.S. Army Traffic Control Centre.

DC 3.4 (5.5 km) **F 1484.6** (2389.2 km) **Historical Mile 3. The Trading Post** to east. See display ad this section.

DC 9.5 (15.3 km) **F 1478.5** (2379.3 km) Golf course, driving range and RV park.

Farmington Fairways and Campground. 9-hole par-36 golf course, grass greens, treed fairways. Driving range, licensed club house, rentals available. 28-site shaded campground, firepits, tables, pit toilets and sani-station. RV park with 23 pull-through hookups. Camp under the trees and golf at your leisure. (604) 843-7774. (VISA and MasterCard.) Enjoy super, natural scenic adventure. [ADVERTISEMENT] ▲

DC 11.2 (18 km) **F 1476.8** (2376.6 km) Turnout with litter barrels to west.

DC 11.5 (18.5 km) **F 1476.5** (2376.1 km) Turnout with litter barrels to east.

DC 13.1 (21.1 km) **F 1474.9** (2373.5 km) **Historic Milepost 13** "Start of Storms Contracting Co. Ltd. contract."

DC 14.8 (24 km) **F 1473.2** (2370.8 km) Farmington (unincorporated).

DC 15.2 (24.5 km) **F 1472.8** (2370.2 km) Farmington store to west; gas, groceries, phone.

DC 17.3 (27.8 km) **F 1470.7** (2366.8 km) Exit east for loop road to Kiskatinaw Provincial Park. Follow good 2-lane paved road (old Alaska Highway) 2.5 miles/4 km for Kiskatinaw Provincial Park. This interesting side road gives travelers the opportunity to drive the original old Alaska Highway and to cross the historic curved wooden Kiskatinaw River bridge. Sign at bridge notes that this 531-foot-/162-m-long structure is the only original timber bridge built along the Alaska Highway that is still in use today. The provincial park has 28 campsites, drinking water, firewood, picnic tables, fire rings, outhouses and garbage containers. Camping fee $7 to $12. ▲

DC 17.5 (28.2 km) **F 1470.5** (2366.5 km) Distance marker indicates Fort St. John 29 miles/47 km.

DC 19.4 (31.2 km) **F 1468.6** (2363.4 km) Large turnout to east.

DC 19.8 (31.9 km) **F 1468.2** (2362.8 km) Highway descends northbound to Kiskatinaw River.

DC 20.9 (33.6 km) **F 1467.1** (2361 km) Kiskatinaw River bridge. *CAUTION: Strong crosswinds on bridge.* Turnout with litter barrel and picnic tables to east at north end of bridge. View of unique bridge support.

DC 21.6 (34.5 km) **F 1466.4** (2359 km) Loop road to Kiskatinaw Provincial Park and Kiskatinaw River bridge (see **Milepost DC 17.3**).

DC 25.4 (41 km) **F 1462.6** (2353.8 km) NorthwesTel microwave tower to east. Alaska Highway travelers will be seeing many of these towers as they drive north. The Northwest Communications System was constructed by the U.S. Army in 1942–43. This land line was replaced in 1963 with the construction of 42 microwave relay stations by Canadian National Telecommunications (Cantel, now NorthwesTel) between Grande Prairie, AB, and the YT–AK border.

DC 30.5 (49.1 km) **F 1457.5** (2345.5 km) Turnout to east with litter barrels. Turnout to west with litter barrels, pit toilet and historical marker about explorer Alexander Mackenzie.

Highway begins steep winding descent northbound to the Peace River bridge. *CAUTION: Trucks check your brakes.* Good views to northeast of Peace River valley and industrial community of Taylor. Some wide gravel shoulder next 4 miles/6.4 km for northbound traffic to pull off.

DC 32.1 (51.6 km) **F 1455.9** (2343 km) Large turnout with litter barrels. Viewpoint with information panel.

DC 33.8 (54.4 km) **F 1454.2** (2340.2 km)

Pingle Creek.

DC 34 (54.7 km) **F 1454** (2339.9 km) Access to Taylor Landing Provincial Park; boat launch, parking and fishing. A **Peace River** jet boat outfitter operates backcountry tours from here. Also access to Peace Island Regional Park, 0.5 mile/0.8 km west of the highway, situated on an island in the Peace River connected to the south shore by a causeway. Peace Island has 35 shaded campsites with gravel pads, firewood, fire rings, picnic tables, picnic shelter, toilets, potable water, playground and horseshoe pits. There are also 4 large picnic areas and a tenting area. Camping fee. Open Memorial Day to Labour Day. Nature trail, good bird watching and good fishing in clear water. Boaters should use caution on the Peace River since both parks are downstream from the W.A.C. Bennett and Peace Canyon dams and water levels may fluctuate rapidly. ▲

Backcountry Adventure Tours. See display ad this section.

DC 34.4 (55.4 km) **F 1453.6** (2339.3 km) Peace River bridge. Gas pipeline bridge visible to east.

Bridging the Peace was one of the first goals of Alaska Highway engineers in 1942. Traffic moving north from Dawson Creek was limited by the Peace River crossing, where 2 ferries with a capacity of 10 trucks per hour were operating in May. Three different pile trestles were constructed across the Peace River, only to be washed out by high water. Work on the permanent 2,130-foot suspension bridge began in December 1942 and was completed in July 1943. One of 2 suspension bridges on the Alaska Highway, the Peace River bridge collapsed in 1957 after erosion undermined the north anchor block of the bridge. The cantilever and truss type bridge that crosses the Peace River today was completed in 1960.

DC 35 (56.3 km) **F 1453** (2338.3 km) **Historic Milepost 35** at **TAYLOR** (pop. 821; elev. 1,804 feet/550m), located on the north bank of the Peace River. **Visitor Information**: On left northbound (10114–100 St.); phone (604) 789-9015. Inquire here about industrial tours of Canadian Forest Products, Fiberco Pulpmill and Greenhouse Complex. Taylor is an industrial community clustered around a Westcoast Energy Inc. gas-processing plant and large sawmill. Established in 1955 with the discovery and development of a natural gas field in the area, Taylor is the site of a pulp mill and plants that handle sulfur processing, gas compressing, high-octane aviation gas production and other byproducts of natural gas. The Westcoast Energy natural gas pipeline reaches from here to Vancouver, BC, with a branch to western Washington.

The fertile Taylor Flats area has several market gardens and roadside stands in summer. A hotel, motels, cafes, grocery store, private RV park, gas station and post office are located here. Free municipal dump station and potable water located behind the Petro–Canada gas station. Taylor holds an annual Class A World Gold Panning Championship in August. Recreation facilities include an 18-hole golf course, a motorcross track and a recreation complex with swimming pool, and district ice centre for skating and curling (open year-round). ▲

Fairway Trailer & R.V. Park. See display ad this section. ▲

Lone Wolf Golf Club. See display ad this section.

Redwood Esso and Taylor Lodge. See display ad this section.

DC 36.3 (58.4 km) **F 1451.7** (2336.2 km) Railroad tracks.

DC 40 (64.5 km) **F 1448** (2330.3 km) **Historical Mile 41.** Post office; private campground. ▲

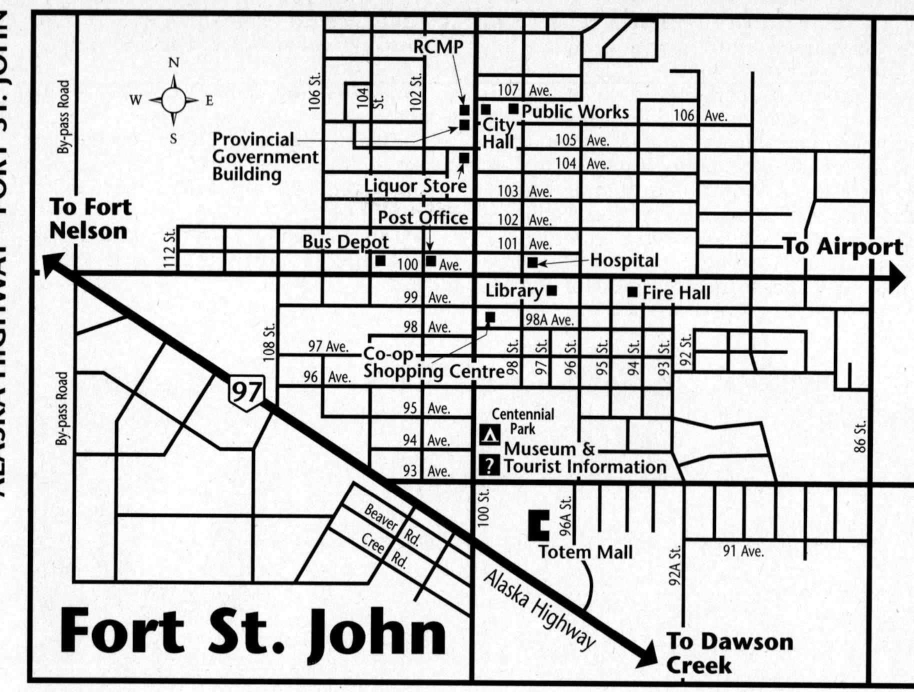

DC 40.3 (64.9 km) **F 1447.7** (2329.8 km) Exit east for Fort St. John airport.

DC 40.4 (65 km) **F 1447.6** (2329.6 km) B.C. Railway overhead tracks.

DC 40.9 (65.8 km) **F 1447.1** (2328.8 km) **Historic Milepost 42** "Access Road to Fort St. John Airport."

DC 41.3 (66.5 km) **F 1446.7** (2328.2 km) **Historical Mile 42.3. The Honey Place** to west. See display ad this section.

DC 43.7 (70.3 km) **F 1444.3** (2324.3 km) Miniature golf, driving range and proposed RV park.

DC 44.6 (71.7 km) **F 1443.4** (2322.9 km) Access to Fort St. John via 86th Street. Private RV Park. ▲

DC 45.7 (73.5 km) **F 1442.3** (2321.1 km) **Historic Milepost 47**, Fort St. John/"Camp Alcan" sign. In 1942 Fort St. John "exploded." What had been home to 200 became a temporary base for more than 6,000.

DC 45.8 (73.7 km) **F 1442.2** (2320.9 km) South access to Fort St. John via 100th Street. Exit east for visitor information and downtown Fort St. John.

DC 47 (75.6 km) **F 1441** (2319 km) **Historical Mile 48.** North access to Fort St. John via 100th Avenue to downtown. Truck stop with 24-hour gas and food.

Fort St. John

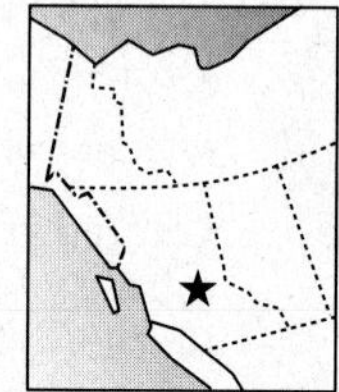

DC 47 (75.6 km) **F 1441** (2319 km) Located approximately 236 miles/ 380 km south of Fort Nelson. **Population:** 15,500; area 40,000. **Emergency Services: RCMP**, phone (604) 785-6617. **Fire Department:** phone (604) 785-2323. **Ambulance**, phone (604) 785-2079. **Hospital**, on Centre (100th) Avenue and 96th Street, phone (604) 785-6611.

Visitor Information: Visitor Infocentre located behind the 150-foot oil derrick in the museum, 9323 100th St. (Fort St. John, BC V1J 4N4); phone (604) 785-3033. Open year-round: 8 A.M. to 8 P.M. in summer, 8:30 A.M. to 5 P.M. the rest of the year. Visitors may also contact the Ministry of Environment & Parks, Parks and Outdoor Recreation Division, regarding wilderness hiking opportunities along the Alaska Highway. The Ministry is located at 10003–110 Ave., Room 250, Fort St. John, BC V1J 6M7; phone (604) 787-3407.

Elevation: 2,275 feet/693m. **Radio**: CKNL 560. **Television**: Cable. **Newspaper**: *Alaska Highway News* (daily), *The Northerner* (weekly).

Private Aircraft: Fort St. John airport, 3.8 miles/6.1 km east; elev. 2,280 feet/695m; length 6,900 feet/2,103m and 6,700 feet/ 2,042m; asphalt; fuel 80, 100. Charlie Lake airstrip, 6.7 miles/10.8 km northwest; elev. 2,680 feet/817m; length 1,800 feet/549m; gravel; fuel 80, 100.

Visitor services are located just off the Alaska Highway and in the city centre, a few blocks north of the highway. Fort St. John is a large modern city with all services available.

Fort St. John is set in the low, rolling hills of the Peace River Valley. The original Fort St. John was established in 1806 on the muddy banks of the Peace River, about 10 miles south of the present townsite, as a trading post for the Sikanni and Beaver Indians. The earlier Rocky Mountain Fort site, near the mouth of the Moberly River, dates from 1794. (Fort St. John celebrated its 200th birthday in 1994.) A granite monument, located on Mackenzie Street (100th Street) in Fort St. John's Centennial Park, is inscribed to Sir Alexander Mackenzie, who camped here on his journey west to the Pacific Ocean in 1793. Mackenzie was looking for trade routes for the North West fur company. He reached Bella Coola on July 22, 1793.

FORT ST. JOHN ADVERTISERS

Alaska Highway Bed & Breakfast......................Ph. (604) 785-3532
Caravan Motel..................Ph. (604) 787-1191
City of Fort St. John..........Ph. (604) 785-6037
Coachman Inn..................Ph. (604) 787-0651
Fort St. John Motor Inn................Behind the courthouse
Fort St. John-North Peace Museum.................1 blk. N. of Alaska Hwy.
Husky Car and Truck Wash....................Across from McDonald's
North Peace Cultural Centre............................10015 100th Ave.
Rapid Lube & Wash............11204 100th Ave.
Totem Mall..................................Alaska Hwy.

In 1942, Fort St. John became field headquarters for U.S. Army troops and civilian engineers working on construction of the Alaska Highway in the eastern sector. It was the largest camp, along with Whitehorse (headquarters for the western sector), of the dozen or so construction camps along the highway. Much of the field housing, road building equipment and even office supplies were scrounged from old Civilian Conservation Corps camps and the Work Projects Administration.

As reported by Theodore A. Huntley of the Public Roads Administration, "A narrow winter road from Fort St. John to Fort Nelson, 256 miles north, provided the only access to the forest itself. From Fort St. John north and west for almost 1,500 miles the wilderness was broken only by dog and pack trails or short stretches of winter road, serviceable only until made impassable by the spring thaw. Within 6 months the first vehicle to travel overland to Alaska would roll into Fairbanks. Thus was a highway born."

The Alaska Highway was opened to the traveling public in 1948, attracting vacationers and homesteaders. An immense natural oil and gas field discovered in 1955 made Fort St. John the oil capital of British Columbia. Land of the New Totems, referring to the many oil rigs, became the slogan for the region.

An extension of the Pacific Great Eastern Railway, now called British Columbia Railway, from Prince George in 1958 (continued to Fort Nelson in 1971), gave Fort St. John a link with the rail yards and docks at North Vancouver.

Today, Fort St. John is the hot spot in North America for natural gas, but it also depends on other industries, including forestry and agriculture. Farms in the North Peace region raise grain and livestock, such as sheep and cattle. Bison are also raised locally. The fields of clover and alfalfa have also attracted bees, and honey is produced for both local markets and export.

TRANSPORTATION

Air: Canadian Regional Airlines and Central Mountain Air to Fort Nelson, Whitehorse, Vancouver, Grande Prairie, Edmonton and Prince George. **Bus**: Coachways service to Prince George, Vancouver, Edmonton and Whitehorse; depot at 10355 101st Ave., phone (604) 785-6695.

ACCOMMODATIONS/VISITOR SERVICES

Numerous major motels, hotels, restaurants, fast-food outlets, and full-service gas stations are located on the Alaska Highway and in town. Other services include supermarkets, laundromats, several banks (automatic teller machines at Totem Mall and downtown at Charter Banks), a car wash and shops. The Totem Mall is located on the Alaska Highway. Indoor public pool, skating and curling at North Peace Recreation Centre, phone (604) 785-6148 for schedule. The North Peace Cultural Centre has a library, a 413-seat theatre and a gallery/gift shop.

Fort St. John RV Park, located at the east end of Centennial Park behind the visitor centre and museum, has 35 sites, showers, a laundry, dump station and hookups; senior citizen rates. Fresh water fill-up and dump station located at the northwest corner of 86th Street and the Alaska Highway. Also camping north of the city at Beatton and Charlie Lake provincial parks, and at private and Rotary campgrounds at Charlie Lake. ▲

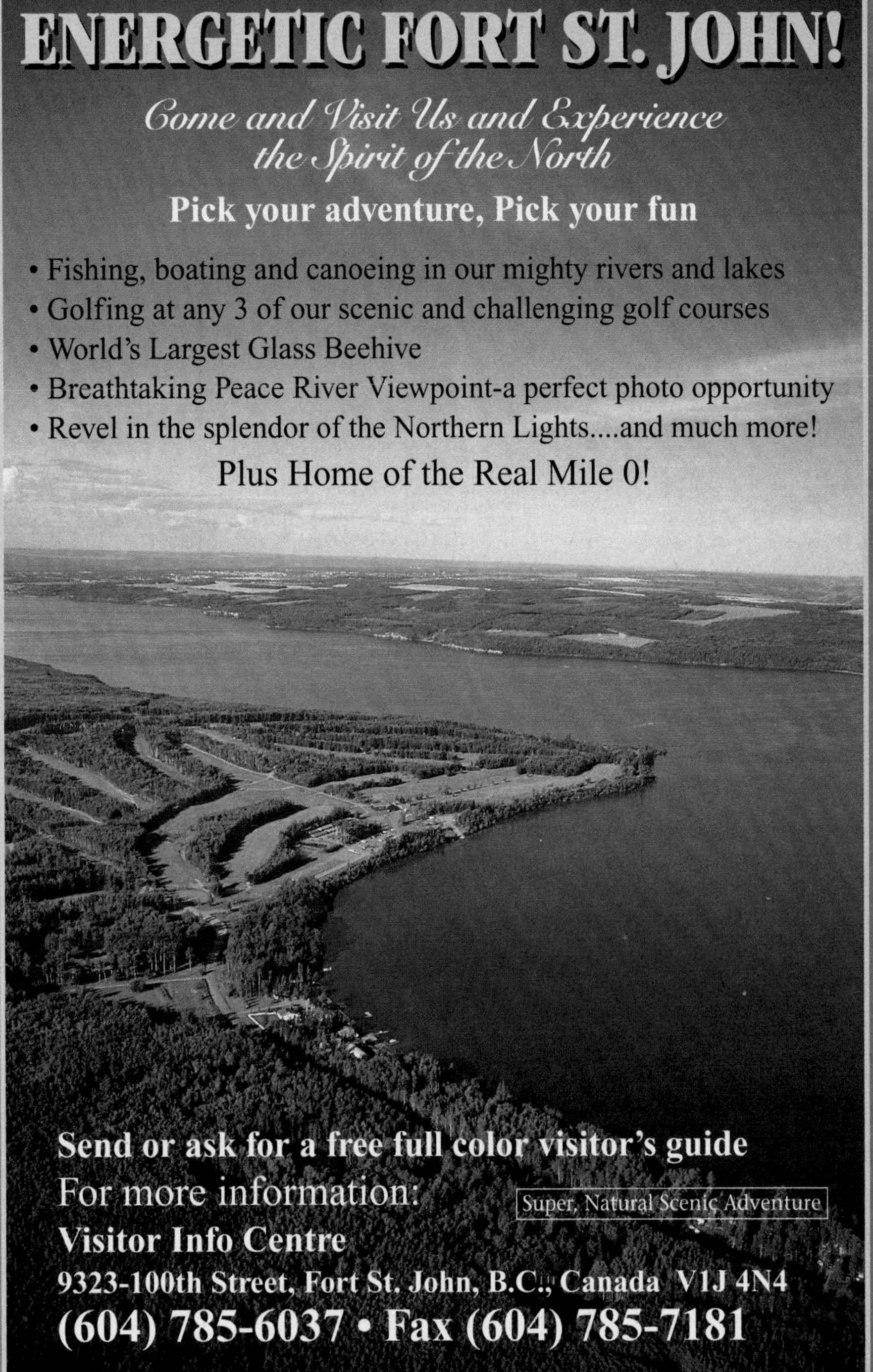

ATTRACTIONS

Centennial Park, located on 100th Street, has a museum, the Visitor Information Centre and an RV park. The Fort St. John–North Peace Museum houses more than 6,000 artifacts from the region, including items from Finch's Store (the first store in Fort St. John), an 1806 Fort St. John post, a trapper's cabin and early-day schoolroom. Inquire at the Visitor Information Centre about local hiking trails, fishing, boat tours, trail rides and the lily farm. The tourist centre and museum are open 8 A.M. to 8 P.M. daily in summer.

Directly in front of the Visitor Information Centre is a 150-foot oil derrick, presented to the North Peace Historical Society and the people of Fort St. John. The derrick is especially resplendent in winter when it is decorated with Christmas lights, making it the tallest Christmas tree in northern British Columbia. Check with the North Peace Museum at (604) 787-0430 about summer entertainment at the derrick.

Play golf. Fort St. John's only in-town golf course is Links Golf Course, just off the Bypass Road at 86 Street; 9 holes, pro shop and lounge. Phone (604) 785-9995. The Lakepoint Golf Course, on Golf Course Road at Charlie Lake, is rated one of the nicest courses in British Columbia. Open 8 A.M. to 9 P.M. daily; 18 holes, pro shop, lounge and restaurant. Phone (604) 785-5566.

Industry and agriculture of the area are showcased for the public at various places. Check with the Infocentre for directions and details. Canada Forest Products offers tours of their mills, phone (604) 785-8906 for details. The Honey Place, just south of town on the Alaska Highway, offers guided tours, fresh honey for sale, and the world's Largest Glass Beehive for viewing year-round; phone (604) 785-4808.

Fish Creek Community Forest, adjacent Northern Lights College, has 3 interpretive trails to view forest management activities and learn more about the forest. Cross-country ski trails in winter. From the Alaska Highway follow 100th Street north 1.2 miles/2 km to parking area at college.

W.A.C. Bennett Dam is a major attraction in the area. For an interesting side trip, drive north from Fort St. John on the Alaska Highway to **Milepost DC 53.7** and take Highway 29 west 40.3 miles/74.0 km to Hudson's Hope. Highway 29 follows the original Canadian government telegraph trail of 1918. Hudson's Hope, formerly a pioneer community established in 1805 by explorer Simon Fraser, grew with construction of the W.A.C. Bennett Dam, which is located 13.5 miles/21.7 km west of town. B.C. Hydro's Peace Canyon dam is located approximately 4 miles/6.4 km south of Hudson's Hope. Turn to the HUDSON'S HOPE LOOP section for more information.

Alaska Highway Log

(continued)

Distance* from Dawson Creek (DC) is followed by distance from Fairbanks (F). Original mileposts are indicated in the text as Historical Mile.

*Mileages from Dawson Creek are based on actual driving distance. Kilometres from Dawson Creek are based on physical kilometreposts. Please read Mileposts and Kilometreposts in the introduction for an explanation of how this highway is logged.

DC 45.8 (73.7 km) **F 1442.2** (2320.9 km) South access to Fort St. John via 100th Street.

DC 47 (75.6 km) **F 1441** (2319 km) **Mile 48.** North access to Fort St. John via 100th Avenue.

DC 48.6 (78.2 km) **F 1439.4** (2316.4 km) **Historic Milepost 49** commemorates "Camp Alcan."

DC 49.5 (79.6 km) **F 1438.5** (2315 km) Exit for Beatton Provincial Park, 5 miles/8 km east via paved road; 37 campsites, picnic shelter, wood stove, horseshoe pits, volleyball net, playground, baseball field, sandy beach, swimming and boat launch. Camping fee $7 to $12. Fishing for northern pike, walleye (July best) and yellow perch in **Charlie Lake.**

DC 50.6 (81.4 km) **F 1437.4** (2313.2 km) **CHARLIE LAKE** (unincorporated), gas, diesel and propane, grocery, pub, post office, private RV parks and Ministry of Energy, Mines and Petroleum. Access to lakeshore east side of highway; boat launch, no parking. At one time during construction of the Alaska Highway, Charlie Lake was designated Mile 0, as there was already a road between the railhead at Dawson Creek and Fort St. John, the eastern sector headquarters for troops and engineers.

Charlie Lake General Store. See display ad this section.

Rotary R.V. Park. See display ad this section.

DC 51.2 (82.4 km) **F 1436.8** (2312.2 km) **Historic Milepost 52.** Charlie Lake Mile 0 Army Tote Road. Site of a major distribution camp for workers and supplies heading north. 12 American soldiers also drowned here in 1942 while crossing the lake aboard pontoon barges.

DC 51.5 (82.9 km) **F 1436.5** (2311.7 km) **Ron's R.V. Park. Historical Mile 52.** Treed sites with complete RV hookups, shaded lawned tenting areas, picnic tables, firepits, firewood provided. Walking trails, playground, flush toilets, hot showers, laundromat, pay phone, ice. Shaded full-hookup pull-throughs, good drinking water. Large boat launching facilities nearby. Boat rentals. Quiet location away from hectic city confusion. Post office, golf course, fishing licenses, Red Barn Pub nearby. Charlie Lake, world famous for walleye and northern pike fishing. Phone (604) 787-1569. [ADVERTISEMENT]

DC 52 (83.7 km) **F 1436** (2311 km) Exit east on Charlie Lake Road for lakeshore picnicking.

DC 53.6 (86.3 km) **F 1434.4** (2308.4 km) Truck weigh scales east side of highway.

DC 53.7 (86.4 km) **F 1434.3** (2308.2 km) **Junction** with Highway 29 and truck stop with restaurant, gas and diesel. Highway 29 leads west to Hudson's Hope and the W.A.C. Bennett Dam, then south to connect with the Hart Highway (97) at Chetwynd. (See HUDSON'S HOPE LOOP section.) Truck stop to west.

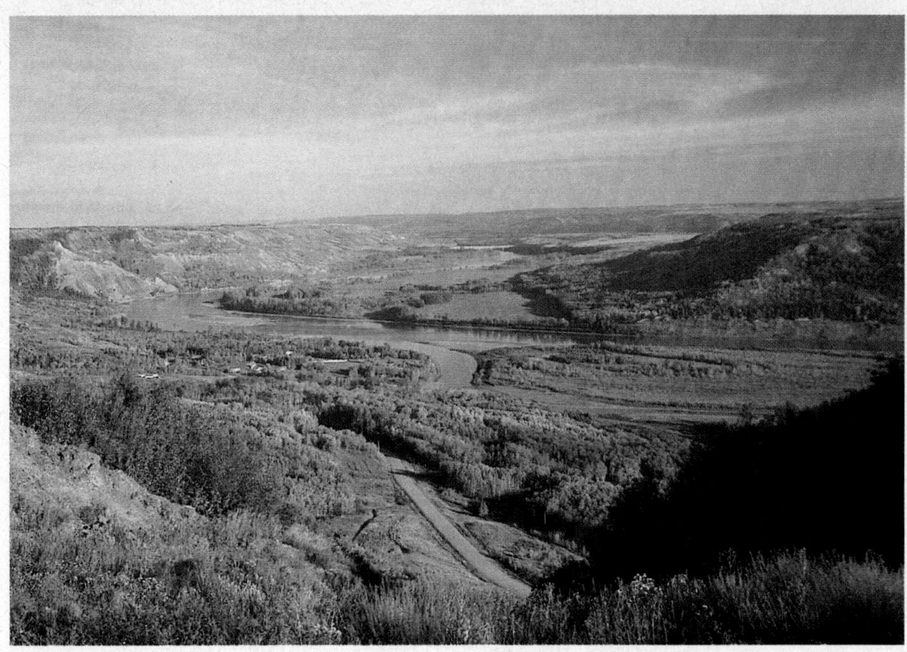

Fertile Peace River valley from lookout near Fort St. John. Farms in the area raise grain and livestock. (Earl L. Brown, Staff)

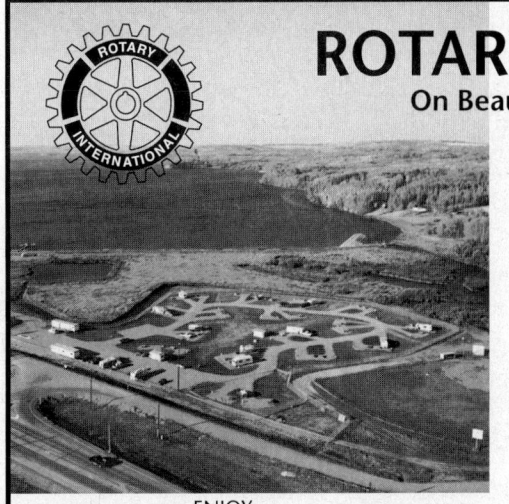

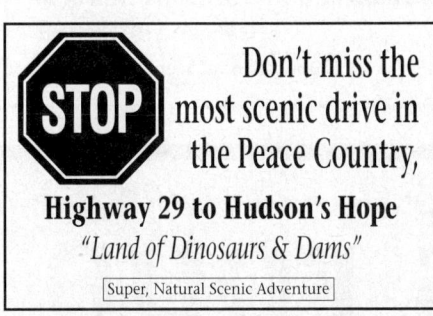

Turn east for Charlie Lake Provincial Park, just off highway: paved loop road (with speed bumps) leads through campground. There are 58 shaded sites, picnic tables, kitchen shelter with wood stove, firepits, firewood, outhouses, dump station, water and garbage. Level gravel sites, some will accommodate 2 large RVs. Camping fee $7 to $12. Playfield, playground, horseshoe pits, volleyball net and a 1.2-mile/2-km hiking trail down to lake. Watch for wildflowers: because of the wide variety of plants here, including some that may not be seen elsewhere along the Alaska Highway, Verna E. Pratt's *Wildflowers Along the Alaska Highway* includes a special list of species for this park. Fishing in **Charlie Lake** for walleye, northern pike and yellow perch. Access to the lake for vehicles and boats is from the Alaska Highway just east of the park entrance. Boat launch and picnic area at lake.

DC 63.6 (102 km) **F 1424.4** (2292.3 km) Microwave tower to east.

DC 65.4 (105 km) **F 1422.6** (2289.4 km) Turnout with litter barrel to west.

DC 71.7 (115.4 km) **F 1416.3** (2279.3 km) **Historical Mile 72.** Food, gas, camping, lodging and crafts store. ▲

Northern Expressions Gifts is a point of interest along the Alaska Highway. It is a log cabin you would expect to see in the Last Frontier. There is easy access for motorhomes, plenty of parking and a nice restful place to stop. The old-fashioned shop will give you the feeling of old and possibly better days. Bring this ad in and receive 10 percent

off your purchase of T-shirts, jewelry, moccasins, stuffed animals, postcards, candy and much more! A favorite gift shop on the Alaska Highway! [ADVERTISEMENT]

DC 71.7 (115.4 km) **F 1416.3** (2279.3 km) **The Shepherd's Inn.** We specialize in making folks at home, offering regular and breakfast specials, complete lunch and dinner menu. Low-fat buffalo burgers. Our specialties: homemade soups, home-baked sweet rolls, cinnamon rolls, blueberry and bran muffins, bread, biscuits and trappers bannock. Delicious desserts, rhubarb-strawberry, Dutch apple and chocolate dream pie, cherry and strawberry cheesecake. Hard ice cream. Specialty coffees: Norwegian Mint, Swiss Almond. Herb teas. Refreshing fruit drinks from local fruits: blueberry and raspberry coolers. Caravaners and bus tours ... a convenient and delightful stop on your Alaska Highway adventure! You may reserve your stop–break with us. Full RV hookups, motel service 24 hours. Quality Husky products. Your "Husky Buck" is a great traveling idea. Phone (604) 827-3676. An oasis on the Alcan at Mile 72. Enjoy Super, Natural Scenic Adventure. [ADVERTISEMENT] ▲

DC 72.8 (117.1 km) **F 1415.2** (2277.5 km) **Historic Milepost 73** commemorates Beatton River Flight Strip, 1 of 4 gravel airstrips built for American military aircraft during WWII. Road to Prespetu and Buick Creek.

DC 79.1 (127.3 km) **F 1408.9** (2267.3 km) **Historical Mile 80** paved rest area to west with litter barrels, picnic tables, water and flush toilets. Information panel on Alaska Highway parks.

DC 91.4 (147.1 km) **F 1396.6** (2247.5 km) **Historical Mile 92**. Westcoast Energy compressor station to west.

DC 94.6 (152.2 km) **F 1393.4** (2242.4 km) Oil pump east of highway behind trees.

DC 101 (161.7 km) **F 1387** (2232.1 km) **Historic Milepost 101. WONOWON** (pop. 150), unincorporated, has 3 gas stations (gas, diesel, propane), 3 restaurants, 2 motels, camping, a food store, pub and post office. Formerly known as Blueberry, Wonowon was the site of an official traffic control gate during WWII. Wonowon Horse Club holds an annual race meet and gymkhana at the track beside the highway, where the community club holds its annual snowmobile rally in February. ▲

The historic sign and interpretive panel here commemorate Blueberry Control Station, "site of the Blueberry Control Gate, a 24-hour military checkpoint operated by U.S. army personnel through the war years."

The Alaska Highway follows the Blueberry and Prophet river drainages north to Fort Nelson. The Blueberry River, not visible from the highway, lies a few miles east of Wonowon.

Hall's Food & Gas. See display ad this section. ▲

DC 101.5 (163.3 km) **F 1386.5** (2231.3 km) Food, diesel, gas, camping and lodging to east; open year-round. ▲

102 Husky. See display ad this section. ▲

DC 103.5 (166.5 km) **1384.5** (2228.1 km) **Historic Milepost 104** marks start of Adolphson, Huseth, Layer & Welch contract during Alaska Highway construction.

DC 114 (183.2 km) **F 1374** (2211.2 km) Paved turnout with litter barrel to east.

DC 124.3 (200 km) **F 1363.7** (2194.6 km) The Cut (highway goes through a small rock cut). Relatively few rock cuts were necessary during construction of the Alaska Highway in 1942–43. However, rock excavation was often made outside of the roadway to obtain gravel fill for the new roadbed.

DC 135.3 (217.7 km) **F 1352.7** (2176.9 km) Gravel turnout to east.

CAUTION: Northbound travelers watch for moose next 15 miles/24 km, especially at dusk and at night.

DC 140.4 (225.9 km) **F 1347.6** (2168.7 km) **Historical Mile 143. PINK MOUNTAIN** (pop. 99, area 300; elev. 3,600 feet/1,097m). Post office, grocery, motels, restaurant, campgrounds, gas stations (gas, diesel, propane) with minor repair service. Bus depot at Pink Mountain Motor Inn east side of highway. Pink Mountain is home to Darryl Mills, Canadian champion bullrider.

Pink Mountain Campsite & R.V. Park, on the left northbound. Take it easy folks, you've arrived at one of the nicest campgrounds on the highway ... coffee's always on. Unleaded Tempo gas, diesel, metered propane for RVs and auto. Post office, general store, liquor store, fishing and hunting licenses. Souvenirs—you'll like our prices. Shaded campsites, picnic tables, firepits and firewood. Tents and RVs welcome. Full hookups, power hookups, water and sani-

dump. Pull-throughs. Something for everyone. Cabins available $15–$20, reservations recommended. Laundromat and clean showers. Open year-round. VISA and MasterCard. Phone and fax (604) 774-1033. Your hosts, Ron and Pat. Enjoy Super, Natural Scenic Adventure. [ADVERTISEMENT] ▲

Pink Mountain Motor Inn. Mile 143, a welcome stopping point for all travelers. 34 fully modern rooms, Get and Go groceries, gift shop, and licensed restaurant with pies and pastries and home-cooked meals. The perfect lunch break stop for bus tours. Ample parking space, picnic tables. For RVs, electric hookups, gravel sites. Treed camping sites with good gravel parking. Picnic tables. Water, hot showers, laundromat. Dump station. Caravans welcome, reservations recommended. Full line of Esso products. We hope you're enjoying your Super, Natural Scenic Alaska Highway Adventure! Fax (604) 774-1071. Phone (604) 772-3234. [ADVERTISEMENT] ▲

DC 144.1 (231.9 km) F 1343.9 (2162.7 km) **Historical Mile 147.** Sportsman Inn to east with food, lodging, souvenirs, RV park, gas and diesel. ▲

Sportsman Inn to east. See display ad this section. ▲

DC 144.5 (232.5 km) **F 1343.5** (2162.1 km) **Historical Mile 147.** Restaurant and vehicle repair (towing service).

Mae's Kitchen and Ed's Garage to east. See display ad this section.

DC 144.7 (232.9 km) **F 1343.3** (2161.8 km) **Historic Milepost 148** commemorates Suicide Hill, one of the most treacherous hills on the original highway noted for its ominous greeting: "Prepare to meet thy maker." Beatton River bridge. The Beatton River was named for Frank Beatton, a Hudson's Bay Co. employee. The Beatton River flows east and then south into the Peace River system.

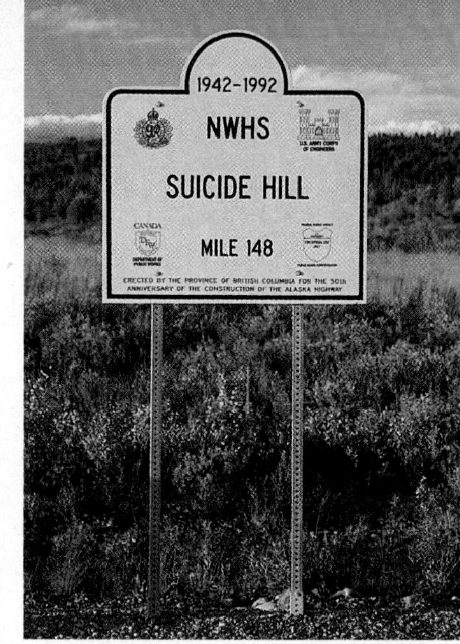

1942-1992
NWHS
SUICIDE HILL
MILE 148
ERECTED BY THE PROVINCE OF BRITISH COLUMBIA FOR THE 50th ANNIVERSARY OF THE CONSTRUCTION OF THE ALASKA HIGHWAY

Sign commemorates Suicide Hill at Historic Milepost 148. (Earl L. Brown staff)

DC 146 (234 km) **F 1342** (2159.7 km) **Private Aircraft:** Sikanni Chief flight strip to east; elev. 3,258 feet/993m; length, 6,000 feet/1,829m; gravel; not maintained in winter, soft in spring. Well-known local pilot Jimmy "Midnight" Anderson used the Sikanni Chief airstrip.

DC 150.3 (241.9 km) **F 1337.7** (2152.8 km) *CAUTION: Southbound travelers watch for moose next 15 miles/24 km, especially at dusk and at night.*

DC 155.6 (250.4 km) **F 1332.4** (2144.2 km) Large double-ended, gravel turnout with litter barrels. *CAUTION: Slow down! Watch for loose gravel.*

DC 156.6 (252 km) **F 1331.4** (2142.6 km) Sikanni Hill. *CAUTION: Slow down for hill.*

DC 159.2 (256.2 km) **F 1328.8** (2138.4 km) Sikanni Chief River bridge (elev. 2,662 feet/811m). To the west you may see steel stanchions, all that remains of the historic wooden Sikanni bridge, which was destroyed by arson July 10, 1992. The original timber truss bridge built across the Sikanni Chief River in the spring of 1943 was the first permanent structure completed on the Alaska Highway. Highway construction crews rerouted much of the pioneer road built in 1942 and replaced temporary bridges with permanent structures in 1943. The Sikanni Chief River flows east and then north into the Fort Nelson River, which flows into the Liard River and on to the Mackenzie River, which empties into the Arctic Ocean. Check at the lodge for information on Sikanni River Falls (see **Milepost DC 168.5**).

Sikanni Chief River, fair fishing at mouth of tributaries in summer for pike; grayling to 2½ lbs.; whitefish to 2 lbs.

DC 159.4 (256.5 km) **F 1328.6** (2138.1 km) **Historical Mile 162. SIKANNI CHIEF.** Food, gas, lodging and camping.

Sikanni River RV Park. This riverside RV park offers a beautiful, natural setting for your enjoyment, with easy access to well graveled, long sites. It's reputation for both cleanliness and beauty has made it a popular destination. Make it a must on your list when only the best will do. Reservations recommended. Resident owners. Clean, safe, secure. Recommended as a fueling stop in Alaska Highway—an Insiders Guide for 6 years. Located at the bottom of Sikanni River Hill. (604) 774-1028. Enjoy Super, Natural Scenic Adventure. [ADVERTISEMENT] ▲

DC 160 (257.5 km) **F 1328** (2137.2 km) "Drunken forest" on hillside to west is shallow-rooted black spruce trees growing in unstable clay-based soil that is subject to slide activity in wet weather.

DC 160.4 (258.1 km) **F 1327.6** (2136.5 km) Section of the old Alaska Highway is visible to east; no access.

DC 168.5 (271.2 km) **F 1319.5** (2123.5 km) Gravel road west to Sikanni River Falls. This private road is signed "Travel at own risk." Drive in 10.5 miles/16.9 km to parking area with picnic tables at B.C. Forest Service trailhead; 10-minute hike in on well-marked trail to view falls. Gravel access road has some steep hills and a single-lane bridge. *CAUTION: Do not travel in wet weather. Not recommended for vehicles with trailers.*

*IMPORTANT: Watch for moose on highway northbound to **Milepost DC 200**, especially at dusk. Drive carefully!*

DC 172.5 (277.6 km) **F 1315.5** (2117 km) Polka Dot Creek.

DC 173.1 (278.6 km) **F 1314.9** (2116 km) Buckinghorse River bridge; access to river at north end of bridge.

DC 173.2 (278.7 km) **F 1314.8** (2115.9 km) **Historical Mile 175.** Inn with gas and camping to east at north end of bridge. Also turnoff east for Buckinghorse River Provincial Park. Follow the narrow gravel road past the gravel pit 0.7 mile/1.1 km along river to camping and picnic area. Camping fee $7 to $12. The park has 30 picnic tables, side-by-side camper parking, firewood, fire rings, water pump, outhouses and garbage containers. Poor fishing for grayling in **Buckinghorse River**. Swimming in downstream pools. ▲

DC 173.4 (279 km) **F 1314.6** (2115.6 km) **Historical Mile 175. Buckinghorse River Lodge**, on left northbound. Motel, cafe with home cooking, hard ice cream and ice cream novelties. Bed and breakfast available. Service station, large parking area, free camping. Look forward to our friendly atmosphere. Picnic tables and beautiful scenery. A great spot to take a break for fishing or walking. Enjoy Super, Natural Scenic Adventure. (604) 773-6468. [ADVERTISEMENT] ▲

DC 176 (283.2 km) **F 1312** (2111.4 km) South end of 27-mile/43-km Trutch Mountain bypass. Completed in 1987, this section of road rerouted the Alaska Highway around Trutch Mountain, eliminating the steep, winding climb up to Trutch Summit (and the views). Named for Joseph W. Trutch, civil engineer and first governor of British Columbia, Trutch Mountain was the second highest summit on the Alaska Highway with an elevation of 4,134 feet/1,260m. The new roadbed cuts a wide swath through the flat Minaker River valley. The river, not visible to motorists, is west of the highway; it was named for local trapper George Minaker. Trutch Mountain is to the east of the highway. Motorists can see part of the old highway on Trutch Mountain.

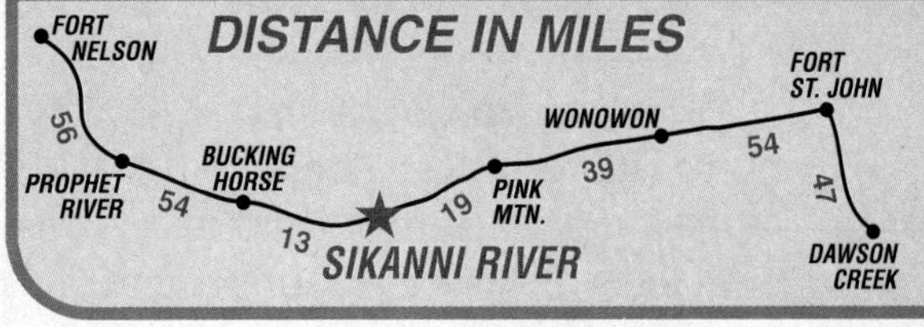

DC 182.8 (294.2 km) **F 1305.2** (2100.4 km) Large gravel turnout with litter barrel to west.

DC 199.1 (320 km) **F 1288.9** (2074.2 km) Large gravel turnout with litter barrels.

DC 202.5 (325.5 km) **F 1285.5** (2068.8

Buckinghorse River Lodge
MILE 175, ALASKA HIGHWAY
125 Miles North of Fort St. John / 125 Miles South of Fort Nelson
"Your halfway stop between Fort Nelson and Fort St. John"
Modern Motel • Cafe • Ice • Hard Ice Cream
Unleaded Gas • Showers • Public Phone •
Free Camping
Get Your Buck's Worth at the Buck!
VISA
MasterCard
Bus Tours Welcome by Reservation
Drop in and see Paul & Barb
Phone/Fax (604) 773-6468
Super, Natural Scenic Adventure

km) Turnout with litter barrels at north end of Trutch Mountain bypass (see **Milepost** DC 176).

CAUTION: Southbound travelers watch for moose on highway, especially at dusk, to Sikanni Chief. Drive carefully!

DC **204.2** (328 km) **F 1283.8** (2066 km) **Beaver Creek**; fishing for grayling to 2½ lbs. 

DC **217.2** (349.3 km) **F 1270.8** (2045.1 km) Turnoff to west for Prophet River Provincial Park, 0.4 mile/0.6 km via gravel road. Side-by-side camper parking (36 sites), picnic tables, firewood, fire rings, water pump, outhouses and garbage containers. Camping fee $7 to $12. The park access road crosses an airstrip (originally an emergency airstrip on the Northwest Air Staging Route) and part of the old Alaska Highway (the Alcan). This provincial park is also the first stop on the self-guided Forest Ecology Tours (Ecotours) established by the Fort Nelson Forest District. A pamphlet, available from their office in Fort Nelson (phone 604/774-3936), describes the forests at various sites along the Alaska Highway. This Ecotour stop is noted for its trembling aspen stands and mature white spruce. 

The Alaska Highway roughly parallels the Prophet River from here north to the Muskwa River south of Fort Nelson.

Private Aircraft: Prophet River emergency airstrip; elev. 1,954 feet/596m; length 6,000 feet/1,829m; gravel.

DC **218.2** (350.7 km) **F 1269.8** (2043.5 km) View of Prophet River to west.

DC **222.3** (357.2 km) **F 1265.7** (2036.9 km) Bougie Creek bridge; turnout with litter barrel beside creek at south end of bridge. At this Ecotour stop, note the typical climax white spruce stand and trees of a variety of ages.

CAUTION: Watch for rough road approaching Bougie Creek bridge from either direction.

DC **224.8** (360.6 km) **F 1263.2** (2032.8 km) Microwave tower to east.

DC **226.2** (363.4 km) **F 1261.8** (2030.6 km) Prophet River Indian Reserve to east.

DC **226.5** (363.9 km) **F 1261.5** (2030.1 km) St. Paul's Roman Catholic Church to east.

DC **227** (364.7 km) **F 1261** (2029.3 km) **Historical Mile 233. PROPHET RIVER**, gas, diesel, propane, food, camping and lodging. Prophet River Services is on the left northbound; Prophet River Inn on right. Southbound travelers note: Next service 68 miles/109 km. ▲

Prophet River Services. See display ad this section. ▲

DC **227.6** (366.3 km) **F 1260.4** (2028.4 km) **Historic Milepost 234**, Adsett Creek Highway Realignment. This major rerouting eliminated 132 curves on the stretch of highway that originally ran between Miles 234 and 275. Turnout with litter barrels.

DC **227.7** (366.4 km) **F 1260.3** (2028.2 km) Adsett Creek.

DC **230.7** (371.3 km) **F 1257.3** (2023.3 km) Natural gas pipeline crosses beneath highway.

DC **232.9** (374.8 km) **F 1255.1** (2019.8 km) Turnout to west with litter barrels.

DC **235.5** (378.4 km) **F 1252.5** (2015.6 km) Mesalike topography to the east is Mount Yakatchie.

DC **241.5** (388 km) **F 1246.5** (2006 km) Parker Creek.

DC **245.9** (395.7 km) **F 1242.1** (1998.9 km) Gravel turnout with litter barrels.

DC **261.1** (420.2 km) **F 1226.9** (1974.4 km) Turnout with litter barrels to east.

DC **264.6** (425.2 km) **F 1223.4** (1968.8 km) Jackfish Creek bridge. Ecotour stop; note the variety of trembling aspen stands and the white spruce seedlings under them.

DC **265.5** (426.5 km) **F 1222.5** (1967.4 km) Turnoff to east for Andy Bailey Lake Provincial Park (day use only) via 6.8-mile/11-km dirt and gravel access road. (Large RVs and trailers note: only turnaround space on access road is approximately halfway in.) The park is located on **Andy Bailey Lake** (formerly Jackfish Lake); picnic tables, fire rings, firewood, water, outhouses, garbage containers, boat launch (no powerboats), swimming and fair fishing for northern pike. Bring insect repellent!

DC **270.8** (435.1 km) **F 1217.2** (1958.8 km) Gas pipeline crosses highway overhead.

DC **271** (435.4 km) **F 1217** (1958.5 km) Westcoast Energy gas processing plant to east. Petrosul (sulfur processing) to west.

DC **272.4** (437.6 km) **F 1215.6** (1956.3 km) Access to downhill skiing to east.

DC **276.2** (443.8 km) **F 1211.8** (1950 km) Rodeo grounds to west. The rodeo is held in August.

DC **276.7** (444.6 km) **F 1211.3** (1949.3 km) Railroad tracks. Microwave tower at Muskwa Heights.

DC **277.5** (446.2 km) **F 1210.5** (1948 km) Muskwa Heights (unincorporated), an industrial area with rail yard, plywood plant, sawmill and bulk fuel outlet. More than 7,000 carloads of logs were shipped from here in 1995.

DC **277.9** (447.2 km) **F 1210.1** (1947.4 km) Truck stop with gas, restaurant and RV campground.

Husky 5th Wheel Truck Stop and RV Park. See display ad this section. ▲

DC **278.1** (447.5 km) **F 1209.9** (1947.1 km) Truck scales to west. Turnoff for Chopstick manufacturing plant. This plant produces 6 million pairs of chopsticks a day.

Tours by appointment only.

DC **278.4** (448 km) **F 1209.6** (1946.6 km) **Trapper's Den.** Owned and operated by a local trapping family. Moose horns, diamond willow, northern novelties and artwork. Best seller books. World famous porcupine quill-decorated birchbark baskets. Moose hair tuftings. Deerskin and moosehide slippers and gloves. Fur hats, mitts and earmuffs. Professionally tanned furs. See our

"Muskwa River Pearls." Museum-like atmosphere—no charge for admission. Photographers welcome. Located ½ mile north of Husky 5th Wheel RV Park on the Alaska Highway. VISA, MasterCard. Mail orders. Open 9 A.M. to 8 P.M. daily. John, Cindy and Mandy Wells. Box 1164, Fort Nelson, BC V0C 1R0. (604) 774-3400. Recommended. [ADVERTISEMENT]

DC **279** (448.6 km) **F 1209** (1945.6 km) Site of oriented strand board plant (opening 1996), which will process aspen and balsam poplar. This 400,000-square-foot building is the largest industrial building of its kind in the province.

DC **279.5** (449.8 km) **F 1208.5** (1944.8 km) **Klahanie Trailer and RV Park** If you want to be packed shoulder-to-shoulder this isn't the place for you. Only 20 quiet secluded sites for tenting and smaller RVs. Showers, laundromat, phone available. Electrical hookup. $15 includes GST and showers. An attendant will register you in the evening. [ADVERTISEMENT] ▲

DC **281** (451.4 km) **F 1207** (1942.4 km) **Muskwa River** bridge, lowest point on the Alaska Highway (elev. 1,000 feet/305m). The Muskwa River flows to the Fort Nelson River. Fair fishing at the mouth of tributaries for northern pike; some goldeye. The Fort Nelson River is too muddy for fishing. The Muskwa River valley exhibits typical river-bottom balsam poplar and white spruce stands, according to the Fort Nelson Forest District's Forest Ecology Tours pamphlet.

The Alaska Highway swings west at Fort Nelson above the Muskwa River, winding southwest then northwest through the Canadian Rockies.

DC **283** (454.3 km) **F 1205** (1939.2 km) Entering Fort Nelson northbound. Fort Nelson's central business district extends along the highway from the private campground at the east end of the city to the private campground at the west end. Businesses and services are located both north and south of the highway.

Fort Nelson

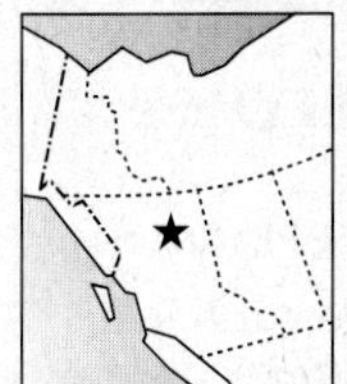

DC **283** (454.3 km) **F 1205** (1939.2 km) **Historical Mile 300. Population:** 3,804; area 5,500. **Emergency Services: RCMP,** phone (604) 774-2777. **Fire Department**, phone (604) 774-2222. **Hospital,** 35 beds, phone (604) 774-6916. **Ambulance**, phone (604) 774-2344. Medical, dental and optometric clinics. Visiting veterinarians and chiropractors.

Visitor Information: Located in the

Aerial view shows Fort Nelson's forestry products industrial area south of town.
(Earl L. Brown, staff)

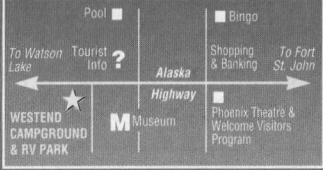

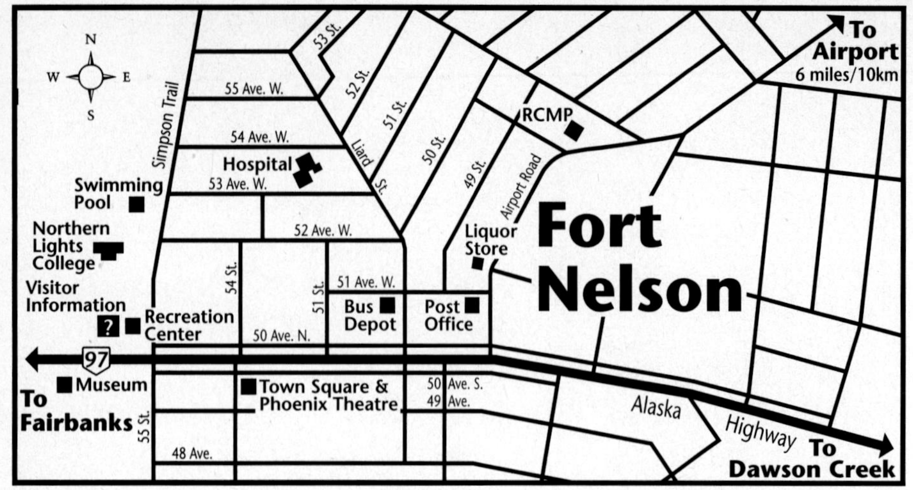

Recreation Centre at the west end of town, open 8 A.M. to 8 P.M. Inquire here about local industrial tours, and also about road conditions on the Liard Highway. Fort Nelson Heritage Museum across the highway from the infocentre. Contact the Town of Fort Nelson by writing Bag Service 399, Fort Nelson, BC V0C 1R0; phone (604) 774-6400 (seasonal) or 774-2541 (all year).

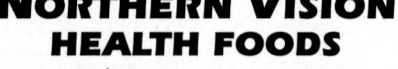

Elevation: 1,383 feet/422m. **Climate**: Winters are cold with short days. Summers are hot and the days are long. In mid-June (summer solstice), twilight continues throughout the night. The average number of frost-free days annually is 116. Last frost occurs about May 11, and the first frost Sept. 21. Average annual precipitation of 16.3 inches. **Radio**: CFNL 590, CBC 1610. **Television**: Channels 8, 13 and cable. **Newspaper**: *Fort Nelson News* (weekly).

Transportation: **Air**—Scheduled service to Edmonton and Grande Prairie, and to Prince George and Vancouver via Canadian Regional Airlines. Charter service available. **Bus**—Greyhound service. **Railroad**—B.C. Railway (freight service only).

Private Aircraft: Fort Nelson airport, 3.8 air miles/6.1 km east northeast; elev. 1,253 feet/382m; length 6,400 feet/1,950m; asphalt; fuel 80, 100, Jet B. Gordon Field, 4 miles/6.4 km west; elev. 1,625 feet/495m approximately; length 2,000 feet/610m; turf; fuel 80.

Fort Nelson is located in the lee of the Rocky Mountains, surrounded by the Muskwa, Nelson and Prophet rivers. The area is heavily forested with white spruce, poplar and aspen. Geographically, the town is located about 59° north latitude and 122° west longitude.

Flowing east and north, the Muskwa, Prophet and Sikanni Chief rivers converge to form the Fort Nelson River, which flows into

FORT NELSON ADVERTISERS

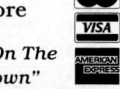

Bennetts Travel Time Inc..Ph. (604) 774-6144
Bluebell Inn, The ....S. end of town
Coachouse Inn ....Ph. (604) 774-3911
Dan's Neighbourhood Pub ......S. end of town
Dixie Lee.......................................Downtown
Fabric Fun.......................New Landmark Plaza
Fort Nelson Bed & Breakfast.....................Ph. (604) 774-6050
Fort Nelson Heritage Museum ....Across from travel infocentre
Home on the Hill Bed & Breakfast...........Ph. (604) 774-3000
KaCee's Koin Kleaners..Next to IGA Foodstore
Mini-Price Inn ....Ph. (604) 774-2136
Northern Husky.............................Downtown
Northern Lights Deli.........Ph. (604) 774-3311
Northern Vision Health Foods.........................New Landmark Plaza
Pioneer Motel ....Ph. (604) 774-6459
Poplar Hills Golf & Country Club ....Ph. (604) 774-3862
Provincial Motel ....S. end of town
Red Rose Convenience Store ....S. end of town
Sann's Place ....Downtown
Shannon Motel.......................N. end of town
Smi-Dee's Gourmet.........New Landmark Plaza
Town of Fort Nelson..................Town Square
Westend R.V. Campground and Mini-Golf ....N. end of town

the Liard River, then on to the Mackenzie River, which empties into the Arctic Ocean. Rivers provided the only means of transportation in both summer and winter in this isolated region until 1922, when the Godsell Trail opened, connecting Fort Nelson with Fort St. John. The Alaska Highway linked Fort Nelson with the Outside in 1942.

In the spring, the Muskwa River frequently floods the low country around Fort Nelson and can rise more than 20 feet/6m. At an elevation of 1,000 feet/305m, the Muskwa (which means "bear") is the lowest point on the Alaska Highway. There was a danger of the Muskwa River bridge washing out every June during spring runoff until 1970, when a higher bridge—with piers arranged to prevent log jams—was built.

Fort Nelson's existence was originally based on the fur trade. In the 1920s, trapping was the main business in this isolated pioneer community populated with less than 200 Indians and a few white men. Trappers still harvest beaver, wolverine, weasel, wolf, fox, lynx, mink, muskrat and marten. Other area wildlife includes black bear, which are plentiful, some deer, caribou and a few grizzly bears. Moose remains an important food source for the Indians.

Fort Nelson aboriginal people are mostly Slave (slay-vee), who arrived here about 1775 from the Great Slave Lake area and speak an Athabascan dialect.

Fort Nelson was first established in 1805 by the North West Fur Trading Co. The post, believed to have been located about 80 miles/129 km south of Nelson Forks, was named for Lord Horatio Nelson, the English admiral who won the Battle of Trafalgar.

A second Fort Nelson was later located south of the first fort, but was destroyed by fire in 1813 after Indians massacred its 8 residents. A third Fort Nelson was established in 1865 on the Nelson River's west bank (1 mile from the present Fort Nelson airport) by W. Cornwallis King, a Hudson's Bay Co. clerk. This trading post was built to keep out the free traders who were filtering in from the Mackenzie River and Fort St. John areas. The free traders' higher fur prices were a threat to the Hudson's Bay Co., which in 1821 had absorbed the rival North West Fur Trading Co. and gained a monopoly on the fur trade in Canada.

This Hudson's Bay Co. trading post was destroyed by a flood in 1890 and a fourth Fort Nelson was established on higher ground upstream and across the river, which is now known as Old Fort Nelson. The present town of Fort Nelson is the fifth site.

Fort Nelson saw its first mail service in 1936. Scheduled air service to Fort Nelson—by ski- and floatplane—also was begun in the 1930s by Yukon Southern Air (which was later absorbed by CPAir, now Canadian Airlines International and Canadian Regional Airlines). The Canadian government began construction of an airport in 1941 as part of the Northwest Air Staging Route, and this was followed by perhaps the biggest boom to Fort Nelson—the construc-

Trapper's cabin is one of the displays at Fort Nelson Heritage Museum, which also features pioneer artifacts. *(Earl L. Brown, staff)*

tion of the Alaska Highway in 1942. About 2,000 soldiers were bivouacked in Fort Nelson, which they referred to as Zero, as it was the beginning of a road to Whitehorse and another road to Fort Simpson. Later Dawson Creek became Mile 0 and Fort Nelson Mile 300.

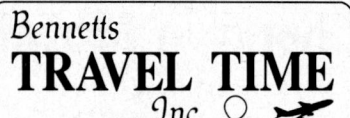

Fort Nelson expanded in the 1940s and 1950s as people came here to work for the government or to start their own small businesses: trucking, barging, aviation, construction, garages, stores, cafes, motels and sawmills. It is surprising to consider that as recently as the 1950s, Fort Nelson was still a pioneer community without power, phones, running water, refrigerators or doctors. Interesting recollections of Fort Nelson's early days may be found in Gerri Young's book *The Fort Nelson Story*; available at the museum.

Fort Nelson was an unorganized territory until 1957 when it was declared an Improvement District. Fort Nelson took on village status in 1971 and town status in 1987.

Forestry is a major industry here with a veneer plant, plywood plant, oriented strand board plant and sawmill complex. Chopsticks are manufactured at a local plant for export to Asian markets. Check with the infocentre about scheduled industrial tours.

Forestry products are shipped south by truck and rail. Fort Nelson became a railhead in 1971 with the completion of a 250-mile extension of the Pacific Great Eastern Railway (now British Columbia Railway) from Fort St. John.

Agriculture is under development here with the recent establishment of the 55,000-acre McConachie Creek agricultural subdivision.

Northeastern British Columbia is the only sedimentary area in the province currently producing oil and gas. Oil seeps in the Fort Nelson area were noted by early residents. Major gas discoveries were made in the 1960s when the Clarke Lake, Yoyo/Kotcho, Beaver River and Pointed Mountain gas reserves were developed. The Westcoast Energy natural gas processing plant at Fort Nelson, the largest in North America, was constructed in 1964. This plant purifies the gas before sending it south through the 800-mile-long pipeline that connects the Fort Nelson area with the British Columbia lower mainland. Sulfur, a byproduct of natural gas processing, is processed in a recovery plant and shipped to outside markets in pellet form.

ACCOMMODATIONS/VISITOR SERVICES

Fort Nelson has 9 hotels/motels, 2 bed and breakfasts, several gas stations and restaurants, a pub, fast food, deli and health food outlets; an auto supply store, department stores and other services, most located north and south just off the Alaska Highway. The post office and liquor store are on Airport Drive. There are 2 banks, both with bank machines, on the business frontage road north of the highway. Fresh water fill-up and free municipal dump station adjacent the blue chalet near the museum. Inquire at the infocentre for location of local churches and their hours of worship.

Fort Nelson has 4 campgrounds: one is located at the north (or west) end of town near the museum; one is at the south (or east) end of town; and the others are in the Muskwa Heights area south of Fort Nelson.▲

Fort Nelson Bed & Breakfast. (Non-smoking). For your convenience and privacy, our B&B is a self-contained unit on one side of our duplex. En suite bathrooms. Home-style breakfast. Laundry facilities. Cable TV. "Come and be spoiled." Your hosts, Doug and Renee. Box 58, Fort Nelson, BC V0C 1R0. (604) 774-6050. VISA. Open year-round. (Member—Northern Network of B&B's). [ADVERTISEMENT]

Westend R.V. Campground and Mini-Golf welcome you to Fort Nelson! Located in town, next to the museum, only a few short minutes walk from restaurants, banking, bingo, local stores and services and the free welcome visitors program. Overnight

and extended stay parking with a selection of over 130 sites. Lots of shade and grass, gravelled sites with many full hookups and pull-throughs. Grassy tenting areas with cooking shelter, and a playground for the kids. Caravans welcomed, covered meeting place, handicap facilities, free carwash and firewood. Drinking water, coin-op hot showers and laundry. Pay phones. CAA/AAA and Woodall's approved. Confectionary, ice, souvenirs and gift shop with local Indian arts and crafts and tanned furs. Open April 1–Oct. 31. Your hosts, Chris and Sandra Brown, invite you to take a look at their beautiful wild animal displays. We hope you enjoy our northern hospitality and Super, Natural Scenic Adventure. Phone (604) 774-2340. [ADVERTISEMENT] ♿▲

ATTRACTIONS

Fort Nelson offers travelers a free

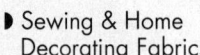

"Welcome Visitor Program" on summer evenings (Monday through Thursday in 1995) at 6:45 P.M. at the Phoenix Theatre. These interesting and entertaining presentations are put on by local residents and range from slide shows to talks on items of local interest. Check with the travel infocentre or at the Town Square for details.

The Fort Nelson Heritage Museum, across the highway from the travel infocentre, has excellent displays of pioneer artifacts, Alaska Highway history, wildlife (including a white moose), a spruce bark canoe and souvenirs and books for sale. This non-profit museum charges a modest admission fee. Native crafts are displayed at the Fort Nelson–Liard Native Friendship Centre, located on 49th Avenue.

The recreation centre, across from the museum, has tennis courts; hockey and curling arena for winter sports. Swimming pool, swirl pool, sauna and gym located in the Aqua Centre on Simpson Trail. For golfers, the Poplar Hills Golf and Country Club just north of town on the Old Alaska Highway, has grass greens; open daily.

A community demonstration forest is open to the public. There is a forest trail (0.6 mile/1 km, half-hour walk), a silviculture trail (1.9 miles/3 km, 45-minute walk), and a Native trail. Located off the Simpson Trail via Mountainview Drive; check at the infocentre for trail guide.

Fort Nelson hosts a number of annual benefits, dances, tournaments and exhibits. Check locally for details and dates on all events. Summer events include a rodeo in August. Winter events include a big cash prize curling bon spiel in February, Trapper's Rendezvous in March, and the Canadian Open Sled Dog Races in December (with local racers from the well-known Streeper Kennels). Eddy Streeper is a two-time World Champion (Anchorage) and also an Open North American Champion (Fairbanks) sled dog racer. Streeper Kennels is located on Radar Road.

Alaska Highway Log

(continued)

Distance* from Dawson Creek (DC) is followed by distance from Fairbanks (F). Original mileposts are indicated in the text as Historical Mile.

*Mileages from Dawson Creek are based on actual driving distance. Kilometres from Dawson Creek are based on physical kilometreposts. Please read Mileposts and Kilometreposts in the introduction for an explanation of how this highway is logged.

DC 284 (456.4 km) **F 1204** (1937.6 km) **Historic Milepost 300**, historic sign and interpretive panel at west end of Fort Nelson. Visitor information in the Recreation Centre north side of highway, log museum south side of highway. Private campground adjacent museum. ▲

Northbound: Watch for sections of rough, narrow, winding road and breaks in surfacing between Fort Nelson and the BC–YT border (approximately next 321 miles/516.5 km).

Southbound: Good pavement, wider road, next 284 miles/457 km (to Dawson Creek).

DC 284.5 (457.5 km) **F 1203.5** (1936.8 km) Fort Nelson Forest District Office to north provides a pamphlet of self-guided Forest Ecology Tours on the Alaska and Liard highways; phone (604) 774-3936.

DC 284.7 (458.2 km) **F 1203.3** (1936.5 km) **Junction** with south end of Old Alaska Highway (Mile 301–308). The Muskwa Valley bypass between Mile 301 and 308 opened in 1992.

DC 287.9 (462.6 km) **F 1200.1** (1931.3 km) Access to Poplar Hills Golf and Country Club, located on Old Alaska Highway; 9 hole golf course, driving range, grass greens, clubhouse (licensed), golf club rentals. Open 8 A.M. to dusk, May to October.

DC 291 (467.6 km) **F 1197** (1926.3 km) Parker Lake Road. **Junction** with north end of Old Alaska Highway (Mile 308–301).

DC 292 (469.9 km) **F 1196** (1924.7 km) Private airstrip alongside highway; status unknown.

DC 301 (483.5 km) **F 1187** (1910.2 km) **Junction** with Liard Highway (BC Highway 77) north to Fort Liard, Fort Simpson and other Northwest Territories destinations. See LIARD HIGHWAY section and the MACKENZIE ROUTE section for details.

DC 304.1 (489.4 km) **F 1183.9** (1905.3

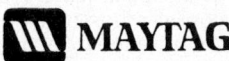

km) **Historic Milepost 320**. Sign marks start of Reese & Olson contract during construction of the Alaska Highway.

DC 308.2 (495.3 km) **F 1179.8** (1898.7 km) Raspberry Creek. Turnout with garbage barrels to south.

DC 316.6 (506.2 km) **F 1171.4** (1885.1 km) Turnout with litter barrel to south.

DC 318.4 (509.1 km) **F 1169.6** (1882.2 km) Kledo Creek bridge.

DC 318.7 (509.5 km) **F 1169.3** (1881.8 km) Kledo Creek wayside rest area to north (unmaintained).

DC 322.7 (516 km) **F 1165.3** (1875.3 km) Steamboat Creek bridge. Highway begins climb northbound up Steamboat Mountain; some 10 percent grades.

DC 329 (526.1 km) **F 1159** (1865.2 km) Pull-through turnout with litter barrel to south.

DC 333 (532.5 km) **F 1155** (1858.7 km) **Historic Milepost 351. STEAMBOAT** (unincorporated), lodge with food, gas, diesel and camping to south; open year-round. Historical sign marks start of Curran & Briggs Ltd. contract during construction of the Alaska Highway. ▲

DC 333.7 (533.5 km) **F 1154.3** (1857.6 km) Winding road ascends Steamboat Mountain westbound. Views of the Muskwa River valley and Rocky Mountains to the southwest from summit of 3,500-foot/1,067-m Steamboat Mountain, named because of its resemblance to a steamship. *CAUTION: Narrow road; watch for sharp curves and rough spots.*

DC 334.3 (534.5 km) **F 1153.7** (1856.6 km) Turnout with view and litter barrel to south.

NOTE: Watch for road construction northbound between Kilometreposts 535 and 539 in 1996.

DC 336.7 (538.5 km) **F 1151.3** (1852.8 km) Turnout to south with litter barrels and pit toilets. Highway descends for westbound travelers.

DC 339.1 (542.5 km) **F 1148.9** (1848.9 km) Drinking water to north. *CAUTION: Hairpin curve!*

DC 342.8 (548 km) **F 1145.2** (1843 km) View of Indian Head Mountain, a high crag resembling the classic Indian profile.

DC 343.4 (549 km) **F 1144.6** (1842 km) Turnout with litter barrel, outhouse and point of interest sign to south.

IMPORTANT: BEWARE OF BEARS! Two bear attacks along the Alaska Highway, between Fort Nelson and Liard River Hot Springs in 1994, were blamed on the roadside feeding of bears. While bear-human encounters were down in 1995, remember: DO NOT FEED BEARS!

DC 345 (551.5 km) **F 1143** (1839.4 km) Scenic Teetering Rock viewpoint with litter barrel and outhouses to north. Teetering Rock is in the distance on the horizon. Fort Nelson Forest District (phone 604/774-3936) has developed a 7.6-mile-/12.3-km-long trail to Teetering Rock; steep climbs. Stay on well-marked trails, keep pets on leash; it is easy to get lost in this country.

DC 346.4 (553.9 km) **F 1141.6** (1837.2 km) Mill Creek, which flows into the Tetsa River. The highway follows the Tetsa River westbound. The Tetsa heads near Summit Lake in the northern Canadian Rockies.

Bare peaks of the Canadian Rockies tower above campground at Summit Lake, Milepost DC 373.6. (Earl L. Brown staff)

Tetsa River, good fishing for grayling to 4 lbs., average $1^1/_2$ lbs., flies or spin cast with lures; Dolly Varden to 7 lbs., average 3 lbs., spin cast or black gnat, coachman, Red Devils, flies; whitefish, small but plentiful, use flies or eggs, summer.

DC 346.5 (554 km) **F 1141.5** (1837 km) Turnoff to south for Tetsa River Provincial Park, 1.2 miles/1.9 km via gravel road. Grass tenting area, 25 level gravel sites in trees, picnic tables, fire rings, firewood, outhouses, water and garbage containers. Camping fee $7 to $12. ▲

DC 351 (561.2 km) **F 1137** (1829.8 km) *CAUTION: Slow down, dangerous curve!*

DC 357.5 (571.5 km) **F 1130.5** (1819.3 km) **Historical Mile 375.** Gas, store, cabins and private campground. Trail rides by reservation; phone (604) 774-1005. ▲

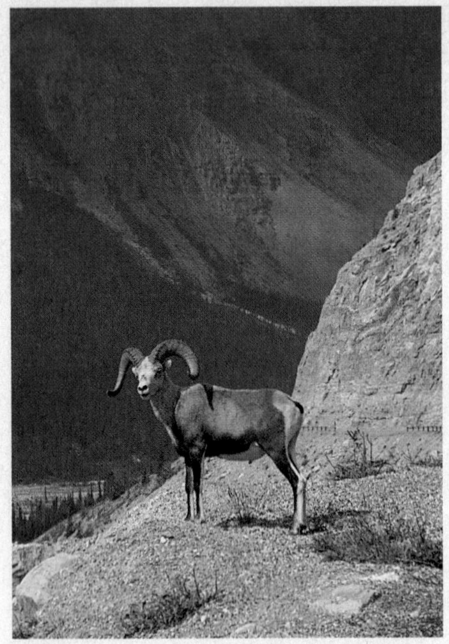

Stone sheep ram photographed near Milepost DC 377. (Earl L. Brown, staff)

cabins with kitchenettes. Bed and breakfast. Great fishing! Licenses and local information. Local arts and handiwork. Experience Rocky Mountain wilderness by horseback. (Reservations recommended.) Working guest ranch. Overnight horse boarding. Enjoy Super, Natural Scenic Adventure. (604) 774-1005. [ADVERTISEMENT] ▲

DC 358.6 (573.3 km) **F 1129.4** (1817.5 km) Highway follows Tetsa River westbound. Turnouts next 0.2 mile/0.3 km south to river.

DC 360.2 (575.9 km) **F 1127.8** (1815 km) Turnout with litter barrel, picnic site. Ecotour stop: Note the aspen-dominated slopes on the north side of the Tetsa River, and the white spruce on the south side.

DC 364.4 (582.6 km) **F 1123.6** (1808.2 km) Gravel turnout to south.

DC 365.6 (584.6 km) **F 1122.4** (1806.3 km) Tetsa River bridge No. 1, clearance 17 feet/5.2m.

DC 366 (585.4 km) **F 1122** (1805.6 km) Pull-through turnout with litter barrel to north.

DC 367.3 (587.3 km) **F 1120.7** (1803.5 km) Tetsa River bridge No. 2.

The high bare peaks of the central Canadian Rockies are visible ahead westbound.

DC 371.5 (594.2 km) **F 1116.5** (1796.8 km) South boundary of Stone Mountain Provincial Park. Stone sheep are indigenous to the mountains of northern British Columbia and southern Yukon Territory. They are darker and somewhat slighter than the bighorn sheep found in the Rocky Mountains. Dall or white sheep are found in the mountains of Yukon, Alaska and Northwest Territories.

CAUTION: Northbound, watch for caribou and stone sheep along the highway. DO NOT FEED WILDLIFE. DO NOT STOP VEHICLES ON THE HIGHWAY TO TAKE PHOTOS; use shoulders or turnouts.

DC 372.7 (596 km) **F 1115.3** (1794.9 km) Pull-through turnout with litter barrel to north.

DC 373.3 (597 km) **F 1114.7** (1793.9 km) **Historical Mile 392. SUMMIT LAKE** (unincorporated), lodge with gas, diesel, propane, cafe, camping and lodging. The peak behind Summit Lake is Mount St. George (elev. 7,419 feet/2,261m) in the Stone Mountain range. The Summit area is known for dramatic and sudden weather changes. ▲

Summit Lodge. See display ad this section. ▲

DC 373.5 (597.4 km) **F 1114.5** (1793.5 km) Rough gravel side road leads 1.5 miles/2.5 km to Flower Springs Lake trailhead, 4.3 miles/7 km to microwave tower viewpoint. Not suitable for motorhomes, trailers or low clearance vehicles.

DC 373.6 (597.6 km) **F 1114.4** (1793.4 km) Gravel turnout and Summit Lake provincial campground to south at east end of Summit Lake. **Historic Milepost 392** sign and interpretive panel mark the highest summit on the Alaska Highway, elev. 4,250 feet/1,295m. A very beautiful area of bare rocky peaks (which can be snow-covered anytime of the year). The provincial campground has 28 level gravel sites; picnic tables; water and garbage containers; information shelter; boat launch. Camping fee $7 to $12. Hiking trails to Flower Springs Lake and Summit Peak. Fair fishing for lake trout, whitefish and rainbows in **Summit Lake.** ▲

DC 375.6 (600.8 km) **F 1112.4** (1790.2 km) Turnout to north.

DC 375.9 (601.3 km) **F 1112.1** (1789.7 km) Picnic site to south with tables and litter barrel on Rocky Crest Lake.

DC 376 (601.5 km) **F 1112** (1789.5 km) Erosion pillars north of highway (0.6-mile/1-km hike north); watch for caribou. Northbound, the highway winds through a rocky limestone gorge, before descending into the wide and picturesque MacDonald River valley. Turnouts next 2.5 miles/4 km northbound with views of the valley. Watch for Stone sheep along rock cut.

DC 378.2 (605.1) **F 1109.8** (1786 km) Baba Canyon to north.

DC 378.6 (605.7 km) **F 1109.4** (1785.4 km) **Historical Mile 397.** Rocky Mountain Lodge to south; gas, lodging, store and camping. ▲

Rocky Mountain Lodge. See display ad this section. ▲

DC 379.7 (607.4 km) **F 1108.3** (1783.6 km) Turnout to south.

DC 380.7 (609 km) **F 1107.3** (1782 km) North boundary of Stone Mountain Provincial Park. *CAUTION: Southbound, watch for wildlife alongside and on the road. DO NOT FEED WILDLIFE.*

DC 381.2 (611.2 km) **F 1106.8** (1781.2 km) Highway winds along above the wide rocky valley of MacDonald Creek.

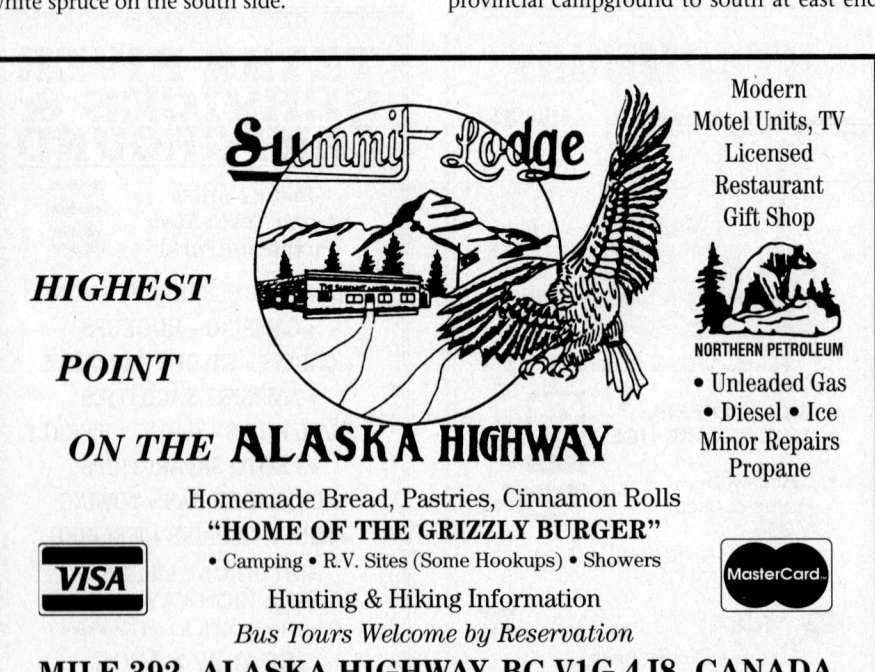

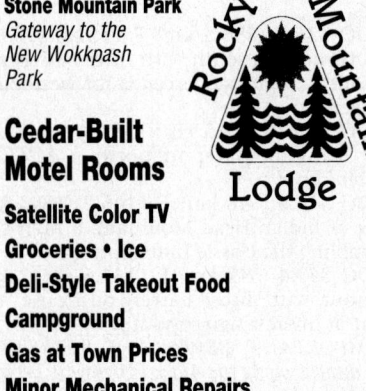

MacDonald Creek and river were named for Charlie McDonald, a Cree Indian credited with helping Alaska Highway survey crews locate the best route for the pioneer road. More history on McDonald may be found in *Alcan Trail Blazers* (648th Memorial Fund) and *Northwest Epic — The Building of the Alaska Highway* by Heath Twichell.

DC 382.2 (612.8 km) **F 1105.8** (1779.5 km) Trail access via abandoned Churchill Mines Road (4-wheel drive only beyond river) to Wokkpash Recreation Area, located 12 miles/20 km south of the highway, which adjoins the southwest boundary of Stone Mountain Provincial Park. This remote area features extensive hoodoos (erosion pillars) in Wokkpash Gorge, and the scenic Forlorn Gorge and Stepped Lakes. Contact the Parks District Office in Fort St. John before venturing into this area; phone (604) 787-3407.

DC 383.3 (614.6 km) **F 1104.7** (1777.8 km) 113 Creek. The creek was named during construction of the Alaska Highway for its distance from Mile 0 at Fort Nelson. While Dawson Creek was to become Mile 0 on the completed pioneer road, clearing crews began their work at Fort Nelson, since a rough winter road already existed between Dawson Creek and Fort Nelson. Stone Range to the northeast and Muskwa Ranges of the Rocky Mountains to the west.

DC 384.2 (615.4 km) **F 1103.8** (1776.3 km) 115 Creek provincial campground to southwest, adjacent highway; double-ended entrance. Side-by-side camper parking (8 sites), water, garbage containers, picnic tables. Camping fee $7 to $12. Access to the riverbank of 115 Creek and **MacDonald Creek.** Beaver dams nearby. Fishing for grayling and Dolly Varden.

DC 385.4 (616.6 km) **F 1102.6** (1774.4 km) 115 Creek bridge. Turnout to south at east end of bridge with tables and litter barrels. Like 113 Creek, 115 Creek was named during construction of the pioneer road for its distance from Fort Nelson, Mile 0 for clearing crews.

DC 390.5 (624.8 km) **F 1097.5** (1766.2 km) **Historical Mile 408.** MacDonald River Services (closed in 1995; current status unknown).

DC 392.5 (627.8 km) **F 1095.5** (1763 km) MacDonald River bridge, clearance 17 feet/5.2m. Highway winds through narrow valley.

MacDonald River, fair fishing from May to July for Dolly Varden and grayling.

DC 394.8 (631.8 km) **F 1093.2** (1759.3 km) Turnout with litter barrel to east.

DC 396.1 (633.8 km) **F 1091.9** (1757.2 km) Folding rock formations on mountain face to west. The Racing River forms the boundary between the Sentinel Range and the Stone Range, both of which are composed of folded and sedimentary rock.

DC 399.1 (638.6 km) **F 1088.9** (1752.4 km) Stringer Creek.

DC 400.7 (641.1 km) **F 1087.3** (1749.8 km) Racing River bridge, clearance 17 feet/5.2m. River access to north at east end of bridge. Ecotour stop: note the open south-facing slopes on the north side of the river that are used as winter range by stone sheep, elk and deer. Periodic controlled burns encourage the growth of forage grasses and shrubs, and also allow chinook winds to clear snow from grazing grounds in winter.

Racing River, grayling to 16 inches; Dolly Varden to 2 lbs., use flies, July through September.

DC 404.6 (647.4 km) **F 1083.4** (1743.5 km) **Historical Mile 422. TOAD RIVER** (unincorporated), situated in a picturesque valley. Highway maintenance camp, school and private residences on north side of highway. Toad River Lodge on south side of highway with cafe, gas, tire repair, propane, camping and lodging. Ambulance service. Toad River Lodge is open year-round. The lodge is known for its collection of hats, which numbers more than 3,800. Also, inquire at the lodge about good wildlife viewing locations nearby.

Toad River Lodge. See display ad this section.

Private Aircraft: Emergency gravel airstrip; elev. 2,400 feet/732m; length 2,300 feet/701m.

DC 405.5 (648.8 km) **F 1082.5** (1742.1 km) Turnout to south with **Historic Milepost 422.** Sign and interpretive panel commemorate Toad River/Camp 138 Jupp Construction.

DC 406.3 (650.1 km) **F 1081.7** (1740.8 km) Turnout with litter barrels to north.

DC 407.5 (652 km) **F 1080.5** (1738.8 km) **Historical Mile 426.** Food, gas, propane, tire repair, cabins and camping south side of highway. Inquire here about local hiking trails.

The Poplars Campground. See display ad this section.

DC 409.2 (654.6 km) **F 1078.8** (1736.1 km) South boundary of Muncho Lake Provincial Park.

DC 410.6 (656.8 km) **F 1077.4** (1733.9 km) Turnout with information panel on area geology. Impressive rock folding formation on mountain face, known as Folded Mountain.

DC 411 (657.4 km) **F 1077** (1733.2 km) Beautiful turquoise-coloured Toad River to north. The highway now follows the Toad River westbound.

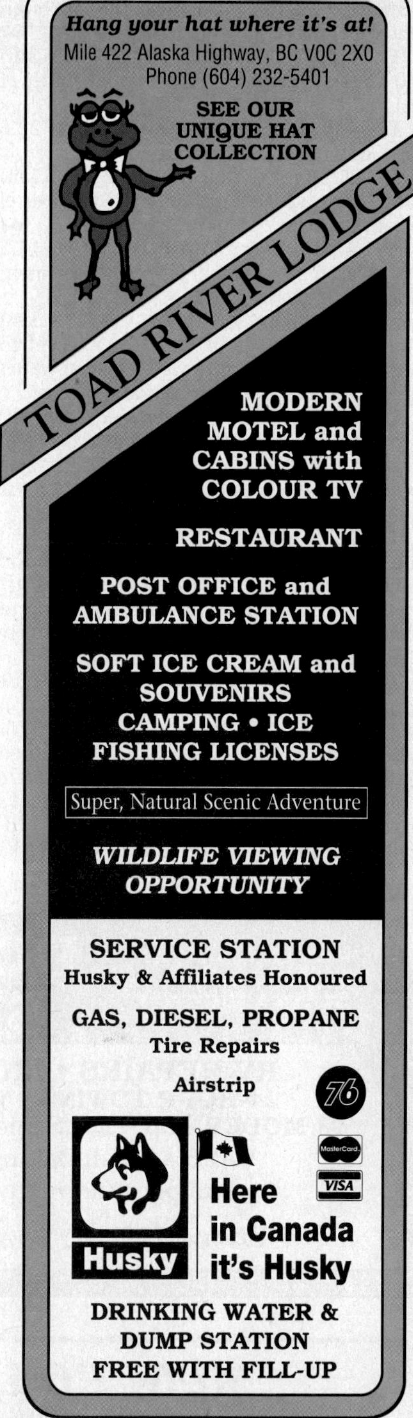

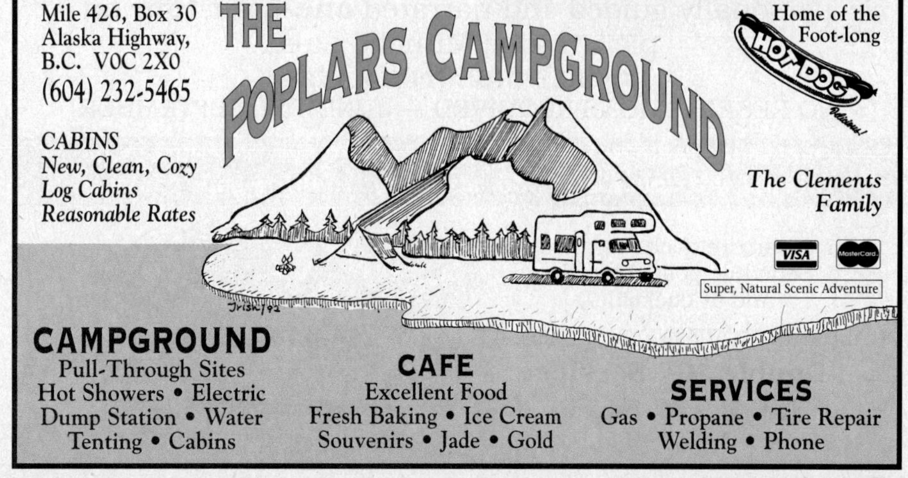

Toad River, grayling to 16 inches; Dolly Varden to 10 lbs., use flies, July through September.

DC 415.5 (664.7 km) **F 1072.5** (1726 km) 150 Creek bridge. Creek access to south at east end of bridge.

DC 417.6 (668.2 km) **F 1070.4** (1722.6 km) Centennial Falls to south.

DC 419.8 (671.7 km) **F 1068.2** (1719 km) **Toad River** bridge. Turnout with litter barrel to south at west end of bridge; fishing.

DC 422.6 (676.2 km) **F 1065.4** (1714.5 km) Watch for moose in pond to north; morning or evening best.

DC 423 (676.8 km) **F 1065** (1713.9 km) Double-ended turnout with litter barrel to north. Excellent wildlife viewing area; watch for Stone sheep, caribou, bear and moose.

CAUTION: Watch for Stone sheep along the highway (or standing in the middle of the highway). DO NOT FEED WILDLIFE. Do not stop vehicles on the highway to take photos; use shoulders or turnouts.

DC 423.1 (677 km) **F 1064.9** (1713.7 km) The highway swings north for Alaska-bound travelers. Highway climbs next 6 miles/9.7 km northbound. For Dawson Creek-bound travelers, the highway follows an easterly direction.

DC 424.1 (678.7 km) **F 1063.9** (1712.1 km) **Historic Milepost 443** at Peterson Creek No. 1 bridge. The creek was named for local trapper Pete Peterson, who helped Alaska Highway construction crews select a route through this area. Historic sign marks start of Campbell Construction Co. Ltd. contract during construction of the Alaska Highway.

DC 424.3 (679 km) **F 1063.7** (1711.8 km) The Village; gas, snacks and camping. ▲

DC 429.5 (688.9 km) **F 1058.5** (1703.4 km) Viewpoint to east with information shelter and litter barrels. Information panel on geology of "Sawtooth Mountains."

DC 436.5 (698.5 km) **F 1051.5** (1692.2 km) **Historic Milepost 456.** Entering **MUNCHO LAKE** (pop. 24; elev. 2,700 feet/823m). Muncho Lake businesses extend from here north along the east shore of Muncho Lake to approximately **Milepost DC 443.7.** Businesses in Muncho Lake include 4 lodges, gas stations with towing and repair, restaurants, cafes and campgrounds. The post office is located at Double G Service; open year-round. ▲

A historic sign and interpretive panel mark Muncho Lake/Refueling Stop, Checkpoint during Alaska Highway construction. The road around the lake was a particular challenge. Workers had to cut their way through the lake's rocky banks. Horses were used to haul away the rock. The Muncho Lake area offers hiking in the summer and cross-country skiing in the winter. Narrated boat tours of Muncho Lake are available in summer; check with Double G Service. This highly recommended tour highlights the history and geography of the area. Boat rentals are available from J&H Wilderness Resort and Highland Glen Lodge. Flightseeing and fly-in fishing service available from Liard Air at Highland Glen Lodge. An annual lake trout derby is held in June; inquire locally for dates.

Alaska Highway follows the Toad River north to Muncho Lake. (Earl L. Brown, staff)

CAUTION: Watch for Stone sheep and caribou on the highway north of here. Please DO NOT FEED WILDLIFE. Please do not stop on the highway to take photos; use shoulders or turnouts.

Double G Service, located at the south end of beautiful Muncho Lake, offers you "one stop" service. Have your vehicle repaired in our mechanic's shop or stay for the night in the campground or motel. Our cozy cafe has delicious homemade bread and pastries to go, or stay in and try our hearty soups, stews and chili. Full grocery store. Your children will enjoy our playground and there is excellent hiking just out the back door. For a more relaxed outing, pick up your tickets for the Muncho Lake boat tour aboard the MV *Sandpiper*. Your hosts, The Gunness Family, invite you to stop and check the cleanliness, comfort and friendliness yourself. [ADVERTISEMENT]

Muncho Lake Tours. See display ad this section.

DC 436.9 (699.2 km) **F 1051.1** (1691.5 km) Gravel airstrip to west; length 1,200 feet/366m. View of Muncho Lake ahead northbound. The highway along Muncho Lake required considerable rock excavation by the Army in 1942. The original route went along the top of the cliffs, which proved particularly hazardous. (Portions of this hair-raising road can be seen high above the lake.) The Army relocated the road by benching into the cliffs a few feet above lake level.

Muncho Lake, known for its beautiful deep green and blue waters, is 7 miles/11 km in length, and 1 mile/1.6 km in width; elevation of the lake is 2,680 feet/817m. The colours are attributed to copper oxide leaching into the lake. Deepest point has been reported to be 730 feet/223m, although recent government tests have not located any point deeper than 400 feet/122m. The lake drains the Sentinel Range to the east and the Terminal Range to the west, feeding the raging Trout River in its 1,000-foot/305-m drop to the mighty Liard River. The mountains surrounding the lake are approximately

7,000 feet/2,134m high.

Muncho Lake, fishing for Dolly Varden; some grayling; whitefish to 12 inches; lake trout (record to 50 lbs.), use spoons, spinners, diving plug or weighted spoons, June and July best. The lake trout quota is 3 trout per person; minimum size 15¾ inches. Make sure you have a current British Columbia fishing license and a copy of the current regulations. Also rainbow trout.

DC 437.7 (700.5 km) **F 1050.3** (1690.2 km) Strawberry Flats Campground, Muncho Lake Provincial Park; 15 sites on rocky lakeshore, picnic tables, outhouses, garbage containers. Camping fee $7 to $12. ▲

CAUTION: Watch for bears in area.

DC 442.2 (707.9 km) **F 1045.8** (1683 km) **Historical Mile 462.** Highland Glen Lodge with cabins, restaurant, gas and camping west side of highway. Flying service for sightseeing and fly-in fishing. ▲

DC 442.9 (709 km) **F 1045.1** (1681.9 km) Turnoff to west for MacDonald campground, Muncho Lake Provincial Park; 15 level gravel sites, firewood, picnic tables, outhouses, boat launch, information shelter, pump water, on Muncho Lake. Camping fee $7 to $12. *CAUTION: Watch for bears in area.* ▲

DC 443.6 (710.1 km) **F 1044.4** (1680.8 km) **Historical Mile 463.** Muncho Lake Lodge; gas, propane, food, camping and lodging. ▲

DC 443.7 (710.3 km) **F 1044.3** (1680.6 km) **Historical Mile 463.1.** J&H Wilderness Resort; food, gas, store, boat rentals, tackle, lodging and camping available. Muncho Lake businesses extend south to **Milepost DC 436.5.** ▲

J&H Wilderness Resort. See display ad this section. ▲

DC 444.9 (712.2 km) **F 1043.1** (1678.7 km) Muncho Lake viewpoint to west with information panel, large parking area, picnic tables, litter barrels and outhouses. View of Peterson Mountain at south end of lake.

NOTE: Watch for Stone sheep on highway next 10 miles/16 km northbound.

DC 453.3 (725.6 km) **F 1034.7** (1665.1 km) Turnout with litter barrel to east.

NOTE: Watch for Stone sheep on highway next 10 miles/16 km southbound.

DC 455.5 (729.2 km) **F 1032.5** (1661.6 km) Turnout with litter barrel and message board to west.

DC 457.7 (732.7 km) **F 1030.3** (1658.1 km) Trout River bridge. The Trout River drains into the Liard River. The highway follows the Trout River north for several miles.

Trout River, grayling to 18 inches; whitefish to 12 inches, flies, spinners, May, June and August best.

DC 458.9 (734.6 km) **F 1029.1** (1656.1 km) Gravel turnout to east.

DC 460.7 (737.4 km) **F 1027.3** (1653.2 km) Prochniak Creek bridge. The creek was named for a member of Company A, 648th Engineers Topographic Battalion, during construction of the Alaska Highway. North boundary of Muncho Lake Provincial Park.

DC 463.3 (741.6 km) **F 1024.7** (1649 km) Watch for curves next 0.6 mile/1 km northbound.

DC 465.6 (745.3 km) **F 1022.4** (1645.3 km) Turnout with litter barrel to east.

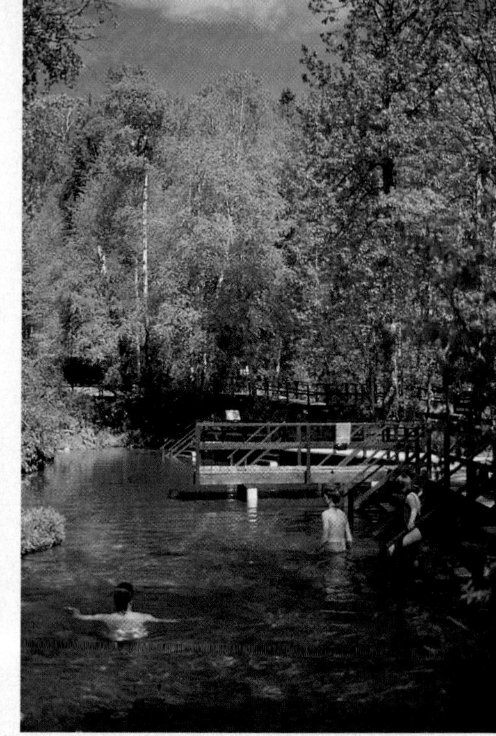

Alpha pool at Liard Hotsprings Provincial Park is 1 of 2 hot pools open year-round for bathing. (Earl L. Brown, staff)

DC 466.3 (746.3 km) **F 1021.7** (1644.2 km) *CAUTION: Dangerous curves next 3 miles/5 km northbound.*

DC 468.9 (749.5 km) **F 1019.1** (1640 km) Pull-through turnout with litter barrel to east. This Ecotour stop shows the extent of the 1959 fire that swept across the valley bottom. Lodgepole pine, trembling aspen and paper birch are the dominant species re-establishing this area.

DC 471 (754.1 km) **F 1017** (1636.7 km) First glimpse of the mighty Liard River for northbound travelers. Named by French-Canadian voyageurs for the poplar ("liard") that line the banks of the lower river. The Alaska Highway parallels the Liard River from here north to Watson Lake. The river offered engineers a natural line to follow during routing and construction of the Alaska Highway in 1942.

DC 472.2 (756 km) **F 1015.8** (1634.7 km) Washout Creek.

DC 474.3 (759.5 km) **F 1013.7** (1631.3 km) Turnout with litter barrel to west.

DC 476.7 (763 km) **F 1011.3** (1627.5 km) Lower Liard River bridge. This is the only suspension bridge on the Alaska Highway. The 1,143-foot suspension bridge was built by the American Bridge Co. and McNamara Construction Co. of Toronto in 1943.

The **Liard River** flows eastward toward the Fort Nelson River and parallels the Alaska Highway from the Lower Liard River bridge to the BC–YT border. The scenic Grand Canyon of the Liard is to the east and not visible from the highway. Good fishing for Dolly Varden, grayling, northern pike and whitefish.

DC 477.1 (763.8 km) **F 1010.9** (1626.8 km) **Historical Mile 496. LIARD RIVER**

(unincorporated), lodge with gas, store, pay phone, food, camping and lodging to west; open year-round. ▲

Liard River Lodge. See display ad this section. ▲

DC 477.7 (764.7 km) **F 1010.3** (1625.9 km) **Historic Milepost 496.** Turnoff to north for Liard River Hotsprings Provincial Park, long a favorite stop for Alaska Highway travelers. The park has become so popular in recent years that the campground fills up very early each day in summer. Overflow parking area across highway from park entrance. The park is open year-round. This well-developed provincial park has 53 large, shaded, level gravel sites (some will accommodate 2 RVs), picnic tables, picnic shelter, water, garbage containers, firewood, fire rings, playground and heated restrooms with wheelchair accessible toilet. Camping fees to $15.50. Pay phone at park entrance. ▲

A boardwalk leads to the pools, crossing a wetlands environment that supports more than 250 boreal forest plants, including 14 orchid species and 14 plants that survive at this latitude because of the hot springs. Also watch for moose feeding in the pools. There are 2 hot springs pools. Nearest is the Alpha pool with a children's wading area. Beyond the Alpha pool is Beta pool, which is larger and deeper. Both have changing rooms. Beta pool is about a 0.4-mile/0.6-km walk. Plenty of parking at trailhead.

Excellent interpretive programs and nature walks in summer; check schedule posted at park entrance and at information shelter near trailhead. Emergency phone at park headquarters. *CAUTION: BEWARE OF BEARS!*

DC 477.8 (764.9 km) **F 1010.2** (1625.7 km) **Historical Mile 497.** Liard Hotsprings Lodge (open year-round) with food, gas, lodging and camping. ▲

Trapper Ray's Liard Hotsprings Lodge. See display ad this section. ▲

DC 482.8 (772.9 km) **F 1005.2** (1617.7 km) Teeter Creek. A footpath leads upstream; 10-minute walk to falls. Grayling fishing.

DC 485.4 (777 km) **F 1002.6** (1613.5 km) Small turnout overlooking the Liard River.

DC 489 (783.6 km) **F 999** (1607.7 km) **Private Aircraft:** Liard River airstrip; elev. 1,400 feet/427m; length 4,000 feet/1,219m; gravel.

NOTE: Northbound travelers watch for road construction between Kilometreposts 787 and 823 in 1996. Also watch for sections of rough surface, gravel breaks and loose gravel next 118.5 miles/190.7 km (to BC–YT border).

DC 495 (792.3 km) **F 993** (1598 km) **Historic Milepost 514. Smith River** bridge, clearance 17 feet/5.2m. Access to Smith River Falls via 1.6-mile/2.6-km gravel road; not recommended for large RVs or trailers or in wet weather. There is a hiking trail down to 2-tiered Smith River Falls from the parking area. Grayling fishing.

The historic sign here commemorates Smith River Airport Road. The old airstrip, part of the Northwest Staging Route, is located in a burned-over area about 25 miles/40 km from the highway (accessible by 4-wheel drive only).

DC 509.4 (815.6 km) **F 978.6** (1574.9 km) Large turnout with litter barrel to east.

DC 513.9 (822.8 km) **F 974.1** (1567.6 km) **Historical Mile 533. COAL RIVER,** lodge with gas, diesel, food, camping and lodging. ▲

Coal River Lodge (1994). See display ad this section. ▲

DC 514.2 (823.2 km) **F 973.8** (1567.1 km) **Historical Mile 533.2.** Coal River bridge. The Coal River flows into the Liard River south of the bridge.

DC 519.5 (831.4 km) **F 968.5** (1558.6 km) Sharp easy-to-miss turnoff to west for undeveloped "do-it-yourself campsite" (watch for sign). Small gravel parking area with outhouse, litter barrels, and beautiful view of the Liard River (not visible from the highway). Although signed "Whirlpool Canyon," this scenic stretch of the Liard River has been identified by one astute reader as Mountain Portage Rapids, with Whirlpool Canyon being located farther downriver. ▲

DC 524.2 (839.2 km) **F 963.8** (1551 km) **Historical Mile 543. FIRESIDE** (unincorporated). Highway maintenance camp and truck stop with gas, diesel, major repairs, cafe and RV parking (open April to Sept.). *CAUTION: Keep pets in vehicles; unfriendly local animals.* This community was partially destroyed by fire in the summer of 1982. Evidence of the fire can be seen from south of Fireside north to Lower Post. The 1982 burn, known as the Eg fire, was the second largest fire in British Columbia history, destroying more than 400,000 acres.

Fireside Car/Truck Stop. See display ad this section.

NOTE: Watch for road construction northbound between Kilometreposts 839 and 845.

DC 524.7 (840 km) **F 963.3** (1550.2 km) Good view of Liard River and Cranberry Rapids to west.

DC 527.7 (845 km) **F 960.3** (1545.4 km) *IMPORTANT:* Rerouting of the Alaska Highway was under way in 1995 for the next 12.7 miles/20.4 km. The new highway will bypass the dangerous curves in the LeQuil Creek area and shorten the road by approximately 2 miles/3.2 km. In 1996, watch for continued road construction, soft spots and gravel surfacing on new highway section.

DC 530 (848.7 km) **F 958** (1541.7 km) Gravel turnout with litter barrels to south.

DC 540.4 (865.3 km) **F 947.6** (1525 km) North end of rerouting of Alaska Highway (see **Milepost DC 527.7**).

DC 545.9 (874.2 km) **F 942.1** (1516.1 km) Turnout with litter barrel to west overlooking the Liard River.

DC 550.9 (882.2 km) **F 937.1** (1508 km) **Historical Mile 570.** Allen's Lookout; very large pull-through turnout with picnic tables, outhouse and litter barrel to west overlooking the Liard River. Goat Mountain to west. Legend has it that a band of outlaws took advantage of this sweeping view of the Liard River to attack and rob riverboats.

DC 555 (888.8 km) **F 933** (1501.5 km) Good berry picking in July among roadside raspberry bushes; watch for bears.

DC 556 (890.4 km) **F 932** (1499.9 km) Highway swings west for Alaska-bound travelers.

DC 562.5 (900.8 km) **F 925.5** (1489.4 km) Large gravel turnout with litter barrel.

DC 567.9 (909.4 km) **F 920.1** (1480.7 km) **Historic Milepost 588.** Contact Creek bridge. Turnout to south at east end of bridge with tables, toilets, litter barrels and information shelter. Contact Creek was named by soldiers of the 36th Regiment from the south and the 340th Regiment from the north who met here Sept. 24, 1942, completing the southern sector of the Alaska Highway. Historic sign and interpretive panel.

DC 568.3 (910.2 km) **F 919.7** (1480.1 km) First of 7 crossings of the BC–YT border. Large gravel turnout to north with point of interest sign about the Yukon Territory. "The Yukon Territory takes its name from the Indian word *Youcon,* meaning 'big river.' It was first explored in the 1840s by the Hudson's Bay Co., which established several trading posts. The territory, which was then considered a district of the Northwest Territories, remained largely untouched until the Klondike gold rush, when thousands of people flooded into the country and communities sprang up almost overnight. This sudden expansion led to the official formation of the Yukon Territory on June 13, 1898."

DC 570 (912.9 km) **F 918** (1477.3 km) **Historical Mile 590. CONTACT CREEK,** lodge open year-round; food, gas, diesel, car repair, towing, car wash and pay phone.

Contact Creek Lodge. See display ad this section.

DC 573.9 (918.9 km) **F 914.1** (1471.1 km) Irons Creek bridge. Turnout with litter barrel to south at east end of bridge. According to the folks at Iron Creek Lodge, Irons Creek was named during construction of the Alaska Highway for the trucks that stopped here to put on tire irons (chains) in order to make it up the hill.

DC 575.9 (922 km) **F 912.1** (1467.8 km) **Historical Mile 596.** Iron Creek Lodge; food, gas, diesel, dump station, lodging and camping. Private stocked lake at campground. ▲

Iron Creek Lodge. See display ad this section. ▲

NOTE: Watch for road construction northbound between Kilometreposts 922 and 931 in 1996.

DC 582 (931.8 km) **F 906** (1458 km) NorthwesTel microwave tower.

DC 585 (937 km) **F 903** (1453.2 km) **Hyland River** bridge; good fishing for rainbow, Dolly Varden and grayling.

NOTE: Watch for logging trucks northbound to Watson Lake.

DC 585.3 (937.2 km) **F 902.7** (1452.7 km) **Historical Mile 605.9.** Hyland River bridge. The Hyland River is a tributary of the Liard River. The river was named for Frank Hyland, an early-day trader at Telegraph Creek on the Stikine River. Hyland operated trading posts throughout northern British Columbia, competing successfully with the Hudson's Bay Co., and at one time printing his own currency.

DC 598.7 (957.5 km) **F 889.3** (1431.2 km) Access to **LOWER POST** (unincorporated), at **Historical Mile 620**, via short gravel road; cafe and store. A B.C. Forest Service field office is located here. This British Columbia settlement is a historic Hudson's Bay Co. trading post and the site of an Indian village. The Liard and Dease rivers meet near here. The Dease River, named for Peter Warren Dease, a fur trader for the Hudson's Bay Co., heads in Dease Lake to the southwest on the Cassiar Highway.

DC 605.1 (967.6 km) **F 882.9** (1420.8 km) **Historic Milepost 627** marks official BC–YT border; Welcome to the Yukon sign. Monitor CB Channel 9 for police. The Alaska Highway dips back into British Columbia several times before making its final crossing into the Yukon Territory near Morley Lake (**Milepost DC 751.5**).

NOTE: Kilometreposts on the Yukon Territory portion of the highway reflect historical mileposts. Kilometreposts on the British Columbia portion of the highway reflect actual driving distance. There is approximately a 40-kilometre difference at the BC–YT border between these measurements.

Northbound: Good paved highway with wide shoulders next 380 miles/611.5 km to Haines Junction, with the exception of some short sections of narrow road and occasional gravel breaks.

Southbound: Watch for rough, narrow, winding road and breaks in surfacing between border and Fort Nelson (approximately 321 miles/516.6 km).

DC 606.9 (1011.9 km) **F 881.1** (1418 km) Lucky Lake picnic area to south; ball diamond and 1.2-mile/2-km hiking trail to Liard River Canyon (watch for signs), observation platform with information panels at river. **Lucky Lake** is a popular local swimming hole for Watson Lake residents, who installed a water slide here. Relatively shallow, the lake warms up quickly in summer, making it one of the few area lakes where swimming is possible. Stocked with rainbow trout.

According to R. Coutts in *Yukon Places & Names*, Lucky Lake was named by American Army Engineer troops working on construction of the Alaska Highway in 1942: "A young woman set up a tent business and clients there referred to transactions as 'a change of luck.'"

DC 609.2 (1015.5 km) **F 878.8** (1414.3 km) Rest area with litter barrel and outhouses to north.

DC 610.4 (1017.5 km) **F 877.6** (1412.3 km) Weigh station.

DC 610.5 (1017.7 km) F 877.5 (1412.2 km) Mile 632.5. Campground Services at Mile 632.5 is the largest and best equipped RV park in Watson Lake, the gateway to the Yukon. The park features full or partial hookups and pull-throughs, tent sites, showers, a laundry, car wash and playground, firepits and a screened kitchen.

Good Sam Park. A food market stocks groceries, "chester fried" chicken, convenience items, fishing tackle, licenses and ice. Husky gasoline and diesel and ICG propane are available at the self-serve pumps. A licensed mechanic is available for repairs, alignments, tire changes, etc. Agents for Western Union money transfers. Open for business year-round, serving the traveler's needs for over 25 years! Phone (403) 536-7448. [ADVERTISEMENT] ▲

Yukon flag's 3 colour panels represent the territory's rivers and lakes (blue), forests (green) and snow (white). (Earl L. Brown, staff)

Official formation of Yukon Territory took place on June 13, 1898.

Watson Lake

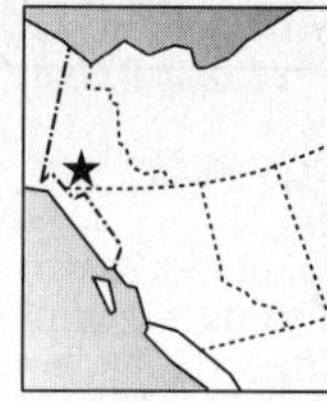

DC 612.9 (1021 km) F 875.1 (1408.3 km). **Historic Milepost 635.** "Gateway to the Yukon," located 329 miles/529 km from Fort Nelson, 274 miles/441 km from Whitehorse. **Population:** 1,749. **Emergency Services: RCMP,** phone (403) 536-5555 (if no answer call toll-free 1-403-667-5555). **Fire Department,** phone (403) 536-2222. **Ambulance,** phone (403) 536-4444. **Hospital,** phone (403) 536-4444.

Visitor Information: Located in the Alaska Highway Interpretive Centre behind the Signpost Forest, north of the Alaska Highway; access to the centre is from the Campbell Highway. Phone (403) 536-7469. The town of Watson Lake provides a toll-free number (Lower 48 only) for information on local attractions; phone 1-800-663-5248.

Elevation: 2,265 feet/690m. **Climate:** Average temperature in January is -15°F/-26°C, in July 57°F/14°C. Record high temperature 93°F/34°C in June 1950, record low -74°F/-59°C in January 1947. Annual snowfall is 90.6 inches. Driest month is April, wettest month is September. Average date of last spring frost is June 2; average date of first fall frost is Sept. 14. **Radio:** CBC 990, CKYN-FM 96.1 (Visitor Radio CKYN is broadcast from the visitor information centre from mid-May to mid-September). **Television:** Channel 8 and cable.

Private Aircraft: Watson Lake airport, 8 miles/12.9 km north of Campbell Highway; elev. 2,262 feet/689m; length 5,500 feet/1,676m and 3,530 feet/1,076m; asphalt; fuel 100, jet. Heliport and floatplane bases also located here. The Watson Lake airport terminal building was built in 1942. The log structure has been designated a Heritage Building. In the late 1800s, Watson Lake was known as Fish Lake. The lake was later renamed Watson, for Frank Watson of Yorkshire, England. He gave up on the gold rush in 1898 to settle here on its shores with his Indian wife. Today, Watson Lake is an important service stop on the Alaska and Campbell highways (Campbell Highway travelers, fill your gas tanks here!); a communication and distribution centre for the southern Yukon; a base for trappers, hunters and fishermen; and a supply point for area mining and mineral exploration.

Watson Lake businesses are located along either side of the Alaska Highway. The lake itself is not visible from the Alaska Highway. Access to the lake, airport, hospital and Mount Maichen ski hill is via the Campbell Highway (locally referred to as Airport Road). The ski area is about 4 miles/6.4 km out the Campbell Highway from town.

Watson Lake was an important point during construction of the Alaska Highway in 1942. The airport, built in 1941, was one

WATSON LAKE ADVERTISERS

Belvedere Motor Hotel.....Ph. (403) 536-7712
Big Horn Hotel & Tavern..Ph. (403) 536-2020
Campground Services Ltd. .....E. edge of town
Cedar Lodge Motel..........Ph. (403) 536-7406
Downtown R.V. Park ....Ph. (403) 536-2646
Gateway Motor Inn ....Ph. (403) 536-7744
Green Valley Trailer Park....................Kmpost 1032 Alaska Hwy.
Grunow Motors ....Ph. (403) 536-2272
Hougens Department Store ....Alaska Hwy.
Jer-Cal Holdings Ltd.......................Downtown
Napa Auto Parts ....Ph. (403) 536-2521
O'Neill Repairs........1 blk. S. of Signpost Forest
Rudy's Towing ....Ph. (403) 536-2123
Signpost Services..Across from Signpost Forest
Totem Oil.........................Ph. 1-800-661-0550
Town of Watson Lake.......Ph. (403) 536-7778
Watson Lake Chevron................Downtown
Watson Lake Hotel ..Next to Signpost Forest
Watson Lake Rodeo........Ph. (403) 536-2272

of the major refueling stops along the Northwest Staging Route, the system of airfields through Canada to ferry supplies to Alaska and later lend-lease aircraft to Russia. Of the nearly 8,000 aircraft ferried through Canada, 2,618 were Bell P-39 Airacobras. A full-scale replica of the P-39 Airacobra is displayed at the Alaska Highway Interpretive Centre by the Signpost Forest.

The Alaska Highway helped bring both people and commerce to this once isolated settlement. A post office opened here in July 1942. The economy of Watson Lake is based on services and also the forest products industry. White spruce and lodgepole pine are the two principal trees of the Yukon and provide a forest industry for the territory. White spruce grows straight and fast wherever adequate water is available, and it will grow to extreme old age without showing decay. The lodgepole pine developed from the northern pine and can withstand extreme cold, grow at high elevations and take full advantage of the almost 24-hour summer sunlight of a short growing season.

ACCOMMODATIONS/VISITOR SERVICES

There are several hotels/motels, restaurants and gas stations with unleaded, diesel and propane, automotive and tire repair. Dump stations available at local campgrounds and service stations. There are department, variety, grocery and hardware stores. A complex on the north side of the highway contains the post office, fire hall, government liquor store and library. (The Watson Lake Library has a Northern video and display; library hours are posted.) The RCMP office is east of town centre on the Alaska Highway. There is 1 bank in Watson Lake, Canadian Imperial Bank of Commerce; it is open Monday through Thursday from 10 A.M. to 3 P.M., Friday 10 A.M. to 6 P.M., closed holidays. Automatic teller machine available 24 hours. Check at the Visitor Information Centre for locations of local churches. Dennis Ball Memorial Swimming Pool is open weekdays in summer. (The pool staff operates the Lucky Lake waterslide on weekends in summer from 1–4 P.M.)

Belvedere Motor Hotel, located in the centre of town, is Watson Lake's newest and finest hotel. It offers such luxuries as Jacuzzi tubs in the rooms, waterbeds, and cable TV, and all at competitive prices. Dining is excellent, whether you decide to try the superb dining room menu, or the coffee shop menu. Phone (403) 536-7712, fax (403) 536-7563. [ADVERTISEMENT]

Big Horn Hotel & Tavern. New in 1993. 29 beautiful rooms. Centrally located on the Alaska Highway in downtown Watson Lake, YT. Our rooms are quiet, spacious, clean and they boast queen-size beds and complimentary coffee. You get quality at a reasonable price. Available to you are king-size motionless waterbeds, Jacuzzi rooms, kitchenette suites. We know you'll enjoy staying with us. Book ahead. Phone (403) 536-2020, fax (403) 536-2021. [ADVERTISEMENT]

Watson Lake Hotel. The historic "Watson Lake Hotel." We're right in the heart of Watson Lake's historical "Signpost Forest." Enjoy northern hospitality at its finest. Ample parking on our 6 acres of property. Quiet outside modern units, (renovated May 1993), boardwalk gift shops and espresso bar. Senior, government, military and corporate discounts. Present this editorial for your 5-cent coffee in "Watson's Daytime Grill." (See our display ad.) Phone (403) 536-7781. [ADVERTISEMENT]

The turnoff for Watson Lake Yukon government campground is 2.4 miles/3.9 km west of the Signpost Forest via the Alaska Highway; see description at **Milepost DC 615.3.** There is a private campground at **Milepost DC 619.6,** 4.3 miles/6.9 km past the turnoff for the government campground; a private campground 2.4 miles/3.9 km east of the Signpost Forest on the Alaska Highway (see **Milepost DC 610.5**); and an RV park located downtown. ▲

Downtown R.V. Park, situated in the centre of town. 71 full hookup stalls, 19 with pull-through parking; showers; laundromat. Free truck/trailer, motorhome wash with overnight stay. Easy walking distance to stores, garages, hotels, restaurants, liquor store, banking, churches, information centre and the world-famous Signpost Forest. Just across the street from Wye Lake Park. Excellent hiking trails. Phone (403) 536-2646 in summer, 536-2224 in winter. [ADVERTISEMENT] ▲

TRANSPORTATION

Air: Scheduled service to Whitehorse via Alkan Air; to Prince George, Vancouver, Victoria, Smithers and Dease Lake via Central Mountain Air. Helicopter charters available from Frontier Helicopters and Trans North Helicopters. **Bus:** Scheduled service to Edmonton and Whitehorse via Coachways. **Taxi** and **Car Rental:** Available.

ATTRACTIONS

The **Alaska Highway Interpretive Centre**, operated by Tourism Yukon, is well worth a visit. Located behind the Signpost Forest, north of the Alaska Highway. Excellent slide presentation and displays, including photographs taken in the mid-1940s showing the construction of the Alaska Highway in this area, and a brief Alaska Highway video. Full-scale reproduction of a P-39 Airacobra fighter plane on display just outside the centre. Visitor information is available at the Interpretive Centre; pick up your free Yukon Gold Explorer's Passport here. The passport features 13 sites in the Yukon; you may get your passport stamped at each site (starting with Watson Lake). Also check at the interpretive centre for the location of the Watson Lake Historical Displays or watch for signs. The centre is open daily, May to mid-Sept. Free admission. Phone (403) 536-7469.

The Watson Lake Signpost Forest, seen at the north end of town at the junction of the Alaska and Robert Campbell highways, was started by Carl K. Lindley of Danville, IL, a U.S. Army soldier in Company D, 341st

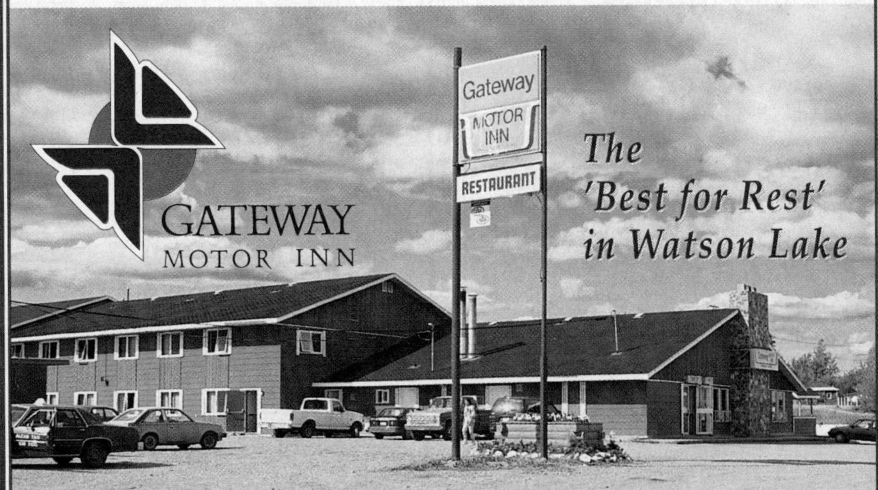

Engineers, working on the construction of the Alaska Highway in 1942. (Mr. Lindley made his first visit back to Watson Lake since 1942 for the 1992 Alaska Highway anniversary.) Travelers are still adding signs to the collection, which numbers well over 25,000. Visitors are encouraged to add a sign to the Signpost Forest. **Historic Milepost 635** is located at the Signpost Forest. A sign and interpretive panel explain the Northwest Staging Route.

Special Events. The 3rd annual Watson Lake Rodeo (NRA-approved) will be held at Lucky Lake July 6-7, 1996. A parade, 8 main events and junior events will be featured.

Wye Lake Park offers a picnic area and boardwalk trails for viewing birds. There is also a bandshell, kitchen shelter and handicap-accessible restrooms. The lake attracts both migrating birds (spring and fall) and resident species, such as nesting grebes. Native plants and flowers are identified by plaques. The development of this park was initiated by a local citizens group.

St. John the Baptist Anglican Church has a memorial stained-glass window designed by Yukon artist Kathy Spalding. Titled "Our Land of Plenty," the window features a scene just north of Watson Lake off the Campbell Highway.

Famous Watson Lake Signpost Forest. (© Chris Sharp)

Drive the Campbell Highway. This good gravel road offers an excellent wilderness highway experience. Motorists can travel the entire 373 miles/600 km of the Campbell Highway, stopping at Ross River and Faro en route, to junction with the Klondike Highway at Carmacks. Or drive north 52 miles/83 km from Watson Lake to Simpson Lake for picnicking, fishing and camping. (See CAMPBELL HIGHWAY section for details.)

Play golf at Upper Liard, 6 miles/9.6 km north of Watson Lake on the Alaska Highway. The 9-hole, par-35 course has grass greens and is open daily May through September. Phone (403) 536-2477.

Explore the area. Take time to fish, canoe a lake, take a wilderness trek or flightsee by helicopter. Outfitters in the area offer guided fishing trips to area lakes. Trips can be arranged by the day or by the week. Check with the visitor information centre.

AREA FISHING: Boat charters available locally, check with Watson Lake Boat Charters (403) 536-2138. **Watson Lake** has grayling, trout and pike. **McKinnon Lake** (walk-in only), 20 miles/32 km west of Watson Lake, pike 5 to 10 lbs. **Toobally Lake** and string of lakes 14 miles/23 km long, 90 air miles/145 km east, lake trout 8 to 10 lbs.; pike 5 to 10 lbs.; grayling 1 to 3 lbs. **Stewart Lake**, 45 air miles/72 km north northeast; lake trout, grayling.

Alaska Highway Log

(continued)

Distance* from Dawson Creek (DC) is followed by distance from Fairbanks (F). Original mileposts are indicated in the text as Historical Mile.

*Mileages from Dawson Creek are based on actual driving distance. Kilometres from Dawson Creek are based on physical kilometreposts. Please read Mileposts and Kilometreposts in the introduction for an

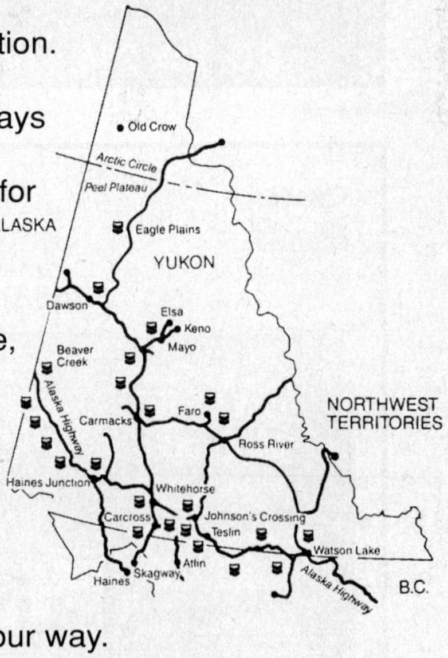

explanation of how this highway is logged.

DC 612.9 (1021 km) **F 875.1** (1408.3 km) Watson Lake Signpost Forest at the **junction** of the Campbell Highway (Yukon Route 4) and Alaska Highway. The Campbell Highway leads north to Ross River and Faro (see CAMPBELL HIGHWAY section), to junction with the Klondike Highway to Dawson City. Campbell Highway travelers should fill gas tanks in Watson Lake. The first 6 miles/9.7 km of the Campbell Highway is known locally as Airport Road; turn here for access to visitor information (in the Alaska Highway Interpretive Centre), airport, hospital and ski hill.

DC 615.3 (1025 km) **F 872.7** (1404.4 km) Turnoff to north for Watson Lake Recreation Park. Drive in approximately 2 miles/3 km for Watson Lake Yukon government campground; 55 gravel sites, most level, some pull-through, drinking water, kitchen shelters, outhouses, firepits, firewood and litter barrels. Camping fee $8. ▲

There is a separate group camping area and also a day-use area (boat launch, swimming, picnicking at Watson Lake). Follow signs at fork in access road. Trails connect all areas.

DC 618.5 (1030 km) **F 869.5** (1399.3 km) Watch for livestock.

DC 619.6 (1032 km) **F 868.4** (1397.5 km) **Green Valley R.V. Park.** Phone (403) 536-2276. Just 7 miles west of Watson Lake, quiet greenbelt area along Liard River. Friendly service, clean facilities. Pay phone. Serviced and unserviced sites, dump station, grassy tent sites, riverside camping, firepits, car wash, laundry, showers, grocery, coffee, pastries, ice, souvenirs, free gold panning, game room, fishing licenses and tackle. Fish for grayling and dollies. Pick wild strawberries and raspberries in season. Cold beer and off sales. Bikers welcome. Your hosts: Ralph and Marion Bjorkman. [ADVERTISEMENT] ▲

DC 620 (1032.4 km) **F 868** (1396.9 km) Upper Liard River bridge. The Liard River heads in the St. Cyr Range in southcentral Yukon Territory and flows southeast into British Columbia, then turns east and north to join the Mackenzie River at Fort Simpson, NWT.

Liard River, grayling, lake trout, whitefish and northern pike.

DC 620.2 (1032.7 km) **F 867.8** (1396.5 km) **Historical Mile 642. UPPER LIARD VILLAGE**, site of Our Lady of the Yukon Church. Gas, food, lodging and camping; open year-round. ▲

DC 620.3 (1033 km) **F 867.7** (1396.4 km) Greenway's Greens golf course to south with 9 holes, par 35, grass greens, open daily in summer.

DC 620.8 (1033.7 km) **F 867.2** (1395.6 km) Albert Creek bridge. Turnout with litter barrel to north at east end of bridge. A sign near here marks the first tree planting project in the Yukon. Approximately 200,000 white spruce seedlings were planted in the Albert Creek area in 1993.

DC 626.2 (1043 km) **F 861.8** (1386.9 km) **Historic Milepost 649. Junction** with the Cassiar Highway, which leads south to Yellowhead Highway 16 (see CASSIAR HIGHWAY section). Services here include towing, gas, store with souvenirs, propane, car repair, car wash, laundromat, cafe, camping and lodging. ▲

Junction 37 Services. See display ad this section.

DC 627 (1043.9 km) **F 861** (1385.6 km) **Alaska Highway's Best Coffee Stop.** See display ad this section.

The Northern Beaver Post. Historical Mile 649.9. As with trading posts of the past, The Northern Beaver Post is an essential stop for any traveler. Here you will find unique, quality items which are often as useful as they are decorative. In the friendly atmosphere of the Post, discover a fine selection of Native crafts, jewellery, gold, jade, authentic Eskimo carvings, furs, woolens, northern art, tufting, sweatshirts and tees, cards, gifts, and more. Show us this editorial and receive 10 percent off your purchase of a Beaver Post T-shirt or sweat shirt. Open 7 A.M. to 10 P.M. 7 days a week, May through Oct. Caravans and bus tours welcome. Free overnight RV parking. Don't miss "Alaska Highway's Best Coffee Stop" next door—fresh home baking. VISA, MasterCard, Discovery. Phone (403) 536-2307, fax (403) 536-7667. [ADVERTISEMENT]

DC 627.3 (1044.5 km) **F 860.7** (1385.1 km) Large gravel turnout and rest area with litter barrels and pit toilets.

DC 630 (1050.8 km) **F 858** (1380.8 km) Several hundred rock messages are spelled out along the highway here. The rock messages were started in summer 1990 by a Fort Nelson swim team.

DC 633 (1055.6 km) **F 855** (1375.9 km) Gravel turnout to north.

NOTE: Watch for road construction northbound between Kilometreposts 1056 and 1076 in 1996.

DC 637.8 (1063.3 km) **F 850.2** (1368.2 km) NorthwesTel microwave tower access road to north.

DC 639.8 (1066.5 km) **F 848.2** (1365 km) Hill and sharp curve.

DC 647.2 (1078.5 km) **F 840.8** (1353.1 km) Turnout with litter barrel on Little Rancheria Creek to north.

DC 647.4 (1079 km) **F 840.6** (1352.8 km) Little Rancheria Creek bridge. Sign reads: "Northbound winter travelers put on chains here."

DC 650.6 (1084 km) **F 837.4** (1347.6 km) Highway descends westbound to Big Creek.

DC 651.1 (1084.8 km) **F 836.9** (1346.8 km) Big Creek bridge, clearance 17.7 feet/5.4m. Turnout at east end of bridge.

DC 651.2 (1085 km) **F 836.8** (1346.7 km) Turnoff to north for Big Creek Yukon gov-

Improved section of Alaska Highway winds through Rancheria River valley.

(© Carmen Scott)

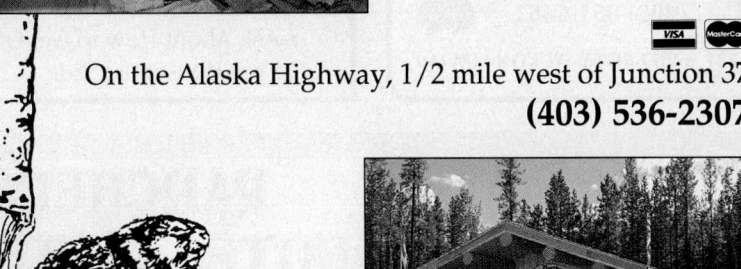

ernment day-use area, adjacent highway on Big Creek; gravel loop road, outhouses, firewood, kitchen shelter, litter barrels, picnic tables, drinking water.

DC 652.5 (1087.3 km) **F 835.5** (1344.6 km) Sign reads: "Northbound winter travelers chains may be removed."

DC 658.4 (1096.7 km) **F 829.6** (1335.1 km) Pull-through turnout south side of highway.

DC 662.3 (1102.9 km) **F 825.7** (1328.8 km) NorthwesTel microwave tower road to north.

DC 664.1 (1105.8 km) **F 823.9** (1325.9 km) Double-ended turnout to north to Lower Rancheria River.

DC 664.3 (1106.2 km) **F 823.7** (1325.6 km) Bridge over Lower Rancheria River. For northbound travelers, the highway closely follows the Rancheria River west from here to the Swift River.

Legendary Northern bush pilot Les Cook was credited with helping General Hoge find the best route for the Alaska Highway between Watson Lake and Whitehorse. According to John Schmidt's *"This Was No ΦΥΧΝΗ Picnic!"*, Cook's Rancheria River route saved engineers hundreds of miles of highway construction over the original plan.

Rancheria River, fishing for Dolly Varden and grayling.

DC 665.1 (1110.4 km) **F 822.9** (1324.3 km) Scenic viewpoint.

DC 667.2 (1113.7 km) **F 820.8** (1320.9 km) Turnout to south.

DC 667.6 (1114.3 km) **F 820.4** (1320.2 km) Large double-ended turnout with litter barrel to south.

DC 671.9 (1118.7 km) **F 816.1** (1313.3 km) Spencer Creek.

DC 673.4 (1121 km) **F 814.6** (1310.9 km) Improved highway and view of Cassiar Mountains westbound.

DC 677 (1126.9 km) **F 811** (1305.1 km) Turnout with litter barrel to south overlooking the Rancheria River. Trail down to river.

According to R.C. Coutts, author of *Yukon: Places & Names,* the Rancheria River was named by Cassiar miners working Sayyea Creek in 1875, site of a minor gold rush at the time. Rancheria is an old Californian or Mexican miners' term from the Spanish, meaning a native village or settlement. It is pronounced Ran-che-RI-ah.

DC 678.5 (1129.3 km) **F 809.5** (1302.7 km) George's Gorge, culvert.

DC 683.2 (1137 km) **F 804.8** (1295.2 km) NorthwesTel microwave tower to south.

DC 684 (1138.4 km) **F 804** (1293.9 km) Turnout with litter barrel overlooking Rancheria River. *CAUTION: Watch for livestock on or near highway in this area.*

DC 687.2 (1143.8 km) **F 800.8** (1288.7 km) **Historic Milepost 710.** Rancheria Hotel–Motel to south; gas, food, camping and lodging. Open year-round. Historic sign and interpretive panel on highway lodges. ▲

Rancheria Hotel–Motel. See display ad this section. ▲

DC 687.4 (1143.9 km) **F 800.6** (1288.4 km) Turnoff to south for private campground (formerly Rancheria Yukon government campground) adjacent highway overlooking Rancheria River. The Rancheria is a tributary of the Liard River. ▲

DC 689.2 (1146.6 km) **F 798.8** (1285.5 km) Canyon Creek.

DC 690 (1148 km) **F 798** (1284.2 km) Highway follows the Rancheria River. This stretch of highway was reconstructed in 1995.

DC 692.5 (1152 km) **F 795.5** (1280.2 km) Young Creek.

DC 694.2 (1155 km) **F 793.8** (1277.5 km) **Historical Mile 717.5.** Abandoned building.

DC 695.2 (1156.5 km) **F 792.8** (1275.8 km) Rancheria Falls recreation site has a good gravel and boardwalk trail to the falls; easy 10-minute walk. Large parking area with toilets and litter barrels at trailhead.

DC 697.4 (1160 km) **F 790.6** (1272.3 km) Beautiful view of the Cassiar Mountains.

DC 698.4 (1161.6 km) **F 789.6** (1270.7 km) **Historical Mile 721.** Walker's Continental Divide; gas, food, camping and lodging. ▲

Walkers Continental Divide. Fresh baking daily, mouthwatering cinnamon rolls, rhubarb pie, muffins, tarts & donuts. Breakfast served all day—try our sourdough pancakes. Gift shop, hard ice cream. Motel with clean, comfortable, cozy rooms. Proposed for 1996—full service RV park with laundromat, showers and trailer dump. Clean washrooms. Hospitality spoken here, free of charge. [ADVERTISEMENT] ▲

DC 698.7 (1162 km) **F 789.3** (1270.2 km) Upper Rancheria River bridge, clearance 17.7 feet/5.4m. For northbound travelers, the highway leaves the Rancheria River.

DC 699.1 (1162.8 km) **F 788.9** (1269.6 km) Large gravel turnout to north with point of interest signs, outhouses and litter barrels. This marks the Continental Divide, the water divide between rivers that drain into the Arctic Ocean via the Mackenzie River system and those that drain into the Pacific Ocean via the Yukon River system. All rivers crossed by the Alaska Highway between here and Fairbanks, AK, drain into the Yukon River.

DC 699.6 (1163.3 km) **F 788.4** (1268.8 km) **Historic Milepost 722.** Pine Lake airstrip to north (status unknown).

DC 702.2 (1168 km) **F 785.8** (1264.6 km) Swift River bridge. For northbound travelers, the highway now follows the Swift River west to the Morley River.

DC 706.2 (1174.5 km) **F 781.8** (1258.2 km) Steep hill for westbound travelers.

DC 709.7 (1180 km) **F 778.3** (1252.5 km) Seagull Creek.

DC 710 (1180.9 km) **F 778** (1252 km) **Historic Milepost 733, SWIFT RIVER.** Lodge with food, gas, lodging, car repair, pay phone and highway maintenance camp. Open year-round.

Swift River Lodge. Friendly haven in a beautiful mountain valley. Tasty cooking with a plentiful supply of coffee. Mouthwatering homemade pies and pastries fresh daily. Wrecker service, welding and repairs. Reasonable rates. Gas and diesel at some of the best prices on the highway. Clean restrooms, gifts and public phone. [ADVERTISEMENT]

DC 710.5 (1181.5 km) **F 777.5** (1251.2 km) **Historical Mile 733.5.** The highway reenters British Columbia for approximately 42 miles/68 km northbound.

DC 712.7 (1185 km) **F 775.3** (1247.7 km) Partridge Creek.

DC 716 (1190.3 km) **F 772** (1242.4 km) Gravel turnout with litter barrels.

DC 718.5 (1194.2 km) **F 769.5** (1238.3 km) Screw Creek.

DC 719.6 (1196 km) **F 768.4** (1236.6 km) **Historical Mile 743.** Turnout with litter barrel to south on **Swan Lake.** Fishing for trout and whitefish. The pyramid-shaped mountain to south is Simpson Peak.

DC 724.2 (1203.7 km) **F 763.8** (1229.2 km) Pull-through turnout to south.

DC 727.9 (1209.5 km) **F 760.1** (1223.2 km) Logjam Creek.

DC 735.8 (1222.5 km) **F 752.2** (1210.5 km) Smart River bridge. The Smart River flows south into the Cassiar Mountains in British Columbia. The river was originally called Smarch, after the Indian family of that name who lived and trapped in this area. The Smarch family currently includes well-known carver Keith Smarch.

DC 741.4 (1231.7 km) **F 746.6** (1201.5 km) Microwave tower access road to north.

DC 744.1 (1236 km) **F 743.9** (1197.2 km) Upper Hazel Creek.

DC 745.2 (1238 km) **F 742.8** (1195.4 km) Lower Hazel Creek.

DC 746.9 (1240.7 km) **F 741.1** (1192.6 km) Turnouts both sides of highway; litter barrel at south turnout.

DC 749 (1245 km) **F 739** (1189.3 km) Andrew Creek.

DC 751.5 (1249.2 km) **F 736.5** (1185.2 km) Morley Lake to north. The Alaska Highway re-enters the Yukon Territory northbound. This is the last of 7 crossings of the YT–BC border.

DC 752 (1250 km) **F 736** (1184.4 km) Sharp turnoff to north for **Morley River** Yukon government day-use area; large gravel parking area, picnic tables, kitchen shelter, water, litter barrels and outhouses. Fishing.

DC 752.3 (1251 km) **F 735.7** (1184 km) Morley River bridge; turnout with litter barrel to north at east end of bridge. Morley River flows into the southeast corner of Teslin Lake. The river, lake and Morley Bay (on Teslin Lake) were named for W. Morley Ogilvie, assistant to Arthur St. Cyr on the 1897 survey of the Telegraph Creek–Teslin Lake route.

Morley Bay and **River,** good fishing near mouth of river for northern pike 6 to 8 lbs., best June to August, use small Red Devils; grayling 3 to 5 lbs., in May and August, use small spinner; lake trout 6 to 8 lbs., June to August, use large spoon.

DC 752.9 (1252 km) **F 735.1** (1183 km) **Historic Milepost 777.7.** Morley River Lodge, food, gas, diesel, towing, tires, camping and lodging. Open year-round. ▲

Morley River Lodge. See display ad this section. ▲

DC 754.8 (1256 km) **F 733.2** (1179.9 km) *CAUTION: Watch for livestock on highway.*

DC 757.9 (1261 km) **F 730.1** (1174.9 km) Small marker to south (no turnout) reads: "In memory of Max Richardson 39163467,

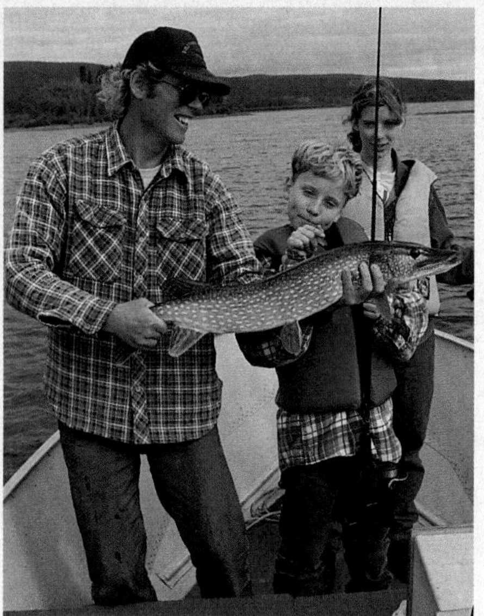

Guided fishing trip out of Teslin lands a pike. (Earl L. Brown, staff)

Corporal Co. F 340th Eng. Army of the United States; born Oct. 10, 1918, died Oct. 17, 1942. Faith is the victory."

DC 761.5 (1267.9 km) **F 726.5** (1169.1 km) Strawberry Creek.

DC 764.1 (1273.7 km) **F 723.9** (1165 km) Hayes Creek.

DC 769.6 (1282.5 km) **F 718.4** (1156.1 km) **Historical Mile 797.** Food, lodging and camping. ▲

Dawson Peaks Northern Resort. Slow down folks! No need to drive any farther. Fishing's good, coffee's on, camping is easy and the rhubarb pie can't be beat. Couple that with our renowned Yukon hospitality and you'll have one of the best experiences on your trip. We're looking forward to seeing you this summer. [ADVERTISEMENT] ▲

DC 776 (1292 km) **F 712** (1145.8 km) Nisutlin Bay (Nisutlin River) bridge, longest water span on the Alaska Highway at 1,917 feet/584m. The Nisutlin River flows into Teslin Lake here. Good view northbound of the village of Teslin and Teslin Lake. Teslin Lake straddles the BC–YT border; it is 86 miles/138 km long, averages 2 miles/3.2 km across, and has an average depth of 194 feet/59m. The name is taken from the Indian name for the lake—Teslintoo ("long, narrow water").

Turnout with litter barrel and point of interest sign at south end of bridge, east side of highway.

Historic Milepost 804 at the north end of the bridge, west side of the highway; historic sign and interpretive panel, parking area, marina and day-use area with picnic tables and boat ramp. Turn west on side road here for access to Teslin village (description follows).

DC 776.3 (1294 km) **F 711.7** (1145.3 km) Entering Teslin **(Historic Milepost 804)** at north end of bridge. Gas, food, camping and lodging along highway.

Yukon Motel, just right (northbound) on the north side of Nisutlin Bridge. An excellent stop for a fresh lake trout dinner (or full menu), accompanied by good and friendly service topped off with a piece of fantastic rhubarb and strawberry pie (lots of fresh baking). Soft ice cream. Recently renovated. Three satellite TV channels. Open year-round, summer hours 6-11. New lakeshore RV park (mosquito control area), 70 sites, full and partial hookups. "Good Sam Park" — washhouse rated TL 10. A real home away from home on the shore of beautiful Nisutlin Bay. (403) 390-2575. [ADVERTISEMENT] ▲

Teslin

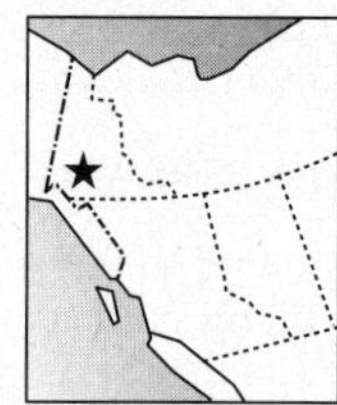

Located at **Historic Milepost 804,** 111 miles/179 km southeast of Whitehorse, 163 miles/263 km northwest of Watson Lake. **Population:** 465. **Emergency Services: RCMP**, phone (403) 390-5555 (if no answer call toll free 1-403-667-5555). **Fire Department,** phone (403) 390-2222. **Nurse**, phone (403) 390-4444.

Elevation: 2,239 feet/682.4m. **Climate:** Average temperature in January, -7°F/-22°C, in July 57°F/14°C. Annual snowfall 66.2 inches/168.2 cm. Driest month April, wettest month July. Average date of last spring frost is June 19; first fall frost Aug. 19. **Radio:** CBC 940. **Television:** Channel 13.

The village of Teslin, situated on a point of land at the confluence of the Nisutlin River and Teslin Lake, began as a trading post in 1903. Today the community consists of a trading post, Catholic church, health centre and post office. There is a 3-sheet regulation curling rink and a skating rink.

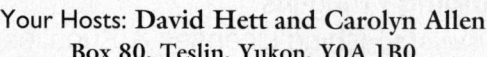

TESLIN ADVERTISERS

George Johnston Museum	Ph. (403) 390-2550
Nisutlin Trading Post	Ph. (403) 390-2521
Teslin Lake Motors	Ph. (403) 390-2551
Yukon Motel	Ph. (403) 390-2575

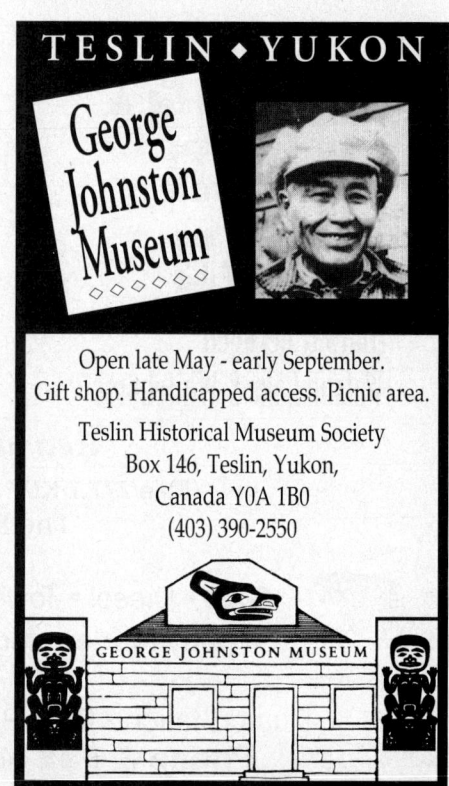

Teslin has one of the largest Native populations in Yukon Territory and much of the community's livelihood revolves around traditional hunting, trapping and fishing. In addition, some Tlingit residents are involved in the development of Native woodworking crafts (canoes, snowshoes and sleds); traditional sewn art and craft items (moccasins, mitts, moose hair tufting, gun cases); and the tanning of moose hides.

George Johnston Museum, renovated in 1991, is located on the right on the way into the village. The museum, run by the Teslin Historical Museum Society, is open daily, 9 A.M. to 7 P.M. in summer; minimal admission fee, wheelchair accessible. (Get your Yukon Gold Explorer's Passport stamped at the museum.) The museum displays items from gold rush days and the pioneer mode of living, Indian artifacts and many items of Tlingit culture. A Tlingit Indian, George Johnston (1884–1972) was an innovative individual, known for his trapping as well as his photography. With his camera he captured the life of the inland Tlingit people of Teslin and Atlin between 1910 and 1940. Johnston also brought the first car to Teslin, a 1928 Chevrolet. Since the Alaska Highway had not been built yet, George built a 3-mile road for his "Teslin taxi." In winter, he put chains on the car and drove it on frozen Teslin Lake. The '28 Chevy has been restored and is now on permanent display at the museum. For more information, write the Teslin Historical Museum Society, Box 146, Teslin, YT Y0A 1B0; phone (403) 390-2550, or fax 390-2828. ♿

Teslin is located west of the Alaska Highway, accessible via a short side road from the north end of Nisutlin Bay bridge. Nisutlin Trading Post in the village has groceries and general merchandise. Gas, diesel and propane, car repair, gift shop, restaurants and motels are found along the Alaska Highway. There is 1 bank, located in the Tlingit Band office building; open Wednesday, Thursday and Friday, noon to 3 P.M., in summer. The Teslin area has an air charter service, boat rentals and houseboat tours.

Nisutlin Trading Post, on short loop road, left northbound in Teslin Village. A pioneer store established in 1928, and located on the shore of Nisutlin Bay, an "arm" of Teslin Lake. This store handles a complete line of groceries, general merchandise including clothing, hardware, fishing tackle and licenses. Open all year 9 A.M. to 5:30 P.M. Closed Sunday. Founded by the late R. McCleery, Teslin pioneer, the trading post is now operated by Mr. and Mrs. Bob Hassard. Phone 390-2521, fax 390-2103. [ADVERTISEMENT]

Teslin Lake, fishing for trout, grayling,

View of Nisutlin Bay bridge from marina on Teslin Lake. (© Beth Davidow)

Yukon Territory is larger than all the New England states combined.

pike and whitefish. King salmon in August. Guides and boats available at Nisutlin Bay Marina.

Alaska Highway Log

(continued)

Distance* from Dawson Creek (DC) is followed by distance from Fairbanks (F). Original mileposts are indicated in the text as Historical Mile.

*Mileages from Dawson Creek are based on actual driving distance. Kilometres from Dawson Creek are based on physical kilometreposts. Please read Mileposts and Kilometreposts in the introduction for an explanation of how this highway is logged.

DC 777 (1295 km) **F 711** (1144.2 km) **Historic Milepost 805. Private Aircraft:** Teslin airstrip to east; elev. 2,313 feet/705m; length 5,500 feet/1,676m; gravel; fuel 100, jet. Runway may be unusable during spring breakup.

DC 779.1 (1298.5 km) **F 708.9** (1140.8 km) **Historical Mile 807.** Halsteads' gas, food, camping and lodging. Microwave tower on hillside to northwest. ▲

Halsteads'. See display ad this section. ▲

DC 779.5 (1299 km) **F 708.5** (1140.2 km) Fox Creek.

DC 784.3 (1306.7 km) **F 703.7** (1132.5 km) **Historical Mile 812.** Mukluk Annie's; food, lodging and camping. ▲

Mukluk Annie's Salmon Bake. See display ad this section. ▲

DC 785.2 (1308 km) **F 702.8** (1131 km) **Historical Mile 813.** Teslin Lake Yukon government campground to west; 27 sites (some level) in trees on **Teslin Lake,** water pump, litter barrels, kitchen shelter, firewood, firepits, picnic tables. Camping fee $8. Fishing. Boat launch 0.3 mile/0.5 km north of campground. ▲

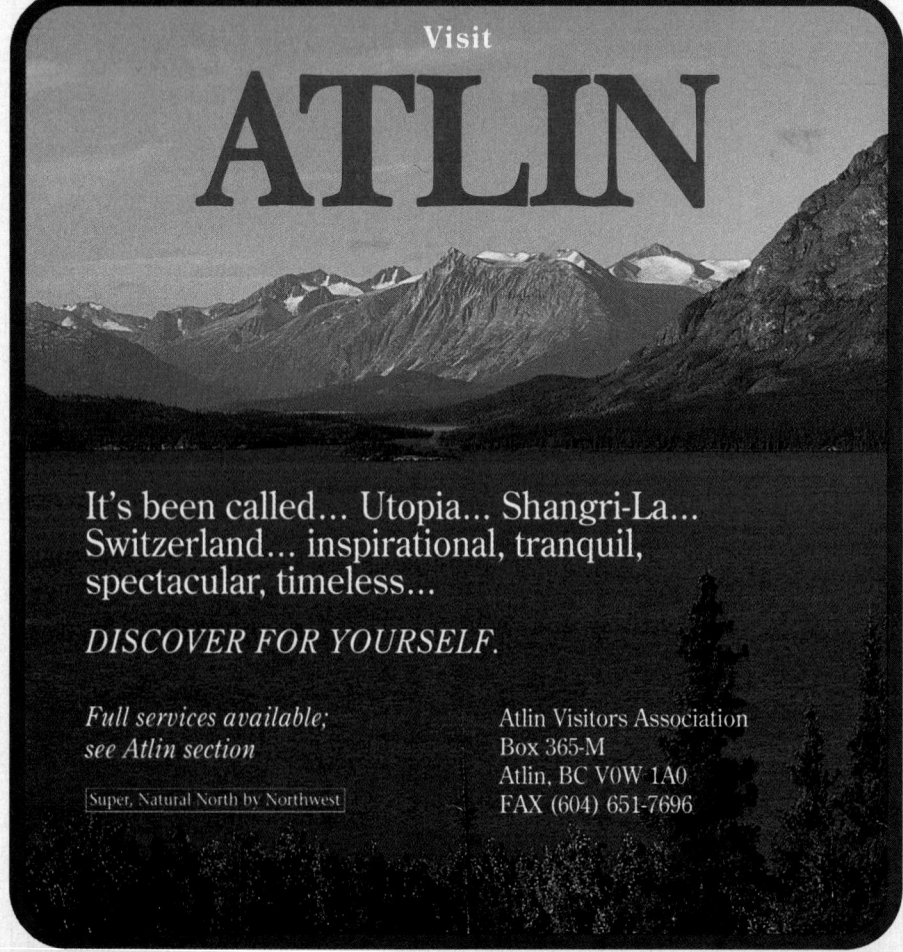

DC 785.3 (1308.2 km) **F 702.7** (1130.8 km) Tenmile Creek.

DC 788.9 (1314 km) **F 699.1** (1125 km) Lone Tree Creek.

DC 794.6 (1323 km) **F 693.4** (1115.9 km) Deadman's Creek.

DC 800.8 (1333.3 km) **F 687.2** (1105.9 km) Robertson Creek.

DC 801.6 (1334.4 km) **F 686.4** (1104.6 km) **Historic Milepost 829.** Brooks' Brook. According to R.C. Coutts in *Yukon: Places & Names,* this stream was named by black Army engineers who completed this section of road in 1942, for their company officer, Lieutenant Brooks.

DC 808.2 (1345 km) **F 679.8** (1094 km) **Junction** with the Canol Road (Yukon Highway 6) which leads northeast to the Campbell Highway. (See the CANOL ROAD section for details.) Historic sign and interpretive panel about the Canol Project.

The Canol (Canadian Oil) Road was built in 1942–44 to provide access to oil fields at Norman Wells, NWT. Conceived by the U.S. War Dept., the $134 million project was abandoned soon after the war ended in 1945. Canol truck "graveyard" nearby.

DC 808.6 (1345.6 km) **F 679.4** (1093.3 km) Teslin River bridge, third longest water span on the highway (1,770 feet/539m), was constructed with a very high clearance above the river to permit steamers of the British Yukon Navigation Co. to pass under it en route from Whitehorse to Teslin. River steamers ceased operation on the Teslin River in 1942. Before the construction of the Alaska Highway, all freight and supplies for Teslin traveled this water route from Whitehorse.

DC 808.9 (1346 km) **F 679.1** (1092.9 km) **Historic Milepost 836. JOHNSON'S CROSSING** to east at north end of bridge; store, food and camping. One of the original lodges on the Alaska Highway, the history of Johnson's Crossing is related in Ellen Davignon's *The Cinnamon Mine.* Access to Teslin River; boat launch, no camping on riverbank. ▲

Johnson's Crossing Campground Services. Located across the Teslin River bridge, home of the "world famous cinnamon buns," including a small store with a full array of mouth-watering baked goods, souvenirs and groceries. Full-service RV campground facilities include treed pull-throughs, complete laundry and washhouse facilities, Chevron gasoline products, cold beer and ice, and great fishing. Treat yourselves to the historically scenic Km 1347 (Mile 836) Alaska Highway, Yukon Y1A 9Z0. (403) 390-2607. [ADVERTISEMENT] ▲

Teslin River, excellent grayling fishing from spring to late fall, 10 to 15 inches, use spinner or red-and-white spoons for spinning or black gnat for fly-fishing. King salmon in August.

Canoeists report that the Teslin River is wide and slow, but with gravel, rocks and weeds. Adequate camping sites on numerous sand bars; boil drinking water. Abundant wildlife—muskrat, porcupine, moose, eagles and wolves—also bugs and rain. Watch for bear. The Teslin enters the Yukon River at Hootalinqua, an old steamboat landing and supply point (under restoration). Roaring Bull rapids: choppy water. Pull out at Carmacks. Inquire locally about river conditions before setting out.

DC 809.1 (1346.5 km) **F 678.9** (1092.5 km) Access road east to the Teslin River. The Big Salmon Range, also to the east, parallels the Teslin. For Alaska-bound travelers, the highway now swings west.

DC 812.8 (1352.5 km) **F 675.2** (1086.6 km) Little Teslin Lake on south side of highway.

DC 819.8 (1364 km) **F 668.2** (1075.3 km) In mid-June, the roadside is a profusion of purple Jacob's ladder and yellow dandelions.

DC 820.3 (1364.8 km) **F 667.7** (1074.5 km) Seaforth Creek bridge.

DC 820.4 (1365 km) **F 667.6** (1074.4 km) Large turnout to south; picnic area.

DC 820.6 (1365.3 km) **F 667.4** (1074 km) Squanga Lake to northwest. Named Squanga by Indians for a type of whitefish of the same name found in the lake. Watch for **Historic Milepost 843,** with historic sign about Squanga Lake flightstrip. Look for the eagle's nest in the old observation tower.

DC 821 (1366 km) **F 667** (1073.4 km) Turnoff to northwest to **Squanga Lake** Yukon government campground: 13 sites, kitchen shelter, drinking water. Small boat launch. Fishing for northern pike, grayling, whitefish, rainbow and burbot. ▲

DC 827.5 (1376.8 km) **F 660.5** (1062.9 km) White Mountain, to the southeast, was named by William Ogilvie during his 1887 survey, for Thomas White, then Minister of the Interior. The Yukon government introduced mountain goats to this area in 1981.

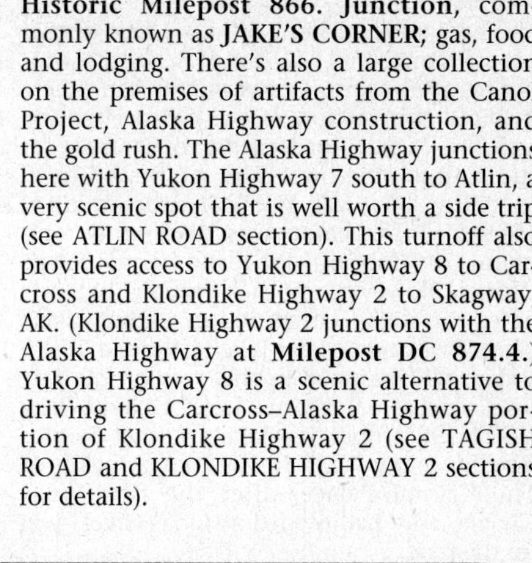

DC 836.8 (1392.5 km) **F 651.2** (1048 km) **Historic Milepost 866. Junction,** commonly known as **JAKE'S CORNER;** gas, food and lodging. There's also a large collection on the premises of artifacts from the Canol Project, Alaska Highway construction, and the gold rush. The Alaska Highway junctions here with Yukon Highway 7 south to Atlin, a very scenic spot that is well worth a side trip (see ATLIN ROAD section). This turnoff also provides access to Yukon Highway 8 to Carcross and Klondike Highway 2 to Skagway, AK. (Klondike Highway 2 junctions with the Alaska Highway at **Milepost DC 874.4.**) Yukon Highway 8 is a scenic alternative to driving the Carcross–Alaska Highway portion of Klondike Highway 2 (see TAGISH ROAD and KLONDIKE HIGHWAY 2 sections for details).

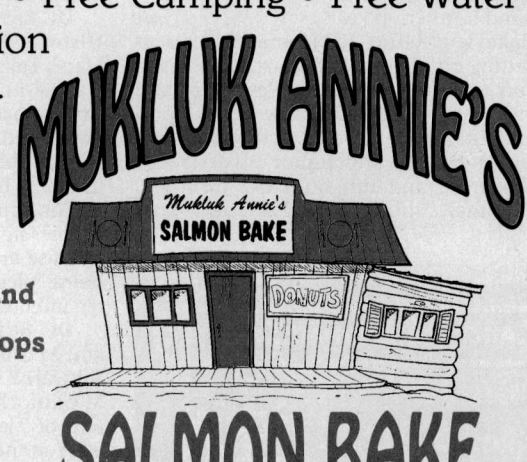

Jake's Corner Inc. See display ad this section.

There are 2 versions of how Jake's Corner got its name. In 1942, the U.S. Army Corps of Engineers set up a construction camp here to build this section of the Alcan Highway and the Tagish Road cutoff to Carcross for the Canol pipeline. (The highway south to Atlin, BC, was not constructed until 1949–50.) The camp was under the command of Captain Jacobson, thus Jake's Corner. However, another version that predates the Alcan construction is that Jake's Corner was named for Jake Jackson, a Teslin Indian who camped in this area on his way to Carcross. Roman "Jake" Chaykowsky (1900–1995) operated Jake's Corner Service here for many years. It was known locally as The Crystal Palace, after the first lodge Chaykowsky had owned at Judas Creek, just up the road.

DC 843.2 (1402.7 km) **F 644.8** (1037.7 km) Judas Creek bridge.

DC 850 (1413.5 km) **F 638** (1026.7 km) Turnoff to west for Lakeview Resort on Marsh Lake; camping, lodging, restaurant, boat rentals and boat launch. ▲

Marsh Lake, excellent fishing for grayling and northern pike.

Lakeview Resort & Marina, a spectacular setting on the shore of Marsh Lake, just 2 km off the Alaska Highway. Restaurant and lounge with panoramic view of lake and mountains. Motel rooms, cabins, convenience store, ice and liquor off-sales. RV park, partial and full hookups, camping, laundromat, showers, marina and boat rentals. Budget friendly rates. Km 1414, Alaska Highway, Yukon. Mailing address—P.O. Box 4759, Whitehorse, YT Y1A 4N6. Phone (403) 399-4567, Fax (403) 399-4747. [ADVERTISEMENT] ▲

DC 851.6 (1416 km) **F 636.4** (1024.1 km) Several access roads along here which lead to summer cottages. Marsh Lake is a popular recreation area for Whitehorse residents.

DC 852.7 (1417.8 km) **F 635.3** (1022.4 km) Good view of Marsh Lake to west. The highway parallels this beautiful lake for several miles. Marsh Lake (elev. 2,152 feet/656m) is part of the Yukon River system. It is approximately 20 miles/32 km long and was named in 1883 by Lt. Frederick Schwatka, U.S. Army, for Yale professor Othniel Charles Marsh.

DC 854.4 (1421 km) **F 633.6** (1019.6 km) **Historic Milepost 883**, Marsh Lake Camp historic sign. Boat ramp turnoff to west.

DC 854.8 (1421.2 km) **F 633.2** (1019 km) Caribou Road leads northwest to Airplane Lake; hiking trail, good skiing and snowmachining in winter. This road was bulldozed out to get men and equipment into a small lake where an airplane had made an emergency landing.

DC 859.9 (1432 km) **F 628.1** (1010.8 km) **Historical Mile 890.** Turnoff to west for Marsh Lake Yukon government campground via 0.4-mile/0.6-km gravel loop road: 47 sites, most level, some pull-through; outhouses, firewood, firepits, litter barrels, picnic tables, kitchen shelter, water pump. Camping fee $8. ▲

For group camping and day-use area, follow signs near campground entrance. Day-use area includes sandy beach, change house, picnic area, playground, kitchen shelter and boat launch.

DC 861.1 (1433.9 km) **F 626.9** (1008.9 km) M'Clintock River, named by Lieutenant Schwatka for Arctic explorer Sir Francis M'Clintock. This river flows into the north end of Marsh Lake. Boat ramp turnoff to west at north end of bridge. M'Clintock River is narrow, winding and silty with thick brush along shoreline. However, it is a good river for boat trips, especially in late fall.

DC 864.3 (1437 km) **F 623.7** (1003.7 km) Bridge over Kettley's Canyon.

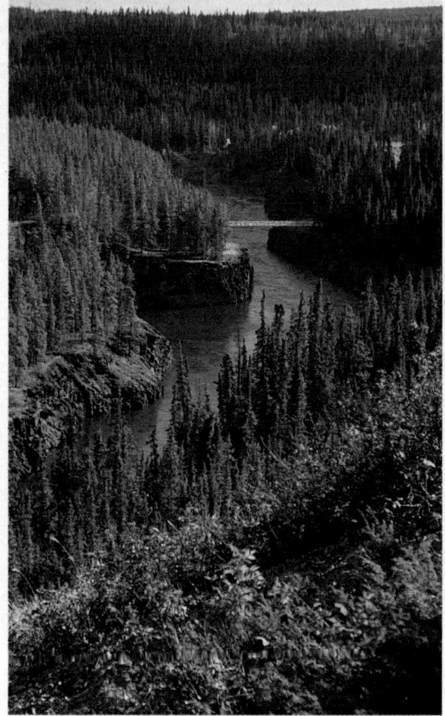

Turn off at Milepost DC 881.7 for this scenic view of Miles Canyon.
(© Carmen Scott)

DC 867.3 (1441.8 km) **F 620.7** (998.9 km) **Historic Milepost 897.** Yukon River bridge. Turnout to north for day-use area and boat launch on **Yukon River** at Marsh Lake bridge near Northern Canada Power Commission (NCPC) control gate. Point of interest sign and litter barrels. From here (elev. 2,150 feet/645m) the Yukon River flows 1,980 miles/3,186 km to the Bering Sea. Good fishing for grayling, jackfish and some trout.

DC 873.5 (1453.3 km) **F 614.5** (988.9 km) **Historical Mile 904.** Sourdough Country Campsite to east. ▲

Sourdough Country Campsite. See display ad this section. ▲

DC 874.4 (1455 km) **F 613.6** (987.5 km) **Historical Mile 905. Junction** with Klondike Highway 2 (Carcross Road) which leads south to Carcross and Skagway. (See KLONDIKE HIGHWAY 2 section.) Restaurant, convenience store, gas, diesel, propane, car repair and rock shop here.

Carcross Corner Services. See display ad this section.

Yukon Rock Shop. See display ad this section.

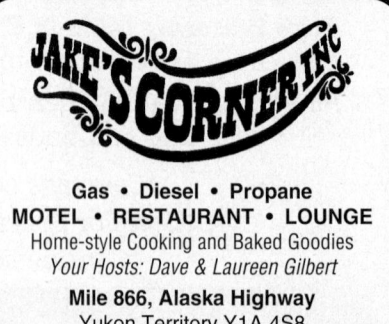

DC 874.6 (1455.3 km) **F 613.4** (987.1 km) Whitehorse city limits. Incorporated June 1, 1950, Whitehorse expanded in 1974 from its original 2.7 square miles/6.9 square kilometres to 162 square miles/421 square kilometres.

DC 875.6 (1456.9 km) **F 612.4** (985.5 km) Kara Speedway to west.

DC 875.9 (1457.4 km) **F 612.1** (985 km) Cowley Creek.

DC 876.8 (1459 km) **F 611.2** (983.6 km) **Historical Mile 906.** Wolf Creek Yukon government campground to east. An 0.8-mile/1.3-km gravel loop road leads through this campground: 49 sites, most level, some pull-through; kitchen shelters, water pumps, picnic tables, firepits, firewood, outhouses, litter barrels, playground. Wolf Creek self-guiding trail; varied and abundant plant life, views of and access to Yukon River. Camping fee $8. Fishing in **Wolf Creek** for grayling. ▲

DC 879.4 (1463 km) **F 608.6** (979.4 km) Highway crosses abandoned railroad tracks of the White Pass & Yukon Route (WP&YR) narrow-gauge railroad. Construction of the WP&YR began in May 1898 at the height of the Klondike gold rush. Completion of the railway in 1900 linked the port of Skagway, AK, with Whitehorse, YT, providing passenger and freight service for thousands of gold seekers. The WP&YR ceased operation in 1982, but started limited service again in 1988 between Skagway and Fraser. See the WHITE PASS & YUKON ROUTE section for more information and current schedule.)

DC 879.6 (1463.3 km) **F 608.4** (979.1 km) Point of interest sign about 135th meridian to east; small turnout. Gas station.

DC 879.8 (1463.7 km) **F 608.2** (978.8 km) **Historic Milepost 910.** Historic sign reads: "McCrae originated in 1900 as a flag stop on the newly-constructed White Pass & Yukon Railway. During WWII, this area served as a major service and supply depot, a major construction camp and a recreation centre." McCrae truck stop to east.

DC 880.4 (1464.5 km) **F 607.6** (977.8 km) Turnoff to west for Whitehorse Copper Mines (closed). Road to east leads to Yukon River.

DC 881 (1465.5 km) **F 607** (976.8 km) **Historic Milepost 911.** Site of Utah Construction Co. Camp. Pioneer RV Park, store and self-serve gas to east. ▲

Pioneer R.V. Park. See display ad this section. ▲

DC 881.3 (1466 km) **F 606.7** (976.4 km) White Pass & Yukon Route's Utah siding to east. This was also the site of an Army camp where thousands of soldiers were stationed during construction of the Alaska Highway.

DC 881.7 (1466.6 km) **F 606.3** (975.7 km) Sharp turnoff to east (watch for camera viewpoint sign) to see Miles Canyon. Drive down side road 0.3 mile/0.5 km to fork. The right fork leads to Miles Canyon parking lot. From the parking area it is a short walk to the Miles Canyon bridge; good photo spot. Cross bridge for easy hiking trails overlooking Yukon River. A 1.1-mile/1.7-km hiking trail from the bridge leads to the historic site of **CANYON CITY**, a gold rush settlement that existed from 1897 to 1900 as a portage point around Miles Canyon and Whitehorse Rapids. Two tramways, each several miles long, transported goods along the east and west sides of the river. Completion of the White Pass & Yukon Route in 1900 made the trams obsolete, and the settlement was abandoned. Canyon City is currently undergoing archaeological excavation. Interepreter on site weekdays in July and part of August. No restrooms or litter barrels available at site; plan accordingly.

The left fork on this side road leads to Schwatka Lake Road, which follows the lake and intersects the South Access Road into Whitehorse. Turnouts along road overlook Miles Canyon.

DC 881.9 (1466.9 km) **F 606.1** (975.4 km) Riding stable with daily trail rides in summer.

DC 882.6 (1468 km) **F 605.4** (974.3 km) **Historical Mile 912.** RV service and supply.

Philmar RV Service and Supply. See display ad this section.

DC 882.9 (1468.5 km) **F 605.1** (973.8 km) **Mountain Ridge Motel & R.V. Park.** See display ad this section. ▲

DC 883.2 (1468.9 km) **F 604.8** (973.3 km) **Historical Mile 913.** Gas, diesel and mini-mart.

Whitehorse Shell. See display ad this section. ▲

DC 883.7 (1469.7 km) **F 604.3** (972.5 km) Turnout to east with litter barrel, outhouses and information sign.

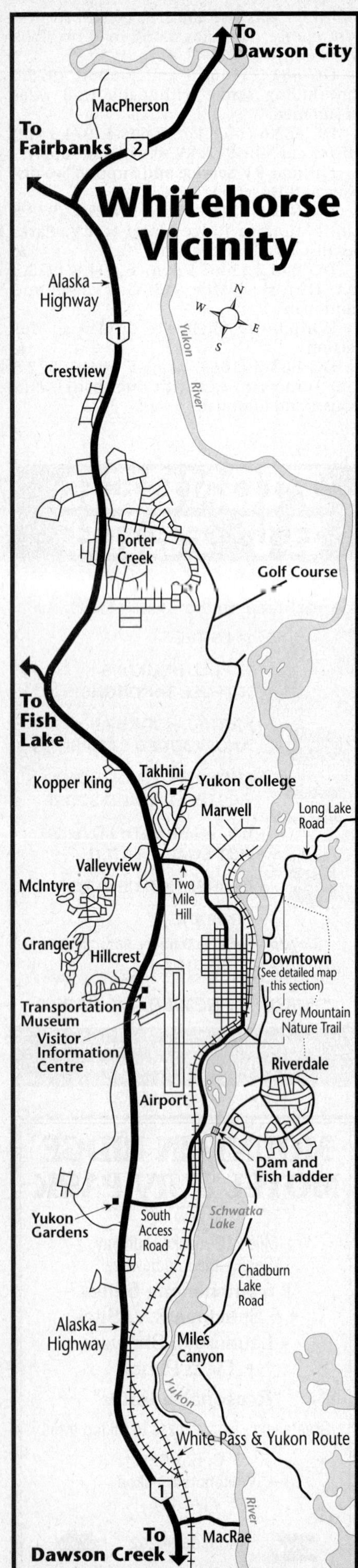

Douglas DC-3 in front of Whitehorse airport is the world's largest weathervane.
(© Beth Davidow)

DC 884 (1470.2 km) **F 604** (972 km) **Hi-Country R.V. Park.** Good Sam. New facilities to serve the traveler. Large wooded sites, electric and water hookups, dump station, hot showers. Picnic tables and firepits, gift shop with wildlife display. Propane. Conveniently located on the highway at the south access to Whitehorse, next to beautiful Yukon Gardens. Toll-free reservations: from Alaska, 1-800-764-7604; from Yukon, Alberta, British Columbia and Northwest Territories, 1-800-661-0539. [ADVERTISEMENT] ▲

DC 884 (1470.2 km) **F 604** (972 km) First exit northbound for Whitehorse. Exit east for South Access Road to Whitehorse via 4th Avenue and 2nd Avenue. At the turnoff is Yukon Gardens botanical exhibit. At Mile 1.4/2.3 km on this access road is the side road to Miles Canyon and Schwatka Lake; at Mile 1.6/2.6 km is Robert Service Campground (tent camping only) with a picnic area for day use; at Mile 2.6/4.2 km is the SS *Klondike* National Historic Site, turn left for downtown Whitehorse. ▲

DC 884.5 (1471.1 km) **F 603.5** (971.2 km) Government weigh scale and vehicle inspection station to west.

DC 885.7 (1472.9 km) **F 602.3** (969.3 km) Yukon Visitors Reception Centre, open mid-May to mid-September, 8 A.M. to 8 P.M. daily; phone (403) 667-2915. Wheelchair accessible, pets welcome. Preview Yukon attractions on laser disc player. Enjoy an outstanding multi-image slide presentation on Yukon National Parks and historic sites. Radio CKYN "Yukon Gold," 96.1-FM, broadcasts from the centre. Get your Yukon Gold Explorer's Passport stamped here. If you don't have an Explorer's Passport, you can get one at visitor reception centres and at most museums in the Yukon. (A new visitor center, scheduled to open in 1997, is under construction in downtown Whitehorse near the Yukon Government Building.) ♿

DC 885.8 (1473.1 km) **F 602.2** (969.1 km) Yukon Transportation Museum features exhibits on all forms of transportation in the North (see Attractions in the WHITEHORSE section for more details). A mural on the front of the museum depicts the methods of transportation used in construction of the Alaska Highway in 1942. The 16-by-60-foot/5-by-8-m mural was painted by members of the Yukon Art Society. Open mid-May to mid-Sept. Admission fee. (Get your Yukon Gold Explorer's Passport stamped here.)

Cairns in front of the museum commemorate 18 years of service on the Alaska Highway (1946–64) by the Corps of Royal Canadian Engineers. Near this site, the U.S. Army officially handed over the Alaska Highway to the Canadian Army on April 1, 1946.

The Yukon Transportation Museum. See display ad this section.

DC 886.2 (1473.8 km) **F 601.8** (968.5 km) Turnoff to east for Whitehorse International Airport. Built for and used by both U.S. and Canadian forces during WWII. Watch for the DC-3 weathervane (see Attractions in the WHITEHORSE section for details).

DC 887.4 (1475.6 km) **F 600.6** (966.5 km) Second (and last) exit northbound for Whitehorse. North access road to Whitehorse (exit east) is via Two-Mile Hill and 4th Avenue. Access to private RV park. At Mile 1.2/1.9 km on this access road is Qwanlin Mall.

Alaska Highway log continues on page 143. Description of Whitehorse follows.

Whitehorse

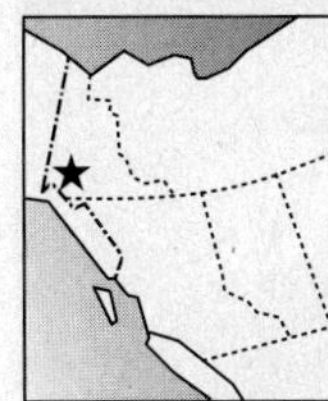

Historic Milepost 918. Located on the upper reaches of the Yukon River in Canada's subarctic at latitude 61°N. Whitehorse is 100 miles/160 km from Haines Junction; 109 miles/175 km from Skagway, AK; 250 miles/241 km from Haines, AK; and 396 miles/637 km from Tok, AK. **Population:** 22,911. **Emergency Services: RCMP, Fire Department, Ambulance, Hospital,** phone 911.

Visitor Information: Tourism Yukon's Visitor Reception Centre is located on the Alaska Highway at **Milepost DC 885.7**, adjacent the Transportation Museum. An excellent multi-image slide presentation on Yukon National Parks and historical sites is presented at the Centre, and Yukon attractions can be previewed on a laser disc player. Radio CKYN "Yukon Gold," 96.1-FM, is broadcast from the centre. The centre is open from mid-May to mid-September; phone (403) 667-2915. You may also pick up a Yukon Gold Explorer's Passport at the Centre and get it stamped at various sites in Whitehorse and throughout the Yukon. For additional visitor information contact the Whitehorse Chamber of Commerce, Suite 101, 302 Steele St., Whitehorse, YT Y1A 2C5, phone (403) 667-7545. The chamber is open year-round 9 A.M. to 5 P.M. weekdays, extended hours in summer. Free information is also available from the territorial government by writing Tourism Yukon, Box 2703, Whitehorse, YT Y1A 2C6. Canadian government topographic maps are available at Jim's Toy and Gift on Main Street. Parks Canada is located in the Federal Bldg. at 4th and Main; phone (403) 668-2116. The Parks office has information on hiking the Chilkoot Trail.

Elevation: 2,305 feet/703m. **Climate:** Wide variations are the theme here with no two winters alike. The lowest recorded temperature is -62°F/-52°C and the warmest 94°F/35°C. Mean temperature for month of January is -6°F/-21°C and for July 57°F/14°C. Annual precipitation is 10.3 inches, equal parts snow and rain. On June 21 Whitehorse enjoys 19 hours, 11 minutes of daylight and on Dec. 21 only 5 hours, 37 minutes. **Radio:** CFWH 570, CBC network with repeaters throughout territory; CBC Montreal; CKRW 610, local; CKYN-FM 96.1, summer visitor information station, "Yukon Gold," broad-

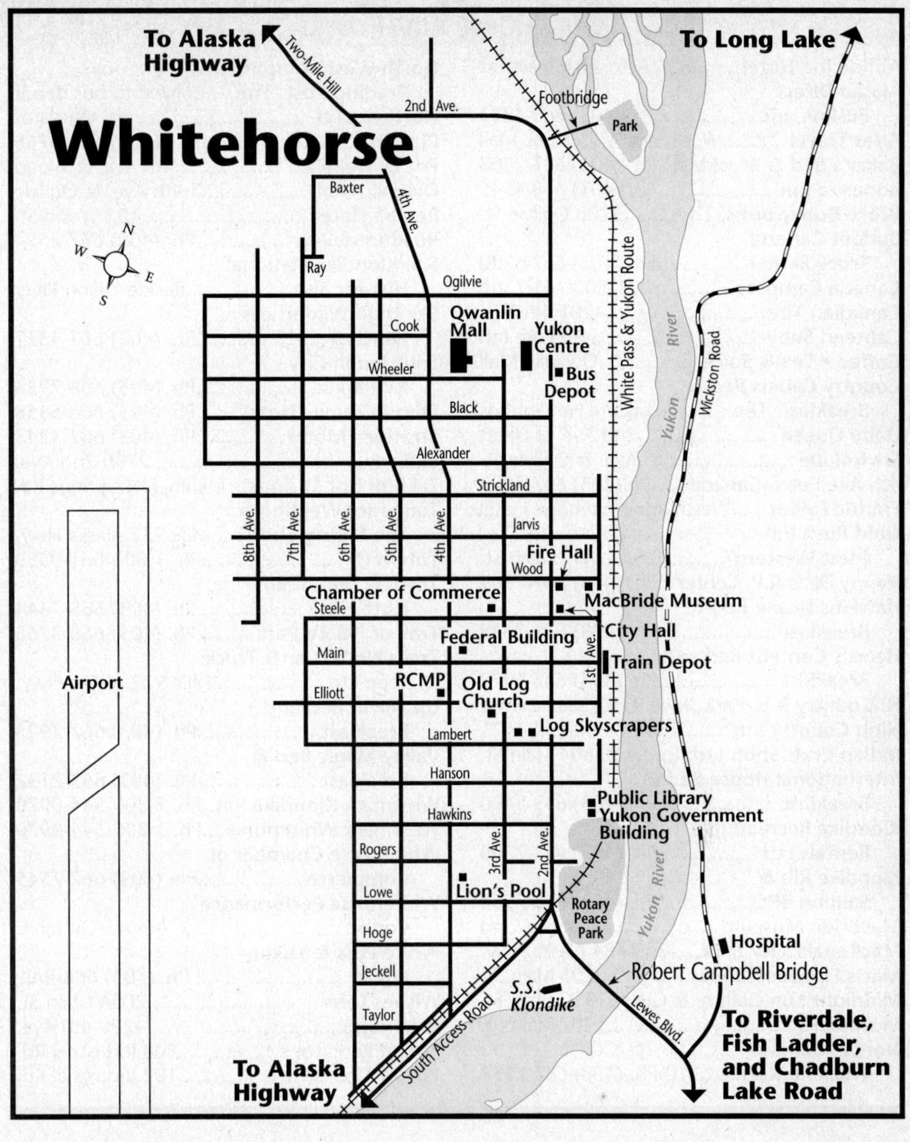

WHITEHORSE ADVERTISERS

Airline Inn Hotel ....Across from airport
Alaska Direct Busline, Inc. ....Ph. (403) 668-4833
Atlas Travel ....Westmark Whitehorse Mall
Baker's Bed & Breakfast ..Ph. (403) 633-2308
Bonanza Inn ....Ph. (403) 668-4545
Broke Bookworms, The.........210B Ogilvie St.
Budget Car and Truck Rental ....Ph. (403) 667-6200
Canada Campers ....Ph. 1-800-461-7368
Canadian Tire..........................4201 4th Ave.
Canteen Show.........................Gold Rush Inn
Coffee • Tea & Spice ....Qwanlin Mall
Country Cabins Bed & Breakfast, The............Takhini Hot Springs
Dairy Queen.......................2nd Ave. at Elliott
Envirolube ....5th Ave. & Ogilvie St.
4th Ave Petro-Canada ......Ph.(403) 667-4003
Frantic Follies......Westmark Whitehorse Hotel
Gold Rush Inn (Best Western).....................411 Main St.
Happy Daze R.V. Center...Ph. (403) 667-7069
Hawkins House Bed & Breakfast ....Ph. (403) 668-7638
Heart's Content Bed and Breakfast ....Ph. (403) 667-4972
Hi-Country R.V. Park..Mile 913.4 Alaska Hwy.
High Country Inn ....Ph. 1 800 554-4471
Indian Craft Shop Ltd. ....504 Main St.
International House Bed & Breakfast ....Ph. (403) 633-5490
Klondike Recreational Rentals Ltd. ....Ph. (403) 668-2200
Klondike Rib & Salmon BBQ ....Ph. (403) 667-7554
MacBride Museum ....1st & Wood
MacKenzie's RV Park....Km 1484 Alaska Hwy.
Mac's Fireweed Books..................203 Main St.
Midnight Sun Gallery & Gifts..205C Main St.
Murdoch's.................................207 Main St.
Norcan Car and Truck Rentals............Ph. (403) 668-2137
North West Company Trading Post, The.........Next to bus depot
NorthwesTel ....Ph. Operator
Pizza Hut ....Ph. (403) 667-6766
Pot O' Gold ....4th Ave. & Wood
Qwanlin Mall ....4th Ave. & Ogilvie
Regina Hotel...........................102 Wood St.
Roadhouse Inn ....Ph. (403) 667-2594
S.S. Klondike National Historic Site.................Beside Yukon River
Sky High Wilderness Ranches ....Ph. (403) 667-4321
Sourdough City RV Park......................Ph. (403) 668-7938
Stop In Family Hotel........Ph. (403) 668-5558
Stratford Motel ....Ph. (403) 667-4243
Subway.......................................2190 2nd Ave.
Takhini Hot Springs...Takhini Hot Springs Rd.
Tamarack Welding & The Spring Shop......Mile 922 Alaska Hwy.
Totem Oil.......................Ph. 1-800-661-0550
Town & Mountain Hotel, The ....Ph. (403) 668-7644
Trail of '98 RV Park..........Ph. (403) 668-3768
Trails North Car & Truck Stop Ltd. ....Mile 922 Alaska Hwy.
Up North Bed and Breakfast ....Ph. (403) 667-7905
Valley Magic Bed & Breakfast ....Ph. (403) 667-2132
Westmark Klondike Inn..Ph. 1-800-544-0970
Westmark Whitehorse....Ph. 1-800-544-0970
Whitehorse Chamber of Commerce................Ph. (403) 667-7545
Whitehorse Performance Centre ....4th Ave. at Jarvis
White Pass & Yukon Route ....Ph. (403) 668-RAIL
Wishes Gifts ....206A Main St.
Yukon Inn...............................4220 4th Ave.
Yukon Radiator..................108 Industrial Rd.
Yukon Tire Centre ....107 Industrial Rd.

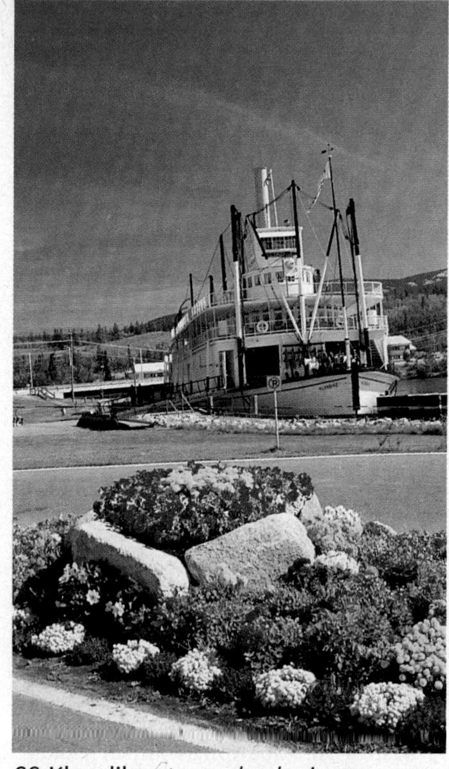

SS Klondike *stern-wheeler is a Whitehorse landmark.* (Earl L. Brown, staff)

casts mid-May to mid-September; CHON-FM 98.1. **Television:** CBC–TV live, colour via ANIK satellite, Canadian network; WHTV, NADR (First Nation issues), local cable; CanCom stations via satellite, many channels. **Newspapers:** *Whitehorse Star* (weekdays); *Yukon News* (twice-weekly).

Private Aircraft: Whitehorse International Airport, 3 runways; has approach over city and an abrupt escarpment; elev. 2,305 feet/703m; main runway length 7,200 feet/2,195m; surfaced; fuel 80, 100, jet fuel available. Customs clearance available.

Floatplane base on Schwatka Lake above Whitehorse Dam (take the South Access Road from Alaska Highway and turn on road by the railroad tracks).

TRAILS NORTH CAR & TRUCK STOP LTD.
Located 4 miles north of Whitehorse • Mile 922 Alaska Hwy, Yukon

FULL SERVICE STATION
• Clean Fuel
• Diesel
• Propane

RESTAURANT
• Full Service
• Licensed
• Home Cooked Meals

ACCOMMODATION
• Clean
• Modern Rooms
• Reasonable rates

STORE
• Cigarettes
• Souvenirs
• Confectionary
• Film • Ice
• Fishing Licenses

PACKAGED LIQUOR TO GO
• Cold Beer & Wines
• Liquor

RV'S & CAMPERS
• Parking
• Dump Station
• RV Repair Adjacent

OPEN YEAR ROUND
Phone (403) 633-2327 • FAX (403) 633-6637

Enjoy the atmosphere of country living with the luxury of a beautifully furnished private cabin in the woods.
10 minutes to Takhini Hot Springs.
Amenities include large private cabin, use of outdoor hot tub, delicious full breakfast or fruits, muffins, breads and Yukon spreads!
Evening snacks and friendly hosts.
Shelley & Murray Williamson
Site 15 #144, Whitehorse, Yukon
Canada Y1A 5W9
Phone: (403) 667-4972

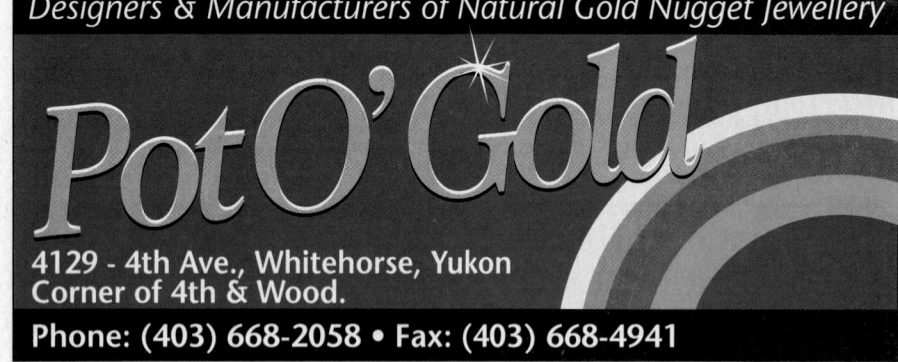

DESCRIPTION

Whitehorse has been the capital of Yukon Territory since 1953, and serves as the centre for transportation, communications and supplies for Yukon Territory and the Northwest Territories.

The downtown business section of Whitehorse lies on the west bank of the Yukon River. The Riverdale subdivision is on the east side. The low mountains rising behind Riverdale are dominated by Canyon Mountain, known locally as Grey Mountain. Wolf Creek, Hillcrest and Granger subdivisions lie south of the city; McIntyre subdivision is to the west; and Porter Creek, Takhini and Crestview subdivisions are north of the city. The Takhini area is the location of the Yukon College campus.

Downtown Whitehorse is flat and marked at its western limit by a rising escarpment dominated by the Whitehorse International Airport. Originally a woodcutter's lot, the airstrip was first cleared in 1920 to accommodate 4 U.S. Army planes on a test flight from New York to Nome. Access to the city is by Two-Mile Hill from the north and by access road from the south; both connect with the Alaska Highway.

In 1974, the city limits of Whitehorse were expanded from the original 2.7 square miles/6.9 square kilometres to 162 square miles/421 square kilometres making Whitehorse at one time the largest metropolitan area in Canada. More than two-thirds of the population of Yukon Territory live in the city. Whitehorse is the hub of a network of about 2,664 miles/4,287 km of all-weather roads serving Yukon Territory.

HISTORY, ECONOMY

When the White Pass & Yukon Route railway was completed in July 1900, connecting Skagway with the Yukon River, Whitehorse came into being as the northern terminus. Here the famed river steamers connected the railhead to Dawson City, and some of these boats made the trip all the way to St. Michael, a small outfitting point on Alaska's Bering Sea coast.

Klondike stampeders landed at Whitehorse to dry out and repack their supplies after running the famous Whitehorse Rapids. (The name Whitehorse was in common use by the late 1800s; it is believed that the first miners in the area thought that the foaming rapids resembled white horses' manes and so named the river rapids.) The

Yukon Archives Photo, #5538

rapids are no longer visible since construction of the Yukon Energy Corporation's hydroelectric dam on the river. This dam created man-made Schwatka Lake, named in honour of U.S. Army Lt. Frederick Schwatka, who named many of the points along the Yukon River during his 1883 exploration of the region.

The gold rush brought stampeders and the railroad. The community grew as a transportation centre and transshipment point for freight from the Skagway–Whitehorse railroad and the stern-wheelers plying the Yukon River to Dawson City. The river was the only highway until WWII, when military expediency built the Alaska Highway in 1942.

Whitehorse was headquarters for the western sector during construction of the Alaska Highway. Fort St. John was headquarters for the eastern sector. Both were the largest construction camps along the highway.

The first survey parties of U.S. Army engineers reached Whitehorse in April of 1942. By the end of August, they had constructed a pioneer road from Whitehorse west to White River, largely by following an existing winter trail between Whitehorse and Kluane Lake. November brought the final breakthrough on the western end of the highway, marking completion of the pioneer road.

During the height of the construction of the Alaska Highway, thousands of American military and civilian workers were employed in the Canadian North. It was the second boom period for Whitehorse.

There was an economic lull following the war, but the new highway was then opened to civilian travel, encouraging new development. Mineral exploration and the development of new mines had a profound effect on the economy of the region, as did the steady growth of tourism. The Whitehorse Copper Mine, located a few miles south of the city in the historic Whitehorse copper belt, is now closed. The Grum Mine site north of Faro produced lead, silver and zinc concentrates for Cyprus-Anvil (1969-1982) and Curragh Resources (1986-1992). It was reopened

MacBride Museum features Yukon's cultural and natural history. (Earl L. Brown, staff)

in 1994 by Anvil Range Mining Corp. (mine tours available). Gold mining activity has been taking place southwest of Whitehorse in the last few years. Stop by the Yukon Chamber of Mines office on Main Street for information on mining and rockhounding in Yukon Territory. The Chamber of Mines log building also houses a mineral display.

Because of its accessibility, Whitehorse became capital of the Yukon Territory (replacing Dawson City in that role) on March 31, 1953.

Bridges built along the highway to Dawson City, after Whitehorse became capital of the territory, were too low to accommodate the old river steamers, and by 1955 all steamers had been beached. After her last run in 1960, the SS *Keno* was berthed on the riverbank in Dawson City where she became a national historic site in 1962. The SS *Klondike* was moved through the streets of Whitehorse in 1966 to its final resting place as a riverboat museum beside the Robert Campbell bridge.

ACCOMMODATIONS/VISITOR SERVICES

Whitehorse offers 22 hotels and motels for a total of about 840 rooms. Several hotels include conference facilities; most have cocktail lounges, licensed dining rooms and taverns. Rates range from $60 to $150 for a double room with bath. Bed-and-breakfast

The Royal Canadian Mounted Police (RCMP) is the only police force in Yukon Territory. The RCMP is headquartered in Whitehorse, YT.

accommodations are also available.

The city has 31 restaurants downtown and in surrounding residential subdivisions that serve meals ranging from French cuisine to fast food; 14 have liquor licenses.

Whitehorse has a downtown shopping district stretching 6 blocks along Main Street. The Qwanlin Mall at 4th Avenue and Ogilvie has a supermarket and a variety of shops. The Yukon Centre Mall on 2nd Avenue has a liquor store. The Riverdale Mall is located on the east side of the river in the Riverdale subdivision. Another shopping mall is located in the Porter Creek subdivision north of the city on the Alaska Highway.

In addition to numerous supermarkets, garages and service stations, there are churches, movie houses, beauty salons and a covered swimming pool. Whitehorse also has several banks with automatic teller machines. (Many businesses in Whitehorse participate in the Fair Exchange Program, which guarantees an exchange rate within 4 percent of the bank rate set once a week on Mondays. Participating businesses display the Fair Exchange logo.)

NOTE: There is no central post office in Whitehorse. Postal services are available in Qwanlin Mall at Coffee, Tea & Spice; The Hougen Centre on Main Street (lower floor below Shoppers Drugs); and in Riverdale and Porter Creek subdivisions. Stamps are available at several locations. General delivery pickup at corner of 3rd Avenue and Wood Street.

Specialty stores include gold nugget and ivory shops where distinctive jewelry is manufactured, and Indian craft shops specializing in moose hide jackets, parkas, vests, moccasins, slippers, mukluks and gauntlets. Inuit and Indian handicrafts from Canada's Arctic regions are featured in some stores.

Baker's Bed & Breakfast. Make Baker's Bed & Breakfast your home away from home. Hosts are longtime residents of Yukon. Friendly, cozy home, decorated with country crafts, and located in quiet area. Enjoy large yard and fireplace. Hearty, variety breakfasts served with fresh fruit. We look forward to sharing our home with you. Phone (403) 633-2308. 84 – 11th Ave., Whitehorse, YT Y1A 4J2. [ADVERTISEMENT]

Hawkins House Bed & Breakfast. Enjoy the Yukon's most luxurious accommoda-

Main Street in downtown Whitehorse. (© Doug Wilson)

tions in our new Victorian home in downtown Whitehorse. Turn-of-the-century charm includes a grand foyer, guest parlor, high ceilings, balconies, hardwood floors, and historical and cultural themes. First-class rooms feature private bath, telephone, cable TV and VCR, bar sink and fridge, table and chairs, top quality beds, soundproofing and a great view of the downtown and surrounding mountains. Jacuzzis® and claw foot tub available. Breakfast is a feast of local and international delicacies. Enjoy a 5-minute walk to Main Street shops and restaurants, historic attractions, pool, river, 24-hour groceries, etc. Non-smoking. Open year-round. Français, Deutsch. Phone (403) 668-7638 or write 303 Hawkins St., Whitehorse, YT, Canada Y1A 1X5. [ADVERTISEMENT]

High Country Inn. During your stay in Whitehorse, relax and enjoy real northern hospitality at the High Country Inn. The Inn offers over 100 rooms with a wide choice of comfortable, affordable lodging close to downtown and major attractions. Select from economical single rooms to large, deluxe suites, complete with kitchen. Great views, elevators, guest laundry, health

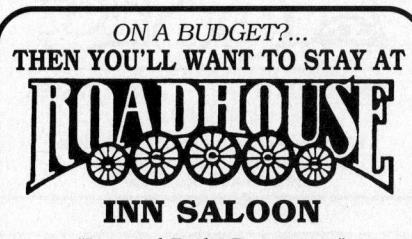

See the GENERAL INFORMATION section for details on holidays, driving regulations, money and customs requirements in Canada.

spa, senior discounts and the most delightful lobby, restaurant, outdoor deck and cocktail lounge in Whitehorse. Just good old-fashioned quality at surprisingly low prices. (Reservations recommended.) Phone (403) 667-4471, fax (403) 667-6457, 1-800-554-4471. [ADVERTISEMENT]

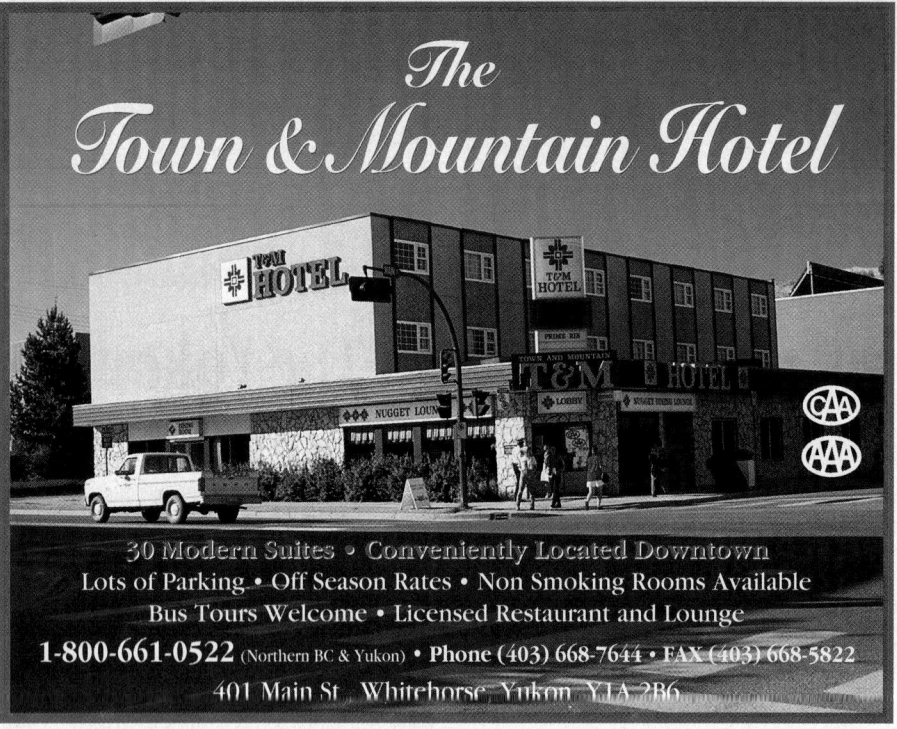

International House Bed & Breakfast. Enjoy a clean, quiet, cozy country style home of charm and hospitality. Lots of great food, full breakfast, home baked goodies at night. Quiet neighborhood, walking and x-country skiing, on bus route, 2 short blocks off Alaska Highway. Pickup available. Non-smoking. Enjoy one of the finest bed and breakfasts anywhere. Your hosts Al and Ann Dibbs. Open year-round. VISA. (403) 633-5490. Fax (403) 668-4751. [ADVERTISEMENT]

Klondike Rib & Salmon BBQ. Located in two of the oldest buildings in Whitehorse at Second and Steele, across from the Frantic Follies and Westmark Hotel. A delicious salmon BBQ, and Texas BBQ ribs, English-style fish and chips, and specialty northern food like bison burgers, caribou, musk-ox and fresh bannock. Just some of the mouth-watering fare served in a unique historic Klondike Airways Building with historical exhibits as part of the fascinating decor. (403) 667-7554. [ADVERTISEMENT]

Up North Bed and Breakfast offers you friendly, family service, a full-cooked breakfast and evening snack. We are located on the Yukon River 3 minutes from downtown. We have a full canoe rental service for Yukon's rivers and lakes. We look forward to meeting you. Phone Stenzigs (403) 667-7905 or fax (403) 667-6334. Box 5418, 86 Wickstrom Road, Whitehorse, YT Y1A 5H4. [ADVERTISEMENT]

There is a private RV park on the north access road (Two Mile Hill) and on 2nd Avenue downtown. Tent camping only is available at Robert Service Park on the South Access Road. There are 4 private campgrounds south of downtown Whitehorse on the Alaska Highway (see **Mileposts DC 873.5**, **881**, **882.9** and **883.7** in the highway log), and 1 private campground 6 miles/9.6 km north of the city on the highway (see **Milepost DC 891.9**). Wolf Creek Yukon government campground is 7 miles/11 km south of Whitehorse on the Alaska Highway. A private campground and Yukon government campground are located at Marsh Lake. Takhini Hot Springs on the Klondike Loop is also a popular camping spot (1/2-hour drive from Whitehorse). ▲

IMPORTANT: RV caravans should contact

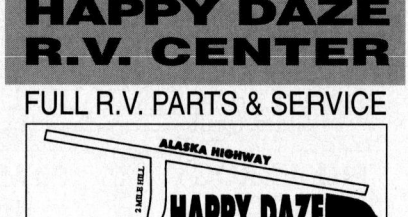

private campground operators well in advance of arrival regarding camping arrangements. At our press time, there was no designated RV parking in downtown Whitehorse.

TRANSPORTATION

Air: Service by Canadian Airlines International and Alkan Air daily to major cities and Yukon communities. Air North to Dawson City, Old Crow, Juneau and Fairbanks, AK. (Air North offers a 21-day Klondike Explorer's Pass between Juneau, Old Crow, Fairbanks, Whitehorse and Dawson City.) Whitehorse International Airport is reached from the Alaska Highway.

Seaplane dock on Schwatka Lake just above the Whitehorse Dam (take the South Access Road from Alaska Highway and turn right on road by the railroad tracks to reach the base). Flightseeing tours available.

Trans North Air offers helicopter sightseeing tours from the airport.

Bus: Greyhound service to Watson Lake, Dawson Creek, Prince George and other points in southern Canada. Norline serves Mayo and Dawson City. Alaska–Yukon Motorcoaches serves Skagway, Haines, Tok, Anchorage and Fairbanks. Alaska Direct to Anchorage, Skagway and Haines, phone 1-800-288-1305 or contact office at 4th Avenue Residence. North West Stage Lines to Haines Junction, Beaver Creek, Faro, Carmacks and Ross River. Alaska Direct Busline to Skagway, Haines, Anchorage and Fairbanks; phone (403) 668-4833.

Whitehorse Transit Commission operates bus service around city and suburbs from Qwanlin Mall.

Railroad: Arrangements for White Pass & Yukon Route rail trips may be made by phoning WP&YR in Whitehorse at (403) 668-RAIL, or contacting local travel agencies. (See WHITE PASS & YUKON ROUTE section.)

Taxi: 5 taxi companies operate in Whitehorse.

Car, Truck, Motorhome and Camper Rentals: Several local and national agencies are located in Whitehorse.

ATTRACTIONS

The SS *Klondike* National Historic Site is hard to miss. This grand old stern-wheeler sits beside the Yukon River near the Robert Campbell bridge. After carrying cargo and

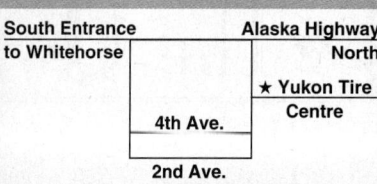

passengers between Whitehorse and Dawson City from 1937 until the 1950s, the SS *Klondike* went into permanent retirement on the bank of the Yukon River, donated to the people of Canada by White Pass & Yukon Route. Refurbished by Parks Canada, the stern-wheeler is open to the public. Built by British Yukon Navigation Co., the SS *Klondike* is 210 feet/64m long and 41.9 feet/12.5m wide. Visitor information centre, gift shop and public parking at the site. A film on the history of riverboats is shown continuously in a tent theatre adjacent the boat. Tours of the stern-wheeler leave on the half hour. The 20-minute film is shown prior to each tour. Admission fee charged. Large groups are advised to book tours in advance. Contact Canadian Identity, 300 Main St., Room 105, Whitehorse, YT Y1A 2B5; phone (403) 667-3970, fax (403) 668-3769. The SS *Klondike* visitor centre and stern-wheeler are open from mid-May to mid-Sept.

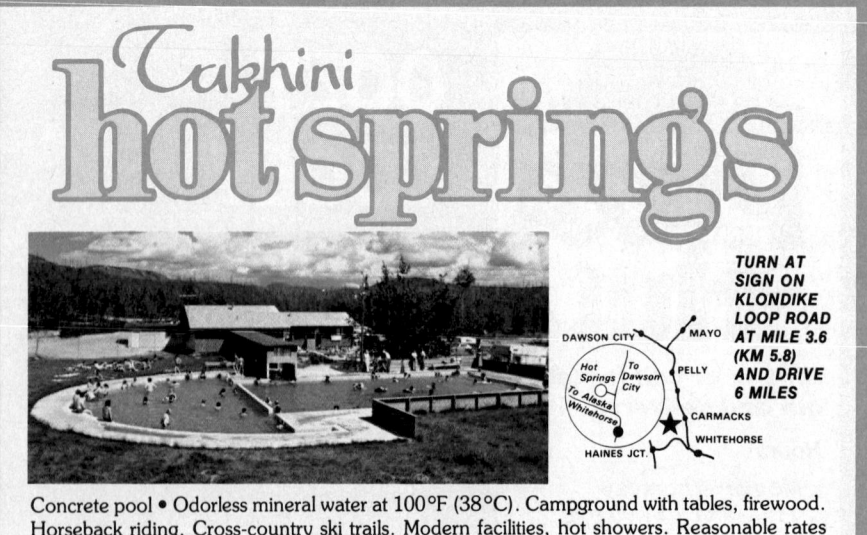

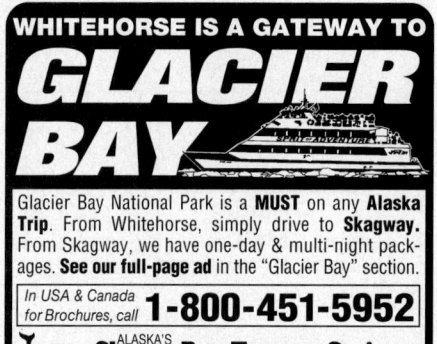

Live Shows. Frantic Follies, a very popular vaudeville stage show, is held nightly June through mid-Sept, at the Westmark Whitehorse Hotel. 1997 marks the 27th season for this 1½-hour show which features entertainers, a high-kicking chorus line, rousing music, hilarious skits from Robert W. Service ballads and plenty of laughs for the whole family. Visitors are advised to get tickets in advance. Tickets are available at the box office in the Westmark or contact phone (403) 668-2042, fax 633-4363.

The Canteen Show, held at the Gold Rush Inn, is a light-hearted revue of 1940s Whitehorse and the construction of the Alaska Highway. Tickets at the box office at the Gold Rush Inn; phone (403) 668-4500, fax 668-7432.

Special Events. A major attraction in winter is the Sourdough Rendezvous, held the last week in February. During this annual event local citizens wear the garb of trappers, miners and saloon hall girls, and menus feature moose stew and sourdough pancakes. Among the many activities are sled dog races, a beard-judging contest and a flour-packing competition.

Whitehorse is also the start and/or finish of the annual Yukon Quest Sled Dog Race in February. This 1,000-mile race between Whitehorse and Fairbanks, AK, takes mushers from 10 to 14 days. The race alternates starting points each year between the 2 cities.

Tour boat cruises the Yukon River to Miles Canyon. (Earl L. Brown, staff)

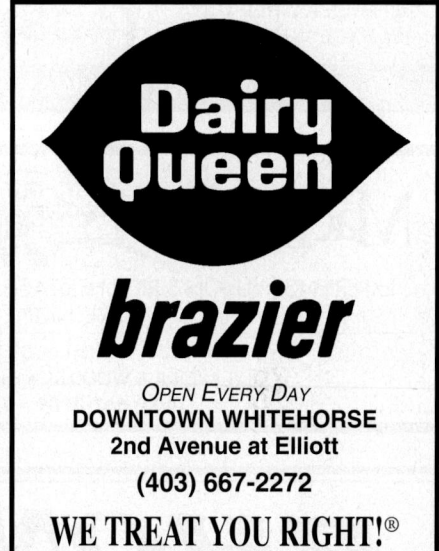

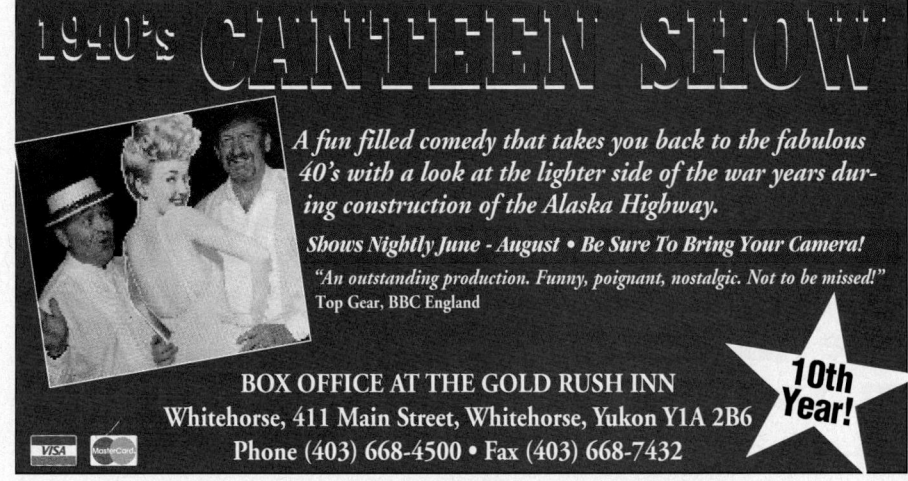

A grueling race for humans is the 110-mile Klondike Trail of '98 International Road Relay between Skagway, AK, and Whitehorse, held in Sept. Teams of 6 to 10 runners run 10 legs of varying lengths along Klondike Highway 2.

Take a hike with the Yukon Conservation Society (YCS). Every summer the society offers free guided nature walks, ranging in difficulty from easy to strenuous, from July to late August. Trips are 1 to 6 hours in length and informative guides explain the local flora, fauna, geology and history along the trails. The YCS conducts interpretive walks at Canyon City (see **Milepost DC 881.7**) during the summer on a regular basis, including evenings and weekends. For a schedule of hikes, contact the Yukon Conservation Society, at 302 Hawkins St.; phone (403) 668-5678.

World's largest weathervane. Located in front of the Whitehorse International Airport is the world's largest weathervane—a Douglas DC-3. This vintage plane (registration number CF-CPY) flew for several Yukon airlines from 1946 until 1970, when it blew an engine during takeoff. The plane was restored by Joe Muff with the help of the Yukon Flying Club and the Whitehorse community. It is now owned and managed by the Yukon Transportation Museum. The restored plane was mounted on a rotating pedestal in 1981 and now acts as a weather-vane, pointing its nose into the wind.

The Yukon Transportation Museum, located on the Alaska Highway adjacent to the Whitehorse Airport (see **Milepost DC 885.8**), features exhibits on all forms of transportation in the North. Housed in a former RCAF recreation centre, the outside front of the building is covered by an enormous mural depicting methods of transportation used in construction of the Alaska Highway in 1942: a Fairchild '71, P-40s, boats and pack horses. Working from archival photos, the project took almost 2,000 hours to complete and involved 9 artists from the Yukon Art Society. Displays inside include the full-size replica of the *Queen of the Yukon* Ryan monoplane, sister ship to Lindbergh's *Spirit of St. Louis;* railway rolling stock; Alaska Highway vintage vehicles, dogsleds and stagecoaches. Also featured are the Chilkoot Trail, the Canol Highway and bush pilots of the North. The museum includes video theatres and a gift shop. Plenty of parking. Admission charged. Open daily, 9 A.M. to 6 P.M., mid-May to mid-Sept. Write P.O. Box 5867, Whitehorse, YT Y1A 5L6 or phone (403) 668-4792, fax 633-5547.

Historical walking tours of Whitehorse are conducted by the Yukon Historical & Museums Assoc. These walks take in the city's heritage buildings. Meet at the Donnenworth House, 3126 3rd Ave.; phone 667-4704. Fee charged. There are tours daily from July to the end of August. For self-guided tours, *A Walking Tour of Yukon's Capital* is available from local stores or from the Yukon Historical & Museums Assoc., Box 4357, Whitehorse, YT Y1A 3T5.

MacBride Museum, on 1st Avenue between Steele and Wood streets, showcases Yukon's cultural and natural history in 4 indoor galleries and outdoor displays. The

Yukon wildlife exhibit includes bears, wolverine, caribou, Dall sheep and bowhead whale. A photo exhibit features Yukon personalities and the history of Whitehorse. New exhibits cover the 100-year history of the Mounted Police in Yukon and feature the only public collection of gold in the Yukon. Outside the museum is Sam McGee's real cabin, an old telegraph office and White Pass steam engine and stage coaches. The Museum Shop features books, local carts and crafts and northern souvenirs. Admission charged. Open daily late-May to Labour Day. Phone (403) 667-2709, fax 633-6607 or write Box 4037, Whitehorse, YT Y1A 3S9. ♿

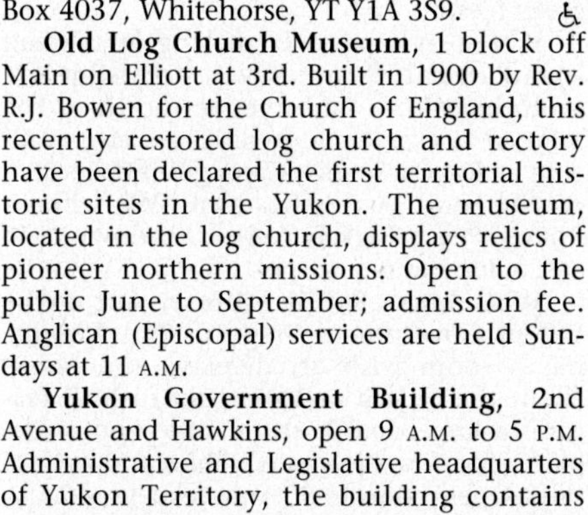

Old Log Church Museum, 1 block off Main on Elliott at 3rd. Built in 1900 by Rev. R.J. Bowen for the Church of England, this recently restored log church and rectory have been declared the first territorial historic sites in the Yukon. The museum, located in the log church, displays relics of pioneer northern missions. Open to the public June to September; admission fee. Anglican (Episcopal) services are held Sundays at 11 A.M.

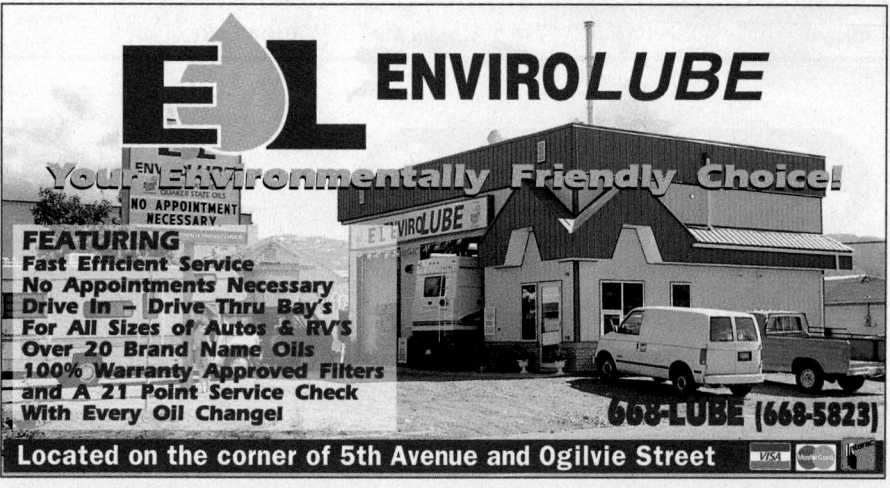

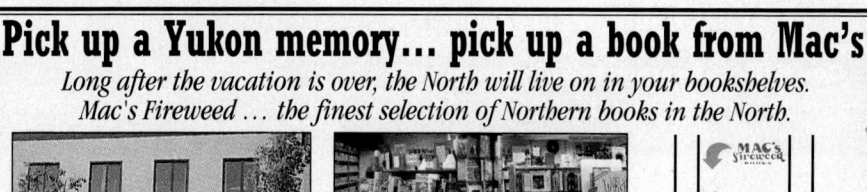

Yukon Government Building, 2nd Avenue and Hawkins, open 9 A.M. to 5 P.M. Administrative and Legislative headquarters of Yukon Territory, the building contains some notable artworks. On the main floor mall is an acrylic resin mural, 120 feet/37m long, which portrays the historical evolution of the Yukon. The 24 panels, each measuring 4 by 5 feet/1.2 by 1.5m, highlight events such as the arrival of Sir John Franklin at Herschel Island in 1825, the Klondike gold rush, and the coming of the automobile. The mural was created by Vancouver, BC, artist David MacLagen.

In the Legislative Chamber, an 18-by-12-foot/5-by-4m tapestry is an abstraction of the fireweed plant, Yukon's floral emblem. The Yukon Women's Tapestry, 5 panels each 7-by-13-feet/2-by-4m, hangs in the legislative library lounge. The wool panels portray the role of women in the development of the territory, depicting the 5 seasons of the North; spring, summer, autumn, winter and "survival," the cold gray season between winter and spring and fall and winter. Begun by the Whitehorse Branch of the Canadian Federation of Business and Professional Women in 1976 to mark International Women's Year, the wall hangings were stitched by some 2,500 Yukoners.

Yukon Gardens, located at the junction of the Alaska Highway and South Access Road, is the only formal northern botanical garden. The 22-acre site features more than 100,000 wild and domestic flowers; vegetables, herbs and fruits; scenic pathways and floral displays; a children's "Old MacDonald's farm"; gift shop; and fresh produce in summer. Open daily in summer. Admission charged.

Whitehorse Rapids Fishway. The fish ladder was built in 1959 to provide access for chinook (king) salmon and other species above the Yukon Energy Corporation hydroelectric dam. Displays installed and viewing area improved in 1992. Located at the end of Nisutlin Drive in the Riverdale suburb. Open daily, 9 A.M. to 5 P.M. from May 25 to July 1, 8 A.M. to 10 P.M. from July to September. Interpretive displays and viewing decks.

Mountain View Public Golf Course, located in Porter Creek subdivision on the Yukon River, is accessible via the Porter Creek exit off the Alaska Highway or from Range Road. Eighteen holes, grass greens; green fees.

Picnic in a park. Picnicking on a small island in the Yukon River, accessible via footbridge from 2nd Avenue, north of the railroad tracks. Picnic facilities are also available at Robert Service Campground, located on the South Access Road into Whitehorse. Rotary Peace Park is central to downtown and a popular picnic spot.

Whitehorse Public Library, part of the Yukon Government Bldg. on 2nd Avenue, has a room with art displays and books about the Yukon and the gold rush. It features a large double stone and copper fireplace, comfortable chairs, tables and helpful staff. Open noon to 9 P.M. weekdays, 10 A.M. to 6 P.M. Saturday, 1-9 P.M. Sunday and closed holidays.

Yukon Archives is located adjacent Yukon College at Yukon Place. The archives was established in 1972 to acquire, preserve and make available the documented history of the Yukon. The holdings, dating from 1845, include government records, private manuscripts, corporate records, photographs, maps, newspapers (most are on microfilm), sound recordings, university theses, books, pamphlets and periodicals. Visitors are welcome. Phone (403) 667-5321 for hours, or write Box 2703, Whitehorse, YT Y1A 2C6, for more information.

Boat Tours. The MV *Youcon Kat,* docked across from the MacBride Museum, offers

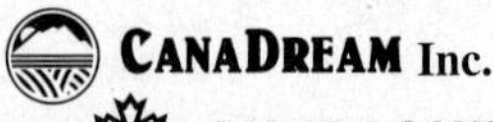

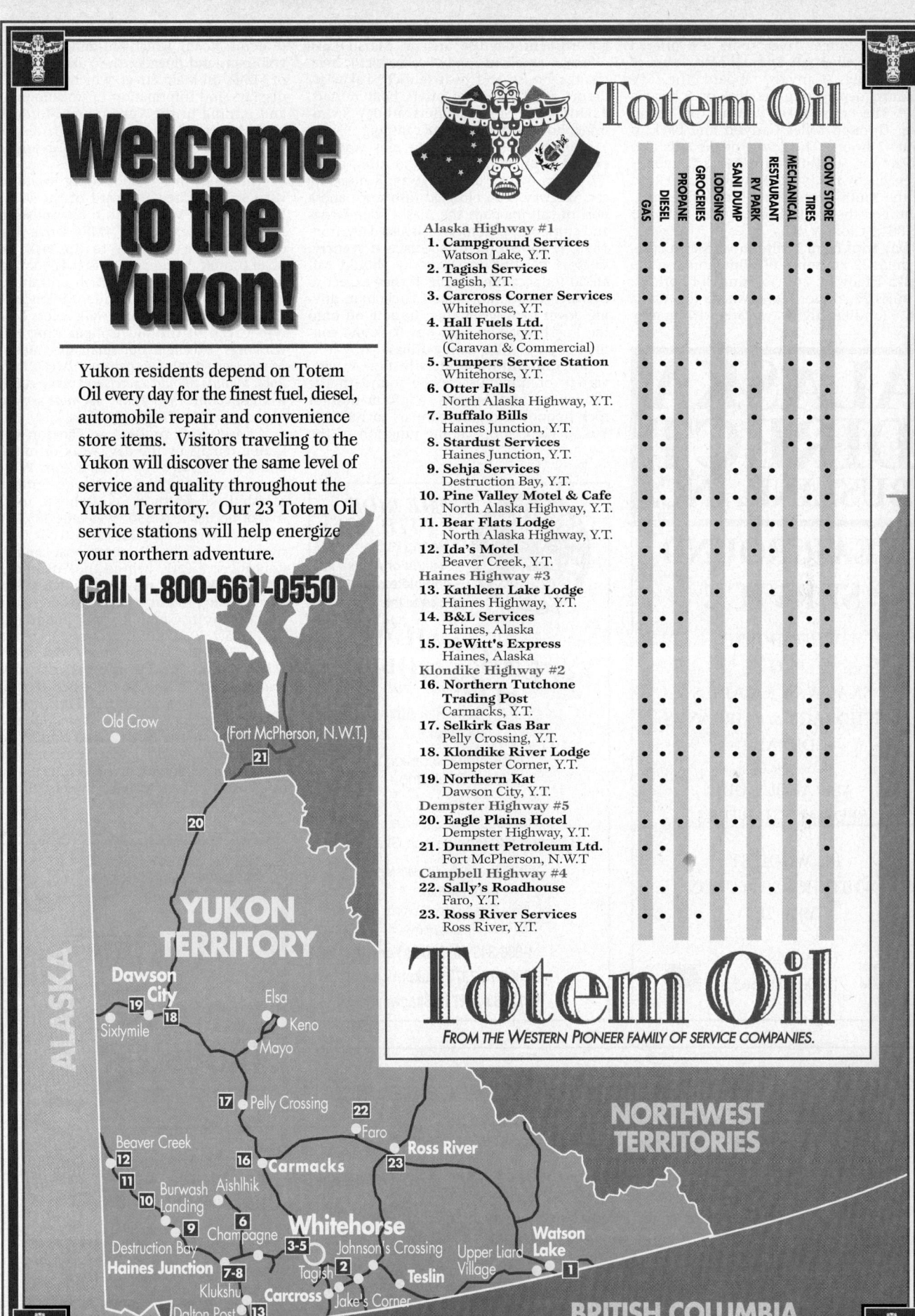

2½-hour trips down the Yukon River. 4-hour and longer river tours are offered aboard the river raft *Emerald Mae*. Tours of scenic Miles Canyon, aboard the MV *Schwatka,* depart from the dock on Schwatka Lake. The cruise takes you up the Yukon River through Miles Canyon and back in about 2 hours. The *Queen of the Mile* also operates on Schwatka Lake. Miles Canyon is accessible by road: take Schwatka Lake Road off the South Access Road into Whitehorse, or turn off the Alaska Highway (see **Milepost DC 881.7**); follow signs.

Day trips from Whitehorse. Marsh Lake, 24 miles/39 km south of Whitehorse on the Alaska Highway, and Takhini Hot Springs, 17 miles/27 km north of town via the Alaska and Klondike highways, are within easy driving distance of Whitehorse. The Yukon government day-use area at Marsh Lake offers an excellent sandy beach, picnic area, change house and boat launch. Lakeview Resort at Marsh Lake offers boat rentals. Takhini Hot Springs offers all-day swimming, horseback riding and camping.

Longer trips (which you may want to extend to an overnight) are to Atlin, about 2½ hours by car, and Skagway, 3 hours by car. Skagway is an old gold rush town and a port of call for both the Alaska state ferries and cruise ships. Atlin, which also dates from 1898, is known for its spectacular scenery. Visitors heading for Skagway should call ahead for accommodations if they expect to overnight. You may make a circle tour, driving down to Skagway then turning off onto the Tagish Road on your way back and continuing on to Atlin via the Atlin Road.

Rockhounding and Mining. A wide variety of minerals can be found in the Whitehorse area. Sources of information for rock hounds and gold panners include the Yukon Rock Shop, at the junction of the Alaska Highway and Klondike Highway 2 (Carcross Road), which has mineral samples, gold pans and nuggets; the Yukon Chamber of Mines on Main Street, which has mineral displays and information on rockhounding and mining in the Yukon; and Murdoch's gem shop on Main Street, which displays gold nugget jewellery and gold rush artifacts and photos.

The following rockhounding location is suggested by Fred Dorward of the Whitehorse Gem & Mineral Club (26 Sunset Dr. N., Whitehorse, YT Y1A 4M8). Drive north on the Alaska Highway to the Fish Lake Road turnoff (**Milepost DC 889.4**), located 2 miles/3.2 km from the north entrance to Whitehorse. About 0.5 mile/0.8 km in on Fish Lake Road, park and walk across McIntyre Creek to the old Copper King mine workings. Excellent but small specimens of brown garnet, also serpentine. *IMPORTANT: Rock hounds should exercise extreme caution when exploring. Do not enter old mine workings. Please respect No Trespassing signs.*

Canoe, Raft or Boat to Dawson City. Canoe rentals by the day, week or month, and guide services are available in Whitehorse. From the Yukon River's outlet at Marsh Lake south of Whitehorse to the Alaska border it is 530 river miles/853 km; from Whitehorse to Dawson City it is 410 river miles/660 km. There is a boat launch at Rotary Peace Park, behind the Yukon Government Bldg. You may also launch at Deep Creek Campground on Lake Laberge. Contact Up North Canoe Rentals, phone (403) 667-7905.

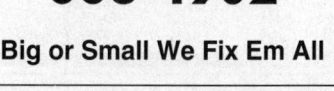

NOTE: Before leaving on any river or other wilderness trip, for your own protection, report your plans and itinerary to the RCMP. Be guided by the advice in government publications regarding travel on the Yukon's rivers and lakes. Do not attempt the Five Finger Rapids on the Yukon River without qualified advice. For more information on wilderness travel, contact Tourism Yukon office, located between 2nd and

3rd on Hawkins; phone (403) 667-5340. Hikers planning to do the Chilkoot Trail should check with Parks Canada, in the Federal Bldg. at 4th and Main; phone (403) 668-2116.

Mount McIntyre Recreation Centre, 0.9 mile/1.5 km west of the Alaska Highway (see **Milepost DC 887.6**), has 70 kilometres of groomed cross-country ski trails (open for hiking, running and mountain biking in summer). Contact Whitehorse Cross-Country Ski Club, P.O. Box 4639, Whitehorse, YT Y1A 3Y7.

Sportsmen can obtain complete information on fishing and hunting in the Whitehorse area by writing Tourism Yukon, Box 2703, Whitehorse, YT Y1A 2C6. They will provide lists of guides and advise what licenses are required.

AREA FISHING: Fish for rainbow and coho salmon in the following lakes: **Hidden, Scout, Long, Jackson** and **McLean.** Inquire locally for directions. Nearby fly-in fishing lakes are accessible by charter plane; see advertisements in this section. **Yukon River,** fish for grayling below the dam and bridge. Fishing below the dam prohibited in August during the salmon run.

Alaska Highway Log

(continued from page 127)

Distance* from Dawson Creek (DC) is followed by distance from Fairbanks (F). Original mileposts are indicated in the text as Historical Mile.

*Mileages from Dawson Creek are based on actual driving distance. Kilometres from Dawson Creek are based on physical kilometreposts. Please read Mileposts and Kilometreposts in the introduction for an explanation of how this highway is logged.

DC 887.4 (1475.6 km) **F 600.6** (966.5 km) First exit southbound for Whitehorse. North access road to Whitehorse (exit east) is via Two-Mile Hill and 4th Avenue.

DC 887.6 (1476 km) **F 600.4** (966.2 km) Turnoff to west on Hamilton Boulevard for Mount McIntyre Recreation Centre (0.9 mile/1.5 km); 70 kilometres of cross-country ski trails (summer hiking and biking), chalet for indoor waxing, curling and bonspiels. Truck weigh scales west side of highway.

DC 888.6 (1477.5 km) **F 599.4** (964.6 km) **Historical Mile 918.3.** Turnoff for Kopper King restaurant, motel, grocery, gas and diesel.

Kopper King. See display ad this section.

DC 889.3 (1478.6 km) **F 598.7** (963.5 km) McIntyre Creek.

DC 889.4 (1478.8 km) **F 598.6** (963.3 km) Turnoff to west for Fish Lake Road. Follow paved road west 2.5 miles/4 km to historic information sign about copper mining in this area. Road continues 10.5 miles/17 km (winding gravel) to Jackson Lakes (named Franklin and Louise).

DC 890.1 (1479.9 km) **F 597.9** (962.2 km) Rabbit's Foot Canyon.

DC 890.5 (1480.6 km) **F 597.5** (961.6 km) Turnoff to Porter Creek to east.

DC 891 (1481.4 km) **F 597** (960.8 km) Porter Creek grocery.

DC 891.3 (1482 km) **F 596.7** (960.3 km) **Historical Mile 921,** laundromat, gas and other businesses.

DC 891.5 (1482.3 km) **F 596.5** (959.9 km) Clyde Wann Road and Porter Creek subdivision, a residential suburb of Whitehorse. Access to Range Road and Mountain View Golf Course (18 holes).

DC 891.6 (1482.4 km) **F 596.4** (959.8 km) **Historical Mile 922.** Trails North Car & Truck Stop, and Tamarack Welding and Spring Shop are located here.

DC 891.8 (1482.5 km) **F 596.2** (959.5 km) MacDonald Road to north; auto repair.

DC 891.9 (1484 km) **F 596.1** (959.3 km) **Historical Mile 922.5.** Access to MacKenzie's RV Park. Azure Road. ▲

DC 894.3 (1486.4 km) **F 593.7** (955.4 km) Turnoff east to Cousins dirt airstrip.

DC 894.5 (1486.7 km) **F 593.5** (955.1 km) Rest area to west with litter barrels, outhouses, information sign and pay phone.

DC 894.8 (1487.2 km) **F 593.2** (954.6 km) **Junction** with Klondike Highway 2 to Dawson City (see KLONDIKE LOOP section). Turn off on Klondike Highway 2 for Takhini Hot Springs (swimming, camping), 3.8 miles/6.1 km north. ▲

For Alaska-bound travelers, the highway now swings west.

DC 895.5 (1488.3 km) **F 592.5** (953.5 km) Turnoff to south for Haeckel Hill. Not recommended for hiking as this area is used for target practice.

DC 899.1 (1495.4 km) **F 588.9** (947.7 km) Turnoff for 3-mile/4.8-km loop drive on old section of Alaska Highway. Access to stocked lake.

DC 901.6 (1499.3 km) **F 586.4** (943.7 km) Turnoff to north to sled dog track.

DC 905.4 (1507.1 km) **F 582.6** (937.6 km) **Historic Milepost 937.** Camera viewpoint turnout to north with point of interest sign about the old Dawson Trail. There were at least 50 stopping places along the old Dawson Trail winter stagecoach route between Whitehorse and Dawson City, and from 1 to 3 roadhouses at each stop. At this point, the stagecoach route crossed the Takhini River. This route was discontinued in 1950 when the Mayo–Dawson Road (now Klondike Highway 2) was constructed.

DC 908.7 (1512.4 km) **F 579.3** (932.3 km) Private farm and windmill; good example of Yukon agriculture. Facilities for overnighting large livestock.

DC 914.7 (1525 km) **F 573.3** (922.6 km) Takhini River bridge. According to R. Coutts in *Yukon: Places & Names,* the name Takhini derives from the Tagish Indian *tahk,* meaning mosquito, and *heena,* meaning river.

DC 922.7 (1535 km) **F 565.3** (909.7 km) Watch for horses and other livestock grazing on open range near highway.

DC 924.5 (1538.4 km) **F 563.5** (906.8 km) Stoney Creek.

DC 924.7 (1538.7 km) **F 563.3** (906.5 km) View of Mount Bratnober.

DC 926 (1540.8 km) **F 562** (904.4 km) Turnout to south with litter barrels and information panels on Takhini River valley, Kusawa Lake, and the changing landscape and wildlife of the area. Point of interest sign about 1958 burns; more than 1.5 million acres/629,058 hectares of Yukon forest lands were burned in 1958. Campfires were responsible for most of these fires.

DC 927.3 (1542.9 km) **F 560.7** (902.3 km) Turnoff to south for viewpoint (1.9 miles/3 km) and Kusawa Lake Yukon government campground (15 miles/24 km). Access road to campground is a narrow, winding gravel road, very slippery when wet; not recommended for long trailers or heavily loaded vehicles. ▲

Day-use area with sandy beach, boat dock, kitchen shelter and drinking water; boat launch 0.6 mile/1 km south. Campground at north end of lake has 32 sites, kitchen shelter, firepits and drinking water. Camping fee $8.

Kusawa Lake (formerly Arkell Lake), located in the Coast Mountains, is 45 miles/72 km long and averages 2 miles/3.2 km wide, with a shoreline perimeter of 125 miles/200 km. An access road to the lake was first constructed by the U.S. Army in 1945 to obtain bridge timbers for Alaska Highway construction.

Kusawa Lake, lake trout to 20 lbs., good to excellent; also grayling and pike.

DC 936.8 (1558 km) **F 551.2** (887 km) Mendenhall River bridge. A tributary of the Takhini River, the Mendenhall River—like the Mendenhall Glacier outside Juneau, AK—was named for Thomas Corwin Mendenhall (1841–1924), superintendent of the U.S. Coast & Geodetic Survey.

DC 939.5 (1562.3 km) **F 548.5** (882.7 km) View of 3 prominent mountains northbound (from left to right): Mount Kelvin; center mountain unnamed; and Mount Bratnober.

DC 942.2 (1566.5 km) **F 545.8** (878.4 km) Native traditional camp interpretive site; fee charged, open May to Oct.

Reconstruction of historic Canyon Creek bridge at Milepost DC 965.6. (Earl L. Brown, staff)

Traditional First Nations Camp. See dipslay ad this section.

DC 942.8 (1567.6 km) **F 545.2** (877.4 km) NorthwesTel microwave tower to south.

DC 943.5 (1568.5 km) **F 544.5** (876.3 km) **Historic Milepost 974.** Historic sign and interpretive panel about **CHAMPAGNE.** Originally a camping spot on the Dalton Trail to Dawson City, established by Jack Dalton in the late 1800s. In 1902, Harlow "Shorty" Chambers built a roadhouse and trading post here, and it became a supply centre for first the Bullion Creek rush and later the Burwash Creek gold rush in 1904. The origin of the name is uncertain, although one account is that Dalton's men—after successfully negotiating a herd of cattle through the first part of the trail—celebrated here with a bottle of French champagne. Today, it is home to members of the Champagne-Aishihik Indian Band.

There is an Indian cemetery on right westbound, just past the log cabin homes; a sign there reads: "This cemetery is not a tourist attraction. Please respect our privacy as we respect yours."

For northbound travelers, the Alaska Highway parallels the Dezadeash River (out of view to the south) from here west to Haines Junction. The Dezadeash Range is to the south and the Ruby Range to the north.

DC 944.4 (1570 km) **F 543.6** (874.8 km) Gravel turnout with litter barrel.

DC 955.8 (1588 km) **F 532.2** (856.5 km) First glimpse northbound of Kluane Range.

DC 957 (1590 km) **F 531** (854.5 km) **Historic Milepost 987.** Cracker Creek. Former roadhouse site on old stagecoach trail. Watch for "Old Man Mountain" on right northbound (the rocky crags look like a face, particularly in evening light).

DC 964.6 (1602.2 km) **F 523.4** (842.3 km) **Historical Mile 995.** Otter Falls Cutoff, **junction** with Aishihik Road. Gas station, store and camping to south, Aishihik Road turnoff to north. ▲

Otter Falls Cutoff. See display ad this section. ▲

Aishihik Road leads 84 miles/135 km north to the old Indian village of Aishihik (AYSH-ee-ak, means high place). Northern Canada Power Commission built a 32-megawatt dam at the foot of Aishihik Lake in 1976 to supply power principally to the mining industry. Flow hours for the Otter Falls hydro project are given at the start of Aishihik Road. This is a narrow, gravel road, maintained for summer travel only to the government campground. Aishihik Road is not recommended for large RVs and trailers.

There is a day-use recreation site at Otter Falls, 18.6 miles/30 km distance; picnic shelter, tables, outhouses and boat ramp.

The Yukon government Aishihik Lake Campground is located at the south end of Aishihik Lake, approximately 26 miles/41.8 km distance; 13 sites, drinking water, picnic tables, firepits, kitchen shelter, boat launch and playground. Camping fee $8. ▲

Aishihik Lake, fishing for lake trout and grayling. As with most large Yukon lakes, ice is not out until late June. Low water levels may make boat launching difficult. *WARNING: Winds can come up suddenly on this lake.* **Pole Cat Lake,** just before the Aishihik weather station; fishing for pike.

CAUTION: Bears in area. Other wildlife includes eagles, moose and caribou.

DC 965.6 (1603.8 km) **F 522.4** (840.7 km) **Historic Milepost 996.** Turnoff to north at east end of Aishihik River bridge (watch for camera viewpoint sign) to see Canyon Creek bridge. The original bridge was built about 1920 by the Jacquot brothers to move freight and passengers across the Aishihik River to Silver City on Kluane Lake, and from there by boat to Burwash Landing. The bridge was reconstructed in 1942 by Army Corps of Engineers during construction of the Alaska Highway. It was rebuilt again in 1987.

DC 965.7 (1604 km) **F 522.3** (840.5 km) Aishihik River bridge.

DC 966.3 (1605 km) **F 521.7** (839.6 km) View of impressive Kluane Range ice fields straight ahead northbound between Kilometreposts 1604 and 1616.

DC 974.9 (1619 km) **F 513.1** (825.7 km) Turnout to south on Marshall Creek.

DC 977.1 (1622.4 km) **F 510.9** (822.2 km) Double-ended turnout to north with information plaques about the Kluane Ranges. The rugged snowcapped peaks of the Kluane Icefield Ranges and the outer portion of the St. Elias Mountains are visible to the west, straight ahead northbound.

The Kluane National Park Icefield Ranges are Canada's highest and the world's largest nonpolar alpine ice field, forming the interior wilderness of the park. In clear weather, Mount Kennedy and Mount Hubbard, 2 peaks that are twice as high as the front ranges seen before you, are visible from here.

DC 979.3 (1626 km) **F 508.7** (818.6 km) Between Kilometreposts 1626 and 1628, look for the NorthwesTel microwave repeater station on top of Paint Mountain. The station was installed with the aid of helicopters and supplied by the tramline carried by high towers, which is also visible from here.

DC 980.8 (1628.4 km) **F 507.2** (816.2 km) Turnoff to north for Yukon government Pine Lake recreation park and campground. Day-use area has sandy beach, boat launch and dock, group firepits, drinking water and 7 tent sites near beach. The Pine Lake Regatta, held here in mid-July, is the "biggest beach party in the Yukon." The campground, adjacent **Pine Lake** with a view of the St. Elias Mountains, has 33 sites, outhouses, firewood, litter barrels, kitchen shelter, playground and drinking water. Camping fee $8. Fishing is good for lake trout, northern pike and grayling. ▲

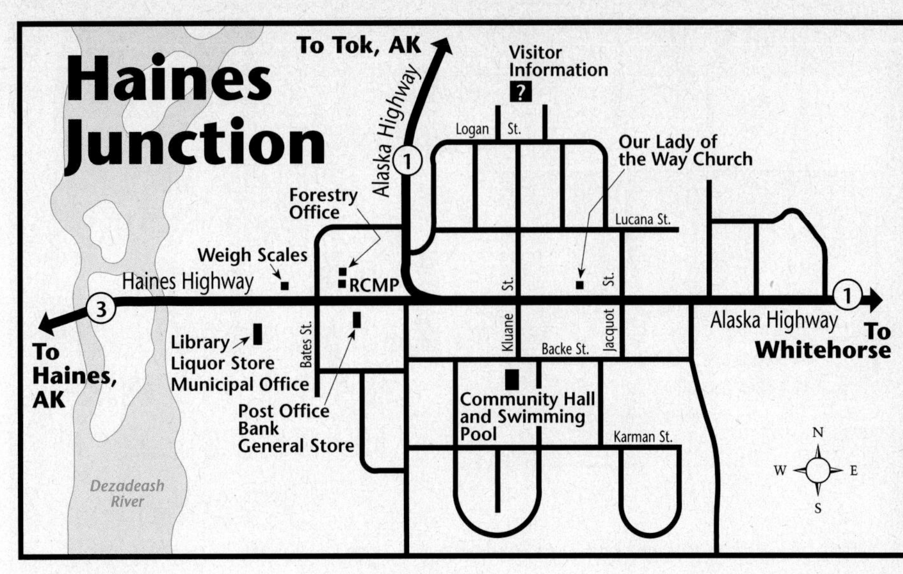

DC 980.9 (1628.5 km) **F 507.1** (816.1 km) Access road to floatplane dock.

DC 982.2 (1630.8 km) **F 505.8** (814 km) Turnoff to north for Haines Junction airport. Flightseeing tours of glaciers, fly-in fishing and air charters available; fixed-wing aircraft or helicopters. **Private Aircraft:** Haines Junction airstrip; elev. 2,150 feet/655m; length 5,000 feet/1,524m; gravel. Fuel sales (100LL) from Sifton Air.

Highway swings to south for last few miles into Haines Junction, offering a panoramic, close-up view of the Auriol Range straight ahead.

DC 984.8 (1635 km) **F 503.2** (809.8 km) Northbound travelers turn right (southbound travelers turn left) on Kluane Street for Kluane National Park Visitor Centre.

DC 985 (1635.3 km) **F 503** (809.5 km) **Historic Milepost 1016, junction** of Alaska Highway and Haines Highway (Haines Road).

IMPORTANT: THIS JUNCTION CAN BE CONFUSING; CHOOSE YOUR ROUTE CAREFULLY! Fairbanks- and Anchorage-bound travelers TURN RIGHT at this junction for continuation of Alaska Highway (Yukon Highway 1); highway log follows description of Haines Junction, YT. Continue straight ahead (south) on the Haines Highway (Yukon Highway 3) for port of Haines, AK; see HAINES HIGHWAY section. (Haines-bound motorists note: It is a good idea to fill up with gas in Haines Junction. Gas is available en route only at Kathleen Lake Lodge.)

Haines Junction

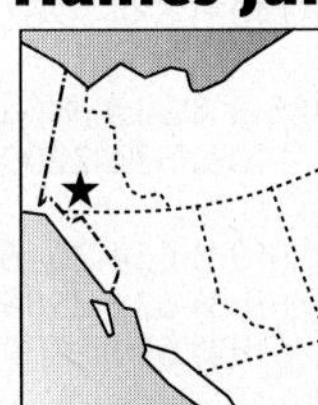

DC 985 (1635.3 km) **F 503** (809.5 km) **Historic Milepost 1016,** at the **junction** of the Alaska Highway (Yukon Highway 1) and the Haines Highway (Yukon Highway 3, also known as the Haines Road). Driving distance to Whitehorse, 100 miles/161 km; YT–AK border, 205 miles/330 km; Tok, 296 miles/476 km; and Haines, 150.5 miles/242 km. **Population:** 796. **Elevation:** 1,956 feet/596m. **Emergency Services: RCMP,** phone (403) 634-5555. **Fire Department,** phone (403) 634-2222. **Nursing Centre,** phone (403) 634-4444. **Radio:** 106.1 FM.

Visitor Information: At the Kluane National Park and Yukon government visitor information centre, 0.2 mile/0.3 km east of the junction just off the Alaska Highway. Phone (403) 634-2345. Interpretive exhibits, displays and an outstanding multi-image slide presentation are featured. The centre is open daily from May to Sept.

Haines Junction was established in 1942 during construction of the Alaska Highway. The first buildings here were Army barracks for the U.S. Army Corps of Engineers. The engineers were to build a new branch road connecting the Alaska Highway with the port of Haines on Lynn Canal. The branch road—today's Haines Highway—was completed in 1943.

The Our Lady of the Way Catholic mission in Haines Junction was built in 1954, using parts from an old Army hut left from highway construction days. The octagonal log St. Christopher's Anglican Church was built in 1987, replacing a 1955 structure built from an old garage used in the pipeline project.

Haines Junction is still an important stop for travelers on the Alaska and Haines highways. Services are located along both highways, and clustered around Village Square at the junction, where a 24-foot monument depicts area wildlife.

Haines Junction offers an excellent range of accommodations. Visitor services include motels, bed and breakfasts, restaurants, gas stations, garage services, groceries, souvenirs and a bakery that last summer hosted a popular "coffee house" on Monday nights, with an open mike for traveling musicians. There

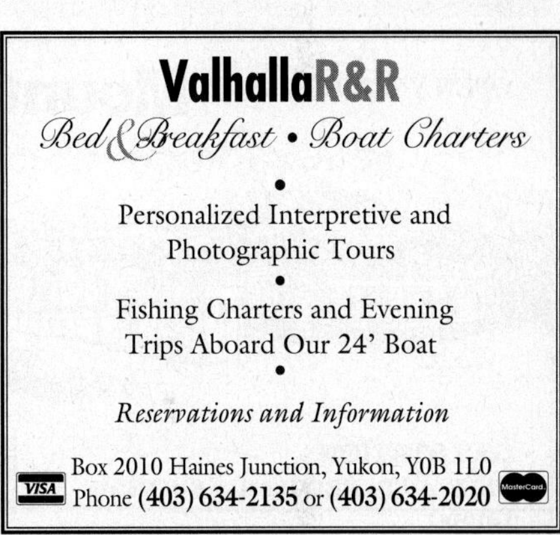

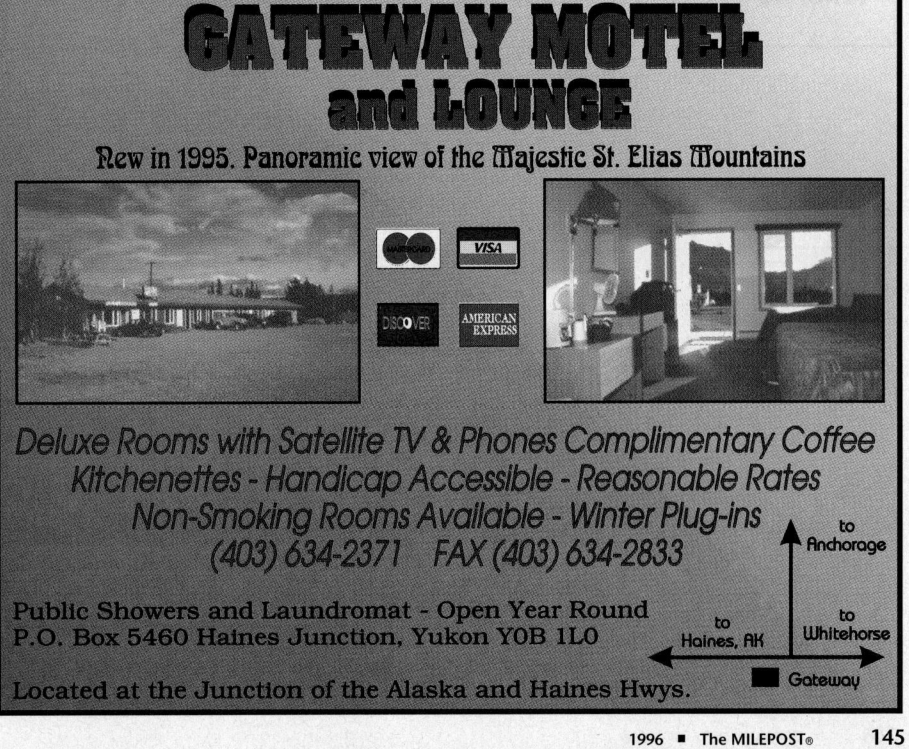

is a full-facility indoor heated swimming pool with showers available; open daily from May to Sept., fee charged. Also here are a RCMP office, Lands and Forest District Office and health centre. The post office and bank are located in Madley's General Store. (Banking service weekdays, 12:30-4:30 P.M.; extended hours on Fridays.) The Commissioner James Smith Administration Bldg., at Kilometre 255.6 Haines Road, 0.2 mile/0.3 km south from the Alaska Highway junction, contains the government liquor store and public library. The airport is located on the Alaska Highway just east of town (see **Milepost DC 982.2**).

Haines Junction is on the eastern boundary of Kluane National Park Reserve. Administration offices and the visitor centre for the park are located in town; the park warden and general works station are located just north of town. Kluane (pronounced kloo-WA-nee) National Park Reserve encompasses extensive ice fields, mountains and wilder-

HAINES JUNCTION ADVERTISERS

Alcan Fuels ....Ph. (403) 634-2268
Cabin Crafts.............Across from visitor centre
Cozy Corner Motel & Restaurant ....Ph. (403) 634-2511
Gateway Motel ....Ph. (403) 634-2371
Junction Cycle. ....Ph. (403) 634-2453
Kluane Machine ....Ph. (403) 634-2115
Kluane Park Adventure Center ....Ph. (403) 634-2313
Kluane Park Inn Ltd. ....Ph. (403) 634-2261
Kluane R.V. Kampground ....Mile 985.3 Alaska Hwy.
Madley's General Store ....Ph. (403) 634-2200
Mountain View Motor Inn ....Ph. (403) 634-2646
North Country R.V. Park...Ph. (403) 634-2505
Raven, The ....Ph. (403) 634-2500
Stardust Motel & R.V. Park ....Mile 985.9 Alaska Hwy.
Trans North Helicopters ....At the airport
Valhalla R&R ....Ph. (403) 634-2135
Village Bakery ....Next to visitor centre
Village of Haines Junction ....Ph. (403) 634-2291

ness. There is one campground, Kathleen Lake, located 16 miles/27 km south of town on the Haines Highway. There are numerous hiking trails of varying degrees of difficulty; check with the park visitor centre or see Vivien Lougheed's *Kluane Park Hiking Guide* (1992). Flightseeing the park by fixed-wing aircraft or helicopter from Haines Junction is a popular way to see Kluane's scenery; check with charter services at the airport.

The park was first suggested in 1942, and in 1943 land was set aside and designated the Kluane Game Sanctuary. A formal park region was established in 1972 and the national park boundaries were official in 1976. In 1980, Kluane National Park Reserve, along with Wrangell–St. Elias National Park in Alaska, became a joint UNESCO World Heritage Site. Kluane has become a world-class wilderness destination among outdoor recreation enthusiasts. Hikers note: There is mandatory registration (fee charged) for overnight trips into the park.

For more information on Kluane National Park Reserve, stop by the excellent visitor centre and see the exhibits and the award-winning multi-image slide presentation (shown on the hour and half hour). Also check at the visitor centre for a schedule of guided hikes and walks; these interpretive programs are available daily from the third week in June through August. Fees are charged for the slide show and all other interpretive events. Contact Kluane National Park at Box 5495, Haines Junction, YT Y0B 1L0, or phone (403) 634-2251, fax 634-2686.

Haines Junction is also headquarters for the new Tatshenshini-Alsek Wilderness Park. Created in 1993, the park protects the magnificent Tatshenshini and Alsek rivers area in Canada, where the 2 rivers join and flow (as the Alsek) to the Gulf of Alaska at Dry Bay. Known to riverrunners as "the Tat," the Tatshenshini is famous for its whitewater rafting, stunning scenery and wildlife. Due to a dramatic increase in river traffic in

Village monument in Haines Junction. (© Carmen Scott)

Silver City, an early trading post, north of Haines Junction at Milepost DC 1020.3.
(Earl L. Brown, staff)

recent years, permits are required from the park agencies (the National Park Service in Alaska and B.C. Parks in Canada). Locally, Kluane Park Adventure Center (403/634-2313) offers rafting trips to the Tatshenshini. For more information about the park, contact Tatshenshini-Alsek Wilderness Park, Box 5495, Haines Junction, YT Y0B 1L0; phone (403) 634-2251, fax (403) 634-2686.

Picnicking available at day-use area on the Dezadeash River, located at the west edge of town on the Haines Highway, which also has a wheelchair-accessible trail. Other outdoor recreation available locally includes guided fishing and boating (canoe and boat rentals available). ♿

RV camping available at several campgrounds in and near town. Dump stations and water are also available at local service station and campgrounds. Yukon government campground located 4.2 miles/6.7 km east of junction on the Alaska Highway at Pine Lake. ▲

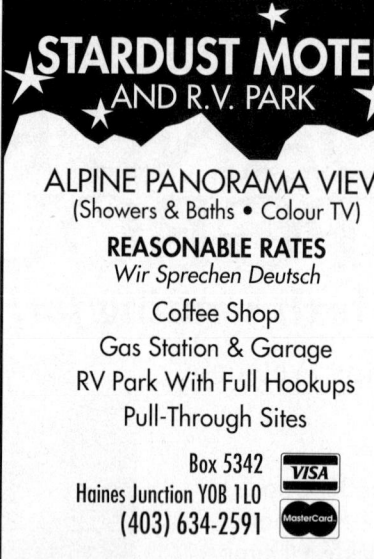

Special events in Haines Junction include the Alsek Music Festival held June 7-8, 1996, and the Pine Lake Regatta in July (see **Mile-**

post DC 980.8). Also remember that July 1st is Canada Day (the anniversary of Canada's confederation) and is celebrated with parades and flags. The Dalton Trail Gymkhana and Jackpot Rodeo is scheduled for early August.

Bicycling offers several events, including the Trail of '42 Road Race (May 25, 1996) and the Kluane to Chilkat International Bike Relay (June 22, 1996), which attracted 650 cyclists last year. Junction Cycle (403-634-2453) has details on other bike rallies in 1996, including the Bayshore Classic. *IMPORTANT: Watch for cyclists on the Alaska and Haines highways during these events.*

Alaska Highway Log

(continued)

Distance* from Dawson Creek (DC) is followed by distance from Fairbanks (F). Original mileposts are indicated in the text as Historical Mile.

*Mileages from Dawson Creek are based on actual driving distance. Kilometres from Dawson Creek are based on physical kilometreposts. Please read Mileposts and Kilometreposts in the introduction for an explanation of how this highway is logged.

DC 985 (1635.3 km) **F 503** (809.5 km) **Junction** of the Alaska Highway (Yukon Highway 1) and the Haines Highway (Yukon Highway 3). Markers indicate distance to Destruction Bay 67 miles/108 km, Beaver Creek 186 miles/299 km.

Northbound: From Haines Junction to the YT–AK border, the Alaska Highway is in fair to good condition but narrow, often without shoulders. Watch for frost heaves north from Destruction Bay and extremely poor surfacing north from Beaver Creek to the YT-AK border.

Southbound: Good paved highway with wide shoulders next 380 miles/611.5 km (from here to Watson Lake) with the exception of some short sections of narrow road and occasional gravel breaks. *NOTE: This junction can be confusing; choose your route carefully!* Whitehorse-bound travelers TURN LEFT at junction for continuation of Alaska Highway (Yukon Highway 1); highway log follows description of Haines Junction. TURN RIGHT for the Haines Highway (Yukon Highway 3) to the port of Haines, AK; see HAINES HIGHWAY section for log. (Haines-bound motorists note: Next gas 119 miles/191.5 km.)

DC 985.3 (1635.9 km) **F 502.7** (809 km) Kluane RV Kampground; RV and tent camping, gas, diesel, dump station, pay phone. ▲

DC 985.8 (1636.5 km) **F 502.2** (808.2 km) **Historical Mile 1017.** Alcan Fuels; gas, diesel, propane, auto repair and towing. Open daily. Open year-round.

DC 985.9 (1636.7 km) **F 502.1** (808 km) Stardust Motel and RV Park. ▲

DC 986.6 (1637.8 km) **F 501.4** (806.9 km) Highway follows the Kluane Ranges which are to the west. Livestock open range in this area: Watch for horses and cattle!

DC 987.8 (1639.8 km) **F 500.2** (805 km) **Historical Mile 1019.** Kluane National Park warden headquarters. (Visitor information in Haines Junction at the visitor centre.)

DC 988.3 (1640.6 km) **F 499.7** (804.1 km) Rest area to west with pit toilets.

DC 991.4 (1645.6 km) **F 496.6** (799.1 km) Photo stop on right northbound. A short hike uphill leads to lookout and information sign about ancient lakes in the area.

Highway climbs next 9 miles/14.5 km northbound to Bear Creek Summit.

DC 991.6 (1645.9 km) **F 496.4** (798.9 km) **Historic Milepost 1022,** Mackintosh Trading Post historic sign. Lodge to east; food, gas, lodging and camping. Helicopter flightseeing service across from lodge. Trailhead to west for Alsek Pass trail; 18 miles/29 km long, suitable for shorter day hikes, mountain bikes permitted. ▲

Mackintosh Lodge offers something for everyone, from our delicious homemade meals and fresh baking from "Gramma's Kitchen" to our comfy rooms with handmade quilts. A favorite stopping spot for Alaskan travelers. Across from the lodge, the Alsek Trail leads to Kluane National Park, a world heritage site. "Majestic mountains make for Mackintosh miracles." [ADVERTISEMENT]

DC 1000.1 (1660 km) **F 487.9** (785.2 km) Bear Creek Summit (elev. 3,294 feet/1,004m), highest point on the Alaska Highway between Whitehorse and Fairbanks.

Glimpse of Kloo Lake to north of highway between Kilometreposts 1660 and 1662.

DC 1003.5 (1665.4 km) **F 484.5** (779.7 km) Jarvis Creek.

DC 1003.6 (1665.6 km) **F 484.4** (779.5 km) **Historic Milepost 1035.** Turnout to west next to Jarvis Creek. Pretty spot for a picnic. Trail rides may be available here with Ruby Range Trail Rides.

Jarvis Creek, grayling 8 to 16 inches, good all summer; Dolly Varden 8 to 10 inches, best in early summer.

DC 1013.6 (1682 km) **F 474.4** (763.5 km) Beautiful view to west of the snow-covered Kluane Ranges. For northbound travelers, the Alaska Highway parallels the Kluane Ranges from Haines Junction to Koidern, presenting a nearly unbroken chain of 7,000- to 8,000-foot/2,134- to 2,438-m summits interrupted only by a few large valleys cut by glacier-fed rivers and streams. West of the Kluane Ranges is the Duke Depression (not visible from the highway), a narrow trough separating the Kluane Ranges from the St. Elias Mountains. Major peaks in the St. Elias (not visible from the highway) are: Mount Logan, Canada's highest peak, at 19,545 feet/5,959m (recalculated in 1992 from 19,520 feet by a scientific expedition); Mount St. Elias, 18,008 feet/5,489m; Mount Lucania, 17,147 feet/5,226m; King Peak, 16,971 feet/5,173m; Mount Wood, Mount Vancouver, Mount Hubbard and Mount Steele, all over 15,000 feet/4,572m. Mount Steele (16,664 feet/5,079m) was named for Superintendent Sam Steele of the North West Mounted Police. As commanding officer of the NWMP in the Yukon in 1898, Steele established permanent detachments at the summits of the White and Chilkoot passes to ensure not only that gold stampeders obeyed Canadian laws, but also had sufficient supplies to carry them through to the gold fields.

DC 1016.5 (1686.7 km) **F 471.5** (758.8 km) Turnout to west with view of Kluane Ranges.

DC 1017.2 (1687.8 km) **F 470.8** (757.7 km) Christmas Creek.

DC 1019.8 (1692 km) **F 468.2** (753.5 km) First glimpse of Kluane Lake for northbound travelers at Boutillier Summit (elev. 3,293 feet/1,003m), second highest point on the highway between Whitehorse and Fairbanks.

DC 1020 (1692.5 km) **F 468** (753.2 km) Turnout to east with information plaques on area history and geography.

DC 1020.3 (1693 km) **F 467.7** (752.7 km) **Historic Milepost 1053.** Historic sign and interpretive panel at turnoff for Silver City. Access to a bed and breakfast. Follow dirt and gravel road east 3.1 miles/5 km to ruins of Silver City. This old trading post, with roadhouse and North West Mounted Police barracks, was on the wagon road from Whitehorse to the placer goldfields of Kluane Lake (1904–24). Good photo opportunities.

Kluane Bed and Breakfast. Just 3 miles off the highway at historical Silver City on the shore of Kluane Lake. Private heated A-frame cabins with mountain view, cooking and shower facilities, full family-style breakfast. Your hosts—The Sias Family, a sixth generation Yukon family. Contact mobile operator, 2M 3924, Destruction Bay channel. Reservations recommended. C/o Box 5459, Haines Junction, Yukon Y0B 1L0. [ADVERTISEMENT]

DC 1020.9 (1694 km) **F 467.1** (751.7 km) Silver Creek.

DC 1022.5 (1696.5 km) **F 465.5** (749.1 km) Turnoff to east for Kluane Lake Research Station; station and airstrip are 0.9 mile/1.4 km via a straight gravel road. This research station is sponsored by the Arctic Institute of North America, University of Calgary.

Highway follows west shore of Kluane Lake next 39 miles/63 km northbound to Burwash Landing.

DC 1023.7 (1698.5 km) **F 464.3** (747.2 km) **Historical Mile 1056.** Kluane Camp commemorative plaque. Kluane Lake Lodge (closed in 1995, current status unknown). Trans North helicopter base; flightseeing in summer. These highly recommended flightseeing trips offer spectacular views of the Slims River Valley and Kaskawulsh Glacier.

Trans North Helicopters. See display ad this section.

DC 1026.8 (1703.4 km) **F 461.2** (742.2 km) Slim's River East trail turnoff (2-mile/3.3-km access road, not recommended for motorhomes); parking at trailhead. This 12.4-mile/20-km trail is rated "easy" by the *Kluane Hiking Guide.*

DC 1027.8 (1705 km) **F 460.2** (740.6 km) Slim's River bridge (clearance 17.7 feet/5.4m). Slim's River, which flows into Kluane Lake, was named for a packhorse that drowned here during the 1903 Kluane gold rush. Sheep Mountain is directly ahead for northbound travelers. The highway winds along Kluane Lake: Drive carefully!

DC 1029 (1706.8 km) **F 459** (738.7 km) Sheep Mountain visitor information centre. Excellent interpretive programs, laser disc information videos, parking and outhouses are available. Open mid-May to mid-Sept. Hours are 9 A.M. to 6:30 P.M. June through Aug., 9:30 A.M. to 5 P.M. in May and Sept. Stop here for information on Kluane National Park's flora and fauna. A viewing telescope is set up to look for sheep on Sheep Mountain. This is the sheep's winter range; best chance to see them is late Aug. and Sept., good chance in late May to early June. Slim's River West trail; trailhead adjacent visitor information centre.

The small white cross on the side of Sheep Mountain marks the grave of Alexander Clark Fisher, a prospector who came into this area about 1906.

DC 1030.7 (1709.5 km) **F 457.3** (735.9 km) **Historic Milepost 1061.** Soldier's Summit. The Alaska Canada Military Highway was officially opened with a ribbon-cutting ceremony here on blizzardy Nov. 20, 1942. A rededication ceremony was held Nov. 20, 1992, commemorating the 50th anniversary of the highway. A trail leads up to the original dedication site from the parking area.

Several turnouts overlooking Kluane Lake next mile northbound. This beautiful lake is the largest in Yukon Territory, covering approximately 154 square miles/400 square km. The Ruby Range lies on the east side of the lake. Boat rentals are available at Destruction Bay and Burwash Landing.

Kluane Lake, excellent fishing for lake trout, northern pike and grayling.

DC 1031.9 (1711.7 km) **F 456.1** (734 km) **The Bayshore,** where Yukon Jim and Sheep Mountain Shirley want your stop to be one of the highlights of your trip. Enjoy our friendly hospitality and fabulous food in a spectacular lakeside setting surrounded by majestic mountains. See for yourself why the Bayshore is one of the most popular spots in the Yukon. [ADVERTISEMENT] ▲

Flightseeing Kaskawulsh Glacier. (Carol Murdock)

DC 1034.5 (1715.8 km) **F 453.5** (729.8 km) Williscroft Creek.

DC 1034.9 (1717 km) **F 453.1** (729.2 km) **Historical Mile 1067.** Cottonwood campground to east. ▲

Cottonwood RV Park and Campground. See display ad this section. ▲

DC 1039.7 (1724.7 km) **F 448.3** (721.4 km) Congdon Creek trailhead to west; 16-mile/26-km hike to Sheep Mountain.

DC 1039.9 (1725 km) **F 448.1** (721.1 km) **Historical Mile 1072.** Turnoff to east for Congdon Creek Yukon government campground on Kluane Lake. Drive in 0.4 mile/0.6 km via gravel loop road; tenting area, 77 level sites (some pull-through), outhouses, kitchen shelters, water pump, firewood, firepits, picnic tables, sandy beach, interpretive talks, playground, boat launch. Camping fee $8. ▲

DC 1040.4 (1725.6 km) **F 447.6** (720.3 km) Congdon Creek. According to R. Coutts, *Yukon: Places & Names,* Congdon Creek is believed to have been named by a miner after Frederick Tennyson Congdon. A lawyer from Nova Scotia, Congdon came to the Yukon in 1898 and held various political posts until 1911.

DC 1046.9 (1735.3 km) **F 441.1** (709.9 km) Nines Creek. Turnout to east.

DC 1047.3 (1736.2 km) **F 440.7** (709.2 km) Mines Creek.

DC 1048.9 (1739 km) **F 439.1** (706.6 km) Bock's Brook.

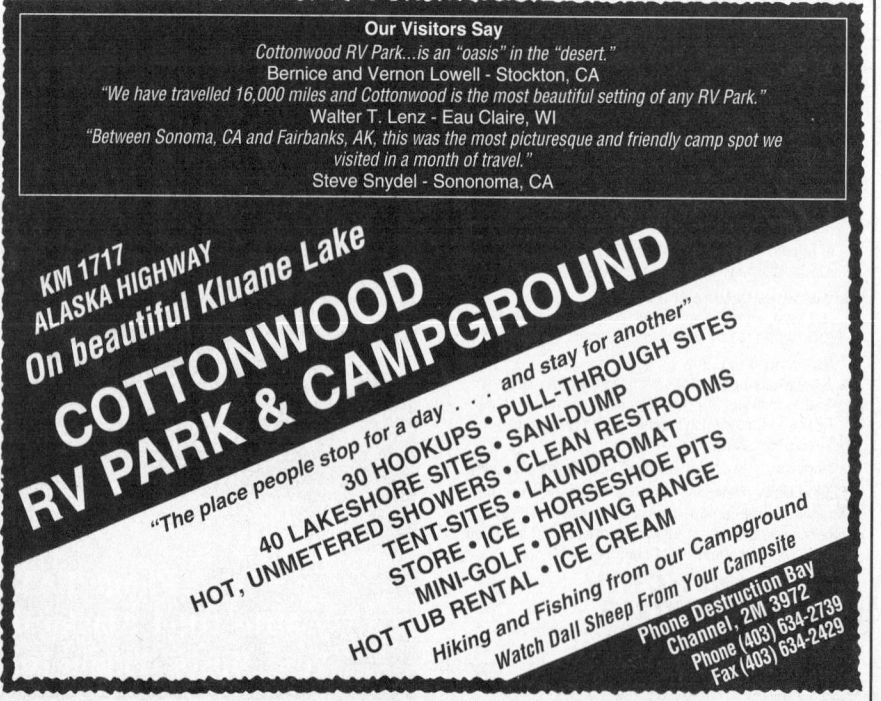

DC 1051.5 (1743 km) **F 436.5** (702.5 km) **Historic Milepost 1083. DESTRUCTION BAY** (pop. less than 100). **Emergency Services: RCMP**, phone collect (403) 634-5555. **Health clinic**, phone (403) 841-4444; **Ambulance**, phone (403) 841-3333; **Fire Department**, phone (403) 841-2221. Located on the shore of Kluane Lake, Destruction Bay is one of several towns that grew out of the building of the Alaska Highway. It earned its name when a storm destroyed buildings and materials here. Destruction Bay was one of the many relay stations spaced at 100-mile intervals to give truck drivers a break and a chance to repair their vehicles. Historic sign adjacent historic milepost. A highway maintenance camp is located here. Destruction Bay has camping, boat launch, boat rentals and guided fishing tours. A fishing derby is held first weekend in July. Food, gas, camping and lodging available at the Talbot Arm (open year-round) and Sehja Services. Glacier flightseeing trips available. ▲

Talbot Arm Motel in Destruction Bay at historic Mile 1083 Alaska Highway has been offering Yukon visitors a modern, clean and friendly stop since 1967. Built and managed by the Van der Veen family, Talbot Arm has been setting the standard for rural lodges. In 1988 we were recognized by our peers for our efforts by winning the Sourdough Award from Tourism Industry Association and Customers Service Award from Chevron. Recently we have added 2 attractions to our list of services: Ruby Range Airways Ltd. is headquartered at Talbot Arm and is offering glacier flights in Kluane National Park and surrounding area. Enjoy a scenic flight over the largest non-polar icefield in the world and Canada's most majestic peaks in a Cessna 182P piloted by Neil Hardy. Talbot Arm Fishing Tours are also arranged at the lodge. Our 3 available guides have over 50 years total experience hunting the huge Kluane Lake trout. A day in a boat on our crystal clear waters in the best scenery in the Yukon won't soon be forgotten. [ADVERTISEMENT]

DC 1051.7 (1743.3 km) **F 436.3** (702.1 km) **Sehja Services & RV Park.** Historical mile "1083"—original equipment site of camp 1083 and the first full service lodge on the Alcan Highway. Beautifully nestled against the St. Elias mountains overlooking Kluane (clue-ah-knee) Lake. Reasonable rates, clean facilities, home cooking with 5 star service. Please come and visit us. Your hosts Loren & Kevin. Phone (403) 841-4807, fax (403) 841-4909. [ADVERTISEMENT] ▲

DC 1051.9 (1743.6 km) **F 436.1** (701.8 km) Rest area with litter barrels and toilet.

DC 1055.1 (1748.8 km) **F 432.9** (696.7 km) Lewes Creek.

DC 1058.3 (1753.9 km) **F 429.7** (691.5 km) Halfbreed (Copper Joe) Creek trailhead.

DC 1061.3 (1758.7 km) **F 426.7** (686.7 km) Store, post office and general auto repairs.

DC 1061.5 (1759 km) **F 426.5** (686.4 km) **Historic Milepost 1093.** Turnoff to east for **BURWASH LANDING**, a resort with 24-hour gas, food, camping and lodging on Kluane Lake. Boat rentals and Kluane Lake fishing trips available. Helicopter flightseeing trips of Kluane National Park are also

Beautiful Kluane Lake is the largest lake in Yukon Territory. (Earl L. Brown, staff)

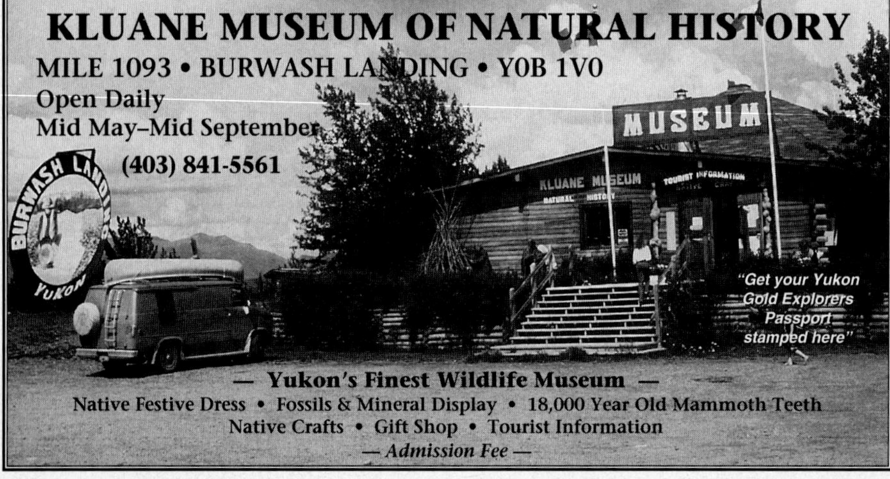

available out of Burwash Landing.

Burwash Landing was settled in 1904 by the Jacquot brothers, Louis and Eugene, as a supply centre for local miners. The log mission here, Our Lady of the Holy Rosary, was built in 1944. The historic sign here reads: "After months of rough camp life, American soldiers were surprised and delighted when they reached this prosperous little settlement which seemed like an oasis in the wilderness. Burwash also became the home of Father Eusebe Morisset, an Oblate Missionary, who served as an auxiliary chaplain with the American Army."

The highly recommended Kluane Museum of Natural History is located on the east side of the highway at the turnoff; open 9 A.M. to 9 P.M. in summer; phone (403) 841-5561. The museum features wildlife, minerals and other natural history exhibits, and has a souvenir shop. Admission is charged. Yukon Gold Explorer's Passports are stamped here. Next to the museum is the world's largest gold pan, measuring 28 feet/ 8m high.

Burwash Landing Resort & RV Park. See display ad this section. ▲

Kluane Museum of Natural History. See display ad this section.

DC 1062 (1759.8 km) **F 426** (685.5 km) **Dalan Campground.** Turn off north, to Dalan Campground, 1 km off the Alaska Highway on the shores of beautiful Kluane Lake, "largest lake in the Yukon." Owned and operated by Kluane First Nation, this campground offers 25 individual private campsites, RVs welcome! Firewood, water pump, picnic tables, firepits and dump station are available. For additional information, call (403) 841-4274. [ADVERTISEMENT] ▲

DC 1062.7 (1761 km) **F 425.3** (684.4 km) **Historic Milepost 1094. Private Aircraft:** Burwash Yukon government airstrip to north; elev. 2,643 feet/806m; length 6,000 feet/1,829m; gravel, no fuel.

DC 1067 (1768.8 km) **F 421** (677.5 km) Duke River bridge (clearance 17.7 feet/5.4m). The Duke River flows into Kluane Lake; named for George Duke, an early prospector.

DC 1071.9 (1776.5 km) **F 416.1** (669.6 km) Turnout to north. Burwash Creek, named for Lachlin Taylor Burwash, a mining recorder at Silver City in 1903.

DC 1076.7 (1784.1 km) **F 411.3** (661.9 km) Sakiw Creek.

DC 1077.3 (1785.1 km) **F 410.4** (660.5 km) Rest area with information panels and observation platform overlooking Kluane River.

DC 1078.5 (1787 km) **F 409.5** (659 km) Buildings to west belong to Hudson Bay Mining and Smelting Co.'s Wellgreen Nickel Mines, named for Wellington Bridgeman Green, the prospector who discovered the mineral showing in 1952. During the mine's operation, from May 1972 to July 1973, three shiploads of concentrates (averaging 13,000 tons each) were trucked to Haines, AK. The material proved to be too insufficient to be economical. No facilities or services.

NOTE: Watch for road construction between Kilometreposts 1787 and 1797 in 1996.

DC 1079.4 (1788.5 km) **F 408.6** (657.6 km) Quill Creek.

DC 1080.9 (1791 km) **F 407.1** (655.1 km) Glacier Creek. Kluane River to east of highway.

DC 1083.5 (1795.5 km) **F 404.5** (651 km) **Historic Milepost 1117.** Turnout. Sign commemorates 1st Lt. Roland Small, of the 18th Engineers Regiment, who died in a jeep accident near this site during construction of the Alaska Highway in 1942. Short road to Kluane River; no turnaround.

DC 1084.6 (1797.2 km) **F 403.4** (649.2 km) **Historical Mile 1118.** Kluane Wilderness Village; gas, restaurant, camping and lodging. Open year-round. Viewing platform of: Mount Kennedy, Mount Logan and Mount Lucania. Halfway mark between Whitehorse and Tok. ▲

Kluane Wilderness Village offers all amenities to modern day travelers. 24-hour service station and one-stop grocery, full-menu restaurant, "Scully's Saloon" and comfortable accommodation. Our Good Sam R.V. Park (with Satellite TV) is the ideal resting location between Whitehorse and Tok, nestled in the beautiful Kluane Mountains. See our display ad for more. [ADVERTISEMENT] ▲

DC 1086.6 (1799.5 km) **F 401.4** (646 km) Swede Johnson Creek. Turnout to east.

DC 1087.4 (1801.7 km) **F 400.6** (644.7 km) *CAUTION: Rough road northbound next 168 km (104 miles), maximum 70 kmph (about 45 mph), some gravel patches, some winding*

Donjek River bridge at Milepost DC 1100. (Earl L. Brown, staff)

sections. Drive carefully, especially vehicles with trailers. Road surface can be particularly hard on trailer hitches. Various road construction projects may be under way between the Donjek River at Kilometrepost 1822 and Kilometrepost 1915 in 1996.

DC 1091.3 (1808 km) **F 396.7** (638.4 km) Buildings to east are a dormant pump station once used to pressure up fuel being transferred from Haines to Fairbanks.

DC 1095 (1814 km) **F 393** (632.4 km) NorthwesTel microwave tower visible ahead northbound.

DC 1095.4 (1814.6 km) **F 392.6** (631.8 km) Abandoned Mountain View Lodge. View of Donjek River Valley.

Alaska Highway workers faced one of their toughest construction jobs during completion of the Alaska Highway in 1943 from the Donjek River to the Alaska border. Swampy ground underlain by permafrost, numerous creeks, lakes and rivers, plus a thick insulating ground cover made this section particularly difficult for road builders.

DC 1096.3 (1816 km) **F 391.7** (630.4 km) Turnout to west with view of Donjek River Valley and the Icefield Ranges of the St. Elias Mountains. Interpretive display.

DC 1099.7 (1819.5 km) **F 388.3** (624.9 km) **Historic Milepost 1130.** Turnout with interpretive panel on the Donjek River bridge. Sign reads: "Glacial rivers, like the Donjek, posed a unique problem for the builders of the Alaska Highway. These braided mountain streams would flood after a heavy rainfall or rapid glacial melt, altering the waters' course and often leaving bridges crossing dry ground."

NOTE: Watch for road construction between Kilometreposts 1822 and 1844 in 1996.

DC 1100 (1820 km) **F 388** (624.4 km) Donjek River bridge (clearance 17.4 feet/5.3m). Access to river at north end of bridge on west side of highway. This wide silty river is a major tributary of the White River. According to R. Coutts, *Yukon: Places & Names,* the Donjek is believed to have been named by Charles Willard Hayes in 1891 from the Indian word for a peavine that grows in the area.

DC 1113.5 (1844.4 km) **F 374.5** (602.7 km) **Edith Creek** bridge, turnout to west. Try your hand at gold panning here, "colours" have been found. Grayling fishing, June through September. *CAUTION: WATCH FOR BEARS!* Local dump in area.

DC 1113.8 (1844.8 km) **F 374.2** (602.2 km) **Historical Mile 1147. Pine Valley Motel and Cafe.** Thanks to all our customers for your patronage from your hosts Carmen and Dave. Don't let the construction get you down, drop in for a relaxing break. We have unleaded and diesel available (seniors gas discount). Tire repairs, towing available, minor repairs and welding. RV park and campground, pull-throughs, water and power hookups, hot showers included, dump station, picnic tables, firepits. Caravan discounts. Gold panning and good fishing at Edith Creek. Motel units, cabins with colour TV. Newly renovated licensed cafe with full menu and bakery, featuring hearty soups, homemade bread, pies and pastries, fresh daily. Enjoy a scenic view of the mountains while our friendly morning cook prepares you up a mean breakfast, or sink your teeth into some of Carmen's wonderful sweet rolls. Take-out for cold beer, wine and spirits. Pay phone, cubed ice, fishing license and tackle, souvenirs. Book exchange available. Harleys welcome. Free cup of coffee in the morning to get you going with your overnight stay. MasterCard, Discover and VISA. Bonjour et bon vacances! Phone/fax (403) 862-7407.

[ADVERTISEMENT] ▲

DC 1118.3 (1852.2 km) **F 369.7** (595 km) Koidern River bridge No. 1.

NOTE: Watch for road construction between Kilometreposts 1852 and 1872 in 1996.

DC 1118.8 (1853 km) **F 369.2** (594.2 km) **Historical Mile 1152.** Lake Creek Yukon government campground just west of highway; 30 large level sites (6 pull-through), water pump, litter barrels, firewood, firepits, picnic tables, kitchen shelter and outhouses. Camping fee $8. ▲

DC 1122.7 (1859.5 km) **F 365.3** (587.9 km) **Historical Mile 1156.** Longs Creek.

DC 1125 (1863.5 km) **F 363** (584.2 km) Turnout to east with litter barrel.

DC 1125.7 (1864.7 km) **F 362.3** (583 km) **Pickhandle Lake** to west, good fishing from boat for northern pike all summer; also grayling, whitefish and lingcod.

DC 1128 (1868.4 km) **F 360** (579.3 km) Aptly named Reflection Lake to west mirrors the Kluane Ranges. The highway parallels this range between Koidern and Haines Junction.

DC 1130.6 (1872.6 km) **F 357.4** (575.2 km) **Historical Mile 1164.** Lodge. There are 2 "lodges" at Koidern; continue north past Koidern River bridge No. 2 for Bear Flats Lodge at Koidern.

DC 1130.7 (1872.8 km) **F 357.3** (575 km) Koidern River bridge No. 2.

DC 1133.7 (1877.6 km) **F 354.3** (570.2 km) **Historic Milepost 1167.** Bear Flats Lodge; gas, food, camping and lodging.

Bear Flats Lodge offers a relaxing and refreshing change for the travel weary. Licensed dining room, pizza, cold beer to go, ice, excellent well water. Tour buses are welcome. Our cottages have private baths, fully-serviced RV parking, gas, diesel, minor repairs. Dump station and campground with tables and firewood. We also provide a book trading shelf and souvenirs. Winter plug-ins available. A dedicated service to travelers. Phone (403) 862-7401. [ADVERTISEMENT] ▲

DC 1135 (1880 km) **F 353** (568 km) **Historical Mile 1169.** White River Motor Inn; food, gas, lodging and camping. Open year-round. ▲

White River Motor Inn. See display ad this section.

DC 1135.6 (1881 km) **F 352.4** (567.1 km) White River bridge, clearance 17.1 feet/5.2m. The White River, a major tributary of the Yukon River, was named by Hudson's Bay Co. explorer Robert Campbell for its white colour, caused by the volcanic ash in the water. *This river is considered very dangerous; not recommended for boating.*

CAUTION: Slow down for sharp turn in road at north end of bridge.

NOTE: Watch for road construction northbound between Kilometreposts 1882 and 1915 in 1996.

DC 1141.5 (1890.5 km) **F 346.5** (557.6 km) **Moose Lake** to west, grayling to 18 inches, use dry flies and small spinners, midsummer. Boat needed for lake.

DC 1144.3 (1895 km) **F 343.7** (553.1 km) Sanpete Creek, named by an early prospector after Sanpete County in Utah.

DC 1147.5 (1900.3 km) **F 340.5** (548 km) Dry Creek No. 1. Turnout to east.

DC 1149.8 (1904 km) **F 338.2** (544.3 km) *CAUTION: Slow down for bumpy banked descent to Dry Creek No. 2.*

DC 1150.3 (1904.5 km) **F 337.7** (543.5 km) **Historical Mile 1184.** Dry Creek No. 2. Historical marker to west about the Chrisna gold rush.

DC 1155 (1911.8 km) **F 333** (535.9 km) Small Lake to east.

DC 1155.2 (1913 km) **F 332.8** (535.6 km) **Historical Mile 1188.** Turnoff for Snag Junction Yukon government campground, 0.4 mile/0.6 km in on gravel loop road. There are 15 tent and vehicle sites (some level), a kitchen shelter, outhouses, picnic tables, firewood, firepits and litter barrels. Camping fee $8. Small-boat launch. Swimming in Small Lake. A dirt road (status unknown) connects the Alaska Highway here with the abandoned airfield and Indian village at Snag to the northeast. ▲

DC 1162.1 (1924.5 km) **F 325.9** (524.5 km) Inger Creek.

DC 1165.7 (1930 km) **F 322.3** (518.7 km) View of Nutzotin Mountains to northwest, Kluane Ranges to southwest. On a clear day you should be able to see the snow-clad Wrangell Mountains in the distance to the west.

DC 1167.2 (1932.4 km) **F 320.8** (516.3 km) Beaver Creek plank bridge, clearance 17.1 feet/5.2m.

Canada-U.S. international border north of Beaver Creek. (Earl L. Brown, staff)

Beaver Creek

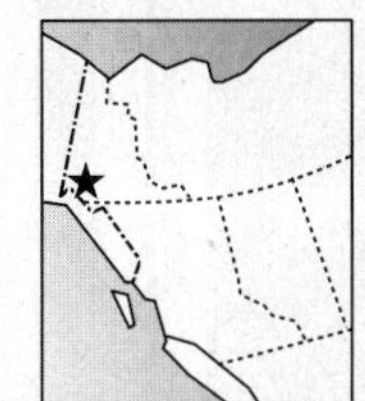

DC 1168.5 (1934.5 km) **F 319.5** (514.2 km) **Historic Milepost 1202.** Driving distance to Haines Junction, 184 miles/295 km; to Tok, 113 miles/182 km; to Haines, 334 miles/537.5 km. **Population:** 143. **Emergency Services:** RCMP, phone (403) 862-5555. **Ambulance,** phone (403) 862-3333. **Visitor Information:** Yukon government visitor information centre, open daily late May through mid-September. Phone (403) 862-7321. The visitor centre has a book of dried Yukon wildflowers for those interested in the flora of the territory. Get your Yukon Gold Explorer's Passport stamped here.

Site of the old Canadian customs station. Local residents were pleased to see customs relocated north of town in 1983, having long endured the flashing lights and screaming sirens set off whenever a tourist forgot to stop.

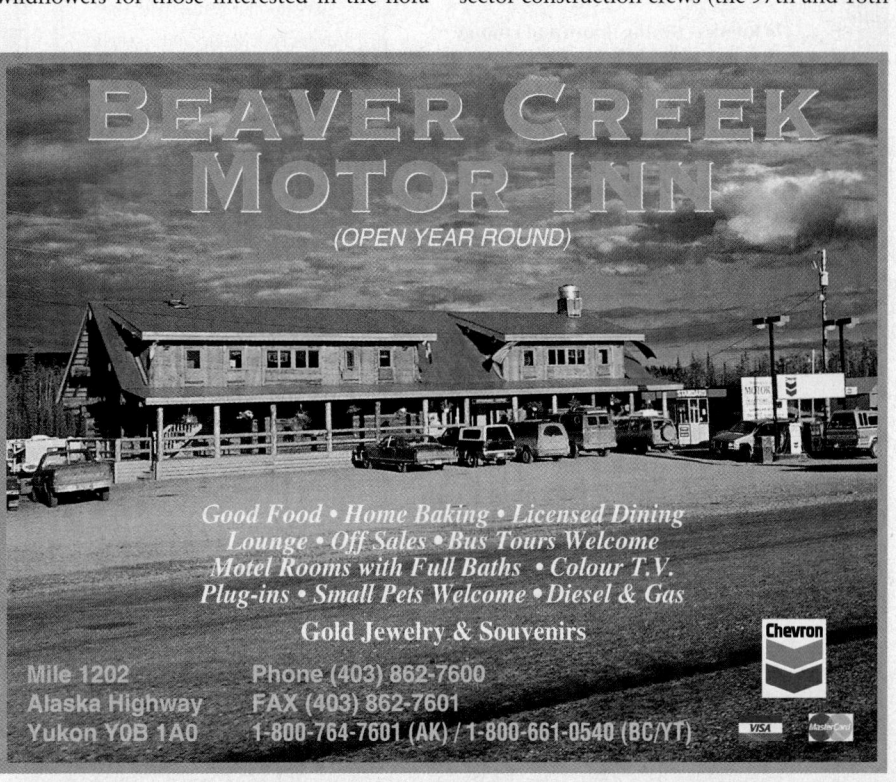

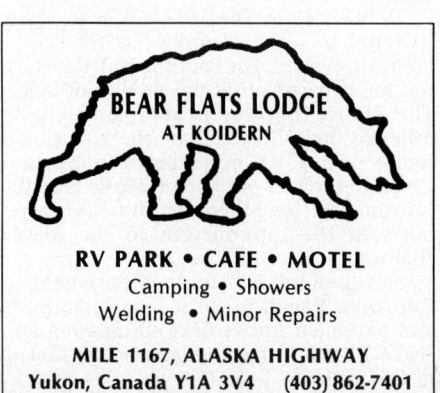

Beaver Creek is 1 of 2 sites where Alaska Highway construction crews working from opposite directions connected the highway. In October 1942, Alaska Highway construction operations were being rushed to conclusion as winter set in. Eastern and western sector construction crews (the 97th and 18th

Engineers) pushed through to meet at a junction on Beaver Creek on Oct. 28., thus making it possible for the first time for vehicles to travel the entire length of the highway. East–west crews had connected at Contact Creek on Sept. 24, 1942.

Motels, gas stations with repair service, a post office and licensed restaurants are located here. Beaver Creek is also an overnight stop for bus travelers. Private RV park with hookups, hot showers, store, laundry and dump station. ▲

The interesting looking church here is Our Lady of Grace mission. Built in 1961, it is 1 of 3 Catholic missions on the north Alaska Highway (the others are in Burwash Landing and Haines Junction). Services from the last Sunday of May to first Sunday of September. There is a public swimming pool beside the community club. Check with the information centre about the live stage show at the Westmark Inn, evenings in summer; admission charged.

Beaver Creek Motor Inn. See display ad this section.

Westmark Inn. See display ad this section.

Alaska Highway Log

(continued)

Distance* from Dawson Creek (DC) is followed by distance from Fairbanks (F). Original mileposts are indicated in the text as Historical Mile.

*Mileages from Dawson Creek are based on actual driving distance. Kilometres from Dawson Creek are based on physical kilometreposts. Please read Mileposts and Kilometreposts in the introduction for an explanation of how this highway is logged.

DC 1169.7 (1936.3 km) **F 318.3** (512.2 km) Rest area to west with litter barrels and outhouses.

DC 1170.3 (1937.3 km) **F 317.7** (511.3 km) **Private Aircraft:** Beaver Creek airstrip; elev. 2,129 feet/649m; length 3,740 feet/1,140m; gravel; no fuel. Airport of entry for Canada customs.

DC 1170.5 (1937.6 km) **F 317.5** (511 km) Beaver Creek Canada customs station; phone (403) 862-7230. Open 24 hours a day year-round. All traffic entering Canada must stop here for clearance. (See Customs Requirements in the GENERAL INFORMATION section.)

CAUTION: Narrow winding road from here to border northbound (next 19.4 miles/31.2 km). Watch for bad corners, rough spots, gravel road surface. Highway reconstruction may be under way in 1996 as part of the ongoing Shakwak Highway Reconstruction Project. Watch for construction crews and equipment between Beaver Creek and the border.

DC 1175.4 (1945.5 km) **F 312.6** (503.1 km) Snag Creek plank bridge.

DC 1176.3 (1946.9 km) **F 311.7** (501.6 km) Mirror Creek.

DC 1178.3 (1952 km) **F 309.7** (498.4 km) Lake to east, turnout to west.

DC 1186 (1963 km) **F 302** (486 km) Little Scottie Creek.

DC 1189.5 (1967.5 km) **F 298.5** (480.4 km) **Historic Milepost 1221.** Turnout with plaque and other markers at Canada–U.S. international border. Litter barrels. From the viewing decks, note the narrow clearing marking the border. This is part of the 20-foot-/6-m-wide swath cut by surveyors from 1904 to 1920 along the 141st meridian (from Demarcation Point on the Arctic Ocean south 600 miles/966 km to Mount St. Elias in the Wrangell Mountains) to mark the Alaska–Canada border. This swath continues south to mark the boundary between southeastern Alaska and Canada. Portions of the swath are cleared periodically by the International Boundary Commission.

TIME ZONE CHANGE: Alaska observes Alaska time; Yukon Territory observes Pacific time. See Time Zones in the GENERAL INFORMATION section for details.

DC 1189.8 (1968 km) **F 298.2** (479.9 km) **Historical Mile 1221.8.** U.S. customs border station.

IMPORTANT: *The MILEPOST®* log now switches to physical mileposts for northbound travelers. For southbound travelers, the log is based on actual driving distance. The Alaska Highway is approximately 32 miles/51 km shorter than the traditional figure of 1,221.8 miles between Dawson Creek and the YT–AK border. Please read the information on Mileposts and Kilometreposts in the introduction to the Alaska Highway.

Northbound: Fair to good pavement to Fairbanks. Watch for frost heaves, potholes and pavement breaks next 40 miles/64 km. *NOTE: Watch for road construction northbound to Tok.*

Southbound: Narrow, winding road to

Haines Junction. Poor pavement to Beaver Creek, fair to good pavement to Haines Junction. Watch for frost heaves, rough spots, gravel breaks and road construction.

ALASKA ROUTE 2
Distance* from Dawson Creek (DC) is followed by distance from Fairbanks (F).
*Mileages from Dawson Creek and Fairbanks are based on physical mileposts in Alaska. Kilometres given are the metric equivalents of these mileages.

DC 1221.8 (1966.3 km) **F 298.2** (479.9 km) Port Alcan U.S. Customs and Immigration Service border station, open 24 hours a day year-round; pay phone (credit card and collect calls only) and restrooms. All traffic entering Alaska must stop for clearance. Phone (907) 774-2242; emergencies, 774-2252. Read through the GENERAL INFORMATION section for details on alcoholic beverages, holidays, customs requirements, fishing regulations, driving and other aspects of travel in Alaska and Canada.

Border Branch U.S. post office is located here (ZIP 99764); ask for directions at the custom office.

DC 1222.5 (1967.4 km) **F 297.5** (478.8 km) Tetlin National Wildlife Refuge boundary sign to west.

DC 1223.4 (1968.9 km) **F 296.6** (477.3 km) Scotty Creek bridge.

DC 1224.6 (1970.7 km) **F 295.4** (475.4 km) Double-ended gravel turnout to southwest at Highway Lake with USF&WS interpretive sign on wetlands. Beaver lodges southwest side of highway.

DC 1225.4 (1972 km) **F 294.6** (474.1 km) USF&WS Desper Creek parking area and canoe launch.

DC 1225.5 (1972.2 km) **F 294.5** (473.9 km) **Border City Lodge.** See display ad this section. ▲

DC 1226 (1973 km) **294** (473.1 km) **Scottie Creek Services.** See display ad this section.

DC 1227.8 (1975.9 km) **F 292.2** (470.2 km) Large double-ended paved parking area to southwest with litter barrels and USF&WS interpretive sign on migratory birds and area geography. View to south of lakes in Chisana (SHOE-sanna) River valley along Scotty Creek and west to the Wrangell Mountains. The Chisana gold rush took place in 1913. A mining camp was established on Cross Creek near the Chisana River, 38 miles southeast of Nabesna in the Wrangell Mountains. The settlement's population peaked at 148 in 1920.

DC 1229 (1977.8 km) **F 291** (468.3 km) USF&WS log cabin visitor center to south. Viewing deck and outdoor displays on wildlife and other subjects. Indoor wildlife displays and mounts. Deckside nature talks given twice daily. Restrooms (wheelchair accessible). Open 7 A.M. to 7 P.M. Memorial Day to Labor Day. Current highway conditions and fishing information posted on bulletin board. ♿

CAUTION: Watch for frost heaves, patches and potholes northbound and southbound.

DC 1230.9 (1980.9 km) **F 289.1** (465.3 km) View of Island Lake.

DC 1233.3 (1984.7 km) **F 286.7** (461.4 km) Large paved double-ended parking area to northeast on old alignment; litter barrels. Watch for bears.

DC 1237 (1990.7 km) **F 283** (455.4 km) Trail to **Hidden Lake** (1 mile/1.6 km); rainbow fishing. USF&WS interpretive signs on rainbow trout and black spruce bogs.

DC **1240** (1995.5 km) F **280** (450.6 km) Turnout to west; no easy turnaround. Access to **Willow Lake** for fishing.

DC **1240.3** (1996 km) F **279.7** (450.1 km) Vertical culverts on either side of highway are an experiment to keep ground from thawing and thus prevent frost heaves.

DC **1243.6** (2001.3 km) F **276.4** (444.8 km) Paved turnout. Scenic viewpoint to south on loop road has a litter barrel and USF&WS interpretive signs on fire management and the effects of forest fires on the natural history of area.

DC **1246.6** (2006.1 km) F **273.4** (440 km) **Historic Milepost 1248. Gardiner Creek** bridge; parking to west at south end of bridge. Grayling fishing.

DC **1247.6** (2007.8 km) F **272.4** (438.4 km) Paved double-ended viewpoint to east with litter barrels.

DC **1249.3** (2010.5 km) F **270.7** (435.6 km) **Historic Milepost 1254. Deadman Lake** USF&WS campground, 1.2 miles/1.9 km in on dirt road. Turnout at highway junction with campground access road. The campground has 18 sites on long loop road, firepits, toilets, picnic tables, no drinking water, boat ramp, interpretive signs, information board and self-guided nature trail. Scenic spot. Swimming and fishing. Northern pike average 2 feet, but skinny (local residents call them "snakes"); use wobbling lures or spinners.

Pavement patches next mile northbound.

DC **1250.1** (2011.8 km) F **269.9** (434.3 km) Rest area to west. Double-ended paved parking area, 4 picnic tables, litter barrels, concrete fireplaces, toilets, no water.

DC **1252.2** (2015.2 km) F **267.8** (431 km) Double-ended gravel turnout to southwest with USF&WS interpretive sign on solar basins (warm ponds and shallow marshes).

DC **1253** (2016.5 km) F **267** (429.7 km) Views of lakes and muskeg in Chisana River valley.

DC **1253.6** (2017.4 km) F **266.4** (428.7 km) **Frontier Surplus.** Military surplus goods. Clothing, sleeping bags, extreme cold weather "bunny boots," military tents, ammunition, tanned furs. Alaska T-shirts and caps. Local crafts, shed moose and caribou antlers. Antler products, belt buckles, bolo ties, hat racks, handmade ulus.

"Moosquitoes," diamond willow lamps and canes, finished or unfinished. Used Alaska license plates, cold pop. Open late every day. Motorhome and RV loop. Phone (907) 778-2274. [ADVERTISEMENT]

DC **1256.3** (2021.7 km) F **263.7** (424.4 km) Northway state highway maintenance camp; no services.

DC **1256.7** (2022.5 km) F **263.3** (423.7 km) Lakeview USF&WS campground on beautiful Yarger Lake; 8 sites, tables, toilets, firepits, firewood, no drinking water. Interpretive signs. *NOTE: No turnaround space. Not recommended for trailers, 5th wheelers or large RVs. (Large vehicles use Deadman Lake Campground at* ***Milepost DC 1249.3.****)*

This is a good place to view ducks and loons. Look for the St. Elias Range to the

Waterfowl, like this pintail, are common on lakes in the Tetlin refuge. (© Chris Sharp)

south, Wrangell Mountains to the southwest and Mentasta Mountains to the west.

Roadside wildflowers include sweet pea, pale yellow Indian paintbrush, yarrow and Labrador tea.

DC 1258 (2024.5 km) **F 262** (421.6 km) Watch for rough patches in pavement.

DC 1260.2 (2028 km) **F 259.8** (418.1 km) 1260 Inn roadhouse (closed in 1995, current status unknown).

Southbound: Watch for frost heaves, potholes and pavement breaks next 40 miles/64 km to border. Expect road construction.

DC 1263 (2032.5 km) **F 257** (413.6 km) **Wrangell View Service Center.** See display ad this section.

DC 1263.5 (2033.4 km) **F 256.5** (412.8 km) Chisana River parallels the highway to the southwest. This is the land of a thousand ponds, most unnamed. Good trapping country. In early June, travelers may note numerous cottony white seeds blowing in the wind; these seeds are from a species of willow.

DC 1264 (2034.2 km) **F 256** (412 km) **Northway Junction.** Campground, gas, laundromat, store and Native arts and crafts shop located at junction. An Alaska State Trooper is also stationed here. ▲

Naabia Niign Campground & Athabascan Indian Crafts. See display ad this section. ▲

A 7-mile/11.3-km side road leads south across the Chisana River bridge to the community of Northway (description follows). A boat launch at Chisana River bridge is one of 3 boat access points to Tetlin National Wildlife Refuge.

Northway

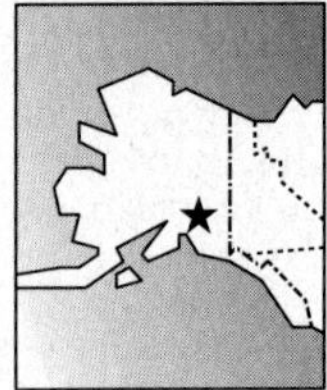

Located 7 miles/11.3 km south of the Alaska Highway via a side road. **Population:** 364 (area). **Emergency Services: Alaska State Troopers,** phone (907) 778-2245. **EMS,** phone (907) 778-2211. **Fire Department, Clinic.**

Elevation: 1,710 feet/521m. **Climate:** Mean monthly temperature in July, 58.5°F/15°C. In January, -21°F/-30°C. Record high 91°F/33°C in June 1969; record low -72°F/-58°C in January 1952.

Private Aircraft: Northway airport, adjacent south; elev. 1,716 feet/523m; length 5,147 feet/1,569m; asphalt; fuel 100LL, Jet B, MOGAS; customs available.

Northway has a community hall, post office and modern school. FAA station and customs office are at the airport. Visitor services include motels, grocery, liquor store, propane, gas stations and air taxi service.

Historically occupied by Athabascan Indians, Northway was named to honor the village chief who adopted the name of a riverboat captain in the early 1900s. (Chief Walter Northway died in 1993. He was thought to be 117 years old.) The rich Athabascan traditions of dancing, crafts and hunting and trapping continue today in Northway Village. Local Athabascan handicrafts available for purchase include birchbark baskets, beadwork accessories, and moose hide and fur items such as moccasins, mukluks, mittens and hats.

Northway's airport was built in the 1940s as part of the Northwest Staging Route. This cooperative project of the United States and Canada was a chain of air bases from Edmonton, AB, through Whitehorse, YT, to Fairbanks. This chain of air bases helped build up and supply Alaska defense during WWII and also was used during construction of the Alcan and the Canol project. Lend-lease aircraft bound for Russia were flown up this route to Ladd Field (now Fort Wainwright) in Fairbanks. Northway is still an important port of entry for air traffic to Alaska, and a busy one.

Northway is located within Tetlin National Wildlife Refuge. Established in 1980, the 730,000-acre refuge stretches south from the Alaska Highway and west from the Canadian border. The major physical features include rolling hills, hundreds of small lakes and 2 glacial rivers (the Nabesna and Chisana) which combine to form the Tanana River. The refuge has a very high density of nesting waterfowl. Annual duck production in favorable years exceeds 50,000. Among the larger birds using the refuge are trumpeter swans, sandhill cranes, Pacific and common loons, osprey, bald eagles and ptarmigan. Other wildlife includes moose, black and grizzly bear, wolf, coyote, beaver, red fox and lynx. Activities allowed on the refuge include wildlife observation, hunting, fishing, camping, hiking and trapping. Check with refuge personnel at the USF&WS office in Tok prior to your visit for more detailed information. Write Refuge Manager, Tetlin National Wildlife Refuge, Box 779, Tok, AK 99780; or phone

(907) 883-5312. Information on the refuge is also available at the USF&WS visitor center at **Milepost DC 1229** on the Alaska Highway.

Confluence of Moose Creek and Chisana River, about 0.8 mile/1.3 km downstream from Chisana River bridge on Northway Road, south side of river, northern pike to 15 lbs., use red-and-white spoon, spring or fall. **Chisana River**, downstream from bridge, lingcod (burbot) to 8 lbs., use chunks of liver or meat, spring. **Nabesna Slough**, south end of runway, grayling to 3 lbs., use spinner or gold flies, late May.

Northway Airport Lodge & Motel. See display ad this section.

Alaska Highway Log

(continued)

DC 1267.4 (2039.6 km) **F 252.6** (406.5 km) *CAUTION: Slow down for a big bump in the road known as "Beaver Slide."*

Wonderful view of the Tanana River.

DC 1268.1 (2040.8 km) **F 251.9** (405.4 km) Beaver Creek bridge. The tea-colored water flowing in the creek is the result of tannins absorbed by the water as it flows through muskeg. This phenomenon may be observed in other Northern creeks.

DC 1269 (2042.2 km) **F 251** (403.9 km) **Historic Milepost 1271.** Scenic viewpoint. Double-ended gravel turnout to west has a litter barrel and USF&WS interpretive sign about the Tanana River, largest tributary of the Yukon River.

DC 1269.1 (2042.4 km) **F 250.9** (403.8 km) Slow down for bad pavement break.

DC 1272.7 (2048.2 km) **F 247.3** (398 km) Scenic viewpoint. Double-ended paved turnout to west with litter barrels. USF&WS interpretive sign on pond ecology and mosquitoes.

To the northwest the Tanana River flows near the highway; beyond, the Kalutna River snakes its way through plain and marshland. Mentasta Mountains are visible to the southwest.

DC 1273.9 (2050.1 km) **F 246.1** (396 km) Paved parking area with litter barrel to west by Tanana River.

In June, wild sweet peas create thick borders along the highway. This is rolling country, with aspen, birch, cottonwood, willow and white spruce.

DC 1275.5 (2052.7 km) **F 244.5** (393.5 km) Slide area next 0.3 mile/0.5 km northbound.

DC 1279 (2058.3 km) **F 241** (387.8 km) Highway cuts through sand dune stabilized by aspen and spruce trees.

DC 1281 (2061.5 km) **F 239** (384.6 km) Rough road, pavement cracks.

DC 1284.2 (2066.7 km) **F 235.8** (379.5 km) Tetlin National Wildlife Refuge boundary sign.

DC 1284.6 (2067.3 km) **F 235.4** (378.8 km) Large double-ended paved turnout to east.

DC 1285.7 (2069.1 km) **F 234.3** (377.1 km) Granite intrusion in older metamorphosed rock is exposed by road cut.

DC 1289 (2074.4 km) **F 231** (371.7 km) First view northbound of 3.4-mile-/5.5-km-long Midway Lake.

DC 1289.4 (2075 km) **F 230.6** (371.1 km) **Historic Milepost 1292.** Turnout uphill on east side of highway with litter barrels, view of Midway Lake and the Wrangell Mountains. USF&WS interpretive signs on Wrangell-St. Elias National Park and Native peoples.

NOTE: Difficult access for large vehicles and trailers, easier access from southbound lane.

Chisana River valley view from the Alaska Highway near Northway. (© Carmen Scott)

DC 1290 (2076 km) **F 230** (370.1 km) Beautiful view of Midway Lake southbound.

DC 1292.4 (2079.8 km) **F 227.6** (366.3 km) Paved turnout west side.

DC 1293.7 (2081.9 km) **F 226.3** (364.2 km) Paved turnout west side.

DC 1294.3 (2082.9 km) **F 225.7** (363.2 km) Bad pavement break.

DC 1301.7 (2094.8 km) **F 218.3** (351.3 km) **Historic Milepost 1306. Tetlin Junction,** Alaska Highway and Taylor Highway (Alaska Route 5) junction. 40 Mile Roadhouse; status of services unknown. The Taylor Highway (gravel, open summer only) heads northeast via Jack Wade Junction to Eagle (see TAYLOR HIGHWAY section) and to Yukon Highway 9 (Top of the World Highway) to Dawson City. (See KLONDIKE LOOP section for log of Yukon Highway 9 and description of Dawson City.)

NOTE: If you are traveling to Dawson City, keep in mind that both the Canada and U.S. customs stations are closed at night; you CANNOT cross the border unless customs stations are open. Proposed customs hours in summer 1996: 8 A.M. *to 9* P.M. *Alaska time, 9* A.M. *to 10* P.M. *Pacific time on the Canadian side.*

DC 1302.7 (2096.4 km) **F 217.3** (349.7 km) Scenic viewpoint at paved turnout to southwest.

DC 1303.4 (2097.5 km) **F 216.6** (348.6 km) Tanana River bridge. Informal parking area and boat launch to east at north end of bridge. Tanana (TAN-uh-naw), an Indian name, was first reported by the Western Union Telegraph Expedition of 1886. According to William Henry Dall, chief scientist of the expedition, the name means "mountain river." The Tanana is the largest tributary in Alaska of the Yukon River. From here the highway parallels the Tanana to Fairbanks. The Alaska Range looms in the distance.

DC 1304.6 (2099.5 km) **F 215.4** (346.6 km) Evidence of 1990 burn from here north to Tok. The Tok River fire occurred in July of 1990 and burned 97,352 acres. The fire closed the Alaska and Glenn highways at times and threatened the town of Tok. There is an interpretive display on the Tok River fire at the Alaska Public Lands Information Center in Tok.

DC 1306.6 (2102.7 km) **F 213.4** (343.4 km) Road east to lake.

DC 1308.5 (2105.7 km) **F 211.5** (340.4 km) Weigh station and turnoff to U.S. Coast Guard loran-C station and signal towers.

This loran (long range navigation) station is 1 of 7 in Alaska. A series of 4 700-foot/213-m towers suspends a multi-element wire antenna used to transmit navigation signals. These signals may be used by air, land and sea navigators as an aid in determining their position. This station is located here as necessary for good geometry with 2 Gulf of Alaska loran transmitting stations.

DC 1308.8 (2106.3 km) **F 211.2** (339.9 km) Paved turnout to west.

Porcupines are common in wooded areas. (© Beth Davidow)

DC 1309.2 (2106.9 km) F 210.8 (339.2 km) Tok River State Recreation Site; 25 campsites, overflow parking, tables, firepits, toilets (wheelchair accessible), litter barrels, nature trail and boat launch. Check bulletin board for schedule of interpretive programs. Camping fee $8/night or annual pass. *CAUTION: Swift water.* ♿▲

Annual passes good for unlimited camping at all Alaska state parks within a calendar year are available for $75 for Alaska residents and $100 for nonresidents. Annual daily parking pass is $25, annual boat launch pass is $50. Super Pass (camping, boat launch and parking) is available to Alaska residents only for $135. Passes may be purchased at the Alaska Public Lands Information Center in Tok.

DC 1309.4 (2107.2 km) F 210.6 (338.9 km) Tok River bridge.

DC 1312.7 (2112.5 km) F 207.3 (333.6 km) Tok community limits. Mountain views ahead northbound.

Wayfarer's Motel. See display ad this section.

DC 1312.8 (2112.7 km) F 207.2 (333.4 km) Tok Dog Mushers Assoc. track and buildings. Paved bike trail from Tok ends here.

DC 1313 (2113 km) F 207 (333.1 km) Airstrip. See Private Aircraft information in Tok section. Entering Tok (northbound), description follows. Tok is located at the junction of the Alaska Highway and Tok Cutoff (Glenn Highway). Anchorage-bound travelers turn west on the Tok Cutoff (see the TOK CUTOFF/GLENN HIGHWAY section). Fairbanks-bound travelers continue north on the Alaska Highway.

Southbound travelers: Driving distance from Tok to Beaver Creek is 113 miles/182 km; Haines Junction 296 miles/476 km; Haines (departure point for Alaska state ferries) 446.5 miles/718.5 km; and Whitehorse 396 miles/637 km.

NOTE: Watch for road construction southbound to the AK-YT border in 1996.

DC 1313.1 (2113.1 km) F 206.9 (332.9 km) **Tok Gateway Salmon Bake and RV Park.** Vacationers should not miss Tok's Gateway Salmon Bake, featuring outdoor flame-grilled Alaska king salmon, halibut, ribs and reindeer sausage. Buffalo burgers. Chowder. Good food, friendly people; casual

dining at its best. Open 11 A.M. to 9 P.M., except Sunday 4-9 P.M. Free shuttle bus service from local hotels and RV parks. Wooded RV and tent sites with tables, clean restrooms, dump station and water. Free dry camping with dinner. Phone (907) 883-5555. [ADVERTISEMENT] ▲

DC 1313.2 (2113.3 km) F 206.8 (332.8 km) **Willard's Full Service Repair**. See display ad this section.

DC 1313.3 (2113.5 km) F 206.7 (332.6 km) **Eska Trading Post**, on the left northbound. Home of frozen yogurt and premium quality hand-dipped Alaskan ice cream. Along with our audio books for sale and book swap, check out our video and Nintendo rentals, popcorn, candy, pop and "hex" tanning unit. See display ad this section. [ADVERTISEMENT]

DC 1313.3 (2113.5 km) F 206.7 (332.6 km) **Young's Motel and Fast Eddy's Restaurant.** A touch of Alaskana in a modern setting. Affordable, clean and spacious. We cater to the independent highway traveler. Open year-round with all the

amenities: telephones, private baths, satellite TV, ample parking. Check in at Fast Eddy's full-service restaurant, open 6 A.M. to midnight. Reserve early! P.O. Box 482, Tok, AK 99780. (907) 883-4411; fax (907) 883-5023. [ADVERTISEMENT]

DC 1313.3 (2113.5 km) F 206.7 (332.6 km) **Village Texaco Foodmart.** Filtered unleaded and premium gas and diesel. Lubricants and propane. Automatic teller machine, laundromat, phone cards, pay phones and clean restrooms. Chicken, burritos, mojos, snacks, pop, ice, milk shakes and ice cream. RV supplies. Alaskan souvenirs. Across highway from Tok RV Village. See display ad this section. [ADVERTISEMENT]

DC 1313.3 (2113.5 km) F 206.7 (332.6 km) **The Bull Shooter Sporting Goods & RV Park,** Tok, Alaska. Fishing and hunting licenses. Sporting goods. Large selection of fishing gear and tackle. Camping supplies. Guns and ammo. Plan to stay at the Bull Shooter's nice, quiet RV park. 30 spaces, 24 pull-throughs. Full or partial hookups, 30-amp electric, dump station, good drinking water. Non-metered showers, restrooms, ice and phone. We accept VISA and MasterCard. Welcome to Alaska! We are on the left as you come into Tok. P.O. Box 553, Tok, AK 99780. Reservations accepted. Call (907) 883-5625. See display ad in Tok section. [ADVERTISEMENT] ▲

DC 1313.4 (2113.6 km) F 206.6 (332.5 km) **Tok RV Village.** Alaska's finest. Good Sam or KOA cards honored. Convenient pull-through spaces with 30-amp power. Full and partial hookups, clean restrooms and showers, dump station, laundry, vehicle wash, picnic tables, public phones. Gift shop. RV supplies, ice. MasterCard, VISA and Discover. Located across highway from Village Texaco Foodmart. Restaurants, liquor store, night club, hardware store, 1-hour photo processing and oil change and lube service station nearby. See display ad in Tok section. [ADVERTISEMENT] ▲

DC 1313.9 (2114.5 km) F 206.1 (331.7 km) **Iron Dog Outfitters/Tok Northern Exposures.** 1-hour photo developing. Your first stop in Tok for RV maintenance needs. Oil change, lubrication, machine shop and

certified welder; (907) 883-5670. Get your film developed next door and have your "olde tyme" portrait taken. Film, albums, frames, gifts; (907) 883-5424. On your left northbound. See display ad. [ADVERTISEMENT]

DC 1314.1 (2114.8 km) F 205.9 (331.3 km) Alaska Public Lands Information Center and Tok Mainstreet Visitor Center.

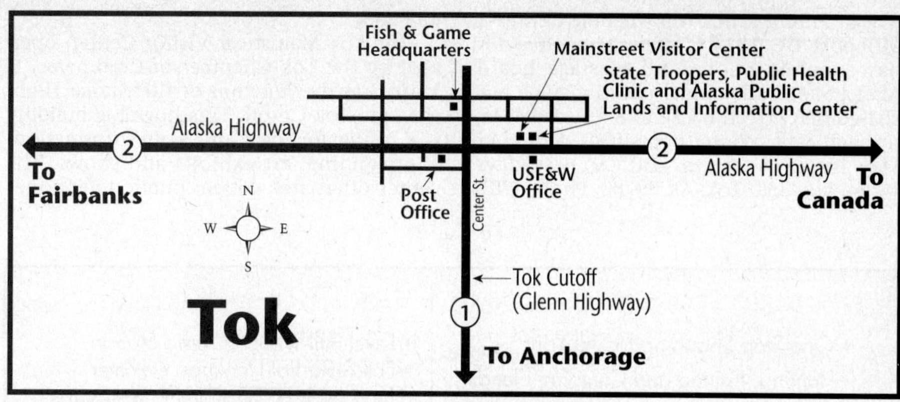

Tok

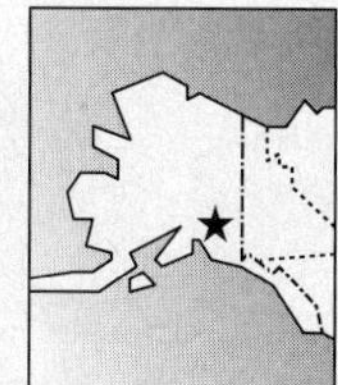

DC 1314.2 (2115 km) F 205.8 (331.2 km) At the junction of the Alaska Highway and Tok Cutoff (Glenn Highway) between the Tanana River to the north and the Alaska Range to the southwest. **Population:** 1,405. **Emergency Services: Alaska State Troopers,** phone (907) 883-5111. **Fire Department,** phone (907) 883-2333. **Community Clinic,** across from the fire hall on the Tok Cutoff, phone (907) 883-5855 during business hours. **Ambulance,** phone (907) 883-2300 or 911. EMT squad and air medivac available. **Public Health Clinic,** next to the Alaska State Troopers at **Milepost 1314.1,** phone (907) 883-4101.

Visitor Information: The state-operated

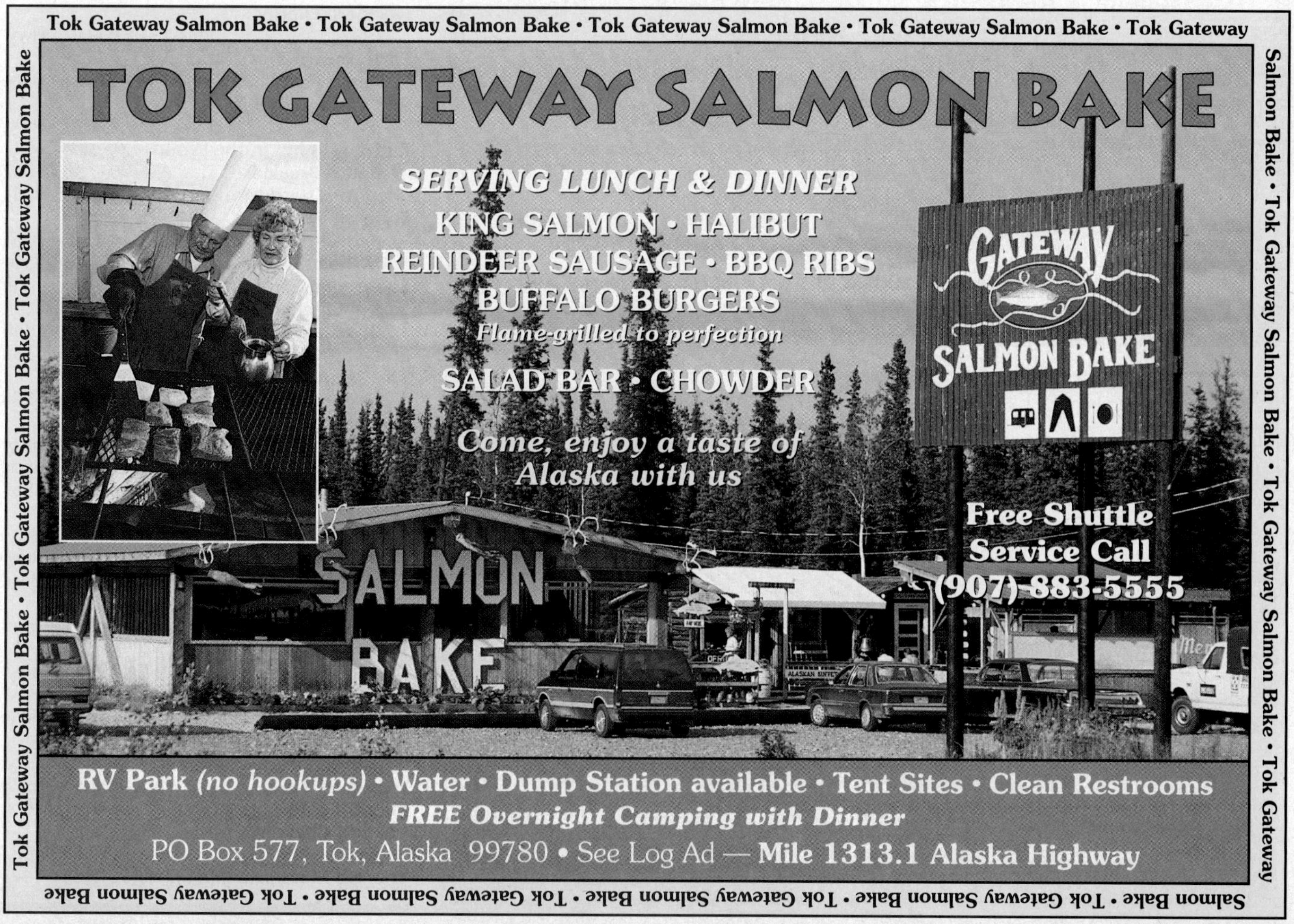

Alaska Public Lands Information Center at **Milepost DC 1314.1** offers free coffee and has a public phone and message board. Alaska State Park annual passes may be purchased here. Open 8 A.M. to 8 P.M. daily May through Sept. Winter hours (Oct. 1 through May 15) are 8 A.M. to 4:30 P.M., weekdays. Write: Box 359, Tok, AK 99780. Phone (907) 883-5667.

The Tok Mainstreet Visitor Center, operated by the Tok Chamber of Commerce, is located at the junction of the Alaska Highway and Tok Cutoff. This huge log building is a center for local and state information, trip planning, art exhibits and shows. The center offers free coffee, public telephones and restrooms, a message board and gift shop. It is open daily 7 A.M. to 9 P.M., May 1 to Oct. 1. Write Box 389, Tok, AK 99780; phone (907) 883-5775 or 883-5887.

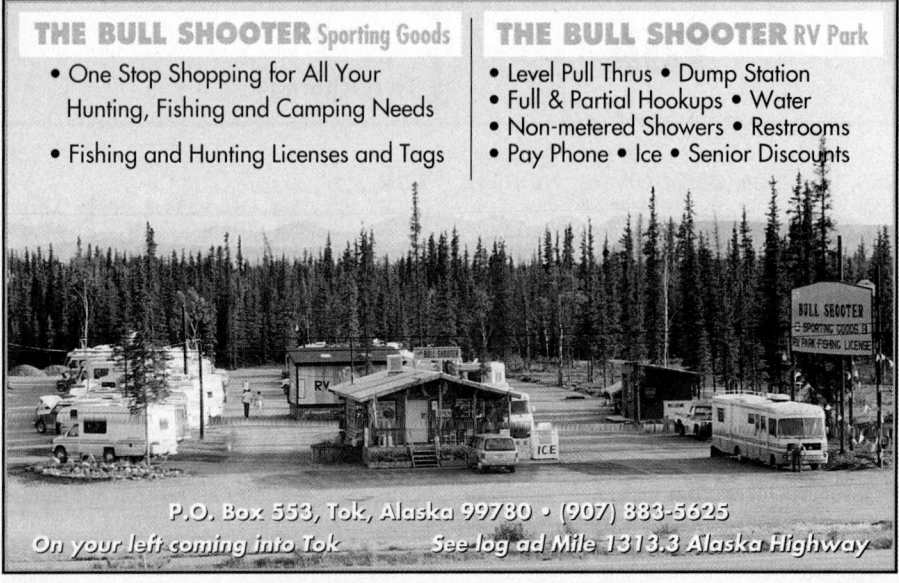

The U.S. Fish & Wildlife Service office is located directly across the highway from the Public Lands Information Center. Visitors are welcome. Check with them regarding Tetlin National Wildlife Refuge. Office hours

TOK ADVERTISERS

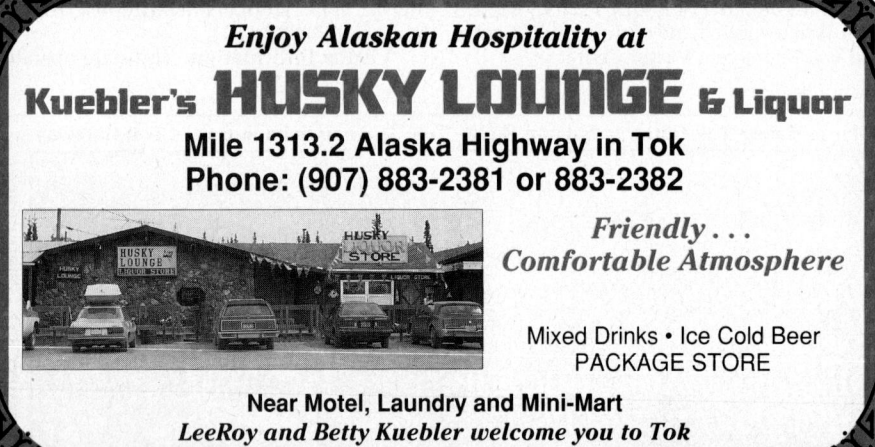

"A Tent in Tok" .... P.O. Box 110
A WinterCabin Bed & Breakfast .... Ph. (907) 883-5655
All Alaska Gifts & Crafts .... N. corner of junction
Bull Shooter Sporting Goods & RV Park, The .... Mile 1313.3 Alaska Hwy.
Burnt Paw .... Adjacent post office
Cheryl's Old Fashion Bed & Breakfast Cabin .... Mile 1315.7 Alaska Hwy.
Eska Trading Post ...... Mile 1313.3 Alaska Hwy.
Faith Chapel .... First & Center
Fast Eddy's Restaurant .... Mile 1313.3 Alaska Hwy.
First Baptist Church .... Downtown
Golden Bear Motel, Restaurant, RV Park .... Ph. (907) 883-2561
Golden Dreams Bed and Breakfast .... Ph. (907) 883-5659
Grizzly Auto Repair ..... 1 mile S. on Tok Cutoff
Hayner's Trading Post .... Mile 1.7 Tok Cutoff
International Cabana ... Mile 1313.8 Alaska Hwy.
Iron Dog Outfitters .... Ph. (907) 883-5670
Kuebler's Husky Lounge & Liquor .... Ph. (907) 883-2381
Lois's Bed & Breakfast ...... Ph. (907) 883-5647
Mukluk Land .... Mile 1317 Alaska Hwy.
Northern Energy Corp. .... Mile 1314.8 Alaska Hwy.
Plaza Texaco Truck Stop and Restaurant .... Mile 1313.8 Alaska Hwy.
Rita's Campground/ RV Park .... Mile 1315.7 Alaska Hwy.
Ruth Ann's Inn-In-the-Woods Bed & Breakfast .... Ph. (907) 883-5532
Shamrock Hardware .... Ph. (907) 883-2161
Snowshoe Fine Arts and Gifts .... Mile 1314 Alaska Hwy.
Snowshoe Motel .... Ph. (907) 883-4511
Sourdough Campground .. Mile 1.7 Tok Cutoff
Sourdough Pancake Breakfast .... Mile 1.7 Tok Cutoff
Stage Stop, The .... Ph. (907) 883-5338
Tok Chamber of Commerce .... Ph. (907) 883-5775
Tok Gateway Salmon Bake .... Mile 1313.1 Alaska Hwy.
Tok Liquor & Mini-Mart ... Adjacent Tok Lodge
Tok Lodge .... Ph. (907) 883-2851
Tok Norther Exposures .... Mile 1313.9 Alaska Hwy.
Tok RV Center .... Mile 1313.6 Alaska Hwy.
Tok RV Village .... Mile 1313.4 Alaska Hwy.
Tok Saveway Motel, Groceries & Gas .... Downtown on Tok Cutoff
Tundra Lodge and RV Park .... Mile 1315 Alaska Hwy.
Village Texaco Foodmart .... Across from Tok RV Village
Wadsworth's Department Store .... Mile 1313.8 Alaska Hwy.
Westmark Tok .... Ph. 1-800-544-0970
Young's Cafe .... At the junction
Young's Chevron Service .... Ph. (907) 883-2821
Young's Motel .... Ph. (907) 883-4411

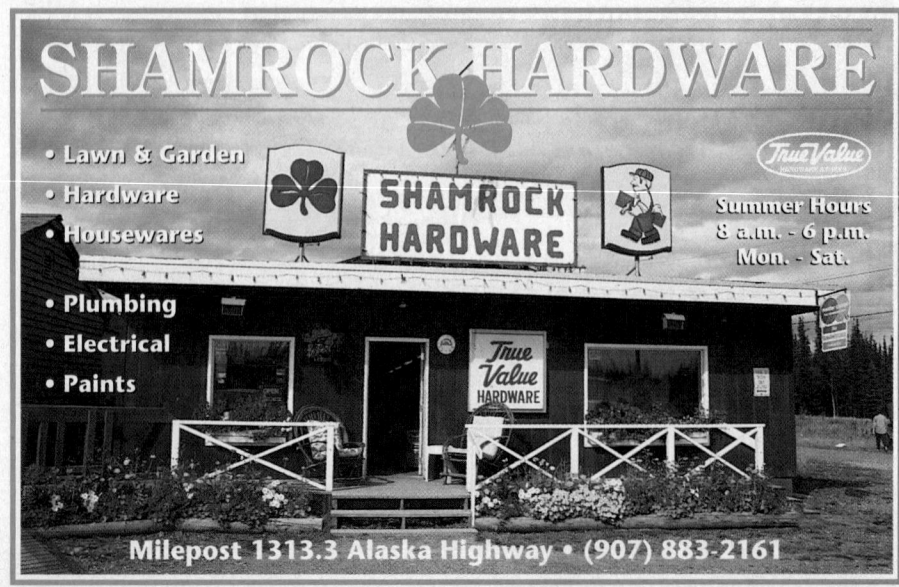

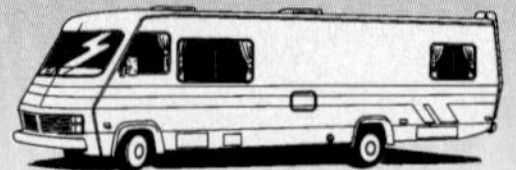

Mounted musk ox head at Tok visitor center. (© Carmen Scott)

are 8 A.M. to noon and 1-4:30 P.M., weekdays. Write Box 155, Tok, AK 99780, or phone (907) 883-5312.

Elevation: 1,635 feet/498m. **Climate:** Mean monthly temperature in January, -19°F/-29°C; in July 59°F/14°C. Record low was -71°F/-57°C in January 1965; record high, 96°F/36°C in June 1969. **Radio:** FM stations are 90.5, 91.1 (KUAC-FM, University of Alaska Fairbanks) and 101.5. **Television:** Satellite channel 13. **Newspaper:** *Mukluk News* (twice monthly).

Private Aircraft: Tok Junction, 1 mile/1.6 km east; elev. 1,630 feet/497m; length 2,510 feet/765m; asphalt; fuel 100 LL; unattended. Tok airstrip, 2 miles/3.2 km south; elev. 1,670 feet/509m; length 1,690 feet/515m; gravel; no fuel, unattended. Tok NR 2 airstrip across the highway to the west

Drive with your headlights on at all times for safety.

Raising sled dogs is a popular pastime in Tok. (Michael N. Dill)

of Tok airstrip, is private.

Tok had its beginnings as a construction camp on the Alcan Highway in 1942. Highway engineer C.G. Polk was sent to Fairbanks in May of 1942 to take charge of Alaskan construction, and start work on the road between Tok Junction and Big Delta. Work was also under way on the Gulkana–Slana–Tok Junction road (now the Tok Cutoff on the Glenn Highway to Anchorage). But on June 7, 1942, a Japanese task force invaded Attu and Kiska islands in the Aleutians, and the Alcan took priority over the Slana cutoff.

The name Tok is believed to be derived from Tokyo Camp, patriotically shortened during WWII to Tok. But there exist at least three other versions of how Tok (pronounced to rhyme with poke) got its name.

Because Tok is the major overland point of entry to Alaska, it is primarily a trade and service center for all types of transportation, especially for summer travelers coming up the Alaska Highway. A stopover here is a good opportunity to meet other travelers and swap experiences. Tok is the only town in Alaska that the highway traveler must pass through twice—once when arriving in the state and again on leaving the state. The governor proclaimed Tok "Mainstreet Alaska" in 1991. Townspeople are proud of this designation and work hard to make visitors happy and to represent their community and state.

Tok's central business district is at the junction of the Alaska Highway and Tok Cutoff (Glenn Highway). From the junction, homes and businesses spread out along both highways on flat terrain dotted with densely timbered stands of black spruce.

Tok has 13 churches, a public library, an elementary school, a 4-year accredited high school and a University of Alaska extension program. Local clubs include the Lions, Disabled American Veterans, Veterans of Foreign Wars and Chamber of Commerce

ACCOMMODATIONS/VISITOR SERVICES

There are 8 hotels/motels, a variety of restaurants and several gas stations in town, as well as bed and breakfasts in Tok, just north of Tok Junction along the Alaska Highway and south on the Glenn Highway (Tok Cutoff). Also here are grocery, hardware and sporting goods stores, bakery, beauty

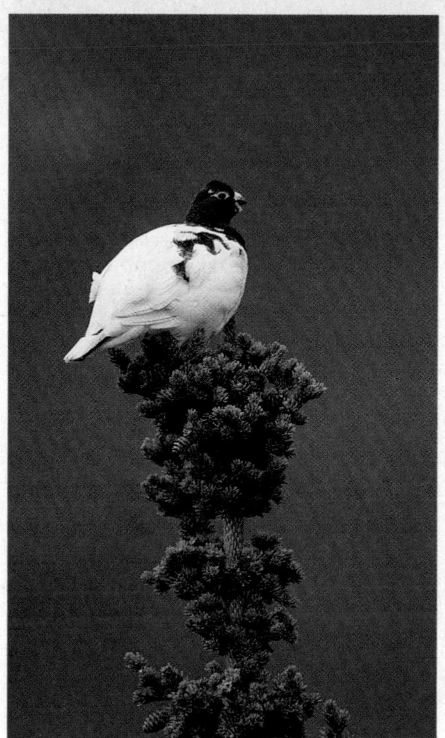

The willow ptarmigan is the state bird.
(© Bruce M. Herman)

shop, gift shops, liquor stores, auto repair and auto parts stores, wrecker service, laundromats and a post office. The bank is located across the highway from the Public Lands Information Center. There is an automatic teller machine at Village Texaco.

Tok AYH youth hostel is located on Pringle Road, 0.8 mile/1.3 km south of **Milepost DC 1322.6**; phone (907) 883-3745.

There are several private RV parks in Tok. Nearby state campgrounds include: Tok River State Recreation Site at **Milepost DC 1309.2** and Moon Lake State Recreation Site at **Milepost DC 1331.9** Alaska Highway; and Eagle Trail State Recreation Site at **Milepost GJ 109.3** Tok Cutoff (Glenn Highway) 16 miles/25 km west. ▲

A WinterCabin Bed & Breakfast. New log cabins with sun porch. Quiet surroundings on original site of the world famous "Tent In Tok." Owned and operated by author/Poet Laureate Donna Blasor-Bernhardt. Share the atmosphere various media personalities (including Charles Kuralt's T.V. crew) have found so inviting. Ample parking, picinic tables, continental-plus breakfast. Shared bathouse, oversize bathtub. Non-smoking. (907) 883-5655. See display ad. [ADVERTISEMENT]

Golden Bear Motel. Quiet location, 62 deluxe units, RV park with wooded pull-through sites, heated bathhouse, laundry; fine restaurant with cocktails available. Open 6 A.M. to 11 P.M. Our gift shop carries an extensive selection of Alaskana, jewelry, T-shirts and souvenirs. The friendly atmosphere you came to Alaska to find! See display ad this section. [ADVERTISEMENT] ▲

Golden Dreams Bed and Breakfast will begin your Alaskan adventure. Awaiting you are personalized photo albums depicting 20 years of gold mining, dog mushing and trapping adventures. Our hot breakfast, served on fine china and crystal, will leave our guests feeling pampered and loved. Group and senior discounts. Warm hospitality with your comfort our priority. Hebrews 13:2. Smoke and alcohol-free. (907) 883-5659 or 1-800-880-5659; Box 106, Tok, AK 99780. 3.5 miles west of Tok. [ADVERTISEMENT]

Ruth Ann's Inn In-the-Woods Bed & Breakfast. Come share our modern home-in-the-woods, located within walking distance of Tok. Comfortable, quiet atmosphere. Clean rooms. Personalized service provided by 2 young retired Alaskan teachers. Full breakfast featuring regional specialties and homemade breads. Very reasonable rates. (907) 883-5532. See display ad this section. [ADVERTISEMENT]

Sourdough Campground's Pancake Breakfast, served 7–11 A.M. Genuine "Sourdough"! Full and partial RV hookups. Dry campsites. Showers included. High-pressure car wash. Open-air museum with gold rush memorabilia. Free evening video program. Located 1.7 miles from the junction toward Anchorage on Tok Cutoff (Glenn Highway). See display ad this section. [ADVERTISEMENT] ▲

Snowshoe Motel. 24 units with private baths. Excellent accommodations for families or two couples traveling together. In-room phones, satellite TV. Free continental breakfast served summers only. Our guests are invited to enjoy panoramic mountain views and sunsets from our Midnight Sun Room and deck. We provide barbecue facilities and a place to make your own cocktails. 1-800-478-4511 or (907) 883-4511. See display ad this section. [ADVERTISEMENT]

The Stage Stop, bed and breakfast for people and horses. Private cabin and 3 large rooms with king and queen beds, one with

Central mounted wildlife display at Tok visitor center. (Earl L. Brown, staff)

private bath, plus full breakfast. Quiet location Mile 1.7 Tok Cutoff highway. New barn and corrals for horses. Reasonable rates from $35. Open all year. Mary Underwood, Box 69, Tok, AK 99780. Phone (907) 883-5338. In Alaska, 1-800-478-5369. [ADVERTISEMENT]

Tok Lodge, located on Glenn Highway, 1 block from junction. Alcan Room serves buses, leaving full-service restaurant open for car traffic. 36 new motel rooms. Common comments are: "nicest rooms on the highway" and "best meal since leaving home." Locally owned by Pam and Bud Johnson for 22 years. Mini-Mart and liquor store located on premises. See display ad this section. [ADVERTISEMENT]

Tundra Lodge & RV Park offers spacious, tree-shaded camping sites. Full and partial hookups. Tent sites. Pull-throughs. Clean restrooms and showers included in price. Picnic tables, fire rings and wood. Dump station. Laundromat. Vehicle wash. Pay phone. Ice. Lounge and meeting room. See display ad Mile 1315 Alaska Highway. [ADVERTISEMENT] ▲

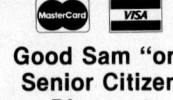

TRANSPORTATION

Air: Charter air service available; inquire at Tok state airstrip (Milepost DC 1313). Charter flightseeing and fly-in fishing trips available. Scheduled passenger and freight service between Tok, Delta Junction and Fairbanks four days a week via 40-Mile Air.

Bus: See Bus Lines in the GENERAL INFORMATION section for scheduled service to other communities.

ATTRACTIONS

Alaska Public Lands Information Center has a large floor map, trip-planning center, and a historical timeline room. There is an award-winning interpretive display on the 1990 Tok River fire. Wildlife displays at the museum include an 8-foot grizzly bear, a wolf, wolverine, lynx, walrus, Dall sheep, musk-ox, a caribou head mount and moose rack. Also on display are examples of baleen (part of the food-filtering apparatus of the bowhead whale, from which fine Alaskan jewelry is now made). Restrooms, pay phone and message board located here.

Tok Mainstreet Visitor Center. This 7,000-square-foot building was built using local timber and local labor. Huge natural spruce logs support an open-beamed, cathedral ceiling. Large picture windows frame the Alaska Range. Displays at the center include: the gold rush; rocks, gems and fossils; Alaskan wildlife; waterfowl; and Alaska Highway memorabilia. Built in a modified T shape, 3 of the 4 wings are devoted to the visitor, with displays, restrooms and trip planning. Tok's community library is housed in the fourth wing. Free Alaska videos shown. A Sourdough Show is given at 1 P.M. Sundays.

The aurora borealis, also called the Northern Lights, occur most often in the spring and fall months. They often appear as arcs or draperies of green, red, blue and purple in the nighttime skies.

Donna Bernhardt, an Alaskan writer and TV personality, can frequently be seen in the summer months in live performances at the center.

Local Events: There are a variety of things to do in Tok, thanks to local individuals, businesses and clubs. Local campgrounds offer slide shows, movies, gold panning, a salmon bake, miniature golf and sourdough pancake breakfasts. Sled dog demonstrations are given at Burnt Paw gift shop and at the Westmark.

Other local events include bingo games and softball games at the local field. Visitors are welcome at the senior citizens center. The Tok triathlon (12 miles of biking, 10 of canoeing and 5 of jogging) and Tok Trot are both held annually. Tok's Fourth of July celebration is a major event, complete with a parade, picnic and games. Check at the Mainstreet Visitor Center for more information on these local events.

Bike Trail: A wide paved bike trail extends southeast from Tok on the Alaska Highway as far east as the Dog Mushers

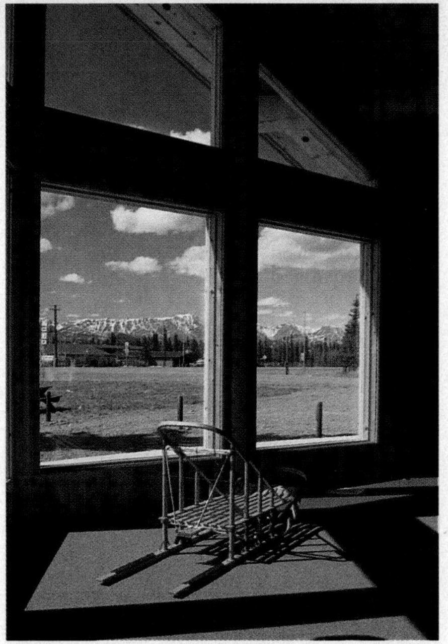

Large picture windows at Tok visitor center offer a view of surrounding mountains. (© Carmen Scott)

Assoc. track, and as far west as Tanacross Junction; approximate length is 13.2 miles/ 21.2 km. You may also bike out the Tok Cutoff past Sourdough Campground. Travelers may park their vehicles in and around Tok and find a bike trail nearby leading into or out of Tok.

Native Crafts: Tok is a trade center for the Athabascan Native villages of Tanacross, Northway, Tetlin, Mentasta, Dot Lake and Eagle. Several of the Native women make birch baskets, beaded moccasins, boots and beaded necklaces. Examples of Native work may be seen at the Native-operated gift shop at Northway junction and at several gift shops and other outlets in Tok.

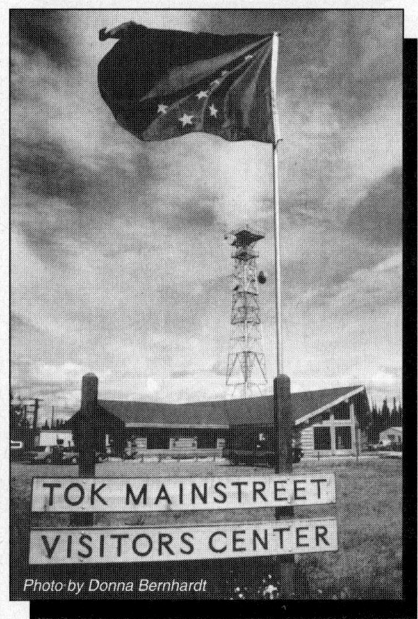

The state of Alaska has a crafts identification program which identifies authentic

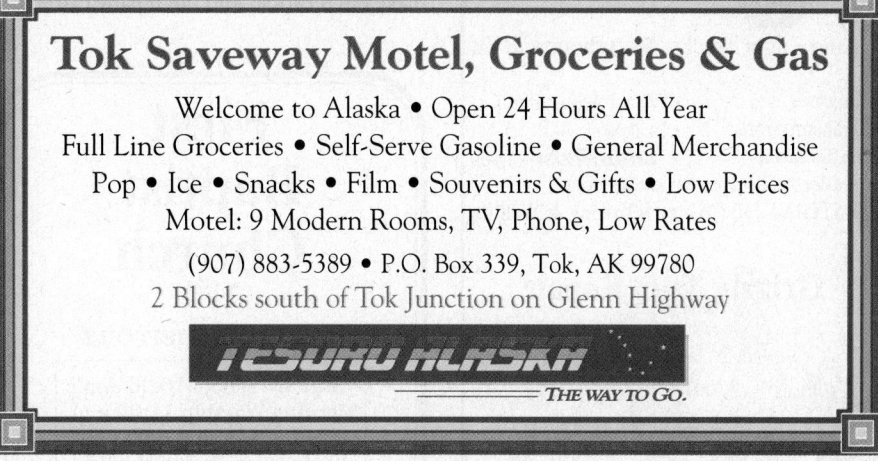

Native and Alaskan handicrafts. This symbol is of a polar bear.

Birch baskets were once used in the Native camps and villages. Traditionally they had folded corners, which held water, and were even used for cooking by dropping heated stones into the liquid in the baskets. The baskets are made by peeling the bark from the birch trees, usually in the early summer months. The bark is easiest to work with when moist and pliable. It is cut into shape and sewn together with strips of spruce root dug out of the ground and split. If the root is too dry it is soaked until it is manageable. Holes are put in the birch bark with a punch or screwdriver and the spruce root is laced in and out. Native women dye the spruce root with food coloring, watercolors or berry juice. A few Natives also make birch canoes and birch baby carriers.

Many of the moccasins and mukluks for sale in Tok are made with moose hide that has the "Native tan." This means moose hide tanned by the Native. First the excess fat and meat is scraped off the hide, then it is soaked in a soap solution (some use a mixture of brains and ashes). After soaking, all the moisture is taken out by constant scraping with a dull knife or scraper. The hide is then scraped again and rubbed together to soften it. Next it is often smoke-cured in rotted spruce wood smoke. The tanning process takes from a few days to a week.

Beading can be a slow and tedious pro-

Alaska became the 49th state on January 3, 1959.

Alaska Public Lands Information Center has displays and a message board.

(© Carmen Scott)

cess. Most women say if they work steadily all day they can put the beading on one moccasin, but usually they do their beadwork over a period of several days, alternating it with other activities.

Snowshoe Fine Arts and Gifts invites you to come browse and shop in our gift store. See our gallery of art prints, figurines, Alaska Native-made carvings, masks, dolls, birch and grass baskets and beadwork. Jewelry made of natural Alaska gemstones, ivory

and gold nugget. Lots of caps, T-shirts and sweatshirts. Souvenir items and Alaska-made products. Fur hats, earmuffs and bronzes by Alaskan artists Sue and Frank Entsminger. Phone (907) 883-4181. See display ad this

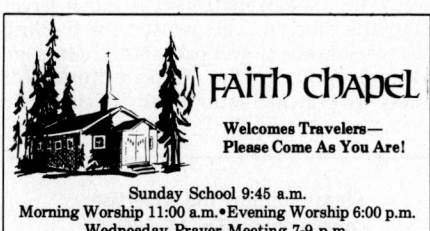

Alaska has 19 mountains over 14,000 feet. Mount McKinley is the highest peak.

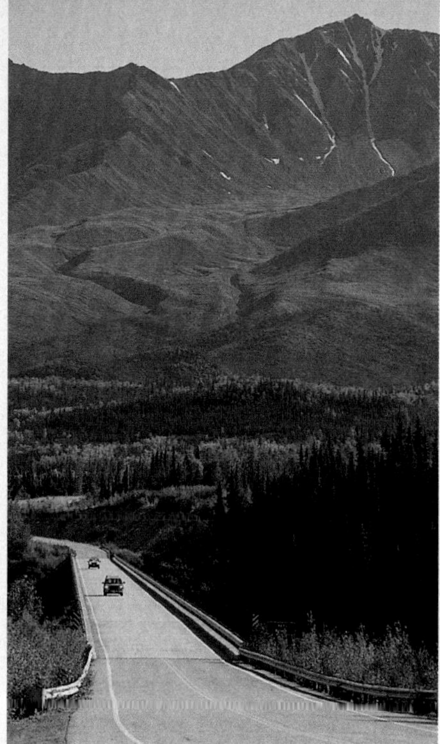

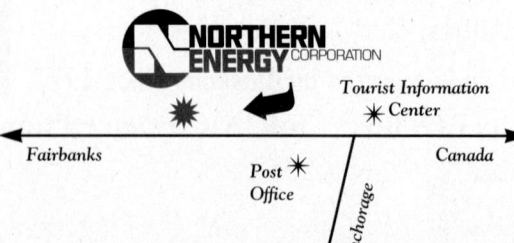

Mentasta Mountains along the Alaska Highway north of Tok. (Jerrianne Lowther, staff)

section. [ADVERTISEMENT]

All Alaska Gifts and Crafts. A unique full-service Alaskan gift store featuring Alaskan craftsmen, artists, wildlife, Eskimo

dolls, stuffed animals, jade and Alaska Native products. We have a large selection of quality Alaskan T-shirts and jewelry. Free coffee. Free Tolkat grizzly bear with any purchase of $99. You'll like our price and quality. [ADVERTISEMENT]

Sled Dog Breeding and Training: Dog mushing is Alaska's official state sport, and Tok has become known as the "Sled Dog Capital of Alaska," with at least 1 out of every 3 people in town involved in some way with raising dogs. Kennels range in size from 100 dogs to a single family pet. Visitors who come to Tok seeking either a pet or a racing sled dog will probably find what they are looking for here.

The Siberian husky is the most popular sled dog and oftentimes has distinctive blue eyes. The Alaskan malamute is much larger than the Siberian and is used for hauling heavy loads at a slower pace. Both breeds are AKC recognized. The Alaskan husky (or husky) is a catchall term for any of the arctic breeds or northern types of dogs and is usually a cross. Sled dogs may be any registered breed or crossbreed, since mushers look for conformation, attitude and speed when putting together a working team rather than pedigrees. Common strains in racing dogs have included Irish setter, Labrador and wolf, among others.

Sled Dog Trails and Races: Tok boasts a well-known and long-established dog mushing trail, which draws many world-class and recreational mushers. The 20.5-mile/33-km trail begins at the rustic log Tok Dog Mushers Assoc. building at **Milepost DC 1312.8** on the Alaska Highway. The trail is a favorite with spectators because it affords many miles of viewing from along the Alaska Highway.

Racing begins in late Nov. and extends through the end of March. Junior mushers include 1-, 2-, 3- and 5-dog classes; junior adult mushers include 5- and 8-dog classes. Open (unlimited) classes can run as many as 16 dogs.

The biggest race of the season in Tok is the Race of Champions, held in late March, which also has the largest entry of any sprint race in Alaska. Begun in 1954 as a bet between 2 roadhouse proprietors, today the Race of Champions includes over 100 teams in 3 classes competing for prize money and trophies. It is considered to be the third leg of sled dog racing's "triple crown," following the Fur Rendezvous in Anchorage and the Fairbanks North American Championship. Visitors are also welcome to attend the Tok Native Assoc.'s potlatch, held the same weekend as the race, in the Tok school gym.

AREA FISHING: Fly-in fishing to area lakes for northern pike, grayling and lake trout; inquire at Tok state airstrip. There are 43 lakes in the Delta-Tok area that are stocked by the Alaska Dept. of Fish and Game. Lakes are stocked primarily with rainbow trout; other stocked species include arctic grayling, lake trout, arctic char and king salmon. Most of these lakes are located close to the road system, but there are walk-in lakes available as well. Most easily accessible are **North Twin, South Twin** and **Mark Lake.** There is a trailhead 0.5 mile/0.8 km east of the Gerstle River bridge for **Big Donna Lake** (3.5-mile/5.6-km hike) and **Little Donna Lake** (4.5 miles/7.2 km). **Quartz Lake,** north of Delta Junction, is a popular spot for rainbow trout and silver salmon. Consult ADF&G offices in Tok or Delta Junction for other locations.

Alaska Highway Log

(continued)

DC 1315 (2116.2 km) **F 205** (329.9 km) **Tundra Lodge and RV Park.** See display ad on page 179. ▲

DC 1315.7 (2117.3 km) **F 204.3** (328.8 km) **Rita's Campground RV Park and Cheryl's Old Fashion Bed & Breakfast Cabin.** See display ad on page 179. ▲

DC 1316.6 (2118.8 km) **F 203.4** (327.3 km) Scoby Road, Sundog Trail. Access to bed and breakfast.

DC 1317 (2119.4 km) **F 203** (326.7 km) **Mukluk Land.** See display ad this section.

DC 1322.6 (2128.5 km) **F 197.4** (317.7 km) Pringle Road. Tok youth hostel, housed in a wall tent, is located 0.8 mile/1.3 km south; 10 beds, tent space available.

DC 1324.6 (2131.7 km) **F 195.4** (314.5 km) Tanacross fireguard station.

DC 1324.7 (2131.8 km) **F 195.3** (314.3 km) Gravel access road to Tanacross airstrip. (See also **Milepost DC 1325.7**)

DC 1325.6 (2133.3 km) **F 194.4** (312.8 km) **Historic Milepost 1328.**

DC 1325.7 (2133.4 km) **F 194.3** (312.7 km) **Tanacross Junction.** End of paved bike trail from Tok and access to Tanacross.

Drive in 1.2 miles/1.9 km on gravel road to junction, turn left for village of TANACROSS (pop. 106), home of the once numerous branch of the Tanah, or Tinneh, Indians. This village of colorful modern houses is built on a short 0.7-mile/1.1-km loop road. Turn right at junction and drive 0.2 mile/0.3 km for access road to airstrip, or 0.3 mile/0.5 km to reach Tanana River and view across river of the white church steeple in the old village of Tanacross which burned down in 1979. Road eventually dead ends in residential area.

Private Aircraft: Tanacross airstrip; elev. 1,549 feet/472m; 2 runways, length 5,000 feet/1,524m and 5,100 feet/1,554m; asphalt; unattended.

DC 1327.4 (2136.2 km) **F 192.6** (310 km) Parking area at lake to north.

DC 1328 (2137.2 km) **F 192** (309 km) Watch for sections of patched pavement and frost heaves northbound to Dot Lake.

DC 1330.1 (2140.5 km) **F 189.9** (305.6 km) Paved turnout with litter container to east. View of Alaska Range to the west.

DC 1330.7 (2141.5 km) **F 189.3** (304.6 km) Paved turnout with litter barrels to east.

DC 1331.9 (2143.5 km) **F 188.1** (302.7 km) Moon Lake State Recreation Site, 0.2 mile/0.3 km north off highway; 15 campsites, toilets, tables, water, firepits, swimming (watch for floatplanes). Camping fee $8/night or annual pass. ▲

DC 1333.6 (2146.2 km) **F 186.4** (300 km) **Historic Milepost 1339.** Yerrick Creek bridge.

DC 1335 (2148.4 km) **F 185** (297.7 km) Watch for moose.

DC 1338.2 (2153.5 km) **F 181.8** (292.6 km) Highway crosses Cathedral Creeks 3 times between here and **Milepost DC 1339.**

DC 1342.2 (2160 km) **F 177.8** (286.1 km) Sheep Creek culvert.

DC 1344.5 (2163.8 km) **F 175.5** (282.4 km) **Historic Milepost 1352.** Double-ended paved parking area to east. Interpretive panel on the "father of the international highway," Donald MacDonald. Mentasta Mountains to the south. Good photo stop.

DC 1347.2 (2168 km) **F 172.8** (278 km) **Forest Lake** trailhead; 6 mile/9.6 km ATV trail (not easy access) to lake stocked with rainbow trout.

DC 1347.3 (2168.2 km) **F 172.7** (277.9 km) Entering Game Management Unit 20D northbound, Unit 12 southbound.

DC 1347.5 (2168.5 km) **F 172.5** (277.6 km) Robertson River bridge. The river was named by Lt. Henry T. Allen for a member of his 1885 expedition.

DC 1348 (2169.3 km) **F 172** (276.8 km) Bad frost heaves.

DC 1348.1 (2169.5 km) **F 171.9** (276.6 km) Side road west to parking lot at old Haines pipeline right-of-way. Hike in 0.3 mile/0.5 km for **Robertson No. 2 Lake;** rainbow fishing.

DC 1348.8 (2170.6 km) **F 171.2** (275.5 km) Bad frost heaves.

DC 1350.5 (2173.3 km) **F 169.5** (272.8 km) Double-ended paved turnout with litter barrels to west. Rough road next mile northbound.

DC 1353.7 (2178.5 km) **F 166.3** (267.6 km) Jan Lake Road. Drive in 0.5 mile/0.8 km to parking area with boat launch and toilets. No overnight camping, carry out garbage. **Jan Lake** is stocked with rainbow; use spinners, flies, or salmon eggs with bobber. Dot Lake Native Corp. land, limited public access.

DC 1357.3 (2184.4 km) **F 162.7** (261.8 km) Bear Creek bridge. Paved turnout to west.

DC 1358.7 (2186.6 km) **F 161.3** (259.6 km) Chief Creek bridge. Paved turnout to west at north end of bridge.

DC 1361.3 (2190.2 km) **F 158.7** (255.4 km) **DOT LAKE** (pop. 70). Gas, groceries, lodge restaurant, car wash, motel, camping and post office. Headquarters for the Dot Lake (Athabascan) Indian Corp. Homesteaded in the 1940s, a school was established here in 1952. Dot Lake's historic chapel was built in 1949.

Dot Lake Lodge. See display ad this section.

DC 1361.6 (2191 km) **F 158.4** (254.9 km) **Historic Milepost 1368.** Gravel turnout by lake to east. Rough narrow road northbound.

DC 1370.2 (2205.1 km) **F 149.8** (241.1 km) Double-ended paved parking area to east.

DC 1370.5 (2205.4 km) **F 149.5** (240.6 km) **Historic Milepost 1376.** Alaska Highway interpretive panel on "the Crooked Road."

DC 1371.5 (2207.2 km) **F 148.5** (239 km) Berry Creek bridge. Parking area to west.

DC 1374.2 (2211.5 km) **F 145.8** (234.6 km) Sears Creek bridge. Parking area to west.

DC 1376 (2214.4 km) **F 144** (231.7 km) Entering Tok Management Area, Tanana State Forest southbound.

DC 1378 (2217.6 km) **F 142** (228.5 km) Bridge over Dry Creek. Evidence of forest fire next mile northbound.

DC 1379 (2219.2 km) **F 141** (226.9 km) Double-ended paved turnout with mountain views to west.

Canoeing at Moon Lake State Recreation Site, Milepost DC 1331.9.

(Jerrianne Lowther, staff)

DC 1380.5 (2221.6 km) **F 139.5** (224.5 km) Johnson River bridge. A tributary of the Tanana River, the Johnson River was named by Lt. Henry T. Allen in 1887 for Peder Johnson, a Swedish miner and member of his party.

DC 1381.1 (2222.6 km) **F 138.9** (223.5 km) Paved turnout to west. Access road to **Lisa Lake** (stocked).

DC 1383.9 (2227.1 km) **F 136.1** (219 km) **Craig Lake** access west side of highway via 0.5-mile/0.8-km trail; rainbow trout fishing.

DC 1385 (2228.9 km) **F 135** (217.3 km) Double-ended gravel turnout. Tanana River access.

CAUTION: Watch for major road construction between ***Mileposts DC 1386 and 1398*** *in 1996.*

DC 1388.4 (2234.4 km) **F 131.6** (211.8

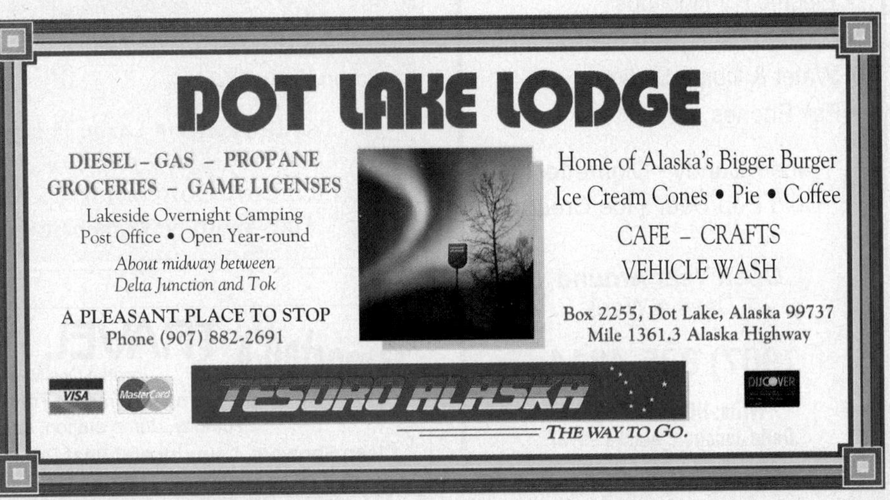

km) Little Gerstle River bridge.

DC 1391.9 (2240 km) **F 128.1** (206.2 km) Trailhead to **Big Donna Lake**, 3.5 miles/5.6 km, and **Little Donna Lake**, 4.5 miles/7.2 km; stocked with rainbow.

DC 1392.3 (2240.6 km) **F 127.7** (205.5 km) Cummings Road through Delta barley project. *CAUTION: Watch for buffalo (bison) on highway between here and Delta Junction.*

On the southwest side of the Alaska Highway approaching Delta Junction is the Bison Sanctuary. This range provides the bison herd with autumn and winter grazing on over 3,000 acres of grassland. It was developed to reduce agricultural crop depredation by bison.

DC 1392.7 (2241.3 km) **F 127.3** (204.9 km) Gerstle River Black Veterans Recognition bridge. The river was named for Lewis Gerstle, president of the Alaska Commercial Co., by Lt. Henry T. Allen, whose 1885 expedition explored the Copper, Tanana and Koyukuk river regions for the U.S. Army Dept. of the Columbia.

DC 1395.5 (2245.8 km) **124.5** (200.4 km) Evidence of 1994 forest fire southwest side of highway next 32 miles/4.8 km northbound.

DC 1398 (2249.8 km) **F 122** (196.5 km) Watch for bison next 15 miles/24 km northbound.

CAUTION: Watch for major road construction next 12 miles/19 km southbound in 1996.

DC 1401.2 (2255 km) **F 118.8** (191.2 km) Double-ended gravel turnout to northeast.

DC 1403.6 (2258.8 km) **F 116.4** (187.3 km) Sawmill Creek Road to northeast. This rough gravel road goes through the heart of the Delta barley fields. A sign just off the highway explains the barley project. Visiting farmers are welcome to talk with local farmers along the road, except during planting (May) and harvesting (August or September) when they are too busy.

DC 1403.9 (2259.3 km) **F 116.1** (186.8 km) Sawmill Creek bridge.

DC 1408 (2265.9 km) **F 112** (180.2 km) Access to University of Alaska Agricultural and Forestry Experiment Station. Major research at this facility concentrates on agricultural cropping, fertilization and tillage management.

DC 1410 (2269.1 km) **F 110** (177 km) Access road north to Delta barley project.

DC 1411 (2270.7 km) **F 109** (175.4 km) Look for wild irises in roadside ditches in June.

DC 1411.7 (2271.8 km) **F 108.3** (174.3 km) Double-ended gravel turnout. Scenic view of Alaska Range to south.

DC 1412.5 (2273.2 km) **F 107.5** (173 km) **Cherokee Lodge & RV Park.** You won't regret this stop! Owned and operated by a lifelong Alaskan, offering true Alaskan hospitality and food. Full menu, including rein

deer sausage breakfasts, "Blue Ribbon Chili"! (Grand Champion—winner at Deltana State Fair Chili Cook-off for last 3 years.) Try our halibut! Hand-picked right off the fishing boats and a favorite among locals, visitors and truckers. Well-stocked cocktail lounge and liquor store. Ice cold beer and spirits "to go." Clean, reasonable rooms, pay phones, ice. Shaded RV park includes electric hookups, water, dump station, fire pits and picnic tables. See the "Arctic Train" with tires over 9 feet high and 4 feet wide. Sack lunches made to order for fire fighters, construction crews, bird and bison hunters. Hunters, please call Gary for hunting and weather updates. Open daily year-round. Your host: Gary Schoening (907) 895-4814. [ADVERTISEMENT] ▲

DC 1413.3 (2274.4 km) **F 106.7** (171.7 km) Grain storage facility.

DC 1414.9 (2277 km) **F 105.1** (169.1 km) Clearwater Road leads north past farmlands to Clearwater State Recreation Site campground and junctions with Remington Road. Stay on pavement leading to Jack Warren Road, which goes west to the Richardson Highway at **Milepost DC 1424.3 (V 268.3).** Good opportunity to see area agriculture; see Delta Vicinity map this section.

To reach the state campground, follow Clearwater Road 5.2 miles/8.4 km north to junction with Remington Road; turn right and drive 2.8 miles/4.5 km east for Clearwater state campground on bank of stream. There are 15 campsites, toilets, tables, firepits, water and boat ramp. Camping fee $8/night or annual pass. ▲

Delta–Clearwater River (boat needed for best fishing), beautiful spring-fed stream, grayling and whitefish; silver salmon spawn here in Oct. **Goodpaster River**, accessible by boat via Delta–Clearwater and Tanana rivers; excellent grayling fishing.

DC 1415.4 (2277.8 km) **F 104.6** (168.3 km) Dorshorst Road; access to homestead farm and private museum, open to public June 1 to Sept. 15, admission charged.

Alaska Homestead & Historical Museum. See display ad this section.

DC 1420.7 (2286.3 km) **F 99.3** (159.8 km) Alaska State Troopers.

DC 1420.9 (2286.7 km) **F 99.1** (159.5 km) **Bergstad's Travel and Trailer Court.** See display ad this section. ▲

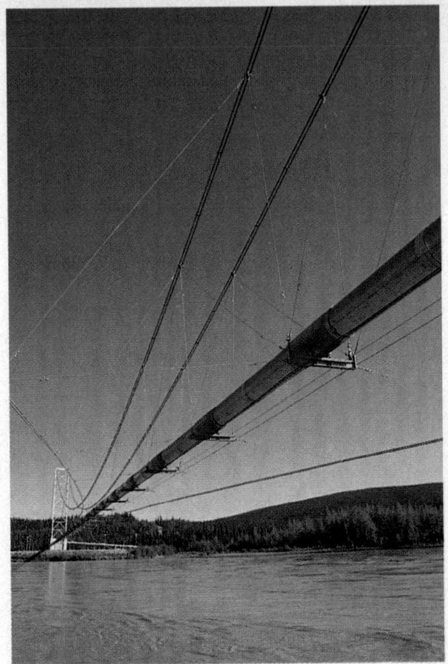

Trans-Alaska pipeline spans the Tanana River at Milepost V 275.4.
(© Barbara Harn)

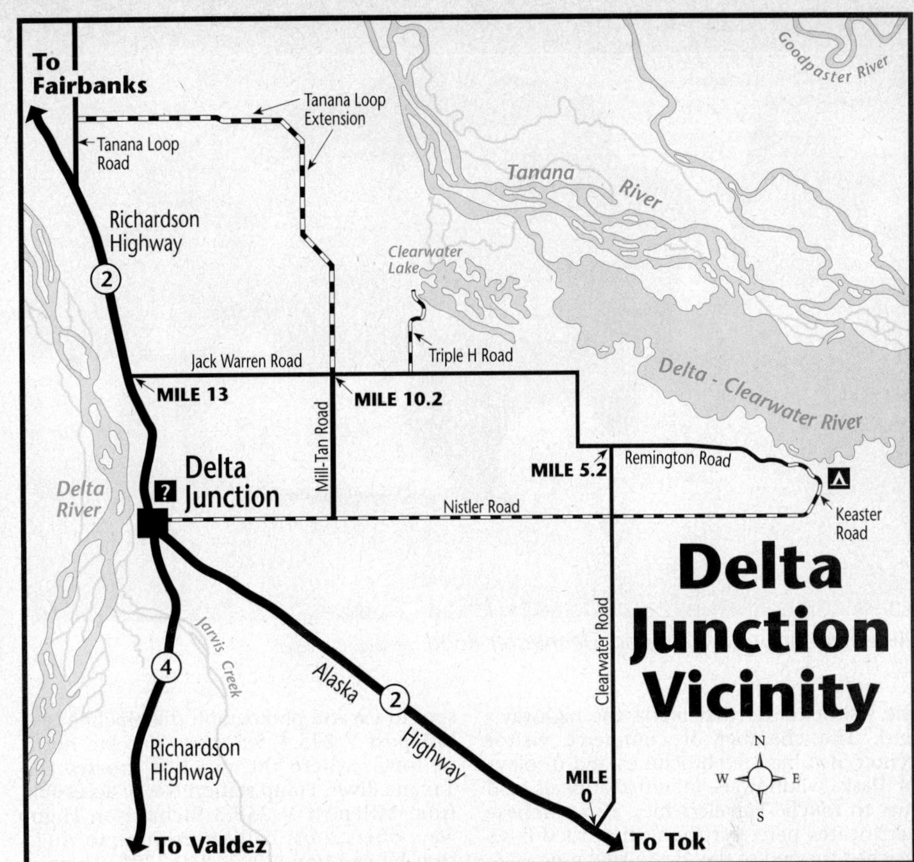

Delta Junction

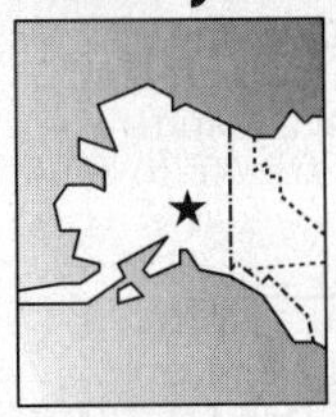

DC 1422 (2288.4 km) **F 98** (157.7 km) **V 266** (428.1 km). Located at the junction of the Alaska and Richardson highways. **Population:** 736. **Emergency Services:** Emergencies only phone 911. **Alaska State Troopers,** in the Jarvis Office Center at **Milepost DC 1420.5**, phone (907) 895-4800. **Fire Department** and **Ambulance Service,** emergency only phone 911. **Clinics.** One doctor and a dentist in private practice.

Visitor Information: Visitor Center junction of Alaska and Richardson highways, open daily 8:30 A.M. to 7:30 P.M., mid-May to mid-Sept.; phone (907) 895-9941. The visitor center has a garden with local grains, flowers and vegetables, and a pay phone. Highway information, phone (907) 451-2207. Dept. of Fish and Game at north edge of town, **Milepost DC 1422.8**; phone (907) 895-4632.

City Hall and the Delta Junction Library, located at **Milepost V 266.5**, are also good sources of information. City Hall, open 9 A.M. to 5 P.M. weekdays, has a pay phone, public restrooms, a notary public and can give local directions. The library has a free paperback book and magazine exchange, Anchorage newspaper, public fax and copier service. The library, open 11 A.M. to 6 P.M. Monday through Thursday and 11 A.M. to 4 P.M. Friday and Saturday, also offers free Alaska video programs to any traveler waiting for vehicle repairs in Delta (ask at the circulation desk).

Elevation: 1,180 feet/360m. **Climate:** Mean monthly temperature in January, -15°F/-26°C; in July 58°F/14°C. Record low was -66°F/-54°C in Jan. 1989; record high was 88°F/31°C in Aug. 1990. Mean monthly precipitation in July, 2.57 inches/6.5cm. **Radio:** KUAC-FM 91.7 broadcasts from University of Alaska Fairbanks; Fort Greely broadcasts on 90.5 FM. **Television:** Three channels from Fairbanks.

Private Aircraft: Delta Junction airstrip, 1 mile/1.6 km north; elev. 1,150 feet/350m; length 2,400 feet/731m; gravel. Allen Army Airfield, 3 miles/4.8 km south; elev. 1,277 feet/389m; 3 asphalt-surfaced runways available, length to 7,500 feet/2,286m; fuel J4; joint-use military/civil airport (prior permission required).

Delta Junction is at the actual end of the Alaska Highway. From here, the Richardson Highway leads to Fairbanks. (*The MILEPOST*® logs this stretch of highway as a continuation of the Alaska Highway.) Have your picture taken with the monument in front of

American bison graze along Clearwater Road. (© Susan Cole Kelly)

the visitor center that marks the highway's end. The chamber of commerce visitor center also has free brochures and displays of Alaska wildflowers, mounted animals, and furs to touch. Travelers may also purchase certificates here, certifying that they have reached the end of the Alaska Highway.

Delta Junction is also the first view of the trans-Alaska pipeline for travelers coming up the Alaska Highway from Canada. A good spot to see and photograph the pipeline is at **Milepost V 275.4**, 9.5 miles/15.3 km north of town, where the pipeline crosses the Tanana River. Pump station No. 9, accessible from **Milepost V 258.3** Richardson Highway, offers tours daily from June to Aug.; stop by or phone (907) 869-3270. There is also an interesting display of pipe used in 3 Alaska pipeline projects outside the visitor center in Delta Junction.

Named after the nearby Delta River, Delta Junction began as a construction camp on the Richardson Highway in 1919. (It was first known as Buffalo Center because of the American bison that were transplanted here in the 1920s.)

The Richardson Highway, connecting Valdez at tidewater with Fairbanks in the Interior, predates the Alaska Highway by 20 years. The Richardson was already a wagon road in 1910, and was updated to automobile standards in the 1920s by the Alaska Road Commission (ARC).

Since the late 1970s, the state has encouraged development of the agricultural industry in the Delta area. They have conducted a dozen land disposal programs involving more than 112,000 acres. These programs generated 37 farms averaging 2,310 acres and 169 small farms averaging 161 acres.

In 1995, nearly 42,000 acres were in some form of agricultural use (including production of barley, oats, wheat, forage, pasture, grass seed, canola, potatoes, field peas, forage brassicas) and conservation use. Barley is the major feed grain grown in Delta. It is an excellent energy feed for cattle, hogs and sheep. Production acreages are determined by the anticipated in-state demand for barley.

Delta barley is stored on farms or in a local co-op elevator, sold on the open market, or used to feed livestock. Small-scale farming of vegetables, 3 commercial potato farms, 5 active dairies, a dairy processing center, 6 beef producers, 2 beef feedlots, 3 swine producers, 3 bison ranches and 4 commercial greenhouses all contribute to Delta Junction's agriculture.

Congratulations... you have reached the

END of the ALASKA HIGHWAY...

Delta Junction, Alaska

End of the Alaska Highway certificates available, $1

- Delta Deep Freeze Classic
- Festival of Lights - February
- Memorial Day Buffalo Wallow Square Dance Jamboree
- July 4th Buffalo Barbecue
- Deltana Fair, last weekend in July

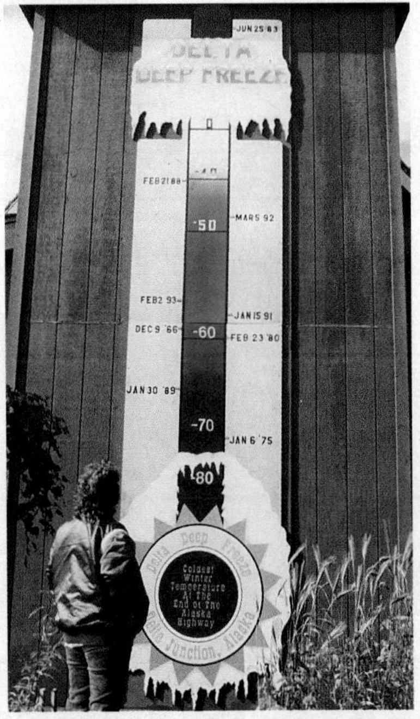

- Delta Agricultural Project
- Farmer's Market
- Pipeline Pump Station Tours
- Historical Sites
- Fine dining, hotels and motels
- Great fishing, hunting in season
- Hiking throughout the season

- Quartz Lake: fishing, hiking, camping, picnics
- Two state camp grounds
- Several private RV parks with full hookups
- Largest free-roaming bison herd in Alaska

Alaska's Friendly Frontier

For further information contact:
Delta Chamber of Commerce
PO Box 987MP
Delta Junction, Alaska 99737
(907) 895-5068 (year 'round)
(907) 895-5069 (summer only)

ACCOMMODATIONS/VISITOR SERVICES

There are 14 hotels/motels, several bed Delta Junction has motels, restaurants, gas stations, a laundromat and dry cleaners, a coin-operated car wash, a shopping center, post office, bank and other businesses. There are several churches. Delta Community Park, on Kimball Street one block off the highway, has softball and soccer fields.

Delta international hostel north of town: turn at **Milepost V 271.7** (Tanana Loop Road), drive 1 mile/1.6 km and turn right on Tanana Loop Extension then left on a gravel road named Main Street, USA (follow signs). Sleeping bags are required. Fee: $7 per night. Hostel open Memorial Day through Labor Day; phone (907) 895-5074.

There are private RV parks just south and just north of town. 2 public campgrounds are located nearby: Delta state campground at **Milepost V 267.1**, and Clearwater state campground on Remington Road (see **Milepost DC 1414.9** and **V 268.3**). ▲

Alaska 7 Motel, 16 large, clean, comfortable rooms with full bath and showers. Color TV and courtesy coffee in each room. Kitchenettes and phone available. Comfort at a comfortable price. Open year-round. Major credit cards accepted. Milepost 270.3 Richardson–Alaska Highway. Phone (907) 895-4848. See display ad this section. [ADVERTISEMENT]

Tanana Bed and Breakfast. Climb aboard for the experience of a lifetime. Take a 1/2 hour scenic boat ride to a real Alaskan homestead in the bush. Comfortable log home with queen size beds, blue ribbon grayling fishing, sourdough breakfast, television, and hiking trails. Coast guard licensed and approved. Your host: Brooks Ludwig, P.O. Box 682, Delta Junction, AK 99737. (907) 388-5500. [ADVERTISEMENT]

Delta Junction's End of the Alaska Highway monument. (Michael N. Dill)

TRANSPORTATION

Air: Scheduled service via 40-Mile Air from Tok to Fairbanks; Delta stop on request. Local air service available. **Bus:** See Bus Lines in the GENERAL INFORMATION section for scheduled service to other communities.

ATTRACTIONS

Buffalo Herd. American bison were transplanted into the Delta Junction area in the 1920s. Because the bison have become costly pests to many farmers in the Delta area, the 90,000-acre Delta Bison Sanctuary was created south of the Alaska Highway in 1980. However, keeping the bison on their refuge and out of the barley fields is a continuing problem. Summer visitors who wish to look at the bison are advised to visit the viewpoint at **Milepost V 241.3** on the Richardson Highway; use binoculars. The herd contained 482 bison in 1992 when the last census was taken by the ADF&G.

Special Events: Delta Junction celebrates a traditional Fourth of July with a Buffalo Barbecue, sponsored by the Pioneers. Buffalo Wallow, a 4-day square dance festival hosted by Buffalo Squares, is held every Memorial Day weekend. The Buffalo Squares also sponsor a campout and dance at Delta state campground the second Saturday in July.

The Deltana Fair is held the last weekend in July. The fair includes a barbecue, Lions' pancake breakfast, local handicrafts, horse show, livestock display and show, games, concessions, contests and a parade. A highlight of the fair is the Great Alaska Outhouse Race, held on Sunday, in which 4 pushers and 1 sitter compete for the coveted "Golden Throne" award.

A Festival of Lights is held each Feb. in Delta Junction. This special event, designed to break up the monotony of long winter nights, features a parade of lights where the local citizenry builds and decorates floats with lights. There are also dog races, fireworks, square dancing, ice sculpting and more. It was -40°F/-40°C for the 1994 festival—an evening to remember, according to residents!

Area Museums. Alaska Homestead & Historical Museum, located approximately 6 miles/9.6 km east of town at **Milepost DC 1415.4** Alaska Highway, offers guided tours of an authentic Alaska homestead farm. There's also a large collection of historical farming equipment. Open June 1 to Sept. 15, daily 10 A.M. to 7 P.M. North of town about 8 miles/12.9 km at **Milepost V 275** Richardson (Alaska) Highway is Rika's Roadhouse at Big Delta State Historical Park. This restored roadhouse was built in 1910. Guides in period costumes tour the grounds, which include other historic structures. Open daily in summer.

Tour the agriculture of the area by driving Sawmill Creek Road (turn off at **Milepost DC 1403.6** Alaska Highway) and Clearwater Road (see **Milepost DC 1414.9**). Sawmill Creek Road goes through the heart of the grain-producing Delta Ag Project and local farmers welcome visiting farmers' questions in between planting and harvesting. Along Clearwater and Remington roads you may view the older farms, which produce forage crops and livestock. Tanana Loop Road (**Milepost V 271.7**), Tanana Loop Extension and Mill–Tan Road also go past many farms. The visitor information center in downtown Delta Junction can answer many questions on local agriculture.

AREA FISHING: **Delta–Clearwater River,** grayling and whitefish; silver salmon spawn here in Oct. Access via Clearwater Road or Jack Warren Road (see Delta Vicinity map). (Although USGS topographic maps show this tributary of the Tanana River as Clearwater Creek, local residents refer to the stream as the Delta–Clearwater River.) **Goodpaster River,** accessible by boat via Delta–Clearwater and Tanana rivers; excellent grayling fishing.

There are 43 lakes in the Delta-Tok area that are stocked by the Alaska Dept. of Fish and Game. Lakes are stocked primarily with rainbow trout, and also with arctic grayling, lake trout, arctic char and king salmon. Most of these lakes are located close to the road system, but there are walk-in lakes available as well. **Quartz Lake,** at **Milepost V 277.7** north of Delta Junction, one of the most popular fishing lakes in the Delta area, is also the largest and most easily accessed of area lakes; angler success is excellent. Consult ADF&G offices in Delta or Tok for other locations.

Richardson–Alaska Highway Log

Although logged here as a natural extension of the Alaska Highway, the highway between Delta Junction and Fairbanks is designated as part of the Richardson Highway, with existing mileposts showing distance from Valdez.

Distance from Valdez (V) is followed by distance from Dawson Creek (DC) and distance from Fairbanks (F).

V 266 (428 km) **DC 1422** (2288.5 km) **F 98** (157.7 km) Delta Junction visitor information center sits at the junction of the Alaska and Richardson highways. Turn south for Valdez (see RICHARDSON HIGHWAY section). Continue north for Fairbanks.

V 266.3 (428.6 km) **DC 1422.3** (2289 km) **F 97.7** (157.2 km) Delta Junction post office.

V 266.4 (428.7 km) **DC 1422.4** (2289.1 km) **F 97.6** (157.1 km) City Park Carwash.

V 266.5 (428.9 km) **DC 1422.5** (2289.2 km) **F 97.5** (156.9 km) Delta Junction library and city hall. Library hours are 11 A.M. to 6 P.M. Mon. through Thurs. and 11 A.M. to 4 P.M. Fri. and Sat.; free paperback book and magazine exchange, Alaska videos, public fax and copier service. City Hall is open 9 A.M. to 5 P.M. weekdays; pay phone and public restrooms.

V 266.8 (429.4 km) **DC 1422.8** (2289.7 km) **F 97.2** (156.4 km) Alaska Dept. of Fish and Game office.

V 267 (429.7 km) **DC 1423** (2290 km) **F 97** (156.1 km) BLM airstrip; current status unknown.

V 267.1 (429.8 km) **DC 1423.1** (2290.2 km) **F 96.9** (155.9 km) Delta state campground to east; 24 sites, water, tables, shelter with covered tables, toilets, $8 nightly fee or annual pass. Large turnout at campground entrance. Turnout on west side of highway on bank of the Delta River offers excellent views of the Alaska Range. ▲

V 267.2 (430 km) **DC 1423.2** (2290.4 km) **F 96.8** (155.7 km) Alaska Division of Forestry office.

V 267.3 (430.2 km) **DC 1423.3** (2290.5 km) **F 96.7** (155.6 km) Medical clinic.

V 267.5 (430.5 km) **DC 1423.5** (2290.9 km) **F 96.5** (155.3 km) Laundromat with showers, thrift store.

V 268 (431.3 km) **DC 1424** (2291.6 km) **F 96** (154.5 km) **Smith's Green Acres RV Park & Campground.** Avoid the rush and the crowds, stay with us. One of Alaska's finest RV parks. 9.5 Good Sam rating. From a guest: "One of the best we've seen in Alaska." Great trout and grayling fishing nearby. See display ad in Delta Junction section. [ADVERTISEMENT] ▲

V 268.3 (431.7 km) **DC 1424.3** (2292.1 km) **F 95.7** (154 km) **Junction** with Jack Warren Road (see Delta Vicinity map this section). Turn here for access to Clearwater state campground (10.5 miles/16.9 km).

On the banks of the Tanana River at ***BIG DELTA STATE HISTORICAL PARK,*** enjoy

RIKA'S ROADHOUSE & LANDING

"Best food in all 1,488 miles of the Alaska Highway . . ." *Seattle Times-Seattle Post-Intelligencer*

Roadhouse & Historical Buildings clustered in 10-acre Park

RATED #1 ON THE ALASKA HIGHWAY BY MAJOR TOUR COMPANIES

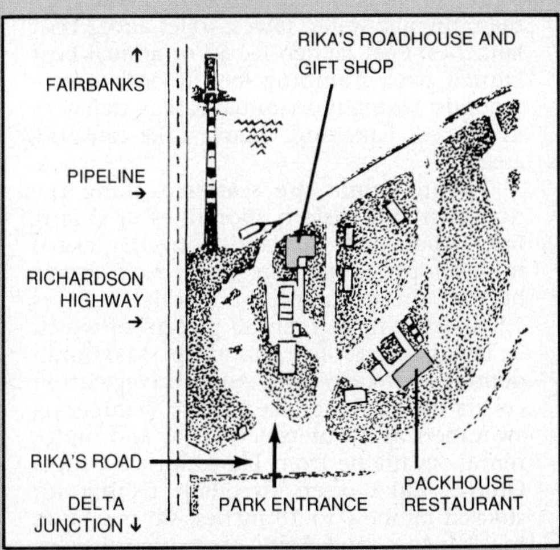

Tour Buses Welcome
Free Admission, Parking and Tours

THE ROAD HOUSE GIFT SHOP
Specializing in Alaskan-made gifts of
Gold Nugget Jewelry, Wood Puzzles,
Finished Fur Apparel & Diamond Willow,
Souvenir Shirts, Cards & Postcards

WORLDWIDE POSTAL SERVICE

ALASKAN RANCH-RAISED FURS
from **Whitestone Furs of Alaska**
featured in The Roadhouse Gift Shop
Fur & Leather Coats, Jackets, Stoles,
Flings, Clings & Collars,
Hats, Hand Muffs & Ear Muffs
Fur Items Made To Order

Staff Attired in Period Costumes

PACKHOUSE RESTAURANT

- Seating for over 150 for Breakfast and Lunch (Dinners for Special Functions)
- Homemade Soups
- Fresh Salads & Sandwiches
- Fresh Baked Pies, Breads & Cookies from **The Alaska Baking Company**

Park Hours 8–8 Daily
Restaurant 9–5 Daily

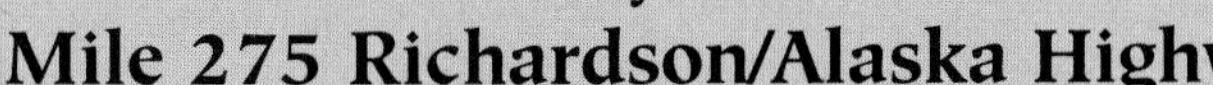

Mile 275 Richardson/Alaska Highway

Just upstream from the Trans-Alaska Pipeline Tanana River Crossing

Call (907) 895-4201 or (907) 895-4938 Anytime
P.O. Box 1229, Delta Junction, Alaska 99737

See our log ad at Mile 275 Richardson/Alaska Highway • Brochure Available

VISA

Clearwater campground has toilets, tables, water and boat launch; pleasant campsites on bank of river. Camping fee $6/night or annual pass. ▲

Driving this loop is a good opportunity to see local homesteads. Note that mileposts on these paved side roads run backward from Mile 13 at this junction to Mile 0 at the junction of Clearwater Road and the Alaska Highway.

V **270.3** (435 km) **DC 1426.3** (2295.3 km) **F 93.7** (150.8 km) Motel.

V **271** (436.1 km) **DC 1427** (2296.5 km) **F 93** (149.7 km) Medical clinic.

V **271.7** (437.2 km) **DC 1427.7** (2297.6 km) **F 92.3** (148.5 km) Tanana Loop Road. Turn here for Delta Junction youth hostel. To make a loop drive through farmlands, follow Tanana Loop Road approximately 1 mile/1.6 km, turn right on Tanana Loop Extension, which connects with Jack Warren Road. Turn west on Jack Warren Road to return to highway.

V **272.1** (437.9 km) **DC 1428** (2298 km) **F 92** (148 km) Fire station.

V **274.5** (441.8 km) **DC 1430.5** (2302.1 km) **F 89.5** (144 km) **Big "D" Bar.** See display ad this section.

V **275** (442.6 km) **DC 1431** (2303.9 km) **F 89** (143.2 km) **The Tanana Trading Post.** See display ad this section.

V **275** (442.6 km) **DC 1431** (2303.9 km) **F 89** (143.2 km) **Rika's Roadhouse at Big Delta State Historical Park.** Turn northeast at Rika's Road for Rika's Roadhouse and Landing on the banks of the Tanana River. Tour buses welcome. Parking areas with restrooms at both park entrances. The newly renovated Rika's Roadhouse offers worldwide postal service and gift shop specializing in fox furs, gold, diamond willow and interlocking wood puzzles. Visit the sod-roofed museum, barn, Signal Corp station and other historic structures. Local artisans at work. Live farm animals. Guides in period costumes are available to walk with you through the history of this important crossroads on the Valdez–Fairbanks trail.

Meals served 9 A.M. to 5 P.M. in our Packhouse Restaurant, home of the Alaska Baking Co. Try our famous bear claws and homemade muffins. The Packhouse Restaurant also offers homemade soups, fresh salads and sandwiches. Guests rave about our homemade pies, featuring strawberry–rhubarb, pecan, chocolate truffle and coconut cream. Overnight RV parking and dump station. After the dust of the highway, the green gardens of the 10-acre park are a welcome haven. Brochure available. P.O. Box 1229, Delta Junction, AK 99737. Phone (907) 895-4201 or 895-4938 anytime. Free admission. Handicapped access. See displayad this section. [ADVERTISEMENT] ♿▲

Rika's Roadhouse, which reopened in 1986 after extensive restoration, was built in 1910 by John Hajdukovich. In 1923, Hajdukovich sold it to Rika Wallen, a Swedish immigrant who had managed the roadhouse since 1917. Rika ran the roadhouse into the late 1940s and lived there until her death in 1969. Big Delta State Historical Park campground; camping fee $8/vehicle, dump station ($3). ▲

V **275.4** (443.2 km) **DC 1431.4** (2303.6 km) **F 88.6** (142.6 km) Big Delta Bridge across the Tanana River; spectacular view of pipeline suspended across river. Slow down for parking area at south end of bridge with litter barrels and interpretive sign about pipeline.

From here to Fairbanks there are views of the Tanana River and the Alaska Range to the south. Farming community of **BIG DELTA** (pop. 400); gas, store, 2 bars, a church, Kenner Sawmill and Tanana River boat landing.

The Fur Shack. See display ad this section.

V **277.7** (446.9 km) **DC 1433.7** (2307.2 km) **F 86.3** (138.9 km) Turnoff to east for Quartz Lake Recreation Area. Drive in 2.5 miles/4 km on gravel road to intersection: turn left for Lost Lake, continue straight ahead for Quartz Lake (another 0.3 mile/0.5 km). Lost Lake, 0.2 mile/0.3 km from intersection, has 8 campsites with picnic tables, toilet and a large parking area with tables and litter barrels. A shallow, picturesque lake with no fish. Quartz Lake has more developed campsites on good loop road, firepits, water, tables, toilet and 2 boat launches. Boat launch fee $3 or annual boat launch pass. Camping fees at both campgrounds: $8/night or annual pass. A trail connects Lost Lake and Quartz Lake camping areas. ▲

Private cabins are scattered along the northern and eastern shorelines of Quartz Lake. About half the land along the lake is undeveloped and there is no road access beyond the campground. The lake covers 1,500 acres, more than 80 percent of which is less than 15 feet/5m deep. Maximum depth is 40 feet/12m. Aquatic vegetation covers most of the lake surface, hampering swimmers and waterskiers. Boat and motor rentals available from Black Spruce Lodge. **Quartz Lake** offers excellent fishing for stocked rainbow to 18 inches, silver salmon to 13 inches, and Arctic char; use spinners, plugs and artificial flies. Ice fishing in winter. For more information phone the ADF&G office in Delta at (907) 895-4632.

V **277.9** (447.2 km) **DC 1433.9** (2307.5 km) **F 86.1** (138.6 km) Former U.S. Army petroleum station, now closed. Pay phone beside highway.

V **278.2** (447.7 km) **DC 1434.2** (2308 km) **F 85.8** (138.1 km) South end of long double-ended turnout to west. Several of these long turnouts northbound are old sections of the Alaska Highway.

V **280.3** (451.1 km) **DC 1436.3** (2311.4 km) **F 83.7** (134.7 km) Gravel turnout to east.

V **284** (457 km) **DC 1440** (2317.4 km) **F 80** (128.7 km) Watch for moose.

V **286.6** (461.2 km) **DC 1442.6** (2321.6 km) **F 77.4** (124.6 km) Shaw Creek bridge; boat launch.

V **286.7** (461.4 km) **DC 1442.7** (2321.7 km) **F 77.3** (124.4 km) **Shaw Creek** road. Good to excellent early spring and fall grayling fishing; subject to closure (check locally). Good view northbound of Tanana River which parallels the highway.

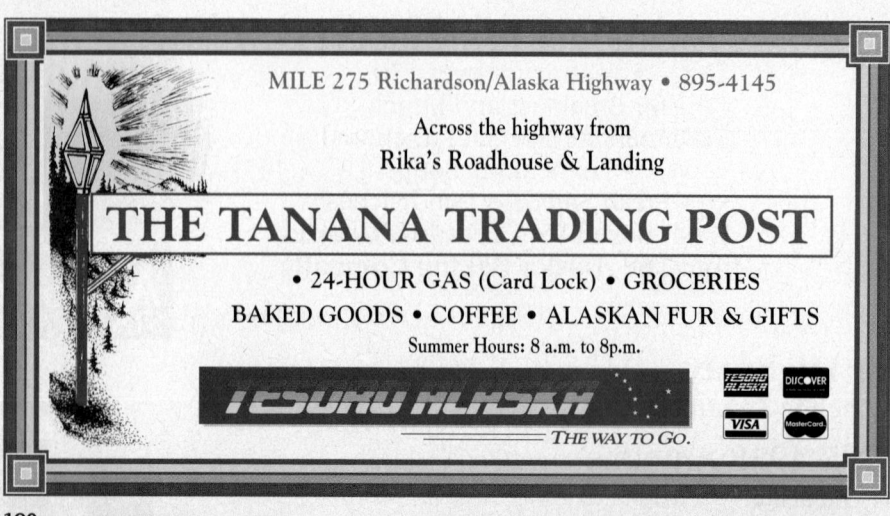

V **287.2** (462.2 km) **DC 1443.2** (2322.5 km) **F 76.8** (123.6 km) Turnout and road to slough to east. Birch trees are thick along this stretch of highway.

V 288 (463.5 km) **DC 1444** (2323.8 km) **F 76** (122.3 km) Panoramic view to the south with vistas of 3 great peaks of the Alaska Range: Mount Hayes, elev. 13,832 feet/4,216m, almost due south; Hess Mountain, elev. 11,940 feet/3,639m, to the west (right) of Mount Hayes; and Mount Deborah, elev. 12,339 feet/3,761m, to the west (right) of Hess Mountain. Mount Hayes is named for Charles Hayes, an early member of the U.S. Geological Survey. Mount Deborah was named in 1907 by the famous Alaskan Judge Wickersham for his wife.

V 289.8 (466.4 km) **DC 1445.8** (2326.7 km) **F 74.2** (119.4 km) Paved double-ended turnout to east.

V 291.8 (469.6 km) **DC 1447.8** (2329.9 km) **F 72.2** (116.2 km) Northbound truck lane begins.

V 292.8 (471.2 km) **DC 1448.8** (2331.5 km) **F 71.2** (114.6 km) Truck lane ends. View of Tanana River valley.

V 294 (473.1 km) **DC 1450** (2333.5 km) **F 70** (112.7 km) Paved double-ended turnout.

V 294.2 (473.5 km) **DC 1450.2** (2333.8 km) **F 69.8** (112.3 km) Southbound truck lane begins.

V 294.9 (474.6 km) **DC 1450.9** (2334.9 km) **F 69.1** (111.2 km) Game Management Unit boundary between 20B and 20D. Entering Fairbanks North Star borough northbound.

V 295 (474.7 km) **DC 1451** (2335.1 km) **F 69** (111 km) Site of the original old Richardson Roadhouse, which burned down in December 1982.

V 295.4 (475.4 km) **DC 1451.4** (2335.7 km) **F 68.6** (110.4 km) Banner Creek bridge; historic placer gold stream.

V 296.4 (477 km) **DC 1452.4** (2337.3 km) **F 67.6** (108.8 km) Paved turnout to west; view of Alaska Range and Tanana River to south.

V 297.7 (479.1 km) **DC 1453.7** (2339.4 km) **F 66.3** (106.7 km) Large gravel parking area to west below highway; good scenic viewpoint. Paved access road to Tanana River.

V 298.2 (479.9 km) **DC 1454.2** (2340.2 km) **F 65.8** (105.9 km) Scenic viewpoint; paved double-ended turnout to west.

V 301.7 (485.5 km) **DC 1457.7** (2345.9 km) **F 62.3** (100.3 km) South end of long double-ended turnout to west.

V 304.3 (489.7 km) **DC 1460.3** (2350 km) **F 59.7** (96.1 km) Small paved turnout to east.

V 305.2 (491.2 km) **DC 1461.2** (2351.5 km) **F 58.8** (94.6 km) Birch Lake Road to east; access to military recreation area (restricted).

V 306 (492.4 km) **DC 1462** (2352.8 km) **F 58** (93.3 km) Large parking area to east overlooking **Birch Lake**; unimproved gravel boat launch and beach; fish from shore in spring, from boat in summer, for rainbow and silver salmon. Many Fairbanks residents have summer homes at Birch Lake.

V 306.1 (492.6 km) **DC 1462.1** (2352.9 km) **F 57.9** (93.2 km) Turnoff to west for **Lost Lake**. Drive in 0.7 mile/1.1 km on dirt road; silver salmon fishing.

V 307.2 (494.3 km) **DC 1463.2** (2354.7 km) **F 56.8** (91.4 km) Birch Lake highway maintenance station.

V 308.4 (496.3 km) **DC 1464.4** (2356.6 km) **F 55.6** (89.5 km) South end of long double-ended turnout to east.

V 310 (498.9 km) **DC 1466** (2359.2 km) **F 54** (86.9 km) Double-ended paved parking area to west.

V 313 (503.7 km) **DC 1469** (2364 km) **F 51** (82.1 km) Paved double-ended turnout to west. Access to **Silver Fox Pond**; stocked with arctic char.

V 314.8 (506.6 km) **DC 1470.8** (2366.9 km) **F 49.2** (79.2 km) **Midway Lodge** is open 7 A.M. to 11 P.M. daily. Bar open till ?. Breakfast anytime, famous homemade chili, royal ½-pound hamburgers, fresh pies. Clean rooms starting at $35. Showers. Gifts. We are a family-oriented stop on the Alaska Highway and welcome your visit. 11191 Richardson Highway, Salcha, AK 99714. Phone (907) 488-2939. [ADVERTISEMENT]

V 317.9 (511.6 km) **DC 1473.9** (2371.9 km) **F 45.4** (73.1 km) Double-ended gravel turnout to west.

V 319.3 (513.8 km) **DC 1475.3** (2374.2 km) **F 44.7** (71.9 km) Access road leads east to Harding Lake summer homes.

V 319.8 (514.7 km) **DC 1475.8** (2375 km) **F 44.2** (71.1 km) Second access road northbound leads east to Harding Lake summer homes. Access to **Little Harding Lake**, king salmon fishing.

V 321.5 (517.4 km) **DC 1477.5** (2377.8 km) **F 42.5** (68.4 km) **Harding Lake** State Recreation Area turnoff; drive east 1.5 miles/2.4 km on paved road to campground. Park headquarters, drinking water fill-up and dump station ($3 charge) at campground entrance. Picnic grounds on lakeshore, swimming, boat ramp ($3 launch fee or annual boat launch pass), ball fields and about 80 campsites. Camping fee $8/night or annual pass. Fishing for lake trout, arctic char, burbot, northern pike and salmon. Lake is reported to be "hard to fish." Worth the drive! *Bring your insect repellent. You may need it!*

V 322.2 (518.5 km) **DC 1478.2** (2378.9 km) **F 41.8** (67.3 km) Salcha post office and lodge with food, gas and camping.

Salcha River Lodge. Alaskan hospitality. Gas, diesel, propane, RV parking, clean showers, modern motel, groceries, restaurant, gift shop, post office. Ice cream cones, shakes, sundaes, homemade pie. Also stop and visit the Whimsical Whittler Shop. Finest diamond willow work in the Interior. Close to rivers and lakes; excellent fishing. 9162 Richardson Highway, Salcha, AK 99714. Phone (907) 488-2233. [ADVERTISEMENT]

V 323.1 (520 km) **DC 1479.1** (2380.3 km) **F 40.9** (65.8 km) **Salcha River** State Recreation Site; large parking area with 75 sites, boat ramp ($3 launch fee or annual boat launch pass), picnic area, toilets and water. Camping fee $8/night per vehicle or annual pass. Fishing for king and chum salmon, grayling, sheefish, northern pike and burbot.

V 323.4 (520.4 km) **DC 1479.4** (2380.8 km) **F 40.6** (65.3 km) Salcha River bridge.

V 324 (521.4 km) **DC 1480** (2381.7 km) **F 40** (64.4 km) Clear Creek bridge.

V 324.6 (522.4 km) **DC 1480.6** (2382.7 km) **F 39.4** (63.4 km) Double-ended gravel turnout to east.

V 324.8 (522.7 km) **DC 1480.8** (2383 km) **F 39.2** (63.1 km) Munsons Slough bridge.

V 325.5 (523.8 km) **DC 1481.5** (2384.2 km) **F 38.5** (62 km) The community of **SALCHA** (pop. 354) stretches along the highway in both directions. The elementary school is located here. The post office (ZIP 99714) is at **Milepost V 322.2.**

V 326.4 (525.3 km) **DC 1482.4** (2385.6 km) **F 37.6** (60.5 km) Salcha Baptist log church to west.

V 327 (526.2 km) **DC 1483** (2386.6 km) **F 37** (59.5 km) Picturesque log home to west.

V 327.7 (527.4 km) **DC 1483.7** (2387.7 km) **F 36.3** (58.4 km) Little Salcha River bridge.

V 328.3 (528.3 km) **DC 1484.3** (2388.7 km) **F 35.7** (57.4 km) **Salcha Store and Service.** See display ad this section.

V 330.4 (531.7 km) **DC 1486.4** (2392.1 km) **F 33.6** (54.1 km) Johnson Road. Access to Pump Station 8.

V 331.7 (533.8 km) **DC 1487.7** (2394.2 km) **F 32.3** (52 km) Salcha Fairgrounds.

V 332.2 (534.6 km) **DC 1488.2** (2395 km) **F 31.8** (51.2 km) Access east to **31-Mile Pond**; stocked with arctic char.

V 332.3 (534.8 km) **DC 1488.3** (2395.1 km) **F 31.7** (51 km) **The Knotty Shop.** Stop and be impressed by a truly unique Alaskan gift shop and wildlife museum. Jim and Paula have attempted to maintain a genuine Alaskan flavor—from the unusual burl construction to the Alaskan wildlife displayed in a natural setting to the handcrafted Alaskan gifts. Don't miss the opportunity to stop and browse. See display ad this section. Show us *The MILEPOST®* advertisement for a free small ice cream cone. [ADVERTISEMENT]

V 334.5 (538.3 km) **DC 1490.5** (2398.7 km) **F 29.5** (47.5 km) Public dumpster at gravel pit.

V 334.7 (538.6 km) **DC 1490.7** (2399 km) **F 29.3** (47.2 km) South boundary of Eielson AFB. Watch for various military aircraft taking off and landing to the east. Aircraft include Air Force F-16s, F-15s, KC-135s, C-130s, C-141s, OA-10s, Navy A-6s, F-14s and others.

V 335.1 (539.3 km) **DC 1491.1** (2399.6 km) **F 28.9** (46.5 km) Access east to **28-Mile Pond;** stocked with rainbow and silver salmon.

V 340.7 (548.3 km) **DC 1496.7** (2408.6 km) **F 23.3** (37.5 km) Divided highway begins for northbound traffic. *CAUTION: Watch for heavy traffic southbound turning east into the base, 7-8 A.M., and merging northbound traffic, 3:45-5:30 P.M., weekdays.*

V 341 (548.8 km) **DC 1497** (2409.1 km) **F 23** (37 km) Entrance to **EIELSON AIR FORCE BASE,** constructed in 1943 and named for Carl Ben Eielson, a famous Alaskan bush pilot. A weekly tour is offered for groups of 10 or more. Phone the Public Affairs office at (907) 377-1410 for reservations and more information.

Moose may be seen year-round in Interior and Southcentral Alaska. (© Michael DeYoung)

V 343.7 (553.1 km) **DC 1499.7** (2413.5 km) **F 20.3** (32.7 km) Moose Creek Road and general store; diesel, gas, wrecker service.

Moose Creek General Store. See display ad this section.

Piledriver Slough parallels the highway from here north, flowing into the Tanana River. It is stocked with rainbow trout. Check with general store for access and fishing information. **Bathing Beauty Pond,** stocked with rainbow, arctic char and grayling, is accessible via Eielson Farm Road off Moose Creek Road.

V 344.7 (554.7 km) **DC 1500.7** (2415 km) **F 19.3** (31.1 km) Moose Creek bridge.

V 345.5 (556 km) **DC 1501.5** (2416.4 km) **F 18.5** (29.8 km) *CAUTION: Highway crosses Alaska Railroad tracks.*

V 346 (556.8 km) **DC 1502** (2417.2 km) **F 17.9** (28.8 km) Chena Flood Channel bridge. Upstream dam is part of flood control project initiated after the Chena River left its banks and flooded Fairbanks in 1967.

V 346.7 (558 km) **DC 1502.7** (2418.4 km) **F 17.3** (27.8 km) Laurance Road. Turn right northbound for Chena Lakes Recreation Area (follow signs, 2.2 miles/3.5 km to entrance). Constructed by the Army Corps of Engineers and run by Fairbanks North Star Borough, the recreation area has 80 campsites, 92 picnic sites (some with handicap access), pump water, volleyball courts, and a 250-acre lake with swimming beach. **Chena Lake** is stocked with silver salmon, arctic char, grayling and rainbow trout. Nonmotorized boats may be rented from a concessionaire. The **Chena River** flows through part of the recreation area and offers good grayling fishing and also northern pike, whitefish and burbot. Hiking and self-guiding nature trails. Open year-round. Fee charged Memorial Day to Labor Day; day use $3 per vehicle, camping $6 per day.

V 347.1 (558.6 km) **DC 1503.1** (2419 km) **F 16.9** (27.2 km) Newby Road.

V 347.7 (559.6 km) **DC 1503.7** (2419.9 km) **F 16.3** (26.2 km) Exit west for St. Nicholas Lane, east for Dawson Road.

V 348.7 (561.2 km) **DC 1504.7** (2421.5 km) **F 15.3** (24.6 km) North Pole Visitor Information Center; open 8 A.M. to 7 P.M. daily, Memorial Day to mid-Sept. Turn right on Mission Road for radio station KJNP, turn left northbound for 5th Avenue businesses, RV park and Santa Claus House.

Santaland RV Park. Good Sampark. New 1992. Center of North Pole, next to Santa Claus House, home of Dancer and Prancer, North Pole's resident reindeer. Water and electric, pull-throughs, full hookups and limited dry. RV and car wash. Private bathrooms, laundry, pay phones, facilities for handicapped. Malls and churches within walking distance. Daily shuttle bus to Fairbanks points of interest. Tour sales and reservations for your convenience. See display ad or call (907) 488-9123. [ADVERTISEMENT]

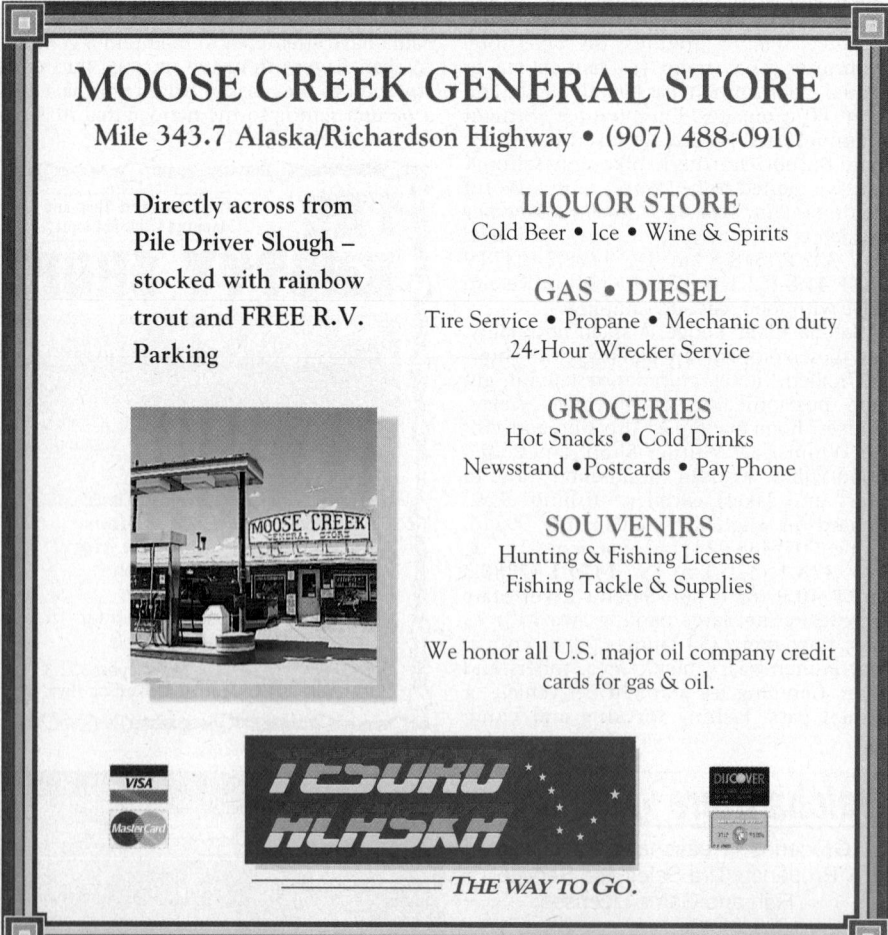

V 349 (561.6 km) **DC 1505** (2422 km) **F 15** (24.1 km) **Santa Claus House.** In 1949, Con Miller began wearing a Santa Claus suit on business trips throughout the territory, bringing the spirit of St. Nicholas to hundreds of children for the first time. Here the Miller family continues this tradition. Ask about Santa's Christmas letter. Mail your cards and letters here for authentic North Pole postmark. Enjoy the unique gift shop and exhibits. Summer hours: 8 A.M.–8 P.M. daily, Memorial Day through Labor Day. Ride the Snowy River Railroad daily except Sun., summers only. Visit with Santa Claus 10 A.M–6 P.M. except Tues. and Wed. Summers and Christmas season only. Santa's reindeer, Dancer and Prancer, live on the grounds all summer long. Santa Claus House winter hours: 10 A.M.–6 P.M. (closed January and February for Santa's annual vacation). See display ad this section. [ADVERTISEMENT]

V 349.5 (562.3 km) **DC 1505.5** (2422.8 km) **F 14.5** (23.3 km) North Pole and North Pole Plaza to the left northbound via Santa Claus Lane; Badger Road to the right. Truck stop with diesel, 2 small shopping malls, motel and other businesses are located on Badger Road. Santa Claus Lane has several businesses along it, and connects with 5th Avenue, which loops back to the highway at **Milepost V 348.6.** Badger Road is a loop road leading 12 miles/19.3 km along Badger Slough. It reenters the Alaska Highway 7 miles/11.3 km outside of Fairbanks at **Milepost V 357.1.**

North Pole

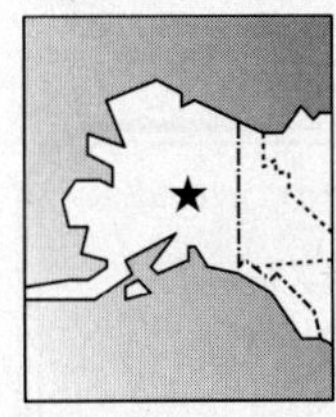

V 349.5 (562.3 km) **DC 1505.5** (2422.8 km) **F 14.5** (23.3 km) West of the Alaska Highway. **Population:** 1,456. **Emergency Services:** Emergencies only phone 911. **Police,** phone (907) 488-6902. **Alaska State Troopers,** phone (907) 452-2114. **Fire Department,** phone (907) 488-2232.

Visitor Information: At **Milepost V 348.7.** Open 8 A.M. to 7 P.M. daily, Memorial Day to mid-Sept.

Elevation: 500 feet/152m. **Radio:** KJNP-AM 1170, KJNP-FM 100.3; also Fairbanks stations.

NORTH POLE ADVERTISERS

Alaskan's Lazy Daze Bed & Breakfast....................Mile 6 Badger Rd.
Beaver Lake Resort Motel.........................Ph. (907) 488-9600
Birch Tree Bed & Breakfast.....................Ph. (907) 488-4667
Bo's Logos............................North Pole Plaza
Elf's Den, The.................Next to visitor center
Food Factory.................101 Santa Claus Lane
Jolly Acres Motel...................3068 Badger Rd.
KJNP...Mission Rd.
North Pole Chamber of Commerce..............Ph. (907) 488-2242
North Pole Coffee Roasting Company...............................220 Parkway
Riverview RV Park.......Mile 357.1 Alaska Hwy.
Santa Claus House..................St. Nicholas Dr.
Santaland RV Park and Campground..............St. Nicholas Dr.

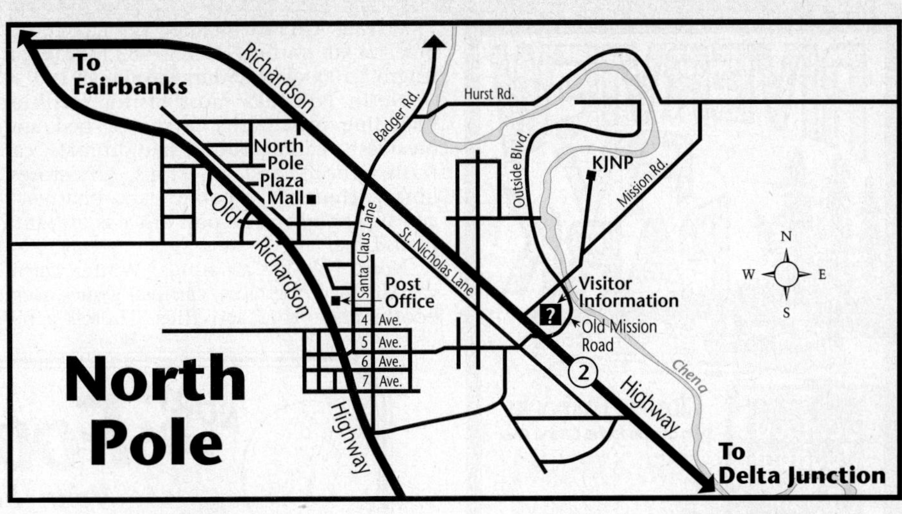

Private Aircraft: Bradley Sky Ranch, 0.9 mile/1.4 km northwest; elev. 483 feet/147m; length 4,100 feet/1,250m; gravel; fuel 100.

North Pole has most visitor facilities including restaurants, a motel, bed and breakfasts, campgrounds, laundromats, car wash, grocery and gas stops, gift stores, library, churches, a public park, pharmacy and supermarket. The post office is on Santa Claus Lane.

North Pole has an annual Winter Carnival with sled dog races, carnival games, food booths and other activities. There's a big summer festival weekend celebration, held July 5–7, 1996, with carnival rides, food booths, arts and crafts booths and a parade.

In 1944 Bon V. Davis homesteaded this area. Dahl and Gaske Development Co. bought the Davis homestead, subdivided it, and named it North Pole, hoping to attract a toy manufacturer who could advertise products as being made in North Pole.

North Pole is the home of many Fairbanks commuters. It has an oil refinery that produces heating fuel, jet fuel and other products. Eielson and Wainwright military

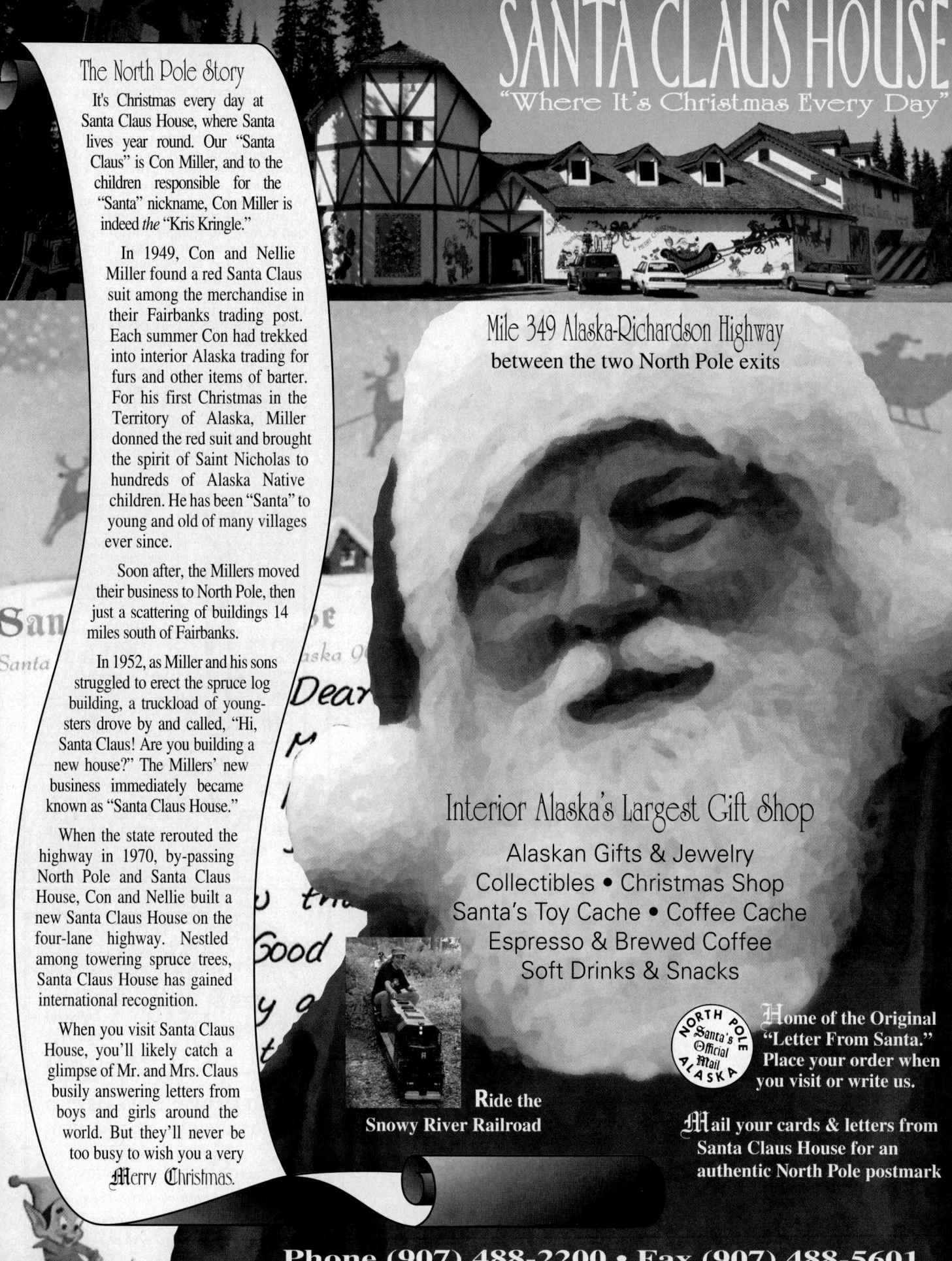

bases are nearby.

Radio station KJNP, operated by Calvary's Northern Lights Mission, broadcasts music and religious programs on 1170 AM and 100.3 FM. They also operate television station KJNP Channel 4. Visitors are welcome between 8 A.M. and 10 P.M.; tours may be arranged. KJNP is located on Mission Road about 0.6 mile/1 km northeast of the Alaska Highway. The missionary project includes a dozen hand-hewn, sod-roofed homes and other buildings constructed of spruce logs.

Full-service campgrounds downtown at Santaland RV Park and Campground, at **Milepost V 356** Alaska-Richardson Highway and at Riverview RV Park on Badger Road. North Pole Public Park, on 5th Avenue, has tent sites in the trees along a narrow dirt road; no camping fee. Dump station available at North Pole Plaza. ▲

North Pole Coffee Roasting Company offers gourmet coffee beans from around the world roasted right here in North Pole. Coffee shop, espresso bar, pastries, breakfast, lunches. Gifts and T-shirts. Mail order. From exit, turn south on Santa Claus Lane. We're at 220 Parkway, on your right, just beyond North Pole Plaza Mall. (907) 488-7190. See display ad, North Pole section. [ADVERTISEMENT]

Richardson–Alaska Highway Log *(continued)*

V 350.6 (564.2 km) **DC 1506.6** (2424.6 km) **F 13.4** (21.6 km) *CAUTION: Highway crosses Alaska Railroad tracks.*

V 351 (564.9 km) **DC 1507** (2425.3 km) **F 13** (20.9 km) Twelvemile Village exit. Greenhouse with floral displays.

V 354.4 (570.3 km) **DC 1510.4** (2430.7 km) **F 9.6** (15.4 km) Old Richardson Highway exit.

V 356 (572.9 km) **DC 1512** (2433.3 km) **F 8** (12.9 km) **Road's End RV Park.** Just 6.5 miles south of Fairbanks. Full hook-ups, showers. Reasonable rates. Weekly and monthly rates available. (907) 488-0295. [ADVERTISEMENT] ▲

V 357.1 (574.7 km) **DC 1513.1** (2435 km) **F 6.9** (11.1 km) Badger Road. This loop road connects with the Alaska Highway again at North Pole. Motel, RV park, salmon bake, bed and breakfasts and other businesses are located on Badger Road.

V 357.6 (575.5 km) **DC 1513.6** (2435.8 km) **F 6.4** (10.3 km) Weigh stations both sides of highway.

V 358.6 (577.1 km) **DC 1514.6** (2437.4 km) **F 5.4** (8.7 km) Entrance to Fort Wainwright.

V 359.2 (578.1 km) **DC 1515.2** (2438.4 km) **F 4.8** (7.7 km) *CAUTION: Highway crosses Alaska Railroad tracks.*

V 359.6 (578.7 km) **DC 1515.6** (2439.1 km) **F 4.4** (7.1 km) West truck route (Old Richardson Highway) exit for westbound traffic only. Access to motels, restaurants and Cushman Street business area.

V 360.6 (580.3 km) **DC 1516.6** (2440.7 km) **F 3.4** (5.5 km) Denali Park/Parks Highway (Alaska Route 3) exit northbound to bypass Fairbanks via the Robert J. Mitchell expressway. Hospital this exit.

V 361 (581 km) **DC 1517** (2441.4 km) **F 3** (4.8 km) Exit via 30th Avenue to Big Bend business area for east and westbound traffic. Access to motels, restaurants, Old Richardson Highway, Van Horn Road, Cushman Street and downtown Fairbanks.

V 361.3 (581.4 km) **DC 1517.3** (2441.8 km) **F 2.7** (4.3 km) 30th Avenue overpass; exits both sides of highway. A heart-shaped picture created from plantings of yellow flowers represents the Golden Heart of Fairbanks.

V 363 (584.2 km) **DC 1519** (2444.6 km) **F 1** (1.6 km) Turn right on Gaffney Road for Fort Wainwright; left on Airport Way for downtown Fairbanks, University of Alaska, Alaskaland and George Parks Highway (Alaska Route 3). Follow city center signs to downtown Fairbanks and visitor information center. Go straight ahead on the Steese Expressway for Gavora Mall, Bentley Mall, Fox, Steese and Elliott highways and Chena Hot Springs Road.

V 363.3 (584.7 km) **DC 1519.3** (2445 km) **F 0.7** (1.1 km) 10th Avenue exit to Fairbanks.

V 363.6 (585.1 km) **DC 1519.6** (2445.6 km) **F 0.4** (0.6 km) Steese Expressway crosses Chena River.

V 363.9 (585.6 km) **DC 1519.9** (2446 km) **F 0.1** (0.2 km) 3rd Street exit. Gavora Mall.

V 364 (585.8 km) **DC 1520** (2446.2 km) **F 0 FAIRBANKS.** College Road exit route to University of Alaska, Bentley Mall and city center (turn left). For details see FAIRBANKS section.

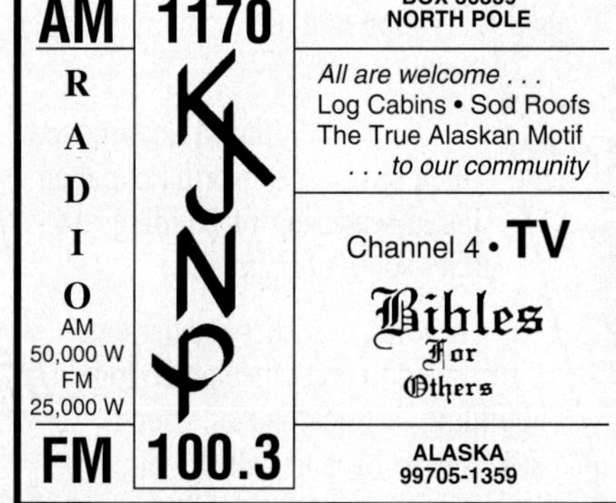

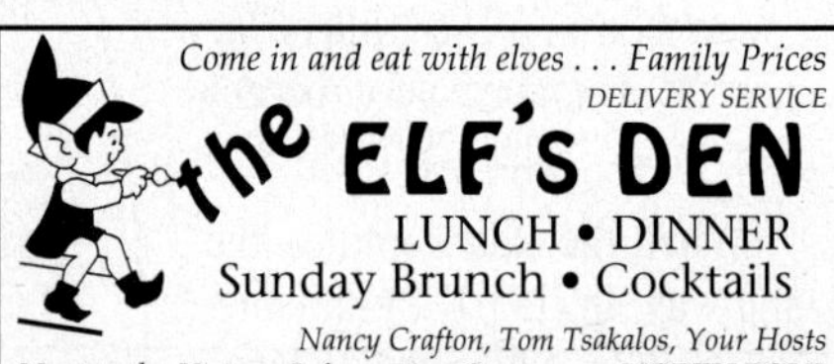

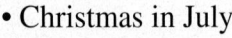

LIARD HIGHWAY

Junction with Alaska Highway to Mackenzie Highway Junction
BC Highway 77, NWT Highway 7

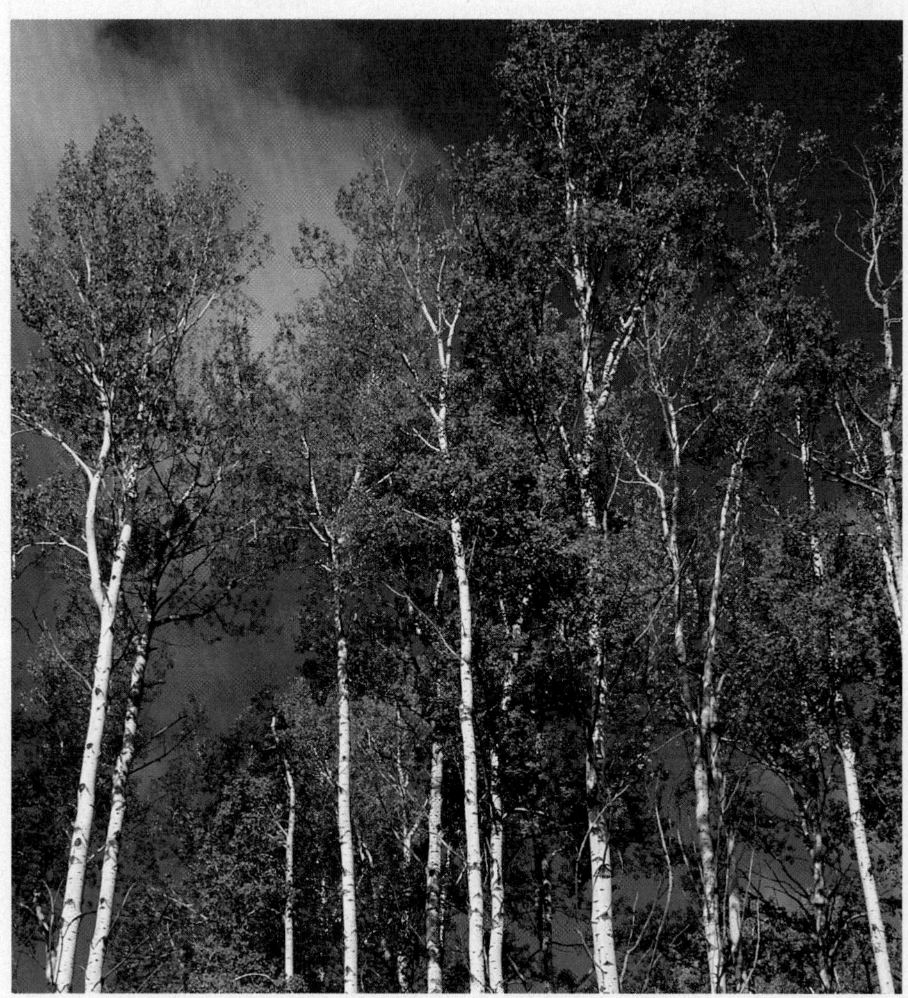

Aspens along the Liard Highway near Fort Liard. (© Stephanie Satter)

The Liard Highway, also called the Liard Trail or "Moose Highway" (after the road sign logo), is named for the Liard River Valley through which it runs for most of its length. The Liard Highway begins about 17 miles/27 km north of Fort Nelson on the Alaska Highway and leads northeast through British Columbia and Northwest Territories for 244.4 miles/393.4 km to junction with the Mackenzie Highway (NWT Highway 1).

The Liard is a relatively straight 2-lane gravel road through boreal forest and muskeg. In French, Liard means "black poplar," and this wilderness highway (officially opened in June 1984) is a corridor through a forest of white and black spruce, trembling aspen and balsam poplar.

The road can be dusty when dry and very muddy when wet. Poor road conditions (potholes, lack of grading) were reported on the BC portion of the Liard Highway in 1995. The NWT portion of the highway is well-maintained. Travelers may check current road conditions on the BC section of the highway (first 85 miles/136.8 km of road) by inquiring at the visitor information centre in Fort Nelson, BC. Travel information for the Northwest Territories is available from Northwest Territories Tourism; phone toll-free weekdays 1-800-661-0788. Food, gas and lodging are available at Fort Liard. Gas is also available at the Mackenzie Highway junction. It is a good idea to fill up in Fort Nelson.

Although the Northwest Territories portion of the Liard Highway parallels the Liard River, there is little access to the river. Travelers may enhance their trip by visiting Blackstone Territorial Park and exploring Nahanni National Park by air charter out of Fort Liard, Fort Simpson or Fort Nelson. Blackstone Territorial Park is accessible by road. Along the highway, travelers may walk the cut lines, drive to abandoned construction camps, swim in the borrow pits and bird watch at the barge landings. Remember to bring along lots of insect repellent! (Black flies are worst in September.)

Fishing the highway streams is only fair, but watch for wildlife such as moose, black bear, wood bison and grouse.

Liard Highway Log

Physical kilometreposts are up on the British Columbia portion of the highway about every 5 kilometres, starting with km 0 at the Alaska Highway junction and ending at the BC–NWT border. Kilometreposts are up about every 2 kilometres on the Northwest Territories portion of the highway, starting with Km 0 at the BC–NWT border and ending at the junction with the Mackenzie Highway.

Distance from the junction with the Alaska Highway (A) is followed by distance from the Mackenzie Highway junction (M).

A 0 M 244.4 (393.4 km) **Junction** with the Alaska Highway.

A 6.2 (10.1 km) **M 238.2** (383.3 km) Beaver Creek.

A 6.4 (10.3 km) **M 238** (383.1 km) Short side road east to Beaver Lake recreation site; 2 picnic tables, litter barrels, pit toilets, firewood, turnaround space. Short hike downhill through brush to floating dock; limited lake access.

A 14.3 (23.1 km) **M 230.1** (370.3 km) Stanolind Creek. Beaver dams to west.

A 15.6 (25.2 km) **M 228.8** (368.2 km) Gravel pit to west.

A 17.5 (28.2 km) **M 226.9** (365.2 km) Pond to west and cut line through trees shows Cat access in summer, ice road in winter.

A 21.1 (34 km) **M 223.3** (359.4 km) Westcoast Transmission Pipeline crossing. Pipeline transports natural gas from Pointed Mountain near Fort Liard to the company's gas plant on the Alaska Highway just south of Fort Nelson.

A 23.9 (38.4 km) **M 220.5** (355 km) Gravel pit to west.

A 24.2 (38.9 km) **M 220.2** (354.5 km) Road begins descent northbound to Fort Nelson River.

A 26.4 (42.5 km) **M 218** (350.9 km) Fort Nelson River bridge, single lane, reduce speed. The Nelson bridge is the longest Acrow bridge in the world at 1,410 feet/430m. It is 14 feet/4m wide, with a span of 230 feet/70m from pier to pier. The Acrow bridge, formerly called the Bailey bridge after its designer Sir Donald Bailey, is designed of interchangeable steel panels coupled with pins for rapid construction.

A 26.6 (42.9 km) **M 217.8** (350.5 km) Turnout at north end of bridge with pit

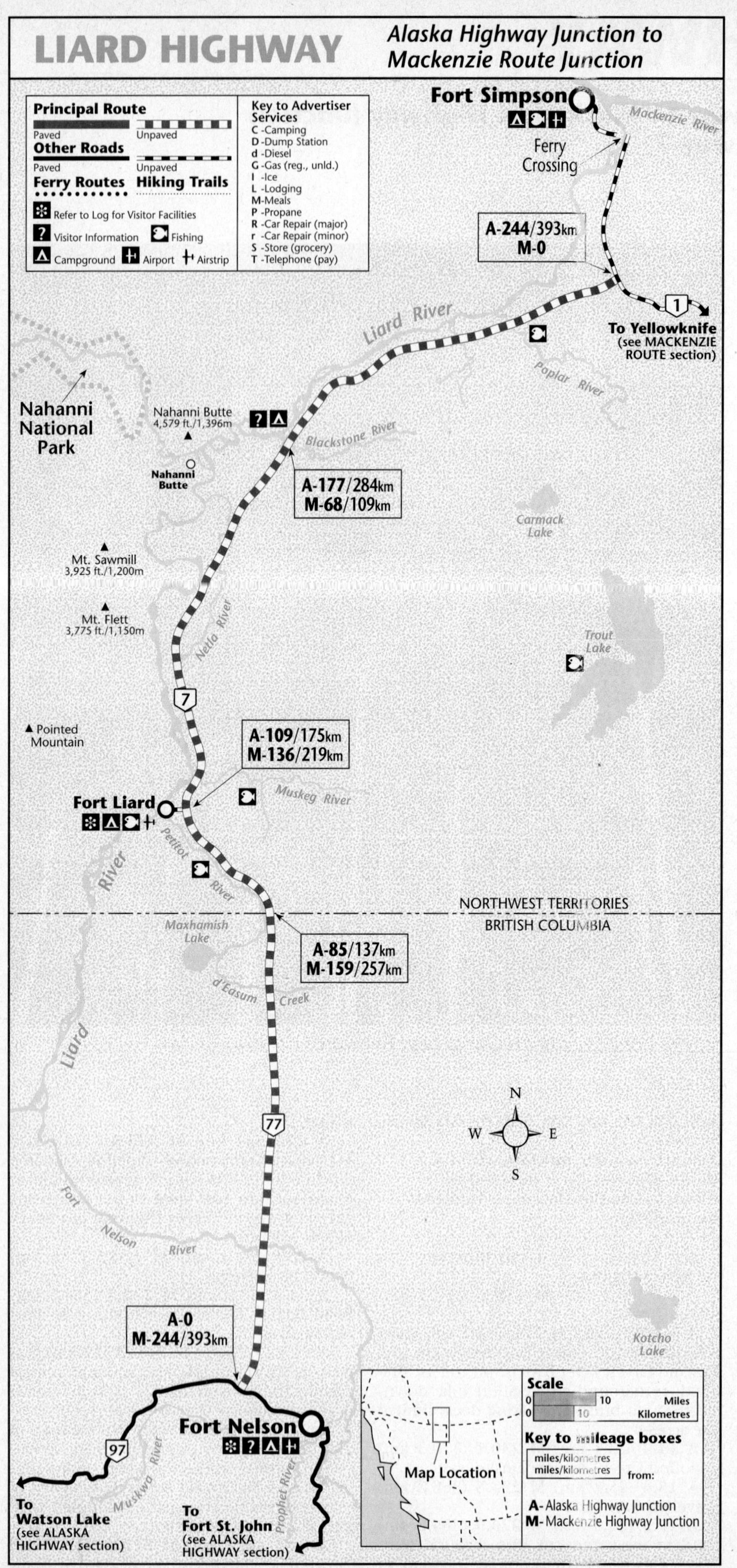

toilet, table and garbage container.

A 39.7 (63.9 km) **M 204.7** (329.5 km) **Tsinhia Creek**, grayling run for about 2 weeks in spring.

A 43.4 (69.8 km) **M 201** (323.5 km) Trapper's cabin to east.

A 51.8 (83.3 km) **M 192.6** (310.1 km) Side road leads west 1.9 miles/3 km to Tsinhia Lake and dead-ends in soft sandy track. A recreation site is planned at Tsinhia Lake.

A 59.2 (95.3 km) **M 185.2** (298.1 km) Concrete beams on west side of highway were dropped from a truck during construction of the Petitot River bridge, setting completion of the bridge back a year. Referred to locally as the "million-dollar garbage heap."

There are several winter roads in this area used by the forest, oil and gas industries. To most summer travelers these roads look like long cut lines or corridors through the Bush.

The Liard Highway replaced the old Fort Simpson winter road that joined Fort Nelson and Fort Simpson. The original Simpson Trail was first blazed in Nov. 1942 by Alaska Highway engineers, including the 648th, Company A detachment.

A 69.4 (111.7 km) **M 175** (281.7 km) Bridge over d'Easum Creek. Good bird-watching area.

A 71.4 (115 km) **M 173** (278.4 km) Access to Maxhamish Lake via 8-mile/13-km winter road accessible in summer by all-terrain vehicles only. A recreation site is planned for Maxhamish Lake.

A 74 (119.1 km) **M 170.4** (274.3 km) Wide unnamed creek flows into Emile Creek to east. Good bird-watching area, beaver pond.

A 75.4 (121.4 km) **M 169** (272 km) Highway emerges from trees northbound; view west of Mount Martin (elev. 4,460 feet/1,360m) and the Kotaneelee Range.

A 80.6 (129.7 km) **M 163.8** (263.7 km) View northwest of mountain ranges in Northwest Territories.

A 81.2 (130.7 km) **M 163.2** (262.6 km) Highway begins descent (7 percent grade) northbound to Petitot River.

A 82.8 (133.2 km) **M 161.6** (260.2 km) Petitot River bridge. The **Petitot River** is reputed to have the warmest swimming water in British Columbia (70°F/21°C). A 9-hour canoe trip to Fort Liard is possible from here (some sheer rock canyons and rapids en route). Good bird-watching area. Also freshwater clams, pike and pickerel; short grayling run in spring.

The Petitot River was named for Father Petitot, an Oblate missionary who came to this area from France in the 1860s.

The Petitot River bridge was the site of the official opening of the Liard Highway on June 23, 1984. The ceremony was marked by an unusual ribbon-cutting: A 1926 Model T Ford, carrying dignitaries, was driven through the ribbon (which stretched for about 20 feet before snapping) while a guard of kilted pipers from Yellowknife played. The Model T, driven by Marl Brown of Fort Nelson, had been across this route in March 1975 just weeks after the bush road had been punched through by Cats and seismic equipment. This earlier trip, in which Mr. Brown was accompanied by Mickey Hempler, took 44 hours from Fort Nelson to Fort Simpson.

A 84.1 (135.4 km) **M 160.3** (258 km) Crest of Petitot River hill (10 percent grade).

A 85 (136.8 km) **M 159.4** (256.6 km) BC–NWT border. TIME ZONE CHANGE:

British Columbia observes Pacific time, Northwest Territories observes Mountain time.

Northwest Territories restricts liquor importation as follows: 1 40-oz. hard liquor or 1 40-oz. wine or 1 dozen bottles of beer per person.

A 85.2 (137.1 km) **M 159.2** (256.2 km) Turnout to east with litter barrels.

A 107 (172.2 km) **M 137.4** (221.1 km) Vehicle inspection station and weigh scales to east.

A 108.6 (174.8 km) **M 135.8** (218.5 km) **Junction** with side road that leads 4 miles/6.4 km to Fort Liard (description follows). Gas and diesel available at junction. Current status of proposed tourist centre here unknown.

Views from road into Fort Liard across the Liard River of Mount Coty (elev. 2,715 feet/830m) and Pointed Mountain (elev. 4,610 feet/1,405m) at the southern tip of the Liard Range.

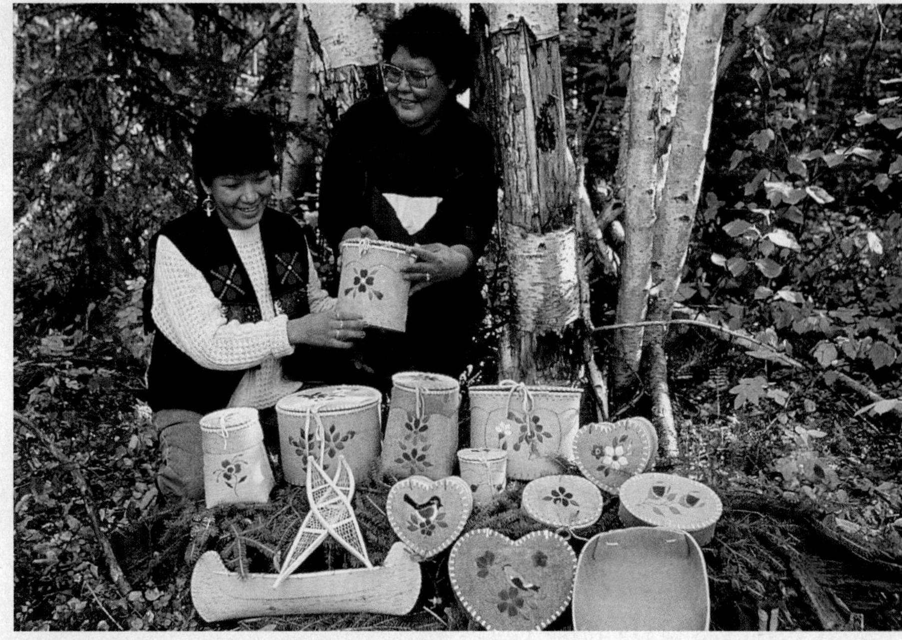

Birch-bark baskets from Acho Dene crafts shop in Fort Liard. (© Lyn Hancock)

Fort Liard

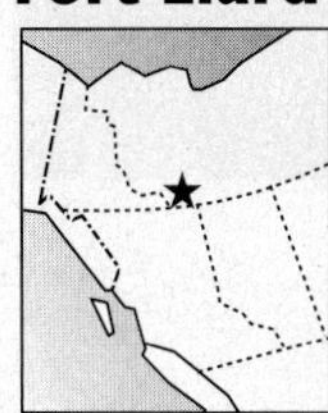

Located on the south bank of the Liard River near its confluence with the Petitot River (known locally as Black River because of its colour), about 50 miles/80 km south of Nahanni Butte. **Population:** 428. **Emergency Services: RCMP**, phone (403) 770-4221. **Fire Department**, phone (403) 770-4241. **Nursing Station**, phone (403) 770-4301.

Elevation: 700 feet/213m. **Climate:** There is no permafrost here. Good soil and water, a long summer season with long hours of daylight, and comparatively mild climate considering Fort Liard's geographical location. Several luxuriant local gardens. The Liard River here is approximately 1,500 feet/450m wide, fairly swift and subject to occasional flooding. **Radio** and **Television:** CBC radio (microwave), a Native language station from Yellowknife and a community radio station; 4 channels plus CBC Television (Anik) and private satellite receivers.

Private Aircraft: Fort Liard airstrip; elev. 700 feet/213m; length 2,950 feet/899m; gravel; fuel 100/130 (obtain from Deh Cho Air Ltd.).

Transportation: Air–Charter service year-round via Deh Cho Air. **Barge**–Non-scheduled barge service in summer from Fort Nelson and Hay River.

This small, well-laid-out settlement of traditional log homes and new modern housing is located among tall poplar, spruce and birch trees on the south bank of the Liard River. The residents live a comparatively traditional life of hunting, trapping, fishing and making handicrafts, although there are more people taking jobs in construction and highway maintenance. Fort Liard residents are well known for the high quality of their birch-bark baskets and porcupine quill workmanship.

Recreation and sightseeing in the area include swimming and fishing (for pike, pickerel, goldeye and spring grayling) at the confluence of the Liard and Petitot rivers; air charter or canoe trip to Trout Lake, Bovie Lake, Fisherman's Lake, 300-foot-/91-m-high Virginia Falls in Nahanni National Park, Tlogotsho Plateau, or scenic Liard and Kotaneelee mountain ranges. Good viewing for Dall sheep, grizzly bear and caribou. Canoe rentals available from Deh Cho Air Ltd. Also check with Deh Cho Air about adventure tours. The traditional Dene settlement of **TROUT LAKE** (pop. 60) is also accessible by air from Fort Liard.

FORT LIARD ADVERTISERS

Acho Dene Native Crafts ..Ph. (403) 770-4161
Deh Cho Air Ltd. ....Ph. (403) 770-4103
Hamlet of Fort Liard ....Ph. (403) 770-4104
Liard Valley General Store
& Motel Ltd. ....Ph. (403) 770-4441

The North West Co. established a trading post near here at the confluence of the Liard and Petitot rivers called Riviere aux Liards in 1805. The post was abandoned after the massacre of more than a dozen residents by Indians. It was reestablished in 1820, then taken over by the Hudson's Bay Co. in 1821 when the 2 companies merged. The well-known geologist Charles Camsell was born at Fort Liard in 1876.

Facilities here include a motel with 8 rooms, 6 with kitchenettes (reservations suggested), 2 general stores, playground, outdoor rink, curling rink, craft shop (open 1-5 P.M. weekdays), the modern Acho Dene

School and a Roman Catholic mission. There is no bank in Fort Liard. The community centre has a snack bar. Gas and diesel available at highway junction.

Community-run Hay Lake Campground located just off the access road into Fort Liard; campsites, picnic tables, toilets and floating dock. Campground road may be slippery when wet. ▲

Liard Highway Log

(continued)

A 113.3 (182.4 km) **M 131.1** (211 km) **Muskeg River** bridge; turnout at north end. Gravel bars on the river make a good rest stop. Trapper's cabin on left. Fishing for pike, pickerel and freshwater clams. The Muskeg River is the local swimming hole for Fort Liard residents.

A 124.9 (201 km) **M 119.5** (192.4 km) Rabbit Creek bridge. Highway now runs close to the Liard River with good views of Liard Range to the west and northwest for the next 13 miles/21 km northbound.

A 128 (206 km) **M 116.4** (187.4 km) Kilometrepost 70.

A 131.1 (211 km) **M 113.3** (182.4 km) Good view of Mount Flett (elev. 3,775 feet/1,150m) ahead northbound.

A 136.7 (220 km) **M 107.7** (173.4 km) Access to Liard River (15-minute hike) via Paramount Mine winter road, an abandoned exploration road across the Liard River into the Liard Range.

A 146.9 (236.4 km) **M 97.5** (157 km) Short road west to locally named Whissel Landing on the Liard River, where road construction materials were brought in by barge during construction of the Liard Highway.

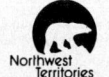

Liard River sunset photographed from Lindberg Landing. (© Lyn Hancock)

A 147.3 (237 km) **M 97.1** (156.4 km) Road widens for an emergency airstrip.

A 157.8 (253.9 km) **M 86.6** (139.5 km) Netla River bridge. The Netla River Delta is an important waterfowl breeding habitat and Indian fishing and hunting area.

A 163.7 (263.4 km) **M 80.7** (130 km) Road widens for an emergency airstrip.

A 165.9 (267 km) **M 78.5** (126.4 km) Turnoff to west for winter ice road that leads 13.8 miles/22.3 km to the Dene settlement of **NAHANNI BUTTE** (pop. 87), at the confluence of the South Nahanni and Liard rivers. Summer access by boat or floatplane.

A 171.8 (276.5 km) **M 72.6** (116.8 km) Creek Bridge, once called Scotty's Creek after an old trapper who had a cabin upstream. There are many such cabins in this area that once belonged (and still do) to prospectors and trappers, but they are not visible to the motorist. Stands of white spruce, white birch and balsam poplar along highway.

A 176.3 (283.7 km) **M 68.1** (109.7 km) Bridge over Upper Blackstone River. Picnic area on riverbank with tables, firewood, firepits and garbage containers.

A 176.6 (284.2 km) **M 67.8** (109.2 km) Blackstone River bridge.

A 179.1 (288.3 km) **M 65.3** (105.1 km) Entrance to Blackstone Territorial Park; 19 campsites with tables and firepits; firewood, water and garbage containers, and boat dock. State-of-the-art restroom, designed by Yellowknife architect Gino Pin, referred to locally as the "half-million-dollar toilet and shower." The boat launch here is usable only in high water early in the season; use boat launch at Cadillac Landing, **Milepost A 182.9**, during low water. The visitor information building, built with local logs, is located on the bank of the Liard River with superb views of Nahanni Butte (elev. 4,579 feet/1,396m). The centre is open mid-May to mid-Sept. ▲

A 180.9 (291.2 km) **M 63.5** (102.2 km) Entrance to Lindberg Landing, the homestead of Liard River pioneers Edwin and Sue Lindberg. The Lindbergs offer a bed and breakfast; rustic accommodations, bring your own sleeping bag. By appointment only. Contact Mobile Telephone JR36644 Arrowhead Channel, or write Sue and Edwin Lindberg, Box 28, Fort Simpson, NWT XOE ONO.

Blackstone Aviation operates floatplane flightseeing trips of Nahanni National Park from here. (See description of Nahanni National Park under Fort Simpson attractions in the MACKENZIE ROUTE section.)

A 182.9 (294.3 km) **M 61.5** (99.1 km) Barge landing once used to service Cadillac Mine and bring in construction materials. Access to river via 0.6-mile/0.9-km road (muddy when wet).

A 192.8 (310.3 km) **M 51.6** (83.1 km) Road widens for emergency airstrip.

A 197.8 (318.4 km) **M 46.6** (75 km) Kilometrepost 180.

A 211.3 (340.1 km) **M 33.1** (53.3 km) Bridge over Birch River.

A 216.7 (348.8 km) **M 27.7** (44.6 km) Kilometrepost 210.

A 222.8 (358.5 km) **M 21.6** (34.9 km) Good grayling and pike fishing in **Poplar River** culverts.

A 223 (358.8 km) **M 21.4** (34.6 km) Dirt road on left northbound leads 4 miles/6.4 km to Liard River; 4-wheel drive recommended. Wide beach, good spot for viewing wildlife.

A 228.1 (367.1 km) **M 16.3** (26.3 km) Microwave tower to east. Vegetation changes northbound to muskeg with black spruce, tamarack and jackpine.

A 235.6 (379.2 km) **M 8.8** (14.2 km) Kilometrepost 240.

A 244.2 (393 km) **M 0.2** (0.4 km) Road maintenance camp.

A 244.4 (393.4 km) **M 0 Junction** with the Mackenzie Highway (NWT 1). "Checkpoint": 24-hour gas, diesel, propane; licensed restaurant. Phone (403) 695-2953. Turn right (south) for Hay River and Yellowknife; turn left (north) for Fort Simpson. See **Milepost G 550.6** on the Mackenzie Highway in the MACKENZIE ROUTE section for log.

MACKENZIE ROUTE

Valleyview, Alberta, to Yellowknife, Northwest Territories
Alberta Highways 2, 35, 43, NWT Highways 1, 2, 3, 4, 5 and 6
(See maps, pages 202-203)

Named for explorer Alexander Mackenzie, who in 1779 navigated Great Slave Lake and sailed to the mouth of the Mackenzie River seeking a trade route for the Hudson's Bay Co., the Mackenzie Route is an adventure for modern explorers. It is not a trip for the impulsive. While there are accommodations, gas stations and other services in cities and settlements along the highways, long distances require that motorists plan in advance.

The Mackenzie Route covers the following highways: Alberta Highway 35 and NWT Highway 1 to Fort Simpson (Mackenzie Highway) and the new (1994) extension to Wrigley; Highway 2 to Hay River; Highway 3 to Yellowknife; Highway 4 (Ingraham Trail); Highway 5 to Fort Smith; and Highway 6 to Fort Resolution. NWT Highway 7, the Liard Highway, connecting the Mackenzie Highway with the Alaska Highway north of Fort Nelson, is covered in the LIARD HIGHWAY section. The Dempster Highway (NWT Highway 8) to Inuvik is covered in the DEMPSTER HIGHWAY section.

Allow at least 2 weeks to travel the entire route. For general information on travel in the Northwest Territories, phone Northwest Territories Tourism toll free at 1-800-661-0788 during business hours on weekdays.

Most Northwest Territories highways are gravel. Asphalt chip seal surfacing is under way on Highways 1 and 3. Gravel road is treated with calcium chloride to control the dust; wash your vehicle when possible. For road conditions phone 1-800-661-0750.

In summer, the Northwest Territories government provides free ferry service for cars and passengers across the Mackenzie River to Fort Providence, across the Liard River to Fort Simpson and across the Mackenzie River to Wrigley. In winter, traffic crosses on the ice. For current ferry information call (403) 873-7799 in Yellowknife, or 1-800-661-0751.

The Mackenzie Highway begins at Grimshaw, AB. There are several routes to Grimshaw to choose from (see map). *The MILEPOST®* logs the Valleyview–Peace River route to the Mackenzie Highway via Highways 43 and 2.

Cirque of the Unclimbables in the Ragged Range of the Mackenzie Mountains is a favorite helitour destination out of Fort Simpson. (© Lyn Hancock)

Log of the Valleyview–Peace River Route to the Mackenzie Highway

Distance from Valleyview (V) is followed by distance from Mackenzie Highway (MH).

HIGHWAY 43

V 0 MH 101.1 (162.7 km) **Junction** of Highways 34 and 43. Follow Highway 43 north.

V 0.6 (1 km) **MH 100.5** (161.6 km) Turnoff to west for downtown Valleyview (see description of Valleyview in the EAST ACCESS ROUTE section).

V 2.2 (3.5 km) **MH 98.9** (159.3 km) **Junction** with Secondary Road 669 which leads east 20 miles/32 km to Sunset House Community Campground on Snipe Lake; 20 sites, firewood, playground, boat launch, camping fee. ▲

V 4 (6.4 km) **MH 97.1** (156.3 km) Sturgeon Creek.

V 18 (29 km) **MH 83.1** (133.7 km) East Dollar Lake to west.

V 23.1 (37.2 km) **MH 78** (125.6 km) Entering Midnight Twilight Tourist Zone northbound, entering Game Country Tourist Zone southbound.

V 25.1 (40.4 km) **MH 76** (122.3 km) **Junction** with Secondary Road 676 to Whitmud Creek, 14 miles/22 km west.

V 28.3 (45.6 km) **MH 72.8** (117.3 km) Entering Grande Prairie Forest southbound.

V 29.1 (46.8 km) **MH 72** (115.8 km) Little Smokey River bridge. Little Smokey River provincial recreation area to west on south bank of river; 12 sites, shelters, picnic tables, camping fee. ▲

V 30.3 (48.8 km) **MH 70.8** (114 km) **Junction** with Highway 2A east, a spur road which leads 17 miles/27 km to junction with Highway 2.

V 31.3 (50.4 km) **MH 69.8** (112.3 km) Turnout with litter barrels to east.

V 32.4 (52.1 km) **MH 68.7** (110.6 km) Entering Peace River Forest northbound.

V 36.4 (58.6 km) **MH 64.7** (104.2 km) Community of **GUY** (pop. 57) to east; pay phone. Access road leads west 7 miles/11 km to Five Star Golf Course; 9 holes, grass greens, pro shop.

V 40.5 (65.2 km) **MH 60.6** (97.5 km) **Junction** with Secondary Road 679 to Highway 2 and Winigami Lake Provincial Park (19 miles/30.5 km east).

V 48.7 (78.4 km) **MH 52.4** (84.4 km) **Donnelly Corners, junction** of Highways 2 and 49. **DONNELLY** (pop. 450) has a hotel, restaurants, stores, service stations with repair facilities, and a library. Historic site 3 miles/5 km south of town features a fully operational 1904 Case Steam Engine. Highway 43 ends northbound. Continue on Highway 2 North.

HIGHWAY 2

V 61 (98.1 km) **MH 40.1** (64.5 km) Access leads west 7 miles/11 km to **JEAN COTE** (pop. 65), and 18 miles/28 km to Rainbow Trout Park and Campground; 55

MACKENZIE ROUTE *Valleyview, AB, to Steen River, AB*

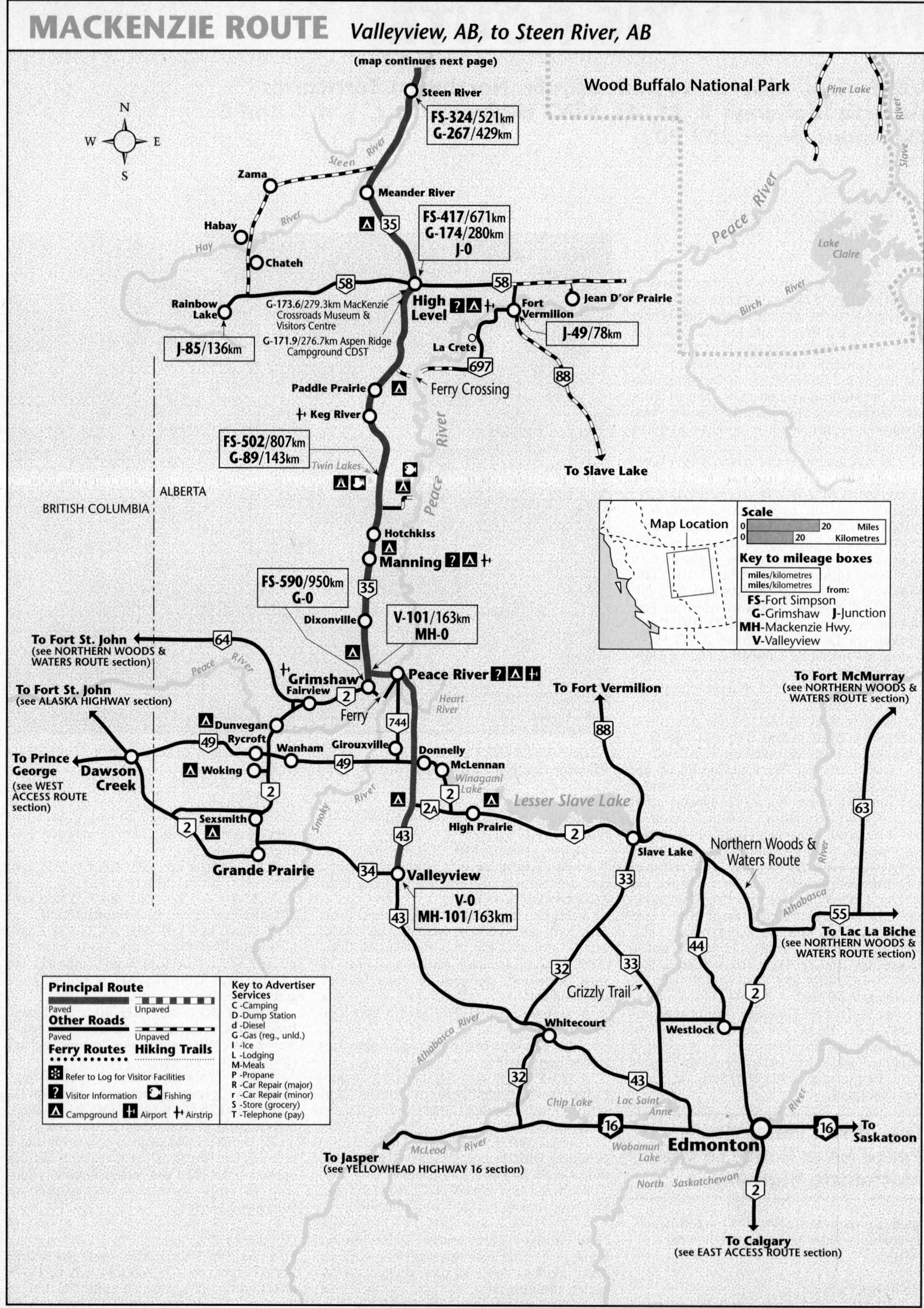

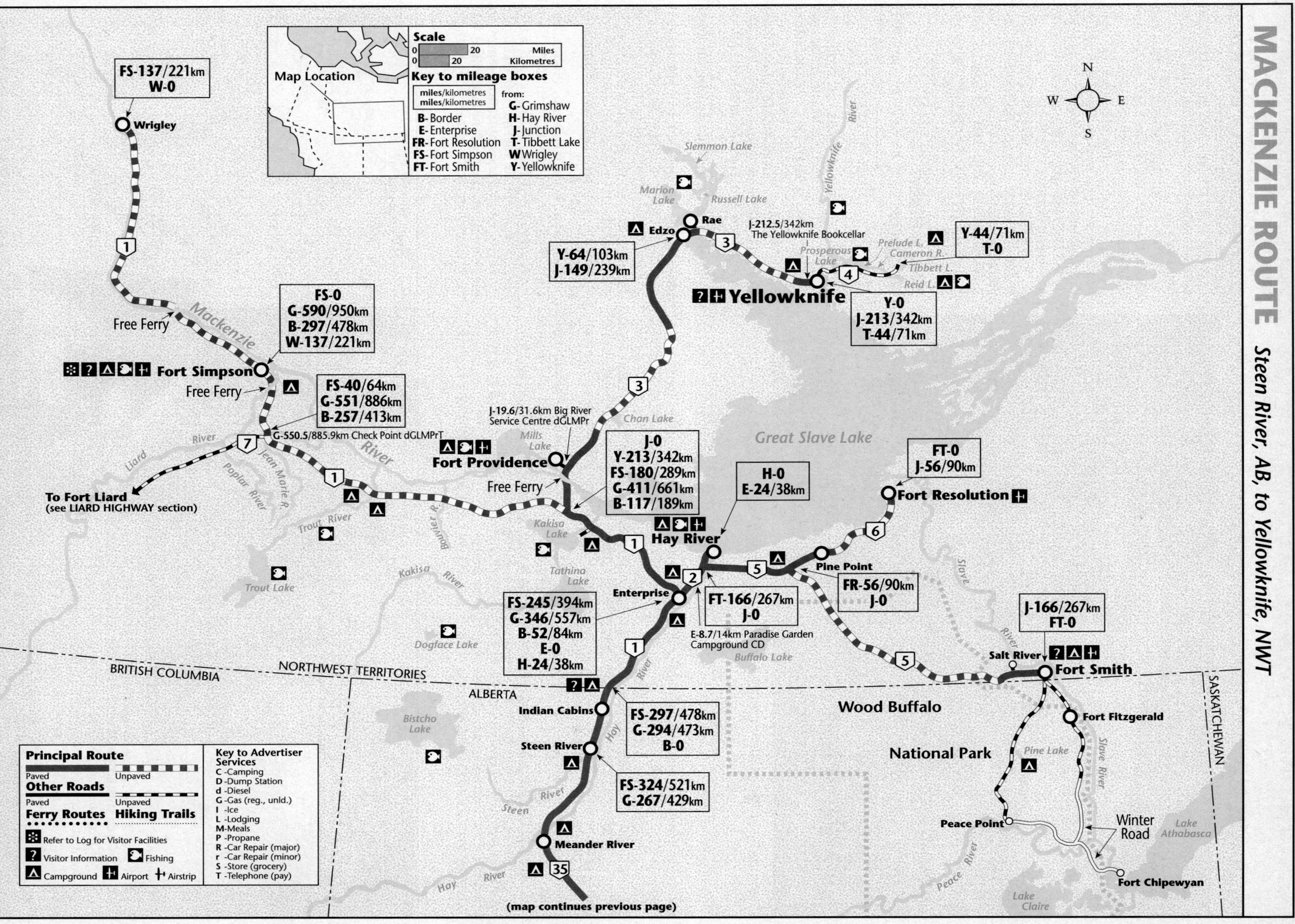
MACKENZIE ROUTE
Steen River, AB, to Yellowknife, NWT
Scale
Miles
Kilometres
Map Location
Key to mileage boxes
miles/kilometres
from:
B-Border
E-Enterprise
FR-Fort Resolution
FS-Fort Simpson
FT-Fort Smith
G-Grimshaw
H-Hay River
J-Junction
T-Tibbett Lake
W-Wrigley
Y-Yellowknife
FS-137/221km W-0
Wrigley
Free Ferry
Mackenzie
FS-0 G-590/950km B-297/478km W-137/221km
Fort Simpson
Free Ferry
FS-40/64km G-551/886km B-257/413km
G-550.5/885.9km Check Point dGLMPrT
River
Liard
Poplar River
Jean Marie R.
To Fort Liard (see LIARD HIGHWAY section)
Trout River
Trout Lake
Bouvier R.
Kakisa River
Dogface Lake
Bistcho Lake
J-19.6/31.6km Big River Service Centre dGLMPr
Mills Lake
Fort Providence
Free Ferry
Chan Lake
J-0 Y-213/342km FS-180/289km G-411/661km B-117/189km
Kakisa Lake
Tathina Lake
Hay River
H-0 E-24/38km
Great Slave Lake
Enterprise
FS-245/394km G-346/557km B-52/84km E-0 H-24/38km
FT-166/267km J-0
E-8.7/14km Paradise Garden Campground CD
Buffalo Lake
Pine Point
FR-56/90km J-0
FT-0 J-56/90km
Fort Resolution
Slave
River
Salt River
J-166/267km FT-0
Fort Smith
Fort Fitzgerald
Slave River
Pine Lake
Wood Buffalo
National Park
Peace Point
Peace River
Winter Road
Lake Athabasca
Fort Chipewyan
Lake Claire
SASKATCHEWAN
BRITISH COLUMBIA
NORTHWEST TERRITORIES
ALBERTA
Indian Cabins
FS-297/478km G-294/473km B-0
Steen River
FS-324/521km G-267/429km
Steen River
Hay River
Meander River
(map continues previous page)
Edzo
Rae
Y-64/103km J-149/239km
Marion Lake
Slemmon Lake
Russell Lake
Yellowknife River
J-212.5/342km The Yellowknife Bookcellar
Prosperous Lake
Prelude L.
Cameron R.
Tibbett L.
Reid L.
Y-44/71km T-0
Yellowknife
Y-0 J-213/342km T-44/71km
N
E
S
W
Principal Route
Paved
Unpaved
Other Roads
Paved
Unpaved
Ferry Routes
Hiking Trails
Refer to Log for Visitor Facilities
Visitor Information
Fishing
Campground
Airport
Airstrip
Key to Advertiser Services
C -Camping
D -Dump Station
d -Diesel
G -Gas (reg., unld.)
I -Ice
L -Lodging
M-Meals
P -Propane
R -Car Repair (major)
r -Car Repair (minor)
S -Store (grocery)
T -Telephone (pay)

Community of Peace River on the banks of the Peace River. (Fred Chapman, Diarama)

sites, hookups, picnic tables, shelter, firewood, playground, rental cabins, mini-golf, horseshoe pits. Camping fee $9. ▲

V 66.1 (106.5 km) **MH 35** (56.3 km) Entering Land of the Mighty Peace Tourist Zone northbound, Midnight Twilight Tourist Zone southbound.

V 67.2 (108.1 km) **MH 33.9** (54.6 km) Access road leads east 5.5 miles/9 km to Reno.

V 70.7 (113.8 km) **MH 30.4** (49 km) Nampa visitor centre and museum to west. **NAMPA** (pop. 500) was founded in 1917 when the East Dunvegan and BC Railway Company built a line through the area. Visitor facilities include a hotel, motel, restaurants, grocery and retail stores, service stations with repair facilities, and a library. Recreational facilities include a curling rink, ball diamonds and tennis courts. Heart River Golf Club, 5 miles/8 km northeast, has 9 holes. Camping at Mill Brown Memorial Park. ▲

V 71.3 (114.7 km) **MH 29.8** (48 km) **Junction** with Secondary Road 683 which leads west 6 miles/10 km to Secondary Road 744 to Marie Reine.

V 72.1 (116 km) **MH 29** (46.6 km) Heart River bridge.

V 73.4 (118.1 km) **MH 27.7** (44.6 km) South Harmon Road east to Harmon Valley Fairgrounds (14 miles/23 km).

V 73.5 (118.3 km) **MH 27.6** (44.4 km) Access road leads east 3 miles/5 km to Harmon Valley Golf Course.

V 75.3 (121.2 km) **MH 25.8** (41.6 km) Grain storage equipment on both sides of highway.

V 79.6 (128.1 km) **MH 21.5** (34.6 km) North Harmon Valley Road east to Harmon Valley Fairgrounds (12 miles/20 km).

V 84.3 (135.7 km) **MH 16.8** (27 km) **Junction** with Secondary Road 688 (Three Creeks Road) which leads east 5 miles/8 km to **ST. ISIDORE** (pop. 180); gas station, pay phone and library.

V 85 (136.8 km) **MH 16.1** (25.9 km) Highway begins descent northbound into Peace River Valley.

V 87.6 (141 km) **MH 13.5** (21.7 km) Turnout to east with information sign about Peace River.

Peace River

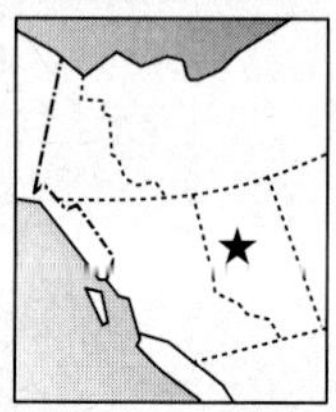

V 88.4 (142.3 km) **MH 12.7** (20.5 km) Located on the banks of the Peace River, 15 miles/24 km northeast of Grimshaw (Mile 0 of the Mackenzie Highway). **Population:** 6,700. **Emergency Services: RCMP**, phone (403) 624-6611. **Hospital**, phone (403) 624-7500. **Ambulance** and **Fire Department**, phone (403) 624-3911.

Visitor Information: Tourist Information Booth housed in log cabin next to the trestle at the east end of town; phone (403) 624-2044. Open mid-May to mid-Sept., 9 A.M. to 9 P.M. The Mighty Peace Tourist Assoc., at the north end of Main Street in the restored railway station, also has information on northern Alberta destinations; phone (403) 624-4042.

Elevation: 1,066 feet/325m. **Private Aircraft:** Peace River airport, 7 miles/11.2 km west; elev. 1,873 feet/571m; length 5,000 feet/1,524m; asphalt; fuel 80, 100, Jet B.

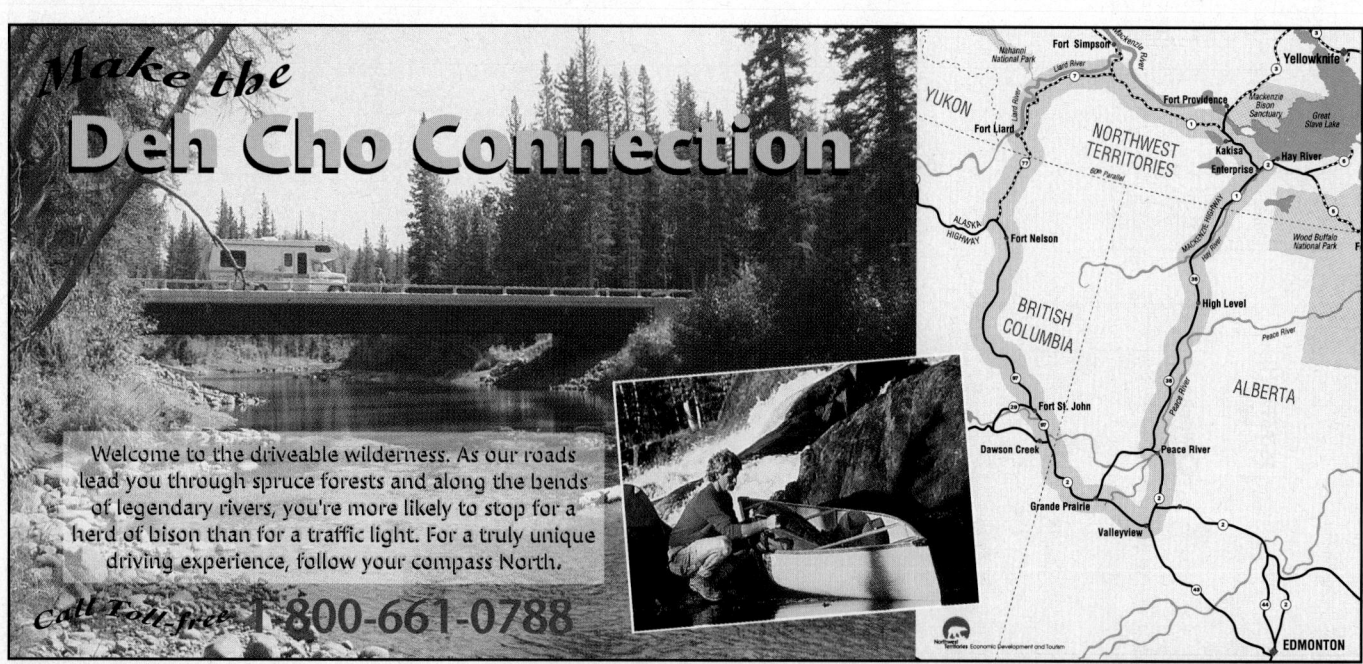

An important transportation centre on the Peace River, the town of Peace River was incorporated in 1919, 3 years after the railroad reached Peace River Crossing. Today, Peace River is a centre for government services in the region. Area industry includes Peace River Pulp, Shell Canada and farming.

Visitor facilities include 3 hotels, a motel and many restaurants. Camping at Lions Club Campground on the west side of the river; 85 sites, hookups, restrooms, dump station and laundry. ▲

There are 9 campgrounds along the Peace River. For details, contact the Peace Valley Conservation, Recreation and Tourism Society, phone (403) 835-2616 or fax 835-3131.

The Centennial Museum (on the south side of town along the river) houses archives and exhibits on Sir Alexander Mackenzie, the fur trade and local history. Historical reenactments in summer. Open 9 A.M. to 5 P.M. Mon. to Wed., noon to 8 P.M. Thurs. to Sat. (May 1 to Aug. 31); 9 A.M. to 5 P.M. weekdays Sept. 1 to April 31. Rail transportation exhibit at restored NAR railway station. Museum phone (403) 624-4261.

Visitors can take the Historic Mackenzie Moose Walking Trail by following the moose tracks from the Centennial Museum to various points of interest around town. The tour includes the statue of Twelve-Foot Davis, a gold miner who struck it rich on a 12-foot strip of land between 2 larger claims in the Cariboo gold fields. He invested his $15,000 in gold in a string of trading posts along the Peace. He is buried on Grouard Hill overlooking the Peace River Valley.

Log of Valleyview–Peace River Route

(continued)

V 89.2 (143.5 km) **MH 11.9** (19.1 km) Peace River bridge.

V 90 (144.8 km) **MH 11.1** (17.9 km) **Junction** with Secondary Road 684 which leads southwest 15 miles/24 km to Secondary Road 740 and the Shaftsbury Ferry Crossing of the Peace River.

V 90.8 (146.1 km) **MH 10.3** (16.5 km) **Junction** with Secondary Road 743 which leads north 10 miles/16 km to Secondary Road 686 to the Mackenzie Highway. Access to Peace View golf course, 2.5 miles/4 km north; 9 holes, sand greens, pro shop.

V 91.6 (147.4 km) **MH 9.5** (15.3 km) Turnout to south with information sign about Peace River.

V 94.7 (152.4 km) **MH 6.4** (10.3 km) Peace River airport to south.

V 96 (154.5 km) **MH 5.1** (8.2 km) **Roma Junction, junction** with Highway 2A to Grimshaw (7 miles/12 km southwest).

V 97.1 (156.3 km) **MH 4** (6.5 km) Access road leads 1.2 miles/2 km to Mighty Peace golf course; 18 holes, licensed dining room, pro shop, camping.

V 99.1 (159.5 km) **MH 2** (3.2 km) Access road leads south 0.6 mile/1 km to Wilderness Park; picnic tables, outhouses, hiking trails.

V 101.1 (162.7 km) **MH 0 Junction** with Highway 35 (Mackenzie Highway).

Fields of rapeseed are a common sight in northern Alberta's prairie country.
(© Lyn Hancock)

Mackenzie Highway Log

ALBERTA HIGHWAY 35
Distance from Grimshaw (G) is followed by distance from Fort Simpson (FS).

Grimshaw

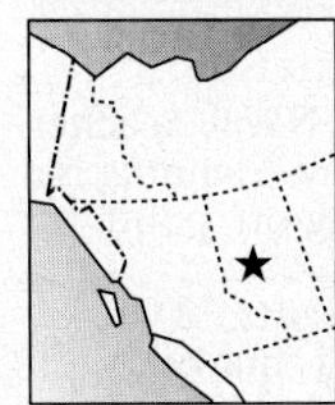

G 0 FS 590.4 (950.2 km) Mile 0 of the Mackenzie Highway. **Population:** 2,812. **Emergency Services:** RCMP, phone (403) 332-4666. **Hospital** and **Ambulance**, phone (403) 332-1155. **Fire Department**, phone (403) 332-4430. **Visitor Information:** In the NAR railway car located adjacent the centennial monument marking Mile 0 of the Mackenzie Highway.

Named for pioneer doctor M.E. Grimshaw, who established a practice at Peace River Crossing in 1914, Grimshaw developed as a community centre for area farmers and as a shipping point with the arrival of the railroad in 1921. Scheduled air service from Edmonton and High Level to Peace River airport, 8 miles/12.8 km east.

Grimshaw became a town in Feb. 1953. Local resources are wheat and grains, livestock, gravel, lumber, gas and oil.

Grimshaw has 1 motel, 2 hotels, 6 service stations, 2 car washes, a laundromat and all other visitor facilities. RV dump station and drinking water located south of the Mile 0 marker and 2 blocks east. Camping just north of town (see **Milepost G 1.9**). There are also an outdoor swimming pool, tennis courts, golf course and seasonal market garden located here.

Mackenzie Highway Log

(continued)

G 0.2 (0.4 km) **FS 590.2** (949.8 km) **Private Aircraft:** Airstrip to west; elev. 2,050 feet/625m; length, 3,000 feet/914m; turf; fuel 80, 100.

G 1.9 (3 km) **FS 588.5** (947.2 km) Grimshaw provincial campsite and Queen Elizabeth Provincial Park to west. Grimshaw campsite has 20 sites, picnic shelter, firepits, firewood, tables, outhouses, water pump and no camping fee. Queen Elizabeth park (located 3 miles/5 km west) on Lac Cardinal has 56 campsites, picnic shelter, firewood, firepits, toilets, playground and swimming. ▲

G 2.8 (4.6 km) **FS 587.6** (945.6 km) **Junction** of Highways 35 and 2 East.

G 3.4 (5.5 km) **FS 587** (944.7 km) Sign about construction of the Mackenzie Highway.

G 4.1 (6.6 km) **FS 586.3** (943.6 km) Turnout to east with litter barrels.

G 5 (8 km) **FS 585.4** (942.1 km) **Junction** with Chinook Valley Road to east.

G 6.9 (11.1 km) **FS 583.5** (939.1 km) Truck scales to west.

G 7.8 (12.5 km) **FS 582.6** (937.6 km) Bear Creek Drive and Bear Creek golf course to west; 9 holes, sand greens, clubhouse.

G 8.6 (13.8 km) **FS 581.8** (936.3 km) **Junction** with Secondary Road 737 (Warrensville) to west.

G 12.3 (19.8 km) **FS 578.1** (930.3 km) Road widens to 4 lanes northbound.

G 12.6 (20.3 km) **FS 577.8** (929.8 km) **Junction** with Secondary Road 686 to east.

G 13 (20.9 km) **FS 577.4** (929.2 km) Road narrows to 2 lanes northbound.

G 19 (30.6 km) **FS 571.4** (919.5 km) Entering Manning Ranger District northbound.

G 20.8 (33.5 km) **FS 569.6** (916.7 km) Chinook Valley to east; cafe, pay phone and 24-hour gas station with tire repair.

G 21 (33.8 km) **FS 569.4** (916.3 km) Chinook Valley Road to east.

G 23 (37 km) **FS 567.4** (913.1 km) Whitemud River.

G 25.1 (40.4 km) **FS 565.3** (909.8 km) **DIXONVILLE** (pop. 200) has a post office, gas station, souvenir shop, museum, store and cafe. Sulphur Lake provincial camp-

Highway 58 West Log

Distance is measured from junction with the Mackenzie Highway (J).

J 0 Junction with Mackenzie Highway at High Level.

J 6.1 (9.8 km) High Level Sporting Assoc. and Gun Club to north.

J 27.2 (43.8 km) Paved turnout with litter barrels to south.

J 31.2 (50.2 km) Entering Rainbow Lake Ranger District westbound.

J 44.2 (71.1 km) Bridge over Chinchaga River.

J 46.3 (74.5 km) Large turnout and gravel stockpiles to south.

J 50 (80.5 km) Bridge over East Sousa Creek.

J 56.5 (90.9 km) Bridge over West Sousa Creek.

J 56.9 (91.6 km) **Junction** with secondary road north to communities of Chateh, Habay and Zama.

J 59.7 (96.1 km) North Canadian Oils Ltd. wells and equipment to north.

J 60.7 (97.7 km) Oil pumping station to north.

J 63.3 (101.8 km) Paved turnout with litter barrel to north.

J 65.3 (105.1 km) Power station to north.

J 70.3 (113.1 km) Side road leads north to the Zama Tower.

J 70.7 (113.8 km) Esso Resources Canada oil production plant to north.

J 71.5 (115 km) Rainbow Lake Field Office to north.

J 76.8 (123.6 km) Side road leads north to Rainbow Lake gas plant.

J 80.5 (129.5 km) Oil station to south. Side road leads south to Rainbow Processing Plant.

J 82.5 (132.8 km) Turnout with picnic table to south.

J 83.3 (134 km) Rainbow Lake city limits.

J 84.5 (136 km) **RAINBOW LAKE** (pop. 1,146). **Emergency Services: RCMP**, phone (403) 321-3753. **Nursing Station**, phone (403) 356-3646. **Fire Department**, phone (403) 956-3934. **Radio:** 103.7-FM.

Private Aircraft: Rainbow Lake airport 0.8 mile/1.3 km west, 0.5 mile/0.8 km south on Frontage Road; elev. 1,100 feet/335m; length 4,550 feet/1,390m; asphalt; fuel 80, 100, Jet B.

A service community for oil and natural gas development in the region. The first oil well was brought in by Banff Oil and Gas in 1965 at the Rainbow field. (The Zama field was discovered in 1967.)

Visitor facilities include a hotel, motel with licensed restaurant, 3 gas stations and a bank. The community also supports a school, 3 churches, 2 car washes, a grocery store, gift shop, laundromat and a 9-hole golf course. Rainbow Lake Campground is located 14 miles/24 km south of town via a secondary road.

Return to Milepost G 173.3 Mackenzie Highway

ground is located 34 miles/55 km west via Highway 689 (the first 14 miles/22.5 km are paved, the remainder is gravel to the campground).

G 26.9 (43.3 km) **FS 563.5** (906.8 km) Sulphur Lake Road leads west to junction with Highway 689 from Dixonville.

G 38.4 (61.8 km) **FS 552** (888.4 km) **Junction** with Secondary Road 690 east to Deadwood (6.8 miles/11 km). There is a private exotic bird farm located 2 miles/3.2 km east then 1 mile/1.6 km south. The Bradshaws have geese, peacocks, turkeys, pheasants and other birds; visitors welcome.

G 44.4 (71.5 km) **FS 546** (878.7 km) Buchanan Creek.

G 46.8 (75.4 km) **FS 543.6** (874.8 km) Community of **NORTH STAR** (pop. 52) to east.

Manning

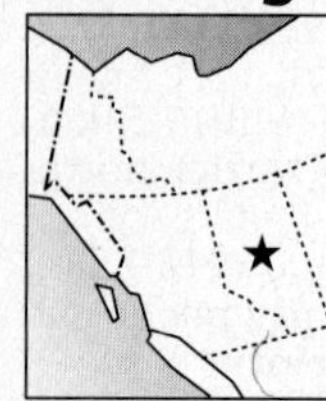

G 50.6 (81.4 km) **FS 539.8** (868.8 km) Located on the Notikewin River at the junction of Highways 35 and 691. **Population:** 1,260. **Emergency Services: RCMP**, phone (403) 836-3007. **Hospital** and **Ambulance**, phone (403) 836-3391. **Fire Department**, phone (403) 836-3000.

Visitor Information: In the information centre. There is a playground adjacent the centre and a dump station across the street.

Named for an Alberta premier, Manning was established in 1947. The railway from Roma, AB, to Pine Point, NWT, reached Manning in Sept. 1962. Today, Manning is a service centre and jumping-off point for hunters and fishermen.

Manning has 5 restaurants, 3 hotel/motels, a pharmacy, food market, golf course, swimming pool and ice rink. Attractions here include the Battle River Pioneer Museum, located on the grounds of the Battle River Agricultural Society, 0.6 mile/1 km east via Highway 691. The museum, which features tools and machinery from the pioneer days, is open daily 1-5 P.M., from June 1 to mid-Sept. A small ski hill is located 12.5 miles/20 km northeast of town via Highways 691 and 741; 1 T-lift and 3 runs.

Turn east at the information centre for Manning municipal campground; 14 sites on the banks of the Notikewin River, fireplaces, tables, water and flush toilets. ▲

NOTE: Last sizable community with all facilities for the next 123 miles/198 km northbound.

Mackenzie Highway Log

(continued)

G 50.7 (81.6 km) **FS 539.7** (868.5 km) Downtown Manning; bridge over the Notikewin River.

G 52.9 (85.1 km) **FS 537.5** (865.1 km) **Private Aircraft:** Manning airstrip to west; elev. 1,611 feet/491m; length 5,577 feet/1,700m; asphalt; fuel 100/130, Jet B.

G 53.2 (85.6 km) **FS 537.2** (864.5 km) Hotel, restaurant and service station to west.

G 54.6 (87.8 km) **FS 535.8** (862.4 km) Community of Notikewin to west.

G 60.6 (97.6 km) **FS 529.8** (852.6 km) Hotchkiss River bridge.

G 60.8 (97.8 km) **FS 529.6** (852.4 km) Hotchkiss Provincial Park to east; 10 sites, picnic shelter, tables, firepits, fishing, outhouses and water pump. No camping fee. ▲

G 61.3 (98.6 km) **FS 529.1** (851.6 km) Community of **HOTCHKISS** to east, golf course to west. Hotchkiss has a post office, service station, pay phone, coffee bar, grocery, and fuel and propane available. Condy Meadow golf course; 9 holes, grass greens, pro shop.

G 63.3 (101.8 km) **FS 527.1** (848.3 km) Large lumber plant to west.

G 66.9 (107.6 km) **FS 523.5** (842.6 km) Meikle River bridge.

G 71.2 (114.6 km) **FS 519.2** (835.5 km) Turnout with litter barrel to west.

G 74.3 (119.5 km) **FS 516.1** (830.7 km) **Junction** with Highway 692 and access to Notikewin Provincial Park (18.6 miles/30 km) on the Notikewin and Peace rivers. Highway 692 is fairly straight with pavement for the first 8 miles/13 km followed by good gravel surface to the park, although the road narrows and the surfacing may be muddy in wet weather as you approach the park. Just past the entrance to the park is the Top of Hill trailer drop off site; 10 campsites with tables, toilets, water pump and garbage container. The park road then winds down the hill for 1.4 miles/2.2 km (not recommended for trailers, slippery when wet) to the riverside campground and day-use area; 19 campsites on the **Notikewin River** and 6 picnic sites on the **Peace River**; facilities include tables, water pump, pit toilets, garbage containers, firepits, boat launch and fishing. *CAUTION: Bears in area.* ▲

G 88.4 (142.3 km) **FS 502** (807.9 km) Twin Lakes Lodge to east; gas, food, lodging, pay phone and fishing supplies.

G 88.9 (143 km) **FS 501.5** (807.2 km) Twin Lakes Campground to west; 30 shaded sites, picnic shelter, fireplaces, firewood, tables, outhouses, water; beach, boat launch (no gas motors). No camping fee. **Twin Lakes** is stocked with rainbow; good fishing June to Sept. ▲

G 95.8 (154.1 km) **FS 494.6** (796.1 km) Turnout to west.

G 102.9 (165.6 km) **FS 487.5** (784.6 km) Kemp Creek.

G 111.2 (179 km) **FS 479.2** (771.2 km) **Junction** with Highway 695 East which leads 24 miles/38 km to community of **CARCAJOU** (pop. 50). Access to Keg River airstrip 0.4 mile/0.6 km east. **Private Aircraft**: Keg River airstrip; elev. 1,350 feet/410m; approximate length 2,700 feet/ 832m; turf; emergency only.

G 112.3 (180.8 km) **FS 478.1** (769.4 km) Keg River bridge. The community of **KEG RIVER** (area pop. 400) just north of the bridge has a gas station, post office, grocery, cafe, motel, pay phone and airstrip.

G 115.6 (186 km) **FS 474.8** (764 km) **Junction** with Secondary Road 695 West. This paved road leads 9 miles/14.5 km to Keg River Post.

G 124 (199.6 km) **FS 466.4** (750.6 km) Boyer River bridge.

G 129.5 (208.4 km) **FS 460.9** (741.8 km) **PADDLE PRAIRIE** (pop. 164) has a gas station, grocery store and cafe. Paddle Prairie is a Metis settlement. The Metis culture, a combination of French and Amerindian, played a key role in the fur trade and development of northwestern Canada.

G 134.2 (216 km) **FS 456.2** (734.2 km) Turnout to west with litter barrels.

G 135.1 (217.4 km) **FS 455.3** (732.7 km) Boyer River Campground to east; 8 sites, tables, firewood, firepits, picnic shelter, toilets and water pump. ▲

G 136.2 (219.2 km) **FS 454.2** (731 km) **Junction** with Secondary Road 697, which leads northeast 75 miles/121 km to junction with Highway 88 near Fort Vermilion (see description of Fort Vermilion in the HIGHWAY 58 EAST side road log on page 208). This is a 2-lane, mostly paved road with a ferry crossing of the Peace River at Tompkin's Landing, 11 miles/18 km east from here. The ferry operates 24 hours a day, except in heavy fog, and carries 6 cars or 4 trucks. Highway 697 provides access to **BUFFALO HEAD PRAIRIE** (pop. 453), 43.6 miles/70.2 km east, which has a small store and gas. Also access to **LA CRETE** (pop. 902), 53.8 miles/86.6 km east and north, Canada's most northerly agricultural community. La Crete has a motel, 3 restaurants, service stations with repair facilities, car wash, grocery, hardware and retail stores, a laundromat and bank. Recreation facilities include a golf course and a sports complex with hockey, curling and bowling.

This is the ferry crossing of the Peace River on Secondary Road 697 to La Crete. *(© Lyn Hancock)*

G 141 (226.9 km) **FS 449.4** (723.2 km) Entering High Level Ranger District northbound.

G 146.3 (235.4 km) **FS 444.1** (714.7 km) Chuckegg Creek.

G 153.5 (247 km) **FS 436.9** (703.2 km) Turnout with litter barrel to west. Watch for waterfowl in small lakes along highway.

G 161.2 (259.4 km) **FS 429.2** (690.7 km) Bede Creek.

G 161.9 (260.5 km) **FS 428.5** (689.6 km) Parma Creek.

G 165.5 (266.3 km) **FS 424.9** (683.9 km) Melito Creek.

G 170.6 (274.6 km) **FS 419.8** (675.6 km) Turnout with litter barrel to west.

G 171.9 (276.7 km) **FS 418.5** (673.5 km) Private campground with hot showers and electrical hookups.

Aspen Ridge Campground. See display ad this section. ▲

G 173.3 (278.9 km) **FS 417.1** (671.3 km) **Junction** with Highway 58 West, which leads 84.5 miles/136 km to Rainbow Lake. See side road log of HIGHWAY 58 WEST on page 206.

High Level

G 173.6 (279.3 km) **FS 416.8** (670.9 km) Located at the junction of Highways 35 and 58. **Population:** 3,004. **Emergency Services: RCMP,** phone (403) 926-2226. **Hospital,** 25 beds, 6 doctors, phone (403) 926-3791. **Ambulance,** phone (403) 926-2545. **Fire Department,** phone (403) 926-3141.

Visitor Information: The visitors centre and Mackenzie Crossroads Museum are located at the south end of town. Open year-round. Summer hours 9 A.M. to 9 P.M. daily. Includes displays, souvenirs and rest area. RV dump at Shell station. **Radio:** 530 AM, 89.9, 104.1-FM.

Begun as a small settlement on the Mackenzie Highway after WWII, High Level grew with the oil boom of the 1960s and completion of the railroad to Pine Point. High Level has a strong agricultural economy and boasts the most northerly grain elevators in Canada. The community is also supported by a sawmill complex and serves as a transportation centre for the northwestern Peace River region. There is scheduled air service to Edmonton daily.

Visitor facilities include a hotel, 6 motels, restaurants and service stations with major repair. There are also an ice arena and curling rink, golf course, swimming pool, playgrounds, banks, schools and churches. Recreation includes hunting (moose, caribou, deer) and fishing for northern pike, perch, walleye, whitefish, goldeye and grayling.

There is a private campground at the south edge of town. A campground operated by the local Lions Club is located just east of town on Highway 58. ▲

Mackenzie Crossroads Museum and Visitors Centre is a must-see. Open year-round, the centre features tourist information, museum, interpretive centre and outdoor rest area. Displays include the "Northern Trading Post," farming, trapping and an outstanding collection of historical photographs. Souvenir items for sale. Summer hours 9 A.M.–9 P.M. 7 days/week. Phone (403) 926-4811, fax (403) 926-3044. [ADVERTISEMENT]

Mackenzie Highway Log

(continued)

G 173.6 (279.3 km) **FS 416.8** (670.9 km) Downtown High Level.

G 174 (280 km) **FS 416.4** (670.2 km) **Junction** with Highway 58 East to Jean D'or Prairie and Highway 88 to Fort Vermilion. See side road log of HIGHWAY 58 EAST on page 208.

G 176.2 (283.5 km) **FS 414.2** (666.7 km) High Level golf and country club to east. Open daily, May 1 to first snow, until midnight. Clubhouse, grass greens and 9 holes.

G 181.1 (291.5 km) **FS 409.3** (658.7 km) **Private Aircraft**: High Level airport; elev. 1,110 feet/338m; length 5,000 feet/1,524m; asphalt; fuel 80, 100, Jet B. Floatplane base at Footner Lake, 0.6 mile/1 km west.

G 193.4 (311.2 km) **FS 397** (639 km) Turnoff to west for Hutch Lake Recreation Area; parking, 8 picnic sites with tables and firepits, toilets. Short path leads down to lake. Bring mosquito repellent.

G 196 (315.5 km) **FS 394.4** (634.7 km) Hutch Lake provincial campground, 2.9 miles/4.6 km west; 12 sites, firepits, firewood, tables, toilets. Beach and boat launch on Hutch Lake. Hiking trails. Good spot for bird watchers. Camping fee $7.50. ▲

G 196.8 (316.7 km) **FS 393.6** (633.5 km) Turnouts with litter barrels both sides of highway.

G 207.3 (333.6 km) **FS 383.1** (616.6 km) Wooden railway bridge to east.

Highway 58 East Log

Distance is measured from junction with the Mackenzie Highway (J).

J 0 Junction with Mackenzie Highway at High Level.

J 0.2 (0.4 km) High Level Lions Club Campground to south; 33 sites, no camping fee, picnic shelter, stoves, firewood, tables, toilets, water pump. ▲

J 0.4 (0.6 km) High Level rodeo grounds to north.

J 1.5 (2.5 km) Bushe River bridge.

J 2.4 (3.8 km) Small grocery and gas pumps to north.

J 15.3 (24.7 km) Turnoff to south for Machesis Lake Campground, 16 miles/27 km via gravel road; 21 sites, picnic shelter, firepits, firewood, tables, toilets, water. Fishing for rainbows in **Machesis Lake.** ▲

J 20.3 (32.7 km) Turn south for Eleske Shrine (5 miles/8 km), Child Lake Reserve Native church and burial grounds. The Eleske Shrine, on the banks of the Boyer River, was built in 1950 and dedicated to St. Bernadette in hopes that the grotto would cure a tuberculosis epidemic in the community.

J 22.3 (35.9 km) Entering Fort Vermilion Ranger District eastbound.

J 27 (43.5 km) Turnout with litter barrels to north.

J 27.4 (44.1 km) Side road leads south 3.7 miles/6 km to Rocky Lane; museum located in school.

J 28 (45 km) Ponton River bridge.

J 35.4 (57 km) **Junction** of Highways 58 and 88. From this junction, Highway 58 turns to gravel road and continues 37 miles/59 km east to junction with a 5-mile/8-km side road to Jean D'or Prairie (no services). Highway 88 (renumbered and renamed the Bicentennial Highway to commemorate the 200th anniversary of Fort Vermilion in 1988) leads south to Fort Vermilion (log follows), then continues 255 miles/410 km to Slave Lake. Highway 88 is paved to Fort Vermilion; the 150-mile/242-km section to Red Earth Creek is gravel; the remaining 105 miles/168 km to Slave Lake are paved. There are no services along the road south of Fort Vermilion, and travel is not recommended on the gravel portion in wet weather.

HIGHWAY 88

J 40 (64.3 km) Boyer River bridge.

J 42.6 (68.5 km) Side road leads west 8.5 miles/14 km to Rocky Lane.

J 43.1 (69.3 km) Historical sign about Fort Vermilion and access to Fort Vermilion provincial campground (0.1 mile/0.2 km east); 16 sites, picnic shelter, fireplace, firewood, tables, toilets, water, no camping fee. ▲

J 43.4 (69.8 km) Fort Vermilion Bridge over the Peace River.

J 45.2 (72.7 km) **Junction** with Secondary Road 697 which leads south to Le Crete (21.5 miles/34.6 km) and rejoins the Mackenzie Highway at **Milepost G 136.2** (75.3 miles/121.2 km from here).

J 48 (77.2 km) **Junction** with Highway 88 south to Red Earth and Slave Lake (255miles/410 km). Continue straight ahead for Fort Vermilion (description follows).

J 48.5 (78 km) **FORT VERMILION** (pop. 850), located on the Peace River. **Emergency Services: RCMP,** phone (403) 927-3258. **Hospital,** St. Theresa phone (403) 927-3761. A trading post was established near here by the North West Co. in 1786. By 1831, the Hudson's Bay Co. had established a prosperous trading enterprise at Fort Vermilion. The area's farming potential gained attention when Fort Vermilion's wheat took top prize at the 1893 Chicago World's Fair. Transportation to the community was by riverboat until the Mackenzie Highway was built in the 1950s. The Peace River bridge was completed in 1974.

Visitor facilities include a hotel, motel, 3 restaurants, service stations, bank, laundromat and liquor store. The airport is located just east of town. Attractions include historic homes and buildings dating back to the mid-1800s. Pick up a walking tour brochure from the visitor centre; phone (403) 927-3216.

Return to Milepost G 174
Mackenzie Highway

G 219.3 (352.9 km) **FS 371.1** (597.3 km) **MEANDER RIVER** (pop. 340) has a post office, gas, grocery store and confectionary with pay phone.

G 221.5 (356.4 km) **FS 368.9** (593.7 km) Mission Creek.

G 223.8 (360.1 km) **FS 366.6** (590.1 km) The Mackenzie Highway crosses the Hay River here and follows it north into Northwest Territories.

G 227.5 (366.2 km) **FS 362.9** (584 km) Railway bridge over Hay River to east. Construction of the Great Slave Lake Railway (now part of Canadian National Railway's Peace River Division) was one of the largest railway construction projects since the boom of the first transcontinental railway lines in the late 1800s and early 1900s in Canada. The line extends 377 miles/607 km from Roma Junction near Peace River, AB, to Hay River, NWT, on the shore of Great Slave Lake. (A 54-mile/87-km branch line extended the line to the now-defunct lead–zinc mine at Pine Point, NWT.) Opened for traffic in 1964, the line carries mining shipments south and supplies north to Hay River.

G 228.1 (367.1 km) **FS 362.3** (583.1 km) Gravel road leads west 39 miles/63 km to **ZAMA** (pop. 200), an oil field community. Drilling and related operations take place at Zama in winter. Zama is the southern terminal of the interprovincial pipeline, carrying Norman Wells crude to Edmonton refineries.

G 231.5 (372.5 km) **FS 358.9** (577.6 km) Slavey Creek.

G 241.2 (388.2 km) **FS 349.3** (562 km) Rough patch in pavement. Watch for frost heaves north to NWT border.

G 243.5 (391.9 km) **FS 346.9** (558.3 km) Paved turnout with litter barrels to west.

G 250.2 (402.6 km) **FS 340.2** (547.5 km) Lutose Creek.

G 263.3 (423.7 km) **FS 327.1** (526.5 km) Steen River bridge.

G 266.7 (429.2 km) **FS 323.7** (521 km) **STEEN RIVER** (pop. 25) to east; no services.

G 266.9 (429.5 km) **FS 323.5** (520.7 km) Steen River Forestry Tanker Base to west. Grass airstrip.

G 268.1 (431.5 km) **FS 322.3** (518.7 km) Sams' Creek.

G 270.1 (434.7 km) **FS 320.3** (515.4 km) Jackpot Creek.

G 276.2 (444.5 km) **FS 314.2** (505.6 km) Bannock Creek.

G 283.3 (455.9 km) **FS 307.1** (494.2 km) Indian Cabins Creek.

G 284 (457 km) **FS 306.4** (493.2 km) **INDIAN CABINS** (pop. 10) to east has a gas station, cafe, grocery, pay phone and historic log church. The old Indian cabins that gave this settlement its name are gone, but nearby is an Indian cemetery with spirit houses.

NOTE: No services next 61 miles/98 km northbound.

G 285.3 (459.1 km) **FS 305.1** (491 km) Delphin Creek.

G 293.7 (472.7 km) **FS 296.7** (477.5 km) 60th parallel. Border between Alberta and Northwest Territories. The Mackenzie Highway now changes from Alberta Highway 35 to NWT Highway 1.

NWT HIGHWAY 1

Highway 1 begins its own series of kilometre markers, starting with Kilometre 0 at the border, which appear about every 2 kilometres.

Distance from Grimshaw (G) is followed by distance from Fort Simpson (FS) and distance from the AB–NWT border (B).

G 293.7 (472.7 km) **FS 296.7** (477.5 km) **B 0** AB–NWT border, 60th Parallel. A government visitor information centre here has brochures, maps, fishing licenses, camping permits, a dump station and emergency radiophone. Déne (Indian) arts and crafts are on display. Also check here on road and ferry conditions before proceeding. The visitor centre is open May 15 to Sept. 15 from 8 A.M. to 10 P.M.

60th Parallel Campground and picnic area adjacent visitor centre. Facilities include 12 campsites, 5 picnic sites, kitchen shelter and drinking water. The park overlooks the Hay River and canoeists may launch here. ▲

Driving distances from the border to destinations in Northwest Territories are as follows (see individual highway logs this section for details): Hay River 76 miles/122 km; Fort Simpson 297 miles/478 km; Wrigley 430 miles/694 km; Fort Providence 140 miles/225 km; Yellowknife 330 miles/531 km; Fort Smith 238 miles/383 km.

G 295.5 (475.6 km) **FS 294.9** (474.6 km) **B 1.8** (2.9 km) Reindeer Creek.

G 318.5 (512.6 km) **FS 271.9** (437.6 km)

B 24.8 (39.9 km) Grumbler Rapids, just off highway, is audible during low water periods in late summer.

G 319.1 (513.5 km) FS 271.3 (436.6 km) B 25.4 (40.8 km) Swede Creek.

G 319.8 (514.6 km) FS 270.6 (435.5 km) B 26.1 (42 km) Large turnout and gravel stockpile to west.

G 334.2 (537.8 km) FS 256.2 (412.4 km) B 40.5 (65.1 km) Mink Creek.

G 335.5 (539.9 km) FS 254.9 (410.2 km) B 41.8 (67.3 km) Large turnout and gravel stockpile to west.

G 338.8 (545.3 km) FS 251.6 (404.9 km) B 45.1 (72.6 km) Alexandra Falls picnic area to east. Paved parking area and gravel walkway to falls viewpoint, overlooking the Hay River, which plunges 109 feet/33m to form Alexandra Falls. Excellent photo opportunities; easy hike down to top of falls. A walking trail connects with Louise Falls.

G 340.3 (547.6 km) FS 250.1 (402.6 km) B 46.6 (74.9 km) Turnoff to east for Louise Falls picnic area and territorial campground; 18 campsites, 6 picnic sites, kitchen shelters, tables, toilets, firepits, firewood, water. Hiking trails to viewpoint overlooking 3-tiered Louise Falls, which drops 50 feet/15m. (It is not advisable to walk down to the water.) Hike along bluff 3 miles/5 km for Alexandra Falls. ▲

G 341.9 (550.2 km) FS 248.5 (400 km) B 48.2 (77.5 km) Escarpment Creek picnic area; tables, shelter, toilets, firepits, garbage container, water pump. Spectacular series of waterfalls downstream.

G 342.1 (550.5 km) FS 248.3 (399.7 km) B 48.4 (77.8 km) Highway crosses Escarpment Creek.

G 345.4 (555.9 km) FS 245 (394.3 km) B 51.7 (83.2 km) Truck weigh scales to east, service station to west. Entering Enterprise northbound.

G 345.8 (556.5 km) FS 244.6 (393.7 km) B 52.1 (83.8 km) **Junction** of Highway 1 and Highway 2. Highway 2 leads 23.6 miles/38 km from here to **HAY RIVER** (pop. 2,891), the hub for transportation on Great Slave Lake and a major service centre with all visitor facilities (see HAY RIVER HIGHWAY log on page 212 for details on Hay River). Continue on Highway 1 for Enterprise (description follows) and Fort Simpson.

ENTERPRISE (pop. 56), a highway community with food, grocery store, gas, diesel and lodging. Pay phone. It is a good idea to fill up gas tanks here. View of Hay River Gorge just east of the highway.

G 369.3 (594.3 km) FS 221.1 (355.8 km) B 75.6 (121.6 km) Turnout to north with view of McNally Creek Falls.

Highway crosses McNally Creek northbound.

G 370.5 (596.2 km) FS 219.9 (353.9 km) B 76.8 (123.6 km) Large paved turnout to north with litter barrels and scenic view.

G 374.7 (603 km) FS 215.7 (347.2 km) B 81 (130.3 km) Easy-to-miss Hart Lake Fire Tower access road turnoff leads 0.5 mile/0.8 km to picnic area and forest fire lookout tower. Panoramic view over more than 100 square miles/259 square km of forest to Great Slave Lake and Mackenzie River. Path to ancient coral reef. *CAUTION: Keep the fly repellent handy and stay away from the edge of escarpment.*

G 378.9 (609.8 km) FS 211.5 (340.4 km) B 85.2 (137.1 km) Crooked Creek.

G 379.4 (610.5 km) FS 211 (339.7 km) B 85.7 (137.8 km) Trapper's cabin to north.

G 385.6 (620.5 km) FS 204.8 (329.6 km) B 91.9 (147.9 km) Side road to highway maintenance camp.

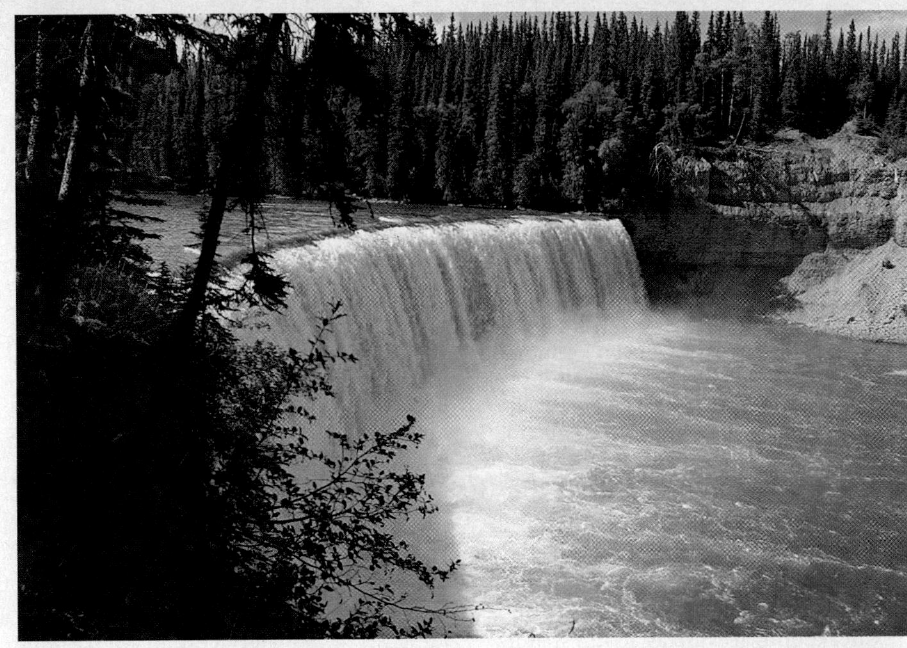

Lady Evelyn Falls on the Kakisa River at Milepost G 398.7 Mackenzie Highway.
(© Lyn Hancock)

G 391.7 (630.3 km) FS 198.7 (319.9 km) B 98 (157.6 km) Turnout with litter barrels.

G 398.2 (640.8 km) FS 192.2 (309.3 km) B 104.5 (168.2 km) Highway maintenance camp and stockpiles to north.

G 398.7 (641.7 km) FS 191.7 (308.5 km) B 105 (169 km) Access road leads south 4.5 miles/7.2 km to Lady Evelyn Falls where the Kakisa River drops 49 feet/15m over an escarpment. Staircase down to viewing platform. Hiking trail to base of falls; swimming and wading. Ample parking, interpretive display, territorial campground with 10 tent sites, 18 RV sites and 5 picnic sites; tables, firepits, firewood, garbage containers, water pump, kitchen shelters. At end of road, 4 miles/6.4 km past campground, is Slavey Indian village and **Kakisa Lake**; fair fishing for walleye, pike and grayling. ▲

G 399.6 (643.1 km) FS 190.8 (307.1 km) B 105.9 (170.4 km) Kakisa River bridge.

G 399.8 (643.4 km) FS 190.6 (306.8 km) B 106.1 (170.7 km) Kakisa River bridge picnic area with 10 sites, tables, fireplaces and firewood. Hiking trails along river lead upstream to Lady Evelyn Falls. Fair fishing in **Kakisa River** for grayling.

G 410.5 (660.6 km) FS 179.9 (289.5 km) B 116.8 (187.9 km) Turnout with litter barrels, log cabin, outhouse, picnic tables and map display on Highways 1 and 3.

G 410.9 (661.2 km) FS 179.5 (289 km) B 117.2 (188.5 km) **Junction** of Highway 1 and Highway 3. Highway 3 (paved and gravel) leads 212.5 miles/342 km north to Yellowknife, capital of Northwest Territories (see YELLOWKNIFE HIGHWAY log on page 212). Highway 1 (gravel) leads west 179.5 miles/289 km to Fort Simpson. Continue with this log for Fort Simpson.

G 411.1 (661.6 km) FS 179.3 (288.5 km) B 117.4 (188.9 km) Pavement ends, gravel begins, westbound.

G 438.4 (705.5 km) FS 152 (244.7 km) B 144.7 (232.8 km) Emergency survival cabin and turnout with litter barrels and outhouse to south.

G 450.5 (725 km) FS 139.9 (225.1 km) B 158.6 (255.3 km) Turnout to north with parking and scenic view.

G 456.3 (734.3 km) FS 134.1 (215.8 km) B 162.6 (261.6 km) Dust-free passing zone.

G 466.2 (750.3 km) FS 124.2 (199.9 km) B 172.5 (277.6 km) Bouvier River.

G 467.2 (751.9 km) FS 123.2 (198.3 km) B 173.5 (279.2 km) Emergency survival cabin and turnout with litter barrels to south.

G 471.9 (759.5 km) FS 118.5 (190.7 km) B 180.1 (289.8 km) Turnout to north.

G 473.9 (762.6 km) FS 116.5 (187.6 km) B 180.2 (289.9 km) Wallace Creek. Scenic canyon to north.

G 477 (767.6 km) FS 113.4 (182.6 km) B 183.3 (294.9 km) Highway maintenance camp to south.

G 477.6 (768.6 km) FS 112.8 (181.6 km) B 183.9 (295.9 km) Redknife River.

G 488.7 (786.4 km) FS 101.7 (163.8 km) B 195 (313.7 km) Morrissey Creek.

G 491.7 (791.8 km) FS 98.7 (158.8 km) B 199.8 (321.6 km) Winter ice road leads south 78 miles/126 km to **TROUT LAKE** (pop. 66), a Déne settlement.

G 494.1 (795.3 km) FS 96.3 (155 km) B 202 (325.1 km) Trout River bridge.

G 495 (796.3 km) FS 95.4 (153.5 km) B 202.8 (326.4 km) Turnout to south with litter barrels.

G 495.7 (797.8 km) FS 94.7 (152.4 km) B 202 (325 km) Whittaker Falls (Saanba Deh) Territorial Park, located on a bluff overlooking the **Trout River**. There are 3 picnic sites, 9 campsites, tables, litter barrels, showers, kitchen shelter, firepits and firewood. Walk along the river to view large deposits of shale and limestone. Grayling fishing, use dry flies in deep pools. Hike to Coral Falls. ▲

G 498.1 (801.6 km) FS 92.3 (148.5 km) B 206.1 (331.7 km) Emergency survival cabin and turnout with litter barrels to north.

G 523.7 (842.8 km) FS 66.7 (107.3 km) B 229.9 (370 km) **Ekali Lake** access; pike and pickerel fishing.

G 527.4 (848.7 km) FS 63 (101.4 km) B 233.6 (376 km) Winter ice road leads 17 miles/27 km to **JEAN MARIE RIVER** (pop. 67), a traditional Slavey community known for its hand-crafted moose hide clothing decorated with moose tufting, porcupine quilling and embroidery. Accessible in summer by plane or boat from Fort Simpson. This winter road is being upgraded to all-weather standards and is scheduled for completion in 1996.

G 530.5 (853.7 km) **FS 59.9** (96.5 km) **B 236.8** (381 km) Emergency survival cabin and turnout to north with outhouse and litter barrels.

G 534.8 (860.7 km) **FS 55.6** (89.5 km) **B 241.1** (388 km) I.P.L. pipeline camp and pump station to north. Highway crosses pipeline.

G 536.3 (863 km) **FS 54.1** (87 km) **B 242.6** (390.4 km) Microwave tower to south.

G 550.4 (885.8 km) **FS 40** (64.4 km) **B 256.7** (413.1 km) Jean Marie Creek bridge.

G 550.5 (885.9 km) **FS 39.9** (64.3 km) **B 256.8** (413.2 km) "Checkpoint"; 24-hour gas, diesel, propane, licensed restaurant. Phone (403) 695-2953. Open year-round.

Checkpoint. See display ad this section.

G 550.6 (886.1 km) **FS 39.8** (64.1 km) **B 256.9** (413.4 km) **Junction** with the Liard Highway (NWT Highway 7), which leads south to Fort Liard and junctions with the Alaska Highway near Fort Nelson. See the LIARD HIGHWAY section for details.

G 552 (888.4 km) **FS 38.4** (61.8 km) **B 258.3** (415.7 km) Turnout to east.

G 563.7 (907.1 km) **FS 26.7** (43.1 km) **B 270** (434.4 km) Emergency survival cabin and turnout with litter barrels and outhouse to west.

G 577.8 (929.8 km) **FS 12.6** (20.4 km) **B 284.1** (457.1 km) Highway crests hill; view of Liard River ahead. Ferry landing 3,280 feet/1,000m.

G 578.2 (930.5 km) **FS 12.2** (19.7 km) **B 284.5** (457.8 km) Liard River Campground to accommodate travelers who miss the last ferry at night, has 5 sites, tables, firepits, outhouse and garbage container. ▲

G 578.5 (930.9 km) **FS 11.9** (19.3 km) **B 284.8** (458.2 km) Free government-operated Liard River ferry operates daily May through Oct. from 8 A.M. to 11:40 P.M., 7 days a week. Crossing time is 6 minutes. Capacity is 8 cars or 2 trucks, with a maximum total weight of 130,000 lbs./59,090 kg. An ice bridge opens for light vehicles in late Nov. and heavier vehicles as ice thickens. *NOTE: No crossing possible during breakup (about mid-April to mid-May) and freezeup (mid-Oct. to mid-Nov.).* For ferry information phone (403) 873-7799 or 1-800-661-0751.

G 580.7 (934.6 km) **FS 9.7** (15.6 km) **B 287** (461.9 km) Fort Simpson airport. See Private Aircraft information in Fort Simpson.

G 588.1 (946.4 km) **FS 2.3** (3.8 km) **B 294.4** (473.7 km) **Junction** with Fort Simpson access road which leads 2.3 miles/3.8 km to Fort Simpson (description follows). The extension of NWT Highway 1 to Wrigley was completed in 1994; see WRIGLEY EXTENSION log following Fort Simpson description.

G 589.7 (949 km) **FS 0.7** (1.2 km) **B 296** (476.3 km) Causeway to Fort Simpson Island.

G 590.1 (949.6 km) **FS 0.3** (0.6 km) **B 296.4** (476.9 km) Turnoff for village campground. ▲

Fort Simpson

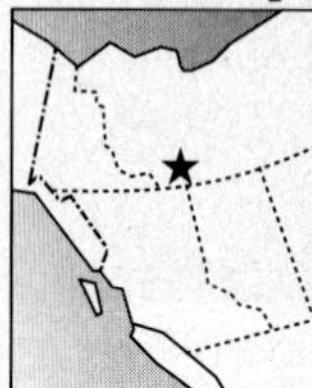

G 590.4 (950.2 km) **FS 0 B 296.7** (477.5 km) Located on an island at the confluence of the Mackenzie and Liard rivers. **Population:** 1,150. **Emergency Services: RCMP**, phone (403) 695-3111. **Hospital** (12 beds), for medical emergency phone (403) 695-2291. **Fire Department** (volunteer), phone (403) 695-2222.

Visitor Information: Village office operates a visitor booth June through Aug. The visitor information centre is open until 8 P.M., 7 days a week in summer; closed Sundays in winter. Nahanni National Park information centre on Main Street has a photo exhibit and films. The centre is open 8:30 A.M. to 5 P.M., 7 days a week in July and Aug., weekdays the rest of the year.

Television: Channels 2, 4, 6, 7, 9, 11. **Transportation:** Scheduled service to Yellowknife via Buffalo Airways and Ptarmigan Air. Fixed wing and helicopter charters available. **Rental cars**–Available. **Taxi service**–Available.

Private Aircraft: Fort Simpson airport; elev. 554 feet/169m; length 6,000 feet/1,829m; asphalt; fuel 100, Jet B. Fort Simpson Island; elev. 405 feet/123m; length 3,000 feet/914m; gravel; fuel 100, Jet B.

Fort Simpson is a full-service community. There is a motel with kitchenettes and a hotel; dining at the hotel (licensed premises) and 2 restaurants in town; gas stations with repair service (unleaded, diesel and propane available); 2 grocery stores, department store, hardware store, a bank, laundromat, post office, crafts shop and sports shop. Small engine repair shop and mechanics available. Fort Simpson has grade schools, churches (Anglican, Catholic and Pentecostal), the Stanley Isaiah Senior Citizen's Centre (designed by Gino Pin), and various territorial and federal offices. Recreational facilities include an arena, curling rink, gym, ball diamond, tennis, small indoor pool and a boat launch at government wharf. A number of community activities are held at the Papal Site, a large field with a cross, log tepee and stone monument commemorating Pope John Paul II's visit here in 1987.

Public campground at edge of town in wooded area has 30 campsites and 4 picnic sites. ▲

Fort Simpson is the oldest continuously occupied site on the Mackenzie River, dating from 1804 when the North West Co. established its Fort of the Forks. There is a historical marker on the bank of the Mackenzie. The Hudson's Bay Co. began its post here in 1821. At that time the fort was renamed after Sir George Simpson, one of the first governors of the combined North West Co. and Hudson's Bay Co. Fort Simpson served as the Mackenzie District headquarters for the Hudson's Bay Co. fur-trading operation. Its key location on the Mackenzie River also made Fort Simpson an important transportation centre. Anglican and Catholic missions were established here in 1858 and 1894.

Fort Simpson continues to be an important centre for the Northwest Territories water transport system. Visitors may walk along the high banks of the Mackenzie River and watch the boat traffic and floatplanes. According to resident Lyn Hancock, one of the easiest places to get down to the water is by Alfred Faille's cabin on Mackenzie Drive. Faille was a well-known Fort Simpson pioneer and prospector.

For visitors, Fort Simpson has Slavey crafts, such as birch-bark baskets and beadwork. Fort Simpson is also the jumping-off point for jet boat trips on the North Nahanni River; Mackenzie River traffic; and

Flightseeing passengers have dinner at Virginia Falls before returning to Fort Simpson. (© Lyn Hancock)

fly-in trips to Nahanni National Park.

The 4,766-square-km **NAHANNI NATIONAL PARK,** listed as a unique geological area on the UNESCO world heritage site list, is accessible only by nonpowered boat or aircraft. Located southwest of Fort Simpson near the Yukon border, day-trip flightseeing tours of the park may be arranged in Fort Simpson, Fort Liard and Yellowknife, and from Fort Nelson, BC, and Watson Lake, YT. Highlights include the spectacular Ram Plateau and Virginia Falls (300 feet/90m, twice as high as Niagara Falls). One of the most popular attractions in the park is running the South Nahanni River or its tributary, the Flat River. The South Nahanni River route stretches about 186 miles/300 km from Rabbitkettle Lake to the eastern park boundary. Rabbitkettle Hot Springs, a major feature on the upper section of the river, is reached by trail (restricted access, hikers must be guided by park staff). Near the east park boundary is Kraus Hot Springs, on the remains of the old Kraus homestead. The Flat River route stretches 80 miles/128 km from Seaplane Lake to the confluence with the South Nahanni. Charter air service for canoe drop-offs is available in Fort Simpson.

In order to evenly distribute visitor use and maintain ecological integrity within Nahanni National Park Reserve, the park has implemented a mandatory reservation system for overnight use. Two non-guided departures with a maximum group size of 6 each are allowed each day. (Groups larger than 6 are required to reserve 2 departure units with a maximum group size of 12.) The maximum length of stay at Virginia Falls is 2 nights. Reservations may be made by telephone or fax. User fees are charged. The seasonal overnight use fee is $50, payable by VISA or MasterCard at the time a reservation is made. (Seasonal user fees are transferable to any national park in Northwest Territories.) A day-use fee of $10 per person is charged to those visitors flying into Virginia Falls for a day trip. Reservations are not required for day trips. Contact Nahanni National Park Reserve, Box 348, Fort Simpson, NT X0E 0N0; phone (403) 695-2310, fax 695-2446.

AREA FISHING: Willow, Dogface and **Trout lakes** accessible by air. Good fishing for trout and grayling. Inquire locally.

Mackenzie Highway Log

(continued)

WRIGLEY EXTENSION

Improved to all-weather road standards, this former trail to Wrigley officially opened in 1994 as part of Highway 1 (although it's still referred to locally as the road to Wrigley). Slippery when wet. Use caution approaching all bridges. Driving time is approximately 3 hours between Fort Simpson and Wrigley. Allow at least 2 hours from Wrigley to the Camsell ferry crossing.

Distance from Fort Simpson (FS) is followed by distance from Wrigley (W).

FS 0 W 137 (220.5 km) **Junction** with Fort Simpson access road.

FS 9.5 (15.3 km) **W 127.5** (205.2 km) Single-lane bridge over Martin River. *CAUTION: Slow down for steep descent to bridge.*

FS 17.9 (28.8 km) **W 119.1** (191.7 km) Creek crossing. *CAUTION: Slow down, steep drop-offs and no guardrails.*

FS 33.4 (53.7 km) **W 103.6** (166.7 km) Single-lane bridge over Shale Creek.

FS 34 (54.7 km) **W 103** (165.8 km) Turnout to east.

FS 46.6 (75 km) **W 90.4** (145.5 km) Ferry crossing of the Mackenzie River at Camsell Bend (Ndulee Crossing). Ferry operates daily, 9 A.M. to 11 A.M. and 2 P.M. to 8 P.M. Capacity is 6 cars or 4 trucks. NOTE: There are no overnight facilities for anyone missing the ferry. Ferry does not operate in fog. Be prepared to wait and not to wait.

FS 71 (114.3 km) **W 66** (106.2 km) Mackenzie Mountains come into view to the west, northbound.

FS 73.5 (118.3 km) **W 63.5** (102.2 km)

Highway maintenance camp to east.

FS 94.2 (151.6 km) **W 42.8** (68.9 km) Willowlake River bridge, longest bridge in the Northwest Territories.

FS 95.2 (153.2 km) **W 41.8** (67.3 km) Highway climbs steep hill northbound.

FS 97.7 (157.2 km) **W 39.3** (63.2 km) Turnout to west at top of hill with litter barrels and scenic view of the Mackenzie River.

FS 110.9 (178.5 km) **W 26.1** (42 km) Single-lane wooden bridge over the "River Between Two Mountains."

FS 112.6 (181.2 km) **W 24.4** (39.3 km) Scenic view of the Mackenzie River to west.

FS 121.5 (195.5 km) **W 15.5** (25.1 km) Wrigley interprovincial pipeline pump station and radio tower to east.

FS 128.9 (207.4 km) **W 8.1** (13 km) Single-lane bridge over Smith's Creek.

FS 131.1 (211 km) **W 5.9** (9.5 km) Highway maintenance camp to west.

FS 132.2 (212.7 km) **W 4.8** (7.7 km) **Junction** with winter ice road to east which leads north to Fort Norman, Norman Wells, Fort Franklin and Fort Good Hope. Winter road mileages are as follows: Wrigley to Fort Norman, 148 miles/238 km; Fort Norman to Norman Wells, 50 miles/80 km; Norman Wells to Fort Good Hope, 91 miles/147 km; Norman Wells to Franklin, 68 miles/110 km.

FS 132.9 (213.9 km) **W 4.1** (6.6 km) Turnoff to west for Wrigley airport. **Private Aircraft:** Wrigley airport, 4 miles/7 km south of town; elev. 493 feet/142m; length 3,500 feet/1,148m; gravel; fuel 80.

FS 137 (220.5 km) **W 0 WRIGLEY** (pop. 180). **Emergency Services: RCMP**, phone (403) 581-3411. **Nursing Station**, phone (403) 587-3441. **Fire Department**, phone (403) 581-3333.

The Hudson's Bay Co. built a trading post here in 1870 called Fort Wrigley. The fort was abandoned in 1910 due to disease and famine, and the inhabitants moved down river. Although a church and school were built at that site in 1957, the community decided to move to higher ground in 1965. 15 homes were built at the "new" townsite of present-day Wrigley. The church, school and other buildings were moved from the old townsite by boat.

Visitor facilities here include a small coop motel ($120/night/bed; you might share the room), restaurant, 2 stores, the school and nursing station.

Hay River Highway Log

NWT HIGHWAY 2

Highway 2 is paved from Enterprise to Hay River; watch for rough spots in the surfacing. Kilometreposts along the highway reflect distance from Enterprise.

Distance from Enterprise (E) is followed by distance from Hay River (H).

E 0 H 23.6 (38 km) **Junction** of Highways 1 and 2.

E 8.7 (14 km) **H 14.9** (24 km) Private campground 0.7 mile/1.1 km east. Market garden in season. ▲

E 11.6 (18.6 km) **H 12** (19.4 km) Sawmill Road to east.

E 16 (25.7 km) **H 7.6** (12.3 km) Gravel road leads east 0.6 mile/1 km to Hay River golf course; large log clubhouse, driving range, 9 holes (par 36), artificial greens. Site of the NWT Open every second year in late August.

E 20 (32.3 km) **H 3.6** (5.7 km) **Junction** with Highway 5 to Fort Smith (see Fort Smith Highway Log this section).

E 22.4 (36 km) **H 1.2** (2 km) Chamber of Commerce Welcome to Hay River sign. Parking area to east.

Hay River

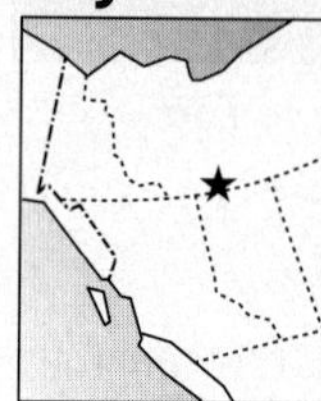

E 23.6 (38 km) **H 0** Located on the south shore of Great Slave Lake at the mouth of the Hay River, on both the mainland and Vale Island. **Population:** 2,891. **Emergency Services: Police**, phone (403) 874-6555, **Fire Department**, phone (403) 874-2222. **Hospital**, phone (403) 874-2565.

Visitor Information: Visitor information centre, just east of the highway, is housed in a 2-story brown structure. The centre is open daily, late May to early Sept.; 9 A.M. to 9 P.M.. There is a dump station located here. Write the Chamber of Commerce at Box 1278, Hay River, NT X0E 0R0; phone (403) 874-6160.

Radio: CKHR-FM 107.3, 93.7, 100.1-FM. **Television:** Channels 2, 6, 7, 10 and 12 via satellite. **Newspaper:** *The Hub* (weekly). **Transportation: Air**–Canadian Airlines International, Ptarmigan Airways, Landa Aviation, Carter Air and Buffalo Airways. **Bus**–Coachways. **Rental cars**–Available.

Private Aircraft: Hay River airport; elev. 543 feet/165m; length 6,000 feet/1,830m, paved; 4,000 feet/1,219m, gravel; fuel 100, Jet B.

Hay River was established in 1868 with the building of a Hudson's Bay Co. post. Today's economy combines transportation, communications, commercial fishing and service industries.

The community is the transfer point from highway and rail to barges on Great Slave Lake bound for arctic and subarctic communities. Hay River harbour is also home port of the Mackenzie River barge fleet that plies the river in summer. World-class jet boat racing takes place on the Mackenzie River in July each year. The turnaround point is Hay River Gorge.

The airstrip was built in 1942 on Vale Island by the U.S. Army Corps of Engineers. Vale Island was the townsite until floods in 1951 and 1963 forced evacuation of the population to the mainland townsite, where most of the community is now concentrated. Vale Island, referred to as "Old Town," is bounded by Great Slave Lake and the west and east channels of the Hay River.

The town boasts the tallest building in the Northwest Territories—a 17-story apartment high-rise that can be seen for miles around—and a purple high school designed by Douglas Cardinal. Hay River also has Paradise Gardens, the largest market-gardening operation in Northwest Territories, and Perron's Funny Farm, one of the few livestock producers in the territories.

There are 10 restaurants, gas stations with unleaded gas, propane and repair service, and grocery stores. Reservations are a must at the town's 5 hotels/motels; lodgings are booked solid in the busy summer season by construction and transportation workers. There is also a bed and breakfast. Other facilities include 2 banks, 2 laundromats and a variety of gift and arts and crafts shops.

Hay River has schools, churches, a civic centre with a swimming pool (1 of only 2 year-round swimming pools in Northwest Territories), curling sheets, hockey arena and dance hall. Northwest Territories Centennial Library headquarters is located here. There is a public boat launch at Porritt Landing on Vale Island.

There is a public campground on Vale Island (follow the signs; it is about 6 miles/10 km past the information centre). There are 21 sites (4 with electrical hookups), showers, firewood and firepits, picnic area, playground and horseshoe pit. Camping fee is $10 per night. Open mid-May to mid-Sept. ▲

Great sportfishing area with fly-in fishing camps (check with the chamber of commerce). Boat rentals on nearby **Great Slave Lake**, where northern pike up to 40 lbs. are not unusual. Inconnu (sheefish), pickerel and grayling also found here.

Yellowknife Highway Log

NWT HIGHWAY 3

Distance from the junction of Highways 1 and 3 (J) is followed by distance from Yellowknife (Y).

J 0 Y 212.5 (342 km) **Junction** of Highways 1 and 3. Turn right northbound for Fort Providence, Rae–Edzo and Yellowknife.

The first 59.5 miles/95.8 km of Highway 3 are paved. The remainder of the highway is gravel to Yellowknife, with the exception of 2 stretches of pavement. Plans call for extending the paved portion of this highway in the coming years.

J 4.8 (7.7 km) **Y 207.7** (334.3 km) Chikilee Creek.

J 4.9 (7.9 km) **Y 207.6** (334.1 km) Wolf Skull Creek.

J 9.1 (14.7 km) **Y 203.4** (327.3 km) Dory Point maintenance camp to west.

J 10.6 (17 km) **Y 201.9** (324.9 km) Turnoff for winter ice crossing to east.

J 13.2 (21.2 km) **Y 199.3** (320.8 km) Dory Point picnic area to east with 5 sites and kitchen shelter, no drinking water; overlooking Mackenzie River with view of passing riverboats.

J 13.9 (22.4 km) **Y 198.6** (319.6 km) Campground with hookups, service station with regular, unleaded and diesel, and restaurant. ▲

J 14.5 (23.3 km) **Y 198** (318.6 km) Dory Point marine access camp to west.

J 15.1 (24.3 km) **Y 197.4** (317.7 km) Free government-operated Mackenzie River ferry operates daily May through Oct. or Nov. from 6 A.M. to midnight. Crossing time is 8 minutes. Capacity is 10 cars or 4 trucks, with a maximum total weight of 220,000 lbs./100,000 kg. An ice bridge opens for light vehicles in Dec. and heavier vehicles as ice thickens. *NOTE: No crossing possible during* *breakup (about April to mid-May).* Ice breaking procedures now keep the channel open for the ferry during freezeup while an ice bridge is being constructed. For ferry information phone (403) 873-7799 or 1-800-661-0751.

J 15.9 (25.6 km) **Y 196.6** (316.4 km) Sign indicates Mackenzie Wood Bison Sanctuary. The wood bison are not often seen along the highway; however, sandhill cranes, squirrels, spruce grouse and ptarmigan may be seen in season.

J 19.4 (31.2 km) **Y 193.1** (310.8 km) Motel, restaurant and service station with unleaded, diesel and propane. Pay phone.

J 19.6 (31.6 km) **Y 192.9** (310.4 km) **Junction** with access road which leads 2.8 miles/4.5 km west to Fort Providence (description follows). Gas station with unleaded, diesel, propane, restaurant and tire repair. There is an airstrip located 0.4 mile/0.6 km west on the access road. *NOTE: It is a good idea to fill gas tanks here if you are bound for Yellowknife. Next gas available is in Rae–Edzo.*

Big River Service Centre. See display ad this section.

Fort Providence territorial campground is located 0.7 mile/1.1 km west of the highway on the access road; 30 sites, tables, firewood, kitchen shelter, garbage container, pump water and dump station. Situated on the banks of the Mackenzie River. Rental boats, boat launch and fishing nearby. ▲

Entering Mackenzie Bison Sanctuary northbound.

Fort Providence

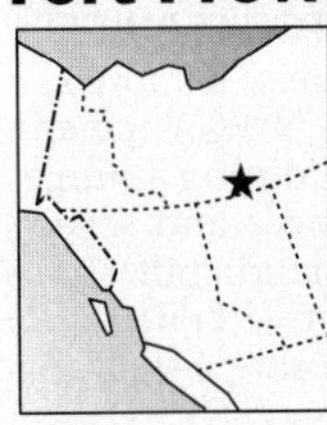

Located on the Mackenzie River, 2.8 miles/4.5 km northwest of Highway 3. **Population:** 688. **Emergency Services: Police,** phone (403) 699-3291. **Fire Department**, phone (403) 699-4222. **Nursing station,** phone (403) 699-4311.

Elevation: 550 feet/168m. **Radio:** 1230. **Television:** Channels 6 and 13 (CBC). **Transportation:** Air–Air Providence and charter service. **Bus**–Coachways.

Private Aircraft: Fort Providence airstrip; elev. 530 feet/162m; length 3,000 feet/915m; gravel; fuel emergency only.

Facilities include 2 motels, 2 restaurants, gas stations with minor repair service, grocery and general stores.

A Roman Catholic mission was established here in 1861. Although noted for its early agricultural endeavors, Fort Providence is traditionally a trapping community. Three historical markers in the community commemorate the roles of the church and explorer Alexander Mackenzie in settling the area.

Unique and popular with northern collectors is the moose hair embroidery found in local gift shops. Local craftswomen are also noted for their porcupine quill work. Along with seeing the crafts, visitors may cruise the Mackenzie River. Spectacular photo opportunities here for sunsets on the Mackenzie.

Good to excellent fishing in **Mackenzie River**; guides and cabins available, also boats and air charter trips. Northern pike to 30 lbs., May 30 to Sept., use large Red Devils; grayling and pickerel from 1 to 6 lbs., June to Sept., use anything (small Red Devils will do).

Roman Catholic mission church on the main street of Rae-Edzo. (© Lyn Hancock)

Yellowknife Highway Log

(continued)

J 26.4 (42.5 km) **Y 186.1** (299.5 km) Side road west to highway maintenance camp and stockpiles.

J 27.5 (44.3 km) **Y 185** (297.7 km) Bluefish Creek.

J 37 (59.5 km) **Y 175.5** (282.4 km) Large turnout to east at sand and gravel stockpiles.

J 38.7 (62.3 km) **Y 173.8** (279.7 km) Small gravel turnout to east.

J 42.3 (68.1 km) **Y 170.2** (273.9 km) Turnout to east with litter barrels and sign about Mackenzie Bison Sanctuary.

J 51.7 (83.2 km) **Y 160.8** (258.8 km) Turnout to west.

J 59.2 (95.3 km) **Y 153.3** (246.7 km) Telecommunications building to east.

J 69.6 (112 km) **Y 142.9** (230 km) Pavement ends, gravel begins, northbound.

J 75.6 (121.6 km) **Y 136.9** (220.4 km) Chan Lake picnic area to east with kitchen shelter, tables, firepits and firewood. No drinking water. Watch for waterfowl.

J 76.1 (122.5 km) **Y 136.4** (219.5 km) Turnout with litter barrels to east.

J 100 (160.9 km) **Y 112.5** (181.1 km) Turnout with litter barrels, outhouse and highway map sign to east. Watch for buffalo.

J 104.4 (168 km) **Y 108.1** (174 km) Telecommunications building to east.

J 116.2 (187 km) **Y 96.3** (155 km) Gravel ends, pavement begins, northbound.

J 124.7 (200.7 km) **Y 87.8** (141.3 km) Entering Yellowknife District northbound.

J 129.7 (208.8 km) **Y 82.8** (133.2 km) Turnout with litter barrels to east. Northbound travelers may notice the trees are getting shorter as you move farther north.

J 140.2 (225.7 km) **Y 72.3** (116.3 km) Turnout to east. Highway descends northbound to Mosquito Creek.

J 141.2 (227.3 km) **Y 71.3** (114.7 km) Highway crosses **Mosquito Creek**. Fishing for pickerel and whitefish, May and June.

J 144.2 (232 km) **Y 68.3** (110 km) North Arm Territorial Park on the shores of Great Slave Lake. Campground with kitchen shelter, tables, toilets, firewood, firepits and boat launch *(CAUTION: Reefs)*. Lowbush cranberries and other berries in area. *Beware of bears.* ▲

J 148.3 (238.6 km) **Y 64.2** (103.3 km) **Junction** with winter ice road north to communities of Lac La Marte and Rae Lakes.

J 148.5 (239 km) **Y 64** (103 km) **Junction** with access road west to community of Edzo (see description at **Milepost J 152.2**).

J 148.8 (239.5 km) **Y 63.7** (102.5 km) Picnic area to west. Pickerel fishing in **West Channel** in spring.

J 149.3 (240.2 km) **Y 63.2** (101.8 km) West Channel.

J 151.5 (243.8 km) **Y 61** (98.2 km) Bridge over **Frank Channel**, which extends from the head of the North Arm of Great Slave Lake to the Indian village of Rae. Watch for turnoff to Rabesca's Bear Healing Rock; lodging, mud baths, boating and fishing for whitefish.

J 152.2 (245 km) **Y 60.3** (97 km) **Junction** with road which leads west 7 miles/11.2 km to community of Rae (description follows).

RAE–EDZO (pop. about 2,000). **Emergency Services: RCMP**, in Rae, phone 392-6181. **Nursing station** in Edzo, phone 371-3551. **Radio:** 105.9-FM. The 2 hamlets of Rae and Edzo contain the territories' largest Déne (Indian) community. The Rae area, where most of the community resides, is an old Indian hunting spot and was the site of 2 early trading posts. The Edzo site was developed in 1965 by the government to provide schools and an adequate sanitation system. Rae has grocery stores, a post office, Native crafts shop, 2 hotels, food ser-

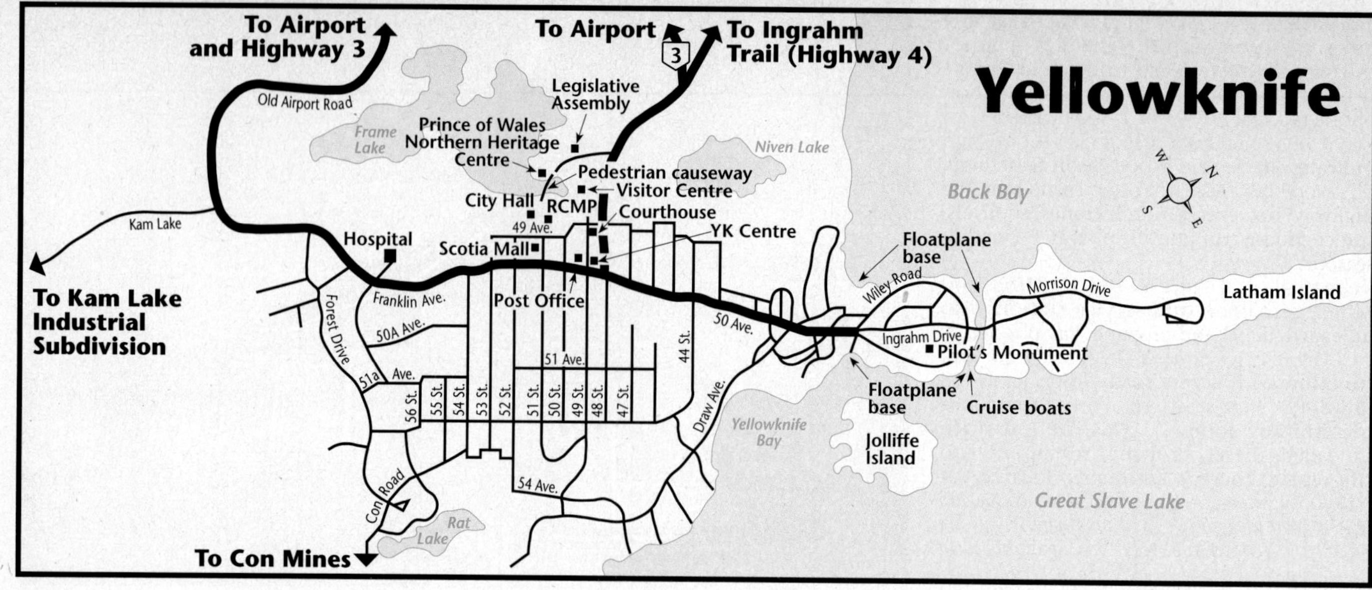

vice and gas stations with regular, unleaded and diesel. Pay phones are located at the community sports centre and at the cafe.

J 152.3 (245.1 km) **Y 60.2** (96.9 km) Pavement ends, gravel begins, eastbound.

J 159.8 (257.2 km) **Y 52.7** (84.8 km) Stagg River bridge. After crossing the North Arm of Great Slave Lake, the highway swings southeast toward Yellowknife. Winding road to Yellowknife, good opportunities to see waterfowl in the many small lakes.

J 160.4 (258.1 km) **Y 52.1** (83.9 km) Turnout with litter barrels to south.

J 189.2 (304.5 km) **Y 23.3** (37.5 km) Turnout with litter barrels to north.

J 189.5 (304.9 km) **Y 23** (37.1 km) Boundary Creek.

J 203.8 (328 km) **Y 8.7** (14 km) Yellowknife city limits.

J 208.5 (335.5 km) **Y 4** (6.5 km) Gravel ends, pavement begins.

J 208.7 (335.8 km) **Y 3.8** (6.2 km) Yellowknife Golf Club to north; 9 holes, sand greens, pro shop, licensed clubhouse. Built on the Canadian Shield, the course is mostly sand and bedrock. Each player gets a small piece of carpet to take along on the round as their own portable turf. Site of the June 21 Midnight Tournament. Some modified rules have been adopted by this Far North golf course, among them: "No penalty assessed when ball carried off by raven."

J 209.8 (337.7 km) **Y 2.7** (4.3 km) Yellowknife airport to south.

J 210 (338 km) **Y 2.5** (4 km) Fred Henne Recreational Park on Long Lake. Attractive public campground with 82 sites, water, firewood, firepits, picnic area, boat launch, snack bar, showers and pay phone. Daily and seasonal rates available; open from mid-May to mid-Sept. Sandy beach and swimming in Long Lake. Interpretive trail. ▲

J 210.5 (338.7 km) **Y 2** (3.3 km) Old Airport Road access to Yellowknife. Just past the turnoff is the Welcome to Yellowknife sign and the hard-to-miss Wardair Bristol freighter to the south. A historical plaque commemorates the Bristol freighter, which was the first wheel-equipped aircraft to land at the North Pole. Picnic sites nearby.

J 211.4 (340.2 km) **Y 1.1** (1.8 km) Stock Lake to south.

J 211.7 (340.7 km) **Y 0.8** (1.3 km) **Junction** of Highway 3 and Highway 4 (Ingraham Trail); see log this section.

Yellowknife

J 212.5 (342 km) **Y 0** On the north shore of Great Slave Lake, approximately 940 miles/1513 km from Edmonton, AB. **Population:** 17,500. **Emergency Services: RCMP**, phone (403) 920-8311. **Fire Department** and **Ambulance**, phone (403) 873-3434 or 873-2222. **Hospital,** Stanton Yellowknife, phone (403) 920-4111.

Visitor Information: Northern Frontier Regional Visitors Centre, showcasing the culture and crafts of the area, is located at 4807 49th St. Reservation desk for booking tours. Open daily year-round; summer hours 8 A.M. to 8 P.M. Phone (403) 873-4262. Information also available from Northwest Territories Tourism, P.O. Box 1320, Yellowknife, NT X1A 2L9. Or write the Chamber of Commerce, Box 906, Yellowknife, NT X1A 2N7; phone (403) 920-4944.

Radio: 1240, 1340, 101.1-FM. **Television:** Channel 8; 15 cable channels. **Newspapers:** *News/North* (weekly); *Yellowknifer* (twice weekly).

Private Aircraft: Yellowknife airport; elev. 674 feet/205m; length 7,500 feet/2,286m; asphalt; fuel 100/130, Jet B. Floatplane bases located at East Bay and West Bay of Latham Island.

Yellowknife, capital of Northwest Territories and considered the only "city" in Northwest Territories, is a relatively new community. White settlers arrived in the 1930s with the discovery of gold in the area and radium at Great Bear Lake.

Cominco poured its first gold brick in 1938. WWII intervened and gold mining was halted until Giant Yellowknife Mines began milling May 12, 1948. It was not until 1960 that the road was completed connecting the city with the provinces. Yellowknife became capital of the Northwest Territories in 1967.

The most recent mining boom in Yellowknife was the discovery of diamonds north of Yellowknife at Lac de Gras in 1992. The find set off a rush of claim stakers. An estimated 150 companies have staked claims in an area stretching from north of Yellowknife to the Arctic coast, and east from the North Arm of Great Slave Lake to Hudson Bay.

For 2 to 6 weeks each spring, vehicle traffic to Yellowknife is cut off during breakup on the Mackenzie River crossing near Fort Providence. All fresh meat, produce and urgent supplies must be airlifted during this period, resulting in higher prices.

Yellowknife has continued to develop as a mining, transportation and government administrative centre for the territories.

ACCOMMODATIONS/VISITOR SERVICES

Acommodations at 6 hotels, 3 motels, 7 bed and breakfasts, and the YWCA (co-ed). There are 14 restaurants, 3 dining lounges (no minors), 8 cocktail lounges and several shopping malls. Northern handicraft shops for fur parkas and other Native crafts are a specialty here, and there are shops specializing in Northern art.

TRANSPORTATION

Air: Scheduled air service to Edmonton via NWT Airways and Canadian Airlines International; Winnipeg via NWT Airways. Carriers serving Yellowknife and arctic communities are NWT Airways, Canadian Airlines International, Ptarmigan Airways, Simpson Air, Air Providence and First Air. Charter service available. **Bus:** Greyhound from Edmonton with connections at Enterprise. **Rentals:** Several major car rental agencies; boat and canoe rentals.

ATTRACTIONS

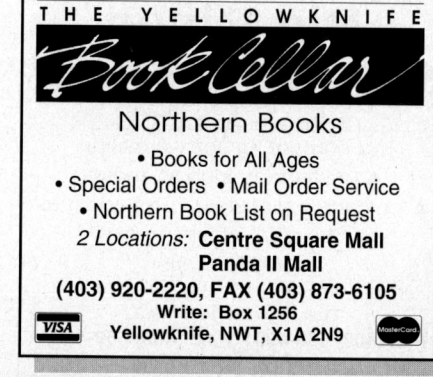

Northern Frontier Regional Visitors Centre. (MP5)#4, 4807 - 49th St., Yellowknife, Northwest Territories X1A 3T5. Featuring interpretive displays, exhibits and a bush plane elevator ride. Information on things to see and do. A tour reservation desk operates during the summer. Open year-round, 7 days a week (8 A.M. to 8 P.M. summer hours). Phone (403) 873-4262, fax 873-3654.

Prince of Wales Northern Heritage Centre. Opened in 1979, this large museum complex was built to collect, preserve, document, exhibit, study and interpret the North's natural and cultural history. For visitors there are a variety of temporary exhibits ranging from Inuit stone sculpture to historical photographs, and permanent exhibits in the galleries. The orientation gallery gives general background on the Northwest Territories; the south gallery tells the story of the land and the Déne and Inuit people; the north gallery shows the arrival of the Euro–Canadians. The centre is located on Frame Lake, accessible via 48th Street or by way of a pedestrian causeway behind City Hall.

Tours. There are a variety of local tours offered. Public tours of the Legislative Assembly are available by calling the Coordinator of Public Information at (403) 669-2230. Visitors may take a 2- or 3-hour tour of the city or a 2-hour cruise on Great Slave Lake. Local tour operators also offer tours out Ingraham Trail (NWT Highway 4).

Explore Yellowknife. Walk along the popular Frame Lake Trail with its views of Yellowknife's skyline, including the new Armed Forces Northern Headquarters and Legislative Assembly buildings. The trail is a favourite with dog walkers, bicyclists, birdwatchers and commuters. Drive or walk down the hill and around the "Rock" where the original town sprang up on Yellowknife Bay and where there are now barges, fishing boats and a large floatplane base; climb steps to the cairn on top of the rock, a tribute to early-day bush pilots who opened up this country in the 1930s and 1940s. The log Wildcat Cafe at the bottom of the rock is open May to Sept. Drive out to Old Town on Latham Island to see some of the creative solutions builders have found to the problem of building on solid rock.

The Yellowknife Bookcellar. See display ad this section.

View of Yellowknife's modern skyline. (© Lyn Hancock)

Ingraham Trail Log

NWT HIGHWAY 4

NWT Highway 4 begins in Yellowknife and extends 44 miles/71 km along an almost continuous chain of lakes and streams, ending at Tibbett Lake. In winter, this highway is used as part of the 380-mile/612-km ice road to Lupin gold mine. The winter road also serves Lac de Gras, heart of the diamond rush.

Distance from Yellowknife (Y) is followed by distance from Tibbett Lake (T).

Y 0 T 44.1 (70.9 km) **Junction** of Highways 3 and 4.

Y 1.9 (3.1 km) **T 42.2** (67.9 km) Giant Yellowknife Mines main office. The mine has been operating since 1947.

Y 3.1 (5 km) **T 41** (66 km) Side road leads north 3 miles/5 km to Vee Lake.

Y 4.7 (7.5 km) **T 39.4** (63.4 km) Single-lane bridge across the **Yellowknife River.** Historical sign at north end of bridge about the Ingraham Trail. Picnic area with tables and boat launch. Good fishing for northern pike, lake trout and grayling.

Y 6.1 (9.8 km) **T 38** (61.2 km) Turnoff to south by 2 transmission towers for 7-mile/11-km road to Detah Indian village; no services.

Y 11.9 (19.2 km) **T 32.2** (51.7 km) **Prosperous Lake** picnic area and boat launch to north. Fishing for northern pike, whitefish and lake trout.

Y 14.9 (24 km) **T 29.2** (46.9 km) **Madeline Lake** picnic area and boat launch to north. Fishing for northern pike, whitefish, cisco and yellow perch.

Y 16.4 (26.4 km) **T 27.7** (44.5 km) **Pontoon Lake** picnic area and boat launch to south. Fishing for northern pike, whitefish, cisco and suckers.

Y 17.5 (28.2 km) **T 26.6** (42.7 km) Side road leads north 1 mile/1.6 km to Prelude Lake territorial campground with 28 campsites, 20 picnic sites, boat launch and swimming. Prelude Wildlife Trail is a 1½-hour walk. The trail has 15 interpretive stations showing the adaptations and relationships of wildlife in the North. Boat rentals, cabins and a restaurant located here.

Fishing in **Prelude Lake** for lake trout, grayling, whitefish, cisco, burbot, suckers and northern pike.

Good views of Prelude Lake from the highway next 10 miles/16 km eastbound.

Y 28.6 (46 km) **T 15.5** (24.9 km) Powder Point on Prelude Lake to north; parking area. Boat launch for canoeists doing the route into Hidden Lake Territorial Park, Lower Cameron River, or 4-day trip to Yellowknife River bridge.

Y 30.1 (48.4 km) **T 14** (22.5 km) Cameron River Falls trailhead to north; parking. This 0.6-mile/1-km trail leads to cliffs overlooking Cameron River Falls.

Y 35.4 (57 km) **T 8.7** (13.9 km) Single-lane Bailey bridge across Cameron River; parking area, picnicking, canoeing and swimming.

Y 37.9 (61 km) **T 6.2** (9.9 km) **Reid Lake** territorial campground with 27 campsites, 10 picnic sites, kitchen shelter, swimming, hiking trail, boat launch and fishing. Canoe launch point for Upper Cameron River and Jennejohn Lake routes. *CAUTION: Watch for bears.*

Y 44.1 (70.9 km) **T 0** Tibbett Lake. End of road. Launch point for Pensive Lakes canoe route (advanced canoeists only).

Fort Smith Highway Log

NWT HIGHWAY 5

Distance from Highway 2 junction (J) followed by distance from Fort Smith (FT).

J 0 FT 166 (267.2 km) Highway 5 begins its own series of markers giving distances in kilometres.

J 1.3 (2.2 km) **FT 164.7** (265 km) Railroad and auto bridge crosses Hay River.

J 1.5 (2.5 km) **FT 164.5** (264.7 km) Access road leads north 3.7 miles/5.9 km to Hay River reserve.

The first 37.7 miles/60.8 km of Highway 5 are paved. Watch for construction and rough spots in surfacing. There are no services or gas available until Fort Smith.

J 5.4 (8.8 km) **FT 160.6** (258.4 km) Highway crosses Sandy Creek.

J 11 (17.7 km) **FT 155** (249.5 km) Highway maintenance yard to south.

J 17.3 (27.9 km) **FT 148.7** (239.3 km) Birch Creek bridge.

J 23.7 (38.2 km) **FT 142.3** (229 km) Highway crosses Twin Creek.

J 30.3 (48.8 km) **FT 135.7** (218.4 km) Good gravel road leads 1 mile/1.6 km north to **Polar Lake.** Lake is stocked with rainbow; no motorboats allowed. Good bird watching.

J 33.8 (54.4 km) **FT 132.2** (212.7 km) Buffalo River bridge.

J 34.1 (55 km) **FT 131.9** (212.2 km) Turnout to north with litter barrel.

J 37.3 (60 km) **FT 128.7** (207.1 km) **Junction** with Highway 6 east to Pine Point and Fort Resolution (see log this section). Highway 5 turns south for Fort Smith (continue with this log). Highway maintenance camp.

J 54 (87 km) **FT 112** (180.2 km) Turnoff for **Sandy Lake,** 8 miles/13 km south; swimming, sandy beach, fishing for northern pike.

J 54.2 (87.2 km) **FT 111.8** (180 km) Pavement ends, gravel begins, southbound. Dust-free zone to Fort Smith.

J 59.6 (96 km) **FT 106.4** (171.2 km) Entrance to Wood Buffalo National Park. Established in 1922 to protect Canada's only remaining herd of wood bison, **WOOD BUFFALO NATIONAL PARK** (a UNESCO world heritage site) is a vast wilderness area of 44,800 square kilometres with the greater portion located in the northeast corner of Alberta. Park headquarters and Visitor Reception Centre are located in Fort Smith and Fort Chipewyan; excellent audio-video presentations, exhibits and visitor information are available. Or write the Superintendent, Wood Buffalo National Park, Box 750, Fort Smith, NT X0E 0P0; or phone (403) 872-2349 Fort Smith or (403) 697-3662 Fort Chipewyan.

The wood bison, a slightly larger and darker northern relative of the Plains bison, numbered about 1,500 in the area, representing the largest free-roaming herd in Canada at the time the park was established. Soon after this more than 6,600 Plains bison were moved from southern Alberta to the park. Today's herd of about 3,500 bison is considered to be mostly hybrids.

Also found within the park are many species of waterfowl and the world's only remaining natural nesting grounds of the endangered whooping crane.

The park is open year-round, with an interpretive program offered from June to Sept. Check the schedule of events at the park office.

J 63.8 (102.7 km) **FT 102.2** (164.4 km) Paralleling most of the highway to Fort Smith are hydro transmission power lines carrying power to Fort Smith, Pine Point and Fort Resolution that is generated at the Taltson Dam in the Canadian Shield north of the Slave River.

Much of the flora along this stretch of highway is new growth following the devastating forest fires of 1981. *NOTE: To report a forest fire, call the operator toll free and ask for Zenith 5555.*

J 66 (106.2 km) **FT 100** (160.9 km) Picnic area with tables to north at Angus Fire Tower. The sinkhole seen here is an example of karst topography. Sinkholes are formed when the roofs of caves (formed by underground water dissolving bedrock) collapse.

Buffalo wallow beside highway from here to approximately **Milepost J 98.9.**

J 74 (119.2 km) **FT 92** (148 km) Highway crosses Nyarling River, which runs under the dry creekbed.

J 74.2 (119.4 km) **FT 91.8** (147.7 km) Turnout to south with litter barrel.

J 98.9 (159.2 km) **FT 67.1** (108 km) Highway maintenance building to north.

J 110.8 (178.4 km) **FT 55.2** (88.8 km) Highway crosses Sass River. Shallow lakes from here south to Preble Creek provide nesting areas for whooping cranes.

J 116.2 (187 km) **FT 49.8** (80.1 km) Highway crosses Preble Creek.

J 130.5 (210 km) **FT 35.5** (57.1 km) The highway leaves and reenters Wood Buffalo National Park several times southbound.

J 131 (211 km) **FT 34.9** (56.1 km) Little Buffalo River bridge. Camping and picnic area. ▲

J 142.5 (229.4 km) **FT 23.5** (37.8 km) Turnoff for Parsons Lake Road (narrow gravel) which leads south 8 miles/13 km to Salt Plains overlook. Interpretive exhibit and viewing telescope. Springs at the edge of a high escarpment bring salt to the surface and spread it across the huge flat plain; only plants adapted to high salinity can grow here. Fine view of a unique environment. Gravel parking area with tables, firepits and toilets at overlook; hiking trail down to Salt Plains (bring boots). *CAUTION: Parsons Lake Road beyond the overlook may be impassable in wet weather.*

J 144.7 (232.8 km) **FT 21.4** (34.4 km) Turnout to south and gravel stockpile.

J 147.3 (237 km) **FT 18.7** (30.1 km) Pavement begins eastbound into Fort Smith.

J 147.9 (238 km) **FT 18.1** (29.1 km) Salt River bridge.

J 151.6 (244 km) **FT 14.4** (23.2 km) Thebacha (Salt River) private campground and picnic area 10 miles/16 km north via good gravel road. Located on the **Salt River;** 8 sites, toilets, parking, small-boat launch (cruise down to Slave River), and fishing for pike, walleye, inconnu and goldeye. ▲

J 163.4 (263 km) **FT 2.6** (4.2 km) Turnoff to north for Fort Smith airport and Queen Elizabeth Park campground with 19 campsites, 15 picnic sites, water, kitchen shelter, showers and dump station. Short hike from campground to bluff overlooking Rapids of the Drowned on the Slave River; look for pelicans feeding here. ▲

Fort Smith

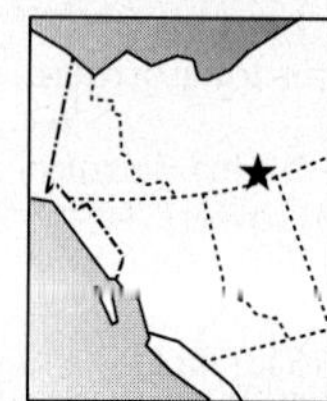

J 166 (267.2 km) **FT 0 Population:** 2,460. **Emergency Services: RCMP,** phone (403) 872-2107. **Fire Department,** phone (403) 872-6111. **Health Centre,** phone (403) 872-2713. **Visitor Information:** Chamber of commerce information centre in Conibear Park, open June to Sept. For general information on the area, contact the Economic Development and Tourism Office, Box 390, Fort Smith, NT X0E 0P0.

Climate: Mean high temperature in July 75°F/24°C; mean low 48°F/9°C. **Radio:** 860, 101.9-FM. **Television:** Channels 12 (local) and 5 (CBC) plus 6 cable channels. **Newspaper:** *Slave River Journal.*

Transportation: Air—Canadian Airlines International provides scheduled service; there are also 3 charter air services here. **Bus**—Available. **Rental cars**—Available.

Private Aircraft: Fort Smith airport; elev. 666 feet/203m; length, 6,000 feet/1,829m; asphalt; fuel 80, 100.

Fort Smith began as a trading post at a favorite campsite of the portagers traveling the 1,600-mile/2575-km water passage from Fort McMurray to the Arctic Ocean. The 4 sets of rapids, named (south to north) Cassette, Pelican, Mountain and the Rapids of the Drowned, separate the Northwest Territories from Alberta. In 1874 Hudson's Bay Co. established a permanent post, and the Roman Catholic mission was transferred here in 1876. By 1911 the settlement had become a major trading post for the area.

There are a hotel, a motel, 2 groceries, a takeout outlet, 3 bars, 3 convenience stores, and gas stations with unleaded gas and repair service.

Wood Buffalo National Park headquarters is located in the Federal Bldg. on McDougal Road, which also houses the post office. The multi-image presentation here is highly recommended. Exhibit area and trip planning assistance available at the visitor reception area. You can drive from Fort Smith to Peace Point via an all-weather gravel road. There are several hiking trails off the road, a picnic area at the Salt River, and a 36-site campground at Pine Lake, 38 miles/61 km south of Fort Smith. There is also a good opportunity for seeing bison on the road between Pine Lake and Peace Point. Contact the park office, phone (403) 872-2349.

Other attractions in Fort Smith include Northern Life Museum, which features a comprehensive view of the area's Indian culture and life of the white settlers since the mid-19th century.

Fort Resolution Highway Log

NWT HIGHWAY 6
Distance from junction with Highway 5 (J) is followed by distance from Fort Resolution (FR).

J 0 FR 55.9 (90 km) **Junction** of Highways 5 and 6. The first 14.7 miles/23.7 km of the highway is paved; the rest is gravel to Fort Resolution. Narrow shoulders.

J 13.2 (21.3 km) **FR 42.7** (68.7 km) Main access road north to **PINE POINT;** no services. A mining town, Pine Point was built in the 1960s by Cominco Ltd. The open-pit lead–zinc mine shut down in 1987. Once a community of almost 2,000 residents, most people moved out in 1988 and houses and structures have been moved or destroyed. The Great Slave Lake Railway (now CNR) was constructed in 1961 from Roma, AB, to Pine Point to transport the lead–zinc ore to market.

J 14.6 (23.6 km) **FR 41.3** (66.4 km) Secondary access road to Pine Point.

J 14.7 (23.7 km) **FR 41.2** (66.3 km) Pavement ends, gravel begins, eastbound. Dust-free zone to Fort Resolution.

J 15.8 (25.5 km) **FR 40.1** (64.5 km) Pine Point airport to north, microwave and satellite dish to south.

J 24.6 (39.6 km) **FR 31.3** (50.3 km) Tailing piles from open-pit mining to south.

J 32.3 (52 km) **FR 23.6** (38 km) Turnoff to north for Dawson Landing viewpoint on Great Slave Lake, accessible via a 25-mile/40-km bush road (not recommended in wet weather).

J 36.5 (58.8 km) **FR 19.4** (31.2 km) Turnout to north with litter barrel.

J 37.8 (60.8 km) **FR 18.1** (29.1 km) Glimpse of Great Slave Lake to north.

J 41.4 (66.7 km) **FR 14.5** (23.3 km) Bridge over **Little Buffalo River.** Good fishing for northern pike and walleye.

J 42.4 (68.3 km) **FR 13.5** (21.7 km) Access road to Little Buffalo River Indian village.

J 54.5 (87.7 km) **FR 1.4** (2.2 km) Campground to west; 5 gravel sites, outhouses, tables and firepits. ▲

J 55.9 (90 km) **FR 0 FORT RESOLUTION** (pop. 447), located on the south shore of Great Slave Lake on Resolution Bay. **Emergency Services: RCMP,** phone (403) 394-4111. This historic community grew up around a Hudson's Bay Co. post established in 1786, and was named Fort Resolution in 1821 when the Hudson's Bay Co. and North West Co. united. Missionaries settled in the area in 1852, establishing a school and hospital to serve the largely Chipewyan population. Walking tours through the village may be arranged. The road connecting Fort Resolution with Pine Point was built in the 1960s.

Today's economy is based on trapping and a logging and sawmill operation. There are a small motel, 2 general stores, a gas station with minor repair service, a post office and cafe. Meals are also available at the community hall.

YELLOWHEAD HIGHWAY 16

Edmonton, Alberta, to Prince Rupert, British Columbia

(See maps, pages 218–220)

Yellowhead Highway 16 is a paved trans-Canada highway extending from Winnipeg, MB, through Saskatchewan, Alberta, and British Columbia to the coastal city of Prince Rupert. (The highway connecting Masset and Queen Charlotte on Graham Island has also been designated as part of Yellowhead Highway 16.) *The MILEPOST®* logs Yellowhead Highway 16 from Edmonton, AB, to Prince Rupert, BC, a distance of 906 miles/ 1,458 km.

Yellowhead Highway 16 terminates at Prince Rupert, BC, where you may connect with the Alaska Marine Highway System to southeastern Alaska cities, and the British Columbia ferry system to Port Hardy on Vancouver Island (see MARINE ACCESS ROUTES section).

This is a major east–west route, providing access to a number of attractions in Alberta and British Columbia. Yellowhead Highway 16 is also a very scenic highway, passing through both forest and farmland. Visitor services are readily available in towns along the way, and campsites may be found in towns and along the highway at both private and provincial park campgrounds. (It is unsafe and illegal to overnight in rest areas.)

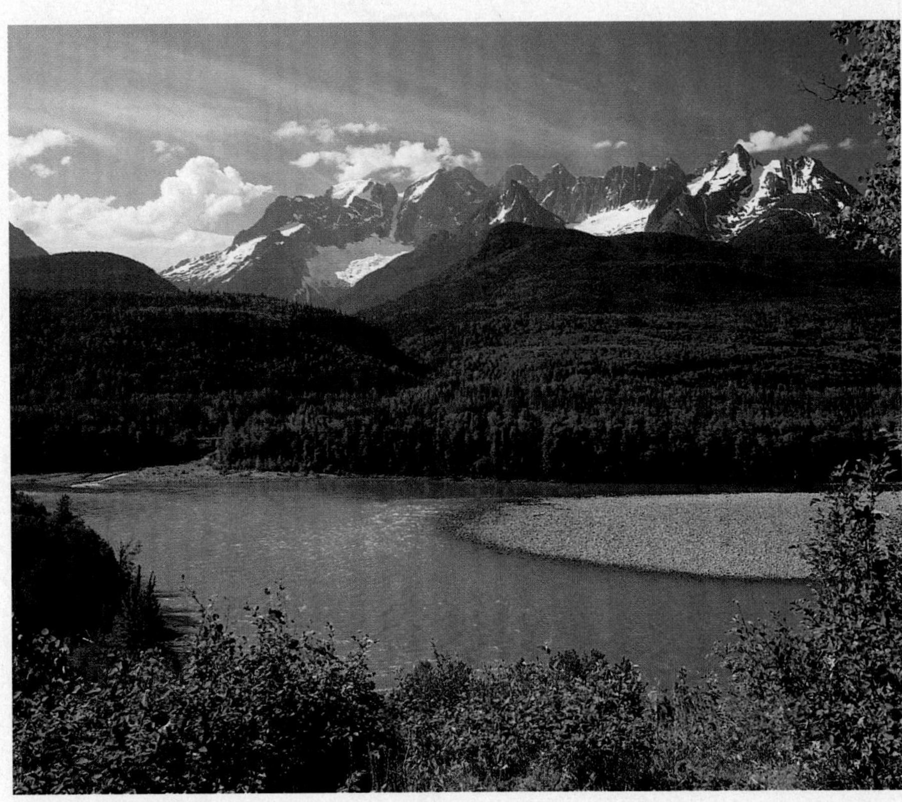

Seven Sisters peaks and the Skeena River near Kitwanga. (West Bergen, Diarama)

Yellowhead Highway 16 Log

The Yellowhead Highway log is divided into 2 sections: Edmonton to Prince George, and Prince George to Prince Rupert. Kilometreposts on Yellowhead reflect distances within highway maintenance districts; *The MILEPOST®* periodically notes these physical posts as reference points.

This section of the log shows distance from Edmonton (E) followed by distance from Prince George (PG).

E 0 PG 450 (724.2 km) **EDMONTON** city limit. See EAST ACCESS ROUTE section for description of city.

E 4 (6.4 km) **PG 446** (717.8 km) **Junction** of Highways 16 West and 60 (Devon Overpass); access to Glowing Embers Travel Centre campground with 273 sites. ▲

E 12 (19.3 km) **PG 438** (704.9 km) **SPRUCE GROVE** (pop. 13,076). All visitor facilities including motels, restaurants, gas and service stations, grocery stores, farmer's market, shopping malls and all emergency services. Recreational facilities include a golf course, swimming pool, 2 ice skating rinks, a curling rink, and extensive walking and cycling trails. The chamber of commerce tourist information booth, located on Highway 16, is open year-round; phone (403) 962-2561.

E 18.1 (29.1 km) **PG 431.9** (695.1 km) **STONY PLAIN** (pop. 7,800). All visitor facilities including hotels, restaurants, supermarkets, shopping mall and gas stations with major repair service; RCMP and hospital; outdoor swimming pool and 18-hole golf course. The Multicultural Heritage Centre nearby has historical archives, a craft shop and home-cooked meals. Other attractions include 16 outdoor murals; a new teahouse; Oppertshauser Art Gallery; the Andrew Wolf Winery; and the Pioneer Museum at Exhibition Park. Visitor information centres at Rotary Park and rest area. Camping at Lions RV Park and Campground; 26 sites. ▲

Bears & Bedtime Mfg. See display ad this section.

Stony Plain Highway Inn. See display ad this section.

Country Lace Cottage. Featuring hearty,

YELLOWHEAD HIGHWAY 16 *Edmonton, AB, to Prince George, BC*

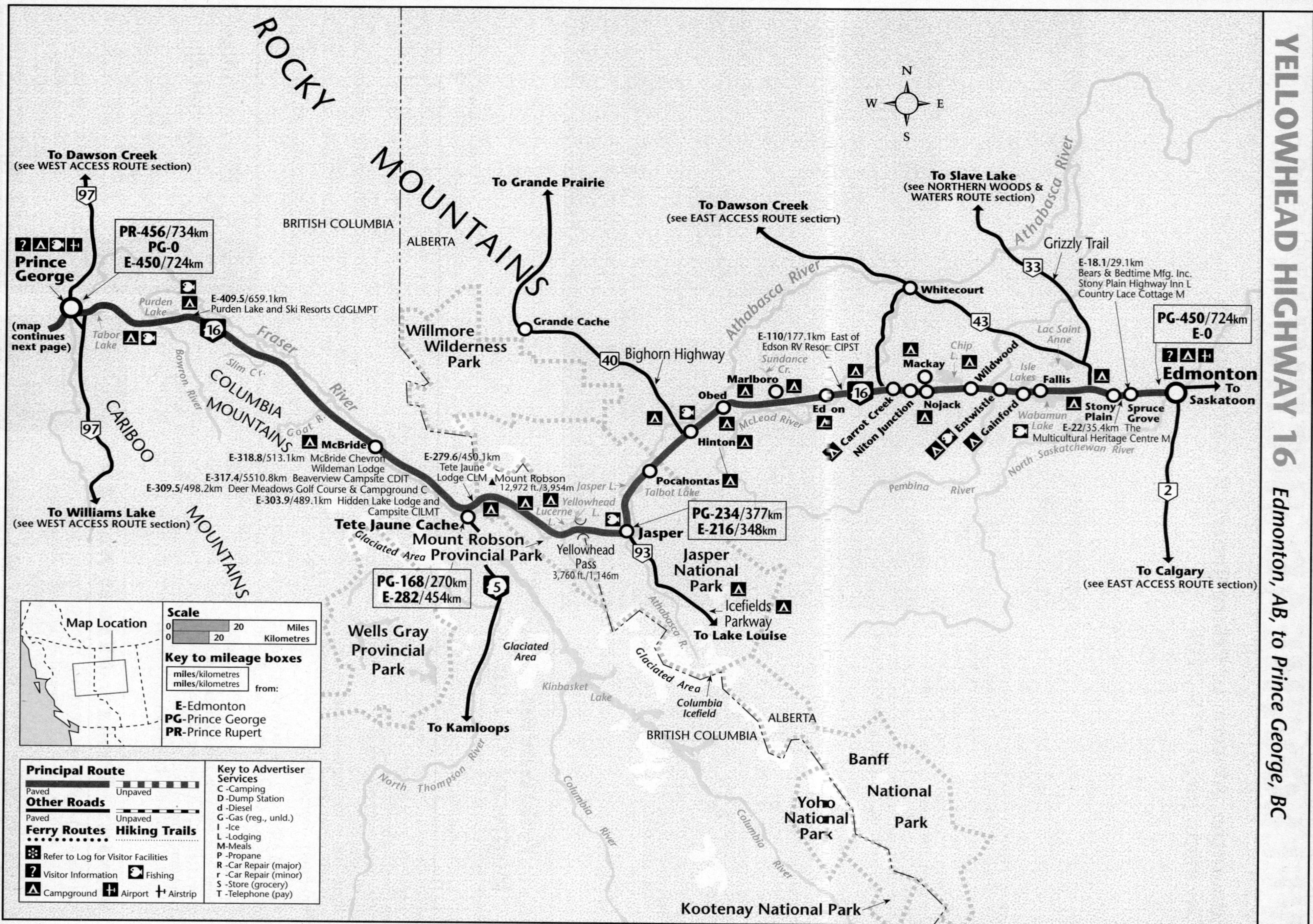

YELLOWHEAD HIGHWAY 16 *Prince George, BC, to Topley, BC*

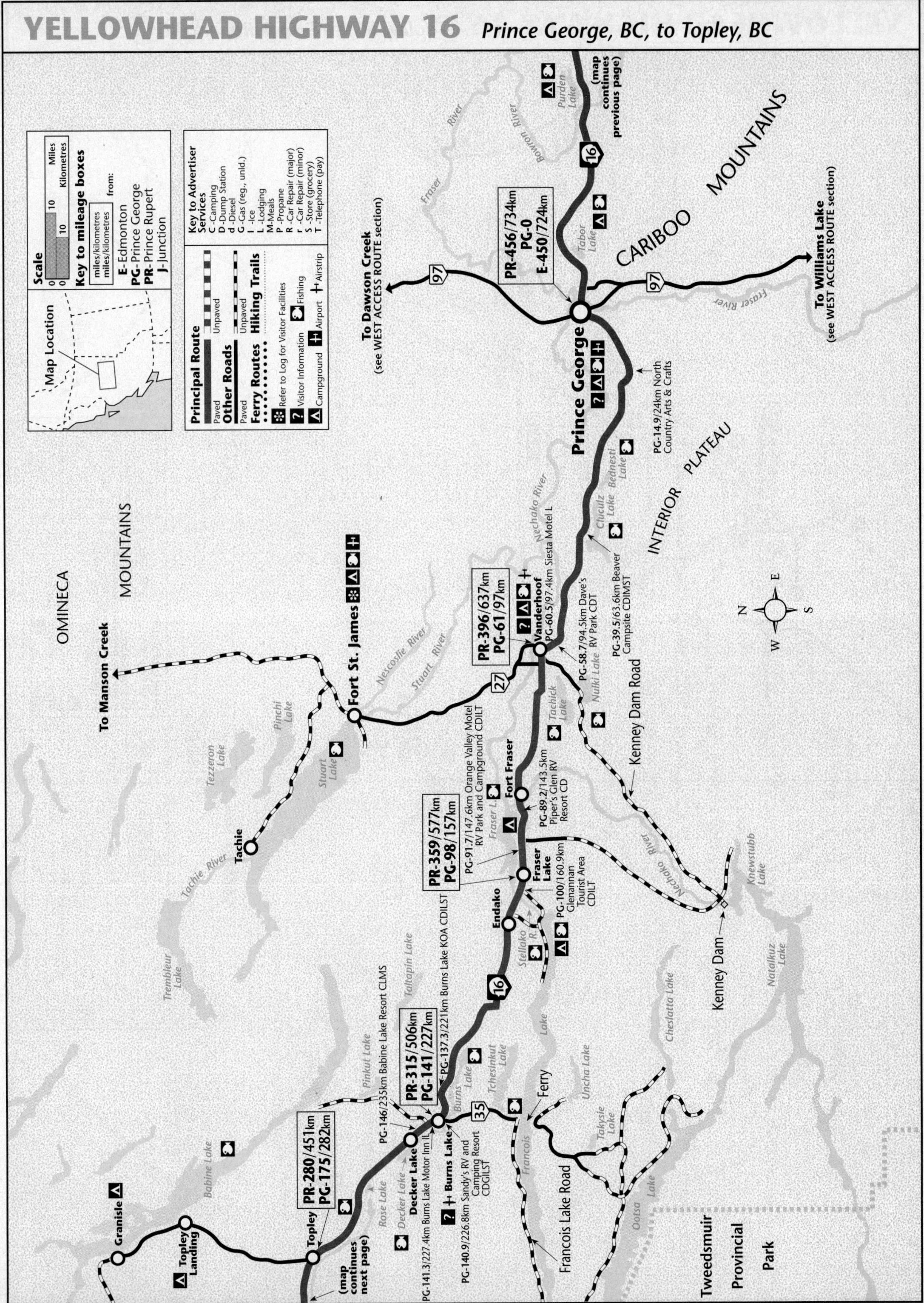

YELLOWHEAD HIGHWAY 16 *Topley, BC, to Prince Rupert, BC*

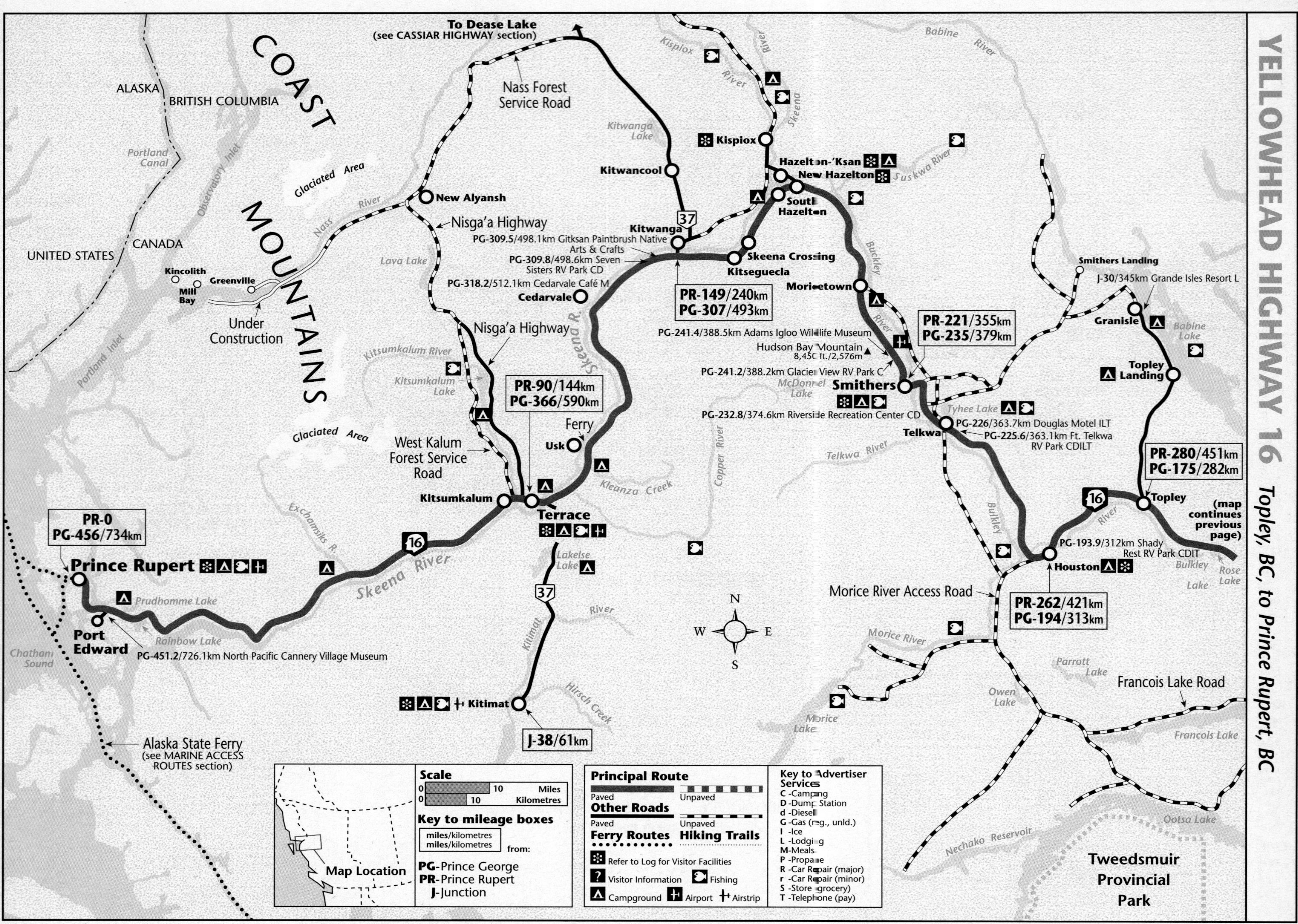

homemade soups, sandwiches, seasonal fruit and cream pies. Generous portions. Outdoor patio. Take out. Bring your container for 10% discount. Decorated by local crafters. Free book exchange. Mon-Sat 8 A.M. to 5 P.M.; Sun 10 A.M. to 2 P.M.; Holiday hours vary. 4805–52 Ave., Stony Plain, AB. T7Z IC4. (403) 968-2222. [ADVERTISEMENT]

E 19 (30.6 km) PG 431 (693.6 km) Private campground, 1.9 miles/3.1 km north. ▲

E 19.6 (31.5 km) PG 430.4 (692.7 km) Turnoff to south for Edmonton Beach and campground. ▲

E 20.1 (32.3 km) PG 429.9 (691.9 km) Hubbles Lake turnoff to north.

E 21.2 (34.1 km) PG 428.8 (690.1 km) Restaurant, gas station and store to north.

E 21.7 (35 km) PG 428.3 (689.2 km) Andrew Wolf Winery; visitors welcome.

E 22 (35.4 km) PG 428 (688.8 km) **The Multicultural Heritage Centre.** Features a regional museum, unique restaurant, a public art gallery featuring Canadian artists, as well as both local and imported craft shops. Award-winning grounds and historically significant buildings complete this rewarding experience. Open Monday to Saturday 10 A.M. to 4 P.M., Sunday 10 A.M. to 6:30 P.M. Phone (403) 963-2777. Address: 5411 - 51 St. [ADVERTISEMENT]

E 25 (40.2 km) PG 425 (684 km) **Junction** with Highway 43. Turn north for access to Alaska Highway (see EAST ACCESS ROUTE section) and Northwest Territories (see MACKENZIE ROUTE section). Continue west for Prince George.

E 25.5 (41 km) PG 424.5 (683.2 km) Hubbles Lake to north.

E 30.3 (48.8 km) PG 419.7 (675.4 km) Gas and groceries south side of road at junction.

E 30.9 (49.8 km) PG 419.1 (674.4 km) Sign: Watch for moose.

E 33 (53.1 km) PG 417 (671.1 km) **Wabamun Lake** Provincial Park, 1 mile/1.6 km south on access road; 288 campsites, fishing, boating and swimming. ▲

E 34.7 (55.9 km) PG 415.3 (668.3 km) Village of **WABAMUN** with gas, convenience store, car wash, laundromat, dump station, hotel and post office. Park with shelter, tables, litter barrels, washroom and flush toilets. Also located here is Trans Alta Utilities generating station, which generates electricity from coal.

E 38.5 (61.9 km) PG 411.5 (662.3 km) Emergency phone to south. Propane, fuel and groceries.

E 42.5 (68.4 km) PG 407.5 (655.8 km) **FALLIS** (pop. 190); no services. Strip mining of coal on north side of highway.

E 46.2 (74.4 km) PG 403.8 (649.8 km) Private campground/RV park, open year-round. ▲

E 48.7 (78.3 km) PG 401.3 (645.9 km) **GAINFORD** (pop. 205). Cafe, hotel and post office. Free public campground at west end of town with 8 sites, firewood, tables, pit toilets and water. ▲

E 56.6 (91.1 km) PG 393.4 (633.1 km) **ENTWISTLE** (pop. 477). Restaurants, gas station, 2 motels, post office, swimming pool and grocery store. **Pembina River** Provincial Park, 1.9 miles/3.1 km north; 129 campsites, firewood, tables, pit toilets, water and dump station. Camping fee $11. Fishing, swimming, playground and phone. ▲

E 66.2 (106.5 km) PG 383.8 (617.7 km) **WILDWOOD** (pop. 375), the "Bingo Capital of Canada." Post office, hotel, gas station, restaurants and shops. Campground at **Chip Lake** with 14 sites, tables, firewood, pit toilets, water, fishing, swimming and boat launch. ▲

E 68.7 (110.6 km) PG 381.3 (613.6 km) View of Chip Lake to north.

E 81.5 (131.1 km) PG 368.5 (593.1 km) **NOJACK** and **MACKAY** (pop. 250). Grocery, post office, restaurant and gas station with towing, diesel and major repair service. Mackay is 1.9 miles/3.1 km north of Nojack on a gravel road. Campgrounds 1 mile/1.6 km and 3 miles/4.8 km west of town on Highway 16. ▲

E 81.6 (131.4 km) PG 368.4 (592.8 km) Emergency phone.

E 84.6 (136.1 km) PG 365.4 (588.1 km) Private campground to north. ▲

E 89.5 (144 km) PG 360.5 (580.2 km) **NITON JUNCTION.** Hamlet has 2 gas stations with tires and parts, diesel, propane, car wash, pay phone, groceries, post office, 2 restaurants, lounge, motel. Private campground with full hookups. ▲

E 93.7 (150.8 km) PG 356.3 (573.4 km) **CARROT CREEK**, post office, grocery store, gas station, car wash and phone.

E 97.5 (157 km) PG 352.5 (567.2 km) **Junction** with Highway 32 which leads to Whitecourt and Highway 43, 42 miles/67.6 km north on paved road. (See **Milepost E 112.7** in the EAST ACCESS ROUTE section.)

E 102.1 (164.4 km) PG 347.9 (559.8 km) Wolf Lake public campground, 33 miles/53 km south on gravel road; 14 sites, pit toilets, tables, litter barrels. ▲

E 105 (169 km) PG 345 (555.2 km) Edson rest area to south with flush toilets, water, tables, shelter, phone and sani-dump.

E 106 (170.6 km) PG 344 (553.6 km) Rosevear Road; eastbound access to Edson rest area.

E 110 (177.1 km) PG 340 (547.1 km) **East of Edson RV Resort.** 8 km (5 miles) east of Edson on Highway 16. Open May to October. Full services in the wilderness. Long drive-through sites with 30/15-amp service. Coin-op hot showers. Laundromat. Small store. Public phone. Walkways. Recreation activities. Security gate. Pets welcome. Reservations (403) 723-2287. Box 7378, Edson, AB T7E 1V6. [ADVERTISEMENT] ▲

E 113.1 (182 km) PG 336.9 (542.2 km) McLeod River bridge.

E 114.9 (185 km) PG 335.1 (539.2 km) **EDSON** (pop. 7,323). Large highway community with 14 motels, many restaurants and gas stations; 18-hole golf course, indoor pool; hospital and RCMP post. Tourist information to south; turn left west bound onto 55th Street. There is camping at Lions Club Campground east of town (42 sites), and at Willmore Recreation Park, 3.7 miles/6 km south of town on the McLeod River. Campground resort, 5 miles/8 km east of Edson, with full hookups; open May to Oct. Edson's economy is based on coal mining, forestry, oil, natural gas and manufacturing. ▲

E 123.2 (198.3 km) PG 326.8 (525.9 km) Food, gas, lodging and phone.

E 128 (206 km) PG 322 (518.2 km) Government campground to north adjacent to highway. ▲

E 133 (214 km) PG 317 (510.2 km) Small community of Marlboro to north. First view of Canadian Rockies westbound.

E 140.8 (226.6 km) PG 309.2 (497.6 km) Westbound-only turnout with picnic tables, pit toilets and litter barrels; generous, paved parking area.

E 142.7 (229.6 km) PG 307.3 (494.6 km) Eastbound-only turnout with litter barrels.

E 148.1 (238.3 km) PG 301.9 (485.9 km) Obed Lake public campground to north; 13 sites, firewood, tables, pit toilets and water. ▲

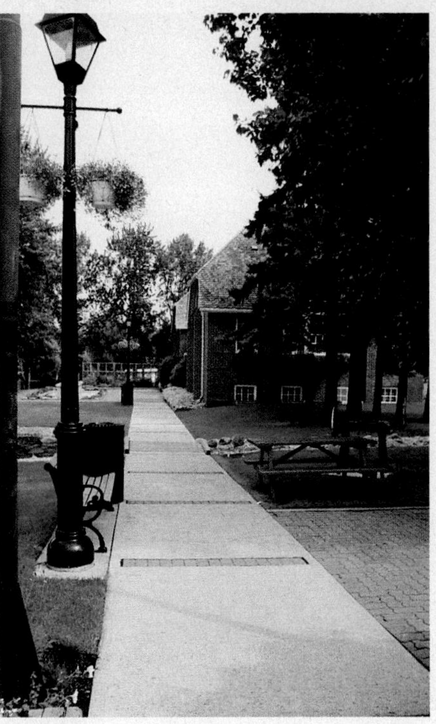

Stony Plain's Multicultural Heritage Centre. *(Judy Parkin, staff)*

E 150.3 (241.9 km) PG 299.7 (482.3 km) **OBED**. Phone, gas and groceries.

E 156.4 (251.8 km) PG 293.6 (472.4 km) Obed Summit, highest elevation on the Yellowhead Highway at 3,819 feet/1,164m. Paved turnout with picnic tables, toilets and litter barrels; good view of the Rockies, weather permitting.

E 157.7 (253.9 km) PG 292.3 (470.3 km) Treed roadside turnout; generous parking area, picnic tables, toilets and litter barrels.

E 160.8 (258.8 km) PG 289.2 (465.4 km) Motel to south.

E 166.7 (268.3 km) PG 283.3 (455.9 km) **HINTON** (pop. 8,537). All visitor facilities including hotels and motels, golf course, hospital, dentist, RCMP and recreation complex with indoor pool. Campground with 50 sites, hookups and dump station. Site of St. Regis (Alberta) Ltd. pulp mill; tours of mill complex may be arranged. ▲

E 171 (275.3 km) PG 279 (448.9 km) South **junction** with Highway 40.

E 172.2 (277.1 km) PG 277.8 (447.1 km) **Junction** with Bighorn Highway 40, which leads north 90 miles/145 km (paved) to Grande Cache then another 117 miles/188 km (gravel) to Grande Prairie. See BIG HORN HIGHWAY log on page 33. William A. Switzer Provincial Park 16.8 miles/27 km north; camping, picnicking, fishing. ▲

E 176.8 (284.5 km) PG 273.2 (439.7 km) Maskuta Creek picnic area with tables, shelter, toilets and litter barrels.

E 177.8 (286.2 km) PG 272.2 (438 km) Weigh scales and pay phone.

E 179 (288.1 km) PG 271 (436.1 km) Public campground 3.1 miles/5 km north. ▲

E 181.5 (292.2 km) PG 268.5 (432 km) Private campground, pay phone. ▲

E 182.4 (293.6 km) PG 267.6 (430.6 km) Point of interest sign about Athabasca River to north.

E 182.9 (294.4 km) PG 267.1 (429.8 km)

William A. Switzer Provincial Park on Gregg Lake is 17 miles/27 km north of Milepost E 172.2 on Highway 40. (© Stephanie Satter)

Resort with lodging to north.

E 184.2 (296.5 km) **PG 265.8** (427.7 km) East entrance to Jasper National Park; public phones. Park fees charged on a per-person basis and must be paid by all visitors using facilities in Rocky Mountain national parks.

Highway 16 has restricted speed zones where wildlife sightings are frequent. Drive carefully and watch out for moose, elk, white-tailed and mule deer, mountain goats, bighorn sheep, and black and grizzly bears. *NOTE: It is illegal to feed, touch, disturb or hunt wildlife in the national park. All plants and natural objects are also protected and may not be removed or destroyed.*

E 185.6 (298.8 km) **PG 264.4** (425.4 km) Fiddle River bridge.

E 187.6 (302 km) **PG 262.4** (422.2 km) Weather permitting, layering in mountains is quite apparent. It is speculated that the Rockies were once part of a sea bed that was lifted from the water and folded. The visible layers are sedimentary deposits laid on the bottom of the sea.

E 189 (304.2 km) **PG 261** (420 km) **POCAHONTAS.** Grocery, motel, cafe and gas station with minor repair service. **Junction** with Miette Hot Springs Road, which leads 0.6 mile/1 km south to Park Service campground (140 sites) and 11 miles/17.7 km south to Miette Hot Springs and resort. There are 2 thermal pools; towels and bathing suits for rent; admission fee. Beautiful setting, look for mountain goats. ▲

E 192 (309 km) **PG 258** (415.2 km) Turnout with cairn to south. Mineral lick here is frequented by goats and sheep. Watch for wildlife, especially at dawn and dusk. Many turnouts next 25 miles/40 km westbound.

E 193 (310.6 km) **PG 257** (413.6 km) First Rocky River bridge westbound.

E 194.3 (312.7 km) **PG 255.7** (411.5 km) Second Rocky River bridge westbound.

E 203 (326.7 km) **PG 247** (397.5 km) Two bridges spanning the Athabasca River. Watch for elk and stone sheep.

E 205.1 (330.1 km) **PG 244.9** (394.1 km) Snaring River bridge.

E 206.7 (332.7 km) **PG 243.3** (391.5 km) Jasper airfield to south.

E 208.1 (335 km) **PG 241.9** (389.2 km) Snaring overflow camping south. ▲

E 208.4 (335.4 km) **PG 241.6** (388.8 km) Snaring rest area to south.

E 208.8 (336 km) **PG 241.2** (388.2 km) Palisades picnic area.

E 212.9 (342.6 km) **PG 237.1** (381.6 km) Access road to Jasper Park Lodge, Maligne Lake and park office. The area is home to a large population of harlequin ducks, endangered elsewhere.

E 215.8 (347.3 km) **PG 234.2** (376.9 km) **Junction** with Highway 93A. Lodging and restaurant to south.

E 216.6 (348.6 km) **PG 233.4** (375.6 km) Access to Jasper and **junction** with Highway 93, the scenic Icefields Parkway, south to Banff past Columbia Icefield.

Many residents in this area maintain hummingbird feeders. The 2 species of hummingbirds found in the Canadian Rockies are the Rufous and the Calliope.

Jasper is also in elk territory. Elk can be dangerous during calving (May through June) and mating (Aug. through Oct.), so stay back at least 40 paces.

NOTE: No fuel next 62.5 miles/100.6 km westbound.

E 217.1 (349.5 km) **PG 232.9** (374.7 km) Miette River.

E 222.2 (357.6 km) **PG 227.8** (366.6 km) Paved turnout to north with outhouses, litter barrels and interpretive sign about Yellowhead Pass. Many turnouts next 25 miles/40 km eastbound.

E 223.2 (359.3 km) **PG 226.8** (364.9 km) Meadow Creek.

E 223.4 (359.5 km) **PG 226.6** (364.7 km) Trailhead for Virl Lake, Dorothy Lake and Christine Lake.

E 226.1 (363.9 km) **PG 223.9** (360.3 km) Clairvaux Creek.

E 229.4 (369.3 km) **PG 220.6** (354.9 km) West entrance to Jasper National Park; park fee must be paid by all visitors using facilities in Rocky Mountain national parks.

E 231.6 (372.7 km) **PG 218.4** (351.5 km) Yellowhead Pass (elev. 3,760 feet/1,146m), Alberta–British Columbia border. Named for an Iroquois trapper and guide who worked for the Hudson's Bay Co. in the early 1800s. His light-colored hair earned him the name Tete Jaune ("yellow head") from the French voyageurs.

East entrance to Mount Robson Provincial Park. Portal Lake picnic area with tables, toilets, information board and hiking trail.

TIME ZONE CHANGE: Alberta observes Mountain standard time. Most of British Columbia observes Pacific standard time. Both observe daylight saving time. See Time Zones in the GENERAL INFORMATION section for details.

E 232.8 (374.7 km) **PG 217.2** (349.5 km) Kilometrepost 75. Kilometreposts on Yellowhead Highway 16 reflect distances within highway maintenance districts; *The MILEPOST®* periodically notes these physical posts as reference points.

E 235.8 (379.6 km) **PG 214.2** (344.6 km) Rockingham Creek.

E 236.2 (380.1 km) **PG 213.8** (344.1 km) **Yellowhead Lake**; picnic tables, viewpoint, boat launch and fishing.

E 238 (383 km) **PG 212** (341.2 km) Lucerne Campground; 32 sites, picnic tables, drinking water, firewood and swimming; camping fee charged. ▲

E 239.3 (385.2 km) **PG 210.7** (339 km) Fraser Crossing rest area to south; litter barrels and toilets.

E 239.4 (385.3 km) **PG 210.6** (338.9 km) Fraser River bridge No. 1.

E 242.4 (390.1 km) **PG 207.6** (334.1 km) Fraser River bridge No. 2.

E 245.2 (394.6 km) **PG 204.8** (329.6 km) Kilometrepost 55.

E 246.2 (396.2 km) **PG 203.8** (328 km) Grant Brook Creek.

E 249 (400.8 km) **PG 201** (323.4 km) Moose Creek bridge.

E 251.1 (404.2 km) **PG 198.9** (320 km) Turnout at east end of Moose Lake; information kiosk, tables, litter barrels, toilet and boat launch.

E 255.5 (411.2 km) **PG 194.5** (313 km) Turnout with litter barrels.

E 257.5 (414.4 km) **PG 192.5** (309.8 km) Kilometrepost 35.

E 263.7 (424.4 km) **PG 186.3** (299.8 km) Paved turnout with litter barrels.

E 268 (431.3 km) **PG 182** (292.9 km) Overlander Falls rest area to south; pit toilets and litter barrels. Hiking trail to Overlander Falls, about 30 minutes round-trip.

E 268.8 (432.7 km) **PG 181.2** (291.4 km) Viewpoint of Mount Robson (elev. 12,972 feet/3,954m), highest peak in the Canadian Rockies, and visitor information centre. Parking, picnic tables, restrooms, litter barrels, gas and restaurant. Berg Lake trailhead; hike-in campgrounds. Private campground north of highway. Robson Meadows government campground south of highway with 125 sites, dump station, showers, pay phone, interpretive programs, tables, firewood, flush toilets, water and horseshoe pits; group camping; camping fee charged. ▲

E 269.4 (433.6 km) **PG 180.6** (290.6 km) Robson River government campground to north with 19 sites (some wheelchair-accessible), tables, firewood, pit toilets, showers, water and horseshoe pits; camping fee charged. ♿▲

E 269.8 (434.3 km) **PG 180.2** (289.9 km) Kilometrepost 15.

E 269.9 (434.4 km) **PG 180.1** (289.8 km) Robson River bridge. Look for Indian paintbrush June through Aug. The bracts are orange-red while the petals are green.

E 270.3 (435.1 km) **PG 179.7** (289.1 km) West entrance to Mount Robson Provincial Park. Turnout with litter barrels and statue.

E 270.5 (435.3 km) **PG 179.5** (288.9 km) Gravel turnout to south.

E 271.4 (436.8 km) **PG 178.6** (287.4 km) Swift Current Creek.

E 274.4 (441.7 km) **PG 175.6** (282.5 km) Mount Terry Fox Provincial Park picnic area with tables, restrooms and viewing telescope. The information board here points out the location of Mount Terry Fox in the Selwyn Range of the Rocky Mountains. The peak was named in 1981 to honour cancer victim Terry Fox, who, before his death from the disease, raised some $25 million for cancer research during his attempt to run across Canada.

E 276.3 (444.7 km) **PG 173.7** (280.5 km) Gravel turnout to north with Yellowhead Highway information sign.

E 276.4 (444.9 km) **PG 173.6** (280.3 km) Rearguard Falls Provincial Park picnic area. Easy half-hour round-trip to falls viewpoint. Upper limit of 800-mile/1,300-km migration of Pacific salmon; look for chinook in late summer.

E 277.8 (447.1 km) **PG 172.2** (277.1 km) Gravel turnout to south overlooking Fraser River.

E 278.2 (447.8 km) **PG 171.8** (276.4 km) Weigh scales.

E 278.7 (448.6 km) **PG 171.3** (275.6 km) Tete Jaune Cache rest area with tables, litter barrels and toilets.

E 279 (449.1 km) **PG 171** (275.1 km) **Junction** with Yellowhead Highway 5 to the small community of Tete Jaune Cache (0.5 mile/0.8 km south of junction) and Kamloops (208 miles/335 km south), British Columbia's fourth largest settlement. Food, gas and lodging just west of the junction. Yellowhead Highway 5 opened in 1969. A year earlier, construction of the section of the highway east from Prince George to Tete Jaune Cache had connected Highway 16 with a rough road east to Jasper National Park. The final link in Northern Transprovincial Highway 16 (now Yellowhead Highway 16)—between Prince George and Edmonton—officially opened in 1969.

E 279.1 (449.2 km) **PG 170.9** (275 km) Turnoff for gas, general store and deli, camping, and lodging.

NOTE: No fuel eastbound next 62.5 miles/100.6 km.

E 279.6 (450.1 km) **PG 170.4** (274.1 km) Private lodging, restaurants.

E 283.1 (455.7 km) **PG 166.9** (268.5 km) Spittal Creek Interpretive Forest; hiking trails, tables, litter barrels and toilets. Kilometrepost 140.

E 288.2 (463.8 km) **PG 161.8** (260.4 km) Private resort. Lodging, restaurant.

E 289.1 (465.3 km) **PG 160.9** (258.9 km) Small River rest area by stream with tables, toilets and litter barrels.

E 293.6 (472.5 km) **PG 156.4** (251.7 km) Horsey Creek.

E 295.4 (475.5 km) **PG 154.6** (248.7 km) Kilometrepost 120.

E 300 (482.9 km) **PG 150** (241.3 km) Turnoff to south for settlement of Dunster; gas and general store.

Mount Robson, elev. 12,972 feet, is the highest peak in the Canadian Rockies.
(Fred Chapman, Diarama)

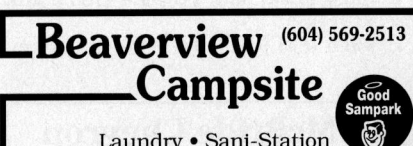

E 303.8 (489 km) **PG 146.2** (235.2 km) Holiday Creek rest area with toilets, picnic tables, litter barrel and hiking trails.

E 303.9 (489.1 km) **PG 146.1** (235.1 km)

E 304.3 (489.7 km) **PG 145.7** (234.5 km) Baker Creek rest area with tables, litter barrels and toilets.

E 308.5 (496.6 km) **PG 141.5** (227.6 km) Kilometrepost 100.

E 308.9 (497.2 km) **PG 141.1** (227 km) Nevin Creek.

E 309.5 (498.2) **PG 140.5** (226 km)

E 312 (502.1 km) **PG 138** (222.1 km) Turnouts at both ends of Holmes River bridge.

E 317.4 (510.8 km) **PG 132.6** (213.4 km) **Beaverview Campsite.** See display ad this section. ▲

E 317.9 (511.6 km) **PG 132.1** (212.6 km) Fraser River bridge. A forest fire swept through the Robson Valley in 1912. As you look at the sides of the mountain to the north of the highway, it is possible to distinguish the new growth which has taken place in the last 81 years.

E 318.2 (512.1 km) **PG 131.8** (212.1 km) Turnout to north with litter barrels.

E 318.8 (513.1 km) **PG 131.2** (211.1 km) **McBRIDE** (pop. 700; elev. 2,369 feet/722.1m), located in the Robson Valley by the Fraser River. The Park Ranges of the Rocky Mountains are to the northeast and the Cariboo Mountains are to the southeast. A road leads to Teare Mountain lookout for a spectacular view of countryside. The village of McBride was established in 1913 as a divisional point on the railroad and was named for Richard McBride, then premier of British Columbia. Forest products are a major industry here today.

Visitor Information: Travel Infocentre located in railcar on south side of Highway 16. Look for the carved grizzly bear family in front. When the Infocentre isn't open, try the McBride Village Office. Located beside the railcar in the same parking lot, it is open 9 A.M. to 5 P.M.

McBride has all visitor facilities, including 5 hotels/motels, a bed and breakfast, 2 supermarkets, convenience/video store, clothing stores, restaurants, pharmacy, hospital and gas stations. A library, museum and neighborhood pub are 1.9 miles/3 km from town. There is a private campground just east of town. Dump station located at the gas station.

While in McBride, watch wood ducks, scoters, teals and more at the Horseshoe Lake Bird Watch. In late summer, see the salmon run in the Holmes River. In winter, go cross-country skiing on developed trails and snowmobiling in the backcountry. Helicopter service available for fly-in skiing and hiking.

McBride Chevron. See display ad this section.

Wildeman Lodge. Lodge, B&B, Cabins —6 paved km from McBride. Overnight, weekly, weekend rates. Quality rooms.

Meals. Guest laundry. Cabin/bunkhouse, wilderness cabin. Country setting. Summer/winter destination recreational packages. BC Adventure Tours 6–12 persons 10-plus days. Open year-round. VISA, MasterCard. Phone (604) 569-2529, fax (604) 569-2619. Box 124, McBride, BC V0J 2E0. Super, Natural North by Northwest. [ADVERTISEMENT]

NOTE: Next gas westbound is 90.7 miles/146 km from here (Purden Lake).

E 321.9 (518.1 km) **PG 128.1** (206.1 km) Dore River bridge.

E 326.7 (525.8 km) **PG 123.3** (198.4 km) Macintosh Creek.

E 328.8 (529.2 km) **PG 121.2** (195 km) Clyde Creek.

E 333.1 (536.2 km) **PG 116.9** (188 km) Kilometrepost 60.

E 336.9 (542.3 km) **PG 113.1** (181.9 km) West Twin Creek bridge.

E 343.6 (553.1 km) **PG 106.4** (171.1 km) Goat River bridge. Paved rest area to north with tables, toilets and litter barrels.

E 346.7 (558 km) **PG 103.3** (166.2 km) Little LaSalle Recreation Area and BC Forest Service site. Small lake, small wharf, toilet.

E 351.2 (565.2 km) **PG 98.8** (159 km) Snowshoe Creek.

E 351.8 (566.2 km) **PG 98.2** (158 km) Kilometrepost 30.

E 354.9 (571.2 km) **PG 95.1** (153 km) Catfish Creek.

E 360.7 (580.6 km) **PG 89.3** (143.6 km) Ptarmigan Creek bridge.

E 363.8 (585.6 km) **PG 86.2** (138.6 km) Turnout with litter barrels to north.

E 369.2 (594.1 km) **PG 80.8** (130.1 km) Dome Creek.

E 371.5 (597.9 km) **PG 78.5** (126.3 km) Food, phone.

E 373.3 (600.8 km) **PG 76.7** (123.4 km) Slim Creek paved rest area to south with information kiosk, tables, playground, litter barrels and wheelchair-accessible toilets. Watch for bears.

E 373.4 (601 km) **PG 76.6** (123.2 km) Ministry of Highways camp.

E 374.1 (602.1 km) **PG 75.9** (122.1 km) Slim Creek bridge.

E 382.5 (615.6 km) **PG 67.5** (108.6 km) Kilometrepost 100.

E 385.6 (620.7 km) **PG 64.4** (103.5 km) Driscol Creek.

E 386.4 (621.9 km) **PG 63.6** (102.3 km) Forests in this area have been destroyed by the hemlock looper, an insect which has killed or damaged over 45.9 million cubic feet/1.3 million cubic metres of wood in British Columbia.

E 387.6 (623.9 km) **PG 62.4** (100.3 km) Gravel turnout with litter barrel to north.

E 388.9 (626 km) **PG 61.1** (98.2 km) Lunate Creek.

E 391.8 (630.6 km) **PG 58.2** (93.6 km) Grizzly hiking trail to south.

E 392 (630.9 km) **PG 58** (93.3 km) Hungary Creek. Watch for Ministry of Forests signs indicating the year in which a logged area was replanted. Wildflowers include fireweed, mid-July through Aug.

E 394.8 (635.4 km) **PG 55.2** (88.8 km) Kilometrepost 80.

E 395.8 (637 km) **PG 54.2** (87.2 km) Sugarbowl Creek.

E 400.5 (644.6 km) **PG 49.5** (79.6 km) Paved turnout with litter barrel to north.

E 407 (655.1 km) **PG 43** (69.1 km) Kilometrepost 60.

E 408.2 (657 km) **PG 41.8** (67.2 km) Kenneth Creek.

E 408.4 (657.4 km) **PG 41.6** (66.8 km) Purden Mountain ski resort.

E 409.5 (659.1 km) **PG 40.5** (65.1 km) Purden Lake resort with gas, phone, lodging and camping. ▲

Purden Lake and Ski Resorts. Campground with lakefront camping; hook-ups. Cabin rentals, boat rentals, boat launch. Good rainbow trout fishing. Cafe, gas station (propane, diesel, unleaded). Cafe and gas open 6 A.M. to 8 P.M. Ski area with 20 runs, 2 double chairs, T-bar, day lodge, ski rentals, ski school, cafeteria. P.O. Box 1239, Prince George, BC V2L 4V3. (604) 565-7777. [ADVERTISEMENT] ▲

NOTE: Next gas eastbound is 90.7 miles/146 km from here (McBride).

E 411.2 (661.9 km) **PG 38.8** (62.3 km) **Purden Lake** Provincial Park, 1.9 miles/3 km from highway; 78 campsites, 48 picnic sites, tables, water, dump station, firewood, playground and horseshoe pits. This recreation area offers a sandy beach, change houses, swimming, walking trails, waterskiing and boat launch. Good rainbow fishing to 4 lbs., trolling. ▲

E 412.6 (664.1 km) **PG 37.4** (60.1 km) Bowron River bridge. Paved rest area to north beside river, on west side of bridge; toilets, tables and litter barrels. Entrance on curve; use care.

E 420.7 (677.1 km) **PG 29.3** (47.1 km) Kilometrepost 40.

E 421 (677.6 km) **PG 29** (46.6 km) Vama Vama Creek.

E 424 (682.4 km) **PG 26** (41.8 km) Wansa Creek.

E 427.1 (687.4 km) **PG 22.9** (36.8 km) Willow River bridge. Rest area at west end of bridge beside river; tables, litter barrels, toilets and nature trail. The 1.2-mile-/1.9-km-long Willow River Forest Interpretation Trail is an easy 45-minute walk.

E 429.5 (691.3 km) **PG 20.5** (32.9 km) Bowes Creek.

E 429.7 (691.6 km) **PG 20.3** (32.6 km) Turnout to north with litter barrels and information board on 1961 forest fire and moose habitat. Circle trail to moose observation site.

E 433 (697 km) **PG 17** (27.2 km) Kilometrepost 20.

E 435.2 (700.5 km) **PG 14.8** (23.7 km) Tabor Mountain ski hill.

E 435.4 (700.8 km) **PG 14.6** (23.4 km) Gravel turnout to north with litter barrels.

E 437.6 (704.3 km) **PG 12.4** (19.9 km) Access to **Tabor Lake**; good fishing for rainbow in spring. ▲

E 444.8 (715.9 km) **PG 5.2** (8.3 km) **Junction**, Highway 16B with Highway 97 south bypass.

E 450 (724.2 km) **PG 0 PRINCE GEORGE** (see description, pages 56-59). **Junction** with Highway 97 north to Dawson Creek and the beginning of the Alaska Highway.

See WEST ACCESS ROUTE section for details on Prince George and the log of Highway 97 north. Continue west for Prince Rupert (log follows).

Yellowhead Highway 16 Log

(continued)

This section of the log shows distance from Prince George (PG) followed by distance from Prince Rupert (PR).

PG 0 PR 456 (733.8 km) From Prince George to Prince Rupert, Highway 16 is a 2-lane highway with 3-lane passing stretches. Fairly straight, with no high summits, the highway follows the valleys of the Nechako, Bulkley and Skeena rivers, paralleling the Canadian National Railway route. There are few services between towns.

PG 1.4 (2.3 km) **PR 454.6** (731.6 km) **Junction** with Domano Blvd.; access to bed and breakfast.

PG 3 (4.8 km) **PR 453** (729 km) Private RV park. ▲

PG 4.8 (7.7 km) **PR 451.2** (726.1 km) **West Lake** Provincial Park 8 miles/12.9 km south; day-use area with swimming, fishing and boat launch.

PG 14.9 (24 km) **PR 441.1** (709.9 km) **North Country Arts & Crafts.** See display ad this section.

PG 32.1 (51.7 km) **PR 423.9** (682.2 km) Rest area to north with picnic tables, toilets and litter barrels.

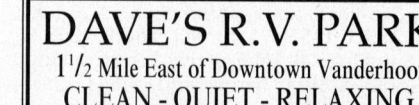

PG 38 (61.2 km) **PR 418** (672.7 km) Access to lakeside resort and fishing at **Cluculz Lake** (not visible from highway). Rainbow to 3³/₄ lbs. by trolling, use snell hook and worms; kokanee to 1¹/₂ lbs., troll with snell hook and worms, in spring; char to 57 lbs., use large flatfish, spoons, plugs and weights, early spring and late fall; whitefish to 5 lbs., year-round. Very good fishing in spring; ice goes out about the first week of May. Good ice fishing Dec. to March. In September kokanee are at their peak. *Lake gets rough when windy.* ▲

PG 39.1 (62.9 km) **PR 416.9** (670.9 km) Cluculz rest area to south with flush toilets (summer only), picnic tables and litter barrels.

PG 39.5 (63.6 km) **PR 416.5** (670.3 km) **Beaver Campsite & Cafe.** 35 restful creekside sites in quiet pine forest. Eight pull-throughs. Electric hookups, laundromat, hot coin-op showers, sani-station. Ice. Store. Cafe with delicious home cooking. Playground. Water. One kilometre from Cluculz Lake with fishing and boat rentals. On site hairdresser proposed for 1996. Your hosts Mathew and Lorri Johnson. RR 1, Site 16, Comp. 36, Vanderhoof, BC V0J 3A0. (604) 441-3385. [ADVERTISEMENT] ▲

PG 58.7 (94.5 km) **PR 397.3** (639.4 km) **Dave's RV Park.** See display ad this section. ▲

Vanderhoof

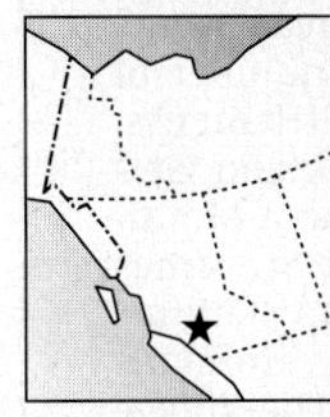

PG 60.5 (97.4 km) **PR 395.5** (636.5 km). **Population:** 4,025; area 12,000. **Emergency Services: Police,** phone (604) 567-2222. **Fire Department**, phone (604) 567-2345. **Ambulance,** phone 112-562-7241. **Hospital**, St. John's, Northside District, phone (604) 567-2211.

Visitor Information: Travel Infocentre downtown on Burrard Avenue, 1 block off Highway 16. Write Vanderhoof & District Chamber of Commerce, Box 126-MP, Vanderhoof, BC V0J 3A0; phone (604) 567-2124.

Elevation: 2,086 feet/636m. **Radio:** CJCI 620, CFPR-FM 96.7, CKPG 550, CIVH 1340, CIRX-FM 95.9. **Television:** Channels 2, 4, 5, 6, 8. **Newspapers:** *Omineca Express–Bugle* (weekly). **Transportation: Air**—Vanderhoof airport, 2 miles/3.2 km from intersection of Highways 16 and 27; 5,000-foot/1,524-m paved runway. Seaplane landings on Nechako River at corner of View Street and Boundary Avenue. **Railroad**—VIA Rail, station at 2222 Church Ave. **Bus**—Greyhound.

Vanderhoof was named for Chicago publisher Herbert Vanderhoof, who founded the village in 1914 when he was associated with the Grand Trunk Development Co. Today, Vanderhoof is the supply and distribution centre for a large agricultural, lumbering and mining area.

The community's history is preserved at Vanderhoof Heritage Village Museum, just off Highway 16. Relocated pioneer structures furnished with period artifacts recall the early days of the Nechako Valley.

Located on the Nechako River, Vanderhoof is a stopping place in April and September for thousands of migrating waterfowl. The river flats upstream of the bridge are a bird sanctuary. Pelicans have been spotted feeding at Tachick Lake south of town.

There are 7 hotels and motels and 16 restaurants in the town. All shopping facilities and several gas stations. Dump station at Dave's RV Park. Municipal campground is on Burrard Avenue close to downtown; second municipal campground west of town on Highway 16. Nine-hole, par 35 golf course located 1.9 miles/3.1 km north of town. ▲

Area attractions include Fort St. James (see description page 226), Tachick Lake and Kenney Dam. Follow the gravel road southwest from Vanderhoof 60 miles/97 km to Kenney Dam. At the time of its construction in 1951, it was North America's largest earth-filled dam. Near the dam site are Cheslatta Falls and Nechako River canyon (good area for rockhounding). Beautiful Tachick Lake (18 miles/29 km south) has a modern log building fishing resort and a lodge which serves European food. Also access to Sai' Kuz Park on Nulki Lake, with annual fishing derby, Native dancers, Native crafts and gambling, and more (phone 604/567-4916); see fishing information following. Kenney Dam Road turnoff is at the Kwik-Save gas station on Highway 16.

Nulki Lake, 10 miles/16 km west on Kenney Dam Road, rainbow to 6 or 7 lbs., average 2 lbs., use worms, year-round. **Tachick Lake,** 18 miles/29 km south on Kenney Dam Road, rainbow 2 to 7 lbs. year-round, largest fish in the area were taken from this lake; several small lakes in the area abound with rainbow and kokanee. Fishing charters available at Vanderhoof airport.

Siesta Motel. See display ad this section.

Yellowhead Highway 16 Log

(continued)

PG 60.5 (97.4 km) **PR 395.5** (636.5 km) First **junction** westbound with Highway 27, which extends north from Vanderhoof several hundred miles. The 37 miles/60 km to Fort St. James are fully paved; see page 226.

PG 61.1 (98.3 km) **PR 394.9** (635.5 km) Vanderhoof Municipal Campground, pleasantly situated on a creek. ▲

PG 64.7 (104.1 km) **PR 391.3** (629.7 km) Second **junction** westbound with Highway 27 (see description at **Milepost PG 60.5**). This route skirts Vanderhoof. Truck weigh scales to north.

PG 72.8 (117.2 km) **PR 383.2** (616.7 km) Restaurant with pay phone and RV parking.

PG 73.7 (118.6 km) **PR 382.3** (615.2 km) Sawmill to south.

PG 83.8 (134.9 km) **PR 372.2** (599 km) Turnout to south with view of Nechako River. The Grand Trunk Pacific Railway was completed near this site in 1914. The railroad (later the Canadian National) linked Prince Rupert, a deep-water port, with interior British Columbia. Entering Lakes District. This high country has over 300 freshwater lakes.

PG 84.3 (135.7 km) **PR 371.7** (598.2 km) **FORT FRASER** (pop. 600). **Radio:** CBC-FM 102.9. Small community with food, gas, propane, lodging and first-aid station. Gas station with hot showers, convenience store and restaurant. Named for Simon Fraser, who established a trading post here in 1806. Now a supply centre for surrounding farms and sawmills. The last spike of the Grand Trunk Railway was driven here on April 7, 1914.

Farmland along Yellowhead Highway 16 near Vanderhoof. (© Carmen Scott)

PG 85.1 (137 km) **PR 370.9** (596.9 km) Nechako River bridge. Turnout to south with parking, litter barrels and access to **Nechako River;** fishing for rainbow and Dolly Varden, June to fall. At the east end of Fraser Lake, the Nautley River—less than a mile long—drains into the Nechako River.

PG 87 (140 km) **PR 369** (593.8 km) Beaumont Provincial Park, on beautiful **Fraser Lake,** north side of highway; site of original Fort Fraser. Boat launch, swimming, hiking, fishing, 49 campsites, picnic tables, firewood, flush toilets, water, playground, horseshoe pits, dump station. Fishing for rainbow and lake trout, burbot, sturgeon and Dolly Varden. ▲

PG 89.2 (143.5 km) **PR 366.8** (590.3 km) **Pipers Glen RV Resort**. See display ad this section. ▲

PG 90.7 (146 km) **PR 365.3** (587.9 km) Dry William Lake rest area to south with picnic tables, toilets and litter barrels.

PG 91.7 (147.6 km) **PR 364.3** (586.3 km) **Orange Valley Motel, RV Park and Campground.** Easy access featuring level sites, large pull-throughs, electricity, water, some with sewer. Free showers, flush toilets, sani-

Fort St. James

Fort St. James

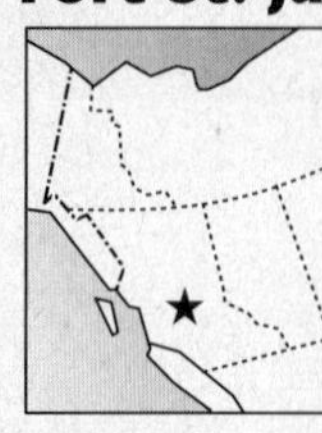

Located 37 miles/59.5 km north of Vanderhoof on Highway 27. **Population:** 1,983. **Emergency Services: Police,** phone (604) 996-8269. **Ambulance:** phone 1-562-7241. **Elevation:** 2,208 feet/673m. **Radio:** CKPG 550, CJCI 1480; CBC-FM 107.0.

Fort St. James is the home of **FORT ST. JAMES NATIONAL HISTORIC SITE.** Established in 1806 by Simon Fraser as a fur trading post for the Northwest Co., Fort St. James served throughout the 19th century as headquarters for the Hudson's Bay Co.'s New Caledonia fur trade district. The fur warehouse, fish cache, men's house, officers' dwelling and trade shop have been restored in 1896-style and are open to the public. Check with the visitor centre regarding tours and interpretive programs.

Costumed docents are part of summer interpretive program at Fort St. James National Historic Park. *(John K. Nakata)*

From mid-May through June and in September, visitors may take guided tours. In July and August, visitors may explore the grounds on their own. Staff members are dressed in period costumes as part of a living history program; hours are 9 A.M. to 5 P.M. daily. For the remainder of the year, the site is closed. Admission fee.

The historic site and village are located on Stuart Lake. Named for John Stuart, the man who succeeded Simon Fraser as head of the New Caledonia district, the 59-mile-/95-km-long lake is the southernmost in a 3-lake chain which provides hundreds of miles of boating and fishing. Fort St. James also boasts the Nation Lakes, a chain of 4 lakes (Tsayta, Indata, Tchentlo and Chuchi) connected by the Nation River.

Attractions include the Our Lady of Good Hope Catholic Church and the Chief Kwah burial site. The recently renovated church is one of the oldest in British Columbia. Open for summer evening services only, check schedule. Chief Kwah was one of the first Carrier Indian chiefs to confront early white explorers. His burial site is located on the Nak'azdli Indian Reserve at the mouth of the Stuart River. At Cottonwood Park on the shore of Lake Stuart, look for a model of a Junkers airplane, which depicts the Fort's major role in early bush flying in Northern British Columbia.

Fort St. James has a hotel, lodge, resort, 4 motels, 2 bed and breakfasts, 3 private campgrounds and a number of surrounding lodges and settlements, such as Tachie, Manson Creek and Germansen Landing in the Omineca Mountains. Other services in Fort St. James include 4 gas stations, 4 dump stations, 2 government marinas, 2 private marinas and several restaurants. The village also has a theatre and 2 shopping centres. Picnicking and swimming at Cottonwood Park on Stuart Lake. A new 9-hole, par 5 golf course now overlooks Stuart Lake; rentals available. Murray Ridge ski area, a 20-minute drive from town, has 21 downhill ski runs and 18.5 miles/30 km of cross-country ski trails. ▲

Stuart River Campgrounds. Treed sites, tenting to full hookups, showers and laundry, firepits and firewood, pay phone. Playgrounds, horseshoe pits; marina with launching ramp and moorage space. Great fishing! Boat rentals, river and lake charters, fishing licenses and tackle. Your hosts, George and Heather Malbeuf, Box 306, Fort St. James, BC V0J 1P0. (604) 996-8690. Super, Natural North by Northwest. [ADVERTISEMENT] ▲

Camping is also available at **Paarens Beach** Provincial Park, located 6.8 miles/10.9 km off Highway 27 on Sowchea Bay Road; 36 campsites, picnic shelter, picnic tables, toilets, water, firepits, boat launch and swimming; camping fee. Sowchea Bay Recreation Area, located 10.6 miles/17.1 km off Highway 27 on Sowchea Bay Road, has 30 campsites, camping fee, picnic tables, toilets, water, firepits boat launch and swimming. ▲

Good fishing in **Stuart Lake** for rainbow and char (to trophy size), kokanee and Dolly Varden.

Return to Milepost PG 60.5 or PG 64.7 Yellowhead Highway 16

FORT ST. JAMES ADVERTISERS

Douglas Lodge ....Ph. (604) 996-7080
Fort St. James Chamber of Commerce ....Ph. (604) 996-7023
Stuart River Campgrounds ....Ph. (604) 996-8690

British Columbia's capital is Victoria.

dump, treed shaded sites with picnic tables. Firepits, firewood; freezer space available. Quiet relaxed setting. Pay phone, hiking trails, beaver dam. Phone (604) 699-6350. [ADVERTISEMENT] ▲

PG 93.8 (151 km) **PR 362.2** (582.9 km) Fraser Lake sawmill to north.

PG 95.5 (153.7 km) **PR 360.5** (580.2 km) Rest area to north. Trail to Fraser Lake.

PG 97.5 (156.9 km) **PR 358.5** (576.9 km) **FRASER LAKE** (pop. 1,400; elev. 2,580 feet/786m). **Visitor Information:** Travel Infocentre and museum in log building at east edge of town. **Radio:** CJCI 1450. Small community with all facilities. Created by Endako Mines Ltd. in 1964 on an older townsite; named after the explorer Simon Fraser. Endako Mines Ltd. began operating in 1965 and was Canada's largest molybdenum mine until production slowed in 1982. Mining resumed in 1986. Mine tours are available on Wednesdays; check with the Travel Infocentre for reservations. Also located here is Fraser Lake Sawmills, the town's largest employer.

PG 100 (160.9 km) **PR 356** (572.9 km) **Junction** with main access road south to scenic Francois Lake; also accessible via roads from Burns Lake to Houston. Francois Lake Road (gravel) leads south 7 miles/11 km to the east end of Francois Lake (where the Stellako River flows from the lake) and back to Highway 16 at Endako. Molyhills golf course and several resorts with camping, cabins and boats are located on this scenic rural road through the Glenannan area. ▲

Glenannan Tourist Area. See display ad this section.

Francois Lake, good fishing for rainbow to 5 lbs., May to Oct.; kokanee to 3/4 lb., use flashers, willow leaf, flashers with worms, flatfish or spinners, Aug. and Sept.; char to 30 lbs., use large flatfish or spoon, June and July. **Stellako River** is considered one of British Columbia's better fly-fishing streams with rainbow over 2 lbs., all summer; whitefish averaging 1 lb., year-round.

PG 100.1 (161.1 km) **PR 355.9** (572.7 km) Bridge over Stellako River. Highway passes through the Stellako Indian Reserve.

PG 105.9 (170.4 km) **PR 350.1** (563.4 km) **ENDAKO.** A small highway community with grocery (closed Sunday), post office, pub and gas station with minor repair service. Turnoff for molybdenum mine just east of town. Several private campgrounds are located along Francois Lake Road to the south in the Glenannan area. ▲

PG 107 (172.2 km) **PR 349** (561.6 km) Endako River bridge.

PG 110.5 (177.8 km) **PR 345.5** (556 km) Savory rest area to north beside Watskin Creek.

PG 113.3 (182.3 km) **PR 342.7** (551.5 km) Ross Creek.

PG 122.1 (196.5 km) **PR 333.9** (537.3 km) Paved turnout to south.

PG 126.1 (202.9 km) **PR 329.9** (530.9 km) Babine Forest Products sawmill to south.

PG 128.7 (207.1 km) **PR 327.3** (526.7 km) Pay phone to south.

PG 133.7 (215.2 km) **PR 322.3** (518.7 km) Rest area to south with toilet, tables, litter barrels and Tintagel Cairn point of interest.

PG 137.3 (221 km) **PR 318.7** (512.9 km) **Burns Lake K.O.A.**, a day's drive from Prince Rupert ferry. Cabins, tenting to full hookups, store, heated showers, laundromat, game room, playground. Mini-golf, canoe rentals, lake swimming. Open May 1 to Sept. 30. Pay phone. Your host, Ed Brown, Box 491, Burns Lake, BC V0J 1E0. (604) 692-3105, 1-800-562-0905. [ADVERTISEMENT] ▲

Scenic view from Tintagel Cairn rest area at Milepost PG 133.7. (© Carmen Scott)

PG 139.9 (225.1 km) **PR 316.1** (508.7 km) Welcome to Burns Lake sign.

PG 140.9 (226.8 km) **PR 315.1** (507.1 km) **Junction** with scenic Highway 35 (paved) south to **Tchesinkut, Francois, Takysie** and **Ootsa lakes**; lodging, camping and fishing. Another of the Yellowhead's popular fishing areas with a variety of family-owned camping and cabin resorts. ▲

Sandy's RV and Camping Resort. Comfortable, casual atmosphere where you'll be welcomed with northern hospitality. Located on a true fishing lake: catch freshwater ling cod, kokanee, rainbow and lake trout. Over 50 full-service sites to accommodate the largest RV, with easy access, pull-through and a view of the water. Partial hookups, camping and firewood available. Fully equipped cabins with heat, electricity, water, linens and utensils. Hot showers, laundromat, playground, recreation centre, telephones. Boat and fishing equipment rental. Sheltered marina with boat launch, fuel and moorage. On Highway 35, 18 paved miles south of Burns Lake on Francois Lake. Pets welcome. May 15–Oct. 15. Phone/fax (604) 695-6321. Your hosts Chris and Sheila, Box 42, Burns Lake, BC V0J 1E0. Super Natural North by Northwest. [ADVERTISEMENT] ▲

Burns Lake

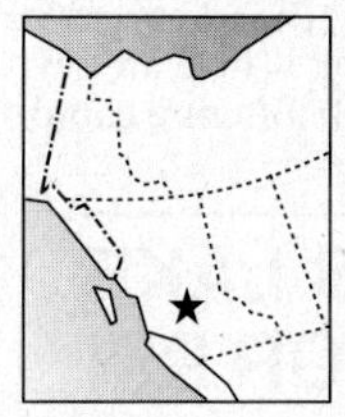

PG 141.3 (227.4 km) **PR 314.7** (506.4 km) **Population:** 2,300; area 10,000. **Visitor Information:** Government Travel Infocentre along Highway 16 on the west side of the village. The infocentre also houses a museum, art gallery and the chamber of commerce.

Elevation: 2,320 feet/707m. **Radio:** CFLD 730, CJFW-FM 92.9, CBC-FM 99.1.

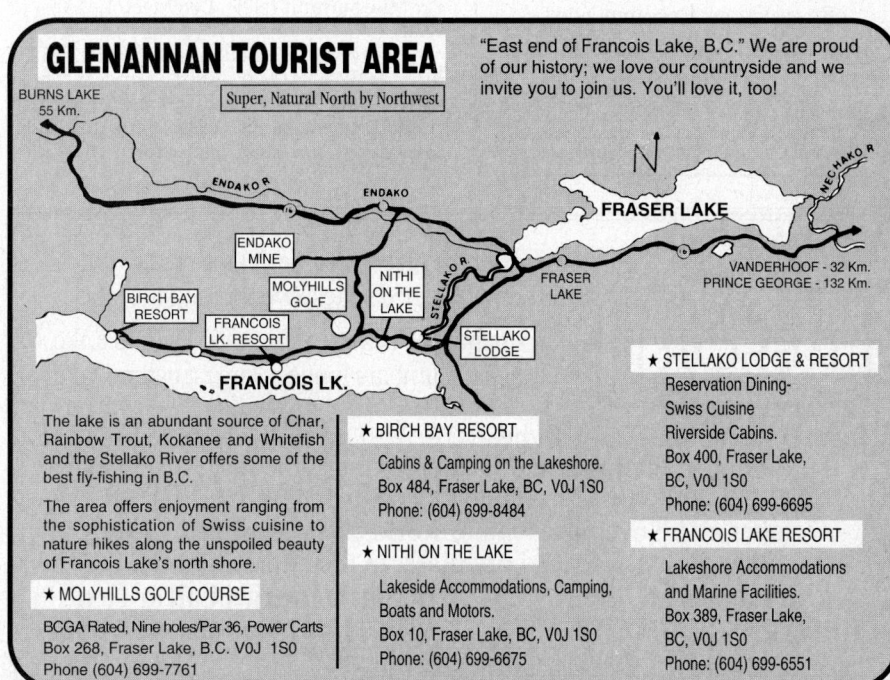

Transportation: Greyhound Bus, VIA Rail.

Burns Lake began about 1911 as a construction camp for the Grand Trunk Pacific Railway. Forestry is the economic mainstay of the area today, with ranching and tourism also important.

Located in the heart of the Lakes District, Burns Lake boasts "3,000 miles of fishing." Species include rainbow trout, char and salmon. Small family-owned fishing resorts offering lodging and camping are tucked along these lakes, offering quality vacation experiences.

Burns Lake is also the gateway to Tweedsmuir Provincial Park, 50 miles/80 km south. This huge wilderness park is accessible by boat, trail and air.

Rock hounds can visit Eagle Creek opal deposits, a short drive south of Burns Lake (not recommended for motorhomes).

There are 4 gas stations, a dump station on Railway Avenue, 5 hotels/motels, 4 bed and breakfasts, 12 restaurants, several gift shops—many of which feature local crafts and artists—and shopping malls.

The Burns Lake Municipal Park, located next to the civic centre, offers a pleasant setting for a picnic. On the north shore of the lake, the park has picnic tables and a small pier.

Travelers can also visit Nourse Creek Falls, take a self-guided forest tour or go hiking.

From Burns Lake, Highway 35 (paved) extends south 18 miles/29 km past **Tchesinkut Lake** to **Francois Lake** ferry landing. A free 36-car ferry departs from the south shore on the hour, from the north shore on the half-hour. From the south shore of Francois Lake, Highway 35 continues to **Takysie Lake** and **Ootsa Lake,** with access to a number of other fishing lakes. There are several resorts along Highway 35 offering camping and lodging. Gas stations, stores and food service are also available.

Burns Lake Motor Inn. See display ad this section.

Yellowhead Highway 16 Log

(continued)

PG 146 (235 km) **PR 310** (498.9 km) Side road leads north to **Babine Lake**, the longest natural lake in the province. One of British Columbia's most important salmon producing lakes, Babine Lake drains into the Skeena River. Excellent fishing for char and trout in summer. At Mile 15/24.1 km on this road is Ethel F. Wilson Provincial Park on **Pinkut Lake**; 10 campsites, fishing, swimming, drinking water, toilets, firewood, picnic tables, boat launch. Tours of nearby Pinkut Fish Hatchery available. Look for pictographs on cliffs across from hatchery. Pendleton Bay Provincial Park on Babine Lake, open May to October, offers 20 campsites, picnic tables, fishing, swimming and boat launch. Resorts with cabins and camping on Babine Lake.

PG 150 (241.4 km) **PR 306** (492.4 km) Small community of **DECKER LAKE.**

Decker Lake, good char and trout fishing; fly-fishing in **Endako River,** which joins Decker and Burns lakes.

PG 153.3 (246.7 km) **PR 302.7** (487.1 km) Palling rest area with picnic tables, toilets and litter barrels.

PG 157.1 (252.8 km) **PR 298.9** (481 km) Baker Lake airstrip to south is used by firefighting tankers. Weather station.

PG 160.2 (257.8 km) **PR 295.8** (476 km) Rose Lake to south.

PG 165.2 (265.9 km) **PR 290.8** (468 km) **Broman Lake,** rainbow and char to 4 lbs., use white-winged flies, spring and summer.

PG 169.1 (272.1 km) **PR 286.9** (461.7 km) Six Mile Summit (elev. 4,669 feet/1,423m) to west.

PG 175.5 (282.4 km) **PR 280.5** (451.4 km) **TOPLEY** (pop. 300). Grocery, post office, cafe, motel and gas station. Turn north here for Babine Lake Recreation Area. This paved side road leads north to Topley Landing and Granisle on Babine Lake (descriptions follow). From its junction with the highway at Topley, mileages are as follows: Mile 23.6/38 km, private lodge; Mile 24.4/39.3 km, turnoff to village of Topley Landing; Mile 28.8/46.3 km, Fulton River spawning channel; Mile 28/45.1 km, Red Bluff Provincial Park with 43 campsites, picnicking and day-use facilities, boat launch, drinking water, toilets, firewood, swimming, fishing and hiking; Mile 31.4/50.5 km, Granisle; Mile 33.4/53.8 km, begin 16-mile/25.7-km gravel road to Smithers Landing Road, which connects Smithers Landing and Smithers. *CAUTION: Watch for moose along road.*

TOPLEY LANDING has several resorts and an unmaintained provincial park. The government-operated Fulton River spawning channel has 2 major spawning channels on the river that connect Fulton Lake and Babine Lake. **Babine Lake,** which flows into the Skeena River, is one of the largest fresh-water habitats for sockeye salmon. The salmon enhancement project at Fulton River produces about 95 million sockeye fry annually. The sockeye run takes place in August and September. Tours may be available at hatchery office.

GRANISLE (pop. 600) was established in 1965 as a company town for the Granisle Copper Mine. In 1972, Noranda Bell Mines Copper Division went into operation. Granisle Copper was closed in 1982 and the Noranda mine was closed in 1992. Granisle has become a retirement community and remains a resort area for fishing, boating, waterskiing and camping on Babine Lake. Facilities at Granisle include a convenience store, liquor outlet and hotel. Dump station, showers, laundromat and fresh water available at the Travel Infocentre.

Grand Isles Resort. See display ad this section.

Babine Lake, rainbow 6 to 8 lbs.; lake trout to 40 lbs., use spoons, flashers and red-and-white spoons, May through Nov. When fishing early in the year, use a short troll.

PG 175.8 (282.9 km) **PR 280.2** (450.9 km) Rest area to south with view of coastal mountains.

PG 193.9 (312 km) **PR 262.1** (421.8 km) **Shady Rest RV Park.** See display ad this section.

Houston

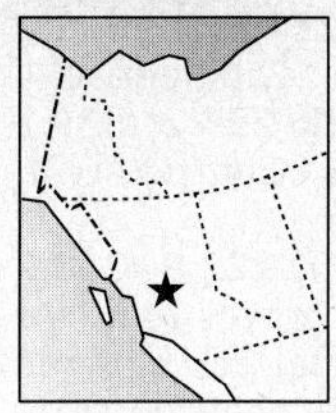

PG 194.3 (312.7 km) **PR 261.7** (421.2 km) **Population:** 3,960. **Emergency Services: Police,** phone (604) 845-2204. **Ambulance,** phone 112-562-7241. **Visitor Information:** Travel Infocentre in log building on Highway 16 across from the mall; open year-round. Write Houston Travel Infocentre, Box 396, Houston, BC V0J 1Z0, or phone (604) 845-7640.

Elevation: 1,949 feet/594m. **Radio:** CFBV 1450, CFPR-FM 102.1, CJFW-FM 105.5. **Transportation:** Greyhound bus, VIA Rail.

Established in the early 1900s, Houston was a tie-cutting centre during construction of the Grand Trunk Pacific Railway in 1912. It was named for Prince Rupert newspaperman John Houston, the former mayor of Nelson, BC. Logging continued to support the local economy with the rapid growth of mills and planer mills in the 1940s and 1950s. Houston was incorporated as a village in 1957.

The Equity Silver Mine began production in 1980. Production ceased in January 1994 and equipment was dismantled.

Today, the main industry in Houston is forest products. The 2 large sawmills here, Houston Forest Products and Northwood Pulp and Timber, offer forestry-awareness tours. The chamber of commerce and Travel Infocentre arrange tours of the sawmills and also offer a day-long tour through the area's forests to provide a first-hand look at the forest industry.

Hunting, canoeing, cross-country skiing and especially sportfishing are major attractions here with the Bulkley River, nearby Morice River and several lakes. Look for the World's Largest Fly Fishing Rod on display at the Travel Infocentre. The 60-foot-long anodized aluminum fly rod was designed by a local avid fly fisherman and built by local volunteers. (The 21-inch fly is a fluorescent "Skykomish Sunrise.")

Houston has all visitor facilities, including motels, campgrounds, restaurants, gas stations, a shopping centre and golf courses. ▲

Yellowhead Highway 16 Log

(continued)

PG 197.4 (317.7 km) **PR 258.6** (416.2 km) **Junction** with the Morice River access road which extends 52 miles/84 km south to Morice Lake. Approximately 20 miles/32 km along the Morice River Road you can turn east on a gravel road which leads past Owen Lake and Nadina River Road to Francois Lake. From Francois Lake ferry landing Highway 35 leads north to Burns Lake.

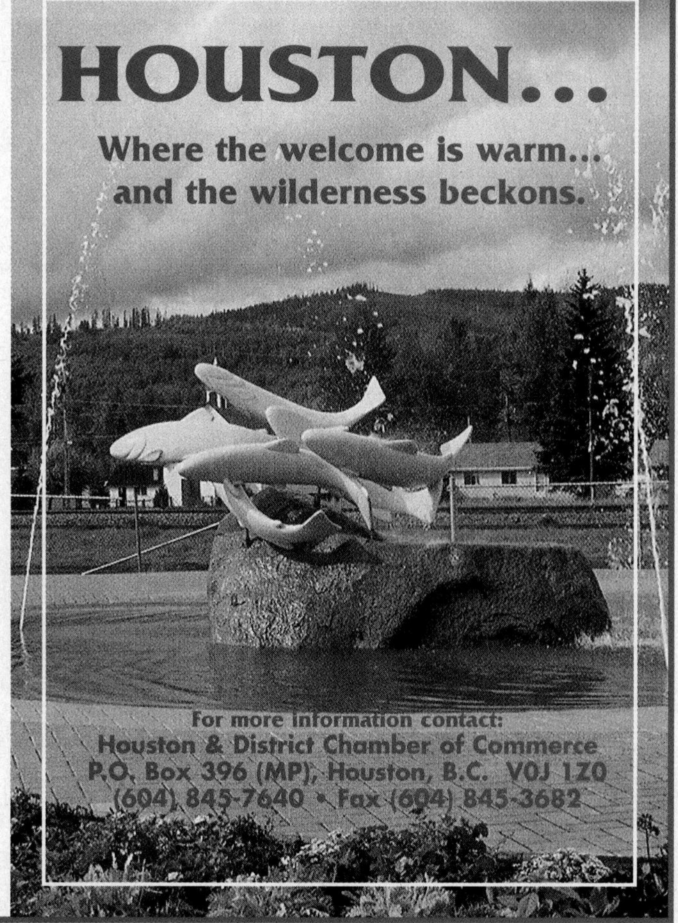

The 2 famous salmon and steelhead streams, **Morice** and **Bulkley**, unite near Houston and it is possible to fish scores of pools all along the Morice River. *NOTE: Special requirements apply to fishing these streams; check with Fish and Game office.*

PG 198.5 (319.4 km) **PR 257.5** (414.4 km) Bulkley River bridge; picnic spot with tables, litter barrel and toilets.

PG 202.5 (325.9 km) **PR 253.5** (408 km) View of Morice River valley eastbound. Westbound travelers are in the Bulkley River valley.

PG 205.3 (330.4 km) **PR 250.7** (403.5 km) Hungry Hill Summit (elev. 2,769 feet/844m). To the north are the snow-capped peaks of the Babine Mountains, to the west is the Hudson Bay Range.

PG 222.8 (358.6 km) **PR 233.2** (375.3 km) Bulkley View paved rest area with picnic tables, toilets and litter barrels.

PG 225.6 (363.1 km) **PR 230.4** (370.8 km) **Ft. Telkwa R.V. Park.** See display ad this section. ▲

PG 226 (363.7 km) **PR 230** (370.1 km) **TELKWA** (pop. 959). A pleasant village at the confluence of the Telkwa and Bulkley rivers (you can fish from Riverside Street or the riverbanks). Travel Infocentre at the village office and museum. Facilities include a grocery, post office and a gas station with auto repair. Lodging at Douglas Motel, dining at 3 restaurants. A unique shop found here is Horsfield Leather, which specializes in handmade fishing rod cases, leather water bottles and other leather goods. Fishing and hunting information, licenses and supplies available at the general store. Kinsmen Barbecue is held over Labour Day weekend; games, contests and demolition derby. Eddy Park, on the western edge of town beside the Bulkley River, is a good spot for picnicking (look for the wishing well). St. Stephen's Anglican Church was built in 1911 and the bell and English gate added in 1921. Other Heritage Bldgs. date back to 1908.

Douglas Motel beside beautiful Bulkley River. Riverview units, suites, log cabin with fireplace in relaxing resort atmosphere. Hot pool, sauna complex, kitchens, cablevision, queen beds, electric heat, summer ceiling fans, picnic area, firepit, barbecues, horseshoe pitch, summer outdoor sports equipment. Salmon and steelhead fishing. Walking distance to stores, restaurants and lake. VISA and MasterCard. Douglas Family, (604) 846-5679. [ADVERTISEMENT]

Carved alpenhorn player in downtown Smithers. *(Wes Bergen, Diarama)*

PG 226.5 (364.5 km) **PR 229.5** (369.3 km) Turnoff to north for **Tyhee Lake** Provincial Park; 55 campsites, 20 picnic tables, dump station, hiking trails, fishing, swimming, boat launch. Seaplane base at lake; charter fly-in fishing. ▲

Also turnoff here on the Telkwa High Road, which intersects with Babine Lake access road (gravel), which leads 46 miles/74 km north to Smithers Landing on Babine Lake and 56 miles/90 km to Granisle.

Tyhee Lake, rainbow and lake trout to 2 lbs., June through August; Kamloops trout to 2 lbs. **Babine River**, steelhead to 40 lbs., late fall. **Telkwa River**, spring and coho salmon to 24 lbs., summer to fall.

PG 231.5 (372.6 km) **PR 224.5** (361.3 km) Second turnoff westbound for Babine Lake.

PG 232.8 (374.6 km) **PR 223.2** (359.2 km) Riverside Recreation Centre; golf, restaurant and campground. ▲

PG 233.1 (375.1 km) **PR 222.9** (358.7 km) Turnoff to north on gravel road for Driftwood Canyon Provincial Park; picnic area and toilets. Fossil beds in shale outcroppings along creekbank. This gravel side road continues north to Smithers Landing.

PG 233.7 (376.1 km) **PR 222.3** (357.7 km) Bridge over Bulkley River.

Smithers

PG 235.4 (378.8 km) **PR 220.6** (355 km). **Population:** 5,000; area 30,000. **Emergency Services: Police,** phone (604) 847-3233. **Hospital** and **Poison Centre,** 3950 8th Ave., phone (604) 847-2611. **Ambulance,** phone 1-562-7241. **Visitor Information:** Travel Infocentre at the intersection of Highway 16 and Main Street, east side of highway, in the railcar adjacent to the museum; open daily June through Aug. The chamber of commerce, located above the museum in the Central Park Building, provides information year-round.

Elevation: 1,621 feet/494m. **Climate:** Relatively warmer and drier than mountainous areas to the west, average temperature in July is 58°F/14°C, in January 14°F/-10°C; annual precipitation, 13 inches. **Radio:** CFBV 1230, CFPR-FM 97.5. **Television:** Channels 5, 13 and cable. **Newspaper:** *Interior News* (weekly).

Transportation: Air—Scheduled service to Vancouver and Terrace via Canadian Airlines International. Daily flights to Prince George, Terrace and Burns Lake via Central Mountain Air. **Railroad**—VIA Rail. **Bus**—Greyhound. **Car Rentals**—Available.

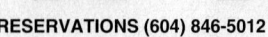

Sitting amidst rugged mountains, the alpine flavour of the town has been enhanced by Swiss-style storefronts that have been added to many of the buildings. Reconstructed in 1979, Main Street offers many shops and restaurants. Incorporated as a village in 1921, Smithers officially became a town in Canada's centennial year, 1967. The original site was chosen in 1913 by construction crews working on the Grand Trunk Pacific Railway (the town was named for one-time chairman of the railway A.W. Smithers). Today it is a distribution and supply centre for farms, mills and mines in the area.

Smithers is the largest town in the Bulkley Valley and the site of Hudson Bay Mountain, a popular ski area (skiing from November to mid-April).

ACCOMMODATIONS/VISITOR SERVICES

Smithers has several motels, gas stations, restaurants and good shopping. Government liquor store located on Queen Street at Broadway Avenue. There are 2 18-hole golf courses, both with rentals and clubhouses.

There is a municipal campground with security and firewood (no hookups) at Riverside Park on the Bulkley River; turn north at the museum across from Main Street and drive up the hill about a mile and watch for sign. There are private campgrounds located east and west of town; see highway log. A dump station is located beside the railcar Infocentre on the corner of Highway 16 and Main Street. ▲

ATTRACTIONS

The Art Gallery and Museum, in the Central Park Bldg. at the corner of Main Street and Highway 16, displays both local and traveling art shows in addition to artifacts from the early days of the Bulkley Valley.

Bulkley Valley Fall Fair is held on the last weekend in August each year, and is one of the largest agricultural exhibitions in the province.

The Midsummer Music Festival, June 23-25, 1996, features local, regional and national artists.

Area Attractions. Smithers offers a number of scenic drives. Hudson Bay Mountain (elev. 8,700 feet/2,652m) is a 14-mile/23-km drive from Highway 16; the plateau above timberline at the ski area is a good spot for summer hikes. In the winter months, Smithers boasts one of the largest ski hills in northern British Columbia. A 6,000-foot/1,829-m triple chair and 2 T-bars climb the 1,750-foot/533-m vertical, offering skiers 18 different runs.

Fossil hunters should drive to Driftwood Canyon Provincial Park; turn off Highway 16 just east of the Bulkley River bridge (travelers are advised to stop first at the visitor information centre in town for a map and directions). A display at the park illustrates the fossils, such as metasequoia, a type of redwood which occurs in the shale formation.

Adams Igloo Wildlife Museum, just west of town on Highway 16, has an excellent display of mammals found in British Columbia.

A beautiful spot not to be missed is Twin Falls and Glacier Gulch. Take the 4-mile-/6.4-km-long gravel road (steep in places) from Highway 16 on the western edge of town.

A 2.2-mile-/3.5-km-long interpretive nature trail with native wildlife and plant species is 10 miles/16 km west of Smithers on the Hudson Bay Mountain Ski Hill road in Smithers Community Forest. This trail can also be used in winter for cross-country skiing, and connects to other cross-country ski trails. Detailed maps of the area showing all hiking trails are available at the information centre.

Fishing: An extensive list of lake and river fishing spots in the area, with information on boat launches and boat rentals, is available from the Smithers District Chamber of Commerce, Box 2379, Smithers, BC V0J 2N0; phone (604) 847-9854; or ask at the Travel Infocentre.

Hunting: Moose, mule deer, grizzly and

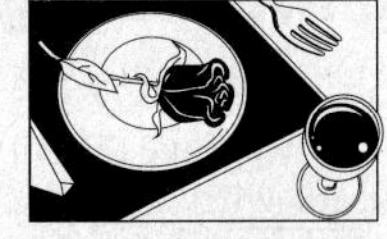

This region's mining and logging history are recalled at New Hazelton visitor centre. (© Carmen Scott)

black bears, mountain goats and caribou are found in the area, and guides and outfitters are available locally. All species of grouse can be hunted in the Bulkley Valley during the fall. Information is available from the Fish and Wildlife Branch office in Smithers.

Yellowhead Highway 16 Log

(continued)

PG 237.8 (382.7 km) **PR 218.2** (351.1 km) Paved access road to Lake Kathlyn. There is a municipal park with small beach and boat launch located here. Powerboats not permitted. Closed to waterfowl hunting. Side road continues 4 miles/6.4 km (gravel) to Twin Falls and Glacier Gulch.

PG 238.9 (384.5 km) **PR 217.1** (349.4 km) Road to north leads to Smithers airport.

PG 241.2 (388.2 km) **PR 214.8** (345.7 km) **Glacier View RV Park.** Wake up to panoramic views of the Kathlyn Glacier and Hudson Bay Mountain. Reasonably priced level sites for self-contained units. 40- and 60-foot pull-throughs with picnic tables. Toilets. Water tap for guest use. Reservations: R.R. 1 S9 C31, Smithers, BC VOJ 2NO, or call (604) 847-3961. [ADVERTISEMENT] ▲

PG 241.4 (388.5 km) **PR 214.6** (345.4 km) **Adams Igloo Wildlife Museum.** The finest collection of big game animals, furbearers and birds native to British Columbia. Mounted life-size and displayed in their natural habitat. The inside mural, painted by leading wildlife artist Tom Sander, gives a 3-dimensional impression for realism. Stop at the White Dome, 6 miles west of Smithers beside one of the highway's most beautiful viewpoints. Fur rugs and souvenirs for sale. Ted Moon, Curator. Super, Natural North by Northwest. [ADVERTISEMENT]

PG 241.5 (388.6 km) **PR 214.5** (345.2 km) Hudson Bay rest area to west with picnic tables, toilets and litter barrels. Beautiful view of Hudson Bay Mountain.

PG 249.5 (401.5 km) **PR 206.5** (332.3 km) Trout Creek bridge. Store with groceries, post office and phone; fishing licenses available.

PG 255.5 (411.2 km) **PR 200.5** (322.7 km) Turnout to north with picnic tables and view of Bulkley River and Moricetown Canyon; good photo stop.

PG 255.7 (411.5 km) **PR 200.3** (322.3 km) Short side road on the north side of the highway leads to Moricetown Canyon and Falls on the Bulkley River and Moricetown campground. For centuries a famous Indian fishing spot, Indians may still be seen here gaffing, jigging and netting salmon in July and August. A worthwhile stop. ▲

PG 257.9 (415 km) **PR 198.1** (318.8 km) **MORICETOWN** (pop. 680; elev. 1,341 feet/409m). **Radio:** CBC-FM 96.5. Moricetown has a gas station with minor repair service and diesel fuel. There is a handicraft store. A campground is located in Moricetown Canyon (turnoff at **Milepost PG 255.7**). Moricetown is an Indian reserve and village, the oldest settlement in the Bulkley Valley. Traditionally, the Native people (Wet'su-wet'en) took advantage of the narrow canyon to trap salmon. The centuries-old Indian settlement ('Kyah Wiget) is now named after Father A.G. Morice, a Roman Catholic missionary. Born in France, Father Morice came to British Columbia in 1880 and worked with the Indians of northern British Columbia from 1885 to 1904. He achieved world recognition for his writings in anthropology, ethnology and history.

PG 271.5 (436.9 km) **PR 184.5** (296.9 km) Turnoff to north for Forest Service campsite (7.5 miles/12.1 km) with pit toilets, tables and litter barrels. Fishing in **Suskwa River;** coho salmon to 10 lbs., use tee-spinners in July; steelhead to 20 lbs., use Kitamat #32 and soft bobbers in late fall. ▲

PG 276.5 (445 km) **PR 179.5** (288.9 km) Turnoff to north for Ross Lake Provincial Park; 25 picnic sites, boat launch (no powerboats), swimming. Fishing at **Ross Lake** for rainbow to 4 lbs.

PG 278.5 (448.2 km) **PR 177.5** (285.7 km) Turnout with litter barrel and Hazelton area map.

PG 278.8 (448.7 km) **PR 177.2** (285.2 km) Entering New Hazelton, the first of 3 communities westbound sharing the name Hazelton; the others are Hazelton and South Hazelton.

New Hazelton

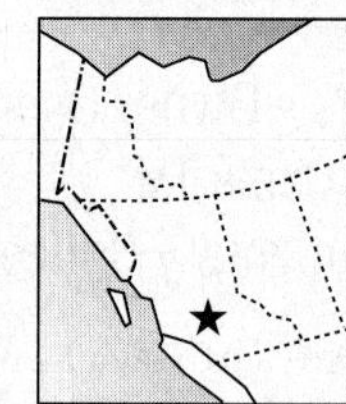

PG 279 (449 km) **PR 177** (284.8 km) **Junction** of Highway 16 and Highway 62 to Hazelton, 'Ksan and Kispiox. **Population:** area 1,300. **Emergency Services: Police,** phone (604) 842-5244. **Visitor Information:** Travel Infocentre in 2-story log building at the junction. Look for the 3 statues representing the gold rush packer Cataline, the Northwest miner, and the Upper Skeena logger. Museum located in Infocentre.

Elevation: 1,150 feet/351m. **Radio:** CBC 1170. **Transportation:** VIA Rail. Greyhound bus.

This small highway community has gas stations, major auto repair, restaurants, cafes, post office, general store, a hotel and a motel. Laundromat, propane, sporting goods, and hunting and fishing licenses available in town. Mount Rocher Deboule, elev. 8,000 feet/2,438m, towers behind the town.

Attractions here include historic Hazelton, the Indian village of 'Ksan and sportfishing the Bulkley and Kispiox rivers. Descriptions follow.

HAZELTON. Situated at the confluence

of the Skeena and Bulkley rivers, Hazelton grew up at "The Forks" as a trans-shipping point at the head of navigation on the Skeena and a wintering place for miners and prospectors from the rigorous Interior. Thomas Hankin established a Hudson's Bay Co. trading post here in 1868. The name Hazelton comes from the numerous hazelnut bushes growing on the flats.

Cataline, famous pioneer packer and traveler, is buried near here. Jean Caux (his real name) was a Basque who, from 1852 to 1912, with loaded mules plodding 12 miles/19 km a day, supplied mining and construction camps from Yale and Ashcroft northward through Hazelton, where he often wintered. His mule trails became roads; his exploits are legends.

For some years, before the arrival of railroad and highways, supplies for trading posts at Bear and Babine lakes and the Omineca goldfields moved by riverboat from the coast to Hazelton and from there over trails to the backcountry. Some of the Yukon gold rushers passed through Hazelton on their way to the Klondike, pack trains having made the trip from Hazelton to Telegraph Creek over the old Telegraph Trail as early as 1874.

This community has reconstructed much of what the town was like in the 1890s. Look for the antique machinery downtown. The history of the Hazelton area can be traced by car on the Hand of History tour. Pick up a brochure from the Travel Infocentre showing the location of the 19 historic sites on the driving tour.

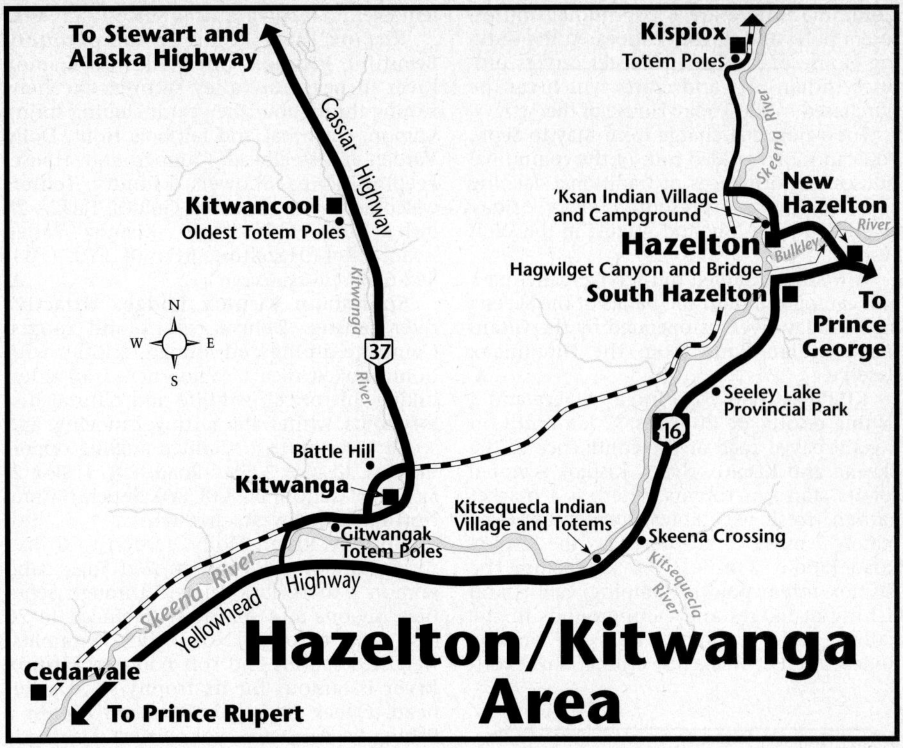

'KSAN INDIAN VILLAGE Museum, a replica Gitksan Indian village, is 4.5 miles/7.2 km from Highway 16. It was constructed at the junction of the Bulkley and Skeena rivers by the 'Ksan Assoc. with the assistance of the governments of Canada and British

Hazelton/Kitwanga Area

To Stewart and Alaska Highway
Cassiar Highway
Kitwancool
Oldest Totem Poles
Kitwanga River
37
Battle Hill
Kitwanga
Gitwangak Totem Poles
Skeena River
Yellowhead Highway
Cedarvale
To Prince Rupert
Kispiox
Totem Poles
Skeena River
'Ksan Indian Village and Campground
New Hazelton
Hazelton
Bulkley River
Hagwilget Canyon and Bridge
South Hazelton
To Prince George
Seeley Lake Provincial Park
16
Kitsequecla Indian Village and Totems
Skeena Crossing
Kitsequecla River

Columbia. There are 6 communal houses, totem poles and dugout canoes. At the Carving House of All Times, master carvers produce Indian arts and crafts which can be purchased in the Today House of the Arts.

For a nominal charge from May to Sept., you can join a guided tour of the communal houses. Performances of traditional dancing and singing are presented every Friday evening during July and August in the Wolf House.

A well-maintained full-service trailer park and campground on the banks of the Skeena and Bulkley rivers is operated by the Gitanmaax Indian Band from the Gitanmaax Reserve. ▲

KISPIOX (pop. 825) Indian village and 3 fishing resorts are 20 miles/32 km north on a good paved road at the confluence of the Skeena and Kispiox rivers. Kispiox is noted for its stand of totems. There is a market garden (fresh vegetables) located approximately 7 miles/11 km north on the Kispiox Road (about 2 miles/ 3.2 km before the Kispiox totem poles). Camping, cabins and fishing at lodges and campgrounds in the valley. Valley residents host the Kispiox Rodeo the first weekend of June. This excellent event has run annually since 1952. ▲

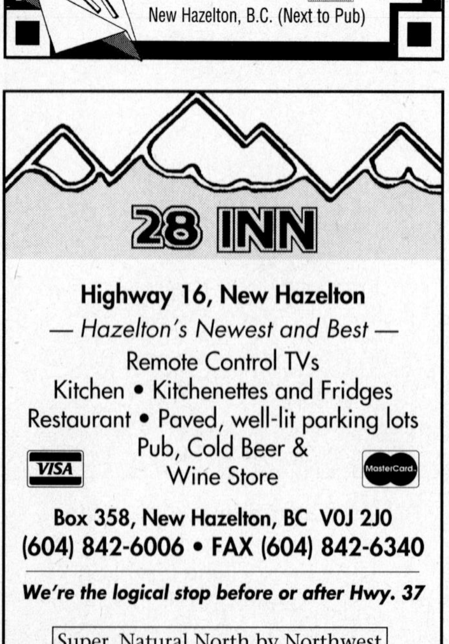

Kispiox River Resort & Campground. Beautiful location on banks of Kispiox River in peaceful valley setting. Excellent fishing throughout the year including spring salmon, cutthroat and rainbow trout, Dolly Varden and steelhead. Campground. Housekeeping cabins. Showers. Laundry. Tenters welcome. Fishing licenses. Guides. Tackle. 26 miles from Highway 16. Kispiox Valley Road. RR 1, Hazelton, BC V0J 1Y0. (604) 842-6182. [ADVERTISEMENT] ▲

Sportsman Kispiox Lodge. Attractive river setting. Deluxe cabins and rooms. Complete dining and lounge facilities with homecooked meals. Wilderness trail rides, hiking, historical, wildlife and natural history tours, whitewater rafting, canoeing, and scenic river tours. Unlimited angling opportunities. Kispiox Valley Road, R.R. 1, Box 2, Site M, Hazelton, BC V0J 1Y0. Super, Natural North by Northwest. [ADVERTISEMENT]

Bulkley River, Dolly Varden to 5 lbs.; spring salmon, mid-July to mid-Aug.; coho salmon 4 to 12 lbs., Aug. 15 through Sept., flies, spoons and spinners; steelhead to 20 lbs., July through Nov., flies, Kitamats, weighted spoons and soft bobbers. **Kispiox River** is famous for its trophy-sized steelhead. Check on regulations and obtain a fishing license before your arrival. Fishing is done with single-hook only, with catch-release for steelhead between Aug. 15 and Sept. 30. Season is July 1 to Nov. 30 for salmon, trout and steelhead. Excellent fly-fishing waters: spring salmon, July to early Aug.; coho salmon, late Aug. to early Sept.; steelhead from Sept. until freezeup. Sizable Dolly Vardens and cutthroat. Steelhead average 20 lbs., with some catches over 30 lbs.

Yellowhead Highway 16 Log

(continued)

PG 281.4 (452.9 km) **PR 174.6** (281 km) Turnoff to north for 2-mile/3.2-km loop road through small community of **SOUTH HAZELTON**; restaurant, general store, gas station with minor repair, lodging.

PG 285 (458.7 km) **PR 171** (275.2 km) **Seeley Lake** Provincial Park; 20 campsites, drinking water, toilets, firewood, sani-dump, day-use area with picnic tables, swimming, fishing. ▲

PG 294.7 (474.3 km) **PR 161.3** (259.6 km) Skeena Crossing. Historic Canadian National Railways bridge (see plaque at Kitseguecla).

PG 295.9 (476.2 km) **PR 160.1** (257.6 km) **KITSEGUECLA,** Indian village. Totem poles throughout village are classic examples, still in original locations. Historical plaque about Skeena Crossing.

PG 306.6 (493.4 km) **PR 149.4** (240.4 km) Gas station and cafe at **junction** with Cassiar Highway (BC Highway 37). Bridge across Skeena River to Kitwanga and Cassiar Highway to Stewart, Hyder, AK, and Alaska Highway. This is the principal access to the Cassiar Highway. Alternate access via Nass Road at **Milepost PG 369.3.** See CASSIAR HIGHWAY section.

Highway passes Seven Sisters peaks; the highest is 9,140 feet/2,786m.

PG 309.5 (498.1 km) **PR 146.5** (235.8 km) **Gitksan Paintbrush Native Arts & Crafts.** Silver and gold jewelry: rings, earrings, bracelets. Limited edition prints and originals. Smoked moosehide moccasins, beaded leatherwork. Wood carvings, cedar baskets. Clothing and souvenirs. Quality merchandise, most from local artists. Excellent prices. Easy access. Summer hours 9 A.M.–7 P.M. P.O. Box 97, Kitwanga, BC V0J 2A0. Phone or fax (604) 849-5085. [ADVERTISEMENT]

PG 309.8 (498.6 km) **PR 146.2** (235.3 km) **Seven Sisters RV Park and Campground.** Outstanding value. Beautiful park-like setting. Many treed sites. Fresh water, sani-dump, picnic tables at every site, flush toilets, shower, firepits with free firewood, all for $8. Excellent salmon fishing close by. Tenters and cyclists welcome. (604) 849-5489 for reservations. Box 338, Kitwanga, BC V0J 2A0. [ADVERTISEMENT] ▲

PG 312.4 (502.7 km) **PR 143.6** (231.1 km) Boulder Creek rest area; parking for large vehicles; toilets, litter barrels and picnic tables.

PG 316.5 (509.3 km) **PR 139.5** (224.5 km) Gravel turnout to north with litter barrel.

PG 318.2 (512.1 km) **PR 137.8** (221.8 km) **CEDARVALE,** cafe. Loop road through rural setting. Historical plaque about Holy City.

Cedarvale Café. Specializing in quality food and friendly, efficient service. Delicious daily specials. Relaxing atmosphere, camping spots and picnic tables. Children's playground with volleyball net and basketball. Summer hours: Monday–Friday 7 A.M.–10 P.M., Saturday and Sunday 10 A.M.–8 P.M. Winters hours: Monday–Friday 9 A.M.–9 P.M., Saturday and Sunday 10 A.M.–8 P.M. (604) 849-5539. [ADVERTISEMENT]

PG 322.9 (519.6 km) **PR 133.1** (214.2 km) Gravel turnout to north on Skeena River.

PG 324.8 (522.7 km) **PR 131.2** (211.1 km) Turnout with historical plaque about Skeena riverboats. Watch for bears fishing the river for salmon in late July and early August.

PG 329.3 (529.9 km) **PR 126.7** (203.9 km) Gravel turnout to north with litter barrel.

PG 335.8 (540.4 km) **PR 120.2** (193.4 km) Watch for fallen rock on this stretch of highway.

PG 345.2 (555.5 km) **PR 110.8** (178.3 km) Rest area on river with water pump, picnic tables, toilets and litter barrels. Historical plaque about Skeena River steamboats.

PG 345.5 (556 km) **PR 110.5** (177.8 km) Skeena Cellulose private bridge across Skeena River to access tree farms on north side.

PG 352.6 (567.4 km) **PR 103.4** (166.4 km) Tiny chapel to south serves small community of **USK;** the village is reached via the reaction ferry seen to north. The nondenominational chapel is a replica of the pioneer church that stood in Usk until 1936, when the Skeena River flooded, sweeping away the village and the church. The only item from the church to survive was the Bible, which was found floating atop a small pine table.

PG 354.9 (571.1 km) **PR 101.1** (162.7 km) Side road leads 0.5 mile/0.8 km south to **Kleanza Creek** Provincial Park; 21 campsites, 25 picnic sites, fishing, drinking water, toilets, firewood, wheelchair access. Short trail to remains from Cassiar Hydraulic Mining Co. gold-sluicing operations here (1911–14). ▲

PG 360.7 (580.5 km) **PR 95.3** (153.4 km) Gas and lodging. **Copper (Zymoetz) River,** can be fished from Highway 16 or follow local maps. Coho salmon to 10 lbs., use tee-spinners in July; steelhead to 20 lbs., check locally for season and restrictions.

PG 362.4 (583.2 km) **PR 93.6** (150.6 km) Turnout to north with tourist information sign and area map.

PG 365.1 (587.6 km) **PR 90.9** (146.3 km)

Highway 37 South Log

Distance is measured from the junction with Yellowhead Highway 16 (J).

J 0.9 (1.4 km) Krumm Road. Turn east for golf course.

J 3.1 (5 km) Terrace–Kitimat airport access road.

J 7.9 (12.7 km) Lakelse Lake Provincial Park parking area and trail to Gruchy's Beach.

J 8.7 (14 km) Lakelse Lake Provincial Park parking areas and picnic area; tables, toilets, showers, changehouses and beach. Park headquarters located here.

J 10.6 (17.1 km) Waterlily Bay; food, lodging, boat launch.

J 11.4 (18.3 km) Lakelse Lake Provincial Park Furlong Bay Campground and picnic area; 156 campsites, nature trail, swimming beach, flush toilets, dump station, boat launch, drinking water, wheelchair access, firewood and interpretive programs.

13.8 (22.2 km) Onion Lake hiking and ski trails to west.

J 20.6 (33.2 km) Access to Kitimat River.

J 27.4 (44.1 km) Kitimat Airpark landing strip for small planes.

J 34.8 (56 km) Hirsch Creek Park to west; picnic area, camping, fishing and hiking.

J 35 (56.3 km) Hirsch Creek bridge.

J 35.8 (57.6 km) Kitimat Travel Infocentre to east.

J 36.2 (58.3 km) Minette Bay Road leads east to MK Bay Marina.

J 36.6 (58.9 km) Viewpoint of Douglas Channel and city map. Picnic tables, garden.

Kitimat

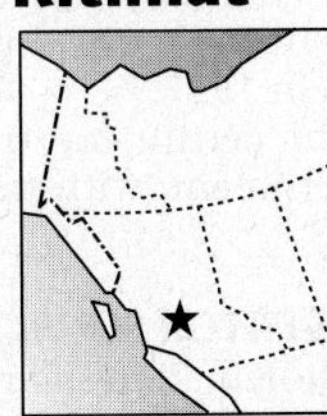

J 37.6 (60.5 km) Located at the head of Douglas Channel. **Population:** 12,000. **Emergency Services: RCMP,** phone (604) 632-7111. **Fire Department,** phone (604) 639-9111. **Ambulance,** phone (604) 632-5433. **Hospital,** phone (604) 632-2121. **Radio:** CKTK 1230; CBC-FM 101.1, CJFW-FM 103.1. **Newspaper:** *The News Advertiser* (weekly); *Northern Sentinel* (weekly).

This community was planned and built in the early 1950s when the B.C. government attracted Alcan (Aluminum Co. of Canada) to establish a smelter here. Today, Kitimat is a major port and home to several industries. Free tours are available (primarily in summer, reservations recommended) at Alcan, (604) 639-8259; Eurocan Pulp and Paper, (604) 632-6111; Methanex Corp., (604) 639-9292; and Kitimat fish hatchery, (604) 639-9616. Tour Mike's Wildlife Museum to see over 100 mounts; admission fee; (604) 632-7083.

Kitimat's location at the head of Douglas Channel makes it a popular boating, fishing and scuba diving destination. There are several charter operators.

Kitimat has all visitor facilities, including a modern shopping mall, restaurants and motels; library, theatre, swimming pool and gym; and an 18-hole golf course. Many scenic hiking trails are available. The Centennial Museum is located at city centre. For further information contact the Chamber of Commerce, Box 214 (M), Kitimat, BC V8C 2G7; phone 1-800-664-6554 or (604) 632-6294; fax (604) 632-4685.

There is camping at Radley Park in town; electrical hookups, showers, fishing, toilets, playground and dump station. (Radley Park—on the other side of the river—is also the site of a 165-foot/50-m Sitka spruce, largest of its kind in the province.) There is also camping at Hirsch Creek Park on the edge of town and private campgrounds.

Local fishermen line the banks of the **Kitimat River** in May for the steelhead run. Chinook salmon run in June and July. Coho run from Aug. into Sept.

Return to Milepost PG 365.1 Yellowhead Highway 16

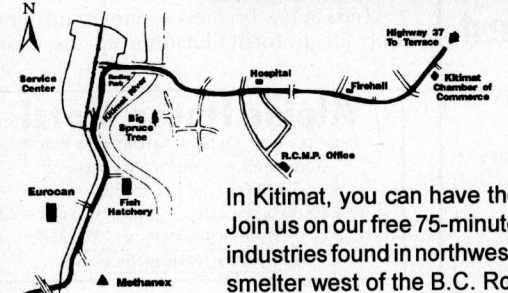

Four-way stop; east access to Terrace and **junction** with Highway 37 south to Kitimat. For access to downtown Terrace, turn north here and continue over 1-lane bridge. For west access to Terrace and continuation of Yellowhead Highway 16 westbound, go straight at intersection. Turn south for Kitimat (see log of HIGHWAY 37 SOUTH page 235).

PG 365.6 (588.4 km) **PR 90.4** (145.5 km) Bridge over Skeena River. Ferry Island municipal campground; 68 sites, some electrical hookups. Covered picnic shelters, barbecues, walking trails and a fishing bar are also available. ▲

Westbound, highway crosses railway overpass.

PG 366.2 (589.3 km) **PR 89.8** (144.5 km) Terrace Chamber of Commerce Travel Infocentre.

PG 366.3 (589.5 km) **PR 89.7** (144.4 km) Stoplight; west access to Terrace. Turn north at intersection for downtown (description of Terrace follows).

Continue through intersection on Highway 16 westbound for Prince Rupert, eastbound for Prince George.

CAUTION: No gas or services available between Terrace and Prince Rupert.

Original log buildings and artifacts are found at Terrace's Heritage Park.
(Fred Chapman, Diarama)

Terrace

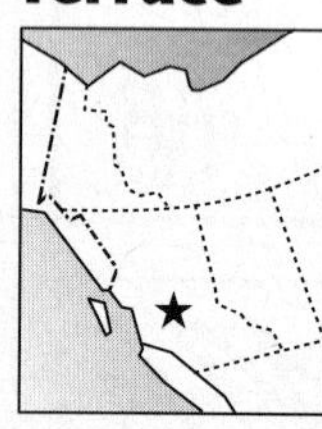

Located on the Skeena River. City centre is located north of Highway 16: Exit at overpass (**PG 366.3**) or at Highway 37 junction (**PG 365.1**). **Population:** 12,000; area 17,000. **Emergency Services:** Police, fire and ambulance located at intersection of Eby Street and Highway 16. **Police,** phone (604) 635-4911. **Fire Department,** phone (604) 638-8121. **Ambulance,** phone (604) 638-1102. **Hospital,** 2711 Tetrault St., phone (604) 635-2211.

Visitor Information: Travel Infocentre located in the chamber of commerce log building at **Milepost PG 366.2.** Open in summer daily, 9 A.M. to 8 P.M.; in winter, Monday through Friday, 9 A.M. to 5 P.M. Write Box 107, Terrace, BC V8G 4A2; phone (604) 635-2063. Information also available from Municipal Hall, #5-3215 Eby St.; open weekdays, phone (604) 635-6311.

Elevation: 220 feet/67m. **Climate:** Average summer temperature is 69°F/21°C; yearly rainfall 36 inches, snowfall 71.5 inches. **Radio:** CFTK 590; CFPR-FM 95.3, CJFW-FM 103.9. **Television:** 8 channels (cable). **Newspapers:** *Terrace Standard* (weekly).

Transportation: Air—Canadian Airlines International, Air BC and Central Mountain Air from Terrace-Kitimat airport on Highway 37 South. **Railroad**—VIA Rail, 4531 Railway Ave. **Bus**—Farwest Bus Lines and Greyhound. **Car Rentals**—Available.

Terrace has become an important service stop for motorists heading up the Cassiar Highway to the Alaska Highway. It is the last large retail-commercial centre for travelers until they reach the similar-sized community of Whitehorse, YT.

Tom Thornhill, the first white settler, found an Indian village just east of the present location of Terrace in 1892. When stern-wheelers were plying the Skeena, the first farmer in the area, George Little, gave land to the community that became a port of call and post office in 1905. Originally it was known as Little Town, and later was named Terrace because of the natural terraces cut by the river. The village site was laid out in 1910 and the Grand Trunk Pacific Railway reached Terrace in 1914. The municipality was incorporated in 1927.

Terrace is a regional centre for trade, entertainment and government, with ties to the forestry industry.

ACCOMMODATIONS/VISITOR SERVICES

There are 14 motels/hotels, 20 restaurants and 2 shopping centres. The government

TERRACE ADVERTISERS

liquor store is at 3250 Eby St. There are 4 laundromats. The community has a library and art gallery, indoor swimming pool, tennis courts and a golf course.

Public campgrounds are located at Ferry Island, turn off at Skeena River bridge (**Milepost PG 365.6**); Kleanza Creek, 10 miles/16.1 km east of Terrace; and Lakelse Lake, 11.7 miles/18.8 km south. There are 4 private campgrounds, 1 on the Skeena River, 1 at the east edge of the city (follow signs at junction of Highways 16 and 37), and 2 affiliated with motels on the west side of Terrace. Fisherman's Park on the east side of the Kalum River, at its junction with the Skeena, provides picnic facilities. ▲

ATTRACTIONS

Heritage Park is a collection of original log buildings from this region. Chosen to represent both the different aspects of pioneer life, as well as different log building techniques, the structures include a trapper's cabin, miner's cabin and lineman's cabin. The 9 structures also house artifacts from the period. Managed by the Terrace Regional Museum Society; guided tours available in summer, admission charged.

Lakelse Lake Provincial Park at Furlong Bay, 11.4 miles/18.3 km south of Highway 16 on Highway 37, offers 156 vehicle and tent campsites, day-use facilities, drinking water, flush and pit toilets, wheelchair access, firewood, dump station, boat launch, showers, sandy beaches, swimming, nature trails and interpretive programs. ♿▲

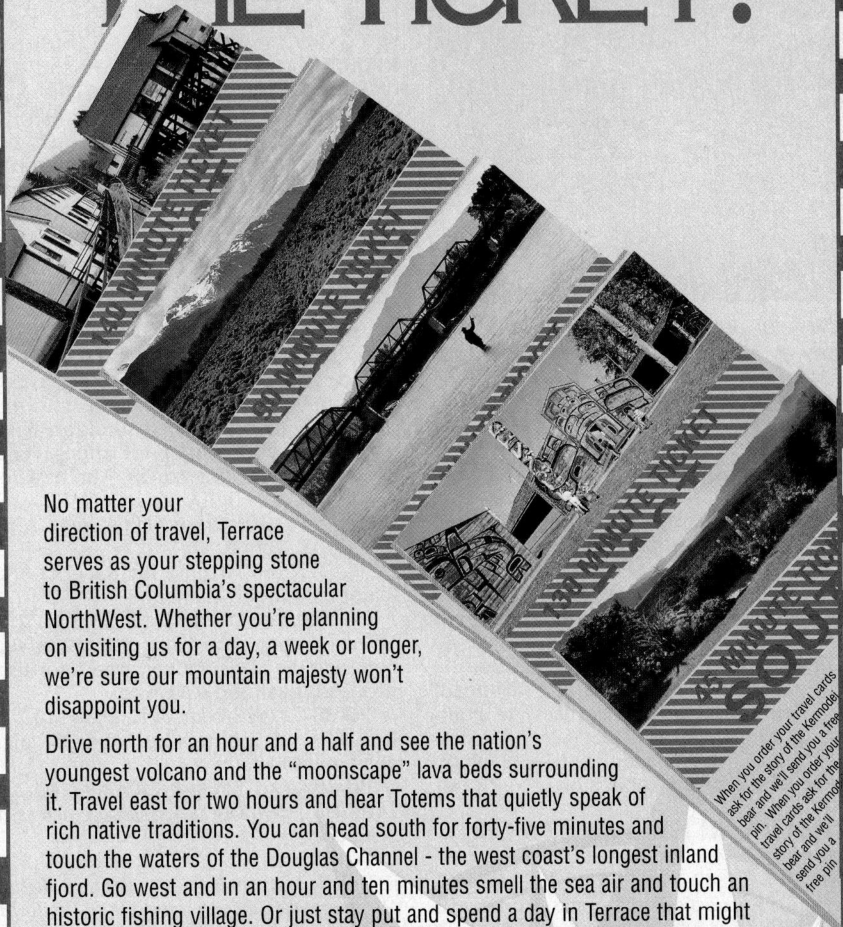

Hiking trails in the Terrace area range from easy to moderate. Terrace Mountain Nature Trail is a 3.2-mile/5.1-km uphill hike which offers good views of the area; it begins at Halliwell and Anderson streets. Check with the Travel Infocentre for details on other area trails.

Special events in Terrace include the Skeena Valley Fall Fair, Labour Day weekend; and River Boat Days, B.C. Day weekend.

Nisga'a Memorial Lava Bed Provincial Park. The lava beds are 42 miles/67 km north of Terrace via the Nisga'a Highway (see page 239). Limited picnic spots; no camping; interesting hikes. Canada's youngest volcano last erupted approximately 300 years ago, burying 2 Indian villages. The cooled lava makes the valley look

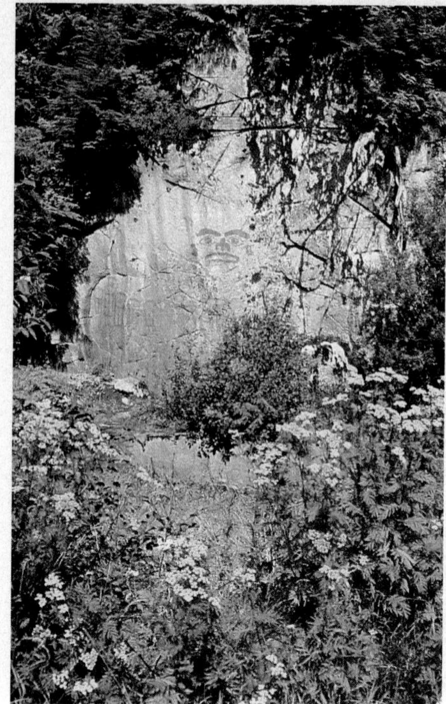

Watch for pictograph eastbound on highway near Milepost PG 435.
(Judy Parkin, staff)

like the surface of the moon.

Sportfishing. Fish on the banks of the province's second largest river, the **Skeena.** Terrace is ideally situated for sportfishing, with easy access to the **Copper, Kalum, Kitimat** and **Lakelse rivers.** Cutthroat, Dolly Varden and rainbow are found in all lakes and streams; salmon (king and coho) from May to late autumn. Kings average 40 to 70 lbs.; coho 14 to 20 lbs. Check locally for season and restrictions on steelhead. Information and fishing licenses are available from B.C. Government Access Centre, 3220 Eby St., Terrace (phone 604/638-3200), and at most sporting goods stores.

Yellowhead Highway 16 Log

(continued)

PG 366.3 (589.5 km) **PR 89.7** (144.4 km) Stoplight; west access to Terrace. Turn north at intersection for downtown. Continue through intersection eastbound for Prince George, westbound for Prince Rupert.

PG 366.5 (589.8 km) **PR 89.5** (144 km) **Junction** with Nisga'a Highway (Kalum Lake Road) to **NEW AIYANSH.** Nisga'a Highway is paved until the junction with Nass Road. Beyond here the highway is a gravel road used by logging trucks as an alternate to Cassiar Highway. (The paved portion of Nisga'a Highway is recommended over the Nass Road, which is a gravel logging road.) See NISGA'A HIGHWAY/NASS ROAD log opposite page.

PG 367.9 (592.1 km) **PR 88.1** (141.8 km) Access road to boat launch (fee charged) on the Kitsumkalum River downstream from Highway 16 bridge; RV parking.

Leaving Terrace, Highway 16 is in good condition westbound although the few straightaways are interrupted by some amazing 70-degree zigzags as the highway crosses the railroad tracks. The section of highway along the Skeena River is spectacular, with waterfalls cascading down the steep rock faces.

PG 369.3 (594.3 km) **PR 86.7** (139.5 km) **KITSUMKALUM.** Grocery store and House of Sim-oi-Ghets craft center. This Native enterprise on reserve land handles only authentic arts and crafts such as totem poles, leather goods and local carvings. This is also the **junction** with West Kalum Forest Service Road, which leads north 15 miles/24 km to Kitsumkalum Provincial Park with 20 campsites. This narrow gravel logging road joins the Nisga'a Highway, which turns into another forest service road, Nass Road, that joins the Cassiar Highway. (Nisga'a Highway, also known as Kalum Lake Road from Terrace, past the community college is paved to the junction with Nass Road.) ▲

Beyond the Nass Road junction Nisga'a Highway is a narrow gravel and pavement road used by logging trucks. The best route to the Cassiar Highway is from Kitwanga, **Milepost PG 306.6.** For details, see CASSIAR HIGHWAY section.

PG 373 (600.3 km) **PR 83** (133.6 km) Shames Mountain Ski Area.

PG 380.2 (611.9 km) **PR 75.8** (122 km) Paved turnout with litter barrels to south alongside the Skeena River; watch for fishermen during salmon season.

PG 387.2 (623.1 km) **PR 68.8** (110.7 km) Rest area on left westbound with picnic tables and toilets.

PG 393.1 (632.6 km) **PR 62.9** (101.2 km) *CAUTION! Highway turns sharply across railroad tracks.*

PG 395.2 (636 km) **PR 60.8** (97.8 km) *CAUTION: Carwash Rock overhangs highway. Water cascades down mountain and onto highway during heavy rains.*

PG 395.5 (636.5 km) **PR 60.5** (97.4 km) Sharp curves and falling rocks approximately next mile westbound.

PG 397.2 (639.2 km) **PR 58.8** (94.6 km) *CAUTION: Slow down for sharp curve and steep grade.*

PG 400.6 (644.7 km) **PR 55.4** (89.2 km) **Exchamsiks River** Provincial Park; 20 campsites and 20 picnic sites among old-growth Sitka spruce. Open May to Oct., camping fee, water and pit toilets. Good salmon fishing in Exchamsiks River. Access to Gitnadoix River canoeing area across Skeena River. ▲

PG 401.1 (645.5 km) **PR 54.9** (88.4 km) Very pleasant rest area north side of road at west end of bridge; boat launch on Exchamsiks River.

PG 402.4 (647.6 km) **PR 53.6** (86.3 km) Conspicuous example of Sitka spruce on north side of highway. Aboriginal people ate its inner bark fresh or dried in cakes, served with berries. As you travel west, the vegetation becomes increasingly influenced by the maritime climate.

PG 406 (653.4 km) **PR 50** (80.5 km) Kasiks River; boat launch.

PG 416.4 (670.1 km) **PR 39.6** (63.7 km) Kwinitsa River bridge and boat launch. No public moorage.

PG 421.1 (677.7 km) **PR 34.9** (56.2 km) Telegraph Point rest area to south on bank of Skeena River; paved turnout with outhouses, picnic tables, litter barrels and water pump. Watch for seals and sea lions in spring and during salmon season.

PG 427.8 (688.5 km) **PR 28.2** (45.4 km) Basalt Creek rest area to south with picnic tables.

PG 432.5 (696 km) **PR 23.5** (37.8 km) Turnout to south.

PG 435 (700 km) **PR 21** (33.8 km) Watch for pictograph, visible from the road for eastbound traffic only, possibly a boundary marker for Chief Legaic over 150 years ago. It was rediscovered in the early 1950s by Dan Lippett of Prince Rupert.

PG 435.5 (700.9 km) **PR 20.5** (33 km) Scenic viewpoint to south with litter barrels and historical plaque about Skeena River. Highway leaves Skeena River westbound. Abandoned townsite of Port Essington visible on opposite side of river.

PG 440.5 (708.9 km) **PR 15.5** (24.9 km) Rainbow Summit, elev. 528 feet/161m.

PG 442.8 (712.6 km) **PR 13.2** (21.2 km) Side road south to Rainbow Lake Reservoir; boat launch. The reservoir water is used by the pulp mill on Watson Island.

PG 445.4 (716.8 km) **PR 10.6** (17.1 km) **Prudhomme Lake** Provincial Park; 24 campsites, well water, toilets, firewood, fishing, camping fee. ▲

PG 446.3 (718.2 km) **PR 9.7** (15.6 km) Turnoff for Diana Lake Provincial Park, 1.5 miles/2.4 km south via single-lane gravel road (use turnouts). Day-use facility. Very pleasant grassy picnic area on lakeshore with 50 picnic tables, kitchen shelter, firewood, grills, wheelchair access, outhouses, water pump and garbage cans. Parking for 229 vehicles. The only freshwater swimming beach in the Prince Rupert area. Fish viewing at Diana Creek on the way into the lake; 2 hiking trails.

PG 451.2 (726.1 km) **PR 4.8** (7.7 km) **Junction.** Turnoff for **PORT EDWARD,** pulp mill and historic cannery. The North Pacific Cannery Village and Fishing Museum at Port Edward is open daily in summer. Built in 1889, this is the oldest cannery village on the north coast. Phone (604) 628-3538 for more information.

North Pacific Cannery Village Museum. See display ad this section.

PG 451.3 (726.3 km) **PR 4.7** (7.6 km) Galloway Rapids. Bridge crossing to Prince Rupert, on Kaien Island.

PG 451.5 (726.6 km) **PR 4.5** (7.2 km)

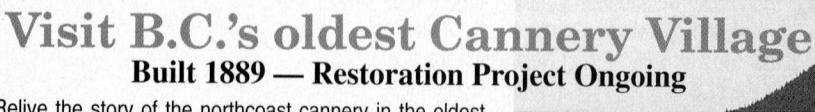

Nisga'a Highway/Nass Road Log

The Nisga'a Highway/Nass Forest Service Road junctions with Yellowhead Highway 16 west of Terrace at **Milepost PG 366.5** and travels north to the join the Cassiar Highway at **Milepost J 44.9**. Total driving distance is 98.6 miles/158.7 km and the first 39.2 miles/63.2 km are paved; the remainder is gravel. Services along this route are limited. Grading on the gravel sections often turns up sharp rocks, especially in the lava sections, and travelers are advised to carry a spare tire. Portions of the road are narrow and winding and there are many 1-lane bridges. Fuel is available at New Aiyansh, which is the major settlement on this route. Limited campsites are available.

The Nisga'a Highway is named after the people of the First Nations, who have for centuries lived in the villages in the Nass River Valley. Villages include New Aiyansh, which is on this route, Greenville, Gitwinksihlkw (formerly Canyon City) and Kincolith. (There is currently no road access to Kincolith, but a 16 mile/26 km road-building project is underway which will provide a link).

The most prominent feature of this route is the Nisga'a Memorial Lava Bed Park with the Tseax Lava Flow. The park commemorates the destruction of 2 Nisga'a villages and the deaths of more than 2,000 people in an eruption which took place approximately 300 years ago. The eruption also dammed the valley to form Lava Lake. The park is co-managed by BC Parks and the local Nisga'a Tribal Council.

There is active logging in the area and travelers share the route with logging and local traffic. Motorists are advised to exercise caution and drive with headlights on. Between New Aiyansh and the Cassiar Highway, there are a number of Y-intersections and, in most instances, the route is signed; however, if in doubt, follow the road which parallels the hydro lines.

Yellow kilometre markers begin at **Milepost J 58.5** and continue to the Cassiar Highway. These markers are used by loggers when reporting their road positions and marker '0' is at the Ginlulak log dump near Greenville. During winter, depending on logging activity, the eastern portion of the road may not be maintained (plowed). Call Nass Camp (604) 633-2434) to inquire about winter road conditions before setting out.

Distance is measured from junction (J) with Yellowhead Highway 16.

J 0 Junction with Yellowhead Highway 16 at **Milepost PG 366.5.**

J 7 (11.2 km) Finlay Lake to west.

J 13.7 (22 km) Kitsumkalum River to west.

J 17.4 (28 km) View of Kitsumkalum Lake to west.

J 19.8 (31.9 km) Paved turnout to west overlooking Kitsumkalum Lake.

J 23 (37 km) Rosswood settlement at the head of the lake, named for Annie Ross, who homesteaded here with her 4 children at the turn of the century.

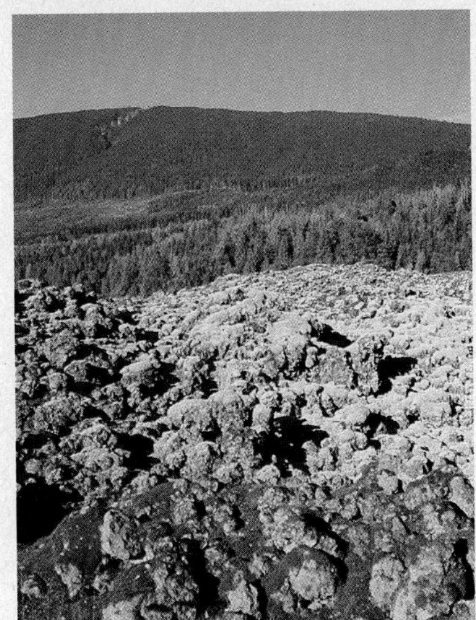

Tseaux lava flow. *(Judy Parkin, staff)*

J 25.8 (41.5 km) Rosswood General Store; groceries, fishing tackle (open year-round).

J 30.4 (48.9 km) Entering Skeena Cellulose Tree Farm License #1. Twenty-five year tree farm licenses are issued by the Crown and define the terms of timber harvest, including taxation, reforestation and long-term planning requirements.

J 31.4 (50.5 km) One-lane bridge crosses Cedar River.

J 37 (59.6 km) Sand Lake, marshy area to south. Watch for wildlife.

J 39.3 (63.2 km) Pavement ends, gravel begins, northbound.

J 39.5 (63.6 km) Gainor Lake west.

J 42.2 (67.9 km) Southern park boundary for Nisga'a Memorial Lava Bed Park. Lava Lake to west. Narrow winding road next 6.2 miles/10 km northbound. *Note: Removal of lava prohibited; stay on designated trails and roads.*

The flow is thought to be the most recent volcanic eruption in Canada, originating in a small valley east of the highway. It covers an area approximately 6.3 miles/10 km long and 1.8 miles/3 km wide and was created by a volcano less than 361 foot/100m high. The eruption produced little ash or cinder, and large quantities of basalt.

The flow entered the Tseax Valley, filling it to depths of more than 98 feet/30m, and blocking the upper section of the valley. Waters from the surrounding drainage filled the valley to form the 180 foot/55m-deep Lava Lake, which in turn drains into the permeable lava flow and reappears approximately 1.2 miles/2 km downstream as the Tseax River and Vetter Creek.

J 46 (74.1 km) Access to Lava Lake on west side of road.

J 48.3 (77.8 km) North end of Lava Lake. Sil Tax picnic site; toilets, litter barrels, tables, park information. No overnight camping.

J 48.7 (78.4 km) Lava flow to east. Interpretive sign, trail (0.6 mile/1 km) and photo viewpoint.

J 50.1 (80.6 km) One-lane wooden bridge.

J 54.7 (88 km) Beaupre Falls trail (10 minutes round trip).

J 56.2 (90.5 km) Vetter Falls viewpoint and "phantom fish." Near Vetter Falls the Tseax River divides; the eastern channel flows into the Nass River. The eastern channel flows over Vetter Falls to join Vetter Creek. Just east of the Vetter Falls campsite, the runoff sinks into channels below the lava. Often, steelhead spawning in the Tseax River return to the ocean; occasionally the fish take the eastern channel and go over the falls, becoming trapped in this section of the river. They starve and become "snake-like" in appearance. Locals refer to them as "phantom fish."

J 58.5 (94.1 km) **Junction** with road to Gitwinksihlkw (Canyon City) and Greenville. Information sign. Road presently ends at Greenville. Vetter Falls campsite to northwest; tables, fire rings, and toilets. Water from creek; recommend boiling. ▲

Nisga'a Enterprises operates a fishing lodge at Nass Harbour with good fishing and ocean kayaking.

J 59.6 (95.9 km) Northern boundary for Nisga'a Memorial Lava Bed Park; information, toilets, viewpoint. Turnout by creek to south. One-lane wooden bridge.

J 60.1 96.7 km) RCMP station to north.

J 60.2 (96.9 km) Village of **NEW AIYANSH** to south. Repairs, gas, grocery and convenience stores, a school, post office, first aid, fire and police stations, post office and gift shop are available. Area bed and breakfast and lodge operators offer meals and accommodation. Limited campsites are available. ▲

J 67.7 (109 km) Northbound: Highway becomes Nass Forest Service Road at Y-intersection. Keep left for Nass Camp/Bill-Nor Tillicum Lodge (all visitor services), keep right for Cassiar Highway.

J 71.3 (114.7 km) BC Forest Recreation Site on Dragon Lake. A medium, semi-open, user-maintained site with good water and broad access; mixed forest; boat launch. ▲

J 73.7 (118.6 km) Y-intersection: Keep to right for Cassiar Highway, left for Alice Arm/Kitsault. Follow hydro lines.

J 80.5 (129.5 km) One-lane wooden bridge with turnouts at each end. Leaving Skeena Tree Fall License #1 northbound.

J 94.8 (152.5 km) Y-intersection: Follow yellow kilometreposts on right side of road for Cassiar Highway.

J 98.6 (158.7 km) **Junction** with Cassiar Highway 37 (see Cassiar Highway section).

Return to Milepost PG 366.5 Yellowhead Highway or J46.8 Cassiar Highway

Historic North Pacific Cannery at Port Edward, just east of Prince Rupert.
(Wes Bergen, Diarama)

Galloway Rapids rest area to south with litter barrels, picnic tables and visitor information sign. View of Watson Island pulp mill.

PG 453 (729 km) **PR 3** (4.8 km) Ridley Island access road. Ridley Island is the site of terminals used for the transfer of coal and grain from—respectively, the North East Coal resource near Dawson Creek and Canada's prairies—to ships.

PG 453.4 (729.7 km) **PR 2.6** (4.2 km) Oliver Lake rest area to south just off highway; picnic tables, grills, firewood. Point of interest sign about bogs.

PG 454.1 (730.8 km) **PR 1.9** (3.1 km) Mount Oldfield and Butze Rapids hiking trails.

PG 455.4 (732.9 km) **PR 0.6** (1 km) Turnoff to north for viewpoint of Butze Rapids, a series of reversing rapids. The action of the tidal waters creates quantities of foam as the waters flow through the rapids. It is from these "foaming waters" that the island takes its Indian name *Kaien.*

PG 456 (733.8 km) **PR 0** Prince Rupert industrial park on the outskirts of Prince Rupert. Continue straight ahead 3 miles/ 4.8 km for the Travel Infocentre in downtown Prince Rupert. Yellowhead Highway 16 becomes McBride Street as you enter the city centre.

CAUTION: No gas or services available eastbound between Prince Rupert and Terrace.

Prince Rupert

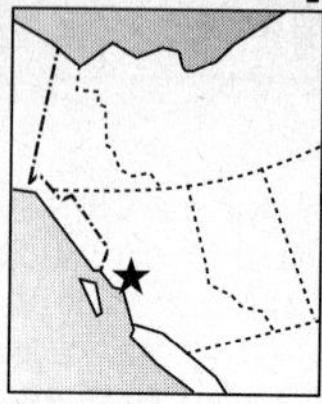

Located on Kaien Island near the mouth of the Skeena River, 90 miles/ 145 km by air or water south of Ketchikan, AK. **Population:** 17,500; area 25,000. **Emergency Services:** Phone 911 for **Police, Ambulance** and **Fire Department. RCMP,** 6th Avenue and McBride Street, non-emergency phone (604) 624-2136. **Hospital,** Prince Rupert Regional, phone (604) 624-2171.

Visitor Information: Travel Infocentre at 1st Avenue and McBride Street. Open daily in summer, 9 A.M. to 9 P.M. Travel information is also available at the Park Avenue Campground; open daily in summer, 9 A.M. to 9 P.M., and until midnight for B.C. Ferry arrivals. Write Box 669-MP, Prince Rupert, BC V8J 3S1, phone (800) 667-1994 and (604) 624-5637, fax (604) 627-8009.

Elevation: Sea level. **Climate:** Temperate with mild winters. Annual precipitation 95.4 inches. **Radio:** CHTK 560, CBC 860; CJFW-FM 101.9. **Television:** 12 channels, cable. **Newspaper:** *The Prince Rupert Daily News, Prince Rupert This Week* (weekly).

Prince Rupert, "Gateway to Alaska," was surveyed prior to 1905 by the Grand Trunk Pacific Railway (later Canadian National Railways) as the terminus for Canada's second transcontinental railroad.

Twelve thousand miles/19,300 km of survey lines were studied before a final route along the Skeena River was chosen. Some 833 miles/1,340 km had to be blasted from solid rock, 50 men drowned, and costs rose to $105,000 a mile (the final cost of $300 million was comparable to Panama Canal construction) before the last spike was driven near Fraser Lake on April 7, 1914. Financial problems continued to plague the company, forcing it to amalgamate to become part of the Canadian National Railways system in 1923.

Charles M. Hays, president of the company, was an enthusiastic promoter of the new terminus, which was named by competition from 12,000 entries. While "Port Rupert" had been submitted by two contestants, "Prince Rupert" (from Miss

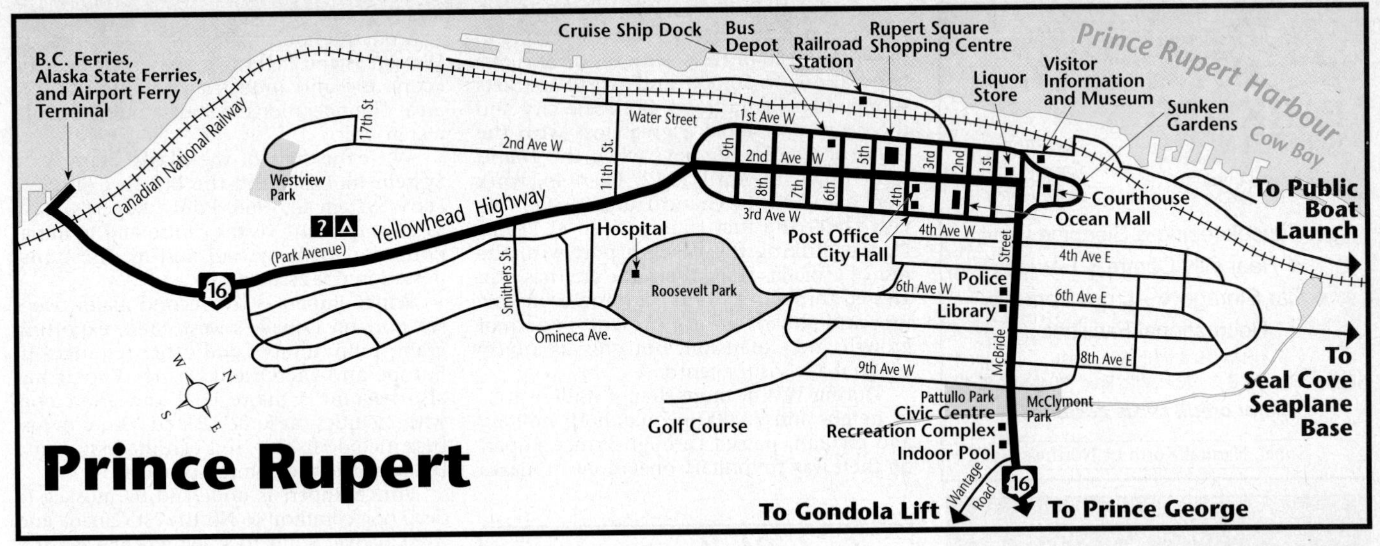

Eleanor M. Macdonald of Winnipeg) called to mind the dashing soldier–explorer, cousin to Charles II of England and first governor of the Hudson's Bay Co., who had traded on the coast rivers for years. Three first prizes of $250 were awarded and Prince Rupert was officially named in 1906.

Prince Rupert's proposed port and adjacent waters were surveyed by G. Blanchard Dodge of the Hydrographic branch of the Marine Dept. in 1906, and in May the little steamer *Constance* carried settlers from the village of Metlakatla to clear the first ground on Kaien Island. Its post office opened Nov. 23, 1906, and Prince Rupert, with a tent-town population of 200, began an association with communities on the Queen Charlotte Islands, with Stewart served by Union steamships and Canadian Pacific Railways boats, and with Hazelton 200 miles/322 km up the Skeena River on which the stern-wheelers of the Grand Trunk Pacific and the Hudson's Bay Co. traveled.

PRINCE RUPERT ADVERTISERS

Aleeda Motel ....Ph. (604) 963-6300
Anchor Inn........................Ph. (604) 627-8522
Archaeology Tours, Museum
of Northern B.C...........Ph. (604) 624-3207
Best Western
Highliner Inn..............Ph. 1-800-668-3115
Breakers Pub....................Ph. (604) 624-5990
City of Prince Rupert ....Ph. 1-800-667-1994
Crest Motor Hotel..................222 1st Ave. W.
Eagle Bluff
Bed and Breakfast.......Ph. 1-800-833-1550
Harbour Air Ltd. ....Ph. (604) 627-1341
Inland Air Charters Ltd. ..Ph. (604) 624-2577
Inn On The Harbour ....Ph. 1-800-663-8155
Moby Dick Inn ....Ph. (604) 624-6961
Park Avenue Campground.......1750 Park Ave.
Parkside Resort Motel.......Ph. (604) 624-9131
Rose's Bed & Breakfast .....Ph. (604) 624-5539
Seashore Charters...........Ph. 1-800-667-4393
Skeena Valley
Wilderness Tours ....Ph. (604) 624-5700
Starline Water Tours.........Ph. (604) 624-5421
Taquan Air ....Ph. 1-800-770-8800
Totem Lodge Motel ....1335 Park Ave.
Wagilsla Air Inc. ....Ph. (604) 627-1955

Incorporated as a city March 10, 1910, Prince Rupert attracted settlers responding to the enthusiasm of Hays, with his dreams of a population of 50,000 and world markets supplied by his railroad. Both the city and the railway suffered a great loss with the death of Charles M. Hays when the *Titanic* went down in April 1912. Even so, work went ahead on the Grand Trunk Pacific. Two years later the first train arrived at Prince Rupert, linking the western port with the rest of Canada. Since then, the city has progressed through 2 world wars and economic ups and downs to its present period of growth and expansion, not only as a busy port but as a visitor centre.

During WWII, more than a million tons of freight and 73,000 people, both military and civilian, passed through Prince Rupert on their way to military operations in Alaska and the South Pacific.

Construction of the pulp operations on Watson Island in 1951 greatly increased the economic and industrial potential of the area. The operations include a pulp mill and a kraft mill.

With the start of the Alaska State Ferry System in 1963, and the British Columbia Ferry System in 1966, Prince Rupert's place as an important visitor centre and terminal point for highway, rail and marine transportation was assured.

Prince Rupert is the second major deep-sea port on Canada's west coast, exporting grain, pulp, lumber and other resources to Europe and the Orient. Prince Rupert has also become a major coal and grain port with facilities on Ridley Island. Other industries include fishing and fish processing and the manufacture of forest products.

Prince Rupert is underlaid by muskeg (a deep bog common to Northwest Canada and Alaska) over solid rock, which makes for a difficult foundation to build on. Many sites are economically unfeasible for development as they would require pilings 70 feet/21m or more into the muskeg to provide a firm foundation. Some of the older buildings have sagged slightly as a result of unstable foundations.

ACCOMMODATIONS/VISITOR SERVICES

More than a dozen hotels and motels accommodate the influx of ferry passengers each summer. Many restaurants feature fresh local seafood in season.

Modern supermarkets, shopping centres and a hospital are available. Government

Prince Rupert has an 18-hole golf course. (Fred Chapman, Diarama)

liquor store is at the corner of 2nd Avenue and Highway 16. There are 5 main banks, the Civic Centre Recreation Complex, 18-hole golf course, racquet centre, bowling alley, a swimming pool and tennis courts.

Park Avenue Campground on Highway 16 in the city has 87 campsites with hookups, unserviced sites, restrooms with hot showers, coin-operated laundry facilities, children's play area and picnic shelters. There are 24 campsites at Prudhomme Lake Park, 12.5 miles/20.1 km east on Highway 16. A private RV park on McBride Street offers camper and trailer parking. ▲

TRANSPORTATION

Air: Harbour Air, Wagair and Inland Air Charters to outlying villages and Queen Charlotte Islands; Canadian Airlines International daily jet service to Terrace and Vancouver; Taquan Air daily floatplane service to Ketchikan, AK; and Air BC to Vancouver with connecting flights to Victoria.

Prince Rupert airport is located on Digby Island, which is connected by city-operated ferry to Prince Rupert. There is a small terminal at the airport. The airport ferry leaves from the Fairview dock, next to the Alaska State ferry dock; fare is charged for the 20-minute ride. Check with the Canadian Airlines International office at the downtown Rupert Mall (office is open for passenger check-in only when planes are arriving or departing). Air BC check-in at corner of 6th Street and 1st Avenue West. Bus service to airport from airline check-in areas.

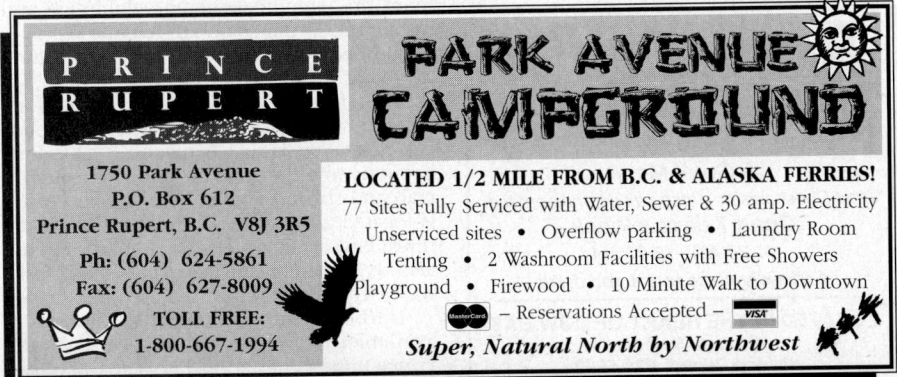

There is a seaplane base at Seal Cove with airline and helicopter charter services.

Ferries: British Columbia Ferry System, Fairview dock, phone (604) 624-9627, provides automobile and passenger service from Prince Rupert to Port Hardy, and between Prince Rupert and Skidegate in the Queen Charlotte Islands. For details, see MARINE ACCESS ROUTES section.

Alaska Marine Highway System, Fairview dock, phone (604) 627-1744, provides automobile and passenger service to southeastern Alaska. See MARINE ACCESS ROUTES section.

NOTE: Vehicle storage is available; inquire at the Information Centre.

Car Rentals: Tilden, phone (604) 624-5318, and Budget, phone (604) 627-7400.

Taxi: Available. Prince Rupert taxi cabs are powered by LNG (liquefied natural gas); phone (604) 624-2185.

Railroad: VIA Rail, in British Columbia, phone 1-800-561-8630 (from Manitoba west to British Columbia) or 1-800-561-3949 (from the United States).

Bus: Greyhound, phone (604) 624-5090. Farwest Bus Lines, phone (604) 624-6400. Charter sightseeing tours available.

ATTRACTIONS

Take a Tour. Tour the city's historic and scenic points of interest. Maps are available at the Travel Infocentre. Scattered throughout the city are 18 large cedar totem poles, each with its own story. Most are reproductions by Native craftsmen of the original Tsimshian (SHIM shian) poles from the mainland and the Haida (HI duh) carvings from the Queen Charlotte Islands. The originals are now in the British Columbia Provincial Museum in Victoria. Several totem poles may be seen at Service Park, near 3rd Avenue W. and Fulton.

Check with the Museum of Northern British Columbia (1st and McBride) about tours of area archaeological sites. Included is a stop at "Old" Metlakatla in Prince Rupert harbour ("new" Metlakatla is located on Annette Island near Ketchikan, AK; see METLAKATLA section).

Prince Rupert Grain on Ridley Island (turn off Highway 16 at **Milepost PG 453**) offers a look at Canada's most advanced grain-cleaning terminal. Tours may be arranged through the Travel Infocentre.

Cannery Tour. North Pacific Cannery Village Museum at Port Edward (turn off Highway 16 at **Milepost PG 451.2**). Built in 1889, this restored heritage site has dozens of displays on this once–major regional industry. A live performance highlights the history of the cannery. Open daily in summer, closed Mondays and Tuesdays Oct. through April; admission charged.

Watch the Seaplanes. From McBride Street, head north on 6th Avenue E. (watch for signs to seaplane base); drive a few miles to Solly's Pub, then turn right to Seal Cove seaplane base. Visitors can spend a fascinating hour here watching seaplanes loading, taking off and landing. Helicopter and seaplane tours of the area are available at Seal Cove.

Visit the Queen Charlotte Islands. Ferry service is available between Prince Rupert and Skidegate on Graham Island, largest of the 150 islands and islets that form the Queen Charlotte Islands. Located west of Prince Rupert—a 6- to 8-hour ferry ride—Graham Island's paved road system connects Skidegate with Masset, the largest town in the Queen Charlottes. Scheduled flights from Prince Rupert to Sandspit and Masset are available. Island attractions include wild beaches, Haida culture, flora and fauna. Read THE QUEEN CHARLOTTES on opposite page for more information.

Kwinitsa Station Railway Museum. Built in 1911, Kwinitsa Station was one of nearly 400 identical stations along the Grand Trunk Pacific Railway line. In 1985 the station was moved to the Prince Rupert waterfront. Restored rooms, exhibits and videos tell the story of early Prince Rupert and the role the railroad played in the city's development. Open daily in summer; contact the Museum of British Columbia for more information.

Museum of Northern British Columbia/Art Gallery displays an outstanding collection of artifacts depicting the settlement history of British Columbia's north coast. Traveling art collections are displayed in the gallery, and works by local artists are available for purchase. Centrally located at 1st Avenue and McBride Street, marked by several tall totem poles. Summer hours 9 A.M. to 8 P.M. Monday through Saturday; winter hours 10 A.M. to 5 P.M. Monday through Saturday. Phone (604) 624-3207.

"Photographs and Memories" is a well done multimedia production on Prince Rupert's history. The exhibit's location for 1996 was undetermined at press time. Contact the Infocentre for details.

Performing Arts Centre offers both professional and amateur theatre, with productions for children, and classical and contemporary plays presented. The 700-seat facility may be toured in summer; phone (604) 627-8888.

Special Events. Seafest is a 4-day celebration, held the second weekend in June, which includes a parade and water-jousting competition. Indian Culture Days, a 2-day event held during Seafest, features Native food, traditional dance, and arts and crafts. The All Native Basketball Tournament, held in February, is the largest event of its kind in Canada.

The Civic Centre Recreation Complex located on McBride Street (Highway 16) welcomes visitors. Activities include fitness gym, squash, basketball and volleyball. Supervised children's activities during summer. Ice skating and roller skating rinks also located at the centre. Phone (604) 624-6707 for more information.

Swim at Diana Lake. This provincial park, about 13 miles/21 km from downtown on Highway 16, offers the only freshwater swimming in the Prince Rupert area. Picnic tables, kitchen shelter, parking and beach.

Swim at Earl Mah Aquatic Centre, located next to the Civic Centre Recreation Complex. There is an indoor swimming pool, tot pool, weight room, saunas, showers, whirlpool, slides and diving boards. Access for persons with disabilities. Phone (604) 627-7946. An admission fee is charged.

Golf Course includes 18-hole course, resident pro, equipment rental, clubhouse and restaurant. Entrance on 9th Avenue W.

Go Fishing. Numerous freshwater fishing areas are available near Prince Rupert. For information on bait, locations, regulations and licensing, contact local sporting goods stores or the Travel Infocentre. This area abounds in all species of salmon, steelhead, crab and shrimp. Public boat launch facility is located at Rushbrook Public Floats at the north end of the waterfront. Public floats are also available at Fairview, past the Alaska state ferry terminal near the brewater.

Harbour Tours and Fishing Charters are available. For information, contact the Prince Rupert charter operators at 1-800-667-1994.

The Queen Charlottes

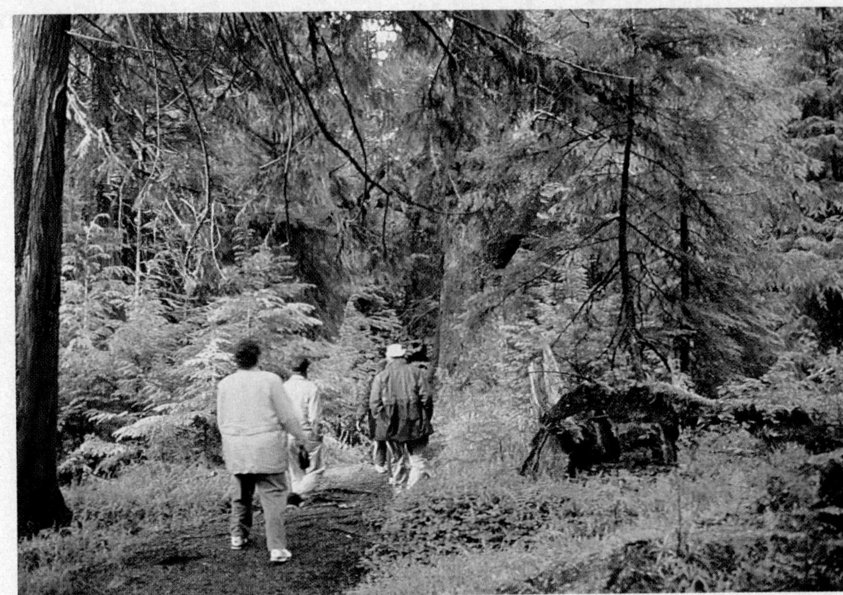

Walking through old-growth forest on Graham Island. (Judy Parkin, staff)

Also called Haida Gwaii (a Haida Indian expression meaning "islands of the people"), the Queen Charlotte Islands are situated 50 miles/80 km off the west coast of British Columbia. To get the most from a trip to the Queen Charlottes, some fairly extensive planning is required. But for those who make the effort, and also enjoy a more rustic experience, the results can be very satisfying.

There are 150 islands in the Queen Charlottes archipelago. The 2 largest islands are Graham and Moresby. Most of the Charlottes 6,000 residents live on Graham. Tourism to the Charlottes began with the introduction of ferry service in 1980.

The climate is moderated by the Japanese current. Summers are predictably dry and sunny, with temperatures reaching 64° F/17° C. Winters are wet and often mild, averaging 40° F/4° C. The annual precipitation is 53.4 inches/1356 mm, and since the islands lie in one of the windiest regions of Canada, there is usually a coastal breeze. Visitors should take note that the weather can change very rapidly and is given to extremes.

The islands are sometimes referred to as the Canadian Galapagos because of the unique adaptations that have evolved in some species. Portions of the islands seem to have remained ice-free during glaciation, and it is speculated that some of today's flora and fauna may have existed continuously for the last 100,000 years.

The Golden Spruce is one of the most famous and easier-to-reach natural attractions, 4 miles/6 km south of Port Clements on Graham Island. The 300-year-old golden-needled tree stands 165 feet/49.5m high. A rare mutation, this excellent specimen is one of only a few such trees known to exist.

Also of particular interest are the wild beaches. Naikoon Provincial Park, encompassing the northeast corner of Graham Island, conserves sandy beach and dunes from Tlell to the northern tip of the island.

Haida culture is a major attraction in the Charlottes. Although nature has reclaimed old villages depopulated by smallpox in the 19th century, the Haida culture continues to thrive: new poles and canoes are carved, and long house architecture is adapted to today's needs. Argillite sculpture, prints, and weavings of contemporary Haida artists are found in shops and studios.

The Queen Charlotte Island Museum at Skidegate, rated as a '"must see" attraction, has exhibits on Haida culture, natural history and island geology. The logging museum at Port Clements describes the modern settlement history.

Fishing is also an attraction, with charter boats, floating and on-shore lodges for saltwater salmon fishing, and river fishing for steelhead, Dolly Varden, coho and cutthroat trout.

The islands are rich with birdlife; some 132 species have been recorded in the Delkatla Wildlife Sanctuary, located near Masset village on Graham Island.

The leeward side of Moresby Island and the protected island passages of the Charlottes offer spectacular sea kayaking. Kayak rentals, pick-ups and drop-offs are available.

Many visitors elect wilderness drives and camping. There are approximately 90 miles/145 km of paved highway on Graham and Moresby islands, and hundreds of miles of unpaved logging roads. Private logging roads provide recreational access to wilderness areas, like Rennell Sound on the rugged west coast on Graham Island. Visitors should check with logging companies to find out what haul roads are active, to pick up maps, and to receive briefing on logging road etiquette before setting out.

Gwaii Haanas ("place of wonder") National Park Reserve/Haida Heritage Site encompasses the lower half of Moresby Island and surrounding islands. It offers a diversity of landscapes and natural features. Special protected areas include the Haida village sites at Skedans, Tanu, and Ninstints on Sgan Gwaii (Anthony Island), a UNESCO World Heritage Site. Travel in this remote and rugged area is not for the inexperienced. There are no roads to or in the park and no developed facilities. Reservations and registration are required. Contact Parks Canada at P.O. Box 37, Queen Charlotte, BC, VOT lS0; phone (604) 559-8818; Email: gwaiicomm@? island.net.ca. Tour companies registered to operate in the area offer a range of services. User fees are proposed for 1997.

Accommodations, restaurants, groceries, fuel and repair services are available in Masset, Queen Charlotte, Port Clements and Sandspit. Limited services in smaller communities. Most island businesses are owner-operated, and business hours vary; plan accordingly. The number of hotel/motel rooms is limited, but bed and breakfasts are a good alternative. There are bank machines and medical facilities in both Masset and Queen Charlotte.

Camping is available at Agate Beach in Naikoon Park; in Masset; at Misty Meadows in Tlell; in Queen Charlotte at Rennell Sound; and at Gray Bay on Moresby. Hookups are available in Masset, Queen Charlotte and Sandspit.

The B.C. Ferry Corporation provides year-round sailings between Prince Rupert and Skidegate on Graham Island. Travelers are strongly urged to make advance reservations. The crossing time is approximately 6 hours.

To reach Moresby Island, there is scheduled service between Skidegate and Alliford Bay aboard the car-carrying MV *Kwuna* ferry. The crossing takes 20 minutes. A paved 6.8-mile/11 km road connects Aliford Bay and Sandspit.

Canadian Airlines International offers jet service between Vancouver and Sandspit on Moresby Island. From Prince Rupert, Harbour Air provides scheduled service to Masset, Sandspit and Queen Charlotte.

Budget and Tilden car rentals are available in Masset and Queen Charlotte on Graham Island and Sandspit on Moresby. While there is shuttle service between Queen Charlotte and the airport at Sandspit, there is no scheduled public transit between other island communities. Taxis are available for hire in Masset, Queen Charlotte and Sandspit.

For more information on travel in the Queen Charlottes, contact the following: Visitor InfoCentre, c/o Joy's Island Jewellers, P.O. Box 819, Queen Charlotte, BC V0T 1S0, phone (604) 559-4742; the Queen Charlotte Islands Chamber of Commerce, P.O. Box 38, Masset, BC V0T 1M0, phone/fax (604) 626-3300.

CASSIAR HIGHWAY

Junction with Yellowhead Highway 16, British Columbia, to Junction with the Alaska Highway
BC Highway 37
(See map, page 247)

Meziadin Lake is one of several scenic lakes on the Cassiar Highway.
(Wes Bergen, Diarama)

The Cassiar Highway junctions with Yellowhead Highway 16 at the Skeena River bridge (**Milepost PG 306.6** in the YELLOWHEAD HIGHWAY 16 section) and travels north to the Stewart, BC–Hyder, AK, access road and Dease Lake, ending at the Alaska Highway 13.3 miles/21.4 km west of Watson Lake, YT (See **Milepost DC 626.2** in the ALASKA HIGHWAY section). Total driving distance is 446.1 miles/718 km. Travelers driving between Prince George and the junction of the Alaska and Cassiar highways will save 123.5 miles/198.7 km by taking the Cassiar Highway. (Yellowhead–Cassiar route is 752.7 miles/1,211.4 km; Alaska Highway route is 876.2 miles/1,410.1 km.) The Cassiar is a rougher road with fewer facilities than the Alaska Highway, but the Cassiar Highway offers a most enjoyable adventure drive with outstanding and varied scenery.

Completed in 1972, much of the Cassiar has been leveled, straightened and brought up to all-weather standards. The highway is paved from **Milepost J 0** to Meziadin junction. From Meziadin junction to the Alaska Highway, the highway is surfaced (pavement or seal coat) with the exception of 4 short gravel sections totaling 80.9 miles/130.2 km. About 80 percent of the Cassiar is surfaced, with various ongoing improvement projects in summer. On gravel stretches watch for washboard and potholes. Gravel road may be dusty in dry weather and muddy in wet weather. Seal coat is subject to deterioration from weather and traffic. A few bridges are still single lane. Watch for potholes at bridge ends and slippery bridge decks. Drive with your headlights on. The Cassiar Highway is the route of commercial truckers headed north of 60°.

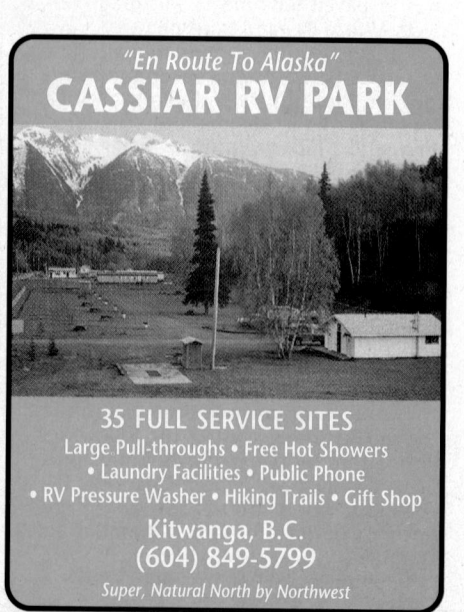

Watch for logging trucks on the lower Cassiar Highway and freight trucks anywhere on the highway. *WARNING: Exercise extreme caution when passing or being passed by these trucks; reduce speed and allow trucks adequate clearance.*

Increasingly popular with motorists in recent years, both because of its savings in travel time and its diverse scenery, the Cassiar also provides access to Hyder and Stewart. These communities are described in detail in this section beginning on page 250.

Food, gas and lodging are available along the Cassiar Highway, but check the highway log for distances between services. Be sure your vehicle is mechanically sound with good tires. It is a good idea to carry a spare tire and extra fuel, especially in the off-season. In case of emergency, motorists are advised to flag down trucks to radio for help. It is unlawful to camp overnight in turnouts and rest areas unless otherwise posted. Camp at private campgrounds or in provincial park campgrounds.

NOTE: According to the Ministry of Highways, litter barrels on the Cassiar Highway are often moved to areas which are being used more frequently. Litter barrels may not be in the same location from season to season. The MILEPOST® log indicates their location as of summer 1995.

For a recorded message on road conditions on the Cassiar Highway, in Canada phone 1-900-451-4997 (75 cents per minute charged). Current road conditions are also available by phoning the Highways Maintenance Contractor at (604) 771-3000 (if no answer, contact the District Highways office at 604/771-4511).

Cassiar Highway Log

BC HIGHWAY 37
Kilometreposts are along the Cassiar Highway every 5 km. Because the posts do not always accurately reflect driving distance, mileages from the Yellowhead Highway 16 junction are based on actual driving distance while kilometres are based on physical kilometreposts as they occurred in summer 1995.
Distance from junction with the Yellowhead Highway (J) is followed by distance from Alaska Highway (AH).

J 0 AH 446.1 (718 km) **Junction** with Yellowhead Highway 16 (see **Milepost PG 306.6** in the YELLOWHEAD HIGHWAY 16 section). Gas station. Bridge across Skeena River from Yellowhead Highway 16 to start of Cassiar Highway.

J 0.2 (0.4 km) **AH 445.9** (717.6 km) Turn east on side road to view totem poles of **GITWANGAK.** The Native reserve of Gitwangak was renamed after sharing the name Kitwanga with the adjacent white settlement. Gitwangak has some of the finest authentic totem poles in the area. Also here is St. Paul's Anglican Church (the original old bell tower standing beside the church dates back to 1893) and one of the last existing Grand Trunk Pacific railway stations.

J 2.5 (4 km) **AH 443.6** (714 km) Kitwanga post office, a private RV park, and a bed and breakfast. ▲

Cassiar RV Park. See display ad this section. ▲

J 2.6 (4.2 km) **AH 443.5** (713.8 km) South

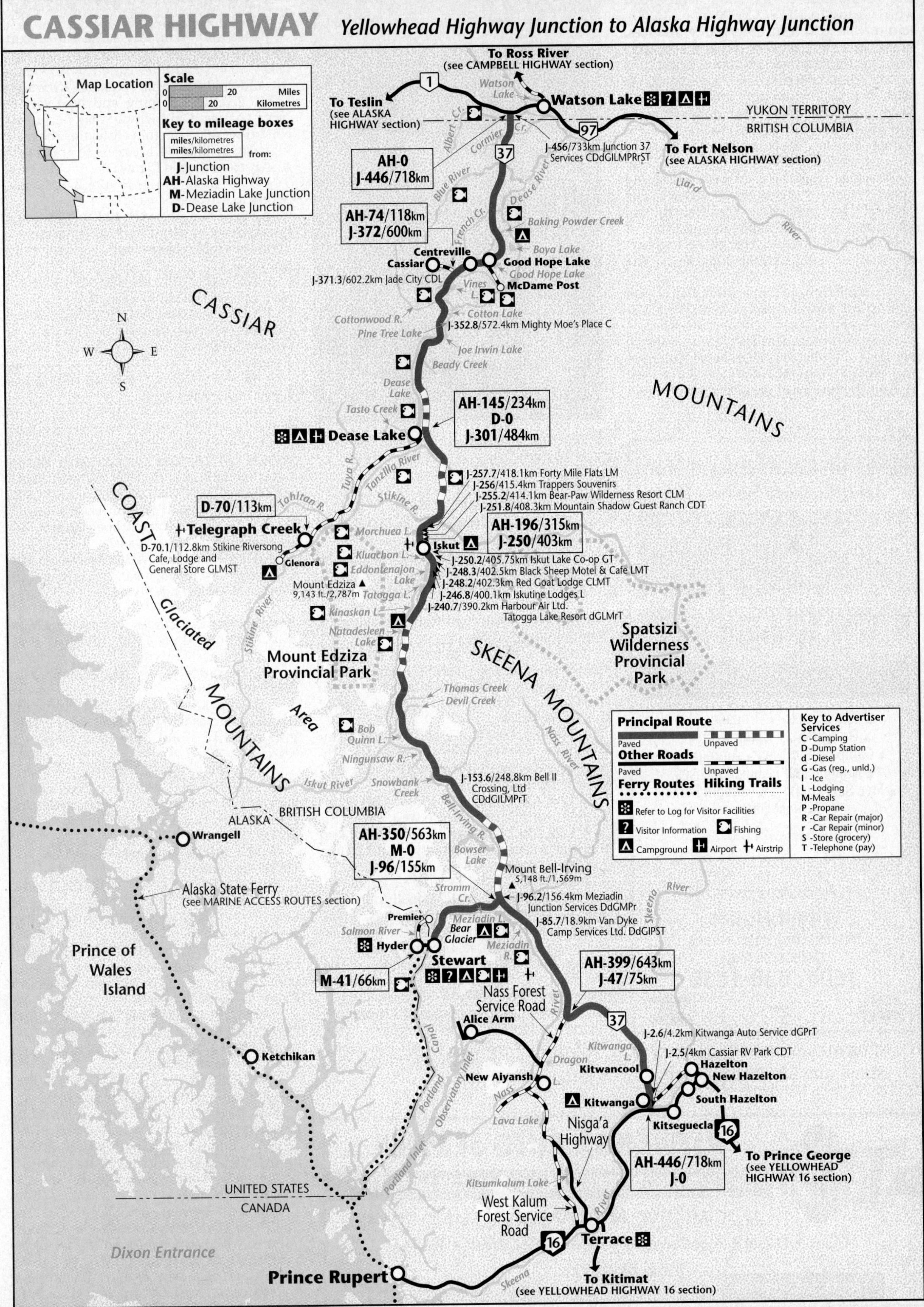
CASSIAR HIGHWAY
Yellowhead Highway Junction to Alaska Highway Junction
Map Location
Scale
0 20 Miles
0 20 Kilometres
Key to mileage boxes
miles/kilometres
miles/kilometres
from:
J-Junction
AH-Alaska Highway
M-Meziadin Lake Junction
D-Dease Lake Junction
To Ross River
(see CAMPBELL HIGHWAY section)
To Teslin
(see ALASKA HIGHWAY section)
Watson Lake
Watson Lake
YUKON TERRITORY
BRITISH COLUMBIA
To Fort Nelson
(see ALASKA HIGHWAY section)
J-456/733km Junction 37
Services CDdGILMPRrST
AH-0
J-446/718km
Albert Cr.
Cormier Cr.
Blue River
Dease River
Liard River
AH-74/118km
J-372/600km
French Cr.
Baking Powder Creek
Boya Lake
Centreville
Cassiar
Good Hope Lake
Good Hope Lake
McDame Post
J-371.3/602.2km Jade City CDL
Vines L.
Cotton Lake
Cottonwood R.
Pine Tree Lake
J-352.8/572.4km Mighty Moe's Place C
Joe Irwin Lake
Beady Creek
CASSIAR
MOUNTAINS
N
W
E
S
Dease Lake
Tasto Creek
AH-145/234km
D-0
J-301/484km
Dease Lake
Tuya R.
Tanzilla River
J-257.7/418.1km Forty Mile Flats LM
J-256/415.4km Trappers Souvenirs
J-255.2/414.1km Bear-Paw Wilderness Resort CLM
J-251.8/408.3km Mountain Shadow Guest Ranch CDT
Stikine R.
Tahltan R.
D-70/113km
Telegraph Creek
D-70.1/112.8km Stikine Riversong Cafe, Lodge and General Store GLMST
Glenora
Morchuea L.
Kluachon L.
Eddontenajon Lake
Iskut
AH-196/315km
J-250/403km
J-250.2/405.75km Iskut Lake Co-op GT
J-248.3/402.5km Black Sheep Motel & Cafe LMT
J-248.2/402.3km Red Goat Lodge CLMT
J-246.8/400.1km Iskutine Lodges L
J-240.7/390.2km Harbour Air Ltd.
Tatogga Lake Resort dGLMrT
Mount Edziza
9,143 ft./2,787m
Tatogga L.
Kinaskan L.
Natadesleen Lake
COAST
Glaciated
Area
MOUNTAINS
Stikine River
Mount Edziza Provincial Park
SKEENA MOUNTAINS
Spatsizi Wilderness Provincial Park
Thomas Creek
Devil Creek
Bob Quinn L.
Ningunsaw R.
Nass River
Iskut River
Snowbank Creek
J-153.6/248.8km Bell II Crossing, Ltd CDdGILMPrT
Bell-Irving R.
BRITISH COLUMBIA
ALASKA
Wrangell
AH-350/563km
M-0
J-96/155km
Bowser Lake
Mount Bell-Irving
5,148 ft./1,569m
Strohm Cr.
J-96.2/156.4km Meziadin Junction Services DdGMPr
J-85.7/18.9km Van Dyke Camp Services Ltd. DdGIPST
Alaska State Ferry
(see MARINE ACCESS ROUTES section)
Premier
Salmon River
Meziadin L.
Bear Glacier
Meziadin R.
Hyder
Stewart
Skeena River
Prince of Wales Island
M-41/66km
AH-399/643km
J-47/75km
Nass Forest Service Road
Alice Arm
J-2.6/4.2km Kitwanga Auto Service dGPrT
J-2.5/4km Cassiar RV Park CDT
Kitwanga L.
Dragon L.
Kitwancool
Hazelton
New Hazelton
Ketchikan
Portland Canal
Observatory Inlet
New Aiyansh
Nass
Kitwanga
South Hazelton
Lava Lake
Nisga'a Highway
Kitseguecla
To Prince George
(see YELLOWHEAD HIGHWAY 16 section)
AH-446/718km
J-0
Portland Inlet
Kitsumkalum Lake
UNITED STATES
CANADA
West Kalum Forest Service Road
River
Terrace
Dixon Entrance
Prince Rupert
Skeena
To Kitimat
(see YELLOWHEAD HIGHWAY 16 section)
Principal Route
Paved
Unpaved
Other Roads
Paved
Unpaved
Ferry Routes
Hiking Trails
Refer to Log for Visitor Facilities
Visitor Information
Fishing
Campground
Airport
Airstrip
Key to Advertiser Services
C-Camping
D-Dump Station
d-Diesel
G-Gas (reg., unld.)
I-Ice
L-Lodging
M-Meals
P-Propane
R-Car Repair (major)
r-Car Repair (minor)
S-Store (grocery)
T-Telephone (pay)

end of 1.6-mile/2.5-km loop access road which leads to **KITWANGA** (pop. 1,200). **Radio:** CBC 630 AM. **Emergency Services:** Ambulance. The business area of Kitwanga has a visitor information booth (open June to Aug., local crafts for sale), gas station, car wash, a general store and small restaurant. There is a free public campground. Hunting and fishing licenses may be purchased at Kitwanga Video. After hours, phone Rose McLeod, (604) 849-5589. ▲

Kitwanga is at the crossroads of the old upper Skeena "grease trail" trade. The "grease" was eulachon (candlefish) oil, which was a trading staple among tribes of the Coast and Interior. The grease trails are believed to have extended north to the Bering Sea.

A paved turnout with litter barrel and sign on the Kitwanga access road mark Kitwanga Fort National Historic Site, where a wooden fortress and palisade once crowned the large rounded hill here. Seven interpretive panels along the trail up Battle Hill explain the history of the site. Kitwanga Fort was the first major western Canadian Native site commemorated by Parks Canada.

Kitwancool has some fine old totems.
(© Carmen Scott)

Kitwanga Auto Service. See display ad this section.

J 4 (6.5 km) **AH 442.1** (711.5 km) North end of 1.6-mile/2.6-km loop access road (Kitwanga North Road) to Kitwanga; see description preceding milepost.

J 4.1 (6.6 km) **AH 442** (711.4 km) **Junction** with alternate access route (signed Hazelton–Kitwanga Road) from Hazelton to the Cassiar Highway via the north side of the Skeena River.

J 5 (8 km) **AH 441.1** (710 km) The mountain chain of Seven Sisters is visible to southwest (weather permitting) next 4 miles/6.4 km northbound.

J 12.5 (20.2 km) **AH 433.6** (697.9 km) Turnout with litter barrels to west.

J 12.6 (20.3 km) **AH 433.5** (697.7 km) Highway follows Kitwanga River and former grease trail route.

J 13 (21 km) **AH 433.1** (697.1 km) South access to **KITWANCOOL**, a small Indian village with many fine old totems, some recently restored. Guided tours of the totem poles may be available; inquire at the Travel Infocentre. A Native craft shop in the village sells local art. The village of Kitwancool was originally called Gitanyow, meaning place of many people, but was renamed Kitwancool, meaning place of reduced number, after many of its inhabitants were killed in raids.

J 16.1 (26.1 km) **AH 430** (692.1 km) North access to Kitwancool.

J 18.8 (30.4 km) **AH 427.3** (687.8 km) Bridge over Moonlit Creek.

J 18.9 (30.7 km) **AH 427.2** (687.5 km) Rest area north of creek, east of road, with tables, toilets and litter barrels. Road west is the old highway and access to **Kitwanga Lake.** Fishing, camping and boat launch spots on lake. Old highway may be in poor condition; drive carefully. It rejoins the main highway at Mile 24.1. Access to the lake is strictly from the old highway. ▲

J 19.9 (32.2 km) **AH 426.2** (686 km) Access to Kitwanga Lake.

J 21.3 (34.5 km) **AH 424.8** (683.7 km) Good views of Kitwanga Lake to west; old highway visible, below west, winding along lakeshore.

J 26.1 (42.2 km) **AH 420** (676 km) Kitwancool Forest Road to west.

J 38.8 (62.9 km) **AH 407.3** (655.5 km) **Cranberry River** bridge No. 1. A favorite salmon stream in summer; consult fishing regulations.

J 46.5 (75.3 km) **AH 399.6** (643.2 km) Paved turnout to west.

J 46.8 (75.9 km) **AH 399.3** (642.6 km) **Junction** with the Nass Forest Service Road to **NEW AIYANSH** (38.4 miles/61.8 km) and Terrace. *NOTE: This intersection is easy to miss.* See NISGA'A HIGHWAY/NASS ROAD log on page 239. A B.C. Forest campsite is 27 miles/44 km west at Dragon Lake; room for 10 to 12 vehicles, cartop boat launch. Bed and breakfast at New Aiyansh.

J 47.1 (76.3 km) **AH 399** (642.2 km) Cranberry River bridge No. 2. Turnout with toilets, tables and litter barrels.

J 53.1 (86 km) **AH 393** (632.6 km) BC Hydro power line crosses and parallels highway. Completed in 1990, this line links Stewart to the BC Hydro power grid. Previously, Stewart's power was generated by diesel fuel.

Entering Kalum Forest District northbound. Watch for signs telling dates of logging activity, and observe patterns of regrowth.

J 58.6 (94.9 km) **AH 387.5** (623.7 km) Kelly Lake rest area at north end of lake on west side of highway, with tables, toilet and litter barrels. First view northbound of Nass River.

J 64.1 (103.8 km) **AH 382** (614.9 km) Paved turnout.

J 65.6 (106.4 km) **AH 380.5** (612.4 km) View of Nass River to west. The Nass River is one of the province's prime producers of sockeye salmon.

J 66.4 (107.7 km) **AH 379.7** (611.1 km) Views northbound (weather permitting) of the Coast Mountains to the west. Watch for Cambrian ice field to west.

J 70.1 (113.6 km) **AH 376** (605.2 km) Paved turnout with litter barrel to west.

J 78.7 (127.4 km) **AH 367.4** (591.3 km) Paved turnout with litter barrel.

J 85 (137.8 km) **AH 361.1** (581.2 km) Paved turnout with litter barrels to west.

J 85.7 (138.9 km)**AH 360.4** (580.1 km) Elsworth logging camp; open to public; fuel, groceries, dump station, hunting and fishing licenses, emergency phone. Private airstrip.

Meziadin Lake General Store. See display ad this section.

J 87.9 (142.4 km) **AH 358.2** (576.6 km) *CAUTION: 1-lane bridge over Nass River.* Paved rest area with picnic tables, toilets and litter barrel to east at south end of bridge. A plaque at the north end commemorates bridge opening in 1972 that joined roads to form Highway 37. The gorge is almost 400 feet/122m wide; main span of bridge is 186 feet/57m. Bridge decking is 130 feet/40m above the riverbed.

J 89.4 (145 km) **AH 356.7** (574.1 km) Tintina Logging Road.

J 93.1 (151 km) **AH 353** (568.1 km) Tintina Creek. Along with Hanna Creek, this stream produces 40 percent of the sockeye salmon spawning in the Meziadin Lake watershed.

J 94.3 (152.8 km) **AH 351.8** (566.3 km) Large gravel turnout to west with litter barrels.

J 94.4 (153 km) **AH 351.7** (566 km) Bridge over Hanna Creek South. Sockeye salmon spawn here in autumn and can be observed from creek banks and bridge deck. It is illegal to fish for or harass these fish. *CAUTION: Watch for bears.*

J 95.6 (155.3 km) **AH 350.5** (564.2 km) **Meziadin Lake** Provincial Park; 46 campsites (many on lake), drinking water, toilets, wheelchair access, day-use facilities, swimming, firewood, garbage containers, boat launch. The lake has a significant fish population, including rainbow trout, mountain whitefish and Dolly Varden. Fishing is especially good at the mouths of small streams draining into Meziadin Lake. *CAUTION: Watch for bears. The hills around the lake are prime bear habitat.*

J 96.2 (156.4 km) **AH 349.9** (563.1 km) **Meziadin Lake Junction** (Mezy-AD-in); Cassiar Highway junctions with the access road to Stewart, BC, and Hyder, AK. Fuel, propane, minor car repair, food, laundry, RV parking and dump station. See page 250 for log of STEWART, BC–HYDER, AK, ACCESS ROAD.

NOTE: This junction can be confusing. Choose your route carefully.

Meziadin Junction Services. See display ad this section.

J 97.5 (158.5 km) **AH 348.6** (561.1 km) Travelers will notice large areas of clear-cut along the southern half of the Cassiar Highway. Bark beetle infestation necessitated the harvest of timber along this particular stretch of highway. After logging, it was reforested.

J 100.8 (164.8 km) **AH 345.3** (555.8 km) Hanna Creek North river and bridge. Gravel turnout at north end of bridge on west side of road with litter barrel.

J 104.1 (169.2km) **AH 342** (550.5 km) Large paved turnout to west with litter barrels.

J 109.8 (178.5 km) **AH 336.3** (541.3 km) Northbound: Pavement ends, gravel begins.

NOTE: There was considerable construction northbound to the Belll-Irving River bridge in 1995. Driving distance over this stretch may vary from log due to detours. Project is scheduled for completion in summer 1998.

Southbound: Pavement begins, gravel ends.

J 116 (189.2 km) **AH 330.1** (531.3 km) Bell I rest area at north end of Bell–Irving bridge; picnic tables, pit toilets, litter barrels.

J 118.2 (192.2 km) **AH 327.9** (527.7 km) Spruce Creek bridge.

J 122.8 (198.9 km) **AH 323.3** (520.3 km) Bell–Irving River parallels highway.

J 125.1 (202.5 km) **AH 321** (516.7 km) Cousins Creek.

J 126.7 (205.2 km) **AH 319.4** (514.1 km) Ritchie Creek bridge, wooden-decked, slippery when wet.

J 130.4 (211.2 km) **AH 315.7** (508.1 km) Taft Creek bridge, wooden-decked, slippery when wet.

J 136.1 (220.4 km) **AH 310** (499 km) Deltaic Creek.

J 141.5 (229.2 km) **AH 304.6** (490.3 km) Glacier Creek.

J 142 (230 km) **AH 304.1** (489.5 km) Northbound: Seal coat begins, gravel ends.

Southbound: Gravel begins, seal coat ends.

J 143.6 (232.7 km) **AH 302.5** (486.8 km) Skowill Creek.

J 145.1 (235 km) **AH 301** (484.5 km) Large gravel turnout with litter barrels.

J 148.1 (239.8 km) **AH 298** (479.7 km) Oweegee Creek.

J 152.1 (246.2 km) **AH 294** (473.2 km) Provincial rest area by **Hodder Lake;** information kiosk, tables, litter barrels, pit toilets, cartop boat launch. Fly or troll for small rainbows.

J 153.6 (248.8 km) **AH 292.5** (470.7 km) Food, gas, diesel, propane, pay phone and lodging.

Bell II Crossing Ltd. See display ad this section.

J 153.8 (249.3 km) **AH 292.3** (470.5 km) Second crossing northbound of Bell–Irving River.

J 156.8 (254.2 km) **AH 289.3** (465.6 km) Large gravel turnout with litter barrel.

J 159.2 (258.1 km) **AH 286.9** (461.7 km) Snowbank Creek.

J 161.2 (261.1 km) **AH 284.9** (458.6 km) Avalanche area: No stopping in winter or spring. Avalanche chutes are visible on slopes to west in summer. Highway serves as emergency airstrip. Watch for aircraft landing or taking off; keep to side of road!

J 161.6 (261.8 km) **AH 284.5** (457.9 km) Redflat Creek.

J 164.1 (266 km) **AH 282** (453.8 km) Revision Creek.

J 165.1 (267.6 km) **AH 281** (452.2 km) Fan Creek.

J 167.3 (271 km) **AH 278.8** (448.7 km) Avalanche area. No stopping.

J 168.7 (273.2 km) **AH 277.4** (446.5 km) Turnout with litter barrels to east overlooking large moose pasture, beaver ponds.

J 169.6 (274.9 km) **AH 276.5** (445 km) Ningunsaw Pass (elev. 1,530 feet/466m). Nass–Stikine water divide; turnout with litter barrels to west beside **Ningunsaw River**. Mountain whitefish and Dolly Varden. The highway parallels the Ningunsaw northbound. Watch for fallen rock on road through the canyon. The Ningunsaw is a tributary of the Stikine watershed.

J 169.9 (275.4 km) **AH 276.2** (444.5 km) Beaverpond Creek.

J 170.3 (276 km) **AH 275.8** (443.9 km) Liz Creek.

J 172.7 (279.9 km) **AH 273.4** (440 km) Alger Creek. The massive piles of logs and debris in this creek are from a 1989 avalanche. Avalanche chutes visible to west.

J 173 (280.3 km) **AH 273.1** (439.5 km) Large gravel turnout to east with litter barrel.

J 174.8 (283.2 km) **AH 271.3** (436.7 km)

(Continues on page 253)

Stewart, BC–Hyder, AK, Access Road Log

HIGHWAY 37A
Distance is measured from Meziadin Lake Junction (M).

M 0 Junction with Cassiar Highway at **Milepost J 96.2**. Visitor information cabin, status unconfirmed at press time.

M 4.8 (7.7 km) Picnic area with tables, toilets, litter barrels and boat launch.

M 7.7 (12.4 km) Surprise Creek bridge.

M 10.1 (16.3 km) Turnout to south with view of hanging glaciers.

M 11.5 (18.5 km) Windy Point bridge.

M 13 (20.9 km) Cornice Creek bridge.

M 13.5 (21.7 km) Strohn Creek bridge.

M 14.7 (23.7 km) Rest area with litter barrels, view of Bear Glacier.

M 15.8 (25.4 km) Turnouts along lake into which Bear Glacier calves its icebergs. Watch for falling rock from slopes above road in spring. Morning light is best for photographing spectacular Bear Glacier. At one time the glacier reached this side of the valley; the old highway can be seen hundreds of feet above the present road.

M 18.4 (29.6 km) Cullen River bridge.

M 18.9 (30.4 km) Huge delta of accumulated avalanche snow. Narrow road with little shoulder; no stopping.

M 21.5 (34.6 km) Argyle Creek.

M 23.2 (37.3 km) Narrow, steep-walled Bear River canyon. Watch for rocks on road.

M 24.5 (39.4 km) Turnout with litter barrel to north.

M 24.8 (39.9 km) Bear River bridge.

M 30.1 (48.4 km) Bitter Creek bridge.

M 32.5 (52.3 km) Wards Pass cemetery. The straight stretch of road along here is the former railbed from Stewart.

M 36.9 (59.4 km) Bear River bridge and welcome portal to Stewart.

M 38.5 (62 km) Highway joins main street of Stewart (description follows).

M 40.9 (65.8 km) U.S.–Canada border. Hyder (description follows).

TIME ZONE CHANGE: Stewart observes Pacific time, Hyder observes Alaska time. See Time Zones in the GENERAL INFORMATION section.

Stewart, BC–Hyder, AK

Stewart is at the head of Portland Canal on the AK–BC border. **Hyder** is 2.3 miles/3.7 km beyond Stewart. **Population: Stewart** about 1,000; **Hyder** 85. **Emergency Services:** In Stewart, **RCMP**, phone (604) 636-2233. EMS personnel and Medivac helicopter in Hyder. **Fire Department**, phone (604) 636-2345. **Hospital** and **Ambulance**, Stewart Health Care Facility (3 beds), phone (604) 636-2221.

Visitor Information: Stewart Travel Infocentre (Box 306, Stewart, BC V0T 1W0), located in Chamber of Commerce/Infocentre Bldg. on 5th Avenue; phone (604) 636-9224 or fax (604) 636-2199. Limited off-season hours. Hyder Information Center and Museum is located on the right as you drive into Hyder.

Elevation: Sea level. **Climate:** Maritime, with warm winters and cool rainy summers. Summer temperatures range from 41°F/5°C to 57°F/14°C; winter temperatures range from 25°F/-4°C to 43°F/6°C. Average temperature in January is 27°F/-3°C; in July, 67°F/19°C. Reported record high 89°F/32°C, record low -18°F/-28°C. Slightly less summer rain than other Northwest communities, but heavy snowfall in winter. **Radio:** CFPR 1450, CJFW-FM 92.9, CFMI-FM 101. **Television:** Cable, 15 channels.

Private Aircraft: Stewart airport, on 5th Street; elev. 10 feet/3m; length 3,900 feet/1,189m; asphalt; fuel 80, 100.

Stewart and Hyder are on a spur of the Cassiar Highway, at the head of Portland Canal, a narrow saltwater fjord approximately 90 miles/145 km long. The fjord forms a natural boundary between Alaska and Canada. Stewart has a deep harbour and boasts of being Canada's most northerly ice-free port.

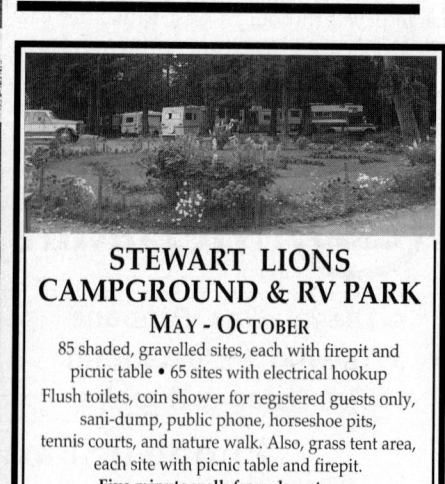

Prior to the coming of the white man, Nass River Indians knew the head of Portland Canal as *Skam-A-Kounst,* meaning safe place, probably referring to the place as a retreat from the harassment of the coastal Haidas. The Nass came here annually to hunt birds and pick berries. Little evidence of their presence remains.

In 1896, Captain D.D. Gaillard (after whom the Gaillard Cut in the Panama Canal was later named) explored Portland Canal for the U.S. Army Corps of Engineers. Two years after Gaillard's visit, the first prospectors and settlers arrived. Among them was D.J. Raine, for whom a creek and mountain in the area were named. The Stewart brothers arrived in 1902 and in 1905 Robert M. Stewart, the first postmaster, named the town Stewart. Hyder was first called Portland City. It was then renamed Hyder, after Canadian mining engineer Frederick B. Hyder, when the U.S. Postal Authority told residents there were already too many cities named Portland.

Gold and silver mining dominated the early economy. Hyder boomed with the discovery of rich silver veins in the upper Salmon River basin in 1917–18. Hundreds of pilings, which supported structures during this boom period, are visible on the tidal flats at Hyder.

Hyder became an access and supply point for the mines, while Stewart served as the centre for Canadian mining activity. Mining ceased in 1956, with the exception of the Granduc copper mine, which operated until 1984. Currently, Westmin Resources Ltd. operates a gold and silver mine. Today the economy is driven by forestry, mining

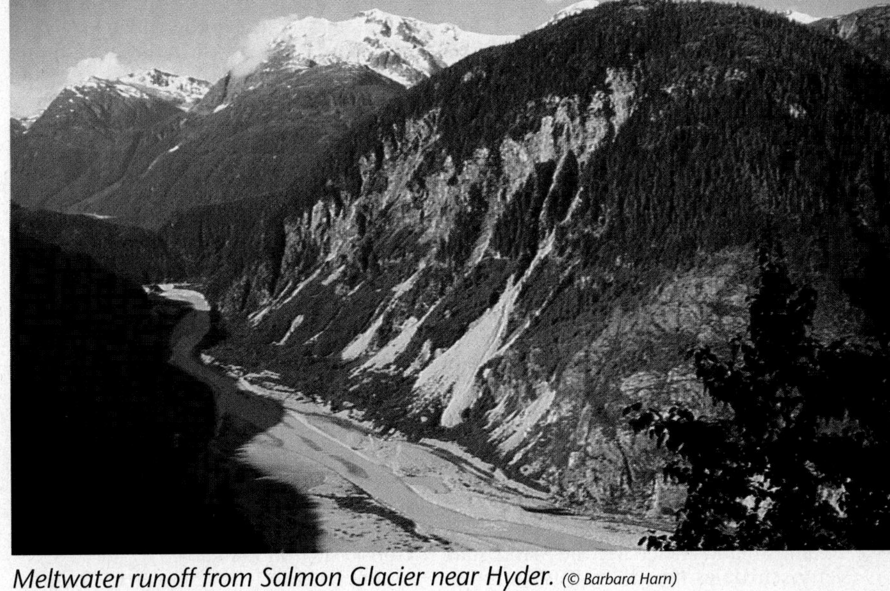

Meltwater runoff from Salmon Glacier near Hyder. (© Barbara Harn)

and tourism.

ACCOMMODATIONS/VISITOR SERVICES

Stewart: Three hotels/motels, 3 restaurants, 1 grocery store, 2 churches, service stations, dry cleaners, laundromat, pharmacy, post office, a bank (open 10 A.M. to 3 P.M. Monday through Thursday, Friday until 6 P.M.), liquor store and other shops. Camping at 2 campgrounds/RV parks with washrooms, showers and hookups. ▲

Hyder: 2 groceries, 3 gift shops, a post office, 3 cafes, a Baptist church, 2 motels and 2 bars. There is no bank in Hyder. There are no automatic teller machines in Stewart/Hyder.

TRANSPORTATION

Air: Taquan Air scheduled service from Hyder to Ketchikan. **Bus:** Limousine service to Terrace. **Ferry:** Once-a-week (Tuesday) seasonal service between Ketchikan and Hyder. See the Alaska state ferry schedules (Southern Panhandle) in the MARINE ACCESS ROUTES section. *IMPORTANT: Check ferry departure times carefully!*

ATTRACTIONS

Historic Buildings: In Stewart, the former fire hall at 6th and Columbia streets built in 1910, which now houses the Historical Society Museum; the Empress Hotel (now occupied by a hardware store) on 4th Street; and St. Mark's Church (built in 1910) on 9th Street at Columbia. On the border at Eagle Point is the stone storehouse built by Captain D.D. Gaillard of the U.S. Army Corps of Engineers in 1896. This is the oldest masonry building in Alaska. Originally 4 of these buildings were built to hold exploration supplies. This one was subsequently used as a cobbler shop and jail. Storehouses Nos. 3 and 4 are included on the (U.S.) National Register of Historic Places.

Stewart Historical Society Museum, in the fire hall, has a wildlife exhibit on the main floor and an exhibit of historical items on the top floor. Included is a display on movies filmed here: "Bear Island" (1978), John Carpenter's "The Thing" (1981), and "The Ice Man" (1982).

Hyder's night life is well-known, and has helped Hyder earn the reputation and town motto of "The Friendliest Little Ghost Town in Alaska."

Recreation in Stewart includes winter spots at the indoor skating rink; swimming in the Paddy McNeil Memorial Swimming Pool (indoor); an outdoor tennis court; ball parks; and hiking trails.

Fjording Ventures, Breakfast & Dinner Cruises. Join the captain for a 4-hour cruise down the quiet, protected waters of Portland Canal aboard the beautiful 60 ft. Swedish motorsailor, *Fjording*. Covered dining provided for all-weather cruising past quiet inlets and beautiful glaciers, May 15th through September 30th. Reservations required. 1-800-916-0250. [ADVERTISEMENT]

Sightseeing tours of the area take in active and abandoned mine sites, such as Granduc, and glaciers, including the spectacular Salmon Glacier. Other sights include nearby Fish Creek and Summit Lake at the toe of Salmon Glacier. Once a year, usually in August, the ice dam holding back Summit Lake breaks, and the force of the meltwater results in a spectacular flooding of the Salmon River valley at Hyder. Chum and pink salmon are seen in their spawning colors in Fish Creek during August; they ascend the streams and rivers in great numbers to spawn. Visitors may photograph feeding bald eagles and black bears which are drawn to the streams by the salmon.

Visit the old mines. A 30-mile-/48-km-long road leads to movie locations and former mine sites. *CAUTION: The road is narrow and winding.* Access to Premier Mine, Big Missouri Mine and

Salmon Glacier. Inquire at the Stewart Infocentre for more information.

International Days. Fourth of July begins July 1 as Stewart and Hyder celebrate Canada Day and Independence Day. Parade and fireworks.

Charter trips by small boat on Portland Canal and vicinity available for sightseeing and fishing. Flightseeing air tours available.

AREA FISHING: Portland Canal, salmon to 50 lbs., use herring, spring and late fall; coho to 12 lbs. in fall, fly-fishing. *(NOTE: Alaska or British Columbia fishing license required, depending on whether you fish U.S. or Canadian waters in Portland Canal.)* **Fish Creek,** up the Salmon River road from Hyder, Dolly Varden 2 to 3 lbs. on salmon eggs and lures, best in summer. Fish Creek is a fall spawning ground for some of the world's largest chum salmon; it is illegal to kill chum in fresh water in British Columbia. It is legal to harvest chum from both salt and fresh water in Alaska.

Return to Milepost J 96.2 on the Cassiar Highway

Watch for bears along the Cassiar Highway. (© Carmen Scott)

(Continued from page 249)
Gamma Creek.

J 175.6 (284.5 km) **AH 270.5** (435.4 km) Bend Creek.

J 176.9 (286.9 km) **AH 269.2** (433.2 km) Ogilvie Creek.

J 177.8 (288.2 km) **AH 268.3** (431.9 km) Point of interest sign about Yukon Telegraph line. The 1,900-mile/3,057-km Dominion Telegraph line linked Dawson City with Vancouver. Built in 1899–1901, the line was a route for prospectors and trappers headed to Atlin, BC; it was replaced by radio in the 1930s.

J 178 (288.6 km) **AH 268.1** (431.5 km) Echo Lake. Flooded telegraph cabins are visible in the lake below. Good view of Coast Mountains to west. Spectacular cliffs seen to the east are part of the Skeena Mountains (Bowser Basin).

J 181 (293.7 km) **AH 265.1** (426.6 km) Bob Quinn Forest Service Road, under construction as the Iskut Mining Road, will provide year-round access to goldfields west of the Ningunsaw River. The road will follow the Iskut River Valley toward the Stikine River, with a side branch to Eskay Creek gold deposit.

J 181.5 (294.4 km) **AH 264.6** (425.9 km) **Little Bob Quinn Lake,** rainbow and Dolly Varden, summer and fall. Access to Bob Quinn Lake at **Milepost J 183.3.**

J 182.2 (295.3 km) **AH 263.9** (424.7 km) Bob Quinn flight airstrip. This is a staging site for supplies headed for the Stikine/Iskut goldfields. Paved rest area with litter barrels, picnic tables and toilet.

J 183.3 (297 km) **AH 262.8** (423 km) Bob Quinn highway maintenance camp; helicopter base. Emergency assistance. Access to Bob Quinn Lake; toilet, picnic table, cartop boat launch.

J 187 (303.1 km) **AH 259.1** (417 km) Gravel turnout with litter barrels on both sides of road.

J 188.3 (305.2 km) **AH 257.8** (415 km) Old kilometrepost 150, which reflects distance from Meziadin Junction.

J 190.2 (308.4 km) **AH 255.9** (411.8 km) Devil Creek Canyon bridge.

J 191.1 (309.7 km) **AH 255** (410.5 km) Gravel turnout with litter barrel to west.

J 191.6 (310.7 km) **AH 254.5** (409.6 km) Devil Creek Forest Service Road.

J 193.6 (313.9 km) **AH 252.5** (406.4 km) Thomas Creek.

Highway passes through Iskut burn, where fire destroyed 78,000 acres in 1958. This is also British Columbia's largest huckleberry patch.

Northbound, the vegetation begins to change to northern boreal white and black spruce. This zone has cold, long winters and low forest productivity. Look for trembling aspen and lodgepole pine.

Southbound, the vegetation changes to become part of the interior cedar–hemlock zone. Cool wet winters and long dry summers produce a variety of tree species including western hemlock and red cedar, hybrid white spruce and subalpine fir.

J 196.3 (318.1 km) **AH 249.8** (402 km) Large gravel turnout with litter barrel to west.

J 197.3 (319.6 km) **AH 248.8** (400.5 km) Slate Creek.

J 198.4 (321.74 km) **AH 247.7** (398.6 km) Gravel turnout with litter barrels to east.

J 199.7 (323.7 km) **AH 246.4** (396.6 km) Durham Creek.

J 203.7 (330.2 km) **AH 242.4** (390.1 km) Northbound: Gravel begins, seal coat ends.

Southbound: Gravel ends, seal coat begins.

J 204 (330.6 km) **AH 242.1** (389.7 km) Gravel turnout with litter barrels to west.

J 205.1 (332.4 km) **AH 241** (387.9 km) Single-lane bridge crosses Burrage River, northbound traffic yields. Note the rock pinnacle upstream to east.

J 205.5 (333 km) **AH 240.6** (387.2 km) Iskut River to west.

J 206.8 (335 km) **AH 239.3** (385.2 km) Gravel turnout to west.

J 207.8 (336.6 km) **AH 238.3** (383.6 km) Emergency airstrip crosses road; no stopping, watch for aircraft.

J 213 (345.4 km) **AH 233.1** (375.1 km) Rest area by Eastman Creek; picnic tables, outhouses, litter barrels and information sign with map and list of services in Iskut Lakes Recreation Area. The creek was named for George Eastman (of Eastman Kodak fame), who hunted big game in this area before the highway was built.

J 216 (350.2 km) **AH 230.1** (370.3 km) Slow down for 1-lane bridge across Rescue Creek, northbound traffic yields.

J 217.7 (352.9 km) **AH 228.4** (367.6 km) Slow down for 1-lane bridge over Willow Creek, northbound traffic yields.

J 218.3 (353.9 km) **AH 227.8** (366.6 km) Willow Creek Forest Service Road.

J 219.9 (356.6 km) **AH 226.2** (364 km) Gravel turnout with litter barrels to east.

J 220.6 (357.7 km) **AH 225.5** (362.9 km) Natadesleen Lake trailhead to west; toilets and litter barrel. Hike 0.6 mile/1 km west to lake.

J 222.6 (360.9 km) **AH 223.5** (359.7 km) Gravel turnout to west.

J 223.9 (362.9 km) **AH 222.2** (357.7 km) Snapper Creek.

J 225.1 (365 km) **AH 221** (355.7 km) Entrance to Kinaskan campground with 50 sites, outhouses, firewood, picnic and day-use area, wheelchair access, swimming, 2 hiking trails, drinking water and boat launch on **Kinaskan Lake;** rainbow fishing, July and Aug. Start of 15-mile/24.1-km hiking trail to Mowdade Lake in Mount Edziza Provincial Park. ▲

J 225.2 (365.2 km) **AH 220.9** (355.5 km) Northbound: Seal coat begins, gravel ends.

Southbound: Gravel begins, seal coat ends.

J 230.1 (373.1 km) **AH 216** (347.6 km) Turnout with litter barrel and view of Kinaskan Lake to west.

J 231.1 (374.6 km) **AH 215** (346.1 km) Small lake to east.

J 233.1 (377.9 km) **AH 213** (342.8 km) Gravel turnout with litter barrels to east.

J 233.4 (378.4 km) **AH 212.7** (342.3 km) Todagin Creek 1-lane bridge, northbound traffic yields.

J 239.4 (388.1 km) **AH 206.7** (332.7 km) Gravel turnout to west.

J 240.7 (390.2 km) **AH 205.4** (330.6 km) **Harbour Air Ltd.** See display ad this section.

Tatogga Lake Resort. See display ad this section. ▲

J 240.8 (390.3 km) **AH 205.3** (330.5 km) Jackman Creek.

J 241.3 (391.1 km) **AH 204.8** (329.7 km) Coyote Creek.

J 241.9 (392.1 km) **AH 204.2** (328.7 km) Ealue Lake (EE-lu-eh) turnoff. Small B.C. Forest Service recreation area, 7.5 miles/12 km off highway on gravel access road. Rustic sites, picnic tables, rock fire rings (bring own firewood), user-maintained, no fee. ▲

J 244.5 (396.4 km) **AH 201.6** (324.5 km) Turnout with litter barrel.

J 244.6 (396.6 km) **AH 201.5** (324.3 km) Spatsizi trailhead to east.

Turnout with litter barrel beside **Eddontenajon Lake** (Ed-don-TEN-ajon). It is unlawful to camp overnight at turnouts. People drink from the lake; be careful not to contaminate it. Use dump stations. Breakup in late May; freezeup early November. Rainbow fishing July and August.

J 246.8 (400.1 km) **AH 199.3** (320.8 km) **Iskutine Lodge**—featuring 5–12 day guided adventure tours via mountain bike, canoe, kayak, hike—breathtaking scenery, abundant fish/wildlife, small group size, nutritious food, high environmental standards, knowledgeable guides—$150–$200/day inclusive—equals exceptional value! "Accommodation only" packages available. Reservations required. No RVs please! Box 39, Iskut, BC V0J 1K0. (604) 234-3456. [ADVERTISEMENT]

J 248.2 (402.3 km) **AH 197.9** (318.6 km) **Red Goat Lodge** is a complete wilderness resort offering first-class lakeshore camping for RVs and tenters, and a bed and breakfast with an unparalleled reputation. The crushed gravel RV sites are landscaped to the same exacting standards used by B.C. Parks, with TV, deluxe hot showers, washrooms, laundry and phone. We have canoe rentals, canoe tours, and instruction. Fishing is excellent from shore, easy boat launch, licenses available. Choose Red Goat for real quality. AAA approved and undoubtedly the best facility on Highway 37. May–Sept. Tony and Doreen Shaw, Iskut, BC. Phone and fax (604) 234-3261. Pre-season information available from Box 8749, Victoria, BC V8W 3S3. Phone and fax (604) 383-1805. Super, Natural North by Northwest. [ADVERTISEMENT] ▲

J 248.3 (402.5 km) **AH 197.8** (318.4 km) **Black Sheep Motel & Cafe.** See display ad this section.

J 250 (405.4 km) **AH 196.1** (315.6 km) B.C. Hydro generating plant, supplies power for Iskut area.

J 250.2 (405.7 km) **AH 195.9** (315.3 km) **ISKUT** (pop. 300). Small Tahltan Indian community with post office, grocery store, public phone, motel and gas station. Quality beaded moccasins available locally. Camping and cabins available at local lodges and guest ranches. Horse trips, canoe rentals and river rafting may be available; inquire at local lodges and resorts. Clinic open 1–3 P.M., 5 days a week. ▲

Stikine River bridge at Milepost J 269.5. (© Steven Seiller)

Iskut Lake Co-op. See display ad this section.

Private Aircraft: Eddontenajon airstrip, 0.6 mile/1 km north of Iskut; elev. 3,100 feet/945m; length 3,000 feet/914m; gravel; fuel available at Trans-Provincial Airlines base south on Eddontenajon Lake.

J 251.8 (408.3 km) **AH 194.3** (312.7 km) **Mountain Shadow Guest Ranch.** Located in a quiet, secluded parklike setting with scenic mountain and lake views. We offer long RV pull-throughs with hookups, cabins and beautiful private wooded campsites with picnic tables and firepits. Short nature walk to Kluachon Lake. Excellent fishing from lakeshore or canoe. Explore wilderness trails by hiking or mountain bike. Guided trail-rides with prior notice. [ADVERTISEMENT] ▲

J 255.2 (414.1 km) **AH 190.9** (307.2 km) **Bear Paw Wilderness Resort.** Experience our 16-suite Alpine Hotel c/w hot tub, saunas, gourmet reserved dining, lounge and

souvenir shop. Relax on our large picturesque sundeck. Join our outdoor BBQs, but plan on more than an overnight stay. We offer guided tours of Mount Edziza and the Spatsizi Plateau. You can pan for gold, jet boat on the Stikine River or fish for prize rainbow trout. Deluxe accommodations, guest cabins, licensed dining, tenting, horseback riding and tours. VISA, MasterCard. Super, Natural Scenic Adventure. [ADVERTISEMENT] ▲

J 256 (415.4 km) **AH 190.1** (306 km) **Trappers Souvenirs.** See display ad this section.

J 257.7 (418.1 km) **AH 188.4** (303.3 km) **Forty Mile Flats.** See display ad this section. ▲

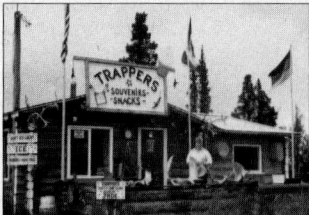

J 260.6 (423 km) **AH 185.5** (298.5 km) Turnout with litter barrels to west. From here the dormant volcano of Mount Edziza (elev. 9,143 feet/2,787m) and its adjunct cinder cone can be seen to the southwest. The park, not accessible by road, is a rugged wilderness with a glacier, cinder cones, craters and lava flows. Panoramic view of Skeena and Cassiar mountains for next several miles northbound. Information signs.

J 261.8 (424.9 km) **AH 184.3** (296.6 km) Turnoff to Morchuea Lake B.C. Forest Service campsite. Rustic, some tables, rock fire rings (bring firewood), no fee. ▲

J 263.3 (427.3 km) **AH 182.8** (294.2 km) Northbound: Gravel begins, seal coat ends.

Southbound: Gravel ends, seal coat begins.

J 264 (428.4 km) **AH 182.1** (293.1 km) Entering Stikine River Recreation Area.

J 266.3 (432.1 km) **AH 179.8** (289.4 km) Steep grade. Winding road next 1.2 miles/2 km northbound.

J 267.2 (433.6 km) **AH 178.9** (287.9 km) Hairpin turn: Keep to right. Highway descends to Stikine River in switchbacks.

J 269 (436.6 km) **AH 177.1** (285 km) Turnout with litter barrels and toilets to south. Tourist map and services directory for area located here.

J 269.5 (437.3 km) **AH 176.6** (284.3 km) Stikine River bridge.

Drive with your headlights on at all times! Reduce your speed on gravel road. Watch for potholes.

J 271.3 (440.2 km) **AH 174.8** (281.4 km) Turnout to east with litter barrel.

J 273.4 (443.6 km) **AH 172.7** (278 km) Leaving Stikine River Recreation Area northbound.

J 274.1 (444.8 km) **AH 172** (276.8 km) Northbound: Seal coat begins, gravel ends.

Southbound: Gravel begins, seal coat ends.

J 277.3 (450 km) **AH 168.8** (271.6 km) Turnout on Upper Gnat Lake; tables, toilets, litter barrels. Long scar across Gnat Pass valley to east is grading preparation for B.C. Railway's proposed Dease Lake extension from Prince George. Construction was halted in 1977. Grade is visible for several miles northbound.

J 279 (452.7 km) **AH 167.1** (268.9 km) Large gravel turnout with litter barrel to east.

J 282 (457.6 km) **AH 164.1** (264.1 km) Gravel turnout with litter barrel to east.

J 283.9 (460.7 km) **AH 162.2** (261.1 km) Gravel turnout to east.

J 284.2 (461.3 km) **AH 161.9** (260.5 km) Upper Gnat Rest Area.

J 284.5 (461.7 km) **AH 161.6** (260.1 km) Wilderness trail rides.

J 285.8 (463.8 km) **AH 160.3** (258 km) Turnout overlooking **Lower Gnat Lake,** abundant rainbow.

J 287.9 (467.1 km) **AH 158.2** (254.7 km) Turnout with litter barrel.

J 288.7 (468.5 km) **AH 157.4** (253.3 km) Gnat Pass Summit.

J 291.7 (473.3 km) **AH 154.4** (248.5 km) Steep grade, 8 percent downhill.

J 295.2 (479.1 km) **AH 150.9** (242.8 km) **Tanzilla River bridge.** Pleasant rest area with picnic tables and outhouses at north end of bridge beside river. Fishing for grayling to 16 inches, June and July; use flies.

J 296.5 (481.2 km) **AH 149.6** (240.7 km) Dalby Creek.

J 298.4 (484.1 km) **AH 147.7** (237.8 km) Turnout with litter barrel to west.

J 300.2 (487.1 km) **AH 145.9** (234.9 km) Divide (elev. 2,690 feet/820m) between Pacific and Arctic ocean watersheds.

J 300.9 (488.3 km) **AH 145.2** (233.7 km) **Junction** with Telegraph Creek Road and access to Dease Lake (description follows). See TELEGRAPH CREEK ROAD log on opposite page.

Dease Lake

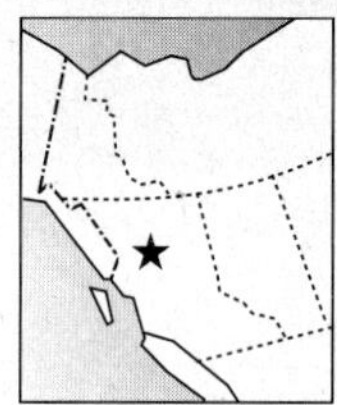

Located just west of the Cassiar Highway. **Emergency Services: RCMP** detachment. **Private Aircraft:** Dease Lake airstrip, 1.5 miles/2.4 km south; elev. 2,600 feet/792m; length 6,000 feet/1,829m; asphalt; fuel JP4, 100. **Visitor Information:** Write Dease Lake and Tahltan District Chamber of Commerce, Box 338, Dease Lake, BC V0C 1L0. Phone (604) 771-3900.

Dease Lake has motels, gas stations (with regular, unleaded, diesel, propane and minor repairs), food stores, restaurant, a post office, hardware/sporting goods, highway maintenance centre and government offices. Charter flights and regular air service to Terrace and Smithers. Information kiosks at south entrance to town. ▲

A Hudson's Bay Co. post was established by Robert Campbell at Dease Lake in 1838, but abandoned a year later. The lake was named in 1834 by John McLeod of the Hudson's Bay Co. for Chief Factor Peter Warren Dease. Laketon, on the west side of the lake (see **Milepost J 327.7**), was a centre for boat building during the Cassiar gold rush of 1872–80. In 1874, William Moore, following an old Indian trail, cut a trail from Telegraph Creek on the Stikine River to the

(Continues on page 258)

DEASE LAKE ADVERTISERS

Dease Lake RV Park .... Ph. (604) 771-4666
Goodacre's Store Ltd. .... Ph. (604) 771-4381
Northway Motor Inn & Restaurant .... Ph. (604) 771-5341
The Other Place .... Ph. (604) 771-3667
Trapper's Den Gift Shoppe .... Ph. (604) 771-3224

Telegraph Creek Road Log

Built in 1922, this was the first road in the vast Cassiar area of northern British Columbia. The scenery is remarkable and the town of Telegraph Creek is a picture from the turn of the century. *CAUTION: Telegraph Creek Road has some steep narrow sections and several sets of steep switchbacks; it is not recommended for trailers or large RVs. Car and camper drivers who are familiar with mountain driving should have no difficulty, although some motorists consider it a challenging drive even for the experienced. DRIVE CAREFULLY! Use caution when road is wet or icy. Very slippery when wet. Watch for rocks and mud.* There are no visitor facilities en route. Allow a minimum of 2 hours driving time with good conditions. Check road conditions at highway maintenance camp or RCMP office in Dease Lake before starting the 70.1 miles/112.8 km to Telegraph Creek. According to a Telegraph Creek resident, weather varies considerably: It may be raining in Dease Lake, but clear and sunny in Telegraph Creek. You may phone the Stikine Riversong Cafe (604) 235-3196 for weather and road conditions.

Distance from Dease Lake junction (D) on the Cassiar Highway is shown.

D 0 Dease Lake junction, Milepost J 300.9 Cassiar Highway.

D 0.9 (1.4 km) **Junction** with road to Dease Lake. Turn left for Telegraph Creek.

D 1.4 (2.3 km) Entrance to airport.

D 3.1 (5 km) Pavement ends, gravel begins westbound.

D 5 (8 km) Entering Tanzilla Plateau.

D 7.2 (11.6 km) Tatsho Creek (Eightmile).

D 15.9 (25.6 km) 16 Mile Creek.

D 17.1 (27.5 km) Augustchilde Creek, 1-lane bridge.

D 18.8 (30.3 km) 19 Mile Creek.

D 20.2 (32.5 km) 22 Mile Creek. Turnout with litter barrels south.

D 22.4 (36 km) View of Tanzilla River to south.

D 35.7 (57.5 km) Cariboo Meadows. Entering old burn area for 12 miles/19.3 km.

D 36.7 (59.1 km) Entering Stikine River Recreation Area. Tuya River valley viewpoint to north; turnout with litter barrels. Short walk uphill for good views and photographs.

D 37.7 (60.6 km) Approximate halfway point to Telegraph Creek from Dease Lake. Turnout with litter barrels to north.

D 45.5 (73.2 km) Begin 18 percent grade as road descends canyon; steep and narrow with switchbacks.

D 46 (74.1 km) Turnout with litter barrels to south.

D 47.2 (76 km) Tuya River bridge.

D 47.7 (76.8 km) End of burn area.

D 49 (78.9 km) Road makes Y-intersection. Old road to left; keep right for newer section.

D 50.4 (81.1 km) Old road rejoins newly constructed section.

D 50.8 (81.7 km) Golden Bear Mine access road. Private.

D 51.1 (82.2 km) Twenty percent downhill grade for approximately 0.6 mile/1 km. Day's Ranch on left.

D 54.2 (87.3 km) Rest area with table, toilet and litter barrel; overlooks river gorge.

D 55.7 (89.7 km) Road runs through lava beds, on narrow promontory about 50 feet/15m wide, dropping 400 feet/122m on each side to Tahltan and Stikine rivers. Sudden 180-degree right turn begins steep descent to Tahltan River and Indian fishing camps. Excellent views of the Grand Canyon of the Stikine and Tahltan Canyon can be seen by walking a short distance across lava beds to promontory point. Best views of the river canyon are by flightseeing trip. The Stikine River canyon is only 8 feet/2.4 m wide at its narrowest point.

D 56.1 (90.3 km) Sudden 180-degree turn begins 18 percent downhill grade to Tahltan River.

D 56.5 (90.9 km) Tahltan River bridge. Turnout with litter barrel south, on north side of bridge. Traditional communal Indian smokehouses adjacent to road at bridge. Smokehouse on north side of bridge is operated by a commercial fisherman; fresh and smoked salmon sold. There is a commercial inland fishery on the Stikine River, one of only a few such licensed operations in Canada.

D 57.5 (92.6 km) Start of very narrow road on ledge rising steeply up the wall of the Stikine Canyon for 3 miles/4.8 km, rising to 400 feet/122m above the river.

D 60 (96.6 km) Ninemile Creek.

D 60.1 (96.7 km) Old Tahltan Indian community above road. Private property: No trespassing! Former home of Tahltan bear dogs. The Tahltan bear dog, believed to be extinct, was only about a foot high and weighed about 15 pounds. Short-haired, with oversize ears and shaving-brush tail, the breed was recognized by the Canadian Kennel Club. First seen by explorer Samuel Black in 1824, the dogs were used to hunt bears.

D 61.8 (99.5 km) Eightmile Creek bridge. Spectacular falls into canyon on left below. Opposite the gravel pit at the top of the hill there is a trailhead and parking on the west side of the creek.

D 63.1 (101.5 km) Turnout. Good photos of Stikine Canyon to east.

D 69.1 (111.2 km) Indian community. Road follows steep winding descent into old town, crossing a deep narrow canyon via a short bridge. Excellent picture spot 0.2 mile/0.3 km from bridge. Glenora Road **junction** on right.

D 70.1 (112.8 km) **TELEGRAPH CREEK** (pop. 300; elev. 1,100 feet/335m). Former head of navigation on the Stikine and once a telegraph communication terminal. An important centre during the gold rush days on the Telegraph trail to the Atlin and Klondike goldfields, and also during construction of the Alaska Highway.

There are a cafe, lodge, general store, post office, and a public school and nursing station here. Gas, minor auto and tire repair are available. Stikine River trips and charter flights are available.

Residents make their living fishing commercially for salmon, doing local construction work and guiding visitors on hunting, fishing and river trips. Telegraph Creek is becoming a jumping-off point for wilderness hikers headed for Mount Edziza Provincial Park.

The scenic view along the main street bordering the river has scarcely changed since gold rush days. The turn-of-the-century Hudson's Bay Co. post, which now houses the Riversong Cafe, is a recognized Heritage Bldg. Historic St. Aidan's Church (Anglican) is also located here.

A 12-mile/19.3-km road continues west to Glenora, site of attempted railroad route to the Yukon and limit of larger riverboat navigation. There are 2 primitive B.C. Forest Service campsites on the road to Glenora. Several spur roads lead to the Stikine River and to Native fish camps. ▲

Stikine Riversong Cafe, Lodge & General Store. See display ad this section.

Return to Milepost J 300.9
Cassiar Highway

Ghost town of Laketon on Dease Lake, Milepost J 327.7. (© Carmen Scott)

(Continued from page 256)

gold rush settlement on Dease Lake. This trail became Telegraph Creek Road, which was used in 1941 to haul supplies for Alaska Highway construction and Watson Lake Airport to Dease Lake. The supplies were then ferried down the Dease River.

Today, Dease Lake is a government centre and supply point for the district. The community has dubbed itself the "jade capital of the province." Jade is available locally. It is a popular point from which to fly in to Mount Edziza and Spatsizi wilderness parks or pack in by horse.

Trapper's Den Gift Shoppe. Quality Canadian and British Columbian gift items ranging from local jade to native moccasins and cottage crafts. Come visit the "Trapper" in his "den." Very reasonable jade prices. VISA/MasterCard accepted. Located around the corner from the grocery store, just 200 feet off Highway 37. Box 70, Dease Lake, BC

V0C 1L0. (604) 771-3224. [ADVERTISEMENT]

Cassiar Highway Log

(continued)

J 300.9 (488.3 km) **AH 145.2** (233.7 km) **Dease Lake Junction.** Junction with access road to Dease Lake and Telegraph Creek Road (see log page 257).

J 301.7 (489.6 km) **AH 144.4** (232.4 km) Hotel Creek.

J 308.8 (501.3 km) **AH 137.3** (220.9 km) Turnout with litter barrel to west.

J 309.6 (502.5 km) **AH 136.5** (219.7 km) Serpentine Creek.

J 309.8 (502.9 km) **AH 136.3** (219.3 km) Seal coat ends northbound, gravel begins and extends 16.4 miles/26.4 km. Seal coat southbound extends 35.7 miles/57.5 km.

J 313.5 (508.7 km) **AH 132.6** (213.5 km) Gravel turnout to west with litter barrel.

J 314.1 (509.8 km) **AH 132** (212.4 km) Good views of Dease Lake, limited access to lake shore.

J 315.7 (512.3 km) **AH 130.4** (209.9 km) Gravel turnout to west.

J 316.3 (513.3 km) **AH 129.8** (208.9 km) Halfmoon Creek.

J 318.8 (517.4 km) **AH 127.3** (204.9 km) Rabid Grizzly rest area with picnic tables, travel information signs, litter barrels and outhouses. View of Dease Lake.

J 322.1 (522.8 km) **AH 124** (199.5 km) Gravel turnout to west.

J 324.2 (526.1 km) **AH 121.9** (196.2 km) Black Creek.

J 326.2 (529.4 km) **AH 119.9** (192.9 km) Pavement begins northbound and extends to end of highway at Alaska Highway junction; watch for resurfacing project. Pavement ends southbound; gravel begins and extends 16.4 miles/26.4 km.

J 326.3 (529.5 km) **AH 119.8** (192.8 km) Sawmill Point Recreation Site to west; side road leads to **Dease Lake** for fishing. Lake trout to 30 lbs., use spoons, plugs, spinners, June to Oct., deep trolling in summer, spin casting in fall.

J 327.2 (531.2 km) **AH 118.9** (191.4 km) Dorothy Creek.

J 327.7 (532 km) **AH 118.4** (190.5 km) The site of the ghost town Laketon lies across the lake at the mouth of Dease Creek. Laketon was the administrative centre for the district during the Cassiar gold rush (1872–80). Boat building was a major activity along the lake during the gold rush years, with miners heading up various creeks and rivers off the lake in search of gold. Today's miners ford the lake when the water is low to reach claims on the northwest side.

J 330.2 (535.9 km) **AH 115.9** (186.5 km) Beady Creek. Entering the Cassiar Mountains northbound.

J 333.5 (541.1 km) **AH 112.6** (181.3 km) Turnout to west with litter barrels.

J 333.8 (541.7 km) **AH 112.3** (180.7 km) Turnout with litter barrel to west. **Dease River** parallels the highway. Grayling to 17 inches; Dolly Varden and lake trout to 15 lbs.; northern pike 8 to 10 lbs., May through Sept.

Marshy areas to west; good moose pasture. Watch for wildlife, especially at dawn and dusk.

J 334.4 (542.7 km) **AH 111.7** (179.7 km) Packer Tom Creek, named for a well-known Indian who lived in this area.

J 336.1 (545.4 km) **AH 110** (177 km) Elbow Lake.

J 342 (554.7 km) **AH 104.1** (167.5 km) Pyramid Creek.

J 342.4 (555.6 km) **AH 103.7** (166.9 km) Dease River 2-lane concrete bridge.

J 343.9 (558 km) **AH 102.2** (164.5 km) Beale Creek.

J 344.3 (558.6 km) **AH 101.8** (163.9 km) Turnout beside **Pine Tree Lake.** Good grayling and lake char fishing.

J 351 (569.5 km) **AH 95.1** (153.1 km) Burn area. An abandoned campfire started the fire in July 1982.

J 352.8 (572.4 km) **AH 93.3** (150.2 km) **Mighty Moe's Place.** (Under new management.) "Wilderness Camping at its Best." RV parking, tenting, cabins; free, clean, hot showers, and coffee, for guests; convenience foods, fishing, hiking, canoe rentals, boat launch. For information or reservations, write or call Larry and Lynne Sketchley, Box 299, Dease Lake, BC V0C 1L0, Radio phone 604 N416219 Chicken Neck (voice call). [ADVERTISEMENT] ▲

J 353.7 (573.9 km) **AH 92.4** (148.7 km) Gravel turnout with litter barrels to east. Views of Needlenose Mountain southbound.

J 357.9 (580.9 km) **AH 88.2** (141.9 km) **Cottonwood River** bridge; rest area 0.4 mile/0.6 km west on old highway on south side of river. Fishing for grayling and whitefish. Early summer runs of Dolly Varden.

J 358.7 (582 km) **AH 87.4** (140.7 km) Cottonwood River rest area No. 2 is 0.5 mile/0.8 km west on old highway on north side of river.

J 363.6 (589.8 km) **AH 82.5** (132.8 km) Turnout to west beside **Simmons Lake;** information kiosk, picnic tables, picnic shelter, toilets, small beach and dock. Fishing for lake trout.

J 365.3 (592.7 km) **AH 80.8** (130 km) Road runs on causeway between Twin Lakes.

J 365.8 (593.5 km) **AH 80.3** (129.2 km) **Vines Lake,** named for bush pilot Lionel

Vines; fishing for lake trout.

J 366.9 (595.3 km) **AH 79.2** (127.4 km) Limestone Creek.

J 367.3 (595.9 km) **AH 78.8** (126.8 km) Lang Lake and creek. Needlepoint Mountain visible straight ahead southbound.

J 369.8 (599.9 km) **AH 76.3** (122.8 km) Cusak gold mine visible on slopes to east. Gold mined on the far side of the mountain is processed in the mill here.

J 370.1 (600.3 km) **AH 76** (122.3 km) Side road east leads to McDame Lake.

J 370.9 (601.6 km) **AH 75.2** (121 km) Trout Line Creek.

J 371.1 (601.9 km) **AH 75** (120.7 km) **JADE CITY** (pop. 12), named for the jade deposits found to the east of the highway community. The huge jade boulders that visitors can see being cut here are from the Princess Jade Mine, 82 miles/132 km east, one of the largest jade claims in the world.

J 371.3 (602.2 km) **AH 74.8** (120.4 km) Jade store and RV park.

Jade City. See display ad this section.

J 372.5 (604.1 km) **AH 73.6** (118.5 km) **Cassiar junction.** Cassiar Road to west leads 9.7 miles/15.6 km to the former Cassiar townsite and Cassiar Asbestos Mine. Continue straight ahead for Alaska Highway.

CASSIAR (pop. 25) was the company town of Cassiar Mining Corp. Much of the world's high-grade chrysotile asbestos came from Cassiar. The mine closed in March 1992, and the site is closed to visitors. It is now the site of a B.C. Chrysotile Corp. reclamation project. No services available.

J 372.7 (604.4 km) **AH 73.4** (118.2 km) Snow Creek.

J 372.8 (605.6 km) **AH 73.3** (117.9 km) Gravel turnout with litter barrel to east.

J 373.5 (606.1 km) **AH 72.6** (116.8 km) Deep Creek.

J 377.4 (612.2 km) **AH 68.7** (110.6 km) No. 3 North Fork Creek.

J 378.4 (613.9 km) **AH 67.7** (108.9 km) No. 2 North Fork Creek.

J 381 (618 km) **AH 65.1** (104.7 km) Historic plaque about Cassiar gold.

CENTREVILLE (pop. 2; elev. 2,600 feet/792m), a former gold rush town of 3,000, was founded and named by miners for its central location between Sylvester's Landing (later McDame Post) at the junction of McDame Creek with the Dease River, and Quartzrock Creek, the upstream limit of pay gravel on McDame Creek. A miner named Alfred Freeman washed out the biggest all-gold (no quartz) nugget ever found in British Columbia on a claim near Centreville in 1877; it weighed 72 ounces. Active mining in area.

J 381.1 (618.2 km) **AH 65** (104.6 km) No. 1 North Fork Creek.

J 385.2 (625 km) **AH 60.9** (98 km) **GOOD HOPE LAKE** (pop. 100), Indian village with limited services; fuel may be available.

Turn east on Bush Road and drive 9 miles/14.5 km for **McDAME POST**, an early Hudson's Bay post, at the **confluence of Dease River and McDame Creek.** Good fishing and hunting here.

J 386.9 (627.7 km) **AH 59.2** (95.3 km) Turnout to east alongside Aeroplane Lake.

J 387.7 (629 km) **AH 58.4** (94 km) Dry Creek.

J 389.5 (631.9 km) **AH 56.6** (91.1 km) Mud Lake to east.

J 393.6 (638.5 km) **AH 52.5** (84.5 km) Turnout with litter barrels at entrance to **Boya Lake** Provincial Park. The park is 1.6 miles/2.6 km east of highway; 44 campsites, picnic area on lakeshore, boat launch, toilets, wheelchair access, walking trails, drinking water, firewood and swimming. Fishing for lake char, whitefish, grayling and burbot. Attendant on duty during summer.

J 393.7 (638.6 km) **AH 52.4** (84.4 km) Turnout. Horseranch Range may be seen on the eastern horizon northbound. These mountains date back to the Cambrian period, or earlier, and are the oldest in northern British Columbia. According to the Canadian Geological Survey, this area contains numerous permatites with crystals of tourmaline, garnet, feldspar, quartz and beryl. Road crosses Baking Powder Creek and then follows Dease River.

J 397.9 (645.4 km) **AH 48.2** (77.6 km) Camp Creek.

J 399.4 (648 km) **AH 46.7** (75.1 km) Beaver Dam Creek.

J 400.3 (649.4 km) **AH 45.8** (73.7 km) Beaver Dam rest area with visitor information sign to west.

J 400.6 (649.8 km) **AH 45.5** (73.3 km) Leaving Cassiar Mountains, entering Yukon Plateau, northbound.

J 402.5 (652.9 km) **AH 43.6** (70.2 km) Baking Powder Creek.

J 410.9 (666.5km) **AH 35.2** (56.7 km) Gravel access road to French Creek B.C. Forest Service campsite 0.6 miles/1 km from highway. Rustic. Tables, rock fire ring (bring firewood), small boat launch into Dease River, no fee.

J 411.2 (667 km) **AH 34.9** (56.1 km) French Creek 2-lane concrete bridge.

J 417.5 (677.2 km) **AH 28.6** (46.1 km) Twentyeight Mile Creek. Cassiar Mountains rise to south.

J 420.2 (681.8 km) **AH 25.9** (41.6 km) Wheeler Lake to west.

J 422.9 (686.1 km) **AH 23.2** (37.3 km) Blue River Forest Service Road to east.

J 426.3 (691.5 km) **AH 19.8** (31.9 km) Blue River 2-lane concrete bridge.

J 429.7 (697.1 km) **AH 16.4** (26.4 km) Turnout at **Blue Lakes;** litter barrels, picnic tables and fishing for pike and grayling.

J 431.5 (700 km) **AH 14.6** (23.5 km) Mud Hill Creek.

J 436 (707.4 km) **AH 10.1** (16.2 km) Old Faddy Forest Service Road.

J 440.1 (714 km) **AH 6** (9.6 km) Turnout with litter barrels beside Cormier Creek.

J 443.8 (720 km) **AH 2.3** (3.7 km) Leaving British Columbia northbound; leaving Yukon Territory southbound.

J 444 (720.3 km) **AH 2.1** (3.4 km) Turnout to west at BC–YT border, 60th parallel. Information sign. *NOTE: Drive with headlights on at all times in Yukon Territory.*

J 445.3 (722.5 km) **AH 0.8** (1.2 km) **Albert Creek.** Good grayling fishing. Yukon Territory fishing license required.

J 446.1 (723.7 km) **AH 0 Junction** of Cassiar Highway with Alaska Highway. Gas, store, campground and RV park, cafe, souvenirs, laundromat, camp-style motel, saloon, propane, towing and car repair at junction. Turn left for Whitehorse, right for Watson Lake, 13.6 miles/21.9 km southeast. Watson Lake is the nearest major community.

Junction 37 Services. See display ad this section.

Turn to **Milepost DC 626.2** in the ALASKA HIGHWAY section (page 116) for log of Alaska Highway from this junction.

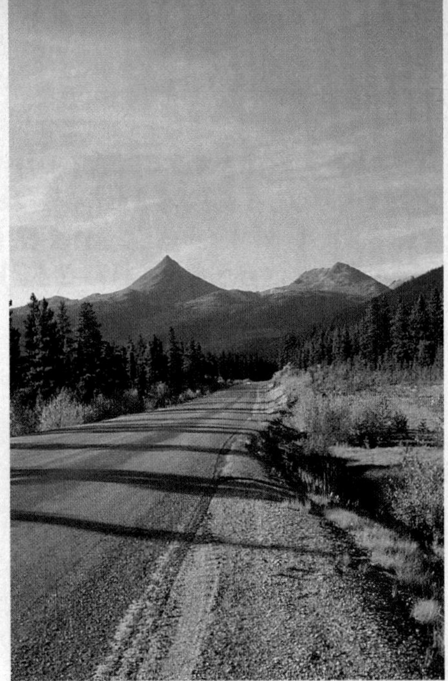

Needlepoint Mountain, Milepost J 367.3. (Judy Parkin, staff)

KLONDIKE LOOP

Alaska Highway Junction to Taylor Highway Junction via Dawson City, Yukon Territory Yukon Highways 2 and 9 (Top of the World Highway)

(See maps, pages 261–262)

A windy day on Lake Laberge, Milepost J 20.4. (Earl L. Brown, staff)

The Klondike Loop refers to the 327-mile/526-km-long stretch of the Klondike Highway (Yukon Highway 2) from its junction with the Alaska Highway north of Whitehorse to Dawson City; the 65-mile/105-km Top of the World Highway (Yukon Highway 9); and 109 miles/175 km of the Taylor Highway (Alaska Route 5).

All of the Klondike Highway between the Alaska Highway junction and Dawson City is asphalt-surfaced. Beware of Yukon Alaska Transport trucks, each carrying up to 50 tons of lead–zinc concentrates, operating between Faro on the Campbell Highway and the port of Skagway on the south Klondike Highway. The trucks are 8½ feet wide and 85 feet long. Drive with your headlights on at all times.

Watch for road construction on the Top of the World Highway (Yukon Highway 9). This is a gravel road with some hills; a truly scenic route, but slippery in wet weather with some steep grades and winding sections. *CAUTION: Road conditions on some sections of the Alaska portion of this road were in rough condition in 1995!* The top of the World Highway is also scheduled for gravel surfacing in 1996 between kilometreposts 60 and 105 on the Canadian side (miles 38 to 66). Check with the Dawson City Visitor Centre for current road and weather conditions; phone (403) 993-5566. Drive with your headlights on. The Taylor Highway (Alaska Route 5) is a narrow, gravel road with some steep, winding sections and washboard (see the TAYLOR HIGHWAY section). Both the Taylor and Top of the World highways are not maintained from mid-Oct. to April and the arrival of snow effectively closes the roads for winter. Yukon Highway 2 is open year-round.

Alaska-bound motorists may turn off the Alaska Highway north of Whitehorse (**Milepost DC 894.8**); follow the Klondike Highway to Dawson City; ferry from there across the Yukon River; drive west via the Top of the World Highway into Alaska; then take the Taylor Highway south back to the Alaska Highway near Tok (**Milepost DC 1301.7**). Total driving distance is 502 miles/808 km. (Driving distance from Whitehorse to Tok via the Alaska Highway is approximately 396 miles/637 km.)

Although this loop avoids construction on the Alaska Highway, travelers should be aware that the Top of the World Highway (reached by ferry from Dawson City) may not open until late spring. In heavy traffic, there may be a wait of 3 hours or longer for the ferry. Customs stations are open in summer only, 13 hours a day: most likely 8 A.M. to 9 P.M. Alaska time, and 9 A.M. to 10 P.M. Pacific time. There are no restrooms, services or currency exchanges available at the border.

The highway between Skagway and the Alaska Highway, sometimes referred to as the South Klondike, is also designated Klondike Highway 2 (see KLONDIKE HIGHWAY 2 section for log of that road).

Kilometreposts along the highway to Dawson City reflect distance from Skagway. Our log's driving distances were measured in miles from the junction of the Alaska Highway to Dawson City by our field editor. These mileages were converted into kilometres with the exception of the kilometre distance following Skagway (S). That figure reflects the physical location of the kilometrepost and is not necessarily an accurate conversion of the mileage figure.

The route from Whitehorse to Dawson City began as a trail used by miners and trappers at the turn of the century. Steamships also provided passenger service between Whitehorse and Dawson City. A road was built connecting the Alaska Highway with the United Keno Hill Mine at Mayo in 1950. By 1955, the Mayo Road had been upgraded for automobile traffic and extended to Dawson City. In 1960, the last of 3 steel bridges, crossing the Yukon, Pelly and Stewart rivers, was completed. The only ferry crossing remaining is the Yukon River crossing at Dawson City. Mayo Road (Yukon Highway 11) from Stewart Crossing to Mayo, Elsa and Keno was redesignated the Silver Trail in 1985 (see SILVER TRAIL section for road log).

Emergency Medical Services: On Yukon Highway 2 from **Milepost J 0** to **J 55.6** (Whitehorse to Braeburn Lodge), phone Whitehorse Ambulance toll free 1-667-3333 or RCMP 1-667-3333. From **Milepost J 55.6** to **J 169.4** (Braeburn Lodge to Pelly Crossing), phone Carmacks Medical Emergency (403) 863-4444 or RCMP (403) 863-5555. From **Milepost J 169.4** to **J 242.9** (Pelly Crossing to McQuesten River Lodge), phone Mayo Medical Emergency (403) 996-4444 or RCMP (403) 996-5555. From **Milepost J 242.9** to **J 327.2** and on Yukon Highway 9 from **Milepost D 0** to **D 66.1** (McQuesten River Lodge to Dawson City to Alaska border), phone Dawson City Medical Emergency (403) 993-4444 or RCMP (403) 993-5555. From **Milepost D 66.1** to **D 78.8** (Alaska border to Taylor Highway), phone Tok Area EMS at 911 or (907) 883-5111.

Klondike Loop Log

YUKON HIGHWAY 2
This section of the log shows distance from junction with the Alaska Highway (J) followed by distance from Dawson City (D) and distance from Skagway (S). Physical kilometreposts show distance from Skagway.

J 0 D 327.2 (526.6 km) **S 119.2** (191.8 km) **Junction** with the Alaska Highway (**Milepost DC 894.8**).

KLONDIKE LOOP *Milepost J 0 to Milepost J 296*

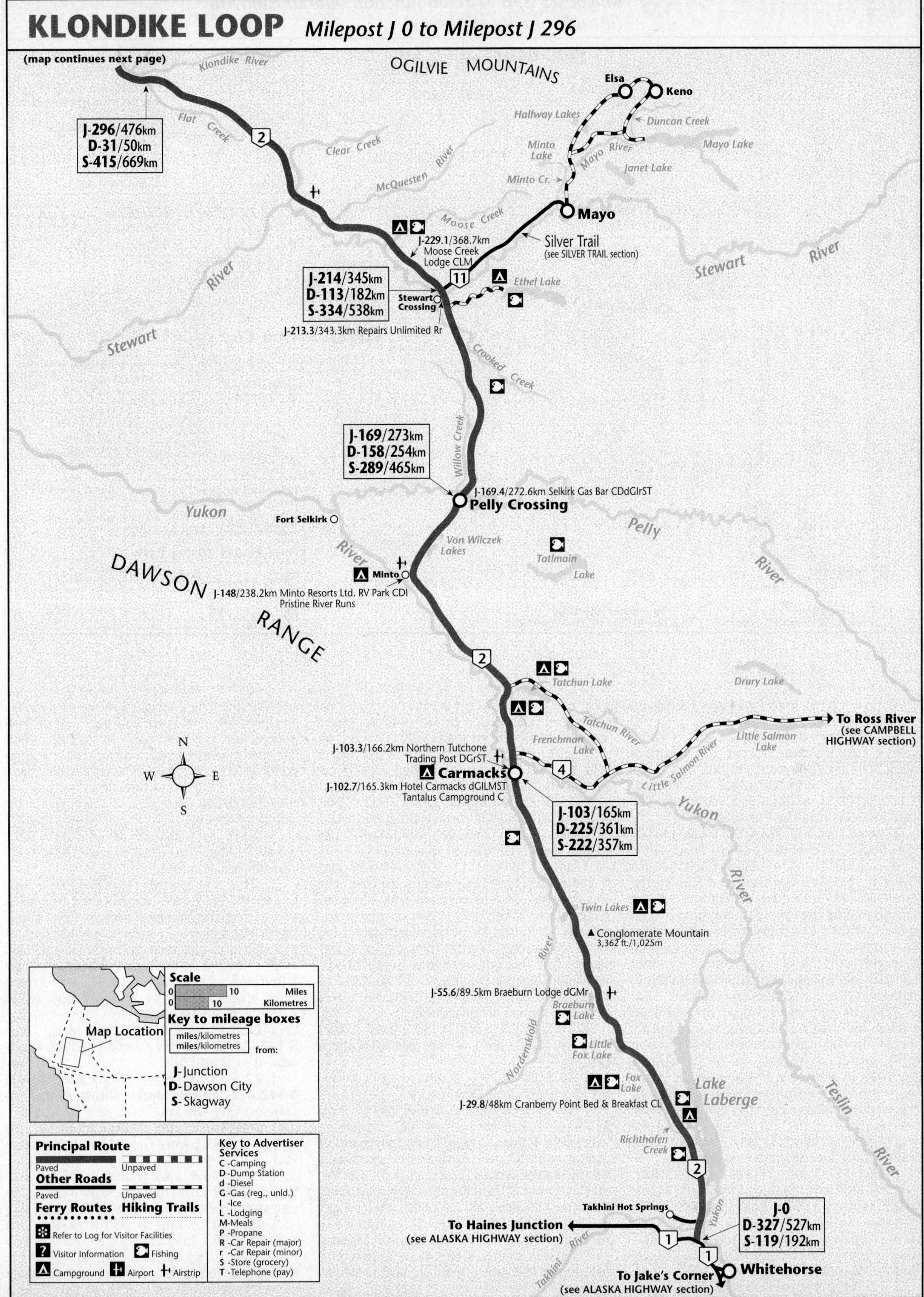

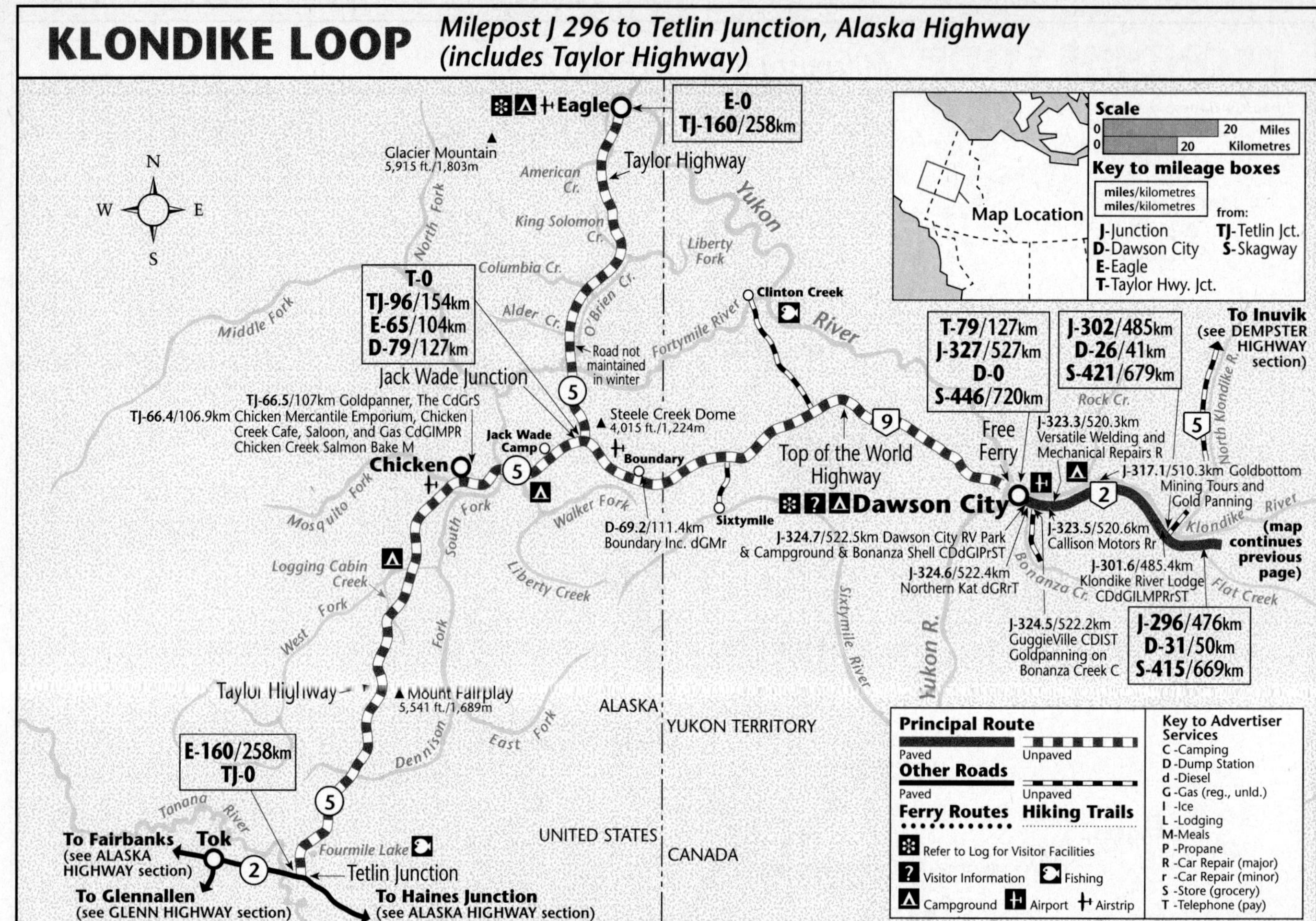

J 0.6 (1 km) **D 326.6** (525.6 km) **S 119.8** (192.8 km) Road west leads to McPherson subdivision.

J 1 (1.6 km) **D 326.2** (525 km) **S 120.2** (193.4 km) Ranches, farms and livestock next 20 miles/32 km northbound.

J 2.3 (3.7 km) **D 324.9** (522.9 km) **S 121.5** (195.5 km) Takhini River bridge. The Takhini flows into the Yukon River.

J 3.8 (6.1 km) **D 323.4** (520.4 km) **S 123** (197.9 km) Takhini Hot Springs Road. Drive west 6 miles/9.7 km via paved road for Takhini Hot Springs; bed and breakfasts, camping, cafe, trail rides, ski trails in winter. The source of the springs maintains a constant 117°F/47°C temperature and flows at 86 gallons a minute. The hot springs pool averages 100°F/38°C year-round. The water contains no sulfur. The chief minerals present are calcium, magnesium and iron.

Trappers and Indians used these springs around the turn of the century, arriving by way of the Takhini River or the old Dawson Trail. During construction of the Alaska Highway in the early 1940s, the U.S. Army maintained greenhouses in the area and reported remarkable growth regardless of the season.

J 9.4 (15.1 km) **D 317.8** (511.4 km) **S 128.6** (207 km) Sawmill to west.

J 10.7 (17.2 km) **D 316.5** (509.3 km) **S 129.9** (209 km) Shallow Bay Road. Access to Northern Splendor Reindeer Farm. This reindeer farm is 0.8 mile/1.3 km east. The farm is open to visitors in summer from 7 A.M. to 6 P.M.; there is an admission charge. Pull-through drive for big rigs.

J 12.7 (20.4 km) **D 314.5** (506.1 km) **S 131.9** (212.2 km) Horse Creek Road leads east to Lower Laberge Indian village and lakeshore cottages. **Horse Creek**; good grayling fishing from road.

J 15.1 (24.3 km) **D 312.1** (502.3 km) **S 134.3** (216.1 km) Access to bed and breakfast, 0.9 miles/1.5 km west.

J 15.8 (25.4 km) **D 311.4** (501.1 km) **S 135** (217.2 km) Microwave site near road.

J 16.8 (27 km) **D 310.4** (499.5 km) **S 136** (219.1 km) Large turnout to west.

J 17.4 (28 km) **D 309.8** (498.6 km) **S 136.6** (220 km) Lake Laberge to east. The Yukon River widens to form this 40-mile-/64-km-long lake. Lake Laberge was made famous by Robert W. Service with the lines: "The Northern Lights have seen queer sights. But the queerest they ever did see, was that night on the marge of Lake Lebarge I cremated Sam McGee," (from his poem "The Cremation of Sam McGee").

J 18.2 (29.3 km) **D 309** (497.3 km) **S 137.4** (221.1 km) Gravel pit turnout to east.

J 20.3 (32.7 km) **D 306.9** (493.9 km) **S 139.5** (224.5 km) Deep Creek.

J 20.4 (32.8 km) **D 306.8** (493.7 km) **S 139.6** (224.6 km) Historical marker at turnoff for **Lake Laberge** Yukon government campground. On the campground road are a bakery, canoe rentals, emergency phone and message post. The campground is situated 1.8 miles/2.9 km east on Lake Laberge next to Deep Creek; 22 RV sites, $8 camping fee, resident campground host, group camping area, kitchen shelter, water, boat launch, and fishing for lake trout, grayling and northern pike.

CAUTION: Storms can blow up quickly and without warning on Lake Laberge as on other northern lakes. Canoes and other small craft should stay to the west side of the lake, where the shoreline affords safe refuges should a storm come up. The east side of the lake is lined with high rocky bluffs, and there are few places to pull out. Small craft should not navigate the middle of the lake.

J 20.9 (33.6 km) **D 306.3** (492.9 km) **S 140.1** (225.5 km) View of Lake Laberge for southbound travelers.

J 21.2 (34.1 km) **D 306** (492.4 km) **S 140.4** (225.9 km) Northbound the highway enters the Miners Range, plateau country of the Yukon, an immense wilderness of forested dome-shaped mountains and high ridges, dotted with lakes and traversed by tributaries of the Yukon River. To the west, Pilot Mountain in the Miners Range (elev. 6,739 feet/2,054m) is visible.

J 22.8 (36.7 km) **D 304.4** (489.9 km) **S 142** (228.5 km) **Fox Creek**; grayling, excellent in June and July.

J 23.5 (37.8 km) **D 303.7** (488.7 km) **S 142.7** (229.8 km) Marker shows distance to Dawson City 486 km.

J 26.9 (43.3 km) **D 300.3** (483.3 km) **S 146.1** (235.1 km) Gravel pit turnout to east.

J 28.8 (46.3 km) **D 298.4** (480.2 km) **S 148** (238.2 km) Highway now follows the east shoreline of Fox Lake northbound.

J 29.4 (47.3 km) **D 297.8** (479.2 km) **S 148.6** (239.1 km) Turnout to west on Fox Lake. Historic sign here reads: "In 1883, U.S. Army Lt. Frederick Schwatka completed a survey of the entire length of the Yukon

Montague House, a typical early-day roadhouse, at Milepost J 81.4. (Earl L. Brown, staff)

River. One of many geographical features that he named was Fox Lake, which he called Richthofen Lake, after geographer Freiherr Von Richthofen. Known locally as Fox Lake, the name was adopted in 1957. The Miners Range to the west was named by geologist/explorer George Mercer Dawson in 1887 'for the miners met by us along the river.' "

J 29.8 (48 km) **D 297.4** (478.6 km) **S 149** (239.8 km) **Cranberry Point Bed & Breakfast.** Open year-round. Wonderful northern wilderness experience, right on beautiful Fox Lake. Woodstove cooking, full breakfast, other meals arranged! Comfortable guestroom and cabin. Limited dry camping. Reservations recommended: radio phone Whitehorse mobile operator, JJ3-9257 Fox Lake Channel. Km 240 Klondike Hwy., Site 15, #91, Whitehorse, Yukon Y1A 5W8. [ADVERTISEMENT]

J 34.8 (56 km) **D 292.4** (470.6 km) **S 154** (247.8 km) Turnoff west for **Fox Lake** Yukon government campground; 30 RV and 3 tent-only sites, $8 camping fee, kitchen shelter, drinking water and boat launch. Good fishing for lake trout and burbot from the shore at the campground; excellent grayling year-round.

J 35.2 (56.6 km) **D 292** (469.9 km) **S 154.4** (248.5 km) Turnout with view of Fox Lake. Good photo spot.

J 39.8 (64.1 km) **D 287.4** (462.5 km) **S 159** (255.8 km) North end of Fox Lake.

J 42 (67.6 km) **D 285.2** (459 km) **S 161.2** (259.4 km) **Little Fox Lake** to west; lake trout 3 to 8 lbs., fish the islands.

J 43.8 (70.5 km) **D 283.4** (456.1 km) **S 163** (262.1 km) Double-ended/turnout with litter barrel to west beside Little Fox Lake. Small boat launch.

J 49.5 (79.7 km) **D 277.7** (446.9 km) **S 168.7** (271.5 km) Large turnout to west.

J 50.1 (80.6 km) **D 277.1** (445.9 km) **S 169.3** (272.4 km) First glimpse of Braeburn Lake for northbound travelers.

J 52.5 (84.5 km) **D 274.7** (442.1 km) **S 171.7** (276.3 km) Gravel pit turnout to east.

J 55.6 (89.5 km) **D 271.6** (437.1 km) **S 174.8** (281.5 km) Braeburn Lodge to west; food, gas, lodging and minor car repairs. One Braeburn Lodge cinnamon bun will feed 4 people. The lodge is also home of the 200-mile/320-km "Cinnamon Bun" Dog Sled Race, held the first weekend in February.

Braeburn Lodge. See display ad this section.

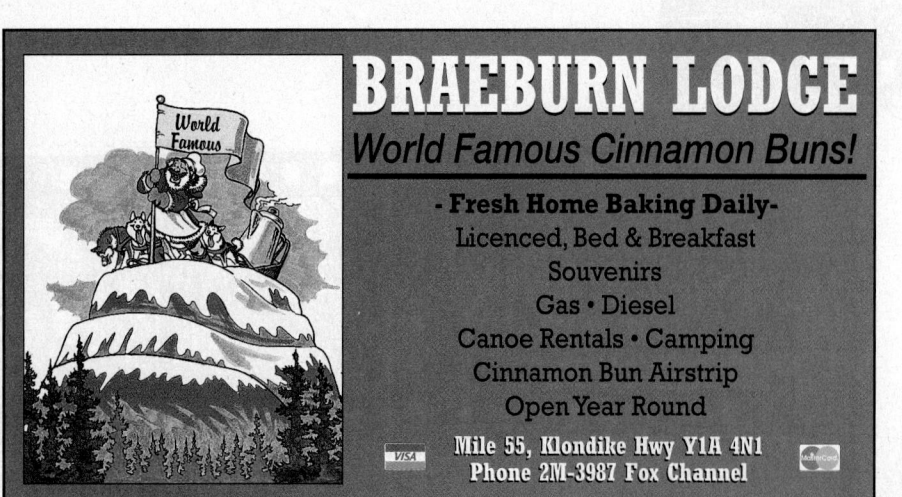

Private Aircraft: Braeburn airstrip to east, dubbed Cinnamon Bun Strip; elev. 2,350 feet/716m; length 3,000 feet/914m; dirt strip; wind sock.

J 66.3 (106.7 km) **D 260.9** (419.9 km) **S 185.5** (298.5 km) Photo stop; pull-through turnout on east side of highway with information sign about Conglomerate Mountain (elev. 3,361 feet/1,024m). Sign reads: "The Laberge Series was formed at the leading edge of volcanic mud flows some 185 million years ago (Early Jurassic). These flows solidified into sheets several kilometres long and about 1 km wide and 100m thick. This particular series of sheets stretches from Atlin, BC, to north of Carmacks, a distance of about 350 km. Other conglomerates of this series form Five Finger Rapids."

Rock hounds can find pieces of conglomerate in almost any borrow pit along this stretch of highway.

J 71.6 (115.2 km) **D 255.6** (411.3 km) **S 190.8** (307 km) Turnouts on both sides of highway between Twin Lakes. These 2 small lakes, 1 on either side of the road, are known for their beauty and colour.

J 72.3 (116.4 km) **D 254.9** (410.2 km) **S 191.5** (308.2 km) Turnoff to west for **Twin Lakes** Yukon government campground; 18 sites, $8 camping fee, drinking water, boat launch. Lake is stocked. Enjoyable fishing for lake trout, grayling and pike. Good swimming for the *hardy!*

J 81.4 (131 km) **D 245.8** (395.6 km) **S 200.6** (323 km) Large turnout with litter barrel to east at remains of Montague House, a typical early-day roadhouse which offered lodging and meals on the stagecoach route between Whitehorse and Dawson City. A total of 52 stopping places along this route were listed in the Jan. 16, 1901, edition of the *Whitehorse Star* under "On the Winter Trail between White Horse and Dawson Good Accommodations for Travellers." Montague House was listed at Mile 99. Good photo stop.

J 87.4 (140.7 km) **D 239.8** (385.9 km) **S 206.6** (332.5 km) Small lake to west.

J 93.7 (150.8 km) **D 233.5** (375.8 km) **S 212.9** (343.9 km) Side road to east, information sign about agate deposits.

J 100.1 (161.1 km) **D 227.1** (365.5 km) **S 219.3** (352.9 km) Carmacks town limits.

J 101.3 (163 km) **D 225.9** (363.5 km)

S 220.5 (354.8 km) **Nordenskiold River** to west was named by Lt. Frederick Schwatka, U.S. Army, for Swedish arctic explorer Erik Nordenskiold. Good grayling and pike fishing all summer. This river, which parallels the highway for several miles, flows into the Yukon River at Carmacks.

J 101.5 (163.3 km) **D 225.7** (363.2 km) **S 220.7** (355.2 km) Pull-through rest area to east with large mural of *Moment at Tantalus Butte.* Litter barrels and outhouses.

Carmacks

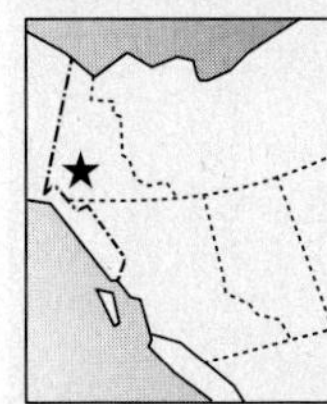

J 102.7 (165.3 km) **D 224.5** (361.3 km) **S 221.9** (357.1 km). Located on the banks of the Yukon River, Carmacks is the only highway crossing of the Yukon River between Whitehorse and Dawson City. **Population:** 489. **Emergency Services: RCMP**, phone (403) 863-5555. **Fire Department**, phone (403) 863-2222. **Nurse**, phone (403) 863-4444. **Ambulance**, phone (403) 863-444. **Forest Fire Control**, (403) 863-5271.

Private Aircraft: Carmacks airstrip; elev. 1,770 feet/539m; length 5,200 feet/1,585m; gravel; no fuel.

Carmacks was once an important stop for Yukon River steamers traveling between Dawson City and Whitehorse, and it continues as a supply point today for modern river travelers. Carmacks has survived—while other river ports have not—as a service centre for highway traffic and mining interests. Carmacks was also a major stopping point on the old Whitehorse to Dawson Trail. It was named for George Carmack; see feature in this section. (For more on George Carmack read *Carmack of the Klondike* by James Albert Johnson.)

Traveler facilities include a hotel, motel, bed and breakfast, Carmacks Municipal Campground and several territorial campgrounds; restaurant, gas bar, general store (with groceries, bakery and hardware) and laundromat at Hotel Carmacks; post office and bank (both with limited hours), general store, gas bar and dump station at Northern Tutchone Trading Post. The trading post also has some Native crafts for sale. There are also churches, a school, swimming pool, service centre, cafe and a community library. ▲

In 1995, a 1.2-mile/2-km interpretive boardwalk was constructed, making it possible to enjoy a stroll along the Yukon River;

GEORGE CARMACK

In the summer of 1896, while prospecting on Rabbit Creek, George Washington Carmack unearthed a 5-dollar pan of coarse gold, during a time when a 10-cent pan was considered a good find. That same winter, more than a ton of gold was extracted from Rabbit Creek (which Carmack renamed Bonanza) and its tributary, Eldorado. The next spring, when word finally reached the States, more than 100,000 adventurers set off for the Klondike. Carmack, who for 11 years had lucklessly prospected the Yukon, had begun the last great gold rush.

George Carmack
(Photo courtesy of Alaska State Library, Early Prints Collection)

Carmack had arrived in Juneau, AK, in 1885, hoping to strike it rich and return to California to marry his sweetheart. The next 10 years were marked by Carmack's repeated failures in prospecting and his remarkable persistence and ingenuity in continuing his quest. Finding himself broke in Juneau, he hunted deer and sold the meat to survive. Later, he worked as a packer alongside Tagish Indians, one of the few white men ever to take on this crushing occupation. For 10 dollars, each man would haul a 100-lb. pack across the Chilkoot Trail for the miners' expeditions. Whenever Carmack scraped together enough money, he and his 2 Tagish partners, Skookum Jim and Tagish Charley, would prospect for themselves.

To his own surprise, Carmack eventually realized that he was no part-time gold seeker in the North—his life was in the Yukon. He lived for a time among the Tagish Indians (he had received word that his California girlfriend had left him), picking up their language and learning how to survive in the North. By the time he struck gold in the Klondike, he had become a remarkable outdoorsman. He married a Tagish woman, Kate with whom he had a daughter.

Carmack eventually returned to Seattle as a rich man. While most of the other original stakers on the Bonanza managed to dissipate their fortunes with astounding speed, Carmack invested in real estate and other mining prospects (he mined in Western Washington almost to the day of his death in 1922). He left an estate worth $150,000 (a fortune in 1922), which was divided between his second wife, Marguerite, and his daughter by Kate (whom he divorced in 1900), Graphie Gracey.

KLONDIKE GOLD RUSH CENTENNIAL 1896 • 1996 THE DISCOVERY

The town of Carmacks is named after him. It had been a trading post he established shortly before his gold strike. In 1896, the post had gone bankrupt, but Carmack, undaunted, decided to move his family to Fortymile where he could fish to eat and cut timber to sell. That same summer he become the owner of Discovery Claim on the richest goldfield in the North.

beautiful view of countryside and Tantalus Butte, gazebo and park at end, wheelchair accessible.

Carmacks is also an excellent area for rock hounds. There are 5 agate trails in the area, which can double as good, short hiking trails.

Check locally for boat tours to Five Finger and Rink rapids and Fort Selkirk. Fort Selkirk was an important trading post and subsequent RCMP post (see **Milepost J 148.6**). Helicopter service and local canoe and hiking tours available. Abundant fishing in area rivers and lakes: salmon, grayling, northern pike, lake and rainbow trout, whitefish and ling cod.

Hotel Carmacks. See display ad this section.

Tantalus Campground. See display ad this section.

Canoeing into the midnight sunset on the Yukon River. (© Rich Reid)

Klondike Loop Log

(continued)

J 103.2 (166.1 km) **D 224** (360.5 km) **S 222.4** (357.9 km) Yukon River bridge. Turnout and parking area at south end of bridge; 2.3-mile-/3.7-km-long trail to Coal Mine Lake.

J 103.3 (166.2 km) **D 223.9** (360.3 km) **S 222.5** (358.1 km) Trading post with store, gas and diesel, vehicle repair and post office at north end of Yukon River bridge. Fishing tackle and licenses available.

Northern Tutchone Trading Post. See display ad this section.

J 104.4 (168 km) **D 222.8** (358.6 km) **S 223.6** (359.8 km) **Junction** with Campbell Highway (Yukon Highway 4), also known as Watson Lake–Carmacks Road, which leads east and south to Faro, Ross River and Watson Lake. See CAMPBELL HIGHWAY section.

J 105.1 (169.1 km) **D 222.1** (357.4 km) **S 224.3** (361 km) Side road east to Tantalus Butte Coal Mine; the coal was used in Cyprus Anvil Mine's mill near Faro for drying concentrates. The butte was named by Lt. Frederick Schwatka because it is seen many times before it is actually reached.

J 105.4 (169.6 km) **D 221.8** (356.9 km) **S 224.6** (361.4 km) Turnout to west with litter barrels, information sign, view of Yukon River Valley.

J 108 (173.8 km) **D 219.2** (352.8 km) **S 227.2** (365.3 km) Side road west to agate site for rock hounds.

J 110 (177 km) **D 217.2** (349.5 km) **S 229.2** (368.8 km) Small lake to west.

J 117.5 (189.1 km) **D 209.7** (337.5 km) **S 236.7** (378.5 km) Pull-through rest area to west with toilets, litter barrels and viewing platform for Five Finger Rapids. Information sign here reads: "Five Finger Rapids named by early miners for the 5 channels, or fingers, formed by the rock pillars. They are a navigational hazard. The safest passage is through the nearest, or east, passage." Stairs (219 steps) lead down to a closer view of the rapids.

J 118.9 (191.3 km) **D 208.3** (335.2 km) **S 238.1** (380.6 km) Tatchun Creek. Side road to Five Finger Rapids boat-tour operator.

J 119 (191.5 km) **D 208.2** (335.1 km) **S 238.2** (380.8 km) First turnoff (northbound) to east for **Tatchun Creek** Yukon government campground; 12 sites, $8 camping fee, kitchen shelter and drinking water. Good fishing for grayling, June through Sept.; salmon, July through Aug.

J 119.1 (191.7 km) **D 208.1** (334.9 km) **S 238.3** (380.9 km) Second turnoff (northbound) east for Tatchun Creek Yukon government campground.

J 119.6 (192.5 km) **D 207.6** (334.1 km) **S 238.8** (381.8 km) Side road leads east to **Tatchun Lake.** Follow side road 4.3 miles/6.9 km east to boat launch and pit toilets. Continue past boat launch 1.1 miles/1.8 km for Tatchun Lake Yukon government campground with 20 sites, $8 camping fee, pit toilets, firewood, litter barrels and picnic tables. Fishing for northern pike, best in spring or fall.

This maintained side road continues east past Tatchun Lake to Frenchman Lake, then loops south to the Campbell Highway, approximately 25 miles/40 km distance. The main access to Frenchman Lake is from the Campbell Highway.

J 121.8 (196 km) **D 205.4** (330.6 km) **S 241** (388 km) Tatchun Hill.

J 126.6 (203.7 km) **D 200.6** (322.8 km) **S 245.8** (395.8 km) Large turnout overlooking Yukon River.

J 126.9 (204.2 km) **D 200.3** (322.3 km) **S 246.1** (396.3 km) Highway descends hill, northbound. Watch for falling rocks.

J 132 (212.4 km) **D 195.2** (314.1 km) **S 251.2** (404.5 km) McGregor Creek.

J 135 (217.3 km) **D 192.2** (309.3 km) **S 254.2** (409.4 km) Northbound, first evidence of the huge forest fires of 1995. The fires started on June 12, one burning on either side of the Yukon River. The fires were finally extinguished at the end of July, after they had consumed 325,000 acres of forest.

J 136.6 (219.8 km) **D 190.6** (306.7 km) **S 255.8** (411.9 km) Good representation of White River ash layer for approximately next mile northbound. About 1,250 years ago a layer of white volcanic ash coated a third of the southern Yukon, or some 125,000 square miles/323,725 square km, and it is easily visible along many roadcuts. This distinct line conveniently provides a division used by archaeologists for dating artifacts: materials found below this major stratigraphic marker are considered to have been deposited before A.D. 700, while those found above the ash layer are postdated A.D. 700. The small amount of data available does not support volcanic activity in the White River area during the same period. One theory is that the ash could have spewn forth from a single violent volcanic eruption. The source may be buried under the Klutlan Glacier in the St. Elias Mountains in eastern Alaska.

J 144 (231.7 km) **D 183.2** (294.8 km) **S 263.2** (423.8 km) McCabe Creek.

J 148 (238.2 km) **D 179.2** (288.4 km) **S 267.2** (430.4 km) **Minto Resorts Ltd. R.V. Park.** 1,400-foot Yukon River frontage. Halfway between Whitehorse and Dawson City on the Old Stage Road, Minto was once a steamboat landing and trading post. 27 sites, wide easy access, picnic tables, firepits, souvenirs, fishing licenses, ice, snacks, pop. Coin-op showers and laundry, clean restrooms, dump station, and water. Bus tour buffet, reservation only. Caravans welcome. Wildlife viewing opportunities. Try fishing the river. Owned and operated by Yukoners. Come and visit us! See display ad this section. [ADVERTISEMENT] ▲

J 148 (238.2 km) **D 179.2** (288.4 km) **S 267.2** (430.4 km) **Pristine River Runs.** See display ad this section.

J 148.6 (239.1 km) **D 178.6** (287.4 km) **S 267.8** (431.4 km) Minto Road, a short loop road, leads west to location of the former riverboat landing and trading post of **MINTO.** Drive in 1.2 miles/1.9 km for Minto Landing Yukon government campground situated on the scenic, grassy banks of the Yukon River; 10 sites, kitchen shelter and drinking water. Camping fee $8. Large flat grassy area may be used for parking. This campground is used as a put in and takeout site by river travelers. Check with Pristine River Runs about river tours to Sheep Mountain and Fort Selkirk leaving daily from Minto Resorts. ▲

Fort Selkirk, 25 river miles/40 km from here, was established by Robert Campbell in 1848 for the Hudson's Bay Co. In 1852, the fort was destroyed by Chilkat Indians, who had dominated the fur trade of central Yukon–trading here with the Northern Tutchone people (Selkirk First Nation), who used the area as a seasonal home and exchanged furs for the Chilkats' coastal goods–until the arrival of the Hudson's Bay Co. The site was occupied sporadically by traders, missionaries and the RCMP until the 1950s. About 40 buildings still stand in good repair. A river trip to Fort Selkirk lets travelers see the fort virtually unchanged since the turn of the century.

Private Aircraft: Minto airstrip; elev. 1,550 feet/472m; length 5,000 feet/1,524m; gravel.

J 160.3 (258 km) **D 166.9** (268.6 km) **S 279.5** (450.5 km) Side road east to Von Wilczek Lakes.

J 162.8 (262 km) **D 164.4** (264.6 km) **S 282** (454.5 km) Northern limits of damage from 1995 fires.

J 163.4 (263 km) **D 163.8** (263.6 km) **S 282.6** (455.5 km) Rock Island Lake to east.

J 164.2 (264.2 km) **D 163** (262.3 km) **S 283.4** (456.8 km) Turnout. Small lake to west.

J 168.7 (271.5 km) **D 158.5** (255.1 km) **S 287.9** (464 km) Road west to garbage dump.

J 169.4 (272.6 km) **D 157.8** (253.9 km) **S 288.6** (465 km) Side road to **PELLY CROSSING** (pop. about 290). RCMP, phone (403) 537-5555. There are a nursing station, post office and trading post, general store with phone, campgrounds, and gas station with unleaded, diesel, tire repair and dump station. ▲

Selkirk Gas Bar. See display ad this section.

This Selkirk Indian community attracted residents from Minto when the highway to Dawson City was built. School, mission and sawmill located near the big bridge. The local economy is based on hunting, trapping, fishing and guiding. The Selkirk Indian Band has erected signs near the bridge on the history and culture of the Selkirk people.

J 169.7 (273.1 km) **D 157.5** (253.5 km) **S 288.9** (465.5 km) Pelly River bridge.

J 170.4 (274.2 km) **D 156.8** (252.3 km) **S 289.6** (467 km) Turnout with litter barrel to east. View of Pelly Crossing and river valley. A historical marker here honours the Canadian Centennial (1867–1967). The Pelly River was named in 1840 by explorer Robert Campbell for Sir John Henry Pelly, governor of the Hudson's Bay Co. The Pelly heads near the Northwest Territories border and flows approximately 375 miles/603 km to the Yukon River.

J 171.5 (276 km) **D 155.7** (250.6 km) **S 290.7** (468.6 km) **Private Aircraft:** Airstrip to east; elev. 1,870 feet/570m; length 3,000 feet/914m; gravel. No services.

J 179.6 (289 km) **D 147.6** (237.5 km) **S 298.8** (481.7 km) Pull-through turnout to east.

J 180.9 (291.1 km) **D 146.3** (235.4 km) **S 300.1** (483.8 km) Small lake to west.

J 183.8 (295.8 km) **D 143.4** (230.8 km) **S 303** (488.6 km) Large turnout to west. Bridge over Willow Creek.

J 185.5 (298.5 km) **D 141.7** (228 km) **S 304.7** (491.3 km) Side road west to Jackfish Lake.

J 195.6 (314.8 km) **D 131.6** (211.8 km) **S 314.8** (506.6 km) Access road west to **Wrong Lake** (stocked); fishing.

J 197.4 (317.7 km) **D 129.8** (208.9 km) **S 316.6** (511 km) Turnout with litter barrel to west. Winding descent begins for northbound traffic.

J 203.6 (327.7 km) **D 123.6** (198.9 km) **S 322.8** (521 km) Pull-through turnout to east.

J 205.9 (331.4 km) **D 121.3** (195.2 km) **S 325.1** (524.6 km) **Crooked Creek**; pike; grayling, use flies, summer best.

J 207.2 (333.4 km) **D 120** (193.1 km) **S 326.4** (526.7 km) Pull-through turnout with litter barrel to east at turnoff for **Ethel Lake** Yukon government campground. Drive in 16.6 miles/26.7 km on narrow and winding side road (not recommended for large RVs) for campground; 14 sites, boat launch, fishing. Camping fee $8. ▲

J 213.3 (343.3 km) **D 113.9** (183.3 km) **S 332.5** (535.1 km) **Repairs Unlimited**. See display ad this section.

J 213.8 (344.1 km) **D 113.4** (182.5 km) **S 333** (537.3 km) Stewart Crossing government maintenance camp to east.

J 213.9 (344.2 km) **D 113.3** (182.3 km) **S 333.1** (537.5 km) Stewart Crossing Lodge (camping, food, lodging), private RV park and campground, and gas station east side of highway. Turnout with information sign west side of highway; Silver Trail information booth. ▲

In 1886 **STEWART CROSSING** was the site of a trading post established by Arthur Harper, Alfred Mayo and Jack McQuesten to support gold mining in the area. Later a roadhouse was built here as part of the Whitehorse to Dawson overland stage route. Stewart Crossing also functioned as a fuel stop for the riverboats and during the 1930s was a transfer point for the silver ore barges from Mayo.

Harper, Mayo and McQuesten are 3 prominent names in Yukon history. Harper, an Irish immigrant, was one of the first white men to prospect in the Yukon, although he never struck it rich. He died in 1898 in Arizona. (His son, Walter Harper, was on the first complete ascent of Mount McKinley in 1913. Walter died in 1918 in the SS *Princess Sophia* disaster off Juneau.)

Mayo, a native of Maine, explored, prospected and traded in the Yukon until his death in 1924.

McQuesten, like Harper, worked his way north from the California goldfields. Often referred to as the "Father of the Yukon" and a founding member of the Yukon order of Pioneers, Jack Leroy Napoleon McQuesten ended his trading and prospecting days in 1898 when he moved to California. He died in 1909 while in Seattle for the Alaska–Yukon–Pacific Exposition.

J 214.3 (344.9 km) **D 112.9** (181.7 km) **S 333.5** (538 km) Stewart River bridge. The Stewart River flows into the Yukon River upstream from Dawson City.

J 214.4 (345 km) **D 112.8** (181.5 km) **S 333.6** (538.2 km) **Silver Trail (Stewart Crossing) Junction** at north end of Stewart River bridge. Marker shows distance to Dawson 182 km. The Silver Trail Information Centre is located in the restored Binet House in Mayo; phone (403) 996-2926 in summer. The Silver Trail (Yukon Highway 11) leads northeast to Mayo, Elsa and Keno; see SILVER TRAIL section.

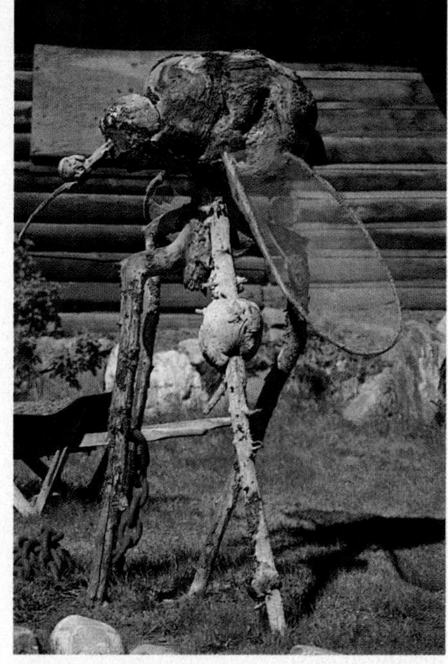
Moose Creek Lodge's Max the Mosquito. (© Carmen Scott)

Yukon Gold Explorer's Passports are stamped at the Keno City Mining Museum and the Binet House in Mayo, 2 of 14 passport stamp locations.

J 214.8 (345.7 km) **D 112.4** (180.9 km) **S 334** (538.8 km) View to west of Stewart River and mountains as highway climbs northbound.

J 220.8 (355.3 km) **D 106.4** (171.2 km) **S 340** (545.1 km) Dry Creek.

J 224.4 (361.1 km) **D 102.8** (165.4 km) **S 343.6** (556.2 km) Access to Stewart River to west. Historical information sign about Stewart River. A major tributary of the Yukon River, the Stewart River was named for James G. Stewart, who discovered it in 1849. Stewart was assistant to Robert Campbell of the Hudson's Bay Co.

J 229.1 (368.7 km) **D 98.1** (157.9 km) **S 348.3** (561.9 km) **Moose Creek Lodge**. A must for Yukon travelers! An authentic trapper's cabin featuring a large selection of Northern books, souvenirs and crafts. In our cozy cafe, enjoy a hearty sourdough pancake breakfast, our scrumptious cinnamon buns, homebaked sourdough bread. Hearty homemade soups, delicious belt-bustin' sandwiches and burgers, mouthwatering homebaked pies. Try our Triple Berry Crumble or Chocolate Heaven ice cream dessert. Meet Max the Mosquito and Murray the Moose! Smokehouse. Cozy rustic economical log cabins. For reservations, dial 1311 and ask for JL3-9570 on Stewart Channel or write, Bag 1, Mayo, YT Y0B 1M0. Moose Creek is also serving group tours in their beautiful open-air gazebo, reservations a must. RV park proposed for 1996. VISA and MasterCard. Your hosts, the Lefler family. [ADVERTISEMENT]

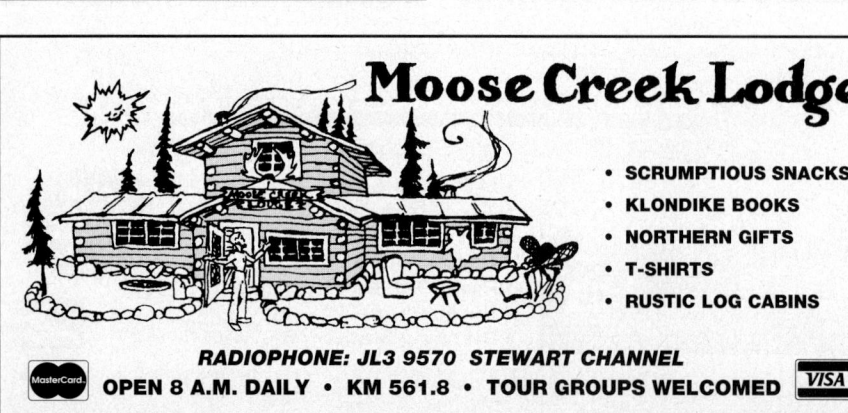

J 229.2 (368.9 km) **D 98** (157.7 km) **S 348.4** (562 km) Moose Creek bridge.

J 229.5 (369.3 km) **D 97.7** (157.2 km) **S 348.7** (562.4 km) Turnout to west at turnoff for Moose Creek Yukon government campground adjacent to **Moose Creek** and Stewart River; good picnic spot. There are 30 RV sites, 6 tent-only sites, kitchen shelter, playground and playfield. Camping fee $8. Short trail to Stewart River. Good fishing for grayling, 1 to 1¼ lbs. ▲

J 242.7 (390.6 km) **D 84.5** (136 km) **S 361.9** (583.7 km) McQuesten River, a tributary of the Stewart River, named for Jack (Leroy Napoleon) McQuesten.

J 242.9 (390.9 km) **D 84.3** (135.7 km) **S 362.1** (584 km) McQuesten, a lodge with cafe, cabins and RV sites. Site of Old McQuesten River Lodge to east. ▲

J 247.5 (398.3 km) **D 79.7** (128.3 km) **S 366.7** (590.1 km) Partridge Creek Farm. Organic vegetables in season.

J 249.3 (401.2 km) **D 77.9** (125.4 km) **S 368.5** (594 km) **Private Aircraft:** McQuesten airstrip 1.2 miles/1.9 km west; elev. 1,500 feet/457m; length 5,000 feet/1,524m; gravel and turf. No services.

J 251.3 (404.4 km) **D 75.9** (122.1 km) **S 370.5** (596.5 km) Clear Creek, access via side road west.

J 260.4 (419.1 km) **D 66.8** (107.5 km) **S 379.6** (612 km) Barlow Lake, access via 0.6-mile-/1-km-long side road west.

J 263.7 (424.4 km) **D 63.5** (102.2 km) **S 382.9** (617.2 km) Beaver Dam Creek.

J 266 (428.1 km) **D 61.2** (98.5 km) **S 385.2** (621 km) Willow Creek.

J 268.5 (432.1 km) **D 58.7** (94.5 km) **S 387.7** (625 km) Flat Hill.

J 268.8 (432.6 km) **D 58.4** (94 km) **S 388** (625.5 km) Gravel Lake to east.

J 272.1 (437.9 km) **D 55.1** (88.7 km) **S 391.3** (630.8 km) Meadow Creek.

J 272.5 (438.5 km) **D 54.7** (88 km) **S 391.7** (631.4 km) Rest area with litter barrel to south.

J 276.5 (445 km) **D 50.7** (81.6 km) **S 395.7** (637.9 km) French Creek.

J 279.7 (450.1 km) **D 47.5** (76.4 km) **S 398.9** (643.1 km) Stone Boat Creek.

J 288.9 (464.9 km) **D 38.3** (61.6 km) **S 408.1** (657.9 km) Rest area.

J 289.3 (465.6 km) **D 37.9** (61 km) **S 408.5** (658.5 km) Geologic point of interest turnout, with information sign, to east overlooking Tintina Trench. This geologic feature, which extends hundreds of miles across Yukon and Alaska, provides visible proof of plate tectonics.

J 295.1 (474.9 km) **D 32.1** (51.7 km) **S 414.3** (667.8 km) Flat Creek.

J 295.9 (476.2 km) **D 31.3** (50.4 km) **S 415.1** (669 km) Klondike River to east.

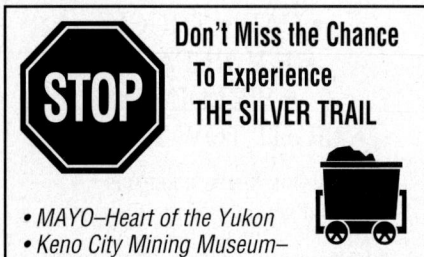

J 297.6 (478.9 km) **D 29.6** (47.6 km) **S 416.8** (671.9 km) Large turnout to east with historic sign about Klondike River and information sign on Dempster Highway.

J 298 (479.6 km) **D 29.2** (47 km) **S 417.2** (672.5 km) Watch for livestock.

J 301.6 (485.4 km) **D 25.6** (41.2 km) **S 420.8** (678.5 km) **Dempster Corner, junction** of Klondike Highway and the Dempster Highway (Yukon Highway 5). Klondike River Lodge east side of highway just north of the junction; open year-round, food, lodging, gas, diesel and propane. The Dempster Highway leads northeast to Inuvik, NWT. See DEMPSTER HIGHWAY section for log of that road. (Details on the Dempster are also available from the Western Arctic Information Centre in Dawson City.)

Klondike River Lodge. See display ad this section.

J 307.3 (494.5 km) **D 19.9** (32 km) **S 426.5** (687.4 km) Goring Creek.

J 308.4 (496.3 km) **D 18.8** (30.3 km) **S 427.6** (689.2 km) Turnout to north with access to the Klondike River.

J 315.2 (507.3 km) **D 12** (19.3 km) **S 434.4** (700 km) Turnoff to north for **Klondike River** Yukon government campground, located on Rock Creek near the Klondike River; 38 sites, kitchen shelter, drinking water, playground. Camping fee $8. ▲

J 315.7 (508.1 km) **D 11.5** (18.5 km) **S 434.9** (700.8 km) Dawson City airport to south. **Private Aircraft:** Runway 02-20; elev. 1,211 feet/369m; length 5,000 feet/1,524m; gravel; fuel 80 (in drums at Dawson City), 100, JP4. Flightseeing trips and air charters available.

J 317.1 (510.3 km) **D 10.1** (16.3 km) **S 436.3** (703.4 km) Hunker Creek Road to south. Access to Goldbottom Mining Tours, 9 miles/15km south, a family-run placer mine offering tours and gold panning; fee charged.

Goldbottom Mining Tours and Gold Panning. See display ad this section.

J 318.4 (512.4 km) **D 8.8** (14.2 km) **S 437.6** (705.4 km) Turnout to south with point of interest sign about Hunker Creek. Albert Hunker staked the first claim on Hunker Creek Sept. 11, 1896. George Carmack made the big discovery on Bonanza Creek on Aug. 17, 1896. Hunker Creek is 16 miles/26 km long, of which 13 miles/21 km was dredged between 1906 and 1966.

J 318.9 (513.2 km) **D 8.3** (13.4 km) **S 438.1** (706.1 km) Bear Creek Road.

J 319.6 (514.3 km) **D 7.6** (12.2 km) **S 438.8** (707.2 km) Turnout with historic sign about the Yukon Ditch and tailings to north. To the south is Bear Creek historical site, operated by Parks Canada. Open 9:30 A.M. to 5 P.M. daily in summer, with scheduled tours. Admission: adults $2.25, children 12 and under free. This 62-acre compound of the Yukon Consolidated Gold Corp. features complete blacksmith and machinery shops and Gold Room.

J 323.3 (520.3 km) **D 3.9** (6.3 km) **S 442.5** (712 km) Collison industrial area; charter helicopter service, bulk fuel plant and heavy equipment repairs.

Versatile Welding and Mechanical Repairs. See display ad this section.

J 323.5 (520.6 km) **D 3.7** (6 km) **S 442.7** (712.4 km) **Callision Motors.** Located in the Callison Industrial Subdivision. The public is served by certified mechanics for automotive, and recreational vehicle repairs, along with tire repair and 24-hour towing services. National Auto League-approved roadside service. Phone (403) 993-6953, fax (403) 993-5731. VISA and MasterCard accepted. Open year-round for your convenience. [ADVERTISEMENT]

J 324.5 (522.2 km) **D 2.7** (4.3 km) **S 443.7** (714 km) Bonanza Creek Road to Discovery Claim and historic Dredge No. 4, largest wooden hull dredge in North America. Restoration of the dredge is under way. Interpretive centre on site; tours 9 A.M. to 5 P.M. daily June through Aug. Admission: adults $2.25, children 12 and under free. Bonanza Creek Road is maintained for 10 miles/16.1 km. Commercial RV park and gold panning at junction. ▲

GuggieVille. Good Sam. This clean, attractive campground is built on dredge tailings at the former site of the Guggenheim's mining camp. 72 RV sites with water and electricity, 28 unserviced sites,

public showers ($2 each). Rates include tax. Car wash, dump station and laundromat are available. A mining display is open to the public free of charge. Gold panning discount

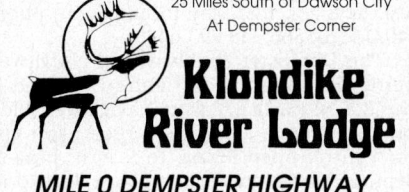

View from Dome Road of tailings from Bonanza Creek mining. (Earl L. Brown, staff)

Drive with your headlights on at all times.

for those staying at GuggieVille. Phone (403) 993-5008. Fax (403) 993-5006. [ADVERTISEMENT]▲

J 324.5 (522.2 km) D 2.7 (4.3 km) S 443.7 (714 km) **Bonanza Creek Goldpanning.** See display ad this section. ▲

J 324.6 (522.4 km) D 2.6 (4.2 km) S 443.8 (714.2 km) **Northern Kat.** See display ad on page 269.

J 324.7 (522.5 km) D 2.5 (4 km) **S 443.9** (715.3 km) Campground, gas station and store. ▲

Dawson City R.V. Park & Campground and **Bonanza Shell.** See display ad this section. ▲

J 324.8 (522.7 km) D 2.4 (3.9 km) S 444 (715.5 km) Klondike River bridge.

J 325.3 (523.5 km) D 1.9 (3.1 km) S 444.5 (716.4 km) Large turnout with information sign and map.

J 325.8 (524.3 km) D 1.4 (2.3 km) S 445 (717.2 km) Dome Road to north leads 5.7 miles/9.2 km to Dome Mountain (elev. 2,911 feet/887m), which offers views of Dawson City, the Yukon and Klondike rivers, Bonanza Creek and the Ogilvie Mountains.

J 325.9 (524.5 km) D 1.3 (2.1 km) S 445.1 (717.4 km) Trans North Helicopter base on left northbound; Klondike goldfield tours. Rock face on right northbound is known locally as Crocus Bluff; short, interpretive foot trail leads to viewpoint overlooking Klondike River and Dawson City.

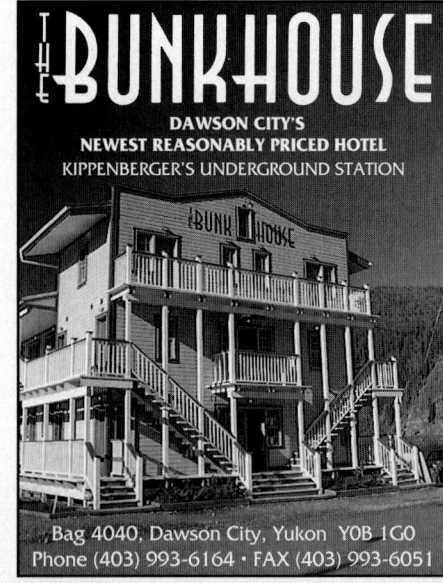

J 326.1 (524.8 km) **D 1.1** (1.8 km) **S 445.3** (717.7 km) Fifth Avenue. Turnout with sign about the Klondike River to south: "With headwaters in the Ogilvie Mountains, the Klondike River and its tributaries gave birth to the world's greatest gold rush—the Klondike Gold Rush of '98."

J 327.2 (526.6 km) **D 0 S 446.4** (719.5 km) Dawson City, ferry at Yukon River. *Description of Dawson City follows. Log of Klondike Loop continues page 278.*

Dawson City

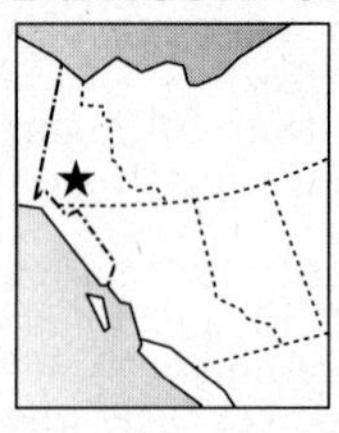

J 327.2 (526.6 km) **D 0 S 446.4** (719.5 km) Located 165 miles/266 km south of the Arctic Circle on the Yukon River at its junction with the Klondike River. **Population:** 2,019. **Emergency Services: RCMP,** 1st Avenue S., phone (403) 993-5555. **Fire Department,** phone (403) 993-2222. **Nursing station,** phone (403) 993-4444. **Ambulance,** phone (403) 993-4444.

Visitor Information: Visitor Reception Centre, operated by Tourism Yukon and Parks Canada, at Front and King streets, in a replica of the 1897 Alaska Commercial Co. store. Yukon information and a Dawson City street map are available. Video disks on a variety of subjects, particularly Dawson attractions and history. Walking tours are part of the daily schedule. Get your Yukon Gold Explorer's Passport stamped here and at the Dawson City Museum. Open daily, 8 A.M. to 8 P.M. mid-May to mid-Sept., phone (403) 993-5566, fax 993-6449.

The Dempster Highway and Northwest Territories Information Centre is located in the B.Y.N. (British Yukon Navigation) Bldg. on Front Street, across from the Yukon visitor centre; open 9 A.M. to 9 P.M., June to Sept. Information on Northwest Territories and the Dempster Highway. Phone (403) 993-6167, fax 993-6334.

Elevation: 1,050 feet/320m. **Climate:** There are 20.9 hours of daylight June 21, 3.8 hours of daylight on Dec. 21. Mean high in

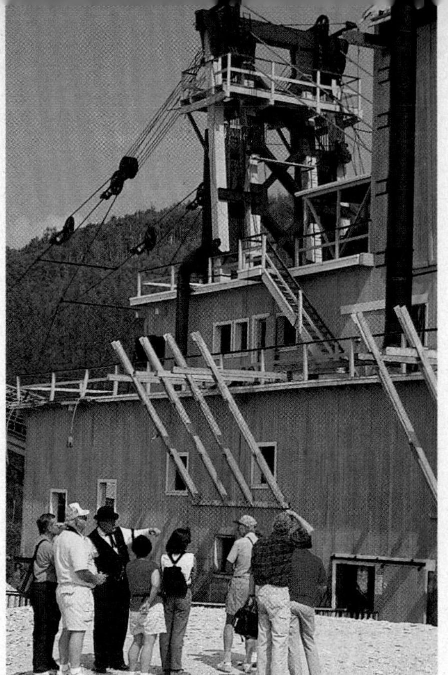

Historic Dredge No. 4 on Bonanza Creek Road. (© Beth Davidow)

July, 72°F/22.2°C. Mean low in January, -30.5°F/-34.7°C. First fall frost end of August, last spring frost end of May. Annual snowfall 59.8 inches. **Radio:** CBC 560; CFYT-FM 106, CKYN-FM 96.1 (summer visitor station). **Television:** CBC Anik Channel 7 and 14 other channels via cable. **Newspaper:** *Klondike Sun* (monthly).

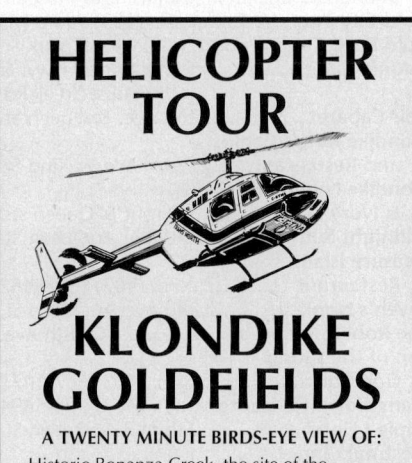

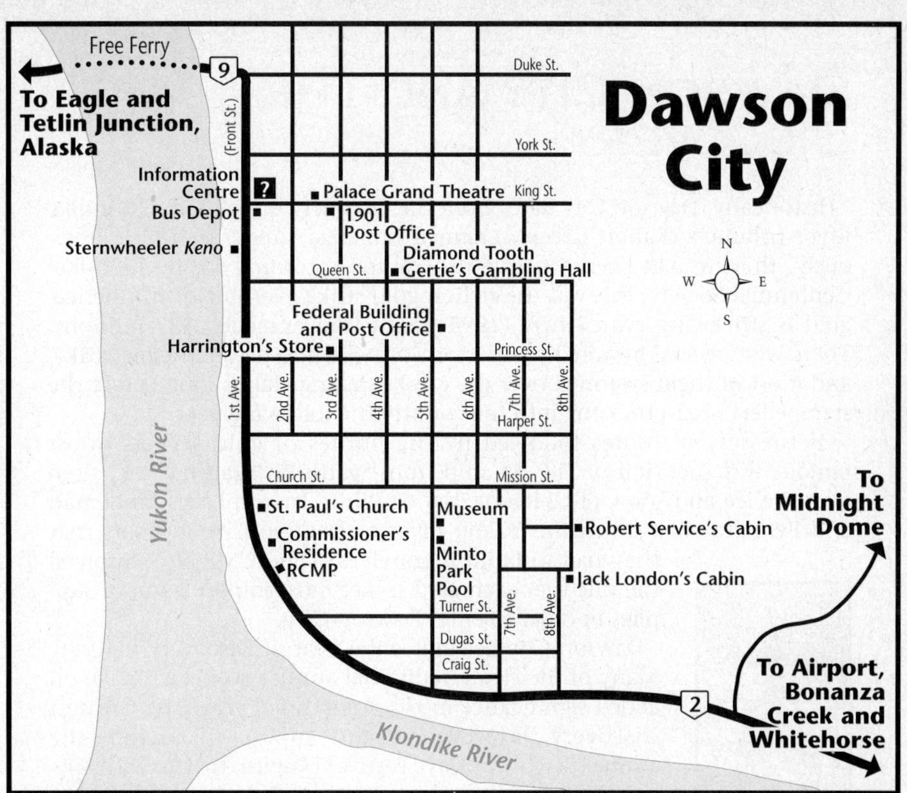

Dawson City and The Discovery

Historically, Dawson City dates from the discovery of gold on a Klondike River tributary (Rabbit Creek, renamed Bonanza Creek) in 1896. Previously, the site had been a native fish camp. According to the Klondike Centennial Society, this was the richest gold strike ever in North America; gold is still being mined here (1994 production exceeded $37 million). There were several hundred prospectors in the region before the big strike, and most of them swarmed over the creeks staking claims long before the stampeders began trickling into the country the following year.

Of the several routes followed by the hordes of gold seekers, most famous was the Trail of '98: by ship from Seattle to Skagway, AK, then over the ice and snow of Chilkoot Pass or White Pass to Lakes Lindeman and Bennett, then down the Yukon River to Dawson City in boats that they had to build themselves. The RCMP also enforced the rule that each gold seeker must import 1 ton of supplies in order to enter Dawson City.

Klondike Gold Rush Centennial 1896 • 1996 The Discovery

Dawson City celebrates the Year of Discovery in 1996. Many of the city's traditional annual events will take on added significance in this Centennial year. The Greatest Discovery Days Ever (August 16-25) will include the annual Discovery Days Festival (August 16-19), with special Centennial events such as the dedication of the Discovery Claim Interpretive Site at Bonanaza Creek, and the World Gold Panning Championship (August 19-25). Other special events celebrating gold are the International Gold Show (May 17-18) and the Yukon Gold Panning Championships (July 1).

Private Aircraft: Dawson City airport located 11.5 miles/18.5 km southeast (see **Milepost J 315.7**). Customs available.

Originally laid out to serve 30,000 people, Dawson City today still occupies much of the original townsite but with only a fraction of the buildings and people. In summer the city is crowded with visitors and miners headed for the goldfields.

The townsite was prepared by Joe Ladue, a trader and sawmill operator, and surveyed by William Ogilvie. The town was named for George Mercer Dawson of the Geological Survey of Canada. Trading companies moved to Dawson City from Fortymile and Circle City and established warehouses along the waterfront. Food and mining supplies sufficient for their normal trade with Indian trappers and the 200 white men in the watershed at the time were not enough for the masses of people who had arrived by winter 1897. While additional steamers did start from St. Michael with extra cargo, at least 3 were frozen into the ice 200 miles/322 km before Dawson City and forced to remain until the ice went out in May 1898. Men who said that gold would buy anything had not reckoned with Dawson City in 1897—it had nothing to sell.

The next summer, when the great rush to the Klondike got into full swing, there was sufficient shipping to move the freight required to create a city in a wilderness

DAWSON CITY ADVERTISERS

Art's Gallery............3rd Ave.
Bonanza Aviation Ltd.......Ph. (403) 993-6904
Bunkhouse, The............Ph. (403) 993-6164
Cruise the Yukon River.....Ph. (403) 993-5599
Dawson City Bed and Breakfast.......Ph. (403) 993-5649
Dawson City Museum...5th Ave. & Church St.
Dawson Trading Post.....5th Ave. & Harper St.
Downtown Hotel...........2nd Ave. & Queen St.
Eldorado Hotel, The.....3rd Ave. & Princess St.
Farmer's Market............2nd Ave.
5th Avenue Bed and Breakfast............Adjacent to museum
Gold City Tours............Ph. (403) 993-5175
Gold Rush Campground....5th Ave. & York St.
GuggieVille............Jct. of Klondike Hwy. & Bonanza Creek Rd.
Hair Cabaret............2nd Ave. & Queen St.
Klondike Kate's Cabins and Restaurant............3rd Ave. & King St.
Klondike Nugget & Ivory Shop............Front & Queen sts.
Midnight Sun Hotel.......3rd Ave. & Queen St.
Pleasure Island Restaurant............Ph. (403) 993-5482
Raven's Nook............2nd Ave. & Queen St.
The Robert Service Show............8th Ave.
Top of the World Golf Course............Ph. (403) 667-1472
Trans North Helicopters...Ph. (403) 993-5494
Triple J Hotel............5th Ave. & Queen St.
Westmark Inn Dawson City............5th Ave. & Harper St.
White Ram Manor Bed & Breakfast........7th Ave. & Harper St.

where every stick, nail and scrap of paper had to be brought in. By 1900 Dawson City was the largest city west of Winnipeg and north of San Francisco.

These were the conditions and the days that built Dawson City. They prevailed until 1903, when stampedes to Nome and other Alaska points drew off the froth from Dawson society, leaving a sturdy government-cum-mining fraternity that maintained an aura of big city worldliness until WWI.

By 1953, Whitehorse—on the railway and the highway, and with a large airport—was so much the hub of activity that the federal government moved the capital from Dawson City, along with 800 civil servants, and years of tradition and pride. Some recompense was offered in the form of a road linking Whitehorse with the mining at Mayo and Dawson City. With its completion, White Pass trucks replaced White Pass river steamers.

New government buildings were built in Dawson, including a fire hall. In 1962 the federal government reconstructed the Palace Grand Theatre for a gold rush festival that featured the Broadway musical, *Foxy*, with Bert Lahr. A museum was established in the Administration Bldg. and tours and entertainments were begun, which continue today.

Dawson City was declared a national historic site in the early 1960s. Parks Canada is currently involved with 35 properties in Dawson City. Many buildings have been restored, some reconstructed and others stabilized. Parks Canada offers an interpretive

Yukon Territory's flag was chosen in 1967 from a territory-wide design competition, and officially approved March 1, 1968.

program each summer for visitors to this historic city.

From 1993 to 2002, Dawson City is hosting a "Decade of Centennials." Highlights include the centennials of the discovery of gold in 1996, the great Klondike gold rush in 1998, and the completion of the White Pass and Yukon Route Railway in 2000. For further information, contact the Klondike Centennial Society, Bag 1996, Dawson City, YT Y0B 1G0.

ACCOMMODATIONS/VISITOR SERVICES

Accustomed to a summer influx of visitors, Dawson has modern hotels and motels (rates average $75 and up) and several bed and breakfasts. The community has a bank, automatic teller machine, restaurants, 5 laundromats (4 with showers), 2 grocery stores (with bakeries), general stores, souvenir shops, churches, art galleries, post office, government offices, government liquor store, information centre, hostel, swimming pool and plenty of entertainment. Many Dawson City merchants abide by the Fair Exchange Policy, offering travelers an exchange rate within 4 percent of the banks'. Dawson City's hotels and motels fill up early, especially at times of special events. Reservations are a must from June through Aug.

5th Avenue Bed and Breakfast. Located adjacent to the museum overlooking Victory Gardens. A modern home with a historic finish, serving a hearty, healthy, all-you-can-eat breakfast. We guarantee comfort, cleanliness and courteous service along with the most convenient location in town. VISA. Call or write Larry and Pat Vezina, Box 722, Dawson City, YT Y0B 1G0. Phone (403) 993-5941. [ADVERTISEMENT]

Klondike Kate's Cabins and Restaurant. We offer you charming, clean and affordable accommodations with private bath. Located near all major attractions. Enjoy the friendly atmosphere of our restaurant, set in a 1902 historic building. Dine inside or on our outdoor patio. We serve ethnic foods, espresso coffees and feature a $3.99 breakfast special. Box 417 Dawson City, YT Y0B 1G0. Phone (403) 993-6527. Fax (403) 993-6044. [ADVERTISEMENT]

There are 2 Yukon government (YTG) campgrounds in the Dawson area. Yukon River YTG campground is across the Yukon River (by ferry) from town, adjacent to the west-side ferry approach (see **Milepost D 0.2** on Top of the World Highway log, following Dawson City section). Klondike River YTG campground is southeast of town near the airport (see **Milepost J 315.2**). Private RV parks in the Dawson area include Gold Rush Campground, downtown at 5th and York; GuggieVille, east of town at **Milepost J 324.5**; and Dawson City R.V. Park and Campground at **Milepost J 324.7**. ▲

TRANSPORTATION

Air: Dawson City airport is 11.5 miles/18.5 km southeast of the city. Alkan Air provides scheduled service to Inuvik, NWT, Old Crow, Mayo and Whitehorse. Air North connects Dawson City with Whitehorse (daily service in summer); with Old Crow and Juneau (3 times weekly in summer); and Fairbanks (4 times weekly in summer). Charter and flightseeing tours available from Bonanza Aviation. Helicopter tours from Trans North Air and Fireweed.

Ferry: The Yukon government operates a free 24-hour ferry, the *George Black,* across the Yukon River from about the third week in May to mid-Oct. (depending upon breakup and freezeup); ferry departs Dawson City on demand. The ferry carries vehicles and passengers across to the public campground and is the only connection to the Top of the World Highway (Yukon Highway 9). Be prepared to wait 3 hours or more during peak traffic.

Taxi: Airport taxi service available from downtown hotels. Scheduled and charter limo service available from Gold City Tours.

Reconstructed Palace Grand Theatre hosts Dawson's "Gaslight Follies."
(Earl L. Brown, staff)

Bus: Service between Whitehorse and Dawson City, and to Inuvik, NWT by Norline coaches; 3 times weekly June through Sept. (check with agent at Gas Shack or Gold City Tours).

Boat: Service to Eagle, AK, on the *Yukon Queen*. Canoe rentals available from Dawson Trading Post.

ATTRACTIONS

Take a Walking Tour. Town-core tours leave the Visitor Reception Centre 2 times daily in summer. The Fort Herchmer Northwest Mounted Police walking tour starts outside the restored Commissioner's Residence (rededication scheduled for August 1996) on Front Street. This handsome building was once the residence of Hon. George Black, M.P., Speaker of the House of Commons, and his famous wife, Martha Louise, who walked to Dawson City via the Trail of '98 and stayed to become the First Lady of the Yukon. Pierre Berton's boyhood home has also been restored and will be dedicated in August. Berton is the author of Klondike Lost, and account of the Klondike Gold Rush. Pick up a schedule of daily events at the Visitor Reception Centre.

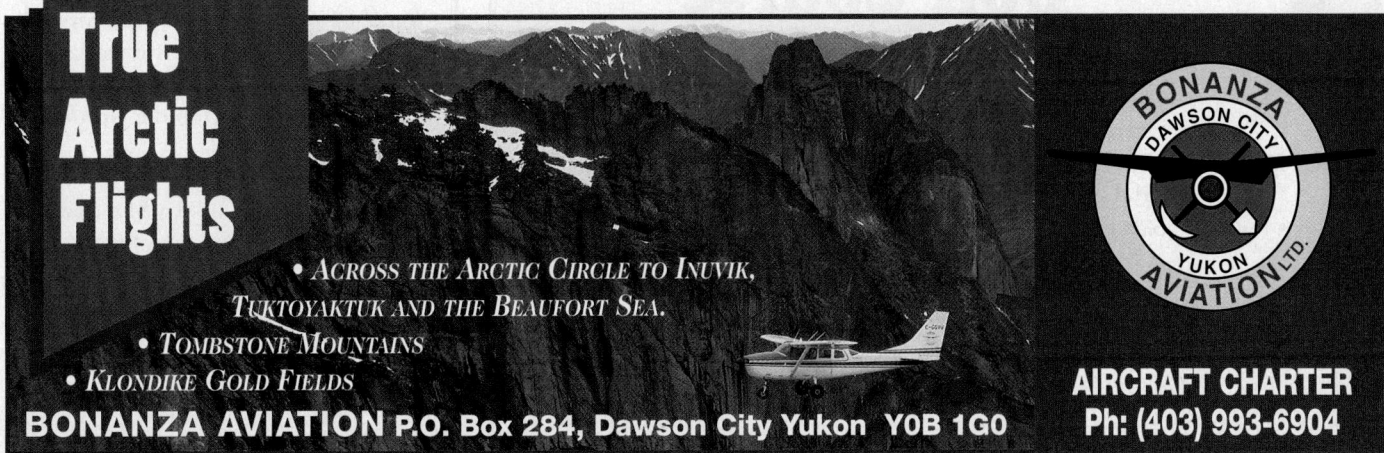

Take a Bus Tour. Motorcoach and van tours of Klondike creeks, goldfields and Dawson City are available; inquire at Gold City Tours (ask about step-on guide service, too). For a panoramic view of Dawson City, the Klondike River, Bonanza Creek and Yukon River, take the bus or drive the 5 miles/8 km to the top of Dome Mountain (elev. 2,911 feet/887m).

Take a River Tour: Yukon River Cruises offers tours aboard the miniature sternwheeler launch *Yukon Lou* leaving the dock behind Birch Cabin booking office near SS *Keno* at 1 P.M. daily in summer, and traveling to Pleasure Island and the stern-wheeler graveyard. Cruise takes 1½ hours. Westours (Grayline Yukon) operates the *Yukon Queen* on the Yukon River between Dawson City and Eagle, AK; check with the Grayline Yukon office about tickets. One-way and round-trip passage is sold on a space-available basis. The trip takes 4 hours downstream to Eagle, and 6 hours back to Dawson. Yukon River Sightseeing Tours offers raft trips on the RR *Cleo Maria* between Carcross and Dawson City.

Cruise the Yukon River. Cruise from Dawson City down the famous Yukon River to Eagle, Alaska. Retrace the old sternwheeler route of this historic Gold Rush area as you cruise past abandoned settlements among the forested hills. A hearty prospector's meal is included. Daily departures. Roundtrip fare is $135 U.S. per person. Prices subject to change. Call (403) 993-5599. [ADVERTISEMENT]

Pleasure Island Restaurant. Don't miss the riverboat cruise on the MV *Yukon Lou*. See the old stern-wheeler shipyard, historic Native village of Moosehide and stop in at Pleasure Island for an all-you-can-eat smoked salmon barecue. Dinner includes garden fresh salad and slow-baked potatoes, topped off by homemade chocolate cake. Steak available on request. This is a "must" when in Dawson City. For reservations: (403) 993-5482 or (907) 488-4602. Group rates. [ADVERTISEMENT]

Visit the Palace Grand Theatre. This magnificently reconstructed theatre, now a national historic site, is home to the "Gaslight Follies," a turn-of-the-century entertainment. Performances nightly except Tuesday, from late May to early Sept. Arizona Charlie Meadows opened the Palace Grand in 1899, and today's visitors, sitting in the curtained boxes around the balcony, will succumb to the charm of this beautiful theatre. Tours of the building are conducted once daily by Parks Canada, June through Sept. Films and presentations daily in summer.

Gambling. Klondike Visitors Assoc. (a nonprofit community organization) operates Diamond Tooth Gertie's Gambling Hall, open May 16 to Sept. 21, 1996. There are Klondike gambling tables (specially licensed in Yukon), 52 "Vegas-style" slot machines, bar service and floor shows nightly. You may have a soft drink if you prefer, and still see the cancan girls present their floor show. Persons under 19 not admitted. Gertie's hosts Yukon Talent Night Aug. 26, 1996. Diamond Tooth Gerties celebrates its silver anniversary May 21-26, 1996, with a reunion of past casino headliners and can can girls.

Visit the Dawson City Museum. Housed in the renovated Territorial Administration Bldg. on 5th Avenue, the museum is open daily from 10 A.M. to 6 P.M., mid-May through early Sept.; by appointment year-round. Featured are the Kings of the Klondike and City Life Galleries, hourly audiovisual and dramatic presentations, and the museum's collection of narrow-gauge locomotives, including a Vauclain-type Baldwin engine, the last one in existence in Canada. Weekly lecture series during summer; check for schedule. The films "City of Gold" and "The Yukoner" are shown daily. A selection of silent film serials, news and documentary reels from 1903 to 1929 is shown in the gallery. Also take part in the "Meet a Klondike Character" show and explore the "Klondike Gold" CD Rom.

The museum has a gift shop, wheelchair ramp, resource library, genealogy service and an extensive photography collection. A nominal admission fee is charged. For more information write the museum at Box 303, Dawson City, YT Y0B 1G0; phone (403) 993-5291, fax 993-5839. ♿

Art's Gallery offers limited edition and original works by Northern artists, and specializes in Yukon-made crafts; pottery, baskets, moosehair tuftings. Featuring soapstone carvings and unique creations from Canada's Arctic. Mastodon, antler, silver jewellery, and a wide selection of Klondike and illustrated children's books also offered, with post and art cards too! We ship everywhere! Third Ave. across from Old Post Office. (403) 993-6967. [ADVERTISEMENT]

SS *Keno* National Historic Site. The SS *Keno* was the last steamer to run the Yukon River when she sailed from Whitehorse in 1960 to her present berth on the riverbank next to the bank. Although she is closed to the public, an interpretive display is set up beside the site.

Historic Harrington's Store, 3rd Avenue and Princess Street, houses a photographic exhibit entitled "Dawson As They Saw It". Open daily.

Visit Robert Service's Cabin. Highly recommended. On the hillside on 8th Avenue, the author–bank clerk's cabin has been restored by Parks Canada. Stories and poetry recitals (by actor Tom Byrne) are offered daily in summer at 10 A.M. and 3 P.M. Photos are welcomed, but no videotaping. Audio and video cassettes may be purchased at downtown retail outlets. Visitors come from every part of the world to sign the guest book on the rickety desk where Service wrote his famous poems, including "The Shooting of Dan McGrew" and "The Cremation of Sam McGee". Open 9 A.M. to noon and 1-5 P.M. daily. Admission: adults $2.25, children 12 and under free.

Visit the Historic Post Office, where you may buy stamps; all first-class mail sent from here receives the old hand-cancellation stamp. Open daily.

Fire Fighters Museum, located at the fire hall at 5th Avenue and King Street, is open Monday through Saturday, 11 A.M. to 5 P.M.

The George Black ferry crossing the Yukon River. (John K. Nakata)

Visit the Jack London Interpretive Centre: Along 8th Avenue and past Service's home is Jack London's cabin, built from half of the logs saved from the original cabin in the Bush where the writer stayed on his way to the Klondike. Also at the site are a cache for perishables and a museum with photos and memorabilia. Interpretation daily at 1 P.M. No admission charged.

Special Events. Dawson City hosts a number of unique and unusual celebrations during the year. The Commissioner's Ball is held June 1, 1996. This gala event, commemorating Yukon becoming a territory in 1898, features turn-of-the-century fashion. The Yukon Gold Panning Championship is held July 1 each year in Dawson City ind in 1996 the city will host the World Gold Panning Championship, Aug. 19-25. Then on July 20, 1996, it's the Canadian Airlines International Dome Race, which attracts over 200 runners each year from all over the world. The 4.6-mile/7.4-km course rises a total elevation of 1,850 feet/564m.

The 18th Annual Dawson City Music Festival, July 19–21, 1996, features entertainers and artists from Canada and the United States, free workshops, dances and dinners. Tickets and information from the Music Festival Assoc., Box 456, Dawson City, YT Y0B 1G0. Phone (403) 993-5584.

If you are near Dawson Aug. 16–19, 1996, be sure to join the Discovery Days fun when Yukon Order of Pioneers stages its annual parade. This event is a Yukon holiday commemorating the Klondike gold discovery of Aug. 17, 1896. 1996 marks the centennial year and additional festivities are planned.

The Great Klondike International Outhouse Race and Bathroom Wall Limerich Contest, held the Sunday of Labour Day weekend (Sept. 1, 1996), is a race of outhouses (on wheels) over a 1.9 mile/3-km course through the streets of Dawson City; before the race, all contestants must recite original limericks. Gerties Darts International Tournament is held the second weekend of Sept.

See the Midnight Sun: If you are in Dawson City on June 21, be sure to make it to the top of the Dome by midnight, when the sun barely dips behind the 6,000-foot/1,829-m Ogilvie Mountains to the north—the picture of a lifetime. There's quite a local celebration on the Dome on June 21, so for those who don't like crowds, a visit before or after summer solstice will also afford fine views and photos. Turnoff for Dome Mountain is at **Milepost J 325.8**; it's about a 5-mile/8-km drive.

Pan for Gold: The chief attraction for most visitors is panning for gold. There are several mining operations set up to permit you to actually pan for your own "colours" under friendly guidance. Take Bonanza Creek Road from **Milepost J 324.5** up famous Bonanza Creek, past Dredge No. 4, Discovery Claim and miles of gravel tailings worked over 2 and 3 times in the continuing search for gold. The Klondike Visitors Assoc. sponsors a public panning area at No. 6 above Discovery, 13 miles/21 km from

Dawson City on Bonanza Creek Road. Check with the Visitor Reception Centre for more information.

Bear Creek Camp, (see **Milepost J 319.6** on the Klondike Highway), was operated by Yukon Consolidated Gold Corp. until 1966. Tours are conducted by Parks Canada interpreters; check with the Visitor Reception Centre for current tour schedule. The compound features the Gold Room, where the gold was melted and poured into bricks, complete blacksmith and machinery shops, and other well-preserved structures. Open 9:30 A.M. to 5 P.M. from mid-June to late Aug. Admission: adults $2.25, children 12 and under free.

Klondike Loop Log

(continued)

YUKON HIGHWAY 9

The Top of the World Highway (Yukon Highway 9) connects Dawson City with the Taylor Highway (Alaska Route 5). A free ferry carries passengers and vehicles from Dawson City across the Yukon River to the beginning of the Top of the World Highway. The ferry wait in heavy traffic may be 3 hours or longer. The Alaska Highway is 174.5 miles/280.8 km from here; Eagle, AK, is 143.4 miles/230.8 km from here. Allow plenty of time for this drive; average speed for this road is 25 to 40 mph/40 to 64 kmph. DRIVE WITH YOUR HEADLIGHTS ON! Yukon Highway 9 and the Taylor Highway (Alaska Route 5) in Alaska are not maintained from mid-Oct. to April and the arrival of snow effectively closes the roads for winter.

CAUTION: Road conditions on some sections of the Alaska portion of this road were rough in 1995. The Top of the World Highway is also scheduled for gravel surfacing in 1996 between kilometreposts 60 and 105 on the Canadian side (Mile 38 to 66). Check with the Dawson City Visitor Reception Centre for current road and weather conditions; phone (403) 993-5566.

*IMPORTANT: U.S. and Canada customs are open from about May 15 to Sept. 15 for 13 hours a day. (Probable customs hours for summer 1996 are 9 A.M. to 10 P.M. Pacific time on the Canadian side; 8 A.M. to 9 P.M. Alaska time.) Check with the RCMP or Visitor Reception Centre in Dawson City to make certain the border crossing at **Milepost D 66.1** will be open. Serious fines are levied for crossing the border without clearing customs! There are no restrooms, services or currency exchanges available at the border.*

This section of the log shows distance from Dawson City (D) followed by distance from junction with the Taylor Highway (T) at Jack Wade Junction. Physical kilometreposts show distance from Dawson City.

D 0 T 78.8 (126.8 km) **DAWSON CITY.** Free ferry crosses the Yukon River daily in summer.

D 0.2 (0.3 km) **T 78.6** (126.5 km) **Yukon River** government campground on riverbank opposite Dawson City; 74 RV sites, 24 tent-only sites, 2 kitchen shelters, playground and drinking water. Camping fee $8. Within walking distance of stern-wheeler graveyard. Put in and takeout spot for Yukon River travelers. ▲

D 2.7 (4.4 km) **T 76.1** (122.5 km) Access to 9-hole golf course via 3.2-mile/5.1-km gravel road; rentals.

D 2.9 (4.6 km) **T 75.9** (122.1 km) Turnout for viewpoint overlooking Dawson City and the Yukon and Klondike rivers.

D 3.2 (5 km) **T 75.6** (121.7 km) Turnout with good view of Yukon River and river valley farms.

D 9 (12.4 km) **T 69.8** (112.3 km) Rest area with pit toilets, picnic tables, litter barrels and information sign about Top of the World Highway (also has ferry information for travelers to Dawson City).

D 11 (15.6 km) **T 67.8** (109.1 km) "Top of the World" view as highway climbs above tree line.

D 16.4 (26.2 km) **T 62.4** (100.4 km) Snow fence along highway next 8 miles/13 km westbound.

D 18.4 (29.4 km) **T 60.4** (97.2 km) Large turnout on left.

D 29.2 (47 km) **T 49.6** (79.8 km) Evidence of 1989 burn.

D 32.1 (51.2 km) **T 46.7** (75.2 km) First outcropping (westbound) of Castle Rock. Turnout to south with panoramic view of countryside.

D 33.1 (52.8 km) **T 45.7** (73.5 km) Distance marker shows customs 52 km, Dawson City 53 km.

D 35.2 (56 km) **T 43.6** (70.2 km) Main outcropping of Castle Rock; lesser formations are also found along this stretch. Centuries of erosion have created these formations. Turnout on left westbound.

D 37.4 (59 km) **T 41.4** (66.6 km) Unmaintained road leads 25 miles/40 km to the former settlement of Clinton Creek, which served the Cassiar Asbestos Mine from 1967–79. There are no facilities or services available there. Distance marker shows U.S. border 43 km.

The confluence of the Yukon and Fortymile rivers is 3 miles/4.8 km below the former townsite of Clinton Creek. Clinton Creek bridge is an access point on the Fortymile River National Wild and Scenic River system, managed by the Bureau of Land Management. The Fortymile River offers intermediate and advanced canoeists over 100 miles/160 km of challenging water.

Yukon River, near Clinton Creek, grayling to 3 lbs. in April; chum salmon to 12 lbs. in August; king salmon to 40 lbs., July and August. **Fortymile River**, near Clinton Creek, grayling to 3 lbs. during spring breakup and fall freezeup; inconnu (sheefish) to 10 lbs. in July and August.

D 54 (85.6 km) **T 24.8** (39.9 km) Old sod-roofed cabin on right westbound, originally a supply and stopping place for the McCormick Transportation Co.

D 54.3 (86.1 km) **T 24.5** (39.4 km) Road forks left westbound to old mine workings at Sixtymile, which have been reactivated by Cogasa Mining Co. Keep to right for Alaska. The road winds above timberline for many miles. The lack of fuel for warmth and shelter made this a perilous trip for the early sourdoughs.

D 64.1(101.9 km) **T 14.7** (23.7 km) large gravel turnout. Information sign about Top of the World Highway viewpoint.

D 65.2 (103.7 km) **T 13.6** (21.9 km) Pull-through rest area with toilet and litter barrels; good viewpoint. Just across the highway, short hike to cairn, excellent viewpoint. Highest point on Top of the World Highway (elev. 4,515 feet/1,376 m).

Note: Last public facilities available to those traveling to the United States—none available at border.

D 66.1 (105.1 km) **T 12.7** (20.4 km) U.S.–Canada border (elev. 4,127 feet/1,258m). Canada Customs and Immigration Little Gold Creek office is open 9 A.M. to 10 P.M. (Pacific time) from about May 15 to Sept. 15. All traffic entering Canada must stop here. The U.S. border station Poker Creek office, just past the Canadian station, is open 8 A.M. to 9 P.M. (Alaska time) from about May 15 to Sept. 15. All traffic entering the United States must stop here. Both stations are closed in winter. A short hike up the hill behind U.S. border station provides good viewpoint.

TIME ZONE CHANGE: Alaska observes Alaska time; Yukon Territory observes Pacific time. See Time Zones in GENERAL INFORMATION section for details.

D 67.1 (108 km) **T 11.7** (18.8 km) Double-ended turnout to north with viewing platform to see mountains; toilet, litter barrel, aluminum can recycling bin.

Note: last public facilities available to those traveling to Canada—none available at border.

D 69.2 (111.4 km) **T 9.6** (15.4 km) **BOUNDARY.** Boundary Lodge was one of the first roadhouses in Alaska; food, gas, emergency phone and lodging.

Boundary Inc. See display ad this section.

Watch your gas supply. Between here and Tetlin Junction on the Alaska Highway, gas is available again only at Chicken, **Milepost TJ 66.5**. From here to Eagle, gas may be available at O'Brien Creek Lodge, **Milepost TJ 125.4**. Gas is available in Eagle.

Private Aircraft: Boundary airstrip; elev. 2,940 feet/896m; length 2,100 feet/640m; earth and gravel; fuel 80; unattended.

D 78 (125.6 km) **T 0.8** (1.3 km) Viewpoint.

D 78.8 (126.9 km) **T 0 Jack Wade Junction, Milepost TJ 95.7** on the Taylor Highway. The Taylor Highway (Alaska Route 5), also known as the Eagle Road or Eagle Cutoff, leads north 64.6 miles/104 km to Eagle, AK, or south 95.7 miles/154 km to Tetlin Junction, just east of Tok, on the Alaska Highway. *CAUTION: The Taylor Highway is a narrow, winding, mountain road, not well-maintained. Drive carefully!*

*NOTE: Eagle-bound and Alaska Highway-bound travelers turn to **Milepost TJ 95.7** on page 282 in the TAYLOR HIGHWAY section to continue log. Eagle-bound travelers continue with log forward from **Milepost TJ 95.7**. Alaska Highway-bound travelers read log backward from **Milepost TJ 95.7**.*

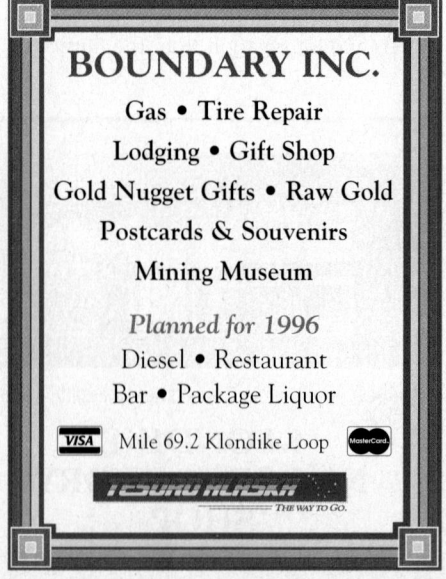

TAYLOR HIGHWAY

Tetlin Junction to Eagle, Alaska
Alaska Route 5
(See map, page 262)

The Taylor Highway is narrow and hilly. (© Michael DeYoung)

The 160.3-mile/258-km Taylor Highway (Alaska Route 5) begins at Tetlin Junction on the Alaska Highway and ends at the small town of Eagle on the Yukon River. This is a beautiful "top of the world" drive, and Eagle is well worth a visit. Construction of the Taylor Highway began in 1946, and was completed to Eagle in late 1953, providing access to the historic Fortymile Mining District.

The highway also provides river runners with access to the Fortymile River National Wild and Scenic River system. A brochure on access points and float times is available from the Bureau of Land Management, 1150 University Ave., Fairbanks, AK 99709-3844; phone (907) 474-2350.

The Taylor Highway is a narrow, winding, dusty mountain road with many steep hills and some hairpin curves. Allow plenty of time to drive its length. The road surface is gravel, with sporadic soft spots during breakup or after heavy rains. Road surface ranges from very poor to good depending on maintenance. Shoulders are narrow and may be unstable. Large RVs and trailers especially should use caution in driving this road. Watch for large tanker trucks, some with double trailers, hauling fuel between Tetlin Junction and Boundary. (Your best defense is to pull over and stop, if possible.) The Taylor Highway is not maintained from mid-Oct. to April, and the arrival of snow effectively closes the road for winter.

*NOTE: Watch for major road construction between **Milepost TJ 0** and **TJ 23** in 1996.*

The Taylor is the shortest route to Dawson City, YT, from Alaska. Drive 95.7 miles/154 km north on the Taylor Highway to Jack Wade Junction, and turn east on the Top of the World Highway (Yukon Highway 9) for Dawson City. (See end of KLONDIKE LOOP section for log of Yukon Highway 9.)

Dawson City-bound travelers keep in mind that gas is available only at Chicken and at Boundary Lodge. Also, the U.S. and Canadaian customs offices at the border are open 13 hours a day from about mid-May to mid-September. Probable customs hours for summer 1996 are 8 A.M. to 9 P.M. Alaska time, 9 A.M. to 10 P.M. Pacific time on the Canadian side. There are no restrooms, services or currency exchanges available at the border.

IMPORTANT: You cannot cross the border unless the customs office for the country you are entering is open. Severe fines are levied for crossing without clearing customs. Officials at Canadian customs are concerned about child abductions. If you are traveling with children, remember to bring identification for them. (See GENERAL INFORMATION section for specific customs restrictions.)

NOTE: All gold-bearing ground in area is claimed. Do not pan in streams.

Emergency medical services: Between Tetlin Junction and O'Brien Creek bridge at **Milepost TJ 113.2**, phone the Tok Area EMS at 911 or (907) 883-5111. Between O'Brien Creek bridge and Eagle, phone the Eagle EMS at (907) 547-2300 or (907) 547-2211. Use CB channel 21.

Taylor Highway Log

Distance from Tetlin Junction (TJ) is followed by distance from Eagle (E).

TJ 0 E 160.3 (258 km) **Tetlin Junction. Junction** with the Alaska Highway at **Milepost DC 1301.7**. 40-Mile Roadhouse Service Station; gas, diesel, towing.

NOTE: Watch for major road construction next 23 miles/37 km northbound in 1996.

Begin 9 miles/14.5 km of winding road up out of the Tanana River valley. Highway traverses stabilized sand dunes first 5 miles/ 8 km.

TJ 4.5 (7.2 km) **E 155.8** (250.7 km) Gravel turnout to east. A 0.7-mile/1.1-km trail leads to **Four Mile Lake;** rainbow trout and sheefish.

TJ 5.4 (8.7 km) **E 154.9** (249.3 km) Evidence of 1990 forest fire known as the Porcupine burn.

TJ 5.9 (9.5 km) **E 154.4** (248.5 km) Entering Tok Management Area, Tanana Valley State Forest, northbound.

TJ 6 (9.7 km) **E 154.3** (248.3 km) Double-ended turnout to east, easy for trailers but can be soft or bumpy.

Wildflowers along the highway include arnica, chiming bells, wild roses and Labrador tea. As the name suggests, Labrador tea leaves (and flowers) may be steeped in boiling water to make tea. However, according to Janice Scofield, author of *Discovering Wild Plants*, Labrador tea contains a narcotic toxin that can cause ill effects if used too frequently or in high concentrations.

NOTE: Winding road northbound. Watch for ruts and soft spots and for loose gravel on curves.

TJ 9.4 (15.1 km) **E 150.9** (242.8 km) Entering Game Management Unit 20E northbound; entering GMU 12 southbound. Road begins gradual climb of Mount Fairplay for northbound travelers.

TJ 12.1 (19.5 km) **E 148.2** (238.5 km) Entering Tok Management Area, Tanana State Forest, southbound.

TJ 14.6 (23.5 km) **E 145.7** (234.5 km) Small turnout to west. Blueberries in season.

TJ 16 (25.7 km) **E 144.3** (232.2 km) Parking at one of Mount Fairplay's several summits.

Panoramic view of the Alaska Range from Milepost TJ 38. (© Carmen Scott)

TJ 18 (29 km) **E 142.3** (229 km) *NOTE: Watch for soft spots after rain.*

TJ 21.2 (34.1 km) **E 139.1** (223.9 km) Long descent from Mount Fairplay summit northbound.

TJ 23 (37 km) **E 137.3** (221 km) Scenic views, Alaska Range to west. *NOTE: Watch for major road construction next 23 miles/37 km southbound in 1996.*

TJ 27 (43.5 km) **E 133.3** (214.5 km) Small turnout to west.

TJ 28.3 (45.5 km) **E 132** (212.4 km) Turnout with view to west.

TJ 32.8 (52.8 km) **E 127.5** (205.2 km) Turnout to west.

TJ 34.4 (55.4 km) **E 125.9** (202.6 km) Double-ended turnout with view to west. Nine-percent downgrade northbound.

TJ 35.1 (56.5 km) **E 125.2** (201.5 km) Entering Fortymile Mining District northbound. The second-oldest mining district in Alaska, gold was first discovered here in 1886. Claims were filed in both Canada and Alaska due to boundary uncertainties.

Double-ended turnout to east near summit of Mount Fairplay (elev. 5,541 feet/1,689m). Interpretive sign, viewing platform, litter barrels, aluminum recycling, toilet, wheelchair accessible. ♿

Highway descends a 9-percent grade northbound. Southbound, the road descends for the next 25 miles/40 km from Mount Fairplay's summit, winding through heavily forested terrain. Panoramic views of the Fortymile River forks' valleys. Views of the Alaska Range to the southwest.

TJ 39.1 (62.9 km) **E 121.2** (195 km) Large turnout to west, no easy turnaround.

TJ 43 (69.2 km) **E 117.3** (188.8 km) Logging Cabin Creek bridge; small turnout to west at south end of bridge. Side road to creek. This is the south end of the Fortymile River National Wild and Scenic River system managed by BLM.

TJ 49 (78.9 km) **E 111.3** (179.1 km) Loop roads through BLM West Fork Recreation Site; 25 sites (7 pull-through sites), tables, firepits, no water, covered tables, toilets, dumpsters. Access point of Fortymile River canoe trail. Improved campground. ▲

TJ 49.3 (79.3 km) **E 111** (178.6 km) Bridge over West Fork of the Dennison Fork of the Fortymile River. Access point for Fortymile River National Wild and Scenic River system.

TJ 50.5 (81.3 km) **E 109.8** (176.7 km) Taylor Creek bridge. Watch for potholes and rough road as bridge approaches. All-terrain vehicle trail to Taylor and Kechumstuk mountains; heavily used in hunting season.

TJ 57 (91.7 km) **E 103.3** (166.2 km) Scenic viewpoint turnout to east, no easy turnaround.

TJ 58.9 (94.8 km) **E 101.4** (163.2 km) Scenic viewpoint turnout to east.

TJ 62.5 (100.6 km) **E 97.8** (157.4 km) Turnout to west. Drive-in, no easy turnaround.

TJ 63.2 (101.7 km) **E 97.1** (156.3 km) View of Chicken.

TJ 63.3 (101.9 km) **E 97** (156.1 km) Turnout to west. Drive-in, no easy turnaround.

TJ 63.7 (102.5 km) **E 96.6** (155.5 km) Steep descent northbound to Mosquito Fork.

TJ 64.1 (103.2 km) **E 96.2** (154.8 km) Well-traveled road leads to private buildings, not into Chicken.

TJ 64.3 (103.5 km) **E 96** (154.5 km) Bridge over Mosquito Fork of the Fortymile River; day-use area with table, toilet and litter barrel at north end of bridge. The Mosquito Fork is a favorite access point for the Fortymile National Wild and Scenic River system, according to the BLM.

TJ 64.4 (103.6 km) **E 95.9** (154.3 km) Turnout with pit toilets.

TJ 66 (106.2 km) **E 94.3** (151.8 km) Entering **CHICKEN** (pop. 37), northbound. *(NOTE: Driving distance between* ***Mileposts TJ 66*** *and* ***67*** *is 0.7 mile.)* This is the newer commercial settlement of Chicken. The original mining camp (abandoned, private property) is north of Chicken Creek (see **Milepost TJ 67**). Chicken is a common name in the North for ptarmigan. One story has it that the early miners wanted to name their camp ptarmigan, but were unable to spell it and settled for Chicken. Access point for the Fortymile River canoe trail is below Chicken airstrip.

Fuel is available in Chicken. Your next opportunity will be at O'Brien Creek Lodge, en route to Eagle, **Milepost TJ 125.4**; in Boundary, en route to Canada (Top of the World Highway, **Milepost D 69.2**); or in Tetlin junction en route to Alaskan Highway **(Milepost TJ 0)**.

TJ 66.3 (106.7 km) **E 94** (151.3 km) Chicken post office (ZIP code 99732) located on hill beside the road. The late Ann Purdy lived in this area. The book *Tisha* is based on her experiences as a young schoolteacher in the Alaska Bush.

TJ 66.4 (106.9 km) **E 93.9** (151.1 km) Airport Road. Access to Chicken airstrip and "downtown" Chicken. Combination grocery store, restaurant, bar and gas station located here.

Private Aircraft: Chicken airstrip, adjacent southwest; elev. 1,640 feet/500m; length 2,500 feet/762m; gravel; maintained year-round.

The Chicken Creek Salmon Bake uses only wild Alaska Yukon king salmon. Besides salmon, we also feature halibut, barbeque chicken, buffalo and reindeer burgers, homemade beans, our famous potato salad and salmon chowder. All are offered daily

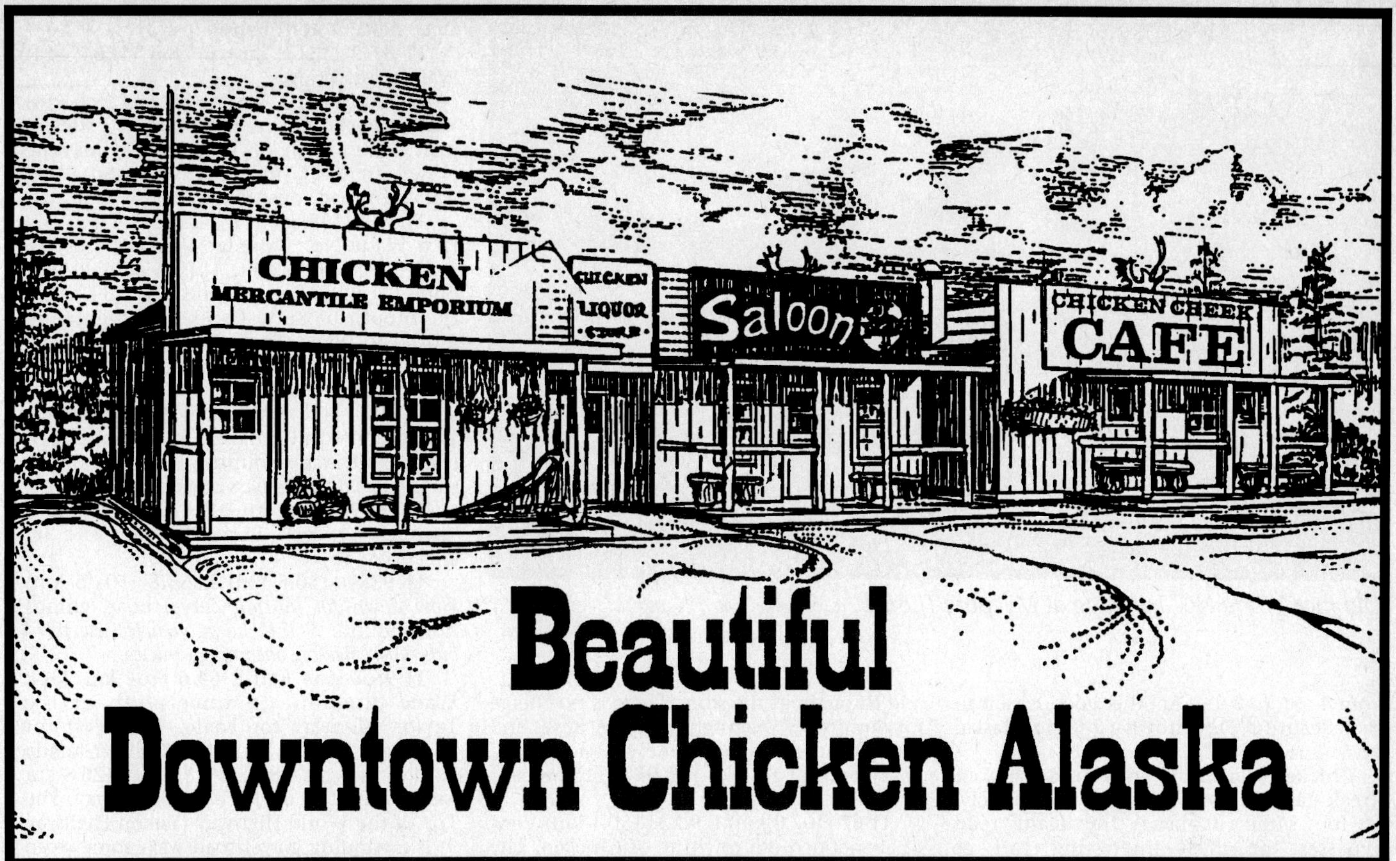

Beautiful Downtown Chicken Alaska

CHICKEN CREEK CAFE

GREAT HOMEMADE FOOD!

Hamburgers - Pies
Pastries and Cinnamon Buns

Chicken Mercantile Emporium

World Famous Chicken T-Shirts
Chicken Souvenirs, Local Gold

Tisha Books

CHICKEN CREEK SALMON BAKE

Wild Yukon King Salmon
Halibut

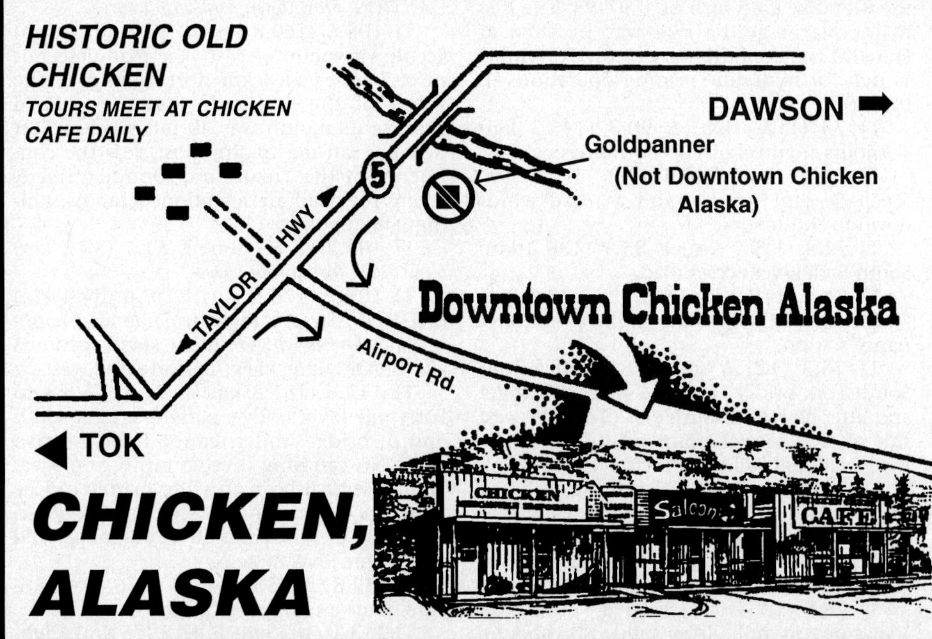

CHICKEN GAS

Always the Lowest Priced Gas, and Friendliest Service in CHICKEN

Propane **Diesel**

REMEMBER!

To find *REAL* Downtown Chicken Alaska you have to Turn Off the Taylor Hwy.

Old Jack Wade No. 1 dredge at Milepost TJ 86.1. (*Earl L. Brown, staff*)

from 4 P.M. to 8 P.M. Another good reason to visit Beautiful Downtown Chicken Alaska! [ADVERTISEMENT]

Chicken Mercantile Emporium, Chicken Creek Cafe, Saloon and Gas. Unfortunately, as too often happens, the main road bypasses the most interesting part of Chicken. If it's modern facilities you are looking for, original Chicken is not for you. The Chicken Creek Saloon and Cafe are some of the last remnants of the old frontier Alaska. It is a trading post where local miners (some straight out of Jack London) trade gold for supplies and drink. Tisha's schoolhouse and other historic buildings may be seen on the walking tour of old Chicken, meeting daily at the Chicken Creek Cafe at 1 P.M. It's also possible to purchase an autographed copy of *Tisha* at the Chicken Mercantile Emporium. Hunting and fishing licenses are for sale at the Emporium. A wealth of gifts abound in the Chicken Mercantile Emporium and the cafe is famous throughout Alaska for its excellent food, homemade pies, pastries and cinnamon buns. For a bird's-eye view of this spectacular country and fantastic photo opportunities, check out the local flightseeing service. Chicken Creek Saloon, Cafe and Mercantile Emporium are a rare treat for those with the courage to stray just a few hundred yards from the beaten path. Major credit cards accepted. Note: The Goldpanner, located on the main road, is not the same as "Beautiful Downtown Chicken, Alaska." [ADVERTISEMENT]

TJ 66.5 (107 km) **E 93.8** (151 km) **The Goldpanner.** Owners Bill, Mary, Grant and Dana Morris welcome you to Chicken. We have lots of parking and turnaround space. Our station has gas, diesel, tire repair and minor repairs. The store carries some groceries, staples, snacks, cold pop, canned meats and souvenirs. Chicken souvenirs include T-shirts, sweatshirts, hats, spoons, cups, patches, magnets, bumper stickers, postcards and hatpins. We also carry many other articles including the book *Tisha.* Try your hand at our free gold panning or get your local gold already in vials, nuggets or jewelry. For the sportsman, hunting and fishing licenses are available. For those interested in local history, old bones, rocks and mining artifacts are on display on the porch and throughout the store. There is no charge for our dry RV overnight parking. Buses and caravans are always welcome. [ADVERTISEMENT] ▲

TJ 66.6 (107.2 km) **E 93.7** (150.8 km) Chicken Creek bridge.

TJ 67 (107.8 km) **E 93.3** (150.1 km) View of abandoned old townsite of Chicken. The road in is blocked off, and the dozen or so old buildings are owned by a mining company. Private property, do not trespass. Guided walking tours available; inquire at Chicken Creek Cafe. Look upstream (northwest) on Chicken Creek to see the old gold dredge, which was shut down in the 1960s.

TJ 68.2 (109.8 km) **E 92.1** (148.2 km) BLM Chicken field station; information and emergency communications. Trailhead for Mosquito Fork Dredge trail (3 miles/4.8 km round-trip). *NOTE: Watch for potholes and soft spots.*

TJ 68.9 (110.9 km) **E 91.4** (147.1 km) Lost Chicken Creek. Site of Lost Chicken Hill Mine, established in 1895. Mining was under way in this area several years before the Klondike gold rush of 1897–98. The first major placer gold strike was in 1886 at Franklin Gulch, a tributary of the Fortymile. Watch for hydraulic mining operations in the creek.

TJ 70 (112.7 km) **E 90.3** (145.3 km) Turnouts at gravel pits on both sides of road.

TJ 71.7 (115.4 km) **E 88.6** (142.6 km) Steep descent northbound as road winds down to South Fork.

TJ 74.4 (119.7 km) **E 85.9** (138.2 km) South Fork River access road.

TJ 74.5 (119.9 km) **E 85.8** (138.1 km) South Fork DOT/PF state highway maintenance station.

TJ 75.3 (121.2 km) **E 85** (136.8 km) South Fork bridge. Day-use area with toilet and litter barrels at south end of bridge, west side of road. Access point for the Fortymile River National Wild and Scenic River system. The muddy, bumpy road leading into the brush is used by miners.

TJ 76.8 (123.6 km) **E 83.5** (134.4 km) Turnout with litter barrels to west. View of oxbow lakes in South Fork valley.

TJ 78.5 (126.3 km) **E 81.8** (131.6 km) Views of Fortymile River valley northbound to **Milepost TJ 82.**

TJ 78.8 (126.8 km) **E 81.5** (131.2 km) Steep descent northbound.

TJ 81.9 (131.8 km) **E 78.4** (126.2 km) Walker Fork bridge.

TJ 82.1 (132.1 km) **E 78.2** (125.8 km) Walker Fork BLM campground (16 sites, 2 picnic sites with covered tables) may be closed in 1996 for reconstruction. Also watch for road construction in this area.

TJ 86.1 (138.6 km) **E 74.2** (119.4 km) Old Jack Wade No. 1 dredge in creek next to road. Turnout to east. This is actually the Butte Creek Dredge, installed in 1934 below the mouth of Butte Creek and eventually moved to Wade Creek. This was one of the first bucketline dredges used in the area, according to the BLM.

TJ 90 (144.8 km) **E 70.3** (113.1 km) Jack Wade, an old mining camp that operated until 1940. Active mining is under way in this area. *Do not trespass on mining claims.*

TJ 91.9 (147.9 km) **E 68.4** (110.1 km) Turnout to east. Primitive campsite by stream.

TJ 93.5 (150.5 km) **E 66.8** (107.5 km) *Slow down for hairpin curve.* Road climbs northbound. *NOTE: Large vehicles use turnouts when meeting oncoming vehicles.*

TJ 95.7 (154 km) **E 64.6** (104 km) **Jack Wade Junction.** Continue north on the Taylor Highway for Eagle. Turn east for Boundary Lodge and the Alaska–Canada border. Dawson City is 78.8 miles/126.8 km east via the Top of the World Highway. The Top of the World Highway (Yukon Highway 9) is a winding gravel road with some steep grades. Slippery in wet weather, closed by snow. Road conditions in 1995 on some sections of the Alaska portion were rough, so drive carefully.

Dawson City-bound travelers turn to the end of the KLONDIKE LOOP section (page 278) and read the Top of the World Highway log back to front. Eagle-bound travelers continue with this log.

TJ 96 (154.5 km) **E 64.3** (103.5 km) Turnout. View to the north-northeast of Canada's Ogilvie Mountains in the distance.

TJ 99.5 (160.1 km) **E 60.8** (97.8 km) Road winds around the summit of Steele Creek Dome (elev. 4,015 feet/1,224m) visible directly above the road to the east. *CAUTION: Road is slippery when wet.*

TJ 99.6 (160.3 km) **E 60.7** (97.7 km) *CAUTION: Slow down for hairpin curve.*

TJ 105.5 (169.8 km) **E 54.8** (88.2 km) Scenic viewpoint to east. The road descends next 7 miles/11.3 km northbound to the valley of the Fortymile River, so named because its mouth was 40 miles below Fort Reliance, an old trading post near the confluence of the Yukon and Klondike rivers. Along the road are abandoned cabins, tailings and dredges.

TJ 109.2 (175.7 km) **E 51.1** (82.2 km) *Slow down for hairpin curve!*

TJ 109.7 (176.5 km) **E 50.6** (81.4 km) *CAUTION: Steep, narrow, winding road northbound. Slow down!* Frequent small turnouts and breathtaking views to north and west.

TJ 112.6 (181.2 km) **E 47.7** (76.8 km) Fortymile River bridge; parking area at south end of bridge, toilet, canoe launch, trash cans. No camping. Active mining in area. Nearly vertical beds of white marble can be seen on the northeast side of the river. Access to the Fortymile River National Wild and Scenic River system.

TJ 112.8 (181.5 km) **E 47.5** (76.4 km) Private home and mining camp.

TJ 113.1 (182 km) **E 47.2** (76 km) Highway maintenance camp located here.

TJ 113.2 (182.2 km) **E 47.1** (75.8 km)

O'Brien Creek bridge. Access to creek.

TJ 114.2 (183.8 km) **E 46.8** (75.3 km) Winding road northbound with rock slide areas to **Milepost TJ 116**; highway parallels O'Brien Creek to Liberty Fork; several turnouts. *CAUTION: Watch for small aircraft using road as runway.*

TJ 117.2 (188.6 km) **E 43.1** (69.4 km) Alder Creek bridge.

TJ 118.2 (190.2 km) **E 42.1** (67.8 km) Road narrows northbound: Watch for falling rock next 1.5 miles/2.4 km northbound.

TJ 119.7 (192.6 km) **E 40.6** (65.3 km) Slide area, watch for rocks.

TJ 124.6 (200.5 km) **E 35.7** (57.5 km) Columbia Creek bridge.

TJ 125.4 (201.8 km) **E 34.9** (56.2 km) Lodge with gas. Nearest gas stations in Eagle, Chicken and Boundary.

TJ 131.5 (211.6 km) **E 28.8** (46.3 km) King Solomon Creek bridge. Primitive camping (no facilities) at south end of bridge, east side of road, at site of former BLM campground. Highway follows King Solomon Creek next 0.5 mile/0.8 km northbound. (The creek has a tributary named Queen of Sheba.)

TJ 135.7 (218.4 km) **E 24.6** (39.6 km) *CAUTION: Slow down for hairpin curve.*

TJ 135.8 (218.5 km) **E 24.5** (39.4 km) North Fork Solomon Creek bridge.

TJ 141 (226.9 km) **E 19.3** (31.1 km) Glacier Mountain management area; walk-in hunting only. Top of the world views to west.

TJ 143.2 (230.5 km) **E 17.1** (27.5 km) Turnout on summit. Top of the world views. Road begins winding descent northbound to Yukon River.

TJ 149.1 (239.9 km) **E 11.2** (18 km) Bridge over Discovery Fork.

TJ 150.7 (242.5 km) **E 9.6** (15.4 km) Old cabin by creek to west is a local landmark. Private property.

TJ 151.8 (244.3 km) **E 8.5** (13.7 km) American Creek bridge No. 1. Outcroppings of asbestos, greenish or gray with white, and serpentine along creekbank. Doyon Ltd. claims ownership of surface and mineral estates on these lands; do not trespass.

TJ 152.5 (245.4 km) **E 7.8** (12.6 km) Bridge No. 2 over American Creek.

TJ 153.2 (246.5 km) **E 7.1** (11.4 km) Small turnout. Springwater piped to road.

TJ 153.6 (247.2 km) **E 6.7** (10.8 km) Small turnout. Springwater piped to road.

TJ 159.3 (256.4 km) **E 1** (1.6 km) Gas station.

TJ 159.7 (257 km) **E 0.6** (1 km) Turnout with historical sign about the settlement of Eagle.

TJ 160.3 (258 km) **E 0** Fourth Avenue, Eagle (description follows). Eagle school to east. Side road to west leads 1 mile/1.6 km to Fort Egbert mule barn, officers' quarters and parade ground. The U.S. Army established Fort Egbert in 1899, then abandoned it in 1911. From here a road leads 0.8 mile/1.3 km to Eagle Campground; 13 sites. ▲

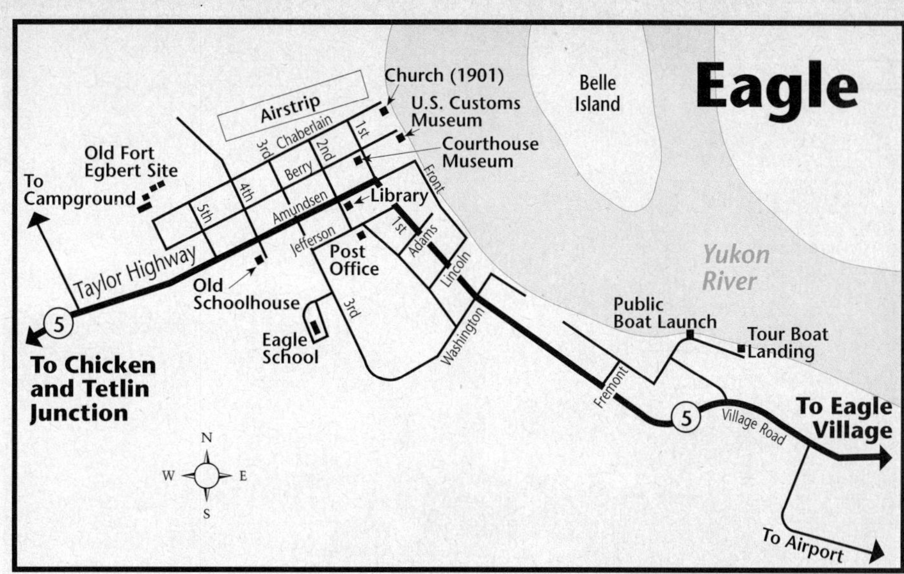

Eagle

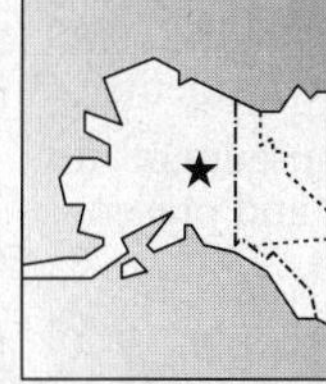

Population: 139. **Emergency Services:** Eagle EMS (907) 547-2300 or (907) 547-2211; use CB channel 21; Eagle health clinic. **Visitor Information:** Contact the Eagle Historical Society (Box 23, Eagle 99738; phone 907/547-2325) for information on area tours, museums and events.

The National Park Service office, headquarters for Yukon–Charley Rivers National Preserve, is located on the banks of the Yukon River at the base of Fort Egbert. Reference library available to the public. Office hours are 8 A.M. to 5 P.M. weekdays. The National Park Service Visitor Center offers maps and books for sale. Also a video on the preserve is shown on request. Informal talks and interpretive programs available. Visitor center hours are 8 A.M. to 5 P.M. daily in

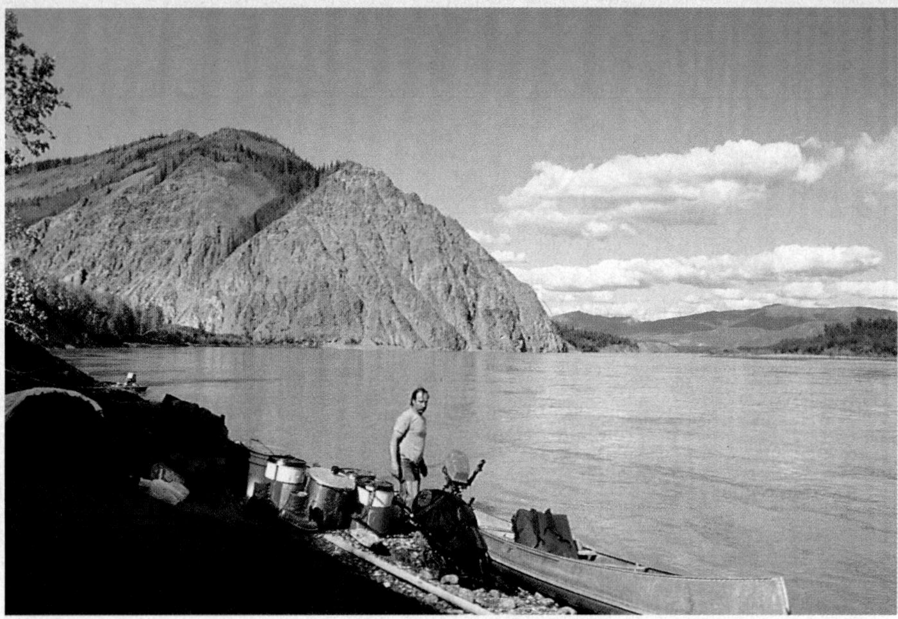

On the bank of the Yukon River with Eagle Bluff in background. (© Ruth von Spalding)

summer (Memorial Day weekend through Labor Day weekend). Check at the visitor center for information on the Yukon River, Yukon–Charley Rivers National Preserve and other parklands in Alaska. (Write them at Box 167, Eagle 99738, or phone 907 547-2233.)

Elevation: 820 feet/250m. **Climate:** Mean monthly temperature in July 59°F/15°C; in January -13°F/-25°C. Record low -71°F/-57°C in January 1952; record high 95°F/35°C in July 1925. July also has the greatest mean number of days (21) with temperatures above 70°F/21°C. Mean precipitation in July, 1.94 inches; in December, 10.1 inches. Record snow depth 42 inches in April 1948.

Transportation: By road via the Taylor Highway (closed by snow Oct. to April); air taxi, scheduled air service; dog team and snow machine in winter. Eagle is also accessible via the Yukon River. U.S. customs available at post office for persons entering Alaska via the Yukon River or by air.

Private Aircraft: Eagle airstrip, 2 miles/3.2 km east; elev. 880 feet/268m; length 3,500 feet/1,067m, gravel, unattended.

This small community was once the supply and transportation center for miners working the upper Yukon and its tributaries. Francois Mercier established his Belle Isle trading post here in the 1880s. By 1898, Eagle's population was 1,700. Gold strikes in Fairbanks and Nome lured away many, and by 1910, the population had dwindled to 178.

In the center of town stands a windmill and wellhouse (hand-dug in 1901); the well still provides water for over half the town's population. There are gas stations, restaurants, gift shops, museum store, post office, showers, laundromat, hardware store and mechanic shop with tire repair. Groceries and sundries are available. Fax service is available at both stores. Overnight accommodations at motels, rental cabins and bed and breakfasts. RV parking with hookups is available or stay at Eagle BLM campground just outside town (turn left on 4th Avenue and left again along airstrip at Fort Egbert). Eagle Village, an Athabascan settlement, is 3 miles/4.8 km from Eagle. ▲

Eagle, perched on the south bank of the Yukon River below Eagle Bluff (elev. 1000 feet/305m), remains relatively untouched. Locals still practice traditional subsistence activities—fishing with nets, gathering berries, gardening and handcrafting necessities—and many of the town's original cabins, over 100 years old, are used today.

Eagle also boasts the largest museum system in the state. Walking tours, offered by the Eagle Historical society, include the Wickersham courthouse, Waterfront Customs House and the mule barn, water wagon shed and NCO quarters at Fort Egbert. Tours are guided by long-time Eagle residents and begin at 9 A.M. daily (from in front of the courthouse), Memorial Day through Labor Day; cost is $3, members of Eagle Historical Society and children under 12 free (annual society membership, $5). Special tours may be arranged. Books, maps and gifts available at the museum store in the courthouse. For more information, contact the Eagle Historical Society (Box 23, Eagle 99738). Fort Egbert, renovated and restored by the Bureau of Land Management, has an interpretive exhibit and a photo display showing the stages of reconstruction. Videos of the Eagle area are shown every Monday at 7 P.M. in the public library, which also conducts lectures, slide presentations and other features every Thursday at 7 P.M.

Historically an important riverboat landing, Eagle is still a popular jumping-off point for Yukon River travelers. Most popular is a summer float trip from Eagle downriver through the **YUKON–CHARLEY RIVERS NATIONAL PRESERVE** to Circle. Length of the Eagle–Circle trip is 154 river miles/248 km, with most trips averaging 5 to 10 days. Float trips may also be made from Dawson City, YT, to Circle (252 miles/406 km, 7 to 10 days) with a halfway stop at Eagle. Boaters also often float the Fortymile to the Yukon River, then continue to the boat landing at Eagle to take out. Commercial boat trips are also available. Westours (Gray Line Yukon) operates the *Yukon Queen* daily boat service between Eagle and Dawson City, YT. Breakup on the Yukon is in May; freezeup in October. For details on weather, clothing, gear and precautions, contact the National Park Service, Box 167, Eagle 99738; phone (907) 547-2233.

Eagle Canoe Rentals. Canoe rentals on the Yukon River between Dawson City, Yukon Territory; Eagle City, Alaska; and Circle City. Brochures available, or call for details. From April to October: Dawson City River Hostel, Dieter Reinmuth, Box 32, Dawson City, YT, Y0B 1G0; (403) 993-6823 or Eagle Canoe Rentals, Mike Sager, Box 4, Eagle, AK 99738; (907) 547-2203. [ADVERTISEMENT]

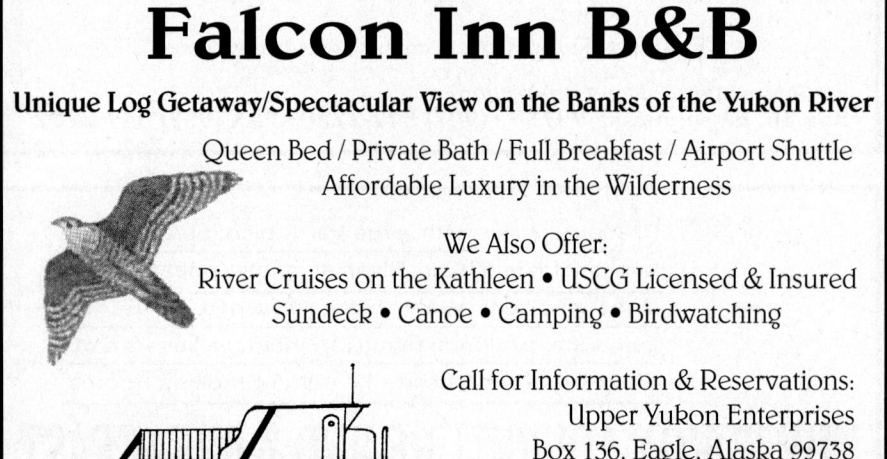

GLENN HIGHWAY/TOK CUTOFF

Tok to Anchorage, Alaska
Alaska Route 1
(See maps, pages 286–287)

The Glenn Highway/Tok Cutoff (Alaska Route 1) is the principal access route from the Alaska Highway west to Anchorage, a distance of 328 miles/527.8 km. This route includes the 125-mile/201-km Tok Cutoff, between Tok and the Richardson Highway junction; a 14-mile/22.5-km link via the Richardson Highway; and the 189-mile/304-km Glenn Highway, between the Richardson Highway and Anchorage.

It is a full day's drive between Tok and Anchorage on this paved all-weather highway. There is some spectacular scenery along the Glenn Highway with mountain peaks to the north and south. Road conditions are generally good. The highway between Tok and Glennallen has some very narrow sections with no shoulders. There is also winding road without shoulders from about Tahneta Pass to Palmer. Watch for frost heaves and pavement breaks along the entire highway. Watch for road construction. Slow down at signs saying Bump—they mean it!

Four side roads are logged in this section: the Nabesna Road to the old Nabesna Mine, which also provides access to Wrangell-St. Elias National Park and Preserve; Lake Louise Road to Lake Louise Recreation Area; the Hatcher Pass Road, connecting the Glenn and George Parks highways to Independence Mine State Historical Park; and the Old Glenn Highway, an alternate route between Palmer and Anchorage.

Emergency medical services: Between Tok and Duffy's Roadhouse at **Milepost GJ 63**, phone the Alaska State Troopers at 911 or (907) 883-5111. Between Duffy's and Gakona Junction, phone the Copper River EMS at Glennallen at (907) 822-3203 or 911. From Gakona Junction to Anchorage phone 911. CB channel 9 between **Milepost A 30.8** and Anchorage.

Mountain views dominate the scenery along the Glenn Highway. (© Ruth von Spalding)

Tok Cutoff Log

Physical mileposts read from **Milepost 125** at Tok to **Milepost 0** at Gakona Junction, the north junction with the Richardson Highway.

Distance from Gakona Junction (GJ) is followed by distance from Anchorage (A) and distance from Tok (T).

GJ 125 (201.2 km) **A 328** (527.8 km) **T 0** Tok (see description in the ALASKA HIGHWAY section).

GJ 124.2 (199.9 km) **A 327.2** (526.6 km) **T 0.8** (1.3 km) Tok Community Center.

GJ 124.1 (199.7 km) **A 327.1** (526.4 km) **T 0.9** (1.4 km) Tok Community Clinic, Tok Fire Station.

GJ 124 (199.6 km) **A 327** (526.2 km) **T 1** (1.6 km) Dept. of Natural Resources.

GJ 123.9 (199.4 km) **A 326.9** (526.1 km) **T 1.1** (1.8 km) Dept. of Transportation and Public Facilities, Tok Station.

GJ 123.7 (199.1 km) **A 326.7** (525.8 km) **T 1.3** (2.1 km) Borealis Avenue.

GJ 123.3 (198.4 km) **A 326.3** (525.1 km) **T 1.7** (2.7 km) **Hayner's Trading Post.** Alaskan handmade jewelry and gifts, beads and supplies, greeting and note cards. Sporting goods and black powder supplies. Custom leather work and repairs. Free coffee and tea. Open year-round. Summer hours 10 A.M. to 8 P.M. Rocky and Sue Hayner, owners. (907) 883-5536. See display ad in Tok in the ALASKA HIGHWAY section. [ADVERTISEMENT]

GJ 122.8 (197.6 km) **A 325.8** (524.3 km) **T 2.2** (3.5 km) **Sourdough Campground's Pancake Breakfast** served 7-11 A.M. Genuine "Sourdoughs." Full and partial RV hookups. Dry campsites. Showers included. High-pressure car wash. Free evening video program. Located 1.7 miles from the junction toward Anchorage on Tok Cutoff (Glenn Highway). See display ad in Tok in the ALASKA HIGHWAY section. [ADVERTISEMENT] ▲

GJ 122.6 (197.3 km) **A 325.6** (524 km) **T 2.4** (3.9 km) Bayless and Roberts Airport. Paved bike trail from Tok ends here.

GJ 116.7 (187.8 km) **A 319.7** (514.5 km) **T 8.3** (13.4 km) Entering Tok Management Area, Tanana Valley State Forest, westbound.

GJ 113 (181.9 km) **A 316** (508.5 km) **T 12** (19.3 km) Beautiful mountain views westbound.

GJ 110 (177 km) **A 313** (503.7 km) **T 15** (24.1 km) Flashing lights are from U.S. Coast Guard loran station at **Milepost DC 1308.5** on the Alaska Highway. Watch for frost heaves westbound.

GJ 109.3 (175.9 km) **A 312.3** (502.6 km) **T 15.7** (25.3 km) Eagle Trail State Recreation Site; 40 campsites, 15-day limit, 4 picnic sites, water, toilets, firepits, pay phone, rain shelter, hiking trail, Clearwater Creek. Camping fee $8/night or annual pass. The access road is designed with several loops to aid larger vehicles. A 0.9-mile/1.4-km section of the pioneer trail to Eagle is signed for hikers; trailhead near covered picnic tables. The historic Tok–Slana Cutoff road goes through this campground. ▲

GJ 104.5 (168.2 km) **A 307.5** (494.9 km) **T 20.5** (33 km) Small paved turnout to north. **Little Tok River** overflow runs under highway in culvert; fishing for grayling and Dolly Varden.

GJ 104.1 (167.5 km) **A 307.1** (494.2 km) **T 20.9** (33.6 km) Bridge over Tok River, side road north to riverbank and boat launch.

Wildlife is abundant from here west to Mentasta Summit. Watch for moose in roadside ponds, bears on gravel bars, and Dall sheep on mountainsides. For best wildlife viewing, stop at turnouts and use good binoculars. Wildflowers include sweet peas, chiming bells, arnica, oxytrope and lupine.

GJ 103.5 (166.6 km) **A 306.5** (493.3 km)

GLENN HIGHWAY

Tok Cutoff (GJ-125 to GJ-0) to Milepost A 160

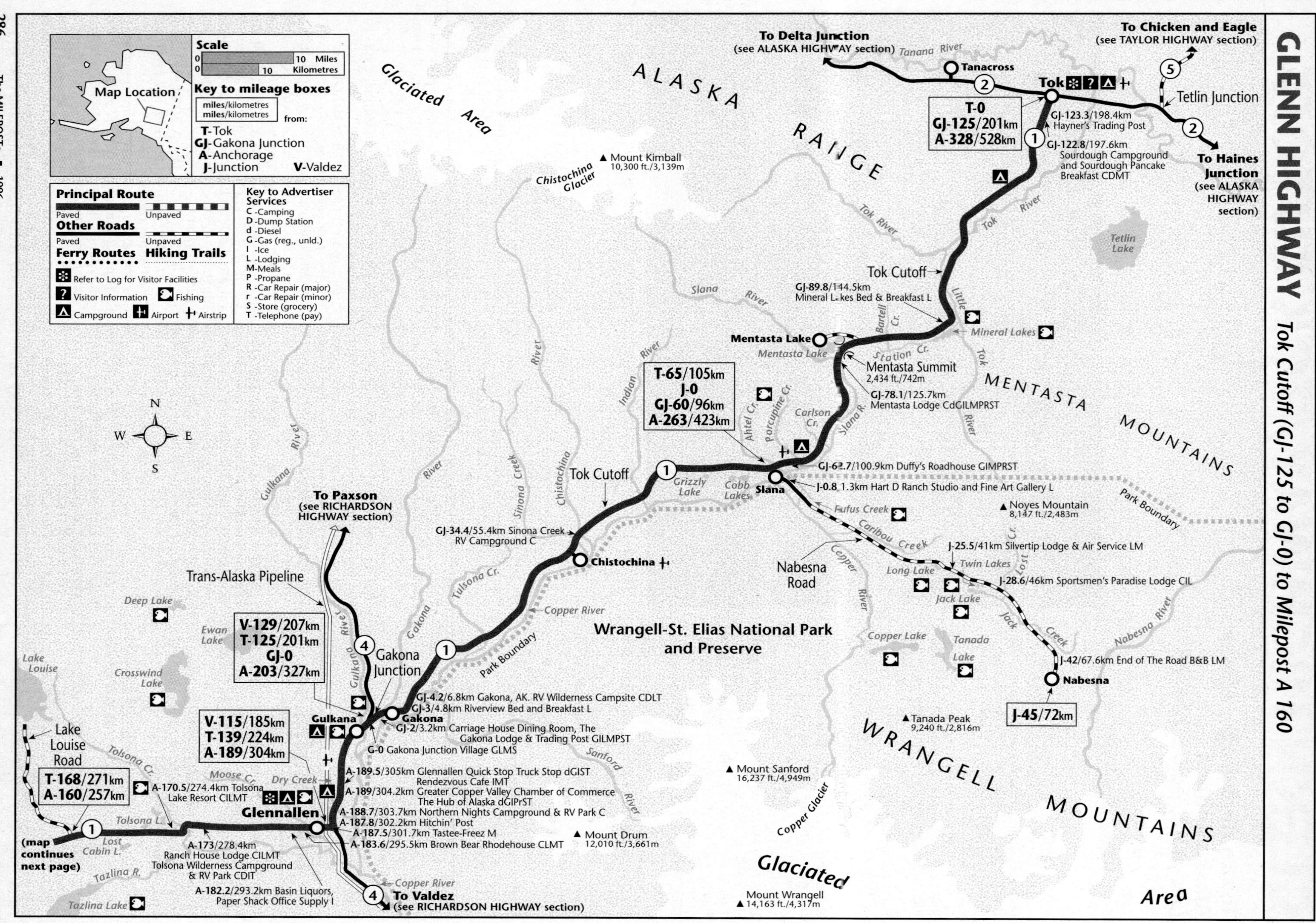

GLENN HIGHWAY *Milepost A 160 to Anchorage, AK*

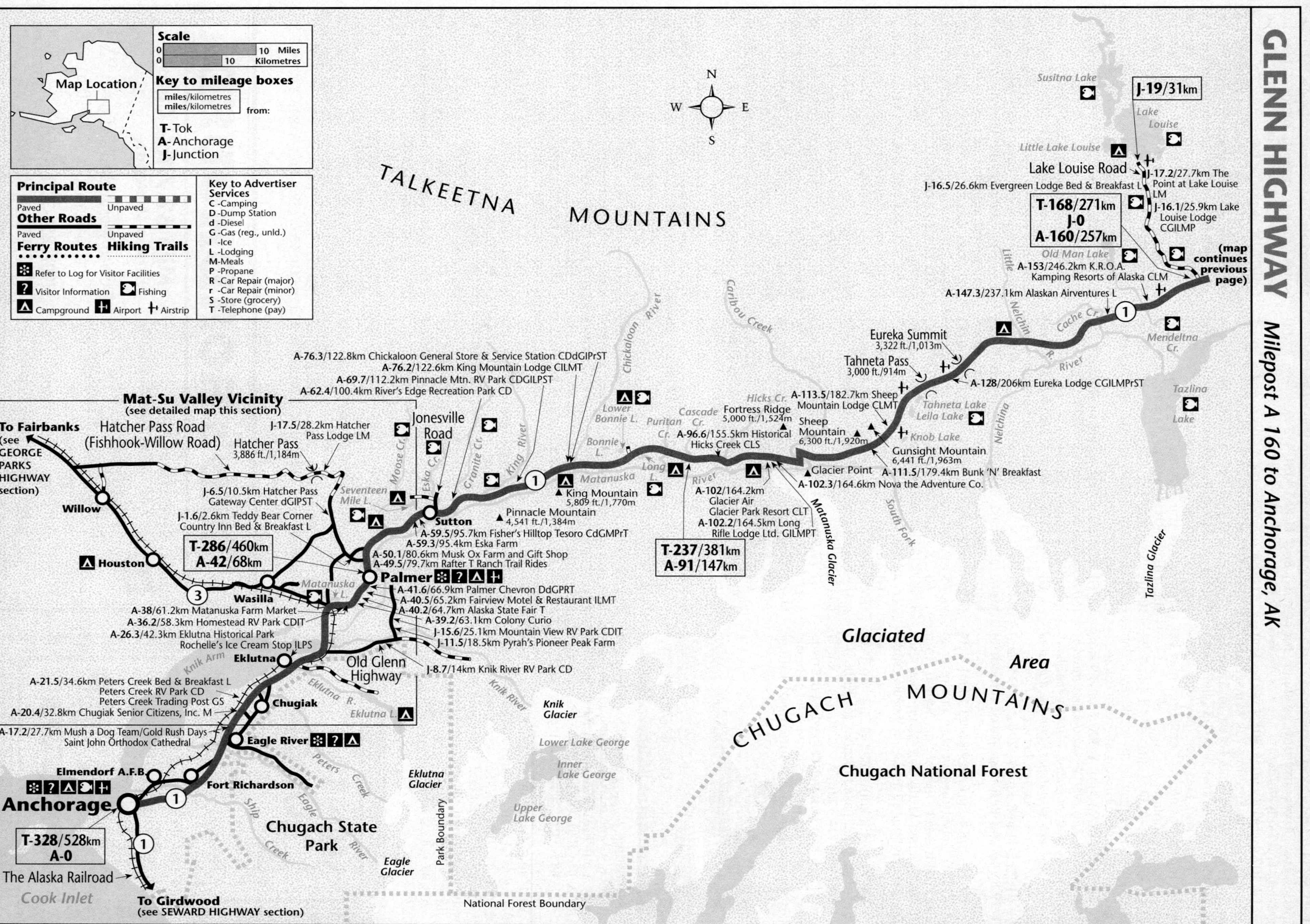

T 21.5 (34.6 km) Paved turnout to north. **Little Tok River** overflow; fishing for grayling and Dolly Varden.

GJ 102.4 (164.8 km) **A 305.4** (491.5 km) **T 22.6** (36.4 km) Entering Tok Management Area, Tanana Valley State Forest, eastbound.

GJ 99.3 (159.8 km) **A 302.3** (486.5 km) **T 25.7** (41.4 km) Rest area; paved double-ended turnout to north. Cranberries may be found in late summer.

GJ 98 (157.7 km) **A 301** (484.4 km) **T 27** (43.5 km) Bridge over Little Tok River, which parallels highway. Parking at end of bridge.

GJ 97.7 (157.2 km) **A 300.7** (483.9 km) **T 27.3** (43.9 km) *NOTE: Westbound travelers watch for sections of narrow highway (no shoulders); some gravel patches, bumps, dips and pavement breaks; and frost heaves.*

GJ 95.2 (153.2 km) **A 298.2** (479.9 km) **T 29.8** (48 km) Rest area; paved turnout to south.

GJ 91 (146.4 km) **A 294** (473.1 km) **T 34** (54.7 km) Gravel turnout with dumpster to north. Side road with bridge (weight limit 20 tons) across **Little Tok River;** good fishing for grayling, 12 to 14 inches, use small spinner.

GJ 90 (144.8 km) **A 293** (471.5 km) **T 35** (56.3 km) Small paved turnout to south.

GJ 89.8 (144.5 km) **A 292.8** (471.2 km) **T 35.2** (56.6 km) **Mineral Lakes Bed & Breakfast.** Cabins on lake with sourdough breakfast. Open year-round. Northern pike fishing

trips, boating, walking trails, RV parking and gift shop. Come relax—an Alaskan rural getaway. Your hosts, Gary and Patty Stender. HC72, Box 830, Tok, AK 99780-9410. Phone (907) 883-5498. Fall hunters welcomed. [ADVERTISEMENT]

GJ 89.5 (144 km) **A 292.5** (470.7 km) **T 35.5** (57.1 km) **Mineral Lakes.** These are sloughs of the Little Tok River and provide both moose habitat and a breeding place for waterfowl. Good fishing for northern pike and grayling.

GJ 89 (143.2 km) **A 292** (469.9 km) **T 36** (57.9 km) Small paved turnout to south.

GJ 86.7 (139.5 km) **A 289.7** (466.2 km) **T 38.3** (61.6 km) Good place to spot moose.

GJ 85.7 (137.9 km) **A 288.7** (464.6 km) **T 39.3** (63.2 km) Turnout to north.

GJ 83.2 (133.9 km) **A 286.2** (460.6 km) **T 41.8** (67.3 km) Bridge over Bartell Creek. Just beyond is the divide between the drainage of the Tanana River, tributary of the Yukon River system flowing into the Bering Sea, and the Copper River system, emptying into the North Pacific near Cordova.

GJ 81 (130.4 km) **A 284** (457 km) **T 44** (70.8 km) Access road to **MENTASTA LAKE** (pop. 72), a Native village.

GJ 79.4 (127.8 km) **A 282.4** (454.5 km) **T 45.6** (73.4 km) Mentasta Summit (elev. 2,434 feet/742m). Watch for Dall sheep on mountainsides. Boundary between Game Management Units 12 and 13C and Sportfish Management Units 8 and 2. Mountain views westbound.

GJ 78.1 (125.7 km) **A 281.1** (452.4 km) **T 46.9** (75.5 km) **Mentasta Lodge**. See display ad this section.

GJ 78 (125.5 km) **A 281** (452.2 km) **T 47** (75.6 km) View for westbound traffic of snow-covered Mount Sanford (elev. 16,237 feet/4,949m).

GJ 77.9 (125.4 km) **A 280.9** (452.1 km) **T 47.1** (75.8 km) Paved turnout to north by Slana Slough; salmon spawning area in August. Watch for beavers.

GJ 76.3 (122.8 km) **A 279.3** (449.5 km) **T 48.7** (78.4 km) Bridge over Mabel Creek. Mastodon flowers (marsh fleabane) in late July; very large (to 4 feet) with showy seed heads.

GJ 76 (122.3 km) **A 279** (449 km) **T 49** (78.8 km) Bridge over Slana Slough.

GJ 75.6 (121.7 km) **A 278.6** (448.3 km) **T 49.4** (79.5 km) Bridge over Slana River. Rest area to south with large paved parking area, dumpsters, toilets and picnic tables along the river. This river flows from its source glaciers some 55 miles/88.5 km to the Copper River.

GJ 74 (119.1 km) **A 277** (445.8 km) **T 51** (82.1 km) Large paved turnout to south overlooking Slana River.

GJ 69 (111 km) **A 272** (437.7 km) **T 56** (90.1 km) Turnout to north.

GJ 68 (109.4 km) **A 271** (436.1 km) **T 57** (91.7 km) Carlson Creek bridge. Paved turnout to south at west end of bridge.

GJ 65.5 (105.4 km) **A 268.5** (432.1 km) **T 59.5** (95.8 km) Paved turnout to south; viewpoint.

GJ 64.2 (103.3 km) **A 267.2** (430 km) **T 60.8** (97.8 km) Bridge over Porcupine Creek. State Recreation Site 0.2 mile/0.3 km from highway; 12 campsites, 15-day limit, $8 nightly fee or annual pass, drinking water, firepits, toilets, picnic tables and dumpster. Lowbush cranberries in fall. *CAUTION: Watch for bears.*

GJ 63 (101.4 km) **A 266** (428 km) **T 62** (99.8 km) Scenic viewpoint with view of Wrangell Mountains. The dominant peak to the southwest is Mount Sanford, a dormant volcano; the pinnacles of Capital Mountain can be seen against its lower slopes. Mount Jarvis (elev. 13,421 feet/4,091m) is visible to the south behind Mount Sanford; Tanada Peak (elev. 9,240 feet/2,816m) is more to the south. (Tanada Peak is sometimes mistaken for Noyes Mountain.)

Walk up the gravel hill behind the sign to view Noyes Mountain (elev. 8,147 feet/2,483m), named for U.S. Army Brig. Gen. John Rutherford Noyes, a one-time commissioner of roads in the territory of Alaska. Appointed adjutant general of the Alaska National Guard in 1953, he died in 1956 from injuries and frostbite after his plane crashed near Nome.

GJ 62.7 (100.9 km) **A 265.7** (427.6 km) **T 62.3** (100.3 km) **Duffy's Roadhouse**. See display ad this section.

Private Aircraft: Duffy's Tavern airstrip; elev. 2,420 feet/737m; length 900 feet/274m; gravel; fuel 100LL; unmaintained.

GJ 60.8 (97.8 km) **A 263.8** (424.6 km) **T 64.2** (103.3 km) Bridge over **Ahtell Creek;** grayling. Parking area to north at east end of bridge. This stream drains a mountain area of igneous rock, where several gold and silver-lead claims are located.

GJ 59.8 (96.2 km) **A 262.8** (422.9 km) **T 65.2** (104.9 km) **Junction** with Nabesna Road. See NABESNA ROAD log page 290.

GJ 59.7 (96.1 km) **A 262.7** (422.8 km) **T 65.3** (105.1 km) Gravel turnout to south. View of Tanada Peak, Mount Sanford, Mount Blackburn and Mount Drum to the south and southwest. The Mentasta Mountains are to the east.

GJ 57 (91.7 km) **A 260** (418.4 km) **T 68** (109.4 km) Cobb Lakes.

GJ 55.2 (88.8 km) **A 258.2** (415.5 km) **T 69.8** (112.3 km) Tanada Peak viewpoint; gravel turnout to south.

GJ 53 (85.3 km) **A 256** (412 km) **T 72** (115.9 km) Grizzly Lake. Watch for horses on road.

GJ 44.6 (71.8 km) **A 247.6** (398.5 km) **T 80.4** (129.4 km) Turnout to north. Eagle Trail access (not marked).

GJ 43.8 (70.5 km) **A 246.8** (397.1 km) **T 81.2** (130.6 km) Bridge over Indian River. This is a salmon spawning stream, usually late June through July. Picnic site to south at west end of bridge with tables, 2 firepits, litter container, toilets.

GJ 43.4 (69.8 km) **A 246.4** (396.5 km)

Scenery along the Tok Cutoff near Glennallen. (© Ruth von Spalding)

T 81.6 (131.3 km) Double-ended gravel turnout to south.

GJ **41.2** (66.3 km) **A 244.2** (393 km) **T 83.8** (134.8 km) Long, double-ended turnout overlooking pond.

GJ **40.1** (64.5 km) **A 243.1** (391.2 km) **T 84.9** (136.6 km) Small paved turnout to south. Fish Creek BLM trailhead.

GJ **39** (62.8 km) **A 242** (389.5 km) **T 86** (138.4 km) Views of the Copper River valley and Wrangell Mountains. Looking south, peak on left is Mount Sanford and on right is Mount Drum (elev. 12,010 feet/3,661m).

Look for cotton grass and mastodon flowers in late July and Aug.

CAUTION: Rough road next 2 miles/3.2 km eastbound.

GJ **38.7** (62.2 km) **A 241.7** (389 km) **T 86.3** (138.8 km) Paved turnout to north. Mankoman Lake trail.

GJ **35.5** (57.1 km) **A 238.5** (383.8 km) **T 89.5** (144 km) Chistochina River Bridge No. 2. Mount Sanford is first large mountain to the southeast, then Mount Drum.

GJ **35.4** (57 km) **A 238.4** (383.7 km) **T 89.6** (144.2 km) Chistochina River Bridge No. 1; parking at west end. Chistochina River trailhead. This river heads in the Chistochina Glacier on Mount Kimball (elev. 10,300 feet/3,139m). Chistochina is thought to mean marmot creek.

GJ **34.7** (55.8 km) **A 237.7** (382.5 km) **T 90.3** (145.3 km) Posty's Sinona Creek Trading Post (current status unknown).

GJ **34.6** (55.7 km) **A 237.6** (382.4 km) **T 90.4** (145.5 km) Bridge over Sinona Creek. Sinona is said to mean place of the many burls, and there are indeed many burls on area spruce trees.

GJ **34.4** (55.4 km) **A 237.4** (382 km) **T 90.6** (145.8 km) **Sinona Creek RV Campground.** See display ad this section. ▲

GJ **34.1** (54.9 km) **A 237.1** (381.6 km) **T 90.9** (146.3 km) Chistochina ball fields.

GJ **32.9** (52.9 km) **A 235.9** (379.6 km) **T 92.1** (148.2 km) Road access to Native village of **CHISTOCHINA** (pop. 43) .

Private Aircraft: Barnhart airstrip, 3 miles/4.8 km north; elev. 1,930 feet/588m; length 2,500 feet/762m; earth; unattended. Chistochina airstrip, adjacent southwest; elev. 1,850 feet/564m; length 2,000 feet/610m; turf and gravel.

GJ **32.8** (52.8 km) **A 235.8** (379.5 km) **T 92.2** (148.4 km) Chistochina Lodge.

GJ **30.1** (48.4 km) **A 233.1** (375.1 km) **T 94.9** (152.7 km) Paved turnout to south. Road narrows eastbound; no shoulders. Watch for frost heaves.

GJ **28.1** (45.2 km) **A 231.1** (371.9 km) **T 96.9** (155.9 km) Double-ended paved parking area to south with a marker on the Alaska Road Commission. The ARC was established in 1905, the same year the first automobile arrived in Alaska at Skagway. The ARC operated for 51 years, building roads, airfields, trails and other transportation facilities. It was replaced by the Bureau of Public Roads (referred to by some Alaskans at the time as the Bureau of Parallel Ruts) in 1956. In 1960 the Bureau of Public Roads was replaced by the Dept. of Public Works.

GJ **24** (38.6 km) **A 227** (365.3 km) **T 101** (162.5 km) Large rest area to south with paved double-ended parking area, toilets, picnic tables, litter container and firepits on grass under trees; paths lead to Copper River. Mount Sanford is to the southeast, Mount Drum to the south.

GJ **21.3** (34.3 km) **A 224.3** (361 km) **T 103.7** (166.9 km) Buster Gene trailhead to south.

GJ **20.9** (33.6 km) **A 223.9** (360.3 km) **T 104.1** (167.5 km) Turnout to south.

GJ **17.8** (28.6 km) **A 220.8** (355.3 km) **T 107.2** (172.5 km) **Tulsona Creek** bridge. Good grayling fishing.

GJ **11.6** (18.7 km) **A 214.6** (345.4 km) **T 113.4** (182.5 km) Yellow pond lily *(Nuphar polysepalum)* in ponds along highway.

GJ **9.4** (15.1 km) **A 212.4** (341.8 km) **T 115.6** (186 km) Paved turnout to north by lake. Fox Lake BLM trailhead.

GJ **8.8** (14.2 km) **A 211.8** (340.8 km) **T 116.2** (187 km) Paved turnout to north. BLM trailhead.

GJ **6.3** (10.1 km) **A 209.3** (336.8 km) **T 118.7** (191 km) Paved turnout to southeast.

GJ **4.2** (6.8 km) **A 207.2** (333.4 km) **T 120.8** (194.4 km) **Gakona, AK. R.V. Wilderness Campsite.** See display ad this section. ▲

GJ **3** (4.8 km) **A 206** (331.5 km) **T 122** (196.3 km) **Riverview Bed and Breakfast.** See display ad this section.

(Continues on page 291)

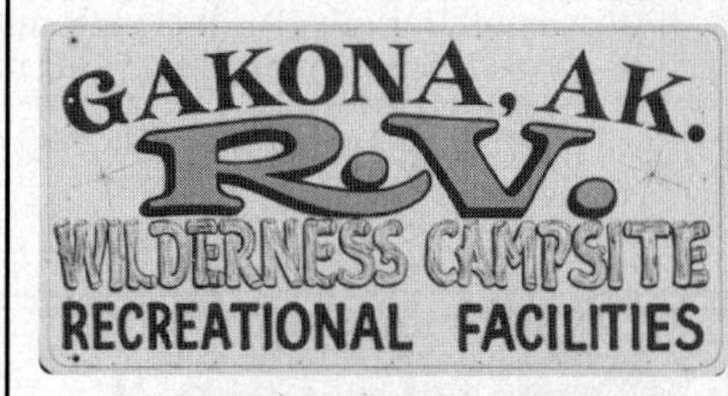

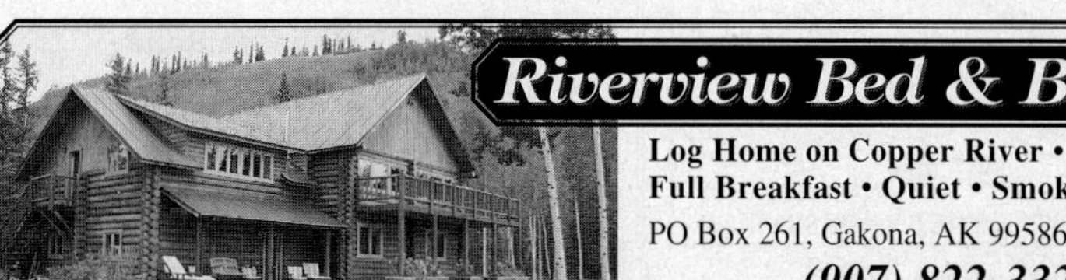

Nabesna Road Log

The Nabesna Road leads 45 miles/ 72.4 km southeast from **Milepost GJ 59.8** Glenn Highway (Tok Cutoff) to the mining community of Nabesna. This side trip can be enjoyable for campers; there are no formal campgrounds but there are plenty of beautiful spots to camp. The area also offers good fishing. Horses are permitted on all trails. Off-road vehicles must have permits. The Nabesna Road provides access to the northwest corner of Wrangell–St. Elias National Park and Preserve. The National Park Service ranger station at Slana has information on current Nabesna Road conditions and on backcountry travel in the park. (The Wrangell–St. Elias National Park visitor center is in Copper Center on the Richardson Highway.) The first 4 miles/6.4 km of road is chip seal surface, the remainder is gravel. Beyond **Milepost J 28.6** the road becomes rough and crosses several creeks which may be difficult to ford. Four-wheel drive only is recommended beyond **Milepost J 42.**

Distance is measured from the junction with the Glenn Highway (J).

J 0.1 (0.2 km) Highway maintenance station.

J 0.2 (0.3 km) Slana NPS ranger station; information on road conditions and on Wrangell–St. Elias National Park and Preserve. Open 8 A.M. to 5 P.M. daily, June 1 through Sept. USGS maps and natural history books for sale. For more information contact: Superintendent, Wrangell–St. Elias National Park and Preserve, P.O. Box 439, Copper Center, AK 99573; phone (907) 822-5234.

J 0.8 (1.3 km) The Slana post office is located at the picturesque Hart D Ranch, home of artist Mary Frances DeHart.

Hart D Ranch Studio and Fine Art Gallery. See display ad this section.

J 1 (1.6 km) **SLANA** (pop. 39), once an Indian village on the north bank of the Slana River, now refers to this general area. Besides the Indian settlement, Slana boasted a popular roadhouse, now a private home. Slana elementary school is located here.

J 1.5 (2.4 km) Slana River Bridge; undeveloped camping area. Boundary between Game Management Units 11 and 13C.

J 2 (3.2 km) BLM homestead area next 2 miles/3.2 km southbound. Blueberries in the fall; grouse are seen in this area.

J 3.9 (6.2 km) Entering Wrangell–St. Elias National Park and Preserve. The Glenn Highway follows the northern boundary of the preserve between Slana and Gakona Junction; Nabesna Road provides access to the northwest corner of the park.

J 4 (6.4 km) Turnouts. Hard surface ends, gravel begins, southbound.

J 7 (11.3 km) Road crosses **Rufus Creek** culvert. Dolly Varden to 8 inches, June to Oct. Watch out for bears, especially during berry season.

J 8.9 (14.3 km) Rough turnout.

J 11 (17.7 km) Suslota Lake trailhead No. 1 to north.

J 11.4 (18.3 km) Gravel pit, room to park or camp.

J 12.2 (19.6 km) Road crosses Caribou Creek culvert.

J 12.5 (20.1 km) Turnout to southeast; Copper Lake trailhead.

J 13 (20.9 km) Suslota Lake trailhead No. 2 to north.

J 15 (24.1 km) Turnout.

J 15.4 (24.8 km) Beautiful views of Mount Sanford and Tanada Peak in the Wrangell Mountains, across the great plain of the Copper River.

J 16 (25.7 km) Turnout to northeast.

J 16.6 (26.7 km) Turnout to southwest.

J 16.9 (27.2 km) Turnout by large lake which reflects Mount Sanford.

J 18 (29 km) Pond to northeast. The highly mineralized Mentasta Mountains are visible to the north. This is sparsely timbered high country.

J 18.8 (30.3 km) Caribou Creek culvert.

J 19.3 (31.1 km) Turnout at gravel pit to northwest. Look for poppies, lupine, arnica and chiming bells in season.

J 21.2 (34.1 km) Turnout at gravel pit to northwest.

J 21.8 (35.1 km) Rock Creek culvert.

J 22.3 (35.9 km) Rock Lake; turnouts both sides of road.

J 22.9 (36.8 km) Long Lake.

J 23.4 (37.7 km) Turnout. Floatplane landing.

J 24.4 (39.3 km) Turnout to southwest with view of Wrangell Mountains. Tanada Lake trail.

J 25.2 (40.6 km) Boundary between Sportfish Areas C and K, and Game Management Areas 11 and 12.

J 25.5 (41 km) Lodge. Glimpse of Tanada Lake beneath Tanada Peak to the south.

Silvertip Lodge & Air Service. See display ad this section.

J 25.9 (41.7 km) Little Jack Creek.

J 26.1 (42 km) Access road to private campground and floatplane service at Jack Lake; no turnaround. ▲

J 27 (43.5 km) Turnout to north.

J 28.2 (45.4 km) Turnouts at Twin Lakes; primitive campsite, good place to observe waterfowl. Wildflowers in June include Lapland rosebay, lupine and 8-petalled avens.

AREA FISHING: Twin Lakes, grayling 10 to 18 inches, mid-May to Oct., flies or small spinner; also burbot. **Copper Lake** (fly in from Long Lake or Jack Lake), lake trout 10 to 12 lbs., mid-June to Sept., use red-and-white spoon; kokanee 10 to 12 inches, mid-June to July, use small spinner; grayling 12 to 20 inches, July through Sept.; also burbot. **Long** and **Jack lakes,** grayling fishing. **Tanada Lake** (fly in from Long Lake or Jack Lake), grayling and lake trout.

J 28.6 (46 km) **Sportsmen's Paradise Lodge** is located 28.6 miles from the Glenn Highway on the Nabesna Gold Mine Road. Miles of magnificent views on this old road to the former Nabesna

Gold Mine. Free camper parking, sandwiches, bar, air taxi service, fishing, boating, hunting. A side trip not to miss. Fly-in fishing to Copper Lake, boats, motors, light-housekeeping cabins available. Dick and Lucille Frederick, your hosts. Phone (907) 822-5288 (radiophone). [ADVERTISEMENT] ▲

J 28.6 (46 km) The road deteriorates beyond this point and you may have to ford several creeks. Inquire at lodge here or Slana Ranger Station about road conditions.

J 29.6 (47.6 km) Trail Creek crosses road; no culvert but road has gravel base here. Easy to drive through creek, especially in fall. Overnight hikers may hike up Lost Creek and return via Trail Creek.

J 31.4 (50.5 km) Road crosses Lost Creek, a very wide expanse of water in spring and may remain difficult to cross well into summer. Loose gravel makes it easy to get stuck in creek if you spin your wheels. Scout it out first. If you hesitate once in the creek, wheels may dig in. The road crosses several more creeks beyond here; these may also be difficult to ford.

J 31.6 (50.9 km) Boyden Creek (may have to ford after rain or during spring melt).

J 32.4 (52.1 km) Chalk Creek culvert.

J 33 (53.1 km) Big Grayling Lake hiking trail. Horses allowed.

J 34.1 (54.9 km) Radiator Creek culvert.

J 35 (56.3 km) Creek (must ford).

J 36 (57.9 km) Jack Creek Bridge.

J 36.1 (58.1 km) Informal campsite. The road crosses 5 creeks the next 4.3 miles/6.9 km southbound. Watch for loose gravel in creekbeds.

J 41 (66 km) A marked trail, approximately 5 miles/8 km long, leads to Nabesna River and old Reeves Field airstrip, once used to fly gold out and supplies in to mining camps. Devil's Mountain is to the left of the trail. The trail on the river also leads to the old Indian village of Khiltat.

J 41.4 (66.6 km) Skookum Creek in culvert.

J 42 (67.6 km) Devil's Mountain Lodge (private property). Four-wheel-drive vehicles only beyond this point.

End of the Road B&B. See display ad this section.

J 45 (72.4 km) **NABESNA** (area pop. less than 25; elev. 3,000 feet/914m). No facilities. This region has copper reserves, as well as gold in the streams and rivers, silver, molybdenum and iron ore deposits. Tailings deposits here are currently closed to the public. Nabesna gold mine is located here. Area residents subsist on caribou, Dall sheep, moose, bear, fish and small game. Fire fighting and trapping also provide some income. Big game hunting is popular in this area and several outfitters have headquarters along Nabesna Road.

Return to Milepost GJ 59.8
Glenn Highway (Tok Cutoff)

(Continued from page 289)

GJ 2.7 (4.3 km) **A 205.7** (331 km) **T 122.3** (196.8 km) **GAKONA** (area pop. 200). The village of Gakona lies between the Gakona and Copper rivers (Gakona is Athabascan for "rabbit"). Originally Gakona was a Native wood and fish camp, and fish wheels are still common. The post office is located on the highway here.

GJ 2 (3.2 km) **A 205** (330 km) **T 123** (198 km) Gakona Lodge, entered on the National Register of Historic Places in 1977. Originally one of several roadhouses providing essential food and lodging for travelers, it opened in 1905 and was first called Doyle's Ranch. The original carriage house is now a restaurant.

Gakona Lodge & Trading Post and **The Carriage House Dining Room.** See display ad this section.

GJ 1.8 (2.9 km) **A 204.8** (329.6 km) **T 123.2** (198.3 km) Bridge over Gakona River. Entering Game Management Unit 13B westbound and 13C eastbound. The highway climbs a short hill and joins the Richardson Highway 1.8 miles/2.9 km from this bridge. From the hill there is a fine view of the many channels where the Gakona and Copper rivers join.

GJ 1 (1.6 km) **A 204** (328.3 km) **T 124** (200 km) Rest area to south has paved turnout overlooking the valley of the Gakona and Copper rivers; picnic tables and litter barrels. View of Mount Drum and Mount Sanford. Good photo stop.

GJ 0 A 203 (326.7 km) **T 125** (201.2 km) **Gakona Junction.** Lodge. Junction of Tok Cutoff (Alaska Route 1) with the Richardson Highway (Alaska Route 4); the 2 roads share a common alignment for the next 14 miles/22.5 km westbound.

Turn north here for Delta Junction via the Richardson Highway (see **Milepost V 128.6** in the RICHARDSON HIGHWAY section). Turn south for Anchorage or Valdez. *NOTE: This junction can be confusing. Choose your route carefully.*

Gakona Junction Village, king salmon fishing headquarters for the Copper Valley, is one-stop shopping for the Alaska traveler. Located at the junction of the Richardson Highway and Tok Cut-Off, we offer beautiful rooms, great food, Texaco gas, groceries, gifts, gallery and king salmon fishing guides. Reservations: 1-800-962-1933; general information: (907) 822-3664 and fax (907) 822-3696 [ADVERTISEMENT]

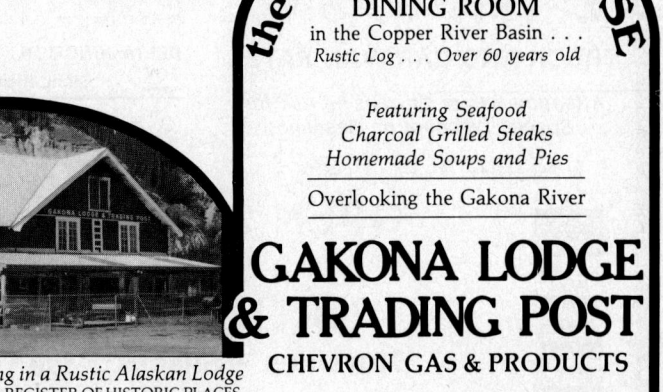

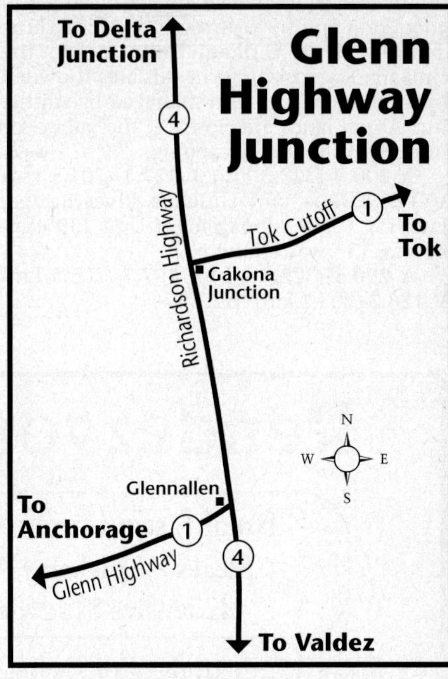

Richardson Highway Log

ALASKA ROUTE 4

Physical mileposts for the next 14 miles/22.5 km southbound give distance from Valdez. **Distance from Anchorage (A) is followed by distance from Tok (T) and distance from Valdez (V).**

A 203 (326.7 km) **T 125** (201.2 km) **V 128.6** (207 km) **Junction** of the Tok Cutoff with the Richardson Highway at Gakona Junction. Watch for frost heaves between here and **Milepost V 124.**

A 201 (323.5 km) **T 127** (204.4 km) **V 126.9** (204.2 km) Access road to **GULKANA** (pop. 100) on the bank of the Gulkana River. Camping is permitted along the river by the bridge. Grayling fishing and good king and sockeye salmon fishing (June and July) in the **Gulkana River.** Most of the Gulkana River frontage in this area is owned by Gulkana village and managed by Ahtna, Inc. Ahtna lands are closed to the public for hunting, fishing and trapping.

A 200.9 (323.3 km) **T 127.1** (204.5 km) **V 126.8** (204 km) Gulkana River Bridge. Entering Game Management Unit 13B eastbound, 13A westbound.

A 200.3 (322.3 km) **T 127.7** (205.5 km) **V 126.2** (203.1 km) Inn.

A 200.1 (322 km) **T 127.9** (205.8 km) **V 126** (202.8 km) Paved double-ended turnout to north.

A 197.3 (317.5 km) **T 130.7** (210.3 km) **V 123.2** (198.3 km) Large paved turnout to south.

A 192.1 (309.1 km) **T 135.9** (218.7 km) **V 118.1** (190 km) **Private Aircraft:** Gulkana airstrip; elev. 1,578 feet/481m; length 5,000 feet/1,524m; asphalt; fuel 100. Flying service located here.

A 192 (309 km) **T 136** (218.9 km) **V 118** (189.9 km) Dry Creek State Recreation Site; 58 campsites, 15-day limit, $10 nightly fee or annual pass, 4 picnic sites, toilets, picnic shelter. *Bring mosquito repellent!*

A 189.5 (305 km) **T 138.5** (222.9 km) **V 115.5** (185.9 km) **Glennallen Quick Stop Truck Stop.** Stop for friendly family service, gas, diesel, convenience store with ice, pop, snacks, postcards, ice cream, specialty items, pay phone and free coffee. Truck, caravan, senior citizen discounts. Several interesting items on display, including an authentic Native Alaskan fish wheel. Full-service restaurant adjacent. See display ad this section. [ADVERTISEMENT]

A 189.5 (305 km) **T 138.5** (222.9 km) **V 115.5** (185.9 km) **Rendezvous Cafe.** See display ad this section.

A 189 (304.2 km) **T 139** (223.7 km) **V 115** (185.1 km) **Junction** of the Richardson Highway (Alaska Route 4) with the Glenn Highway (Alaska Route 1). Turn south here on the Richardson Highway for Valdez (see **Milepost V 115** in the RICHARDSON HIGHWAY section). Continue west on the Glenn Highway for Anchorage. *NOTE: This junction can be confusing. Choose your route carefully. See map page 291.*

Greater Copper Valley Chamber of Commerce visitor information center and gas station. Alaska State Troopers, Dept. of Motor Vehicles, Fish and Wildlife Protection and courthouse located on east side of highway.

Greater Copper Valley Chamber of Commerce Visitor Center in log cabin; open 8 A.M. to 7 P.M. daily in summer. There's also a convenience grocery and a gas station (with diesel) at junction.

Greater Copper Valley Chamber of Commerce. See display ad this section.

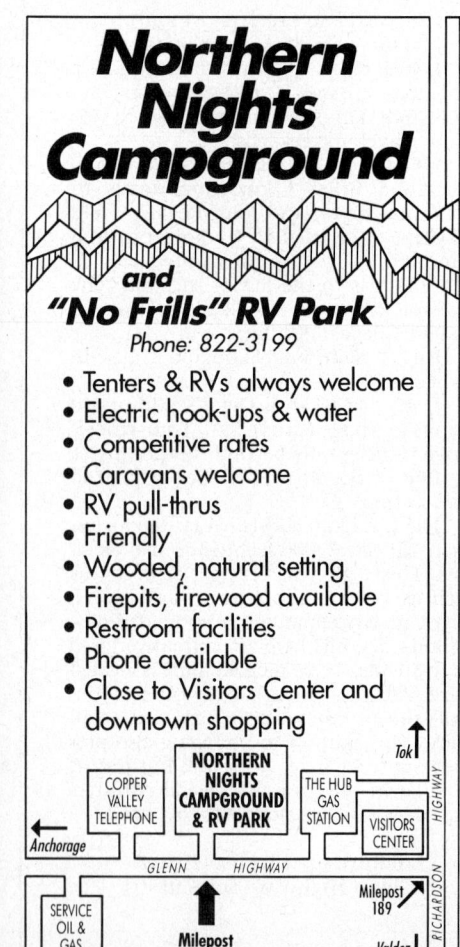

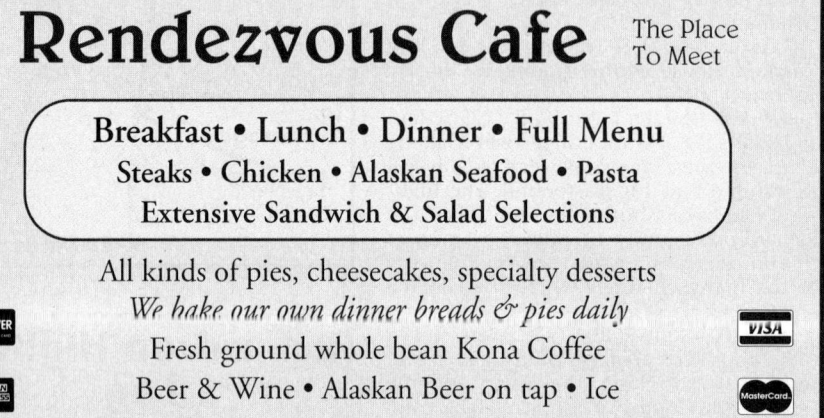

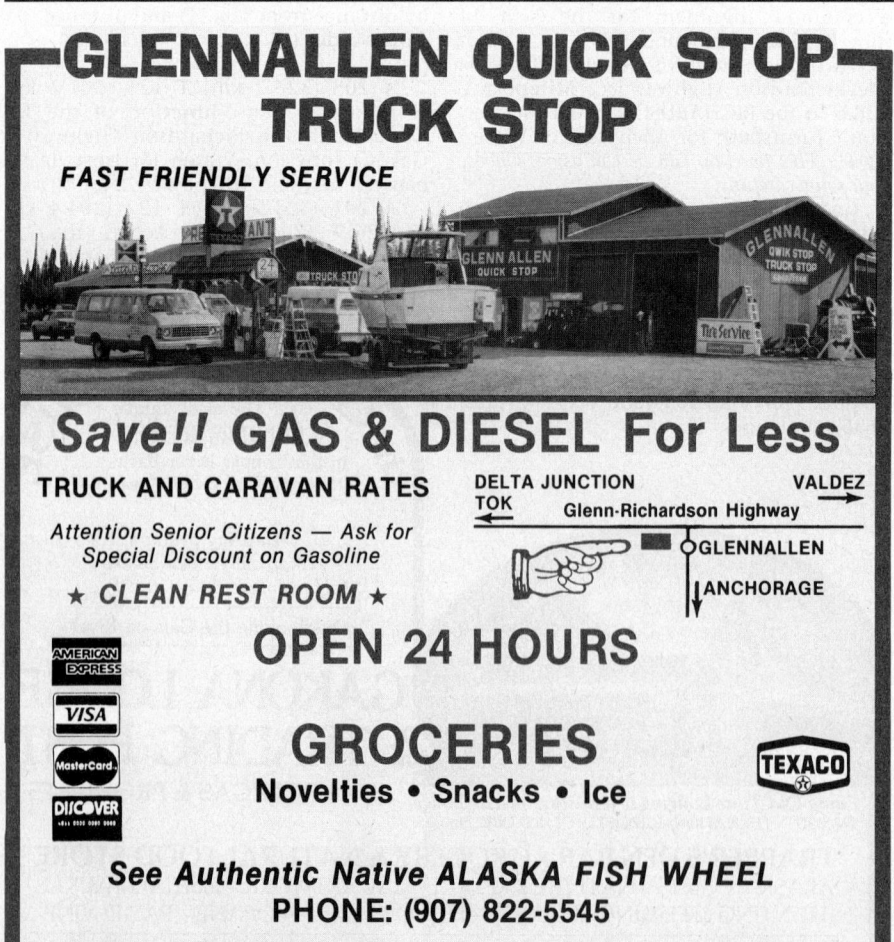

The Hub of Alaska. See display ad this section.

Glenn Highway Log

ALASKA ROUTE 1
Physical mileposts between Glennallen and Anchorage show distance from Anchorage. **Distance from Anchorage (A) is followed by distance from Tok (T).**

A 188.7 (303.7 km) **T 139.3** (224.2 km) **Northern Nights Campground and "No Frills" RV Park.** See display ad this section. ▲

A 188.3 (303 km) **T 139.7** (224.8 km) Trans-Alaska pipeline passes under the highway.

A 187.8 (302.2 km) **T 140.2** (225.6 km) **The Hitchin' Post.** The little place with the big reputation. Known for our great fries, KC style BBQ ribs on Saturday nights, and our big breakfasts. Enjoy the picnic tables, eat indoors, or stop at our drive through. Located across from the car wash and RV park. See display ad. [ADVERTISEMENT]

A 187.5 (301.7 km) **T 140.5** (226.1 km) **Tastee-Freez.** This popular spot features an excellent menu of fast food, including breakfast, with some of the lowest prices on the highway. We satisfy appetites of all sizes, from a quick taco to double cheeseburgers, cooked fresh and fast. Our comfortable dining room displays a selection of the finest original drawings and handmade gifts. Plan to stop! See display ad in Glennallen section. [ADVERTISEMENT]

Aurora borealis photographed in winter from the Glenn Highway. (© Michael DeYoung)

A 187.2 (301.3 km) **T 140.8** (226.6 km) National Bank of Alaska; 24-hour automatic teller machine. Post office a block north of highway. Description of Glennallen follows.

Glennallen

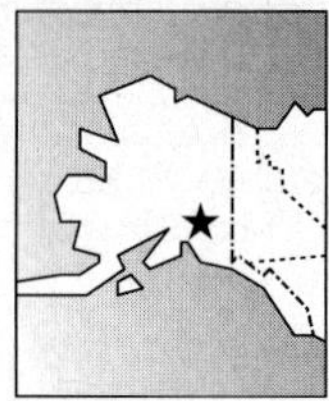

A 187 (300.9 km) **T 141** (226.9 km) Near the south junction of Glenn and Richardson highways. **Population:** 928. **Emergency Services: Alaska State Troopers, Milepost A 189**, phone (907) 822-3263. **Fire Department**, phone 911. **Ambulance**, Copper River EMS, phone (907) 822-3203 or 911. **Clinic, Milepost A 186.6**, phone (907) 822-3203. **Road Conditions**, phone (907) 822-5511.

Visitor Information: The Greater Copper Valley Chamber of Commerce Visitor Center is located in the log cabin at the junction of the Glenn and Richardson highways. **Milepost A 189;** open 8 A.M. to 7 P.M. daily in summer, phone (907) 822-5555. The Alaska Dept. of Fish and Game office is located at **Milepost A 186.2** on the Glenn Highway, open weekdays 8 A.M. to 5 P.M.; phone (907) 822-3309.

Elevation: 1,460 feet/445m. **Climate:** Mean monthly temperature in Jan. -10°F/-23°C; in July, 56°F/13°C. Record low was -61°F/-52°C in Jan. 1975; record high,

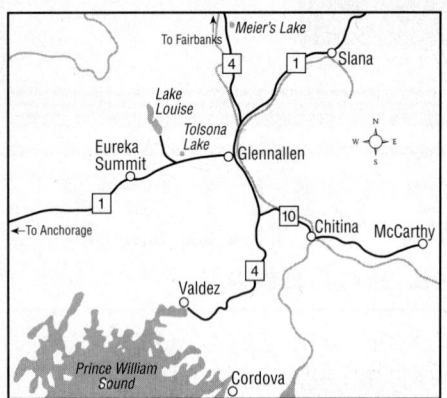

GLENNALLEN ADVERTISERS

90°F/32°C in June 1969. Mean precipitation in July, 1.53 inches/3.9cm. Mean precipitation (snow/sleet) in Dec., 11.4 inches/29cm. **Radio:** KCAM 790, KOOL 107.1, KUAC-FM 92.1. **Television:** KYUK (Bethel) and Wrangell Mountain TV Club via satellite; Public Broadcasting System.

Private Aircraft: Gulkana airstrip, 4.3 miles/6.9 km northeast of Glennallen at **Milepost A 192.1**; elev. 1,578 feet/481m; length 5,000 feet/1,524m; asphalt; fuel 100. Parking with tie downs. Mechanic available.

The name Glennallen is derived from the combined last names of Capt. Edwin F. Glenn and Lt. Henry T. Allen, both leaders in the early exploration of the Copper River region.

Glennallen lies at the western edge of the huge Wrangell–St. Elias National Park and Preserve. It is a gateway to the Wrangell Mountains and the service center for the Copper River basin. Glennallen is also a fly-in base for several guides and outfitters.

Four prominent peaks of the majestic Wrangell Mountains are to the east; from left they are Mounts Sanford, Drum, Wrangell and Blackburn. The best views are on crisp winter days at sunset. The rest of the countryside is relatively flat.

The main business district is 1.5 miles/2.4 km west of the south junction of the Glenn and Richardson highways. There are also several businesses located at the south junction. About two-thirds of the area's residents are employed by trade/service firms;

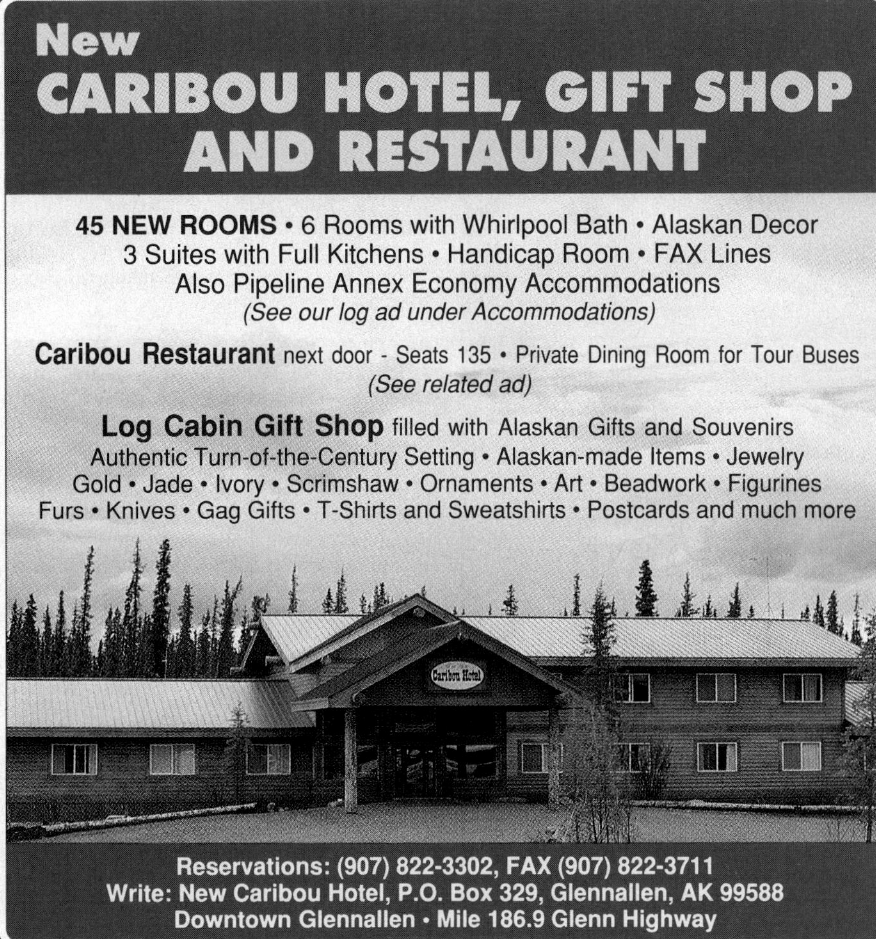

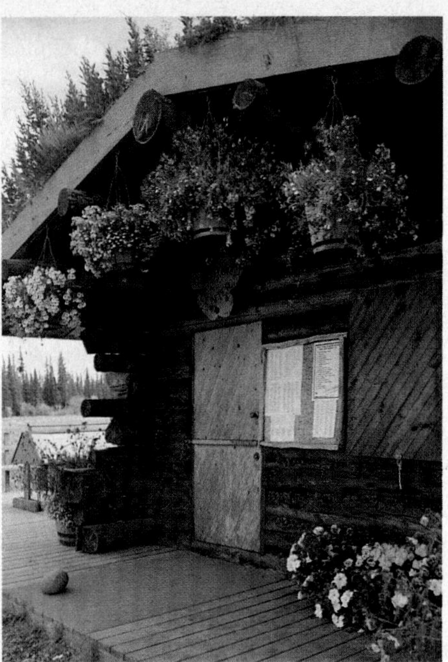

Copper Valley Visitor Center at Milepost A 189 (© Carman Scott)

the balance hold various government positions. Offices for the Bureau of Land Management, the Alaska State Troopers and Dept. of Fish and Game are located here. There are several small farms in the area. There is a substantial Native population in the area and the Native-owned Ahtna Corp. has its headquarters near Glennallen on the Richardson Highway.

Also headquartered here is KCAM radio, which broadcasts on station 790. KCAM broadcasts area road condition reports daily and also airs the popular "Caribou Clatter," which will broadcast personal messages. Radio messages are still a popular form of communication in Alaska and a necessary one in the Bush. Similar programs throughout the state are KJNP's "Trapline Chatter"; KYAK's "Bush Pipeline"; KHAR's "Northwinds"; and KIAK's "Pipeline of the North." KFAR in Fairbanks broadcast "Tundra Topics" for 37 years; it was taken off the air in 1980.

ACCOMMODATIONS/VISITOR SERVICES

Because of its strategic location, most traveler services are available. During summer months reservations are advised for visitor accommodations. Glennallen has several lodges and motels and a variety of restaurants. Auto parts, groceries, gifts, clothing, propane, sporting goods and other supplies are available at local stores. Services include a bank and automatic teller machine, a dentist, several churches, a chiropractic center, a laundromat, gas stations and major auto repair.

New Caribou Hotel, Gift Shop and Restaurant. The New Caribou Hotel in downtown Glennallen, on the edge of the largest national park in America, was completed fall of 1990. This 45-unit modern facility features custom built furniture, state-of-the-art color coordinated Alaskan decor, 6 rooms with 2-person whirlpool baths, 2-bedroom fully furnished suites with kitchens and cooking facilities. Alaskan art, handicap facilities, conference rooms, phones and fax lines, satellite TV. Winter snow machine rentals. Large full menu restaurant with banquet room, unique Alaskan gift shop (a must stop in your travels). All major credit cards accepted. Tour buses welcome. Airport transportation. Ask us for travel and visitor information. Open year-round. Phone (907) 822-3302. Toll-free in Alaska (800) 478-3302, fax (907) 822-3711. [ADVERTISEMENT] ♿

There are private campgrounds west of town on the Glenn Highway (see **Milepost A 173** and **A 170.5**) and east of town at **Milepost A 188.7**. There are 2 private RV parks in Glennallen and at **Milepost V 110.5** Richardson Highway (4.5 m/7.2 km south of the junction). Northeast of Glennallen 5 miles/8 km is Dry Creek state campground (see **Milepost A 192**). ▲

TRANSPORTATION

Bus: Scheduled service between Anchorage and Whitehorse via Glennallen. Bus service between Glennallen and McCarthy via Copper Center and Chitina in summer.

ATTRACTIONS

Fourth of July weekend is a major event in Glennallen. Activities include the Ahtna Arts and Crafts Fair, a music festival, raft race, parade and salmon bake.

Recreational opportunities in the Glennallen area include hunting, river running, bird watching and fishing. According to the ADF&G, approximately 50 lakes in the Glennallen area are stocked with grayling, rainbow trout and coho salmon. A complete list of lakes, locations and species is available at the Copper River Valley Visitor Center at **Milepost A 189**, or from the ADF&G office at **Milepost A 186.2.** Locally, there's good grayling fishing in **Moose Creek; Tulsona Creek** to the east at **Milepost GJ 17.5**; west on the Glenn Highway at **Tolsona Creek, Milepost A 173**; and **Mendeltna Creek,**

Milepost A 152.8. Lake Louise, approximately 27 miles/43 km west and 19 miles/30.5 km north from Glennallen, offers excellent grayling and lake trout fishing.

Many fly-in lakes are located in the Copper River basin and Chugach Mountains near Glennallen. **Crosswind Lake,** large lake trout, whitefish and grayling, early June to early July. **Deep Lake,** all summer for lake trout to 30 inches. **High Lake,** lake trout to 22 inches, June and early July with small spoons; some rainbow, fly-fishing; cabin, boats and motors rental. **Tebay Lakes,** excellent rainbow fishing, 12 to 15 inches, all summer, small spinners; cabin, boats and motors rental. **Jans Lake,** 12- to 14-inch silver salmon, June, spinners; also rainbow. **Hanagita Lake,** excellent grayling fishing all summer; also lake trout and steelhead in September. **Minnesota Lake,** lake trout to 30 inches, all summer; boat only, no cabins.

Glenn Highway Log

(continued)

A 186.6 (300.3 km) **T 141.4** (227.6 km) Cross Road Medical Center clinic. Alaska Bible College, the state's only accredited resident 4-year bible college, is located behind the clinic.

A 186.4 (300 km) **T 141.6** (227.9 km) Bureau of Land Management district office; phone (907) 822-3217.

A 186.2 (299.7 km) **T 141.8** (228.2 km) Alaska State Dept. of Fish and Game; phone (907) 822-3309.

A 186.1 (299.5 km) **T 141.9** (228.4 km) Copper Valley library.

A 186 (299.3 km) **T 142** (228.5 km) **Moose Creek** culvert; good grayling fishing in spring.

A 183.6 (295.5 km) **T 144.4** (232.4 km) **Brown Bear Rhodehouse.** Because of the excellent food, reasonable prices and Alaskan hospitality, this famous old lodge is a favorite eating and gathering place for local people and travelers alike. If eating in the Glennallen area, we recommend stopping here, and if coming from south it is well worth the extra few minutes wait. Superb steaks and seafood are the specialties, along with broasted chicken and the widest sandwich selection in the area. Your hosts, Doug and Cindy Rhodes, have managed to take one of the largest grizzly-brown bear photograph collections anywhere. So, if not dining, you will enjoy just stopping and looking at the many photographs that cover the walls or listening to a few bear tales in the lounge. This is the only place in the area that with one stop you have a campground, rustic cabins, modern rooms, restaurant and bar. This is also the only place on the highway to get a bucket of golden brown broasted chicken to go. Phone (907) 822-3663. [ADVERTISEMENT] ▲

A 183 (294.5 km) **T 145** (233.3 km) Watch for frost heaves.

A 182.2 (293.2 km) **T 145.8** (234.6 km) **Basin Liquors, Paper Shack Office Supply.** Liquor store opens 8 A.M., 7 days a week, 365 days a year. Liquor, snacks, ice, cigarettes. We

invite you to take a break; walk around in one of the most beautiful yards on the Glenn Highway, longtime home of pioneer resident "Gramma Ole" Hanson. [ADVERTISEMENT]

A 176.6 (284.2 km) **T 151.4** (243.6 km) Paved turnout to south with interpretive sign about the Wrangell Mountains and view east across the Copper River valley to Mount Drum. Northeast of Mount Drum is Mount Sanford and southeast is Mount Wrangell (elev. 14,163 feet/4,317m), a semi-active volcano. Mount Wrangell last erupted in 1912 when lava flowed to its base and ash fell as far west as this point.

Wildflowers growing along the roadside include lupine, cinquefoil, oxytrope, Jacob's ladder and sweet pea.

A 174.7 (281.1 km) **T 153.3** (246.7 km) Double-ended paved turnout to south.

A 173 (278.4 km) **T 155** (249.4 km) **Tolsona Wilderness Campground & RV Park.** AAA approved, Good Sam Park. This

beautiful campground, located three-quarter mile north of the highway, is surrounded on 3 sides by untouched wilderness. Each shady campsite is situated beside sparkling Tolsona Creek and is complete with table, litter barrel and fireplace. It is a full-service campground with tent sites, restrooms, dump station, coin-op showers, laundromat, water and electric hookups for RVs. While there, browse through their collection of neat old stuff from the turn of the century. These relics from Grandma's kitchen and Grandpa's workshop in a logging or sawmill camp will bring back memories of a simpler time. See how many items you can identify. Public phone. Open from May 20 through Sept. 10. $10 to $15 per night. Phone (907) 822-3865. [ADVERTISEMENT] ♿▲

Tolsona Creek, grayling to 16 inches, use mosquito flies in still, clear pools behind obstructions, June, July and Aug. Best fishing 1.5 miles/2.4 km upstream from highway. **Tolsona** and **Moose lakes,** rainbow trout, burbot, grayling to 16 inches, all summer; good ice fishing for burbot in winter; boats, food and lodging.

A 173 (278.4 km) **T 155** (249.4 km) **Ranch House Lodge,** established 1958. Enjoy friendly hospitality in an authentic rustic atmosphere in Alaska's most beautiful

log lodge. Superb steaks and seafood. Our

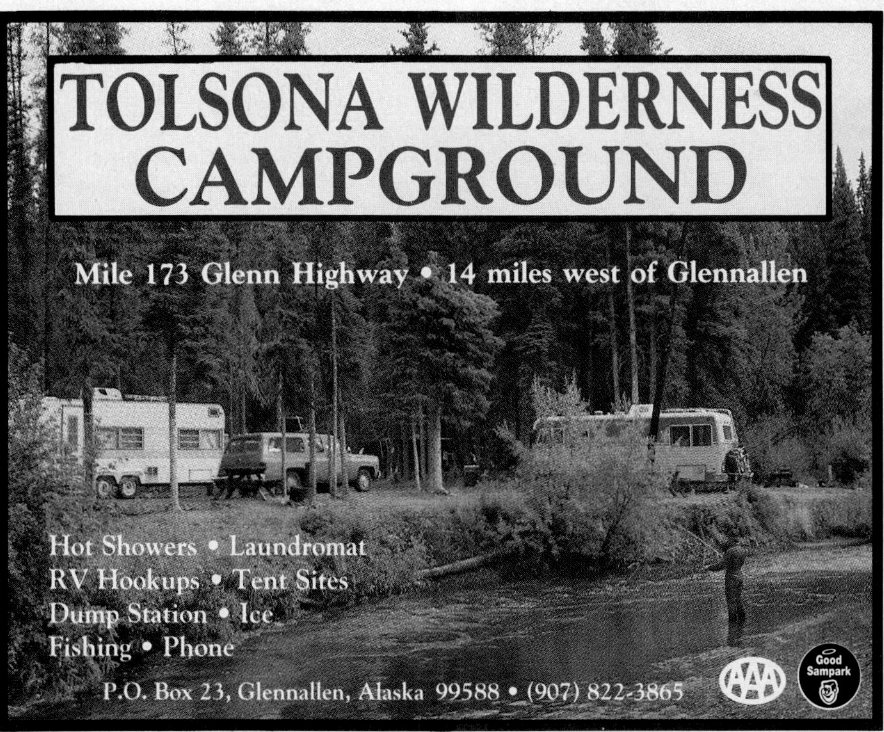

TOLSONA WILDERNESS CAMPGROUND
Mile 173 Glenn Highway • 14 miles west of Glennallen
Hot Showers • Laundromat
RV Hookups • Tent Sites
Dump Station • Ice
Fishing • Phone
AAA
Good Sampark
P.O. Box 23, Glennallen, Alaska 99588 • (907) 822-3865

Lake Louise Road Log

This 19.3-mile-/31-km-long scenic gravel road from the Glenn Highway north to Lake Louise Recreation Area is open year-round. Lake Louise is known for its good lake trout fishing; ice fishing in winter. Excellent cross-country skiing. Many turnouts and parking areas along the road; views of Tazlina Glacier and Lake; berry picking for wild strawberries and blueberries (July and Aug.), and cranberries (Sept.).

Distance is measured from the junction with the Glenn Highway (J).

J 0.2 (0.3 km) **Junction Lake** to east; grayling fishing.

J 1.1 (1.8 km) Turnout with view of Tazlina Glacier and Crater Lake.

J 1.2 (1.9 km) Double-ended turnout to west. Just north is the road west to **Crater Lake.** There are a number of small lakes along the road with good fishing for grayling and rainbow.

J 5.2 (8.4 km) **Old Road Lake and Round Lake** trails to east; rainbow fishing.

J 6 (9.7 km) **Mendeltna Creek** trail to west (0.5 mile/0.8 km); grayling fishing.

J 7 (11.2 km) **Forgotten Lake** trail to east (0.1 mile/0.2 km); grayling fishing.

J 9.4 (15.1 km) Beautiful pothole lakes. First view of Lake Louise northbound.

J 11 (17.7 km) Good view on clear days of the Alaska Range and Susitna River valley.

J 11.5 (18.5 km) Road west to **Caribou Lake;** grayling fishing. Turnout to east by Elbow Lake.

J 14 (22.5 km) Boundary of Matanuska–Susitna Borough.

J 15.5 (24.9 km) Gas station, public dumpster.

J 16 (25.7 km) **North and South Jan's Lakes** trails to north (0.4 mile/0.6 km); fishing.

J 16.5 (26.6 km) **Evergreen Lodge Bed & Breakfast.** See display ad this section.

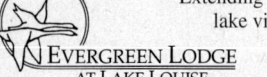

Blueberry and bearberry in fall.
(© Michael DeYoung)

J 16.8 (27 km) **Conner Lake**, rainbow and grayling fishing.

J 17.2 (27.7 km) Side road to lodge and Lake Louise State Recreation Area's Army Point and Lake Louise campgrounds; 52 campsites on 2 loop roads, firepits, toilets (handicap accessible), covered picnic tables at lakeshore and a boat launch. Well water. Camping fee $6/night or annual pass. Swimming in Lake Louise. Winter ski trail access.

J 17.2 (27.7 km) **The Point at Lake Louise.** See display ad this section.

J 17.6 (28.3 km) Turnout to west. Winter ski trail access.

J 18.8 (30.3 km) Airport road to west. **Private Aircraft:** Lake Louise airstrip; elev. 2,450 feet/747m; length 2,000 feet/610m; gravel. Seaplane base adjacent.

J 19.3 (31 km) Road ends at Lake Louise rest area; picnic tables, fireplaces, toilets, parking, boat launch.

Lake Louise, excellent grayling and lake trout fishing; lake trout 20 to 30 lbs., average 10 lbs., good year-round, best spring through July, then again in late Sept.; early season use herring or whitefish bait, cast from boat; later (warmer water) troll with #16 red-and-white spoon, silver Alaskan plug or large silver flatfish; grayling 10 to 12 inches, casting flies or small spinners, June, July and August; in winter jig for lake trout.

Susitna Lake can be reached by boat across Lake Louise; burbot, excellent lake trout and grayling fishing. Both lakes can be rough; underpowered boats not recommended. **Dinty Lake**, access by boat across Lake Louise; grayling and lake trout fishing.

Return to Milepost A 159.8 Glenn Highway

Ranchburgers are built on custom-made buns and are famous statewide. Cocktails over solid log bar. Rustic log cabins. Liquor store. Ice. Camping on beautiful Tolsona Creek. Your host: Burt Ward. Phone (907) 822-3882 or write HC-01 Box 1980, Glennallen, AK 99588. [ADVERTISEMENT] ▲

A 170.5 (274.4 km) **T 157.5** (253.5 km) **Tolsona Lake**, grayling to 16 inches, burbot, rainbow. **Crosswind Lake**, 18 miles/ 29 km north by floatplane, excellent fishing for lake trout, grayling and whitefish.

Tolsona Lake Resort. See display ad this section. ▲

A 169.3 (272.3 km) **T 158.7** (255.4 km) **Mae West Lake** trail. Paved double-ended turnout to south. The long narrow lake, fed by Little Woods Creek, is a little less than 1 mile/1.6 km away. Grayling fishing.

CAUTION: Watch for frost heaves next several miles westbound.

A 168 (270.4 km) **T 160** (257.5 km) Rough road, patched pavement and frost heaves westbound. Soup Lake to north. Trumpeter swans can sometimes be seen in lakes and ponds along this section of highway. In June and July look for wildflowers such as sweet pea, fireweed, lupine, cinquefoil, oxytrope, Jacob's ladder and milk-vetch.

A 166.1 (267.3 km) **T 161.9** (260.5 km) Atlasta House, a local landmark, was named by the homesteader who was happy to have a real house at last.

A 166 (267.2 km) **T 162** (260.7 km) Tolsona Mountain (elev. 2,974 feet/906m), a prominent ridge just north of highway, is a landmark for miles in both directions. This area is popular with berry-pickers in late summer and early fall. Varieties of wild berries include blueberries, lowbush cranberries and raspberries.

A 165.9 (267 km) **T 162.1** (260.9 km) Paved double-ended turnout to south and 2-mile/3.2-km trail to **Lost Cabin Lake**; grayling fishing.

Watch for frost heaves.

A 162.3 (261.2 km) **T 165.7** (266.7 km) Paved turnout to south.

A 162 (260.7 km) **T 166** (267.1 km) **Tex Smith Lake** to north; stocked with rainbow.

A 161 (259 km) **T 167** (268.7 km) Bad frost heaves next 0.4 mile/0.6 km eastbound.

A 159.8 (257.2 km) **T 168.2** (270.7 km) **Junction** with Lake Louise Road to Lake Louise Recreation Area. See LAKE LOUISE ROAD log on page opposite.

A 159.6 (256.8 km) **T 168.4** (271 km) **Little Junction Lake** trailhead, 0.3-mile/0.4-km hike south; grayling.

A 159 (255.8 km) **T 169** (272 km) Watch for bumps in pavement and frost heaves westbound to **Milepost A 133.**

A 157.2 (253 km) **T 170.8** (274.9 km) Trails to south to **DJ Lake** (rainbow fishing) and **Sucker Lake** (grayling and burbot).

A 156 (251.1 km) **T 172** (276.8 km) Tazlina Glacier, seen to the east, feeds into 20-mile-/32-km-long Tazlina Lake at its foot. **Buffalo Lake**; stocked with rainbow.

A 156.2 (251.4 km) **T 171.8** (276.5 km) Tazlina Glacier Lodge.

A 156 (251 km) **T 172** (276.8 km) **Private Aircraft:** Tazlina airstrip; elev. 2,450 feet/747m; length 1,200 feet/366m; gravel; unattended.

A 155.8 (250.7 km) **T 172.2** (277.2 km) **Arizona Lake** to south; fishing for grayling.

A 155.6 (250.4 km) **T 172.4** (277.4 km) Paved turnout to south.

Little Nelchina River recreation site at Milepost A 137.6. (© Rick Ebrecht)

A 155.2 (249.8 km) **T 172.8** (278.1 km) **Gergie Lake** to south; fishing for grayling and rainbow.

A 153 (246.2 km) **T 175** (281.6 km) **K.R.O.A. Kamping Resorts of Alaska** on the Little Mendeltna, a natural spring-fed stream. Excellent fishing for grayling, whitefish and others. Many lakes nearby. Fishing, hunting guides available. Gateway to Tazlina Lake and Glacier. Ski, hiking, snow machine trails. Modern hookups. Pull-throughs. Laundromat. Hot showers. Can handle any size caravan. Rustic cabins. Brick-oven fresh dough pizza. Homemade cinnamon rolls. Museum of Alaska's Drunken Forest, a large collection of unusual and artistic natural designs of trees. Minerals. Artifacts of Alaska's drunken forest. Free. [ADVERTISEMENT] ▲

A 152.8 (245.9 km) **T 175.2** (282 km) Mendeltna Creek bridge.

AREA FISHING: Mendeltna Creek, good fishing north to Old Man Lake; watch for bears. (The Mendeltna Creek drainage is closed to the taking of salmon.) Excellent fishing for grayling to 17½ inches, May to Nov., use spinners and flies; whitefish to 16 inches; burbot to 30 inches, May to Nov., use spinners or flies; rainbow, from May to Nov., use spinners or flies. Walk or boat away from the bridge.

A 152.7 (245.7 km) **T 175.3** (282.1 km) Paved double-ended rest area to north with picnic tables, dumpster and toilets. Rough road.

A 150 (241.4 km) **T 178** (286.4 km) Eastbound view of Mount Sanford and Mount Drum straight ahead.

A 149 (239.8 km) **T 179** (288.1 km) **Mirror Lake**; fishing for grayling, whitefish and rainbow.

A 147.3 (237.1 km) **T 180.7** (290.8 km) **Alaskan Airventures.** See display ad this section.

A 147.3 (237.1 km) **T 180.7** (290.8 km) **Cache Creek** culvert. Grayling in late May and June. Trail leading from parking area to lake, approximately 0.5 mile/0.8 km. Small picnic area on east side of highway. Steep approach.

A 147 (236.6 km) **T 181** (291.3 km) Very bad frost heaves next 0.7 mile/1.1 km westbound.

A 144.9 (233.2 km) **T 183.1** (294.7 km) Lottie Sparks (Nelchina) Elementary School.

A 141.2 (227.2 km) **T 186.8** (300.6 km) Nelchina state highway maintenance station. Slide Mountain trailhead located behind station.

A 137.6 (221.4 km) **T 190.4** (306.4 km) Little Nelchina State Recreation Site 0.3 mile/0.5 km from highway; 11 campsites, 15-day limit, no camping fee, no drinking water, tables, firepits, toilet, boat launch. Watch for moose and bear. ▲

A 137.5 (221.3 km) **T 190.5** (306.6 km) Little Nelchina River bridge.

A 137 (220.5 km) **T 191** (307.4 km) Boundary of Matanuska–Susitna Borough.

A 135.7 (218.4 km) **T 192.3** (309.5 km) Small paved turnout. Highway widens eastbound.

*NOTE: Watch for major road construction to **Milepost A 127** in 1996.*

A 134.8 (216.9 km) **T 193.2** (310.9 km) Watch for livestock on highway.

A 132.1 (212.6 km) **T 195.9** (315.2 km) Caribou crossing. Gravel turnout to north. View of Mount Sanford eastbound. Caribou and moose seen in this area in winter. The Nelchina caribou herd passes through here in Oct.–Nov. Watch for caribou westbound.

A 131 (210.8 km) **T 197** (317 km) View west to the notch of Gunsight Mountain. From here to Eureka Summit there are views of the Wrangell and Chugach mountains.

A 130.3 (209.7 km) **T 197.7** (318.2 km) Old Man Creek trailhead parking to north. Old Man Creek 2 miles/3 km; Crooked Creek 9 miles/14.5 km; Nelchina Town 14.5 miles/23 km. Established trails west from here to Palmer are part of the Chickaloon–Knik–Nelchina trail system.

A 129.3 (208.1 km) **T 198.7** (319.8 km) Eureka Summit (elev. 3,322 feet/1,013m). Highest point on the Glenn Highway, near timberline, with unobstructed views south toward the Chugach Mountains. The Nelchina Glacier winds downward through a cleft in the mountains. To the northwest are the peaks of the Talkeetnas, and to the west the highway descends through river valleys which separate these 2 mountain ranges. This is the divide of 3 big river systems: Susitna, Matanuska and Copper.

A 128 (206 km) **T 200** (321.9 km) Site of the first lodge on the Glenn Highway, the Eureka Roadhouse, which was opened in 1937 by Paul Waverly and has operated continuously ever since. The original log building is next to Eureka Lodge.

Eureka Lodge. See display ad this section.

Private Aircraft: Skelton airstrip; elev. 3,289 feet/1,002m; length 2,400 feet/732m; gravel; fuel mogas; unattended.

*NOTE: Watch for road construction eastbound to **Milepost A 135.7** in 1996.*

A 127 (204.4 km) **T 201** (323.4 km) Gravel turnout to south.

A 126.4 (203.4 km) **T 201.6** (324.4 km) Watch closely for turnout to Belanger Creek–Nelchina River trailhead parking to south. Eureka Creek 1.5 miles/2.4 km; Goober Lake 8 miles/13 km; Nelchina River 9 miles/14.5 km.

A 125 (201.2 km) **T 203** (326.7 km) Gunsight Mountain (elev. 6,441 feet/1,963m) is visible to the west for the next few miles to those approaching from Glennallen. The notch or "gunsight" is plain if one looks closely. Eastbound views of snow-covered Mount Sanford (weather permitting), Mount Drum, Mount Wrangell and Mount Blackburn.

A 123.3 (198.4 km) **T 204.7** (329.4 km) Belanger Pass trailhead: Belanger Pass 3 miles/5 km; Alfred Creek 6.5 miles/10.5 km; Albert Creek 8 miles/13 km.

A 123.1 (198.1 km) **T 204.9** (329.8 km) Old Tahneta Inn (closed).

Private Aircraft: Tahneta Pass airstrip; elev. 2,960 feet/902m; length 1,100 feet/335m; gravel/dirt. Floatplanes land on Tahneta Lake.

A 122.9 (197.8 km) **T 205.1** (330 km) Gunsight Mountain Lodge (current status unknown).

A 122 (196.3 km) **T 206** (333.5 km) Tahneta Pass (elev. 3,000 feet/914m). Double-ended paved turnout to north. **Leila Lake** trailhead (unsigned) on old alignment to north; grayling 8 to 14 inches abundant through summer, best fishing June and July. Burbot, success spotty for 12 to 18 inches in fall and winter.

A 120.8 (194.4 km) **T 207.2** (333.4 km) Boundary of Sportfish Management Area 2 and Sheep Mountain Closed Area.

A 120.3 (193.6 km) **T 207.7** (334.3 km) View eastbound overlooks Tahneta Pass. The largest lake is Leila Lake; in the distance is Tahneta Lake. Drive carefully along the southern part of Tahneta Pass.

*NOTE: Watch for road construction westbound to **Milepost A 109** in 1996.*

A 118.6 (190.9 km) **T 209.4** (337 km) Double-ended gravel turnout to south.

A 118.5 (190.7 km) **T 209.5** (337.1 km) FAA road south to communication towers.

A 118.3 (190.4 km) **T 209.7** (337.5 km) Large gravel turnout to south.

A 117.8 (189.5 km) **T 210.2** (338.2 km) Turnout with viewpoint. Looking southeast of the highway, a tip of a glacier can be seen coming down South Fork Canyon. Knob Lake and the "knob" (elev. 3,000 feet/914m) can be seen to the northeast.

A 117.6 (189.3 km) **T 210.4** (338.6 km) Squaw Creek trailhead: Squaw Creek 3.5 miles/5.6 km; Caribou Creek 9.5 miles/15 km; Alfred Creek 13 miles/21 km; Sheep Creek 15 miles/24 km.

A 115 (185 km) **T 213** (342.8 km) Between **Mileposts A 115** and **116** there are three turnouts with views of mineralized Sheep Mountain and Matanuska Glacier area.

A 114.5 (184.3 km) **T 213.5** (343.6 km) In season, on slopes adjacent the highway and along old creek beds back from the road, are many kinds of flowers, including lupine, Labrador tea, bluebells, fireweed, chiming bells and large patches of forget-me-nots, Alaska's state flower.

A 114.3 (183.9 km) **T 213.7** (343.9 km) For Anchorage-bound travelers a vista of incomparable beauty as the road descends in a long straightaway toward Glacier Point, also known as the Lion Head, an oddly formed rocky dome. No turnouts for 1 mile/1.6 km.

A 114 (183.5 km) **T 214** (344.4 km) Winding road, long stretches without shoulders, watch for rocks and frost heaves westbound between here and Palmer.

A 113.5 (182.7 km) **T 214.5** (345.2 km) **Sheep Mountain Lodge.** Our charming log lodge, established in 1946, has been serving travelers for half a century. We're famous for our wholesome homemade food, fresh baked breads, pastries and desserts. Our comfortable guest cabins, all with private bathrooms, boast spectacular mountain views. We also have RV hookups, full bar, liquor store and Alaskan gifts. You can watch Dall Sheep through our telescope and relax in the hot tub or sauna after a day of traveling or hiking. HC03 Box 8490, Palmer, AK 99645. Phone (907) 745-5121; fax (907) 745-5120. See display ad this section. [ADVERTISEMENT] ▲

Private Aircraft: Sheep Mountain airstrip; elev. 2,750 feet/838m; length 2,300 feet/701m; gravel/dirt; unattended.

A 113.5 (182.7 km) **T 214.5** (345.2 km) As the highway descends westbound into the valley of the Matanuska River, there is a view of the great glacier which is the main headwater source and gives the water its milky color.

A 113 (181.9 km) **T 215** (346 km) Gravel turnout.

A 112.5 (181.1 km) **T 215.5** (346.8 km) View to north of Sheep Mountain (elev. 6,300 feet/1,920m) for 11 miles/17.7 km between Tahneta Pass and Caribou Creek. Sheep are often seen high up these slopes. The area surrounding Sheep Mountain is closed to the taking of mountain sheep.

A 112 (180.2 km) **T 216** (347.6 km) Gravel turnout by creek. View westbound of Lion Head and first view of Matanuska Glacier.

A 111.5 (179.4 km) **T 216.5** (348.4 km) **Bunk 'N' Breakfast.** Rustic homestead accommodations below Sheep Mountain Preserve. Bring sleeping bag. Sleeps 6. $15/person, group rates. Complimentary morning beverage. Within 10 miles of Matanuska Glacier, hiking, fishing, horseback tours, rafting, flightseeing, cross-country skiing and snowmobiling. Dee Larson, HC03, Box 8488A, Palmer, AK 99645. (907) 745-5143. [ADVERTISEMENT]

A 111 (178.6 km) **T 217** (349.2 km) Sharp curves and falling rocks for the next mile westbound.

A 110.3 (177.5 km) **T 217.7** (350.3 km) Watch for mountain sheep.

A 109.7 (176.5 km) **T 218.3** (351.3 km) Paved turnout to south.

A 109.5 (176.2 km) **T 218.5** (351.6 km) Paved turnout to south.

A 109 ((175.4 km) **T 219** (352.4 km) *NOTE: Watch for road construction eastbound to* ***Milepost A 118*** *in 1996.*

A 108.4 (174.4 km) **T 219.6** (353.4 km) Large gravel turnout to south.

A 107.8 (173.5 km) **T 220.2** (354.4 km) Turnout with view of Glacier Point (Lion Head) and Matanuska Glacier. Exceptional picture stop.

A 107.1 (172.4 km) **T 220.9** (355.5 km) Large gravel turnouts to south, viewpoint.

A 106.8 (171.9 km) **T 221.2** (356 km) Caribou Creek Bridge and Caribou Creek trailhead. Hiking distances: Squaw Creek 9 miles/14.5 km; Alfred Creek 13 miles/21 km; Sheep Creek 15 miles/24 km; and Squaw Creek trailhead 18.5 miles/30 km. Caribou Creek trail zigzags up the mountainside between the highway and the creek and leads back behind Sheep Mountain. A pleasant hike for good walkers.

Highway makes a steep descent (from both directions) down to Caribou Creek. The banks of this stream provide good rockhounding, particularly after mountain storms. There are turnouts on both sides of the highway here. Fortress Ridge (elev. 5,000 feet/1,524m) above the highway to the north. Sheep Mountain reserve boundary.

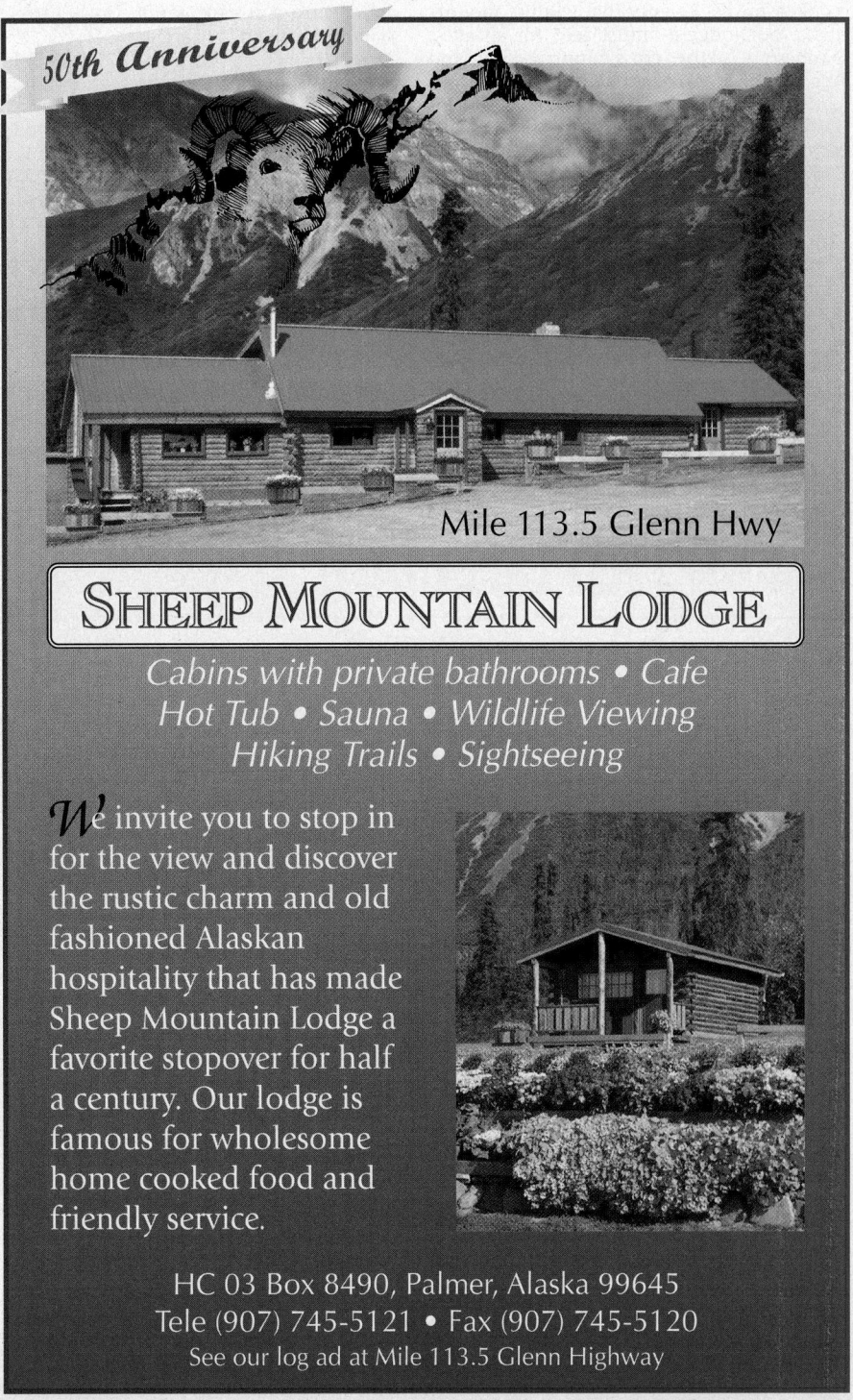

A 106 (170.6 km) **T 222** (357.3 km) Large gravel turnout overlooking Caribou Creek canyon. Steep descent eastbound.

A 105.8 (170.3 km) **T 222.2** (357.6 km) Road (closed to public) to FAA station on flank of Glacier Point. Mountain sheep occasionally are seen on the upper slopes.

A 105.5 (169.8 km) **T 222.5** (358.1 km) Gravel turnout to south.

A 105.3 (169.4 km) **T 222.7** (358.4 km) Turnout with views of Matanuska Glacier and the FAA station on Glacier Point.

A 104.1 (167.5 km) **T 223.9** (360.3 km) Access to Glacier View School, which overlooks Matanuska Glacier.

A 104 (167.4 km) **T 224** (360.5 km) From here to **Milepost A 98** several kinds of wild orchids and other wildflowers may be found along the trails into the roadside brush.

A 102.8 (165.4 km) **T 225.2** (362.4 km) Gravel turnout to south with view of Matanuska Glacier.

A 102.3 (164.6 km) **T 225.7** (363.2 km) **NOVA the Adventure Co.**. Since 1975. Join us on the most popular whitewater trip in Alaska. Lion Head, a rock wall wrestling with the converging Matanuska Glacier, produces several miles of non-stop class IV whitewater. Includes a refreshment stop and hike on the moraine for a fantastic overview of the glacier. Suitable for first-timers. Minimum age 12. Call 1-800-746-5753 for information and reservations. Main office: Mile 76 Glenn Highway. [ADVERTISEMENT]

A 102.2 (164.5 km) **T 225.8** (363.4 km) **Long Rifle Lodge**. Welcome to Alaska's most fabulous dining view of the Matanuska Glacier. We offer a complete breakfast, lunch and dinner menu, specializing in home-cooked meals. Twenty-five wildlife mounts make our lodge a "must see" for all ages. Numerous hiking, cross-country skiing and snowmobile trails surround the area. In addition, we have motel rooms, gasoline, 24-hour wrecker service, laundry, showers, gift shop and a full-service lounge. Phone 1-800-770-5151. See display ad this section. [ADVERTISEMENT]

A 102 (164.2 km) **T 226** (363.7 km) Access to foot of Matanuska Glacier via Glacier Park Resort. Admission fee charged.

Glacier Air. See display ad this section.

Glacier Park Resort. We would like to invite you to experience the Matanuska Glacier, at Glacier Park of Alaska. A 540-acre private resort located at the terminus of the Matanuska Glacier, in the heart of the Chugach Mountains. This is a great addition to your vacation. We offer glacier tours, hiking, flightseeing, backcountry adventures, recreation camping, tent camping, gift shop, rooms, laundry, showers, liquor store, film, snack foods, picnic area, snow machining, cross-country skiing. Motorcoaches and tours welcome. Open all year. Access at Milepost 102 Glenn Highway. HC03 Box 8449, Palmer, AK 99645. Phone (907) 745-2534. [ADVERTISEMENT] ▲

A 101.7 (163.7 km) **T 226.3** (364.2 km) Paved turnout with good view of Matanuska Glacier, which heads in the Chugach Mountains and trends northwest 27 miles/43.5 km. Some 18,000 years ago the glacier reached all the way to the Palmer area. The glacier's average width is 2 miles/3.2 km; at its terminus it is 4 miles/6.4 km wide. The glacier has remained fairly stable the past 400 years. At the glacier terminus meltwater drains into a stream which flows into the Matanuska River.

A 101 (162.5 km) **T 227** (365.3 km) Matanuska Glacier State Recreation Site; 12 campsites on loop drive, 3-day limit, $10 nightly fee or annual pass, water and toilets. Excellent views of the glacier from hiking trails along the bluff. (Use caution when walking near edge of bluff.) Wildflowers here in late July include fireweed, yarrow and sweet peas. ▲

A 100.8 (162.2 km) **T 227.2** (365.6 km) Large gravel turnout to south.

A 99.2 (159.6 km) **T 228.8** (368.2 km) Gravel turnout to south, viewpoint. Pinochle–Hicks Creek trail.

Winding road with steep grades westbound.

A 97 (156 km) **T 231** (371.7 km) Gravel turnout to north.

A 96.6 (155.5 km) **T 231.4** (372.4 km) Private campground, lodge and store. Hicks Creek was named by Captain Glenn in 1898 for H.H. Hicks, the guide of his expedition. Ridges back from here, right side Anchorage-bound, are good rockhound areas. Anthracite Ridge has jasper, rosy-banded agate, petrified wood and rock crystal. Difficult to reach on foot.

Historical Hicks Creek. See display ad this section. ▲

A 96.4 (155.1 km) **T 231.6** (372.7 km) Small gravel turnout to south.

A 94.9 (152.7 km) **T 233.1** (375.1 km) Victory Road. Slide area. Look for lupine and wild sweet pea.

A 93.4 (150.3 km) **T 234.6** (377.5 km) Cascade state highway maintenance camp.

A 93 (149.7 km) **T 235** (378.2 km) Gravel turnouts both sides of highway. Views of Amulet Peak and Monument Glacier and Valley.

A 91.3 (146.9 km) **T 236.7** (380.9 km) Cascade Creek culvert.

A 91 (146.4 km) **T 237** (381.4 km) First view eastbound of Matanuska Glacier.

A 90.6 (145.8 km) **T 237.4** (382 km) Paved turnout to south.

A 90.1 (145 km) **T 237.9** (382.9 km) Turnout to south.

A 89 (143.2 km) **T 239** (384.6 km) Purinton Creek trailhead. Bridge over Purinton Creek. Good blueberry patches in season if you can beat the bears to them. The stream heads on Anthracite Ridge and flows into the Matanuska River. Westbound, watch for coal seams along the highway.

A 87.8 (141.3 km) **T 240.2** (386.5 km) Two small gravel turnouts to south.

A 87.6 (141 km) **T 240.4** (386.9 km) Large gravel turnout above Weiner Lake.

A 87.4 (140.6 km) **T 240.6** (387.2 km) **Weiner Lake** access; fishing for rainbow and grayling.

A 87.3 (140.5 km) **T 240.7** (387.4 km) Turnout. Highway descends eastbound.

A 86.8 (139.7 km) **T 241.2** (388.2 km) Slide area: Watch for falling rock.

A 86.5 (139.2 km) **T 241.5** (388.6 km) Good gravel turnout overlooking Long Lake to south.

A 85.3 (137.3 km) **T 242.7** (390.6 km) **Long Lake,** in a narrow canyon below the highway, is a favorite fishing spot for Anchorage residents. Fair for grayling to 18 inches, spring through fall; fish deeper as the water warms in summer. Good ice fishing in winter for burbot, average 12 inches. Long Lake State Recreation Site has 9 campsites, 15-day limit, no camping fee, no water, tables, firepits and toilets. Wildflowers include roses, sweet pea, paintbrush and lupine. Long upgrade begins eastbound. ▲

A 84.6 (136.1 km) **T 243.4** (391.7 km) There are several gravel turnouts westbound.

A 84.3 (135.7 km) **T 243.7** (392.2 km) Large double-ended turnout. View of Matanuska River and unnamed mountains.

A 84.1 (135.3 km) **T 243.9** (392.5 km) Large double-ended gravel turnout.

CAUTION: Watch for road equipment in slide areas next 4 miles/6.4 km eastbound.

A 83.2 (133.9 km) **T 244.8** (394 km) Narrow gravel road to Ravine and Lower Bonnie lakes. (Side road not signed.) Drive in 0.8 mile/1.3 km on side road to reach **Ravine Lake**; fishing from shore for rainbow. **Lower Bonnie Lake** is a 2-mile/3.2-km drive from the highway; Bonnie

Lake State Recreation Site has 8 campsites, 15-day limit, no camping fee, no water, toilets and boat launch. Fishing for grayling and rainbow. Steep and winding road beyond Ravine Lake is not recommended for large vehicles or trailers; during rainy season this side road is not recommended for any vehicle. ▲

A **82** (132 km) T **246** (395.9 km) Pyramid-shaped King Mountain is to the right (westbound) of the milepost as you look across the canyon. Several small gravel turnouts westbound.

A **80.8** (130 km) T **247.2** (397.8 km) Entering Matanuska Valley Moose Range westbound. Large gravel turnout to south.

A **79.5** (127.9 km) T **248.5** (399.9 km) Views of King Mountain (elev. 5,809 feet/ 1,770m).

A **79.1** (127.3 km) T **248.9** (400.6 km) Gravel turnout to south.

A **78.2** (125.8 km) T **249.8** (402 km) Gravel turnout with view of King Mountain and Matanuska River.

A **77.7** (125 km) T **250.3** (402.8 km) Chickaloon River bridge. Gravel turnout. Boundary between Game Management Units 13 and 14. The old Chickaloon Road winds upstream. Travelers have reported seeing no trespassing and private property signs a short distance up this road, indicating Native land claims along the road and river. Inquire locally about public access to the Chickaloon River via this side road before driving in.

A **77.5** (124.7 km) T **250.5** (403.1 km) Gravel turnout to south. Steep ascent eastbound. Highway parallels Matanuska River.

A **76.5** (123.1 km) T **251.5** (404.7 km) Gravel turnout by river.

A **76.3** (122.8 km) T **251.7** (405.1 km) **CHICKALOON** (pop. 145); general store, gas station and river runner.

Chickaloon General Store and Service Station. See display ad this section.

A **76.2** (122.6 km) T **251.8** (405.2 km) **King Mountain Lodge.** See display ad this section.

A **76.1** (122.5 km) T **251.9** (405.4 km) King Mountain State Recreation Site. Pleasant campground on the banks of the Matanuska River with 22 campsites, 2 picnic sites, fireplaces, picnic tables, water, toilets. Camping fee $10/night or annual pass; 15-day limit. King Mountain to the southeast. ▲

CAUTION: Watch for road equipment in slide areas westbound to ***Milepost A 60.***

A **73** (117.5 km) T **255** (410.4 km) Ida Lake/Fish Lake subdivision. Chickaloon River loop road.

A **72.3** (116.4 km) T **255.7** (411.5 km) Ida Lake is visible to the west.

A **71.2** (114.6 km) T **256.8** (413.3 km) End slide area. Beaver pond to north.

A **71** (114.3 km) T **257** (413.6 km) Turnouts to south by Matanuska River.

A **70.6** (113.6 km) T **257.4** (414.2 km) Access to Matanuska River to south.

A **69.7** (112.2 km) T **258.3** (415.7 km) Chickaloon post office (ZIP code 99674), private campground. ▲

A **68.6** (110.4 km) T **259.4** (417.5 km) Slide areas. Several gravel turnouts; watch for soft shoulders along highway.

A **68** (109.4 km) T **260** (418.4 km) Pinnacle Mountain (elev. 4,541 feet/1384m) rises directly southeast of the highway—easy to identify by its unusual top. Cottonwoods and aspen along the highway. Talkeetna Mountains to the north.

A **66.5** (107 km) T **261.5** (420.8 km) King River bridge. Turnouts both sides of road.

AREA FISHING: King River (Milepost A 66.5), trout, early summer best, use eggs. **Granite Creek (Milepost A 62.4)**, small Dolly Varden and trout, spring or early summer, use flies or single eggs. **Seventeenmile Lake (Milepost A 57.9 or 60.9)**, small grayling, early spring, use flies or spinners; trout, early spring, use eggs. **Eska Creek (Milepost A 60.8)**, small Dolly Varden, spring, use flies or single eggs; silver salmon, Aug. or Sept., use eggs. **Moose Creek (Milepost A 54.6)**, trout and Dolly Varden, summer, use eggs.

A **66.4** (106.8 km) T **261.6** (421 km) King River trailhead (unsigned in 1993); King River Crossing 5 miles/8 km.

A **62.7** (100.9 km) T **265.3** (426.9 km) Large gravel turnout to south along Matanuska River. Dwarf fireweed and sweet pea in June.

A **62.4** (100.4 km) T **265.6** (427.4 km) Granite Creek bridge and access to private campground. ▲

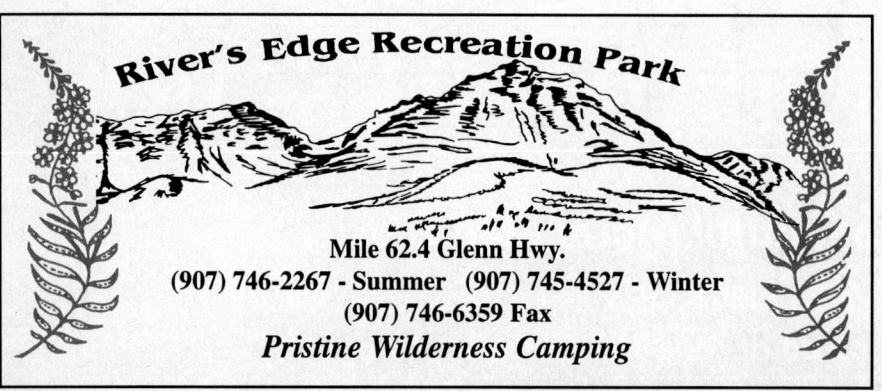

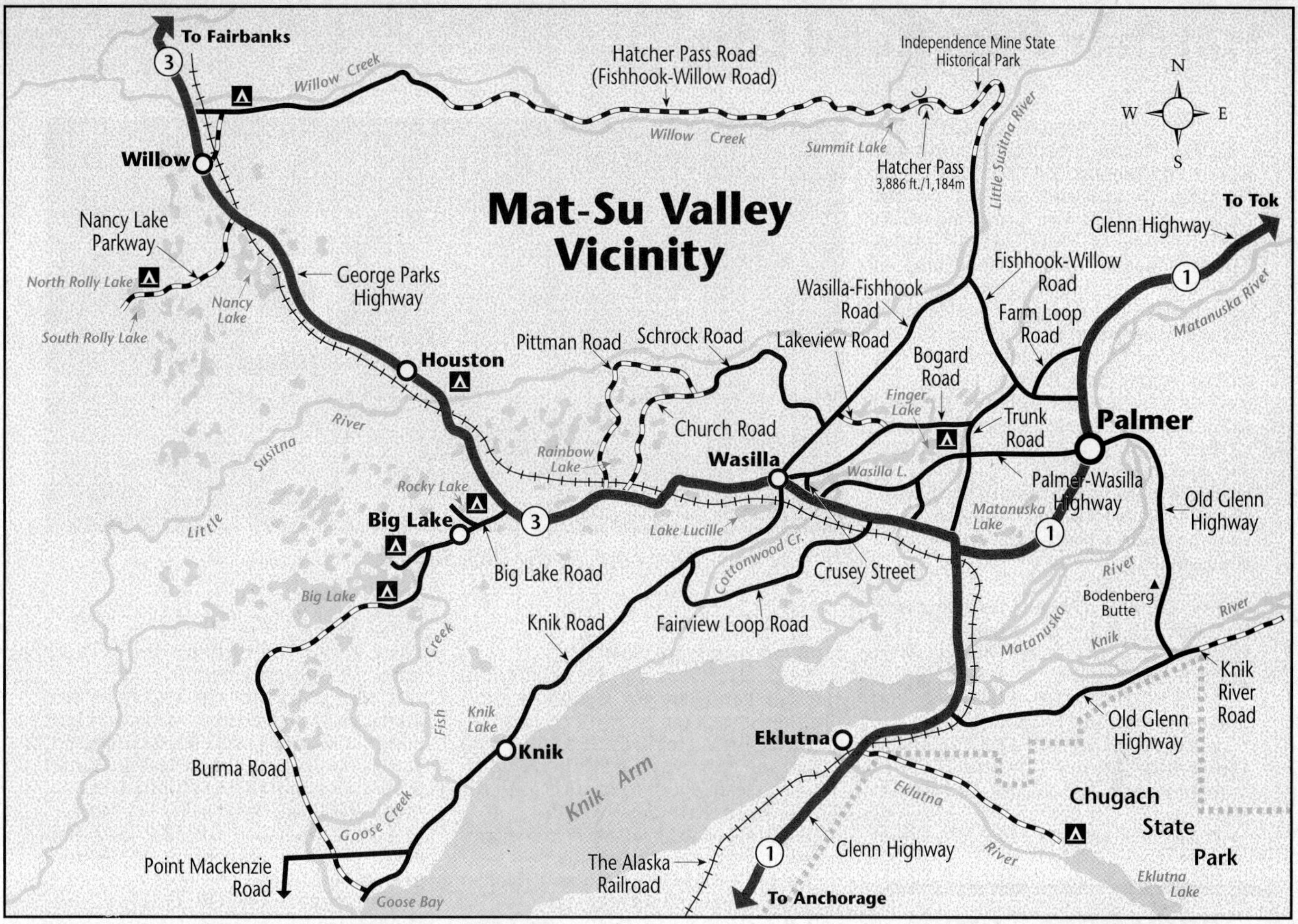

Mat-Su Valley Vicinity
To Fairbanks
Willow Creek
Hatcher Pass Road (Fishhook-Willow Road)
Independence Mine State Historical Park
N
W
E
S
Willow
Willow Creek
Summit Lake
Hatcher Pass 3,886 ft./1,184m
Little Susitna River
To Tok
Nancy Lake Parkway
Glenn Highway
North Rolly Lake
Nancy Lake
George Parks Highway
Fishhook-Willow Road
Wasilla-Fishhook Road
Farm Loop Road
Matanuska River
South Rolly Lake
Pittman Road
Schrock Road
Lakeview Road
Bogard Road
Houston
Finger Lake
River
Church Road
Trunk Road
Palmer
Susitna
Rainbow Lake
Wasilla
Wasilla L.
Rocky Lake
Palmer-Wasilla Highway
Old Glenn Highway
Big Lake
Matanuska Lake
Little
Lake Lucille
Cottonwood Cr.
Crusey Street
Big Lake Road
River
Bodenberg Butte
Big Lake
River
Knik Road
Fairview Loop Road
Matanuska
Knik
Creek
Knik River Road
Fish
Knik Lake
Old Glenn Highway
Eklutna
Knik
Burma Road
Knik Arm
Chugach State Park
Eklutna
Goose Creek
Point Mackenzie Road
The Alaska Railroad
Glenn Highway
River
Eklutna Lake
Goose Bay
To Anchorage

CAMP. [ADVERTISEMENT] ▲

A 62.2 (100.1 km) **T 265.8** (427.7 km) Sutton post office. Sign in at their guest book.

A 61.6 (99.1 km) **T 267.6** (430.6 km) Alpine Historical Park, an open-air museum. featuring the concrete ruins of the Sutton Coal Washery (1920–22). Access via Elementary School Road. The museum is still under development. Donations accepted.

A 61 (98.2 km) **T 267** (429.7 km) **SUTTON** (pop. 340) was established as a railroad siding about 1918 for the once-flourishing coal industry and is now a small highway community. Sutton has a fire department, general store, post office and gas station. Fossilized shells and leaves can be found in this area 1.7 miles/2.7 km up the Jonesville Road. Inquire locally for directions.

A 60.9 (98 km) **T 267.1** (429.8 km) Jonesville Road. Access to Coyote Lake Recreation Area (3 miles/4.8 km); day-use area with pavilion, covered picnic tables, toilets, fireplaces, trails and swimming. Also access to Seventeenmile Lake (for recommended access see **Milepost A 57.9**). Drive north 1.7 miles/2.7 km to end of pavement; continue straight ahead for residential area and old Jonesville and Eska coal mines; turn left where pavement ends for Seventeenmile Lake. From the turnoff on Jonesville Road it is 3.1 miles/5 km via a rough dirt road (may be muddy) to **Seventeenmile Lake;** undeveloped parking area on lakeshore, boat launch, good grayling fishing. Inquire at local businesses about road conditions.

A 60.8 (97.8 km) **T 267.2** (430 km) Eska Creek bridge.

A 60.7 (97.7 km) **T 267.3** (430.2 km) Paved double-ended turnout to south; pavement break.

A 60 (96.6 km) **T 268** (431.3 km) Long winding descent eastbound.

*CAUTION: Watch for road equipment in slide areas eastbound to **Milepost A 76.***

A 59.5 (95.7 km) **T 268.5** (430.5 km) **Fisher's Hilltop Tesoro**. See display ad this section.

A 59.3 (95.4 km) **T 268.7** (432.4 km) **Eska Farm.** Fresh, locally-grown vegetables and berries in season. We grow Alaska's best tomatoes. Locally made crafts and gifts. Visit our farm market gardens and greenhouses. Our picnic area makes a perfect lunch stop. Take a short nature walk to a scenic view point with a beautiful view of the Matanuska River and the Chugach Mountains. Owned and operated by long-time Alaskans. Easy access for RVs. See display ad this section. [ADVERTISEMENT]

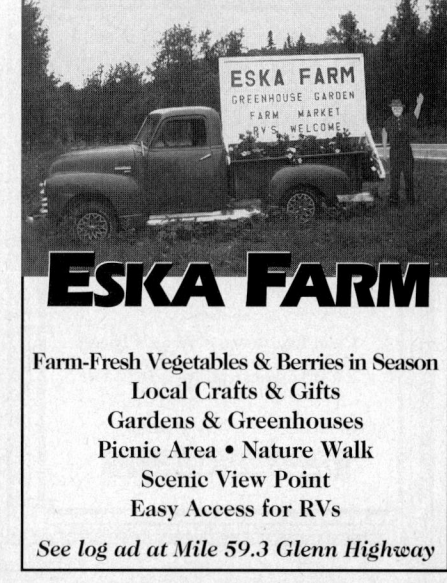

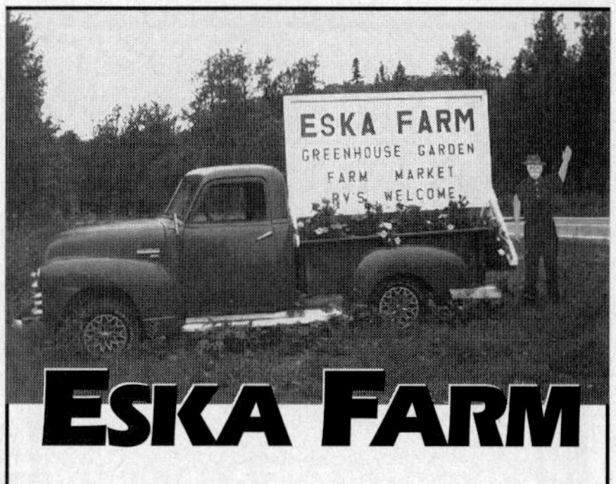

A 58.6 (94.3 km) **T 269.4** (433.5 km) Small gravel turnout to south. View of Matanuska River.

A 57.9 (93.2 km) **T 270.1** (434.7 km) 58 Mile Road. Access to Palmer Correctional

ESKA FARM
GREENHOUSE GARDEN
FARM MARKET
RVS WELCOME

Hatcher Pass Road Log

The 49-mile-/79-km-long Hatcher Pass (Fishhook–Willow) Road leads north and west from **Milepost A 49.5** on the Glenn Highway to **Milepost A 71.2** on the George Parks Highway, providing access to Independence Mine State Historical Park (see Mat-Su Valley Vicinity map on page 287). It is a mostly gravel road, not recommended for large RVs or trailers beyond **Milepost J 14**. The road usually does not open until late June or early July and snow may close the pass in Sept. The road stays open to the historical park and to Hatcher Pass Lodge in winter, a popular winter sports area for snowmobiling and cross-country skiing.

Distance from junction with the Glenn Highway (J) is followed by distance from junction with the George Parks Highway (GP).

Hatcher Pass Road parallels the Little Susitna River. (© Carmen Scott)

J 0 GP 49.1 (79 km) **Junction** with the Glenn Highway at **Milepost A 49.5.** Fishhook–Willow Road heads west through farm country.

J 1.4 (2.3 km) **GP 47.7** (76.8 km) **Junction** with Farm Loop Road.

J 1.6 (2.6 km) **GP 47.5** (76.4 km) **Teddy Bear Corner Country Inn Bed and Breakfast.** See display ad this section.

J 2.4 (3.9 km) **GP 46.7** (75.2 km) **Junction** with Trunk Road.

J 6.5 (10.5 km) **GP 42.5** (68.4 km) **Hatcher Pass Gateway Center**. See display ad this section.

J 6.8 (10.9 km) **GP 42.3** (68.1 km) **Junction** with Wasilla–Fishhook Road. This road leads south to connect with the George Parks Highway at Wasilla.

J 7.2 (11.6 km) **GP 41.9** (67.4 km) Edgerton Parks Road to Wasilla.

J 8.1 (13 km) **GP 41** (66 km) Hatcher Pass Management Area boundary.

J 8.5 (13.7 km) **GP 40.6** (65.3 km) Little Susitna River bridge. Pavement ends, gravel begins, northbound. *Watch for continued paving next 5.5 miles/8.8 km in 1996.* Road parallels river. Several turnouts westbound.

J 9 (14.5 km) **GP 40.1** (64.5 km) Entering Hatcher Pass public-use area westbound. No flower picking or plant removal without a permit in public-use area.

J 14 (22.5 km) **GP 35.1** (56.5 km) Side road to lodges and access to mine and trails. Trailhead parking for Gold Mint and Arkose Ridge trails.

Motherlode Lodge. See display ad this section.

Hatcher Pass Road begins climb to Hatcher Pass via a series of switchbacks. There are several turnouts the next 2.4 miles/3.9 km westbound.

J 14.6 (23.5 km) **GP 34.5** (55.5 km) Archangel Valley Road to Mabel and Fern mines and Reed Lakes. Road crosses private property (do not trespass). Winter trails (snowmobiles prohibited east of Archangel Road). Reed Lakes Trail access.

J 16.4 (26.4 km) **GP 32.7** (52.6 km) Parking lot to east, snowmobile trail to west.

J 17.3 (27.8 km) **GP 31.8** (51.2 km) Gold Cord Road provides year-round access to lodge and Independence Mine State Historical Park (1.5 miles/2.4 km). The 271-acre **INDEPENDENCE MINE STATE HISTORICAL PARK** includes several buildings and old mining machinery. Park visitor center is housed in the red-roofed building, which was built in 1939 to house the mine manager. The visitor center and assay office are open 11 A.M. to 7 P.M. daily from June through Labor Day; weekends the rest of the year. (Hours and days may vary.) Guided tours of the bunkhouse, mess hall and warehouse are given from June to Labor Day (weather permitting) for a nominal fee; phone visitor center at (907) 745-2827 or phone 745-3975 in Palmer for current

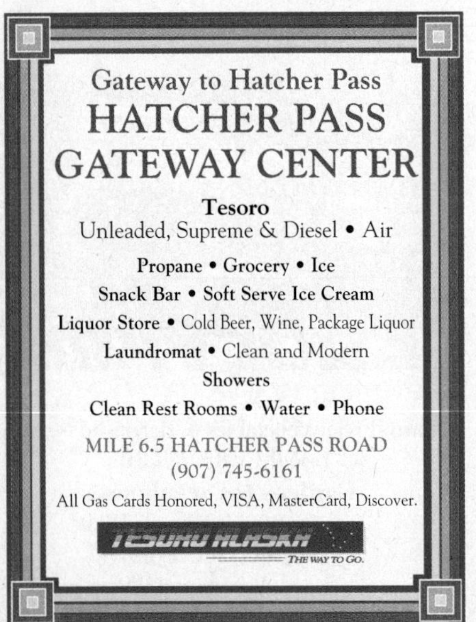

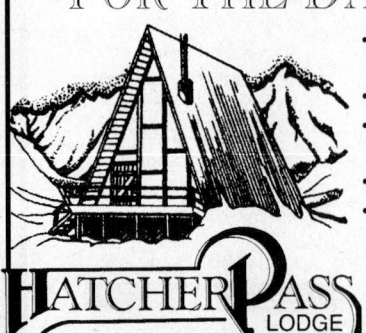

information. Groups of 20 or more call ahead for tours. Office hours and tour times may vary, but visitors are always welcome to explore on their own.

Alaska Pacific Consolidated Mine Co., one of the largest gold producers in the Willow Creek mining district, operated here from 1938 through 1941. The Gold Cord Mine buildings (private property) are visible on the hill above and to the north of Independence Mine.

Recreational gold panning is permitted in the park. Some pans are available for loan at the visitor center.

Snowmobiling is prohibited in the park.

J 17.5 (28.2 km) **GP 31.6** (50.8 km) **Hatcher Pass Lodge.** See display ad this section.

J 18.7 (30.1 km) **GP 30.4** (48.9 km) Entering Summit Lake State Recreation Site; no ground fires permitted.

J 18.9 (30.4 km) **GP 30.1** (48.4 km) Hatcher Pass Summit (elev. 3,886 feet/ 1,184m). Several turnouts westbound.

J 19.2 (30.9 km) **GP 29.8** (48 km) Summit Lake, headwaters of Willow Creek. Summit Lake State Recreation Site under development. The road follows Willow Creek from here to the George Parks Highway. There are several old and new mines in the area.

J 20.4 (32.8 km) **GP 28.6** (46 km) Upper Willow Creek Valley Road to mine.

J 23.8 (38.3 km) **GP 25.3** (40.7 km) Craigie Creek Road (very rough) leads to mine sites. Remains of historic Lucky Shot and War Baby mines on hillside are visible on hillside ahead westbound.

J 24.3 (39.1 km) **GP 24.8** (39.9 km) Beaver lodges and dams.

J 25.6 (41.2 km) **GP 23.5** (37.8 km) View of Beaver Ponds to west; mine site visible to south below road. Road begins descent westbound into Little Willow Creek valley; numerous turnouts.

J 30.3 (48.8 km) **GP 18.7** (30.1 km) Leaving Hatcher Pass public-use area westbound.

J 34.2 (55 km) **GP 14.9** (24 km) Little Willow Creek bridge; large parking area.

J 38.9 (62.6 km) **GP 10.2** (16.4 km) Gravel ends, pavement begins, westbound.

J 47.9 (77.1 km) **GP 1.2** (1.9 km) Willow Creek State Recreation Area Deception Creek Campground; 7 campsites, 15-day limit, $10 nightly fee per vehicle or annual pass, covered picnic tables, water, toilets (handicap accessible). ♿▲

J 48 (77.2 km) **GP 1.1** (1.8 km) Deception Creek Bridge.

J 48.2 (77.5 km) **GP 0.9** (1.4 km) Deception Creek picnic area. Back road into Willow from here.

J 48.5 (78.1 km) **GP 0.6** (1 km) Road crosses Alaska Railroad tracks.

J 49.1 (79 km) **GP 0 Junction** with George Parks Highway at **Milepost A 71.2.** (Turn to the GEORGE PARKS HIGHWAY section.)

Return to Milepost A 49.5
Glenn Highway

Center. Alternate access (see also **A 60.9**) to Seventeenmile Lake. Drive north 0.5 mile/ 0.8 km; turn right and drive 1.7 miles/ 2.7 km; turn left, drive 0.3 mile/0.5 km; turn right, drive 0.2 mile/0.3 km; turn right again and drive 0.2 mile/0.3 km to lake. Undeveloped camping on lakeshore.

A 56.7 (91.2 km) **T 271.3** (436.6 km) Entering Matanuska Valley Moose Range eastbound.

A 54.6 (87.9 km) **T 273.4** (440 km) Bridge over Moose Creek. Highway ascends steeply from creek in both directions. Moose Creek State Recreation Site; 12 campsites, 7-day limit, $10 nightly fee or annual pass, 4 picnic sites, water, covered tables, firepits and toilets (wheelchair accessible). Look for fossils in the road bank on the west side of the highway. ♿▲

A 54 (86.9 km) **T 274** (440.9 km) Truck lane starts westbound.

A 53.6 (86.3 km) **T 274.4** (441.6 km) Truck lane ends westbound.

A 53 (85.3 km) **T 275** (442.6 km) Side road to Buffalo Coal Mine. Access to Wishbone Lake 4-wheel-drive trail. Wild rose, geranium and chiming bells bloom along this section of highway.

A 52.3 (84.2 km) **T 275.7** (443.7 km) Soapstone Road. Wild geraniums in June.

A 51.2 (82.4 km) **T 276.8** (445.5 km) Fire station.

A 50.9 (81.9 km) **T 277.1** (445.9 km) Farm Loop Road, a 3-mile/4.8-km loop road connecting with Fishhook–Willow Road.

A 50.1 (80.6 km) **T 277.9** (447.2 km) Turn here for the Musk Ox Farm.

Musk Ox Farm and Gift Shop. The world's only domestic musk-oxen farm. The animals are combed for the precious qiviut, which is then hand-knit by Eskimos in

isolated villages, aiding the Arctic economy. During the farm tours in the summer, you can see these shaggy ice age survivors romping in beautiful pastures with Pioneer Peak as a backdrop. Open May to September Phone (907) 745-4151. P.O. Box 587, Palmer, AK 99645. [ADVERTISEMENT]

A 49.5 (79.7 km) **T 278.5** (448.2 km) **Junction** with Hatcher Pass (Fishhook–Willow) Road which leads west and north over Hatcher Pass to connect with the George Parks Highway at **Milepost A 71.2** north of Willow. See HATCHER PASS ROAD log opposite page.

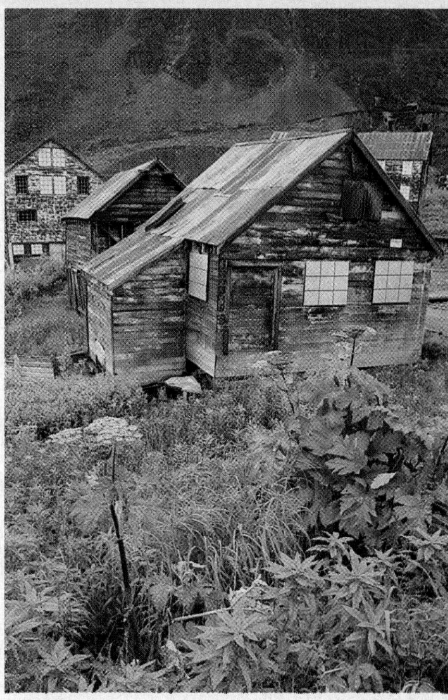

Independence Mine State Historical Park is accessible via Hatcher Pass Road. (© George Wuerthner)

Rafter T Ranch Trail Rides. See display ad this section.

A 49 (78.9 km) **T 279** (449 km) Entering Palmer, which extends to **Milepost A 41.** Actual driving distance between **Milepost 49** and **42** is 1 mile/1.6 km. Just beyond here the highway emerges on a hill overlooking

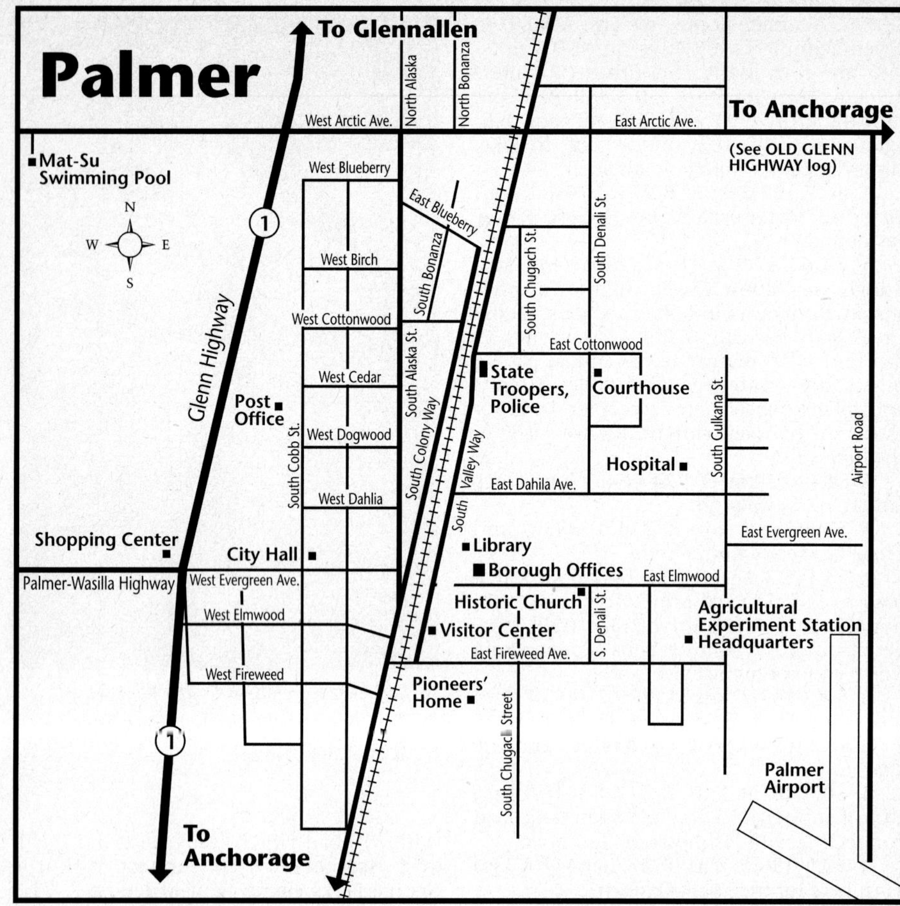

the Matanuska Valley, a view of the farms and homes of one of Alaska's agricultural areas, and the business center of Palmer.

A **42.1** (67.8 km) T **285.9** (460.1 km) Arctic Avenue leads east through Palmer to the Old Glenn Highway, a scenic alternate route to Anchorage that rejoins the highway at **Milepost A 29.6.**

Highlights along the old Glenn Highway include the original Matanuska Colony Farms, U-pick vegetable farms, campgrounds and salmon-spawning viewing areas. See OLD GLENN HIGHWAY log on page 312 (Anchorage-bound travelers read log back to front).

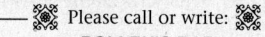

Access to Palmer High School west at this junction.

Palmer

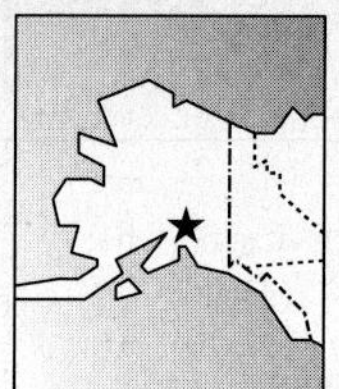

A **42** (67.6 km) T **286** (460.3 km) In the Matanuska Valley northeast of Anchorage. The city extends from about **Milepost A 49** to **A 41,** an actual driving distance of 2.1 miles/3.4 km. **Population:** 4,100. **Emergency Services:** Phone 911. **Alaska State Troopers,** phone (907) 745-2131. **City Police,** phone (907) 745-4811. **Fire Department** and **Ambulance,** phone (907) 745-3271. **Valley Hospital,** 515 E. Dahlia, phone (907) 745-4813.

Visitor Information: Visitor center in log cabin across the railroad tracks on South Valley Way at East Fireweed Avenue. Pick up a brochure and map of downtown Palmer's historic buildings. Open daily 8 A.M. to 7 P.M. May to Sept. 15; weekdays 9 A.M. to 4 P.M. mid-Sept. to May. Pay phone. Small museum in basement; Alaskan-made gifts may be for sale on main floor. Mailing address: Chamber of Commerce, P.O. Box 45, Palmer, AK 99645. Matanuska Valley Agricultural Showcase adjacent visitor center features flower and vegetable gardens.

Excellent local library, located at 655 S. Valley Way; open Monday through Friday. Paperback and magazine exchange. Wheelchair accessible. ♿

Elevation: 240 feet/74m. **Climate:** Temperatures range from 4° to 21°F/-16° to -6°C in Jan. and Dec., with a mean monthly snowfall of 8 to 10 inches. Record low was -40°F/-40°C in Jan. 1975. Temperatures range from 44° to 68°F/7° to 20°C in June and July, with a mean monthly precipitation of 2 inches. Record high was 89°F/32°C in

PALMER ADVERTISERS

Blueberry Cottage Gifts and Collectables Shop ....Mile 3.2 Palmer/Wasilla Hwy
City of Palmer ....231 W. Evergreen Ave.
Colony Inn ....325 Elmwood St.
Dee's Truck & Equipment Inc. ....Ph. (907) 745-1900
Gold Miner's Hotel ....Ph. 1-800-725-2752
Mountain View RV Park....Off Old Glenn Hwy.
Musk Ox Farm & Gift Shop ....Mile 50.1 Glenn Hwy.
Pioneer Motel & Apt. ....Ph. (907) 745-3425
Pollen's B & B ....Ph. (907) 745-8920
Tara Dells Bed & Breakfast.....................Ph. (907) 745-0407
Valley Hotel...........................606 S. Alaska St.
Wash Day Too.......................127 S. Alaska St.

June 1969. Mean annual rainfall is 15.5 inches, with 50.7 inches of snow. **Radio:** Anchorage stations; KMBQ (Wasilla). **Television:** Anchorage channels and cable. **Newspaper:** *The Frontiersman* (twice weekly).

Private Aircraft: Palmer Municipal Airport, adjacent southeast; elev. 232 feet/71m; length 6,000 feet/1,829m; asphalt; fuel 100LL, Jet A1, B. Butte Municipal, 6 miles/9.7 km southeast; elev. 64 feet/19m; length 1,800 feet/549m; gravel; unattended. Seaplane base on Finger Lake.

Palmer is a commercial center for the Matanuska and Susitna valleys (collectively referred to as the Mat–Su valleys). The town was established about 1916 as a railway station on the Matanuska branch of the Alaska Railroad.

In 1935, Palmer became the site of one of the most unusual experiments in American history: the Matanuska Valley Colony. The Federal Emergency Relief Administration, one of the many New Deal relief agencies created during Franklin Roosevelt's first year in office, planned an agricultural colony in Alaska to utilize the great agricultural potential in the Matanuska–Susitna valleys, and to get some American farm families—struck by first the dust bowl, then the Great Depression—off the dole. Social workers picked 203 families, mostly from the northern counties of Michigan, Wisconsin and Minnesota, to join the colony, because it was thought that the many hardy farmers of Scandinavian descent in those 3 states would have a natural advantage over other ethnic groups. The colonists arrived in Palmer in the early summer of 1935, and though the failure rate was high, many of their descendants still live in the Matanuska Valley. Palmer gradually became the unofficial capital of the Matanuska Valley, acting as headquarters for a farmers cooperative marketing organization and as the business and social center for the state's most productive farming region.

Palmer is Alaska's only community that developed primarily from an agricultural economy. (Real estate now takes a close second to agriculture.) The growing season averages 80 to 110 days a year, with long hours of sunshine. The University of Alaska Fairbanks has an Agricultural and Forestry Experiment Station Office and a district Cooperative Extension Service Office here. The university also operates its Matanuska Research Farm, located on Trunk Road off the George Parks Highway, about a 7-mile/11.3-km drive from Palmer. The university farm conducts research in agronomy, horticulture, soil science and animal science.

The community has a hospital, the Mat–Su College (University of Alaska), a library, banks, the Mat-Su Borough offices, borough school district and several other state and federal agency offices. Palmer has churches representing most denominations. The United Protestant Church in Palmer, the "church of a thousand logs," dates from Matanuska Colony days and is one of the oldest churches in Alaska still holding services. It is included in the National Register of Historic Places.

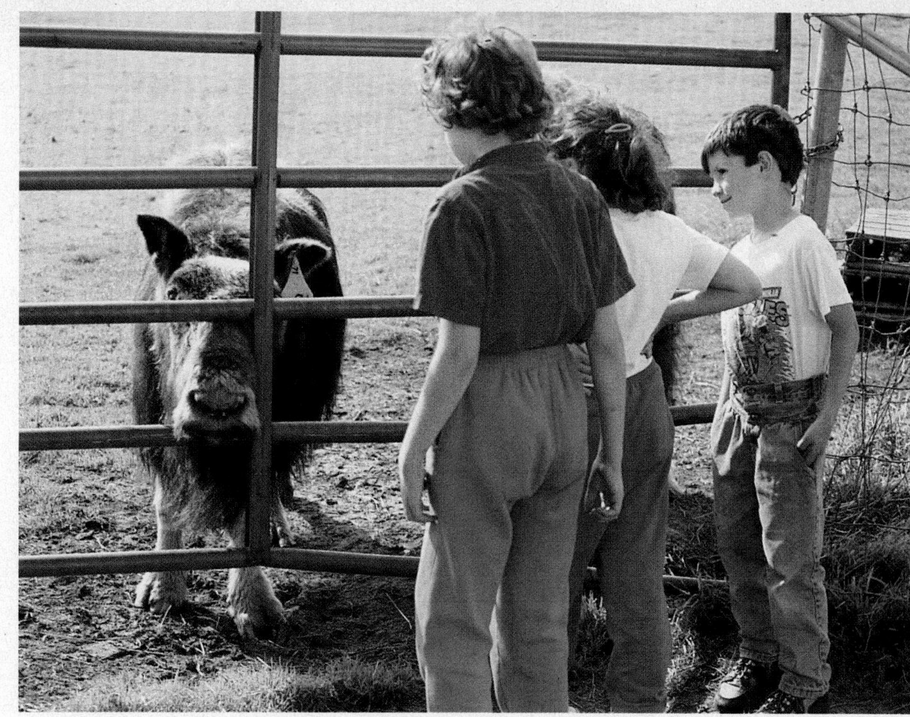

Children get a close-up view of a young musk ox. (© Ruth von Spalding)

ACCOMMODATIONS/VISITOR SERVICES

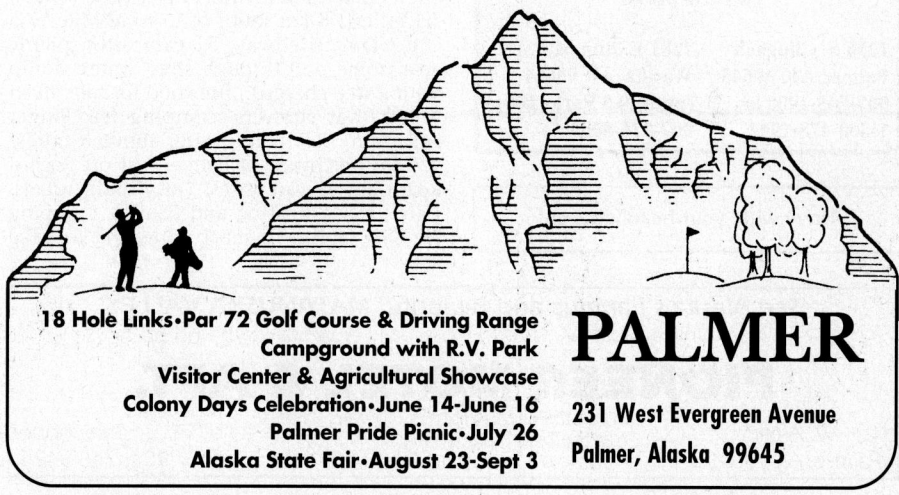

Palmer has all visitor facilities including 3 hotels, 2 motels, bed and breakfasts, gas sta-

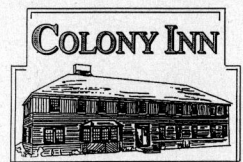

Fun and colorful Alaska State Fair is an annual event in Palmer. (© Ruth von Spalding)

tions, grocery stores, laundromat, auto repair and parts, and shopping. The Matanuska Valley region has several lake resorts offering boat rentals, golf, fly-in fishing, hunting and horseback riding.

There is a private RV park on Smith Road off the Old Glenn Highway. There are also private campgrounds on the Glenn Highway a few miles west of Palmer. The Mat–Su Borough operates Matanuska River Park, located 1.1 miles/1.8 km south of town at Mile 17.5 Old Glenn Highway; 51 campsites, picnic area, some pull-through sites, water, dump station (fee charged), firewood for sale, flush toilets, hot showers, camping fee. Finger Lake State Recreation Site, about 6 miles/ 9.7 km northwest of Palmer just off Bogard Road, has 69 campsites, 7-day limit, toilets, water, trails, boating and fishing. Camping fee $10/night. To reach Finger Lake, take Palmer–Wasilla Highway north 4 miles/6.4 km from **Milepost A 41.8** to Trunk Road, then follow Trunk Road to Bogard Road. ▲

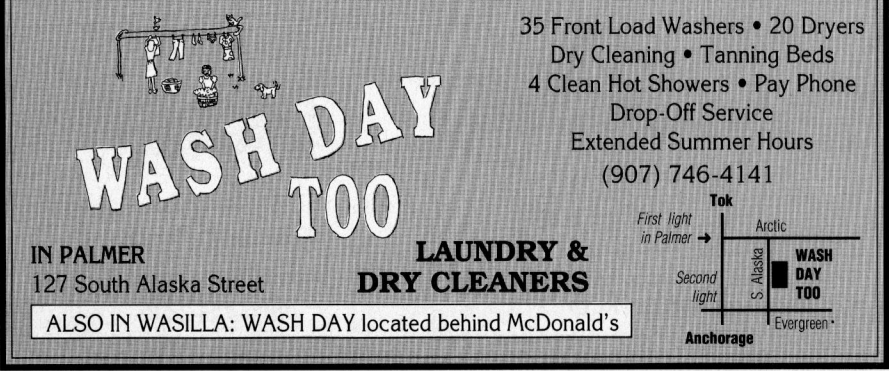

Blueberry Cottage Gift and Collectibles Shop. Mile 3.2 Palmer/Wasilla Hwy. Cold drinks, specialty foods, coffee, teas and candies. Relax and browse through our unique gifts and distinctive Alaskan Artisan creations. Open Monday–Friday 10 A.M. to 6 P.M. and Saturday 10 A.M. to 5 P.M. Phone (907) 745-8850. "Look for us in the Big Blue Colonial House." [ADVERTISEMENT]

Mountain View RV Park offers breathtaking views of the Matanuska mountains. Watch wildlife from your door. Full hookups, hot showers included. New bathrooms and laundromat, dump station. Good Sam Park. Call (907) 745-5747 for reservations. Mail forwarding. Write P.O. Box 2521, Palmer, AK 99745. From Mile A 42.1 Glenn

Highway (Arctic), follow Old Glenn Highway 2.8 miles. Turn east on Smith Road, drive 0.6 mile, turn right (0.3 mile). We're 3.7 miles from the Glenn Highway. See display ad this section. [ADVERTISEMENT] ♿▲

TRANSPORTATION

Air: No scheduled service, but the local airport has a number of charter operators. **Bus**: Charter service only.

ATTRACTIONS

Go Swimming: The 25-m swimming pool is open to the public 6 days a week (closed Sundays)—$4 for adults and showers are available. The pool is located at Palmer High School; phone (907) 745-5091.

Get Acquainted: Stop at the visitor information center, a log building just off the "main drag" (across the railroad tracks at the intersection of East Fireweed Avenue and South Valley Way). The center includes a museum, artifacts, a gift shop and agricultural showcase garden.

Visit the Musk Ox Farm. Located east of Palmer on the Glenn Highway at **Milepost 50.1**, the Musk Ox Farm is the only place in the world these exotic animals are raised domestically. Hunted to near extinction in Alaska in 1865, the species was reintroduced in the 1930s. The farm is open May to Sept.; admission is charged.

Visit a Reindeer Farm, located 8.1 miles/ 11.5 km south of Palmer via the Old Glenn Highway to Bodenburg Loop Road. This commercial reindeer farm is open daily in summer; admission is charged.

Play Golf. Palmer links golf course has 18 holes (par 72, USGA rated), rental carts and clubs, driving range and clubhouse. Phone (907) 745-4653.

Enjoy Water Sports. Fishing, boating, waterskiing and other water sports are popular in summer at Finger Lake west of Palmer. Kepler–Bradley Lakes State Recreation Area on Matanuska Lake has canoe rentals; turn off the Glenn Highway at **Milepost A 36.4.**

The Alaska State Fair, an 11-day annual

Drive with your headlights on!

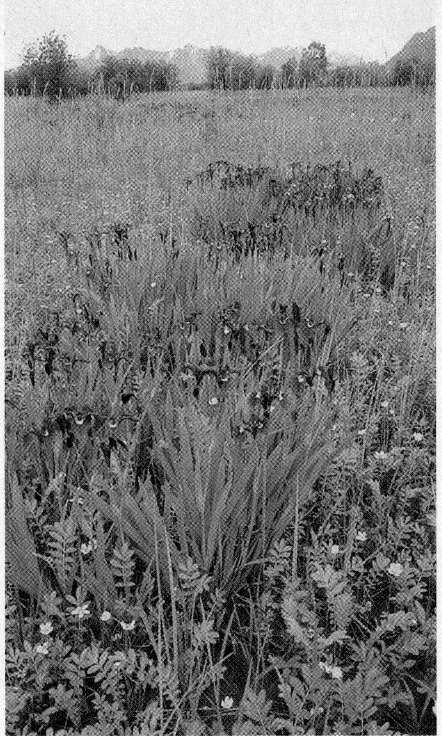

Wild iris grow in Palmer Hay Flats refuge. (© Michael DeYoung)

event ending on Labor Day (Aug. 23 to Sept. 2, 1996), has agricultural exhibits from farms throughout Alaska. There are also food booths, games and rides. This is a very popular event, and fairgoers from Anchorage can tie up traffic. But it's worth the drive just to see the huge vegetables. Phone (907) 745-4827.

Visit Scenic Hatcher Pass: A 6- to 8-hour drive from **Milepost A 49.5** near Palmer that climbs through the beautiful Hatcher Pass Recreation Area and connects with the George Parks Highway at **Milepost A 71.2.** Access to Independence Mine State Historical Park. See HATCHER PASS ROAD this section.

See the Matanuska Glacier: Drive 50 miles/80 km east on the Glenn Highway from Palmer to visit this spectacular 27-mile-/43.5-km-long glacier, one of the few you can drive to and explore on foot. Access to the foot of the glacier is through a private campground at **Milepost A 102**; admission charged. If you're not interested in getting close, there are several vantage points along the highway and from trails at Matanuska Glacier Campground, **Milepost A 101.**

Glenn Highway Log

(continued)

A 41.8 (67.3 km) **T 286.2** (460.6 km) **Junction** with Palmer–Wasilla Highway. Gas station and shopping mall. West Evergreen Avenue access to downtown Palmer.

Palmer–Wasilla Highway leads northwest 10 miles/16 km to the George Parks Highway. It provides access to a car wash, several other businesses, Mat–Su College, Finger Lake State Recreation Site (via Trunk and Bogard roads) and Wolf Lake State Recreation Site. At Mile 1.9 on the Palmer–Wasilla Highway is the Crevasse Moraine trailhead; parking, picnic tables, fireplaces and access to 5 loop hiking trails.

Carrs Pioneer Square shopping mall, located at this junction, is the site of a bronze sculpture by Jacques and Mary Regat dedicated to the Matanuska Valley pioneers.

A 41.6 (66.9 km) **T 286.4** (460.9 km) **Palmer Chevron.** See display ad this section.

A **41.2** (66.3 km) **T 286.8** (461.5 km) First access road to Palmer business district for eastbound travelers.

A 40.5 (65.2 km) **T 287.5** (462.7 km) **Fairview Motel & Restaurant.** See display ad this section.

A 40.2 (64.7 km) **T 287.8** (463.2 km) Main entrance to fairgrounds (site of Alaska State Fair) and Herman Field (home of the Mat–Su Miners baseball team). Alaska State Fair is held the end of August to Labor Day (Aug. 23 to Sept. 2, 1996).

Alaska State Fair. See display ad this section.

A 39.2 (63.1 km) **T 288.8** (464.8 km) Outer Springer Loop. Gift shop. Short, steep trail to **Meiers Lake**; grayling fishing.

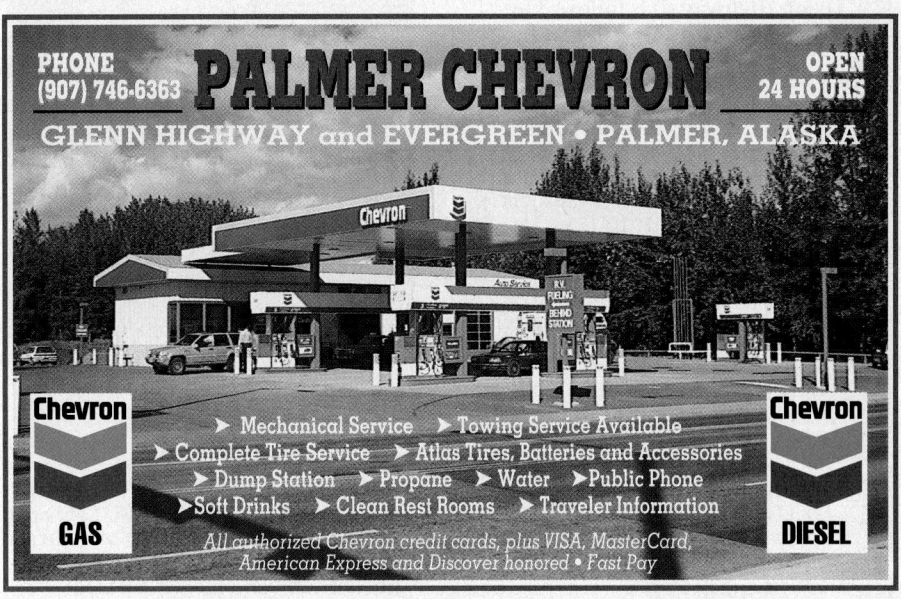

Old Glenn Highway (Palmer Alternate) Log

This 18.6-mile/29.9-km paved road is a scenic alternate route between Palmer and Anchorage, exiting the Glenn Highway at **Milepost A 29.6** and rejoining the Glenn Highway at **Milepost A 42.1**. The Old Glenn Highway goes through the heart of the original Matanuska Colony agricultural lands.

Distance from south junction with the Glenn Highway (J) is followed by distance from Palmer (P).

J 0 P 18.6 (29.9 km) Exit from Glenn Highway at **Milepost A 29.6.**

J 6.1 (9.8 km) **P 12.3** (19.8 km) Goat Creek Bridge.

J 7.2 (11.6 km) **P 11.4** (18.3 km) View of Bodenburg Butte across Knik River.

J 8.6 (13.8 km) **P 10** (16.1 km) **Junction** with Knik River Road, a gravel side road which leads to view of Knik Glacier. Pioneer Ridge/Knik River trailhead 3.6 miles/5.8 km from bridge. Knik River Road dead ends 11.4 miles/18.3 km from here.

J 8.7 (14 km) **P 9.9** (15.9 km) Knik River bridge; parking at east end of bridge.

Knik River RV Park. See display ad this section. ▲

J 11.4 (18.3 km) **P 7.2** (11.6 km) Butte branch U.S. post office. Pioneer Peak dominates the skyline for southbound travelers.

J 11.5 (18.5 km) **P 7.1** (11.4 km) South **junction** with Bodenburg Butte Loop Road which leads west (see description following), and **junction** with Plumley Road to east. Plumley Road provides access to **Jim Creek** trail off Caudill Road; fishing for Dolly Varden, silver and red salmon.

The 5.8-mile/9.3-km Bodenburg Butte Road rejoins the Old Glenn Highway opposite Dack Acres Road (**Milepost J 12.6**). The **BODENBURG BUTTE** area (pop. 1,232) has original Matanuska Colony farms and a commercial reindeer farm (visitors welcome, fee charged).

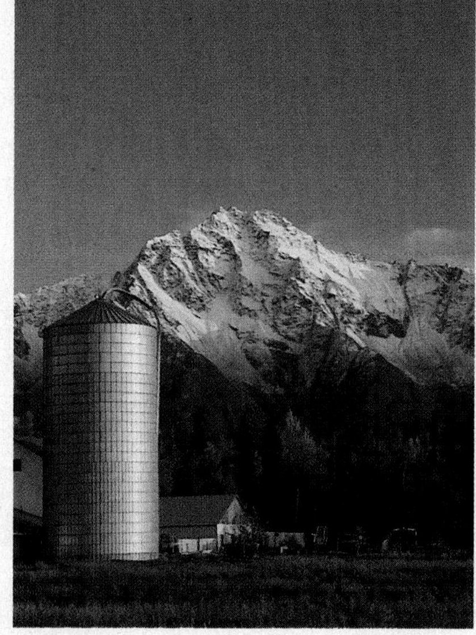
Palmer-area farm. (© Harry M. Walker)

Measuring mileages from the south junction, look for these attractions: Mile 0.6/1 km, Matanuska Colony log house and Bodenburg Butte trailhead; and Mile 0.8/1.3 km, reindeer farm.

Pyrah's Pioneer Peak Farm. See display ad this section.

J 12.6 (20.3 km) **P 6** (9.7 km) **Junction** with Dack Acres Road, north end of Bodenburg Butte Loop Road (see **Milepost J 11.5**).

J 13.3 (21.4 km) **P 5.3** (8.5 km) Turnout to west. Bodenburg Creek parallels highway next 0.7 mile/1.1 km northbound; red and pink salmon spawn here from late Aug. through Sept. Eagles nest across the creek. *CAUTION: Use turnouts and watch for heavy traffic.*

J 14.5 (23.3 km) **P 4.1** (6.6 km) Maud Road. Access to **Mud Lake** (4 miles/6.4 km); fishing for Dolly Varden.

J 15.6 (25.1 km) **P 3** (4.8 km) **Junction** with Smith Road. Access to private campground. Trail rides available at a nearby ranch.

Mountain View RV Park. See display ad this section. ▲

J 16.1 (25.9 km) **P 2.5** (4 km) Clark-Wolverine Road; access to Lazy Mountain recreation area hiking trails. Drive in 0.7 mile/1.1 km; turn right on Huntly Road at T; drive 1 mile/1.6 km on gravel road and take right fork to recreation area and overlook. Picnic tables, toilets, good berry picking.

J 16.8 (27 km) **P 1.8** (2.9 km) Matanuska River bridge. Access to river.

J 17.5 (28.2 km) **P 1.1** (1.8 km) Matanuska River Park; 51 campsites, picnic area, some pull-through sites, water, fireplaces, dump station, flush toilets, hot showers. Camping, shower and dump station fees charged. ▲

J 18.6 (29.9 km) **P 0 Junction** of Old Glenn Highway (Arctic Avenue) at Palmer, **Milepost A 42.1** Glenn Highway.

Return to Milepost A 42.1 or A 29.6 Glenn Highway

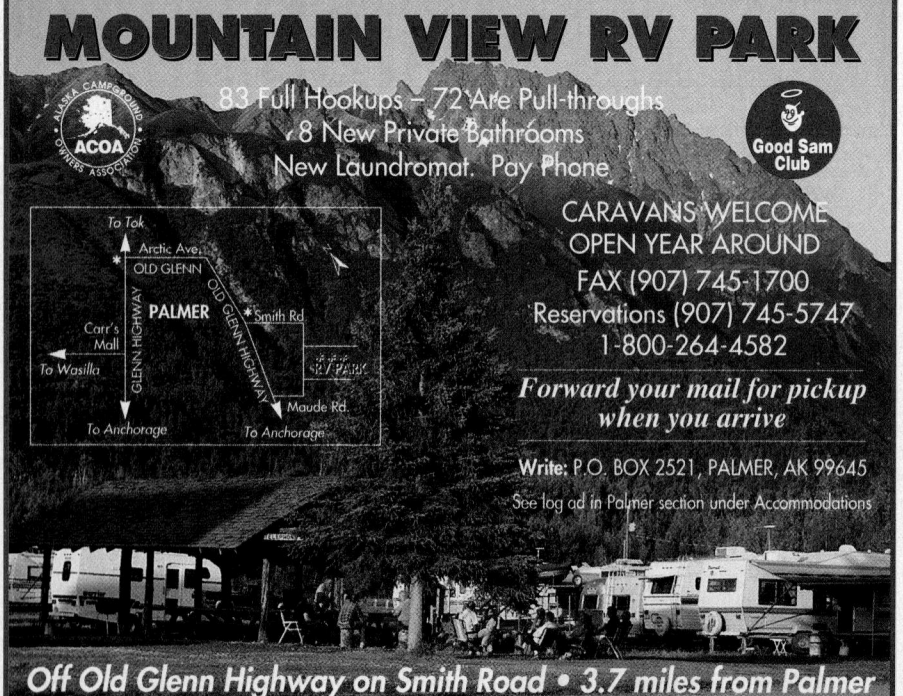

Colony Curio. A unique Alaskan gift shop with something for everyone. Two Matanuska Colony homes are located on the original Meiers' homestead, with Alaskan farm implements, Alaskan gardens and our

10-foot carved bear. Our shop carries a large selection of made-in-Alaska products, including items made right here in our factory. Also enjoy our wide selection of local crafts. Stop in for the friendly atmosphere you visit Alaska to find. See display ad this section. [ADVERTISEMENT]

A 38 (61.2 km) **T 290** (466.7 km) **Matanuska Farm Market.** See display ad this section.

A 37.4 (60.2 km) **T 290.6** (467.7 km) Kepler Drive; access to private campground and lake. ▲

A 37.2 (59.9 km) **T 290.8** (468 km) **Echo Lake** turnout; parking and trail to lake. Fishing for landlocked salmon and rainbow.

A 37 (59.5 km) **T 291** (468.3 km) Echo Lake Road.

A 36.4 (58.6 km) **T 291.6** (469.3 km) Kepler–Bradley Lakes State Recreation Area on Matanuska Lake; day-use area with water, toilets, parking, picnic tables, canoe rentals, fishing and hiking. The lakes are **Matanuska Lake, Canoe Lake, Irene Lake** and **Long Lake.**

A 36.2 (58.3 km) **T 291.8** (469.6 km) **The Homestead RV Park.** Wooded pull-throughs to 70 feet, tent sites. Very clean restrooms and showers. Electric and water hookups; dump station; also, on-site portable dumping. Laundry. Picnic tables, pay phone. Area tours, evening entertainment. Square dancing Thursday nights. Enclosed pavilion and amphitheatre. Walking and jogging trails, trout fishing nearby. Good Sam park. 60 sites. Handicap access. Beautiful view. Commuting distance to Anchorage. Caravans welcome. Phone (907) 745-6005. Toll-free in Alaska 1-800-478-3570. See display ad this section. [ADVERTISEMENT] ▲

A 35.3 (56.8 km) **T 292.7** (471.1 km) *CAUTION: Traffic signal at busy **junction** of the Glenn Highway and George Parks Highway (Alaska Route 3), which form a common highway into Anchorage.* If headed for Fairbanks or Mount McKinley turn north on the George Parks Highway. See **Milepost A 35** GEORGE PARKS HIGHWAY section for details.

A 34.9 (56.2 km) **T 293.1** (471.7 km) *CAUTION: Highway crosses the Alaska Railroad tracks.*

A 34 (54.7 km) **T 294** (473.1 km) Paved double-ended turnout west side of highway. Rabbit Slough.

A 32.4 (52.1 km) **T 295.6** (475.7 km) Palmer Hay Flats state game refuge. According to the ADF&G, this is the most heavily utilized waterfowl hunting area in Alaska. Access to the refuge is via Fairview Loop Road off the George Parks Highway.

A 31.5 (50.7 km) **T 296.5** (477.2 km) Bridge over the Matanuska River, which is fed by the Matanuska Glacier.

A 30.8 (49.6 km) **T 297.5** (478.8 km) There are 2 Knik River bridges. Exits to parking areas below highway between the bridges. The Knik River comes down from the Knik Glacier to the east and splits into several branches as it approaches Knik Arm. Game Management Unit 14C boundary. Also boundary of Matanuska–Susitna Borough.

Moose winter in this area and the cows and calves may be seen early in the morning and in the evening as late as early July. In winter, watch for moose on the road between here and Anchorage.

A 29.6 (47.6 km) **T 298.4** (480.2 km) Exit to the Old Glenn Highway (Palmer Alternate). See OLD GLENN HIGHWAY log on opposite page.

A 27.3 (43.9 km) **T 300.7** (483.9 km) The

Athabascan spirit houses at Eklutna cemetery. (Jerrianne Lowther, staff)

highway crosses a swampy area known locally as Eklutna Flats. These flats are a protected wildflower area (picking flowers is strictly prohibited). Look for wild iris, shooting star, chocolate lily and wild rose in early June.

A 26.8 (43.1 km) **T 301.2** (484.7 km) Highway crosses Alaska Railroad via overpass.

A 26.3 (42.3 km) **T 301.7** (485.5 km) Eklutna overpass, exits both sides of highway. Access to Eklutna Road (description follows), the village of Eklutna and also access to Thunderbird Falls (see **Milepost A 25.3**) for Anchorage-bound travelers. West of the highway is the Indian village of **EKLUTNA** (pop. 25), site of Eklutna Village Historical Park, which preserves the heritage and traditions of the Athabascan Alaska Natives. Attractions include the historic St. Nicholas Russian Orthodox Church and a hand-built Siberian prayer chapel. Admission fee charged. Open daily mid-May to mid-Sept. The bright little grave houses or spirit houses in the cemetery are painted in the family's traditional colors.

Eklutna Historical Park. See display ad this section.

Eklutna Road leads east 10 miles/16.1 km to Eklutna Lake Recreation Area in Chugach State Park. General store at Mile 9. The recreation area has a campground, picnic area and hiking trails. The campground has 50 sites, drinking water, pit toilets and a 15-day limit. Camping fee $10/night or annual pass. The 32-unit picnic area is located at the trailhead parking lot, which will accommodate 80 cars and has a boat launch for hand-carried boats. Three trails branch off the trailhead: Twin Peaks, Lakeside and Bold Ridge. The Lakeside trail skirts Eklutna Lake and gives access to Eklutna Glacier (12.7 miles/20.4 km). **Eklutna Lake** is the largest lake in Chugach State Park, measuring approximately 7 miles long by a mile wide. Fed by Eklutna Glacier, it offers fair fishing for Dolly Varden. *CAUTION: Afternoon winds can make the lake dangerous for boaters.* Interpretive displays on wildlife and a telescope for viewing Dall sheep, eagles and other wildlife are located at the trailhead.

A 25.7 (41.3 km) **T 302.3** (486.5 km) Highway crosses Eklutna River.

A 25.3 (40.7 km) **T 302.7** (487.1 km) Thunderbird Falls exit (northbound traffic only) and northbound access to Eklutna Road (see **Milepost A 26.3** for description). Drive about 0.3 mile/0.5 km to parking area. Thunderbird Falls is about 1 mile/1.6 km from the highway. The scenic trail to the falls winds through private property on a 25-foot right-of-way and follows a hillside down to Thunderbird Creek. The falls are just upstream. *CAUTION: Do not climb the steep cliffs overhanging the falls!*

A 24.5 (39.4 km) **T 303.5** (488.4 km) Southbound exit to Edmonds Lake residential area and Mirror Lake picnic wayside. The shallow, 73-acre Mirror Lake is located at the foot of Mount Eklutna.

A 23.6 (38 km) **T 304.4** (489.9 km) Access to Mirror Lake picnic wayside for northbound traffic only.

A 23 (37 km) **T 305** (490.8 km) North Peters Creek overpass, exits both sides of highway.

A 21.5 (34.6 km) **T 306.5** (493.3 km) South Peters Creek underpass, exits both sides of highway. Access to Peters Creek and portion of the Old Glenn Highway, which parallels the newer highway south to Eagle River, and provides access to a number of local services. **PETERS CREEK** services include gas stations, grocery, car wash, body repair shop and restaurant.

Peters Creek RV Park. See display ad this section.

Peters Creek Trading Post. See display ad this section.

A 21.2 (34.1 km) **T 306.8** (493.7 km) Peters Creek bridge.

A 20.9 (33.6 km) **T 306.9** (493.9 km) North Birchwood Loop Road underpass, exits both sides of highway; turn east for community of **CHUGIAK** and for portion of Old Glenn Highway, which leads south to Eagle River and north to Peters Creek. There are many services and attractions in the Peters Creek–Chugiak–Eagle River area.

A 20.4 (32.8 km) **T 307.6** (495 km) Exit for North Birchwood Loop Road, Chugiak post office and services.

A 17.2 (27.7 km) **T 310.8** (500.2 km) South Birchwood Loop Road underpass, exits both sides of highway. Access to St. John Orthodox Cathedral, sled dog demonstrations, Chugiak High School and Old Glenn Highway.

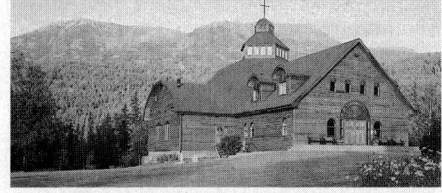

A 15.3 (24.6 km) **T 312.7** (503.2 km) Exits for Fire Lake residential area, Old Glenn Highway and Eagle River.

A 13.4 (21.6 km) **T 314.6** (506.3 km) Eagle River overpass. Exit east for community of Eagle River (all visitor services), the North Anchorage Visitor Information Center (located at Valley River Mall in Eagle River) and Eagle River Road to Chugach State Park visitor center (a highly recommended stop); descriptions follow.

Eagle River

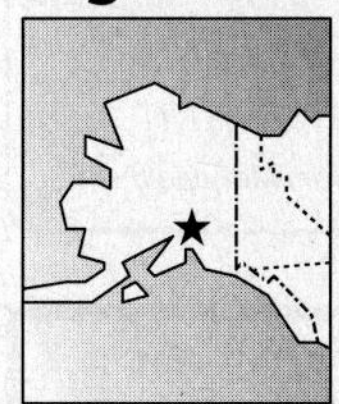

A 13.4 (21.6 km) **T 314.6** (506.3 km) **Population:** Area 18,040. **Emergency Services: Clinic,** phone (907) 694-2807. **Visitor Information:** The Anchorage Convention and Visitors Bureau North Anchorage Visitor Information Center is located in the Parkgate Bldg., along with the Southcentral Alaska Museum of Natural History, in downtown Eagle River. Stop by for information on Anchorage events, parking maps and brochures, or phone (907) 696-4636. For information on Eagle River, contact the Chugiak–Eagle River Chamber of Commerce, P.O. Box 770353, Eagle River, AK 99577; phone (907) 694-4702. You can also visit the Chamber office at 11401 Old Glenn Highway, Ste. 110A, in the Eagle River Shopping Center.

The Chugiak–Eagle River area was home-

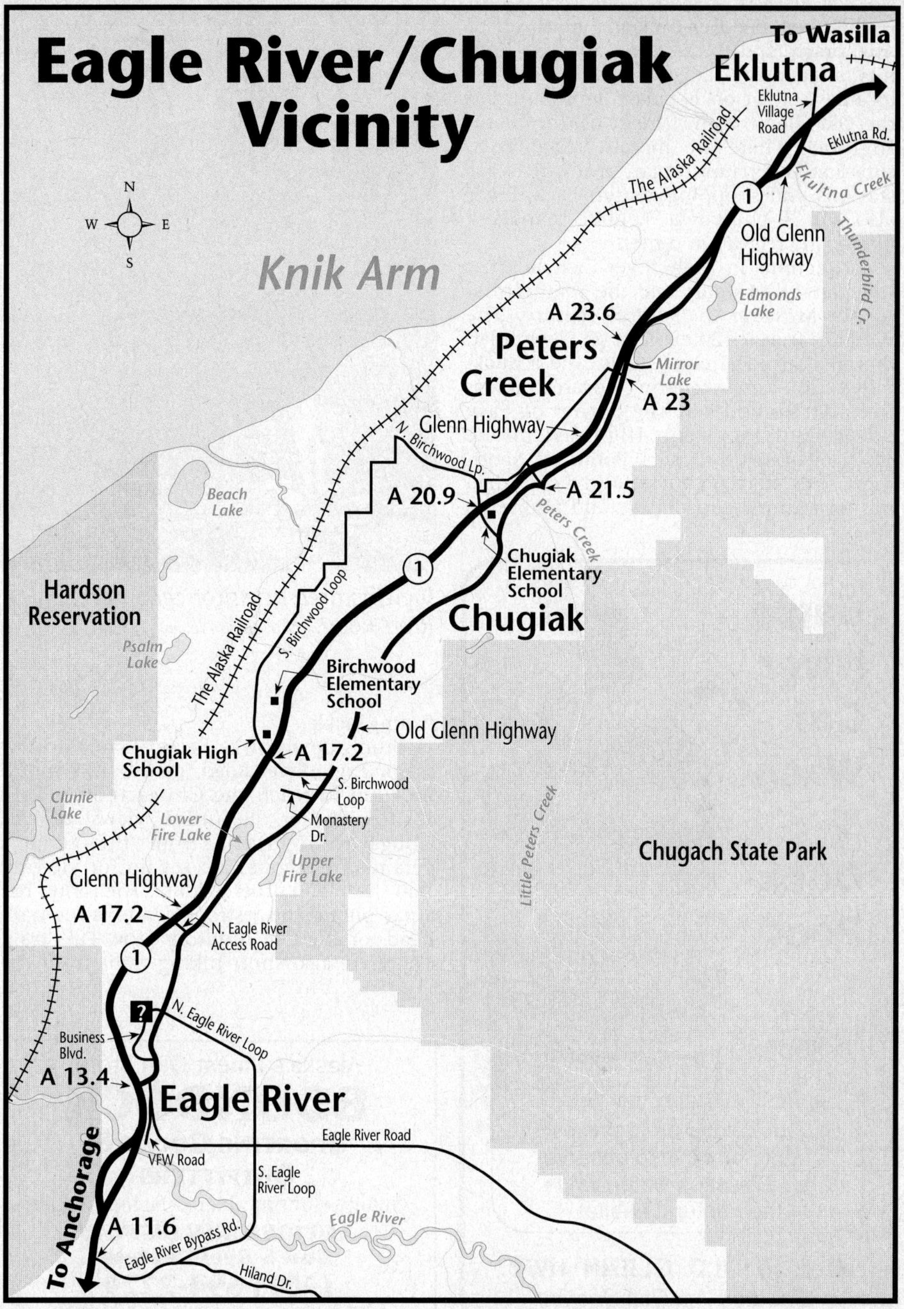

Eagle River/Chugiak Vicinity

To Wasilla
Eklutna
Eklutna Village Road
Eklutna Rd.
Eklutna Creek
The Alaska Railroad
Old Glenn Highway
Thunderbird Cr.
Knik Arm
Edmonds Lake
A 23.6
Peters Creek
Mirror Lake
A 23
Glenn Highway
N. Birchwood Lp.
A 20.9
A 21.5
Beach Lake
Peters Creek
Chugiak Elementary School
Hardson Reservation
S. Birchwood Loop
Chugiak
Psalm Lake
Birchwood Elementary School
Old Glenn Highway
Chugiak High School
A 17.2
S. Birchwood Loop
Monastery Dr.
Clunie Lake
Lower Fire Lake
Upper Fire Lake
Little Peters Creek
Chugach State Park
Glenn Highway
A 17.2
N. Eagle River Access Road
N. Eagle River Loop
Business Blvd.
A 13.4
Eagle River
Eagle River Road
VFW Road
S. Eagle River Loop
To Anchorage
A 11.6
Eagle River Bypass Rd.
Eagle River
Hiland Dr.

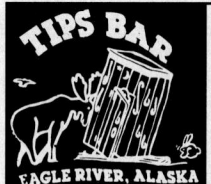

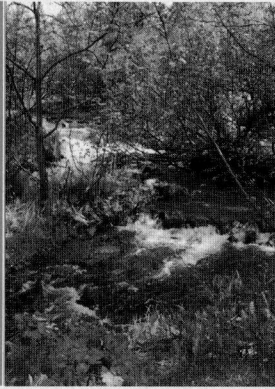

steaded after WWII when the new Glenn Highway opened this rural area northeast of Anchorage. Today, the Eagle River community offers a full range of businesses, most located near or on Business Boulevard and the Old Glenn Highway east off the Glenn Highway. There are motels, restaurants, supermarkets, laundromat, post office, gas stations and shopping center. Eagle River also has 30 churches, 9 public schools, a library and recreation center.

Attractions in Eagle River include artist Jon Van Zyle's studio and the Southcentral Alaska Museum of Natural History. The museum features 20 exhibits on Cook Inlet, dioramas of local ecosystems, and a duck-billed dinosaur skeleton. Located across from McDonald's at the corner of Easy Street and Old Glenn Highway; phone (907) 694-0819 for hours. Boondock Sporting Goods store on Eagle River Loop Road has an antique gun display and also rents

Viewing area at visitor center on Eagle River Road. (© Michael DeYoung)

fishing tackle.

From downtown Eagle River, follow scenic Eagle River Road (paved) 12.7 miles/20.4 km to reach the Chugach State Park Visitor Center. Beautiful views of the Chugach Mountains from the center's veranda; telescopes are set up for viewing Dall sheep and other wildlife. The center has a pay phone and restrooms, and is the trailhead for the Old Iditarod–Crow Pass trail. There are also short hiking trails from the center and scheduled ranger-led hikes and naturalist programs. The center is staffed part time; hours vary in summer and winter. Phone (907) 694-2108 for current information.

Kayaks, rafts and canoes can put in at Mile 7.5 Eagle River Road at the **North Fork Eagle River** access/day-use area with paved parking, toilets, fishing for rainbow trout, Dolly Varden and a limited king salmon fishery, along with cross-country skiing and snow machining in winter. The Eagle River offers class II, III and IV float trips. Check with rangers at Chugach State Park for infor-

EAGLE RIVER ADVERTISERS

Alaska Bubbling Brook B&B .... Ph. 1-800-244-5103
Alaska Limited Editions ..... Ph. (907) 688-3627
Anchorage Convention & Visitors Bureau .... Ph. (907) 696-4636
Boondock Sporting Goods & Outfitters .... Eagle River Loop Rd.
Chugiak-Eagle River Chamber of Commerce .... Ph. (907) 694-4702
Competitive Edge, The ...... Ph. (907)696-3566
Eagle River Car Wash and Duck Pond .... Old Glenn Hwy.
Eagle River Driving Tour .... Palmer Visitors Center
Eagle River Motel/Hotel ... Ph. (907) 694-5000
Hidden Haven RV Park ..... Ph. (907) 694-7275
Laundry Basket, The .... Business Blvd
Southcentral Alaska Museum of Natural History .... Old Glenn Hwy.
Tips Bar & Cafe .... Old Glenn Hwy.

mation on river conditions.

The Competitive Edge. Full service bicycle, ski and skate shop, specializing in mountain bikes, Nordic skis and inline skates. Sales. Service. Rental. Certified technicians. Same day service available. Open 7 days a week, year-round. Easy access off the Glenn Highway. Located in downtown Eagle River. 11925 Old Glenn Highway. (907) 696-3566. [ADVERTISEMENT]

Eagle River Car Wash and Duck Pond. Facilities available for washing cars, campers, trucks, boats and travel homes. Vacuums available. A duck pond on the premises is open to the public and features cedar viewing decks for observing some of the natural wild Alaskan waterfowl in their natural habitat. Mile 15.5 Old Glenn Highway. Turn off at North Eagle River access for car wash. See display ad this section. [ADVERTISEMENT]

Glenn Highway Log

(continued)

A 12.8 (20.6 km) **T 315.2** (507.3 km) Eagle River Bridge.

A 11.6 (18.7 km) **T 316.4** (509.2 km) Hiland Road exit. Access to Alaska State Forest Nursery and Eagle River Campground in Chugach State Park. The nursery welcomes visitors; phone (907) 694-5880 for tours.

Eagle River Campground, 1.4 miles/2.3 km from the highway, has 58 campsites, walk-in tent camping, a 4-day camping limit, picnic shelter (may be reserved in advance), dump station, pay phones, flush toilets and drinking water. Camping fee $15/night. Day-use fee $3. Canoe/kayak staging area. This is one of the most popular campgrounds in the state. Phone the state park office at (907) 345-5014 for information. ▲

A 10.6 (17.1 km) **T 317.4** (510.8 km) Truck weigh stations on both sides of highway. Pay phones.

The last 9 miles/14.5 km of the Glenn Highway has been designated the Veterans' Memorial Parkway.

A 7.5 (12.1 km) **T 320.5** (515.8 km) Southbound exit to **FORT RICHARDSON** and Arctic Valley road. *CAUTION: Watch for moose.*

A 6.1 (9.8 km) **T 321.9** (518 km) Northbound exit to Fort Richardson and Arctic Valley Road. Road to Arctic Valley Ski Area is steep and winding but offers spectacular views of Anchorage and Cook Inlet. It is approximately 7.5 miles/12 km to the ski area. Good berry picking in summer. Not recommended for large vehicles.

A 6 (9.7 km) **T 322** (518.2 km) Ship Creek.

A 4.4 (7.1 km) **T 323.6** (520.8 km) Muldoon Road overpass. (Exit here to connect with Seward Highway via Muldoon and Tudor roads bypass.) U.S. Air Force Hospital and Bartlett High School to the north, Muldoon Road to the south. Exit south on Muldoon for Centennial Park municipal campground. To reach the campground, go south on Muldoon to first left (Boundary); go about 100 yards then make a second left; continue about quarter-mile to campground entrance. There is a bicycle trail from Muldoon Road to Mirror Lake, **Milepost A 23.6.** ▲

A 3 (4.8 km) **T 325** (523 km) Boniface Parkway; access to businesses. Russian Jack Springs city campground is located south of the Glenn Highway on Boniface Parkway just north of DeBarr. Turn north for Elmendorf AFB.

A 1.8 (2.9 km) **T 326.2** (525 km) Bragaw Street.

A 0.7 (1.1 km) **T 327.3** (526.7 km) Reeve Boulevard; access to **ELMENDORF AFB.**

A 0.3 (0.5 km) **T 327.7** (527.4 km) Concrete Street. Access to Elmendorf AFB.

A 0 **T 328** (527.9 km) The Glenn Highway ends at Medfra Street. Continue straight ahead on 5th Avenue (one way westbound) to downtown Anchorage. Turn left at Gambell Street (one way southbound) for the Seward Highway and Kenai Peninsula. See ANCHORAGE section following for description of city.

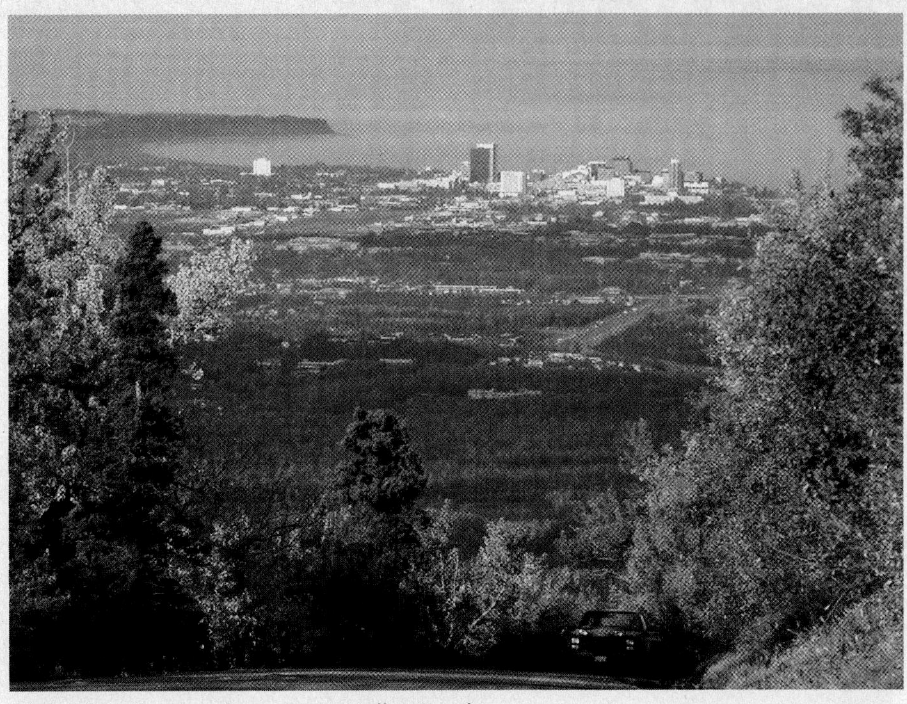

View of Anchorage from Arctic Valley Road. (© Carmen Scott)

ANCHORAGE

(See maps, pages 319–320)

Photographer's double-exposure puts a full moon over the Chugach Mountains behind Anchorage. (© Michael DeYoung)

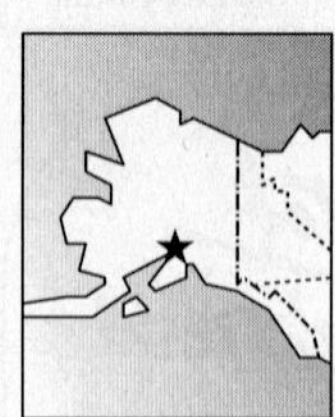

Located on the upper shores of Cook Inlet, at 61° north latitude and 150° west longitude, Anchorage is in the heart of Alaska's southcentral gulf coast. The townsite is on a low-lying alluvial plain bordered by mountains, dense forests of spruce, birch and aspen, and water. Cook Inlet's Turnagain Arm and Knik Arm define the broad peninsula on which the city lies. Anchorage is situated 358 miles/576 km south of Fairbanks via the George Parks Highway; 304 miles/489 km from Valdez, southern terminus of the trans-Alaska pipeline, via the Glenn and Richardson highways; 2,459 driving miles/3,957 km via the West Access Route, Alaska Highway and Glenn Highway/Tok Cutoff, 1,644 nautical miles/2,646 km, and 3 hours flying time from Seattle. Anchorage has been called the "Air Crossroads of the World." In terms of nonstop air mileages, Anchorage is the following distance from each of these cities: Amsterdam, 4,475/7,202 km; Chicago, 2,839/4,569 km; Copenhagen, 4,313/6,941 km; Hamburg, 4,430/7,129 km; Honolulu, 2,780/4,474 km; London, 4,487/7,221 km; Paris, 4,683/7,536 km; San Francisco, 2,015/3,243 km; Seattle, 1,445/2,325 km; Tokyo, 3,460/5,568 km.

Population: Anchorage Municipality 257,780. **Emergency Services: Police, Fire Department, Ambulance** and **Search & Rescue**, phone 911, CB Channel 9. **Police**, phone (907) 786-8500. **Alaska State Troopers**, phone (907) 269-5511. **Hospitals:** Alaska Regional Hospital, phone (907) 276-1131; Alaska Native Medical Center, phone (907) 279-6661; Providence, Alaska Medical Center, phone (907) 562-2211; U.S. Air Force, phone (907) 552-5555. **Dental Emergencies**, phone (907) 279-9144 (24-hour service). **Emergency Management**, phone (907) 267-4904. **Crisis Line**, phone 1-800-478-2221 or (907) 563-3200 (24-hour service). **Rape & Assault**, phone (907) 276-7273. **Battered Women**, phone (907) 272-0100. **Pet Emergency**, phone (907) 274-5636. **Poison Control**, phone (907) 261-3193. **Road Conditions**, statewide, phone 1-800-478-7675 or (907) 273-6037.

Visitor Information: Log Cabin Visitor Information Center, operated by the Anchorage Convention and Visitors Bureau, is at 4th Avenue and F Street; open daily, year-round. Hours are 7:30 A.M. to 7 P.M. June through August; 8 A.M. to 6 P.M. in May and September; and 9 A.M. to 4 P.M. the remainder of the year. The cabin offers a wide assortment of free brochures and maps. Mailing address is 1600 A St., Suite 200, Anchorage 99501; phone (907) 274-3531; Internet, http://www.alaska.net/~acvb.;e-mail at acvb@alaska.net. The bureau also operates a year-round visitor information phone with a recorded message of the day's special events and attractions, including films, plays, sports events and gallery openings, and it produces several publications including 2 visitor guides, a restaurant directory, a fall/winter discount book and a monthly calendar of events; phone (907) 276-3200. Additional visitor information centers are open daily at Anchorage International Airport, one on the lower level for passengers arriving on domestic flights; another in the customs-secured area of the International concourse; and a third in the lobby of the International terminal. The North Anchorage Visitor Information Center is located in the Parkgate Bldg., just off the Glenn Highway at 11723 Old Glenn Highway. The Anchorage Convention and Visitors Bureau offers information on community events, phone (907) 276-4118.

The Alaska Public Lands Information Center, 605 W. 4th, in the historic Federal Bldg., has extensive displays and information on outdoor recreation lands in Alaska; phone (907) 271-2737. (See detailed description under Attractions, this section.)

Elevation: 38 to 120 feet/16 to 37m, with terrain nearly flat throughout the bowl area.

Climate: Anchorage has a climate closely resembling that of the Rocky Mountains area. Shielded from excess Pacific moisture by the Kenai Mountains to the south, the city has an annual average of only 15.9 inches of precipitation. Winter snowfall averages about 70 inches per year, with snow on the ground typically from Oct. to April. Anchorage is in a transition zone, between the moderating influence of the Pacific Ocean and the extreme temperatures found in interior Alaska. The average temperature in January (coldest month) is 15°F/-9°C; in July (warmest month), 58°F/14°C. A record 40 days of 70°F/21°C temperatures or higher was set in 1936, according to the National Weather Service. Record high was 85°F/29°C in June of 1969. Record low was

(Continues on page 322)

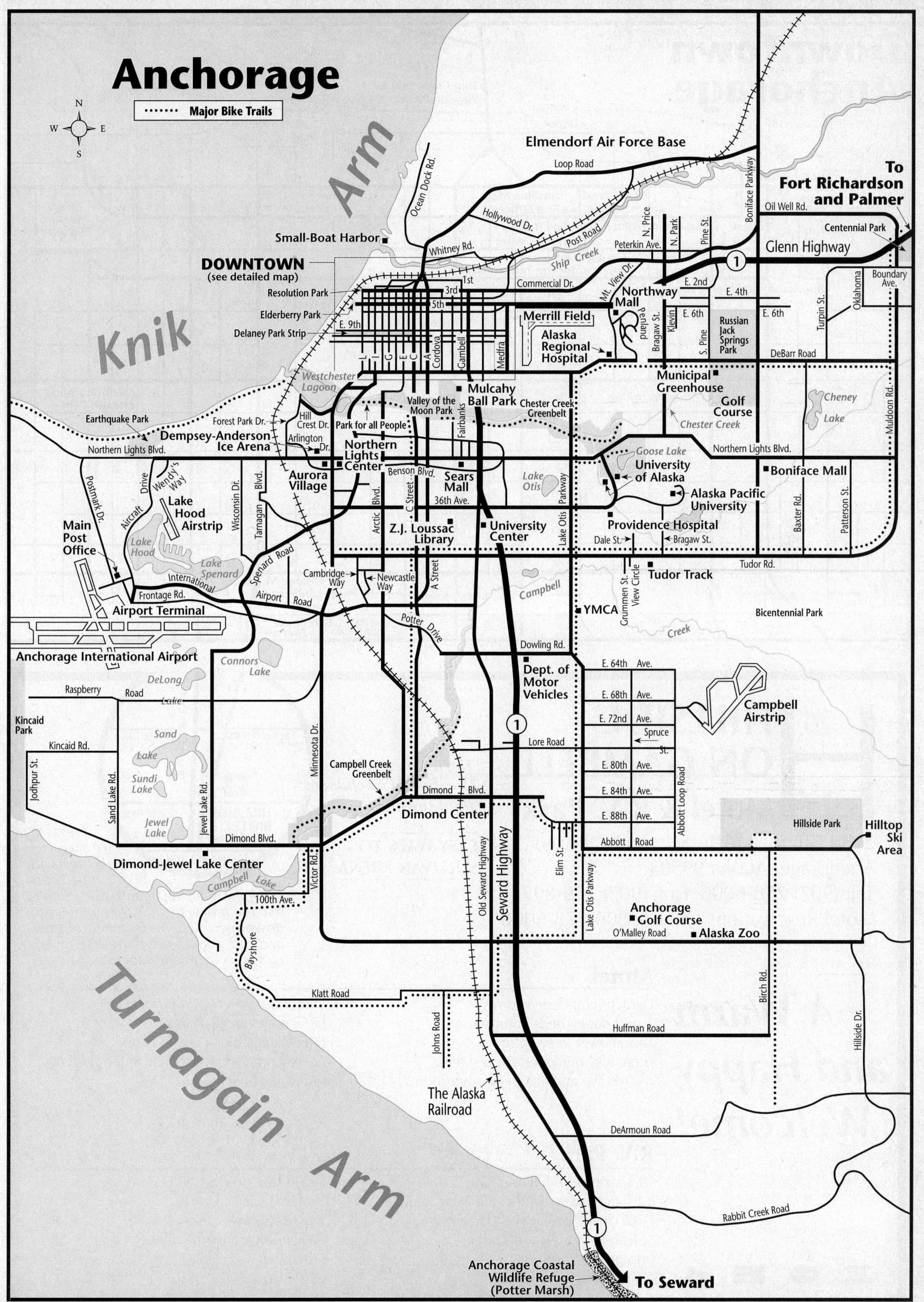
Anchorage
Major Bike Trails
N
S
E
W
Knik
Arm
Turnagain
Arm
Elmendorf Air Force Base
Loop Road
Ocean Dock Rd.
Hollywood Dr.
Small-Boat Harbor
Whitney Rd.
Post Road
Ship Creek
DOWNTOWN
(see detailed map)
Resolution Park
Elderberry Park
Delaney Park Strip
E. 9th
3rd
5th
1st
Commercial Dr.
Merrill Field
Alaska Regional Hospital
Mt. View Dr.
Northway Mall
Peterkin Ave.
N. Price
N. Park
Pine St.
Boniface Parkway
To Fort Richardson and Palmer
Oil Well Rd.
Centennial Park
Glenn Highway
1
E. 2nd
E. 4th
E. 6th
Russian Jack Springs Park
Boundary Ave.
Turpin St.
Oklahoma
DeBarr Road
Muldoon Rd.
Westchester Lagoon
Mulcahy Ball Park
Valley of the Moon Park
Park for all People
Chester Creek Greenbelt
Municipal Greenhouse
Golf Course
Chester Creek
Cheney Lake
Earthquake Park
Forest Park Dr.
Hill Crest Dr.
Dempsey-Anderson Ice Arena
Arlington Dr.
Northern Lights Center
Northern Lights Blvd.
Goose Lake
University of Alaska
Boniface Mall
Alaska Pacific University
Providence Hospital
Postmark Dr.
Aircraft Drive
Wendy's Way
Lake Hood Airstrip
Lake Hood
Lake Spenard
Wisconsin Dr.
Tarnagan Blvd.
Aurora Village
Benson Blvd.
Sears Mall
36th Ave.
Lake Otis
Lake Otis Parkway
Z.J. Loussac Library
University Center
Arctic Blvd.
C Street
Fairbanks
Gambell
Cordova
Medfra
Dale St.
Bragaw St.
Baxter Rd.
Patterson St.
Main Post Office
Spenard Road
International
Frontage Rd.
Airport Terminal
Airport Road
Cambridge Way
Newcastle Way
A Street
Tudor Track
Tudor Rd.
Grummen St.
View Circle
Campbell
Creek
YMCA
Bicentennial Park
Anchorage International Airport
Connors Lake
DeLong Lake
Potter Drive
Dowling Rd.
Dept. of Motor Vehicles
E. 64th Ave.
E. 68th Ave.
E. 72nd Ave.
Campbell Airstrip
Raspberry Road
Kincaid Park
Kincaid Rd.
Sand Lake
Sundi Lake
Jewel Lake
Jodhpur St.
Sand Lake Rd.
Jewel Lake Rd.
Minnesota Dr.
Campbell Creek Greenbelt
Lore Road
Spruce St.
E. 80th Ave.
E. 84th Ave.
E. 88th Ave.
Abbott Loop Road
Abbott Road
Dimond Blvd.
Dimond Center
Hillside Park
Hilltop Ski Area
Dimond-Jewel Lake Center
Campbell Lake
Victor Rd.
100th Ave.
Old Seward Highway
Seward Highway
Elim St.
Lake Otis Parkway
Anchorage Golf Course
O'Malley Road
Alaska Zoo
Bayshore
Klatt Road
Johns Road
Huffman Road
Birch Rd.
Hillside Dr.
The Alaska Railroad
DeArmoun Road
Rabbit Creek Road
Anchorage Coastal Wildlife Refuge (Potter Marsh)
To Seward

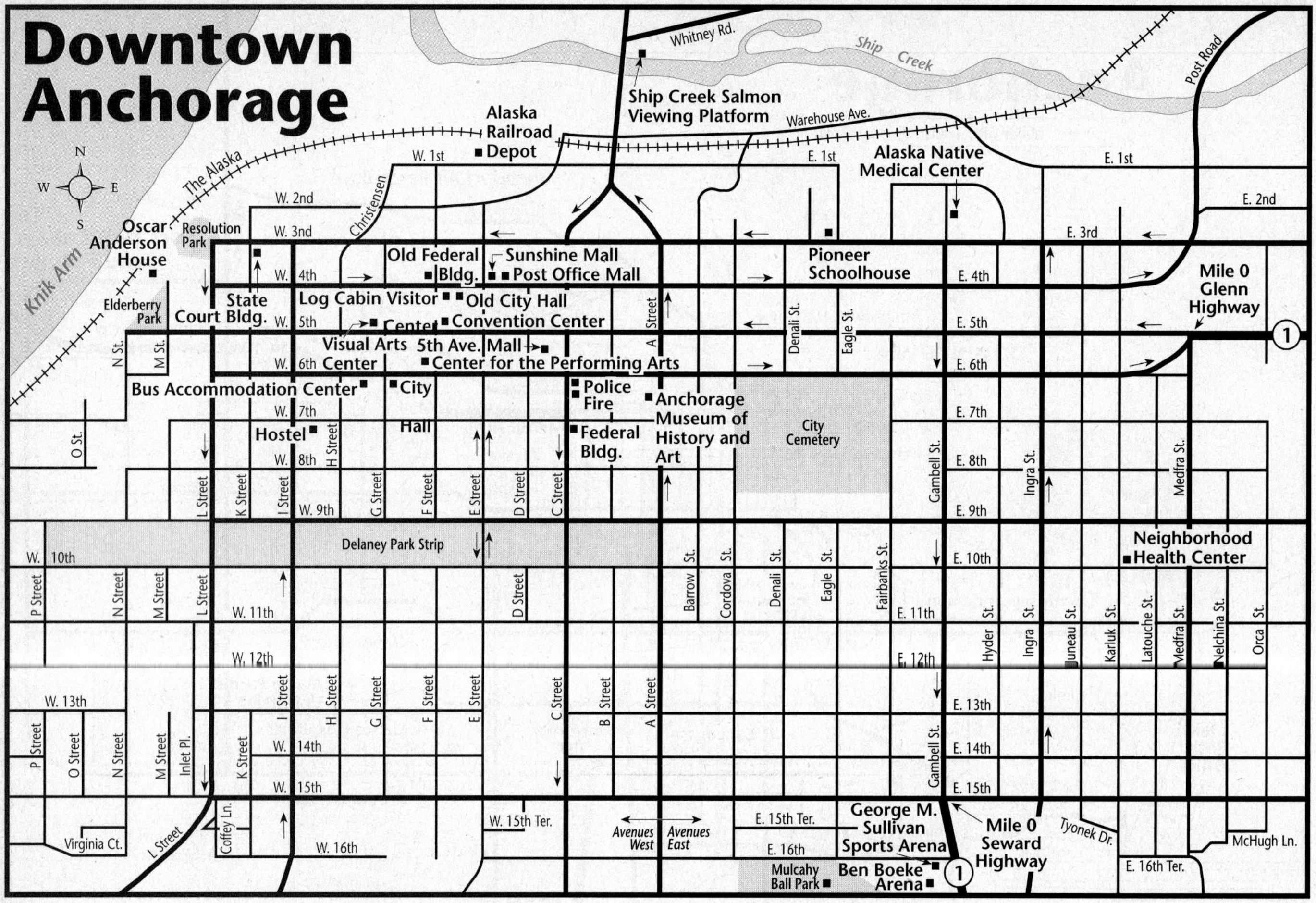

Downtown Anchorage

Ship Creek Salmon Viewing Platform
Alaska Railroad Depot
Alaska Native Medical Center
Oscar Anderson House
Resolution Park
Elderberry Park
State Court Bldg.
Old Federal Bldg.
Sunshine Mall
Post Office Mall
Log Cabin Visitor Center
Old City Hall
Convention Center
Visual Arts Center
5th Ave. Mall
Center for the Performing Arts
Bus Accommodation Center
City Hall
Police
Fire
Federal Bldg.
Anchorage Museum of History and Art
Hostel
Pioneer Schoolhouse
City Cemetery
Mile 0 Glenn Highway
Neighborhood Health Center
Delaney Park Strip
George M. Sullivan Sports Arena
Ben Boeke Arena
Mulcahy Ball Park
Mile 0 Seward Highway
Avenues West
Avenues East

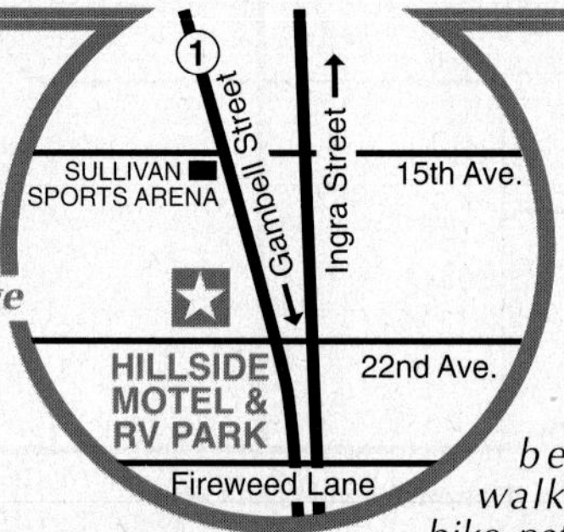

Apone's T-Shirt Cache
BIGGEST and BEST selection of T-SHIRTS
& SWEATSHIRTS in the Universe (we've checked)
436 W 4TH AVE
(4th Ave. & E St)
ANCHORAGE, AK
99501-2364
FREE
Catalogue
1-800-770-1007
PH 907-272-1007
FAX 907-272-1019
Alaska
ALASKA
Alaska
Footprints of the Endangered
ALASKA
Alaska
WAY TO A MAN'S HEART
IS THROUGH HIS FLY
Alaska
ALASKA
NIVERSITY
UNIVERSITY OF ALASKA
AD SUMMUM
1917
I fish
therefore,
I LIE!
Alaska
COUNT THE ANIMALS
LEGENDS LIVE WHERE LEGENDS ROAM
HARLEY-DAVIDSON
ALASKA

(Continued from page 318)

-34°F/-37°C in January 1975. The growing season in the area is 100 to 120 days and typically extends from late May to early Sept. Anchorage has a daily maximum of 19 hours, 21 minutes of daylight in summer, and 5 hours, 28 minutes in winter. Prevailing wind direction is north.

Radio: KENI 550, KHAR 590, KYAK 650, KBYR 700, KFQD 750, KLEF 98.1, KFFR 1020, KKSD 1080, KRUA-FM 88.1, KATB-FM 89.3, KSKA-FM 91.1, KJMM-FM 94.5, KEAG-FM 97.3, KYMG-FM 98.9, KBFX-FM 100.5, KGOT-FM 101.3, KKRD-FM 102.1, KMXS-FM 103.1, KBRJ-FM 104.1, KNIK-FM 105.3, KWHL-FM 106.5, KASH-FM 107.5. **Television:** KTUU (NBC), Channel 2; KTBY (Fox), Channel 4; KYES (independent), Channel 5; KAKM (PBS), Channel 7; KTVA (CBS), Channel 11; KIMO (ABC), Channel 13; and UHF channels. Pay cable television is also available. **Newspapers:** *Anchorage Daily News* (daily); *Alaska Journal of Commerce, Anchorage*

ANCHORAGE ADVERTISERS

Press (weekly); *Chugiak-Eagle River Star* (semi-weekly).

Private Aircraft: Anchorage airports provide facilities and services to accommodate all types of aircraft. Consult the *Alaska Supplement,* the *Anchorage VFR Terminal Area Chart* and *Terminal Alaska Book* for the following airports: Anchorage International, Merrill Field, Campbell airstrip, and Lake Hood seaplane and strip.

HISTORY AND ECONOMY

In 1914 Congress authorized the building of a railroad linking an ocean port with the interior river shipping routes. The anchorage at the mouth of Ship Creek was chosen as the construction camp and headquarters for the Alaskan Engineering Commission. By the summer of 1915 the camp's population, housed mainly in tents, had grown to about 2,000.

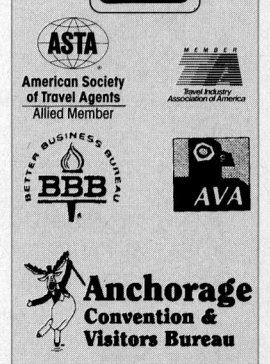

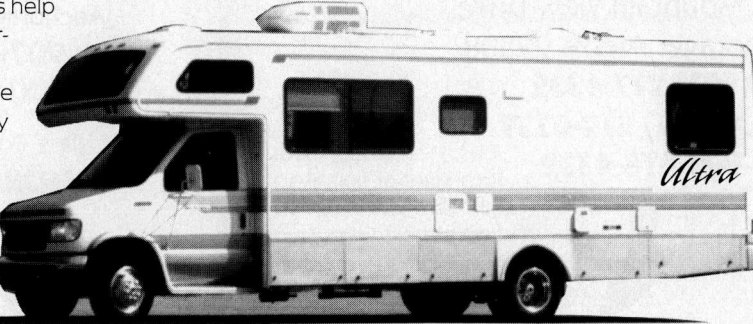

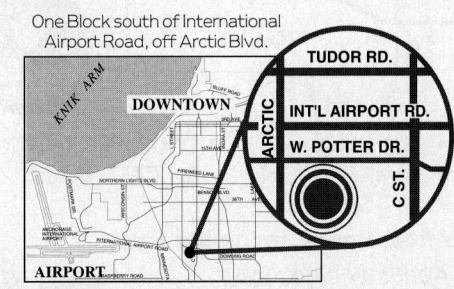

The name Anchorage (earlier names included Woodrow, Ship Creek, Ship Creek Landing and Knik Anchorage) was chosen by the federal government when the first post office opened in May 1915. A few months later the bluff south of the creek was cleared and surveyed, and 655 lots, on 347 acres, were auctioned off by the General Land Office for $148,000. The intersection of 4th Avenue and C Street was regarded as the center of the business district, and by late summer about 100 wooden structures had been built. Anchorage continued to prosper and was incorporated in 1920.

Anchorage's growth has been in spurts, propelled by: (1) construction of the Alaska Railroad and the transfer of its headquarters from Seward to Anchorage in 1917; (2) colonization of the Matanuska Valley, a farming region 45 miles/72 km to the north, in 1935; (3) construction of Fort Richardson and Elmendorf Field in 1940; (4) oil discoveries between 1957 and 1961 in Cook Inlet; and (5) the development of North Slope oil fields and the construction of the trans-Alaska pipeline—all since 1968.

The earthquake of March 27, 1964, which caused millions of dollars in damage, resulted in a flurry of new construction. Government relief funds (in the form of Small Business Administration loans) were offered to those who wished to rebuild. Most did, and a distinctly new Anchorage began to emerge.

In the 1970s and 1980s, Anchorage underwent a population and construction boom tied to oil production. Oil companies located their headquarters in Anchorage. ARCO completed its 21-story office tower in 1983. The decline in oil prices in recent years has brought about a slower economy than was enjoyed in those "boom" years. Today, Anchorage is a center of commerce and distribution for the rest of Alaska.

DESCRIPTION

Anchorage is a sprawling city, bordered on the east by the stunningly beautiful Chugach Mountain Range and on the west by Knik Arm of Cook Inlet. On a clear day, you can catch a tantalizing glimpse of Mount McKinley, 135 miles/217 km to the north.

Many new buildings dot the Anchorage skyline. Millions of dollars were allocated by the legislature for Project 80s, the largest construction program in Anchorage's history. Perhaps best known is the Alaska Center for the Performing Arts, located at the corner of 5th Avenue and F Street. Con-

struction costs on the center grew from an original estimate of $22 million to more than $70 million. Visitors may notice the fences on the center's roof: these had to be added to prevent snow from sliding off the steep pitch of the roof and onto pedestrians below. Other completed projects include the George M. Sullivan Sports Arena, William A. Egan Civic and Convention Center, Z.J. Loussac Public Library, and a major expansion and renovation of the Anchorage Museum of History and Art.

"Whaling Wall" by artist Wyland in downtown Anchorage. (© Michael DeYoung)

With its curious mixture of the old frontier and the jet age, Anchorage is truly a unique place. In profile, the town has:

• About 80 schools, including special education and alternative public programs and a number of privately operated schools, also the University of Alaska, Alaska Pacific University and Alaska Business College.

• More than 200 churches and temples.

• Z.J. Loussac Public Library, plus 4 branch libraries, National Bank of Alaska Heritage Library Museum, Dept. of the Interior's Alaska Resource Library, the Oil Spill Public Information Center, Alaska State Library Services for the Blind and the University of Alaska Library.

• Municipal bus service and 7 taxi services.

• In the arts—**Dance:** Alaska Center for

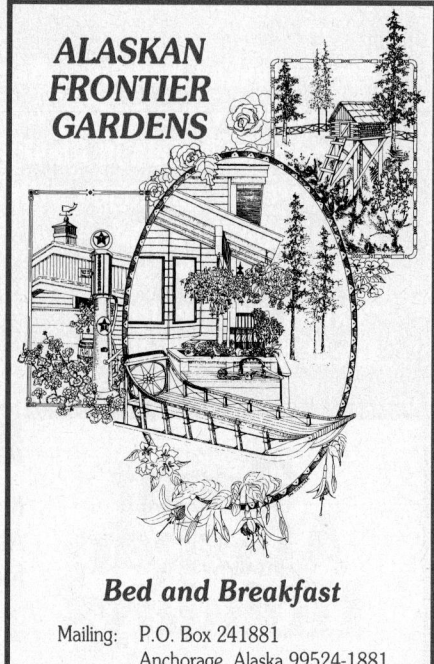

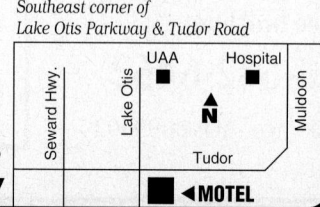

Performing Arts; Alaska Dance Theatre; Anchorage Concert Assoc.; Anchorage Opera; Ballet Alaska. **Music:** Alaska Airlines Autumn Classics; Anchorage Concert Chorus; Anchorage Community Concert Band; Anchorage Concert Assoc.; Anchorage Children's Choir; Anchorage Symphony Orchestra; Anchorage Festival of Music; Sweet Adelines (Cheechako and Sourdough chapters); University of Alaska Anchorage Singers; Young People's Concerts. **Theater:** Out North Theater Company; Alaska Junior Theater; Alaska Theatre of Youth; Anchorage Community Theatre; Alaska Stage Company; Valley Performing Arts; UAA Theatre; Alaska Festival Theatre; Cyrano's Off Center Playhouse. **Art:** About 20 art galleries.

ACCOMMODATIONS/VISITOR SERVICES

There are more than 70 motels and hotels in the Anchorage area with prices for a double room ranging from $50 to $70 and up. Reservations are a must. Bed-and-breakfast accommodations are also available in more than 100 private residences.

Hostelling International–Anchorage is located at 700 H St., 1 block from the People Mover Transit Center in downtown Anchorage. The hostel is open 8 A.M. to noon and 5-12 P.M.; cost for members is $15 per night, nonmembers $18. American Youth Hostel cards available at the hostel or by mail. The hostel is open year-round and has dormitory rooms with bunkbeds, kitchen facilities, common rooms, laundry room and TV room. For information or to make reserva-

tions no less than 1 day in advance with VISA or MasterCard, phone (907) 276-3635, or write for reservations (prepayment required): 700 H St., Anchorage 99501.

Restaurants number more than 600, with many major fast-food chains, formal dining rooms and specialty establishments including Italian, Japanese, Korean, Chinese (Cantonese and Mandarin), Mexican, Polynesian, Greek, German, Sicilian, Thai, soul food, seafood, smorgasbord and vegetarian.

Alaska Sunset Inn Bed & Breakfast. 340 E. 2nd Ct., Anchorage, Alaska 99501. (907) 272-1321, fax (907) 272-0840. Downtown location—beautiful rooms/suites with private baths, continental breakfast. Available: laundry, fax, phones. Open year-round, business or pleasure. [ADVERTISEMENT]

Alaskan Frontier Gardens Bed and Breakfast. Elegant Alaska hillside estate on peaceful scenic three acres by Chugach State Park, 20 minutes from downtown. Spacious luxury suites with big Jacuzzi, sauna, and fireplace, laundry facility. Great for honeymooners. Gourmet breakfast, museum-like environment with Alaskan hospitality and exceptional comfort. Truly Alaska's finest. Year-round service. Credit cards accepted. P.O. Box 241881, Anchorage, AK 99524-1881. (907) 345-6556 or 345-6562. Fax (907) 562-2923. [ADVERTISEMENT]

Arctic Fox Bed & Breakfast Inn. 326 E. 2nd Ct., Anchorage, AK 99501. Phone (907) 272-4818, fax (907) 272-4819. Quiet, convenient, downtown location with beautiful inlet view. Tastefully decorated rooms and corporate suites with moderate summer rates, low winter rates. Near all major downtown hotels, restaurants, museum, bike trail, train station and Ship Creek (salmon fishing). Laundry facilities, private baths, TV and phone in rooms. [ADVERTISEMENT]

Caribou Inn. 501 L Street, Anchorage, AK 99501. Clean, comfortable rooms in an excellent downtown Anchorage location. Shared or private bath, some with kitchenettes. Daily or weekly rates, major credit cards accepted. For reservations or information phone (907) 272-0444 or fax (907) 274-4828. [ADVERTISEMENT]

Glacier Way Bed & Breakfast. 2051 Glacier St., Anchorage, Alaska. Five luxurious rooms, hilltop setting, quiet, close to town. Stay includes: jacuzzi, Habitat, pool, table tennis at no extra charge. Back yard accesses 180 miles of bike trails, ski trails. $65 single, $75 doubles and special rates for off season. Call (907) 337-5201, (907) 277-7148 or Wayne at (907) 279-1994. [ADVERTISEMENT]

Missy's B&B. Private lodging for the business professional. Quiet, clean rooms, private bath. Executive suite. Smoke-free. Private phone. Sourdough pancakes. Cable TV. Laundry facilities. Open year around.

MasterCard, VISA. Located off Northern Lights Boulevard near Providence Hospital. "For Real Alaskan Hospitality." 4919 Wesleyan Dr., Anchorage, AK 99508. Phone/fax (907) 338-4309. [ADVERTISEMENT]

North Country Castle Bed & Breakfast. Luxuriate in our spacious, sunny, warm Victorian home! Relax on any of 4 decks with sparkling mountain and Cook Inlet views. Explore moose trails on our forested acreage or amble down our country road to nearby hiking paths. Only minutes from major Anchorage attractions and the wilds of Alaska. Bounteous breakfasts. Year-round. P.O. Box 111876, Anchorage, AK 99511. (907) 345-7296. [ADVERTISEMENT]

Potter's Inn Bed and Breakfast. 2120 Tudor Hills Court, Anchorage, AK 99507. Perfect for groups of 4–6 travelers seeking peaceful, garden environment. Three-bedroom suite, in elegant midtown residence. Luxury bath with double Jacuzzi, kitchenette, private entrance, video library, phone. Single rooms also. Reservations recommended. Phone (907) 562-5464 or fax (907) 258-6613. [ADVERTISEMENT]

Puffin Inn. Experience comfortable, quality accommodations and exceptional service at reasonable rates. Our friendly Alaskan hospitality includes complimentary coffee, muffin and daily newspaper. Located near Lake Hood floatplane airport with courtesy airport shuttle, non-smoking rooms, cable TV and freezer space for your hunting and fishing needs. Handicap accessible. 4400 Spenard Rd., Anchorage, AK 99517. Phone (907) 243-4044. Fax (907) 248-6853. (800) 4PU-FFIN. [ADVERTISEMENT] ♿

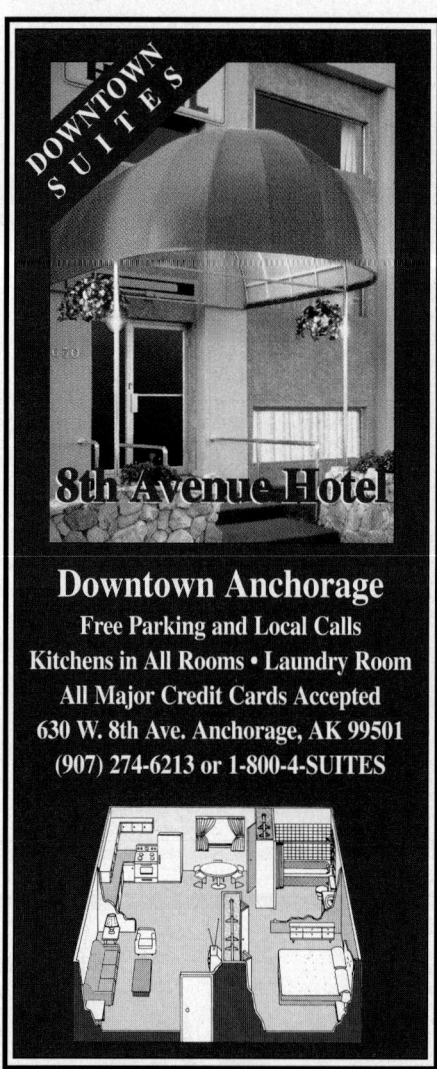

Puffin Place Studios & Suites. Relax and enjoy 1 of our 38 attractively furnished studios and 1-bedroom suites featuring fully equipped kitchens with microwaves. Within walking distance of restaurants, shopping and Tony Knowles Coastal Trail, our amenities include: courtesy airport shuttle, non-smoking rooms, laundry facility, freezer space, cable TV. Weekly and monthly rates offered October–May. 1058 W. 27th, Anchorage, AK 99503 (907) 279-1058. Fax (907) 257-9595. (800) 71-PLACE. [ADVERTISEMENT]

Sharon's Place "An Anchorage B&B." Enjoy a clean, quiet, relaxing stay, surrounded by antique furnishings, with mountain and lake views. Queen bed, private bath, in-room cable TV/VCR, delicious continental breakfast. Seven minutes from airport. For reservations and information, call (907) 243-7374. 2751 Pelican Dr., Anchorage, 99515. [ADVERTISEMENT]

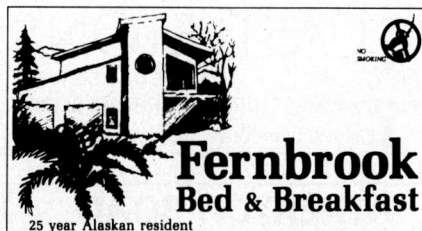

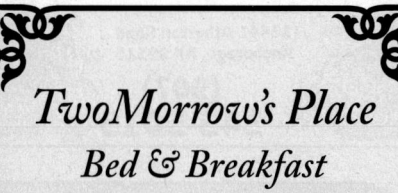

Sixth & B Bed and Breakfast. Prime downtown location on the corner of 6th Avenue and B Street in the middle of downtown Anchorage. Free bicycles at Downtown Bicycle Rental. Casual, comfortable, clean. Breakfast anytime. Flexible check in/check out. Cable TV. Low winter rates: $38-63. Summer rates: $78-105. No bed tax. For informative brochure with photos, write: 145 W. 6th Avenue, Anchorage, AK 99501. [ADVERTISEMENT]

Susie's Lake View Bed & Breakfast. Enjoy the quiet setting overlooking scenic Campbell Lake. Unwind with a leisure tour of our quaint garden setting. The large deck areas offer comfortable privacy for an individual or big enough for a family barbecue. Start or end your day with a steamy hot tub—available 24 hours a day and located where it should be ... outside. Continental or traditional breakfast. Business travelers welcome. Located only 11 minutes from the airport. VISA and MasterCard accepted. 9256 Campbell Terrace, Anchorage, AK 99515. Phone (907) 243-4624. [ADVERTISEMENT]

The Teddy Bear House Bed & Breakfast. Experience a traditional home stay in our uniquely decorated home in a quiet south Anchorage neighborhood, 15 minutes from airport and downtown. Close to Anchorage

- Spectacular view of Alaska Range
- Peaceful accommodations
- Open all year
- Winter aurora viewing
- Smoke free environment
- Private & shared bath
- Business travelers welcome
- Laundry & freezer facilities

6720 Cloudcroft Lane
Anchorage, Alaska 99516
(907) 345-1001

Welcome to the North Country!

CAMPING
Just 5 miles from downtown Anchorage
Close to stores, gas stations and bus stop

CENTENNIAL CAMPER PARK

90 Spaces
Showers • Dump Station
Picnic Tables • 40 Tent Spaces
50-meter Pool 1/2 mile away

Turn south off Glenn Highway onto Muldoon Road, then turn east on Boundary Avenue.

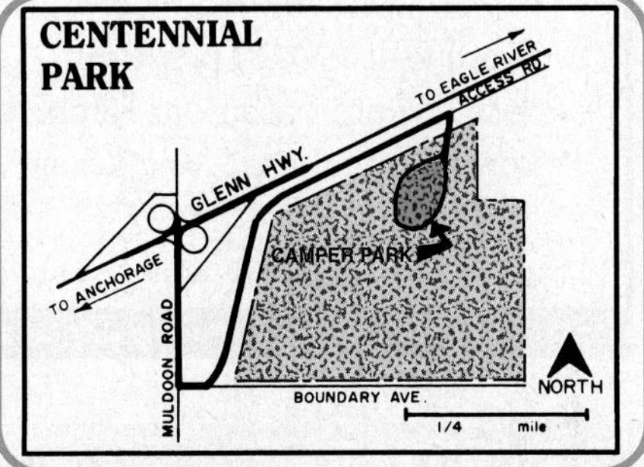

WATCH FOR THE SIGNS!
Parks are open May-September
Phone: 333-9711
"MUNICIPALITY OF ANCHORAGE"

GARDEN BEDS
A BED & BREAKFAST

A Most Charming Place To

Delightful, private suites offering lovely garden walks
Convenient Anchorage location
Telephone • Laundry Facilities

Rebecca Fox-Krogstad
3105 West 29th Avenue
Anchorage, Alaska 99517
(907) 243-8880

Zoo and shopping. Twin or queen beds. Private and shared bath. Continental or traditional breakfast. Large deck for your relaxation. Open year-round. No smoking. P.O. Box 190265, Anchorage, AK 99519 (907) 344-3111. [ADVERTISEMENT]

Anchorage has 2 public campgrounds: Centennial Park, open from May through Sept., and Lions Camper Park, open July and part of August on an as-needed basis. Fees for both are $13 for non-Alaskans and $11 for Alaska residents and seniors holding a Golden Age Pass. To reach Centennial Park, take the Muldoon Road exit south off the Glenn Highway, take the first left onto Boundary, take the next left and follow the signs. Lions Camper Park is located at 5800 Boniface Parkway, half a mile south of the Glenn Highway. Centennial, recommended for large RVs, has 90 RV sites and 40 tent sites. Lions has 50 tent sites. Both feature barracks-type showers, flush toilets, water and dump stations and no hookups. Between May and Sept., phone (907) 333-9711 for details on either park. In the off-season, phone (907) 248-4346.

Chugach State Park has campgrounds located near Anchorage at Bird Creek (Seward Highway), and at Eagle River and Eklutna Lake (Glenn Highway). Anchorage also has several private campgrounds. ▲

TRANSPORTATION

Air: More than a dozen international and domestic air carriers and numerous intrastate airlines serve Anchorage International Airport, located 6.5 miles/10.5 km from downtown. Limousine service to and from major downtown hotels is available. Bus service to downtown is via People Mover (follow signs for city bus from baggage claim area to bus stop).

Ferry: There is no ferry service to Anchorage. The nearest port is Whittier on Prince William Sound, served by Alaska state ferry from Cordova and Valdez. Whittier is accessible by train from either Anchorage or Portage on the Seward Highway. See the Southwestern Ferry Schedules in the MARINE ACCESS ROUTES section for details.

Cruise Ships: See Cruise Ships in the MARINE ACCESS ROUTES section for ships making Anchorage a port of call.

Railroad: The Alaska Railroad offers daily passenger service in summer from Anchorage to Seward and to Fairbanks via Denali National Park (Mount McKinley). In addition, a shuttle train for both foot passengers and vehicles operates daily between Portage and Whittier, connecting with the Alaska Marine Highway to Valdez and Cordova. Winter service is reduced. *NOTE: Rail transportation is NOT available between Anchorage and Portage.*

See the ALASKA RAILROAD section for passenger schedules. For more information, write the railroad at Passenger Services Dept., Box 107500, Anchorage 99510; phone 1-800-544-0552 or (907) 265-2494, fax 265-2323.

The Alaska Railroad depot is located on 1st Avenue, within easy walking distance of downtown.

Town Square Park in downtown Anchorage. (© Michael DeYoung)

Bus: Local service via People Mover, which serves most of the Anchorage bowl from Peters Creek to Oceanview. Fares are $1 for adults, 50¢ for youth 5 to 18, 25¢ for senior citizens and disabled citizens with transit identification. Monthly passes are sold at the Transit Center (6th Avenue and H Street), the Dimond Transit Center and municipal libraries. Day passes are also available for $2.50 at the Transit Center, Dimond Transit Center and 7-11 stores. For bus route information, phone the Rideline at (907) 343-6543.

Taxi: There are 7 taxi companies.

Car and Camper Rentals: There are more than 2 dozen car rental agencies located at the airport and downtown. There are also several RV rental agencies (see advertisements this section).

RV Parking: The Anchorage Parking Authority offers a lot with spaces for oversized vehicles (motorcoaches, campers, large trucks) at 3rd Avenue, north of the Holiday Inn, between A and C streets. Parking is $5 per space, per day. For more information, phone (907) 276-PARK or (800) 770-ACAR.

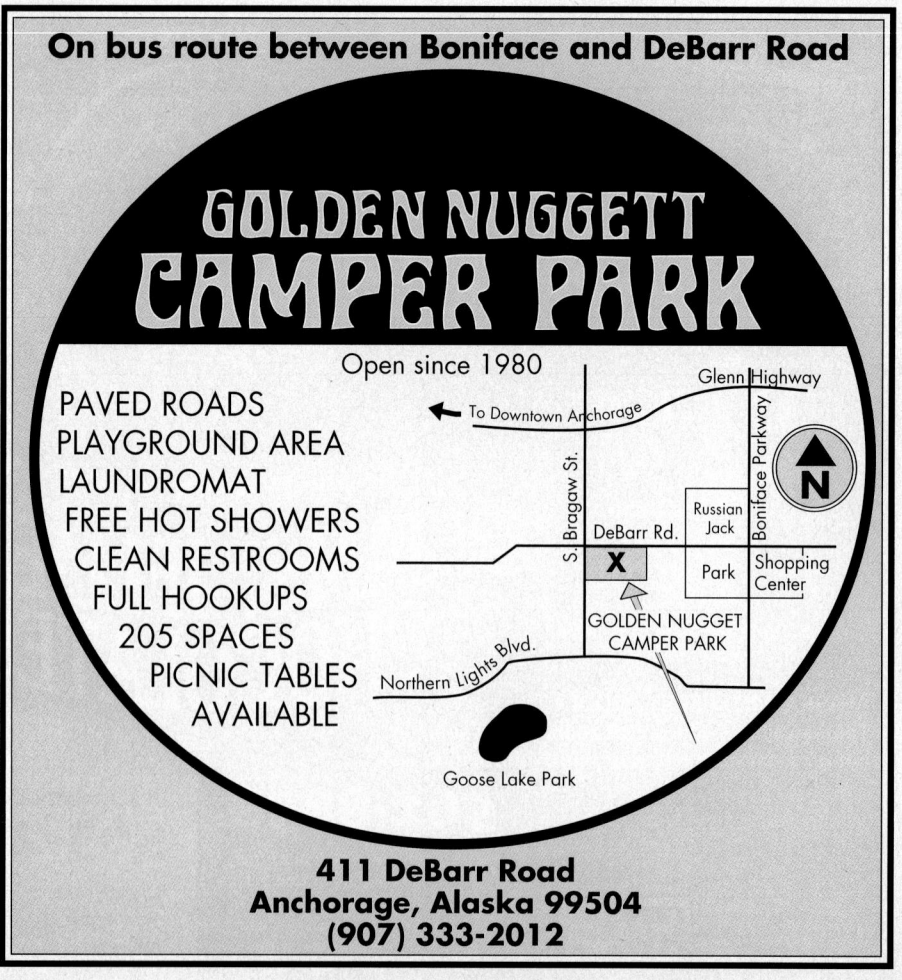

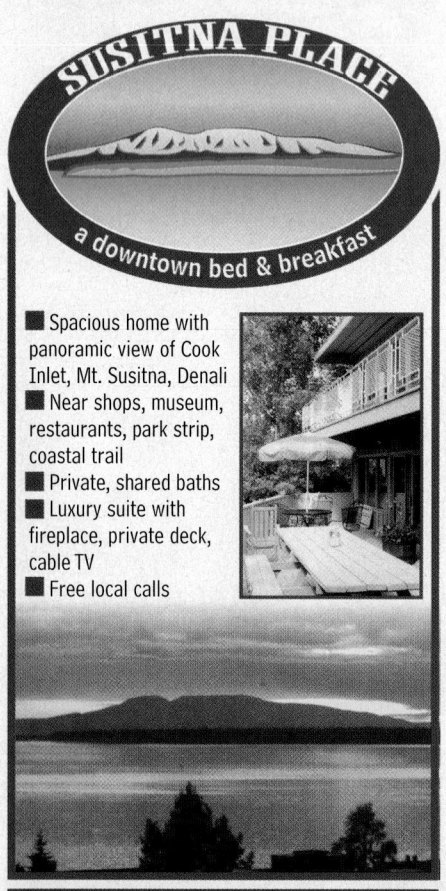

Highway: Anchorage can be reached via the Glenn Highway and the Seward Highway. See GLENN HIGHWAY and SEWARD HIGHWAY sections for details.

ATTRACTIONS

Get Acquainted: Start at the Log Cabin Visitor Information Center at 4th Avenue and F Street, open 7:30 A.M. to 7 P.M. June through August; 8 A.M. to 6 P.M. in May and September; and 9 A.M. to 4 P.M. the remainder of the year; phone (907) 274-3531. Free visitor guidebooks.

Take a Historic Walking Tour: Start at the Log Cabin Visitor Information Center at 4th Avenue and F Street. The Anchorage Convention and Visitors Bureau's *Anchorage Visitors Guide* suggests an excellent downtown walking tour.

Take a Tour: Several tour operators offer local and area sightseeing tours. These range from a 1-hour narrated trolley tour of Anchorage to full-day tours of area attractions such as Portage Glacier and Alyeska Resort. Two-day or longer excursions by motorcoach, rail, ferry and air to nearby attractions such as Prince William Sound or remote areas are also available. Inquire at your hotel, see ads this section, or contact a travel agent.

Anchorage City Trolley Tours. It's fun. It's 1-hour. It's only $10. A lively, informative, 1-hour sightseeing tour of Alaska's

largest city. Located at the historic Fourth Avenue Theatre between F and G streets. Departs hourly. 9 A.M.–5 P.M. The theatre also offers the only dinner show that brings Alaska right to your table for just $19.95. 630 West 4th Avenue #1, Anchorage, Alaska 99501. (907) 257-5603. [ADVERTISEMENT]

The Alaska Public Lands Information Center, located in the historic Federal Bldg.

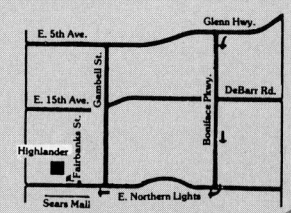

on 4th Avenue and F Street, offers a wide variety of information on all of Alaska's state and federal parks, forests and wildlife refuges. Displays, video programs and computers permit self-help trip-planning. Expert staff provide additional assistance and supply maps, brochures and other aids. Federal passports (Golden Age, Eagle and Access) and state park passes are available. Reservations may be made here (in person or by mail only) for U.S. Forest Service cabins throughout the state. The center is open year-round. Summer hours are 10:30 A.M. to 5:30 P.M. daily; open in winter 9 A.M. to 5:30 P.M. Monday through Friday, closed weekends and holidays. Phone (907) 271-2737 or write the center at 605 W. 4th Ave., Suite 105, Anchorage 99501, for more information.

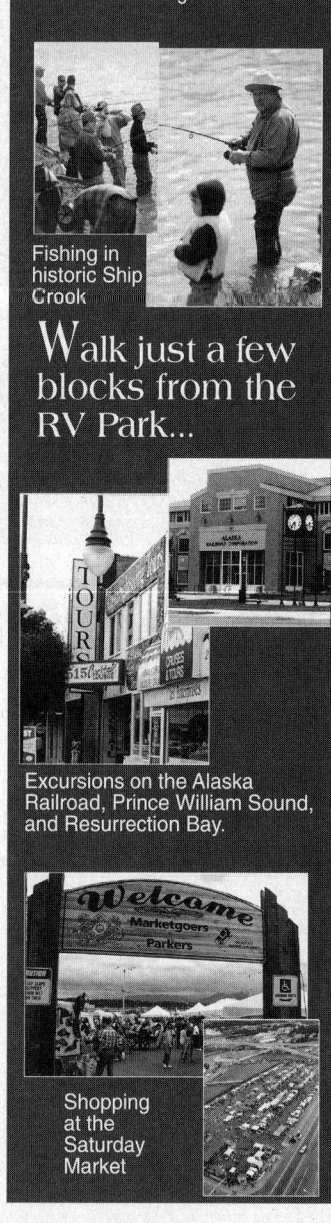

The Anchorage Museum of History and Art, located at 121 W. 7th Ave., is a must stop. One of the most visited attractions in Anchorage, the museum features permanent displays of Alaska's cultural heritage and artifacts from its history. The 15,000-square-foot/1,400-square-meter Alaska Gallery on the second floor is the museum's showcase, presenting Alaska Native cultures—Aleut, Eskimo and Indian—and displays about the Russians, New England whalers, also gold rush, WWII, statehood and Alaska today. Displays include full-scale dwellings and detailed miniature dioramas. The gallery contains some 300 photographs, more than 1,000 artifacts, 33 maps and specially made ship and aircraft models. The main floor of the museum consists of 6 connecting galleries displaying Alaska art, such as works by Sydney Laurence. Also on the 1st floor are a Children's Gallery and 3 temporary

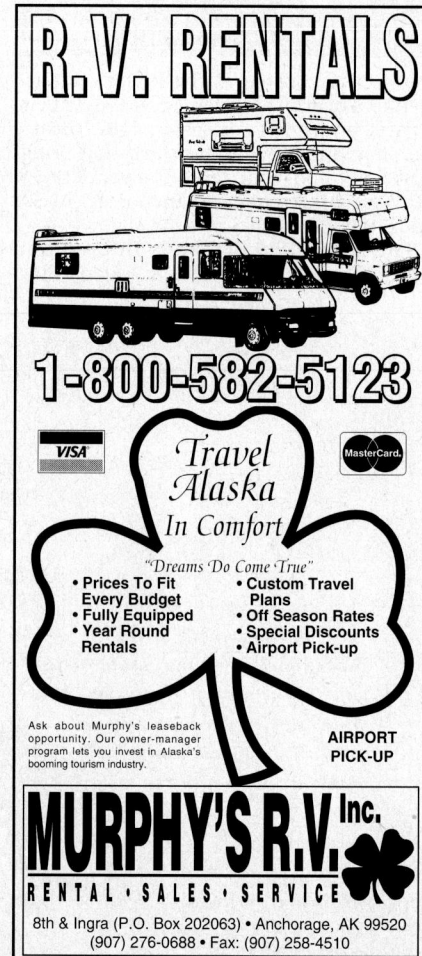

ALASKA RAILROAD

(See maps, pages 361-362 and 472)

The Alaska Railroad operates year-round passenger and freight service between Anchorage and Fairbanks, Portage and Whittier. In summer, passenger service is daily between Anchorage and Fairbanks via Denali Park; Portage and Whittier; and between Anchorage and Seward. Reduced service in winter. For additional information on the Alaska Railroad, write Passenger Services Dept., Box 107500, Anchorage 99510. Phone 1-800-544-0552 or (907) 265-2494; fax 265-2323.

Construction of the railroad began in 1915 under Pres. Woodrow Wilson. On July 15, 1923, Pres. Warren G. Harding drove the golden spike at Nenana, signifying completion of the railroad. The main line extends from Seward to Fairbanks, approximately 470 miles/756 km.

The Alaska Railroad accommodates visitors with disabilities. Six coaches feature wheelchair lifts. Coaches have provisions for occupied wheelchairs, and restrooms are accessible. With advance notice, sign language interpreters are available. ♿

Following are services, schedules and fares available on Alaska Railroad routes. Keep in mind that schedules and fares are subject to change without notice.

ANCHORAGE–DENALI PARK–FAIRBANKS (Express Service)

Passenger service between Anchorage, Denali Park and Fairbanks is offered daily from May 18 to Sept. 18, 1996. The express service operates with a food service car, a vista-dome for all passengers to share, and coaches with comfortable reclining seats. Travel along the 350-mile/1563-km route between Anchorage and Fairbanks is at a leisurely pace with comfortable window seats and good views of the countryside.

Luxury railcars are available on the Anchorage–Denali Park–Fairbanks route through Gray Line of Alaska (Holland America Lines/Westours) and Princess Tours. These tour companies operate (respectively) the *McKinley Explorer* and *Midnight Sun Express.* Both cars, which are coupled onto the end of the regular Alaska Railroad train, are glass-domed and offer gourmet cuisine along with other amenities. Higher priced than the regular Alaska Railroad cars, tickets are sold on a space-available basis. Packages with a Denali Park overnight are also available. Phone Princess Tours at (800) 835-8907, or Gray Line of Alaska at (800) 544-2206 for details.

The summer schedule is: Northbound express trains depart Anchorage at 8:30 A.M., arrive Denali Park at 4 P.M., and arrive Fairbanks at 8:30 P.M. Southbound express trains depart Fairbanks at 8:30 A.M., arrive Denali Park at 12:30 P.M., and arrive Anchorage at 8:30 P.M.

One-way fares are as follows: Anchorage–Denali Park, $96; Fairbanks–Denali Park, $50; Anchorage–Fairbanks, $135. Children aged 2 through 11 ride for approximately half fare, under 2 ride free.

During fall, winter and spring, weekend-only rail service is provided between Anchorage and Fairbanks. The train travels from Anchorage to Fairbanks on Saturday and returns on Sunday.

Reservations: Reservations should be made 40 days prior to travel. Write the Alaska Railroad, Passenger Services Dept., Box 107500, Anchorage 99510; phone 1-800-544-0552 or (907) 265-2623; fax 265-2323. Your letter should include the dates you plan to travel, points of departure and destination, the number of people in your party and your home phone number. Tickets may be purchased in advance by mail if you desire.

Baggage: Each adult is allowed 2 pieces of luggage to a maximum combined weight of 100 lbs. Children are allowed 2 pieces of baggage to a maximum combined weight of 75 lbs. Excess baggage may be checked for a nominal fee. Bicycles are accepted for a charge of $20 per station, on a space-available basis on the day of travel. Keep in mind that baggage, including backpacks, must be checked before boarding, and it is not accessible during the trip. Canoes, motors, motorcycles, items weighing over 150 lbs., etc., are not accepted for transportation on passenger trains. These items are shipped via freight train.

LOCAL SERVICE

Local rural service between Anchorage and Hurricane Gulch operates Thursday, Saturday and Sunday each week between May 18 and Sept. 18, 1996. This 1-day trip takes you past breathtaking views of Mount McKinley into some remote areas and provides an opportunity to meet local residents who use the train for access. Local service uses self-propelled rail diesel cars and has vending-machine snacks available.

PORTAGE–WHITTIER

The Portage–Whittier shuttle train carries passengers and vehicles between Portage on the Seward Highway and Whittier on Prince William Sound. Portage, which has no facilities other than the railroad's vehicle loading ramp, is 47 miles/75 km south of Anchorage at **Milepost S 80.3** on the Seward Highway. Whittier, on Prince William Sound, is port to the Alaska Marine Highway's ferry MV *Bartlett,* which provides passenger and vehicle service to Cordova and Valdez. The Portage–Whittier railway line is 12.4 miles/20 km long, includes 2 tunnels (one 13,090 feet/3,990m long, the other 4,910 feet/1,497m long). Called the Whittier Cutoff, the line was constructed in 1942–43 as a safeguard for the flow of military supplies. It is a 35-minute train ride.

The shuttle makes several round trips daily between Portage and Whittier, from mid-May through mid-Sept., connecting with Alaska Marine Highway ferry sailings and other vessels which operate between Whittier and Valdez. (Remember that ferry tickets are purchased separately from train tickets; see MARINE ACCESS ROUTES section, Southwest Ferry System.)

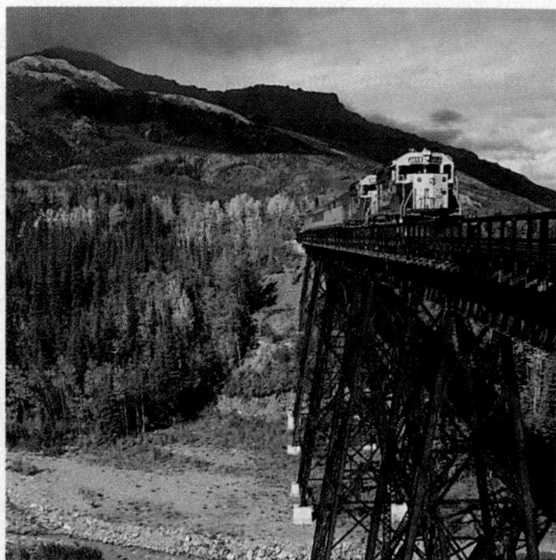

Alaska Railroad train crossing Riley Creek bridge. (© Bruce M. Herman)

Train tickets for the Whittier shuttle may be purchased from ticket sellers at Portage. Reservations are not accepted for the shuttle train, although passengers with confirmed ferry connections are given priority boarding on the 1:20 P.M. shuttle between Portage and Whittier, if vehicles are at Portage by no later than 12:30 P.M. Standard vehicles under 24 feet/7m in length are charged $70, round-trip, between Portage and Whittier; includes driver fare. Other adult passengers in the vehicle are charged $16 round-trip; children (2 through 11 years of age) pay $8 round-trip. Vehicle rates are based upon length. Some height and width restrictions apply.

During fall, winter and spring, service to Whittier is provided on Wednesday, Friday, Saturday and Sunday.

ANCHORAGE–SEWARD

Rail passenger service between Anchorage and Seward operates daily between May 18 and Sept. 2, 1996. (Weekend service to Seward is available May 11-12 and Sept. 7-8 and 14-15.) The 230-mile/370-km excursion follows Turnagain Arm south from Anchorage and passes through some of the most beautiful scenery to be found along the railroad. Travel is aboard classic passenger coaches. Food service is available in the bar/deli car. Departs Anchorage at 6:45 A.M., arrives Seward at 11 A.M. The return trip departs Seward at 6 P.M., arriving Anchorage at 10 P.M. Reservations are required. The round-trip fare is $80 for adults; half fare for children 2 through 11. Overnight tours which include hotel and Resurrection Bay boat excursions are available from the railroad ticket office.

GEORGE PARKS HIGHWAY

Anchorage to Fairbanks, Alaska
Alaska Route 3
(See maps, pages 361–362)

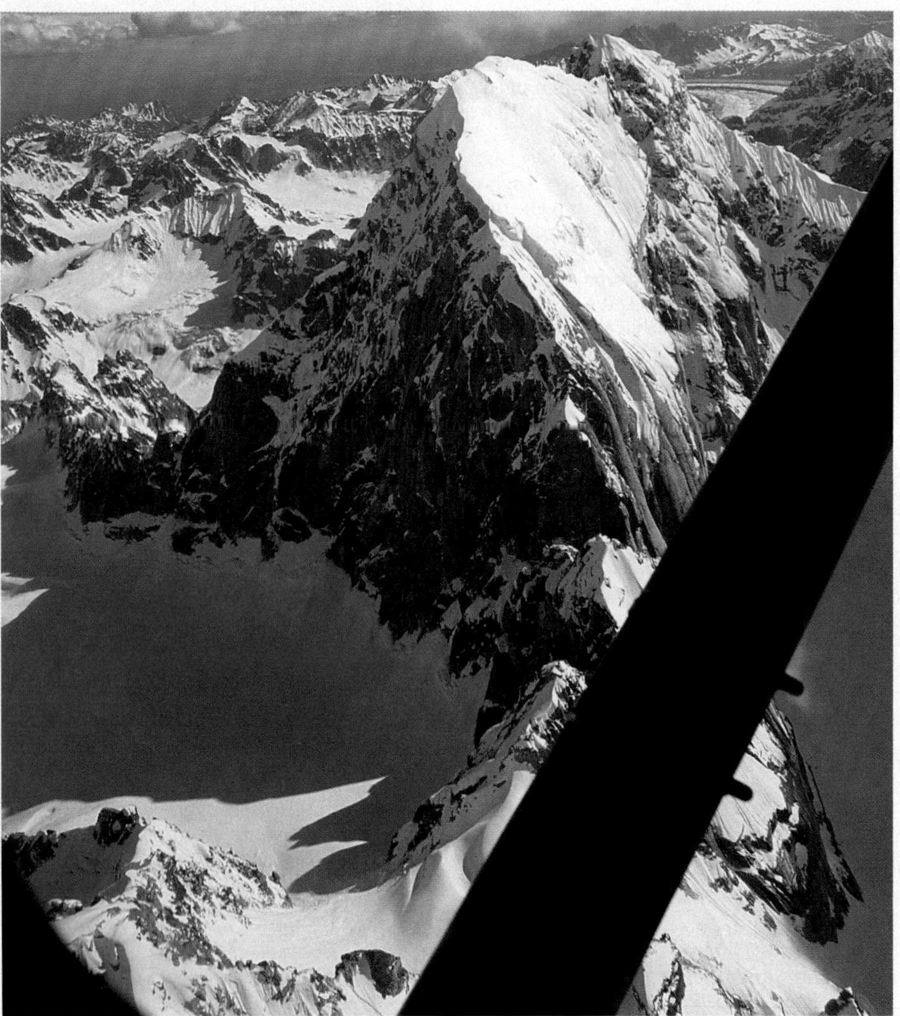

Flightseeing Mount McKinley and the Alaska Range is a popular attraction. Several communities along the George Parks Highway offer these tours.
(© Gene & Judy Wright, Diamond Photo)

The George Parks Highway connects Anchorage and Fairbanks, Alaska's largest population centers. The route, called the Anchorage–Fairbanks Highway after its completion in 1971, was renamed in July 1975, in honor of George A. Parks (1883–1984), the territorial governor from 1925 to 1933.

The highway runs 358 miles/576.1 km through some of the grandest and most rugged land that Alaska has to offer. The road is a modern paved highway, maintained year-round. The highway is mostly in good condition with some pavement breaks and frost heaves.

Motorists who plan to drive the highway during the winter (roughly from Oct. 1 to June 1) should check highway conditions before proceeding. Severe winter storms and extremely low temperatures can create hazardous driving conditions. Contact the Alaska Dept. of Transportation or the Alaska State Troopers in Anchorage or Fairbanks.

Some facilities along the highway north of the Talkeetna turnoff (**Milepost A 98.7**) and south of Nenana (**Milepost A 304.5**) are open in summer only.

From approximately **Milepost A 70** north of Anchorage there are many places where Mount McKinley—also called Denali—(elev. 20,320 feet/6,194m) is visible from the highway, weather permitting.

The George Parks Highway provides the most direct highway access to Denali National Park and Preserve (formerly Mount McKinley National Park) from either Anchorage or Fairbanks. Driving distance to the park entrance is 237.3 miles/381.9 km from Anchorage and 120.7 miles/194.2 km from Fairbanks. See DENALI NATIONAL PARK section for details.

Emergency medical services: Between the Glenn Highway junction and **Milepost A 202.1**, phone 911. Between **Milepost A 174** at Hurricane Gulch bridge and **Milepost A 224** at Carlo Creek bridge, phone the Cantwell ambulance at 768-2982 or the state troopers at 768-2202. Between **Milepost A 224** and Fairbanks, phone 911.

George Parks Highway Log

ALASKA ROUTE 1
Distance from Anchorage (A) is followed by distance from Fairbanks (F).

A 0 F 358 (576.1 km) **ANCHORAGE.** Follow the Glenn Highway (Alaska Route 1) north 35 miles/56.3 km to junction with the George Parks Highway. (Turn to the end of the GLENN HIGHWAY section and read log back to front from Anchorage to junction with the George Parks Highway.)

ALASKA ROUTE 3

A 35 (56.3 km) **F 323** (519.8 km) Traffic light at **junction** of the George Parks Highway (Alaska Route 3) and the Glenn Highway (Alaska Route 1).

A 35.4 (57 km) **F 322.6** (519.2 km) Trunk Road. Turn right, northbound, for Mat–Su College and the University of Alaska Fairbanks' Matanuska Research Farm. The Matanuska Research Farm conducts research in agronomy, horticulture, soil science and animal science. No formal tours are conducted.

A 35.5 (57.1 km) **F 322.5** (519 km) Welcome Way; access to Mat–Su Visitors Center,

GEORGE PARKS HIGHWAY *Anchorage, AK, to Milepost A 169*

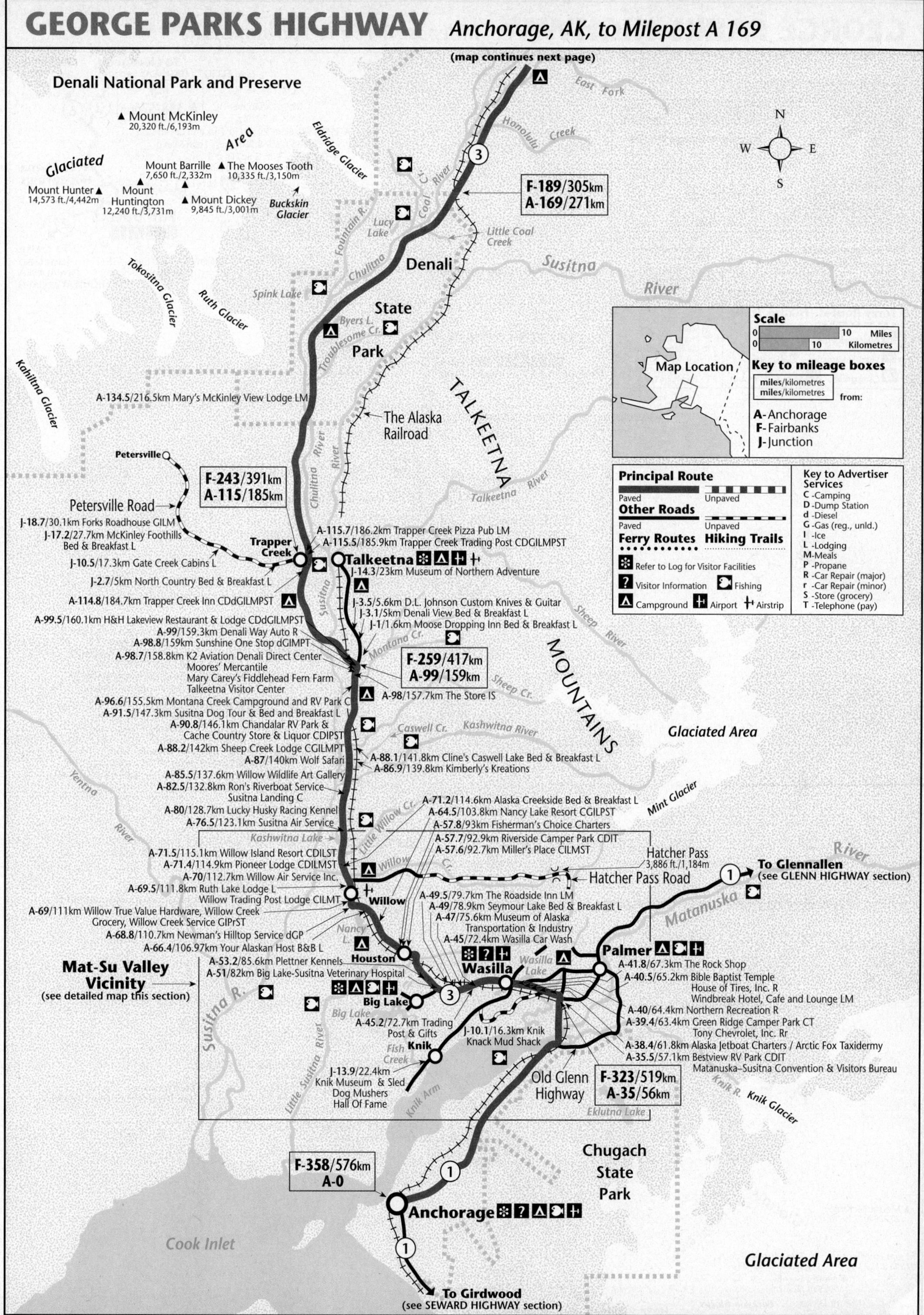

GEORGE PARKS HIGHWAY *Milepost A 169 to Fairbanks, AK*

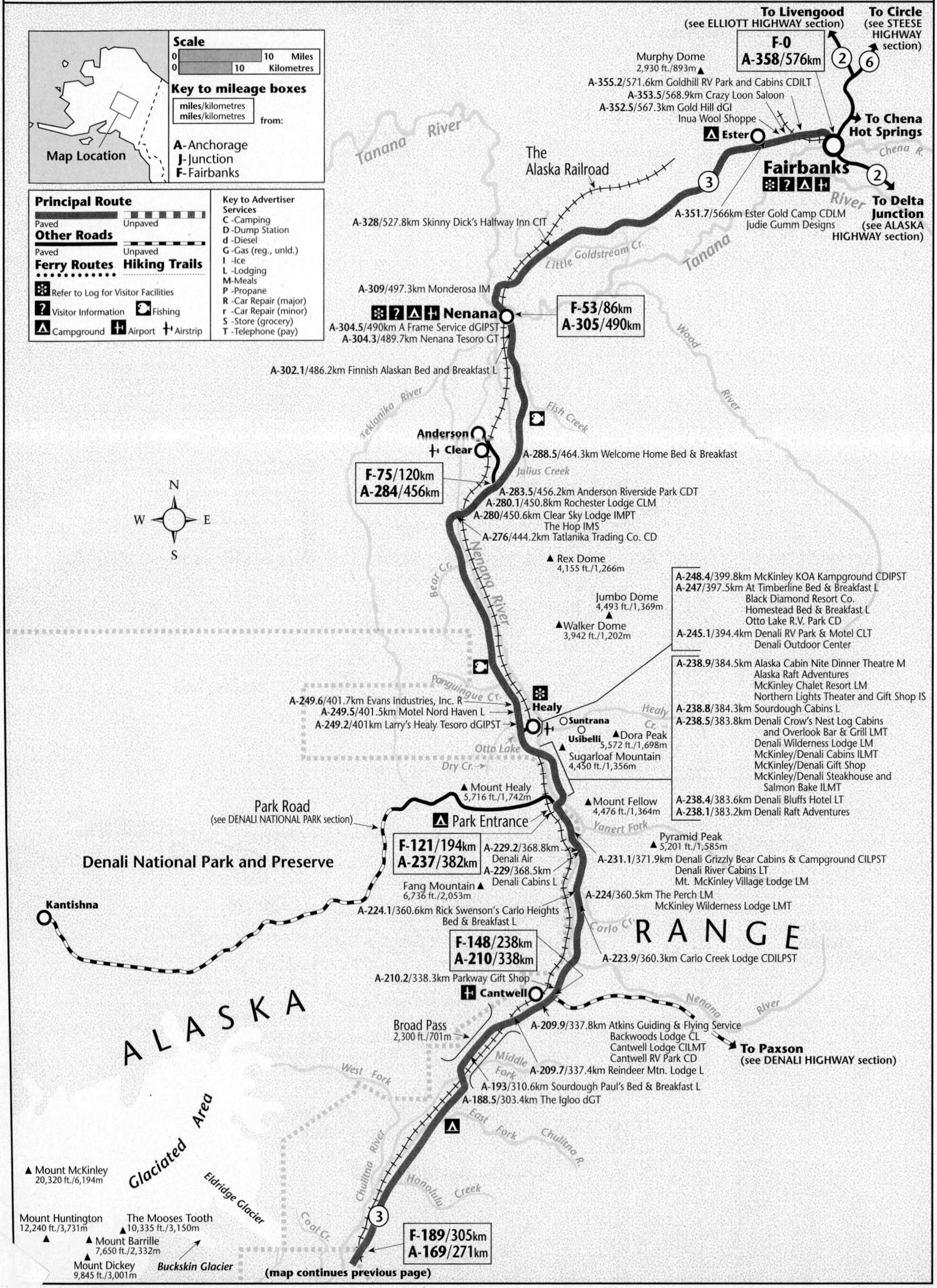

Scale
0 10 Miles
0 10 Kilometres

Map Location

Key to mileage boxes
miles/kilometres
miles/kilometres from:
A-Anchorage
J-Junction
F-Fairbanks

Principal Route
Paved / Unpaved
Other Roads
Paved / Unpaved
Ferry Routes
Hiking Trails
Refer to Log for Visitor Facilities
Visitor Information
Fishing
Campground
Airport
Airstrip

Key to Advertiser Services
C -Camping
D -Dump Station
d -Diesel
G -Gas (reg., unld.)
I -Ice
L -Lodging
M-Meals
P -Propane
R -Car Repair (major)
r -Car Repair (minor)
S -Store (grocery)
T -Telephone (pay)

To Livengood (see ELLIOTT HIGHWAY section)
To Circle (see STEESE HIGHWAY section)
F-0
A-358/576km
Murphy Dome 2,930 ft./893m
A-355.2/571.6km Goldhill RV Park and Cabins CDILT
A-353.5/568.9km Crazy Loon Saloon
A-352.5/567.3km Gold Hill dGI
Inua Wool Shoppe
Ester
To Chena Hot Springs
Fairbanks
Chena R.
To Delta Junction (see ALASKA HIGHWAY section)
A-351.7/566km Ester Gold Camp CDLM
Judie Gumm Designs
Tanana River
The Alaska Railroad
A-328/527.8km Skinny Dick's Halfway Inn CIT
Little Goldstream Cr.
Tanana River
A-309/497.3km Monderosa IM
Nenana
F-53/86km
A-305/490km
A-304.5/490km A Frame Service dGIPST
A-304.3/489.7km Nenana Tesoro GT
A-302.1/486.2km Finnish Alaskan Bed and Breakfast L
Wood River
Teklanika River
Fish Creek
Anderson
Clear
A-288.5/464.3km Welcome Home Bed & Breakfast
Julius Creek
F-75/120km
A-284/456km
A-283.5/456.2km Anderson Riverside Park CDT
A-280.1/450.8km Rochester Lodge CLM
A-280/450.6km Clear Sky Lodge IMPT
The Hop IMS
A-276/444.2km Tatlanika Trading Co. CD
N W E S
Rex Dome 4,155 ft./1,266m
Bear Cr.
Nenana River
Jumbo Dome 4,493 ft./1,369m
Walker Dome 3,942 ft./1,202m
A-248.4/399.8km McKinley KOA Kampground CDIPST
A-247/397.5km At Timberline Bed & Breakfast L
Black Diamond Resort Co.
Homestead Bed & Breakfast L
Otto Lake R.V. Park CD
A-245.1/394.4km Denali RV Park & Motel CLT
Denali Outdoor Center
A-238.9/384.5km Alaska Cabin Nite Dinner Theatre M
Alaska Raft Adventures
McKinley Chalet Resort LM
Northern Lights Theater and Gift Shop IS
A-238.8/384.3km Sourdough Cabins L
A-238.5/383.8km Denali Crow's Nest Log Cabins and Overlook Bar & Grill LMT
Denali Wilderness Lodge LM
McKinley/Denali Cabins ILMT
McKinley/Denali Gift Shop
McKinley/Denali Steakhouse and Salmon Bake ILMT
A-238.4/383.6km Denali Bluffs Hotel LT
A-238.1/383.2km Denali Raft Adventures
Panguingue Cr.
A-249.6/401.7km Evans Industries, Inc. R
A-249.5/401.5km Motel Nord Haven L
A-249.2/401km Larry's Healy Tesoro dGIPST
Healy
Suntrana
Usibelli
Healy Cr.
Dora Peak 5,572 ft./1,698m
Otto Lake
Sugarloaf Mountain 4,450 ft./1,356m
Dry Cr.
Mount Healy 5,716 ft./1,742m
Park Road (see DENALI NATIONAL PARK section)
Park Entrance
Mount Fellow 4,476 ft./1,364m
Yanert Fork
Pyramid Peak 5,201 ft./1,585m
F-121/194km
A-237/382km
A-229.2/368.8km Denali Air
A-229/368.5km Denali Cabins L
A-231.1/371.9km Denali Grizzly Bear Cabins & Campground CILPST
Denali River Cabins LT
Mt. McKinley Village Lodge LM
Denali National Park and Preserve
Fang Mountain 6,736 ft./2,053m
A-224/360.5km The Perch LM
McKinley Wilderness Lodge LMT
Kantishna
A-224.1/360.6km Rick Swenson's Carlo Heights Bed & Breakfast L
Carlo Cr.
RANGE
F-148/238km
A-210/338km
A-223.9/360.3km Carlo Creek Lodge CDILPST
A-210.2/338.3km Parkway Gift Shop
Cantwell
Nenana River
ALASKA
Broad Pass 2,300 ft./701m
A-209.9/337.8km Atkins Guiding & Flying Service
Backwoods Lodge CL
Cantwell Lodge CILMT
Cantwell RV Park CD
To Paxson (see DENALI HIGHWAY section)
Middle Fork
West Fork
A-209.7/337.4km Reindeer Mtn. Lodge L
A-193/310.6km Sourdough Paul's Bed & Breakfast L
A-188.5/303.4km The Igloo dGT
Glaciated Area
East Fork
Chulitna R.
Chulitna River
Mount McKinley 20,320 ft./6,194m
Eldridge Glacier
Honolulu Creek
Mount Huntington 12,240 ft./3,731m
The Mooses Tooth 10,335 ft./3,150m
Mount Barrille 7,650 ft./2,332m
Mount Dickey 9,845 ft./3,001m
Buckskin Glacier
Coal Cr.
F-189/305km
A-169/271km
(map continues previous page)

operated by the Mat–Su Convention & Visitors Bureau. Open May 15 to Sept. 15, 8 A.M. to 6 P.M. daily. This large center offers a wide variety of displays and information on the Mat–Su Valley; pay phone, gift shop. Write HC01, Box 6166J21, Palmer, AK 99645; or phone (907) 746-5000. The visitors bureau also operates a booking and reservation service.

Best View RV Park. See display ad this section. ▲

Matanuska-Susitna Convention & Visitors Bureau. See display ad this section.

A 36.2 (58.3 km) **F 321.8** (517.9 km) Highway narrows to 2 lanes northbound.

A 37.4 (60.2 km) **F 320.6** (515.9 km) Air Road; road to airstrip.

A 37.8 (60.8 km) **F 320.2** (515.3 km) Hyer Road. Wasilla Creek bridge. Turnout.

A 38 (61.2 km) **F 320** (515 km) Fairview Loop Road to west leads 11 miles/17.7 km to connect with Knik Road. Access to Palmer Hay Flats State Game Refuge.

A 38.4 (61.8 km) **F 319.6** (514.3 km) **Alaska Jetboat Charters, Arctic Fox Taxidermy.** Fishing charters, taxidermy shop, Alaska Jetboat Charters (907) 376-4776. Offers guided full-day or half-day fishing trips for king salmon May 25 to July 14. Silver, red, pink and chum salmon July 15 to September. Arctic Fox Taxidermy, a full service taxidermy shop, specializes in Alaskan fish and big game mounts. (907) 376-4776. [ADVERTISEMENT]

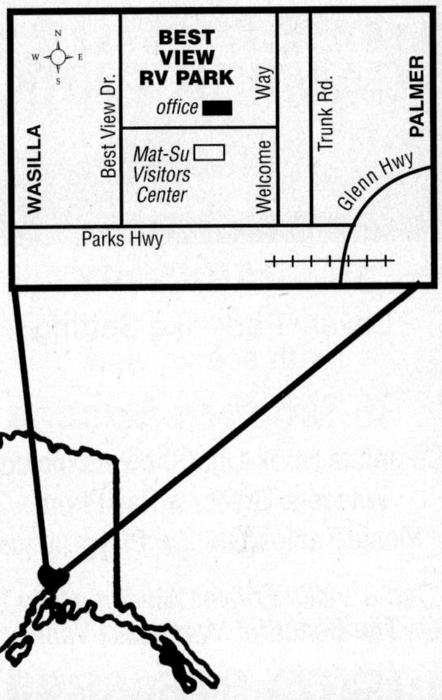

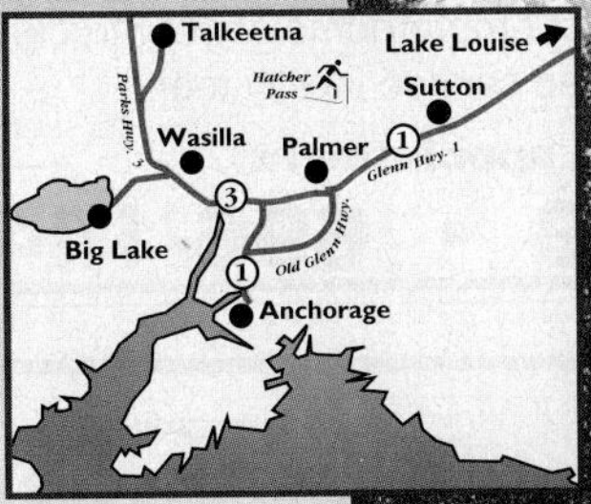

A 39.4 (63.4 km) **F 318.6** (512.7 km) Seward Meridian Road, which junctions with the Palmer–Wasilla Highway, which leads east to Palmer and provides access to Finger Lake State Recreation Site (see **Mile-**

post A 41.1). Shopping center.

Green Ridge Camper Park. See display ad this section. ▲

Tony Chevrolet Inc. See display ad this section.

A **39.5** (63.6 km) F **318.5** (512.6 km) Wasilla city limits; medical clinic (376-1276). Wasilla shopping, services and attractions are located along the highway (from here north to **Milepost A 45**) and at Main Street in Wasilla city center.

A **40** (64.4 km) F **318** (511.8 km) **Northern Recreation.** See display ad this section.

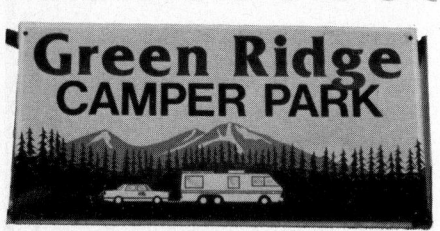

A **40.5** (65.2 km) F **317.5** (511 km) Tire and auto repair, church, hotel, cafe and lounge.

Bible Baptist Temple. See display ad this section.

House of Tires, Inc. See display ad this section.

The Windbreak. See display ad this section.

A **40.9** (65.8 km) F **317.1** (510.3 km) Cottonwood Creek bridge.

A **41.1** (66.1 km) F **316.9** (510 km) **Junction** with Palmer–Wasilla Highway, which leads east 10 miles/16 km to the Glenn Highway at Palmer. It provides access to several businesses, Finger Lake state recreation site and a day-use area with picnic sites and playground.

A **41.7** (67 km) F **316.3** (509 km) Park with picnic shelter, restrooms, playground and swimming beach on Wasilla Lake; limited parking. Monument to George Parks.

A **41.8** (67.3 km) F **316.2** (508.9 km) Crusey Street, access to Bogard Road, a resort with motel and dining, and Finger Lake state recreation site. Turn right (northbound) and drive 3.7 miles/6 km via Crusey Street and Bogard Road to reach Finger Lake. (The recreation site is also accessible from Palmer–Wasilla Highway, or turn east at **Milepost A 42.2** and drive 0.3 mile/0.5 km to intersection of Wasilla–Fishhook and Bogard roads, then follow Bogard Road 4.1 miles/6.6 km to Finger Lake.) Finger Lake has picnic tables, campsites, water, toilets and a boat launch. Camping fee $10. Also access to Wolf Lake state recreation site, off Bogard Road, which has picnic sites, toilets and hiking trail. ▲

A **42** (67.6 km) F **316** (508.5 km) Art gallery and food market.

A **42.1** (67.8 km) F **315.9** (508.4 km) Boundary Street, Lake Lucille Park.

A **42.2** (67.9 km) F **315.8** (508.2 km) Wasilla's Main Street; visitor center and museum 1 block north; post office 2 blocks north (ZIP code 99687). Access to Hatcher Pass and Knik from this intersection. Turn

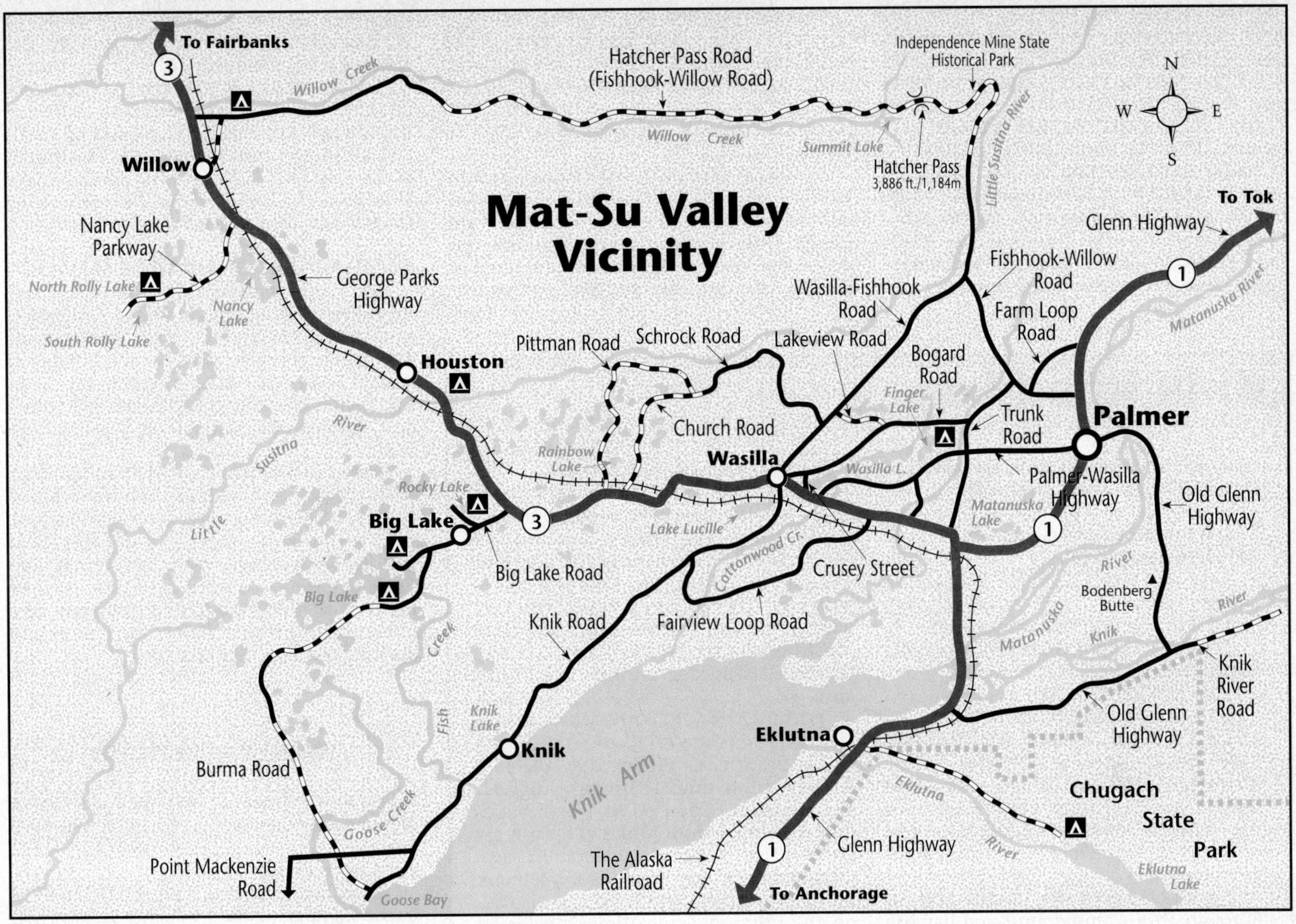

Mat-Su Valley Vicinity

south across railroad tracks for Knik Road to Knik, the "Dog Mushing Center of the World" (see KNIK ROAD log on page 366). Turn north on Wasilla's Main Street for downtown Wasilla and Hatcher Pass. Description of Wasilla follows. ▲

Wasilla–Fishhook Road leads northeast about 10 miles/16 km to junction with the Hatcher Pass (Fishhook–Willow) Road to Independence Mine State Historical Park; turn to the Hatcher Pass side road log in the GLENN HIGHWAY section, page 306, for a description of the road to Hatcher Pass from this junction (J 6.8 in that log). See also the map above. The 49-mile/79-km Hatcher Pass Road junctions with the George Parks Highway at **Milepost A 71.2.**

Wasilla

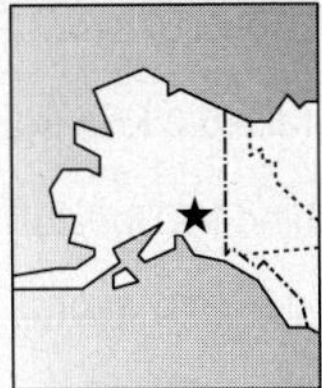

A 42.2 (67.9 km) **F 315.8** (508.2 km). Located between Wasilla and Lucille lakes in the Susitna Valley, about an hour's drive from Anchorage. **Population:** 4,635. **Emergency Services: City Police,** phone (907) 745-2131, emergency only phone 911. **Fire Department** and **Ambulance,** phone (907) 376-5320, emergency only phone 911. **Hospital,** in Palmer. **Doctor** on Seward Meridian Road, **Milepost A 39.5,** phone (907) 376-1276, and at West Valley Medical Center, E. Bogard Road, phone (907) 376-5028. Chiropractic clinics, phone (907) 373-2022.

Visitor Information: At the Dorothy G. Page Museum and Old Wasilla Town Site Park on Main Street just off the George Parks

Highway, phone (907) 373-9071, fax 373-9072. Or contact the chamber of commerce, Box 871826, Wasilla 99687, phone (907) 376-1299. Mat-Su Visitors Center at **Milepost A 35.5**, write Mat-Su Convention & Visitors Bureau, HC 01, Box 6166J21-MP, Palmer, AK 99645; phone (907) 746-5000.

Radio and **Television** via Anchorage stations; KNBZ-FM 99.7. **Newspapers:** *The Valley Sun* (weekly); *The Frontiersman* (semiweekly). **Transportation: Air**–Charter service available. **Railroad**–Alaska Railroad. **Bus**–Matanuska Valley commuter to Anchorage.

Private Aircraft: New Wasilla airstrip, 3 miles/4.8 km southwest; elev. 348 feet/106m; length 3,700 feet/1,128m; gravel; unattended. Wasilla Lake seaplane base, 0.9 mile/1.4 km east; elev. 330 feet/100m. Numerous private airstrips and lakes in vicinity.

Wasilla is one of the Matanuska–Susitna Valley's pioneer communities, supplying mines and farms in the area. Long before the George Parks Highway was built, local residents and visitors bound for Lake Lucille, Wasilla Lake, Big Lake and Knik, drove over the valley roads from Palmer to the village of Wasilla. Wasilla became a station on the Alaska Railroad about 1916.

Today, Wasilla is the largest community on the George Parks Highway between Anchorage and Fairbanks. Shopping malls and businesses here offer a wide assortment of services. *NOTE: There are no banks between Wasilla and Fairbanks, but automatic teller machines are available and noted in the log.*

ACCOMMODATIONS/VISITOR SERVICES

All visitor facilities are available here, including sporting goods stores, post office, gas stations, tire and RV repair, laundromats and other services. Mat–Su Ice Arena, at Bogard Road and Crusey Street, has ice skating, picnic area and fitness court. Swimming and showers are available at Wasilla High School.

Knik Road Log

Distance is measured from the junction (J) with George Parks Highway.

J 0 Junction with George Parks Highway, **Milepost A 42.2.**

J 0.1 (0.2 km) *CAUTION: Road crosses railroad tracks.*

J 0.2 (0.3 km) VFW Post No. 9365.

J 0.7 (1.1 km) Glenwood Avenue, Senior center.

J 1.5 (2.4 km) Gas station.

J 2.1 (3.4 km) Smith ball fields.

J 2.2 (3.5 km) Iditarod Trail Sled Dog Race® headquarters and visitor center; historical displays, films, dogs and musher, souvenir shop. Open 8 A.M. to 5 P.M., daily in summer, weekdays the rest of the year. Adjacent Lake Lucille campground.

J 2.3 (3.7 km) **Lake Lucille** Mat–Su Borough Park Campground and day-use area 0.6 mile/1 km north via gravel road; 64 campsites, pavilion with covered picnic tables, firepits, parking. Camping fee charged. Fishing for landlocked silver salmon. Non-motorized lake access.

J 4.1 (6.6 km) **Junction** with Fairview Loop Road, which joins the Parks Highway at **Milepost A 38**; access to Palmer Hay Flats State Game Refuge. Shopping center with gas and groceries at this junction.

J 7 (11.3 km) Knik fire hall.

J 8 (12.9 km) Settlers Bay, a housing development built around a lodge; golf course and stables.

J 10.1 (16.3 km) Turnoff for Homestead Museum, with a large collection of early Alaskan memorabilia, and gift shop.

Knik Knack Mud Shack. See display ad this section.

J 11.1 (17.9 km) Laurence airport.

J 13 (20.9 km) Knik Kennels.

J 13.3 (21.4 km) **KNIK** on **Knik Lake.** There is a bar here with a pay phone, a liquor store, gas station and private campground. Lake fishing for rainbow; inquire at the Knik Bar. Knik is a checkpoint on the Iditarod Trail Sled Dog Race® route and is often called the "Dog Mushing Center of the World"; many famous Alaskan dog mushers live in this area.

J 13.9 (22.4 km) Knik Museum and Sled Dog Mushers' Hall of Fame, open noon to 5 P.M. Wednesday through Sunday, from June 1 through Aug. 31. The museum is housed in 1 of 2 buildings remaining from Knik's gold rush era (1898–1916). Regional memorabilia, artifacts, archives, dog mushing equipment, mushers' portraits and historical displays on the Iditarod Trail. Admission fee $2 for adults, $1.50 for seniors, free for children under 18. Phone (907) 376-7755, from Sept. through May call 376-2005.

Traditional Athabascan graveyard with fenced graves and spirit houses next to Knik Museum. The gravesite can be observed from the Iditarod Trail.

Knik Museum and Sled Dog Mushers' Hall of Fame. See display ad this section.

J 16.1 (25.9 km) **Fish Creek** bridge; parking, fishing for silver salmon.

J 17.2 (27.7 km) Goose Bay Point Road to Little Susitna River public-use facility at state game refuge (12 miles/19.3 km); 83 parking spaces, 65 campsites, boat ramps, dump station, water, tables, toilets. Also access to Point Mackenzie.

J 18.5 (29.8 km) Pavement ends at small bar beside road. Road continues into rural area.

Return to Milepost A 42.2
George Parks Highway

WASILLA ADVERTISERS

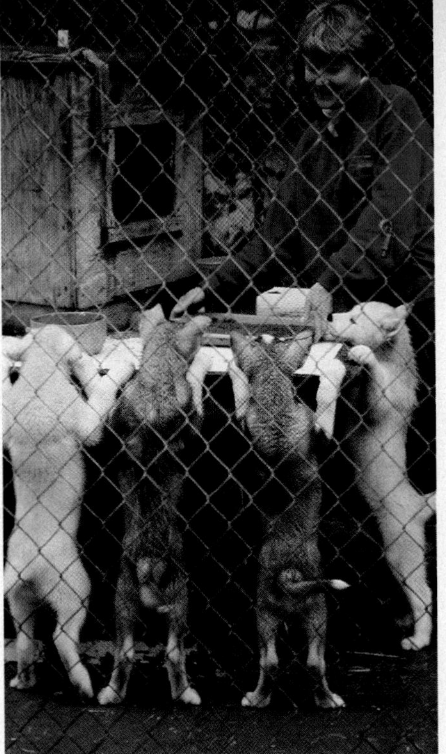

Feeding husky pups at Knik Networking kennels on Knik Road. (© Carmen Scott)

Peak A View Bed and Breakfast uniquely offers a large cozy room, ideal for families or travelers who want all the comforts of home. Two queen-size beds, day bed,

private bath, telephone, microwave, and refrigerator. Enjoy the continental breakfast at your own leisure. Large deck with panoramic mountain view. 5731 Portage Dr., Wasilla, AK 99654. 1-800-776-6259. (907) 376-6259. [ADVERTISEMENT]

St. David's Episcopal Church, phone (907) 373-0625. Sunday morning worship is at 10:30 A.M. We are located at Mile 2.2 Wasilla-Fishhook Road. Turn north on Main Street from the Parks Highway. Go past the post office and bear left on Wasilla-Fishhook Road for 2.2 miles. Come as you are. [ADVERTISEMENT]

Valley Chiropractic Clinic Inc. Phone (907) 373-2022. 24-hour emergency service. Complete modern facility, same day emergency care. Reasonable fees with VISA and MasterCard accepted. We're accustomed to treating travelers' needs. We're located at 400 N. Main St., in Wasilla. Turn north on to Main Street from the Parks Highway and go up 2 blocks on the left, directly across the street from the post office. [ADVERTISEMENT]

ATTRACTIONS

On the town's Main Street, north of the Parks Highway, are the Dorothy G. Page Museum and Visitors Information Center, the library and the post office. The museum is open daily year-round, 10 A.M. to 6 P.M. in summer, 8 A.M. to 5 P.M. in winter; admission fees are $3 adults, $2.50 senior citizens; under 18 years free. Included in the price of admission to the museum is entrance to the Old Wasilla Town Site Park, located behind the museum. Picnic tables and museum shop on site. Local Farmer's Market on Wednesdays in summer. The historical park has 7 renovated buildings from before, during and after Wasilla's pioneer days, including Wasilla's first schoolhouse (built in 1917). Adjacent to the park is the Herning/Teeland Country Store, which is currently under restoration. The log museum building, school, store and nearby railroad depot are on the National Register of Historic Sites.

Wasilla is home to the Iditarod Trail Sled Dog Race® headquarters. The internationally known 1,150-mile Iditarod Trail Sled Dog Race® between Anchorage and Nome takes place in March. The Iditarod headquarters and visitors center is located at Mile 2.2 Knik Road. The center has historical displays on the Iditarod, videos, an Iditarod musher and dog teams, and a gift shop with unique souvenirs. Open daily in summer, weekdays in winter, from 8 A.M. to 5 P.M. Large tours are welcome, phone (907) 376-5155 in advance. Circular drive for buses and motorhomes, camping at adjacent Lake Lucille campground. No fee for museum or film. Fee charged for rides on wheeled dogsled.

Historical displays on Alaskan mushers and sled-dog trails can be found at the Knik Museum at Mile 13.9 Knik Road (see KNIK ROAD log this section). The museum is open from noon to 5 P.M. daily except Monday and Tuesday in summer. Admission fee $2 adults.

Iditarod Days is held in conjunction with the Iditarod Race in March. Other area winter events include ice golf at Mat-Su Resort and ice bowling at Big Lake. Check with the chamber of commerce about summer events.

Bear Air. Air taxi service from Wasilla lakes/airport. Open year-round. Glacier flightseeing, drop-off hunting, fishing, wilderness cabin rental, complete air charter services. Specializing in Knik/Colony Glacier, Mount McKinley, Prince William Sound and Historic Iditarod Trail tours. Experienced pilot with 35 years accident-free flying. Call (907) 373-3373. [ADVERTISEMENT]

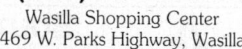

Cheechako: a newcomer, greenhorn or tenderfoot; the opposite of a sourdough or oldtimer.—*ALASKA A TO Z*

Town Square Art Gallery. Fine art and gifts by Alaskan artists, antler baskets, jewelry, pottery. Tremendous selection of art representing the best of Alaskan Mill Pond Press and Greenwich Workshop artists. We gladly pack and ship your purchases. Credit cards, layaways, and phone orders are welcome. Open Monday–Friday 10–6, Saturday 10–5 and seasonally on Sundays 1–5 (summer and Christmas). Carrs Wasilla Mall. 591 E. Parks Hwy #406, Wasilla, AK 99654. (907) 376-0123. [ADVERTISEMENT]

George Parks Highway Log

(continued)

A 42.7 (68.7 km) **F 315.3** (507.4 km) Airport Drive; food and shopping.

A 43.5 (70 km) **F 314.5** (506.1 km) Lucas Road; Hallea Lane access to Lake Lucille.

A 43.9 (70.6 km) **F 314** (505.5 km) Divided highway ends northbound.

A 44.4 (71.4 km) **F 313.6** (504.7 km) Church Road.

A 45 (72.4 km) **F 313** (503.7 km) Wasilla city limits. Shopping and services are located along the highway to **Milepost A 39.5** and at Main Street in Wasilla city center.

Wasilla Car Wash. See display ad on page 370.

A 45.2 (72.7 km) **F 312.8** (503.4 km) **Trading Post & Gifts.** Near bear encounters! Take home bear stories, fish stories, only available here. Capture your Alaskan experience with our camera, photos in 3 minutes. Another option, still pictures from your video. Photos of your Alaskan experience that last forever. All made possible through

our on site taxidermy business, tours available. Enjoy the wildlife display outside but, don't forget inside, you'll find game mounts to view, a large selection of furs, Native handcrafts, jewelry, Alaskan keepsakes. Easy access for motorhomes. Alaskan owned and operated. Open year-round. May–August hours: Monday–Saturday 9 A.M.–8 P.M. Located west of Wasilla on the Parks Highway Frontage Road. (907) 376-1327. [ADVERTISEMENT]

A 46.7 (75.2 km) **F 311.3** (501 km) *CAUTION: Railroad crossing.*

A 47 (75.6 km) **F 311** (500.5 km) Neuser Road. Turnoff for the Museum of Alaska Transportation and Industry, open 10 A.M. to 6 P.M. daily in summer, and 9 A.M. to 5 P.M. Tuesday–Saturday in winter. The museum features historic aircraft, railroad equipment, old farm machinery and heavy equipment. Steam train rides on selected Saturdays. Admission fees in summer are $5 adults, $7 families. Group tours by arrangement.

Museum of Alaska Transportation & Industry. See display ad this section.

A 48.8 (78.5 km) **F 309.2** (497.6 km) Turnoff on Pittman Road to Rainbow Lake. Medical center, convenience store, gas station, cafe and Meadow Lakes post office.

A 49 (78.9 km) **F 309** (497.3 km) **Seymour Lake Bed & Breakfast.** See display ad this section.

A 49.5 (79.7 km) **F 308.5** (496.5 km) **The Roadside Inn.** See display ad this section.

A 50.1 (80.6 km) **F 307.9** (495.5 km) **Blodgett Lake Bed and Breakfast.** See display ad this section.

A 51 (82 km) **F 307** (494 km) **Big Lake–Susitna Veterinary Hospital.** See display ad this section.

A 52.3 (84.2 km) **F 305.7** (492 km) **Junction** with Big Lake Road. Meadowood shopping mall located here with a service station, hardware store, automatic teller machine, grocery and emergency phone (dial 911). See BIG LAKE ROAD log page this section.

A 53.2 (85.6 km) **F 304.8** (490.5 km) **Plettner Kennels.** A full service Iditarod sled dog training facility. Year-round sled dog rides, guided kennel tours, play with puppies, learn to mush dogs, dog team boarding, sales and leases, sled shop, and mushers newspaper. RV, tour bus, and handicapped accessible. P.O. Box 878586, Wasilla, AK 99687-8586; (907) 892-6944. [ADVERTISEMENT]

A 53.3 (85.8 km) **F 304.7** (490.4 km) Houston High School and Wasilla Senior Center. Turnout to west with map and information sign.

A 56.1 (90.3 km) **F 301.9** (485.8 km) Miller's Reach Road.

A 56.4 (90.8 km) **F 301.6** (485.4 km) *CAUTION: Railroad crossing.*

A 57.1 (91.9 km) **F 300.9** (484.2 km) Bridge over the Little Susitna River; turnouts either side. This river heads at Mint Glacier in the Talkeetna Mountains to the northeast and flows 110 miles/177 km into Upper Cook Inlet.

A 57.3 (92.4 km) **F 300.7** (483.9 km) Turnoff to Houston city-operated Little Susitna River Campground. Large, well-maintained campground with 86 sites (many wide, level gravel sites); camping fee, water, restrooms, covered picnic area, 10-day limit. Off-road parking lot near river with access to river. Follow signs to camping and river. Day-use area with water and toilets west side of highway.

The **Little Susitna River** has a tremendous king salmon run and one of the largest silver salmon runs in southcentral Alaska. Kings to 30 lbs. enter the river in late May and June, use large red spinners or salmon eggs. Silvers to 15 lbs., come in late July and Aug., with the biggest run in Aug., use small weighted spoons or fresh salmon roe. No bait is allowed and artificials are required during the early weeks of the fishery in the first part of Aug. Also red salmon to 10 lbs., in mid-July, use coho flies or salmon eggs. Charter boats nearby.

A 57.5 (92.5 km) **F 300.5** (483.6 km) **HOUSTON** (pop. 956) has a grocery store, restaurant (open daily), laundromat, gift shop, inn with food, lodging and pay phone, a campground and gas station. Post office located in the grocery store. Fishing charter operators and marine service are located here. Emergency phone at Houston fire station.

Homesteaded in the 1950s, incorporated as a city in 1966. Houston is a popular fishing center for anglers on the Little Susitna River.

A 57.6 (92.7 km) **F 300.4** (483.4 km) **Miller's Place.** Don't miss this stop! Groceries, post office, laundry, RV parking, cabin rentals, tenting on riverbank. Gift shop, fishing tackle and licenses, fresh salmon eggs. Ice, sporting goods sales and rental, pay phone. Fishing charters available; full day only $45. Probably the best soft ice cream and hamburgers in Alaska. Clean restrooms. Visitor information experts. Family-run Christian business. Gary and Debbie Miller. (907) 892-6129. [ADVERTISEMENT]

(Continues on page 372)

Big Lake Road Log

The 6.5-mile/10.5-km Big Lake Road leads south from the George Parks Highway junction at **Milepost A 52.3** to **BIG LAKE** (pop. 2,333), a recreation area with swimming, camping, boating, fishing, jet skiing and tour boat rides in summer. Wintersports include snowmachining. Businesses are found along Big Lake Road and along North Shore Drive, which forks off Big Lake Road at Mile J 3.6. **Distance is measured from the junction (J) with the George Parks Highway.**

J 0 Junction with George Parks Highway. Meadowood Mall and gas station; automatic teller machine.

J 3.4 (5.5 km) Beaver Lake Road turnoff. Lions Club dump station at gas station located at intersection. Turn right here for public and private campgrounds. Drive 0.5 mile/0.8 km on Beaver Lake Road (gravel) for Rocky Lake state recreation site; 10 campsites, $10 nightly fee or annual pass, toilets, firepits, water and boat launch. ▲

J 3.6 (5.8 km) Fisher's Y; gas station and Big Lake post office (ZIP code 99652). Big Lake Road forks here: Go straight ahead for North Shore Drive (description follows); keep to left for south Big Lake Road businesses and Big Lake South state recreation site (continue with this log).

North Shore Drive provides access to Klondike Inn and restaurant (1.4 miles/2.3 km) and Big Lake North state recreation site (1.6 miles/2.6 km), which has parking for 120 vehicles, overnight RV parking, tent sites, $10 nightly fee per vehicle or annual pass, covered picnic tables, water, toilets, dumpsters, boat launch ($5 fee) and sandy beach. Day-use parking $2. ▲

Big Lake Houseboat Rental. Watch the sunset in a secluded cove or cruise 53 miles of scenic shoreline aboard a comfortable, easy to handle houseboat. Fully equipped galley, bath, shower. Models to

accommodate 2 to 6 persons. Jet skis and fishing gear available. Anchorage transportation arranged. VISA/MasterCard. 1-800-770-9187, (907) 892-9187. [ADVERTISEMENT]

J 3.7 (6 km) Shopping mall.

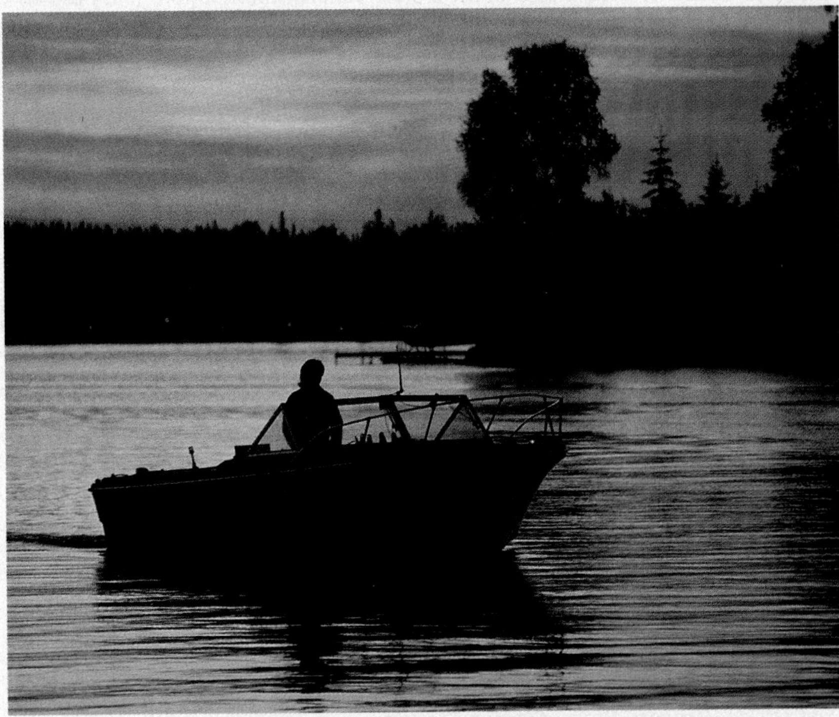

Boating at sunset—which is about 11 P.M. in summer—on Big Lake.
(Jerrianne Lowther, staff)

J 3.9 (6.3 km) Big Lake fire station.

J 4 (6.4 km) East Lake Mall; visitor information center, restaurant and grocery.

J 4.7 (7.6 km) Aero Drive and Big Lake airport. Big Lake is a 15-minute flight from Anchorage.

Private Aircraft: 1 mile/1.6 km southeast; elev. 150 feet/46m; length 2,400 feet/732m; gravel; fuel 100LL.

J 5 (8 km) Big Lake Motel. Bridge over Fish Creek. Fish Creek park picnic area; fish weir with salmon spawning view area. Fishing prohibited.

J 5.1 (8.2 km) Private RV park. ▲

J 5.2 (8.4 km) Big Lake South state recreation site; 13 campsites, 6 picnic sites, toilets, water, dumpsters, boat ramp ($5 fee). Camping fee $10/night per vehicle or annual pass. Day-use fee $2. ▲

J 5.3 (8.5 km) Double-ended turnout with picnic tables and water.

J 5.7 (9.2 km) Gravel turnout, Echo Lake Road. Dog mushers' race track.

J 6.5 (10.5 km) Pavement ends. Burma Road continues into rural area, providing access to the former Point MacKenzie dairy project and Little Susitna River public-use facility at state game refuge (also accessible via Knik Road); parking, camping, boat ramps.

Big Lake is connected with smaller lakes by dredged waterways. It is possible to boat for several miles in the complex. Fish in Big Lake include lake trout, Dolly Varden, rainbow, red and coho salmon, and burbot.

Return to Milepost A 52.3
George Parks Highway

BIG LAKE ADVERTISERS

(Continued from page 370)

A 57.7 (92.9 km) F **300.3** (483.3 km) **Riverside Camper Park.** See display ad this section. ▲

A 57.8 (93 km) F 300.2 (483.1 km) **Fisherman's Choice Charters.** Guided trips on the Little Susitna and Talkeetna Rivers. Trophy kings, silvers, reds, rainbow trout, Dolly Varden. Drop-offs available. May through September. We furnish the highest quality equipment available. 20 years experience. Free overnight parking with water and electric hookups for our fishing clients. Reservations, information: (907) 892-8707. Raymond Blodgett, Box 940276, Houston, AK 99694. See display ad. [ADVERTISEMENT]

A **64.5** (103.8 km) F **293.5** (472.3 km) **Nancy Lake Resort.** See display ad this section.

A **66.4** (106.9 km) F **291.6** (469.3 km) **Your Alaskan Host B&B.** See display ad this section.

A **66.7** (107.3 km) F **291.3** (468.8 km) Highway crosses Alaska Railroad tracks. Turnoff (not well marked) for Nancy Lake state recreation site; 30 campsites, 30 picnic sites, toilets, boat launch, horseshoe pits. Camping fee $10/night or annual pass. ▲

A **67.2** (108.1 km) F **290.8** (468 km) Wide gravel road into Nancy Lake Recreation Area in the mixed birch and spruce forest of the Susitna River valley (good mushroom hunting area). At Mile 2.5/4 km on the access road there is a well-marked nature trail, toilets and parking area. At Mile 4.7/7.6 km there is a canoe launch, toilet and parking area. At Mile 5.7/9.2 km a hiking trail leads 3 miles/4.8 km to Chicken Lake, 5.5 miles/8.9 km to Red Shirt Lake. At Mile 6.2/10 km is South Rolly Lake overlook (day use only) with barbecues, 11 picnic tables, litter barrels and toilets. There are 106 campsites at South Rolly Lake Campground, at Mile 6.6/10.6 km, with firepits, toilets, water, canoe rentals and boat launch; firewood sometimes is provided. Camping fee $10/night or annual pass. ▲

South Rolly Lake, small population of rainbow, 12 to 14 inches.

A **68.8** (110.7 km) F **289.2** (465.4 km) Miner's Last Stand Museum of Hatcher Pass, gas, diesel and gift shop.

Newman's Hilltop Service. See display ad this section.

A **69** (111 km) F **289** (465.1 km) **WILLOW** (pop. 368). Visitor facilities include 2 gas stations, grocery, hardware and notions store, air taxi service, lodges, RV parks, video rental and restaurants. The Willow civic organization sponsors an annual Winter Carnival in January.

Willow extends about 2.5 miles/4 km north along the George Parks Highway. The community is also a stop on the Alaska Railroad. Willow had its start about 1897, when gold was discovered in the area. In the early 1940s, mining in the nearby Talkeetna Mountains slacked off, leaving Willow a virtual ghost town. The community made a comeback upon completion of the Parks Highway in 1972.

In 1976, Alaska voters selected the Willow area for their new capital site. However, funding for the capital move from Juneau to Willow was defeated in the November 1982 election.

Willow True Value Hardware, Willow Creek Grocery and **Willow Creek Service.** See display ad this section.

A 69.2 (111.4 km) **F 288.8** (464.8 km) Long Lake Road. Alternate access to Deshka Landing Cafe.

A 69.5 (111.8 km) **288.5** (464.3 km) Short road to Willow post office, lodge, trading post with cabins and camper spaces, and Alaska Railroad depot. ▲

Ruth Lake Lodge. See display ad this section.

Willow Trading Post Lodge. See display ad this section. ▲

A 69.6 (112 km) **F 288.4** (464.1 km) Willow elementary school.

A 69.7 (112.2 km) **F 288.3** (464 km) Willow Community Center, open daily, has a large parking area, commercial kitchen, showers, covered picnic pavilion, grills, ball court, boat launch and pay phone. (Available for rent to groups, 500-person capacity; phone 907/495-6633.) Willow library.

A 69.9 (112.5 km) **F 288.1** (463.6 km) Fire station.

A 70 (112.7 km) **F 288** (463.5 km) **Private Aircraft:** Willow airport; elev. 220 feet/67m; length 4,200 feet/1,280m; gravel; fuel 100LL.

A 70 (112.7 km) **F 288** (463.5 km) **Willow Air Service Inc.** See display ad this section.

A 70.8 (113.9 km) **F 287.2** (462.2 km) Willow Creek Parkway (**Susitna River** access road) to Willow Creek state recreation area (4 miles/6.4 km); camping $10/night, parking, litter barrels, trail to mouth of creek. Access to Deshka Landing boat launch. Fishing for king and silver salmon, rainbow trout. ▲

A 71 (114.3 km) **F 287** (461.9 km) Willow DOT/PF highway maintenance station.

A 71.2 (114.6 km) **F 286.8** (461.5 km) **Junction** with Hatcher Pass (Fishhook–Willow) Road. This road leads east and south across Hatcher Pass 49 miles/79 km to junction with the Glenn Highway. Independence Mine State Historical Park is 31.8 miles/51.2 km from here. Turn to the Hatcher Pass side road in the GLENN HIGHWAY section, page 306, for log of this road. (Parks Highway travelers should read that log back to front.) See also the Mat–Su Valley Vicinity map page 365. Hatcher Pass Road is mostly gravel with some steep, narrow, winding sections.

Access to Willow Creek state recreation area via Hatcher Pass Road. Deception Creek main campground, with 17 campsites, is located 1.2 miles/1.9 km from this junction via Hatcher Pass Road. Additional campsites and a picnic area are located 0.8 mile/1.3 km east. Both sites have tables, firepits and toilets. Camping fee $10/night or annual pass. Bed and breakfast located 2 miles/3.2 km east of highway past the campground. ▲

Alaska Creekside Bed & Breakfast. See display ad this section.

A **71.4** (114.9 km) **F 286.6** (461.2 km) Lodge. Bridge over **Willow Creek.** This stream heads in Summit Lake, west of Hatcher Pass on the Hatcher Pass Road, and is a favorite launch site for airboat enthusiasts. Excellent king salmon fishing; also silvers, rainbow. Inquire at either lodge or resort for information. Entering Game Management Subunit 14B northbound, 14A southbound. From here to Denali National Park and Preserve watch for views of the Alaska Range to the east of the highway.

Pioneer Lodge. One of Alaska's oldest, original log lodges. Restaurant with full bar overlooking Willow Creek. Liquor store. Full RV hookups $12, campground—tent sites $8, showers, laundromat, dump station.

Rooms. Fishing, hunting charters, drop offs, wilderness tours, fly-ins, bank fishing—4 types of salmon, rainbows, grayling. Hiking trails. Boat launch. Bait, tackle, fishing rentals. Groceries, ice, gift shop. (907) 495-6883. See display ad. [ADVERTISEMENT] ▲

A **71.5** (115.1 km) **F 286.5** (461.1 km) **Willow Island Resort.** Scenic riverside RV park, cabins and campground. Great salmon and trout fishing from the banks of crystal clear Willow Creek. Full hookups on level

riverbank sites. Hot showers, laundry, dump station, tackle, mini-grocery, good water. Excellent king and silver salmon fishing. Rainbows to 10 lbs. Scenic fishing and hunting charters. Guided fishing charters available. Close to Hatcher Pass; 3 hours from Denali National Park. Plan to stay awhile. Write: P.O. Box 85, Willow, AK 99688 or call (907) 495-6343. See display ad this section [ADVERTISEMENT] ▲

A **74.7** (120.2 km) **F 283.3** (455.9 km) Bridge over **Little Willow Creek.** Large undeveloped parking areas below highway on either side of creek. Fishing for salmon and trout.

A **76.4** (122.9 km) **F 281.6** (453.2 km) Paved double-ended turnout to west by **Kashwitna Lake.** Stocked with rainbow trout. Small planes land on lake. Good camera viewpoints of lake and Mount McKinley (weather permitting).

A **76.5** (123.1 km) **F 281.5** (453 km) **Susitna Air Service.** See display ad this section.

A **80** (128.7 km) **F 278** (447.4 km) **Lucky Husky Racing Kennel.** Come, visit Ruth Hirsiger's sled dog kennel. Experience a true Alaskan lifestyle. Meet Ruth's sled dog family. Kennel tours with Iditarod checkpoint display, souvenirs, movies, puppies. Learn about care, nutrition, breeding, raising, training and racing. Cuddle future champions! Get dressed in original mushers clothes. Take pictures with your favorite husky. Action all year! Open 10 A.M. to 6 P.M. May through September. By reservation only, November through March. Closed October and April. See display ad. [ADVERTISEMENT]

A **81.3** (130.8 km) **F 276.7** (445.3 km) **Grey's Creek,** gravel turnouts both sides of highway. Fishing for salmon and trout.

A **82.5** (132.8 km) **F 275.5** (443.4 km) Susitna Landing, 1 mile/1.6 km on side road; boat launch, camping, handicap-accessible restrooms, bank fishing, riverboat service. Concessionaire-operated (ADF&G land) boat launch on **Kashwitna River,** just upstream of the **Susitna River;** access to both rivers on site. The Susitna River heads at Susitna Glacier in the Alaska Range to the northeast and flows west then south for 260 miles/418 km to Cook Inlet. ▲

Ron's Riverboat Service. See display ad this section.

Susitna Landing. Scenic riverside, handicap accessible campground. Bank fishing on Susitna and Kashwitna rivers. Guided fishing charters, scenic river trips and canoe drop-off and pick-up available. Espresso, snacks, tackle and gifts. Planning for 1996: RV electrical hookups and covered day-use picnic area. More information call (907) 495-5000,

(907) 373-6700. [ADVERTISEMENT]

A 83.2 (133.9 km) **F 274.8** (442.2 km) Bridge over the **Kashwitna River**; parking areas located at both ends of bridge. Salmon and trout fishing. The river heads in a glacier in the Talkeetna Mountains and flows westward 60 miles/ 96.5 km to enter the Susitna River 12 miles/19 km north of Willow.

A 84.1 (135.3 km) **F 273.9** (440.8 km) Large paved turnout to west.

A 84.3 (135.7 km) **F 273.7** (440.5 km) Gravel turnout to west. Walk-in for fishing at **Caswell Creek**; kings, silvers, pinks and rainbow.

A 85.1 (137 km) **F 272.9** (439.2 km) Caswell Creek, large gravel turnout.

A 85.5 (137.6 km) **F 272.5** (438.5 km) Gift shop and art gallery.

Willow Wildlife Art Gallery. Features Alaskan wildlife and sled dog art, as well as locally handcrafted gifts. Meet artist Dave Totten in his home studio/gallery. "From Anchorage to Fairbanks ... best gallery," Jerry Griswold, *L.A. Times,* August 1, 1993. Free coffee and wildberry muffins. (907) 495-

1090. Open all year. [ADVERTISEMENT]

A 86 (138.4 km) **F 272** (437.7 km) Public access road leads 1.3 miles/2.1 km to mouth of Sheep Creek public boat launch and Bluffs on Susitna. **Sheep Creek** has parking, toilets, dumpster and wheelchair accessible trail to mouth of creek; fishing for kings, silvers, pinks and rainbow. Bluffs on Susitna is the site of an annual bluegrass festival.

A 86.9 (139.8 km) **F 271.1** (436.3 km) **Kimberly's Kreations.** The ultimate Eskimo workshop. The Native crafts, ivory, bead work and ceramics are made by Alaska Eskimos. Workshop tours. See the originality in Eskimo doll making, ivory carving and in pouring of Alaska native clay. Select from a wide variety of original Native crafts. See our unique gifts in our handpeeled log cabin

showroom. Truly owned and operated by Alaska Eskimos. Buy directly from artists and receive possibly the lowest prices in Alaska. Open 8 A.M. to 8 P.M. year-round. (907) 278-3655. Mail: 425 E St., Anchorage, AK 99501. [ADVERTISEMENT]

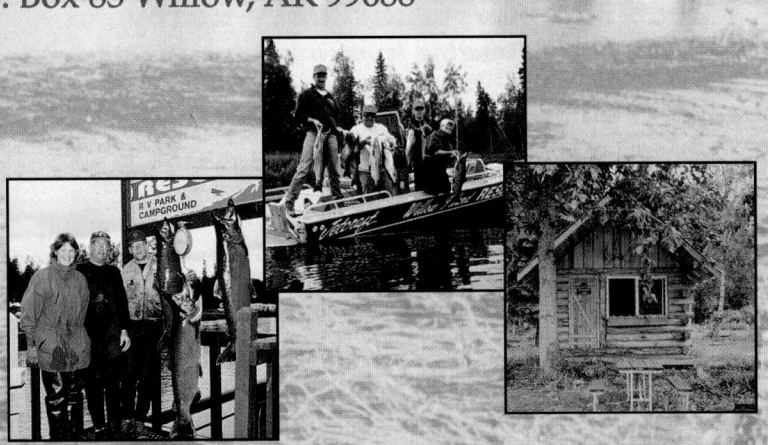

A 87 (140 km) **F 271** 436.1 km) **Wolf Safari**, an educational facility and home of the "Kissing Wolves." 30 hybrid wolves on hand for your viewing and petting pleasure on a guided tour. Cameras welcome. Memento shop and free picnic area. Open every day. No backing up RV parking and pull-through. Remember, "You Getta

Pettum." (907) 495-5874. [ADVERTISEMENT]

A 88.1 (141.8 km) F 269.9 (434.4 km) **Cline's Caswell Lake Bed & Breakfast.** See display ad this section.

A 88.2 (142 km) F 269.8 (434.2 km) **Sheep Creek Lodge.** Beautiful log lodge, built with Alaskan white spruce logs, some over 200 years old. Fine dining, cocktail lounge, serving breakfast, lunch and dinner. Warm cozy cabins, creekside RV parking or camping. Excellent salmon and trout fishing within walking distance of lodge. Package liquor store, ice, fuel and propane. Gift shop featuring unique local Alaskan gifts, many Alaskan wildlife mounts and local tour information. Open year-round with winter activities including cross-country skiing, marked snow machine trails, ice fishing and dog mushing. Phone (907) 495-6227. See display ad this section. [ADVERTISEMENT] ▲

A 88.6 (142.6 km) F 269.4 (433.5 km) Bridge over **Sheep Creek.** Unimproved picnic area on west side below bridge by creek. Fishing for salmon and trout.

A 90.8 (146.1 km) F 267.2 (430 km) **Chandalar RV Park & Cache Country Store & Liquor.** See display ad this section. ▲

A 91.5 (147.3 km) F 266.5 (428.9 km) **Susitna Dog Tours & Bed and Breakfast.** Easy access to this newly built log home offering a unique blend of Alaskan living and wilderness sled dog mushing or just a peaceful night's rest. Hot showers, sauna. Trails and seminars available for cross-country skiing, skijoring, dog mushing. Located within striking distance of Talkeetna and Denali National Park. Your hosts: Iditarod Veterans Bill & Rhodi Davidson and 50 sled dogs. Open year-round (907) 495-6324. [ADVERTISEMENT]

A 91.7 (147.6 km) F 266.3 (428.5 km) *CAUTION: Railroad crossing.*

A 93.4 (150.3 km) F 264.6 (425.8 km) Gravel turnouts both sides of highway.

A 93.5 (150.5 km) F 264.5 (425.7 km) **Goose Creek** culvert; gravel turnout. Fishing.

A 93.6 (150.6 km) F 264.4 (425.5 km) Goose Creek community center; park pavilion, picnic tables, grills, litter barrels.

A 95.1 (153 km) F 262.9 (423.1 km) **Private Aircraft:** Montana Creek airstrip; elev. 250 feet/76m; length 2,400 feet/731m; gravel; fuel 80, 100.

A 96.6 (155.5 km) F 261.4 (420.7 km) Bridge over Montana Creek. Homesteaders settled in the area surrounding this creek in the 1950s. Today, about 200 families live in the area. Camping and picnic areas on both sides of **Montana Creek**; excellent king salmon fishing, also silvers, pinks (even-numbered years), grayling, rainbow and Dolly Varden.

A **96.6** (155.5 km) F **261.4** (420.7 km) **Montana Creek Campground and RV Park.** Located on both the north and south sides of Montana Creek, all campsites in these private campgrounds are scenic, with many overlooking one of Alaska's best salmon and trout fishing streams. Picnic tables, campfires, toilets, tackle shop and snacks. Only a short walk to the Susitna River. Conveniently located within 3 miles of grocery store, cafe, laundromat and showers. [ADVERTISEMENT]

A **97.8** (157.4 km) F **260.2** (418.7 km) Denali Medical Center and Alaska State Troopers post (phone 907/733-2556 or 911 for emergencies).

A **98** (157.7 km) F **260** (418.4 km) For weather information, tune your radio to 830-AM (99.7-FM).

The Store. See display ad this section.

A **98.3** (158.2 km) F **259.7** (417.9 km) Large gravel turnout to east.

A **98.4** (158.3 km) F **259.6** (417.8 km) Susitna Valley High School; 3.1-mile/5-km trail for running in summer, cross-country skiing in winter. Senior Center.

A **98.7** (158.8 km) F **259.3** (417.3 km) **Junction** with Talkeetna Spur Road; visitor information cabin. Access to hardware, lumber and feed store with automatic teller machine. Turn right northbound on paved spur road that leads 14.5 miles/23.3 km to Talkeetna (description begins on page 378). See TALKEETNA SPUR ROAD log on page 378. Continue straight ahead on the George Parks Highway for Fairbanks.

Experience Alaska! Talkeetna Visitor Information Center. Staffed by knowledgeable local residents. Information and bookings of area recreational activities, including fishing, flightseeing, lodging and Denali

Park. Large garden and picnic area. Public restrooms. E-mail access. ATM. Parks Highway at Talkeetna Junction. Write Box 688, Talkeetna, AK 99676. Phone 1-800-660-2688 or (907) 733-2688. [ADVERTISEMENT]

Mary Carey's Fiddlehead Fern Farm. See display ad this section.

Moores' Mercantile. See display ad this section.

K2 Aviation Denali Direct Center. Talkeetna, Denali Park and vicinity information. Central booking for McKinley flightseeing, glacier landings, summit overflights, river cruises, lake cabins, and other accommodations. Enjoy an espresso, a McKinley photograph and art display, get current McKinley weather, glacier conditions and flight schedules. Find out what Talkeetna offers. Inquire about flying to Kantishna/Wonder Lake, a Denali Park fly-drive-rail overnight adventure triangle. Make your park arrangements here. Watch for the K2 flag at the center; when it is flying high, most of McKinley is clear and K2 can fly you there. Denali gifts, modern restrooms, and knowledgeable staff. Phone: (907) 733-2295. Mile 98.7 George Parks Highway (Route 3). [ADVERTISEMENT]

A **98.8** (159 km) F **259.2** (417.1 km) **Sunshine One Stop/Tesoro Alaska.** See display ad this section.

(Continues on page 383)

Talkeetna Spur Road Log

Distance from George Parks Highway junction (J) at Milepost A 98.7 is shown.

J 0 Junction with the George Parks Highway; visitor center.

J 1 (1.6 km) **Moose Dropping Inn.** See display ad this section.

J 3.1 (5 km) Turn west on Jubilee Road for bed and breakast. Turn east on Yoder Road for Benka Lake (private property).

Denali View B&B. This cozy cedar home, off Jubilee Road to west, offers hunting and fishing motif, antiques, great homemade breakfasts. Private baths. Located 12 miles south of Talkeetna and midway between Anchorage and Denali

Park. View Denali from your room. Lush gardens. Aurora viewing in winter. Cross-country ski trails. Wonderful, friendly atmosphere. A must for the discerning traveler. Open year-round. Let us book your Talkeetna experience. Resident hosts, 25-year Alaskans LesLee and Norm Solberg. HC 89 Box 8360, Talkeetna, AK 99676. Phone or fax (907) 733-2778. [ADVERTISEMENT]

J 3.5 (5.6 km) **D. L. Johnson Knives & Guitars.** Visit our family-owned and operated shop and showroom where we handcraft fine knives with the sportsman in mind. We also design and build custom flat-top and archtop steel string acoustic guitars. Please stop in. We would like to meet you. (907) 733-2777. [ADVERTISEMENT]

J 5.3 (8.5 km) Answer Creek. Sunshine Community Health Center.

J 7.1 (11.4 km) Question Lake.

J 7.8 (12.6 km) Paradise Lodge.

J 9.2 (14.8 km) Fish Lake private floatplane base.

J 11.5 (18.5 km) Bays Bed and Breakfast.

J 12 (19.3 km) Turn east on paved Comsat Road (unmarked) for **Christianson Lake;** drive in 0.7 mile/1.1 km on Comsat Road, turn left at Christianson Lake Road sign onto gravel road and drive 0.7 mile/1.1 km, turn right and follow signs to floatplane base. Fishing for silvers and rainbow. Good place to observe loons and waterfowl.

J 13 (20.9 km) Large gravel double-ended turnout with interpretive sign and viewpoint at crest of hill. Splendid views of Mount McKinley, Mount Foraker and the Alaska Range above the Susitna River. A must photo stop when the mountains are out. *CAUTION: Watch for traffic.*

J 13.3 (21.4 km) *CAUTION: Alaska Railroad crossing.*

J 13.5 (21.7 km) Talkeetna public library. Gas station

J 13.8 (22.2 km) Restaurant and motel VFW Post No. 3836 is 2 blocks west.

J 13.9 (22.4 km) RV park.

J 14 (22.5 km) East Talkeetna Road leads to state airport, municipal campground and boat launch on Talkeetna River and businesses.

J 14.2 (22.9 km) Talkeetna post office (ZIP code 99676).

J 14.3 (23 km) Welcome to Beautiful Downtown Talkeetna sign and Talkeetna Historical Society visitor center log cabin; walking tour brochures available. (Description of Talkeetna follows.)

Museum of Northern Adventure. Highlighting Alaska's exciting history in 24 realistic dioramas, featuring life-sized figures and sounds. Entertaining and educational for all ages. Meander through the historic railroad building, experiencing Alaskana at every turn: homesteading, prospecting, wildlife, famous characters, and more. Open daily year-round with special group/family rates. Clean restrooms. Gift shop featuring Eskimo dolls and totems. Carved grizzly and prospector outside to greet you. Main Street, Talkeetna (907) 733-3999. Handicap accessible. [ADVERTISEMENT]

J 14.5 (23.3 km) Talkeetna Spur Road ends at Talkeetna River Park.

Talkeetna

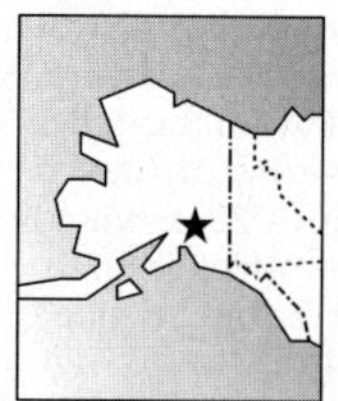

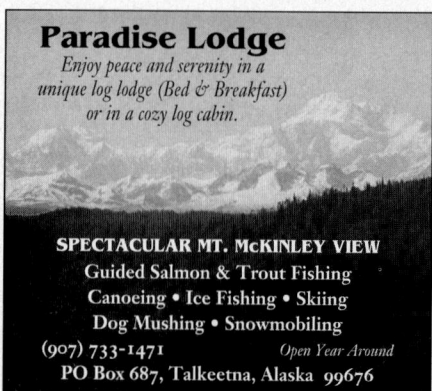

Located on a spur road, north of **Milepost A 98.7** George Parks Highway. **Population:** 441. **Emergency Services: Alaska State Troopers, Fire Department** and **Ambulance,** phone 911 or 733-2556. **Doctor,** phone 733-2708.

Visitor Information: Stop by the Talkeetna Historical Society Museum one block off Main Street opposite the Fairview Inn. Visitor information also available at log cabin at junction of Parks

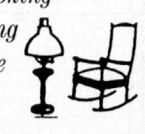

Highway and spur road. Or, write the Chamber of Commerce, P.O. Box 334, Talkeetna 99676.

The National Park Service maintains a ranger station that is staffed full time from mid-April through mid-Sept. and intermittently during the winter. Mountaineering rangers provide information on Denali National Park and climbing within the Alaska Range. A reference library and video program are available to climbers. Mountaineering regulations and information may be obtained from Talkeetna Ranger Station, P.O. Box 588, Talkeetna, AK 99676; phone (907) 733-2231.

Elevation: 346 feet/105m. **Radio:** KSKA-FM (PBS). **Television:** Channels 4, 6, 9.

Private Aircraft: Talkeetna airstrip (state airport), adjacent east; elev. 358 feet/109m; length 3,500 feet/1,067m; paved; fuel 100LL, Jet B. Talkeetna village airstrip on Main Street; elev. 346 feet/105m; length 1,200 feet/366m; gravel; village airstrip not recommended for transient aircraft or helicopters (watch for closures and poor conditions).

A Welcome to Beautiful Downtown Talkeetna sign is posted at the town park as you enter Talkeetna's old-fashioned Main Street, the only paved street in town. Log cabins and clapboard homes and businesses line Main Street, which dead ends at the Susitna River.

Talkeetna is the jumping-off point for many climbing expeditions to Mount McKinley. Most climbing expeditions use the West Buttress route, pioneered by Bradford Washburn, flying in in specially equipped ski-wheel aircraft to Kahiltna Glacier. The actual climb on Mount McKinley is made from about 7,000 feet/2,134m (where the planes land) to the summit of the South Peak (elev. 20,320 feet/6,194m). Several air services based in Talkeetna specialize in the glacier landings necessary to ferry climbers and their equipment to and from the mountain. The climb via the West Buttress route usually takes 18 to 20 days. Flightseeing the mountain is also popular (and easier!).

ACCOMMODATIONS/VISITOR SERVICES

Talkeetna has 5 motels/hotels, several bed and breakfasts, 6 restaurants, 2 gas stations, laundromats, gift and clothing shops, grocery and general stores. Dump station located at Three Rivers Tesoro.

There is a campground with toilets and shelters at the public boat launch (fee charged) just beyond the Swiss Alaska Inn; take East Talkeetna Road (a right turn at Mile 14 on the Spur Road as you approach Talkeetna). ▲

Talkeetna Motel, Restaurant and Lounge. Built in 1964 by "Evil Alice" and Sherm Powell, the "Tee-Pee" (nicknamed by oldtimers) became known for its excellent food, fast service and sincere Alaskan hospitality. Today, we also offer private baths, color TV in rooms and lounge, full menu for casual and fine dining. MasterCard/VISA welcome. See display ad this section. [ADVERTISEMENT]

Talkeetna Roadhouse. Located on the edge of wilderness in a living pioneer village the Talkeetna Roadhouse (Frank Lee cabin, circa 1917) has served the territory since early gold rush days. Still family owned, operated and occupied, this historic restaurant and lodge is known worldwide for its fine home-style cooking and frontier hospitality. Slow down to "Talkeetna time," relax amidst the rustic charm and listen to the stories these old walls have to tell! Rooms start at $45. Restaurant features daily specialties from 1902 sourdough pancakes to mouth watering ribs smoked with our own Homestead BBQ sauce. (907) 733-1351. [ADVERTISEMENT]

TRANSPORTATION

Air: There are 4 air taxi services in Talkeetna. Charter service, flightseeing and glacier landings are available. **Railroad:** The Alaska Railroad.

ATTRACTIONS

The Talkeetna Historical Society Museum is located 1 block off Main Street opposite the Fairview Inn. The original 1-room schoolhouse, built in 1936, exhibits historical items, local art, a historical library and a display on the late Don Sheldon, famous Alaskan bush pilot. In the Railroad Section House see the impressive 12-foot-by-12-foot scale model of Mount McKinley (Denali) with photographs by Bradford Washburn. A mountaineering display features pioneer and recent climbs of Mount McKinley. The Ole Dahl cabin, an early trapper/miner's cabin located on the museum grounds, is furnished with period items. Admission: $1 adult, under 12 free. Pick up a walking tour map of Talkeetna's historic sites here. Picnic area adjacent museum. Museum buildings open 10 A.M. to 5 P.M. daily in summer. Reduced hours other seasons. Phone (907) 733-2487. Privately operated guided history tours.

Miners Day. Held the weekend before Memorial Day, this family event has a trade and craft fair, local cancan dancers, softball tournament, a thrilling outhouse race, street dance and parade.

Annual Moose Dropping Festival is held second Saturday in July as a fund-raising project for the museum. Activities include a 5-km run and walk, a parade, entertainment, music, barbecue, food and game booths, and, of course, a moose dropping throwing contest.

Riverboat tours up Talkeetna Canyon, Devils Canyon, Chulitna River and Tokositna River are available. Several guides also offer riverboat fishing trips from Talkeetna. Inquire locally for details.

TALKEETNA ADVERTISERS

Chinook Winds Cabins	Ph. (907) 733-1899
Denali Dry Goods	Main St.
Denali Floats	Ph. (907) 733-2384
Doug Geeting Aviation	Ph. (907) 733-2366
Hudson Air Service, Inc.	Ph. (907) 733-2321
K2 Aviation	State Airport
Latitude 62° Lodge/Motel	Mile J 13.8
Mahay's Riverboat Service	Ph. (907) 733-2223
McKinley Air Service	State Airport
McKinley View Jetboat Safari	Ph. (907) 733-2223
Mountain Gift Shop/Visitor Information Cabin	Main St.
Mt. McKinley Flight Tours	Main St.
Museum of Northern Adventure	Mile J 14.3
Paradise Lodge	Ph. (907) 733-1471
Ptarmigan View	Ph. (907) 733-2376
Swiss-Alaska Inn	Ph. (907) 733-2424
Talkeetna Air Taxi	Ph. (907) 733-2218
Talkeetna & Beyond Bed & Breakfast	Ph. (907) 733-3050
Talkeetna Gifts and Collectables	Mile J 14.3
Talkeetna Motel	Ph. (907) 733-2323
Talkeetna River Guides	Main St.
Talkeetna Riverboat Service	Main St.
Talkeetna Roadhouse	Main St.
Three Rivers Accommodation	Ph. (907) 733-2741
Three Rivers Tesoro	Main St.
TransNorthern Aviation	State Airport
Trapper John's Bed & Breakfast	Ph. (907) 733-2354
Village Arts & Craft	Ph. (907) 733-2281
Whistle Stop Bed & Breakfast	Ph. (907) 733-1515

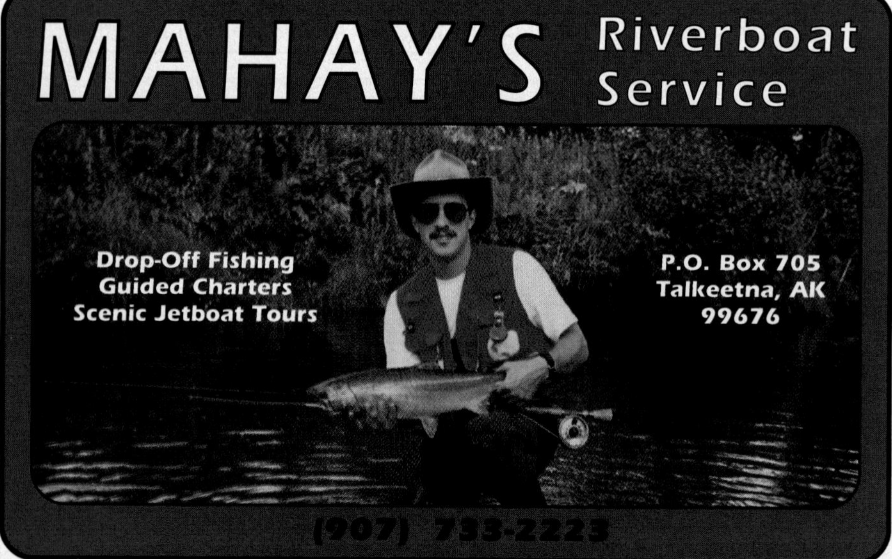

Hudson Air Service, Inc., Talkeetna's senior air taxi, provides unique guided tours of "Denali" with running commentary on the points of interest, wildlife and history of the area. Cliff Hudson helped pioneer Mount McKinley flights and glacier landings. Our family-owned business, in continuous operation since 1948, now has 2 generations of pilots flying. Highly skilled and knowledgeable, with many years of accident-free flying, their safety records speak for them. We specialize in scenic flights, Mount McKinley glacier landings and scenic wildlife tours. We can make your trip to Alaska and Mount McKinley a memorable one. Fly with us for a once-in-a-lifetime Alaskan experience. Reservations and information: 1-800-478-2321 or (907) 733-2321. Fax (907) 733-2333. P.O. Box 648, Talkeetna, AK 99676. [ADVERTISEMENT]

Mt. McKinley Flight Tours. Experience a flight with renowned glacier and flying expert Doug Geeting, who knows the climbers and all the lore and legend of Denali (the great one). You can experience a glacier landing and look up at 5,000-foot walls of ice and rock that will astound the most world-weary traveler. This flight will definitely be the high point of all your Alaska adventures! Intercom-equipped. Group rates available. Guest house available, $65 per night. Fly-in fishing cabins. Open year-round. For reservations and prices write or call Doug Geeting Aviation, Box 42 MP, Talkeetna, AK 99676; (800) 770-2366 or (907) 733-2366. Fax (907) 733-1000. See display ad in the DENALI NATIONAL PARK section. [ADVERTISEMENT]

K2 Aviation. Always something to see—every day, every season. Let K2 help you discover hidden Alaska: mile-high rock walls, icy peaks, twisting glaciers, salmon-filled rivers, hillsides of bear, caribou and sheep, meadows of moose and wildflowers, clear winter days, sunny summer nights. All in the shadow of Mount McKinley. Jim Okonek's K2 Aviation offers: experienced McKinley pilots, glacier landings, fly-in fishing and hunting, remote cabins, climbing expedition air support, scenic flights, headphones for every passenger, natural history and local lore. Denali Park Grand Tour, Summit Overflight, Wildlife Air Safari and Overnight Park Package. Office at Talkeetna airport. P.O. Box 545, Talkeetna, AK 99676. Phone (907) 733-2291, fax (907) 733-1221. Alaska 800-478-2291. [ADVERTISEMENT]

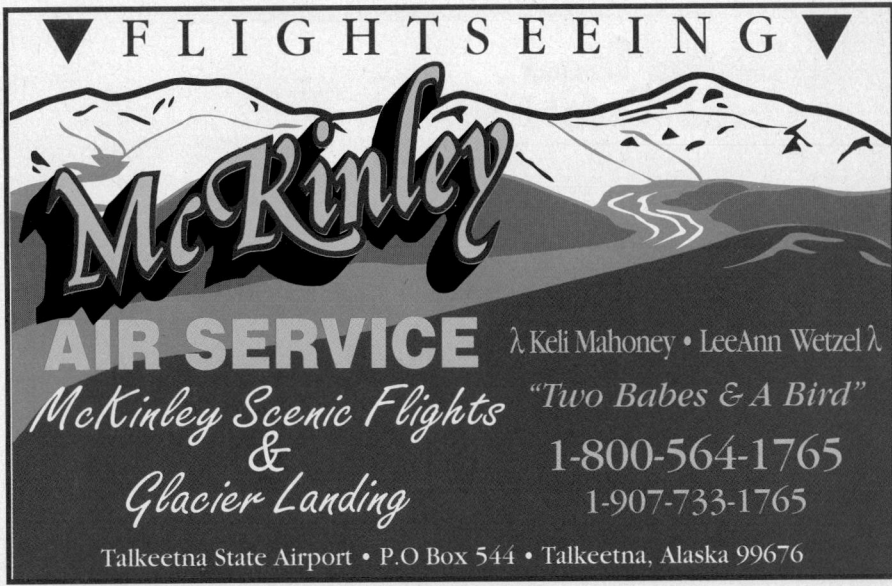

Talkeetna Spur Road Log (continued)

Mahay's Riverboat Service. Fish clear-water streams for all 5 species of Pacific salmon and trout. Custom-designed jet boats allow access to over 200 miles of prime fishing territory. Guided fishing charters include all equipment needed. Fishing packages are also available that include accommodations, meals and all the "extras." Spend the afternoon exploring an authentic trapper's cabin, viewing nesting bald eagles and sightseeing on the McKinley View River Cruise. Drop-off fishing also available at reasonable rates. Credit cards accepted. (907) 733-2223, fax (907) 733-2712. In Alaska, 1-800-736-2210. [ADVERTISEMENT]

Mountain Gift Shop/Visitor Information Cabin. Near the famous "Welcome to Beautiful Downtown Talkeetna" sign. Enjoy shopping for mountain theme items: books, maps, posters, T-shirts, flags, colorful gemstone necklaces and quill jewelry handmade in Alaska. Moose nugget items our specialty. Open summer 10-5:30. Free town map. Information, reservation (907) 733-1686. [ADVERTISEMENT]

Talkeetna Air Taxi. Fly Mount McKinley. Glacier landing, wildlife tours, aerial photography. Climbing expedition support. In business since 1947. Office in log building at state airport. Write Box 73-MP, Talkeetna, AK 99676. For information, reservations, call ahead (907) 733-2218 collect. [ADVERTISEMENT]

Talkeetna Gifts & Collectables. "One of the nicest and most complete gift shops in Alaska" located in a spacious log building with handmade keepsakes, souvenirs, jewelry, books, Alaskana, birch bowls, quilts, and other treasures. Fur slippers/accessories, beautiful sweatshirts, sweaters, plush toys, puppets and huggable Eskimo dolls. Alaskan foods and sourdough. Suzy's exclusive "Alaska Map" cross-stitch pattern. Quality merchandise with friendly service. We mail purchases. Goldpanning, with gold guaranteed! Open daily year-round. Main Street, Talkeetna. (907) 733-2710. [ADVERTISEMENT]

Takeetna River Guides. Fish with a recognized leader for salmon and trout in our exciting, area streams and rivers. Guided charters start at $109 and include all equipment and use of our specialized jet boats. Drop-off fishing available as well. Also, join us on a wildlife, natural history float trip. 2, 4, and 6-hour tours available daily. 1-800-353-2677. See display ad. [ADVERTISEMENT]

Fishing. A Calico (chum) Salmon Derby is held the first 3 weeks of Aug. The **Susitna River** basin offers many top fishing streams and lakes, either accessible by road, plane or riverboat.

Return to Milepost A 98.7
George Parks Highway

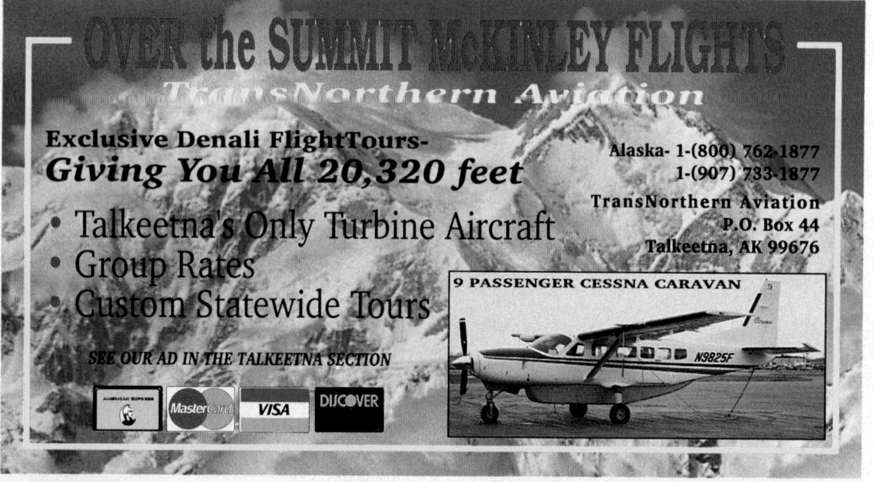

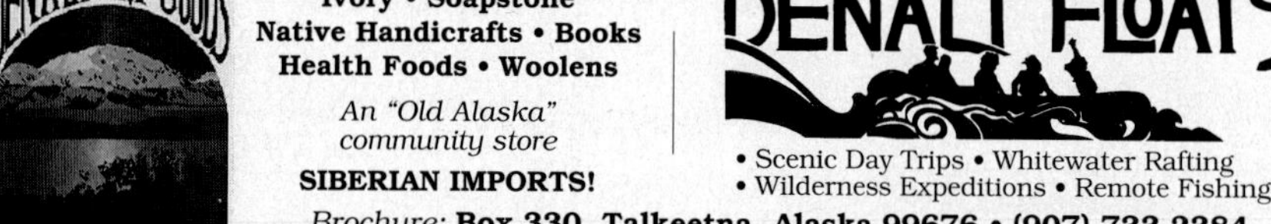

(Continued from page 377)

A 99 (159.3 km) **F 259** (416.8 km) **Denali Way Auto.** See display ad this section.

A 99.3 (159.8 km) **F 258.7** (416.3 km) **Montana and Little Montana lakes** on opposite sides of highway, stocked with rainbow. Watch for floatplanes.

A 99.5 (160.1 km) **F 258.5** (416 km) **H&H Lakeview Restaurant & Lodge**, serving travelers since 1965. Feast your senses in our spacious lakeside dining room, hidden away from the busy highway by a birch grove. You'll love our omelettes. Great hamburgers and steaks. Prime rib and

seafood, too. Our bread pudding is famous statewide. Take home a taste of Alaska in jellies from our gift shop. We make the jellies from Alaska berries, each with its own distinct flavor. Lakeside RV parking and camping. Hear the loons and watch beavers from your motorhome. Gerald and Sherry Berryman, proprietors since 1977. See display ad for details. [ADVERTISEMENT] ▲

A 99.8 (160.6 km) **F 258.2** (415.5 km) Access road to YMCA camp on Peggy Lake.

A 100.4 (161.6 km) **F 257.6** (414.6 km) *CAUTION: Railroad crossing.*

A 102 (164.1 km) **F 256** (412 km) Paved double-ended turnout to east.

A 102.6 (165.1 km) **F 255.4** (411 km) Turnout at Sunshine Road; access to **Sunshine Creek** for fishing via dirt road.

A 104.2 (167.7 km) **F 253.8** (408.4 km) Entering Game Management Unit 16A, northbound, Unit 14B southbound.

A 104.3 (167.8 km) **F 253.7** (408.3 km) Bridge over Big Susitna River. State rest area to west on south bank of river; loop road, parking area, tables, firepits, toilets, no drinking water. ▲

Some of the finest stands of white birch in Alaska may be seen for several miles on both sides of the river. This area is also noted for its fiddlehead ferns. The ferns (lady fern, ostrich fern and shield fern) are harvested in the spring, when their young shoots are tightly coiled, resembling a fiddle's head. The fiddleheads should be picked clean of the brown flakes which coat them. (Of the 3 ferns, ostrich fern is favored because it has the least amount of this coating.) Fiddleheads should be cooked before consumption.

A 104.6 (168.3 km) **F 253.4** (407.8 km) Rabideaux Creek access; parking, 0.3 mile/0.5 km trail to mouth of creek. Watch for seasonal flooding.

A 104.8 (168.7 km) **F 253.2** (407.5 km) Double-ended turnout to west.

A 105.9 (170.4 km) **F 252.1** (405.7 km) Rabideaux Creek access and bridge.

A 107.6 (173.2 km) **F 250.4** (403 km) View of Mount McKinley for northbound travelers.

A 114.8 (184.7 km) **F 243.2** (391.4 km) Cluster of businesses serving highway travelers and Trapper Creek the next mile northbound include: lodges with gift shops, gas and restaurant; RV park; laundromats; and flightseeing service. ▲

Trapper Creek Inn & General Store. Gateway to Denali, visitors information

Driving with headlights on at all times is the law in Alaska.

center, Tesoro gas, diesel, deluxe lodging, large RV campground, full hook-ups, dump station, propane, showers, restrooms, laundry, pay phone, deli, groceries, coffee, ice, etc. Fishing and hunting supplies and charters. Flightseeing Mount McKinley. Major credit cards accepted. Phone (907) 733-2302. Fax (907) 733-1002. Tour buses welcome. See large display ad this section. [ADVERTISEMENT] ▲

A 114.9 (184.9 km) **F 243.1** (391.2 km) **TRAPPER CREEK** (area pop. about 700), at **junction** with Petersville Road. Trapper Creek post office (ZIP code 99683). Miners built the Petersville Road in the 1920s and federal homesteading began here in 1948, with settlement continuing through the 1950s and 1960s. The George Parks Highway opened as far as Trapper Creek in 1967. Today it is the southern gateway to Denali Park and the Alaska Range, with access via the Petersville Road (description follows). Trapper Creek businesses are located along the Parks Highway and up Petersville Road.

Petersville Road leads west and north from Trapper Creek approximately 40 miles/64 km (no winter maintenance beyond Mile 14). This scenic gravel road (with excellent views of Mount McKinley) goes through a homestead and gold mining area that also contains some new subdivisions. Berry picking in season. There are several bed and breakfasts along the road. The Forks Roadhouse is at Mile 18.7/30.1 km. Turn down the right fork for the former mining camp of Petersville (4-wheel drive recommended). *Please respect private property.* The left fork leads 0.2 mile/0.3 km to **Peters Creek** stream. Fishing for salmon and trout. The road to Petersville is rough and used primarily by miners and trappers beyond The Forks Roadhouse. ▲

North Country Bed and Breakfast (Mile 2.7 Petersville Road). Nestled on a lake with a spectacular view of Mount McKinley. Five first-class rooms with private bathrooms and private entries. Mount McKinley flightseeing trips available at the lake by appointment. Bird watching, wildlife, paddleboating and horseshoes available. Your hosts—Mike and Sheryl Uher. Phone (907) 733-3981. [ADVERTISEMENT]

Gate Creek Cabins modern log cabins, equipped for comfortable stay of day, week or longer. Located mile 10.5 on Historic Petersville Road, with year around access. Furnished with linens, dishes, utensils, stove, refrigerator, TV, VCR, showers, sauna, BBQ grill. Bring your personal items, food, and recreation equipment. Fishing, mountain viewing, hiking, biking, photography, berry picking, canoeing, paddle boating on our small lake; cross-country skiing, snowmobiling, with rentals and guided tours available. Rates: $38/person/night, children 12 and under free, 5 percent bed tax. Weekly rate. Family pets welcome. Your hosts, Gary and Dorothy Rawie, reservations (907) 733-1393 (cabins), (907) 248-2765 (Anchorage). [ADVERTISEMENT]

McKinley Foothills Bed and Breakfast. Off Mile 17.2 Petersville Road. Furnished, secluded log cabins in a rural setting, 2 with

kitchenettes. Full breakfast. Great food and hospitality. Great view of Mount McKinley. Bird watching. Fishing nearby. Open year-round. Winter wonderland for skiers, snowmachiners. VISA, MasterCard. Phone or fax (907) 733-1454. P.O. Box 13089, Trapper

Creek, AK 99683. [ADVERTISEMENT]

The Forks Roadhouse. See display ad this section.

A 115.2 (185.4 km) **F 242.8** (390.7 km) Trapper Creek community park.

A 115.5 (185.9 km) **F 242.5** (390.2 km) **Trapper Creek Trading Post.** See display ad this section. ▲

A 115.6 (186 km) **F 242.4** (390.1 km) Highway crosses Trapper Creek.

Excellent views of Mount McKinley (weather permitting) northbound.

A 115.7 (186.2 km) **F 242.3** (390 km) **Trapper Creek Pizza Pub.** See display ad this section.

A 121.1 (194.9 km) **F 236.9** (381.2 km) Chulitna highway maintenance camp.

A 121.5 (195.5 km) **F 236.5** (380.6 km) Easy-to-miss large paved double-ended rest area to east with tables, firepits, drinking water, toilet and interpretive bulletin board. Shade trees; cow parsnip grows lush here.

A 123.4 (198.6 km) **F 234.6** (377.5 km) Wooded area with many dead trees covered with "conks" (a term applied to a type of bracket fungus).

A 126.6 (203.7 km) **F 231.4** (372.4 km) Large paved turnout to east.

A 128.4 (206.6 km) **F 229.6** (369.5 km) Undeveloped parking area below highway by creek.

A 132 (212.4 km) **F 226** (363.7 km) Boundary of Denali State Park (see description next milepost).

A 132.7 (213.6 km) **F 225.3** (362.6 km) Denali State Park entrance sign. This 325,460-acre park has 48 miles/77.2 km of hiking trails. Camping at Troublesome Creek (**Milepost A 137.3**) and at Byers Lake (**Milepost A 147**). Hunting is permitted in the park, but discharge of firearms is prohibited within 0.3 mile of highway, and 0.5 mile of a developed facility or 0.5 mile of trail around Byers Lake.

A 132.8 (213.7 km) **F 225.2** (362.4 km) **Chulitna River** bridge. Fishing for grayling, rainbow. Game Management Unit 13E, leaving unit 16A, northbound.

CAUTION: Watch for construction trucks entering and exiting highway here.

A 134.5 (216.5 km) **F 223.5** (359.7 km) **Mary's McKinley View Lodge.** Located on Mary Carey's original homestead. Spectacular view of McKinley from every room, especially the glass-walled restaurant. Mary, famous for Alaskan books, homesteaded before the state park was created. She fought for highway completion to share her magnificent view with travelers. Enjoy dining, browse the gift shop or spend a pleasant night in the modern rooms. Call (907) 733-1555. See display ad this page. [ADVERTISEMENT]

A 134.8 (216.9 km) **F 223.2** (359.2 km) Small turnout to east. Springwater piped to road.

A 135.2 (217.6 km) **F 222.8** (358.6 km) Large paved turnout with litter barrels, toilet and view of 20,320-foot/6,194-m Mount McKinley; a display board here points out peaks. From here northbound for many miles there are views of glaciers on the southern slopes of the Alaska Range to the west. Ruth, Buckskin and Eldridge glaciers are the most conspicuous.

Ruth Glacier trends southeast through the Great Gorge for 31 miles/50 km. The glacier was named in 1903 by F.A. Cook for his daughter. The Great Gorge was named by mountain climbers in the late 1940s. Nicknamed the Grand Canyon of Alaska, peaks on either side of the gorge tower up to 5,000 feet/1,500m above Ruth Glacier. The gorge opens into Don Sheldon Amphitheater, at the head of Ruth Glacier, where the

Fishing from a canoe on Byers Lake, Milepost A 147. (© Michael DeYoung)

Don Sheldon mountain house sits. Donald E. Sheldon (1921–75) was a well-known bush pilot who helped map, patrol and aid search and rescue efforts in this area.

Flightseeing trips can be arranged that take you close to Mount McKinley, into the Don Sheldon Amphitheater, through the Great Gorge and beneath the peak of The Mooses Tooth. Inquire at Trapper Creek Inn, **Milepost A 114.8**, or with air taxi operators in Talkeetna and in the national park.

Peaks to be sighted, left to right, along the next 20 miles/32.2 km to the west are: Mount Hunter (elev. 14,573 feet/4,442m); Mount Huntington (elev. 12,240 feet/ 3,731m); Mount Barrille (elev. 7,650 feet/ 2,332m); and Mount Dickey (elev. 9,845 feet/3,001m).

A 137.3 (221 km) **F 220.7** (355.1 km) Troublesome Creek bridge. Lower Troublesome Creek state recreation site has 10 campsites, $6/night camping fee per vehicle or annual pass, day-use area with sheltered picnic sites, toilets, water and litter barrels. Lower Troublesome Creek trailhead. This is usually a clear runoff stream, not silted by glacial flour. The stream heads in a lake and flows 14 miles/22.5 km to the Chulitna River. ▲

Troublesome Creek, rainbow, grayling and salmon (king salmon fishing prohibited); June through Sept.

A 137.6 (221.4 km) **F 220.4** (354.7 km) Upper Troublesome Creek trailhead and parking area. Trails to Byers Lake (15 miles/ 24 km) and Tarn Point, elev. 2,881 feet/ 878m (10.8 miles/17.3 km). *NOTE: Trailhead and trail to Mile 5.5 closed from mid-July to Sept. 1 due to the high concentration of bears feeding on spawning salmon.*

A 139.9 (225.1 km) **F 218.1** (351 km) Paved turnout to west.

A 143.9 (231.6 km) **F 214.1** (344.6 km) Bridge over Byers Creek.

A 145.7 (234.5 km) **F 212.3** (341.6 km) Paved turnout to west.

A 147 (236.6 km) **F 211** (339.6 km) **Byers Lake** state campground with 66 sites, $12/night camping fee or annual pass, picnic tables, firepits, water, toilets (wheelchair accessible) and access to Byers Lake (electric motors permitted). Fishing for grayling, burbot, rainbow, lake trout and whitefish. Remote campsite 1.8-mile/2.9-km hike from campground (see directions posted on bulletin board). Hiking trail to Curry Ridge and south to Troublesome Creek. *CAUTION: Black bears frequent campground. Keep a clean camp.* ▲

A 147.2 (236.9 km) **F 210.8** (339.2 km) Alaska Veterans Memorial turnoff. This concrete memorial honoring the armed forces is scheduled to be closed in 1996 for rehabilitation.

A 155.6 (250.4 km) **F 202.4** (325.7 km) For the next mile northbound, there are views of Eldridge Glacier to the left. The face of the glacier is 6 miles/9.7 km from the road. The Fountain River heads at the terminus of the glacier and flows into the Chulitna.

A 157.7 (253.8 km) **F 200.3** (322.3 km) Small paved turnout to west.

A 159.4 (256.5 km) **F 198.6** (319.6 km) Double-ended paved turnout to west.

A 159.9 (257.3 km) **F 198.1** (318.8 km) Parking area east side of highway by Horseshoe Creek.

A 160.8 (258.8 km) **F 197.2** (317.4 km) The highway makes a steep descent northbound with moderate S-curves to Little Coal Creek.

A 161 (259.1 km) **F 197** (317 km) Large gravel turnout to east.

A 162.4 (261.4 km) **F 195.6** (314.8 km) Large paved turnout with litter barrels to west; Denali viewpoint.

A 162.5 (261.5 km) **F 195.5** (314.6 km) Denali View North campground (scheduled to open July 1, 1996); 20 sites, camping fee charged, day-use parking, toilets (handicap accessible), water, interpretive kiosks, spotting scope, short loop trail. Overlooks Chulitna River. Views of Denali, Mooses Tooth, Mount Huntington and Alaska Range peaks above Hidden River valley. ▲

A 162.7 (261.8 km) **F 195.3** (314.3 km) Small paved turnout to east. Watch for beaver pond to west northbound.

A 163.1 (262.5 km) **F 194.9** (313.6 km) Large double-ended paved turnout to west.

A 163.2 (262.6 km) **F 194.8** (313.5 km) Bridge over Little Coal Creek.

Coal Creek, rainbow, grayling and salmon, July through Sept.

A 163.8 (263.6 km) **F 194.2** (312.5 km) Little Coal Creek trailhead and parking area. According to park rangers, this trail offers easy access (1½-hour hike) to alpine country. It is a 27-mile/43.5-km hike to Byers Lake via Kesugi Ridge.

A 165.6 (266.5 km) **F 192.4** (309.6 km) A small stream passes under the road; paved turnouts on both sides of highway. Good berry picking in the fall.

A 168.5 (271.2 km) **F 189.5** (305 km) Denali State Park boundary sign.

A 169 (272 km) **F 189** (304.2 km) *CAUTION: Railroad crossing.* A solar collector here helps power the warning signals.

Denali State Park boundary (leaving park northbound, entering park southbound).

A 170.3 (274 km) **F 187.7** (302.1 km) Paved viewpoint area to west.

A 171 (275.2 km) **F 187** (300.9 km) There are several small turnouts next 5 miles/8 km northbound.

A 174 (280 km) **F 184** (296.1 km) Bridge over Hurricane Gulch; rest area. From the south end of the bridge, scramble through alders up the east bank of the gulch to find photographers' trail (unmarked). A 0.3-mile/ 0.4-km trail along edge of Hurricane Gulch offers good views of the bridge span and gulch. A pleasant walk, good berry picking in the fall. *Do not go too near the edge.* Parking areas at both ends of bridge.

Construction costs for the bridge were approximately $1.2 million. The 550-foot/ 168-m deck of the bridge is 260 feet/79m above Hurricane Creek, not as high as the railroad bridge that spans the gulch near the Chulitna River. From this bridge the highway begins a gradual descent northbound to Honolulu Creek.

A 176 (283.2 km) **F 182** (292.9 km) Paved turnout to east. There are several small turnouts next 5 miles/8 km southbound.

A 176.5 (284 km) **F 181.5** (292.1 km) Double-ended gravel turnout to west with view of the Alaska Range. Highway descends long grade northbound.

A 177.8 (286.1 km) **F 180.2** (290 km) Paved turnout and view of eroded bluffs to west.

A 178.1 (286.6 km) **F 179.9** (289.5 km) Bridge over Honolulu Creek. The highway begins a gradual ascent northbound to Broad Pass, the gap in the Alaska Range crossed by both the railroad and highway. Undeveloped parking areas below highway on the creek.

A 179.5 (288.9 km) **F 178.5** (287.3 km) Paved turnout to west by small lake. In early September blueberries are plentiful for the next 25 miles/40 km.

A 180 (289.7 km) **F 178** (286.5 km) Small paved turnout to west by small lake. Short trail to **Mile 180 Lake**, stocked with grayling.

A 183.2 (294.8 km) **F 174.8** (281.3 km) Large paved double-ended turnout to west of highway. Look to the west across the Chulitna River for dramatic view of the Alaska Range.

A 184.5 (296.9 km) **F 173.5** (279.2 km) Paved turnout to west.

A 185 (297.7 km) **F 173** (278.4 km) East Fork DOT/PF highway maintenance station.

A 185.1 (297.9 km) **F 172.9** (278.3 km) Bridge over East Fork Chulitna River.

A 185.6 (298.7 km) **F 172.4** (277.4 km) East Fork rest area (no sign at turnoff) on right northbound. A 0.5-mile/0.8-km paved loop gives access to a gravel picnic area with overnight parking, 23 tables, concrete fireplaces and picnic shelter. No restrooms or toilet facilities were open here in 1995; current status of facilities unknown. The rest area is in a bend of the East Fork Chulitna River amid a healthy growth of Alaskan spruce and birch. Cut wood is often available. ▲

A 186.4 (300 km) **F 171.6** (276.2 km) Small paved turnout to east.

A 187.5 (301.8 km) **F 170.5** (274.4 km) Paved double-ended turnout to west; small paved turnout east side of highway.

A 188.5 (303.4 km) **F 169.5** (272.8 km) **The Igloo**, an Alaskan landmark, 50 miles south of entrance to Denali National Park. New ownership. Unleaded, regular and diesel fuels. Ask for 5¢ discount for cash fill-ups. Caravan discounts. Espresso, postcards,

candy, snacks, soft drinks. Unique Alaskan art, gifts and souvenirs not seen elsewhere. Open year-round. (907) 768-2622. See display ad. [ADVERTISEMENT]

A 189.9 (305.6 km) **F 168.1** (270.5 km) Gravel double-ended turnout. Watch for beaver dam to east northbound.

A 191.5 (308.2 km) **F 166.5** (267.9 km) Large paved turnout to west. Look for cotton grass.

A 193 (310.6 km) **F 165** (265.5 km) **Sourdough Paul's Bed and Breakfast.** Rustic Alaskan atmosphere, scenic, private setting with Mount McKinley view, less than 1 hour from Denali Park's main gate. Log home with Finnish sauna and bath house, hot rocks at foot of bed, mints on pillows.

Overnight camping available. Full breakfast, Alaskan sourdough hotcakes. Guided summer and winter tours through historical Alaskan gold mining areas. Watch the famous Alaska Railroad trains. Headquarters for sightseeing, flightseeing, Chulitna River float trips, sportfishing, gold panning, blueberries. Best snowmachining in Alaska. Extreme Northern Lights viewing. Horses and guides available. Reservations: (907) 768-2020. Lifetime Alaskan jeweler Paul Miebs, P.O. Box 213, Cantwell, AK 99729. [ADVERTISEMENT]

A 194.3 (312.7 km) **F 163.7** (263.4 km) *CAUTION: Railroad crossing.*

A 194.5 (313 km) **F 163.5** (263.1 km) Bridge over Middle Fork Chulitna River. Undeveloped parking area southwest of bridge below the highway. *CAUTION: Windy area through Broad Pass.*

A 195 (313.8 km) **F 163** (262.3 km) Entering Broad Pass northbound. Good views of Broad Pass.

A 201.1 (323.6 km) **F 156.9** (252.5 km) Large paved parking area to east with mountain view.

A 201.3 (324 km) **F 156.7** (252.2 km) Summit of Broad Pass (not signed). Broad Pass is one of the most beautiful areas on the George Parks Highway. A mountain valley, bare in some places, dotted with scrub spruce in others, and surrounded by mountain peaks, there's a top-of-the-world feeling for the traveler, although it is one of the lowest summits along the North American mountain system. Named in 1898 by George Eldridge and Robert Muldrow, the 2,300-foot/701-m pass, sometimes called Caribou Pass, marks the divide between the drainage of rivers and streams that empty into Cook Inlet and those that empty into the Yukon River.

Orange towers of weather service station building west of highway.

A 202.3 (325.6 km) **F 155.7** (250.6 km) Boundary of Matanuska–Susitna and Denali boroughs.

Burls, used in crafts, grow on spruce trees. (© Susan Cole Kelly)

A 203.1 (326.9 km) **F 154.9** (249.3 km) *CAUTION: Railroad crossing.*

A 203.6 (327.7 km) **F 154.4** (248.5 km) Paved parking area with view to east.

A 208 (334.7 km) **F 150** (241.4 km) Turnout to west at end of bridge over Pass Creek; blueberries in season.

A 209.4 (337 km) **F 148.6** (239.1 km) Large gravel parking area to east.

*NOTE: Watch for guardrail construction northbound to **Milepost A 276** in 1996.*

A 209.5 (337.1 km) **F 148.5** (239 km) Bridge over Jack River; paved turnout.

A 209.7 (337.4 km) **F 148.3** (238.7 km) **Reindeer Mtn. Lodge.** Lodging, towing, gifts, snacks and furs. Beautiful view of Mount McKinley. Rooms have private baths and color TV. Beautiful log office has ornate wood carvings and 2 stuffed moose on porch. Open year-round. Wildlife, scenery, skiing, snowmobiling, fishing, hunting, hiking or relaxing. Call (907) 768-2420 or fax (907) 768-2942. Write Box 7, Cantwell, AK 99729. [ADVERTISEMENT]

A 209.9 (337.8 km) **F 148.1** (238.3 km) **Junction** of the George Parks Highway with the Denali Highway. **CANTWELL** post office and school, as well as a motel, lodge, restaurant, grocery and gas stations are located here. An RV park is located 0.3 mile/0.5 km west of the junction. **Emergency Services: Alaska State Troopers**, phone (907) 768-2202. **Ambulance**, phone (907) 768-2982. The original town of Cantwell, 1.8 miles/2.9 km west of this junction, has a cafe, bar and

See the GENERAL INFORMATION section for a Calendar of Events.

liquor store. Turn west on the Denali Highway for Cantwell, turn east for Paxson (see DENALI HIGHWAY section for description of Cantwell and Denali Highway log). ▲

Atkins Guiding & Flying Service. See display ad this section.

Backwoods Lodge. See display ad this section.

Cantwell Lodge. See display ad this section.

Cantwell RV Park. See display ad this section. ▲

A 210 (338 km) **F 148** (238.2 km) Cantwell post office (ZIP code 99729).

A 210.2 (338.3 km) **F 147.8** (237.9 km) **Parkway Gift Shop.** See display ad this section.

A 211.5 (340.4 km) **F 146.5** (235.8 km) Paved double-ended parking area to west.

A 212.7 (342.3 km) **F 145.3** (233.8 km) Gravel turnout to west by Nenana River. Watch for large beaver dam to west. Slide area northbound.

A 213.9 (344.2 km) **F 144.1** (231.9 km) Paved double-ended turnout to west among tall white spruce and fireweed.

A 215.3 (346.5 km) **F 142.7** (229.6 km) Access road to Nenana River, which parallels the highway northbound.

A 215.7 (347.1 km) **F 142.3** (229 km) First bridge northbound over the Nenana River. Highway narrows northbound.

A 216.2 (347.9 km) **F 141.8** (228.2 km) Entering Game Management Unit 20A and leaving unit 13E northbound.

A 216.3 (348.1 km) **F 141.7** (228 km) Paved double-ended turnout to west. Good spot for photos of Panorama Mountain (elev. 5,778 feet/1,761m), the prominent peak visible to the east.

A 217.6 (350.2 km) **F 140.4** (225.9 km) Small gravel turnout to west.

A 218.6 (351.8 km) **F 139.4** (224.3 km) Paved double-ended turnout to west with beautiful view of Nenana River.

A 219 (352.4 km) **F 139** (223.7 km) Slide area: Watch for rocks next 0.4 mile/0.6 km northbound.

A 219.8 (353.7 km) **F 138.2** (222.4 km) Paved double-ended turnout to west overlooking Nenana River.

A 220 (354 km) **F 138** (222.1 km) Slime Creek.

A 220.2 (354.4 km) **F 137.8** (221.8 km) Wide gravel turnout to east.

A 222.2 (357.6 km) **F 135.8** (218.5 km) Large, paved double-ended turnout to west beside Nenana River slough. Snow poles beside roadway guide snowplows in winter.

A 223.9 (360.3 km) **F 134.1** (215.8 km) **Carlo Creek Lodge.** Located 12 miles south of Denali Park entrance. 32 wooded acres bordered by beautiful Carlo Creek, the Nenana River and Denali National Park. Cozy creekside log cabins with own bathroom, showers. RV park, dump station, potable water, propane. Clean bathroom, showers. Dishwashing facility. Individual sheltered tent sites each with picnic table and firepit. Unique gift shop. Small store. Information. Pay phone. You won't be disappointed. It's a beautiful place to be. HC 2, Box 1530, Healy, AK 99743. (907) 683-2576, 683-2573. [ADVERTISEMENT] ▲

A 224 (360.5 km) **F 134** (215.7 km) **The Perch.** A beautiful, established restaurant-bar perched on a private hill. Spectacular dining, specializes in freshly baked bread, seafood and steaks. Also, take-out giant cinnamon rolls. Breakfast 6 P.M. to 11 A.M. Open for dinner daily 5 P.M. to 10 P.M., mid-May

through September. Sleeping cabins with central bath, some with private baths, beside Carlo Creek. Owners/operators, Jerry and Elaine Pollock. (907) 683-2523. HC2 Box 1525, Healy, AK 99743. See display ad in the DENALI NATIONAL PARK section. [ADVERTISEMENT]

A 224 (360.5 km) **F 134** (215.7 km) Bridge over Carlo Creek.

McKinley Wilderness Lodge and Tumbling B Ranch, on the banks of Carlo Creek. Cabins with private bath, economy cabins with central bath. 1- to 4-hour fully guided trail rides. 2- to 5-day pack trips. Restaurant. (907) 683-2277; fax (907) 683-1558. PO Box 89, Denali Park, AK 99755. See display ad in Denali National Park section. [ADVERTISEMENT]

A 224.1 (360.6 km) **F 133.9** (215.5 km) **Rick Swenson's Carlo Heights Bed and Breakfast and Sled Dog School.** Open year around, this establishment offers privacy, seclusion and spectacular views of the Alaska Range. Accommodations include 2 double rooms and an executive suite, full kitchen and laundry facilities. The sled dog school offers dog mushing courses and tours. Reservations recommended. Phone (907) 683-1615. [ADVERTISEMENT]

A 225 (362.1 km) **F 133** (214 km) Beautiful mountain views southbound.

A 226 (363.7 km) **F 132** (212.4 km) Fang Mountain (elev. 6,736 feet/2,053m) may be visible to the west through the slash in the mountains.

A 229 (368.5 km) **F 129** (207.6 km) **Denali Cabins.** Private cabins with bath, outdoor hot tubs, complimentary coffee and extensive information about Denali National Park. Seasonal service mid-May through mid-September. VISA, MasterCard accepted. Winter: (907) 258-0134 or summer: (907) 683-2643. Brochure: 200 W. 34th Ave. #362, Anchorage, AK 99503. Fax (907) 243-2062 or summer (907) 683-2595. See display ad in DENALI NATIONAL PARK section. [ADVERTISEMENT]

A 229.2 (368.8 km) **F 128.8** (207.3 km) Private airstrip. Flightseeing trip.

Denali Air. We fly you closer to Denali's beauty on our 1-hour aerial tours of Mount McKinley and Denali National Park. Flights

PHOTO: Johnny Johnson

originate from the airstrip here or from main office next to Denali Park railroad depot. Three person minimum. Reservations: (907) 683-2261. See display ad in the DENALI NATIONAL PARK section. [ADVERTISEMENT]

A 229.7 (369.7 km) **F 128.3** (206.5 km) Paved turnout to west.

A 231.1 (371.9 km) **F 126.9** (204.2 km) **McKinley Village Lodge**, is convenient to all Denali National Park activities. Located on a quiet stretch of the Nenana River, the 50-room lodge is complete with a lovely cafe, lounge, gift shop and tour desk to arrange area tour and rafting activities. Our outdoor pavilion, overlooking the Nenana River, is host to evening barbecues and live entertainment. (800) 276-7234; Anchorage: 276-7234. [ADVERTISEMENT]

Visitors have a good chance of seeing grizzly bears in Denali National Park. (© Loren Taft, Alaskan Images)

Denali Grizzly Bear Cabins & Campground. South boundary Denali National Park. AAA approved. Drive directly to your individual kitchen, sleeping, or tent cabin with its old-time Alaskan atmosphere overlooking scenic Nenana River. Two conveniently located buildings with toilets, sinks, coin-operated hot showers. Advance cabin reservations suggested. Tenting and RV campsites also available in peaceful lower wooded area. Hookups. Propane. Caravans welcome! Hot coffee and rolls, ice cream, snacks, groceries, ice, liquor store, Alaskan gifts. Specialty sweatshirts. VISA and MasterCard accepted. Owned and operated by a pioneer Alaskan family. Reservations (907) 683-2696 (summer); (907) 457-2924 (winter). See display ad in DENALI NATIONAL PARK section. [ADVERTISEMENT] ▲

Denali River Cabins. Located on the banks of the Nenana River, 5 minutes away from the Visitor Center, our cedar cabin resort offers the ideal base for your Denali Park experience. Our cabins are situated both on and off river with an extra large hot tub and riverside sauna. The new cozy cedar cabins are fully furnished all with private bath. There are 3 sun decks right on the riverbank, looking into Denali Park. We also offer exclusive Fairbanks day tours and Kantishna tours inside Denali National Park. (907) 683-2500 for reservations year-round. See display ad, DENALI NATIONAL PARK section. [ADVERTISEMENT] ▲

A 231.3 (372.2 km) **F 126.7** (203.9 km) Crabb's Crossing, second bridge northbound over the Nenana River.

At the north end of this bridge is the boundary of Denali National Park and Preserve. From here north for 6.8 miles/10.9 km the George Parks Highway is within the boundaries of the park and travelers must abide by park rules. No discharge of firearms permitted.

A 233.1 (375.1 km) **F 124.9** (201 km) Gravel turnout to east.

A 234.1 (376.7 km) **F 123.9** (199.4 km) Double-ended turnout with litter barrels to east; scenic viewpoint. No overnight parking or camping. Mount Fellows (elev. 4,476 feet/1,364m) to the east. The constantly changing shadows make this an excellent camera subject. Exceptionally beautiful in the evening. To the southeast stands Pyramid Peak (elev. 5,201 feet/1,585m).

A 235.1 (378.4 km) **F 122.9** (197.8 km) *CAUTION: Railroad crossing.*

A 236.7 (380.9 km) **F 121.3** (195.2 km) Alaska Railroad crosses over highway. From this point the highway begins a steep descent northbound to Riley Creek.

A 237.2 (381.7 km) **F 120.8** (194.4 km) Riley Creek bridge.

A 237.3 (381.9 km) **F 120.7** (194.2 km) Entrance to **DENALI NATIONAL PARK AND PRESERVE** (formerly Mount McKinley National Park) to west. Fresh water fill-up hose and dump station 0.2 mile/0.3 km from junction on Park Road; Visitor Center is 0.5 mile/0.8 km from the highway junction. Campsites within the park are available on a first-come, first-served basis; sign up at the visitor center. You may also pick up schedules for the shuttle bus service at the visitor center (private vehicle access to the park is restricted). See DENALI NATIONAL PARK section for details.

Clusters of highway businesses north and south of the park entrance between Cantwell and Healy offer a variety of services to the highway traveler and park visitor. Services include river running, gift shops, accommodations, restaurants and entertainment.

A 238 (383 km) **F 120** (193.4 km) Third bridge northbound over the Nenana River. The 4.8 miles/7.7 km of road and 7 bridges in the rugged Nenana Canyon cost $7.7 million to build. Sugarloaf Mountain (elev. 4,450 feet/1,356m), to the east, is closed to the hunting of Dall sheep, which are regularly sighted in the early and late summer months. Mount Healy (elev. 5,716 feet/1,742m) is to the west.

Southbound for 6.8 miles/10.9 km the George Parks Highway is within the boundaries of Denali National Park and Preserve and travelers must abide by park rules. No discharge of firearms.

A 238.1 (383.2 km) **F 119.9** (193 km) **Denali Raft Adventures.** Come with the original Nenana River rafters! Paddleboats, too! Age 5 or older welcome, 7 departures daily. White water or scenic floats. Get away

to untouched wilderness! 2-hour, 4-hour and 6-hour trips. Also available: Full-day fly-in raft trips on the Yanert River. See display ad in DENALI NATIONAL PARK section. Phone (907) 683-2234. VISA, MasterCard accepted. [ADVERTISEMENT]

A 238.3 (383.5 km) **F 119.7** (192.6 km) Kingfisher Creek.

A 238.4 (383.6 km) **F 119.6** (192.5 km) **Denali Bluffs Hotel.** Opening 1996. The newest and closest hotel to the Denali National Park and Preserve entrance. 100 rooms, each room features 2 double beds, a private balcony or patio, and numerous other amenities. Most of the rooms have spectacular views of the Alaska Range. The lodge features a large stone fireplace and cathedral ceilings. There are comfortable sitting areas inside the lodge or outside on the deck to enjoy the panoramic views. Gift shop and coin-operated laundry. Shuttle service to visitor center and rail depot. Complete tour and activity desk. Handicap accessible. Open mid-May through mid-September. Credit cards accepted. PO Box 72460, Fairbanks, AK 99707. Phone (907) 488-7000 (winter) or (907) 683-7000 (summer). See display ad in the DENALI NATIONAL PARK section. [ADVERTISEMENT]

A 238.5 (383.8 km) **F 119.5** (192.3 km) Alaska flag display features a 10-by-15-foot/3-by-5-m state flag and plaques detailing history of flag design and song.

A 238.5 (383.8 km) **F 119.5** (192.3 km) **McKinley/Denali Steakhouse and Salmon Bake.** Satisfy that hearty Alaskan appetite at a real home-style barbecue restaurant, featuring char-broiled burgers, steaks, sandwiches,

fresh salmon and halibut, tender beef ribs, barbecued chicken with rice pilaf, baked beans, extensive salad bar, homemade soups and desserts. Cocktails. Rustic heated indoor seating with majestic view of mountains. Free shuttle from all local hotels. Sourdough breakfasts. Large selection of postcards in our upstairs gift shop. T-shirts, sweatshirts and ice for sale. Pay phone. Open daily 5 A.M. to 11 P.M. in summer. Phone (907) 683-2733. See display ad in the DENALI NATIONAL PARK section. [ADVERTISEMENT]

McKinley/Denali Gift Shop. Largest giftshop in park area—upstairs at McKinley/Denali Steakhouse and Salmon Bake. Largest selection of Mount McKinley and Denali National Park T-shirts and sweatshirts. Hundreds of souvenirs and gifts. Photo calendars and postcards. Open 5 A.M. to 11 P.M. Call for free shuttle service. [ADVERTISEMENT]

McKinley/Denali Cabins. Economy tent cabins with electric heat and lights from $65. Closest full-service facility to park entrance, wildlife shuttles. Close to raft trips, store, gift shop, gas. Beds, linens, blankets. Central showers. Pay phone. Some cabins with private baths. Shuttle to visitor center, railroad depot available. Free visitor information. Call us for reservations on many area activities. Reservations: (907) 683-2258 or 683-2733 or write: Box 90M, Denali Park, AK 99755. See display ad in DENALI NATIONAL PARK section. [ADVERTISEMENT]

Denali Crow's Nest Log Cabins and the Overlook Bar & Grill. Open mid-May to mid-September, offering the finest view in area. Close to park entrance. Authentic Alaska log cabins with hotel comforts; all rooms with private bath. Courtesy trans-

portation. Hot tubs, tour bookings. Dine on steaks, seafood, burgers, salmon and halibut indoors or on the deck at The Overlook Bar & Grill. 64 varieties of beer, 6 draft beers; meals 11 A.M. to 11 P.M. Bar open till midnight. For restaurant courtesy shuttle from all local hotels, call (907) 683-2723, fax (907) 683-2323. See display ad in DENALI NATIONAL PARK section. [ADVERTISEMENT]

Denali Wilderness Lodge is Alaska's historic fly-in wilderness lodge—an authentic bush homestead nestled in the pristine Wood River Valley just outside Denali Park. The bush plane flight to the lodge, over the mountains and glaciers of the Alaska Range,

is spectacular. Comfortable accommodations, gourmet meals, naturalist programs, horseback riding, nature/photo walks and hikes, bird-watching, wildlife museum. This is the Alaska of your dreams. Overnight packages and day trips available. Free brochure. 1-800-541-9779. See display ad: DENALI NATIONAL PARK section. [ADVERTISEMENT]

A 238.6 (384 km) **F 119.4** (192.2 km) Denali Princess (formerly Harper) Lodge.

A 238.7 (384.1 km) **F 119.3** (192 km) Mt. McKinley Motor Lodge.

A 238.8 (384.3 km) **F 119.2** (191.8 km) **Sourdough Cabins.** Office and front desk are located adjacent to the McKinley Raft Tours office. Sourdough offers individual heated cabins, nestled in a spruce forest located below the office, away from the highway noise. Phone (907) 683-2773, fax (907) 683-2357. VISA, MasterCard, American Express accepted. See display ad in the DENALI NATIONAL PARK section. [ADVERTISEMENT] ▲

A 238.9 (384.5 km) **F 119.1** (191.7 km) **Alaska Cabin Night Dinner Theater** has 2 evening shows. Expect an all you can eat dinner featuring salmon and ribs, served family style followed by a rousing musical revue depicting the exciting gold rush days. Located at McKinley Chalet Resort in a beautiful handcrafted log cabin. For reservations call (800) 276-7234; in Anchorage 276-7234 or stop by the tour desk located in the lobby of the McKinley Chalet Resort. [ADVERTISEMENT]

Alaska Raft Adventures, offers two wonderful rafting experiences complete with experienced guides and all equipment needed to enjoy a great Nenana River adventure. Our Wilderness Run floats through a glacial valley offering unparalleled scenery. Our Canyon Run offers exciting whitewater action, (class III & IV rapids). Both adventures depart three times daily, and courtesy transportation is available between area hotels and the Alaska Railroad Depot. Allow for a total of three hours. Call 1-800-276-7234; in Anchorage (907) 276-7234 or stop by the tour desk at the McKinley Chalet Resort. [ADVERTISEMENT]

Denali Outdoor Center. Denali's most diversified river outfitter. Oarboats, paddleboats, inflatable kayak tours and comprehensive whitewater kayak school. Whitewater or scenic wilderness trips daily. 2-hour, 4-hour, 1/2 day and full day guided trips. All gear and custom drysuits provided! Ages 5 and up. Call for reservations (907) 683-1925. Major credit cards accepted. [ADVERTISEMENT]

McKinley Chalet Resort, offers 343 mini-suites overlooking the Nenana River. We offer fine dining, lounge, gift shop and full service tour desk. The Chalet Center Cafe treats you to fresh muffins, sandwiches, salads, soups, a specialty drink bar, indoor pool, sauna, jacuzzi and local artist's gallery. Also the home of Alaska Cabin Nite Dinner Theater and Alaska Raft Adventures. (800) 276-7234; in Anchorage 276-7234. [ADVERTISEMENT]

Northern Lights Theatre and Gift Shop. Come experience a Northern Lights or Denali Park Photo Symphony on a 34-foot-wide screen. These 2 multi-image presentations are one of a kind, entertaining and informative displays of the aurora borealis or Denali National Park. Stop by for show times and tickets. Don't miss Denali's largest gift

shop in a beautiful, natural log building next door, specializing in quality Alaskan gifts. Full mount, world class polar bear on display. Groceries at Denali General Store. Located 1.5 miles north of park entrance. Large parking area. VISA/MasterCard. Dont miss this attraction! P.O. Box 65, Denali Park, AK 99755. Phone (907) 683-4000. Mention this ad for 10 percent discount. [ADVERTISEMENT]

A 240.1 (386.4 km) **F 117.9** (189.7 km) Bridge over Ice Worm Gulch. *CAUTION: Rock slide area. Slow down.* High winds in the Nenana Canyon can make this stretch of road dangerous for campers and motorhomes.

WARNING: The highway has many sharp curves. Do not park along the highway. Use the many parking areas provided.

A 240.2 (386.6 km) **F 117.8** (189.6 km) Hornet Creek bridge. Paved double-ended turnout to west beside Nenana River.

A 240.5 (387 km) **F 117.5** (189.1 km) Large gravel parking area to west by river.

A 240.7 (387.4 km) **F 117.3** (188.8 km) Paved double-ended turnout to west beside river.

A 241 (387.7 km) **F 117** (188.3 km) Paved turnout to west.

A 241.2 (388.2 km) **F 116.8** (188 km) Bridge over Fox Creek; gravel road to creek. Large gravel turnout to west. Slide area next 0.4 mile/0.6 km northbound.

A 241.7 (389 km) **F 116.3** (187.2 km) Large gravel turnout to west.

A 242.3 (389.9 km) **F 115.7** (186.2 km) Paved double-ended turnout to west.

A 242.4 (390.1 km) **F 115.6** (186 km) Dragonfly Creek bridge; paved double-ended turnout to west.

A 242.8 (390.7 km) **F 115.2** (185.4 km) Paved double-ended turnout to west. *CAUTION: Windy area next mile northbound.*

A 242.9 (390.9 km) **F 115.1** (185.2 km) Moody Bridge. This 4th bridge northbound over the Nenana River. Measures 174 feet/53m from its deck to the bottom of the canyon. Dall sheep can be spotted from the bridge. Entering Game Management Unit 20A northbound, 20C southbound.

A 243.6 (392 km) **F 114.4** (184.1 km) Bridge over Bison Gulch. Paved viewpoint to east. A steep grade follows northbound, end wind area.

A 244.1 (392.8 km) **F 113.9** (183.3 km) Paved turnout to east. Watch for frost heaves next 1 mile/1.6 km northbound.

A 244.6 (393.6 km) **F 113.4** (182.5 km) Bridge over Antler Creek.

A 245.1 (394.4 km) **F 112.9** (181.7 km) **Denali RV Park & Motel.** 90 full and partial RV hookups, 30-amp electric. Level sites,

pull-throughs, easy highway access. Individual restrooms with private showers, flush toilets. Dump station. Caravans welcome! 14 motel rooms: Central bath $45, private bath $65, family units with full kitchen $90. Outdoor cooking area, pay phones, gift shop, general store. Located 8 miles north of park entrance. Close to all park facilities. Beautiful mountain views. Hiking trails. Reasonable rates. VISA/MasterCard. Box 155, Denali Park, AK 99755. 1-907-683-1500. 1-800-478-1501 (in Alaska). See display ad in the DENALI NATIONAL PARK section. [ADVERTISEMENT] ▲

A 245.6 (395.2 km) **F 112.4** (180.9 km) Watch for rough road, frost heaves and dips 0.4 mile/0.6 km northbound.

A 246.9 (397.3 km) **F 111.1** (178.8 km) Paved turnout to east and beautiful view of Healy area.

A 247 (397.5 km) **F 111** (178.6 km) Side road leads 1 mile/1.6 km to **Otto Lake**, 5 miles/8 km to Black Diamond Coal Mine. Primitive parking area on lakeshore (0.8-mile/1.3-km drive in) with toilet, litter barrels, shallow boat launch. Stocked with rainbow and coho. Denali hostel. Access to bed and breakfasts, golf driving range and RV park. ▲

At Timberline Bed & Breakfast. The view is simply spectacular. Just minutes from Denali. We have 3 rooms with queen beds. Continental breakfast included. The hospitality is warm and our comfortable rooms are very affordable. Your hosts are Dick and Kim White. Dick was born and raised in Alaska and Kim relocated here in 1987 from Wisconsin. Open year around with fantastic viewing of the Northern Lights from our 16-by-32-foot deck. Reservations strongly suggested but not required. Box 13, Healy, Alaska 99743. Phone (907) 683-2757. Fax (907) 683-2767. See display ad in DENALI NATIONAL PARK section. [ADVERTISEMENT]

Black Diamond Resort Co. Come visit us on the greens! We have a beautiful golf driving range open for your pleasure this summer. Look for us in the future with our 9-hole course under current construction. 1 mile west down the Otto Lake Road. Club rentals available. [ADVERTISEMENT]

Otto Lake R.V. Park and Campground. Beautiful mountain views from primitive lakeside RV and tent sites, 1/2 mile west of Parks Highway on Otto Lake Road. Spacious and secluded sites with picnic tables, firepits, firewood, potable water, toilets, dump station and pay phone. Boat rentals. Located 9.7 miles north of Denali National Park entrance. [ADVERTISEMENT] ▲

Homestead Bed & Breakfast. See display ad this section.

A 248.4 (399.8 km) **F 109.6** (176.4 km) **McKinley KOA Kampground.** One of the nicest campgrounds around; 92 sites and utilities available. Come let our family help your family have a great vacation. ... We will help you experience the sights and sounds of Denali. We book camping, rafting, horseback riding, dinner, flightseeing and

shows. We offer our guests free showers, dump station, wooded landscape, a movie on Alaska, miniature golf, fax service and propane. Caravans–groups welcome. Peaceful setting, spectacular view and beautiful open skies. Come let us make you feel at home. Reservations recommended. Write Box 340MP, Healy, AK 99743. Phone: (907) 683-2379. Fax: (907) 683-2281. National (800) 478-AKOA. See display ad in the DENALI NATIONAL PARK section. [ADVERTISEMENT] ▲

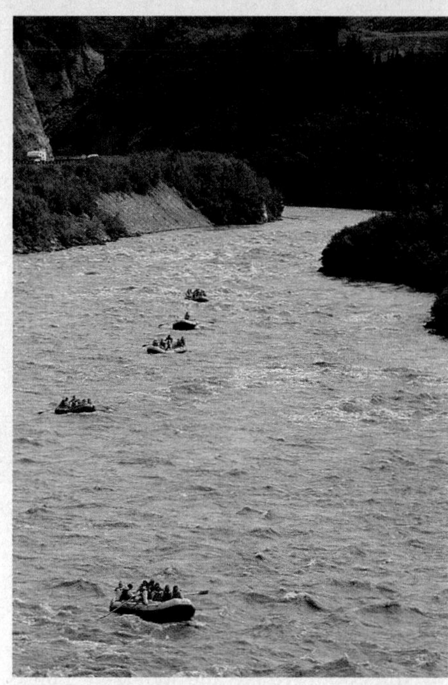

Rafting trips down the Nenana River are available. (Jerrianne Lowther, staff)

A 248.5 (399.9 km) **F 109.5** (176.2 km) Paved turnout to east. River rafting service office. Looking south, Mount Healy is visible just west of the highway; first mountain east of the highway is Sugarloaf; to the northeast is Dora Peak (elev. 5,572 feet/1,698m).

A 248.7 (400.2 km) **F 109.3** (175.9 km) **Junction** with spur road to community of Healy (see description following **Milepost A 248.8**). Homes and businesses of this Alaska community are dispersed along the highway from here north to **Milepost A 249.6** and in the first mile east along the spur road toward the Nenana River. Hotel and motel accommodations are available at the highway junction, and several bed and breakfasts are located along the spur road.

A 248.8 (400.4 km) **F 109.2** (175.7 km) North side of Healy spur road intersection.

Denali North Star Inn. Located at Healy intersection, Mile 248.8 Parks Highway. Comfortable, reasonably priced rooms, finest dining in the Denali Park area. Information and reservations for Denali Park tours. Area shuttle service, authentic Alaskan gifts, beauty salon, barber shop, tanning beds. Recreation and exercise areas, saunas, self-service laundry. 11 miles to Denali Park entrance. 1-800-684-1560. See display ad in DENALI NATIONAL PARK section. [ADVERTISEMENT]

The Siberian aster is Alaska's most common aster and a harbinger of autumn.
(Jerrianne Lowther, staff)

Denali Wings. The most comprehensive Air Tour of Denali National Park. Your 1-hr, 10-minute narrated fight to Mt. McKinley overflies both remote and well-known areas of the Park. Views of glaciers, mountains and wildlife not seen on ground tours. When you visit Denali, See Denali!! (907) 683-2245. Reservation desk at Stampede Lodge, Mile 248.8 Parks Highway. [ADVERTISEMENT]

Stampede Lodge and Bushmaster Grill. Historic Alaskan Lodge and Restaurant completely remodeled in 1995. Warm, comfortable atmosphere located 10 minutes away from the congestion of the Park entrance. Private baths and phones in all rooms. Free train station pick-up. Restaurant open 6 A.M.–10 P.M. 7 days a week. 1-800-478-2370, (907) 683-2242, fax (907) 683-2243. [ADVERTISEMENT]

Healy

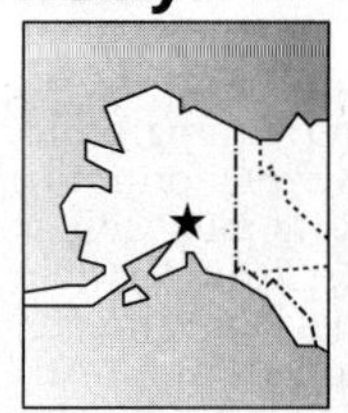

Located on a spur road just east of the George Parks Highway **junction. Population:** 605. **Emergency Services: Alaska State Troopers,** phone (907) 683-2232. **Fire Department,** Tri–Valley Volunteer Fire Dept., phone 911 or (907) 683-2223. **Clinic,** Healy Clinic, located on 2nd floor of Tri–Valley Community Center at Mile 0.5 Usibelli Spur Road, phone (907) 683-2211 or 911 (open 24 hours).

Visitor Information: Available at the Healy Senior Center, located on Healy Spur Road behind the grocery store. Open 11 A.M. to 7 P.M., year-round; phone (907) 683-1317.

Elevation: 1,294 feet/394m. **Radio:** KUAC-FM 101.7. **Private Aircraft:** Healy River airstrip adjacent north; length 2,800 feet/853m; gravel; unattended.

Healy's power plant has the distinction of being the largest coal-fired steam plant in Alaska, as well as the only mine-mouth power plant. This plant is part of the Golden Valley Electric Assoc., which furnishes electric power for Fairbanks and vicinity. The Fairbanks–Tanana Valley area uses primarily coal and also oil to meet its electrical needs.

Across the Nenana River lie the mining settlements of Suntrana and Usibelli. Dry Creek, Healy and Nenana river valleys comprise the area referred to as Tri–Valley. Coal mining began here in 1918 and has grown to become Alaska's largest coal mining operation. Usibelli Coal Mine, the state's only commercial coal mine, mines about 800,000 tons of coal a year, supplying South Korea, the University of Alaska, the military and other Fairbanks-area utilities. The Usibelli Coal Mine began a successful reclamation program in 1971; Dall sheep now graze where there was once evidence only of strip mining.

From the highway, you may see a 33-cubic-yard walking dragline (named Ace in the Hole by local schoolchildren in a contest) removing the soil, or overburden, to expose the coal seams. This 4,275,000-pound machine, erected in 1978, moves an average of 24,000 cubic yards each 24 hours. Private vehicles are not allowed into the mining area and no tours are available.

Alaksan Chateau Bed and Breakfast, set on two wooded acres with hiking and biking trails. Just minutes to Denali National Park entrance. Private baths, entrances and sun decks, mini kitchens and barbecue pit. Satellite TV available. Continental-plus breakfast. Families welcome. Hosts Teresa Chepoda and Alaskan-born John Usibelli will provide an environment of elegance, hospitality and congeniality. Call (907) 683-1377 or write PO Box 187, Healy, AK 99743. See display ad in DENALI NATIONAL PARK section. [ADVERTISEMENT]

HEALY ADVERTISERS

Alaskan Chateau Bed & Breakfast	Ph. (907) 683-1377
Denali Dome Home Bed and Breakfast	Ph. (907) 683-1239
Denali North Star Inn	Mile 248.8 Parks Hwy.
Denali Suites	Ph. (907) 683-2848
Denali Wings	Mile 248.8 Parks Hwy.
GrandView Bed & Breakfast	Ph. (907) 683-2468
Pat & Windell's Bed and Breakfast	Ph. (907) 683-2472
Stampede Lodge	Mile 248.8 Parks Hwy.
Totem Inn	Mile 248.7 Parks Hwy.
Valley Vista Bed & Breakfast	Ph. (907) 683-2842

Denali Dome Home Bed, Breakfast and Hospitality is a 7,200-foot geodesic home run year-round by the Miller Family and located one turn and 15 minutes from Denali National Park. The Dome has 9 bedrooms, 7 baths, 2 living rooms, sauna, fireplaces, decks, and large off-street parking on 2.75 wooded acres. The Millers are happy to advise or arrange your Denali Park vacation. Very reasonable rates. MasterCard and VISA accepted. Call (907) 683-1239 or write Box 262, Healy, AK 99743 for information. [ADVERTISEMENT]

Denali Suites. Located 15 minutes north of entrance to Denali National Park on Healy Spur Road. Units include 2 or 3 bedrooms, kitchen and dining area, living room with queen-sized hide-a-bed, TV and VCR, and private baths. Coin-operated laundry facilities. Clean, comfortable, affordable. Each unit accommodates up to 6 people, one accommodates 8, with 2 private baths; families welcome. VISA, MasterCard, Discover. Open all year. Call (907) 683-2848 or write Box 393, Healy, AK 99743. See display ad in the DENALI NATIONAL PARK section. [ADVERTISEMENT]

GrandView Bed & Breakfast. Located 12 miles from the entrance to Denali National Park. Relax and enjoy the spectacular view of the Alaska Range. Deck, barbecue, sitting area. Continental breakfast. Open year-round. VISA/MasterCard. Write GrandView Bed & Breakfast, Box 109, Healy, AK 99743 or call (907) 683-2468. See display ad in DENALI NATIONAL PARK section. [ADVERTISEMENT]

George Parks Highway Log

(continued)

A 248.8 (400.4 km) **F 109** (175.7 km) Healy spur road junction, north side of intersection; food and lodging.

A 249 (400.7 km) **F 109** (175.4 km) Suntrana Road, post office and Tri–Valley School.

A 249.2 (401 km) **F 108.8** (175.1 km) **Larry's Healy Tesoro.** See display ad this section.

A 249.3 (401.2 km) **F 108.7** (174.9 km) Dry Creek Bridge No. 1.

A 249.4 (401.4 km) **F 108.6** (174.8 km) Lester Road.

A 249.5 (401.5 km) **F 108.5** (174.6 km) **Motel Nord Haven.** Built in 1994 with your motoring family in mind. West side of highway in the trees. Peaceful and secluded. 12 miles north of Denali National Park entrance. Each room has 2 queen beds, private bath, television and telephone. Open year-round. MasterCard and VISA. Phone (907) 683-4500. Fax (907) 683-4503. [ADVERTISEMENT]

A 249.6 (401.7 km) **F 108.4** (174.4 km) **Evans Industries, Inc.** See display ad this section.

A 249.8 (402 km) **F 108.2** (174.1 km) Dry Creek bridge No. 2. Good berry picking area first part of August.

A 251.1 (404.1 km) **F 106.9** (172 km) Stampede Road to west. Lignite Road to east.

A 251.2 (404.3 km) **F 106.8** (171.9 km) Paved turnout to west. Coal seams visible in bluff to east. Cotton grass and lupine along roadside in June, fireweed in July.

A 252.4 (406.2 km) **F 105.6** (169.9 km) Gravel turnout to west.

A 252.5 (406.4 km) **F 105.5** (169.8 km) Bridge over **Panguingue Creek;** turnout at end. Moderate success fishing for grayling. This stream, which flows 8 miles/13 km to the Nenana River, was named for a Philippine card game.

CAUTION: Watch for frost heaves northbound.

A 259.4 (417.5 km) **F 98.6** (158.7 km) Large paved turnout to east. Views of Rex Dome to the northeast. Walker and Jumbo domes to the east. Liberty Bell mining area lies between the peaks and highway.

A 261.1 (420.2 km) **F 96.9** (155.9 km) Gravel turnout to east. Look for bank swallows, small brown birds that nest in clay and sand banks near streams and along highways.

A 262 (421.6 km) **F 96** (154.5 km) Watch for rough patches in pavement and gravel shoulders, northbound. Watch for frost heaves southbound.

A 263 (423.2 km) **F 95** (152.9 km) Small gravel turnout to east. Wildflowers include sweet pea and oxytrope.

A 264.5 (425.7 km) **F 93.5** (150.5 km) Paved turnout to west.

A 269 (432.9 km) **F 89** (143.2 km) June Creek rest area and picnic spot to east; large gravel parking area. Gravel road leads down to lower parking area on June Creek (trailers and large RVs check turnaround space before driving down). Wooden stairs lead up to the picnic spot and a view of the Nenana River. There are picnic tables, fireplaces, toilets, a litter bin and a sheltered table. Cut wood may be available.

A 269.3 (433.4 km) **F 88.7** (142.8 km) Bridge over Bear Creek. Gravel turnout to east.

A 271.4 (436.8 km) **F 86.6** (139.4 km) Paved turnout to west. Highway northbound leads through boggy area with few turnouts.

A 275.6 (443.5 km) **F 82.4** (132.6 km) Entering Game Management Unit 20A northbound, 20C southbound.

A 275.8 (443.9 km) **F 82.2** (132.3 km) Rex Bridge over Nenana River.

A 276 (444.2 km) **F 82** (132 km) **Tatlanika Trading Co.** Located in a beautiful pristine wilderness setting. Tent sites and RV parking with electricity, water, dump station, showers, TV. 39 miles from Denali National Park on the Nenana River. Our gift shop features a gathering of handmade art/crafts/artifacts from various villages. See the rare Samson fox, along with relics and antiques from Alaska's colorful past in a museum atmosphere. Many historical and educational displays. Nothing sold from overseas. Visitor information. Coffee, pop, juice, snacks. Clean restrooms. This is a must stop. See display ad this section. [ADVERTISEMENT] ▲

A 276.5 (445 km) **F 81.5** (131.2 km) *CAUTION: Railroad crossing.*

NOTE: Watch for guardrail construction southbound to Cantwell in 1996.

A 280 (450.6 km) **F 78** (125.5 km) Lodge with dining and a cafe/grocery.

Clear Sky Lodge. See display ad this section.

The Hop. See display ad this section.

CAUTION: Watch for dips in road next 5 miles/8 km northbound.

A 280.1 (450.8 km) **F 77.9** (125.4 km) **Rochester Lodge.** See display ad this section.

A 280.4 (451.2 km) **F 77.6** (124.9 km) Entering Clear Air Force Station northbound.

A 283.5 (456.2 km) **F 74.5** (119.9 km) Access road west to **ANDERSON** (pop. 626) and **CLEAR.** Clear is a military installation (ballistic missile early warning site), and a sign at turnoff states it is unlawful to enter without permission. However, you can drive into Anderson without permission. Located 6 miles/9.7 km northwest of Clear, Anderson has a city campground in an 80-acre park with 10 sites on the Tanana River. RV dump station, toilets, showers. The community also has churches, a restaurant, softball fields and shooting range. For more information call the city office at (907) 582-2500. Emergency aid is available through the Clear Air Force Site Fire Department; phone (907) 585-6321. ▲

Anderson Riverside Park. Come enjoy our city's 616 beautiful acres located along

the bank of the Tanana River! Featuring restrooms, showers, RV dump station, electrical hook-ups. Riverside campsites, rustic campsites with barbecue pits, picnic area with covered pavilion, fireplace. Shooting range, bandstand, telephone. Home of the annual Anderson Bluegrass Festival, held the last weekend in July. City of Anderson, P.O. Box 3100, Anderson, AK 99744. Phone (907) 582-2500; fax (907) 582-2496. [ADVERTISEMENT]

Private Aircraft: Clear airstrip, 2.6 miles/4.2 km southeast; elev. 552 feet/168m; length 3,900 feet/1,189m; gravel; unattended. Clear Sky Lodge airstrip, 4.3 miles/6.9 km south; elev. 650 feet/198m; length 2,500 feet/762m; gravel, earth.

A 285.7 (459.8 km) **F 72.3** (116.3 km) Julius Creek bridge.

A 286.3 (460.7 km) **F 71.7** (115.4 km) View of Mount McKinley southbound.

A 286.8 (461.5 km) **F 71.2** (114.6 km) Double-ended paved parking area to east. Watch for frost heaves northbound.

A 288 (463.5 km) **F 70** (112.7 km) Entering Clear Military Reservation southbound.

A 288.5 (464.3 km) **F 69.5** (111.8 km) **Welcome Home Bed and Breakfast.** See display ad this section.

A 296.7 (477.5 km) **F 61.3** (98.7 km) Bridge over **Fish Creek.** Small gravel turnout with litter barrels by creek. Access to creek at south end of bridge; moderate success fishing for grayling.

A 302.1 (486.2 km) **F 55.9** (90 km) **Finnish Alaskan Bed and Breakfast.** See display ad this section.

A 302.9 (487.4 km) **F 55.1** (88.7 km) Nenana municipal rifle range.

A 303.7 (488.7 km) **F 54.3** (87.4 km) Nenana airport (see Private Aircraft information in Nenana).

A 304.3 (489.7 km) **F 53.7** (86.4 km) **Nenana Tesoro.** See display ad this section.

A 304.5 (490 km) **F 53.5** (86.1 km) **A Frame Service.** See display ad this section.

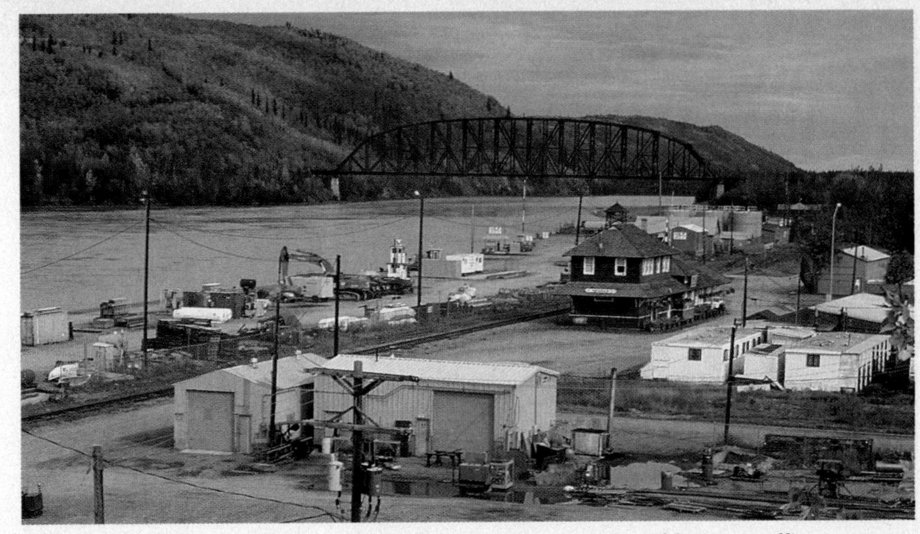

View of Nenana's riverfront, a staging area for railroad and barge traffic.
(© George Wuerthner)

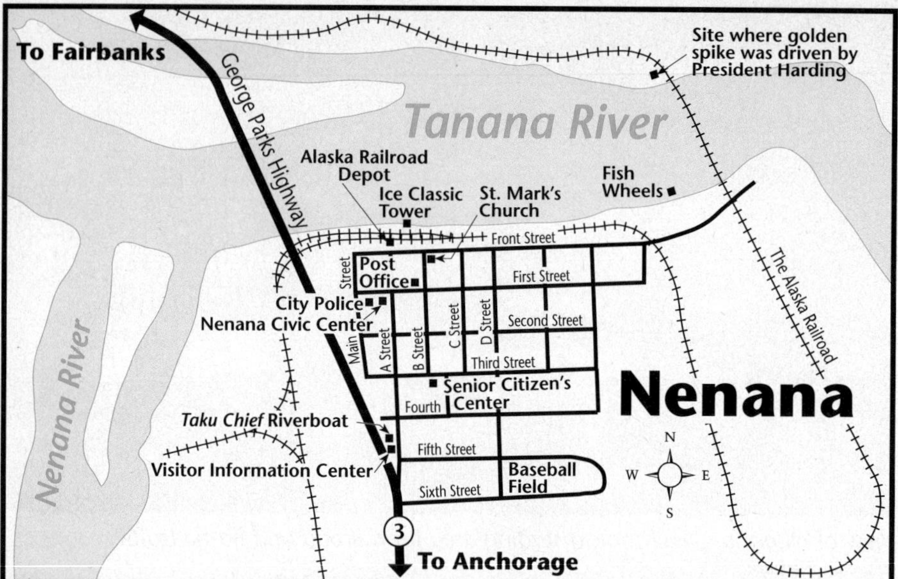

Nenana

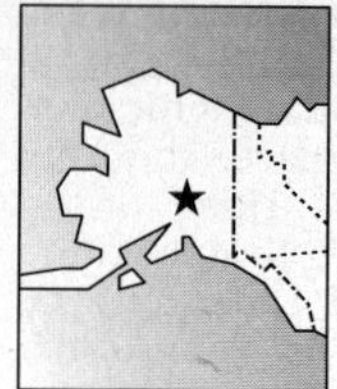

A 304.5 (490 km) **F 53.5** (86.1 km) Located at the confluence of the Tanana and Nenana rivers. **Population:** 361. **Emergency Services:** Emergency only (fire, police, ambulance), phone 911. **Alaska State Troopers,** phone (907) 832-5554, at **Milepost A 310** George Parks Highway. **City Police,** phone (907) 832-5632. **Fire Department,** phone (907) 832-5632.

Visitor Information: In a picturesque log cabin with sod roof at junction of the highway and A Street, phone (907) 832-9953. Open 8 A.M. to 6 P.M., 7 days a week, Memorial Day to Labor Day. Pay phone and ice for sale. Ice Classic tickets may be purchased here.

Marge Anderson Senior Citizen Center, located on 3rd Street between Market and B streets, also welcomes visitors.

Elevation: 400 feet/122m. **Radio:** KIAM 630, KUAC-FM 91.1. **Transportation: Air–** Nenana maintains an FAA-approved airport. **Railroad–**The Alaska Railroad.

Private Aircraft: Nenana Municipal Airport, 0.9 mile/1.4 km south; elev. 362 feet/110m; length 5,000 feet/1,524m; asphalt; fuel 100, Jet B. Floatplane and skiplane strip.

The town got its name from the Indian word *Nenana,* which means "a good place to camp between the rivers." It was first known as Tortella, a white man's interpretation of the Athabascan word *Toghotthele.* In 1902 Jim Duke built a roadhouse and trading post here, trading with Indians and supplying river travelers with goods and lodging.

Nenana boomed as a construction base for the Alaska Railroad. Today, Nenana is home port of the tug and barge fleet that in summer carries tons of freight, fuel and supplies to villages along the Tanana and Yukon rivers. Because the Tanana is a wide, shallow, muddy river, the barges move about 12 mph downstream and 5 mph upstream. The dock area is to the right of the highway northbound. Behind the Nenana visitor information center is the *Taku Chief:* This old tug, which has been renovated, once pushed barges on the Tanana.

On July 15, 1923, Pres. Warren G. Harding drove the golden spike at Nenana, signifying completion of the Alaska Railroad. A monument to the event stands east of the depot here. The Nenana Railroad Depot, located at the end of Main Street, is on the National Register of Historic Places. Built in 1923 and renovated in 1988, the depot has a pressed metal ceiling and houses the state's Alaska Railroad Museum; open 9 A.M. to 6 P.M. daily.

One block from the depot is St. Mark's Mission Church. This Episcopal church was built in 1905 upriver from Nenana; it was

NENANA ADVERTISERS

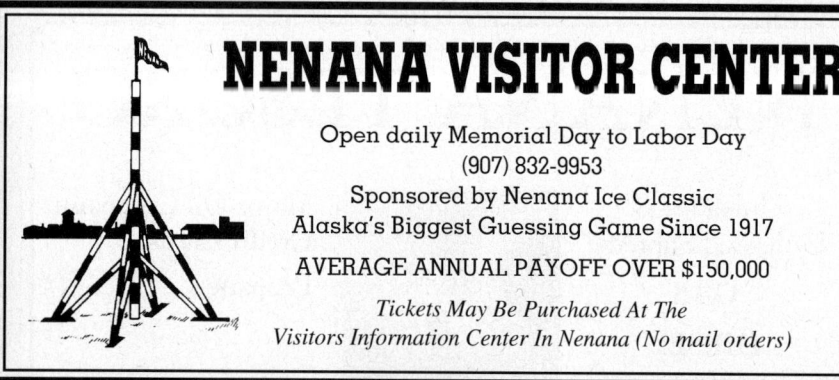

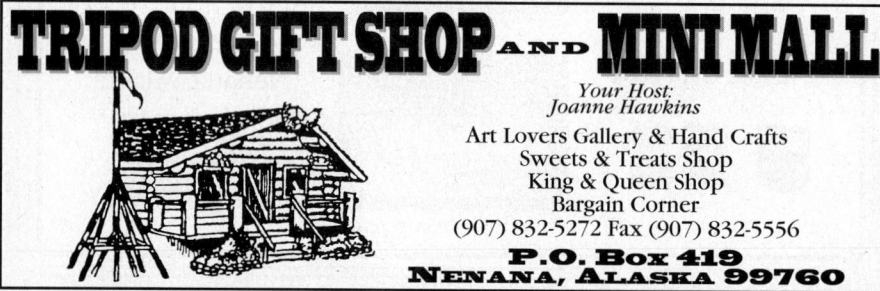

Bed & Maybe Breakfast....Ph. (907) 832-5272
Coghill's General Merchandise......Downtown
Nenana Inn..................................2nd & A St.
Nenana Valley RV Park & Campground...............................4th St.
Nenana Visitor Center..................Downtown
Tripod Gift Shop and Mini Mall....................Ph. (907) 832-5272

moved to its present location in the 1930s when riverbank erosion threatened the structure. A school was located next door to the mission until the 1940s, and pupils were brought in by tug from villages along the river. The restored log church has pews with hand-carving and an altar covered with Native beadwork-decorated moosehide.

Nenana is perhaps best known for the Nenana Ice Classic, an annual event that offers cash prizes to the lucky winners who can guess the exact minute of the ice breakup on the Tanana River. Ice Classic festivities begin the last weekend in February with the Tripod Raising Festival and Nenana Ice Classic Dog Race, and culminate at breakup time (late April or May) when the surging ice on the Tanana River dislodges the tripod. A line attached to the tripod stops a clock, recording the official breakup time.

Nenana celebrates River Daze the first weekend in June. The main event is "The Annihilator," the toughest 10-kilometer foot race in Alaska, over Tortella Hill.

Nenana has an auto repair shop, radio station, several churches, restaurants, a laundromat, gift shops, a grocery and general store. Accommodations at local motel, inn and bed and breakfast; access to wilderness lodge. RV facilities include an RV park with electric hookups and camping. River charters and guide service available. Picnic tables and rest area beside the restored *Taku Chief* are behind the visitor information center. ▲

George Parks Highway Log
(continued)

A 305.1 (491 km) **F 52.9** (85.1 km) Tanana River bridge. Large paved turnout to west at north end of bridge. The Tanana is formed by the joining of the Chisana and the Nabesna rivers near Northway and flows 440 miles/708 km westward to the Yukon River. From the bridge, watch for freight-laden river barges bound for the Yukon River. North of this bridge, fish wheels sometimes may be seen in action and occasionally fish may be purchased from the owners of the wheels.

Entering Game Management Unit 20B northbound, 20A southbound.

A 305.5 (491.6 km) **F 52.5** (84.5 km) Paved turnout to west by Tanana River. There is a Native cemetery 0.6 mile/1 km to east on side road.

A 305.6 (491.8 km) **F 52.4** (84.3 km) Paved turnout to west overlooking Tanana River.

A 305.9 (492.3 km) **F 52.1** (83.8 km) Double-ended gravel turnout to east.

A 308.9 (497.1 km) **F 49.1** (79 km) *CAUTION: Railroad crossing.*

A 309 (497.3 km) **F 49** (78.9 km) **Monderosa.** See display ad this section.

A 314.6 (506.3 km) **F 43.4** (69.8 km) Paved double-ended turnout to west.

A 314.8 (506.6 km) **F 43.2** (69.5 km) Bridge over Little Goldstream Creek.

A 315.4 (507.6 km) **F 42.5** (68.6 km) Truck lane next 2.8 miles/4.5 km northbound.

A 318.8 (513 km) **F 39.2** (63.1 km) Paved double-ended turnout to west with scenic view. The view is mostly of bogs, small lakes and creeks, with names like Hard Luck Creek, Fortune Creek, All Hand Help Lake and Wooden Canoe Lake.

Southbound travelers will see the Tanana River on both sides of the highway. It follows a horseshoe-shaped course, the top of the closed end being the bridge at Nenana.

A 321 (516.6 km) **F 37** (59.5 km) Fairbanks-bound traffic: Highway climbs a steep grade with sweeping curves next 1 mile/1.6 km; truck lane next mile northbound. Mount McKinley is visible to the southwest on a clear day.

A 323 (519.8 km) **F 35** (56.3 km) Tanana River visible to east in valley below highway.

A 323.8 (521.1 km) **F 34.2** (55 km) Truck lane next 0.3 mile/0.5 km northbound.

A 324.5 (522.2 km) **F 33.5** (53.9 km) Paved double-ended turnout to east with scenic view to south.

A 325 (523 km) **F 33** (53.1 km) This stretch of highway is often called Skyline Drive; views to west. Downgrade northbound.

A 325.7 (524.1 km) **F 32.3** (52 km) Entering Fairbanks North Star Borough northbound.

A 328 (527.8 km) **F 30** (48.2 km) **Skinny Dick's Halfway Inn.** See display ad this section.

A 328.3 (528.3 km) **F 29.7** (47.8 km) Truck lane next 3 miles/4.8 km southbound.

A 331.6 (533.6 km) **F 26.4** (42.5 km) Long paved double-ended turnout to east. Intermittent truck lanes northbound to Fairbanks.

A 338.2 (544.3 km) **F 19.8** (31.9 km) Wide view to east. Look for Murphy Dome (elev. 2,930 feet/893m) with white communication installations on summit to west.

A 339.3 (546 km) **F 19.7** (30.1 km) Viewpoint and sign to east. This is the south end of a 1-mile/1.6-km scenic loop road that rejoins the highway at **Milepost A 339.9**. Highway begins downgrade northbound.

A 339.9 (547 km) **F 18.1** (29.1 km) Turnoff (unmarked) for Bonanza Experimental Forest via 1-mile/1.6-km loop road east; scenic viewpoint.

A 342.2 (550.7 km) **F 15.8** (25.4 km) Rosie Creek Road.

A 342.4 (551 km) **F 15.6** (25.1 km) Old Nenana Highway.

A 344.2 (553.9 km) **F 13.8** (22.2 km) Monument in honor of George Alexander Parks, former governor of Alaska. Also here is a Blue Star Memorial highway plaque honoring the armed forces. Viewpoint and litter barrels to east. Tanana River can be seen below the Parks monument.

A 349 (561.6 km) **F 9** (14.5 km) Cripple Creek Road to south, Park Ridge Road to north. Truck lane next 4.2 miles/6.8 km southbound.

A 350 (563.3 km) **F 8** (12.9 km) Alder Creek.

A 351.2 (565.2 km) **F 6.8** (10.9 km) Old gold dredges visible to the east.

A 351.7 (566 km) **F 6.3** (10.1 km) Turnoff to west for Ester (description follows).

Ester

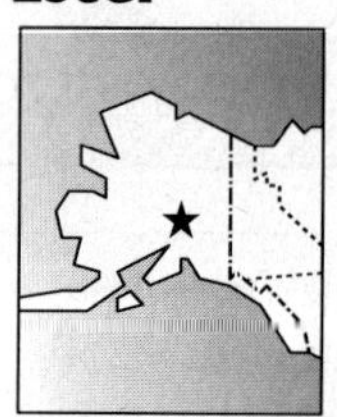

Located 0.6 mile/1 km west of highway. **Population:** 211. **Emergency Services:** Emergency only, phone 911. **Fire Department**, phone (907) 479-6050. A former gold mining camp and current visitor attraction, Ester has a hotel, RV camping, 2 saloons, 3 gift shops and a post office. A village sign on Main Street locates these services.

Ester was a raucous mining camp in 1906, with a population of some 5,000 miners. Today a quiet bedroom community of Fairbanks, Ester's heydays are relived in music, song and dance at the Malemute Saloon. Active gold mining is still under way in the area. One of the best preserved gold dredges from the gold rush days can be seen from **Milepost A 351.2**.

The Malemute Saloon is an Ester landmark. (Mike Mathers)

Ester Gold Camp. At the turn-of-century, discovery of gold in the Ester region drew hundreds of prospectors to seek their fortunes. In 1936, the Fairbanks Exploration Company built Ester Camp to support a large scale gold dredge operation. After twenty years of operation, the camp was closed. It opened again in 1958, but this time as a summer visitor attraction. Today, Ester Gold Camp, on the National Register of Historic Places, provides services for another kind of prospector: those seeking accommodations, excellent food and a fun-filled night of entertainment. Open late May through early September. See display ad. [ADVERTISEMENT] ▲

Judie Gumm Designs. Noted for her sculptural interpretations of northern images, her work has been featured in many national publications. Priced moderately; easy to pack—her jewelry makes a perfect remembrance of your adventure North. Follow the signs in Ester. Weekdays 10–6. Saturday 12–5. Catalog available. P.O. Box 169, Ester, AK 99725. Phone: (907) 479-4568. See display ad. [ADVERTISEMENT]

George Parks Highway Log
(continued)

A 351.8 (566.2 km) **F 6.2** (10 km) Weigh stations.

A 352.5 (567.3 km) **F 5.5** (8.8 km) Gold Hill Road.

Gold Hill. See display ad this section.

Inua Wool Shoppe. On Gold Hill Road, .3 mile to Henderson, 1.0 mile to 202 Henderson Road, a beautiful hand hewn log house that is home of Inua Wool Shoppe, Interior Alaska's most complete knitting shoppe. Fabulous selection of Quiviuq, wool, cotton, silk, linen, alpaca, hand-painted yarn and more. Browse through large selection of Alaskan, Norwegian and American patterns, needlepoints, buttons, books and yarns. Hand carved ivory and antler needles and crochet hooks. Black walnut, birch and

Inox knitting needles. Come enjoy a unique and complete knitting shoppe. Open 10–6 Monday–Saturday. (907) 479-5830. (Alaska 800-478-9848). VISA and MasterCard welcome. [ADVERTISEMENT]

A 353.5 (568.9 km) **F 4.5** (7.2 km) Gas station and store. Public dumpster.

Crazy Loon Saloon & Music House. Bar and music hall features Alaskan beer, other microbrews, live music, dancing. Grounds include volleyball courts, campfire and picnic area. Ample parking, RVs welcome. The bar hosts concerts, private parties, and other special events year-round. Casual atmosphere, snacks, souvenirs. (907) 455-4487. [ADVERTISEMENT]

A 355.2 (571.6 km) **F 2.8** (4.5 km) **Goldhill RV Park and Cabins.** See display ad this section. ▲

A 355.8 (572.6 km) **F 2.2** (3.5 km) Sheep Creek Road and Tanana Drive. Road to Murphy Dome (a restricted military site).

A 356.8 (574.2 km) **F 1.2** (1.9 km) Turnoff to University of Alaska, Geist Road, Chena Ridge Loop and Chena Pump Road.

A 357.6 (575.5 km) **F 0.4** (0.6 km) Bridge over Chena River.

A 357.7 (575.6 km) **F 0.3** (0.5 km) Fairbanks airport exit.

A 358 (576.1 km) **F 0** Fairbanks exit; George Parks Highway (Robert J. Mitchell Expressway) continues to Richardson Highway, bypassing Fairbanks. Take Fairbanks exit to Airport Way for University Avenue (access to University of Alaska and Chena River state recreation site); Peger Road (access to private campground, flying service and Alaskaland); and Cushman Street turnoff to downtown and to connect with the Richardson Highway and Steese Expressway. (See Fairbanks Vicinity map in the FAIRBANKS section.)

NOTE: There are no banks between Fairbanks and Wasilla at ***Milepost A 42.2****. Automatic teller machines are noted in the log.*

FAIRBANKS

(See maps, page 406)

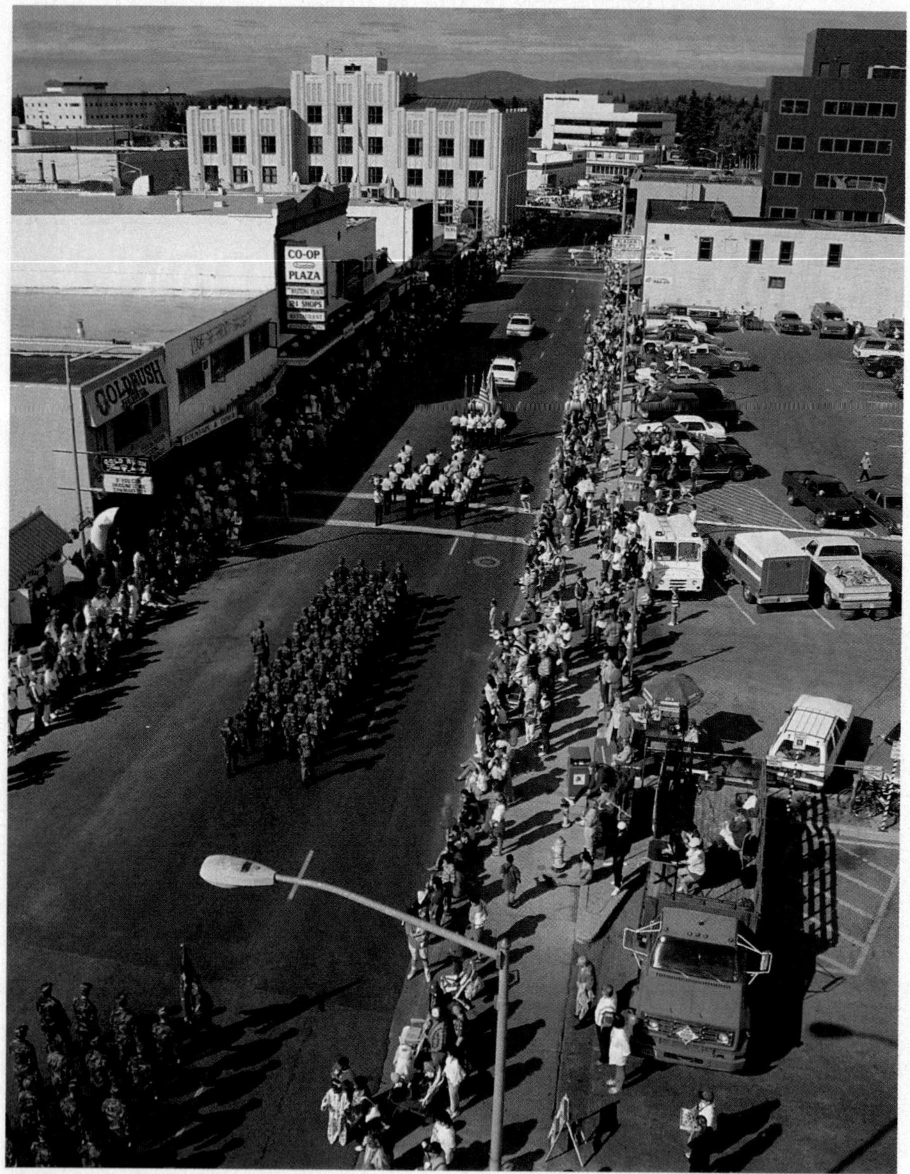

Golden Days parade on Second Avenue. This July event celebrates the city's heritage. (© Steven Seiller)

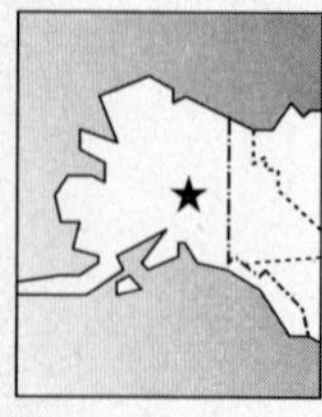

Located in the heart of Alaska's Great Interior country. By highway, it is approximately 1,488 miles/2,395 km north of Dawson Creek, BC, the start of the Alaska Highway (traditional milepost distance is 1,523 miles); 98 miles/158 km from Delta Junction (official end of the Alaska Highway); 358 miles/576 km from Anchorage via the George Parks Highway; and 2,305 miles/3,709 km from Seattle.

Population: Fairbanks–North Star Borough, 84,380. **Emergency Services: Alaska State Troopers**, 1979 Peger Road, phone (907) 451-5333; for nonemergencies, (907) 451-5100; and using TTY service, (907) 451-5344. **Fairbanks Police**, 656 7th Ave., phone 911 or, for nonemergencies, phone (907) 459-6500. **Fire Department** and **Ambulance Service**, phone 911. **Hospitals**, Fairbanks Memorial, 1650 Cowles St., phone (907) 452-8181; Bassett Army Hospital, Fort Wainwright, phone (907) 353-5143; Eielson Clinic, Eielson AFB, phone (907) 377-2259. **Women's Crisis Line**, phone (907) 452-2293. **Civil Defense**, phone (907) 459-1481 or (907) 474-7721 (24-hour line). **Borough Information**, phone (907) 459-1000.

Visitor Information: Fairbanks Visitor Information Center at 550 1st Ave. (at Cushman Street, where a riverside marker shows the distance of Fairbanks from some 75 cities); phone (907) 456-5774 or 1-800-327-5774. In summer, open 8 A.M. to 8 P.M. daily; in winter, open 8 A.M. to 5 P.M. weekdays, closed weekends. Phone (907) 456-INFO for daily recorded information.

Visitor information is also available at Fairbanks International Airport in the baggage claim area, at the Alaska Railroad depot at the University of Alaska Museum and at Alaskaland.

For information on Alaska's state parks, national parks, national forests, wildlife refuges and other outdoor recreational sites, visit the Alaska Public Lands Information Center downstairs in historic Courthouse Square at 250 N. Cushman St. The center is a free museum featuring films on Alaska, interpretive programs, lectures, exhibits, artifacts, photographs and short video programs on each region in the state. The exhibit area and information desk are open 7 days a week in summer; Tuesday through Saturday in winter. Phone (907) 456-0527. For recorded information on Denali National Park, phone (907) 456-0510. TDD information line is (907) 456-0532.

Elevation: 436 feet/133m at Fairbanks International Airport. **Climate:** January temperatures range from -2°F/-19°C to -19°F/-28°C. The lowest temperature ever recorded was -62°F/-52°C in Dec. 1961. July temperatures average 62°F/17°C, with a record high of 99°F/37°C in July 1919. In June and early July daylight lasts 21 hours—and the nights are really only twilight. Annual precipitation is 10.9 inches, with an annual average snowfall of 65 inches. The record for snowfall is 147.3 inches, set the winter of 1990–91. **Radio:** KSUA-FM, KFAR, KCBF, KAKQ, KWLF-FM, KIAK, KIAK-FM, KJNP-AM and FM (North Pole), KUAC-FM 104.7. **Television:** Channels 2, 4, 7, 9, 11 and cable. **Newspapers:** *Fairbanks Daily News–Miner*.

Private Aircraft: Facilities for all types of aircraft. Consult the *Alaska Supplement* for information on the following airports: Eielson AFB, Fairbanks International, Fairbanks International Seaplane, Chena Marina Air Field and Fort Wainwright. For more information phone the Fairbanks Flight Service Station at (907) 474-0137.

HISTORY

In 1901, Captain E.T. Barnette set out from St. Michael on the stern-wheeler *Lavelle Young*, traveling up the Yukon River with supplies for his trading post, which he proposed to set up at Tanana Crossing

(Continues on page 407)

RIVERBOAT DISCOVERY

Riverboat Discovery III

The Riverboat Discovery is the one adventure you won't want to miss when you travel to Fairbanks. Owned and operated by the Binkley family, whose river boating experience in Alaska spans four generations and almost 100 years, the Riverboat Discovery tour has been rated the top boating attraction in North America in *Travel Weekly Magazine*. Captain Jim Binkley and his crew of children, grandchildren and native Alaskans takes you back to the heyday of sternwheelers, to an era when prospectors, fur traders and Native people of the Interior relied on rivers as their only link to the outside world.

Passengers relax in the comfort of glass enclosed or open decks as the Discovery III winds its way down the Chena and Tanana Rivers. Drawing on their knowledge of Alaskan history, the Binkley family entertains listeners with witty descriptions of Alaskan life during the four hour narrated cruise. The Discovery makes a brief stop at the river front home of veteran Iditarod Dog Musher, Susan Butcher, where visitors hear tales of Susan's Iditarod adventures and are introduced to her champion sled dogs.

One of the highlights of the trip is a stop ashore at the Old Chena Indian Village. Here passengers disembark for a guided tour. Alaskan Natives share their culture as they recount how their ancestors hunted, fished, sewed clothing and built shelters to survive for centuries in the harsh Alaskan wilderness. At the village a dog mushing demonstration with Susan Butcher's long distance racing team gives passengers a "close-up" view of an actual mushing kennel.

The Discovery departs from Steamboat Landing, off Dale Road. daily at 8:45 AM and 2:00 PM, mid-May through mid-September. Reservations are recommended. Call 907-479-6673 for further information.

Steamboat Landing is also the home of the Discovery Trading Post, Fairbanks' premiere gift shop. Visitors while away the time between Discovery III departures, browsing among one of a kind souvenirs, Alaskan clothing and gifts. Next door, the Susan Butcher Gallery is filled with Susan's Iditarod memorabilia as well as an exclusive line of Susan Butcher clothing. Open 8:00 AM to 8:00 PM daily. Wheelchair accessible.

Steamboat Landing

EL DORADO GOLD MINE

Pan for gold at the El Dorado Gold Mine. Join the Binkley family for another Alaskan experience that can't be missed! El Dorado Gold Mine is an exciting hands-on adventure for the whole family. Visitors learn about the history of mining in Alaska, experience a modern day mining operation and pan for gold, while enjoying famous Alaskan hospitality.

El Dorado Gold Mine

The two hour tour to a working gold mine begins when passengers board the Tanana Valley Railroad for a narrated trip through the original gold fields of the Interior that were once part of Alaska's richest mining district.

Passengers ride the narrow-gauge rails though a permafrost tunnel where miners with head lamps and pick-axes seek out the rich gold veins, reminiscent of mining days gone by. Winding through the valley, the train comes to a halt as a prospector crouches down to dip his gold pan into cold, clear waters of Fox Creek in search of the sparkle of gold.

At El Dorado Camp, local miners "Yukon Yonda" and her husband Dexter Clark are on hand to conduct a guided tour through a working gold mine. Visitors gather around to watch the operation of a modern day sluice box and enjoy stories about life in Alaskan mining camps.

A crash course in gold panning is followed by the real thing! Visitors grab a poke filled with pay dirt right from the sluice box and try their hand at panning for gold. And when they strike it rich, they keep the gold!

The next stop is the assay office where visitors, while enjoying complementary home-made cookies and coffee, weigh their gold and assay its market value. The "all aboard" call gathers everyone onto the train for the short ride back to the station.

Daily tours for the El Dorado Gold Mine depart from the old train station at 1.3 mile Elliott Highway, just past Fox, Alaska, nine miles north of Fairbanks. Reservations are recommended. Call 907-479-7613 for further information. Wheelchair accessible.

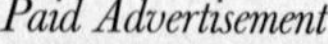

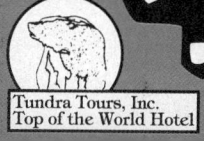

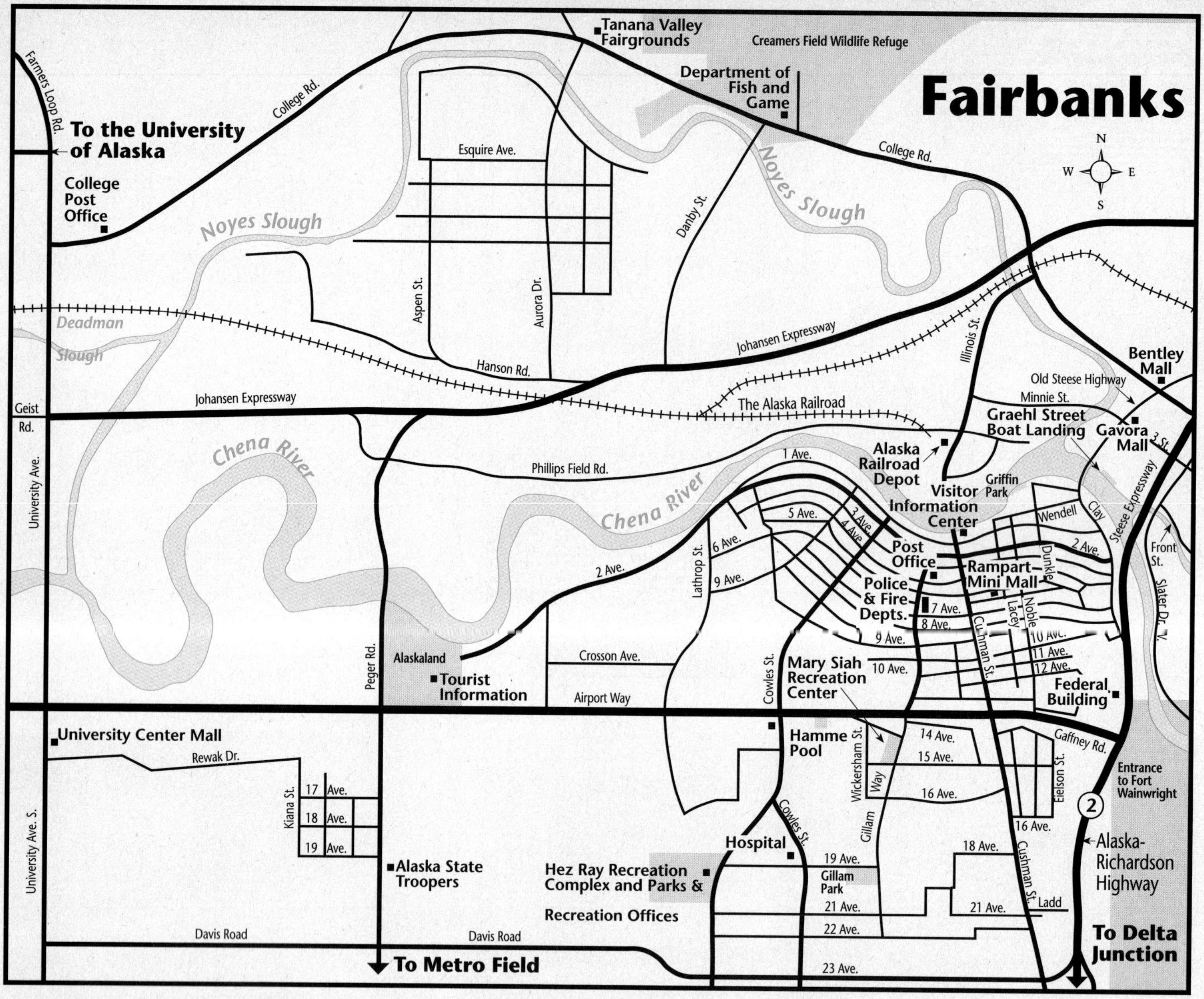

Fairbanks

Tanana Valley Fairgrounds
Creamers Field Wildlife Refuge
Department of Fish and Game
Farmers Loop Rd.
To the University of Alaska
College Rd.
College Post Office
Esquire Ave.
Noyes Slough
Danby St.
College Rd.
Aspen St.
Aurora Dr.
Deadman Slough
Hanson Rd.
Johansen Expressway
Illinois St.
Bentley Mall
Old Steese Highway
Minnie St.
Geist Rd.
Johansen Expressway
The Alaska Railroad
Graehl Street Boat Landing
Gavora Mall
3 St.
Chena River
Phillips Field Rd.
1 Ave.
Alaska Railroad Depot
Visitor Information Center
Griffin Park
Steese Expressway
University Ave.
Chena River
5 Ave.
3 Ave.
4 Ave.
Wendell
Clay
Front St.
6 Ave.
Post Office
2 Ave.
2 Ave.
Lathrop St.
9 Ave.
Police & Fire Depts.
Rampart Mini Mall
Dunkle
Slater Dr.
7 Ave.
8 Ave.
Cushman St.
Lacey
Noble
9 Ave.
10 Ave.
11 Ave.
12 Ave.
Alaskaland
Crosson Ave.
Peger Rd.
Tourist Information
Airport Way
Cowles St.
Mary Siah Recreation Center
10 Ave.
Federal Building
University Center Mall
Hamme Pool
Gaffney Rd.
Rewak Dr.
14 Ave.
15 Ave.
Wickersham St.
Way
Eielson St.
Entrance to Fort Wainwright
17 Ave.
18 Ave.
19 Ave.
Kiana St.
16 Ave.
Cowles St.
16 Ave.
Gillam
2
University Ave. S.
Alaska-Richardson Highway
Hospital
18 Ave.
Alaska State Troopers
Hez Ray Recreation Complex and Parks & Recreation Offices
19 Ave.
Gillam Park
Cushman St.
21 Ave.
21 Ave.
Ladd
22 Ave.
Davis Road
Davis Road
To Metro Field
23 Ave.
To Delta Junction

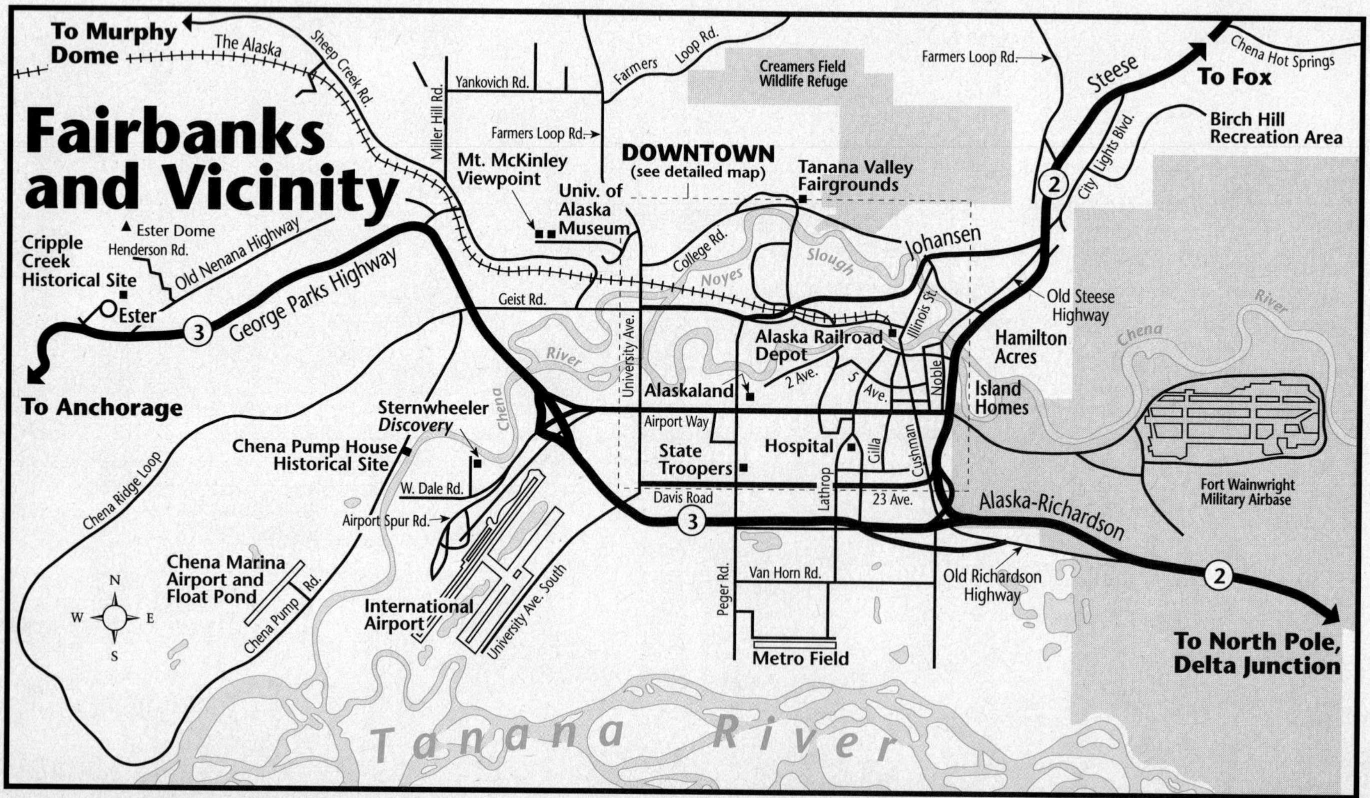

Fairbanks and Vicinity

To Murphy Dome
The Alaska
Sheep Creek Rd.
Yankovich Rd.
Farmers Loop Rd.
Creamers Field Wildlife Refuge
Farmers Loop Rd.
Steese
Chena Hot Springs
To Fox
Miller Hill Rd.
Farmers Loop Rd.
Birch Hill Recreation Area
Mt. McKinley Viewpoint
DOWNTOWN (see detailed map)
Tanana Valley Fairgrounds
2
City Lights Blvd.
Univ. of Alaska Museum
Ester Dome
Cripple Creek Historical Site
Henderson Rd.
Old Nenana Highway
George Parks Highway
College Rd.
Noyes
Slough
Johansen
Old Steese Highway
River
Geist Rd.
Illinois St.
Ester
3
Alaska Railroad Depot
Hamilton Acres
Chena
River
University Ave.
2 Ave.
S Ave.
Noble
Island Homes
To Anchorage
Alaskaland
Sternwheeler *Discovery*
Chena
Airport Way
Hospital
Chena Pump House Historical Site
State Troopers
Gilla
Cushman
Fort Wainwright Military Airbase
W. Dale Rd.
Chena Ridge Loop
Davis Road
Lathrop
23 Ave.
Alaska-Richardson
Airport Spur Rd.
3
Chena Marina Airport and Float Pond
Van Horn Rd.
Old Richardson Highway
2
Chena Pump Rd.
International Airport
University Ave. South
Peger Rd.
Metro Field
To North Pole, Delta Junction
Tanana River

(Continued from page 400)
(Tanacross), the halfway point on the Valdez–Eagle trail. But the stern-wheeler could not navigate the fast-moving, shallow Tanana River beyond the mouth of the Chena River. The stern-wheeler's captain finally dropped off the protesting Barnette on the Chena River, near the present site of 1st Avenue and Cushman Street. A year later, Felix Pedro, an Italian prospector, discovered gold about 16 miles/26 km north of Barnette's temporary trading post. The opportunistic Barnette quickly abandoned his original plan to continue on to Tanana Crossing.

In September 1902, Barnette convinced the 25 or so miners in the area to use the name "Fairbanks" for the town that he expected would grow up around his trading post. The name had been suggested that summer by Alaska Judge James Wickersham, who admired Charles W. Fairbanks, the senior senator from Indiana. The senator later became vice president of the United States under Theodore Roosevelt.

The town grew, largely due to Barnette's promotion of gold prospects and discoveries in the area, and in 1903 Judge Wickersham moved the headquarters of his Third Judicial District Court (a district which encompassed 300,000 square miles) from Eagle to Fairbanks.

Thanks to Wickersham, the town gained government offices and a jail. Thanks to Barnette, it gained a post office and a branch of the Northern Commercial Company, a large Alaska trading firm based in San Francisco. In addition, after Barnette became the first mayor of Fairbanks in 1903, the town acquired telephone service, set up fire protection, passed sanitation ordinances and contracted for electric light and steam heat. In 1904, Barnette started a bank.

The town of "Fairbanks" first appeared in the U.S. Census in 1910 with a population of 3,541. Miners living beside their claims on creeks north of town brought the area population figure to about 11,000.

Barnette stayed in Fairbanks until late 1910, when he resigned the presidency of the Washington–Alaska Bank and moved to

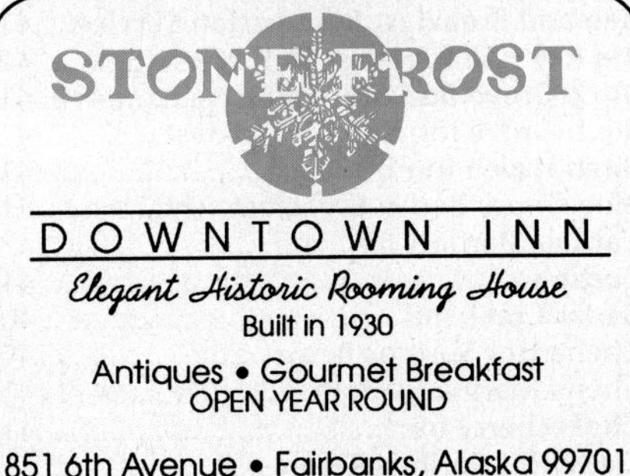

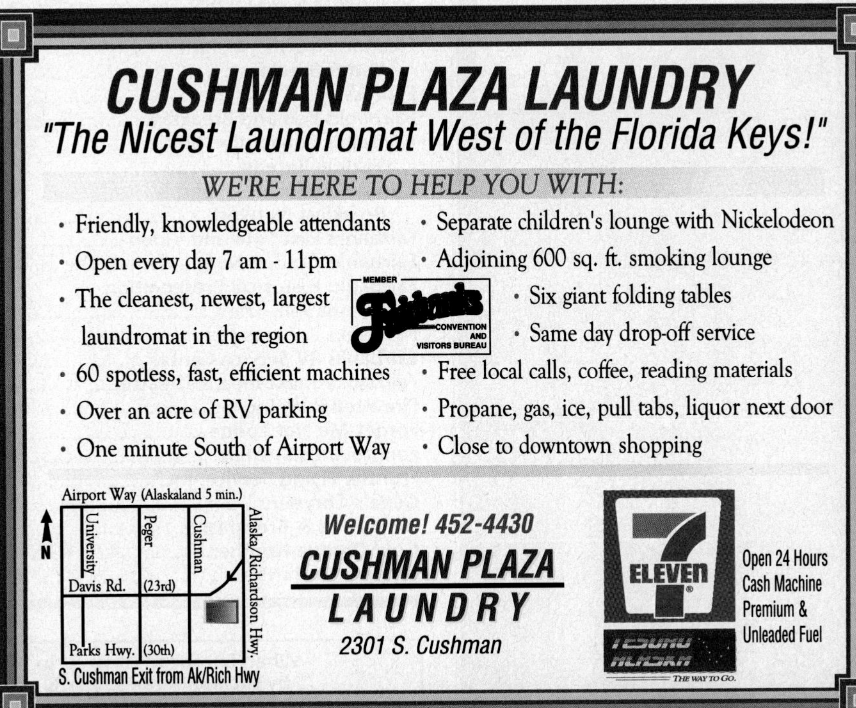

California. When the bank collapsed early in 1911, the people of Fairbanks blamed Barnette. The tale of the "most hated man in Fairbanks" is told in *E.T. Barnette, The Strange Story of the Man Who Founded Fairbanks.*

ECONOMY

The city's economy is linked to its role as a service and supply point for Interior and Arctic industrial activities. Fairbanks played a key role during construction of the trans-Alaska pipeline in the 1970s. The Dalton Highway (formerly the North Slope Haul Road) to Prudhoe Bay begins about 75 miles/121 km north of town. Extractive industries such as oil and mining continue to play a major role in the economy.

Government employment contributes significantly to the Fairbanks economy. Including military jobs, 50 percent of employment in Fairbanks is through the government. Fort Wainwright (formerly Ladd Field) was the first Army airfield in Alaska, begun in 1938. The fort currently employs 4,600 soldiers and 1,600 civilians, and it houses 6,200 family members. Fort Wainwright also provides emergency services by assisting with search and rescue operations. Eielson Air Force Base, located 25

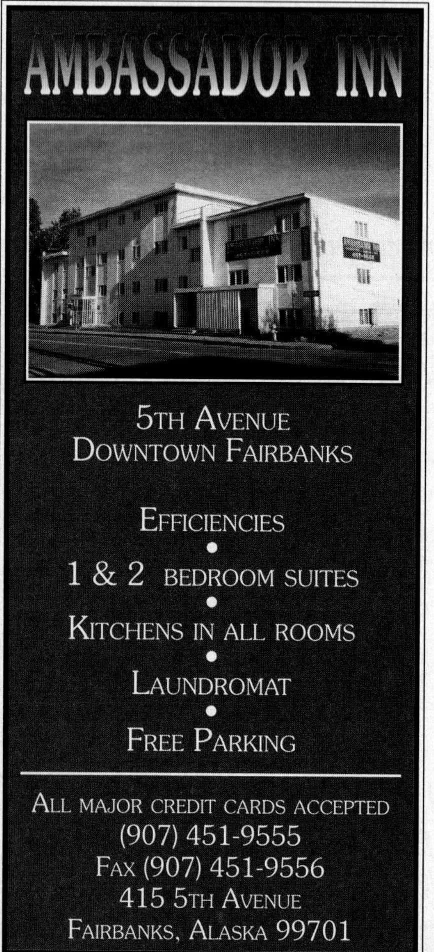

FAIRBANKS ADVERTISERS

When Europeans arrived in Alaska in 1741, the land was populated by the indigenous Eskimo, Indian and Aleut peoples, all of whom had distinct and complex cultures.—*ALASKA A TO Z*

miles/40 km southeast of Fairbanks on the Richardson–Alaska Highway, also has a strong economic impact on the city. Eielson has about 2,700 military personnel and approximately 4,200 family members assigned, with about 1,200 military personnel and family members living off base.

Also boosting the Fairbanks economy are the University of Alaska Fairbanks, and trade and service industries such as retail sales and tourism.

DESCRIPTION

Alaska's second largest city and the administrative capital of the Interior, Fairbanks lies on the flat valley floor of the Tanana River on the banks of the Chena River. Good views of the valley are available from Chena Ridge Road to the west and Farmers Loop Road to the north.

The city is a blend of old and new: Modern hotels and shopping malls stand beside log cabins and historic wooden buildings.

Fairbanks is bounded to the north, east and west by low rolling hills of birch and white spruce. To the south is the Alaska Range and Denali National Park, about a 2½-hour drive via the George Parks Highway. The Steese and Elliott highways lead north to the White Mountains.

ACCOMMODATIONS/VISITOR SERVICES

Fairbanks has about 2 dozen hotels and motels and more than 100 bed and breakfasts during the summer. Rates vary widely, from a low of about $40 for a single to a high of $150 for a double. Reservations for accommodations are suggested during the busy summer months.

There are several private campgrounds in the Fairbanks area. Chena River recreation site, a state campground, is located on University Avenue by the Chena River bridge. The campground has 57 sites, tables, firepits, toilets, water and a dump station. Camping fee $15/night or annual pass; $3 for use of dump station; and $5 for use of boat launch.

There is overnight camping at Alaskaland for self-contained RVs only with a 4-night limit, $9 fee and use of the Borough dump station on 2nd Avenue. ▲

Fairbanks has more than 100 restaurants ranging from deluxe to fast food.

Ah, Rose Marie Bed and Breakfast. Historic 1928 Fairbanks home. Very centrally located in downtown neighborhood. Full hearty breakfasts. Friendly cat and dog. Outdoor smoking areas. Singles, couples, triples, families welcomed. Open year-round. Extraordinary hospitality. Single $50 up, doubles $65 up. Wow! John E. Davis, 302 Cowles St., Fairbanks, AK 99701. (907) 456-2040. [ADVERTISEMENT]

Applesauce Inn B&B. Friendly crew of 6 (half of them cats) ensures a memorable stay! Hearty breakfast features reindeer sausage. Peaceful, woodsy neighborhood 5 minutes from town. Private 3 bedroom living area for families and groups. Also available: Cedar Creek Inn, vacation home to yourself. Brochures. 119 Gruening Way, Fairbanks, AK 99712. Phone (907) 457-3392, within Alaska 1-800-764-3392. Fax (907) 457-3332. See display ad this section. [ADVERTISEMENT]

Bear Paw B&B. Share our warm and friendly family atmosphere and lovable cocker spaniel! Our private residence provides convenient in-town location, walking distance to Alaskaland, churches, restaurants and comfortable, clean quiet rooms. Private and semiprivate baths available. Reasonable

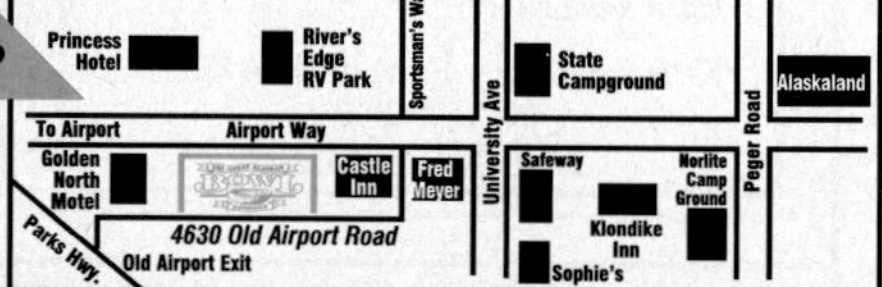

rates. Teachers and quilters are our specialty. Call/write Renée Kappen, 1101 Kodiak St., Fairbanks, AK 99709. Phone (907) 474-4275. [ADVERTISEMENT]

Birch Grove B&B. In the hills, 15 minutes north of Fairbanks. Clean, cozy rooms in the guest house. Private or shared bath, laundry, kitchen, TV/VCR or your own private chalet with kitchenette. We live next door. Just close enough to brag on Alaska, far enough to give you your privacy. 50 year residents. 1-800-53-BIRCH, US/Canada/ Alaska, (907) 457-2981. [ADVERTISEMENT]

Chena Marina RV Park guests speak: "RV having fun? Yes—Thanks to folks like you! ... 'Dankeschon' services really special ... Nice, clean, green—you care for it as you would your own home ... Captured our hearts ... People who take time to care ... One of the best—location, spacious, landscaped ... Beautiful ... First-rate." (907) 479-GOLD. 1145 Shypoke Dr., Fairbanks, AK 99709. See map at picture ad for directions. [ADVERTISEMENT]

The Cushman Plaza Laundry appreciates notes from travellers from Florida to Texas, complimenting us as "The nicest laundromat anywhere," "Spotless!" "Just like home." "All the machines work!!" "So Spacious." On the Alaska/Richardson Highway,

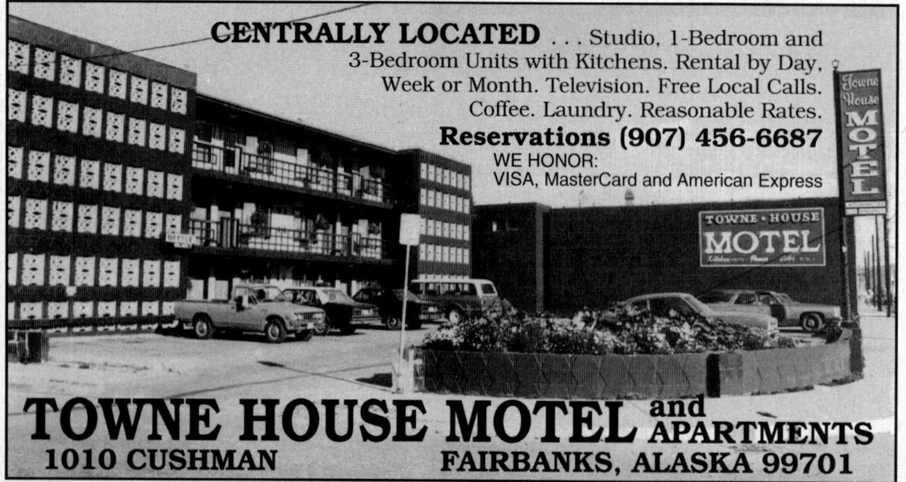

adjacent to Tesoro, 7-11, propane and nearby downtown shopping. 23rd and Cushman. (Please see our display ad this section.) Phone (907) 452-4430. [ADVERTISEMENT]

Fairbanks Bed And Breakfast. Barbara Neubauer, hostess and 26-year resident, has many bear and gold mining tales. The quiet historical neighborhood is walking distance to town on bus route. Our home has many interesting ivory artifacts and Alaskan art. Private bath, large yard and deck. Smoking. Hearty breakfast and laundry facilities for fee plus ample parking. 902 Kellum St. (907) 452-4967, fax (907) 451-6955. [ADVERTISEMENT]

Fairbanks Princess Hotel. Interior Alaska's newest hotel located on the banks of the Chena River. Terraced deck area, gift shop, fine or casual dining, tour desk, health club. Five minutes from downtown Fairbanks International Airport. Free airport shuttle. Meeting rooms accommodate up to 435 guests. Open year-round. Write 2815 2nd Ave., Suite 400, Seattle, WA 98121-1299, or call (800) 426-0500. [ADVERTISEMENT]

Fountainhead Hotels. Our hotel hotline, 1-800-528-4916, accesses more than 500 rooms at 3 of Fairbanks' best hotels: Sophie Station, Wedgewood Resort, and the Bridgewater Hotel. Varying locations and features assure that we will have the right room for you. Our staff will gladly assist you in selecting the best accommodations. Each property offers dining facilities, laundry services, and free local calls. For color brochure call our hotline, or write: 1717 University Ave., Fairbanks, AK 99709. [ADVERTISEMENT]

Geni's Bed & Breakfast. Country hospitality May to September. Two bedrooms with queen-sized beds, shared full bath. No

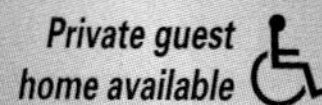

pets, smoking on deck only. Continental or full country breakfast. Affordable accommodations in woodland setting 15 minutes from Fairbanks at Mile 5.3 Chena Hot

Springs Road. Handmade Alaska crafts available. George and Nila Lyle, P.O. Box 10352, Fairbanks, AK 99710; phone (907) 488-4136. [ADVERTISEMENT]

Goldhill RV Park & Cabins is proud to be Fairbanks' only park successfully combining nature with modern conveniences. Located on the northwest side of Fairbanks, Goldhill is convenient to all attractions, shopping and the University of Alaska. Nestled in a spruce forest on 12.5 acres of an old F.E. Co. mining claim, Goldhill is ideally situated for family fun and safety. Goldhill's policy of cleaning and disinfecting the private showers after each use and their sparkling clean laundry and restrooms are popular with all family members. Personal, friendly service is always first at Goldhill. See display ad this section. [ADVERTISEMENT] ▲

Goldstream Valley Bed and Breakfast Association. Stay in beautiful Goldstream Valley northwest of Fairbanks, and marvel in the sense of Alaska wilderness. Two informal family residences provide all the ammenities plus valley views while soaking in the hot tub. Specialties are day tours in nordic and alpine skiing, dog mushing, hiking and bicycling. Liz Ofelt, Wildrose Bed and Breakfast, P.O. Box 82385, Fairbanks, AK 99708, (907) 455-7469 and Mary Mathews, Spinach Creek Bed & Breakfast, 3872 Frenchman Rd., Fairbanks, AK 99709, (907) 455-6311. [ADVERTISEMENT]

Marilyn's Bed and Breakfast. Located in downtown Fairbanks. Enjoy true pioneer friendliness in a comfortable, homey atmosphere. Continental breakfast with homemade jams. Perhaps you may persuade Marilyn to fix waffles made from her 1877 sourdough starter. No smoking. Off-street parking. For reservations, Marilyn Nigro, 651 9th Ave., Fairbanks, AK 99701. (907) 456-1959. [ADVERTISEMENT]

Norlite Campground, Inc. Centrally located within Fairbanks city limits just 0.3 mile south off Airport Road on Peger Road, Norlite is the most complete of all Fairbanks' campgrounds. City water, sewer and electric hookups, showers, dump station, tour tickets, laundry, truck/car wash, snack and ice cream bar and grocery store are all on the grounds. (907) 474-0206, fax (907) 474-0992. (See ad in this section.) [ADVERTISEMENT] ▲

River's Edge RV Park & Campground. Beautiful setting on the Chena River and within walking distance of major shopping centers. 180 spacious wooded sites. Wide pull-throughs; 30 amp electric; dump station; full and partial hookups, free showers, gifts, free shuttle to Riverboat *Discovery* and Alaskaland Salmon Bake. Tour arrangements featuring Point Barrow and Arctic Circle. Immaculate facilities. [ADVERTISEMENT] ▲

7 Gables Inn. Central to major attractions, this remodeled fraternity house is between the University campus and the airport. The spacious Tudor-style house features a floral solarium, stained-glass foyer with indoor waterfall, cathedral ceilings, banquet/conference facilities. Gourmet breakfast served daily. Cable TV, VCR, phone in each room, laundry, bikes, canoes and skis. Winter rates $50–75; 4312 Birch Lane, Fairbanks, AK 99709. Phone (907) 479-0751. [ADVERTISEMENT]

Wildview Cabin is your own log home away from home! On a private wooded 12 acre lot, your cabin is fully furnished and outfitted for short stays or long visits. Available May through August. Exceptional rates, so book early! Wildview Cabin, 891 Goldpan Road, Fairbanks, AK 99712. (907) 457-1154. [ADVERTISEMENT]

TRANSPORTATION

Scheduled Air Carriers: Several international, interstate and intra-Alaska carriers serve Fairbanks; see Air Travel in the GENERAL INFORMATION section.

Charter Flights: Air charter services are available for flightseeing, fly-in fishing and hunting, and trips to bush villages; see ads.

Warbelow's Air Ventures, Inc. Local scheduled and charter air service. Get off the beaten path and experience the ultimate in bush excursions! Available daily: bush mail flights, Arctic Circle tours, hot springs fly-in packages, flightseeing. Located at 3758 University Ave. S., Fairbanks, AK 99709; phone (907) 474-0518. In business for almost 40 years. [ADVERTISEMENT]

Alaska Railroad: Passenger depot at 280 N. Cushman St. in the downtown area. Daily passenger service in summer between Fairbanks and Anchorage with stopovers at Denali National Park; less frequent service in winter. For details see the ALASKA RAILROAD section, or phone (907) 456-4155.

Bus: Scheduled motorcoach service to Anchorage and points south. Local daily bus service by Metropolitan Area Commuter Service (MACS), and regular MACS service is also now available to North Pole weekdays; no service on Sundays and some legal holidays. Drivers do not carry change, and exact change or tokens must be used. Fares are: $1.50 or 1 token. Tokens are available at Transit Park, the UAF Woodcenter, Fred Meyer west, Bentley Hall and North Pole Plaza. Information is available via the Transit Hotline, phone (907) 459-1011, or from MACS offices at 3175 Peger Road, phone (907) 459-1002.

Tours: Local and area sightseeing tours are available; see ads in this section.

Nicholas Tours. Classic, guided, "see-everything" city tours, 7 persons maximum. Town, countryside. Pan for gold where Felix Pedro found it. Must-sees; unique sights. Personal service, can start/finish at Riverboat. Also: Twilight tours, up unfading boreal slopes. Chena Hot Springs trips. Wintertime aurora tours. Gracious host. Phone (907) 451-1125. [ADVERTISEMENT]

Train to Denali. Ride the luxurious private domed railcars of the McKinley Explorer to Denali National Park from either Anchorage or Fairbanks. Overnight packages in Denali with round-trip train service are available from only $255 ppdo. Prices subject to change. Call Gray Line of Alaska at (907) 456-7741 for train and package tour options. [ADVERTISEMENT]

Taxi Service: 9 cab companies.

Car, Camper and Trailer Rentals: Several companies rent cars, campers and trailers; see ads in this section.

ATTRACTIONS

Get Acquainted: A good place to start is the visitor information center at 550 1st Ave., where you'll find free brochures, maps and tips on what to see and how to get there. Phone (907) 456-5774, (907) 456-INFO, or 1-800-327-5774 for a recording of current daily events.

Next to the log cabin visitor information center is Golden Heart Park, site of the 18-foot/5-m bronze monument, "Unknown First Family." The statue, by sculptor Malcolm Alexander, and park were dedicated in July 1986 to celebrate Fairbanks' history and heritage.

The Alaska Public Lands Information Center, located in the lower level of historic Courthouse Square at 3rd Avenue and Cushman Street, is a free museum and information center featuring Alaska's natural history, cultural artifacts and recreational opportunities. In addition to detailed information on outdoor recreation in the state, the center offers films, interpretive programs, lectures and a book shop.

Tour the University of Alaska Fairbanks, situated on a 2,250-acre ridge overlooking the city and Tanana River valley. The campus has all the features of a small town, including a fire station, post office, radio and TV stations, medical clinic and a 1,000-seat concert hall.

UAF offers special tours and programs from June through August. Free guided tours of the campus are provided Monday through Friday at 10 A.M.; tours begin at the UA Museum. Also offered are tours of the Large Animal Research Station, Poker Flat Research Range and a slide show and tour at the Geophysical Institute, where research and study range from the center of the earth to the center of the sun. Films on mining in Alaska are also shown. Visitors can take a guided tour or tour on their own at the Agricultural and Forestry Experiment Station's Georgeson Botanical Garden, which is open to the public June through September. Phone (907) 474-7581 for information on any tour.

The University of Alaska Museum is a must stop for Fairbanks visitors. The museum features cultural and natural history displays from all the state's regions. The 5 galleries explore Alaska's history, Native culture, art, natural phenomena, wildlife, birds, geology and prehistoric past. Highlights include a 36,000-year-old Steppe bison mummy, the state's largest gold display, the trans-Alaska pipeline story, and a special section on the northern lights. The museum grounds hold sculptures, totem poles, a Russian blockhouse, and a nature trail with signs identifying local vegetation. The museum's special summer exhibit in 1996 will be "A Legacy of Arctic Art," an examination of Native art in the era preceding its popularity. Free summer programs include presentations on natural and cultural history topics and Alaska Native Elders discussing traditional and contemporary lifestyles. Summer shows include "Northern Inua," a 50-minute show of northern athletic games, dance and creation stories produced by the World Eskimo-Indian Olympics, and "Dynamic Aurora," a 50-minute show on the scientific and Alaska Native understanding of the northern lights. Admission is charged for these shows; call for times. Hours are: May and September, 9 A.M. to 5 P.M.; June through Aug., 9 A.M. to 7 P.M.; Oct. through April, weedkays, 9 A.M. to 5 P.M., weekends, noon to 5 P.M. Museum admission fees: adults, $5; seniors, $4.50; youth (12 to 17), $3; children under 12, free. For 24-hour information, call (907) 474-7505.

Take in Some Local Events: Fairbanks has several unique summer celebrations. Late June is a busy time as Fairbanks celebrates the longest day of the year (summer solstice is June 21). The Midnight Sun Baseball Game will be played at 10:45 P.M. on June 21, 1996, without artificial lights. The Yukon 800 also gets under way; it is a marathon outboard boat race of 800 miles/1287 km on the Chena, Tanana and Yukon rivers to Galena and back. A Midnight Sun 10K Fun Run begins at 10 P.M.

Golden Days, when Fairbanksans turn out in turn-of-the-century dress and celebrate the gold rush, is July 8-21, 1996. Golden Days starts off with a Felix Pedro look-alike taking his gold to the bank and includes a parade and rededication of the Pedro Monument honoring the man who started it all when he discovered gold in the Tanana Hills. Other events include pancake breakfasts, a dance, canoe and raft races, and free outdoor concerts.

The World Eskimo and Indian Olympics, with Native competition in such events as the high kick, greased pole walk, stick pull, fish

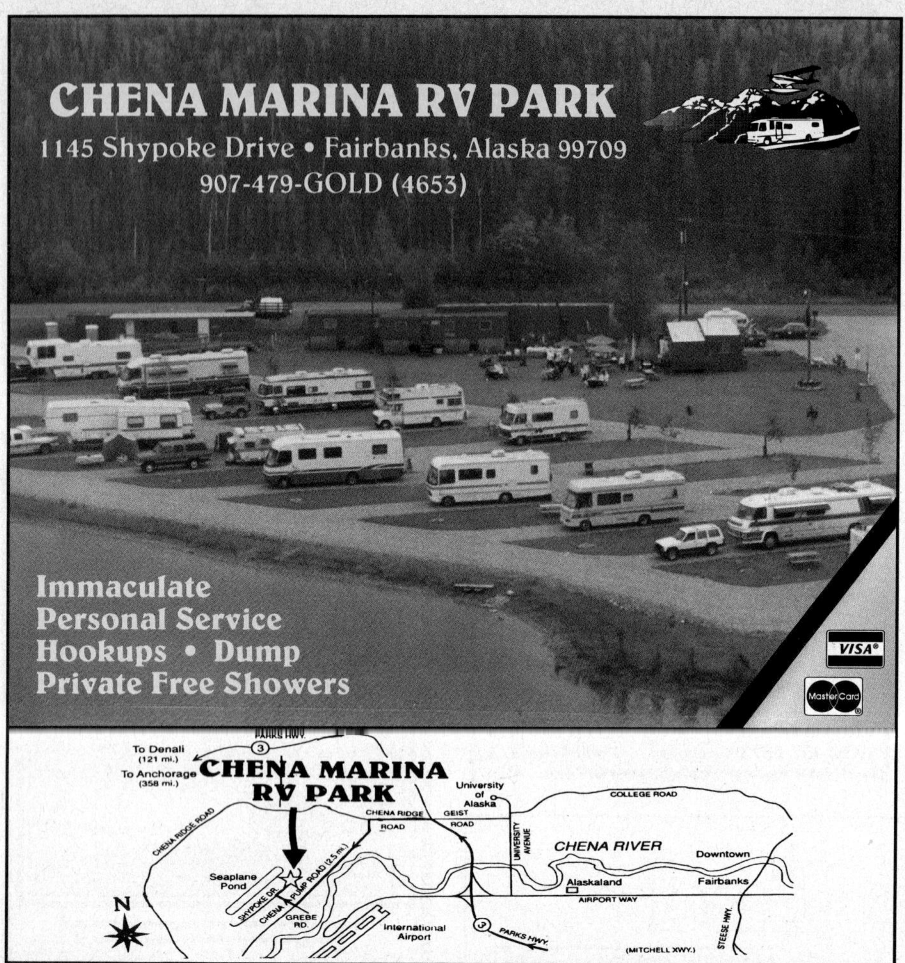

cutting, parka contest and muktuk-eating contest will be held July 19–23, 1996.

The annual Tanana Valley State Fair will be held Aug. 2–10, 1996. Alaska's oldest state fair, the Tanana Valley State Fair features agricultural exhibits, arts and crafts, food booths, a rodeo and other entertainments.

Fairbanks Summer Arts Festival, 2 weeks of workshops and concerts including music from jazz to classics, dance, theater and the visual arts, will be held July 26 to Aug. 6, 1996.

Check with the Fairbanks visitor information center for more information on local events.

Besides these special events, summer visitors can take in a semipro baseball game at Growden Park where the Fairbanks Goldpanners take on other Alaska league teams.

The Fairbanks Shakespeare Theatre, now entering their fourth season, presents "Merry Wives of Windsor." This production is held in the outdoor setting of Birch Hill Recreation Area, a few easy miles from Fairbanks off the Steese Highway. July 9–Aug. 4; shows 8 P.M. Wednesdays–Sundays. For information call 457-POET. [ADVERTISEMENT]

Visit Creamer's Field. Follow the flocks of waterfowl to Creamer's Field Migratory Waterfowl Refuge. Located 1 mile/1.6 km from downtown Fairbanks, this 1,800-acre refuge managed by the Alaska Dept. of Fish and Game offers opportunities to observe large concentrations of ducks, geese, shorebirds and cranes in the spring and fall. Throughout the summer, sandhill cranes eat in the planted barley fields.

Explore the 2-mile/3.2-km self-guided nature trail and the renovated historic farmhouse that serves as a visitor center. Stop at 1300 College Road to find the trailhead, viewing areas and brochures on Creamer's Field. For more information, phone (907) 452-1531.

Creamer's Field Migratory Waterfowl Refuge–where nature is at its best. Summer visitor center hours, 10-5, closed Sunday and Monday. June–August, guided walks leave front parking lot on College Road Tuesday and Thursday at 7 P.M.; Wednesday and Saturday at 9 A.M. No charge and the refuge is always open. (907) 452-5162. [ADVERTISEMENT]

A Walk in the Woods. Would you enjoy a guided walk in the last great forest on earth—a quiet opportunity to feel the peace of Nature and learn how life adapts to the northern challenges? Please join us for a comfortable 2 or 3 hour walking tour. For reservations, phone or fax (907) 455-6469 or write P.O. Box 80961, Fairbanks, AK 99708. [ADVERTISEMENT]

SS *Nenana*. A premier attraction. Voices from Alaska's past echo from the 5 decks of the SS *Nenana*, a National Historic Landmark. Fully restored and permanently berthed at Alaskaland, the last overnight packet sternwheeler remaining in America has begun her final and most important voyage. By telling her story through the art form of her incredibly detailed diorama, she will transport visitors back in time from 1847 to 1932 along the mighty Yukon River system, where the lure and mystique of the North cast its spell on the early sourdoughs. Nothing will equal the unique and unforgettable experience aboard the steamer *Nenana*, the second largest wooden vessel in existence most appropriately called: "The Last

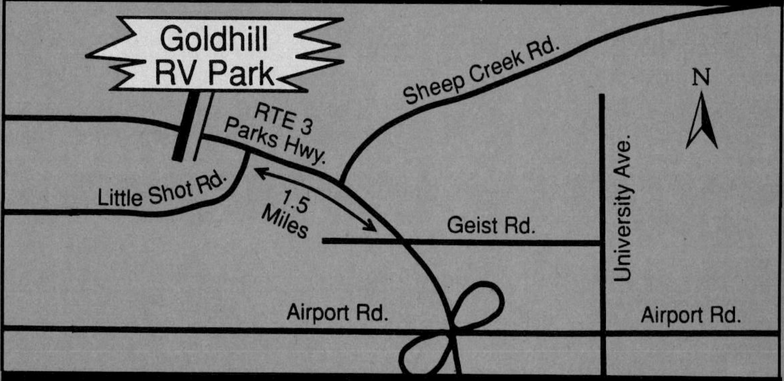

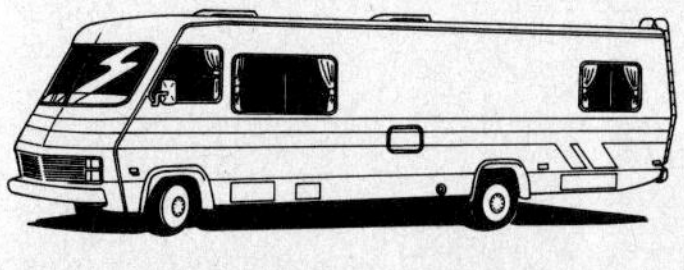

Lady of the River." [ADVERTISEMENT]

Tanana Valley Farmers Market. Visit Alaska's premier Farmers Market, located next to the Fairgrounds on College Road, open from May through September. Vendors offer "thousands of miles fresher" Alaska-grown vegetables; blue-ribbon bouquets;

Alaskan meats, fish, honey, jams and syrups; made in Alaska handcrafts and baked goods. Look for our Farmers Market brochure at

Distinctive sod-roofed Fairbanks Log Cabin Visitor Center at Cushman Street bridge. (© Steven Seiller)

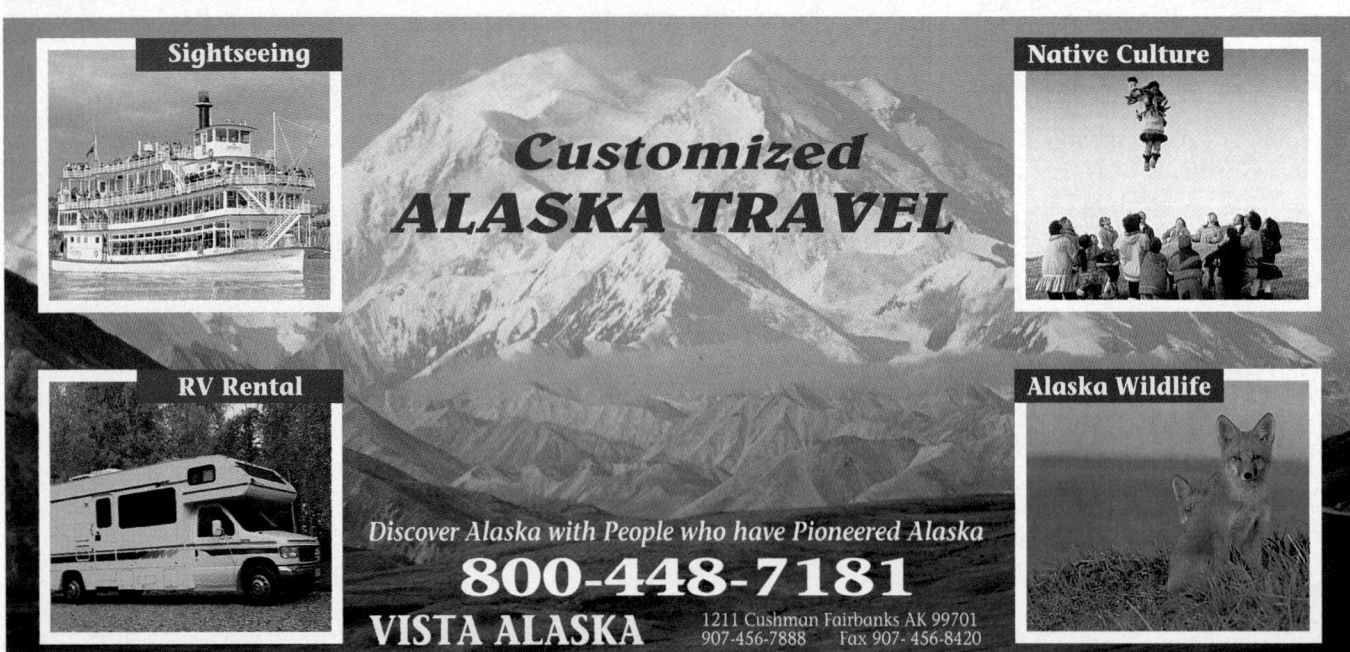

local Visitor's Centers. Market hours are Wednesdays noon to 5 P.M. and Saturdays 10 A.M. to 5 P.M.; there's plenty of parking. Stop by the Market and support Alaska grown. ... Meet you at the Market! [ADVERTISEMENT]

The Alaska Rag Co. A must-see for Fairbanks travelers. This unique Alaskan gift shop manufactures beautiful handwoven rag rugs from 100 percent recycled clothing. The store also features works from many Alaskan artists. Items include jewelry, pottery, paintings, stained glass, qiviut, dog hair hats, mittens and much more. Stop in, meet our weavers, and see their work. 552 2nd Ave., Fairbanks, AK 99701. Phone (907) 451-4401. [ADVERTISEMENT]

The Great Alaskan Bowl Company. A mile from the airport, the Great Alaskan Bowl Company is one of only 2 mills in the country still turning out 1-piece wooden bowls. Watch demonstrations using 1800s ingenuity and 1990s technology from our large viewing area and learn about Alaska's forests. Open year-round. (907) 474-9663, 1-800-770-4222. 4630 Old Airport Rd., Fairbanks, AK 99706. [ADVERTISEMENT]

Chena Pump House National Historic Site. Built in 1931–33 by the Fairbanks Exploration Co. to pump water from the Chena River to dredging operations at Cripple Creek, the pump house was remodeled in 1978 and now houses a restaurant and saloon. The sheet metal cladding, interior roof and some equipment (such as the

intake ditch) are from the original pump house, which shut down in 1958 when the F.E. Co. ceased its Cripple Creek dredging operations. The pump house is located at Mile 1.3 Chena Pump Road.

Sled Dog Racing. The Alaska Dog Mushers' Assoc. hosts a series of dog races beginning in mid-December with preliminary races, and ending in March with the Open North American Championship. The Open is a 3-day event with 3 heats (of 20, 20 and 30 miles) with teams as large as 24 dogs; this race is considered by many to be the "granddaddy of dog races." Fairbanks also hosts the 1,000-mile/1,609-km Yukon Quest Sled Dog Race between Fairbanks and Whitehorse, YT. The Yukon Quest alternates start and finish between the 2 cities: The race started in Fairbanks in February 1996. For more information, contact the Alaska Dog Mushers' Assoc. at (907) 457-MUSH, or the Yukon Quest office at (907) 451-8985.

Alaskan Tails of the Trail. Mary Shields, celebrated musher and author, welcomes you to her log home. Enjoy a hands-on experience with the friendly huskies and hang on to your heart if there are puppies! Learn about the joys of dog mushing with this personal visit. Call (907) 457-1117 for reservations or write P.O. Box 80961-p, Fairbanks, AK 99708. [ADVERTISEMENT]

See Bank Displays: The Key Bank, at 1st Avenue and Cushman Street, has a display of gold nuggets and several trophy animals. Mount McKinley Mutual Savings Bank features a display of McKinley prints and the original cannonball safe used when the bank opened. The bank is at 531 3rd Ave.

Visit Historic Churches: St. Matthew's Episcopal, 1029 1st Ave., was originally built in 1905, but burned in 1947 and was rebuilt the following year. Of special interest is the church's intricately carved altar, made in 1906 of interior Alaska birch and saved from the fire.

Fairbanks Convention & Visitors Bureau

Your information source for Fairbanks and Alaska!

We can answer your questions on where to stay, what to see, how to get around, or when to visit because answering questions is our business!

Just ask us!

Call or write for your FREE Visitors Guide packed with information on Fairbanks and Alaska's Interior.

When in Fairbanks stop by our Log Cabin Visitors Center. Talk with our friendly staff, browse the brochures, look at sample menus, or check the vacancy listings. Bring this ad and receive a FREE gift!

Fairbanks Convention & Visitors Bureau
550 First Ave., Ste. 307
Fairbanks, AK 99701 (907) 456-5774

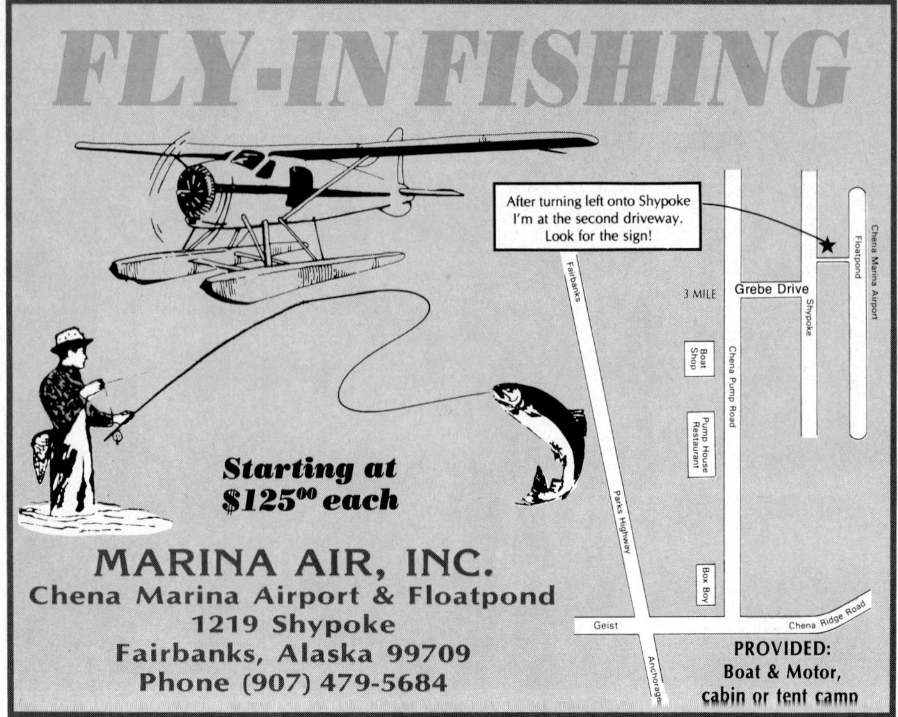

Immaculate Conception Church, on the Chena River at Cushman Street bridge, was drawn by horses to its present location in the winter of 1911 from its original site at 1st Avenue and Dunkel Street.

See the Pipeline: Drive about 10 miles/ 16 km north from downtown on the Steese Highway to see the trans-Alaska pipeline. Clearly visible are the thermal devices used to keep the permafrost frozen around the pipeline support columns.

View Mount McKinley: The best spot to see Mount McKinley is from the University of Alaska Fairbanks campus (on Yukon Drive, between Talkeetna and Sheenjek streets) where a turnout and marker define the horizon view of Mount Hayes (elev. 13,832 feet/4,216m); Hess Mountain (elev. 11,940 feet/3,639m); Mount Deborah (elev. 12,339 feet/3,761m); and Mount McKinley (elev. 20,320 feet/6,194m). Distant foothills

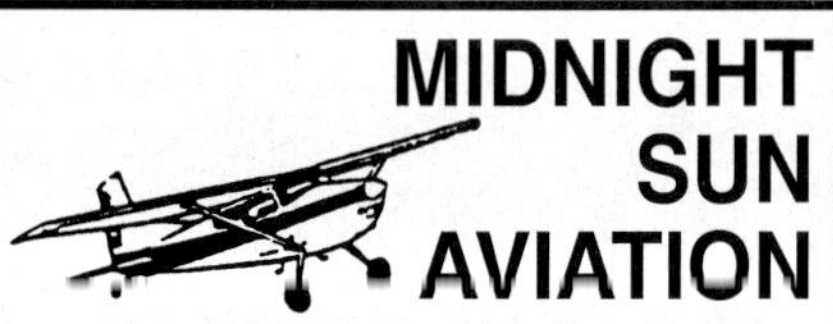

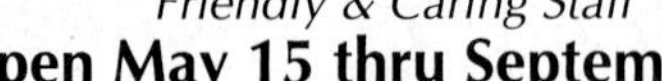

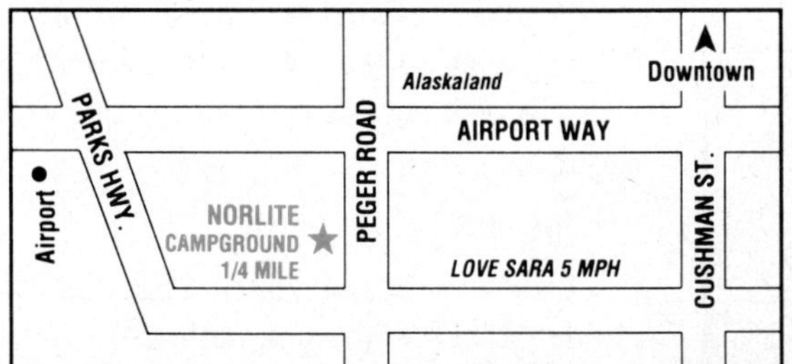

VISA

are part of the Wood River Butte.

Cruise Aboard the Riverboat *Discovery*: Every day at 8:45 A.M. and 2 P.M. in summer, the riverboat *Discovery* departs for a half-day cruise on the Chena and Tanana rivers. Drive out Airport Road, turn south at Dale Road and continue 0.5 mile/0.8 km on Dale to Discovery Drive. Reservations are advised, as this is one of the most popular attractions in town. For the first leg of the trip, the *Discovery* winds its way down the meandering Chena River, its banks lined by old homesteads, modern homes and bush planes. The Chena River also joins with Cripple Creek, the Interior's richest gold rush stream. On the Tanana River, fish wheels turn in the swift glacial water, scooping up salmon to be dried and smoked for winter food. Returning up the Tanana River, the boat stops at Old Chena Indian Village, where passengers have the opportunity to see Susan Butcher's Iditarod-champion dog team in action. After the demonstration, passengers disembark for a tour of the village. Guides from the *Discovery*, who are of Indian or Eskimo heritage, are on hand to explain past and present Native culture. For more information on the riverboat *Discovery*, contact Alaska Riverways, Inc., 1975 Discovery Dr., Fairbanks, AK 99709; phone (907) 479-6673, fax 479-4613.

Visit Alaskaland Pioneer Park. Visitors will find a relaxed atmosphere at Alaskaland, a pleasant park with historic buildings, small shops, food, entertainment, playgrounds and 4 covered picnic shelters. The park—which has no admission fee—is open year-round.

To drive to Alaskaland (at Airport Way and Peger Road), take Airport Way to Wilbur, turn north onto Wilbur, then immediately west onto access road, which leads to Alaskaland enclosure.

The 44-acre historic park was created in 1967 as the Alaska Centennial Park to commemorate the 100th year of statehood. Designed to provide a taste of interior Alaska history, visitors may begin their visit at the information center, which is located just inside the park's main gate. Walk through Gold Rush Town, a narrow winding street of authentic old buildings that once graced downtown Fairbanks and now house gift shops. Here you will find: the Kitty Hensley and Judge Wickersham houses, furnished with turn-of-the-century items; the First Presbyterian Church, constructed in 1906; and the Pioneers of Alaska Museum, dedicated to those who braved frontier life to found Fairbanks. Free guided historical walking tours take place each afternoon.

The park is home to the newly renovated SS *Nenana,* a national landmark. Cared for by the Fairbanks Historical Preservation Foundation, the *Nenana* is the largest sternwheeler ever built west of the Mississippi: and the second largest wooden vessel in existence. The Foundation also displays a 300-foot/91-m diorama of life along the Tanana and Yukon rivers in the early 1900s.

The top level of the Civic Center houses an art gallery, featuring rotating contemporary exhibits and paintings; 11 A.M. to 9 P.M. daily, Memorial Day through Labor Day; noon to 8 P.M. daily, except Monday, during the rest of the year.

Behind the Civic Center, you'll find the

Historic river steamer SS Nenana *at Alaskaland.* (© Steven Seiller)

Pioneer Air Museum, which features antique aircraft and stories of their Alaskan pilots, with displays from 1913–48. Phone (907) 451-0037, Memorial Day through Labor Day, for information. Admission is $1.

At the rear of the park is the Native Village Museum and Kashims with Native wares, artifacts, crafts and exhibitions of Native dancing. Across from the Native Village is Mining Valley, with displays of

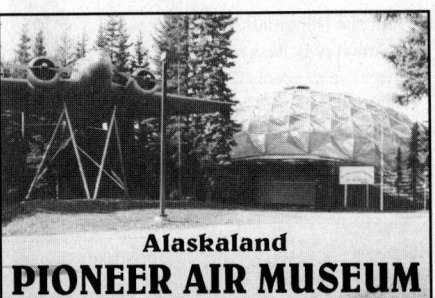

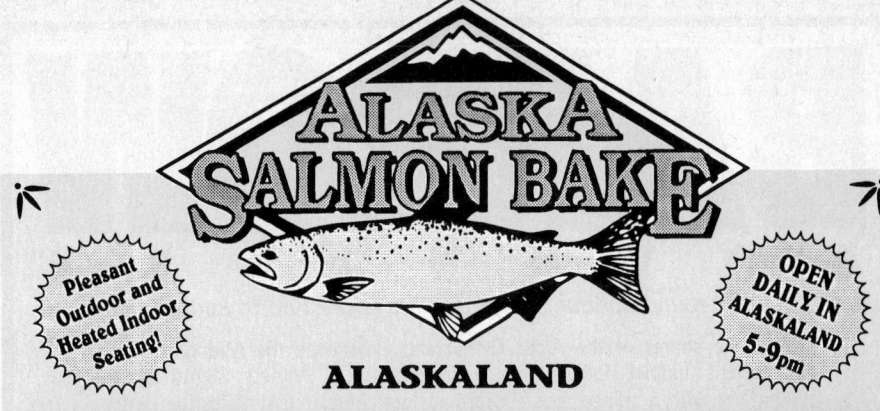

The largest gold nugget found in Alaska weighed 107 ounces.

gold-mining equipment. The Salmon Bake, with both outdoor and heated indoor seating areas, is also part of Mining Valley. A popular feature, the Salmon Bake is open daily for lunch from noon to 2 P.M. (June 10 to Aug. 15), and for dinner from 5–9 P.M. (end of May to mid-Sept.). Salmon, barbecued ribs, halibut and 16-oz. porterhouse steaks are served, rain or shine.

There's entertainment 7 nights a week starting at 8:15 P.M. at the Palace Theatre & Saloon, featuring a musical comedy review about life in Fairbanks titled "Golden Heart Review." "Riversong," a musical about Native lifestyles, is performed in the Civic Center Theater at 8 P.M. nightly. The Big Stampede show in Gold Rush Town is a theater in the round presenting the paintings of Rusty Heurlin which depicts the trail of '98; narrative by Ruben Gaines.

The Crooked Creek & Whiskey Island Railroad, a 30-gauge train, takes passengers for a 12-minute ride around the park. Other types of recreational activities available at Alaskaland include miniature golf, an antique carousel and picnicking in covered shelters. A public dock is located on the Chena River at the rear of the park.

Visitors are welcome to take part in square and round dances year-round at the Alaskaland Dance Center. Phone (907) 452-5699 evenings for calendar of events. For more information about Alaskaland, phone (907) 459-1087.

Area Attractions: Fairbanks is a good jumping-off point for many attractions in Alaska's Interior. Head out the Steese Highway for swimming at Chena Hot Springs or Circle Hot Springs. At Fox, 11 miles/17.7 km north of Fairbanks, the Steese Highway intersects with the Elliott Highway, which leads to the start of the Dalton Highway (formerly the North Slope Haul Road). Popular attractions in this area include Gold Dredge Number 8 (take Goldstream Road exit to Old Steese Highway), a historic 5-deck, 250-foot dredge, and Little El Dorado Gold Mine at Mile 1.2 Elliott Highway. Both offer gold mining demonstrations and gold panning. See highway sections for details.

Gold Dredge Number 8. Turn left on Goldstream Road, then left again on the Old Steese Highway. Drive 0.3 mile to Gold

Dredge Number 8 on your right. Tours of Dredge Number 8 and gold panning are one of the Interior's top attractions. Visit Gold Dredge Number 8 early on while in Fairbanks. It's so interesting and so authentic that many people come back again and

Gold Dredge No. 8 ...

... it's the kind of experience you should

Gold Dredge No. 8 is open from 9 a.m. to 6 p.m., 7 Days a Week, from May 31 to September 15. Tours are offered every 45 minutes and include unlimited gold panning. Cost is $10 per person with free admission for children 8 and under.

expect to have in Alaska.

The Dredge is a 250-foot vessel displacing 1,065 tons and standing as tall as a five-story building. Gold Dredge No. 8 was designated a National Historic Mechanical Engineering Landmark by the American Society of Mechanical Engineers in 1986. John and Ramona Reeves take great pride in being the stewards of one of the few privately-owned National Historic Districts in America.

From Fairbanks, take the Steese Highway north to Goldstream Road, then follow then follow the signs. It's about 10 minutes from downtown.

There's still gold in Alaska, and plenty of it. Located amidst the spectacular venues and rugged frontier that draws people the world over to Alaska, is gold. Gold Dredge No. 8 is your gateway to a truly authentic gold mining experience. John and Ramona Reeves are your hosts at this "must do" Fairbanks attraction you'll remember for a lifetime.

Gold Dredge No. 8 is a gold processing ship built in 1928 that unearthed millions of ounces of gold during the heyday of large-scale placer gold mining in Alaska. The Reeves' acquired Gold Dredge No. 8 in 1982, and have brought back the excitement of real gold prospecting as it was then – and still is today. Gold Dredge No. 8 is the only gold dredge in Alaska open to the public. It is listed in the National Register of Historic Sites, the National Register of Historic Objects, and the National Register of Historic Districts.

In addition to an informative tour of Gold Dredge No. 8 led by very competent, friendly and knowledgeable guides, visitors can pan for gold to their heart's content. We provide everything you'll need – hardhats, pans, shovels and directions on what to do and where to look. You keep all the gold you find! And we'll weigh it for you in our assay office!

"This is the real deal," says John Reeves. "We've got 60 acres of paydirt in front of the dredge. Our visitors aren't going to clean us out... but we want you to try and have a great time doing it!"

The Gold Dredge No. 8 grounds are packed with nostalgic relics, buildings and equipment. In fact, the Dredge is home to an extensive collection of mastodon and woolly mammoth bones and tusks from when dinosaurs roamed the Alaskan frontier. The film presentation "*Alaskan Gold*" runs continuously. Our gift shop has an excellent variety of uniquely Alaskan items, many of which are hand crafted by Fairbanks area artisans. There's a great museum, as well as a snack bar featuring coffee roasted on premises, fresh baked goodies, and a nice selection of Alaskan beers.

This year, make Gold Dredge No. 8 part of your Fairbanks travel plans and enjoy this informative, fun-filled, authentic gold mining experience. But we should warn you... Gold Fever is extremely catching.

"You'll get a gold rush without going bust!"

Acres of RV Parking

See log ad under Attractions

P.O. Box 81941
Fairbanks, Alaska 99708
TEL (907) 457-6058
FAX (907) 457-8888

again. Families love it. See display ad in this section. [ADVERTISEMENT]

Denali National Park is a 2½-hour drive, or a 3½-hour train trip via the Alaska Railroad, from Fairbanks. Once there, take the shuttle bus or guided tour through the park. For road conditions on the George Parks Highway between Fairbanks and Denali, phone the Dept. of Transportation at (907) 451-2200.

Eielson AFB, 25 miles/40 km southeast of Fairbanks on the Richardson–Alaska Highway, was built in 1943. Originally a satellite base to Ladd Field (now Fort Wainwright) and called Mile 26, it served as a storage site for aircraft on their way to the Soviet Union under the WWII Lend–Lease program. Closed after WWII, the base was reactivated in 1946 and renamed Eielson AFB, after Carl Ben Eielson, the first man to fly from Alaska over the North Pole to Greenland. A tour of

University of Alaska Fairbanks campus.
(© Harry M. Walker)

in this section or consult local travel services.

Play Tennis: There is 1 outdoor court at Hez Ray Recreation Complex, 19th Avenue and Lathrop Street. There are 6 outdoor asphalt courts at the Mary Siah Recreation Center, 1025 14th Ave. No fees or reservations. For more information phone (907) 459-1070.

Play Golf: Maintaining a scenic 9-hole course with artificial greens, the Fairbanks Golf and Country Club (public is invited) is

the base is offered every Friday during the summer months from 9–10 A.M.; phone the public affairs office at (907) 377-2116 for reservations and more information.

There are 1-day or longer sightseeing trips to Point Barrow, Prudhoe Bay, Fort Yukon and other bush destinations. See ads

west of the downtown area at Farmers Loop and Ballaine Road; phone (907) 479-6555 for information and reservations. The 9-hole Chena Bend Golf Course is located on Fort Wainwright; phone (907) 355-6749. North Star Golf Club, located 10 minutes north of downtown on the Old Steese Highway, also offers a regulation 9-hole course; phone (907) 457-4653 or (907) 452-2104.

Ride Bikes Around Fairbanks: There are many day-touring choices in Fairbanks. A round-trip tour of the city, the University of Alaska and the College area can be made by leaving town on Airport Way and returning on College Road. The Farmers Loop Road or a ride out the Old Steese Highway toward Fox are easy tours.

Go Skiing: Fairbanks has several downhill ski areas: Cleary Summit, **Milepost F 20.3** Steese Highway; Skiland, **Milepost F 20.9** Steese Highway; Eielson AFB and Fort

Wainwright ski hills; Moose Mountain Ski Resort, Spinach Creek Road on Murphy Dome; and an alpine ski hill at Chena Hot Springs Resort at **Milepost J 56.5** Chena Hot Springs Road.

Cross-country ski trails are at Birch Hill Recreation Area; drive 2.8 miles/4.5 km north of Fairbanks via Steese Expressway to a well-marked turnoff, then drive in 2.3 miles/3.7 km. University of Alaska–Fairbanks has 26 miles/42 km of cross-country ski trails. The trail system is quite extensive; you may ski out to Ester Dome.

Go Swimming. Fairbanks North Star Borough Parks and Recreation Dept. offers 3 pools: Mary Siah Recreation Center, 1025 14th Ave., phone (907) 459-1082; Robert Hamme Memorial Pool, 901 Airport Way, phone (907) 459-1086; and Robert Wescott Memorial Pool, 8th Avenue in North Pole, phone (907) 488-9402.

Chena Lakes Recreation Area. This 2,178-acre park, located 17.3 miles/27.8 km southeast of Fairbanks on the Richardson–Alaska Highway, offers a wide assortment of outdoor recreation. There are 80 campsites for both RV and tent camping, including campsites on an island; canoe, sailboat and rowboat rentals; bike paths and trails for nature hikes, skiing, skijoring and dog mushing; and boat ramp access to the nearby Chena River. Admission to the park, maintained by the Fairbanks North Star Borough, is $3 per vehicle between Memorial Day and Labor Day. No admission is charged the rest of the year.

Go Fishing: There are several streams and lakes within driving distance of Fairbanks, and local fishing guides are available. **Chena Lake,** about 20 miles/32 km southeast of the city via the Richardson–Alaska Highway at Chena Lakes Recreation Area, is stocked with rainbow trout, silver salmon and arctic char. The **Chena River** and its tributaries offer fishing for sheefish, whitefish, northern pike and burbot. The Chena River flows through Fairbanks. Chena Hot Springs Road off the Steese Highway provides access to fisheries in the Chena River Recreation Area (see the STEESE HIGHWAY section). The Steese Highway also offers access to the **Chatanika River** for northern pike and burbot fishing. Special regulations apply in these waters for grayling and salmon fishing. Phone the ADF&G office at (907) 456-4359.

Air taxi operators and guides in Fairbanks offer short trips from the city for rainbow trout, grayling, northern pike, lake trout and sheefish in lakes and streams of the Tanana and Yukon river drainages. Some operators have camps set up for overnight trips while others specialize in day trips. The air taxi operators usually provide a boat and motor for their angling visitors. Rates are reasonable, and vary according to the distance from town and type of facilities offered.

DENALI NATIONAL PARK

(Formerly Mount McKinley National Park)
Includes log of Park Road
(See map, page 438)

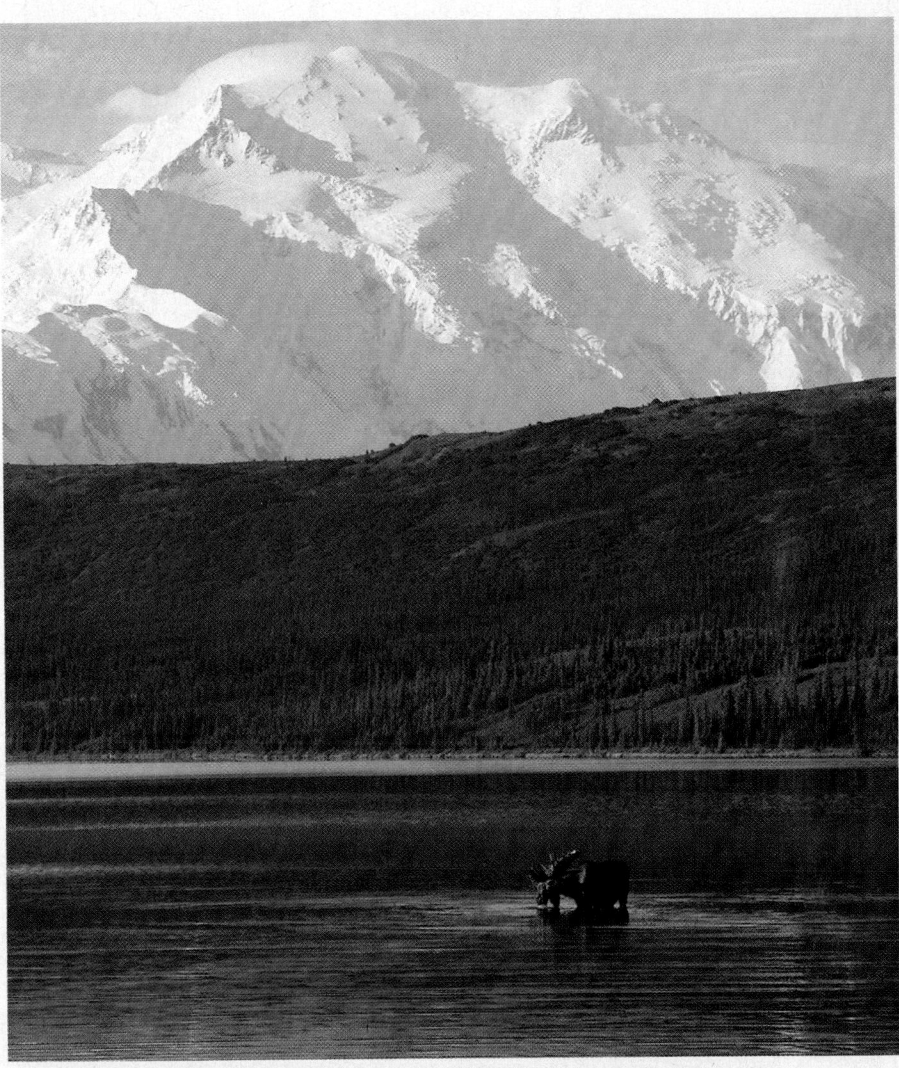

Bull moose in Wonder Lake with Mount McKinley in background.
(© Loren Taft, Alaskan Images)

Denali National Park and Preserve (formerly Mount McKinley National Park) lies on the north flank of the Alaska Range, 250 miles/402 km south of the Arctic Circle. The park entrance, accessible by highway, railroad and aircraft, is 237 highway miles/381 km north of Anchorage, and about half that distance from Fairbanks.

The park is open year-round to visitors, although the hotel, most campgrounds, and food and shuttle bus service within the park are available only from late May or early June to mid-Sept. (Opening dates for facilities and activities for the summer season are announced in the spring by the Park Service and depend mainly on snow conditions in May.)

When you arrive be sure to stop at the Visitor Center, near the park entrance. The center offers information and limited reservations for campgrounds in the park; maps, brochures and schedules of events; details on campfire talks, hikes, nature walks, sled dog demonstrations and wildlife tours; and shuttle bus schedules and ticket reservations (2 days in advance). Also available are National Park passes. The center is open daily in summer, generally from early morning into the evening.

Parking space is limited at the Visitor Center. Overflow parking is available at Riley Creek Campground (walk or mini-shuttle to Visitor Center).

Lodging and camping are available outside the park on the George Parks Highway, and there are a variety of activities—river rafting, hikes and ranger programs—to enjoy. Check with operators outside the park and with personnel at the Visitor Center about programs and activities.

First-time visitors should be particularly aware of the controlled-access system for Park Road use. Private vehicle traffic on the 91-mile/146-km road into the park is restricted beyond the Savage River check station (**Milepost J 14.8**). Campers must reserve campsites by phone or at the Visitor Center; see Visitor Services this section for details on the Reservation System. The shuttle bus system and concession-operated tours are available to allow visitors a means of viewing the park without disturbing the wildlife; see Transportation this section for details on the shuttle service.

In an effort to preserve wildlife viewing opportunities for the public, the National Park Service has set road traffic limits. Traffic will be held to the 1984 averages. Consequently, there are limited bus seats available. When planning trips to the park, visitors should reserve shuttle bus tickets in advance by phone or plan activities in the entrance area, such as attending naturalist programs, for the first 1 or 2 days, until bus seats can be obtained.

An admission fee of $3 per person ($5 per family) is charged to visitors traveling beyond the Savage River checkpoint at Mile 14.8 on the Park Road (see log this section). The fee is collected when visitors obtain shuttle bus tickets and campground permits at the Visitor Center. Persons 16 years of age or less, and U.S. citizens 62 years or older, are exempt from the admission fee. (A $15 annual park pass and the $25 Golden Eagle Pass, are valid for admission.)

For information about the park, write Denali National Park and Preserve, Box 9, Denali Park, AK 99755; winter phone (907) 683-2294, summer phone (907) 683-1266 or 1267.

One of the park's best-known attractions is Mount McKinley, North America's highest mountain at 20,320 feet/6,194m. On a clear day, Mount McKinley is visible from Anchorage. However, cloudy, rainy summer weather frequently obscures the mountain, and travelers have about a 20 percent chance of seeing it.

First mention of Mount McKinley was in 1794, when English explorer Capt. George Vancouver spotted a "stupendous snow mountain" from Cook Inlet. Early Russian explorers and traders called the peak *Bolshaia Gora,* or "Big Mountain." The Tanana Indian name for the mountain is *Denali,* said to mean "high one." The mountain was named McKinley in 1896 by a Princeton-educated prospector named William A. Dickey for presidential nominee William McKinley of Ohio. Even today, the mountain has two names: Mount McKinley according to USGS maps, and Denali according to the state Geographic Names Board.

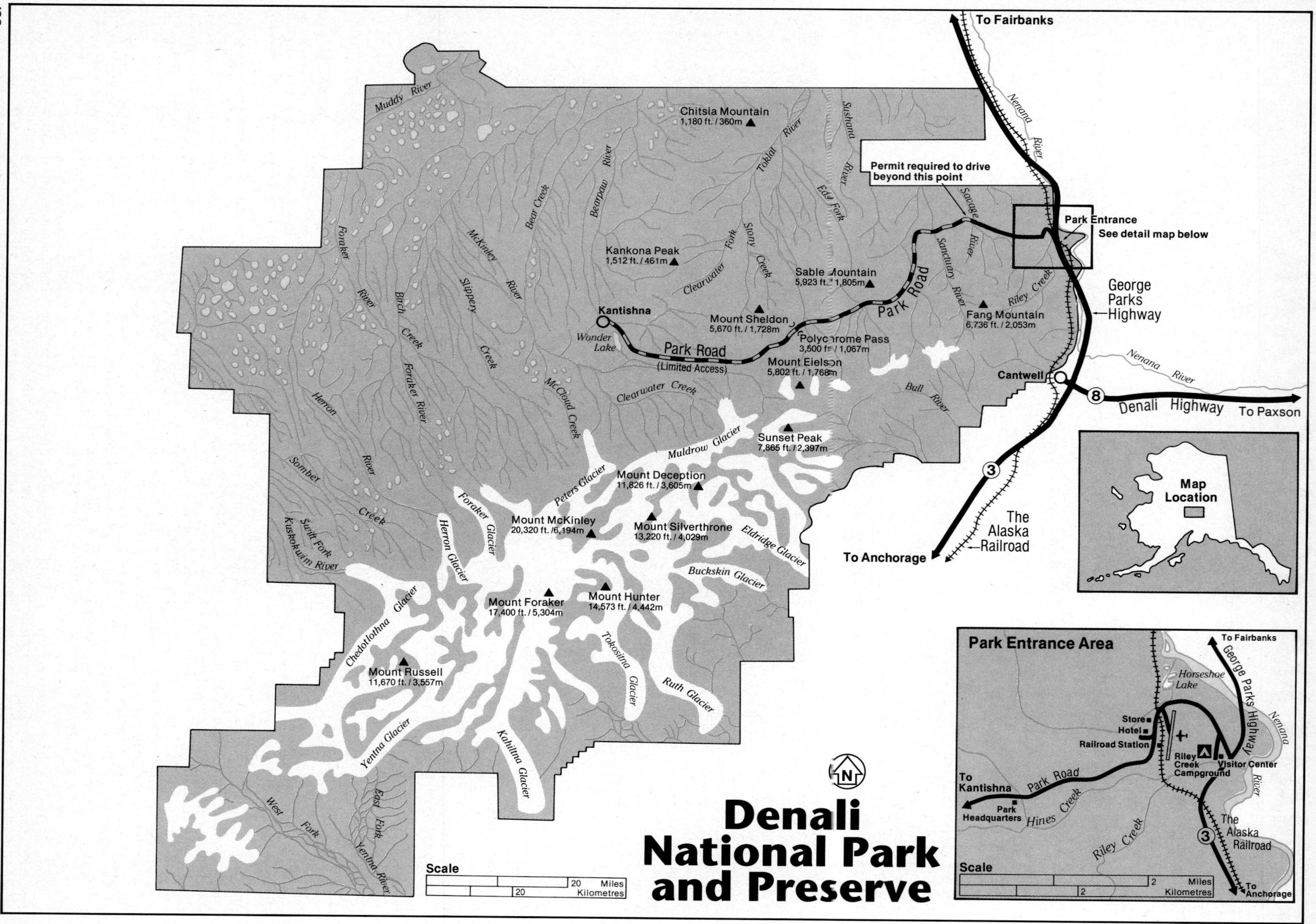
Denali
National Park
and Preserve
To Fairbanks
Permit required to drive
beyond this point
Park Entrance
See detail map below
George
Parks
Highway
Chitsia Mountain
1,180 ft. / 360m
Kankona Peak
1,512 ft. / 461m
Sable Mountain
5,923 ft. / 1,805m
Kantishna
Mount Sheldon
5,670 ft. / 1,728m
Polychrome Pass
3,500 ft. / 1,067m
Fang Mountain
6,736 ft. / 2,053m
Wonder
Lake
Park Road
(Limited Access)
Mount Eielson
5,802 ft. / 1,768m
Cantwell
Denali Highway
To Paxson
Sunset Peak
7,865 ft. / 2,397m
Mount Deception
11,826 ft. / 3,605m
Mount McKinley
20,320 ft. /6,194m
Mount Silverthrone
13,220 ft. / 4,029m
Mount Foraker
17,400 ft. / 5,304m
Mount Hunter
14,573 ft. / 4,442m
Mount Russell
11,670 ft. / 3,557m
To Anchorage
The
Alaska
Railroad
Map
Location
Muddy River
Foraker River
Birch Creek
Slippery Creek
McKinley River
Bear Creek
Bearpaw River
Toklat River
Sushana River
Eldi Fork
Stony Creek
Clearwater Fork
Savage River
Sanctuary River
Riley Creek
Nenana River
Bull River
Clearwater Creek
McCloud Creek
Herron River
Somber Creek
Swift Fork
Kuskokwim River
Muldrow Glacier
Peters Glacier
Foraker Glacier
Herron Glacier
Eldridge Glacier
Buckskin Glacier
Chedotlothna Glacier
Tokositna Glacier
Ruth Glacier
Kahiltna Glacier
Yentna Glacier
West Fork
East Fork
Yentna River
Scale
20 Miles
20 Kilometres
Park Entrance Area
To Fairbanks
George Parks Highway
Horseshoe
Lake
Nenana River
Store
Hotel
Railroad Station
Riley
Creek
Campground
Visitor Center
To
Kantishna
Park Road
Park
Headquarters
Hines Creek
Riley Creek
The
Alaska
Railroad
To
Anchorage
Scale
2 Miles
2 Kilometres

The history of climbs on McKinley is as intriguing as its many names. In 1903, Judge James Wickersham and party climbed to an estimated 8,000 feet/2,438m, while Dr. Frederick A. Cook and party reached the 11,000-foot/3,353-m level. In 1906, Cook returned to the mountain and made 2 attempts at the summit—the first unsuccessful, and the second (according to Cook) successful. Cook's vague description of his ascent route and a questionable summit photo led many to doubt his claim. Tom Lloyd, of the 1910 Sourdough Party (which included Charles McGonagall, Pete Anderson and Billy Taylor), claimed they had reached both summits (north and south peaks) but could not provide any photographic evidence. (Much later it was verified that they had reached the summit of the lower north peak.) The first complete ascent of the true summit of Mount McKinley was made in 1913 by Hudson Stuck, Harry Karstens and Walter Harper.

Today, close to a thousand people attempt to climb Mount McKinley each year between April and June, most flying in to base camp at 7,000 feet/2134m. (The first airplane landing on the mountain was flown in 1932 by Joe Crosson.) Geographic features of McKinley and its sister peaks bear the names of many early explorers: Eldridge and Muldrow glaciers, after George Eldridge and Robert Muldrow of the U.S. Geographic Service who determined the peak's altitude in 1898; Wickersham Wall; Karstens Ridge; and Mount Carpe and Mount Koven, named for

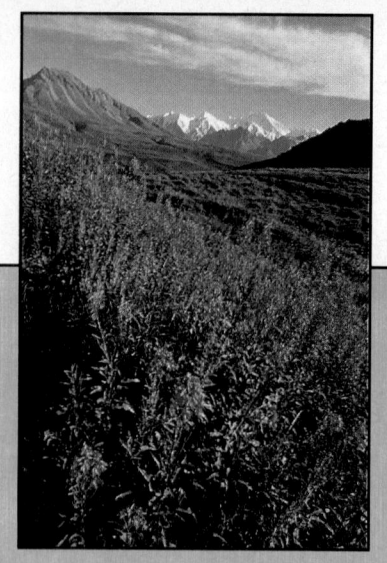

Allen Carpe and Theodore Koven, both killed in a 1932 climb.

The National Park Service maintains a ranger station in Talkeetna that is staffed full time from mid-April through mid-Sept. and intermittently during the winter. Mountaineering rangers provide information on climbing within the Alaska Range. A reference library and slide/tape program are available for climbers. Mountaineering regulations and information may be obtained from: Talkeetna Ranger Station, P.O. Box 588, Talkeetna, AK 99676; phone (907) 733-2231.

Timberline in the park is 2,700 feet/823m. The landscape below timberline in this subarctic wilderness is called taiga, a term of Russian origin that describes the scant growth of trees. Black and white spruce, willow, dwarf birch and aspen grow at lower elevations. The uplands of alpine tundra are carpeted with lichens, mosses, wildflowers and low-growing shrubs. Wildflowers bloom in spring, usually peaking by early July.

Denali National Park represents one of the last intact ecosystems in the world, according to the Park Service. Here visitors have the opportunity to observe the natural behavior of wild animals. Grizzly bears, caribou, wolves and red foxes freely wander over the tundra. Moose wade through streams and lake shallows. A few lynx pursue snow-

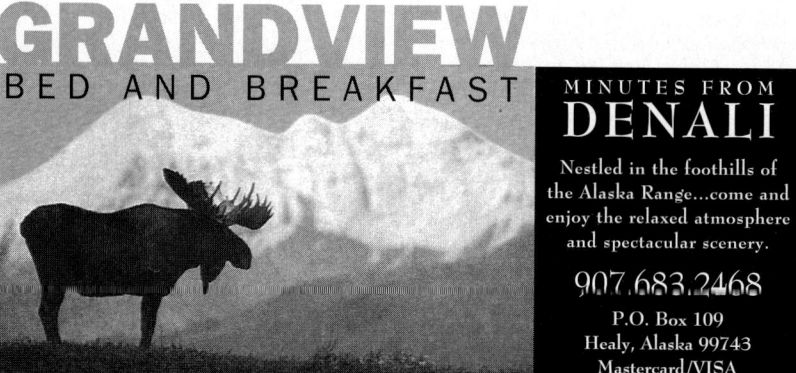

DENALI PARK AREA ADVERTISERS

shoe hare in taiga forests. Marmots, pikas and Dall sheep inhabit high, rocky areas. The arctic ground squirrel's sharp warning call is heard throughout the park.

Migratory bird life encompasses species from 6 continents, including waterfowl, shorebirds, songbirds and birds of prey. Ptarmigan, gray jays and magpies are year-round residents.

The park's silty glacial rivers are not an angler's delight, but grayling, Dolly Varden and lake trout are occasionally caught in streams and small lakes.

Emergency Services: Within Denali National Park, phone (907) 683-2294.

ACCOMMODATIONS/VISITOR SERVICES

There is only 1 hotel within the park, but several motels will be found outside the park along the George Parks Highway (turn to **Milepost A 237.3** in the GEORGE PARKS HIGHWAY section). Accommodations are also available in the Kantishna area. *NOTE: Visitors should make reservations for lodging far in advance.* The park hotel and area motels are often filled during the summer. Visitors must book their own accommodations. See ads for accommodations this section.

Visitor services are available from late May to mid-Sept., depending on weather. The Denali National Park Hotel has a gift shop, restaurant, snack bar and saloon. Limited groceries and showers are available at a small store near the hotel. Gas is no longer available inside the park. Gas service 1 mile/1.6 km north of the Park Road junction, May to mid-Sept. The post office is

A group of caribou gathered on Park Road. (© Beth Davidow)

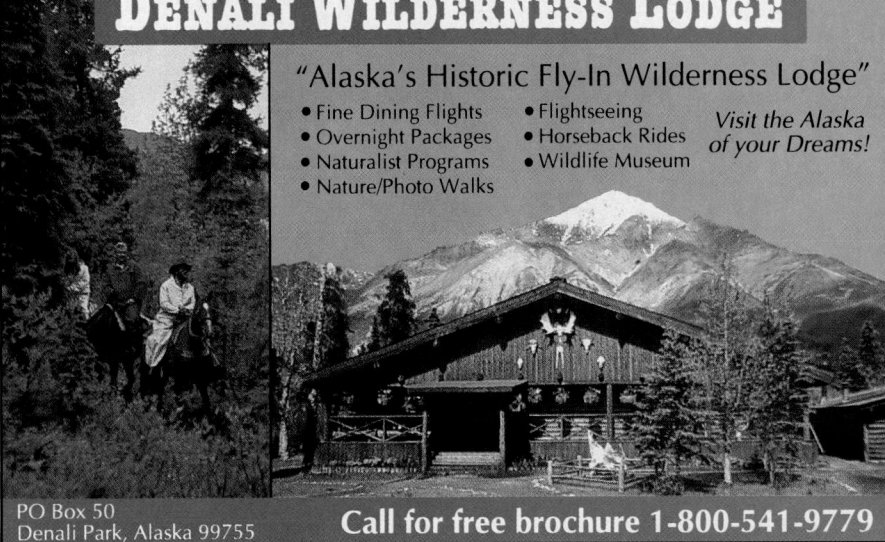

near the hotel. There is a dump station near Riley Creek Campground.

NOTE: There are no food services in the park after you leave the headquarters entrance area.

Campers should bring a gasoline or propane stove or purchase firewood from concessionaire; a tent or waterproof shelter because of frequent rains; and rain gear.

There are 7 campgrounds in the park along the 87-mile/140-km Park Road (see log of Park Road in this section for most locations). Wonder Lake, Sanctuary River and Igloo Creek campgrounds are tent only and accessible only by shuttle bus. Riley Creek, Savage River and Teklanika are available for both RV and tent camping. Morino is for those without vehicles only and is not on the reservation system. ▲

The campgrounds are open from about late May to early Sept., except for Riley Creek, which is open year-round (snow-covered and no water, flush toilets or dump station in winter). There is a fee and a 14-day limit at all campgrounds in summer. There is a 3-night minimum stay requirement at Teklanika River Campground, and also a limit of 1 round-trip to this campground for registered campers with vehicles. Additional travel to and from Teklanika is by shuttle bus. See chart for facilities at each campground. *(NOTE: Campground fees are subject to change!)*

Campground	Spaces	Tent	Trailer	Pit toilets	Flush toilets	Tap water	Fee
Morino	60	•		•			$ 6
Riley Creek	102	•	•		•	•	$12
Savage River	33	•	•		•	•	$12
Sanctuary River	7	•		•		•	$ 6
Teklanika River	50	•	•	•		•	$12
Igloo Creek	7	•		•		•	$ 6
Wonder Lake	28	•			•	•	$12

Several private campgrounds are located outside the park along the George Parks Highway. See display ads this section.

For area accommodations, also turn to pages 387–391 in the GEORGE PARKS HIGHWAY section.

Reservation System: One-third of the park's campsites may be reserved through a nationwide, toll-free number, 1-800-622-7275 (PARK). (Anchorage residents and foreign visitors phone 907/272-7275 for reservations.) The phone-in reservation system opens around mid-January. The remaining campsite reservations will be available up to 2 days in advance at the Visitor Center at **Milepost J 0.5** Park Road. During peak season, campgrounds fill up by midmorning for the following day and, on occasion, the day after.

Denali Backcountry Lodge. Don't pass up a visit to this lodge if you want to escape the park's crowded east entrance and immerse yourself deep within the park for a few days. The lodge is located at the end of the 97-mile park road. Full-service accommodations feature a comfortable wilderness lodge, cozy cedar cabins, dining room and lounge. One- to 4-night all-inclusive stays include round-trip transportation from the train depot, all meals and lodging, guided hikes, wildlife viewing, bicycling, photography, and natural history programs. Credit cards accepted. P.O. Box 189, Denali Park, AK 99755. Call (800) 841-0692. See display ad this section. [ADVERTISEMENT]

Denali Bluffs Hotel. Opening 1996. The newest and closest hotel to the Denali National Park and Preserve entrance. 100 rooms, each room featuring 2 double beds, a private balcony or patio, and numerous other amenities. Most of the rooms have spectacular views of the Alaska Range. The lodge features a large stone fireplace and cathedral ceilings. There are comfortable sitting areas inside the lodge or outside on the deck to enjoy the panoramic views. Gift shop and coin-operated laundry. Shuttle service to visitor center and rail depot. Complete tour and activity desk. Handicap accessible. Open mid-May through mid-September. Credit cards accepted. P.O. Box 72460, Fairbanks, AK 99707. Phone (907) 488-7000 (winter) or (907) 683-7000 (summer). [ADVERTISEMENT] ♿

Denali National Park Hotel, located in park, this 100-room hotel is the bustling center for visitor activities and accommodations. The hotel is a 5 minute walk from the rail depot, provides fine dining, snack shop, gift shop, railcar lounge and grocery store (propane available). The hotel auditorium is the center for national park interpretive services. All accommodations for the hotel, McKinley Chalet (at **Milepost A 238.9** Parks Highway), McKinley Village Lodge (at **Milepost A 229** Parks Highway), wildlife and history tours, rafting adventures, dinner theater and transportation can be arranged by calling (800) 276-7234; in Anchorage 276-7234. [ADVERTISEMENT]

Denali National Park Wilderness Centers–Camp Denali, begun in 1951, is known as a premier national park wilderness vacation lodge and nature center. Its 17 guest cabins dot a hillside looking out onto an expansive view of Mount McKinley and the Alaska Range. Activities: guided hiking with experienced naturalists, wildlife observation, photography, canoeing, biking, rafting, flightseeing, evening natural history programs and periodic summer seminars. Central dining. All expense. See display ad. [ADVERTISEMENT]

Denali National Park Wilderness Centers–North Face Lodge is a small, well-appointed North Country inn in the heart of Denali National Park with a spectacular view of Mount McKinley. It features 15 guest rooms with private baths, dining room and living room. Activities: guided hiking with experienced naturalists, wildlife observation, canoeing, biking, flightseeing and evening natural history programs. All expense. See display ad. [ADVERTISEMENT]

Denali Princess Lodge. Most modern accommodations in area. 280 rooms and suites with phones and TVs. Free shuttle to rail depot and park activities. Spas, gift shop, fine dining and cafe. Handicap accommodations. Seasonal service mid-May to mid-Sept. VISA, MasterCard and American Express. Write 2815 2nd Ave., Suite 400, Seattle, WA 98121-1299, or call (800) 426-0500. [ADVERTISEMENT] ♿

Denali RV Park and Motel. 90 full and partial RV hookups, 30-amp electric. Level sites, pull-throughs, easy highway access. Individual restrooms with private showers, flush toilets. Dump station. Caravans welcome! 14 motel rooms: central bath $45, private bath $65, family units with full kitchens $90. Gift shop, general store, outdoor cooking area, pay phones. Close to all park facilities. Beautiful mountain views. Hiking trails. Reasonable rates. VISA/MasterCard. Box 155, Denali Park, AK 99755. Located 8 miles north of park entrance, Mile 245.1 Parks Highway. (907) 683-1500. 1-800-478-1501 (in Alaska). See display ad this section. [ADVERTISEMENT] ▲

Denali Wilderness Lodge is Alaska's historic fly-in wilderness lodge—an authentic bush homestead nestled in the pristine Wood River Valley. Comfortable accommodations, gourmet meals, naturalist programs, horseback riding, nature/photo walks and hikes, bird watching, wildlife museum. This is the Alaska so many hope to see but few ever experience! Overnight packages and day trips available. Free brochure. 1-800-541-9779. See display ad this section. [ADVERTISEMENT] ▲

Kantishna Roadhouse. Premier wilderness lodge located at the quiet west end of Denali National Park offers opportunities to view, photograph and explore the park. Packages include comfortable log cabins with private baths, guided hiking, gold panning, horses, fishing, fine meals and Alaskan hospitality. P.O. Box 130, Denali Park, AK 99755. Phone 1-800-942-7420. [ADVERTISEMENT]

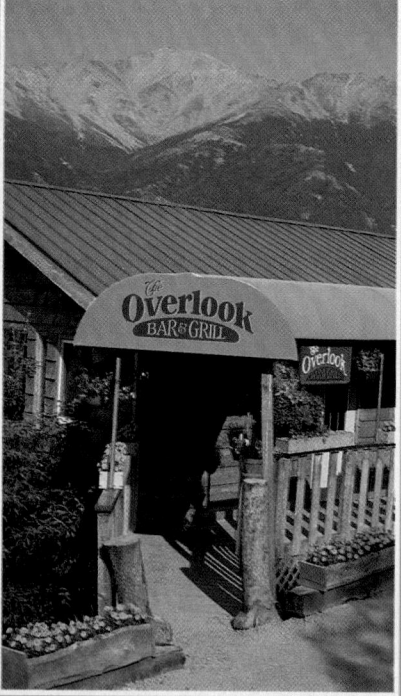

Lynx Creek Pizza. "The Best Pizza in Alaska!" We also offer Mexican specialties, hand-dipped ice cream, espresso, extensive beer/wine selection. In addition, great campground and grocery store. Only 1 mile north of park entrance (Mile 238.6 Parks High-

DENALI PARK RESORTS

Stay for the Adventure

Unbelievable scenery, amazing wildlife and exciting activities await you at Denali National Park. It is nature at its grandest. And Denali Park Resorts is dedicated to helping you enjoy everything about this majestic experience. That's why we offer you a choice of comfortable accommodations, excellent restaurants, evening entertainment, and a full range of outdoor adventures.

After an adventurous day touring the Park, unwind in our indoor swimming pool, hot tub and sauna.

Alaska Cabin Nite Dinner Theater is a treat for all ages: songs, stories and an all-you-can eat Alaskan-style barbecue.

Your Wilderness Home

McKinley Chalet Resort offers you Alaskan hospitality at its best featuring more than 300 rooms with warm, pine wood interiors. Plus, a complete restaurant, dinner theater, lounge, and gift shop.

Denali National Park Hotel, with 100-rooms "inside" the Park, is the bustling center for visitor activities. In addition to our dining room, snack shop, gift shop and lounge, the hotel is home to a 300-seat auditorium for National Park Service programs.

McKinley Village Lodge rests quietly on the banks of the Nenana River. The 50-room lodge has a full-service cafe, gift shop and cozy lounge with river-rock fireplace for your relaxation.

Activities Abound

At Denali Park Resorts we help you experience this amazing wilderness area with a variety of entertaining and exciting activities. Photograph Alaska wildlife, massive mountains, and taiga forests on one of our special park tours. Travel a wild Alaska river by raft, flightsee, enjoy a unique dinner theater presentation. The activities are endless, simply stop by the tour desk at any of our hotels.

Guest rooms compliment the warmth and charm of the wilderness.

There are numerous hiking and scenic spots to explore in Denali and we can show them to you.

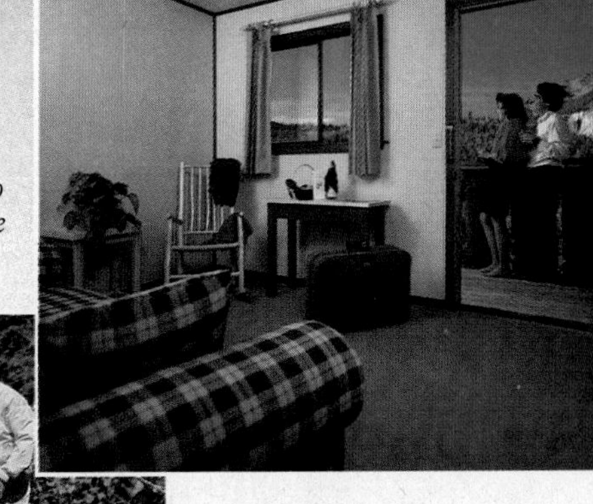

If you really want to enjoy the whole Denali experience, let us help. Denali Park Resorts has 20 years of experience in Alaska's premiere National Park, and we're ready to put that knowledge to work for you.

Denali Park Resorts
For Information And Reservations
(907) 276-7234
(800) 276-7234

P.O. Box 202516
Anchorage, AK., 99520

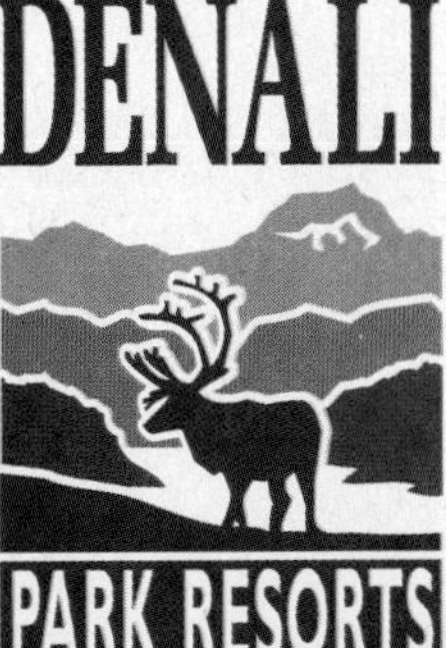

MORE THAN THE MOUNTAIN

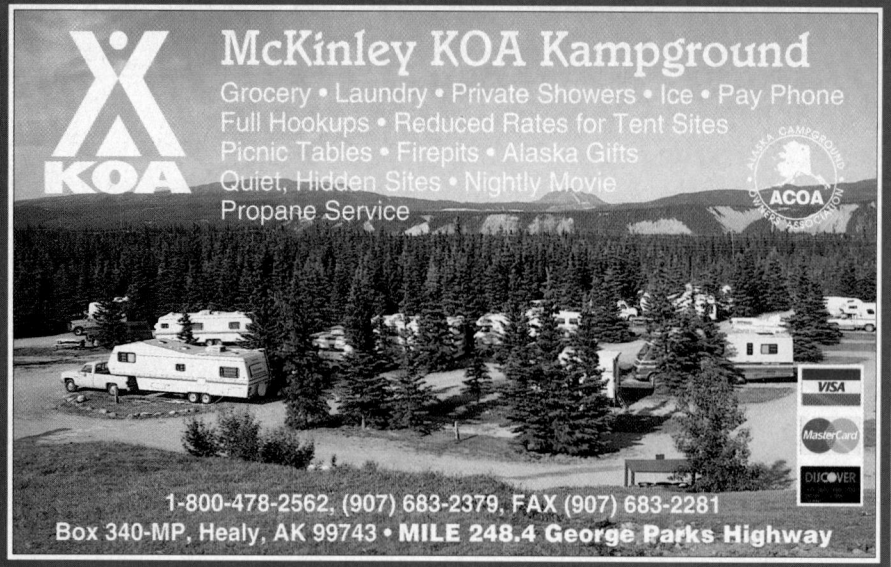

way). In Denali, call (907) 683-2547. [ADVERTISEMENT] ▲

McKinley/Denali Cabins at McKinley/Denali Steakhouse and Salmon Bake. Economy tent cabins with electric heat and lights from $65. Some cabins with private baths. Closest full-service facility to park entrance, wildlife shuttles. Close to raft trips, store, gas. Largest T-shirt selection in park area on premises. Shuttle to visitor center, railroad depot available. Free visitor information. Reservations: (907) 683-2258 or (907) 683-2733 or write P.O. Box 90M, Denali Park, AK 99755. See display ad this section. [ADVERTISEMENT]

White Moose Lodge. 1-800-481-1232. This is a small Alaskan frontier-style motel with hanging baskets, wildflowers and a rustic deck, set in a quiet wooded environment. Each newly decorated room has 2

double beds, private bath and a mountain view. A central location to services and activities, and reasonable rates make this a good place to stay while visiting Denali. Mile 248.1 Parks Highway. [ADVERTISEMENT]

ATTRACTIONS

Organized activities put on by the Park Service include ranger-led nature hikes; sled dog demonstrations at park headquarters; campfire programs at Riley Creek, Savage

River, Teklanika River and Wonder Lake campgrounds; and interpretive programs at the hotel auditorium.

Private operators in the park offer flightseeing tours, bus tours, raft tours and wintertime dogsled tours. Cross-country skiing and snowshoeing are also popular in winter.

There are few established trails in the park, but there is plenty of terrain for cross-country hiking. Free permits are required for any overnight hikes.

Permits and information on ranger-led hikes and other activities are available at the Visitor Center near the park entrance.

TRANSPORTATION

Highway: Access via the George Parks Highway and the Denali Highway.

The Park Road runs westward 92 miles/148.1 km from the park's east boundary to Kantishna. The road is paved only to Savage River (**Milepost J 14.7**). Private vehicle travel is restricted beyond the Savage River checkpoint at Mile 14.8. Mount McKinley is first visible at about **Milepost J 9** Park Road, but the best views begin at about **Milepost J 60** and continue with few interruptions to Wonder Lake. At the closest point, the summit of the mountain is 27 miles/43.5 km from the road. See log this section.

Shuttle bus: The National Park Service provides shuttle bus service from the Visitor Center to Toklat, Eielson Visitor Center and Wonder Lake. One-third of all shuttle bus tickets are available through a nationwide, toll-free number, 1-800-622-7275 (PARK). (Anchorage residents and foreign visitors phone 907/272-7275 for reservations.) The remaining shuttle bus tickets will be available on a walk-in basis, up to 2 days in advance, at the Visitor Center at **Milepost J 0.5** Park Road. During peak season, bus tickets for the next day's shuttles are generally gone by mid-morning. Shuttle buses pick up and drop off passengers along the Park Road on a space-available basis, and stop for scenic and wildlife viewing as schedules permit. A round-trip between the Visitor Center and Eielson Visitor Center takes approximately 8 hours. The round-trip to Wonder Lake takes about 11 hours. Bring a lunch, camera, binoculars, extra film, warm clothes and rain gear. Buses run daily from approximately Memorial Day through Labor Day, weather permitting.

Air: Charter flights are available from most nearby towns with airfields, and flightseeing tours of the park are offered by operators from the park area or out of Talkeetna, Anchorage or Fairbanks. A round-trip air tour of the park from Anchorage takes 3 to 4 hours. See ads this section.

Alaska Ridge Riders. Enjoy adventurous, guided fishing, wildlife and bird watching tours from comfort of enclosed, 8-wheeled all-terrain vehicle. Fish for grayling and trout at 8-Mile Lake. Travel to a ridge top for wildlife and McKinley views. Journey along Stampede Trail to Savage River for McKinley views, birds, fishing, animal track casting. Limit 5–10 passengers per tour. Light refresh-

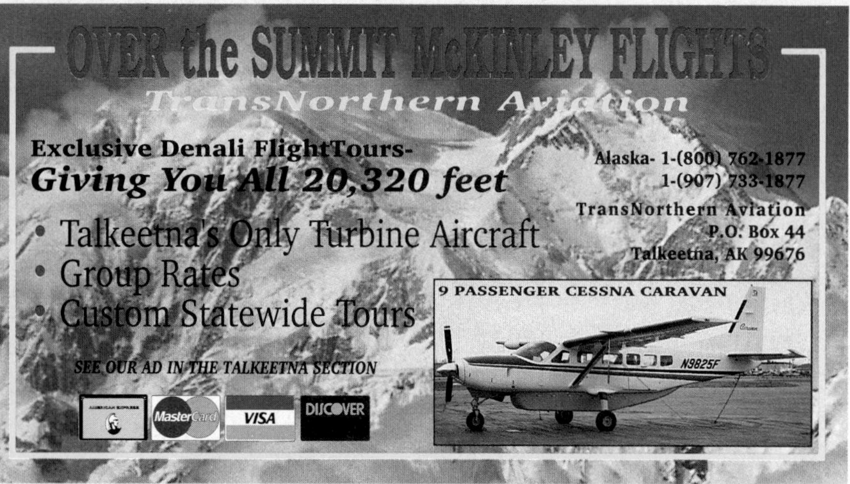

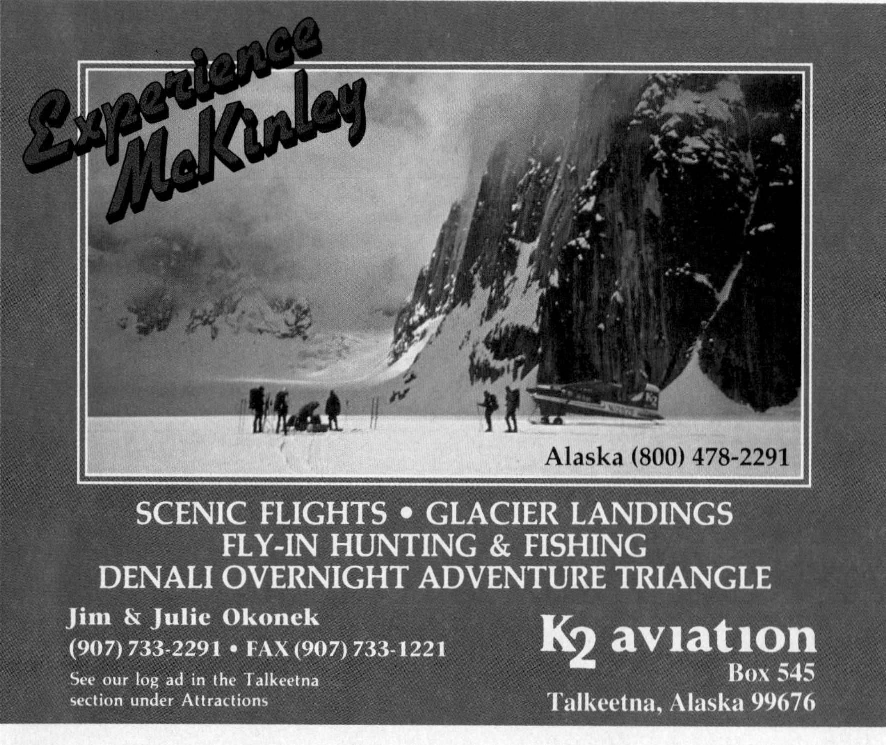

See the GENERAL INFORMATION section for details on daylight hours and driving.

ments, courtesy transportation. Custom guided bird-watching tours in Denali and Denali Highway areas arranged on request. Call (907) 683-2580 or write P.O. Box 357, Healy, AK 99743. October–April: 3020 Issaquah-Pine Lake Rd., Suite 483, Issaquah, WA 98029. See display ad this section. [ADVERTISEMENT]

Era Helicopters. Enjoy an eagle-eyed view of the grandeur of Denali National Park and Mt. McKinley with Alaska's most experienced helicopter company. Look for moose, sheep and bear in the valleys and mountainsides below. Located 1/2 mile north of the park entrance. Phone 1-800-843-1947 or (907) 683-8574 May to September.

Fly Denali. Denali Park's highest rated flightseeing tour. Local, experienced pilot. Naturalists give you more than just an airplane ride. Our aircraft get you 30 miles closer than helicopters! We're located at Mile 238.9 across from the McKinley Chalets, next to Northern Lights Gift Shop. (907) 683-2889 (April–October). See display ad. [ADVERTISEMENT]

Railroad: The Alaska Railroad offers daily northbound and southbound trains between Anchorage and Fairbanks, with stops at Denali Park Station, during the summer season. For details on schedules and fares see the ALASKA RAILROAD section.

Midnight Sun Express®. Daily rail service

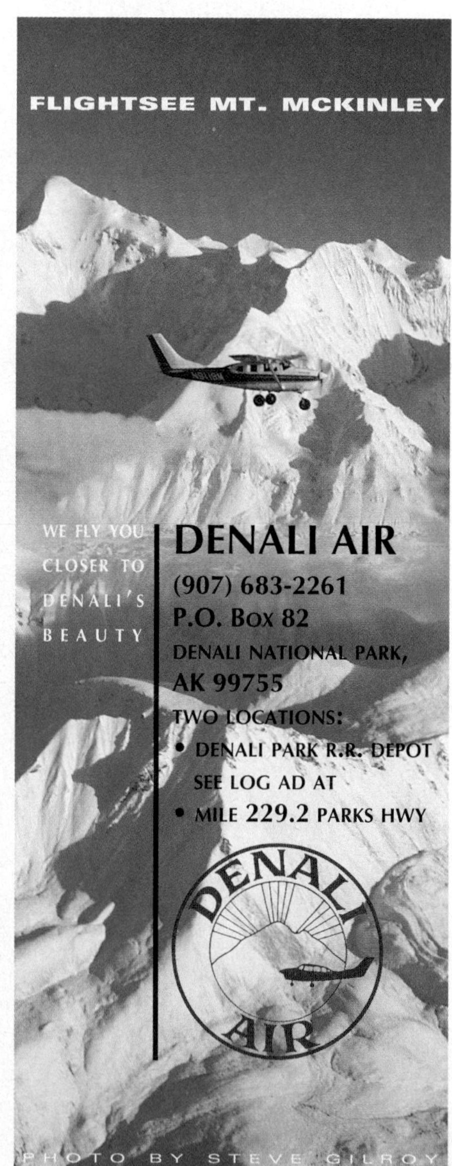

aboard the private, fully-domed ULTRA DOME® rail cars between Anchorage, Denali National Park and Fairbanks. Enjoy on-board dining prepared fresh-to-order and the only outdoor viewing platform on the Alaska Railroad system. Overnight accommodations available at Denali Park. Seasonal service mid-May through mid-September. Write 2815 2nd Ave., Suite #400, Seattle, WA 98121-1299 or call 1-800-835-8907 year-round. [ADVERTISEMENT]

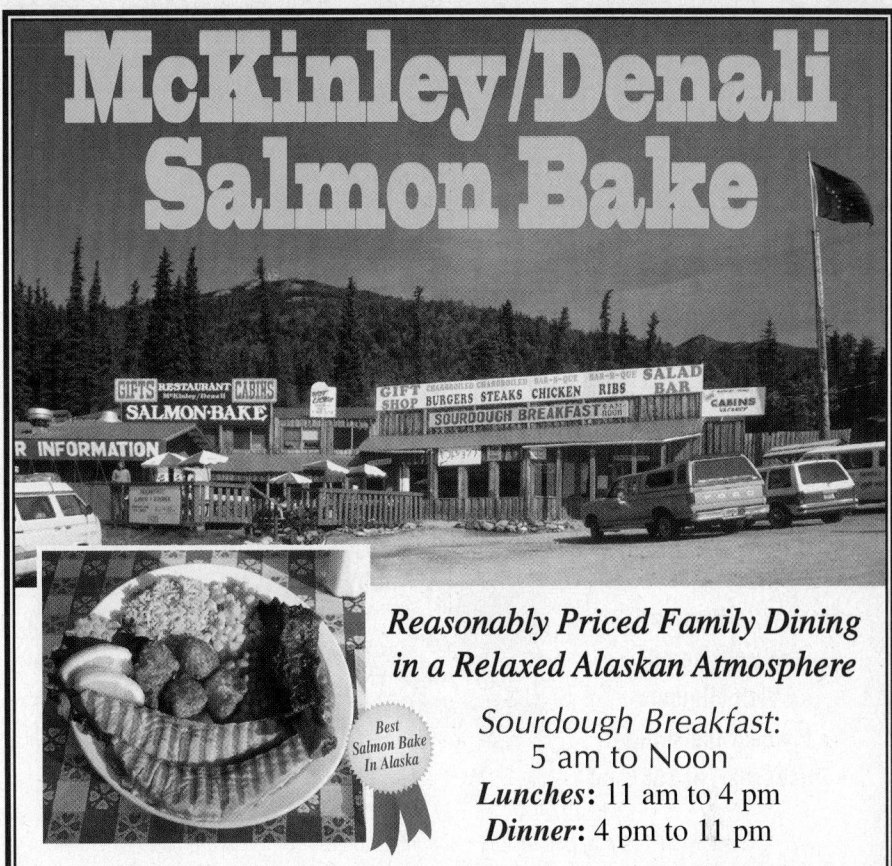

Bus: Daily bus service to the park is available from Anchorage and Fairbanks, and special sightseeing tours are offered throughout the summer months. A 6- to 8-hour guided bus tour of the park is offered by the park concessionaire. Tickets and information are available in the hotel lobby at the front desk tour window.

A FEW SPECIAL NOTES FOR VISITORS

The 1980 federal legislation creating a much larger Denali National Park and Preserve also changed some rules and regulations normally followed in most parks. The following list of park rules and regulations apply in the Denali Wilderness Unit—the part of the park that most visitors come to. Contact the Superintendent at Denali (Box 9, Denali Park, 99755) for more information on regulations governing the use of aircraft, firearms, snow machines and motorboats in the park additions and in the national preserve units.

For those driving: The Park Road was built for scenic enjoyment and not for high speed. Maximum speed is 35 mph/56 kmp except where lower limits are posted. Fast driving is dangerous to you and the wildlife you have come to see.

Your pets and wildlife don't mix. Pets are allowed only on roadways and in campgrounds and must be leashed or in a vehicle at all times. Pets are not allowed on shuttle buses, trails or in the backcountry.

Hikers who stay overnight *must obtain a backcountry permit* and return it when the trip is completed. Backpacking permits must be obtained in person (no phone-ins) up to 1 day in advance at the Visitor Center, **Milepost J 0.5** Park Road. There may be a fee.

Mountaineering expeditions are required to acquire a permit and pay a $150 fee. Before climbing Mount McKinley or Mount Foraker. Permit applications must be received at least 60 days prior to the start of the expedition. Contact the Talkeetna Ranger Station, Box 588, Talkeetna, AK 99676; phone (907) 733-2231.

Natural features: The park was established to protect a natural ecosystem. Destroying, defacing or collecting plants, rocks and other features is prohibited. Capturing, molesting, feeding or killing any animal is prohibited.

Firearms and hunting are not allowed in the wilderness area.

Fishing licenses are not required in the wilderness area; state law is applicable on all other lands. Limits for each person per day are: lake trout (2 fish); grayling and other fish (10 fish or 10 lbs. and 1 fish). Fishing is poor because most rivers are silty and ponds are shallow.

Motor vehicles of any type, including trail bikes, motorcycles and mopeds, may not leave the Park Road.

Feeding wildlife is prohibited. Wild animals need wild food; your food will not help them.

Park Road Log

Distance from the junction (J) with George Parks Highway is shown.

J 0 Junction. Turn west off the George Parks Highway (Alaska Route 3) at **Milepost A 237.3** onto the Park Road. The Park Road is paved to the Savage River bridge.

J 0.2 (0.3 km) Turnoff for Riley Creek Campground and overflow parking area. A dump station is also located here. ▲

J 0.5 (0.8 km) Visitor Center has information on all visitor activities as well as shuttle bus tickets and camping and overnight hiking permits. A park orientation program is available in the theater. The center is open daily. This is also the shuttle bus departure point.

J 1.2 (1.9 km) Alaska Railroad crossing. Horseshoe Lake trailhead.

J 1.4 (2.3 km) Convenience store showers.

J 1.5 (2.4 km) **Denali National Park Hotel,** located in Denali National Park, this 100 room hotel is the bustling center for visitor activities. The hotel is proud to offer a full-service dining room, snack shop, railcar lounge and grocery store (propane available). The hotel auditorium is the center for national park interpretive services. The hotel is a 5 minute walk from the rail depot. Wilderness activities include wildlife and natural history bus tours, rafting and flightseeing. All arrangements can be made by calling (800) 276-7234; in Anchorage 276-7234, or by contacting the hotel tour desk staff. [ADVERTISEMENT]

J 1.6 (2.6 km) Denali Park Station (elev. 1,730 feet/527m), where visitors can make train connections to Anchorage and Fairbanks, daily service during the summer. Denali National Park Hotel is across from the depot. The post office and a flying service office are located in the hotel area.

Private Aircraft: McKinley Park airstrip, 1.7 miles/2.7 km northeast of park headquarters; elev. 1,720 feet/524m; length 3,000 feet/914m; gravel; unattended.

J 3.5 (5.6 km) Park headquarters. This is the administration area for Denali National Park and Preserve. In winter, information on all visitor activities can be obtained here. Report accidents and emergencies to the rangers; phone (907) 683-9100.

J 5.5 (8.9 km) Paved turnout with litter barrel. Sweeping view of countryside. There are numerous small turnouts along the Park Road.

J 12.8 (20.6 km) Savage River Campground (elev. 2,780 feet/847m). Wildlife in the area includes moose, grizzly bear and fox. ▲

J 14.7 (23.7 km) Bridge over the Savage River. Blacktop pavement ends. Access to river, toilet and picnic tables at east end of bridge.

J 14.8 (23.8 km) Savage River check station. PERMIT REQUIRED BEYOND THIS POINT.

NOTE: Road travel permits for access to the Kantishna area are issued at park headquarters only under special conditions.

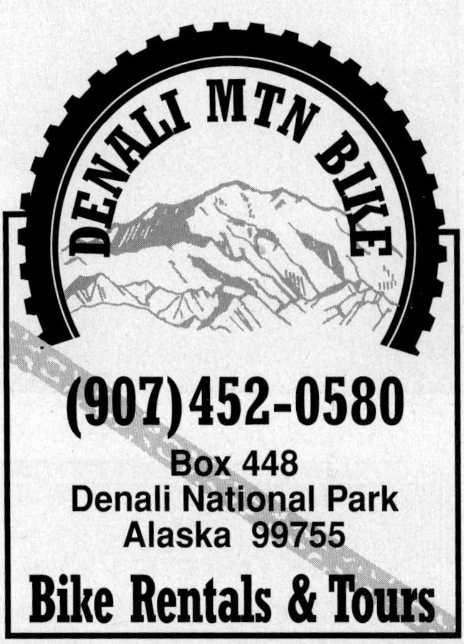

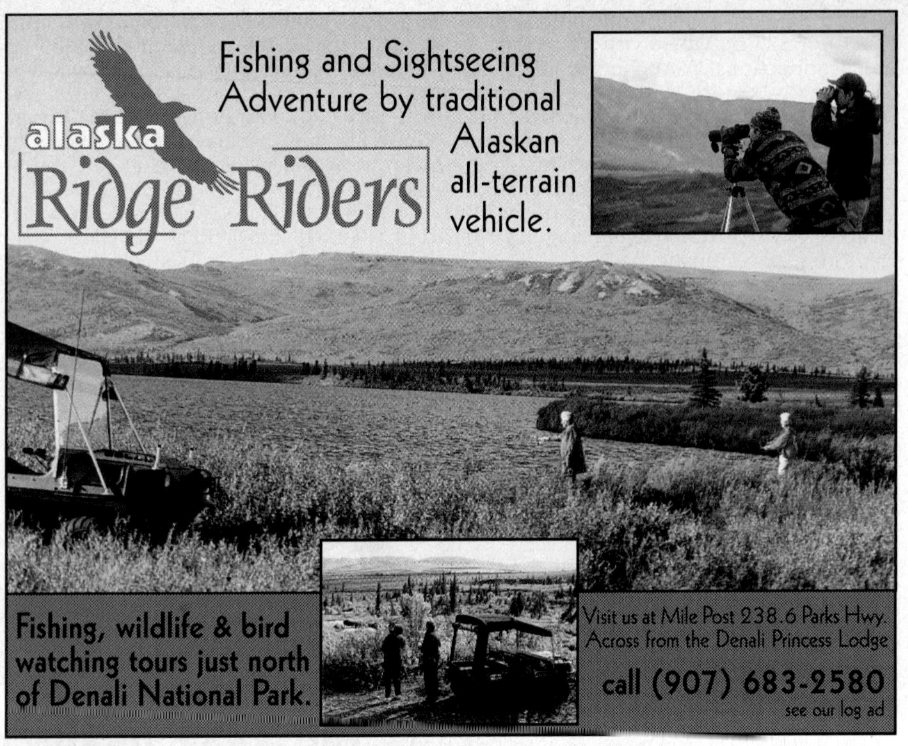

J **17.3** (27.8 km) Viewpoint of the Alaska Range and tundra.

J **21.3** (34.3 km) Hogan Creek bridge.

J **22** (35.4 km) Sanctuary River bridge, ranger station and campground (tents only). Wildlife: moose, fox, grizzly bear, wolf. ▲

J **29.1** (46.8 km) Teklanika River Campground (elev. 2,580 feet/786m). Grizzly bears may sometimes be seen on the gravel bars nearby. ▲

J **30.7** (49.4 km) Rest area with chemical toilets.

J **31.3** (50.4 km) Bridge over Teklanika River.

J **34.1** (54.9 km) Igloo Creek Campground (tents only); accessible by shuttle bus only. Wildlife in the area includes Dall sheep, grizzly bear, moose, fox and wolf. ▲

J **37** (59.5 km) Igloo Creek bridge. *NOTE: The area within 1 mile/1.6 km of each side of the Park Road from* **Milepost J 38.3** *to* **J 42.9** *is*

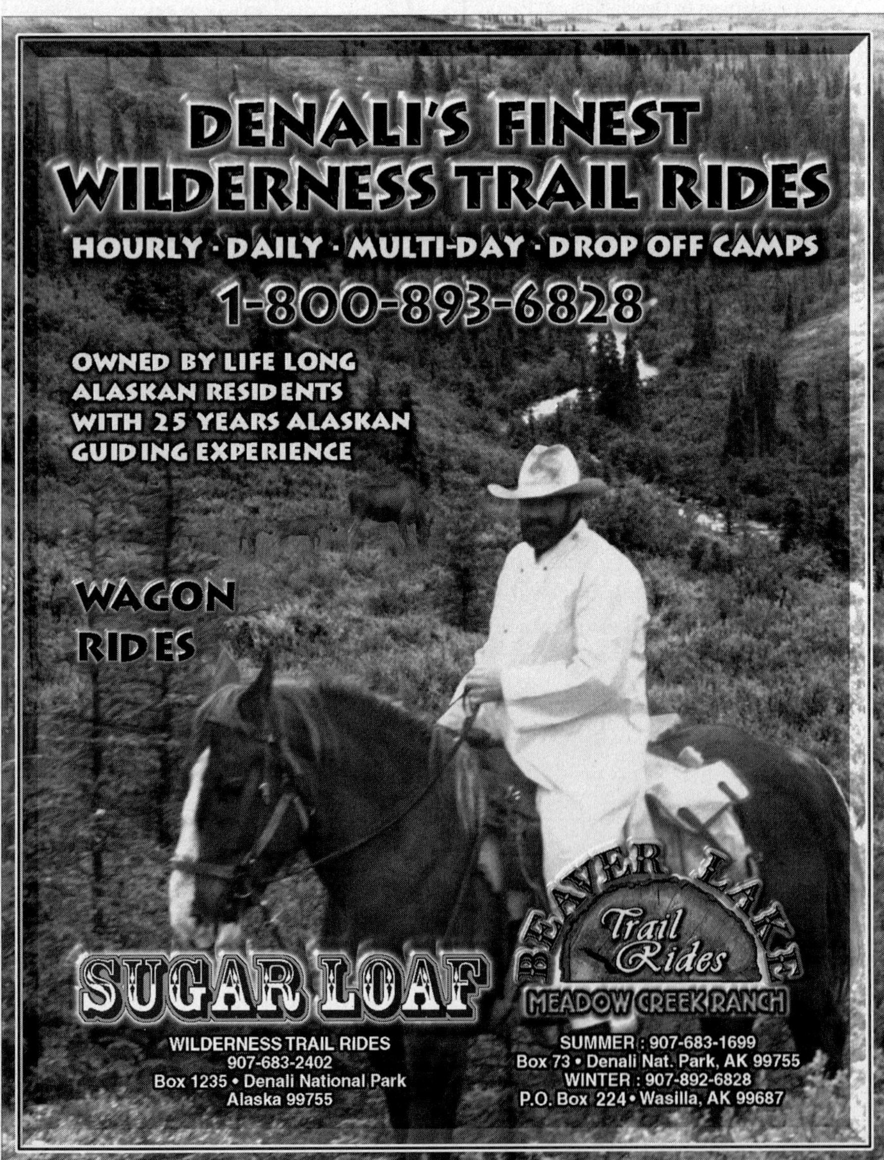

closed to all off-road foot travel as a special wildlife protection area. Toklat grizzlies are often seen in the area.

J 39.1 (62.9 km) Sable Pass (elev. 3,900 feet/1,189m).

J 43.4 (69.8 km) Bridge over East Fork Toklat River. Views of Polychrome Mountain, the Alaska Range and several glaciers are visible along the East Fork, from open country south of the road.

J 45.9 (73.9 km) Summit of Polychrome Pass (elev. 3,700 feet/1,128m); rest stop with toilets. The broad valley of the Toklat River is visible below to the south. Good hiking in alpine tundra above the road. Wildlife: wolf, grizzly bear, Dall sheep, marmot, pika, eagle and caribou.

J 53.1 (85.5 km) Bridge over the Toklat River. The Toklat and all other streams crossed by the Park Road drain into the Tanana River, a tributary of the Yukon River.

J 53.7 (86.4 km) Ranger station.

J 58.3 (93.8 km) Summit of Highway Pass (elev. 3,980 feet/1,213m). This is the highest point on the Park Road.

J 61 (98.2 km) Stony Hill (elev. 4,508 feet/1,374m). A good view of Mount McKinley and the Alaska Range on clear days. Wildlife: grizzly bear, caribou, fox and birds.

J 62 (99.8 km) Viewpoint.

J 64.5 (103.8 km) Thorofare Pass (elev. 3,900 feet/1,189m).

J 66 (106.2 km) Eielson Visitor Center. Ranger-led hikes, nature programs, displays, restrooms and drinking water. Film, maps and natural history publications for sale. Report accidents and emergencies here.

Excellent Mount McKinley viewpoint. On clear days the north and south peaks of Mount McKinley are visible to the southwest. The impressive glacier, which drops from the mountain and spreads out over the valley floor at this point, is the Muldrow. Wildlife: grizzly bear, wolf, caribou.

For several miles beyond the visitor center the road cut drops about 300 feet/91m to the valley below, paralleling the McKinley River.

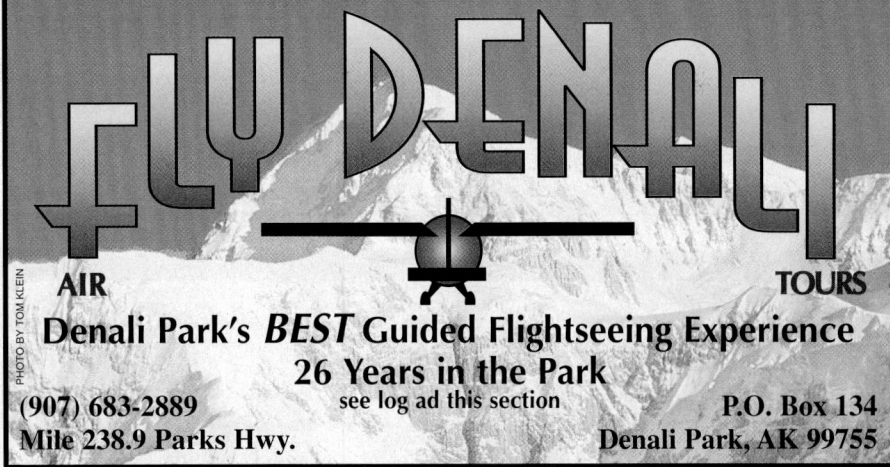

Look for Dall sheep on the mountainsides. (© Bruce M. Herman)

J 84.6 (136.1 km) Access road leads left, westbound, to Wonder Lake Campground (elev. 2,090 feet/637m). Tents only; campground access by shuttle bus only. An excellent Mount McKinley viewpoint. ▲

The road continues to Wonder Lake, where rafting and canoeing are permitted (no rental boats available). Wildlife: grizzly bear, caribou, moose, beaver, waterfowl.

J 85.6 (137.8 km) Reflection Pond, a kettle lake formed by a glacier.

J 86.6 (139.4 km) Wonder Lake ranger station.

J 87.7 (141.1 km) Bridge over Moose Creek.

J 88 (141.6 km) North Face Lodge.

J 88.2 (141.9 km) Camp Denali.

J 91 (146.4 km) **KANTISHNA** (pop. 2 in winter, 135 in summer; elev. 1,750 feet/533m). Established in 1905 as a mining camp at the junction of Eureka and Moose creeks. Most of the area around Kantishna is private property and there may be active mining on area creeks in summer. Kantishna Roadhouse, which consists of a dozen log guest cabins and a dining hall, comprise the townsite of Kantishna.

Private Aircraft: Kantishna airstrip, 1.3 miles/2.1 km northwest; elev. 1,575 feet/480m; length 1,850 feet/564m; gravel; unattended, no regular maintenance.

J 92 (148.1 km) Denali Backcountry Lodge.

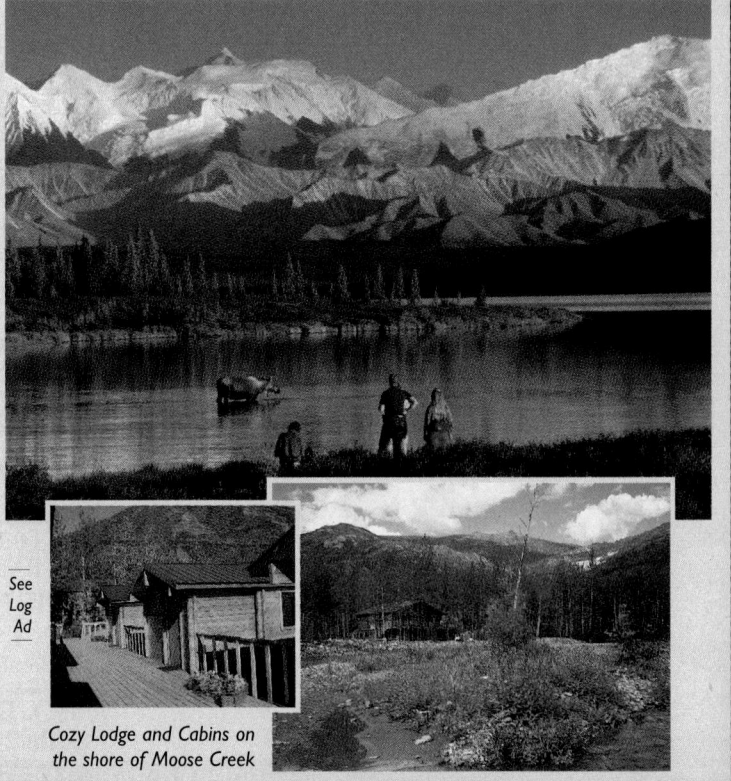

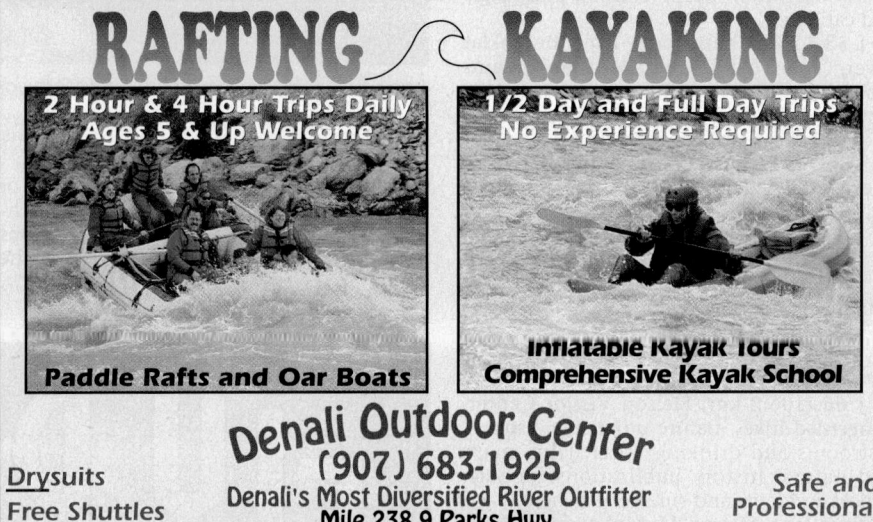

DENALI HIGHWAY

Paxson to Cantwell, Alaska
Alaska Route 8
(See map, page 456)

Although gravel, the rolling Denali Highway is popular because of its scenery and light traffic. (© Doug Wilson)

The Denali Highway extends 135.5 miles/218.1 km from Paxson at **Milepost V 185.5** on the Richardson Highway to Cantwell, about 2 miles/3.2 km west of **Milepost A 209.9** on the George Parks Highway. The first 21 miles/33.8 km from Paxson are paved and the rest is gravel. The highway is closed from October to mid-May.

The condition of the gravel portion of the highway varies, depending on highway maintenance, weather and the opinion of the driver. The road surface is rough; washboard can develop quickly. Much of the road is in need of gravel, but the roadbed is solid. This can be a dusty and bumpy drive in dry weather. Watch for potholes in wet weather.

There are dozens of primitive campsites and turnouts along the highway (heavily used by hunters in the fall). Excellent fishing in lakes and streams accessible on foot or via designated off-road vehicle trails. The Denali Highway is popular with mountain bikers. There are also many unmarked trails leading off into the Bush. Inquire locally and carry a good topographic map when hiking off the highway.

The Denali Highway has very beautiful scenery and some interesting geography. Glacier-formed features visible from the road include: moraines (drift deposited by glaciers); kames (conical hills or terraces of gravel and sand); kettle lakes (holes formed by blocks of ice melting); and eskers (ridges of gravel formed by streams flowing under glaciers).

Tangle Lakes Archaeological District lies between **Milepost P 17** and **P 35**. Within this 226,000-acre area, more than 400 archaeological sites chronicle man's seasonal exploitation of the local natural resources. For more than 10,000 years, hunter-gatherers have dug roots, picked berries, fished and hunted big game (primarily caribou) in this area. You may hike along the same high, gravel ridges once used by prehistoric people and used today by modern hunters, anglers and berry pickers. Off-road vehicles are permitted within the district, although some restrictions are in effect spring through fall. Information on Tangle Lakes Archaeological District and off-road vehicle use is available at the lodges along the Denali Highway and at the Bureau of Land Management office in Glennallen. Write BLM, Box 147, Glennallen, AK 99588; or phone (907) 822-3217.

The Denali Highway was the only road link to Denali National Park and Preserve (formerly Mount McKinley National Park) prior to completion of the George Parks Highway in 1972. Before the Denali Highway opened in 1957, Denali National Park was accessible only via the Alaska Railroad.

Emergency medical services: Between Paxson and **Milepost P 77.5** (Susitna Lodge), phone 911 or the state troopers at (907) 822-3263. Between **Milepost P 77.5** and Cantwell, phone the Cantwell ambulance at (907) 768-2982 or the state troopers at (907) 768-2202.

Denali Highway Log

Distance from Paxson (P) is followed by distance from Cantwell (C).

P 0 C 135.5 (218.1 km) **PAXSON** (pop. 33; elev. 2,650 feet/808m). A lodge with restaurant, gas station, post office and small grocery store is located here. Wilderness tours; inquire at lodge. Wildlife often seen near here: grizzly bear, moose and porcupine.

Private Aircraft: Paxson airstrip, adjacent south; elev. 2,653 feet/809m; length 2,800 feet/853m; gravel; emergency fuel; attended.

Paxson Alpine Tours. See display ad this section.

Paxson Lodge. See display ad this section.

P 0.2 (0.3 km) **C 135.3** (217.7 km) Gulkana River bridge; parking at west end. In season, spawning salmon may be seen here. This portion of the Gulkana River is off-limits to salmon fishing.

P 0.3 (0.5 km) **C 135.2** (217.6 km) Entering Paxson Closed Area westbound. This area is closed to the taking of all big game. Side road leads south to Mud Lake.

Westbound, there are many long steep upgrades and many turnouts the next 21 miles/33.8 km. Wildflowers carpet the tundra in the spring and summer.

P 1.1 (1.8 km) **C 134.4** (216.3 km) **Mud Lake** below highway; early grayling fishing.

P 3.6 (5.8 km) **C 131.9** (212.3 km) Paved turnout to south. Several more turnouts next 2.5 miles/4 km with views of Summit Lake to the north. Gakona Glacier to the north-

DENALI HIGHWAY *Paxson, AK, to Cantwell, AK*

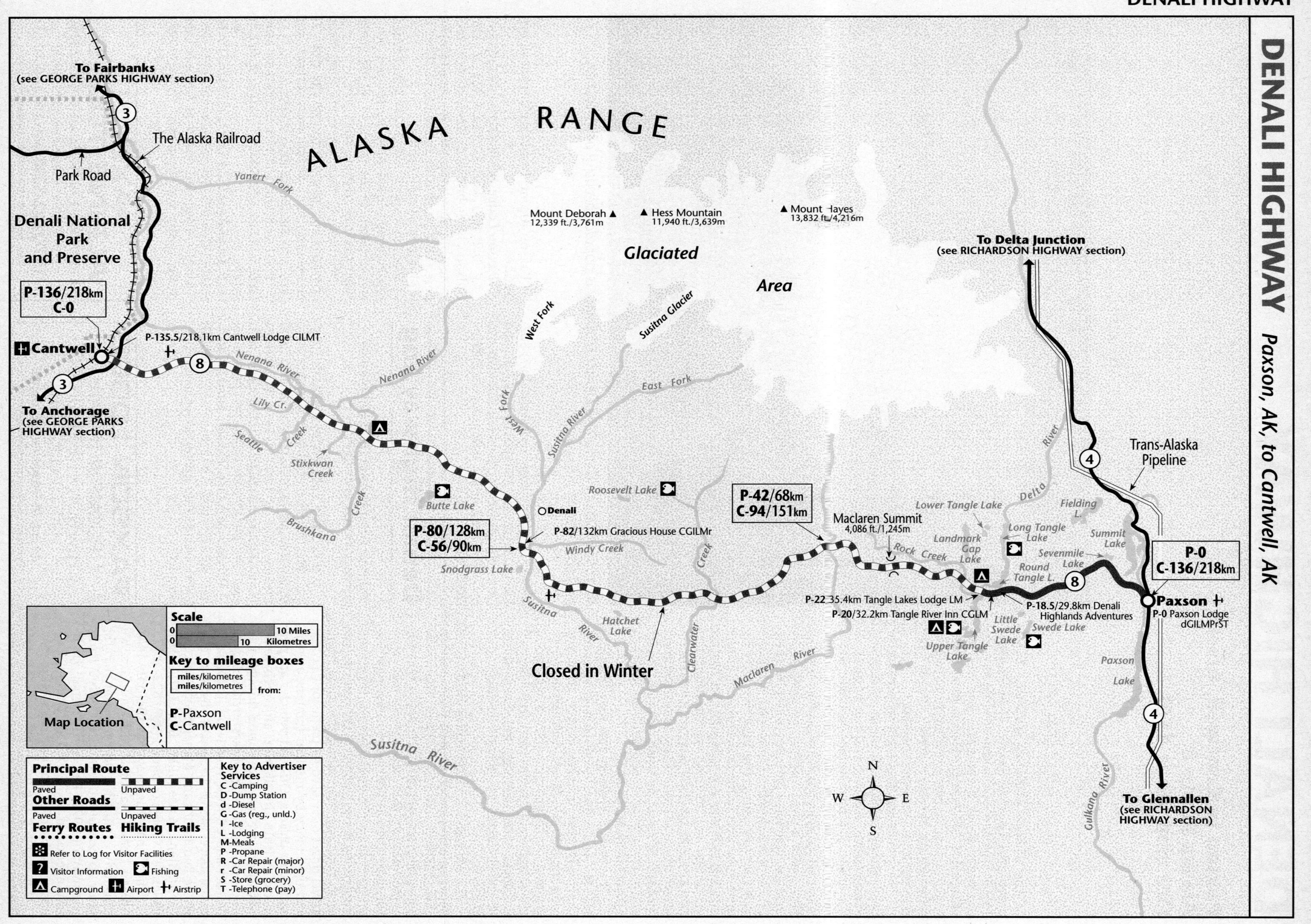

To Fairbanks
(see GEORGE PARKS HIGHWAY section)
The Alaska Railroad
Park Road
Denali National Park and Preserve
P-136/218km C-0
Cantwell
P-135.5/218.1km Cantwell Lodge CILMT
To Anchorage
(see GEORGE PARKS HIGHWAY section)
ALASKA RANGE
Yanert Fork
Mount Deborah 12,339 ft./3,761m
Hess Mountain 11,940 ft./3,639m
Mount Hayes 13,832 ft./4,216m
Glaciated Area
West Fork
Susitna Glacier
Nenana River
East Fork
Susitna River
Lily Cr.
Seattle Creek
Stixkwan Creek
Brushkana Creek
Butte Lake
Roosevelt Lake
Denali
P-80/128km C-56/90km
P-82/132km Gracious House CGILMr
Windy Creek
Snodgrass Lake
Susitna River
Hatchet Lake
Clearwater Creek
Closed in Winter
Maclaren River
P-42/68km C-94/151km
Maclaren Summit 4,086 ft./1,245m
Rock Creek
Lower Tangle Lake
Landmark Gap Lake
Long Tangle Lake
Delta River
Fielding L.
Summit Lake
Sevenmile Lake
Round Tangle L.
P-22 35.4km Tangle Lakes Lodge LM
P-20/32.2km Tangle River Inn CGLM
P-18.5/29.8km Denali Highlands Adventures
Little Swede Lake
Swede Lake
Upper Tangle Lake
To Delta Junction
(see RICHARDSON HIGHWAY section)
Trans-Alaska Pipeline
P-0 C-136/218km
Paxson
P-0 Paxson Lodge dGILMPrST
Paxson Lake
Gulkana River
To Glennallen
(see RICHARDSON HIGHWAY section)
Susitna River
N W E S
Map Location
Scale
0 10 Miles
0 10 Kilometres
Key to mileage boxes
miles/kilometres
miles/kilometres
from:
P-Paxson
C-Cantwell
Principal Route
Paved Unpaved
Other Roads
Paved Unpaved
Ferry Routes
Hiking Trails
Refer to Log for Visitor Facilities
Visitor Information
Fishing
Campground
Airport
Airstrip
Key to Advertiser Services
C -Camping
D -Dump Station
d -Diesel
G -Gas (reg., unld.)
I -Ice
L -Lodging
M-Meals
P -Propane
R -Car Repair (major)
r -Car Repair (minor)
S -Store (grocery)
T -Telephone (pay)

east and Icefall Peak to the west of the glacier. West of Icefall Peak is Gulkana Glacier.

P 6.1 (9.8 km) **C 129.4** (208.2 km) Paved turnout to north; views of Gulkana and Gakona glaciers.

P 6.7 (10.8 km) **C 128.8** (207.3 km) Paved turnout to south.

P 6.8 (10.9 km) **C 128.7** (207.1 km) Access to **Sevenmile Lake** 0.8 mile/1.3 km north; excellent fishing for lake trout in summer.

P 7.1 (11.4 km) **C 128.4** (206.6 km) Paved turnout to south.

P 7.3 (11.7 km) **C 128.2** (206.3 km) Gravel turnout overlooking Sevenmile Lake. Two Bit Lake is the large lake to the north; Summit Lake is to the northeast.

P 7.5 (12.1 km) **C 128** (206 km) Paved turnout to north overlooking Sevenmile Lake. Summit Lake visible to east.

P 8.2 (13.2 km) **C 127.3** (204.9 km) Paved turnout to north; small lakes (not visible from highway) in Hungry Hollow to the south.

P 9 (14.5 km) **C 126.5** (203.6 km) Gravel turnout. Entering BLM public lands westbound.

P 10.1 (16.3 km) **C 125.4** (201.8 km) Paved turnout to south overlooking **Ten Mile Lake**. Short hike downhill to outlet. Fishing for lake trout, grayling and burbot in summer.

P 10.6 (17.1 km) **C 124.9** (201 km) Paved turnout overlooking **Teardrop Lake** to south. Short hike down steep hill to lake; lake trout, grayling and burbot in summer.

For the next 4 miles/6.4 km westbound, there are wide-open spaces with magnificent views of the great Denali country. Look for kettle lakes and kames.

P 11.1 (17.9 km) **C 124.4** (200.2 km) Paved turnout and trail to **Octopus Lake** 0.3 mile/0.5 km south; lake trout, grayling, whitefish.

P 13.1 (21.1 km) **C 122.4** (197 km) Viewpoint at summit; interpretive plaque. In the spring from this spot a traveler can count at least 40 lakes and potholes. To the southeast are Mount Sanford, Mount Drum and Mount Wrangell in the Wrangell Mountain range.

Highway begins descent westbound to Tangle Lakes area. Lupine blooms alongside the road in late June.

P 15 (24.1 km) **C 120.5** (193.9 km) Fourteenmile Lake lies about 1.5 miles/2.4 km north of the highway, beyond 8 smaller ponds.

P 16.8 (27 km) **C 118.7** (191 km) **16.8 Mile Lake** to north (walk up creek 200 yards); lake trout and grayling. **Rusty Lake**, 0.5 mile/0.8 km northwest of 16.8 Mile Lake; lake trout and grayling. Swede Lake trail, 3 miles/4.8 km long, to south; **Little Swede Lake**, 2 miles/3.2 km. This trail connects with the Middle Fork Gulkana River branch trail (access to Dickey Lake and Meier Lake trail) and the Alphabet Hills trail. **Big Swede Lake** has excellent fishing for lake trout, grayling, whitefish and burbot. Little Swede Lake excellent for lake trout. Inquire at Tangle River Inn for directions.

P 17 (27.4 km) **C 118.5** (190.7 km) **17 Mile Lake** to north, turnout at west end of lake; lake trout and grayling fishing.

P 18.2 (29.3 km) **C 117.3** (188.8 km) Bad frost heave.

P 18.4 (29.6 km) **C 117.1** (188.4 km) Gravel turnout by **Denali–Clearwater Creek**; grayling fishing.

P 18.5 (29.8 km) **C 117** (188.3 km) **Denali Highlands Adventures.** See display ad this section.

P 20 (32.2 km) **C 115.5** (185.9 km) **Tangle River Inn** overlooking Tangle Lakes. Home-style cooking and desserts. Motel rooms starting at $45 double. Log cabin bunkhouse with restroom inside for groups. Beautiful views. Hiking and canoe trails, fishing for grayling and lake trout. Local talent, prospectors, artist and "liars" on premises. Karaoke bar. See display ad. ▲ [ADVERTISEMENT]

P 20.1 (32.3 km) **C 115.4** (185.7 km) Large paved turnout to north overlooking lake.

P 20.6 (33.2 km) **C 114.9** (184.9 km) Paved parking area with toilets to north.

P 21 (33.8 km) **C 114.5** (184.3 km) The Nelchina caribou herd travels through this area, usually around the end of Aug. or early in Sept.

P 21.3 (34.3 km) **C 114.2** (183.8 km) Pavement ends westbound.

P 21.4 (34.4 km) **C 114.1** (183.6 km) One-lane bridge over Tangle River.

P 21.5 (34.6 km) **C 114** (183.5 km) Tangle Lakes BLM campground and wayside, 0.7 mile/1.1 km north from highway on shore of Round Tangle Lake; 13 sites, toilets, boat launch, picnicking, hiking (no thick brush, good views). Blueberry picking in August. ▲

Easy access to boat launch for Delta River

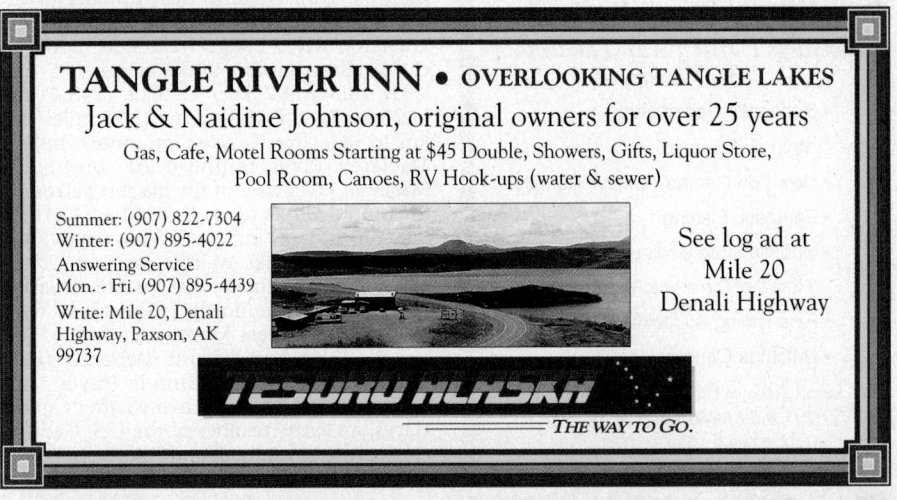

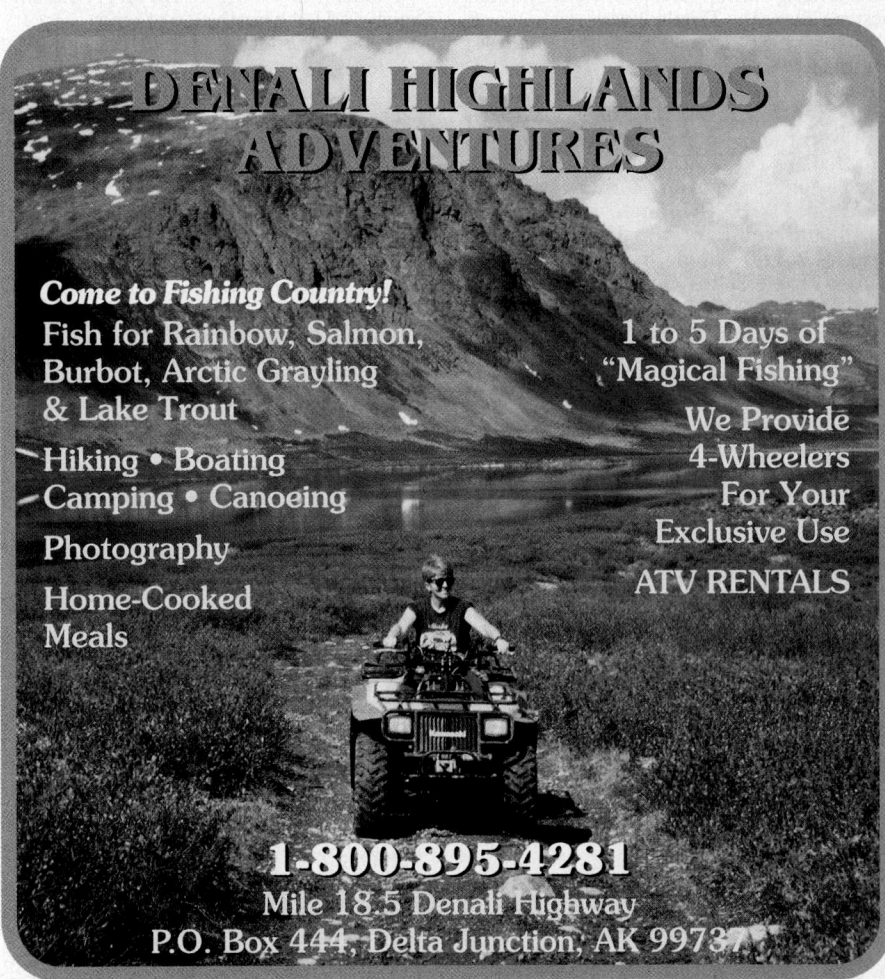

canoe trail, which goes north through Tangle Lakes to the Delta River. The 2- to 3-day float to the take-out point on the Richardson Highway requires 1 portage. The Delta National Wild, Scenic and Recreational River system is managed by the BLM. For details on this river trail or the Gulkana River trail, contact the BLM, Box 147, Glennallen, AK 99588; phone (907) 822-3217.

Watershed divide. The Gulkana River joins the Copper River, which flows into Prince William Sound. The Delta River joins the Tanana River, which flows into the Yukon River. The Yukon flows into the Bering Sea.

P 21.7 (34.9 km) **C 113.8** (183.1 km) Tangle River BLM campground; toilets, water pump, boat launch. Watch for caribou on surrounding hills. Watch for arctic warblers nesting along the Tangle River. ▲

The name Tangle is a descriptive term for the maze of lakes and feeder streams contained in this drainage system. Access to Upper Tangle Lakes canoe trail, which goes south through Tangle Lakes (portages required) to Dickey Lake, then follows the Middle Fork to the main Gulkana River.

AREA FISHING: Tangle Lakes system north and south of the highway (**Long Tangle, Round Tangle, Upper Tangle** and **Lower Tangle Lake**). Good grayling, burbot and lake trout fishing. Fishing begins as soon as the ice goes out, usually in early June, and continues into Sept. Good trolling, and some fish are taken from the banks. Early in season, trout are hungry and feed on snails in the shallows at the outlet. Inquire at Tangle Lakes Lodge or Tangle River Inn for information and assistance in getting to where the fish are.

P 22 (35.4 km) **C 113.5** (182.6 km) **Tangle Lakes Lodge**, originally known as Butcher's Hunting Camp, was built in 1952, the first lodge on the Denali Highway. It is quickly becoming a popular birding destination. Arctic warblers, Smith's longspurs, gyrfalcons and ptarmigan are some of the local favorites. The owners, Rich and Linda Holmstrom, are avid birders and provide the most accurate information available for this area of Alaska. Most of the Nelchina caribou herd can be seen in the area at most times of the season. This is also a favorite moose calving area. The Denali Highway has undergone many upgrades over the years. Although a gravel road, it is well maintained and easily traveled by any type of vehicle. Discover the real Alaska. Drop by Tangle Lakes Lodge and find the finest food, local information and hospitality in the area. [ADVERTISEMENT]

P 22.3 (35.9 km) **C 113.2** (182.2 km) Trail to south along esker.

P 24.8 (39.9 km) **C 110.7** (178.1 km) Landmark Gap BLM trail to north open to ORVs to **Landmark Gap Lake**. Grayling in stream at trail end; trout in main lake. Mountain biking is also popular on this trail.

P 24.9 (40.1 km) **C 110.6** (178 km) **Rock Creek** 1-lane bridge; parking and informal campsites at both ends of bridge. Fair grayling fishing. Landmark Gap Lake lies north of highway between the noticeable gap in the mountains (a caribou migration route).

P 28.1 (45.2 km) **C 107.4** (172.8 km) Downwind Lake north side of road.

P 30.6 (49.2 km) **C 104.9** (168.8 km) Cat trail leads 2 miles/3.2 km north to **Glacier Lake**; lake trout, grayling.

P 32 (51.5 km) **C 103.5** (166.6 km) Amphitheater Mountains rise above High Valley to the north. Glacier Lake is visible in the gap in these mountains.

P 35.2 (56.6 km) **C 100.3** (161.4 km) Turnout at Maclaren Summit (elev. 4,086 feet/1,245m). Highest highway pass in Alaska (not including 4,800-foot/1,463-m Atigun Pass on the Dalton Highway, formerly the North Slope Haul Road). A profusion of flowers—notably the various heaths and frigid shooting star.

P 36 (57.9 km) **C 99.5** (160.1 km) **36 Mile Lake** 0.5-mile/0.8-km hike north; lake trout and grayling.

P 36.4 (58.6 km) **C 99.1** (159.5 km) Entering Clearwater Creek controlled-use area westbound. Closed to motorized hunting.

P 36.6 (58.9 km) **C 98.9** (159.2 km) Osar Lake ORV trail south; 5 miles/8 km.

P 37 (59.5 km) **C 98.5** (158.5 km) Turnout with view of Susitna River valley, Mount Hayes and the Alaska Range. Osar Lake trail leads 5 miles/8 km south toward the Alphabet Hills; Maclaren Summit trail leads 3 miles/4.8 km north to good view of Alaska Range; mountain biking. Osar Lake was first named Asar Lake, the Scandinavian word for esker. (An esker is a ridge of sand and gravel marking the former stream channel of a glacier.)

P 39.8 (64.1 km) **C 95.7** (154 km) Sevenmile Lake ORV trail to north; 6.5 miles/10.5 km long, parallels Boulder Creek, crosses peat bog.

P 42 (67.6 km) **C 93.5** (150.5 km) Maclaren River and bridge, a 364-foot/111-m multiple span crossing this tributary of the Susitna River. Parking and litter barrels. Maclaren River Lodge west side. Look for cliff swallows nesting under bridge.

P 43.3 (69.7 km) **C 92.2** (148.4 km) Maclaren River Road leads north 12 miles/19.3 km to Maclaren Glacier; mountain biking. Maclaren River trailhead to south. The Maclaren River rises in the glaciers surrounding Mount Hayes (elev. 13,832 feet/4,216m). For the next 60 miles/96.6 km westbound, the highest peaks of this portion of the mighty Alaska Range are visible, weather permitting, to the north. From east to west: Mount Hayes, Hess Mountain (elev. 11,940 feet/3,639m) and Mount Deborah (elev. 12,339 feet/3,761m). Mount Hayes, first climbed in Aug. 1941, is named after Charles Hayes, an early member of the U.S. Geological Survey. Mount Deborah, first climbed in Aug. 1954, was named in 1907 by Judge Wickersham after his wife.

P 44.1 (71 km) **C 91.4** (147.1 km) Small turnout to south. Beaver lodge and dam.

P 44.6 (71.8 km) **C 90.9** (146.3 km) Highway crosses Crazy Notch gap.

P 46.9 (75.5 km) **C 88.6** (142.6 km) Road north to **46.9 Mile Lake**; fishing for grayling in lake and outlet stream.

P 47 (75.6 km) **C 88.5** (142.4 km) Beaver dam. Excellent grayling fishing in **Crooked Creek**, which parallels the highway.

P 48.6 (78.2 km) **C 86.9** (139.8 km) Informal campsite by small lake.

P 49 (78.8 km) **C 86.5** (139.2 km) The road follows an esker between 4 lakes. Parts of the highway are built on eskers. Watch for ptarmigan, swans, arctic terns, ducks and beaver. Look for a pingo (earth-covered ice hill) at lakeshore.

P 49.7 (80 km) **C 85.8** (138.1 km) Turnout to north overlooks lake. Interpretive plaque on glacial topography and wildlife, including trumpeter swans and loons.

P 51.8 (83.4 km) **C 83.7** (134.7 km) Private hunting camp to south. Trail to north.

P 56.1 (90.3 km) **C 79.4** (127.8 km) **Clearwater Creek** 1-lane bridge and rest area with toilets and litter barrels. Informal camping. Cliff swallows nest under bridge. Grayling fishing in summer.

P 58.2 (93.7 km) **C 77.3** (124.4 km) Clearwater Creek walk-in (no motorized vehicles) hunting area north of highway.

P 58.8 (94.6 km) **C 76.7** (123.4 km) Road winds atop an esker flanked by kames and kettle lakes. Watch for moose.

P 64 (103 km) **C 71.5** (115.1 km) Road descends westbound into Susitna Valley. Highest elevation of mountains seen to north is 5,670 feet/1,728m.

P 65.7 (105.7 km) **C 69.8** (112.3 km) Waterfall Creek.

P 68.9 (110.9 km) **C 66.6** (107.2 km) Raft Creek. Hatchet Lake lies about 2 miles/3.2 km south of highway. Inquire at Gracious House, **Milepost P 82**, for directions.

P 71.5 (115.1 km) **C 64** (103 km) Moose often sighted in valley below road.

P 72.2 (116.2 km) **C 63.3** (101.9 km) Nowater Creek.

P 72.8 (117.2 km) **C 62.7** (100.9 km) Swampbuggy Lake.

P 75 (120.7 km) **C 60.5** (97.4 km) Clearwater Mountains to north; watch for bears on slopes. View of Susitna River in valley below.

P 77.5 (124.7 km) **C 58** (93.3 km) Clear Water Mountain Resort, formerly Susitna Lodge; current status of services unknown.

Private Aircraft: Private airstrip, adjacent west; elev. 2,675 feet/815m; length 2,000 feet/610m; gravel.

P 78.8 (126.8 km) **C 56.7** (91.2 km) Valdez Creek Road. Former mining camp of Denali, about 6 miles/10 km north of the highway via a gravel road, was first established in 1907. Active mining area; watch for large trucks and equipment on road. Do not trespass on private mining claims. Fair fishing reported in **Roosevelt Lake** and area creeks. Watch for bears.

P 79.3 (127.6 km) **C 56.2** (90.4 km) Susitna River 1-lane bridge, a combination multiple span and deck truss, 1,036 feet/316m long. Butte Creek trailhead.

The Susitna River heads at Susitna Glacier in the Alaska Range (between Mounts Hess and Hayes) and flows southwest 260 miles/418 km to Cook Inlet. Downstream through Devil's Canyon it is considered unfloatable. The river's Tanaina Indian name, said to mean "sandy river," first appeared in 1847 on a Russian chart.

Entering Game Management Unit 13E westbound, leaving unit 13B eastbound.

P 81 (130.4 km) **C 54.5** (87.7 km) Snodgrass Lake (elev. 2,493 feet/760m) is about 2 miles/3.2 km south of the highway. Check with Gracious House, **Milepost P 82,** for directions. *CAUTION: Watch for horses.*

P 82 (132 km) **C 53.5** (86.1 km) **Gracious House.** Centrally located on the shortest, most scenic route to Denali National Park. 16 modern cabins or motel units, most with private baths, bar, cafe featuring ice cream and home-baked pies. Tent sites, parking for self-contained RVs overlooking lake. Water, restrooms and showers available at lodge. "Cash" gas, towing, welding, mechanical repairs, tire service. Air taxi, guide service available in a variety of combinations serving the sportsman, tourist, photographer, families with tours and outings to individual desires, from campouts to guided hunts. Same owners/operators for 38 years. Reasonable rates. For brochure on hunting and fishing trips, write to the Gracious Family. Summer address: P.O. Box 88, Cantwell, AK 99729. Winter address: 859 Elaine Dr., Anchorage, AK 99504. Message phone (907) 333-3148 or call (907) 822-7307 (let ring, radio phone). [ADVERTISEMENT] ▲

P 83 (133.6 km) **C 52.5** (84.5 km) Visible across the Susitna River is Valdez Creek mining camp at the old Denali townsite. Valdez Creek Mine is operated by Cambior Alaska, Inc. *CAUTION: Watch for truck traffic.*

P 84 (135.2 km) **C 51.5** (82.9 km) **Stevenson's Lake** 0.5 mile/0.8 km south; grayling fishing.

P 88.7 (142.7 km) **C 46.8** (75.3 km) Large turnout by pond. Good stop for pictures of the Alaska Range (weather permitting).

P 90.5 (145.6 km) **C 45** (72.4 km) A major water drainage divide occurs near here. East of the divide, the tributary river system of the Susitna flows south to Cook Inlet. West of the divide, the Nenana River system flows north to the Yukon River, which empties into the Bering Sea.

P 91.2 (146.8 km) **C 44.3** (71.3 km) Turnout and access to small lake beside road.

P 93.8 (151 km) **C 41.7** (67.1 km) **Butte Lake,** 5 miles/8 km south of highway. Motorized access by tracked vehicle. Best fishing June through Sept. Lake trout to 30 lbs., troll with red-and-white spoons or grayling remains; grayling to 20 inches, small flies or spinners; burbot to 12 lbs., use bait on bottom.

P 94.3 (151.8 km) **C 41.2** (66.3 km) Short road leads to parking area above pond. View of Monahan Flat and Alaska Range to the north. Interpretive plaque on earthquakes.

P 94.8 (152.6 km) **C 40.7** (65.5 km) Bridge over Canyon Creek.

P 96.1 (154.7 km) **C 39.4** (63.4 km) Good viewpoint of the West Fork Glacier. Looking north up the face of this glacier, Mount Deborah is to the left and Mount Hess is in the center.

P 97 (156.1 km) **C 38.5** (62 km) Looking at the Alaska Range to the north, Mount Deborah, Mount Hess and Mount Hayes are the highest peaks to your right; to the left are the lower peaks of the Alaska Range and Mount Nenana.

P 99.5 (160.1 km) **C 36** (57.9 km) Lodge (closed in 1995, current status unknown).

P 100 (160.9 km) **C 35.5** (57.1 km) Residents of this area say it is a wonderful place for picking cranberries and blueberries in August.

P 103 (165.8 km) **C 32.5** (52.3 km) Highway is built on an esker between kettle lakes.

P 104.6 (168.3 km) **C 30.9** (49.7 km) **Brushkana River** bridge and BLM campground; 12 sites beside river, tables, firepits, toilets, litter barrels and water. Fishing for grayling and Dolly Varden. Watch for moose. ▲

P 106.6 (171.6 km) **C 28.9** (46.5 km) **Canyon Creek,** grayling fishing.

P 107.2 (172.5 km) **C 28.3** (45.5 km) **Stixkwan Creek** flows under highway in culvert. Grayling.

P 111.2 (179 km) **C 24.3** (39.1 km) **Seattle Creek** 1-lane bridge. Fishing for grayling and Dolly Varden.

P 112 (180.2 km) **C 23.5** (37.8 km) Lily Creek. Matanuska–Susitna Borough boundary.

P 113.2 (182.2 km) **C 22.3** (35.9 km) View to east of the Alaska Range and extensive rolling hills grazed by caribou.

P 115.7 (186.2 km) **C 19.8** (31.9 km) Large gravel turnout with beautiful view of the Nenana River area.

P 117.1 (188.4 km) **C 18.4** (29.6 km) Log cabin beside Nenana River.

P 117.5 (189.1 km) **C 18** (29 km) Leaving BLM public lands westbound.

P 117.7 (189.4 km) **C 17.8** (28.6 km) Highway parallels the Nenana River, which flows into the Tanana River at the town of Nenana.

P 120 (193.1 km) **C 15.5** (24.9 km) A variety of small water birds, including ducks, snipes and terns, can be observed in the marshy areas along both sides of the road for the next 1 mile/1.6 km westbound.

P 122.3 (196.8 km) **C 11.3** (18.2 km) View (westbound) of Mount McKinley.

P 125.7 (202.3 km) **C 9.8** (15.8 km) **Joe Lake,** about 0.5 mile/0.8 km long (large enough for floatplane), is south of highway. **Jerry Lake** is about 0.2 mile/0.3 km north of the highway. Two small turnouts provide room for campers and fishermen. Both lakes have grayling.

P 128.1 (206.2 km) **C 7.4** (11.9 km) Fish Creek bridge. Access to creek and informal campsite at east end of bridge.

P 128.2 (206.3 km) **C 7.3** (11.7 km) Beautiful view of Talkeetna Mountains to the south.

P 128.6 (207 km) **C 6.9** (11.1 km) Small pond just off highway. Good berry picking in the fall. Fishing for grayling in unnamed creek.

P 130.3 (209.7 km) **C 5.2** (8.4 km) The small town of Cantwell, nestled at the foot of the mountains, can be seen across a long, timbered valley dotted with lakes. Excellent view of Mount McKinley, weather permitting.

P 131.5 (211.6 km) **C 4** (6.4 km) Airstrip; current status unknown.

P 132 (212.4 km) **C 3.5** (5.6 km) Good grayling fishing in stream beside road.

P 133 (214 km) **C 2.5** (4 km) Cantwell Station highway maintenance camp.

P 133.1 (214.2 km) **C 2.4** (3.9 km) **Junction** with old Anchorage–Fairbanks Highway; turn right westbound for Alaska State Troopers complex located approximately 0.2 mile/0.3 km north on left side of road.

P 133.7 (215.2 km) **C 1.8** (2.9 km) **Junction** of Denali and George Parks highways. Cantwell post office and school, a lodge, RV park with hookups, 2 restaurants, mini-grocery, gas stations and gift shop are located here. Continue straight ahead 1.8 miles/2.9 km for the original town of Cantwell. Turn left (south) for Anchorage or right (north) for Denali National Park and Fairbanks. See **Milepost A 209.9** in the GEORGE PARKS HIGHWAY section for details.

Cantwell

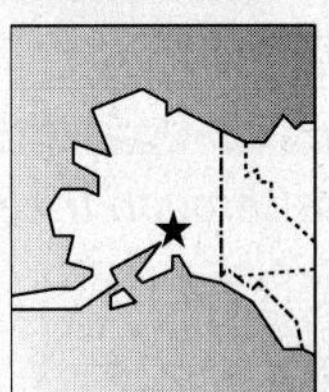

P 135.5 (218.1 km) **C 0** Western terminus of the Denali Highway. **Population:** 200 to 300. **Emergency Services: Alaska State Troopers,** business phone (907) 768-2202, emergency phone (907) 451-5333. **Fire Department,** emergency only phone (907) 768-2240. **Ambulance,** phone (907) 768-2982.

Elevation: 2,190 feet/668m. **Television:** Channel 2. **Private Aircraft:** Cantwell airport, adjacent north; elev. 2,190 feet/668m; length 2,100 feet/640m; gravel, dirt; fuel 100LL.

Cantwell began as a railroad flag stop between Seward on Prince William Sound and Fairbanks on the Chena River. The Alaska Railroad now serves Cantwell several times a week on its Anchorage to Fairbanks run during summer. The village was named for the Cantwell River, which is the former name of the Nenana River.

Cantwell's newer businesses are located at the intersection of the Denali and George Parks highways. An RV park with hookups is located west of the junction. Cantwell Lodge, with cafe, bar and laundry, is located in the older section of Cantwell, along the railroad tracks 1.8 miles/2.9 km west of intersection.

Cantwell Lodge. See display ad this section. ▲

STEESE HIGHWAY

Fairbanks to Circle, Alaska
Alaska Routes 2 and 6
Includes logs of Chena Hot Springs Road and Circle Hot Springs Road

The Steese Highway winds through the scenic Chatanika River valley. (© Steven Seiller)

The Steese Highway connects Fairbanks with Chena Hot Springs (61.4 miles/98.8 km) via Chena Hot Springs Road; the town of Central (127.5 miles/205.2 km); Circle Hot Springs (136.1 miles/219 km) via Circle Hot Springs Road; and with Circle, a small settlement 162 miles/260.7 km to the northeast on the Yukon River and 50 miles/80.5 km south of the Arctic Circle. The scenery alone makes this a worthwhile drive.

The first 44 miles/70.8 km of the Steese Highway are paved. Beyond this it is wide gravel road into Central, where there is a stretch of paved road. From Central to Circle, the highway is a narrow, winding road with gravel surface. *NOTE: Watch for road construction between* ***Milepost F 81*** *and* ***F*** *125 in 1996.*

The highway is open year-round; check with the Dept. of Transportation in Fairbanks regarding winter road conditions. The Steese Highway was completed in 1927 and named for Gen. James G. Steese, U.S. Army, former president of the Alaska Road Commission.

Among the attractions along the Steese are Eagle Summit, highest pass on the highway, where there is an unobstructed view of the midnight sun at summer solstice (June 21); the Chatanika River and Chena River recreation areas; and Chena and Circle hot springs.

Emergency medical services: Between Fairbanks and Circle, phone the state troopers at 911 or (907) 452-1313. Use CB Channels 2, 19, 22.

Steese Highway Log

ALASKA ROUTE 2
Distance from Fairbanks (F) is followed by distance from Circle (C).

F 0 C 162 (260.7 km) **FAIRBANKS. Junction** of Airport Way, Richardson–Alaska Highway and the Steese Expressway. Follow the 4-lane Steese Expressway north.

F 0.4 (0.6 km) **C 161.6** (260.1 km) Tenth Avenue exit.

F 0.6 (1 km) **C 161.4** (259.7 km) Expressway crosses Chena River.

F 0.9 (1.4 km) **C 161.1** (259.3 km) Third Street exit.

F 1 (1.6 km) **C 161** (259.1 km) College Road exit to west and access to Bentley Mall and University of Alaska.

F 1.4 (2.3 km) **C 160.6** (258.5 km) Trainer Gate Road; access to Fort Wainright.

F 2 (3.2 km) **C 160** (257.5 km) Johansen Expressway (Old Steese Highway) to west, City Lights Boulevard to east.

F 2.8 (4.5 km) **C 159.2** (256.2 km) Fairhill Road; access to Birch Hill Recreation Area, 2.3 miles/3.7 km from the highway via a paved road. Access to Farmers Loop Road to west; residential areas of Birch Hill, Fairhill, Murray Highlands and View Crest to east. Birch Hill Recreation Area is mainly for winter use as a cross-country ski area; open from 8 A.M. to 10 P.M.; picnic areas, toilets, firepits and hiking trails. Day-use only.

F 4.9 (7.9 km) **C 157.1** (252.8 km) Chena Hot Springs Road underpass, exits both sides of highway. Turn east at exit for Chena Hot Springs Road; see CHENA HOT SPRINGS ROAD log this section. Turn west for grocery, gas and pay phone at Old Steese Highway.

F 6.4 (10.3 km) **C 155.6** (250.4 km) Steele Creek Road. Exit for Bennett Road, Hagelbarger Road, Old Steese Highway and Gilmore trail. Exit to left northbound for scenic view of Fairbanks.

F 7 (11.3 km) **C 155** (249.4 km) View of pipeline from top of hill.

F 7.6 (12.2 km) **C 154.4** (248.4 km) Watch for frost heaves.

F 8 (12.9 km) **C 154** (247.8 km) End 4-lane divided highway, begin 2 lanes, northbound. *CAUTION: Watch for moose.*

F 8.4 (13.5 km) **C 153.6** (247.2 km) Trans–Alaska pipeline viewpoint with interpretive displays. Excellent opportunity for pipeline photos. Alyeska Pipeline Service Co. visitor center open May to Sept., 7 days a week. Free literature and information; phone (907) 456-9391. Highway parallels pipeline.

F 9.5 (15.3 km) **C 152.5** (245.4 km) Goldstream Road exit to Old Steese Highway and Gold Dredge Number 8. The dredge, built in 1928, was added to the list of national historic sites in 1984 and designated a National Historical Mechanical Engineering Landmark in 1986. The 5-deck, 250-foot-long dredge operated until 1959; it is now privately owned and open to the public for tours (admission fee).

F 10.4 (16.7 km) **C 151.6** (244 km) Road to permafrost tunnel to east (research area, not open to public). Excavated in the early 1960s, the tunnel is maintained cooperatively by the University of Alaska Fairbanks and the U.S. Army Cold Regions Research and Engineering Laboratory.

F 11 (17.7 km) **C 151** (243 km) End of Steese Expressway. Weigh station. Check here for current information on Dalton Highway conditions. Turn east at this junction for continuation of Steese Highway, which now becomes Alaska Route 6 (log

(Continues on page 463)

STEESE HIGHWAY *Fairbanks, AK to Circle, AK*

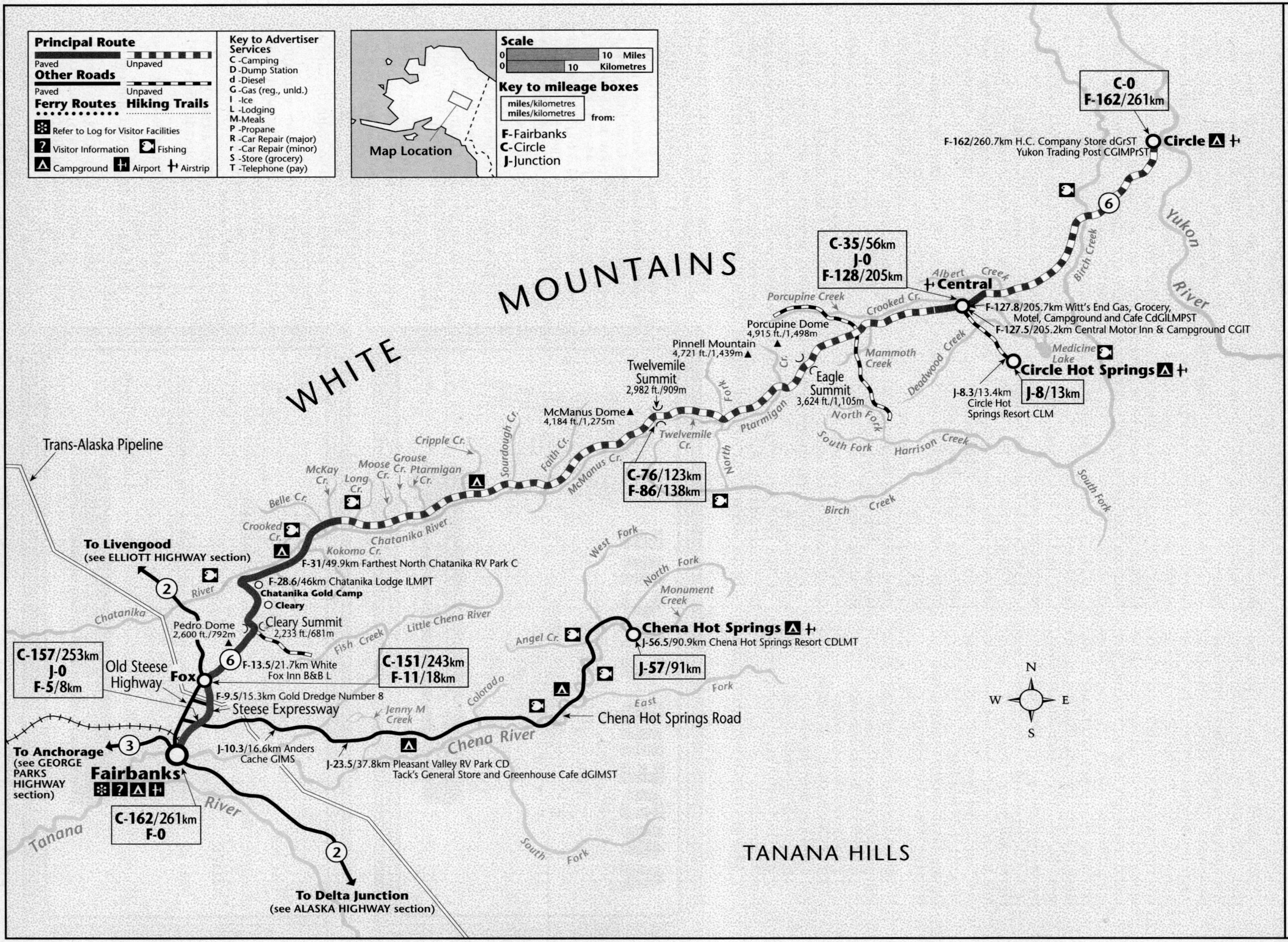

Principal Route
Paved Unpaved
Other Roads
Paved Unpaved
Ferry Routes **Hiking Trails**
Refer to Log for Visitor Facilities
Visitor Information
Fishing
Campground
Airport
Airstrip

Key to Advertiser Services
C -Camping
D -Dump Station
d -Diesel
G -Gas (reg., unld.)
I -Ice
L -Lodging
M -Meals
P -Propane
R -Car Repair (major)
r -Car Repair (minor)
S -Store (grocery)
T -Telephone (pay)

Map Location

Scale
0 10 Miles
0 10 Kilometres

Key to mileage boxes
miles/kilometres
miles/kilometres
from:
F-Fairbanks
C-Circle
J-Junction

C-0
F-162/261km
F-162/260.7km H.C. Company Store dGrST
Yukon Trading Post CGIMPrST
Circle
Yukon River
Birch Creek
6

C-35/56km
J-0
F-128/205km
Central
Albert Creek
Crooked Cr.
F-127.8/205.7km Witt's End Gas, Grocery, Motel, Campground and Cafe CdGILMPST
F-127.5/205.2km Central Motor Inn & Campground CGIT
Medicine Lake
Circle Hot Springs
J-8/13km
J-8.3/13.4km Circle Hot Springs Resort CLM
Porcupine Creek
Porcupine Dome
4,915 ft./1,498m
Mammoth Creek
Deadwood Creek
Pinnell Mountain
4,721 ft./1,439m
Eagle Summit
3,624 ft./1,105m
North Fork
South Fork
Harrison Creek
Twelvemile Summit
2,982 ft./909m
Twelvemile Cr.
Ptarmigan
North Fork
McManus Dome
4,184 ft./1,275m
C-76/123km
F-86/138km
Birch Creek
South Fork

WHITE MOUNTAINS

Trans-Alaska Pipeline
Cripple Cr.
Sourdough Cr.
Faith Cr.
McManus Cr.
McKay Cr.
Moose Cr.
Grouse Cr.
Ptarmigan Cr.
Long Cr.
Belle Cr.
Crooked Cr.
Chatanika River
Kokomo Cr.
F-31/49.9km Farthest North Chatanika RV Park C
To Livengood
(see ELLIOTT HIGHWAY section)
2
River
F-28.6/46km Chatanika Lodge ILMPT
Chatanika Gold Camp
Cleary
Chatanika
Pedro Dome
2,600 ft./792m
Cleary Summit
2,233 ft./681m
Fish Creek
Little Chena River
6
F-13.5/21.7km White Fox Inn B&B L
C-151/243km
F-11/18km
C-157/253km
J-0
F-5/8km
Old Steese Highway
Fox
F-9.5/15.3km Gold Dredge Number 8
Steese Expressway
To Anchorage
(see GEORGE PARKS HIGHWAY section)
3
Fairbanks
C-162/261km
F-0
Tanana River
2
To Delta Junction
(see ALASKA HIGHWAY section)
J-10.3/16.6km Anders Cache GIMS
Jenny M Creek
Colorado
J-23.5/37.8km Pleasant Valley RV Park CD
Tack's General Store and Greenhouse Cafe dGIMST
Chena River
Chena Hot Springs Road
East Fork
Angel Cr.
West Fork
North Fork
Monument Creek
Chena Hot Springs
J-56.5/90.9km Chena Hot Springs Resort CDLMT
J-57/91km
N
W E
S
South Fork

TANANA HILLS

Chena Hot Springs Road Log

This paved road, open year-round, leads 56.5 miles/90.9 km east to Chena Hot Springs, a private resort open daily year-round. Chena Hot Springs Road passes through the middle of Chena River Recreation Area, 254,000 acres of mostly undeveloped river bottom and alpine uplands. This is an exceptional year-round recreation area with picnic sites, campgrounds, hiking trails and easy access to the Chena River, one of the most popular grayling fisheries in the state. *IMPORTANT: Check current ADF&G regulations regarding the taking of any fish*

*NOTE: Watch for paving under way between **Mileposts J 7** and **J 22** in 1996. Also watch for trucks and crews doing erosion control and flood repair work between **Mileposts J 28*** and ***J 48.***

Distance is measured from junction with the Steese Highway (J).

J 0 Chena Hot Springs Road exit at **Milepost F 4.9** Steese Highway.

J 0.5 (0.8 km) Bad frost heaves.

J 1.8 (2.9 km) Bennett Road.

J 3.5 (5.6 km) Steele Creek Road.

J 4 (6.4 km) Frost heaves.

J 6.3 (10.1 km) Nordale Road.

J 8.3 (13.4 km) Paved double-ended turnout to south.

J 10.3 (16.6 km) Mini-mart, public dumpster.

Anders Cache. See display ad this section.

J 11.9 (19.2 km) Bridge over Little Chena River. Water gauging station in middle of bridge. This Army Corps of Engineers flood control project, completed in 1979, was designed to prevent floods such as the one which devastated Fairbanks in 1967.

J 14 (22.5 km) Bumpy paved double-ended turnout to south.

J 15 (24.1 km) Rough road next 2 miles/3.2 km eastbound.

J 18 (29 km) Watch for moose.

J 18.6 (29.9 km) Two Rivers Road. Access to Two Rivers School and Two Rivers Recreation Area (maintained by Fairbanks North Star Borough) with cross-country ski and hiking trails. Public dumpster.

J 20.1 (32.3 km) Jenny M. Creek. Some 2,000 people reside along the road between here and its junction with the Steese Highway.

J 20.2 (32.5 km) Large, double-ended paved parking area to south.

J 23.4 (37.7 km) Grocery with gas; public dumpster.

J 23.5 (37.8 km) Store and RV park. Two Rivers post office is in store.

Tacks' General Store and Greenhouse Cafe. See display ad this section.

J 25.6 (41.2 km) HIPAS Observatory, UCLA Plasma Physics Lab (Geophysical Institute Chena Radio Facility).

J 25.7 (41.4 km) Road passes sloughs and ponds of the Chena River area. Fine place for berry pickers, furred and human.

J 26.1 (42 km) Entering **Chena River** Recreation Area. No shooting except at target range. Grayling fishing (check current regulations).

J 26.5 (42.6 km) Flat Creek culvert.

J 26.7 (43 km) Paved turnout to south for picnic area with tables and toilets.

J 27 (43.5 km) Rosehip state campground to south; 25 sites, picnic tables, firepits, toilets, water, $8 nightly fee or annual pass. Large, flat, gravel pads and an easy 0.7-mile/1.1-km loop road make this a good campground for large RVs and trailers. ▲

Canoe exit point. The Chena is popular with paddlers, but should not be underestimated: The river is cold and the current very strong. Watch for river-wide logjams and sweepers. Secure your gear in waterproof containers. Local paddlers suggest a float from **Milepost J 39.5** to **J 37.9** for easy paddling; **J 44** to **J 37.9** for a longer float; and **J 52.3** to **J 47.3** for paddlers with more skill. Allow about an hour on the river for each road mile traveled.

J 27.5 (44.3 km) Paved turnout to south.

J 27.9 (44.9 km) Toilets and access to river via road to south which leads 0.9 mile/1.4 km to large parking area with picnic tables, dumpster, loop turnaround. Canoe exit point.

J 28.8 (46.3 km) Access road to river, drive 0.7 mile/1.1 km south to canoe launch in brushy area along river; picnic table, toilet, dumpster, parking.

J 29.4 (47.3 km) Pleasant double-ended paved turnout to south on Chena River; picnic table.

J 30 (48.3 km) Outdoor education camp (available for rent by groups). Small lake stocked with grayling.

J 31.3 (50.4 km) Bridge over Colorado Creek. River access.

J 31.5 (50.7 km) River access.

J 31.8 (51.2 km) Colorado Creek ATV trail.

J 33.9 (54.6 km) Fourmile Creek flows under the road.

J 35.8 (57.6 km) Paved turnout to south.

J 36.5 (58.7 km) Target shooting range to north. ORV trails, toilets and picnic tables. Cathedral Bluffs view.

J 37.9 (61 km) First bridge over the **North Fork Chena River.** Water gauge in

center of bridge. There are 3 stream flow meters on the upper Chena. Grayling fishing (check current special regulations).

Side road leaves highway to the south and forks. Left fork is a short road to the river and toilet; right fork leads 0.2 mile/0.3 km to picnic tables by the river. Canoe launch. This road is bordered by dense underbrush which may scratch wide vehicles.

J 39.2 (63.1 km) Paved turnout to south.

J 39.5 (63.6 km) Second bridge over North Fork Chena River. Loop road through Granite Tors trail state campground; 20 large sites among tall spruce trees, parking area, water, toilets, tables, firepits, $8 nightly fee or annual pass. Canoe launch. Picnic area on loop road along river. ▲

Trailhead for Granite Tors trail; follow dike (levee) on west side upstream 0.3 mile/0.5 km to trail sign. It is a 6-mile/9.7-km hike to the nearest tors, 8 miles/12.9 km to the main grouping. Tors are high, isolated pinnacles of jointed granite jutting up from the tundra.

J 39.7 (63.9 km) A 0.2-mile/0.3-km side road leads south to Chena River picnic area with tables, toilets and a riverbank of flat rocks ideal for sunbathing.

J 39.8 (64.1 km) Campground loop road exit; toilet beside road.

J 41.8 (67.3 km) Paved turnout to south by slough.

J 42.1 (67.8 km) Large turnout south of road. Watch for muskrats and beaver in ponds here.

J 42.8 (68.9 km) Mile 43 Red Squirrel picnic area to north, one of the nicest on this road, with covered tables, firepits, toilets, water and dumpster. Located on edge of small lake stocked with grayling. Watch for moose.

J 42.9 (69 km) Gravel turnouts to south.

J 43.8 (70.5 km) Small lake to north stocked with grayling.

J 44.1 (71 km) Third bridge over North Fork Chena River. Picnic area with tables and toilets to north at east end of bridge. A favorite place to sunbathe and fish. Canoe launch.

J 45.7 (73.5 km) Fourth bridge over North Fork Chena River.

J 46 (74 km) Paved turnout to south.

J 46.8 (75.3 km) Chena River flows alongside the road; good access point for fishermen. Paved parking to south opposite river.

J 47.3 (76.1 km) Access to river north side of road.

J 47.9 (77.1 km) Side road leads 0.1 mile/0.2 km south to **48-Mile Pond.** Stocked with grayling; picnic tables, informal campsites.

J 48.8 (78.5 km) Watch for people and horses next mile eastbound.

J 48.9 (78.7 km) Angel Rocks trailhead; table, toilet, dumpster. Angel Rocks trail is a 3.5-mile/5.6-km loop trail to spectacular rock outcroppings; strenuous hike.

J 49 (78.9 km) Fifth bridge over **North Fork Chena River;** parking. Excellent fishing from here.

J 49.1 (79 km) Lower Chena Dome trailhead. Side road leads 0.2 mile/0.3 km north to trailhead, parking, water, dumpster and toilets.

J 49.3 (79.3 km) Cathedral Bluffs, an unusual rock formation to southeast.

J 49.9 (80.3 km) Paved turnout to north. **Angel Creek,** grayling 12 to 17 inches.

J 50.5 (81.3 km) Chena Dome trailhead; this 29-mile/47-km loop trail exits at **Milepost J 49.1.** Angel Creek Cabin ATV trailhead (6 miles/10 km). Parking, toilets. Bring mosquito repellent!

J 50.7 (81.6 km) Chena River Recreation Area boundary.

J 52.3 (84.2 km) Bridge over West Fork Chena River. Gravel side road leads south to parking area along the river. *CAUTION: Abrupt approaches to bridge.*

J 55.3 (89 km) North Fork Chena River bridge. Double-ended paved turnout to south.

J 56.5 (90.9 km) **CHENA HOT SPRINGS:** food, lodging, camping, bar and swimming. To phone ahead, call (907) 452-7867. These mineral hot springs were first reported in 1904 by the U.S. Geological Survey's field teams. The springs take their name from the nearby Chena River, which flows southwest. There is an airstrip at the lodge. ▲

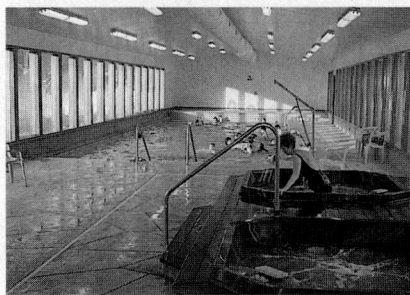

Return to Milepost F 4.9
Steese Highway

(Continued from page 460)
follows). Continue straight ahead (north) on Alaska Route 2, which now becomes the Elliott Highway, for access to Dalton Highway and Manley Hot Springs (see ELLIOTT HIGHWAY section for details).

Turn west for Old Steese Highway and for **FOX,** a once famous mining camp established before 1905 and named for nearby Fox Creek. Gas, food and lodging.

ALASKA ROUTE 6

F 13.5 (21.7 km) **C 148.5** (239 km) **White Fox Inn Bed & Breakfast.** See display ad this section.

F 13.6 (21.9 km) **C 148.4** (238.8 km) Eisele Road; turnoff on right northbound for NOAA/NESDIS Command and Data Acquisition Station at Gilmore Creek. This facility monitors 2 polar orbiting satellites. Tours of the satellite tracking station are available 9 A.M. to 4 P.M., Monday through Saturday, from June through August. Phone (907) 451-1200 for more information.

F 16.4 (26.4 km) **C 145.6** (234.3 km) Turnout by gold-bearing creek. Now privately claimed; no recreational gold panning permitted.

F 16.5 (26.6 km) **C 145.5** (234.2 km) Gravel turnout to west. Monument to Felix Pedro, the prospector who discovered gold on Pedro Creek in July 1902 and started the rush that resulted in the founding of Fairbanks.

F 17.4 (28 km) **C 144.6** (232.7 km) Gravel turnout to east. Winding ascent northbound to Cleary Summit area.

F 19.6 (31.5 km) **C 142.4** (229.2 km) Large gravel turnout to east.

F 20.3 (32.7 km) **C 141.7** (228 km) Cleary Summit (elev. 2,233 feet/681m) has a weekend ski area in winter. Named for early prospector Frank Cleary. On a clear day there are excellent views of the Tanana Valley and Mount McKinley to the south and the White Mountains to the north. Road north to Pedro Dome military site.

Fairbanks Creek Road to the south leads several miles along a ridge crest; access to Fish Creek Road and dirt roads leading to Solo Creek, Bear Creek and Fairbanks Creek.

Highway descends steep grade northbound. Watch for frost heaves.

F 20.6 (33.2 km) **C 141.4** (227.6 km) Very rough turnout next to ski area buildings;

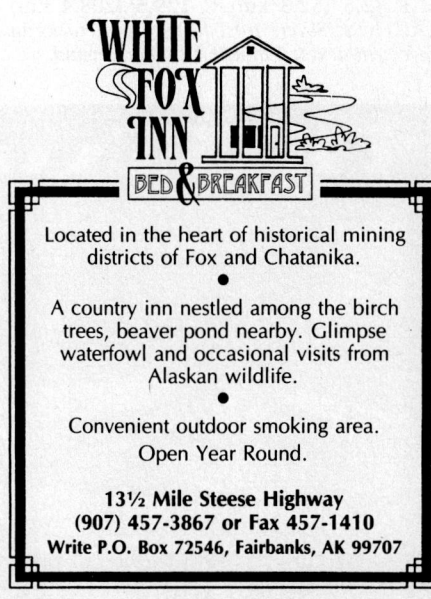

view of current mining operation and old buildings from early mining and dredging on Cleary Creek below.

F 23.9 (38.5 km) **C 138.1** (222.2 km) Gravel turnout to east. Watch for frost heaves.

F 27.6 (44.4 km) **C 134.4** (216.3 km) Tailings (gravel and boulders of dredged streambeds) from early mining activity which yielded millions of dollars in gold. There is quite a bit of mining in the Chatanika area now.

F 27.9 (44.9 km) **C 134.1** (215.8 km) Sharp right turn up hill for historic Fairbanks Exploration Co. gold camp at **CHATANIKA**, built in 1925 to support gold dredging operations in the valley. Between 1926 and 1957 the F.E. Co. removed an estimated $70 million in gold. Chatanika Gold Camp, on the National Register of Historic Places, offers food and lodging year-round.

F 28.6 (46 km) **C 133.4** (214.7 km) Old gold dredge behind tailing piles to west (private property, *DO NOT TRESPASS*). Lodge to east with meals and lodging.

Chatanika Lodge. Cafe open 9 A.M. daily (year-round). Halibut/catfish fry Friday and Saturday, country-fried chicken on Sunday, served family-style, all you can eat. Diamond Willow Lounge. Rustic atmosphere, Alaska artifacts. Historic Alaska gold dredge across from lodge, plus aurora borealis videos on big-screen TV. Good grayling fishing. Rooms $45 to $50. See display ad this section. [ADVERTISEMENT]

F 29.5 (47.5 km) **C 132.5** (213.2 km) Neal Brown Road to Poker Flat rocket facility; off-limits except to authorized personnel. The Poker Flat rocket range, operated by the Geophysical Institute, University of Alaska, is dedicated to unclassified auroral and upper atmospheric research. It is the only university-owned sounding rocket range in the world and the only high latitude and auroral zone launch facility on U.S. soil. Tours for interested groups may be arranged by calling (907) 474-7634.

Fishing at gravel pit ponds from here north to **Milepost F 39.5**. Ponds are stocked with grayling. (Watch for green signs at access points.)

F 31 (49.9 km) **C 131** (210.8 km) **Farthest North Chatanika RV Park.** See display ad this section. ▲

F 32.3 (52 km) **C 129.7** (208.7 km) Captain Creek bridge.

F 32.5 (52.3 km) **C 129.5** (208.4 km) *CAUTION: Severe frost heaves and cracks in pavement next 0.2 mile/0.3 km northbound.*

F 35 (56.3 km) **C 127** (204.4 km) Access to Chatanika River. Double-ended paved turnout to west.

F 36.5 (58.7 km) **C 125.5** (202 km) Gravel turnout alongside ponds to west. Pond stocked with grayling.

F 37.1 (59.7 km) **C 124.9** (201 km) *CAUTION: Severe frost heaves and dips in pavement next 0.1 mile/0.2 km northbound.*

F 37.3 (60 km) **C 124.7** (200.7 km) Kokomo Creek bridge.

F 39 (62.8 km) **C 123** (197.9 km) Chatanika River bridge. Upper Chatanika River State Recreation Site, just north of the bridge, is a beautiful state campground on the riverbank. There are 25 sites with fireplaces, and a gravel parking area near the bridge. A water pump is at the entrance. Firewood is usually available during the summer. Camping fee $8/night or annual pass. Look for wild roses here in June. ▲

Boats can be launched on the gravel bars by the river. Bring your mosquito repellent. This is an access point to the Chatanika River canoe trail. See **Milepost F 60** for more information on canoeing this river.

Chatanika River, grayling 8 to 20 inches, use flies or spinners, May to Sept.

F 39.5 (63.5 km) **C 122.5** (197.1 km) 39.3 Mile Pond, to west, is stocked with grayling.

F 40.2 (64.7 km) **C 121.8** (196 km) *CAUTION: Watch for severe dips in highway surface.*

F 40.4 (65 km) **C 121.6** (195.7 km) Bridge over Crooked Creek.

F 41.5 (66.8 km) **C 120.5** (193.9 km) Bridge over Belle Creek. Most homes here are those of permanent residents.

F 42.7 (68.7 km) **C 119.3** (192 km) Bridge over McKay Creek.

F 42.9 (69 km) **C 119.1** (191.7 km) Turnout to east.

F 43.8 (70.5 km) **C 118.2** (190.2 km) Pavement ends; it is good gravel road to Circle with the exception of a short stretch of blacktop at Central. Highway parallels the Chatanika River for the next 10 miles/16 km.

F 45.4 (73.1 km) **C 116.6** (187.6 km) **Long Creek** bridge. Grayling 8 to 14 inches, use spinners or flies, May to Sept. Beautiful view of Chatanika River.

F 49 (78.9 km) **C 113** (181.9 km) View down Chatanika River valley to east.

F 53.5 (86.1 km) **C 108.5** (174.6 km) Ptarmigan Creek in valley below highway.

F 57.1 (91.9 km) **C 104.9** (168.8 km) White Mountains National Recreation Area (BLM). Access to this area's trails and cabins is from the Elliott Highway.

F 57.3 (92.2 km) **C 104.7** (168.5 km) U.S. Creek to west. The large pipe near U.S. Creek was part of the Davidson Ditch, built in 1925 by the Fairbanks Exploration Co., to carry water to float gold dredges. The 83-mile-/133.6-km-long ditch, designed and engineered by J.B. Lippincott, begins near **Milepost F 64** on the Steese Highway and ends near Fox. A system of ditches and inverted siphons, the pipeline was capable of carrying 56,100 gallons per minute. After the dredges closed, the water was used for power until 1967, when a flood destroyed a bridge and flattened almost 1,000 feet/305m of pipe.

All-weather road leads 6 miles/9.7 km west to Nome Creek; recreational gold panning. There are some mining claims on Nome Creek. No dredges allowed. The road to Nome Creek is very steep and not recommended for large or underpowered vehicles. Nome Creek is a historic mining area; additional recreational facilities are under development by the BLM.

F 59 (94.9 km) **C 103** (165.8 km) Wide double-ended gravel parking area to east.

F 60 (96.6 km) **C 102** (164.1 km) Cripple Creek BLM campground (7-day limit), 6 tent, 15 trailer sites; water pumps, fireplaces, toilets, tables, nature trail. Parking for walk-in campers. Firewood is usually available all summer. Recreational gold panning permitted. *Bring mosquito repellent!* ▲

Access to Cripple Creek BLM recreation cabin. Preregister and pay $10 fee at BLM office, 1150 University Ave., Fairbanks 99709; phone (907) 474-2200.

Cripple Creek bridge is the uppermost access point to the Chatanika River canoe trail (follow side road near campground entrance to canoe launch site). *CAUTION: This canoe trail may not be navigable at low water.* The Chatanika River is a clear-water Class II stream. The Steese Highway parallels the river for approximately 28 miles/45 km and there are many access points to the highway downstream from the Cripple Creek bridge. No major obstacles on this canoe trail, but watch for overhanging trees. Downstream pullout points are Perhaps Creek, Long Creek and Chatanika Campground.

F 62.3 (100.3 km) **C 99.7** (160.4 km) Viewpoint to east overlooking Chatanika River.

F 63.4 (102 km) **C 98.6** (158.7 km) View of historic Davidson Ditch pipeline.

F 65 (104.6 km) **C 97** (156.1 km) Side road east to viewpoint.

F 65.6 (105.6 km) **C 96.4** (155.1 km) Sourdough Creek bridge.

F 65.7 (105.7 km) **C 96.3** (155 km) Mile 66. Double-ended turnout to east; Davidson Ditch viewpoint. Hendrickson's Miracle Mile Lodge.

F 66 (106.2 km) **C 96** (154.5 km) Sourdough Creek Road (unmarked) to north.

F 69 (111 km) **C 93** (149.7 km) Faith

Creek bridge and road. Creek access to east at north end of bridge. Large parking area to west.

F 72 (115.9 km) **C 90** (144.8 km) View ahead for northbound travelers of highway route along mountains, McManus Creek below.

F 73.8 (118.8 km) **C 88.2** (141.9 km) Faith Creek Road to west.

F 79.1 (127.3 km) **C 82.9** (133.4 km) Road widens for parking next 500 feet/152m.

F 80.1 (128.9 km) **C 81.9** (131.8 km) Montana Creek state highway maintenance station. Montana Creek runs under road and into McManus Creek to the east. McManus Dome (elev. 4,184 feet/1,275m) to west.

F 81.2 (130.7 km) **C 80.8** (130 km) Turnout to east. Spring water (untested) piped to roadside. Wide gravel highway begins ascent to Twelvemile Summit. *NOTE: Watch for road construction northbound to **Milepost F 125** in 1996.*

F 83 (133.6 km) **C 79** (127.1 km) Sharp turn to right northbound. Watch for the hoary marmot and other small mammals.

F 85.5 (137.6 km) **C 76.5** (123.1 km) Large parking area and viewpoint to east at Twelvemile Summit (elev. 2,982 feet/909m) on the divide of the Yukon and Tanana river drainages. Wildflowers carpet the alpine tundra slopes. Entering Game Management Unit 25C, leaving unit 20B, northbound. Fairbanks–North Star Borough limits. This is caribou country; from here to beyond Eagle Summit (**Milepost F 108**) migrating bands of caribou may be seen from late July through mid-September.

Access to Pinnell Mountain national recreation trail (Twelvemile Summit trailhead). The trail is also accessible from **Milepost F 107.1.** Named in honor of Robert Pinnell, who was fatally injured in 1952 while climbing nearby Porcupine Dome. This 27-mile-/43-km-long hiking trail winds through alpine terrain, along mountain ridges and through high passes. Highest elevation point reached is 4,721 feet/1,439m. The trail is marked by rock cairns. Shelter cabins at Mile 10.7 and Mile 17.7. Vantage points along the trail with views of the White Mountains, Tanana Hills, Brooks Range and Alaska Range. Watch for willow ptarmigan, hoary marmot, rock pika, moose, wolf and caribou. Mid-May through July is the prime time for wildflowers, with flowers peaking in mid-June. Carry drinking water and insect repellent at all times. Additional information on this trail is available from the Bureau of Land Management, 1150 University Ave., Fairbanks, AK 99708-3844; phone (907) 474-2350.

F 88 (141.6 km) **C 74** (119.1 km) Twelvemile Creek to east below road.

F 88.7 (142.7 km) **C 73.3** (118 km) Bridge over Reed Creek.

F 90.5 (145.6 km) **C 71.5** (115.1 km) Double-ended turnout to east.

F 93.4 (150.3 km) **C 68.6** (110.4 km) Bridge over the North Fork Twelvemile Creek. Nice picnic spot to west below bridge.

F 94 (151.3 km) **C 68** (109.4 km) Side road leads 0.2 mile/0.3 km down to north fork of Birch Creek; parking area and canoe launch for Birch Creek canoe trail. This is the main put in point for canoeing Birch Creek, a Wild and Scenic River. Undeveloped campsite by creek. Extensive mining in area. **Birch Creek**, grayling to 12 inches; use flies, June to Oct.

F 95.8 (154.2 km) **C 66.2** (106.5 km) Bridge over Willow Creek.

Much gold mining activity along this part of the highway. These are private mining claims. *IMPORTANT: Do not trespass. Do not approach mining equipment without permission.*

F 97.7 (157.2 km) **C 64.3** (103.5 km) Bridge over Bear Creek.

F 98 (157.7 km) **C 64** (103 km) Gold mine and settling ponds in creek valley to east.

F 99.8 (160.6 km) **C 62.2** (100.1 km) Bridge over Fish Creek. Privately owned cabins.

F 101.5 (163.3 km) **C 60.5** (97.4 km) Bridge over Ptarmigan Creek (elev. 2,398 feet/731m). Alpine meadows carpeted with wildflowers in spring and summer for next 9 miles/14.5 km.

F 102.3 (164.6 km) **C 59.7** (96.1 km) Ptarmigan Creek access to west.

F 103 (165.8 km) **C 59** (94.9 km) Good view of mining operation next mile northbound.

F 104.6 (168.3 km) **C 57.4** (92.4 km) Snowpoles guide snowplows in winter.

F 105.4 (169.6 km) **C 56.6** (91.1 km) Large gravel parking area to west.

F 107.1 (172.4 km) **C 54.9** (88.4 km) Parking area to west. Pinnell Mountain trail access (Eagle Summit trailhead); see description at **Milepost F 85.5.**

F 108 (173.8 km) **C 54** (86.9 km) Eagle Summit (elev. 3,624 feet/1,105m) to the east. Steep, narrow, rocky side road leads from the highway 0.8 mile/1.3 km to the summit. This is the third and highest of 3 summits (including Cleary and Twelvemile) along the Steese Highway. *NOTE: Gates across the highway may be closed in bad weather.* Favorite spot for local residents to observe summer solstice (weather permitting) on June 21. Best wildflower viewing on Alaska highway system.

Scalloped waves of soil on hillsides to west are called solifluction lobes. These are formed when meltwater saturates the thawed surface soil, which then flows slowly downhill.

Wildflowers found here include: dwarf forget-me-nots, alpine rhododendron or rosebay, rock jasmine, alpine azalea, arctic bell heather, mountain avens, Jacob's ladder, anemones, wallflowers, Labrador tea, lupine, oxytropes, gentians and louseworts. The museum in Central has a photographic display of Eagle Summit alpine flowers to help highway travelers identify the wildflowers of this area.

F 109.2 (175.7 km) **C 52.8** (85 km) Large parking area to east with view down into Miller Creek far below. Excellent wildflower display. Highway begins steep descent northbound.

F 114.2 (183.8 km) **C 47.8** (76.9 km) Parking area to east looking down onto the Mastodon and Mammoth creeks area.

F 114.4 (184.1 km) **C 47.6** (76.6 km) Side road to east leads to Mammoth and Mastodon creeks; active gold placer mining areas.

F 116.2 (187 km) **C 45.8** (73.7 km) Road east to creek.

F 116.4 (187.3 km) **C 45.6** (73.4 km) Bridge over Mammoth Creek. Near here fossil remains of many species of preglacial Alaskan mammals have been excavated and may be seen at the University of Alaska museum in Fairbanks and at the museum in Central.

F 117 (188.3 km) **C 45** (72.4 km) Highway crosses over Stack Pup. From here the highway gradually descends to Central.

F 117.6 (189.3 km) **C 44.4** (71.5 km) Parking area to west.

F 119.1 (191.7 km) **C 42.9** (69 km) Bedrock Creek.

F 119.2 (191.8 km) **C 42.8** (68.9 km) Narrow dirt road leads to site of former Bedrock Creek BLM campground; closed.

F 121 (194.7 km) **C 41** (66 km) Bridge over Sawpit Creek.

F 122.5 (197.1 km) **C 39.5** (63.6 km) Road west to parking space by pond.

F 125.4 (201.8 km) **C 36.6** (58.9 km) Bridge over Boulder Creek.

F 126.8 (204.1 km) **C 35.2** (56.6 km) Paved highway begins and continues through Central. *NOTE: Road construction ends northbound, 1996.*

F 127.1 (204.5 km) **C 34.9** (56.2 km) Central elementary school.

F 127.5 (205.2 km) **C 34.5** (55.5 km) **CENTRAL** (pop. approximately 400 in summer, 150 in winter; elev. 965 feet/294m). **Radio:** KUAC-FM 91.7. This small community, formerly called Central House, is situated on Crooked Creek along the Steese Highway.

Central is the central point in the huge Circle Mining District, one of the oldest and still one of the most active districts in the state. The annual Circle Mining District Picnic for local miners and their families is held in Aug.

Central has many facilities for the visitor: state airstrip (see **Milepost F 128.3**), cafes and bars, motel cabins, laundromat, showers, groceries, gas, tire repair, welding, pay phone and post office (ZIP code 99730). Report fires to BLM field station at **Milepost F 127.8.** Picnic area at Central Park.

The Circle District Historical Society museum has displays covering the history of the Circle Mining District and its people. Also here are a photo display of wildflowers, fossilized remains of preglacial mammals, a minerals display, library and archives, gift shop and visitor information. Admission is $1 for adults, 50¢ for children under 12; members free. Open daily noon to 5 P.M., Memorial Day through Labor Day.

Central Motor Inn and Campground. See display ad this section.

F 127.8 (205.7 km) **C 34.2** (55 km) **Witt's End Gas, Grocery, Motel, Campground and Cafe.** Jim and Mari Witt offer gas, propane, cafe, bar, package store. Fresh beef

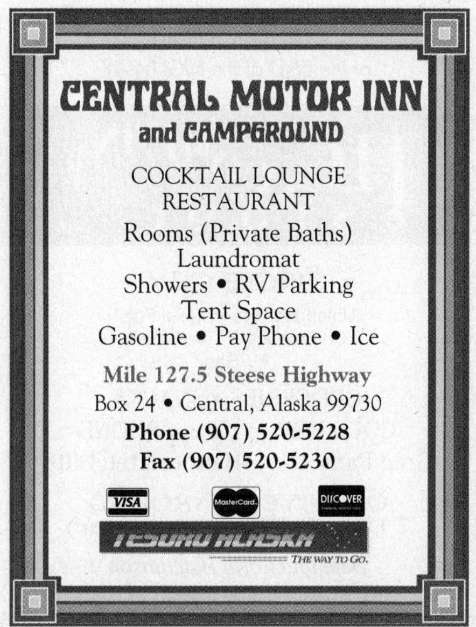

hamburgers. RV parking. Fresh water. Laundromat. Complete variety of grocery items

including mosquito repellents. Pay phone. Open daily. (907) 520-5115. The place to eat in Central! [ADVERTISEMENT] ▲

F 127.8 (205.7 km) **C 34.2** (55 km) **Junction** with Circle Hot Springs Road; see CIRCLE HOT SPRINGS ROAD log this section.

BLM Alaska Fire Services office.

F 127.9 (205.8 km) **C 34.1** (54.9 km) Bridge over Crooked Creek. Site of Central House roadhouse on south side of bridge.

F 128.1 (206.2 km) **C 33.9** (54.6 km) Central DOT/PF highway maintenance station.

F 128.3 (206.5 km) **C 33.7** (54.2 km) **Private Aircraft**: Central state-maintained airstrip, adjacent north; elev. 932 feet/284m; length 2,700 feet/823m; gravel; unattended.

Pavement ends northbound. Watch for soft spots, curves and little or no shoulder between here and Circle; otherwise, the road is in good shape. Wildlife is frequently sighted between Central and Circle.

F 130.5 (210 km) **C 31.5** (50.7 km) Pond frequented by a variety of ducks.

F 131.2 (211.1 km) **C 30.8** (49.6 km) Albert Creek bridge. Small parking area with litter barrel at end of bridge.

F 133 (214 km) **C 29** (46.7 km) Repair shop.

F 147.1 (236.7 km) **C 14.9** (24 km) One-lane bridge over Birch Creek; clearance 13 feet, 11 inches. Turnouts, undeveloped campsites, both ends of bridge. Usual take-out point for the Birch Creek canoe trail.

F 147.6 (237.5 km) **C 14.4** (23.2 km) Turnout to east.

F 155.9 (250.9 km) **C 6.1** (9.8 km) Diamond (Bebb) willow along road. Diamond willow is used to make walking sticks.

F 156.7 (252.2 km) **C 5.3** (8.5 km) Large turnout opposite gravel pit. Look for bank swallow nests in cliffs.

F 159.6 (256.8 km) **C 2.4** (3.9 km) Old Indian cemetery to east.

Circle Hot Springs Road Log

Distance is measured from junction with Steese Highway (J).

J 0 Pavement extends next 0.3 mile/0.5 km.

J 0.9 (1.4 km) Graveyard Road, 0.5 mile/0.8 km to cemetery.

J 1.9 (3.1 km) Deadwood Creek Road.

J 2.9 (4.7 km) Bridge over Deadwood Creek.

J 5.7 (9.2 km) Bridge over Ketchem Creek. Primitive camping at site of former Ketchem Creek BLM campground on right before bridge; no facilities.

J 8.3 (13.4 km) **CIRCLE HOT SPRINGS**; year-round swimming, lodging, food and RV parking. A popular spot with Alaskans.

According to research done by Patricia Oakes of Central, the hot springs were used as a gathering place by area Athabascans before the gold rush. Local prospectors probably used the springs as early as the 1890s. Cassius Monohan homesteaded the site in 1905, selling out to Frank Leach in 1909. Leach built the airstrip, on which Noel Wien landed in 1924. (Wien pioneered many flight routes between Alaska communities.)

Circle Hot Springs Resort, historic hotel with hostels, restaurant, cabins, saloon and outdoor Olympic-sized pool

fed by natural hot springs. RV parking and state-maintained 3,600-foot lighted airstrip. The lodge is open year-round. Call (907) 520-5113 or write Circle Hot Springs Resort, Box 254, Central, AK 99730. [ADVERTISEMENT]

Private Aircraft: Circle Hot Springs state-maintained airstrip; elev. 956 feet/291m; length 3,600 feet/1,097m; gravel; lighted, unattended.

Return to Milepost F 127.8 Steese Highway

Circle

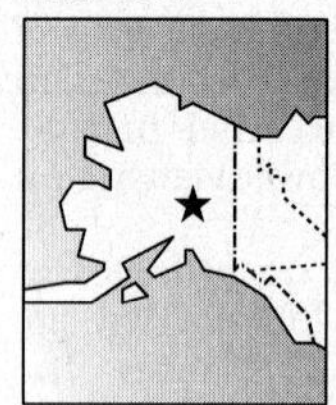

F 162 (260.7 km) **C 0** Located on the banks of the Yukon River, 50 miles/80.5 km south of the Arctic Circle. The Yukon is Alaska's largest river; the 2,000-mile/3,219-km river heads in Canada and flows west into Norton Sound on the Bering Sea. **Population**: 94.

Elevation: 700 feet/213m. **Climate**: Mean monthly temperature in July 61.4°F/16.3°C, in Jan. -10.6°F/-23.7°C. Record high 91°F/ 32.8°C July 1977, record low -60°F/-51.1°C in Dec. 1961, Feb. 1979 and Jan. 1983. Snow from Oct. (8 inches) through April (2 inches). Precipitation in the summer averages 1.45 inches a month.

Private Aircraft: Circle City state-maintained airstrip, adjacent west; elev. 610 feet/186m; length 3,000 feet/914m; gravel; fuel 100LL.

Before the Klondike gold rush of 1898, Circle City was the largest gold mining town on the Yukon River. Prospectors discovered gold on Birch Creek in 1893, and the town of Circle City (so named because the early miners thought it was located on the Arctic Circle) grew up as the nearest supply point to the new diggings on the Yukon River.

Today, Circle serves a small local population and visitors coming in by highway or by river. Gas, groceries, snacks and sundries are available at 2 local stores. The trading post houses the post office, cafe and liquor store. Hunting and fishing licenses are also available at the trading post. There's a lot of summer river traffic here: canoeists put in and take out; the tug *Brainstorm* docks here on its trip from Fort Yukon; Yutana Barge Lines docks here; and floatplanes land on the river.

The old Pioneer Cemetery, with its markers dating back to the 1800s, is an interesting spot to visit. Walk a short way upriver (past the old machinery) on the gravel road to a barricade: You will have to cross through a private front yard (please be respectful of property) to get to the trail. Walk straight ahead on the short trail, which goes through dense under brush (many mosquitoes), for about 10 minutes. Watch for a path on your left to the graves, which are scattered among the thick trees.

Camping on the banks of the Yukon at the end of the road; tables, toilets, parking area. In 1989, when the Yukon flooded, water covered the bottom of the welcome sign at the campground entrance. From the campground you are looking at one channel of the mighty Yukon. ▲

H.C. Company Store. See display ad this section.

Yukon Trading Post. See display ad this section.

ELLIOTT HIGHWAY

Fox to Manley Hot Springs, Alaska
Alaska Route 2
(See map, page 468)

The Elliott Highway leads 152 miles/244.6 km from its junction with the Steese Highway at Fox (11 miles/17.7 km north of Fairbanks) to Manley Hot Springs, a small settlement near the Tanana River with a natural hot springs. The highway was named for Malcolm Elliott, president of the Alaska Road Commission from 1927 to 1932.

The first 28 miles/45.1 km of the Elliott Highway are paved; the remaining 124 miles/200 km are gravel. The highway is wide, hard-based gravel to the Dalton Highway junction. (The road is treated with calcium chloride for dust control; wash your vehicle after travel to prevent corrosion.) From that junction until Manley, the road is narrower but fairly smooth with some soft spots and a roller-coaster section near Manley. Gas is available at **Milepost F 5.5**, probably at **Milepost F 49.5** and at Manley.

*NOTE: Watch for major road construction between **Mileposts F 120 and F 127** in 1996.*

Watch for heavy truck traffic. Drivers pulling trailers should be especially cautious when the road is wet. The highway is open year-round; check with the Dept. of Transportation in Fairbanks regarding winter road conditions.

The Elliott Highway also provides access to 4 trailheads in the White Mountains National Recreation Area. These hiking trails are managed by the BLM in Fairbanks.

Emergency medical services: Between Fox and Manley Hot Springs, phone the state troopers at 911 or (907) 452-1313. Use CB channels 9, 14, 19.

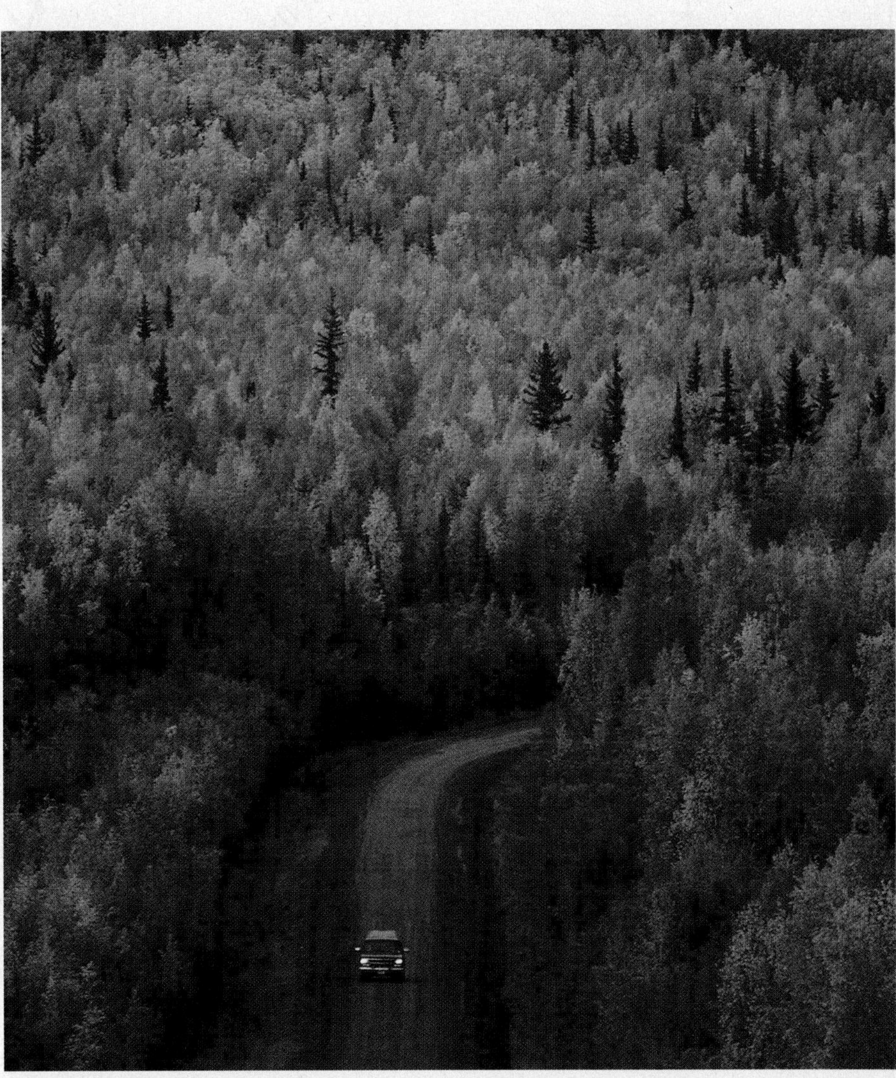

Typical Interior forest of spruce, birch and aspen along the Elliott Highway.
(© Steven Seiller)

Elliott Highway Log

Distance from Fox (F) is followed by distance from Manley Hot Springs (M).

F 0 M 152 (244.6 km) **FOX. Junction** of the Steese Highway with the Elliott Highway. Weigh station.

F 0.4 (0.6 km) **M 151.6** (244 km) Fox Spring picnic area; 2 tables, spring water.

F 1.2 (1.9 km) **M 150.8** (242.7 km) Turnoff for Little El Dorado Gold Mine, a commercial gold mine offering tours and gold panning to the public; admission charged.

F 3.4 (5.5 km) **M 148.6** (239.1 km) Rough side road leads west to Murphy Dome, 28 miles/45 km away. Road is signed "restricted military site."

F 5.5 (8.9 km) **M 146.5** (235.8 km) **Hilltop Truck Stop.** See display ad this section.

F 7.5 (12.1 km) **M 144.5** (232.5 km) Views to the east of Pedro Dome and Dome Creek. Buildings of Dome and Eldorado

ELLIOTT HIGHWAY *Fox, AK, to Manley Hot Springs, AK*

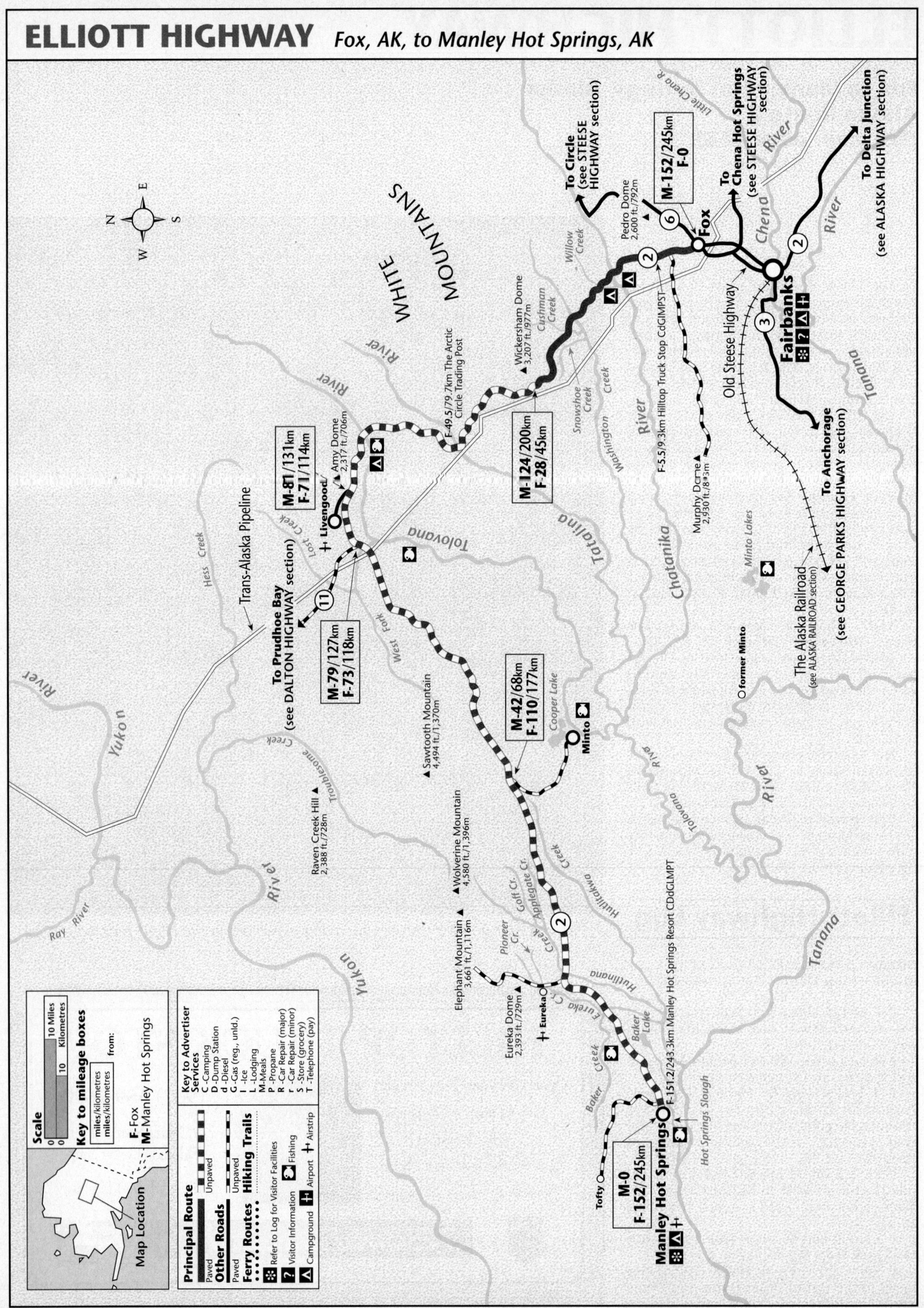

WHITE MOUNTAINS
To Circle (see STEESE HIGHWAY section)
M-152/245km F-0
To Chena Hot Springs (see STEESE HIGHWAY section)
To Delta Junction (see ALASKA HIGHWAY section)
Pedro Dome 2,600 ft./792m
Fox
Fairbanks
Old Steese Highway
To Anchorage (see GEORGE PARKS HIGHWAY section)
The Alaska Railroad (see ALASKA RAILROAD section)
Wickersham Dome 3,207 ft./977m
F-49.5/79.7km The Arctic Circle Trading Post
M-124/200km F-28/45km
F-5.5/9.3km Hilltop Truck Stop CdGIMPST
Murphy Dome 2,930 ft./893m
Minto Lakes
former Minto
Amy Dome 2,317 ft./706m
M-81/131km F-71/114km
Livengood
Trans-Alaska Pipeline
To Prudhoe Bay (see DALTON HIGHWAY section)
M-79/127km F-73/118km
M-42/68km F-110/177km
Cooper Lake
Minto
Sawtooth Mountain 4,494 ft./1,370m
Raven Creek Hill 2,388 ft./728m
Wolverine Mountain 4,580 ft./1,396m
Elephant Mountain 3,661 ft./1,116m
Eureka Dome 2,393 ft./729m
Eureka
F-151.2/243.3km Manley Hot Springs Resort CDdGLMPT
Hot Springs Slough
Tofty
M-0 F-152/245km
Manley Hot Springs
Map Location
Scale
10 Miles
10 Kilometres
Key to mileage boxes
miles/kilometres from:
F-Fox
M-Manley Hot Springs
Principal Route Paved Unpaved
Other Roads Paved Unpaved
Ferry Routes
Hiking Trails
Refer to Log for Visitor Facilities
Visitor Information
Fishing
Campground
Airport
Airstrip
Key to Advertiser Services
C -Camping
D -Dump Station
d -Diesel
G -Gas (reg., unld.)
I -Ice
L -Lodging
M -Meals
P -Propane
R -Car Repair (major)
r -Car Repair (minor)
S -Store (grocery)
T -Telephone (pay)

camps are in the valley below to the east (best view is southbound).

F 9.2 (14.8 km) **M 142.8** (229.8 km) Olnes, former railroad station of Tanana Valley Railroad and mining camp. Old tailings and abandoned cabins.

F 10.6 (17.1 km) **M 141.4** (227.6 km) Lower Chatanika River State Recreation Area Olnes Creek Campground, 1 mile/1.6 km west of highway on loop road; 50 campsites, toilets, water, tables, group area with campfire ring and benches. Camping fee $8/night or annual pass. ▲

F 11 (17.7 km) **M 141** (226.9 km) Chatanika River bridge. Lower Chatanika State Recreation Area Whitefish Campground at north end of bridge; picnic area (wheelchair accessible) with covered picnic tables, campsites, toilets, firepits, water, litter barrels, river access and boat launch. Camping fee $8/night or annual pass. ♿▲

F 11.5 (18.5 km) **M 140.5** (226.1 km) General store.

F 13.1 (21.1 km) **M 138.9** (223.5 km) Willow Creek bridge.

F 13.4 (21.6 km) **M 138.6** (223 km) Old log cabin to west is a landmark on the Elliott Highway.

F 18.3 (29.5 km) **M 133.7** (215.2 km) Double-ended paved turnout to west.

F 18.5 (29.8 km) **M 133.5** (214.8 km) Washington Creek. Parking area below bridge east of road; undeveloped campsite.

F 20.1 (32.3 km) **M 131.9** (212.3 km) Beaver pond with dam and lodge to east.

F 20.3 (32.7 km) **M 131.7** (212 km) Cushman Creek Road.

F 23.5 (37.8 km) **M 128.5** (206.8 km) Large double-ended turnout with view of forested valley to west.

F 24.2 (38.9 km) **M 127.8** (205.7 km) Double-ended gravel turnout to east at top of hill. Snowshoe Creek parallels the road.

F 24.7 (39.7 km) **M 127.3** (204.9 km) Long paved double-ended turnout to east.

F 27.7 (44.6 km) **M 124.3** (200 km) Large double-ended paved turnout to west. Highway winds around the base of Wickersham Dome (elev. 3,207 feet/977m). Views of the White Mountains, a range of white limestone mountains (elev. 5,000 feet/1,524m). Entering Livengood/Tolovana Mining District northbound, Fairbanks Mining District southbound.

Trailhead for White Mountains–Wickersham Creek trail and White Mountains–Summit trail to Borealis–LeFevre BLM cabin. The Wickersham Creek route is 20 miles/32 km in length; ATVs are permitted. The Summit route is 22 miles/35.4 km long and ATVs are prohibited. For more information and cabin registration, contact the BLM office in Fairbanks at 1150 University Ave.; phone (907) 474-2350.

Pipeline access restricted to ensure public safety and security, and to protect the reseeding and restoration of construction areas.

F 28 (45.1 km) **M 124** (199.6 km) Pavement ends.

F 29.1 (46.8 km) **M 122.9** (197.8 km) Sled Dog Rocks ahead northbound.

F 29.5 (47.5 km) **M 122.5** (197.1 km) Double-ended gravel turnout to east.

F 29.8 (48 km) **M 122.2** (196.7 km) Turnouts to west. Spring water piped to road.

F 30.4 (48.9 km) **M 121.6** (195.7 km) Rough double-ended turnout to west. Fairbanks–North Star Borough boundary.

F 31 (49.9 km) **M 121** (194.7 km) Long double-ended gravel turnout to east.

F 31.8 (51.2 km) **M 120.2** (193.4 km) Double-ended turnout to west.

F 34.7 (55.8 km) **M 117.3** (188.8 km) Good view of pipeline; creek.

F 36.4 (58.6 km) **M 115.6** (186 km) Large double-ended turnout to east.

F 37 (59.5 km) **M 115** (185.1 km) Globe Creek bridge. Steep access road to parking area next to bridge.

F 38 (61.2 km) **M 114** (183.5 km) Highway follows pipeline. View of Globe Creek canyon. Grapefruit Rocks to east.

F 39 (62.8 km) **M 113** (181.9 km) Double-ended turnout to east.

F 39.3 (63.2 km) **M 112.7** (181.4 km) Double-ended turnout to west.

F 40.6 (65.3 km) **M 111.4** (179.3 km) Scenic view from double-ended turnout to east at top of hill.

F 41.2 (66.3 km) **M 110.8** (178.3 km) Drive-in parking area to east; no easy turnaround.

F 42.8 (68.9 km) **M 109.2** (175.7 km) Pipeline pump station No. 7 to west.

F 44.8 (72.1 km) **M 107.2** (172.5 km) Tatalina Creek bridge; rest area to east at south end of bridge. The Tatalina is a tributary of the Chatanika.

F 47.1 (75.8 km) **M 104.9** (168.8 km) Turnout to east.

F 49.9 (80.3 km) **M 102.1** (164.3 km) Northern Lights School. This 2-room public school has an enrollment of 22 students.

F 51.9 (83.5 km) **M 100.1** (161.1 km) Double-ended parking area, water. View of White Mountains to northeast and the Elliott Highway descending slopes of Bridge Creek valley ahead. Bridge Creek flows into the Tolovana River.

F 52 (83.7 km) **M 100** (160.9 km) Grizzly and black bear are sometimes seen in this area.

F 57.1 (91.9 km) **M 94.9** (152.7 km) **Tolovana River** bridge. Grayling to 11 inches; whitefish 12 to 18 inches; northern pike.

Colorado Creek trail to Colorado Creek and Windy Gap BLM cabins. Check with BLM office in Fairbanks for details.

F 58 (93.3 km) **M 94** (151.3 km) Highway winds around Amy Dome (elev. 2,317 feet/706m) to east. The Tolovana River flows in the valley to the southwest, paralleling the road.

F 59.3 (95.4 km) **M 92.7** (149.2 km) Parking area to west by stream.

F 59.9 (96.4 km) **M 92.1** (148.2 km) Double-ended turnout to west.

F 62.3 (100.3 km) **M 89.7** (144.4 km) Access to Fred Blixt BLM cabin, east side of road. Preregister at BLM office in Fairbanks.

F 70.1 (112.8 km) **M 81.9** (131.8 km) Livengood Creek, 2-lane bridge. Money Knob to northeast.

F 70.8 (113.9 km) **M 81.2** (130.7 km) Double-ended turnout at **junction** with Livengood access road. Drive 2 miles/3.2 km to former mining camp of **LIVENGOOD** (area pop. about 100); state highway maintenance station and EMT squad.

The settlement of Livengood began in July 1914 with the discovery of gold by Nathaniel R. Hudson and Jay Livengood. A lively mining camp until 1920, some $9.5 million in gold was sluiced out by miners. Large-scale mining was attempted in the late 1930s and again in the 1940s, but both operations were eventually shut down and Livengood became a ghost town.

With the building of the trans-Alaska pipeline and the North Slope Haul Road (now the Dalton Highway) in the 1970s, the town was revitalized as a construction camp. In 1977 a mining corporation acquired much of the gold-rich Livengood Bench. *NO TRESPASSING* on mining claims.

F 71.1 (114.4 km) **M 80.9** (130.2 km) Large double-ended turnout to south.

F 73.1 (117.6 km) **M 78.9** (127 km) **Junction** with the Dalton Highway (see DALTON HIGHWAY section); turn left (west) for Manley Hot Springs.

F 74.1 (119.2 km) **M 77.9** (125.4 km) Alyeska pipeline access road (restricted). Pipeline stretches for miles to the east.

F 74.3 (119.6 km) **M 77.7** (125 km) Site of old Livengood pipeline camp.

F 74.7 (120.2 km) **M 77.3** (124.4 km) Camping spot at west end of **Tolovana River** bridge; grayling to 15 inches, use spinners or flies. ▲

F 76.3 (122.8 km) **M 75.7** (121.8 km) Cascaden Ridge (low hills to north).

F 79 (127.1 km) **M 73** (117.5 km) Travelers should appreciate the abundance of dragonflies seen along the Elliott Highway: their main food is mosquitoes.

F 85.5 (137.6 km) **M 66.5** (107 km) Looking south toward the Tolovana River valley, travelers should be able to see Tolovana Hot Springs Dome (elev. 2,386 feet/727m). (Hot springs are on the other side of dome; no road access.)

F 93.7 (150.8 km) **M 58.3** (93.8 km) Watch for foxes from here to top of hill. Wild rhubarb and fireweed border roadsides for miles.

F 94.5 (152.1 km) **M 57.5** (92.5 km) Long double-ended turnout to south. Good vantage point to view Minto Flats, Tanana River and foothills of the Alaska Range to south.

F 97 (156.1 km) **M 55** (88.5 km) The mountains to the north are Sawtooth (elev. 4,494 feet/1,370m); Wolverine (elev. 4,580 feet/1,396m); and Elephant (elev. 3,661 feet/1,116m). To the south are Tolovana River flats and Cooper Lake. Wild rhubarb and fireweed grow in old burn area.

F 98.3 (158.2 km) **M 53.7** (86.4 km) Turnout to southwest with view of Minto Lakes.

F 100.4 (161.6 km) **M 51.6** (83 km) Turnout to east in former gravel pit.

F 106.8 (171.9 km) **M 45.2** (72.7 km) Turnout with view of Sawtooth Mountains to north.

F 110 (177 km) **M 42** (67.6 km) **Junction** with Minto Road which leads 11 miles/17.7 km to the Indian village of **MINTO** (pop. 233). The village was moved to its present location on the Tolovana River from the east bank of the Tanana River in 1971 because of flooding. Minto has a lodge with accommodations and meals and a general store. Most Minto residents make their living by hunting and fishing. Some local people also work in the arts and crafts center, making birch-bark baskets and beaded skin and fur items. Temperatures here range from 55°F to 90°F/13°C to 32°C in summer, and from 32°F to -50°F/0°C to -46°C in winter. Minto Flats is one of the most popular duck hunting spots in Alaska in terms of number of hunters, according to the ADF&G.

Private Aircraft: Minto airstrip 1 mile/1.6 km east; elev. 460 feet/140m; length 2,000 feet/610m; gravel; unattended.

Minto Lakes, pike to 36 inches, use wobblers, bait, red-and-white spoons, good all summer. Also grayling, sheefish and whitefish. Name refers to all lakes in this lowland area. Accessible only by plane or boat; best to fly in.

F **113** (181.9 km) **M 39** (62.8 km) Evidence of 1983 burn.

F **113.5** (182.7 km) **M 38.5** (62 km) West Fork Hutlitakwa Creek.

F **119** (191.5 km) **M 33** (53.1 km) The road travels the ridges and hills, providing a "top of the world" view of hundreds of square miles in all directions.

F **119.5** (192.3 km) **M 32.5** (52.3 km) Eureka Dome (elev. 2,393 feet/729m) to north.

F **120** (193.1 km) **M 32** (51.5 km) *CAUTION: Watch for major road construction westbound to* ***Milepost F 127*** *in 1996.*

F **121.1** (194.9 km) **M 30.9** (49.7 km) To the north, travelers look down into the draws of Applegate and Goff creeks.

F **123.2** (198.3 km) **M 28.8** (46.3 km) Small turnout to north. Road begins descent into the Eureka area.

F **123.7** (199.1 km) **M 28.3** (45.5 km) Dugan Hills visible to the south at this point.

F **129.3** (208.1 km) **M 22.7** (36.5 km) Hutlinana Creek bridge.

F **131.3** (211.3 km) **M 20.7** (33.3 km) Eureka Road turnoff; access to private ranch. Active mining is taking place in this area. *NO TRESPASSING* on private claims. A trail leads to the former mining camp of Eureka, at the junction of Pioneer and Eureka creeks, 3 miles/4.8 km south of Eureka Dome.

Private Aircraft: Eureka Creek airstrip; elev. 700 feet/213m; length 1,500 feet/457m; turf; unattended.

F **137.4** (221.1 km) **M 14.6** (23.5 km) One-lane bridge over **Baker Creek.** Grayling 5 to 20 inches, use flies, black gnats, mosquitoes, May 15 to Sept. 30.

Winding road with many ups and downs.

F **138.4** (222.7 km) **M 13.6** (21.9 km) Highway goes over Overland Bluff and through a 1968 burn area. Bracket fungus is growing on the dead birch trees.

F **150** (241.4 km) **M 2** (3.2 km) *NOTE: This part of the road can be extremely slick after heavy rains. Drive with caution.*

F **151.1** (243.2 km) **M 0.9** (1.4 km) Manley DOT/PF highway maintenance station.

F **151.2** (243.3 km) **M 0.8** (1.3 km) **Junction** with Tofty Road, which leads 16 miles/25.7 km to former mining area of Tofty, founded in 1908 by pioneer prospector A.F. Tofty. Mining activity in area.

The hot springs is on a hillside on the right before entering the town. One spring runs 35 gallons a minute with a temperature of 136°F/58°C, another runs 110 gallons per minute at 135°F/57°C.

F **151.2** (243.3 km) **M 0.8** (1.3 km) **Manley Hot Springs Resort.** Open year-round. Swim in hot mineral spring-fed pool. Rooms with half baths, full baths or double Jacuzzis; log cabins, restaurant, bar, RV park, dump station, laundromat, showers, gift shop. Gas and diesel, boats available for grayling, northern pike, sheefish. Riverboat charters available. All our tours are to authentic operating fish camps, gold mines. See the real Interior Alaska lifestyle. River tours include visits to fish camp (operating fish wheel). Dogsled rides cross-country in winter. Crystal clear winter nights for viewing aurora borealis. Cross-country skiing, snowshoeing, ice skating. We can accommodate up to 65 guests. Write Box 28, Manley Hot Springs Resort, Manley Hot Springs, AK 99756 or phone (907) 672-3611. Fax (907) 672-3461. [ADVERTISEMENT]

Manley Hot Springs

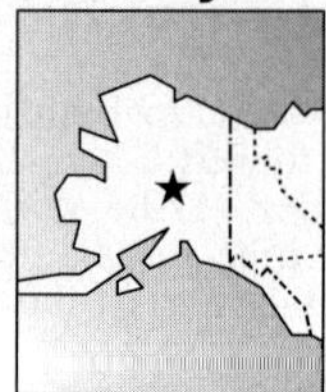

F **152** (244.6 km) **M 0** Located at the end of the Elliott Highway on Hot Springs Slough. **Population:** 88. **Elevation:** 330 feet/101m. **Climate:** Mean temperature in July is 59°F/15°C, in January -10.4°F/-23.6°C. Record high 93°F/33.9°C in June 1969, record low -70°F/-56.7°C in Jan. 1934. Precipitation in summer averages 2.53 inches a month. Snow from Oct. through April, with traces in Sept. and May. Greatest mean monthly snowfall in Jan. (11.1 inches). Record snowfall 49 inches in Jan. 1937.

Private Aircraft: Manley Hot Springs civil airstrip (open year-round), adjacent southwest; elev. 270 feet/82m; length 2,900 feet/884m; gravel; fuel 100.

A pocket of "Pioneer Alaska." J.F. Karshner homesteaded here in 1902, about the same time the U.S. Army Signal Corps established a telegraph station nearby. The location soon became known as Baker Hot Springs, after nearby Baker Creek. Frank Manley built a 4-story resort hotel here in 1907. The settlement's name was changed to Manley Hot Springs in 1957. Once a busy trading center during peak activity in the nearby Eureka and Tofty mining districts, Manley Hot Springs is now a quiet settlement with a trading post, roadhouse, airfield and hot springs resort. Many residents are enthusiastic gardeners, and visitors may see abundant displays of vegetables and berries growing around homes and businesses. Outstanding display of wild irises at the airstrip in June.

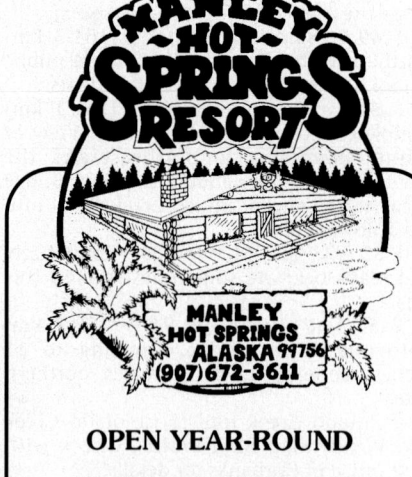

A restaurant, bar and overnight accommodations are at the roadhouse. The post office, gas station and grocery are at the trading post. There is an air taxi service here and scheduled service from Fairbanks.

The Manley Roadhouse. Come visit one of Alaska's oldest original roadhouses from the gold rush era. See the many prehistoric and Alaskana artifacts on display. The Manley Roadhouse is a great place to meet local miners, dog mushers, trappers or fishermen enjoying a cup of coffee. The Manley Roadhouse specializes in traditional Alaska home-style hospitality, fresh-baked pies, giant cinnamon rolls and good food. Largest liquor selection in Alaska. Stop by and see us. See display ad this section. [ADVERTISEMENT]

Manley Hot Springs Park Assoc. maintains a public campground near the bridge in town; fee $5 (pay at roadhouse). The hot springs are a short walk from the campground. There's a nice grassy picnic area on the slough near the campground. A boat launch is also nearby.

Manley Hot Springs Slough, pike 18 to 36 inches, use spinning and trolling lures, May through September. Follow the dirt road from the old Northern Commercial Co. store out of town for 2.5 miles/4 km to reach the Tanana River; king, silver and chum salmon from 7 to 40 lbs., June 15 to Sept. 30. Fish wheels and nets are used.

MANLEY HOT SPRINGS ADVERTISERS

Kenai Peninsula
SEWARD HIGHWAY

Anchorage to Seward, Alaska
Alaska Routes 1 and 9
(See map, page 472)

The 127-mile-/204-km-long Seward Highway connects Anchorage with the community of Seward on the east coast of the Kenai Peninsula. It has been called one of the most scenic highways in the country, and has been designated a National Forest Scenic Byway. Leaving Anchorage, the Seward Highway follows the north shore of Turnagain Arm through Chugach State Park and Chugach National Forest, permitting a panoramic view of the south shore and the Kenai Mountains.

The Seward Highway provides access to Alyeska ski resort, the Hope Highway, Portage Glacier and Kenai Fjords National Park. There is a bike trail between Anchorage and Girdwood. The bike route is marked by signs. Numerous hiking trails branch off the highway.

The Seward Highway junctions with the other major Kenai Peninsula route, the Sterling Highway (see STERLING HIGHWAY section) at Tern Lake. Both these highways offer hiking, fishing and camping opportunities, and beautiful scenery.

Physical mileposts on the Seward Highway show distance from Seward. The Seward Highway is a paved, 2-lane highway with passing lanes. It is open all year. There are no gas stations on the Seward Highway between **Milepost S 90** (Girdwood turnoff) and **Milepost S 6.6**, just outside Seward. Some sections of the highway are subject to avalanches in winter. Check Anchorage news sources for winter road conditions. In 1996, expect major road construction projects along the Seward Highway between **Milepost S 97** and **S 90** (Girdwood turnoff) and between **Milepost S 59** and **S 53** (Hope Highway cutoff).

CAUTION: The Seward Highway from Anchorage to just past Girdwood statistically has one of the highest number of traffic accidents in the state. DRIVE CAREFULLY! Motorists must drive with headlights on at all times.

Emergency medical services: Phone 911 or use CB channels 9, 11 or 19. Cellular phone service is available as far south as Girdwood and is also available in Seward.

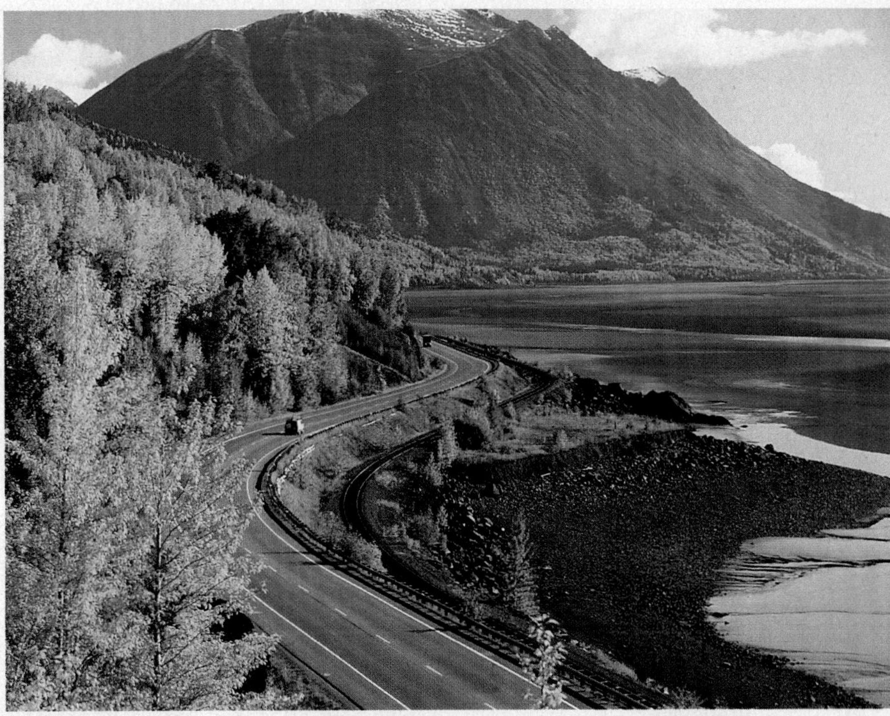

The Seward Highway winds along Turnagain Arm south of Anchorage.
(© Michael DeYoung)

Seward Highway Log

ALASKA ROUTE 1
Distance from Seward (S) is followed by distance from Anchorage (A). Physical mileposts show distance from Seward.

S 127 (204.4 km) **A 0** Gambell Street and 10th Avenue in Anchorage. The Seward Highway (Gambell Street) connects with the Glenn Highway in Anchorage via 5th Avenue (westbound) and 6th Avenue (eastbound). (See area map in the ANCHORAGE section.) Follow Seward Highway signs south on Gambell.

S 126.7 (203.9 km) **A 0.3** (0.5 km) 15th Avenue (DeBarr Road).

S 126.6 (203.7 km) **A 0.4** (0.6 km) 16th Avenue; access to Sullivan sports arena, ice rinks and baseball stadium.

S 126 (202.8 km) **A 1** (1.6 km) Fireweed Lane.

S 125.8 (202.4 km) **A 1.2** (1.9 km) Northern Lights Boulevard (one-way westbound). Access to shopping centers.

S 125.7 (202.3 km) **A 1.3** (2.1 km) Benson Boulevard (one-way eastbound).

S 125.4 (201.8 km) **A 1.6** (2.6 km) Southbound access only to Old Seward Highway.

S 125.3 (201.6 km) **A 1.7** (2.7 km) 36th Avenue; hospital to east.

S 125.2 (201.5 km) **A 1.8** (2.9 km) Freeway begins southbound. There are no services or facilities along the new Seward Highway. However, there are several exits in the next 7.5 miles/12.1 km to the Old Seward Highway (which parallels the new Seward Highway) where traveler services are available.

S 124.7 (200.7 km) **A 2.3** (3.7 km) Tudor Road overpass; exits both sides of highway. (Tudor Road is used as a bypass route for northbound travelers, connecting them with the Glenn Highway via Muldoon Road.)

S 124.2 (199.8 km) **A 2.8** (4.5 km) Campbell Creek bridge.

S 123.7 (199.1 km) **A 3.3** (5.3 km) Dowling Road underpass; exits on both sides of highway.

S 122.7 (197.5 km) **A 4.3** (6.9 km) 76th Avenue exit, southbound traffic only.

S 122.2 (196.7 km) **A 4.8** (7.7 km) Dimond Boulevard underpass; exits on both sides of highway.

S 120.8 (194.4 km) **A 6.2** (10 km) O'Malley Road underpass; exits on both sides of highway. Turn east on O'Malley Road and drive 2 miles/3.2 km to reach the Alaska Zoo. Turn west for access to Old Seward Highway and major shopping area on Dimond Boulevard. Views of Chugach Mountains along this stretch.

S 119.7 (192.6 km) **A 7.3** (11.7 km) Huffman Road underpass; exits on both sides of highway.

S 118.5 (190.7 km) **A 8.5** (13.7 km) De Armoun Road overpass, exits both sides of highway.

S 117.8 (189.6 km) **A 9.2** (14.8 km) Overpass: Exits both sides of highway for Old

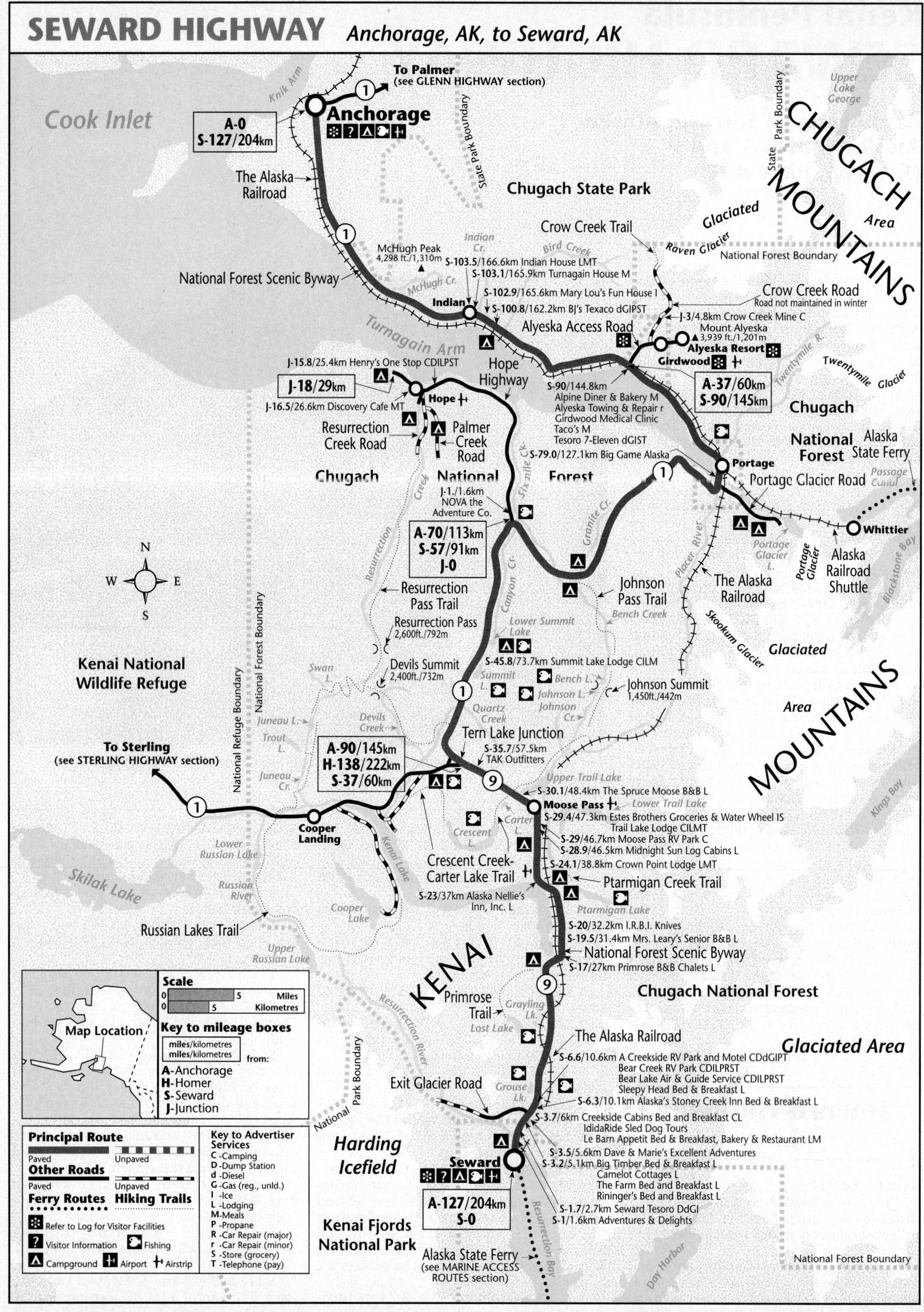
SEWARD HIGHWAY
Anchorage, AK, to Seward, AK
To Palmer
(see GLENN HIGHWAY section)
Knik Arm
Cook Inlet
A-0
S-127/204km
Anchorage
State Park Boundary
The Alaska Railroad
Chugach State Park
CHUGACH MOUNTAINS
Glaciated Area
Upper Lake George
State Park Boundary
Crow Creek Trail
Raven Glacier
National Forest Boundary
McHugh Peak
4,298 ft./1,310m
Indian Cr.
Bird Creek
National Forest Scenic Byway
McHugh Cr.
S-103.5/166.6km Indian House LMT
S-103.1/165.9km Turnagain House M
S-102.9/165.6km Mary Lou's Fun House I
S-100.8/162.2km BJ's Texaco dGIPST
Indian
Crow Creek Road
Road not maintained in winter
J-3/4.8km Crow Creek Mine C
Mount Alyeska
3,939 ft./1,201m
Alyeska Access Road
Alyeska Resort
Girdwood
Turnagain Arm
Twentymile R.
Twentymile Glacier
J-15.8/25.4km Henry's One Stop CDILPST
Hope Highway
J-18/29km
Hope
J-16.5/26.6km Discovery Cafe MT
S-90/144.8km
Alpine Diner & Bakery M
Alyeska Towing & Repair r
Girdwood Medical Clinic
Taco's M
Tesoro 7-Eleven dGIST
A-37/60km
S-90/145km
Chugach National Forest
Resurrection Creek Road
Palmer Creek Road
Alaska State Ferry
Six-mile Ck.
S-79.0/127.1km Big Game Alaska
Portage
Passage Canal
Portage Glacier Road
Chugach National Forest
J-1./1.6km
NOVA the Adventure Co.
Creek
Granite Cr.
Whittier
A-70/113km
S-57/91km
J-0
Placer River
Portage Glacier L.
Portage Glacier
Alaska Railroad Shuttle
Blackstone Bay
N
W
E
S
Resurrection
Resurrection Pass Trail
Canyon Cr.
Johnson Pass Trail
The Alaska Railroad
Bench Creek
Resurrection Pass
2,600ft./792m
Lower Summit Lake
Skookum Glacier
Glaciated Area
Kenai National Wildlife Refuge
Devils Summit
2,400ft./732m
Swan L.
S-45.8/73.7km Summit Lake Lodge CILM
Summit L.
Bench L.
Johnson L.
Johnson Summit
1,450ft./442m
National Refuge Boundary
National Forest Boundary
Juneau L.
Devils Creek
Quartz Creek
Johnson Cr.
MOUNTAINS
Trout L.
Tern Lake Junction
To Sterling
(see STERLING HIGHWAY section)
A-90/145km
H-138/222km
S-37/60km
S-35.7/57.5km
TAK Outfitters
Juneau Cr.
Upper Trail Lake
S-30.1/48.4km The Spruce Moose B&B L
Kings Bay
Moose Pass
Lower Trail Lake
S-29.4/47.3km Estes Brothers Groceries & Water Wheel IS
Trail Lake Lodge CILMT
S-29/46.7km Moose Pass RV Park C
S-28.9/46.5km Midnight Sun Log Cabins L
Cooper Landing
Lower Russian Lake
Kenai Lake
Crescent L.
Carter L.
Crescent Creek-Carter Lake Trail
S-24.1/38.8km Crown Point Lodge LMT
Ptarmigan Creek Trail
Skilak Lake
Russian River
S-23/37km Alaska Nellie's Inn, Inc. L
Ptarmigan Lake
Cooper Lake
Russian Lakes Trail
S-20/32.2km I.R.B.I. Knives
S-19.5/31.4km Mrs. Leary's Senior B&B L
National Forest Scenic Byway
Upper Russian Lake
S-17/27km Primrose B&B Chalets L
KENAI
Chugach National Forest
Scale
0 5 Miles
0 5 Kilometres
Map Location
Key to mileage boxes
miles/kilometres
miles/kilometres
from:
A-Anchorage
H-Homer
S-Seward
J-Junction
Primrose Trail
Grayling Lk.
Lost Lake
Resurrection River
The Alaska Railroad
S-6.6/10.6km A Creekside RV Park and Motel CDdGIPT
Bear Creek RV Park CDILPRST
Bear Lake Air & Guide Service CDILPRST
Sleepy Head Bed & Breakfast L
Glaciated Area
Park Boundary
Exit Glacier Road
Grouse Lk.
S-6.3/10.1km Alaska's Stoney Creek Inn Bed & Breakfast L
National
S-3.7/6km Creekside Cabins Bed and Breakfast CL
IdidaRide Sled Dog Tours
Le Barn Appetit Bed & Breakfast, Bakery & Restaurant LM
Principal Route
Paved
Unpaved
Other Roads
Paved
Unpaved
Ferry Routes
Hiking Trails
Refer to Log for Visitor Facilities
Visitor Information
Fishing
Campground
Airport
Airstrip
Key to Advertiser Services
C -Camping
D -Dump Station
d -Diesel
G -Gas (reg., unld.)
I -Ice
L -Lodging
M -Meals
P -Propane
R -Car Repair (major)
r -Car Repair (minor)
S -Store (grocery)
T -Telephone (pay)
Harding Icefield
Seward
S-3.5/5.6km Dave & Marie's Excellent Adventures
S-3.2/5.1km Big Timber Bed & Breakfast L
Camelot Cottages L
The Farm Bed and Breakfast L
Rininger's Bed and Breakfast L
A-127/204km
S-0
S-1.7/2.7km Seward Tesoro DdGI
S-1/1.6km Adventures & Delights
Kenai Fjords National Park
Resurrection Bay
Alaska State Ferry
(see MARINE ACCESS ROUTES section)
Day Harbor
National Forest Boundary

Seward Highway (west); access to Rabbit Creek Road (east). The picturesque Chapel by the Sea overlooks Turnagain Arm. The church is often photographed because of its unique setting and its display of flowers.

S 117.6 (189.3 km) **A 9.4** (15.1 km) View of Turnagain Arm and Mount Spurr.

S 117.4 (188.9 km) **A 9.6** (15.4 km) Rabbit Creek Rifle Range to west. Boardwalk Wildlife Viewing exit leads east to Potter Point State Game Refuge. This is a very popular spot for bird watching. From the parking lot, an extensive boardwalk crosses Potter Marsh, a refuge and nesting area for waterfowl. The marsh was created when railroad construction dammed a small creek in the area. Today, the marsh is visited by arctic terns, Canadian geese, trumpeter swans, many species of ducks, and other water birds. Bring binoculars.

S 117.3 (188.8 km) **A 9.7** (15.6 km) Highway narrows to 2 lanes southbound.

S 117.2 (188.6 km) **A 9.8** (15.8 km) Small paved turnout at end of boardwalk.

S 116.1 (186.8 km) **A 10.9** (17.5 km) Paved double-ended turnout to east. Highway parallels Alaska Railroad southbound to **Milepost S 90.8.**

S 115.4 (185.7 km) **A 11.6** (18.7 km) **Junction** with Old Seward Highway; access to Potter Valley Road. Old Johnson trail begins 0.5 mile/0.6 km up Potter Valley Road; parking at trailhead. Only the first 10 miles/16 km of this state park trail are cleared. Moderate to difficult hike; watch for bears.

The natural gas pipeline from the Kenai Peninsula emerges from beneath Turnagain Arm here and follows the roadway to Anchorage.

WARNING: When the tide is out, the sand in Turnagain Arm might look inviting. DO NOT go out on it. Some of it is quicksand. You could become trapped in the mud and not be rescued before the tide comes in, as happened to a victim in 1989.

S 115.3 (185.6 km) **A 11.7** (18.8 km) Entering Chugach State Park southbound. Potter Section House, Chugach State Park Headquarters (phone 907/345-5014) to west; pay phone, snack and gift shop, large parking lot, wheelchair-accessible toilets. Open daily in summer, Monday to Friday 8 A.M. to 4:30 P.M. year-round. The renovated Potter Section House, dedicated in October 1986, was home to a small crew of railroad workers who maintained the Alaska Railroad tracks between Seward and Anchorage in the days of coal- and steam-powered locomotives. Displays here include photographs from the National Archives, a vintage snowblower and working model railroad. ♿

S 115.1 (185.2 km) **A 11.9** (19.2 km) Potter Creek trailhead to east.

S 115 (185 km) **A 12** (19.3 km) Watch for rockfalls. Avalanche area and hazardous driving conditions during winter for the next 25 miles/40.2 km.

From here to **Milepost S 90** there are many turnouts on both sides of the highway, some with scenic views of Turnagain Arm. An easterly extension of Cook Inlet, Turnagain Arm was called Return by the Russians. Captain Cook, seeking the fabled Northwest Passage in 1778, called it Turnagain River, and Captain Vancouver, doing a more thorough job of surveying in 1794, gave it the present name of Turnagain Arm.

S 114.7 (184.6 km) **A 12.3** (19.8 km) Weigh station and pay phone to east.

S 114.5 (184.3 km) **A 12.5** (20.1 km) Double-ended gravel turnout to east. From here to **Milepost S 104**, patches of harebells (Bluebells of Scotland) can be seen in late July and early August.

S 113.3 (182.3 km) **A 13.7** (22.1 km) Large paved turnout for slow vehicles.

S 113.1 (182 km) **A 13.9** (22.4 km) Small gravel turnout to east at McHugh boulder area. Watch for rock climbers practicing on the steep cliffs alongside the highway. The cliffs are part of the base of McHugh Peak (elev. 4,298 feet/1,310m).

S 111.8 (179.9 km) **A 15.2** (24.5 km) McHugh Creek state wayside to east with 30 picnic sites. A stream and waterfall make this a very refreshing place to stop. *CAUTION: Steep but paved road into this picnic site. Be sure you have plenty of power and good brakes for descent, especially if you are towing a trailer.* There is also a parking area beside the highway. Good berry picking in season near the stream for wild currants, blueberries and watermelon berries. A 1-mile portion of the Old Johnson trail here is wheelchair accessible. ♿

S 111.6 (179.6 km) **A 15.4** (24.8 km) Double-ended gravel turnout to east. There are numerous turnouts southbound to Indian.

S 110.3 (177.5 km) **A 16.7** (26.9 km) Beluga Point scenic viewpoint and photo stop has a commanding view of Turnagain Arm. A good place to see bore tides and beluga whales. (The only all-white whale, belugas are easy to identify.) Large paved double-ended turnout to west with tables, benches, telescopes and interpretive signs on orcas, bore tides, mountain goats, etc.

WARNING: Do not go out on the mud flats at low tide. The glacial silt and water can create a dangerous quicksand.

Turnagain Arm is known for having one of the world's remarkably high tides, with a diurnal range of more than 33 feet/10m. A bore tide is an abrupt rise of tidal water just after low tide, moving rapidly landward, formed by a flood tide surging into a constricted inlet such as Turnagain Arm. This foaming wall of water may reach a height of 6 feet/2m and is very dangerous to small craft. To see a bore tide, check the Anchorage-area tide tables for low tide, then add approximately 2 hours and 15 minutes to the Anchorage low tide for the bore to reach points between 32 miles/51.5 km and 37 miles/59.5 km south of Anchorage on the Seward Highway. Visitors should watch for bore tides from Beluga Point south to Girdwood.

S 109.2 (175.7 km) **A 17.8** (28.6 km) Paved turnout to west. Spring water is piped to the highway.

S 108.5 (174.6 km) **A 18.5** (29.8 km) Rainbow Road to Rainbow Valley.

S 108.4 (174.4 km) **A 18.6** (29.9 km) Rainbow trailhead and parking; access to Old Johnson trail.

S 107.3 (172.7 km) **A 19.7** (31.7 km) Gravel turnout to east. Rock climbers practice on the cliffs here.

S 107 (172.2 km) **A 20** (32.2 km) From here to Girdwood, in summer when snow is still on the peaks or after heavy rainfall, watch for many small waterfalls tumbling down the mountainsides to Turnagain Arm.

S 106.9 (172 km) **A 20.1** (32.3 km) Scenic

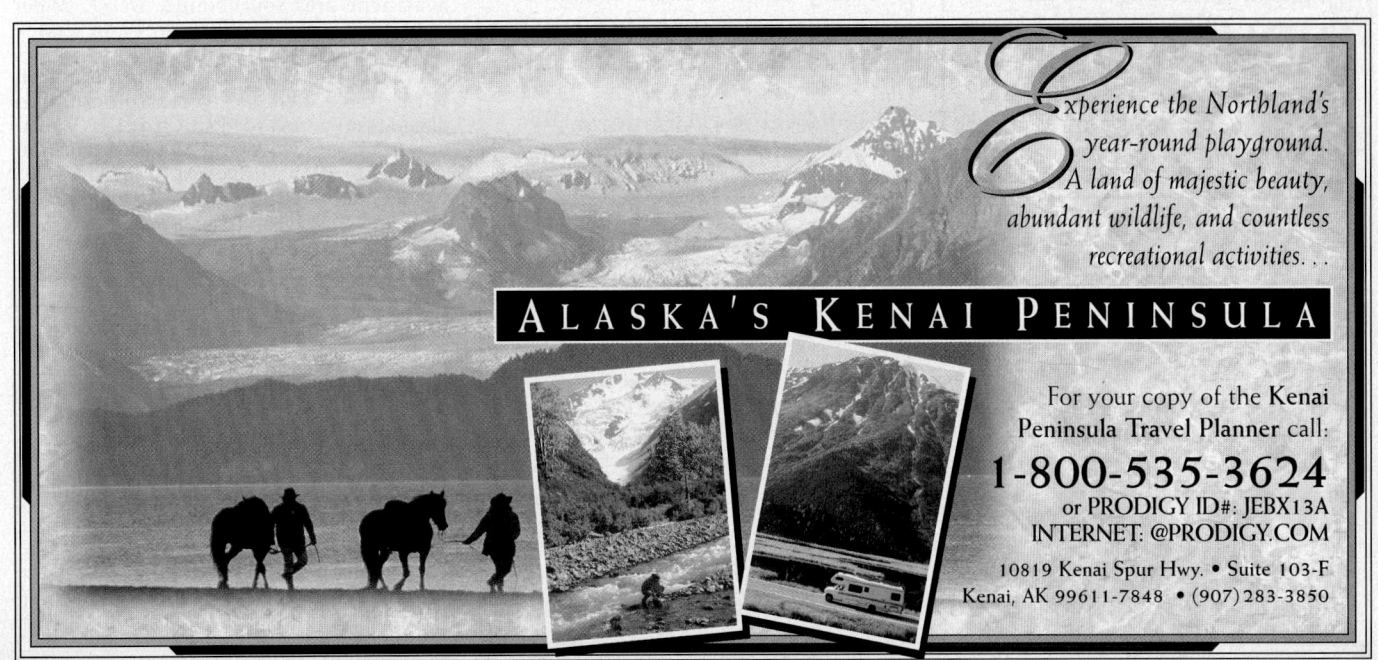

viewpoint. Double-ended paved turnout to west; Old Johnson trail access. Watch for Dall sheep near road. *NOTE: DO NOT FEED WILDLIFE.*

S 106.7 (171.7 km) **A 20.3** (32.7 km) Paved turnout to east; Windy trailhead.

S 106.6 (171.5 km) **A 20.4** (32.8 km) Large paved turnout to west; watch for Dall sheep.

S 105.7 (170.1 km) **A 21.3** (34.3 km) Falls Creek trailhead and parking to east; Old Johnson trail access.

S 104 (167.4 km) **A 23** (37 km) Indian Valley Mine National Historic Site.

S 103.9 (167.2 km) **A 23.1** (37.2 km) Indian Road and Indian Valley businesses on east side of highway.

S 103.5 (166.6 km) **A 23.5** (37.8 km) **INDIAN.** Restaurants, motel and gift shop south from here along the highway.

The Indian House, Indian, Alaska, is a 15 mile scenic drive south of Anchorage. From the lounge and restaurant you can experience the majestic view of the Turnagain Arm where whales follow the salmon and Captain Cook turned again in 1778. The full-service family restaurant includes reindeer sausage with eggs, buffalo burgers, Alaskan salmon and halibut. Join us at The Indian House and share the beauty and history of Alaska. [ADVERTISEMENT]

S 103.1 (165.9 km) **A 23.9** (38.5 km) Bore Tide Road, also called Ocean View Road. Turnagain House restaurant.

Turnagain House, Milepost 103.1 Seward Highway at Indian, AK. Fresh Alaskan seafood, fine steaks and baby back ribs. Located 16 miles south of Anchorage. Excellent view of Turnagain Arm and bore tides. Rustic and casual atmosphere. The Turnagain House is a year-round favorite of Anchorage residents and is considered one of the finest restaurants in the area. Major credit cards accepted. Reservations: (907) 653-7500. [ADVERTISEMENT]

S 103 (165.8 km) **A 24** (38.6 km) Bridge over Indian Creek.

Indian Creek, heavily fished! Pink salmon, sea-run Dolly Varden, few coho (silver) salmon and rainbow, June to Sept.; pink salmon run from latter part of July to mid-Aug. in even-numbered years. **Bird Creek,** same fishing as Indian Creek, except heavier run of pink salmon in July and August.

S 102.9 (165.6 km) **A 24.1** (38.8 km) Indian Creek rest area to west; wheelchair accessible toilets and parking. Bar and liquor store to east. Pay phone.

Mary Lou's Fun House. See display ad this section.

S 102.1 (164.3 km) **A 24.9** (40.1 km) Bird Ridge trailhead and parking; Old Johnson trail access.

S 101.5 (163.3 km) **A 25.5** (41 km) Bridge over Bird Creek; parking. Watch for pedestrians next mile southbound.

S 101.2 (162.9 km) **A 25.8** (41.5 km) Bird Creek State Recreation Site with picnic sites and 19 campsites, firepits, pay phone, covered picnic tables, toilets and water. Firewood is sometimes available. Camping fee $10/night or annual pass. A pleasant campground densely wooded but cleared along the high banks of Turnagain Arm. Paved bike trail goes through campground (nice ride along Turnagain Arm). Great spot for sunbathing. This campground is full most weekends in the summer.

WARNING: Do not go out on the mud flats at low tide. The glacial silt and water can create a dangerous quicksand.

S 100.8 (162.2 km) **A 26.2** (42.2 km) **BJ's Texaco.** See display ad this section.

S 100.5 (161.7 km) **A 26.5** (42.6 km) To the east is the Bird House Bar, a local landmark.

S 99.8 (160.6 km) **A 27.2** (43.8 km) Paved turnout to west. Southbound traffic entering avalanche area, northbound traffic leaving avalanche area.

S 99.3 (159.8 km) **A 27.7** (44.6 km) Large gravel turnout to west with view across Turnagain Arm to the cut in the mountains where Sixmile Creek drains into the arm; the old mining settlement of Sunrise was located here. The town of Hope is to the southwest. The peak visible across Turnagain Arm between here and Girdwood is Mount Alpenglow in the Kenai mountain range. Avalanche gates.

S 99.2 (159.6 km) **A 27.8** (44.7 km) Avalanche gun emplacement (motorists will notice several of these along the highway southbound).

S 97.2 (156.4 km) **A 29.8** (48 km) Southbound traffic leaving winter avalanche area, northbound traffic entering avalanche area.

S 96.8 (155.8 km) **A 30.2** (48.6 km) *CAUTION: Watch for road construction next 7 miles/11.3 km southbound in 1996; possible traffic delays.* Winter avalanche area. There are many gravel turnouts the next 5 miles/8 km southbound.

S 95.5 (153.7 km) **A 31.5** (50.7 km) Turnout to west; avalanche gun emplacement. European elder bushes on slopes; white blossoms in spring, red berries (not edible) in fall.

S 94.4 (151.9 km) **A 32.6** (52.5 km) Gravel turnout to west. Avalanche safety zone.

S 90.8 (146.1 km) **A 36.2** (58.3 km) *CAUTION: Railroad crossing and very bad curve.*

S 90.6 (145.8 km) **A 36.4** (58.6 km) Bridge crosses Tidewater Slough. Avalanche gun emplacement at south end of bridge.

S 90.4 (145.5 km) **A 36.6** (58.9 km) Leaving Chugach State Park southbound. The 1964 Good Friday earthquake caused land to sink in the Turnagain Arm area, particularly apparent from here to **Milepost S 74.** As a result, many trees had their root systems invaded by salt water, as seen by the stands of dead spruce trees along here. Good bird watching, including bald eagles, arctic terns and sandhill cranes.

S 90.2 (145.2 km) **A 36.8** (59.2 km) Girdwood highway maintenance station. End avalanche area southbound. *NOTE: Major road construction northbound 1996, next 7 miles/11.3 km.*

S 90 (144.8 km) **A 37** (59.5 km) **Junction** with 3-mile/4.8-km Alyeska (pronounced al-ee-ES-ka) access road to Crow Creek road and mine, Girdwood and Alyeska Recreation Area. Worth the drive! ALYESKA ACCESS ROAD log starts on opposite page. This

(Continues on page 478)

Alyeska Access Road Log

This 3-mile/4.8-km spur road provides access to Crow Creek Road, Girdwood and Alyeska Resort. There are many restaurants, gift shops, accommodations and attractions in the Girdwood/Alyeska area. **Distance is measured from junction with Seward Highway (J).**

J 0 **Junction** with Seward Highway at **Milepost S 90.** Towing service. Girdwood Station Mall: 24-hour convenience store and gas station, medical clinic with emergency services, chiropractic clinic, 2 restaurants and a gift shop.

Glacier Gifts. See display ad this section.

Taco's. See display ad this section.

J 0.2 (0.3 km) Bridge over Alaska Railroad tracks. Paved bike trail to Alyeska Resort begins.

J 0.4 (0.6 km) Forest Station Road. Chugach National Forest Glacier Ranger District office (P.O. Box 129, Girdwood, AK 99587; phone 907/783-3242). Open 8 A.M. to 5 P.M. Monday to Friday year-round; also 9 A.M. to 5 P.M. weekends Memorial Day through Labor Day. Maps and information available here.

J 0.5 (0.8 km) **Alaska Candle Factory.** One-half mile off Seward Highway on Alyeska. Home of handcrafted candles made in the form of Alaska wild animals.

Hand-dipped tapers and molded candles made daily. All candles have unique individual designs. Open 7 days a week, 10 A.M. to 6 P.M., in summer until 7 P.M. Visitors welcome. (907) 783-2354. P.O. Box 786, Girdwood, AK 99587. [ADVERTISEMENT]

J 1.6 (2.6 km) **Junction** with Brenner Road.

J 1.9 (3.1 km) **Junction** with Crow Creek Road. Two restaurants and Raven Glacier Lodge are located 0.2 mile/0.3 km up Crow Creek Road. This single-lane dirt road leads 3.1 miles/5 km to Crow Creek Mine, 7 miles/11.3 km to Crow Pass trailhead. In winter, the road is not maintained past Mile 0.6. Crow Creek Mine is a national historic site. The authentic gold mine and 8 other buildings at the mine are open to the public (fee charged).

Crow Creek Mine. Visit this historic 1898 mining camp located in the heart

of Chugach National Forest. Drive 3 miles up Crow Creek Road (Old Iditarod trail). Eight original buildings. Pan for gold. Visit our gift shop. Enjoy beautiful grounds, ponds, flowers. Animals and friendly people. Campground for tents and self-contained vehicles. Open May 15–Sept. 15, 9 A.M. to 6 P.M. daily. Phone (907) 278-8060 (messages). [ADVERTISEMENT] ▲

Crow Pass and Old Iditarod trailhead at Mile 7 Crow Creek Road. Crow Pass trail climbs steeply 3 miles/4.8 km to ruins of an old gold mine and a USFS public-use cabin at Crow Pass near Raven Glacier; hiking time approximately 2½ hours. The Old Iditarod trail extends 22.5 miles/36.2 km north from Crow Pass down Raven Creek drainage to the Chugach State Park Visitor Center on Eagle River Road. All of the hiking trail, from Crow Creek Road trailhead to the state park visitor center, is part of the Iditarod National Historic Trail used in the early 1900s. Trail is usually free of snow by mid-June. Closed to motorized vehicles; horses prohibited during early spring due to soft trail conditions.

J 2 (3.2 km) California Creek bridge.

J 2.1 (3.4 km) **GIRDWOOD** (area pop. 1,500), at the junction of Alyeska access road and Hightower Road. **Emergency Services: Alaska State Troopers, EMS** and **Fire Department**, phone 911 or (907) 783-2704 (message only) or 269-5711. Located here are a post office, restaurants, vacation rental offices, laundromat, grocery store with gas, a rafting business, small shops and fire hall. Girdwood is a popular resort area for winter sports enthusiasts and for summer activities. There are many fine summer homes here and a substantial year-round community.

Girdwood Community Center offers tennis courts, pay phone, Kinder Park day-care center and picnic area, and is the site of the Girdwood midsummer crafts fair. The town was named after Col. James Girdwood, who established a mining operation near here in 1901.

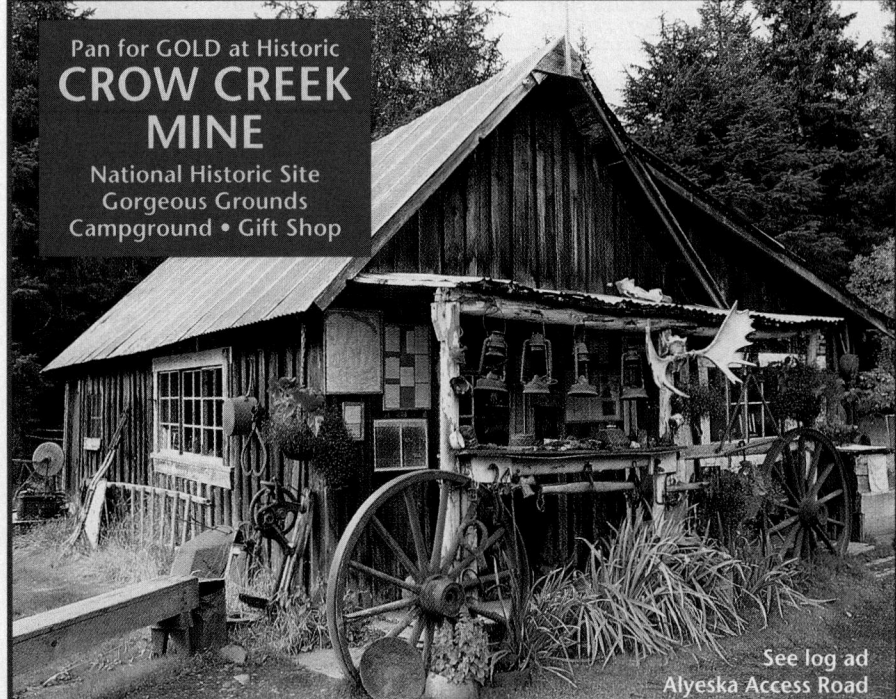

Alyeska Booking Co. offers free reservation service for travelers. They offer affordable lodging at local bed and breakfasts, luxury condos and chalets; either nightly or weekly. Girdwood makes a great base camp for glacier cruises out of Whittier or Seward. Alyeska Booking Co. always has the best price and selection on glacier cruises. They also offer rafting, flightseeing and mountain bike rentals. Call the friendly staff at (907) 783-4386. [ADVERTISEMENT]

Chair Five Restaurant. A favorite of locals and travelers since 1983, Chair Five offers quality food at affordable prices. Renowned for its famous tundra steak with buffalo and reindeer, always fresh

GIRDWOOD / ALYESKA ADVERTISERS

Alaska Candle Factory.............Mile 0.5 Alyeska Access Rd.
Alaskana Haus...................Ph. (907) 783-2481
Alpina Inn and Alpina Tours ....Ph. (907) 783-2482
Alpine Air Inc.......................Girdwood Airport
Alyeska Accommodations.....................Mile 3 Alyeska Access Rd.
Alyeska Air Service............Ph. (907) 783-2163
Alyeska Booking Co. ....Ph. (907) 783-4386
Alyeska Resort........................1-800-880-3880
Alyeska View B & B...........Ph. (907) 783-2747
Bake Shop, The..........................Alyeska Resort
Chair 5 Restaurant.......................Linblad Ave.
Crow Creek Mercantile ....Mile 2.1 Alyeska Access Rd.
Crow Creek Mine ....Crow Creek Rd.
Delphinium House............Ph. (907) 783-3435
Fireweed Inn B & B...........Ph. (907) 783-3153
Glacier Gifts......................Ph. (907) 783-1226
Kobuk Valley Jade Co. ....Mile 3 Alyeska Access Rd.
Spotted Dog Aviation ....Girdwood Airport
Taco's...........................Girdwood Station Mall
Timberline B & B ....Ph. (907) 783-2917

halibut and pasta dishes. They also offer gourmet fresh-dough pizza that gets rave reviews. Over 60 beer varieties and 30-plus single malt scotch selections round out a great cocktail menu. Open 11–11 daily. MasterCard/VISA/American Express. Phone (907) 783-2500. Mile 2.1 Alyeska Access Road; turn on Hightower Road.
[ADVERTISEMENT]

Spotted Dog Aviation. Alaska's mountain flying expert. Glacier landings from $49. No need to get a group, singles for the same price. Fly in the legendary "Super Cub" for a real Alaskan experience

or ride in our special photography airplane with the largest flightseeing windows in Alaska. Special $25 introductory flight for those who have never been in an Alaskan bush plane and just want to take a short ride to see what all the excitement is about. Located at the Girdwood Airport. Open year-round. Senior and children under 12 discount, physically challenged welcomed. Drop in or

Alyeska Access Road Log (continued)

call (907) 522-5101. [ADVERTISEMENT]

J 2.3 (3.7 km) Glacier Creek bridge.

J 2.6 (4.2 km) Donner access to Airport Road. **Private Aircraft:** Girdwood landing strip; elev. 150 feet/46m; length 2,100 feet/640m; gravel; unattended.

Alpine Air Inc. Scenic flights in spacious, intercom-equipped wheel/ski planes into the Chugach Mountains, Prince William Sound and McKinley

areas. Glacier landings are our specialty! Charters throughout the state available. We are federally licensed, fully insured, and proud of our flawless safety record. Visitors welcome year-round to drop in at our hangar office on the Girdwood airport, last blue hangar, north end. Phone (907) 783-2360. [ADVERTISEMENT]

J 2.7 (4.3 km) Timberline Drive.

Delphinium House Bed & Breakfast. See display ad this section.

J 3 (4.8 km) **ALYESKA** Resort and recreation area at Mount Alyeska (elev. 3,939 feet/1,201m). Road forks: To right are the day lodge and ski lift in the base area. To the left is Alyeska business district with jade shop, gift and craft shops, restaurant and ski resort.

Alyeska Resort is Alaska's largest ski area and a year-round resort. Owned and operated by Seibu Alaska Inc. since 1980.

Ski season is generally from early Nov. through April. Facilities include a high-speed detachable bubble quad, 2 fixed-grip quads, 3 double chair lifts and 2 pony tows. Night skiing available during holiday periods in November and December, and Wednesday through Saturday from January through March. Ski school, ski rental shop and sports shops. Wheelchair-accessible mountaintop cafeteria, restaurant and lounge (open year-round) accessed by a 60-passenger tram. ♿

Winter activities include cross-country skiing, dogsled rides, heli-skiing, ice fishing and snowmachining. Summer activities available are glacier skiing, hiking, mountain biking, flightseeing, canoeing, tennis, gold panning and river rafting.

J 4 (6.4 km) Parking for shuttle to hotel and tram to top of mountain and Skyride restaurant.

J 4.5 (7.2 km) Alyeska Prince Hotel and Glacier Terminal (tram). Opened in 1994, the 307-room Alyeska Prince Hotel has 4 restaurants, 2 lounges and a fitness center with indoor swimming pool. The beautiful chalet-style hotel has wood-paneled interior and cost $80 million to build. For more information on the hotel or Alyeska Resort phone (907) 754-1111 or 1-800-880-3880.

Return to Milepost S 90
Seward Highway

intersection is "old" Girdwood: railroad station, school, towing service and shopping center located here. Girdwood Station Mall houses a 24-hour Tesoro 7-Eleven gas station; medical and chiropractic clinic, 2 restaurants and a gift shop. After the 1964 earthquake, Girdwood moved up the access road 2.1 miles/3.4 km. *NOTE: Next gas available southbound on the Seward Highway is at* ***Milepost S 6.6****; next gas available westbound on Sterling Highway is at* ***Milepost S 45*** *(Sunrise).*

Alpine Diner & Bakery. See display ad this section.

Alyeska Towing & Repair. See display ad this section.

Girdwood Medical Clinic. See display ad this section.

Tesoro 7-Eleven. See display ad this section.

Taco's at Mile 90 features authentic Sonoran-style Mexican food. Tacos, Burritos, Nachos, Tamales and Alaska Supreme Ice Cream. One free coffee if you mention this ad in *The MILEPOST®*. Alaska's only taco shop! Home of 55 hot sauces from all over the world. "We've got the hots for you!" So don't run for the border, run to Girdwood Station Mall. Girdwood's sizzlin' hot stop! [ADVERTISEMENT]

S 89.8 (144.5 km) **A 37.2** (59.9 km) Glacier Creek bridge.

S 89.1 (143.4 km) **A 37.9** (61 km) Virgin Creek bridge. View of 3 glaciers to east.

S 89 (143.2 km) **A 38** (61.2 km) Wide straight highway from here to Portage. The Alaska Railroad parallels the highway.

S 88.2 (141.9 km) **A 38.8** (62.4 km) Turnout to east.

S 87.5 (140.8 km) **A 39.5** (63.6 km) Avalanche gun emplacement.

S 86.1 (138.6 km) **A 40.9** (65.8 km) Small gravel turnout by ocean. Chugach National Forest boundary sign.

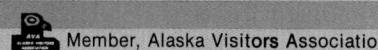

S 84.1 (135.3 km) **A 42.9** (69 km) Peterson Creek. View of Blueberry Mountain.

S 82.3 (132.4 km) **A 44.7** (71.9 km) Turnout to east.

S 81 (130.4 km) **A 46** (74 km) BLM observation platform with informative plaques on Twentymile River wetlands and wildlife. Watch for dip-netters in the spring fishing for hooligan (also known as eulachon or candlefish), a smelt. Road access east to Twentymile River.

Twentymile River, good hooligan fishing in May. These smelt are taken with long-handled dip nets. Pink, red and silver (coho) salmon 4 to 10 lbs., use attraction lures, best in August. Dolly Varden 4 to 10 lbs., eggs best, good all summer in clear-water tributaries.

S 80.7 (129.9 km) **A 46.3** (74.5 km) Bridge over Twentymile River, which flows out of the Twentymile Glacier and other glaciers through a long green valley at the edge of the highway. Twentymile Glacier can be seen at the end of the valley to the northeast. Twentymile River is a popular windsurfing area in summer. Gravel turnout west side of highway.

S 80.3 (129.2 km) **A 46.7** (75.2 km) Access to the Alaska Railroad motor vehicle loading area for ferry traffic taking the shuttle train to Whittier. Ticket office and pay phone. Small visitor information center and gift shop in station. Connections at Whittier with Alaska Marine Highway; regular ferry service is provided across Prince William Sound past the spectacular Columbia Glacier to Valdez. For details see the ALASKA RAILROAD and PRINCE WILLIAM SOUND sections.

S 80.1 (128.9 km) **A 46.9** (75.5 km) **PORTAGE.** No facilities here. The 1964 earthquake caused the land to drop between 6 and 12 feet along Turnagain Arm here. High tides then flooded the area, forcing the estimated 50 to 100 residents of Portage to move. Some old buildings are visible; more evidence of trees killed by the invading salt water. Leaving Game Management Unit 14C, entering unit 7, southbound.

S 80 (128.7 km) **A 47** (75.6 km) Second access to motor vehicle loading ramps and passenger parking for Alaska Railroad shuttle train from Portage to Whittier.

S 79.4 (127.8 km) **A 47.6** (76.6 km) Bridge No. 2 southbound over Portage Creek. Parking and interpretive sign to west at south end of bridge. This gray-colored creek carries the silt-laden glacial meltwater from Portage Glacier and Portage Lake to Turnagain Arm. Mud flats in Turnagain Arm are created by silt from the creek settling close to shore.

S 79 (127.1 km) **A 48** (77.2 km) Bridge No. 1 southbound over Portage Creek. Drive-through wildlife park and gift shop.

Big Game Alaska. See display ad this section.

S 78.9 (127 km) **A 48.1** (77.4 km) **Junction** with Portage Glacier access road. Portage Glacier is one of Alaska's most popular attractions. See PORTAGE GLACIER ROAD log on page 480. *NOTE: There is no gas or lodging available at the glacier.* Tidewater Cafe south side of junction.

S 78.4 (126.1 km) **A 48.6** (78.2 km) Bridge over Placer River; boat launch. Second bridge over Placer River at **Milepost S 77.9.** Turnouts next to both bridges. Between Placer River and Ingram Creek, there is an excellent view on clear days of Skookum Glacier to the northeast. To the north across Turnagain Arm is Twentymile Glacier. Arctic terns and waterfowl are often seen in the slough here.

Placer River has good hooligan fishing in May. These smelt are taken with long-handled dip nets. Silver salmon may be taken in Aug. and Sept.

S 77.9 (125.4 km) **A 49.1** (79 km) Bridge over Placer River overflow. Paved turnout to south.

S 77 (123.9 km) **A 50** (80.5 km) Boundary of Chugach National Forest.

S 75.5 (121.5 km) **A 51.5** (82.9 km) Paved double-ended scenic viewpoints both sides of highway.

S 75.2 (121 km) **A 51.8** (83.4 km) Bridge over **Ingram Creek**; pink salmon fishing (even years).

S 75 (120.7 km) **A 52** (83.7 km) Paved turnout to west. Welcome to the Kenai Peninsula sign. Highway begins ascent to Turnagain Pass southbound. Passing lane next 5 miles/8 km southbound.

S 74.5 (119.9 km) **A 52.5** (84.5 km) Double-ended paved turnout to east. Several kinds of blueberries, together with false azalea blossoms, are seen along here during summer months.

S 72.5 (116.7 km) **A 54.5** (87.7 km) Double-ended paved turnout to east.

S 71.5 (115.1 km) **A 55.5** (89.3 km) Double-ended paved turnout to west.

S 71.2 (114.6 km) **A 55.8** (89.8 km) Double-ended paved turnout to west.

S 71 (114.3 km) **A 56** (90.1 km) Paved turnout to east. The many flowers seen in surrounding alpine meadows here include yellow and purple violets, mountain heliotrope, lousewort and paintbrush.

S 69.9 (112.5 km) **A 57.1** (91.9 km)

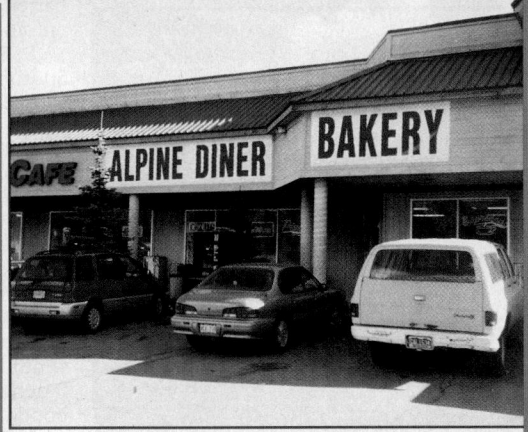

Portage Glacier Road Log

Distance from the junction with the Seward Highway (J).

J 0 Junction with Seward Highway at **Milepost S 78.9.** *CAUTION: Alaska Railroad tracks, rough crossing.*

J 2 (3.2 km) Portage Glacier Work Center (USFS); no services available.

J 2.4 (3.8 km) Paved turnout. Explorer Glacier viewpoint on right.

J 3.1 (5 km) Bridge. Beaver dam visible from road.

J 3.7 (5.9 km) Black Bear USFS campground; 12 sites (2 will accommodate medium-sized trailers), toilets, water, firepits, dumpsters, tables, $6 fee. Pleasant wooded area. ▲

J 4.1 (6.6 km) Bridge over Williwaw Creek. USFS campground, south of road below Middle Glacier; 38 campsites, toilets, dumpsters, water, firepits, tables, $6 fee. Beautiful campground. Campfire programs in the amphitheater; check bulletin board for schedule. Spawning red salmon and dog salmon can be viewed (from late July to mid Sept.) from Williwaw Creek observation deck near campground entrance. Self-guided Williwaw nature trail off the campground loop road goes through moose and beaver habitat. ▲

J 5.2 (8.4 km) Paved road forks at Portage Glacier Lodge; left fork leads to visitor center (description follows). Take right fork 0.8 mile/1.3 km to parking lot; 1.2 miles/1.9 km to Byron Glacier overlook; and 1.5 miles/2.4 km to MV *Ptarmigan* sightseeing boat cruise dock and passenger waiting facility.

J 5.5 (8.8 km) Begich, Boggs Visitor Center at Portage Glacier and Portage Lake. Open daily in summer (9 A.M.–6 P.M.); weekends in winter (10 A.M.–4 P.M.). Phone the visitor center at (907) 783-2326 or the U.S. Forest Service district office at (907) 783-3242 for current schedule.

Forest Service naturalists are available to answer questions and provide information about Chugach National Forest resources. There are displays on glaciers and on the natural history of the area. The award-winning film *Voices from the Ice* is shown in the theater hourly. Schedules of hikes and programs led by naturalists are posted at the center. One of the most popular activities is the iceworm safari. (Often regarded as a hoax, iceworms actually exist; the small, black worms thrive at temperatures just above freezing.) A self-guided interpretive trail about glacial landforms begins just south of the visitor center.

Large paved parking area provides views of Portage Lake. There are several excellent spots in the area to observe salmon spawning (August and September) in Portage Creek and its tributaries.

Return to Milepost S 78.9 Seward Highway

Scenic viewpoint with double-ended parking area to west. The highway traverses an area of mountain meadows and parklike stands of spruce, hemlock, birch and aspen, interlaced with glacier-fed streams. Lupine and wild geranium grow profusely here in the summer.

S 69.2 (111.4 km) **A 57.8** (93 km) Paved turnout to east.

S 69.1 (111.2 km) **A 57.9** (93.2 km) Passing lane ends southbound.

S 68.9 (110.9 km) **A 58.1** (93.5 km) Divided highway begins southbound, ends northbound.

S 68.5 (110.2 km) **A 58.5** (94.1 km) Turnagain Pass Recreation Area (elev. 988 feet/301m). Parking area, restrooms and dumpster (southbound lane); emergency call box. U-turn. Turnagain Pass Recreation Area is a favorite winter recreation area for snowmobilers (west side of highway) and cross-country skiers (east side of highway). Snow depths here frequently exceed 12 feet/4m.

S 68.1 (109.6 km) **A 58.9** (94.8 km) Parking area, restrooms and dumpster for northbound traffic. U-turn.

S 67.8 (109.1 km) **A 59.2** (95.3 km) Bridge over Lyon Creek.

S 67.6 (108.8 km) **A 59.4** (95.6 km) Divided highway ends southbound, begins northbound.

S 66.8 (107.5 km) **A 60.2** (96.9 km) Paved double-ended turnout with litter barrel to east.

S 65.3 (105.1 km) **A 61.7** (99.3 km) Bridge over Bertha Creek. Bertha Creek USFS campground; 12 sites, water, toilets, firepits, table, dumpsters and $6 fee. ▲

S 64.8 (104.3 km) **A 62.2** (100.1 km) Bridge over Spokane Creek.

S 64 (102.9 km) **A 63** (101.3 km) Granite Creek fireguard station.

S 63.7 (102.5 km) **A 63.3** (101.9 km) Johnson Pass north trailhead. This 23-mile-/37-km-long trail is a fairly level good family trail, which follows a portion of the Old Iditarod trail which went from Seward to Nome. See **Milepost S 32.6.**

Johnson Pass trail leads to **Bench Lake,** which has arctic grayling, and **Johnson Lake,** which has rainbow trout. Both lakes are about halfway in on trail.

S 63.3 (101.9 km) **A 63.7** (102.5 km) Bridge over Granite Creek. Traditional halfway point on highway between Anchorage and Seward.

S 63 (101.4 km) **A 64** (103 km) Granite Creek USFS campground, 0.8 mile/1.3 km from main highway; 19 sites (most beside creek), water, toilets, dumpsters, tables, firepits and $6 fee. **Granite Creek,** small Dolly Varden. ▲

S 62 (99.8 km) **A 65** (104.6 km) Bridge over East Fork Sixmile Creek.

S 61 (98.2 km) **A 66** (106.2 km) Bridge over Silvertip Creek.

S 59.7 (96.1 km) **A 67.3** (108.3 km) Gravel turnout next to Granite Creek. Excellent place to photograph this glacial stream. Beaver dam.

S 58.8 (94.6 km) **A 68.2** (109.8 km) Large gravel turnout to west. There are several turnouts along this stretch of highway.

S 57.6 (92.7 km) **A 69.4** (111.7 km) Bridge over Dry Gulch Creek.

S 57 (91.7 km) **A 70** (112.7 km) Bridge over Canyon Creek.

NOTE: Watch for road construction next 7 miles/11.3 km southbound in 1996.

S 56.8 (91.4 km) **A 70.2** (113 km) State wayside with picnic tables, toilets and litter barrels. Travelers sometimes confuse wayside entrance with Hope Highway turnoff.

S 56.7 (91.2 km) **A 70.3** (113.1 km) Southbound **junction** with Hope Highway to historic mining community of Hope. See HOPE HIGHWAY log on opposite page.

NOTE: Southbound travelers may find this junction confusing. Hope Highway veers right; Seward Highway veers left.

S 56.6 (91.1 km) **A 70.4** (113.3 km) Northbound **junction** with Hope Highway. Numerous gravel turnouts next 6 miles/9.7 km southbound.

S 50.1 (80.6 km) **A 76.9** (123.8 km) Begin improved highway southbound with wide shoulders and passing lanes. Winter avalanche area next 1.5 miles/2.4 km southbound.

Truck lane next 2 miles/3.2 km northbound.

S 48 (77.2 km) **A 79** (127.1 km) Fresno Creek bridge; turnout to east at south end of bridge.

S 47.6 (76.6 km) **A 79.4** (127.8 km) Double-ended paved turnout to east on lake.

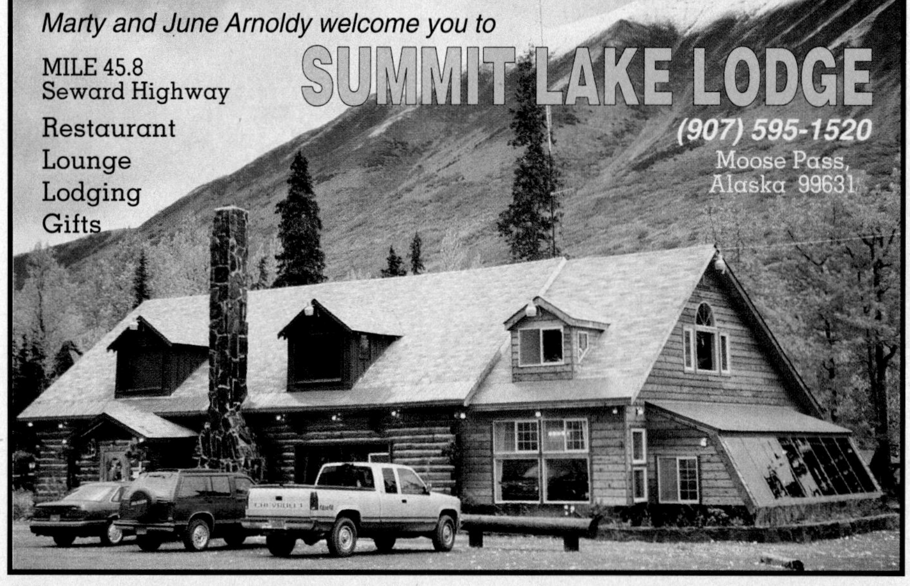

S 47.2 (76 km) **A 79.8** (128.4 km) Paved double-ended turnout to east next to Lower Summit Lake; a favorite photo stop. Extremely picturesque with lush growth of wildflowers in summer.

Upper and Lower Summit lakes, good spring and fall fishing for landlocked Dolly Varden (goldenfins), ranging in size from 6 to 11 inches, flies and single salmon eggs.

S 46.6 (74.7 km) **A 80.6** (129.7 km) Double-ended paved turnout to east on lake.

S 46 (74 km) **A 81** (130.4 km) Colorado Creek bridge. Tenderfoot Creek USFS campground 0.6 mile/0.9 km from highway; 28 sites, water, toilets (wheelchair accessible), dumpsters, tables, firepits, boat launch, $6 fee. ▲

S 45.8 (73.7 km) **A 81.2** (130.7 km) Summit Lake Lodge; open year-round. Emergency radio. Winter avalanche area begins southbound.

Summit Lake Lodge. Genuine hospitality on the north shore of Summit Lake in

Alaska's most beautiful log lodge. Located in the heart of Chugach National Forest, it is a landmark for many. The view is spectacular and the food excellent. Complete menu from eye-opening omelettes to mouth-watering steaks. Enjoy our cozy motel and relaxing lounge. Open year-round. Fishing, hiking, photography, cross-country skiing, snowmobiling. It's a must stop for every visitor in the last frontier. See display ad this section. [ADVERTISEMENT] ▲

S 45.5 (73.2 km) **A 81.5** (131.2 km) Upper Summit Lake. Paved turnout to east.

S 44.5 (71.6 km) **A 82.5** (132.7 km) Large paved double-ended turnout with interpretive sign to east at end of Upper Summit Lake.

S 44.3 (71.3 km) **A 82.7** (133.1 km) Beaver dams.

S 44 (70.8 km) **A 83** (133.6 km) Gravel turnout to east. Avalanche gun emplacement.

S 43.8 (70.5 km) **A 83.2** (133.9 km) Winter avalanche area begins northbound. Avalanche gates.

S 43.7 (70.3 km) **A 83.3** (134.1 km) Paved

Hope Highway Log

The paved 17.7-mile/28.5-km Hope Highway leads northwest to the historic community of Hope on the south side of Turnagain Arm and provides access to the Resurrection Creek area.

Distance is measured from junction with the Seward Highway (J).

J 0 Junction with Seward Highway at **Milepost S 56.7.**

J 0.1 (0.2 km) Silvertip highway maintenance station.

J 0.6 (1 km) Double-ended paved turnout to east; road access to creek. Highway parallels Sixmile Creek, a glacial stream. There are many paved turnouts along the Hope Highway, some with views of Turnagain Arm.

J 1 (1.6 km) **NOVA the Adventure Co.** Since 1975. Sixmile Creek, Alaska's premier whitewater trip! Class IV and V. This is the most challenging raft trip in the state. Spectacular canyons and thrilling participatory whitewater. Granite Creek, a whitewater primer for the first-timer. Includes the class IV canyon of the Six-Mile trip plus a very scenic float down Turnagain Pass. Call 1-800-746-5753 for information and reservations. P.O. Box 1129, Chickaloon, AK 99674. [ADVERTISEMENT]

J 1.4 (2.3 km) Beaver marsh to east.

J 2.3 (3.7 km) Large paved turnout to east. Moose may often be seen in Sixmile Creek valley below. The old gold mining town of Sunrise City, with a population of 5,000, was founded in 1895 at the mouth of Sixmile Creek. The present community of Sunrise has a population of about 20.

J 3.4 (5.5 km) Large paved turnout to east; trail access to creek.

J 3.9 (6.3 km) Large paved turnout to east; trail access to creek.

J 10 (16.1 km) Double-ended paved turnout to east overlooking Turnagain Arm.

J 11.1 (17.9 km) Large paved turnout to east overlooking Turnagain Arm.

J 11.8 (19 km) Double-ended paved turnout to east overlooking Turnagain Arm.

J 15.8 (25.4 km) **Henry's One Stop.** See display ad this section. ▲

J 15.9 (25.6 km) Bear Creek Lodge.

J 16.2 (26 km) Turn left (south) for Hope airport; USFS Resurrection Pass trailhead, 4 miles/6.4 km south on Resurrection Creek Road; Paystreke, a privately owned gold mining town (burned down 1993), 4.6 miles/7.4 km; and Coeur d'Alene Campground on Palmer Creek Road, 7.6 miles/12.2 km. ▲

The 38-mile-/61-km-long Resurrection Pass USFS trail climbs from an elevation of 400 feet/122m at the trailhead to Resurrection Pass (elev. 2,600 feet/792m) and down to the south trailhead at **Milepost S 53.1** on the Sterling Highway. There are 8 cabins on the trail. Parking area at the trailhead.

Coeur d'Alene, former USFS campground (semi-developed), has 5 sites (not recommended for large RVs or trailers); primitive camping only; no maintained facilities; no water, no camping fee. Palmer Creek Road continues past the campground to alpine country above 1,500 feet/457m elevation, and views of Turnagain Arm and Resurrection Creek valley. The road past the old campground is rough and narrow and not recommended for low-clearance vehicles.

J 16.5 (26.6 km) Turn on Hope Road for downtown **HOPE** (pop. 224). Hope Road leads past the post office down to the waterfront, a favorite fishing spot near the ocean; motel, cafe, grocery store and gift shop.

This historic mining community was founded in 1896 by gold seekers working Resurrection Creek and its tributary streams. Today, many Anchorage residents have vacation homes here.

Discovery Cafe. See display ad this section.

J 17 (27.3 km) Road to historic Hope townsite. Interpretive sign at intersection. The original townsite of Hope City was founded in 1896. Portions of the town destroyed by the 1964 earthquake are marked with dotted lines on the map sign.

J 17.1 (27.5 km) Resurrection Creek bridge.

J 17.7 (28.4 km) Gas station.

J 17.8 (28.6 km) Hope Highway ends at Porcupine USFS campground; 24 sites, tables, tent spaces, toilets, firepits, dumpster, drinking water and $6 fee. Gull Rock trailhead. ▲

Return to Milepost S 56.7
Seward Highway

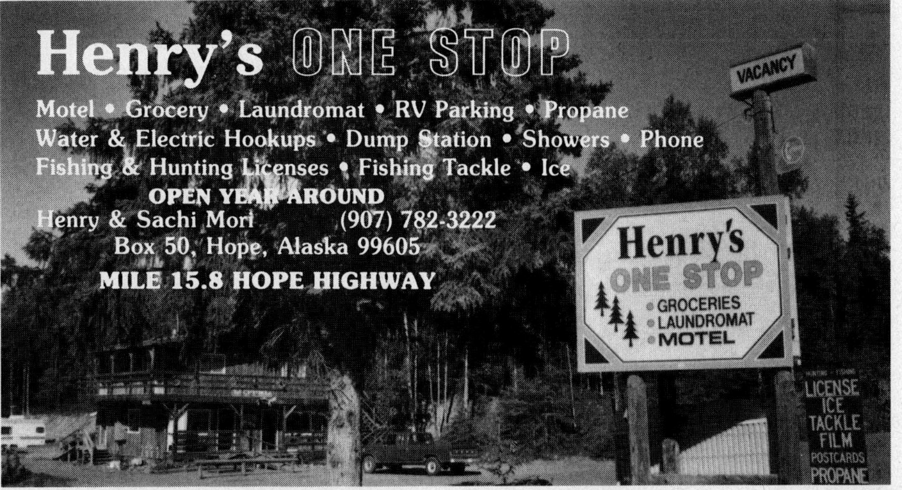

double-ended turnout to east.

S 42.6 (68.6 km) **A 84.4** (135.8 km) Summit Creek bridge.

S 42.2 (67.9 km) **A 84.8** (136.5 km) Quartz Creek bridge.

S 41.4 (66.6 km) **A 85.6** (137.8 km) Passing lane next 1 mile/1.6 km northbound.

S 39.6 (63.7 km) **A 87.4** (140.7 km) Avalanche gates.

S 39.4 (63.4 km) **A 87.6** (141 km) Devils Pass trailhead; parking area and toilets to west. This USFS trail starts at an elevation of 1,000 feet/305m and follows Devils Creek to Devils Pass (elev. 2,400 feet/732m), continuing on to Devils Pass Lake and Resurrection Pass trail. Hiking time to Devils Pass is about 5½ hours.

S 39 (62.8 km) **A 88** (141.6 km) Truck lane extends northbound to **Milepost S 39.3**.

S 38.6 (62.1 km) **A 88.4** (142.3 km) Paved turnout to west adjacent **Jerome Lake**, rainbow and Dolly Varden to 22 inches, use salmon egg clusters, year-round, still fish. A sign here explains rainbow plant in lake.

S 38.3 (61.6 km) **A 88.7** (142.7 km) Paved double-ended turnout to west overlooking Jerome Lake. USFS interpretive sign about sticklebacks.

S 38.2 (61.5 km) **A 88.8** (142.9 km) Truck lane ends northbound.

S 37.7 (60.7 km) **A 89.3** (143.7 km) **Junction.** First southbound exit (one-way road) for Sterling Highway (Alaska Route 1) on right. Continue straight ahead on Alaska Route 9 for Seward.

If you are bound for Soldotna, Homer, or other Sterling Highway communities and attractions, turn to page 503 in the STERLING HIGHWAY section and begin that log. Continue with this log if you are going to Seward.

ALASKA ROUTE 9

S 37.2 (59.9 km) **A 89.8** (144.5 km) Paved turnout to west overlooking Tern Lake for Seward-bound travelers.

S 37 (59.5 km) **A 90** (144.8 km) **Tern Lake Junction.** Second southbound turnoff on right (2-way road) for Sterling Highway (Alaska Route 1) and access to Tern Lake USFS campground and salmon spawning channel. To reach campground, drive 0.4 mile/0.6 km around Tern Lake; 25 sites, water, toilets, picnic tables, firepits, canoe launch, $6 fee. Tern Lake is a good spot for bird watching in summer. See STERLING HIGHWAY section. ▲

Continue straight ahead on Alaska Route 9 for Seward.

S 36.7 (59.1 km) **A 90.3** (145.3 km) Truck lane begins northbound.

S 36.4 (58.6 km) **A 90.6** (145.8 km) Avalanche gates.

S 35.7 (57.5 km) **A 91.3** (146.9 km) Outfitter for guided horse pack trips.

TAK Outfitters. See display ad this section.

S 35.3 (56.8 km) **A 91.7** (147.6 km) End avalanche area southbound.

S 35 (56.3 km) **A 92** (148 km) For the next 3 miles/4.8 km many small waterfalls tumble down the brushy slopes. Winter avalanche area between **Milepost S 35.3** and **34.6.** You are driving through the Kenai mountain range.

S 33.1 (53.3 km) **A 93.9** (151.1 km) Carter Lake USFS trailhead No. 4 to west, parking and toilets. Trail starts at an elevation of 500 feet/152m and climbs 986 feet/300m to **Carter Lake** (stocked with rainbow trout). Trail is good, but steep; hiking time about 1½ hours. Good access to sheep and mountain goat country. Excellent snowmobiling area in winter.

S 32.6 (52.5 km) **A 94.4** (151.9 km) Johnson Pass USFS south trailhead with parking area, toilet. North trailhead at **Milepost S 63.7.**

S 32.5 (52.3 km) **A 94.5** (152.1 km) Large paved double-ended turnout; USFS information sign on life cycle of salmon; short trail to observation deck on stream where spawning salmon may be seen in August.

S 32.4 (52.1 km) **A 94.6** (152.2 km) Cook Inlet Aquaculture Assoc. Trail Lake fish hatchery on Moose Creek. Display room and restrooms. Open 8 A.M. to 5 P.M. daily. Tours available daily at 10 A.M. June 1 to Sept. 15; phone (907) 288-3688 to confirm tour times or for more information.

S 31.8 (51.1 km) **A 95.2** (153.2 km) Paved double-ended rest area to east on Upper Trail Lake; toilets, picnic tables.

S 30 (48.3 km) **A 97** (156.1 km) Short side road to large undeveloped gravel parking area on Upper Trail Lake, boat launch.

S 29.9 (48.1 km) **A 97.1** (156.3 km) Gravel turnout by Trail Lake.

S 29.4 (47.3 km) **A 97.6** (157.1 km) Large working waterwheel that turns a grindstone, built by Ed Estes, on way into Moose Pass. Parking area and sign at waterwheel which reads: "Moose Pass is a peaceful little town. If you have an ax to grind, do it here."

MOOSE PASS (pop. 145) has a motel, bed and breakfast, log cabins for rent, RV park, general store, gift shop, restaurant, salmon bake, post office and highway maintenance station. Pay phone outside GTE building. Alaska State Troopers, emergency only phone 911. This mountain village on Upper Trail Lake was a construction camp on the Alaska Railroad in 1912. Local resident Ed Estes attributes the name Moose Pass to a 1904 observation by Nate White of the first moose recorded in this area. Another version holds that "in 1903, a mail carrier driving a team of dogs had considerable trouble gaining the right-of-way from a giant moose." A post office was established in 1928. ▲

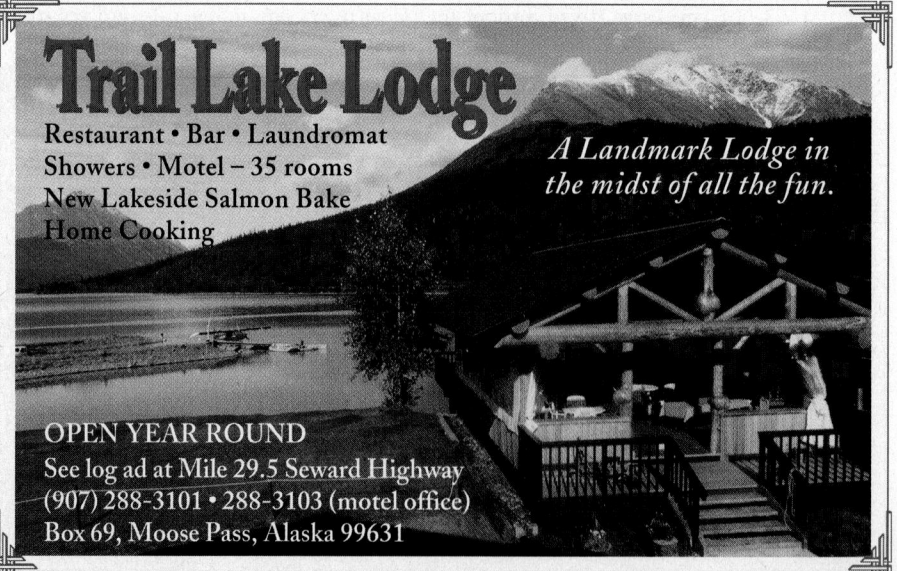

Moose Pass has a 1.3-mile-/2.1-km-long paved bike trail which winds along Trail Lake from the Moose Pass ball diamond to the McFadden house on the south. Gravel turnout by lake.

The main street of town is the site of the Annual Moose Pass Summer Festival, a community-sponsored event which takes place the weekend nearest summer solstice (June 21). The festival features a triathlon, arts and crafts booths, a barbecue, auction and other events.

Estes Brothers Groceries & Water Wheel. See display ad this section.

Trail Lake Lodge. Home cooking, friendly staff and clean facilities welcome you to this landmark lodge "in the midst of all the fun." Conveniently located in the

heart of the Chugach National Forest trail system, close to Seward and the famed Kenai River. Moderate motel rates. Menu offers unique selections as well as Alaskan seafood and steaks. Real sourdough hotcakes and muffins. (907) 288-3101 or (motel) (907) 288-3103. [ADVERTISEMENT]

S 29 (46.7 km) **A 98** (157.1 km) **Moose Pass RV Park.** New! 25 spaces and growing. Electric hookups planned for 1996. Scenic campground-like setting. Close to restaurant, laundromat. More information available from Trail Lake Lodge, (907) 288-3103. [ADVERTISEMENT]

S 28.9 (46.5 km) **A 98.1** (157.9 km) **Midnight Sun Log Cabins.** See display ad this section.

S 26 (41.8 km) **A 101** (162.5 km) Lower Trail Lake. Timbered slopes of Madson Mountain (elev. 5,269 feet/1,605m) to the west. Crescent Lake lies just west of Madson.

S 25.8 (41.5 km) **A 101.2** (162.9 km) Gravel turnout to west.

S 25.4 (40.9 km) **A 101.6** (163.5 km) Bridge over Trail River.

S 25 (40.2 km) **A 102** (164.1 km) Bridge over Falls Creek.

S 24.8 (39.9 km) **A 102.2** (164.5 km) Gravel turnout to west.

S 24.2 (38.9 km) **A 102.8** (165.4 km) Side road leads 1.2 miles/1.9 km to Trail River USFS campground; $6 fee, 64 sites, picnic tables, firepits, dumpsters, toilets, and volleyball and horseshoe area. Day-use group picnic area; for reservations, call Seward District office, (907) 224-3374. Spacious, wooded campsites in tall spruce on shore of Kenai Lake and Lower Trail River. Pull-through sites available. Campground host may be in residence during summer, providing fishing and hiking information. Good spot for mushrooming and berry picking in August. ▲

Lower Trail River, lake trout, rainbow and Dolly Varden to 25 inches, July, Aug. and Sept., use salmon eggs, small spinners. Access via Lower Trail River campground road. **Trail River,** Dolly Varden 12 to 20 inches, spring and fall, use fresh eggs; rainbow 12 to 20 inches, spring, use fresh eggs.

S 24.1 (38.8 km) **A 102.9** (165.6 km) **Crown Point Lodge.** Let our staff plan your fishing, hunting, sightseeing or flightseeing while you dine on our true home-cooked meals, pies and breads in an Alaska setting. Clean, comfortable rooms are available at moderate costs. We offer package prices for lodging, meals and charters. Phone (907) 288-3136 or 1-800-764-0054. Y'all come! [ADVERTISEMENT]

S 23.4 (37.7 km) **A 103.6** (166.7 km) *CAUTION: Railroad crossing.* USFS Kenai Lake work center (no information services available). Report forest fires here.

Private Aircraft: Lawing landing strip; elev. 475 feet/144m; length 2,300 feet/701m; gravel; unattended.

S 23.1 (37.1 km) **A 103.9** (167.2 km) **Ptarmigan Creek** bridge and USFS picnic area and campground with 16 sites, water, toilets, tables, firepits and dumpsters, $6 fee. Fair to good fishing in creek and in lake outlets at **Ptarmigan Lake** (hike in) for Dolly Varden. Watch for spawning salmon in Ptarmigan Creek in Aug. ▲

Ptarmigan Creek USFS trail No. 14 begins at campground (elev. 500 feet/152m) and leads 3.5 miles/5.6 km to Ptarmigan Lake (elev. 755 feet/230m). Trail is steep in spots; round-trip hiking time 5 hours. Good chance of seeing sheep, goats, moose and bears. Carry insect repellent. Trail is poor for winter use due to avalanche hazard.

S 23 (37 km) **A 104** (167.3 km) Turnoff for Alaska Nellie's Homestead. The late Nellie Neal–Lawing arrived in Alaska in 1915. Her colorful life included cooking for the railroad workers and big game hunting and guiding. She converted a roadhouse at Lawing into a museum to house the trophies and souvenirs she and her husband, Billie

Beautiful mountain and lake scenery on the Kenai Peninsula. (© Doug Wilson)

Lawing, gathered on their travels.

Alaska Nellie's Inn, Inc. See display ad this section.

S 22.9 (36.9 km) **A 104.1** (167.5 km) Viewpoint to west overlooking Kenai Lake. This lake (elev. 436 feet/132m) extends 24 miles/39 km from the head of the Kenai River on the west to the mouth of Snow River on the east. A sign here explains how glacier meltwater gives the lake its distinctive color.

Winter avalanche area next 3 miles/4.8 km southbound.

S 22.5 (36.2 km) **A 104.5** (168.2 km) Rough gravel double-ended turnout to east.

S 21.3 (34.3 km) **A 105.7** (170.1 km) Gravel turnout to east overlooking lake.

S 20.2 (32.5 km) **A 106.8** (171.9 km) Avalanche gun emplacement.

S 20.1 (32.3 km) **A 106.9** (172 km) Gravel turnout. Avalanche area ends southbound.

S 20 (32.2 km) **A 107** (172.2 km) **I.R.B.I. Knives.** See display ad this section.

S 19.5 (31.4 km) **A 107.5** (173 km) Victor Creek bridge. Victor Creek USFS trail No. 23 begins here. A 2-mile/3.2-km hike with good view of mountains.

Mrs. Leary's Senior B&B located just south of the Victor Creek Bridge at Milepost 19.5 will make you feel right at home. Country comfort in over-stuffed furniture, satin bed linens for sensitive skin, a private bathroom and your own thermostat. I serve a full breakfast of salmon, scrambled eggs, sliced fresh fruit, bagels & cream cheese, wild berry jam, and robust coffee or herbal teas. Smokers welcome! $75/night, May through September. (907) 288-3168. [ADVERTISEMENT]

S 17.7 (28.5 km) **A 109.3** (175.9 km) Bridge over center channel of Snow River. This river has 2 forks that flow into Kenai Lake.

S 17 (27 km) **A 110** (177 km) Turn west for Primrose USFS campground, 1 mile/1.6 km from the highway. (Campground access road leads past private homes. Drive carefully!) The campground, overlooking Kenai Lake, has 10 sites, toilets, dumpsters, tables, firepits, boat ramp, water, $6 fee. Primrose trail (6.5 miles/10.5 km) starts from the campground and connects with Lost Lake trail (7 miles/11.2 km). High alpine hike, trail is posted. ▲

Bridge over south channel of Snow River.

Primrose B&B Chalets. See display ad this section.

S 16.2 (26.1 km) **A 110.8** (178.3 km) Gravel turnout to east.

S 16 (25.7 km) **A 111** (178.6 km) Snow River hostel.

S 15 (24.1 km) **A 112** (180.2 km) Watch for moose in ponds and meadows.

S 14.9 (24 km) **A 112.1** (180.4 km) Gravel turnout to east.

S 14 (22.5 km) **A 113** (181.9 km) *CAUTION: Railroad crossing.*

S 13.3 (21.4 km) **A 113.7** (183 km) Grayling Lake USFS trailhead to west, large paved parking area to east. Grayling Lake trail No. 20, 1.6 miles/2.6 km, connects with trails to Meridian and Leech lakes. Good spot for photos of Snow River valley. Watch for moose. **Grayling Lake,** 6- to 12-inch grayling, use flies, May to Oct.

S 12 (19.3 km) **A 115** (185.1 km) Alaska Railroad crosses under highway.

S 11.6 (18.6 km) **A 115.4** (185.7 km) Gravel parking area to west and USFS trail No. 6 to **Golden Fin Lake,** Dolly Varden averaging 8 inches. This is a 0.6-mile/1-km hike on a very wet trail: wear rubber footwear.

S 10.8 (17.4 km) **A 116.2** (187 km) Large gravel turnout to east.

S 8.5 (13.6 km) **A 118.5** (190.7 km) Gravel turnout to west.

S 8.3 (13.4 km) **A 118.7** (191 km) Paved turnout by creek to east. Leaving Chugach National Forest land southbound.

S 8 (12.9 km) **A 119** (191.5 km) **Grouse Creek** bridge. Dolly Varden fishing.

S 7.4 (11.9 km) **A 119.6** (192.5 km) **Grouse Lake** access road. Good ice fishing for Dolly Varden in winter.

S 7.1 (11.4 km) **A 119.9** (193 km) Old Mill subdivision.

S 6.6 (10.6 km) **A 120.4** (193.7 km) Bear Creek bridge and Bear Lake Road; access to gas station, 2 private RV parks, bed and breakfast, and a flying service. Drive in 0.7 mile/1.1 km on Bear Lake Road to see a state-operated fish weir. Silver and red (sockeye) salmon are trapped to provide life-cycle data and also eggs for the state's salmon stocking program.

A Creekside Park & Motel. Bear Lake Road. Full and partial RV hookups, dry camping, tent sites. Dump station, restrooms, showers, laundry. Free shower with hookups, free firewood. Gas, diesel, propane, ice, pay phone. Senior citizen discounts. Family owned and operated. Located on salmon spawning stream. Bring your camera. Fishing for Dolly Varden, rainbow trout and grayling in the park. Fishing charters for salmon and halibut arranged. Check in at Gary's Independent Gas. See display ad this section. [ADVERTISEMENT] ▲

Bear Creek RV Park, drive 1/2 mile on Bear Lake Road. Good Sam Park has full and partial hookups, dump station, 2 private restrooms with showers, cable TV, travelers lounge, propane, laundry, convenience store, ice, video rentals. 2 free showers per site. Pay phone inside. Excellent water. (907) 224-5725. Fax service available. Bunkhouse for rent. Free shuttle when reservations are booked through our office for glacier and fishing trips. Auto and RV repair and service. RV and boat storage. High pressure wash. Short walk to fish weir. Bear Creek RV Park is not to be mistaken for A Creekside RV Park located at the gas station on the corner of the Seward Highway and Bear Lake Road. See display ad this section. [ADVERTISEMENT] ▲

Bear Lake Air & Guide Service. See display ad this section.

Sleepy Head Bed & Breakfast. See display ad this section.

S 6.3 (10.1 km) **A 120.7** (194.2 km) Lake Drive; access to bed and breakfasts.

Alaska's Stoney Creek Inn Bed & Breakfast. See display ad this section.

S 5.9 (9.4 km) **A 121.1** (194.8 km) **Salmon Creek** bridge. Good fishing in stream for sea-run Dolly Varden averaging 10 inches, use single salmon eggs, begins about Aug. 1.

S 5.2 (8.4 km) **A 121.8** (196 km) Bear Creek volunteer fire department.

S 3.8 (6.1 km) **A 123.2** (198.3 km) Clear Creek bridge.

S 3.7 (6 km) **A 123.3** (198.4 km) Turnoff for Exit Glacier Road. Access to restaurant, health food store, dogsled rides, and bed and breakfasts; turn right onto loop road (old Exit Glacier Road) immediately after turning off highway.

The 9-mile/14.5-km Exit Glacier Road (open May to Nov., depending on snow) is paved for the first 4 miles/6.4 km; expect road construction on the last 5 miles/8 km in 1996. The road ends at a parking lot with toilets and picnic area next to Exit Glacier ranger station in Kenai Fjords National Park. Look for bears high on the hillside opposite the ranger station. Walk-in campground with 9 sites. A public-use cabin is available; access in winter by cross-country skis, dogsled or snowmachine; permit required, phone (907) 224-3175. The National Park Service operates a visitor center at the ranger station (seasonal). The flat, easy 0.8-mile Lower Loop trail leads through alder forest to outwash plain; pick your own route to base of glacier. The longer 1-mile/1.6-km Upper Loop trail is no longer a loop, since the glacier overran the trail, but it does lead to a glacier overlook. The first 0.2 mile/0.3 km of this trail is paved and wheelchair accessible. There is also an easy 0.8 mile/1.3 km nature trail loop

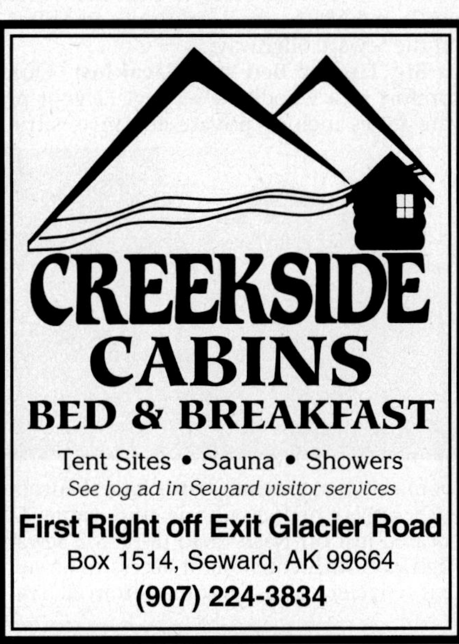

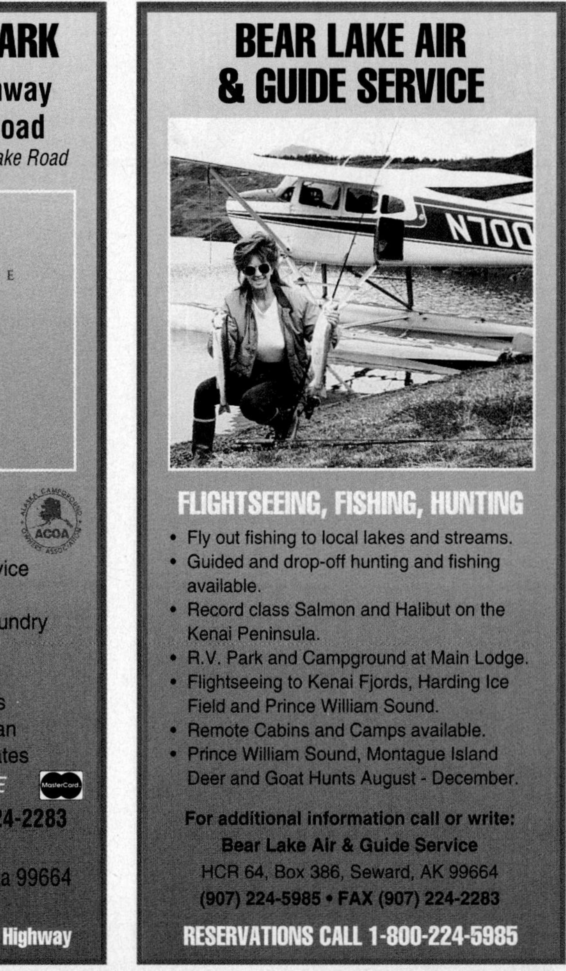

with 10 interpretive signs on forest succession. A strenuous 3.5-mile/5.6-km trail leads to Harding Icefield from the parking lot. Summer activities include ranger-led walks to the glaciers and all-day hikes to Harding Icefield. Worth the drive to see an active glacier up close. *CAUTION: Falling ice at face of glacier, stay behind warning signs.* ♿

On the drive out, note the finger dikes built along the road to protect it from erosion by the Resurrection River. The trailhead for Resurrection River trail is located just before crossing the Resurrection River bridge on the access road. The 16-mile/25.7-km USFS trail ties in with the Russian Lakes trail. It is part of the 75-mile/121-km Hope-to-Seward route. *CAUTION: Black and brown bears also use this trail.*

Creekside Cabins Bed & Breakfast. See display ad on page 485.

Le Barn Appétit Bed & Breakfast. See display ad this section.

IdidaRide Sled Dog Tours. See display ad this section.

S 3.5 (5.6 km) **A 123.5** (198.7 km) **Dave & Marie's Excellent Adventures.** See display ad this section.

S 3.2 (5.1 km) **A 123.8** (199.2 km) Nash Road; access to bed and breakfasts. It is a scenic 5-mile/8-km drive out Nash Road to Seward's Marine Industrial Center in the Fourth of July Creek valley. Fine views along the way and from Kertulla Point of Resurrection Bay and the city of Seward. At Mile 2.1 Nash Road is the trailhead for the Iditarod Trail, which begins at the ferry terminal in downtown Seward. Hike to Bear Lake; from north end of lake, trail continues to Mile 12 on the Seward Highway.

Big Timber Bed and Breakfast. Quiet comfort in a woodland setting. Elegant private suites include private entrance, sitting

room, kitchen, private bath, large bedroom with queen bed(s), phone and cable TV. Located just off Nash Road (Mile 3.2 Seward Highway) with convenient access to Seward, Exit Glacier, and famous Iditarod Trail. Hosted by Tom and Sharon Shirk, P.O. Box 2014, Seward, AK 99664. Open year-round. Brochures/reservations (907) 224-5429. VISA/MasterCard accepted. [ADVERTISEMENT]

Camelot Cottages. See display ad this section.

The Farm Bed & Breakfast. Turn off Seward Highway on Nash Road, turn left immediately on Salmon Creek Road, and follow the signs to "The Farm." Tranquil country setting on acres of trees and green grass. Elegantly casual rooms, private baths,

decks and entrances. Cable TV, barbecues. Smoking restricted. Delightful continental breakfast. "We are not in the middle of everything." Reservations welcome. VISA and MasterCard accepted. Call (907) 224-5691, fax (907) 224-2300. Your host: Jack Hoogland. P.O. Box 305, Seward, AK 99664. Open year-round. See display ad in Seward section. [ADVERTISEMENT]

Rininger's Bed & Breakfast (Mile 1.6 Nash Road) is located on Rabbit Run Road (left at fork). Open year-round. Large, sunny room with skylights and handcrafted furnishings. Private bath and kitchenette; sleeping loft, separate entrance. Breakfast in room at your leisure. Outdoor wood-heated sauna. Hiking and cross-country ski trails nearby. A

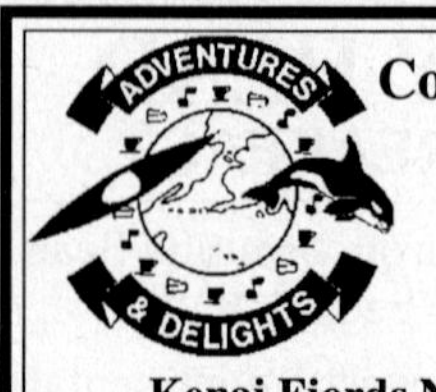

perfect weekend getaway. Families welcome. Sleeps up to 8. Kent and Lisa Rininger, P.O. Box 548, Seward, AK 99664. (907) 224-5918. [ADVERTISEMENT]

S 3 (4.8 km) **A 124** (199.6 km) Resurrection River, 3 channels and 3 highway bridges. This river, formed by snowmelt from the Harding Icefield, empties into Resurrection Bay just northeast of Seward.

Seward city limits.

S 2.7 (4.3 km) **A 124.3** (200 km) Turnoff for Seward airport.

S 2.4 (3.9 km) **A 124.6** (200.5 km) Forest Acres municipal campground; water, flush toilets, 14-day limit. No tables. ▲

S 2.1 (3.4 km) **A 124.9** (201 km) U.S. Air Force and U.S. Army Seward Recreation Area.

S 2 (3.2 km) **A 125** (201.1 km) Seward Chamber of Commerce-Convention and Visitors Bureau visitor center.

S 1.7 (2.7 km) **A 125.3** (201.6 km) **Seward Tesoro.** See display ad this section.

S 1.6 (2.6 km) **A 125.4** (201.8 km) Seward High School.

S 1.2 (1.9 km) **A 125.8** (202.4 km) Large parking area to west with memorial to Benny Benson, who designed the Alaska state flag.

S 1 (1.6 km) **A 126** (202.8 km) Main entrance to boat harbor.

Adventures & Delights. See display ad this section.

S 0.3 (0.5 km) **A 126.7** (203.9 km) Intersection of 3rd Avenue (Seward Highway) and Jefferson. Post office 1 block east. Hospital 2 blocks west. Information Cache railcar at intersection.

Seward

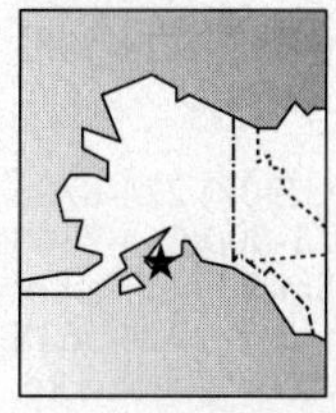

S 0 A 127 (204.4 km) Located on Resurrection Bay, east coast of Kenai Peninsula; 127 miles/204.4 km south of Anchorage by road, or 35 minutes by air. **Population:** 3,000. **Emergency Services: Police, Fire Department** and **Ambulance**, emergency only, phone 911. **State Troopers**, phone (907) 224-3346. **Hospital**, Seward General, 1st Avenue and Jefferson Street, phone (907) 224-5205. **Maritime Search and Rescue**, phone 1-800-478-5555.

Visitor Information: Available at 2 locations, operated by the Seward Chamber of Commerce-Convention and Visitors Bureau.

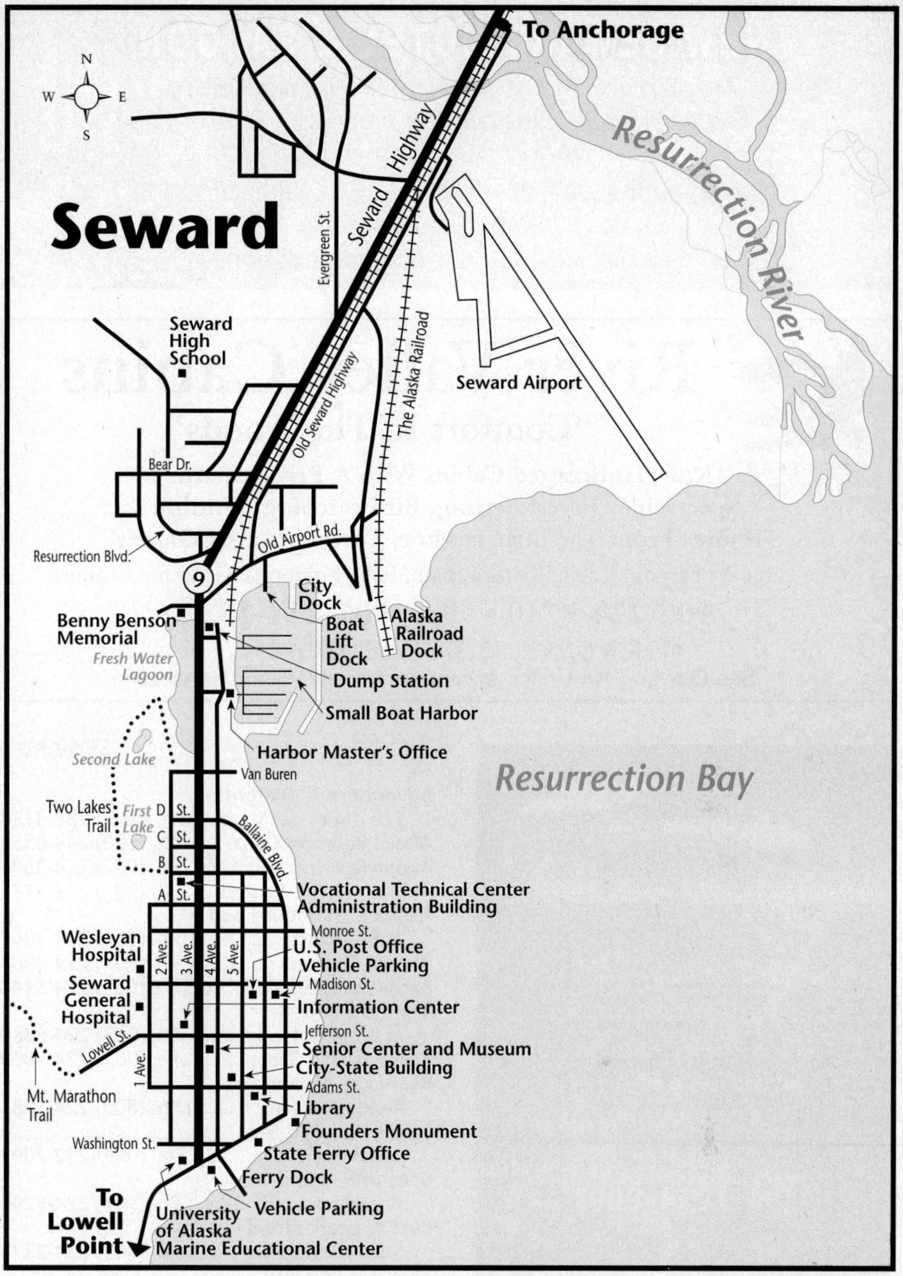

Seward

To Anchorage
Resurrection River
Seward Highway
Evergreen St.
Seward High School
Seward Airport
The Alaska Railroad
Old Seward Highway
Bear Dr.
Resurrection Blvd.
Old Airport Rd.
City Dock
Benny Benson Memorial
Boat Lift Dock
Alaska Railroad Dock
Fresh Water Lagoon
Dump Station
Small Boat Harbor
Second Lake
Harbor Master's Office
Van Buren
Resurrection Bay
Two Lakes Trail
First Lake
D St.
C St.
B St.
A St.
Ballaine Blvd.
Vocational Technical Center Administration Building
Monroe St.
Wesleyan Hospital
2 Ave.
3 Ave.
4 Ave.
5 Ave.
U.S. Post Office Vehicle Parking
Madison St.
Seward General Hospital
Information Center
Lowell St.
Jefferson St.
Senior Center and Museum
City-State Building
1 Ave.
Mt. Marathon Trail
Adams St.
Library
Founders Monument
Washington St.
State Ferry Office
Ferry Dock
To Lowell Point
University of Alaska Marine Educational Center
Vehicle Parking

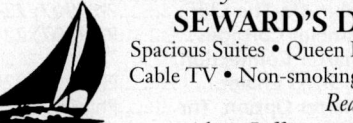

The visitor center at **Milepost S 2** Seward Highway (2001 Seward Highway) is open 7 days a week from Memorial Day through Labor Day, weekdays the rest of the year; phone 224-8051. The Information Cache, located in the historic railroad car *Seward* at 3rd and Jefferson Street, is open daily from 11 A.M. to 5 P.M., June through Aug.; write Box 749, Seward 99664.

Kenai Fjords National Park Visitor Center, 1212 4th Ave. (in the Small Boat Harbor), is open 8 A.M. to 7 P.M. daily, Memorial Day to Labor Day; 8:30 A.M. to 5 P.M. weekdays the remainder of the year. Information on the park, slide show, interpretive programs and bookstore. Phone (907) 224-3175 or write P.O. Box 1727, Seward 99664.

Chugach National Forest, Seward Ranger District office, is located at 334 4th Ave. USFS personnel can provide information on hiking, camping and fishing opportunities on national forest lands. Open weekdays, 8 A.M. to 5 P.M. Mailing address: P.O. Box 390, Seward 99664. Phone (907) 224-3374.

Elevation: Sea level. **Climate:** Average daily maximum temperature in July, 62°F/17°C; average daily minimum in Jan., 18°F/-7°C. Average annual precipitation, 67 inches; average snowfall, 80 inches. **Radio:**

SEWARD ADVERTISERS

Adventures & Delights Eco Tours ....Ph. 1-800-288-3134
Alaska Railroad Corp. ....Ph. (800) 544-0552
Alaska Renown Charters...Ph. (907) 224-3806
Alaska Wildlife Cruises....Ph. (907) 272-9775
Alaska's Treehouse Bed & Breakfast ....Ph. (907) 224-3867
Aurora Charters ....Ph. (907) 224-3968
Bardarson Studio ....Ph. (907) 224-5448
Bay Vista Bed & Breakfast ....Ph. (907) 224-5880
Beach House, The ....Ph. (907) 224-7000
Bear Lake Air and Guide Service....Ph. (800) 224-5985
Bear's Den Bed & Breakfast....Ph. 1-800-232-7099
Benson Bed and Breakfast....Ph. (907) 224-5290
Best Western Hotel Seward....Ph. (907) 224-2378
Bluefield Bed and Breakfast....Ph. (907) 224-8732
Breeze Inn Motel....Small Boat Harbor
Brown and Hawkins ....4th Ave.
Cabin-On-The-Cliff....Ph. (907) 224-8001
Camelot Cottages....Ph. (907) 224-3039
Charter Connection/ Swiss Chalet....Ph. (907) 224-4446
Charter Option, The ....Ph. (907) 224-2026
Chinook's....Small Boat Harbour
Clear Creek Cottage ....Ph. (907) 224-3968
Command Charters ....Ph. (800) 770-2833
Creekside Cabins Bed and Breakfast....Ph. (907) 224-3834
Eagle Song Bed & Breakfast....Ph. (907) 224-8755
Falcon's Way Bed & Breakfast....Ph. (907) 224-5757
Fantasea Charters ....Ph. (907) 345-0100
Farm Bed & Breakfast, The....Ph. (907) 224-5691
Fifth Avenue Lodging ....Ph. (907) 224-3412
Fish House, The ....Small Boat Harbor
Harborview Bed and Breakfast....Ph. (907) 224-3217
Harmony Bed & Breakfast....Ph. (907) 224-3661
House of Diamond Willow....2 locations—See ad
IdidaRide Sled Dog Tours..Ph.(907) 224-8607
Kenai Fjords RV Park ....Small Boat Harbor
Kenai Fjords Tours ....Ph. 1-800-478-8068
Kenai Fjords Wilderness Lodge....Ph. (907) 224-5271
Le Barn Appétit Restaurant, Bakery, Health Food Store and Bed and Breakfast ....Ph. (907) 224-8706
Major Marine Tours....Ph. 1-800-764-7300
Mariah Tours & Charters ....Small Boat Harbor
Marina Motel....Ph. (907) 224-5518
Miller's Landing....Lowell Point Rd.
Morning Calm Bed & Breakfast....Ph. (907) 224-3049
Murphy's Motel ....4th Ave. & D St.
New Seward Hotel & Saloon....Ph. (907) 224-8001
Northern Nights Bed & Breakfast....Ph. (907) 224-5688
Oldow Family Charters....Ph. (907) 563-6336
Quarterdeck B&B, The....Ph. (907) 224-2396
Ranting Raven Bakery, The ....228 4th Ave.
Ray's Waterfront ....Small Boat Harbor
Resurrect Art Coffee House Gallery....320 3rd Ave.
River Valley Cabins ....Ph. (907) 224-5740
Sablefish Charters....Ph. (907) 224-3283
Sea Lion Sports....Ph. (907) 224-7171
Seward Chamber of Commerce....Ph. (907) 224-8051
Seward Drug Co. ....Downtown
Seward Laundry ....806 4th Ave.
Seward Waterfront Lodging ....Ph. (907) 224-5563
Seward's Downtown Lodging ....Ph. (907) 224-3939
Seward's Port-of-Call Bed & Breakfast ....Ph. (907) 224-5663
Seward's Visitor Automated Helpline....Ph. 1-800-844-2424
6 Mile Bed and Breakfast ....Mile 6.3 Seward Hwy.
Taroka Inn....Ph. (907) 224-8975
Van Gilder Hotel....308 Adams St.

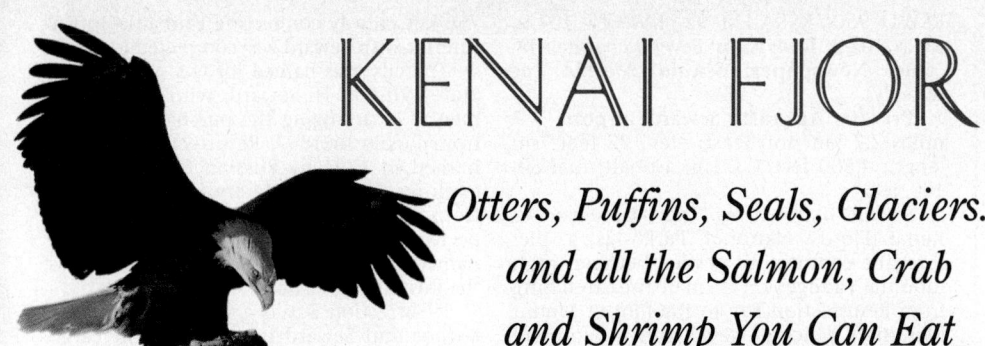

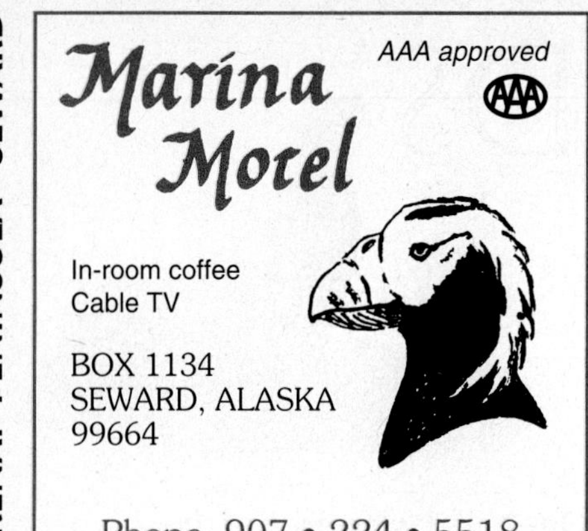

KSWD 950, KSKA-FM 92, KWAVE 104.9, KPEN 102.3. **Television:** Several channels by cable. **Newspaper:** *Seward Phoenix Log* (weekly).

Private Aircraft: Seward airport, 1.7 miles/2.7 km northeast; elev. 22 feet/7m; length 4,500 feet/1,371m; asphalt; fuel 80, 100, jet.

Seward—known as the "Gateway to Kenai Fjords National Park"—is a picturesque community nestled between high mountain ranges on a small rise stretching from Resurrection Bay to the foot of Mount Marathon. Thick groves of cottonwood and scattered spruce groves are found in the immediate vicinity of the city, with stands of spruce and alder growing on the surrounding mountainsides.

Downtown Seward (the main street is 4th Avenue) has a frontier-town atmosphere with some homes and buildings dating back to the early 1900s. The town was established in 1903 by railroad surveyors as an ocean terminal and supply center. The 470-mile/756-km railway connecting Fairbanks in the Interior with Seward was completed in 1923.

The city was named for U.S. Secretary of State William H. Seward, who was instrumental in arranging the purchase of Alaska from Russia in 1867. Resurrection Bay was named in 1791 by Russian fur trader and explorer Alexander Baranof. While sailing from Kodiak to Yakutat he found unexpected shelter in this bay from a storm and named the bay Resurrection because it was the Russian Sunday of the Resurrection.

Resurrection Bay is a year-round ice-free harbor and Seward is an important cargo port and fishing port. The Alaska state ferry MV *Tustumena* calls at Seward.

Seward's economic base includes tourism, a coal terminal, sawmill, fisheries and government offices. The Alaska Vocational Technical Center is located here.

ACCOMMODATIONS/VISITOR SERVICES

All visitor facilities, including hotels, motels, bed and breakfasts, cafes and restaurants, post office, grocery stores, drugstore, travel agencies, gift shops, gas stations, bars, laundromats, churches, bowling alley and theater.

The Harbormaster Building has public restrooms and pay showers, mailbox and pay phones. Weather information is available here during the summer. Public restrooms and pay showers on Ballaine Boulevard along the ocean between the boat harbor and town. Dump station and drinking water fill-up at the Small Boat Harbor at the end of 4th Avenue (see city map). There are picnic areas with covered tables along Ballaine Blvd. just south of the harbor, and at Adams Street.

Seward has made a good effort to provide overnight parking for self-contained RVs. There are designated camping areas along the shore south of Van Buren; camping fee

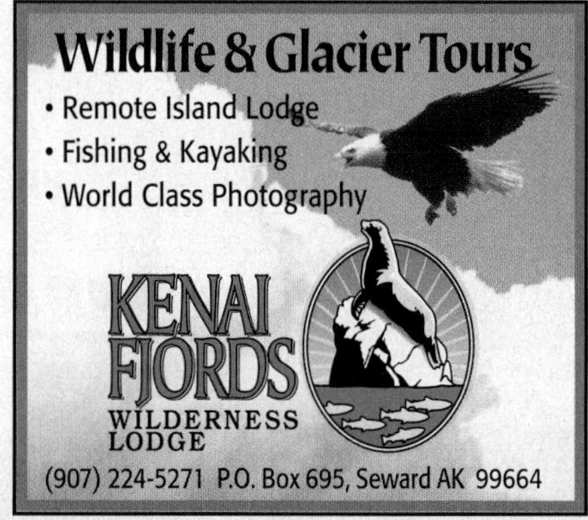

charged. RV parking is marked by signs. (Caravans: contact the City Parks and Recreation Dept. for reservations, phone 907/ 224-3331.) Forest Acres municipal campground is at **Milepost S 2.4** Seward Highway. Private RV parks at Small Boat Harbor, at **Milepost S 6.6** and on Lowell Point Road. Tent camping also available at Exit Glacier (turnoff at **Milepost S 3.7** Seward Highway). ▲

Alaska's Treehouse Bed and Breakfast. Nestled in the trees at the edge of town. Spectacular views of the Chugach Mountains from the solarium. Hiking and skiing trails at your doorstep, fishing nearby. Relax in the hand-built, wood-fired sauna. Breakfast—hearty Alaskan sourdough pancakes and waffles served with local wild berry sauces. Hosted by long-time Alaskans. Large, comfortable, smoke-free rooms. Accommodating singles to small groups. Open year-round. Phone (907) 224-3867; P.O. Box 861, Seward, AK 99664. [ADVERTISEMENT]

Bay Vista Bed & Breakfast is nestled at the bottom of Mount Marathon with a spectacular panoramic view of Resurrection Bay. Two private suites with a spacious sitting room, phone, TV/VCR, fridge, microwave, and private entrance. Walk to harbor, train, bus/trolley. Shared and private baths. Open year-round! Jeff and Vera Johnson, P.O. Box 1232, Seward, AK 99664. (907) 224-5880. [ADVERTISEMENT]

Benson Bed and Breakfast. Family atmosphere, smoke-free. Queen/double beds, private baths. Full breakfast. Quiet neighborhood near harbor, groceries, bike path, bus, train, visitor center. Hosts: Rich and Sandy Houghton, long-time Alaskans with 8 years experience living and teaching above the Arctic Circle at Kivalina and Noatak. Open year-round. 209 Benson, P.O. Box 3506, Seward, AK 99664. (907) 224-5290. [ADVERTISEMENT]

Best Western Hotel Seward. Enjoy being in the center of activity, yet in a quiet setting overlooking Resurrection Bay. Our 1991 extensive expansion includes breathtaking view rooms with in-room coffee and your own refrigerator. And check this out! For your in-room entertainment, all rooms include (1) remote control TVs with cablevision, (2) remote control VCRs with videotape rental available and (3) 2 channels of free in-room movies featuring the latest hits! Complimentary scheduled shuttle bus service for our guests to boat harbor, train depot and airport. We accept all major credit cards. Reservations (907) 224-2378 or (800) 478-4050 inside Alaska. Fax (907) 224-3112. See display ad this section. [ADVERTISEMENT]

Bluefield Bed and Breakfast, found in a quiet neighborhood at the foot of Mt. Marathon, surrounded by lovely gardens. Easy walking distance to boat harbor, railroad depot, shops and fine restaurants. Private entrance to your spacious room with king bed and double-futon sitting area. Tea cart, jacuzzi in private bath. Breakfast table in room serving a hearty, gourmet, continental breakfast at your leisure. Liz, Duane and Darcy Harp, P.O. Box 2068, Seward, AK 99664; (907) 224-8732. [ADVERTISEMENT]

Camelot Cottages. 1.4 Mile Salmon Creek Road: Affordable, clean, cozy furnished cabins with private baths and fully equipped kitchenettes. Linens, housekeeping services provided. Nestled in a natural woodland setting, the smaller cabins sleep 2-4 comfortably, the beautiful natural wood Chalet sleeps up to 8. Private, family friendly, owned and operated by longtime Alaskans. 1-800-739-3039, (907) 346-3039 Anchorage, (907) 224-3039 Seward. See display ad Mile 3.2 Seward Highway. [ADVERTISEMENT]

Chinook's Waterfront Restaurant, an unforgettable Alaskan experience in dining. We specialize in fresh Alaskan seafood. Chinook's offers the most spectacular view in Seward. You will often see sea lions, eagles, otters, salmon and seals right from your table. Located in the small boat harbor. (907) 224-2207; Box 2786, Seward, AK

99664. [ADVERTISEMENT]

Clear Creek Cottage. Fully furnished smoke-free 2-bedroom cabin, full kitchen. Sleeps up to 8. Clean, comfortable, affordable rates. Perfect hideaway for couples, families, small groups. On the banks of Clear Creek, on Resurrection River Road to Exit Glacier, Mile 3.7 Seward Highway. 7 minutes to downtown Seward. (907) 224-3968. Fax (907) 224-7230. P.O. Box 241, Seward, AK 99664. [ADVERTISEMENT]

Creekside Cabins Bed and Breakfast. Nonsmoking. Clean, cozy cabins; tent sites. Central heated restrooms with sauna and showers. Located on beautiful Clear Creek, surrounded by tall spruce. Peaceful country setting for a relaxing stay. Phone (907) 224-3834. See display ad Mile 3.7 Seward Highway. Take first right off Exit Glacier Road, follow signs. Also available: cozy, fully-equipped, 2-bedroom log home. Beautiful view. Nightly or weekly rentals. Separate location. [ADVERTISEMENT] ▲

Eagle Song Bed & Breakfast is located in a peaceful country setting in the shadow of an active bald eagles' nest, easy 15 minute

commute from Seward. We offer 4 bedrooms, with queen size beds, 2 shared baths, full country breakfast, smoking outside, no alcohol, adults only. VISA and MasterCard. (907) 224-8755, P.O. Box 2231, Seward, AK 99664. [ADVERTISEMENT]

Harborview Bed and Breakfast. 900 3rd and C Street. New rooms with private entrances, private baths, color cable television, telephone, Alaska Native fine art. Just 10-minute walk to: tour boats, fishing charters, downtown and laundromat. Ask about "Seaview," our newly remodeled 2-bedroom apartments on the beachfront, breathtaking view of snowcapped mountains and bay. All nonsmoking. $85. Early reservations advised. Alaska Native hostess. Phone/fax (907) 224-3217; P.O. Box 1305, Seward, AK 99664. [ADVERTISEMENT]

Harmony Bed & Breakfast, nestled peacefully in Forrest Acres and conveniently close to town and harbor. Private entrance, private bath. Very clean, new rooms with all the comforts of home. Open year-round with reasonable rates. Call Carol for information and reservations. (907) 224-3661. P.O. Box 1606, Seward, AK 99664. [ADVERTISEMENT]

Kenai Fjords Wilderness Lodge. Remote island lodge overlooking the Kenai Fjords National Park. Guided wildlife, natural history and glacier tours daily deep into the Kenai Fjords. Experience calving glaciers, whales, sea otters, puffins, eagles and much more. Sea kayaking, hiking, canoeing and excellent fishing. Photographer's paradise. P.O. Box 695, Seward, AK 99664, phone (907) 224-5271. [ADVERTISEMENT]

Le Barn Appétit Restaurant, Bakery, Health Food Store and Bed and Breakfast. Creekside setting in the trees; beautiful views. Nonsmoking, nonalcoholic. Families welcome. Petting park for small children. Giant teeter-totter. Breakfast, lunch and dinner. Continental cuisine. Omelettes, crépes, quiches, seafood specialties. European-style coffees and teas. VISA, MasterCard accepted. Your hosts: Yvon and Janet Van Driessche, P.O. Box 601, Seward, AK 99664. Phone (907) 224-8706 or (907) 224-3462. Fax (907) 224-8461. Mile 3.7 Seward Highway, first right off Exit Glacier Road. [ADVERTISEMENT]

Miller's Landing. Alaskan family operated fishing, tent/RV campground located on family homestead. Boat and pole rentals, fishing/sightseeing charters (full and half day), water taxi service to remote fishing areas, boat launch, kayak dropoffs to Aialik Glacier, Holgate Arm, Fox Island. Catch king salmon, Dolly Varden, pink, silver, chum salmon from beach, catch halibut from boat rentals or charters. Scenic campground located on Resurrection Bay. See sea otters, eagles, seals from camp. Private beaches. Hiking trail to Caine's Head State Park. Cozy cabin rentals, $40. Country store sells bait, tackle, ice, fishing licenses, T-shirts, hats, gifts. Pull-through electric RV sites, 20/30/50 amps; large tent sites. Beach sites or forested sites. Showers (included in camping cost). Phone. Mike Miller homesteaded here. He's an expert on fishing advice and visitor information. Survived 1964 earthquake. Free coffee. Fishing advice 5¢. Guaranteed effective or your nickel back! Down-home Alaskan atmosphere. Reservations accepted/advisable for guaranteed arrivals only. $12.50 dry camp, $17.50 electric. Box 81, Seward, AK 99664. (907) 224-5739. [ADVERTISEMENT] ▲

Morning Calm Bed and Breakfast. A touch of the Orient in Alaska. Quiet residential neighborhood near the visitor center, small boat harbor and railroad depot. Nonsmoking. Two rooms, queen and twin beds,

shared bath. Hot tub. In-room TV/VCR. Open year-round. The Martins, P.O. Box 816, Seward, AK 99664. (907) 224-3049. [ADVERTISEMENT]

New Seward Hotel & Saloon. Centrally located in downtown Seward, within walking distance of shops, ferry, bus terminal, boat harbor; 35 rooms featuring TV, phones, free videos. Some kitchenettes. Salmon and halibut fishing charters or Kenai Fjords tours available. Year-round service. Brochure. All major credit cards accepted. Reservations (907) 224-8001. Fax (907) 224-3112. See display ad this section. [ADVERTISEMENT]

River Valley Cabins. New handcrafted cabins paneled in knotty pine, open beam ceiling. Large bedroom, bath, sitting room, phone, carpet, electric heat, continental

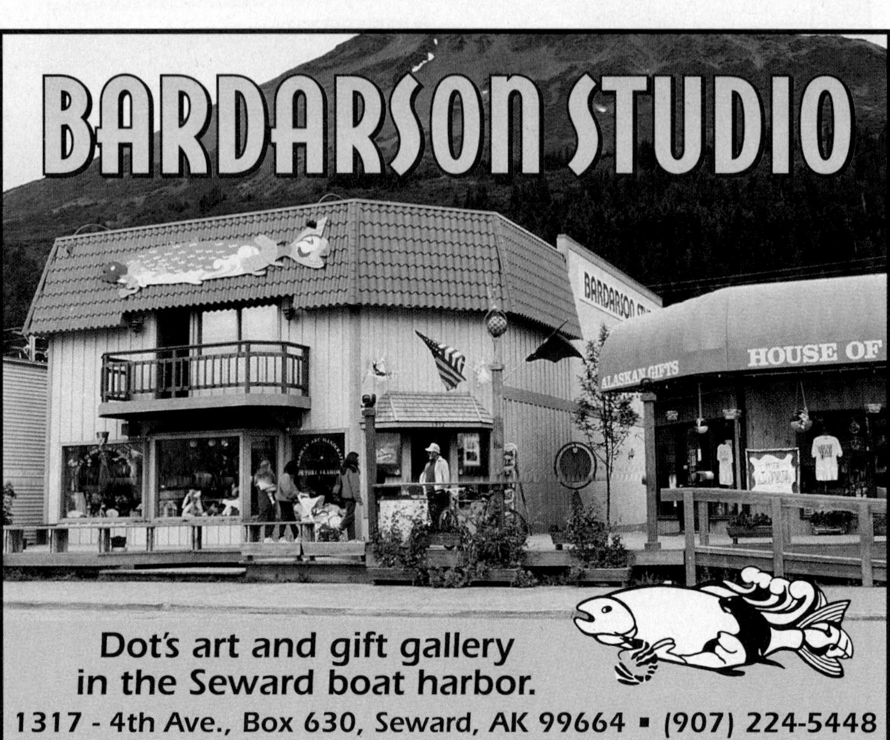

Bear's Den Bed & Breakfast

• Luxurious studio-style B&B • Sleeps up to 6 • Spectacular view of Resurrection Bay
• Guest deck • Private entry • Private bath • Kitchenette • Cable TV
• Continental breakfast • Evening popcorn • Coffee & Tea • Smoking outside only

1-800-232-7099 • (907) 224-3788

Richard & Shareen Adelmann • Box 2142, Seward, AK 99664

SEWARD WATERFRONT LODGING

Bed and Breakfast

Downtown ✳ Open Year-Round

550 Railway • Overlooking The Bay

Hosted By 30-Year Alaskans

(907) 224-5563 ✳ Fax (907) 224-2397

VISA PO Box 618, Seward, AK 99664 

The Beach House

(907) 224-7000

Your Own House At B&B Prices

200′ From Bay On Magical Lowell Pt.

True Family Value—Sleeps 6

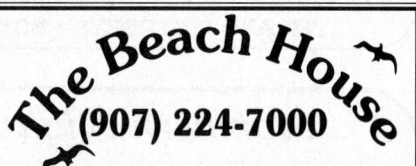

Kenai Fjords RV Park

30 Spaces with electric hookups

24-hour registration

Fishing & sightseeing information

Phone (907) 224-8779 • PO Box 2772, Seward, Alaska 99664

Small Boat Harbor • Mile 1 Seward Highway

FANTASEA CHARTERS

Resurrection Bay ❖ Seward, Alaska

Halibut ❖ Salmon ❖ Bottom Fish

Best Private Charter Rates

(907) 345-0100

Mail: 5131 Metz Court, Anchorage, AK 99516

breakfast. Secluded on 7 acres of forested land. Open year-round. Large, cozy 2-bedroom cabin, kitchen, bath, fully equipped. Non-smoking. Take Exit Glacier turnoff, then first road to the right, drive 3/4 mile. Look for our sign on the right. HCR 64, Box 3517, Seward, AK 99664. Phone (907) 224-5740, fax (907) 224-2333. [ADVERTISEMENT]

6 Mile Bed & Breakfast, Lake Drive. Antiques and quilts furnish spacious, skylit room in farm setting of Alaskan gardens. Birdwatch from private balcony. Country breakfast featuring award-winning berry products, served on local pottery. Private bath with handcrafted cabinetry and tile. Separate entrance. Sleeps up to 8. Families welcome! Open year-round. Walkers, Box 112, Seward, AK 99664; (907) 224-3848. [ADVERTISEMENT]

Taroka Inn. Clean, homey units with equipped kitchens, private bathrooms, color cable TV. Queen beds, one in separate bedroom. Suitable for larger parties (up to 7 adults), longer stays, or for those wishing to save by dining in. Pets, upon approval. Convenient downtown location. Our rates are among the most reasonable in Seward. (907) 224-8975. See display ad this section. [ADVERTISEMENT]

Van Gilder Hotel. Seward's favorite small hotel, built in 1916 and completely renovated for the 1990s. Now a National Historic Site, it retains its original Edwardian charm. Centrally located at 308 Adams Street in downtown Seward within easy walking distance of restaurants and shops. Clean, casual, comfortable rooms for tourists and business travelers. For hotel reservations call 1-800-204-6835. P.O. Box 2, Seward, AK, 99664. Fax (907) 224-3689. Our tour desk can book your tours, charters or complete itinerary. Tour desk: 1-800-204-2404. See display ad this section. [ADVERTISEMENT]

TRANSPORTATION

Air: Seward airport is reached by turning east on Airport Road at **Milepost S 2.7** on the Seward Highway. Scheduled daily service to Anchorage; charters also available.

Highway: Seward is reached via the 127-mile/203.2-km Seward Highway from Anchorage.

Ferry: Alaska Marine Highway office on Cruise Ship Dock; phone (907) 224-5485. The Alaska ferry MV *Tustumena* departs Seward for Kodiak and Valdez. See the MARINE ACCESS ROUTES section for schedule.

Bus: Scheduled service to Anchorage.

Railroad: The Alaska Railroad connects Seward to Anchorage and Fairbanks. See the ALASKA RAILROAD section.

Taxi: Service available.

ATTRACTIONS

The Railcar *Seward* houses the chamber of commerce information center. Located at 3rd and Jefferson Street, this railcar was the Seward observation car on the Alaska Railroad from 1936 until the early 1960s. Information and detailed map of the city are available.

Walking Tour of Seward encompasses more than 30 attractions including homes and businesses that date back to the early 1900s; some are still being used, while others have been restored as historic sites. A brochure containing details on all the attractions of the tour is available at the railcar information center. The complete tour covers about 2 miles/3.2 km and takes about 1 to 2 hours, depending upon how much time you wish to spend browsing.

Marine Educational Center, maintained by the University of Alaska, has laboratories, aquaculture ponds and the vessel *Alpha Helix,* which carries on oceanographic research in Alaskan waters. There is a marine display here. Open 1–5 P.M. weekdays, 10 A.M. to noon and 1–5 P.M. on Saturday, June through August.

Visit the Small Boat Harbor. This municipal harbor, built after the 1964 earthquake, is home port to fishing boats, charter boats and sightseeing boats. The harbor is also home to sea otters; watch for them! Visitors may notice the great number of sailboats moored here: many are members of the William H. Seward Yacht Club, which sponsors an annual sailboat and yacht show.

Seward Museum, at Jefferson and 3rd Avenue, is operated by the Resurrection Bay Historical Society (Box 55, Seward 99664). The museum features artifacts and photographs from the 1964 earthquake, WWII, the founding days of Seward, and other highlights of Seward's history. Also on display is a collection of Native baskets and ivory carvings. The museum is open daily, 11 A.M. to 5 P.M., May 15 to Sept. 30. Open reduced hours remainder of year; check locally, or phone (907) 224-3902. A modest admission fee is charged.

Seward Community Library, across from the City–State Bldg., presents (on request) short slide/sound shows on a variety of subjects and has some informative displays. A program on the 1964 earthquake is shown daily at 2 P.M. (except Sunday) from June 15 through the first Saturday in Sept.

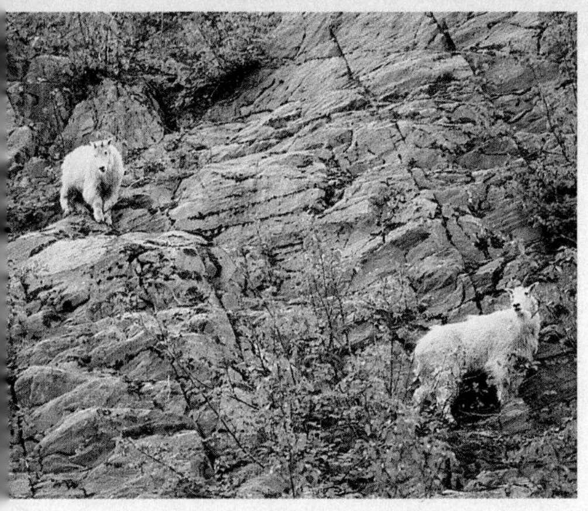

Mountain goats at Exit Glacier.
(© Rich Reid)

Library hours are 1–8 P.M. Monday through Friday, 1–6 P.M. Saturday.

St. Peter's Episcopal Church is 3 blocks west of the museum at the corner of 2nd Avenue and Adams Street. It was built in 1906 and is considered the oldest Protestant church on the Kenai Peninsula. A feature is the unique painting of the Resurrection, for which Alaskans were used as models and Resurrection Bay as the background. Well-known Dutch artist Jan Van Emple was commissioned to paint the picture in 1925 when he was living in Seward. Obtain key to church from the Information Cache in season.

Hiking Trails. Two Lakes trail is an easy mile-long loop trail along the base of Mount Marathon. The trail passes through a wooded area and follows what used to be Hemlock Street. Beautiful view of marina below and north end of Resurrection Bay. Start at First Lake, behind the Alaska Vocational and Technical Center Administration Bldg. at 2nd Avenue and B Street.

The National Historic Iditarod Trail begins at the ferry terminal and follows a marked course through town, then north on the Seward Highway. At Mile 2.1 Nash Road (turn off at **Milepost S 3.2** Seward Highway), the trail continues from a gravel parking area on the east side of Sawmill Creek north to Bear Lake. The trail eventually rejoins the Seward Highway at **Milepost S 12.**

Caines Head State Recreation Area, 6 miles/9.6 km south of Seward, is accessible by boat or via a 4.5-mile/7.2-km beach trail (low tide only). The trailhead/parking is located about Mile 2 Lowell Point Road. The Caines Head area has bunkers and gun emplacements that were used to guard the entrance to Resurrection Bay during WWII.

Mount Marathon Race™, Seward's annual Fourth of July endurance race to the top and back of Mount Marathon (elev. 3,022 feet/921m), is a grueling test for athletes. The race is said to have begun in 1909 with a wager between 2 sourdoughs as to how long it would take to run up and down Mount Marathon. The first year of the official race is uncertain, but records indicate either 1912 or 1915. Fastest recorded time is 43 minutes, 23 seconds set in 1981 by Bill Spencer, who broke his own 1974 record. The descent is so steep that it's part run, part jump, and part slide. The race attracts competitors from all over, and thousands of spectators line the route each year.

Kenai Fjords National Park

Alaska's #1 Glacier and Wildlife Cruise

Superlatives come easy in Alaska. The biggest, the highest, and so on. However, it's almost impossible to use too many superlatives when describing the beauty encountered while visiting Kenai Fjords National Park. It's an awe-inspiring combination of scenery and activity: the most magnificent coastal mountains, the most spectacular glaciers, and home to an astounding variety of Alaska's watchable wildlife. The best way to experience this incredible part of Alaska is by taking a day cruise with the "Fjord Experts" at Kenai Fjords Tours.

A Bit of History

About 20 years ago, Pamela Oldow and her good friend Sheila Scoby began operating tours (mostly for "birding groups") of the area, even before it was a national park. Pam and Sheila ran most of the cruises themselves. In 1978, Cecil Andrus, then U.S. Secretary of the Interior under President Carter, rode with Pam to evaluate the Kenai Fjords for national park status. The steep-sided fjords, massive glaciers, and rich animal habitat were so outstanding that the Kenai Fjords were set aside in 1980 as a national park. "Pam and Sheila's love for the area was evident on every cruise," commented Tom Tougas, Kenai Fjords Tours' present owner. That same love for the fjords still drives the company's operation today.

High Concentrations of Marine Mammals

All of Kenai Fjords Tours' captains are trained and experienced naturalists who provide cruise commentary and scout for wildlife. Seeing both marine and land mammals on a Kenai Fjords Tours cruise is not uncommon. "Whales seem to be on the top of everyone's list. We see gray whales in the spring, humpback whales throughout the summer, and both transient and resident pods of orcas (killer whales). Even when we don't happen to come upon a whale, we're sure to see Steller sea lions, otters, seals, maybe a group of harbor porpoise—we never know exactly what we're going to see on any given day, but it's always a great experience," says Captain Eric Olsen, manager of Kenai Fjords Tours' vessel operations. In the spring, mountain goat with their newborn can be seen at the shoreline. On occasion, black bear can even be viewed from the vessels.

Puffins, Puffins, and a Lot More!

Avid birders and casual bird-watchers alike appreciate the variety of species found in the area. Biologists have counted over 100 different types of birds in the Kenai Fjords, including the colorful tufted and horned puffins, black oystercatchers, bald eagles, cormorants, murres, and kittiwakes. Captain Olsen says his skippers think nothing of going out of their way to find a particular species of bird for a passenger with a "life list" of birds they have spotted.

Harding Ice Field: Birthplace of Glaciers

The Kenai Fjords were formed by glaciers. The whole park is capped by the Harding Ice Field, one of the last remaining ice fields in the world today. Within the 580,000-acre park there are over 40 glaciers, many of them cascading all the way down to the sea. "We spend quite a bit of time on our cruises at the face of tidewater glaciers. They put on a magnificent show, 'calving' ice right into the ocean," says Tougas. "Holgate and Northwestern Glaciers are just two of the most spectacular ones we visit."

Why Kenai Fjords Tours is Alaska's #1 Choice

Over the years, Kenai Fjords Tours has kept with its tradition of offering a consistently high-quality experience. Many Alaskan families enjoy cruising with Kenai Fjords Tours every summer. It's fun, educational, and no two cruises are ever exactly the same. Kenai Fjords Tours has the finest cruise vessels, custom-built for up-close glacier and wildlife viewing. "Investing in new boats means that we can offer our passengers an experience that's totally unique to our company. All vessels are stabilized for a smoother ride. We've also built our boats with a balance of inside seating area and lots of outside deck space. Deck accessibility is important because that's where you can take the best photos, and see and hear all of the action," says Tougas. Most of the boats are 90–95 feet in length, handicapped-accessible, and have spacious seating.

How to Get to Kenai Fjords

The community of Seward, Alaska is the gateway to the fjords. It's located in the southcentral region of Alaska, on the Kenai Peninsula. From Anchorage, visitors can reach Seward easily in 3–4 hours by car, bus, or via the Alaska Railroad. It's one of the most popular day trips from Anchorage.

Kenai Fjords Tours cruises from the Seward small boat harbor every day, May 1st through October 1st. A variety of cruises is offered, including: specialty cruises in April to watch for the annual northbound migration of Pacific gray whales, 4-hour Resurrection Bay tours, 6- and 8-1/2-hour cruises that focus on both the glaciers and wildlife of the national park, 9-hour cruises to cathedral-like Northwestern Fjord, and afternoon and evening dinner cruises featuring fresh Alaska seafood. New for 1996, the company will offer a special salmon barbecue included with Resurrection Bay cruises, served to guests on a secluded private island. Cost for cruises ranges from $49 to $129, and reservations are highly recommended. Special children's rates and transportation packages are available. For more information, contact Kenai Fjords Tours at 1-800-478-8068. Outside of the U.S., call 907-224-8068.

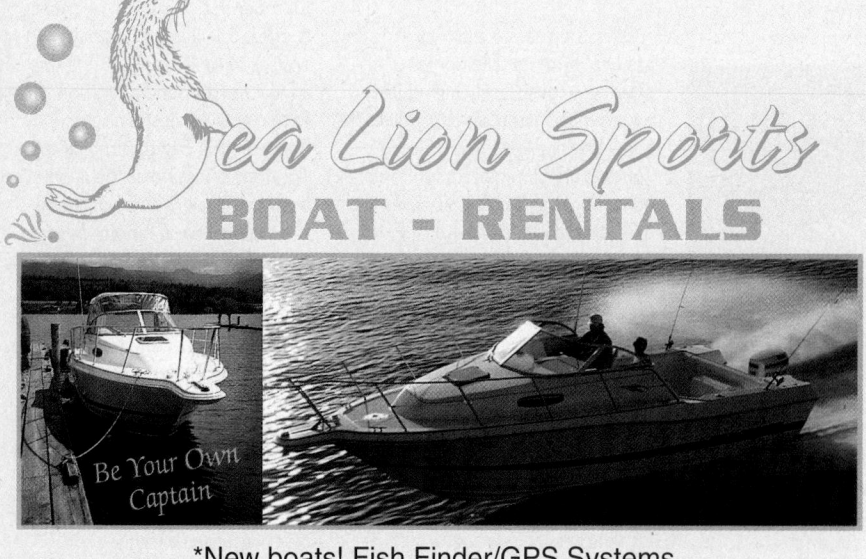

Annual Seward Silver Salmon Derby™ in Aug. is one of the largest sporting events in Alaska. It is held over 9 days, starting the second Saturday in Aug. through Sunday of the following weekend. 1996 will be the derby's 41st year. Record derby catch to date is a 20.59-lb. salmon caught off Twin Rocks by John Westlund of Anchorage.

There is more than $140,000 in prizes for the derby, including $10,000 in cash for the largest fish. Also part of the derby are the sought-after tagged silvers worth as much as $25,000. Prizes are sponsored by various merchants and the chamber of commerce.

The town fills up fast during the derby: Make reservations! For more information contact the Seward Chamber of Commerce; phone (907) 224-8051.

Annual Seward Halibut Jackpot Tournament runs the entire month of July. First, second and third place prizes awarded for heaviest fish. In 1994 the winner weighed in at 232 lbs. A 360-lb. halibut was reeled in in 1993. That was the largest halibut reported caught in southcentral Alaska that year.

Kenai Fjords National Park. Seward is the gateway to this popular 650,000-acre national park. Dominant feature of the park is the Harding Icefield, a 700-square-mile vestige of the last ice age. Harding Icefield can be reached by a strenuous all-day hike from the base of Exit Glacier or by a charter flightseeing trip out of Seward.

The fjords of the park were formed when glaciers flowed down to the sea from the ice field and then retreated, leaving behind the deep inlets that characterize the coastline here. Substantial populations of marine mammals inhabit or migrate through the park's coastal waters, including sea otters, Steller sea lions, dolphins and whales. Icebergs from calving glaciers provide ideal refuge for harbor seals, and the rugged coastline provides habitat for more than 100,000 nesting birds. The park's spectacular scenery and wildlife may be viewed by daily tour and charter boats or by charter planes. Four public-use cabins along the coast are available in summer by reservation; kayakers can also camp on beaches. *NOTE: Private boaters should consult with local outfitters and charter operators for detailed information on boating conditions.*

Seward's busy harbor is port to fishing boats, pleasure crafts, tour boats and visiting cruise ships. (Jerrianne Lowther, staff)

Exit Glacier is the most accessible of the park's glaciers. Turn at **Milepost S 3.7** on the Seward Highway and follow Exit Glacier Road to the visitor center parking area. There are several trails through the outwash plain of Exit Glacier that afford excellent views of the ice and surrounding mountains. A 0.2-mile paved trail is wheelchair accessible and leads from the parking lot to an information display. Ranger-led hikes are available in summer at Exit Glacier, where there are a picnic area and walk-in campground. Visitor information is available at the Exit Glacier ranger station and visitor center; open summer only. Exit Glacier is accessible in winter by skis, dogsled or snow machine. A public-use cabin is available by permit; phone (907) 224-3175. *CAUTION: Active glacier with unstable ice. Do not walk past warning signs!* ♿

Slide programs, videos, exhibits and information on Kenai Fjords National Park and organized activities at the park are available at the park visitor center on 4th Avenue in the Small Boat Harbor area next to the Harbormaster's office. The center is open daily from Memorial Day to Labor Day; hours are 8 A.M. to 7 P.M. The remainder of the year hours are 8 A.M. to 5 P.M. (subject to change) weekdays. Phone (907) 224-3175 or write the park superintendent, Box 1727, Seward 99664.

Adventures & Delights Eco Tours. Alaskan coastal kayaking in Kenai Fjords, Prince William Sound, Shuyiak and the Aleutian Islands. Paddle amongst ice laden fjords and along pristine waterways, where

the observation of whales, seals, sea lions, otters, and a remarkable variety of seabirds is a rewarding possibility. No experience necessary on guided tours. Rentals for experienced sea kayakers. Free brochures. 414 "K" Street, Suite MP, Anchorage, AK 99501. Toll free 1-800-288-3134. [ADVERTISEMENT]

Alaska Wildlife Cruises. Our low-priced 4½-hour cruises of the Kenai Fjords feature incredible glaciers and up-close wildlife—otters, sea lions, puffins, eagles, porpoises, whales and more. Cruise aboard a 115-foot boat with reserved seating and inside heated cabin. Close-up wildlife viewing and photography is easy from our outside decks. Snacks and full-beverage service on board. The tour departs from Seward's Boat Harbor at noon and 6 P.M. Cost: $64. Rail and bus packages available from Anchorage. Reservations/free brochure, call: (907) 272-9775. Alaska Wildlife Cruises, 509 West 3rd, Anchorage, AK 99501. [ADVERTISEMENT]

Bardarson Studio. In Seward find Bardarson Studio on the prettiest boardwalk in the boat harbor area, with the best selection of Alaska art and fine crafts set to music. Bardarson Studio recognizes that shopping is entertainment for travelers, providing a Kiddie-Kave for children, and a video room for your non-shopper. Public restroom and postal service available. 1317 4th Avenue. Phone 1-800-354-0141. [ADVERTISEMENT]

Bear Lake Air and Guide Service. Exclusive floatplane service from beautiful Bear Lake. Flightseeing, air charters, fly-in day fishing. Guiding services for big game hunting. Bunkhouse for rent. Shuttle service available. Reservations welcome, 1-800-224-5985. Bear Lake Air Service office located at Bear Creek RV Park, Mile 6.6 Seward Highway, drive 1/2 mile on Bear Lake Road. [ADVERTISEMENT]

Command Charters. Sportfishing for halibut, silver salmon, rockfish in beautiful Resurrection Bay/Kenai Fjords. Sightseeing and hunting. USCG licensed. Individuals and small parties welcome. All gear provided. May to Oct. In Alaska phone (907) 694-2833 or 1-800-770-2833. [ADVERTISEMENT]

The Fish House. First and finest fishing charter service in Seward! Record class halibut and silver salmon fishing charters available now. While fishing, enjoy the scenic

beauty of the Kenai Fjords National Park—glaciers, mountains, puffins, whales, sea otters and seals. The Fish House also supplies a complete line of fishing tackle, bait, ice and outboard motor repairs. Come, fish Alaska's biggest salmon derby with more than $100,000 in cash and prizes. Derby begins 2nd Saturday in Aug. Call now for reservations or information on fishing the scenic waters surrounding Seward, Alaska. 1-800-257-7760 or (907) 224-3674. Halibut charters: May 1–Oct. 1; Halibut Derby July 1–July 31. Salmon charters: July 1–Sept. 20. P.O. Box 1209, Seward, AK 99664. See display ad this section. [ADVERTISEMENT]

IdidaRide Sled Dog Tours. Experience dog mushing, summer style, on a 2-mile wilderness dog sled ride at Iditarod racer Mitch Seavey's training location. Informative tour includes 80-husky kennel, cuddly puppies, arctic equipment demonstration. P.O. Box 2906, Seward, AK 99664. (907) 224-8607, fax (907) 224-8608. Off Exit Glacier Road. See display ad Mile 3.7 Seward Highway. [ADVERTISEMENT]

Kenai Fjords Tours. The excitement begins the moment you pull away from the Seward boat harbor! You'll be greeted by playful sea otters, look for whales and porpoise, photograph colorful puffins, bald eagles, and watch a calving glacier. Kenai Fjords Tours is the original Kenai Fjords National Park tour, and continues to be the

most popular. Our comfortable cruisers have walk-around decks, so you can easily watch and photograph the magnificent scenery. Our captains are experienced naturalists, so you'll learn all about this coastal wilderness from guides who really know the area. Lunches and beverages served on board. For reservations or more information about how you can enjoy Alaska's finest nature tour, call toll-free 1-800-478-8068. Our office is located in The Landing at the Seward Small Boat Harbor. Look for our display ad in this section. [ADVERTISEMENT]

Major Marine Kenai Fjords Wildlife Tours. Join us for Seward's famous wildlife cruises of the Kenai Fjords. We offer two wonderful cruise options: 1) A 4 1/2-hour wildlife cruise of the Kenai Fjords, and 2) An 8-hour wildlife cruise of the Kenai Fjords National Park and Chiswell Islands National Wildlife Refuge, narrated by a Kenai Fjords National Park Ranger. Both cruises include incredible glaciers and up-close wildlife—otters, sea lions, puffins, eagles, porpoises, whales, bird colonies and more. The tour boats feature reserved table seating, inside heated cabins and multiple outside decks for close-up wildlife viewing and photography. The 4 1/2-hour cruise features an all-you-can-eat salmon, crab and shrimp buffet with dessert bar. On the 8-hour cruise, you'll be served an all-you-can-eat salmon buffet with all the trimmings. Both cruises sail from Seward's boat harbor May to late Sept. The 8-hour cruise departs at 10:30 A.M. and costs $99. The 4 1/2-hour cruise departs at 12 P.M. ($79) and 6 P.M. ($69). For reservations or free brochure, call: 1-800-764-7300 or (907) 274-7300. Major Marine Tours, 509 West 3rd, Anchorage, AK 99501. Ticket office also located on Seward boardwalk: (907) 224-8030 (May to Sept.). [ADVERTISEMENT]

Mariah Tours & Charters offers 16 years experience of guided tours to Kenai Fjords National Park and the Chiswell Islands Wildlife Refuge. Our custom-built 22 passenger ships offer the small ship alternative to

Kenai Fjords National Park, for a more personalized, uncrowded tour. Also featuring tours to spectacular Northwestern Glacier via Granite Passage, the most scenic area within Kenai Fjords National Park. Popular exclusive tours for birding and naturalist groups and other interested parties. Operating April 20–Sept. 30. For reservations: 1-800-270-1238. In Anchorage: (907) 243-1238. See display ad this section. [ADVERTISEMENT]

AREA FISHING: Resurrection Bay, coho (silver) salmon to 22 lbs., use herring, troll or cast, July to Oct.; king salmon to 45 lbs., May to Aug.; also bottom fish, flounder, halibut to 300 lbs. and cod, use weighted spoons and large red spinners by jigging, year-round. Charter and rental boats are available.

Kenai Peninsula
STERLING HIGHWAY

Junction with Seward Highway to Homer, Alaska
Includes Seldovia
Alaska Route 1
(See maps, pages 504–505)

The Sterling Highway begins 90 miles/145 km south of Anchorage at its junction with the Seward Highway and travels 142.5 miles/229.3 km west and south to the community of Homer. The Sterling Highway junctions with several major Kenai Peninsula side roads: Skilak Lake Loop Road, Swanson River Road, Kenai Spur Highway, Kalifornsky Beach Road, Cohoe Loop Road and Anchor River Beach Road.

From its junction with the Seward Highway at Tern Lake (see SEWARD HIGHWAY section), the Sterling passes through Chugach National Forest and Kenai National Wildlife Refuge. The Kenai Mountains are home to Dall sheep, mountain goats, black and brown bears, and caribou. The many lakes, rivers and streams of the Kenai Peninsula are famous for their sportfishing. The highway also provides access to the Resurrection Pass Trail System.

From Soldotna south, the Sterling Highway follows the west coast of the peninsula along Cook Inlet. There are beautiful views on clear days of volcanic peaks on the Alaska Peninsula.

Physical mileposts on the Sterling Highway show distance from Seward. The Sterling Highway is a paved 2-lane highway, open year-round.

Emergency medical services: phone 911 or use CB channels 9, 11 or 19.

Viewing platform at Tern Lake offers scenic mountain views and wildlife watching. *(© Michael DeYoung)*

Sterling Highway Log

Distance from Seward (S) is followed by distance from Anchorage (A) and distance from Homer (H). Physical mileposts show distance from Seward.

S 37.7 (60.7 km) **A 89.3** (143.7 km) **H 141.8** (228.2 km) **Junction** with Seward Highway. First exit southbound (1-way road) for Sterling Highway.

S 37 (59.5 km) **A 90** (144.8 km) **H 142.5** (229.3 km) **Tern Lake Junction.** Second southbound exit (2-way road) for Sterling Highway. This exit provides access to Tern Lake Campground (see description next milepost). Gravel turnout beside Tern Lake with interpretive boardwalk and viewing platforms. Information signs on area birds and wildlife.

S 37.4 (60.2 km) **A 90.4** (145.5 km) **H 142.1** (228.7 km) USFS Tern Lake Campground; 25 campsites, toilets, water, picnic tables, firepits, $6 camping fee. USFS spawning channel for king salmon on Daves Creek at outlet of Tern Lake. Short viewing trail with information signs illustrating use of log weirs and stream protection techniques. ▲

S 38 (61.1 km) **A 91** (146.4 km) **H 141.5** (227.7 km) Avalanche gates. Gravel turnouts.

S 38.3 (61.6 km) **A 91.3** (146.9 km) **H 141.2** (227.2 km) Gravel turnout. Emergency call box.

S 39 (62.8 km) **A 92** (148 km) **H 140.5** (226.1 km) **Daves Creek,** an unusually beautiful mountain stream which flows west into Quartz Creek. Dolly Varden and rainbow averaging 14 inches, June through Sept. A good place to view spawning salmon in late July and Aug.

S 40.5 (65.2 km) **A 93.5** (150.5 km) **H 139** (223.7 km) Double-ended gravel turnout to south.

S 40.9 (65.8 km) **A 93.9** (151.1 km) **H 138.6** (223 km) Bridge over Quartz Creek. This stream empties into Kenai Lake. You are now entering one of Alaska's best-known lake and river fishing regions, across the center of the Kenai Peninsula. The burn on the hillsides to the south was part of a Forest Service moose habitat improvement program.

S 41.1 (66.1 km) **A 94.1** (151.4 km) **H 138.4** (222.7 km) Cooper Landing Closed Area. This area is closed to the hunting of Dall sheep. The ridges to the north are a lambing ground for Dall sheep.

S 42.8 (68.9 km) **A 95.8** (154.2 km) **H 136.7** (220 km) Gravel turnouts on Quartz Creek.

S 43.1 (69.4 km) **A 96.1** (154.6 km) **H 136.4** (219.5 km) Double-ended gravel turnout to east on Quartz Creek.

S 43.5 (70 km) **A 96.5** (155.3 km) **H 136** (218.9 km) Double-ended gravel turnout to east.

S 44 (70.8 km) **A 97** (156.1 km) **H 135.5** (218.1 km) Gravel turnout on Quartz Creek.

S 44.3 (71.3 km) **A 97.3** (156.6) **H 135.2** (217.6 km) Solid waste transfer site to east; public dumpsters.

S 45 (72.4 km) **A 98** (157.7 km) **H 134.5** (216.5 km) Quartz Creek Road to Quartz Creek Recreation Area. Quartz Creek Campground, 0.3 mile/0.5 km from the highway, has 31 sites, boat launch, flush toilets, firepits and a $7 camping fee. Crescent Creek Campground, 3 miles/4.8 km from the highway, has 9 sites, tables, water and pit toilets; $6 fee. Crescent Creek USFS trail leads 6.2 miles/10 km to the outlet of Crescent Lake. The trailhead is about 1 mile/1.6 km from Crescent Creek Campground. A public-use cabin is located at the lake; permit required for use; not accessible in

(Continues on page 506)

STERLING HIGHWAY *Tern Lake Junction to Soldotna, AK*

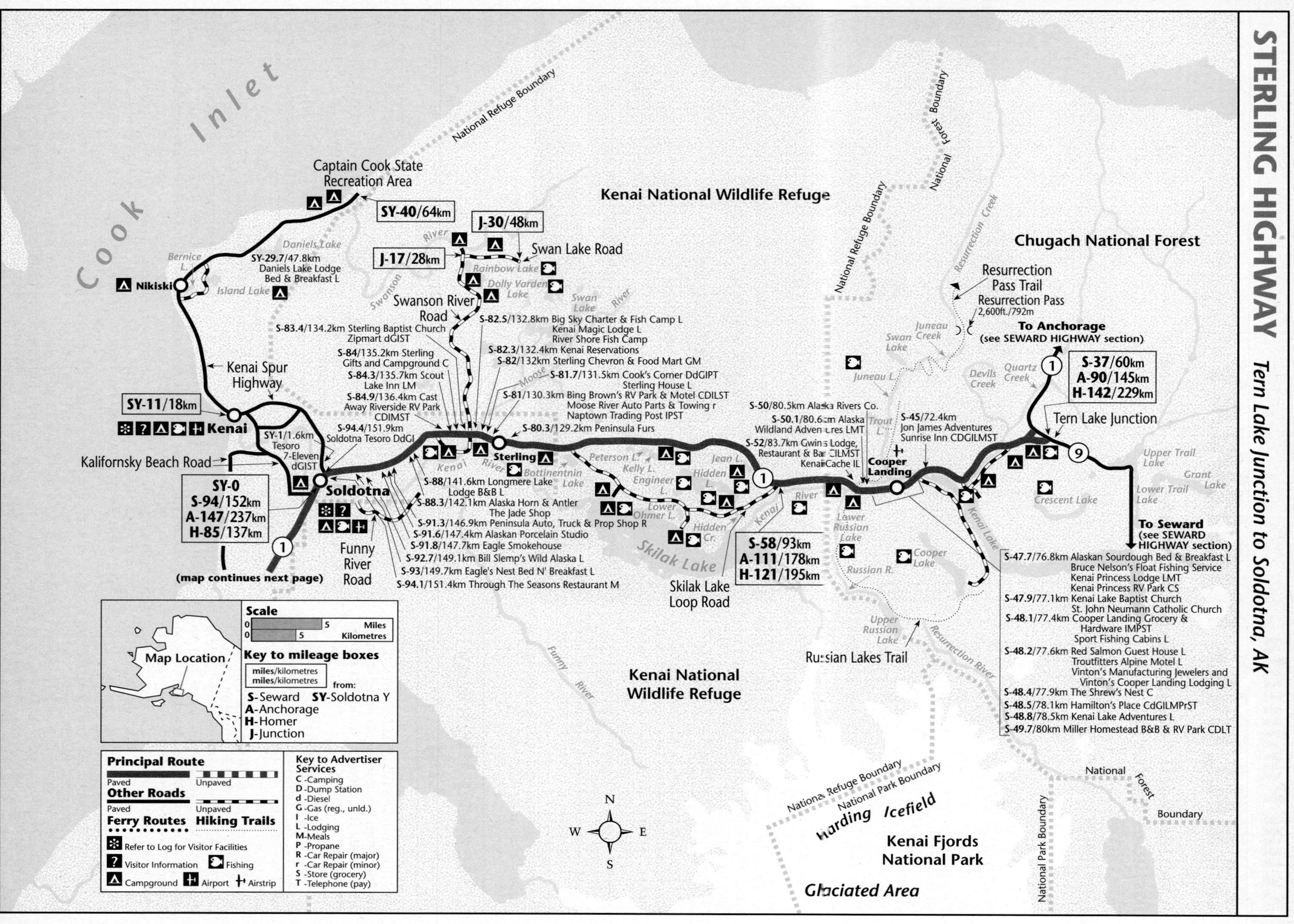

STERLING HIGHWAY Soldotna, AK, to Homer, AK

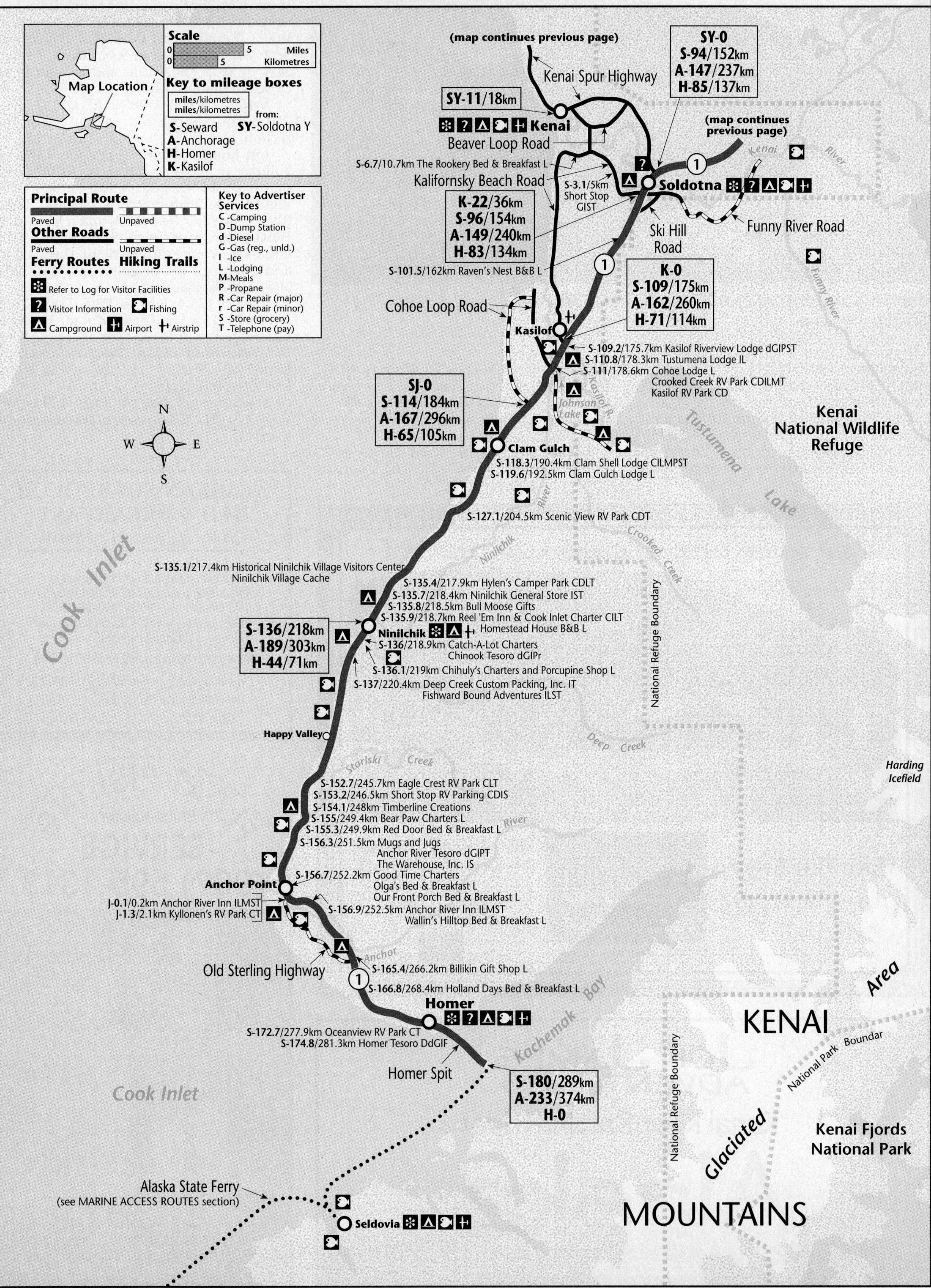

Crescent Lake, reached by trail from Quartz Creek Campground, has grayling fishing. (© Bill Sherwonit)

(Continued from page 503)
winter or early spring due to extreme avalanche danger. ▲

The Sterling Highway from the junction with the Seward Highway west to Sterling takes the traveler through the heart of some prime fishing country, and provides access to numerous fishing lakes and rivers. *NOTE: The diversity of fishing conditions and frequent regulation changes in all Kenai waters make it advisable to consult locally for fishing news and regulations.*

Beautiful views of Kenai Lake next 3 miles/4.8 km westbound. The lake's unusual color is caused by glacial silt.

Quartz Creek, rainbow, midsummer; Dolly Varden to 25 inches, late May through June. **Crescent Lake**, grayling, July 1 to April 14 (2 grayling daily bag and possession limit). **Kenai Lake**, lake trout, May 15 to Sept. 30; trout, May to Sept.; Dolly Varden, May to Sept. Kenai Lake and tributaries are closed to salmon fishing.

S 45 (72.4 km) **A 98** (157.7 km) **H 134.5** (216.5 km) **Sunrise Inn.** See display ad this section.

Jon James Adventures, Cooper Landing. Full-day or half-day rafting or fishing trips on the Upper Kenai River. Full-day and overnight scenic floats down the beautiful Kenai River Canyon. Gear and lunch provided. Flexible departure times. Personalized service enhances your enjoyment of the scenery and wildlife of this beautiful area. Call (907) 595-1598. [ADVERTISEMENT]

S 45.6 (73.4 km) **A 98.6** (158.7 km) **H 133.9** (215.5 km) Large turnout. This is an observation point for Dall sheep on near mountain and mountain goats on Cecil Rhode Mountain (directly across Kenai Lake); use binoculars.

S 46.2 (74.3 km) **A 99.2** (159.6 km) **H 133.3** (214.5 km) Small gravel turnout to east.

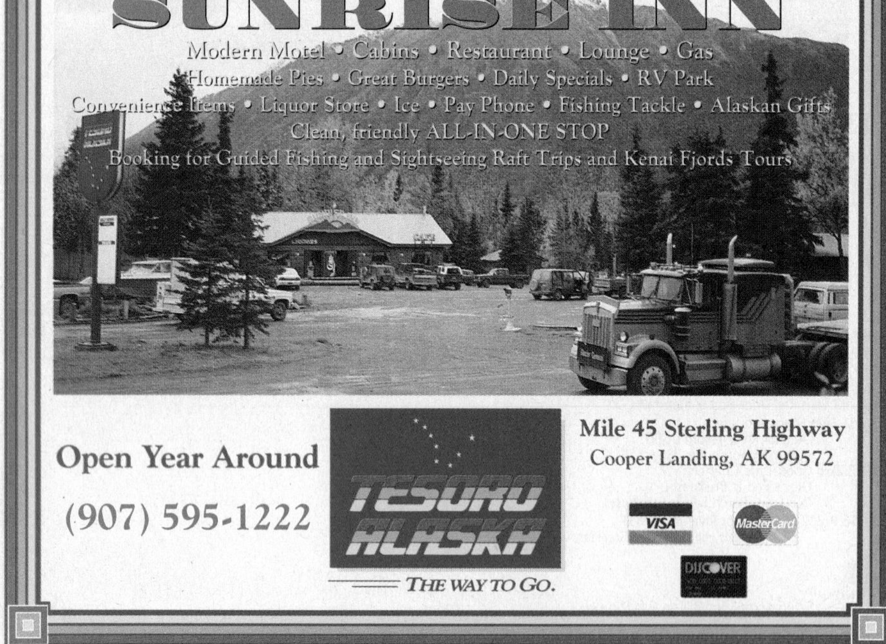

S 47 (75.6 km) **A 100** (160.9 km) **H 132.5** (213.2 km) Turnout to east.

S 47.1 (75.8 km) **A 100.1** (161.1 km) **H 132.4** (213.1 km) Kenai Lake Lodge.

S 47.3 (76.1 km) **A 100.3** (161.4 km) **H 132.2** (212.7 km) Bed and breakfast on Kenai Lake.

S 47.7 (76.8 km) **A 100.7** (162 km) **H 131.8** (212.1 km) Bean Creek Road, access to a bed and breakfast and the Kenai Princess Lodge and RV Park on the Kenai River. The lodge has an interesting chandelier made from antlers in the lobby. ▲

Alaskan Sourdough Bed & Breakfast. See display ad this section.

Bruce Nelson's Float Fishing Service. See display ad this section.

Kenai Princess Lodge at Cooper Landing. 70 private bungalows with sun porches, wood stoves, TVs and phones. Located on the Kenai River with outdoor deck, gift shop, dining room, lounge, hot tubs and tour office. River rafting, flightseeing and fishing. Seasonal service March to Jan. Meeting space available. Rates from $79. VISA, MasterCard, American Express. Write 2815 2nd Ave., Suite #400, Seattle, WA 98121-1299, or call (800) 426-0500 year-round. [ADVERTISEMENT]

Kenai Princess RV Park at Cooper Landing on the Kenai River. Water, power and septic at each site. General store, showers, laundry and hotel service. Adjacent to Kenai Princess Lodge. Access to all hotel facilities. Hiking, fishing, river rafting. Seasonal service mid-May to late September. $20 per night. VISA, MasterCard, American Express accepted. Write 2815 2nd Ave., Suite #400, Seattle, WA 98121-1299, or call (800) 426-0500 year-round. [ADVERTISEMENT] ▲

S 47.8 (76.9 km) **A 100.8** (162.2 km) **H 131.7** (211.9 km) Kenai River bridge. A new boat launch and parking area with restrooms may be under construction here in 1996; boaters may launch on the north side of the bridge at the unimproved launch.

The Kenai River flows directly alongside the highway for the next 10 miles/16 km with several gravel turnouts offering good views. (A proposed plan to reroute this portion of the Sterling Highway away from the Kenai River and into the mountains is under consideration.)

Kenai River from Kenai Lake to Skilak Lake, including Skilak Lake within a half mile of the Kenai River inlet, closed to king salmon fishing; closed to all fishing April 15 through June 10. Silver salmon 5 to 15 lbs., Aug. through Oct.; pink salmon 3 to 7 lbs., July and Aug.; red salmon 3 to 12 lbs., June 11 through mid-Aug.; rainbow and Dolly Varden, June 11 through Oct. *IMPORTANT: Be familiar with current regulations on closed areas; dates given here are subject to change!*

S 47.9 (77.1 km) **A 100.9** (162.4 km) **H 131.6** (211.8 km) Snug Harbor Road. This side road leads 12 miles/19.3 km to Cooper Lake and trailhead for 23-mile/37-km USFS trail to Russian River Campground (see **Milepost S 52.6**). A Baptist church and the St. John Neumann Catholic Church, named after one of the first American saints, are on Snug Harbor Road.

Kenai Lake Baptist Church. See display ad this section.

St. John Neumann Catholic Church. See display ad this section.

S 48.1 (77.4 km) **A 101.1** (162.7 km) **H 131.4** (211.7 km) **Sport Fishing Cabins.** See display ad this section.

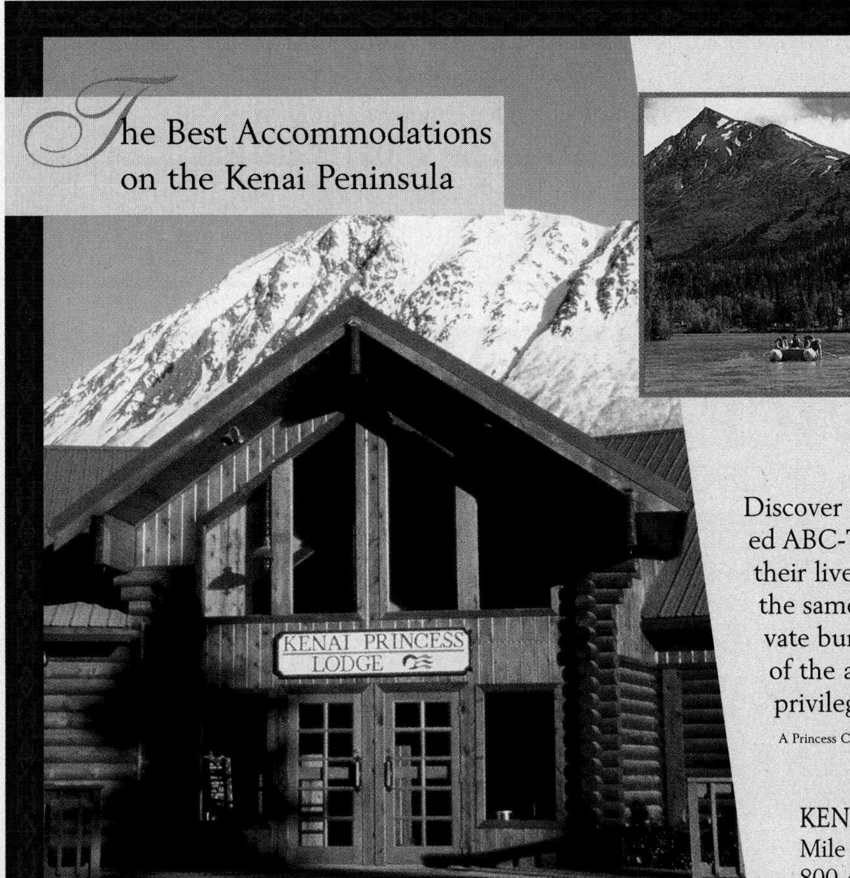

Cooper Landing Grocery & Hardware, the only full-service store between Anchorage and Soldotna. New owners in 1995 have made this the store to stop at on your trip through the Kenai Peninsula. Located in Cooper Landing, 1/2 mile from the bridge over the Kenai River and Lake. Friendly folks will provide you with the latest fishing news and visitor information. Hunting and fishing licenses are available, along with all the preferred tackle to fish the Kenai and Russian Rivers. A large selection of groceries and fresh produce and everyday low prices eliminate the need to "stock up" before heading south from Anchorage. Ice cream parlor and deli. Fried chicken and pizza to go. RV supplies and hardware for minor repairs. VISA and MasterCard accepted at no extra charge. Wayne and Glenda Mitchell, (907) 595-1677. See display ad. [ADVERTISEMENT]

S 48.2 (77.6 km) **A 101.2** (162.9 km) **H 131.3** (211.3 km) **Red Salmon Guest House.** See display ad this section.

Troutfitters Alpine Motel. See display ad this seciton.

Vinton's Manufacturing Jewelers and Vinton's Cooper Landing Lodging. Gold nugget jewelry manufactured on premises. Custom orders. Ivory, jade, Alaskan gifts. Three modern bunkhouses with large kitchens and baths each sleep 5 to 6. Freezers for your fish. $125 to $150 per day. Turn on to Edwards Street between Cooper Landing Grocery and Troutfitters Alpine Motel. Phone (907) 595-1227, fax (907) 595-1640. P.O. Box 760, Cooper Landing, AK 99572. [ADVERTISEMENT]

S 48.4 (77.9 km) **A 101.4** (163.2 km) **H 131.1** (211 km) **COOPER LANDING** (pop. 386) stretches along several miles of the highway. All visitor facilities. Cooper Landing ambulance, phone (907) 595-1255.

The Shrew's Nest, Last Resort RV Park and Landing Latté. See display ad this section.

Private Aircraft: Quartz Creek (Cooper Landing) airstrip, 4 miles/6.4 km west; elev. 450 feet/137m; length 2,200 feet/671m; gravel; unattended.

S 48.5 (78.1 km) **A 101.5** (163.3 km) **H 131** (210.8 km) **Hamilton's Place** river resort, only complete stop on the upper Kenai River. Information center for

the famous Russian River and surrounding area. Centrally located for day trips to Seward, Soldotna/Kenai, Homer. Make us your Kenai Peninsula headquarters. Tesoro services, 24-hour recovery and transport (flatbed) service, propane. (All emergency road service providers.) General store, groceries, licenses, tackle, ice, liquor store.

Swanson River and Swan Lake Roads Log

Swanson River Road leads north 17.2 miles/27.7 km, where it junctions with Swan Lake Road, which leads east 12.7 miles/20.4 km and dead ends at Paddle Lake. Both roads provide access to fishing, hiking trails and canoe trails. *CAUTION: Do not leave valuables in vehicles at canoe trailheads.*

Distance from junction with the Sterling Highway (J) is shown.

J 0 Junction with Sterling Highway at **Milepost S 83.4.** Swanson River Road is a good gravel road but can be rough in spots; slow speeds are advised. There are numerous turnouts suitable for overnight camping in self-contained RVs.

J 0.7 (1.1 km) Robinson Loop Road; rejoins Sterling Highway at **Milepost S 87.5.**

J 1.3 (2.1 km) Airstrip.

J 4.4 (7.1 km) Entering Kenai National Wildlife Refuge.

J 7.9 (12.7 km) **Mosquito Lake,** turnout; 0.5-mile trail to lake. Rainbow trout.

J 9.1 (14.6 km) **Silver Lake** trailhead and parking: 1-mile/1.6-km hike to lake. Rainbow trout and arctic char.

J 9.8 (15.8 km) **Finger Lake** trailhead: 2.3-mile/3.7-km hike to lake. Good arctic char fishing.

J 10.6 (17.1 km) **Forest Lake** wayside, parking: 0.3-mile/0.5-km trail to lake. Rainbow trout; best fished from canoe or raft.

J 13 (20.9 km) **Weed Lake** wayside: small turnout by lake. Rainbow trout.

J 13.3 (21.4 km) **Drake** and **Skookum lakes** trailhead and parking; 2-mile/3.2-km trail. Rainbow trout and arctic char.

J 14 (22.5 km) Access to Breeze Lake.

J 14.2 (22.9 km) **Dolly Varden Lake** Campground; 15 sites, water, toilets, boat launch. Large RVs and trailers note: 0.5-mile/0.8-km access road to campground is narrow and bumpy; check turnaround space before driving in. Fishing for Dolly Varden and rainbow; best in late Aug. and Sept.

J 14.9 (24 km) Access road to canoe trails to east. Oil field road to west closed to private vehicles. The Swanson River Road was originally built as an access road to the Swanson River oil field. Chevron operated the field from 1958 to 1986; it is currently operated by Unocal.

J 15.7 (25.2 km) **Rainbow Lake** Campground; small 3-unit camping area on lakeshore with toilets, water and boat launch. Fishing for Dolly Varden and rainbow trout. *CAUTION: Steep road; difficult turnaround. Large RVs: check visually before driving in.*

J 17.2 (27.7 km) **Junction** with Swan Lake Road. Continue north 0.5 mile/0.8 km for Swanson River Landing at end of Swanson River Road; camping area with picnic tables, firepits, water, toilets, boat launch, large gravel parking area. This is the terminus of the Swanson River canoe route, which begins at Paddle Lake at the end of Swan Lake Road. Log now follows Swan Lake Road east.

J 17.3 (27.8 km) Kenai National Wildlife Refuge Outdoor Environmental Education Center. Reservation required. Educational group-use permits obtained at Kenai National Wildlife Refuge Visitor Center in Soldotna.

J 20.2 (32.5 km) **Fish Lake**; 3 sites, tables, firepits, toilets. Fishing for Dolly Varden.

J 21.2 (34 km) **Canoe Lake**, parking. West entrance to Swan Lake canoe route. Fishing for Dolly Varden.

J 21.8 (35.1 km) Sucker Creek wayside; campsite, table, fireplace. **Sucker Lake**, rainbow trout.

J 23.3 (37.5 km) **Merganser Lakes**, 0.5 mile/0.8 km south; rainbow trout.

J 25.4 (40.9 km) Nest Lakes trail, 0.5-mile/0.8-km hike north.

J 26.9 (43.3 km) Large turnout and toilet to west.

J 27 (43.5 km) **Portage Lake.** East entrance to Swan Lake canoe route. Lake is stocked with coho salmon.

J 27.3 (43.9 km) Informal pullout on lake.

J 29.4 (47.3 km) Y in road; bear left.

J 29.9 (48.1 km) End of road. **Paddle Lake** entrance to Swanson River canoe route; parking, picnic table, water and toilet. Fishing for rainbow and Dolly Varden.

Return to Milepost S 83.4 Sterling Highway

Loop Road 1.6 miles/2.6 km to turnoff for Morgan's Landing: follow side road 2.4 miles/3.9 km to reach Morgan's Landing State Recreation Area; $10 nightly fee per vehicle or annual pass, 40 developed campsites with 10 pull-through sites and some double sites, toilets and water. Alaska State Parks area headquarters is located here.

Cast Away Riverside RV Park. See display ad this section.

Good access from Morgan's Landing to the **Kenai River**, king salmon from mid-June through July, average 30 lbs. Red (sockeye) salmon average 8 lbs., use flies in July and Aug.; silver (coho) salmon to 15 lbs., Aug.and Sept., use lure; pink salmon average 4 lbs. with lure, best in July, even-numbered years only; rainbow and Dolly Varden, use lure, June through Aug.

Divided highway ends southbound.

S 87.5 (140.8 km) **A 140.5** (226.1 km) **H 92** (148.1 km) Robinson Loop Road.

S 88 (141.6 km) **A 141** (226.9 km) **H 91.5** (147.3 km) St. Theresa's Drive.

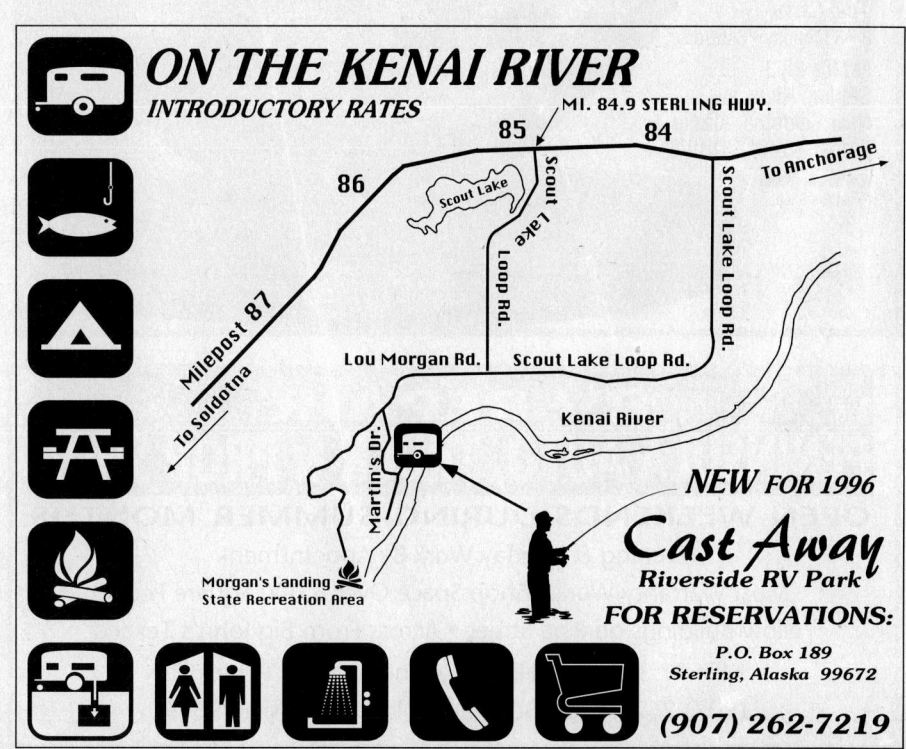

S 88.3 (142.1 km) **A 141.3** (227.4 km) **H 91.2** (146.8 km) **Alaska Horn & Antler.** See display ad this section.

The Jade Shop at Alaska Horn and Antler features raw jade, finished pieces, clocks, novelties. Also, Alaskan marble and petrified wood from Kachemak Bay. Antler buttons, bolos, earrings, letter openers, souvenir pins, antler baskets, Alaska back-scratchers. We buy antlers. Watch Tom Cooper carve here. Closed Sunday. See display ad. [ADVERTISEMENT]

S 91.3 (146.9 km) **A 144.3** (232.2 km) **H 88.2** (141.9 km) Gas station, RV repair and store.

Peninsula Auto, Truck & Prop Shop. See display ad this section.

S 91.6 (147.4 km) **A 144.6** (232.7 km) **H 87.9** (141.5 km) **Alaska Porcelain Studios.** See display ad this section.

S 91.8 (147.7 km) **A 144.8** (233 km) **H 87.7** (141.1 km) **Eagle Smokehouse.** We will smoke (kipper) or pickle your salmon or halibut for you. We also vacuum pack and freeze your fresh fish. No luck fishing? We have all of the above for sale plus our smoked salmon/cream cheese spread in 2 flavors, pickled and fresh Alaskan shrimp and 4 flavors of smoked salmon jerky. All our products are all natural with no artificial colors, flavors or preservatives—no nitrites. We box and ship. Free samples. Box 4085, Soldotna, AK 99669. Phone and fax (907) 262-7007. [ADVERTISEMENT]

S 92 (148 km) **A 145** (233.3 km) **H 87.5** (140.8 km) Public golf course, driving range and cottages.

S 92.5 (148.9 km) **A 145.5** (234.2 km) **H 87** (140 km) State Division of Forest, Land and Water Management. Fire danger indicator sign.

S 92.7 (149.1 km) **A 145.7** (234.5 km) **H 86.8** (139.7 km) Mackey Lake Road. Private lodging is available on this side road.

Bill Slemp's Wild Alaska. See display ad this section.

S 93 (149.7 km) **A 146** (235 km) **H 86.5**

CABIN RENTALS
Bill Slemp's Wild Alaska
P.O. Box 963, Soldotna, AK 99669
(907) 262-7409 or (907) 262-2463
Mile 92.7 Sterling Highway Turn On Mackey Lake Road 2.3 Miles

ALASKA PORCELAIN STUDIOS
FACTORY OUTLET
Locally Made – FINE PORCELAIN
"Our Porcelain has been Selected by Discriminating Collectors Worldwide!"
Milepost 91.6
P.O. Box 1550, Soldotna, AK 99669
(907) 262-5626

EAGLES' NEST
BED N' BREAKFAST
MILE 93
STERLING HIGHWAY
SOLDOTNA, ALASKA
JUST ONE MILE TO WORLD FAMOUS
KENAI RIVER
907-262-5396
PO BOX 1040
SOLDOTNA, AK 99669

RV REPAIR
PENINSULA AUTO, TRUCK & PROP SHOP
OPEN WEEKENDS DURING SUMMER MONTHS
Evening & Holiday Work By Appointment
Most Warranty Work • Shop Space Over 6,000 Square Feet
Yellow Buildings on Pine Street • Across From Big John's Texaco
Mile 91.3 Sterling Highway, on the Kenai Peninsula
(907) 262-6440 • Box 956, Soldotna, Alaska 99669

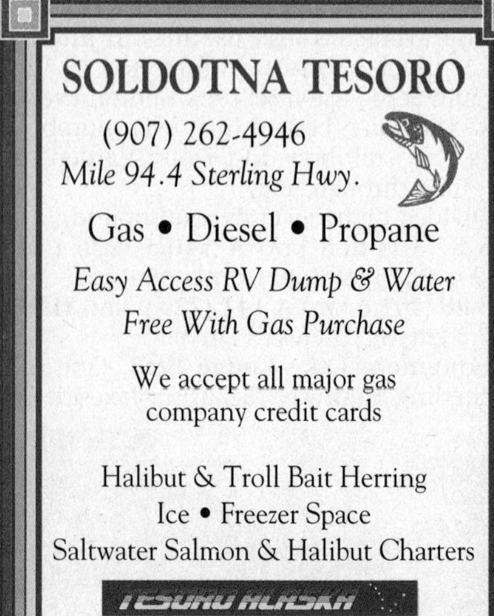

(139.2 km) **Eagles' Nest Bed N' Breakfast.** See display ad this section.

S 93.1 (149.8 km) **A 146.1** (235.1 km) **H 86.4** (139 km) Loren Lake.

S 94 (151.2 km) **A 147** (236.6 km) **H 85.5** (137.6 km) Four-lane highway begins and leads through Soldotna.

S 94.1 (151.4 km) **A 147.1** (236.7 km) **H 85.4** (137.4 km) Restaurant. Turn on East Redoubt Street and follow the gravel road 0.5 mile/0.8 km for Swiftwater Park municipal campground. The municipal campground has 20 spaces on **Kenai River** (some pull-throughs), some tables, firepits, firewood, phone, dump station, 2-week limit, litter barrels, toilets, boat landing, fee charged, good fishing.

Through the Seasons Restaurant specializes in fine dining in pleasant surroundings. Open daily for lunch and dinner. Lunch: homemade breads, gourmet soups, sandwiches made with freshly roasted meats. Dinner: seafoods, homemade pasta, steak and nightly specials. Through the Seasons cheesecakes. Fine wines and imported beers. See display ad in Soldotna section. [ADVERTISEMENT]

S 94.2 (151.6 km) **A 147.2** (236.9 km) **H 85.3** (137.3 km) **Junction** with Kenai Spur Highway. This junction is called the Soldotna Y.

There are 2 ways to reach the city of Kenai (see description of city on page 528): Turn right (westbound) at the Y, physical **Milepost S 94.2**, and continue 11 miles/17.7 km northwest to Kenai via the Kenai Spur Highway; or continue on the Sterling Highway to **Milepost S 96.1** and turn right (southbound) on the Kalifornsky Beach Road and continue 9.3 miles/14.9 km to Kenai via the Warren Ames Memorial Bridge. For details see KENAI SPUR HIGHWAY log on page 527 and KALIFORNSKY BEACH ROAD log on page 532. Description of Soldotna follows.

S 94.4 (151.9 km) **A 147.4** (237.2 km) **H 85.1** (137 km) Soldotna DOT/PF highway maintenance station, gas station. Turn east here for access to Soldotna Creek Park (day use only). Follow road behind restaurant.

Soldotna Tesoro. See display ad this section.

S 95 (152.9 km) **A 148** (238.2 km) **H 84.5** (136 km) Soldotna city center; Peninsula Center shopping mall. Turn on Binkley Street for access to fire station, police station and post office. See description of city following. See city map this page.

Homer-bound travelers continue south across the Kenai River bridge past visitor center, then turn west on Kalifornsky Road for Soldotna city campground; turn east off the Sterling Highway on Funny River Road for airport. See descriptions at **Milepost S 96.1** on page 531.

Log of the Sterling Highway continues on page 531.

Soldotna

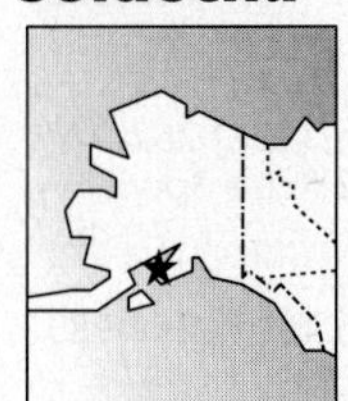

S 95.2 (153.2 km) **A 148.2** (238.5 km) **H 84.3** (135.7 km) On the western Kenai Peninsula, the city stretches over a mile southwest along the Sterling Highway and northwest along the Kenai Spur Highway. **Population:** 3,900; Kenai Peninsula Borough 44,411. **Emergency Services:** Phone 911 for all emergency services. **Alaska State Troopers** at Mile 22 Kalifornsky Beach Road just off

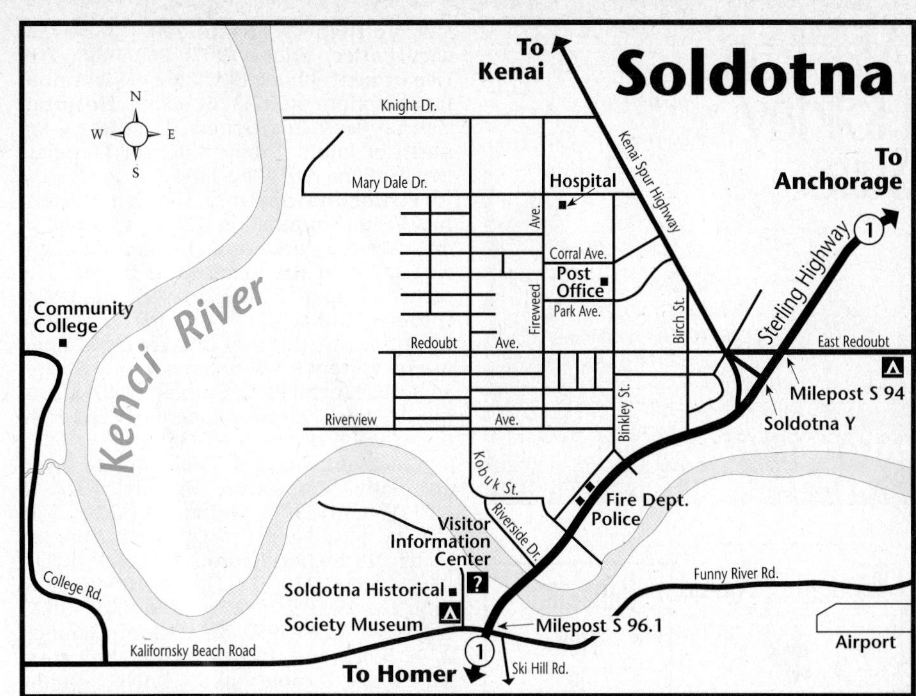

Sterling Highway, phone (907) 262-4453. **City Police**, phone (907) 262-4455. **Fire Department**, phone (907) 262-4792. **Ambulance**, phone (907) 262-4500. **Hospital**, Central Peninsula General, 1 mile/1.6 km north of Public Safety Bldg. off Marydale Drive, phone (907) 262-4404.

Visitor Information: The Kenai Peninsula Visitor Information Center is located in downtown Soldotna on the Sterling Highway south of the Kenai River bridge. The center is open 7 days a week, mid-May through mid-Sept., 9 A.M. to 7 P.M. The remainder of the year the center is open weekdays from 9 A.M. to 5 P.M. Write: Greater Soldotna Chamber of Commerce, Box 236-MP, Soldotna 99669; phone (907) 262-1337 or 262-9814, fax (907) 262-3566.

Elevation: 115 feet/35m. **Climate:** Average daily temperature in July, 63°F to 68°F/17°C to 20°C; January, 19°F to 23°F/-7°C to -5°C. Annual precipitation, approximately 18 inches. **Radio:** KGTL 620, KFQD 750, KSRM 920, KGTL-FM 100.9/103.5, MBN-FM 95.3/97.7, KWHQ-FM 1001, KPEN-FM 101-7, KZXX 980. **Television:** Channels 2, 4, 9, 12 and 13 via booster line from Anchorage, cable and KANG public education channel. **Newspapers:** *Peninsula Clarion* (daily), *The Dispatch* (weekly).

Private Aircraft: Soldotna airstrip, 0.9 mile/1.4 km southeast; elev. 107 feet/32m; length 5,000 feet/1,524m; asphalt; fuel 100LL; unattended.

The town of Soldotna was established in the 1940s because of its strategic location at the Sterling–Kenai Spur Highway junction. (Visitors may see the homestead cabin, which became Soldotna's first post office in 1949, at its original location on the Kenai Spur Highway at Corral Street.) Soldotna was named for a nearby stream; it is a Russian word meaning "soldier," although some believe the name came from an Indian word meaning the "stream fork."

Today, Soldotna is a business center, sportfishing capital of the Kenai Peninsula and the community of choice for workers in the oil-related industry in Cook Inlet.

Soldotna was incorporated as a first-class city in 1967. It has a council–manager form of government. Kenai Peninsula Borough headquarters and state offices of the depts. of Highways, Public Safety, Fish and Game, and Forest, Land and Water Management are located here. Soldotna is also headquarters for the Kenai Peninsula Borough school district. There are 3 elementary schools, a junior high school and 2 high schools. University of Alaska Kenai Penin-

SOLDOTNA ADVERTISERS

Accommodations on the Kenai ....Ph. (907) 262-2139
Across The River RV Park ....Mile 13.8 Funny River Rd.
Alaska Recreational Rentals ....Ph. (907) 262-2700
Alaskan Holiday Suites ....Ph. (907) 262-9635
Alaska's Kenai Peninsula B&B/ Lodging ....Ph. (907) 262-1002
Antler Art ....Next to Dairy Queen
Beemun's V & S Variety Store ....35277 Kenai Spur Hwy.
Best Western King Salmon Motel, Restaurant & RV Park ....Kenai Spur Hwy.
Birch Tree Gallery ....Mile 0.2 Funny River Rd.
Blazy's B & B ....Ph. (907) 262-4591
Bo's Fishing Guide Service ....Ph. (907) 262-5154
Cashman's Lodging ....Ph. (907) 262-4359
China Sea Restaurant ....Blazy's Soldotna Mall
Donna's Country & Victorian Gifts ....Blazy's Soldotna Mall
Edgewater RV Park ....Ph. (907) 262-7733
Fenton Bros. Guided Sportfishing ....Ph. (907) 262-2502
First Baptist Church ....159 Binkley St.
Frames & Things Gallery West ....Blazy's Soldotna Mall
Foto Quick ....Ph. (907) 262-4279
Greater Soldotna Chamber of Commerce ....Sterling Hwy. & Kenai River Bridge
Hardy's Alaskan Adventures ....Ph. (907) 262-9881
Harry Gaines Kenai River Fishing Guide ....Ph. (907) 262-5097
Jim Rusk Fishing Guide ....Ph. (907) 262-4911
Jimmie Jack Charters ....Ph. (907) 283-6488
Johnson Bros. Guides & Outfitters ....Downtown
Kenai Custom Seafoods ....Mile 14.4 Kalifornsky Beach Rd.
Kenai Peninsula Condos ....Ph. (907) 262-1383
Kenai River Lodge ....Kenai River Bridge
Kenai River Retreat ....Ph. (907) 262-1361
King's Budget Charters ....Ph. (907) 262-4564
Knight Manor Bed & Breakfast ....Ph. (907) 262-2438
Lottie's Place Bed and Breakfast ....Ph. (907) 283-8707
Moose Hollow Bed & Breakfast ....Ph. (907) 262-7526
Mykel's Restaurant & Lounge ....Mile 0.2 Kenai Spur Hwy.
Northcountry Fair ....Ph. (907) 262-7715
Northland Gallery & Wildlife Studio ....At the Y
Northstar ....Ph. (800) 869-9418
Oil Exchange, The ....Mile 1 Kenai Spur Hwy.
Orca Lodge ....Ph. (907) 262-5649
Peninsula Center Mall ....Downtown
Poppy Ridge Bed & Breakfast ....Ph. (907) 262-4265
Posey's Kenai River Hideaway ....Ph. (907) 262-7430
Rise and Shine Bed & Breakfast ....Ph. (907) 262-9049
River Quest RV Park ....Ph. (907) 283-4991
River Terrace RV Park ....Ph. (907) 262-5593
Riverside Auto Supply Inc. ....Kenai River Bridge
RiverSide House & RV Park, The ....Ph. (907) 262-0500
Riverside Resort Bed and Breakfast ....355 Riverside Dr.
Rod 'N Real Charters ....Ph. (907) 262-6064
Slammin Salmon Charters ....Ph. (907) 262-5661
Sohi Lane Lodging ....Ph. (907) 262-7572
Soldotna Bed & Breakfast Lodge ....Ph. (907) 262-4779
Soldotna Inn ....Mile 0.2 Kenai Spur Hwy.
Soldotna Wash & Dry ....At the Y
Spruce Avenue Bed & Breakfast ....Ph. (907) 269-9833
Thompson's Log Gift & Jewelry ....Mile 94 Sterling Hwy.
Through the Seasons Restaurant ....At the Y

sula College is also located in Soldotna.

Area terrain is level and forested, with many streams and lakes nearby. Large rivers of the area are the Swanson River, the Moose River, and the Kenai River, which empties into Cook Inlet just south of Kenai. The area affords a majestic view of volcanic mountains across Cook Inlet. Always snow-covered, they are Mount Spurr (elev. 11,100 feet/3,383m), which erupted in 1992; Mount Iliamna (elev. 10,016 feet/3,053m), which has 3 smaller peaks to the left of the larger one; and Mount Redoubt (elev. 10,197 feet/3,108m), which was identified by its very regular cone shape until it erupted in Dec. 1989.

The Soldotna–Kenai area offers a wide variety of recreation and all goods and services. Many fishing guides operate out of Soldotna; write the chamber of commerce for more information.

ACCOMMODATIONS/VISITOR SERVICES

All modern conveniences and facilities are available, including supermarkets, banks, hotels/motels, restaurants and drive-ins, medical and dental clinics, bowling alley, golf course, veterinarians, churches and a library. Two shopping malls are located on the Sterling Highway near the center of town. Bed-and-breakfasts, cabin rentals and lodges also offer accommodations.

Accommodations on the Kenai. Your one-stop reservation service for bed and breakfast inns, lodges, cabins and condos. Hotels and motels, too. Personally inspected by AOK staff. Let us book your halibut, salmon and fly-in fishing charters. Deposit required to confirm reservations. Phone (907) 262-2139. P.O. Box 2956MP, Soldotna, AK 99669. [ADVERTISEMENT]

Alaskan Holiday Suites. Two-bedroom, 2-bath suites, with fully equipped kitchens. Suites accommodate up to 6. Convenient location, close to all services and just a short walk to the famous Kenai River. Continental breakfast. Free local calls. Cable TV. Guide reservations available. VISA/MasterCard accepted. Reservations: (907) 694-7615 or (907) 262-9635. See display ad. [ADVERTISEMENT]

Alaska's Kenai Peninsula B&B/Lodging. Downtown Soldotna. Walk to Kenai River, city parks, restaurants, shopping malls. Private apartment; living room, bathroom, fully-equipped kitchenette, queen, twin beds; or individual bedrooms, shared bathroom, kitchenette. In-room telephone, TV. Quiet, clean. Maid service. Same location 18 years. Affordable rates. VISA, MasterCard. 162 South Birch Street, Soldotna, AK 99669. Phone (907) 262-1002. [ADVERTISEMENT]

Best Western King Salmon Motel, Restaurant and RV Park downtown Soldotna on Kenai Spur Highway. Large rooms, queen beds, some kitchenettes, cable TV, phones. Free in-room coffee. Restaurant serves early fisherman's breakfast, lunch, dinner. Steaks, seafood, salad bar. Beer and wine available. Fishing licenses, ice. Fish processing close by. RV park with 39 pull-through spaces, full hookups, restrooms, coin-operated showers and laundry. Phone (907) 262-5857; fax (907) 262-9441. See display ad this section. [ADVERTISEMENT] ▲

Drive with your headlights on at all times.

Cashman's Lodging. Finest lodging on the Kenai Peninsula. Spacious cabins on the Kenai River. Also, condos with 1 to 3 bedrooms, 1 or 2 baths, complete kitchens. Laundry facilities available. Centrally located

in Soldotna. Complete services for fishing or hunting. Groups and combination packages our specialty. (907) 262-4359. Write Box 3143, Soldotna, AK 99669. [ADVERTISEMENT]

Kenai River Retreat. Vacation condos on the Kenai River are nonsmoking and include well-supplied kitchens, master bedroom, cable TV, telephone, laundry facilities, large freezer, and great Alaskan hospitality! Relax on your secluded deck overlooking the river, walk down and fish from our bank or hike on nearby trails. Kenai River Retreat offers an Alaskan adventure—in style. For reservations, call (907) 262-1361 or write 360 W. Endicott–MP, Soldotna, AK 99669. [ADVERTISEMENT]

Lottie's Place Bed and Breakfast. Located Mile 12.3 Kalifornsky Beach Road, halfway between the Kenai and Kasilof rivers. Walk the beach, relax by the fireplace. Barbecue available for your catch of the day. Continental or full breakfast. Queen–size beds, satellite TV. Honeymoon bedroom with fireplace. Owned and operated by long-time Alaskans. Reservations: (907) 283-8707. See display ad in Soldotna section. [ADVERTISEMENT]

Orca Lodge. Beautiful, luxurious, handcrafted Kenai riverfront log cabins. Roomy cabins with loft and full bath accommodate up to 4. Community picnic area for outdoor

cooking. Great bank fishing or hire our professional guides and catch the trophy of a lifetime. Ideal base camp for hunters. Hunter booking service. Open year-round. (907) 262-5649. [ADVERTISEMENT]

RiverSide House Hotel & RV Park. Hotel, restaurant, lounge, and RV park on the banks of the Kenai River. Clean rooms, cable TV, Alaska cuisine, cocktails, dancing, fishing on premises. RV electrical hook-ups; water and dump station in park. Guide service, individual, groups, fishing. 44611 Sterling Hwy, Soldotna, AK 99669. (907) 262-0500, fax (907) 262-0406, 1-800-200-0504. [ADVERTISEMENT] ▲

Riverside Resort Bed and Breakfast. Stay in a beautiful log home overlooking famous Kenai River. Two rooms overlook river, third has private bath. All rooms have antique or brass furnishings, color cable TV, and ceiling fans. Full breakfast from menu and/or sack lunch. Airport/guide transportation, excellent bank fishing, freezer storage, and laundry facilities. Walk-ins welcome. Phone/fax (907) 262-5371 or write 355 Riverside Dr., Soldotna, AK 99669. [ADVERTISEMENT]

Sohi Lane Lodging. 2- and 3-bedroom apartments. Fully furnished with hide-a-bed in living room. Fully-equipped kitchen, cable TV, phone. Close to famous Kenai River fishing and other activities. Fishing guides available. Family and group rates. Discounts for June reservations. Early reservations suggested. Call (907) 262-7572. P.O. Box 958, Soldotna, AK 99669. [ADVERTISEMENT]

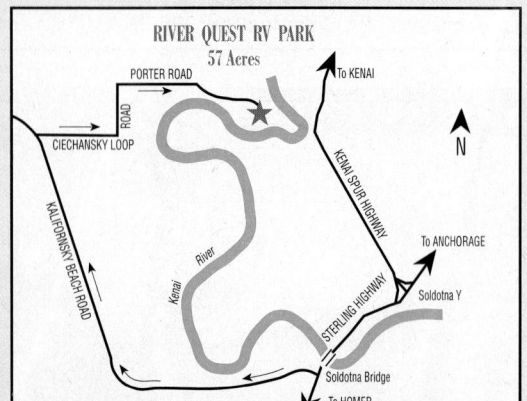

Spruce Avenue Bed and Breakfast. Native Alaskan art decorates large, nonsmoking residence. Delicious breakfasts feature Finnish fare hosted by retired Alaskan teachers. Moderate rates $50–$80. Paintings and Native art for sale. Send for Recipe/Story Collection, $9 ppd. Sharon and Richard Waisanen, 35985 Pioneer Dr., Soldotna, AK 99669; (907) 262-9833. [ADVERTISEMENT]

For Swiftwater Campground, turn on East Redoubt Street at **Milepost S 94.1** Sterling Highway. Centennial Park Campground is 0.1 mile/0.2 km from the Sterling Highway just south of the Kenai River bridge on Kalifornsky Beach Road; turn west at **Milepost S 96.1.** Both campgrounds are owned by the City of Soldotna. Register for camping at either park; camping fees charged. Dump station available at Centennial Park Campground. These campgrounds are heavily used; good idea to check in early. There are several private campgrounds located in and near Soldotna; see ads this section or contact the chamber of commerce. ▲

Across The River RV Park. Bank fishing for reds, rainbows, silvers. Guided fishing for Kenai River kings, silvers. Public boat launch close by. Fish cleaning facility, ice, freezer, water, dump station. Electric hookups, laundry, showers, phone, ice, tackle. 1-800-276-2434, summer (907) 262-0458. Box 2193, Soldotna, AK 99669. Mile 13.8 Funny River Road. See display ad. [ADVERTISEMENT] ▲

Edgewater RV Park on the banks of world famous Kenai River, across from the Soldotna visitors' center. Full and partial hookups, laundry, showers, grassy sites, picnic tables, local guide service and fish cleaning facilities. Bank fishing. Walk to stores, restaurants. Reservations and information (907) 262-7733. P.O. Box 3391, Soldotna, AK 99669. [ADVERTISEMENT]

River Quest Resort and RV Park is located on the world-famous Kenai River, with water frontage. Fully furnished cabins with kitchens for rent. Water and electric hookups, pull-throughs, laundry, shower, phones, boat gas, propane, convenience store and snack bar, all available on location. Boat launching, fishing charter and in-state tour booking service, fish weighing and cleaning facilities. Your hosts: Kathy and Vern Davidhizar. For information or reservations, call (907) 283-4991 or write P.O. Box 3457, Soldotna, AK 99669. See display ad this section. [ADVERTISEMENT] ▲

River Terrace RV Park features 1,100 feet of Kenai River frontage in Soldotna at the bridge. Walking distance to Kenai Peninsula Visitor Center, restaurants, groceries and downtown shopping malls. Full and partial hookups, riverfront sites. Heated

restrooms, showers with unlimited hot water, laundry. World-famous red salmon fishing from the riverbank. 1,004,214 salmon swam by our property in 1994, by Alaska State Fish and Game sonar count. Tackle shop, ice, fish processing and taxidermy available on premises. Let our park resident master guides provide custom king and silver salmon charters on the Kenai and Kasilof rivers. Reserve early to avoid disappointment. Phone (907) 262-5593; fax (907) 262-9229; write P.O. Box 322, Soldotna, AK 99669. [ADVERTISEMENT] ▲

TRANSPORTATION

Air: Charters available. Soldotna airport is south of Soldotna 2 miles/3.2 km off the Sterling Highway; at **Milepost S 96.1**, just after crossing Kenai River bridge, turn left (east) on Funny River (Airport) Road 2 miles/3.2 km.

Local: Taxi service, car rentals, vehicle leasing, boat rentals and charters.

ATTRACTIONS

Join in Local Celebrations. July's big event is the annual Soldotna Progress Days, held during the 4th weekend of the month. Activities include a parade, 2 days of rodeo, autocross competition, car show, barbecues, dance, arts and crafts show, and other events.

During the month of Aug. (16-25, 1996), the Kenai River Guides Assoc. sponsors the annual Soldotna Silver Salmon Derby. 1996 marks the 10th year for this event. Daily prizes are awarded for the heaviest silver salmon caught, in addition to other categories. Several thousand dollars in cash and merchandise is awarded in this exciting event. The Peninsula Winter Games take place in February in Soldotna. Activities include an ice sculpture contest, cross-country ski race, ice bowling and snow volleyball. Games, booths, concessions and demonstrations are held throughout the weekend. The Alaska State Championship Sled Dog Races and Dog Weight Pull Contest take place during the Winter Games.

Donna's Country & Victorian Gifts at Blazy's Soldotna Mall. A shopper's delight, a fisherman's wife's revenge. This is the perfect place to spend an afternoon while your

husband goes fishing. Roomfuls of wonderful things, constantly changing. Enjoy our cozy, relaxing atmosphere. Don't miss our Santa room! You'll find things in our shoppe you never thought you'd find in Alaska! [ADVERTISEMENT]

Fish the Kenai River. Soldotna is one of Alaska's best-known sportfishing headquarters, and many claim that some of the world's best fishing is here at the Kenai River, which flows next to town. Many charter boats and fishing guides for Kenai River fishing are located in the Soldotna area. In May 1985, Les Anderson of Soldotna landed a 97-lb., 4-oz. king salmon, a new world's record. The mounted fish is on display at the visitor center.

Soldotna gets very busy during fishing season, and for those fishermen who want a more remote fishing spot—or for visitors who want to see wildlife and glaciers—there are fly-in fishing trips for rainbow, grayling,

Wilderness canoeing on the Swan Lake canoe route, Kenai NWR. (© Michael DeYoung)

salmon and Dolly Varden, and flightseeing trips to see Tustumena Lake, the Harding Icefield and wildlife, through local outfitters.

In Soldotna, the early run of kings begins about May 15, with the peak of the run occurring between June 12 and 20. The late run enters the river about July 1, peaking between July 23 and 31; season closes July 31. The first run of red salmon enters the river during early June and is present in small numbers through the month; the second run enters about July 15 and is present through early Aug. In even years pink salmon are present from early through mid-Aug. The early silver salmon run arrives in early Aug., peaks in mid-Aug, and is over by the end of the month. Late run silver salmon enter the Kenai in early Sept., peak in mid- to late Sept., and continue to enter the river through October. Dolly Varden and rainbow trout can be caught all summer.

Day-use Parks. Soldotna Creek Park, located off the Sterling Highway on the Kenai River, behind Hutchings Chevrolet at the Y, has covered picnic tables, grills, playground and trails. Facilities include wheelchair-accessible toilets and a boardwalk with handicapped accessibility for bank fishing. Airport Rotary Park, at Mile 4 Funny River Road, also has a wheelchair-accessible boardwalk with excellent bank fishing during the red salmon run.

Central Peninsula Sports Center, on

Kalifornsky Beach (K-Beach) Road, has an Olympic-sized hockey rink, a jogging track, 2 racquetball/volleyball courts, a weight and exercise room, dressing rooms and showers. The Sports Center also has convention facilities and meeting rooms. Phone (907) 262-3150 for more information.

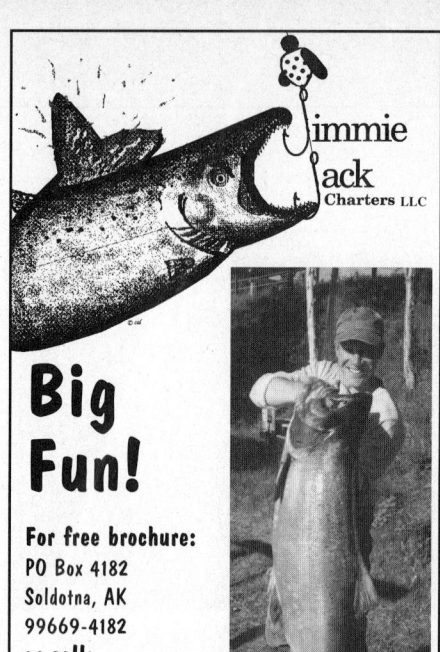

Soldotna Historical Society Museum, located on Centennial Park Road, features a wildlife museum and historic log village. Among the log buildings is the last territorial school (built in 1958). Soldotna's founding settlers arrived in 1947. The "habitable dwellings" that entitled 2 of these first homesteaders to 160 acres from what is now mid-town Soldotna are part of the village. How these latter-day pioneers lived is revealed in a collection of homestead artifacts and photos in the former Soldotna Chamber of Commerce log tourist center. Damon Hall, a large building constructed for the Alaska Centennial, features an outstanding display of wildlife mounts with a background mural of these species' natural habitat. Open 10 A.M. to 4 P.M., Tuesday through Saturday and noon to 4 P.M. Sunday in summer.

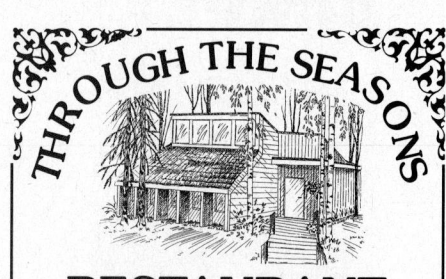

Joyce Carver Memorial Library offers temporary cards for visitors; large sunlit reading areas for both adults and children; Alaska videos on summer Saturday afternoons at 2 P.M. Open 9 A.M. to 8 P.M. Monday through Thursday, noon to 6 P.M. Friday, and 9 A.M. to 6 P.M. Saturdays. 235 Binkley St., Soldotna, phone (907) 262-4227.

Kenai National Wildlife Refuge Visitor Center, located at the top of Ski Hill Road (see **Milepost S 97.9**) and also accessible from Funny River Road (see **Milepost S 96.1**), hosts some 25,000 visitors annually. This modern center has dioramas containing lifelike mounts of area wildlife in simulated natural settings. There is a free video about the refuge shown on the hour, between noon and 4 P.M., weekdays in summer. Free wildlife films are shown on the hour every weekend from noon to 5 P.M. Information available here on canoeing, hiking and camping. There is a 1-mile-/1.6-km-long nature trail with an observation platform and spotting scope on Headquarters Lake. The Alaska Natural History Assoc. has a sales outlet here with books, posters and slide sets. Pay phone located in center. Open weekdays 8 A.M. to 4:30 P.M., and weekends 10 A.M. to 6 P.M. No admission fee.

The refuge was created in 1941 when Pres. Franklin D. Roosevelt set aside 1,730,000

Slikok Valley School, the last of the Alaska Territorial log schools, was built by homesteaders in 1958. (Photo courtesy of Soldotna Historical Society)

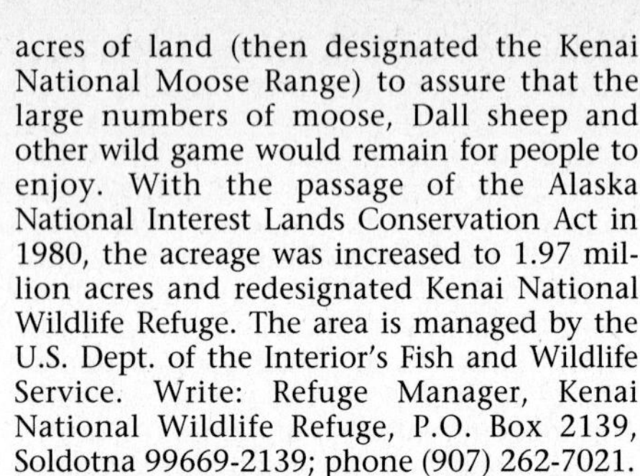

acres of land (then designated the Kenai National Moose Range) to assure that the large numbers of moose, Dall sheep and other wild game would remain for people to enjoy. With the passage of the Alaska National Interest Lands Conservation Act in 1980, the acreage was increased to 1.97 million acres and redesignated Kenai National Wildlife Refuge. The area is managed by the U.S. Dept. of the Interior's Fish and Wildlife Service. Write: Refuge Manager, Kenai National Wildlife Refuge, P.O. Box 2139, Soldotna 99669-2139; phone (907) 262-7021.

Take a Canoe Trip on one of several routes available in this part of the Kenai Peninsula. Enjoyment of wildlife in their natural habitat, true wilderness scenery, camping, and fishing for trout and salmon are a few highlights of a canoe trip.

Established canoe trails include the Swanson River route (80 miles/129 km) and Swan Lake route (60 miles/97 km). Complete information on Kenai Peninsula canoe trails is available at the USF&WS information cabin at Mile 58 Sterling Highway, the Kenai NWR information center in Soldotna and at chamber of commerce visitor centers in Kenai and Soldotna.

Kenai Spur Highway Log

Distance from Soldotna Y (SY). The Kenai Spur Highway branches off the Sterling Highway at the Soldotna Y.

SY 0 Junction with Sterling Highway at **Milepost S 94.2.**

SY 0.7 (1.1 km) Hospital, Soldotna High School.

SY 1 (1.6 km) Fishing licenses, tackle, 24-hour gas.

Tesoro 7-Eleven. See display ad this section.

SY 1.8 (2.8 km) Big Eddy Road to west. Access to Big Eddy state recreational site on Kenai River with wheelchair-accessible toilets, fishing guides, private camping, moorage, boat launches and rental facilities.

SY 2.2 (3.5 km) Big Eddy second access.

SY 2.5 (4 km) Sport Lake Road; access to bed and breakfast.

SY 4 (6.4 km) Kenai city limits.

SY 5.9 (9.4 km) Dogwood Street.

SY 6.1 (9.8 km) Beaver Creek Park (day use only); parking, toilets, picnic tables, playground, basketball court, covered table, litter barrels.

SY 6.4 (10.3 km) Twin City Raceway. South **junction** with Beaver Loop Road: Drive 2.5 miles/4 km on Beaver Loop Road and turn south (left fork), crossing Warren Ames Memorial Bridge, to connect with Kalifornsky Beach Road. Turn north (right fork) for return to Kenai Spur Highway at Mile 10.9.

SY 9.3 (14.9 km) Tinker Lane. Access to Peninsula Oilers baseball park, municipal golf course and junior high school.

SY 10.2 (16.4 km) Airport Road (right), Walker Road (left). Begin divided 4-lane highway, 35-mph/56-kmph zone, through Kenai business area.

SY 10.5 (16.9 km) Bridge Access Road; north **junction** with Beaver Loop Road. Access south to Bridge Access Road and Port of Kenai; public boat launch with parking and toilets available. Road crosses Warren Ames Bridge and junctions with Kalifornsky Beach Road. Kenai River Flats state recreation site south of bridge has toilets and dumpster. Good spot to see migrating waterfowl.

SY 11 (17.7 km) **KENAI** (description of city begins on page 528). Carr's/Kmart shopping complex. Willow Street access to Kenai Municipal Airport 1 mile northeast.

SY 12.1 (19.5 km) Forest Drive. Scenic viewpoint overlooking Cook Inlet.

SY 12.4 (20 km) C Plaza; shopping.

SY 15 (24.1 km) Kenai city limits.

SY 21.3 (34.3 km) Miller Loop Road, connects with Island Lake Road.

SY 22.1 (35.5 km) **NIKISKI** (pop. 5,000). **Emergency Services,** phone 911 for fire and paramedics. Also known as Port Nikiski and Nikishka, this area was homesteaded in the 1940s and grew with the discovery of oil on the Kenai Peninsula in 1957. By 1964, oil-related industries here included Unocal Chemical, Phillips LNG, Chevron and Tesoro. Oil docks servicing offshore drilling platforms today include Rigtenders, Standard Oil, Phillips 66 and Union Collier Chemical. Commercial fishing, hunting and trapping are still a source of income for some residents.

SY 22.5 (36.2 km) Access to Nikiski Rigtenders dock; tankers may be seen next to dock.

SY 23.5 (37.8 km) North Peninsula Recreation Area and Nikiski elementary school. Dome-shaped building in trees near highway is the Nikiski recreational swimming pool, renovated (1994) with indoor slide and hot tub; visitor observation area at pool. Other facilities include an ice rink, hiking and ski trails, a picnic area and ball fields. Phone (907) 776-8800.

SY 25.8 (41.5 km) Island Lake Road.

SY 26.6 (42.8 km) Nikishka Mall shopping, restaurant, supermarket, gas station and Nikiski branch Kenai post office.

SY 26.7 (43 km) Nikiski Beach Road; views of Nikishka Bay and Cook Inlet. Nikiski Fire Station No. 2.

SY 29.7 (47.8 km) Halbouty Road.

Daniels Lake Lodge Bed & Breakfast. See display ad this section.

SY 30 (48.2 km) Daniels Lake.

SY 32.5 (52.3 km) Turnout west opposite Twin Lakes.

SY 35.6 (57.3 km) Entering Captain Cook State Recreation Area.

SY 35.9 (57.8 km) Bishop Creek State Recreation Site; 15 campsites, parking, toilets, water, picnic area and trail to beach. Camping fee $8/night or annual pass. Watch for spawning red salmon in creek in July and August, silvers August to Sept. Closed to salmon fishing. ▲

SY 36.5 (58.7 km) Access to **Stormy Lake** swimming area, changehouse, toilet, water, parking and rainbow and arctic char fishing.

SY 36.7 (59.1 km) Stormy Lake overlook; large paved turnout to east.

SY 36.9 (59.4 km) Stormy Lake picnic area; water, toilets, covered tables.

SY 37.8 (60.8 km) Stormy Lake boat launch; water, toilets, parking.

SY 38.6 (62.1 km) Swanson River canoe landing area; drive 0.6 mile/1 km east to parking and toilets, river access.

SY 38.7 (62.3 km) Clint Starnes Memorial Bridge crosses **Swanson River**; parking next to bridge for fishing access, toilets, view of Mount Spurr. Fishing for silver and red salmon, and rainbow.

SY 39 (62.8 km) Pavement ends at T. Take left fork for Discovery Campground (Captain Cook SRA); 53 campsites, picnic area, Maggie Yurick Memorial hiking trail, water, beachcombing for agates. Right fork leads to additional parking. Camping fee $10/night or annual pass. ▲

SY 39.6 (63.7 km) Picnic area with tables and toilets, on bluff overlooking ocean at end of Kenai Spur Highway.

Return to Milepost S 94.2 Sterling Highway

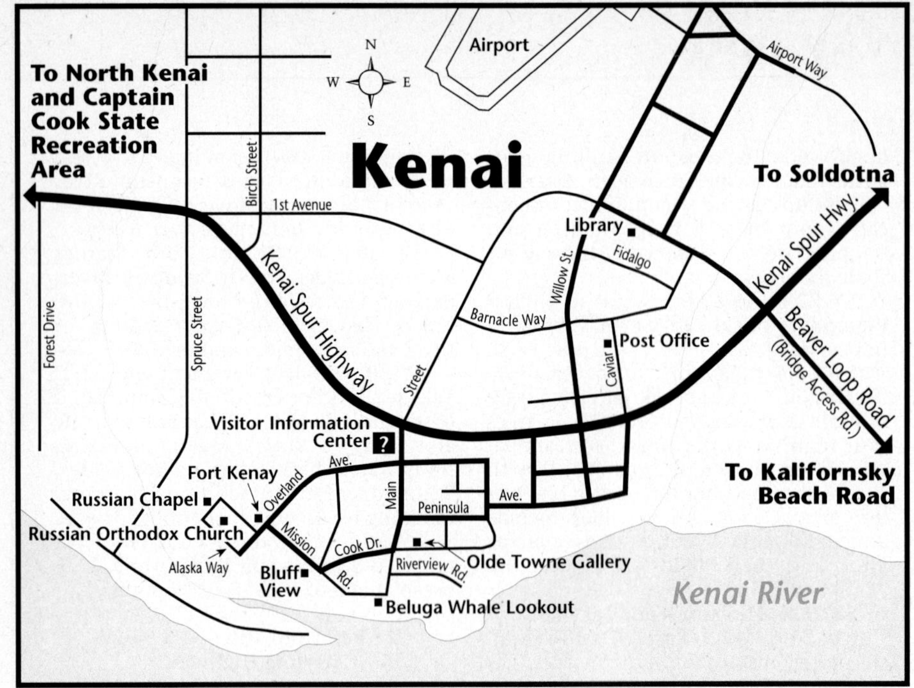

Kenai

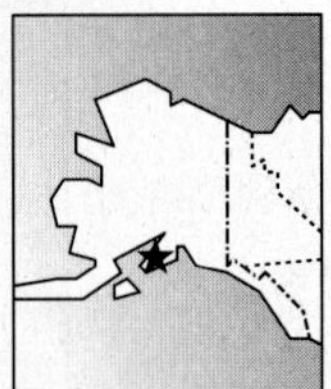

SY 11 (17.7 km). On the western Kenai Peninsula. Reached via the Kenai Spur Highway, or 9.3 miles/14.9 km from Soldotna via the Kalifornsky Beach Road, 158.5 miles/255 km from Anchorage, 89.3 miles/143.7 km from Homer. **Population:** 6,613.

Emergency Services: Phone 911 for all emergency services. **Alaska State Troopers** (in Soldotna), phone (907) 262-4453. **Kenai City Police**, phone (907) 283-7879. **Fire Department** and **Ambulance**, phone 911. **Hospital** (in Soldotna), phone (907) 262-4404. **Maritime Search and Rescue**, dial 0 for Zenith 5555, toll free.

Visitor Information: The Kenai Bicentennial Visitors and Cultural Center, located in downtown Kenai, provides brochures and other visitor information. The center features a cultural museum, wildlife displays and movies (in summer). For a full list of visitor services available in Kenai, write the Kenai Visitors and Cultural Center, 11471 Kenai Spur Highway, Kenai, AK 99611; phone (907) 283-1991, fax 283-2230.

Elevation: 93 feet/28m. **Climate:** Average daily maximum temperature in July, 61°F/16°C; Jan. temperatures range from 11° to -19°F/-12° to -28°C. Lowest recorded temperature in Kenai was -48°F/-44°C. Average annual precipitation, 19.9 inches (68.7 inches of snowfall). **Radio:** KCSY 1140, KENI 550, KGTL 620, KSRM 920, KWVV 105, KGTL 100.9/103.5, MBN-FM 95.3/97.7, KENY 980, KWHQ-FM 100.1, KPEN-FM 101.7. **Television:** Several channels and cable. **Newspaper:** *Peninsula Clarion* (daily).

Private Aircraft: Kenai Municipal Airport, adjacent north; elev. 92 feet/28m; length 7,575 feet/2,309m; asphalt; fuel 100LL; attended. Transient tie-down fees $2/day. Adjacent floatplane base offers 3,500-foot/1,067-m basin with 35 slips.

Kenai is situated on a low rise overlooking the mouth of the Kenai River where it empties into Cook Inlet. It is the largest city on the Kenai Peninsula. Prior to Russian Alaska, Kenai was a Dena'ina Native community. The Dena'ina people fished, hunted, trapped, farmed and traded with neighboring tribes here. In 1791 it became the second permanent settlement established by the Russians in Alaska, when a fortified post called Fort St. Nicholas, or St. Nicholas Redoubt, was built near here by Russian fur traders. In 1848, the first Alaska gold discovery wqas made on the Russian River. In 1869 the U.S. Army established Fort Kenai (Kenay); in 1899 a post office was authorized.

Oil exploration began in the mid-1950s, with the first major discovery in this area, the Swanson River oil reserves, 20 miles/32.2 km northeast of Kenai in 1957. Two years later, natural gas was discovered in the Kalifornsky Beach area 6 miles/9.6 km south of the city of Kenai. Extensive exploration offshore in upper Cook Inlet has established that Cook Inlet's middle-ground shoals contain one of the major oil and gas fields in the world.

KENAI ADVERTISERS

Alaska's Reservation Central .... Kenai Airport
Beaver Creek Cabin Rentals .... Ph. (907) 283-4262
Beluga Lookout RV Park ... Ph. (907) 283-5999
Captain Bligh's "Beaver Creek Lodge" & Guide Services .... Ph. (907) 283-7550
Inlet Card & Craft .. Mile 12.4 Kenai Spur Hwy.
Lottie's Place Bed and Breakfast .... Mile 12.3 Kalifornsky Beach Rd.
Katmai Hotel .... Main St. & Kenai Spur Hwy.
Kenai Golf Course .... 1420 Lawton Dr.
Kenai Kings Inn .... Ph. (907) 283-6060
Kenai Merit Inn .... Ph. (800) 227-6131
Kenai Visitors & Convention Bureau, Inc. .... 11471 Kenai Spur Hwy.
Overland RV Park and Gift Shop .... Mile 11.5 Kenai Spur Hwy.

The industrial complex on the North Kenai Road is the site of Unocal Chemicals, which produces ammonia and urea for fertilizer. Phillips Petroleum operates a liquid natural gas plant. Tesoro has a refinery here.

Offshore in Cook Inlet are 15 drilling platforms, all with underwater pipelines bringing the oil to the shipping docks on both sides of Cook Inlet for loading onto tankers.

Federal and state agencies based in and around Kenai contribute to the local economy. Next to oil, tourism, fishing and fish processing are the leading industries.

ACCOMMODATIONS/VISITOR SERVICES

Kenai has all shopping facilities and conveniences. Medical and dental clinics, banks, laundromats, theaters, pharmacies, supermarkets and numerous gift and specialty shops are located on and off the highway and in the shopping malls. Several motels and hotels and about a dozen restaurants and drive-ins are located in Kenai. Local artists are featured at the Kenai Fine Arts Center on Cook Street. Showers, sauna, weight room, racquetball courts and gym at Kenai Recreation Center, on Caviar Street. Open 6 A.M. to 10 P.M. Monday through Saturday, Sunday 1 to 10 P.M. Phone (907) 283-3855. For joggers there's the Bernie Huss Memorial Trail, a 0.5-mile jogging and exercise course located just off the Kenai Spur Highway on Main Street Loop. Dump stations located at several local service stations and city dock.

City of Kenai public boat ramp on Boat Launch Road off Bridge Access Road has 24-hour parking, restrooms with flush toilets, pay phone.

Kenai City Park has covered picnic tables and fireplaces. Arrangements for caravan camping may be made in advance through the Kenai Visitors and Cultural Center. Tent camping and private RV parks available in and near shopping areas. Ask at the Visitors Center for directions. ▲

Drive north of town on the Kenai Spur Highway for more lodging and camping.

Beluga Lookout RV Park, 2 blocks from Kenai Visitors Center, downtown Kenai. Overlooking bluff with fantastic view of beluga whales, Kenai River, Cook Inlet, Mount Redoubt. The historic Russian Orthodox Church, Fort Kenay are next door. Restaurants, shopping 2 blocks. New 1995 log lodge, private bathrooms and hot showers, laundry, free coffee. Charter and tour bookings. Service with a smile. 75 level full-hookup spaces, cable TV, picnic tables, gas grills, pull-throughs, 30-50 amp power. Caravans welcome. Good Sam Club. VISA, MasterCard accepted. Reservations 1-800-745-5999 or (907) 283-5999. See display ad this section. [ADVERTISEMENT] ▲

Kenai Merit Inn. Conveniently located in downtown Kenai. $80–$90 June–August. $50–$60 September–May. Same rates single or double occupancy. Tour groups welcome year-round. Large parking area. Group meals to fit your schedule. 58 clean, quiet, comfortable rooms, Cable TV, phone, private bath. Free local calls. Full-service restaurant and lounge. Breakfast served all day. Laundromat, vehicle services nearby. Walk to see: Beluga Whales in the famous Kenai River, local commercial fishing fleet, Russian Orthodox church tours, Visitor Center displays and information. 5 minutes to beautiful 18-hole golf course. 15 minutes to Nikiski indoor pool and 136 foot water slide. Book adventures. Credit cards accepted. 1-800-227-6131. [ADVERTISEMENT]

Lottie's Place Bed and Breakfast. Located Mile 12.3 Kalifornsky Beach Road, halfway between the Kenai and Kasilof rivers. Walk the beach, relax by the fireplace. Barbecue available for your catch of the day. Continental or full breakfast. Queen-size beds, satellite TV. Honeymoon bedroom with fireplace. Owned and operated by longtime Alaskans. Reservations: (907) 283-8707. See display ad in Soldotna section. [ADVERTISEMENT]

Overland RV Park and Gift Shop, next to Kenai Visitors Center, downtown Kenai, within a block of everything: Kenai River bluff view, Russian Orthodox Church, restaurants, shopping. 50 full hookups, 30-amp power, level spaces, pull-throughs; picnic tables at each site. Dump station, clean restrooms, hot showers, laundry for guests only. Daily, weekly, monthly rates. Caravans welcome. We can arrange fishing charters or tell you where to bank fish. Quality gifts and souvenirs at affordable prices. Alaska Native handicrafts, T-shirts and postcards, too. VISA, MasterCard accepted. (907) 283-4512 (summer); (907) 283-4227 (winter). See display ad this section. [ADVERTISEMENT] ▲

TRANSPORTATION

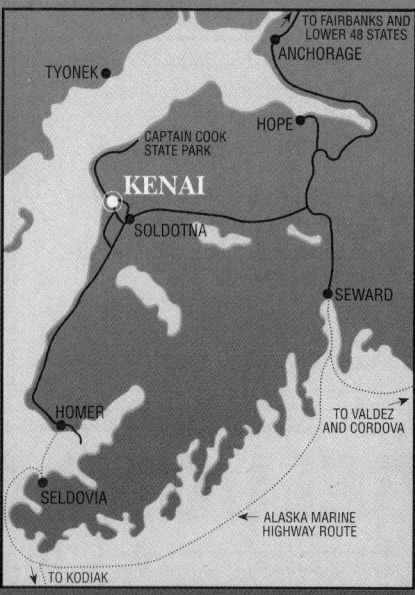

Air: Kenai is served by MarkAir and Era–Alaska. Several firms offer charter service out of Kenai. Kenai Municipal Airport (see description under Private Aircraft) is approx-

Kenai's St. Nicholas Chapel, built in 1906. (© Harry M. Walker)

imately 2 blocks west of the Carr's/Kmart complex on the Kenai Spur Highway. **Local:** Limousine and taxi service is available as well as car rentals, vehicle leasing, boat rentals and charters.

ATTRACTIONS

Get Acquainted. Pick up a brochure at the Kenai Visitors and Cultural Center. The center houses a cultural museum, which has wildlife displays and information on local activities. The center also shows films on Alaska daily in summer.

Kenai River Flats is a must stop for bird-watchers. Great numbers of Siberian snow geese and other waterfowl stop to feed on this saltwater marsh in the spring. The state recreation site on Bridge Access Road at Warren Ames Bridge has parking and interpretive signs. Boardwalk for wildlife-watchers. Also watch for caribou on the Kenai Flats.

Beluga Whale Watching on the Kenai River beach at the west end of Main Street. Beluga whales are the only all-white whale. The beach also offers a good view of Kenai's fish-processing industry.

Watch Baseball or Play Golf. Some fine semipro baseball is played at the Peninsula Oilers ball park on Tinker Lane. Golfers may try the 18-hole Kenai golf course on Lawton Drive.

Fort Kenay was the first American military installation in the area, established in 1869. More than 100 men were stationed here in the 1½ years it officially served to protect American citizens in the area. A replica of the fort's barracks building was built as an Alaskan Purchase Centennial project by Kenai residents in 1967. It is opeated by the Holy Assumption Russian Orthodox Church.

Holy Assumption Russian Orthodox Church is across from Fort Kenay. The original church was founded in 1846 by a Russian monk, Egumen Nicolai. The present church was built some 50 years after the original and with its 3 onion-shaped domes is considered one of the finest examples of a Russian Orthodox church built on a vessel or quadrilateral ground plan. It is one of the oldest Russian Orthodox churches in Alaska. In 1971 it was designated a national historic landmark. An 1847 edition of the book of the Holy Gospel of the 4 evangelists—Matthew, Mark, Luke and John—with 5 enameled icons on the cover, is awaiting restoration (not on display). Regular church services are held here, and tours are available; inquire at the church. Donations accepted.

St. Nicholas Chapel, built in 1906, west of the Russian church, marks the burial location of Father Egumen Nicolai and other Russian Orthodox Church workers.

Sterling Highway Log

(continued from page 517)

S 95.9 (154.3 km) **A 148.9** (239.6 km) **H 83.6** (134.5 km) Kenai River bridge.

Entering Soldotna northbound. Description of city begins on page 517.

S 96 (154.5 km) **A 149** (239.8 km) **H 83.5** (134.4 km) Soldotna visitor center at south end of Kenai River bridge.

S 96.1 (154.7 km) **A 149.1** (239.9 km) **H 83.4** (134.2 km) **Junction.** Funny River Road to east, Kalifornsky Beach Road to west. Kalifornsky Beach Road rejoins the Sterling Highway at **Milepost S 108.8.** (See KALIFORNSKY BEACH ROAD log on page 532.)

Centennial Park campground, 0.1 mile/0.2 km west, on the banks of the Kenai River. There are 126 campsites (some on river), tables, firepits, firewood provided, water, restrooms, dump station, pay phone, 2-week limit. Boat launch and favorite fishing site at far end of campground. Register at campground entrance.

Funny River (Airport) Road leads east 2 miles/3.2 km to Soldotna airport, 4 miles/6.4 km to Airport Rotary Park (day-use only) and 11.5 miles/18.5 km to Funny River State Recreation Site; 12 campsites, $8 nightly fee per vehicle or annual pass, picnic tables, water, toilets, river access. Salmon and trout fishing at the confluence of the **Kenai** and **Funny rivers** at the recreation area. Turn on Funny River Road and take first right (Ski Hill Loop Road) for USF&WS visitor center. Funny River Road dead ends 17.2 miles/27.7 km from the highway. Private RV park located at Mile 13.8.

S 97.9 (157.6 km) **A 150.9** (242.8 km) **H 81.6** (131.3 km) Sky View High School. Easy-to-miss turnoff for Kenai National Wildlife Refuge headquarters and information center: Turn east off highway and drive 1 mile/1.6 km on Ski Hill Road, which loops back to Funny River Road (see preceding milepost). Nature trail with wildlife observation platform and spotting scope on Headquarters Lake. The center is open 8 A.M. to 4:30 P.M. on weekdays, 10 A.M. to 6 P.M. weekends.

S 99.9 (160.8 km) **A 152.9** (246.1 km) **H 79.6** (128.1 km) Echo Lake Road to west.

S 101.5 (163.3 km) **156.1** (251.2 km) **H 78** (125.5 km) Goldust Avenue.

S 108.8 (175 km) **A 161.8** (260.4 km) **H 70.7** (113.8 km) South **junction** with Kalifornsky Beach Road. (See KALIFORNSKY

BEACH ROAD log this section.) Drive west 3.6 miles/5.8 km to Beach Road for access to beach, Kasilof small-boat harbor and Kasilof River. This loop road rejoins Sterling Highway at **Milepost S 96.1.**

KASILOF (kuh-SEE-lawf; pop. 383; elev. 75 feet/23m) was originally a settlement established in 1786 by the Russians as St. George. An Indian fishing village grew up around the site, but no longer exists. Native inhabitants of the peninsula are mostly Kanai Indians, a branch of the great Athabascan family. The population is spread out over the general area which is called Kasilof. The area's income is derived from fishing and fish processing.

Kasilof River. The red salmon dip-net fishery here is open by special announcement for Alaska residents only. Check with the ADF&G for current regulations.

Private Aircraft: Kasilof airstrip, 1.7 miles/2.7 km north; elev. 125 feet/38m; length 2,300 feet/701m; gravel; unattended.

S 109 (175.4 km) **A 162** (260.7 km) **H 70.5** (113.5 km) Grocery store.

S 109.2 (175.7 km) **A 162.2** (261 km) **H 70.3** (113.1 km) **Kasilof Riverview.** See display ad this section.

S 109.4 (176.1 km) **A 162.4** (261.3 km) **H 70.1** (112.8 km) Bridge over Kasilof River, which drains Tustumena Lake, one of the largest lakes on the Kenai Peninsula. Kasilof River State Recreation Site; 16 campsites, $8 nightly fee or annual pass, 5 picnic sites on riverbank, picnic tables, toilets and water are on the south side of the bridge. Boat launch $5 fee or annual pass. Entering Game Management Subunit 15C southbound, 15B northbound.

S 110 (177 km) **A 163** (262.3 km) **H 69.5** (111.8 km) Tustumena Elementary School and north end of Tustumena Lake Road. This is the first turnoff southbound for access to Johnson and Tustumena lakes. Also turn off here for picnic area with covered picnic tables, toilets (wheelchair accessible), firepits, water and dumpster. There is a huge metal T at Tustumena Lake Road, just beyond the picnic area: Turn east at the T for Johnson and Tustumena lakes. **Johnson Lake** is 0.3 mile/0.5 km from the highway. Johnson Lake state campground has 50 sites (some double and some pull-throughs), $10 nightly fee or annual pass, water, toilets, boat launch and firewood. Lake is stocked with rainbow. Watch for beaver, moose, and king salmon migrating up Crooked Creek. **Tustumena Lake** is 6.4 miles/10.3 km from the highway; a campground on the Kasilof River near the lake has 10 sites, toilets and boat launch. Fishing for lake trout and salmon. Tustumena Lake is closed to king and sockeye salmon fishing.

CAUTION: This lake is 6 miles/10 km wide and 25 miles/40 km long and subject to severe winds.

S 110.5 (177.8 km) **A 163.5** (263.1 km) **H 69** (111 km) Double-ended paved parking by Crooked Creek.

S 110.8 (178.3 km) **A 163.8** (263.6 km) **H 68.7** (110.6 km) **Tustumena Lodge.** Motel, cocktail lounge, fishing guides. Phone (907) 262-4216. Clean, affordable rooms at half the price of town. Some kitchenettes. Friendly Alaskan atmosphere where a cold drink, light snack and good fish stories are always available. Monday night–prime rib, $7. Friday night–New York Steak, $6. See the world's largest razor clam. Look for a hat from your hometown among the over 6,500 hats in our pending Guinness record collection. [ADVERTISEMENT]

S 111 (178.6 km) **A 164** (263.9 km) **H 68.5** (110.2 km) Cohoe Loop Road north **junction** (turnoff to west). Crooked Creek State Recreation Site (camping and fishing) 1.8 miles/2.8 km west on Cohoe Loop Road.

Kalifornsky Beach Road Log

Also called K–Beach Road, Kalifornsky Beach Road leads west and south from the Sterling Highway at Soldotna, following the shore of Cook Inlet to Kasilof. **Distance from the Sterling Highway junction at Milepost S 96.1 at Soldotna (S) is followed by distance from Sterling Highway junction at Milepost S 108.8 at Kasilof (K). Mileposts run south to north.**

S 0 K 22.2 (35.7 km) **Junction** with Sterling Highway at **Milepost S 96.1.**

S 0.1 (0.2 km) **K 22.1** (35.6 km) Soldotna Alaska Purchase Centennial Park Campground, operated by the city of Soldotna. Kenai River access for bank fishing, boat launch (fee charged).

S 0.2 (0.3 km) **K 22** (35.4 km) Alaska State Troopers.

S 0.4 (0.6 km) **K 21.8** (35.1 km) Rodeo grounds.

S 0.6 (1 km) **K 21.6** (34.8 km) Central Peninsula Sports Center; hockey, ice skating, jogging track and other sports available; phone (907) 262-3150 for more information. Senior center.

S 1.7 (2.7 km) **K 20.5** (33 km) Kenai Peninsula Community College access road. Also access to Slikok Creek State Recreation Site, 0.7 mile/1.1 km north; day use only with 12-hour parking, wheelchair accessible toilets, picnic tables, information kiosk and trails. No fires or ATVs.

S 2.9 (4.7 km) **K 19.3** (31.1 km) K–Beach center. ADF&G office; stop in here for current sportfishing information.

S 3.1 (5 km) **K 19.1** (30.7 km) Grocery and gas.

Short Stop. See display ad this section.

S 3.5 (5.6 km) **K 18.7** (30.1 km) Red Diamond shopping center, Duck Inn Motel and restaurant.

S 4.6 (7.4 km) **K 17.6** (28.3 km) Firehouse.

S 4.7 (7.6 km) **K 17.5** (28.2 km) Ciechansky Road leads 2.2 miles/3.5 km to Ciechansky State Recreation Site, a day-use only picnic area with tables, toilets, dumpster and Kenai River access. Also access to private campgrounds with RV hookups on the Kenai River.

S 6 (9.7 km) **K 16.2** (26.1 km) Turnoff for city of Kenai, 3.1 miles/5 km north via the Warren Ames Memorial Bridge.

S 6.7 (10.8 km) **K 15.5** (24.9 km) **The Rookery B&B** sits atop the bluff, offering a panoramic view of the Kenai River, National Snow Goose Preserve and Alaska Range. Moose, caribou and eagles are often seen. Three bedrooms, large recreation room, pool table, TV, VCR and full kitchen. A real Alaskan breakfast is served. (907) 283-9410; fax (907) 283-9354. [ADVERTISEMENT]

S 6.8 (10.9 km) **K 15.4** (24.8 km) Magnificent beaver dam and lodge, lupine display in June.

S 7.6 (12.2 km) **K 14.6** (23.5 km) Robinsons mini-mall.

S 7.8 (12.5 km) **K 14.4** (23.2 km) Kenai Custom Seafoods.

S 8 (12.9 km) **K 14.2** (22.9 km) Cafe.

S 8.9 (14.3 km) **K 12.3** (19.8 km) Bed and breakfast.

S 13 (20.9 km) **K 9.2** (14.8 km) Scenic viewpoint overlooking Cook Inlet.

S 17.4 (28 km) **K 4.8** (7.7 km) Kasilof Beach Road.

S 20.1 (32.3 km) **K 2.1** (3.4 km) Kasilof Airfield Road.

S 22.1 (35.6 km) **K 0.1** (0.2 km) Kasilof post office.

S 22.2 (35.7 km) **K 0 Junction** with Sterling Highway at **Milepost S 108.8** at Kasilof.

Return to Milepost S 96.1 or S 108.8 Sterling Highway

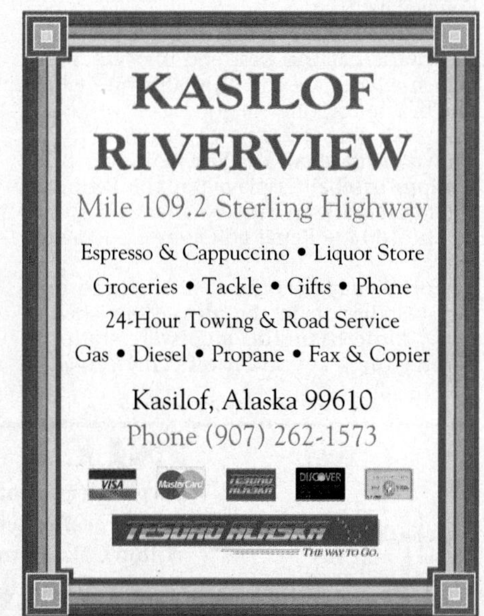

South end of Tustumena Lake Road (to east) for Johnson and Tustumena lakes (see description at **Milepost S 110**). Cohoe Loop Road rejoins the Sterling Highway at **Milepost S 114.3** (see COHOE LOOP ROAD log this section).

Just east of the highway on the Johnson and Tustumena lakes access road is Crooked Creek fish hatchery, open 8 A.M. to 5 P.M.; a sign explains the chinook and sockeye salmon operation here. For further information, contact Cook Inlet Aquaculture Assoc., phone (907) 283-5761. The hatchery-produced salmon create a popular fishery at the confluence of Crooked Creek and the Kasilof River, accessible via the Cohoe Loop Road. Just past the hatchery is Crooked Creek Road, and just beyond is a huge metal T at Tustumena Lake Road. Continue past this monument for a picnic area, and return to Sterling Highway at **Milepost S 110**; turn at the T for lakes and camping. ▲

Cohoe Lodge. See display ad this section.

Crooked Creek RV Park & Guide Service. See display ad this section. ▲

Kasilof RV Park. 1/2 mile off the Sterling Highway on Crooked Creek Road. View peaceful Johnson Lake while being centrally located for all your Kenai Peninsula vacation activities. Electrical hookups, dump station, sparkling fresh well-water, pull-throughs, showers, modern bathrooms, laundry room. (907) 262-0418. [ADVERTISEMENT] ▲

S 114.3 (183.9 km) **A 167.3** (269.2 km) **H 65.2** (104.9 km) Cohoe Loop Road south **junction** with the Sterling Highway. The 13-mile/21-km road loops north to **Milepost S 111.** See COHOE LOOP ROAD log this section.

S 117.4 (188.9 km) **A 170.4** (274.2 km) **H 62.1** (99.9 km) Clam Gulch State Recreation Area (watch for easy-to-miss sign) is 0.5 mile/0.8 km from highway; picnic tables, picnic shelter, toilets, water, 116 campsites, $8 nightly fee or annual pass. *CAUTION: High ocean bluffs are dangerous.* Short access road to beach (recommended for 4-wheel-drive vehicles only, limited turnaround space). ▲

Clam digging for razor clams on most of the sandy beaches of the western Kenai Peninsula from Kasilof to Anchor Point can be rewarding. Many thousands of clams are dug each year at Clam Gulch. You must have a sportfishing license to dig, and these are available at most sporting goods stores. The bag limit is 60 clams regardless of size (always check current regulations). There is no legally closed season, but quality of the clams varies with month; check locally. Good clamming and fewer people in March and April, although there may still be ice on the beach. Any tide lower than a minus 1-

Cohoe Loop Road Log

The Cohoe Loop Road loops south 15.3 miles/24.7 km from **Milepost S 111** on the Sterling Highway. The popular Crooked Creek fishing and camping area is at the top or north end of the loop. The bottom (or south) 10 miles of the Cohoe Loop Road travels through mostly undeveloped parcels of land; no services, views or recreation. Motorists may wish to use the north junction approach.

Distance from north junction with the Sterling Highway (NJ) at Milepost S 111 is followed by distance from south junction (SJ) at Milepost S 114.3. Mileposts run south to north.

NJ 0 SJ 15.3 (24.6 km) **Junction** with Sterling Highway at **Milepost S 111.**

NJ 1.8 (2.9 km) **SJ 13.5** (21.7 km) Crooked Creek/Rilinda Drive; access to private RV park and Crooked Creek State Recreation Site at the confluence of Crooked Creek and the Kasilof River. The recreation site has 83 campsites, 36 day-use sites, toilets and water trails to Kasilof River for fishermen. Camping fee $8/night or annual pass, day-use fee $5/vehicle or annual pass. ▲

Fishing in **Crooked Creek** closed to king salmon fishing and closed to all fishing near hatchery. Fishing access to confluence of Crooked Creek and Kasilof River is through the state recreation site. *NOTE: Fishing access to Crooked Creek frontage above confluence is through a private RV park; fee charged.* Fishing in the **Kasilof River** for king salmon, late May through July, best in mid-June; coho salmon, mid-August to September, use salmon egg clusters, wet flies, assorted spoons and spinners.

NJ 2.4 (3.9 km) **SJ 12.9** (20.7 km) Webb–Ramsell Road. Kasilof River access across private property, fee charged.

NJ 5.3 (8.5 km) **SJ 10** (16 km) Cohoe Spur Road **junction.** A post office was established in 1950 at **COHOE** (area pop. 508), originally an agricultural settlement.

NJ 5.6 (9 km) **SJ 9.7** (15.6 km) T intersection; go west 0.8 mile/1.3 km for beach and boat launch. Private campground on Madsen Road. Cohoe Loop Road continues north. Pavement begins northbound. ▲

NJ 15.3 (24.6 km) **SJ 0 Junction** with Sterling Highway at **Milepost S 114.3.**

Return to Milepost S 114.3 or Milepost S 111 Sterling Highway

foot tide is enough to dig clams; minus 4- to 5-foot tides are best. The panoramic view of Mount Redoubt, Mount Iliamna and Mount Spurr across Cook Inlet and the expanse of beach are well worth the short side trip even during the off-season.

S 118.2 (190.2 km) **A 171.2** (275.5 km) **H 61.3** (98.7 km) **CLAM GULCH** (pop. 79) post office, lodge and a sled dog racing outfitters shop.

S 118.3 (190.4 km) **A 171.3** (275.7 km) **H 61.2** (98.5 km) **Clam Shell Lodge.** See display ad this section.

S 119.6 (192.5 km) **A 172.6** (277.8 km) **H 59.9** (96.4 km) **Clam Gulch Lodge, Bed & Breakfast.** We welcome guests to our

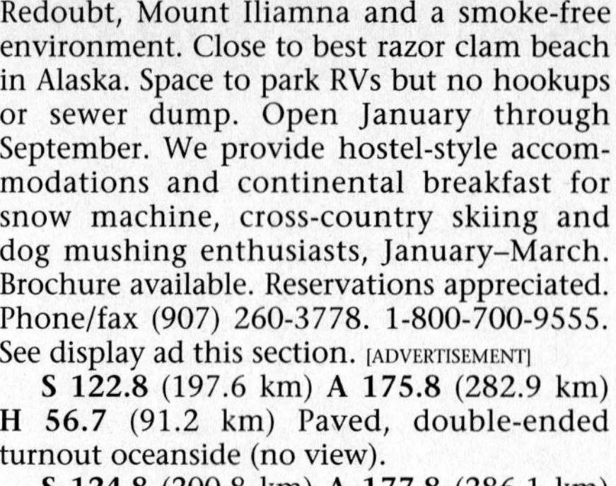

home with breathtaking views of Mount Redoubt, Mount Iliamna and a smoke-free environment. Close to best razor clam beach in Alaska. Space to park RVs but no hookups or sewer dump. Open January through September. We provide hostel-style accommodations and continental breakfast for snow machine, cross-country skiing and dog mushing enthusiasts, January–March. Brochure available. Reservations appreciated. Phone/fax (907) 260-3778. 1-800-700-9555. See display ad this section. [ADVERTISEMENT]

S 122.8 (197.6 km) **A 175.8** (282.9 km) **H 56.7** (91.2 km) Paved, double-ended turnout oceanside (no view).

S 124.8 (200.8 km) **A 177.8** (286.1 km) **H 54.7** (88 km) Paved, double-ended turnout oceanside with view of Cook Inlet.

S 126.8 (204.1 km) **A 179.8** (289.4 km) **H 52.7** (84.8 km) Double-ended paved scenic wayside overlooking upper Cook Inlet. Polly Creek, due west across Cook Inlet, is a popular area for clam diggers (fly in). Across the inlet is Mount Iliamna; north of Iliamna is Mount Redoubt.

S 127.1 (204.5 km) **A 180.1** (289.8 km) **H 52.4** (84.3 km) Double-ended paved scenic viewpoint to west with interpretive display on Mount Redoubt and Mount Spurr volcanoes. Private RV park.

Scenic View RV Park. Spectacular view of Mount Redoubt, Cook Inlet. Ten minutes to Deep Creek for halibut, salmon fishing and clamming. Visit Homer, Kenai, Soldotna and return to peaceful Scenic View sunsets. Hookups, tenting, showers, laundry, local charters. Weekly, monthly rates. Pay phone. 27 spaces. Friendly family atmosphere. Tackle, soft drinks, snacks, gifts available. See display ad this section. [ADVERTISEMENT]

S 132.2 (212.7 km) **A 185.2** (298 km) **H 47.3** (76.1 km) Pay phone at bar.

S 134.5 (216.4 km) **A 187.5** (301.7 km) **H 45** (72.4 km) Ninilchik State Recreation Area. Ninilchik River Scenic Overlook: $8/camping fee, $3/day-use fee. Ninilchik River Campground: $10 camping fee, 43 sites, water, toilets and tables. Trail to **Ninilchik River;** fishing for king and silver salmon, steelhead and Dolly Varden. Ninilchik Beach Campground: $8 camping fee, 50 campsites, toilets, water. Popular beach for razor clamming. Access to the clamming beds adjacent to the campgrounds during minus tides. *CAUTION: Drownings have occurred here. Be aware of tide changes when clam digging. Incoming tides can quickly cut you off from the beach.*

S 134.7 (216.8 km) **A 187.7** (302 km) **H 44.8** (72.1 km) Coal Street; access west to Ninilchik's historic Russian Orthodox Church at top of hill; plenty of parking and turnaround space.

S 134.8 (216.9 km) **A 187.8** (302.2 km) **H 44.7** (71.9 km) Large double-ended gravel turnout.

S 135.1 (217.4 km) **A 188.1** (302.7 km) **H 44.4** (71.4 km) Double-ended gravel turnout and dumpsters at north end of Ninilchik River bridge. Side road leads to **NINILCHIK VILLAGE,** the original village of Ninilchik, and to the beach. Access to mouth of **Ninilchik River;** fishing. A short road branches off this side road and leads into the old village of Ninilchik. Continue straight on side road for motel, beach, overnight RV parking, camping and toilets (follow signs). Sea breezes here keep the beach free of mosquitoes. Historic signs near beach and at village entrance tell about Ninilchik Village, which includes several old dovetailed log buildings. A walking tour brochure is available from businesses in the village and along the highway. Present-day Ninilchik is located at **Milepost S 135.5.** A beautiful white Russian Orthodox church sits on a hill overlooking the sea above the historic old village. Trail leads up to it from the road into town (watch for sign just past the old village store). The church and cemetery are still in use. You are welcome to walk up to it but use the well-defined path behind the store (please do not walk through private property), or drive up using the Coal Street access at **Milepost S 134.7.**

The Historical Ninilchik Village Visitors Center, located in Ninilchik Village just off the Sterling Highway, provides information and history on Ninilchik. Director/resident Michele Vaughan offers referrals to local lodging, camping and fishing charter businesses. The center also offers local art, snacks and sodas. Open year-round. Call at (907) 567-3500. [ADVERTISEMENT]

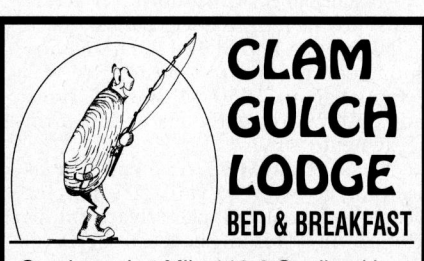

Ninilchik Village Cache, in the old village. Finest selection of "unique" Russian and original Alaskan Native artworks for the collector. Free walking tour map of old village site. Planned for 1996: 11-room lodge and Russian tea room with Cook Inlet View. Reservations (907) 567-1028. See display ad this section. [ADVERTISEMENT]

S 135.3 (217.7 km) **A 188.3** (303 km) **H 44.2** (71.1 km) Gravel turnout to west.

S 135.4 (217.9 km) **A 188.4** (303.2 km) **H 44.1** (71 km) Kingsley Road; access to Ninilchik post office and 2 private campgrounds. Ninilchik View state campground is across the highway overlooking the village and sea; 12 campsites, water, toilets, litter disposal, 2 dump stations ($5 fee), drinking water fill-up. Camping fee $10/night or annual pass. Foot trail from campground down to beach and village. DOT/PF road maintenance station. ▲

Hylen's Camper Park. Next to post office and Senior Center. Fish Deep Creek and Ninilchik River for kings, silvers; Cook Inlet for record halibut, king salmon, May–September. Great clamming. Fish cleaning tables. Smoker. Local businesses, fishing charter discounts. Full, partial or no hookups. No tents. Daily, weekly, plus 30 monthly/seasonal-rated sites. Housekeeping cottages, showers, laundry, storage, social room. Horseshoes. Pay phone. Clean, friendly, reasonable rates. [ADVERTISEMENT] ▲

Ninilchik's historic Russian Orthodox Church at Milepost S 134.7. (© Steven Seiller)

Ninilchik

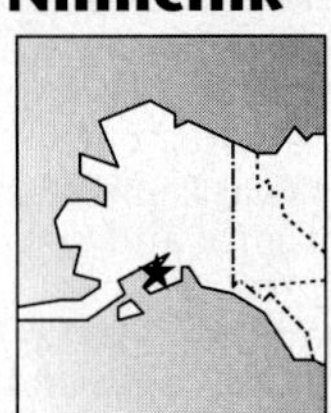

S 135.5 (218 km) **A 188.5** (303.4 km) **H 44** (70.8 km) Pronounced Nin-ILL-chick. **Population:** 456. **Emergency services:** Phone 911. **Clinic and ambulance,** phone (907) 567-3412. **Visitor Information:** At Ninilchik Library, **Milepost S 135.6.** Local businesses are also very helpful. **Private Aircraft:** Ninilchik airstrip, 6.1 miles/9.8 km southeast; elev. 276 feet/84m; length 2,400 feet/732m; dirt; unattended.

Restaurant, lodging and charter service east side of road are part of the community of Ninilchik. Ninilchik extends roughly from Ninilchik State Recreation Area to the north to Deep Creek to the south, with services (grocery stores, gas stations, campgrounds, etc.) located at intervals along the highway. The original village of Ninilchik (signed

NINILCHIK ADVERTISERS

Alexander CM Charters....Ph. (907) 567-3600
Chinook Tesoro............Mile 136 Sterling Hwy.
Deep Creek B&B ....Mile 140 Sterling Hwy.
Hylen's Camper Park ....Ph. (907) 567-3393
Ninilchik Cabins & Fish Camp ....Ph. (907) 567-3645
Ninilchik Chamber of Commerce ....Ph. (907) 567-3571
Ninilchik Charters ....Ph. (907) 248-3507
Ninilchik General Store ....Mile 135.7 Sterling Hwy.
Ninilchik Saltwater Charters ....Ph. (907) 567-3611
Reel 'Em Inn and Cook Inlet Charters......................Ph. (907) 567-7335

Ninilchik Village) is reached by a side road from **Milepost S 135.1.**

On Memorial Day weekend, Ninilchik is referred to as the third biggest city in Alaska, as thousands of Alaskans arrive for the fishing (see Area Fishing following). The Kenai Peninsula Fair is held at Ninilchik the third weekend in Aug. Dubbed the "biggest little fair in Alaska," it features a parade, horse show, livestock competition and exhibits ranging from produce to arts and crafts. Pancake breakfasts, bingo and other events, such as the derby fish fry, are held at the fairgrounds throughout the year. The king salmon derby is held from May to June 11. A halibut derby, sponsored by the Ninilchik Chamber of Commerce, runs from Father's Day through Labor Day. There is an active senior center offering meals and events. Swimming pool at the high school.

AREA FISHING: Well-known area for saltwater king salmon fishing and record halibut fishing. Charter services available. (Combination king salmon and halibut charters are available and popular.) Salt water south of the mouth of **Deep Creek** has produced top king salmon fishing in late May, June and July. Kings 50 lbs. and over are frequently caught. "Lunker" king salmon are available 1 mile/1.6 km south of Deep Creek in **Cook Inlet** from late May through July. Trolling a spinner or a spoon from a boat is the preferred method. Silver, red and pink salmon are available in salt water between Deep Creek and the Ninilchik River during July. A major halibut fishery off Ninilchik has produced some of the largest trophy halibut found in Cook Inlet, including a 466-lb. unofficial world record sport-caught halibut.

Sterling Highway Log

(continued)

S 135.6 (218.2 km) **A 188.6** (303.5 km) **H 43.9** (70.6 km) Ninilchik High School. Ninilchik Library and visitor information center, open 10 A.M. to 4 P.M. daily in the summer.

S 135.7 (218.4 km) **A 188.7** (303.7 km) **H 43.8** (70.5 km) **Ninilchik General Store.** Open every day for all your travel needs. Offering groceries, bait, tackle, licenses, rain gear, ice, film, gifts, books, T-shirts, gold nugget jewelry, hardware and a snack bar. Try our Fisherman's Bag Lunch. Stop in for free information packet on the Ninilchik area. You'll like our prices and service. Ask your friends who have met us. We compete for your business, we don't just wait for it to happen. See display ad this section. [ADVERTISEMENT]

S 135.8 (218.5 km) **A 188.8** (303.7 km) **H 43.7** (70.3 km) **Bull Moose Gifts.** One of the nicest gift shops on the Kenai Peninsula, offering a wide selection of gifts and souvenirs. Alaskan and Russian arts and crafts, fine art prints, jewelry, including Alaskan gold nuggets, caps, postcards, notecards, and over 50 Alaskan designs of T-shirts and sweatshirts. Easy access for large RVs, lots of parking and clean restroom. See display ad this section. [ADVERTISEMENT]

S 135.9 (218.7 km) **A 188.9** (304 km) **H 43.6** (70.2 km) **Homestead House B&B.** See display ad this section.

Reel 'Em Inn/Cook Inlet Charters. East 1 mile on Oilwell Road at the Chinook Tesoro. Owned and operated by Alaskan family with the knowledge to show you how to experience the area's attractions. Full-service facility. Fishing charters, lodging, RV hookups. Equipment rental—fishing poles, raingear, boots, clam shovels. Check us out, you will not be sorry! Reservations welcome. (907) 567-7335. See display ad. [ADVERTISEMENT]

S 136 (218.9 km) **A 189** (304.1 km) **H 43.5** (70 km) **Catch-A-Lot Charters.** Fish minutes from launch at Deep Creek for trophy halibut and Kenai king salmon in our 28-foot deluxe boats, the largest allowed in Ninilchik. Large, fully-enclosed cabins, marine bathrooms. Quality rods and reels provided. Free fish cleaning. Vacuum packing, freezing, shipping available. Call ahead for reservations and lodging referrals: (907)

567-7345; Fax (907) 567-7346. [ADVERTISEMENT]

Chinook Tesoro. Ninilchik. 24-hour card lock. Open year-round. Self-serve gasoline, propane, filtered diesel. Auto/RV mechanics, tire repair, water/air for RVs. Bait, ice, market items. Free tide books, visitor information on clamming and guided fishing. Tesoro, VISA, MasterCard, Discover. All major oil company cards welcome. See display ad this section. [ADVERTISEMENT]

S 136.1 (219 km) **A 189.1** (304.3 km) **H 43.4** (69.8 km) **Chihuly's Charters** and **Porcupine Shop.** See display ad this section.

S 136.2 (219.2 km) **A 189.2** (304.5 km) **H 43.3** (69.7 km) Peninsula Fairgrounds.

S 136.7 (219.9 km) **A 189.7** (305.3 km) **H 42.8** (68.9 km) Bridge over Deep Creek. Developed sites on both sides of creek: Deep Creek North Scenic Overlook and Deep Creek South Scenic Overlook. Both have $8/camping fee, $3/day-use fee, restrooms, water, interpretive kiosks, tables and fireplaces. Deep Creek South offers camping May and June only, day-use only rest of summer. ▲

Freshwater fishing in **Deep Creek** for king salmon up to 40 lbs., use spinners with red bead lures, Memorial Day weekend and the 4 weekends following; Dolly Varden in July and Aug.; silver salmon to 15 lbs., Aug. and Sept.; steelhead to 15 lbs., late Sept. through Oct. No bait fishing permitted after Aug. 31. Mouth of Deep Creek access from Deep Creek State Recreation Area turnoff at **Milepost S 137.3.**

S 137 (220.4 km) **A 190** (305.8 km) **H 42.5** (68.4 km) Cannery and sports shop with tackle and clam shovel rentals west side of road.

Fishward Bound Adventures. See display ad this section.

Deep Creek Custom Packing, Inc. Just south of Deep Creek bridge in Ninilchik. Home of the finest gourmet smoked salmon and halibut in the world. Free samples and coffee. Seafood display includes locally caught scallops, razor clams, crab, halibut and salmon. Sport fishermen take their own catch in to be hand-packed, frozen, canned or smoked to their specifications. Mail order service available for gift packs, fresh Alaskan seafood, canned salmon, smoked salmon and halibut. State-of-the-art insulated packaging. Overnight delivery, door-to-door, anywhere in the U.S. Visitor information on the best charters, clam digging and fishing. Stop in and see this truly traditional Alaskan business. See display ad this section. [ADVERTISEMENT]

S 137.3 (220.9 km) **A 190.3** (306.2 km) **H 42.2** (67.9 km) Deep Creek State Recreation Area on the beach at the mouth of Deep Creek; parking for 300 vehicles, overnight camping, water, tables, dumpsters, toilets and fireplaces. Drive 0.5 mile/0.8 km down paved road. Camping fee $10/night per vehicle or annual pass, day-use fee $5 or annual pass. Favorite area for surf fishing and to launch boats. Boat launch $5 fee or annual pass. Private boat launch service here uses tractors to launch boats from beach into Cook Inlet. Seasonal checks by U.S. Coast Guard for personal flotation devices, boating safety. Good bird watching in wetlands behind beach; watch for eagles. Good clamming at low tide. The beaches here are lined with coal, which falls from the exposed seams of high cliffs. ▲

CAUTION: Rapidly changing tides and weather. Although the mouth of Deep Creek affords boaters good protection, low tides may prevent return; check tide tables.

S 138.6 (223 km) **A 191.6** (308.3 km) **H 40.9** (65.8 km) Solid waste transfer site; public dumpsters.

S 140.3 (225.8 km) **A 193.3** (311.1 km) **H 39.2** (63.1 km) Double-ended turnout with scenic view to west.

S 142.7 (229.6 km) **A 195.7** (314.9 km) **H 36.8** (59.2 km) Double-ended paved turnout with dumpster, view of Mount Iliamna across the inlet.

S 143.8 (231.4 km) **A 196.8** (316.7 km) **H 35.7** (57.4 km) Happy Valley Creek. The area surrounding this creek is known locally as the Happy Valley community.

S 148 (238.1 km) **A 201** (323.5 km) **H 31.5** (50.7 km) Scenic viewpoint. Sign here reads: "Looking westerly across Cook Inlet, Mt. Iliamna and Mt. Redoubt in the Chigmit Mountains of the Aleutian Range can be seen rising over 10,000 feet above sea level. This begins a chain of mountains and islands known as the Aleutian Chain extending west over 1,700 miles to Attu beyond the International Date Line to the Bering Sea, separating the Pacific and Arctic oceans. Mt Redoubt on the right, and Iliamna on the left, were recorded as active volcanoes in the mid-18th century. Mt. Redoubt had a minor eruption in 1966."

Mount Redoubt had a major eruption in Dec. 1989. The eruptions continued through April 1990, then subsided to steam plumes. Mount Redoubt is still considered active.

S 150.9 (242.8 km) **A 203.9** (328.1 km) **H 28.6** (46 km) Bridge over Stariski Creek.

S 151.9 (244.4 km) **A 204.9** (329.7 km) **H 27.6** (44.4 km) Stariski Creek State Recreation Site on bluff overlooking Cook Inlet; 13 campsites, $10 nightly fee or annual pass, toilets (wheelchair accessible) and well water. ♿▲

S 152.7 (245.7 km) **A 205.7** (331 km) **H 26.8** (43.1 km) **Eagle Crest RV Park & Cabins.** See display ad this section. ▲

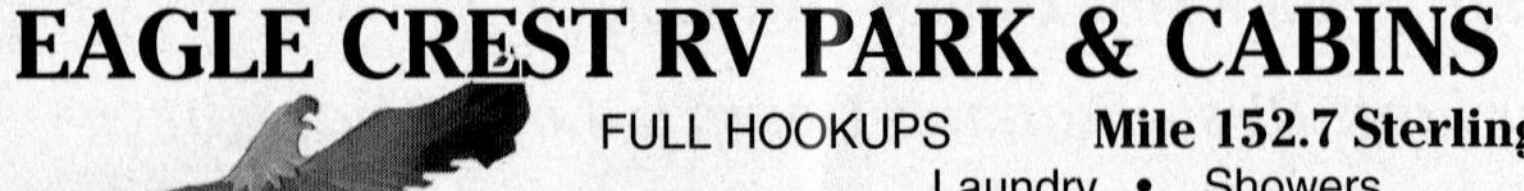

S 153.2 (246.5 km) **A 206.2** (331.8 km) **H 26.3** (42.3 km) **Short Stop RV Parking.** See display ad this section. ▲

S 154.1 (248 km) **A 207.1** (333.3 km) **H 25.4** (40.9 km) **Timberline Creations.** See display ad this section.

S 155 (249.4 km) **A 208** (334.7 km) **H 24.5** (39.4 km) **Bear Paw Charters.** This Anchor Point location is only minutes from trophy halibut and salmon fishing. All equipment provided plus free filleting. Small groups and personalized service are the focus of this family-owned and operated business. Lodging also available in private, fully equipped log cabin. You'll like the gift shop. Phone (907) 235-5399. See display ad this section. [ADVERTISEMENT]

S 155.3 (249.9 km) **A 208.3** (335.2 km) **H 24.2** (38.9 km) **Red Door Bed & Breakfast.** See display ad this section.

S 156.3 (251.5 km) **A 209.3** (336.8 km) **H 23.2** (37.3 km) **Anchor River Tesoro**. See display ad this section.

Mugs and Jugs. See display ad this section.

The Warehouse, Inc. See display ad this section.

S 156.7 (252.2 km) **A 209.7** (337.5 km) **H 22.8** (36.7 km) Anchor Point post office at turnoff for Milo Fritz Road to west and North Fork Road to east, an 18-mile/29-km loop which rejoins the Sterling Highway at **Milepost S 164.3.** Post office is open 9 A.M. to 5 P.M. weekdays, 9 A.M. to noon on Saturday.

ANCHOR POINT (pop. 866) has groceries, gas stations with major repair service, motel, restaurant and fast-food stands, liquor store, clinic, sporting goods, gift shops and ceramic studio. Volunteer fire department and ambulance, phone 911. **Visitor Information:** Located in the log cabin just off the Sterling Highway on Old Sterling Highway. Open 10 A.M. to 4 P.M., Friday through Monday, from Memorial Day weekend through Labor Day. The center is manned by volunteers from Anchor Point Senior Citizens, Inc.

Good Time Charters. See display ad this section.

Olga's Bed and Breakfast. Quiet country setting. Our rooms are neat and clean. Country- or Russian-style breakfast. Walk to Anchor River, beach and best fishing. Close

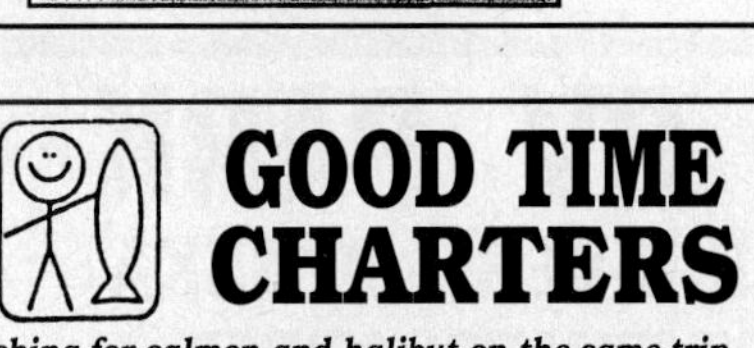

The first gold discovery in Alaska was on the Kenai Peninsula in 1849.

Anchor River (Beach) Road Log

MILEPOST® field editor Jerrianne Lowther at the westernmost highway point in North America. (Jerrianne Lowther, staff)

Turn off the Sterling Highway at **Milepost S 156.9** on to the Old Sterling Highway and continue past the Anchor River Inn to the Anchor River. Just beyond the bridge is the turnoff for Anchor River (Beach) Road, a 1.2-mile/1.9-km spur road providing access to Anchor River recreation area.
Distance from junction (J) is shown.

J 0 Junction of Old Sterling Highway and Sterling Highway at **Milepost S 156.9**.

J 0.1 (0.2 km) School Road. Anchor River visitor information center. A plaque across from the visitor center marks the westernmost point on the contiguous North American Highway system.

Anchor River Inn, overlooking beautiful Anchor River and in business for 20 years, has the finest family restaurant on the peninsula, where you can see one of the largest displays of collectible plates in Alaska. Serving breakfast, lunch and dinner. Large cocktail lounge has a wide-screen TV, pool tables, dance floor and video games. 20 modern motel units with phones; 10 spacious units with color TV and two queen-sized beds, and 10 smaller units overlooking the river. Our fully stocked liquor, grocery store and gift shop serve the Anchor Point area year-round. Write: Box 154, Anchor Point, AK 99556; phone 1-800-435-8531 in USA, or (907) 235-8531; fax (907) 235-2296. Your hosts: Bob and Simonne Clutts. [ADVERTISEMENT]

J 0.3 (0.5 km) Anchor River bridge, also known as "the erector set bridge."

J 0.4 (0.6 km) Road forks: Old Sterling Highway continues south and rejoins Sterling Highway at **Milepost S 164.8**. Turn right for Anchor River (Beach) Road.

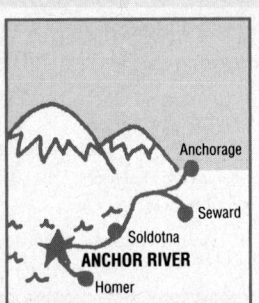

Access to Silverking campground (Anchor River State Recreation Area); RV camping, toilets, dumpster, $8 nightly fee or annual pass. ▲

J 0.6 (1 km) Coho campground (Anchor River SRA); camping, toilets, $8 nightly fee or annual pass. ▲

J 0.7 (1.1 km) Anchor Point Chamber of Commerce Salmon Derby Weigh-in and information.

J 0.7 (1.1 km) Tackle shop.

J 0.8 (1.3 km) Steelhead campground (Anchor River SRA); camping, toilets, $10 nightly fee or annual pass. ▲

J 1.1 (1.8 km) Slidehole campground (Anchor River SRA); 30 campsites, $10 nightly fee or annual pass, shelter with tables, public water source for campers, special senior/handicapped camping area, large day-use parking lot, trail access to river. ♿▲

J 1.3 (2.1 km) **Kyllonen's RV Park**, a few steps from famous Anchor River and picturesque Cook Inlet. Providing spring water, electricity and sewer. Additional amenities include fish cleaning station, BBQ pits, free firewood and picnic tables. Showers, restrooms. Gift shop and Espresso Bar. Fishing licenses. We book fishing charters and area sightseeing tours. May through September. Year-round area information center, phone/fax (907) 235-7762, fax (907) 235-6435. See display ad this section. [ADVERTISEMENT] ▲

J 1.5 (2.4 km) Halibut campground (Anchor River SRA); camping, toilets, $8 nightly fee or annual pass. ▲

J 1.6 (2.6 km) Road deadends on shore of Cook Inlet; beach access, 12-hour parking. Private tractor boat launch service. Signs here mark the most westerly point on the North American continent accessible by continuous road system and depict outlines of Cook Inlet volcanoes.

The Anchor Point area is noted for seasonal king and silver salmon, steelhead and rainbow fishing. Saltwater trolling for king salmon to 80 lbs., halibut to 200 lbs., spring through fall. **Anchor River**, king salmon fishing permitted only on 5 consecutive weekends, beginning Memorial Day weekend; trout and steelhead from July to October; closed to all fishing Dec. 31 to June 30, except for king salmon weekends. Fishermen report excellent fishing for 12- to 24-inch sea-run Dollies in July and late summer. During the August silver runs, fishing with high tides is usually more productive, because the Anchor River's water level is lower at that time of year.

Anchor River King Salmon Derby is usually held the last weekend in May and the first 4 weekends in June. Prizes for first fish caught and heaviest fish, each weekend, plus a mystery fish special prize. A silver salmon derby is held in August.

Return to Milepost S 156.9 Sterling Highway

to great clam beaches. Turn west by Billie's Video on Milo Fritz Road, right on Granross, left on Laida. (907) 235-6654. See display ad.

[ADVERTISEMENT]

Our Front Porch Bed & Breakfast. See display ad this section.

S 156.9 (252.5 km) **A 209.9** (337.8 km) **H 22.6** (36.4 km) **Junction** with Old Sterling Highway; access to Anchor River businesses and Anchor River (Beach) Road. See ANCHOR RIVER (BEACH) ROAD log this section.

Anchor River Inn. See display ad this section.

Wallin's Hilltop Bed & Breakfast. See display ad this section.

S 157.1 (252.8 km) **A 210.1** (338.1 km) **H 22.4** (36 km) Anchor River bridge.

S 160.9 (258.9 km) **A 213.9** (344.2 km) **H 18.6** (29.9 km) Side road to artist Norman Lowell's studio and KWLS radio station.

S 161 (259.1 km) **A 214** (344.4 km) **H 18.5** (29.8 km) Anchor River bridge.

S 164.3 (264.4 km) **A 217.3** (349.7 km) **H 15.2** (24.5 km) North Fork Loop Road to Anchor River.

S 164.8 (265.2 km) **A 217.8** (350.5 km) **H 14.7** (23.7 km) Old Sterling Highway leads 9.4 miles/15.1 km northwest in a loop to Anchor River (Beach) Road, which provides access to Cook Inlet, Anchor River recreation and Anchor Point businesses. See ANCHOR RIVER (BEACH) ROAD log this section and **Milepost S 156.9**.

S 165.4 (266.2 km) **A 218.4** (351.5 km) **H 14.1** (22.7 km) **Billikin Gift Shop.** See display ad this section.

S 166.8 (268.4 km) **A 219.8** (353.7 km) **H 12.7** (20.4 km) Virginia Avenue.

Holland Days Bed & Breakfast. See display ad this section.

S 167.1 (268.9 km) **A 220.1** (354.2 km) **H 12.4** (20 km) Diamond Ridge Road.

S 168.5 (271.2 km) **A 221.5** (356.5 km) **H 11** (17.7 km) Alaska State Parks' South District office is located on the bluff here. A small parking lot is adjacent to the log office where visitors may obtain information on Kachemak Bay state park, as well as other southern Kenai Peninsula state park lands.

S 169 (271.9 km) **A 222** (357.2 km) **H 10.5** (16.9 km) Homer DOT/PF highway maintenance station. *NOTE: Watch for road construction southbound next 5 miles/8 km in 1996.*

S 169.6 (272.9 km) **A 222.6** (358.2 km) **H 9.9** (15.9 km) Two viewpoints overlooking Kachemak Bay.

S 170 (273.6 km) **A 223** (358.9 km) **H 9.5** (15.3 km) Bay View Inn.

S 171.2 (275.5 km) **A 224.2** (360.8 km) **H 8.3** (13.4 km) Land fill road.

S 171.9 (276.6 km) **A 224.9** (361.9 km) **H 7.6** (12.2 km) West Hill Road; access to bed and breakfasts. Connects to Skyline Drive and East Hill Road for scenic drive along Homer Bluff.

S 172.5 (277.6 km) **A 225.5** (362.9 km) **H 7** (11.3 km) Hotel.

S 172.6 (277.8 km) **A 225.6** (363 km) **H 6.9** (11.1 km) Homer Junior High School.

S 172.7 (277.9 km) **A 225.7** (363.2 km) **H 6.8** (10.9 km) **Oceanview RV Park.** See display ad this section. ▲

S 172.8 (278.1 km) **A 225.8** (363.4 km) **H 6.7** (10.8 km) Exit onto Pioneer Avenue for downtown **HOMER** (description follows). Drive 0.2 mile/0.3 km on Pioneer Avenue and turn left on Bartlett Avenue for the Pratt Museum (see Attractions in the Homer section) and Homer city campground (follow signs). Pioneer Avenue continues through downtown Homer to Lake Street and to East Hill Road. ▲

S 173.1 (278.6 km) **A 226.1** (363.9 km) **H 6.4** (10.3 km) Homer Chamber of Commerce Visitor Center at Main Street; access to food, lodging, dump station and other services. Bishop's Beach Park.

S 173.5 (279.2 km) **A 226.5** (364.5 km) **H 6** (9.7 km) Eagle Quality Center; shopping, groceries.

S 173.7 (279.5 km) **A 226.7** (364.8 km) **H 5.8** (9.3 km) Heath Street. Post office (ZIP code 99603).

S 173.9 (279.9 km) **A 226.9** (365.2 km) **H 5.6** (9 km) Lake Street. Access to downtown Homer and Lakeside Center.

S 174 (280 km) **A 227** (365.3 km) **H 5.5** (8.9 km) Beluga Lake floatplane base.

S 174.4 (280.7 km) **A 227.4** (366 km) **H 5.1** (8.2 km) Lambert Lane, access to floatplane base.

S 174.7 (281.1 km) **A 227.7** (366.4 km) **H 4.8** (7.7 km) Alaska Dept. of Fish and Game office.

S 174.8 (281.3 km) **A 227.8** (366.6 km) **H 4.7** (7.6 km) **Homer Tesoro.** See display ad this section.

S 175 (281.6 km) **A 228** (366.9 km) **H 4.5** (7.2 km) Airport Road. Sterling Highway crosses onto Homer Spit.

A series of boardwalks along the Spit house shops, charter services, food outlets, etc. Also on the Spit: a resort hotel, restaurants, seafood markets, private campgrounds, and public camping areas (check in with camping registration office on the Spit); the harbormaster's office, small boat basin, shore fishing for salmon in the Fishing Hole, Alaska Marine Highway ferry terminal and a boat ramp. ▲

S 179.5 (288.9 km) **A 232.5** (374.2 km) **H 0** Sterling Highway ends at Land's End Resort and Campground at the tip of Homer Spit.

Homer

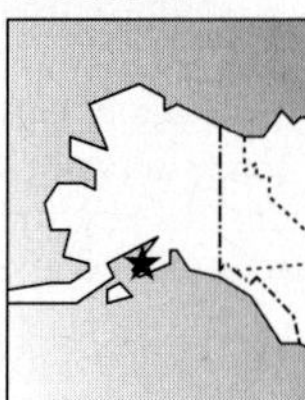

Located on the southwestern Kenai Peninsula on the north shore of Kachemak Bay at the easterly side of the mouth of Cook Inlet; 226 miles/364 km by highway or 40 minutes by jet aircraft from Anchorage. **Population:** 4,349. **Emergency Services:** Phone 911 for all emergency services. **City Police,** phone (907) 235-3150. **Alaska State Troopers,** in the Public Safety Bldg., phone (907) 235-8239. **Fire Department** and **Ambulance,** phone (907) 235-3155. **Coast Guard,** phone Zenith 5555. (Coast Guard Auxiliary, phone (907/235-7277.) **Hospital,** South Peninsula, phone (907) 235-8101. **Veterinary Clinic,** phone (907) 235-8960.

Visitor Information: Chamber of Commerce Visitor Center is located on the Homer Bypass at Main Street. Open from Memorial Day to Labor Day. Contact the Homer Chamber of Commerce, Box 541, Homer 99603; phone during business hours (907) 235-7740 or 235-5300.

The Pratt Museum Visitor Information Center is open daily 10 A.M. to 6 P.M. from May through Sept.; open noon to 5 P.M. Tuesday through Sunday from Oct. through April; closed in Jan. Contact the Pratt Museum, 3779 Bartlett St., Homer 99603. Phone (907) 235-8635.

Elevation: Sea level to 800 feet/244m. **Climate:** Winter temperatures occasionally fall below zero, but seldom colder. The Kenai Mountains north and east protect Homer from severe cold, and Cook Inlet provides warming air currents. The highest temperature recorded is 81°F/27°C. Average annual precipitation is 27.9 inches. Prevailing winds are from the northeast, averaging 6.5 mph/10.5 kmph. **Radio:** KGTL 620, KWAV 103.5/104.9/106.3, MBN-FM 107.1/96.7/95.3, KBBI 890, KPEN-FM 99.3/100.9/102.3, KWHQ-FM 98.3. **Television:** KENI Channel 2, KTVA Channel 4, KAKM Channel 7, KIMO Channel 13. **Newspaper:** *Homer News* (weekly), *Homer Tribune* (weekly).

Private Aircraft: Homer airport, 1.7 miles/2.7 km east; elev. 78 feet/24m; length 7,400 feet/2,255m; asphalt; fuel 100LL, Jet A; attended.

In the late 1800s, a coal mine was operating at Homer's Bluff Point, and a railroad carried the coal out to the end of Homer Spit. (The railroad was abandoned in 1907.) Gold seekers debarked at Homer, bound for the goldfields at Hope and Sunrise. The community of Homer was established about 1896 and named for Homer Pennock.

Coal mining operations ceased about WWI, but settlers continued to trickle into the area, some to homestead, others to work in the canneries built to process Cook Inlet fish.

Today, Homer's picturesque setting, mild climate and great fishing (especially for halibut) attract thousands of visitors each year. In addition to its tourist industry and role as a trade center, Homer's commercial fishing industry is an important part of its economy. Homer calls itself the "Halibut Fishing Capital of the World." Manufacturing and seafood processing, government offices, trades and construction are other key industries.

Rising behind the townsite are the gently sloping bluffs which level off at about 1,200 feet/366m to form the southern rim of the western plateau of the Kenai. These green slopes are tinted in pastel shades by acres of wildflowers from June to Sept.; fireweed predominates among scattered patches of geranium, paintbrush, lupine, rose and many other species. Two main roads (East Hill Road and West Hill Road) lead from the Homer business section to the "Skyline Drive" along the rim of the bluffs, and other roads connect with many homesteads on the "Hill."

The name *Kachemak* (in Aleut dialect said to mean "smoky bay") was supposedly derived from the smoke which once rose from the smoldering coal seams jutting from the clay bluffs of the upper north shore of Kachemak Bay and the cliffs near Anchor Point. In the early days many of the exposed coal seams were slowly burning from causes unknown. Today the erosion of these bluffs drops huge fragments of lignite and bituminous coal on the beaches, creating a plentiful supply of winter fuel for the residents. There are an estimated 400,000,000 tons of coal deposit in the immediate vicinity of Homer.

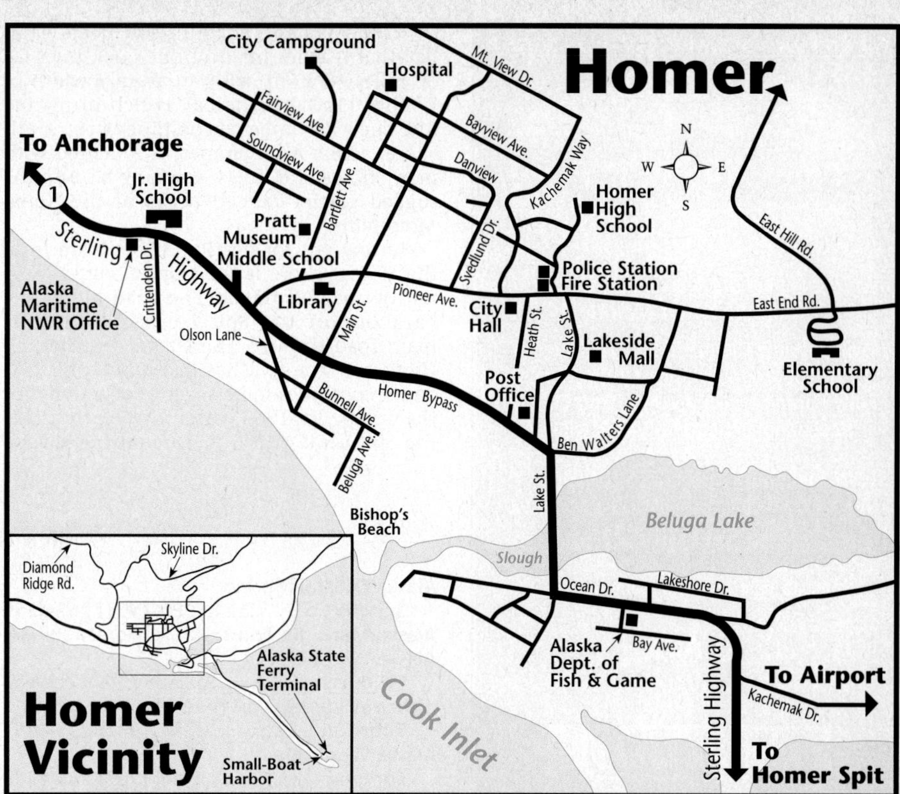

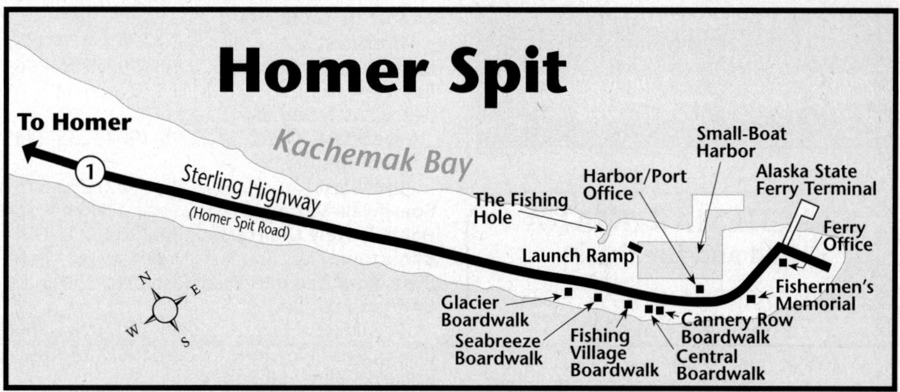

Kachemak is a magnificent deep-water bay that reaches inland from Cook Inlet for 30 miles/48.3 km, with an average width of 7 miles/11.3 km. The bay is rich in marine life. The wild timbered coastline of the south shore, across from Homer, is indented with many fjords and inlets, reaching far into the rugged glacier-capped peaks of the Kenai Mountains.

Jutting out for nearly 5 miles/8 km from the Homer shore is the Homer Spit, a long, narrow bar of gravel. The road along the backbone of the Spit connects with the main road through Homer (all the Sterling Highway). The Spit has had quite a history, and it continues to be a center of activity for the town. In 1964, after the earthquake, the Spit sank 4 to 6 feet, requiring several buildings to be moved to higher ground. Today, the Spit is the site of a major dock facility for boat loading, unloading, servicing and refrigerating. The deep-water dock can accommodate up to 2 340-foot vessels with 30-foot drafts at the same time, making it accessible to cruise and cargo ships. It is also home port to the Alaska Marine Highway ferry MV *Tustumena*. The small-boat harbor on the Spit has a 5-lane load/launch ramp. Also in the small-boat harbor area are the harbormaster's office, canneries, parking/camping areas, charter services, small shops, live theatre, restaurants and a motel.

In summer, the Homer Spit bustles with activity: people fish from its shores for salmon; fishermen come and go in their

HOMER ADVERTISERS

boats; cars, trucks and trailers line the road; tent camps are set up on the beach; and boat builders and repairers are busy at their craft. Fresh crab, shrimp and halibut, as well as smoked fish, can be purchased from seafood shops on the Spit or sometimes from the fishermen themselves. Seafood processors on Homer Spit offer custom smoking, freezing and air shipping for sport-caught fish. It is also possible to trade your sport-caught fish for similar fish already processed and ready to ship or take with you.

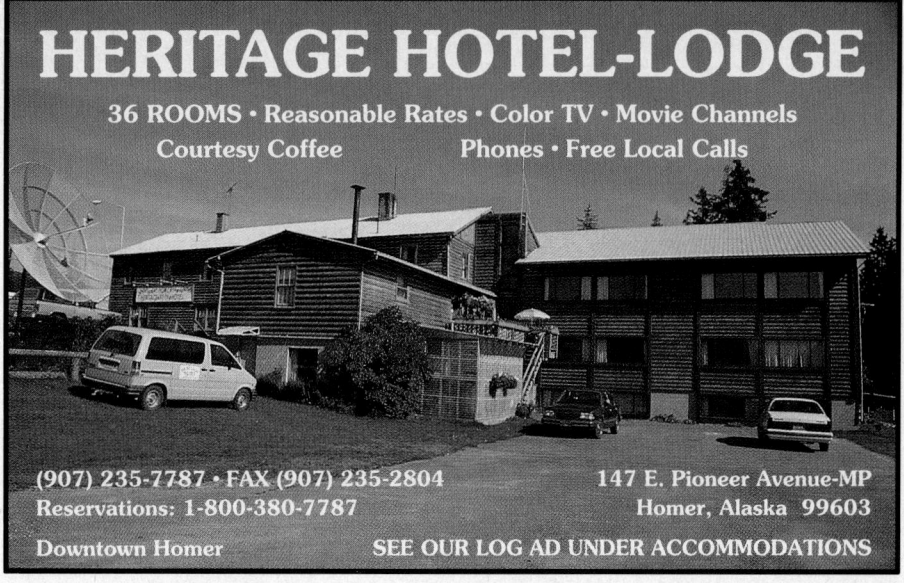

ACCOMMODATIONS/VISITOR SERVICES

Homer has hundreds of small businesses offering a wide variety of goods and services. There are many hotels, motels and bed and breakfasts for lodging. Nearly 40 restaurants offer meals ranging from fast food to fine dining. Travelers are advised to book overnight accommodations well in advance during the busy summer months. Homer has a post office, library, museum, laundromats, gas stations with propane and dump stations, banks, a hospital and airport terminal. There are many boat charters, boat repair and storage facilities, marine fuel at Homer marina, bait, tackle and sporting goods stores, and also art galleries, gift shops and groceries.

Homer Spit has both long-term parking and camping. Camping and parking areas are well-marked. Camping fees are $7 per night for RVs and $3 per night for tents. Camping permits are available at the camper registration office on the Spit. There is a 14-day limit; restrooms, water and garbage

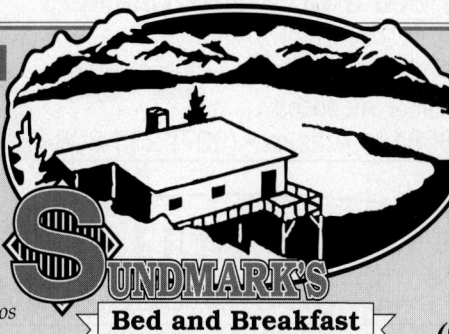

View of Homer Spit and Kachemak Bay from East Hill Road. (© Steven Seiller)

available. Check with the harbormaster's office or the camper registration office on the Spit if you have questions on rules and regulations pertaining to camping, campfires, long-term parking, boat launching and moorage. Homer City Campground, on a hill overlooking town, is reached via Bartlett Avenue (follow signs). ▲

Following are paid advertisements for campgrounds and lodging. A number of other services and stores are listed under Attractions.

Homer Spit Campground and Lodging. Beachfront and ocean view campsites at the end of the Homer Spit on Kachemak Bay. Harbor, restaurants and boardwalk shops within a minute's walk. Daily, weekly, overnight room accommodations with beach frontage or ocean view. Travel trailers with kitchenettes for rent on site. Clean restrooms, unmetered hot showers. Electrical hookups, dump station, Alaskan gift shop; cheerful, complete visitor information. Reservations advised. Call us to book your halibut charters, wildlife boat tours or any other recreational activities. Over 20 years of reliable service. John and Peggy Chapple, owner-managers. P.O. Box 1196, Homer, AK 99603; phone (907) 235-8206. [ADVERTISEMENT] ▲

Land's End RV Park. On the water's edge, at the tip of Homer Spit. Truly the most spectacular spot on the Kenai Peninsula. Gorgeous mountain views and sunsets. Minutes from the Spit's boardwalks and small-boat harbor. Electric hookups, laundry. Showers, ice, sundries. Open May through Sept. (907) 235-2525. P.O. Box 273, Homer, AK 99603. [ADVERTISEMENT] ▲

Oceanview RV Park just past Best Western Bidarka Inn on your right coming into Homer. Spectacular view of Kachemak Bay, beachfront setting. 85 large pull-through spaces in terraced park. Full/partial hookups, heated restrooms, free showers, laundry, pay phone, free cable TV, picnic area. Walking distance to downtown Homer. Special halibut charter rates for park guests. Phone (907) 235-3951. See display ad at Mile 172.7 Sterling Highway. [ADVERTISEMENT] ▲

Alaska Woodside Lodging. Your host, Merle Meisinger, a 25-year Alaska resident, will welcome you with hospitality and a wealth of local information. Offering plush, spacious condos for your comfort, with furnished kitchens and bathrooms, linens, phones and TV. Laundry facilities. Conveniently located right in downtown Homer.

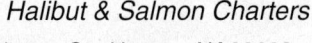

Bed and breakfast rooms also available. Quiet, reasonable rates. We can make all your reservations for halibut or salmon fishing, lodging, sightseeing or wildlife tours. All you need for your Alaskan adventure. Southbound on Sterling Highway, turn left onto Pioneer Avenue, immediately turn left on Woodside Avenue (behind Intermediate School). See Homer map. Phone: (907) 235-8389. See display ad. [ADVERTISEMENT]

Alaska's Pioneer Inn. 244 Pioneer Ave., in downtown Homer. Clean, comfortable 1-bedroom suites with private baths and

furnished kitchens. Sleeps up to 4. Complimentary coffee. Single guest rooms available. Year-round. Homer's best value. Credit cards accepted. Brochure: P.O. Box 1430, Homer, AK 99603. (907) 235-5670. Toll-free from continental U.S. 1-800-STAY-655. In Alaska, 1-800-478-8765. [ADVERTISEMENT]

Almost Home Bed and Breakfast. Nestled in the trees on the bluff overlooking the mountains and the bay. Mini-kitchen, shared bath and continental breakfast. Clean, comfortable, affordable and friendly! Open year-round. Fishing charters available for halibut and salmon. Reservations recommended. (907) 235-2553. In Alaska: 1-800-478-2352; 1269 Upland Court, Homer, AK 99603. [ADVERTISEMENT]

Bay View Inn. Spectacular panoramic view from the top of the hill as you enter Homer. Every room overlooks the shimmering waters of Kachemak Bay, and the Kenai Mountains. Immaculately clean rooms, nonsmoking, firm comfortable beds, color TV, private bathrooms, and outside entrances. Options include kitchenettes, suite with fireplace, and secluded honeymoon cottage. Serene setting, spacious lawn, picnic tables, Adirondack chairs, and freshly brewed morning coffee. Friendly staff offering local tour information and activity recommendations. Mile 170 Sterling Highway. P.O. Box 804, Homer, AK 99603. Phone (907) 235-8485. Fax (907) 235-8716. In Alaska 1-800-478-8485. See display ad this section. [ADVERTISEMENT]

Brass Ring Bed and Breakfast. Alaskan log home. Walk to shops, restaurants, and museum. Full breakfasts. No smoking or pets, please. Children over 6. Private guest house with panoramic view of Kachemak Bay, Kenai Mountains and Grewingk Glacier also available. Outdoor hot tub. Coin laundry. Limited freezer space. Hosts: Vicki and Dave Van Liere. P.O. Box 2090, Homer, AK 99603. (907) 235-5450. [ADVERTISEMENT]

Bridge Creek Bed and Breakfast. Located 4 miles above Homer on 16 wooded acres overlooking Kachemak Bay. Private 2 bedroom suites with full kitchen and bath or comfortable single rooms available. Experience the panoramic view of Alaskan glaciers, mountains and Kachemak Bay. Homemade breakfasts served with Alaska's freshest fare. Smoke-free environment. P.O. Box 2555, Homer, AK 99603. Phone (907) 235-7590. Fax (907) 235-7941. [ADVERTISEMENT]

Cranes' Crest B&B. Unobstructed 225-degree view of Kachemak Bay from 1,200-foot elevation is breathtaking, awe-inspiring, even for long-time Homerites. Sandhill cranes, moose, coyotes visit regularly, for your viewing pleasure. Myriad wildflowers and birds abound. Glaciers galore. Dietary considerations easily accommodated. Open year 'round. 59830 Sanford Drive. (907) 235-2969. [ADVERTISEMENT]

Driftwood Inn. Charming, historic beachfront hotel/motel, B&B, RV parking. Spectacular view overlooking beautiful Kachemak Bay, mountains, glaciers. Quiet downtown location. Completely renovated, color TVs, immaculately clean, unique rooms. Free coffee, tea, local pickup/delivery, local information. Comfortable common areas with TV, fireplace, library, microwave, refrigerator, barbecue, shellfish cooker, fish cleaning area, freezer, picnic and laundry facilities. Continental breakfast available. Friendly, knowledgeable staff, specializing in helping make your stay in Homer the best possible. Reasonable, seasonal rates. Open year-round. Write, call for brochure. 135 W. Bunnell Ave., MP, Homer, AK 99603. (907) 235-8019. In Alaska 1-800-478-8019. [ADVERTISEMENT]

Heritage Hotel-Lodge. One of Alaska's finest log hotels, conveniently located in the heart of Homer. Walking distance to beach, shops, museum. Accommodations: 36 rooms including suite with 2-person Jacuzzi. Reasonable rates. Color TV, movie channels. Phones, free local calls. Courtesy coffee. Restaurants adjacent. Alaskan hospitality. Open year-round. 147 E. Pioneer Ave., phone (907) 235-7787. Reservations 1-800-380-7787. Fax (907) 235-2804. See display ad this section. [ADVERTISEMENT]

Holland Days Bed and Breakfast offers a private cabin with 2 separate units, each with its own kitchenette and bathroom. The other cabin is log and was built in 1995. Your hosts are Al and Marcia Veldstra (907) 235-7604. Located off Virginia Avenue about 1/4 mile from the Sterling Highway at Mile 166.8. (See display ad there.) [ADVERTISEMENT]

Homer Referral Agency/Seekins. We do it all with one phone call—booking for bed and breakfasts, some furnished with kitchens; cabins, apartments and houses. In-town, out-of-town. Fantastic views of bay, mountains and glaciers. Private baths, saunas, hot tubs, Jacuzzis. Full-day, half-day fishing charters for halibut and salmon. Sightseeing by van, bus, boat, plane or helicopter. Trips to Halibut Cove, Seldovia and the Center for Alaskan Coastal Studies. These bookings are made at no charge to the client.

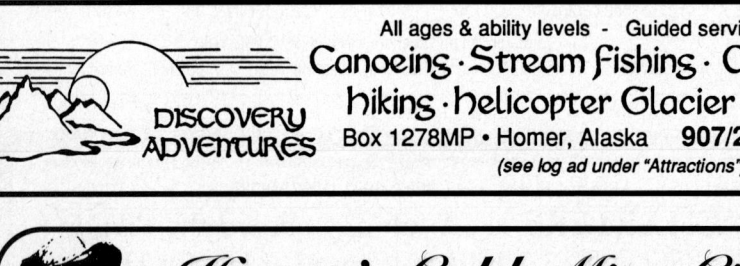

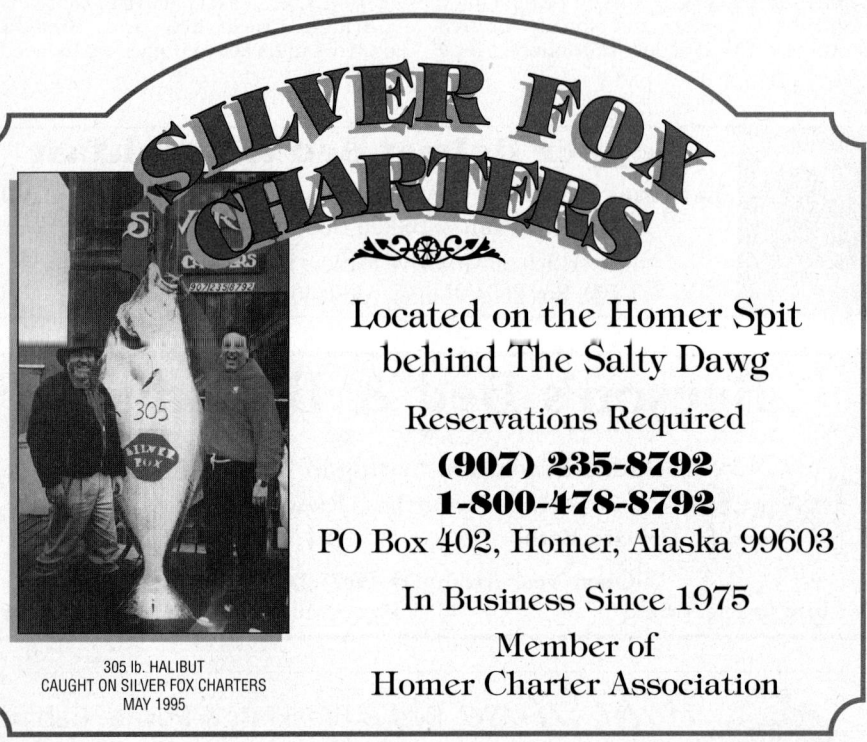

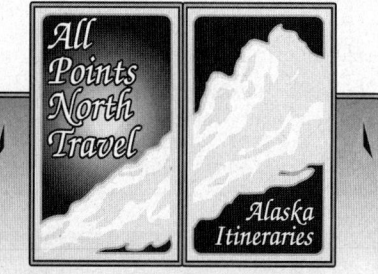

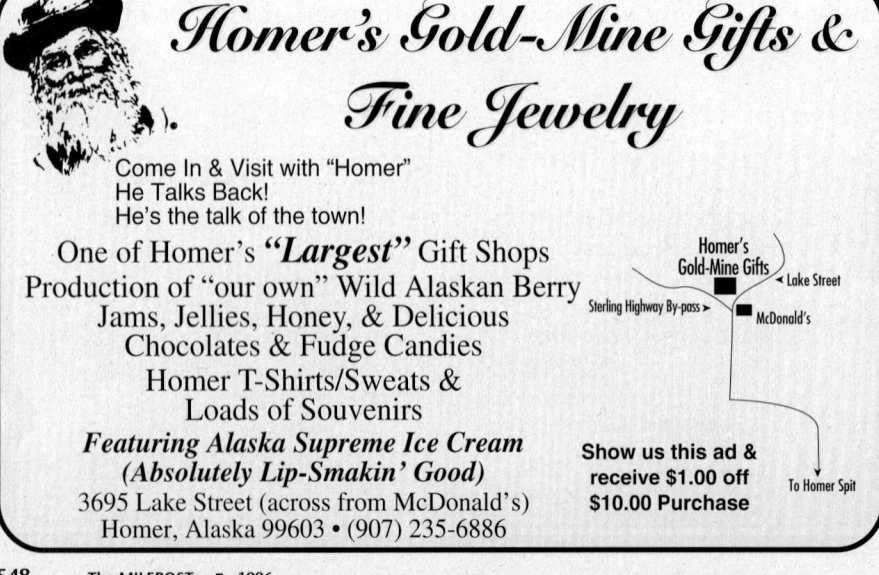

Your hosts, Floyd and Gert, moved to Homer in 1969 from Wisconsin and Minnesota. Box 1264, Homer, AK 99603. (907) 235-8996 or 235-8998. Fax (907) 235-2625. [ADVERTISEMENT]

Journeymen's B & B. Join us for some down-Homer hospitality in our spacious 1-level home, Mile 3.8 East Road. Families welcome. Nonsmoking, no alcohol. Full breakfast, home-baked goodies. Fresh raspberries in August. Third night half-price. Winter rates. Phone (907) 235-8238; P.O. Box 3106-MP, Homer, AK 99603. See display ad. [ADVERTISEMENT] ♿

Kachemak Shores Bed and Breakfast. On Kachemak Drive, convenient to airport. Single rooms and apartment-size units. Kitchenette, satellite TV. Can accommodate parties of 1 to 6 persons. Beach access. Captivating view of Kachemak Bay, romantic harbor lights, glaciers. Watch seals and majestic bald eagles from your window or deck. Reservations: (907) 235-6864 or (907) 235-8234. See Kachemak Shores display ad this section. We also book for Lottie's Place in the Kenai-Soldotna area. [ADVERTISEMENT]

Land's End Resort. Open year-round! Homer Spit's only hotel, on the water, at the tip of Homer Spit. Breathtaking views! Watch seals, otters, various seabirds and other sea life as you have lunch or cocktails on our spacious outdoor deck. The Chartroom restaurant is famous for its locally caught seafood. The Wheelhouse Lounge provides lighter meals. Rates are 30 percent off between Oct. 1 and April 30. Truly an Alaskan landmark! (907) 235-2500 or 1-800-478-0400 (AK). 4786 Homer Spit Rd., Homer, AK 99603. [ADVERTISEMENT]

Manley's Bed and Breakfast. Conveniently located Homer Spit, airport, downtown. First-class accommodations overlooking Beluga Lake. Private guesthouse, sleeps 4, complete kitchen, bath, TV, telephone, fax. Enjoy greenhouse fruit trees, flower, vegetable gardens, berry patches, available in season. Jim, Louise Manley. Box 955, Homer, AK 99603. (907) 235-6766. [ADVERTISEMENT]

The Ocean Shores Motel, under new ownership, has completed a series of brand new, spacious accommodations available for the 1996 season. These are all within 100 feet of the ocean with a spectacular view of Kachemak Bay, the Kenai Mountains and their residing glaciers. This is in a quiet location with easy access to our private beach yet only 3 blocks to downtown Homer and next door to the Kachemak Bay Park visitors center. A full variety of kitchenettes and standard rooms are available and all at reasonable prices. (907) 235-7775. [ADVERTISEMENT]

Old Inlet Trading Post Bed & Breakfast. A restored historic building on the shore of

Kachemak Bay. Sunny, clean and elegant, our antique-appointed rooms, reasonable rates and old-fashioned hospitality welcome you. Bunnell Street Gallery and Two Sisters Bakery downstairs. The perfect beachwalkers retreat. 106-D West Bunnell Ave., Homer, AK 99603, (907) 235-7558. [ADVERTISEMENT]

Seaside Farms. Hostel bunkhouse, guest cottages, tent campground with picnic area, BBQ, beach trails. For budget-minded travelers, backpackers, nature lovers, families wanting a friendly, fun, informal atmosphere. Beautiful gardens, scenic horse pastures, raspberry patch, birds, ducks, farm pets. Drop-ins welcome. 58335 East End Rd., Homer, AK 99603; phone (907) 235-7850. [ADVERTISEMENT]

Sundmark's B & B (formerly Seekins Homer B & B). Our guests enjoy one of Homer's best views of the Homer Spit, Kachemak Bay and the mountains and glaciers beyond. Our accommodations vary to meet the needs of our guests. Private cabin, private apartments, rooms with shared or private bath, furnished kitchens, cable TV. We serve a large, hearty breakfast every day. Children welcome. Reasonable rates. Nonsmoking. Open year-round. Hosts: Teresa, Dean and Dillon Sundmark, and friendly dog, Jessi. Brochure available. P.O. Box 375, Homer, AK 99603. (907) 235-5188 phone/fax. 2 miles up East Hill Road. [ADVERTISEMENT]

TRANSPORTATION

Air: Regularly scheduled air service to Anchorage. Several charter services also operate out of Homer.

Ferry: The Alaska State ferry *Tustumena* serves Seldovia, Kodiak, Seward, Port Lions, Valdez and Cordova from Homer with a limited schedule to Sand Point, King Cove and Dutch Harbor. Natural history programs offered on ferry in summer by Alaska Maritime National Wildlife Refuge naturalists. See MARINE ACCESS ROUTES section for details, or contact the offices of the Alaska Marine Highway System at the City Dock, phone (907) 235-8449. Tour boats offer passenger service to Seldovia and Halibut Cove.

Local: 2 major rental car agencies and several taxi services.

ATTRACTIONS

The **Pratt Museum**, focusing on the natural and cultural history of southcentral Alaska, is located at 3779 Bartlett St. Exhibits include artifacts from the area's first Native people, thousands of years ago, to homesteaders of the 1930s and 1940s. Excellent aquariums and a touch-tank feature live Kachemak Bay sea creatures. Also exhibited are Alaskan birds and land and sea mammals, including the complete skeletons of a Bering Sea beaked whale and a beluga whale.

Changing exhibits feature Alaskan artwork and other topics of special interest. Beautiful handmade quilts depict local natural history themes. Summer visitors may take a self-guided tour through the botanical garden for a look at local wild plants. The Museum Store features books and Alaskan collectibles.

The Pratt Museum is sponsored by the Homer Society of Natural History. All facilities are handicap accessible. A 45-minute taped audiotour is available. Admission charged; children under 18 years free, members and their guests free. Summer hours (May through September), 10 A.M. to 6 P.M. daily. Winter hours (Oct. through April), noon to 5 P.M., Tuesday through Sunday. Closed Jan. Phone (907) 235-8635. ♿

The U.S. Fish and Wildlife Alaska Maritime National Wildlife Refuge protects the habitats of seabirds and marine mammals on 3,500 islands and rocks along the coastline from Ketchikan to Barrow. The visitor center is open in summer from 9 A.M. to 6 P.M.

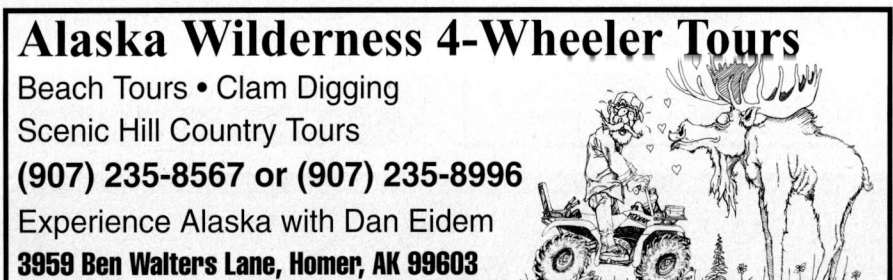

daily. Winter hours are 2–5 P.M. Tuesday through Thursday. The center has displays focusing on the marine environment, videos and a small shop selling books and pamphlets. Wildlife programs include guided bird walks and beach walks, special slide presentations and a children's nature hour. Join the naturalists at the visitor center for an informative day. Naturalists are also on board the state ferry runs to Seldovia, Dutch Harbor and Kodiak. Information on the latest bird sightings can be obtained by calling the Bird Hotline at (907) 235-PEEP (7337). The visitor center is located at 509 Sterling Hwy., Homer, AK 99603; phone (907) 235-6961.

The Kachemak Bay Shorebird Festival celebrates the arrival of 100,000 migrating shorebirds to the tidal flats of Kachemak Bay. The 4th annual festival is scheduled for May 10–12, 1996. The event promotes awareness of this critical shorebird habitat that provides a final feeding and resting place for at least 20 species of shorebirds on the last leg of their journey from Central and South America to breeding grounds in western and northen Alaska. Festival highlights include guided bird walks, classes for beginning and advanced birders, children's activities and more. Sponsored by the Homer Chamber of Commerce and U.S. Fish & Wildlife Service; phone (907) 235-7740 for more details.

Fish the Homer Halibut Derby. The annual Jackpot Halibut Derby, sponsored by the Homer Chamber of Commerce, runs from May 1 through Labor Day. The state's largest cash halibut derby ($85,000) provides 4 monthly cash prizes, tagged fish and final jackpot prize. Tickets are $5 and available at the Jackpot Halibut Derby headquarters on Homer Spit, visitor center or local charter service offices. Phone (907) 235-7740.

Charter Boats, operating out of the boat harbor on Homer Spit, offer sightseeing and halibut fishing trips. (Charter salmon fishing trips, clamming, crabbing, and sightseeing charters are also available.) These charter operators provide gear, bait and expert knowledge of the area. Homer is one of Alaska's largest charter fishing areas (most charters are for halibut fishing). Charter boats for halibut fishermen cost about $120 to $155 a day. Several sightseeing boats operate off the Homer Spit, taking visitors to view the bird rookery on Gull Island, to Halibut Cove and to Seldovia. (Most sightseeing trips are available Memorial Day to Labor Day.)

AREA FISHING: The Kachemak Bay and Cook Inlet area is one of Alaska's most popular spots for halibut fishing, with catches often weighing 100 to 200 lbs. Guides and charters are available locally. Halibut up to 350 lbs. are fished from June through Sept., fish the bottom with herring. Year-round trolling for king salmon is popular, use small herring. King salmon may also be taken during late May and June in area streams. Pink salmon (4 to 5 lbs.) may be caught in July and Aug.; use winged bobbers, small weighted spoons and spinners. Similar tackle or fresh roe will catch silver salmon weighing 6 to 8 lbs. in Aug. and Sept. Dolly Varden are taken throughout the area April to Oct.; try single eggs or wet flies. Steelhead/rainbow are available in local streams, but for conservation purposes, must be immediately released unharmed.

Fishermen have had great success in recent years casting from the shore of Homer Spit for king salmon. The Fishing Hole (also referred to as the Fishing Lagoon or Spit Lagoon) on the Homer Spit supports a large run of hatchery-produced kings and silvers beginning in late May and continuing to Sept. Kings range from 20 to 40 lbs. The fishery is open 7 days a week in season.

Regulations vary depending on species and area fished, and anglers are cautioned to consult nearby tackle shops or Fish and Game before fishing.

Take a Scenic Drive. East End Road, a 20-mile/32-km drive from downtown Homer, climbs through hills and forests toward the head of Kachemak Bay; pavement ends at Mile 12.5, beautiful views of the bay. Or turn off East End Road on to East Hill Road and drive up the bluffs to Skyline Drive; beautiful views of the bay and glaciers. Return to town via West Hill Road, which intersects the Sterling Highway at **Milepost S 167.1**.

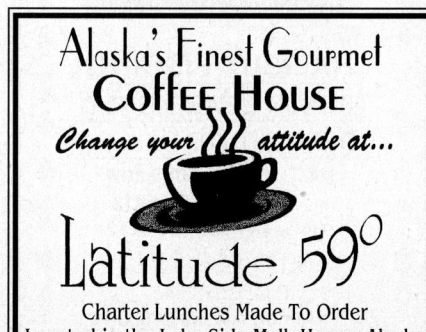

The glaciers that spill down from the Harding Icefield straddling the Kenai Mountains across the bay create an ever-changing panorama visible from most points in Homer, particularly from the Skyline Drive. The most spectacular and largest of these glaciers is Grewingk Glacier in Kachemak Bay State Park, visible to the east directly across Kachemak Bay from Homer. The glacier was named by Alaska explorer William H. Dall in 1880 for Constantin Grewingk, a German geologist who had published a work on the geology and volcanism of Alaska. The Grewingk Glacier has a long gravel bar at its terminal moraine, behind which the water draining from the ice flows into the bay. This gravel bar, called Glacier Spit, is a popular excursion spot, and may be visited by charter plane or boat. (There are several charter plane operators and charter helicopter services in Homer.) Portlock and Dixon glaciers are also visible directly across from the spit.

Kachemak Bay State Park is located on the south shore of the bay and includes glaciers, alpine tundra, forests, fjords, bays and high-country lakes. Recently the state enlarged this park by the purchase of 23,802 additional acres of land with funds from the settlement of the Exxon Valdez oil spill. The existing trail system offers hiking from Glacier Spit to China Poot Peak. An extensive new trail system is under construction. Campsites are currently available on Glacier Spit, Halibut Cove Lagoon and China Poot Lake. Additional campsites and public-use cabins are planned. Inquire locally about transportation to the park. Phone the district office at (907) 235-7024 for more information or stop by the state park office at **Milepost S 168.5.**

McNeil River State Game Sanctuary. Homer is the main base for visitors flying across Cook Inlet to the sanctuary, where the world's largest concentration of bears in a natural area this size is found. Brown bears congregate near the mouth of the river, where a falls slows down migrating salmon, making fishing easy for the bears. Visits to the game sanctuary are on a permit basis; a drawing for the limited number of permits is held in March each year. Permit applications are available from the Alaska Dept. of Fish and Game, Attn: McNeil River, 333 Raspberry Road, Anchorage 99518. Phone (907) 267-2180.

Study Marine Environment. The Center for Alaskan Coastal Studies is located across Kachemak Bay from Homer. Volunteer naturalists lead a day tour which includes Gull Island bird rookery, coastal forest and intertidal areas. Write the Center for Alaskan Coastal Studies, P.O. Box 2225-MP, Homer 99603; phone (907) 235-6667. Reservations, phone (907) 235-7272.

Alaska Maritime Tours. Enjoy the only half-day wildlife tour from Homer to Seldovia which includes Gull Island bird rookery. Top quality, personal service is provided aboard the 50-foot MV *Denaina*. Two daily departures: 8 A.M. and 1:30 P.M. Weekly all-day birding trips to Barren Islands scheduled June–August. Bring camera, extra film, warm jacket, light rain gear to be prepared to spend time outside on deck for close-up views of puffins, sea otters and occasional whales. Located on Homer Spit Road. Call (907) 235-2490 or in Alaska 1-800-478-2490 for reservations or brochure. See display ad this section. [ADVERTISEMENT]

Alaska Wild Berry Products, celebrating 50 years in downtown Homer, invites you to see our wild berry jams, jellies and chocolates handmade the old-fashioned way. Delicious free samples at our taster's stand. Gift shop. Picnic area. Open year around, 528

East Pioneer Avenue. See display ad this section. [ADVERTISEMENT]

Bald Mountain Air. All-day brown bear photo safari from Homer via floatplane landing in Katmai National Park. Let life-long Alaskans, Gary and Jeanne Porter, give you an unforgettable adventure. Scenic wildlife glacier tours. See the best of Alaska! Hunting and fishing also. P.O. Box 3134, Homer, AK 99603. 1-800-478-7969. [ADVERTISEMENT]

The Bookstore, located in Eagle Quality Center, specializes in Alaskan, nature, cooking and children's books. It is acclaimed as one of the nicest bookstores in the state. Besides a great selection of paperback books, it features the most original card selection on the Peninsula (many by local artists) and a very special kids' corner. While browsing, check out the view and ask for our Alaskana catalog. Hours 10 A.M. to 7 P.M. 436 Sterling Highway. (907) 235-7496. [ADVERTISEMENT]

Brown Bear Viewing. Fly across Cook Inlet in a Kachemak Air Service, Inc. floatplane to see Alaskan brown bears as they walk along beaches and fish streams for salmon. Inquire about these flights; or about a 5-day Bear Viewing Cruise; or about guided trips to view bears. Write or phone Kachemak Air Service, Inc., P.O. Box 1769, Homer, AK 99603, phone: (907) 235-8924. Brochures available. [ADVERTISEMENT]

Central Charters Booking Agency Inc. We offer full-service bookings for charter fishing, wildlife tours, lodging, ferries to Halibut Cove (*Danny-J*), Seldovia and Kachemak Bay State Park, and complete fishing and lodging packages. See our selection of T-shirts, sweatshirts, Alaskan gifts and postcards. Also available are bait, ice, fishing licenses, sundries, shipping boxes and derby tickets. Free information and maps. Saltwater aquarium. Located on the Homer Spit. See display ad this section. [ADVERTISEMENT]

Coastal Outfitters: Share the adventure of a lifetime with us! Fly, via floatplane, to our 96 foot vessel in the pristine waters along the coast of Katmai National Park and stay overnight or longer. From June through September, enjoy world class bear viewing, superior halibut and salmon fishing, breathtaking scenery, and a variety of birds and marine mammals. October through December, we specialize in deer and elk hunts at Kodiak, Afognak, and Shuyak Islands. See display ad. Call (907) 235-8492. [ADVERTISEMENT]

Discovery Adventures offers a day to warm your heart; all ages and ability levels. Hiking, heli-hiking, tide pooling, stream fishing, clamming, canoeing, helicopter glacier tours. Your enthusiasm is all that is needed. A guide/naturalist shares a love for the natural wonders, going at your pace, giving instruction whenever needed. Wildlife viewing/photography opportunities. Box 1278MP, Homer, AK 99603. (907) 235-6942. See display ad this section. [ADVERTISEMENT]

Homer's Gold-Mine Gifts & Fine Jewelry. Located on the corner of Lake Street and the Sterling Bypass. Al and Jan Waddell, old-time Alaskans, offer a wonderful selection of Alaskan made as well as other gifts and souvenirs, fine jewelry, and now are in full-swing production of their wild berry jams, jellies and honey. Also they're cooking wonderful chocolates and fudge candies with wild berries and nuts. Plenty of RV parking. Ice. Come visit them and share their Alaskan hospitality. Enjoy some old fashioned Alaskan-made ice cream. [ADVERTISEMENT]

Hughes Float Plane Service, Beluga Lake, (907) 235-4229. "Take off for adventure!" Fly across Smoky Bay. Whisper past pristine mountain lakes. Ascend the glaciers over the Harding Ice Fields and descend over waterfalls to the Kenai Fjords and the Pacific.

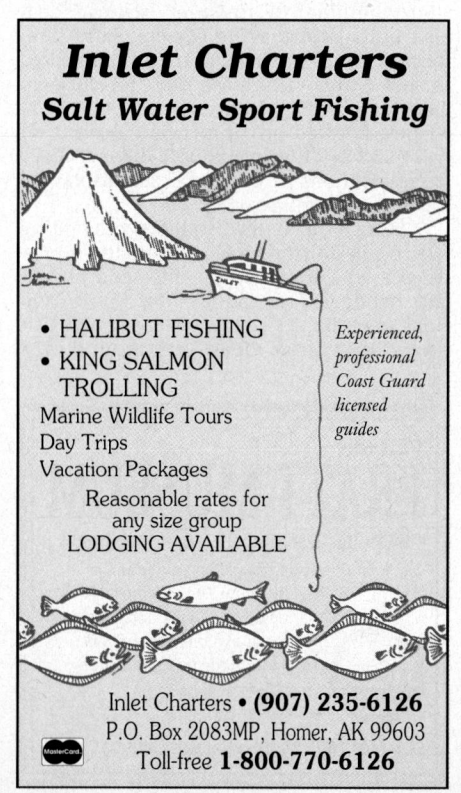

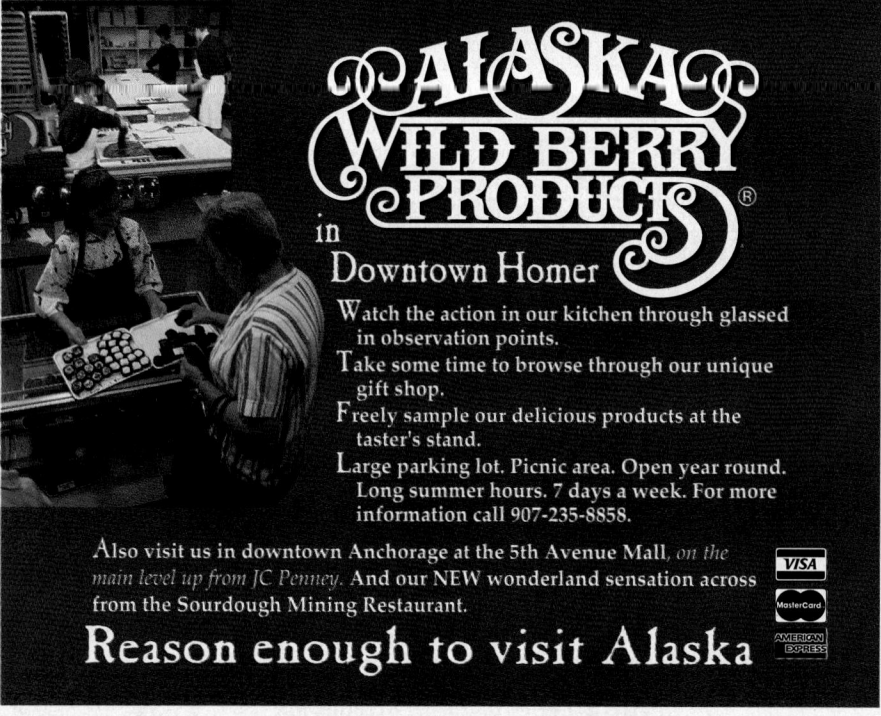

See native fishing villages and in the distance Kodiak, the Barren Islands and the volcanoes. Don't forget your camera. We are your time machine into the past and beyond the Alaskan frontier. Listen to the history, geology and ecology of Kachemak Bay. Experience the excitement and romance of the float plane. Certified Air Taxi Owner/Operator. See display ad. [ADVERTISEMENT]

Kachemak Air Service, Inc. has been in business in Homer for 30 years. They can take you on a sightseeing trip to view glaciers and wildlife across Kachemak Bay or over Kenai Fjords National Park in their Havilland Beaver and Otter floatplanes; also special flights in a 1929 Travel Air cabin seaplane. P.O. Box 1769, Homer, AK 99603; phone (907) 235-8924. [ADVERTISEMENT]

The Kachemak Goldsmith. On the corner of Pioneer and Main. Also at Dockside Village on Homer Spit. Specializing in unique custom jewelry, silver ethnic jewelry, and Alaskan animal charms. Also a unique selection of Alaskan Nugget jewelry. Find that special gift from Alaska at the Kachemak Goldsmith. Phone (907) 235-7803. Open Monday through Saturday, 10 A.M. to 6 P.M. [ADVERTISEMENT]

Anglers line up to catch silver salmon at the Homer Spit Lagoon. (© Bill Sherwonit)

NOMAR (Northern Marine Canvas Products) began business the summer of 1978 in a yellow school bus. Today, visit our manufacturing facility and manufacturer's outlet store at 104 E. Pioneer Ave., downtown Homer. NOMAR manufactures a wide variety of products for our Alaskan lifestyles. Softsided 'Laska Luggage® that's stuffable and floatplane friendly. Watertight bags for kayak tours or whitewater expeditions. Warm polar fleece clothing to keep you warm, no matter what the adventure, and well-made, Homer-made, packable, mailable, useful gifts for everyone on the "list." Park in our spacious, paved parking lot and take a walk around our town. We'll gladly ship your purchases for you. See display ad this section. [ADVERTISEMENT]

North Country Charters, originally owned and operated by Sean and Gerri Martin since 1979, has brought in some of the largest halibut catches ever landed in Homer. Two 50-foot boats for large groups from 16 to 20 passengers. Three 6-passenger boats. All twin-engine, Coast Guard-equipped, heated cabins, full restrooms. See display ad. [ADVERTISEMENT]

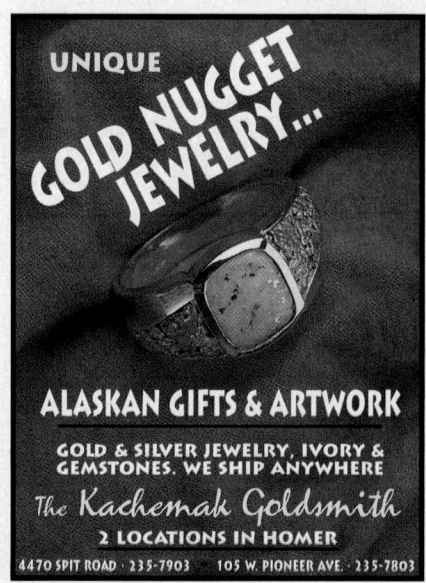

Pier One Theatre. Local talent lights up an intimate stage in an Alaskan-friendly waterfront atmosphere halfway out of

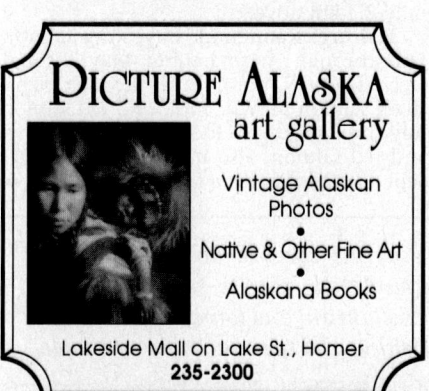

Homer Spit. Plays, new productions, readings, dance theatre, musicals. Offered summer weekends with some midweek shows. Season information locally. Phone (907) 235-7333. [ADVERTISEMENT]

Sorry Charlie Charters. Come and enjoy some fantastic halibut fishing with us! We believe in providing quality, personalized service at affordable rates. The captain has over 12 years experience and operates a clean, 28-foot *Baha* with heated cabins for up to 6 passengers. Reservations recommended. (907) 235-2553. In Alaska: 1-800-478-2352; 1269 Upland Court, Homer, AK 99603. B&B also available. [ADVERTISEMENT]

Trail's End Horse Adventures. Horses and Alaska are my life. Join me in my 11th season offering trail rides in the Homer Hills. Day trips and pack adventures to the head of Kachemak Bay. View mountains and glaciers. Gentle Alaskan horses. Located at Mile 11.2 East End road. Write Mark Marette, Box 1771, Homer, Alaska 99603 or call (907) 235-6393. [ADVERTISEMENT]

Seldovia

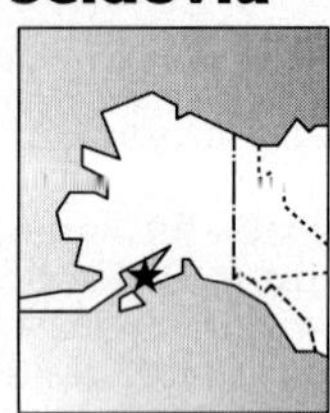

Reached by air, tour boat or ferry. Located on the southwestern Kenai Peninsula on Seldovia Bay, an arm of Kachemak Bay, 16 miles/25.7 km southwest of Homer. **Population:** 403. **Emergency Services: City Police, Ambulance, Fire** and **Rescue**, emergency only, phone 911, monitor CB Channel 9. **Seldovia Medical Clinic**, phone (907) 234-7825. Seldovia has a resident doctor and visiting dentists.

Visitor Information: Seldovia Chamber of Commerce, Drawer D, Seldovia, AK 99663. Information cache at Synergy Art Works on Main Street, across from the boat harbor. You may also stop by the Seldovia Native Assoc. office on Main Street. The office features a small museum with Native artifacts.

Elevation: Sea level. **Climate:** Rather mild for Alaska, with a year-round average temperature of about 39°F/4°C. Annual precipitation, 28 inches. Wind is a small factor due to the protecting shield of the Kenai Mountains. **Radio:** Homer stations. **Television:** KENI Channel 2, KTVA Channel 4, KAKM Channel 7, KIMO Channel 13.

Private Aircraft: Seldovia airport, 0.6 mile/1 km east; elev. 29 feet/9m; length 2,000 feet/610m; gravel; unattended.

Seldovia is a small community connected to Homer by the Alaska Marine Highway Southwest ferry system. Because it is removed from Kenai Peninsula highways, Seldovia has retained much of its old Alaska charm and traditions (its historic boardwalk dates from 1931). There are some areas just outside town, accessible by car, that have been called "Alaska's hidden paradises." A good place to observe bald eagles, seabirds, and sea otters, Seldovia is included as a stop on some tour boat cruises out of Homer.

The name Seldovia is derived from Russian *Seldevoy,* meaning "herring bay." Between 1869 and 1882, a trading station was located here. A post office was established in Nov. 1898.

ACCOMMODATIONS/VISITOR SERVICES

Seldovia has most visitor facilities, including a hotel, 7 bed and breakfasts, a lodge, general store, 3 restaurants and a variety of shops. The post office is in the center of town. Public restrooms, showers, and pay phone in front of the boat harbor near town center. Pay phones are also located at the ferry dock outside ferry office, at the airport, and library.

Seldovia's Boardwalk Hotel. Waterfront view. 14 lovely rooms with private baths. Large harbor view deck. In-room phones. Near bike rental and Otterbahn Trail. Free airport or harbor pickup. Friendly service. Romantic getaway. Package prices from Homer. P.O. Box 72, Seldovia, AK 99663. (907) 234-7816. [ADVERTISEMENT]

Gerry's Place. Bed and breakfast 1 block from harbor. Convenient for fishermen and divers. Private entrance. Close to everything. Air fills available. Rates for families. Freshly baked continental breakfast. Accommodates 6, share bathroom. Box 74, Seldovia, AK 99663. (907) 234-7471. [ADVERTISEMENT]

Harmony Point Wilderness Lodge. Easily reached by sea or air from Homer. We offer sea kayaking, boating, mountain biking, fishing, hiking, wildlife, sauna and fun. Private guest cabins and local seafood served in a new, handcrafted lodge. Come, explore or relax. Call (907) 234-7858 or write Box 110, Seldovia, AK 99663. [ADVERTISEMENT]

Seldovia, City of Secluded Charm, is still the unspoiled Alaska you dream of. Easily reached by commercial tour boat, airline or state ferry, Seldovia is an affordable step beyond the end of the road. For brochure, information call (907) 234-7625 or write Seldovia Chamber of Commerce, Drawer L, Seldovia, AK 99663. [ADVERTISEMENT]

Seldovia Lodge. Newly remodeled restaurant, lounge and lodgings. Featuring the finest breakfast, lunch and dinner in town. Lounge has a unique after hours "cook your own" style barbecue grill. Lodgings offer private entrance, bath and reasonable rates. Halibut fishing and tour packages available. Close to all outdoor activities. P.O. Box 185, Seldovia, AK 99663. (907) 234-7654. [ADVERTISEMENT]

Undeveloped campground for tent camping only at Outside Beach; picnic tables, litter containers, pit toilet. RV camping at the city-owned Seldovia Wilderness Park located just outside the city. From downtown, drive 1 mile/1.6 km out via Anderson Way to fork in road; turn left and drive 0.9 mile/1.4 km to beach. ▲

TRANSPORTATION

Air: Scheduled and charter service. **Ferry:** Alaska's Southwestern Marine Highway system serves Seldovia, with connections to and from Homer, Port Lions, Kodiak, Valdez, Cordova and Seward. See MARINE ACCESS ROUTES section for schedules. **Charter and Tour Boats:** Available for passenger service; inquire locally and in Homer.

ATTRACTIONS

Special Events. Just about the whole town participates in Seldovia's old-fashioned Fourth of July celebration. The holiday includes food booths, parade, games and contests. Seldovia also holds a summer-long fishing derby. Check with the chamber of commerce for details.

Scenic Drives. Outside Beach, a beautiful spot with undeveloped tent camping, beachcombing, surf fishing, rockhounding, and a view of Kachemak Bay and the volcanoes St. Augustine, Mount Iliamna and Mount Redoubt, is 1.9 miles/3.1 km from town. Drive out Anderson Way from downtown 1 mile/1.6 km to a fork in the road by a gravel pit; turn left and drive 0.9 mile/1.4 km to beach.

Continue on Anderson Way (past the Outside Beach turnoff) to hilly and unpaved Jakolof Bay Road, which offers panoramic views of Kachemak Bay, McDonald Spit, Jakolof Bay and Kasitsna Bay. At Mile 7.5, steps lead down to 1.5-mile-long McDonald Spit, a favorite spot for seabirds and marine life. Spend an afternoon exploring the spit, or continue out to Jakolof Bay, where the road offers many opportunities to get onto the beach. The road becomes impassable to vehicles at Mile 13.

It is a pleasant drive out to Seldovia's refuse dump, with wonderful blueberry picking in the fall. From downtown, cross the bridge over Seldovia Slough; then turn right on North Augustine Avenue, then left on Rocky Street for the dump. This is a 1.4-mile/2.3-km drive.

Fishing: Kachemak Bay, king salmon, Jan. through Aug.; halibut May through Oct.; Dolly Varden, June through Sept.; silver salmon in Aug. and Sept.; red salmon, July through Aug. **Seldovia Bay,** king, silver and red salmon, also halibut, May through Sept. Excellent bottom fishing.

SELDOVIA ADVERTISERS

KODIAK

(See map, page 563)

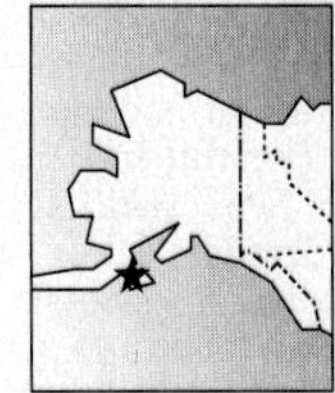

The Kodiak Island group lies in the Gulf of Alaska, south of Cook Inlet and the Kenai Peninsula. The city of Kodiak is located near the northeastern tip of Kodiak Island, at the north end of Chiniak Bay. By air it is 60 minutes from Anchorage. By ferry from Homer it is 10 hours.

Population: 15,575 Kodiak Island Borough. **Emergency Services in Kodiak:** Dial 911 for emergencies. **Alaska State Troopers,** phone (907) 486-4121. **Police,** phone (907) 486-8000. **Fire Department,** phone (907) 486-8040. **Hospital,** Kodiak Island Hospital, Rezanof Drive, phone (907) 486-3281. **Coast Guard,** Public Affairs Officer, phone (907) 487-5542. **Crime Stoppers,** phone (907) 486-3113.

Visitor Information: Located at 100 Marine Way; open year-round. Hours in June, July and August are: 8 A.M. to 5 P.M. weekdays, 10 A.M. to 3 P.M. Saturday, 1–5 P.M. Sunday (and later for arriving ferries). Knowledgeable local staff will answer your questions and help arrange tours and charters. Free maps, brochures, hunting and fishing information. For information, contact the Kodiak Island Convention & Visitors Bureau, Dept. MP, 100 Marine Way, Kodiak 99615; phone (907) 486-4782.

Elevation: Sea level. **Climate:** Average daily temperature in July is 54°F/12°C; in Jan., 30°F/1°C. Sept., Oct. and May are the wettest months in Kodiak, with each month averaging more than 6 inches of rain. **Radio:** KVOK 560, KMXT-FM 100.1, KJJZ-FM 101.1, KPEN-FM 102.3, KWVV-FM 105. **Television:** Via cable and satellite. **Newspapers:** *The Kodiak Daily Mirror* (daily except Saturday and Sunday).

Private Aircraft: Kodiak state airport, 3 miles/4.8 km southwest; elev. 73 feet/22m; length 7,500 feet/2,286m; asphalt; fuel 100LL, Jet A-1. Kodiak Municipal Airport, 2 miles/3.2 km northeast; elev. 139 feet/42m; length 2,500 feet/762m; paved; unattended. Kodiak (Lilly Lake) seaplane base, 1 mile/1.6 km northeast; elev. 130 feet/40m. Inner Harbor seaplane base, adjacent north, on Near Island Channel; unattended, docks; watch for boat traffic; no fuel. A new seaplane base is scheduled to open in spring 1996 at Trident Basin on Near Island.

Gravel airstrips at Akhiok, length 3,000 feet/914m; Karluk, length 1,900 feet/579m; Larsen Bay, length 2,400 feet/732m; Old Harbor, length 2,000 feet/610m; Ouzinkie, length 2,500 feet/762m; and Port Lions, length 2,600 feet/792m.

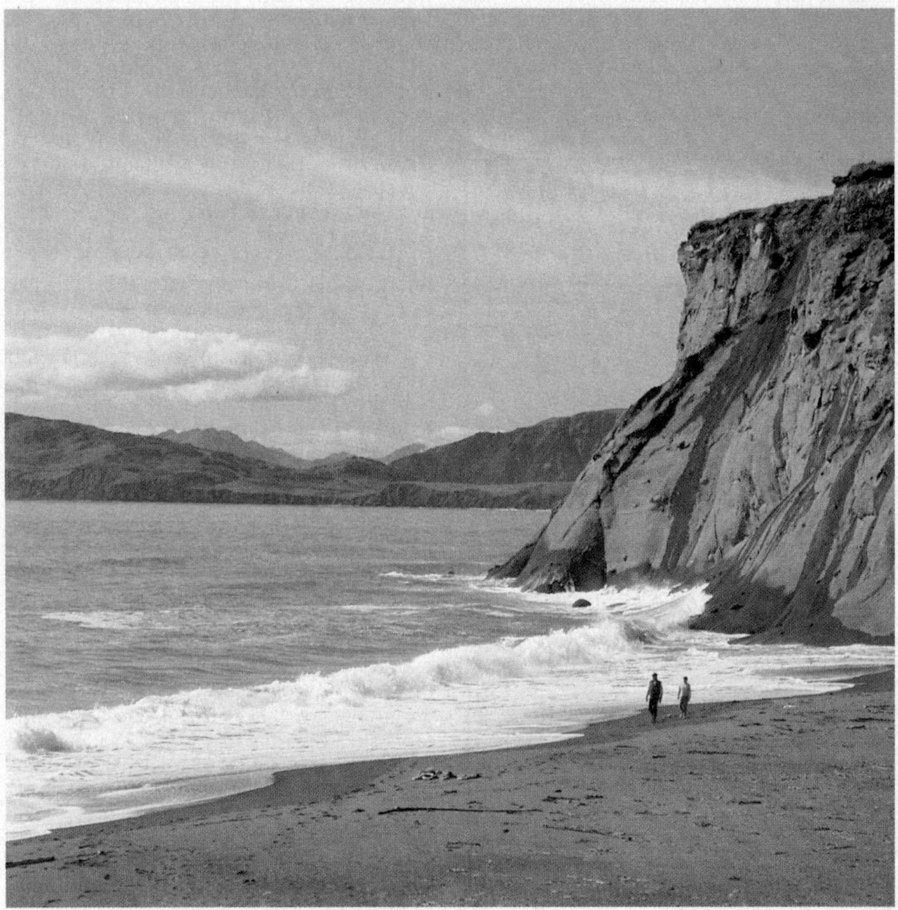

Walking Fossil Beach at the end of Pasagshak Bay Road. (© Harry M. Walker)

Kodiak Island, home of the oldest permanent European settlement in Alaska, is about 100 miles/161 km long. Known as "the emerald isle," Kodiak is the largest island in Alaska and the second largest island in the U.S. (after Hawaii), with an area of 3,588 square miles and about 87 miles/140 km of road (see logs this section). The Kodiak Borough includes some 200 islands, the largest being Kodiak, followed in size by Afognak, Sitkalidak, Sitkinak, Raspberry, Tugidak, Shuyak, Uganik, Chirikof, Marmot and Spruce islands. The borough has only one unincorporated townsite: **KARLUK** (pop. 65), located on the west coast of Kodiak Island, 75 air miles/121 km from Kodiak.

The six incorporated cities in the Kodiak Island Borough are: **KODIAK** (pop. 7,428) on Chiniak Bay, with all visitor services (see Visitor Services, Transportation and Attractions this section); **AKHIOK** (pop. 86) at Alitak Bay on the south side of Kodiak Island, 80 miles/129 km southwest of Kodiak; **LARSEN BAY** (pop. 153) on the northwest coast of Kodiak Island, 62 miles/100 km southwest of Kodiak; **OLD HARBOR** (pop. 311) on the southeast side of Kodiak Island, 54 miles/87 km from Kodiak; **OUZINKIE** (pop. 221) on the west coast of Spruce Island; and **PORT LIONS** (pop. 264) on Settler Cove on the northeast coast of Kodiak Island.

Kodiak Island was originally inhabited by the Alutiiq people, who were maritime hunters and fishermen. More than 7,000 years later, the Alutiiq still call Kodiak home.

In 1763, the island was discovered by Stephen Glotov, a Russian explorer. The name Kodiak, of which there are several variations, was first used in English by Captain Cook in 1778. Kodiak was Russian Alaska's first capital city, until the capital was moved to Sitka in 1804.

Kodiak's turbulent past includes the 1912 eruption of Novarupta Volcano, on the nearby Alaska Peninsula, and the tidal wave of 1964. The Novarupta eruption covered the island with a black cloud of ash. When the cloud finally dissipated, Kodiak was buried under 18 inches of drifting pumice. On Good Friday in 1964 the greatest earthquake ever recorded in North America (9.2 on the Richter scale) shook the Kodiak area. The tidal wave that followed virtually leveled downtown Kodiak, destroying the fishing fleet, processing plants, canneries and 158 homes.

Because of Kodiak's strategic location for defense, military facilities were constructed on the island in 1939. Fort Abercrombie, now a state park and a national historic landmark, was one of the first secret radar installations in Alaska. Cement bunkers still remain for exploration by the curious.

The Coast Guard occupies the old Kodiak Naval Station. Kodiak is the base for the Coast Guard's North Pacific operations; the U.S. Coast Guard cutters *Yocona, Storis, Ironwood* and *Firebush* patrol from Kodiak to seize foreign vessels illegally fishing U.S. waters. (The 200-mile/322-km fishing limit went into effect in March 1977.) A 12-foot star, situated halfway up the side of Old Woman Mountain overlooking the base, was rebuilt and rededicated in 1981 in memory of military personnel who have lost their lives while engaged in operations from Kodiak. Originally erected in the 1950s, the star is lit every year between Thanksgiving and Christmas.

Kodiak's St. Paul harbor is home port to 800 local fishing boats and serves about 2,000 outside vessels each year.

Commercial fishing is the backbone of Kodiak's economy. Kodiak is one of the largest commercial fishing ports in the U.S. Some 3,000 commercial fishing vessels use the harbor each year, delivering salmon, shrimp, herring, halibut and whitefish, plus king, tanner and Dungeness crab to the 15 seafood processing companies in Kodiak. Cannery tours are not available. Kodiak's famous seafood is premarketed, with almost all the commercially caught seafood exported. (Kodiak is the only city in Alaska with more tonnage exported than imported.) You can celebrate Kodiak's main industry at the Kodiak Crab Festival, May 23–27, 1996.

Kodiak is also an important cargo port and transshipment center. Container ships stop here to transfer goods to smaller vessels bound for the Aleutians, the Alaska Peninsula and other destinations.

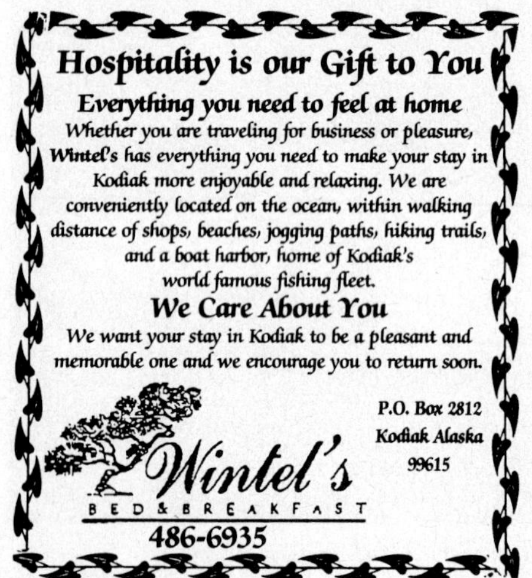

ACCOMMODATIONS/VISITOR SERVICES

There are 4 hotels/motels in Kodiak and more than a dozen bed-and-breakfasts. A variety of restaurants offers a wide range of menus and prices. Shopping is readily available for gifts, general merchandise and sporting goods. There is a movie theater and 750-seat performing arts center.

There are 3 state campgrounds: Fort Abercrombie, north of town (see Rezanof–Monashka Bay Road log); Buskin River state recreation site, south of town (see Chiniak Road log); and Pasagshak River state recreation site at the end of Pasagshak Bay Road (see log). City campground (established for transient process workers) at Gibson Cove has showers and restrooms, $2 per person/night camping fee. ▲

Dump stations are located at the Buggy Banya station on Mill Bay Road, at the Union 76 service station in downtown Kodiak, and at Buskin River state recreation site at Mile 4.4 Chiniak Road.

There are 23 remote fly-in hunting and fishing lodges in the Kodiak area; several roadhouses on the island road system; public-use cabins available within Kodiak National Wildlife Refuge, Shuyak Island and Afognak Island state parks; and private wilderness camps and cabin rentals available throughout the Kodiak area.

TRANSPORTATION

Air: Scheduled service via MarkAir Express, Era Aviation and Alaska Airlines.

Ferry: The Alaska state ferry MV *Tustumena* serves Kodiak from Homer (9½-hour ferry ride) and Seward (13 hours). It also stops at Port Lions. Ferry terminal is downtown; phone (907) 486-3800 or toll free in the U.S. 1-800-526-6731. See MARINE ACCESS ROUTES section for details.

Highways: There are 4 roads on Kodiak Island (see logs this section). The 11.3-mile/18.2-km Rezanof–Monashka Bay Road leads from downtown Kodiak north to Fort Abercrombie and Monashka Bay. Chiniak Road leads 42.8 miles/68.9 km south from Kodiak along the island's eastern shore to Chiniak Point and Chiniak Creek (it is a beautiful drive!). Anton Larsen Bay Road leads 11.8 miles/19 km from junction with Chiniak Road near Kodiak airport to Anton Larsen Bay. Pasagshak Bay Road branches off Chiniak Road and leads 16.5 miles/26.6 km to Fossil Beach at Pasagshak Point.

IMPORTANT: Most of the land along the road system is privately owned. Using land owned by Leisnoi, Inc. requires a nonfee user permit, available at the Leisnoi office in Kodiak at 202 Center Ave.; phone (907) 486-8191.

Car Rental and Taxi: Available.

ATTRACTIONS

State Fair and Rodeo held Labor Day weekend, at the fairgrounds in Womens Bay, includes all-state competitions in crafts, gardening, 4-H livestock raising and home products. Stock car races are held at the fairgrounds on weekends during the summer.

St. Herman's Day, Aug. 9, is of particular

significance to the Kodiak community as Father Herman, the first saint of the Russian Orthodox Church in North America, was canonized in Kodiak in 1970. Father Herman arrived in Kodiak in 1794.

The Baranov Museum (Erskine House), maintained by the Kodiak Historical Society (101 Marine Way, Kodiak 99615; phone 907/486-5920), is open in summer, 10 A.M. to 4 P.M. weekdays, and noon to 4 P.M. Saturday and Sunday. (Winter hours 11 A.M. to 3 P.M. weekdays, except Thursday and Sunday, and noon to 3 P.M. Saturday. Closed in February.) The building was originally a fur warehouse built in the early 1800s by Alexsandr Baranov. It is one of just 4 Russian-built structures in the United States today. Purchased by the Alaska Commercial Co. around 1867, the building was sold to W.J. Erskine in 1911, who converted it into a residence; it was then referred to as the Erskine House. In 1962 it was declared a national historic landmark. Many items from the Koniag and Russian era are on display. In the gift shop, Russian samovars, Russian Easter eggs, Alaska Native baskets and other items are for sale. A walking tour map of Kodiak is available here. Donations accepted, $2 per adult, children under 12 free.

Picnic on the Beach. There are some outstandingly beautiful beaches along Chiniak Road (see log this section). These unpopulated beaches are also good for beachcombing. Watch for Sitka deer and foxes.

Go for a Hike. Hiking trails around the Kodiak area provide access to alpine areas, lakes, coastal rainforests and beaches. Trail guide available for $5 at the visitors center, (907) 486-4782. Pay attention to notes regarding footwear and clothing, tides, bears, trailhead access and weather conditions.

Go Mountain Biking. Kodiak is fast becoming known for its premier mountain biking, attracting racers and enthusiasts from around the country. Bike rentals are available year-round for half-days, weekends and weekly rates. For information on upcoming bike races, call (907) 486-4219.

Kodiak Tribal Council's Barabara sod house is an authentic Alutiiq dwelling that features presentations of Alutiiq dancing. The Kodiak Alutiiq Dancers form the only Alutiiq dance group in Alaska. The dances have been re-created from stories passed down through generations of the Alutiiq people, who have inhabited Kodiak Island for more than 7,000 years. Dance performances are held in summer, Monday through Saturday at 3:30 P.M., at the barabara located at 713 Rezanof Drive. Phone (907) 486-4449 to confirm performance times.

City Parks and Recreation Dept. maintains a swimming pool year-round, and the school gyms are available on a year-round basis for community use. The town has 8 parks and playgrounds including the 7-acre Baranof Park with 4 tennis courts, baseball field, track, playgrounds and picnic areas.

Bear Valley Golf Course. The 9-hole Bear Valley Golf Course is located on the Anton Larsen Bay Road. Owned and operated by the U.S. Coast Guard, the course has a driving range, putting green and pro shack. The course is open to the public from approximately June until October, depending on weather. The pro shack carries golf clothing, items and rental equipment, and serves food and beer. Hours of operation vary according to weather and daylight hours. Call (907) 486-7561 or 487-5108.

Fort Abercrombie State Park. Site of a WWII coastal fortification, bunkers and other evidence of the Aleutian campaign. The park is located north of Kodiak on scenic Miller Point. Picnicking and camping in a setting of lush rain forest, wildflowers, seabirds and eagles.

The U.S. Coast Guard Winter Recreation Area is located on the Anton Larsen Bay Road and has a lighted downhill ski slope with rope-tow lift, a separate sledding area and a ski chalet that serves refreshments. Open to the public, depending on weather and snow conditions. Call (907) 487-5108.

Alutiiq Museum Archaeological Repository Center in downtown Kodiak houses artifacts from coastal sites around Kodiak Island. The Alutiiq are descendants of the Pacific Eskimos, whom Russian explorers encountered and referred to as the Koniag people, many of whom lived in the Karluk area on Kodiak's west coast around 1200 A.D. However, some of the items found date to 3,000 and even 7,000 years ago. The Karluk area is billed as one of the most amazing archaeological finds in Alaska because of the level of preservation of the artifacts and because of the abundance of items used in daily life.

Shuyak Island State Park encompasses 11,000 acres and is located 54 air miles north of Kodiak. Access is by boat or by plane only. Hunting, fishing and kayaking are the major recreational activities. Four public-use cabins are available at $30 per

KODIAK ADVERTISERS

Afognak Wilderness Lodge..........Ph. (800) 478-6442
Alaska Marine Highway...Ph. (800) 526-6731
Baranov Museum..........101 Marine Way
Beryl's..........202 Center Ave.
Budget..........Ph. (907) 487-2220
Cy's Sporting Goods & Outfitters..........202 Shelikof
Inlet Guest Rooms..........Ph. (907) 486-4004
King's Diner..........Ph. (907) 486-4100
Kodiak Bed and Breakfast..........Ph. (907) 486-5367
Kodiak–Katmai Outdoors Incorporated..........Ph. (907) 486-2628
Kodiak VFW Post 7056 RV Park.......Mile 7 Monashka Bay Rd.
La Fiesta..........1517 Mill Bay Rd.
Mack's Sport Shop Inc........117 Lower Mill Bay
Norman's "on the Mall"........414 Marine Way
Northern Exposure Gallery.......103 Center St.
Port of Kodiak Gifts..........516 Marine Way
Rent-A-Heap..........Ph. (907) 486-5200
Russian Heritage Inn.........Ph. (907) 486-5657
Sea Hawk Air..........Ph. (800) 770-HAWK
Uyak Air Service..........Ph. (907) 486-3407
Wintel's Bed & Breakfast..........Ph. (907) 486-6935

The ferry MV Tustumena, *also known as the "trusty Tusty," serves Kodiak from Kenai Peninsula ports.* (© Ruth Fairall)

night, December through May, and $50 per night, June through November. Cabins are 12 feet by 20 feet and sleep up to 8 people. Reservations accepted up to 6 months in advance with a full nonrefundable payment. Call (907) 486-6339 or 762-2261.

Holy Resurrection Russian Orthodox Church. Orthodox priests, following Russian fur traders from Siberia, arrived in Kodiak and established the first Russian Orthodox Church in North America in Sept. 1794. The original church was built on a bluff overlooking St. Paul Harbor in 1796. A second church was built on the same location. The bluff was leveled during reconstruction following the earthquake and tsunami in 1964.

Three churches have been built on the present site. The first appears on an 1869 map of Fort Kodiak. Another church was begun in 1874 and survived until destroyed by fire in 1943. The present church was built in 1945 and is listed on the National Register of Historic Places.

The church interior provides a visual feast, and the public is invited to attend services. A church visit is included in guided tours of Kodiak, or visitors may visit on weekdays in summer between 1–3 P.M.; donation $1. (The church will close to visitors during special services.) In winter, call the parish priest at (907) 486-3854 to arrange for a tour.

A scale replica of the original (1796) church building was completed in May 1994 and is located on the grounds of St. Herman's Theological Seminary on Mission Road.

Arrange a Boat or air charter, or guide for fishing and hunting trips, adventure tours, sightseeing and photography. There are several charter services in Kodiak.

See Kodiak by Kayak. One of the best ways to experience Kodiak's beautiful coastline, and view marine mammals and seabirds, is from a kayak. Day tours around the nearby islands are available for all skill levels, or schedule an extended tour.

Kodiak National Wildlife Refuge encompasses 2,491 square miles on Kodiak Island, Uganik Island, Afognak Island and Ban Island. The refuge was established in 1941 to preserve the natural habitat of the famed Kodiak bear and other wildlife. Biologists estimate that more than 3,000 bears inhabit Kodiak Island. Most bears enter dens by December and remain there until April. Bears are readily observable on the refuge in July and August when they congregate along streams to feed on salmon. At other times they feed on grasses or berries.

Native wildlife within the refuge includes the red fox, river otter, short-tailed weasel, little brown bat and tundra vole. Introduced mammals include the Sitka black-tailed deer, beaver, snowshoe hare and mountain goat. On Afognak Island, an introduced band of elk share the island with the bears. The coastline on the Kodiak refuge shelters a large population of waterfowl and marine mammals. Bald eagles are common nesting birds on the refuge, along with 215 other bird species that have been seen on the island.

Visitors to the refuge typically go to fish, observe/photograph wildlife, backpack, kayak, camp and hunt.

NOTE: The refuge is accessible only by floatplane or boat. There are public-use cabins available; applications must be made in advance to the refuge manager. For more information contact the Kodiak National Wildlife Refuge Manager, 1390 Buskin River Road, Kodiak, AK 99615; phone (907) 487-2600. You may also stop by the U.S. Fish and Wildlife Service Visitor Center at Mile 4.4 Chiniak Road. The center features exhibits and films on Kodiak wildlife, and is open weekdays year-round, and also Saturdays April through September; hours are variable.

Wildlife Watching. The best time to observe animals is when they are most active: at daybreak. Bald eagles can be seen near the city of Kodiak from January through March, and nesting near water in the summer. Peregrine falcons are spotted frequently from the road in October. In the summer, puffins can be seen at Miller Point on calm days. Narrow Cape, Spruce Cape and Miller Point are good stakeout points in the spring for those in search of gray whales. Womens Bay is home to a variety of migrating geese in April.

Kodiak is a gateway to Katmai National Park and Preserve, well-known for its bear-viewing and sportfishing, as well as for an abundance of other wildlife and activities. There is a National Park Service information office in Kodiak, and local air taxi operators offer direct flights to King Salmon and also to the remote Katmai coast.

Bear-viewing Trips. To see brown bears, it's best to leave the road system and travel to the Bush by plane or boat. Almost all the air charter services offer some sort of bear-viewing excursion, ranging from half-day trips to multiple-day visits in cabins or tent-camps. Many lodge operations and licensed guides/outfitters also provide bear-viewing trips.

AREA FISHING: Kodiak Island is in the center of a fine marine and freshwater fishery and possesses some excellent fishing for rainbow, halibut, Dolly Varden and 5 species of Pacific salmon. Visiting fishermen will have to charter a boat or aircraft to reach remote lakes, rivers and bays, but the island road system offers many good salmon streams in season. Roads access red salmon fisheries in the Buskin and Pasagshak rivers. Pink and silver salmon are also found in the **Buskin** and **Pasagshak rivers**, and **Monashka, Pillar, Russian, Salonie, American, Olds, Roslyn** and **Chiniak creeks**.

Afognak and Raspberry islands, both approximately 30 air miles/48 km northeast of Kodiak, have lodges and offer excellent remote hunting and fishing. Both islands are brown bear country. Hikers and fishermen should make noise as they travel and carry a .30-06 or larger rifle. Stay clear of bears. If you take a dog, make sure he is under control. Dogs can create dangerous situations with bears.

CAUTION: A paralytic-shellfish-poisoning alert is in effect for all Kodiak Island beaches. This toxin is extremely poisonous. There are no approved beaches for clamming on Kodiak Island. For more current information, call the Dept. of Environmental Conservation in Anchorage at (907) 349-7343.

Rezanof–Monashka Bay Road Log

Distance is measured from the junction of Rezanof Drive and Marine Way in downtown Kodiak (K).

K 0.1 (0.2 km) Mill Bay Road access to library, post office and Kodiak businesses.

K 0.4 (0.6 km) Entrance to Near Island bridge to North End Park, a city park with trails and picnic areas; St. Herman Harbor, boat launch ramp, fish-cleaning station; and Fishery Industrial Technology Center, phone (907) 486-1500 for tours. Also access to Trident Basin seaplane base, located beyond the Technology Center on Trident Way.

K 1.5 (2.4 km) Kodiak Island Hospital on left.

K 2 (3.2 km) Benny Benson Drive. Turnoff left to Kodiak College and beginning of paved bicycle trail, which parallels main road to Fort Abercrombie State Historic Park. Excellent for walking, jogging and bicycling.

K 3.4 (5.5 km) Turnout and gravel parking area to right for Mill Bay Park. Scenic picnic spot with picnic tables, barbecue grates. Good ocean fishing from beach.

K 3.9 (6.3 km) Road right to Fort Abercrombie State Historic Park. Drive in 0.2 mile/0.3 km to campground; 13 campsites with 7-night limit at $10 per night, water, toilets, fishing, swimming and picnic shelter. Extensive system of scenic hiking trails. No off-road biking. View of bay and beach, WWII fortifications. Miller Point Bunker open Monday, Friday and Sunday at 2:30 P.M. for public viewing. Saturday evening naturalist programs June 1 to Aug. 30. Just beyond the campground entrance is the Alaska State Parks ranger station, open weekdays 8 A.M. to 5 P.M.; pay phone, public restrooms, park information. ▲

K 4.6 (7.4 km) Monashka Bay Park left at junction with Otmeloi Way. Playground equipment, covered picnic area, barbecue grates.

K 6.3 (10.1 km) Kodiak Island Borough baler/landfill facility. Recycling center.

K 6.4 (10.3 km) Pavement ends. Excellent gravel road.

K 6.8 (10.9 km) Gravel turnout to right.

K 6.9 (11.1 km) Good view of Three Sisters mountains.

K 7.1 (11.4 km) Road on right leads to VFW RV park with camping facilities, scenic views, restaurant and lounge, (907) 486-3195; Kodiak Island Sportsman's Association shooting range, (907) 486-8566. ▲

K 7.6 (12.2 km) Pillar Creek bridge and Pillar Creek Hatchery to left.

K 8.3 (13.3 km) Road to right leads to Pillar Beach. Beautiful black-sand beach at mouth of creek. Scenic picnic area. Dolly Varden fishing.

K 9.2 (14.8 km) Pullout to right. Scenic overlook and panoramic views of Monashka Bay and Monashka Mountain.

K 10.1 (16.3 km) Gravel pullout and parking to right. Access to North Sister trailhead directly across road.

K 11.2 (18 km) Bridge over Monashka Creek.

K 11.3 (18.2 km) Road ends. Large turnaround parking area. Paths to right lead through narrow band of trees to secluded Monashka Bay beach. Large, sweeping sandy beach. Excellent for picnics. Fishing off beach for Dolly Varden, pink salmon. To north of parking area is trailhead for Termination Point hike, a beautiful 6-mile loop trail along meadows and ocean bluffs, and dense Sitka spruce forest. *NOTE: Leisnoi user-*

permit required to hike this trail.

Chiniak Road Log

Distance from Kodiak's U.S. post office building (K).

K 0 Kodiak U.S. post office building.

K 2.2 (3.5 km) Gibson Cove campground, operated by City Parks & Recreation, with showers and restrooms. Fee $2 per person/night; $3/vehicle; $5/trailer. ▲

K 2.4 (3.9 km) Gravel turnout to left with panoramic view of Kodiak, Chiniak Bay and nearby islands.

K 3.8 (6.1 km) **Boy Scout Lake**, stocked; gravel turnout and parking to left.

K 4.4 (7.1 km) U.S. Fish and Wildlife Service Visitor Center and Kodiak National Wildlife Refuge headquarters; open weekdays year-round, 8 A.M. to 4:30 P.M., weekends, noon to 4:30 P.M. Exhibits and films on Kodiak wildlife. Road on left to Buskin River state recreation site; 15 RV campsites with a 14-night limit at $10/night, picnic tables and shelter, water, pit toilets, trails, beach access and dump station. Fishing along **Buskin River** and on beach area at river's mouth for red, silver and pink salmon and trout. Handicapped-accessible fishing platform. Parking for fishermen. ▲

K 5 (8 km) Unmarked turnoff on right for Anton Larsen Bay Road (see log this section).

K 5.1 (8.2 km) Kodiak airport.

K 5.5 (8.9 km) *CAUTION: Jet blast area at end of runway. Stop here and wait if you see a jet preparing for takeoff.*

K 5.7 (9.2 km) Gravel turnout and limited parking to access Barometer Mountain. Steep, straight, well-trodden trail to 2,500-foot peak. Beautiful panoramic views. To access trailhead, cross paved road and walk halfway back to jet blast area.

K 6.6 (10.6 km) Entrance to U.S. Coast Guard station.

K 7.2 (11.6 km) Road continues around Womens Bay. The drive out to Chiniak affords excellent views of the extremely rugged coastline of the island.

K 9.3 (15 km) Turnoff to right to state fair and rodeo grounds. Excellent bird watching on tideflats to Salonie Creek.

K 10.1 (16.3 km) **Sargent Creek** bridge. Good fishing for pink salmon in Aug.

K 10.3 (16.6 km) Russian River and Bell Flats Road.

K 10.6 (17.1 km) Pavement ends; gravel begins. *NOTE: Be sure you have a spare tire. It is the law in Alaska to drive with headlights on at all times.*

K 10.7 (17.2 km) Grocery and liquor store, diesel and unleaded gas.

K 10.8 (17.4 km) View of Bell Flats.

K 10.9 (17.5 km) Store and gas station (diesel and unleaded), tire repair.

K 12 (19.3 km) Salonie Creek.

K 12.4 (20 km) Kodiak Island Sportsman's Association rifle range turnoff to right.

K 12.6 (20.3 km) Pull off to left; beach access.

K 12.8 (20.6 km) Remnants on beach of WWII submarine dock. Begin climb up Marine Hill.

K 13.6 (21.9 km) Good turnout to left with panoramic view of Mary Island, Womens Bay, Bell Flats, Kodiak. Mountain goats visible with binoculars in spring and fall in mountains behind Bell Flats.

K 14.4 (23.2 km) Pullout and limited parking to right to access **Heitman Lake** trailhead. Beautiful views. Stocked with rainbow trout.

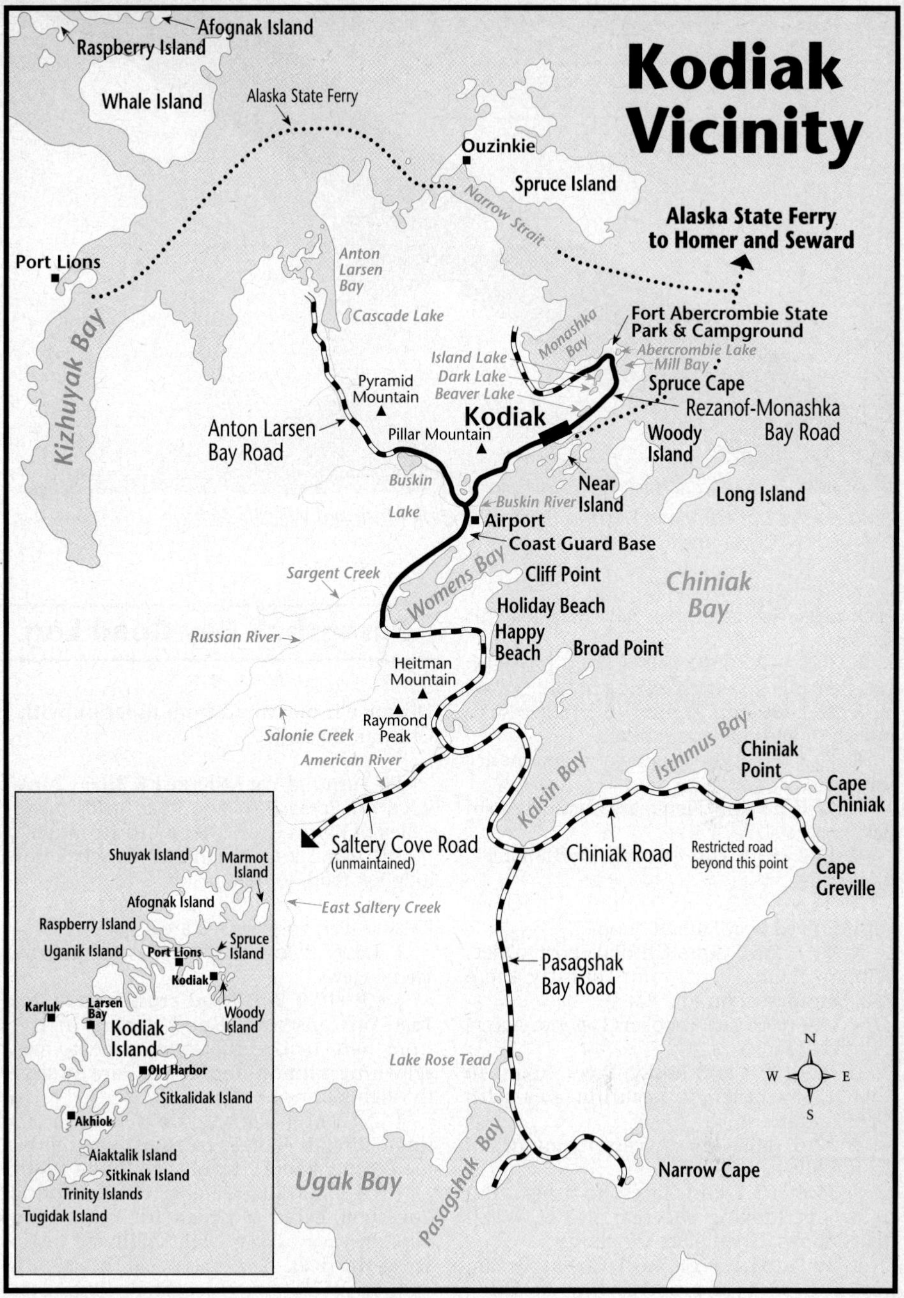

K 15 (24.1 km) View of Long Island.

K 16.2 (26 km) Turnout to left.

K 16.7 (26.9 km) Road east to Holiday Beach. Closed to public. Permission by USCG required for access.

K 17.1 (27.5 km) USCG communication facility; emergency phone.

K 17.8 (28.6 km) View of Middle Bay.

K 19 (30.6 km) Undeveloped picnic area in grove of trees along beach of Middle Bay; easy access to beach. Watch for livestock.

K 19.6 (31.5 km) Small Creek bridge.

K 20 (32.2 km) Salt Creek bridge. Excellent bird watching on tideflats to left.

K 20.8 (33.5 km) American River bridge. River empties into Middle Bay.

K 20.9 (33.6 km) Unimproved road on right, marginal for 4-wheel-drive vehicles, leads toward Saltery Cove. *NOTE: NOT RECOMMENDED FOR MOST VEHICLES AND DRIVERS. Check in Kodiak for road conditions before driving.*

K 21 (33.8 km) Felton Creek Bridge.

K 23.2 (37.3 km) Pullout to left. Foot access to gravel beach; nice picnic site.

K 24.1 (38.8 km) *CAUTION: Steep switchbacks. Slow to 10 mph.*

K 24.5 (39.4 km) Pullout to right, limited parking. Access to Mayflower Lake. Stocked with landlocked silver salmon.

K 24.6 (39.6 km) Mayflower Beach.

K 25.3 (40.7 km) View of Kalsin Bay.

K 27.1 (43.6 km) Turnout to right.

K 28.2 (45.4 km) Steep, narrow, winding road drops down to head of Kalsin Bay; sheer cliffs on both sides of road.

K 28.9 (46.5 km) Kalsin Bay Inn; food, bar, laundromat, showers, tire repair; open year-round. ▲

K 29.2 (47 km) Deadman Creek Bridge.

K 29.9 (48.1 km) Olds River.

K 30.2 (48.6 km) Kalsin River (creek) bridge. Slow down for cattle guard in road just before bridge.

K 30.6 (49.2 km) Road forks: Turn left for Chiniak, right for Pasagshak Bay. Northland Ranch Resort; food, lodging and horse-

Bald eagles are common nesting birds in Kodiak National Wildlife Refuge. (© Michael DeYoung)

back rides. See Pasagshak Bay Road log this section.

K 30.9 (49.7 km) Kalsin Pond on right; excellent silver salmon fishing in fall.

K 31.1 (50 km) Turnoff to left; access to mouth of Olds River and beach.

K 31.5 (50.7 km) Highway maintenance station.

K 32 (51.5 km) Picnic area beside Kalsin Bay.

K 33.2 (53.4 km) Turnoff Myrtle Creek, picnic site.

K 34.9 (56.2 km) Thumbs Up Cove. Unimproved boat launch ramp.

K 35.1 (56.5 km) Chiniak post office. Window hours Tuesday and Thursday 4 to 6 P.M., Saturday noon to 2 P.M.

K 35.9 (57.8 km) Brookers Lagoon. Access to gravel beach.

K 36.9 (59.4 km) Roslyn River. Access to Roslyn Bay beach, a beautiful area with picnic tables.

K 37.6 (60.5 km) Access to mouth of Roslyn River.

K 39.6 (63.7 km) Access to a beautiful point overlooking the sea; site of WWII installations. Good place for photos.

K 39.9 (64.2 km) Twin Creeks Beach, beautiful dark-sand and rolling breakers. Park in pullout area. Do not drive onto soft beach sand.

K 40.4 (65 km) Twin Creek.

K 40.7 (65.5 km) Silver Beach.

K 40.8 (65.7 km) **Pony Lake** (stocked).

K 41.3 (66.4 km) Chiniak wayside. A borough park with picnic benches in beautiful setting.

K 41.5 (66.8 km) Chiniak school, public library, playground and ballfield. Baseball diamond, play area, picnic tables.

K 41.7 (67.1 km) Turnoff to right onto King Crab Way. Location of Tsunami Evacuation Center.

K 42.4 (68.2 km) Road's End lounge and restaurant. Excellent whalewatching for gray whales in April, across road from restaurant; phone (907) 486-2885.

K 42.5 (68.4 km) Chiniak Point. State-maintained road ends. Unmaintained road continues as public easement across Leisnoi Native Corp. land. Public access discouraged beyond Chiniak Creek.

K 42.8 (68.9 km) Public road ends at **Chiniak Creek.** Pink salmon fishing in midsummer. View of Chiniak Point. Turnaround point.

Pasagshak Bay Road Log

Distance is measured from junction with Chiniak Road (J).

J 0 Turn right at **Milepost K 30.6** Chiniak Road for Pasagshak Bay. Road leads up the valley of Kalsin Creek past a private ranch.

J 0.1 (0.2 km) Northland Ranch Resort; lodging, food, lounge.

J 1.2 (1.9 km) Pull off to right to access Kalsin River, good picnic area.

J 4.5 (7.2 km) Top of Pasagshak Pass; scenic views.

J 6.8 (10.9 km) Road crosses Lake Rose Tead on causeway. Good fishing in river from here to ocean. Good place to view spawning salmon and eagles late summer through fall.

J 7.1 (11.4 km) Combined barn and single aircraft hangar to right. Remnant of Joe Zentner Ranch, established in the 1940s.

J 8.4 (13.5 km) Derelict wooden bridge once connected old road to Portage Bay, now an easy hiking trail. Trailhead begins across the river.

J 8.9 (17.5 km) Pasagshak River State Recreation Site: 7 campsites with a 14-night limit (no fee), toilets, water, picnic sites, fishing and beach access.

J 9.3 (15 km) Mouth of Pasagshak River, view of Pasagshak Bay.

J 9.6 (15.4 km) Turnout at Boat Bay, traditional gravel boat launch ramp and mooring area. Four-wheel drive vehicles required to use launch ramp.

J 10.3 (16.6 km) Turnoff to right takes you to Pasagshak Point, 2 trout lakes, nice vistas.

J 11.1 (17.9 km) Entrance to Kodiak Cattle Co. grazing lease. Public land—hunting, fishing, hiking, but keep vehicle on road.

J 11.4 (18.3 km) Turnout to right provides panoramas of Narrow Cape, Ugak Island, Pasagshak Point, Sitkalidik Island. Good beachcombing on sandy beaches.

J 12.3 (19.8 km) Beach access to the right. *CAUTION: Do not approach free-ranging buffalo on foot. They can be dangerous.*

J 14.6 (23.5 km) Entrance to Kodiak Cattle Co. Ranch; guided horseback riding, fishing, camping, hunting; phone (907) 486-3705.

J 14.9 (24 km) Entrance at right to USCG Narrow Cape Loran Station. No public access. *NOTE: Minimal road maintenance from here to end of road. Drive with caution and have a good spare tire.*

J 16.2 (26.1 km) **Twin Lakes** to the left and right of road. Trout in lake to the left.

J 16.5 (26.6 km) Road ends at Fossil Cliffs. Fossils imbedded in cliffs are visible along Fossil Beach to left and right. *CAUTION: Cliffs are extremely unstable. Do not approach cliff face, and watch for falling rocks at all times.* Beautiful vistas and views of WWII observation bunkers on Narrow Cape to the left.

Anton Larsen Bay Road Log

Distance is measured from the turnoff (T) at Milepost K 5 Chiniak Road.

T 0 Unmarked turnoff for Anton Larsen Bay Road at **Milepost K 5** on Chiniak Road immediately before crossing the Buskin River bridge.

T 0.6 (1 km) **Buskin River** bridge No. 6. Parking area to left accessing fishing along river. Road to the right leads to good fishing holes.

T 0.7 (1.1 km) Pavement ends.

T 0.9 (1.4 km) Enter posted restricted-access area in USCG antenna field. Do not leave road for approximately next 1.5 miles.

T 1.5 (2.4 km) **Buskin River** bridge No. 7. Turnoff to left before crossing bridge accesses river and outlet of Buskin Lake. Good fishing for Dolly Varden, salmon.

T 1.6 (2.6 km) Immediately after crossing bridge, paved road to right leads to USCG communications site. Turn on gravel road to left to Anton Larsen Bay. Beautiful drive, berry picking, mountain views, wildflowers, boat launch ramp. Excellent kayaking in bay and around outer islands.

T 2 (3.2 km) High hill on right is Pyramid Mountain (elev. 2,420 feet/738m).

T 2.4 (3.9 km) End restricted access area.

T 2.9 (4.7 km) Bear Valley Golf Course. Driving range, parking on left. Nine-hole course operated by USCG. Open to the public April to Oct., weather permitting. Phone (907) 486-7561 or 486-4782.

T 3.2 (5.1 km) Turnout to left to unimproved trailhead of Buskin Lake. Watch for bears.

T 4.2 (6.8 km) Steep switchback.

T 5.8 (9.3 km) Buskin Valley Winter Recreation Area. Phone (907) 487-5274 or 486-4782. To right is large parking area and trailhead to top of 2,400-foot Pyramid Mountain. Trail follows ridgeline. Great vistas from top.

T 7.3 (11.7 km) Red Cloud River bridge. Small, unimproved campsite is adjacent to river on right.

T 9 (14.5 km) **Cascade Lake** trail to right. Approximately 5 miles round-trip. Rubber boots recommended to cross tidal areas. Watch for bears. Lake is stocked.

T 9.3 (15 km) Head of Anton Larsen Bay. Fox, land otters and deer can be seen in this area. Good bird watching along tidal flats.

T 10.1 (16.3 km) Public small-boat launch adjacent to road. Road continues on left side of bay for about 1.5 miles/2.4 km.

T 11.8 (19 km) Road ends. A foot-path continues beyond this point. Parking area to right.

PRINCE WILLIAM SOUND

Includes Columbia Glacier, Whittier, Valdez and Cordova

(See map, page 622)

A cruise ship approaches Harvard (left) and Yale (right) glaciers in College Fjord. *(Michael N. Dill)*

Southcentral Alaska's Prince William Sound lies at the north extent of the Gulf of Alaska. It is just as spectacular as southeastern Alaska's Inside Passage. The area is also rich in wildlife. Visitors may see Dall sheep, mountain goats, sea lions, sea otters, whales, harbor seals, bald eagles and other birds. The waters carry all species of Pacific salmon; king, Dungeness and tanner crab; halibut; and rockfish.

This section includes: Columbia Glacier; Whittier; Valdez, start of the Richardson Highway; and Cordova, start of the Copper River Highway.

There are several ways to explore Prince William Sound. From Anchorage, drive south on the Seward Highway 47 miles/75.6 km to Portage and board the Alaska Railroad shuttle train for a 35-minute ride to Whittier (presently there is no road connection to Whittier), or take the Alaska Railroad train from Anchorage to Whittier. (See the ALASKA RAILROAD section.) You may also start your trip across Prince William Sound from Valdez by driving 304 miles/498.2 km from Anchorage to Valdez via the Glenn and Richardson highways (see GLENN HIGHWAY and RICHARDSON HIGHWAY sections).

From Whittier or Valdez, board the ferry or one of the privately operated excursion boats to tour Prince William Sound. Flightseeing trips are also available. Depending on your itinerary and type of transportation, you may see the glacier and return to Anchorage in a day or have to stay overnight along the way. All-inclusive tours of Prince William Sound are available out of Anchorage.

Plan your trip in advance. Reservations for the ferry or cruise boats are necessary. The Alaska Railroad does not take reservations, although passengers with confirmed ferry reservations are given first priority when loading.

Columbia Glacier

Star attraction of Prince William Sound is Columbia Glacier, one of the largest and most magnificent of the tidewater glaciers along the Alaska coast. The Columbia Glacier has an area of about 440 square miles/1144 square km. The glacier is more than 40 miles/64 km long; its tidewater terminus, which visitors to Prince William Sound will see, is about 3 miles/4.8 km across. Columbia Glacier has receded more than 5 miles/8 km since the early 1980s, and is expected to leave behind a 26-mile/42-km-long fiord. A bay area has formed between its face and terminal moraine (where it rested prior to retreat). This bay has been filled with ice during the retreat, keeping boats away from the glacier's face. However, in late 1995, the icebergs had cleared enough so that boats were again able to approach and watch ice calving from the face. Check with tour operators regarding access in 1996.

The face of the glacier varies in height above sea level from 25 to 200 feet/8 to 61m, and reaches 1,000 feet/305m or more below sea level. An abundance of plankton thrives here attracting great numbers of fish which attract bald eagles, kittiwakes, gulls and harbor seals. Seals can usually be seen resting on ice floes or swimming in the icy waters.

The glacier was named by the Harriman Alaska expedition in 1899 for Columbia University in New York City. The glacier's source is Mount Einstein (elev. 11,552 feet/3,521m) in the Chugach Mountains.

There are daily and weekly charters by yacht or sailboat and flightseeing trips over the glacier. (See the ads in Whittier, Valdez and Cordova in this section for charter boats offering sightseeing trips and flying services offering flightseeing trips.) See the MARINE ACCESS ROUTES section for ferry schedule.

Whittier

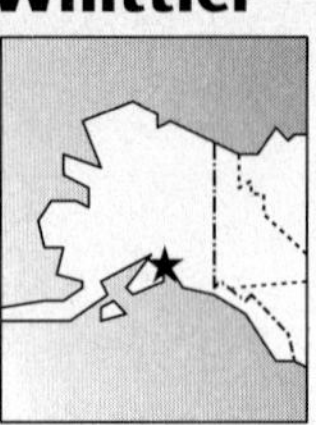

Located at the head of Passage Canal on Prince William Sound, 75 miles/121 km southeast of Anchorage. **Population:** 243. **Emergency Services: Police, Fire** and **Medical**, phone (907) 472-2340. **Visitor Information:** Information kiosk at the Harbor Triangle.

Elevation: 30 feet/9m. **Climate:** Normal daily temperature for July is 56°F/13°C; for Jan., 25°F/-4°C. Maximum temperature is 84°F/29°C and minimum is -29°F/-2°C. Mean annual precipitation is 174 inches, including 260 inches of snow. Winter winds can reach 60 mph.

Private Aircraft: Airstrip adjacent northwest; elev. 30 feet/9m; length 1,100 feet/335m; gravel; no fuel; unattended.

Named after the poet John Greenleaf Whittier, Whittier is nestled at the base of mountains that line Passage Canal, a fjord that extends eastward into Prince William Sound. The community is connected to the Seward Highway by railroad, where you can ride the train in your car as a foot passenger, and to other Prince William Sound communities by ferry and charter air service. No roads lead to Whittier, although a plan for an access road extending the existing Portage Glacier Road to connect with Whittier via the railroad tunnel is under consideration.

Alaska state ferry E.L. Bartlett *serves Prince William Sound ports.* (© Ruth Fairall)

The city of Whittier was created by the U.S. Army during WWII as a port and petroleum delivery center tied to bases farther north by the Alaska Railroad and later a pipeline. The railroad spur from Portage was completed in 1943, and Whittier became the primary debarkation point for cargo, troops and dependents of the Alaska Command. Construction of the huge buildings that dominate Whittier began in 1948 and the Port of Whittier, strategically valuable for its ice-free deep-water port, remained activated until 1960, at which time the population was 1,200. The city of Whittier was incorporated in 1969. The government tank farm is still located here.

The 14-story Begich Towers, formerly the Hodge Bldg., houses more than half of Whittier's population. Now a condominium, the building was used by the U.S. Army for family housing and civilian bachelor quarters. The building was renamed in honor of U.S. Rep. Nick Begich of Alaska, who, along with Rep. Hale Boggs of Louisiana, disappeared in a small plane near here in 1972 while on a campaign tour.

The Buckner Bldg., completed in 1953, was once the largest building in Alaska and was called the "city under one roof." It is now privately owned and is to be renovated.

Whittier Manor was built in the early 1950s by private developers as rental units for civilian employees and soldiers who were ineligible for family housing elsewhere. In early 1964, the building was bought by another group of developers and became a condominium, which now houses the remainder of Whittier's population.

Since military and government activities ceased, the economy of Whittier rests largely on the fishing industry, the port and increasingly on tourism.

Annual events in Whittier include a Fourth of July parade, barbecue and fireworks; a Fish Derby, held Memorial Day weekend to Labor Day weekend; and Regatta, at the end of April or beginning of May, when residents boat to Valdez for Casino Night and then bus or fly back to Whittier.

Whittier has 2 inns providing accommodations, a bed and breakfast, several restaurants, 2 bars, gift shops, laundry facilities, 2 general stores, video rental, gas station, post office, library and a school (preschool through grade 12), and a camper park for tents and self-contained RVs ($5 nightly fee). Fishing licenses may be purchased locally. There is no bank in Whittier. ▲

Whittier also has a harbor office, marine services and repairs, marine supply store, boat launch and lift, freight services, dry storage and self-storage units.

WHITTIER ADVERTISERS

Anchor Inn........................Ph. (907) 472-2354
Honey Charters................Ph. (907) 344-3340
Irma's Outpost.................Ph. (907) 472-2461

Valdez

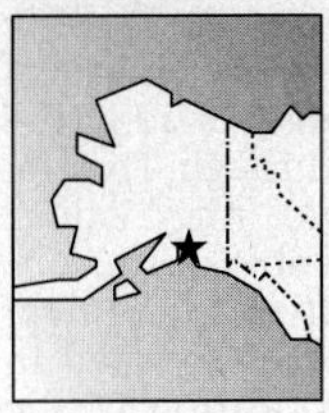

Located on Port Valdez (pronounced val-DEEZ), an estuary off Valdez Arm in Prince William Sound. Valdez is 115 air miles/185 km and 304 highway miles/489 km from Anchorage, 368 highway miles/592 km from Fairbanks. Valdez is the southern terminus of the Richardson Highway and the trans-Alaska pipeline. **Population:** 4,068.

Emergency Services: Alaska State Troopers, phone (907) 835-4359 or 835-4350. **City Police, Fire Department** and **Ambulance**, emergency only phone 911. **Hospital**, Valdez Community, phone (907) 835-2249. **Maritime Search and Rescue**, dial 0 for Zenith 5555, toll free. Report oil spills to Dept. of Environmental Conservation, dial 0 and ask for Zenith 9300.

Visitor Information: The visitor information center, located opposite city hall at 200 Chenega St., is open 7 days a week from 8 A.M. to 8 P.M. The visitor center offers a self-guided tour map of historic homes moved from old Valdez. Write: Valdez Convention and Visitors Bureau, Box 1603-MP, Valdez 99686; or phone (907) 835-2984, fax 835-4845. Visitors may also check the community calendar at the Valdez Civic Center by phoning the hotline at (907) 835-3200.

Elevation: Sea level. **Climate:** Record high was 81°F/27°C in Aug. 1977; record low -20°F/-29°C in Jan. 1972. Normal daily maximum in Jan., 30°F/-1°C; daily minimum 21°F/-6°C. Normal daily maximum in July, 61°F/16°C; daily minimum 46°F/8°C. Average snowfall in Valdez from Oct. to May is 303 inches, or about 25 feet. (By comparison, Anchorage averages about 6 feet in that period.) New snowfall records were set in January 1990, with snowfall for one day at 47½ inches and snowfall for the month at 134 inches. Record monthly snowfall is 174.5 inches in Feb. 1928. Windy (40 mph/64 kmph) in late fall. **Radio:** KCHU 770, KVAK 1230. **Television:** Seven channels via cable and satellite. **Newspapers:** *Valdez Vanguard* (weekly) and *Valdez Star* (weekly).

Private Aircraft: Valdez, 3 miles/4.8 km east; elev. 120 feet/37m; length 6,500feet/1,981m; asphalt; fuel 100LL, Jet B; attended.

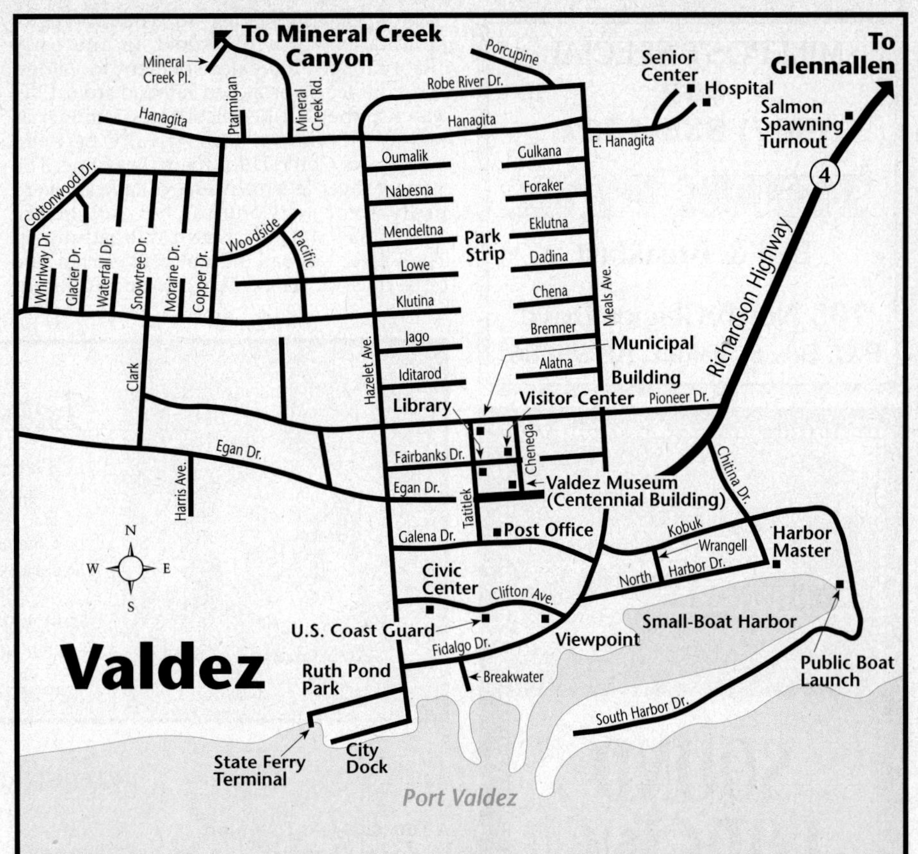

Flanked by the Alp-like Chugach Mountains, Valdez is often called Alaska's "Little Switzerland." The city lies on the north shore of Port Valdez, an estuary named in 1790 by Spanish explorer Don Salvador Fidalgo for Antonio Valdes y Basan, a Spanish naval officer.

Valdez was established in 1897–98 as a port of entry for gold seekers bound for the Klondike goldfields. Thousands of stampeders arrived in Valdez to follow the Valdez trail to the Eagle mining district in Alaska's Interior, and from there up the Yukon River to Dawson City and the Klondike. The Valdez trail was an especially deadly route, the first part of it leading over Valdez Glacier, where the early stampeders faced dangerous crevasses, snowblindness and exhaustion.

Copper discoveries in the Wrangell Mountains north of Valdez in the early 1900s brought more development to Valdez, and conflict. A proposed railroad from tidewater to the rich Kennicott copper mines at McCarthy began a bitter rivalry between Valdez and Cordova for the railway line. The Copper River & Northwestern Railway eventually went to Cordova, but not before Valdez had started its own railroad north. The Valdez railroad did not get very far: The only trace of its existence is an old hand-drilled railway tunnel at **Milepost V 14.9** on the Richardson Highway.

The old gold rush trail out of Valdez was developed into a sled and wagon road in the early 1900s. It was routed through Thompson Pass (rather than over the Valdez Glacier) by Captain Abercrombie of the U.S. Army, who was commissioned to connect Fort Liscum (a military post established in 1900 near the present-day location of the pipeline terminal) with Fort Egbert in Eagle. Colonel Wilds P. Richardson of the Alaska

VALDEZ ADVERTISERS

A Touch O' Old Town Inn Bed & Breakfast	Ph. (907) 835-5684
Alaska Charter Reservation Services	Ph. (907) 835-4634
Anadyr Adventures	Ph. (907) 835-2814
Angie's DownHome Bed & Breakfast	Ph. (907) 835-2832
Anna's Bed & Breakfast	Ph. (907) 835-2202
Bear Paw R.V. Park	Small Boat Harbor
Bear Paw Trading Post	Small Boat Harbor
Best of All Bed and Breakfast	Ph. (907) 835-4524
Boat House Bed and Breakfast, The	Ph. (907) 835-4407
Capt. Jim's Great Alaska Charter Company	Ph. (907) 835-2282
Capt'n Joe's Tesoro	Next to Eagle's Rest RV Park
Casa de LaBellezza Bed & Breakfast	Ph. (907) 835-4489
Chapel of the Sea	Ph. (907) 835-5141
Downtown B & B Inn	Ph. 1-800-478-2791
Eagle's Rest RV Park	Richardson Hwy. & Pioneer Dr.
Easy Living Bed & Breakfast	Ph. (907) 835-4208
Era Helicopters	Ph. 1-800-843-1947
France Inn Bed & Breakfast	714 N. Snowtree
Glacier Charter Service	Behind Totem Inn
Gussie's Lowe St. Inn	Ph. (907) 835-4448
Harbor Landing General Store	Harbor Court
Head Hunters Inn	Ph. (907) 835-2900
Homeport Bed & Breakfast	Ph. (907) 835-5545
Hook Line and Sinker	Chitina & Kobuk sts.
Ivy Rose Bed & Breakfast	Ph. (907) 835-3804
Ketchum Air Service, Inc.	Ph. 1-800-433-9114
Keystone Hotel	Ph. (907) 835-3851
Keystone Raft & Kayak Adventures Inc.	Ph. (907) 835-2606
L&L's B&B	Ph. (907) 835-4447
Lake House Bed & Breakfast	Mile 6 Richardson Hwy.
Last Frontier Gallery	Across from City Museum
Luck of the Irish Charters	Ph. (907) 835-4338
Lu-Lu Belle	Behind Totem Inn
Mike's Palace	201 N. Harbor Dr.
Misty's Bed Breakfast	Ph. (907) 835-3865
Northern Comfort Bed & Breakfast	Ph. (907) 835-4649
Northern Country Inn Bed & Breakfast	Ph. (907) 835-2630
Northern Magic Charters and Tours	Ph. 1-800-443-3543
One Call Does It All	Ph. (907) 835-4988
Prince William Sound Cruise	Ph. (907) 835-2357
Prospector Apparel & Sporting Goods, The	141 Galena St.
PWS Express	Ph. (907) 835-5807
Raven Customized Sailing Charters	Slip C-19, Small Boat Harbor
Sandie's Dragons & Dreams	Ph. (907) 835-2465
Sea Otter RV Park	South Harbor Dr.
Snowtree Inn Bed & Breakfast	Ph. (907) 835-4399
Stan Stephens Cruises	Westmark Dock
Think Pink Bed & Breakfast	Ph. (907) 835-4367
Totem Inn	Ph. (907) 835-4443.
Valdez Christian Book & Coffee Shoppe	126 Pioneer St.
Valdez Convention and Civic Center	Ph. (907) 835-3200
Valdez Convention & Visitors Bureau	Ph. (907) 835-2984
Valdez Drug & Photo	321 Fairbanks Dr.
Valdez Red Apple Market	Egan Dr.
Valdez Tesoro	Meals Ave. and Egan Dr.
Valdez Tours	Ph. (907) 835-2686
Valdez Village Inn	Richardson Hwy. at Meals Ave.
Village Pharmacy	Meals Ave. & Pioneer Dr.
Westmark Valdez	Ph. 1-800-544-0970

Road Commission further developed the wagon road, building an automobile road from Valdez to Fairbanks which was completed in the early 1920s.

Old photos of Valdez show Valdez Glacier directly behind the town. This is because until 1964 Valdez was located about 4 miles east of its present location, closer to the glacier. The 1964 Good Friday earthquake, the most destructive earthquake ever to hit southcentral Alaska, virtually destroyed Valdez. The quake measured between 8.4 and 8.6 on the Richter scale (since revised to 9.2) and was centered in Prince William Sound. A series of local waves caused by massive underwater landslides swept over Valdez wharf and engulfed the downtown area. Afterward, it was decided that Valdez would be rebuilt at a new townsite. By late August 1964, reconstruction projects had been approved for Valdez and relocation was under way. The last residents remaining at "old" Valdez moved to the new town in 1968.

Since its days as a port of entry for gold seekers, Valdez has been an important gateway to interior Alaska. As the most northerly ice-free port in the Western Hemisphere, and connected by the Richardson Highway to the Alaska highway system, Valdez has evolved into a shipping center, offering the shortest link to much of interior Alaska for seaborne cargo.

Construction of the trans-Alaska pipeline was begun in 1974 and completed in 1977 (the first tanker load of oil shipped out of Valdez on Aug. 1, 1977). The 1,000-acre site at Port Valdez was chosen as the pipeline terminus; tours of the marine terminal are available (see Attractions).

From Prudhoe Bay on the Arctic Ocean, the 48-inch-diameter, 800-mile-/1287-km-long pipeline follows the Sagavanirktok River and Atigun Valley, crossing the Brooks Mountain Range at 4,739-foot/1,444-m Atigun Pass. South of the Brooks Range it passes through Dietrich and Koyukuk valleys and crosses the hills and muskeg of the Yukon–Tanana uplands to the Yukon River. South of the Yukon the line passes through more rolling hills 10 miles/16 km east of Fairbanks, then goes south from Delta Junction to the Alaska Range, where it reaches an elevation of 3,420 feet/1,042m at Isabel Pass

Pipeline terminal at Port Valdez. (© W. Wright-Diamond Photo)

before descending into the Copper River basin. It crests the Chugach Mountains at Thompson Pass (elev. 2,812 feet/857m) and descends through the Keystone Canyon to Valdez, where it is fed by gravity into tanks or directly into waiting oil tankers at the marine terminal.

Because of varying soil conditions along its route, the pipeline is both above and below ground. Where the warm oil would cause icy soil to thaw and erode, the pipeline goes above ground to avoid thawing. Where the frozen ground is mostly well-drained gravel or solid rock, and thawing not a problem, the line is underground.

The line was designed with 11 pump stations (although Pump Station 11 was never built) and numerous large valves to control the flow of oil. The entire system can operate on central computer control from Valdez or independent local control at each pump station.

National attention was focused on Valdez and the pipeline when the oil tanker *Exxon Valdez* ran aground in March 1989, causing an 11-million-gallon oil spill.

Valdez's economy depends on the oil industry, the Prince William Sound fishery and tourism. The city limits of Valdez comprise an area of 274 square miles/712 square km, including all surrounding mountains to timberline. Valdez has long been known for its beautiful setting, with the Chugach Mountains rising behind the city, and the small-boat harbor in front. The town has wide streets and open spaces, with the central residential district built around a park strip which runs from the business district almost to the base of the mountains behind town.

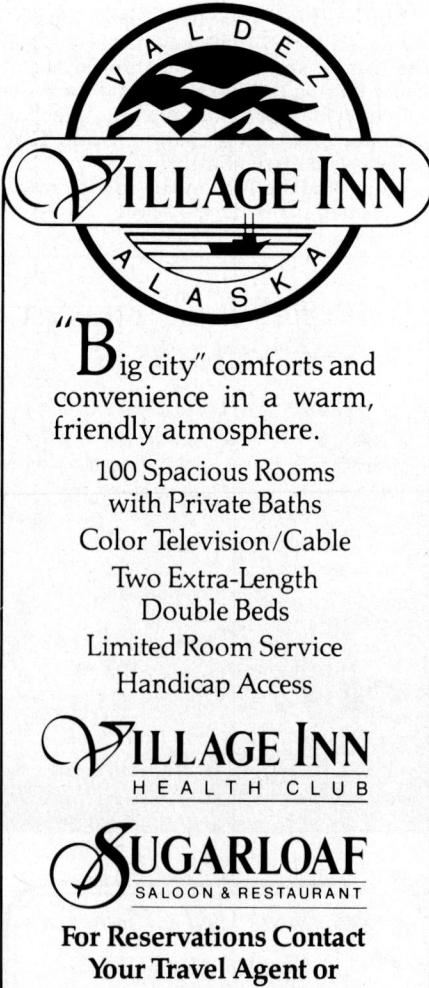

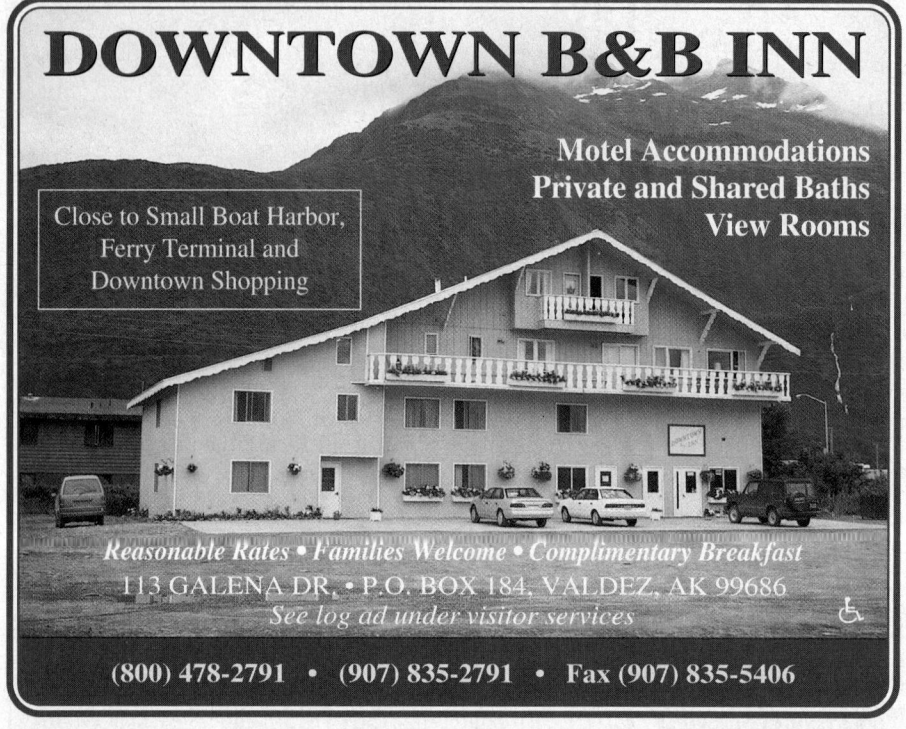

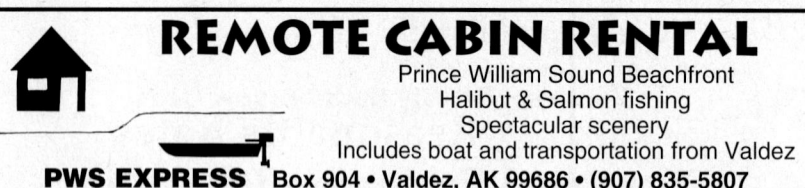

ACCOMMODATIONS/VISITOR SERVICES

Services in Valdez include several restaurants and bars, grocery stores, sporting goods stores, gift shops, 4 service stations, hardware, hair stylists, 1 drugstore, 2 pharmacies and numerous churches.

Valdez has 7 motel/hotel facilities and numerous bed and breakfasts. You are advised to make reservations well in advance. Summer tourist season is also the peak work season, and accommodations fill up quickly. Expect to pay $100 and up for a double motel room with bath, $65 to $85 for a bed and breakfast.

Casa de LaBellezza Bed & Breakfast in Valdez. Elegant, first-class, non-smoking, accommodations located within the city; straight up the street from the ferry dock. Friendly, comfortable, quiet, peaceful, immaculate rooms. Queen beds. (Twin, family only.) Private or shared bath. Beautiful, private backyard and deck. Gourmet breakfast at your convenience. Homemade pastries and pizzelles. We aspire to make your stay in Valdez a memorable one. Phone (907) 835-4489. Fax (907) 835-5450. See display ad this section. [ADVERTISEMENT]

Downtown B & B Inn. Motel accommodations, 113 Galena Dr. Centrally located near small-boat harbor, museum, ferry terminal, downtown shopping. View rooms, private and shared baths, coin-op laundry, TV and phones in rooms. Wheelchair accessible. Complimentary breakfast. Reasonable rates. Single, double, family rooms. (800) 478-2791 or (907) 835-2791. See display ad this section. [ADVERTISEMENT] ♿

Keystone Hotel. Located downtown (corner of Egan and Hazelet) within walking distance to ferry terminal, shops and restaurants. 107 newly remodeled rooms with private baths, cable TV, phones, non-smoking or smoking, handicap access, coin-op laundry facilities. Continental breakfast included with room. Comfortable, clean rooms at reasonable rates. (907) 835-3851. See display ad this section. [ADVERTISEMENT] ♿

The Lake House Bed & Breakfast. Comfortable and quiet, this very large home is located only 10 minutes from Valdez's city center. Excellent bird and wildlife viewing and dramatic alpine scenery. Spacious rooms, most with private bath. Continental breakfast. Brochure available. P.O. Box 1499, Valdez, AK 99686; phone (907) 835-4752. Mile 6 Richardson Highway. [ADVERTISEMENT]

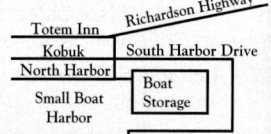

One Call Does It All. Free reservation service for Valdez, Kennicott, Cordova and the Greater Copper Valley. Lodging, glacier cruises, extended cruises, fishing charters. Flightseeing, rafting, kayaking, car and RV rentals. VISA, MasterCard accepted. For the spectacular Prince William Sound, One Call Does It All! (907) 835-4988. See display ad this section. [ADVERTISEMENT]

Totem Inn, completely remodeled restaurant and lounge featuring an Old Town look with a New Town taste. Diners are surrounded by famous works of Alaska art. Restaurant opens at 5 A.M., serving breakfast, lunch and dinner. The lounge offers tall tales and a wide variety of libations. The motel provides deluxe rooms with private baths, satellite TV, phones, handicap access. Ask for rooms or suites in our brand new annex. Motel reservations suggested. Ample parking available. Open year-round. Phone (907) 835-4443, fax (907) 835-5751. See display ad this section. [ADVERTISEMENT] ♿

Valdez Village Inn, downtown Valdez: 100 modern rooms. Cable TV, private baths. Cottages with kitchenettes. Handicap access. Fitness center, sauna, Jacuzzi. Sugarloaf Restaurant & Saloon. Room/Glacier Cruise packages. Phone (907) 835-4445, fax (907) 835-2437. See display ad this section. [ADVERTISEMENT] ♿

There are 3 private RV parks with hookups near the small-boat harbor. Dump station and diesel at Valdez Tesoro. Dump station at Bear Paw R.V. Park for registered guests.

The nearest public campground is Valdez Glacier campground, at the end of the airport road, about 6 miles/9.7 km from town; turn left at **Milepost NV 3.4** on the Richardson Highway. This city-operated campground has 101 sites, tent-camping areas, picnic areas, firepits, tables, litter barrels, water and toilets; 15-day limit, $7 fee charged. ▲

Bear Paw R.V. Park, centrally located on scenic North Harbor Drive overlooking the boat harbor, puts you within easy walking distance of museums, shops, restaurants, entertainment, charter boats—no need to unhook and drive to grocery stores or points

of interest. Full, partial or no hookups; immaculate private restrooms with hot showers. Dump station and coin-operated launderette for guests. Also available, for

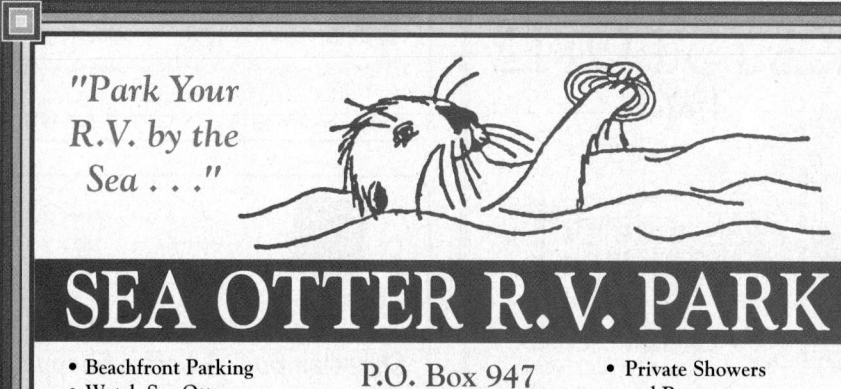

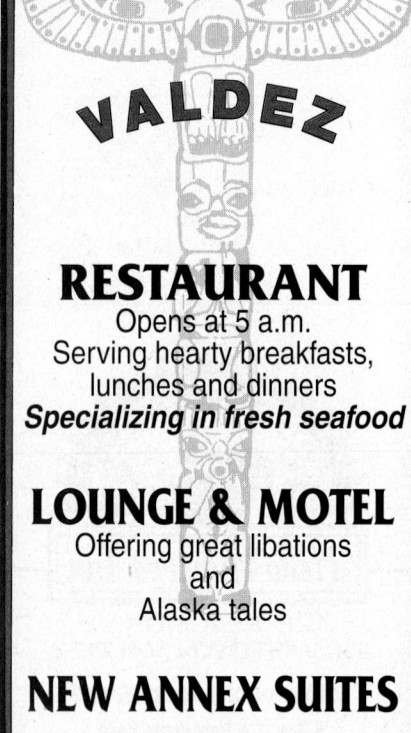

adults only, waterfront full-hookup RV sites. Very nice, quiet, wooded tent sites, some platforms, among the salmonberries on Porcupine Hill. Fish-cleaning table and freezer available. Don't miss the Bear Paw Trading Post Gift Shop. Let us book your glacier tour at the reservations desk in our spacious office lounge, where the coffee pot is always on. Advance reservations recommended: (907) 835-2530. (Bear Paw does fill up!) Let us know if you're coming in on the evening ferry and we'll be there to help you get parked. See our large display ad this section. [ADVERTISEMENT] ▲

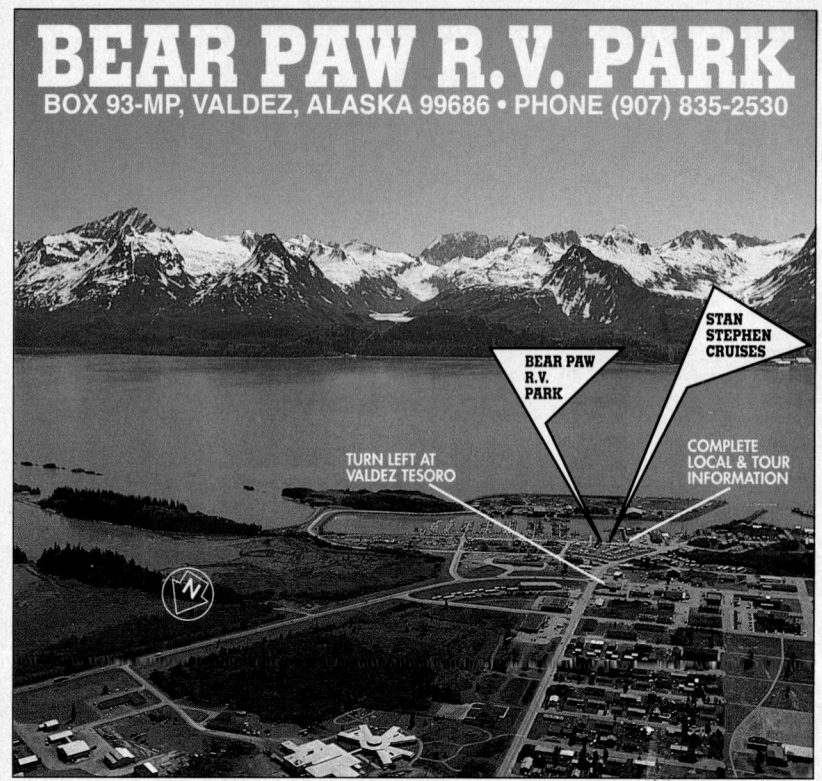

Eagle's Rest RV Park, the newest RV park in downtown Valdez, offers you Good Sam Park service with a smile. Let Herb, Jeff or Laura take care of all your bookings on

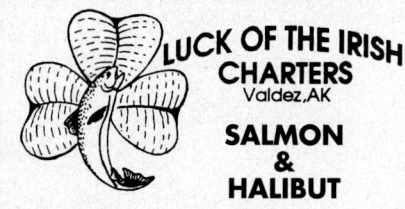

cruises, tours and charters. Enjoy the beautiful panoramic view of our mountains and glaciers right off our front porch! We also can let you know where the hottest fishing spots are or the quietest walking trails! Fish-cleaning table and freezer available. Capt'n Joe's Tesoro next door offers gas, diesel, propane; free sewer dump with fill-up. Parking with us puts you within walking distance of our museum, gift shops, banks and even the largest grocery store on our same block. Shuttle service for glacier cruises. No charge to wash your RV at your site. Call us for reservations, 1-800-553-7275 or (907) 835-2373. Fax (907) 835-KAMP (835-5267). Stay with us and leave feeling like family. See display ad this section. [ADVERTISEMENT] ▲

Glacier Day
Meares Glacier
Glacier Night

Cordova

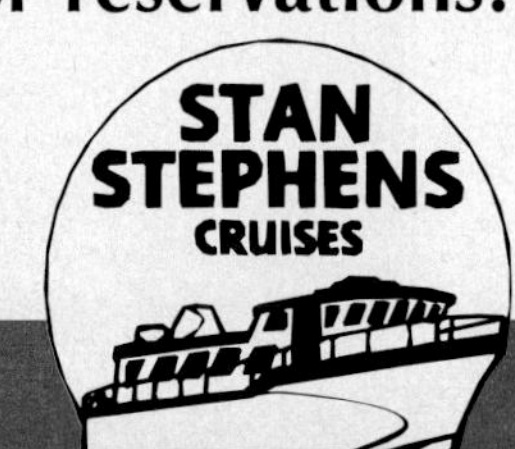
STAN
STEPHENS
CRUISES

TRANSPORTATION

Air: Daily scheduled service via Alaska Airlines and Era Aviation. Air taxi and helicopter services available.

Highway: The Richardson Highway extends north from Valdez to the Glenn Highway and the Alaska Highway. See the RICHARDSON HIGHWAY section.

Ferry: Scheduled state ferry service to Cordova, Whittier and Seward. Phone (907) 835-4436. Reservations are a must! See MARINE ACCESS ROUTES section.

Bus: Regularly scheduled service to Anchorage and Fairbanks.

Taxi: One local taxi service.

Car Rental: Two companies offer car rentals; available at airport terminal.

ATTRACTIONS

Celebrate Gold Rush Days. Held Aug. 7–11, 1996, this celebration includes a parade, contests and a casino night. During the celebration cancan girls meet the cruise ships and a jail is pulled through town by "deputies" who arrest citizens without beards and other suspects.

Visit Valdez Museum, located at 217 Egan Dr. Exhibits depict lifestyles and workplaces from 1898 to present. Displays include a beautifully restored 1907 Ahrens steam fire engine, the original Cape Hinchinbrook lighthouse lens, a Civil War-era field cannon, and an illuminated model of the Alyeska Marine Terminal. Interpretive exhibits explain the impact of the 1964 earthquake, the construction of the trans-Alaska oil pipeline, and the 1989 *Exxon Valdez* oil spill cleanup. Visitors can touch Columbia Glacier ice, play slot machines (for entertainment only!), sing along with the jukebox in the Pinzon Bar exhibit, and feel the luxurious softness of a sea otter pelt. The museum's William A. Egan Commons provides a showcase setting for the Ahrens steam fire engine, models of antique aircraft, and the lighthouse lens. Outside exhibits include displays of local wildflowers, an oil pipeline "pig" and a unique snow tractor. Valdez Museum is open year-round: daily during summer months (May to Sept.); Tuesday through Saturday during off-season (Oct. to April). Children free; $2 for adults (18 and older). Call (907) 835-2764 for more information.

Tour the oil pipeline terminus. The marine terminal of the Alyeska pipeline is across the bay from the city of Valdez. Bus tours of the pipeline terminal are available daily, from May to Sept., from Valdez Tours Co.; fee charged, reservations suggested, cameras welcome. Phone (907) 835-2686 for details.

While entry to the terminal is restricted to authorized bus tours only, the drive out to the terminal is worthwhile. From Meals Avenue drive 6.8 miles/10.9 km out the Richardson Highway and turn right on the terminal access road (Dayville exit). The 5.4-mile/8.7-km road leading to the terminal passes Solomon Gulch dam and a spectacular view of Solomon Gulch Falls. There is also excellent fishing in season at Allison Point for pink and silver salmon. Entrance to the pipeline terminal is at the end of the road.

Outside the marine terminal gate is a

bronze sculpture commemorating the efforts of men and women who built the trans-Alaska oil pipeline. Dedicated in Sept. 1980, the sculpture was created by Californian Malcolm Alexander. It is composed of 5 figures representing various crafts and skills employed in the construction project. The work is the focal point of a small park from which visitors can watch tankers loading Alaska crude oil at the terminal. A small parking lot accommodates about 30 cars, and a series of signs explains the pipeline and terminal operations.

Take a boat tour to see Columbia Glacier, Shoup Glacier and other Prince William Sound attractions. Columbia Glacier, a tidewater glacier in Columbia Bay 28 miles/45 km southwest of Valdez, has become one of Alaska's best-known attractions. See ads in this section.

Raft and kayak trips of Prince William Sound, Keystone Canyon and surrounding rivers are available.

Go flightseeing and see Columbia Glacier, spectacular Prince William Sound and the surrounding Chugach Mountains from the air. There are several air charter services and 2 helicopter services in Valdez; see ads in this section.

Our Point of View, an observation platform offering views of the original Valdez townsite, pipeline terminal and the town, is located by the Coast Guard office.

Valdez Consortium Library, located on Fairbanks Street, has a magazine and paperback exchange for travelers. A trade is appreciated but not required. The library also has music listening booths, public computers, typewriters and a photocopier. Wheelchair

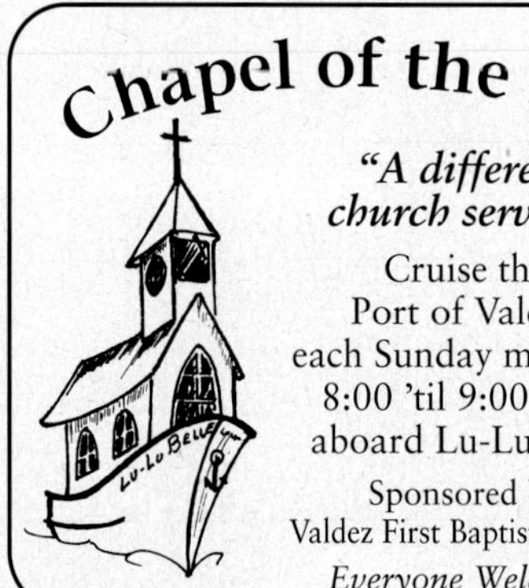

accessible. Open Monday and Friday 10 A.M. to 6 P.M., Tuesday through Thursday, 10 A.M. to 8 P.M., and Saturday, noon to 6 P.M. ♿

Visit Prince William Sound Community College, located at 303 Lowe St. Two huge wooden carvings on campus (1 located in the dorms on Pioneer Street), by artist Peter Toth, are dedicated to the Indians of America. An Elderhostel is held at Prince William Sound Community College from mid-June through mid-Aug. This educational program (college credit given) is available for people over age 55. Subjects include Alaska history, wildlife and fisheries of Prince William Sound, and Alaska literature. Contact Elderhostel, 80 Boylston St., Suite 400, Boston, MA 02116, for more information on its Alaska programs. The fourth annual theatre conference sponsored by the college will be held Aug. 14–18, 1996, at the Valdez Civic Center. For the last 3 years Pulitzer playwright Edward Albee has been featured. For more information contact PWSCC, P.O. Box 97, Valdez, AK 99686.

View salmon spawning at Crooked Creek. From Meals Avenue drive 0.9 mile/1.4 km out the Richardson Highway to the Crooked Creek salmon spawning area and hatchery. A U.S. Forest Service information station, open Memorial Day to Labor Day, has interpretive displays, and information on cultural history and recreation. An observation platform gives a close-up look at salmon spawning in midsummer and fall. This is also a waterfowl sanctuary and an excellent spot for watching various migrating birds.

Fish a Derby. The Valdez Chamber of Commerce holds a halibut, silver salmon and pink salmon derby every year, with cash prizes awarded to the first through third place winners for all 3 derbies. The Halibut Derby will be held May 5 through Sept. 1, 1996; the Silver Salmon Derby July 29 through Sept. 1, 1996; the Pink Salmon Derby June 29 through July 27, 1996. For further information contact the Valdez Chamber of Commerce at (907) 835-2330.

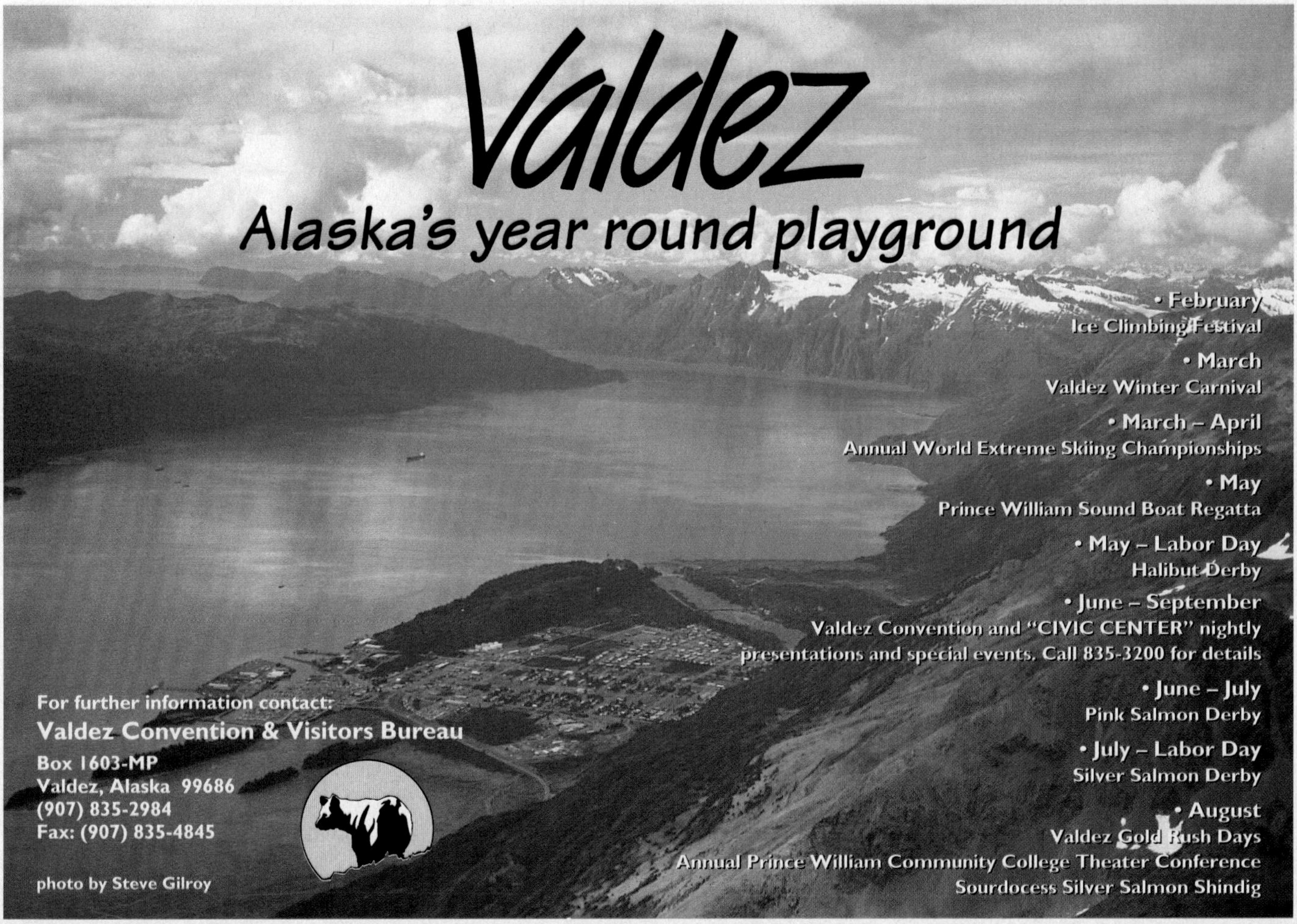

Drive Mineral Creek Road. A 5.5-mile/8.9-km drive behind town leading northwest through the breathtaking alpine scenery along Mineral Creek. *Drive carefully!* This is a narrow road; conditions depend on weather

and how recently the road has been graded. Bears are frequently sighted here. To reach Mineral Creek Road drive to the end of Hazelet Street toward the mountains and turn left on Hanagita then right on Mineral Creek Road. Excellent view of the city from the water tower hill just to the right at the start of Mineral Creek Road.

Valdez Arm supports the largest sport fishery in Prince William Sound. Important species include pink salmon, coho (silver) salmon, halibut, rockfish and Dolly Varden. Charter boats are available in Valdez. A hot fishing spot near Valdez accessible by road is the **Allison Point** fishery (or "Winnebago Point" as it is known locally) created by the Solomon Gulch Hatchery, which produces major pink and silver salmon returns annually. Turn off the Richardson Highway at **Milepost V 2.9.** It is one of the largest pink salmon fisheries in the state. Pink salmon returns are best in odd years, but with hatchery production good pink runs are anticipated every year. Pinks average 3 to 5 lbs., from late June to early Aug. Silvers from 6 to 10 lbs., late July into Sept.

Anadyr Adventures offers 3-hour to 10-day guided sea kayaking eco-tours throughout Prince William Sound. Paddle amongst icebergs. See whales, otters, seals, birds. Hike,

fish, beachcomb. Lodge, cabin, motor vessel-support. Kayak rentals. No experience necessary. Children welcome. 203 N Harbor Drive, Box 1821, Valdez, AK 99686. Phone/fax (907) 835-2814 or 1-800-TO-KAYAK. [ADVERTISEMENT]

Bear Paw Trading Post Gift Shop, next to Bear Paw RV Park on Harbor Drive, features fine Alaska Native arts and crafts. Carved walrus ivory, scrimshaw, soapstone carvings, Native masks, fur items. Gold nugget jewelry, jade, hematite. Prints and books by Doug and Patti Lindstrand. Film, postcards, souvenirs, Alaska books. Phone (907) 835-2530. [ADVERTISEMENT]

Capt. Jim's Great Alaska Charter Company offers marine wildlife tours and cruises to spectacular Columbia Glacier and Meares Glacier. Your trip to Prince William Sound won't be complete until you've seen our humpback whales, orcas, porpoise, sea lions, sea otters, eagles, puffins and more. See it all from the comfort of our 65-foot *Orca Princess* with beverages and hot lunch. Columbia Glacier and Meares Glacier are two of

Alaska's most spectacular glaciers. We offer tours to each glacier. Watch as huge slabs of blue ice crash into the Sound's emerald green waters. Watch for seals and sea otters that frequent icebergs in surrounding waters. Make reservations today. Call 1-800-997-6722. Ask about our whale boat discount. [ADVERTISEMENT]

Era Helicopters. Fly over Valdez and the Prince William Sound with Alaska's most experienced helicopter company. Soar over the breathtaking Columbia Glacier. Land at the face of Shoup Glacier or feast on Alaskan seafood at a rustic island camp. Phone (800) 843-1947 or (907) 835-2595 locally. Tours also available in Anchorage, Juneau and Mount McKinley. [ADVERTISEMENT]

Ketchum Air Service, Inc. Alaska's outdoor specialists. Floatplane tours/charters into Prince William Sound, Wrangell–St. Elias park. Day fishing/fully equipped. Columbia Glacier tour. Drop-off cabins. Kennecott Mine visit! Floatplane tour office located small-boat harbor Valdez. Call or write for brochure. VISA, MasterCard. Phone (907) 835-3789 or (800) 433-9114. Box 670, Valdez, AK 99686. [ADVERTISEMENT]

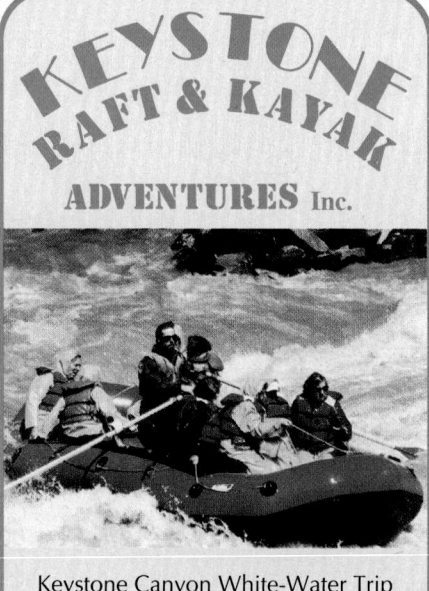

Lu-Lu Belle. The motor yacht *Lu-Lu Belle* is probably the cleanest, plushest tour vessel you will ever see! When you come aboard and see all the teak, mahogany and oriental rugs, you will understand why Captain Rodolf asks you to wipe your feet before boarding. The *Lu-Lu Belle* has wide walk-around decks thus assuring everyone ample opportunity for unobstructed viewing and photography, and is equipped with 110-volt outlets for battery chargers. Captain Fred Rodolf has logged over 2,500 Columbia Glacier cruises since 1979 and he will personally guide and narrate every cruise. The Columbia Glacier cruise of Prince William Sound is awesome. Puffins, Steller sea lions, sea otters, seals and bald eagles are seen on every cruise. Dall porpoise, orca, humpback

and minke whales, black bear, Sitka black-tail deer, Dall sheep and mountain goats are often seen as the *Lu-Lu Belle* cruises from Valdez to Columbia Glacier on the protected, calm waters of the Sound. Columbia is the most active retreating calving tidewater glacier in North America, retreating back 6 miles from where it was when Captain Vancouver's expedition first saw it in 1794. In November 1995, the 16-square-mile ice jam in front of its face disappeared, thus allowing us to take you right up to the calving face. Boarding at 7:45 A.M. and 1:45 P.M. each day from Memorial Day to Labor Day. (No morning cruise on Sunday.) The cost is $70 per person (with a cash discount price of $65). The cruise is approximately 5 hours. During the trip the crew prepares fresh-baked goods in the galley. Friendliness and gracious hospitality on a beautiful yacht with small intimate groups. No wonder people refer to the *Lu-Lu Belle* as the limousine of Prince William Sound. Join us for an extra special day and see why Captain Rodolf refers to Switzerland as being the "Valdez of Europe!" There is also RV parking (full hookups only) and the best dog-gone critter sitters at the office lot. Call 1-800-411-0090 or (907) 835-5141. Winter phone (206) 842-9123. [ADVERTISEMENT]

Northern Magic Charters and Tours offers one of the finest personalized tours in Valdez. You'll enjoy the spacious luxury of our custom-built, 43-foot ship, the *Viking*. The 360-degree wrap-around deck makes it ideal for close-up wildlife viewing and photography. See it up close and in comfort aboard our 20-passenger vessel for a more relaxed, uncrowded tour. It's the small ship alternative. Two of our more popular sight-seeing and wildlife tours are the 2 1/2 hour Shoup Glacier and Port of Valdez historic harbor tour or our 5 1/2 hour Columbia Glacier tour. We also offer customized tours and halibut fishing throughout Prince William Sound. Locally owned and operated. For more information or reservations, call 1-800-443-3543 or (907) 835-4433. Or write P.O. Box 1559, Valdez, AK 99686. See display ad. [ADVERTISEMENT]

Prince William Sound Cruise. Experience the spectacular beauty of Prince William Sound aboard the *Glacier Queen II*. This Gray Line of Alaska tour cruises past Columbia Glacier, the largest glacier in Prince William Sound. Watch for abundant marine life as you travel round-trip between Valdez and Whittier. Two meals are included. This 12-hour tour departs daily from Valdez and costs $110 per person. Prices subject to change. Call (907) 835-2357. [ADVERTISEMENT]

Raven Sailing Charters. Cruise in comfort aboard our handsome 50-foot ketch on 1–10 day trips personalized to fulfill your interests. View wildlife, marine life, glaciers and secluded bays. Involve yourself in wilderness hiking, photography and beach-combing. Hot showers, prepared meals, fresh linens and central heating are some of the amenities offered aboard. Complete safety and navigation equipment. Small group of 1–6 persons. (907) 835-5863, (907) 835-4960 message. See display ad this section. [ADVERTISEMENT]

Stan Stephens Cruises. Let Alaskans show you Alaska. This Alaskan, family-owned business offers a variety of cruises in Prince William Sound to and from Valdez, Cordova and Whittier. Our most popular tour is an 8 1/2 hour Columbia Glacier cruise including an all-you-can-eat Alaskan buffet at Growler Island. Our buffet features salads, soup, halibut, salmon, chicken, beef and all the trimmings. After eating, explore the beaches and intertidal zone. New in

1996, we will be offering a daily 11-hour tour to Meares and Columbia glaciers, including the meal at Growler Island. The longer excursions offer greater opportunity to view the wildlife of the Sound (sea otters, seals, sea lions, porpoise and the possibility of spotting orca, humpback or minke

whales). The ultimate wilderness experience is to stay overnight in a heated tent-cabin at Growler Island Wilderness Camp in view of the largest tidewater glacier in Prince William Sound. Add an overnight at Growler Island to any of our tours except the economy trip. The Growler Island overnight price includes all meals, accommodation plus use of canoes and paddle boats. The economy tour departs Valdez daily, does not include a stop on Growler Island, but gives a quality 5 1/2 hour tour. Our 2-day Cordova and Childs Glacier Adventure departs Valdez each Thursday at 7:45 A.M. Day one of this trip includes a picnic lunch on the banks of the Copper River across from the actively calving Childs Glacier; day two features Columbia Glacier and Growler Island. Our daily Valdez–Whittier connection includes Columbia and Blackstone glaciers and a hot meal on board. We are successful at accommodating most physically-challenged travelers. Call toll free or write for schedules, prices and a brochure. P.O. Box 1297, Valdez, AK, 99686. Call 1-800-992-1297 or (907) 835-4731; fax (907) 835-3765. See our full-page display ad for photos. [ADVERTISEMENT] ♿

Valdez Convention and Civic Center. Visit the elegant "Civic Center" at 110 Clifton Drive, up the hill to the west of the boat harbor. Nightly presentations June through September, and other intermittent entertainment events. Call the HOTLINE at 835-3200 or the office at 835-4440 for details. The Civic Center is perched on the hill overlooking the bay. For great pictures with a 360-degree view of Valdez, climb the stairs to the overlook in back of the Civic Center. Then walk down and enjoy Ruth Pond below the Civic Center. [ADVERTISEMENT]

Cordova

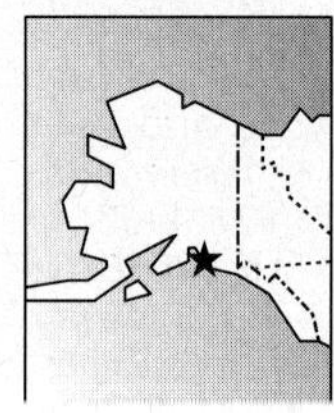

Located on the east side of Prince William Sound on Orca Inlet. **Population:** 2,585. **Emergency Services: Alaska State Troopers**, phone (907) 424-7331, emergency phone 911. **Police, Fire Department, Ambulance**, phone (907) 424-6100, emergency phone 911. **Hospital**, phone (907) 424-8000.

Visitor Information: Information kiosk at the ferry office. Chamber of Commerce office on 1st Street inside the Union Hall Bldg.; phone (907) 424-7260 or write Box 99, Cordova, AK 99574. There is also a visitor information center at the museum. A one-hour audiotaped, self-guided walking tour of downtown Cordova is available for rent from the Chamber of Commerce. A self-guided walking tour map of Cordova, prepared by the Cordova Historical Society, is also available.

Chugach National Forest Cordova Ranger District office is located at 612 2nd St. USFS personnel can provide information on trails, cabins and other activities on national forest lands. The office is open weekdays from 8 A.M. to 5 P.M. Write P.O. Box 280, Cordova 99574, or phone (907) 424-7661.

Elevation: Sea level to 400 feet/122m. **Climate:** Average temperature in July is 54°F/12°C, in Jan. 21°F/-6°C. Average annual precipitation is 167 inches. Prevailing winds are easterly at about 4 knots. **Radio:** KLAM-AM, KCHU-FM (National Public Radio). **Television:** Cable. **Newspaper:** *Cordova Times* (weekly).

Private Aircraft: Merle K. "Mudhole" Smith Airport, 11.3 miles/18.2 km southeast; elev. 42 feet/13m; length 7,500 feet/2,286m; asphalt; attended. Cordova Municipal (city air field), 0.9 mile/1.4 km east; elev. 12 feet/4m; length 1,900 feet/579m; gravel; fuel 100, 100LL; unattended. Eyak Lake seaplane base, 0.9 mile/1.4 km east.

It was the Spanish explorer Don Salvador Fidalgo who named the adjacent water Puerto Cordoba in 1790. The town was named Cordova by Michael J. Heney, builder of the Copper River & Northwestern Railway. By 1889, the town had grown into a fish camp and cannery site. A post office was established in 1906. Cordova was incorporated in 1909.

One of the first producing oil fields in Alaska was located at Katalla, 47 miles/76 km southeast of Cordova on the Gulf of Alaska. The discovery was made in 1902 and the field produced until 1933.

The town was chosen as the railroad terminus and ocean shipping port for copper ore shipped by rail from the Kennecott mines near Kennicott and McCarthy. The railroad and town prospered until 1938 when the mine closed.

Commercial fishing has now supplanted mining as the basis of the town's economy. The fishing fleet can be seen at Cordova harbor, home port of the MV *Bartlett* and the USCG cutter *Sweetbrier*. Also at the harbor is the Cordova Fishermen's Memorial, *The Southeasterly*.

The fishing and canning season for salmon runs from about May to Sept., with red, king and silver (coho) salmon taken from the Copper River area, chum, red and pink salmon from Prince William Sound. Black cod, crab and shrimp season runs during winter. Dungeness crab season runs during the summer and early fall months. Razor clams, halibut and scallops are also processed.

ACCOMMODATIONS/VISITOR SERVICES

Cordova has 2 motels and 2 hotels, 8 bed and breakfasts, 12 restaurants, a laundromat and a variety of shopping facilities.

A Peaceful Night, private lodging. One and 2 bedroom apartments with full kitchen. Complimentary coffee and juice. Located in a quiet neighborhood, close to town. Mountain view. Laundry facilities and freezer space available. Families with children welcome. Please no smoking inside building. Dave and Kathy Sjostedt, P.O. Box 1028, Cordova, AK 99574. (907) 424-5702,

fax (907) 424-3994. [ADVERTISEMENT]

Cordova Rose Lodge. Historical 1924 landlocked barge and lighthouse. Former fishtrap setter, cannery, recluse home, machine shop and houseboat. Unique B&B in barge decor; nautical artifacts with a touch of whimsy. Guests from around the world "cruise" on the renovated barge. Alaskan ambiance and hospitality the moment you go on board. (907) 424-7673; 1315 Whitshed Road. See display ad. [ADVERTISEMENT]

Cordova has one campground, Odiak Camper Park, located on Whitshed Road and operated by the city. The camper park has 24 RV sites and a tenting area. Free shower tokens are available for paying campers. Contact Cordova's city hall at (907) 424-6200. ▲

The historic Skater's Cabin on Eyak Lake is available for rent from the city. The rustic cabin has a woodstove and outhouse. The fee is $25 per night. Contact Bidarki Recreation Center, phone (907) 424-7282.

The U.S. Forest Service maintains 17 cabins in the Cordova district. Three are accessible by trail, the rest by boat or plane. Phone (907) 424-7661 for current fees, reservations and information.

TRANSPORTATION

Air: Scheduled service via Alaska Airlines and Era Aviation. Several air taxi services based at the municipal airport, Mile 13 airport and Eyak Lake offer charter and flightseeing service.

Ferry: The Alaska Marine Highway system ferries connect Cordova with Valdez, Whittier and Seward. Phone (907) 424-7333. See the MARINE ACCESS ROUTES section for details.

Taxi: Local service available.

Car Rental: Available locally.

Highways: The Alaska state highway system does not connect to Cordova. The Copper River Highway leads 48 miles/77 km east and north of Cordova, ending at the Million Dollar Bridge and Childs Glacier. (See the COPPER RIVER HIGHWAY section.)

Private Boats: Cordova has an 850-slip boat harbor serving recreational boaters as well as the commercial fishing fleet. Berth arrangements may be made by contacting the harbormaster's office at (907) 424-6400 or on VHF Channel 16.

ATTRACTIONS

Cordova's Museum and Library, at 622 1st St., are connected by a central entryway. "Where Cultures Meet" is the theme of the museum. Native artifacts such as stone implements, a dugout canoe and skin bidarka (kayak) represent the rich Native culture. One display tells of early explorers to the area, including Vitus Bering, who

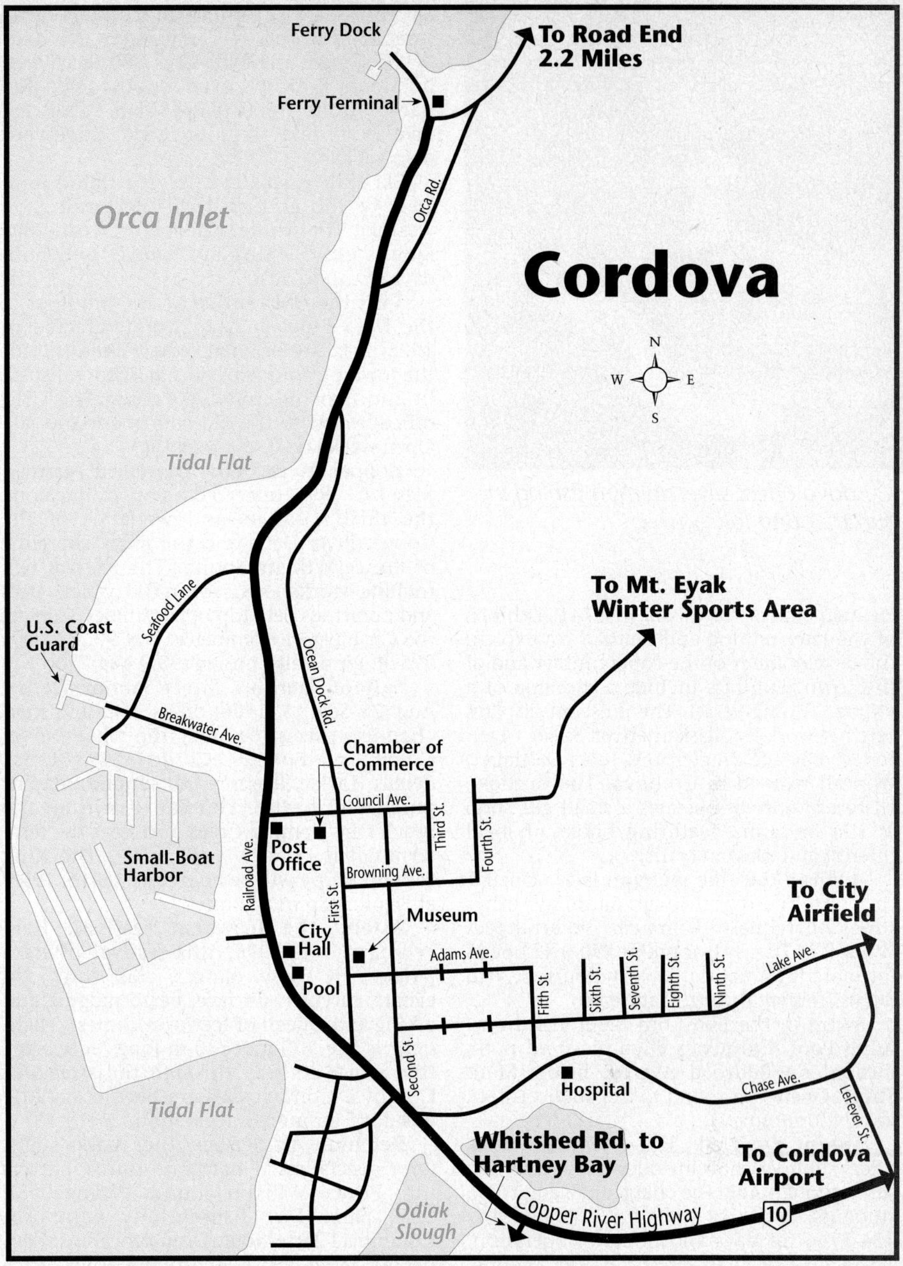

Cordova

Ferry Dock
To Road End 2.2 Miles
Ferry Terminal
Orca Inlet
Orca Rd.
N W E S
Tidal Flat
To Mt. Eyak Winter Sports Area
Seafood Lane
U.S. Coast Guard
Ocean Dock Rd.
Breakwater Ave.
Chamber of Commerce
Council Ave.
Third St.
Fourth St.
Small-Boat Harbor
Railroad Ave.
Post Office
Browning Ave.
First St.
Museum
To City Airfield
City Hall
Pool
Adams Ave.
Fifth St.
Sixth St.
Seventh St.
Eighth St.
Ninth St.
Lake Ave.
Second St.
Hospital
Chase Ave.
Lefevier St.
Tidal Flat
Whitshed Rd. to Hartney Bay
To Cordova Airport
Odiak Slough
Copper River Highway
10

CORDOVA ADVERTISERS

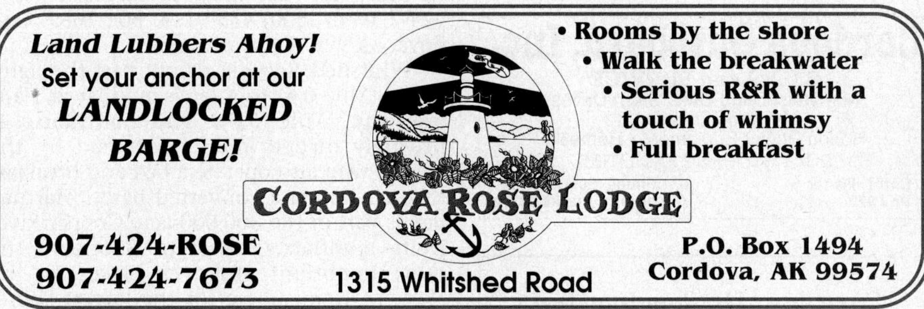

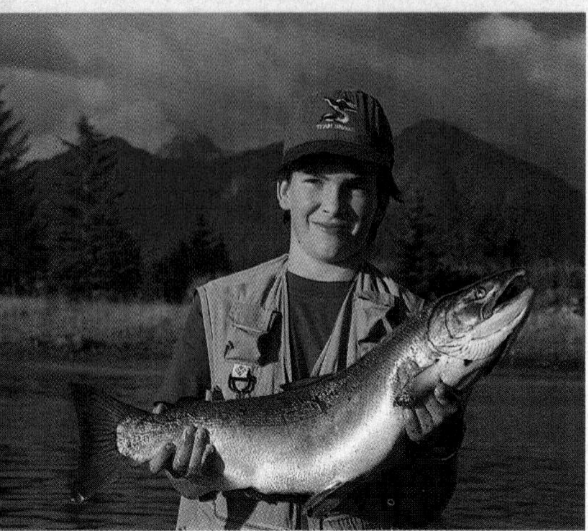

Cordova offers silver salmon fishing in summer and fall. (Joe Prax)

claimed Alaska for Russia in 1741. Exhibits of the later mining and railroad era explain the development of the copper mines and of the town. Exhibits include a diorama of a vintage fishing vessel. The museum displays original work by Alaskan artists Sydney Laurence, Eustace Ziegler and Jules Dahlager, who all worked in Cordova. The Cordova Historical Society operates a small gift shop at the museum, featuring books of local interest and Alaskan crafts.

Admission to the museum is $1. Open 1 to 5 P.M. Tuesday through Saturday; other times on request. Tours can be arranged. Write P.O. Box 391 or phone (907) 424-6665 for more information. Library hours are 1 to 8 P.M. Tuesday through Saturday.

Swim in the Bob Korn Memorial Swimming Pool, Cordova's Olympic-sized pool, located on Railroad Avenue below Main Street. Open year-round to the public. Check locally for hours.

Mount Eyak. Ski Hill on Mount Eyak offers summer chair lift rides for sightseeing, June through Aug. Fee charged: $7 adults, $5 students, under 12 years free. Phone (907) 424-7766 for days and hours of operation. To reach the chair lift from 4th Avenue, take Council Avenue 1 block, then follow Ski Hill Road to top (about 1 mile/1.6 km from Main Street).

The single chair lift rises 880 feet/268m up Mount Eyak and overlooks the town and harbor from 1,600 feet/488km. Walk up, take a cab, take the tour bus or drive your own vehicle.

Ski Hill is usually open for skiing mid-Dec. to the end of April, depending on weather. The winter schedule is Wednesday (adults only), Saturday, Sunday and holidays, 9 A.M. to dusk.

Visit the USFS office on the 3rd floor of the USFS Bldg. at 612 2nd St. Erected in 1925, it is the original federal building for the town of Cordova. Natural history display in 2nd floor Interpretive Center. The USFS office is next to the old courtroom and jail. Open weekdays 8 A.M. to 5 P.M.

Copper River Delta Shorebird Festival, May 1–5, 1996, offers 5 days of birding along the tidal mudflats and wetlands of the Copper River Delta and the rocky shoreline of Prince William Sound. The festival will include workshops, community activities and numerous field trip opportunities. Contact the Chamber of Commerce, Box 99, Cordova 99574, for details; phone (907) 424-7260.

Salmon Derbies. Silver Salmon Derby, Aug. 23–Sept. 3, 1996, offers cash and merchandise prizes. Contact the Chamber of Commerce, Box 99, Cordova 99574, for details. Tackle, licenses and supplies may be purchased locally. You can fish from the beach (the Fleming Creek area near the ferry terminal is especially popular). The King Salmon Derby will be held June 15–16, 1996, at Fleming Spit/Orca Inlet.

Attend the Iceworm Festival: Held February 2–4, 1996, this festival offers a parade, art show, dances, craft show, ski events, survival suit race, beard judging and a King and Queen of Iceworm contest. Highlight is the 100-foot-/30-m-long "iceworm" that winds its way through the streets of Cordova. Contact Barbara Beedle at (907) 424-3527 for more information.

Whitshed Road leads out past the lighthouse (Mile 0.4) to a large mudflat at Hartney Bay (Mile 5.5). The lighthouse is privately owned and maintained by the Gleins, who also operate a bed and breakfast in their home: a converted barge. Hartney Bay is part of the 300,000-acre Copper River Delta mudflats. The delta is one of the most important stopover places in the Western Hemisphere for the largest shorebird migration in the world. Birders can view up to 31 different species as millions of shorebirds pass through the delta each spring.

Power Creek Road, from the corner of Lake and Chase avenues, leads out past the municipal airport to Crater Lake trailhead and Skaters Cabin picnic area (Mile 1.2), continues to Hatchery Creek salmon spawning channel (Mile 5.7), and ends at the Power Creek trailhead (Mile 6.9). The Crater Lake trailhead is directly northwest of the Eyak Lake Skaters Cabin. The 2.4-mile/3.8-km trail climbs to 1,500 feet/457m. Excellent views, alpine lake with fishing for cutthroat trout. Watch for bears. Visitors may view spawning salmon at the Hatchery Creek channel in July and Aug. Power Creek trail, 4.2 miles/6.7 km long, accesses both the USFS public-use cabin in Power Creek Basin and a ridge that connects with the Crater Lake trail creating a 12-mile/19.3-km loop. Power Creek trail offers spectacular scenery, with waterfalls, hanging glaciers and views of Power Creek Basin (called "surprise valley" by locals), the Chugach Range and Prince William Sound. Excellent berry picking. Watch for bears.

Drive the Copper River Highway to see the Million Dollar Bridge, Childs Glacier and the Copper River Delta. The 48-mile/77-km highway leads east from Cordova through the Delta to the historic Million Dollar Bridge, built in 1909–10, and Childs Glacier. Viewing platform and picnic area at Childs Glacier. Wildlife seen along the highway includes brown and black bear, moose, beaver, mountain goats, trumpeter swans, and numerous other species of birds. See COPPER RIVER HIGHWAY section for log of road.

AREA FISHING: According to the ADF&G, "Saltwater fishing in **Orca Inlet** and adjacent western Prince William Sound is accessible from Cordova. Species include halibut, rockfish and 5 species of salmon. Trolling for salmon is best for kings in the winter and spring, and silvers in the summer and fall. Boat charters are available locally. Road-accessible fishing opportunities exist for salmon in salt water at **Fleming Spit/Lagoon**, near the ferry terminal off Orca Bay Road. Strong runs of hatchery-enhanced kings (in the spring) and silvers (August and September) return to this terminal fishery. The Chamber of Commerce sponsors a fishing derby for both the king and silver fisheries. Road-accessible freshwater fishing is also good in the Cordova Area. **Eyak Lake** and **Eyak River** support strong returns of sockeye during June and July and silvers in Aug. and Sept. The area at the outlet of the lake, where the road crosses, is fly-fishing only. Several streams along the **Copper River** Highway between Eyak Lake and the Million Dollar Bridge also support runs of sockeye and coho. These streams include **Clear Creek**, **Alaganik Slough**, **Eighteen-mile Creek** and **Twenty-mile Creek**. In addition, cutthroat trout and Dolly Varden are present in most of these streams. Lake fishing for sockeye salmon, Dolly Varden and cutthroat trout is available in **McKinley Lake** and the **Pipeline Lake** system. Arctic grayling are stocked in several gravel-pit ponds developed by the U.S. Forest Service. Fly-out fishing from Cordova is also popular for salmon, Dolly Varden and cutthroat trout. Charter operators are available locally." See also the COPPER RIVER HIGHWAY section for area fishing.

RICHARDSON HIGHWAY

Valdez to Delta Junction, Alaska
Alaska Route 4
(See map, page 586)

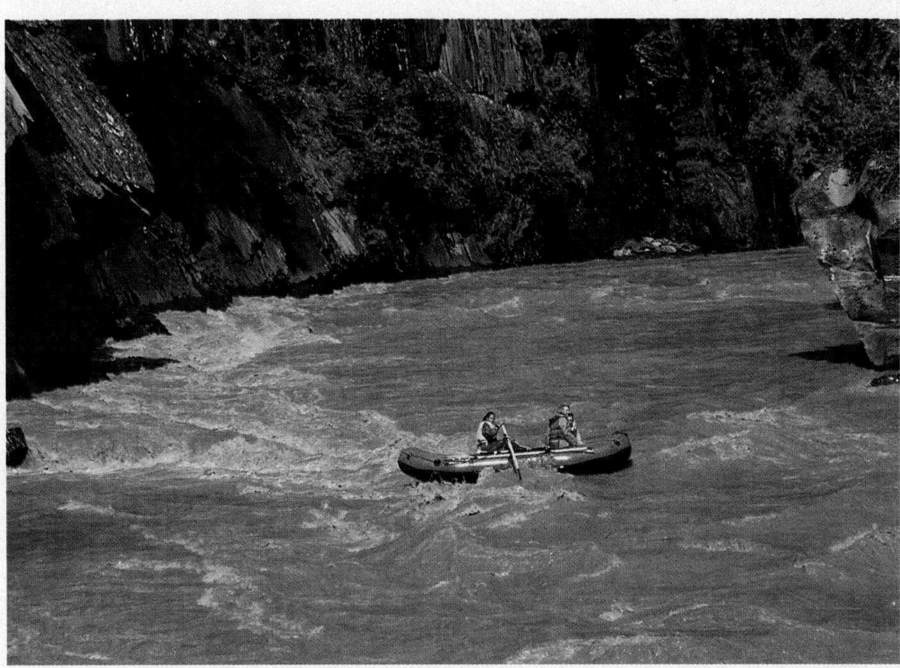

Rafters on the Lowe River in Keystone Canyon. (© Bruce M. Herman)

The Richardson Highway extends 368 miles/592 km from Valdez to Fairbanks. This section logs the first 270 miles/434.5 km of the Richardson Highway from Valdez to Delta Junction (the remaining 98 miles/157.7 km from Delta Junction to Fairbanks are logged in the ALASKA HIGHWAY section). Southbound travelers read log back to front.

The Richardson is a wide paved highway in good condition except for sporadic frost heaving. *NOTE: Watch for road repair crews between* **Milepost V 15** *and* **V 76** *in 1996.*

A new section of highway completed in 1989 bypasses the historic community of Copper Center. *The MILEPOST®* logs the old highway through town. The "new" Richardson Highway (bypass route) is of equal distance—6.5 miles/10.5 km—with no notable features. You must exit the highway (watch for signs) to see Copper Center.

The Richardson Highway is a scenic route through the magnificent scenery of the Chugach Mountains and Alaska Range. It passes many fine king salmon streams, including the Gulkana and Tonsina rivers.

The Richardson Highway was Alaska's first road, known to gold seekers in 1898 as the Valdez to Eagle trail. The gold rush trail led over the treacherous Valdez Glacier, then northeast to Eagle and the Yukon River route to the Klondike goldfields. Captain W.R. Abercrombie of the U.S. Army rerouted the trail in 1899 through Keystone Canyon and over Thompson Pass, thus avoiding the glacier. As the Klondike gold rush waned, the military kept the trail open to connect Fort Liscum in Valdez with Fort Egbert in Eagle. In 1903, the U.S. Army Signal Corps laid the trans-Alaska telegraph line along this route.

Gold stampeders started up the trail again in 1902, this time headed for Fairbanks, site of a big gold strike. The Valdez to Fairbanks trail became an important route to the Interior, and in 1910 the trail was upgraded to a wagon road under the direction of Gen. Wilds P. Richardson, first president of the Alaska Road Commission. The ARC updated the road to automobile standards in the 1920s. The Richardson Highway was hard-surfaced in 1957.

Emergency medical services: Phone 911 anywhere along the highway.

Richardson Highway Log

Mileposts on the Richardson Highway were erected before the 1964 Good Friday earthquake and therefore begin 4 miles/6.4 km from present-day downtown Valdez near the Old Valdez townsite (destroyed during the earthquake).

Distance from New Valdez (NV) is followed by distance from Old Valdez (OV).

NV 0 OV 4 (6.4 km) Intersection of Meals Avenue and the Richardson Highway.

NV 0.4 (0.6 km) **OV 3.6** (5.8 km) Paved double-ended turnout to north with Valdez information kiosk, maps, brochures, pay phones.

NV 0.5 (0.8 km) **OV 3.5** (5.6 km) DOT/PF district office.

NV 0.6 (1 km) **OV 3.4** (5.5 km) Valdez highway maintenance station.

NV 0.9 (1.4 km) **OV 3.1** (5 km) Double-ended turnout to north with litter barrels at Crooked Creek salmon spawning area and hatchery. Viewing platform offers close-up look at salmon spawning in midsummer and fall. U.S. Forest Service information station is staffed Memorial Day through Labor Day; interpretive displays, history and recreation. Migrating birds such as Canada geese and various ducks are often here. It is a game sanctuary; no shooting is allowed. Good spot for pictures.

NV 1.3 (2.1 km) **OV 2.7** (4.3 km) Paved turnout to south.

NV 2 (3.2 km) **OV 2** (3.2 km) Paved turnout to south.

NV 2.1 (3.4 km) **OV 1.9** (3.1 km) Mineral Creek Loop Road through business and residential area on outskirts of Old Valdez comes out at **Milepost NV 3.4**. Access to Port of Valdez container terminal and grain elevators.

NV 3.4 (5.5 km) **OV 0.6** (1 km) Road leads north 0.6 mile/1 km to Valdez Airport, 2 miles/3.2 km to Valdez Glacier campground, and 3.9 miles/6.3 km to a parking area next to the glacial moraine of Valdez Glacier. Good views of the glacier area are *not* available from this spot, nor is Valdez Glacier a very spectacular glacier. Valdez Glacier campground has 101 sites, tent camping, covered picnic area, litter barrels, water, toilets and fireplaces; 15-day limit, camping fee. *CAUTION: Beware of bears.* ▲

Mineral Creek Loop Road leads south to the original townsite of Valdez, destroyed during the Good Friday earthquake on March 27, 1964. A few homes and businesses are here now; there is little evidence of the earthquake's destruction.

NV 4 (6.4 km) **OV 0** Former access road to Old Valdez, now blocked off. Milepost 0 of the Richardson Highway is located here.

(Southbound travelers note: Physical mileposts end here, it is 4 miles/6.4 km to downtown Valdez.)

Distance from Old Valdez (V) is followed by distance from Fairbanks (F). Physical mileposts begin northbound showing distance from Old Valdez.

V 0 F 364 (585.8 km) **Milepost 0** of the Richardson Highway is located here at the

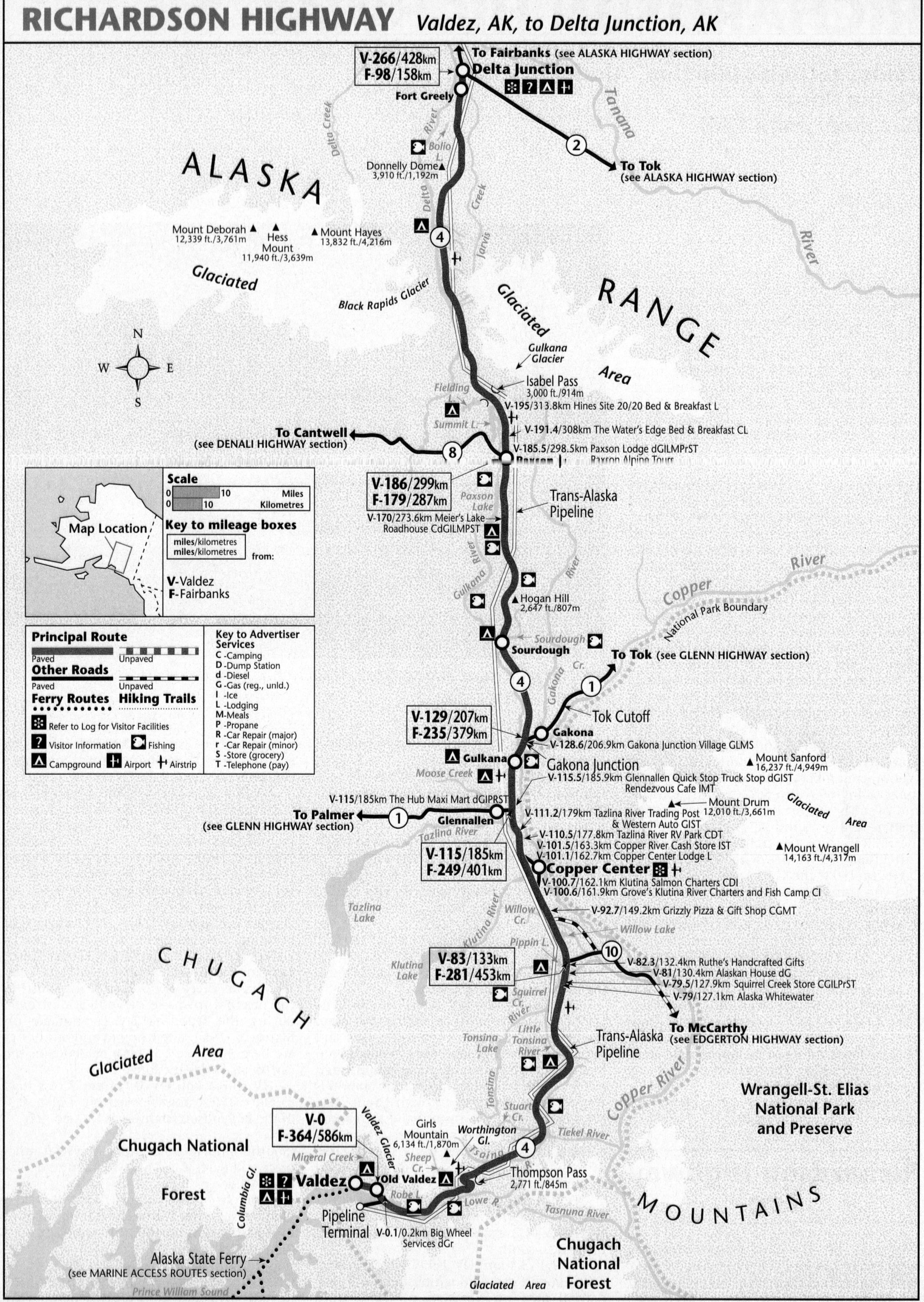
RICHARDSON HIGHWAY Valdez, AK, to Delta Junction, AK
To Fairbanks (see ALASKA HIGHWAY section)
V-266/428km
F-98/158km
Delta Junction
Fort Greely
Delta Creek
Tanana
To Tok
(see ALASKA HIGHWAY section)
Bolio L.
Donnelly Dome
3,910 ft./1,192m
ALASKA
RANGE
Delta River
Jarvis Creek
River
Mount Deborah
12,339 ft./3,761m
Hess Mount
11,940 ft./3,639m
Mount Hayes
13,832 ft./4,216m
Glaciated
Black Rapids Glacier
Glaciated
Area
Gulkana Glacier
Isabel Pass
3,000 ft./914m
Fielding
V-195/313.8km Hines Site 20/20 Bed & Breakfast L
Summit L.
V-191.4/308km The Water's Edge Bed & Breakfast CL
To Cantwell
(see DENALI HIGHWAY section)
V-185.5/298.5km Paxson Lodge dGILMPrST
Paxson
Paxson Alpine Tours
V-186/299km
F-179/287km
Paxson Lake
Trans-Alaska Pipeline
V-170/273.6km Meier's Lake Roadhouse CdGILMPST
Gulkana River
Hogan Hill
2,647 ft./807m
Copper River
National Park Boundary
Sourdough
Sourdough
To Tok (see GLENN HIGHWAY section)
Gakona Cr.
Tok Cutoff
V-129/207km
F-235/379km
Gakona
V-128.6/206.9km Gakona Junction Village GLMS
Gulkana
Gakona Junction
Moose Creek
V-115.5/185.9km Glennallen Quick Stop Truck Stop dGIST
Rendezvous Cafe IMT
Mount Sanford
16,237 ft./4,949m
V-115/185km The Hub Maxi Mart dGIPRST
To Palmer
(see GLENN HIGHWAY section)
Glennallen
Tazlina River
Mount Drum
12,010 ft./3,661m
V-111.2/179km Tazlina River Trading Post & Western Auto GIST
V-110.5/177.8km Tazlina River RV Park CDT
V-101.5/163.3km Copper River Cash Store IST
V-101.1/162.7km Copper Center Lodge L
V-115/185km
F-249/401km
Copper Center
V-100.7/162.1km Klutina Salmon Charters CDI
V-100.6/161.9km Grove's Klutina River Charters and Fish Camp CI
Glaciated Area
Mount Wrangell
14,163 ft./4,317m
Tazlina Lake
Klutina River
Willow Cr.
V-92.7/149.2km Grizzly Pizza & Gift Shop CGMT
Willow Lake
Pippin L.
CHUGACH
Klutina Lake
V-83/133km
F-281/453km
V-82.3/132.4km Ruthe's Handcrafted Gifts
V-81/130.4km Alaskan House dG
V-79.5/127.9km Squirrel Creek Store CGILPrST
V-79/127.1km Alaska Whitewater
Squirrel Cr.
River
To McCarthy
(see EDGERTON HIGHWAY section)
Tonsina Lake
Little Tonsina River
Trans-Alaska Pipeline
Glaciated
Area
Tonsina
Copper River
Wrangell-St. Elias National Park and Preserve
Stuart Cr.
Tiekel River
V-0
F-364/586km
Valdez Glacier
Girls Mountain
6,134 ft./1,870m
Worthington Gl.
Chugach National Forest
Mineral Creek
Sheep Cr.
Tsaina R.
Thompson Pass
2,771 ft./845m
Valdez
Old Valdez
Columbia Gl.
Robe L.
Lowe R.
Tasnuna River
MOUNTAINS
Pipeline Terminal
V-0.1/0.2km Big Wheel Services dGr
Chugach National Forest
Alaska State Ferry
(see MARINE ACCESS ROUTES section)
Prince William Sound
Glaciated Area
N
W
E
S
Map Location
Scale
0 10 Miles
0 10 Kilometres
Key to mileage boxes
miles/kilometres
miles/kilometres
from:
V-Valdez
F-Fairbanks
Principal Route
Paved
Unpaved
Other Roads
Paved
Unpaved
Ferry Routes
Hiking Trails
Refer to Log for Visitor Facilities
Visitor Information
Fishing
Campground
Airport
Airstrip
Key to Advertiser Services
C -Camping
D -Dump Station
d -Diesel
G -Gas (reg., unld.)
I -Ice
L -Lodging
M -Meals
P -Propane
R -Car Repair (major)
r -Car Repair (minor)
S -Store (grocery)
T -Telephone (pay)

former access road to Old Valdez.

V 0.1 (0.2 km) **F 363.9** (585.6 km) **Big Wheel Services.** See display ad this section.

V 0.9 (1.4 km) **F 363.1** (584.4 km) The highway passes over the terminal moraine of the Valdez Glacier, bridging several channels and streams flowing from the melting ice.

V 1.4 (2.3 km) **F 362.6** (583.5 km) Valdez Trapshooting Range.

V 1.5 (2.4 km) **F 362.5** (583.4 km) City of Valdez Goldfields Recreation Area; trails, ponds, swimming, picnic sites and baseball field.

V 2.2 (3.5 km) **F 361.8** (582.2 km) Dylen Drive.

V 2.4 (3.9 km) **F 361.6** (581.9 km) Paved turnout to west.

V 2.5 (4 km) **F 361.5** (581.8 km) Valdez cemetery to east.

V 2.7 (4.3 km) **F 361.3** (581.5 km) Large paved double-ended turnout to west beside Robe River. During Aug. and early Sept. watch for pink and silver salmon spawning in roadside creeks and sloughs. *DO NOT* attempt to catch or otherwise disturb spawning salmon. *CAUTION: Beware of bears.*

V 2.9 (4.7 km) **F 361.1** (581.1 km) Turnoff for Old Dayville Road to Trans-Alaska Pipeline Valdez Marine Terminal and access to Allison Point fishery. This 5.4-mile/8.7-km paved road (open to the public) crosses the Lowe River 4 times. At Mile 2.4/3.9 km the road parallels the bay and there is excellent fishing in season at Allison Point, especially for pink and silver salmon; also watch for sea otters and bald eagles along here. At Mile 4.1/6.6 km is the Solomon Gulch water project and a spectacular view of Solomon Gulch Falls; a fish hatchery is located across from the water project. Entrance to the pipeline terminal is at the end of the road. Supertankers load oil pumped from the North Slope to this facility via the trans-Alaska pipeline. Bus tours of the terminal are available; see the VALDEZ section for details.

V 3 (4.8 km) **F 361** (581 km) Weigh station.

V 3.4 (5.5 km) **F 360.6** (580.3 km) A 0.5-mile/0.8-km gravel road to Robe Lake and floatplane base. Watch for cow parsnip and river beauty (dwarf fireweed). Also watch for bears!

V 4.7 (7.5 km) **F 359.3** (578.2 km) Turnout to east. Access to **Robe River**; Dolly Varden, red salmon (fly-fishing only, mid-May to mid-June).

V 5.3 (8.5 km) **F 358.7** (577.3 km) Salmonberry Ridge ski area road to west.

V 7.3 (11.7 km) **F 356.7** (574 km) Lowe River parallels the highway next mile northbound.

V 9.6 (15.4 km) **F 354.4** (570.3 km) Fire station.

V 11.6 (18.7 km) **F 352.4** (567.1 km) Large paved turnout to east.

V 12.8 (20.6 km) **F 351.2** (565.2 km) Here the Lowe River emerges from Keystone Canyon. The canyon was named by Captain William Ralph Abercrombie, presumably for Pennsylvania, the Keystone State. In 1884, Abercrombie had been selected to lead an exploring expedition up the Copper River to the Yukon River. Although unsuccessful in his attempt to ascend the Copper River, he did survey the Copper River Delta and a route to Port Valdez. He returned in 1898 and again in 1899, carrying out further explorations of the area. The Lowe River is named for Lt. Percival Lowe, a member of his expedition. Glacier melt imparts the slate-gray color to the river.

V 13.5 (21.7 km) **F 350.5** (564.1 km) Horsetail Falls; large paved turnout to west.

CAUTION: Watch for pedestrians.

V 13.7 (22 km) **F 350.3** (563.7 km) Goat trail is visible on the west side of the highway; see description of this landmark at **Milepost V 15.2.**

V 13.8 (22.2 km) **F 350.2** (563.6 km) Bridal Veil Falls; large paved turnout to west.

V 14.9 (24 km) **F 349.1** (561.8 km) Lowe River bridge (first of 3 bridges northbound); view of Riddleston Falls. About 175 yards east of this bridge and adjacent to the highway is an abandoned hand-drilled tunnel. Large paved turnout with historical marker. Sign reads: "This tunnel was hand cut into the solid rock of Keystone Canyon and is all that is left of the railroad era when 9 companies fought to take advantage of the short route from the coast to the copper country. However, a feud interrupted progress. A gun battle was fought and the tunnel was never finished."

V 15.2 (24.5 km) **F 348.8** (561.3 km) Small gravel turnout. On the far side just above the water are the remains of the old sled trail used in the early days. This trail was cut out of the rock just wide enough for 2 horses abreast. 200 feet above can be seen "the old goat trail." This road was used until 1945.

V 15.3 (24.6 km) **F 348.7** (561.2 km) Lowe River bridge No. 2, built in 1980, replaced previous highway route through the long tunnel visible beside highway. Turnout at south end of bridge. Traces of the old trail used by horse-drawn sleds can be seen about 200 feet/61m above the river.

V 15.9 (25.6 km) **F 348.1** (560.2 km) Leaving Keystone Canyon northbound, entering Keystone Canyon southbound. Raft trips of Keystone Canyon are available; check with visitor center in Valdez.

V 16.2 (26.1 km) **F 347.8** (559.7 km) Avalanche gun emplacement.

V 16.3 (26.2 km) **F 347.7** (559.6 km) Lowe River bridge No. 3.

V 18 (29 km) **F 346** (556.8 km) Large paved turnouts both sides of road.

V 18.6 (29.9 km) **F 345.4** (555.8 km) Sheep Creek bridge.

Truck lane begins northbound as highway ascends 7.5 miles/12 km to Thompson Pass. This was one of the most difficult sections of pipeline construction, requiring heavy blasting of solid rock for several miles. The pipeline runs under the cleared strip beside the road. Low-flying helicopters often seen along the Richardson Highway are usually monitoring the pipeline.

V 21.6 (34.8 km) **F 342.4** (551 km) Paved turnout to east.

V 23 (37 km) **F 341** (548.8 km) Large gravel turnout to east.

V 23.4 (37.7 km) **F 340.6** (548.1 km) Large paved turnout to east with view.

V 23.6 (38 km) **F 340.4** (547.8 km) Loop road past Thompson Lake to Blueberry Lake and state recreation site; see **Milepost V 24.1.**

V 23.8 (38.3 km) **F 340.2** (547.5 km) Small paved turnout to east.

V 24.1 (38.8 km) **F 339.9** (547 km) Loop road to Blueberry Lake State Recreation Site; drive in 1 mile/1.6 km. Tucked into an alpine setting between tall mountain peaks, this is one of Alaska's most beautifully situated campgrounds; 10 campsites, 4 covered picnic tables, toilets, firepits and water. Camping fee $10/night or annual pass. ▲

Blueberry Lake, and **Thompson Lake** (formerly Summit No. 1 Lake). Good grayling and rainbow fishing all summer.

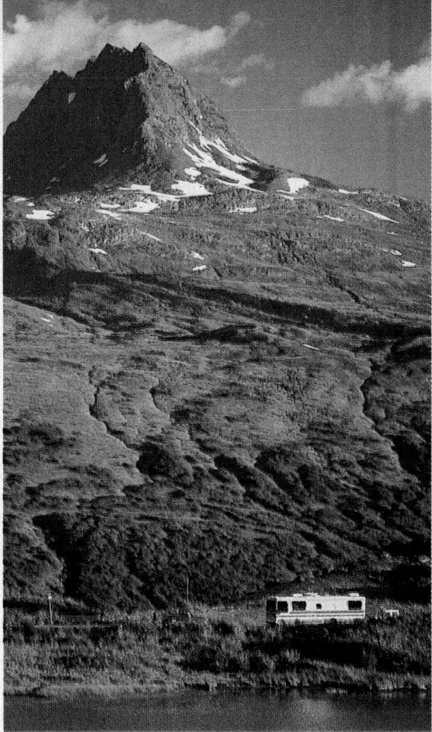

Blueberry Lake State Recreation Site at Milepost V 24.1. (Jerrianne Lowther, staff)

V 24.4 (39.3 km) **F 339.6** (546.5 km) Large paved turnout to west. Bare bone peaks of the Chugach Mountains rise above the highway. Thompson Pass ahead; Marshall Pass is to the east.

During the winter of 1907, the A.J. Meals Co. freighted the 70-ton river steamer *Chitina* (or *Chittyna*) from Valdez over Marshall Pass and down the Tasnuna River to the Copper River. The ship was moved piece by piece on huge horse-drawn freight sleds and assembled at the mouth of the Tasnuna. The 110-foot-/34-m-long ship navigated 170 miles/274 km of the Copper and Chitina rivers above Abercrombie Rapids, moving supplies for construction crews of the Copper River & Northwestern Railway. Much of the equipment for the Kennicott mill and tram was moved by this vessel.

V 25.5 (41 km) **F 338.5** (544.7 km) Large

paved turnout to west. Entering Game Management Unit 13D, leaving unit 6D, northbound.

V 25.7 (41.4 km) **F 338.3** (544.4 km) Large paved turnout to west with view; Keystone Glacier to the south.

V 26 (41.8 km) **F 338** (543.9 km) Thompson Pass (elev. 2,678 feet/816m) at head of Ptarmigan Creek. Truck lane ends northbound; begin 7.5-mile/12-km descent southbound.

Thompson Pass, named by Captain Abercrombie in 1899, is comparatively low elevation but above timberline. A wildflower lover will be well repaid if he rambles over the rocks in this area: tiny alpine plants may be in bloom, such as Aleutian heather and mountain harebell.

The National Climatic Center credits snowfall extremes in Alaska to the Thompson Pass station, where record measurements are: 974.5 inches for season (1952-53); 298 inches for month (Feb. 1953); and 62 inches for 24-hour period (Dec. 1955). Snowpoles along the highway mark the road edge for snow plows.

Private Aircraft: Thompson Pass airstrip; elev. 2,080 feet/634m; length 2,500 feet/762m, turf, gravel, unattended.

V 27 (43.5 km) **F 337** (542.3 km) Thompson Pass highway maintenance station.

V 27.5 (44.3 km) **F 336.5** (541.5 km) Steep turnout to east by **Worthington Lake**; rainbow fishing.

V 27.7 (44.6 km) **F 336.3** (541.2 km) Good viewpoint of 27 Mile Glacier.

V 28 (45.1 km) **F 336** (540.7 km) Paved turnout to east.

V 28.6 (46 km) **F 335.4** (539.8 km) Paved turnout to west.

V 28.7 (46.2 km) **F 335.3** (539.6 km) Worthington Glacier State Recreation Site; large viewing shelter, interpretive displays, toilets, picnic sites, parking and pay phone. According to state park rangers, this is the most visited site in the Copper River Basin. The glacier, which heads on Girls Mountain (elev. 6,134 feet/1,870m), is accessible via a short road to the left. It is possible to drive almost to the face of the glacier. Care should be exercised when walking on ice because of numerous crevasses.

V 30.2 (48.6 km) **F 333.8** (537.2 km) Large paved turnout both sides of highway. Excellent spot for photos of Worthington Glacier.

V 31.1 (50 km) **F 332.9** (535.7 km) Small turnout to east. Avalanche gun emplacement.

V 32 (51.5 km) **F 332** (534.3 km) Highway parallels Tsaina River. Long climb up to Thompson Pass for southbound motorists.

V 33.6 (54.1 km) **F 330.4** (531.7 km) Tsaina River access to west.

V 34.7 (55.8 km) **F 329.3** (529.9 km) Tsaina Lodge.

V 36.5 (58.7 km) **F 327.5** (527 km) Pipeline runs under highway.

V 37 (59.5 km) **F 327** (526.2 km) Entering BLM public lands northbound.

V 37.3 (60 km) **F 326.7** (525.8 km) Tsaina River bridge at Devil's Elbow; turnout at south end of bridge.

V 40.5 (65.2 km) **F 323.5** (520.6 km) Pipeline passes under highway. Avalanche gun emplacement.

V 40.8 (65.7 km) **F 323.2** (520.1 km) Gravel turnout to west.

V 42 (67.6 km) **F 322** (518.2 km) Buried pipeline. View of waterbars (ridges on slope designed to slow runoff and control erosion).

V 43.3 (69.7 km) **F 320.7** (516.1 km) Long double-ended turnout.

V 43.5 (70 km) **F 320.5** (515.8 km) Small turnout to east.

V 45.6 (73.4 km) **F 318.4** (512.4 km) Large paved turnout to east at north end of Stuart Creek bridge.

V 45.8 (73.7 km) **F 318.2** (512.1 km) Watch for moose next 20 miles/32 km northbound.

V 46.9 (75.5 km) **F 317.1** (510.3 km) **Tiekel River** bridge; small Dolly Varden. Small turnout at north end of bridge.

V 47.9 (77.1 km) **F 316.1** (508.7 km) Large paved rest area by Tiekel River; covered picnic sites, toilets, no drinking water. Viewpoint and historical sign for Mount Billy Mitchell.

Lieutenant William "Billy" Mitchell was a member of the U.S. Army Signal Corps, which in 1903 was completing the trans-Alaska telegraph line (Washington–Alaska Military Cable and Telegraph System) to connect all the military posts in Alaska. The 2,000 miles/3,200 km of telegraph wire included the main line between Fort Egbert in Eagle and Fort Liscum at Valdez, and a branch line down the Tanana River to Fort Gibson and on to Fort St. Michael near the mouth of the Yukon and then to Nome. Mitchell was years later to become the "prophet of American military air power."

V 50.7 (81.6 km) **F 313.3** (504.1 km) Bridge over Tiekel River. Dead spruce trees in this area were killed by beetles.

V 53.8 (86.6 km) **F 310.2** (499.2 km) Squaw Creek culvert.

V 54.1 (87.1 km) **F 309.9** (498.7 km) Large paved turnout to east by Tiekel River. Look for lupine in June, dwarf fireweed along river bars in July.

V 54.3 (87.4 km) **F 309.7** (498.4 km) Old beaver lodge. Beaver may inhabit the same site for generations.

V 54.5 (87.7 km) **F 309.5** (498.1 km) Moose often seen here in the evenings.

V 55.1 (88.7 km) **F 308.9** (497.1 km) Large paved turnout to east by Tiekel River.

V 56 (90.1 km) **F 308** (495.7 km) Tiekel River Lodge.

V 56.3 (90.6 km) **F 307.7** (495.2 km) Large paved turnout to east by Tiekel River.

V 57 (91.7 km) **F 307** (494.1 km) Old beaver lodge and dams in pond to east. Tireless and skillful dam builders, beavers construct their houses in the pond created by the dam. Older beaver dams can reach 15 feet in height and may be hundreds of feet long. The largest rodent in North America, beaver range south from the Brooks Range. They eat a variety of vegetation, including aspen, willow, birch and poplar.

V 58.1 (93.5 km) **F 305.9** (492.3 km) Wagon Point Creek culvert.

V 60 (96.6 km) **F 304** (489.2 km) Large paved turnout to east. Highway parallels **Tiekel River**; fishing for small Dolly Varden.

V 62 (99.7 km) **F 302** (486 km) Ernestine Station highway maintenance camp.

V 62.4 (100.4 km) **F 301.6** (485.4 km) Boundary for Sport Fish Management areas. Entering Upper Susitna/Copper River Area N northbound, Prince William Sound southbound.

V 64.7 (104.1 km) **F 299.3** (481.7 km) Pump Station No. 12 to east. Interpretive viewpoint and parking to west. Short walk to viewpoint from parking area.

V 65 (104.6 km) **F 299** (481.2 km) Little Tonsina River.

V 65.1 (104.8 km) **F 298.9** (481 km) **Little Tonsina River** State Recreation Site with 10 campsites, firepits, water, litter barrels and toilets. Camping fee $6/night or annual pass. Dolly Varden fishing. Road to right as you enter wayside dead ends, road to left goes to the river (no turnaround space); follow loop road for easy access. Good berry picking in fall. *CAUTION: Beware of bears!*

Watch for moose next 20 miles/32 km southbound.

V 66.2 (106.5 km) **F 297.8** (479.2 km) Double-ended gravel turnout to west.

V 68.1 (109.6 km) **F 295.9** (476.2 km) Site of former Tonsina Camp (Alyeska Pipeline Service Co.) used during pipeline construction. These camps have been completely removed.

V 70.5 (113.5 km) **F 293.5** (472.3 km) Trans-Alaska pipeline follows base of mountains across valley.

V 71.2 (114.6 km) **F 292.8** (471.2 km) Long double-ended paved turnout to east.

V 72 (115.9 km) **F 292** (469.9 km) Double-ended paved turnout to west. Leaving BLM public lands northbound. View of trans-Alaska pipeline across the valley.

V 74.4 (119.7 km) **F 289.6** (466.1 km) Paved double-ended turnout to west. Vehicle access to Little Tonsina River.

V 78.9 (127 km) **F 285.1** (458.8 km) Bernard Creek trail. According to the BLM, this 15-mile loop road—which was originally part of the WAMCATS line—provides mountain bikers with an uphill ride on hard-pack dirt to near Kimball Pass.

V 79 (127.1 km) **F 285** (458.7 km) Tonsina Lodge. **Private Aircraft:** (Upper) Tonsina airstrip, adjacent south of lodge; elev. 1,500 feet/457m; length 1,400 feet/426m; turf; fuel 80; unattended.

V 79.2 (127.5 km) **F 284.8** (458.3 km) Bridge over Tonsina River, which rises in Tonsina Lake to the southwest.

V 79.5 (127.9 km) **F 284.5** (457.8 km) **Squirrel Creek Store.** See display ad this section.

V 79.6 (128.1 km) **F 284.4** (457.7 km) Bridge and Squirrel Creek state campground. Pleasant campsites on the bank of Squirrel Creek, some pull-through spaces; $10/night or annual pass; dumpster, boat launch, water, toilets and firepits. Rough access road through campground; low-clearance vehicles use caution. Large vehicles note: Limited

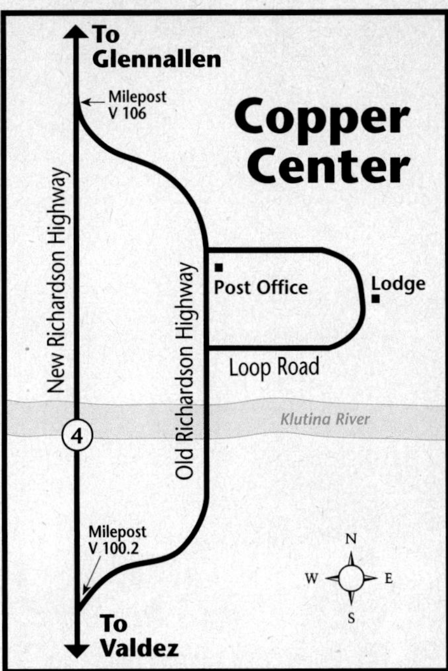

turnaround on back loop road. ▲

Mouth of **Squirrel Creek** at Tonsina River. Some grayling and salmon; grayling, small, use flies or eggs, all season; salmon, average size, egg clusters and spoons, all season. Also try the gravel pit beside the campground; according to state park rangers, some fishermen have good luck catching rainbow and grayling here using flies, eggs and spinners.

V 79.7 (128.3 km) **F 284.3** (457.5 km) Begin 1.3-mile/2.1-km truck lane northbound up Tonsina Hill. Hill can be slippery in winter. Watch for severe frost heaves.

V 81 (130.4 km) **F 283** (455.4 km) **Alaskan House.** See display ad this section.

V 82.3 (132.4 km) **F 281.7** (453.3 km) **Ruthe's Handcrafted Gifts.** Stop by our cabin for a visit and see quilts and critters, one-of-a-kind wearing apparel, and many other functional and attractive gifts. For a unique remembrance of Alaska, take hoone one of my handcrafted treasures. We also feature one of the largest antique and collectible bottle inventories in Alaska. [ADVERTISEMENT]

V 82.6 (132.9 km) **F 281.4** (452.9 km) **Junction** with the Edgerton Highway. The Edgerton Highway leads east to Chitina and connects with the McCarthy Road to McCarthy in Wrangell–St. Elias National Park and Preserve (see EDGERTON HIGHWAY section).

V 83 (133.6 km) **F 281** (452.2 km) Small paved turnout to west beside Pippin Lake.

V 87.7 (141.1 km) **F 276.3** (444.6 km) Paved double-ended turnout to east at Willow Lake. On a clear day this lake mirrors the Wrangell Mountains which lie within Wrangell–St. Elias National Park and Preserve. The park visitor center is at **Milepost V 105.1** and there is a good mountain viewpoint at **V 112.6.**

V 88.5 (142.4 km) **F 275.5** (443.4 km) Pipeline parallels road. Interpretive viewpoint to west on pipeline (1 of 3 Alyeska pipeline displays along this highway). National Park Service plaque with schematic diagram of Wrangell Mountains.

V 90.8 (146.1 km) **F 273.2** (439.7 km) Large paved turnout to west by Willow Creek culvert; thick patches of diamond willow in woods off highway (and thick clouds of mosquitoes!).

V 91.1 (146.6 km) **F 272.9** (439.2 km) Turnoff to east is an 8-mile/12.9-km gravel cutoff that intersects Edgerton Highway at **Milepost J 7.3.** This is a drive through the rolling hills of homestead country and heavy thickets of birch and spruce.

V 92.7 (149.2 km) **F 271.3** (436.6 km) **Grizzly Pizza & Gift Shop.** See display ad this section.

V 98.1 (157.9 km) **F 265.9** (427.9 km) Microwave tower.

V 100.2 (161.2 km) **F 263.8** (424.5 km) IMPORTANT: South **junction** with Copper Center Bypass (New Richardson Highway). Northbound travelers TURN OFF onto Old Richardson Highway for scenic route through historic Copper Center (log and description follow). *The MILEPOST®* does not log the bypass route (New Richardson Highway), which is the same distance as the old highway (6.5 miles/10.5 km) with no notable features. Although according to the BLM, there is an old 4-wheel-drive road to Klutina Lake (25 miles/40 km) which is appropriate for mountain bikes. Turn west at Brenwick–Craig Road sign on the bypass and cross under pipeline. The old highway rejoins the bypass route at **Milepost V 106.**

V 100.6 (161.9 km) **F 263.4** (423.9 km) **Grove's Klutina River Charters and Fish Camp.** One of the friendliest places around. Great king and red salmon fishing. Also Dolly Varden, grayling and lake trout. Camping and RV parking on the south bank of the Klutina River. Electrical hookups and potable water. Headquarters in historic log cabin on premises. Call 1-800-770-5822. See Klutina River Services ad in Copper Center. [ADVERTISEMENT] ▲

V 100.7 (162.1 km) **F 263.3** (423.7 km) Klutina River bridges. Excellent fishing in the **Klutina River** for red (sockeye) and king (chinook) salmon. Also grayling and Dolly Varden. Kings to 50 lbs., average 30 lbs.;

from June 15 to Aug. 10, peaking in mid-July. Red's peak run is from late June to early Aug.; fish from either bank downstream from the new bridge to the mouth of the Copper River. *NOTE: Most riverfront property is privately owned. Inquire at the tackle shop about river access.* Two campgrounds and fishing charter services are located here.

V **100.7** (162.1 km) F **263.3** (423.7 km) **Klutina Salmon Charters.** See display ad on page 589.

Copper Center

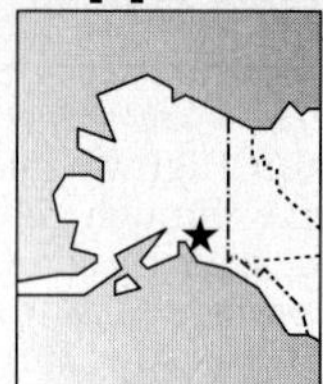

V **100.8** (162.2 km) F **263.2** (423.6 km) The community of Copper Center extends down the road to the east then north through the trees and along the highway. An inner loop road leads through Copper Center and rejoins the Richardson Highway at **Milepost V 101.1. Population:** 449. **Emergency Services:** Phone 911. **Ambulance** in Glennallen, phone 911. **Elevation:** 1,000 feet/305m.

Private Aircraft: Copper Center NR 2 airstrip, 1 mile/1.6 km south; elev. 1,150 feet/351m; length 2,500 feet/762m; gravel; unattended.

Facilities include lodging, private campgrounds, meals, groceries, liquor store, gas station, general store, post office and gift shops. Fishing charters, tackle, riverboat services and guides available.

With the influx of gold seekers following the trail from Valdez to the Klondike, a trading post was established in Copper Center in

Pioneer buildings in Copper Center.
(© Barbara Harn)

COPPER CENTER ADVERTISERS

1898. A telegraph station and post office were established in 1901 and Copper Center became the principal settlement and supply center in the Nelchina–Susitna region.

Copper Center Lodge on the inner loop road, selected by the Alaska Centennial Commission as a site of historic importance (a plaque is mounted to the right of the lodge's entrance), had its beginning as the Holman Hotel and was known as the Blix Roadhouse during the gold rush days of 1897–98. It was the first lodging place in the Copper River valley and was replaced by the Copper Center Lodge in 1932.

The George I. Ashby Memorial Museum, operated by the Copper Valley Historical Society, is housed in the bunkhouse annex at the Copper Center Lodge. It contains early Russian religious articles, Athabascan baskets, telegraph and mineral displays, copper and gold mining memorabilia and trapping articles from early-day Copper Valley. Hours vary. Donations appreciated.

Historic buildings in Copper Center are located on private property. Please do not trespass.

The Copper River reportedly carries the highest sediment load of all Alaskan rivers. The river cuts through the Chugach Mountains and connects the interior of southcentral Alaska with the sea; it is the only corridor of its kind between Cook Inlet and the Canadian border.

Richardson Highway Log

(continued)

V 101 (162.5 km) **F 263** (423.3 km) A visitor attraction in Copper Center is the log Chapel on the Hill built in 1942 by Rev. Vince Joy with the assistance of U.S. Army volunteers stationed in the area. The chapel is open daily and there is no admission charge. A short slide show on the Copper River area is usually shown to visitors in the chapel during the summer. A highway-level parking lot is connected to the Chapel on the Hill by stairs.

V 101.1 (162.7 km) **F 262.9** (423 km) Turnoff on inner loop road to historic Copper Center Lodge and other businesses.

Copper Center Lodge. Beautifully rustic historic landmark, serving the public since 1897; 21 rooms, private or shared baths. Century-old sourdough starter hotcakes, homemade rolls and pies. Restaurant serving breakfast, lunch, dinner. Wine and beer served. Located near the base of the Wrangell–St. Elias National Park and next to the Copper and Klutina rivers. See display ad. [ADVERTISEMENT]

V 101.4 (163.2 km) **F 262.6** (422.6 km) Post office to east; outside mailbox.

V 101.5 (163.3 km) **F 262.5** (422.4 km) **Copper River Cash Store**, established in 1896, sits on part of the first farm started in Alaska. The center of the building is the original structure. Behind the store is the old jail, bars still on windows. Open 6 days a week, all year. Complete line of groceries, general merchandise, RV supplies, video rentals. [ADVERTISEMENT]

V 101.9 (164 km) **F 262.1** (421.8 km) Parking area. Historical marker about Copper Center reads: "Founded in 1896 as a government agriculture experiment station, Copper Center was the first white settlement in this area. The Trail of '98 from Valdez over the glaciers came down from the mountains and joined here with the Eagle Trail to Forty Mile and Dawson. 300 miners, destitute and lonely, spent the winter here. Many suffered with scurvy and died. Soon after the turn of the century, the Washington Alaska Military Cable and Telegraph System, known as WAMCATS, the forerunner of the Alaska communications system, operated telegraph service here between Valdez and Fairbanks."

V 102 (164.1 km) **F 262** (421.6 km) Brenwick–Craig Road. Access to Klutina River Bed & Breakfast.

V 102.2 (164.5 km) **F 261.8** (421.3 km) Copper Center Community Chapel and Indian graveyard.

V 102.5 (165 km) **F 261.5** (420.8 km) Fish wheel may sometimes be seen here operating in Copper River to east. The old school is a local landmark.

V 104 (167.4 km) **F 260** (418.4 km) Ahtna building houses Copper River Native Assoc.

V 104.5 (168.2 km) **F 259.5** (417.6 km) Silver Springs Road. Copper Center school.

V 104.8 (168.7 km) **F 259.2** (417.1 km) Paved turnout to east. Watch for horses.

V 105.1 (169.1 km) **F 258.9** (416.6 km) National Park Service headquarters and visitor center for Wrangell–St. Elias National Park and Preserve. Access to Wrangell–St. Elias National Park and Preserve is via the Edgerton Highway and McCarthy Road (see EDGERTON HIGHWAY section) and the Nabesna Road off the Tok Cutoff (see the GLENN HIGHWAY section). Ranger on duty, general information available. A 10-minute video is shown; additional video programs shown on request. Maps and publications are for sale. Open 9 A.M. to 6 P.M. daily, Memorial Day through Labor Day. Winter hours are 8 A.M. to 5 P.M. weekdays. For more information write P.O. Box 439, Copper Center, AK 99573; or phone (907) 822-5234.

V 106 (170.6 km) **F 258** (415.2 km) IMPORTANT: North **junction** with Copper Center Bypass (New Richardson Highway). Southbound travelers TURN OFF on to Old Richardson Highway for scenic route through historic Copper Center (see description this section). *The MILEPOST®* does not log the bypass route (New Richardson Highway), which is the same distance as the old highway (6.5 miles/10.5 km) but without notable features. The old highway rejoins the bypass route at **Milepost V 100.2.**

V 110 (177 km) **F 254** (408.8 km) Dept. of Highways Tazlina station and Dept. of Natural Resources office. Report forest fires here or phone (907) 822-5533.

V 110.5 (177.8 km) **F 253.5** (408 km) Pipeline storage area. Turn west on pipeline storage area road and take second right for private RV park.

V 110.5 (177.8 km) **F 253.5** (408 km) **Tazlina River RV Park.** See display ad this section. ▲

V 110.6 (178 km) **F 253.4** (407.8 km) Rest area to east on banks of Tazlina River; large paved surface, 2 covered picnic tables, water, toilets.

V 110.7 (178.2 km) **F 253.3** (407.6 km) Tazlina River bridge. *Tazlina* is Indian for "swift water." The river flows eastward from the glacier of the same name into the Copper River.

V 111.2 (179 km) **F 252.8** (406.8 km) Community college and trading post; groceries and gas.

Tazlina River Trading Post & Western Auto. See display ad this section.

V 111.7 (179.8 km) **F 252.3** (406 km) Copperville access road. Developed during pipeline construction, this area has a church and private homes. Glennallen fire station.

V 112.3 (180.7 km) **F 251.7** (405 km) Steep grade southbound from Tazlina River to the top of the Copper River bluffs.

V 112.6 (181.2 km) **F 251.4** (404.6 km) Paved parking area with historical information sign on the development of transportation in Alaska. Short (0.1 mile) walk to good viewpoint on bluff with schematic diagram of Wrangell Mountains: Mount Sanford (elev. 16,237 feet/4,949m); Mount Drum (elev. 12,010 feet/3,661m); Mount Wrangell (elev. 14,163 feet/4,317m); and Mount Blackburn (elev. 16,390 feet/4,996m).

Sign at viewpoint reads: "Across the Copper River rise the peaks of the Wrangell Mountains. The 4 major peaks of the range can be seen from this point, with Mount Drum directly in front of you. The Wrangell Mountains, along with the St. Elias Mountains to the east, contain the most spectacular array of glaciers and ice fields outside polar regions. The Wrangell Mountains are part of Wrangell–St. Elias National Park and Preserve, the nation's largest national park. Together with Kluane National Park of Canada, the park has been designated a World Heritage site by the United Nations."

Visitor information for Wrangell–St. Elias National Park is available at **Milepost V 105.1** Old Richardson Highway.

V 115 (185 km) **F 249** (400.7 km) **South junction** of Richardson and Glenn highways at Glennallen. Greater Copper Valley Visitor Information Center at service center at junction, open daily in summer; pay phone, gas, groceries. The town of Glennallen extends west along the Glenn Highway from here, with businesses located at the junction and along the Glenn Highway. Anchorage is 189 miles/304 km, Tok 139 miles/224 km, from here.

Offices of the Alaska State Troopers (phone 907/822-3263), Dept. of Fish and

Wildlife, Dept. of Motor Vehicles, Alaska Court and community college located on east side of highway.

For the next 14 miles/22.5 km northbound the Richardson and Glenn highways share a common alignment. They separate at **Milepost V 128.6.**

NOTE: Anchorage- or Tok-bound travelers turn to ***Milepost A 189*** *in the GLENN HIGHWAY section on page 292. Valdez- or Fairbanks-bound travelers continue with this log.*

The Hub Maxi Mart. See display ad this section.

V 115.5 (185.9 km) **F 248.5** (399.9 km) **Rendezvous Cafe.** See display ad this section.

V 115.5 (185.9 km) **F 248.5** (399.9 km) **Glennallen Quick Stop Truck Stop.** Stop for friendly family service. Gas, diesel. Convenience store contains ice, pop, snacks, postcards, ice cream, specialty items, pay phone and free coffee. Senior citizen, truck and caravan discounts. Several interesting items on display, include an authentic Native Alaskan fish wheel. Full-service restaurant adjacent. [ADVERTISEMENT]

V 118 (189.9 km) **F 246** (395.9 km) Dry Creek State Recreation Site; 51 campsites, walk-in tent camping, water, tables, toilets, firepits, 15-day limit. Camping fee $10/night or annual pass. *Bring mosquito repellent!* Old ore car here was once used to haul gravel to Tonsina. ▲

V 118.1 (190.1 km) **F 245.9** (395.7 km) **Private Aircraft**: Gulkana airport; elev. 1,579 feet/481m; length 5,000 feet/1,524m; asphalt; fuel 100.

V 123.2 (198.3 km) **F 240.8** (387.5 km) Large paved turnout to east and well-defined 1.5-mile/2.4-km trail east side of road to the mouth of the **Gulkana River** (see **Milepost V 126.9** for details on access and permits). Excellent fishing mid-June to mid-July for king salmon to 50 lbs. (average is 30 lbs.), and red salmon to 6 lbs. Use bright colored yarn or flies, half-inch hook. Heavy tackle with 25- to 30-lb.-test line recommended for kings. Check special regulations before fishing the Gulkana River.

V 126 (202.8 km) **F 238** (383 km) Paved double-ended turnout to west.

V 126.8 (204.1 km) **F 237.2** (381.7 km) Gulkana River bridge. Entering Game Management Unit 13B, leaving unit 13A, northbound.

V 126.9 (204.2 km) **F 237.1** (381.6 km) Access road to **GULKANA** (pop. 100) on the bank of the Gulkana River. Camping is permitted along the river by the bridge. ▲

NOTE: Gulkana River frontage from 2 miles/3.2 km downstream of Sourdough Campground to the mouth of the Gulkana River is owned by Gulkana Village and managed by Ahtna, Inc. There are public easements along the Richardson Highway between Sourdough Campground and the bridge.

V 128.6 (206.9 km) **F 235.4** (378.8 km) **North junction** (Gakona Junction) of the Richardson Highway and Tok Cutoff (Glenn Highway), known locally as Gulkana Junction. Gas, food and lodging. Tok Cutoff leads east 125 miles/201 km to Tok on the Alaska Highway. The Richardson Highway crosses the Gulkana River bridge and continues straight ahead north.

Gakona Junction Village, king salmon fishing headquarters for the Copper Valley, is one-stop shopping for the Alaska traveler. Located at the junction of the Richardson Highway and Tok Cut-Off, we offer beautiful rooms, great food, Texaco gas, groceries, gifts, gallery and king salmon fishing guides. Reservations: 1-800-962-1933; general information: (907) 822-3664 and fax (907) 822-3696 [ADVERTISEMENT]

NOTE: Tok-bound travelers turn to ***Milepost A 203*** *on page 291 in the GLENN HIGHWAY section. Valdez- or Fairbanks-bound travelers continue with this log.*

V 129.2 (207.9 km) **F 234.8** (377.9 km) Pond with lily pads and occasionally a floatplane.

V 129.4 (208.2 km) **F 234.6** (377.5 km) Paved turnout to west. Sailor's Pit (gravel pit opposite lake to west); BLM trail across to **Gulkana River.** Fishing for rainbow trout, grayling, king and red salmon. Highway follows the Gulkana River.

V 132.1 (212.6 km) **F 231.9** (373.2 km) Paved turnout to west.

V 134.6 (216.6 km) **F 229.4** (369.2 km) Paved double-ended turnout with view of Gulkana River to west.

V 135.5 (218.1 km) **F 228.5** (367.7 km) Watch for caribou.

V 135.8 (218.5 km) **F 228.2** (367.2 km) Paved turnout to east. Old beaver pond; 1 mile/1.6 km winter trail to Gulkana River.

V 136.4 (219.5 km) **F 227.6** (366.3 km) Coleman Creek bridge.

V 136.7 (220 km) **F 227.3** (365.8 km) Side road west to **Gulkana River** fishing access: Poplar Grove/Gulkana River BLM-marked vehicle trail, 1 mile/1.6 km. Informal campsites along river.

V 138.1 (222.2 km) **F 225.9** (363.5 km)

Poplar Grove Creek bridge; spring grayling fishing. Paved turnout to west at north end of bridge.

V 139 (223.7 km) **F 225** (362.1 km) Watch for frost heaves.

V 139.4 (224.3 km) **F 224.6** (361.4 km) Paved turnout to west with view of Gulkana River.

V 140.6 (226.3 km) **F 223.4** (359.5 km) Paved turnout to east.

V 141.2 (227.2 km) **F 222.8** (358.6 km) Side road west to Gulkana River fishing access. Informal campsites along river.

V 141.4 (227.6 km) **F 222.6** (358.2 km) Paved double-ended scenic viewpoint to west. One-mile/1.6-km trail to Gulkana River.

V 146 (234.9 km) **F 218** (350.8 km) Lakes and potholes next 9 miles/14.5 km northbound; watch for waterfowl. Views of Chugach Mountains southbound.

V 146.4 (235.6 km) **F 217.6** (350.2 km) Entering BLM public lands northbound.

V 147.1 (236.7 km) **F 216.9** (349.1 km) Double-ended paved scenic viewpoint.

V 147.6 (237.5 km) **F 216.4** (348.3 km) **SOURDOUGH.** BLM Sourdough Creek Campground; 60 sites, good king salmon fishing. Access to **Gulkana River**, marked trail to Sourdough Creek. Across the bridge (load limit 8 tons) and to the right a road leads to parking, toilets and boat launch on river. Watch for potholes in access roads. Native lands; check for restrictions.

The Sourdough Roadhouse, destroyed by fire in December 1992, stood next to the creek. It was established in 1903. A gas station was operating here in 1995. The old Valdez trail runs 150 yards/137m behind the few buildings left standing.

The Gulkana River is part of the National Wild and Scenic Rivers System managed by the BLM. A popular float trip for experienced canoeists begins at Paxson Lake and ends at Sourdough Campground. See description at **Milepost V 175.**

Gulkana River above Sourdough Creek, grayling 9 to 21 inches (same as Sourdough Creek below), rainbow 10 to 24 inches, spinners, June through Sept.; red salmon 8 to 25 lbs. and king salmon up to 62 lbs., use streamer flies or spinners, mid-June through mid-July. **Sourdough Creek**, grayling 10 to 20 inches, use single yellow eggs or corn, fish deep early May through first week in June, use spinners or flies mid-June until freezeup.

V 150.7 (242.5 km) **F 213.3** (343.3 km) Large gravel turnout to east.

V 151 (243 km) **F 213** (342.8 km) Private gravel driveway to west by large pond; please do not trespass.

V 153.8 (247.5 km) **F 210.2** (338.3 km) Highway passes through boggy terrain; watch for caribou. *CAUTION: No turnouts, little shoulder. Watch for dips and rough patches in highway next 10 miles/16 km northbound.*

V 154.2 (248.2 km) **F 209.8** (337.6 km) Double-ended gravel turnout to east.

V 156.4 (251.7 km) **F 207.6** (334.1 km) As the highway winds through the foothills of the Alaska Range, over a crest called Hogan Hill (elev. 2,647 feet/807m), there are magnificent views of 3 mountain ranges: the Alaska Range through which the highway leads, the Wrangell Mountains to the southeast and the Chugach Mountains to the southwest. To the west is a vast wilderness plateau where the headwaters of the big Susitna River converge to flow west and south into Cook Inlet, west of Anchorage.

V 156.7 (252.2 km) **F 207.3** (333.6 km) Good view of pothole lakes to west.

Trans-Alaska pipeline parallels the Richardson Highway. (© George Wuerthner)

V 157 (252.7 km) **F 207** (333.1 km) Good long-range viewpoints from highway. Moose and other game may be spotted from here (use binoculars).

V 158.9 (255.7 km) **F 205.1** (330.1 km) Sweeping view of the Glennallen area to the south.

V 160.7 (258.6 km) **F 203.3** (327.2 km) **Haggard Creek** BLM marked trailhead; grayling fishing. Access to Gulkana River 7 miles/11.3 km to west.

V 162.2 (261 km) **F 201.8** (324.8 km) Double-ended gravel turnout to east.

V 166.5 (267.9 km) **F 197.5** (317.8 km) Jane Lake trail; 1 mile/1.6 km to west.

V 168.1 (270.5 km) **F 195.9** (315.3 km) **Gillespie Lake** trailhead and parking to west. Walk up creek 0.3 mile/0.5 km to lake; grayling fishing.

V 169.3 (272.5 km) **F 194.7** (313.3 km) Large gravel pit. Turnout to west.

V 169.4 (272.6 km) **F 194.6** (313.2 km) Middle Fork BLM-marked trail to Meier's Lake and Middle Fork Gulkana River.

V 170 (273.6 km) **F 194** (312.2 km) Roadhouse with gas, food, lodging and camping. **Meier's Lake**; parking area, good grayling fishing.

Meier's Lake Roadhouse. See display ad this section.

V 171.6 (276.2 km) **F 192.4** (309.6 km) Gravel turnout by river to west. Long upgrade begins northbound.

V 172.7 (277.9 km) **F 191.3** (307.9 km) Small turnout to west, view of pipeline to east.

V 173.3 (278.9 km) **F 190.7** (306.9 km) **Dick Lake** to the east via narrow side road (easy to miss); no turnaround space. Good grayling fishing in summer. View of trans-Alaska oil pipeline across the lake. Good spot for photos.

V 175 (281.6 km) **F 189** (304.2 km) BLM Paxson Lake Campground turnoff. Wide gravel road (full of potholes if not recently graded) leads 1.5 miles/2.4 km to large camping area near lakeshore; 50 campsites, some pull-throughs, spaces for all sizes of vehicles but some sites on slope (RVs may need leveling boards); toilets, water, tables, firepits, dump station and concrete boat launch. Parking for 80 vehicles. Bring mosquito repellent. *CAUTION: Watch for bears.* Fishing in **Paxson Lake** for lake trout, grayling, red salmon and burbot.

This is the launch site for floating the Gulkana River to Sourdough Campground at **Milepost V 147.6.** Total distance is about 50 miles/80 km and 4 days travel, according to the BLM, which manages this national wild river. While portions of the river are placid, the Gulkana does have Class II and III rapids, with a gradient of 38 feet/mile in one section. Canyon Rapids may be Class IV depending on water levels (there is a portage). Recommended for experienced boaters only. For further information on floating the Gulkana, contact the BLM at Box 147, Glennallen 99588, or phone (907) 822-3217.

V 177.1 (285 km) **F 186.9** (300.8 km) Small gravel turnout to west with view of Paxson Lake.

V 177.5 (285.7 km) **F 186.5** (300.1 km) Turnout to east. Trans-Alaska oil pipeline may be seen on the ridge northwest of the highway.

V 178.7 (287.6 km) **F 185.3** (298.2 km) Small gravel turnout to east.

V 179 (288.1 km) **F 185** (297.7 km) Gravel turnout overlooking Paxson Lake. The lake was named for the owner of the roadhouse (still Paxson Lodge) about 1906.

V 179.2 (288.4 km) **F 184.8** (297.4 km) Gravel turnout to west overlooking Paxson Lake.

V 182.1 (293 km) **F 181.9** (292.7 km)

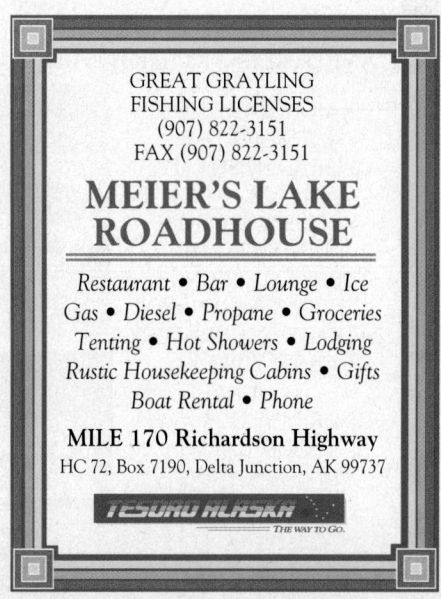

Large gravel turnout at head of Paxson Lake. Rough gravel trail to lake.

V 183.2 (294.8 km) **F 180.8** (291 km) Entering Paxson Closed Area northbound (closed to taking of all big game).

V 184.4 (296.8 km) **F 179.6** (289 km) Large gravel turnout to west.

V 184.7 (297.2 km) **F 179.3** (288.6 km) One Mile Creek bridge.

V 185.5 (298.5 km) **F 178.5** (287.3 km) **Junction** with Denali Highway to Denali National Park and George Parks Highway (see DENALI HIGHWAY section for details) at **PAXSON** (pop. 33), site of a lodge with gas station (open year-round), restaurant and small grocery store. Wilderness tours, inquire at lodge. Sled dog racing first weekend in April. Paxson Mountain (elev. 5,200 feet/1,585m) is 3 miles/4.8 km west-southwest.

V 185.5 (298.5 km) **F 178.5** (287.3 km) **Paxson Lodge.** See display ad this section.

Private Aircraft: Paxson airstrip (Hufman Field), adjacent south; elev. 2,653 feet/809m; length 2,800 feet/853m; gravel; emergency fuel; attended.

V 185.7 (298.9 km) **F 178.3** (286.9 km) Site of original Paxson Lodge.

V 185.8 (299 km) **F 178.2** (286.8 km) Paxson Station highway maintenance camp.

V 186.4 (300 km) **F 177.6** (285.8 km) Leaving BLM public lands northbound.

V 188.3 (303 km) **F 175.7** (282.8 km) Large paved double-ended rest area to east across from Gulkana River; tables, fireplaces, toilets, dumpster and water. The Gulkana River flows south to the Copper River.

V 189.6 (305.1 km) **F 174.4** (280.7 km) Long paved double-ended turnout to west.

V 190.4 (306.4 km) **F 173.6** (279.4 km) Paved parking area by Gulkana River with picnic tables, dumpster and view of Summit Lake and pipeline. Access to Summit Lake. Interpretive sign about red salmon. Salmon spawning area; fishing for salmon prohibited. Access to **Fish Creek** at north end of turnout; grayling fishing. Access to Fish Lake is via trail paralleling creek for 2 miles/3.2 km, according to the ADF&G.

V 191 (307.4 km) **F 173** (278.4 km) Summit Lake to west; turnout at head of stream.

V 191.1 (307.5 km) **F 172.9** (278.2 km) Double-ended turnout to west.

V 192.2 (309.3 km) **F 171.8** (276.5 km) Turnout with table and boat launch on **Summit Lake;** lake trout, grayling, burbot and red salmon.

V 192.6 (310 km) **F 171.4** (275.8 km) Large gravel turnout on Summit Lake.

V 193.3 (311.1 km) **F 170.7** (274.7 km) Gravel turnout to west by Summit Lake.

V 194.1 (312.4 km) **F 169.9** (273.4 km) Gravel turnout on Summit Lake.

V 195 (313.8 km) **F 169** (271.9 km) Large gravel turnout at **Summit Lake** (elev. 3,210 feet/978m). Bed and breakfast. This lake, 7 miles/11.3 km long, is named for its location near the water divide between the Delta and Gulkana rivers. The Gulkana River flows into the Copper River, which flows into Prince William Sound. The Delta River is part of the Yukon River drainage. Fishing for lake trout, grayling, red salmon and burbot.

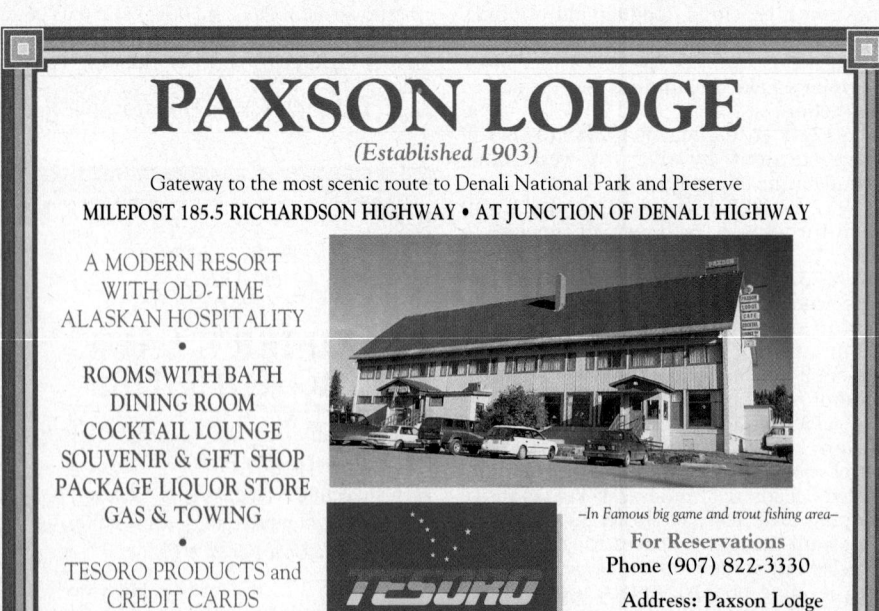

V 195 (313.8 km) **F 169** (272 km) Summit Lake Lodge; burned down in November 1993. Current status unknown.

V 196.8 (316.7 km) **F 167.2** (269.1 km) Gunn Creek bridge. View of Gulkana Glacier to the northeast. This glacier, perched on 8,000-foot/2,438-m Icefall Peak, feeds streams that drain into both Prince William Sound and the Yukon River.

V 197.6 (318 km) **F 166.4** (267.8 km) Large gravel turnout. Memorial monument honoring Gen. Wilds P. Richardson, for whom the highway is named, at summit of Isabel Pass (elev. 3,000 feet/914m). Sign here reads: "Captain Wilds P. Richardson presented the need for roads to Congress in 1903. His familiarity with Alaska impressed Congress with his knowledge of the country and his ability as an engineer. When the Act of 1905 became a law, he was placed at the head of the Alaska Road Commission in which position he served for more than a decade. The Richardson Highway, from Valdez to Fairbanks, is a fitting monument to the first great road builder of Alaska."

Entering Sport Fish Management Area C southbound.

V 198.5 (319.4 km) **F 165.5** (266.3 km) Gravel turnout to west.

V 200.4 (322.5 km) **F 163.6** (263.3 km) Gravel side road leads west 1.5 miles/2.4 km to **Fielding Lake** Campground. Pleasant area above tree line; 7 campsites, no water, no camping fee, picnic tables, pit toilets, large parking areas and boat ramp. Good fishing for lake trout, grayling and burbot.

Snow poles along highway guide snowplows in winter.

V 201.5 (324.3 km) **F 162.5** (261.5 km) Phelan Creek bridge. Buried section of pipeline to west is a large animal crossing.

V 202 (325.1 km) **F 162** (260.7 km) Trans-Alaska oil pipeline parallels the highway above ground here. Entering BLM public lands northbound.

V 202.5 (325.9 km) **F 161.5** (259.9 km) McCallum Creek bridge, highway follows Phelan Creek northbound. This stream heads in Gulkana Glacier and flows northwest to the Delta River.

V 203.5 (327.5 km) **F 160.5** (258.3 km) Watch for beaver ponds (and beaver); lupine in June.

V 204 (328.3 km) **F 160** (257.5 km) Spring water piped to east side of highway; paved turnout.

V 204.7 (329.4 km) **F 159.3** (256.4 km) Large gravel turnouts both sides of highway.

V 205.3 (330.4 km) **F 158.7** (255.4 km) Small gravel turnout by stream. Good place for pictures of the pipeline up a steep hill.

V 206.4 (332.2 km) **F 157.6** (253.6 km) Double-ended turnout with picnic tables, litter barrels and view of mineralized Rainbow Ridge to northeast. Wildflowers include yellow arnica and sweet pea.

V 207 (333.1 km) **F 157** (252.7 km) Good gravel turnout to west. There are frequent turnouts the next 6 miles/9.6 km northbound.

V 207.8 (334.4 km) **F 156.2** (251.4 km) Turnout. Rock slide and avalanche area next mile northbound; watch for rocks on road.

V 208.1 (334.9 km) **F 155.9** (250.9 km) Turnout to west by river. Look for wild, or Alaskan, rhubarb (*P. alaskanum*), a member of the buckwheat family. Grows to 6 feet with showy clusters of small yellowish-white flowers.

V 211.7 (340.7 km) **F 152.3** (245.1 km) Side roads signed APL are Alyeska pipeline access roads and closed to the public.

V 213.2 (343.1 km) **F 150.8** (242.7 km) Gravel turnout to west along Phelan Creek.

V 213.6 (343.7 km) **F 150.4** (242 km) Gravel turnout and road to gravel pit to east. Avalanche area ends northbound.

V 214 (344.4 km) **F 150** (241.4 km) Double-ended paved turnout with picnic tables and litter barrels. Highway follows Delta River northbound, Phelan Creek southbound.

V 215.1 (346.2 km) **F 148.9** (239.6 km) Pipeline crosses Miller Creek right next to bridge. Parking at both ends of bridge, access to creek.

V 215.9 (347.4 km) **F 148.1** (238.3 km) Pipeline interpretive viewpoint with information sign.

V 216.3 (348.1 km) **F 147.7** (237.7 km) Gravel turnout to east.

V 216.7 (348.7 km) **F 147.3** (237 km) Lower Miller Creek. Turnouts at both ends of bridge. This is a pipeline interpretive viewpoint and one of the best spots on the highway to photograph the pipeline.

V 217.2 (349.5 km) **F 146.8** (236.2 km) Castner Creek; parking at both ends of bridge, west side of road.

V 218.2 (351.1 km) **F 145.8** (234.6 km) Trims Station DOT/PF highway maintenance camp.

V 218.8 (352.1 km) **F 145.2** (233.7 km) Bridge over Trims Creek, parking. Wildflowers in the area include lupine, sweet pea and fireweed. Watch for caribou on slopes.

V 219.2 (352.8 km) **F 144.8** (233 km) Access to Pipeline Pump Station No. 10.

V 219.3 (352.9 km) **F 144.7** (232.9 km) Small gravel turnout. Note the flood control dikes (also called finger dikes) in stream to slow erosion.

V 219.9 (353.9 km) **F 144.1** (231.9 km) Michael Creek bridge; parking at both ends of bridge. Buried pipeline to west. Southbound drivers have a spectacular view of Pump Station No. 10 and the surrounding mountains.

V 220.9 (355.5 km) **F 143.1** (230.3 km) Flood Creek bridge; parking.

V 223 (358.9 km) **F 141** (226.9 km) Whistler Creek bridge; parking. Watch for frost heaves.

V 223.8 (360.2 km) **F 140.2** (225.6 km) Boulder Creek bridge; parking.

V 224.5 (361.3 km) **F 139.5** (224.5 km) Lower Suzy Q Creek bridge; parking.

V 224.8 (361.8 km) **F 139.2** (224 km) Suzy Q Creek bridge. Double-ended gravel turnout.

V 225.2 (362.4 km) **F 138.8** (223.4 km) Large gravel turnout to east.

V 225.4 (362.7 km) **F 138.6** (223.1 km) Double-ended paved turnout with picnic table and litter barrels to west. Historical marker here identifies the terminal moraine of Black Rapids Glacier to the west. Currently a retreating glacier with little ice visible, this glacier was nicknamed the Galloping Glacier when it advanced more than 3 miles/4.8 km during the winter of 1936–37.

Black Rapids Lake trail begins across from historical sign (0.3 mile/0.4 km to lake). Look for river beauty and wild sweet pea blooming in June.

Private Aircraft: Black Rapids airstrip, adjacent north; elev. 2,125 feet/648m; length 2,200 feet/671m; gravel.

V 226 (363.7 km) **F 138** (222.1 km) Good gravel turnout by river to west.

V 226.3 (364.2 km) **F 137.7** (221.6 km) Falls Creek bridge.

V 226.7 (364.8 km) **F 137.3** (221 km) Black Rapids U.S. Army training site at Fall Creek. Boundary between Game Management Units 20D and 13.

V 227 (365.3 km) **F 137** (220.5 km) Gunnysack Creek. View of Black Rapids Glacier to west.

V 227.4 (366 km) **F 136.6** (219.8 km) Old Black Rapids Lodge. Dirt airstrip.

V 228.4 (367.6 km) **F 135.6** (218.2 km) Parking beside One Mile Creek bridge.

V 230.4 (370.8 km) **F 133.6** (215 km) Large paved turnout overlooks Delta River.

V 231 (371.7 km) **F 133** (214 km) Darling Creek. Gravel turnout to east.

V 233.3 (375.5 km) **F 130.7** (210.3 km) Bear Creek bridge; turnouts at either end, access to creek. Wildflowers include pale oxytrope, yellow arnica, fireweed, wild rhubarb and cow parsnip.

V 234.2 (376.9 km) **F 129.8** (208.9 km) Double-ended gravel turnout to east.

V 234.5 (377.4 km) **F 129.5** (208.4 km) Paved turnout with litter barrels to west. Pipeline access road. Pipeline comes up out of the ground here and goes through forest.

V 234.8 (377.9 km) **F 129.2** (207.9 km) Ruby Creek bridge; parking to west.

V 237.9 (382.9 km) **F 126.1** (202.9 km) Loop road (watch for potholes) through Donnelly Creek State Recreation Site; 12 campsites, tables, firepits, toilets and water. Camping fee $8/night or annual pass. ▲

V 238.7 (384.1 km) **F 125.3** (201.6 km) Watch for frost heaves northbound.

V 239.1 (384.8 km) **F 124.9** (201 km) Small gravel turnout to east.

V 241.3 (388.3 km) **F 122.7** (197.5 km) Large paved turnout to west with litter barrel.

V 242 (389.5 km) **F 122** (196.3 km) Pipeline parallels highway. Donnelly Dome ahead northbound. Watch for pavement dips.

V 242.1 (389.6 km) **F 121.9** (196.2 km) Coal Mine Road (4-wheel-drive vehicles only) leads east to fishing lakes; **Last Lake**, arctic char; **Coal Mine No. 5 Lake**, lake trout; **Brodie Lake** and **Pauls Pond**, grayling and lake trout. Check with the ADF&G for details.

V 243.4 (391.7 km) **F 120.6** (194.1 km) Pipeline viewpoint with interpretive signs. Good photo stop.

V 243.9 (392.5 km) **F 120.1** (193.3 km) Paved double-ended turnout with litter barrels to east. The trans-Alaska oil pipeline snakes along the ground and over the horizon. Zigzag design of pipeline converts pipe thermal expansion, as well as movement from other forces (like earthquakes), into a controlled sideways movement. A spectacular view to the southwest of 3 of the highest peaks of the Alaska Range. From west to south they are: Mount Deborah (elev. 12,339 feet/3,761m); Hess Mountain (elev. 11,940 feet/3,639m), center foreground; and Mount Hayes (elev. 13,832 feet/4,216m).

In spring look for wild sweet pea, chiming bells, lupine, lousewort and bluebell for the next 3 miles/4.8 km.

V 244.3 (393.2 km) **F 119.7** (192.6 km) Gravel turnout to east. Trail to **Donnelly Lake**; king and silver salmon, rainbow trout. Donnelly Dome ahead northbound.

V 245 (394.3 km) **F 119** (191.5 km) Gravel turnout to east overlooking lake.

V 245.2 (394.4 km) **F 118.9** (191.3 km) Large gravel turnout to east; ponds.

V 246 (395.9 km) **F 118** (189.9 km) Donnelly Dome immediately to the west (elev. 3,910 feet/1,192m), was first named Delta Dome. For years the mountain has been used to predict the weather: "The first snow on the top of the Donnelly Dome means snow in Delta Junction within 2 weeks."

V 246.9 (397.3 km) **F 117.1** (188.4 km) Gravel turnout to east.

V 247 (397.5 km) **F 117** (188.3 km) Cutoff to Old Richardson Highway loop to west; access to fishing lakes.

V 247.3 (398 km) **F 116.7** (187.8 km) From here northbound the road extends straight as an arrow for 4.8 miles/7.7 km.

V 249.3 (401.2 km) **F 114.7** (184.6 km) Bear Drop Zone. Military games area. Controlled access road: No trespassing.

V 252.8 (406.8 km) **F 111.2** (179 km) Scenic viewpoint to west with picnic tables and litter barrels.

V 253.9 (408.6 km) **F 110.1** (177.2 km) Good view of Pump Station No. 9 if southbound.

V 256 (412 km) **F 108** (173.8 km) Fort Greely Ridge Road to west.

V 257.6 (414.6 km) **F 106.4** (171.2 km) Entrance to U.S. Army Cold Regions Test Center at Fort Greely.

Meadows Road (4-wheel-drive vehicles only) leads west to fishing lakes. Access to **Bolio Lake**; grayling, rainbow, lake trout. Rainbow-producing **Mark Lake** is 4.5 miles/7.2 km along this road. Meadows Road junctions with the Old Richardson Highway loop. Check with the ADF&G for details on fishing lakes.

V 258.3 (415.7 km) **F 105.7** (170.1 km) Pump Station No. 9 access road to east. Tours of Pump Station 9 are offered daily from June to Aug. Phone (907) 869-3270 or 456-9391 for more information and tour reservations.

V 261.2 (420.3 km) **F 102.8** (165.4 km) **FORT GREELY** (restricted area) main gate. Fort Greely was named for A.W. Greely, arctic explorer and author of *Three Years of Arctic Service*.

V 262.6 (422.6 km) **F 101.4** (163.2 km) Double-ended paved turnout with scenic view. Watch for bison. Wind area next 2 miles/3.2 km northbound.

V 262.7 (422.8 km) **F 101.3** (163 km) FAA buildings. Big Delta.

V 264.9 (426.3 km) **F 99.1** (159.5 km) Jarvis Creek, rises near Butch Lake to the east and flows into the Delta River. Buffalo (bison) may be seen in this area.

V 266 (428 km) **F 98** (157.7 km) **Junction** of the Richardson Highway and the Alaska Highway, **Milepost DC 1422,** at Delta Junction. Visitor center is located at junction. Turn to page 183 for description of Delta Junction services and continuation of highway log to Fairbanks (the remaining 98 miles/157.7 km of the Richardson Highway leading into Fairbanks are logged in the ALASKA HIGHWAY section).

COPPER RIVER HIGHWAY

Cordova, Alaska, to the Million Dollar Bridge Alaska Route 10

View of Sheridan Glacier from Milepost 16 on the Copper River Highway. (© Ruth Fairall)

The Copper River Highway leads 48.1 miles/77.4 km northeast from Cordova to the Million Dollar Bridge at the Copper River.

Construction of the Copper River Highway began in 1945. Built along the abandoned railbed of the Copper River & Northwestern Railway, the highway was to extend to Chitina (on the Edgerton Highway), thereby linking Cordova to the Richardson Highway.

Construction was halted by the 1964 Good Friday earthquake, which severely damaged the highway's roadbed and bridges. The quake also knocked the north span of the Million Dollar Bridge into the Copper River and distorted the remaining spans. The 48 miles of existing highway have been repaired and upgraded since the earthquake, but repairs to the Million Dollar Bridge remain temporary and travel across the bridge and beyond is not recommended.

Copper River Highway Log

Distance is measured from Cordova (C).

C 0 **CORDOVA.** See description in PRINCE WILLIAM SOUND section. The Copper River Highway starts at the ferry terminal and leads east through town.

C **1.4** (2.3 km) Whitshed Road on right leads 0.5 mile/0.8 km to Odiak municipal camper park (24 sites, tenting area, obtain shower tokens at City Hall), 5.5 miles/8.9 km to **Hartney Bay.** Fishing from Hartney Bay bridge for Dolly Varden from May; pink and chum salmon, mid-July through Aug.; closed for salmon upstream of bridge. Use small weighted spoons, spinners and eggs. Clam digging at low tide (license required). Shorebird migration in early spring.

C **2.1** (3.4 km) Powder House Bar and Liquor Store (restaurant) overlooking Eyak Lake. Site of CR&NW railway powder house.

C **2.3** (3.7 km) Paved turnout to north by Eyak Lake. Heney Range to the south. Mount Eccles (elev. 2,357 feet/718m) is the first large peak. Pointed peak beyond is Heney Peak (elev. 3,151 feet/960m).

C **3.7** (5.9 km) Large paved turnout with litter barrels by Eyak Lake.

C **4.1** (6.6 km) Historical marker on left gives a brief history of the CR&NW railway. Also here is a monument erected by the railroad builder M.J. Heney in memory of those men who lost their lives during construction of the CR&NW. Begun in 1907 and completed in 1911, the CR&NW railway connected the port of Cordova with the Kennecott Copper Mines near Kennicott and McCarthy. The mine and railway ceased operation in 1938.

For the next 2 miles/3.2 km, watch for bears during early morning and late evening (most often seen in June).

C **5.3** (8.5 km) Paved turnout on lake to north.

C **5.6** (9 km) Paved turnout at lake to north.

C **5.7** (9.2 km) Bridge over Eyak River, access to Eyak River trail. This is a good spot to see waterfowl feeding near the outlet of Eyak Lake. An estimated 100 trumpeter swans winter on Eyak Lake.

Eyak River trailhead is on the west bank of the river. The 2.2-mile/3.5-km trail, much of which is boardwalk over muskeg, is popular with fishermen.

C **6** (9.7 km) **Eyak River**, outhouse and boat launch. Dolly Varden; red salmon, June–July; silvers, Aug.–Sept. Also pinks and chums. Use Vibrax spoon, spinner or salmon eggs. Fly-fishing only for salmon within 200 yards of weir.

C **7.4** (11.9 km) Paved turnout. *CAUTION: High winds for next 4 miles/6.4 km.* In January and February, these winds sweep across this flat with such velocity it is safer to pull off and stop.

C **7.6** (12.2 km) Bridge over slough.

C **7.7** (12.4 km) First bridge across Scott River.

C **8.1** (13 km) Bridge over slough waters. Gravel turnout; access to slough.

C **8.4** (13.5 km) Scott River bridge.

C **9** (14.5 km) Between **Mileposts 9** and **10** there are 4 bridges across the Scott River and the slough. Sloughs along here are from the runoff of the Scott Glacier, visible to the northeast. Bear and moose are often seen, especially in July and August. In May and August, thousands of dusky Canada geese nest here. This is the only known nesting area of the dusky geese, which winter in Oregon's Willamette Valley. Also watch for swans.

Moose feed in the willow groves on either side of the highway. Moose are not native to Cordova; the mountains and glaciers prevent them from entering the delta country. Today's herd stems from a transplant of 26 animals made between 1949 and 1959.

C **10.4** (16.7 km) Scott River bridge. Watch for old and new beaver dams and lodges beside the highway.

C **10.7** (17.2 km) U.S. Forest Service information pavilion (8 interpretive plaques) and large paved turnout with litter barrel to south. Game management area, 330,000 acres. Trumpeter swans and Canada geese. Look for arctic terns here.

C **10.8** (17.4 km) Bridge, beaver lodge.

C **11.1** (17.9 km) Elsner River bridge.

C **11.5** (18.5 km) Look for brown bears feeding in the outwash plains of Scott Glacier. Thousands of salmon swim up nearby rivers to spawn. There are numerous

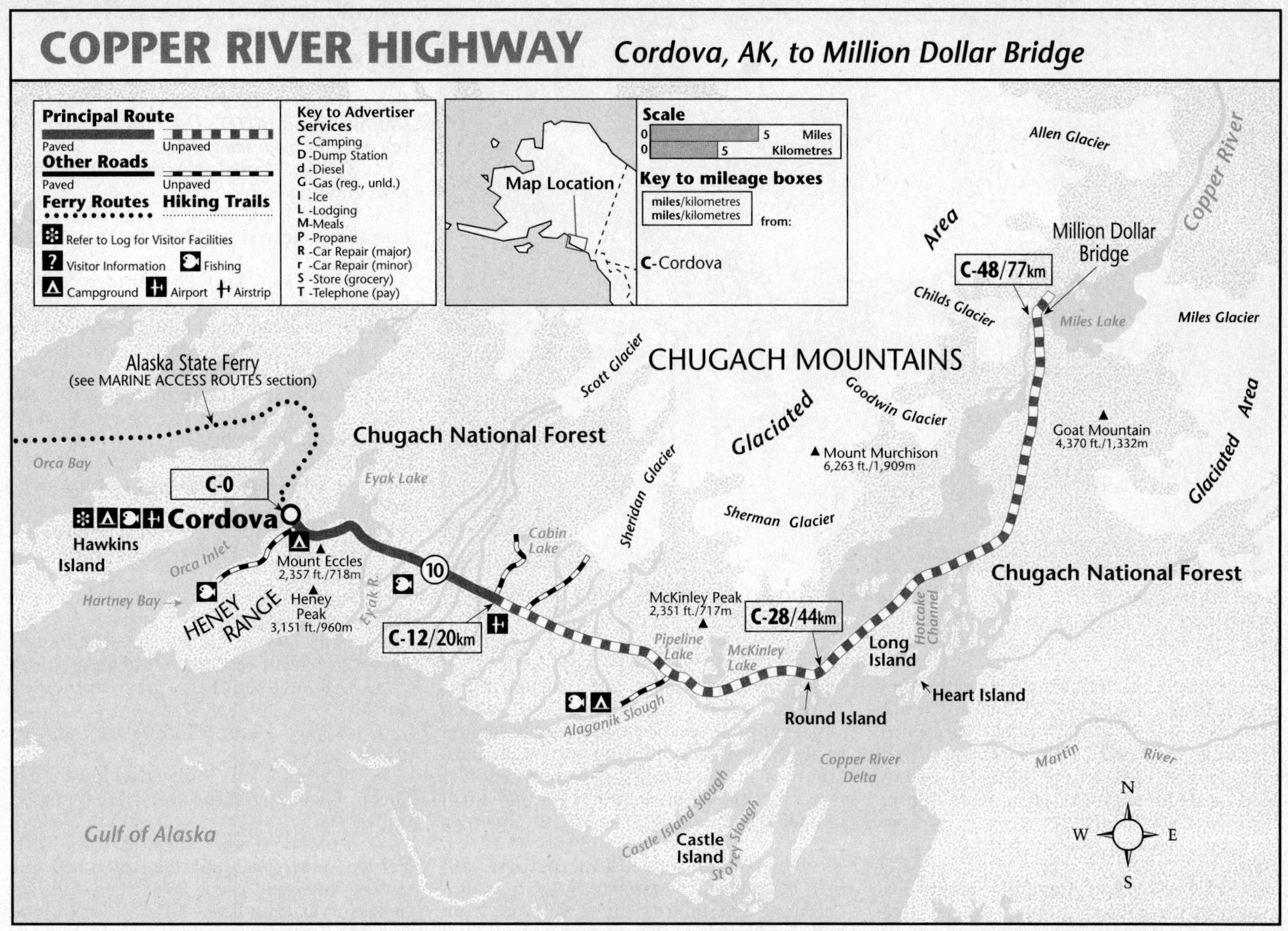

beaver lodges on both sides of the highway.

C 11.8 (19 km) State of Alaska Cordova highway maintenance station to northeast. U.S. Coast Guard station.

C 12.1 (19.5 km) Cordova airport and access to Cabin Lake Recreation Area. Drive north 2.8 miles/4.5 km for recreation area (gravel access road forks 0.3 mile/0.5 km in; right fork leads to gravel pit, continue straight ahead for recreation area). *CAUTION: Narrow road, no directional signs, active logging and logging trucks.* Picnic tables, toilet, litter barrel and firepits at **Cabin Lake**; cutthroat fishing.

C 12.4 (20 km) Pavement ends, gravel begins. Watch for potholes.

C 13 (20.9 km) Keep a lookout for snowshoe hare and birds of prey.

C 13.7 (22 km) Sheridan Glacier access road leads 4.3 miles/6.9 km to the terminus of Sheridan Glacier. *CAUTION: Narrow road, watch for logging trucks.* The glacier was named by U.S. Army explorer Capt. Abercrombie for Gen. Philip H. Sheridan of Civil War fame. Sheridan Mountain trailhead, several picnic tables, litter barrels and a partial view of the glacier are available at the end of the access road. It is about a 0.5-mile/0.8-km hike to the dirt-covered glacial moraine.

C 14.8 (23.8 km) Bridge over Sheridan River. Raft takeout point. View of Sheridan Glacier. To the east of Sheridan Glacier is Sherman Glacier.

Winter moose range next 8 miles/13 km eastbound.

C 15 (24.1 km) Silver salmon spawn during Sept. and Oct. in the stream beside the highway.

C 16 (25.7 km) Beautiful view of Sheridan Glacier to the northeast.

C 16.3 (26.2 km) Second bridge over Sheridan River.

C 16.9 (27.2 km) Turnoff for **Alaganik Slough**, Chugach National Forest Recreation Area. Drive south 3 miles/4.8 km via gravel road; picnic tables, firepits, wheelchair accessible toilets, litter barrel, information kiosk and boat launch. Wheelchair-accessible interpretive boardwalk with viewing blind for watching birds and other wildlife. No water, informal camping. Interpretive plaque on side road reads: "Why are Delta moose the largest and healthiest? This moose herd, first introduced in 1949, maintains its vitality primarily due to its abundant willow supply. As part of a normal cycle, accelerated by the 1964 earthquake, much of the willow is becoming unavailable to moose. As the willow grows tall, the moose can no longer reach the tender new shoots. In the future this could cause a decrease in the numbers of moose on the delta. To slow the cycle down, the Forest Service is experimenting in this area, cutting back the shrubs. This should increase the amount of available willow browse. Biologists will evaluate the response of moose to new willow growth." Fishing for Dolly Varden, sockeye (July) and silver salmon (Aug. and Sept.).

C 17.4 (28 km) Trumpeter swans may be seen in pond beside highway. One of the largest of all North American waterfowl (6–8 foot wingspan), it has been almost completely eliminated in the Lower 48 and Canada. Alaska harbors more than 80 percent of breeding trumpeters and more than 7 percent of the world population breeds in the Copper River Delta.

C 18 (29 km) For the next mile look for silver salmon spawning in streams during September. To the left and on the slopes above timberline mountain goats may be seen. The mountain to the left of the road ahead eastbound is McKinley Peak (elev. 2,351 feet/717m).

C 18.1 (29.1 km) Entering Chugach National Forest eastbound.

C 18.2 (29.3 km) Gravel road leads south to small picnic area with table, firepit, litter barrel and toilet.

C 18.5 (29.8 km) Road narrows. *NOTE: Road not maintained in winter (after Nov. 1) beyond this point.*

C 18.8 (30.3 km) Turnout to north access to Muskeg Meander cross-country ski trailhead; length 2.5 miles/4 km. According to the USFS district office, this trail offers a beautiful view of the Copper River Delta.

C 19.2 (30.9 km) Haystack trailhead to south. Easy 0.8-mile/1.2-km trail leads to delta overlook with interpretive signs. Excellent place to see moose and bear according to the USFS district office in Cordova.

C 20.1 (32.3 km) Large gravel turnout to south; beaver dam, fishing.

C 21.4 (34.4 km) **Pipeline Lakes** trailhead to north, parking to south. The 1.8-mile/2.9-km trail was originally built as a water pipeline route to supply locomotives on the CR&NW railway. Segments of the pipeline are still visible. Fishing for grayling and cutthroat, fly or bait. Trail joins McKinley Lake trail. Rubber boots are necessary.

C 21.6 (34.8 km) **McKinley Lake** trail to

The north span of the Million Dollar Bridge collapsed during the 1964 earthquake.
(© Ruth Fairall)

north; easy 2.1-mile/3.4-km hike with excellent fishing for sockeye, Dolly Varden and cutthroat. Access to USFS public-use cabins: McKinley Trail cabin (100 yards from highway) and McKinley Lake cabin (45-minute walk in from highway; also accessible by boat via Alaganik Slough).

C **22** (35.4 km) Double-ended turnout to north.

C **22.1** (35.5 km) **Alaganik Slough** boat ramp, picnic tables, firepits, toilets, litter barrel, wildflowers, interpretive signs on local cultural history and fishing access to south at west side of Alaganik Slough river bridge. Sockeye (red) and coho (silver) salmon, July to Sept. Also boat access to McKinley Lake.

C **23.7** (38.1 km) Salmon Creek bridge, parking. Beaver lodge.

C **24.6** (39.6 km) One-mile/1.6-km road north leads to Saddlebag Glacier trailhead and parking area; access to canoe route. According to the USFS office in Cordova, this is an easy 3-mile/4.8-km trail to Saddlebag Lake. View of Saddlebag Glacier and icebergs; look for goats on surrounding mountains. *CAUTION: Watch for bears.*

C **24.8** (39.9 km) Channel to beaver pond for spawning salmon. A plaque here reads: "Pathway to salmon rearing grounds. Channel provided access to beaver pond (north side of road) for coho fry. Beaver pond can support up to 25,400 young salmon. Fallen trees and brush provide cover from predators."

C **25.4** (40.9 km) Small gravel turnout by 2 spawning channels with weirs. Interpretive signs along a short trail here explain the project: "Channel built by USDA Forest Service to provide high quality spawning habitat for coho and sockeye salmon. Before construction, the streambed was muddy and the stream dried up during low flow periods. Fish spawned in the streams but few eggs survived. Improved channel is deeper and ensures a consistent flow. Adjustable weirs control water depth. Clean gravels placed in the channel make better spawning conditions while large rip-rap on streambanks prevent erosion.

"Can you see small circles of gravel which appear to have been turned over? These are salmon 'redds,' or nests in which female salmon lay their eggs. Female salmon create the redds by digging with their tails. Environmental conditions and predators take a heavy toll on salmon eggs and small fry. Of the 2,800 eggs which the average female coho salmon lays, only about 14 will survive to adulthood. Most of these will then be caught by commercial, sport or subsistence fishermen. Only 2 salmon from each redd will actually return to spawn and complete their life cycle."

Near here was the cabin of Rex Beach, author of *The Iron Trail,* a classic novel about the building of the CR&NW railway.

C **26.4** (42.5 km) Flag Point. Turnout with view of the Copper River which empties into the Gulf of Alaska. Downriver to the southwest is Castle Island Slough. Storey Slough is visible a little more to the south. Castle Island and a number of small islands lie at the mouth of the Copper River. Monument on the riverbank is dedicated to the men who built these bridges and "especially to the crane crew who lost their lives on July 21, 1971."

CAUTION: Extreme high winds next 10 miles/16 km in fall and winter. Stay in your vehicle.

C **26.7** (43 km) Two bridges cross the Copper River to Round Island, a small island with sand dunes and a good place to picnic.

In midsummer the Copper River has half a million or more red (sockeye) and king salmon migrating 300 miles/483 km upstream to spawn in the river's clear tributaries. There is no sportfishing in this stretch of the Copper River because of glacial silt.

Candlefish (eulachon) also spawn in the Copper River. Candlefish oil was once a significant trade item of the Coastal Indians. These fish are so oily that when dried they can be burned like candles.

C **27.5** (44.3 km) Copper River Bridge No. 3 from Round Island to Long Island. The 6.2 miles/10 km of road on Long Island pass through a sandy landscape dotted with dunes. Long Island is in the middle of the Copper River.

C **27.9** (44.9 km) Double-ended turnout to north; primitive campsite, beaver lodge.

C **28.5** (45.9 km) Lake to south is stocked with grayling.

C **30.8** (49.5 km) Watch for nesting swans, other birds and beaver in slough to south of road. *NOTE: Use extreme caution if you drive off road: sandy terrain.*

C **31** (49.9 km) Lakes to south stocked with grayling.

C **33** (53.1 km) View of 2 glaciers to the northwest; nearest is Goodwin, the other is Childs.

C **33.3** (53.6 km) First bridge leaving Long Island. View to south down Hotcake Channel to Heart Island. Road built on top of a long dike which stretches across the Copper River Delta. From here to **Milepost C 37.7** there are 7 more bridges across the delta. The Copper River channels have changed and many bridges now cross almost dry gulches.

C **34.2** (55 km) Large gravel turnout to north.

C **34.3** (55.2 km) Copper River bridge.

C **35.7** (57.5 km) Large gravel turnout to north.

C **36.8** (59.2 km) Bridge crossing main flow of the Copper River (this is the 5th bridge after leaving Long Island eastbound). Access to river at east end of bridge.

C **37.8** (60.8 km) Large gravel turnout to north.

C **38.8** (62.4 km) Childs Glacier directly ahead.

C **39.9** (64.2 km) Milky glacial waters of Sheep Creek pass through large culvert under road.

C **40.5** (65.2 km) **Clear Creek;** Dolly Varden, cutthroat, red salmon (July) and silvers (Aug.–Sept.). Use flies, lures, spinners or eggs. Watch for bears.

C **41.1** (66.1 km) Park on old railroad grade to south for access to Clear Creek.

C **41.7** (67.1 km) Goat Mountain (elev. 4,370 feet/1,332m) rises to the east of the highway. To the west parts of the Sherman and Goodwin glaciers flow down the sides of Mount Murchison (elev. 6,263 feet/1,909m).

C **42.1** (67.7 km) Side road to gravel pit, pond, informal camping and picnic site by Goat Mountain.

C **48** (77.2 km) Access to Childs Glacier Recreation Area with handicap-accessible covered viewing platform, picnic sites, covered tables, toilets and trails. No water. Limited RV parking. U.S. Forest Service hosts on site in summer. Childs Glacier was named by Capt. W.R. Abercrombie (1884 expedition) for George Washington Childs of Philadelphia. The glacier face is approximately 350 feet/107m high and very active. *CAUTION: Calving ice may cause waves to break over the beach and into the viewing area. Be prepared to run to higher ground!*

C **48.1** (77.4 km) The Million Dollar Bridge; viewing platform. The north span collapsed during the 1964 earthquake. Temporary repairs were made and people have been driving across it, but driving across the bridge and beyond is definitely a "drive at your own risk" venture. Primitive road extends only about 10 miles/16 km beyond the bridge to the Allen River. Heavy snow blocks road in winter; road may not be open until June. Proposed extension of the Copper River Highway to Chitina is currently under debate.

From here there is a view of Miles Glacier to the east. This glacier was named by Lieutenant Allen (1885 expedition) for Maj. Gen. Nelson A. Miles.

EDGERTON HIGHWAY/ McCARTHY ROAD

Richardson Highway Junction to McCarthy, Alaska
Alaska Route 10
(See map, page 601)

The Edgerton Highway, known locally as the Edgerton Cutoff, is a scenic paved road leading 35.1 miles/56.5 km east from its junction with the Richardson Highway to Chitina, then across the Copper River bridge to the start of the McCarthy Road. The gravel McCarthy Road leads 58.3 miles/93.8 km east and dead ends at the Kennicott River, about 1 mile/1.6 km west of the settlement of McCarthy. Total driving distance from the Richardson Highway turnoff to the end of the McCarthy Road is 93.4 miles/150.3 km.

The Edgerton Highway is paved with some long, steep grades. From **Milepost R 7.3**, the Edgerton Highway follows the approximate route of the old pack trail that once connected Chitina with Copper Center. The Edgerton Highway is named for U.S. Army Maj. Glenn Edgerton of the Alaska Territorial Road Commission.

The McCarthy Road is recommended for the adventurous traveler and only in the summer. Allow 4 hours driving time, with a maximum speed of 20 mph/32 kmph. Maintained by the state Dept. of Transportation, the road is suitable for most vehicles to **Milepost J 13.3** (Strelna Creek). The road is very narrow and may be dusty in dry weather and muddy in wet weather.

Increased tourist and truck traffic on the McCarthy Road resulted in alternate hourly closures of the road to passenger vehicles and logging trucks in summer 1995 to avoid collisions. Also be aware that the Kennicott River crossing is by hand-pulled cable tram, there is currently no vehicle access across the river; see description at **Milepost J 58.2**. Keep in mind that there may be long lines at the tram crossing on holiday weekends. The state plans to install a bridge here.

Motorists with large vehicles or trailers exercise caution, especially in wet weather. Watch for old railroad spikes in roadbed. Unless recently graded, watch for potholes, soft spots and severe washboard. Tire repair and mechanical light-towing service are available at Silver Lake Campground, **Milepost J 9.3**. The National Park Service ranger station in Chitina has information on current road conditions and also on backcountry travel in Wrangell–St. Elias National Park and Preserve. Most land along the McCarthy Road is either privately- or publicly-held. Local residents have asked that visitors please help protect water sources from contamination.

The McCarthy Road follows the right-of-way of the old Copper River & Northwestern Railway. Begun in 1907, the CR&NW (also referred to as the "can't run and never will") was built to carry copper ore from the Kennecott Mines to Cordova. It took 4 years to complete the railway. The railway and mine ceased operation in 1938.

View of the Copper River and Mount Drum from Milepost R 21 on the Edgerton Highway. (Jerrianne Lowther, staff)

The solitude and scenery of McCarthy, along with the historic Kennecott Mine and surrounding wilderness of Wrangell–St. Elias National Park and Preserve, have drawn increasing numbers of visitors to this area. It is a 126-mile/202-km drive from Glennallen to McCarthy, 315 miles/507 km from Anchorage.

Emergency medical services: Between the junction of the Richardson and Edgerton highways and McCarthy, contact the Copper River EMS in Glennallen, phone 911 or (907) 822-3203.

Edgerton Highway Log

Distance from junction with Richardson Highway (R) is followed by distance from junction with McCarthy Road (M).

R 0 M 35.1 (56.5 km) **Junction** at **Milepost V 82.6** Richardson Highway. Begin long downgrade eastbound. Watch for horses.

Excellent view of Mount Drum (to the northeast), a 12,010-foot/3,661-m peak of the Wrangell Mountains. Mount Wrangell (elev. 14,163 feet/4,317m) and Mount Blackburn (elev. 16,390 feet/4,996m) are visible straight ahead.

R 5.2 (8.4 km) **M 29.9** (48.1 km) Kenny Lake School.

Rather Rough-It Adventures. See display ad this section.

R 5.3 (8.5 km) **M 29.8** (48 km) Paved turnout to north.

R 7.2 (11.6 km) **M 27.9** (44.9 km) **Kenny Lake Mercantile & RV Park.** See display ad on page 600. ▲

The Nugget Cafe & Rooms. See display ad on page 600.

R 7.3 (11.7 km) **M 27.8** (44.7 km) Old Edgerton Loop Road (gravel) leads from here 8 miles/12.9 km through homestead and farm country to the Richardson Highway at **Milepost V 91.1.**

R 7.5 (12.1 km) **M 27.6** (44.4 km) Kenny Lake community hall, fairgrounds.

R 7.7 (12.4 km) **M 27.4** (44.1 km) Spacious double-ended paved rest area to south with picnic table on shore of Kenny Lake.

R 12.3 (19.8 km) **M 22.8** (36.7 km) Paved turnout to south. Tonsina River BLM trailhead, 2 miles/3.2 km (marked, brushed trail; good hike).

R 12.5 (20.1 km) **M 22.6** (36.4 km) Paved turnout to north. Copper River BLM trailhead, 5 miles/8 km.

Scenic Liberty Falls at Milepost R 23.7.
(© George Wuerthner)

R 13 (20.9 km) **M 22.2** (35.7 km) **Tonsina Native Arts & Crafts.** See display ad this section.

R 18 (29 km) **M 17.1** (27.5 km) Steep downhill grade eastbound. Views of the Copper River and bluffs. A buffalo herd in the area can be seen occasionally on the bluffs across the river.

R 19.3 (31 km) **M 15.8** (25.4 km) Site of the settlement of Lower Tonsina, formerly a roadhouse for travelers using the Copper River. Tonsina and Copper rivers are visible here. Beyond are the Wrangell Mountains.

The road continues from here east up a steep bluff. Much of the highway has been hewn from solid rock, leaving great cuts on either side. Pockets of pure peat moss are evident in breaks in the rock walls along the road. *CAUTION: Peat fires can be a serious problem; be careful with campfires.*

R 19.4 (31.2 km) **M 15.7** (25.3 km) Tonsina River bridge. Former Lower Tonsina townsite to west of bridge.

R 19.5 (31.4 km) **M 15.6** (25.1 km) Turnout to south.

R 19.6 (31.5 km) **M 15.5** (24.9 km) Double-ended turnout at lake to north.

R 21 (33.8 km) **M 14.2** (22.9 km) Gravel turnout to north overlooking the Copper River.

R 21.6 (34.8 km) **M 13.5** (21.7 km) Paved viewpoint to north above Copper River.

R 21.9 (35.2 km) **M 13.3** (21.4 km) Small gravel turnout to north.

R 22 (35.4 km) **M 13.1** (21.1 km) Top of hill, steep descents both directions.

R 23.5 (37.8 km) **M 11.6** (18.7 km) Liberty Falls Creek BLM trailhead to south.

R 23.7 (38.1 km) **M 11.4** (18.3 km) Liberty Creek bridge (8-ton load limit) and Liberty Falls State Recreation Site. The campground is just south of the highway on the banks of Liberty Creek, near the foot of the thundering falls. Scenic spot. Loop road through campground (large RVs and trailers check road before driving in); 5 sites, no water, no camping fee. Berry picking; watch for bears. ▲

R 28.4 (45.7 km) **M 6.7** (10.8 km) Small gravel turnout to north overlooking river.

R 28.5 (45.9 km) **M 6.6** (10.6 km) Pavement break. Side road north to Chitina DOT/PF maintenance station and airstrip. ADF&G office.

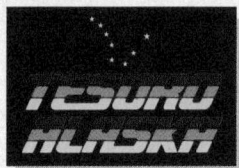

EDGERTON HIGHWAY/McCARTHY ROAD

Richardson Highway to McCarthy, AK

To Glennallen (see RICHARDSON HIGHWAY section)
Copper Center
Mount Wrangell 14,163 ft./4,317m
WRANGELL MOUNTAIN
Old Edgerton Loop Road
R-5.2/8.4km Rather Rough-It Adventures
R-7.2/11.6km Kenny Lake Mercantile & RV Park CDGIPST
The Nugget Cafe and Rooms LM
R-13/20.9km Tonsina Native Arts & Crafts
Mount Blackburn 16,390 ft./4,996m
Glaciated Area
R-0 M-35/57km RE-93/150km
R-35/57km M-0 J-0 RE-58/94km
Lower Tonsina
Chitina
J-9.3/15km Silver Lake Campground Clr
J-58.2/93.7km Copper Oar Rafting
Roadside Potatohead M
The Tram Station CrT
J-15/24.1km McCarthy Road Farm and Rides CL
R-33/53.1km Chitina Fuel & Grocery & Chitina Motel dGILPS
Spirit Mountain Artworks
Trans-Alaska Pipeline
R-33/53km M-2/3km
The McCarthy Road
J-58/94km RE-0
Kennicott
McCarthy
J-55.2/88.8km Willow Herb Mountain Depot GLr
To Valdez (see RICHARDSON HIGHWAY section)
Wrangell-St. Elias National Park and Preserve

Scale: 0–10 Miles; 0–10 Kilometres

Key to mileage boxes: miles/kilometres from: J-Junction, M-McCarthy Road Junction, R-Richardson Highway Junction, RE-Road End

Principal Route: Paved, Unpaved. Other Roads: Paved, Unpaved. Ferry Routes. Hiking Trails. Refer to Log for Visitor Facilities. Visitor Information. Fishing. Campground. Airport. Airstrip.

Key to Advertiser Services: C-Camping, D-Dump Station, d-Diesel, G-Gas (reg., unld.), I-Ice, L-Lodging, M-Meals, P-Propane, R-Car Repair (major), r-Car Repair (minor), S-Store (grocery), T-Telephone (pay)

Private Aircraft: Chitina Municipal Airfield; elev. 556 feet/169m; length 2,800 feet/853m; gravel; unattended.

R 29.5 (47.5 km) **M 5.7** (9.2 km) Small gravel turnout by Threemile Lake.

R 29.7 (47.8 km) **M 5.4** (8.7 km) Paved turnout by **Threemile Lake;** good grayling and rainbow trout fishing.

R 30.1 (48.4 km) **M 5** (8 km) Small turnout to south by **Twomile Lake;** good grayling and rainbow trout fishing, canoe launch.

R 30.6 (49.2 km) **M 4.5** (7.2 km) Large paved turnout at end of Twomile Lake.

R 31.9 (51.3 km) **M 3.2** (5.1 km) Onemile Lake (also called First Lake). Access road to boat launch at east end of lake.

Chitina

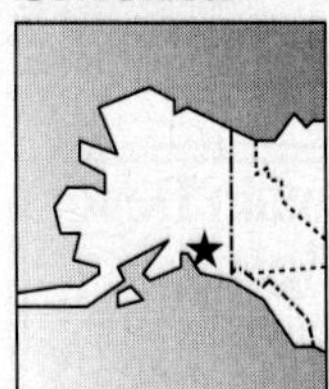

R 33 (53.1 km) **M 2.1** (3.4 km). Located about 120 miles/193 km northeast of Valdez, and about 66 miles/106 km southeast of Glennallen. **Population:** 49. **Emergency Services:** Copper River EMS, phone (907) 822-3203.

Visitor Information: National Park Service ranger station for Wrangell–St. Elias National Park and Preserve in Chitina is staffed by volunteers. Hours were 9:30 A.M. to 6 P.M., daily, in 1995; hours may vary. Open Memorial Day to Labor Day. A slide show on the McCarthy Road is available. Write Box 439, Copper Center, AK 99573, or phone (907) 822-5234 (park headquarters); Chitina ranger station, phone (907) 823-2205.

Chitina has a post office, store, 2 gas stations, bar, restaurant, tire repair service and phone service. The National Park Service ranger station is housed in a historic cabin. Follow signs to public well and toilets. One of the first buildings in Chitina, a hardware and sheet metal shop now on the National Register of Historic Places, houses an art gallery. A public pay phone is located beside the highway between the NPS ranger station and Town Lake. There is also a pay phone at the Chitina Saloon.

Chitina (pronounced CHIT-na) was established about 1908 as a railroad stop on the Copper River & Northwestern Railway and as a supply town for the Kennecott Copper Mines at McCarthy. The mine and railroad were abandoned in 1938. The McCarthy Road east of town follows the old railroad bed, which is listed on the National Register of Historic Places.

Inquire locally about informal camping areas: Much of the land around Chitina is owned by the Chitina Native Corp. and is posted no trespassing. Primitive camping is available along the Edgerton Highway at Onemile and Twomile lakes. There is an 8-site state campground east of Chitina across the Copper River bridge and a private campground on the McCarthy Road.

A big attraction in Chitina for fishermen and spectators is the seasonal salmon run (reds, kings or silvers), which draws hundreds of dip-netters to the **Copper River.** The dip-net fishery for salmon runs June through September (depending on harvest levels), and it's worth the trip to see fish wheels and dip nets in action. O'Brien Creek Road provides a state right-of-way access to popular fishing areas on large sandbars along the Copper River. This fishery is open only to Alaska residents with a personal-use or subsistence permit. Check with the Chitina ADF&G office for details and current regulations.

Chitina Fuel & Grocery and Chitina Motel. See display ad this section.

Spirit Mountain Artworks. See display ad this section.

Edgerton Highway Log

(continued)

R 33.6 (54.1 km) **M 1.6** (2.6 km) Pavement ends eastbound. No road maintenance east of here between Oct. 15 and May 15.

R 33.8 (54.4 km) **M 1.4** (2.3 km) Turnout overlooking the Copper River.

R 34.1 (54.9 km) **M 1.1** (1.8 km) Turnout overlooking the Copper River. Access to river.

R 34.7 (55.8 km) **M 0.5** (0.8 km) Copper River bridge. Completed in 1971, this 1,378-foot/420-m steel span was designed for year-round use. The $3.5 million bridge reestablished access across the river into the McCarthy–Kennicott area.

R 35.1 (56.5 km) **M 0 Junction** with McCarthy Road (log follows). Dept. of Transportation campground on the **Copper River**; 8 sites, picnic tables, fireplaces, toilets, boat launch, no water. Fishing for red and king salmon. Travelers are now within Wrangell–St. Elias National Park and Preserve.

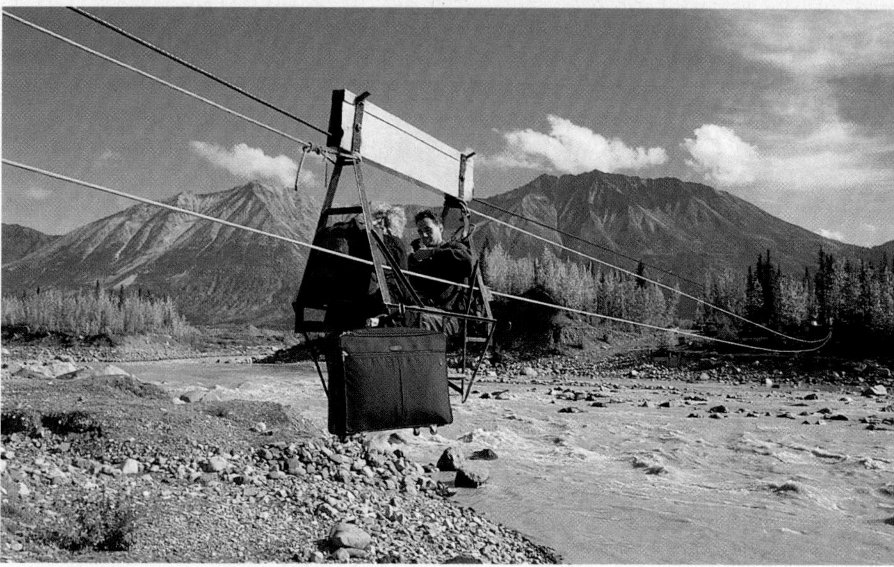

Visitors use hand-pulled tram to cross the Kennicott River. (© George Wuerthner)

McCarthy Road Log

Distance from junction with the Edgerton Highway (J) is followed by distance from road end (RE). Traditional mileposts used by local residents are indicated in the log.

J 0 RE 58.3 (93.8 km) **Junction** with the Edgerton Highway.

J 3.7 (6 km) **RE 54.6** (87.9 km) Turnout overlooking the Chitina River.

J 8.3 (13.4 km) **RE 50** (80.5 km) **Milepost 10.** Physical mileposts indicate distance from Chitina. Trail opposite homestead leads 0.3 mile/0.5 km north to **Strelna Lake**; rainbow trout and silver salmon. (Private property adjacent trail.)

J 9.3 (15 km) **RE 49** (78.9 km) **Milepost 11.** Private campground on **Silver Lake;** rainbow trout fishing, boat and canoe rentals, boat launch, tire repair. Trail access to **Van Lake,** located south of Silver Lake; good rainbow trout fishing.

J 10.8 (17.4 km) **RE 47.5** (76.4 km) **Milepost 12. Sculpin Lake** (also known as Nelson Lake); rainbow trout fishing.

J 13 (20.9 km) **RE 45.3** (72.9 km) Access road leads north 2.3 miles/4 km to trailheads for Dixie Pass, Kotsina and Nugget Creek trails. *NOTE: Access road crosses private homesteads. Please do not trespass.*

J 13.3 (21.4 km) **RE 45** (72.4 km) **Milepost 15. Strelna Creek** (culvert); fair fishing for Dolly Varden.

J 16 (25.7 km) **RE 42.3** (68.1 km) Kuskulana bridge. This old railroad bridge (built in 1910) is approximately 525 feet/160m long and 385 feet/117m above the river below. It is a narrow 3-span steel railway bridge with wood decking. Rehabilitated in 1988 for vehicle traffic.

Large gravel turnout at east end of bridge, small turnout at west end.

J 22.3 (35.9 km) **RE 36** (57.9 km) Large gravel turnout to south with view of Wrangell Mountains. There are several turnouts between here and the Kennicott River.

J 22.5 (36.2 km) **RE 35.8** (57.6 km) Boundary between park and preserve lands (unmarked). Wrangell–St. Elias National Park and Preserve allows sport hunting with a valid Alaska state license.

J 23.5 (37.8 km) **RE 34.8** (56 km) **Lou's Lake** to north; silver salmon and grayling fishing.

J 25.5 (41 km) **RE 32.8** (52.8 km) Chokosna River bridge.

J 27.7 (44.6 km) **RE 30.6** (49.2 km) One-lane bridge over Gilahina River. Old railroad trestle and parking.

J 40.3 (64.9 km) **RE 18** (29 km) Crystal Lake.

J 41.4 (66.6 km) **RE 16.9** (27.2 km) Double-ended turnout with view to south.

J 42.9 (69 km) **RE 15.4** (24.8 km) One-lane bridge over Lakina River, access to river at east end.

J 44.1 (71 km) **RE 14.2** (22.9 km) Long Lake Wildlife Refuge next 2.6 miles/4.2 km eastbound.

J 44.2 (71.1 km) **RE 14.1** (22.7 km) Watch for salmon spawning in Long Lake outlet (no fishing at outlet within 300 feet/91m of weir).

J 44.7 (71.9 km) **RE 13.6** (21.9 km) Turnout on **Long Lake**; lake trout, silver salmon, grayling, Dolly Varden, burbot.

J 54.9 (88.4 km) **RE 3.4** (5.5 km) Swift Creek culvert.

and much more. Gas and tire repair available. Rent our beautiful, handscribed log cabins by the night. Secluded, wood heat, light breakfast provided. Terry and Dee Frady, proprietors. MasterCard, VISA. (907) 554-4420. [ADVERTISEMENT]

J 58.1 (93.5 km) **RE 0.2** (0.3 km) Local parking lot for Kennicott and McCarthy residents.

J 58.2 (93.7 km) **RE 0.1** (0.2 km) Parking lot and Tram Station for visitors crossing Kennicott River; $5/day for parking, $10/day for parking and camping. ▲

The Tram Station, constructed from salvaged timbers from the Nizina River railroad bridge, houses the parking concession, tour booking service, snack shop and gift shop.

A hand-pulled, open-platform, cable tram carries passengers across the first part of the Kennicott River. (There is a footbridge across the river's second channel, unless it has been washed out.) The state plans to install a footbridge or suspension bridge over the main channel in 1996 or 1997. If the tram is still in use, keep in mind that you must pull yourself across 300 feet of river. It takes about 1/2 hour, less time if someone helps from the other bank. (Kids were helping for tips in 1995.) Wear gloves. The tram is open 24-hours a day. Expect long lines Fourth of July weekend and other holidays. *CAUTION: DO NOT attempt to wade across this glacial river; strong currents and cold water make it extremely treacherous.*

A CB radio at the Tram Station has instructions for calling businesses in McCarthy and Kennicott (they monitor Channel 5 when the Tram Station is closed).

Parking on the riverbank is not recommended in July or early August because of flooding.

Copper Oar Rafting. See display ad this section.

Roadside Potatohead, a welcome sight for hungry travelers after their adventurous journey down the McCarthy Road. Your hosts, Kathleen, Denise, Yoshi and LuLu offer a variety of fabulous food that won't bust your budget. Specialty items include fresh-cut curly fries with various toppings, homemade burritos (try our breakfast burrito), brats and kraut, sandwiches, Starbucks coffee, baked goods and more! Catering to vegetarians and wranglers, open 7 days a week. Come join us at the end of the road for a unique experience at the "Home of the Flying Potato." [ADVERTISEMENT]

Downtown McCarthy. (© George Wuerthner)

The Tram Station. Let the friendly folks at this uniquely Alaskan visitor center answer all of your questions at the end of the road. We can arrange hiking tours, lodging, flightseeing, rafting and provide you with a virtual "copper mine" of information. Check out our campground or stay in one of our spacious wall tents on the river bank beneath the towering Root Glacier. We also offer parking, snacks, gifts, tires, gas, emergency repairs and telephone service. Open late every day, May–September. Phone (907) 554-4490. [ADVERTISEMENT]

J 58.3 (93.8 km) **RE 0** McCarthy Road dead ends at Kennicott River. On the east side of the river, follow the road for about 1/2 mile to a fork; the right fork leads to McCarthy (less than a mile) and the left fork goes to Kennicott (about 5 miles).

McCarthy

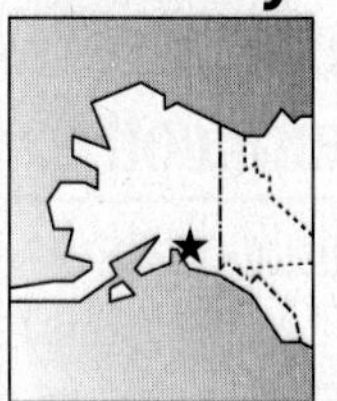

Located within the Wrangell–St. Elias National Park and Preserve 61 miles/98.1 km east of Chitina. **Population:** 25. **Transportation:** Scheduled van service between Glennallen and McCarthy/Kennicott and Valdez. Daily shuttle to Chitina; phone (907) 822-5292. **Radio:** KCAM (Glennallen).

There is shuttle service between McCarthy and Kennicott. Lodging is available in McCarthy at the McCarthy Lodge, which also offers food service and a bar. The McCarthy area has flightseeing services, a bed and breakfast, a pizza restaurant and an operating gold mine. Check with lodges about activities in the area. Two wilderness guide services operate here. McCarthy does not have a post office, school, or television.

Private Aircraft: McCarthy airstrip, 1 mile/1.6 km south; elev. 1,494 feet/455m; length 1,400 feet/427m; turf, gravel; unattended. McCarthy Nr 2, 1 mile/1.6 km northeast; elev. 1,531 feet/467m; length 3,400 feet/1,036m; gravel; unattended.

The town of McCarthy is in a beautiful

area of glaciers and mountains. The Kennicott River flows by the west side of town and joins the Nizina River which flows into the Chitina River. The local museum, located in the railway depot, has historical artifacts and photos from the early mining days.

It is 4.5 miles/7.2 km from McCarthy at the end of the CR&NW railroad bed to the old mining town of **KENNICOTT** (pop. 8 to 15). Perched on the side of a mountain next to Kennicott Glacier, the town was built by Kennecott Copper Corp. between 1910 and 1920. (An early-day misspelling made the mining company Kennecott, while the region and settlement are Kennicott.) The richest copper mine in the world until its closure in 1938, Kennicott's mill processed more than 591,535 tons of copper ore and employed some 800 workers in its heyday. Today, a lodge is located here. The 3 dozen barn-red mine buildings are on private land. Kennecott Copper Mine is a National Historic Site.

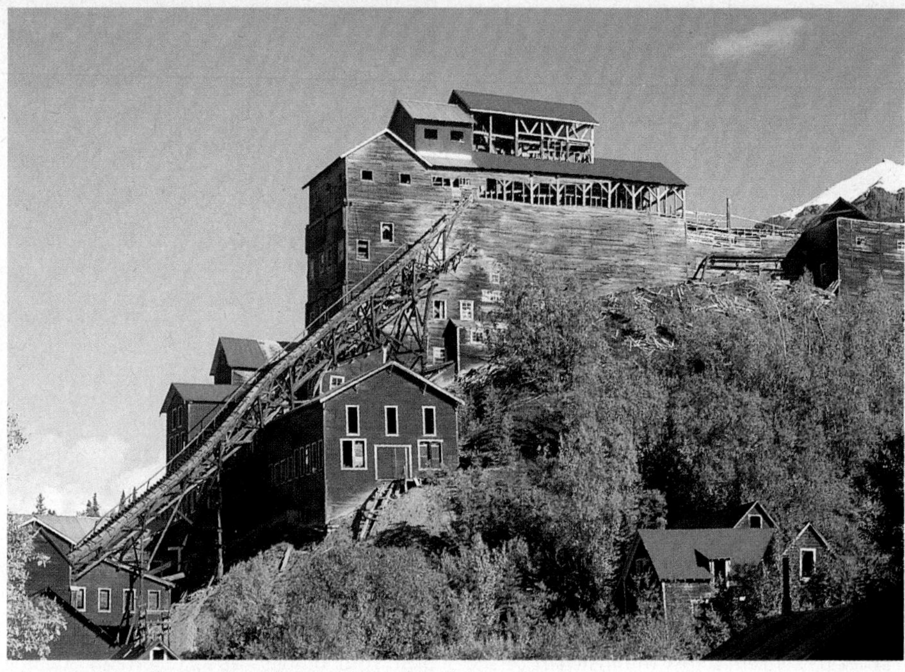

Historic Kennicott mine is on private land. (© George Wuerthner)

Kennicott Glacier Lodge, located in the ghost town of Kennicott, offers the area's finest accommodations and dining. Built in 1987, this new lodge has 25 clean, delightful guest rooms, 2 living rooms, a spacious dining room, and a 180-foot front porch with a spectacular panoramic view of the Wrangell Mountains, Chugach Mountains and Kennicott Glacier. The homemade food, served family-style, has been called "wilderness gourmet dining." Guest activities at this destination resort include glacier trekking, flightseeing, photography, alpine hiking, historical and nature tours, rafting. May 15 to Sept. 20. (800) 582-5128. See display ad. [ADVERTISEMENT]

McCarthy lies within **WRANGELL–ST. ELIAS NATIONAL PARK AND PRESERVE.** This 13.1 million acre park encompasses the southeast corner of the Alaska mainland, stretching from the Gulf of Alaska to the Copper River basin. Access to the park is by way of the McCarthy Road, the Nabesna Road (off the Tok Cutoff) and out of Yakutat. This vast unspoiled wilderness offers backpacking, mountaineering, river running, hunting and sportfishing. For more information, contact: Superintendent, Wrangell–St. Elias National Park and Preserve, P.O. Box 439, Copper Center, AK 99573; phone (907) 822-5234.

Wrangell Mountain Air offers daily flights as a convenient alternative to driving the McCarthy Road. Park your car or RV in Chitina at the end of the paved road and enjoy a spectacular flight through the Wrangell Mountains. Fly-in hiking, rafting, glacier trekking are also available. All aircraft are high wing for great viewing and equipped with headsets for each passenger. Call toll free for reservations. 1-800-478-1160 or (907) 554-4411. See display ad. [ADVERTISEMENT]

McCARTHY/KENNICOTT ADVERTISERS

Backcountry Connection ....Ph. (907) 822-5292
Kennicott Glacier Lodge ....Ph. 1-800-582-5128
McCarthy Air ....Ph. 1-800-245-6909
Wrangell Mountain Air ....Ph. (907) 554-4411

MARINE ACCESS ROUTES

Alaska ports via BC Ferries, Alaska State Ferries and Cruise Ships
Includes: SOUTHEAST ferry system connecting Bellingham, WA, Port Hardy and Prince Rupert, BC, to Ketchikan and other Southeastern Alaska ports
(See maps, pages 606–607)
SOUTHCENTRAL/SOUTHWEST ferry system connecting Kenai Peninsula, Kodiak and Prince William Sound ports
(See map, page 622)

Alaska state ferries provide transportation for people and vehicles via the Inside Passage through Southeast Alaska. (© Adrienne DeLiso)

Much of Alaska's southeastern region, with its thousands of islands, bays and steep, mountainous shorelines, prohibits building highways from city to city. The Alaska Marine Highway—which stretches almost 1,000 nautical miles from Bellingham, WA, to Skagway, AK—provides the vital link for people and their vehicles.

Many visitors to Alaska use the Alaska Marine Highway as an alternative route to driving to Alaska. Travelers often drive one direction and take the Marine Highway the other. This option not only eliminates the necessity of driving the road system twice, but affords the traveler the opportunity to take in the magnificent scenery and picturesque communities of Southeast Alaska and the Inside Passage.

The Alaska state ferries depart from Bellingham, WA (85 miles north of Seattle on Interstate 5, Exit 250), or Prince Rupert, BC, for Southeast Alaska communities. (Bellingham is accessible by Amtrak and bus. Fairhaven Station, a new transportation center next to the Bellingham Cruise Terminal at 401 Harris Ave. in south Bellingham, provides a central location for rail, bus, airporter, taxi and ferry services.) Alaska state ferries out of Bellingham do not stop in Canada. The cruise route goes up the famed Inside Passage through several hundred miles of forested islands and deep fjords in Canada and southeastern Alaska. Ferries out of Prince Rupert follow the same route as the ferries out of Bellingham from Chatham Sound north. Ketchikan (the first stop for both) is a 36-hour ferry ride from Bellingham and about 6 hours by ferry from Prince Rupert. There is also ferry service between Ketchikan, AK, and Stewart, BC/Hyder, AK, and feeder service between southern and northern panhandle communities. Descriptions of Southeast Alaska communities start on page 629. Details on the Alaska State Ferry System begin on page 614; schedules begin on page 610.

BC Ferries provides year-round service on 25 routes throughout coastal British Columbia, with a fleet of 40 passenger- and vehicle-carrying ferries. There are 3 northern routes operated by BC Ferries. The 15-hour Inside Passage cruise from Port Hardy on Vancouver Island to Prince Rupert is often combined with a trip on the Alaska Marine Highway by travellers wanting to see all of the Inside Passage. A second route provides service between Prince Rupert and the Queen Charlotte Islands (see Prince Rupert description and Queen Charlottes sidebar in the YELLOWHEAD HIGHWAY section). And new in the summer of 1996, BC Ferries is adding a mid-coast route which will link Port Hardy and Bella Coola. Some sailings will stop at Namu, Bella Bella, Shearwater, Ocean Falls, Finn Bay and Klemtu along the way, and shore excursions will be available.

Cruise ships offer a variety of itineraries from West Coast ports through the Inside Passage and to Southcentral Alaska.

BC Ferries

BC Ferries provides marine transportation for passengers and vehicles between Port Hardy, at the north end of Vancouver Island, and Prince Rupert, at the end of Yellowhead Highway 16, which is also the southern port for most Alaska state ferries.

BC Ferries also provides service on 24 other routes throughout coastal British Columbia. They include 3 major routes that

(Continues on page 608)

MARINE ACCESS ROUTES *Washington and British Columbia from Puget Sound to Hecate Strait*

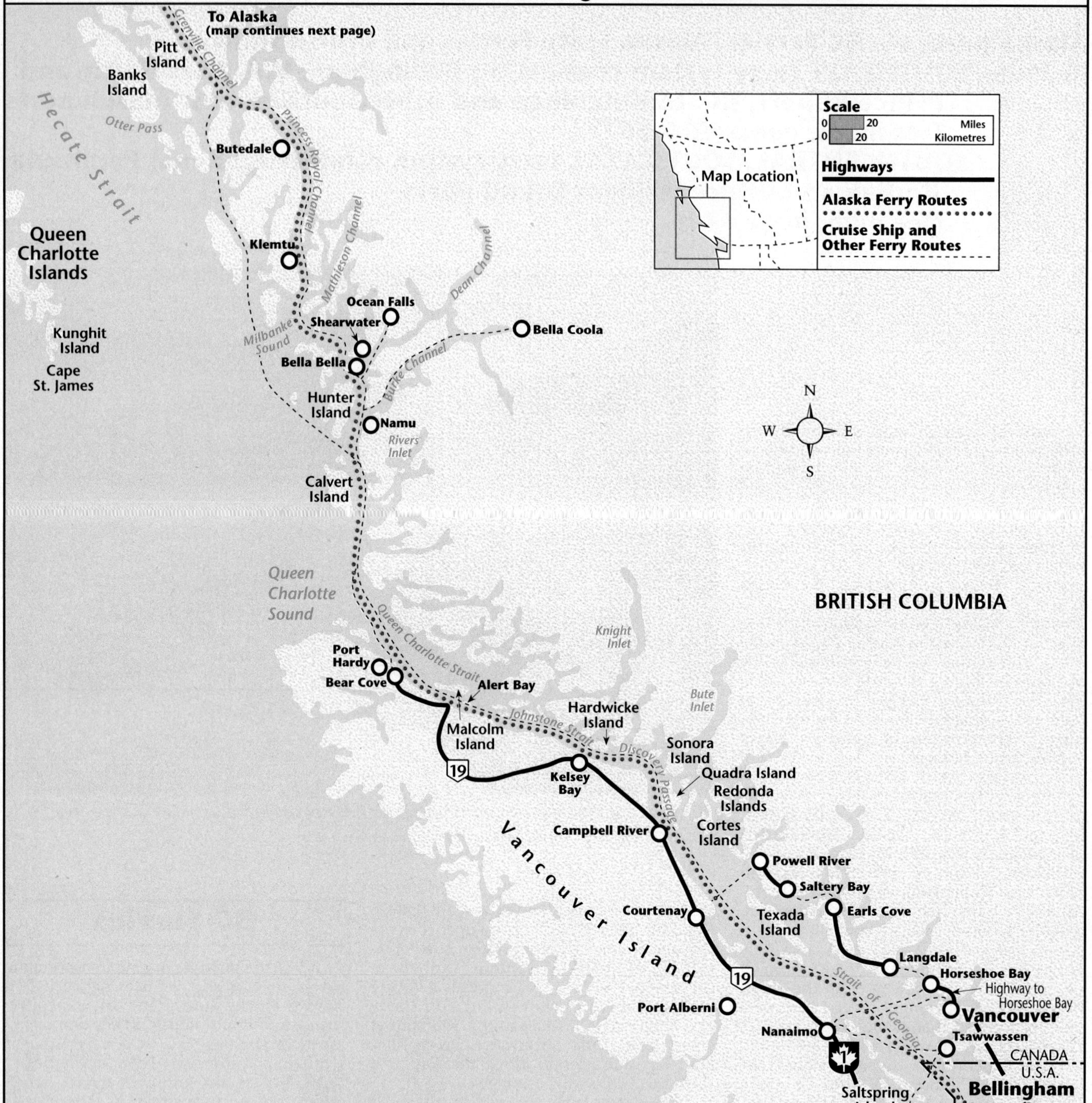

To Alaska
(map continues next page)

Scale
0 20 Miles
0 20 Kilometres
Highways
Alaska Ferry Routes
Cruise Ship and Other Ferry Routes
Map Location

Pitt Island
Banks Island
Grenville Channel
Hecate Strait
Otter Pass
Butedale
Princess Royal Channel
Queen Charlotte Islands
Klemtu
Mathieson Channel
Dean Channel
Ocean Falls
Shearwater
Bella Coola
Milbanke Sound
Bella Bella
Burke Channel
Kunghit Island
Cape St. James
Hunter Island
Namu
Rivers Inlet
Calvert Island
N
W
E
S
Queen Charlotte Sound
BRITISH COLUMBIA
Queen Charlotte Strait
Knight Inlet
Port Hardy
Bear Cove
Alert Bay
Bute Inlet
Hardwicke Island
Johnstone Strait
Malcolm Island
Discovery Passage
Sonora Island
19
Kelsey Bay
Quadra Island
Redonda Islands
Campbell River
Cortes Island
Vancouver Island
Powell River
Saltery Bay
Courtenay
Texada Island
Earls Cove
Langdale
Horseshoe Bay
Highway to Horseshoe Bay
Strait of Georgia
Port Alberni
Vancouver
Nanaimo
1
Tsawwassen
CANADA
U.S.A.
Bellingham
Saltspring Island
Swartz Bay
Sidney
Anacortes
CANADA
U.S.A.
Victoria
Pacific Ocean
San Juan Islands
5
Strait of Juan de Fuca
Port Angeles
Everett
WASHINGTON
Seattle
Puget Sound

MARINE ACCESS ROUTES

British Columbia and Southeastern Alaska from Prince Rupert, BC, to Skagway, AK

To Alaska Highway
To Alaska Highway
CANADA
U.S.A.
Haines Highway (see HAINES HIGHWAY section)
7
Skagway
2
Klondike Highway 2 (see KLONDIKE HIGHWAY 2 section)
White Pass & Yukon Route
Haines
Glaciated Area
Glacier Bay National Park and Preserve
Glacier Bay
Lynn Canal
Glaciated Area
Map Location
Scale
0 20 Miles
0 20 Kilometres
Highways
Alaska Ferry Routes
Cruise Ship and Other Ferry Routes
Bartlett Cove
Gustavus
Auke Bay Ferry Terminal
Juneau
Taku Inlet
Cross Sound
Icy Strait
Pelican
Hoonah
Douglas Island
Gastineau Channel
BRITISH ALASKA
Chichagof Island
Tenakee Springs
Admiralty Island
Tracy Arm
Chatham Strait
Stephens Passage
Endicott Arm
N
W
E
S
Angoon
Glaciated Area
Alexander Archipelago
Sitka
Frederick Sound
Baranof Island
Kake
Kuiu Island
Kupreanof Island
Stikine River
BRITISH COLUMBIA
Petersburg
Mitkof Island
Sumner Strait
Zarembo Island
Wrangell
Wrangell Island
BRITISH COLUMBIA ALASKA
Etolin Island
Clarence Strait
Thorne Bay
Misty Fiords
Hyder
Klawock
Revillagigedo Island
Craig
Hollis
Behm Canal
National
Hydaburg
Prince of Wales Island
Ketchikan
Gravina Island
Revillagigedo Channel
Monument
Portland Canal
Metlakatla
Annette Island
U.S.A.
CANADA
Chatham Sound
Dixon Entrance
Dundas Island
Pacific Ocean
Prince Rupert
16
Yellowhead Highway 16 (see YELLOWHEAD HIGHWAY 16 section)
Skeena River
Masset
Graham Island
Porcher Island
Kitimat
Hecate Strait
Grenville Channel
Queen Charlotte Islands
Queen Charlotte City
Skidegate
Sandspit
Banks Island
Pitt Island
Morseby Island
Otter Pass

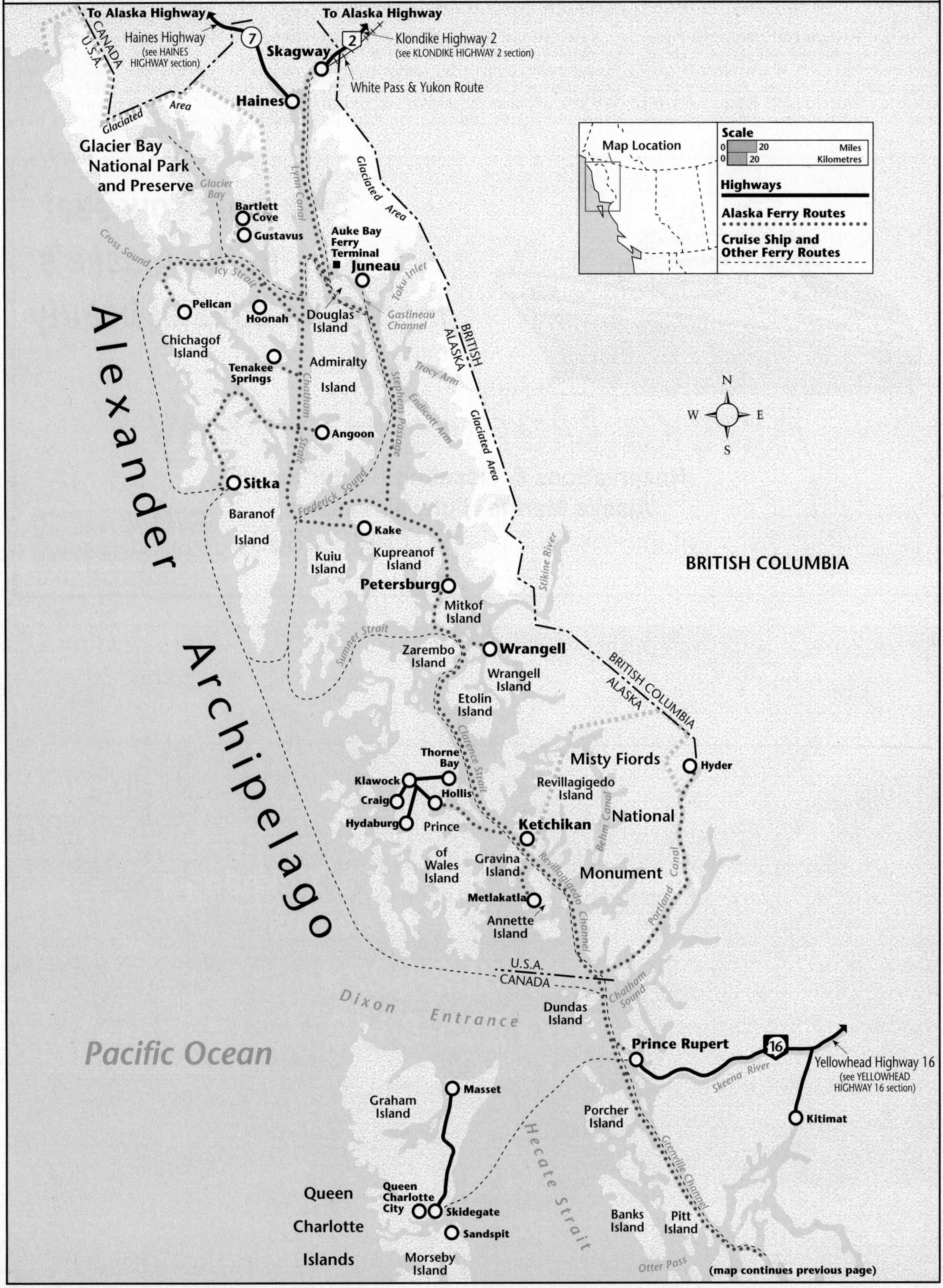

(map continues previous page)

(Continued from page 605)
link mainland British Columbia and Vancouver Island: Tsawwassen–Swartz Bay, Tsawwassen–Nanaimo and Horseshoe Bay–Nanaimo.

Service between Port Hardy and Prince Rupert during the summer season is aboard the *Queen of the North,* which carries 750 passengers and 157 vehicles. The ferry has a cafeteria, buffet dining room, news/gift shop, licensed and view lounges, children's playroom, day cabins and staterooms (for round-trip use). Summer service on this route is during daylight hours to make the most of the scenery, so cabins are not necessary.

Reservations: Strongly recommended for passengers and vehicles on the Inside Passage route. Contact BC Ferries Reservations Centre, 1112 Fort St., Victoria, BC V8V 4V2, or phone the reservation office in Vancouver (604) 669-1211, in Victoria (604) 386-3431.

Schedules and fares: The 1996 Inside Passage summer sailing schedule is shown here. Rates current at time of printing (subject to change) are as follows (1-way, in Canadian funds): Adult passenger, $100; child (5 to 11 years), $50; car, $206; camper/RV (up to 20 feet in length, over 6 feet 8 inches in height), $344; additional length, $17.20 per foot; motorcycle, $103; bicycle, $6.50. Service during the fall, winter

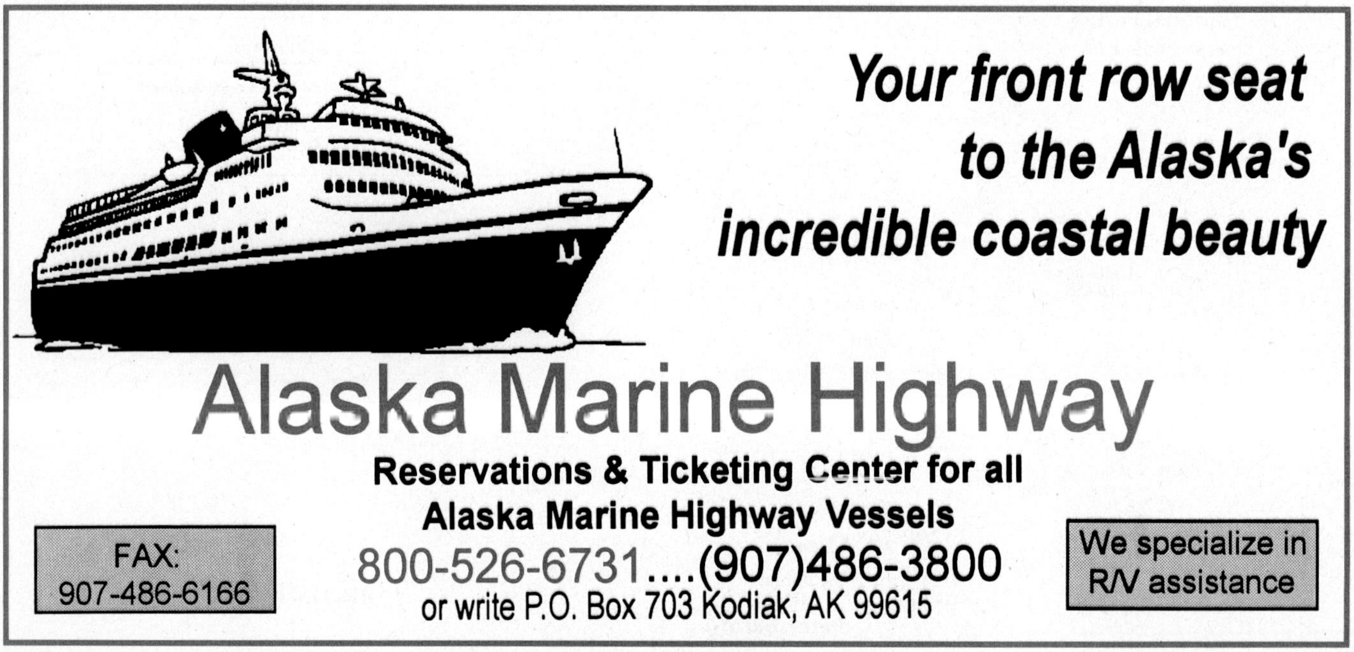

BC FERRIES SCHEDULE

PORT HARDY TO PRINCE RUPERT

May 25 to Sept. 26, 1996

NORTHBOUND	SOUTHBOUND
Departs: Port Hardy 7:30 A.M.	**Departs:** Prince Rupert 7:30 A.M.
Arrives: Prince Rupert 10:30 P.M.	**Arrives:** Port Hardy 10:30 P.M.
Dates: May 25, 27, 29, 31	**Dates:** May 26, 28, 30
June, July, September (even-numbered days)	June, July, September (odd-numbered days)
August (odd-numbered days)	August (even-numbered days)

and spring is less frequent and fares are reduced. Contact BC Ferries for details.

Check-in time is 1½ hours before sailing. Cancellations made less than 30 days prior to departure are subject to a cancellation fee.

Prince Rupert is located 450 miles/724 km west of Prince George via the Yellowhead Highway (see YELLOWHEAD HIGHWAY 16 section). Port Hardy is approximately 307 miles/494 km north of Victoria via Trans-Canada Highway 1 and BC Highway 19. From Nanaimo it is 236 miles/380 km—or about 5 hours' driving time—to Port Hardy. If you are driving from Victoria, allow at least 8 hours (the route is almost all 2-lane highway between Victoria and Campbell River). Or, take your time and spend several days exploring island communities along the way. Keep in mind that there are limited services between Campbell River and Port Hardy, a distance of 145 miles/233 km. The Port Hardy ferry terminal is located at Bear Cove, 4 miles/7 km from downtown Port Hardy.

To reach Vancouver Island from the lower British Columbia mainland, take BC Ferries from either Tsawwassen or Horseshoe Bay. Follow Highway 99 through Vancouver for the Horseshoe Bay terminal, 13 miles/21 km northwest of the city, and ferry service to Nanaimo (crossing time: 1½ hours). Or turn off Highway 99 approximately 17 miles/27 km north of the U.S. border for the Tsawwassen terminal and service to Swartz Bay near Victoria (1½-hour crossing) and to Nanaimo (2-hour crossing). There are a minimum of 16 round trips daily during summer between Tsawwassen and Swartz Bay, and 8 round trips daily year round between Tsawwassen and Nanaimo. Reservations are not accepted for passengers or vehicles on these routes.

There are several ways to reach Vancou-

(Continues on page 612)

1996 Southeast Ferry Schedules

May 1996 Northbound Schedule

LEAVE BELLINGHAM	LEAVE PRINCE RUPERT	LEAVE STEWART/HYDER	METLAKATLA	KETCHIKAN	HOLLIS	WRANGELL	PETERSBURG	KAKE	ARRIVE SITKA	ANGOON	TENAKEE	HOONAH	JUNEAU/ AUKE BAY	HAINES	ARRIVE SKAGWAY
			SEE M/V AURORA SCHEDULE BELOW		SEE M/V AURORA SCHEDULE BELOW		W1 11:00A	W1 4:15P	TH2 12:30A	TH2 9:15A		TH2 2:15P	TH2 11:30P	F3 5:00A	F3 6:00A
	F3 11:30A			F3 5:45P		S4 12:30A	S4 4:15A		S4 2:15P				SU5 5:45A	SU5 12:15P	SU5 1:15P
								Lv. Sitka	S4 10:30A	S4 4:45P	S4 8:00P	SU5 12:15A	SU5 3:30A		
										Lv. Pelican	SU5 3:30P		SU5 10:00P		
F3 6:30P				SU5 8:00A		SU5 1:45P	SU5 5:30P		M6 2:45A				M6 4:45P	M6 11:45P	T7 12:45A
								Lv. Sitka	M6 6:00P	T7 12:15A	T7 3:30A	T7 7:45A	T7 11:00A		
	T7 9:00A			T7 3:30P		T7 10:15P	W8 2:00A						W8 11:45A	W8 5:45P	W8 6:45P
							W8 11:15P	TH9 4:15A	TH9 12:30P	TH9 9:15P		F10 2:15A	F10 6:30A	F10 11:55A	F10 1:00P
	F10 11:55A			F10 6:15P		S11 1:00A	S11 4:45A		S11 3:00P				SU12 5:15A	SU12 11:45A	SU12 12:45P
								Lv. Sitka	S11 11:45P	SU12 6:00A	SU12 9:15A	SU12 1:30P	SU12 4:45P		
F10 6:30P				SU12 5:45A		SU12 11:30A	SU12 5:15P		M13 4:15A				M13 6:00P	T14 1:00A	T14 2:00A
								Lv. Sitka	M13 1:15P	M13 7:30P	M13 11:00P	T14 4:00A	T14 7:15A		
	T14 9:00A			T14 3:30P		T14 10:15P	W15 2:00A						W15 11:45A	W15 5:45P	W15 6:45P
		T14 3:45P		W15 1:30A			W15 5:45P	W15 10:45P	TH16 7:00A	TH16 3:15P		TH16 8:15P	F17 12:30A	F17 6:00A	F17 7:00A
	*W15 9:45A			W15 4:45P		W15 11:30P	TH16 4:30A		TH16 7:15P				F17 8:45A	F17 2:15P	F17 3:15P
	*F17 11:30A			F17 5:45P		S18 12:30A	S18 4:15A		S18 2:15P				SU19 3:15A	SU19 9:15A	SU19 10:15A
								Lv. Sitka	S18 10:30A	S18 4:45P	S18 8:00P	SU19 12:15A	SU19 3:30A		
										Lv. Pelican	SU19 3:30P		SU19 10:00P		
	SU19 9:15A			SU19 3:45P									M20 9:00A	M20 4:15P	M20 5:15P
*F17 6:00P				SU19 7:30A		SU19 1:15P	SU19 5:00P		M20 2:45A				M20 4:45P	M20 11:45P	T21 12:45A
								Lv. Sitka	M20 6:00P	T21 12:15A	T21 3:45A	T21 8:00A	T21 11:15A		
	T21 [illegible]			T21 3:30P		T21 10:15P	W22 2:00A						W22 11:45A	W22 5:45P	W22 6:45P
		T21 3:45P		W22 1:30A			W22 10:15P	TH23 3:15A	TH23 11:30A	TH23 8:00P		F24 1:00A	F24 5:15A	F24 10:45A	F24 11:45A
	W22 9:45A			W22 4:15P		W22 11:00P	TH23 4:00A		TH23 5:45P				F24 8:00A	F24 2:00P	F24 3:00P
	F24 10:45A			F24 5:00P		F24 11:45P	S25 3:30A		S25 1:45P				SU26 2:45A	SU26 9:15A	SU26 10:15A
								Lv. Sitka	S25 10:15P	SU26 4:30A	SU26 7:45A	SU26 11:55A	SU26 3:15P		
	SU26 9:15A			SU26 3:45P									M27 10:45A	M27 4:15P	M27 5:15P
F24 6:30P				SU26 8:00A		SU26 1:45P	SU26 5:30P		M27 2:45A				M27 5:30P	M27 11:30P	T28 12:30A
								Lv. Sitka	M27 11:45A	M27 6:00P	M27 9:30P	T28 1:45A	T28 5:00A		
	T28 8:30A			T28 2:30P		T28 9:15P	W29 1:00A		W29 11:00A				TH30 1:30A	TH30 9:00A	TH30 10:00A
							W29 4:30P	W29 9:30P	TH30 5:45A	TH30 2:15P		TH30 7:15P	TH30 10:30P		
	W29 9:45A			W29 4:15P		W29 11:00P	TH30 4:00A		TH30 6:00P				F31 8:00A	F31 2:00P	F31 3:00P
	TH30 9:00P			F31 3:30A		F31 10:30A	F31 2:15P	F31 7:00P					S1 3:45A	S1 9:45A	S1 10:45A
F31 6:30P				SU2 7:00A		SU2 12:45P	SU2 4:30P		M3 1:45A				M3 3:45P	M3 10:45P	M3 11:45P

*THE FOLLOWING EVENT MAY AFFECT AVAILABILITY OF SPACE: LITTLE NORWAY FESTIVAL MAY 16-19 PETERSBURG

HOW TO READ YOUR SCHEDULE

1. Reading across the top of each page, find the month you wish to travel, and refer to either the Northbound or Southbound schedule. (Using the example of traveling from Skagway to Juneau/Auke Bay, you would read the Southbound schedule on the right-hand page.)
2. Reading across the top of the schedule, find the city from which you wish to depart (e.g. Leave Skagway).
3. Read down the column to locate your desired departure date. For example: Leave Skagway SU2 (Sunday, the 2nd) 8:45 p.m..
4. Beginning with departure date, read horizontally from left to right for dates and times of departure from various ports. For example: After departing Skagway, ferry will dock in Haines, and after a short time in port it will depart Haines on SU2 (Sunday, the 2nd) at 11:15 p.m. for Juneau/Auke Bay. Refer to the Running Time Table on page 612 to calculate the time in port and approximate unlisted arrival time.
5. The color of the horizontal bars indicates the ship on which you will travel.

Example

LEAVE SKAGWAY	HAINES	JUNEAU/ AUKE BAY	HOONAH	TENAKEE	ANGOON	ARRIVE SITKA	KAKE	PETERSBURG	WRANGELL	HOLLIS	KETCHIKAN	METLAKATLA	ARRIVE STEWART/HYDER	ARRIVE PRINCE RUPERT	ARRIVE BELLINGHAM
F31 6:00P	F31 8:30P	S1 2:30A						S1 11:30A	S1 3:30P		S1 11:00P			SU2 6:00A	
S1 1:45P	S1 4:15P	S1 10:15P				SU2 7:45A	SU2 7:45P	M3 12:30A	M3 4:15A		M3 11:15A			M3 6:15P	
SU2 8:45P	SU2 11:15P	M3 5:15A						M3 1:45P	M3 5:30P		T4 1:15A			T4 8:30A	

Day of week — Day of month — AM or PM — Time

VESSEL COLOR CODING

Aurora · Columbia · Le Conte · Malaspina · Matanuska · Taku

The state reserves the right to revise or cancel schedules and rates without prior notice and assumes no responsibility for delays and/or expenses due to such modifications.

Alaska state ferry schedules reprinted courtesy of Alaska Marine Highway

May 1996 Southbound Schedule

LEAVE SKAGWAY	HAINES	JUNEAU/ AUKE BAY	HOONAH	TENAKEE	ANGOON	ARRIVE SITKA	KAKE	PETERSBURG	WRANGELL	HOLLIS	KETCHIKAN	METLAKATLA	ARRIVE STEWART/HYDER	ARRIVE PRINCE RUPERT	ARRIVE BELLINGHAM
W1 8:45P	W1 11:15P	TH2 5:15A						TH2 1:45P	TH2 5:30P	SEE M/V AURORA SCHEDULE BELOW	F3 1:30A	SEE M/V AURORA SCHEDULE BELOW		F3 8:30A	
F3 7:30A	F3 9:30A	F3 3:30P	F3 7:45P	F3 11:45P	S4 3:00A	S4 8:00A									
SU5 4:15P	SU5 7:15P	M6 3:45A						M6 12:15P	M6 4:00P		M6 11:30P			T7 6:30A	
		SU5 7:00A	Ar. Pelican	SU5 1:30P											
		SU5 11:15P	M6 3:30A	M6 7:30A	M6 10:45A	M6 3:45P									
T7 3:45A	T7 7:15A	T7 1:45P				T7 10:15P		W8 3:00P	W8 6:30P		TH9 1:00A				F10 11:00A
		T7 2:30P	T7 6:45P		T7 11:45P	W8 4:45A	W8 4:45P	W8 8:45P							
W8 9:45P	TH9 12:15A	TH9 6:45A						TH9 3:15P	TH9 7:00P		F10 2:00A			F10 9:00A	
F10 2:30P	F10 4:30P	F10 10:00P	S11 2:15A	S11 6:30A	S11 9:45A	S11 2:45P									
SU12 3:45P	SU12 6:45P	M13 1:15A						M13 9:45A	M13 1:45P		M13 9:15P			T14 5:45A	
		SU12 6:30P	SU12 10:45P	M13 2:45A	M13 5:45A	M13 10:45A					T14 1:45A		T14 1:00P		
T14 5:00A	T14 8:30A	T14 3:00P				T14 11:45P		W15 2:00P	W15 5:30P		W15 11:55P				F17 10:00A
		*T14 9:30A	T14 1:45P		T14 6:45P	T14 11:45P	W15 11:55A	W15 4:00P							
*W15 9:45P	TH16 12:15A	TH16 6:15A						TH16 2:45P	TH16 6:30P		F17 1:30A			F17 8:30A	
F17 8:30A	F17 10:30A	F17 4:00P	F17 8:15P	S18 12:15A	S18 3:15	S18 8:15A									
*F17 6:15P	F17 8:30P	S18 2:30A						S18 11:30A	S18 3:45P		S18 11:15P			SU19 6:15A	
*SU19 1:15P	SU19 3:45P	SU19 9:45P						M20 6:15A	M20 10:15A		M20 8:15P			T21 5:45A	
		SU19 7:00A	Ar. Pelican	SU19 1:30P							T21 1:45A		T21 1:00P		
		SU19 11:00P	M20 3:15A	M20 7:15A	M20 10:30A	M20 3:30P									
M20 8:15P	M20 10:15P	T21 4:15A						T21 1:15P	T21 5:15P		W22 12:15A			W22 7:15A	
T21 3:45A	T21 7:15A	T21 1:45P				T21 10:15P		W22 2:00P	W22 5:30P		W22 11:55P				F24 10:00A
		T21 2:00P	T21 6:15P		T21 11:15P	W22 4:15A	W22 4:45P	W22 8:45P							
W22 9:45P	TH23 12:15A	TH23 6:15A						TH23 2:45P	TH23 6:30P		F24 1:30A			F24 8:30A	
F24 1:15P	F24 3:15P	F24 8:45P	S25 1:00A	S25 5:15A	S25 8:30A	S25 1:30P									
F24 6:00P	F24 8:30P	S25 2:30A						S25 11:30A	S25 3:30P		S25 11:00P			SU26 6:00A	
SU26 1:15P	SU26 4:15P	SU26 11:45P						M27 8:30A	M27 12:30P		M27 9:30P			T28 5:45A	
		SU26 5:00P	SU26 9:15P	M27 1:15A	M27 4:15A	M27 9:15A									
M27 7:45P	M27 9:45P	T28 3:45A						T28 12:45P	T28 4:45P		T28 11:45P			W29 6:45A	
T28 3:30A	T28 7:00A	T28 1:30P				T28 10:30P		W29 2:00P	W29 5:30P		W29 11:55P				F31 10:00A
		T28 8:15A	T28 12:30P		T28 5:30P	T28 10:30P	W29 10:45A	W29 2:45P							
TH30 1:00P	TH30 5:15P	F31 1:15A						F31 10:00A	F31 2:00P		F31 10:30P			S1 5:45A	
		F31 2:15P	F31 6:30P	F31 10:45P	S1 2:00A	S1 7:00A									
F31 6:00P	F31 8:30P	S1 2:30A						S1 11:30A	S1 3:30P		S1 11:00P			SU2 6:00A	

ALL TIMES SHOWN ARE LOCAL TIMES

M/V AURORA Southern Panhandle Summer 1996

How To Use This Schedule

The M/V AURORA operates a daily schedule between Ketchikan, Metlakatla and Hollis (Gateway to Prince of Wales Island). There are several sailings to and from these communities each day. To determine the best one for your trip, use this table. Please allow enough time to make appropriate connections with the mainline sailings from Ketchikan (see tables above).

EFFECTIVE MAY 1 - SEPTEMBER 19

Sun	Lv Hollis	6:15AM
	Ar Ketchikan	9:00AM
	Lv Ketchikan	12:15PM
	Ar Metlakatla	1:30PM
	Lv Metlakatla	2:15PM
	Ar Ketchikan	3:30PM
	Lv Ketchikan	6:15PM
	Ar Hollis	9:00PM
Mon	Lv Hollis	6:15AM
	Ar Ketchikan	9:00AM
	Lv Ketchikan	12:15PM
	Ar Metlakatla	1:30PM
	Lv Metlakatla	2:15PM
	Ar Ketchikan	3:30PM
	Lv Ketchikan	6:15PM
	Ar Hollis	9:00PM
*Tue	Lv Hollis	9:15AM
	Ar Ketchikan	11:55AM
	Lv Ketchikan	6:15PM
	Ar Hollis	9:00PM
Wed	Lv Hollis	6:15AM
	Ar Ketchikan	9:00AM
	Lv Ketchikan	12:15PM
	Ar Metlakatla	1:30PM
	Lv Metlakatla	2:15PM
	Ar Ketchikan	3:30PM
	Lv Ketchikan	6:15PM
	Ar Hollis	9:00PM
Thu	Lv Hollis	9:15AM
	Ar Ketchikan	11:55AM
	Lv Ketchikan	6:15PM
	Ar Hollis	9:00PM
Fri	Lv Hollis	6:15AM
	Ar Ketchikan	9:00AM
	Lv Ketchikan	12:15PM
	Ar Metlakatla	1:30PM
	Lv Metlakatla	2:15PM
	Ar Ketchikan	3:30PM
	Lv Ketchikan	6:15PM
	Ar Hollis	9:00PM
	Lv Hollis	10:00PM
Sat	Ar Ketchikan	12:45AM
Sat	Lv Ketchikan	6:15AM
	Ar Metlakatla	7:30AM
	Lv Metlakatla	8:15AM
	Ar Ketchikan	9:30AM
	Lv Ketchikan	10:30AM
	Ar Hollis	1:15PM
	Lv Hollis	2:15PM
	Ar Ketchikan	5:00PM
	Lv Ketchikan	6:45PM
	Ar Metlakatla	8:00PM
	Lv Metlakatla	8:45PM
	Ar Ketchikan	10:00PM
	Lv Ketchikan	11:00PM
Sun	Ar Hollis	1:45AM

*TUESDAY - MAY 14, 21

Mon	Lv Hollis	10:00PM
Tue	Ar Ketchikan	12:45AM
	Lv Ketchikan	1:45AM
	Ar Stewart/Hyder	1:00PM
	Lv Stewart/Hyder	3:45PM
Wed	Ar Ketchikan	1:30AM
	Lv Ketchikan	2:30AM
Wed	Ar Hollis	5:15AM

RECORDED ARRIVAL / DEPARTURE INFORMATION

Southeast Alaska Offices

Bellingham ....(360) 676-8445
24-hour recorded info. ..(360) 676-0212
Prince Rupert ....(604) 627-1744
Ketchikan ....(907) 225-6181
Wrangell ....(907) 874-3711
Petersburg ....(907) 772-3855
Sitka ....(907) 747-3300
Juneau ....(907) 465-3940
Haines ....(907) 766-2113
Skagway ....(907) 983-2229

Southcentral / Southwest

Anchorage ....(907) 272-4482
Cordova ....(907) 424-7333
Homer ....(907) 235-8449
Kodiak ....(907) 486-3800
Seldovia ....(907) 234-7868
Seward ....(907) 224-5485
Valdez ....(907) 835-4436

June 1996 Northbound Schedule

LEAVE BELLINGHAM	LEAVE PRINCE RUPERT	LEAVE STEWART/HYDER	METLAKATLA	KETCHIKAN	HOLLIS	WRANGELL	PETERSBURG	KAKE	ARRIVE SITKA	ANGOON	TENAKEE	HOONAH	JUNEAU/ AUKE BAY	HAINES	ARRIVE SKAGWAY
	TH30 9:00P		SEE M/V AURORA SCHEDULE BELOW	F31 3:30A	SEE M/V AURORA SCHEDULE BELOW	F31 10:30A	F31 2:15P	F31 7:00P					S1 3:45A	S1 9:45A	S1 10:45A
	S1 8:30A			S1 3:00P		S1 9:45P	SU2 1:30A						SU2 10:45A	SU2 4:45P	SU2 5:45P
								Lv. Sitka	S1 9:30A	S1 3:45P	S1 7:00P	S1 11:45P	SU2 3:00A		
										Lv. Pelican	SU2 2:15P		SU2 9:00P		
	SU2 9:15A			SU2 3:45P									M3 10:45A	M3 4:15P	M3 5:15P
F31 6:30P				SU2 7:00A		SU2 12:45P	SU2 4:30P		M3 1:45A				M3 3:45P	M3 10:45P	M3 11:45P
	M3 8:30P			T4 3:30A		T4 10:30A	T4 2:15P						T4 11:00P	W5 4:30A	W5 5:30A
								Lv. Sitka	M3 11:15P	T4 5:15A		T4 10:15A	W5 2:30A	W5 8:00A	W5 9:00A
	T4 11:30A			T4 7:30P		W5 2:30A	W5 6:30A		W5 4:30P				TH6 5:30A	TH6 11:30A	TH6 12:30P
		T4 3:45P		W5 1:30A				Lv. Sitka	TH6 1:30P	TH6 7:30P	TH6 10:45P	F7 3:00A	F7 6:15A		
	W5 11:45A			W5 6:15P		TH6 1:15A	TH6 6:00A		TH6 5:15P				F7 7:30A	F7 1:00P	F7 2:00P
	TH6 9:00P			F7 4:45A		F7 11:30A	F7 4:30P	F7 9:30P					S8 5:45A	S8 11:15A	S8 12:15P
								Lv. Sitka	S8 3:30P	S8 9:45P	SU9 1:00A	SU9 5:45A	SU9 9:00A		
	S8 8:30A			S8 3:00P		S8 9:45P	SU9 1:30A						SU9 10:45A	SU9 4:45P	SU9 5:45P
	SU9 9:15A			SU9 3:15P									M10 10:15A	M10 3:45P	M10 4:45P
F7 6:30P				SU9 8:00A		SU9 2:00P	SU9 5:45P		M10 3:00A				M10 4:30P	M10 11:30P	T11 12:30A
							M10 6:00P		T11 4:00A	T11 12:30P		T11 5:30P	W12 9:45A	W12 3:15P	W12 4:15P
	M10 8:30P			T11 2:45A		T11 9:30A	T11 1:15P						T11 10:00P	W12 3:30A	W12 4:30A
	T11 11:30A			T11 5:30P		W12 12:15A	W12 4:00A		W12 2:00P				TH13 4:30A	TH13 11:00A	TH13 11:55A
								Lv. Sitka	TH13 8:30P	F14 2:15A	F14 5:30A	F14 9:45A	F14 1:00P		
	W12 10:30A			W12 4:30P		W12 11:15P	TH13 4:00A		TH13 6:00P				F14 8:00A	F14 2:00P	F14 3:00P
	TH13 9:00P			F14 3:30A		F14 10:30A	F14 2:30P	F14 7:30P					S15 2:45A		
								Lv. Sitka	S15 9:45A	S15 4:00P	S15 7:15P	S15 11:55P	SU16 3:15A		
	S15 8:30A			S15 3:00P		S15 9:45P	SU16 1:30A						SU16 10:15A		SU16 3:15P
										Lv. Pelican	SU16 2:00P		SU16 8:45P		
													M17 12:45A	M17 6:15A	M17 7:15A
F14 6:30P				SU16 7:00A		SU16 12:45P	SU16 4:30P		M17 1:45A				M17 3:45P	M17 10:45P	M17 11:45P
	SU16 8:00P			M17 2:30A		M17 9:15A	M17 1:00P						M17 8:45P		
	M17 12:30P			M17 7:00P		T18 1:45A	T18 6:30A						T18 4:30P	T18 10:30P	T18 11:30P
		T18 3:45P		W19 1:30A				Lv. Sitka	M17 11:00P	T18 5:00A		T18 10:00A	W19 2:15A	W19 7:45A	W19 8:45A
	T18 9:30P			W19 3:30A		W19 10:15A	W19 2:00P						W19 11:45P	TH20 6:15A	TH20 7:15A
	W19 7:30A			W19 2:00P		W19 9:00P	TH20 1:00A	TH20 6:00A					TH20 2:15P	TH20 7:45P	TH20 8:45P
													F21 3:45A	F21 9:15A	F21 10:15A
								Lv. Sitka	TH20 12:45P	TH20 6:30P	TH20 9:45P	F21 2:00A	F21 5:15A		
	TH20 4:30P			TH20 11:00P		F21 5:45A	F21 12:15P		F21 11:15P				S22 12:30P	S22 6:00P	S22 7:00P
								Lv. Sitka	S22 1:30P	S22 8:00P	S22 11:15P	SU23 3:30A	SU23 6:45A		
	S22 8:30A			S22 3:00P		S22 9:45P	SU23 1:30A						SU23 10:15A		SU23 3:15P
													M24 12:45A	M24 6:15A	M24 7:15A
F21 6:00P				SU23 6:30A		SU23 12:15P	SU23 4:00P		M24 1:15A				M24 2:30P	M24 9:30P	M24 10:30P
	SU23 8:45P			M24 2:45A		M24 9:30A	M24 1:15P						M24 9:00P		
	M24 12:30P			M24 7:00P		T25 1:45A	T25 6:30A						T25 4:30P	T25 10:30P	T25 11:30P
							T25 4:30A		T25 2:30P	T25 11:55P		W26 5:00A	W26 10:15A	W26 3:45P	W26 4:45P
	T25 9:30P			W26 3:30A		W26 10:15A	W26 2:00P						TH27 12:45A	TH27 7:15A	TH27 8:15A
	W26 8:00A			W26 2:30P		W26 9:15P	TH27 1:00A	TH27 6:00A					TH27 2:15P	TH27 7:45P	TH27 8:45P
													F28 4:15A	F28 9:45A	F28 10:45A
								Lv. Sitka	TH27 7:00P	F28 12:45A	F28 4:00A	F28 8:15A	F28 11:30A		
	TH27 4:30P			TH27 11:00P		F28 6:00A	F28 11:00A		F28 11:30P				S29 1:15P	S29 6:45P	S29 7:45P
								Lv. Sitka	S29 8:30A	S29 2:30P	S29 5:45P	S29 10:30P	SU30 1:45A		
	S29 8:30A			S29 3:00P		S29 9:45P	SU30 1:30A						SU30 10:15A		SU30 3:15P
										Lv. Pelican	SU30 3:15P		SU30 10:00P		
F28 6:00P				SU30 6:15A		SU30 11:55A	SU30 3:45P		M1 1:00A				M1 2:45P	M1 9:45P	M1 10:45P
	SU30 9:00P			M1 3:00A		M1 9:45A	M1 1:30P						M1 9:15P		

RUNNING TIME TABLE

INSIDE PASSAGE ROUTE:

Bellingham — Ketchikan	37 hrs.
Prince Rupert — Ketchikan	6 hrs.
Stewart/Hyder — Ketchikan	9 hrs. 45 min.
Ketchikan — Wrangell	6 hrs.
Wrangell — Petersburg	3 hrs.
Petersburg — Sitka	10 hrs.
Petersburg — Juneau/Auke Bay	8 hrs.
Sitka — Juneau/Auke Bay	8 hrs. 45 min.
Juneau/Auke Bay — Haines	4 hrs. 30 min.
Haines — Skagway	1 hr.

SOUTHCENTRAL ROUTE:

Whittier — Valdez	6 hrs. 45 min.
Valdez — Cordova	5 hrs. 30 min.
Cordova — Whittier	7 hrs.
Cordova — Seward	11 hrs.
Valdez — Seward	11 hrs.
Homer — Seldovia	1 hr. 30 min.

SOUTHCENTRAL/SOUTHWEST ROUTE CONNECTIONS:

Homer — Kodiak	9 hrs. 30 min.
Homer — Port Lions	10 hrs.
Seward — Kodiak	13 hrs. 15 min.

SOUTHWEST ROUTES:

Kodiak — Port Lions	2 hrs. 30 min.
Kodiak — Chignik	18 hrs. 30 min.
Chignik — Sand Point	9 hrs. 15 min.
Sand Point — King Cove	6 hrs. 30 min.
King Cove — Cold Bay	2 hrs.
Cold Bay — False Pass	4 hrs. 15 min.
False Pass — Akutan	10 hrs. 30 min.
Akutan — Unalaska	3 hrs. 30 min.

For more accurate arrival times, please contact the local Marine Highway office on the day of arrival.

(Continued from page 609)
ver Island from Washington. If you are traveling with a vehicle, you can take the Washington state ferry from Anacortes, WA, to Sidney, BC (near Victoria), cruising through the San Juan Islands; or you can take the MV *Coho* from Port Angeles, WA, to Victoria. Reservations are not accepted for passengers or vehicles on either service. Anacortes is 85 miles/137 km north of Seattle, WA, via Interstate 5. Port Angeles is about 2 hours west of Seattle by ferry and highway. The Anacortes crossing to Sidney is approximately 3 hours. The Port Angeles crossing is $1^1/_2$ hours. For the Washington state ferries, phone (206) 464-6400 in Seattle or 1-800-843-3779 state-wide. For the MV *Coho*, contact Black Ball Transport, 430 Belleville St., Victoria, BC V8V 1W9; phone (206) 622-2222 in the Seattle area, (360) 457-4491 in Port Angeles, or (604) 386-2202 in Victoria.

Passenger-only service between Seattle
(Continues on page 614)

Aurora | Columbia | Le Conte | Malaspina | Matanuska | Taku

June 1996 Southbound Schedule

LEAVE SKAGWAY	HAINES	JUNEAU/ AUKE BAY	HOONAH	TENAKEE	ANGOON	ARRIVE SITKA	KAKE	PETERSBURG	WRANGELL	HOLLIS	KETCHIKAN	METLAKATLA	ARRIVE STEWART/HYDER	ARRIVE PRINCE RUPERT	ARRIVE BELLINGHAM
										SEE M/V AURORA SCHEDULE BELOW		SEE M/V AURORA SCHEDULE BELOW			
F31 6:00P	F31 8:30P	S1 2:30A						S1 11:30A	S1 3:30P		S1 11:00P			SU2 6:00A	
S1 1:45P	S1 4:15P	S1 10:15P				SU2 7:45A	SU2 7:45P	M3 12:30A	M3 4:15A		M3 11:15A			M3 6:15P	
SU2 8:45P	SU2 11:15P	M3 5:15A						M3 1:45P	M3 5:30P		T4 1:15A			T4 8:30A	
		SU2 6:00A	Ar. Pelican	SU2 12:45P							T4 1:45A		T4 1:00P		
		SU2 10:00P	M3 2:15A	M3 6:30A	M3 9:45A	M3 2:45P									
M3 8:15P	M3 10:15P	T4 4:15A						T4 1:15P	T4 5:30P		W5 1:30A			W5 8:30A	
T4 2:45A	T4 6:15A	T4 12:30P				T4 9:00P		W5 2:00P	W5 5:30P		W5 11:55P				F7 10:00A
W5 8:30A	W5 10:30A	W5 4:00P						TH6 12:45A	TH6 4:30A		TH6 11:55A			TH6 7:00P	
W5 10:30A	W5 12:30P	W5 8:15P	TH6 1:00A		TH6 6:00A	TH6 11:00A									
TH6 3:30P	TH6 6:00P	TH6 11:55P						F7 8:45A	F7 12:45P		F7 9:45P			S8 5:30A	
		F7 2:15P	F7 6:30P	F7 10:45P	S8 2:00A	S8 7:00A									
F7 5:00P	F7 7:00P	S8 1:00A						S8 10:00A	S8 2:15P		S8 11:00P			SU9 6:00A	
S8 3:15P	S8 5:15P	S8 11:15P				SU9 8:00A	SU9 8:00P	M10 12:45A	M10 4:30A		M10 11:30A			M10 6:30P	
		SU9 10:00A	SU9 2:15P	SU9 6:30P	SU9 9:45P	M10 2:45A		M10 3:45P							
SU9 8:45P	SU9 11:15P	M10 5:15A						M10 1:45P	M10 5:30P		T11 1:15A			T11 8:30A	
M10 7:45P	M10 9:45P	T11 3:15A						T11 12:15P	T11 4:30P		W12 12:30A			W12 7:30A	
T11 3:30A	T11 7:00A	T11 1:30P				T11 10:15P		W12 1:00P	W12 5:00P		W12 11:55P				F14 10:00A
W12 5:45P	W12 7:45P	TH13 3:15A	TH13 8:00A		TH13 1:00P	TH13 6:00P									
W12 7:15A	W12 9:15A	W12 2:45P						W12 11:30P	TH13 3:30A		TH13 11:00A			TH13 6:00P	
TH13 3:00P	TH13 6:00P	F14 1:30A						F14 10:00A	F14 1:45P		F14 10:15P			S15 5:30A	
		F14 2:30P	F14 6:45P	F14 11:00P	S15 2:15A	S15 7:15A									
F14 6:00P	F14 8:30P	S15 3:15A				S15 1:30P		SU16 11:30A	SU16 3:45P		SU16 11:45P			M17 6:45A	
		S15 3:45A					S15 11:55A	S15 4:45P	S15 8:30P		SU16 4:00A			SU16 11:00A	
		SU16 5:45A	Ar. Pelican	SU16 12:30P											
SU16 4:45P	SU16 6:45P	SU16 11:15P													
		SU16 9:45P	M17 2:00A	M17 6:15A	M17 9:30A	M17 2:30P					T18 1:45A		T18 1:00P		
M17 10:15A	M17 12:15P	M17 6:15P						T18 2:45A			T18 11:30A			T18 6:30P	
T18 2:45A	T18 6:15A	T18 12:45P				T18 9:15P		W19 1:00P	W19 4:30P		W19 11:00P				F21 10:00A
		M17 10:45P					T18 7:00A	T18 11:45A	T18 3:30P		T18 10:30P			W19 5:30A	
W19 2:30A	W19 4:30A	W19 10:00A						W19 7:00P	W19 11:00P		TH20 6:30A			TH20 1:30P	
W19 10:15A	W19 12:15P	W19 7:30P	TH20 12:15A		TH20 5:15A	TH20 10:15A									
TH20 11:15A	TH20 2:15P	TH20 10:45P						F21 7:30A	F21 11:30A		F21 8:30P			S22 5:30A	
TH20 9:45P		F21 2:45A													
F21 1:00P	F21 3:00P	F21 8:30P				S22 5:15A	S22 5:15P	S22 10:15P	SU23 2:15A		SU23 10:30A			SU23 5:30P	
		F21 11:45A	F21 4:30P	F21 8:45P	F21 11:55P	S22 5:00A									
S22 10:00P	S22 11:55P	SU23 5:30A						SU23 2:30P	SU23 6:30P		M24 1:30A			M24 8:45A	
		SU23 2:15P	SU23 6:30P	SU23 10:45P	M24 2:00A	M24 7:00A		T25 3:00A							
SU23 4:45P	SU23 6:45P	SU23 11:15P													
M24 10:15A	M24 12:15P	M24 6:15P						T25 2:45A			T25 11:30A			T25 6:30P	
T25 1:30A	T25 5:00A	T25 11:30A				T25 8:15P		W26 10:00A	W26 2:00P		W26 9:30P				F28 10:00A
		M24 10:45P					T25 7:00A	T25 11:45A	T25 3:30P		T25 10:30P			W26 5:30A	
W26 2:30A	W26 4:30A	W26 10:00A						W26 7:00P	W26 11:00P		TH27 6:30A			TH27 1:30P	
W26 6:15P	W26 8:15P	TH27 2:00A	TH27 6:15A		TH27 11:15A	TH27 4:30P									
TH27 12:15P	TH27 3:15P	TH27 11:45P						F28 8:45A	F28 12:45P		F28 9:45P			S29 5:30A	
TH27 9:45P		F28 2:45A													
F28 1:45P	F28 3:45P	F28 9:15P				S29 6:00A	S29 6:00P	S29 10:45P	SU30 2:30A		SU30 10:30A			SU30 5:30P	
		F28 1:15P	F28 5:30P	F28 9:45P	S29 1:00A	S29 6:00A									
S29 10:15P	SU30 12:15A	SU30 5:45A						SU30 2:45P	SU30 7:00P		M1 2:00A			M1 9:00A	
		SU30 7:00A	Ar. Pelican	SU30 1:45P											
SU30 4:45P	SU30 6:45P	SU30 11:15P													

ALL TIMES SHOWN ARE LOCAL TIMES

M/V AURORA Southern Panhandle Summer 1996

How To Use This Schedule

The M/V AURORA operates a daily schedule between Ketchikan, Metlakatla and Hollis (Gateway to Prince of Wales Island). There are several sailings to and from these communities each day. To determine the best one for your trip, use this table. Please allow enough time to make appropriate connections with the mainline sailings from Ketchikan (see tables above).

EFFECTIVE MAY 1 - SEPTEMBER 19

Sun	Lv Hollis	6:15AM
	Ar Ketchikan	9:00AM
	Lv Ketchikan	12:15PM
	Ar Metlakatla	1:30PM
	Lv Metlakatla	2:15PM
	Ar Ketchikan	3:30PM
	Lv Ketchikan	6:15PM
	Ar Hollis	9:00PM
Mon	Lv Hollis	6:15AM
	Ar Ketchikan	9:00AM
	Lv Ketchikan	12:15PM
	Ar Metlakatla	1:30PM
	Lv Metlakatla	2:15PM
	Ar Ketchikan	3:30PM
	Lv Ketchikan	6:15PM
	Ar Hollis	9:00PM
*Tue	Lv Hollis	9:15AM
	Ar Ketchikan	11:55AM
	Lv Ketchikan	6:15PM
	Ar Hollis	9:00PM
Wed	Lv Hollis	6:15AM
	Ar Ketchikan	9:00AM
	Lv Ketchikan	12:15PM
	Ar Metlakatla	1:30PM
	Lv Metlakatla	2:15PM
	Ar Ketchikan	3:30PM
	Lv Ketchikan	6:15PM
	Ar Hollis	9:00PM
Thu	Lv Hollis	9:15AM
	Ar Ketchikan	11:55AM
	Lv Ketchikan	6:15PM
	Ar Hollis	9:00PM
Fri	Lv Hollis	6:15AM
	Ar Ketchikan	9:00AM
	Lv Ketchikan	12:15PM
	Ar Metlakatla	1:30PM
	Lv Metlakatla	:15PM
	Ar Ketchikan	:30PM
	Lv Ketchikan	6:15PM
	Ar Hollis	9:00PM
	Lv Hollis	10:00PM
Sat	Ar Ketchikan	12:45AM
Sat	Lv Ketchikan	6:15AM
	Ar Metlakatla	7:30AM
	Lv Metlakatla	8:15AM
	Ar Ketchikan	9:30AM
	Lv Ketchikan	10:30AM
	Ar Hollis	1:15PM
	Lv Hollis	2:15PM
	Ar Ketchikan	5:00PM
	Lv Ketchikan	6:45PM
	Ar Metlakatla	8:00PM
	Lv Metlakatla	8:45PM
	Ar Ketchikan	10:00PM
	Lv Ketchikan	11:00PM
Sun	Ar Hollis	1:45AM

*TUESDAY - JUN 4, 18

Mon	Lv Hollis	10:00PM
Tue	Ar Ketchikan	12:45AM
	Lv Ketchikan	1:45AM
	Ar Stewart/Hyder	1:00PM
	Lv Stewart/Hyder	3:45PM
Wed	Ar Ketchikan	1:30AM
	Lv Ketchikan	2:30AM
Wed	Ar Hollis	5:15AM

July 1996 Northbound Schedule

SEE M/V AURORA SCHEDULE BELOW (Metlakatla and Hollis)

LEAVE BELLINGHAM	LEAVE PRINCE RUPERT	LEAVE STEWART/HYDER	METLAKATLA	KETCHIKAN	HOLLIS	WRANGELL	PETERSBURG	KAKE	ARRIVE SITKA	ANGOON	TENAKEE	HOONAH	JUNEAU/ AUKE BAY	HAINES	ARRIVE SKAGWAY
													M1 12:45A	M1 6:15A	M1 7:15A
F28 6:00P				SU30 6:15A		SU30 11:55A	SU30 3:45P		M1 1:00A				M1 2:45P	M1 9:45P	M1 10:45P
	SU30 9:00P			M1 3:00A		M1 9:45A	M1 1:30P						M1 9:15P		
	M1 12:30P			M1 7:00P		T2 1:45A	T2 6:30A						T2 4:30P	T2 10:30P	T2 11:30P
		T2 3:45P		W3 1:30A				Lv. Sitka	M1 10:30P	T2 4:30A		T2 9:30A	W3 2:15A	W3 7:45A	W3 8:45A
	T2 9:30P			W3 3:30A		W3 10:15A	W3 2:00P						TH4 12:45A	TH4 7:15A	TH4 8:15A
	W3 8:00A			W3 2:30P		W3 9:15P	TH4 1:00A	TH4 6:00A					TH4 2:15P	TH4 7:45P	TH4 8:45P
													F5 4:00A	F5 9:30A	F5 10:30A
								Lv. Sitka	TH4 12:45P	TH4 6:30P	TH4 9:45P	F5 2:00A	F5 5:15A		
	TH4 4:00P			TH4 10:00P		F5 5:00A	F5 12:45P		F5 11:15P				S6 12:45P	S6 6:15P	S6 7:15P
								Lv. Sitka	S6 1:45P	S6 8:30P	S6 11:45P	SU7 4:00A	SU7 7:15A		
	S6 8:30A			S6 4:30P		S6 11:30P	SU7 3:15A						SU7 11:55A		SU7 5:00P
													M8 2:30A	M8 8:00A	M8 9:00A
F5 6:30P				SU7 6:30A		SU7 12:15P	SU7 4:00P		M8 1:15A				M8 2:45P	M8 9:45P	M8 10:45P
	SU7 9:00P			M8 3:00A		M8 9:45A	M8 1:30P						M8 9:15P		
	M8 12:30P			M8 7:00P		T9 1:45A	T9 6:30A						T9 4:30P	T9 10:30P	T9 11:30P
							M8 10:45P		T9 8:45A	T9 6:30P		T9 11:55P	W10 4:15A	W10 9:45A	W10 10:45A
	T9 10:30P			W10 4:30A		W10 11:15A	W10 3:00P						TH11 1:45A	TH11 8:15A	TH11 9:15A
	W10 8:00A			W10 2:30P		W10 9:15P	TH11 1:00A	TH11 6:00A					TH11 2:15P	TH11 7:45P	TH11 8:45P
													F12 4:15A	F12 9:45A	F12 10:45A
								Lv. Sitka	TH11 1:15P	TH11 7:00P	TH11 10:15P	F12 3:00A	F12 6:15A		
	TH11 6:00P			F12 1:00A		F12 8:00A	F12 1:00P		F12 11:45P				S13 1:30P	S13 7:00P	S13 8:00P
								Lv. Sitka	S13 8:45A	S13 3:00P	S13 6:15P	S13 11:00P	SU14 2:15A		
	S13 8:30A			S13 3:00P		S13 9:45P	SU14 1:30A						SU14 10:15A		SU14 3:15P
										Lv. Pelican	SU14 3:15P		SU14 10:00P		
													M15 12:45A	M15 6:15A	M15 7:15A
F12 6:00P				SU14 6:30A		SU14 12:15P	SU14 4:00P		M15 1:15A				M15 2:30P	M15 9:30P	M15 10:30P
	SU14 9:30P			M15 3:30A		M15 10:15A	M15 2:00P						M15 9:45P		
	M15 12:30P			M15 7:00P		T16 1:45A	T16 6:30A						T16 4:00P	T16 10:00P	T16 11:00P
		T16 3:45P		W17 1:30A				Lv. Sitka	M15 10:15P	T16 4:15A		T16 9:15A	W17 2:00A	W17 7:30A	W17 8:30A
	T16 9:30P			W17 3:30A		W17 10:15A	W17 2:00P						TH18 12:45A	TH18 7:15A	TH18 8:15A
	W17 8:00A			W17 2:00P		W17 8:45P	TH18 12:30A	TH18 5:15A					TH18 1:30P	TH18 7:00P	TH18 8:00P
													F19 3:00A	F19 8:30A	F19 9:30A
								Lv. Sitka	TH18 11:55A	TH18 5:45P	TH18 9:00P	F19 1:15A	F19 4:30A		
	TH18 3:30P			TH18 9:30P		F19 4:15A	F19 9:15A		F19 10:00P				S20 11:15A	S20 4:45P	S20 5:45P
								Lv. Sitka	S20 12:30P	S20 7:00P	S20 10:15P	SU21 2:30A	SU21 5:45A		
	S20 8:30A			S20 3:00P		S20 9:45P	SU21 1:30A						SU21 10:15A		SU21 3:15P
													M22 12:45A	M22 6:15A	M22 7:15A
F19 6:30P				SU21 8:30A		SU21 2:30P	SU21 6:30P		M22 5:00A				M22 6:45P	T23 1:45A	T23 2:45A
	SU21 6:00P			SU21 11:55P		M22 7:30A	M22 11:55A						M22 7:45P		
	M22 12:30P			M22 7:00P		T23 1:45A	T23 6:30A						T23 4:00P	T23 9:30P	T23 10:30P
							M22 8:15P		T23 6:15A	T23 4:00P		T23 9:30P	W24 1:45A	W24 7:15A	W24 8:15A
	T23 9:30P			W24 3:30A		W24 10:15A	W24 2:00P						TH25 12:45A	TH25 7:15A	TH25 8:15A
	W24 8:00A			W24 2:00P		W24 8:45P	TH25 12:30A	TH25 5:15A					TH25 1:30P	TH25 7:00P	TH25 8:00P
													F26 3:00A	F26 8:30A	F26 9:30A
								Lv. Sitka	TH25 11:15A	TH25 5:15P	TH25 8:30P	F26 1:15A	F26 4:30A		
	TH25 6:00P			F26 1:00A		F26 7:45A	F26 12:30P		F26 10:15P				S27 11:45A	S27 5:15P	S27 6:15P
								Lv. Sitka	S27 7:15A	S27 1:30P	S27 4:45P	S27 9:30P	SU28 12:45A		
	S27 8:30A			S27 3:00P		S27 9:45P	SU28 1:30A						SU28 10:15A		SU28 3:15P
										Lv. Pelican	SU28 3:15P		SU28 10:00P		
													M29 12:45A	M29 6:15A	M29 7:15A
F26 6:30P				SU28 8:30A		SU28 2:30P	SU28 6:30P		M29 5:15A				M29 7:00P	T30 2:00A	T30 3:00A
	SU28 6:30P			M29 12:30A		M29 7:15A	M29 11:55A						M29 7:45P		
	M29 11:00A			M29 5:30P		T30 12:15A	T30 5:00A						T30 3:00P	T30 9:00P	T30 10:00P
		T30 3:45P		W31 1:30A				Lv. Sitka	M29 9:30P	T30 3:30A		T30 8:30A	W31 1:15A	W31 6:45A	W31 7:45A
	T30 9:30P			W31 3:30A		W31 10:15A	W31 2:00P						TH1 12:45A	TH1 7:15A	TH1 8:15A
	W31 8:00A			W31 2:00P		W31 8:45P	TH1 12:30A	TH1 5:15A					TH1 1:30P	TH1 7:00P	TH1 8:00P

SEE M/V AURORA SCHEDULE BELOW

(Continued from page 612)
and Victoria is available on the *Victoria Clipper* ferry daily from Pier 69. The cruise takes 2½ hours. For schedules and fares, contact Victoria Clipper, 2701 Alaskan Way, Pier 69, Seattle, WA 98121; phone (206) 448-5000.

Between May and September, round-trip passenger and vehicle service between Seattle and Victoria are offered on the Victoria Line's *Royal Victorian*. Phone 1-800-668-1167 for recorded message, (206) 625-1880 in Seattle or (604) 480-5555 in Victoria for reservation information.

Bus service is available between Vancouver and Victoria, from Pacific Coach Lines, 150 Dunsmuir St., Vancouver; phone (604) 662-8074. Bus service between Victoria and Port Hardy is provided by Island Coach Lines, 700 Douglas St., Victoria, BC V8W 2B3; phone (604) 388-5248. Canadian Regional Airlines, Orca Air and Pacific Coastal Airlines have scheduled air service to Port Hardy.

Alaska State Ferries

The main office of the Alaska Marine Highway is in Juneau. Write P.O. Box 25535, Juneau, AK 99802-5535; phone toll free 1-800-642-0066, fax (907) 277-4829, TDD 1-800-764-3779. Local reservation numbers in Juneau (907/465-3941) and in Anchorage (907/272-7116).

The Alaska State Ferry System is divided into 2 different systems serving 2 different areas: Southeast and Southcentral/Southwest. These 2 systems *DO NOT* connect.

If you are headed for Alaska from Bellingham, WA, or Prince Rupert, BC, via the Alaska Marine Highway, you'll take the Southeast system, which stops at mainline Southeast Alaska port cities from Ketchikan to Skagway. Keep in mind that only 2 major Southeast communities are connected to the Alaska Highway: Haines, via the Haines Highway; and Skagway, via Klondike Highway 2. (See the HAINES HIGHWAY and KLONDIKE HIGHWAY 2 sections.) Stewart/Hyder is also accessible via the Stewart–Cassiar Highway. From May through Sept., the Southeast system also includes feeder service between Ketchikan and Stewart/ Hyder; Ketchikan and Hollis; Ketchikan and Metlakatla; and Juneau and Pelican. Other Southeast

(Continues on page 616)

Aurora Columbia Le Conte Malaspina Matanuska Taku

July 1996 Southbound Schedule

LEAVE SKAGWAY	HAINES	JUNEAU/ AUKE BAY	HOONAH	TENAKEE	ANGOON	ARRIVE SITKA	KAKE	PETERSBURG	WRANGELL	HOLLIS	KETCHIKAN	METLAKATLA	ARRIVE STEWART/HYDER	ARRIVE PRINCE RUPERT	ARRIVE BELLINGHAM
		M1 3:15A	M1 7:30A	M1 11:45A	M1 3:00P	M1 8:00P				SEE M/V AURORA SCHEDULE BELOW	T2 1:45A	SEE M/V AURORA SCHEDULE BELOW	T2 1:00P		
M1 10:15A	M1 12:15P	M1 6:15P						T2 2:45A			T2 11:30A			T2 6:30P	
T2 1:45A	T2 5:15A	T2 11:45A				T2 8:30P		W3 1:00P	W3 4:30P		W3 11:00P				F5 10:00A
		M1 10:45P					T2 7:15A	T2 11:55A	T2 3:45P		T2 10:45P			W3 5:45A	
W3 2:30A	W3 4:30A	W3 10:00A						W3 7:00P	W3 11:00P		TH4 6:00A			TH4 1:00P	
W3 10:15A	W3 12:15P	W3 7:15P	W3 11:55P		TH4 5:00A	TH4 10:00A									
TH4 11:15A	TH4 2:15P	TH4 10:45P						F5 7:30A	F5 11:30A		F5 8:30P			S6 5:30A	
TH4 9:45P		F5 2:45A													
F5 1:15P	F5 3:15P	F5 8:45P				S6 5:30A	S6 5:30P	S6 10:15P	SU7 2:00A		SU7 11:00A			SU7 6:00P	
		F5 11:55A	F5 4:45P	F5 9:00P	S6 12:15A	S6 5:15A									
S6 10:15P	SU7 12:15A	SU7 6:00A						SU7 3:00P	SU7 7:00P		M8 2:00A			M8 9:00A	
		SU7 2:45P	SU7 7:00P	SU7 11:15P	M8 2:30A	M8 7:30A		M8 8:15P							
SU7 6:30P	SU7 8:30P	M8 1:00A													
M8 11:55A	M8 2:00P	M8 8:00P						T9 4:30A			T9 1:00P			T9 8:00P	
T9 1:45A	T9 5:15A	T9 11:45A				T9 8:45P		W10 10:15A	W10 2:00P		W10 9:00P				F12 10:00A
		M8 11:15P					T9 7:30A	T9 12:30P	T9 4:15P		T9 11:15P			W10 6:15A	
W10 2:30A	W10 5:00A	W10 11:30A						W10 8:30P	TH11 12:30A		TH11 8:00A			TH11 3:00P	
W10 12:15P	W10 2:15P	W10 8:15P	TH11 12:30A		TH11 5:30A	TH11 10:45A									
TH11 12:15P	TH11 3:45P	F12 12:15A						F12 9:00A	F12 1:00P		F12 10:00P			S13 5:30A	
TH11 9:45P		F12 2:45A													
F12 1:45P	F12 3:45P	F12 9:30P				S13 6:15A	S13 6:15P	S13 11:00P	SU14 3:00A		SU14 11:00A			SU14 6:00P	
		F12 1:30P	F12 5:45P	F12 10:00P	S13 1:15A	S13 6:15A									
S13 10:30P	SU14 12:30A	SU14 6:00A						SU14 3:00P	SU14 7:00P		M15 2:30A			M15 9:30A	
		SU14 7:00A	Ar. Pelican	SU14 1:45P											
SU14 4:45P	SU14 6:45P	SU14 11:15P													
		M15 2:45A	M15 7:00A	M15 11:15A	M15 2:30P	M15 7:45P					T16 1:45A		T16 1:00P		
M15 10:15A	M15 12:15P	M15 6:15P						T16 2:45A			T16 11:30A			T16 6:30P	
T16 1:30A	T16 5:00A	T16 11:30A				T16 8:15P		W17 12:15P	W17 4:00P		W17 11:00P				F19 10:00A
		M15 11:15P					T16 7:30A	T16 12:15P	T16 4:00P		T16 11:00P			W17 6:00A	
W17 2:00A	W17 4:00A	W17 9:30A						W17 6:30P	W17 10:30P		TH18 5:30A			TH18 12:30P	
W17 10:00A	W17 11:55A	W17 6:30P	W17 11:15P		TH18 4:15A	TH18 9:15A									
TH18 11:15A	TH18 2:15P	TH18 9:45P						F19 6:30A	F19 10:30A		F19 8:30P			S20 5:30A	
TH18 9:00P		F19 2:00A													
F19 11:55A	F19 2:00P	F19 7:30P				S20 4:15A	S20 4:00P	S20 9:00P	SU21 1:00A		SU21 8:00A			SU21 3:00P	
		F19 10:45A	F19 3:30P	F19 7:45P	F19 11:00P	S20 4:00A									
S20 8:45P	S20 11:15P	SU21 5:15A						SU21 2:15P	SU21 6:30P		M22 2:00A			M22 9:00A	
		SU21 12:30P	SU21 4:45P	SU21 9:00P	M22 12:15A	M22 5:15A		M22 6:00P							
SU21 4:45P	SU21 6:45P	SU21 11:15P													
M22 10:15A	M22 12:15P	M22 6:15P						T23 2:45A			T23 11:30A			T23 6:30P	
T23 5:45A	T23 9:15A	T23 3:45P				W24 1:00A		W24 3:00P	W24 6:30P		TH25 12:30A				F26 10:30A
		M22 10:15P					T23 6:30A	T23 11:30A	T23 3:15P		T23 10:30P			W24 5:30A	
W24 1:30A	W24 3:30A	W24 9:30A						W24 6:45P	W24 11:00P		TH25 7:15A			TH25 2:15P	
W24 9:45A	W24 11:45A	W24 6:30P	W24 10:45P		TH25 3:45A	TH25 8:45A									
TH25 11:15A	TH25 2:15P	TH25 10:15P						F26 7:00A	F26 11:00A		F26 8:30P			S27 5:30A	
TH25 9:00P		F26 2:00A													
F26 12:30P	F26 2:30P	F26 8:00P				S27 4:45A	S27 4:45P	S27 9:45P	SU28 1:30A		SU28 9:30A			SU28 4:30P	
		F26 11:45A	F26 4:00P	F26 8:15P	F26 11:30P	S27 4:45A									
S27 9:15P	S27 11:15P	SU28 4:45A						SU28 1:45P	SU28 5:45P		M29 1:30A			M29 8:30A	
		SU28 7:00A	Ar. Pelican	SU28 1:45P											
SU28 4:45P	SU28 6:45P	SU28 11:15P													
		M29 2:15A	M29 6:30A	M29 10:45A	M29 2:00P	M29 7:00P									
M29 10:15A	M29 12:15P	M29 6:15P						T30 2:45A			T30 11:30A			T30 6:30P	
T30 6:00A	T30 9:30A	T30 4:00P				W31 1:30A		W31 3:00P	W31 6:30P		TH1 1:00A				F2 11:00A
		M29 10:00P					T30 6:15A	T30 11:00A	T30 3:00P		T30 10:30P			W31 5:30A	
W31 1:00A	W31 3:00A	W31 8:30A						W31 5:30P	W31 9:30P		TH1 4:30A			TH1 11:30A	
W31 9:15A	W31 11:15A	W31 6:00P	W31 10:45P		TH1 3:45A	TH1 8:45A									

M/V AURORA Southern Panhandle Summer 1996

How To Use This Schedule

The M/V AURORA operates a daily schedule between Ketchikan, Metlakatla and Hollis (Gateway to Prince of Wales Island). There are several sailings to and from these communities each day. To determine the best one for your trip, use this table. Please allow enough time to make appropriate connections with the mainline sailings from Ketchikan (see tables above).

EFFECTIVE MAY 1 - SEPTEMBER 19

**Sun	Lv Hollis	6:15AM
	Ar Ketchikan	9:00AM
	Lv Ketchikan	12:15PM
	Ar Metlakatla	1:30PM
	Lv Metlakatla	2:15PM
	Ar Ketchikan	3:30PM
	Lv Ketchikan	6:15PM
	Ar Hollis	9:00PM
Mon	Lv Hollis	6:15AM
	Ar Ketchikan	9:00AM
	Lv Ketchikan	12:15PM
	Ar Metlakatla	1:30PM
	Lv Metlakatla	2:15PM
	Ar Ketchikan	3:30PM
	Lv Ketchikan	6:15PM
	Ar Hollis	9:00PM
*Tue	Lv Hollis	9:15AM
	Ar Ketchikan	11:55AM
	Lv Ketchikan	6:15PM
	Ar Hollis	9:00PM
Wed	Lv Hollis	6:15AM
	Ar Ketchikan	9:00AM
	Lv Ketchikan	12:15PM
	Ar Metlakatla	1:30PM
	Lv Metlakatla	2:15PM
	Ar Ketchikan	3:30PM
	Lv Ketchikan	6:15PM
	Ar Hollis	9:00PM
Thu	Lv Hollis	9:15AM
	Ar Ketchikan	11:55AM
	Lv Ketchikan	6:15PM
	Ar Hollis	9:00PM
Fri	Lv Hollis	6:15AM
	Ar Ketchikan	9:00AM
	Lv Ketchikan	12:15PM
	Ar Metlakatla	1:30PM
	Lv Metlakatla	2:15PM
	Ar Ketchikan	3:30PM
	Lv Ketchikan	6:15PM
	Ar Hollis	9:00PM
	Lv Hollis	10:00PM
Sat	Ar Ketchikan	12:45AM
**Sat	Lv Ketchikan	6:15AM
	Ar Metlakatla	7:30AM
	Lv Metlakatla	8:15AM
	Ar Ketchikan	9:30AM
	Lv Ketchikan	10:30AM
	Ar Hollis	1:15PM
	Lv Hollis	2:15PM
	Ar Ketchikan	5:00PM
	Lv Ketchikan	6:45PM
	Ar Metlakatla	8:00PM
	Lv Metlakatla	8:45PM
	Ar Ketchikan	10:00PM
	Lv Ketchikan	11:00PM
Sun	Ar Hollis	1:45AM

***TUESDAY - JUL 2, 16, 30**

Mon	Lv Hollis	10:00PM
Tue	Ar Ketchikan	12:45AM
	Lv Ketchikan	1:45AM
	Ar Stewart/Hyder	1:00PM
	Lv Stewart/Hyder	3:45PM
Wed	Ar Ketchikan	1:30AM
	Lv Ketchikan	2:30AM
Wed	Ar Hollis	5:15AM

**LOGGING SHOW & FAIR - JULY 27-28 AT THORNE BAY (HOLLIS)

August 1996 Northbound Schedule

LEAVE BELLINGHAM	LEAVE PRINCE RUPERT	LEAVE STEWART/HYDER	METLAKATLA	KETCHIKAN	HOLLIS	WRANGELL	PETERSBURG	KAKE	ARRIVE SITKA	ANGOON	TENAKEE	HOONAH	JUNEAU/ AUKE BAY	HAINES	ARRIVE SKAGWAY
	T30 9:30P		SEE M/V AURORA SCHEDULE BELOW	W31 3:30A	SEE M/V AURORA SCHEDULE BELOW	W31 10:15A	W31 2:00P						TH1 12:45A	TH1 7:15A	TH1 8:15A
	W31 8:00A			W31 2:00P		W31 8:45P	TH1 12:30A	TH1 5:15A					TH1 1:30P	TH1 7:00P	TH1 8:00P
													F2 3:00A	F2 8:30A	F2 9:30A
								Lv. Sitka	TH1 11:30A	TH1 5:15P	TH1 8:30P	F2 12:45A	F2 4:00A		
	TH1 2:00P			TH1 8:00P		F2 2:45A	F2 7:30A		F2 10:00P				S3 11:15A	S3 4:45P	S3 5:45P
	S3 8:30A			S3 4:00P		S3 11:00P	SU4 2:45A						SU4 11:30A		SU4 4:30P
								Lv. Sitka	S3 7:15P	SU4 1:30A	SU4 4:45A	SU4 9:00A	SU4 12:15P		
													M5 2:00A	M5 7:30A	M5 8:30A
F2 6:30P				SU4 8:00A		SU4 2:00P	SU4 6:00P		M5 5:45A				M5 7:30P	T6 2:30A	T6 3:30A
	SU4 9:30P			M5 4:00A		M5 10:45A	M5 2:30P						M5 10:15P		
	M5 12:30P			M5 7:00P		T6 1:45A	T6 6:30A						T6 3:30P	T6 9:00P	T6 10:00P
							T6 3:15A		T6 1:15P	T6 11:00P		W7 4:30A	W7 8:45A	W7 2:15P	W7 3:15P
	*T6 10:00P			W7 4:00A		W7 10:45A	W7 2:30P						TH8 1:15A	TH8 7:45A	TH8 8:45A
	*W7 10:00A			W7 4:30P		W7 11:15P	TH8 3:00A	TH8 8:00A					TH8 4:45P	TH8 10:45P	TH8 11:45P
													*F9 8:45A	F9 2:45P	F9 3:45P
								*Lv. Sitka	TH8 6:00P	TH8 11:45P	F9 3:00A	F9 7:15A	F9 11:55A	F9 4:30P	
													*S10 12:45A	S10 6:45A	S10 7:45A
	TH8 4:45P			TH8 10:45P		F9 5:45A	F9 10:45A		F9 10:30P				S10 12:15P	S10 5:45P	S10 6:45P
	S10 8:30A			S10 3:00P		S10 9:45P	SU11 1:30A						SU11 10:15A		SU11 3:15P
								Lv. Sitka	S10 7:45P	SU11 2:00A	SU11 5:15A	SU11 9:30A	SU11 1:45P	SU11 6:15P	
													M12 12:45A	M12 6:15A	M12 7:15A
F9 6:30P				SU11 5:00A		SU11 10:45A	SU11 2:30P		SU11 11:55P				M12 1:45P	M12 8:45P	M12 9:45P
	M12 11:45A			M12 5:45P		T13 12:30A	T13 5:15A						T13 1:15P		
	M12 8:30P			T13 3:30A		T13 10:30A	T13 2:15P						T13 11:00P	W14 4:30A	W14 5:30A
		T13 3:45P		W14 1:30A				Lv. Sitka	T13 3:45A	T13 10:15A		T13 3:45P	W14 8:45A	W14 2:15P	W14 3:15P
	T13 9:30P			W14 3:30A		W14 10:15A	W14 2:00P						TH15 12:45A	TH15 7:15A	TH15 8:15A
								Lv. Sitka	TH15 5:00P	TH15 10:45P	F16 2:00A	F16 6:45A	F16 10:00A		
	W14 9:00P			TH15 3:30A		TH15 10:30A	TH15 3:15P		F16 2:30A				F16 4:00P	F16 9:30P	F16 10:30P
	TH15 10:00P			F16 5:30A		F16 12:30P	F16 4:30P	F16 9:30P					S17 6:15A	S17 11:45A	S17 12:45P
								Lv. Sitka	S17 11:45A	S17 5:45P	S17 9:00P	SU18 1:45A	SU18 5:00A		
	S17 8:30A			S17 2:30P		S17 9:15P	SU18 1:30A						SU18 10:45A	SU18 4:45P	SU18 5:45P
										Lv. Pelican	SU18 3:15P		SU18 10:00P		
	SU18 3:00P			SU18 9:00P									M19 4:00P	M19 9:30P	M19 10:30P
F16 6:30P				SU18 7:00A		SU18 12:45P	SU18 4:30P		M19 4:00A				M19 5:30P	T20 12:30A	T20 1:30A
	M19 10:00P			T20 4:00A		T20 10:45A	T20 2:30P						T20 11:15P	W21 4:45A	W21 5:45A
							T20 10:15A	T20 3:15P	T20 11:30P	W21 8:00A		W21 1:00P	W21 4:15P		
	T20 11:30A			T20 7:30P		W21 2:30A	W21 6:30A		W21 6:00P				TH22 7:15A	TH22 1:15P	TH22 2:15P
								Lv. Sitka	TH22 3:30P	TH22 9:15P	F23 12:30A	F23 4:45A	F23 8:00A		
	W21 5:15P			TH22 1:15A		TH22 8:45A	TH22 2:15P		F23 2:00A				F23 3:30P	F23 9:00P	F23 10:00P
	TH22 9:00P			F23 3:30A		F23 10:15A	F23 2:00P	F23 6:45P					S24 3:00A	S24 8:30A	S24 9:30A
	S24 8:30A			S24 2:30P		S24 9:15P	SU25 1:30A						SU25 10:45A	SU25 4:45P	SU25 5:45P
								Lv. Sitka	S24 6:00P	SU25 12:15A	SU25 3:30A	SU25 8:15A	SU25 11:30A		
	SU25 5:30P			M26 1:45A									M26 8:45P	T27 2:15A	T27 3:15A
F23 6:30P				SU25 8:30A		SU25 2:30P	SU25 6:30P		M26 5:00A				M26 6:45P	T27 1:45A	T27 2:45A
	M26 5:30P			M26 11:30P		T27 7:15A	T27 11:00A						T27 7:45P	W28 1:15A	W28 2:15A
		T27 3:45P		W28 1:30A			T27 4:30A	T27 10:00A	T27 6:45P	W28 3:15A		W28 8:15A	W28 11:30A		
	T27 10:30A			T27 4:30P		T27 11:15P	W28 3:00A		W28 1:00P				TH29 3:45A	TH29 10:15A	TH29 11:15A
								Lv. Sitka	TH29 10:15A	TH29 4:15P	TH29 7:30P	TH29 11:45P	F30 3:00A		
	W28 3:15P			TH29 12:15A		TH29 8:00A	TH29 1:30P		F30 2:15A				F30 3:45P	F30 9:15P	F30 10:15P
	TH29 8:00P			F30 2:30A		F30 9:15A	F30 1:00P	F30 5:45P					S31 2:00A	S31 7:30A	S31 8:30A
								Lv. Sitka	S31 11:45A	S31 5:45P	S31 9:00P	SU1 1:45A	SU1 5:00A		
	S31 8:30A			S31 3:45P		S31 10:30P	SU1 2:15A						SU1 11:15A	SU1 5:15P	SU1 6:15P
F30 6:30P				SU1 7:30A		SU1 1:30P	SU1 5:30P		M2 4:15A				M2 6:00P	T3 1:00A	T3 2:00A

*THE FOLLOWING EVENT MAY AFFECT THE AVAILABILITY OF SPACE: SOUTHEAST ALASKA STATE FAIR AUG. 7-11 HAINES

(Continued from page 614)
communities are accessible only by ferry or by air.

The Southcentral/Southwest system serves coastal communities from Prince William Sound to the Aleutian Islands. With the exception of Cordova, Seldovia and Kodiak, Southcentral communities on the ferry system are also accessible by highway. These road-accessible ports are Valdez, Seward and Homer. Whittier is accessible to vehicles only via shuttle train. Communities on the Southwest system are accessible only by ferry or air.

Travel on the Alaska state ferries is at a leisurely pace, with observation decks, food service and vehicle decks on all ferries. Cabins are available only on 4 Southeast ferries and 1 Southwest ferry.

Keep in mind that the state ferries are not cruise ships: They do not have beauty salons, gift shops, deck games, telephones and the like. The small stores on the larger ferries are open limited hours and sell a limited selection of items.

Food service varies from vessel to vessel. There's dining room service on the *Columbia, Tustumena* and *Bartlett*. The *Columbia* also has a 24-hour snack bar. Cafeteria service is available on all other ferries. Cocktail lounges on board the larger vessels are open from late morning to midnight.

It's a good idea to bring your own snacks, books, games and toiletries, since these are not always available on board.

Season: The Alaska Ferry System has 2 seasons—April 1 to Sept. 30 (spring/summer), when sailings are most frequent, and Oct. 1 to March 31 (fall/winter), when departures are somewhat less frequent. Schedules and information appearing in this section are for the summer season only.

Contact the Alaska Marine Highway office for fall/winter/spring schedules, fares and information. Fares are normally reduced and crowds are virtually nonexistent.

Reservations: Required on all vessels. The Alaska state ferries are very popular in summer. Reservations should be made as far in advance as possible to get the sailing dates you wish. Cabin space on summer sailings is often sold out by early December on the Bellingham sailings. Requests for space are accepted year-round and held until reservations open. For reservations, write the Alaska Marine Highway, P.O. Box 25535, Juneau, AK 99802-5535; phone toll free 1-800-642-0066, or fax (907) 277-4829.

(Continues on page 619)

Aurora Columbia Le Conte Malaspina Matanuska Taku

August 1996 Southbound Schedule

LEAVE SKAGWAY	HAINES	JUNEAU/ AUKE BAY	HOONAH	TENAKEE	ANGOON	ARRIVE SITKA	KAKE	PETERSBURG	WRANGELL	HOLLIS	KETCHIKAN	METLAKATLA	ARRIVE STEWART/HYDER	ARRIVE PRINCE RUPERT	ARRIVE BELLINGHAM
T30 6:00A	T30 9:30A	T30 4:00P				W31 1:30A		W31 3:00P	W31 6:30P	SEE M/V AURORA SCHEDULE BELOW	TH1 1:00A	SEE M/V AURORA SCHEDULE BELOW			F2 11:00A
W31 1:00A	W31 3:00A	W31 8:30A						W31 5:30P	W31 9:30P		TH1 4:30A			TH1 11:30A	
W31 9:15A	W31 11:15A	W31 6:00P	W31 10:45P		TH1 3:45A	TH1 8:45A									
TH1 11:15A	TH1 2:15P	TH1 8:45P						F2 5:30A	F2 9:30A		F2 8:30P			S3 5:30A	
TH1 9:00P		F2 2:00A													
F2 11:55A	F2 2:00P	F2 7:30P				S3 4:15A	S3 4:15P	SU4 12:30A	SU4 4:15A		SU4 11:30A			SU4 6:30P	
		F2 5:15P	F2 10:00P	S3 2:15A	S3 5:30A	S3 10:30A									
S3 8:45P	S3 11:00P	SU4 5:00A						SU4 2:15P	SU4 6:30P		M5 2:00A			M5 9:00A	
SU4 6:00P	SU4 8:00P	M5 12:30A													
		SU4 7:30P	SU4 11:45P	M5 4:00A	M5 7:15A	M5 12:15P		T6 12:45A							
M5 11:30A	M5 1:30P	M5 7:00P						T6 3:30A			T6 11:55A			T6 7:00P	
T6 6:30A	T6 10:00A	T6 4:30P				W7 1:30A		W7 3:15P	W7 6:45P		TH8 1:00A				F9 11:00A
		T6 12:15A					T6 8:30A	T6 1:15P	T6 5:00P		T6 11:55P			W7 7:00A	
W7 1:00A	W7 3:15A	W7 9:15A						W7 6:15P	W7 10:15P		TH8 6:45A			TH8 1:45P	
W7 4:45P	W7 6:45P	TH8 1:15A	TH8 5:30A		TH8 10:30A	TH8 3:30P									
TH8 11:45A	TH8 2:45P	TH8 10:15P						F9 7:00A	F9 11:00A		F9 8:30P			S10 5:30A	
F9 12:45A	F9 2:45A	F9 7:15A													
F9 4:45P	F9 6:45P	F9 11:15P													
	F9 5:30P	F9 11:55P	S10 4:45A	S10 9:00A	S10 12:15P	S10 5:15P									
S10 10:45A	S10 1:15P	S10 7:15P				SU11 5:00A	SU11 5:00P	SU11 10:00P	M12 2:00A		M12 9:00A			M12 4:00P	
*S10 9:45P	S10 11:45P	SU11 5:15A						SU11 3:15P	SU11 7:15P		M12 2:15A			M12 9:15A	
*SU11 4:15P	SU11 6:15P	SU11 10:45P													
	*SU11 7:15P	M12 1:45A	M12 6:00A	M12 10:15A	M12 1:30P	M12 6:45P					T13 1:45A		T13 1:00P		
M12 10:15A	M12 12:15P	M12 6:15P						T13 2:45A			T13 11:30A			T13 6:30P	
T13 12:45A	T13 4:15A	T13 10:45A				T13 7:15P		W14 11:30A	W14 3:30P		W14 10:00P				F16 10:00A
		T13 3:15P						W14 12:15A	W14 4:15A		W14 11:15A			W14 6:15P	
W14 8:30A	W14 10:30A	W14 4:00P						TH15 12:45A	TH15 4:30A		TH15 11:30A			TH15 6:30P	
W14 4:45P	W14 6:45P	TH15 12:15A	TH15 4:30A		TH15 9:30A	TH15 2:30P									
TH15 11:15A	TH15 2:15P	TH15 8:45P						F16 5:15A	F16 9:15A		F16 8:30P			S17 5:30A	
		F16 4:30P	F16 8:45P	S17 1:00A	S17 4:15A	S17 9:15A									
S17 1:30A	S17 3:30A	S17 9:00A						S17 6:00P	S17 10:00P		SU18 5:00A			SU18 11:55A	
S17 3:45P	S17 6:15P	SU18 12:30A				SU18 9:45A	SU18 9:30P	M19 2:15A	M19 6:00A		M19 1:00P			M19 8:00P	
		SU18 7:00A	Ar. Pelican	SU18 1:45P											
SU18 8:45P	SU18 11:15P	M19 5:15A						M19 1:45P	M19 5:30P		T20 1:30A			T20 8:30A	
		SU18 11:45P	M19 4:00A	M19 8:15A	M19 11:30A	M19 4:30P	T20 4:30A	T20 8:30A							
T20 1:30A	T20 3:30A	T20 9:00A						T20 6:00P	T20 10:15P		W21 5:15A			W21 12:15P	
T20 4:30A	T20 8:00A	T20 2:30P				T20 11:15P		W21 12:30P	W21 4:30P		W21 11:00P				F23 10:00A
W21 8:45A	W21 10:45A	W21 4:15P						TH22 12:45A	TH22 4:30A		TH22 11:30A			TH22 6:30P	
		W21 10:45P	TH22 3:00A		TH22 8:00A	TH22 1:00P									
TH22 5:15P	TH22 7:45P	F23 2:45A						F23 11:30A	F23 3:30P		F23 10:30P			S24 5:30A	
		F23 4:30P	F23 8:45P	S24 1:00A	S24 4:15A	S24 9:30A									
S24 1:00A	S24 3:30A	S24 9:30A						S24 6:30P	S24 10:30P		SU25 5:30A			SU25 12:30P	
S24 12:15P	S24 2:15P	S24 7:45P				SU25 4:30A	SU25 4:30P	SU25 9:15P	M26 1:00A		M26 8:00A			M26 3:00P	
SU25 8:45P	SU25 11:15P	M26 5:15A						M26 1:45P	M26 5:30P		T27 1:00A			T27 8:00A	
		SU25 12:30P	SU25 4:45P	SU25 9:00P	M26 12:15A	M26 5:15A	M26 11:30P	T27 3:30A			T27 1:45A		T27 1:00P		
T27 5:15A	T27 7:15A	T27 12:45P						T27 9:45P	W28 2:00A		W28 9:00A			W28 4:00P	
T27 5:45A	T27 9:15A	T27 3:45P				W28 12:30A		W28 2:00P	W28 5:30P		W28 11:55P				F30 10:00A
W28 5:15A	W28 7:45A	W28 1:45P						W28 10:30P	TH29 2:30A		TH29 10:00A			TH29 5:00P	
		W28 5:30P	W28 9:45P		TH29 2:45A	TH29 7:45A									
TH29 2:15P	TH29 5:15P	F30 12:45A						F30 9:30A	F30 1:30P		F30 10:15P			S31 5:30A	
		F30 4:30P	F30 8:45P	S31 1:00A	S31 4:15A	S31 9:15A									
S31 1:15A	S31 3:15A	S31 8:45A						S31 5:45P	S31 9:45P		SU1 4:45A			SU1 11:45A	
S31 11:30A	S31 1:30P	S31 7:00P				SU1 3:45A	SU1 4:45P	SU1 11:00P	M2 2:45A		M2 10:00A			M2 5:00P	

ALL TIMES SHOWN ARE LOCAL TIMES

M/V AURORA Southern Panhandle Summer 1996

How To Use This Schedule

The M/V AURORA operates a daily schedule between Ketchikan, Metlakatla and Hollis (Gateway to Prince of Wales Island). There are several sailings to and from these communities each day. To determine the best one for your trip, use this table. Please allow enough time to make appropriate connections with the mainline sailings from Ketchikan (see tables above).

EFFECTIVE MAY 1 - SEPTEMBER 19

Sun	Lv Hollis	6:15AM
	Ar Ketchikan	9:00AM
	Lv Ketchikan	12:15PM
	Ar Metlakatla	1:30PM
	Lv Metlakatla	2:15PM
	Ar Ketchikan	3:30PM
	Lv Ketchikan	6:15PM
	Ar Hollis	9:00PM
Mon	Lv Hollis	6:15AM
	Ar Ketchikan	9:00AM
	Lv Ketchikan	12:15PM
	Ar Metlakatla	1:30PM
	Lv Metlakatla	2:15PM
	Ar Ketchikan	3:30PM
	Lv Ketchikan	6:15PM
	Ar Hollis	9:00PM
*Tue	Lv Hollis	9:15AM
	Ar Ketchikan	11:55AM
	Lv Ketchikan	6:15PM
	Ar Hollis	9:00PM
Wed	Lv Hollis	6:15AM
	Ar Ketchikan	9:00AM
	Lv Ketchikan	12:15PM
	Ar Metlakatla	1:30PM
	Lv Metlakatla	2:15PM
	Ar Ketchikan	3:30PM
	Lv Ketchikan	6:15PM
	Ar Hollis	9:00PM
Thu	Lv Hollis	9:15AM
	Ar Ketchikan	11:55AM
	Lv Ketchikan	6:15PM
	Ar Hollis	9:00PM
Fri	Lv Hollis	9:15AM
	Ar Ketchikan	11:55AM
	Lv Ketchikan	12:15PM
	Ar Metlakatla	1:30PM
	Lv Metlakatla	2:15PM
	Ar Ketchikan	3:30PM
	Lv Ketchikan	6:15PM
	Ar Hollis	9:00PM
	Lv Hollis	10:00PM
Sat	Ar Ketchikan	12:45AM
Sat	Lv Ketchikan	6:15AM
	Ar Metlakatla	7:30AM
	Lv Metlakatla	8:15AM
	Ar Ketchikan	9:30AM
	Lv Ketchikan	10:30AM
	Ar Hollis	1:15PM
	Lv Hollis	2:15PM
	Ar Ketchikan	5:00PM
	Lv Ketchikan	6:45PM
	Ar Metlakatla	8:00PM
	Lv Metlakatla	8:45PM
	Ar Ketchikan	10:00PM
	Lv Ketchikan	11:00PM
Sun	Ar Hollis	1:45AM

***TUESDAY - AUG 13, 27**

Mon	Lv Hollis	10:00PM
Tue	Ar Ketchikan	12:45AM
	Lv Ketchikan	1:45AM
	Ar Stewart/Hyder	1:00PM
	Lv Stewart/Hyder	3:45PM
Wed	Ar Ketchikan	1:30AM
	Lv Ketchikan	2:30AM
Wed	Ar Hollis	5:15AM

September 1996 Northbound Schedule

LEAVE BELLINGHAM	LEAVE PRINCE RUPERT	LEAVE STEWART/HYDER	METLAKATLA	KETCHIKAN	HOLLIS	WRANGELL	PETERSBURG	KAKE	ARRIVE SITKA	ANGOON	TENAKEE	HOONAH	JUNEAU/ AUKE BAY	HAINES	ARRIVE SKAGWAY
	S31 8:30A		SEE M/V AURORA SCHEDULE BELOW	S31 3:45P	SEE M/V AURORA SCHEDULE BELOW	S31 10:30P	SU1 2:15A						SU1 11:15A	SU1 5:15P	SU1 6:15P
								Lv. Sitka	S31 11:45A	S31 5:45P	S31 9:00P	SU1 1:45A	SU1 5:00A		
										Lv. Pelican	SU1 3:15P		SU1 10:00P		
	SU1 2:45P			SU1 8:45P									M2 3:45P	M2 9:15P	M2 10:15P
F30 6:30P				SU1 7:30A		SU1 1:30P	SU1 5:30P		M2 4:15A				M2 6:00P	T3 1:00A	T3 2:00A
	M2 8:00P			T3 2:30A		T3 9:15A	T3 1:00P						T3 9:45P	W4 3:15A	W4 4:15A
		T3 3:45P		W4 1:30A			T3 10:45A	T3 3:45P	W4 12:15A	W4 8:45A		W4 1:45P	W4 5:00P		
	T3 10:15A			T3 4:15P		T3 11:00P	W4 2:45A		W4 12:45P				TH5 3:00A	TH5 9:30A	TH5 10:30A
								Lv. Sitka	TH5 4:15P	TH5 10:00P	F6 1:15A	F6 5:30A	F6 8:45A		
	W4 3:00P			W4 9:00P		TH5 3:45A	TH5 8:30A		TH5 7:45P				F6 9:30A	F6 3:00P	F6 4:00P
	TH5 9:00P			F6 3:00A		F6 10:00A	F6 1:45P	F6 6:30P					S7 2:45A	S7 8:15A	S7 9:15A
	S7 8:30A			S7 3:00P		S7 9:45P	SU8 1:30A						SU8 10:45A	SU8 4:15P	SU8 5:15P
								Lv. Sitka	S7 6:15P	SU8 12:15A	SU8 3:30A	SU8 8:15A	SU8 11:30A		
	SU8 9:15A			SU8 3:15P									M9 10:15A	M9 3:45P	M9 4:45P
F6 6:30P				SU8 7:30A		SU8 1:30P	SU8 5:30P		M9 5:00A				M9 6:45P	T10 1:45A	T10 2:45A
	M9 6:00P			M9 11:55P		T10 6:45A	T10 10:30A						T10 7:15P	W11 12:45A	W11 1:45A
		T10 3:45P		W11 1:30A			T10 5:15A	T10 10:15A	T10 6:30P	W11 3:00A		W11 8:00A	W11 11:15A		
								Lv. Sitka	TH12 9:45A	TH12 3:45P	TH12 7:00P	TH12 11:15P	F13 2:30A		
	W11 10:30A			W11 5:30P		TH12 12:30A	TH12 5:30A		TH12 7:15P				F13 8:45A	F13 2:15P	F13 3:15P
	TH12 7:00P			F13 1:15A		F13 8:00A	F13 11:45A	F13 4:30P					S14 12:45A	S14 6:15A	S14 7:15A
								Lv. Sitka	S14 11:00A	S14 5:00P	S14 8:15P	SU15 1:00A	SU15 4:15A		
										Lv. Pelican	SU15 2:45P		SU15 9:30P		
	SU15 10:15A			SU15 5:15P									M16 12:15P	M16 5:45P	M16 6:45P
F13 6:30P				SU15 7:30A		SU15 1:30P	SU15 5:30P		M16 2:45A				M16 4:30P	M16 11:30P	T17 12:30A
	M16 8:00P			T17 2:00A		T17 8:45A	T17 12:30P						T17 9:15P	W18 2:45A	W18 3:45A
							T17 9:00A	T17 2:00P	T17 10:15P	W18 7:00A		W18 11:55A	W18 3:15P		
								Lv. Sitka	TH19 1:45P	TH19 7:30P	TH19 10:45P	F20 3:00A	F20 6:15A		
	W18 3:15P			W18 10:45P		TH19 5:30A	TH19 10:45A		TH19 11:55P				F20 1:30P	F20 7:00P	F20 8:00P
	TH19 9:00P			F20 3:00A	F20 6:45A	F20 2:00P	F20 5:45P						S21 2:30A	S21 8:00A	S21 9:00A
								Lv. Sitka	S21 4:15P	S21 10:15P	SU22 1:45A	SU22 6:00A	SU22 9:15A		
	SU22 12:30P			SU22 6:30P									M23 1:30P	M23 7:00P	M23 8:00P
F20 6:30P				SU22 7:30A		SU22 1:30P	SU22 5:30P		M23 3:45A				M23 5:15P	T24 12:15A	T24 1:15A
	M23 7:00P			T24 1:00A		T24 7:45A	T24 11:30A						T24 8:15P	W25 1:45A	W25 2:45A
			T24 2:00P	T24 4:45P	T24 7:30P										
			W25 1:30P	W25 4:45P	W25 7:30P										
	W25 3:15P			W25 10:15P		TH26 6:45A	TH26 11:45A		F27 1:15A				F27 2:45P	F27 8:15P	F27 9:15P
				TH26 8:15A			TH26 5:45P	TH26 4:45P	F27 11:15P	F27 7:30A		F27 3:45P	F27 8:45P	F27 11:55P	
	TH26 9:00P			F27 3:00A	F27 6:45A	F27 2:00P	F27 5:45P						S28 2:30A	S28 8:00A	S28 9:00A
								Lv. Sitka	S28 11:00P	SU29 5:00A	SU29 8:30A	SU29 12:45P	SU29 4:00P		
	SU29 12:30P			SU29 6:30P									M30 1:30P	M30 7:00P	M30 8:00P

*THE FOLLOWING EVENT MAY AFFECT AVAILABILITY OF SPACE: KLONDIKE TRAIL OF '98 INTERNATIONAL ROAD RELAY SEP 6-7 SKAGWAY

Aurora | Columbia | Le Conte | Malaspina | Matanuska | Taku

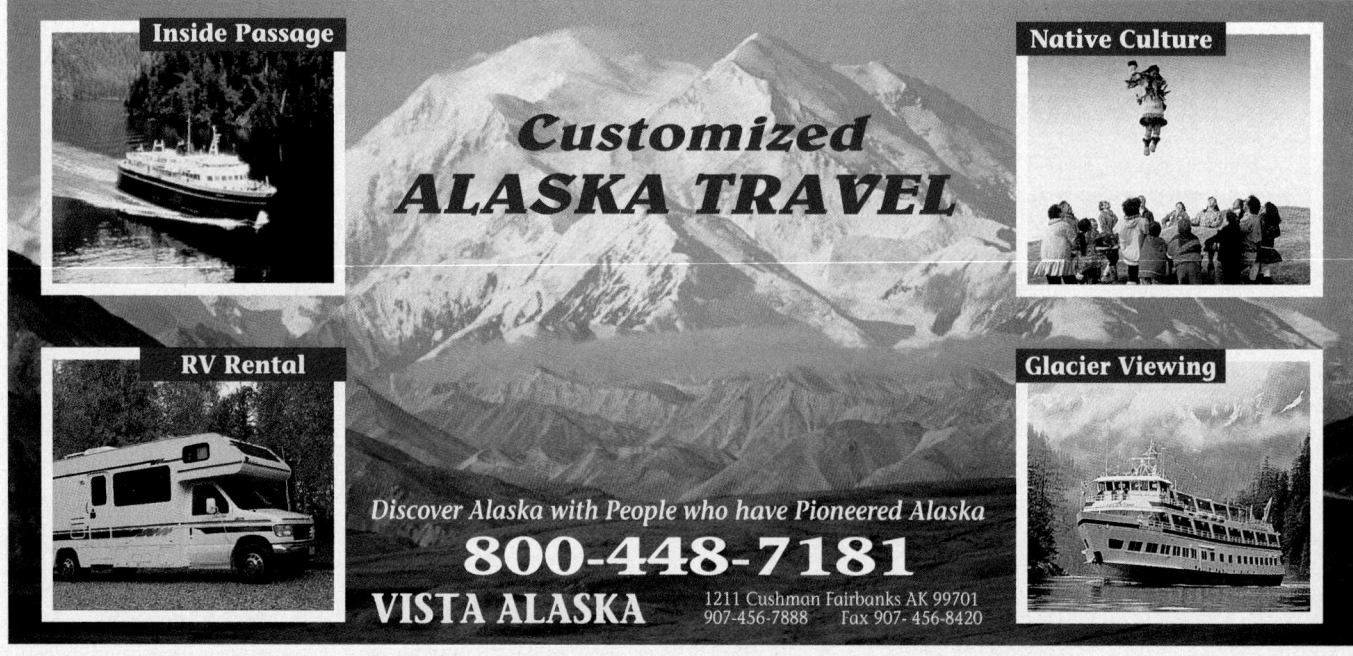

September 1996 Southbound Schedule

LEAVE SKAGWAY	HAINES	JUNEAU/ AUKE BAY	HOONAH	TENAKEE	ANGOON	ARRIVE SITKA	KAKE	PETERSBURG	WRANGELL	HOLLIS (SEE M/V AURORA SCHEDULE BELOW)	KETCHIKAN	METLAKATLA (SEE M/V AURORA SCHEDULE BELOW)	ARRIVE STEWART/HYDER	ARRIVE PRINCE RUPERT	ARRIVE BELLINGHAM
S31 11:30A	S31 1:30P	S31 7:00P				SU1 3:45A	SU1 4:45P	SU1 11:00P	M2 2:45A		M2 10:00A			M2 5:00P	
SU1 9:15P	SU1 11:15P	M2 5:15A						M2 1:45P	M2 5:30P		T3 12:30A			T3 7:30A	
		SU1 7:00A	Ar. Pelican	SU1 1:45P											
		SU1 11:45P	M2 4:00A	M2 8:15A	M2 11:30A	M2 4:45P	T3 5:00A	T3 9:00A			T3 1:45A		T3 1:00P		
T3 1:15A	T3 3:15A	T3 8:45A						T3 5:45P	T3 10:00P		W4 5:00A			W4 11:55A	
T3 5:00A	T3 8:30A	T3 3:00P				T3 11:55P		W4 1:15P	W4 5:00P		W4 11:55P				F6 10:00A
W4 7:15A	W4 9:15A	W4 2:45P						W4 11:15P	TH5 3:00A		TH5 11:00A			TH5 6:00P	
		W4 11:30P	TH5 3:45A		TH5 8:45A	TH5 1:45P									
TH5 1:30P	TH5 4:30P	TH5 11:55P						F6 8:45A	F6 12:45P		F6 10:15P			S7 5:30A	
		F6 4:45P	F6 9:00P	S7 1:15A	S7 4:30A	S7 9:45A									
F6 7:00P	F6 9:00P	S7 2:30A						S7 11:30A	S7 3:30P		S7 10:30P			SU8 5:30A	
S7 12:15P	S7 2:15P	S7 7:45P				SU8 4:30A	SU8 4:30P	SU8 9:15P	M9 1:00A		M9 8:00A			M9 3:00P	
*SU8 8:15P	SU8 10:15P	M9 4:15A						M9 12:45P	M9 4:30P		M9 10:30P				
		SU8 12:30P	SU8 4:45P	SU8 9:00P	M9 12:15A	M9 5:15A	M9 11:30P	T10 3:30A			T10 1:45A		T10 1:00P		
M9 7:45P	M9 9:45P	T10 3:15A						T10 12:15P	T10 4:30P		W11 12:30A			W11 7:30A	
T10 5:45A	T10 9:15A	T10 3:45P				W11 12:15A		W11 1:45P	W11 5:30P		W11 11:55P				F13 10:00A
W11 4:45A	W11 6:45A	W11 12:45P						W11 9:30P	TH12 1:30A		TH12 9:00A			TH12 4:00P	
		W11 5:00P	W11 9:15P		TH12 2:15A	TH12 7:15A									
		F13 3:30P	F13 7:45P	F13 11:55P	S14 3:15A	S14 8:30A									
F13 6:15P	F13 8:15P	S14 2:00A						S14 11:00A	S14 3:00P		S14 10:00P			SU15 5:00A	
S14 10:00A	S14 11:55A	S14 5:30P				SU15 2:15A	SU15 2:15P	SU15 11:00P	M16 2:45A		M16 9:45A			M16 4:45P	
		SU15 6:30A	Ar. Pelican	SU15 1:15P											
		SU15 10:30P	M16 2:45A	M16 7:00A	M16 10:15A	M16 3:30P	T17 3:45A	T17 7:45A							
M16 9:45P	M16 11:45P	T17 5:15A						T17 2:15P	T17 6:30P		W18 1:30A			W18 8:30A	
T17 3:30A	T17 7:00A	T17 1:30P				T17 10:00P		W18 12:30P	W18 4:30P		W18 11:00P				F20 10:00A
W18 6:45A	W18 8:45A	W18 2:15P						TH19 1:00A	TH19 4:45A		TH19 11:55A			TH19 7:00P	
		W18 8:45P	TH19 1:00A		TH19 6:00A	TH19 11:15A									
		F20 3:30P	F20 7:45P	F20 11:45P	S21 3:00A	S21 7:45A									
F20 11:00P	S21 1:00A	S21 6:30A						S21 3:30P	S21 7:30P		SU22 2:30A			SU22 9:30A	
S21 11:00A	S21 1:00P	S21 6:30P				SU22 3:15A	SU22 5:45P	SU22 9:30P	M23 5:00A		M23 9:00A			M23 4:00P	
		SU22 11:45A	SU22 4:00P	SU22 8:00P	SU22 11:30P	M23 4:15A	M23 4:00P	M23 9:00P		T24 8:00A	T24 11:45A	T24 1:00P			
M23 10:30P	T24 12:30A	T24 6:00A						T24 3:00P	T24 7:15P		W25 3:15A			W25 10:15A	
T24 4:15A	T24 7:45A	T24 2:15P				T24 11:15P		W25 1:45P	W25 5:30P		W25 11:55P				F27 10:00A
W25 4:45A	W25 6:45A	W25 12:30P						W25 9:00P	TH26 12:45A	TH26 8:15A	TH26 11:55A			TH26 7:00P	
										W25 7:30A	W25 11:15A	W25 12:30P			
										W25 9:00P	W25 11:45P				
S28 12:15A	S28 2:15A	S28 7:45A						S28 4:45P	S28 8:45P		SU29 3:45A			SU29 10:45A	
		S28 4:00A	S28 8:15A	S28 12:15P	S28 3:30P	S28 8:30P									
S28 10:30A	S28 12:30P	S28 6:00P				SU29 2:45A		SU29 5:00P	SU29 8:45P	M30 4:15A	M30 9:00A			M30 4:00P	
		SU29 5:15P	SU29 9:30P	M30 1:30A	M30 5:00A	M30 9:45A	M30 9:30P	T1 1:30A							

ALL TIMES SHOWN ARE LOCAL TIMES

M/V AURORA Southern Panhandle Summer 1996

How To Use This Schedule

The M/V AURORA operates a daily schedule between Ketchikan, Metlakatla and Hollis (Gateway to Prince of Wales Island). There are several sailings to and from these communities each day. To determine the best one for your trip, use this table. Please allow enough time to make appropriate connections with the mainline sailings from Ketchikan (see tables above).

EFFECTIVE SEPTEMBER 1 - SEPTEMBER 19

Sun	Lv Hollis	6:15AM
	Ar Ketchikan	9:00AM
	Lv Ketchikan	12:15PM
	Ar Metlakatla	1:30PM
	Lv Metlakatla	2:15PM
	Ar Ketchikan	3:30PM
	Lv Ketchikan	6:15PM
	Ar Hollis	9:00PM
Mon	Lv Hollis	6:15AM
	Ar Ketchikan	9:00AM
	Lv Ketchikan	12:15PM
	Ar Metlakatla	1:30PM
	Lv Metlakatla	2:15PM
	Ar Ketchikan	3:30PM
	Lv Ketchikan	6:15PM
	Ar Hollis	9:00PM
*Tue	Lv Hollis	9:15AM
	Ar Ketchikan	11:55AM
	Lv Ketchikan	6:15PM
	Ar Hollis	9:00PM
Wed	Lv Hollis	6:15AM
	Ar Ketchikan	9:00AM
	Lv Ketchikan	12:15PM
	Ar Metlakatla	1:30PM
	Lv Metlakatla	2:15PM
	Ar Ketchikan	3:30PM
	Lv Ketchikan	6:15PM
	Ar Hollis	9:00PM
Thu	Lv Hollis	9:15AM
	Ar Ketchikan	11:55AM**
	Lv Ketchikan	6:15PM
	Ar Hollis	9:00PM
Fri	Lv Hollis	6:15AM
	Ar Ketchikan	9:00AM
	Lv Ketchikan	12:15PM
	Ar Metlakatla	1:30PM
	Lv Metlakatla	2:15PM
	Ar Ketchikan	3:30PM
	Lv Ketchikan	6:15PM
	Ar Hollis	9:00PM
	Lv Hollis	10:00PM
Sat	Ar Ketchikan	12:45AM
Sat	Lv Ketchikan	6:15AM
	Ar Metlakatla	7:30AM
	Lv Metlakatla	8:15AM
	Ar Ketchikan	9:30AM
	Lv Ketchikan	10:30AM
	Ar Hollis	1:15PM
	Lv Hollis	2:15PM
	Ar Ketchikan	5:00PM
	Lv Ketchikan	6:45PM
	Ar Metlakatla	8:00PM
	Lv Metlakatla	8:45PM
	Ar Ketchikan	10:00PM
	Lv Ketchikan	11:00PM
Sun	Ar Hollis	1:45AM

***TUESDAY - SEP 3, 10**

Mon	Lv Hollis	10:00PM
Tue	Ar Ketchikan	12:45AM
	Lv Ketchikan	1:45AM
	Ar Stewart/Hyder	1:00PM
	Lv Stewart/Hyder	3:45PM
Wed	Ar Ketchikan	1:30AM
	Lv Ketchikan	2:30AM
Wed	Ar Hollis	5:15AM

** TO OVERHAUL SEPTEMBER 19 UPON ARRIVAL KETCHIKAN 11:55AM

(Continued from page 616)

Reservation requests must include departure dates and ports of embarkation/debarkation; full names of all members of the party, and the ages of those under 12 years; width, height and overall length (including hitch if with trailer) of vehicles; mailing address and phone number; alternate dates in the event cabin or vehicle space is not available on your first choice; and approximate date you will be leaving home.

Persons with disabilities requiring special accommodations should include this information when making reservations. Also notify the purser upon boarding the vessel. ♿

If you are unable to obtain reservations at the time of advance booking, you may be waitlisted. If a cancellation occurs you will be notified of confirmation of space. You may also choose to go standby, which is literally standing in line until all reserved passengers and vehicles are on board; if there is space, standbys may board. Standbys are subject to off-loading at each port of call!

If cabin space is filled, you may go deck

(Continues on page 621)

1996 Southeast Alaska Passenger and Vehicle Tariffs

ADULT 12 YEARS OR OVER (Meals and Berth NOT included) **ITEM ADT**

BETWEEN / AND	BELLINGHAM	PRINCE RUPERT	STEWART/HYDER	KETCHIKAN	METLAKATLA	HOLLIS	WRANGELL	PETERSBURG	KAKE	SITKA	ANGOON	HOONAH	JUNEAU	HAINES	SKAGWAY	PELICAN
KETCHIKAN	164	38	40													
METLAKATLA	168	42	44	14												
HOLLIS	178	52	54	20	22											
WRANGELL	180	56	58	24	28	24										
PETERSBURG	192	68	70	38	42	38	18									
KAKE	202	80	82	48	52	48	34	22								
SITKA	208	86	88	54	58	54	38	26	24							
ANGOON	222	100	102	68	72	68	52	40	28	22						
HOONAH	226	104	106	74	78	74	56	44	38	24	20					
JUNEAU	226	104	106	74	78	74	56	44	44	26	24	20				
HAINES	240	118	120	88	92	88	70	58	58	40	38	34	20			
SKAGWAY	246	124	126	92	96	92	76	64	64	44	42	40	26	14		
PELICAN	248	126	128	96	100	96	78	66	52	40	38	22	32	46	54	
TENAKEE	226	104	106	74	78	74	56	44	32	22	16	16	22	34	40	32

CHILD 2 THROUGH 11 YEARS (Under 2 Transported Free) **ITEM CHD**

BETWEEN / AND	BELLINGHAM	PRINCE RUPERT	STEWART/HYDER	KETCHIKAN	METLAKATLA	HOLLIS	WRANGELL	PETERSBURG	KAKE	SITKA	ANGOON	HOONAH	JUNEAU	HAINES	SKAGWAY	PELICAN
KETCHIKAN	82	18	20													
METLAKATLA	84	20	22	8												
HOLLIS	88	26	28	12	14											
WRANGELL	90	28	30	12	14	12										
PETERSBURG	96	34	36	20	22	20	10									
KAKE	102	40	42	24	26	24	18	12								
SITKA	104	42	44	26	28	26	20	14	12							
ANGOON	110	50	52	34	36	34	26	20	14	12						
HOONAH	114	52	54	38	40	38	28	22	20	12	10					
JUNEAU	114	52	54	38	40	38	28	22	22	12	12	10				
HAINES	120	60	62	44	46	44	36	30	30	20	20	18	10			
SKAGWAY	124	62	64	46	48	46	38	32	32	22	22	20	14	8		
PELICAN	126	64	66	48	50	48	40	34	26	20	20	12	16	24	28	
TENAKEE	114	52	54	38	40	38	28	22	16	12	8	8	12	18	20	16

ALTERNATE MEANS OF CONVEYANCE (Bicycles, Small Boats and Inflatables) **ITEM AMC**

BETWEEN / AND	BELLINGHAM	PRINCE RUPERT	STEWART/HYDER	KETCHIKAN	METLAKATLA	HOLLIS	WRANGELL	PETERSBURG	KAKE	SITKA	ANGOON	HOONAH	JUNEAU	HAINES	SKAGWAY	PELICAN
KETCHIKAN	28	10	11													
METLAKATLA	29	11	12	7												
HOLLIS	30	12	13	8	9											
WRANGELL	31	13	14	9	10	9										
PETERSBURG	32	14	15	11	12	11	8									
KAKE	34	16	17	12	13	12	10	8								
SITKA	35	17	18	13	14	13	11	9	8							
ANGOON	37	19	20	15	16	15	13	11	9	7						
HOONAH	38	20	21	16	17	16	14	12	11	8	8					
JUNEAU	38	20	21	16	17	16	14	12	12	9	9	8				
HAINES	39	22	23	18	19	18	16	14	14	11	10	10	8			
SKAGWAY	40	23	24	19	20	19	17	15	15	12	11	11	9	7		
PELICAN	41	23	24	19	20	19	17	15	13	11	10	8	10	12	13	
TENAKEE	38	20	21	16	17	16	14	12	10	8	7	7	9	10	11	10

TWO WHEELED MOTORCYCLES (Without Trailers - Driver **NOT** included) **ITEM 705**

BETWEEN / AND	BELLINGHAM	PRINCE RUPERT	STEWART/HYDER	KETCHIKAN	METLAKATLA	HOLLIS	WRANGELL	PETERSBURG	KAKE	SITKA	ANGOON	HOONAH	JUNEAU	HAINES	SKAGWAY	PELICAN
KETCHIKAN	133	28	31													
METLAKATLA	140	32	35	8												
HOLLIS	146	40	44	16	17											
WRANGELL	150	45	47	20	23	20										
PETERSBURG	160	54	58	30	33	30	14									
KAKE	169	66	68	40	44	40	26	17								
SITKA	174	70	72	45	48	45	30	20	18							
ANGOON	186	82	84	56	60	56	43	32	22	16						
HOONAH	191	86	89	61	64	61	46	36	30	18	15					
JUNEAU	191	86	89	61	64	61	46	36	36	20	18	15				
HAINES	204	98	100	72	76	72	58	47	47	31	30	26	15			
SKAGWAY	208	104	105	77	81	77	62	53	53	36	35	31	20	8		
PELICAN	210	106	107	79	83	79	64	53	41	32	30	17	26	38	44	
TENAKEE	191	86	89	61	64	61	46	36	25	17	13	13	17	28	32	26

VEHICLES UP TO 10 FEET (Driver **NOT** Included) **ITEM 710**

BETWEEN / AND	BELLINGHAM	PRINCE RUPERT	STEWART/HYDER	KETCHIKAN	METLAKATLA	HOLLIS	WRANGELL	PETERSBURG	KAKE	SITKA	ANGOON	HOONAH	JUNEAU	HAINES	SKAGWAY	PELICAN
KETCHIKAN	218	45	50													
METLAKATLA	223	53	56	14												
HOLLIS	238	66	71	26	29											
WRANGELL	243	73	76	31	38	31										
PETERSBURG	259	89	94	49	54	49	23									
KAKE	275	105	110	65	71	65	43	28								
SITKA	284	114	118	73	79	73	49	33	30							
ANGOON	303	133	136	91	98	91	69	53	36	26						
HOONAH	310	140	144	99	105	99	75	59	49	30	25					
JUNEAU	310	140	144	99	105	99	75	59	59	33	30	24				
HAINES	330	160	163	118	124	118	94	76	76	51	49	43	25			
SKAGWAY	338	168	170	125	131	125	101	85	85	59	56	51	33	14		
PELICAN	341	171	174	129	134	129	104	86	68	53	49	29	43	63	71	
TENAKEE	310	140	144	99	105	99	75	59	41	28	20	20	28	45	53	43

VEHICLES UP TO 15 FEET (Driver **NOT** Included) **ITEM 715**

BETWEEN / AND	BELLINGHAM	PRINCE RUPERT	STEWART/HYDER	KETCHIKAN	METLAKATLA	HOLLIS	WRANGELL	PETERSBURG	KAKE	SITKA	ANGOON	HOONAH	JUNEAU	HAINES	SKAGWAY
KETCHIKAN	374	75	83												
METLAKATLA	372	84	95	21											
HOLLIS	394	107	119	41	46										
WRANGELL	405	117	129	51	61	51									
PETERSBURG	433	145	158	80	90	80	35								
KAKE	460	174	187	109	119	109	70	44							
SITKA	473	187	200	122	132	122	80	52	49						
ANGOON	505	220	233	155	164	155	116	86	60	41					
HOONAH	534	240	246	168	177	168	126	98	82	49	39				
JUNEAU	534	240	246	168	177	168	126	98	98	52	47	38			
HAINES	568	273	278	200	210	200	158	129	129	85	80	71	39		
SKAGWAY	581	286	291	213	224	213	172	143	143	99	94	85	53	21	
PELICAN	570	285	298	220	228	220	176	147	114	86	80	47	70	104	119

VEHICLES UP TO 19 FEET (Driver **NOT** Included) **ITEM 719**

BETWEEN / AND	BELLINGHAM	PRINCE RUPERT	STEWART/HYDER	KETCHIKAN	METLAKATLA	HOLLIS	WRANGELL	PETERSBURG	KAKE	SITKA	ANGOON	HOONAH	JUNEAU	HAINES	SKAGWAY
KETCHIKAN	445	90	99												
METLAKATLA	443	100	113	25											
HOLLIS	470	128	141	49	55										
WRANGELL	482	139	153	61	73	61									
PETERSBURG	515	172	188	95	107	95	42								
KAKE	548	207	223	130	141	130	83	52							
SITKA	563	223	238	145	157	145	96	63	58						
ANGOON	602	261	277	184	196	184	138	103	71	49					
HOONAH	636	285	292	200	211	200	150	117	97	58	47				
JUNEAU	636	285	292	200	211	200	150	117	117	62	56	45			
HAINES	676	325	331	238	250	238	188	154	154	101	95	84	46		
SKAGWAY	692	341	347	254	267	254	205	171	171	117	112	101	63	25	
PELICAN	679	339	354	261	271	261	210	175	136	103	95	56	83	124	141

VEHICLES UP TO 21 FEET (Driver **NOT** Included) **ITEM 721**

BETWEEN / AND	BELLINGHAM	PRINCE RUPERT	STEWART/HYDER	KETCHIKAN	METLAKATLA	HOLLIS	WRANGELL	PETERSBURG	KAKE	SITKA	ANGOON	HOONAH	JUNEAU	HAINES	SKAGWAY
KETCHIKAN	557	112	127												
METLAKATLA	572	129	145	31											
HOLLIS	606	164	182	62	70										
WRANGELL	622	179	197	78	93	78									
PETERSBURG	665	222	242	122	137	122	53								
KAKE	707	267	287	167	182	167	107	67							
SITKA	727	287	307	187	202	187	123	80	74						
ANGOON	777	337	357	237	252	237	177	132	91	63					
HOONAH	821	368	377	257	272	257	193	150	125	74	60				
JUNEAU	821	368	377	257	272	257	193	150	150	79	72	57			
HAINES	872	419	427	307	322	307	242	198	198	130	122	108	59		
SKAGWAY	893	440	447	327	344	327	264	220	220	151	144	130	81	31	
PELICAN	877	437	457	337	350	337	270	225	175	132	122	71	107	159	182

All tariffs and rates are quoted in U.S. dollars.

Vehicles over 21 feet - Contact any Marine Highway office for information. Vessels in Southeast Alaska can load vehicles up to 70 feet long with special arrangements. Maximum length on the M/V TUSTUMENA is 40 feet. Fares are based on vehicle length and width. Fares for towed vehicles or trailers are calculated at combined connected length of both vehicles. Vehicles may not be disconnected for travel at separate rates on the same sailing.

Minimum Rates - Vehicles with high centers of gravity (commercial highway vans, loaded flat bed trailers) are charged a minimum rate which is equal to the fare for a 25-foot van. If the vehicle is over 25 feet, the appropriate rate for the vehicle length applies. If your vehicle fits this category, contact our commerical booking desk (907) 465-8816 for information and reservations.

1996 Southeast Alaska Cabin Rates

FOUR BERTH CABIN/SITTING ROOM - OUTSIDE/COMPLETE FACILITIES **ITEM 4BS**
M/V COLUMBIA - M/V MALASPINA

BETWEEN AND	BELLINGHAM	PRINCE RUPERT	KETCHIKAN	HOLLIS	WRANGELL	PETERSBURG	KAKE	SITKA	JUNEAU	HAINES
KETCHIKAN	272	63		N			N			
WRANGELL	300	89	58	O			O			
PETERSBURG	318	103	71		47					
SITKA	351	128	91	S	71	60	S			
JUNEAU	371	145	107	T	91	78	T	54		
HAINES	392	164	129	O	108	97	O	74	51	
SKAGWAY	392	164	129	P	108	97	P	74	51	39

FOUR BERTH CABIN - OUTSIDE/COMPLETE FACILITIES **ITEM 4BF**
M/V COLUMBIA - M/V MALASPINA - M/V MATANUSKA - M/V TAKU

BETWEEN AND	BELLINGHAM	PRINCE RUPERT	KETCHIKAN	HOLLIS	WRANGELL	PETERSBURG	KAKE	SITKA	JUNEAU	HAINES
KETCHIKAN	248	58								
HOLLIS	266	71	48							
WRANGELL	274	80	53	50						
PETERSBURG	289	92	65	56	41					
KAKE	304	104	75	65	53	48				
SITKA	319	114	84	74	64	55	50			
JUNEAU	337	128	100	90	80	69	63	48		
HAINES	362	152	121	110	100	90	77	67	45	
SKAGWAY	362	152	121	110	100	90	77	67	45	35

FOUR BERTH CABIN - INSIDE/COMPLETE FACILITIES **ITEM 4BI**
M/V COLUMBIA - M/V MALASPINA - M/V MATANUSKA - M/V TAKU

BETWEEN AND	BELLINGHAM	PRINCE RUPERT	KETCHIKAN	HOLLIS	WRANGELL	PETERSBURG	KAKE	SITKA	JUNEAU	HAINES
KETCHIKAN	210	50								
HOLLIS	229	57	42							
WRANGELL	233	69	48	43						
PETERSBURG	250	80	57	49	39					
KAKE	262	90	64	56	46	40				
SITKA	275	100	75	65	56	48	42			
JUNEAU	292	112	88	78	69	60	55	42		
HAINES	311	131	106	96	88	79	69	59	39	
SKAGWAY	311	131	106	96	88	79	69	59	39	31

THREE BERTH CABIN - OUTSIDE/COMPLETE FACILITIES **ITEM 3BF**
M/V COLUMBIA - M/V MATANUSKA

BETWEEN AND	BELLINGHAM	PRINCE RUPERT	KETCHIKAN	HOLLIS	WRANGELL	PETERSBURG	KAKE	SITKA	JUNEAU	HAINES
KETCHIKAN	202	45		N			N			
WRANGELL	222	63	44	O			O			
PETERSBURG	232	72	52		35					
SITKA	254	90	67	S	52	45	S			
JUNEAU	271	102	77	T	62	55	T	40		
HAINES	294	119	91	O	74	67	O	53	37	
SKAGWAY	294	119	91	P	74	67	P	53	37	30

TWO BERTH - OUTSIDE/COMPLETE FACILITIES **ITEM 2BF**
M/V COLUMBIA - M/V MALASPINA - M/V MATANUSKA - M/V TAKU

BETWEEN AND	BELLINGHAM	PRINCE RUPERT	KETCHIKAN	HOLLIS	WRANGELL	PETERSBURG	KAKE	SITKA	JUNEAU	HAINES
KETCHIKAN	177	43								
HOLLIS	188	50	35							
WRANGELL	193	58	37	36						
PETERSBURG	204	67	46	44	33					
KAKE	216	76	54	46	40	34				
SITKA	227	84	61	58	47	40	36			
JUNEAU	243	97	72	70	58	50	45	37		
HAINES	263	113	84	82	69	62	60	48	34	
SKAGWAY	263	113	84	82	69	62	60	48	34	27

TWO BERTH CABIN - INSIDE/COMPLETE FACILITIES **ITEM 2BI**
M/V COLUMBIA - M/V MALASPINA - M/V MATANUSKA - M/V TAKU

BETWEEN AND	BELLINGHAM	PRINCE RUPERT	KETCHIKAN	HOLLIS	WRANGELL	PETERSBURG	KAKE	SITKA	JUNEAU	HAINES
KETCHIKAN	156	38								
HOLLIS	164	44	27							
WRANGELL	174	53	34	28						
PETERSBURG	180	60	41	36	29					
KAKE	189	68	48	42	36	30				
SITKA	199	74	53	47	41	35	32			
JUNEAU	211	83	63	60	51	44	40	33		
HAINES	227	98	76	73	63	57	56	44	31	
SKAGWAY	227	98	76	73	63	57	56	44	31	25

(Continued from page 619)
passage. This means you'll be sleeping on lounge chairs or on the deck itself. There is a limited number of recliner chairs and spaces to roll out sleeping bags. Small, free-standing tents are permitted on back decks if space allows. Beware of wind. Pillows and blankets are available for rent from the purser on most sailings.

Fares and fare payment: See page 620 for Southeast passenger and vehicle, above chart for cabin rates; see page 623 for Southwest passenger, vehicle and cabin rates. Fares are charged for passengers, vehicles and cabins on a port to port basis. If you are traveling from Ketchikan to Skagway with a stopover at Juneau, you are charged from Ketchikan to Juneau and Juneau to Skagway, with the total ticket cost being slightly higher than if you were not stopping off in Juneau.

Special fares are available for senior citizens and persons with disabilities. Contact the Alaska Marine Highway System for fares and restrictions.

Full payment is required on or before the due date stated at the time of reservations. Bookings will be cancelled if reservations are not paid for by the payment due date. Payment may be made by mail with certified or cashier's check, or money order. Personal checks are not accepted unless written on an Alaska bank. Credit cards (VISA, MasterCard, American Express, Discover and Diners

(Continues on page 625)

Enjoying the solarium aboard the Alaska state ferry. (© Chris Sharp)

SOUTHCENTRAL/SOUTHWEST FERRY SYSTEM

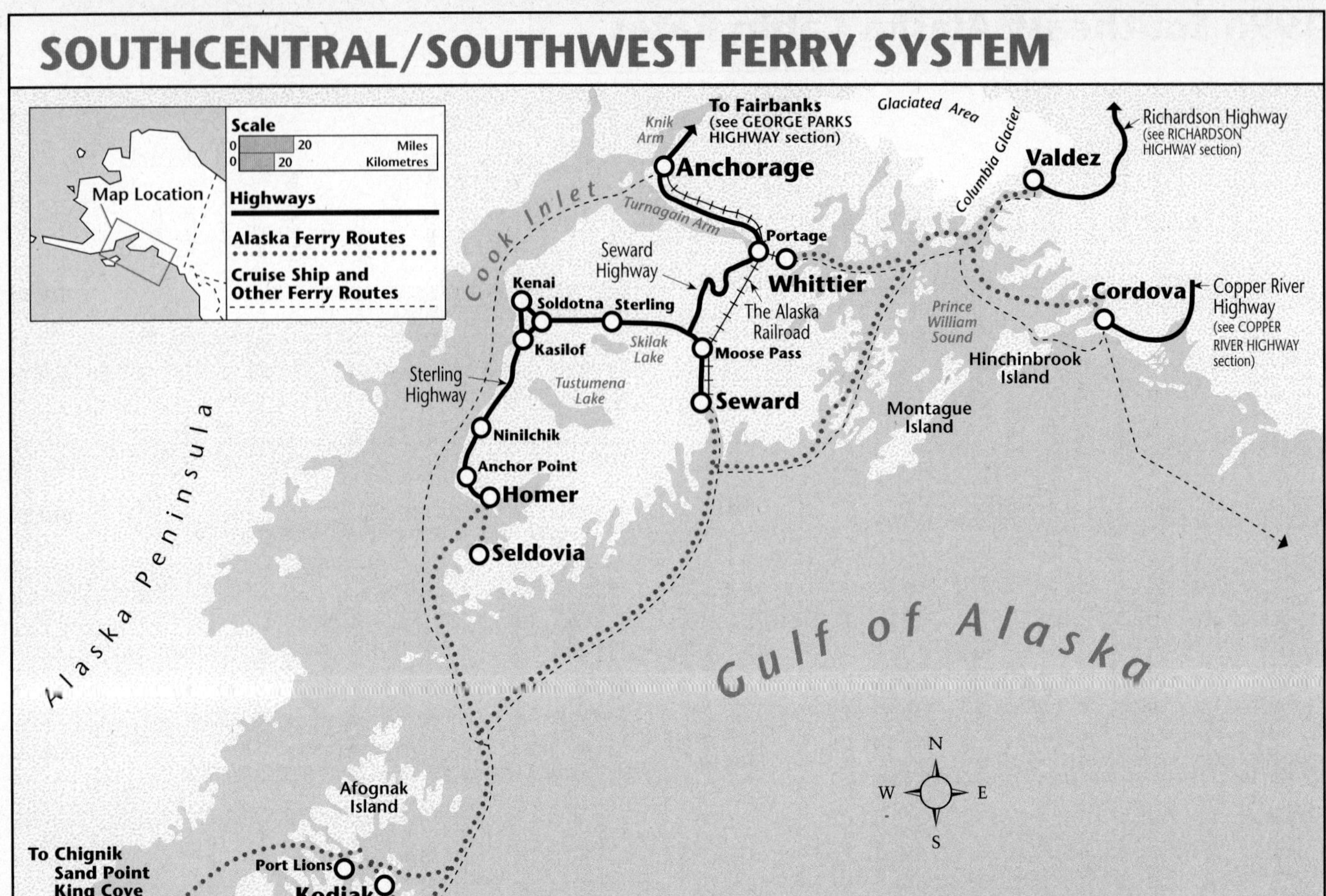

M/V BARTLETT–ALASKA RAILROAD Schedule • Effective May 1, 1996

The M/V BARTLETT serves the port of Whittier using the Alaska Railroad shuttle between Portage and Whittier. In Portage, passengers and their vehicles load on an Alaska Railroad flatcar for a 40-minute sight-filled trip through mountain tunnels to Whittier, a former military town. Ferry service from Whittier is available to Cordova and Valdez.

PORTAGE TO WHITTIER*
Alaska Railroad Service

LV PORTAGE	10:15 A.M.
AR WHITTIER	10:55 A.M.
LV PORTAGE	1:20 P.M.
AR WHITTIER	2:00 P.M.

*Check-in time in Portage is 1 hour earlier than departure.

WHITTIER TO PORTAGE
Alaska Railroad Service

LV WHITTIER	3:30 P.M.
AR PORTAGE	4:10 P.M.
LV WHITTIER	6:15 P.M.
AR PORTAGE	6:55 P.M.

PORTAGE TO WHITTIER ALASKA RAILROAD SHUTTLE PRICES (1-Way)

Adult Vehicle Occupants Other than Driver	$13.00
Vehicles to 23 feet	56.00
Child 6-11 (under 6 free)	6.00
Vehicles to 40 feet	75.00
Motorcycles and Kayaks	25.00

Southcentral/Southwest Alaska – M/V Bartlett Schedule

Effective May 1 — May 31, 1996 AND August 30 — September 13, 1996

MON	LV	CORDOVA	7:00 AM	
	AR	WHITTIER	2:00 PM	
	LV	WHITTIER	2:45 PM	
	AR	CORDOVA	9:45 PM	
TUE	LV	CORDOVA	12:30 AM	
	AR	VALDEZ	6:15 AM	
	LV	VALDEZ	7:15 AM	
	AR	WHITTIER	2:00 PM	
	LV	WHITTIER	2:45 PM	
	AR	VALDEZ	9:30 PM	
* WED	LV	VALDEZ	6:45 AM	**
	AR	CORDOVA	1:45 PM	
	LV	CORDOVA	6:30 PM	**
THU	AR	VALDEZ	1:30 AM	
THU	LV	VALDEZ	7:15 AM	
	AR	WHITTIER	2:00 PM	
	LV	WHITTIER	2:45 PM	
	AR	VALDEZ	9:30 PM	
FRI	LV	VALDEZ	12:15 AM	
	AR	CORDOVA	6:00 AM	
	LV	CORDOVA	7:00 AM	
	AR	WHITTIER	2:00 PM	
	LV	WHITTIER	2:45 PM	###
	AR	CORDOVA	9:45PM	
SAT	LV	CORDOVA	12:30 AM	***
	AR	VALDEZ	6:15 AM	
	LV	VALDEZ	7:15 AM	
	AR	WHITTIER	2:00 PM	
	LV	WHITTIER	2:45 PM	
	AR	VALDEZ	9:30 PM	
SUN	LV	VALDEZ	7:15 AM	
	AR	WHITTIER	2:00 PM	
	LV	WHITTIER	2:45 PM	
	AR	VALDEZ	9:30 PM	
	LV	VALDEZ	11:45 PM	
MON	AR	CORDOVA	5:30 AM	

* Schedule begins here May 1, 1996.
** Tatitlek Whistle Stops available by notifying Valdez or Cordova terminal.
+++Switch to this schedule at Whittier, Friday May 31.
###Switch to this schedule at Whittier. Friday August 30.

Effective May 31, 1996 — August 30, 1996

MON	LV	VALDEZ	7:15 AM	
	AR	WHITTIER	2:00 PM	
	LV	WHITTIER	2:45 PM	
	AR	CORDOVA	9:45 PM	
MON	LV	CORDOVA	11:15 PM	**
TUE	AR	VALDEZ	6:15 AM	
	LV	VALDEZ	7:15 AM	
	AR	WHITTIER	2:00 PM	
TUE	LV	WHITTIER	2:45 PM	
	AR	VALDEZ	9:30 PM	
	LV	VALDEZ	11:45 PM	
WED	AR	CORDOVA	5:15 AM	
WED	LV	CORDOVA	7:00 AM	
	AR	WHITTIER	2:00 PM	
	LV	WHITTIER	2:45 PM	
	AR	VALDEZ	9:30PM	
THU	LV	VALDEZ	6:45 AM	**
	AR	CORDOVA	12:30 PM	
	LV	CORDOVA	6:30 PM	
	AR	VALDEZ	11:55 PM	
FRI	LV	VALDEZ	7:15 AM	
	AR	WHITTIER	2:00 PM	
	LV	WHITTIER	2:45 PM	+++
	AR	VALDEZ	9:30 PM	
SAT	LV	VALDEZ	7:15 AM	
	AR	WHITTIER	2:00 PM	
	LV	WHITTIER	2:45 PM	
	AR	VALDEZ	9:30 PM	
SUN	LV	VALDEZ	7:15 AM	
	AR	WHITTIER	2:00 PM	
	LV	WHITTIER	2:45 PM	
	AR	VALDEZ	9:30 PM	

***** PRINCE WILLIAM SOUND GOLD RUSH REGATTA MAY 11, 1996**

SAT	LV	CORDOVA	12:30 AM	AR	WHITTIER	7:30 AM
SAT	LV	WHITTIER	11:00 AM	AR	VALDEZ	6:00 PM

1996 Southcentral/Southwest Passenger and Vehicle Tariffs

PASSENGER 12 YEARS AND OVER (Meals and Berths not included) **ITEM ADT**

BETWEEN / AND	UNALASKA	AKUTAN	FALSE PASS	COLD BAY	KING COVE	SAND POINT	CHIGNIK	KODIAK	PORT LIONS	SELDOVIA	HOMER	SEWARD	WHITTIER	VALDEZ
AKUTAN	16													
FALSE PASS	46	34												
COLD BAY	62	50	18											
KING COVE	74	66	34	18										
SAND POINT	98	90	58	42	32									
CHIGNIK	132	124	92	76	66	42								
KODIAK	202	194	162	146	136	112	76							
PORT LIONS	202	194	162	146	136	112	76	20						
SELDOVIA	246	240	208	192	180	156	122	52	52					
HOMER	242	236	204	188	176	152	118	48	48	18				
SEWARD	250	242	210	194	184	160	124	54	54	100	96			
WHITTIER	316	308	276	260	250	226	190	120	120	166	162			
VALDEZ	292	286	254	238	226	202	168	98	98	142	138	58	58	
CORDOVA	292	286	254	238	226	202	168	98	98	142	138	58	58	30

CHILDREN 2 THROUGH 11 YEARS OLD (Under 2 Transported Free) **ITEM CHD**

BETWEEN / AND	UNALASKA	AKUTAN	FALSE PASS	COLD BAY	KING COVE	SAND POINT	CHIGNIK	KODIAK	PORT LIONS	SELDOVIA	HOMER	SEWARD	WHITTIER	VALDEZ
AKUTAN	8													
FALSE PASS	24	18												
COLD BAY	32	26	10											
KING COVE	38	34	18	10										
SAND POINT	50	46	30	22	16									
CHIGNIK	66	62	46	38	34	22								
KODIAK	102	98	82	74	68	56	38							
PORT LIONS	102	98	82	74	68	56	38	10						
SELDOVIA	124	120	104	96	90	78	62	26	26					
HOMER	122	118	102	94	88	76	60	24	24	10				
SEWARD	126	122	106	98	92	80	62	28	28	50	48			
WHITTIER	158	154	138	130	126	114	96	60	60	84	82			
VALDEZ	146	144	128	120	114	102	84	50	50	70	70	30	30	
CORDOVA	146	144	128	120	114	102	84	50	50	70	70	30	30	16

ALTERNATE MEANS OF CONVEYANCE (Bicycles-Kayaks-Inflatables) **ITEM AMC**

BETWEEN / AND	UNALASKA	AKUTAN	FALSE PASS	COLD BAY	KING COVE	SAND POINT	CHIGNIK	KODIAK	PORT LIONS	SELDOVIA	HOMER	SEWARD	WHITTIER	VALDEZ
AKUTAN	6													
FALSE PASS	10	8												
COLD BAY	12	10	8											
KING COVE	14	12	10	6										
SAND POINT	18	16	12	9	8									
CHIGNIK	23	18	14	15	13	9								
KODIAK	33	23	18	25	23	20	15							
PORT LIONS	33	23	23	25	23	20	15	6						
SELDOVIA	40	33	23	32	30	26	21	11	11					
HOMER	39	40	33	31	29	26	21	10	10	5				
SEWARD	40	39	40	32	30	27	22	11	11	18	17			
WHITTIER	50	44	42	42	40	37	31	21	21	28	27			
VALDEZ	47	54	52	38	37	33	28	18	18	24	24	10	10	
CORDOVA	47	54	52	38	37	33	28	18	18	24	24	10	10	8

TWO-WHEELED MOTORCYCLES (Without trailers - Driver NOT included) **ITEM 705**

BETWEEN / AND	UNALASKA	AKUTAN	FALSE PASS	COLD BAY	KING COVE	SAND POINT	CHIGNIK	KODIAK	PORT LIONS	SELDOVIA	HOMER	SEWARD	WHITTIER	VALDEZ
FALSE PASS	38	N												
COLD BAY	52	O	14											
KING COVE	61		28	14										
SAND POINT	197	V	48	35	25									
CHIGNIK	227	E	78	64	55	35								
KODIAK	171	H	139	125	115	209	64							
PORT LIONS	171	I	139	125	115	209	64	15						
SELDOVIA	210	C	176	162	153	132	102	43	43					
HOMER	207	L	174	160	151	130	99	39	39	12				
SEWARD	213	E	178	164	155	135	105	45	45	84	81			
WHITTIER	265	S	232	219	209	189	160	100	100	139	135			
VALDEZ	246		213	199	190	169	139	82	82	121	118	40	40	
CORDOVA	246		213	199	190	169	139	82	82	121	118	40	40	24

VEHICLES UP TO 10 FEET (Driver NOT included) **ITEM 710**

BETWEEN / AND	UNALASKA	AKUTAN	FALSE PASS	COLD BAY	KING COVE	SAND POINT	CHIGNIK	KODIAK	PORT LIONS	SELDOVIA	HOMER	SEWARD	WHITTIER	VALDEZ
FALSE PASS	61	N												
COLD BAY	84	O	23											
KING COVE	99		45	23										
SAND POINT	133	V	79	56	41									
CHIGNIK	181	E	128	105	90	56								
KODIAK	279	H	225	203	188	154	105							
PORT LIONS	279	I	225	203	188	154	105	25						
SELDOVIA	341	C	286	264	249	215	166	69	69					
HOMER	335	L	281	259	214	210	161	64	64	19				
SEWARD	345	E	290	268	253	219	170	73	76	136	131			
WHITTIER	436	S	383	360	345	311	263	165	165	229	223			
VALDEZ	405		350	328	313	279	230	133	133	196	191	68	68	
CORDOVA	405		350	328	313	279	230	133	133	196	191	68	68	39

VEHICLES UP TO 15 FEET (Driver NOT included) **ITEM 715**

BETWEEN / AND	UNALASKA	AKUTAN	FALSE PASS	COLD BAY	KING COVE	SAND POINT	CHIGNIK	KODIAK	PORT LIONS	SELDOVIA	HOMER	SEWARD	WHITTIER	VALDEZ
FALSE PASS	104	N												
COLD BAY	142	O	38											
KING COVE	168		72	34										
SAND POINT	226	V	131	93	67									
CHIGNIK	311	E	215	177	151	93								
KODIAK	480	H	384	346	320	262	177							
PORT LIONS	480	I	384	346	320	262	177	39						
SELDOVIA	587	C	492	454	428	369	285	116	116					
HOMER	577	L	482	444	418	359	275	106	106	29				
SEWARD	593	E	498	460	434	376	291	122	122	233	223			
WHITTIER	753	S	657	619	593	535	450	281	281	392	382			
VALDEZ	697		602	564	538	480	395	226	226	337	327	112	112	
CORDOVA	697		602	564	538	480	395	226	226	337	327	112	112	64

VEHICLES UP TO 19 FEET (Driver NOT included) **ITEM 719**

BETWEEN / AND	UNALASKA	AKUTAN	FALSE PASS	COLD BAY	KING COVE	SAND POINT	CHIGNIK	KODIAK	PORT LIONS	SELDOVIA	HOMER	SEWARD	WHITTIER	VALDEZ
FALSE PASS	123	N												
COLD BAY	169	O	46											
KING COVE	200		87	41										
SAND POINT	269	V	156	110	80									
CHIGNIK	370	E	257	211	180	110								
KODIAK	571	H	458	412	381	312	211							
PORT LIONS	571	I	458	412	381	312	211	46						
SELDOVIA	699	C	586	540	509	439	339	138	138					
HOMER	687	L	574	528	497	428	327	126	126	35				
SEWARD	706	E	594	548	517	447	347	145	145	277	265			
WHITTIER	896	S	783	737	706	637	536	335	335	467	455			
VALDEZ	830		718	672	641	571	470	269	269	401	389	134	134	
CORDOVA	830		718	672	641	571	470	269	269	401	389	134	134	76

VEHICLES UP TO 21 FEET (Driver NOT included) **ITEM 721**

BETWEEN / AND	UNALASKA	AKUTAN	FALSE PASS	COLD BAY	KING COVE	SAND POINT	CHIGNIK	KODIAK	PORT LIONS	SELDOVIA	HOMER	SEWARD	WHITTIER	VALDEZ
FALSE PASS	158	N												
COLD BAY	217	O	59											
KING COVE	257		111	52										
SAND POINT	347	V	201	142	102									
CHIGNIK	477	E	331	272	232	142								
KODIAK	737	H	591	532	492	402	272							
PORT LIONS	737	I	591	532	492	402	272	59						
SELDOVIA	902	C	756	697	657	567	437	177	177					
HOMER	887	L	741	682	642	552	422	162	162	44				
SEWARD	912	E	766	707	667	577	447	187	187	357	342			
WHITTIER	1157	S	1011	952	912	822	692	432	432	602	587			
VALDEZ	1072		926	867	827	737	607	347	347	517	502	172	172	
CORDOVA	1072		926	867	827	737	607	347	347	517	502	172	172	97

All tariffs and rates are quoted in U.S. dollars.

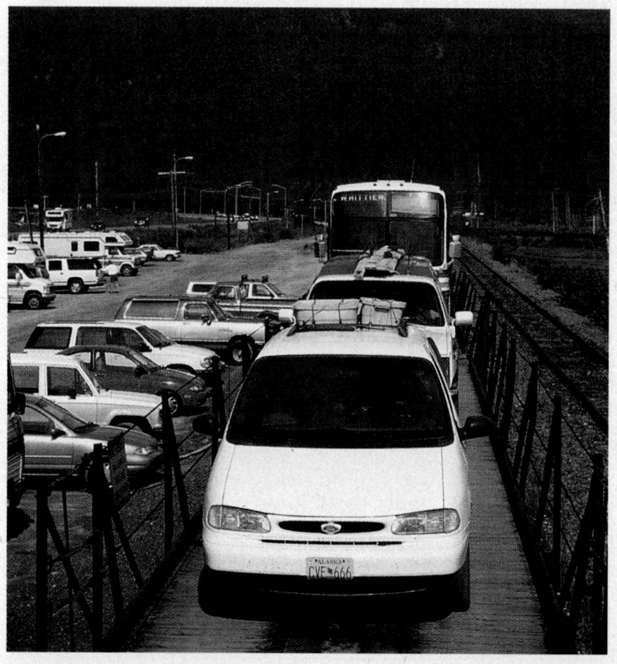

Vehicles on Portage to Whittier train. (© Michael DeYoung)

M/V TUSTUMENA Schedule

MAY EASTBOUND

Leave SELDOVIA	Leave HOMER	PORT LIONS	Arrive KODIAK	Leave SEWARD	Arrive VALDEZ
T30 6:00P	T30 10:00P	W1 8:30A	Lv.W1 5:00P	Ar.TH2 6:15A	
SU5 6:00A	SU5 9:30A		SU5 7:00P		
	M6 11:55A		M6 9:30P		
T7 6:00P	T7 11:30P		W8 9:00A		
	*** FROM ALEUTIAN CHAIN TRIP ***		M13 8:15P		
T14 6:00P	T14 10:00P	W15 8:30A	Lv.W15 5:00P	TH16 10:45A	TH16 10:45P
SU19 6:00A	SU19 9:30A		SU19 7:00P		
	M20 11:55A		M20 9:30P		
*T21 5:00P	W22 1:30A		Lv.W22 5:00P	TH23 10:45A	TH23 10:45P
SU26 5:00A	SU26 8:00A		SU26 5:30P		
	M27 9:30A		M27 7:00P		
T28 7:00P	T28 10:00P	W29 8:30A	Lv.W29 5:00P	TH30 10:45A	TH30 10:45P

* The following event may affect availability of space:
Kodiak King Crab Festival May 21-27

MAY WESTBOUND

Leave VALDEZ	Leave SEWARD	Leave KODIAK	PORT LIONS	Leave HOMER	Arrive SELDOVIA
	F3 9:30P	S4 12:45P	S4 4:00P	SU5 3:30A	SU5 5:00A
		SU5 10:30P		Ar.M6 8:00A	
		M6 11:55P		T7 12:30P	T7 2:00P
		W8 5:00P	*** TO ALEUTIAN CHAIN TRIP ***		
		M13 11:30P		T14 12:30P	T14 2:00P
F17 6:30A	F17 9:30P	S18 12:45P	S18 4:00P	SU19 3:30A	SU19 5:00A
		SU19 10:30P		Ar.M20 8:00A	
		M20 11:55P		T21 11:55A	T21 1:30P
F24 5:00A	F24 8:00P	S25 11:30A	S25 2:30P	SU26 2:30A	SU26 4:00A
		SU26 10:30P		Ar.M27 8:00A	
		*M27 11:55P		T28 2:00P	T28 3:30P
F31 6:30A	F31 9:30P	S1 12:45P	S1 4:00P	SU2 3:30A	SU2 5:00A

JUNE EASTBOUND

Leave SELDOVIA	Leave HOMER	PORT LIONS	Arrive KODIAK	Leave SEWARD	Arrive VALDEZ
SU2 8:00A	SU2 11:55A		SU2 9:30P		
	M3 11:55A		M3 9:30P		
T4 6:00P	T4 10:00P	W5 8:30A	Lv.W5 5:00P	TH6 10:45A	TH6 10:45P
SU9 6:00A	SU9 9:30A		SU9 7:00P		
	M10 11:55A		M10 9:30P		
T11 6:00P	T11 11:30P		W12 9:00A		
	*** FROM ALEUTIAN CHAIN TRIP ***		M17 8:15P		
T18 6:00P	T18 10:00P	W19 8:30A	Lv.W19 5:00P	TH20 10:45A	TH20 10:45P
SU23 6:00A	SU23 9:30A		SU23 7:00P		
	M24 11:55A		M24 9:30P		
T25 6:00P	T25 10:00P	W26 8:30A	Lv.W26 5:00P	TH27 10:45A	TH27 10:45P
SU30 6:00A	SU30 9:30A		SU30 7:00P		

JUNE WESTBOUND

Leave VALDEZ	Leave SEWARD	Leave KODIAK	PORT LIONS	Leave HOMER	Arrive SELDOVIA
		M3 11:55P		T4 12:30P	T4 2:00P
		SU2 10:30P		Ar.M3 8:00A	
F7 6:30A	F7 9:30P	S8 12:45P	S8 4:00P	SU9 3:30A	SU9 5:00A
		SU9 10:30P		Ar.M10 8:00A	
		M10 11:55P		T11 12:30P	T11 2:00P
		W12 5:00P	*** TO ALEUTIAN CHAIN TRIP ***		
		M17 11:30P		T18 12:30P	T18 2:00P
F21 6:30A	F21 9:30P	S22 12:45P	S22 4:00P	SU23 3:30A	SU23 5:00A
		SU23 10:30P		Ar.M24 8:00A	
		M24 11:55P		T25 12:30P	T25 2:00P
F28 6:30A	F28 9:30P	S29 12:45P	S29 4:00P	SU30 3:30A	SU 30 5:00A
		SU30 10:30P		Ar.M1 8:00A	

JULY EASTBOUND

Leave SELDOVIA	Leave HOMER	PORT LIONS	Arrive KODIAK	Leave SEWARD	Arrive VALDEZ
	M1 11:55A		M1 9:30P		
T2 6:00P	T2 10:00P	W3 8:30A	Lv.W3 5:00P	TH4 10:45A	TH4 10:45P
SU7 6:00A	SU7 9:30A		SU7 7:00P		
	M8 11:55A		M8 9:30P		
T9 6:00P	T9 11:30P		W10 9:00A		
	*** FROM ALEUTIAN CHAIN TRIP ***		M15 8:15P		
T16 6:00P	T16 10:00P	W17 8:30A	Lv.W17 5:00P	TH18 10:45A	TH18 10:45P
SU21 6:00A	SU21 9:30A		SU21 7:00P		
	M22 11:55A		M22 9:30P		
T23 6:00P	T23 10:00P	W24 8:30A	Lv.W24 5:00P	TH25 10:45A	TH25 10:45P
SU28 6:00A	SU28 9:30A		SU28 7:00P		
	M29 11:55A		M29 9:30P		
T30 6:00P	T30 10:00P	W31 8:30A	Lv.W31 5:00P	TH1 10:45A	TH1 10:45P

JULY WESTBOUND

Leave VALDEZ	Leave SEWARD	Leave KODIAK	PORT LIONS	Leave HOMER	Arrive SELDOVIA
		M1 11:55P		T2 12:30P	T2 2:00P
F5 6:30A	F5 9:30P	S6 12:45P	S6 4:00P	SU7 3:30A	SU7 5:00A
		SU7 10:30P		Ar.M8 8:00A	
		M8 11:55P		T9 12:30P	T9 2:00P
		W10 5:00P	*** TO ALEUTIAN CHAIN TRIP ***		
		M15 11:30P		T16 12:30P	T16 2:00P
F19 6:30A	F19 9:30P	S20 12:45P	S20 4:00P	SU21 3:30A	SU21 5:00A
		SU21 10:30P		Ar.M22 8:00A	
		M22 11:55P		T23 12:30P	T23 2:00P
F26 6:30A	F26 9:30P	S27 12:45P	S27 4:00P	SU28 3:30A	SU28 5:00A
		SU28 10:30P		Ar.M29 8:00A	
		M29 11:55P		T30 12:30P	T30 2:00P

AUGUST EASTBOUND

Leave SELDOVIA	Leave HOMER	PORT LIONS	Arrive KODIAK	Leave SEWARD	Arrive VALDEZ
SU4 6:00A	SU4 9:30A		SU4 7:00P		
	M5 11:55A		M5 9:30P		
T6 6:00P	T6 11:30P		W7 9:00A		
	*** FROM ALEUTIAN CHAIN TRIP ***		M12 8:15P		
T13 6:00P	T13 10:00P	W14 8:30A	Lv.W14 5:00P	TH15 10:45A	TH15 10:45P
SU18 6:00A	SU18 9:30A		SU18 7:00P		
	M19 11:55A		M19 9:30P		
T20 6:00P	T20 10:00P	W21 8:30A	Lv.W21 5:00P	TH22 10:45A	TH22 10:45P
SU25 6:00A	SU25 9:30A		SU25 7:00P		
	M26 11:55A		M26 9:30P		
T27 6:00P	T27 10:00P	W28 8:30A	Lv.W28 5:00P	TH29 10:45A	TH29 10:45P

AUGUST WESTBOUND

Leave VALDEZ	Leave SEWARD	Leave KODIAK	PORT LIONS	Leave HOMER	Arrive SELDOVIA
F2 6:30A	F2 9:30P	S3 12:45P	S3 4:00P	SU4 3:30A	SU4 5:00A
		SU4 10:30P		Ar.M5 8:00A	
		M5 11:55P		T6 12:30P	T6 2:00P
		W7 5:00P	*** TO ALEUTIAN CHAIN TRIP ***		
		M12 11:30P		T13 12:30P	T13 2:00P
F16 6:30A	F16 9:30P	S17 12:45P	S17 4:00P	SU18 3:30A	SU18 5:00A
		SU18 10:30P		Ar.M19 8:00A	
		M19 11:55P		T20 12:30P	T20 2:00P
F23 6:30A	F23 9:30P	S24 12:45P	S24 4:00P	SU25 3:30A	SU25 5:00A
		SU25 10:30P		Ar.M26 8:00A	
		M26 11:55P		T27 12:30P	T27 2:00P
F30 6:30A	F30 9:30P	S31 12:45P	S31 4:00P	SU1 3:30A	SU1 5:00A

SEPTEMBER EASTBOUND

Leave SELDOVIA	Leave HOMER	PORT LIONS	Arrive KODIAK	Leave SEWARD	Arrive VALDEZ
SU1 6:00A	SU1 9:30A		SU1 7:00P		
	M2 11:55A		M2 9:30P		
T3 6:00P	T3 10:00P	W4 8:30A	Lv.W4 5:00P	TH5 10:45A	TH5 10:45P
SU8 6:00A	SU8 9:30A		SU8 7:00P		
	M9 11:55A		M9 9:30P		
T10 6:00P	T10 11:30P		W11 9:00A		
	*** FROM ALEUTIAN CHAIN TRIP ***		M16 8:15P		
T17 6:00P	T17 10:00P	W18 8:30A	Lv.W18 5:00P	TH19 10:45A	TH19 10:45P
SU22 6:00A	SU22 9:30A		SU22 7:00P		
	M23 11:55A		M23 9:30P		
T24 6:00P	T24 11:30P		W25 9:00A		
	*** FROM ALEUTIAN CHAIN TRIP ***		M30 8:15P		

SEPTEMBER WESTBOUND

Leave VALDEZ	Leave SEWARD	Leave KODIAK	PORT LIONS	Leave HOMER	Arrive SELDOVIA
		SU1 10:30P		Ar.M2 8:00A	
		M2 11:55P		T3 12:30P	T3 2:00P
F6 6:30A	F6 9:30P	S7 12:45P	S7 4:00P	SU8 3:30A	SU8 5:00A
		SU8 10:30P		Ar.M9 8:00A	
		M9 11:55P		T10 12:30P	T10 2:00P
		W11 5:00P	*** TO ALEUTIAN CHAIN TRIP ***		
		M16 11:30P		T17 12:30P	T17 2:00P
F20 6:30A	F20 9:30P	S21 12:45P	S21 4:00P	SU22 3:30A	SU22 5:00A
		SU22 10:30P		Ar.M23 8:00A	
		M23 11:55P		T24 12:30P	T24 2:00P
		W25 5:00P	*** TO ALEUTIAN CHAIN TRIP ***		
		M30 11:30P		T1 12:30P	T1 2:00P

NOTE: Chenega Bay Whistle stops are available by notifying the Seward terminal.

M/V TUSTUMENA Cabin Tariffs

FOUR BERTH CABIN - OUTSIDE/COMPLETE FACILITIES **ITEM 4BF**

BETWEEN / AND	UNALASKA	AKUTAN	FALSE PASS	COLD BAY	KING COVE	SAND POINT	CHIGNIK	KODIAK	PORT LIONS	SELDOVIA	HOMER	SEWARD
AKUTAN	23											
FALSE PASS	80	57										
COLD BAY	109	86	29									
KING COVE	122	129	72	43								
SAND POINT	152	165	108	79	68							
CHIGNIK	194	210	153	124	113	80						
KODIAK	282	295	238	209	194	166	124					
PORT LIONS	282	295	238	209	194	166	124	43				
SELDOVIA	337	350	293	264	250	216	182	96	96			
HOMER	328	342	285	256	242	209	175	88	88	43		
SEWARD	349	362	305	276	262	228	194	98	98	163	155	
VALDEZ	(NO DIRECT SAILINGS)							164	164	216	209	91

FOUR BERTH CABIN - INSIDE/NO FACILITIES**ITEM 4NO**

BETWEEN / AND	UNALASKA	AKUTAN	FALSE PASS	COLD BAY	KING COVE	SAND POINT	CHIGNIK	KODIAK	PORT LIONS	SELDOVIA	HOMER	SEWARD
AKUTAN	19											
FALSE PASS	66	47										
COLD BAY	91	72	25									
KING COVE	102	108	61	36								
SAND POINT	127	138	91	66	57							
CHIGNIK	162	175	128	103	94	67						
KODIAK	235	246	199	174	162	138	103					
PORT LIONS	235	246	199	174	162	138	103	36				
SELDOVIA	281	292	245	220	208	180	152	80	80			
HOMER	274	285	238	213	202	174	146	73	73	36		
SEWARD	291	302	255	230	218	190	162	82	82	136	129	
VALDEZ	(NO DIRECT SAILINGS)							137	137	180	174	76

TWO BERTH CABIN - OUTSIDE/NO FACILITIES**ITEM 2NO**

BETWEEN / AND	UNALASKA	AKUTAN	FALSE PASS	COLD BAY	KING COVE	SAND POINT	CHIGNIK	KODIAK	PORT LIONS	SELDOVIA	HOMER	SEWARD
AKUTAN	13											
FALSE PASS	47	33										
COLD BAY	64	51	17									
KING COVE	75	79	45	28								
SAND POINT	100	97	63	46	40							
CHIGNIK	129	129	95	78	68	43						
KODIAK	179	192	158	141	130	110	76					
PORT LIONS	179	192	158	141	130	110	76	28				
SELDOVIA	213	226	192	175	164	140	115	56	56			
HOMER	208	221	187	170	159	136	111	52	52	28		
SEWARD	218	230	196	179	168	144	119	60	60	101	96	
VALDEZ	(NO DIRECT SAILINGS)							103	103	144	140	54

M/V TUSTUMENA ALEUTIAN CHAIN TRIPS

LV KODIAK	WED	5:00 PM	LV UNALASKA	SAT	11:45 AM
LV CHIGNIK	THU	1:00 PM	LV AKUTAN	SAT	4:00 PM
LV SAND POINT	THU	12:30 AM	LV COLD BAY	SUN	4:45 AM
LV KING COVE	FRI	9:00 AM	LV KING COVE	SUN	7:15 AM
LV COLD BAY	FRI	11:55 AM	LV SAND POINT	SUN	3:00 PM
LV FALSE PASS	FRI	5:30 PM	LV CHIGNIK	MON	1:45 AM
AR UNALASKA	SAT	6:30 AM	AR KODIAK	MON	8:15 PM

(Continued from page 621)
Club) are accepted at all terminals and by phone (some restrictions may apply).

Cancellation fees are charged if a change or cancellation is made within 14 days of sailing.

Vehicle tariffs depend on the size of vehicle. You are charged by how much space you take up, so a car with trailer is measured from the front of the car to the end of the trailer, including hitch space. (In summer, drivers' fares are not included in the vehicle tariff.)

Waterfall in Misty Fiords, 30 miles east of Ketchikan. (© Jason Paur)

Bicycles, kayaks and inflatables are charged a surcharge. Check the Alternate Means of Conveyance charges in the tariff section.

Passenger tariffs are charged as follows: adults and children 12 and over, full fare; children 2 to 11, approximately half fare; children under 2, free. Passenger fares do not include cabins or meals. Special passes and travel rates are available to senior citizens (over 65) and persons with disabilities. Check with the Alaska Marine Highway or consult the official Marine Highway schedule for costs and restrictions.

Cabin rates depend on vessel, size of cabin and facilities. Only 5 vessels have cabins available.

Pick up cabin keys from the purser's office when you board. Cabins are sold as a unit, not on a per berth basis. In other words, the cost of the cabin is the same whether 1 person occupies it or 10 people share it.

All cabins on the Southeast system ferries have a toilet and shower. Linens (towels, sheets, blankets) are provided. Restrooms and shower facilities are available for deck-passage (walk-on) passengers.

Surcharges are assessed on pets ($25 to/from Bellingham, $10 to/from Prince Rupert and to/from Stewart/Hyder) and unattended vehicles ($50 to/from Bellingham, $20 to/from Prince Rupert and to/from Stewart/Hyder, and $10 to/from other ports). The Marine Highway does not provide for loading and off-loading of unattended vehicles.

Check-in times: Summer check-in times for reserved vehicles prior to departure are: Bellingham and Prince Rupert, 3 hours; Ketchikan, Juneau, Haines, Skagway, Homer, Seward, Kodiak, 2 hours; Petersburg, 1½ hours; all other ports, 1 hour. Call the Sitka terminal for check-in time (907/747-3300). Passengers without vehicles must check in 1 hour prior to departure at all ports except Bellingham, where check-in is 2 hours prior to departure. For MV *Bartlett* departures from

Kayakers skim across Portage Cove near Haines. (© Derby Photography)

Whittier, check-in time at the Portage train loading ramp 1 hour prior to train departure.

Local times are shown on all Alaska Marine Highway schedules: Alaska time for Alaska ports on the Southeast and Southcentral/Southwest schedules, Pacific time for Prince Rupert, BC, Bellingham, WA, and Stewart/Hyder on the Southeast schedules.

Luggage: You are responsible for your own luggage! Foot passengers may bring hand luggage only (not to exceed 100 lbs.). There is no limit on luggage carried in a vehicle. Coin-operated storage lockers are available aboard most ships, and baggage carts are furnished on the car deck. Baggage handling is NOT provided by the Marine Highway. Bicycles, small boats and inflatables are not considered baggage and will be charged a fare.

Stopovers: In-port time on all vessels is only long enough to unload and load. A stopover is getting off at any port between your point of origin and final destination and taking another vessel at a later time. For travelers with vehicles and/or cabins this can be done as long as reservations to do so have been made in advance. For example, travelers with a camper may wish to go from Prince Rupert to Haines but stopover at Petersburg for 2 days before continuing to Haines. As long as reservations for Prince Rupert to Petersburg and Petersburg to Haines are made before leaving Prince Rupert, there will be no problems. But you cannot change your mind once you are loaded and under way. Passenger, vehicle and cabin fares are charged on a point-to-point basis, and stopovers will increase the total ticket cost.

NOTE: Check the schedules carefully. Ferries do *NOT* stop at all ports daily, and northbound and southbound routes vary. You may have to wait 3 to 4 days for the next ferry. Also keep in mind that ferries may be late; do not schedule connections too close together.

Vehicles: Reservations are required. Any vehicle that may be driven legally on the highway is acceptable for transport on the 4 larger vessels. Vessels on the Southeast system can load vehicles up to 70 feet/21m long with special arrangements. Maximum length on the *Tustumena* is 40 feet/12m. Vehicle fares are determined by the overall length and width of the vehicle. Vehicles from 8 to 9 feet wide are charged 125 percent of the fare listed for the vehicle length. Vehicles over 9 feet in width are charged 150 percent of the fare listed for vehicle length.

Motorcycles, motorscooters, bicycles and kayaks are charged.

Hazardous materials may not be transported on the ferries. Bottled gas containers must be turned off. Portable containers of fuel are permitted but must be stored with vessel personnel while en route.

The state assumes no responsibility for the loading and unloading of unattended vehicles. If you ship a vehicle on the ferry you must make your own arrangements for loading and unloading. Unaccompanied vehicles are assessed a surcharge of $50 to or from Bellingham, and $20 to or from Prince Rupert and to or from Stewart/Hyder.

Meals: The cost of meals is not included in passenger, cabin or vehicle fares. Food service varies from vessel to vessel, with dining room or cafeteria-style dining on all ferries.

Vehicle deck restrictions: U.S. Coast Guard regulations prohibit passenger access to the vehicle deck while under way, so plan on bringing up items you will need for the voyage soon after boarding the vessel. Passengers can gain access to their vehicle by applying to the purser's desk for an escort. Regulations prohibit sleeping in your vehicle while the vessel is under way.

Pet policy: Dogs and other pets are not allowed in cabins and must be transported on the vehicle deck only—*NO EXCEPTIONS.* (There are special accommodations for animals aiding disabled passengers. Proper paperwork is required.) Animals and pets are to be transported inside a vehicle or in suitable containers furnished by the passenger. Animals and pets must be cared for by the owner. Passengers who must visit pets or animals en route should apply to the purser's office for an escort to the vehicle deck. (On long sailings the purser periodically announces "cardeck calls.") You may walk your pet at port stops. Keep in mind that some port stops are very brief and that sailing time between some ports will be as long as 36 hours (Bellingham to Ketchikan).

Dogs, cats, or larger animals are assessed a charge of $25 to or from Bellingham and $10 to or from Prince Rupert and to or from Stewart/Hyder. This surcharge applies even if the animal is traveling inside the owner's vehicle.

Animal's owner or attendant must possess a current health certificate (within 30 days) for the animal in order to transport it through Canada. (See Customs Requirements in the GENERAL INFORMATION section.)

Deck passage: Because access to the vehicle deck is not permitted and because of the limited number of cabins available, many people ride the ferries overnight without cabin accommodations. This is done by sleeping in one of the reclining lounge chairs or rolling out your sleeping bag in an empty corner or even out on deck. Public washrooms are available.

Crossing the U.S.–Canada border: If any part of your trip is to, from or through Canada, you must report to customs at the port of entry. No passport is required for citizens of either country, but you will be required to furnish proof of citizenship, financial responsibility, and vehicle registration, ownership and liability coverage. Spe-

NEW FOR 1996!

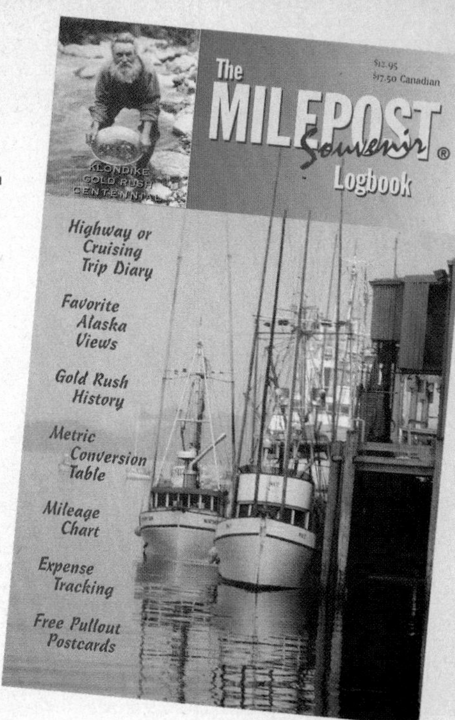

The MILEPOST® Souvenir Logbook

The editors of *The MILEPOST®* family of books have designed a beautiful new logbook for use with *The MILEPOST®*. This logbook contains gorgeous full-color photos of sights that you will actually see when using *The MILEPOST®* to guide your way through northwestern Canada and Alaska.

You'll treasure this beautiful book as a permanent record of your trip to Alaska for years to come. It helps keep track of expenses, lodging, number of miles traveled daily, entertainment and attractions, wildlife sightings, and even addresses and phone numbers of new friends made along the way.

***The MILEPOST® Souvenir Logbook* contains 30 full-color photos, plus 4 FREE pull-out postcards you can send to friends or keep as souvenirs for yourself. It is spiral-bound for easy handling while traveling and is a must-have with your copy of *The MILEPOST®*.**

***The MILEPOST® Souvenir Logbook* also contains ...**

- **Metric conversion chart**
- **Pronunciation guide**
- **Mileage Chart**

$12.95 U.S.

To order see bound-in order envelope in this book.

Gold Discoveries

1897—Klondike gold rush begins

1898—Anvil Creek, AK; Atlin, BC

1899—Nome

1900—Porcupine

1902—Pedro Creek

1906—Chandalar

1907—Ruby

Spectacular Tracy Arm, 50 miles southeast of Juneau, is noted for its large icebergs, waterfalls and striking rock features. (Steve Weber)

cial restrictions govern firearms and animals. (See Customs Requirements in the GENERAL INFORMATION section.)

Information aboard state ferries: Pursers provide general information, and there are also U.S. Forest Service interpreters on duty in summer aboard most vessels to answer questions and provide information about points of interest.

Cruise Ships

From May through September, large luxury cruise ships and small explorer-class ships carry visitors to Alaska from West Coast ports via the Inside Passage. Most ships depart from Vancouver, BC. Other ports of departure include San Francisco and Seattle.

There are 37 ships to choose from and almost as many itineraries. There's also a bewildering array of travel options. Both round-trip and one-way cruises are available, or a cruise may be sold as part of a packaged tour that includes air, rail and/or motorcoach transportation. Various shore excursions may be included in the cruise price or offered to passengers for added cost. Ports of call may depend on length of cruise, which ship you choose, time of sailing or debarkation point. Because of the wide variety of cruise trips available, it is wise to work with your travel agent.

Following is a list of cruise lines serving Alaska in 1996. Included are the names of the line's ships (passenger capacity is shown in parentheses) and proposed Alaska ports of call. Not all ships have the same itinerary. Contact the cruise line directly or your travel agent for more details.

Alaska Sightseeing/Cruise West, 4th & Battery Bldg., Suite 700, Seattle, WA 98121-1438; phone 1-800-426-7702 or (206) 441-8687, fax (206) 441-4757. *Spirit of Glacier Bay* (58 passengers); *Sheltered Seas* (90 passengers, no cabin space); *Spirit of Alaska* (82 passengers); *Spirit of Discovery* (84 passengers), and *Spirit of '98* (101 passengers), *Glacier Seas* (85 passengers). Ports of call: Anchorage, Glacier Bay, Haines, Juneau, Ketchikan, Misty Fiords, Petersburg, Sitka, Skagway, Tracy Arm, Valdez, Wrangell.

Carnival Cruise Line, Carnival Place, 3655 NW 87th Ave., Miami, FL 33178-2428; phone (305) 599-2600. *Tropicale* (1,428 passengers). Ports of call: College Fjord, Haines, Hubbard Glacier, Juneau, Ketchikan, Seward, Sitka, Skagway, Tracy Arm, Valdez.

Celebrity Cruises, Inc., 5200 Blue Lagoon Dr., Miami, FL 33126; phone (305) 262-6677. *Horizon* (1,354 passengers). Ports of call: College Fjord, Glacier Bay, Haines, Hubbard Glacier, Juneau, Ketchikan, Misty Fiords, Seward, Sitka, Skagway, Tracy Arm, Valdez.

Clipper Cruise Lines, Windsor Bldg., 7711 Bonhomme Ave., St. Louis, MO 63105-1956; phone 1-800-325-0010 or (314) 727-2929, fax (314) 727-6576. *Yorktown Clipper* (138 passengers). Ports of call: Glacier Bay, Haines, Juneau, Ketchikan, Misty Fiords, Sitka, Skagway, Tracy Arm, Wrangell.

Crystal Cruises, 2121 Avenue of the Stars, Los Angeles, CA 90067; phone 1-800-446-6620, (310) 785-9300. *Crystal Harmony* (960 passengers). Anchorage, College Fjord, Glacier Bay, Haines, Homer, Hubbard Glacier, Juneau, Ketchikan, Misty Fiords, Seward, Sitka, Skagway, Tracy Arm, Valdez, Wrangell.

Cunard Line Ltd., 555 5th Ave., New York, NY 10017-2453; phone 1-800-5-CUNARD or (212) 949-0915. *Sagafjord* (589 passengers), *Cunard Dynasty* (800 passengers), *Sea Goddess II* (116 passengers). Ports of call: Anchorage, College Fjord, Glacier Bay, Homer, Hubbard Glacier, Juneau, Ketchikan, Misty Fiords, Petersburg, Seward, Sitka, Skagway, Tracy Arm, Valdez, Wrangell.

Glacier Bay Tours & Cruises, 520 Pike St., Suite 1400, Seattle, WA 98101; phone 1-800-451-5952 or (206) 623-2417, fax (206) 623-7809. *Executive Explorer* (49 passengers), *Wilderness Explorer* (36 passengers). Glacier Bay, Haines, Juneau, Ketchikan, Sitka, Skagway

Hanseatic Cruises GmbH, Nagelsweg 55, 20097 Hamburg, Germany; phone 49-40-231603. *Hanseatic*. Ports of call: College Fjord, Glacier Bay, Haines, Juneau, Ketchiakn, Misty Fiords, Seward, Sitka, Skagway, Tracy Arm, Wrangell.

Holland America Westours, 300 Elliott Ave. W., Seattle, WA 98119; phone (206) 281-3535, fax (206) 283-2687. *Statendam* (1,266 passengers), *Nieuw Amsterdam* (1,214 passengers), *Noordam* (1,214 passengers), *Ryndam* (1,266 passengers), *Rotterdam* (1,075 passengers), *Westerdam* (1,494 passengers). Ports of call: College Fjord, Glacier Bay, Hubbard Glacier, Juneau, Ketchikan, Seward, Sitka, Valdez.

Norwegian Cruise Lines, 95 Merrick Way, Coral Gables, FL 33134; phone 1-800-327-7030, (305) 447-9660. *Windward* (1,246 passengers), *Norwegian Crown* (1,052 passengers). Ports of call: Glacier Bay, Haines, Juneau, Ketchikan, Misty Fiords, Sitka, Skagway, Tracy Arm.

Phoenix Reisen GmbH, Kolnstrasse 80, 53111 Bonn, Germany; phone 49-228-726280. *Maxim Gorkiy*. Ports of call: College Fjord, Glacier Bay, Hubbard Glacier, Juneau, Ketchikan, Misty Fiords, Sitka, Skagway, Valdez, Wrangell.

Princess Cruises, 10100 Santa Monica Blvd., Los Angeles, CA 90067; phone (310) 553-1770, fax (310) 277-6175. *Regal Princess* and *Crown Princess* (1,590 passengers), *Star Princess* (1,490 passengers), *Golden Princess* (830 passengers), *Sky Princess* (1,200 passengers) and *Sun Princess* (1,950 passengers). Ports of call: College Fjord, Glacier Bay, Hubbard Glacier, Juneau, Ketchikan, Seward, Sitka, Skagway, Valdez.

Royal Caribbean Cruise Line, 1050 Caribbean Way, Miami, FL 33132; phone 1-800-327-6700. *Legend of the Seas* (1,808 passengers), *Song of Norway* (1,040 passengers). Ports of call: Haines, Hubbard Glacier, Juneau, Ketchikan, Misty Fiords, Sitka, Skagway, Tracy Arm, Wrangell.

Royal Cruise Line, 1 Maritime Plaza, San Francisco, CA 94111; phone (415) 956-7200, fax (415) 956-1656. *Royal Odyssey* (750 passengers). Ports of call: College Fjord, Glacier Bay, Hubbard Glacier, Juneau, Ketchikan, Seward, Sitka, Skagway, Tracy Arm.

Seabourn Cruise Line, 55 Francisco St., San Francisco, CA 94133; phone (415) 391-7444. *Seabourne Pride* (200 passengers). Ports of call: College Fjord, Haines, Hubbard Glacier, Juneau, Ketchikan, Misty Fiords, Petersburg, Seward, Sitka, Skagway, Tracy Arm.

Society Expeditions, 2001 Western Ave., Suite 300, Seattle, WA 98121; phone (206) 728-9400. *World Discoverer* (138 passengers). Ports of call: College Fjord, Homer, Hubbard Glacier, Ketchikan, Misty Fiords, Seward, Sitka, Tracy Arm.

Special Expeditions, 1415 Western Ave., Suite 700, Seattle, WA 98101; phone (206) 382-9593. *Sea Bird* and *Sea Lion* (70 passengers). Ports of call: Glacier Bay, Haines, Juneau, Ketchikan, Sitka, Tracy Arm.

World Explorer Cruises, 555 Montgomery St., Suite 1400, San Francisco, CA 94111; phone 1-800-854-3835, (415) 393-1565. *Universe Explorer* (550 passengers). Ports of call: Glacier Bay, Juneau, Ketchikan, Seward, Sitka, Skagway, Valdez, Wrangell.

INSIDE PASSAGE

Southeastern Alaska communities from Ketchikan to Skagway

(See maps, pages 630–634)

Cruise ships anchored in Juneau's Gastineau Channel. (© Michael DeYoung)

Alaska's Inside Passage, located in the southeastern section of the state, is referred to by many of its residents simply as "Southeast." It is a unique region where industry, transportation, recreation and community planning are dictated by spectacular topography.

The region is accessible by air, land or sea. Jet service is available to Juneau, Ketchikan, Wrangell, Petersburg, Sitka and Gustavus. Smaller communities are served by local commuter aircraft. The port communities of Haines and Skagway offer road connections to the Alaska Highway system via the Haines Highway and Klondike Highway 2. The Alaska Marine Highway moves people and vehicles between ports, and connects the Inside Passage with Prince Rupert, BC, and Bellingham, WA. Several cruise ship lines ply the waterways of the Inside Passage and offer a variety of cruising opportunities. (For details on ferry and cruise ship travel, see the MARINE ACCESS ROUTES section.)

Measuring about 125 by 400 miles/200 by 650 km, 60 percent of the region consists of thousands of islands covered with dense forests of spruce, hemlock and cedar, a result of the mild, moist coastal climate. These islands make up the Alexander Archipelago, and include Prince of Wales Island, the third largest island in the United States (the Big Island of Hawaii is first, followed by Kodiak). The Coast Mountains form the mainland portion of southeastern Alaska.

Southeastern Alaska lies between 54°40' and 60° north latitude, the same as Scotland, Denmark and southern Sweden. The latitude of Scotland's Loch Ness is slightly north of the latitude at Wrangell Narrows. Stockholm and Skagway share the same latitude, and Ketchikan's is a little south of Copenhagen's.

Warmed by ocean currents, this region experiences mild, warm summers, with July temperatures averaging around 60°F/16°C. An occasional heat wave may reach the high 80s. Winters are cool, alternating snow, rain and sunshine; Jan. temperatures average 20° to 40°F/-7° to 4°C. Sub-zero winter temperatures are uncommon. The region receives considerable annual rainfall, from 80 to more than 200 inches (heaviest in late fall, lightest in summer). Populated areas receive 30 to 200 inches of snow annually; the high mountains more than 400 inches a year.

The majority of southeastern Alaska lies within Tongass National Forest, the largest national forest in the United States. (Southeastern Alaska has over 5.6 million acres of wilderness lands.) The forests provide one of the region's major industries. Timber harvesting supplies a pulp mill in Ketchikan and sawmills in Wrangell, Klawock, Metlakatla and Ketchikan.

Commercial fishing and fish processing is another of Southeast's major industries. The numerous rivers and streams, mountains, valleys, melting glaciers and frequent rainfall create ideal spawning grounds for salmon. Local waters harbor an abundance of sea-life, including crab, shrimp, halibut, herring and black cod.

Government is a significant employer throughout the region with federal, state and local government providing the majority of jobs. Juneau serves as the state's capital. Tourism is another major contributor to the region's economy, providing both jobs and revenue.

About 69,000 people live along the Inside Passage, according to 1990 U.S. Census figures. About 70 percent live in the 5 major communities of Juneau (29,228), Sitka (9,194), Ketchikan (15,082), Petersburg (3,350) and Wrangell (2,758). More than 20 percent are Native, mostly Tlingit (KLINK it) Indian, plus Haida (HI duh) and Tsimshian (SHIM shian).

Alaska's Natives, famous for their totem poles, weaving, beading, basketry and dancing, occupied the region long before Vitus Bering discovered Alaska in 1741.

Russia controlled Alaska from the turn of the 19th century until 1867, centering its extensive fur-trading empire in Sitka, the Russian capital of Alaska. Sitka was a port of international trade, controlling trading posts from California to the Aleutians, and was considered cultured because of European influence. At a time when San Francisco was a crude new boom town, Sitka was called the "Paris of the Pacific."

Commercial interest in southeastern

(Continues on page 635)

INSIDE PASSAGE *Prince Rupert, BC to Ketchikan, AK*

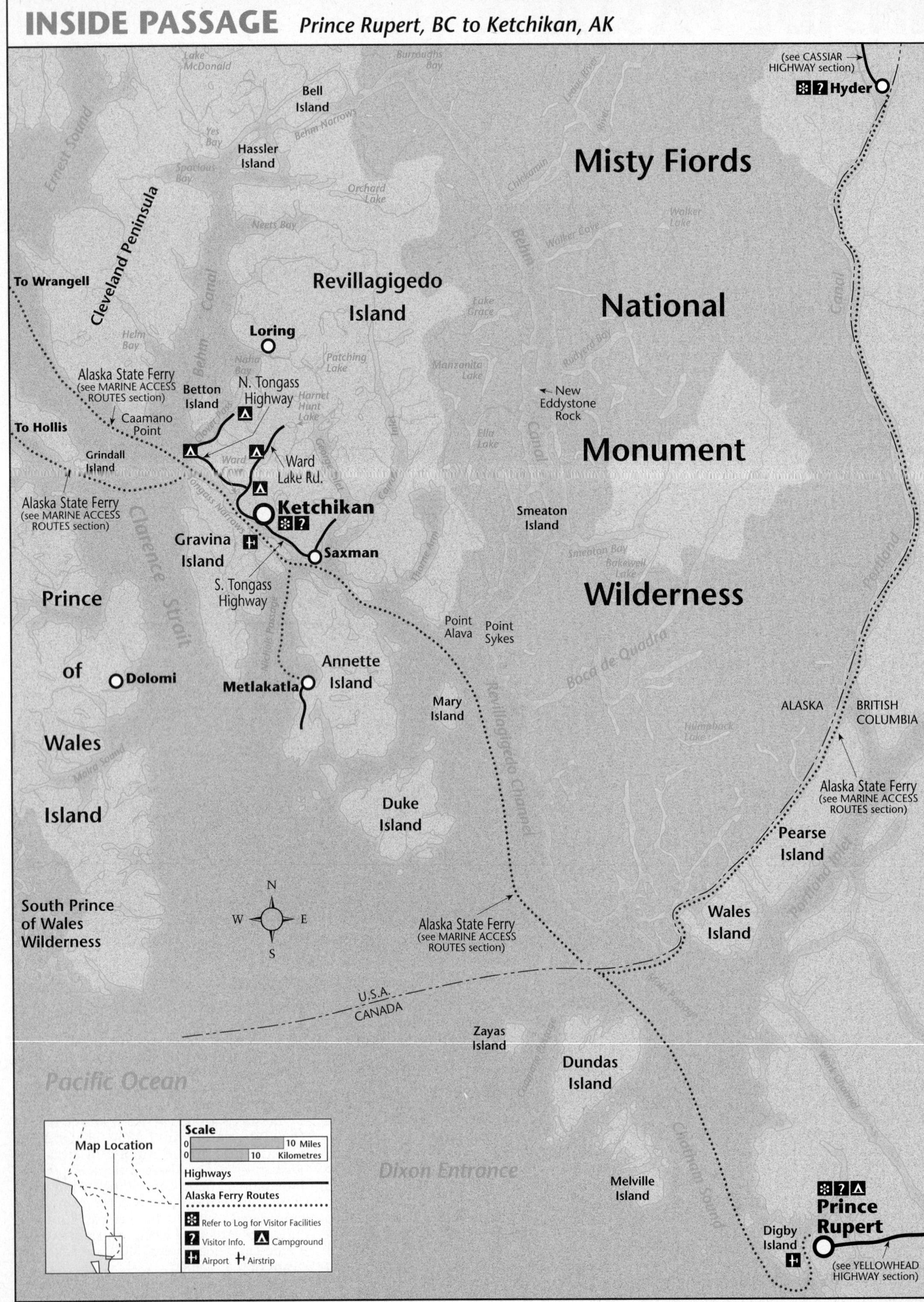

INSIDE PASSAGE *Ketchikan, AK to Wrangell, AK*

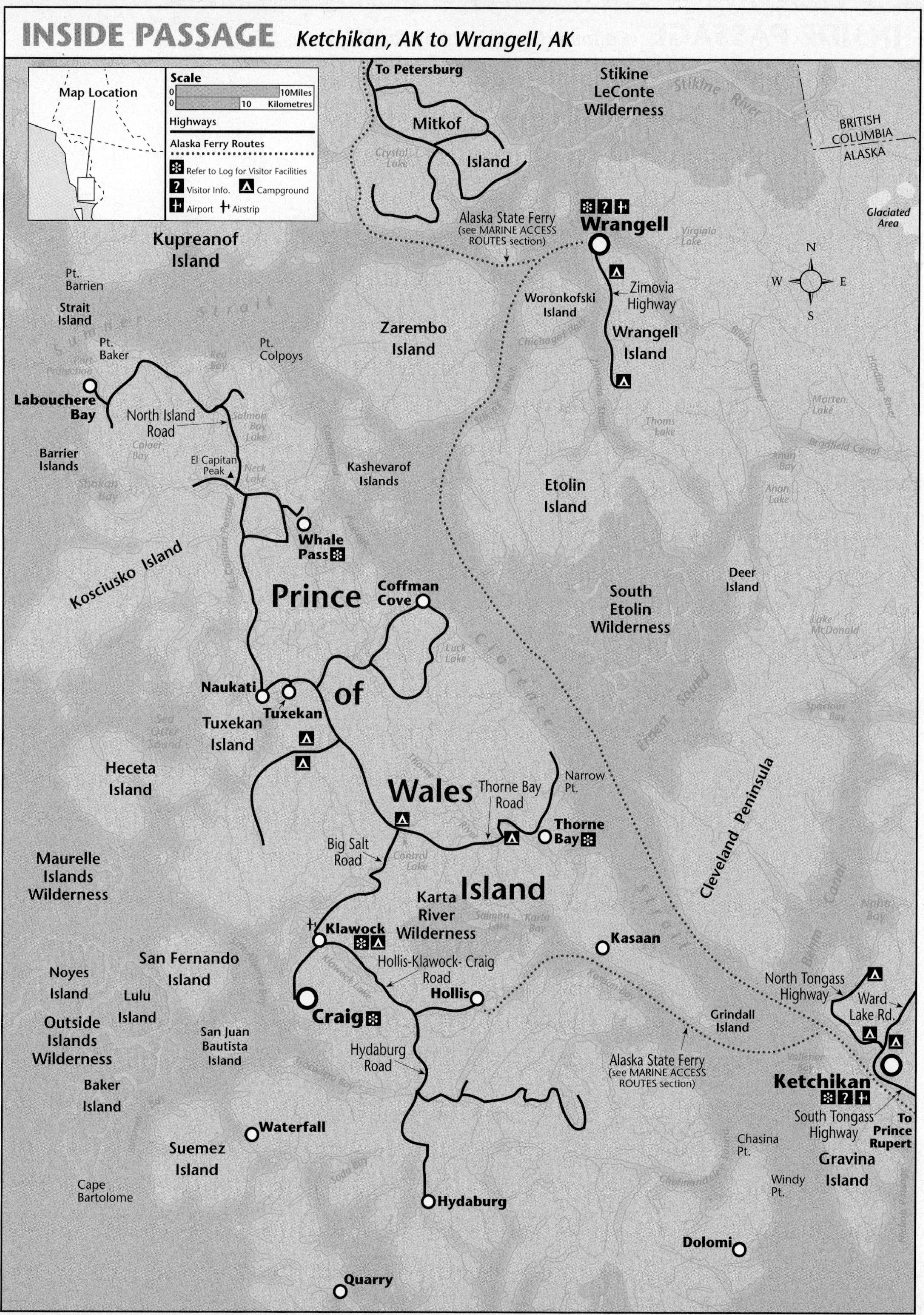
Map Location
Scale
0 10 Miles
0 10 Kilometres
Highways
Alaska Ferry Routes
Refer to Log for Visitor Facilities
Visitor Info.
Campground
Airport
Airstrip
To Petersburg
Mitkof
Island
Crystal Lake
Stikine LeConte Wilderness
Stikine River
BRITISH COLUMBIA
ALASKA
Glaciated Area
Alaska State Ferry (see MARINE ACCESS ROUTES section)
Wrangell
Virginia Lake
Kupreanof Island
Pt. Barrien
Strait Island
Sumner Strait
Pt. Baker
Port Protection
Red Bay
Pt. Colpoys
Zarembo Island
Woronkofski Island
Chichagof Pass
Zimovia Highway
Wrangell Island
Zimovia Strait
Blake Channel
Harding River
Marten Lake
Labouchere Bay
North Island Road
Salmon Bay Lake
Calder Bay
Barrier Islands
El Capitan Peak
Neck Lake
Shakan Bay
Kashevarof Passage
Kashevarof Islands
Stikine Strait
Thoms Lake
Bradfield Canal
Anan Bay
Anan Lake
Etolin Island
Whale Pass
Kosciusko Island
El Capitan Passage
Prince of Wales Island
Coffman Cove
South Etolin Wilderness
Deer Island
Lake McDonald
Luck Lake
Clarence Strait
Ernest Sound
Spacious Bay
Naukati
Tuxekan
Tuxekan Island
Sea Otter Sound
Heceta Island
Thorne River
Narrow Pt.
Thorne Bay Road
Thorne Bay
Cleveland Peninsula
Big Salt Road
Control Lake
Maurelle Islands Wilderness
Karta River Wilderness
Salmon Lake
Karta Bay
Behm Canal
Naha Bay
Klawock
Kasaan
Kasaan Bay
San Fernando Island
Hollis-Klawock- Craig Road
Klawock Lake
San Alberto Bay
Noyes Island
Lulu Island
Craig
Hollis
North Tongass Highway
Ward Lake Rd.
Grindall Island
Outside Islands Wilderness
San Juan Bautista Island
Hydaburg Road
Trocadero Bay
Alaska State Ferry (see MARINE ACCESS ROUTES section)
Vallenar Bay
Ketchikan
Baker Island
Bucareli Bay
Waterfall
South Tongass Highway
To Prince Rupert
Chasina Pt.
Suemez Island
Soda Bay
Cholmondeley Sound
Gravina Island
Windy Pt.
Nichols Passage
Cape Bartolome
Hydaburg
Dolomi
Quarry
N
S
E
W

INSIDE PASSAGE *Coffman Cove, AK to Sitka, AK*

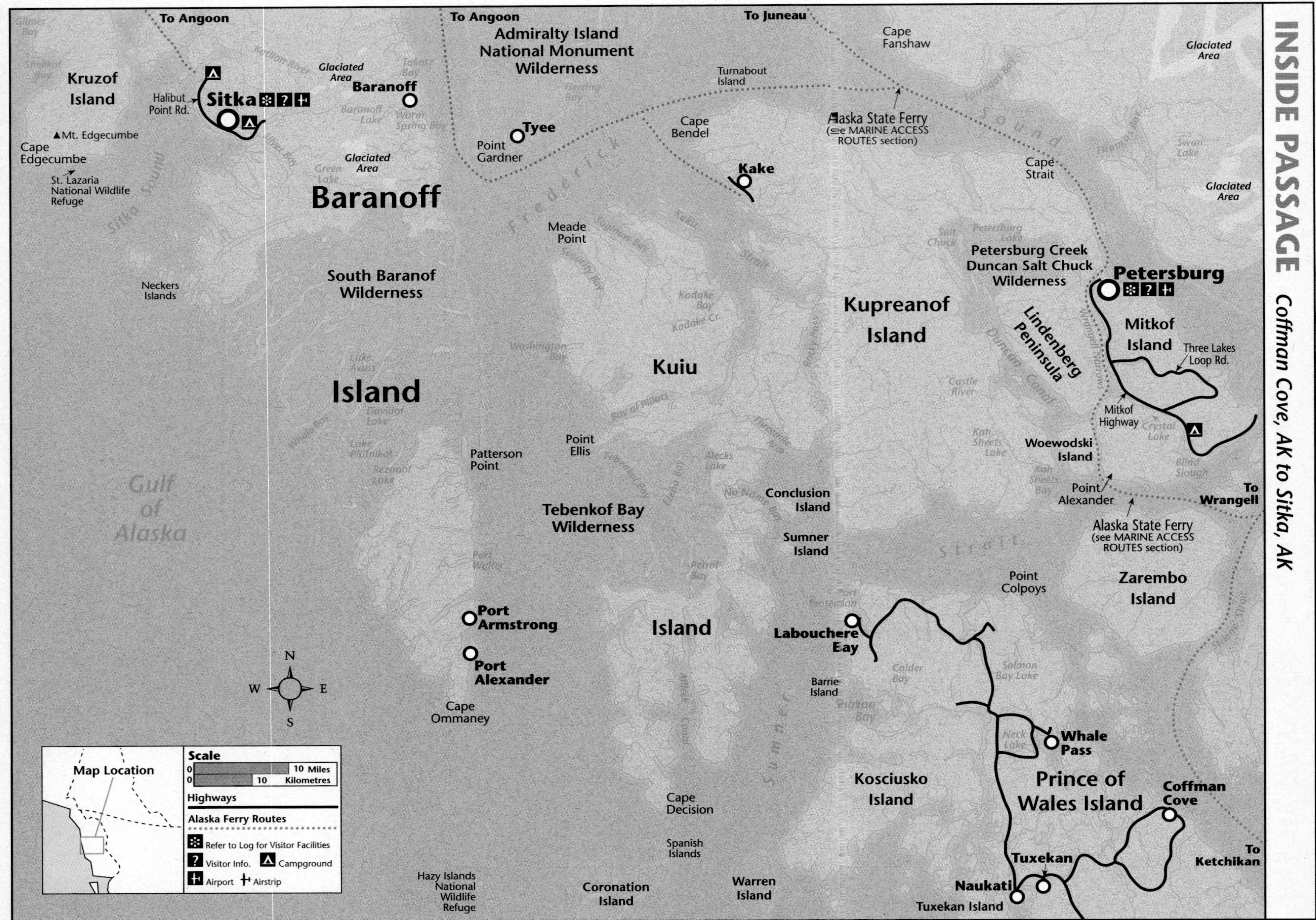
To Angoon
To Angoon
To Juneau
Cape Fanshaw
Admiralty Island National Monument Wilderness
Glaciated Area
Glaciated Area
Glaciated Area
Glaciated Area
Kruzof Island
Halibut Point Rd.
Sitka
Baranoff
Tyee
Point Gardner
Turnabout Island
Cape Bendel
Alaska State Ferry (see MARINE ACCESS ROUTES section)
Kake
Cape Strait
Mt. Edgecumbe
Cape Edgecumbe
St. Lazaria National Wildlife Refuge
Baranoff
Frederick Sound
Meade Point
Petersburg Creek Duncan Salt Chuck Wilderness
Petersburg
Neckers Islands
South Baranof Wilderness
Kupreanof Island
Mitkof Island
Three Lakes Loop Rd.
Lindenberg Peninsula
Kuiu
Island
Mitkof Highway
Patterson Point
Point Ellis
Woewodski Island
Point Alexander
To Wrangell
Gulf of Alaska
Tebenkof Bay Wilderness
Conclusion Island
Sumner Island
Alaska State Ferry (see MARINE ACCESS ROUTES section)
Point Colpoys
Zarembo Island
Port Armstrong
Port Alexander
Island
Labouchere Bay
Cape Ommaney
Barrie Island
Whale Pass
Kosciusko Island
Prince of Wales Island
Coffman Cove
Cape Decision
Spanish Islands
Tuxekan
To Ketchikan
Hazy Islands National Wildlife Refuge
Coronation Island
Warren Island
Naukati
Tuxekan Island
N
W
E
S
Map Location
Scale
0 10 Miles
0 10 Kilometres
Highways
Alaska Ferry Routes
Refer to Log for Visitor Facilities
Visitor Info.
Campground
Airport
Airstrip

INSIDE PASSAGE *Angoon, AK to Juneau, AK*

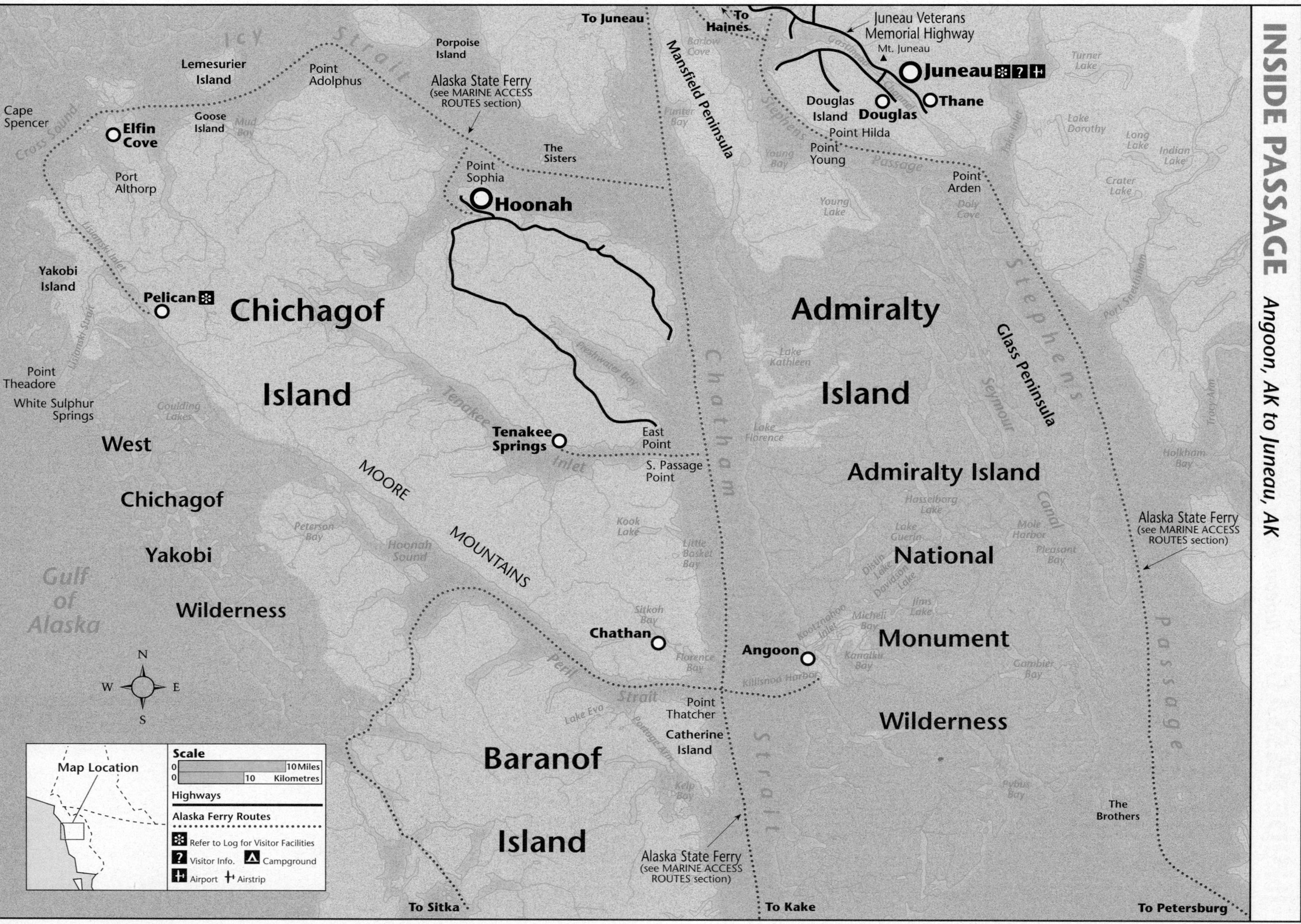
To Juneau
To Haines
Juneau Veterans Memorial Highway
Mt. Juneau
Juneau
Thane
Douglas Island
Douglas
Point Hilda
Point Young
Point Arden
Mansfield Peninsula
Glass Peninsula
Stephens Passage
Icy Strait
Porpoise Island
Lemesurier Island
Point Adolphus
Alaska State Ferry (see MARINE ACCESS ROUTES section)
Cape Spencer
Cross Sound
Elfin Cove
Goose Island
The Sisters
Point Sophia
Hoonah
Port Althorp
Yakobi Island
Pelican
Chichagof Island
Admiralty Island
Point Theadore
White Sulphur Springs
West Chichagof Yakobi Wilderness
Tenakee Springs
Tenakee Inlet
East Point
S. Passage Point
Chatham Strait
Admiralty Island National Monument Wilderness
MOORE MOUNTAINS
Gulf of Alaska
Chathan
Angoon
Peril Strait
Point Thatcher
Catherine Island
Baranof Island
Seymour Canal
The Brothers
To Sitka
To Kake
To Petersburg
N
E
S
W
Map Location
Scale
0 10 Miles
0 10 Kilometres
Highways
Alaska Ferry Routes
Refer to Log for Visitor Facilities
Visitor Info.
Campground
Airport
Airstrip

INSIDE PASSAGE *Juneau, AK to Skagway, AK*

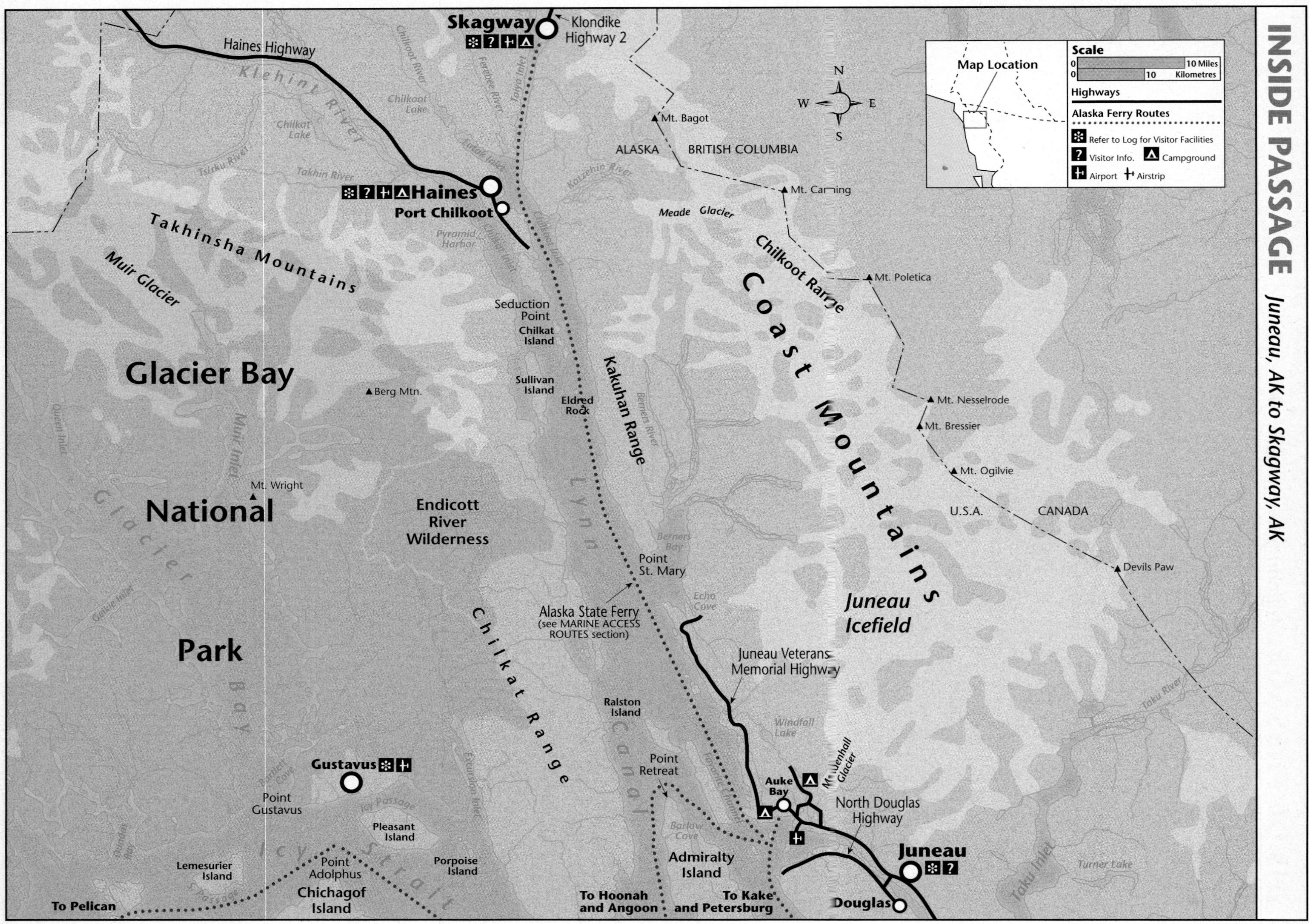
Map Location
Scale
0 10 Miles
0 10 Kilometres
Highways
Alaska Ferry Routes
Refer to Log for Visitor Facilities
Visitor Info.
Campground
Airport
Airstrip
N
W
E
S
Skagway
Klondike Highway 2
Haines Highway
Klehini River
Chilkoot River
Ferebee River
Taiya Inlet
Chilkoot Lake
Chilkat Lake
Tsirku River
Takhin River
Lutak Inlet
Haines
Port Chilkoot
Pyramid Harbor
Chilkat Inlet
Chilkoot Inlet
Takhinsha Mountains
Muir Glacier
Glacier Bay
Berg Mtn.
Queen Inlet
Muir Inlet
Mt. Wright
National
Glacier
Geikie Inlet
Park
Bay
Endicott River Wilderness
Seduction Point
Chilkat Island
Sullivan Island
Eldred Rock
Kakuhan Range
Berners River
Lynn
Canal
Katzehin River
Mt. Bagot
ALASKA
BRITISH COLUMBIA
Mt. Canning
Meade Glacier
Chilkoot Range
Mt. Poletica
Coast Mountains
Mt. Nesselrode
Mt. Bressier
Mt. Ogilvie
U.S.A.
CANADA
Devils Paw
Berners Bay
Point St. Mary
Echo Cove
Juneau Icefield
Alaska State Ferry (see MARINE ACCESS ROUTES section)
Chilkat Range
Juneau Veterans Memorial Highway
Taku River
Windfall Lake
Mendenhall Glacier
Ralston Island
Point Retreat
Favorite Channel
Auke Bay
North Douglas Highway
Barlow Cove
Admiralty Island
Juneau
Douglas
Taku Inlet
Turner Lake
Gustavus
Bartlett Cove
Point Gustavus
Icy Passage
Excursion Inlet
Pleasant Island
Porpoise Island
Dundas Bay
Lemesurier Island
Icy Strait
Point Adolphus
Chichagof Island
S. Passage
To Pelican
To Hoonah and Angoon
To Kake and Petersburg

(Continued from page 629)
Alaska declined with the fur trade, following Alaska's purchase by the United States. Interest in Southeast was rekindled by the salmon industry as canneries were established, the first at Klawock in 1878. Salmon canning peaked in the late 1930s and then declined from overfishing.

But the first significant white populations arrived because of gold. By the time thousands of gold seekers traveled through the Inside Passage in 1898 to Skagway and on to Canada's Klondike (sparking interest in the rest of Alaska), the largest gold ore mine of its day, the Treadwell near Juneau, had been in operation for years.

Juneau became Alaska's capital in 1906,

Whale watching in Stephens Passage between Petersburg and Juneau.
(© Michael DeYoung)

INSIDE PASSAGE ADVERTISERS

and Southeast remained Alaska's dominant region until WWII, when military activity and the Alaska Highway shifted emphasis to Anchorage and Fairbanks.

Additional population growth came to Southeast with new timber harvesting in the 1950s. Increased government activities, as a result of Alaska statehood in 1959, brought even more.

Today, visitors enjoy the many wonders the area offers. Spectacular scenery greets the eye at every turn. Glacier Bay National Park and Preserve, Misty Fiords and Admiralty Island national monuments, Mendenhall Glacier at Juneau, LeConte Glacier near Petersburg and the Stikine River near Wrangell are just a few of the attractions.

The Inside Passage is the last stronghold of the American bald eagle. More than 20,000 eagles reside in the region, and sightings are frequent. Humpback and killer whales, porpoises, sea lions and seals are often observed from ferries, cruise ships and charter boats. Bear viewing opportunities are offered at Pack Creek on Admiralty Island and Anan Creek near Wrangell.

Activities and attractions include Russian and Tlingit dance performances; salmon bakes; historical melodramas; festivals; glacier and icefield flightseeing; sportfishing and wilderness adventure tours by kayak, canoe and raft. Among other attractions are museums, totem poles, hiking trails, colorful saloons and fine dining.

The following sections describe the communities and attractions of Southeast with the exception of Hyder, which is accessible by highway from British Columbia and is included in the CASSIAR HIGHWAY section.

Ketchikan

(See map, pages 630-631)

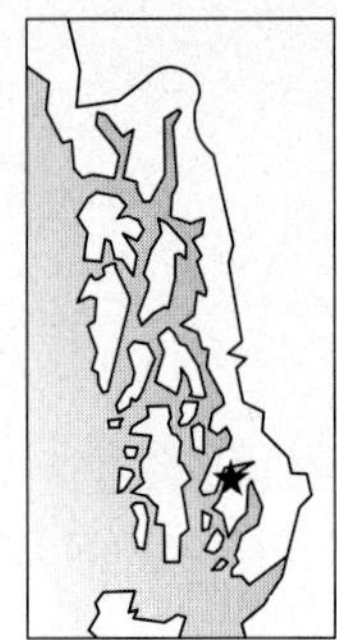

Located on Revillagigedo Island, 235 miles/378 km south of Juneau, 90 miles/145 km north of Prince Rupert, BC. **Population:** Ketchikan Gateway Borough and city, 15,082. **Emergency Services: Alaska State Troopers**, phone (907) 225-5118. **City Police**, phone (907) 225-6631, or 911 for all emergency services. **Fire Department, Ambulance** and **Ketchikan Volunteer Rescue Squad**, phone (907) 225-9616. **Hospital**, Ketchikan General at 3100 Tongass Ave., phone (907) 225-5171. **Maritime Search and Rescue**, call the Coast Guard at (907) 225-5666.

Visitor Information: Ketchikan Visitors Bureau office is located on the downtown dock, open during daily business hours and weekends May through Sept. Write them at 131M Front St., Ketchikan 99901; phone (907) 225-6166 or 1-800-770-2200, fax (907) 225-4250. U.S. Forest Service office for Misty Fiords National Monument and Ketchikan Ranger District is located at 3031 Tongass Ave.; open 8 A.M. to 4:30 P.M. weekdays; phone (907) 225-2148. The Southeast Alaska Visitor Center, located at 50 Main St., is open May 1 to Sept. 30, 8:30 A.M to 4:30 P.M. daily; Oct. 1 to April 30, 8:30 A.M. to 4:30 P.M., Tuesday through Saturday; phone (907) 228-6214, fax 228-6234.

Elevation: Sea level. **Climate:** Rainy. Yearly average rainfall is 162 inches and snowfall is 32 inches. Average daily maximum temperature in July 65°F/18°C; daily minimum 51°F/11°C. Daily maximum in Jan. 39°F/4°C; daily minimum 29°F/-2°C. **Radio:** KTKN 930, KRBD-FM 105.9, KGTW-FM 106.7. **Television:** CFTK (Prince Rupert, BC) and 27 cable channels. **Newspapers:** *Ketchikan Daily News* (daily); *Southeastern Log* (monthly); *New Alaskan* (monthly).

Private Aircraft: Ketchikan International Airport on Gravina Island; elev. 88 feet/27m; length 7,500 feet/2,286m; asphalt; fuel 100LL, A. Ketchikan Harbor seaplane base downtown; fuel 80, 100, A.

Ketchikan is located on the southwest side of Revillagigedo (ruh-vee-uh-guh-GAY-doh) Island, on Tongass Narrows opposite Gravina Island. The name Ketchikan is derived from a Tlingit name, Kitschk-Hin, meaning the creek of the "thundering wings of an eagle." The creek flows through the town, emptying into Tongass Narrows. Before Ketchikan was settled, the area at the mouth of Ketchikan Creek was a Tlingit Indian fish camp. Settlement began with interest in both mining and fishing. The first salmon cannery moved here in 1886, operating under the name of Tongass Packing Co. It burned down in August 1889. Gold was discovered nearby in 1898. This, plus residual effects of the gold, silver and copper mines, caused Ketchikan to become a booming little mining town. It was incorporated in 1901.

As mining waned, the fishing industry

began to grow. By the 1930s more than a dozen salmon canneries had been built; during the peak years of the canned salmon industry, Ketchikan earned the title of "Salmon Capital of the World." Overfishing caused a drastic decline in salmon by the 1940s, and today only 4 canneries and a cold storage plant operate. Trident Seafoods Corp., owner of Ketchikan's oldest and largest cannery, provides lodging for 200-plus salmon processors in a floating bunkhouse. An industry under development is the commercial harvest of abalone near Ketchikan.

As fishing reached a low point, the timber industry expanded. The first sawmill was originally built in 1898 at Dolomi on Prince of Wales Island to cut timber for the Dolomi Mine. It was dismantled and moved to Ketchikan and rebuilt in 1903. A large pulp mill was constructed in 1953 at Ward Cove, a few miles northwest of town.

Tourism is a very important industry here; Ketchikan is Alaska's first port of call for cruise ships and Alaska Marine Highway vessels.

Ketchikan is Alaska's southernmost major city and the state's fourth largest (after Anchorage, Fairbanks and Juneau). The closest city in British Columbia is Prince Rupert. Ketchikan is a linear waterfront city, with much of its 3-mile-/5-km-long business district suspended above water on pilings driven into the bottom of Tongass Narrows. It clings to the steep wooded hillside and has many homes perched on cliffs that are reached by climbing long wooden staircases or narrow winding streets.

The area supports 4 public grade schools, 4 parochial grade schools, a junior high school, 2 high schools and a University of Alaska Southeast campus.

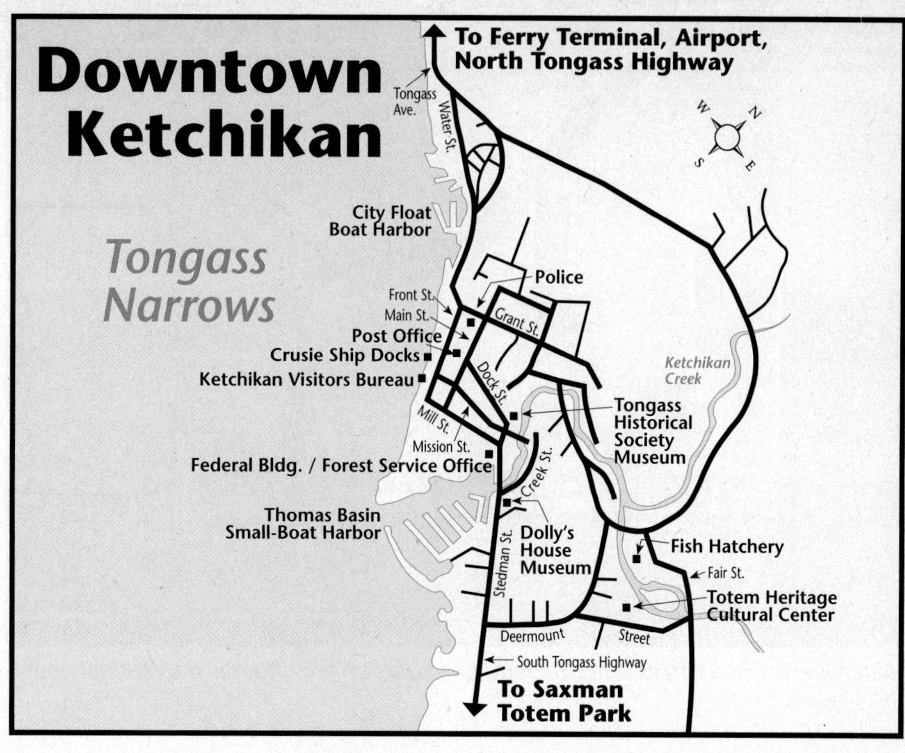

ACCOMMODATIONS/VISITOR SERVICES

Ketchikan has 9 hotels/motels. Bed-and-breakfast and dorm-style accommodations are also available. The major shopping areas are downtown and the west end.

Ketchikan AYH hostel is located at the First United Methodist Church, Grant and Main streets; write Box 8515, Ketchikan, AK 99901; phone (907) 225-3319 (summer only). Open June 1 to Aug. 31, the hostel has showers, sleeping pads (bring sleeping bag) and kitchen facilities. Check-in time is 6 to 11 P.M. Reservations strongly recommended. Cost is $8 per night for members (AYH membership passes may be purchased at the hostel), $11 for nonmembers.

There are 5 campgrounds (4 public campgrounds and a private resort) north of the city on North Tongass Highway and Ward Lake Road. See highway logs in this section. Dump station located at Ketchikan Public Works office, 2 blocks north of state ferry terminal. Contact the visitors bureau for brochure on RV use and parking. ▲

TRANSPORTATION

Air: Daily scheduled jet service is provided from the Ketchikan International Airport by Alaska Airlines to other Southeast cities, Anchorage and Seattle, WA. Com-

Ketchikan's Creek Street, once a "red-light district," now houses art and gift shops. (Michael N. Dill)

muter and charter service to other Southeast communities is available via Ketchikan Air, Taquan Air and Pro-Mech Air. Taquan Air has daily scheduled flights to Prince Rupert, BC.

Airport terminal, across Tongass Narrows on Gravina Island, is reached via shuttle ferry (10-minute ride, $2.50 per person, $5 per vehicle, one way) departing from the ferry terminal on North Tongass Avenue at half-hour intervals. Airporter service between downtown and airport is $11 to $12 (includes ferry fare). Taxi service is also available for about $8 from downtown.

Ferry: Alaska Marine Highway vessels connect Ketchikan with all mainline southeastern Alaska port cities, Prince Rupert, BC, and Bellingham, WA. There are also state ferry connections from Ketchikan to Metlakatla on Annette Island; to Hollis on Prince of Wales Island; and once-weekly service to Hyder in summer. See MARINE ACCESS ROUTES section for schedules.

Terminal building with waiting room, ticket counter and loading area is on North Tongass Avenue (Highway), 2 miles/3.2 km north of downtown. Phone (907) 225-6181. Foot passengers can walk from the ferry to a post office, restaurant and grocery store if stopover time permits. Taxi service available.

Bus: Borough bus returns to every stop at half-hour intervals; operates to city limits only. Schedules available at visitors bureau. Fee charged.

Car Rental: Available at airport and downtown locations.

Taxi: Available at ferry terminal and airport.

Highways: North Tongass, South Tongass, Ward Lake Road and Harriet Hunt Lake Road. See logs this section.

Cruise Ships: Ketchikan is the first port of call for many cruise ships to Alaska. Cruises depart from U.S. West Coast ports and Vancouver, BC. Two cruise lines depart from Ketchikan.

Private Boats: Two public docks downtown, Thomas Basin and City Float, provide transient moorage. In the West End District, 1 mile/1.6 km from downtown, Bar Harbor has moorage, showers. No gas available. Permits required. Moorage space in Ketchikan is limited; all private boats should contact the harbormaster's office at (907) 225-3610 prior to arrival to secure a spot.

ATTRACTIONS

Ketchikan's waterfront is the center of the city. A narrow city on a mountainside, Ketchikan has a waterfront that runs for several miles and consists of docks, stores on pilings, seaplane floats, 3 picturesque boat harbors, a seaplane base and ferry terminal. There is constant activity here as seaplanes take off and vessels move in and out of the harbor. Walking-tour maps are available at the visitors bureau and at the ferry terminal.

Plaza, the. Southeast Alaska's premier shopping center. Two comfort-controlled levels feature a variety of national and local retail shops and services for complete one-stop shopping. Plenty of free parking. Less than a mile south of the ferry terminal. Open every day except major holidays. [ADVERTISEMENT]

Fish Pirate's Daughter, a well-done local musical-comedy melodrama, portrays Ketchikan's early fishing days, with some of the city's spicier history included. Performed 7 P.M. and 8:45 P.M. Fridays, July through Aug. Contact First City Players, 338 Main St., phone (907) 225-4792 or 225-2211, for more information. Admission fee.

Tongass Historical Museum, in the Centennial Bldg., on Dock Street on Ketchikan Creek in central downtown area, featuring an exhibition on Lorin and an exhibit of Native life before the arrival of outsiders. Open in summer from 8 A.M to 5 P.M. daily. Winter (Oct. to mid-May) hours are 1–5 P.M. Wednesday through Friday, 1–4 P.M. Saturday and Sunday. The Raven Stealing the Sun totem stands just outside the entrance. Salmon viewing platforms. Admission fee is $2 for adults; free admission Sunday afternoons. Phone (907) 225-5600 for more information.

Chief Kyan Totem at the top of Main Street is a favorite spot for visitors.

Creek Street is Ketchikan's famous "red-

light district," where Black Mary, Dolly, Frenchie and others plied their trade for over half a century until 1954. Nearly 20 houses lined the far side of Ketchikan Creek; many have been restored. There are also several art and gift shops. Dolly's House, a former brothel, is open during the summer. Admission charged. Creek Street is a wooden street on pilings that begins just past the bridge on Stedman (South Tongass Highway). Watch for salmon in the creek below the bridge in late August.

Totem Heritage Center, at 601 Deermount St., houses 33 totem poles and fragments retrieved from deserted Tlingit and Haida Indian villages. This national landmark collection comprises the largest exhibit of original totems in the United States. Facilities include craft exhibits, craft shops for local artists and reference library. Gift shop, craft demonstrations, videos and guided tours during summer months. Summer admission fee $3. No admission charged off-season. Summer hours are 8 A.M. to 5 P.M. daily. Winter hours (Oct. through May) are 1–5 P.M. Tuesday through Friday. Phone (907) 225-5900.

Deer Mountain Hatchery is located in the city park within walking distance of downtown (take the bridge across Ketchikan Creek from the Totem Heritage Center). The hatchery produces about 150,000 king and 200,000 coho fingerlings annually. Observation platforms and information signs provide education on the life cycles of salmon. Open from 8 A.M. to 4:30 P.M. daily in summer.

The Ketchikan Mural on Stedman Street was created by 21 Native artists in 1978. The 125-by-18-foot/38-by-4-m design is collectively entitled *The Return of the Eagle.*

Fourth of July is a major celebration in Ketchikan. The Timber Carnival takes place over the Fourth of July with events such as ax throwing and chopping, power saw bucking and a tug-of-war. There are also fireworks, the Calamity Race (by canoe and kayak, bicycle and on foot), a parade and other events.

The Blueberry Arts Festival, on Aug. 10, 1996, features arts and crafts, the performing arts and plenty of homemade blueberry pies, blueberry crêpes, blueberry cheesecakes and other culinary delights. Events include a slug race, international bed race, pie-eating contest, trivia contest and spelling bee. A juried art show, fun-run and dance are also part of the festival. Sponsored and coordinated by the Ketchikan Area Arts and Humanities Council, Inc. (338 Main St., Ketchikan 99901; 907/225-2211).

Saxman Totem Park, Milepost 2.5 South Tongass Highway, is included in local sightseeing tours. Open year-round. There is no admission charge, but there is a fee for guided tour (offered May through Sept.). The totem park has 26 totems. The tour includes demonstrations at the Carving Center and performances by the Cape Fox Dancers at the Beaver Tribal House. For more information on hours, tours and events, phone the Cape Fox Tours office at (907) 225-5163, ext. 301 or 304.

Totem Bight community house and totem park, Milepost 9.9 North Tongass Highway, contains an excellent model of a Tlingit community house and a park with 13 totems.

Misty Fiords National Monument, 30 miles/48 km east of Ketchikan, encompasses more than 2 million acres of pristine coastal rain forest and glacially carved fjords. Rich in forests, marine wildlife, waterfalls and spectacular geologic features, the monument offers great scenic and scientific interest for visitors from May to Sept. The Forest Service maintains 25 miles/40 km of trails and several public-use cabins available for rent. Access to the monument is by boat or floatplane from Ketchikan. Floating dock at Naha Bay is 17 miles/27 km north of Ketchikan. Sea kayaking is a popular means of exploring the coastlines and venturing into remote areas. A system of 9 marine buoys is available to saltwater boaters on a first-come, first-served basis; fishing and photography are favorite pastimes in the monument. Cabin reservations, maps and natural history publications are available from the Ketchikan Ranger District, 3031 Tongass Ave., Ketchikan 99901; (907) 225-2148.

Charter boats: About 120 vessels operate out of Ketchikan for half-day, all-day or overnight sightseeing or fishing trips and transport to USFS public-use cabins and outlying communities. See advertisements this section and check with the visitors bureau or at the marinas.

Bare Boat Cruises of Alaska. To see the Inside Passage from Misty Fiords to Skagway or for a few days of fishing, you need a boat. Bare Boat Cruises has new, comfortable, 28-foot cruisers for fishing–cruising the Inside Passage, $235/day. The U-Drive boats are well equipped for extended cruising, just add food and fishing gear. Travel or fish in the comfort and privacy of your own boat. Box 7572, Ketchikan, AK 99901. May–Sept. (907) 225-8885. Anytime 1-800-964-8530. [ADVERTISEMENT]

Fishing resorts in the area are top quality. There are several; the most distant is an hour by floatplane. One resort is located at a renovated fish cannery.

Charter planes operate from the airport and from the waterfront on floats and are available for fly-in fishing, flightseeing or service to lodges and smaller communities.

Picnic areas include Settlers Cove by Settlers Cove Campground, **Milepost 18.2** North Tongass Highway; Refuge Cove, **Milepost 8.7** North Tongass Highway; Rotary Beach at **Milepost 3.5** South Tongass Highway; and Grassy Point and Ward Lake, **Milepost 1.1** Ward Lake Road.

Hiking trails include Deer Mountain trail, which begins at the corner of Fair and Deermount streets. The 3-mile/4.8-km, 3,001-foot/915-m ascent gives trekkers an excellent vantage of downtown Ketchikan and Tongass Narrows. Good but steep trail. Access to Deer Mountain cabin, the only USFS public-use cabin accessible by trail from Ketchikan. Perseverance Lake trail, 2.4 miles/3.8 km from Ward Lake to Perseverance Lake. Connell Lake trail, about 1.5 miles/2.4 km along north shore of Connell Lake, is in poor condition. Silvis Lakes trail, about 2 miles/3.2 km up to Lower Silvis Lake and picnic area. Trail continues to Upper Silvis Lake and Deer Mountain trail, but is very difficult. An easy and informative 1-mile/1.6-km nature trail circles Ward Lake.

Southeast Alaska Visitor Center, 50 Main St., features exhibits on Native cultures, ecosystems, resources and the rainforest in Southeast Alaska. Also 13-minute, multimedia "Mystic Southeast Alaska" program and Alaska Public Lands trip planning room. Open 8:30 A.M. to 4:30 P.M., daily in summer, Tuesday through Saturday in winter.

USFS public-use cabins are available for $25 a night. There are 48 cabins in the Ketchikan management area of the Tongass National Forest. Most are accessible by floatplane, with some accessible by hiking or by boat. Reservations may be made at Ketchikan Ranger Station, 3031 Tongass Ave.; office hours are 8 A.M. to 5 P.M. 5 days a week. Phone (907) 225-2148. For additional information see Cabins in the GENERAL INFORMATION section.

AREA FISHING: Check with the Alaska Dept. of Fish and Game at 2030 Sea Level Dr., Suite 207, or phone (907) 225-2859 for details on fishing in the Ketchikan area. Good fishing spots range from Mountain Point, a 5-mile/8-km drive from Ketchikan on South Tongass Highway, to lakes, bays, and inlets 50 miles/80 km away by boat or by air. Half-day and longer charters and skiff rentals available out of Ketchikan. There are fishing resorts at George Inlet, Yes Bay, Clover Pass and at the entrance to Behm Canal (Salmon Falls Resort); and 8 fishing resorts on Prince of Wales Island. Fish include salmon, halibut, steelhead, Dolly Varden, cutthroat and rainbow, lingcod and rockfish. Ketchikan has 2 king salmon derbies, a silver salmon derby and a halibut derby in summer.

North Tongass Highway Log

The North Tongass Highway is 18.4 miles/29.6 km long with 15.2 miles/24.5 km paved. It begins at the corner of Mill Street and Stedman (at the Federal Bldg.) and pro-

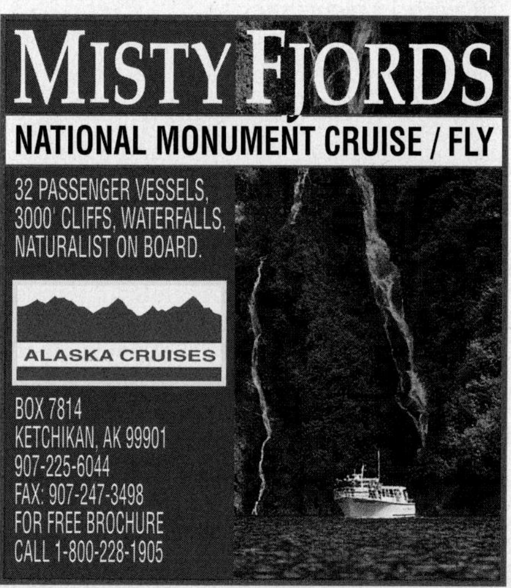

ceeds north to Ward Lake Road, Totem Bight, Clover Pass and Settlers Cove Campground.

0 Federal Bldg. on left with area information display. Proceeding on Mill Street.

0.1 (0.2 km) Southeast Alaska visitor center with information on federal lands in Alaska.

0.2 (0.3 km) Turning right onto Front Street, cruise ship dock on left where passengers disembark from major ships.

0.3 (0.5 km) Tunnel. North of this, Front Street becomes Water Street.

0.5 (0.8 km) City Float on left. Note older vessels, some dating back to the early 1900s.

0.7 (1.1 km) Highway turns left, then right, and becomes Tongass Avenue.

1.2 (1.9 km) West end shopping area begins.

1.7 (2.7 km) Bar Harbor boat basin on left.

2 (3.2 km) Ketchikan General Hospital on right, Ketchikan Ranger Station and Misty Fiords National Monument on left, northbound.

2.3 (3.7 km) Ferry terminals for Alaska Marine Highway.

2.4 (3.9 km) Main branch post office.

2.6 (4.2 km) Carlanna Creek and bridge.

2.7 (4.3 km) Airport shuttle ferry.

3.2 (5.1 km) Almer Wolfe Memorial viewpoint of Tongass Narrows. 24-hour RV parking. Airport terminal is visible across the narrows on Gravina Island.

4 (6.4 km) Hillside on right is a logged area, an example of clear-cut logging method and regrowth.

4.4 (7.1 km) Alaska State Troopers and Highway Dept.

5.5 (8.8 km) Small paved viewpoint overlooking Tongass Narrows and floatplane dock.

6 (9.6 km) Ward Cove Cannery next to road. Cannery Creek and bridge.

6.8 (10.9 km) **Junction** with Ward Lake Road (see log this section).

7 (11.3 km) Ward Creek and bridge; Ketchikan sawmill, owned by Ketchikan Pulp Co. Tours available; see description at mile 7.8 below.

7.3 (11.7 km) **WARD COVE.** Post office, gas station and grocery.

7.8 (12.5 km) Ketchikan Pulp Co. entrance. Pulp mill and high-speed compact sawmills (opened 1989). Tours available May through Aug. Call (907) 225-2151 for times and information or write Box 6600, Ketchikan 99901.

8.7 (14 km) Refuge Cove state recreation site with 14 picnic sites.

9.4 (15.1 km) Mud Bight; "float houses" rest on mud at low tide and float during high tide.

9.9 (15.9 km) Totem Bight state historical park; parking area, restrooms and phones. A short trail leads through the woods to Totem Bight community house and totem park. A striking setting. Don't miss this!

10.8 (17.4 km) Grocery store and gas station.

12.9 (20.8 km) Scenic viewpoint overlooking Guard Island lighthouse built in 1903 and manned until 1969 when finally automated.

14.2 (22.9 km) Clover Pass Resort turnoff. Left, North Point Higgins Road leads 0.6 mile/1 km to turnoff to resort; food, lodging, camping.

Left, then immediately right, is Knudson Cove Road, leading 0.4 mile/0.6 km to Knudson Cove Marina with public float, boat launch and boat rentals. Road rejoins North Tongass Highway at **Milepost 14.8.** ▲

14.8 (23.8 km) Knudson Cove Marina to left 0.5 mile/0.8 km.

15.2 (24.5 km) Pavement ends.

16.6 (26.8 km) Salmon Falls Resort; private fishing lodge with restaurant and boat rentals.

18.2 (29.3 km) Settlers Cove state campground, parking area and picnic area; 9 tent spaces and 7 car and trailer pads. Camping fee $6/night. Tables, water, pit toilets; 12 picnic units along beach to either side of campground. Open year-round. Parking area available for overnight. Good gravel beach for kids and boats. To right of beach is **Lunch Creek** (pink salmon in August), falls and trail. ▲

18.4 (29.6 km) Road end.

Ward Lake Road Log

An 8.3-mile/13.4-km road leading to Ward Lake Recreation Area and Harriet Hunt Road. Motorists and hikers should be aware of private property boundaries, posted by Cape Fox Corp. (CFC), and logging and trucking activities. Campers should be aware of USFS regulations in the Ward Lake Recreation Area: Camping is restricted to developed campgrounds and limited to 7 nights.

0 Right turn northbound from North Tongass Highway at **Milepost 6.8.**

0.1 (0.2 km) Tongass National Forest boundary.

0.4 (0.6 km) Small scenic turnout on right. Pond with lily pads surrounded by pine in muskeg.

0.7 (1.1 km) Signal Creek USFS campground on left; 24 sites with tables, water and pit toilets. Open Memorial Day to Sept. 30. Camping fee. Located among large trees on shore of Ward Lake. One end of nature trail around Ward Lake begins here and encircles lake; a 30- to 50-minute easy walk on well-graveled path. Some sites can be reserved, phone 1-800-280-2267 (CAMP) or TDD 1-800-879-4496. ▲

0.9 (1.4 km) Beginning of Perseverance Lake trail on right. Trailhead is within 100 feet of CCC Campground with parking across road. Site of WWII Aleut internment camp. A 2.4-mile/3.9-km boardwalk trail leads to **Perseverance Lake** (elev. 518 feet/158m); brook trout fishing.

1 (1.6 km) CCC (or Three C's) USFS campground entrance on right; 4 campsites, camping fee, open mid-May to Oct. ▲

1.1 (1.8 km) Ward Creek bridge. Grassy Point USFS picnic area. Several walk-in picnic sites with tables and shelters near road. Footbridge across Ward Creek leads to **Ward Lake** trail; good fly-fishing for steelhead, salmon and Dolly Varden.

Ward Creek and **Ward Lake**, cutthroat and Dolly Varden year-round, best March to June; steelhead to 16 lbs.; silver salmon to 18 lbs. and pink salmon to 5 lbs., August to Oct. (Hatchery-raised coho salmon; bring head of tagged fish to ADF&G.)

1.3 (2.1 km) Ward Lake USFS picnic area; beach, parking area and picnic shelters. One end of nature trail around Ward Lake.

2.9 (4.7 km) Right, Last Chance USFS campground; 19 spaces, tables, pit toilets, water, camping fee. Open mid-June to Sept. 30. ▲

3 (4.8 km) Connell Lake Road, on right, a narrow gravel road extending 0.6 mile/1 km to Connell Lake Reservoir. At Mile 0.4 Connell Lake Road, a bridge passes over large pipe, which carries water from the reservoir to the pulp mill at Ward Cove. Connell Lake trail at reservoir.

3.3 (5.3 km) Turnout.

7.1 (11.4 km) **Junction** with Harriet Hunt Lake Road (log follows), turn left.

8.3 (13.4 km) End public road. Private logging road begins.

Fishing from shore. (© David Job)

Harriet Hunt Lake Road Log

Harriet Hunt Lake Road leads 2.4 miles/3.9 km from **Milepost 7.1** Ward Lake Road to Harriet Hunt Lake; road is on Cape Fox Corp. lands. Watch for logging trucks.

0 Turn left at **Milepost 7.1** Ward Lake Road.

2 (3.2 km) Turnout, alpine meadows.

2.2 (3.5 km) Left, small scenic waterfall.

2.4 (3.9 km) **Harriet Hunt Lake** Recreation Area; pit toilets. Rainbow to 20 inches, May to Nov. Road end and parking area.

South Tongass Highway Log

The South Tongass Highway is a 12.9-mile/20.8-km road (paved for 8.5 miles/13.7 km) leading from the corner of Mill Street and Stedman south to Saxman Totem Park and ending at the power plant.

0 Federal Bldg. on right.

0.1 (0.2 km) Ketchikan Creek and bridge. Beginning of Creek Street boardwalk on left next to bridge.

0.2 (0.3 km) Thomas Street begins on right, a boardwalk street where old-time businesses are located. Thomas Basin boat harbor.

0.5 (0.8 km) Cannery and cold storage plant.

0.9 (1.4 km) U.S. Coast Guard base.

2.5 (4 km) **SAXMAN** (pop. 389) was founded in 1896 by Tlingit Alaska Natives and named after a Presbyterian missionary who served the Tlingit people. The Native village of Saxman has a gas station and convenience store and is the site of Saxman Totem Park. Developed by Cape Fox Corp., this popular attraction includes a carving center and tribal house. Guided tours available from Cape Fox Tours.

2.7 (4.3 km) Gas station.

3.5 (5.6 km) Rotary Beach, public recreation area, contains a shelter and table.

5 (8.1 km) Mountain Point parking area. Good salmon fishing from shore in July and August.

5.6 (9 km) Boat ramp on right.

8.2 (13.2 km) Herring Cove bridge and sawmill. Private hatchery for chum, king and coho salmon on short road to left; no tours.

8.5 (13.7 km) Pavement ends.

8.8 (14.2 km) Whitman Creek and bridge.

9 (14.5 km) Scenic turnout on right. Note different shades of green on trees across the water. Light green are cedar; medium, hemlock; and the darker are spruce. Species grow intermixed.

10.3 (16.6 km) Left, scenic waterfall.

11 (17.7 km) Scenic turnout.

11.8 (19 km) Lodge.

12.9 (20.8 km) Road end, view of power plant, an experimental sockeye salmon hatchery (no tours) and an abandoned cannery. Two-mile/3.2-km walk up gravel road leads to Lower Silvis Lake picnic area. Trail continues to Upper Silvis Lake and joins Deer Mountain trail, which connects to John Mountain National Recreation trail. Trail between Upper and Lower Silvis lakes is very difficult.

Metlakatla

(See map, page 630)

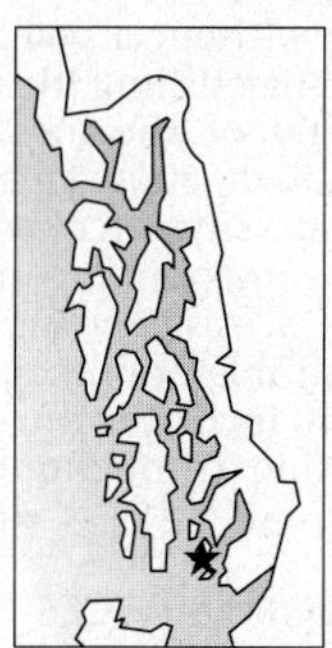

Located on the west coast of Annette Island, 15 miles/24 km south of Ketchikan, Southeastern Alaska's southernmost community. **Population:** 1,540. **Emergency Services: Police, fire** and **ambulance,** emergency only, phone 911. **Visitor Information:** Contact the city clerk, phone (907) 886-4441. A permit from the Metlakatla Indian Community is required for long-term visits.

Elevation: Sea level. **Climate:** Mild and moist. Summer temperatures range from 36°F/12°C to 65°F/18°C; winter temperatures from 28°F/-2°C to 44°F/7°C. Average annual precipitation is 115 inches: October is the wettest month with a maximum of 35 inches of rainfall. Annual snowfall averages 61 inches. **Radio:** KTKN 930 (Ketchikan). **Television:** 20 channels via cable.

Private Aircraft: Floatplane services.

Transportation: Air–Charter and air service. **Ferry**–State ferry from Ketchikan.

Overnight accommodations, restaurant, groceries and banking services available.

Metlakatla was founded in 1887 by William Duncan, a Scottish-born lay minister, who moved here with several hundred Tsimshian Indians from a settlement in British Columbia after a falling-out with church authorities. Congress granted reservation status and title to the entire island in 1891, and the new settlement prospered under Duncan, who built a salmon cannery and sawmill. Today, fishing and lumber continue to be the main economic base of Metlakatla. The community and island also retain the status of a federal Indian reservation, which is why Metlakatla has the only salmon fish traps in Alaska. (Floating fish traps were outlawed by the state shortly after statehood.)

The well-planned community has a town hall, a recreation center with an Olympic-sized swimming pool, well-maintained wood-frame homes, a post office, the mill and cannery. The Metlakatla Indian Community is the largest employer in town, with retail and service trades the second largest. Many residents also are commercial fishermen. Subsistence activities remain an important source of food for residents, who harvest seaweed, salmon, halibut, cod, clams, dungeness crab and waterfowl.

Attractions include the Duncan Museum, the original cottage occupied by Father William Duncan until his death in 1918. A replica of the turn-of-the-century William Duncan Memorial Church, built after the original was destroyed by fire in 1948, is also open to the public.

Prince of Wales Island

(See map, page 631)

Includes Coffman Cove, Craig, Hollis, Hydaburg, Klawock, Thorne Bay and Whale Pass

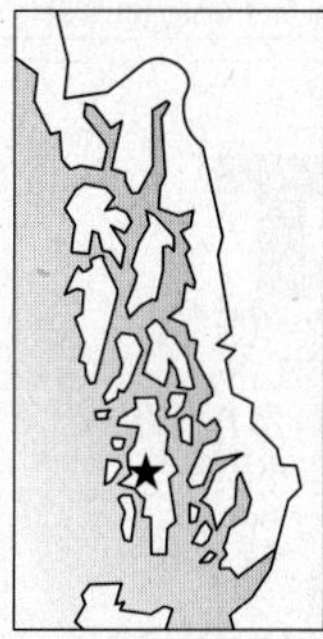

About 15 miles/24.1 km west of Ketchikan. **Population:** Approximately 6,300. **Emergency Services: Alaska State Troopers,** in Klawock, phone (907) 755-2918. **Police,** in Craig, phone (907) 826-3330, emergencies only, phone 911; **Village Public Safety Officers** in Thorne Bay, phone (907) 828-3905; in Hydaburg, phone (907) 285-3321. **Ambulance,** Hydaburg emergency response team, phone 911. **Health Clinics** for all emergencies, phone 911; in Craig, phone (907) 826-3257; in Klawock, phone (907) 755-4800; in Thorne Bay, phone (907) 828-3906; in Hydaburg, phone (907) 285-3462. **Maritime Search and Rescue,** call the Coast Guard at 1-800-478-5555.

Elevation: Sea level to 4,000 feet/1,219m. **Climate:** Mild and moist, but variable due to the island's size and topography. Rainfall in excess of 100 inches per year, with modest snowfall in winter at lower elevations. **Radio:** KRSA 580 (Petersburg), KTKN 930 (Ketchikan), KRBD-FM 90.1 (Ketchikan). **Television:** Via satellite. **Newspaper:** *Island News* (Thorne Bay, weekly).

Private Aircraft: Klawock airstrip, 2 miles/3.2 km northeast; elev. 50 feet/15m; length 5,000 feet/1,524m; lighted and paved; fuel 100LL. (A full instrument landing system was scheduled for completion by 1996). Seaplane bases adjacent to all 4 communities and in several bays.

Heavily forested with low mountains, Prince of Wales Island measures roughly 135 miles/217 km north–south by 45 miles/72 km east–west. The third largest island under the American flag (Kodiak is second, the Big Island of Hawaii is first), it is 2,231 square miles/5,778 square km. The 4 major communities on the island—Craig (the largest with 1,946 residents), Klawock, Thorne Bay and Hydaburg—and the smaller camps and communities of Coffman Cove, Whale Pass, Labouchere Bay and Naukati are connected by road. Among the small scattered villages not connected by road are **KASAAN,** a small Haida village at the head of Kasaan Bay, and **PORT PROTECTION** and **POINT BAKER,** both at the northwest tip of the island. (See *The ALASKA WILDERNESS GUIDE* for details on these communities.)

Prince of Wales Island has been the site of several lumbermills and mining camps since the 1800s. But it was salmon that led to permanent settlement on the island. Klawock was the site of one of Alaska's first canneries, built in 1878. In the following years, some 25 canneries were built on the island to process salmon. Today, logging is prevalent on the island.

Prince of Wales Island offers uncrowded backcountry, fishing for salmon and trout, canoeing waters, opportunities for viewing wildlife (black bears, Sitka black-tailed deer, bald eagles), adequate visitor facilities and some historical attractions. Most of the island is national forest land. The Forest Service manages 5 large, designated wilderness areas on Prince of Wales Island. There are also some Native corporation and private land holdings. Respect No Trespassing signs.

There is a city-run trailer park in Klawock for monthly rentals and a private campground at Mile 0.4 Big Salt Road. RV camping is also available at the Eagle's Nest Campground operated by the USFS just east of the Thorne Bay Road near Control Lake; water, chemical toilets, camping fee $5. Altogether, there are 5 USFS campsites on the island road system. There are also more than 20 USFS cabins (accessible by plane, boat or on foot) available for public use; reservations and a fee are required. Contact the USFS office in Ketchikan or the local ranger districts at Craig (phone 907/826-3271) and Thorne Bay (phone 907/828-3304). Also see Cabins in the GENERAL INFORMATION section. ▲

There are several roadside fishing spots on Prince of Wales Island. See the road logs in this section for details. Lakes and streams support red, pink and silver salmon, cutthroat, rainbow trout and Dolly Varden.

TRANSPORTATION

Air: All communities on the island are served by floatplane, most daily. Wheel planes land at Klawock. Daily scheduled service by Taquan Air from Ketchikan.

Ferry: Alaska Marine Highway ferry operates from Ketchikan to Hollis. Phone Craig office at (907) 826-3432, Hollis terminal at (907) 530-7115. See MARINE ACCESS ROUTES section for rates and schedule. Van taxi service meets ferry at Hollis and offers service to Craig and Klawock.

Car rental: in Klawock at Practical Rent-A-Car, Will Jones; in Craig at Wilderness

Rent-A-Car.

Highways: The most extensive road network in Southeast Alaska. Over 1,100 miles/1,770 km of road allows access to most areas of the island. The island's main roads are the Hollis–Klawock–Craig Highway, Big Salt Road, Thorne Bay Road, Hydaburg Road, Coffman Cove Road and North Island Road (USFS Road No. 20) to Labouchere Bay. See road logs in this section for details.

DRIVER CAUTION: Watch for heavily loaded logging trucks while driving; they have the right-of-way. CB radios are helpful. Carry a spare tire and spare gas. (Gas is available in Coffman Cove, Hydaburg, Craig, Klawock, Whale Pass and Thorne Bay.) Use turnouts and approach hills and corners on your side of the road. Spur roads are *NOT* recommended for large RVs or cars with trailers. Some side roads may be closed intermittently during logging operations or highway construction. Watch for signs posted when roads are closed and expect delays.

ATTRACTIONS

El Capitan Cave. Located just north of Whale Pass off the North Island Road, people have been visiting El Capitan Cave for many years. There is a steep trail (more than 300 steps) leading to the cave entrance. Because of damage to cave formations, a gate has been installed to regulate visitation. There is open visitation to the gate some distance within the cave; guided tours beyond the gate. Tours run May 21 to Sept. 7; Wednesday through Sunday; 8–10 A.M., 10 A.M. to noon, 1–3 P.M. and 3–5 P.M. For guided tours, group size is limited to 6. For reservations write Thorne Bay Ranger District, Box 19001, Thorne Bay 99919; phone (907) 828-3304.

AREA FISHING: Most fish in streams on the island are anadromous (travel upstream to spawn). Try **Klawock Lake** for trout and salmon; **Klawock River** downstream from the hatchery good for trout, steelhead and salmon; **Thorne River** for Dolly Varden and trout; and **Sarkar River** for trout, steelhead and salmon. Freshwater guiding services are available.

World-class saltwater sportfishing abounds immediately offshore and throughout the many smaller islands surrounding Prince of Wales Island. Most communities have boat ramps. For those traveling without a boat, quality half-, full- and multi-day fishing trips are available through many of the local charter operators. 100-lb. halibut, 50-lb. king (chinook) salmon and 15-lb. silver (coho) salmon are not considered uncommon in the sport season, usually May through Aug. due to the weather and fish migration patterns. Abundant bottom fish, including lingcod and red snapper, reside throughout these waters year-round.

DESCRIPTION AND VISITOR SERVICES

COFFMAN COVE (pop. 254), 53 miles/85 km north of Klawock. Formerly one of the largest independent logging camps in Southeast, Coffman Cove is now a second-class city. Recreation includes hunting (deer and bear), good freshwater and saltwater fishing, boating, hiking, and also cable TV and VCRs. Canoe Lagoon Oyster Co. here is the state's oldest and largest oyster producer; fresh oysters available at the Riggin' Shack.

Coffman Cove has a general store, gift shop, gas pump, playground and ballfield. There is a dock and a small beach with access to salt water for canoes and cartop boats. EMTs dispatch from Riggin' Shack.

CRAIG (pop. 1,946), 31 miles/50 km from Hollis, is on the western shore of Prince of Wales Island. The original townsite, on Craig Island, is now connected to Prince of Wales by a short causeway. Craig has 3 hotels, 6 restaurants/eating establishments, a grocery store, clothing and general merchandise stores, a gas station, a laundromat, gift shops, liquor stores, bars, beauty and barber shops, a library, 2 banks and a K–12 school. A swimming pool was constructed in 1995. Propane, towing and auto repair available.

Craig Primary Health Care Facility, commonly known as the Craig clinic, is located just up the hill from the city municipal offices and is currently managed by the Craig Health Corp. The facility is approximately 4,300 square feet and is occupied by a physician and staff, public health nurses and the Craig Native health aide.

The physician services are generally available 24 hours a day except for brief periods of time when the physician is unavailable. An emergency room is provided at the clinic for treatment, minor surgery and stabilization of patients. Medications, emergent pharmaceuticals and medical supplies are available through the clinic (by doctor's prescription only; no retail pharmacies are located on the island). The clinic can take routine X-rays. Clinic hours are 9 A.M. to 5 P.M Monday through Saturday in the summer; 9 A.M. to 5 P.M. weekdays in winter. Emergency Medical Services are available full-time at 911, or call Craig PD at (907) 826-3330. The Craig Native health aide and public health nurse are available weekdays from 9 A.M. to 4 P.M. Craig also has a chiropractic office and 2 dental clinics.

Craig has 2 modern boat harbors, North Cove and South Cove, located on either side of the causeway, a seaplane float, fuel dock, city dock and float, 2 fish-buying docks and an old cannery dock. The Craig harbormaster's office, with public showers and restrooms, is located on the corner close to South Cove; phone (907) 826-3404, VHF Channel 16.

Visitor information is available from Craig City Hall, phone (907) 826-3275, open weekdays 8 A.M. to 5 P.M.; U.S. Forest Service office, open weekdays 8 A.M. to 5 P.M., phone (907) 826-3271; Prince of Wales Chamber of Commerce, phone (907) 826-3870.

Craig was once a temporary fish camp for the Tlingit and Haida Natives of the area. In 1907, with the help of local Natives, William D. Craig Millar established a mildcure station known as Fish Egg for nearby Fish Egg Island. The Tlingit name for Fish Egg Island is "Sheenda" and the townsite was "Sheensit," which is now used by the Native Shaan-Seet Corp. Between 1908 and 1911 a permanent saltery and cold storage facility, along with about 2 dozen homes, were built on the city's present location and named for founder Craig Millar. In 1912 the post office was established, E.M. Streeter opened a sawmill and Craig constructed a salmon cannery. Both businesses peaked during WWI. Craig was incorporated in 1922 and grew throughout the 1930s, with some families relocating from the Dust Bowl.

Although the salmon industry has both prospered and floundered over the years, fishing and fish processing still account for an important part of area employment. In recent years timber harvesting on the island has contributed many jobs in logging and timber processing. The Viking Lumber Co. mill, located between Craig and Klawock, provides year-round employment, producing moulding, window and door stock for the domestic market, and high-grade cants for export. The mill also produces wood chips for the manufacture of pulp. Timber will continue to be a viable economic influence on the island's economy for many years. Mining, transportation and tourism have the potential to become major employers in the foreseeable future. Construction and government jobs will increase as the island and its economy develop.

Craig is the home port of many commercial fishing and charter sportfishing boats due to its proximity to the fertile fishing grounds off the west coast of the island. Halibut, coho and chinook salmon, lingcod and red snapper (yelloweye) are the primary target species. Craig hosts the annual Craig-Klawock King Salmon Derby from April to July 3, followed by a big Fourth of July parade and celebration. In early August the P.O.W. Chamber of Commerce sponsors its annual Fish Egg Seafest, an arts and crafts celebration of the fishing industry.

Alaska Gifts. Featuring the largest selection of Alaskan books in Southeast Alaska. Plus Alaskan-made chocolates, canned smoked salmon, jewelry, gold nuggets, Indian arts and crafts. Also, sweatshirts, T-shirts, paintings and sculptures by Alaskan artists. Souvenirs, cards, gift giving supplies and more. Ask for a free walking-tour map. Phone (907) 826-2991. [ADVERTISEMENT]

HOLLIS (pop. 111), 25 road miles/40 km from Klawock, 35 nautical miles/56 km west of Ketchikan. Hollis was a mining town with a population of 1,000 from about 1900 to 1915. In the 1950s, Hollis became the site of Ketchikan Pulp Co.'s logging camp and served as the base for timber operations on Prince of Wales Island until 1962, when the camp was moved to Thorne Bay. Recent state land sales have spurred the growth of a small residential community here. The ferry terminal and a school are located here.

HYDABURG (pop. 406), 36 miles/58 km from Hollis, 45 miles/72 km from Craig. Hydaburg was founded in 1911 and combined the populations of 3 Haida villages: Sukkwan, Howkan and Klinkwan. President William Howard Taft established an Indian reservation on the surrounding land in 1912, but, at the residents' request, most of the land was restored to its former status as part of Tongass National Forest in 1926. Hydaburg was incorporated in 1927, 3 years after its people became citizens of the United States.

Most of the residents are commercial fishermen, although there are some jobs in construction and the timber industry. Subsistence is also a traditional and necessary part of life here. Hydaburg has an excellent collection of restored Haida totems. The totem park was developed in the 1930s by the Civilian Conservation Corps, which

brought in poles from the three abandoned Haida villages. There is also good salmon fishing here in the fall.

Three boardinghouses provide rooms and meals for visitors. Groceries, hardware and sundry items available locally. There are a gift shop, gas station, video store and cafe. Cable television is available.

KLAWOCK (pop. 759), 24 miles/39 km from Hollis. Klawock originally was a Tlingit Indian summer fishing village; a trading post and salmon saltery were established here in 1868. Ten years later a salmon cannery was built—the first cannery in Alaska and the first of several cannery operations in the area. Over the years the population of Klawock, like other Southeast communities, grew and then declined with the salmon harvest. The local economy is still dependent on fishing and cannery operations, along with timber cutting and sawmilling. A city-operated fish hatchery is located on Klawock Lake, very near the site of a salmon hatchery that operated from 1897 until 1917. Visitors are welcome. Klawock Lake offers good canoeing and boating.

Recreation here includes good fishing for salmon and steelhead in Klawock River, saltwater halibut fishing, and deer and bear hunting. Klawock's totem park contains 21 totems—both replicas and originals—from the abandoned Indian village of Tuxekan (developed by the Civilian Conservation Corps in 1938–40).

Groceries and gas are available in Klawock. Laundromat at Black Bear Quick Stop. Banking service available. Accommodations and meals available at 2 lodges just outside town (Fireweed Lodge and Log Cabin Resort). Log Cabin Resort also offers RV sites. Towing service available. Boat charters and rentals are also available.

Supplies are barged to Southeast communities. (Michael N. Dill)

THORNE BAY (pop. 650), 59 miles/95 km from Hollis. Thorne Bay was incorporated in 1982, making it one of Alaska's newest cities. The settlement began as a logging camp in 1962, when Ketchikan Pulp Co. (a subsidiary of Louisiana Pacific Corp.) moved its operations from Hollis. Thorne Bay was connected to the island road system in 1974. Camp residents created the community—and gained city status from the state—as private ownership of the land was made possible under the Alaska Statehood Act. Employment here depends mainly on the lumber company and the U.S. Forest Service, with assorted jobs in municipal government and in local trades and services. Thorne Bay is centrally located between 2 popular Forest Service recreation areas: Eagle's Nest Campground and Sandy Beach picnic area. The Thorne River offers excellent canoeing and kayaking, and the bay offers excellent sailing and waterskiing (wet suit advised).

There are grocery and hardware stores, gas stations, small-boat repair, tackle shop and gift shop. Accommodations available at several bed and breakfasts, a lodge and rental cabins. Propane is available. Fuel oil is also available. Boat charters and rentals are available. Gas for boats may be purchased at the tackle shack float (unleaded fuel). It is open Monday through Friday from 1–7 P.M.; Saturday and Sunday 11 A.M. to 4 P.M. Aviation fuel available through Petro Alaska. City-operated RV dump station. Facilities include boat dock (with potable water, power, sewer pumpout station and fish cleaning facilities), cement boat-launch ramp, helicopter landing pad, and floatplane float and parking facility.

There is scheduled floatplane service to Thorne Bay from Ketchikan.

WHALE PASS (pop. 92), accessible by loop road from the North Island Road, was the site of a floating logging camp. The camp moved out in the early 1980s, but new residents moved in with a state land sale. The community has a small grocery store and gas pump; cabins and freezer space available. There is also a school, post office and floatplane dock there. Accommodations at Whale Pass Lodge and a bed and breakfast. Good fishing on the loop road into Whale Pass.

Hollis–Klawock–Craig Highway Log

This highway, 31.5 miles/50.7 km long, begins at the ferry landing at Hollis and heads west through Klawock then south to Craig. It is a wide, paved road. Posted speed is 35 to 50 mph/56 to 80 kmph. Takes travelers through the temperate rainforest environment typical of Southeast Alaska. Many roads and trails off highway lead to private property; please respect barricades and No Trespassing signs. *CAUTION: Watch for logging trucks.*

Distance from Hollis (H) is followedby distance from Craig (C). Physical mileposts show distance from Craig.

H 0 C 31.5 (50.7 km) Alaska Marine Highway, Hollis ferry terminal, phone (907) 530-7115, open during ferry arrivals and departures only. Telephone, no other services.

H 0.2 (0.3 km) **C 31.3** (50.4 km) Clark Bay subdivision access to right.

H 1.4 (2.3 km) **C 30.1** (48.4 km) Left 0.3 mile to Hollis townsite. School and USFS office, city harbor and float, floatplane dock, post office, telephone; no other services.

H 2 (3.2 km) **C 29.5** (47.5 km) Alaska Power and Telephone power plant and Alascom satellite station to left. Hollis Fire Department and EMS garage to right.

H 2.4 (3.9 km) **C 29.1** (46.8 km) **Maybeso Creek**, cutthroat; Dolly Varden; pink and silver salmon; steelhead run begins in mid-April. Pools offer the best fishing. Walking good along streambed but poor along bank. Watch for bears.

H 4.2 (6.8 km) **C 27.3** (43.9 km) Turnout left, view of mouth of the Harris River.

H 4.8 (7.7 km) **C 26.7** (43 km) Head left for lower Harris subdivision.

H 5.2 (8.4 km) **C 26.3** (42.3 km) Turnout, one of several slide-damaged areas from Oct. 1993 storm that dumped 11 inches of rain in 24 hours.

H 6.4 (10.3 km) **C 25.1** (40.4 km) Entering Tongass National Forest.

H 6.5 (10.5 km) **C 25** (40.2 km) Head left for upper Harris subdivision.

H 7.7 (12.4 km) **C 23.8** (38.3 km) Turnout, slide damage repaired.

H 8.4 (13.5 km) **C 23.1** (37.2 km) USFS hiking trail to **Harris River** fishing: cutthroat; steelhead run mid-April; salmon and Dolly Varden run beginning in mid-July. Easy walking on the gravel bars in the middle of river.

H 8.5 (13.7 km) **C 23** (37 km) Turnout, slide damage repaired.

H 10.5 (16.9 km) **C 21** (33.8 km) Hydaburg turnoff.

H 11.3 (18.2 km) **C 20.2** (32.5 km) Harris River bridge.

H 12.4 (20 km) **C 19.1** (30.7 km) End of Harris River valley. Island divide is here at 500 feet/152m elev.; streams now flow west.

Turnout left, State DOT gravel storage area.

H 12.6 (20.3 km) **C 18.9** (30.4 km) Leaving Tongass National Forest.

H 13.6 (21.9 km) **C 17.9** (28.8 km) East end of Klawock Lake, about 7 miles/11 km long and up to 1 mile/1.6 km wide. Lake borders the road on the left at several places. Private property; contact Heenya Corp. in Klawock.

H 16.1 (25.9 km) **C 15.4** (24.8 km) Turnout left, boat launch for Klawock Lake.

H 16.2 (26.1 km) **C 15.3** (24.6 km) 35 mph curve; believe the sign.

H 17.6 (28.3 km) **C 13.9** (22.4 km) Turnout left, view of Klawock Lake.

H 20.1 (32.3 km) **C 11.4** (18.3 km) Turnout right, view of Klawock Lake.

H 22 (35.4 km) **C 9.5** (15.3 km) Klawock Hatchery, operated by the city of Klawock and supported by island fishermen and businesses.

H 22.1 (35.6 km) **C 9.4** (15.1 km) Klawock-Heenya Trailer Court to right; turnout left for trail access to Klawock River sportfishing.

H 22.2 (35.7 km) **C 9.3** (15 km) Turnout left, access to Klawock River fishing.

H 22.3 (35.9 km) **C 9.2** (14.8 km) Turnout left, access to Klawock River fishing.

H 22.4 (36 km) **C 9.1** (14.6 km) Turnout left, access to Klawock River fishing.

H 22.5 (36.2 km) **C 9** (14.5 km) Klawock Lake Hatchery, operated by the city of Klawock. The hatchery produces sockeye, coho and steelhead. Visitors welcome Monday through Friday, 8 A.M. to 4:30 P.M.

H 23.3 (37.5 km) **C 8.2** (13.2 km) Belltower Mall, grocery store, liquor store, gift shop, toy store, Papa's Pizza, arcade.

H 23.4 (37.7 km) **C 8.1** (13 km) **Junction** with Big Salt Road; access to Thorne Bay, Coffman Cove, Naukati, Whale Pass and the north end of the island.

H 23.5 (37.8 km) **C 8** (12.9 km) Turnoff right, services available.

H 23.7 (38.1 km) **C 7.8** (12.6 km) Fireweed Lodge to left, St. John's by the Sea Catholic Church to right. St. John's was designed and built with local lumber and materials by the local church community. The stained-glass designs, representing all known Native tribes, were designed and built by local artists. This is a "must-see" structure. Father Jim Blaney and Sister Tish welcome the opportunity to show the church.

H 23.9 (38.5 km) **C 7.6** (12.2 km) Klawock-Heenya Corp. offices.

H 24.2 (38.9 km) **C 7.3** (11.7 km) **Klawock River** bridge spans tidal estuary where river meets salt water. Fishing from bridge.

H 24.3 (39.1 km) **C 7.2** (11.6 km) Klawock Fuels (gas and diesel), Alaska State Troopers and Alaska Dept. of Fish and Game to left.

H 24.5 (39.4 km) **C 7** (11.3 km) Entering village of **KLAWOCK.** State troopers in building on left.

H 24.6 (39.6 km) **C 6.9** (11.1 km) Turnoff right to Phoenix log sort yard, Phoenix shop and Klawock Indian Corp. dock. Oceangoing vessels load locally harvested logs for worldwide transport.

H 25 (40.2 km) **C 6.5** (10.5 km) Viking Lumber Co. mill; produces moulding, window and door stock for the domestic market and high-grade cants for export.

H 26.6 (42.8 km) **C 4.9** (7.9 km) Turnout right, scenic view of Klawock Inlet and San Alberto Bay.

H 27.9 (44.9 km) **C 3.6** (5.8 km) On left is landfill operated by city of Klawock. Bears can usually be seen here.

H 29.1 (46.8 km) **C 2.4** (3.9 km) Crab Creek subdivision.

H 29.3 (47.2 km) **C 2.2** (3.5 km) Crab Creek bridge.

H 29.8 (48 km) **C 1.7** (2.7 km) Shaan-Seet Trailer Court and St. Nicholas Road to left. St. Nicholas Road extends 13 miles around Port St. Nicholas.

H 30.2 (48.6 km) **C 1.3** (2.1 km) Craig schools to left, post office, bank and Thompson House supermarket on right.

H 30.4 (48.9 km) **C 1.1** (1.8 km) North and South Cove Harbors operated by the city of Craig.

H 30.7 (49.4 km) **C 0.8** (1.3 km) Stop sign, downtown **CRAIG.** Turn left 1 block for Craig municipal offices and city gym. Craig clinic is on left, half block past city office. End of highway is 3 blocks right.

H 31 (49.9 km) **C 0.5** (0.8 km) Road dead ends.

Big Salt Road Log

Big Salt Road begins at **Milepost C 8.1** on the Hollis–Klawock–Craig Highway and extends 17.1 miles/27.5 km, ending at its junction with Thorne Bay Road. It is a gravel road with much logging traffic; scheduled for paving in 1997. Top speed for much of the road is 25 mph/40 kmph.

Distance is measured from Klawock.

0 Black Bear Quick Stop: grocery store, laundromat and gas station.

0.1 (0.2 km) Klawock city trailer park on right with some overnight sites; obtain permits from the city clerk. A camping fee is charged. ▲

0.4 (0.6 km) Log Cabin R.V. Park & Resort: tackle store, skiff rentals, lodging and campground. ▲

0.5 (0.8 km) Lodge and restaurant.

2.3 (3.7 km) State highway maintenance facility 0.6 mile/1 km to left, immediately before entering airport.

4 (6.4 km) View of Big Salt Lake and mountains.

8.7 (14 km) Big Salt Lake, actually a saltwater body protected by small islands but permitting tidal flow in and out, is visible to the left from several spots along road. Waterfowl and bald eagles are often observed here. Wreckage of a military aircraft can be seen across lake. The plane crashed in 1969 en route to Vietnam; all aboard survived the crash.

8.9 (14.3 km) Boat ramp and canoe launching area on Big Salt Lake. If boating on this tidal lake, be aware of strong currents.

9.7 (15.6 km) **Black Bear Creek**, cutthroat; Dolly Varden; red, pink, dog and silver salmon, run mid-July to mid-Sept. Except for the lower 2 miles/3.2 km, creek can be fished from the bank. Best at the mouth of stream, 200 yards/183m upstream from the bridge or in large meadow, 1.5 miles/2.4 km from the mouth. Road on right leads to Black Lake. Watch for heavy equipment.

12.6 (20.3 km) **Steelhead Creek**, cutthroat; Dolly Varden; steelhead; pink, dog and silver salmon. Creek can be reached by boat through south entrance to Big Salt Lake. Lake should only be entered during high and low slack tides due to the strong tidal currents. High tide in lake is delayed 2 hours from outside waters. Bank fishing restricted by undergrowth.

16.6 (26.7 km) Short boardwalk on right leads to **Control Lake**, cutthroat; Dolly Varden; pink and silver salmon; good red salmon stream in August. USFS cabin on other side is available for public use. Skiff docked at end of boardwalk is for registered cabin users.

17.1 (27.5 km) **Control Lake Junction.** End of Big Salt Road (SR 929); **junction** with Thorne Bay Road (USFS Road No. 30) and

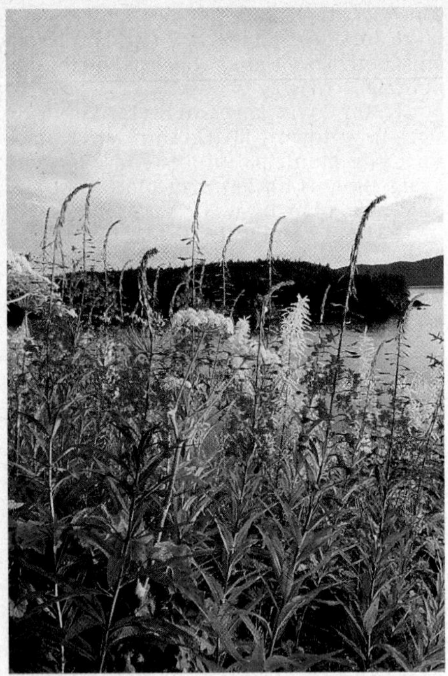

Wildflowers on hillside overlooking Inside Passage. (© David Job)

North Island Road (USFS Road No. 20). Road to Thorne Bay (log follows) is on the right. Road to Labouchere Bay, with access to Whale Pass and Coffman Cove, is on the left; see North Island Road log this section. Turn right for USFS RV park (no services). ▲

Thorne Bay Road Log

Thorne Bay Road extends 18 miles/29 km to Thorne Bay logging camp.
Physical mileposts show distance from Thorne Bay post office.

18 (29 km) **Junction** with Big Salt Road and North Island Road.

16.6 (26.7 km) Eagle's Nest USFS campground; 12 sites, tables, water, toilet and canoe launch. Camping fee $5. **Balls Lake,** cutthroat; Dolly Varden; red, pink and silver salmon. ▲

13 (20.9 km) Bridge. **Rio Roberts** and **Rio Beaver creeks,** cutthroat; pink and silver salmon. A 0.7-mile/1.1-km cedar-chip and double-plank boardwalk leads to a viewing deck overlooking falls and Rio Roberts Fish Pass.

10.7 (17.2 km) Rio Beaver Creek bridge.

6.7 (10.8 km) **Goose Creek,** cutthroat; pink and silver salmon. Excellent spawning stream. Good run of pink salmon in mid-August. Lake Ellen Road on right leads 4.5 miles/7.2 km south to Lake No. 3 USFS campsite; 2 RV sites, pit toilet, 2 fire rings and 2 picnic tables. No water or garbage. Road continues beyond campsite to lake and hiking trail to Salt Chuck. Abandoned Salt Chuck Mine is located here. ▲

6.5 (10.5 km) **Thorne River** runs beside road for the next 0.5 mile/0.8 km. Cutthroat; Dolly Varden; steelhead; rainbow; red, pink, dog and silver salmon. Excellent fishing reported from **Milepost 4.9** to **2.1.**

4.9 (7.9 km) Thorne River bridge. Thorne River now follows road on right.

4.1 (6.6 km) Falls Creek.

4 (6.4 km) Gravelly Creek USFS picnic area; walk in to picnic area on the bank of Thorne River at the mouth of Gravelly Creek; 3 tables, fire rings, vault toilet and open-sided shelter. This site was logged in 1918. Note the large stumps with notches. Notches were used by old-time loggers for spring boards to stand on while sawing or chopping.

3.7 (5.9 km) Gravelly Creek.

2.1 (3.4 km) Right, mouth of Thorne River.

1.7 (2.7 km) Hill on right is an example of a logging cut.

1.3 (2.1 km) Log sorting area. Here different species of logs are sorted for rafting and transporting to mills or for export.

1.2 (1.9 km) Log raft holding area. After logs are sorted and tied into bundles, the bundles are chained together into a raft suitable for towing by tugboat.

0 THORNE BAY. The road extends about 10 miles/16 km beyond the community to Sandy Beach day-use area with picnic shelter, 6 tables, fire rings, vault toilet and RV parking. Good view of Clarence Strait.

Hydaburg Road Log

The Hydaburg Road is 24.6 miles/39.6 km long and begins 11 miles/17.7 km west of the Hollis main ferry terminal on the Hollis–Klawock–Craig Highway. Opened in 1983, the road has been much improved. Road construction may be under way. Some sections of the road are heavily used by logging trucks.

0 Junction with Hollis–Klawock–Craig Highway.

0.5 (0.8 km) Harris River bridge.

2 (3.2 km) Trailhead for One Duck trail to alpine area and cabin. Contact the USFS office for more information.

4.1 (6.6 km) Bridge.

9.8 (15.8 km) Fork in road, keep right for Hydaburg.

11 (17.7 km) Road on left leads to Twelvemile Arm. This logging road leads to Polk Inlet. Watch for logging and construction activity.

11.8 (19 km) Fork in road, keep right for Hydaburg.

13.9 (22.4 km) View of South Pass.

16.9 (27.2 km) Bridge. Take right fork just after crossing bridge for Hydaburg.

23.5 (37.8 km) Keep right at junction.

23.9 (38.5 km) Take right at junction for Hydaburg, left for Saltery.

24.6 (39.6 km) **HYDABURG.**

North Island Road Log

Signed as USFS Road No. 20, this narrow 2-lane road leads north 79.5 miles/127.9 km from its junction with Big Salt and Thorne Bay roads near Control Lake to Labouchere Bay on the northwest corner of the island. The road has a fair to excellent gravel surfacing and some steep grades. Slow down for approaching vehicles. Posted speed is 25 mph/40 kmph. Gas is available at Whale Pass and Coffman Cove.

0 Control Lake Junction, junction with Big Salt and Thorne Bay roads near Control Lake.

4.8 (7.7 km) USFS Road No. 2050 leads west to upper Staney Creek/Horseshoe Hole and loops back to Road No. 20. Access to Staney Bridge campsite. ▲

7.4 (11.9 km) Rock quarry to east.

10.9 (17.5 km) USFS Road No. 2054 leads west to Staney Creek campsite, Staney Creek cabin and access to salt water. ▲

15.5 (24.9 km) **Junction** with Coffman Cove Road (see log this section).

18.4 (29.6 km) Naukati Creek.

19.2 (30.9 km) View to west of Tuxekan Island and Passage.

21 (33.8 km) Logging road leads west to Naukati Bay.

21.4 (34.4 km) Yatuk Creek bridge.

23.3 (37.5 km) **NAUKATI,** established and operating as a mining camp, is 3 miles/4.8 km west. The population has grown due to a state land sale; limited services.

26.5 (42.6 km) **Sarkar Lake** to east. Fishing and boat launch. USFS public-use cabin at east end of lake.

27.9 (44.9 km) Bridge over Sarkar Lake outlet to salt water.

39.7 (63.9 km) USFS Road No. 25 leads east 7 miles/11.3 km past Neck Lake to small settlement of **WHALE PASS;** groceries and gas available, 4 cabins, floatplane dock, post office and school (1 teacher, 13 grades). Whale Pass Road loops back to the main North Island Road at **Milepost 48.6.**

40 (64.4 km) View of Neck Lake to east.

48.6 (78.2 km) Whale Pass loop road to east. Whale Pass is 8 miles/12.9 km from here; Exchange Cove is 16 miles/25.7 km from here.

50.3 (80.9 km) View of El Capitan Passage and Kosciusko Island to west.

51 (82.1 km) Side road leads west 1 mile/1.6 km to USFS El Cap Work Center; access to El Capitan Cave.

55.6 (89.5 km) Summit of the North Island Road (elev. 907 feet/276m).

59.5 (95.8 km) Rough road, heavy truck traffic and 1-lane bridges north from here.

60.6 (97.5 km) Red Creek 1-lane bridge.

61.7 (99.3 km) Big Creek 1-lane bridge.

63.9 (102.8 km) View of Red Bay to north; Red Lake is to the south.

67.6 (108.8 km) Buster Creek 1-lane bridge.

68.3 (109.9 km) Shine Creek 1-lane bridge.

72 (115.9 km) Flicker Creek 1-lane bridge.

72.1 (116 km) Memorial Beach picnic area 1.7 miles/2.7 km north; follow signs to parking area. A short trail leads to picnic tables, pit toilet, memorial plaque and beach. Good view of Sumner Strait and Kupreanof Island. This site is a memorial to 12 victims of a 1978 air crash.

79.5 (127.9 km) **LABOUCHERE BAY,** a small logging camp (no facilities) owned and operated by Louisiana Pacific Corp. The road continues several miles and dead ends at the base of Mount Calder.

Coffman Cove Road Log

Coffman Cove Road branches off the North Island Road (No. 20) at **Milepost 15.5** and leads east and north 20.5 miles/33 km to the logging camp of Coffman Cove. Watch for heavy truck traffic; 25 mph/40 kmph. Slow down for approaching vehicles.

0 Junction with North Island Road.

4.4 (7.1 km) Side road on left (USFS Road No. 30) leads 5 miles/8 km through clear-cut and dead ends.

4.5 (7.2 km) **Logjam Creek** bridge; cutthroat and steelhead; Dolly Varden; pink, silver and sockeye salmon.

9.1 (14.6 km) **Hatchery Creek** bridge; fishing same as Logjam Creek. Trailhead for canoe route to Thorne Bay.

9.4 (15.1 km) Bumpy road on right leads 13 miles/20.9 km to USFS access site; parking area and canoe launch (no trailers) on Luck Lake. Side road then loops north along Clarence Strait to Coffman Cove.

12.1 (19.5 km) View of Sweetwater Lake to left. USFS access site: parking area for Sweetwater public-use cabin, located 0.5 mile/0.8 km along west shore of lake.

17 (27.4 km) Coffman Creek bridge.

19.5 (31.4 km) Chum Creek bridge.

20.2 (32.5 km) **Junction** with Luck Lake loop road.

20.3 (32.7 km) Chum Creek bridge.

20.5 (33 km) **COFFMAN COVE**, a logging and fishing community; groceries, gas, cafe, gifts and local fresh oysters.

Wrangell

(See map, page 631)

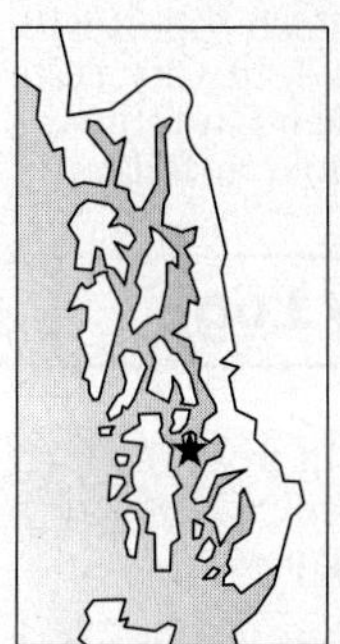

Located at northwest tip of Wrangell Island on Zimovia Strait; 2.5 miles/4 km south of the Stikine River delta; 3 hours by ferry or 32 air miles/51 km southeast of Petersburg, the closest major community; and 6 hours by ferry or 85 air miles/136 km north of Ketchikan. **Population:** 2,758. **Emergency Services:** Phone 911 for all emergencies. **Police,** phone (907) 874-3304. **Fire Department** and **Ambulance,** phone (907) 874-2000. **Hospital,** Wrangell General, 310 Bennett St. just off Zimovia Highway, phone (907) 874-3356. **Maritime Search and Rescue,** contact the Coast Guard at 1-800-478-5555.

Visitor Information: Center located in an A-frame building on the corner of Brueger Street and Outer Drive, next to the city hall; phone 1-800-367-9745 or (907) 874-3901. Write: Chamber of Commerce, Box 49MP, Wrangell 99929. Information is also available at the Wrangell Museum, 318 Church St.

Elevation: Sea level. **Climate:** Mild and moist with slightly less rain than other Southeast communities. Mean annual precipitation is 79.2 inches, with 63.9 inches of snow. Record monthly precipitation, 20.43 inches in Oct. 1961. Average daily maximum temperature in June is 61°F/16°C; in July 64°F/18°C. Daily minimum in Jan. is 21°F/-6°C. **Radio:** KSTK-FM 101.7. **Television:** Cable and satellite. **Newspaper:** *Wrangell Sentinel* (weekly).

Private Aircraft: Wrangell airport, adjacent northeast; elev. 44 feet/13m; length 6,000 feet/1,829m; paved; fuel 100LL, A.

Wrangell is the only Alaskan city to have existed under 4 nations and 3 flags—the Stikine Tlingits, the Russians, the British and the Americans. Wrangell began in 1834 as a Russian stockade called Redoubt St. Dionysius, built to prevent the Hudson's Bay Co. from fur trading up the rich Stikine River to the northeast. The Russians, in a change of policy, leased the mainland of southeastern Alaska to Hudson's Bay Co. in 1840. Under the British the stockade was called Fort Stikine.

The post remained under the British flag until Alaska was purchased by the United States in 1867. A year later the Americans established a military post here, naming it Fort Wrangell after the island, which was named by the Russians after Baron von Wrangel, a governor of the Russian-American Co.

Its strategic location near the mouth of the Stikine River, the fastest free-flowing navigable river in North America, made Wrangell an important supply point not only for fur traders but also for gold seekers following the river route to the goldfields. Today, the Stikine River is a popular hunting and recreation area. Currently, there is an active hard rock mine on the largest tributary of the Stikine, the Iskut. They are extracting gold, silver, copper and traces of other minerals from the site.

Wrangell serves as a hub for goods, services and transportation for outlying fishing villages, and logging and mining camps. The town depended largely on fishing until Japanese interests arrived in the mid-1950s and established a mill downtown (now closed). A small, locally owned mill is now in operation 2 miles/3.2 km beyond the end of Zimovia Highway, off Forest 6265. Fishing is one of Wrangell's largest industries, with salmon the major catch.

To Airport
Wrangell
Ferry Terminal
Stikine Ave. (Airport Rd.)
2 St.
Museum
Library
3 St.
To Airport
Post Office
Reid St.
Bennett St. (Airport Rd.)
Cruise Ship Dock
Front St.
Church St.
City Dock
Hospital
Visitor Information
Outer Dr.
Zimovia Strait
Harbor Entrance
Seaplane Float
Oil Docks
Chief Shakes Island
Zimovia Highway
Peninsula St.
Case Avenue
N
E
S
W
To Shoemaker Bay

ACCOMMODATIONS/VISITOR SERVICES

Wrangell has 4 motels and 4 restaurants downtown, as well as service stations, hardware and appliance stores, banks, drugstore, laundromat, grocery stores (1 with a bakery and deli), a fish market and gift shops. Bed-and-breakfasts are available. Lodges with restaurants are located on Peninsula Street and at Mile 4.4 Zimovia Highway.

RV camping and picnic area at Shoemaker Bay, **Milepost 4.9** Zimovia Highway. Dump stations located at Shoemaker Bay and downtown at the corner of Front Street and Case Avenue. City Park, at **Milepost 1.9** Zimovia Highway, has tent sites, picnic area with tables, flush toilets, shelters and playground.

TRANSPORTATION

Air: Daily scheduled jet service is provided by Alaska Airlines to other Southeast cities with through service to Seattle and Anchorage. Scheduled commuter air service to Petersburg, Kake and Ketchikan. Charter service available.

Airport terminal is 1.1 miles/1.8 km from ferry terminal or 1.1 miles/1.8 km from Zimovia Highway on Bennett Street.

Ferry: Alaska Marine Highway vessels connect Wrangell with all Southeastern Alaska ports plus Prince Rupert, BC, and Bellingham, WA. See MARINE ACCESS ROUTES section for details. Ferry terminal is at the north end of town at the end of Zimovia Highway (also named Church or 2nd Street at this point). Terminal facilities include ticket office, waiting room and vehicle waiting area. Phone (907) 874-3711.

Car Rental: Available.

Taxi: Available to and from airport and ferry terminal.

Highways: Zimovia Highway (see log this section). Logging roads have opened up most of Wrangell Island to motorists. Check with the USFS office at 525 Bennett St. for a copy of the Wrangell Island Road Guide map. (Write USDA Forest Service, Wrangell Ranger District, Box 51, Wrangell 99929; phone 907/874-2323.) Maps are also available at the Chamber of Commerce Visitor Center downtown.

Cruise Ships: Wrangell is a regular port of call in summer for several cruise lines.

Private Boats: Transient float located downtown. Reliance Float is located near Shakes Tribal House.

ATTRACTIONS

Shakes Island and Tribal House, in Wrangell Harbor, is reached by boardwalk. It is the site of several excellent totem poles. The replica tribal house contains Indian working tools, an original Chilkat blanket design and other cultural items. It is listed on the National Register of Historic Places. Open irregular hours during summer (May to Sept.) or by appointment; phone (907) 874-3747. Admission $1.

Totem Poles. The last original totems standing in Wrangell were cut down in November 1981 and removed for preservation. A totem restoration project funded by both state and federal agencies was initiated, and replicas of original totems can be found at Kiksadi Totem Park at the corner of Front and Episcopal streets.

Wrangell Museum, at 318 Church St. (interim site), features items from Wrangell's history, including Tlingit artifacts and petroglyphs. In summer, the museum is open weekdays 10 A.M. to 5 P.M., Saturday 1–6 P.M., and while the ferry is in port Sunday afternoons. Ferry schedules may vary, and staff tries to accommodate visits between 8 A.M. and 6 P.M. Open in winter Monday and Wednesday through Friday from 10 A.M. to 4 P.M., and Sunday when the ferry is in port. Phone (907) 874-3770; fax 874-3785. Admission for adults, $2; children under 16, free.

Our Collections Museum, located on Evergreen Avenue, is a private collection of antiques and Alaska memorabilia. Open when cruise ships and ferries are in port and by special request. Phone (907) 874-3646. Donations accepted.

Sightseeing Tours of attractions and fish bakes are available upon request. Sightseeing buses meet some ferries. Inquire at the visitor center or Wrangell Museum. Flightseeing and jetboat excursions available to Stikine River, Stikine Icefield, Anan Wildlife Observatory and other remote locations.

The Stikine River delta lies north of Wrangell within the Stikine–LeConte Wilderness. It is accessible by boat or by plane only. The delta is habitat for migrating waterfowl, eagles, bears and moose. During the spring run, the largest concentration of bald eagles in the world can be seen in the Stikine River delta. Also watch for seals resting on ice floes from LeConte Glacier (the glacier is at the head of LeConte Bay, just north of the delta), the southernmost tidewater glacier in North America.

Anan Observatory, managed by the U.S. Forest Service, is located 35 miles/56 km southeast of Wrangell; accessible by boat or plane only. During July and Aug., visitors can watch bears catch pink salmon headed for the salmon spawning grounds. Bald eagles, ravens, crows and seals are frequently seen feeding on the fish. Contact the visitor center for list of guides permitted to transport visitors to Anan (1-800-367-9745).

AREA FISHING: Fly in to **Thoms Lake, Long Lake, Marten Lake, Salmon Bay, Virginia Lake** and **Eagle Lake.** Thoms Lake and Long Lake are also accessible via road and trail. **Stikine River** near Wrangell (closed to king salmon fishing), Dolly Varden to 22 inches, and cutthroat to 18 inches, best in midsummer to fall; steelhead to 12 lbs., use bait or lures; coho salmon 10 to 15 lbs., use lures, September and October. Saltwater fishing near Wrangell for king salmon, 20 to 40 lbs., best in May and June. Stop by the Dept. of Fish and Game at 215 Front St. for details.

Wrangell Salmon Derby runs from mid-May to Memorial Day weekend. Kings weighing more than 50 lbs. are not unusual.

Petroglyphs are ancient designs carved into rock faces, usually found between low and high tide marks on beaches. Petroglyph Beach is located 0.7 mile/1.1 km from the ferry terminal; a boardwalk trail leads to the head of the beach from the left of the road. Turn right as you reach the beach and look for petroglyphs between there and a rock outcrop several hundred feet away; at least 40 can be seen. Petroglyphs are also located on the library lawn and are on display in the museum.

Garnet Ledge, a rocky outcrop on the right bank of the Stikine River delta at Garnet Creek, is 7.5 miles/12.1 km from Wrangell Harbor, reached at high tide by small boat. Garnet, a semiprecious stone, can be found embedded in the ledge here. The garnet ledge is on land deeded to the Southeast Council of the Boy Scouts of America by the late Fred Hanford (former mayor of Wrangell). The bequest states that the land shall be used for scouting purposes and the children of Wrangell may take garnets in reasonable quantities (garnets are sold by children at the docks when ships and ferries are in port). Contact the Wrangell Museum (Box 1050-MP, Wrangell 99929; phone 907/874-3770) for information on digging for garnets.

USFS public-use cabins in the Wrangell district are accessible by air or by boat. The 21 USFS cabins are scattered throughout the region. See Cabins in the GENERAL INFORMATION section, and stop by the USFS office at 525 Bennett St.; phone (907) 874-2323. Visitors may also use the white courtesy phone located in the ferry terminal building. Contact the Wrangell Ranger District at Box 51, Wrangell 99929.

Celebrations in Wrangell include a big Fourth of July celebration which begins with a salmon bake. The annual Tent City Festival, celebrated the first weekend in February, commemorates Wrangell's gold rush days.

Zimovia Highway Log

Zimovia Highway leads south from the ferry terminal to Pat Creek at Mile 11, where it connects with island logging roads.

0 Alaska Marine Highway ferry terminal, ticket office and waiting area. There is a bike path to Mile 1.9.

0.3 (0.5 km) St. Rose of Lima Catholic Church, the oldest Roman Catholic parish in Alaska, founded May 2, 1879.

0.4 (0.6 km) First Presbyterian Church has a red-lighted cross, 1 of 2 in the world that serve as navigational aids. This was the first church in Wrangell and is one of the oldest Protestant churches in Alaska (founded in 1877 and built in 1879).

Wrangell Museum interim location situated between the church and Wrangell High School.

0.6 (1 km) Bennett Street (Airport Road) loops north 2.2 miles/3.5 km to the airport and back to the ferry terminal.

0.7 (1.1 km) Public Safety Bldg.

1.9 (3.1 km) City park. Picnic area with shelters, firepits, restrooms, litter barrels. Tent camping only allowed; 24-hour limit.▲

3.6 (5.8 km) Turnout with beach access. Several turnouts along the highway here offer beach access and good spots for bird watching.

4.4 (7.1 km) Lodge on left with restaurant and lounge.

4.9 (7.9 km) Shoemaker Bay small-boat harbor, boat launch, picnic, camping and parking area. Camping area has tent sites, 29 RV sites ($8 per night, with hookups), water, dump station and restrooms. Tennis court, horseshoe pits and children's playground nearby. Rainbow Falls trailhead; 0.5 mile/0.8 km trail to scenic waterfall. Rainbow Falls trail intersects with Institute Creek trail in 0.2 mile/0.3 km, and from there leads 2.7 miles/4.3 km to viewpoint and shelter overlooking Shoemaker Bay. ▲

6.5 (10.5 km) Alaska Pulp Corp.

7.3 (11.7 km) **Milepost 7**, scenic turnout.

8 (12.9 km) Turnout.

8.5 (13.7 km) Turnout, beach access (8 Mile Beach undeveloped recreation area).

10.8 (17.4 km) Access road west to Pat Creek Log Transfer Facility. Road east (Pat Creek Road) leads 0.3 mile/0.5 km to Pat's Lake. This single-lane maintained gravel road continues approximately 6 miles/10 km northeast through logging area.

Pat Creek and **Pat's Lake**, cutthroat, Dolly Varden, pink and silver salmon, spinning gear or flies.

11 (17.7 km) Pat Creek camping area (unmaintained, no facilities); parking for self-contained vehicles. ▲

11.1 (17.9 km) State-maintained highway ends. Begin 1-lane Forest Development Road No. 6265 connecting with other Forest Service logging roads (map showing many island recreation sites and trails available from USFS office in Wrangell). Watch for logging trucks.

The Wrangell logging road system has drive-in roadside fishing. Thoms Lake, Long Lake, Thoms Creek and Salamander Creek for Dolly Varden and cutthroat, best in Aug.; king salmon in Earl West Creek and Salamander Creek in June and July; coho salmon in all of these creeks, Sept. and Oct.

Fishing is the major industry in Petersburg. (© Jason Paur)

Petersburg

(See map, page 632)

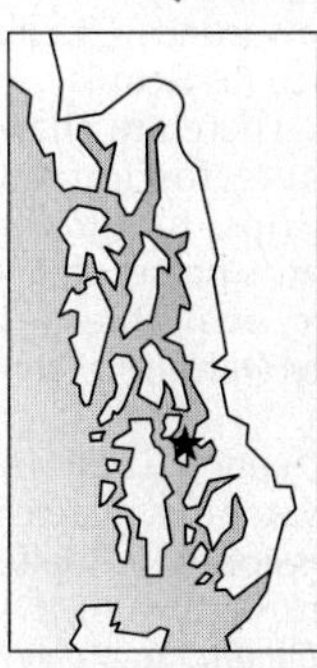

Located on the northwest tip of Mitkof Island at the northern end of Wrangell Narrows, midway between Juneau and Ketchikan. **Population:** 3,350. **Emergency Services:** Phone 911. **Alaska State Troopers,** phone (907) 772-3100. **City Police, Poison Center, Fire Department** and **Ambulance,** phone (907) 772-3838. **Hospital,** Petersburg General, 1st and Fram streets, phone (907) 772-4291. **Maritime Search and Rescue:** contact the Coast Guard at 1-800-478-5555. Harbormaster, phone (907) 772-4688, CB Channel 9, or VHF Channel 16.

Visitor Information: Chamber of Commerce/USFS Information Center located at 1st and Fram streets; open weekdays from 9 A.M. to 5 P.M. spring and summer, 10 A.M. to 2 P.M. fall and winter. Write: Chamber of Commerce, Box 649MP, Petersburg 99833; phone/fax (907) 772-3646. For national forest information, write Petersburg Visitor Information Center, Box 1328, Petersburg 99833; phone/fax (907) 772-4636. Petersburg Museum, 2nd and Fram streets, open daily in summer, limited winter hours; phone (907) 772-3598. Alaska Dept. of Fish and Game, State Office Bldg., Sing Lee Alley; open 8 A.M. to 4:30 P.M., Monday through Friday.

Elevation: Sea level. **Climate:** Average daily maximum temperature in July, 64°F/18°C; daily minimum in Jan., 20°F/-7°C. All-time high, 84°F/29°C in 1933; record low, -19°F/-28°C in 1947. Mean annual precipitation, 105 inches; mean annual snowfall, 119 inches. **Radio:** KRSA 580, KFSK-FM 100.9. **Television:** Alaska Rural Communication Service, Channel 15; KTOO (PBS) Channel 9 and cable channels.

Newspaper: *Petersburg Pilot* (weekly).

Private Aircraft: James A. Johnson Airport, 1 mile/1.6 km southeast; elev. 107 feet/33m; length 6,000 feet/1,829m; asphalt; fuel 100, A. Seaplane base 0.5 mile/0.8 km from downtown.

Petersburg was named for Peter Buschmann, who selected the present townsite for a salmon cannery and sawmill in 1897. The sawmill and dock were built in 1899, and the cannery was completed in 1900. He was followed by other Norwegian–Americans who came to fish and work in the cannery and sawmill. Since then the cannery has operated continuously (with rebuilding, expansion and different owners) and is now known as Petersburg Fisheries Inc., a division of Icicle Seafoods Inc.

Today, Petersburg boasts the largest home-based halibut fleet in Alaska and is also well known for its shrimp, crab, salmon, herring and other fish products. Most families depend on the fishing industry for livelihood. Sportfishing questions should be directed to the Alaska Dept. of Fish and Game's Division of Sportfishing in Ketchikan, phone (907) 225-2859.

ACCOMMODATIONS/VISITOR SERVICES

Petersburg has a hotel, several motels and bed and breakfasts, many restaurants and several fast-food outlets downtown. The 5-block-long commercial area on Main Street (Nordic Drive) has grocery stores, marine and fishing supply stores, hardware, drugstores, travel agency, public showers, banks, gift and variety stores specializing in both Alaskan and Scandinavian items, city hall, post office, gas stations, cocktail bars, a community gym with racquetball courts and a public swimming pool. Petersburg has 17 churches.

There are 3 RV parks, dump station, hookups, showers, laundry; fee charged. There is a tent campground (known locally as Tent City) on Haugen Drive; it is often filled to capacity in summer with young cannery workers. Public campgrounds (1 developed, several undeveloped) are located on Mitkof Highway south of town. ▲

TRANSPORTATION

Air: Daily scheduled jet service by Alaska Airlines to major Southeast cities and Seattle, WA, with connections to Anchorage and Fairbanks. Local and charter service available.

The airport, located 1 mile/1.6 km from the Federal Bldg. on Haugen Drive, has a ticket counter and waiting room.

Ferry: Alaska Marine Highway vessels connect Petersburg with all Southeastern Alaska cities plus Prince Rupert, BC, and Bellingham, WA. (See MARINE ACCESS ROUTES section for schedules.) Terminal at **Milepost 0.8** Mitkof Highway, includes dock, ticket office with waiting room, and parking area. Phone (907) 772-3855.

NOTE: RVs arriving late at night are allowed to park free for up to 8 hours at the south boat harbor parking lot just north of the ferry terminal.

Car Rental: Available at downtown hotels.

Taxi: There are 2 taxi companies. Cab service to and from the airport and ferry terminal.

Highways: Mitkof Highway, Sandy Beach Road and Three Lakes Loop Road (see logs this section).

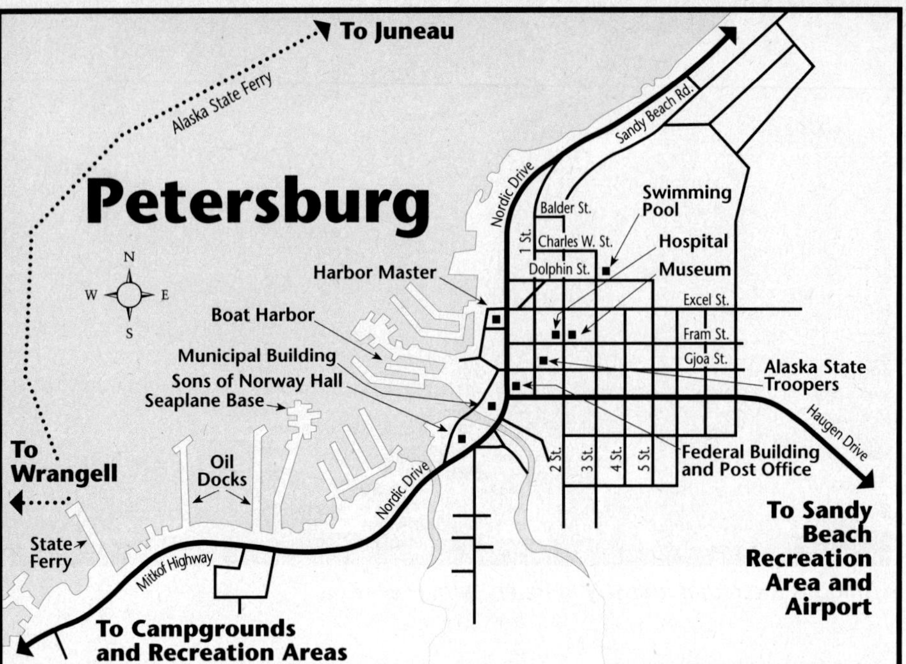

Private Boats: Boaters must check with harbormaster for moorage assignment.

ATTRACTIONS

Clausen Memorial Museum, 203 Fram St., features the world's largest king salmon caught in a fish trap commercially (estimated at 126½ lbs.) and the world-record chum salmon (36 lbs.). It also houses collections of local historical items including a recreation of the office of colorful local cannery owner Earl Ohmer. Open daily in summer; call (907) 772-3598 for updated schedules.

The Fisk, a 10-foot/3-m bronze sculpture commemorating Petersburg's fishing tradition, stands in a working fountain in front of the museum. It was completed during the Alaska centennial year of 1967 by sculptor Carson Boysen.

Sons of Norway Hall, on the National Register of Historic Places, was built in 1912. Situated on pilings over Hammer Slough (a favorite photography subject), its window shutters are decorated with rosemaling (Norwegian tole painting).

Little Norway Festival is scheduled for May 16–19, 1996, as a celebration for Norwegian Independence Day. Pageantry, old-country dress, contests, Vikings, a Viking ship, dancing and a Norwegian "fish feed" for locals and visitors are featured.

LeConte Glacier, in LeConte Bay, 25 miles/40 km east of Petersburg, is the continent's southernmost tidewater glacier. Fast-moving, the glacier continually "calves," creating ice falls from its face into the bay. Seals and porpoises are common; whales are often seen. Helicopters, small aircraft and boats may be chartered in Petersburg or Wrangell to see LeConte Glacier.

Salmon migration and spawning are best observed in the Petersburg area July though Sept. Falls Creek bridge and fish ladder is a good location (silver and pink) as are Blind Slough and the Blind River Rapids area, Petersburg Creek and Ohmer Creek (king, silver, pink and chum).

Crystal Lake Fish Hatchery is at **Milepost 17.5** Mitkof Highway. This hatchery for coho, king and steelhead is operated by the state and used for fish-stocking projects in Southeastern Alaska. It is open for visits, and hatchery personnel will explain the operation, though formal guided tours are not available. Best time to visit is between 8 A.M. and 4 P.M., Monday through Friday.

Falls Creek fish ladder is at **Milepost 10.8** Mitkof Highway. The ladder helps migrating salmon bypass difficult falls on the way to spawning grounds in Falls Creek. It can be observed from the creek bank just off the roadside. Best time is late summer and early fall to observe coho and pink salmon.

Petersburg King Salmon Derby is scheduled for Memorial Day weekend May 24–27, 1996; $30,000 in prizes is awarded. Check with the chamber of commerce for details.

Charter a Boat or Plane. There are charter boat services in Petersburg for guided salt- and freshwater fishing trips. Inquire at the visitor information center. Charter floatplanes and helicopters are available for flightseeing, including whale watching, fly-in fishing and transportation.

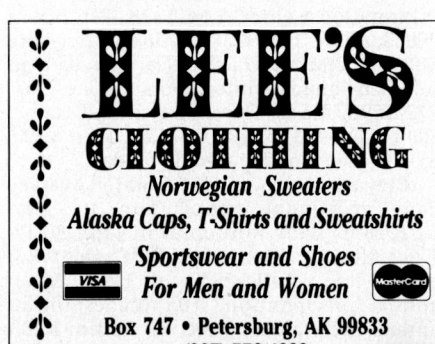

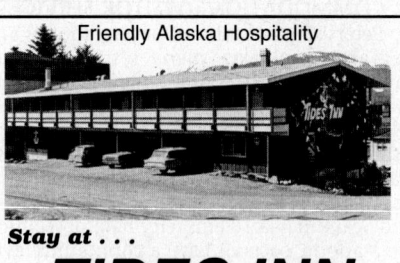

Kaleidoscope Cruises specializes in custom sightseeing, whale-watching, glacier and fishing excursions. Professional biologist and naturalist, Barry Bracken, skipper of the comfortable 28-foot *Island Dream,* has over 25 years experience in Southeast Alaska waters, conducting biological research, exploring, and sportfishing. Half-day, full-day, overnight tours. 1-800-TO-THE-SEA. [ADVERTISEMENT]

AREA FISHING: Salmon, steelhead, cutthroat and Dolly Varden at **Falls Creek, Blind Slough** and **Blind River Rapids;** see log of Mitkof Highway this section. Salmon can be caught in the harbor area and **Scow Bay** area. (Rapid tidal currents in front of the town necessitate the use of an outboard motor.) **Petersburg Creek,** directly across Wrangell Narrows from downtown within Petersburg Creek–Duncan Salt Chuck Wilderness Area, also offers good fishing. Blind Slough, located 15 miles/24 km south of the ferry terminal, offers good drive-up fishing for king salmon. Dolly Varden can be caught from the beach north of town and from downtown docks. Sportfishing opportunities for halibut, rockfish, crab and shrimp. Harvest of mussels, clams and the like is not recommended because of the possibility of paralytic shellfish poisoning. Contact the Sport Fish Division of the Alaska Dept. of Fish and Game (907/225-2859) for additional information.

Wrangell Narrows is a 23-mile-/37-km-long channel between Mitkof and Kupreanof islands. The channel was dredged in the 1940s to a depth of 26 feet/42m. Extremely narrow in places and filled with rocky reefs, islands and strong currents, the narrows is navigated by ships and ferries with the aid of dozens of markers and flashing lights. The 1½-hour run through Wrangell Narrows begins immediately on ferries departing Petersburg southbound, or about 1½ hours after departing Wrangell northbound.

Cabins, canoe and hiking trails managed by the U.S. Forest Service are all within reach of Petersburg, which is the administrative center for the Stikine Area of Tongass National Forest. Stop by the USFS office in the Federal Bldg., or phone (907) 772-3871 for detailed information on cabins and trails. Also consult *The ALASKA WILDERNESS GUIDE*. See also Cabins in the GENERAL INFORMATION section. Information for canoers and kayakers interested in the Stikine River delta or Tebenkof Bay is also available here or at the USFS office in Wrangell.

Sandy Beach Road Log

From Federal Bldg., drive north through town; road leads to Sandy Beach Recreation Area.

0 Federal Bldg. and post office.

0.1 (0.2 km) Petersburg boat harbor 1 block to left, contains one of Alaska's finest fishing fleets.

0.2 (0.3 km) Downtown Petersburg.

0.3 (0.5 km) Petersburg Fisheries Inc., the city's largest processing plant.

Eagles Roost Park. Eagles feed on beach at low tide; best viewing in early summer.

1.2 (1.9 km) Eagle observation point. Eagles can be seen nesting nearby and fishing in Wrangell Narrows. To the northeast is Frederick Sound and the mainland.

2 (3.2 km) Bed and breakfast, sightseeing cruises.

2.8 (4.5 km) Sandy Beach Recreation Area on left; picnic tables, playground, volleyball court, shelter, toilets, limited parking, no camping. **Junction** with Haugen Drive, which loops to airport and back to town.

Just past Sandy Beach Recreation Area is the Fredrick Point boardwalk, a 1-mile/1.6-km trail that leads through the woods to the beach near Fredrick Point. This trail is very popular in summer.

Mitkof Highway Log

The major road on the island, Mitkof Highway leads 33.8 miles/54.4 km south from the Federal Bldg. to the Stikine River delta at the south end of Mitkof Island. The highway is paved to **Milepost 17.5**; good wide gravel to road end.

0 Federal Bldg. and post office.

0.1 (0.2 km) Bridge over Hammer Slough, an intertidal estuary.

0.5 (0.8 km) Harbor parking and RV staging area (8-hour RV parking).

0.6 (1 km) Pier and floatplane base.

0.8 (1.3 km) Alaska Marine Highway ferry terminal, office and waiting area on right.

2.8 (4.5 km) Muskeg meadows on left. Muskeg is a grassy bog, common in Alaska.

2.9 (4.6 km) **Scow Bay**, a wide portion of Wrangell Narrows with king salmon fishing in spring. Scow Bay is noted traditionally as the first election precinct to report its vote in statewide elections. Scow Bay Loop Road rejoins highway at **Milepost 3.1**.

4 (6.4 km) Lodging on right.

4.3 (6.9 km) Turnout on right with view of Wrangell Narrows.

7.5 (12.1 km) Twin Creek RV Park, private campground, small store and phone. ▲

10.7 (17.2 km) North exit to Three Lakes Loop Road (see log this section).

10.8 (17.4 km) **Falls Creek** and fish ladder. Steelhead, April and May; pink salmon below falls in August; coho, August and September; Dolly Varden and cutthroat late summer and fall. No fishing within 300 feet of fish ladder.

11 (17.7 km) Road on right leads 0.5 mile/0.8 km to Papke's Landing; transient boat moorage and boat ramp. USFS Log Transportation Facility.

14.3 (23 km) Entering Tongass National Forest.

14.5 (23.3 km) Blind River Rapids parking area and trail; new outhouse. 0.3-mile/0.4-km boardwalk trail through muskeg meadow to **Blind River Rapids,** hatchery steelhead, mid-April to mid-May; king salmon, June to late July; coho, mid-Aug. to Oct. Also Dolly Varden and cutthroat.

16.3 (26.2 km) Blind Slough waterfowl viewing area on right. Covered platform with interpretive sign on area waterfowl. Trumpeter swans winter in this area.

17.5 (28.2 km) Pavement ends; wide, hard-packed gravel to end of road. Short road leads to Crystal Lake Fish Hatchery and **Blind Slough** Recreation Area with picnic tables, shelter and pit toilets; no overnight camping. Hatchery is open for visiting, though no scheduled tours are available. Fishing for steelhead, best in May; cutthroat and Dolly Varden in summer; coho salmon, mid-Aug. to mid-Sept.; king salmon in June and July.

20 (32.2 km) **Manmade Hole** picnic area with tables, firepits, swimming and short trail. Ice skating in winter. Fishing for cutthroat and Dolly Varden year-round; best in summer and fall.

20.6 (33.1 km) Three Lakes Loop Road begins on left leading to Three Lakes on other side of Mitkof Island, looping back to Mitkof Highway at **Milepost 10.7** near Falls Creek bridge.

21.4 (34.4 km) Woodpecker Cove Road (1-lane) leads about 15 miles/24 km along south Mitkof Island to Woodpecker Cove and beyond. Good views of Sumner Strait. Watch for logging trucks.

21.5 (34.6 km) Ohmer Creek interpretive trail, 0.1 mile/0.2 km long; handicapped accessible. ♿

21.7 (34.9 km) Ohmer Creek Campground, 10 sites (2 are wheelchair accessible), toilets, parking area, picnic tables, drinking water and firepits. Set in meadow area among trees. Open spring to fall; no fee, no restrictions. ♿▲

24 (38.6 km) **Blind Slough** USFS Log Transportation Facility. Excellent fishing from skiff for king salmon in June and July; coho salmon, mid-Aug. to mid-Sept.

26.1 (42 km) Narrow 0.7-mile/1.1-km road on right to Sumner Strait Campground, locally called Green's Camp (undeveloped); must walk in, no facilities. May be inaccessible at high tide. ▲

27 (43.4 km) View of city of Wrangell.

28 (45 km) Wilson Creek state recreation area (undeveloped); picnic tables, parking, outhouse. Good view of Sumner Strait.

28.6 (46 km) Banana Point, boat ramp, outhouse.

31 (49.9 km) Stikine River mud flats, visible on right at low tide. Part of the Stikine River delta, this is the area where Dry Strait meets Sumner Strait.

33.8 (54.4 km) Road ends with turnaround.

Three Lakes Loop Road Log

Access to this 21.4-mile-/34.4-km-long, 1-lane loop road is from **Mileposts 10.7** and **20.6** on the Mitkof Highway. *CAUTION: No services; use turnouts.*

0 Junction at **Milepost 10.7** Mitkof Highway; turn east.

1.4 (2.3 km) View of Wrangell Narrows to west. Older clear-cuts; this area was logged between 1964 and 1968.

4.4 (7.1 km) Falls Creek bridge.

7 (11.3 km) Second-growth stand of spruce-hemlock. First growth was destroyed by fire or wind throw more than 180 years ago. This second-growth stand serves as an example of what a logging unit could look like a century or two after clear-cutting.

9.7 (15.6 km) Directly south is a 384-acre clear-cut logged in 1973 under a contract predating the current policy, which usually limits clear-cut tracts to 100 acres.

10.2 (16.4 km) **Big Creek**; steelhead in April and May; coho late August and September; cutthroat and Dolly Varden, best late summer and fall.

12.3 (19.8 km) Muskeg; view of Frederick Sound.

14.2 (22.8 km) Sand Lake trail. Short boardwalk trail leads to each of the Three Lakes. Tennis shoes are ideal for these short walks, but for areas around the lakes it is advisable to wear rubber boots. A 0.7-mile/1.1-km connecting trail to Hill Lake.

14.7 (23.6 km) Hill Lake trail.

15.1 (24.3 km) Crane Lake trail, 1.3 miles/2.1 km to lake; connecting trail to Hill Lake. USFS skiffs and picnic platforms are located at Sand, Hill and Crane lakes.

Sand, Hill and **Crane lakes,** cutthroat from May through Sept.

16.1 (26.1 km) Dry Straits Road.

21.4 (34.4 km) Second **junction** with Mitkof Highway, at **Milepost 20.6.**

View of Sitka and O'Connell Bridge. (© David Job)

Sitka

(See map, page 632)

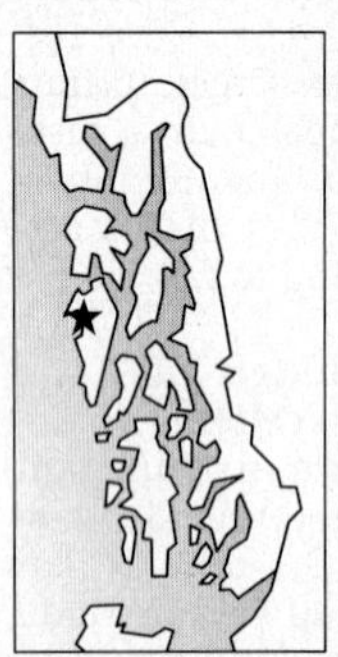

Located on west side of Baranof Island, 95 air miles/153 km southwest of Juneau, 185 air miles/298 km northwest of Ketchikan; 2 hours flying time from Seattle, WA. **Population:** City and Borough, 9,194. **Emergency Services: Alaska State Troopers, City Police, Fire Department,** and **Ambulance,** phone 911. **Hospital,** Sitka Community, 209 Moller Ave., phone (907) 747-3241; Mount Edgecumbe, 222 Tongass Dr., phone (907) 966-2411. **Maritime Search and Rescue,** phone the Coast Guard at 1-800-478-5555.

Visitor Information: Contact the Sitka Convention and Visitors Bureau at Box 1226-MP, Sitka 99835; phone (907) 747-5940. Also available at the Isabel Miller Museum in the Centennial Bldg. on Harbor Drive. Museum hours are 8 A.M. to 5 P.M. in summer, extended hours to accommodate ferry passengers; phone (907) 747-6455. For USDA Forest Service information write the Sitka Ranger District at 201 Katlian Suite 109, Sitka 99835; phone (907) 747-6671. For information on Sitka National Historical Park, write 106 Metlakatla St., Sitka 99835; phone (907) 747-6281.

Elevation: Sea level. **Climate:** Average daily temperature in July, 55°F/13°C; in January, 33°F/1°C. Annual precipitation, 95 inches. **Radio:** KIFW 1230, KRSA-FM 94.9, KSBZ-FM 103.1, KCAW-FM 104.7. **Television:** Cable channels. **Newspaper:** *Daily Sitka Sentinel.*

Private Aircraft: Sitka airport on Japonski Island; elev. 21 feet/6m; length 6,500 feet/1,981m; asphalt; fuel 100, A1. Sitka seaplane base adjacent west; fuel 80, 100.

One of the most scenic of Southeastern Alaskan cities, Sitka rests on the ocean shore protected at the west by myriad small islands and Cape Edgecumbe. Mount Edgecumbe, the Fuji-like volcano (dormant), is 3,201 feet/976m high.

The site was originally occupied by Tlingit Indians. Alexander Baranof, chief manager of the Russian–American Co. with headquarters in Kodiak, built a trading post and fort (St. Michael's Redoubt) north of Sitka in 1799. Indians burned down the fort and looted the warehouses. Baranof returned in 1804, and by 1808 Sitka was capital of Russian Alaska. Baranof was governor from 1790 to 1818. A statue of the Russian governor was unveiled in 1989; it is located outside of the Centennial Bldg. Castle Hill in Sitka is where Alaska changed hands from Russia to the United States in 1867. Salmon was the mainstay of the economy from the late 1800s until the 1950s, when the salmon population decreased. A pulp mill operated at nearby Silver Bay from 1960 to 1993. Today, tourism, commercial fishing, cold storage plants and government provide most jobs.

ACCOMMODATIONS/VISITOR SERVICES

Sitka has several hotels/motels, most with adjacent restaurants. Bed and breakfasts are also available.

Alaska Ocean View Bed & Breakfast. You'll enjoy casual elegance at affordable rates at this superior, quality B&B where guests experience a high degree of personal comfort, privacy and friendly, knowledgeable hosts. Open your day with the tantalizing aroma of fresh bread, fresh ground coffee and a delicious, generous breakfast and close your day with a refreshing soak in the bubbling patio spa. Open year-round, credit cards, smoke-free, on airporter/ferry shuttle route. Business travelers and vacationers rate this lodging a 12 plus! "Delighted beyond our expectations!" Brochure and reservations: 1101 Edgecumbe Drive, Sitka, AK

99835; phone (907) 747-8310. See display ad this section. [ADVERTISEMENT]

Sitka Youth Hostel is located in the United Methodist Church, 303 Kimsham St. (1 1/2 blocks north of McDonald's on Halibut Point Road). Send correspondence to Box 2645, Sitka 99835. Open June 1 to Aug. 31; 20 beds, showers, no kitchen facilities. Phone (907) 747-8356.

An array of businesses cluster in the downtown area, which saw its first traffic light installed in 1992. Services in Sitka's downtown area include restaurants, a laundromat, drugstore, clothing and grocery stores, and gift shops. Shopping and services are also available along Sawmill and Halibut Point roads. Dump stations are located at the Wastewater Treatment Plant on Japonski Island.

Four campgrounds are available in the Sitka area. From the ferry terminal north they are: the Starrigavan Campground (USFS) at **Milepost 7.8** Halibut Point Road, with 32 sites, 2 picnic sites, artesian water, tables, vault toilets, 14-day limit, $8 fee; 4 sites are on the National Forest reservation system (1-800-280-CAMP); Sitka Sportsman's Assoc. RV Park, located 1 block south of the ferry terminal on Halibut Point Road, with 16 RV sites, water and electrical hookups, $14.50 fee, reservations accepted (phone 907/747-6033); Sealing Cove (operated by the City and Borough of Sitka), located adjacent Sealing Cove Boat Harbor on Japonski Island, has overnight parking for 26 RVs, water and electrical hookups, 15-night limit, $16 fee; and Sawmill Creek Campground (USFS) at **Milepost 5.4** Sawmill Creek Road, with 10 sites for self-contained RVs and tenting, vault toilets, boil water, no regular maintenance, no fee, 14-day limit. ▲

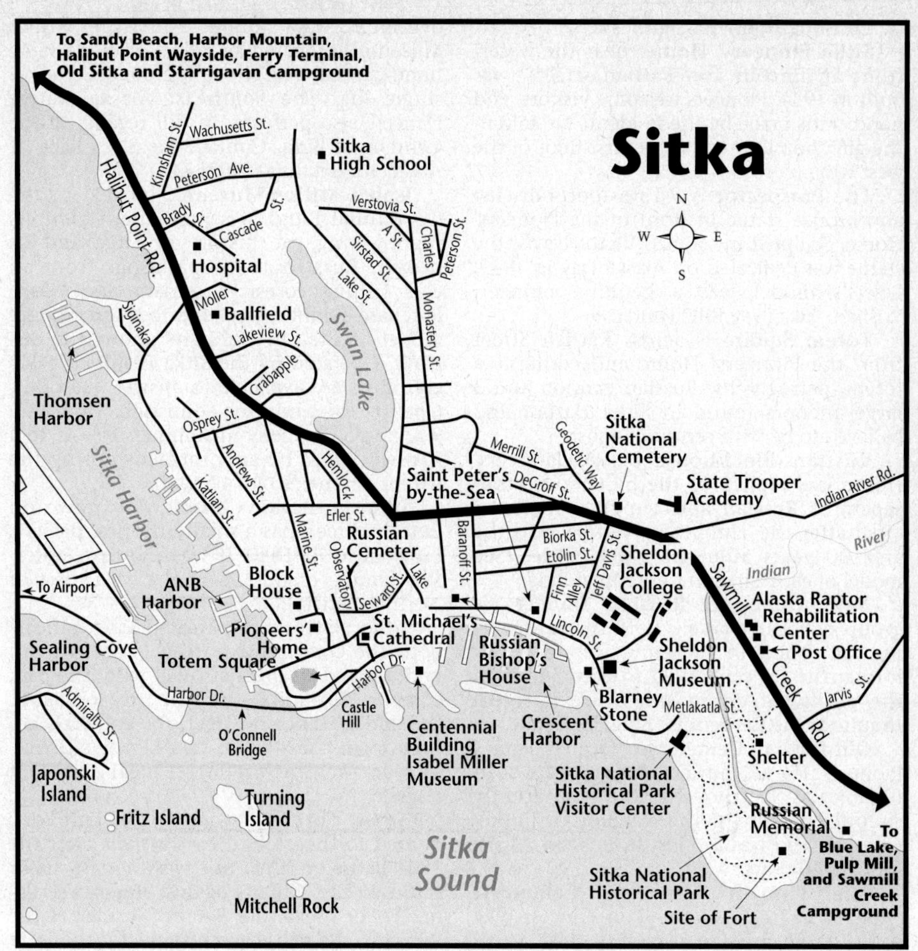

TRANSPORTATION

Air: Scheduled jet service by Alaska Airlines. Charter and commuter service also available. The airport is on Japonski Island, across O'Connell Bridge, 1.7 miles/2.7 km from downtown. Airport facilities include ticket counters, rental cars, small gift shop, restaurant and lounge. Van and taxi service to downtown hotels available.

Ferry: Alaska Marine Highway ferry terminal is located at **Milepost 7** Halibut Point Road; phone (907) 747-8737. Buses for downtown meet all ferries. Van and taxi service also available. Sitka is connected via the Marine Highway to other Southeast ports, Prince Rupert, BC, and Bellingham, WA (see MARINE ACCESS ROUTES section).

Bus: Available to downtown hotels.

Car Rental: At airport.

Taxi: Local service is available.

Highways: Halibut Point Road, 7.9 miles/12.7 km, and Sawmill Creek Road, 7.4 miles/11.9 km; see logs this section.

Cruise Ships: Sitka is a popular port of call for several cruise lines.

Private Boats: Transient moorage available at ANB Harbor, located downtown next to the fuel dock; Thomsen Harbor on Katlian Street, 0.6 mile/1 km from city center; and Sealing Cove on Japonski Island. Moorage is limited during the summer.

ATTRACTIONS

St. Michael's Cathedral is the focal point of Sitka's history as the capital of Russian Alaska. Built in 1844–48 under the direction of Bishop Innocent Veniaminov of the Russian Orthodox Church, one of the finest examples of rural Russian church architecture for 118 years. It was destroyed by fire on Jan. 2, 1966. Priceless icons, some predating 1800, were saved by townspeople and are now back in place in the rebuilt cathedral (an exact replica).

St. Michael's is located in the center of Lincoln Street downtown; a donation is requested when entering to view icons. Open daily June 1 to Sept. 30, 11 A.M. to 3 P.M. St. Michael's currently serves a Russian Orthodox congregation of about 100 families. Visitors are reminded that this is an active parish conducting weekly services.

Castle Hill (Baranof Castle Hill Historic Site) is where Alaska changed hands from Russia to the United States on Oct. 18, 1867. Castle Hill was the site of Baranof's castle. Walkway to site is located on the south side by the bridge (look for sign).

Sitka Pioneers' Home, near the waterfront at Lincoln and Katlian streets, was built in 1934. Pioneers welcome visitors, and handicrafts made by the residents are sold in the gift shop located on the first floor of the west wing.

The Prospector is a 13½-foot/4-m clay and bronze statue in front of the Pioneers' Home. Sculpted by Alonzo Victor Lewis, the statue was dedicated on Alaska Day in 1949. Lewis's model was a genuine pioneer, William "Skagway Bill" Fonda.

Totem Square is across Katlian Street from the Pioneers' Home and contains a totem, petroglyphs, Russian cannon and 3 large anchors found in Sitka Harbor and believed to be 18th century English.

Russian Blockhouse beside Pioneers' Home is a replica of the blockhouse that separated Russian and Tlingit sections of Sitka after the Tlingits moved back to the area 20 years after the 1804 battle. (See model of early Sitka in Centennial Bldg.)

New Archangel Russian Dancers, a group of local women, perform authentic Russian dances in authentic costumes. Performances are scheduled to coincide with the arrival of cruise ships. Fee charged. Inquire at the Centennial Bldg. for details.

Old Russian Cemetery is located behind Pioneers' Home and includes graves of such notables as St. Iahov Netsvetov, a recently canonized saint of the Russian Orthodox Church, who was a priest in Russian Alaska for over 40 years.

The Finnish Lutheran Cemetery, dedicted in 1841, is located on Princess Way next to the Russian cemetery. Just a few steps up the hill from Sitka Lutheran Church, it holds the grave of Princess Maskutov, wife of Alaska's last Russian governor, and other important personages.

Sitka National Cemetery, Milepost 0.5 Sawmill Creek Road, is open 8 A.M. to 5 P.M. daily (maintained by the Veterans Administration). It was known locally as Military Cemetery. In 1924 Pres. Calvin Coolidge designated the site as Sitka National Cemetery, and until WWII it was the only national cemetery west of the Rockies. Civil War veterans, veterans of the Aleutian Campaign in WWII and many notable Alaskans are buried here. One gravestone is dated December 1867, 2 months after the U.S. purchase of Alaska from Russia.

Alaska Day Celebration, Oct. 14–18, celebrates the transfer of Alaska from Russia to the United States with a reenactment of the event, complete with Sitka's own 9th (Manchu) Infantry, authentic uniforms and working muskets of the period. Period costumes and beards are the order of the day. Events ranging from pageant to costume ball and parade highlight the affair.

Annual Sitka Summer Music Festival (June 7–28, 1996). Concerts on Tuesday, Friday and some Saturday evenings in the Centennial Bldg., praised for its excellent acoustics. Emphasizing chamber music, an international group of professional musicians give evening concerts during the festival, plus open rehearsals. Advance tickets are a good idea; the concerts are popular. Dress is informal and concert-goers may have the opportunity to talk with the musicians. Children under 6 years not admitted.

Centennial Building, by the boat harbor on Harbor Drive, is used for Russian dance performances, music festivals, banquets and conventions. Its glass-fronted main hall overlooks Sitka Sound. The Isabel Miller Museum is located here. Nearby is a large hand-carved Tlingit canoe made from a single log. The Southeast Alaska Native Dancers also perform, in full regalia, in the Centennial Bldg. Contact the Sitka tribe of Alaska for details at (907) 747-7290.

Isabel Miller Museum, located in the Centennial Bldg., has permanent exhibits highlighting the history of Sitka and its people. Russian tools, paintings from all eras, fishing, forestry, tourism, and Alaska Purchase exhibits, and an 8-foot-square scale model of Sitka in 1867 are among the displays. Operated by the Sitka Historical Society; hosts are available to answer questions. Open year-round; free admission. Hours are 9 A.M. to 5 P.M. daily in summer; 10 A.M. to 4 P.M. weekdays by appointment during the winter. Phone (907) 747-5940.

Sitka Lutheran Church, downtown on Lincoln Street, has a small historical display. Established in 1840, it was the first Protestant church organized on the west coast of North America.

Sitka National Historical Park reflects both the community's rich Tlingit Indian heritage and its Russian-ruled past. The park consists of 2 units—the Fort Site, located at the end of Lincoln Street, 0.5 mile/0.8 km from town, and the Russian Bishop's House, located on Lincoln Street near Crescent Harbor.

At the Fort Site stood the Tlingit fort, burned to the ground by Russians after the 1804 Battle of Sitka; this was the last major stand by the Tlingits against Russian settlement. For Alexander Baranof, leader of the Russians, the battle was revenge for the 1802 destruction of Redoubt St. Michael by the Tlingits. There is a visitor center here with audiovisual programs and exhibits of Indian artifacts. The Southeast Alaska Indian Cultural Center has contemporary Tlingit artists demonstrate and interpret various traditional arts for visitors.

There is a self-guiding trail through the park to the fort site and battleground of 1804. The National Park Service conducts guided walks; check for schedule. The park's totem pole collection stands near the visitor center and along the trail. The collection includes original pieces collected in 1901–03, and copies of originals lost to time and the elements. The pieces, primarily from Prince of Wales Island, were collected by Alaska Gov. John Brady (now buried in Sitka National Cemetery). The originals were exhibited at the 1904 St. Louis Exposition.

The Russian Bishop's House was built by the Russian–American Co. in 1842 for the first Russian Orthodox Bishop to serve Alaska. It was occupied by the church until 1969, and was added to Sitka National Historical Park in 1972. The house is 1 of 2 Russian log structures remaining in Sitka, and 1 of 4 remaining in North America.

The park's visitor center is open daily, 8 A.M. to 5 P.M., June through Sept.; weekdays, 8 A.M. to 5 P.M., Oct. through May. The park grounds and trails are open daily, 5 A.M. to 10 P.M. in summer; shorter hours in winter. The Russian Bishop's House is open 9:30 A.M. to noon and 1–3 P.M. daily in summer; other times by appointment. The visitor center is closed Thanksgiving, Christmas and New Year's. No admission fee. Phone (907) 747-6281 for more information.

Sheldon Jackson Museum, 104 College Dr., on the Sheldon Jackson College campus, contains some of the finest Native arts and crafts found in Alaska. Much of it was collected by missionary Sheldon Jackson and is now owned by the state of Alaska. Museum shop specializes in Alaska Native arts and crafts: ivory, dolls, masks, silver jewelry, baskets and beadwork. Admission $3, students under 18 free, annual pass $10. Open in summer 8 A.M. to 5 P.M. daily. Winter hours: Tuesday through Saturday, 10 A.M. to 4 P.M. Phone (907) 747-8981.

Blarney Stone, across from Sheldon Jackson College. Believed to originally have been called Baranof's stone and used as a resting stop by Russian–American Co. chief manager Alexander Baranof.

O'Connell Bridge, 1,225 feet/373m long, connecting Sitka with Japonski Island, was the first cable-stayed, girder-span bridge in the United States. It was dedicated Aug. 19, 1972. You'll get a good view of Sitka and the harbors by walking across this bridge.

Old Sitka, at **Milepost 7.5** Halibut Point Road, is a registered national historic landmark and the site of the first Russian settlement in the area in 1799, known then as Fort Archangel Michael. In 1802, in a surprise attack, the Tlingit Indians of the area destroyed the fort and killed most of its occupants, driving the Russians out until Baranof's successful return in 1804.

Visit the Alaska Raptor Rehabilitation Center, located at 1101 Sawmill Creek Road (**Milepost 0.9**) just across Indian River, within easy walking distance of downtown Sitka. This unique facility treats injured eagles, hawks, owls and other birds. Visitors will have the opportunity to see American bald eagles and other raptors close up, review case histories of birds treated at the center and observe medical care being administered to current patients. From May 15 through Sept. the facility is open daily for tours and educational programs; limited hours Oct. to May 15. Phone (907) 747-8662 or fax 747-8397 for times. Admission charged.

Hiking Trails. The Sitka Ranger District office at 201 Katlian, Suite 109, provides information sheets and maps for area trails and remote cabins. Trails accessible from the road include Harbor Mountain Ridge trail,; Mount Verstovia trail; the easy 5-mile/8-km Indian River trail; and the short Beaver Lake trail off Sawmill Creek Road on Blue Lake Road.

AREA FISHING: Sitka holds an annual salmon derby Memorial Day weekend and the weekend following (May 25–27 and June 1–3, 1996). Contact the Sitka Convention and Visitors Bureau for more information; phone (907) 747-5940. Saltwater fishing charters available locally. There are also many lakes and rivers on Baranof Island with good fishing; these range from **Katlian River**, 11 miles/17.7 km northeast of Sitka by boat, to more remote waters such as **Rezanof Lake**, which is 40 air miles/64 km southeast of Sitka. USFS public-use cabins at some lakes (see Cabins in the GENERAL INFORMATION section). Stop by the Dept. of Fish and Game office at 304 Lake St. for details on fishing.

Sawmill Creek Road Log

Sawmill Creek Road is a 7.4-mile/11.9-km road, paved for the first 5.4 miles/8.7 km, which begins at Lake Street and ends beyond the pulp mill (closed) at Silver Bay.

0 Intersection of Lake Street (Halibut Point Road) and Sawmill Creek Road.

0.5 (0.8 km) Sitka National Cemetery.

0.7 (1.1 km) Indian River bridge. Beginning of Indian River trail on left.

0.9 (1.4 km) Alaska Raptor Rehabilitation Center.

1 (1.6 km) Post office.

1.7 (2.7 km) Mount Verstovia trail on left next to supper club. The trail extends 2.5 miles/4 km to summit of Mount Verstovia; strenuous hike, great views.

3.6 (5.8 km) Thimbleberry Creek bridge.

3.7 (6 km) On left past bridge is start of Thimbleberry Lake and Heart Lake trail. Hike in 0.5 mile/0.8 km to **Thimbleberry Lake**, brook trout to 12 inches, May to Sept. *NOTE: Recent changes in regulations make it illegal to use bait in fresh water, except from Sept. 15 to Nov. 15.* Trail continues 1 mile/1.6 km past Thimbleberry Lake to **Heart Lake**, brook trout.

4.4 (7.1 km) Scenic Whale Park viewpoint turnout.

5.3 (8.5 km) Alaska Pulp Corp. (closed).

5.4 (8.7 km) Blue Lake Road on left. Pavement ends on Sawmill Creek Road. Blue Lake Road (narrow dirt) leads 2.2 miles/3.5 km to small parking area and short downhill trail to Blue Lake (no recreational facilities; check with city for information). At Mile 1.5 on right is Sawmill Creek USFS campground (unmaintained). **Blue Lake**, rainbow, May to Sept.; use flies or lure, do not use bait. Lightweight skiff or rubber boat recommended.

5.7 (9.2 km) Sawmill Creek and bridge.

7.2 (11.6 km) Public road ends at Herring Cove near mouth of Silver Bay (boat tours of the bay available in Sitka). City road to hydroelectric power plant continues.

7.4 (11.9 km) Gate marking boundary of city road. No vehicles beyond this point; access for hikers and bicyclists only. No guardrails or road signs to road end.

10.5 (16.9 km) Fish hatchery and gate. Steep grades; watch for rocks on road.

13.7 (22 km) Road end. Green Lake Power Plant.

Halibut Point Road Log

Halibut Point Road (paved) leads northwest from the intersection of Harbor Drive and Lincoln Street past Old Sitka to Starrigavan Creek Campground.

0 Harbor Drive and Lincoln Street. Proceed northwest (road is now Lake Street).

0.1 (0.2 km) Fire station. Intersection with Sawmill Creek Road; keep left.

0.3 (0.5 km) **Swan Lake** to right of road, rainbow from 12 to 14 inches.

0.6 (1 km) Katlian Street on left leads to boat ramp and then to downtown. Hospital to the right.

1.8 (2.9 km) Pioneer Park picnic and day-use area with beach access; parking available.

2.2 (3.5 km) Cascade Creek bridge.

2.3 (3.7 km) Tongass National Forest work center.

2.4 (3.9 km) Sandy Beach; good swimming beach, ample parking, view of Mount Edgecumbe. Whales are sometimes sighted.

3.8 (6.1 km) Viewpoint. On a clear day you can see for 50 miles/80 km.

4.2 (6.8 km) Harbor Mountain Road on right. Steep gravel, accessible to cars. Road leads 5 miles/8 km to road end and Harbor Mountain Ridge trail to lookout at 2,300 feet/701m.

4.4 (7.1 km) Granite Creek bridge. Just beyond the bridge on left is Halibut Point state recreation site with swimming beach, shelters, tables, fireplaces and toilets.

7 (11.3 km) Alaska Marine Highway ferry terminal on left.

7.3 (11.7 km) Boat ramp, litter barrel and pit toilet to left.

7.5 (12.1 km) Old Sitka State Historical Site at left, and Starrigavan Creek bridge just ahead. Old Sitka was the site of the Russian Fort Archangel Michael, established in 1799. Commemorative plaque and historical markers. The site is a registered national historic landmark.

7.6 (12.2 km) Narrow road on right runs along the bank of Starrigavan Creek, where pink salmon spawn in August and September, and continues several miles through Starrigavan River valley. Off-road vehicles permitted.

7.8 (12.6 km) Starrigavan USFS Campground and picnic area; new artesian well with excellent drinking water, hiking trails. Access to beach. **Starrigavan Bay**, Dolly Varden; pink and silver salmon, May to October.

7.9 (12.7 km) Road ends.

Kake

(See map, page 632)

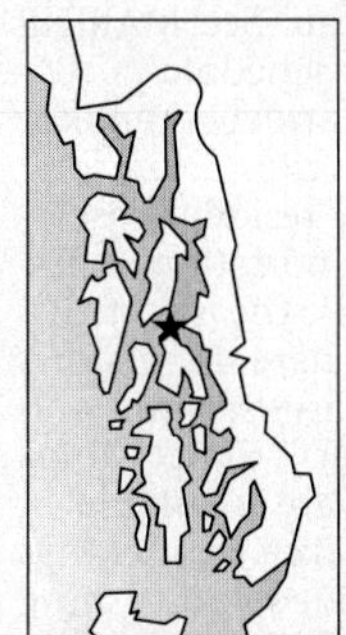

Located on the northwest coast of Kupreanof Island; Petersburg is 40 air miles/64 km or 65 miles/105 km by boat; Juneau is 95 air miles/153 km northeast. **Population:** 696 (approximately 85 percent Native). **Emergency Services:** for all emergencies, 911. **Police,** phone (907) 785-3393. **Public Health Center,** phone (907) 785-3333. **Maritime Search and Rescue**, phone the Coast Guard at 1-800-478-5555.

Visitor Information: City of Kake, Box 500, Kake 99830.

Elevation: Sea level. **Climate:** Less than average rainfall for southeastern Alaska, approximately 50 inches annually. Mild temperatures. January average temperatures are around freezing. Slightly warmer than nearby Petersburg, Kake is noted for being in the "banana belt" of Southeast.

Private Aircraft: Kake seaplane base, located adjacent southeast; fuel 100. Airstrip 1 mile/1.6 km west; elev. 148 feet/45m; length 4,000 feet/1,219m; asphalt; unattended.

Transportation: Air–Scheduled service from Petersburg (15-minute flight), Juneau (45 minutes), Wrangell and Sitka. Scheduled daily charter service provided by L.A.B. Flying Service and Wings of Alaska. **Ferry**–Alaska Marine Highway vessel from Petersburg and Sitka. See MARINE ACCESS ROUTES section for schedule.

Accommodations at local inn and bed and breakfast. There are general, variety and video stores, a cafe and other services. Church groups include Baptist, Salvation Army, Presbyterian and Assembly of God. Kake has an accredited high school, junior high school and elementary.

The town is a permanent village of the Kake (pronounced cake) tribe of the Tlingit Indians. The Tlingits from Kake had a well-earned reputation for aggression in the 18th and 19th centuries. In 1869, the Kakes murdered 2 Sitka traders in revenge for the shooting of a Native by a Sitka sentry. Reprisals taken by the United States resulted in the shelling and destruction of 3 Kake villages. The tribe eventually settled at the present-day site of Kake, where the government established a school in 1891. Residents have historically drawn ample subsistence from the sea. However, with the advent of a cash economy, the community has come to depend on commercial fishing, fish processing (there is a cannery) and logging. The post office was established in 1904, and the city was incorporated in 1952. The city's claim to fame is its totem, reputedly the world's tallest at 132 feet, 6 inches. It was carved for the 1967 Alaska Purchase Centennial Celebration.

Angoon

(See map, page 633)

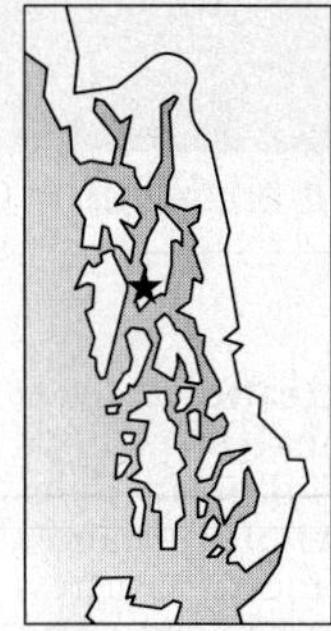

Located on the west coast of Admiralty Island on Chatham Strait, at the mouth of Kootznahoo Inlet. Peril Strait is across Chatham Strait from Angoon. Juneau is 60 air miles/97 km northeast. Sitka is 41 miles/66 km southwest. **Population:** 601. **Emergency Services: Police,** phone (907) 788-3631. **Clinic,** phone (907) 788-3633.

Visitor Information: Local people are happy to help. You may also contact the USFS Admiralty Island National Monument office in Angoon (phone 907/788-3166) or the city of Angoon (phone 907/788-3653).

Elevation: Sea level. **Climate:** Moderate weather with about 40 inches of annual rainfall and mild temperatures.

Private Aircraft: Angoon seaplane base; 0.9 mile/1.4 km southeast; unattended.

Transportation: Air–Scheduled seaplane service from Juneau. **Ferry**–Alaska Marine Highway service. See MARINE ACCESS ROUTES section for schedule.

Accommodations available at a motel and a bed and breakfast. There is a general store. Fuel service available. There are no RV facilities. Charter fishing boats and canoes available. Transient moorage for private boats available.

Angoon is a long-established Tlingit Indian settlement at the entrance to Kootznahoo Inlet. It is the only permanent community on Admiralty Island. On Killisnoo Island, across the harbor from the state ferry landing, a community of mostly summer homes has grown up along the island beaches. The lifestyle of this primarily Tlingit community is heavily subsistence: fish, clams, seaweed, berries and venison. Fishing, mostly hand trolling for king and coho salmon, is the principal industry.

The scenery of Admiralty Island draws many visitors to Angoon. All but the northern portion of the island was declared a national monument in December 1980 and is jointly managed by the U.S. Forest Service and Kootznoowoo Inc. Kootznahoo Inlet and Mitchell Bay near Angoon offer a network of small wooded islands, reefs and channels for kayaking. Mitchell Bay

Kayakers beach at twilight on Seymour Canal, Admiralty Island National Monument. (© Bill Sherwonit)

and Admiralty Lakes Recreational Area are the 2 major recreational attractions within the monument. Wildlife includes many brown bears (Admiralty Island's Indian name, *Kootznoowoo,* means "Fortress of Bears"), Sitka black-tailed deer and bald eagles. There are 12 USFS cabins available for public use in the monument; reservations and fee are required. Contact the U.S. Forest Service in Angoon. Also see Cabins in the GENERAL INFORMATION section.

Local residents can provide directions to the interesting old Killisnoo graveyards, located both on the island and on the Angoon shore of the old Killisnoo settlement, which once was one of the larger communities in southeastern Alaska.

Fishing for salmon is excellent in the Angoon area. (Record kings have been caught in nearby Kelp Bay and in Angoon harbor.) There is also excellent halibut and other bottom fish fishing. Trout (cutthroat and Dolly Varden) fishing in the lakes and streams on Admiralty Island; fair but scattered.

Tenakee Springs

(See map, page 633)

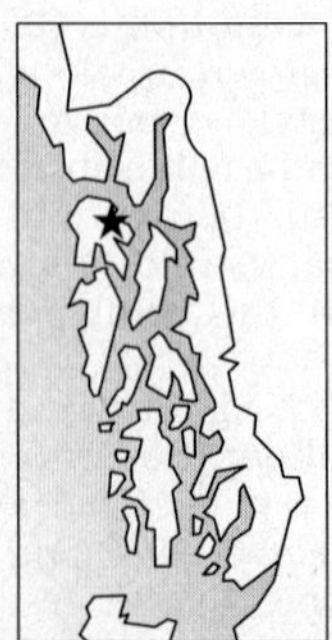

Located on the north shore of Tenakee Inlet on Chichagof Island, 50 miles/81 km northeast of Sitka. **Population:** 107. **Visitor Information:** Can be obtained from city hall, phone (907) 736-2207, or from the town's store, phone (907) 736-2205. **Elevation:** Sea level. **Climate:** Average rainfall 63.2 inches annually, with moderate snowfall. **Private Aircraft:** Seaplane base.

Transportation: Air–Scheduled and charter service available through Wings of Alaska out of Juneau. **Ferry**–Alaska Marine Highway service from Sitka and Juneau. See MARINE ACCESS ROUTES section for schedule.

Tenakee Springs has 1 street—Tenakee Avenue—which is about 3 miles/5 km long and 4 to 12 feet wide. Many residents use 3-wheel motor bikes for transportation, some ride bicycles, but most walk the short distances between buildings. There are a store, cafe, clinic, post office, library, sawmill and city hall. Accommodations at 7 rental cabins (bring your sleeping bag) are available at Snyder Mercantile, and Tenakee Hot Springs Lodge offers rooms and guided sportfishing and sightseeing; phone (907) 736-2400. Tenakee Springs became a city in 1971 and has a mayor, council and planning commission.

The word Tenakee comes from the Tlingit word *tinaghu,* or "Coppery Shield Bay." This refers to 3 copper shields, highly prized by the Tlingits, which were lost in a storm.

The hot springs (temperature from 106°F to 108°F/41°C to 42°C) brought people to Tenakee at the turn of the century. A bathhouse, completed in 1940, located on the waterfront posts times of use for men and women. The facility is maintained by contributions from residents and visitors.

The major industry at Tenakee might be described as relaxation, as many retirees have chosen to live here, away from the bustle of other Southeast cities. There are many summer homes along Tenakee Avenue. During the summer, watch for whales in Tenakee Inlet, which are sometimes spotted from town.

Some logging is under way in the area around Tenakee. Tenakee Inlet produces salmon, halibut, Dungeness and king crab, red snapper and cod. A small fleet of fishing vessels is home-ported in Tenakee's harbor, located about 0.5 mile/0.8 km east of town. Although many visitors come to Tenakee to hunt and fish, there are no hunting guides or rental boats available locally. There are 3 fishing and sightseeing charter services.

Pelican

(See map, page 633)

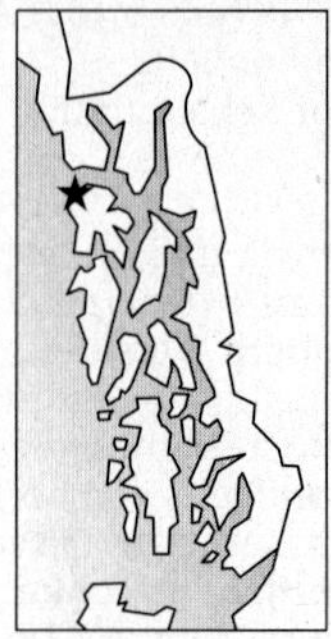

Located on the east shore of Lisianski Inlet on the northwest coast of Chichagof Island; 70 air miles/113 km north of Sitka and 70 air miles/113 km west of Juneau. **Population:** 209. **Emergency Services: Public Safety Officer** and **Fire Department**, phone 911. **Clinic,** phone (907) 735-2250. **Elevation:** Sea level. **Climate:** Average winter temperatures from 21°F/-6°C to 39°F/4°C; summer temperatures from 51°F/11°C to 62°F/17°C. Total average annual precipitation is 127 inches, with 120 inches of snow.

Private Aircraft: Seaplane base; fuel 80, 100. **Transportation: Air**–Scheduled air service from Juneau via Glacier Bay Airlines and Wings of Alaska. Scheduled service from Sitka via Bell Air. **Ferry**–Alaska Marine Highway serves Pelican. See MARINE ACCESS ROUTES section for schedules.

Pelican has 2 bar-and-grills (1 with 4 rooms for rent) and a cafe. Accommodations available at a lodge and bed and breakfast. There are grocery and dry goods stores, laundromats and 2 liquor stores. There is a small-boat harbor, marine repair and a fuel dock.

Established in 1938 by Kalle (Charley) Raatikainen, and named for Raatikainen's fish packer, *The Pelican,* Pelican relies on commercial fishing and seafood processing. Pelican Seafoods processes salmon, halibut, crab, herring, black cod, rockfish, sea urchin and sea cucumber, and is the primary year-round employer. Pelican has dubbed itself "closest to the fish," a reference to its close proximity to the rich Fairweather salmon grounds. Salmon trolling season is from about June to mid-Sept., and the king salmon winter season is from Oct. through April. Pelican's population increases greatly when nonresident fishers work during the salmon seasons. Pelican was incorporated in 1943. Most of Pelican is built on pilings over tidelands. A wooden boardwalk extends the length of the community, and there are about 2 miles of gravel road.

Local recreation includes kayaking, hiking, fishing, and watching birds and marine mammals.

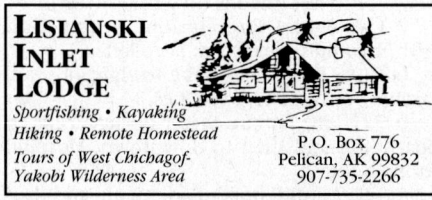

Otter Cove Bed and Breakfast. Explore Pelican's boardwalk, then relax in this secluded, beach retreat room with private bath. Spectacular mountain and water views, and home-cooked breakfasts are yours at a reasonable price. Your host will arrange activities like kayaking, fishing, wildlife viewing and hiking. Relax and refresh yourself in this quiet fishing village. $75–$105. See display ad. [ADVERTISEMENT]

Hoonah

(See map, page 633)

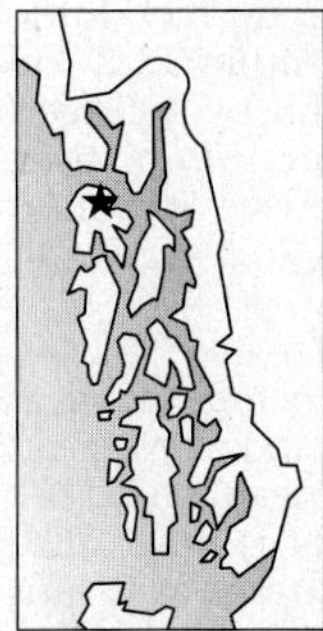

Located on the northeast shore of Chichagof Island, about 40 miles/64 km west of Juneau and 20 miles/32 km south across Icy Strait from the entrance to Glacier Bay. **Population:** 903. **Emergency Services: Alaska State Troopers** and **Hoonah City Police,** phone (907) 945-3655; emergency only phone 911. **Maritime Search and Rescue,** call the Coast Guard at 1-800-478-5555.

Visitor Information: Local business people, city office staff (907/945-3663, weekdays 8 A.M. to 4:30 P.M.) and the postmaster are happy to help. The U.S. Forest Service office in Hoonah (Box 135, Hoonah 99829, phone 907/945-3631) also has visitor information, including a Hoonah area road guide showing forest roads on Chichagof Island.

Elevation: Sea level. **Climate:** Typical Southeastern Alaska climate, with average annual precipitation of 70 inches. Average daily temperature in July, 57°F/13°C; in January, 35°F/1°C. Prevailing winds are southeasterly.

Private Aircraft: Hoonah airport, adjacent southeast; elev. 30 feet/9m; length 3,000 feet/914m; paved. Seaplane base adjacent.

Transportation: Air–Scheduled and charter service from Juneau. Airport is located about 3 miles/5 km from town. **Ferry**–Alaska Marine Highway vessel serves Hoonah. See MARINE ACCESS ROUTES section.

A lodge offers accommodations. Occasional room rentals and bed-and-breakfast lodging are also available. Hoonah has 8 restaurants, 3 grocery stores, a hardware store, a gift shop, a variety store, bank, 2 marine fuel docks, 2 gas pumps and 2 flying services. The marina, with showers and a laundromat, is a popular layover for boaters awaiting permits to enter Glacier Bay.

Hoonah is a small coastal community with a quiet harbor for the seining and trolling fleets. The most prominent structures are a cold storage facility, the lodge, bank, post office and the public school. The village has been occupied since prehistory by the Tlingit people. In the late 1800s, missionaries settled here. Canneries established in the area in the early 1900s spurred the growth of commercial fishing, which remains the mainstay of Hoonah's economy. During the summer fishing season, residents work for nearby Excursion Inlet Packing Co. or Hoonah Cold Storage in town. Halibut season begins in May, and salmon season opens in midsummer and runs through Sept. Logging also contributes to the economy, with employment loading log ships and other industry-related jobs. Subsistence hunting and fishing remain an important lifestyle here, and many families gather food in the traditional way: catching salmon and halibut in summer, shellfish and bottom fish year-round; hunting deer, geese and ducks; berry picking in summer and fall.

Hunting and fishing are the main attractions for visitors. Charter fishing is available locally, with good seasonal king and coho (silver) salmon and halibut fishing as well as crabbing. Guide services are available.

Hoonah is the starting point for an extensive logging and forest road system for northwest Chichagof Island. Island road maps ($3) are available through the USFS in Hoonah, Sitka and Juneau.

Juneau

(See map, pages 633-634)

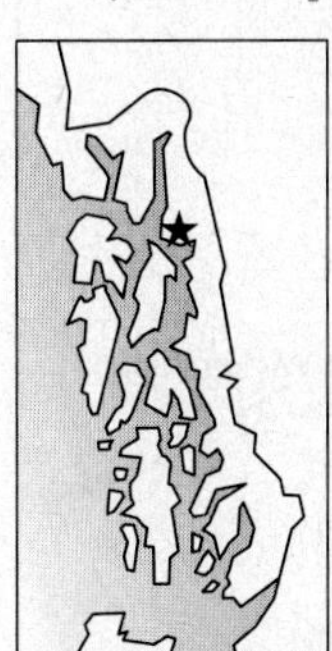

Located on Gastineau Channel; 900 air miles/1,448 km (2 hours, 10 minutes flying time) from Seattle, WA, 650 air miles/1,046 km (1 hour, 25 minutes by jet) from Anchorage. **Population:** Borough 29,228. **Emergency Services:** Phone 911 for all emergencies. **Police,** phone (907) 586-2780. **Fire Department,** phone (907) 586-5245. **Alaska State Troopers,** phone (907) 465-4000. **Poison Center** and **Hospital,** Bartlett Memorial, 3260 Hospital Dr., phone (907) 586-2611. **Maritime Search and Rescue,** Coast Guard, phone (907) 463-2000 or 1-800-478-5555.

Visitor Information: Juneau Convention & Visitors Bureau, Davis Log Cabin Information Center, 134 3rd St., phone (907) 586-2201 or 586-2284; open year-round 8 A.M. to 5 P.M. Monday through Friday; additional hours during the summer, 9 A.M. to 5 P.M. Saturday, Sunday and holidays. To find out about current events in Juneau, phone (907) 586-JUNO for a recorded message. Visitor information kiosk located in Marine Park on waterfront near Merchants Wharf, usually open daily 8:30 A.M. to 6 P.M., from about mid-May to mid-Sept. Information booth at the airport terminal. Visitor information is also available at the cruise ship terminal on S. Franklin Street when cruise ships are in port, and at the Auke Bay ferry terminal. Large groups contact the Davis Log Cabin Information Center in advance for special assistance.

USFS Information Center at Centennial Hall, 101 Egan Dr.; open 8 A.M. to 5 P.M. daily from mid-May to mid-Sept.; 9 A.M. to 5 P.M. Monday through Friday the rest of the year. Phone (907) 586-8751. U.S. Park Service office here open in summer. The center has seasonal features of natural history films. USFS cabins may also be reserved here. The center issues permits for visiting Pack Creek, the bear preserve on Admiralty Island. Juneau Ranger District (USFS), **Milepost 9.4** Glacier Highway (airport area), phone (907) 586-8800; open 8 A.M. to 5 P.M. weekdays. Mendenhall Glacier Visitor Center (USFS), phone (907) 789-0097, open 8:30 A.M. to 5:30 P.M. daily in summer, 9 A.M. to 4 P.M.

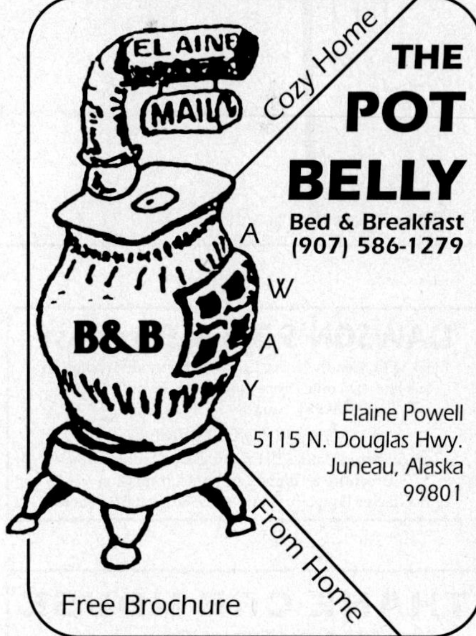

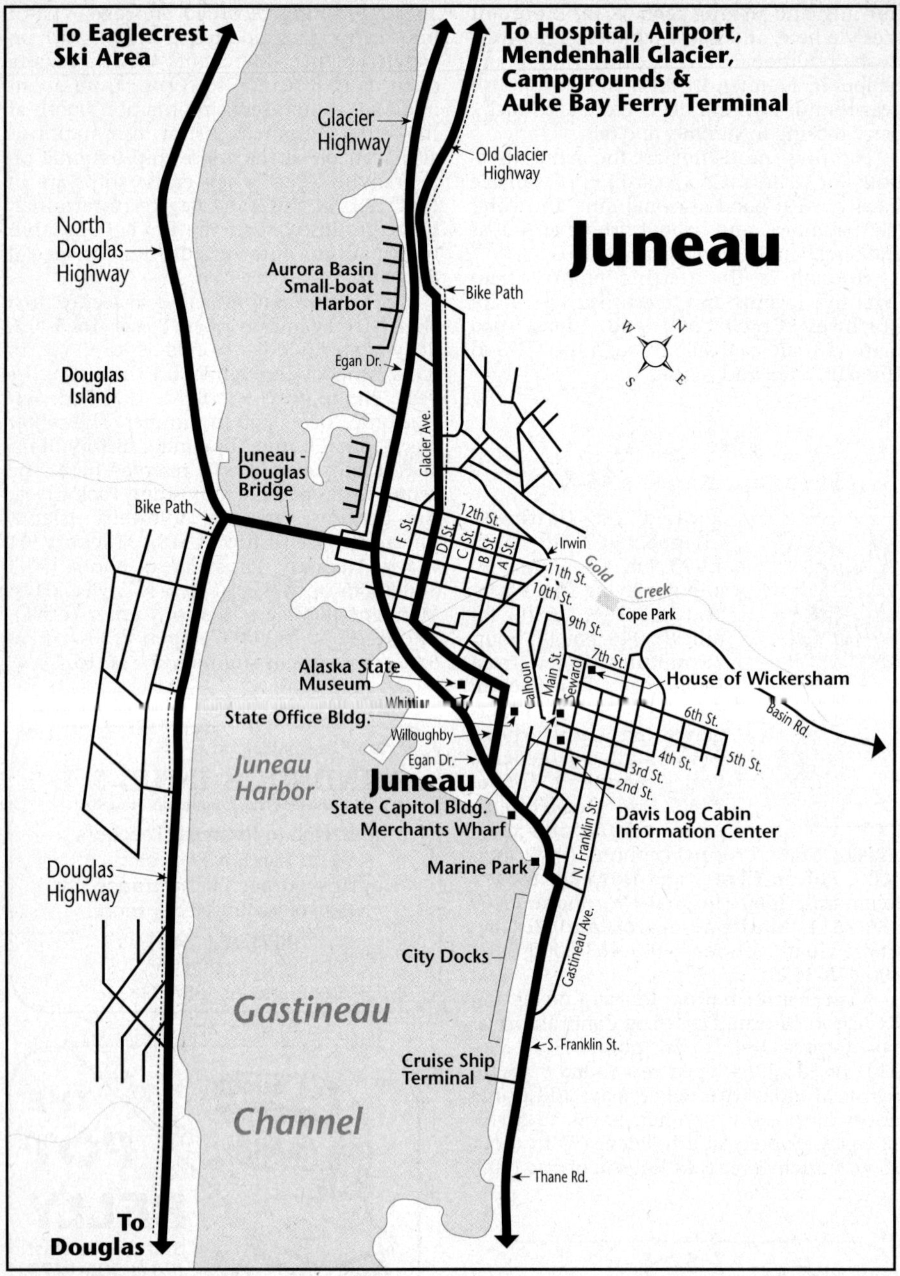

weekends only in winter.

Elevation: Sea level. **Climate:** Mild and wet. Average daily maximum temperature in July, 63°F/17°C; daily minimum in Jan., 20°F/-7°C. Highest recorded temperature, 90°F/32°C in July 1975; the lowest -22°F/-30°C in Jan. 1972. Average annual precipitation, 56.5 inches (airport), 92 inches (downtown); 103 inches of snow annually. Snow on ground intermittently from mid-Nov. to mid-April. Prevailing winds are east-southeasterly. **Radio:** KJNO 630, KINY 800, KTOO-FM 104.3, KTKU-FM 105.1, KSUP-FM 106. **Television:** KJUD Channel 8; JATV cable; KTOO (public television). **Newspapers:** *Juneau Empire* (Sunday through Friday) and *Capital City Weekly*.

Private Aircraft: Juneau International Airport, 9 miles/14.5 km northwest; elev. 18 feet/5m; length 8,456 feet/2,577m; asphalt; fuel 100LL, Jet A. Juneau harbor seaplane base, due east; restricted use, no fuel. International seaplane base, 7 miles/11.3 km northwest; 5,000 feet/1,524m by 450 feet/137m, avgas, Jet A. For more information, phone the Juneau Flight Service Station at (907) 789-6124.

HISTORY AND ECONOMY

In 1880, nearly 20 years before the great gold rushes to the Klondike and to Nome, 2 prospectors named Joe Juneau and Dick Harris found "color" in what is now called Gold Creek, a small, clear stream that runs through the center of present-day Juneau. What they found led to the discovery of one of the largest lodes of gold quartz in the world. Juneau (called Harrisburg the first year) quickly boomed into a gold rush town as claims and mines sprang up in the area.

For a time the largest mine was the Treadwell, across Gastineau Channel south of Douglas (which was once a larger town than Juneau), but a cave-in and flood closed the mine in 1917. In 36 years of operation, Treadwell produced $66 million in gold. The Alaska–Gastineau Mine, operated by Bart Thane in 1911, had a 2-mile shaft through Mount Roberts to the Perseverance Mine near Gold Creek. The Alaska–Juneau (A–J) Mine was constructed on a mountain slope south of Juneau and back into the heart of Mount Roberts. It operated until 1944, when it was declared a nonessential wartime activity after producing over $80 million in gold. Post–WWII wage and price inflation and the fixed price of gold prevented its reopening.

In 1900, the decision to move Alaska's capital to Juneau was made because of the city's growth, mining activity and location on the water route to Skagway and the Klondike; the decline of post-Russian Sitka, as whale and fur trading slackened, secured Juneau's new status as Alaska's preeminent city.

Congress first provided civil government for Alaska in 1884. Until statehood in 1959 Alaska was governed by a succession of presidential appointees, first as the District of Alaska, then as the Territory of Alaska. Between 1867 (when the United States purchased Alaska from Russia) and 1884, the military had jurisdiction over the District of Alaska, except for a 3-year period (1877–79) when Alaska was put under control of the U.S. Treasury Dept. and governed by U.S. Collectors of Customs.

With the arrival of Alaska statehood in

1959, Juneau's governmental role increased even further. In 1974, Alaskans voted to move the capital from Juneau to a site between Anchorage and Fairbanks, closer to the state's population center. In 1976 Alaska voters selected a new capital site near Willow, 65 road miles/105 km north of Anchorage on the George Parks Highway. However, in November 1982, voters defeated funding for the capital move.

Today, government (federal, state and local) comprises an estimated half of the total basic industry. Tourism is the largest employer in the private sector.

Compact downtown Juneau may be seen on a walking tour. (Michael N. Dill)

DESCRIPTION

Juneau, often called "a little San Francisco," is nestled at the foot of Mount Juneau (elev. 3,576 feet/1,091m) with Mount Roberts (elev. 3,819 feet/1,164m) rising immediately to the east on the approach up Gastineau Channel. The residential community of Douglas, on Douglas Island, is south of Juneau and connected by a bridge. Neighboring residential areas around the airport, Mendenhall Valley and Auke Bay lie north of Juneau on the mainland.

Shopping is in the downtown area and at suburban malls in the airport and Mendenhall Valley areas.

Juneau's skyline is dominated by several government buildings, including the Federal Bldg. (1962), the massive State Office Bldg. (1974), the State Court Bldg. (1975) and the older brick, and marble-columned Capitol Bldg. (1931). The modern Sealaska Plaza is headquarters for Sealaska Corp., 1 of the 13 regional Native corporations formed after congressional passage of the Alaska Native Claims Settlement Act in 1971.

To explore downtown Juneau, it is best to park and walk; distances are not great. The streets are narrow and congested with pedestrians and traffic (especially rush hours), and on-street parking is scarce. Visitors should check at the Davis Log Cabin and at the police station to see whether parking permits are available. Public parking lots are located across from Merchants Wharf Mall at Main Street and Egan Drive and south of Marine Park at the Marine Park parking garage; fee required.

The Juneau area supports 35 churches, a

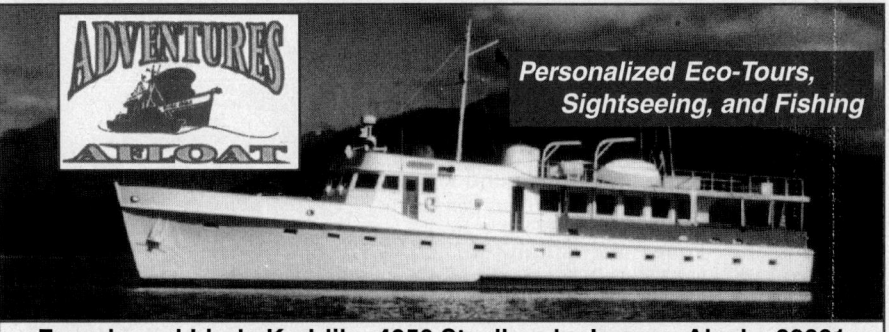

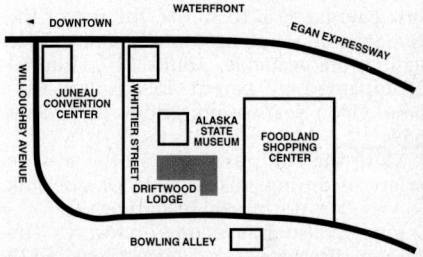

high school, 2 middle schools, several elementary schools and a University of Alaska Southeast campus at Auke Lake. There are 3 municipal libraries and the state library. The Perseverance Theatre, which was established in 1978, provides Juneau with classical and original works, Sept. through May.

The area is governed by the unified city and borough of Juneau, which encompasses 3,108 square miles/8,060 square km. It is the first unified government in the state, combining the former separate and overlapping jurisdictions of the city of Douglas, city of Juneau and greater Juneau borough.

ACCOMMODATIONS/VISITOR SERVICES

Juneau has 11 hotels and motels, most of them downtown. There are also several bed and breakfasts.

The Juneau International Hostel is located at 614 Harris St. (Juneau 99801), 4 blocks northeast of the Capitol Bldg. All ages are welcome. Check-in time is 5–11 P.M. during summer, 5–10:30 P.M. the rest of the year. Showers, cooking, laundry and storage facilities are available. Adults $10, children accompanied by parent $5. Groups welcome. Open year-round. Phone (907) 586-9559.

More than 60 restaurants offer a wide variety of dining. Also watch for sidewalk food vendors downtown in summer.

Juneau also has a microbrewery. The Alaskan Brewing Co., located at 5429 Shaune Dr. in the Lemon Creek area, produces Alaskan Amber Beer and Alaskan Pale Ale. Free tours available. Phone (907) 780-5866 for more information.

Alaska Rainforest Tours/Alaska Bed and Breakfast Association. One call can secure a comfortable B&B, a wilderness or adventure tour, a glacier cruise, and bookings for the rest of Alaska too. For advance planning order "Alaska: The Catalog for Independent Travelers," 88 pages, ($5 postage paid). 369 S. Franklin, Suite 200, Juneau, AK 99801. (907) 463-3466 (tours), (907) 586-2959 (B&Bs), fax (907) 463-4453. [ADVERTISEMENT]

Mt. Juneau Inn is where you'll find comfort and hospitality that makes you feel right at home. From the warm, familiar feel of a plush robe, to the comfortable parlour filled with Native art, books and videos, you're assured that your stay here will be a relaxed and memorable one. But if it's our view of the great outdoors that inspires you, we'll provide bikes, gear and guidance to help you enjoy all that Alaska offers. (See display ad this section.) [ADVERTISEMENT]

Pearson's Pond Luxury B & B Inn. If you want spectacular scenery and quality lodging, you'll find it here at an affordable price. Your suite retreat has all the private comforts of home, away from the crowds, yet close to famous attractions. Soothe your cares in a starlit spa amid lush gardens, wild berries and a glacial duck pond. Dine alfresco on your adjoining deck with the healing sounds of nature and the Mendenhall Glacier as a majestic backdrop. Guests say it is the highest combination of privacy, beauty, comfort and warmth. A year-round, smoke- and pet-free experience. Book far ahead for summer, and plan to stay a week or more. Winner of AAA/ABBA 3-diamond/crown award for excellence. 4541-MP Sawa Circle, Juneau, AK 99801-8723; phone (907) 789-3772, fax (907) 789-6722. Great value. A definite 10! [ADVERTISEMENT]

There are 2 USFS campgrounds: Mendenhall Lake (turn off Glacier Highway at **Milepost 9.4** or **12.2** and continue to Montana Creek Road) and Auke Village (**Milepost 15.4** Glacier Highway). Mendenhall Lake has 60 sites (16 sites accommodate vehicles longer than 20 feet), water, pit toilets, dump station. Ten sites can be reserved; phone 1-800-280-CAMP. Auke Village Campground, 1.5 miles/2.4 km west of the ferry terminal, has 12 campsites, flush and pit toilets, water and firewood: first-come, first-served. There is a private campground with RV hookups located at **Milepost 12.3** Glacier Highway, phone (907) 789-9467. The city and borough of Juneau offers limited RV overnight parking spaces at the Juneau Yacht Club (turnoff at **Milepost 1.7** Egan Drive/Glacier Highway); and at Savikko Park/Sandy Beach (**Milepost 2.5** Douglas Highway), $5 per space, per night, paid at the harbormaster's office; for parking at both yacht club and park, sign in at the harbormaster's office (across from high school on Egan Drive). Contact the visitor information center (907/586-2201) for a brochure on RV facilities. Dump stations are located at Mendenhall Lake campground, Mapco Service Station, Valley Chevron at Mendenhall Center shopping mall in the Mendenhall Valley, and Savikko Park in Douglas. ▲

TRANSPORTATION

Air: Juneau Municipal Airport turnoff is at **Milepost 8.8** Egan Drive (Glacier Highway). Airport terminal contains ticket counters, waiting area, gift shop, rental cars, restaurant, lounge and information booth.

The city express bus stops at the airport weekdays. A Gray Line shuttle, and taxi and van service to downtown are also available. Courtesy vans to some hotels.

Alaska Airlines serves Juneau daily from Seattle, WA, Anchorage, Fairbanks, Ketchikan, Sitka, Yakutat, Cordova, Petersburg and Wrangell. Delta Airlines serves Juneau from Seattle and Fairbanks in summer. MarkAir serves Juneau daily from Seattle and Anchorage. Scheduled commuter service to Haines, Skagway, Sitka, Angoon and other points via several air services. Scheduled service by Summit Air between Juneau and Whitehorse, YT, year-round and between Juneau and Atlin, BC, in summer.

Charter air service (wheel and floatplanes and helicopters) for hunting, fishing, sightseeing and transportation to other communities (see ads in this section).

Loken Aviation, Inc. provides experienced floatplane service to wilderness cabins, Native villages, and fishing lodges in Southeast Alaska. Thirty years of flying experience guarantee personalized, professional sightseeing and wildlife tours. Visit our ticket counter in the Juneau International Airport or phone (907) 789-3331 for further information. [ADVERTISEMENT]

Ferry: Juneau is served by Alaska Marine Highway ferries. See MARINE ACCESS ROUTES section for schedule and fares.

Alaska state ferries dock at the Auke Bay terminal at **Milepost 13.9** Glacier Highway; phone (907) 465-3941 or 789-7453. Taxi service and private shuttle bus is available from Auke Bay terminal to downtown Juneau.

Bus: Capital Transit city bus system runs from the cruise ship terminal downtown and includes Juneau, Douglas, Lemon Creek, Mendenhall Valley and airport area, Auke Bay (the community, which is about 1.5 miles/2.4 km south of the ferry terminal). Hourly service Monday through Saturday, year-round; limited service on Sundays. Route map and schedule available at the visitor information center. Flag buses at any corner except in downtown Juneau, where bus uses marked stops only.

Highways: Longest road is Glacier Highway, which begins in downtown Juneau and leads 40.5 miles/65.3 km north to Echo Cove. Other major roads are Mendenhall Loop Road and Douglas and North Douglas highways. See logs this section.

Taxi: Four companies.

Cruise Ships: Juneau is southeastern Alaska's most frequent port of call. There were 474 port calls by cruise ships in 1995.

The tour boat MV *Fairweather* offers scenic cruises of Lynn Canal between Juneau and Skagway mid-May to mid-Sept. Offered on package tours by Gray Line of Alaska, seats are sold on a space-available basis to visitors not on a package tour. Contact their Juneau office in the Baranof Hotel lobby, phone (907) 586-3773. The MV *Fairweather* departs from Yankee Cove, **Milepost 33** Glacier Highway.

Car Rental: Eight car rental agencies are available at the airport and vicinity; there are none downtown, but most rental agencies will take you to their offices (sometimes

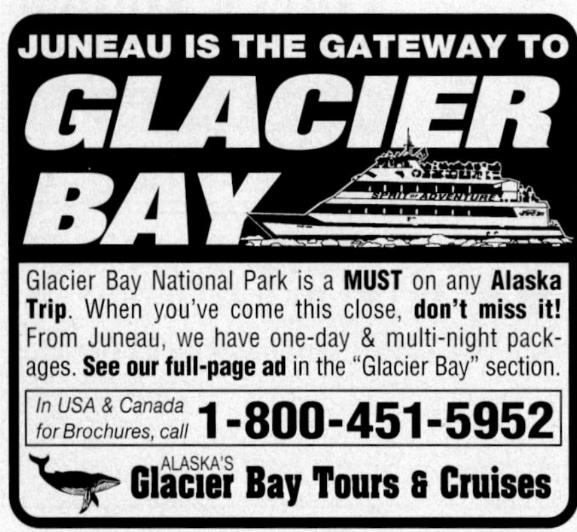

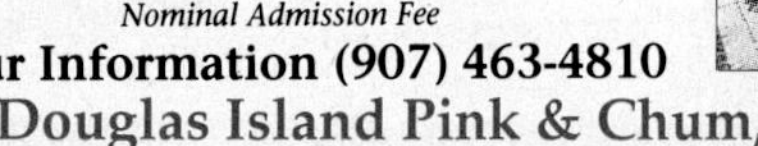

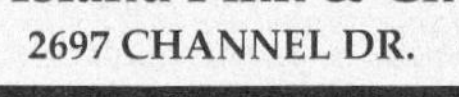

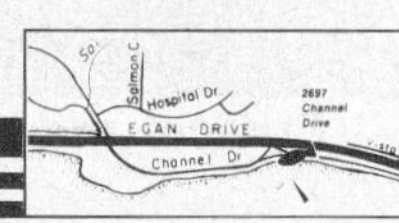

View of Mendenhall Glacier from the scenic turnout on North Douglas Highway.
(© David Job)

at an extra charge). Best to reserve ahead of time because of the great demand for cars.

Private Boats: Transient moorage is available downtown at Harris and Douglas floats and at Auke Bay. Most boaters use Auke Bay. For more information call the Juneau harbormaster at (907) 586-5255 or hail on Channel 16 UHF.

ATTRACTIONS

Juneau walking-tour map (in English, French, Spanish, German, or Japanese) is available from the Davis Log Cabin Information Center at 134 3rd St. and from other visitor information sites and from hotels. See Juneau's many attractions—the St. Nicholas Orthodox Church, totems, Capitol Bldg., Governor's Mansion, historic graves, monuments, state museum, city museum, hatchery and others.

Charter a Boat for salmon and halibut fishing or sightseeing. The visitor information center can provide a list of charter operators; also see ads in this section.

Charter a Plane for fly-in fishing, hunting, transportation to remote lodges and longer flightseeing trips.

Take a Tour. Tours of Juneau and area attractions—by boat, bus, plane and helicopter—can be arranged. These tours range from sightseeing trips out to Mendenhall Glacier to river trips on the Mendenhall River.

Era Helicopters. Soar over the massive Juneau Icefield, viewing 4 unique and distinctive glaciers. Land on a glacier and explore the ancient ice. Fly past historical gold mining areas. Personalized tour with Alaska's most experienced helicopter company. Phone 1-800-843-1947 or (907) 586-2030 locally. Tours also available in Anchorage, Mount McKinley and Valdez. [ADVERTISEMENT]

Visit the Juneau Library. Built on top of the 4-story public parking garage in downtown Juneau, this award-winning library designed by Minch Ritter Voelckers Architects is well worth a visit. Take the elevator to the 5th floor and spend a morning or afternoon reading in this well-lighted and comfortable space with a wonderful view of Juneau, Douglas and Gastineau Channel. Located at South Franklin and Admiralty Way, between Marine Park and the cruise ship terminal.

Juneau–Douglas City Museum, located in the Veteran's Memorial Bldg. across from the State Capitol Bldg. at 4th and Main streets, offers exhibits and audiovisual presentations on the Juneau–Douglas area, featuring gold mining and local cultural history. Displays include a turn-of-the-century store and kitchen, a large relief map, a hands-on history room that's fun for kids of all ages, and a special summer exhibit. Free historical walking-tour maps of Juneau are available. Museum gift shop. Summer hours are 9 A.M. to 5 P.M. weekdays, 10 A.M. to 5 P.M. weekends, mid-May to mid-Sept. Limited hours in winter. Admission $1. Phone (907) 586-3572 or write Parks and Recreation, Attn: Juneau-Douglas City Museum, 155 S. Seward St., Juneau 99801, for more information.

State Capitol Building, at 4th and Main streets, contains the legislative chambers and the governor's office. Free tours available from capitol lobby; most days in summer on the half-hour from 9 A.M. to 5 P.M.. The **State Office Building,** one block west, houses the State Historical Library and Kimball theater organ (free organ concerts at noon Fridays).

Alaska State Museum is a major highlight of Juneau located downtown at 395 Whittier St. Exhibits include dioramas and contain materials from Alaska's Native groups; icons and other artifacts from Russian America days; and a popular life-size eagle nesting tree surrounded by a 2-story high mural of a Southeast Alaska scene. A replica of Capt. George Vancouver's ship, *Discovery,* is located in children's room for kids to explore. During the summer of 1996, a special exhibit commemorating the centennial of the Alaska-Yukon gold rush will be on display. The museum store carries Alaska Native crafts and Alaska books and gifts for all ages. Summer hours are 9 A.M. to 6 P.M. Monday through Friday and 10 A.M. to 6 P.M. weekends. Winter hours are 10 A.M. to 4 P.M. Tuesday through Saturday. General admission is $3. Visitors 18 and under, students with current cards and members of the Friends of the Alaska State Museum are admitted free. A $10 museum pass is also available. Phone (907) 465-2901.

The House of Wickersham, 213 7th St., has an important historical collection dating to the days of the late Judge James Wickersham, one of Alaska's first federal judges, who collected Native artifacts and baskets, as well as many photographs and historical documents concerning Native culture, during his extensive travels throughout the territory early in the century. Afternoon visiting hours in summer except Sunday. Phone (907) 586-9001 for more information. (Steep climb up to Seventh Street.)

The Governor's Mansion at 716 Calhoun Ave. has been home to Alaska's chief executives since it was completed in 1913. The 2 1/2-story structure, containing 12,900 square feet of floor space, took nearly a year to build. Tours may be possible by advance arrangement. Phone (907) 465-3500.

The Gastineau Salmon Hatchery, operated by Douglas Island Pink and Chum, Inc., is located on Channel Drive 2.5 miles from downtown. The hatchery offers visitors a chance to see adult spawning salmon, over 100 species of Southeast Alaska sea-life in saltwater aquariums, aquaculture displays, and other seasonal activities. A variety of smoked salmon products is also available for purchase. Visitor center open in summer 10 A.M. to 6 P.M. Monday through Friday; noon to 5 P.M. Sunday. Incubation-room tours available May 15 through June 30; spawning salmon sights and hatchery operations tour July 1 through Oct. 1. Educational tours provided; nominal admission fee. Phone (907) 463-5114.

See Old Mine Ruins. Remnants from the Treadwell Mine may be seen from a marked trail that starts just south of Sandy Beach on Douglas Island. The impressive remains of the A–J mine mill are located on the hillside along Gastineau Channel just south of downtown Juneau; good views from Douglas Island and from the water. Evidence of the Alaska–Gastineau Mine can be seen south of town along Thane Road. Walking-tour maps of the Treadwell area are available from the city museum and the Davis Log Cabin.

Thane Ore House, Mile 4.4 Thane Road, home of the *Gold Nugget Revue,* featuring the adventures of Joe Juneau, lively cancan dancers and a red hot mama! Enjoy a sumptuous all-you-can-eat buffet of halibut, salmon and BBQ beef ribs, homemade baked beans, corn bread, salad bar and coffee or soft drink. Beer and wine available. Enjoy the indoor/outdoor beachfront facility, a mining museum, horseshoes, beachcombing, nearby fish hatchery, or sitting by the fireplace. The Thane Ore House is open from noon 'til 9 P.M., daily from May through Sept. The "Gold Nugget Revue," a Janice D. Holst production, is great family entertainment. 6:30 P.M. showtime! Bring your camera! For information phone (907) 586-3442 or 586-1462. [ADVERTISEMENT]

Thane Road is a wide, straight paved road beginning just south of downtown Juneau and extending 5.5 miles/8.9 km along Gastineau Channel. Good views of the channel and old mines. Excellent viewpoint for spawning salmon at Sheep Creek bridge and falls, Mile 4.3, in summer.

Marine Park, located at foot of Seward Street, has tables, benches, information kiosk, sculpture of hard-rock miners and lighterage facilities for tour-ship launches. Free concerts on Friday evenings in summer.

Mount Juneau Waterfall, scenic but difficult to photograph, descends 3,576 feet/1,091m from Mount Juneau to Gold Creek behind the city. Best view is from Basin Road. The waterfall is also visible from Marine Park.

Mount Roberts Trail Observation Point offers an elevated view of Juneau. Though the trail extends to the 3,819-foot/1,164-m summit, an excellent observation point above Juneau is reached by a 20-minute hike from the start of Mount Roberts trail at the top of Starr Hill (6th Street).

Mendenhall Glacier is about 13 miles/21 km from downtown Juneau at the end of Mendenhall Glacier Spur Road. Turn right northbound at **Milepost 9.4** Egan Drive (Glacier Highway), and then drive straight for 3.6 miles/5.8 km to the glacier and visitor center. There is a large parking area, and trails lead down to the edge of the lake (a sign warns visitors to stay back; falling ice can create huge waves). The visitor center, a short walk up a paved switchback path (accessible, although steep, for wheelchairs) from the parking area, is open daily from Memorial Day week through Sept., 8:30 A.M. to 5:30 P.M.; weekends only Oct. to May. The visitor center has glacier view, guided hikes and daily video programs in summer; phone (907) 789-0097 or 586-8800. A 0.5-mile/0.8-km self-guiding nature trail starts behind the visitor center. Trailheads for 2 longer trails—

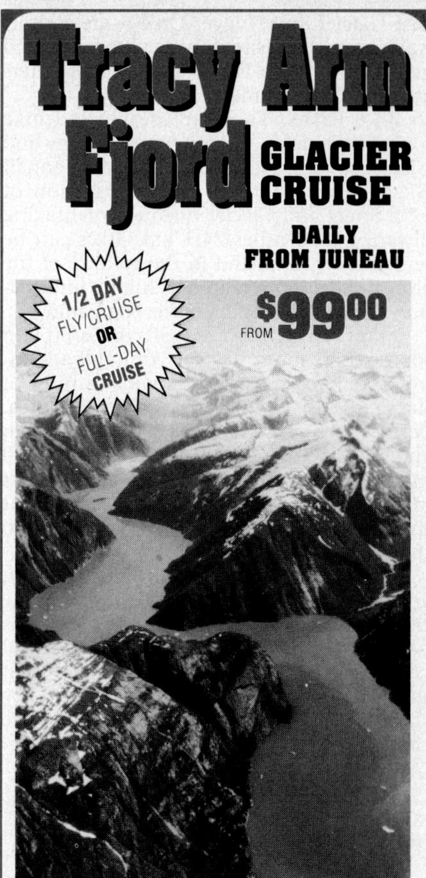

East Glacier and Nugget Creek—are a short walk from the visitor center. Programs and guided hikes with Forest Service interpreters are offered in summer.

Bike Paths. There are designated bike routes to Douglas, to Mendenhall Valley and Glacier, and to Auke Bay. The Mendenhall Glacier route starts at the intersection of 12th Street and Glacier Avenue; total biking distance is 15 miles/24.1 km. Bikes can be rented downtown and in the vicinity of the airport. Bike-route map and hiking information are available at the Davis Log Cabin.

Tracy Arm. Located 50 miles/80 km southeast of Juneau, Tracy Arm and adjoining Endicott Arm are the major features of the Tracy Arm–Fords Terror Wilderness Area. Both Tracy and Endicott arms are long, deep and narrow fjords that extend more than 30 miles/48 km into the heavily glaciated Coast Mountain Range. Active tidewater glaciers at the head of these fjords calve icebergs into the fjords.

Fords Terror, off of Endicott Arm, is an area of sheer rock walls enclosing a narrow entrance into a small fjord. The fjord was named in 1889 for a crew member of a naval vessel who rowed into the narrow canyon at slack tide and was caught in turbulent icy currents for 6 terrifying hours when the tide changed.

Access to this wilderness area is primarily by boat or floatplane from Juneau. Large cruise ships and small cruise ships and charter boats include Tracy Arm and Endicott Arm in their itineraries. It is also a popular destination for sea kayakers.

Tracy Arm Fjord–Adventure Bound, Alaska's greatest combination of mountains, wildlife, icebergs and tidewater glaciers. Best viewed from the *Adventure Bound.* Juneau's favorite because the Weber family doesn't overcrowd and is noted for making people feel welcome. The personal touch makes the difference. Office: 245 Marine Way. Reservations: (907) 790-1966, 1-800-228-3875. [ADVERTISEMENT]

Tracy Arm Adventure Cruise. Travel by small boat (6–15 passengers) with local skippers and naturalists for an intimate tidewater glacier experience. Highlights include glaciers calving, icebergs, winding fjords, waterfalls, seals, and watching for bears, whales and goats. Includes lunch, snacks, beverages. Contact Alaska Rainforest Tours, 369 S. Franklin, Suite 200, Juneau, AK 99801. (907) 463-3466, fax 800-493-4453. [ADVERTISEMENT]

Juneau Icefield, immediately to the east of Juneau, is a 1,500-square-mile/2414 km expanse of glaciated mountains that is the source of all the glaciers in the area, including Mendenhall, Taku, Eagle and Herbert. Best way to experience and photograph it is via charter flightseeing. Flights usually take 30 to 60 minutes. Helicopter tours, which land on the glacier, are also available. Helicopter tours last from about 45 minutes to 1½ hours.

Ski Eaglecrest, Juneau's downhill and cross-country ski area on Douglas Island. Built and maintained by the city of Juneau, the area features a day-lodge, cafeteria, ski school, ski patrol, ski rental shop, 2 chair lifts, a surface lift and runs for experienced, intermediate and beginning skiers. Five miles/ 8 km of maintained cross-country trails available. Open 5 days a week, Dec. to mid-April. The view from the top of the chair lift (operating during ski season only) is worth the visit—Mendenhall Glacier, Juneau Icefield, Lynn Canal, Stephens Passage and more. Drive North Douglas Highway to turnoff left at Eaglecrest sign, then 5.3 miles/8.5 km up the Eaglecrest access road to the lodge. For more information, phone (907) 586-5284 (720-2000 during ski season), or phone (907) 586-5330 for a recorded message about ski conditions.

St. Nicholas Orthodox Church, 5th and Gold streets, a tiny structure built in 1894, is now the oldest original Russian Orthodox church in southeastern Alaska. Visitors are welcome to Sunday services; open daily for summer tours. Phone (907) 586-1023.

Chapel-by-the-Lake (Presbyterian), **Milepost 11.6** Glacier Highway, is a log structure perched above Auke Lake. Its front, made entirely of glass, frames the scenic lake, Mendenhall Glacier and mountains. Popular marriage chapel.

Shrine of St. Terese (Catholic), **Milepost 23.1** Glacier Highway, is a natural stone chapel on its own island, connected to shore by a gravel causeway. A 1 P.M. Sunday mass is during the summer.

Golden North Salmon Derby is a 3-day derby (Aug. 16–18, 1996), offering more than $122,000 in prizes, with a $12,000 first prize for the largest king salmon.

Hiking Trails. *Juneau Trails,* a guidebook of 20-plus area hikes, can be purchased for $4 at Davis Log Cabin Information Center or

State Capitol Building in downtown Juneau. (© Harry M. Walker)

USFS Information Center in Centennial Hall. Juneau Parks and Recreation Dept. offers free organized hikes Wednesday and Saturday, April through Oct.; phone (907) 586-5226 for information.

AREA FISHING: (Several special sportfishing regulations are in effect in the Juneau area; consult current regulations booklet.) Good Dolly Varden fishing available along most saltwater shorelines in Juneau area; pink salmon available about mid-July through Aug., silver and king salmon, best Aug. to mid-Sept. Good fishing by boat from Juneau, Auke Bay or Tee Harbor in **Favorite** and **Saginaw channels, Chatham Strait** and near mouth of **Taku Inlet,** for salmon, Dolly Varden and halibut. Boat in and hike, or fly in to **Turner Lake,** 25 miles/40 km east of Juneau, for kokanee, Dolly Varden and cutthroat (catch and release); USFS public-use cabins available (see Cabins in the GENERAL INFORMATION section).

For up-to-date angling data in the Juneau area, phone (907) 465-4116 for recorded Alaska Dept. of Fish and Game message (April through Oct.). For specific angling information or for a copy of the local sportfishing guide, contact the ADF&G, Division of Sport Fish, Area Management Biologist, P.O. Box 20, Douglas 99824; phone (907) 465-4270. A list of charter boats is available from the Juneau Convention and Visitors Bureau (phone 907/586-2201).

Egan Drive and Glacier Highway/Juneau Veterans' Memorial Highway Log

Egan Drive from downtown Juneau proceeds north to **Milepost 9.4,** then becomes Glacier Highway. Egan Drive is named for William A. Egan (1914–84), first governor of the state of Alaska. From **Milepost 12.2** to road end, Glacier Highway has been renamed the Juneau Veterans' Memorial Highway. The highway ends 40.5 miles/65.3 km north of Juneau near Echo Cove on Berners Bay. It is a scenic drive northward along Favorite Channel.

0 Cruise ship terminal.

0.3 (0.5 km) Parking garage, 3-hour limit.

0.5 (0.8 km) Stoplight. Marine Way and Main Street. Egan Drive begins here.

0.7 (1.1 km) Alaska State Museum, exit east onto Whittier Street.

1.2 (1.9 km) Stoplight. Tenth Street exit east. For access to Douglas Highway and North Douglas Highway, turn west across Juneau–Douglas bridge (see logs this section).

1.3 (2.1 km) Harris Harbor for small boats.

1.5 (2.4 km) Juneau–Douglas High School.

1.7 (2.7 km) Aurora Basin small-boat harbor. Access to Juneau Yacht Club on Harbor Way Road; 10 RV sites, portable toilet and dumpster. No fee; May 1 through Sept.; sign-in at Harbormaster's office for permit (907/586-5255).

3.9 (6.3 km) Stoplight. Picnic tables at Twin Lakes to east. Also exit east for Bartlett Memorial Hospital and Alaska Native Health Center; access to Old Glacier Highway and residential area. Gastineau salmon hatchery to west.

5.5 (8.9 km) Stoplight. Lemon Creek area.

5.9 (9.5 km) Lemon Creek passes beneath highway.

6.1 (9.8 km) Southbound traffic, view area of tidelands; great place to see eagles and waterfowl.

6.7 (10.7 km) Access to Old Glacier Highway and Switzer Creek; exit east. Department store; service station with gas, propane, dump station.

8.1 (13 km) Airport access road.

8.2 (13.2 km) Fred Meyer shopping center.

8.8 (14.2 km) Stoplight; McDonald's. Airport turnoff and access to Nugget Mall and Airport Shopping Center to west. A 0.3-mile/0.5-km loop road (Old Glacier Highway) provides access to malls and to Juneau Municipal Airport. Loop road rejoins Egan Drive at **Milepost 9.4.**

9.4 (15.1 km) Stoplight. **Junction** with Mendenhall Loop Road. Turn west for airport. Turn east for Mendenhall Center shopping mall and post office (just east of junction), and Mendenhall Glacier and visitor center (3.6 miles/5.8 km from junction).

Mendenhall Loop Road is a paved 6.8-mile/10.9-km loop that rejoins Glacier Highway at **Milepost 12.2.** To reach Mendenhall Glacier from here, drive east 2.2 miles/3.5 km and take spur road another 1.4 miles/2.2 km to the glacier and visitor center. The visitor center is open daily in summer from 8:30 A.M. to 5:30 P.M.; weekends only in winter, 9 A.M. to 4 P.M.

Continue on Mendenhall Loop Road past glacier spur road turnoff for Montana Creek Road (3.7 miles/6 km from junction) and access to Mendenhall Lake USFS campground, at Mile 0.4 Montana Creek Road. The campground has 60 sites, tables, fireplaces, water, pit toilets and dump station. Reservations available for some sites; phone 1-800-280 (CAMP). $8 fee. Montana Creek Road dead ends 3.5 miles/5.6 km from Mendenhall Loop Road. ▲

9.7 (15.6 km) Airport area access for southbound travelers via Old Glacier Highway.

9.9 (15.9 km) Mendenhall River and Brotherhood Bridge. The bridge was named in honor of the Alaska Native Brotherhood and is lined by bronze plaques symbolizing the Raven and Eagle clans.

10 (16.1 km) Mendenhall Glacier viewpoint to east; parking area with sign about Brotherhood Bridge and short walking trail.

10.5 (16.9 km) State troopers office.

10.8 (17.4 km) The 2.1-mile/3.4-km Mendenhall Peninsula Road, a 2-lane gravel road, to west. About halfway along this road, Engineer's Cutoff leads 0.3 mile/0.5 km to Fritz Cove Road.

11.4 (18.3 km) Auke Lake scenic wayside to east. Good view of Mendenhall Glacier reflected in the lake. This is one of the most photographed spots in Alaska. Red, pink and coho salmon spawn in Auke Lake system July to Sept. (only limited fishing, for coho in Sept.). Chum salmon are primarily from Auke Creek hatchery program.

11.5 (18.5 km) Fritz Cove Road (paved) leads 2.6 miles/4.2 km west and dead ends at Smuggler's Cove; excellent small-boat anchorage. Scenic viewpoint on Fritz Cove Road at Mile 1.2; Engineer's Cutoff at Mile 1.9 extends 0.3 mile/0.5 km to Mendenhall Peninsula Road.

11.6 (18.7 km) Turnoff to east for Chapel-by-the-Lake and to southeastern branch of University of Alaska.

11.8 (19 km) Short road west to National Marine Fisheries Service biological laboratory (self-guided walking tours between 8 A.M. and 4:30 P.M. Monday through Friday).

12.2 (19.6 km) **Junction** with Mendenhall Loop Road to west. Glacier Highway becomes Juneau Veterans' Memorial Highway and curves around Auke Bay to west. A small-boat harbor with snack shop, skiff and tackle rentals, and boat launch located at the head of the bay. Large schools of herring enter the bay to spawn in the spring.

The 6.8-mile/10.9-km Mendenhall Loop Road rejoins Glacier Highway at **Milepost 9.4.** Motorists may turn east here and follow loop road 3.1 miles/5 km to Montana Creek Road and access to Mendenhall Lake USFS campground, or drive 4.6 miles/7.4 km and turn off on Mendenhall Glacier spur road, which leads another 1.4 miles/2.2 km to the glacier and visitor center. Parking area at Mendenhall Glacier; short, steep path to visitor center. The center is open daily in summer from 8:30 A.M. to 5:30 P.M. ▲

12.3 (19.8 km) Private RV park.

12.4 (20 km) Auke Bay post office to west.

12.6 (20.3 km) Spaulding trailhead to east; 3.5 miles/5.6 km long. Access to John Muir USFS cabin.

12.8 (20.6 km) Waydelich Creek and bridge.

13.8 (22.2 km) Auke Bay ferry terminal exit.

13.9 (22.4 km) Auke Bay ferry terminal entrance. *LeConte* ferry passengers use parking area and terminal on right; all others use parking area and large terminal on left. Visitor information counter staffed in summer; open only for ferry arrivals and departures.

15.1 (24.3 km) Auke Village Recreation Area begins northbound; 5 beachside picnic shelters accessible to west of highway (park on highway shoulder).

15.3 (24.6 km) Auke Village totem pole to east.

15.4 (24.8 km) Auke Village USFS campground; 14 picnic units, 12 campsites, tables, fireplaces, water, flush and pit toilets. $8 fee. Open May 1 to Sept. 30. ▲

16.5 (26.6 km) Lena Point Road, south entrance to loop road.

17 (27.3) Lena Point Road, north entrance to loop road.

17.4 (28.1 km) Lena Beach picnic area.

18.4 (29.6 km) Tee Harbor–Point Stevens Road (gravel) leads 0.3 mile/0.6 km west to public parking area and a private marina and fuel float.

19.2 (30.9 km) Inspiration Point turnout to west with view of the Chilkat Range, and over Tee Harbor and Shelter Island across Favorite Channel. Once a "bread-and-butter" commercial fishing area—hence the name for the strech of shoreline known as "The Breadline"—it is now a popular sportfishing area.

23.1 (37.3 km) Short road west to Catholic Shrine of St. Terese, located on a small island reached by a causeway.

23.3 (37.5 km) Turnout to west and view of island on which Shrine of St. Terese is situated.

23.9 (38.5 km) Peterson Lake trailhead to east; 4 miles/6.4 km long. Access to Peterson Lake USFS cabin. This trail connects with the Spaulding trail (see **Milepost 12.6**).

24.2 (39 km) **Peterson Creek** bridge. View spawning salmon here in late summer and early fall. Trout fishing. Black and brown bears in area.

24.8 (40 km) Gravel road leads 0.6 mile/1 km west to Amalga Harbor; dock, boat launch, bait-casting area. Fireplace and chimney near end of road are remains of an old trapper's cabin.

27.1 (43.7 km) Windfall Lake trailhead to east; 3 miles/4.8 km long.

27.2 (43.9 km) Herbert River bridge.

27.4 (44.2 km) Herbert Glacier trailhead to east; 5 miles/8 km long.

27.7 (44.7 km) Eagle River bridge. Amalga trailhead just across bridge to east; 4 miles/6.4 km long.

28.4 (45.8 km) Eagle Beach picnic area with beachside picnic shelter and 8 picnic sites. View of Chilkat Range across Lynn Canal. Duck hunting on flats in low tide during open season.

28.7 (46.2 km) Scenic viewpoint to west.

29.3 (47.2 km) Scenic viewpoint to west.

32.7 (52.8 km) Turnout to west with view of Benjamin Island to southwest; just beyond it is Sentinel Island lighthouse. Visible to the northwest is North Island and northwest of it is Vanderbilt Reef, site of a great sea disaster. The SS *Princess Sophia,* carrying 288 passengers and 61 crew, ran aground on the Vanderbilt Reef early in the morning of Oct. 24, 1918. All aboard perished when a combination of stormy seas and a high tide forced the *Sophia* off the reef and she sank early in the evening of Oct. 25. The Vanderbilt Reef is now marked by a navigation light.

32.8 (52.9 km) Pavement ends northbound; 2-lane gravel extension of the Glacier Highway begins.

33 (53.1 km) Scenic viewpoint to west. Yankee Cove and beach below this point. The MV *Fairweather,* which cruises between Juneau and Skagway, docks at Yankee Cove.

35.4 (57.1 km) Sunshine Cove public beach access.

37.6 (60.7 km) North Bridget Cove trailhead, Point Bridget State Park. The 2,850-acre park offers meadows, forests, rocky beaches, salmon streams and a trail system. Area is popular for cross-country skiing. Fires allowed on beach.

38.8 (61.3 km) Point Bridget trailhead.

39.4 (63.5 km) Kowee Creek bridge. Large

parking area to west.

40.4 (65 km) Access left to Echo Cove beach. Park area.

40.5 (65.3 km) Road dead ends near Echo Cove on Berners Bay.

Douglas Highway Log

Douglas Highway is a 3-mile/4.8-km paved road beginning on the Juneau side of the Douglas Bridge, crossing to Douglas Island, turning southeast, passing through the city of Douglas to road end and beginning of Treadwell Mine area.

0 Intersection of Egan Drive and Douglas Bridge.

0.5 (0.8 km) Right, Cordova Street leads to Dan Moller trail.

1.5 (2.4 km) Lawson Creek bridge.

2 (3.2 km) Tlingit Indian cemetery and grave houses.

2.5 (4 km) Turn left to boat harbor; dump station and Savikko Park with 4 overnight RV parking spaces without hookups. $5 per night, 3-day limit; obtain permit from Harbormaster's office at 1600 Harbor Way. Short gravel road leads to Juneau Island U.S. Bureau of Mines headquarters. Sandy Beach Recreation Area with water, toilets, play area, tennis courts, track, 2 ball fields, picnic tables, shelters and children's playground. Aptly named, this is one of the few sandy beaches in southeastern Alaska. Highway becomes St. Ann's Avenue.

3 (4.8 km) Road end.

North Douglas Highway Log

North Douglas Highway begins after crossing Douglas Bridge from Juneau and immediately turning right, northwest. **Milepost 1** appears at small bridge on this turn.

0 Douglas Bridge.

0.3 (0.5 km) **Junction** of Douglas Highway and North Douglas Highway.

4.4 (7.1 km) Heliport to right.

6.9 (11.1 km) Eaglecrest Ski Area turnoff on left; drive 5.3 miles/8.5 km on gravel road to ski area. Good blueberry picking in August.

8.3 (13.5 km) Fish Creek bridge. Large parking area on right of bridge. This is a popular roadside fishing spot.

8.6 (13.9 km) Ninemile trail on right; small parking area.

9.5 (15.3 km) Scenic turnout and parking area with excellent view of Mendenhall Glacier; litter barrel. Boat ramp; launch permit required (contact harbormaster before arrival).

10.3 (16.6 km) Small waterfall on left.

11.4 (18.4 km) False Outer Point public beach access. Scenic view of Favorite Channel and Lynn Canal; parking area on right. Near the northern tip of Douglas Island, this is an excellent spot to observe marine activity and eagles.

12.3 (19.8 km) Outer Point trailhead on right.

13.1 (21 km) Road end.

Glacier Bay National Park and Preserve

What Tlingit Indians called "Big Ice-Mountain Bay" in naturalist John Muir's day (1879) is today one of southeastern Alaska's most dramatic attractions, Glacier Bay National Park and Preserve. Muir described Glacier Bay as "a picture of icy wildness unspeakably pure and sublime."

There are no roads to Glacier Bay National Park, except for a 10-mile/16-km stretch of gravel road connecting Bartlett Cove with Gustavus airport. Bartlett Cove is the site of a ranger station and Glacier Bay Lodge. Park naturalists conduct daily hikes and other activities from the visitor center at the lodge, and the excursion boat departs from there. Airlines service Gustavus airport. See Accommodations/Visitor Services and Transportation under Gustavus in this section.

Visitors should contact the Superintendent, Glacier Bay National Park and Preserve, Gustavus, AK 99826-0140, for more information, or check with Glacier Bay tour operators. The national park's headquarters is at Bartlett Cove; phone (907) 697-2230.

Glacier Bay National Park, at the northwest end of Alexander Archipelago, includes not only tidewater glaciers but also Mount Fairweather in the Fairweather Range of the St. Elias Mountains, the highest peak in southeastern Alaska, and also the U.S. portion of the Alsek River.

With passage of the Alaska National Interest Lands Conservation Act in December 1980, Glacier Bay National Monument, established in 1925 by Pres. Calvin Coolidge, became a national park. Approximately 585,000 acres were added to the park/preserve to protect fish and wildlife habitat and migration routes in Dry Bay and along the lower Alsek River, and to include the northwest slope of Mount Fairweather. Total acreage is 3,328,000 (3,271,000 in park, 57,000 in preserve) with 2,770,000 acres designated wilderness.

When the English naval explorer Capt. George Vancouver sailed through the ice-choked waters of Icy Strait in 1794, Glacier Bay was little more than a dent in the coastline. Across the head of this seemingly minor inlet stood a towering wall of ice marking the seaward terminus of an immense glacier that completely filled the broad, deep basin of what is now Glacier Bay. To the north, ice extended more than 100 miles/160 km into the St. Elias Mountains, covering the intervening valleys with a 4,000-foot-/1,219-m-deep mantle of ice.

During the century following Vancouver's pioneering explorations, the glacier retreated some 40 miles/64 km back into the bay, permitting a spruce–hemlock forest to gradually fill the land. By 1916, the Grand Pacific Glacier, which once occupied the entire bay, had receded some 65 miles/105 km from the position observed by Captain Vancouver in 1794. Nowhere else in the world have glaciers been observed to recede at such a rapid pace.

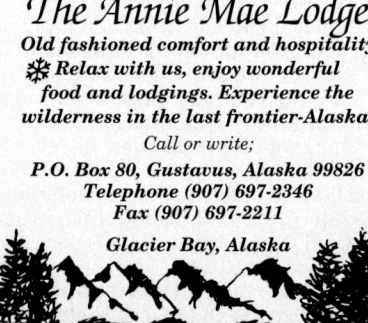

Today, few of the many tributary glaciers that once supplied the huge ice sheet extend to the sea. Glacier Bay National Park encloses 12 active tidewater glaciers, includ-

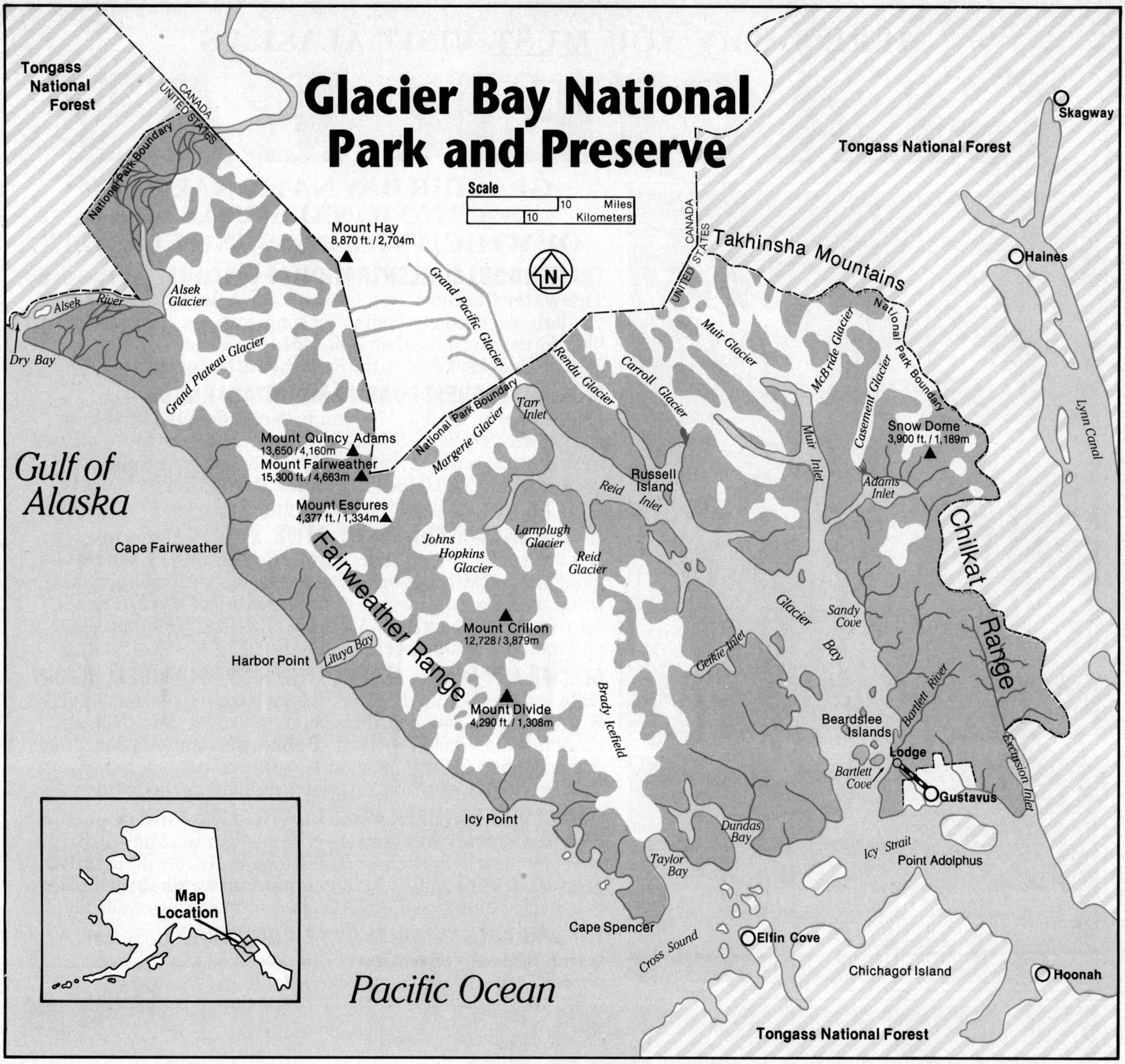

Glacier Bay National Park and Preserve

Scale
10 Miles
10 Kilometers

Tongass National Forest
Skagway
Haines
Takhinsha Mountains
Mount Hay 8,870 ft. / 2,704m
Grand Pacific Glacier
Alsek Glacier
Alsek River
Dry Bay
Grand Plateau Glacier
National Park Boundary
CANADA
UNITED STATES
Muir Glacier
McBride Glacier
Rendu Glacier
Carroll Glacier
Tarr Inlet
Margerie Glacier
Casement Glacier
Snow Dome 3,900 ft. / 1,189m
Lynn Canal
Mount Quincy Adams 13,650 / 4,160m
Mount Fairweather 15,300 ft. / 4,663m
Gulf of Alaska
Mount Escures 4,377 ft. / 1,334m
Russell Island
Reid Inlet
Muir Inlet
Adams Inlet
Chilkat Range
Cape Fairweather
Johns Hopkins Glacier
Lamplugh Glacier
Reid Glacier
Fairweather Range
Mount Crillon 12,728 / 3,879m
Glacier Bay
Sandy Cove
Harbor Point
Lituya Bay
Geikie Inlet
Brady Icefield
Mount Divide 4,290 ft. / 1,308m
Bartlett River
Beardslee Islands
Lodge
Bartlett Cove
Gustavus
Excursion Inlet
Icy Point
Dundas Bay
Taylor Bay
Icy Strait
Point Adolphus
Map Location
Cape Spencer
Cross Sound
Elfin Cove
Chichagof Island
Hoonah
Pacific Ocean

ing several on the remote and seldom-visited western edge of the park along the Gulf of Alaska and Lituya Bay. Icebergs, cracked off from near-vertical ice cliffs, dot the waters of Glacier Bay.

A decline in the number of humpback whales using Glacier Bay for feeding and calf-rearing led the National Park Service to limit the number of boats visiting Glacier Bay from June to Aug. These regulations affect all motorized vessels. Check with the National Park Service for current regulations.

Glacier Bay is approximately 100 miles/160 km from Juneau by boat. Park rangers at Bartlett Cove are available to assist in advising visitors who wish to tour Glacier Bay in private boats or by kayak. Permits are required for motorized pleasure boats between June 1 and Aug. 31. The permits are free. A limited number are available, but rarely are boaters turned away. Permits must be obtained prior to entry into Glacier Bay and Bartlett Cove. Request permits no more than 2 months in advance by writing the National Park Service, Gustavus, AK 99826-0140. For more information, phone (907) 697-2627 (May 1 to Sept. 7).

Glacier Bay Lodge is the only accommodation within the national park, although nearby Gustavus (see description this section) has a number of lodges, inns, bed and breakfasts and rental cabins. Contact Glacier Bay Lodge Inc., 1-800-451-5952, for more information on the concessionaire-operated Glacier Bay Lodge and excursion boat cruises offered from the lodge.

Gasoline and diesel fuel may be purchased at Bartlett Cove, where a good anchorage is available. There are no other

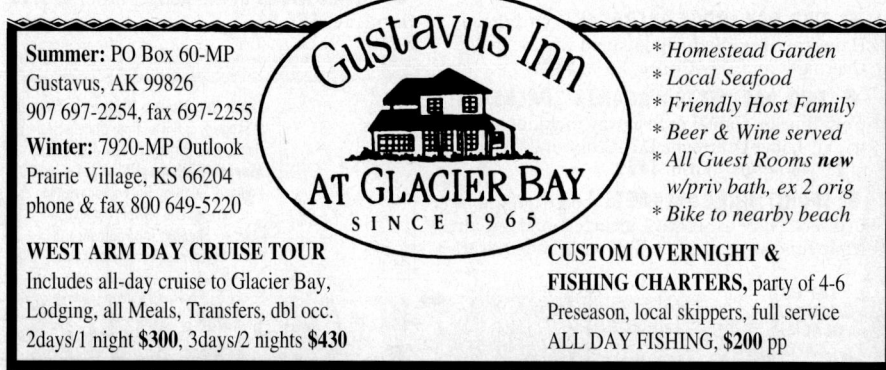

HERE'S WHY YOU MUST VISIT ALASKA'S

GLACIER BAY

EXPERIENCE THE INCREDIBLE BEAUTY
OF ONE OF THE WORLD'S MOST SPECTACULAR PLACES,
GLACIER BAY NATIONAL PARK.

GLACIER BAY NATIONAL PARK IS A "NATIONAL TREASURE" OF WHICH THERE IS "NO EQUAL!"

TREMENDOUS CONCENTRATION OF GLACIERS **16 Massive Tidewater Glaciers** stretch down from the world's most spectacularly glaciated mountains, "calving" icebergs into beautiful blue fjords; plus more than **100 Alpine & Valley Glaciers** create a spectacular backdrop to the Park's **beautiful scenery**.

WORLD'S HIGHEST COASTAL MOUNTAIN RANGE The Fairweather & St. Elias Mountains. **Nowhere else in Alaska** can you see a tidewater glacier flowing from a peak **three miles high** down to sea level, such as Margerie Glacier (see photo) flowing from **15,320 foot high Mt. Fairweather** into Glacier Bay. This kind of "glacial rise" is **unduplicated in the world!**

ABUNDANT WATCHABLE WILDLIFE Plentiful, observable creatures of the wild include: **acrobatic Humpback Whales**, plus Orca and Minke Whales, Porpoises, Stellar Sea Lions; Sea Otters; and **world's largest concentration of Harbor Seals**. Also, Brown & Black Bear; Moose; Wolves; and Mountain Goat; plus more than **200 species of birds**.

GLACIER BAY LODGE, ALASKA'S PREMIER WILDERNESS RESORT **Only lodging** within the Park. **Home base** for all your Glacier Bay Adventures, and departure point for Cruises, Sportfishing, Kayaking and Whale Watching. **Deluxe accommodations**, fine dining, lounge & gift shop. Low-cost **Dormitory** Space. National Park Service displays, audio/visual presentations and nature walks.

DAY CRUISE TO THE GLACIERS & WILDLIFE **Most important part of a Glacier Bay visit** is our daily, Naturalist-narrated day-excursion-boat cruise from the Lodge to where you see the **massive glaciers** close up, and to where the **abundant watchable wildlife** is on display. Multi-night, Small Cruiseship Cruises also available.

THE AMAZING "WHALES OF PT. ADOLPHUS" **Greatest watchable concentration** of Humpback Whales in Southeast Alaska. Twice daily cruises. Whale sightings guaranteed!

BEST WAYS TO EXPERIENCE GLACIER BAY:

- **ONE DAY FLY/CRUISE PACKAGES** from Juneau, Haines or Skagway, include round-trip air and Day-Cruise. From **$299**.
- **TWO DAY LODGE PACKAGES** from Juneau, Haines or Skagway, include round-trip air, Lodge Overnight and Day-Cruise. From **$379**.
- **TWO DAY "EXTRAVAGANZA" PACKAGES** from Juneau, Haines or Skagway, include round-trip air, Lodge Overnight, Day-Cruise and "Whales of Pt. Adolphus." From **$459**.
- **SPORTFISHING PACKAGES** aboard our Cabin Cruisers. Three to Six Days, include round-trip air from Juneau, Haines or Skagway, Lodge overnights & guided sportfishing for trophy-sized halibut or hard-hitting salmon. From **$569**.
- **EXTRA NIGHT** at the Lodge. From **$76.50**. Dorm rate: **$28.00**.

Prices are per person, based on double-occupancy, plus taxes & fees.

HOW TO GET TO GLACIER BAY

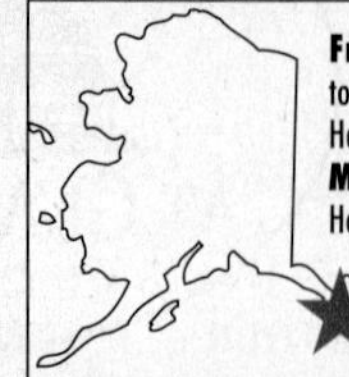

From the Alaska Highway: Proceed to Skagway or Haines from Whitehorse or Haines Junction. **From the "Alaska Marine Highway:"** Proceed to Juneau, Haines or Skagway. Our Packages listed originate in Juneau, Haines and Skagway. Air Packages also available from Major Cities.

FOR RESERVATIONS WHILE IN ALASKA, CONTACT:

Juneau:	Glacier Bay Tour Center, 76 Egan Dr., Suite 130, (907) 463-5510
Haines:	Travel Connection, 301 2nd Ave. S., (907) 755-2681
	Hotel Hälsingland, #13 Fort Seward Dr., (907) 766-2000
Skagway:	Gray Line of Alaska, Westmark Inn, 3rd & Spring, (907) 983-2241
Ketchikan:	Gray Line of Alaska, 3436,Tongass, (907) 225-5930
Sitka:	Sheldon Jackson College Travel, 801 Lincoln St., (907) 747-2540
Anchorage:	Gray Line of Alaska, 745 W. Fourth Ave., (907) 277-5581
Fairbanks:	Gray Line of Alaska, Westmark Hotel, 820 Noble St., (907) 452-2843
	Vista Travel, 1211 Cushman St., (907) 456-7888
Whitehorse:	Gray Line of Alaska, Westmark, 208-G Steele, (403) 668-3225
Prince Rupert:	Seashore Charter Service, 1st & McBride, (604) 624-5645

ALASKA'S **Glacier Bay** TOURS AND CRUISES™
The Authorized Concessionaire of the National Park Service.

LET US SHOW YOU GLACIER BAY!

Phone for Full-Color Brochure and for complete details. **1-800-451-5952** Or Write 520 Pike St., Suite 1400, Seattle, WA 98101

public facilities for boats within park boundaries; Sandy Cove, about 20 miles/32 km from Bartlett Cove, is a popular anchorage. Gustavus has a dock and small-boat harbor.

CAUTION BOATERS: No attempt should be made to navigate Glacier Bay without appropriate charts, tide tables and local knowledge. Floating ice is a special hazard. Because of the danger from waves caused by falling ice, small craft should not approach closer than 0.5 mile/0.8 km from tidewater glacier fronts.

Wildlife in the national park area is protected and hunting is not allowed. Firearms are illegal. *CAUTION: Brown and black bears are present.*

Fishing for silver and king salmon, Dolly Varden and halibut is excellent. A valid Alaska fishing license is required. Charter fishing trips are available.

There is an established campground at Bartlett Cove with 25 sites. Wilderness camping is also available throughout the park. ▲

Tour boat on the West Arm of Glacier Bay National Park. (© David Job)

Gustavus

(See map, page 634)

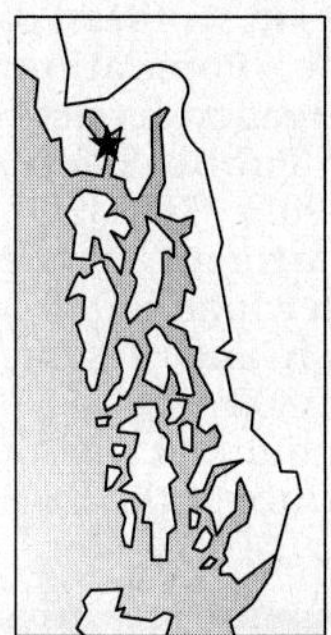

Gateway to Glacier Bay National Park and Preserve, the small community of Gustavus is located just outside the park boundary at the mouth of the Salmon River on the north shore of Icy Passage, 48 miles northwest of Juneau. It is 10 miles/16 km by road from Gustavus to Bartlett Cove within the park. **Population:** 328. **Emergency Services:** Phone 911. **Visitor Information:** Gustavus Visitors Assoc., Box 167, Gustavus 99826.

Surrounded on 3 sides by the snow-covered peaks of the Chilkat Range and the Fairweather Mountains, Gustavus offers miles of level land with expansive sandy beaches, farmland and forest. Homesteaded in 1914 as a small agricultural community, the area was once named Strawberry Point because of its abundant wild strawberries. Today, most residents maintain gardens and make their living by fishing (commercial and subsistence), fish processing, tourism, arts and crafts, and working for the National Park Service and in various local trades.

Besides its proximity to the national park, Gustavus offers a number of attractions. There is fishing for salmon, halibut and trout; excellent berry picking (strawberries, blueberries, nagoonberries and huckleberries); beachcombing; bird watching; whale-watching tours; hiking; and kayaking. Charter boats offer trips into Icy Strait and Glacier Bay.

ACCOMMODATIONS/VISITOR SERVICES

Accommodations in Gustavus include several inns, lodges, bed and breakfasts, and self-sufficient cabins. The lodges and inns serve meals for guests. (Drop-in customers can check for space-available meal reservations.) Taxi service is available. Businesses in Gustavus include a grocery store, art gallery, cafe, gift shop, hardware/building supply store, gas station, auto repair shop and fish-processing facilities. Fishing supplies and licenses may be purchased locally.

Annie Mae Lodge. Old-fashioned good food and good company. Three fine family-style meals using home-baked bread and pastries, fresh caught seafood, berries off the bush, and garden vegetables. We offer beautiful comfortable rooms, peace, quiet, abundant wildlife, wilderness, sportfishing, kayak trips, whale watching. Glacier Bay boat/plane tours. Box 80, Gustavus, AK 99826. Phone (907) 697-2346, fax (907) 697-2211. [ADVERTISEMENT]

Glacier Bay Country Inn and Grand Pacific Charters. Peaceful, storybook accommodations, away from the crowds in a wilderness setting. Cozy comforters, warm flannel sheets, private baths. Superb dining features local seafoods, garden-fresh produce, homebaked breads, spectacular desserts. Fishing, whale watching, sightseeing. Glacier Bay boat/plane tours. Courtesy van, bikes. Box 5MP, Gustavus, AK 99826. Phone (907) 697-2288, fax (907) 697-2289. Winter correspondence (Oct.–April): P.O. Box 2557-MP, St. George, UT 84771. Phone (801) 673-8480, fax (801) 673-8481. [ADVERTISEMENT]

Glacier Bay–Your Way! We provide unforgettable day or overnight tours of Glacier Bay, whale watching, sportfishing, kayaking, hiking. Full-service country inn, B&B accommodations and condominium rentals. Transportation arranged. Full meal packages, bicycles. Box 5MP, Gustavus, AK 99826. Phone (907) 697-2288, fax (907) 697-2289. Winter correspondence (Oct.–April): Box 2557-MP, St. George, UT 84771. Phone (801) 673-8480, fax (801) 673-8481. [ADVERTISEMENT]

Gustavus Inn. Country living, family-style gourmet local seafood meals, cozy bar, kitchen garden, bikes, trout fishing poles, courtesy van, afternoon park naturalist trip. Family-run since 1965. Custom fishing and Glacier Bay sightseeing packages arranged. For map, brochures, please write: Gustavus Inn, Box 60-MP, Gustavus, AK 99826 or call (907) 697-2254. Winter phone and fax (800) 649-5220. [ADVERTISEMENT]

The Puffin. See nearby Glacier Bay and Icy Strait. Stay in your own modern, comfortable, attractively decorated cabin with electricity on quiet wooded homestead. New picturesque central lodge. Complete country breakfast. Bicycles included. Children, pets welcome. Reservations for all charters, Glacier Bay tours. Qualified captains guide fishing, sightseeing charters. Friendly, personal attention. (907) 697-2260, fax (907) 697-2258, e-mail 73654.550@compuserve.com. [ADVERTISEMENT]

Spirit Walker Expeditions. Paddle with whales in Icy Strait! Premium guided sea kayaking trips are the perfect way to really experience Alaska's wilderness scenery, solitude and wildlife. Superb meals, all gear, instruction included. One to 7 days. Beginners, families, custom trips our specialties. Box 240MP, Gustavus, AK 99826. (907) 697-2266 or (800) KAYAKER. [ADVERTISEMENT]

TRI Bed and Breakfast of Glacier Bay. Visit us in our secluded rainforest homesite. Full breakfast with daily fresh eggs, homemade bread/jam. Deluxe and spacious individual cabins with insuite bath. Hiking, kayaking, whale watching, beachcombing, sportfishing, the Glacier Bay day boat or just getting here from Juneau, let us arrange your trip to Glacier Bay/Gustavus. P.O. Box 214MP, Gustavus, AK 99826. (907) 697-2425, fax (907) 697-2450. [ADVERTISEMENT]

TRANSPORTATION

NOTE: There is no state ferry service to Glacier Bay. Closest port of call for state ferries is Hoonah. (Kayakers getting off at Hoonah can expect a 2-day paddle across Icy Strait.)

Air: Glacier Bay may be reached by Alaska Airlines daily jet flights from Juneau and by charter service from Juneau, Sitka, Haines and Skagway to Gustavus airport. Charter air service available in Gustavus. Bus service between the airport and Bartlett Cove is available on jet flights. Taxi service to local facilities and courtesy van service for some lodges are also available.

Rental Cars: Available.

Private Aircraft: Gustavus airport, adjacent northeast; elev. 36 feet/11m; length 6,700 feet/2,042m; asphalt; fuel 100LL, A. Landing within the park is restricted to salt water (Adams Inlet is closed to aircraft landing).

Boat Service: Excursion boats depart daily from Bartlett Cove. You may also charter a boat in Gustavus for sightseeing or fishing. Cruise tours are available from Juneau and Glacier Bay.

Several cruise ships include Glacier Bay cruising in their itineraries. See Cruise Ships in the MARINE ACCESS ROUTES section.

Yakutat

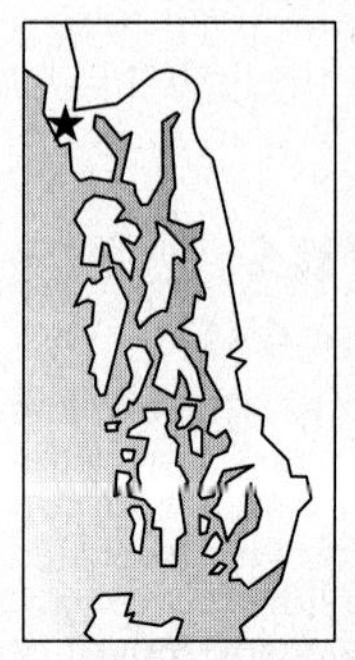

Located on the Gulf of Alaska coast where Southeastern Alaska joins the major body of Alaska to the west; 225 miles/362 km northwest of Juneau, 220 miles/354 km southeast of Cordova and 380 miles/611 km southeast of Anchorage. **Population:** 801. **Emergency Services: Dept. of Public Safety,** phone (907) 784-3206. **Fire Department,** phone 911. **Yakutat Health Center,** phone (907) 784-3275. **Maritime Search and Rescue,** contact the Coast Guard at 1-800-478-5555.

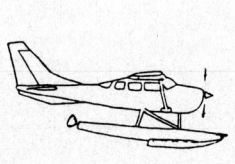

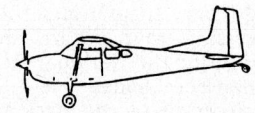

Visitor Information: Inquire at one of the lodges, at the borough office or the USFS office, or write the borough manager at Box 160, Yakutat 99689. For sportfishing information, stop by the ADF&G office at Mile 0.5 Cannon Beach Road, or write Sport Fish Division, Box 49, Yakutat 99689, phone (907) 784-3222.

Elevation: Sea level. **Climate:** Similar to the rest of coastal southeastern Alaska: mild in summer, winters are moderate. Average annual snowfall is 216 inches. Total annual precipitation is about 130 inches. Normal daily maximum in August, 60°F/16°C; minimum in January, 17°F/-8°C. Prevailing winds are southeasterly.

Private Aircraft: Yakutat airport, 3 miles/4.8 km southeast; elev. 33 feet/10m; length 7,700 feet/2,347m; asphalt; fuel 100, A1. Seaplane base 1 mile/1.6 km northwest.

Transportation: Air–Daily jet service from Seattle, Juneau, Anchorage and Cordova. Charter air service available.

Yakutat has 3 lodges, 1 inn, 4 bed and breakfasts, a restaurant, cafe, 2 gift shops, bank, 2 grocery stores, 2 hardware stores, post office, clinic and gas station. Boat rentals, car rentals and cab service are available.

Yakutat Bay is one of the few refuges for vessels along this long stretch of coast in the Gulf of Alaska. The site was originally the principal winter village of the local Tlingit Indian tribe. Sea otter pelts brought Russian to the area in the 19th century. Fur traders were followed by gold seekers, who came to work the black sand beaches. Commercial salmon fishing developed in this century, and the first cannery was built here in 1904. Today's economy is based primarily on fishing and fish processing. Salmon, halibut, crab and black cod make up the fishery. Government and local businesses employ most residents. Subsistence activities are primarily fishing (salmon and shellfish), hunting (moose, bear, goats, ducks and small game), and gathering seaweed and berries. The soil is not suitable for agriculture, and a vegetable garden requires a great deal of preparation to produce small quantities.

While hunting and fishing in particular draw visitors to Yakutat, the surge of Hubbard Glacier in June 1986, which sealed off the mouth of Russell Fiord, drew national attention. Malaspina Glacier, largest on the North American continent, is northwest of town. Nearer to town, Cannon Beach has good beachcombing and a picnic area.

AREA FISHING: Yakutat is considered a world-class sportfishing destination. Steelhead fishing is among the finest anywhere. King and silver (coho) salmon run in abundance in Yakutat area salt water, rivers and streams May through September. The area also boasts red and pink salmon and smelt in season. USFS cabins available on some rivers; check with the Forest Service (907/586-8751).

Lost River and **Tawah Creek,** 10 miles/16 km south of Yakutat on Lost River Road, silver (coho) salmon to 20 lbs., mid-Aug. through Sept. **Situk River,** 12 miles/19.3 km south of Yakutat on the Lost River Road (also accessible by Forest Highway 10), is one of Alaska's top fishing spots spring and fall for steelhead and silver salmon and has one of the best sockeye (red) salmon runs in the state, late June through August; steelhead averaging 10 lbs., April 1 to May 30 for spring run, October and November for fall run; king salmon to 45 lbs., mid-June through July; silver salmon to 23 lbs., mid-August through September; pink salmon run in August, yields Dolly Varden also. **Yakutat Bay**, king salmon 30 to 50 lbs., May through June; silver salmon to 20 lbs., late Aug. through September.

Haines

(See map, page 634)

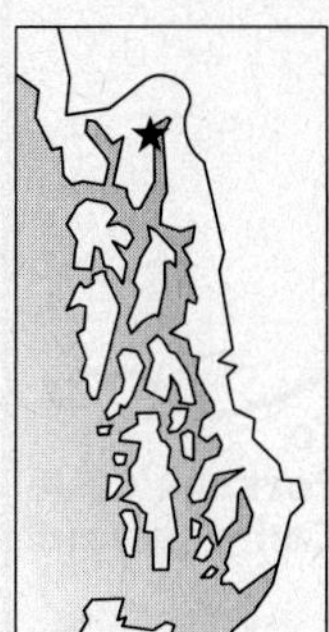

Located on Portage Cove, Chilkoot Inlet, on the upper arm of Lynn Canal, 80 air miles/129 km northwest of Juneau; 151 road miles/243 km southeast of Haines Junction, YT. Southern terminus of the Haines Highway. *NOTE: Although Haines is only 13 miles/21 km by water from Skagway, it is 359 miles/578 km by road!*

Population: 1,363. **Emergency Services: Alaska State Troopers,** phone (907) 766-2552. **City Police,** phone (907) 766-2121. **Fire Department** and **Ambulance,** emergency only phone 911. **Doctor,** phone (907) 766-2521. **Maritime Search and Rescue,** contact the Coast Guard at 1-800-478-5555.

Visitor Information: At 2nd and Willard streets. There are free brochures for all of Alaska and the Yukon. Open daily, 8 A.M. to 8 P.M., June through Aug.; 8 A.M. to 5 P.M. weekdays, Sept. through May. Phone (907) 766-2234; toll free 1-800-458-3579, or from the Yukon and British Columbia 1-800-478-2268. Write the Haines Visitor Bureau at Box 530, Haines 99827. Phone the Alaska Dept. of Transportation at (907) 766-2340.

Elevation: Sea level. **Climate:** Average daily maximum temperature in July, 66°F/19°C; average daily minimum in January, 17°F/-8°C. Extreme high summer temperature, 90°F/32°C; extreme winter low, -16°F/-27°C; average annual precipitation, 59 inches. **Radio:** KHNS-FM 102.3. **Television:** 12 cable channels. **Newspaper:** *Chilkat Valley News* (weekly).

Private Aircraft: Haines airport, 3 miles/4.8 km west; elev. 16 feet/5m; length 3,000 feet/914m; asphalt; fuel 100; unattended.

The original Indian name for Haines was *Dtehshuh,* meaning "end of the trail." It was a trading post for both Chilkat and Interior Indians. The first white man to settle here was George Dickinson, who came as an agent for the North West Trading Co.

The following year S. Hall Young, a Presbyterian missionary, came into Chilkat Inlet with his friend, naturalist John Muir. They planned to build a Christian town, offering

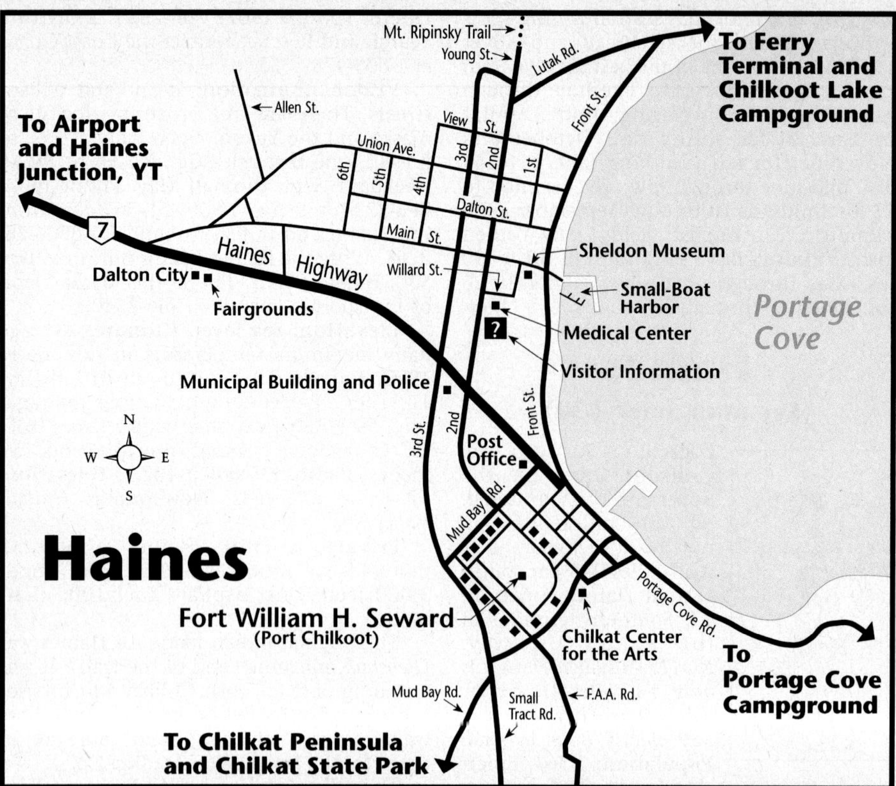

the Chilkat people a missionary and teacher. The site chosen was on the narrow portage between the Chilkat River and Lynn Canal. By 1881, with financial help from Sheldon Jackson, the mission was established. The town was named for Mrs. F.E. Haines, secretary of the Presbyterian National Committee of Home Missions, which raised funds for the new mission.

In 1884 the Haines post office was established, although the settlement was still known locally as Chilkoot. The town became an important outlet for the Porcupine Mining District, producing thousands of dollars' worth of placer gold at the turn of the century. Haines also marked the beginning of the Dalton Trail, which crossed the Chilkat mountain pass to the Klondike goldfields in the Yukon.

Just to the south of Haines city center is Port Chilkoot on Portage Cove. The U.S. government established a permanent military post here in 1904 and called it Fort William H. Seward, in honor of the secretary of state who negotiated the purchase of Alaska from Russia in 1867.

In 1922, the fort was renamed Chilkoot Barracks, after the mountain pass and the Indian tribe on the Chilkoot River. (There are 2 tribes in this area: the Chilkat and the Chilkoot.) Until WWII this was the only U.S. Army post in Alaska. Chilkoot Barracks was deactivated in 1946 and sold in 1947 to a group of enterprising U.S. veterans who had designs of creating a business cooperative on the site. Their original plans were never fully realized, but a few stayed on to convert some of the houses on Officers' Row into permanent homes.

In 1970, Port Chilkoot merged with Haines to become a single municipality, the city of Haines. Two years later, the post was designated a national historic site and became officially known, again, as Fort William H. Seward (although many people still call it Port Chilkoot).

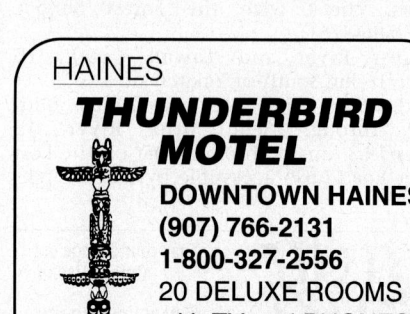

Fishing and gold mining were the initial industries of the Haines area. Haines is also remembered for its famous strawberries, developed by Charles Anway about 1900. His Alaskan hybrid, *Burbank,* was a prize winner at the 1909 Alaska–Yukon–Pacific Exposition in Seattle, WA. A strawberry festival was held annually in Haines for many years, and this local event grew into the Southeast Alaska State Fair, which each summer draws thousands of visitors. Today, halibut and gill-net salmon fishing, lumbering and tourism are the basis of the economy. Haines is an important port on the Alaska Marine Highway System as the southern terminus of the Haines Highway, 1 of the 2 year-round roads linking southeastern Alaska with the Interior.

ACCOMMODATIONS/VISITOR SERVICES

Haines offers travelers comfortable accommodations with 7 hotels/motels and 7 bed and breakfasts. There is a youth hostel (families welcome) with cabin accommodations on Small Tract Road.

Haines has all traveler facilities, including hardware and grocery stores, gift shops and art galleries, automotive repair, laundry, post office and bank. Gift shops and galleries feature the work of local artisans. There are several restaurants, cafes and taverns.

State campgrounds in the area include Portage Cove, Chilkat State Park, Chilkat Lake and Mosquito Lake. ▲

Portage Cove State Recreation Site offers 9 tent sites, half-mile past Fort Seward on Portage Cove. Water and toilets available. Campers enjoy view of the Coast Range and Lynn Canal. Watch for cruise ships, ferries, eagles, whales, porpoises and sea birds. *NOTE: This site is for walk-in and bicyclist camping only.* ▲

Chilkat State Park, with 32 RV sites and 3 tent sites, is about 8 miles/13 km from Haines on Mud Bay Road (from the Haines Highway, bear right at the Y by the Welcome to Haines sign; continue straight past the high school and up the hill, where the road bends to the right; follow signs from hill to Chilkat State Park).

Chilkoot Lake Campground (32 sites) is approximately 10 miles/16 km from Haines on Lutak Road (6 miles/10 km past the ferry terminal; turn right when exiting the ferry for Chilkoot Lake). There are 5 private campgrounds in Haines. ▲

Mosquito Lake State Recreation Site is located on Mosquito Lake Road, 3 miles/6.5 km north of Mile 27 Haines Highway. It has 6 campsites nestled in a wooded setting around Mosquito Lake. Toilets, drinking water, a picnic shelter and boat launch are available. Small store and softball diamond at Mile 27. ▲

TRANSPORTATION

Air: Haines is served regularly by L.A.B. Flying Service, Haines Airways and Wings of Alaska. Haines airport is 3.5 miles/5.6 km from downtown. Commercial airlines provide transportation to and from motels, and some motels offer courtesy car pickup.

Ferry: Alaska Marine Highway vessels

HAINES Valley of the Eagles

The beauty of Southeast Alaska is waiting for you in Haines. Enjoy unique cultural attractions such as the Chilkat Bald Eagle Preserve, Fort William H. Seward—a National Historic Landmark, the Chilkat Indian Dancers, Totem Pole Carvers, Dalton City where the movie "White Fang" was filmed, the American Bald Eagle Foundation, the Haines/S.E. Alaska Rodeo and many talented Alaskan Artists.

ACCOMMODATIONS/RESTAURANTS

① **ALASKA THUNDERBIRD MOTEL** Downtown motel, all ground floor. Clean, comfortable, direct dial phones, color TV, some kitchenettes. (907) 766-2131, or 800-327-2556.

② **BAMBOO ROOM RESTAURANT** Famous for our halibut fish 'n chips, Homemade soups & pies. Daily specials. Seafood & Steaks. Espresso. Open 6 a.m. year round. Full service bar & liquor store. Second Avenue. (907) 766-2800 or 766-2474.

③ **CAPTAIN'S CHOICE INC. MOTEL** Haines finest & most comfortable lodging. Featuring Car Rentals, Room Service, Tour Bookings, Courtesy Transfers. Centrally located. See our display ad. (907) 766-3111 or 800-247-7153 or 800-478-2345 Alaska & Yukon. FAX (907) 766-3332.

④ **CHILKAT BAKERY & RESTAURANT** Bakery products fresh daily. Breakfast-Lunch-Dinner. 7 a.m. - 9 p.m. Plenty of parking. 5th Avenue.

⑤ **CHILKAT VALLEY INN BED & BREAKFAST** 8 miles from downtown Haines on the edge of the Eagle Preserve. 1959 homestead overlooks the Chilkat River Valley. Year round accessibility in a wilderness setting. Ideal location for wildlife photography or quiet retreat. P.O. Box 861, Haines, AK 99827 (8.5 Mile Haines Highway), (907) 766-3331 or 800-747-5528.

⑥ **EAGLE'S NEST MOTEL & CAR RENTAL** Fully modern, quiet rooms, AAA approved. Featuring Chilkoot Lake Tours, fishing & sightseeing trips. P.O. Box 250, Haines, AK 99827, (907) 766-2891 or 800-354-6009.

⑦ **FORT SEWARD CONDOS** Completely furnished, spacious apartments overlooking the bay. 1 and 2 bedrooms, full kitchen, bath and laundry. Will sleep 5. 2 day minimum. No Pets. Reasonable. P.O. Box 75, Haines, AK 99827, (907) 766-2425.

⑧ **FT. SEWARD LODGE & RESTAURANT** Affordable lodging, ocean view kitchenettes, restaurant-saloon, Alaskan cuisine and decor. Military & senior discounts. 1-800-478-7772 (good in Yukon/B.C./AK/& Continental U.S.). See our display ad.

⑨ **HAINES ELKS LODGE #2634** Open Mon.-Sat. 3 p.m - ? Friday nights hamburger feed, Saturday nights steak feed, closed Sundays. Main Street. (907) 766-2289.

⑩ **HOTEL HALSINGLAND** Gracious Victorian Hotel. Renowned Seafood Restaurant. Cocktail lounge. Reasonable rates. See our display ad. 800-542-6363 or Canada 800-478-2525.

⑪ **SUMMER INN BED & BREAKFAST** Charming, historic house. **Open year round.** Full, homemade breakfast, centrally located, clean comfortable rooms, nice views, reasonable rates. Ask about winter rates. See our display ad. **117 Second Avenue North.** (907) 766-2970.

⑫ **THE RIVERHOUSE LUXURY BED & BREAKFAST** The ultimate Alaskan experience. 5 minutes from town, stunning riverside location. Tower bedroom, garden deck, hot tub, full kitchen, bikes & barbeque. Quiet - private - perfect for wildlife photographers and romantics! P.O. Box 1009, Haines, AK 99827. (907) 766-2060 or 800-478-1399.

ART GALLERIES/GIFT SHOPS

⑬ **BELL'S STORE** For the very best Alaskan gifts and a unique shopping experience. FTD service and Fresh Flowers too. OPEN ALL YEAR. Second Ave.

⑭ **KING'S STORE** "Same day" Photo Center. Unique printwear, ivory, gifts & necessities. A browser's paradise. On Main St. across from museum. Help us celebrate our *Golden Anniversary* in 96'. 766-2336.

⑮ **SEA WOLF GALLERY** Artists at work at this fine studio-gallery. Wood carving, prints, & jewelry by local artist, Tresham Gregg. Located at Totem Village, Fort Seward Parade Field.

ATTRACTIONS

⑯ **ALASKA INDIAN ARTS/CHILKAT DANCERS** Traditional Northwest Coast totem carvers, silversmiths & printmakers at work. Home of the Chilkat Dancers who perform several times each week during the summer. At Fort Seward. Box 271, Haines, AK 99827, Phone/FAX (907) 766-2160.

⑰ **FORT WILLIAM H. SEWARD NATIONAL HISTORIC LANDMARK** First Army Post built in Alaska. Totem Village & Arts and Cultural Center. Walking tours available.

⑱ **HAINES/S.E. ALASKA RODEO** Annual authentic Western Rodeo. Featuring professional Alaskan Rodeo riders. Events include: bronc & bull riding, calf roping, barrel racing, pole bending, ribbon & team roping. Many other events. Tentative 1996 date – July 6 & 7. For more information call (907) 766-2202.

⑲ **SHELDON MUSEUM & CULTURAL CENTER** History of the Chilkat Valley and culture of the Tlingit Native People. Chilkat Blankets, Dalton Trail, Ft. Seward. Alaska Book & Gift Store. P.O. Box 269, Haines, AK 99827, (907) 766-2366 or FAX (907) 766-2368.

⑳ **SOUTHEAST ALASKA STATE FAIR & ALASKAN BALD EAGLE MUSIC FESTIVAL** August 7-11, 1996. Great regional & national music, parade, 26th Annual Horse Show, exhibits, logging show, kid's events, food & trade booths. 766-2476.

AUTO SERVICE

㉑ **BIGFOOT AUTO SERVICE** NAPA Parts, RV Service & Towing; A.S.E. Technicians, Gas, Diesel, Goodyear Sales & Service. (907) 766-2458/2459.

㉒ **BUSHMASTER SERVICE & REPAIR** Four wheel alignment, suspension, brakes, major engine & driveline work, electronic engine controls. FACTORY WARRANTY for your new vehicle. Guaranteed service. 4th & Union St. 766-3217.

㉓ **CHARLIE'S REPAIR SERVICE** Auto, marine, R.V., welding; free RV water and dump. 24 Hour Gas with MC-VISA. 766-2794.

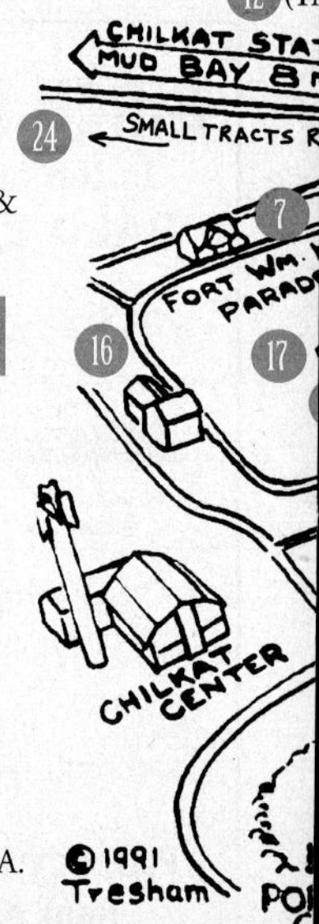

TOURS WILDLIFE VIEWING MUSEUMS HISTORICAL SITES

(24) HAINES MOTORCYCLE AND AUTO REPAIR
2 1/4 Mile Small Tracts Rd., Complete Services, 24 hour towing. 766-3393 Daytime, 766-2061 Evenings.

(25) **THE PARTS PLACE** Auto-RV-Marine. If you need it, we have it or will get it. 206 3rd Ave. S. 766-2940.

(26) **TOTEM OIL** Gas and diesel. Free RV water, dump and coffee. Propane. MasterCard/VISA accepted. At intersection of the Haines Hwy./Main Street. (907) 766-3190.

CAMPER PARKS

(27) **HAINES HITCH-UP RV PARK** 92 Full Service Spaces. 20 Pull-thrus. Level Grassy 25' wide lots. Immaculate Restrooms & Showers. Laundromat and gift shop. (907) 766-2882.

(28) **PORT CHILKOOT CAMPER PARK** Lovely wooded area; full & partial hook-ups; showers, laundry; tents welcome. 800-542-6363 or 800-478-2525 AK & Yukon.

FISHING CHARTERS/LODGES

(29) **BIRCH ISLAND LODGE** Chilkat Lake. Good fishing and good times. All gear provided. P.O. Box 1276, Haines, AK 99827, 767-5656.

GROCERIES/SEAFOOD

(30) **BELL'S SEAFOOD** Alaskan Seafood at its very Best!!! We Pack to Ship. 2nd Avenue next to Bell's Store. Downtown Haines, Alaska. AK 561 • P.O. Box 1189, Haines, AK 99827, 766-2950.

(31) **MOUNTAIN MARKET HEALTH FOOD STORE & DELI**
Espresso Bar • Fresh Baked Goods • Deli Sandwiches • Fresh Soups • Natural & Organic Foods • Vitamins • Health Care Products • Located at the corner of Third Avenue & Haines Hwy. (907) 766-3340.

SERVICES

(32) **E.D. & D.** Cable TV, Computers, Video Tapes, Electronic Parts and Service. Radio Shack Dealer. Mile 1 Haines Highway. 766-2337 or 766-2137

SIGHTSEEING/TRANSPORTATION

(33) **ALASKA NATURE TOURS** Fun & informative excursions into the Chilkat Bald Eagle Preserve guided by top local naturalists. Hiking adventures, wildlife photography, bus & walking tours since 1985. Located behind the Visitor's Center. P.O. Box 491, Haines, AK 99827. Phone/FAX (907) 766-2876.

(34) **CHILKAT GUIDES** Daily 3 1/2 hour float trips through the Bald Eagle Preserve. Also overnight float trips & hiking adventures (907) 766-2491.

(35) **HAINES AIRWAYS** Spectacular flightseeing tours from Haines and Juneau. Scheduled service to Juneau, Haines, Gustavus & Hoonah. (907) 766-2646 or 789-2336.

(36) **HAINES-SKAGWAY WATER TAXI** Two round trips daily between downtown Haines and Skagway. Departures from the Small Boat Harbor. Ask about our discount railroad package to Skagway. $29 RT; $18 OW. Call (907) 766-3395.

(37) **RIVER ADVENTURES** Daily River tours available. Join us as we take you on a journey through the Bald Eagle Preserve and into the wilderness of Alaska. (907) 766-2050, FAX (907) 766-2051.

(38) **SOCKEYE CYCLE/ALASKA BICYCLE TOURS**
Daily 1-3 HR Guided Tours through the Bald Eagle Preserve in the Chilkat Valley. Multi day fully supported MTN. Bike Tours in British Columbia and the Yukon. 2 Full Service bike shops in Haines and Skagway, rentals, sales, service. Brochure, MP. Box 829, Haines, AK 99827, Phone/FAX (907) 766-2869.

(39) **TANANI BAY KAYAK AND CANOE RENTALS**
Sea kayak and canoe rentals. Quality at low prices. Pick-up and delivery available to Chilkoot Lake and other sights in the Lynn Canal area. On Front Street near the corner of Union & Front. Near downtown. (907) 766-2804.

(40) **THE TRAVEL CONNECTION**
Ferry reservations, local sightseeing, Glacier Bay Tours, independent tours for all of Alaska. Box 645, Haines, AK 99827 (across from the Visitors Center). (907) 766-2681 or 800-572-8006.

(41) **WINGS OF ALASKA** Fly the Inside Passage on us. Scheduled, charter, and flightseeing air service. (907) 766-2030 or (907) 789-0790.

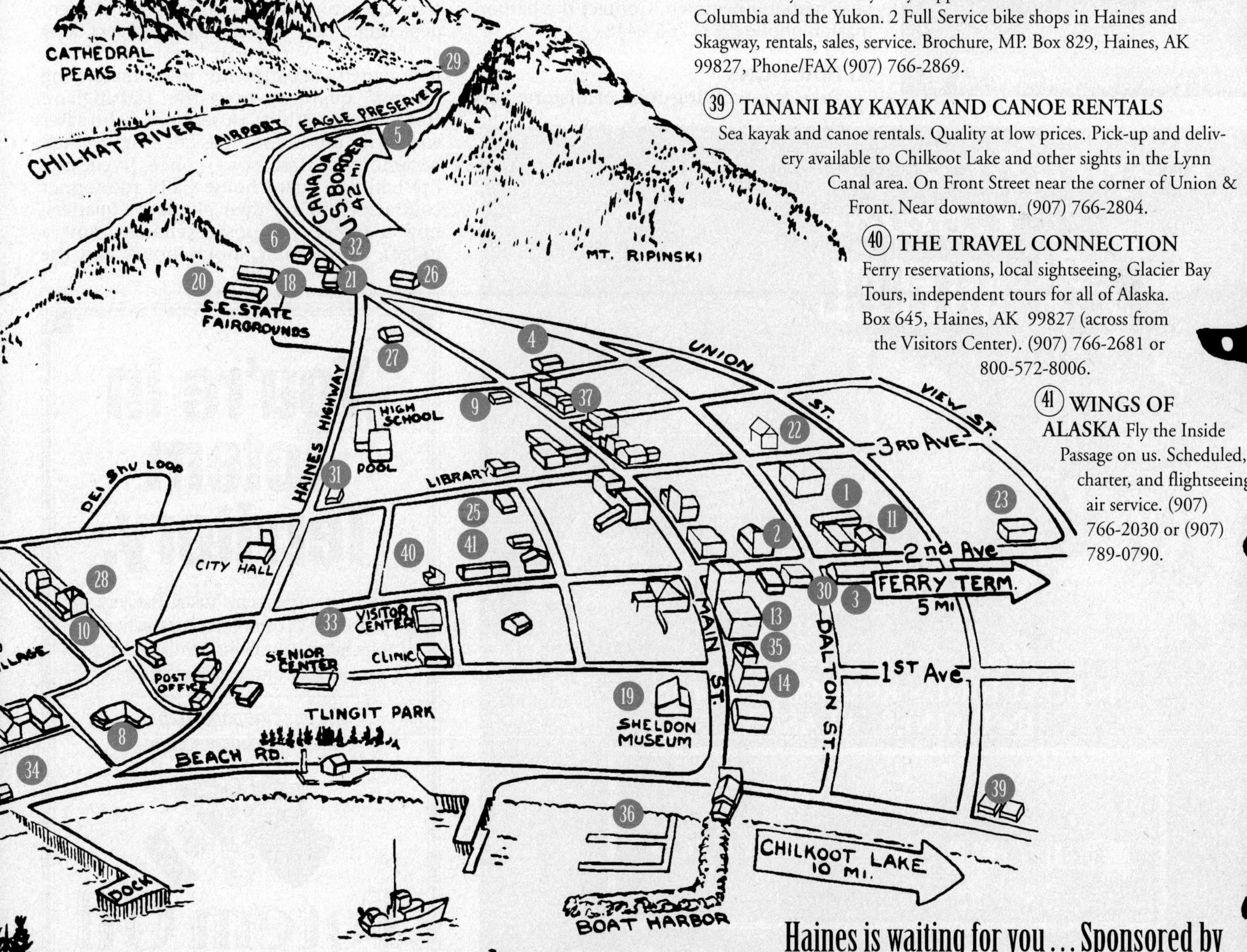

Haines is waiting for you... Sponsored by Haines Chamber of Commerce (907) 766-2202

serve Haines from southeastern Alaska, Prince Rupert, BC, and Bellingham, WA. Alaska state ferries run year-round; phone (907) 766-2111. See MARINE ACCESS ROUTES section for details. Ferries unload at the terminal on Lutak Road, 4.5 miles/7.2 km from downtown Haines. Bus/van service meets all ferries in summer.

The Haines/Skagway Water Taxi provides water-taxi service to Skagway twice daily during the summer; phone (907) 766-3395.

Bus: Local bus service to ferry terminal and guided sightseeing tours are available. Two companies also offer service to and from Anchorage, Fairbanks and Whitehorse, YT, via the Alaska Highway.

Car Rental: Available at Thunderbird Motel, Captain's Choice Motel, Eagle's Nest Motel and Halsingland Hotel.

Taxi: 24-hour service to ferry terminal and airport.

View of Fort Seward at Haines. (© Rich Reid)

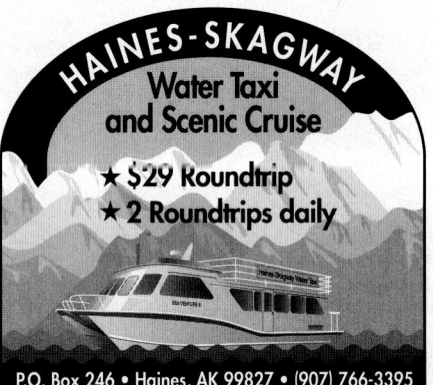

Highways: The Haines Highway connects Haines, AK, with Haines Junction, YT. It is maintained year-round. See HAINES HIGHWAY section for details.

Cruise Ships: Twelve cruise ships make Haines a port of call.

Private Boats: Transient moorage is available at Letnikof Cove and at the small-boat harbor downtown. Contact the harbor-master, phone (907) 766-2448.

ATTRACTIONS

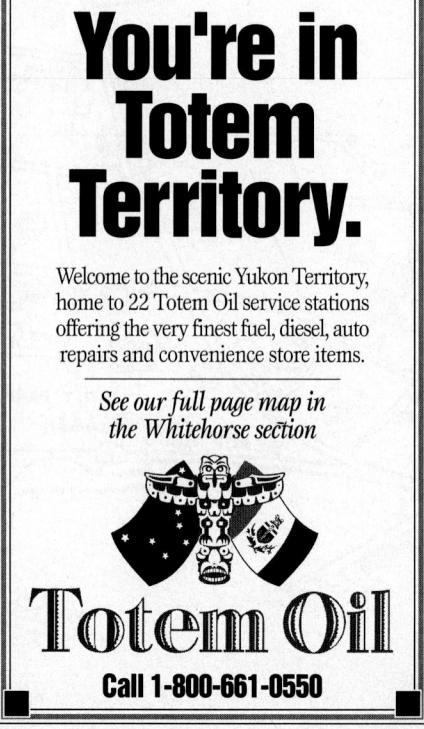

Take the walking tour of historic Fort William H. Seward; details and map are available at the visitor information center and at other businesses. Historic buildings of the post include the former cable office; warehouses and barracks; "Soapsuds Alley," the housing for noncommissioned officers whose wives did washing for the soldiers; the former headquarters building, now a residence, fronted by a cannon and a totem depicting a bear and an eagle; Officers' Row at the "Top O' the Hill," restored houses now rented as apartments; the commanding officers' quarters, now the Halsingland Hotel, where Elinor Dusenbury (who later wrote the music for "Alaska's Flag," which became the state song) once lived; the fire hall; the guard house (jail); the former contractor's office, then plumber's quarters, now a motel; the post exchange (now a lodge), gymnasium, movie house and the mule stables. Look for historic and interpretive signs.

Visit the Chilkat Center for the Arts at the auditorium at Fort Seward. Here, the Chilkat Dancers interpret ancient Tlingit Indian legends, and the production "Smell of the Yukon," a historically based local melodrama, performed by the Lynn Canal Community Players, is sometimes shown. Check with the visitor information center or Alaska Indian Arts Inc. for schedule of performances.

Totem Village, on the former post parade ground, includes a replica of a tribal ceremonial house and a trapper's cabin and cache. There is a salmon bake, the Port Chilkoot Potlatch, held nightly in summer next to the tribal house; reservations recommended. Prior to the establishment of the fort, this area was part of an ancient portage route for Tlingit Indians transporting canoes from the Chilkat River to Lynn Canal.

See the Welcome Totems located at the Y on the Haines Highway. These poles were created by carvers of Alaska Indian Arts Inc. *The Raven* pole is symbolic of Raven, as founder of the world and all his great powers. The second figure is *The Whale,* representing Alaska and its great size. The bottom figure is the head of *The Bear,* which shows great strength. *The Eagle* pole tells of his feeding grounds (the Haines area is noted for its eagles). Top figure is *The Salmon Chief,* who provides the late run of salmon to the feeding grounds. *The Eagle Chief,* head of the Eagle clan, is the third figure, and the bottom figure is *The Brown Bear,* which also feeds on salmon and is a symbol of strength. Inquire at the visitor information center about location of poles.

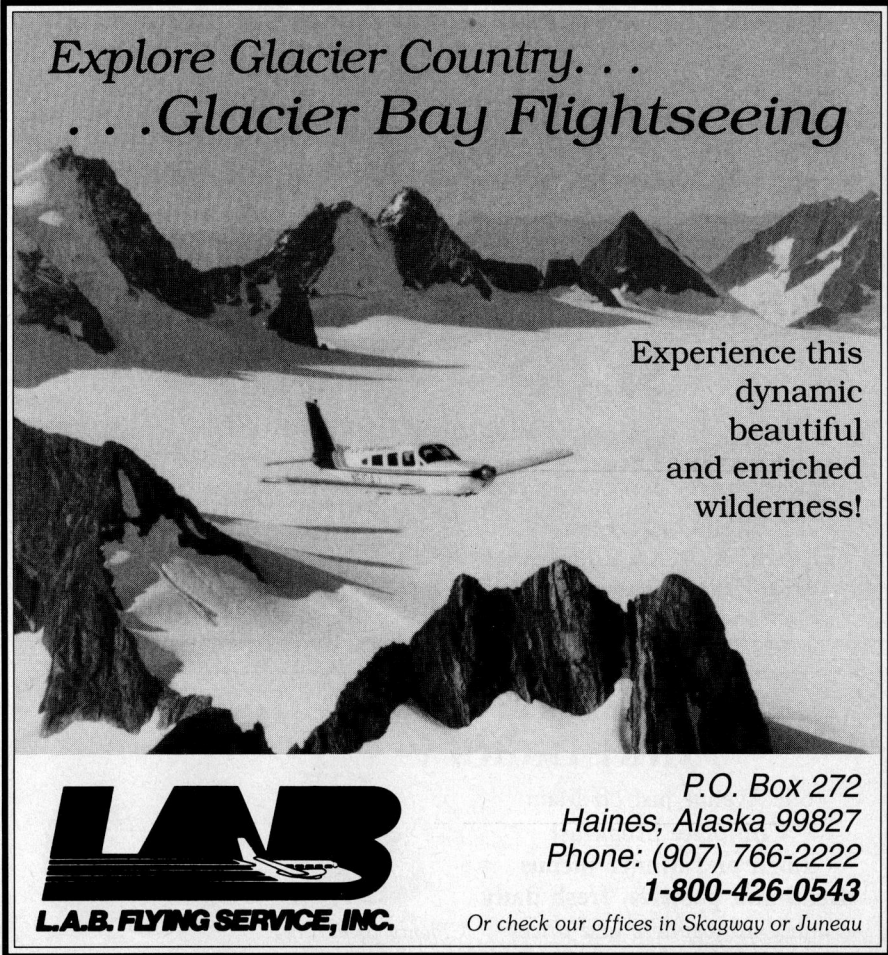

The Sheldon Museum and Cultural Center, at the end of Main Street by the boat harbor, tells through exhibits the pioneer history of the Chilkat Valley and the story and culture of the Tlingit Native people. Chilkat blankets, Russian trunks, blue dishes, eagles (stuffed), Jack Dalton's sawed-off shotgun, photographs and a video on eagles make a fascinating history lesson. Children's "discovery" sheet available. Open daily 1–5 P.M. in summer, plus many mornings and evenings; winter, 1–4 P.M Sunday, Monday and Wednesday, 3–5 P.M. Tuesday,

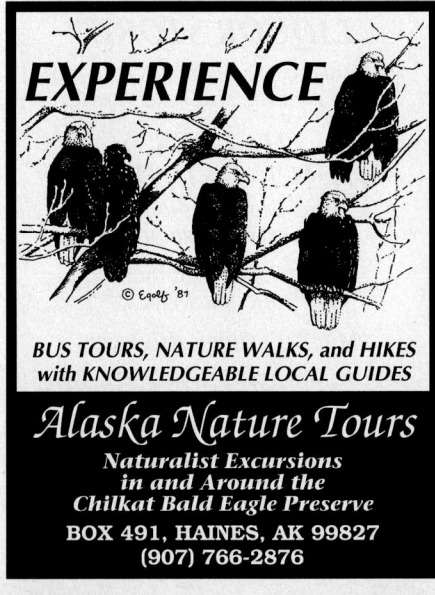

Thursday and Friday. Admission fee $3; children free. Phone (907) 766-2366.

The Haines Rodeo, planned for July 1 and 2, 1996, is an authentic rodeo with the Northern Lights Cowboy Assoc. Events include a barbecue, dance and contests.

Enjoy the Fourth of July celebration, which includes canoe and kayak races on Chilkoot Lake, logging events, bicycle and foot races, pie-eating and other contests, parades and performances at the Chilkat Center for the Arts.

The Southeast Alaska State Fair, held at the fairgrounds in Haines (Aug. 7–11, 1996), features agriculture, home arts, and fine arts and crafts. A big event at the fair is the Bald Eagle Music Festival. There are exhibits of flowers, livestock, baked goods, beer and wine, needlework, quilting, woodworking and over a dozen other categories. There are also a parade, horse show and other events, including pig racing for cookies. Brochures available from the Fair offices. Write to Box 385, Haines 99827, or (907) 766-2476.

Dalton City, opened in 1992, is housed in the "White Fang" Disney film set. It is located at the fairgrounds.

Visit the small-boat harbor at the foot of Main Street for an interesting afternoon outing. Watch gill-net and crab fishermen setting out from here. Good views from Lookout Park and also from the shoreline between Haines and Portage Cove Campground.

Visit State Parks. Chilkoot Lake, at the end of Lutak Road, is worth a visit. Beautiful setting with a picnic area, campground and boat launch. Watch for brown bears in nearby waters in the fall, attracted by spawning salmon. (Private boat tours of Chilkoot Lake are available; check in town.) Chilkat State Park on Mud Bay Road is also a scenic spot with hiking trails, beach access, views of glaciers (Rainbow and Davidson), fishing, camping and picnicking. Both parks are within 10 miles/16 km of downtown Haines.

Go Flightseeing. Local air charter operators offer flightseeing trips for spectacular close-up views of glaciers, ice fields, mountain peaks and bald eagles. Glacier Bay is just west of Haines.

Charter boat operators in Haines offer fishing, sightseeing and photography trips.

Watch totem carvers at the Alaska Indian Arts Inc. workshop, located in the restored hospital at Fort Seward. This nonprofit organization is dedicated to the revival of Tlingit Indian art. Craftsmen also work in silver and stone, and sew blankets. Visitor hours 9 A.M. to noon and 1–5 P.M. weekdays year-round.

Hike Area Trails. Mount Ripinski trail is a strenuous all-day hike, with spectacular views from the summit of mountains and tidal waters. Start at the end of 2nd and Young streets; follow pipeline right-of-way

The Chilkat River at Haines is part of the Alaska Chilkat Bald Eagle Preserve.
(© Loren Taft, Alaskan Images)

about 1.3 miles/2.1 km to trail, which climbs 3.6 miles/5.8 km to the 3,610-foot/1,100-m summit. *CAUTION: This is an unmaintained trail, recommended for experienced hikers only.*

Battery Point trail starts 1 mile/1.6 km beyond Portage Cove Campground and leads about 2 miles/3 km to a primitive camping site on Kelgaya Point overlooking Lynn Canal.

Mount Riley (elev. 1,760 feet/536m) has 3 routes to the summit. The steepest and most widely used trail starts at Mile 3 Mud Bay Road and climbs 2.1 miles/3.4 km to the summit. A second route starts at the end of F.A.A. Road and leads 2 miles/3.2 km along the city water-supply route to connect with the trail from Mud Bay Road to the summit. A third route follows the Battery Point trail for approximately 2 miles/3.2 km, then forks right for a fairly steep climb to the summit of Mount Riley.

Seduction Point, at the southern tip of the Chilkat Peninsula, is accessible from Chilkat State Park via a 6-mile/9.7-km trail; a rolling forest and beach walk. Views of Davidson and Rainbow glaciers.

Observe eagles when the world's greatest concentration of American bald eagles takes place October through January on Chilkat River flats below Klukwan. The eagle viewing area begins at **Milepost H 17** on the Haines Highway. The 48,000-acre Alaska Chilkat Bald Eagle Preserve was established in 1982. The Chilkat Valley at Haines is the annual gathering site of more than 3,000 bald eagles, which gather to feed on the late run of chum salmon in the Chilkat River.

American Bald Eagle Foundation is Haines' newest attraction. Interpretive center shows visitors how the bald eagle interacts with its environment through beautiful exhibits: mounted eagles, a wide variety of mammals, and fish and undersea life. Admission is free, donations welcomed. Open daily 10 A.M. to 6 P.M. in summer. Located at the Haines Highway and 2nd Street, just across 2nd Street from the city/municipal building.

AREA FISHING: Local charter boat operators and freshwater fishing guides offer fishing trips. A sportfishing lodge at Chilkat Lake offers good fishing in a semi-remote setting. Good fishing in the spring for king salmon in **Chilkat Inlet**. Halibut best in summer in **Chilkat**, **Lutak** and **Chilkoot inlets**. Dolly Varden fishing good in all lakes and rivers, and along marine shorelines from early spring to late fall. Great pink salmon fishing in August along the marine shoreline of **Lutak Inlet** and in the **Chilkoot River**. Sockeye salmon in the **Chilkoot River**, late June through Aug. Coho salmon in the **Chilkoot** and **Chilkat rivers**, mid-Sept. through Oct. Cutthroat trout year-round at **Chilkat** and **Mosquito lakes. Herman Lake** is full of hungry grayling stocked there in the mid-1970s. The lake is located off the Sunshine Mountain Road (watch out for logging trucks) accessed from the steel bridge across the Klehini River at **Milepost H 26.3** Haines Highway; get directions locally. For more information, contact the Alaska Deparment of Fish and Game at (907) 766-2625.

Mud Bay Road Log

Mileposts on Mud Bay Road measure distance from its junction with the Haines Highway near Front Street to road end at Mud Bay, a distance of 8 miles/13 km. This road, first paved, then wide gravel, leads to Chilkat State Park, following the shoreline of Chilkat Inlet to Mud Bay on Chilkoot Inlet.
Distance is measured from junction with Haines Highway.

0.1 (0.2 km) Hotel on left, motel and private camper park on right. ▲

0.2 (0.3 km) **Junction** with 3rd Street, which leads back to town.

0.5 (0.8 km) Small Tract Road on left, a 1.9-mile/3.1-km loop road which rejoins Mud Bay Road at **Milepost 2.3.** Small Tract Road leads to private residences and to Bear Creek Camp and Youth Hostel (dorms, cabins and tent camping).

Mud Bay Road leads to the right, following the shoreline of Chilkat Inlet, with views of Pyramid Island. Excellent area for eagle pictures.

2.3 (3.7 km) Stop sign at T intersection: go right for state park, left to return to town via Small Tract Road.

3 (4.8 km) Mount Riley trail on left, parking area on right.

3.9 (6.3 km) View of Pyramid Island and Rainbow Glacier across Chilkat Inlet. Rainbow Glacier, so named because someone once saw a rainbow over it, is a hanging glacier. The ice field moved out over a cliff rather than moving down a valley to the sea. Davidson Glacier is about 2 miles/3.2 km south of Rainbow Glacier.

4.9 (7.9 km) Boat dock on right for small boats (summer tie-off only), boat ramp and pit toilets.

5.2 (8.4 km) Pavement ends, gravel begins.

5.3 (8.5 km) Private road on right to cannery on Letnikof Cove.

6.7 (10.8 km) Turn right and drive in 1.2 miles/1.9 km to entrance of Chilkat State Park (camping area 0.5 mile/0.8 km beyond entrance): 32 campsites, 3 tent sites on beach, $6 nightly fee or annual pass, picnic sites, pit toilets and boat launch. Gravel access road paved and gravel, grades to 11 percent. Drive carefully. Beach access, view of glaciers and hiking trail to Seduction Point at southern tip of Chilkat Peninsula. ▲

8 (12.9 km) Mud Bay Road turns east and crosses Chilkat Peninsula to Flat Bay (commonly called Mud Bay) on Chilkoot Inlet. Road ends at Mud Bay; short walk to rocky beach.

Lutak Road Log

Lutak Road begins at Front Street, and leads north along Chilkoot Inlet past the Alaska Marine Highway ferry terminal, then northwest along Lutak Inlet past Chilkoot Lake Campground to road end, a distance of 10 miles/16 km.
Distance is measured from the junction of Front Street with Lutak Road.

0 Junction, Front Street and Lutak Road.

0.1 (0.2 km) Turnout on right with view of Fort Seward and Lynn Canal.

1.6 (2.6 km) Turnouts along road from here to Mile 7 allow good view of gill-net fleet, July through Sept.

2.4 (3.9 km) Government tank farm, petroleum distribution terminal and beginning of an oil pipeline to Fairbanks. No entry.

3.2 (5.1 km) Dock for oil tankers on right.

3.6 (5.8 km) Alaska Marine Highway ferry terminal on right.

3.8 (6.1 km) City dock on right is used for shipping lumber and also for docking cruise ships and barges.

4.4 (7.1 km) Sawmill.

8.3 (13.4 km) Road on left follows a wide stretch of the Chilkoot River for 1 mile/1.6 km to Chilkoot Lake picnic area and boat launch; state campground with 32 sites just beyond picnic area, 7-day limit, $10 nightly fee or annual pass. ▲

8.4 (13.5 km) Bridge over the mouth of the **Chilkoot River.** Good salmon fishing June through August. Watch for bears.

In 1983, the Chilkoot tribe dedicated Deer Rock here as a historic reminder of the original location of their village.

Road continues to private homes and dead ends; no turnaround.

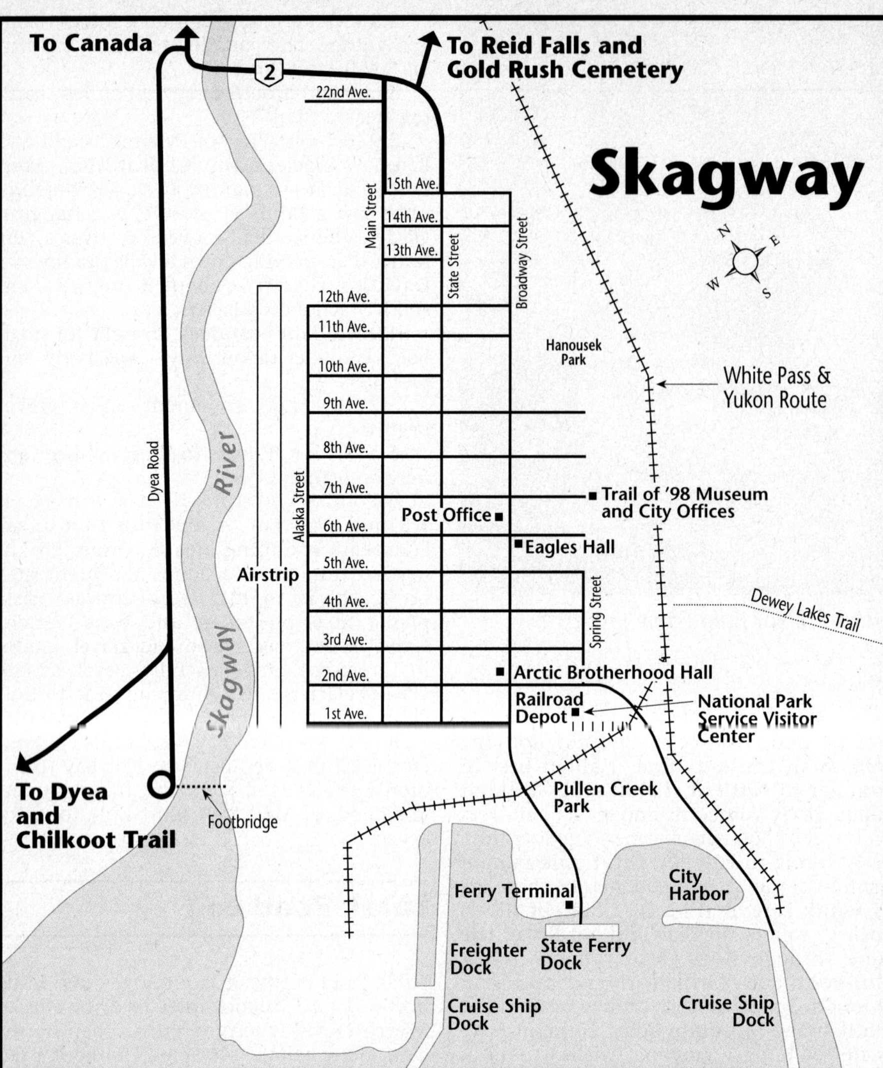

The first boatloads of stampeders bound for the Klondike landed at Skagway in July 1897.

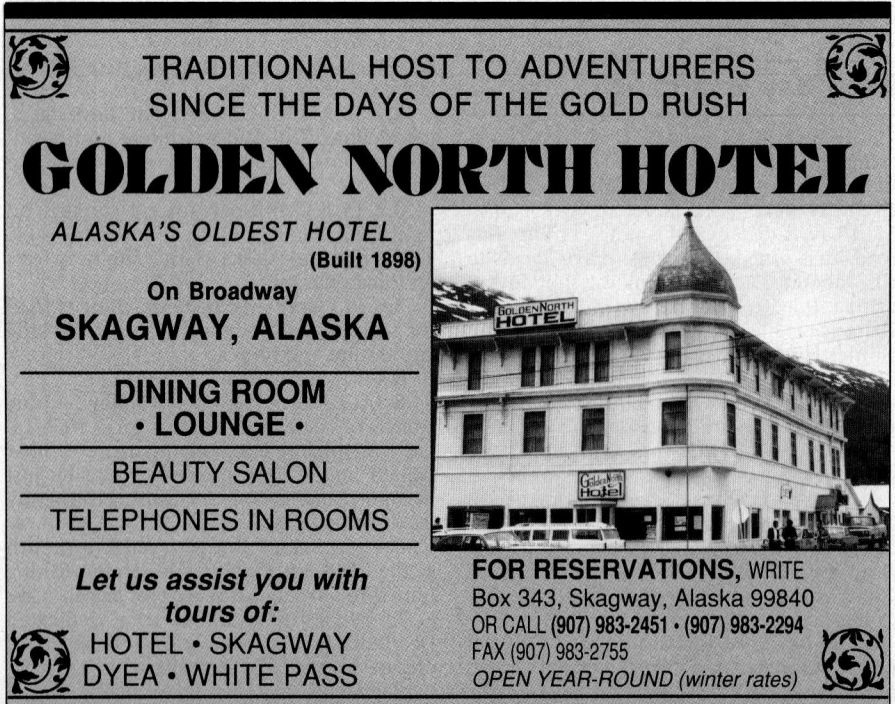

Skagway

(See map, page 634)

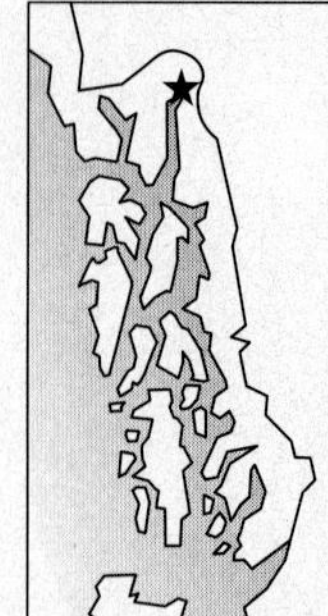

Located on the north end of Taiya Inlet on Lynn Canal, 90 air miles/145 km northwest of Juneau; 108 road miles/174 km south of Whitehorse, YT. The northern terminus of the Alaska Marine Highway Southeast ferry system and southern terminus of Klondike Highway 2 which connects with the Alaska Highway. *NOTE: Although Skagway is only 13 miles/21 km by water from Haines, it is 359 miles/578 km by road!* **Population:** 811. **Emergency Services: Skagway Police Department**, phone (907) 983-2232. **Fire Department** and **Ambulance**, phone 911. **Clinic**, phone (907) 983-2255. **Maritime Search and Rescue**, contact the Coast Guard at 1-800-478-5555.

Visitor Information: Write the Skagway Convention and Visitors Bureau, Box 415MP, Skagway, AK 99840. Phone (907) 983-2854, fax 983-2151. Klondike Gold Rush National Historical Park Visitor Center has exhibits and films on the history of the area and information on hiking the Chilkoot Trail; write Box 517, Skagway, AK 99840; phone (907) 983-2921. Located in the restored railroad depot on 2nd Avenue and Broadway, it is open daily in summer.

Elevation: Sea level. **Climate:** Average daily temperature in summer, 57°F/14°C; in winter, 23°F/-5°C. Average annual precipitation is 29.9 inches. **Radio:** KHNS-FM 91.9. **Newspaper:** *Skagway News* (biweekly).

Private Aircraft: Skagway airport, adjacent west; elev. 44 feet/13m; length 3,700 feet/1,128m; asphalt; fuel 100LL; attended.

The name Skagway (originally spelled Skaguay) is said to mean "home of the north wind" in the local Tlingit dialect. It is the oldest incorporated city in Alaska (incorporated in 1900). Skagway is also a year-round port and 1 of the 2 gateway cities to the Alaska Highway in Southeast Alaska: Klondike Highway 2 connects Skagway with the Alaska Highway. (The other gateway city is Haines, connected to the Alaska Highway via the Haines Highway.)

The first white residents were Capt. William Moore and his son, J. Bernard, who settled in 1887 on the east side of the Skagway River valley (a small part of the Moore homesite was sold for construction of a Methodist college, now the city hall).

But Skagway owes its birth to the Klondike gold rush. Skagway, and the once-thriving town of Dyea, sprang up as thousands of gold seekers arrived to follow the White Pass and Chilkoot trails to the Yukon goldfields.

In July 1897, the first boatloads of stampeders bound for the Klondike landed at Skagway and Dyea. By October 1897, according to a North West Mounted Police report, Skagway had grown "from a concourse of tents to a fair-sized town, with well-laid-out streets and numerous frame buildings, stores, saloons, gambling houses, dance houses and a population of about 20,000." Less than a year later it was reported that "Skagway was little better than a hell on earth." Customs office records for 1898 show that in the month of February alone 5,000 people landed at Skagway and Dyea.

By the summer of 1899 the stampede was all but over. The newly built White Pass & Yukon Route railway reached Lake Bennett, supplanting the Chilkoot Trail from Dyea. Dyea became a ghost town. Its post office closed in 1902, and by 1903 its population consisted of one settler. Skagway's population dwindled to 500. But Skagway persisted, both as a port and as terminus of the White Pass & Yukon Route railway, which connected the town to Whitehorse, YT, in 1900. Cruise ships, and later the Alaska State Ferry System, brought tourism and business to Skagway. Scheduled state ferry service to Southeastern Alaska began in 1963.

Today, tourism is Skagway's main economic base, with Klondike Gold Rush National Historical Park Skagway's major visitor attraction. Within Skagway's downtown historical district, false-fronted buildings and boardwalks dating from gold rush times line the streets. The National Park Service, the city of Skagway and local residents have succeeded in retaining Skagway's Klondike atmosphere.

Skagway has modern schools, churches, a clinic, bank and post office. A U.S. customs office and branch of the U.S. Immigration and Naturalization Service are located at approximately Mile 6.8. Phone or fax customs office at (907) 983-2325, for I.N.S. phone (907) 983-3144. The boat harbor and seaplane base has space for cruisers up to 100 feet/30m. Gas, diesel fuel and water are available.

ACCOMMODATIONS/VISITOR SERVICES

Skagway offers a variety of sleeping accommodations, from gold rush-style hotels and inns to modern motels (reservations are advised in summer).

Historic Skagway Inn Bed & Breakfast, established 1897, located at 7th and Broadway in historic district. Once a gold rush brothel, Victorian-style rooms are comfortable. Hearty breakfast and fresh-ground coffee. Walking distance to shops, museums and trails. Friendly innkeepers can make your reservations for railroad, shows, tours plus arrange transportation to Chilkoot trailhead. Fine dining at Lorna's evenings; Le Cordon Bleu–trained chef. (907) 983-2289. (800) 478-2290 (inside Alaska), fax (907) 983-2713. [ADVERTISEMENT]

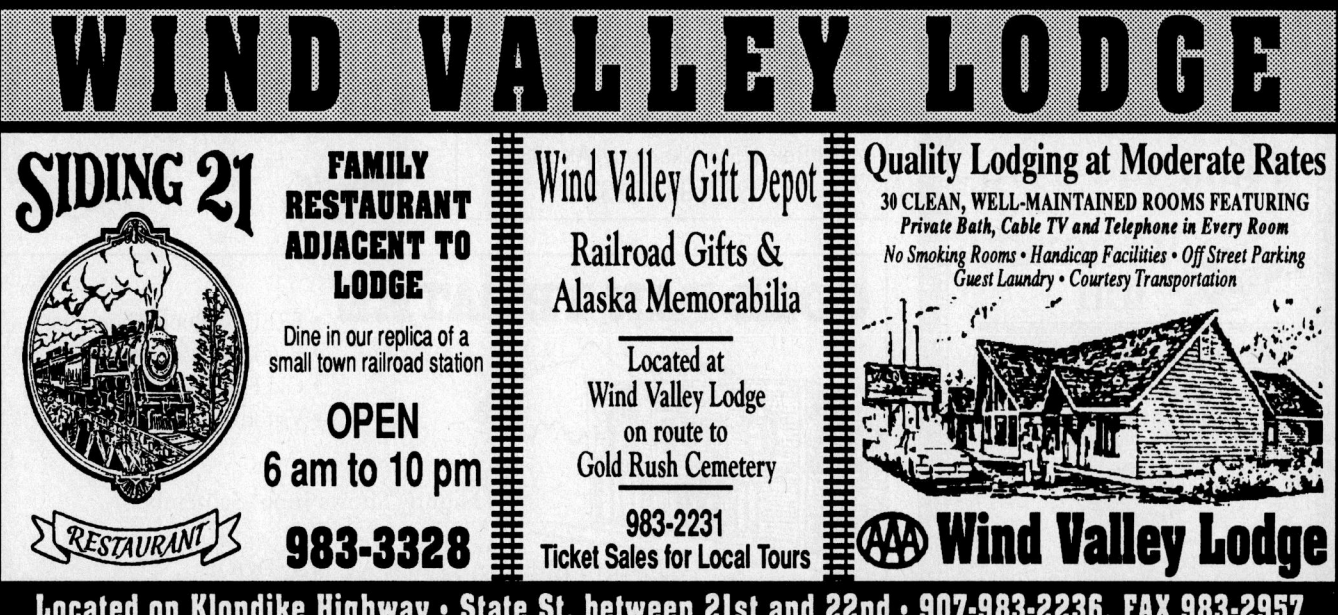

Sergeant Preston's Lodge is the place to stay in Skagway. It's in the heart of turn-of-the century Skagway with 20th century comfort. Very friendly staff who believe in their motto, "We Don't Relax Until You Do." Highly recommended. Rooms start at $60. Phone (907) 983-2521. Fax (907) 983-3500. Open year-round. [ADVERTISEMENT]

There are several restaurants, cafes and bars, grocery, hardware and clothing stores, and many gift and novelty shops offering Alaska and gold rush souvenirs, photos, books, records, gold nugget jewelry, furs and ivory. Propane, marine and automobile gas are available, as is diesel fuel.

There is 1 bank in town (National Bank of Alaska), located at 6th and Broadway; open 10 A.M. to 5 P.M. Monday through Friday in summer.

There are several private campgrounds in Skagway offering hookups, tent sites, restrooms and showers, dump stations and laundromats. A campground for backpackers is located at the Chilkoot Trail trailhead near Dyea. ▲

TRANSPORTATION

Air: Daily scheduled service between Skagway and Haines and Juneau via L.A.B. Flying Service, Skagway Air and Wings of Alaska. Charter service also available between towns and for flightseeing via Skagway Air. Temsco provides helicopter tours. Transportation to and from the airport is provided by the flight services and local hotels.

Bus: Bus/van service to Anchorage, Fairbanks, Haines and Whitehorse, YT.

Car Rental: Three companies.

Taxi: Service in Skagway is tour-oriented. Point-to-point service is limited and not available in winter. Service to Chilkoot Trail trailhead is available.

Highway: Klondike Highway 2 was completed in 1978 and connects Skagway to the Alaska Highway. It is open year-round. See KLONDIKE HIGHWAY 2 section.

Railroad: White Pass & Yukon Route offers 3-hour excursions from Skagway to White Pass Summit and return. Through rail/bus connections are also available daily between Skagway and Whitehorse. See WHITE PASS & YUKON ROUTE section for details.

Ferry: Alaska Marine Highway vessels call regularly year-round, as Skagway is the northern terminus of the Southeast ferry system. See MARINE ACCESS ROUTES section for schedules. The ferry terminal is in the large building on the waterfront (see city map this section); restrooms, pay phone and lockers inside. Ferry terminal office hours vary: opening hours are usually posted at the front door. Phone (907) 983-2941 or 983-2229.

Water-taxi service is available between Haines and Skagway. For schedules and rates, phone (907) 983-2083 in Skagway; 766-3395 in Haines.

Cruise Ships: Skagway is a regular port of call for cruise ships from U.S. and Canadian ports.

The excursion boat MV *Fairweather* cruises to Juneau daily, mid-May to mid-Sept. Operated by Gray Line of Alaska for their package tours, seats may be purchased by the general public on a space-available basis. Contact their Skagway office at the Westmark Hotel (phone 907/983-6000).

Private Boats: Transient moorage is available at the Skagway small-boat harbor. Contact the harbormaster at (907) 983-2628.

ATTRACTIONS

Trail of '98 Museum, owned and operated by the citizens of Skagway, is located at the Arctic Brotherhood Hall on Broadway Street between 2nd and 3rd avenues; open 9 A.M. to 5 P.M. daily in summer (mid-May to mid-Sept.), in winter by appointment; admission is $2 for adults, $1 for students and children. The building is the first granite building constructed in Alaska. It was built by the Methodist Church as a school in 1899–1900 to be known as McCabe College, but public-school laws were passed that made the enterprise impractical, and it was sold to the federal government. For decades it was used as U.S. District Court No. 1 of Alaska, but as the population of the town declined, the court was abandoned and in 1956 the building was purchased by the city.

Sightseers in front of the Arctic Brotherhood Hall on Broadway. (© Barbara Harn)

Since May 1961, the 2nd floor has been open as a museum; the main floor is occupied by City of Skagway offices. The museum's primary interest is to help preserve Alaskan historical material and to display Alaskan pioneer life. The decor of the old courtroom has been preserved, including the judge's bench and chair and some of Soapy Smith's personal items. For more information, phone (907) 983-2420.

Arctic Brotherhood Hall. Located on Broadway between 2nd and 3rd, some 10,000 pieces of driftwood adorn the false front of this 1899 fraternal meeting hall.

See the show *The Days of 1898 Show With Soapy Smith.* This show, produced by Gold Rush Productions, is put on several times a day; summer evening performances (subject to cruise ship arrivals) in Eagles Hall. Check the billboard in front of the hall for show times. The show relates the history of Skagway, from the days of the notorious Soapy Smith. Phone (907) 983-2545.

This show is good family entertainment; bring your camera, gamble with funny money (during evening show only), and enjoy this well-done historical musical comedy. Admission fee charged.

Klondike Gold Rush National Historical Park was authorized in 1976 to preserve and interpret the history of the Klondike gold rush of 1897–98. The park, managed by the National Park Service, consists of 4 units: a 6-block historical district in Skagway's business area; a 1-mile-/1.6-km-wide, 17-mile-/27.4-km-long corridor of land comprising the Chilkoot Trail; a 1-mile-/1.6-km-wide, 5-mile-/8-km-long corridor of land comprising the White Pass Trail; and a visitor center at 117 S. Main St. in Seattle, WA.

In Skagway, the National Park Service offers a variety of free programs in summer. There are daily, guided walking tours of downtown Skagway and ranger talks on a variety of topics. Films are also shown. Check with the Park Service's visitor center in the restored railroad depot on 2nd Avenue and Broadway. Summer (June through August) hours are 8 A.M. to 6 P.M.

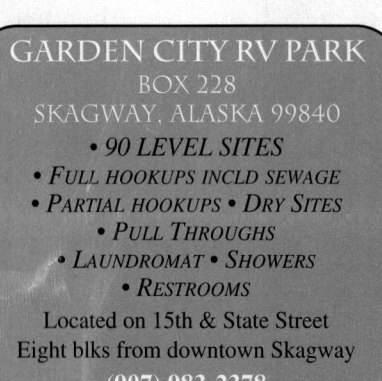

Lynch & Kennedy Dry Goods, established 1908. This historic structure is an original gold rush-era business, restored by the National Park Service and reopened in 1993 by Rosemary and Karl Klupar. Stop by and see the restoration and imagine the hustle and bustle of days gone by. Today the Lynch & Kennedy Dry Goods recreates the excitement of yesteryear and is a fun place to visit. You will find Native art, custom jewelry, quality resort wear, a children's department and home accessories. The Klupars have a special interest in Native art of Alaska. Rosemary has been on buying trips out to most of the remote Native villages, and knows personally the artist's she represents. Everyone at Lynch & Kennedy Dry Goods is there to help you make an informed buying decision; ask for "Little Known Facts about Alaskan Arts & Crafts©" buyers guide. Each piece comes with a biography of the artist and details on how and where the piece was made. The Lynch & Kennedy has made a point of finding quality merchandise not found in every curio shop; many items handcrafted by Alaskan artisans (worthy to be a remembrance of your once-in-a-lifetime trip to the Greatland). Be sure to see Rosemary's Forget-Me-Knot™ line of gold and silver jewelry, a Lynch & Kennedy exclusive. See or be an artist in action! Visit the hand-painted T-shirt section, where you can personalize your own shirt. Enjoy the thrill of printing a custom shirt for yourself or as a one-of-a-kind gift. The staff is trained to assist you in finding something special, answering your questions about their products or Alaska in general. If they don't have what you are looking for, they will find it or refer you to someone who does. All items in the store are available by mail order. Gift wrapping and shipping available. Lynch & Kennedy is open all year. From May 15–Sept. 15, 7 days a week (9 A.M.–10 P.M.) Located at 350 Broadway. Lynch & Kennedy Dry Goods, PO Box 3, Skagway, AK 99840. Phone (907) 983-3034. E-mail to: lynchken@aol.com [ADVERTISEMENT]

McFarlane Trading Co. Alaska. Skagway has a truly excellent shopping district. In terms of diversity, convenience and quality, it is unequaled in Alaska. You find items from all over Alaska in this little port city cradled at the foot of the White Pass and Chilkoot Trail. Among all these "emporia," just 1 door from Skagway's incredible ice cream store, you'll find McFarlane's Trading Company Alaska—a gift shop you must not miss! They have a wide range of genuine Alaskana in jewelry, crafts and carvings, and since Heather McFarlane was a librarian, most items have printed information to go with them. Their special pride is a fantastic collection of scrimshaw, an early American whalers' folk art refined to today's fine art, on fossilized walrus ivory or even mammoth ivory. McFarlane's also has masks and sculptures by Alaska's Eskimos, made from ancient mineralized whalebone, excavated from remote St. Lawrence Island. They also attempt to maintain a wide range of traditionally created Eskimo dolls from all over Alaska. In the summer of 1995, McFarlane's plans to acquire a few fine ivory carvings from Alaska's Eskimo villages. Finally, you'll find dog fur sweaters created by Tagish's Claudia McPhee. McFarlane's has chosen to travel a middle road in terms of price, finding that this is the best way to continue to carry truly Alaskan-made products. (If you are related to the McFarlane Clan, this shop has information on U.S. Clan McFarlane Societies.) [ADVERTISEMENT]

Hike the Chilkoot Trail. This 33-mile/53-km trail begins on Dyea Road (see log this section) and climbs Chilkoot Pass (elev. 3,739 feet/1,140m) to Lake Bennett, following the historic route of the gold seekers of '98. The trail is arduous but offers both spectacular scenery and historical relics. There are several campgrounds and shelters along the route. Hikers planning to take the Chilkoot Trail should check with Parks Canada in Whitehorse, phone (403) 667-

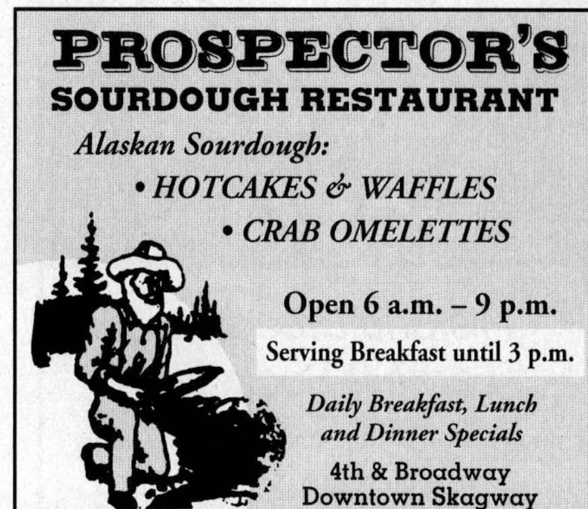

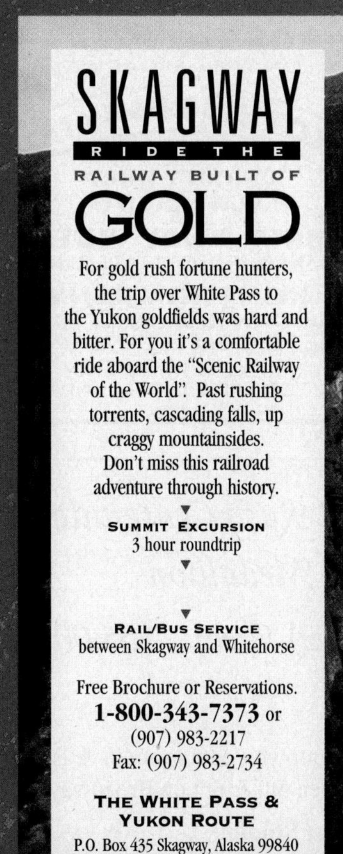

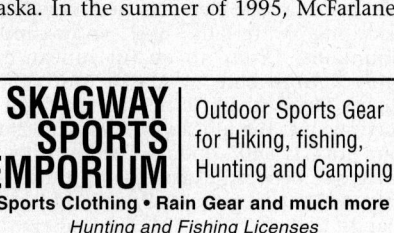

3910. Detailed information and maps of the trail are available from the National Park Service (Box 517, Skagway 99840). *The ALASKA WILDERNESS GUIDE* also has details on the Chilkoot Trail, and "Chilkoot Pass" by Archie Satterfield is a good hiking and history guide to the trail.

Corrington Museum of Alaska History, located at 5th and Broadway, offers a unique record of events from prehistory to the present. Each of the 40 exhibits at the museum features a scene from Alaska history hand-engraved (scrimshawed) on a walrus tusk. The museum is open in summer. Free admission.

Picnic at Pullen Creek Park. This attractive waterfront park has a covered picnic shelter, 2 footbridges and 2 small docks. It is located between the cruise ship and ferry docks, behind the White Pass & Yukon Route depot. Watch for pink salmon in the intertidal waters in August, silver salmon in September.

Helicopter and airplane tours of Skagway and White Pass are available in summer.

Gold Rush Cemetery is 1.5 miles/2.4 km from downtown and makes a nice walk. Go north on State Street to a sign pointing to the cemetery. Follow dirt road across tracks into railroad yard, follow posted direction signs, then continue about 0.4 mile/0.6 km farther to the cemetery. If you drive in, a circular road around the cemetery eliminates having to back up to get out. A path on left at the end of the road leads to the cemetery where the graves of both "bad guy" Soapy Smith and "good guy" Frank Reid are located (both men died in a gunfight in July 1898). Smith's original gravestone was whittled away by souvenir hunters, and the resting place of the feared boss of Skagway is now marked by a metal marker.

Reid Falls are located near Gold Rush Cemetery, and it is only a short hike from Frank Reid's grave to view them.

AREA FISHING: Local charter boat operators offer fishing trips. The ADF&G Sport Fish Division recommends the following areas and species. Dolly Varden: Fish the shore of **Skagway Harbor, Long Bay** and **Taiya Inlet**, May through June. Try the **Taiya River** by the steel bridge in Dyea in early spring or fall; use red and white spoons or salmon eggs. Pink salmon fishing is good at the small local hatchery. Fish **Skagway Harbor** and **Pullen Creek** in town, July and August; use flashing lures. Coho and chum salmon near the steel bridge on the **Taiya River**, mid-Sept. through Oct. Trolling in the marine areas is good but often dangerous for small boats. Trout: A steep trail near town will take you to Dewey lakes, which were stocked with Colorado brook trout in the 1920s. **Lower Dewey Lake,** 1/2-hour to 1-hour hike; heavily wooded shoreline, use raft. The brook trout are plentiful and grow to 16 inches but are well fed, so fishing can be frustrating. **Upper Dewey Lake,** a steep 2 1/2-hour to 4-hour hike to above tree line, is full of hungry brook trout to 11 inches. Use salmon eggs or size #10 or #12 artificial flies. **Lost Lake** is reached via a rough trail near Dyea (ask locals for directions). The lake lies at about elev. 1,300 feet/396m and has a good population of rainbow trout. Use small spinners or spoons. For more information, contact the ADF&G office in Haines at (907) 766-2625.

Dyea Road Log

The Dyea Road begins at **Milepost S 2.3** on Klondike Highway 2. It leads southwest toward Yakutania Point, then northwest past Long Bay and the Taiya River to the beginning of the Chilkoot Trail and to a side road leading to the old Dyea townsite and Slide Cemetery. The Dyea Road is a narrow winding gravel road.

Distance is from the junction with Klondike Highway 2.

0 Junction.

0.1 (0.2 km) Old cemetery on right.

0.4 (0.6 km) View of Reid Falls east across the Skagway River.

1.4 (2.3 km) A scenic wayside with platform on left southbound affords view of Skagway, Taiya Inlet and the Skagway River.

1.7 (2.7 km) A steep, primitive road on left southbound descends 0.4 mile/0.6 km toward bank of the Skagway River, with a view of the Skagway waterfront and Taiya Inlet.

Drive to parking area and walk 0.2 mile/0.3 km to Yakutania Point; horse trail beyond parking area. Bridge at base of hill leads to a short trail back to town. Dyea Road turns northwest along Long Bay at this point.

1.9 (3.1 km) Skyline trailhead (poorly signed). This trail leads to top of AB Mountain (elev. 5,000 feet/1,524m).

2.1 (3.4 km) Head of Long Bay.

4 (6 km) City dump.

4.3 (6.9 km) Taiya Inlet comes into view on left northbound as the road curves away from Long Bay.

5.1 (8.2 km) View of the old pilings in Taiya Inlet. The docks of Dyea used to stretch from the trees to beyond the pilings, which are still visible. These long docks were needed to reach deep water because of the great tidal range in this inlet.

5.7 (9.2 km) Hooligan (smelt) run here in the Taiya River in May and early June. Local swimming hole across the road.

6.5 (10.5 km) Dyea information display.

6.7 (10.8 km) Chilkoot Trail trailhead campground, parking area and ranger station.

7.2 (11.6 km) The Chilkoot Trail begins on right northbound. Bridge over Taiya River.

7.4 (11.9 km) A primitive road on left northbound leads southwest to Slide Cemetery (keep right at forks and follow signs) and old Dyea townsite. The cemetery, reached by a short unmarked path through the woods, contains the graves of men killed in the Palm Sunday avalanche, April 3, 1898, on the Chilkoot Trail. At Dyea townsite, covered with fireweed and lupine in summer, hardly a trace remains of the buildings that housed 8,000 people here during the gold rush. About 30 people live in the valley today.

8.4 (13.5 km) Steel bridge across West Creek. Four-wheel drive recommended beyond this point.

WHITE PASS & YUKON ROUTE

White Pass & Yukon Route train near Summit Lake. (Earl L. Brown, staff)

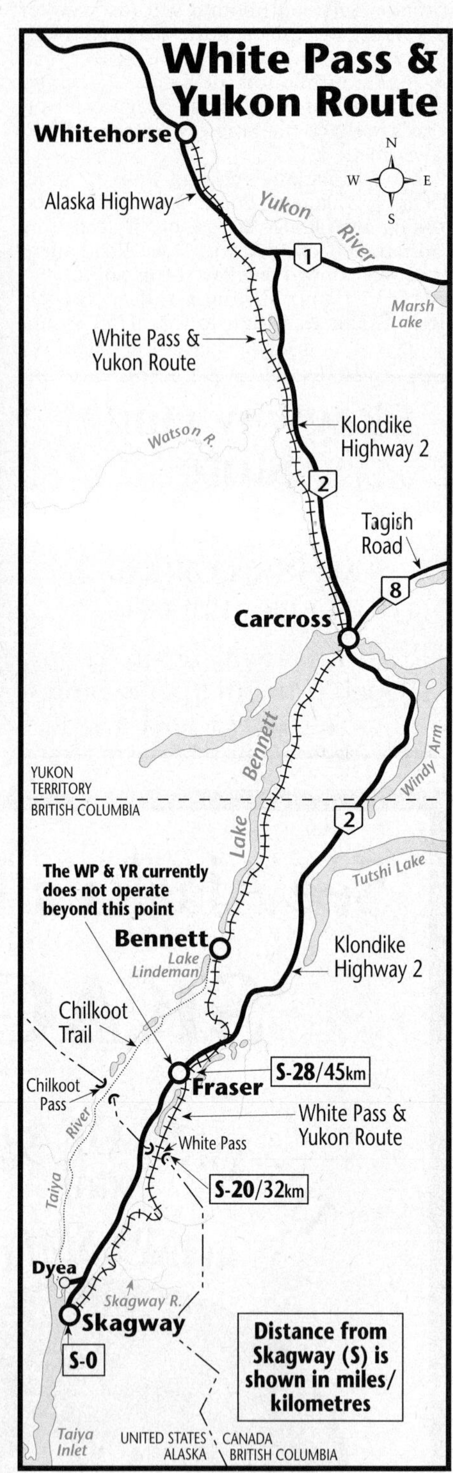

The White Pass & Yukon Route (WP&YR) is a narrow-gauge (36-inch) privately owned railroad built in 1898 at the height of the Klondike gold rush. Between 1900 and 1982, the WP&YR provided passenger and freight service between Skagway, AK, and Whitehorse, YT. The WP&YR no longer offers rail service to Whitehorse.

The WP&YR now operates a 3-hour round-trip train excursion between Skagway and the White Pass Summit, and a combination train and bus trip between Skagway and Whitehorse. In 1994, the White Pass & Yukon Route was declared an International Historic Civil Engineering Landmark, one of only 15 in the world.

Construction of the WP&YR began in May 1898. It was the first railroad in Alaska and at the time the most northern of any railroad in North America. The railroad reached White Pass in February 1899 and Whitehorse in July 1900.

The railroad follows the old White Pass trail. The upper section of the old "Deadhorse" trail near the summit (Mile 19 on the WP&YR railway) is visible beside the tracks. During the Klondike gold rush, thousands of men took the 40-mile/64-km White Pass trail from Skagway to Lake Bennett, where they built boats to float down the Yukon River to Dawson City and the goldfields.

The WP&YR has one of the steepest railroad grades in North America. From sea level at Skagway the railroad climbs to 2,885 feet/879m at White Pass in only 20 miles/32 km of track. Currently, the railroad offers train service on 28 miles/45 km of track between Skagway and Fraser, BC.

Following are services, schedules and fares (U.S. funds) available on the 2 routes offered by White Pass & Yukon Route from mid-May to mid-September 1996. *NOTE: There is no train service to Lake Bennett in 1996.* All times indicated in schedules are local times (Skagway is on Alaska Time, which is 1 hour earlier than Whitehorse, which is on Pacific Time.) Children 12 and under ride for half fare when accompanied by an adult. Children under 2 years ride free if not occupying a seat; half fare for separate seat. Reservations are required. For reservations and information, contact the White Pass & Yukon Route, P.O. Box 435, Skagway, AK 99840. Phone toll free in the U.S. 1-800-343-7373 or (907) 983-2217 in Skagway. Toll free in western Canada, 1-800-478-7373.

SUMMIT EXCURSION

This approximately 3-hour round-trip excursion features the most spectacular part of the WP&YR railway, including the steep climb to White Pass Summit, Bridal Veil Falls, Inspiration Point and Dead Horse Gulch. Offered twice daily from May 13 to Sept. 20, 1996, the morning train departs Skagway at 8:45 A.M. and returns at 11:45 A.M.; the afternoon train departs Skagway at 1:15 P.M. and returns at 4:15 P.M. Fares are $75 for adults and $37.50 for children 12 and under.

SKAGWAY TO WHITEHORSE

Through-service between Skagway, AK, and Whitehorse, YT, is offered daily from May 21 to Sept. 14, 1996. Through passengers travel 28 miles/45km by train between Skagway, AK, and Fraser, BC, and then 87 miles/140 km by bus between Fraser and Whitehorse, YT. The train portion of this trip takes passengers over historic White Pass Summit. Northbound service departs Skagway at 12:40 P.M., and arrives Whitehorse at 6 P.M. Southbound service departs Whitehorse at 8 A.M. and arrives Skagway at noon. One-way fares are $95 for adults and $47.50 for children 12 and under.

HAINES HIGHWAY

Haines, Alaska, to Haines Junction, Yukon Territory
Alaska Route 7, British Columbia Highway 4 and Yukon Highway 3
(See map, page 692)

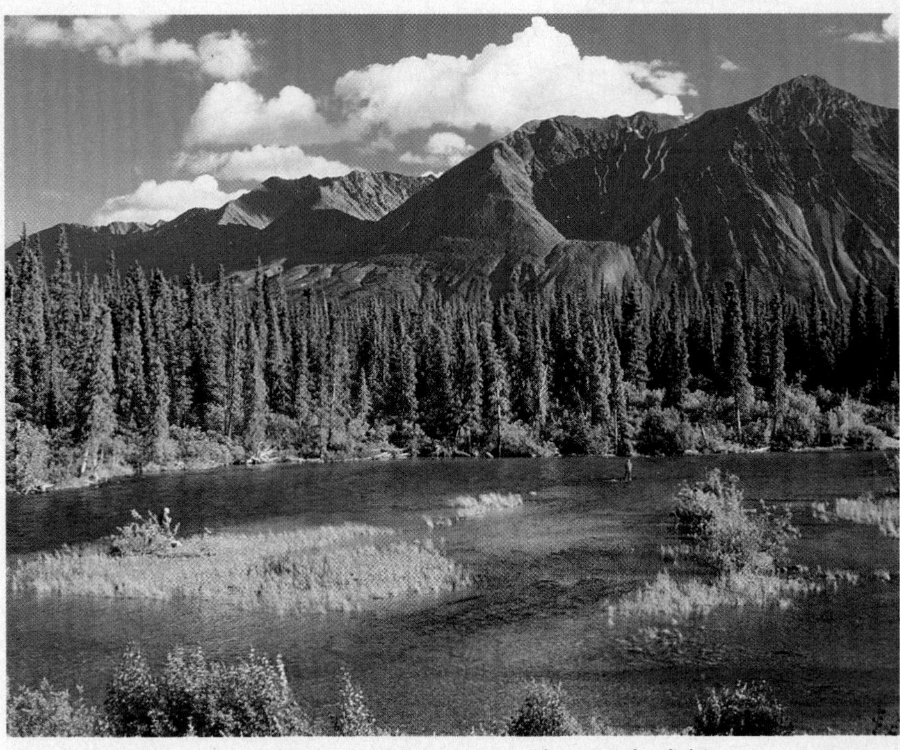

The Kathleen River at Milepost H 135.8 is a popular spot for fishing. (Earl L. Brown, staff)

The paved 151.6-mile-/244-km-long Haines Highway connects Haines, AK (on the state ferry route), at the head of Lynn Canal with the Alaska Highway at Haines Junction, YT. The highway is open year-round. Allow about 4 hours' driving time. Watch for logging and fuel trucks. *NOTE: In summer, gas is available along the highway only at 33 Mile Roadhouse and at Kathleen Lake Lodge,* ***Milepost H 135.2.***

Noted for the grandeur and variety of its alpine scenery, the highway leads from coastal forests near Haines through the Chilkat Eagle Preserve up over the backbone of the St. Elias Mountains, skirting Tatshenshini–Alsek Wilderness Provincial Park, and running along the eastern border of Kluane National Park Reserve and down into the valleys of the Yukon basin. Information on Kluane National Park Reserve is available in Haines Junction, YT.

Part of what is now the Haines Highway was originally a "grease trail" used by the coastal Chilkat Indians trading eulachon oil for furs from the Interior. In the late 1880s, Jack Dalton developed a packhorse trail to the Klondike goldfields along the old trading route. The present road was built in 1943 as a military access highway during WWII to provide an alternative route from the Pacific tidewater into Yukon Territory.

This historic corridor is celebrated each year during Dalton Trail Days, July 1–4. Watch for bikes on the highway during the annual Kluane/Chilkat International Bike Race (June 22, 1996). Some 650 cyclists participated in 1995.

U.S. and Canada customs stations are located about 40 miles/64 km north of Haines. U.S. customs is open from 7 A.M. to 11 P.M. (Alaska time); Canada customs is open from 8 A.M. to midnight (Pacific time). There are no facilities or accommodations at the border. All travelers must stop.

A valid Alaska fishing license is required for fishing along the highway between Haines and the international border at **Milepost H 40.7.** The highway then crosses the northern tip of British Columbia into Yukon Territory. You must have valid fishing licenses for both British Columbia and Yukon Territory if you fish these areas, and a national park fishing license if you fish waters in Kluane National Park.

If you plan to drive the Haines Highway in winter, check road conditions before starting out and carry adequate emergency equipment. In Haines Junction check with the maintenance garage (403/634-2227) or the RCMP (403/634-5555).

Emergency medical services: Between Haines and the U.S.–Canada border at **Milepost H 40.7**, phone 911. Between the U.S.–Canada border and Haines Junction, phone the RCMP at (403) 634-5555.

Haines Highway Log

ALASKA ROUTE 7

Driving distance is measured in miles from Haines, AK. Mileposts are up along the Alaska portion of the highway. The kilometre figures on the Canadian portion of the highway reflect the physical kilometreposts and are not an accurate metric conversion of the mileage figure.

Distance from Haines (H) is followed by distance from Haines Junction (HJ).

H 0 HJ 151.6 (244 km) **HAINES.** See HAINES section for accommodations and facilities.

H 0.2 (0.3 km) **HJ 151.4** (243.7 km) Front Street.

H 0.4 (0.6 km) **HJ 151.2** (243.4 km) Second Street. Turn right northbound (left southbound) for visitor information center and downtown Haines.

H 0.5 (0.8 km) **HJ 151.1** (243.2 km) Third Street. Turn right northbound (left southbound) for downtown Haines.

H 1 (1.6 km) **HJ 150.6** (242.4 km) Haines Hitch–Up RV Park. ▲

H 1.2 (1.9 km) **HJ 150.4** (242.1 km) Main Street Y. If southbound, turn right to Fort William H. Seward, left to downtown Haines.

H 1.3 (2.1 km) **HJ 150.3** (241.9 km) Eagle's Nest Motel.

H 3.3 (5.3 km) **HJ 148.3** (238.7 km) Indian graveyard on the right northbound.

H 3.5 (5.6 km) **HJ 148.1** (238.3 km) **Private Aircraft**: Haines airport; elev. 16 feet/5m; length 3,000 feet/914m; asphalt; fuel 100; unattended.

The Chilkat River estuary, which the highway parallels for the next 15 miles/24 km, flows into Chilkat Inlet of Lynn Canal, a massive fjord about 60 miles/96.5 km long. Lynn Canal was named by English explorer Captain Vancouver for his birthplace (King's Lynn) in England. The yellow signs along the highway indicate mileages on the U.S. Army oil pipeline. The pipeline formerly pumped oil from Haines over the St. Elias Mountains to the Alaska Highway at Haines Junction, YT. These signs were used for aerial checking and monitoring of the line.

H 4.3 (6.9 km) **HJ 147.3** (237 km) Turnout along river.

H 6 (9.6 km) **HJ 145.6** (234.3 km) Picnic spot next to Chilkat River and a clear creek.

H 6.6 (10.6 km) **HJ 145** (233.3 km) Mount Ripinski trailhead.

H 8 (12.8 km) **HJ 143.6** (231.1 km)

HAINES HIGHWAY *Haines, AK, to Haines Junction, YT*

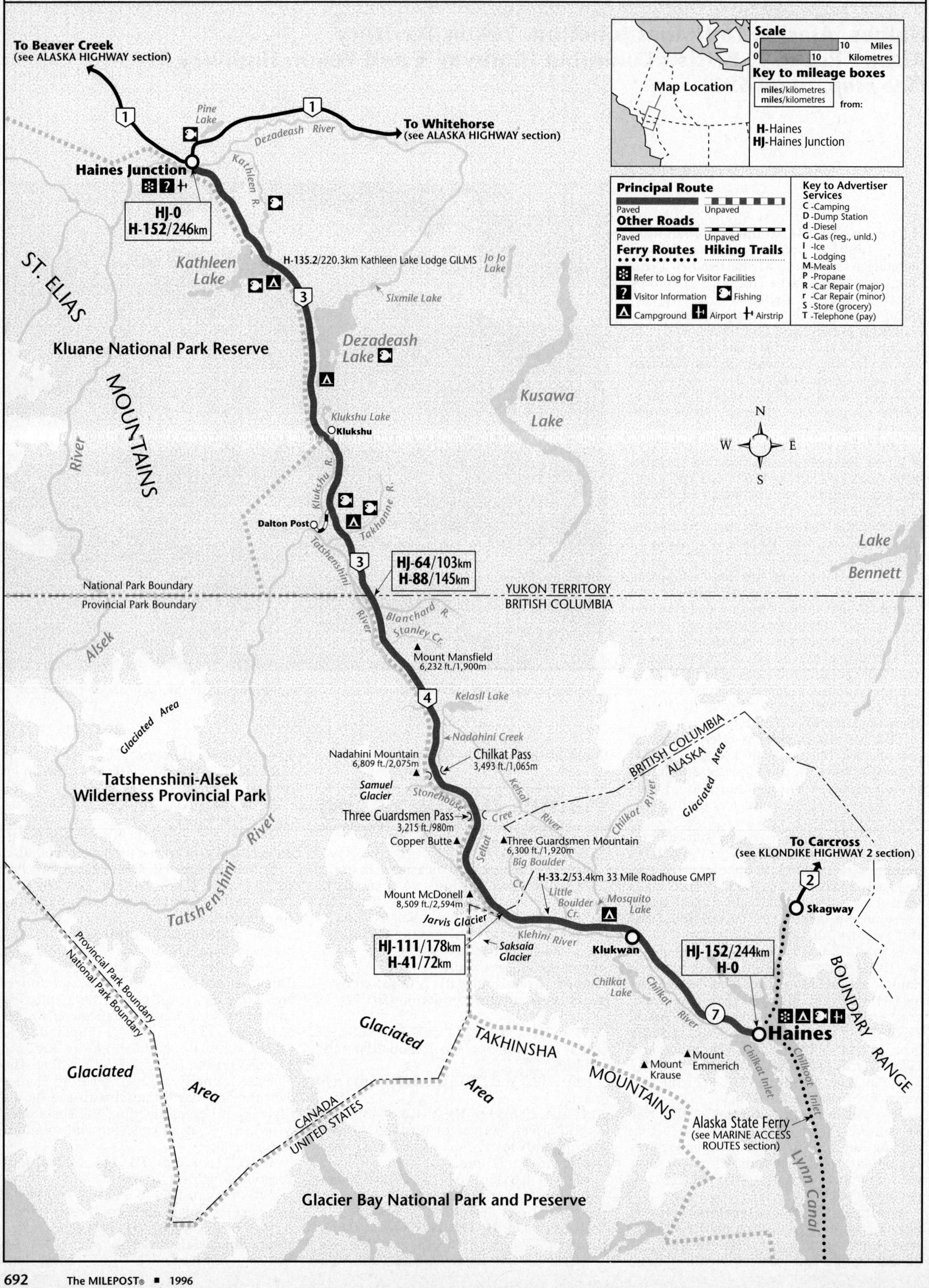

Scale
0 10 Miles
0 10 Kilometres

Key to mileage boxes
miles/kilometres
miles/kilometres
from:
H-Haines
HJ-Haines Junction

Map Location

Principal Route
Paved
Unpaved
Other Roads
Paved
Unpaved
Ferry Routes
Hiking Trails
Refer to Log for Visitor Facilities
Visitor Information
Fishing
Campground
Airport
Airstrip

Key to Advertiser Services
C -Camping
D -Dump Station
d -Diesel
G -Gas (reg., unld.)
I -Ice
L -Lodging
M-Meals
P -Propane
R -Car Repair (major)
r -Car Repair (minor)
S -Store (grocery)
T -Telephone (pay)

To Beaver Creek
(see ALASKA HIGHWAY section)

To Whitehorse
(see ALASKA HIGHWAY section)

Pine Lake
Dezadeash River
Kathleen R.
Haines Junction
HJ-0
H-152/246km
ST. ELIAS
MOUNTAINS
Kathleen Lake
H-135.2/220.3km Kathleen Lake Lodge GILMS
Jo Jo Lake
Sixmile Lake
Kluane National Park Reserve
Dezadeash Lake
Kusawa Lake
Klukshu Lake
Klukshu
River
Klukshu R.
Takhanne R.
Dalton Post
Tatshenshini
HJ-64/103km
H-88/145km
Lake Bennett
National Park Boundary
Provincial Park Boundary
YUKON TERRITORY
BRITISH COLUMBIA
River
Blanchard R.
Stanley Cr.
Alsek
Mount Mansfield
6,232 ft./1,900m
Kelasll Lake
Glaciated Area
Nadahini Creek
Nadahini Mountain
6,809 ft./2,075m
Chilkat Pass
3,493 ft./1,065m
BRITISH COLUMBIA
ALASKA
Glaciated Area
Samuel Glacier
Stonehouse
Kelsal
Tatshenshini-Alsek Wilderness Provincial Park
Three Guardsmen Pass
3,215 ft./980m
Cree
River
Chilkat River
Copper Butte
Three Guardsmen Mountain
6,300 ft./1,920m
Big Boulder Cr.
Seltat
River
Tatshenshini
To Carcross
(see KLONDIKE HIGHWAY 2 section)
H-33.2/53.4km 33 Mile Roadhouse GMPT
Mount McDonell
8,509 ft./2,594m
Little Boulder Cr.
Mosquito Lake
Jarvis Glacier
Skagway
Klehini River
Saksaia Glacier
Klukwan
HJ-111/178km
H-41/72km
HJ-152/244km
H-0
Provincial Park Boundary
National Park Boundary
Chilkat Lake
Chilkat River
BOUNDARY RANGE
Haines
Glaciated Area
TAKHINSHA MOUNTAINS
Glaciated Area
Mount Krause
Mount Emmerich
Chilkat Inlet
Chilkoot Inlet
CANADA
UNITED STATES
Alaska State Ferry
(see MARINE ACCESS ROUTES section)
Lynn Canal
Glacier Bay National Park and Preserve

Watch for subsistence fish camps along the highway in June. Also watch for fish wheels on the river.

H 9.2 (14.8 km) **HJ 142.4** (229.2 km) Entering Alaska Chilkat Bald Eagle Preserve northbound. Established in 1982, the 48,000-acre preserve is the seasonal home to more than 3,000 bald eagles, which gather each year to feed on the late run of chum salmon. Eagle-viewing area begins at **Milepost H 19**; best viewing is mid-October to January.

H 9.6 (15.4 km) **HJ 142** (228.5 km) Magnificent view of Takhinsha Mountains across Chilkat River. This range extends north from the Chilkat Range; Glacier Bay is on the other side. Prominent peaks are Mount Krause and Mount Emmerich (elev. 6,405 feet/1,952m) in the Chilkat Range.

H 14.7 (23.6 km) **HJ 136.9** (220.3 km) Watch for mountain goats on the ridges.

H 17.6 (28.3 km) **HJ 134** (215.6 km) Rustic barn and old cabins. Good photo shots.

H 18.8 (30.3 km) **HJ 132.8** (213.7 km) Slide area.

H 19 (30.6 km) **HJ 132.6** (213.4 km) Begin eagle viewing area (northbound) on Chilkat River flats. Best viewing is mid-October to January. *CAUTION: Eagle watchers, use turnouts and park well off highway!*

H 21.4 (34.4 km) **HJ 130.2** (209.5 km) Turnoff to Indian village of **KLUKWAN**. Gravel access road dead ends at village. No visitor facilities.

H 22 (35.4 km) **HJ 129.6** (208.5 km) Second access northbound to Klukwan (steep grade).

H 23.8 (38.3 km) **HJ 127.8** (205.6 km) Chilkat River bridge. Highway now follows Klehini River. Watch for eagles beginning in late summer.

H 26.3 (42.3 km) **HJ 125.3** (201.6 km) Road west leads across Klehini River; turn off here for jet boat landing on Tsirku River for Birch Island Lodge on Chilkat Lake.

H 27.3 (43.9 km) **HJ 124.3** (200 km) Mosquito Lake State Recreation Site campground; 10 sites, tables, water, toilets, $6/night or annual pass. Mosquito Lake general store. ▲

H 28.8 (46.3 km) **HJ 122.8** (197.6 km) Muncaster Creek bridge.

H 30.9 (49.7 km) **HJ 120.7** (194.2 km) Leaving Alaska Chilkat Bald Eagle Preserve northbound.

H 31.6 (50.9 km) **HJ 120** (193.1 km) Bridge over Little Boulder Creek.

H 33.2 (53.4 km) **HJ 118.4** (190.5 km) Roadhouse with food, gas and phone. Store. *NOTE: Last available gas northbound until Kathleen Lake Lodge. Check your gas tank.*

33 Mile Roadhouse. See display ad this section.

H 33.8 (54.4 km) **HJ 117.8** (189.6 km) Bridge over Big Boulder Creek. Watch for salmon swimming upstream during spawning season. Closed to salmon fishing.

H 36.2 (58.3 km) **HJ 115.4** (185.7 km) View of Saksaia Glacier.

H 40.4 (65 km) **HJ 111.2** (179 km) U.S. customs, Dalton Cache station. All travelers entering United States MUST STOP. Open year-round 7 A.M. to 11 P.M., Alaska time. Restrooms, large parking area.

Jarvis Glacier moraine is visible from the old Dalton Cache (on the National Register of Historic Places), located behind the customs building.

H 40.7 (65.5 km) **HJ 110.9** (178.5 km) U.S.–Canada border. Last milepost marker is Mile 40, first kilometrepost marker is Kilometrepost 74, northbound.

TIME ZONE CHANGE: Alaska observes Alaska time, Canada observes Pacific time. See Time Zones in the GENERAL INFORMATION section.

BC HIGHWAY 4

H 40.8 (71.8 km) **HJ 110.8** (178.3 km) Canada Customs and Immigration office at Pleasant Camp. All travelers entering Canada MUST STOP. Office is open year-round 8 A.M. to midnight, Pacific time. No public facilities.

H 44.9 (78.5 km) **HJ 106.7** (171.7 km) Bridge over Fivemile Creek.

H 49.4 (80.3 km) **HJ 102.2** (164.5 km) Large gravel double-ended turnout at **Historical Mile 48**; information panels on Haines Road history.

Good viewpoint for Tatshenshini–Alsek Wilderness Provincial Park. This new (1993) park encompasses the rugged northwest corner of British Columbia and is dominated by the St. Elias Mountains. It is also habitat for grizzly bears, Dall sheep, the rare "glacier" bear and also rare birds such as the king eider and Stellar's eider. The Tatshenshini and Alsek rivers are famous for their river rafting and sightseeing opportunities.

H 49.7 (86 km) **HJ 101.9** (164 km) Highway crosses Seltat Creek. This is eagle country; watch for them soaring over the uplands. Three Guardsmen Mountain (elev. 6,300 feet/1,920m) to the east.

H 53.9 (92 km) **HJ 97.7** (157.2 km) Three Guardsmen Lake to the east. Glave Peak, part of Three Guardsmen Mountain, rises directly behind the lake.

H 55.1 (94.6 km) **HJ 96.5** (155.3 km) Three Guardsmen Pass to the northeast, hidden by low hummocks along the road. Stonehouse Creek meanders through a pass at the base of Seltat Peak to join the Kelsall River about 6 miles/10 km to the east. To the north is the Kusawak Range; to the south is Three Guardsmen Mountain. The tall poles along the highway indicate the edge of the road for snowplows.

H 55.8 (95.8 km) **HJ 95.8** (154.2 km) Stonehouse Creek culvert.

H 56.2 (96.3 km) **HJ 95.4** (153.5 km) Clear Creek culvert.

H 59.8 (102.1 km) **HJ 91.8** (147.7 km) Double-ended paved turnout on west side of highway at Chilkat Pass, highest summit on this highway (elev. 3,493 feet/1,065m). White Pass Summit on Klondike Highway 2 is 3,290 feet/1,003m. The wind blows almost constantly on the summit and causes drifting snow and road closures in winter. The summit area is a favorite with snow machine and cross-country ski enthusiasts in winter. Snow until late May.

The Chilkat Pass was one of the few mountain passes offering access into the Yukon from the coast. The Chilkat and the Chilkoot passes were tenaciously guarded by Tlingit Indians. These southern Yukon Indians did not want their lucrative fur-trading business with the coastal Indians and Russians jeopardized by white strangers. But the gold rush of 1898, which brought thousands of white people inland, finally opened Chilkat Pass, forever altering the lifestyle of the Interior Natives.

From the Chilkat Pass over Glacier Flats to Stanley Creek, the highway crosses silt-laden streams flowing from the Crestline Glacier. Nadahini Mountain (elev. 6,809 feet/2,075m) to the northwest. Three Guardsmen Mountain to the southeast.

H 63 (107 km) **HJ 88.6** (142.6 km) Chuck Creek culvert.

H 64.4 (109.3 km) **HJ 87.2** (140.3 km) Nadahini River culvert.

H 67.8 (114.7 km) **HJ 83.8** (134.8 km) **Private Aircraft:** Mule Creek airstrip; elev. 2,900 feet/884m; length 4,000 feet/1,219m; gravel. No services.

H 68.9 (116.4 km) **HJ 82.7** (133 km) Mule Creek.

H 73.6 (124.2 km) **HJ 78** (125.5 km) Goat Creek bridge. Watch for horses on road.

H 75.7 (127.3 km) **HJ 75.9** (122.1 km) Holum Creek.

H 80.1 (128.9 km) **HJ 71.5** (115.1 km) Mansfield Creek.

H 81.3 (136.3 km) **HJ 70.3** (113.1 km) Stanley Creek bridge.

H 86.5 (143.6 km) **HJ 65.1** (104.8 km) Blanchard River bridge.

H 87.1 (144.5 km) **HJ 64.5** (103.8 km) Welcome to Yukon sign.

H 87.4 (145 km) **HJ 64.2** (103.3 km) Entering Kluane Game Sanctuary northbound.

H 87.5 (145.2 km) **HJ 64.1** (103.1 km) BC–YT border. Former U.S. Army Alaska–Blanchard River Petroleum pump station, now a highway maintenance camp.

YUKON HIGHWAY 3

H 90.7 (150.7 km) **HJ 60.9** (98 km) Blanchard River Gorge to west.

H 91 (146.4 km) **HJ 60.6** (97.5 km) Large paved turnout.

H 96.2 (159.4 km) **HJ 55.4** (89.1 km) Yukon government Million Dollar Falls Campground on opposite side of Takhanne River; follow access road 0.7 mile/1.1 km west. Boardwalk trail and viewing platform of scenic falls. View of the St. Elias Mountains. Two kitchen shelters, tenting and group firepit, 27 campsites, $8 fee, playground and drinking water (boil water).

Glacier-fed Kathleen Lake offers fishing for lake trout, kokanee and grayling.
(Earl L. Brown, staff)

Walk-in tent sites available. ▲

Good fishing below **Takhanne Falls** for grayling, Dolly Varden, rainbow and salmon. **Takhanne River**, excellent king salmon fishing in early July.

CAUTION: The Takhanne, Blanchard, Tatshenshini and Klukshu rivers are grizzly feeding areas. Exercise extreme caution when fishing or exploring in these areas.

H 96.3 (159.5 km) **HJ 55.3** (89 km) Takhanne River bridge.

H 96.4 (159.7 km) **HJ 55.2** (88.8 km) Parking area at Million Dollar Falls trailhead to west.

H 98.3 (162.6 km) **HJ 53.3** (85.8 km) Large paved turnout with good view of Kluane Range; viewing platform, litter barrels, outhouse.

H 99.5 (164.5 km) **HJ 52.1** (83.8 km) Turnoff to historic Dalton Post, a way point on the Dalton Trail. Steep, narrow, winding access road; four-wheel drive recommended in wet weather. Road not recommended for large RVs or trailers at any time. Several old abandoned log cabins and buildings are located here. Indians once formed a human barricade at Dalton Post to harvest the Klukshu River's run of coho salmon.

Fishing for chinook, coho, sockeye salmon in **Village Creek**. Grayling, Dolly Varden and salmon in **Klukshu River.** Fishing restrictions posted. *CAUTION: Watch for bears.*

H 103.4 (169.7 km) **HJ 48.2** (77.5 km) Viewpoint with information sign to west. Alsek Range to southwest.

H 104 (170.7 km) **HJ 47.6** (76.6 km) Motheral Creek culvert.

H 106.1 (174 km) **HJ 45.5** (73.2 km) Vand Creek.

H 110.8 (181.6 km) **HJ 40.8** (65.6 km) Klukshu Creek.

H 111.6 (183 km) **HJ 40** (64.4 km) Turnoff for **KLUKSHU**, an Indian village, located 0.5 mile/0.8 km off the highway via a gravel road. This summer fish camp and village on the banks of the Klukshu River is a handful of log cabins, meat caches and traditional fish traps. Steelhead, king, sockeye and coho salmon are taken here. Each autumn families return for the annual catch. The site is on the old Dalton Trail and offers good photo possibilities. Museum (open sporadically), picnic spot, souvenirs for sale.

Kluane National Park Reserve borders the highway to the west from here to Haines Junction (the visitor centre there has information on the park). Watch for signs for hiking trails, which are posted 3.1 miles/5 km before trailheads. For more information on the park, contact Kluane National Park Reserve, Parks Canada, Box 5495, Haines Junction, YT Y0B 1L0, phone (403) 634-2251, fax (403) 634-2686. Also visit the park information centre in Haines Junction. Open daily, May to September, the centre has excellent interpretive displays.

H 112.8 (185 km) **HJ 38.8** (62.4 km) Gribbles Gulch.

H 114 (187 km) **HJ 37.6** (60.5 km) Parking area at St. Elias Lake trailhead (4.5-mile/7.2-km round-trip). Novice and intermediate hiking trail winds through subalpine meadow. Watch for mountain goats.

H 117.8 (193 km) **HJ 33.8** (54.4 km) Dezadeash Lodge (closed in 1995, current status unknown). Historically, this spot was known as Beloud Post and is still noted as such on some maps. Mush Lake trail (13.4 miles/21.6 km long) begins behind lodge. It is an old mining road.

NOTE: Watch for horses on highway.

H 119.3 (195 km) **HJ 32.3** (52 km) Turnout along Dezadeash Lake, one of the earliest known features in the Yukon, which parallels the highway for 9 miles/14.5 km northbound, and Dezadeash mountain range. Dezadeash (pronounced DEZ-dee-ash) is said to be the Indian word describing their fishing method. In the spring, the Indians built small fires around the bases of large birch trees, peeled the heat-loosened bark and placed it, shiny white side up, on the bottom of the lake near shore, weighted with stones. From log wharfs built over the white bark Indians waited with spears for lake trout to cross the light area. Another interpretation of Dezadeash relates that Chilkat Indians referred to it as *Dasar-ee-ASH,* meaning "Lake of the Big Winds." Entire tribes were annihilated during mid-19th century Indian wars here.

Dezadeash Lake offers good trolling, also fly-fishing along the shore where feeder streams flow into the lake. There are northern pike, lake trout and grayling in Dezadeash Lake. *CAUTION: This is a mountain lake and storms come up quickly.*

H 119.7 (195.7 km) **HJ 31.9** (51.3 km) Entrance to Yukon government Dezadeash Lake Campground; 20 campsites, $8 fee, kitchen shelter, picnic area, boat launch, no drinking water, pit toilets. ▲

H 123.9 (202.3 km) **HJ 27.7** (44.6 km) Rock Glacier trailhead to west; short 0.5-mile/0.8-km self-guiding trail, partially boardwalk. Interesting walk, some steep sections. Parking area and viewpoint.

H 126.2 (206.9 km) **HJ 25.4** (40.8 km) Dalton Trail Lodge to east with food, lodging and boat rentals.

H 134.7 (216.8 km) **HJ 16.9** (27.2 km) Access to bed and breakfast.

H 134.8 (219 km) **HJ 16.8** (27 km) Access road west to Kathleen Lake, a glacier-fed turquoise-blue lake, nearly 400 feet/122m deep. Access to Kathleen Lake Campground, the only established campground within Kluane National Park; 42 sites and a kitchen area; day-use area with boat launch at lake; campfire programs by park staff. Fees charged for camping ($10), campfire talks and backcountry registration. The 53-mile/85-km Cottonwood loop trail begins here. ▲

NOTE: National parks fishing license required. **Kathleen Lake,** lake trout average 10 lbs., use lures, June and July; kokanee average 2 lbs., June best; grayling to 18 inches, use flies, June to Sept. **Kathleen River,** rainbow to 17 inches, June to Sept.; grayling to 18 inches, July and Aug.; lake trout average 2 lbs., best in September.

H 135.2 (220.3 km) **HJ 16.4** (26.4 km) Kathleen Lake Lodge; food, gas and lodging.

NOTE: Last available gas southbound for next 102 miles. Check your gas tank.

H 135.8 (220.5 km) **HJ 15.8** (25.4 km) **Kathleen River** bridge; a popular spot for rainbow, lake trout and grayling fishing. Some kokanee.

H 139.2 (227 km) **HJ 12.4** (20 km) Turnout to west. Good view of Kathleen Lake. Information plaque on Kluane and Wrangell–St. Elias national parks.

H 143.4 (233.5 km) **HJ 8.2** (13.2 km) Quill Creek trailhead to west (7-mile/11-km trail).

H 147.1 (239.1 km) **HJ 4.5** (7.2 km) Parking area to west at Auriol trailhead (9.3-mile/15-km loop trail); skiing and hiking.

H 148.8 (241.1 km) **HJ 2.8** (4.5 km) Rest stop to east with litter barrels and pit toilets. View of community of Haines Junction and Shakwak Valley.

H 151 (245 km) **HJ 0.6** (1 km) Bridges over Dezadeash River. This river is part of the headwaters system of the Alsek River, which flows into the Pacific near Yakutat, AK.

H 151.6 (246 km) **HJ 0 HAINES JUNCTION,** turn left for Alaska, keep straight ahead for Whitehorse. Turn to Haines Junction (page 145) in the ALASKA HIGHWAY section for description of town and highway log. Whitehorse-bound travelers read log back to front, Alaska-bound travelers read log front to back.

Approximate driving distances from Haines Junction are: Whitehorse 100 miles/161 km; Tok 298 miles/480 km; Fairbanks 504 miles/811 km; and Anchorage 626 miles/1008 km.

KLONDIKE HIGHWAY 2

Skagway, Alaska, to Alaska Highway Junction
(See map, page 696)

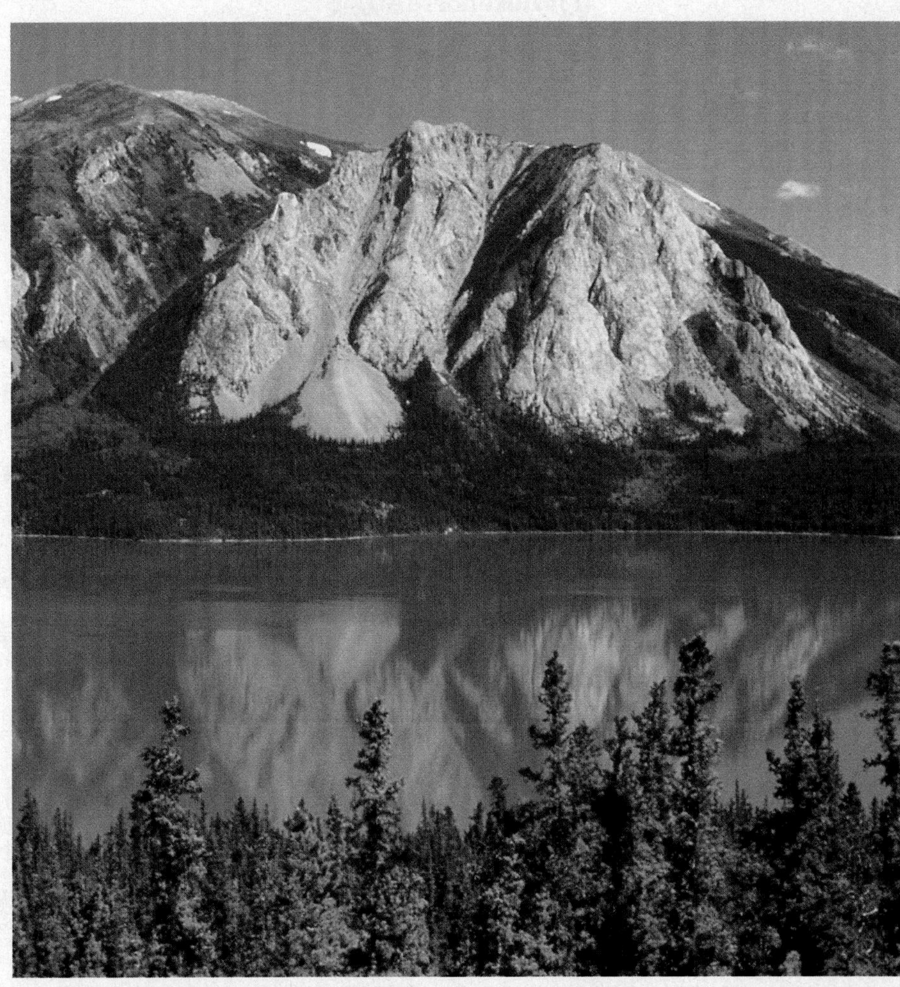

Klondike Highway 2 offers magnificent views of Windy Arm, an extension of Tagish Lake, and Lime Mountain near Milepost S 59.5. (© Rich Reid)

The 98.8-mile-/159-km-long Klondike Highway 2 (also known as the Skagway–Carcross Road and South Klondike Highway) connects Skagway, AK, with the Alaska Highway south of Whitehorse. The highway between Skagway and Carcross (referred to locally as the Skagway Road) was built in 1978 and formally dedicated on May 23, 1981. The highway connecting Carcross with the Alaska Highway (referred to locally as the Carcross Road) was built by the U.S. Army in late 1942 to lay the gas pipeline from Skagway to Whitehorse.

Klondike Highway 2 is a 2-lane, asphalt-surfaced road, open year-round. The road has been improved in recent years and is fairly wide. There is a steep 11.5-mile/18.5-km grade between Skagway and White Pass.

IMPORTANT: If you plan to cross the border between midnight and 8 A.M., call ahead or inquire locally regarding customs stations' hours of operation.

Klondike Highway 2 is one of the two highways connecting ferry travelers with the Alaska Highway; the other is the Haines Highway out of Haines. Klondike Highway 2 offers some spectacular scenery and adds only about 55 miles/89 km to the trip for Alaska-bound motorists compared with the Haines Highway. (The distance from Haines to Tok, AK, is approximately 445 miles/716 km; the distance from Skagway to Tok is 500 miles/805 km.) Klondike Highway 2, like the Haines Highway, crosses from Alaska into British Columbia, then into Yukon Territory.

Klondike Highway 2 continues north of Whitehorse, turning off the Alaska Highway to Dawson City. See the KLONDIKE LOOP section for the log of Klondike Highway 2 between the Alaska Highway and Dawson City.

CAUTION: Watch for ore trucks, 85-foot-long, 8-axle vehicles carrying up to 50 tons of lead–zinc concentrates from Faro mine on the Campbell Highway to Skagway.

Emergency medical services: Between Skagway and the BC–YT border, phone the Skagway Fire Department at (907) 983-2300. Between the border and the Alaska Highway, phone the Whitehorse ambulance at 1-403-667-3333, RCMP at 1-403-667-5555. Police monitor CB Channel 9.

Klondike Highway 2 Log

Mileposts in Alaska and kilometreposts in Canada reflect distance from Skagway. The kilometre distance from Skagway in *The MILEPOST®* log reflects the location of the physical kilometreposts, and is not necessarily an accurate conversion of the mileage figure.

Distance from Skagway (S) is followed by distance from Alaska Highway (AH).

S 0 AH 98.8 (159 km) Ferry terminal in Skagway. See SKAGWAY section for details.

S 1.6 (2.6 km) **AH 97.2** (156.4 km) Skagway River bridge.

S 2.3 (3.7 km) **AH 96.5** (155.3 km) **Junction** with Dyea Road.

S 2.6 (4.2 km) **AH 96.2** (154.8 km) Highway maintenance camp.

S 2.8 (4.5 km) **AH 96** (154.5 km) Plaque to east honoring men and women of the Klondike gold rush, and access to parklike area along Skagway River.

S 2.9 (4.7 km) **AH 95.9** (154.3 km) Access road east to Skagway River. Highway begins steep 11.5-mile/18.5-km ascent northbound from sea level to 3,290 feet/1,003m at White Pass.

S 4.7 (7.6 km) **AH 94.1** (151.4 km) Turnout to west.

S 5 (8 km) **AH 93.8** (151 km) Turnout to east with view across canyon of White Pass & Yukon Route railway tracks and bridge. The narrow-gauge WP&YR railway was completed in 1900 (see the WHITE PASS & YUKON ROUTE sections).

S 5.5 (8.8 km) **AH 93.3** (150.1 km) Turnout to west with historical information signs.

S 6 (9.6 km) **AH 92.8** (149.3 km) Turnout to east.

S 6.8 (10.9 km) **AH 92** (148 km) U.S. customs station; open 24 hours in summer (manned 8 A.M. to midnight, video camera reporting midnight to 8 A.M.). Phone (907) 983-3144 for border crossing (immigration); phone (907) 983-2325 for customs in Skagway. All travelers entering the United States must stop. Have identification ready. Residents of North America must present birth

KLONDIKE HIGHWAY 2

Skagway, AK, to Junction with Alaska Highway (includes Tagish and Atlin Roads)

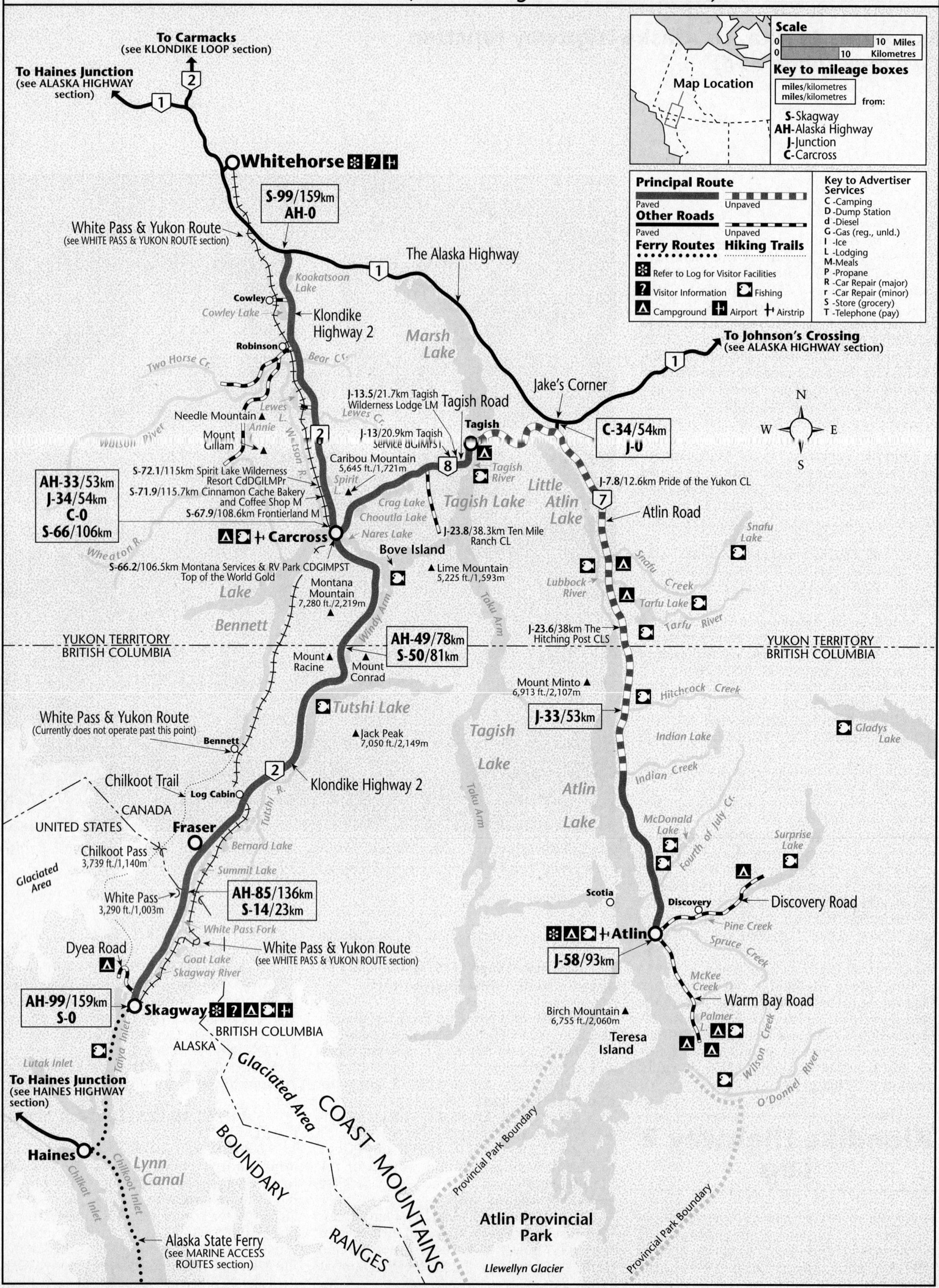

Scale
0 10 Miles
0 10 Kilometres
Key to mileage boxes
miles/kilometres
miles/kilometres
from:
S-Skagway
AH-Alaska Highway
J-Junction
C-Carcross
Map Location
Principal Route
Paved
Unpaved
Other Roads
Paved
Unpaved
Ferry Routes
Hiking Trails
Refer to Log for Visitor Facilities
Visitor Information
Fishing
Campground
Airport
Airstrip
Key to Advertiser Services
C -Camping
D -Dump Station
d -Diesel
G -Gas (reg., unld.)
I -Ice
L -Lodging
M-Meals
P -Propane
R -Car Repair (major)
r -Car Repair (minor)
S -Store (grocery)
T -Telephone (pay)
To Carmacks
(see KLONDIKE LOOP section)
To Haines Junction
(see ALASKA HIGHWAY section)
Whitehorse
S-99/159km
AH-0
White Pass & Yukon Route
(see WHITE PASS & YUKON ROUTE section)
The Alaska Highway
Kookatsoon Lake
Cowley
Cowley Lake
Klondike Highway 2
Marsh Lake
Robinson
Bear Cr.
Two Horse Cr.
To Johnson's Crossing
(see ALASKA HIGHWAY section)
Jake's Corner
J-13.5/21.7km Tagish Wilderness Lodge LM
Tagish Road
Lewes L.
Lewes Cr.
Needle Mountain
Annie
Mount Gillam
Watson River
Watson R.
J-13/20.9km Tagish Service dGIMPST
Tagish
C-34/54km
J-0
N
W
E
S
Caribou Mountain
5,645 ft./1,721m
Tagish River
S-72.1/115km Spirit Lake Wilderness Resort CdDGILMPr
S-71.9/115.7km Cinnamon Cache Bakery and Coffee Shop M
S-67.9/108.6km Frontierland M
Spirit L.
Crag Lake
Chooutla Lake
Nares Lake
Tagish Lake
Little Atlin Lake
J-7.8/12.6km Pride of the Yukon CL
Atlin Road
AH-33/53km
J-34/54km
C-0
S-66/106km
Carcross
J-23.8/38.3km Ten Mile Ranch CL
Snafu Lake
Wheaton R.
Bove Island
S-66.2/106.5km Montana Services & RV Park CDGIMPST
Top of the World Gold
Lime Mountain
5,225 ft./1,593m
Lubbock River
Snafu Creek
Montana Mountain
7,280 ft./2,219m
Lake Bennett
Windy Arm
Taku Arm
Tarfu Lake
Tarfu River
J-23.6/38km The Hitching Post CLS
AH-49/78km
S-50/81km
YUKON TERRITORY
BRITISH COLUMBIA
Mount Racine
Mount Conrad
Mount Minto
6,913 ft./2,107m
Hitchcock Creek
Tutshi Lake
J-33/53km
White Pass & Yukon Route
(Currently does not operate past this point)
Jack Peak
7,050 ft./2,149m
Tagish Lake
Gladys Lake
Indian Lake
Bennett
Chilkoot Trail
Klondike Highway 2
Indian Creek
Log Cabin
Tutshi R.
Atlin Lake
CANADA
UNITED STATES
Fraser
McDonald Lake
Fourth of July Cr.
Surprise Lake
Bernard Lake
Chilkoot Pass
3,739 ft./1,140m
Glaciated Area
Summit Lake
White Pass
3,290 ft./1,003m
AH-85/136km
S-14/23km
Scotia
Discovery
Discovery Road
White Pass Fork
Atlin
Pine Creek
Spruce Creek
Dyea Road
White Pass & Yukon Route
(see WHITE PASS & YUKON ROUTE section)
Goat Lake
Skagway River
J-58/93km
AH-99/159km
S-0
Skagway
McKee Creek
Warm Bay Road
BRITISH COLUMBIA
ALASKA
Birch Mountain
6,755 ft./2,060m
Palmer L.
Taiya Inlet
Teresa Island
Wilson Creek
Lutak Inlet
To Haines Junction
(see HAINES HIGHWAY section)
Glaciated Area
COAST MOUNTAINS
O'Donnel River
BOUNDARY RANGES
Provincial Park Boundary
Haines
Lynn Canal
Chilkoot Inlet
Chilkat Inlet
Alaska State Ferry
(see MARINE ACCESS ROUTES section)
Atlin Provincial Park
Llewellyn Glacier

certificate, driver's license or voter registration. All other foreign visitors must have a passport. Identification is also required for children. See also Customs Requirements in the GENERAL INFORMATION section.

S 7.4 (11.9 km) **AH 91.4** (147.1 km) View to east of WP&YR railway line.

S 7.7 (12.4 km) **AH 91.1** (146.6 km) Good photo stop for Pitchfork Falls, visible across the canyon. Pitchfork Falls flows from Goat Lake.

S 8.1 (13 km) **AH 90.7** (146 km) Turnout to east.

S 9.1 (14.6 km) **AH 89.7** (144.4 km) Paved turnout to east with historical interest signs about the Klondike gold rush trail. Viewpoint looks across the gorge to the WP&YR railway tracks.

S 9.9 (15.9 km) **AH 88.9** (143.1 km) Truck runout ramp to west for large transport units that may lose air brakes on steep descent southbound.

S 11.1 (17.9 km) **AH 87.7** (141.1 km) Captain William Moore Bridge. This unique cantilever bridge over Moore Creek spans a 110-foot-/34-m-wide gorge. Just north of the bridge to the west is a large waterfall. The bridge is named for Capt. Billy Moore, a riverboat captain and pilot, prospector, packer and trader, who played an important role in settling the town of Skagway. Moore helped pioneer this route over White Pass into the Yukon and was among the first to realize the potential of a railroad across the pass.

S 11.6 (18.7 km) **AH 87.2** (140.3 km) Turnouts to east with view of Skagway River gorge, Captain William Moore Bridge and waterfalls, next 0.1 mile/0.2 km northbound.

S 12 (19.3 km) **AH 86.8** (139.7 km) Truck runout ramp to west.

S 12.6 (20.3 km) **AH 86.2** (138.7 km) Posts on east side of road mark highway shoulders and guide rails for snowplows.

S 14.4 (23.2 km) **AH 84.4** (135.8 km) White Pass Summit (elev. 3,290 feet/1,003m). Turnout to west.

CAUTION: Southbound traffic begins steep 11.5-mile/18.5-km descent to Skagway.

Many stampeders on their way to the Klondike goldfields in 1898 chose the White Pass route because it was lower in elevation than the famous Chilkoot Pass trail, and the grade was not as steep. But the White Pass route was longer and the final ascent to the summit treacherous. Dead Horse Gulch (visible from the railway line) was named for the thousands of pack animals that died on this route during the gold rush.

The North West Mounted Police were stationed at the summit to meet every stampeder entering Canada and ensure that each carried at least a year's provisions (weighing about a ton).

S 14.5 (23.3 km) **AH 84.3** (135.7 km) Paved turnout to west.

S 14.9 (24 km) **AH 84** (135.2 km) U.S.–Canada (AK–BC) border. Turnout to west. Monument to east. TIME ZONE CHANGE: Alaska observes Alaska time; British Columbia and Yukon Territory observe Pacific time. See Time Zones in the GENERAL INFORMATION section.

S 16.2 (26.1 km) **AH 82.6** (133 km) Highway winds through rocky valley of Summit Lake (visible to east).

S 18.1 (29.1 km) **AH 80.7** (129.9 km) Summit Creek bridge.

S 18.4 (29.6 km) **AH 80.4** (129.4 km) Summit Lake to east.

S 19.3 (31.1 km) **AH 79.5** (128 km) North end of Summit Lake.

View of Bove Island from turnout at Milepost S 59.5. *(Earl L. Brown, staff)*

S 21.4 (34.4 km) **AH 77.4** (124.5 km) Creek and railroad bridge to east.

S 22.5 (36.2 km) **AH 76.3** (122.8 km) Canada customs at **FRASER** (elev. 2,400 feet/732m), open 24 hours; phone (403) 821-4111. Pay phone. All travelers entering Canada must stop. See Customs Requirements in the GENERAL INFORMATION section.

Old railroad water tower to east, highway maintenance camp to west.

S 22.6 (36.4 km) **AH 76.2** (122.7 km) Beautiful deep-green Bernard Lake to east.

S 22.8 (36.7 km) **AH 76** (122.3 km) Large double-ended turnout with 2 interpretive panels on area attractions and the WP&YR .

S 24.2 (38.9 km) **AH 74.6** (120.1 km) Turnout to east.

S 25.1 (40.4 km) **AH 73.7** (118.6 km) Shallow Lake to east.

S 25.5 (41 km) **AH 73.3** (118 km) Old cabins and buildings to east.

S 25.9 (41.7 km) **AH 72.9** (117.3 km) A-frame structure to east.

S 26.6 (42.8 km) **AH 72.2** (116.2 km) Turnout to east. Beautiful view of Tormented Valley, a rocky desolate "moonscape" of stunted trees and small lakes east of the highway.

S 27.3 (43.9 km) **AH 71.5** (115 km) Highway crosses tracks of the White Pass & Yukon Route at **LOG CABIN**. With completion of the railway in 1900, the North West Mounted Police moved their customs checkpoint from the summit to Log Cabin. There is nothing here today.

NOTE: There are numerous turnouts along the highway between here and Carcross. Turnouts may be designated for either commercial ore trucks or passenger vehicles.

S 30.7 (49.4 km) **AH 68.1** (109.6 km) Tutshi (too-shy) River visible to east.

S 31.1 (50 km) **AH 67.7** (108.9 km) Highway parallels **Tutshi Lake** for several miles northbound. Excellent fishing for lake trout and grayling early in season. Be sure you have a British Columbia fishing license.

S 40.1 (64.5 km) **AH 58.7** (94.5 km) Short, narrow gravel access road to picnic area with pit toilet on Tutshi Lake. Large vehicles check turnaround space before driving in.

S 40.7 (65.5 km) **AH 58.1** (93.5 km) Good views of Tutshi Lake along here.

S 43.7 (70.5 km) **AH 55.1** (88.7 km) Turnout to east with view of Tutshi Lake.

S 46.4 (75.1 km) **AH 52.4** (84.3 km) To the east is the Venus Mines concentrator, with a capacity of 150 tons per day. A drop in silver prices caused the Venus mill's closure in October 1981.

S 48.5 (78.1 km) **AH 50.3** (81 km) South end of Windy Arm, an extension of Tagish Lake.

S 49.2 (79.2 km) **AH 49.6** (79.9 km) Viewpoint to east.

S 49.9 (80.5 km) **AH 48.9** (78.7 km) Dall Creek.

S 50.2 (81 km) **AH 48.6** (78.2 km) BC–YT border. Turnout with picnic table and litter barrel to east overlooking Windy Arm.

S 51.9 (83.5 km) **AH 46.9** (75.5 km) Large turnout to east with litter barrel, picnic table and historical information sign about Venus Mines.

The first claim on Montana Mountain was staked by W.R. Young in 1899. By 1904 all of the mountain's gold veins had been claimed. In 1905, New York financier Col. Joseph H. Conrad acquired most of the Montana Mountain claims, formed Conrad Consolidated Mines, and began exploration and mining. A town of about 300 people sprang up along Windy Arm and an aerial tramway was built from the Conrad townsite up the side of Montana Mountain to the Mountain Hero adit. (This tramline, visible from the highway, was completed in 1906 but was never used to ship ore because the Mountain Hero tunnel did not find a vein.) More tramways and a mill were constructed, but by 1911 Conrad was forced into bankruptcy: The ore was not as rich as estimated and only a small quantity of ore was milled before operations ceased.

Small mining operations continued over the years, with unsuccessful startups by various mining interests. United Keno Hill Mines (Venus Division) acquired the mining claims in 1979, constructed a 100-ton-per-day mill and rehabilitated the old mine workings in 1980.

S 52.9 (85.1 km) **AH 45.9** (73.8 km)

Visitor centre in Carcross is located in the old White Pass & Yukon Route train station. (Earl L. Brown, staff)

Pooly Creek and canyon, named for J.M. Pooly who staked the first Venus claims in 1901.

Access road east to Pooly Point and Venus Mines maintenance garage, trailers and security station. No services, facilities or admittance.

S 54.2 (87.2 km) **AH 44.6** (71.8 km) Venus Mines ore storage bin and foundation of old mill to east. The mill was built in the late 1960s, then disassembled and sold about 1970. A sign here warns of arsenic being present: Do not pick or eat berries.

S 55.7 (89.6 km) **AH 43.1** (69.4 km) Tramline support just east of highway.

S 59.5 (95.8 km) **AH 39.3** (63.3 km) Turnout with historic information sign about Bove Island. Magnificent views along here of Windy Arm and its islands (the larger island is Bove Island). Windy Arm is an extension of Tagish Lake. Lime Mountain (elev. 5,225 feet/1,593m) rises to the east beyond Bove Island.

S 63.5 (102.2 km) **AH 35.3** (56.8 km) Sections of the old government wagon roads that once linked Carcross, Conrad and other mining claims, visible on either side of the highway.

S 65.3 (105.1 km) **AH 33.5** (53.9 km) Private road west to homes, Carcross Tagish First Nation's Band office and Carcross cemetery. Buried at the cemetery are the famous gold discoverers, Skookum Jim, Dawson (or Tagish) Charlie and Kate Carmack; pioneer missionary Bishop Bompas; and Polly the parrot. (Cemetery is closed to visitors during services.)

S 65.9 (106 km) **AH 32.9** (52.9 km) Access road west to Montana Mountain.

S 66 (106.2 km) **AH 32.8** (52.7 km) Nares Bridge crosses the narrows between Lake Bennett to the west and Tagish Lake to the east. Nares Lake remains open most winters, despite air temperatures that drop well below -40°F/-40°C. The larger lakes freeze to an ice depth of more than 3 feet/1m.

Caribou Mountain (elev. 5,645 feet/1,721m) is visible to the east.

S 66.2 (106.5 km) **AH 32.6** (52.4 km) Turnoff west for Carcross (description follows).

Carcross

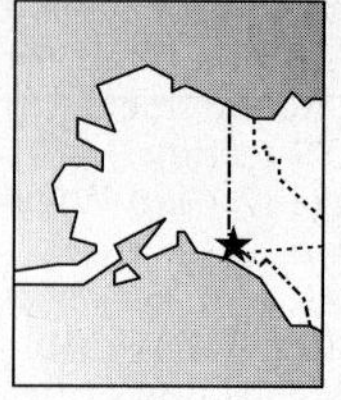

On the shore of Lake Bennett, 44 miles/71 km southeast of Whitehorse. **Population:** 421. **Emergency Services: Police,** phone (403) 821-5555. **Fire Department,** phone (403) 821-2222. **Ambulance,** phone (403) 821-3333. **Health Centre,** phone (403) 821-4444.

Visitor Information: Carcross Visitor Reception Centre, operated by Tourism Yukon, is located in the old White Pass & Yukon Route train station. Model train and lifeboat display. The centre operates daily from 8 A.M. to 8 P.M., mid-May to mid-September; phone (403) 821-4431. Ferry schedules, maps and information on Yukon, British Columbia and Alaska available. Yukon attractions may be previewed on laser disc. Get your Yukon Gold Explorer's Passport stamped here.

Elevation: 2,175 feet/663m. **Climate:** Average temperature in January, -4.2°F/-20.1°C; in July, 55.4°F/13°C. Annual rainfall 11 inches, snowfall 2 to 3 feet. Driest month is April, wettest month August. **Radio:** CKRW, CBC, CKYN-FM 96.1 visitor information station. **Television:** CBC. **Transportation:** Scheduled bus service. Atlin Express Service runs between Atlin and Whitehorse via Tagish and Carcross 3 times weekly.

Private Aircraft: Carcross airstrip, 0.3 mile/0.5 km north of town via highway; elev. 2,161 feet/659m; length 2,000 feet/610m.

There are a hotel, general store, gift shops with Native handicrafts, snack bar and RV park. Gas station with gifts, groceries and cafe located on the highway by the airstrip. ▲

Carcross was formerly known as Caribou Crossing because of the large numbers of caribou that traversed the narrows here between Bennett and Nares lakes. It became a stopping place for gold stampeders on their way to the Klondike goldfields. Carcross was a major stop on the White Pass & Yukon Route railroad from 1900 until 1982, when the railroad ceased operation. (The WP&YR currently operates a limited excursion service; see WHITE PASS & YUKON ROUTE section for details.) Passengers and freight transferred from rail to stern-wheelers at Carcross. One of these stern-wheelers, the SS *Tutshi* (too-shy), was a historic site here in town until it burned down in July 1990.

A cairn beside the railroad station marks the site where construction crews laying track for the White Pass & Yukon Route from Skagway met the crew from Whitehorse. The golden spike was set in place when the last rail was laid at Carcross on July 29, 1900. The construction project had begun May 27, 1898, during the height of the Klondike gold rush.

Other visitor attractions include St. Saviour's Anglican Church, built in 1902; the Royal Mail Carriage; and the little locomotive *Duchess,* which once hauled coal on Vancouver Island. Frontierland, 2 miles/3.2 km north of town on the highway, is also a popular attraction. On sunny days you may sunbathe and picnic at Sandy Beach on Lake Bennett. Behind the post office there is a footbridge across Natasaheenie River. This small body of water joins Lake Bennett and Nares Lake. Check locally for boat tours and boat service on Bennett Lake.

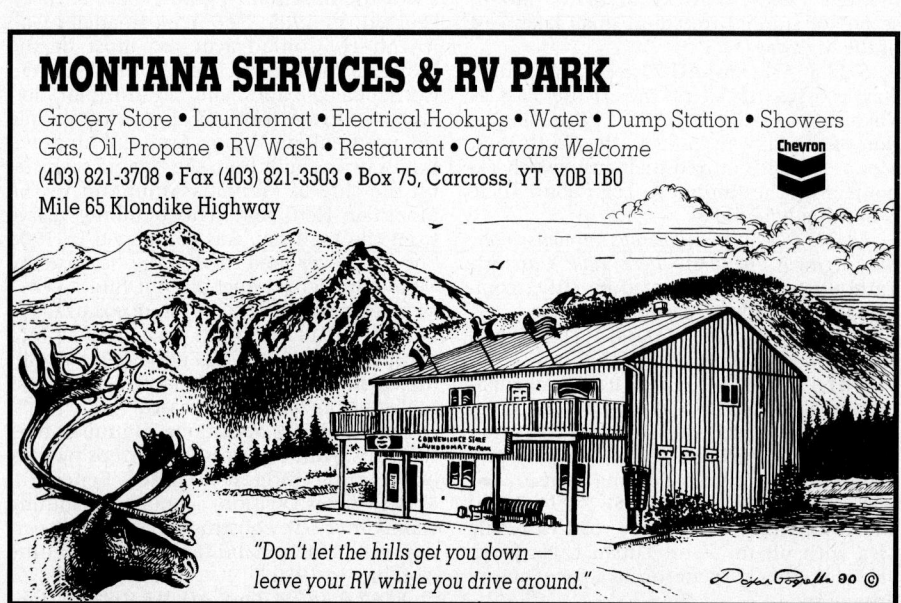

Fishing in **Lake Bennett** for lake trout, northern pike, arctic grayling, whitefish and cisco.

Montana Services & RV Park. See display ad this section.

Top Of The World Gold. A short stroll from downtown Carcross will bring you to our shop overlooking historic Lake Bennett. We find our gold with shovel, sluice, and pan—the old-fashioned way. We make our nugget jewellery and souvenirs by hand—the old-fashioned way. And you'll be welcomed like friends—the old-fashioned way. So drop in for a visit ... We look forward to meeting you, and we're sure you'll find something of interest. Open from mid-June. (VISA) Phone (403) 821-3702. [ADVERTISEMENT]

Klondike Highway 2 Log

(continued)

S 66.4 (106.9 km) **AH 32.4** (52.1 km) Airstrip to east. Turn on access road directly north of airstrip for Carcross Yukon government campground; 14 sites, picnic tables, firewood, drinking water, outhouses, camping fee.

S 66.5 (107 km) **AH 32.3** (52 km) **Junction** with Yukon Highway 8 which leads east to Tagish, Atlin Road and the Alaska Highway at Jake's Corner (see TAGISH ROAD section). Turn east here for alternate access to Alaska Highway and for Yukon government campground on Tagish Road.

S 67.3 (108.3 km) **AH 31.5** (50.7 km) Turnout with point of interest sign about Carcross desert. This unusual desert area of sand dunes, seen east of the highway between Kilometreposts 108 and 110, is the world's smallest desert and an International Biophysical Programme site for ecological studies. The desert is composed of sandy lake-bottom material left behind by a large glacial lake. Strong winds off Lake Bennett have made it difficult for vegetation to take hold here; only lodgepole pine, spruce and kinnikinnick survive. (Kinnikinnick is a low trailing evergreen with small leathery leaves; used for tea.)

S 67.9 (108.6 km) **AH 30.9** (49.7 km) Frontierland (formerly the Museum of Yukon Natural History) features a Yukon wildlife museum, gift shop and coffee house. Displays include a saber-toothed tiger and the world's largest mounted bear—a polar bear.

Frontierland. See display ad this section.

S 70.3 (112.3 km) **AH 28.5** (45.9 km) Dry Creek.

S 71.2 (113.8 km) **AH 27.6** (44.4 km) Carl's Creek.

S 71.9 (115.7 km) **AH 26.9** (43.3 km) **Cinnamon Cache Bakery Coffee Shop.** See display ad this section.

S 72.1 (115 km) **AH 26.7** (43 km) Spirit Lake Wilderness Resort east side of road with food, gas, propane, repairs, lodging, camping and ice cream. Access road east to public use area on Spirit Lake.

Spirit Lake Wilderness Resort. See display ad this section.

S 73.2 (116.8 km) **AH 25.6** (41.2 km) Spirit Lake is visible to the east.

S 73.5 (117.3 km) **AH 25.3** (40.7 km) Large turnout with point of interest sign to west overlooking beautiful Emerald Lake, also called Rainbow Lake by Yukoners. (Good view of lake by climbing the hill across from the turnout.) The rainbowlike colors of the lake result from blue-green light waves reflecting off the white sediment of the lake bottom. This white sediment, called marl, consists of fragments of decomposed shell mixed with clay; it is usually found in shallow, freshwater lakes that have low oxygen levels during the summer months.

S 75.4 (120.3 km) **AH 23.4** (37.7 km) Highway follows base of Caribou Mountain (elev. 5,645 feet/1,721m). View of Montana Mountain to south, Caribou Mountain to east and Gray Ridge Range to the west between Kilometreposts 122 and 128. Flora consists of jack and lodgepole pine.

S 79.8 (127.1 km) **AH 19** (30.6 km) Highway crosses Lewes Creek.

S 85.4 (136.3 km) **AH 13.4** (21.6 km) Access road west leads 1 mile/1.6 km to Lewes Lake.

S 85.6 (136.5 km) **AH 13.2** (21.2 km) Rat Lake to west.

S 86.7 (138.2 km) **AH 12.1** (19.4 km) Bear Creek.

S 87 (140 km) **AH 11.8** (19 km) Access to bed and breakfast and Bear Creek Dog Sled Kennels.

S 87.3 (139.1 km) **AH 11.5** (18.5 km) Access road west to large gravel pull-through with historic information sign about Robinson and view of Robinson. In 1899, the White Pass & Yukon Route built a railroad siding at Robinson (named for Stikine Bill Robinson). Gold was discovered nearby in the early 1900s and a townsite was surveyed. A few buildings were constructed and a post office—manned by Charlie McConnell—operated from 1909 to 1915. Low mineral yields caused Robinson to be abandoned, but postmaster Charlie McConnell stayed and established one of the first ranches in the Yukon. Robinson is accessible from Annie Lake Road (see next milepost).

S 87.5 (139.4 km) **AH 11.3** (18.2 km) Road west to Annie Lake (turn left after crossing the railroad tracks to reach Robinson).

Annie Lake Road (can be rough) leads 0.8 mile/1.4 km to Annie Lake golf course, 1.9 miles/3.1 km to McConnell Lake, and 11 miles/17.7 km to Annie Lake. Beyond Annie Lake the road crosses the Wheaton River. The Wheaton Valley–Mount Skukum area has seen a surge of mineral exploration by private prospectors and mining companies in recent years. For the adventuresome, this is beautiful and interesting country. There are no facilities along Annie Lake Road. *CAUTION: Annie Lake Road can be very muddy during spring breakup or during rain.*

S 93 (148.5 km) **AH 5.8** (9.4 km) Turnoff west for Cowley and for access to Cowley Lake (1.6 miles/2.6 km).

S 95.5 (154.2 km) **AH 3.3** (5.3 km) Turnoff east for Kookatsoon Lake. There is a Yukon government picnic area at Kookatsoon Lake (day use only). The lake is shallow and usually warm enough for swimming in summer. Picnic tables, firepits and pit toilets. Canoe launch.

S 98.4 (156.5 km) **AH 0.4** (0.7 km) Rock shop on east side of road.

S 98.8 (157.1 km) **AH 0 Junction** with the Alaska Highway. Turn left (north) for Whitehorse, right (south) for Watson Lake. Turn to **Milepost DC 874.4** (page 124) in the ALASKA HIGHWAY section: Whitehorse-bound travelers continue with that log; travelers heading south down the Alaska Highway read that log back to front.

TAGISH ROAD

Alaska Highway (Jake's Corner) to Carcross, Yukon Territory
Yukon Highway 8
(See map, page 696)

Marina at the Tagish River bridge, a popular fishing spot. (Earl L. Brown, staff)

The Tagish Road was built in 1942 to lay a gas pipeline. It leads south from the Alaska Highway through the settlement of Tagish to Carcross. This 33.8-mile/54.4-km road connects the Alaska Highway with Klondike Highway 2. The road is good gravel from the Alaska Highway junction to Tagish, asphalt-surfaced between Tagish and Carcross.

If you are traveling Klondike Highway 2 between Skagway and Whitehorse, Tagish Road provides access to Atlin Road and also makes a pleasant side trip. Travelers may wish to use Tagish Road as an alternate route if there is road construction on Klondike Highway 2 between Carcross and the Alaska Highway. This is also a very beautiful drive in the fall; good photo opportunities.

Emergency medical services: Phone the RCMP, 1-403-667-5555; ambulance, phone 1-403-667-3333.

Tagish Road Log

Kilometreposts measure east to west from Alaska Highway junction to Carcross turnoff; posts are up about every 2 kilometres. **Distance from the junction (J) is followed by distance from Carcross (C).**

J 0 C 33.8 (54.4 km) **Junction** with the Alaska Highway at Jake's Corner. Drive south 1.1 miles/1.8 km to junction of Tagish Road and Atlin Road (Highway 7).

J 1.1 (1.8 km) **C 32.7** (52.6 km) **Junction** of Tagish and Atlin roads. Turn southeast for Atlin, BC (see ATLIN ROAD section); head west for Tagish and Carcross.

J 8.8 (14.2 km) **C 25** (40.2 km) For several miles, travelers may see the NorthwesTel microwave tower on Jubilee Mountain (elev. 5,950 feet/1,814m) to the south between Little Atlin Lake and Tagish River. Jubilee Mountain was named by Dr. G.M. Dawson in 1887 in honor of Queen Victoria's Jubilee.

J 12.8 (20.6 km) **C 21** (33.8 km) Tagish Yukon government campground, on **Six Mile River** between Marsh Lake to the north and Tagish Lake to the south. Good fishing, boat launch, picnic area, playground, kitchen shelter, 28 campsites with firepits and tables, drinking water and toilets. Camping fee $8. *CAUTION: Watch for black bears.*

J 13 (20.9 km) **C 20.8** (33.5 km) Marina on north side of road at east end of Tagish bridge has bait, tackle, fishing licenses, boat rental. Gas, oil, minor repairs, snacks and post office. Pay phone on road.

Tagish Service. See display ad this section.

J 13.1 (21 km) **C 20.7** (33.3 km) Tagish bridge. Good fishing is a tradition here; Tagish bridge has an anglers' walkway on the north side. **Tagish River,** lake trout, arctic grayling, northern pike, whitefish and cisco.

West end of bridge has a day-use area with parking, 4 picnic sites and water pump. Gravel ends, pavement begins, westbound.

J 13.5 (21.7 km) **C 20.3** (32.6 km) Improved gravel road leads through parklike area to settlement of **TAGISH** (pop. about 134) on Tagish River between Marsh and Tagish lakes. Express bus service between Atlin and Whitehorse stops here and in Carcross 3 times weekly. Tagish means "fish trap" in the local Indian dialect. It was traditionally an Indian meeting place in the spring on the way to set up fish camps and again in the fall to celebrate the catch. Post office at Tagish Service at east end of Tagish bridge. Wilderness lodge on Taku Arm of Tagish Lake.

Tagish Wilderness Lodge. See display ad this section.

Two miles/3.2 km south of Tagish on the Tagish River is **TAGISH POST,** originally named Fort Sifton, the Canadian customs post established in 1897. Two of the original 5 buildings still stand. The North West Mounted Police and Canadian customs collected duties on thousands of tons of freight carried by stampeders on their way to the Klondike goldfields between September 1897 and February 1898.

J 16.3 (26.2 km) **C 17.5** (28.1 km) Side road leads 1.2 miles/2 km to Tagish Lake and homes.

Tagish Lake, fishing for trout, pike and grayling.

J 23 (37 km) **C 10.8** (17.4 km) Bryden Creek.

J 23.8 (38.3 km) **C 10** (16.1 km) **Ten Mile Ranch.** See display ad this section. ▲

J 24.8 (39.9 km) **C 9** (14.4 km) Crag Lake. Road now enters more mountainous region westbound. Caribou Mountain (elev. 5,645 feet/1,721m) on right.

J 27.2 (43.8 km) **C 6.6** (10.6 km) Porcupine Creek.

J 27.5 (44.3 km) **C 6.3** (10.1 km) **Historic Milepost 7.**

J 28.4 (45.7 km) **C 5.4** (8.7 km) Pain Creek.

J 30.2 (48.6 km) **C 3.6** (5.8 km) Side road to Chooutla Lake.

J 31 (49.9 km) **C 2.8** (4.5 km) First glimpse westbound of Montana Mountain (elev. 7,230 feet/2,204m) across narrows at Carcross.

J 33.8 (54.4 km) **C 0 Junction** with Klondike Highway 2. Westbound travelers turn left for Carcross, right for Whitehorse. See **Milepost S 66.5** (page 699) in the KLONDIKE HIGHWAY 2 section.

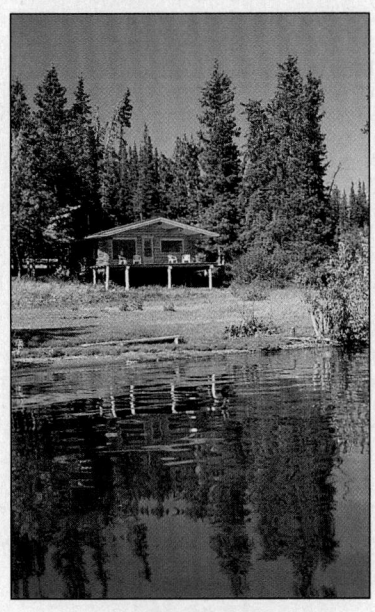

ATLIN ROAD

Tagish Road Junction, Yukon Territory, to Atlin, British Columbia
Yukon/BC Highway 7
(See map, page 696)

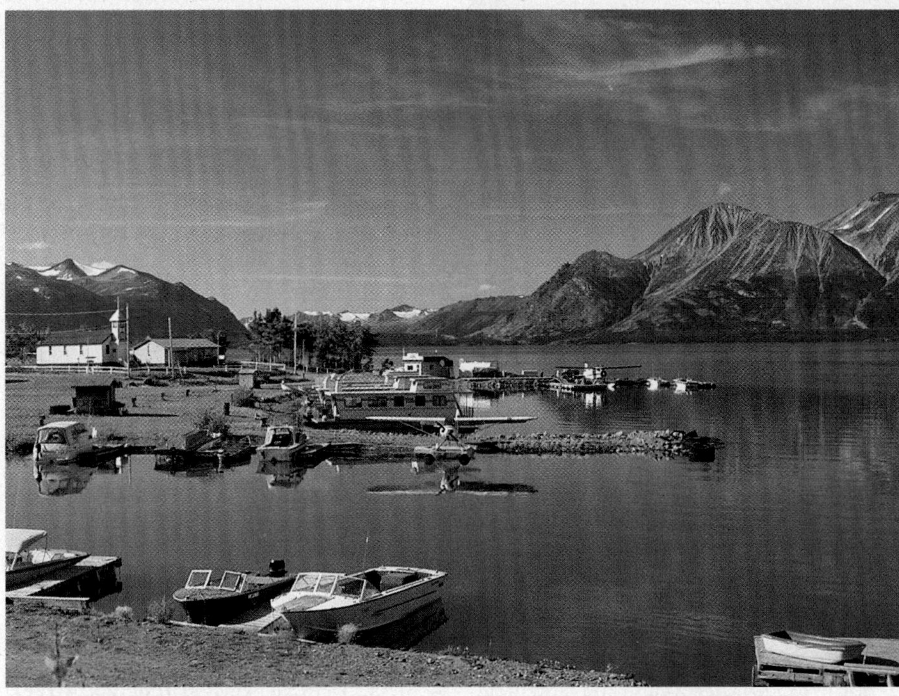

Beautiful Atlin, on the shore of 90-mile-long Atlin Lake. *(Earl L. Brown, staff)*

This 58-mile/93.3-km all-weather road leads south to the pioneer gold mining town of Atlin. Built in 1949 by the Canadian Army Engineers, Atlin Road is a good road, usually in excellent condition, with some winding sections. The first 40 miles/64.4 km are gravel, with the remaining 18 miles/29 km into Atlin paved. Watch for slippery spots in wet weather.

To reach Atlin Road, turn south at Jake's Corner on the Alaska Highway; drive 1.1 miles/1.8 km to the junction of Atlin Road (Highway 7) and Tagish Road (Highway 8); turn left (south) for Atlin.

It is about a 2½-hour drive to Atlin from Whitehorse and the lake scenery from the village is well worth the trip. For more information contact the Atlin Visitors Assoc., Box 365-M, Atlin, BC V0W 1A0; fax (604) 651-7721. Or phone the Atlin museum at (604) 651-7522 for visitor information.

Atlin Road Log

Physical kilometreposts in Yukon Territory and mileposts in British Columbia show distance from Tagish Road junction.
Distance from Tagish Road junction (J) is shown.

J 0 Junction of Tagish and Atlin roads.

J 1.4 (2.3 km) Fish Creek crossing. The road is bordered by many low-lying, boggy areas brilliant green with horsetail *(equisetium).*

J 1.8 (2.9 km) Side road west to Little Atlin Lake. Atlin Road descends along east shoreline of Little Atlin Lake approximately 7.6 miles/12.2 km southbound. During midsummer, the roadsides are ablaze with fireweed and wild roses.

J 2.4 (3.9 km) Large turnout to west on Little Atlin Lake; informal boat launch and camping area. Mount Minto (elev. 6,913 feet/2,107m) can be seen to the southwest. Road climbs southbound.

J 2.8 (4.5 km) Turnout to west. Watch for bald eagles.

J 5 (8 km) Information sign to east about 1983–84 mountain goat transplant. The 12

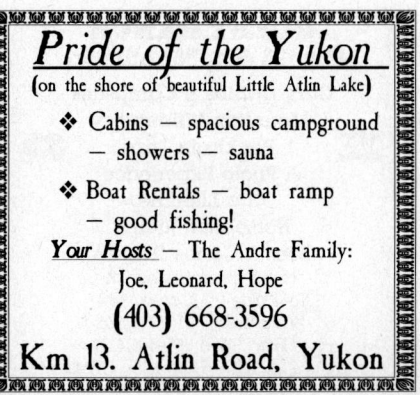

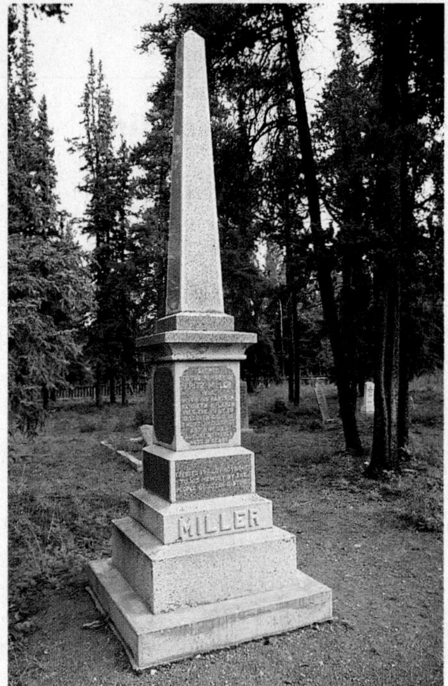
Fritz Miller monument is in Pioneer Cemetery on Discovery Road. (Rollo Pool)

goats were brought from Kluane National Park. They may be observed on the mountainsides.

J 7.8 (12.6 km) Private campground, cabins and boat rentals. ▲

Pride of the Yukon. See display ad on page 701. ▲

J 8.1 (13 km) Greenhouse and farm, roadside vegetable stand in season. Haunka Creek. Turnout to west.

J 8.9 (14.3 km) Good view of Mount Minto ahead southbound.

J 13.8 (22.2 km) Unmarked side road leads 2.4 miles/3.9 km to **Lubbock River**, which connects Little Atlin Lake with Atlin Lake. Excellent for grayling from breakup to mid-Sept.

J 15.5 (24.9 km) Snafu Creek. Turnout to west, north of bridge. According to R. Coutts, author of "Yukon Places & Names," the creek name is an acronym bestowed by army crews who built the road. It stands for Situation Normal—All Fouled Up. (Mr. Coutts resides in Atlin.)

J 16.4 (26 km) Access road leads 0.7 mile/1.1 km to **Snafu Lake** Yukon government campground; 4 sites, $8 camping fee, pit toilets, tables, gravel boat ramp, good fishing. ▲

J 18.6 (29.9 km) Tarfu Creek. Small turnout to east, north of bridge. Creek name is another army acronym. This one stands for Things Are Really Fouled Up.

J 18.7 (30 km) Abandoned cabin and turnout to west.

J 20.4 (32.8 km) Turnoff to east for **Tarfu Lake** Yukon government campground via 2.4-mile/3.8-km side road; 6 sites, $8 camping fee, pit toilets, fishing. Steep grade near campground; not recommended for large RVs or trailers. ▲

J 20.5 (33 km) Short narrow side road leads east to Marcella Lake; good lake for canoeing.

J 21.8 (35.1 km) Turnout to west with view of Atlin Lake, which covers 307 square miles/798 square km and is the largest natural lake in British Columbia. Coast Mountains to the southwest.

J 23.6 (38 km) **The Hitching Post.** See display ad this section. ▲

J 25.8 (41.5 km) BC–YT border. Road follows east shoreline of Atlin Lake into Atlin.

J 26.8 (43.1 km) Survival shelter to east.

J 27 (43.5 km) Mount Minto to west, Black Mountain to east, and Halcro Peak (elev. 5,856 feet/1,785m) to the southeast.

J 28.5 (45.8 km) Slow down for sharp curve.

J 32 (51.5 km) Excellent views of Coast Mountains, southwest across Atlin Lake, next 6 miles/9.7 km southbound.

J 32.7 (52.6 km) **Hitchcock Creek**, grayling to 2 lbs. Survival shelter to east.

J 32.8 (52.7 km) Campground on Atlin Lake; 6 sites, pit toilets, tables, ramp for small boats. ▲

J 36.3 (58.4 km) Turnout with litter barrel to west, south side of Base Camp Creek.

J 36.8 (59.2 km) **Historic Milepost 38.**

J 40 (64.4 km) Indian River. Pull-through turnout south of creek. Highway is paved from here to Atlin.

J 40.2 (64.7 km) Big-game outfitter/guest ranch to east.

J 45.2 (72.7 km) Survival shelter to east.

J 45.3 (72.9 km) Turnout to west.

J 49.8 (80.1 km) Burnt Creek.

J 49.9 (80.3 km) Davie Hall Lake and turnout to west. Waterfowl are plentiful on lake.

J 51.2 (82.4 km) Watch for horses.

J 51.6 (83 km) Ruffner Mine Road leads east 40 miles/64.4 km. Access to **MacDonald Lake**, 2 miles/3.2 km east; bird watching and lake trout fishing from spit.

J 52.8 (85 km) Fourth of July Creek.

J 53.4 (85.9 km) Spruce Mountain (elev. 5,141 feet/1,567m) to west.

J 55.1 (88.7 km) Road skirts east shore of Como Lake next 0.6 mile/1 km southbound.

J 55.2 (88.8 km) Turnout with litter barrel to west on **Como Lake**; good lake for canoeing, also used by floatplanes. Stocked with rainbow.

J 55.7 (89.6 km) South end of Como Lake; boat ramp.

J 57.1 (91.9 km) Atlin city limits.

J 58 (93.3 km) **Junction** of Atlin Road with Discovery Road. Turn right (west) on Discovery Avenue for town of Atlin; description follows. Turn left (east) for Discovery Road and access to Warm Bay Road; see side road logs page 705.

Atlin

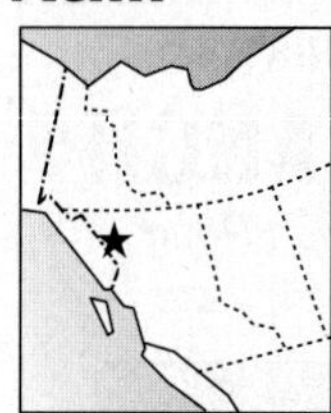

The most northwesterly town in British Columbia, located about 112 miles/180 km southeast of Whitehorse, YT. **Population:** 500. **Emergency Services: Police**, phone (604) 651-7511. **Fire Department**, phone (604) 651-7666. **Ambulance**, phone (604) 651-7700. Red Cross outpost clinic, phone (604) 651-7677.

Visitor Information: Contact the Atlin Visitors Assoc., P.O. Box 365-M, Atlin, BC V0W 1A0, fax (604) 651-7721, phone (604) 651-7522.

Elevation: 2,240 feet/683m. **Radio:** CBC on FM-band. **Television:** Three channels (CBC, BCTV and the Knowledge Network).

Private Aircraft: Peterson Field, 1 mile/1.6 km northeast; elev. 2,348 feet/716m; length 3,950 feet/1,204m; gravel.

Transportation: Air–Regular service from Juneau via Summit Aviation. **Bus**–Service from Whitehorse 3 times a week.

Referred to by some visitors as Shangri-la,

the village of Atlin overlooks the crystal clear water of 90-mile-/145-km-long Atlin Lake and is surrounded by spectacular mountains. On Teresa Island in Atlin Lake is Birch Mountain (elev. 6,755 feet/ 2,060m), the highest point in fresh water in the world.

Atlin was founded in 1898. The name was taken from the Indian dialect and means Big Water. The Atlin Lake area was one of the richest gold strikes made during the great rush to the Klondike in 1897–98. The first claims were registered here on July 30, 1898, by Fritz Miller and Kenneth McLaren.

Pine Creek Falls near Pine Creek campground on Warm Bay Road. (G. Frederick Stork)

VISITOR SERVICES/ACCOMMODATIONS

The village has a hotel, inns, cottages, bed and breakfasts, laundromat (with showers), restaurants, gas stations (propane, diesel and unleaded available), grocery, government liquor store and general stores, and a post office. Atlin branch of Bank of Montreal located at Government Agents Office on 3rd Street; open weekdays 10 A.M. to noon and 1–3 P.M. Dump station at Mile 2.3 Discovery Road. The museum and several shops feature local gold nugget jewelry, arts and crafts, and other souvenirs. Air charter service for glacier tours and fly-in fishing trips. Charter boats and fishing charters available.

Bus tours are welcome, but phone ahead so this small community can accommodate you.

The Noland House. This historic home has been restored to provide luxurious accommodations for 4 guests. Host residence is next door. Private baths and sitting rooms, complimentary wine and snacks, fully equipped kitchen, lake and mountain views, airport and floatplane dock pickup. Single $85, double $95, open May–October. Box 135, Atlin, BC V0W 1A0. (604) 651-7585. [ADVERTISEMENT]

RV park with electric and water hookups, showers and laundry, pay phone and boat moorage downtown on lake. There are several camping areas on Atlin Road, Discovery Road and Warm Bay Road (see logs this section). Atlin community operates the Pine Creek campground at **Milepost J 1.6** Warm Bay Road; 14 sites, $5 fee (pay at any downtown business or at the museum). ▲

ATLIN ADVERTISERS

Atlin Centre	Ph. (800) 651-8882
Atlin General Store	Ph. (604) 651-7555
Atlin Inn, The	Ph. (604) 651-7546
Dragon Studio	Ph. (604) 651-7785
Fireweed Inn, The	Ph. (604) 651-7729
Glacier View Cabins and Sidka Tours	Ph. (604) 651-7691
Glacier Wilderness Ventures	Ph. (604) 651-7466
Kirkwood Cottages	Ph. (604) 651-7546
Noland House, The	Ph. (604) 651-7585
Norseman Adventures Ltd.	Ph. (604) 651-7535
Northern Place, The	Ph. (604) 651-7503
Pine Tree Services	Ph. (604) 651-7636
Quilts & Comforts	Ph. (604) 651-7476
Simply Gold	Ph. (604) 651-7708
Vi & Cor's Food Basket Inc.	Ph. (604) 651-7676

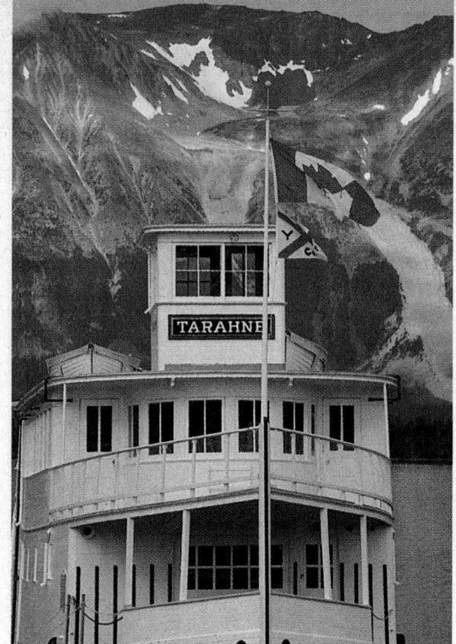

The MV Tarahne *once carried passengers across Atlin Lake.* (© Chris Sharp)

ATTRACTIONS

The MV *Tarahne* (Tah-ron) sits on the lakeshore in the middle of town. Tours daily in summer at 3 P.M.; admission by donation. Built at Atlin in 1916 by White Pass & Yukon Route, she carried passengers and freight from Atlin to Scotia Bay until 1936. (Scotia Bay is across the lake from Atlin and slightly north.) A 2-mile/3.2-km railway connected Scotia Bay on Atlin Lake to Taku Landing on Tagish Lake, where passengers arrived by boat from Carcross, YT. The *Tarahne* was the first gas-driven boat in the White Pass fleet. After she was lengthened by 30 feet in 1927, she could carry up to 198 passengers. In recent years, Atlin residents have launched a drive to restore the boat; they hope to eventually refloat the vessel and offer tours of Atlin Lake.

Atlin Historical Museum, open weekends during June and September, daily July through August. Located in Atlin's original 1-room schoolhouse, the museum has mining artifacts and photo exhibits of the Atlin gold rush. Gift shop features the work of local artisans. Walking-tour guide of Atlin available here. Admission fee; phone (604) 651-7522.

Dragon Studio, located in downtown Atlin above Eggert's Clock, displays original works of art by visual artist Meshell Melvin. Visitors will be welcomed by the brightly coloured characters, in a multitude of mediums. These figures of wonder invite the audience to share in the adventure of the creative mind. Works for sale or commission. Stop in, or call (604) 651-7785 for appointment. [ADVERTISEMENT]

Visit the mineral springs at the north end of town, where you may have a drink of sparkling cold mineral water. The gazebolike structure over the springs was built by White Pass in 1922. Picnic area nearby.

The Pioneer Cemetery, located at **Milepost J 1.1** Discovery Road, contains the weathered grave markers of early gold seekers, including Fritz Miller and Kenneth McLaren, who made the first gold discovery in the Atlin area in July 1898. Also buried here is Walter Gladstone Sweet, reputed to have been a card dealer for Soapy Smith in Skagway.

Public Gold Panning Area has been set aside on Spruce Creek. Turn off Discovery Road at **Milepost J 3.6.** Check at the museum for details. Gold pans available locally for rent or purchase.

Take a Hike. At **Milepost J 2.3** Warm Bay Road are 2 trails: the 3-mile/4.8-km Monarch trail and the short, easy Beach trail. The Monarch trail is a moderately strenuous hike with a steep climb at the end to a bird's-eye view of the area.

Weekend guided nature walks are available at Warm Bay and Warm Springs, late May to early September. Fee charged. Inquire locally for details.

Tours and Rentals. Motorbike rentals, houseboat rentals, boat tours of Atlin and Tagish lakes, guided fishing trips and marine gas are available. Helicopter service, floatplanes for charter hunting and fishing trips and flightseeing trips of Llewellyn Glacier and the Atlin area are also available.

Atlin Provincial Park, accessible by boat or plane only (charters available in Atlin). Spectacular wilderness area; varied topography; exceptional wildlife habitat.

Take a Drive. 13-mile/21-km Discovery Road and 16.5-mile/26.5-km Warm Bay Road are both suitable for passenger cars and RVs, and both offer sightseeing and recreation. See side road logs this section for details.

Atlin Art Centre, located at **Milepost J 2** Warm Bay Road, offers alpine hiking, boating and canoeing adventures to the general public from June to September. The centre is also a summer school and retreat for artists and students, run by Gernot Dick. The centre is designed to allow participants to distance themselves from urban distractions and focus on the creative process. Contact Atlin Art Centre, Monarch Mountain, Atlin, BC V0W 1A0; (800) 651-8882 for more information. Currently, a number of talented artists, authors and other creative people make their home in Atlin.

AREA FISHING: The Atlin area is well known for its good fishing. Fly-in fishing for salmon, steelhead and rainbow, or troll locally for lake trout. Grayling can be caught at the mouths of most creeks and streams or off Atlin docks. Public boat launch on Atlin Lake, south of the MV *Tarahne*. Boat charters available. For information on fishing in the area, contact local businesses. British Columbia fishing licenses are available from the government agent and local outlets. Fresh and smoked salmon may be available for purchase locally in the summer. Annual fishing derby held in June.

Abandoned gold mines and cabins dot the Atlin area. (G. Frederick Stork)

Discovery Road Log

Discovery Road begins 0.4 mile/0.6 km from Atlin's business district at junction with Atlin Road and leads east 13 miles/20.9 km. This is a good, wide, gravel road, bumpy in spots. Posted speed limit is 50 mph/80 kmph, but 40 mph/60 kmph or less is recommended. There is active gold mining under way along the road; watch for large trucks. Beyond Surprise Lake Dam bridge, the road becomes steep and winding for 1.2 miles/1.9 km to road end (large RVs use caution).

Distance is measured from junction with Atlin Road (J).

J 0 Junction of Atlin Road and Discovery Avenue.

J 0.3 (0.5 km) **Junction** with Warm Bay Road.

J 1.1 (1.8 km) Atlin airport to east. Pioneer cemetery to west contains grave markers and monuments to many of Atlin's historical figures.

J 2.3 (3.7 km) Dump station to south.

J 3.5 (5.6 km) Turnout to south with view of Pine Creek and falls.

J 3.6 (5.8 km) Spruce Creek Road leads south 0.9 mile/1.4 km to designated public recreational gold panning area and 1.5 miles/2.4 km to active gold mining on Spruce Creek (no tours but operations can be photographed from the road). This side road is signed as rough and narrow; suitable for cars, vans and pickups.

J 3.9 (6.3 km) Winding road next 1 mile/1.6 km.

J 5.4 (8.7 km) Former townsite of Discovery, originally called Pine Creek, now a ghost town. In its boom days, the town supplied miners working in the area.

J 7 (11.2 km) Active gold mining operation to south can be photographed from the road.

J 8.6 (13.8 km) Slow down for Pine Creek 1-lane bridge. Road follows creek drainage from here to Surprise Lake.

J 9.2 (14.8 km) Small lake to east usually has waterfowl.

J 10.7 (17.2 km) View west of mining road switchbacks on mountainside.

J 11.2 (18 km) Road forks: bear to left. Small lake to west.

J 11.8 (19 km) Surprise Lake Dam bridge. Turnout east side of bridge with litter barrel and view of Surprise Lake.

CAUTION: Steep and winding road next 1.2 miles/1.9 km eastbound to road end.

J 12 (19.3 km) **Surprise Lake** recreation site. One campsite near main road. Steep, bumpy access road leads to more campsites near lake. Pit toilets, picnic tables, firepits. Boat launch for cartop boats and canoes. A gold mining operation is visible across the lake. Fishing for arctic grayling. ▲

J 13 (20.9 km) Road forks and both forks dead end along Boulder Creek. Ample turnaround space for vehicles.

Warm Bay Road Log

Warm Bay Road leads south 16.5 miles/26.5 km to numerous points of interest and 5 camping areas. Warm Bay Road begins at **Milepost J 0.3** Discovery Road, 0.7 mile/1.1 km east of Atlin business district.

Distance is measured from junction with Discovery Road (J).

J 0 Junction with Discovery Road.

J 0.3 (0.5 km) Atlin School.

J 1.5 (2.4 km) Pine Creek 1-lane bridge.

J 1.6 (2.6 km) Pine Creek Campground and picnic area; 14 campsites, tenting area, pit toilets, picnic tables, firepits, some firewood and water. Camping fee: $5/RV, $3/tent; pay at any Atlin business. Short trail to Pine Creek and Pine Creek Falls. ▲

J 2 (3.2 km) Atlin Art Centre (see Attractions in Atlin).

J 2.3 (3.7 km) Trailheads either side of road. Monarch trail is a moderately strenuous 3-mile/4.8-km hike through meadows to scenic vista of Atlin area. Some steep sections; summit of Monarch Mountain at elev. 4,723 feet/1,439m. Beach trail is short and easy.

J 2.5 (4 km) Drinking water from pipe beside road.

J 5.7 (9.2 km) Lina Creek.

J 7 (11.2 km) Viewpoint with litter barrel. Llewellyn Glacier and Atlin Lake are to the southwest. Good photo spot.

J 7.3 (11.7 km) Bed and breakfast, canoe rentals.

J 9.5 (15.3 km) McKee Creek 1-lane bridge. The McKee Creek area has been mined since the 1890s. In July 1981, 2 area miners found what has been dubbed the "Atlin nugget," a 36.86-troy-ounce, hand-sized piece of gold.

J 11.3 (18.2 km) Palmer Lake to east.

J 11.9 (19.1 km) **Palmer Lake** recreation site to east; camping, fishing, picnic tables, pit toilets. No camping fee. ▲

J 13.9 (22.3 km) Warm Bay recreation site on **Atlin Lake**; camping, fishing, picnic tables, pit toilets. No camping fee. Boat launch for small boats. ▲

J 14.4 (23.2 km) Warm Springs to north. This is a small and shallow spring, good for soaking road-weary bones. Large grassy camping area, pit toilet. No camping fee. The meadow streams are lined with watercress. Guided nature walks available; inquire locally for details. ▲

J 16.3 (26.2 km) Grotto recreation site; 2 campsites, picnic tables, pit toilets, firepits, litter barrel. ▲

J 16.4 (26.4 km) "The Grotto" to north. Large turnaround. Water flows through a hole in the rocks from an underground stream. Locals report this is a good place to obtain drinking water.

J 16.5 (26.5 km) Maintained road ends. Steep, bumpy and narrow road continues beyond this point; not recommended for travel.

NORTHERN WOODS & WATERS ROUTE

Saskatchewan Border to Dawson Creek, British Columbia
Alberta Highways 55, 2 and 49
(See maps, pages 707–708)

Northern Alberta agriculture includes fields of canola. (Earl L. Brown, staff)

The Northern Woods & Waters Route is a scenic 489.5-mile/787.8-km route originating at the Saskatchewan–Alberta border that passes the lakes, forests and prairies of northern Alberta before terminating at Dawson Creek, British Columbia.

The Northern Woods & Waters Route follows 3 different highway numbers in Alberta: Highway 55 from the border to Athabasca, Highway 2 from Athabasca to Donnelly Corners, and Highway 49 from Donnelly Corners to Dawson Creek, BC. The highway is paved and is in good to excellent condition.

A full array of visitor facilities is available at the larger communities: Grand Centre, Cold Lake, Lac La Biche, Athabasca, Slave Lake, High Prairie, McLennan and Spirit River. Other visitor facilities are available in most of the smaller communities along the route.

Northern Woods & Waters Route Log

ALBERTA HIGHWAY 55
Distance from the Alberta–Saskatchewan border (B) is followed by distance from Dawson Creek (DC).

B 0 DC 489.5 (787.8 km) Alberta–Saskatchewan border. Head west on Highway 55.

B 8 (12.8 km) **DC 481.6** (775 km) **Junction** with Highway 897 south to Elizabeth Metis settlement.

B 8.5 (13.6 km) **DC 481.1** (774.2 km) **Junction** with Alberta Highway 28 at Beaver Crossing. Tourist information centre for the region is located on the southeast corner of the junction.

B 9.4 (15.2 km) **DC 480.1** (772.6 km) Side road east 1.8 miles/3 km to Grand Centre Golf and Country Club; 9 holes, pro shop, carts for rent and licensed restaurant.

Grand Centre

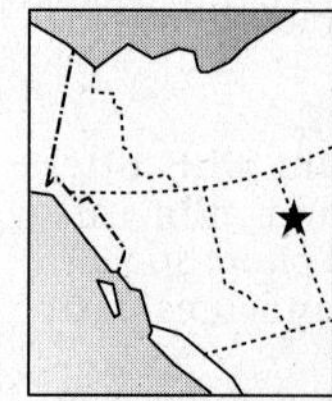

B 11.3 (18.2 km) **DC 478.2** (769.6 km) Located 180 miles/290 km northeast of Edmonton. **Population:** 3,880. **Emergency Services: RCMP**, phone (403) 594-3301. **Hospital and Ambulance**, phone (403) 639-3322. **Fire Department**, phone (403) 594-3100.

Visitor Information: Tourist information centre 3 miles/5 km south at the junction of Highways 55 and 28.

Situated beside one of the largest military bases in Canada (CFB Cold Lake) and immediately south of the community of Cold Lake, Grand Centre is the economic and commercial base of northeast Alberta. Grand Centre, Cold Lake and the military base make up the tri-cities area.

Visitor facilities include 2 hotels, 5 motels, many restaurants, retail and grocery stores, and service stations with major repair facilities. Recreational facilities include a large sports arena, curling rink, tennis courts, public library, ball diamonds and a golf course, 3.6 miles/6 km southeast of town.

Northern Woods & Waters Route Log
(continued)

B 11.7 (18.8 km) **DC 477.8** (769 km) **Junction** with access road west 1.2 miles/2 km to the Cold Lake Air Force Base.

B 11.8 (18.9 km) **DC 477.7** (768.8 km) **Junction** with side road east 11.2 miles/18 km to French Bay Provincial Recreation Area; 10 sites, water pump, partial hookups, public phone, beach, fishing, informal boat launch. Camping fee $5.50. The Kinusoo Lodge Ski Area has 10 runs, artificial snow, equipment rentals and ski lessons.

B 14.8 (23.9 km) **DC 474.7** (764 km) **Junction** of Highways 55 and 28. The highways combine until Highway 28 goes north 1.8 miles/3 km to the community of Cold Lake. If not stopping in Cold Lake, continue on Alberta Highway 55 westbound.

Cold Lake

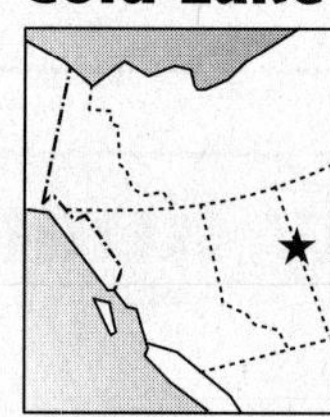

Located at the end of Alberta Highway 28. **Population:** 4,000. **Emergency Services: RCMP**, phone (403) 594-3301. **Hospital and Ambulance**, phone (403) 639-3322. **Fire Department**, phone (403) 639-3131.

Visitor Information: Tourist information booth located on top of a hill in an A-frame overlooking the lake, downtown and marina area. Open May to Sept.

Elevation: 1,780 feet/543m. **Private Aircraft**: Cold Lake Municipal Airport, located 3.7 miles/6 km west of town; elev. 1,787 feet/546m; length 2,953 feet/900m; asphalt; fuel 80, 100, Jet B.

Cold Lake was incorporated in 1957 as a result of construction of the nearby Canadian Forces base. The town is one of the fastest growing communities in the area.

Visitor facilities include 3 motels, several restaurants, retail and grocery stores, and service stations with major repair facilities. Recreational facilities include an ice arena, ball diamonds, tennis courts and public library. **Cold Lake** Provincial Park, 3 miles/5 km east of town via an access road, has 117 campsites, pump and tap water, full hookups, dump station, showers, public phone, beach, fishing and boat launch. Camping fee $13 and up.

NORTHERN WOODS & WATERS ROUTE

Saskatchewan Border to Slave Lake, AB

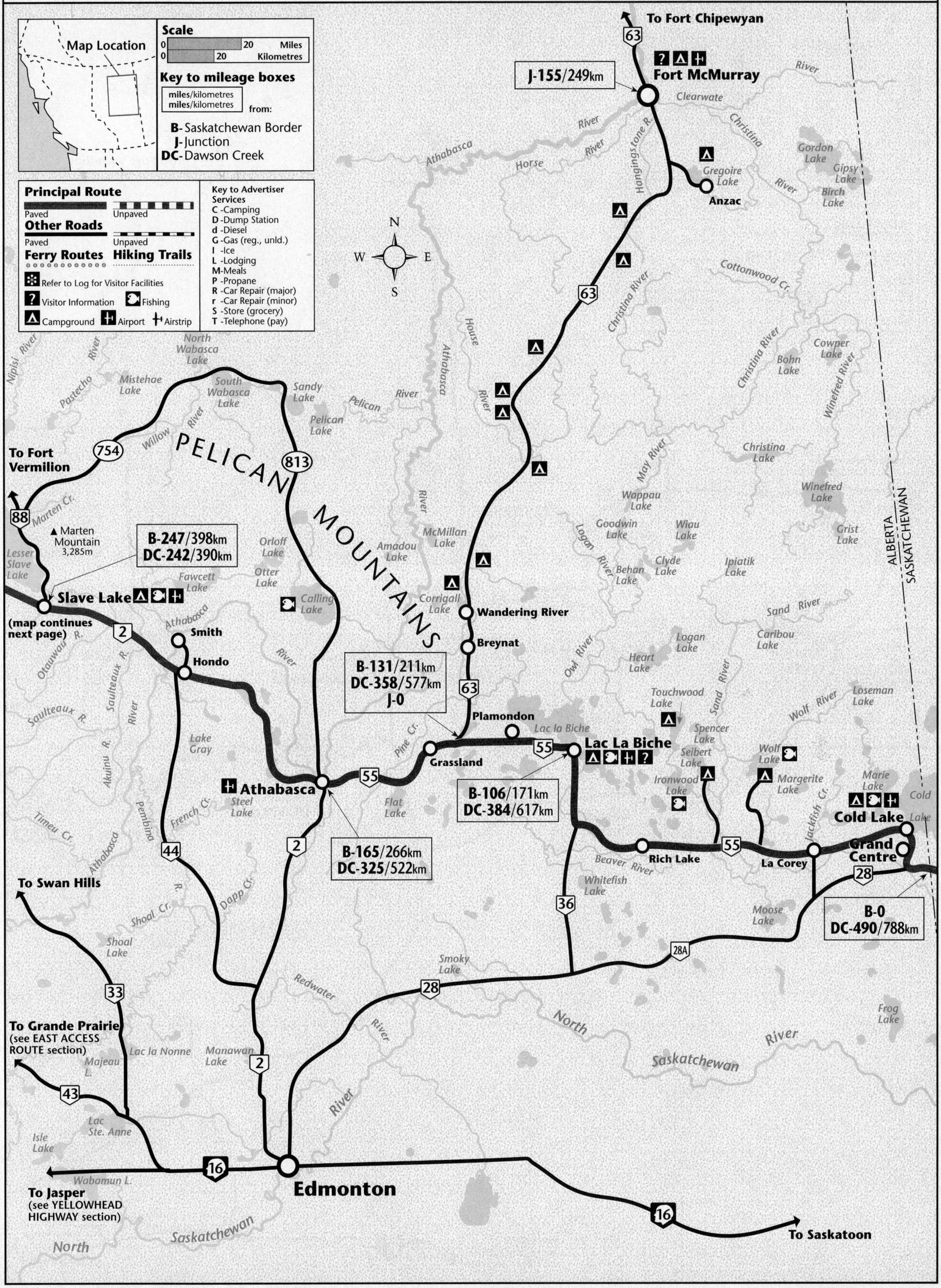

Map Location

Scale
0 — 20 Miles
0 — 20 Kilometres

Key to mileage boxes

miles/kilometres
miles/kilometres
from:

B-Saskatchewan Border
J-Junction
DC-Dawson Creek

Principal Route
Paved
Unpaved
Other Roads
Paved
Unpaved
Ferry Routes
Hiking Trails
Refer to Log for Visitor Facilities
Visitor Information
Fishing
Campground
Airport
Airstrip

Key to Advertiser Services
C -Camping
D -Dump Station
d -Diesel
G -Gas (reg., unld.)
I -Ice
L -Lodging
M-Meals
P -Propane
R -Car Repair (major)
r -Car Repair (minor)
S -Store (grocery)
T -Telephone (pay)

N
W E
S

To Fort Chipewyan
63
J-155/249km
Fort McMurray
Clearwater River
Christina River
Hangingstone R.
Horse River
Athabasca River
Gregoire Lake
Anzac
Gordon Lake
Gipsy Lake
Birch Lake
Cottonwood Cr.
Christina River
Cowper Lake
Bohn Lake
Winefred River
Christina Lake
Winefred Lake
May River
Wappau Lake
Goodwin Lake
Wiau Lake
Grist Lake
Logan River
Behan Lake
Clyde Lake
Ipiatik Lake
ALBERTA
SASKATCHEWAN
House River
Athabasca River
North Wabasca Lake
South Wabasca Lake
Nipisi River
Pastecho River
Mistehae Lake
Sandy Lake
Pelican River
Pelican Lake
Willow River
754
813
PELICAN MOUNTAINS
To Fort Vermilion
88
Marten Cr.
▲ Marten Mountain 3,285m
B-247/398km
DC-242/390km
Lesser Slave Lake
Orloff Lake
Otter Lake
Fawcett Lake
McMillan Lake
Amadou Lake
Calling Lake
Corrigall Lake
Wandering River
Breynat
Slave Lake
(map continues next page)
2
Athabasca River
Smith
Hondo
Otauwau R.
Saulteaux R.
Saulteaux R.
River
B-131/211km
DC-358/577km
J-0
63
Owl River
Heart Lake
Logan Lake
Caribou Lake
Sand River
Sand River
Touchwood Lake
Wolf River
Loseman Lake
Plamondon
Lac la Biche
55
Lac La Biche
Spencer Lake
Seibert Lake
Wolf Lake
Ironwood Lake
Margerite Lake
Marie Lake
Cold Lake
Pine Cr.
Grassland
Lake Gray
Akuinu R.
Pembina
Athabasca
Steel Lake
55
Flat Lake
B-106/171km
DC-384/617km
Cold Lake
Grand Centre
Jackfish Cr.
Rich Lake
55
La Corey
28
Timeu Cr.
Athabasca
French Cr.
44
2
B-165/266km
DC-325/522km
Beaver River
Whitefish Lake
36
Moose Lake
B-0
DC-490/788km
To Swan Hills
Dapp Cr.
Shoal Cr.
Shoal Lake
28A
Smoky Lake
Redwater River
28
33
To Grande Prairie
(see EAST ACCESS ROUTE section)
North Saskatchewan River
Frog Lake
Lac la Nonne
Manawan Lake
Majeau L.
2
River
43
Lac Ste. Anne
Isle Lake
16
Wabamun L.
Edmonton
To Jasper
(see YELLOWHEAD HIGHWAY section)
16
To Saskatoon
North Saskatchewan

NORTHERN WOODS & WATERS ROUTE

Slave Lake, AB, to Dawson Creek, BC

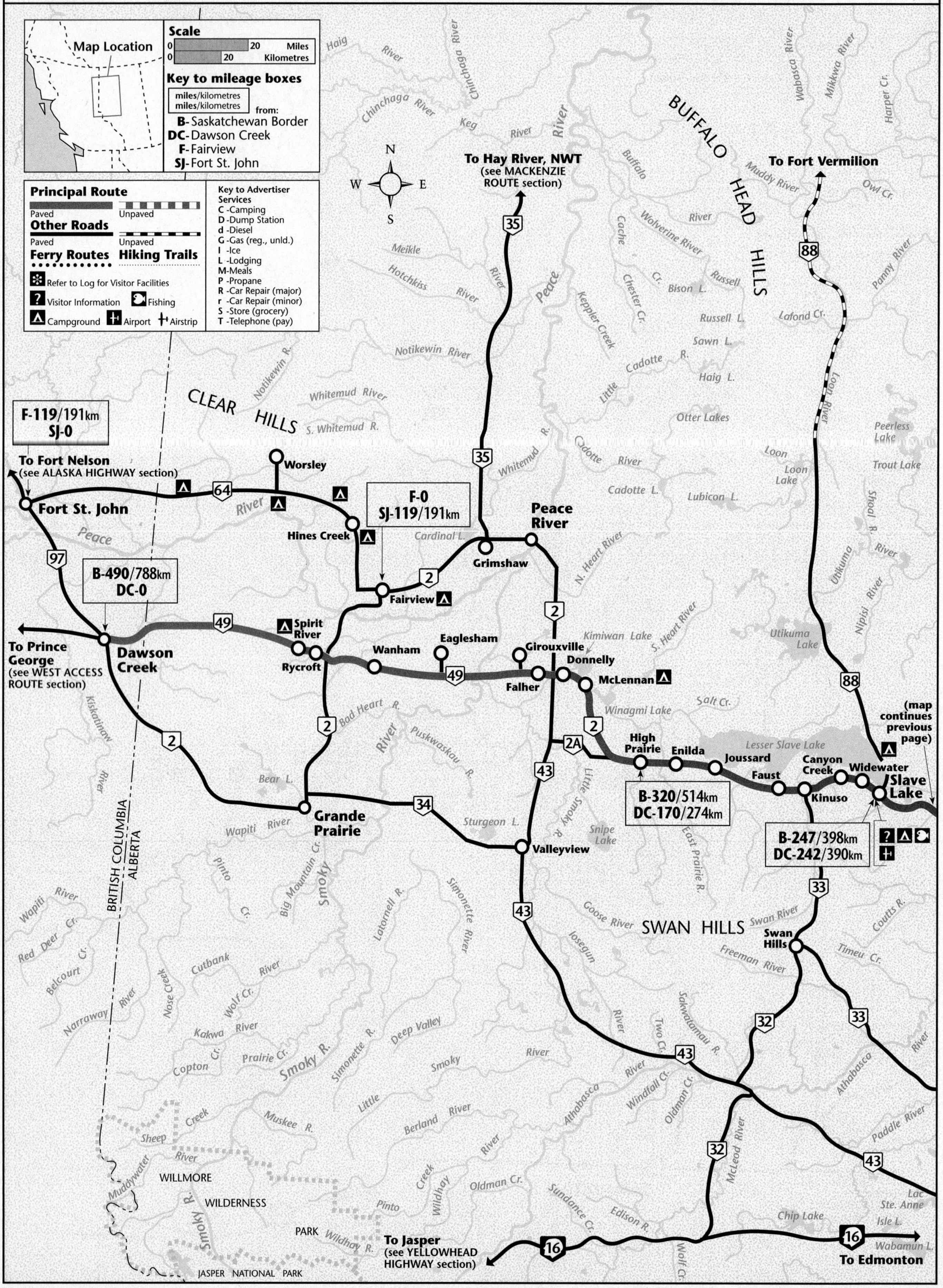

Map Location

Scale
0 — 20 Miles
0 — 20 Kilometres

Key to mileage boxes
miles/kilometres
miles/kilometres
from:
B-Saskatchewan Border
DC-Dawson Creek
F-Fairview
SJ-Fort St. John

Principal Route
Paved
Unpaved
Other Roads
Paved
Unpaved
Ferry Routes
Hiking Trails
Refer to Log for Visitor Facilities
Visitor Information
Fishing
Campground
Airport
Airstrip

Key to Advertiser Services
C -Camping
D -Dump Station
d -Diesel
G -Gas (reg., unld.)
I -Ice
L -Lodging
M -Meals
P -Propane
R -Car Repair (major)
r -Car Repair (minor)
S -Store (grocery)
T -Telephone (pay)

N W E S

F-119/191km
SJ-0

To Fort Nelson
(see ALASKA HIGHWAY section)

Fort St. John

F-0
SJ-119/191km

B-490/788km
DC-0

To Prince George
(see WEST ACCESS ROUTE section)

Dawson Creek

To Hay River, NWT
(see MACKENZIE ROUTE section)

To Fort Vermilion

B-320/514km
DC-170/274km

B-247/398km
DC-242/390km

(map continues previous page)

To Jasper
(see YELLOWHEAD HIGHWAY section)

To Edmonton

Worsley, Hines Creek, Fairview, Grimshaw, Peace River, Spirit River, Rycroft, Wanham, Eaglesham, Girouxville, Donnelly, Falher, McLennan, High Prairie, Enilda, Joussard, Faust, Kinuso, Canyon Creek, Widewater, Slave Lake, Grande Prairie, Valleyview, Swan Hills

35, 64, 97, 2, 49, 2A, 43, 34, 88, 33, 32, 16

CLEAR HILLS, BUFFALO HEAD HILLS, SWAN HILLS, BRITISH COLUMBIA, ALBERTA, WILLMORE WILDERNESS PARK, JASPER NATIONAL PARK

Haig River, Chinchaga River, Keg River, Buffalo River, Wolverine River, Muddy River, Owl Cr., Wabasca River, Mikkwa River, Harper Cr., Meikle River, Hotchkiss River, Peace River, Keppler Creek, Cache Cr., Chester Cr., Bison L., Russell, Russell L., Sawn L., Lafond Cr., Panny River, Notikewin River, Notikewin R., Whitemud River, S. Whitemud R., Little Cadotte R., Haig L., Otter Lakes, Loon River, Peerless Lake, Trout Lake, Loon Lake, Cadotte River, Cadotte L., Lubicon L., Whitemud R., Shoal R., Cardinal L., N. Heart River, Utikuma River, Nipisi River, Utikuma Lake, Kimiwan Lake, S. Heart River, Salt Cr., Winagmi Lake, Lesser Slave Lake, Kiskatinaw River, Bad Heart R., Puskwaskau R., Bear L., Little Smoky R., Sturgeon L., Snipe Lake, East Prairie R., Wapiti River, Pinto Cr., Big Mountain Cr., Smoky, Simonette River, Latornell R., Goose River, Josegun, Swan River, Freeman River, Timeu Cr., Coutts R., Red Deer Cr., Belcourt Cr., Cutbank River, Nose Creek, Wolf Cr., Narraway River, Kakwa River, Deep Valley, Prairie Cr., Copton Cr., Smoky R., Simonette R., Smoky River, Two Cr., Sakwatamau R., Athabasca River, Windfall Cr., Oldman Cr., Little Berland River, Muskeg R., Sheep Creek, Muddywater River, McLeod River, Paddle River, Wildhay River, Creek, Pinto, Wildhay R., Oldman Cr., Sundance Cr., Edison R., Wolf Cr., Chip Lake, Lac Ste. Anne, Isle L., Wabamun L.

Cold Lake M.D. Park in town has 50 sites, tap water, full hookups, dump station, showers, public phone, beach, fishing, boat launch. Camping fee $9 and up.

Northern Woods & Waters Route Log

(continued)

B 17.5 (28.2 km) **DC 471.8** (759.2 km) Cold Lake Municipal Airport to north 2.4 miles/4 km via access road.

B 18.4 (29.6 km) **DC 470.9** (757.8 km) Bridge over Marie Creek.

B 20.6 (33.1 km) **DC 469** (754.7 km) **Junction** with side road north 15 miles/25 km to the Cold Lake fish hatchery and to **English Bay** Provincial Recreation Area; 30 sites, water pump, beach, fishing, boat launch. Camping fee $5.50.

B 21.5 (34.6 km) **DC 468** (753.2 km) **Junction** with Highway 897 (Primrose Lake Road) north 12 miles/20 km to **Ethel Lake** Provincial Recreation Area; 12 sites, water pump, public phone, beach, fishing, boat launch. Camping fee $5.50.

B 21.6 (34.7 km) **DC 467.9** (753.1 km) Riverhurst (no services).

B 26.7 (42.9 km) **DC 462.9** (744.9 km) **Junction** with Highway 892 south 11 miles/18 km to Ardmore and to Alberta Highway 28. **Junction** with side road north 4 miles/6.4 km to **Crane Lake** East Provincial Recreation Area; 28 sites, water pump, beach, fishing and boat launch.

B 29.8 (47.9 km) **DC 459.8** (739.9 km) **Junction** with side road north 3 miles/5 km to **Crane Lake** West Provincial Recreation Area; 27 sites, water pump, public phone, beach, fishing and boat launch.

B 36.5 (58.8 km) **DC 453** (729 km) Bridge over Jackfish Creek.

B 38.3 (61.7 km) **DC 451.2** (726.1 km) **LA COREY** (pop. 62) and **junction** with Alberta Highway 41 south 12 miles/20 km to Bonnyville. La Corey has a small store and service station.

B 44.2 (71.1 km) **DC 445.3** (716.7 km) Iron River (no services).

B 44.4 (71.4 km) **DC 445.1** (716.3 km) **Junction** with access road north 6 miles/10 km to **Manatokan Lake** Provincial Recreation Area; 11 sites, partial hookups, water pump, fishing, boat launch.

B 44.5 (71.6 km) **DC 445** (716.2 km) Entering Improvement District 18 and Lac La Biche National Forest westbound.

B 45.7 (73.5 km) **DC 443.9** (714.3 km) Bridge over Manatokan Creek.

B 47.9 (77.1 km) **DC 441.6** (710.7 km) **Junction** with side road 24 miles/40 km north to **Wolf Lake** and campground; 64 sites, partial hookups, water pump, fishing, boat launch. Camping fee $7.50.

B 56.4 (90.8 km) **DC 433.1** (697 km) Bridge over the Sand River.

B 59.5 (95.8 km) **DC 430** (692 km) **Junction** with access road north 20 miles/32 km to **Seibert Lake** and campground; 43 sites, water pump, partial hookups, fishing, boat launch. Camping fee $5.50.

B 61.2 (98.5 km) **DC 428.3** (689.3 km) **Junction** with Highway 881 south to the communities of Goodridge and Mallaig, and to Alberta Highway 28A.

B 64.1 (103.1 km) **DC 425.5** (684.7 km) Entering Beaver Lake Ranger District westbound.

B 64.2 (103.3 km) **DC 425.3** (684.5 km) Small store, gas station and pay phone to south.

B 69.2 (111.3 km) **DC 420.4** (676.5 km) Access road north 4 miles/6.4 km to Frenchman Lake.

B 70.1 (112.8 km) **DC 419.4** (675 km) **Private Aircraft**: Grass airstrip to south; elev. 1,890 feet/600m; length 1,750 feet/563m; unattended.

B 72.3 (116.3 km) **DC 417.3** (671.5 km) **Junction** with Highway 867, which leads 2.5 miles/4 km to the community of Fork Lake (no services).

B 74.6 (120 km) **DC 415** (667.8 km) **Fork Lake** Campground to south; 46 sites, partial hookups, water pump, phone, beach, fishing, boat launch. Camping fee $7.50.

B 75 (120.7 km) **DC 414.5** (667.1 km) Community of **RICH LAKE** to north; grocery store/confectionery and gas station.

Access road north to Lakeland Provincial Park and Recreation Area, Alberta's third largest park. **Ironwood Lake** Campground, 10 miles/16 km north, has 20 sites, partial hookups, water pump, fishing and boat launch. Camping fee $5.50. **Pinehurst Lake** Campground, located 16 miles/26 km north, has 70 sites, partial hookups, water pump, picnic tables, shelter, beach, fishing and boat launch. Camping fee $5.50. The recreation area is also accessible from **Milepost B 90.1** and from **Milepost B 96.**

B 82.6 (133 km) **DC 406.9** (654.8 km) **Junction** with Highway 866 south to the communities of McRae and Boyne Lake.

B 90.1 (145 km) **DC 399.4** (642.8 km) **Junction** with access road that leads north 3.6 miles/6 km and then east 20 miles/32 km to Lakeland Provincial Park and Recreation Area.

B 93.5 (150.5 km) **DC 396** (637.3 km) **Junction** with Alberta Highway 36 south 11 miles/18 km to the Kikino Metis settlement and then 34 miles/54 km to Alberta Highway 28A.

B 96 (154.5 km) **DC 393.5** (633.3 km) **Junction** with secondary road west to Hylo. A secondary access road to east leads 22 miles/35 km to Lakeland Provincial Park.

B 98.1 (157.8 km) **DC 391.5** (630 km) Bridge over the Beaver River.

B 99.7 (160.5 km) **DC 389.8** (627.3 km) Second bridge over the Beaver River.

B 100.5 (161.8 km) **DC 389** (626 km) **Junction** with access road east 7 miles/12 km to the Spruce Point Campground on **Beaver Lake**; 265 sites, full hookups, water pump, showers, dump station, pay phone, teepee rentals, picnic tables, shelter, beach, fishing, boat launch and boat rentals.

B 101.7 (163.7 km) **DC 387.8** (624.1 km) Third bridge over the Beaver River.

B 104.5 (168.1 km) **DC 385.1** (619.7 km) Roadside turnout with litter barrels and historic plaque.

B 105 (169 km) **DC 384.5** (618.8 km) **Junction** with side road east 2.5 miles/4 km to **Beaver Lake** Provincial Recreation Area; 100 sites, partial hookups, water pump, fishing, boat launch. Camping fee $7.50.

B 105.9 (170.5 km) **DC 383.6** (617.3 km) **Junction** with Highway 881 north 7 miles/11 km to Sir Winston Churchill Provincial Park and Campground; 72 sites, full hookups, pump and tap water, showers, dump station, beach, fishing, boat launch. Camping fee $10.75.

Touchwood Lake Campground is located 8 miles/30 km north and east on Highway 881 and then 18 miles/30 km east on an access road; 75 sites, partial hookups, water pump, beach, fishing, boat launch. Camping fee $7.50.

Downtown Lac La Biche is just east of the Highway 881 junction.

Lac La Biche

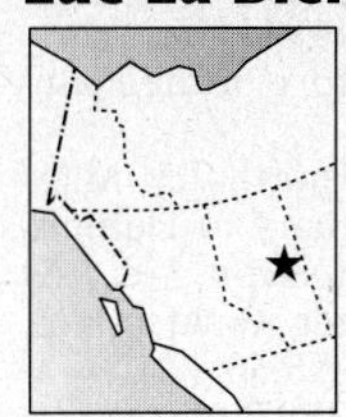

B 106 (170.6 km) **DC 383.5** (617.2 km) Located 134 miles/215 km northeast of Edmonton on Alberta Highway 55. **Population**: 2,550. **Emergency Services: RCMP**, phone (403) 623-4380. **Hospital**, phone (403) 623-4404. **Ambulance**, phone (403) 623-2142. **Fire Department**, phone (403) 623-4311.

Visitor Information: Tourist information booth at the west end of town on Highway 55, phone (403) 623-4804. Open during the summer months only. Town office, located in McArthur Place, phone (403) 623-4323.

Elevation: 1,840 feet/561m. **Private Aircraft**: Lac La Biche Municipal Airport, 1.8 miles/3 km west of town; elev. 1,825 feet/556m; length 3,500 feet/1,067m; asphalt; fuel 80, 100, Jet B.

Lac La Biche's roots go back to 1798 and establishment of a Hudson's Bay Co. trading post. In 1853, Father Albert Lacome built a mission in the area. In 1855 the mission was moved 7 miles east to its present site on the south shore of the lake. Located between the Athabasca, Mackenzie and Churchill river systems, the mission became the transportation centre of the north. Today, Lac La Biche is a major jumping-off point for the surrounding area.

Lakeland Provincial Park is a 15- to 29-mile/24- to 47-km drive east of town (see **Milepost B 75** and **Milepost B 105.9**). The park became Alberta's third largest park in 1992 and showcases some of Alberta's finest wilderness lakes. Two of the park's special features appeal to canoeists and cross country skiers: Alberta's first circle-tour canoe route, developed around a cluster of lakes in the park; and the Shaw Lake Nordic Ski Area, offering 12 miles/20 km of the most scenic groomed trails in Alberta. The adjacent recreation area contains 4 provincial campgrounds, numerous sandy beaches and a designated trophy lake; **Seibert Lake** is accessible by 4-wheel drive only.

Sir Winston Churchill Provincial Park is located on an island in Lac La Biche, joined to the mainland by a causeway (see **Milepost B 105.9**). This island features an old-growth forest that escaped the fires that destroyed the boreal forest growth around the lake. In 1920 the island and the shores of Lac La Biche were designated as a bird sanctuary. Today, bird watchers can view more than 200 species of birds.

Northern Woods & Waters Route Log

(continued)

B 107.4 (172.8 km) **DC 382.2** (615 km) Turnoff to north to Lac La Biche airport.

B 108.7 (174.9 km) **DC 380.8** (612.9 km) **Junction** with Highway 633 southwest 9.3 miles/15 km to **Missawawi Lake** Campground; 20 sites, partial hookups, water pump, fishing, boat launch. Camping fee $5.50.

B 112.4 (180.9 km) **DC 377.1** (606.9 km) Access road north 1.8 miles/3 km to Lac La Biche mission historic site.

B 116 (186.6 km) **DC 373.6** (601.2 km) Old mission road to the north.

B 122.1 (196.5 km) **DC 367.4** (591.3 km) **Junction** with Highway 858 north 1.6 miles/2.6 km to **PLAMONDON** (pop. 260).

Plamondon has a hotel, restaurants, service stations with minor-repair facilities, car wash, curling rink and museum. The museum, a church built in 1911, has many artifacts that depict the history of the Plamondon area.

Highway 858 continues north 7.5 miles/12 km beyond a bird sanctuary to Plamondon Beach Provincial Recreation Area; 69 sites, partial hookups, shelter, water pump, beach, fishing. Camping fee $5.50. ▲

B 130.2 (209.5 km) **DC 359.3** (578.3 km) Atmore; cafe, service station, small store.

B 131.2 (211.2 km) **DC 358.3** (576.6 km) **Junction** with Alberta Highway 63, which leads north 154.5 miles/248.6 km to **FORT McMURRAY** (pop. 34,706). In 1790, the North West Trading Co. established a trading post on the west side of the Athabasca River opposite present-day Fort McMurray. Abandoned after a smallpox epidemic, a new site was chosen in 1870 on the east bank of the Athabasca for a Hudson's Bay Co. tradng post that became a major depot on the supply route from northern Saskatchewan to Lake Athabasca. Today, Fort McMurray's economy is driven by its 2 oil-sands plants, which produce more than 200,000 barrels daily.

A major attraction in Fort McMurray is the Oil Sands Interpretive Centre. The centre features the history, development and technology of Alberta's oil sands industry. Both guided and self-guided tours available. Open year-round; phone (403) 743-7167.

Fort McMurray has all visitor services. There are 9 public campgrounds along Highway 63. ▲

Highway 63 continues north from Fort McMurray as a paved road 38.2 miles/61.4 km to connect with a 99-mile/160-km gravel-dirt winter road/summer trail to **FORT CHIPEWYAN** (pop. 967), the oldest permanentaly inhabited settlement in Alberta. Fort Chipewyan, often referred to as "Fort Chip" or just "Chip" by the locals, has a tourist lodge with 10 rooms and a dining lounge.

B 135.6 (218.2 km) **DC 353.9** (569.6 km) **GRASSLAND** (pop. 66); motel, restaurants, service stations with repair facilities, store.

B 136 (218.8 km) **DC 353.6** (569 km) Small ornate Ukrainian Orthodox church to south.

B 144.4 (232.4 km) **DC 345.1** (555.4 km) Hamlet of Donatville; small store, gas, pay phone. Side road east 12 miles/20 km to North Buck Lake.

B 145.5 (234.1 km) **DC 344.1** (553.7 km) **Junction** with Alberta Highway 63 south 11 miles/17 km to Boyle and 55 miles/89 km to Alberta Highway 28. Hope Lake Campground, located 2 miles/3.2 km south and 2 miles/3.2 km east, has 40 sites, partial hookups, shelter and water pump. ▲

B 147 (236.5 km) **DC 342.6** (551.3 km) Railroad crossing.

B 148 (238.2 km) **DC 341.5** (549.6 km) Side road north 6 miles/10 km to the Alberta Pacific (ALPAC) sawmill complex.

B 148.8 (239.4 km) **DC 340.8** (548.4 km) Bridge over Flat Bed Creek.

B 149.8 (241.1 km) **DC 339.7** (546.7 km) Roadside turnout with a historical plaque describing the former community of Amber Valley to north.

B 150.6 (242.3 km) **DC 338.9** (545.5 km) Bridge over Pine Creek.

B 161.9 (260.6 km) **DC 327.6** (527.2 km) **Junction** with Highway 827 south. Access road north 9 miles/15 km to **Jackfish Lake** Campground; 26 sites, partial hookups, water pump, fishing, boat launch. Camping fee $7. ▲

Pioneer buildings near Athabasca. (Wes Bergen, Diarama)

B 164.7 (265 km) **DC 324.9** (522.8 km) **Junction** with Highway 813 north 38 miles/62 km to the community of Calling Lake and **Calling Lake** Provincial Park; 25 sites, boat launch, firewood, fishing. **Rock Island Lake** and Tanasiuk Campground are located 59 miles/96 km north of this junction; 51 sites, fishing, boat launch. ▲

B 164.9 (265.3 km) **DC 324.7** (522.5 km) Athabasca River visible to north. Athabasca Rivers Edge Campground has 25 sites, partial hookups, tap water, public phone and picnic tables. Camping fee $7. ▲

Athabasca

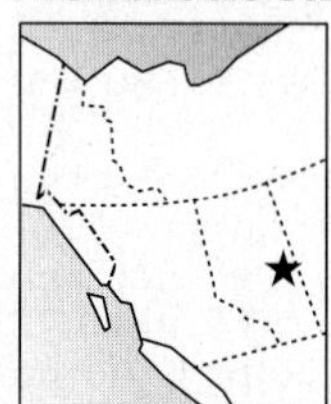

B 165 (265.5 km) **DC 324.5** (522.3 km) Located 91 miles/147 km north of Edmonton at the junction of Highways 55 and 2. **Population:** 2,300. **Emergency Services: RCMP**, phone (403) 675-4252. **Hospital and Ambulance**, phone (403) 675-2261. **Fire Department**, phone (403) 675-2200.

Visitor Information: Tourist information booth along the Athabasca River near the grain elevators in an old train caboose. Open during the summer months only.

Elevation: 1,750 feet/527m. **Private Aircraft**: Athabasca Municipal Airport, 3 miles/5 km east at the junction of Highways 2 and 827; elev. 1,880 feet/574m; length 3,000 feet/914m; asphalt; fuel 80, 100.

Visitor facilities include a hotel, 3 motels, many restaurants, retail and grocery outlets, public library, hockey and curling rink, tennis courts and a swimming pool. An 18-hole golf course is 1.2 miles/2 km north on Highway 813. The course has a clubhouse, driving range and grass greens.

Athabasca Landing was founded by the Hudson's Bay Co. in 1874, when the Athabasca Landing Trail was established and a trading post was constructed. In its early years, Athabasca was a busy transshipment point for freight movement in northwestern Canada. The Athabasca Landing Trail, running from Athabasca south 99 miles/160 km to Edmonton, became in 1880 the first registered highway in Alberta. The railroad arrived in Athabasca in 1912.

The Athabasca Landing Trail, a 76-mile/121 km corridor from Gibbons to Athabasca, runs roughly parallel to Highway 2 and served the Indians long before the arrival of the Europeans. It became the overland route connecting the Athabasca and north Saskatchewan rivers. The Hudson's Bay Co. developed the trail in 1875, and for the next 35 years it played a vital role in the development of the North. The first part of the old trail has been lost to the plough, and today the trail begins 24 miles/40 km north of Edmonton.

Northern Woods & Waters Route Log

(continued)

ALBERTA HIGHWAY 2

B 165.1 (265.7 km) **DC 324.4** (522.1 km) Bridge over the Tawatinaw River.

B 165.8 (266.8 km) **DC 323.7** (521 km) Entrance to Athabasca University to south.

B 173.9 (279.8 km) **DC 315.7** (508 km) **Junction** with side road west to the communities of Baptiste Lake and Sunset Beach.

B 176.3 (283.8 km) **DC 313.2** (504 km) Bridge over Baptiste Creek.

B 179.3 (288.5 km) **DC 310.3** (499.3 km) Access road east 2.5 miles/4 km and then north 5 miles/8 km to **Island Lake** Provincial Recreation Campground; 11 sites, water pump, partial hookups, fishing, boat launch. Camping fee $7. **Chain Lakes** Campground, located another 7 miles/12 km north, has 20 sites, partial hookups, water pump, fishing and boat launch. Electric motors only. Camping fee $5.50. ▲

B 180.6 (290.6 km) **DC 309** (497.2 km) Community of Island Lake South (pop. 122) to east.

B 181.4 (292 km) **DC 308** (495.6 km) North entrance east into Island Lake Recreation Area (see **Milepost B 179.3**).

B 182 (293 km) **DC 307.5** (494.8 km) Island Lake store and gas station to east.

B 183.2 (294.8 km) **DC 306.3** (493 km) Access road east 12 miles/20 km to Chain Lakes.

B 185.6 (298.7 km) **DC 303.9** (489.1 km) Access road west 1.2 miles/2 km to Ghost Lake.

B 193.7 (311.8 km) **DC 295.8** (476 km) **Lawrence Lake** Campground to west; 27

sites, partial hookups, water pump, fishing, boat launch. Camping fee $7.50.

B 199.7 (321.3 km) **DC 289.9** (466.5 km) Creek crossing.

B 201.1 (323.7 km) **DC 288.4** (464.1 km) Secondary side road north 14 miles/23 km to Smith.

B 206.1 (331.7 km) **DC 283.4** (456.1 km) Secondary side road north 5.5 miles/9 km to Hondo.

B 210.2 (338.3 km) **DC 279.3** (449.5 km) **Junction** with Alberta Highway 44 south 66 miles/105 km to Westlock and to Alberta Highway 18. Chisholm Provincial Recreation Area is 6 miles/10 km south; 8 sites, picnic tables, no camping fee.

B 210.8 (339.3 km) **DC 278.7** (448.5 km) Roadside turnout for large trucks on both sides of highway.

B 212.3 (341.6 km) **DC 277.3** (446.2 km) **Junction** with Highway 2A north 1.8 miles/3 km to Hondo (no services) and 9 miles/15 km to **SMITH** (pop. 250). Smith has a hotel, restaurant, small store and service station with minor repair facilities. A secondary road continues north and west out of Smith, along the Slave River, and rejoins the highway at **Milepost B 236.1. Fawcett Lake** Resort is 24 miles/39 km northeast of Smith; 324 sites, dump station, tap water, showers, public phone, laundry, beach, boat launch, fishing, boat and canoe rentals, store, concession/food service. **West Fawcett Lake** Campground, 15 miles/25 km north of Smith, has 28 sites, partial hookups, water pump, fishing and boat launch. Camping fee $7.50.

B 212.5 (341.9 km) **DC 277.1** (445.9 km) Railroad crossing.

B 214.1 (344.6 km) **DC 275.4** (443.2 km) Bridge over the Athabasca River. Entering Slave Lake Ranger District westbound.

B 222.8 (358.6 km) **DC 266.7** (429.2 km) Bridge over the Saulteaux River.

B 230.4 (370.8 km) **DC 259.1** (417 km) Bridge over the Otauwau River.

B 235.5 (379 km) **DC 254** (408.8 km) Divided highway begins westbound.

B 236.1 (380 km) **DC 253.4** (407.8 km) **Junction** with loop road from Smith. **Lesser Slave River** Provincial Recreation Area located 5.5 miles/9 km north on the return road has 11 sites, partial hookups, water pump, fishing and picnic area. Camping fee $5.50.

B 239.5 (385.5 km) **DC 250** (402.3 km) Mitsue Provincial Recreation Area to north; 12 sites, water pump, fishing and picnic tables.

B 245.7 (395.5 km) **DC 243.8** (392.3 km) Heavy-truck inspection and weigh station to south.

B 246.6 (396.8 km) **DC 243** (391 km) **Junction** with Alberta Highway 88 (Bicentennial Highway), which leads north to Lesser Slave Lake Provincial Park (see description following); 105 miles/168 km to the community of Red Earth Creek; and 255 miles/410 km to Fort Vermilion. Highway 88 is paved to Red Earth Creek; the remainder of the road to Fort Vermilion is gravel and in poor condition. In wet weather the road can be slippery, muddy and rutted.

Lesser Slave Lake Provincial Park, along the east shore of Lesser Slave Lake, is divided into 3 different recreational areas. Devonshire Beach day-use area is 3.6 miles/6 km north on Highway 88. Northshore day-use area, 7 miles/11 km north on Highway 88, has 14 picnic sites, shelter, water pump and a fish-cleaning stand. Martin River Campground, 18 miles/30 km north on Highway 88, has 113 sites, dump station, public phone, ski trails, hiking trails, beach, fishing and tap water.

B 247.2 (397.8 km) **DC 242.3** (390 km) Bridge over Sawridge Creek.

Slave Lake

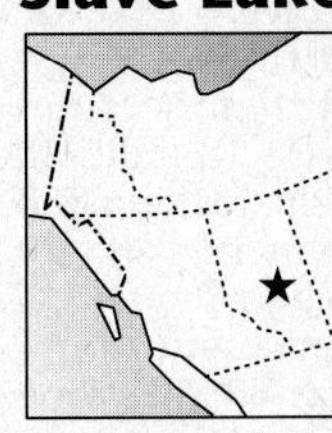

B 247.4 (398.1 km) **DC 242.2** (389.7 km) Located on the southeast shore of Lesser Slave Lake, 152 miles/245 km northwest of Edmonton. **Population**: 5,800. **Emergency Services: RCMP**, phone (403) 849-3045. **Hospital**, phone (403) 849-3732. **Ambulance**, phone (403) 849-3614.

Visitor Information: In a small building on the service road just off Highway 2, phone (403) 849-4611. Open mid-May to mid-Sept. The town office is located at 328 2nd St. NE, phone (403) 849-8000.

Elevation: 1,900 feet/581m. **Private Aircraft**: Slave Lake Airport to north; elev. 1,912 feet/583m; length 5,000 feet/1,524m; asphalt; fuel 100, Jet.

Originally known as Sawridge when it was founded in the 1880s, Slave Lake was an important jumping-off point for steamboat traffic that carried prospectors bound for the Yukon and the Klondike gold rushes. Early settlers included the Metis and Cree Indians. Today, their descendants contribute to the rich cultural heritage of this well-integrated community.

Visitor facilities include 2 hotels, 3 motels, several restaurants and fast-food outlets, numerous stores, service stations with major-repair facilities and car washes.

Recreational facilities include a public library, movie theatre, curling rink, 2 arenas, ball diamonds, racquetball and tennis courts, soccer field, parks, miniature golf course and cross-country ski trails. The Gilwood Golf and Country Club, 6 miles/10 km north on Highway 88, has 9 holes, clubhouse, licensed restaurant, driving range, practice greens, and cart and club rentals.

Lesser Slave Lake Provincial Park, located north of Slave Lake on Highway 88, stretches along the northeastern shore of Lesser Slave Lake, with 5 miles/8 km of beautiful sandy beaches against a backdrop of rolling hills and luxurious growth of spruce, pine and poplar trees. The park consists of a number of campsites and day-use areas (see **Milepost B 246.6**).

Northern Woods & Waters Route Log

(continued)

B 248.2 (399.4 km) **DC 241.3** (388.4 km) Turnoff to Slave Lake industrial area and Sawridge Recreation Area to north. The Sawridge Campground has 32 sites with partial hookups, water pump, showers, picnic tables, fireplaces, firewood, stove, beach, fishing, boat rentals and hiking trails.

B 250.2 (402.7 km) **DC 239.3** (385.1 km) Entering Sawridge Indian Reserve westbound.

B 253.1 (407.3 km) **DC 236.4** (380.5 km) Turnout with litter barrels to north. Leaving Sawridge Indian Reserve westbound.

B 257.6 (414.5 km) **DC 232** (373.3 km) Creek crossing. Entering Kinuso Ranger District westbound.

B 259.1 (417 km) **DC 230.4** (370.8 km) Access road north 0.6 mile/1 km to **WIDEWATER** (pop. 203). Widewater has a small store, gas station and pay phone.

B 261.2 (420.4 km) **DC 228.4** (367.6 km) **CANYON CREEK** (pop. 164) to north; hotel, grocery store, gas station and pay phone.

B 265.6 (427.4 km) **DC 223.9** (360.4 km) Access road north 1.8 miles/3 km to Assineau (no services).

B 266.1 (428.3 km) **DC 223.4** (359.5 km) Assineau River Campground to north; 21 sites, partial hookups, water pump, picnic tables and firewood. Camping fee $5.50.

B 266.2 (428.5 km) **DC 223.3** (359.3 km) Bridge over the Assineau River.

B 272.5 (438.6 km) **DC 217** (349.2 km) Bridge over Eula Creek.

B 273.3 (439.8 km) **DC 216.2** (348 km) **Junction** with Alberta Highway 33 (Grizzly Trail), which leads south 45 miles/72.4 km to **SWAN HILLS** (pop. 2,550) Oil was discovered at Swan Hills in 1957; all visitor facilities are available. Highway 33 also connects with Barrhead (108 miles/174 km south), and junctions with Alberta Highway 43 (136 miles/219 km) west of Edmonton.

B 275.5 (443.3 km) **DC 214.1** (344.5 km) Bridge over the Swan River.

B 275.8 (443.9 km) **DC 213.7** (343.9 km) **Junction** with side road north 1.2 miles/2 km to **KINUSO** (pop. 282); hotel, cafe, store, service station and museum.

B 276.5 (444.9 km) **DC 213.1** (342.9 km) Side road north to Kinuso ranger station.

B 277 (445.7 km) **DC 212.6** (342.1 km) Bridge over Strawberry Creek.

B 278.4 (448 km) **DC 211.1** (339.8 km) Access road north 7 miles/11 km to Spruce Point Park Campground; 126 sites, partial hookups, dump station, water pump, showers, wheelchair-accessible washroom, shelter, store, concession, beach, boat launch, boat rentals, fishing, fireplaces and firewood. Camping fee $10.

B 279.3 (449.5 km) **DC 210.2** (338.3 km) Strawberry Creek Cafe and service station to north.

B 284 (457 km) **DC 205.6** (330.8 km) **FAUST** (pop. 344) to north. Faust has a hotel, restaurant, gas, 2 stores and a laundromat.

B 284.7 (458.2 km) **DC 204.8** (329.6 km) Side road north to the Faust RCMP detachment.

B 289.1 (465.2 km) **DC 200.4** (322.5 km) Creek crossing. Entering Driftpile Indian Reserve westbound.

B 290 (466.4 km) **DC 199.7** (321.4 km) Small cafe and gas station to north.

B 291.3 (468.8 km) **DC 198.2** (319 km) Bridge over the Driftpile River.

B 293 (471.6 km) **DC 196.5** (316.2 km) Leaving Driftpile Indian Reserve westbound.

B 296 (476.7 km) **DC 193.3** (311.1 km) Turnouts with litter barrels on both sides of highway.

B 298 (479.5 km) **DC 191.6** (308.3 km) **JOUSSARD** (pop. 270) to north on access road. Joussard has a small store, service station and cafe. Joussard Lakeshore Campground, located on the south shore of **Lesser Slave Lake**, has 25 sites, full hookups, dump station, tap water, showers, picnic tables, firewood, fishing and boat launch. Camping fee $8 and up.

B 299.9 (482.7 km) **DC 190** (305.1 km) Entering High Prairie Ranger District westbound.

B 304.4 (489.8 km) **DC 185.2** (298 km) Entering Sucker Creek Indian Reserve westbound.

B 305.3 (491.3 km) **DC 184.2** (296.5 km)

Bridge over Sucker Creek.

B 306.3 (492.9 km) **DC 183.2** (294.9 km) Sucker Creek Cafe to north.

B 308.3 (496.2 km) **DC 181.3** (291.7 km) Small cafe and gas station to north.

B 309 (497.2 km) **DC 180.6** (290.7 km) Roadside turnout to north with litter barrels and historical point of interest.

B 309.3 (497.8 km) **DC 180.2** (290 km) **Junction** with Highway 750 northeast to Alberta Highway 88 (Bicentennial Highway), 103 miles/165 km. Highway 750 also provides access to Grouard, 13 miles/21 km north, site of St. Bernard Mission Church and the Native Cultural Arts Museum. Hilliard's Bay Provincial Park, 8 miles/13 km east of Grouard on **Lesser Slave Lake**, has 189 sites, water, phone, beach and fishing.

B 309.8 (498.6 km) **DC 179.7** (289.2 km) Small store and gas to north.

B 312.4 (502.8 km) **DC 177.1** (285 km) **ENILDA** (pop. 128); small store and gas station.

B 313.5 (504.5 km) **DC 176** (283.3 km) East Prairie settlement and sawmill to south. Turnouts on both sides of highway.

B 313.7 (504.8 km) **DC 175.9** (283 km) Bridge over the East Prairie River.

B 318.2 (512 km) **DC 171.4** (275.8 km) High Prairie Lions Campground to north; 14 sites, partial hookups, pump, picnic tables, shelter and firewood. Camping fee $5.

High Prairie

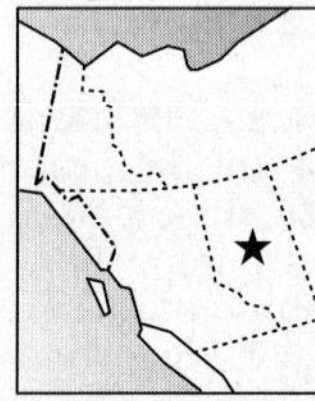

B 319.6 (514.3 km) **DC 169.9** (273.5 km) Located 230 miles/370 km northwest of Edmonton, 78 miles/126 km southeast of Peace River. **Population:** 2,970. **Emergency Services: RCMP**, phone (403) 523-3378. **Hospital and Ambulance**, phone (403) 523-3341. **Fire Department**, phone (403) 523-3388.

Visitor Information: Tourist information centre in the centre of town on the north side of Highway 2. Open summer months only. The High Prairie town office is downtown, phone (403) 523-3388.

Elevation: 1,850 feet/602m. **Private Aircraft**: High Prairie Regional Airport, 3 miles/5 km south on Highway 749; elev. 1,850 feet/602m; length 3,000 feet/914m; asphalt; fuel 80, 100.

While the High Prairie area was being settled by homesteaders in the late 19th century, the arrival of the railroad in 1914 heralded the beginning of High Prairie as a town. A busy agricultural center, this picturesque community of almost 3,000 people also serves the surrounding forest and oil field industries.

Visitor facilities include 4 motels, restaurants, retail and grocery stores, service stations with major-repair facilities, a library, an art gallery and the High Prairie District Museum, located in the centre of town on Highway 2 and part of the library complex. The museum features pioneer artifacts depicting the history of the region. Visitors welcome. Open Tuesday through Saturday 9 A.M. to 5 P.M.; extended hours during the summer.

Recreational facilities include a swimming pool, tennis courts, skating rink, curling rink, hockey arena and ball diamonds. The High Prairie Golf Course, located 5 miles/8 km west of town and south of Highway 2, has 9 holes, driving range, clubhouse with licensed dining, pro shop and carts for rent.

Northern Woods & Waters Route Log

(continued)

B 319.7 (514.5 km) **DC 169.8** (273.3 km) **Junction** with Highway 749 south 20 miles/32 km to Banana Belt Park on the West Prairie River; 6 campsites, picnic tables and water pump. No camping fee.

Highway 749 leads north out of High Prairie 12 miles/20 km and then becomes Highway 679, which leads west 18 miles/30 km and rejoins Highway 2 at **Milepost B 341.9. Winagami Lake** Provincial Park, 20 miles/32 km northwest of High Prairie off Highway 679, is a day-use area and campground. The campground has 63 sites, one site and facility for disabled use, dump station, fishing, boat launch, wading pool, paved trails, bird-viewing platforms with scopes, fireplaces, firewood, shelter and tap water.

Hart River Provincial Recreation Area, 24 miles/40 km northwest of High Prairie, is a day-use area with picnic tables, beach, fishing and boat launch.

B 320.2 (515.3 km) **DC 169.3** (272.5 km) Bridge over the West Prairie River.

B 321.1 (516.8 km) **DC 168.4** (271 km) Railroad crossing.

B 321.1 (521.5 km) **DC 165.5** (266.3 km) Creek crossing.

B 324.7 (522.5 km) **DC 164.9** (265.3 km) High Prairie Golf Course to south.

B 328.8 (529.2 km) **DC 160.7** (258.6 km) **Junction** with Alberta Spur Highway 2A west to Highway 43 (see MACKENZIE ROUTE section). Continue on Highway 2 north to McLennan.

B 329.3 (530 km) **DC 160.2** (257.8 km) Turnout with litter barrels to east.

B 331.4 (533.3 km) **DC 158.1** (254.5 km) Railroad crossing.

B 341.9 (550.3 km) **DC 147.6** (237.5 km) **Junction** with Highway 679 east 7 miles/11 km to **Winagami Lake** Provincial Park (see **Milepost B 319.7**).

B 343 (552 km) **DC 146.5** (235.8 km) Hamlet of Kathleen (no services).

McLennan

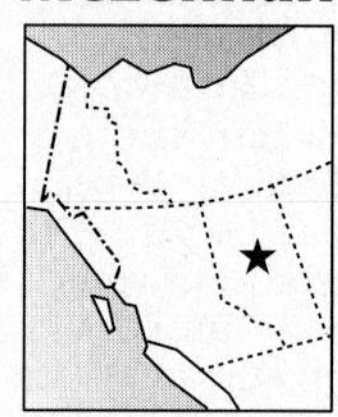

B 350.2 (563.5 km) **DC 139.4** (224.3 km) Located 288 miles/464 km northwest of Edmonton on Highway 2. **Population:** 1,100. **Emergency Services: RCMP**, phone (403) 324-3061. **Hospital and Ambulance**, phone (403) 324-3730. **Fire Department**, phone (403) 324-3811.

Visitor Information: Tourist information centre in town on the north side of Highway 2. Open May to Sept.

Elevation: 1,920 feet/584m. **Private Aircraft**: Smoky River Airport, 8 miles/13 km west on Highway 2 and 0.6 mile/1 km south on access road, 1.2 miles/2 km south of Donnelly; elev. 1,949 feet/592m; length 2,953 feet/900m; asphalt; fuel 100.

McLennan was founded in 1914 as a divisional point for the Edmonton, Dunvegan and British Columbia railway. It was named after John K. McLennan, then secretary of the railway, by his brother-in-law J.D. McArther, the builder of the railway. In the years since, McLennan has developed from a rustic frontier outpost to a modern community. McLennan is the seat of the Roman Catholic Archdiocese of the Grouard-McLennan area and has a beautiful cathedral. Set on the south shore of Kimiwan Lake, which is at the centre of 3 major migration flyways (Mississippi, Pacific and Central), the community has chosen the slogan "Bird Capital of Canada."

Visitor facilities include a hotel, motel, restaurants, grocery and retail stores, service stations with major repair facilities, library, laundromat and a museum housed in an old passenger railcar.

Recreational facilities include an arena, curling rink, tennis courts, ball diamonds and a 9-hole golf course. McLennan Community Campground and Recreation Area, located in town on the south shore of Kimiwan Lake, has 28 sites with hookups, beach, boat launch, licensed dining room and lounge.

Northern Woods & Waters Route Log

(continued)

B 351 (564.8 km) **DC 138.6** (223 km) Smoky River Regional Golf Course to south; 9 holes, pro shop, licensed dining and cart rental. Historical point of interest to north about the Northern Woods & Waters Route.

B 351.5 (565.7 km) **DC 138** (222.1 km) **Junction** with Highway 746 south to Highway 2A.

B 351.6 (565.8 km) **DC 137.9** (222 km) Railroad crossing.

B 358.7 (577.2 km) **DC 130.9** (210.6 km) Donnelly to north, Smoky River Regional Airport to south. **DONNELLY** (pop. 450) has a hotel, restaurants, stores, service stations with repair facilities, and a library. A historic site 3 miles/5 km south of town features a fully operational 1904 Case steam engine.

B 359.7 (578.8 km) **DC 129.9** (209 km) **Junction** of Alberta Highway 49 west, Highway 43 south and Highway 2 north to Peace River and the Mackenzie Highway (see MACKENZIE ROUTE section). The Northern Woods & Waters Route follows Alberta Highway 49 west to Dawson Creek, BC.

ALBERTA HIGHWAY 49

B 361.7 (582.1 km) **DC 127.8** (205.7 km) Large alfalfa-dehydrating plant to the north.

B 362.2 (582.9 km) **DC 127.4** (205 km) Falher Municipal Campground to north; 30 sites, full hookups, tap water, public phone.

B 362.5 (583.3 km) **DC 127.1** (204.5 km) Access road north 1 mile/1.6 km to **FALHER** (pop. 1,200). Falher is known as the "Honey Capital of Canada" and boasts the world's largest replica of a honey bee. The town has 5 grain elevators and 2 alfalfa-processing plantsy. Visitor facilities include a hotel, motel, stores, restaurants and service stations with major repair.

B 367.8 (591.9 km) **DC 121.7** (195.9 km) **Junction** with Highway 744 north 1.8 miles/3 km to Girouxville and on to Peace River. **GIROUXVILLE** (pop. 367). The community has one of the largest museums in Alberta. Opened in 1969, the museum features artifacts recalling Indian life, missionary works, pioneering and trapping, and early machinery and equipment. Open year-round. Small admission fee. Visitor facilities include a hotel, family restaurant, service stations with repair facilities, grocery store, health food store and laundromat.

B 381.3 (613.6 km) **DC 108.2** (174.1 km) Access road north to Peavine Creek day-use area; 10 sites, water pump, shelter, picnic area, fireplaces, firewood and boat launch.

B 381.5 (613.9 km) **DC 108.1** (173.9 km) Bridge over the Smoky River.

B 381.7 (614.3 km) **DC 107.8** (173.5 km) Watino to north. Entering Spirit River Ranger District westbound as the highway ascends a steep hill.

B 383.7 (617.5 km) **DC 105.8** (170.3 km) **Junction** with Highway 740 north 5 miles/8 km to Tangent (no services). Highway 740 continues north 30 miles/49.5 km to the Shaftsbury Ferry crossing of the Peace River.

B 390.9 (629 km) **DC 98.7** (158.8 km) Access road south 0.6 mile/1 km to Lakeside Golf and Country Club; 9 holes and pro shop.

B 391.7 (630.3 km) **DC 97.9** (157.5 km) Eaglesham food and gas station to north.

B 391.9 (630.6 km) **DC 97.7** (157.2 km) **Junction** with Highway 739 north 4 miles/6.4 km to **EAGLESHAM** (pop. 185). Eaglesham has a hotel, motel, restaurant, gas station, library and curling rink. Kieyho Park and day-use area, located 10 miles/16 km north of town on the south shore of the Peace River, has 4 sites, picnic tables, hiking trails and boat launch.

B 404.6 (651.1 km) **DC 84.9** (136.7 km) Access road north to a small ski slope.

B 411.9 (662.8 km) **DC 77.7** (125 km) **Junction** with Highway 733 south 26 miles/42 km to TeePee Creek and 35.4 miles/57 km to Alberta Highway 34. Access road off Highway 49 leads north 0.6 mile/1 km to **WANHAM** (pop. 250); hotel, restaurant, service station with repair facilities, and stores.

B 413.8 (666 km) **DC 75.7** (121.8 km) Access road south 1.8 miles/3 km to **Dreamers Lake** campground and recreation area; 26 sites, water pump, picnic tables, public phone, boat launch, fishing and a 9-hole golf course. Camping fee.

B 416.5 (670.2 km) **DC 73.1** (117.6 km) Railroad crossing.

B 417.8 (672.3 km) **DC 71.8** (115.5 km) Bridge over the Saddle River. Saddle River Campground to south.

B 424.5 (683.2 km) **DC 65** (104.6 km) **Junction** with Alberta Highway 2. Northbound, Highway 2 crosses the Peace River to connect with Alberta Highway 64 to Fort St. John or to Grimshaw at the gateway of the Mackenzie Highway (see MACKENZIE ROUTE section). Southbound, Highway 2 leads through the communities of Sexsmith and Grande Prairie, then west to Dawson Creek (see EAST ACCESS ROUTE section).

Follow Highway 2 north 28 miles/45km for **FAIRVIEW** (pop. 2,500) and Highway 64 west 118.7 miles/191 km to Fort St. John, BC. Fairview, the agricultural centre for the northwest Alberta's Peace River region, has hotels, motels and restaurants. Camping at Cummings Lake recreation area at north end of town; 28 sites, hookups, restrooms, firewood and water. Attractions here include the RCMP Centennial Museum downtown and Fairview College. Highway 64 to Fort St. John is paved with some steep descents westbound and a short section of hairpin turns with intermittent pavement breaks about 10 miles/16 km east of Fort St. John. Public campgrounds are available along Highway 64 at Miles 14.7, 17.6, 26.3, 35.5, 39.6 and 71.1.

Continue on Highway 49 westbound for Dawson Creek.

B 425.6 (684.9 km) **DC 63.9** (102.9 km) Bridge over the Spirit River.

B 425.7 (685 km) **DC 63.9** (102.8 km) **Nardham Lake** Campground to north; 15 sites, hookups, picnic tables, water pump, canoeing, fishing. Camping fee $5.

B 426.1 (685.7 km) **DC 63.4** (102.1 km) Entering **RYCROFT** (pop. 534) westbound. Rycroft is located at the crossroads of Highways 49 and 2, en route to "mile zero" of both the Alaska or Mackenzie highways. Rycroft was established with the coming of the railroad in 1912 and was incorporated on March 15, 1944. Visitor facilities include a motel, restaurants, service stations with major repair facilities, stores, bank, library, ball diamonds, ice arena and tennis courts.

B 427.8 (688.4 km) **DC 61.8** (99.4 km) Access road south 2.4 miles/4 km to golf course; 9 holes, licensed dining, clubhouse, pro shop and carts for rent.

B 429.8 (691.7 km) **DC 59.7** (96.1 km) Spirit River Airport entrance, visitor center and St. Elias Ukrainian Church to north.

Spirit River

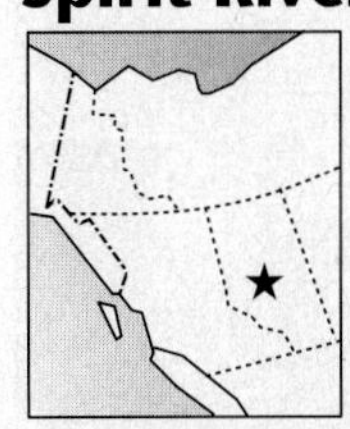

B 430.6 (693 km) **DC 58.9** (94.8 km) Located 221 miles/356 km northwest of Edmonton, 47 miles/76 km north of Grande Prairie, 60 miles/96 km east of Dawson Creek, BC. **Population:** 1,150. **Emergency Services: RCMP**, phone (403) 864-3533. **Hospital**, phone (403) 864-3993. **Ambulance**, phone (403) 864-2453. **Fire Department**, phone (403) 864-3511.

Visitor Information: Tourist information booth located in town on the north side of Highway 49, across from the picturesque St. Elias Ukrainian Orthodox Church. Open summer months only.

Elevation: 2,100 feet/637m. **Private Aircraft**: Spirit River Regional Airport, located on the north side of Highway 49, across from the business district; elev. 2,044 feet/621m; length 3,000 feet/914m; asphalt; no fuel.

In 1891, a trading post was established along both sides of the original settlement of Spirit River. When the railroad came through in 1913, the community established itself as an agricultural centre. Today, Spirit River is a major trading centre for a large rural population.

Visitor facilities include a hotel, motel, restaurants, retail and grocery stores, service stations, bank and public library. A museum houses artifacts of the early days of Spirit River. Recreational facilities include an arena, curling rink, tennis courts, soccer field and ball diamond. Spirit River Municipal Campground, located in town, has 8 sites, partial hookups, tap water, public phone and dump station. Camping fee charged.

Northern Woods & Waters Route Log

(continued)

B 430.9 (693.4 km) **DC 58.7** (94.4 km) **Junction** with Highway 731 south 16 miles/26 km and east 3 miles/5 km to Woking, and then farther east 3 miles/5 km to Alberta Highway 2. Hilltop Recreation Area, located 11.2 miles/18 km south on Highway 731 and then west 7 miles/11 km on Highway 677, and then south 3.6 miles/6 km on Highway 724, has 8 sites, water pump and hiking trails. No camping fee.

Chinook Valley Golf Course, 12 miles/20 km south on Highway 741, has 9 holes, pro shop and licensed dining.

Abundant birdlife along this route includes the red-necked grebe.

(Tom W. Parkin)

B 433.9 (698.3 km) **DC 55.6** (89.5 km) **Junction** with Highway 727 north 6 miles/10 km to Devale.

B 445.7 (717.2 km) **DC 43.9** (70.6 km) Bridge over Ksituan River.

B 446.1 (717.9 km) **DC 43.4** (69.9 km) Access road north 1.8 miles/3 km to Jackbird day-use area.

B 447.1 (719.5 km) **DC 42.4** (68.3 km) **Junction** with Highway 725 north 4 miles/7 km to **Moonshine Lake** Provincial Park and Campground; 110 sites (23 with power), tap water, dump station, public phone, canoeing, fishing, boat launch, shelter, firewood, ball diamond. Electric motors only. Camping fee $10.75.

B 454.6 (731.6 km) **DC 34.9** (56.2 km) Silver Valley Provincial Recreation Area to north; 7 sites, water pump and picnic tables. No camping fee.

B 460.4 (741 km) **DC 29.1** (46.8 km) Gordendale to north (no services).

B 466.5 (750.8 km) **DC 23** (37 km) Pillsworth Road to north leads 21.7 miles/35 km to Cotillian Campsite; 13 sites, tap water, picnic tables, shelter, firewood and boat launch. No camping fee.

B 468.2 (753.5 km) **DC 21.3** (34.3 km) Small airstrip to south.

B 471.6 (759.1 km) **DC 17.8** (28.7 km) **Junction** with Highway 719 north 5 miles/8 km to Bonanza; gas, food, pay phone.

B 474.9 (764.2 km) **DC 14.7** (23.6 km) Baytree to north; gas, food, pay phone.

B 478.2 (769.6 km) **DC 11.3** (18.2 km) Large roadside turnout with litter barrels and bathrooms to south.

B 480 (772.4 km) **DC 9.6** (15.4 km) Alberta–British Columbia border. NOTE: Alberta observes Mountain standard time. Most of British Columbia observes Pacific standard time. Both observe daylight saving time. See Time Zones in the GENERAL INFORMATION section for details.

B 485.5 (781.3 km) **DC 4.6** (7.4 km) Pouce Coupe River bridge.

B 486.3 (782.7 km) **DC 3.2** (5.1 km) **Junction** with access road north 10 miles/16 km to Rolla and on to the crossing of the Peace River and Clayhurst. South from here, the road leads 3 miles/5 km to Pouce Coupe.

B 489.5 (787.8 km) **DC 0** Downtown Dawson Creek, BC. (See the ALASKA HIGHWAY section for description.)

SILVER TRAIL HIGHWAY

Klondike Highway Junction to Keno City, YT
Yukon Highway 11

The Binet House in Mayo offers mineral displays and mining history. (Earl L. Brown, staff)

The Silver Trail leads northeast from the Klondike Highway (see **Milepost J 214.4** in the KLONDIKE LOOP section) to Mayo, Elsa and Keno City. From its junction with the Klondike Highway (Yukon Highway 2), the Silver Trail (Yukon Highway 11) leads 31.9 miles/51.3 km to Mayo; 60.3 miles/97 km to Elsa; and 69.1 miles/111.2 km to Keno City. The Silver Trail also provides access to Duncan Creek Road, the original Silver Trail. It is approximately 140 miles/225 km round-trip to Keno City and an easy day trip for motorists. The road is asphalt-surfaced to Mayo, hard-packed gravel from Mayo to Keno. Watch for soft shoulders, especially in wet weather. Gas is available only at Mayo and at Stewart Crossing.

There is an information kiosk on the Klondike Highway at the south end of Stewart River bridge. Stop at the kiosk for information on the Silver Trail, or visit Binet House in Mayo. Or write Silver Trail Tourism, Box 268, Mayo, YT Y0B 1M0; phone (in summer) (403) 996-2926, winter phone (403) 996-2290.

The Silver Trail to Mayo follows the Stewart River through what has been one of the richest silver mining regions in Canada.

Emergency medical services: In Mayo, phone (403) 996-4444; or phone the RCMP toll free, Yukon-wide, at 1-403-667-5555.

Silver Trail Log

Distance is measured from the junction with the Klondike Highway (J).

J 0 Junction of Silver Trail (Yukon Highway 11) and Klondike Highway.

J 0.2 (0.3 km) Marker shows distance to Mayo 51 km, Elsa 97 km, Keno 110 km.

J 1.2 (2 km) Stewart River to the south.

J 3 (4.8 km) Bad curve. Turnout to south.

J 9.6 (15.4 km) Large gravel pit turnout to south.

J 12 (19.2 km) Large double-ended turnout with litter barrrels overlooking the Stewart River.

J 27.4 (44.1 km) Pull-through rest area; outhouses, litter barrel, picnic tables.

J 30.7 (49.5 km) Winding descent for northeast-bound traffic; good view of valley.

J 31.2 (50.2 km) McIntyre Park picnic area to south on banks of the Mayo River.

J 31.3 (50.3 km) **Mayo River** bridge. Good fishing from bridge for grayling.

J 31.9 (51.3 km) **Junction** with access road to Mayo (description follows). Turn right (south) for Mayo, keep left (north) for road to Elsa and Keno City.

Mayo

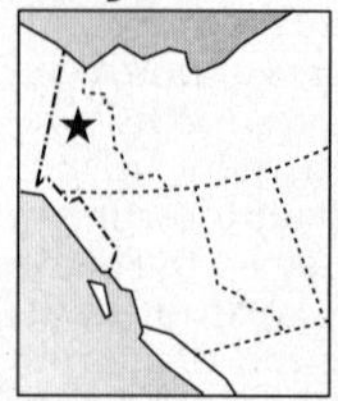

Located on the bank of the Stewart River near its confluence with the Mayo River. **Population:** 500. **Emergency Services: RCMP**, phone (403) 996-5555. **Ambulance**, phone (403) 996-4444. **Visitor Information:** At Binet House Interpretive Centre, open 10:30 A.M. to 6 P.M. in summer, phone (403) 996-2926. Exhibits include floral and mineral displays, silver and galena samples, and information panels on mining and geology. Yukon Gold Explorer's Passport stamped here. **Elevation:** 1,650 feet/503m.**Climate:** Residents claim it's the coldest and hottest spot in Yukon. Record low, -80°F/-62.2°C (February 1947);

SILVER TRAIL HIGHWAY *Klondike Highway Junction to Keno City, YT*

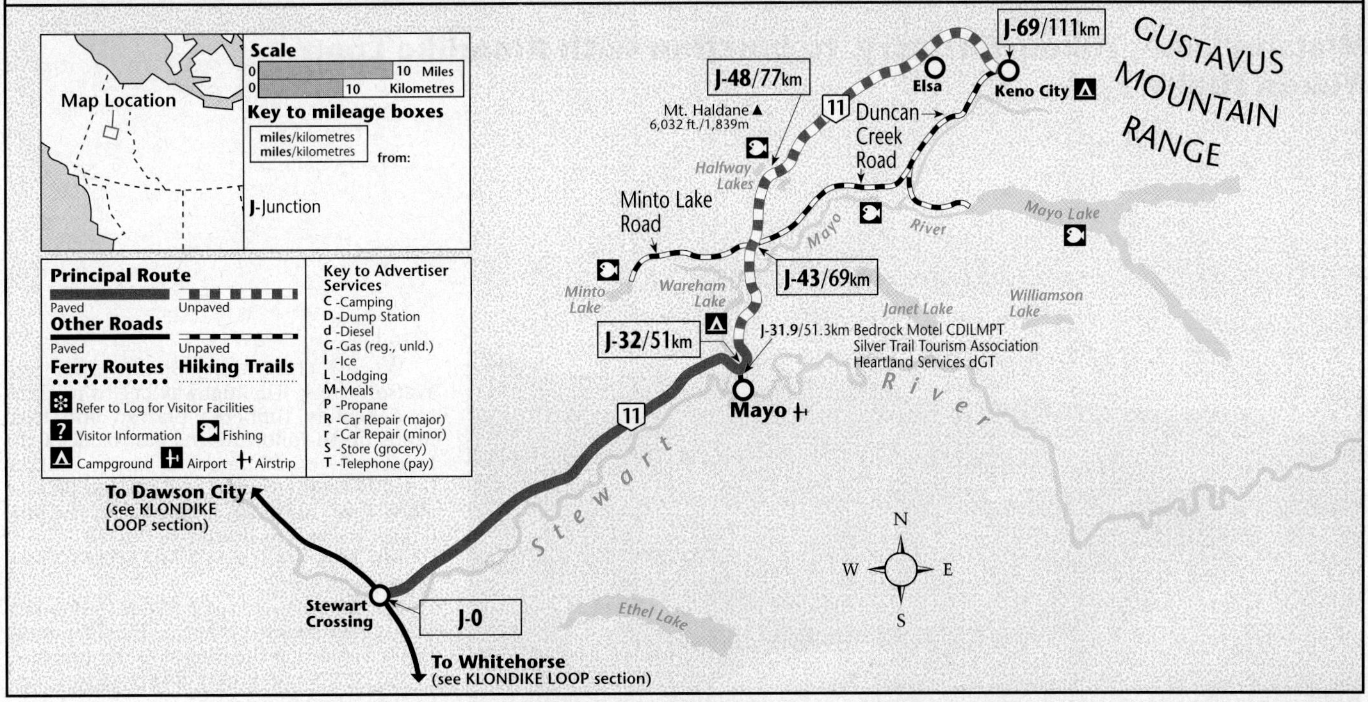

record high, 97°F/36.1°C (June 1969). **Radio:** CBC 1230, CHON-FM 98.5. **Television:** CBC Anik, Channel 7. **Transportation:** Charter floatplane and helicopter service available. Scheduled bus service.

Private Aircraft: Mayo airstrip, 4 miles/ 6.5 km north; elev. 1,653 feet/504m; length 4,850 feet/1,478m; gravel; fuel 100, Jet B.

Mayo has most traveler facilities including 2 motels, 2 bed and breakfasts, cafe, laundromat, gas station with diesel, hardware, grocery and variety stores (closed Sunday). Tire repair and minor vehicle repair are available. Post office, liquor store and library located in the Territorial Bldg. Bank service available 10 A.M. to 1 P.M. Monday, Wednesday and Friday.

Mayo was formerly known as Mayo Landing and began as a river settlement and port for silver ore shipments to Whitehorse. It is now a service centre for mineral exploration in the area. Yukon Electrical Co. Ltd. operates a hydroelectric project here.

Canoeists can put in at Mayo on the Stewart River for a paddle to Stewart Crossing or Dawson City.

The Silver Trail Tourism Association. See display ad this section.

Silver Trail Log

(continued)

J **32.8** (52.8 km) Mayo airport, built in 1928 by the Treadwell Mining Co.

J **34.9** (56.2 km) Side road to Mayo hydro dam, built in 1951 and completed in 1952.

J **35.8** (57.6 km) Turnoff to west for Five Mile Lake Yukon government campground; 20 sites, boat launch, picnic tables, firepits.

J **36.1** (58.1 km) Five Mile Lake day-use area. Pavement ends, gravel begins, northbound.

J **37.6** (60.5 km) Wareham Lake to east, created by the Mayo River power project.

J **38.2** (61.4 km) Survival shelter to east.

J **42.9** (69 km) **Junction** of Yukon Highway 11 with Minto Lake Road and Duncan Creek Road. Turn west (left) and drive 12 miles/19 km for **Minto Lake;** good fishing for lake trout and grayling. Also access to Highet Creek.

Turn east (right) at junction for Duncan Creek Road, which leads to Mayo Lake and Keno City. The original Silver Trail, Duncan Creek Road was used by Treadwell Yukon during the 1930s to haul silver ore from Keno into Mayo, where it was loaded onto riverboats.

This 25-mile/40-km back road is mostly good hard-packed gravel. Motorists note, however, that the last 10 miles/16 km into Keno City via Duncan Creek Road are narrow and winding, slippery when wet, and not recommended for large vehicles or trailers. Heading northeast on Duncan Creek Road, travelers will see the site of Fields Creek Roadhouse at Mile 5, and Stones Roadhouse at Mile 11. At Mile 14 Duncan Creek Road junctions with a 6-mile/10-km side road which leads to **Mayo Lake;** there is good fishing along the **Mayo River** to the dam at the west end of Mayo Lake. At Mile 14.2 there is a private gold mine, Duncan Creek Golddusters, with guided tours and gold panning (fee charged). At Mile 18 are the remains of the Van Cleaves Roadhouse. At Mile 25 Duncan Creek Road junctions with Highway 11 at Keno City.

J **47.1** (77 km) Watch for turnoff for Mount Haldane trail; follow gravel road 2 miles/3.2 km to trailhead. This 4-mile-/6.4-km-long trail leads to summit, elev. 6,023 feet/1,836m.

J **48** (77.2 km) **Halfway Lakes;** fishing for northern pike. Silver Trail Inn; food and lodging in summer.

J **49** (78.8 km) Mount Haldane Lions survival shelter.

J **54.9** (88.3 km) South McQuesten River Road.

J **60.3** (97 km) **ELSA** (pop. 10) was a company town for United Keno Hill Mines, formerly one of the largest silver mines in North America and one of the Yukon's oldest, continuously operating hardrock mines until its closure in 1989. The Elsa claim is a well-mineralized silver vein, located on Galena Hill and named for the sister of prospector Charlie Brefalt, who received $250,000 for Treadwell Yukon's richest mine. A plaque here commemorates American engineer Livingston Wernecke, who came to the Keno Hill area in 1919 to investigate the silver–lead ore discoveries for Treadwell–Yukon Mining Co.

J **63.8** (102.6 km) Side road leads north to Hanson Lakes and McQuesten Lake. Galena Mountains to east. An information sign marks the Wind River trail, a former winter road to oil and mining exploration sites, which leads 300 miles/483 km north to the Bell River. The twin towers are abandoned telephone relays.

J **69.1** (111.2 km) **KENO CITY** (pop. about 50). Originally called Sheep Hill by the early miners, it was renamed Keno—a gambling game—after the Keno mining claim that was staked by Louis Bouvette in July 1919. This enormously rich discovery of silver and galena sparked the interest of 2 large mining companies, the Guggenheims and Treadwell Yukon, who set up camps in the area. During the 1920s, Keno City was a boom town.

Keno has a hotel with a unique bar (no food service available), a coffee shop, and washers, dryers and showers available for the public. There is a city campground located on Lightning Creek.

Well worth a visit here is the Keno Mining Museum, phone (403) 995-2792, fax 395-2730. Photographs and tools recall the mining history of the area. It is open 10 A.M. to 6 P.M. in summer. Be sure to get your Yukon Gold Explorer's Passport stamped at the museum—its location makes it the most exclusive of the 14 passport stamps.

There are a number of hiking trails in the Keno area; inquire at the museum. The Summit trail (can be driven) leads 6.5 miles/10.5 km to the milepost sign on top of Keno Hill, elev. 6,065 feet/1,849m.

CAMPBELL HIGHWAY

Watson Lake, Yukon Territory, to Junction with Klondike Loop
Yukon Highway 4

The gravel Campbell Highway travels 373 miles from Watson Lake to Carmacks.
(Earl L. Brown, staff)

Named for Robert Campbell, the first white man to penetrate what is now known as Yukon Territory, this all-weather gravel road leads 373 miles/600.2 km northwest from the Alaska Highway at Watson Lake, to junction with the Klondike Highway 2 miles/3.2 km north of Carmacks (see the KLONDIKE LOOP section). Gas is available at Watson Lake, Ross River, Faro and Carmacks.

The highway is gravel with the exception of some paved portions between Faro and Carmacks. There is a working mine at Faro; watch for large ore trucks between Faro and Carmacks. Drive with your headlights on at all times.

The Campbell Highway is an alternative route to Dawson City. It is about 20 miles/32 km shorter than driving the Alaska Highway through to Whitehorse, then driving up the Klondike Highway to Dawson City.

The Robert Campbell Highway was completed in 1968 and closely follows sections of the fur trade route established by Robert Campbell. Campbell was a Hudson's Bay Co. trader who was sent into the region in the 1840s to find a route west into the unexplored regions of central Yukon. Traveling from the southeast, he followed the Liard and Frances rivers, building a chain of posts along the way. His major discovery came in 1843, when he reached the Yukon River, which was to become the major transportation route within the Yukon.

Emergency medical services: Phone the RCMP or ambulance in Watson Lake, Ross River or Carmacks. Or phone toll free, Yukon-wide, the RCMP at 1-403-667-5555, or the ambulance at 1-403-667-3333.

Campbell Highway Log

YUKON HIGHWAY 4
Mileages reflect the location of physical kilometreposts; driving distance may vary from log.
Distance from Watson Lake (WL) is followed by distance from junction with the Klondike Highway just north of Carmacks (J).

WL 0 J 373 (600.2 km) **Junction** of the Campbell Highway with the Alaska Highway at Watson Lake (see description of Watson Lake in the ALASKA HIGHWAY section). The famous sign forest is located at this junction. In the parking area off the Campbell Highway (also called Airport Road) is a point of interest sign relating the highway's history. Also located at this junction is the Alaska Highway Interpretive Centre and visitor information.

WL 0.6 (1 km) **J 372.4** (599.3 km) Hospital on right northbound.

WL 4.3 (6.9 km) **J 368.7** (593.3 km) Access road on right northbound to Mount Maichen ski hill.

WL 6.3 (10.1 km) **J 366.7** (590.1 km) Airport Road left to Watson Lake airport. Pavement ends, hard-packed gravel begins, northbound.

WL 6.7 (10.8 km) **J 366.3** (589.5 km) Watson Creek. The highway begins to climb to a heavily timbered plateau and then heads north following the east bank of the Frances River. Tamarack is rare in Yukon, but this northern type of larch can be seen along here. Although a member of the pine family, it sheds its needles in the fall.

WL 10.4 (16.7 km) **J 362.6** (583.5 km) MacDonald Creek.

WL 22.5 (36.2 km) **J 350.5** (564.1 km) Tom Creek, named after an Indian trapper whose cabin is at the mouth of the stream.

WL 27.3 (44 km) **J 345.7** (556.3 km) Sa Dena Hes Mine access.

WL 36.1 (58.1 km) **J 336.9** (542.2 km) Frances River bridge. Turnout at north end of bridge; picnic spot. The highway crosses to west bank and follows the river northward. Named by Robert Campbell for the wife of Sir George Simpson, governor of the Hudson's Bay Co. for 40 years, the Frances River is a tributary of the Liard River. Robert Campbell ascended the Liard River to the Frances River and then went on to Frances Lake and the Pelly River. The Frances River was part of Hudson's Bay Co.'s route into central Yukon for many years before being abandoned because of its dangerous rapids and canyons.

WL 47.2 (76 km) **J 325.8** (524.3 km) Lucky Creek.

WL 49.6 (79.8 km) **J 323.4** (520.4 km) Simpson Creek.

WL 51.8 (83.4 km) **J 321.2** (516.9 km) Access road leads west 1 mile/1.6 km to **Simpson Lake** Yukon government campground: 19 campsites, $8 fee, boat launch, dock, swimming beach, playground, kitchen shelter and drinking water (boil water). Excellent fishing for lake trout, arctic grayling and northern pike.

WL 58.5 (94.2 km) **J 314.5** (506.1 km) Large turnout with litter barrels.

WL 58.7 (94.5 km) **J 314.3** (505.8 km) Access road west to Simpson Lake.

WL 68.5 (110.2 km) **J 304.5** (490 km) **Miner's Junction**, junction with Nahanni Range Road (formerly known as Cantung Junction); no services. Nahanni Range Road leads 125 miles/201.2 km northeast to Tungsten; see NAHANNI RANGE ROAD log this section. The road is not maintained and is not recommended for tourist traffic.

WL 70.3 (113.2 km) **J 302.7** (487.1 km) Yukon government Tuchitua River maintenance camp to east.

WL 70.5 (113.4 km) **J 302.5** (486.8 km) One-lane bridge over Tuchitua River.

WL 91.7 (147.6 km) **J 281.3** (452.7 km) Jules Creek.

WL 100 (160.9 km) **J 273** (439.3 km) 99 Mile Creek.

CAMPBELL HIGHWAY

Watson Lake, YT, to Junction with Klondike Loop (includes Nahanni Range Road)

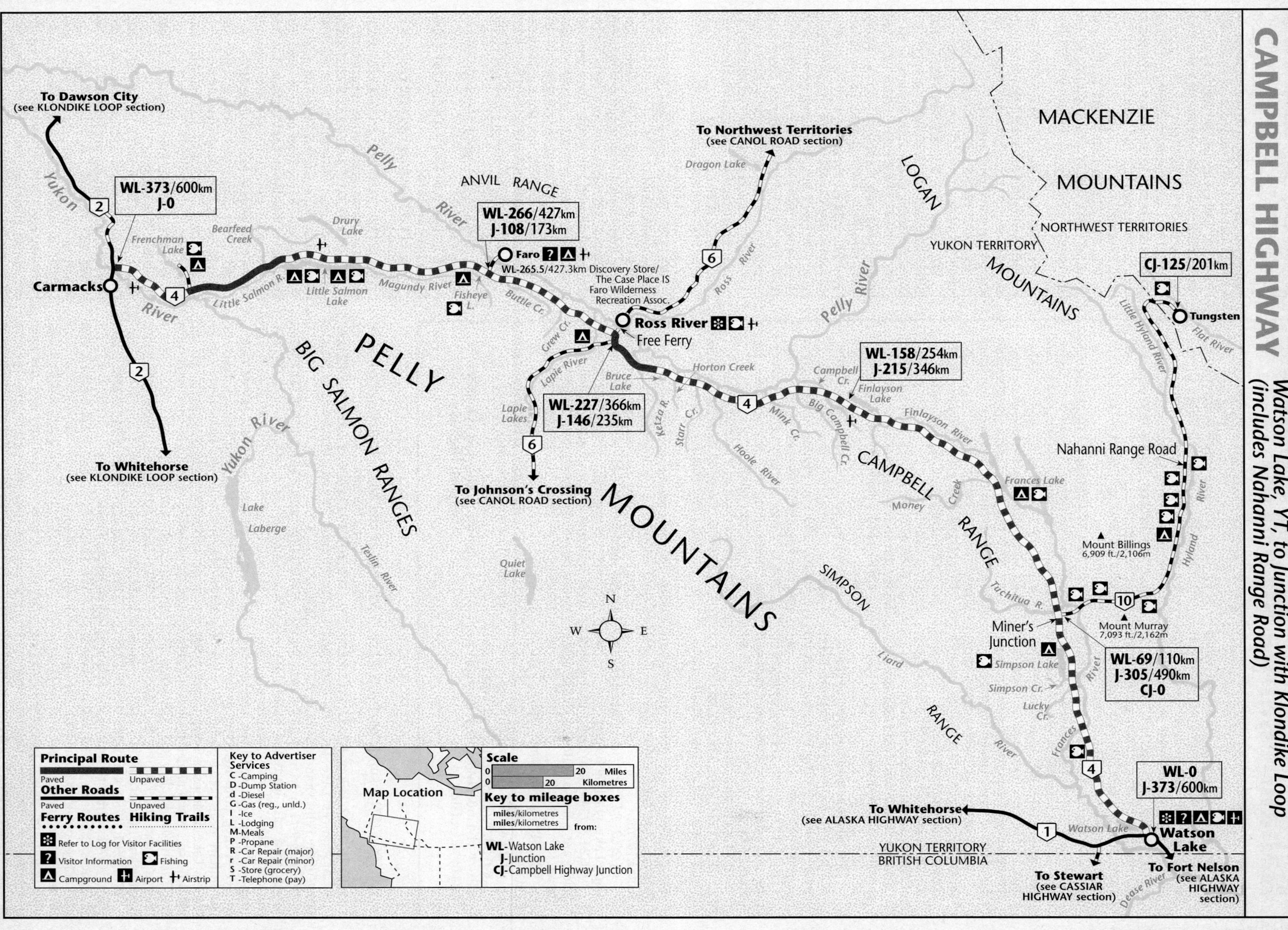

To Dawson City (see KLONDIKE LOOP section)
WL-373/600km
J-0
Carmacks
Yukon
River
Frenchman Lake
Bearfeed Creek
Drury Lake
Little Salmon R.
Little Salmon Lake
To Whitehorse (see KLONDIKE LOOP section)
Pelly River
ANVIL RANGE
WL-266/427km
J-108/173km
Faro
WL-265.5/427.3km Discovery Store/ The Case Place IS Faro Wilderness Recreation Assoc.
Magundy River
Fisheye L.
Buttle Cr.
PELLY
BIG SALMON RANGES
Yukon River
Lake Laberge
Teslin River
Quiet Lake
To Northwest Territories (see CANOL ROAD section)
Dragon Lake
Ross River
Ross River
Free Ferry
Crew Cr.
Lapie River
Lapie Lakes
Bruce Lake
WL-227/366km
J-146/235km
To Johnson's Crossing (see CANOL ROAD section)
MOUNTAINS
Horton Creek
Ketza R.
Starr Cr.
Hoole River
Mink Cr.
LOGAN MOUNTAINS
Pelly River
Campbell Cr.
Big Campbell Cr.
WL-158/254km
J-215/346km
Finlayson Lake
Finlayson River
CAMPBELL RANGE
Money Creek
Frances Lake
MACKENZIE MOUNTAINS
NORTHWEST TERRITORIES
YUKON TERRITORY
CJ-125/201km
Tungsten
Little Hyland River
Flat River
Nahanni Range Road
Hyland River
Mount Billings 6,909 ft./2,106m
Mount Murray 7,093 ft./2,162m
Tuchitua R.
Miner's Junction
Simpson Lake
Simpson Cr.
Lucky Cr.
WL-69/110km
J-305/490km
CJ-0
SIMPSON RANGE
Liard River
Frances River
N E S W
WL-0
J-373/600km
Watson Lake
Watson Lake
To Whitehorse (see ALASKA HIGHWAY section)
YUKON TERRITORY
BRITISH COLUMBIA
To Stewart (see CASSIAR HIGHWAY section)
To Fort Nelson (see ALASKA HIGHWAY section)
Dease River
Principal Route
Paved
Unpaved
Other Roads
Paved
Unpaved
Ferry Routes
Hiking Trails
Refer to Log for Visitor Facilities
Visitor Information
Fishing
Campground
Airport
Airstrip
Key to Advertiser Services
C -Camping
D -Dump Station
d -Diesel
G -Gas (reg., unld.)
I -Ice
L -Lodging
M-Meals
P -Propane
R -Car Repair (major)
r -Car Repair (minor)
S -Store (grocery)
T -Telephone (pay)
Map Location
Scale
0 20 Miles
0 20 Kilometres
Key to mileage boxes
miles/kilometres
miles/kilometres
from:
WL-Watson Lake
J-Junction
CJ-Campbell Highway Junction

Nahanni Range Road Log

The Nahanni Range (Tungsten) Road branches off the Campbell Highway at **Milepost WL 68.5** and leads 125 miles/201.2 km northeast to the former mining town of Tungsten, NWT. It is maintained by the Yukon government from the Campbell Highway junction to **Milepost CJ 82**. The remaining 43 miles/69 km to Tungsten are unmaintained and not recommended for travel. The road to Mile 82 is gravel surfaced with some washouts and soft steep shoulders. *NOTE: The Yukon government does not recommend this road for tourist travel due to lack of services and maintenance.*

Construction of the Nahanni Range Road was begun in 1961 to provide access to the mining property. The road was completed in 1963 with the bridging of the Frances and Hyland rivers.

Distance from Campbell Highway junction (CJ) is shown.

CJ 0 Junction with Campbell Highway.

CJ 5.1 (8.2 km) **Upper Frances River** bridge; good grayling fishing in stream on southeast side.

CJ 7.4 (11.9 km) Good grayling fishing at confluence of **Sequence Creek** and **Frances River.**

CJ 11.8 (19 km) Queen Creek.

CJ 13.1 (21.1 km) King Creek.

CJ 14.2 (22.8 km) Road passes between Mount Billings to the north (elev. 6,909 feet/2,106m) and Mount Murray to the south (elev. 7,093 feet/2,162m).

CJ 20.3 (32.7 km) Short access road to **Long Lake**, grayling fishing.

CJ 21.5 (34.6 km) Long Lake Creek. There are a few private log cabins along here.

CJ 24.1 (38.8 km) Dolly Varden Creek.

CJ 28.4 (45.7 km) French Creek.

CJ 28.9 (46.5 km) Road enters the narrow Hyland River valley through the Logan Mountains.

CJ 32.6 (52.4 km) South Bridge Creek.

CJ 33.2 (53.4 km) North Bridge Creek.

CJ 38.1 (61.3 km) Jackpine Creek.

CJ 40.6 (65.3 km) **Spruce Creek**, good glides and broken pools upstream for grayling fishing.

CJ 42.8 (68.9 km) Short access road to Hyland River.

CJ 45.8 (73.7 km) **Conglomerate Creek**, scenic spot to picnic. Good grayling fishing near small waterfall.

CJ 48 (77.2 km) Mining road to west.

CJ 52.1 (83.8 km) South Moose Creek.

CJ 52.2 (84 km) Yukon government campground (unmaintained); 10 sites, kitchen shelter, picnic tables. ▲

CJ 52.5 (84.5 km) North Moose Creek.

CJ 62.4 (100.4 km) **Flood Creek**, good grayling fishing.

CJ 68.4 (110.1 km) Hyland River bridge; turnout with litter barrel.

CJ 71 (114.2 km) Emergency airstrip to west.

CJ 75.9 (122.1 km) Ostensibility Creek.

CJ 82 (132 km) **Piggott Creek**, good grayling fishing. Outhouse.

NOTE: Yukon government road maintenance ends. Road not recommended for travel beyond this point.

CJ 116.8 (188 km) YT–NWT border.

CJ 125 (201.2 km) **TUNGSTEN,** which was the company town for one of the richest mines in the world and Canada's only tungsten producer, was originally called Cantung (Canada Tungsten Mining Corp. Ltd.). Open-pit mining began here in the early 1960s with the discovery of scheelite in the Flat River area. Scheelite is an ore of tungsten, an oxide used for hardening steel and making white gold. The mine shut down in 1986, and the population of 500 moved out. Only a security staff remains. Hot springs in area.

Return to Milepost WL 68.5 Campbell Highway

WL 106.6 (171.6 km) **J 266.4** (428.7 km) Caesar Creek.

WL 107.1 (172.4 km) **J 265.9** (427.9 km) View of Frances Lake to east, Campbell Range of the Pelly Mountains to west.

WL 108.9 (175.3 km) **J 264.1** (425 km) Access road east leads 0.6 mile/1 km to **Frances Lake** Yukon government campground: 19 campsites, $8 fee, boat launch, kitchen shelter, drinking water (boil water). The solitary peak between the two arms of Frances Lake is Simpson Tower (elev. 5,500 feet/1,676m). It was named by Robert Campbell for Hudson's Bay Co. Governor Sir George Simpson. Fishing for lake trout, grayling and northern pike. ▲

WL 109.1 (175.5 km) **J 263.9** (424.7 km) Money Creek, which flows into the west arm of Frances Lake, one of the Yukon's largest lakes. The creek was named for Anton Money, a mining engineer and prospector who found and mined placer gold in this area between 1929 and 1946. Money later operated "The Village" service station at Mile 442 on the Alaska Highway. He died in 1993, in Santa Barbara, CA.

WL 109.4 (176 km) **J 263.6** (424.2 km) Gravel turnout. View southbound of Frances Lake.

WL 113.8 (183.2 km) **J 259.2** (417.1 km) Dick Creek.

WL 123.8 (199.2 km) **J 249.2** (401 km) Highway descends Finlayson River valley, swinging west away from Frances Lake and following the Finlayson River that may be seen occasionally to the east for about the next 20 miles/32 km. Mountains to the west are part of the Campbell Range.

WL 126.4 (203.5 km) **J 246.6** (396.9 km) Light Creek.

WL 129.1 (207.7 km) **J 243.9** (392.5 km) Van Bibber Creek.

WL 134.1 (215.8 km) **J 238.9** (384.5 km) Wolverine Creek.

WL 147.5 (237.4 km) **J 225.5** (362.9 km) Finlayson Creek, which flows into the river of the same name, drains Finlayson Lake into Frances Lake. Named by Robert Campbell in 1840 for Chief Factor Duncan Finlayson, who later became director of the Hudson's Bay Co. Placer gold mined at the mouth of Finlayson River in 1875 is believed to be some of the first gold mined in the territory. Finlayson Lake (elev. 3,100 feet/945m), on the Continental Divide, separates watersheds of Mackenzie and Yukon rivers.

WL 148.1 (238.4 km) **J 224.9** (361.9 km) Access road north to Finlayson Lake picnic area; litter barrels. To the southwest are the Pelly Mountains.

WL 149 (239.8 km) **J 224** (360.5 km) Turnout with observation platform and information panel on Finlayson caribou herd.

WL 158.1 (254.5 km) **J 214.9** (345.8 km) **Private Aircraft**: Finlayson Lake airstrip to south; elev. 3,300 feet/1,006m; length 2,100 feet/640m; gravel. No services.

WL 163.7 (263.5 km) **J 209.3** (336.8 km) Nancy J. Creek.

WL 164.4 (264.5 km) **J 208.6** (335.7 km) Little Campbell Creek. Robert Campbell followed this creek to the Pelly River in 1840.

WL 170.4 (274.2 km) **J 202.6** (326 km) Bridge over Big Campbell Creek, which flows into Pelly River at Pelly Banks. Robert Campbell named the river and banks after Hudson's Bay Co. Governor Sir John Henry Pelly. Campbell built a trading post here in 1846; never successful, it burned down in 1849. Isaac Taylor and William S. Drury later operated a trading post at Pelly Banks, one of a string of successful posts established by their firm in remote spots throughout the Yukon from 1899 on.

The highway follows the Pelly River for the next 90 miles/145 km.

WL 179 (288.1 km) **J 194** (312.2 km) Mink Creek culvert.

WL 193.9 (312 km) **J 179.1** (288.2 km) Bridge over Hoole Canyon; turnout to north. Confluence of the Hoole and Pelly rivers. Campbell named the Hoole River after his interpreter, Francis Hoole, a half-Iroquois and half-French Canadian employed by the Hudson's Bay Co. Dig out your gold pan—this river once yielded gold.

WL 199.8 (321.6 km) **J 173.2** (278.7 km) Starr Creek culvert.

WL 206.5 (332.3 km) **J 166.5** (267.9 km) Horton Creek.

WL 210.7 (339 km) **J 162.3** (261.2 km) Bruce Lake to south.

WL 211.8 (340.8 km) **J 161.2** (259.4 km) Bruce Creek.

WL 214.9 (345.8 km) **J 158.1** (254.4 km) Pavement begins, gravel ends, westbound.

WL 215.4 (346.6 km) **J 157.6** (253.6 km) Private side road leads south 27.3 miles/44 km to Ketza River Project. The first gold bar was poured at Ketza River mine in 1988. The Ketza River hard-rock gold deposit was first discovered in 1947, but the mine was only recently developed. No visitor facilities.

WL 217.9 (350.7 km) **J 155.1** (249.6 km) Ketza River. St. Cyr Range to southwest.

WL 219.4 (353 km) **J 153.6** (247.2 km) Ketza Creek.

WL 221.4 (356.3 km) **J 151.6** (244 km) Beautiful Creek culvert.

WL 224.8 (361.8 km) **J 148.2** (238.5 km) **Coffee Lake** to south; local swimming hole, picnic tables, trout fishing (stocked).

WL 227.3 (365.8 km) **J 145.7** (234.5 km) **Junction** with South Canol Road (see CANOL ROAD section) which leads south 129 miles/207 km to Johnson's Crossing and the Alaska Highway. Ross River Flying Service; floatplane base on Jackfish Lake here.

WL 227.5 (366.1 km) **J 145.5** (234.1 km) Unmaintained side road on right westbound is continuation of Canol Road to Ross River. Use main Ross River access road next milepost.

WL 232.3 (373.8 km) **J 140.7** (226.4 km) Access road leads 7 miles/11.2 km to Ross River (description follows). Rest area with toilets on highway just north of this turnoff.

Ross River

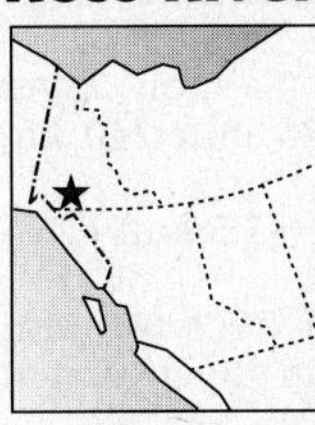

Located on the southwest bank of the Pelly River. **Population:** about 400. **Emergency Services: RCMP**, phone (403) 969-5555. **Hospital**, phone (403) 969-2222. **Radio:** CBC 990, local FM station. **Transportation:** Scheduled air service via Trans North Air.

Private Aircraft: Ross River airstrip; elev. 2,408 feet/734m; length 5,500 feet/1,676m; gravel; fuel 40.

A point of interest sign on the way into Ross River relates that in 1843, Robert Campbell named Ross River for Chief Trader Donald Ross of the Hudson's Bay Co. From 1903, a trading post called Nahanni House (established by Tom Smith and later owned by the Whitehorse firm of Taylor and Drury) located at the confluence of the Ross and Pelly rivers supplied the Indians of the area for nearly 50 years. With the building of the Canol pipeline service road in WWII and the completion of the Robert Campbell Highway in 1968, the community was linked to the rest of the territory by road. Originally situated on the north side of the Pelly River, the town has been in its present location since 1964. Today, Ross River is a supply and communication base for prospectors testing and mining mineral bodies in this region.

Ross River has gas stations with diesel, mechanical and tire repair, grocery stores, 2 motels with dining, and a bed and breakfast. The nearest campground is Lapie Canyon (see **Milepost WL 233.5**). Self-contained RVs may overnight at the gravel parking lot at the end of the pedestrian suspension bridge on the Ross River side.

Ross River is also a jumping-off point for big game hunters and canoeists. There are 2 registered hunting outfitters here. Canoeists traveling the Pelly River can launch just downriver from the ferry crossing. Experienced canoeists recommend camping on the Pelly's many gravel bars and islets to avoid bears, bugs and the danger of accidentally setting tundra fires. The Pelly has many sweepers, sleepers and gravel shallows, some gravel shoals, and extensive channeling. There are 2 sets of rapids between Ross River and the mouth of the Pelly: Fish Hook and Granite Canyon. Water is potable (boil), firewood available and wildlife plentiful. Inquire locally about river conditions before setting out.

Rock hounds watch for coal seams on the access road into Ross River. Also check Pelly River gravels for jaspers and the occasional agate.

The suspension footbridge at Ross River leads across the Pelly River to the site of an abandoned Indian village 1 mile/1.6 km upstream at the mouth of the Ross River.

A government ferry crosses the Pelly River daily in summer, from 8 A.M. to noon and 1–5 P.M. Across the river, the North Canol Road leads 144 miles/232 km to Macmillan Pass at the Northwest Territories border. See the CANOL ROAD section for details.

Campbell Highway Log

(continued)

WL 232.3 (373.8 km) **J 140.7** (226.4 km) Access road leads 7 miles/11.2 km to Ross River (see preceding description).

WL 232.5 (374.2 km) **J 140.5** (226.1 km) Rest area with toilets.

WL 233.4 (375.6 km) **J 139.6** (224.6 km) Lapie River bridge crosses deep gorge of Lapie River, which flows into the Pelly River from Lapie Lakes on the South Canol Road. Highway continues to follow the Pelly River and Pelly Mountains.

WL 233.5 (375.8 km) **J 139.5** (224.5 km) Turnoff to left (south) to Lapie Canyon Yukon government campground adjacent Lapie River: short scenic trails, viewpoint, picturesque canyon; kitchen shelters, firewood, group firepit and picnic area; walk-in tent sites, 14 campsites, $8 fee, drinking water (boil water); boat launch. ▲

WL 236.3 (380.3 km) **J 136.7** (220 km) Danger Creek. In 1905, naturalist Charles Sheldon named this creek after his horse, Danger, supposedly the first horse in this area.

WL 237.1 (381.6 km) **J 135.9** (218.7 km) Pavement ends, gravel begins, westbound.

WL 239.9 (386 km) **J 133.1** (214.2 km) Panoramic view of the Pelly River valley just ahead westbound.

WL 243.6 (392 km) **J 129.4** (208.2 km) *CAUTION: Hill and bad corner.*

WL 244.2 (393 km) **J 128.8** (207.3 km) Highway narrows over Grew Creek, no guide rails. This creek was named for Hudson's Bay Co. trader Jim Grew, who trapped this area for many years before his death in 1906.

WL 249.6 (km) **J 123.4** (km) Pavement begins and extends approximately 1 mile/1.6 km westbound.

WL 251 (404 km) **J 122** (196.3 km) Turnout to north.

WL 260.4 (419 km) **J 112.6** (181.2 km) Buttle Creek, named for Roy Buttle, a trapper, prospector and trader who lived here in the early 1900s, and at one time owned a trading post at Ross River.

WL 264.7 (426 km) **J 108.3** (174.3 km) Across the wide Pelly River valley to the north is a view of the mining community of Faro.

WL 265.5 (427.3 km) **J 107.5** (173 km) Access road on right westbound leads 5.6 miles/9 km to Faro. Point of interest sign about Faro at intersection. Rest area with toilets and litter barrels to south just west of this junction.

Faro

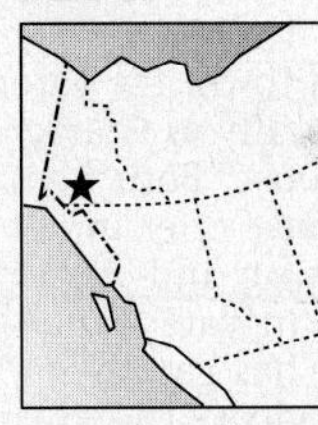

Located in east-central Yukon Territory, 220 road miles/354 km from Whitehorse. **Population:** 1,500. **Emergency Services: RCMP**, phone (403) 994-5555. **Fire Department**, phone (403) 994-2222. **Hospital**, phone (403) 994-4444.

Visitor Information: Centre at the municipal-operated John Connelly RV Park, open June through August. A tourist information phone line has details on wildlife viewing, hiking, biking, horseback trails, town facilities and services, special events

Aerial view of Faro. (Earl L. Brown, staff)

and individual businesses; phone (403) 994-2288, fax (403) 994-3311.

Climate: Temperatures range from -51°F/16°C in winter to a summer maximum of 84°F/29°C. **Radio:** CBC-FM 105.1, CKRW-FM 98.7. **Television:** CBC and 7 cable channels. **Transportation:** Scheduled air service to Whitehorse and Ross River via Alcan Air. Floatplane service from Horizons North.

Private Aircraft: Faro airstrip; 1.5 miles/2.4 km south; elev. 2,351 feet/717m; length 3,000 feet/914m; gravel; fuel 100.

The town of Faro lies on a series of benches or terraces on the northern escarpment of the Tintina Trench. Many places in town offer a commanding view of the Pelly River.

There are 3 restaurants in town, the Faro Hotel, Redmond's (known locally as Cranky Frank's) and Sally's Road House. Both Redmond's and Sally's Road House offer motel accommodations. RV camping and dump station at municipal and private campgrounds. The service station has gas, diesel, propane and full garage services. The area offers excellent fly-in fishing. Other services in town include a large grocery, liquor store, video rental, post office, public library, art gallery, movie theatre and recreation centre with indoor swimming pool, squash courts, and outdoor tennis courts. Catholic and Protestant Sunday services are available. ▲

Faro is named after the card game. The Cyprus Anvil mining and milling operation began producing lead–silver and zinc concentrates in 1969; operation was shut down in 1982 because of depressed metal prices and a poor economic market. Mothballing of the mine began in the spring of 1985, but the mine was reopened in 1986 by Curragh Resources Inc. It closed down again in 1993 and was purchased in June 1994 by Anvil Range Mining Corp. Reopened in 1995, the Faro mine is one of the western world's largest producers of lead and zinc concentrates. Tours are available, phone first to John Connelly RV Park, (403) 994-2288.

Attractions include an all-season observation cabin and isolated photographer's blind, built in 1994, for wildlife viewing. Viewing areas are accessible via a gravel road skirting the Fannin sheep grazing area and are within 4 miles/6.4 km of town. A public boat ramp and canoe rentals are available for exploring the Pelly River.

Discovery Store/The Case Place. See display ad this section.

Faro Wilderness Recreation Association. See display ad this section.

Campbell Highway Log

(continued)

WL 268.4 (432 km) **J 104.6** (168.3 km) Johnson Lake Yukon government campground; 15 sites (7 pull-throughs), $8 fee, toilets, water pump, firewood, picnic shelter, boat launch. ▲

Westbound, the Campbell Highway follows the Magundy River. There are several turnouts.

WL 285.8 (460 km) **J 87.2** (140.3 km) Magundy River airstrip to north; summer use only. Watch for livestock.

WL 288.1 (463.7 km) **J 84.9** (136.6 km) First glimpse of 22-mile-/35-km-long Little Salmon Lake westbound.

WL 299.3 (481.7 km) **J 73.7** (118.6 km) East end of Little Salmon Lake. Highway follows north shore.

WL 300.1 (483 km) **J 72.9** (117.3 km) Short access road south to Drury Creek Yukon government campground, situated on the creek at the east end of **Little Salmon Lake:** boat launch, fish filleting table, kitchen shelter, group firepit, 18 campsites, $8 fee, drinking water. Good fishing for northern pike, grayling, whitefish, lake trout 2 to 5 lbs., June 15 through July. ▲

WL 300.4 (483.5 km) **J 72.6** (116.8 km) Turnout at east end Drury Creek bridge. Yukon government maintenance camp to north.

WL 308.2 (496 km) **J 64.8** (104.3 km) Turnout overlooking lake.

WL 311.3 (501 km) **J 61.7** (99.3 km) *CAUTION: Slow down for curves.* Highway follows lakeshore; no guide rails. Turnouts overlooking Little Salmon Lake next 8.5 miles/13.6 km westbound.

WL 316.9 (510 km) **J 56.1** (90.3 km) **Private Aircraft**: Little Salmon airstrip; elev. 2,200 feet/671m; length 1,800 feet/549m; sand and silt.

WL 321.4 (517.3 km) **J 51.6** (83 km) Steep, narrow, winding road south leads to Yukon government **Little Salmon Lake** campground; boat launch, fishing, 12 campsites, $8 fee, drinking water, picnic tables, outhouses, firepits and kitchen shelter. ▲

WL 323.5 (520.6 km) **J 49.5** (79.7 km) Pavement begins, gravel ends, westbound.

WL 324.7 (522.6 km) **J 48.3** (77.7 km) Bearfeed Creek, a tributary of Little Salmon River, named because of the abundance of bears attracted to the berry patches in this area. Access to creek to north at west end of bridge.

Highway follows Little Salmon River (seen to south) for about 25 miles/40 km westbound.

WL 341 (548.7 km) **J 32** (51.5 km) *CAUTION: Slow down for hill.*

WL 343.8 (553.2 km) **J 29.2** (47 km) Picnic spot on Little Salmon River, which flows into the Yukon River.

WL 347.3 (559 km) **J 25.7** (41.4 km) Access road leads 4.9 miles/8 km north to **Frenchman Lake** Yukon government campground (10 sites), 5.6 miles/9 km to photo viewpoint of lake, and 9.3 miles/15 km to Nunatak Yukon government campground (10 sites, $8 fee). Access road narrows and surface deteriorates beyond Frenchman Lake Campground. South end of this 12-mile-/19-km-long lake offers good fishing for trout, pike and grayling. ▲

WL 348.4 (560.7 km) **J 24.6** (39.6 km) Pavement ends, gravel begins, westbound.

WL 349.5 (562.4 km) **J 23.5** (37.8 km) Turnoff to south for 0.9-mile/1.4-km gravel road to Little Salmon Indian village near confluence of Little Salmon River and Yukon River. There are some inhabited cabins in the area and some subsistence fishing. Private lands, no trespassing.

WL 356.2 (573.2 km) **J 16.8** (27 km) Turnout with point of interest sign overlooking Eagles Nest Bluff (formerly called Eagle Rock), well-known marker for river travelers. One of the worst steamboat disasters on the Yukon River occurred near here when the paddle-wheeler *Columbian* blew up and burned after a crew member accidentally fired a shot into a cargo of gunpowder. The accident, in which 6 men died, took place Sept. 25, 1906.

WL 356.7 (574 km) **J 16.3** (26.2 km) View of the Yukon River. At this point Whitehorse is about 160 miles/258 km upstream and Dawson City is about 300 miles/483 km downriver.

WL 360.4 (580 km) **J 12.6** (20.3 km) Northern Canada Power Commission's transmission poles and lines can be seen along highway. Power is transmitted from Aishihik dam site via Whitehorse dam and on to Cyprus Anvil mine and Faro. Orange balls mark lines where they cross river as a hazard to aircraft.

WL 370 (595.4 km) **J 3** (4.8 km) **Private Aircraft**: Carmacks airstrip to south; elev. 1,770 feet/539m; length 5,200 feet/1,585m; gravel.

WL 370.7 (596.5 km) **J 2.3** (3.7 km) Tantalus Butte coal mine on hill to north overlooking junction of Campbell and Klondike highways. The butte was named by U.S. Army Lt. Frederick Schwatka in 1883, because of its tantalizing appearance around many bends of the river before reaching it.

WL 373 (600.2 km) **J 0 Junction** with the Klondike Highway (Yukon Highway 2), which leads south 2 miles/3.2 km to Carmacks, 103 miles/166 km to the Alaska Highway, and north 221 miles/355 km to Dawson City. (See the KLONDIKE LOOP section.)

CANOL ROAD

Alaska Highway Junction to NWT Border
Yukon Highway 6
(See map, page 722)

The South Canol Road winds along Rose Lake. (*Earl L. Brown, staff*)

The 513-mile-/825-km-long Canol (Canadian Oil) Road was built to provide access to oil fields at Norman Wells, NWT, on the Mackenzie River. Conceived by the U.S. War Dept. to help fuel Alaska and protect it from a Japanese invasion, the road and a 4-inch-diameter pipeline were constructed from Norman Wells, NWT, through Macmillan Pass, past Ross River, to Johnson's Crossing on the Alaska Highway. From there the pipeline carried oil to a refinery at Whitehorse.

Begun in 1942 and completed in 1944, the Canol Project included the road, pipeline, a telephone line, the refinery, airfields, pumping stations, tank farms, wells and camps. Only about 1 million barrels of oil were pumped to Whitehorse before the war ended in 1945 and the $134 million Canol Project was abandoned. (Today, Norman Wells, pop. 757, is still a major supplier of oil with a pipeline to Zama, AB, built in 1985.) The Canol Road was declared a National Historic Site in 1990.

Since 1958, the Canol Road between Johnson's Crossing on the Alaska Highway and Ross River on the Campbell Highway (referred to as the South Canol Road) and between Ross River and the YT–NWT border (referred to as the North Canol Road) has been rebuilt and is open to summer traffic. It is maintained to minimum standards.

The 136.8-mile/220.2-km South Canol Road is a narrow winding road which crests the Big Salmon Range and threads its way above Lapie Canyon via a difficult but scenic stretch of road. Reconstruction on the South Canol has replaced many old bridges with culverts, but there are still a few 1-lane wooden bridges. Driving time is about 4 hours one way. Watch for steep hills and bad corners. There are no facilities along the South Canol Road and it is definitely not recommended for large RVs or trailers. Not recommended for any size vehicle in wet weather. Inquiries on current road conditions should be made locally or with the Yukon Dept. of Highways in Whitehorse (403/667-8215) before driving this road.

The 144.2-mile/232-km North Canol Road is also a narrow, winding road which some motorists have compared to a roller coaster. All bridges on the North Canol are 1-lane, and the road surface can be very slippery when wet. Not recommended during wet weather and not recommended for large RVs or trailers. If mining is under way along the North Canol, watch for large transport trucks.

NOTE: Drive with headlights on at all times!

Our log of the North Canol ends at the YT–NWT border, where vehicles may turn around. Road washouts prohibit travel beyond this point. From the border to Norman Wells it is 230 miles/372 km of unusable road that has been designated the Canol Heritage Trail by the NWT government. Some adventurous travelers have hiked it and report that there are no facilities and river crossings are hazardous, but the route through the Mackenzie Mountains is scenic and there are many relics of the Canol Project.

WARNING: The only facilities on the Canol Road are at Ross River and at Johnson's Crossing on the Alaska Highway.

Emergency medical services: In Ross River, phone (403) 969-2222; or phone the RCMP, (403) 969-5555, or 1-403-667-5555.

South Canol Road Log

Distance from the junction with the Alaska Highway (J) is followed by distance from the Campbell Highway junction (C). Kilometre figures from Alaska Highway junction reflect physical kilometreposts when they occur.

J 0 C 136.8 (220.2 km) **Junction** of the Canol Road (Yukon Highway 6) with the Alaska Highway. Food, gas and camping at Johnson's Crossing at the southwest end of the Teslin River bridge, 0.7 mile/1.1 km from Canol Road turnoff.

J 0.2 (0.3 km) **C 136.6** (219.8 km) Information panel on the history and construction of Canol Road. A short, dirt road (on left, northbound) leads to an auto "boneyard" that includes several WWII Canol Project trucks (all have been significantly cannibalized). Limited turnaround area, not suitable for trailers. Not recommended for any vehicle in wet weather.

J 3.9 (6.2 km) **C 132.9** (213.8 km) Fourmile Creek. Road begins ascent across the Big Salmon Range to the summit (elev. about 4,000 feet/1,219m). Snow possible at summit early October to late spring.

J 6.2 (10 km) **C 130.6** (210.1 km) Beaver Creek.

J 13.9 (22.4 km) **C 122.9** (197.8 km) Moose Creek. Small gravel turnout with litter barrels.

J 17.2 (27.6 km) **C 119.6** (192.4 km) Seventeenmile Creek.

J 19.4 (31.2 km) **C 117.4** (188.9 km) Murphy Creek.

J 19.8 (32 km) **C 117** (188.3 km) Pelly Mountains can be seen in distance northbound.

J 27 (43.4 km) **C 109.8** (176.7 km) One-lane wooden bridge over Evelyn Creek.

J 28.7 (46.2 km) **C 108.1** (174 km) Two-lane bridge over Sidney Creek.

J 30.6 (49.2 km) **C 106.2** (170.9 km) Access road on right northbound leads to Sidney Lake. Nice little lake and good place to camp.

From here northbound the South Canol follows the Nisutlin River, which is to the

CANOL ROAD *Alaska Highway Junction, YT, to NWT Border*

SELWYN MOUNTAINS
BACKBONE RANGES
R-144/232km
Tsichu River
Keele River
Macmillan Pass
Macmillan River
North Macmillan River
ITSI RANGE
South Macmillan River
Ross River
NORTHWEST TERRITORIES
YUKON TERRITORY
Mount Sheldon ▲ 6,937 ft./2,114m
Sheldon Lake
Lewis Lake
Dragon Lake
Pup Cr.
Caribou Cr.
Tay Cr.
Pelly River
ANVIL RANGE
Beaver Creek
LOGA MOUNTAINS
To Carmacks (see CAMPBELL HIGHWAY section)
R-0
Tenas Cr.
Orchie L.
Majorie L.
North Canol Road
PELLY MOUNTAINS
C-0 J-137/220km
Free Ferry
Ross River
Pelly
BIG SALMON RANGE
Fox Creek
Lapie River
Lapie Pass
Lapie Lakes
Pony Cr.
Ground Hog Creek
Caribou Mountain ▲ 6,905 ft./2,105m
▲ Pass Peak 7,194 ft./2,193m
To Watson Lake (see CAMPBELL HIGHWAY section)
CAMPBELL RANGE
Upper Sheep Creek
Rose River
Mount St. Cyr ▲ 6,725 ft./2,050m
Teslin River
Nisutlin River
Nisutlin Lake
Quiet Lake
Cottonwood Cr.
South Canol Road
Sidney Creek
Sidney Lake
Evelyn Cr.
Murphy Cr.
Johnson's Crossing
C-137/220km J-0
To Whitehorse (see ALASKA HIGHWAY section)
Teslin Lake
To Teslin (see ALASKA HIGHWAY section)

Map Location

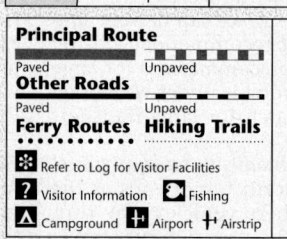

Scale
0 10 Miles
0 10 Kilometres

Key to mileage boxes
miles/kilometres
miles/kilometres
from:
C-Campbell Highway
J-Junction
R-Ross River

Principal Route
Paved
Unpaved
Other Roads
Paved
Unpaved
Ferry Routes
Hiking Trails
Refer to Log for Visitor Facilities
Visitor Information
Fishing
Campground
Airport
Airstrip

Key to Advertiser Services
C -Camping
D -Dump Station
d -Diesel
G -Gas (reg., unld.)
I -Ice
L -Lodging
M -Meals
P -Propane
R -Car Repair (major)
r -Car Repair (minor)
S -Store (grocery)
T -Telephone (pay)

east and can be seen from the road the next 30 miles/48 km until the road crosses the Rose River beyond Quiet Lake.

J 30.9 (49.7 km) **C 105.9** (170.4 km) Turnout with litter barrel to east.

J 36.7 (59 km) **C 100.1** (161.1 km) Coyote Creek, culverts.

J 39.1 (62.9 km) **C 97.7** (157.2 km) Good view of Pelly Mountains ahead. Road crosses Cottonwood Creek.

J 42 (67.6 km) **C 94.8** (152.5 km) Access road on right northbound leads 0.4 mile/0.6 km to Nisutlin River. Good place to camp with tables and outhouse.

J 47.8 (76.9 km) **C 89** (143.2 km) Quiet Lake Yukon government campground; 20 sites, $8 fee, boat launch, picnic tables, kitchen shelter, firewood. Watch for steep hills northbound to Quiet Lake. ▲

J 54.7 (88 km) **C 82.1** (132.1 km) Lake Creek. Road now follows **Quiet Lake** to west; good fishing for lake trout, northern pike and arctic grayling.

J 56 (90.1 km) **C 80.8** (130 km) Turnout with litter barrels and point of interest sign overlooking Quiet Lake. This is the largest of 3 lakes that form the headwaters of the Big Salmon River system. The 17-mile-/28-km-long lake was named in 1887 by John McCormack, 1 of 4 miners who prospected the Big Salmon River from its mouth on the Yukon River to its source. Although they did find some gold, the river and lakes have become better known for their good fishing and fine scenery. Until the completion of the South Canol Road in the 1940s, this area was reached mainly by boating and portaging hundreds of miles up the Teslin and Nisutlin rivers.

J 61.2 (98.5 km) **C 75.6** (121.6 km) Turnoff on left northbound (west) for **Quiet Lake,** day-use area with picnic sites, water, boat launch and fishing. Entry point for canoeists on the Big Salmon River.

J 61.5 (99 km) **C 75.3** (121.2 km) Yukon government Quiet Lake maintenance camp on left northbound. A vintage Canol Project dump truck and pull grader is on display in front of the camp.

J 62.6 (100.7 km) **C 74.2** (119.4 km) Distance marker indicates Ross River 126 km.

J 63.7 (102 km) **C 73.1** (117.6 km) Steep hill and panoramic view of mountains and valley.

J 65.5 (105.4 km) **C 71.3** (114.7 km) One-lane Bailey bridge across Rose River No. 1. The road now follows the valley of the Rose River into Lapie Pass northbound. According to R.C. Coutts in "Yukon Places and Names," Oliver Rose prospected extensively in this area in the early 1900s. He came to the Yukon from Quebec, and was known as a hard-working, solitary and respected man.

J 70.4 (113.3 km) **C 66.4** (106.8 km) Canol Creek culvert.

J 71.9 (115.7 km) **C 64.9** (104.4 km) Deer Creek.

J 75.7 (121.8 km) **C 61.1** (98.3 km) Gravel Creek culvert.

J 81.1 (130 km) **C 55.7** (89.6 km) Road crosses creek (name unknown) in culvert.

J 83.7 (134 km) **C 53.1** (85.4 km) Dodge Creek culvert.

J 87.1 (140 km) **C 49.7** (80 km) Rose River No. 2 culvert.

J 89.7 (144.3 km) **C 47.1** (75.8 km) Rose River No. 3 culverts.

J 91.5 (147.2 km) **C 45.3** (72.9 km) Rose River No. 4 culverts.

J 93.8 (151 km) **C 43** (69.2 km) Rose River No. 5 culverts.

J 94.1 (151.4 km) **C 42.7** (68.7 km) Distance marker indicates Ross River 76 km.

J 95.1 (153 km) **C 41.7** (67.1 km) Upper Sheep Creek joins the Rose River here. To the east is Pass Peak (elev. 7,194 feet/2,193m).

J 96.4 (155.1 km) **C 40.4** (65 km) Rose River No. 6.

J 97.1 (156.2 km) **C 39.7** (63.9 km) Rose Lake to east.

J 97.5 (156.9 km) **C 39.3** (63.2 km) Pony Creek. Caribou Mountain (elev. 6,905 feet/2,105m) to west.

J 101.1 (162.7 km) **C 35.7** (57.4 km) Lakes to west are part of Lapie Lakes chain, headwaters of the Lapie River. These features were named by Dr. George M. Dawson of the Geological Survey of Canada in 1887 for Lapie, an Iroquois Indian companion and canoeman of Robert Campbell, who was the first to explore the Pelly River area in 1843 for the Hudson's Bay Co.

J 101.2 (162.8 km) **C 35.6** (57.3 km) Ground Hog Creek.

J 102.5 (165 km) **C 34.3** (55.2 km) Access road on left northbound leads west a short distance to Lapie Lakes. Good place to camp.

J 107.4 (172.8 km) **C 29.4** (47.3 km) Lapie River No. 1 culverts. Ponds reported good for grayling fishing. Watch for horses on the road.

J 107.5 (173 km) **C 29.3** (47.1 km) Ahead northbound is Barite Mountain (elev. about 6,500 feet/1,981m).

J 110 (177 km) **C 26.8** (43.1 km) Gold Creek.

J 111.4 (179.2 km) **C 25.4** (40.8 km) Bacon Creek.

J 113.4 (182.5 km) **C 23.4** (37.6 km) Boulder Creek.

J 115.6 (186 km) **C 21.2** (34.1 km) Road runs to the east side of Barite Mountain.

J 120.2 (193.4 km) **C 16.6** (26.7 km) Fox Creek culverts.

J 120.7 (194.2 km) **C 16.1** (25.9 km) The road follows the Lapie River Canyon for about the next 11 miles/18 km, climbing to an elevation of about 500 feet/152m above the river. Narrow road, watch for rocks.

J 123.3 (198.4 km) **C 13.5** (21.7 km) Kilometrepost 200. Distance marker indicates Ross River 26 km. Lapie River runs to right side of road northbound.

J 124.7 (200.6 km) **C 12.1** (19.4 km) Glacier Creek.

J 126.3 (203.2 km) **C 10.5** (16.9 km) Turnouts on right side of road northbound overlooking Lapie River Canyon.

J 132.3 (212.9 km) **C 4.5** (7.2 km) Narrow 1-lane bridge over Lapie River No. 2. Point of interest sign on north end of bridge about the Lapie River Canyon. Approximately 100 million years ago, flat horizontal layers of rock were buried several kilometres below the surface of the earth. Movement by rigid plates of the earth's crust subjected the rock to massive compression and strain, and it was deformed into folds. Over millions of years, the rocks rose, exposing the folds in the canyon wall.

J 133 (214 km) **C 3.8** (6.1 km) Erosional features called hoodoos can be seen in the clay banks rising above the road.

J 133.3 (214.5 km) **C 3.5** (5.6 km) Ash layer can be seen in clay bank on right side of road.

J 135.6 (218.2 km) **C 1.2** (1.9 km) Jackfish Lake, below on left northbound, is used for docking floatplanes.

J 136.8 (220 km) **C 0 Junction** of South Canol Road with the Campbell Highway.

Crossing the Lapie River on South Canol Road. (Earl L. Brown, staff)

Approximately straight ahead northbound, across the Campbell Highway, a poorly maintained section of the Canol Road continues to Ross River. Motorists bound for Ross River or the North Canol Road are advised to turn left (west) on the Campbell Highway from the South Canol and drive about 5 miles/8 km to the main Ross River access road (see map).

North Canol Road Log

The North Canol Road leads 144.2 miles/232 km to the NWT border. Physical kilometreposts along the North Canol Road reflect distance from the Alaska Highway junction. *WARNING: There are no services along this road.* **Distance from Ross River (R) is shown.**

R 0 ROSS RIVER (see CAMPBELL HIGHWAY section). Yukon government Ross River ferry (free) crosses the Pelly River. Ferry operates from 8 A.M. to noon and 1–5 P.M. daily from late May to mid-Oct. Those who miss the last ferry crossing of the day may leave their vehicles on the opposite side of the river and use the footbridge to walk into Ross River; vehicles can be brought over in the morning.

R 0.4 (0.6 km) Stockpile to west is barite from the Yukon Barite Mine.

R 0.6 (1 km) Road to east leads to original site of Ross River and Indian village.

R 0.9 (1.4 km) Second access road east to old Ross River and Indian village. Canol Road follows the Ross River.

R 2.1 (3.4 km) *CAUTION: Slide area, watch for falling rocks.*

R 4.7 (7.6 km)) Raspberry patch. Good pickings.

R 6.8 (10.9 km) One-lane bridge over Tenas Creek.

R 10.6 (17 km) Gravel pit to west.

R 17 (27.3 km) Deep Creek.

R 20.9 (33.6 km) **Marjorie Creek.** Locals report good grayling fishing.

R 21 (33.8 km) Access road to west leads to Marjorie Lake. Access road not recommended for large RVs.

R 21.7 (34.9 km) Marjorie Lake to west.

R 27 (43.4 km) Unnamed lake to east.

R 28.1 (45.2 km) Boat launch on Orchie Lake to west.

R 29.8 (48 km) Distance marker indicates NWT border 195 km, Ross River 50 km.

R 31.9 (51.3 km) One-lane bridge over Gravel Creek. The next 15 miles/24 km are excellent moose country.

R 33.4 (53.7 km) One-lane bridge over Flat Creek.

R 37 (59.5 km) One-lane bridge over Beaver Creek.

R 41.8 (67.2 km) One-lane bridge over 180 Mile Creek.

R 43.9 (70.6 km) One-lane bridge over Tay Creek.

R 46.3 (74.5 km) One-lane bridge over Blue Creek.

R 48.1 (77.4 km) Kilometrepost 306. Flood Creek culvert.

R 57.6 (92.7 km) Clifford's Slough to the east.

R 58.6 (94.3 km) Steep hill to 1-lane bridge over Caribou Creek.

R 61.1 (98.3 km) Distance marker indicates NWT border 145 km, Ross River 100 km.

R 61.8 (99.4 km) **B 82.4** (132.6 km) One-lane bridge over Pup Creek.

R 64.8 (104.3 km) Turnout to west. Steep hill.

R 65.1 (104.7 km) Turnout to **Dragon Lake**; overnight parking, litter barrels. Locals report that early spring is an excellent time for pike and trout in the inlet. Rock hounds check roadsides and borrow pits for colorful chert, which can be worked into jewelry.

R 65.4 (105.2 km) Kilometrepost 334. Large, level, gravel turnout to west overlooking Dragon Lake; boat launch.

R 69.6 (112 km) Wreckage of Twin Pioneer aircraft to west. WWII remnants can be found in this area.

R 69.9 (112.5 km) Road to Twin Creek.

R 70.8 (113.9 km) Airstrip.

R 71 (114.2 km) One-lane bridge over Twin Creek No. 1. Yukon government maintenance camp.

R 71.1 (114.4 km) One-lane bridge over Twin Creek No. 2. Good views of Mount Sheldon.

R 75.1 (120.8 km) Kilometrepost 350. Mount Sheldon ahead, located 3 miles/4.8 km north of Sheldon Lake; a very beautiful and distinguishable feature on the Canol Road (elev. 6,937 feet/2,114m). In 1900, Poole Field and Clement Lewis, who were fans of writer Rudyard Kipling, named this peak Kipling Mountain and the lake at its base Rudyard. In 1907, Joseph Keele of the Geological Survey of Canada renamed them after Charles Sheldon, a well-known sheep hunter and naturalist who came to the area to collect Stone sheep specimens for the Chicago Natural History Museum in 1905.

R 76.4 (123 km) Kilometrepost 352. Of the 3-lake chain, Sheldon Lake is farthest north, then Field Lake and Lewis Lake, which is just visible from here. Lewis Lake is closest to the confluence of the Ross and Prevost rivers.

Field Lake and Lewis Lake were named in 1907 by Joseph Keele of the Geological Survey of Canada after Poole Field and Clement Lewis. The 2 partners, who had prospected this country, ran a trading post called Nahanni House at the mouth of the Ross River in 1905.

R 77.6 (124.9 km) Kilometrepost 354. One-lane bridge over Riddell Creek. Tip of Mount Riddell (elev. 6,101 feet/1,859m) can be seen to the west.

R 78.8 (126.8 km) View of Sheldon Lake ahead, Field Lake to right northbound.

R 79.8 (128.4 km) Access road east to Sheldon Lake.

R 82.7 (133.1 km) One-lane bridge over Sheldon Creek. Road climbs, leaving Ross River valley and entering Macmillan Valley northbound.

R 89.3 (143.7 km) Height of land before starting descent northbound into South Macmillan River system.

R 89.7 (144.3 km) Steep hill. Road may wash out during heavy rains. Deep ditches along roadside help channel water.

R 91.4 (147.1 km) One-lane bridge over Moose Creek.

R 91.6 (147.4 km) **B 52.6** (84.6 km) Milepost 230.

R 92.3 (148.5 km) Kilometrepost 378. Peaks of the Itsi Range ahead. Rugged, spectacular scenery northbound.

R 92.7 (149.1 km) Distance marker indicates NWT border 95 km, Ross River 150 km.

R 93.8 (151 km) First of several WWII vehicle dumps to west. To the east is a wannigan, or skid shack, used as living quarters by Canol Road workers during construction of the road. It was too far to return to base camp; these small buildings were strategically located along the route so the workers had a place to eat and sleep at night.

R 94 (151.3 km) To east are remains of a maintenance depot where heavy equipment was repaired. Concrete foundations to west. First glimpse of the South Macmillan River northbound.

R 94.7 (152.4 km) Kilometrepost 382. Another Canol project equipment dump to explore. Watch ditches for old pieces of pipeline.

R 97.8 (157.4 km) One-lane bridge over Boulder Creek.

R 98.5 (158.5 km) Access road west to South Macmillan River where boats can be launched. Locals advise launching boats here rather than from the bridge at **Milepost R 113.6**, which washes out periodically and leaves dangerous debris in the river.

R 100.8 (162.5 km) Kilometrepost 392. Itsi Range comes into view ahead northbound. Itsi is said to be an Indian word meaning "wind" and was first given as a name to Itsi Lakes, headwaters of the Ross River. The road dips down and crosses an unnamed creek.

R 104.5 (168.2 km) Kilometrepost 398. View of the South Macmillan River from here.

R 105.3 (169.4 km) View of Selwyn Mountains, named in 1901 by Joseph Keele of the Geological Survey of Canada for Dr. Alfred Richard Selwyn (1824–1902), a distinguished geologist in England. Dr. Selwyn later became director of the Geological Survey of Australia and then director of the Geological Survey of Canada from 1869 until his retirement in 1895.

R 111 (178.6 km) One-lane bridge over Itsi Creek.

R 112.2 (180.5 km) One-lane bridge over Wagon Creek.

R 113.6 (182.8 km) Turnout to east on South Macmillan River. Good place for a picnic but not recommended as a boat launch. One-lane Bailey bridge over South Macmillan River No. 1.

Robert Campbell, a Hudson's Bay Co. explorer on a journey down the Pelly River in 1843, named this major tributary of the Pelly after Chief Factor James McMillan, who had sponsored Campbell's employment with the company.

R 115.1 (185.2 km) Access road on left northbound leads about 7 miles/11 km to Yukon Barite Mine. Barite is a soft mineral that requires only crushing and bagging before being shipped over the Dempster Highway to the Beaufort Sea oil and gas wells, where it is used as a lubricant known as drilling mud.

R 117.2 (188.6 km) Access road on right northbound to gravel pit.

R 118.8 (191.2 km) Dept. of Public Works maintenance camp; status unknown.

R 118.9 (191.3 km) One-lane bridge over Jeff Creek.

R 121.2 (195 km) One-lane bridge over Hess Creek. Bears in area.

R 123.2 (198.3 km) Gravel turnout on left northbound with RCMP trailer. Distance marker indicates NWT border 45 km, Ross River 200 km. One-lane bridge over Dewhurst Creek.

R 127.5 (205.2 km) Entering Macmillan Pass. At "Mac Pass," the road climbs to elevations above 4,480 feet/1,366m.

R 129.4 (208.2 km) One-lane bridge over Macmillan River No. 2.

R 129.5 (208.4 km) Abandoned Army vehicles from the Canol Project on left northbound.

R 129.6 (208.6 km) Abandoned Army vehicles from the Canol Project on right northbound.

R 133.6 (215 km) To the west is Cordilleran Engineering camp, managers of the mining development of Ogilvie Joint Venture's Jason Project. The Jason deposit is a zinc, lead, silver, barite property. The deposit's size is still uncertain.

One-lane bridge over Sekie Creek No. 1.

R 134.4 (216.3 km) Fuel tanks on left northbound.

R 136.3 (219.3 km) Sekie Creek No. 2 culvert.

R 136.4 (219.5 km) Access to Macmillan airstrip on left northbound. Access road to right to Hudson Bay Mining & Smelting's Tom lead–zinc mineral claims. The Tom is a stratabound silver–lead–zinc deposit and the size is yet to be determined. At one time it was considered to be 9 million tons of 16 percent combined lead–zinc.

R 137.7 (221.6 km) One-lane bridge over Macmillan River No. 3.

R 141.8 (228.2 km) One-lane bridge over Macmillan River No. 4.

R 142.9 (230 km) One-lane bridge over Macmillan River No. 5.

R 144.1 (231.9 km) One-lane bridge over Macmillan River No. 6.

R 144.2 (232 km) YT–NWT border. Sign cautions motorists to proceed at their own risk. The road is not maintained and bridges are not safe beyond this point. Vehicles turn around here.

Ahead is the Tsichu River valley and the Selwyn Mountains. The abandoned North Canol Road continues another 230 miles/372 km from the YT–NWT border to Norman Wells, NWT. Designated the Canol Heritage Trail, it is suitable for hiking, bicycles or motorcycles. There are some river crossings. It is prime grizzly and caribou habitat with exceptional mountain scenery.

DEMPSTER HIGHWAY

Milepost D 25 Klondike Highway 2 to Inuvik, NWT Yukon Highway 5, NWT Highway 8

(See map, page 726)

The Dempster Highway begins 25 miles/40.2 km east of Dawson City, YT, at its junction with Klondike Highway 2, and leads 456.3 miles/734.3 km northeast to Inuvik, NWT.

Construction of the Dempster Highway began in 1959, under the Road to Resources program, and was completed in 1978. A 5-year major reconstruction and surfacing program on the highway concluded in 1988, although freezing weather and heavy truck traffic may erode both road base and surfacing in areas. Calcium chloride is used in some areas to reduce dust and as a bonding agent; wash your vehicle as soon as practical.

The Dempster is a gravel road. There are stretches of clay surface that can be slippery in wet weather. Summer driving conditions on the Dempster vary depending on weather and maintenance. Generally, road conditions range from fair to excellent, with highway speeds attainable on some sections.

Facilities are still few and far between on the Dempster. Full auto services are available at Klondike River Lodge at the Dempster Highway turnoff on Klondike Highway 2. Gas, propane, food and lodging, and car repair are also available at Eagle Plains Hotel, located at about the halfway point on the Dempster. Gas is also available in Fort McPherson. Gas up whenever possible.

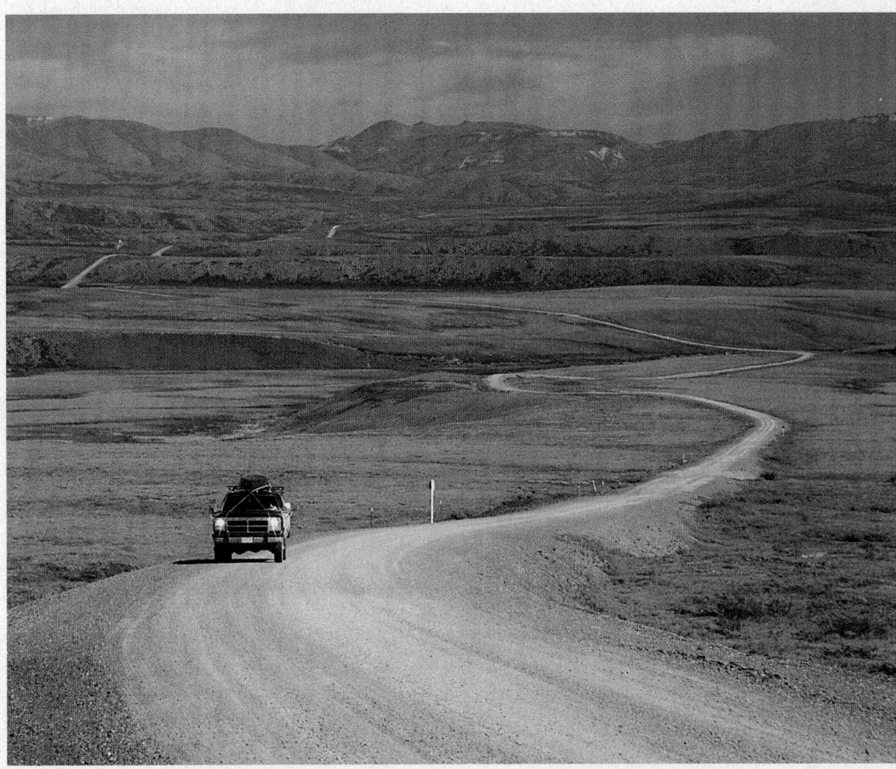

The gravel Dempster Highway winds across the tundra near the Arctic Circle.
(© Michael DeYoung)

The Dempster is open year-round. The highway is fairly well-traveled in summer: A driver may not see another car for an hour, and then pass 4 cars in a row. Locals say the highway is smoother and easier to drive in winter, but precautions should be taken against cold weather, high winds and poor visibility; check road conditions before proceeding in winter. DRIVE WITH YOUR HEADLIGHTS ON!

There are 2 ferry crossings on the Dempster, at **Milepost J 334.9** (Peel River crossing) and **J 377.9** (Mackenzie River and Arctic Red River crossings). Free government ferry service is available 15 hours a day (9 A.M. to 1 A.M. Northwest Territories time, 8 A.M. to midnight Yukon time) during summer (from about June to mid-Oct.). Cross by ice bridge in winter.

General information on Northwest Territories is available by calling the Arctic Hotline at 1-800-661-0788. For recorded messages on ferry service, road and weather conditions, phone 1-800-661-0752. If you are in Dawson City, the Western Arctic Visitor Centre has information on Northwest Territories and the Dempster Highway. Located in the B.Y.N. Bldg. on Front Street, across from the Yukon Visitor Centre, it is open 9 A.M. to 9 P.M., June to September; phone (403) 993-6167. Or write the Western Arctic Tourism Assoc., Box 2600MP, Inuvik, NT X0E 0T0; phone (403) 979-4321, fax (403) 979-2434 for more information.

Dempster Highway Log

YUKON HIGHWAY 5
Driving distance is measured in miles. The kilometre figure on the Yukon portion of the highway reflects the physical kilometreposts and is not necessarily an accurate metric conversion of the mileage figure. Kilometreposts are green with white lettering and are located on the right-hand side of the highway, northbound.
Distance from junction with Klondike Highway 2 (J) is followed by distance from Inuvik (I).

J 0 I 456.3 (734.3 km) **Junction** of Yukon Highways 2 and 5, 25 miles/40.2 km east of Dawson City, also known as Dempster Corner. Lodge with food, gas, propane, lodging, camping and tire repairs; open all year.

J 0.1 (0.2 km) **I 456.2** (734.2 km) Dempster Highway monument with information panels on history and culture, wildlife, ecology and driving tips.

J 0.2 (0.3 km) **I 456.1** (734 km) One-lane wood-planked bridge over Klondike River. The road follows the wooded (spruce and poplar) North Klondike River valley.

J 0.9 (1.4 km) **I 455.4** (732.9 km) Distance marker shows Eagle Plains 363 km (226 miles), Inuvik 735 km (457 miles).

J 3 (5 km) **I 453.3** (729.5 km) Burn area from 1991 fire that burned 5,189 acres/2,100 hectacres.

J 4 (6.4 km) **I 452.3** (727.9 km) The North Fork Ditch channeled water from the North Klondike River to a power plant 15.5 miles/25 km farther west for nearly 60 years, until the 1960s, and it helped to provide electricity and water for huge gold-dredging operations farther down the valley. Watch for salmon migrating upstream from late July through August.

DEMPSTER HIGHWAY *Klondike Highway Junction to Inuvik, NWT*

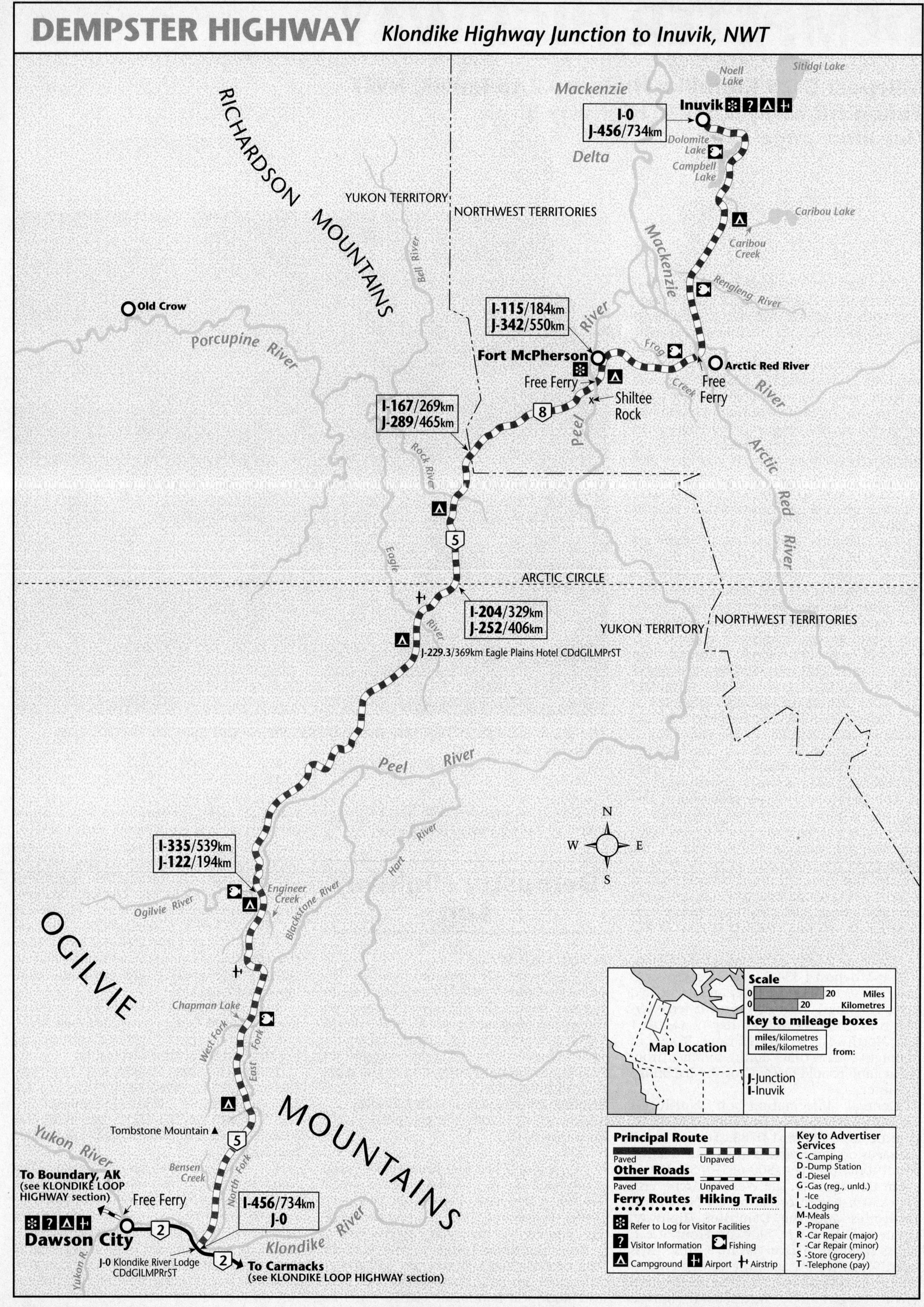

RICHARDSON MOUNTAINS
OGILVIE MOUNTAINS
Mackenzie Delta
Noell Lake
Sitidgi Lake
Inuvik
I-0
J-456/734km
Dolomite Lake
Campbell Lake
Caribou Lake
Caribou Creek
Mackenzie
Rengleng River
YUKON TERRITORY
NORTHWEST TERRITORIES
Bell River
Old Crow
Porcupine River
I-115/184km
J-342/550km
Fort McPherson
Free Ferry
Shiltee Rock
Frog Creek
Arctic Red River
Free Ferry
River
Peel
I-167/269km
J-289/465km
Rock River
Arctic Red River
Eagle River
ARCTIC CIRCLE
I-204/329km
J-252/406km
J-229.3/369km Eagle Plains Hotel CDdGILMPrST
Peel River
Hart River
I-335/539km
J-122/194km
Engineer Creek
Ogilvie River
Blackstone River
Chapman Lake
West Fork
East Fork
Tombstone Mountain
North Fork
Yukon River
Bensen Creek
To Boundary, AK (see KLONDIKE LOOP HIGHWAY section)
Free Ferry
Dawson City
Yukon R.
I-456/734km
J-0
J-0 Klondike River Lodge CDdGILMPRrST
Klondike River
To Carmacks (see KLONDIKE LOOP HIGHWAY section)
Map Location
Scale
0 20 Miles
0 20 Kilometres
Key to mileage boxes
miles/kilometres
miles/kilometres
from:
J-Junction
I-Inuvik
Principal Route
Paved
Unpaved
Other Roads
Paved
Unpaved
Ferry Routes
Hiking Trails
Refer to Log for Visitor Facilities
Visitor Information
Fishing
Campground
Airport
Airstrip
Key to Advertiser Services
C -Camping
D -Dump Station
d -Diesel
G -Gas (reg., unld.)
I -Ice
L -Lodging
M -Meals
P -Propane
R -Car Repair (major)
r -Car Repair (minor)
S -Store (grocery)
T -Telephone (pay)

J 6.5 (10.5 km) **I 449.8** (723.9 km) Antimony Mountain (elev. 6,693 feet/2,040m) about 18.5 miles/30 km away, is one peak of the Ogilvie Mountains and part of the Snowy Range.

J 12.4 (20 km) **I 443.9** (714.4 km) North Klondike Range, Ogilvie Mountains to the west of the highway lead toward the rugged, interior Tombstone Range. These mountains were glaciated during the Ice Age.

J 15.4 (24.5 km) **I 440.9** (709.5 km) Glacier Creek.

J 16.6 (26.7 km) **I 439.7** (707.6 km) Pullout to west.

J 18.1 (29 km) **I 438.2** (705.2 km) Bensen Creek.

J 25.6 (41 km) **I 430.7** (693.1 km) Pea Soup Creek.

J 29.8 (48 km) **I 426.5** (686.4 km) Scout Car Creek.

J 31.7 (51 km) **I 424.6** (683.3 km) Wolf Creek. Trapper's cabin beside creek.

J 34.7 (55.8 km) **I 421.6** (678.5 km) Highway follows North Fork Klondike River.

J 36.6 (58.9 km) **I 419.7** (675.4 km) Grizzly Creek. Mount Robert Service to right northbound.

J 39.6 (63.7 km) **I 416.7** (670.6 km) Mike and Art Creek.

J 40.4 (65 km) **I 415.9** (669.3 km) Klondike Camp Yukon government highway maintenance station. No visitor services but may provide help in an emergency.

J 41.8 (67.3 km) **I 414.5** (667.1 km) First crossing of the North Fork Klondike River. The highway now moves above tree line and on to tundra northbound. At an elevation of approximately 4,003 feet/1,220m, you'll cross the watershed between the Yukon and Mackenzie basins.

J 43 (69.2 km) **I 413.3** (665.2 km) Spectacular first view of Tombstone Range northbound.

J 44.4 (71.5 km) **I 411.9** (662.9 km) Tombstone Mountain Yukon government campground (3,392 feet/1,034m above sea level) with 22 sites, $8 fee, shelter, fireplaces, water, tables, pit toilets. Interpretive centre located at campground is open mid-June to early September; displays, resource library, handouts with area information, campfire talks and nature walks. Good hiking trail begins past the outhouses and leads toward the headwaters of the North Fork Klondike River. ▲

J 46 (74 km) **I 410.3** (660.3 km) Large double-ended pullout. Good views of North Fork Pass and river. To the southwest is Tombstone Mountain (7,195 feet/2,193m). Outstanding aerial view of the mountain available through flightseeing trip out of Dawson City. To the north is the East Fork Blackstone River valley; on each side are the Ogilvie Mountains, which rise to elevations of 6,890 feet/2,100m.

J 48.4 (77.9 km) **I 407.9** (656.4 km) Blackstone River culvert. Tundra in the region indicates permafrost.

J 51 (82 km) **I 405.3** (652.2 km) North Fork Pass Summit, elev. 4,265 feet/1,300m, is the highest point on the Dempster Highway. Wildflowers abundant late June–early July. Descent to the Blackstone River. Good birdwatching area. A hike up to the lower knoll to the right of the main mountain increases chances of seeing pika and marmots.

J 52.2 (84 km) **I 404.1** (650.3 km) Anglecomb Peak (also called Sheep Mountain) is a lambing and nursery habitat for Dall sheep during May and June, as well as a frequent nesting area for a pair of golden eagles.

J 54.2 (87.2 km) **I 402.1** (647.1 km) First crossing of East Fork Blackstone River.

J 56.5 (91 km) **I 399.8** (643.4 km) The Blackstone Uplands, stretching from North Fork Pass to Chapman Lake, are a rich area for birdlife (long-tailed jaegers, gyrfalcons, peregrine falcons, red-throated loons and oldsquaw ducks) and big game hunting for Dall sheep and grizzly bear.

J 63.4 (102 km) **I 392.9** (632.3 km) Distance marker shows Eagle Plains 261 km (162 miles), Inuvik 633 km (393 miles), Dawson 142 km (88 miles), Whitehorse 600 km (373 miles).

J 66.9 (107.6 km) **I 389.4** (626.7 km) Large gravel pullout with litter barrels. Access to Blackstone River.

J 71.5 (115 km) **I 384.8** (619.3 km) First crossing of West Fork Blackstone River. Watch for arctic terns. Good fishing for Dolly Varden and grayling a short distance downstream where the west and east forks of the Blackstone join to form the **Blackstone River**, which the road now follows. After the river crossing, 2 low, cone-shaped mounds called pingos are visible upriver about 5 miles/8 km.

J 72.1 (116 km) **I 384.2** (618.3 km) Commemorative road sign about sled dog patrols of the Royal North–West Mounted Police. Also a sign: Watch for horses. View over Chapman Lake, one of the few lakes close to the highway that is large enough to permit floatplane operations. Porcupine caribou herd often crosses highway in this area in mid-October.

J 77.3 (124.4 km) **I 379** (609.9 km) **Private Aircraft:** Government airstrip (road is part of the strip); elev. 3,100 feet/945m; length 3,000 feet/914m.

J 96 (154.5 km) **I 360.3** (579.8 km) Northbound, highway passes through barren gray hills of Windy Pass. The mountain ridges are the breeding habitat for some species of butterflies and moths not known to exist anywhere else.

J 106 (169.7 km) **I 350.3** (563.7 km) Creek culvert is red from iron oxide. Sulfurous smell is from nearby sulfur springs. Watch for interesting geological features in hills along road.

J 108.1 (173 km) **I 348.2** (560.4 km) Views of red-coloured Engineer Creek, and also erosion pillars and red rock of nearby hills between here and Kilometrepost 182.

J 121.7 (194 km) **I 334.6** (538.5 km) Sapper Hill, named in 1971 in honour of the 3rd Royal Canadian Engineers who built the Ogilvie River bridge. "Sapper" is a nickname for an army engineer. **Engineer Creek** Yukon government campground; 15 sites, $8 fee, fireplaces, water, tables, pit toilets. Grayling fishing. ▲

J 122.9 (195.7 km) **I 333.4** (536.5 km) The 360-foot/110-m Jeckell Bridge spans the Ogilvie River here. Built by the Canadian Armed Forces Engineers as a training exercise, it is named in honour of Allan Jeckell, controller of the Yukon from 1932 to 1946. Fossil coral may be visible in limestone outcrops to the northeast of the bridge.

The Ogilvie River and Ogilvie Mountains were named in honour of William Ogilvie, a highly respected Dominion land surveyor and commissioner of the Yukon during the Klondike gold rush.

J 123 (195.8 km) **I 333.3** (536.4 km) Ogilvie grader station, Yukon government maintenance camp is on north side of the river. Emergency-only gas and minor repairs may be available (not guaranteed).

For the next 25 miles/40 km, the highway follows the narrow valley of the Ogilvie River. For the first 12 miles/20 km, talus slopes edge the road, and game trails are evident along their precipitous sides.

J 124.3 (197.7 km) **I 332** (534.3 km) View of castlelike outcroppings of rock, known as tors, on mountaintops to north.

J 131.9 (209.5 km) **I 324.4** (522.1 km) Between here and Kilometrepost 216, watch for bird nests in the shale embankments along the highway and unusual rock outcroppings and erosion pillars in surrounding hills. Highway crosses rolling plateau country near Kilometrepost 218.

J 137.5 (221.2 km) **I 318.8** (513 km) Small turnout with litter barrels. Easy access to **Ogilvie River**. Good grayling fishing. Elephant Rock may be viewed from right side of road northbound. Fascinating mountain of broken rock and shale near Kilometrepost 224.

J 137.6 (221.5 km) **I 318.7** (512.9 km) Davies Creek.

J 149.1 (235.8 km) **I 307.2** (494.4 km) Ogilvie airstrip, status unknown. The great gray owl, one of Canada's largest, is known to nest as far north as this area.

J 154.4 (244 km) **I 301.9** (485.8 km) Highway climbs away from the Ogilvie River, following a high ridge to the Eagle Plains plateau. One of the few unglaciated areas in Canada, this country is shaped by wind and water erosion rather than by ice. Views of Mount Cronkhite and Mount McCullum to the east.

Seismic lines next 62 miles/100 km provide hiking paths across the tundra. This was the major area of oil and gas exploration activity for which the road was originally built. In season, fields of cotton grass and varieties of tundra plants make good photo subjects. The road continues to follow a high ridge (elev. 1,969 feet/600m) with broad sweeps and easy grades.

J 160.9 (259 km) **I 295.4** (475.4 km) Large double-ended turnout. Panoramic Ogilvie–Peel viewpoint. Lowbush cranberries in August. Outhouse, litter barrels.

J 171.7 (270.6 km) **I 284.6** (458 km) Highway begins descent northbound and crosses fabulous high rolling country above tree line.

J 175.6 (276.7 km) **I 280.7** (451.7 km) Gravel pit full of old oil drums.

J 187.7 (302 km) **I 268.6** (432.3 km) Forest fire burn area; 13,590 acres/5,500 hectacres burned in July–August 1991.

J 204.5 (321 km) **I 256.3** (412.5 km) Road widens to become part of an airstrip.

J 215.6 (347 km) **I 240.7** (387.4 km) Richardson Mountains to the northeast. The thick blanket of rock and gravel that makes up the roadbed ahead is designed to prevent the underlying permafrost from melting. The roadbed conducts heat more than the surrounding vegetation does and must be extra thick to compensate. Much of the highway was built in winter.

J 229.3 (369 km) **I 227** (365.3 km) **Mile 231. EAGLE PLAINS;** hotel, phone (403) 979-4187, fax (403) 979-4187; food, gas, propane, aviation fuel, diesel and lodging. Open year-round.

Built in 1978, just before completion of the Dempster Highway, the hotel here was an engineering challenge. Engineers considered the permafrost in the area and found a place where the bedrock was at the surface. The hotel was built on this natural pad, thus avoiding the costly process of building on pilings as was done at Inuvik.

Artic Circle crossing at Milepost J 252.
(© Michael DeYoung)

Mile 231. Eagle Plains Hotel. Located midway on the Dempster, this year-round facility is an oasis in the wilderness. Modern hotel rooms, plus restaurant and lounge. Full camper services including electrical hookups, laundry, store, dump station, minor repairs, tires, propane and road and area information. Check out our historical photos. See display ad this section. [ADVERTISEMENT] ▲

J 234.8 (377.8 km) **I 221.5** (356.5 km) Short side road to picnic site with information sign about Albert Johnson, "The Mad Trapper of Rat River." Something of a mystery man, Johnson killed 1 mounted policeman and wounded another in 2 separate incidents involving complaints that Johnson was tampering with Native trap lines. The ensuing manhunt became famous in the North, as Johnson eluded Mounties for 48 days during the winter of 1931–32. Johnson was killed in a shoot-out on Feb. 17, 1932. He was buried at Aklavik, a community located 36 miles/58 km by air west of Inuvik.

Dick North, author of 2 books on Johnson (and also author of *The Lost Patrol*), was quoted in the *New York Times* (June 3, 1990) as being 95 percent certain that Johnson, whose true identity has not been known, was a Norwegian-American bank robber named Johnson.

J 234.9 (378 km) **I 221.4** (356.3 km) **Eagle River** bridge. Like the Ogilvie bridge, it was built by the Dept. of National Defence as a training exercise. In contrast to the other rivers seen from the Dempster, the Eagle is a more sluggish, silt-laden stream with unstable banks. It is the main drainage channel for the western slopes of the Richardson Mountains. It and its tributaries provide good grayling fishing. Canoeists leave here bound for Alaska via the Porcupine and Yukon rivers.

J 239.4 (385.3 km) **I 216.9** (349.1 km) Views of the Richardson Mountains (elev. 3,937 feet/1,200m) ahead. Named for Sir John Richardson, surgeon and naturalist on both of Sir John Franklin's overland expeditions to the Arctic Ocean.

J 241.7 (389 km) **I 214.6** (345.4 km) **Private Aircraft:** Emergency airstrip; elev. 2,365 feet/721m; length 2,500 feet/762m; gravel. Used regularly by aircraft hauling freight to Old Crow, a Kutchin Indian settlement on the Porcupine River and Yukon's most northerly community.

J 252 (405.5 km) **I 204.3** (328.8 km) Large double-ended turnout. On June 22, the sun does not fall below the horizon for 24 hours at this latitude. Picnic tables, litter barrels, outhouses nearby. Sign marks Arctic Circle crossing, 66°33'N. Highway crosses arctic tundra on an elevated berm beside the Richardson Mountains; sweeping views.

J 277 (445.8 km) **I 179.3** (288.5 km) Rock River Yukon government campground; 18 sites, $8 fee, tables, kitchen shelter, water, firepits, outhouses. Black flies prevalent; bring repellent. ▲

J 280.1 (450.8 km) **I 176.2** (283.6 km) Turnout. Northbound, the highway winds toward the Richardson Mountains, crossing them at George's Gap near the YT–NWT border. Good hiking area and excellent photo possibilities.

J 288 (463.5 km) **I 168.3** (270.8 km) Turnout; good overnight spot for self-contained vehicles.

J 288.5 (464.3 km) **I 167.8** (270 km) Plaque about Wright Pass, named for Al Wright, a highway engineer with Public Works Canada who was responsible for the routing of the Dempster Highway.

J 288.9 (465 km) **I 167.4** (269.4 km) YT–NWT border. Historical marker. Continental Divide in the Richardson Mountains: West of here, water flows to the Pacific Ocean. East of here, water flows to the Arctic Ocean. Good photo spot.

TIME ZONE CHANGE: Yukon Territory observes Pacific standard time; Northwest Territories is on Mountain time.

NWT HIGHWAY 8

IMPORTANT: Kilometreposts northbound (with white letters on a blue background) indicate distance from YT–NWT border and are indicated at intervals in our log. Highway descends northbound. Watch for change to narrower road surface.

J 297.6 (479 km) **I 158.7** (255.4 km) Kilometrepost 14. **James Creek;** good fishing. Highway maintenance camp. Good spot to park overnight.

J 299 (481.2 km) **I 157.3** (253.1 km) Sign advises no passing next 4.3 miles/7 km; climb to Wright Pass summit.

J 303.7 (488.7 km) **I 152.6** (245.6 km) Wright Pass Summit. From here northbound, the Dempster Highway descends a somewhat rocky, narrow track some 2,300 feet/853m to the Peel River crossing, 32 miles/51 km away.

J 316.3 (509 km) **I 140** (225.3 km) Kilometrepost 44. Side road leads down to Midway Lake.

J 319.4 (514 km) **I 136.9** (220.3 km) **Private Aircraft:** Highway widens to form Midway airstrip; length 3,000 feet/914m.

J 329.3 (530 km) **I 127** (204.4 km) View of Peel River Valley and Fort McPherson to north. Litter barrels.

J 332.4 (535 km) **I 123.9** (199.4 km) Kilometrepost 70. Highway begins descent northbound to Peel River.

J 334.9 (539 km) **I 121.4** (195.4 km) Peel River crossing, called locally Eightmile because it is situated 8 miles/12.8 km south of Fort McPherson. Free government ferry service 15 hours a day during summer (from about early or mid-June to mid-Oct.). Double-ended cable ferry: Drive on, drive off. Light vehicles cross by ice bridge in late November; heavier vehicles cross as ice thickens. *No crossing possible during freezeup or breakup.* Phone (toll free) 1-800-661-0752 for information on ferry crossings, road conditions and weather.

The level of the Peel River changes rapidly in spring and summer in response to meltwater from the mountains and ice jams on the Mackenzie River. The alluvial flood plain is covered by muskeg on the flats, and scrubby alder and stunted black spruce on the valley sides.

Indians from Fort McPherson have summer tent camps on the Peel River. The Indians net whitefish and sheefish (inconnu) then dry them on racks or in smokehouses for the winter.

About 4 miles/6.4 km south upstream is a trail leading to Shiltee Rock, which gives excellent views of the Peel River and the southern end of the Mackenzie.

J 335.9 (540.6 km) **I 120.4** (193.8 km) Nutuiluie territorial campground with 20 sites. (Campground name is from the Gwich'in term *Noo-til-ee,* meaning "fast flowing waters." Information centre open daily June to September. Camping permits, potable water, firewood, pit toilets available. ▲

J 337.4 (543 km) **I 118.9** (191.3 km) Kilometrepost 78.

J 340.4 (547.8 km) **I 115.9** (186.5 km) Access road right to Fort McPherson airport.

J 341.8 (550 km) **I 114.5** (184.3 km) Side road on left to Fort McPherson (description follows).

Fort McPherson

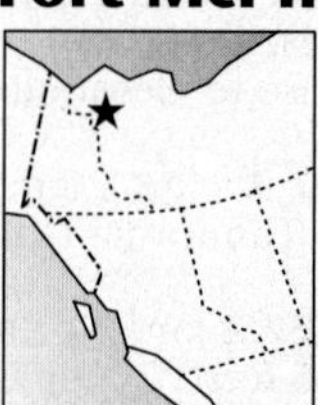

Located on a flat-topped hill about 100 feet/30m above the Peel River, 24 miles/38 km from its junction with the Mackenzie River; 100 miles/160 km southwest of Aklavik by boat along Peel Channel, 31 miles/50 km directly east of the Richardson Mountains. **Population:** 632. **Emergency Services: RCMP,** phone (403) 952-2551. **Health Center,** phone (403) 952-2586.

Visitor Information: Located in the restored log house. **Radio:** CBC 680.

Private Aircraft: Fort McPherson airstrip; 67°24'N 134°51'W; elev. 142 feet/43m; length 3,500 feet/1,067m; gravel.

This Déné Indian settlement has a public phone, cafe, bed and breakfast, 2 general stores and 2 service stations (1 with tire repair). A co-op hotel here offers 8 rooms and a restaurant. Arts and crafts include beadwork and hide garments.

Wildlife watching, adventure tours and canoe trips are popular along the Peel River.

Aklak Air provides scheduled air service from Inuvik.

Fort McPherson was named in 1848 for Murdoch McPherson, chief trader of the Hudson's Bay Co., which had established its first posts in the area 8 years before. Between 1849 and 1859 there were frequent feuds with neighboring Inuit, who later moved farther north to the Aklavik area, where they established a fur-trading post.

In addition to subsistence fishing and hunting, income is earned from trapping (mostly muskrat and mink), handicrafts, government employment, and commercial enterprises such as Fort McPherson Tent and Canvas factory, which specializes in travel bags, tents and tepees. Tours during business hours, 9 A.M. to 5 P.M. weekdays; (403) 952-2179 fax (403) 952-2718.

Photos and artifacts depicting the history and way of life of the community are displayed in the Chief Julius School. Buried in the cemetery outside the Anglican church are Inspector Francis J. Fitzgerald and 3 men from the ill-fated North West Mounted Police patrol of 1910–1911 between Fort McPherson and Dawson.

Inspector Fitzgerald and the men had left Fort McPherson on December 21, 1910, carrying mail and dispatches to Dawson City. By February 20, 1911, the men had not yet arrived in Dawson, nearly a month overdue. A search party led by Corporal W.J.D. Dempster was sent to look for the missing patrol. On March 22, 1911, Dempster discovered their frozen bodies only 26 miles from where they had started. Lack of knowledge of the trail, coupled with too few rations, had doomed the 4-man patrol. One of the last entries in Fitzgerald's diary, quoted in Dick North's *The Lost Patrol*, an account of their journey, read: "We have now only 10 pounds of flour and 8 pounds of bacon and some dried fish. My last hope is gone. ... We have been a week looking for a river to take us over the divide, but there are dozens of rivers and I am at a loss."

Dempster Highway Log
(continued)

J 342.4 (551 km) **I 113.9** (183.3 km) Kilometrepost 86.

J 365.1 (587.6 km) **I 91.2** (146.8 km) **Frog Creek.** Grayling and pike. Road on right northbound leads to picnic area.

J 377.1 (606.8 km) **I 79.2** (127.5 km) Mackenzie River wayside area.

J 377.9 (608.2 km) **I 78.4** (126.2 km) Mackenzie River crossing. Free government ferry service available 15 hours a day during summer (from about early or mid-June to early October). Double-ended ferry: Drive on, drive off. Light vehicles may cross by ice bridge in late November; heavier vehicles can cross as ice thickens. *No crossing possible during freezeup and breakup.*

The ferry travels between landings on either side of the Mackenzie River and also provides access to **TSIIGEHTCHIC (formerly ARCTIC RED RIVER)**, a small Athapaskan community (pop. 140) located at the confluence of the Mackenzie and Arctic Red rivers. Tsiigehtchic has a community-owned grocery store and cafe. The Sunshine Inn provides accommodations for up to 8 people. Boat tours are available through the Band Store or local operators. For more information on lodging or tours call (403) 953-3003 or fax (403) 953-3906.

Tsiigehtchic, which means "mouth of iron river," is one of 4 communities in the Gwich'in Settlement Area. The residents speak a dialect of Gwich'in, one of the Athapaskan languages. They refer to themselves as the Gwichya Gwich'in or "People of the flat land." The Gwich'in Social & Cultural Institute here was formed at an annual assembly in Fort McPherson in 1992 in response to people's concern about the loss of their culture and language.

The Arctic Red River (Tsiigehnjik) was declared a Canadian Heritage River in 1993. Tsiigehnjik, the Gwich'in name for the river, winds it way out of the Mackenzie Mountains and flows into the Mackenzie River at Tsiigehtchic. The Gwichya Gwich'in have long used and travelled the river for fishing, hunting and trapping.

J 399.6 (643 km) **I 56.7** (91.2 km) **Rengling River,** grayling fishing.

J 404.4 (650.8 km) **I 51.9** (83.5 km) Beginning of 13-mile/21-km straight stretch.

J 409.7 (659.3 km) **I 46.6** (75 km) Distance marker shows Inuvik 75 km.

J 426.3 (686 km) **I 30** (48.3 km) Caribou Creek picnic and camping area. ▲

J 431.4 (694.3 km) **I 24.9** (40.1 km) Campbell Lake and Campbell escarpment ahead northbound. Good place to glass for peregrine falcons.

J 440.6 (709 km) **I 15.7** (25.3 km) Cabin Creek picnic spot; pit toilets.

J 442.4 (712 km) **I 13.9** (22.4 km) **Campbell Creek** picnic area; pit toilets. Good fishing for pike and whitefish, some sheefish (inconnu). Creek leads a short distance to Campbell Lake. Boat launch. Bring mosquito repellent.

J 449.9 (724 km) **I 6.4** (10.3 km) Airport Road turnoff; pavement begins.

J 451 (725.8 km) **I 5.3** (8.5 km) Food, gas, and lodging.

J 451.7 (727 km) **I 4.6** (7.4 km) Kilometrepost 262.

J 454 (730.6 km) **I 2.3** (3.7 km) Chuk Park territorial campground; 38 campsites, 20 pull-through, electric hookups, firewood, water, showers, $10 fee. Lookout tower. ▲

J 456.3 (734.3 km) **I 0** Turn left northbound for Inuvik town centre (description follows).

Inuvik

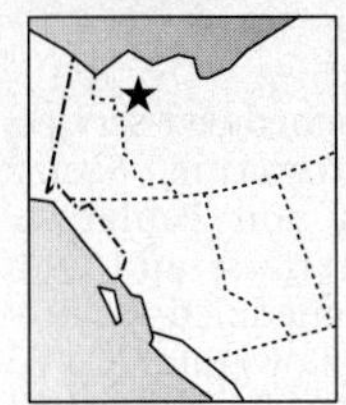

Situated on a flat wooded plateau on the east channel of the Mackenzie River, some 60 air miles/88 km south of the Beaufort Sea, 36 air miles/58 km and 70 water miles/113 km from Aklavik on the western edge of the delta. **Population:** 3,206, Déné, White and Inuvialuit.

Emergency Services: RCMP, phone (403) 979-2935. **Hospital**, Inuvik General, phone (403) 979-2955.

Visitor Information: Western Arctic Regional Visitors Centre is located on Mackenzie Road across from the hospital. The centre is open mid-May to mid-September and features interactive displays. In front of the centre, a green and white Cessna 170 on a mounted display rotates to face into the wind. Phone (403) 979-4727. Or contact the Western Arctic Tourism Assoc., Box 2600MP, Inuvik, NT X0E 0T0, phone (403) 979-4321, fax (403) 979-2434. Visitors are also welcomed to stop by the Ingamo Hall Friendship Centre.

Elevation: 224 feet/68m. **Climate**: Weather information available by calling (403) 979-4381. May 24 marks 57 days of midnight sun. The sun begins to set on July 19; on Dec. 6, the sun sets and does not rise until Jan. 6. Average annual precipitation 4 inches rainfall, 69 inches snowfall. July mean high 67°F/19°C, mean low 45°F/7°C. January mean high -11°F/-24°C, mean low is -30°F/-35°C. **Radio** and **Television:** CBC and local. **Newspaper:** *The Drum* (weekly).

Private Aircraft: Inuvik airstrip; elev. 224 feet/68m; length 6,000 feet/1,829m; asphalt; fuel 80, 100. Townsite airstrip; elev. 10 feet/3m; length 1,800 feet/549m; gravel; fuel 80, 100, Jet B, F40. High pressure refueling.

Inuvik, meaning "The Place of Man," is the largest Canadian community north of the Arctic Circle, and the major government, transportation and communication centre for Canada's western arctic. Construction of the town began in 1955 and was completed in 1961. It was the main supply base for the petrochemical exploration of the delta until Tuktoyaktuk took over that role as activity centered in the Beaufort Sea. In Inuvik some hunting, fishing and trapping is done, but most people earn wages in government and private enterprises, particularly in transportation and construction. With the delta one of the richest muskrat areas in the world, Inuvik is the western centre for shipping furs south.

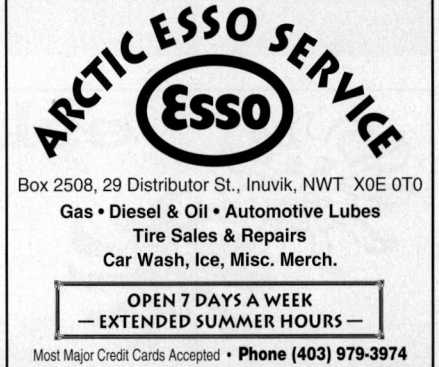

The town's official monument says, in part, that Inuvik was "the first community north of the Arctic Circle built to provide the normal facilities of a Canadian town."

TRANSPORTATION

Air: Aklak Air provides scheduled service between Inuvik and Tuktoyaktuk, Sachs Harbour, Fort McPherson and Paulatuk. Scheduled service to Whitehorse and Old Crow, YT, via Alkan Air. Scheduled service to Edmonton, AB, and to Yellowknife, NWT, via NWT Air and Canadian Airlines International. Scheduled service to Aklavik and Tuktoyaktuk via Arctic Wings. Several air charter services operate out of Inuvik, offering flights to delta communities and charter service for hunting, fishing and camping trips. **Highways:** Dempster Highway from Dawson City. Winter roads (December into April) to Aklavik and Tuktoyaktuk. **Bus:** Service from Dawson City to Inuvik 2 times a week via Arctic Tour Co., phone (403) 979-4100. **Taxi** and **rental cars:** Available.

ACCOMMODATIONS/VISITOR SERVICES

Visitors will find most facilities available, although accommodations should be reserved in advance. Inuvik has 3 hotels, all with dining lounges, and bed and breakfasts. There are also a laundry, post office, territorial liquor store, banks and churches. There are 3 gas stations and a car wash; propane, auto repair and towing are available. Hardware, grocery and general stores and gift shops are here.

Happy Valley territorial campground; 20 RV sites, electrical hookups, 10 tent pads, hot showers, firewood, water, dump station, fee. Chuk Park territorial campground; 20 sites, electrical hookups, firewood, water, showers, $10 fee. ▲

ATTRACTIONS

Igloo Church, painted white with lines to simulate snow blocks, is on Mackenzie Road as you drive in to Inuvik. Inside the church is Inuit painter Mona Thrasher's interpretation of the Stations of the Cross. Visitors are welcome.

Ingamo Hall is a 2-story log community hall that serves the social and recreational needs of Native families. Visitors are welcome. The hall was built by Allan Crich over a 3-year period, using some 1,020 logs that were cut from white spruce trees in the southern part of the Mackenzie River valley and floated down the river to Inuvik.

Tour Western Arctic Communities: Air charter service is available to **AKLAVIK** (pop. 800), an important centre for muskrat harvesting; **TUKTOYAKTUK** (pop. 950), an Inuit village on the Arctic coast and site of oil development; **SACHS HARBOUR** (pop. 158) on Banks Island, an Inuit settlement supported by trapping and some big game outfitters; **PAULATUK** (pop. 255), an Inuit settlement supported by hunting, fishing, sealing and trapping; and **HOLMAN** (pop. 360), an Inuit community on the west coast of Victoria Island, famous for its printmaking. Scheduled air service is also available to **OLD CROW** (pop. 267), an Indian settlement on the Porcupine River in Yukon Territory.

The **Mackenzie River delta**, one of the largest deltas in North America and an important wildlife corridor to the Arctic, is 40 miles/64 km wide and 60 miles/97 km long. A maze of lakes, channels and islands, the delta supports a variety of bird life, fish and muskrats. Boat tours of the Mackenzie River are available.

Arctic Nature Tours, beside the Igloo Church, Arctic wildlife displays, local artwork and crafts. Fly to Tuktoyaktuk on the Arctic coast for a guided tour. Fly to Herschel Island Yukon Park, rich in history and a naturalist's delight. Toast the midnight sun while cruising the Mackenzie River. Try fishing. Call (403) 979-3300, fax (403) 979-3400 or write Box 1530(M), Inuvik, NWT X0E 0T0. [ADVERTISEMENT]

Boreal Books carries a full range of northern books on history, Native studies, exploration and wildlife. Full selection of area postcards, northern posters and local music. Authorized agent for topo maps, marine charts and air charts. Heritage books. Catalogue available. Mail orders welcome. Open all week. Phone (403) 979-2260, fax (403) 979-4429. [ADVERTISEMENT]

Special Events. The annual Northern Games are held in Inuvik or other western Arctic communities in summer. Traditional Inuit and Déné sports, dances, competitions, crafts and Good Woman Contest (where northern women show their talent at animal skinning, bannock baking and other bush skills) are part of the festival. Visitors are welcome to join northerners from Alaska, Yukon Territory, Labrador and the Northwest Territories. For more information, write Northern Games Assoc., Box 1184, Inuvik, NT X0E 0T0.

The 8th annual Great Northern Arts Festival is scheduled for July 1996. The festival features exhibitions, demonstrations, workshops and art sales by Northern artists. For more information contact the Arts Festival, Box 2921, Inuvik, NT X0E 0T0; phone (403) 979-3536.

INUVIK ADVERTISERS

Aklak Air	Ph. (403) 979-3555
Arctic Esso Service	29 Distributor St.
Arctic Nature Tours	Ph. (403) 979-3300
Boreal Books	Ph. (403) 979-2260
Eskimo Inn Ltd.	Ph. (403) 979-2801
Finto Motor Inn	Ph. (403) 979-2647
Great Northern Arts Festival, The	Ph. (403) 979-3536
Mackenzie Hotel, The	Ph. (403) 979-2861
Peppermill Restaurant	Finto Motor Inn
Place of Man	Ph. (403) 979-3381
Robertson's Bed & Breakfast	Ph. (403) 979-3111
Saunatuk Fishing Lodge Ltd.	Ph. (403) 977-2348
Western Arctic Tourism Assoc.	Ph. (403) 979-4321

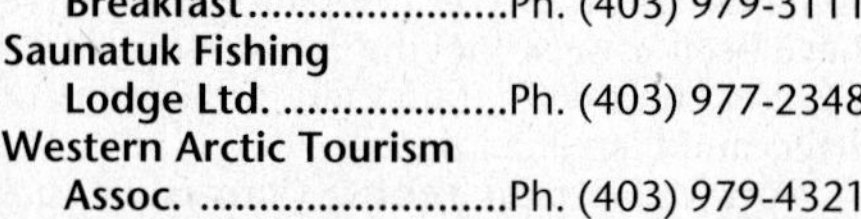

DALTON HIGHWAY

(Formerly the North Slope Haul Road)
Milepost F 73.1 Elliott Highway to Deadhorse, Alaska
Alaska Route 11

The trans-Alaska pipeline parallels the road near Pump Station No. 4 *(Jerrianne Lowther, staff)*

The 414-mile/666.3-km Dalton Highway (still referred to as the "Haul Road") begins at **Milepost F 73.1** on the Elliott Highway and ends—for the general public—at Deadhorse, a few miles from Prudhoe Bay and the Arctic Ocean. (Access to Prudhoe Bay, the largest oil field in North America, is available only through commercial tour operators; private vehicles are not permitted on the oil field.)

Permits are not required to drive the highway to Deadhorse. Public travel on the Dalton Highway was originally restricted. Gov. Hickel moved to open the Dalton Highway to Deadhorse in July 1991, but the opening was delayed until December 1994.

The highway is named for James William Dalton, an arctic engineer involved in early oil exploration efforts on the North Slope. It was built as a haul road between the Yukon River and Prudhoe Bay during construction of the trans-Alaska pipeline, and was originally called the North Slope Haul Road. Construction of the road began April 29, 1974, and was completed 5 months later. The road is 28 feet/9m wide with 3 to 6 feet/1 to 2m of gravel surfacing. Some sections of road are underlain with plastic foam insulation to prevent thawing of the permafrost.

Construction of the 800-mile-/1,287-km-long pipeline between Prudhoe Bay and Valdez took place between 1974 and 1977. The 48-inch-diameter pipeline, of which slightly more than half is above ground, has 10 operating pump stations. The control center is in Valdez. Design, construction and operation of the pipeline are managed by Alyeska Pipeline Service Company, a consortium of 7 oil companies (BP, ARCO, Exxon, Mobil, Amerada Hess, Phillips and Unocal). For more information, contact Public Affairs Dept., Alyeska Pipeline Service Co., 1835 S. Bragaw St., Anchorage, AK 99512.

The Bureau of Land Management (BLM) manages 2.1 million acres of public land along the Dalton Highway between the Yukon and Pump Station No. 3. For information on BLM lands, contact: Arctic District, BLM, 1150 University Ave., Fairbanks, AK 99709; phone (907) 474-2301.

Services along the Dalton Highway are limited. Shop for groceries before departing Fairbanks. There are no convenience stores or grocery stores along the highway or in Deadhorse. Gas, diesel fuel, tire repair, restaurant, motel, phone and emergency communications are available at **Milepost J 56**, just past the Yukon River bridge, and at Coldfoot, **Milepost J 175.** The last dump station northbound is also located at Coldfoot. (Please do NOT dump holding tanks along the road.) Phones at both locations are for credit card and collect calls only. Public phone at Wiseman. Alyeska pump stations do not provide any public services.

IMPORTANT: For emergency services contact the Alaska State Troopers via CB radio, Channel 19, or contact any state highway maintenance camp along the highway. Highway maintenance camps can provide help only in the event of an accident or medical emergency, they cannot fix flat tires nor do they provide gas. Keep in mind that towing fees by private wrecker service can cost $5 a mile, each way.

Road conditions vary depending on weather, maintenance and time of year, but in general the road has a reputation for being rough. Watch for ruts, rocks, dust, soft shoulders and trucks. There are several steep (10 percent) grades. Drive with your headlights on at all times. Slow down and pull over to the side of the road when meeting oncoming trucks. Stop only at turnouts. Carry spare tires.

The Dalton Highway is unique in its scenic beauty, wildlife and recreational opportunities. Travelers are requested to stay on the road and to use the formal turnouts and campgrounds provided to avoid permanently scarring the fragile tundra. Report wildlife violations to Fish and Game at Coldfoot.

All waters between the Yukon River bridge and Dietrich River are part of the Yukon River system, and most are tributaries

DALTON HIGHWAY *Milepost F 73.1 Elliott Highway to Deadhorse, AK*

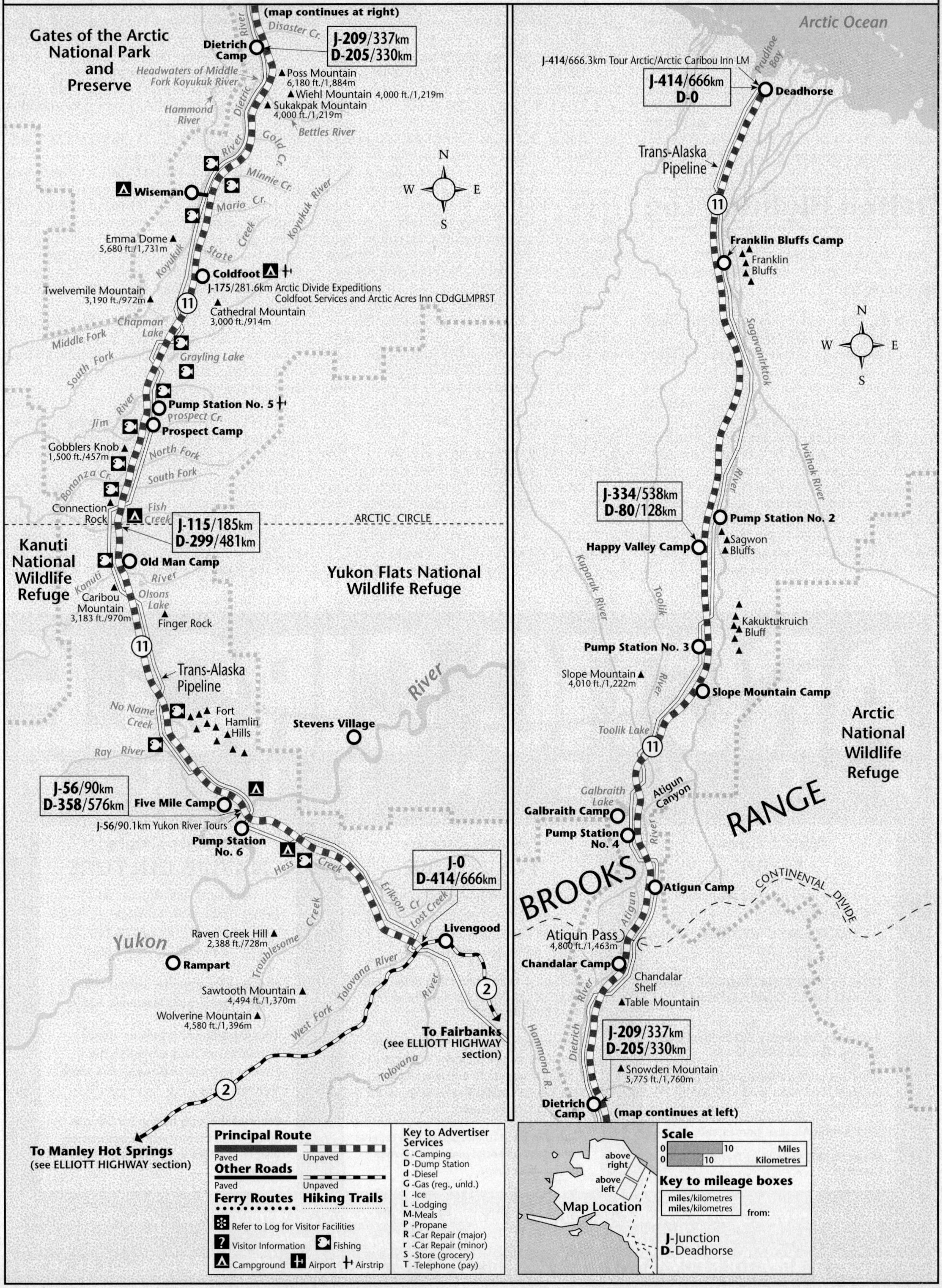

(map continues at right)

Gates of the Arctic National Park and Preserve

Dietrich Camp

J-209/337km
D-205/330km

Disaster Cr.
Headwaters of Middle Fork Koyukuk River
Poss Mountain 6,180 ft./1,884m
Wiehl Mountain 4,000 ft./1,219m
Sukakpak Mountain 4,000 ft./1,219m
Hammond River
Dietrich River
Gold Cr.
Bettles River
Minnie Cr.
Wiseman
Mario Cr.
Koyukuk River
State Creek
Emma Dome 5,680 ft./1,731m
Koyukuk
Coldfoot
J-175/281.6km Arctic Divide Expeditions
Coldfoot Services and Arctic Acres Inn CDdGLMPRST
Twelvemile Mountain 3,190 ft./972m
Cathedral Mountain 3,000 ft./914m
Chapman Lake
Middle Fork
South Fork
Grayling Lake
Pump Station No. 5
Jim River
Prospect Cr.
Prospect Camp
Gobblers Knob 1,500 ft./457m
North Fork
South Fork
Bonanza Cr.
Connection Rock
Fish Creek
ARCTIC CIRCLE

J-115/185km
D-299/481km

Kanuti National Wildlife Refuge
Old Man Camp
Kanuti River
Caribou Mountain 3,183 ft./970m
Olsons Lake
Finger Rock

Yukon Flats National Wildlife Refuge

Trans-Alaska Pipeline
No Name Creek
Fort Hamlin Hills
Ray River
Stevens Village
River

J-56/90km
D-358/576km

Five Mile Camp
J-56/90.1km Yukon River Tours
Pump Station No. 6
Hess Creek
Erikson Cr
Lost Creek

J-0
D-414/666km

Livengood
Yukon
Raven Creek Hill 2,388 ft./728m
Rampart
Troublesome Creek
Tolovana River
Sawtooth Mountain 4,494 ft./1,370m
Wolverine Mountain 4,580 ft./1,396m
West Fork
River
Tolovana

To Fairbanks (see ELLIOTT HIGHWAY section)

To Manley Hot Springs (see ELLIOTT HIGHWAY section)

Arctic Ocean
Prudhoe Bay
J-414/666.3km Tour Arctic/Arctic Caribou Inn LM

J-414/666km
D-0

Deadhorse
Trans-Alaska Pipeline
Franklin Bluffs Camp
Franklin Bluffs
Sagavanirktok River
Ivishak River

J-334/538km
D-80/128km

Pump Station No. 2
Happy Valley Camp
Sagwon Bluffs
Kuparuk River
Toolik River
Kakuktukruich Bluff
Pump Station No. 3
Slope Mountain 4,010 ft./1,222m
Slope Mountain Camp
Toolik Lake

Arctic National Wildlife Refuge

Galbraith Lake
Galbraith Camp
Atigun Canyon
Pump Station No. 4
Atigun River
BROOKS RANGE
Atigun Camp
CONTINENTAL DIVIDE
Atigun Pass 4,800 ft./1,463m
Chandalar Camp
Chandalar Shelf
Table Mountain
Hammond R.
Dietrich River

J-209/337km
D-205/330km

Snowden Mountain 5,775 ft./1,760m
Dietrich Camp
(map continues at left)

Principal Route
Paved — Unpaved
Other Roads
Paved — Unpaved
Ferry Routes — **Hiking Trails**
Refer to Log for Visitor Facilities
Visitor Information — Fishing
Campground — Airport — Airstrip

Key to Advertiser Services
C -Camping
D -Dump Station
d -Diesel
G -Gas (reg., unld.)
I -Ice
L -Lodging
M -Meals
P -Propane
R -Car Repair (major)
r -Car Repair (minor)
S -Store (grocery)
T -Telephone (pay)

Map Location (above right, above left)

Scale
0 — 10 Miles
0 — 10 Kilometres

Key to mileage boxes
miles/kilometres
miles/kilometres
from:
J-Junction
D-Deadhorse

of the Koyukuk River. Fishing for arctic grayling is especially good in rivers accessible by foot from the highway. The large rivers also support burbot, salmon, pike and whitefish. Small Dolly Varden are at higher elevations in streams north of Coldfoot. Fishing for salmon is closed within the trans-Alaska pipeline corridor. According to the Dept. of Fish and Game, anglers should expect high, turbid water conditions throughout much of June as the snowpack melts in the Brooks Range, with the best fishing occurring during July and August.

Dalton Highway Log

Distance from junction with Elliott Highway (J) is followed by distance from Deadhorse (D).

J 0 D 414 (666.3 km) **Junction** with Elliott Highway at **Milepost F 73.1.**

J 4 (6.4 km) **D 410** (659.8 km) Highway descends steeply into the Lost Creek valley. Lost Creek flows into the West Fork Tolovana River. Pipeline is visible stretching across the ridges of the distant hills.

J 5.6 (9 km) **D 408.4** (657.2 km) Lost Creek culvert. Steep hills north- and southbound. Pipeline access road; no public admittance. There are many of these access roads along the highway; all are closed to the public for security and safety concerns.

J 9.8 (15.8 km) **D 404.2** (650.5 km) Road follows a high ridge with spectacular view of Erickson Creek area and pipeline.

J 12 (19.3 km) **D 402** (646.9 km) Small gravel turnouts.

J 12.1 (19.5 km) **D 401.9** (646.8 km) Erickson Creek culvert.

J 20.9 (33.6 km) **D 393.1** (632.6 km) Steep double-ended turnout at gravel pit to west.

J 21 (33.8 km) **D 393** (632.5 km) Descent to Hess Creek begins northbound.

J 23.6 (38 km) **D 390.4** (628.3 km) Pipeline access road, pond.

J 23.8 (38.3 km) **D 390.2** (627.9 km) **Hess Creek** bridge. Campsite in trees. Large gravel bar along creek at north end of bridge. *CAUTION: Sandpit at entrance to gravel bar is an easy place to get stuck.* Bring your mosquito repellent. Whitefish and grayling fishing. Hess Creek, known for its colorful mining history, is the largest stream between the junction and the Yukon River bridge.

J 23.9 (38.5 km) **D 390.1** (627.8 km) Road to west leads 0.2 mile/0.3 km to pond with parking space adequate for camping.

J 25 (40.2 km) **D 389** (626 km) Double-ended rough turnout. Good view of pipeline and remote-operated valve site as the highway crosses Hess Creek and valley.

J 26 (41.8 km) **D 388** (624.4 km) Pipeline parallels highway about 250 feet/76m away.

J 26.3 (42.3 km) **D 387.7** (623.9 km) Turnout.

J 27 (43.4 km) **D 387** (622.8 km) Evidence of 1971 lightning-caused forest fire.

J 28.4 (45.7 km) **D 385.6** (620.5 km) Gravel pit road and pipeline access road to west.

J 33.7 (54.2 km) **D 380.3** (612 km) Turnout at tributary of Hess Creek.

J 35.5 (57.1 km) **D 378.5** (609.1 km) Rough turnout at gravel pit.

J 38.1 (61.3 km) **D 375.9** (604.9 km) Pipeline goes under road. Evidence of the revegetation project undertaken by the oil companies.

J 40.7 (65.5 km) **D 373.3** (600.7 km) Double-ended turnout with litter barrel. Overview of Troublesome and Hess creeks areas. Brush obscures sweeping views.

J 43.1 (69.4 km) **D 370.9** (596.9 km) Isom Creek culvert. Steep ascent from valley north- and southbound.

J 44.6 (71.8 km) **D 369.4** (594.5 km) Turnout with litter barrel.

J 47.9 (77.1 km) **D 366.1** (589.2 km) Highway begins descent to Yukon River.

J 48.5 (78.1 km) **D 365.5** (588.2 km) Pipeline access road. Goalpost-like structures, called "headache bars," guard against vehicles large enough to run into and damage the pipeline.

J 50.1 (80.6 km) **D 363.9** (585.6 km) Turnout.

J 53.2 (85.6 km) **D 360.8** (580.6 km) First view northbound of the Yukon River. As road drops, you can see the pipeline where it crosses the river. Fort Hamlin Hills are beyond the pipeline.

J 54 (86.9 km) **D 360** (579.3 km) **PUMP STATION NO. 6.** Alyeska pump stations monitor the pipeline's oil flow on its journey from Prudhoe Bay to Valdez. No public facilities.

J 54.5 (87.7 km) **D 359.5** (578.5 km) Turnout to west.

J 55.6 (89.5 km) **D 358.4** (576.8 km) Yukon River bridge (formally the E.L. Patton Bridge, named for the president of the Alyeska Pipeline Service Co. after his death in 1982). This wood-decked bridge, completed in 1975, is 2,290 feet/698m long and has a 6 percent grade. The deck was replaced in 1993.

J 56 (90.1 km) **D 358** (576.1 km) Gas, diesel, tire repair, restaurant, motel, phone and emergency communications available at Yukon Ventures Alaska. Tours and charters of the Yukon River include dinner cruise and visit to a working Native fish camp.

This is the southern boundary of BLM-managed lands. The Yukon Crossing Visitor Contact Station here, managed and staffed by the BLM, is open 7 days a week, June through August. There is also an Alyeska pipeline interpretive display here with information on the Yukon River, pipeline construction and related subjects. East of the highway is a camping area with litter barrels. Road closed east of campsite. ▲

J 60.6 (97.5 km) **D 353.4** (568.7 km) Site of **FIVE MILE CAMP**, a former pipeline construction camp. No structures remain at these former construction camps. There is an undeveloped campsite here and an outhouse. Water is available from an artesian well. Highway crosses over buried pipeline.

J 60.8 (97.8 km) **D 353.2** (568.4 km) Five Mile airstrip (length 3,500 feet/1,067m); controlled by Alyeska Security. *CAUTION: Be prepared to stop at control gates at both ends of airstrip.*

J 61.6 (99.1 km) **D 352.4** (567.1 km) View of Fort Hamlin Hills to north, pump station No. 6 to south.

J 61.9 (99.6 km) **D 352.1** (566.6 km) Sevenmile DOT/PF highway maintenance camp.

J 68.4 (110.1 km) **D 345.6** (556.2 km) Highway crosses over buried pipeline.

J 69.2 (111.4 km) **D 344.8** (554.9 km) Double-ended turnout at crest of hill overlooking the Ray River to the north.

J 70 (112.7 km) **D 344** (553.6 km) **Ray River** overlook and turnout. Scenic view of the Ray Mountains to the west. Burbot, grayling and northern pike fishing.

J 72.6 (116.8 km) **D 341.4** (549.4 km) Fort Hamlin Hills Creek bridge and turnout. Winter trail scars are visible here.

J 74.8 (120.4 km) **D 339.2** (545.9 km) Steep descent northbound followed by steep ascent; dubbed the Roller Coaster.

J 79.1 (127.3 km) **D 334.9** (539 km) **No Name Creek** and turnout; burbot, grayling and whitefish.

J 81.6 (131.3 km) **D 332.4** (534.9 km) Fort Hamlin Hills are visible to the southeast. Tree line on surrounding hills is about 2,000 feet/610m.

J 86.5 (139.2 km) **D 327.5** (527 km) Scenic overlook 1 mile/1.6 km west with view of tors to northeast, Yukon Flats Wildlife Refuge to east and Fort Hamlin Hills to southeast. Tors are high, isolated pinnacles of jointed granite jutting up from the tundra and are a residual feature of erosion.

J 88.5 (142.4 km) **D 325.5** (523.8 km) Mackey Hill. Entering Game Management Unit 25D northbound, Unit 20F southbound. The high, unnamed hill east of the road is 2,774 feet/846m in elevation.

J 90.2 (145.2 km) **D 323.8** (521.1 km) Double-ended turnouts both sides of highway. A good photo opportunity of the road and pipeline to the north. The small green structure over the buried pipe is a radio-controlled valve, allowing the pipeline oil flow to be shut down when necessary.

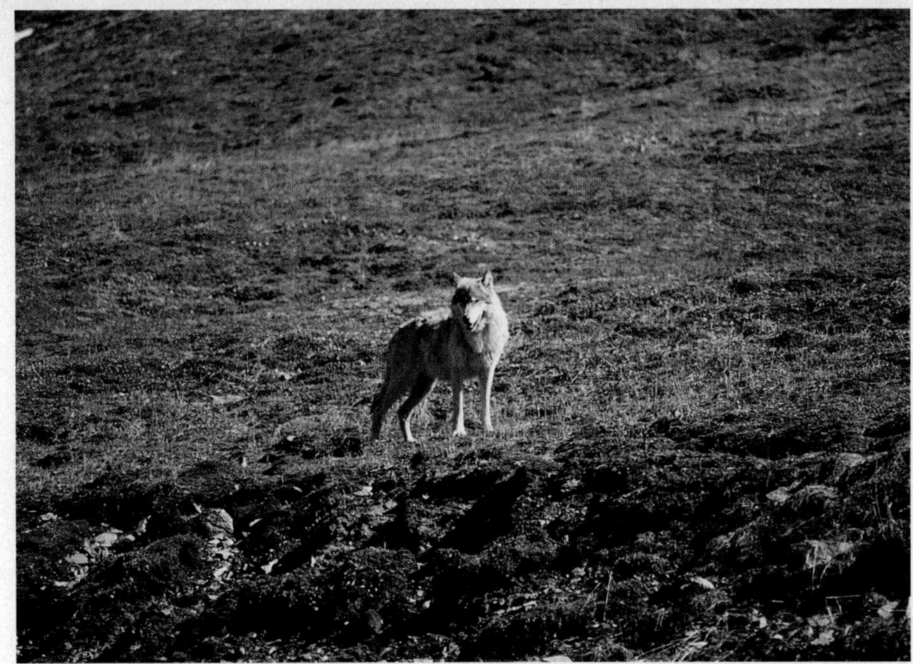

Travelers have a good chance of seeing wildlife–like this wolf–along the highway.
(Jerrianne Lowther, staff)

J 91.1 (146.6 km) **D 322.9** (519.6 km) Culvert directs water from branch of West Fork of Dall River. Watch for soft spots in road.

J 94 (151.3 km) **D 320** (515 km) Turnout at former gravel pit road to west.

J 96 (154.5 km) **D 318** (511.8 km) The road lies above tree line for about 5 miles/8 km. Good opportunities for photos, berry picking (blueberries, lowbush cranberries), wildflower viewing and hiking. Northbound, the terrain becomes more rugged and scenic.

J 97.5 (156.9 km) **D 316.5** (509.3 km) Finger Rock (signed Finger Mountain), a tor, is visible east of the road and most easily seen to the south. Tors are visible for the next 2 miles/3.2 km. Prehistoric hunting sites are numerous in this region. Please do not collect or disturb artifacts.

J 98.2 (158 km) **D 315.8** (508.2 km) Finger Mountain wayside; outhouse, parking, interpretive trail. Caribou Mountain is in the distance to the northwest. Olsens Lake, Kanuti Flats, Kanuti River drainage, and site of former Old Man Camp are visible ahead northbound. The road descends and passes through several miles of valley bottom with excellent mountain views.

J 100.7 (162.1 km) **D 313.3** (504.2 km) Pipeline passes under highway.

J 105.8 (170.3 km) **D 308.2** (496 km) **Kanuti River**, crossing and turnout; burbot, grayling. Abandoned airstrip.

J 107 (172.2 km) **D 307** (494.1 km) Site of **OLD MAN CAMP**, a former pipeline construction camp.

J 109.1 (175.6 km) **D 304.9** (490.7 km) Turnout to west.

J 109.8 (176.7 km) **D 304.2** (489.5 km) Turnout at Beaver Slide. *CAUTION: Road descends very steeply northbound. Watch for soft spots. Slippery when wet.*

J 110 (177 km) **D 304** (489.2 km) Visible against the hillside to the east are water bars constructed to prevent erosion above the buried pipeline.

J 111.5 (179.4 km) **D 302.5** (486.8 km) View of valley and Fish Creek to the north.

J 112.2 (180.6 km) **D 301.8** (485.7 km) Turnout at pipeline access road. Moose and bear frequent willow thickets here.

J 113.9 (183.3 km) **D 300.1** (483 km) Evidence of old winter trail to Bettles is visible here.

J 114 (183.5 km) **D 300** (482.8 km) **Fish Creek** bridge and turnout; grayling 12 to 18 inches.

J 115.3 (185.5 km) **D 298.7** (480.7 km) The Arctic Circle, north latitude 66°33'. BLM wayside with tables, grills, outhouse and interpretive display. Stop and have your picture taken with the sign. This is also a good photo point, with views to the south and to the west. Follow road off turnout 0.6 mile/1 km for undeveloped campsite. If you reach the Alyeska access gate you've gone too far.

J 124.7 (200.7 km) **D 289.3** (465.6 km) Turnout to east at **South Fork Bonanza Creek**; burbot, grayling, whitefish.

J 125.7 (202.3 km) **D 288.3** (464 km) Turnout to east at **North Fork Bonanza Creek**; burbot, grayling, whitefish.

J 127.1 (204.5 km) **D 286.9** (461.7 km) Turnout.

J 127.7 (205.5 km) **D 286.3** (460.7 km) Paradise Hill; blueberries and lowbush cranberries in season.

J 128.9 (207.4 km) **D 285.1** (458.8 km) Gravel pit.

J 129.3 (208.1 km) **D 284.7** (458.2 km) *CAUTION: Long ascent northbound with a short stretch that is very steep. Give trucks plenty of room here!*

J 131.3 (211.3 km) **D 282.7** (454.9 km) Solar-powered communications tower.

J 131.5 (211.6 km) **D 282.5** (454.6 km) View of pump station No. 5 to north.

J 132 (212.4 km) **D 282** (453.8 km) Turnout with litter barrels and outhouse at Gobblers Knob (elev. 1,500 feet/457m) overlooking the Jack White Range, Pope Creek Dome (the dominant peak to the northwest), Prospect Creek drainage, pump station

No. 5, Jim River drainage, South Fork Koyukuk drainage and the Brooks Range on the northern horizon.

J 134.7 (216.8 km) **D 279.3** (449.5 km) Pipeline access road.

J 135.1 (217.4 km) **D 278.9** (448.8 km) **Prospect Creek**; grayling, whitefish and pike. Active gold mining area.

J 135.7 (218.4 km) **D 278.3** (447.9 km) Old winter road goes up creek to mines. Turn left for site of **PROSPECT CAMP**, which holds the record for lowest recorded temperature in Alaska (-80°F/-62°C, Jan. 23, 1971). Rough road leads 0.5 mile/0.8 km to Claja Pond; beaver, ducks. Undeveloped campsite on Jim River. Old winter road to Bettles crosses river here.

J 137.1 (220.6 km) **D 276.9** (445.6 km) **PUMP STATION NO. 5** (signed incorrectly as Prospect Camp). No public access. Side road leads to well. Pump station No. 5 is not actually a pump station, but a "drain down" or pressure relief station for the Alyeska pipeline.

Private Aircraft: Airstrip; length 5,000 feet/1,524m; lighted runway. This airstrip is used as a BLM fire fighting staging area.

J 138.1 (222.2 km) **D 275.9** (444 km) Jim River DOT/PF highway maintenance camp EMT squad. Site of 1988 burn.

J 139 (223.7 km) **D 275** (442.6 km) Road to gravel pit.

J 140.1 (225.5 km) **D 273.9** (440.8 km) Turnout at **Jim River**, bridge No. 1; burbot, chum and king salmon, grayling, pike, whitefish. *CAUTION: Bears here for fall salmon run.*

J 141 (226.9 km) **D 273** (439.3 km) Turnout to east at Jim River, bridge No. 2.

J 141.8 (228.2 km) **D 272.2** (438.1 km) Douglas Creek; blueberries and lowbush cranberries in season.

J 144.1 (231.9 km) **D 269.9** (434.4 km) Bridge No. 3 across main channel of **Jim River**; turnout to east at south end of bridge. See **Milepost J 140.1** for fishing.

J 145.6 (234.3 km) **D 268.4** (431.9 km) Pipeline passes under road. First views northbound of Brooks Range foothills to the north.

J 150.3 (241.9 km) **D 263.7** (424.4 km) **Grayling Lake** to east has good grayling fishing in open water season.

J 150.8 (242.7 km) **D 263.2** (423.6 km) Turnout on Grayling Lake. The road is passing through the foothills of the Brooks Range. There is an active gold mining area behind the hills to the west.

J 155.2 (249.8 km) **D 258.8** (416.5 km) Overlook for the South Fork Koyukuk River valley.

J 156 (251.1 km) **D 258** (415.2 km) Turnout with outhouse at the **South Fork Koyukuk River** bridge; grayling, whitefish, chum and king salmon.

This large river flows past the villages of Bettles, Allakaket, Hughes and Huslia before draining into the Yukon River near Koyukuk.

J 159.1 (256 km) **D 254.9** (410.2 km) Bridge over pipeline.

J 160 (257.5 km) **D 254** (408.8 km) Good view of Chapman Lake 0.5 mile/0.8 km west of road. Old mine trail is visible from the road.

The 2 mountains visible to the north are Twelvemile Mountain (elev. 3,190 feet/972m), left, and Cathedral Mountain (elev. 3,000 feet/914m), on right. The foothills of the Brooks Range are also to the north.

J 163.3 (262.8 km) **D 250.7** (403.5 km) Turnout to west.

J 165.1 (265.7 km) **D 248.9** (400.6 km) Turnout to west with view of pipeline.

J 165.7 (266.7 km) **D 248.3** (399.6 km) Turnout on west side of road overlooking Middle Fork Koyukuk River.

J 167.2 (269.1 km) **D 246.8** (397.2 km) Old winter trail to Tramway Bar.

J 175 (281.6 km) **D 239** (384.6 km) **COLDFOOT**, site of a historic mining camp at the mouth of Slate Creek on the east bank of the Middle Fork Koyukuk River. Coldfoot Services (phone 907/678-5201) offers 3 motels, a 24-hour restaurant, gift shop, general store, trading post, laundromat, fuel facility with gas, diesel and avgas; tire repair, minor vehicle repair; RV park with hookups and dump station; post office, phone and emergency medical service. It is also home of the "farthest North saloon in North America" with "readable walls." Area tours and guided hunting and fishing trips available. ▲

There is a 3,500-foot/1,067-m runway to west, maintained by the state. An Alaska State Trooper, a Fish and Wildlife officer and BLM field station are located at Coldfoot. A visitor center here, operated by the BLM, USF&WS and National Park Service, offers travel information and nightly presentations on the natural and cultural history of the Arctic. It is open from June 1 through Labor Day. Topographic maps for sale.

Originally named Slate Creek, Coldfoot reportedly got its name in 1900 when gold stampeders got as far up the Koyukuk as this point, then got cold feet, turned and departed. The old cemetery still exists. Emma Dome (elev. 5,680 feet/1,731m) is to the west.

Coldfoot Services and Arctic Acres Inn. See display ad this section.

Arctic Divide Expeditions. Rafting the beautiful Koyukuk through the heart of America's northernmost mountains. Day trips and evening midnight sun cruises. Also backpacking and canoeing expeditions, 1–14 days. Discover the splendor of ANWR! 10 years guiding experience in the Brooks Range. We take you where no one else goes. All ages and abilities welcome. Call (906) 521 5962 for a brochure or stop in. [ADVERTISEMENT]

J 179.9 (289.5 km) **D 234.1** (376.7 km) Marion Creek Campground; 26 sites, tables, grills, outhouses, firepits, water, litter barrels, information kiosk. Marion Creek trailhead, RV parking. Fee charged. ▲

J 184.4 (296.7 km) **D 229.6** (369.5 km) Scenic overlook. Excellent view of Middle Fork Koyukuk River and rock slide on adjacent mountain.

J 186 (299.3 km) **D 228** (366.9 km) The historic mining community of Wiseman can be seen across the Koyukuk River to the west. Access to Wiseman from **Milepost J 188.6**.

J 186.7 (300.5 km) **D 227.3** (365.8 km) Turnouts both sides of highway.

J 187.2 (301.3 km) **D 226.8** (365 km) Turnout to west at **Minnie Creek**; burbot, grayling, whitefish.

J 188.5 (303.4 km) **D 225.5** (362.9 km) Turnout at **Middle Fork Koyukuk River** bridge No. 1; Dolly Varden, grayling, whitefish.

J 188.6 (303.5 km) **D 225.4** (362.7 km) Improved access road to **WISEMAN**, a historic mining town. The heyday of Wiseman came in about 1910, after gold seekers abandoned Coldfoot. The Wiseman Trading Co. still stands and houses the town's museum, featuring old photos and mining equipment. About 25 residents live here year-round today, and the population increases in the summer with the arrival of miners. (Note that this is an active mining area and all buildings are privately owned.) Wiseman has a general store, public phone and campground. ▲

J 189 (304.2 km) **D 225** (362.1 km) Finger dikes keep river away from highway and pipeline.

J 190.5 (306.6 km) **D 223.5** (359.7 km) Narrow bridge over Hammond River.

J 190.8 (307.1 km) **D 223.2** (359.2 km) Middle Fork Koyukuk River bridge No. 2.

J 192.8 (310.3 km) **D 221.2** (356 km) Link Up, where 2 sections of pipeline constructed by different crews were joined.

J 194 (312.2 km) **D 220** (354 km) First view northbound of Sukakpak Mountain

Caribou migrate across the North Slope. (© Nancy Faville)

(elev. 4,000 feet/1,219m) to north. Sukakpak Mountain is believed to mark the traditional boundary between Eskimo and Athabascan Indian territories. Wiehl Mountain (elev. 4,000 feet/1,219m) is east of Sukakpak. The high mountain just to the west of the road is unnamed.

J 197 (317 km) **D 217** (349.2 km) Old cabin just west of road is reported to have been constructed in the early 1900s; private property. Gold Creek bridge.

J 197.3 (317.5 km) **D 216.7** (348.7 km) Cat trail to gold mining area.

J 197.7 (318.2 km) **D 216.3** (348.1 km) Turnout east and view of Wiehl Mountain.

J 200 (321.9 km) **D 214** (344.4 km) View of the Middle Fork Koyukuk River, a typical braided river exhibiting frequent changes of the streambed during high water.

J 203.5 (327.5 km) **D 210.5** (338.7 km) Turnout and 0.5-mile/0.8-km footpath to Sukakpak Mountain. The short mounds of earth between the road and Sukakpak are palsas, formed by ice beneath the soil pushing the vegetative mat and soil upward.

J 203.8 (328 km) **D 210.2** (338.3 km) Turnouts next 0.6 mile/1 km northbound.

J 204.3 (328.8 km) **D 209.7** (337.5 km) Middle Fork Koyukuk River bridge No. 3; turnout with outhouses and litter barrels to east.

J 204.5 (329.1 km) **D 209.5** (337.1 km) Middle Fork Koyukuk River bridge No. 4.

J 205.3 (330.4 km) **D 208.7** (335.9 km) Turnout to west. Good view of north side of Sukakpak Mountain.

J 207 (333.1 km) **D 207** (333.1 km) **Dietrich River** bridge, turnout to west at south end; burbot, grayling, whitefish and Dolly Varden.

J 207.5 (333.9 km) **D 206.5** (332.3 km) Small, unnamed lake on east side of road with nice view of Sukakpak Mountain. Dillon Mountain (proposed name) is just to the north.

J 209.1 (336.5 km) **D 204.9** (329.7 km) Site of **DIETRICH CAMP**, a former pipeline construction camp.

J 211 (339.6 km) **D 203** (326.7 km) Disaster Creek. Turnout with litter barrel to east.

J 216 (347.6 km) **D 198** (318.6 km) Snowden Creek culvert. Panorama of Dietrich River valley and Brooks Range north and west of the road.

J 217.1 (349.4 km) **D 196.9** (316.9 km) Rock spire to east is Snowden Mountain (elev. 5,775 feet/1,760m).

J 221.6 (356.6 km) **D 192.4** (309.6 km) Turnout to west is quarry of black marble with white calcite veins.

J 221.8 (356.9 km) **D 192.2** (309.3 km) Turnout at gravel pit to east.

J 224 (360.5 km) **D 190** (305.8 km) Turnout at gravel pit.

J 226 (363.7 km) **D 188** (302.5 km) Pipeline remote valve just west of road. The arch-shaped concrete structures keep pipeline buried in areas of possible flooding.

J 227.3 (365.8 km) **D 186.7** (300.5 km) Nutirwik Creek culvert.

J 228 (366.9 km) **D 186** (299.3 km) Highway parallels Dietrich River.

J 231.4 (372.4 km) **D 182.6** (293.9 km) Small turnouts both sides of highway.

J 234.9 (378 km) **D 179.1** (288.2 km) North Slope Borough boundary. Borough offices are located in Barrow.

J 235.3 (378.7 km) **D 178.7** (287.6 km) Large turnout with litter barrel at foot of Chandalar Shelf and beginning of a long, steep (10 percent) grade. The farthest north spruce tree along the highway is located just south of the turnout. No trees beyond here.

J 236.3 (380.3 km) **D 177.7** (286 km) Turnouts and view of the Dietrich River valley to the south next 0.3 mile/0.5 km.

J 237.1 (381.6 km) **D 176.9** (284.7 km) Turnout at top of Chandalar Shelf; former checkpoint. Headwaters of the Chandalar River are to the east. Table Mountain (elev. 6,425 feet/1,958m) is to the southeast. Dietrich River valley to south.

J 239 (384.6 km) **D 175** (281.6 km) Brown net structure west of road is called a Wyoming Gage; it is used to measure precipitation. Sponsored by the Natural Resources Conservation Service.

J 239.2 (384.9 km) **D 174.8** (281.3 km) Site of **CHANDALAR CAMP**, a former pipeline construction camp, now used as a BLM field station.

J 239.4 (385.3 km) **D 174.6** (281 km) Chandalar highway maintenance station on west side of highway.

J 242.2 (389.8 km) **D 171.8** (276.5 km) West Fork Chandalar River bridge.

J 242.5 (390.2 km) **D 171.5** (276 km) Begin long, steep climb northbound toward Atigun Pass. Winter avalanche area.

J 244.7 (393.8 km) **D 169.3** (272.5 km) Turnout at top of Atigun Pass (elev. 4,800 feet/1,463m), highest highway pass in Alaska; Continental Divide. A Wyoming Gage is located here. Nice example of a cirque, an amphitheater-shaped bowl or depression caused by erosion, in mountain east of road. Endicott Mountains are to the west, Phillip Smith Mountains to the east. James Dalton Mountain is to the left ahead northbound.

Highway descends steeply toward the North Slope. Many mountains in the area exceed 7,000 feet/2,134m in elevation. The pipeline is in a buried, insulated concrete cribbing to the east. Construction in this area was extremely complex, difficult and dangerous.

J 248.4 (399.8 km) **D 165.6** (266.5 km) Turnouts both sides of highway. Good spot to view Dall sheep.

J 249.3 (401.2 km) **D 164.7** (265.1 km) Bridge over Spike Camp Creek. Highway crosses buried pipeline.

J 249.7 (401.8 km) **D 164.3** (264.4 km) Site of **ATIGUN CAMP**, a former pipeline construction camp. Turnouts both sides of highway. View of Atigun River valley. Another Wyoming Gage is located here.

J 251.5 (404.7 km) **D 162.5** (261.5 km) Turnouts next 0.3 mile/0.5 km northbound.

J 253.1 (407.3 km) **D 160.9** (258.9 km) Atigun River crossing No. 1. Highway crosses buried pipeline. *CAUTION: Grizzly bears in area.*

J 258.4 (415.8 km) **D 155.6** (250.4 km) Trevor Creek bridge.

J 258.6 (416.2 km) **D 155.4** (250.1 km) Turnout.

J 261.4 (420.7 km) **D 152.6** (245.6 km) Turnout.

J 265 (426.5 km) **D 149** (239.8 km) Roche Moutonnee Creek bridge.

J 267.5 (430.5 km) **D 146.5** (235.8 km) Bridge over Holden Creek.

J 268 (431.3 km) **D 146** (235 km) Good view of pump station No. 4.

J 269.3 (433.4 km) **D 144.7** (232.9 km) **PUMP STATION NO. 4.** This station has the highest elevation of all the pipeline stations (2,760 feet/841m), and is also a launching and receiving station for special devices called "pigs." A pig consists of spring-mounted scraper blades and/or brushes on a central body which moves through the pipe, cleaning accumulated wax from interior walls and monitoring conditions inside the pipe. There are "dumb" pigs and "smart" pigs. Dumb pigs clean out the pipe of any deposits in the line. Smart pigs scan the pipeline to check welds, wall thickness and other properties to help insure the integrity of the piping and identify maintenance needs.

J 269.5 (433.7 km) **D 144.5** (232.5 km) Highway bridge passes over pipeline.

J 270.9 (436 km) **D 143.1** (230.3 km) Atigun River crossing No. 2. The Arctic National Wildlife Refuge boundary is located 3 miles/4.8 km east along the Atigun gorge. Galbraith Lake may be seen to the west. There are a large number of archaeological sites in this vicinity.

J 274 (440.9 km) **D 140** (225.3 km) View of Galbraith Lake and Galbraith camp.

J 274.7 (442.1 km) **D 139.3** (224.2 km) Road access to **GALBRAITH CAMP**, a construction camp; outhouse, litter barrel. USF&WS field station.

J 276.5 (445 km) **D 137.5** (221.3 km) Island Lake.

J 284.3 (457.5 km) **D 129.7** (208.7 km) Toolik Lake west of road. A former construction camp, it is now the site of Toolik Lake Reserach Camp, run by the Institute of Arctic Biology of the University of Alaska Fairbanks. The field station has no public facilities or services.

J 286.2 (460.6 km) **D 127.8** (205.7 km) Turnout to east at high point in road. View of Brooks Range south and east.

J 288.8 (464.8 km) **D 125.2** (201.5 km) Kuparuk River bridge.

J 289.3 (465.6 km) **D 124.7** (200.7 km) Pipeline crossing. Short, buried section of pipeline to west is called a sag bend and is to allow for wildlife crossing. Watch for caribou northbound.

J 290.4 (467.3 km) **D 123.6** (198.9 km) Turnout to east.

J 294.4 (473.8 km) **D 119.6** (192.5 km) Second sag bend northbound.

J 297.8 (479.2 km) **D 116.2** (187 km) Oxbow Creek culvert. Small turnout to east.

J 301 (484.4 km) **D 113** (181.8 km) Turnout. Slope Mountain (elev. 4,010 feet/ 1,222m) is just west of road. Watch for Dall sheep. This is the northern boundary of BLM-managed land. Land north of here is managed by the state.

J 305.7 (492 km) **D 108.3** (174.3 km) Site of **SLOPE MOUNTAIN CAMP**, a former pipeline construction camp, now Sag River highway maintenance station.

J 309 (497.3 km) **D 105** (169 km) Highway parallels Sagavanirktok River.

J 311.8 (501.8 km) **D 102.2** (164.5 km) **PUMP STATION NO. 3.**

J 319.8 (514.7 km) **D 94.2** (151.6 km) Turnout to east at Oil Spill Hill.

J 320 (515 km) **D 94** (151.3 km) The long range of hills east of the road is the Kakuktukruich Bluff.

J 325.3 (523.5 km) **D 88.7** (142.7 km) Turnout with litter barrel to east at the top of a steep grade called Ice Cut.

J 326.2 (525 km) **D 87.8** (141.3 km) Pipeline crossing.

J 330.7 (532.2 km) **D 83.3** (134.1 km) Dan Creek bridge.

J 334.4 (538.1 km) **D 79.6** (128.1 km) Site of **HAPPY VALLEY CAMP**, a former pipeline construction camp.

J 347.6 (559.4 km) **D 66.4** (106.9 km) Sagwon airstrip. The airstrip is currently not in use in order to protect nesting peregrine falcons in the area.

J 350.5 (564.1 km) **D 63.5** (102.2 km) View of Sagwon Bluffs to the east. The road passes over several low hills that offer views of the surrounding terrain.

J 353 (568 km) **D 61** (98.2 km) Wyoming Gage west of road.

J 355.1 (571.5 km) **D 58.9** (94.8 km) Turnout with litter barrel to east.

J 358.8 (577.4 km) **D 55.2** (88.8 km) **PUMP STATION NO. 2** to the east.

NOTE: The worst winter weather conditions on the Dalton Highway are experienced the next 38 miles/61 km northbound. Blowing snow may obscure visibility and block road.

J 364 (585.8 km) **D 50** (80.5 km) Low hills to the north are the Franklin Bluffs. East of the road, the Ivishak River empties into the Sagavanirktok River on its journey to the Arctic Ocean.

J 365.1 (587.6 km) **D 48.9** (78.7 km) Turnout by pond to west; watch for nesting waterfowl.

J 366 (589 km) **D 48** (77.2 km) Large animal crossing in pipeline for caribou.

J 376 (605.1 km) **D 38** (61.2 km) The small hill that rises abruptly on the horizon about 5 miles/8 km west of the road is called a pingo. Pingos often form from the bed of a lake that has been covered by vegetation. Freezing of the water can raise the surface several hundred feet above the surrounding terrain.

J 377.3 (607.2 km) **D 36.7** (59.1 km) Turnout to east at site of **FRANKLIN BLUFFS CAMP**, a former pipeline construction camp. *CAUTION: Watch for loose, coarse gravel on road.*

J 383 (616.4 km) **D 31** (49.9 km) Franklin Bluffs to the east and a pingo to the west.

J 398.7 (641.6 km) **D 15.3** (24.6 km) Underground pipeline crossing.

J 413.3 (665.1 km) **D 0.7** (1.1 km) Turnout at former highway checkpoint. Oil field activity and equipment become visible along the horizon.

J 414 (666.3 km) **D 0** Security gate at northern limit of state-owned highway at **DEADHORSE** (description follows). Because of safety concerns, private vehicles are not permitted to travel beyond the gates onto the oil field. The Arctic Ocean is about 3 miles away. Public access to the ocean and oil field is available only if you are on a commercial tour. Locally, NANA's Tour Arctic offers a 1-hour shuttle trip to the Arctic Ocean or a 4-hour oil field tour. The airport is about 2 miles/3.2 km ahead. Alaska Airlines, Mark Air, 40 Mile Air and ERA helicopters have offices here.

Accommodations in Deadhorse available at Prudhoe Bay Hotel, Arctic Oilfield Hotel and Arctic Caribou Inn. All serve meals (5:30–8 A.M., 5–8 P.M.). Fuel (gas and diesel) available at Nana Oilfield Services and Petrostar. Petrostar attendant Raymond Greene says, "We have loader tires in abundance (this is an oil field), but anything under 14-inches, bring yourself." There is also a general store and post office.

Deadhorse was established to accommodate Prudhoe Bay oil operations. It is essentially a flat gravel pad in the middle of a tundra bog that serves as a freight depot and service center for the Prudhoe Bay oil fields. Most buildings are prefab metal, with some built on stilts because of the permafrost. The area population, which includes oil and airline-related personnel, varies between 3,500 and 8,600. For security purposes, visitors are not allowed on the docks or on area roads unless they are with a tour.

Scheduled air service from Fairbanks and Anchorage (flying time from Anchorage: 1 hour, 35 minutes). Air taxi service is available at the airport. Packaged tours to the North Slope area are available.

GENERAL INFORMATION

Air Travel

SCHEDULED AIR SERVICE TO ALASKA

Alaska Airlines, Continental Airlines, Delta Air Lines, MarkAir, Northwest Airlines, Reno Air and United Airlines all provide scheduled passenger jet service between Alaska and the Lower 48. Aeroflot Russian Airlines, Alaska Airlines, Cathy Pacific Airways, China Airlines and Korean Air fly to Anchorage with scheduled passenger jet service from other countries. Charter services connecting Anchorage with other states and countries are also available. Contact your travel agent for current schedules and fares.

SCHEDULED AIR SERVICE WITHIN ALASKA

Following are listed many of the carriers offering intrastate scheduled air service. Interline service available to most rural Alaska points; check with carriers. Also check local air taxi operators for charter and commuter service to Alaskan communities.

From ANCHORAGE

Alaska Airlines, 4750 W. International Airport Road, Anchorage 99502; phone (800) 426-0333—To Fairbanks, Prudhoe Bay, Cordova, Yakutat, Juneau, Sitka, Wrangell, Petersburg, Ketchikan, Nome, Kotzebue, Bethel, Dillingham, Dutch Harbor, King Salmon, Kodiak, Barrow and Gustavus/Glacier Bay (summer only).

Delta Air Lines, Anchorage International Airport; (800) 221-1212—To Fairbanks.

Era Aviation (Alaska Airlines commuter), 6160 S. Airpark Dr., Anchorage 99502; phone (800) 866-8394—To Cordova, Kenai, Homer, Kodiak, Valdez and Iliamna plus 17 southwestern Alaska villages from Bethel. Charter service available statewide.

MarkAir, Inc., 4100 W. International Road, Box 196769, Anchorage 99519-6769—To Aniak, Barrow, Bethel, Cold Bay, Cordova, Dillingham, Fairbanks, Homer, Kenai, Dutch Harbor/Unalaska, Galena, King Salmon, Nome, Kotzebue, Kodiak, McGrath, Port Heiden, Prudhoe Bay/Deadhorse, St. George, St. Mary's, St. Paul, Sand Point, Unalakleet and Valdez.

PenAir (Alaska Airlines commuter), 4851 Aircraft Dr., Anchorage 99502, phone (800) 448-4226—To Unalakleet, Dillingham, King Salmon, Dutch Harbor, Akutan, Cold Bay and the Pribilof Islands.

Reeve Aleutian Airways, Inc., 4700 W. International Airport Road, Anchorage 99502; phone (907) 243-1112—To Bethel, King Salmon, Port Heiden, Sand Point, Cold Bay, Unalaska/Dutch Harbor, Adak and St. Paul (special Pribilof Islands tours in summer).

United Airlines, Anchorage International Airport, phone (800) 241-6522—To Fairbanks.

From BARROW

Cape Smythe Air Service, Box 549, Barrow 99723; phone (907) 852-8333—Barrow service to Atqasuk, Wainwright, Point Lay, Point Hope, Nuiqsut, Deadhorse (Prudhoe Bay) and Barter Island. Also office in Kotzebue; phone (907) 442-3020, with service to Buckland, Deering, Ambler, Kiana, Kivalina, Kobuk, Noatak, Noorvik, Point Hope, Selawik and Shungnak. Office in Nome; phone (907) 443-5125, with service to St. Michael, Shishmaref, Stebbins, Teller, Unalakleet, Wales, Shaktoolik, White Mountain, Koyuk, Golovin, Elim, Brevig Mission, Gambell and Savoonga.

From FAIRBANKS

Frontier Flying Service, 3820 University Ave., Fairbanks 99709; phone (907) 474-0014—To 23 Interior and Arctic villages including Gates of the Arctic National Park and the Arctic National Wildlife Refuge.

Larry's Flying Service Inc., 3822 University Ave., Fairbanks 99709; phone (907) 474-9169—To Anaktuvuk Pass, Bettles, Fort Yukon and 13 more villages.

Warbelow's Air Ventures, Inc. 3758 University Ave. S., Fairbanks 99709; phone (907) 474-0518—Scheduled service to Alaska's Interior; Bush mail-plane trips, Arctic Circle tours, hot-springs fly-ins and sightseeing charters also available.

From GLENNALLEN

Gulkana Air Service, Box 342, Glennallen 99588; phone (907) 822-5532—Serves Wrangell–St. Elias National Park and all the Copper River Basin.

From GUSTAVUS (Glacier Bay)

Glacier Bay Airways, Box 34219, Juneau 99803; phone (907) 697-2249—To Juneau, Hoonah, Excursion Inlet, Skagway, Glacier Bay National Park, Haines and other Southeast points.

From HAINES

Haines Airways, Box 470, Haines 99827; phone (907) 766-2646—To Juneau, Hoonah and Gustavus/Glacier Bay.

L.A.B. Flying Service (Alaska Airlines mileage partner), Box 272, Haines 99827; phone (800) 426-0543 or (907) 776-2222—To Juneau, Petersburg, Sitka, Hoonah, Haines, Skagway, Angoon, Tenakee, Kake and Gustavus/Glacier Bay.

From JUNEAU

Air North, 1873 Shell Simmons Dr., Juneau 99801; phone (907) 789-2007—To Whitehorse, YT.

Delta Air Lines, phone (800) 221-1212—Summer flights to Fairbanks.

Glacier Bay Airways, phone (907) 789-9009—To Gustavus/Glacier Bay, Hoonah, Excursion Inlet, Cube Cove, Skagway, Haines and other Southeast locations.

L.A.B. Flying Service (Alaska Airlines mileage partner), Box 2201, Juneau 99803; phone (800) 426-0543—To Haines, Hoonah,

AIR MILEAGES BETWEEN MAJOR POINTS IN ALASKA

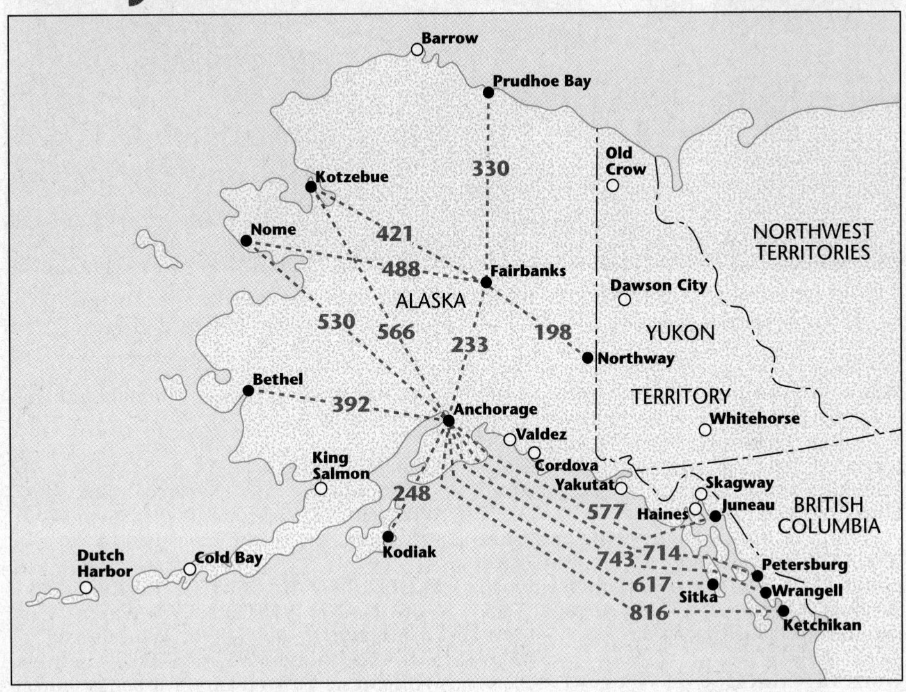

Planes on wheels, skis and floats are used throughout the North. (© Beth Davidow)

Skagway, Petersburg, Sitka, Angoon, Tenakee, Kake and Gustavus/Glacier Bay.

Loken Aviation, 8995 Yandukin Dr., Juneau 99801; phone (907) 789-3331—Schedules and charters to Angoon, Pelican, Elfin Cove and Hobart Bay.

Wings of Alaska Flightseeing and Charters, 1873 Shell Simmons Dr., Juneau 99801; phone (907) 789-0790—To Haines, Hoonah, Skagway, Pelican, Elfin Cove, Angoon, Tenakee and Gustavus/Glacier Bay.

From KETCHIKAN

Ketchikan Air Service, 1600 International Airport, Ketchikan 99901; (800) 656-6608—To Craig, Klawock, Wrangell, Petersburg, Metlakatla, Coffman Cove, Thorne Bay and other southeastern points.

From NOME

Bering Air, Inc., Box 1650, Nome 99762; phone (907) 443-5464, fax 443-5919—From Nome and Kotzebue to western Alaska points and Russian Far East.

From PETERSBURG

Alaska Island Air, Box 508, Petersburg 99833—To Kake and Rowan Bay.

From SKAGWAY

Skagway Air Service, Box 357, Skagway 99840; phone (907) 983-2218—To Juneau, with flag stops in Haines, Hoonah and Gustavus/Glacier Bay.

From WRANGELL

Ketchikan Air Service, Box 847, Wrangell 99929; phone (800) 656-6608—To Petersburg, Ketchikan, Juneau and Kake.

SCHEDULED AIR SERVICE TO/IN YUKON AND WESTERN CANADA

Air North, Box 4998, Whitehorse, YT Y1A 4S2; phone (403) 668-2228—Between Whitehorse, Dawson City, Fairbanks, Juneau and Old Crow.

AirBC, 4740 Agar Dr., Richmond, BC V7B 1A6; for reservations phone Air Canada in British Columbia at (604) 688-5515 or in the United States at 1-800-776-3000—Western Canadian service and service from Vancouver to U.S. destinations of Seattle and Portland.

Alkan Air, P.O. Box 4008, Whitehorse, YT Y1A 3S9; phone (403) 668-2107, fax (403) 667-6117—Between Whitehorse, Dawson City, Old Crow and Inuvik, NWT.

Canadian Airlines International, 206-1030 W. Georgia St., Vancouver, BC V6E 2Y2; phone (604) 279-6611—To Calgary, Edmonton, Vancouver, Prince George, Prince Rupert, Fort St. John, Fort Nelson, Watson Lake, Whitehorse and numerous other points.

CHARTER/AIR TAXI SERVICE WITHIN ALASKA

In addition to scheduled air service, there are more than 200 certified charter/air taxi operators in Alaska.

Air taxi operators conduct their business from a specific base of operations, primarily through the charter of aircraft. Any pilot flying for hire is required to hold a commercial or airline transport pilot certificate. The customer can and should be protected by having the pilot show his/her credentials. A pilot with the necessary credentials will be glad to show them. Do not fly with a pilot who cannot produce certification.

Air taxi rates may vary from carrier to carrier. Most operators charge an hourly rate either per plane load or per passenger; others may charge on a per-mile basis. Flightseeing trips to area attractions are often available at a fixed price per passenger.

Sample per-hour fares for charter planes with varied wheel, float and ski capabilities (luggage space limited and dependent on number of passengers): PA 18 (1 passenger), $160; Cessna 185 (5 passengers), $220; PA 32 (6 passengers), $280; Cessna 207 (6 passengers), $230; Beaver DHC2 (7 passengers), $300; and Otter DHC3 (10 passengers), $500.

PRIVATE AIRCRAFT

The MILEPOST® logs include the location of most airstrips along the Alaska Highway, in Alaskan communities and along other highways in Alaska and northwestern Canada. Airstrips in British Columbia and Alberta are too numerous to be included. Aircraft symbols corresponding to airstrip locations are included on the highway strip maps. The map symbols are a white plane for airports with scheduled service, and a black plane for airstrips with no scheduled service and limited facilities.

Private aircraft information in these logs includes only the name and location of the airstrip, the elevation, length and surface material of the longest runway and the availability of fuel. Many Northland pilots fly jet craft. Jet and other fuel is available at many airports. Fuel sold in Alaska and Canada is almost exclusively 100LL; 80 octane fuel is no longer available, though some airports offer car gasoline.

There are literally thousands of landing areas in the North for amphibious aircraft; *The MILEPOST*® does not include these in the log copy. A Water Aerodrome Supplement is available from the Canada Map Office, Departmentt of Energy, Mines and Resources, 130 Bentley Ave., Nepean, ON K1A 0E9. Phone 1-800-465-6277 or fax 1-800-661-6277.

CAUTION: The brief description of airstrips

FLIGHT TIMES BETWEEN SELECTED CITIES

Between	Time	Between	Time	Between	Time
Anchorage—Bethel	1 hr. 15 min.	Anchorage—Valdez	40 min.	Juneau—Haines	35 min.
Anchorage—Cordova	45 min.	Anchorage—Wrangell	2 hrs. 20 min.	Juneau—Ketchikan	50 min.
Anchorage—Dutch Harbor	2 hrs. 5 min.	Fairbanks—Barrow	1 hr. 20 min.	Juneau—Seattle, WA	2 hrs. 10 min.
Anchorage—Fairbanks	50 min.	Fairbanks—Delta Junction	35 min.	Juneau—Sitka	35 min.
Anchorage—Juneau	1 hr. 35 min.	Fairbanks—Kotzebue	2 hrs. 10 min.	Juneau—Skagway	45 min.
Anchorage—King Salmon	1 hr.	Fairbanks—Nome	2 hrs. 20 min.	Juneau—Whitehorse, YT	1 hr.
Anchorage—Kodiak	55 min.	Fairbanks—Northway	1 hr.	Juneau—Yakutat	45 min.
Anchorage—Kotzebue	1 hr. 30 min.	Fairbanks—Prudhoe Bay	1 hr. 25 min.	Ketchikan—Sitka	50 min.
Anchorage—Nome	1 hr. 30 min.	Fairbanks—Whitehorse, YT	3 hrs. 35 min.	Nome—Kotzebue	40 min.
Anchorage—Petersburg	2 hrs.	(1 stop in Dawson City)		Whitehorse—Dawson City	1 hr. 40 min.
Anchorage—Seattle, WA	3 hrs. 15 min.	Juneau—Glacier Bay	25 min.	Yakutat—Cordova	45 min.

given in The MILEPOST® *is in no way intended as a guide for pilots flying in the North.* In Alaska, up-to-date information on airstrips, fuel, service and radio facilities is published every 8 weeks in accordance with specifications and agreements by the U.S. Dept. of Defense, the Federal Aviation Administration and the Dept. of Commerce. In Canada, this is done by the Minister of Transport and the Chief of the Defense Staff.

Pilots should obtain the latest U.S. government flight information publication, *Alaska Supplement*, by writing: National Oceanic and Atmospheric Administration, N/CG33, Distribution Branch, 6501 Lafayette Ave., Riverdale, MD 20737. Phone (301) 436-6993 or fax (301) 436-6829. Pilots should obtain the Canadian DND flight information publication, *Canada Flight Supplement,* by contacting the Canada Map Office. World Aeronautical Charts and catalogs of charts and related publications are also available from NOAA and CMO. Sectional maps are usually available at aviation stores along the way.

For a packet of free brochures including *Flight Tips for Pilots in Alaska*, write the Federal Aviation Administration, 222 W. 7th Ave., Anchorage, AK 99513.

Pilots may also get in touch with the Alaska Airmen's Assoc., Inc., (907) 272-1251, to buy a copy of the *Alaska Airmen's Logbook for Alaska, Northwest Canada and Russia.*

Two free Canadian publications of interest are *Air Tourist Information—Canada* and *Flying the Alaska Highway in Canada.* Both are available from Transport Canada (AANDHD), Ottawa, ON K1A 0N8.

Alcoholic Beverages

Alaska: Legal drinking age is 21. Packaged liquor, beer and wine are sold by licensed retailers rather than in state liquor stores. The sale and/or importation of alcoholic beverages is prohibited in some 70 bush communities.

Alberta: Legal age is 18. Liquor, beer and wine are sold in private liquor stores open daily. Beer and liquor (take out) are also sold in some taverns.

British Columbia: Legal age is 19. Packaged liquor, beer and wine are sold in government liquor stores (open daily except Sunday and holidays) and in licensed private stores 7 days a week. Sunday serving laws in licensed premises vary from community to community.

Northwest Territories: Legal age is 19. Packaged liquor, beer and wine are sold in government liquor stores at Hay River, Pine Point, Fort Simpson, Fort Smith, Yellowknife, Norman Wells and Inuvik. Beer-only agencies are located in some other places. You can purchase liquor in most hotels for consumption on the premises. The sale and possession of alcohol is prohibited in several communities.

Yukon Territory: Legal age is 19. Packaged liquor, beer and wine are sold in government liquor stores at Watson Lake, Whitehorse, Dawson City and Haines Junction. Some licensed premises have beer and wine for takeout sale.

Arctic Circle

The latitude of the Arctic Circle is approximately 66°33′ north from the equator. We say "approximately" because the Arctic Circle varies a few seconds in latitude from year to year.

During summer solstice, June 20 or 21, the sun does not set at the Arctic Circle (it appears not to set for 4 days because of refraction). Farther north, at Barrow, the sun does not set from May 10 to Aug. 2.

At winter solstice, Dec. 21 or 22, the sun does not rise for 1 day at the Arctic Circle. At Barrow, the sun does not rise for 67 days.

Two highways cross the Arctic Circle. The Dalton Highway starts near Fairbanks and ends at Prudhoe Bay on the Arctic Ocean. The public may travel as far north as Dietrich, 100 miles/161 km north of the Arctic Circle. The Dempster Highway starts near Dawson City, YT, crosses the Arctic Circle after 250 miles/402 km, and ends at Inuvik, NWT, 200 miles/322 km north of the Arctic Circle.

Bears

In Alaska and in Canada, you are treading on bear territory. A true part of this wild country, bears can be a fearsome foe—never a friend. *CAUTION: Do not feed bears!*

There are 3 types of bears found in Alaska: the black bear, brown/grizzly bear and polar bear. Black bears range throughout most of the state, with highest densities in Southeast, Prince William Sound and Southcentral. Black bears can be brown in color, and may be confused with a grizzly, although they are normally smaller than a grizzly, with a more pointed head. Brown/grizzly bears range in color from black to blond, and range over most of the state. Alaska's coastal brown/grizzly bear is the world's largest carnivorous land mammal. (While polar bears are as large or larger, they actually live at sea on the ice, rather than on land.) Grizzlies have a distinct shoulder hump and larger head than black bears. Visitors are most likely to see grizzlies in Denali National Park, McNeil River State Game Sanctuary or Katmai National Park. Brown bear viewing on Kodiak Island, at Anan Bear Observatory near Wrangell and Pack Creek on Admiralty Island.

Bears are large, powerful animals, both unpredictable and dangerous. They will defend their territory, themselves and their young. Like any animal, survival is their most compelling instinct. Avoid surprising them. Avoid close encounters.

They may be any place—in campgrounds, highway rest stops or along hiking trails—so you must always be cautious and alert. Each bear has individual characteristics and behavior and there are no formulas that apply to all bears.

If you are careless and disrespectful you increase the possibility of conflict between people and bears. If you use reasonable judgment and precaution you can reduce the risk to yourself and to the bear.

When hiking, make a lot of noise and avoid dense brush. Hike in the open if possible. Let the bears know where you are. Bears will normally avoid people. Even though their vision is poor, their senses of smell and hearing are excellent. Surprise meetings can occur. Wind and rivers may muffle your noises and you could surprise a bear.

Make noise by talking, ringing a bell or shaking a few pebbles in a can. Make a variety of noises. Talking or singing out loud is one of the best ways to let a bear know you are around.

Dogs are not permitted in national park backcountry. In bear country they can be a liability. Even wolves have difficulty driving bears away. Your pet, when hard pressed, may run to you with a grizzly in close pursuit.

Trouble between you and the grizzly bear can be caused by:

1. Cubs—A small, cuddly looking cub means that a protective mother is usually nearby. She aggressively protects her young, so don't approach.

2. Photography—Taking a close-up photo could lead to disaster. Keep your distance and use a telephoto lens.

3. Camps—Keep your campsite clean. Bears are omnivorous—they eat almost anything. Food and its accompanying odors attract bears. Do not bury trash—carry out everything you carry in.

In campgrounds, store food in vehicles or storage lockers (where provided). When in the backcountry, use bear-resistant food containers for all food and trash. Do not store food in your tent. Eliminate food odor from your camp and from yourself. Wash hands and face before retiring. *(Based on a National Park Service publication.)*

Bicycling in Alaska

Road conditions vary throughout Alaska, from newly paved highways to unimproved dirt roads. In planning your bicycling routes, read the highway logs in *The MILEPOST*® carefully. Abrupt changes in road conditions are generally noted in the log, as are steep grades and whether or not there are shoulders. With the recent popularity of mountain bikes, additional routes are available to the rider who can travel on unimproved dirt roads and trails. Bicyclists will have to share the highways with vehicles, but traffic can be avoided by riding in the early morning and on weekdays. One advantage of touring Alaska in summer is the long daylight hours.

At press time, there were no laws governing bicyclists other than normal vehicle laws. Helmets are recommended.

Boating, Canoeing and Kayaking

Thousands of miles of waterways for both marine boating and lake- and river-boating are available to visitors to the North.

For marine sailors, southeastern Alaska's

Inside Passage offers both recreational boating and a sheltered transportation route. There are numerous marine charter services throughout Southeast for visiting boaters. Most offer sportfishing or sightseeing tours, others have marine craft for charter (most skippered, some bare-boat). Boaters wishing to sail their own craft to Southeast should have the appropriate nautical charts and pilot guides. For U.S. waters, check locally for authorized nautical chart dealers or contact the National Oceanic and Atmospheric Administration; local offices should be listed in the phone book under U.S. Government, Dept. of Commerce, or write NOAA, N/CG33, Distribution Branch, 6501 Lafayette Ave., Riverdale, MD 20737. For Washington and Alaska waters you'll also need the *United States Coast Pilot* (Books 8 and 9). For British Columbia waters you'll need the *British Columbia Sailing Directions* (Volumes I and II). You can get these as well as charts of Canadian coastal waters, tidal tables and other information from the Canadian Hydrographic Service, Chart Sales Office, P.O. Box 6000, 9860 W. Saanich Rd., Sidney, BC V8L 4B2, phone (604) 363-6358.

Marine travelers may also check local bookstores for Alaska cruising titles. Bluewater paddlers should have with them NOAA Tidal Current Tables. Contact the State of Alaska Dept. of Transportation and Public Facilities, Engineering and Operations Division, 3132 Channel Dr., Juneau 99801, for a directory of harbor facilities.

Keep in mind that U.S. visitors entering Canada by private boat must report to Canadian customs immediately upon arrival.

It is possible to travel thousands of miles on Northland river systems by boat, canoe, kayak or raft. In Alaska and Yukon Territory, the Yukon River system provides such an opportunity. In Northwest Territories, the Mackenzie River system provides endless waterways to explore.

River travelers: Keep in mind that proper planning, good skills and common sense can help lessen the chance of capsizing and possible injury or loss of equipment. It is always a good idea to check with local sources, such as sporting goods stores or state and federal agencies, for current information on river conditions.

Canoe trails have been established on Alaskan rivers and lakes near Fairbanks and Anchorage, on Prince of Wales Island and on the Kenai Peninsula.

The Bureau of Land Management maintains 6 rivers that make up the National Wild and Scenic Rivers System. These rivers offer a variety of float trips. Five rivers are in Interior Alaska, near Fairbanks, and 1 is in western Alaska. A 7th river, near Kotzebue in the northwest, is being studied for possible inclusion in the system. BLM offers brochures on the river trails including access points, portages and scale of difficulty. For details on these rivers, write the Bureau of Land Management, 1150 University Ave., Fairbanks 99709-3899, phone (907) 474-2250.

The Alaska Public Lands Information Centers in Fairbanks, Anchorage, Tok and Ketchikan have information on many of Alaska's navigable rivers. Paddling guides, river logs and maps are available. Visit the centers or contact the Alaska Public Lands Information Center at: 250 Cushman St., Suite 1A, Fairbanks 99701, phone (907) 456-0527; 605 W. 4th Ave., Suite 105, Anchorage 99501, phone (907) 271-2737, TDD (907) 271-2738; Box 359, Tok 99780, phone (907) 883-5667; or 50 Main St., Ketchikan 99901, phone (907) 225-8131.

Canoe trails have been established on Prince of Wales Island along the Honker Divide and at Sarkar Lakes. Outstanding sea kayaking opportunities are also available on the west coast of Prince of Wales Island. Contact Craig Ranger District, Tongass National Forest, Box 145, Craig 99921, phone (907) 826-3271. For maps and information contact the Thorne Bay Ranger District, Tongass National Forest, Box 1, Thorne Bay 99950, phone (907) 828-3304.

Canoeing on the Kenai Peninsula's Swan Lake and Swanson River canoe trails starts about late May and continues until late October. For details on the trails write the Refuge Manager, Kenai National Wildlife Refuge, Box 2139, Soldotna 99669.

A sea kayaking/camping map and brochure is available from Misty Fiords National Monument, Tongass National Forest, 3031 Tongass Ave., Ketchikan 99901, phone (907) 225-2148.

In Yukon Territory there are more than a dozen rivers and lakes suitable for canoeing. Write Tourism Yukon, Box 2703, Whitehorse, YT Y1A 2C6.

For information on canoeing in the tundra and subarctic regions of Northwest Territories and the Mackenzie River system write to NWT Toursim Information, The North Group, Box 2107(EX), Yellowknife, NT X1A 2P6.

Bus Lines

Independent travelers wishing to travel by public bus within Alaska and Yukon Territory will generally find routes and services much more limited than in the Lower 48. Scheduled bus service is available within Alaska and Yukon Territory, but scheduled direct bus service to Alaska from the Lower 48 is not available, unless you wish to join an escorted motorcoach tour. If your schedule allows, you can travel from the Lower 48 to Alaska via public bus service by using several carriers. Most scheduled bus service in the North is seasonal.

Contact the following companies for current schedules:

Alaska Direct Bus Line, 102 Wood St., Whitehorse, YT y1A 2E3, phone (800) 780-6652 or (403) 668-4833. Service from Anchorage to Fairbanks, Tok, Whitehorse, Haines, Skagway and Denali.

Alaska Sightseeing/Cruise West, 4th and Battery Bldg., Suite 700, Seattle, WA 98121, phone (907) 276-1305 (summer) or (800) 426-7702 year-round. Motorcoach trips connect Anchorage, Denali National Park and Valdez.

Denali Express Alaska Tours, 405 L St., Anchorage 99501, phone (800) 327-7651 or (907) 274-8539. Service between Anchorage and Denali Park; group tours and special itineraries.

Gray Line of Alaska/Alaskan Express, 300 Elliott Ave. W., Seattle, WA 98119, phone (800) 544-2206 or fax (206) 281-0621. Scheduled service to Anchorage, Fairbanks, Skagway, Whitehorse, Haines and most communities en route. Motorcoach tours to Anchorage, Denali National Park, Fairbanks, Prudhoe Bay, Prince William Sound, Seward and Portage Glacier.

Greyhound Lines of Canada, 2191 2nd Ave., Whitehorse, YT Y1A 3T8, phone (403) 667-2223. Scheduled service to Whitehorse from all U.S.–Canada border crossings; also between Whitehorse and Anchorage, Fairbanks, Skagway and Dawson Creek.

Norline Coaches (Yukon) Ltd., 2191 2nd Ave., Whitehorse, YT Y1A 4T8, phone (403) 668-3355. Service between Whitehorse, Mayo, Carmacks and Dawson City.

Northwest Stage Lines, Box 4932, Whitehorse, YT Y1A 4S2, phone (403) 668-7240. Year-round charter service available.

Parks Highway Express, Box 82884, Fairbanks 99708, phone (907) 479-3065. Service between Anchorage, Denali Park and Fairbanks.

Princess Tours®, 2815 2nd Ave., Suite 400, Seattle, WA 98121, phone 1-800-835-8907. Motorcoach tours include the Klondike in Canada's Yukon, Anchorage, the Kenai Peninsula, Denali National Park, Fairbanks and Prudhoe Bay.

Seward Bus Line, Box 1338, Seward 99664, phone (907) 224-3608. Daily, year-round service between Anchorage and Seward.

Cabins

If you've ever wanted to try living in a log cabin in the wilderness, the USDA Forest Service gives you the opportunity for $25 per night per cabin. There are approximately 200 of these public-use cabins scattered throughout Tongass and Chugach national forests.

Cabins are accessible by air, boat or trail. Average size is 12 by 14 feet. Most cabins have wood stoves, some have oil stoves. Check with the Forest Service to determine what type of stove is provided. All cabins have tables and sleeping room for 4 or more people. You must supply bedding, cookware, stove oil (if necessary) and food. Splitting mauls are provided on site for cutting firewood. There are pit toilets but no garbage dumps (pack garbage out). Skiffs are provided at some cabins.

Permits for use of recreation cabins are issued on either a first-come first-served basis, or by lottery. Applications for permits may be made in person or by mail up to 180 days in advance. You must have a permit for the specific length of occupancy. There is a 3-day limit May 15 to Aug. 31 on hike-in cabins in the Chugach National Forest. There is a 7-day limit on other cabins in the Tongass National Forest from April 1 to Oct. 31, and a 10-day limit Nov. 1 to March 31.

For reservations and information on Chugach National Forest cabins, contact the Alaska Public Lands Information Center, 605 W. 4th Ave., Suite 105, Anchorage 99501, phone (907) 271-2737, TDD (907) 271-2738.

For reservations and information on Tongass National Forest cabins, contact one of the following area offices: Southeast Alaska Visitor Center, 50 Main St., Ketchikan 99901, phone (907) 225-8131; Petersburg Ranger District, Box 309, Petersburg 99833, phone (907) 772-3841; or Sitka Ranger District, 204 Siginaka Way, Sitka 99833, phone (907) 747-6671.

The Bureau of Land Management has public recreation cabins in Alaska, all within 75 miles/120 km of Fairbanks. Cabins must be reserved prior to use and a fee is required. Two are road accessible year-round, 1 can be reached with a 6-mile hike, and 8 are primarily accessed by snow machine, dog team, cross-country skis or snowshoes in winter.

Contact the Bureau of Land Management, 1150 University Ave., Fairbanks 99709-3899, phone (907) 474-2250.

The U.S. Fish and Wildlife Service maintains public-use cabins within Kodiak National Wildlife Refuge. Contact the refuge manager, 1390 Buskin River Rd., Kodiak 99615, phone (907) 487-2600.

The Alaska Division of Parks and Outdoor Recreation maintains several public-use cabins scattered throughout the state. For reservations and information contact the following regional offices: Southcentral, Box 107001, Anchorage 99510, phone (907) 762-2617; Southeast, 400 Willoughby Ave., Juneau 99801, phone (907) 465-4563; and Northern Region, 3700 Airport Way, Fairbanks 99709-4613, phone (907) 451-2695.

This RCMP Musical Ride in Dawson City, YT, in 1995, was a special centennial event. Watch for Klondike Gold Rush Centennial events in 1996–98. (Earl L. Brown, staff)

Calendar of Events—1996

Travelers may wish to take into account some of the North's major celebrations when planning their visit. Following are some of these events listed by month and by place. Additional events are detailed under Attractions for the communities covered in the highway logs. In 1996, watch for events throughout the North that celebrate the centennial of the discovery of gold in the Klondike.

FEBRUARY

Anchorage—Fur Rendezvous. **Cordova**—Iceworm Festival. **Fairbanks/Whitehorse, YT**—Yukon Quest Sled Dog Race. **Nenana**—Tripod Raising Festival. **Whitehorse, YT**—Sourdough Rendezvous.

MARCH

Anchorage—Iditarod Trail Sled Dog Race. **Bethel**—Camai Native Dance Festival. **Fairbanks**—Winter Carnival; North American Sled Dog Championships. **Nome**—Bering Sea Ice Classic Golf Tournament; month of Iditarod events. **North Pole**—Winter Carnival. **Yellowknife, NT**—Caribou Carnival.

APRIL

Girdwood—Alyeska Spring Carnival. **Juneau**—Alaska Folk Festival.

MAY

This month is a busy one for fishing derbies for halibut (Homer, Seldovia and Valdez) and salmon (Ketchikan, Petersburg, Seldovia and Sitka).

Dawson City, YT—International Gold Show. **Delta Junction**—Buffalo Wallow Square Dance Jamboree. **Kodiak**—Crab Festival. **Nome**—Polar Bear Swim. **Petersburg**—Little Norway Festival. **Talkeetna**—Miners Day Festival.

JUNE

Anchorage—Mayor's Midnight Sun Marathon. **Fairbanks**—Midnight Sun Baseball Game. **Nenana**—River Daze. **Nome**—Midnight Sun Festival. **Palmer**—Colony Days. **Sitka**—Summer Music Festival. **Whitehorse, YT**—Yukon International Storytelling Festival.

JULY

Chugiak/Eagle River—Bear Paw Festival. **Dawson City, YT**—Canadian Airlines International Midnight Dome Race; Yukon Gold Panning Championships. **Delta Junction**—Deltana Fair. **Fairbanks**—Golden Days; World Eskimo-Indian Olympics. **Inuvik, NT**—Great Northern Arts Festival. **Seward**—Mount Marathon Race. **Soldotna**—Progress Days. **Talkeetna**—Moose Dropping Festival.

AUGUST

Dawson City, YT—World Gold Panning Championship. **Dawson City and Watson Lake, YT**—Discovery Days. **Fairbanks**—Tanana Valley State Fair. **Haines**—Southeast Alaska State Fair. **Kodiak**—State Fair and Rodeo. **Ninilchik**—Kenai Peninsula State Fair. **Palmer**—Alaska State Fair. **Seward**—Silver Salmon Derby. **Whitehorse/Dawson City, YT**—Annual Sourdough Rendezvous Gold-Rush Bathtub Race.

SEPTEMBER

Dawson City, YT—Great Klondike Outhouse Race and Bathroom Wall Limerick Contest. **Fairbanks**—Equinox Marathon. **Nome**—Great Bathtub Race. **Seldovia**—Blueberry Festival. **Skagway**—Trail of '98 Road Relay to Whitehorse, YT.

OCTOBER

Anchorage—Oktoberfest. **Sitka**—Alaska Day Festival.

NOVEMBER

Anchorage—Great Alaska Shootout.

Camping

The MILEPOST® indicates both private and public campgrounds with tent symbols in the highway logs and on the strip maps for Alaska, Yukon Territory, Northwest Territories and parts of Alberta and British Columbia. Federal, state and provincial agencies offering camping areas are listed here. Reservations are not accepted at any state campgrounds. Keep in mind that government campgrounds do not maintain dump stations (except some British Columbia provincial parks) and few offer electrical hookups. Season dates for most campgrounds in the North depend on weather. Check the highway logs for commercial campgrounds in the North. In Alaska, contact the Alaska Campground Owners Assoc. (ACOA), Box 84884-MP, Fairbanks 99708, for information on private parks.

NOTE: Campers are urged to use established campgrounds. Overnighting in rest areas and turnouts is illegal unless otherwise posted, and may be unsafe. ▲

ALASKA

Alaska Public Lands Information Centers in Anchorage, Fairbanks and Ketchikan provide information on all state and federal campgrounds in Alaska, along with state and national park passes and details on wilderness camping. Visit the centers, or contact the Alaska Public Lands Information Center at: 605 W. 4th Ave., Suite 105, Anchorage 99501, phone (907) 271-2737, TDD (907) 271-2738; 250 Cushman St., Suite 1A, Fairbanks 99701, phone (907) 456-0527; or 50 Main St., Ketchikan 99901, phone (907) 225-8131. (NOTE: At our presstime, the public lands information center in Tok was scheduled to close.)

Alaska Division of Parks and Outdoor Recreation maintains an extensive system of roadside campgrounds and waysides. All are available on a first-come, first-served basis. There is a $6 to $10 per night camping fee charged at all developed state campgrounds, except for $12 at Byers Lake Campground and $15 at Eagle River and Chena River campgrounds. *(NOTE: Rates are subject to change.)* An annual pass, good for unlimited camping in a calendar year, is available for $75 for Alaska residents and $100 for nonresidents. The pass is a windshield decal and is not transferable. There is a day-use parking fee of $2 per vehicle at a small number of state park facilities, including some picnic sites, trailheads and fishing access sites. A full-year parking pass may be purchased for $25. To obtain camping or parking passes, send check or money order payable to the State of Alaska. Mail to Alaska Camping Pass, Division of Parks and Outdoor Recreation, 3601 C Street, Suite 200, Anchorage 99503-5929.

USDA Forest Service provides numerous camping areas in Chugach and Tongass national forests. Most USFS campgrounds charge a fee of under $10 per night depending on facilities. There is a 14-day limit at most campgrounds; this regulation is enforced. For further information write the Office of Information, USDA Forest Service, Box 21628, Juneau 99802.

Bureau of Land Management maintains about 12 campgrounds; fees are charged on some. Unless otherwise posted, all undeveloped BLM public lands are open to free camping, usually for a maximum of 14 days per stay. Write the Bureau of Land Management, 1150 University Ave., Fairbanks 99709-3899, phone (907) 474-2250.

National Park Service maintains 7 campgrounds in Denali National Park and Preserve. There are established hike-in campgrounds at Glacier Bay and Katmai national parks and preserves, and wilderness camping in other national parks and preserves in Alaska. For further information contact the Alaska Public Lands Information Center, 605 W. 4th, Suite 105, Anchorage 99501, phone (907) 271-2737.

U.S. Fish & Wildlife Service manages several camping areas within Kenai National Wildlife Refuge. Contact the Refuge Manager, Kenai National Wildlife Refuge, Box 2139, Soldotna 99669, phone (907) 262-7021.

Two special passes for federal recreation areas are available to U.S. citizens. The Golden Age Passport is for persons 62 and older and costs a 1-time fee of $10. The Golden Access Passport is free for persons with blindness or another permanent disability. Both provide lifetime admittance to federally operated parks, monuments, historic sites, recreation areas and wildlife refuges that charge entrance fees. Accompanying passengers in a private car enter without charge as well. The passport bearer also receives a 50 percent discount on federal use fees charged for facilities and services such as camping, boat launching and parking (exceptions to teh 50 percent discount may apply in government facilities operated by concessionaires, such as the Russian River ferry). These passes must be obtained in person by showing proof of age for a Golden Age Passport, or proof of being medically diagnosed with blindness or another permanent disability for the Golden Access Passport. The passports are available at most of the federal recreation areas where they may be used, so travelers do not need to obtain them in advance. They also can be obtained at Alaska Public Lands Information Centers in Anchorage and Fairbanks.

CANADA

National park campgrounds generally have a per-night fee. Per-night fees range from $6.50 for a tent site to $17 for a full-service site with individual water, sewer and electrical hookups. In addition, a park motor-license sticker is required for motorists staying overnight in the national parks. Electrical service is standard 60 cycle. Wood for campfires is supplied free to all camping and picnicking grounds. Bring your own ax to split kindling. "Serviced" campgrounds have caretakers.

Alberta has 65 **provincial park campgrounds,** some with limited facilities, others with picnic tables, electrical hookups, flush toilets, barbecues and nature programs. There is a fee ranging from $11 to $16 per night for provincial parks, and some accept reservations for an extra fee. There are also limited camping facilities at many of the 236 provincial recreation areas, which have toilets, picnic tables and litter barrels. A nominal fee is charged. Private and public campgrounds are listed in *Campgrounds in Alberta*, available from Travel Alberta (phone 1-800-661-8888).

In British Columbia, **provincial park campgrounds** are indicated 1.2 miles/2 km and 1,312 feet/400m before the entrance along the highways by blue-and-white signs. They are serviced from spring to early fall (however, they may be used throughout the year). Fees range from $6 to $15.50 per night. Gates close from 11 P.M. to 6 A.M. in some parks.

In Northwest Territories: **Territorial campground** fees are $5 or $10 per night, depending upon the site, in attended campgrounds and parks with facilities. Free firewood is supplied for campground use.

Yukon Territory has 43 **Yukon government campgrounds** located along its road system. There is a per-night fee of $8 charged for nonresidents. These well-maintained campgrounds often have kitchen shelters (which may not be used as sleeping accommodations) and free firewood for use at the campground. There is a 14-day limit.

Customs Requirements

Crossing the border into Canada or reentering the United States is a fairly straightforward procedure. However, there are a few items that Alaska-bound travelers should be alerted to.

The first is firearms. Canada has very specific and strict requirements on what firearms may be brought into Canada. If you plan to travel with a firearm, read these requirements carefully.

Certain items, mainly crafts and souvenirs made from parts of wild animals, have caused some problems for travelers to the North in recent years. An item which may be purchased legally in Alaska, for example carved ivory, can be brought back into the Lower 49 but may not be permitted transit through Canada without a permit. Some items which may be purchased legally in parts of Canada may not be allowed into the United States. For example, a seal-fur doll purchased in Inuvik, NWT, would be confiscated by U.S. customs because the import of seal products is restricted except by special permit.

IMPORTANT: You cannot cross the border unless the customs office for the country you are entering is open. Severe fines are levied for crossing without clearing customs. Officials at Canadian customs are concerned about child abductions. If you are traveling with children, remember to bring identification for them.

Read through the following information and contact Canadian or U.S. customs offices directly.

ENTRY INTO CANADA FROM THE UNITED STATES

Your best source of general information on this subject is the Canadian Government Office of Tourism's travel information brochure. To obtain a copy write Tourism Canada, 235 Queen St., Ottawa, ON K1A 0H5. Revenue Canada can also answer travel questions, phone (613) 954-3940. Here are excerpts from the travel brochure.

Citizens or permanent residents of the United States can usually cross the U.S.–Canada border either way without difficulty or delay. They do not require passports or visas. However, to assist officers of both countries in speeding the crossing, native-born U.S. citizens should carry some identifying paper that shows their citizenship, just in case they are asked for it. This would include a driver's license and voters registration (together), passport, or some employment cards with description and photo. Social security cards or driver's licenses alone are not positive identification. Birth certificates of children are sometimes required. Proof of residence may also be required. Naturalized U.S. citizens should carry a naturalization certificate or some other evidence of citizenship. Permanent residents of the United States who are not U.S. citizens are advised to have their Resident Alien Card (U.S. Form 1-151 or Form 1-551).

All persons other than U.S. citizens or legal residents, and residents of Greenland, require a valid passport or an acceptable travel document.

Visitors of the United States who have a single-entry visa should check with an office of the U.S. Immigration and Naturalization Service to ensure that they have all the papers needed to return to the United States.

Persons temporarily in the United States who would require visas if coming to Canada directly from their countries of origin should contact the Canadian Embassy, Consulate or Office of Tourism in their home country before departure for the United States.

NOTE: Canada has been increasingly concerned about child adbuction. Consequently, travelers should carry identification for children, similar to those mentioned above; have a letter of permission from the child's parent or legal guardian when traveling with children who are not legally their own; carry copies of legal documents regarding custody rights if they share custody; and have thier own children in the same vehicle, if traveling in a group of vehicles, when they arrive at the border.

Persons under 18 years of age who are not accompanied by an adult should bring a letter with them from a parent or guardian giving them permission to travel into Canada.

Although there is no set standard for monies required for entrance into Canada, the visitor must have sufficient funds to cover his cost of living per day for the planned length of stay. Consideration in assessing "sufficient funds" includes the locale in which the visitor plans to stay and whether he will be staying with a friend or relative. (Readers report being turned back for lacking $150 in cash; one customs official suggests $500 as an appropriate amount.) The visitor must also have return transportation fare to his country of origin.

Vehicles: The entry of vehicles and trailers into Canada for touring purposes, for periods up to 12 months, is generally a quick, routine matter, without payment of a customs assessment, and any necessary permits are issued at the port of entry. Rental trailers of the U-Haul luggage variety may be subject to a nominal deposit, which is refundable on proof of exportation of trailer. Motor vehicle registration forms should be carried and, if the vehicle is rented from a car rental company, a copy of the rental contract stipulating use in Canada. If a tourist enters Canada using a vehicle not registered in his name, he should carry a letter from its registered owner authorizing the use of the vehicle.

U.S. motorists planning to travel in Canada are advised to obtain a Canadian Nonresident Interprovincial Motor Vehicle Liability Insurance Card, which provides evidence of financial responsibility. This card is available only in the United States through

U.S. insurance companies or their agents. All provinces in Canada require visiting motorists to produce evidence of financial responsibility should they be involved in an accident. Financial responsibility limits vary by province.

All national driver's licenses are valid in Canada.

Trailers: If you plan to leave your vacation trailer in Canada for a season while returning home from time to time, ask Canada customs at the time of entry for a wallet-sized special permit—an E99. Post the permit inside the trailer so that it can be seen easily from outside. You may not store a vacation trailer in Canada during the off-season.

Entry by private boat: Visitors planning to enter Canada by private boat should contact customs in advance for a list of ports of entry that provide customs facilities and their hours of operation. Immediately upon arrival, visitors must report to customs and complete all documentation. In emergency situations, visitors must report their arrival to the nearest regional customs office or office of the RCMP.

Baggage: The necessary wearing apparel and personal effects in use by the visitor are admitted free of duty. Up to 50 cigars, 200 cigarettes (1 carton) and 14 ounces of loose tobacco, and up to 40 ounces of spiritous liquor or wine *OR* 24 12-ounce cans or bottles of beer or ale may be allowed entry in this manner. Additional quantities of alcoholic beverages up to a maximum of 2 gallons may be imported into Canada (except the Northwest Territories) on a payment of duty and taxes plus charges for a provincial permit at port of entry. To import tobacco products a person must be 18 years of age or over and to import alcoholic beverages the importer must have reached the legal age established by authorities of the province or territory into which the alcoholic beverages are being entered.

Recreational Equipment: Visitors may also bring in sporting outfits and other equipment for their own use by declaring them at entry. These can include fishing tackle, portable boats, outboard motors, snowmobiles, equipment for camping, golf, tennis and other games, radios and portable or table-model television sets, musical instruments, typewriters, personal computers and cameras (with a reasonable amount of film and flashbulbs) in their possession on arrival. Although not a requirement, it may facilitate entry if visitors have a list (in duplicate) of each item, including serial numbers when possible. All such articles must be identified and reported when leaving Canada. ▲

Transporting goods through Canada: U.S. citizens from the Lower 49 who wish to transport personally their household or personal effects to Alaska when such goods are not intended for use in Canada, may obtain a temporary admission permit at the border to facilitate the in-transit movements of goods through Canada. A refundable security deposit may be required at time of entry. The traveler should prepare a list of the goods in triplicate, indicating values and serial numbers where applicable.

Firearms: Firearms are divided into 3 categories—prohibited, restricted and non-restricted.

A nonresident importing a non-restricted firearm or moving in transit through Canada with a non-restrcted firearm does not require a Firearms Acquisition Certificate nor a Permit to Transport providing the visitor is 18 years of age or older and the firearm is for sporting or competition use. A non-restricted firearm means a regular hunting rifle or shotgun with a barrel at least 18 1/2 inches/47 cm, and an overall length of 26 inches/66 cm, and which does not fall into the category of a prohibited or restricted firearm.

A prohibited firearm includes any firearm that is capable of firing bullets in rapid succession during 1 pressure of the trigger; any firearm adapted from a rifle or shotgun whether by sawing, cutting or other alteration or modification, that as so adapted, has a barrel that is less than 18 inches/46 cm in length, or that is less than 26 inches/66 cm in overall length; any firearm that is specifically designed as a prohibited weapon by Order in Council (effective Jan. 1, 1995), a number of assault pistols, combat shotguns, assult riffles and carbines become prohibited. Such weapons are not permitted entry into Canada.

A restricted firearm includes any firearm that is not a prohibited weapon, has a barrel less than 18 1/2 inches/47 cm in length and is capable of discharging center-fire ammunition in a semiautomatic manner, or is designed or adapted to be fired when reduced to a length less than 26 inches/66 cm by folding, telescoping or otherwise. Also included would be any firearm designed, altered or intended to be aimed and fired by the action of 1 hand, such as revolvers and handguns (including antique handguns that use rimfire or centre-fire ammunition that is commonly available in Canada).

Tourists or visitors traveling in or through Canada may not import restricted weapons.

The following quantities of explosives (not including hollow-point handgun ammunition) may enter Canada for personal use by hunters and competitive marksmen without a permit issued by the Explosives Branch of the Dept. of Energy, Mines and Resources: 5,000 safety cartridges; 5,000 primers for safety cartridges; 5,000 empty primed safety cartridge cases; 17.6 pounds/8 kg smokeless powder (small-arms nitro compound).

Nonresidents arriving at a Canada customs port must declare all their firearms. Anyone who illegally carries a firearm into Canada is subject to a number of penalties, including seizure of the weapon and the vehicle in which it is carried. All firearms must be transported unloaded.

NOTE: Personal protection devices such as stun-guns, mace and pepper spray are prohibited entry into Canada.

Plants, fruit and vegetables: House plants may be imported without a permit. Some fruits and vegetables may be restricted entry into Canada and all are subject to inspection at the border.

Animals: Dogs and cats (over 3 months of age) from the United States must be accompanied by a certificate issued by a licensed veterinarian of Canada or the United States certifying that the animal has been vaccinated against rabies during the preceding 36 months; such a certificate shall describe the animal and date of vaccination and shall be initialed by inspectors and returned to the owner.

Up to 2 pet birds per family may be imported into Canada. Birds of the parrot family and song birds may be admitted when accompanied by the owner, if the owner certifies in writing that, upon entering the country, the birds have not been in contact with any other birds during the preceding 90 days and have been in the owner's possession for the entire period. All birds of the parrot family, except budgies, cockatiels and Rose-ringed parakeets, are on the CITES endangered species list and require at the minimum a U.S. CITES export permit with some species requiring an additional Canadian CITES import permit. The temporary movement of all parrots through Canada requires a CITES Temporary Import Certificate from the Canadian Wildlife Service. Contact Canadian Wildlife Service, Ottawa, ON K1A 0H3, phone (819) 997-1840.

Endangered species: The importation of certain animals and plants that are on the endangered species list is prohibited. This applies to any recognizable by-product made of the fur, skin, feathers, bone, etc., of these creatures. For example, U.S. citizens transporting carved ivory or parts of lynx, otter, brown/grizzly bear or wolf through Canada must first obtain an export and/or transit permit from the U.S. Fish and Wildlife Service. (Permits are available at 1412 Airport Way in Fairbanks or at any U.S. Fish and Wildlife Refuge office.) Many ivory sellers will furnish a permit upon request. To avoid the need for a permit, either mail the items or travel directly back to the Lower 48. Obtain all necessary permits before importing or exporting the species or product. Request a list of restricted items from Convention Administrator, Canadian Wildlife Service, Environment Canada, Ottawa, ON K1A 0H3.

RE-ENTRY INTO THE UNITED STATES

It is, of course, the responsibility of the traveler to satisfy U.S. immigration authorities of his right to re-enter the United States.

Canadian immigration officers may caution persons entering from the United States if they may have difficulty in returning.

Re-entry to the United States can be simplified if you list all your purchases before you reach the border, keep sales receipts and invoices handy and pack purchases separately.

Within 48 Hours: Residents of the United States visiting Canada for less than 48 hours may take back for personal or household use merchandise to the fair retail value of $200, free of U.S. duty and tax. Any or all of the following may be included, so long as the total value does not exceed $200; 50 cigarettes, 10 cigars (non-Cuban in origin), 4 ounces/150 ml of alcoholic beverages or alcoholic perfume.

If any article brought back is subject to duty or tax, or if the total value of all articles exceeds $200, no article may be exempted from duty or tax. Members of a family household are not permitted to combine the value of their purchases under this exemption.

Persons crossing the International Boundary at one point and re-entering the United States in order to travel to another part of Canada should inquire at U.S. customs regarding special exemption requirements.

After More Than 48 Hours: U.S. residents returning from Canada may take back, once every 30 days, merchandise for personal or household use to the value of $400 free of U.S. duty and tax, provided they have remained in Canada 48 hours. The exemption will be based on the fair retail value of the articles acquired, and goods must accompany the resident upon arrival in the United States. Members of a family household traveling together may combine their personal exemptions—thus a family of 5 would be entitled to a total exemption of $2,000. Up to 100 cigars (non-Cuban in origin) per person may be imported duty-free into the United States by U.S. residents, and also 1 liter of alcoholic beverages if the resident has attained the age of 21 years, and up to 200 cigarettes.

Federal wildlife laws affect what U.S. citizens may bring back into the United States from Canada. The list is extensive, and U.S. visitors to Canada should be particularly aware that the import of the following is restricted except by special permit: products made from sealskin, whalebone and whale and walrus ivory, sea otter, polar bear, most wild bird feathers, mounted birds and skins. Thus, an item that may be purchased legally in parts of Canada, such as a seal-fur doll, may not be allowed into the United States. Also, be aware that wildlife parts and products, whether you bought, found or hunted them, may be restricted from Canadian export without a permit. For a complete list of restricted items and information on import permits, contact the nearest U.S. Fish and Wildlife Service office.

Animals, including those taken out of the country and being returned, must have a valid veterinarian health certificate. Particularly, dogs must have proof of rabies vaccination.

For further information contact the nearest U.S. customs office or write U.S. Customs Service, Box 7407, Washington, D.C., 20229.

Daylight Hours

SUMMER MAXIMUM

	Sunrise	Sunset	Hrs. of daylight
Barrow	May 10	Aug. 2	84 days continuous
Fairbanks	2:59 A.M.	12:48 P.M.	21:49 hours
Anchorage	4:21 A.M.	11:42 P.M.	19:21 hours
Juneau	3:51 A.M.	10:09 P.M.	18:18 hours
Ketchikan	4:04 A.M.	9:32 P.M.	17:28 hours
Adak	6:27 A.M.	11:10 P.M.	16:43 hours

WINTER MINIMUM

	Sunrise	Sunset	Hrs. of daylight
Barrow	Jan. 24 noon	Nov. 18 noon	none
Fairbanks	10:59 A.M.	2:41 P.M.	3:42 hours
Anchorage	10:14 A.M.	3:42 P.M.	5:28 hours
Juneau	8:46 A.M.	3:07 P.M.	6:21 hours
Ketchikan	8:12 A.M.	3:18 P.M.	7:05 hours
Adak	9:52 A.M.	5:38 P.M.	7:46 hours

Disabled Visitor Services

Accommodations and other facilities (public and private) that are equipped for the traveler in a wheelchair are noted with the wheelchair icon ♿. Travelers should be aware, however, that not all facilities carrying this symbol may indeed be wheelchair accessible, and that facilities not carrying this icon may be wheelchair accessible. *The MILEPOST®* is in the process of adding this information to the logs. Readers can help by telling us about disabled visitor services.

For travel to and within Alaska, it is wise to call ahead. With prior notice, most forms of transportation and accommodations are able to facilitate travel, depending upon the flexibility of all parties involved. The Alaska Railroad, the Alaska Marine Highway, many coach services and cruise ships and some taxi, charter boat and flightseeing services are equipped with wheelchair lifts and accessible restrooms. Some businesses offer sign language interpreters, typed transcripts of tours, discounts, ramps, closed caption service, elevators and other enablers.

Alaska Public Lands Information Centers, phone (907) 271-2737 or TDD (907) 271-2738, offer a map and campgrounds guide listing wheelchair-accessible campsites and rest rooms. APLIC can also provide Golden Age and Golden Access passes for senior citizens and qualifying persons with disabilities. Access Alaska, phone (907) 248-4777, provides a free packet of information on accessible services and locations within Alaska. Sign language interpreter referrals are available from the Alaska Center for the Blind and Deaf, phone (907) 277-3323 or TTY (907) 277-0735.

Relay Alaska is a service of GCI, a long-distance telephone carrier certified by the Alaska Public Utilities Commission to provide Telecommunications Relay Service in Alaska. This service for persons with hearing and speech disabilities allows text and voice telephone users to communicate with each other through specially trained GCI assistants. For additional information, phone GCI (800) 770-2234 V/TTY or Alascom (800) 252-7266. ♿

Driving Information

Driving to the North is no longer the ordeal it was in the early days. Those old images of the Alaska Highway with vehicles stuck in mud up to their hubcaps are far removed from the asphalt-surfaced Alaska Highway of today.

Motorists can still expect road construction and some rough road, but have patience! Ongoing projects like the Shakwak Highway Reconstruction Project on the Alaska Highway between Beaver Creek, YT, and the Alaska border, for example, are helping to improve severely deteriorated sections of road.

Highways in the North range from multi-laned paved freeways to 1-lane dirt and gravel roads. Major highways in Alaska are paved with the exception of the following highways that are at least partially gravel: Steese Highway (Alaska Route 6), Taylor Highway (Alaska Route 5), Elliott Highway (Alaska Route 2), Dalton Highway (Alaska Route 11) and Denali Highway (Alaska Route 8).

In Yukon Territory, the Alaska Highway, the Haines Highway and the Klondike Highway from Skagway to Dawson City are asphalt-surfaced. All other roads are gravel.

Major routes through Alberta and British Columbia are paved, with the exception of the Cassiar Highway, which has both gravel and asphalt surfacing. The Cassiar Highway (BC Highway 37) is becoming a popular route to the North.

All highways within Northwest Territories are gravel. Most gravel roads in the North are well-maintained and treated with calcium chloride as a dust-control measure (wash your vehicle as soon as practical).

RV owners should be aware of the height of their vehicles in metric measurements, as bridge heights in Canada are noted in meters.

Know your vehicle and its limitations. Some Northern roads may not be suitable for a large motorhome or trailer, but most roads will present no problem to a motorist who allots adequate time and uses common sense.

NOTE: Driving with the headlights on at all times is the law in Alaska and Yukon Territory.

Auto Preparation: The following recommendations for driving in the North Country in summer are from our *MILEPOST* field editors. One thing to keep in mind is the variable nature of road conditions: Some sections of road may be in poor condition because of construction or weather; other highways—particularly gravel roads closed in winter—may be either very rough or very smooth, depending on when maintenance crews last worked on the road. Another thing to remember is the wide range of roads in the North, from multi-laned freeways to narrow gravel roads. When driving paved rural highways, beware of "frost heaves" caused by subsidence of the ground under the road. The more remote roads, such as the Dempster or Dalton highways, are gravel. Motorists are much farther from assistance and more preparation is required for these roads.

There are some simple preparations that motorists can make for their trip North to make driving easier. First make sure your vehicle and tires are in good condition. An inexpensive and widely available item to include is a set of clear plastic headlight covers (or black metal matte screens). These protect your headlights from flying rocks and gravel. You might also consider a wire-mesh screen across the front of your vehicle to protect paint, grill and radiator from flying rocks. The finer the mesh, the more protection from flying gravel. For those hauling trailers, a piece of quarter-inch plywood fitted over the front of your trailer offers protection.

There is practically no way to protect the windshield, although some motorists have experimented with screen shields that do not seriously impair their vision. These are not recommended nor do you see many of them in the North, but it is, of course, up to the individual motorist whether these are worthwhile.

Crankcases are seldom damaged, but gas tanks can be harmed on rough gravel roads. Sometimes rocks work their way in between the plate and gas tank, wearing a hole in the tank. You may wish to insert a rubber mat between the gas tank and securing straps. However, drivers maintaining safe speeds should have no problems with punctured gas tanks. A high vehicle clearance is best for some of the rougher gravel roads.

Also keep in mind the simple precautions that make driving easier. A visor or tinted glass helps when you're driving into the sun. Good windshield wipers and a full windshield washer (or a bottle of wash and a squeegee) make life easier. Many motorists also find bug screens to be a wise investment.

Dust and mud are generally not a major problem on Northern roads, though you may run into both. Heavy rains combined with a gravel road or roadbed torn up for construction make mud. Mud flaps are suggested. Many gravel roads in the North (such

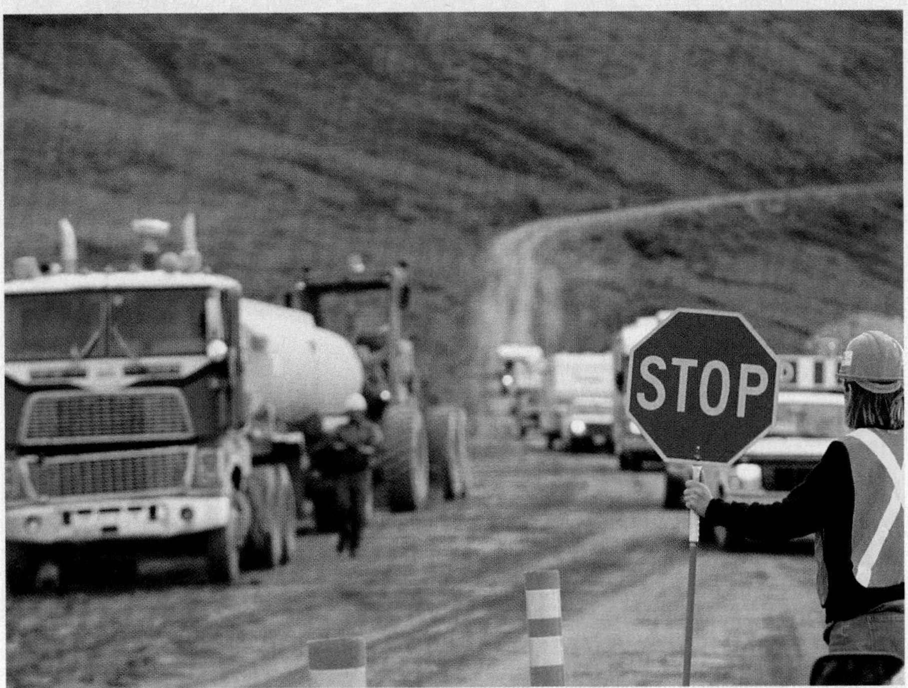

Road construction is a fact of life in the North, where weather and soil conditions can create rough road. (© Doug Wilson)

as the Dalton Highway) are treated with calcium chloride as a dust-control measure. Because calcium chloride tends to eat into paint and metal parts on your vehicle, be sure to thoroughly wash your vehicle. Dust can seep into everything and it's difficult if not impossible to keep it out. Remember to close the windows on your trailer or camper when on a dusty road. It also helps to keep clothes, food and bedding in sealed plastic bags. Also check your air filter periodically.

Driving at slow, safe speeds not only keeps down the dust for drivers behind you, it also helps prevent you from spraying other vehicles with gravel.

Drive with your headlights on at all times. This allows you to be seen easier, especially in dusty conditions, or when approaching vehicles are driving into the sun. It is also the law in Alaska and the Yukon.

NOTE: If driving on a paved surface, it is still necessary to observe "Loose Gravel" signs. Drive slowly.

Although auto shops in Northern communities are generally well-stocked with parts, do carry the following for emergencies and on-the-spot repairs: flares; first-aid kit; trailer bearings; good bumper jack with lug wrench; electrician's tape; small assortment of nuts and bolts; fan belt; 1 or 2 spare tires (2 spares for remote roads); and a simple tool set including crescent wrenches, socket and/or open-end wrenches, hammer, screwdrivers, pliers, wire, and prybar for changing the fan belt.

If you are driving a vehicle which may require parts not readily available up North, add whatever you think necessary. You may wish to carry an extra few gallons of gas and also water, especially on remote roads. You may also wish to carry cans of fluid for brakes, power steering and automatic transmissions.

If your vehicle should break down on the highway and tow truck service is needed, normally you will be able to flag down a passing motorist. Travelers in the North are generally helpful in such situations (traditionally, the etiquette of the country requires one to stop and provide assistance). If you are the only person traveling in the disabled vehicle, be sure to leave a note on your windshield indicating when you left the vehicle and in what direction you planned to travel.

Gasoline: Unleaded gas is widely available in Alaska and is the rule in Canada. Diesel fuel is also commonly available. In Alaska, check with the Alaska State Troopers, and in Canada the RCMP or Visitor Information Centres, about fuel availability. Good advice for Northern travelers: gas-up whenever possible.

Gas prices in the North, as elsewhere, vary. Generally, gas prices are slightly higher in Canada and Alaska than the Lower 48, but this is not a hard and fast rule. You may find gas in Anchorage or elsewhere at the same price—or even lower—than at home. A general rule of thumb is the more remote the gas station, the higher the price. Gas prices may vary considerably from service station to service station within the same community.

It is a good idea to carry cash, since some gas stations in Alaska are independents and do not accept credit cards. Most Chevron, Texaco and Tesoro stations will accept VISA or MasterCard. Also watch for posted gas prices that are for *cash,* but not noted as such. Besides double-checking the posted price before filling up, also ask the attendant which pump is for unleaded, regular or diesel, depending on what you want.

Keep in mind that Canadian gas stations have converted to the metric system; quantity and price are based on liters (see Gas Cost in U.S. Funds Per Gallon chart below). There are 3.785 liters per U.S. gallon, 4.5 liters per imperial gallon. See Metric System

GAS PRICE AVERAGES SUMMER 1995

Alaska Location	Per Gallon U.S. Funds	Canada Location	Per Liter Canadian Funds*
Anchorage	$1.19	Dawson Creek, BC	$.57
Cantwell	1.49	Fort Nelson, BC	.64
Delta Junction	1.37	Haines Junction, YT	.64
Eagle	1.75	Muncho Lake, BC	.67
Fairbanks	1.24	Watson Lake, YT	.63
Fox	1.24	Whitehorse, YT	.62
Glennallen	1.55		
Healy	1.39		
Homer	1.32		
Seward	1.40		
Soldotna	1.36		
Tok	1.38		

*See chart for equivalent cost in U.S. funds for 1 gallon

GAS COST IN U.S. FUNDS PER GALLON

If the Canadian Exchange rate is: / $1.00 U.S. equals Canadian funds:		20% $1.20	25% $1.25	30% $1.30	35% $1.35	40% $1.40
	$.55	$1.73	$1.67	$1.60	$1.54	$1.49
	.56	1.77	1.70	1.63	1.57	1.51
	.57	1.80	1.73	1.66	1.60	1.54
	.58	1.83	1.76	1.69	1.63	1.57
	.59	1.86	1.79	1.72	1.65	1.60
	.60	1.89	1.82	1.75	1.68	1.62
Canadian Price Per Liter	.61	1.92	1.85	1.78	1.71	1.65
	.62	1.96	1.88	1.81	1.74	1.68
	.63	1.99	1.91	1.83	1.77	1.70
	.64	2.02	1.94	1.86	1.79	1.73
	.65	2.05	1.97	1.89	1.82	1.76
	.66	2.08	2.00	1.92	1.85	1.78
	.67	2.11	2.03	1.95	1.88	1.81
	.68	2.14	2.06	1.98	1.91	1.84
	.69	2.18	2.09	2.01	1.93	1.87

For example: If gas costs $0.60 Canadian per liter and the current exchange rate is 30% ($1.00 U.S. equals $1.30 Canadian), using the above chart, the equivalent to 1 U.S. gallon of gas costs $1.75 U.S.

on page 750 for Liters to Gallons conversion chart.

Insurance: Auto insurance is mandatory in all Canadian provinces and territories. Drivers should carry adequate car insurance before entering the country. Visiting motorists are required to produce evidence of financial responsibility should they be involved in an accident. There is an automatic fine if visitors are involved in an accident and found to be uninsured. Your car could be impounded for this. Your insurance company should be able to provide you with proof of insurance coverage (request a Canadian Nonresident Interprovincial Motor Vehicle Liability Insurance Card) that would be accepted as evidence of financial responsibility.

The minimum liability insurance requirement in Canada is $200,000 Canadian, except in the Province of Quebec where the limit is $50,000 Canadian. Further information regarding automobile insurance in Canada may be obtained from The Insurance Bureau of Canada, 181 University Ave., Toronto, ON M5H 3M7. Phone (416) 362-2031 or fax (416) 362-2602.

Tires: On gravel, the faster you drive, the faster your tires will wear out. So take it easy and you should have no tire problems, provided you have the right size for your vehicle, with the right pressure, not overloaded, and not already overly worn. Belted bias or radial ply tires are recommended for gravel roads.

Carry 1 good spare. Consider 2 spares if you are traveling remote gravel roads such as the Dempster or Dalton highways. The space-saver doughnut spare tires found in some passenger cars are not adequate for travel on gravel roads.

In Alaska, studded tires are permitted from Sept. 15 to May 1 (Sept. 30 to April 15 south of 60°N).

Emergency Medical Services

Phone numbers of emergency medical services (if available), such as ambulance and hospital, are listed along with police and fire departments at the beginning of each town or city description in *The MILEPOST®*. Emergency medical services along highways are listed in the highway introductions.

In addition, travelers should note that CB Channels 9 and 11 are monitored for emergencies in most areas, Channels 14 and 19 in some areas. Recommendations for emergency equipment and a list of emergency medical services on Alaska's highways are detailed in a free brochure called *Help Along The Way,* available from the Emergency Medical Services Section, Division of Public Health, Dept. of Health and Social Services, Box 110616, Juneau 99811-0616.

Fires

Travelers are asked to refrain from building campfires on the tundra. Campfires are a common cause of forest fires. Also, fires that escape under the tundra may smolder through the winter and explode in flames the following year. These peat burns are nearly impossible to extinguish. When wildfires threaten inhabited areas, the BLM's Alaska Fire Service (in the northern half of the state) and the State of Alaska Division of Forest (in the southern half of the state) provide fire protection to lands managed by the BLM, National Park Service, U.S. Fish and Wildlife Service, Native corporations and the state.

Unusually dry weather in 1990 made it the most severe fire season on record in Alaska. Lightning was the primary cause of fires with an average of 2,000 strikes a day occurring between June 26 and July 5. In 1995, Yukon Territory experienced the second worst fire in its history: In 2 months, over 325,000 acres of forest were consumed.

Fishing

Throughout *The MILEPOST®* you will find this friendly little symbol. Wherever you see one, you will find a description of the fishing at that point.

Following is a brief summary of fishing license fees, rules and regulations for Alaska and Canada. It is not possible to list all the latest regulations in *The MILEPOST®*, so we urge you to obtain up-to-date information.

Alaska: A nonresident fishing license, valid for the calendar year issued, costs $50. A 1-day nonresident fishing license may be purchased for $10, a 3-day license for $15 and a 14-day license for $30. All anglers fishing for king salmon must also purchase a current year's king salmon tag. A 1-day tag is $10, a 3-day tag is $15 and 14-day/annual tag is $35. Nonresidents under 16 years of age do not need a fishing license or a king salmon tag. Alaska has no discount for senior citizens.

Resident sportfishing licenses cost $15; the king salmon tag is $10 for residents. A resident is a person who has maintained a permanent place of abode within the state for the previous 12 consecutive months and has continuously maintained his voting residence in the state, and any member of the military service who has been stationed in the state for the immediately preceding 12 months.

Nearly all sporting goods stores in Alaska sell fishing licenses. They may also be purchased through the mail by writing or calling the Alaska Dept. of Fish and Game, Licensing Section, Box 25526, Juneau 99802-5526, phone (907) 465-2376. For a variety of published materials for fishers, a price list and free pamphlets, write the Division of Sport Fish at the above address or phone (907) 465-4180. You may contact any regional Sport Fish office throughout Alaska. Be sure you have the most recent edition of the ADF&G regulations booklets for information on bag limits and special permits. The state has 5 separate region booklets.

Canada: A special fishing license is necessary for fishing in Canadian national parks and is good for the entire season in all national parks. These are on sale at park gates.

Alberta: Annual nonresident license (season), $30; limited (5-day) nonresident, $20. Licenses not required for anglers under 16 or residents 65 years of age or more.

British Columbia: Annual nonresident, non-Canadian angler's license, $40; nonresident short-term fishing license, valid for 1 or 8 consecutive days and not valid for steelhead fishing, $10 or $25 respectively. Licenses not required for nonresident anglers under 16 years of age who are accompanied by someone with a license. Special permits required for steelhead and for nonresident fishing lakes and streams classified as "Special Water." Freshwater and saltwater fishing licenses are required of all anglers 16 and older; both are renewable on March 31.

Gold panning is a popular activity in the North. (© Beth Davidow)

Northwest Territories: Annual nonresident fishing license (season), $40; 3-day nonresident license, $30. Nonresident anglers under 16 years of age do not need a license when accompanied by a licensed angler. Fishing licenses are available from the visitor information center at the Alberta–Northwest Territories border on the Mackenzie Highway and in most communities from hardware and sporting goods stores, fishing lodges, RCMP and government wildlife offices.

Yukon Territory: Season fishing license fee for a nonresident is $35, or $20 for 6 days. A 1-day nonresident license is also available for $5. Canadian resident season fee is $25. All persons 16 years of age or over must have a license.

Gold Panning

If you are interested in gold panning, sluicing or suction dredging in Alaska—whether for fun or profit—you'll have to know whose land you are on and familiarize yourself with current regulations. Recreational gold panning is allowed on some state and federal lands. Regulations on use of gold pans and hand shovels, nonmechanized sluice boxes and suction dredges vary depending on where you are.

Throughout Alaska, there are 2 sets of mining regulations to be familiar with—state and federal. Free pamphlets describing the respective requirements of each can be obtained from mining information offices of the State Division of Mining or the Bureau of Land Management. Contact them at: State Division of Mining, P.O. Box 107016, Anchorage 99510-7016, phone (907) 762-2518; Bureau of Land Management, 222 W. 7th Ave. #13, Anchorage 99513-7599, phone (907) 271-5960; State Division of Mining, 3700 Airport Way, Fairbanks 99709, phone

(907) 451-2788; Bureau of Land Management, 1150 University Ave., Fairbanks 99709-3899, phone (907) 474-2250.

Panning, sluicing and suction dredging on private property, established mining claims or Native lands is considered trespassing unless you have the consent of the owner.

You can pan for gold for a small fee by visiting one of the commercial gold panning resorts in Alaska and the Yukon. These include Crow Creek Mine (off Alyeska Access Road, see SEWARD HIGHWAY section); Gold Dredge No. 8 near Fairbanks (see STEESE HIGHWAY section); Little El Dorado, also near Fairbanks (see ELLIOTT HIGHWAY section); and GuggieVille and commercial operations on Bonanza Creek Road outside Dawson City, YT (see the KLONDIKE LOOP section). These resorts rent gold pans and let you try your luck in gold-bearing creeks and streams on their property.

In 1996, look for events throughout the North celebrating the centennial of the discovery of gold in the Klondike.

Hiking

The Alaska Public Lands Information Center, 605 W. 4th, Anchorage 99501, has general information on hiking in all of the National Park Service-administered national parks, preserves and monuments in Alaska.

For details on hiking in Chugach State Park, contact Alaska State Division of Parks, Pouch 7-001, Anchorage 99510. Two excellent brochures, summer and winter guides to Chugach State Park, are available from the park office. Both brochures include a map of the park showing access to trailheads, campgrounds, picnic areas, snow machine and cross-country ski trails, off-road vehicle areas and boating sites from the Glenn Highway, from downtown Anchorage and from the Seward Highway. For visitors to Anchorage, Chugach State Park offers nearby, easily accessible wilderness for day hikes and wildlife viewing.

U.S. Fish and Wildlife Service, 1011 E. Tudor Road, Anchorage 99503, has brochures about the 16 wildlife refuges throughout the state. Only 2 Alaska refuges are accessible by road.

The Bureau of Land Management, 1150 University Ave., Fairbanks 99709-3899, phone (907) 474-2250, has brochures on hiking trails and recreation areas.

The USDA Forest Service Supervisor and District Ranger offices have trail maps and detailed information on hiking trails in Tongass and Chugach national forests.

An extensive system of hiking trails on the Kenai Peninsula is maintained by the Anchorage and Seward Ranger districts of the Chugach National Forest. The most popular trail is the Resurrection Pass trail, a 38.6-mile/62.1-km trail that follows Resurrection Creek from Hope up Resurrection Pass then down Juneau Creek to the Sterling Highway. Other popular Kenai Peninsula trails are Johnson Pass, Crow Pass, Russian Lakes and Ptarmigan Creek. There are public-use cabins along many of the trails; these must be reserved in advance. For general information, write Chugach National Forest, 3301 C St., Suite 300, Anchorage 99503. (For specific information on trails and cabins in Chugach and Tongass national forests, see area office addresses in Cabins this section.)

Yukon Territory has established wilderness trails, too. Information about hiking in Kluane National Park Reserve is available from Parks Canada, Canadian Heritage, 300 Main St., Room 105, Whitehorse, YT Y1A 2B5. For other hiking trails in the Yukon contact Tourism Yukon, Box 2703, Whitehorse, YT Y1A 2C6, phone (403) 667-5340.

Holidays—1996

The following list of observed holidays in Alaska and Canada can help you plan your trip. Keep in mind that banks and other agencies may be closed on these holidays and traffic may be heavier.

ALASKA	
New Year's Day	Jan. 1
Martin Luther King Day	Jan. 15
Presidents' Day	Feb. 19
Seward's Day	March 25
Easter Sunday	April 7
Memorial Day	May 27
Independence Day	July 4
Labor Day	Sept. 2
Columbus Day	Oct. 14
Alaska Day	Oct. 18
Veterans Day	Nov. 11
Thanksgiving Day	Nov. 28
Christmas Day	Dec. 25

CANADA	
New Year's Day	Jan. 1
Yukon Heritage Day	Feb. 23
Good Friday	April 5
Easter Monday	April 8
Victoria Day	May 20
Canada Day	July 1
Alberta Heritage Day	Aug. 5
British Columbia Day	Aug. 5
Discovery Day (YT)	Aug. 19
Labour Day	Sept. 2
Thanksgiving Day	Oct. 14
Remembrance Day	Nov. 11
Christmas Day	Dec. 25
Boxing Day	Dec. 26

Hostels

In Alaska, there are 3 full-service, AYH (American Youth Hostels) hostels; one in Anchorage, Seward and Juneau. Supplemental AYH accommodations can be found in Delta Junction, Girdwood, Ketchikan, Palmer, Sitka and Tok. Other private hostel-style accommodations are available throughout the state.

In Canada, Hostelling International–Canada (HI-C) has 75 hostels coast to coast, with more than a dozen each in Alberta and British Columbia. Yukon Territory has 1 hostel, the Dawson City River hostel in Dawson City. Many hostels in Canada accept advance reservations and payment by credit card. Check with regional hostelling offices or any gateway hostel for details. Keep in mind that you should have a valid hostelling membership from the hostelling association in your own country before you visit Canada. Once in Canada, you can get a free copy of the Hostelling North America official guide to hostels in both Canada and the United States.

For further information, write Hostelling International–Anchorage, 700 H St., Anchorage 99501, phone (907) 276-3635; Hostelling International–U.S.A., Box 37613, Washington, DC 20013-7613, phone (202) 783-6161; Hostelling International–Canada, National Office, 205 Catherine St., Suite 400, Ottawa, ON K2P 1C3, (613) 237-7884.

Hunting

Obtain up-to-date information on fees, licenses, seasons, bag limits and regulations from the following government agencies for Alaska, Alberta, British Columbia, Northwest Territories and Yukon Territory.

Alaska: Alaska Dept. of Fish and Game, Box 25526, Juneau 99802. A complete list of registered Alaska guides is available for $5 from the Dept. of Commerce and Economic Development, Division of Occupational Licensing/Big Game Board, Box 110806, Juneau 99811-0806.

Alberta: Environmental Protection Branch, Information Centre, 9920 108 St., Edmonton, AB T5K 2M4.

British Columbia: Fish and Wildlife Branch, Ministry of Environment, 780 Blanshard St., Victoria, BC V8V 1X4.

Northwest Territories: Dept. of Economic Development and Tourism, Tourism Development and Marketing, Box 1320, Yellowknife, NT X1A 2L9.

Yukon Territory: Yukon Government, Dept. of Renewable Resources, Fish and Wildlife Branch, P.O. Box 2703, Whitehorse, YT Y1A 2C6, phone (403) 667-5221.

Information Sources

Contact the following state and provincial tourism agencies for free maps and brochures and for travel-related questions.

Alaska: Alaska Division of Tourism, Box 110801, Juneau 99811-0801, phone (907) 465-2010.

Alberta: Travel Alberta, 3rd Floor, 10155 102 St., Edmonton, AB T5J 4L6, phone 1-800-661-8888.

British Columbia: Tourism British Columbia, Parliament Bldgs., Victoria, BC V8V 1X4, phone 1-800-663-6000.

Northwest Territories: Dept. of Economic Development and Tourism, Tourism Development and Marketing, Box 1320, Yellowknife, NT X1A 2L9, phone 1-800-661-0788.

Yukon Territory: Tourism Yukon, Box 2703, Whitehorse, YT Y1A 2C6, phone (403) 667-5340; Internet: http://www.parallel.ca/yukon.

Maps

Visitors to Alaska may want more detailed maps of Alaska's backcountry than the highway strip maps and "Plan-A-Trip" Map included in *The MILEPOST*®. Your best source for topographic maps is the U.S. Geological Survey. USGS topographic maps are available in scales. For Alaska, the standard scale is 1:63, 360, 15 minute series, 1-inch to 1 mile. Maps are available by mail from the USGS Distribution Section, Box 25286, Federal Center, Denver, CO 80225. Write for an index of maps for Alaska; the index shows available topographic maps, quadrangle location, name and survey date. (The index and a booklet describing topographic maps are free.)

Sales counters are maintained at USGS offices throughout the country; check the phone book to see if there's an office near you. In Alaska, USGS maps may be purchased over the counter (no mail order) at the USGS office located at 4230 University Dr., Room 101, Anchorage 99508-4664, phone (907) 786-7011. Many commercial dealers also sell USGS maps.

Chugach National Forest maps are available for a small fee from the USDA Forest Service, 3301 C St., Suite 300, Anchorage 99503. Tongass National Forest maps are available from the USDA Forest Service, Box 21628, Juneau 99802. The Alaska Natural History Assoc., 605 W. 4th Ave. Suite 85, Anchorage 99501, also carries Chugach and Tongass National Forest maps, as well as USGS and other recreational maps.

Topographic maps of Canada are available from the Canada Map Office, 130 Bentley Ave., Nepean, ON K1A 0E9. Index maps showing the published topographic maps are available free of charge: Eastern Canada–Index 1, Western Canada–Index 2, Northern Canada–Index 3. Also available is a list of authorized topographic map dealers for each province.

LITERS TO GALLONS

Liters	Gallons	Liters	Gallons	Liters	Gallons
1	.3	21	5.5	41	10.8
2	.5	22	5.8	42	11.1
3	.8	23	6.1	43	11.4
4	1.1	24	6.3	44	11.6
5	1.3	25	6.6	45	11.9
6	1.6	26	6.9	46	12.2
7	1.8	27	7.1	47	12.4
8	2.1	28	7.4	48	12.7
9	2.4	29	7.7	49	12.9
10	2.6	30	7.9	50	13.2
11	2.9	31	8.2	51	13.5
12	3.2	32	8.5	52	13.7
13	3.4	33	8.7	53	14.0
14	3.7	34	9.0	54	14.3
15	4.0	35	9.2	55	14.5
16	4.2	36	9.5	56	14.8
17	4.5	37	9.8	57	15.0
18	4.8	38	10.0	58	15.3
19	5.0	39	10.3	59	15.6
20	5.3	40	10.6	60	15.9

For more precise conversion: 1 liter equals .2642 gallons; 1 gallon equals 3.785 liters.

Metric System

Canada has converted to the metric system. Inches have been replaced with centimeters, feet and yards with meters, miles with kilometers and Fahrenheit with Celsius. Miles, feet, yards and temperatures in all sections of *The MILEPOST®* are followed by the equivalent metric measure. (Equivalents are: 1 mile=1.609 kilometers; 1 kilometer=0.62 miles; 1 yard=0.9144 meters; 1 meter=39.37 inches.)

Money/Credit Cards

The money system in Canada is based on dollars and cents, but the Canadian dollar and the American dollar are separate currencies and the rate of exchange varies. U.S. currency is accepted as payment in Canada, but the best advice for visitors is: exchange your currency for Canadian funds at a bank in Canada. The visitor is then assured of receiving the rate of exchange prevailing on that day. Although businesses in Canada will accept American dollars, they will often give a lower rate of exchange than banks or no exchange rate. However, businesses in some Yukon Territory communities such as Whitehorse participate in the Fair Exchange Program, in which they provide travelers with an exchange rate within 4 percent of the banks.

As you travel north, away from the more populated areas, you will find banks located only in the major cities. Smaller communities may be served by traveling banks or banks open only 1 to 3 days a week for limited hours. Banks in Whitehorse and Dawson City, YT, Yellowknife, NT, and major Alaskan cities are open generally 10 A.M. to 3 P.M. weekdays (open until 6 P.M. on Friday). Also, some Canadian holidays differ from U.S. holidays; see list under Holidays in this section.

Major American bank and credit cards, including most oil company cards and those of retailers who do business in both countries, are accepted in Canada. Credit card purchases are billed at the U.S. dollar equivalent of the Canadian price at the full exchange rate for the day of billing.

Many cities in Alaska and Canada have automated teller machines (ATMs). The MasterCard/Cirrus ATM Network, for example, lists ATMs in 32 Alaska cities, from Ketchikan to Nome, and numerous cities in Alberta and British Columbia. One ATM is listed in Yukon in Whitehorse, and Northwest Territories shows 3 (Fort Smith, Inuvik and Yellowknife).

To find the ATM nearest you, or for a global directory of ATMs, phone 1-800-THE-PLUS.

It is a good idea to carry cash, since some gas stations in Alaska are independents and do not accept oil company credit cards or major-bank credit cards.

Tourists to Canada may be eligible for a rebate on the Goods and Services Tax (GST) paid on certain goods and short term accommodation. Short-term means accommodation for no more than 30 days at any 1 location. The purchase must be for a minimum of $100 to qualify for a refund. Check with tourism or customs authorities for more information.

METRIC CONVERSIONS
Temperatures, distance and speed limits

Fahrenheit	Celsius
122°	50°
120°	49°
110°	43°
104°	40°
100°	38°
90°	32°
86°	30°
80°	27°
70°	21°
68°	20°
60°	16°
50°	10°
40°	4°
32°	0°
30°	-1°
20°	-7°
14°	-10°
10°	-12°
0°	-18°
-4°	-20°
-10°	-23°
-20°	-29°
-22°	-30°
-30°	-34°
-40°	-40°

Miles	Kilometers	Kilometers	Miles
1	1.6	1	0.6
2	3.2	2	1.2
3	4.8	3	1.9
4	6.4	4	2.5
5	8.0	5	3.1
6	9.6	6	3.7
7	11.3	7	4.3
8	12.9	8	5.0
9	14.5	9	5.6
10	16.1	10	6.2
20	32.2	20	12.4
30	48.3	30	18.6
40	64.4	40	24.8
50	80.5	50	31.1
60	96.5	60	37.3
70	112.6	70	43.5
80	128.7	80	49.7
90	144.8	90	55.9
100	160.9	100	62.1

Kilometers Per Hour	30	50	70	90	100
Miles Per Hour	20	30	40	55	60

Mosquitoes

Mosquitoes emerge from hibernation before the snow has entirely disappeared. They peak in about June but continue to harass humans through the fall. Mosquitoes are especially active in the early morning and at dusk. Mosquitoes hatch their eggs in water, so the North—with its marshy tundra and many lakes—is a good breeding ground.

The female mosquito penetrates the skin with a hollow snout to draw blood to nourish her eggs. Mosquito saliva, injected into the wound, is what causes the itch, redness and swelling. Mosquitoes rely on their antennae to smell and are attracted to warmth, moisture, carbon dioxide and dark colors, among other things. Mosquitoes fly into the wind, relying on their senses to pick up a potential meal. They then must home in to within a few inches of the object to determine if it is a good meal. Insect repellents work by jamming the mosquitoes' sensors so they can't tell if you are a meal.

You can't plan your summer vacation around the mosquito. You can take steps to avoid them. The USDA recommends a lightweight parka, tight fitting at the wrists, with a drawstring hood fit snugly around the face, and trousers tucked securely in socks, to reduce biting. Mosquitoes can bite through thin material (such as a cotton shirt), so wear some heavier protection when and where mosquitoes are active. Choose a campsite away from mosquito-breeding areas. According to the USDA, a 5 mph wind velocity grounds most mosquitoes, so locating your campsite where you'll catch a breeze also helps.

According to the USDA, mosquito repellents containing diethyl-meta-toluamide (DEET) are most effective. Make sure you apply repellent to all exposed skin, including hands, ears and feet.

National Parks, Preserves and Monuments

The Alaska National Interest Lands Conservation Act, passed in December 1980, placed more than 97 million acres into new or expanded national parks, monuments, preserves and wildlife refuges. Denali and Glacier Bay national parks and preserves are covered in detail in *The MILEPOST*®. For general information on all of Alaska's national and state parks, refuges and forests, contact the Alaska Public Lands Information Centers either in Anchorage at 605 W. 4th Ave., Suite 105, Anchorage 99510, phone (907) 271-2737; Fairbanks at 250 Cushman St., Suite 1A, Fairbanks 99701, phone (907) 456-0527; or Tok at Box 359, Tok 99780, phone (907) 883-5667.

Alaska's parklands have all varieties of wildlife, from bears to marmots, like this one in Denali National Park. (© Bruce M. Herman)

Pets

Many people travel to the North with their pets, and it is generally not a problem. Keep your pet in your vehicle at highway businesses; local dogs can be aggressive. Also, never approach a chained village dog.

You must have a veterinarian health certificate for your pet to cross the U.S.–Canada border. See Customs Requirements in this section.

Keep your dog on a leash, both for its safety and as a courtesy to other travelers. Dogs are not allowed on national park hiking trails and must be on a leash near your vehicle or confined in your vehicle elsewhere in national parks. Some hotels and motels accept pets, others do not.

Do have identification on your pet should it get lost. However, the best idea is to keep your pet on a leash. There is a great deal of wilderness up North and the chances of recovering a lost dog are slim.

Also keep in mind that not all communities in the North have a resident veterinarian. Pet emergency phone numbers are listed in some places in *The MILEPOST*®.

If you are traveling with your pet on the Alaska state ferry, read the information on pets in the MARINE ACCESS ROUTES section.

Police

Alaska: The Alaska State Troopers are the primary police force in Alaska, and there are city police departments in each of the towns. You will find their phone numbers listed throughout *The MILEPOST*®.

Canada: The Royal Canadian Mounted Police (RCMP) is the primary police force and public safety organization throughout western Canada, although cities and towns in Alberta and British Columbia have their own city or municipal police department. If you are involved in an automobile accident within the city limits of a town in British Columbia, for instance, report the accident to the city police. Outside a city, you should report to the RCMP. The RCMP is the only police force in Yukon Territory and Northwest Territories.

The RCMP plays a major role in relaying urgent messages to visitors; if you need to locate someone in Canada, contact them.

Postal Rates

Alaska: Rates are the same as for all other U.S. states.

Canada: Rates at press time were 45¢ first class (30 grams, about 1 ounce) within Canada, and 52¢ (30 grams) to the United States. U.S. postage stamps may not be used for mailings sent from Canada.

Shipping

Vehicles: Carriers that will ship cars, campers, trailers and motorhomes from Anchorage to Seattle include: Alaska Railroad, Box 107500, Anchorage 99510, phone (907) 265-2490; Alaska Vehicle Transport, Inc., phone 1-800-422-7925; Sea–Land Freight Service, Inc., 1717 Tidewater Ave., Anchorage 99501, phone 1-800-478-2671 or (907) 274-2671; and Totem Ocean Trailer Express (TOTE), 2511 Tidewater, Anchorage 99501, phone (907) 276-5868.

In the Seattle, WA, area, contact A.A.D.A. Systems, Box 2323, Auburn 98071, phone (206) 762-7840 or 1-800-929-2773; Alaska Railroad, 2203 Airport Way S., Suite 215, Seattle 98134, phone (206) 624-4234; Sea–Land Service, Inc., 3600 Port of Tacoma Road, Tacoma 98424, phone (206) 593-8100 or 1-800-426-4512 (outside Washington); or Totem Ocean Trailer Express (TOTE), Box 24908, Seattle 98124, phone (206) 628-9280 or 1-800-426-0074.

Vehicle shipment between southeastern Alaska and Seattle is provided by Alaska Marine Lines, 5615 W. Marginal Way SW, Seattle 98106, phone (206) 763-4244 or toll free (800) 950-4AML (direct service to Ketchikan, Wrangell, Prince of Wales Island, Kake, Petersburg, Sitka, Juneau, Haines, Skagway, Yakutat, Excursion Inlet and Hawk Inlet). Boyer Alaska Barge Line, 7318 4th Ave. S., Seattle 98108, phone (206) 763-8575 (serves Ketchikan, Metlakatla, Prince of Wales Island and Wrangell).

Persons shipping vehicles between Seattle and Anchorage are advised to shop around for the carrier that offers the services and rates most suited to the shipper's needs. Not all carriers offer year-round service and freight charges vary greatly depending upon the carrier and the length and height of the vehicle. Rates increase frequently and the potential shipper is cautioned to call carriers' rate departments for those rates in effect at shipping time. An approximate sample fare to ship a 4-door sedan 1 way is $1000; for a truck, you might pay $1280.

Not all carriers accept rented moving trucks and trailers, and a few of those that do require authorization from the rental company to carry its equipment to Alaska. Check with the carrier and your rental company before booking service.

Book your reservation at least 2 weeks in advance and 3 weeks during summer months, and prepare to have the vehicle at the carrier's loading facility 2 days prior to sailing. Carriers differ on what non-vehicle items they allow to travel inside, from nothing at all to goods packaged and addressed separately. Coast Guard regulations forbid the transport of vehicles holding more than one-quarter tank of gas, and none of the carriers listed above allow owners to accompany their vehicles in transit. Remember to have fresh antifreeze installed in your car or truck prior to sailing!

You may ship your vehicle aboard a state ferry to southeastern ports (at a lesser rate), however, you must accompany your vehicle or arrange for someone to drive it on and off the ferry at departure and arrival ports. See MARINE ACCESS ROUTES section.

Household Goods and Personal Effects: Most moving van lines have service to and from Alaska through their agency connections in most Alaska and Lower 48 cities. To initiate service contact the van line agents nearest your origin point.

Northbound goods are shipped to Seattle and transferred through a port agent to a water vessel for carriage to Alaska. Few shipments go over the road to Alaska. Southbound shipments are processed in a like manner through Alaska ports to Seattle, then on to destination.

U-Haul provides service into the North Country for those who prefer to move their goods themselves. There are 53 U-Haul dealerships in Alaska and northwestern Canada for over-the-road service. In Alaska, there are 8 dealerships in Anchorage, 6 in Fairbanks, 2 in Soldotna, 2 in Eagle River and 1 in each of the following communities: Homer, Juneau,

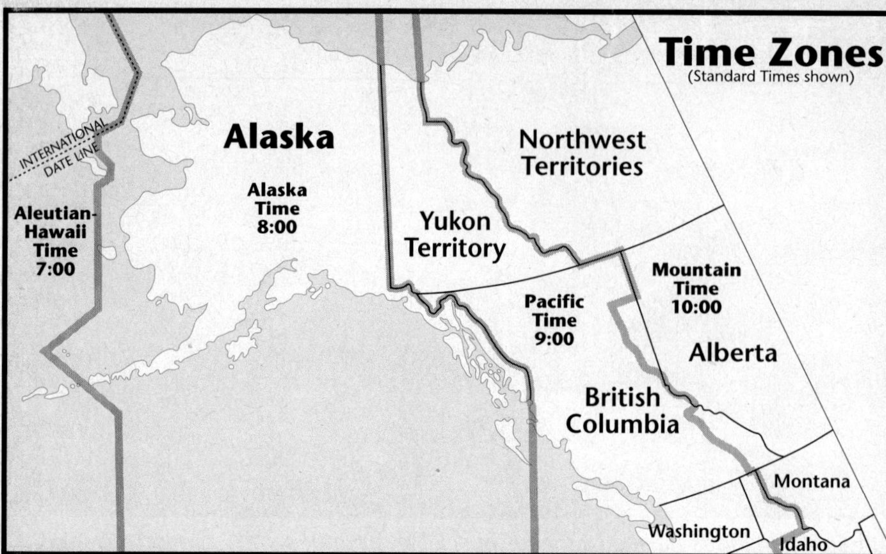

Ketchikan, Delta Junction, Kenai, Palmer, Petersburg, Seward, Tok, Valdez, Wasilla, Sitka and North Pole. In Canada, there are dealerships and ready stations in Dawson City (summer only), Fort St. John, Fort Nelson, Whitehorse and at other locations along the Alaska Highway. There is a dealership in Watson Lake, YT. There are also breakdown stations for service of U-Haul vehicles in Beaver Creek, Swift River and the Kluane Wilderness Area.

It's also possible to ship a rented truck or trailer into southeastern Alaska aboard the water carriers that accept privately owned vehicles (see Shipping Vehicles). A few of the water carriers sailing between Seattle and Anchorage also carry rented equipment. However, shop around for this service, for this has not been common practice in the past, and rates can be very high if the carrier does not yet have a specific tariff established for this type of shipment. You will not be allowed to accompany the rented equipment. Be aware, however, that U-Haul allows its equipment to be shipped on TOTE or Sea-Land, resulting in a 30 percent savings over the price of driving it between Seattle and Anchorage.

Telephone, Telegraph, Money Orders

Alaska: All of Alaska uses the 907 area code.

Telegrams, cablegrams, mailgrams, telex and fax can be sent by telephone from anywhere in Alaska through Western Union. Money transfers can also be sent and received within 15 minutes through Western Union agencies, many with extended hours of operation. Western Union branch offices are located throughout the state and continental United States. To find the Western Union location nearest you, and for hours of operation, phone 1-800-325-6000.

Alberta: All of the province shares the area code 403.

British Columbia: All of the province shares the area code 604. In October 1996, the area code will change for the entire province outside of Vancouver to 250.

Northwest Territories: The territory has 3 area codes. The area code for all communities included in *The MILEPOST®* is 403.

Yukon Territory: All of the territory shares the area code 403 (same as Alberta).

Persons wishing to send telegrams to or from Canada, as well as needing money transfer services, should contact the offices of Western Union at 1-800-325-6000 (the number is valid from the United States and Canada).

Time Zones

At Alaska's request, the federal government reduced the state's time zones from 4 to 2, in 1983. The state is on Alaska time, or 1 hour earlier than Pacific time. The only residents of the state not setting their clocks on Alaska time are in the 4 western Aleutian Island communities of Atka, Adak, Shemya and Attu, which moved from Bering time to Aleutian–Hawaii time.

British Columbia is on Pacific time (daylight saving time in summer), the same as Yukon Territory, except for the area around Dawson Creek and Fort St. John and south from Valemount through Cranbrook, which are on Mountain time. All of Alberta and western Northwest Territories are on Mountain time and observe daylight saving time.

Water

Purify all surface water that is to be used for drinking or cooking. Northern lakes, streams and rivers may be contaminated by the Giardia organism, which can cause the intestinal disorder giardiasis. Giardiasis is characterized by diarrhea, gas, loss of appetite, abdominal cramps and bloating. These symptoms may appear from a few days to a few weeks after ingestion of the organism. To purify water, boil for at least 10 minutes at a full rolling boil. It is a good idea to treat even piped water at campgrounds to be on the safe side. Iodine and chlorine tablets are not effective unless the water is first filtered and allowed to stand for half an hour.

It is also recommended that travelers carry drinking water, and refill containers at safe sources whenever available. RV travelers should consider carrying buckets and funnels for filling tanks at campgrounds with non-standard water faucets.

Swimmers should inquire locally before taking a dip in any gravel pits or roadside lakes. Some of the northern ponds are host to the larvae of schistosomes, which cause "swimmer's itch." Symptoms are redness and itching of the skin, beginning immediately and lasting up to a week.

When to go/What to wear

One of the most often asked questions is "when is the best time to travel?" The high season is June through August, generally the warmest and sunniest months in the North, although July is often one of the wettest months in some regions. The weather is as variable and unpredictable in the North as anywhere else (see Climate Averages chart below). Go prepared for sunny hot days and cold rainy days. Waterproof footwear is always a good idea, as are a warm coat and rain gear. Generally, dress is casual. Comfortable shoes and easy-care clothes are best. There are stores in the North—just like at home—where you can buy whatever you forgot to bring along. There are laundromats (some with showers) in most communities and dry cleaners in the major cities and some smaller towns.

Because most people travel in the summer, filling up hotels, motels, campgrounds and ferries, you might consider an early spring (April or May) or fall (late August into October) trip. There's usually more room at the lodges and campgrounds and on the ferries in these shoulder seasons. The weather can also be quite beautiful in early spring and in the fall. Keep in mind that some tours, attractions, lodges and other businesses operate seasonally. Check the advertisements in *The MILEPOST®* for details on months of operation or call ahead if in doubt.

Normally, May through October is the best time to drive to Alaska. A severe winter or wet spring may affect road conditions and there may be some rough road (especially on highways that are closed in winter) until road maintenance crews get out to upgrade and repair. Motels, hotels, gas stations and restaurants are open year-round in the cities and on many highways. On more remote routes, such as the Cassiar Highway, not all businesses are open year-round. Check ahead for accommodations and gas if traveling these roads in winter.

CLIMATE AVERAGES FOR SELECTED CITIES

	High Temperature	Low Temperature	First Frost	Last Frost	Annual Precipitation
Anchorage, AK	58.4° F/14.7° C	14.9° F/ -9.5° C	N/A	N/A	15.9"/ 40.4 cm
Dawson City, YT	60.1° F/15.6° C	-23.3° F/-30.7° C	Aug. 28	May 28	13.1"/ 33.3 cm
Fairbanks, AK	62.5° F/16.9° C	-10.1° F/-23.4° C	N/A	N/A	10.9"/ 27.7 cm
Juneau, AK	55.9° F/13.3° C	23.1° F/ -4.9° C	N/A	N/A	52.9"/134.4 cm
Whitehorse, YT	57.4° F/14.1° C	-5.3° F/-20.7° C	Aug. 30	June 8	10.3"/ 26.2 cm

N/A = Not Available